Constitutional Law

Constitutional Law

Fourth Edition

Geoffrey R. Stone
Harry Kalven, Jr., Distinguished Service Professor
of Law and Provost
University of Chicago Law School

Louis M. Seidman
Professor of Law
Georgetown University Law Center

Cass R. Sunstein
Karl N. Llewellyn Distinguished Service Professor
of Jurisprudence
University of Chicago Law School and Department
of Political Science

Mark V. Tushnet
Carmack Waterhouse Professor of Constitutional Law
Georgetown University Law Center

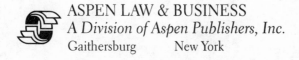

ASPEN LAW & BUSINESS
A Division of Aspen Publishers, Inc.
Gaithersburg   New York

Permissions
Aspen Law & Business
1185 Avenue of the Americas
New York, NY 10036

Printed in the United States of America.

ISBN 0-7355-2016-X

2 3 4 5 6 7 8 9 0

Library of Congress Cataloging-in-Publication Data

Constitutional law / Geoffrey R. Stone . . . [et al.]. — 4th ed.
    p.   cm.
  Includes bibliographical references and index.
  ISBN 0-7355-2016-X (alk. paper)
  1. Constitutional law — United States.   I. Stone, Geoffrey R.

  KF4549.C647   2001
  342.73 — dc21   00-065069

About Aspen Law & Business
Legal Education Division

With a dedication to preserving and strengthening the long-standing tradition of publishing excellence in legal education, Aspen Law & Business continues to provide the highest quality teaching and learning resources for today's law school community. Careful development, meticulous editing, and an unmatched responsiveness to the evolving needs of today's discerning educators combine in the creation of our outstanding casebooks, coursebooks, textbooks, and study aids.

ASPEN LAW & BUSINESS
A Division of Aspen Publishers, Inc.
A Wolters Kluwer Company
www.aspenpublishers.com

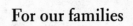

For our families

Summary of Contents

I

The Role of the Supreme Court in the Constitutional Order   1

VI

Implied Fundamental Rights   685

VII

Freedom of Expression   993

VIII

The Constitution and Religion   1411

IX

The Constitution, Baselines, and the Problem of Private Power   1501

Contents

I

The Role of the Supreme Court in the Constitutional Order   1

II

The Powers of Congress   137

III

Judicial Efforts to Protect the Expansion of the Market
against Assertions of Local Power

IV

The Distribution of National Powers   331

V

Equality and the Constitution   421

VI

Implied Fundamental Rights   685

VII

Freedom of Expression   993

VIII

The Constitution and Religion   1411

IX

The Constitution, Baselines, and the Problem of Private Power   1501

Preface

This edition retains its predecessors' emphasis on constitutional theory, interdisciplinary and empirical studies, and comparative constitutional law. The overall presentation has, however, been updated and changed. Developments in constitutional law outside the Supreme Court led to the inclusion of a greatly expanded treatment of impeachment, for example. We have continued to increase the number of references to constitutional law in other nations, with the thought that American constitutional law remains far too insular. Some topics in the law of free expression, previously treated as raising discrete issues, have been integrated into the general treatment of free expression.

The Supreme Court's decisions, particularly on federalism and gender equality, continue to affect the book's content. A new Note on state immunity from suit has been added, for example. The discussion of equality and sexual orientation has been expanded substantially, and the material on race-based districting has been expanded and reorganized. In addition, material on the takings and obligation of contracts clauses has been relocated so that it appears together with the discussion of economic rights in Chapter Six.

Many users will be pleased to learn of another major change in this edition from the preceding one: a significant reduction in length. The reduction was accomplished even as the edition contains substantial treatments of developments since the Third Edition. Cases and notes have been edited more tightly, and some of the less important older material has been reduced or deleted.

We repeat our acknowledgment of our debts to others: We are grateful to the many users of this book, both students and teachers, for their continuing help with this work-in-progress. Fortunately, people have not been reluctant to point to errors, confusions, and possible improvements. We owe a special debt to the hundreds of law teachers on whose work we have drawn throughout this book.

G.R.S.
L.M.S.
C.R.S.
M.V.T.

February 2001

Acknowledgments

We gratefully acknowledge Jessica Barmack, Joshua Davis, Sean Donahue, Jeremy Friedman, Katherine Goodman, Katya Lezin, Brian Polovoy, Nancy Selbst, Jacqueline Shapiro, Rebecca Smith, Kathleen Tenoever, and Élise Tillinghast (and others acknowledged in earlier editions) for the diligent research and editorial assistance; Sandra Leone, Charlotte Maffia, and the members of the Georgetown University Law Center Faculty Support Service for their invaluable secretarial assistance.

Excerpts from the following books and articles appear with the kind permission of the copyright holders:

Ackerman, Bruce. Beyond *Carolene Products*. 98 Harvard Law Review 713 (1985). Copyright © 1985 by the Harvard Law Review Association. Reprinted with permission of the Harvard Law Review Association and the author.

————. Discovering the Constitution. Reprinted by permission of The Yale Law Journal Company and William S. Hein Company from The Yale Law Journal, Vol. 93, pp. 1023-1049.

————. We the People: Foundations. Copyright © 1991 by the President and Fellows of Harvard College. Reprinted with permission of Harvard University Press.

Ackerman, Bruce, and David Golove. Is NAFTA Constitutional? 108 Harvard Law Review 799 (1995). Copyright © 1995 by the Harvard Law Review Association. Reprinted with permission of the Harvard Law Review Association and the authors.

Aleinikoff, Alexander. A Case for Race-Consciousness. This article originally appeared at 91 Colum. L. Rev. 1061 (1991). Reprinted by permission.

Alexander, Larry. What Makes Wrongful Discrimination Wrong? Biases, Preferences, Stereotypes, and Proxies. 141 University of Pennsylvania Law Review 149 (1992). Copyright © University of Pennsylvania Law Review. Reprinted with permission of University of Pennsylvania Law Review and William S. Hein & Company, Inc.

Amar, Akhil Reed. The Bill of Rights and the Fourteenth Amendment. Reprinted by permission of The Yale Law Journal Company and William S. Hein Company from The Yale Law Journal, Vol. 101, pp. 1193-1284.

Auerbach, Carl. The Reapportionment Cases: One Person, One Vote — One Vote, One Value, 1964 Sup. Ct. Rev. 1. © 1964 by The University of Chicago. Reprinted with permission

Baker, C. Edwin. Press Rights and Government Power to Structure the Press. 34 University of Miami Law Review 819 (1980). Reprinted with permission.

_____. Campaign Expenditures and Free Speech. 33 Harvard Civil Rights-Civil Liberties Law Review 1 (1998). Copyright © 1998 by the President and Fellows of Harvard College.

Baker, Lynn A., & Samuel H. Dinkin. The Senate: An Institution Whose Time Has Gone? 13 Journal of Law & Politics 21 (1997). Reprinted with permission.

Balkin, J. M. Tradition, Betrayal, and the Politics of Deconstruction. 11 Cardozo Law Review 1613 (1990). Reprinted with permission.

Bator, Paul. Congressional Power over the Jurisdiction of the Federal Courts. 27 Villanova Law Review 1030 (1982). Reprinted with permission.

Becker, Mary. Obscuring the Struggle: Sex Discrimination, Social Security, and Stone, Seidman, Sunstein, and Tushnet's Constitutional Law. This article originally appeared at 89 Colum. L. Rev. 264 (1989). Reprinted by permission.

_____. The Politics of Women's Wrongs and the Bill of "Rights": A Bicentennial Perspective. 59 University of Chicago Law Review 453 (1992). Reprinted with permission.

_____. Prince Charming: Abstract Equality. 1988 Supreme Court Review 201. Copyright © 1989 by The University of Chicago. Reprinted with permission.

Bell, Derrick. And We Are Not Saved (1987). Copyright © 1987 by Basic Books, Inc. Reprinted with permission of Perseus Books Group.

_____. Brown v. Board of Education and the Interest-Convergence Dilemma. 93 Harvard Law Review 518 (1980). Copyright © 1980 by the Harvard Law Review Association. Reprinted with permission of the Harvard Law Review Association and the author.

Bennett, Robert. The Burger Court and the Poor. In The Burger Court: The Counter-Revolution That Wasn't (V. Blasi ed.). Copyright © 1983 by the Yale University Press. Reprinted with permission.

Berg, Thomas C. Religion Clause Anti-Theories. Volume 72, Issue 3, The Notre Dame Law Review (1997), p. 693. Reprinted with permission. Copyright © by Notre Dame Law Review, University of Notre Dame.

Berger, Raoul. Government by Judiciary (1977). Reprinted with the author's permission.

_____. Impeachment. Copyright © 1973 by the President and Fellows of Harvard College. Reprinted with permission of Harvard University Press.

_____. The Ninth Amendment. 66 Cornell Law Review 1 (1980). Reprinted with permission.

Bernstein, David. Roots of the "Underclass": The Decline of Laissez-Faire Jurisprudence and the Rise of Racist Labor Legislation. 43 American University Law Review 85 (1993). Reprinted with permission.

BeVier, Lillian. Money and Politics: A Perspective on the First Amendment and Campaign Finance Reform. Copyright © 1985 by California Law Review, Inc. Reprinted from California Law Review, Vol. 73, No. 4, July 1985, pp. 1045-1090, by permission.

Bickel, Alexander. The Least Dangerous Branch. Copyright © 1962 by Yale University Press. Reprinted with permission.

———. The Morality of Consent. Copyright © 1975 by Yale University Press. Reprinted with permission.

Black, Charles Lund. Structure and Relationship in Constitutional Law (1969). Reprinted with permission of the Trustees of Princeton University.

Black, Hugo. The Bill of Rights. 35 NYU Law Review 865 (1960). Reprinted with permission.

Blasi, Vincent. How Campaign Spending Limits Can Be Reconciled and the First Amendment. 7 The Responsive Community 1 (1996-1997). Reprinted with permission.

———. The Pathological Perspective and the First Amendment. This article originally appeared in 85 Colum. L. Rev. 449 (1985). Reprinted by permission.

———. Prior Restraint on Demonstrations. 68 Michigan Law Review 1481. Reprinted with permission of the Michigan Law Review Association and the author.

———. Toward a Theory of Prior Restraint: The Central Linkage. 66 Minnesota Law Review 11 (1981). Reprinted with permission of the author.

Bollinger, Lee. Images of a Free Press. Copyright © 1999 by The University of Chicago. Reprinted with permission of The University of Chicago Press.

———. The Skokie Legacy: Reflections on an "Easy Case" and Free Speech Theory. 80 Michigan Law Review 617 (1982). Reprinted with permission of the Michigan Law Review Association and the author.

Bork, Robert. The Impossibility of Finding Welfare Rights in the Constitution. 1979 Washington University Law Quarterly 695. Reprinted with permission of the Washington University Law Quarterly and the author.

———. Neutral Principles and Some First Amendment Problems. 47 Indiana Law Journal 1 (1971). Reprinted with permission.

———. The Tempting of America. Copyright © 1989 by Robert Bork. Reprinted with permission of the Free Press, A Division of Simon & Schuster.

Brest, Paul. Constitutional Citizenship. 34 Cleveland State Law Review 175 (1986). Reprinted with permission of the author.

———. Foreword: In Defense of the Antidiscrimination Principle. 90 Harvard Law Review 1 (1976). Copyright © 1976 by the Harvard Law Review Association. Reprinted with permission of the Harvard Law Review Association and the author.

———. The Substance of Process. Originally published in 42 Ohio St. L.J. 131 (1981). Reprinted with permission of Ohio State Law Journal and the author.

———. Who Decides? 58 Southern California Law Review 661 (1985). Reprinted with the permission of the Southern California Law Review.

Brown, Barbara, Thomas Emerson, Gail Falk, and Ann Freedman. The Equal Rights Amendment: A Constitutional Basis for Equal Rights for Women. Reprinted by permission of The Yale Law Journal Company and William S. Hein Company from The Yale Law Journal, Vol. 80, pp. 871-985.

Burt, Robert. The Constitution in Conflict. Copyright © 1992 by the President and Fellows of Harvard College. Reprinted with permission of Harvard University Press.

_____. The Constitution of the Family. 1979 Supreme Court Review 329. Copyright © 1980 by The University of Chicago. Reprinted with permission.

Caplan, Russell L. The History and Meaning of the Ninth Amendment. 69 Virginia Law Review 223 (1983). Reprinted with the permission of the author.

Carter, Stephen. The Constitutionality of the War Powers Resolution. 70 Virginia Law Review 101 (1984). Reprinted with permission.

_____. Parents, Religion, and Schools: Reflections on *Pierce*, 70 Years Later. 27 Seton Hall Law Review 1194 (1997). Reprinted with permission.

Case, Mary Ann. Of Richard Epstein and Other Radical Feminists. 18 Harvard Journal of Law & Public Policy 369 (1995). Reprinted with permission.

Chaffee, Zechariah. Book Review. 62 Harvard Law Review 891 (1949). Copyright © 1949 by the Harvard Law Review Association. Reprinted with permission of the Harvard Law Review Association.

_____. Free Speech in the United States. Copyright © 1941 by the President and Fellows of Harvard College. Reprinted with permission of Harvard University Press.

Choper, Jesse. Congressional Power to Expand Judicial Definitions of the Substantive Terms of the Civil War Amendments. 67 Minnesota Law Review 299 (1982). Reprinted with permission of the University of Minnesota Law Review and the author.

_____. Judicial Review and the National Political Process. Copyright © 1984 by The University of Chicago Press. Reprinted with permission of The University of Chicago Press.

Clark, Bradford R. Translating Federalism: A Structural Approach. 66 Geo. Wash. L. Rev. 1161 (1998). Copyright © 1998 by The George Washington Law Review. Reprinted with permission of The George Washington Law Review.

Clark, Lorenne. "Liberalism and Pornography." Originally appearing in In Search of the Feminist Perspective: The Changing Potency of Women (Resources for Feminist Research Special Publication #5, Toronto, Spring 1975). Reprinted with permission.

Clune, William H. The Supreme Court's Treatment of Wealth Discriminations under the Fourteenth Amendment, 1985 Supreme Court Review 289. Copyright © 1985 by The University of Chicago. Reprinted with permission

Coase, Ronald. Advertising and Free Speech. 6 Journal of Legal Studies 1 (1977). Copyright © 1977 by The University of Chicago. All rights reserved. Reprinted with permission.

Coenen, Dan T. Business Subsidies and the Dormant Commerce Clause. Reprinted by permission of The Yale Law Journal Company and William S. Hein Company from The Yale Law Journal, Vol. 107, pp. 965-1053 (1998).

Colker, Ruth. Anti-subordination Above All: Sex, Race, and Equal Protection. 61 New York University Law Review 1003 (1986). Reprinted with permission.

Collins, Richard B. Justice Scalia and the Elusive Idea of Discrimination against Interstate Commerce. 20 New Mexico Law Review 555 (1990). Reprinted with permission.

Collins, Ronald, and David Skover. The Death of Discourse (1996). Copyright © 1996 by Perseus Books. Reprinted with permission of the authors.

Conkle, Daniel. The Second Death of Substantive Due Process. 62 Indiana Law Journal 215 (1987). Reprinted with permission.

Corwin, Edward. Liberty Against Government (1948). Reprinted with permission of the Trustees of Princeton University.

Cox, Archibald. Constitutional Adjudication and the Promotion of Human Rights. 80 Harvard Law Review 91 (1966). Copyright © 1966 by the Harvard Law Review Association. Reprinted with permission of the Harvard Law Review Association and the author.

Cross, Frank B. Realism about Federalism. 74 New York University Law Review 1304 (1999) Reprinted with permission.

Cunningham, Clark D., & N. R. Madhava Menon. Race, Class, Caste...? Rethinking Affirmative Action. 97 Michigan Law Review 1296 (1999). Reprinted with permission of the Michigan Law Review Association and the author.

Currie, David. The Constitution in the Supreme Court: Limitations on State Power. 51 University of Chicago Law Review 329 (1983). Reprinted with permission.

_____. The Constitution in the Supreme Court: The Powers of the Federal Courts, 1801-1835. 49 University of Chicago Law Review 646 (1982). Reprinted with permission.

Dailey, Anne C. Federalism and Families. 143 University of Pennsylvania Law Review 1787 (1995). Copyright © University of Pennsylvania Law Review. Reprinted with permission of University of Pennsylvania Law Review and William S. Hein & Company, Inc.

Delgado, Richard. Affirmative Action as a Majoritarian Device: Or, Do You Really Want to Be a Role Model? 89 Michigan Law Review 1222 (1991). Reprinted with permission of the Michigan Law Review Association and the author.

Dellapenna, Joseph W. Nor Piety Nor Wit: The Supreme Court on Abortion. 6 Columbia Human Rights Law Review 379 (1999). Reprinted by permission of the Columbia Human Rights Review.

Dellinger, Walter. The Legitimacy of Constitutional Change: Rethinking the Amendment Process. 97 Harvard Law Review 386 (1983). Copyright © 1983 by the Harvard Law Review Association. Reprinted with permission of the Harvard Law Review Association and the author.

Douglas-Scott, Sionaidh. The Hatefulness of Protected Speech: A Comparison of the American and European Approaches. 7 William & Mary Bill of Rights Journal 305 (1999). Reprinted with permission.

Duncan, Richard. Who Wants to Stop the Church?: Homosexual Rights Legislation, Public Policy, and Religious Freedom. Volume 69, Issue 3, The Notre Dame Law Review (1994), pp. 393, 406, 409. Reprinted with permission. Copyright © 1994 by Notre Dame Law Review, University of Notre Dame.

Dunn, John. Western Political Theory in the Face of the Future. Copyright © 1979 by Cambridge University Press. Reprinted with the permission of Cambridge University Press.

Easterbrook, Frank. Foreword: The Court and the Economic System. 98 Harvard Law Review 4 (1984). Copyright © 1984 by the Harvard Law Review Association. Reprinted with permission of the Harvard Law Review Association and the author.

_____. Substance and Due Process. 1982 Supreme Court Review 85, 112-113. Copyright © 1983 by The University of Chicago. Reprinted with permission.

Eisenberg, Theodore. Congressional Authority to Restrict Lower Federal Court Jurisdiction. Reprinted by permission of The Yale Law Journal Company and William S. Hein Company from The Yale Law Journal, Vol. 83, pp. 499-533.

Eisenstein, Zillah. The Female Body and the Law (1988). Copyright © 1988 University of California Press. Reprinted with permission.

Eisgruber, Christopher L., & Lawrence G. Sager. Unthinking Religious Freedom. 74 Tex. L. Rev. 577 (1996). Copyright © Texas Law Review Association. Reprinted with permission of the Texas Law Review and the authors.

Elhauge, Einer. Does Interest Group Theory Justify More Intrusive Judicial Review? Reprinted by permission of The Yale Law Journal Company and William S. Hein Company from The Yale Law Journal, Vol. 101, p. 31.

Ely, John Hart. Constitutionality of Reverse Racial Discrimination. 41 University of Chicago Law Review 723 (1974). Reprinted with permission.

_____. Democracy and Distrust. Copyright © 1980 by the President and Fellows of Harvard College. Reprinted with permission of Harvard University Press.

_____. Flag Desecration: A Case Study in the Roles of Categorization and Balancing in First Amendment Analysis. 88 Harvard Law Review 1482 (1975). Copyright © 1975 by the Harvard Law Review Association. Reprinted with permission of the Harvard Law Review Association and the author.

_____. Legislative and Administrative Motivation in Constitutional Law. Reprinted by permission of The Yale Law Journal Company and William S. Hein Company from The Yale Law Journal, Vol. 79, pp. 1255-1260

_____. Suppose Congress Wanted a War Powers Act That Worked. This article originally appeared at 88 Colum. L. Rev. 1379 (1988). Reprinted by permission.

_____. The Wages of Crying Wolf. A Comment on *Roe v. Wade*. Reprinted by permission of The Yale Law Journal Company and William S. Hein Company from The Yale Law Journal, Vol. 827, pp. 920-949.

Emerson, Thomas. The Doctrine of Prior Restraint. 20 Law & Contemporary Problems 648 (1955). Reprinted with permission.

Epstein, Richard. Substantive Due Process by Any Other Name: The Abortion Cases. 1973 Supreme Court Review 159. Copyright © 1974 by The University of Chicago. Reprinted with permission.

_____. Toward a Revitalization of the Contracts Clause. 51 University of Chicago Law Review 703 (1984). Reprinted with permission.

_____. Unconstitutional Conditions, State Power, and the Limits of Consent. 102 Harvard Law Review 4 (1988). Copyright © 1988 by the Harvard Law Review Association. Reprinted with permission of the Harvard Law Review Association and the author.

Fairman, Charles. Does the Fourteenth Amendment Incorporate the Bill of Rights? The Original Understanding. 2 Stanford Law Review 5, 132, 137-139 (1949). Copyright © 1949 by the Board of Trustees of the Leland Stanford University. Reprinted with permission of the Stanford Law Review and Fred B. Rothman & Company.

Fallon, Richard. Sexual Harassment, Content-Neutrality, and the First Amendment Dog That Didn't Bark. 1994 Supreme Court Review 1. Copyright © 1995 by The University of Chicago. Reprinted with permission.

Feldman, Stephen M. Principle, History, and Power: The Limits of the First Amendment Religion Clauses. 81 Iowa Law Review 833 (1996). Reprinted with permission.

mission of The Yale Law Journal Company and William S. Hein Company from The Yale Law Journal, Vol. 102, pp. 1611-1644.

Grey, Thomas. Do We Have an Unwritten Constitution? Copyright © 1975 by the Board of Trustees of the Leland Stanford University. Reprinted with permission.

Guinier, Lani. The Tyranny of the Majority: Fundamental Fairness in Representative Democracy. Copyright © 1993 by Lani Guinier. Reprinted with permission of The Free Press, a Division of Simon & Schuster, Inc.

Gunther, Gerald. Foreword: In Search of Evolving Doctrine on a Changing Court: A Model for a Newer Equal Protection. 86 Harvard Law Review 1 (1972). Copyright © 1972 by the Harvard Law Review Association. Reprinted with permission of the Harvard Law Review Association and the author.

_____. Judicial Hegemony and Legislative Autonomy: The Nixon Case and the Impeachment Process. Originally published in 22 UCLA Law Review 30. Copyright © 1982, The Regents of the University of California. All Rights Reserved. Reprinted with permission.

Hall, Timothy. Separating Church and State: Roger Williams and Religious Liberty 158, 159-160 (1998). Permission granted by the University of Illinois Press.

Hellerstein, Walter, and Dan T. Coenen. Commerce Clause Restraints on State Business Development Incentives. 81 Cornell Law Review 789 (1996). Reprinted with permission.

Henkin, Louis. Foreign Affairs and the Constitution (1965). Reprinted by permission from Foundation Press, New York, New York.

_____. Is There a Political Question Doctrine? Reprinted by permission of The Yale Law Journal Company and William S. Hein Company from The Yale Law Journal, Vol. 85, pp. 597-625.

_____. Privacy and Autonomy. This article originally appeared in 74 Columbia Law Review 1410 (1974). Reprinted by permission.

Heymann, Philip, and Douglas Barzelay. The Forest and the Trees: *Roe v. Wade* and Its Critics. 53 Boston University Law Review 765 (1973). Reprinted with permission.

Hundt, Reed. The Public's Airwaves: What Does the Public Interest Require of Television Broadcasters? 45 Duke Law Journal 1080 (1996). Reprinted with permission.

Israel, Jerrold. Selective Incorporation Revisited. 71 Georgetown Law Journal 253 (1982). Reprinted with permission of the author.

Jackson, Vicki C. Federalism and the Uses and Limits of Law: *Printz* and Principle? 111 Harvard Law Review 2180. Copyright © 1998 by the Harvard Law Review Association. Reprinted with permission of the Harvard Law Review Association and the author.

Kaczorowski, Robert. The Politics of Judicial Interpretation: The Federal Courts, the Department of Justice and Civil Rights (1985). Reprinted with permission of Oceana Publications.

Kagan, Elena. The Changing Faces of First Amendment Neutrality. 1992 Supreme Court Review 29. Copyright © 1993 by The University of Chicago Press. Reprinted with permission.

Kalven, Harry. A Worthy Tradition: Freedom of Speech in America (1988).

Copyright © 1988 by The Harry Kalven, Jr. Trust. Reprinted by permission of HarperCollins Publishers, Inc.

Kanowitz, Leo. "Benign" Sex Discrimination: Its Troubles and Their Cure. Copyright © 1980 by University of California, Hastings College of Law. Reprinted from Hastings Law Journal, Vol. 31, pp. 1379, 1394 (1980), by permission.

Karst, Kenneth. Foreword: Equal Citizenship under the Fourteenth Amendment. 91 Harvard Law Review 1. Copyright © 1977 by the Harvard Law Review Association. Reprinted with permission of the Harvard Law Review Association and the author.

_____. Law's Promise, Law's Expression: Visions of Power in the Politics of Race, Gender, and Religion. Copyright © 1993 by Yale University Press. Reprinted with permission.

Karst, Kenneth, and Harold Horowitz. Affirmative Action and Equal Protection. 60 Virginia Law Review 955 (1974). Reprinted with permission.

Kauper, Paul G. Penumbras, Peripheries, Emanations, Things Fundamental and Things Forgotten: The Griswold Case. 64 Michigan Law Review 235 (1965). Reprinted with permission of the Michigan Law Review Association and the author.

Klarman, Michael. Constitutional Fetishism and the Clinton Impeachment Debate. 85 Virginia Law Review 631 (1999). Reprinted with permission.

_____. The Puzzling Resistance to Political Process Theory. 77 Virginia Law Review 747 (1991). Reprinted with permission.

Kluger, Richard. Simple Justice (1976). Copyright © 1975 by Richard Kluger. Reprinted by permission of Alfred A. Knopf Inc.

Koh, Harold. The Coase Theorem and the War Power: A Response. 41 Duke Law Journal 122 (1991). Reprinted with permission.

_____. The National Security Constitution. Copyright © 1990 by Yale University Press. Reprinted with permission.

Komesar, Neil. Taking Institutions Seriously: Introduction to a Strategy for Constitutional Analysis. 51 University of Chicago Law Review 366 (1984). Reprinted with permission.

Koppelman, Andrew. Why Discrimination against Lesbians and Gay Men Is Sex Discrimination. 69 NYU Law Review 197 (1994). Reprinted with permission.

Korobkin, Russell. The Local Politics of Acid Rain: Public Versus Private Decisionmaking and the Dormant Commerce Clause in a New Era of Environmental Law. 75 Boston University Law Review 689 (1995). Reprinted with permission.

Kramer, Larry D. But When Exactly Was Judicially-Enforced Federalism "Born" in the First Place? 22 Harvard Journal of Law & Public Policy 123 (1998). Reprinted with permission.

_____. Putting the Politics Back Into the Political Safeguards of Federalism. This article originally appeared in 100 Colum. L. Rev. 215 (2000). Reprinted by permission.

Krattenmaker, Thomas, and L. A. Powe, Jr. Converging First Amendment Principles for Converging Communications Media. Reprinted by permission of The Yale Law Journal Company and William S. Hein Company from The Yale Law Journal, Vol. 104, pp. 1719-1741.

Krieger, Linda. Civil Rights Perestroika: Intergroup Relations after Affirmative

Action. Copyright © 1998 by California Law Review, Inc. Reprinted from California Law Review Vol. 86, No. 6, December 1998, pp. 1251, 1264, 1267-1268, 1294, 1331 (1998), by permission.

Kurland, Philip. Of Church and State and the Supreme Court. 29 University of Chicago Law Review 1, 5 (1961). Reprinted with permission.

_____. The Religion Clauses and the Burger Court. 34 Catholic University Law Review 1, 13-14 (1984). Reprinted with permission.

Law, Sylvia. Rethinking Sex and the Constitution. 132 University of Pennsylvania Law Review 955 (1984). Copyright © University of Pennsylvania Law Review. Reprinted with permission of University of Pennsylvania Law Review and William S. Hein & Company, Inc.

Lawrence, Charles. The Id, the Ego, and Equal Protection: Reckoning with Unconscious Racism. 39 Stanford Law Review 317, 330, 349 (1987). Copyright © 1987 by the Board of Trustees of the Leland Stanford University. Reprinted with permission of the Stanford Law Review, Fred B. Rothman & Company, and the author.

Lawrence, Michael A. Toward a More Coherent Dormant Commerce Clause: A Proposed Unitary Framework. 21 Harvard Journal of Law & Public Policy 395 (1998). Reprinted with permission.

Laycock, Douglas. "Nonpreferential" Aid to Religion: A False Claim about Original Intent. 27 Wm. & Mary L. Rev. 875 (1986). Reprinted with permission of the author.

_____. Religious Liberty as Liberty. 7 Journal of Contemporary Legal Issues 313 (1996). Copyright © 1996 Journal of Contemporary Legal Issues. Reprinted with the permission of the Journal of Contemporary Legal Issues.

_____. A Survey of Religious Liberty in the United States. Originally published in 47 Ohio St. L.J. 409 (1986). Reprinted with permission of Ohio State Law Journal and the author.

_____. The Underlying Unity of Separation and Neutrality. 46 Emory Law Journal 49 (1997). Reprinted with permission.

Leedes, Gary C. Rediscovering the Link between the Establishment Clause and the Fourteenth Amendment: The Citizenship Declaration. 26 Indiana Law Review 469 (1993). Reprinted with permission.

Lempert, Richard. The Force of Irony: On the Morality of Affirmative Action and United Steelworkers v. Weber. Ethics, Vol. 95, p. 89 (1984). Copyright © 1984 by The University of Chicago Press. Reprinted with permission.

Lessig, Lawrence. Translating Federalism: United States v. Lopez. 1995 Supreme Court Review 125. Copyright © 1995 by The University of Chicago Press. Reprinted with permission.

Levinson, Sanford. 1787: The Constitution in Perspective: Pledging Faith in the Civil Religion; Or, Would You Sign the Constitution? 29 William & Mary Law Review 113 (1987). Reprinted with permission of the author.

Levy, Leonard W. Emergence of a Free Press. Copyright © 1985 by Leonard W. Levy. Used by permission of Oxford University Press, Inc.

Lupu, Ira C. Untangling the Strands of the Fourteenth Amendment. 77 Michigan Law Review 981 (1979). Reprinted with permission of the author.

_____. Where Rights Begin: The Problem of Burdens on the Free Exercise of Religion. 102 Harvard Law Review 933 (1988). Copyright © 1988 by the Harvard Law Review Association. Permission granted by the Harvard Law Review Association and the author.

Lusky, Louis. Footnote Redux: A *Carolene Products* Reminiscence. This article originally appeared in 82 Columbia Law Review 1087(1982). Reprinted by permission.

MacKinnon, Catherine. Feminism Unmodified: Discourses on Life and Law. Copyright © 1987 by the President and Fellows of Harvard College. Reprinted with permission of the author.

———. Not a Moral Issue. 2 Yale Law and Policy Review 321 (1984). Reprinted with permission of the Yale Law and Policy Review and the author.

———. *Roe v. Wade*: A Study in Male Ideology. Reprinted from Abortion: Moral and Legal Perspectives, Jay L. Garfield and Patricia Hennessey, eds. (Amherst: University of Massachusetts Press, 1984). Copyright © 1984 by The University of Massachusetts Press.

———. Sexual Harassment of Working Women (1979). Copyright © 1979 by Yale University Press. Reprinted with permission.

Marcus, Maeva. Truman and the Steel Seizure Case: The Limits of Presidential Power. Copyright © 1977 by Columbia University Press. Reprinted with permission of the author.

Marshall, Thurgood. Commentary: Reflections on the Bicentennial of the United States Constitution. 101 Harvard Law Review 1 (1987). Copyright © 1987 by the Harvard Law Review Association. Reprinted with permission of the Harvard Law Review Association.

Massaro, Toni M. Gay Rights, Thick and Thin. 49 Stanford Law Review 45 (1996). Copyright © 1996 by the Board of Trustees of the Leland Stanford University. Reprinted with permission of the Stanford Law Review, Fred B. Rothman & Company, and the author.

Matsuda, Mari. Public Response to Racist Speech: Considering the Victim's Story. 87 Michigan Law Review 2320 (1982). Reprinted with permission of the author.

McCloskey, Robert. Economic Due Process and the Supreme Court: An Exhumation and Reburial. 1962 Supreme Court Review 34. Copyright © 1963 by The University of Chicago Press. Reprinted with permission.

McConnell, Michael. Accommodation of Religion. 1985 Supreme Court Review 1. Copyright © 1986 by The University of Chicago. Reprinted with permission.

———. Federalism: Evaluating the Founders' Design. 54 University of Chicago Law Review 1484 (1987). Reprinted with permission.

———. The Origins and Historical Understanding of Free Exercise of Religion. 103 Harvard Law Review 1409 (1990). Copyright © 1990 by the Harvard Law Review Association. Reprinted with permission of the Harvard Law Review Association and the author.

McCormack, Wayne. Race and Politics in the Supreme Court, *Bakke* to the Basics. 1979 Utah Law Review 491. Reproduced with permission from the Utah Law Review.

McKay, Robert B. Reapportionment: Success Story of the Warren Court. 67 Michigan Law Review 223. Reprinted with permission of the Michigan Law Review Association.

McLure, Jr. Charles E. Incidence Analysis and the Supreme Court: An Examination of Four Cases from the 1980 Term. 1 Supreme Court Economic Review 69 (1982). Reprinted with permission.

Meese, Edwin. The Law of the Constitution. Originally published in 61 Tul. L.

Rev. 979-990 (1987). Reprinted with the permission of the Tulane Law Review Association, which holds copyright. All rights reserved.

Meiklejohn, Alexander. Free Speech and Its Relation to Self-Government. Reprinted by permission of HarperCollins Publishers, Inc.

Merritt, Deborah Jones. Three Faces of Federalism: Finding a Formula for the Future. 47 Vanderbilt Law Review 1563 (1994). Permission granted by Vanderbilt Law Review.

Michelman, Frank. Foreword: On Protecting the Poor Through the Fourteenth Amendment. 83 Harvard Law Review 7 (1969). Copyright © 1969 by the Harvard Law Review Association. Reprinted with permission of the Harvard Law Review Association and the author.

_____. "Formal and Associational Aims in Procedural Due Process." In NOMOS: Due Process (1977). Reprinted with permission of the New York University Press.

_____. Property, Utility, and Fairness: Comments on the Ethical Foundations of "Just Compensation" Law. 80 Harvard Law Review 1165 (1967). Copyright © 1967 by the Harvard Law Review Association. Reprinted with permission of the Harvard Law Review Association and the author.

_____. The Supreme Court and Litigation Access Fees: The Right to Protect One's Rights — Part II. 1974 Duke Law Journal 527 (1974). Reprinted with permission.

_____. Traces of Self-Government. 100 Harvard Law Review 4 (1996). Copyright © 1986 by the Harvard Law Review Association. Reprinted with permission of the Harvard Law Review Association and the author.

_____. Welfare Rights in a Constitutional Democracy. 1979 Washington University Law Quarterly 659 (1979). Reprinted with permission.

Miller, Arthur. *Dames & Moore v. Regan:* A Political Decision by a Political Court. Originally published in 29 UCLA Law Review 1104. Copyright 1982, The Regents of the University of California. All Rights Reserved. Reprinted with permission.

Miller, Geoffrey. The True Story of *Carolene Products.* 1988 Supreme Court Review 307. Copyright © 1989 by The University of Chicago. Reprinted with permission.

Minow, Martha. When Difference Has Its Home: Group Homes for the Mentally Retarded, Equal Protection and Legal Treatment of Difference. 22 Harvard Civil Rights-Civil Liberties Law Review 111 (1987). Copyright © 1987 by the President and Fellows of Harvard College. Reprinted with permission.

Nagel, Robert F. The Future of Federalism. 46 Case Western Reserve Law Review 643 (1996). Reprinted with permission.

Nagel, Thomas. How Useful Is Judicial Review in Free Speech Cases? 69 Cornell Law Review 302 (1984). Reprinted with permission.

Nagle, John Copeland. The Commerce Clause Meets the Delhi Sands Flower-Loving Fly. 97 Michigan Law Review 174 (1998). Reprinted with permission of the Michigan Law Review Association and the author.

Nelson, William. The Fourteenth Amendment: From Political Principle to Judicial Doctrine. Copyright © 1988 by the President and Fellows of Harvard College. Reprinted with permission of Harvard University Press.

Note, Anti-Pornography Laws and First Amendment Values. 98 Harvard Law Review 460 (1984). Copyright © 1984 by the Harvard Law Review Association. Reprinted with permission of the Harvard Law Review Association.

_____. The Constitutional Imperative of Proportional Representation. Reprinted by permission of The Yale Law Journal Company and William S. Hein Company from The Yale Law Journal, Vol. 94, pp. 163-188.

_____. Developments in the Law — The Constitution and the Family. 93 Harvard Law Review 1156 (1980). Copyright © 1980 by the Harvard Law Review Association. Reprinted with permission of the Harvard Law Review Association.

_____. Irrebuttable Presumptions: An Illusory Analysis. 27 Stanford Law Review 449 (1975). Copyright © 1975 by the Board of Trustees of the Leland Stanford University. Reprinted with permission of the Stanford Law Review and Fred B. Rothman & Company.

_____. Legislative Purpose, Rationality, and Equal Protection. Reprinted by permission of The Yale Law Journal Company and William S. Hein Company from The Yale Law Journal, Vol. 82, pp. 123-154.

_____. The Supreme Court — 1972 Term. 87 Harvard Law Review 57, 66 (1973). Copyright © 1972 by the Harvard Law Review Association. Reprinted with permission of the Harvard Law Review Association and the author.

Olsen, Frances. The Family and the Market: A Study of Ideology and Legal Reform. 96 Harvard Law Review 1497 (1983). Copyright © 1983 by the Harvard Law Review Association. Reprinted with permission of the Harvard Law Review Association and the author.

O'Sullivan, Julie R. The Interaction between Impeachment and the Independent Counsel Statute. 86 Georgetown Law Journal 2193 (1998). Reprinted with permission.

Parker, Richard. The Past of Constitutional Theory — and Its Future. Originally published in 42 Ohio St. L.J. 223 (1981). Reprinted with permission of the Ohio State Law Journal and the author.

Perry, Michael. The Courts, the Constitution, and Human Rights. Copyright © 1982 by Yale University Press. Reprinted with permission.

Posner, Richard. The De Funis Case and the Constitutionality of Preferential Treatment of Racial Minorities. 1974 Supreme Court Review 1. Copyright © 1975 by The University of Chicago. Reprinted with permission.

Post, Robert. The Constitutional Concept of Public Discourse: Outrageous Opinion, Democratic Deliberation and Hustler Magazine v. Falwell. 103 Harvard Law Review 601 (1990). Copyright © 1990 by the Harvard Law Review Association. Reprinted with permission of the Harvard Law Review Association and the author.

_____. Racist Speech, Democracy, and the First Amendment. 32 William & Mary Law Review 267 (1991). Reprinted with permission.

_____. Subsidized Speech. Reprinted by permission of The Yale Law Journal Company and William S. Hein Company from The Yale Law Journal, Vol. 106, pp. 151-195.

Powell, Jefferson. The Oldest Question of Constitutional Law. 79 Virginia Law Review 633 (1993). Reprinted with permission.

powell, john a. As Justice Requires/Permits: The Delimination of Harmful Speech in a Democratic Society. 16 Law & Inequality 97 (1998). Reprinted with permission.

Powell, Lewis F. Carolene Products Revisited. This article originally appeared in 82 Columbia Law Review 1087 (1982). Reprinted by permission.

Rapaczynski, Andrzej. From Sovereignty to Process: The Jurisprudence of Federalism after Garcia. 1985 Supreme Court Review 341. Copyright © 1986 by The University of Chicago. Reprinted with permission.

Regan, Donald. How to Think About the Federal Commerce Power and Incidentally Rewrite *United States v. Lopez.* 94 Michigan Law Review 554 (1995). Reprinted with permission of the Michigan Law Review Association and the author.

———. The Supreme Court and State Protectionism: Making Sense of the Dormant Commerce Clause. 84 Michigan Law Review 1091 (1986). Reprinted with permission of the Michigan Law Review Association and the author.

Richards, David. Sexual Preference as a Suspect (Religious) Classification: An Alternative Perspective on the Unconstitutionality of Anti-Lesbian/Gay Initiatives. Originally published in 55 Ohio St. L.J. 491 (1994). Reprinted with permission of the Ohio State Law Journal and the author.

Robinson, Donald. Slavery in the Structure of American Politics (1971). Reprinted with the author's permission.

Rose-Ackerman, Susan. Risk Taking and Reelection: Does Federalism Promote Innovation? 9 Journal of Legal Studies 593 (1980). Copyright © 1980 by The University of Chicago Press. Reprinted with permission.

Rosberg, Gerald M. The Protection of Aliens from Discriminatory Treatment by the National Government. 1977 Supreme Court Review 275. Copyright © 1977 by The University of Chicago Press. Reprinted with permission.

Rubenfeld, Jed. The Right of Privacy. 102 Harvard Law Review 737 (1989). Copyright © 1989 by the Harvard Law Review Association. Reprinted with permission of the Harvard Law Review Association and the author.

Rubin, Edward L. The Fundamentality and Irrelevance of Federalism. 13 Georgia State Law Review 1009 (1997). Reprinted with permission.

Sager, Lawrence. Fair Measure: The Status of Underenforced Constitutional Norms. 91 Harvard Law Review 1212 (1978). Copyright © 1978 by the Harvard Law Review Association. Reprinted with permission of the Harvard Law Review Association and the author.

Sandalow, Terrance. Constitutional Interpretation. 79 Michigan Law Review 1033 (1971). Reprinted with permission of the Michigan Law Review Association and the author.

Sargentich, Thomas O. The Limits of the Parliamentary Critique of the Separation of Powers. 34 William & Mary Law Review 679 (1993). Reprinted with permission.

Scalia, Antonin. A Matter of Interpretation. Copyright © 1997 by Princeton University Press. Reprinted by permission of Princeton University Press.

Schauer, Frederick. Easy Cases. 58 Southern California Law Review 399 (1985). Reprinted with the permission of the Southern California Law Review.

Schoenbrod, David. Power without Responsibility (1993). Copyright © 1993 by Yale University Press. Reprinted with permission.

Seidman, L. Michael. *Brown* and *Miranda.* Copyright © 1992 by California Law Review Inc. Reprinted from California Law Review, Vol. 80, No. 3, May 1992, pp. 673-756, by permission.

———. Confusion at the Border: *Cruzan,* "The Right to Die," and the Public/Private Distinction. 1992 Supreme Court Review 47. Copyright 1993 by The University of Chicago. Reprinted with permission.

Shapiro, Martin M. Freedom of Speech: The Supreme Court and Judicial Review (1966). Reprinted with permission of Prentice Hall.

Siegan, Bernard. Economic Liberties and the Constitution (1978). Reprinted with permission of author.

Stacy, Tom. Whose Interests Does Federalism Protect? 45 University of Kansas Law Review 1185 (1997). Reprinted with permission of the author.

Stepan, Alfred C. Federalism and Democracy: Beyond the U.S. Model. 10 Journal of Democracy 18 (1999). Copyright © 1999 by Johns Hopkins University Press. Reprinted with permission.

Stone, Geoffrey. The Equal Access Controversy: The Religion Clauses and the Meaning of "Neutrality." Northwestern University Law Review, Volume 81, Issue 1, pp. 168, 169-170 (1986). Reprinted by special permission of Northwestern University School of Law Law Review.

_____. Imagining a Free Press. 90 Michigan Law Review 1246 (1992). Reprinted with permission of the Michigan Law Review Association and the author.

_____. Reflections on the First Amendment: The Evolution of the American Jurisprudence of Free Expression. 131 Proceedings 251 (1987). Reprinted with permission.

_____. Restrictions of Speech Because of Its Content: The Peculiar Case of Subject Matter Restrictions. 46 University of Chicago Law Review 81. Reprinted with permission.

Stout, Lynn. Strict Scrutiny and Social Choice: An Economic Inquiry into Fundamental Rights and Suspect Classifications. 80 Georgetown Law Journal 1787 (1992). Reprinted with permission.

Strauss, David. Abortion, Toleration, and Moral Uncertainty. 1993 Supreme Court Review 1. Copyright © 1994 by The University of Chicago. Reprinted with permission.

_____. Corruption, Equality, and Campaign Finance Reform. This article originally appeared in 94 Columbia Law Review 1369 (1994). Reprinted by permission.

_____. Due Process, Government Inaction, and Private Wrongs. 1989 Supreme Court Review 53. Copyright © 1990 by The University of Chicago. Reprinted with permission.

_____. The Myth of Colorblindness. 1986 Supreme Court Review 99. Copyright © 1987 by The University of Chicago. Reprinted with permission.

_____. Persuasion, Autonomy, and Freedom of Expression. This article originally appeared in 91 Columbia Law Review 334 (1991). Reprinted by permission.

Stromseth, Jane E. Collective Force and Constitutional Responsibility: War Powers in the Post-Cold War Era. 50 Miami Law Review 145 (1995). Reprinted with permission.

Sullivan, Kathleen. Cheap Spirits, Cigarettes, and Free Speech: The Implications of 44 Liquormart. 1996 Supreme Court Review 123. Copyright © 1996 by The University of Chicago Press. Reprinted with permission.

_____. Political Money and Freedom of Speech. This work, copyright 1997 by Kathleen Sullivan was originally published in 30 U.C. Davis L. Rev. 663, 664, 667-673 (1997). Copyright 1997 by the Regents of the University of California. Reprinted with permission.

_____. Sins of Discrimination: Last Term's Affirmative Action Cases. 100 Harvard Law Review 78 (1986). Copyright © 1986 by the Harvard Law Review

Association. Reprinted with permission of the Harvard Law Review Association and the author.

Sunstein, Cass. Democracy and the Problem of Free Speech. Copyright © 1993
by Cass Sunstein. Reprinted with permission of The Free Press, a Division
of Simon & Schuster, Inc.

_____. Free Speech Now. 59 University of Chicago Law Review 255 (1992). Re-
printed with permission.

_____. Homosexuality and the Constitution. 70 Indiana Law Journal 1 (1994).
Reprinted with permission.

_____. Interest Groups in American Public Law. Copyright © 1985 by the
Board of Trustees of the Leland Stanford University. Reprinted with permission of the Stanford Law Review, Fred B. Rothman & Company, and the
author.

_____. Naked Preferences and the Constitution. This article originally ap-
peared in 84 Columbia Law Review 1689 (1984). Reprinted by permission.

_____. Neutrality in Constitutional Law (with Special Reference to Pornogra-
phy, Abortion, and Surrogacy). This article originally appeared in 92 Columbia Law Review 1 (1992). Reprinted by permission.

Swinton, Katherine. The Supreme Court and Canadian Federalism: The Laskin-
Dickson Years (1990). Reprinted with permission of Carswell, a division of
Thomson Canada Limited.

Thompson, Judith Jarvis. A Defense of Abortion. 1 Philosophy & Public Affairs
47 (1971). Copyright © 1971 The Johns Hopkins University Press. Reprinted with permission.

Tooley, Michael. Abortion and Infanticide. Copyright © 1983 by Michael Tooley. Used by permission of Oxford University Press.

Tribe, Laurence. American Constitutional Law (First Edition) (1978). Reprinted
by permission of Foundation Press, New York, New York.

_____. American Constitutional Law (Second Edition) (1988). Reprinted by
permission of Foundation Press, New York, New York.

_____. Constitutional Choices. Copyright © 1985 by the President and Fellows
of Harvard College. Reprinted with permission of Harvard University Press.

_____. A Constitution We Are Amending: In Defense of a Restrained Judicial
Role. 97 Harvard Law Review 433 (1983). Copyright © 1983 by the Harvard
Law Review Association. Reprinted with permission of the Harvard Law Re-
view Association and the author.

_____. Foreword: Toward a Model of Roles in the Due Process of Life and Law.
87 Harvard Law Review 1 (1973). Copyright © 1973 by the Harvard Law
Review Association. Reprinted with permission of the Harvard Law Review
Association and the author.

_____. Structural Due Process. 10 Harvard Civil Rights-Civil Liberties Law Re-
view 269 (1975). Copyright © 1975 by the President and Fellows of Harvard
College. Reprinted with permission.

_____. Taking Text and Structure Seriously: Reflections on Free-Form Method
in Constitutional Interpretation. 108 Harvard Law Review 1221 (1995).
Copyright © 1995 by the Harvard Law Review Association. Reprinted with
permission of the Harvard Law Review Association and the author.

Tribe, Laurence, and Michael Dorf. On Reading the Constitution. Copyright ©
1991 by the President and Fellows of Harvard College. Reprinted with permission of Harvard University Press.

Tushnet, Mark. Following the Rules Laid Down: A Critique of Interpretivism and Neutral Principles. 96 Harvard Law Review 781 (1983). Copyright © 1983 by the Harvard Law Review Association. Reprinted with permission of the Harvard Law Review Association and the author.

————. The Optimist's Tale. 132 University of Pennsylvania Law Review 1257 (1984). Copyright © University of Pennsylvania Law Review. Reprinted with permission of University of Pennsylvania Law Review and William S. Hein & Company, Inc.

————. Why the Supreme Court Overruled *National League of Cities*. 47 Vanderbilt Law Review 1623 (1994). Reprinted with permission.

Ulen, Thomas S. Economic and Public-Choice Forces in Federalism. 6 George Mason Law Review 921 (1998). Reprinted with permission.

Wechsler, Herbert. Principles, Politics, and Fundamental Law. Copyright © 1961 by the President and Fellows of Harvard College Reprinted with permission of the Harvard University Press.

————. Toward Neutral Principles of Constitutional Law. 73 Harvard Law Review 1 (1959). Copyright © 1959 by the Harvard Law Review Association. Reprinted with permission of the Harvard Law Review Association and the author.

Weinberg, Louise. Fear and Federalism. 23 Ohio Northern University Law Review 1295 (1997). Reprinted with permission.

Westen, Peter. The Empty Idea of Equality. 95 Harvard Law Review 537 (1982). Copyright © 1982 by the Harvard Law Review Association. Reprinted with permission of the Harvard Law Review Association and the author.

Williams, David, and Susan Williams. Volitionalism and Religious Liberty. 76 Cornell Law Review 769 (1991). Reprinted with permission.

Williamson, Joel. The Crucible of Race. Copyright © 1984 by Joel Williamson. Used by permission of Oxford University Press, Inc.

Wright, J. Skelly. Politics and the Constitution: Is Money Speech? Reprinted by permission of The Yale Law Journal Company and William S. Hein Company from The Yale Law Journal, Vol. 85, pp. 1005-1019.

Editorial Notice

Throughout this book additions to quoted material are indicated by brackets, and deletions are indicated either by brackets or ellipses. Citations and footnotes are sometimes omitted without notice.

The Constitution of
the United States

We the People of the United States, in Order to form a more perfect Union, establish Justice, insure domestic Tranquility, provide for the common defence, promote the general Welfare, and secure the Blessings of Liberty to ourselves and our Posterity, do ordain and establish this Constitution for the United States of America.

ARTICLE I

Section 1. All legislative Powers herein granted shall be vested in a Congress of the United States which shall consist of a Senate and House of Representatives.

Section 2. [1] The House of Representatives shall be composed of Members chosen every second Year by the People of the several States, and the Electors in each State shall have the Qualifications requisite for Electors of the most numerous Branch of the State Legislature.

[2] No Person shall be a Representative who shall not have attained to the Age of twenty five Years, and been seven Years a Citizen of the United States, and who shall not, when elected, be an Inhabitant of that State in which he shall be chosen.

[3] Representatives and direct Taxes shall be apportioned among the several States which may be included within this Union, according to their respective Numbers, which shall be determined by adding to the whole Number of free Persons, including those bound to Service for a Term of Years, and excluding Indians not taxed, three fifths of all other Persons. The actual Enumeration shall be made within three Years after the first Meeting of the Congress of the United States, and within every subsequent Term of ten Years, in such Manner as they shall by Law direct. The Number of Representatives shall not exceed one for every thirty Thousand, but each State shall have at Least One Representative; and until such enumeration shall be made, the State of New Hampshire shall be entitled to chuse three, Massachusetts eight, Rhode Island and Providence Plantations one, Connecticut five, New York six, New Jersey four, Pennsylvania eight, Delaware one, Maryland six, Virginia ten, North Carolina five, South Carolina five, and Georgia three.

[4] When vacancies happen in the Representation from any State, the Executive Authority thereof shall issue Writs of Election to fill such Vacancies.

[5] The House of Representatives shall chuse their Speaker and other Officers; and shall have the sole Power of Impeachment.

Section 3. [1] The Senate of the United States shall be composed of two Senators from each State, chosen by the Legislature thereof, for six Years; and each Senator shall have one Vote.

[2] Immediately after they shall be assembled in Consequence of the first Election, they shall be divided as equally as may be into three Classes. The Seats of the Senators of the first Class shall be vacated at the Expiration of the second Year, of the second Class at the Expiration of the fourth Year, and of the third Class at the Expiration of the sixth Year, so that one third may be chosen every second Year; and if Vacancies happen by Resignation, or otherwise, during the Recess of the Legislature of any State, the Executive thereof may make temporary Appointments until the next Meeting of the Legislature, which shall then fill such Vacancies.

[3] No Person shall be a Senator who shall not have attained to the Age of thirty Years, and been nine Years a Citizen of the United States, and who shall not, when elected, be an Inhabitant of that State for which he shall be chosen.

[4] The Vice President of the United States shall be President of the Senate, but shall have no Vote, unless they be equally divided.

[5] The Senate shall chuse their other Officers, and also a President pro tempore, in the absence of the Vice President, or when he shall exercise the Office of President of the United States.

[6] The Senate shall have the sole Power to try all Impeachments. When sitting for that Purpose, they shall be on Oath or Affirmation. When the President of the United States is tried, the Chief Justice shall preside: And no Person shall be convicted without the Concurrence of two thirds of the Members present.

[7] Judgment in Cases of Impeachment shall not extend further than to removal from Office, and disqualification to hold and enjoy any Office of honor, Trust or Profit under the United States: but the Party convicted shall nevertheless be liable and subject to Indictment, Trial, Judgment and Punishment, according to Law.

Section 4. [1] The Times, Places and Manner of holding Elections for Senators and Representatives, shall be prescribed in each State by the Legislature thereof; but the Congress may at any time by Law make or alter such Regulations, except as to the Places of chusing Senators.

[2] The Congress shall assemble at least once in every Year, and such Meeting shall be on the first Monday in December, unless they shall by Law appoint a different Day.

Section 5. [1] Each House shall be the judge of the Elections, Returns and Qualifications of its own Members, and a Majority of each shall constitute a Quorum to do Business; but a smaller Number may adjourn from day to day, and may be authorized to compel the Attendance of absent Members, in such Manner, and under such Penalties as each House may provide.

[2] Each House may determine the Rules of its Proceedings, punish its Members for disorderly Behavior, and, with the Concurrence of two thirds, expel a Member.

[3] Each House shall keep a Journal of its Proceedings, and from time to time publish the same, excepting such Parts as may in their Judgment require Secrecy;

and the Yeas and Nays of the Members of either House on any question shall, at the Desire of one fifth of those Present, be entered on the Journal.

[4] Neither House, during the Session of Congress, shall, without the Consent of the other, adjourn for more than three days, nor to any other Place than that in which the two Houses shall be sitting.

Section 6. [1] The Senators and Representatives shall receive a Compensation for their Services, to be ascertained by Law, and paid out of the Treasury of the United States. They shall in all Cases, except Treason, Felony and Breach of the Peace, be privileged from Arrest during their Attendance at the Session of their respective Houses, and in going to and returning from the same; and for any Speech or Debate in either House, they shall not be questioned in any other Place.

[2] No Senator or Representative shall, during the Time for which he was elected, be appointed to any civil Office under the Authority of the United States, which shall have been created, or the Emoluments whereof shall have been encreased during such time; and no Person holding any Office under the United States, shall be a Member of either House during his Continuance in Office.

Section 7. [1] All Bills for raising Revenue shall originate in the House of Representatives; but the Senate may propose or concur with Amendments as on other Bills.

[2] Every Bill which shall have passed the House of Representatives and the Senate, shall, before it becomes a Law, be presented to the President of the United States; If he approve he shall sign it, but if not he shall return it, with his Objections to the House in which it shall have originated, who shall enter the Objections at large on their Journal, and proceed to reconsider it. If after such Reconsideration two thirds of that House shall agree to pass the Bill, it shall be sent, together with the Objections, to the other House, by which it shall likewise be reconsidered, and if approved by two thirds of that House, it shall become a Law. But in all such Cases the Votes of both Houses shall be determined by yeas and Nays, and the Names of the Persons voting for and against the Bill shall be entered on the Journal of each House respectively. If any Bill shall not be returned by the President within ten Days (Sundays excepted) after it shall have been presented to him, the Same shall be a Law, in like Manner as if he had signed it, unless the Congress by their Adjournment prevents its Return, in which Case it shall not be a Law.

[3] Every Order, Resolution, or Vote to Which the Concurrence of the Senate and House of Representatives may be necessary (except on a question of Adjournment) shall be presented to the President of the United States; and before the Same shall take Effect, shall be approved by him, or being disapproved by him, shall be repassed by two thirds of the Senate and House of Representatives, according to the Rules and Limitations prescribed in the Case of a Bill.

Section 8. [1] The Congress shall have Power To lay and collect Taxes, Duties, Imposts and Excises, to pay the Debts and provide for the common Defence and general Welfare of the United States; but all Duties, Imposts and Excises shall be uniform throughout the United States;

[2] To borrow money on the credit of the United States;

[3] To regulate Commerce with foreign Nations, and among the several States, and with the Indian Tribes;

[4] To establish an uniform Rule of Naturalization, and uniform Laws on the subject of Bankruptcies throughout the United States;

[5] To coin Money, regulate the value thereof, and of foreign Coin, and fix the Standard of Weights and Measures;

[6] To provide the Punishment of counterfeiting the Securities and current Coin of the United States;

[7] To establish Post Offices and post Roads;

[8] To promote the Progress of Science and useful Arts, by securing for limited Times to Authors and Inventors the exclusive Right to their respective Writings and Discoveries;

[9] To constitute Tribunals inferior to the supreme Court;

[10] To define and punish Piracies and Felonies committed on the high Seas, and Offenses against the Law of Nations;

[11] To declare War, grant Letters of Marque and Reprisal, and make Rules concerning Captures on Land and Water;

[12] To raise and support Armies, but no Appropriation of Money to that Use shall be for a longer Term than two Years;

[13] To provide and maintain a Navy;

[14] To make Rules for the Government and Regulation of the land and naval Forces;

[15] To provide for calling forth the Militia to execute the Laws of the Union, suppress Insurrections and repel Invasions;

[16] To provide for organizing, arming, and disciplining, the Militia, and for governing such Part of them as may be employed in the Service of the United States, reserving to the States respectively, the Appointment of the Officers, and the Authority of training the Militia according to the discipline prescribed by Congress;

[17] To exercise exclusive Legislation in all Cases whatsoever, over such District (not exceeding ten Miles square) as may, by Cession of particular States, and the Acceptance of Congress, become the Seat of the Government of the United States, and to exercise like Authority over all Places purchased by the Consent of the Legislature of the State in which the Same shall be, for the Erection of Forts, Magazines, Arsenals, dock-Yards, and other needful Buildings; — And

[18] To make all Laws which shall be necessary and proper for carrying into Execution the foregoing Powers, and all other Powers vested by this Constitution in the Government of the United States, or in any Department or Officer thereof.

Section 9. [1] The Migration or Importation of such Persons as any of the States now existing shall think proper to admit, shall not be prohibited by the Congress prior to the Year one thousand eight hundred and eight, but a Tax or duty may be imposed on such Importation, not exceeding ten dollars for each Person.

[2] The privilege of the Writ of Habeas Corpus shall not be suspended, unless when in Cases of Rebellion or Invasion the public Safety may require it.

[3] No Bill of Attainder or ex post facto Law shall be passed.

[4] No Capitation, or other direct, Tax shall be laid, unless in Proportion to the Census or Enumeration herein before directed to be taken.

[5] No Tax or Duty shall be laid on Articles exported from any State.

[6] No Preference shall be given by any Regulation of Commerce or Revenue to the Ports of one State over those of another: nor shall Vessels bound to, or from, one State, be obliged to enter, clear, or pay Duties in another.

[7] No Money shall be drawn from the Treasury, but in Consequence of Appropriations made by Law; and a regular Statement and Account of the Receipts and Expenditures of all public Money shall be published from time to time.

[8] No Title of Nobility shall be granted by the United States: And no Person holding any Office of Profit or Trust under them, shall, without the Consent of the Congress, accept of any present, Emolument, Office, or Title, of any kind whatever, from any King, Prince, or foreign State.

Section 10. [1] No State shall enter into any Treaty, Alliance, or Confederation; grant Letters of Marque and Reprisal; coin Money; emit Bills of Credit; make any Thing but gold and silver Coin a Tender in Payment of Debts; pass any Bill of Attainder, ex post facto Law, or Law impairing the Obligation of Contracts, or grant any Title of Nobility.

[2] No State shall, without the Consent of the Congress, lay any Imposts or Duties on Imports or Exports, except what may be absolutely necessary for executing its inspection Laws: and the net Produce of all Duties and Imposts, laid by any State on Imports or Exports, shall be for the Use of the Treasury of the United States; and all such Laws shall be subject to the Revision and Controul of the Congress.

[3] No State shall, without the Consent of Congress, lay any Duty of Tonnage, keep Troops, or Ships of War in time of Peace, enter into any Agreement or Compact with another State, or with a foreign Power, or engage in War, unless actually invaded, or in such imminent Danger as will not admit of delay.

ARTICLE II

Section 1. [1] The executive Power shall be vested in a President of the United States of America. He shall hold his Office during the Term of four Years, and, together with the Vice President, chosen for the same Term, be elected, as follows:

[2] Each State shall appoint, in such Manner as the Legislature thereof may direct, a Number of Electors, equal to the whole Number of Senators and Representatives to which the State may be entitled in the Congress: but no Senator or Representative, or Person holding an Office of Trust or Profit under the United States, shall be appointed an Elector.

[3] The Electors shall meet in their respective States, and vote by Ballot for two Persons, of whom one at least shall not be an Inhabitant of the same State with themselves. And they shall make a List of all the Persons voted for, and of the Number of Votes for each; which List they shall sign and certify, and transmit sealed to the Seat of the Government of the United States, directed to the President of the Senate. The President of the Senate shall, in the Presence of the Senate and House of Representatives, open all the Certificates, and the Votes shall then be counted. The Person having the greatest Number of Votes shall be the President, if such Number be a Majority of the whole Number of Electors appointed; and if there be more than one who have such Majority, and have an equal Number of Votes, then the House of Representatives shall immediately chuse by Ballot one of them for President; and if no Person have a Majority, then from the five highest on the List the said House shall in like Manner chuse the President. But in chusing the President, the Votes shall be taken by States, the Representation from each State having one Vote, a quorum for this Purpose shall consist of a Member or Members from two thirds of the States, and a Majority of all the States shall be necessary to a Choice. In every Case, after the Choice of the President, the Person having the greatest Number of Votes of the Electors shall be the Vice President. But if there should remain two or

more who have equal Votes, the Senate shall chuse from them by Ballot the Vice President.

[4] The Congress may determine the Time of chusing the Electors, and the Day on which they shall give their Votes; which Day shall be the same throughout the United States.

[5] No person except a natural born Citizen, or a Citizen of the United States, at the time of the Adoption of this Constitution, shall be eligible to the Office of President; neither shall any Person be eligible to that Office who shall not have attained to the Age of thirty five Years, and been fourteen Years a Resident within the United States.

[6] In case of the removal of the President from Office, or of his Death, Resignation or Inability to discharge the Powers and Duties of the said Office, the Same shall devolve on the Vice President, and the Congress may by Law provide for the Case of Removal, Death, Resignation or Inability, both of the President and Vice President, declaring what Officer shall then act as President, and such Officer shall act accordingly, until the Disability be removed, or a President shall be elected.

[7] The President shall, at stated Times, receive for his Services, a Compensation, which shall neither be increased nor diminished during the Period for which he shall have been elected, and he shall not receive within that Period any other Emolument from the United States, or any of them.

[8] Before he enter on the Execution of his Office, he shall take the following Oath or Affirmation: "I do solemnly swear (or affirm) that I will faithfully execute the Office of President of the United States, and will to the best of my Ability, preserve, protect and defend the Constitution of the United States."

Section 2. [1] The President shall be Commander in Chief of the Army and Navy of the United States, and of the Militia of the several States, when called into the actual Service of the United States; he may require the Opinion, in writing, of the principal Officer in each of the executive Departments, upon any subject relating to the Duties of their respective Offices, and he shall have Power to grant Reprieves and Pardons for Offenses against the United States, except in Cases of Impeachment.

[2] He shall have Power, by and with the Advice and Consent of the Senate, to make Treaties, provided two thirds of the Senators present concur; and he shall nominate, and by and with the Advice and Consent of the Senate, shall appoint Ambassadors, other public Ministers and Consuls, Judges of the supreme Court, and all other Officers of the United States, whose Appointments are not herein otherwise provided for, and which shall be established by Law: but the Congress may by Law vest the Appointment of such inferior Officers, as they think proper, in the President alone, to the Courts of Law, or in the Heads of Departments.

[3] The President shall have Power to fill up all Vacancies that may happen during the Recess of the Senate, by granting Commissions which shall expire at the End of their next Session.

Section 3. He shall from time to time give to the Congress Information of the State of the Union, and recommend to their Consideration such Measures as he shall judge necessary and expedient; he may, on extraordinary occasions, convene both Houses, or either of them, and in Case of Disagreement between them, with Respect to the time of Adjournment, he may adjourn them to such Time as he shall think proper; he shall receive Ambassadors and other public

Ministers; he shall take Care that the Laws be faithfully executed, and shall Commission all the Officers of the United States.

Section 4. The President, Vice President and all civil Officers of the United States, shall be removed from Office on Impeachment for, and Conviction of, Treason, Bribery, or other high Crimes and Misdemeanors.

ARTICLE III

Section 1. The judicial Power of the United States, shall be vested in one supreme Court, and in such inferior Courts as the Congress may from time to time ordain and establish. The Judges, both of the supreme and inferior Courts, shall hold their Offices during good Behaviour, and shall, at stated Times, receive for their Services, a Compensation, which shall not be diminished during their Continuance in Office.

Section 2. [1] The Judicial Power shall extend to all Cases, in Law and Equity, arising under this Constitution, the Laws of the United States, and Treaties made, or which shall be made, under their Authority; — to all Cases affecting Ambassadors, other public Ministers and Consuls; — to all Cases of admiralty and maritime Jurisdiction; — to Controversies to which the United States shall be a Party; — to Controversies between two or more States; — between a State and Citizens of another State; — between Citizens of different States; — between Citizens of the same State claiming Lands under Grants of different States, and between a State, or the Citizens thereof, and foreign States, Citizens or Subjects.

[2] In all Cases affecting Ambassadors, other public Ministers and Consuls, and those in which a State shall be a Party, the supreme Court shall have original Jurisdiction. In all the other Cases before mentioned, the supreme Court shall have appellate Jurisdiction, both as to Law and Fact, with such Exceptions, and under such Regulations as the Congress shall make.

[3] The trial of all Crimes, except in Cases of Impeachment, shall be by jury; and such Trial shall be held in the State where the said Crimes shall have been committed; but when not committed within any State, the Trial shall be at such Place or Places as the Congress may by Law have directed.

Section 3. [1] Treason against the United States, shall consist only in levying War against them, or in adhering to their Enemies, giving them Aid and Comfort. No person shall be convicted of Treason unless on the Testimony of two Witnesses to the same overt Act, or on Confession in open Court.

[2] The Congress shall have Power to declare the Punishment of Treason, but no Attainder of Treason shall work Corruption of Blood, or Forfeiture except during the Life of the Person attainted.

ARTICLE IV

Section 1. Full Faith and Credit shall be given in each State to the public Acts, Records, and judicial Proceedings of every other State. And the Congress may by general Laws prescribe the Manner in which such Acts, Records and Proceedings shall be proved, and the Effect thereof.

Section 2. [1] The Citizens of each State shall be entitled to all Privileges and Immunities of Citizens in the several States.

[2] A Person charged in any State with Treason, Felony, or other Crime, who shall flee from Justice, and be found in another State, shall on demand of the executive Authority of the State from which he fled, be delivered up, to be removed to the State having Jurisdiction of the Crime.

[3] No Person held to Service or Labour in one State, under the Laws thereof, escaping into another, shall, in Consequence of any Law or Regulation therein, be discharged from such Service or Labour, but shall be delivered up on Claim of the Party to whom such Service or Labour may be due.

Section 3. [1] New States may be admitted by the Congress into this Union; but no new State shall be formed or erected within the Jurisdiction of any other State; nor any State be formed by the Junction of two or more States, or Parts of States, without the Consent of the Legislatures of the States concerned as well as of the Congress.

[2] The Congress shall have Power to dispose of and make all needful Rules and Regulations respecting the Territory or other Property belonging to the United States; and nothing in this Constitution shall be so construed as to Prejudice any Claims of the United States, or of any particular State.

Section 4. The United States shall guarantee to every State in this Union a Republican Form of Government, and shall protect each of them against Invasion; and on Application of the Legislature, or of the Executive (when the Legislature cannot be convened) against domestic Violence.

ARTICLE V

The Congress, whenever two thirds of both Houses shall deem it necessary, shall propose Amendments to this Constitution, or, on the Application of the Legislatures of two thirds of the several States, shall call a Convention for proposing Amendments, which, in either Case, shall be valid to all Intents and Purposes, as part of this Constitution, when ratified by the Legislatures of three fourths of the several States, or by Conventions in three fourths thereof, as the one or the other Mode of Ratification may be proposed by the Congress; Provided that no Amendment which may be made prior to the Year One thousand eight hundred and eight shall in any Manner affect the first and fourth Clauses in the Ninth Section of the first Article; and that no State, without its Consent, shall be deprived of its equal Suffrage in the Senate.

ARTICLE VI

[1] All Debts contracted and Engagements entered into, before the Adoption of this Constitution, shall be as valid against the United States under this Constitution, as under the Confederation.

[2] This Constitution, and the Laws of the United States which shall be made in Pursuance thereof; and all Treaties made, or which shall be made, under the Authority of the United States, shall be the supreme Law of the Land; and the Judges in every State shall be bound thereby, any Thing in the Constitution or Laws of any State to the Contrary notwithstanding.

[3] The Senators and Representatives before mentioned, and the Members of

the several State Legislatures, and all executive and judicial Officers, both of the United States and of the several States, shall be bound by Oath or Affirmation, to support this Constitution; but no religious Test shall ever be required as a Qualification to any Office or public Trust under the United States.

ARTICLE VII

The Ratification of the Conventions of nine States shall be sufficient for the Establishment of this Constitution between the States so ratifying the Same.

Done in Convention by the Unanimous Consent of the States present the Seventeenth Day of September in the Year of our Lord one thousand seven hundred and Eighty seven and of the Independence of the United States of America the Twelfth.

ARTICLES IN ADDITION TO, AND AMENDMENT OF, THE CONSTITUTION OF THE UNITED STATES OF AMERICA, PROPOSED BY CONGRESS, AND RATIFIED BY THE LEGISLATURES OF THE SEVERAL STATES , PURSUANT TO THE FIFTH ARTICLE OF THE ORIGINAL CONSTITUTION

AMENDMENT I [1791]

Congress shall make no law respecting an establishment of religion, or prohibiting the free exercise thereof; or abridging the freedom of speech, or of the press; or the right of the people peaceably to assemble, and to petition the Government for a redress of grievances.

AMENDMENT II [1791]

A well regulated Militia, being necessary to the security of a free State, the right of the people to keep and bear Arms, shall not be infringed.

AMENDMENT III [1791]

No Soldier shall, in time of peace be quartered in any house, without the consent of the Owner, nor in time of war, but in a manner to be prescribed by law.

AMENDMENT IV [1791]

The right of the people to be secure in their persons, houses, papers, and effects, against unreasonable searches and seizures, shall not be violated, and no Warrants shall issue, but upon probable cause, supported by Oath or affirmation, and particularly describing the place to be searched, and the persons or things to be seized.

Amendment V [1791]

No person shall be held to answer for a capital, or otherwise infamous crime, unless on a presentment or indictment of a Grand Jury, except in cases arising in the land or naval forces, or in the Militia, when in actual service in time of War or public danger; nor shall any person be subject for the same offence to be twice put in jeopardy of life or limb; nor shall be compelled in any criminal case to be a witness against himself, nor be deprived of life, liberty, or property, without due process of law; nor shall private property be taken for public use, without just compensation.

Amendment VI [1791]

In all criminal prosecutions, the accused shall enjoy the right to a speedy and public trial, by an impartial jury of the State and district wherein the crime shall have been committed, which district shall have been previously ascertained by law, and to be informed of the nature and cause of the accusation; to be confronted with the witnesses against him; to have compulsory process for obtaining witnesses in his favor, and to have the Assistance of Counsel for his defence.

Amendment VII [1791]

In Suits at common law, where the value in controversy shall exceed twenty dollars, the right of trial by jury shall be preserved, and no fact tried by a jury, shall be otherwise re-examined in any Court of the United States, than according to the rules of the common law.

Amendment VIII [1791]

Excessive bail shall not be required, nor excessive fines imposed, nor cruel and unusual punishments inflicted.

Amendment IX [1791]

The enumeration in the Constitution, of certain rights, shall not be construed to deny or disparage others retained by the people.

Amendment X [1791]

The powers not delegated to the United States by the Constitution, nor prohibited by it to the States, are reserved to the States respectively, or to the people.

Amendment XI [1798]

The Judicial power of the United States shall not be construed to extend to any suit in law or equity, commenced or prosecuted against one of the United States by Citizens of another State, or by Citizens or Subjects of any Foreign State.

AMENDMENT XII [1804]

The Electors shall meet in their respective states and vote by ballot for President and Vice-President, one of whom, at least, shall not be an inhabitant of the same state with themselves; they shall name in their ballots the person voted for as President, and in distinct ballots the person voted for as Vice-President, and they shall make distinct lists of all persons voted for as President, and of all persons voted for as Vice-President, and of the number of votes for each, which lists they shall sign and certify, and transmit sealed to the seat of the government of the United States, directed to the President of the Senate; — The President of the Senate shall, in the presence of the Senate and House of Representatives, open all the certificates and the votes shall then be counted; — The person having the greatest number of votes for President, shall be the President, if such number be a majority of the whole number of Electors appointed; and if no person have such majority, then from the persons having the highest numbers not exceeding three on the list of those voted for as President, the House of Representatives shall choose immediately, by ballot, the President. But in choosing the President, the votes shall be taken by states, the representation from each state having one vote; a quorum for this purpose shall consist of a member or members from two-thirds of the states, and a majority of all the states shall be necessary to a choice. And if the House of Representatives shall not choose a President whenever the right of choice shall devolve upon them, before the fourth day of March next following, then the Vice-President shall act as President, as in the case of the death or other constitutional disability of the President. — The person having the greatest number of votes as Vice-President, shall be the Vice-President, if such number be a majority of the whole number of Electors appointed, and if no person have a majority, then from the two highest numbers on the list, the Senate shall choose the Vice-President; a quorum for the purpose shall consist of two-thirds of the whole number of Senators, and a majority of the whole number shall be necessary to a choice. But no person constitutionally ineligible to the office of President shall be eligible to that of Vice-President of the United States.

AMENDMENT XIII [1865]

Section 1. Neither slavery nor involuntary servitude, except as a punishment for crime whereof the party shall have been duly convicted, shall exist within the United States, or any place subject to their jurisdiction.

Section 2. Congress shall have power to enforce this article by appropriate legislation.

AMENDMENT XIV [1868]

Section 1. All persons born or naturalized in the United States, and subject to the jurisdiction thereof, are citizens of the United States and of the State wherein they reside. No State shall make or enforce any law which shall abridge the privileges or immunities of citizens of the United States; nor shall any State deprive any person of life, liberty, or property, without due process of law; nor deny to any person within its jurisdiction the equal protection of the laws.

Section 2. Representatives shall be apportioned among the several States according to their respective numbers, counting the whole number of persons in each State, excluding Indians not taxed. But when the right to vote at any election for the choice of electors for President and Vice President of the United States, Representatives in Congress, the Executive and Judicial officers of a State, or the members of the Legislature thereof, is denied to any of the male inhabitants of such State, being twenty-one years of age, and citizens of the United States, or in any way abridged, except for participation in rebellion, or other crime, the basis of representation therein shall be reduced in the proportion which the number of such male citizens shall bear to the whole number of male citizens twenty-one years of age in such State.

Section 3. No person shall be a Senator or Representative in Congress, or elector of President and Vice President, or hold any office, civil or military, under the United States, or under any State, who, having previously taken an oath, as a member of Congress, or as an officer of the United States, or as a member of any State legislature, or as an executive or judicial officer of any State, to support the Constitution of the United States, shall have engaged in insurrection or rebellion against the same, or given aid or comfort to the enemies thereof. But Congress may by a vote of two-thirds of each House, remove such disability.

Section 4. The validity of the public debt of the United States, authorized by law, including debts incurred for payment of pensions and bounties for services in suppressing insurrection or rebellion, shall not be questioned. But neither the United States nor any State shall assume or pay any debt or obligation incurred in aid of insurrection or rebellion against the United States, or any claim for the loss of emancipation of any slave; but all such debts, obligations and claims shall be held illegal and void.

Section 5. The Congress shall have power to enforce, by appropriate legislation, the provisions of this article.

AMENDMENT XV [1870]

Section 1. The right of citizens of the United States to vote shall not be denied or abridged by the United States or by any State on account of race, color, or previous condition of servitude.

Section 2. The Congress shall have power to enforce this article by appropriate legislation.

AMENDMENT XVI [1913]

The Congress shall have power to lay and collect taxes on incomes, from whatever source derived, without apportionment among the several States, and without regard to any census or enumeration.

AMENDMENT XVII [1913]

[1] The Senate of the United States shall be composed of two Senators from each State, elected by the people thereof, for six years, and each Senator shall

have one vote. The electors in each State shall have the qualifications requisite for electors of the most numerous branch of the State legislatures.

[2] When vacancies happen in the representation of any State in the Senate, the executive authority of such State shall issue writs of election to fill such vacancies: *Provided*, That the legislature of any State may empower the executive thereof to make temporary appointments until the people fill the vacancies by election as the legislature may direct.

[3] This amendment shall not be so construed as to affect the election or term of any Senator chosen before it becomes valid as part of the Constitution.

AMENDMENT XVIII [1919]

Section 1. After one year from the ratification of this article the manufacture, sale, or transportation of intoxicating liquors within, the importation thereof into, or the exportation thereof from the United States and all territory subject to the jurisdiction thereof for beverage purposes is hereby prohibited.

Section 2. The Congress and the several States shall have concurrent power to enforce this article by appropriate legislation.

Section 3. This article shall be inoperative unless it shall have been ratified as an amendment to the Constitution by the legislatures of the several States, as provided in the Constitution, within seven years from the date of the submission hereof to the States by the Congress.

AMENDMENT XIX [1920]

[1] The right of citizens of the United States to vote shall not be denied or abridged by the United States or by any State on account of sex.

[2] Congress shall have power to enforce this article by appropriate legislation.

AMENDMENT XX [1933]

Section 1. The terms of the President and Vice President shall end at noon on the 20th day of January, and the terms of Senators and Representatives at noon on the 3d day of January, of the years in which such terms would have ended if this article had not been ratified; and the terms of their successors shall then begin.

Section 2. The Congress shall assemble at least once in every year, and such meeting shall begin at noon on the 3d day of January, unless they shall by law appoint a different day.

Section 3. If, at the time fixed for the beginning of the term of the President, the President elect shall have died, the Vice President elect shall become President. If a President shall not have been chosen before the time fixed for the beginning of his term, or if the President elect shall have failed to qualify, then the Vice President elect shall act as President until a President shall have qualified; and the Congress may by law provide for the case wherein neither a President elect nor a Vice President elect shall have qualified, declaring who shall then act as President, or the manner in which one who is to act shall be selected, and such person shall act accordingly until a President or Vice President shall have qualified.

Section 4. The Congress may by law provide for the case of the death of any of the persons from whom the House of Representatives may choose a President whenever the right of choice shall have devolved upon them, and for the case of the death of any of the persons from whom the Senate may choose a Vice President whenever the right of choice shall have devolved upon them.

Section 5. Sections 1 and 2 shall take effect on the 15th day of October following the ratification of this article.

Section 6. This article shall be inoperative unless it shall have been ratified as an amendment to the Constitution by the legislatures of three-fourths of the several States within seven years from the date of its submission.

Amendment XXI [1933]

Section 1. The eighteenth article of amendment to the Constitution of the United States is hereby repealed.

Section 2. The transportation or importation into any State, Territory, or possession of the United States for delivery or use therein of intoxicating liquors, in violation of the laws thereof, is hereby prohibited.

Section 3. This article shall be inoperative unless it shall have been ratified as an amendment to the Constitution by conventions in the several States, as provided in the Constitution, within seven years from the date of the submission hereof to the States by the Congress.

Amendment XXII [1951]

Section 1. No person shall be elected to the office of the President more than twice, and no person who has held the office of President, or acted as President, for more than two years of a term to which some other person was elected President shall be elected to the office of the President more than once. But this Article shall not apply to any person holding the office of President when this Article was proposed by the Congress, and shall not prevent any person who may be holding the office of President, or acting as President, during the term within which the Article becomes operative from holding the office of President or acting as President during the remainder of such term.

Section 2. This article shall be inoperative unless it shall have been ratified as an amendment to the Constitution by the legislatures of three-fourths of the several States within seven years from the date of its submission to the States by the Congress.

Amendment XXIII [1961]

Section 1. The District constituting the seat of Government of the United States shall appoint in such manner as the Congress may direct:

A number of electors of President and Vice President equal to the whole number of Senators and Representatives in Congress to which the District would be entitled if it were a State, but in no event more than the least populous State; they shall be in addition to those appointed by the States, but they shall be considered, for the purposes of the election of President and Vice President, to be electors appointed by a State; and they shall meet in the District and perform such duties as provided by the twelfth article of amendment.

Section 2. The Congress shall have power to enforce this article by appropriate legislation.

AMENDMENT XXIV [1964]

Section 1. The right of citizens of the United States to vote in any primary or other election for President or Vice President, for electors for President or Vice President, or for Senator or Representative in Congress, shall not be denied or abridged by the United States or any State by reason of failure to pay any poll tax or other tax.

Section 2. The Congress shall have power to enforce this article by appropriate legislation.

AMENDMENT XXV [1967]

Section 1. In case of the removal of the President from office or of his death or resignation, the Vice President shall become President.

Section 2. Whenever there is a vacancy in the office of the Vice President, the President shall nominate a Vice President who shall take office upon confirmation by a majority vote of both Houses of Congress.

Section 3. Whenever the President transmits to the President pro tempore of the Senate and the Speaker of the House of Representatives his written declaration that he is unable to discharge the powers and duties of his office, and until he transmits to them a written declaration to the contrary, such powers and duties shall be discharged by the Vice President as Acting President.

Section 4. Whenever the Vice President and a Majority of either the principal officers of the executive departments or of such other body as Congress may by law provide, transmit to the President pro tempore of the Senate and the Speaker of the House of Representatives their written declaration that the President is unable to discharge the powers and duties of his office, the Vice President shall immediately assume the powers and duties of the office as Acting President.

Thereafter, when the President transmits to the President pro tempore of the Senate and the Speaker of the House of Representatives his written declaration that no inability exists, he shall resume the powers and duties of his office unless the Vice President and a majority of either the principal officers of the executive department or of such other body as Congress may by law provide, transmit within four days to the President pro tempore of the Senate and the Speaker of the House of Representatives their written declaration that the President is unable to discharge the powers and duties of his office. Thereupon Congress shall decide the issue, assembling within forty-eight hours for that purpose if not in session. If the Congress, within twenty-one days after receipt of the latter written declaration, or, if Congress is not in session, within twenty-one days after Congress is required to assemble, determines by two-thirds vote of both Houses that the President is unable to discharge the powers and duties of his office, the Vice President shall continue to discharge the same as Acting President; otherwise, the President shall resume the powers and duties of his office.

AMENDMENT XXVI [1971]

Section 1. The right of citizens of the United States, who are eighteen years of age or older, to vote shall not be denied or abridged by the United States or by any State on account of age.

Section 2. The Congress shall have power to enforce this article by appropriate legislation.

AMENDMENT XXVII [1992]

No law varying the Compensation for the services of the Senators and Representatives shall take effect, unless an election of Representatives shall have intervened.

Biographical Notes

on Selected U.S.

Supreme Court Justices

The brief sketches that follow are designed to offer at least some sense of the background, personality, and intellectual style of the justices who have had the greatest impact on modern constitutional law. Because they are no substitute for serious biography, we have frequently suggested additional sources for further investigation. On less significant justices, see Currie, The Most Insignificant Justice: A Preliminary Inquiry, 50 U. Chi. L. Rev. 466 (1983); Easterbrook, The Most Insignificant Justice: Further Evidence, 50 U. Chi. L. Rev. 481 (1983).

HUGO L. BLACK (1886-1971): In 1937, President Roosevelt chose Hugo Black to fill the first available vacancy on the Court. A southern progressive who had defended the rights of labor organizers and investigated police brutality before coming to Washington, Black served in the U.S. Senate for ten years prior to his appointment. As a senator, he strongly defended New Deal programs, including Roosevelt's "Court-packing" plan. Shortly after his confirmation he became the subject of controversy when it was revealed that he had belonged to the Ku Klux Klan for two years in the 1920s. The controversy subsided after Black, in a dramatic radio address, admitted his prior membership, but added that he had resigned many years before and would comment no further. As a justice, Black was known for his insistence on what he claimed to be literal enforcement of constitutional guarantees, especially the first amendment guarantee of free speech. Although frequently characterized as an "activist" because of his willingness to subject to intensive review legislation that arguably violated express constitutional provisions, Black himself thought that literalism was necessary to confine judicial power. Thus, his insistence that the fourteenth amendment incorporated and made applicable to the states the guarantees of the first eight amendments was premised in part on his belief that any other approach would leave justices free to read their own values into the Constitution. See Adamson v. California, 332 U.S. 46 (1947). Consistent with this view, in cases such as Griswold v. Connecticut, 381 U.S. 479 (1965), Black rejected the notion that the Constitution contained general guarantees of "privacy" or "natural rights" beyond those expressly articulated in the text. See G. Dunne, Hugo Black and the Judicial Revolution (1977).

HARRY A. BLACKMUN (1908-1999): Harry Blackmun was President Nixon's third choice to fill the seat vacated when Abe Fortas resigned in 1970. After failing to secure confirmation of Clement Haynsworth of South Carolina and G. Harrold Carswell of Florida, Nixon announced that the Senate "as it is presently constituted" would not confirm a southerner and turned to Blackmun, a judge on the Eighth Circuit Court of Appeals. A boyhood friend of Chief Justice Burger, Blackmun was quickly dubbed "the Minnesota Twin" by the press. During his early years on the Court, he regularly voted with the chief justice. Later he distanced himself from the Court's conservative bloc and increasingly joined Justices Marshall and Brennan in dissent. Blackmun is best known for his majority opinion in Roe v. Wade, 410 U.S. 113 (1973), upholding the constitutional right of women to decide for themselves whether to have an abortion. It has been suggested that the opinion was influenced by Blackmun's experience before joining the Court as house counsel for the Mayo Clinic, where he frequently advised doctors and defended their right to make medical judgments.

JOSEPH P. BRADLEY (1813-1892): The oldest of eleven children, Joseph Bradley was raised in poverty on a small farm. As a lawyer, he specialized in corporate and commercial law and represented several railroads. A Whig before the Civil War, Bradley was an avid supporter of the Union cause and became identified with the radical wing of the Republican Party in the postwar period. His appointment to the Court by President Grant in 1870 was later the subject of controversy because it made possible the reversal of the Court's earlier decision involving the validity of the Civil War legal tender acts. Compare Hepburn v. Griswold, 75 U.S. (8 Wall.) 603 (1870) with The Legal Tender Cases, 79 U.S. (12 Wall.) 457 (1871). As a justice, Bradley supported the power of Congress to regulate the interstate movement of goods, even if the regulation limited state authority. His dissent in The Slaughter-House Cases, 83 U.S. (16 Wall.) 36 (1873), also showed a willingness to read the newly enacted fourteenth amendment as an important expansion of federal authority. In 1877, Bradley was a last-minute substitute on the electoral commission established to resolve the disputed presidential election of 1876. With the commission deadlocked seven to seven, Bradley cast the deciding vote to make Rutherford B. Hayes the President. See G. White, The American Judicial Tradition ch. 4 (1976); Fairman, Mr. Justice Bradley, in A. Dunham & P. Kurland, Mr. Justice 65-93 (1956).

LOUIS D. BRANDEIS (1856-1941): The son of Jewish immigrants from Bohemia, Louis Brandeis successfully practiced law in Boston for forty years before his nomination to the Court. Although he became wealthy from his practice, Brandeis preferred to live simply and set a ceiling on personal expenditures of one-fifth of his income. Even after his appointment to the Court, he provided financial support for the work of his proteges, one of whom was Felix Frankfurter. He devoted himself to a host of public causes. He defended municipal control of Boston's subway system, opposed monopolistic practices of the New Haven Railroad, arbitrated labor disputes in New York's garment industry, and argued in support of the constitutionality of state maximum hour and minimum wage statutes. His nomination to the Court by President Wilson in 1916 sparked heated opposition, including protests from seven ex-presidents of the American Bar Association. During his long tenure on the Court, Brandeis insisted on respect for jurisdictional and procedural limitations on the Court's power. His distrust of large and powerful institutions, and of dogmatic adherence to the received wisdom, led him to support the constitutional authority of the states to experiment with unconventional social and economic theories. He also frequently dissented from the Court's conservative majority when it blocked efforts of the federal government to intervene in the economy. Some of his most eloquent opinions, however, were written in defense of limits on governmental power when civil liberties were at issue. His famous concurring opinion in Whitney v. California, 274 U.S. 357 (1927), argued for freedom of expression on the ground that "it is hazardous to discourage thought, hope and imagination; that fear breeds repression; that repression breeds hate; that hate menaces stable government; that the path of safety lies in the opportunity to discuss freely supposed grievances and proposed remedies; and that the fitting remedy for evil counsels is good ones." And in Olmstead v. United States, 277 U.S. 438 (1928), Brandeis dissented from the Court's refusal to condemn wiretapping, noting that "[o]ur Government is the potent, the omnipresent teacher. For good or for ill, it teaches the whole people by its example." See L. Paper, Brandeis (1983); M. Urofsky, A Mind of One Piece: Brandeis and American Reform (1971).

WILLIAM J. BRENNAN, JR. (1906-1997): After graduating from Harvard Law School, William Brennan returned to his native Newark, where he joined a prominent law firm and specialized in labor law. As his practice grew, Brennan, a devoted family man, resented the demands it made on his time and accepted an appointment on the New Jersey Superior Court in order to lessen his workload. Brennan attracted attention as an efficient and fair-minded judge and was elevated to the New Jersey Supreme Court in 1952. President Eisenhower appointed him to the Supreme Court in 1956. The appointment was criticized at the time as "political" on the ground that the nomination of a Catholic Democrat on the eve of the 1956 presidential election was intended to win votes. Once on the Court, Justice Brennan firmly established himself as a leader of the "liberal" wing. He authored important opinions in the areas of free expression, criminal procedure, and reapportionment. Often credited with providing critical behind-the-scenes leadership during the Warren Court years, Brennan continued to play a significant role — although more often as a dissenter lamenting what he believed to be the evisceration of Warren Court precedents — as the ideological complexion of the Court shifted in the 1970s and 1980s. Brennan's own spirit is perhaps best captured in his celebration in New York Times v. Sullivan, 376 U.S. 255 (1964), of "our profound national commitment to the principle that debate on public issues should be uninhibited, robust, and wide-open."

STEPHEN G. BREYER (1938-): Prior to his appointment to the Supreme Court, Stephen Breyer had compiled a distinguished record as a legal academic and in all three branches of the federal government. Educated at Oxford and Harvard Law School, he served as law clerk to Justice Arthur Goldberg and in the Justice Department before returning to Harvard to teach. During leaves of absence, he worked for Watergate Special Counsel Archibald Cox and served as chief counsel to the Senate Judiciary Committee. In 1980, President Carter named him to the U.S. Court of Appeals. As chief judge of the First Circuit,

Breyer gained a reputation for his ability to forge consensus and to write opinions that were clear, concise, and trenchant. An expert on administrative law and an author of important works about risk assessment, Breyer is a cautious and thoughtful moderate who is known for his pragmatism, his erudition, and his willingness to rethink old ideas.

WARREN E. BURGER (1907-1995): The son of financially hard-pressed parents, Warren Burger attended college and law school at night while selling life insurance during the day. After graduation, he entered private practice and assisted Harold Stassen in his unsuccessful bid for the Republican presidential nomination in 1948. In 1953, he came to Washington to serve as assistant attorney general for the Civil Division of the Justice Department. While in that post, he attracted public attention by defending the government's dismissal of John F. Peters for disloyalty after Solicitor General Sobeloff refused to argue the case on grounds of conscience. Shortly thereafter President Eisenhower appointed him to the U.S. Court of Appeals for the District of Columbia Circuit. His tenure on that court was marked by sharp clashes with the court's liberal majority, especially over criminal justice issues. In 1969, President Nixon named Burger chief justice to replace Earl Warren. A strong advocate of "strict construction" and a "plain meaning" approach to statutory and constitutional interpretation, Burger firmly identified himself with the Court's conservative wing and often voted to limit Warren Court decisions. But he also authored important opinions upholding the right of trial judges to order busing as a remedy for school segregation, interpreting federal civil rights statutes as imposing an "effects" test for employment discrimination, and upholding the right of the press to remain free of prior restraints in covering criminal trials. Burger wrote for a unanimous Court in United States v. Nixon, 418 U.S. 683 (1974), upholding the subpoena for the Watergate tapes, which a few days later resulted in President Nixon's resignation. The Court's legacy under his leadership is much disputed, with some seeing continuity with the Warren Court years and others claiming that he began a period of substantial retrenchment.

BENJAMIN N. CARDOZO (1870-1938): The son of a Tammany Hall judge who was implicated in the Boss Tweed scandal and resigned, rather than face impeachment, Benjamin Cardozo began his judicial career by narrowly defeating a Tammany candidate for a position on the New York Supreme Court. Shortly thereafter he was appointed to the New York Court of Appeals, where he served for eighteen years, during the last six of which he was chief judge. Cardozo is probably best remembered for his skills as a state common law judge. He was responsible for making the New York Court of Appeals the most respected state court in the country, and his judicial writings and lectures were immensely influential. Upon Justice Holmes's retirement, President Hoover was inundated with requests that Cardozo be elevated to the Supreme Court. But there were already two New Yorkers and one Jew serving on the Court, and Hoover resisted. Only when Justice Stone offered to resign to make way for Cardozo did the President relent. Cardozo was a bachelor who had very few friends and lived for most of his life with his unmarried sister. Called "the hermit philosopher" by some, Cardozo was remembered by others for "the strangely compelling power of [his] reticent, sensitive almost mystical personality." See R. Posner, Cardozo, A Study in Reputation (1990); G. Hellman, Benjamin N. Cardozo (1940).

WILLIAM O. DOUGLAS (1898-1980): Widely regarded as one of the most brilliant, eccentric, and independent persons to serve on the Court, William Douglas sat as an associate justice for thirty-six years, seven months — longer than any other justice. Born in poverty in Minnesota, he spent his early years in Yakima, Washington. Although financially hard pressed, he managed to go east to study law at Columbia Law School, where he taught before joining the Yale faculty in 1929. President Roosevelt named him to the newly created Securities and Exchange Commission in 1934, and Douglas became its chairman in 1937. Roosevelt nominated him to be an associate justice in 1939. Douglas's early opinions gave little hint of the controversy that would surround him in later years. Indeed, Roosevelt came close to choosing him as his running mate in 1944 — a decision that would have made him President on Roosevelt's death a year later. In subsequent years, however, Douglas's controversial statements both on and off the bench, his strong support for unpopular political causes, and his unconventional lifestyle (he was married four times) stirred up a whirlwind of political opposition. Congress twice began impeachment proceedings against him, although neither effort came close to success. A prodigiously rapid worker, Douglas often ridiculed his colleagues for complaining about the Court's workload. By his own account, he once assisted a colleague who had fallen behind in his work by ghost-writing a majority opinion that responded to his own dissent. He often finished his work for the term early and retreated to his nearly inaccessible summer home in Yakima, to which lawyers were forced to trek when emergency matters arose. Critics claimed that his opinions showed the signs of haste; admirers emphasized the forceful, blunt manner in which he cut through legal doctrine to reach the core issue in a case. His opinions were marked by a fierce commitment to individual rights and distrust of government power. See V. Countryman, Douglas of the Supreme Court (1959); W. Douglas, The Court Years 1939-1975 (1980); W. Douglas, Go East Young Man (1974).

STEPHEN J. FIELD (1816-1899): In 1863, Congress authorized an additional seat on the Court in part to assure a majority sympathetic to the Union cause in the Civil War. President Lincoln named Stephen Field, a Democrat who had nonetheless staunchly opposed secession, to fill the seat. Field was part of an illustrious family: His brothers included a well-known politician and lawyer, a widely read author, and a famous entrepreneur; he served for the last seven years of his tenure on the Court with his nephew, Justice Brewer; his niece was Anita Whitney, the left-wing activist who gained notoriety in Whitney v. California, 274 U.S. 357 (1927). Justice Field himself was personally involved in a landmark Supreme Court case. When his personal bodyguard killed former Chief Justice Terry of the California Supreme Court, allegedly while defending Justice Field's life, the ensuing litigation ended in In re Neagle, 135 U.S. 1 (1890). In light of the circumstances surrounding his appointment, it was ironic that, once on the Court, Field tended to defend the South in particular and state sovereignty in general against extension of federal power during the Reconstruction period. In the period before substantive due process secured majority support on the Court, Field sought to provide constitutional protection for business enterprises. His dissenting opinion in The Slaughter-House Cases, 83 U.S. (16 Wall.) 36 (1873), for example, read the fourteenth amendment as providing significant protection to property rights and was an important precursor of Lochner v. New York, 198 U.S. 45 (1905). By the time of his retirement in 1897, Field had surpassed John Marshall's record for length of service. See C. Swisher, Stephen J. Field: Craftsman of the Law (1930).

ABE FORTAS (1910-1984): Founder of the Washington law firm Arnold, Fortas, and Porter, Abe Fortas provided behind-the-scenes advice to Democratic politicians for years before his appointment to the Court in 1965. As a young man, Fortas held a series of jobs in the Roosevelt administration, including under-secretary of the interior under Harold Ickes. After entering private practice, Fortas found time to defend victims of McCarthyism and to litigate several important civil rights cases, including Gideon v. Wainwright, 372 U.S. 335 (1963). In 1948, Fortas successfully represented Congressman Lyndon Johnson when his forty-eight-vote victory in the Democratic senatorial primary was challenged. (The election earned Johnson the nickname "Landslide Lyndon.") Fortas became one of Johnson's close friends, and when Justice Goldberg resigned to become United Nations ambassador, Johnson appointed him to the Court. In 1968, when Chief Justice Warren indicated that he intended to retire, Johnson chose Fortas as Warren's successor. The nomination had long-term consequences that neither man could have foreseen. Republicans and conservative Democrats charged Johnson with "cronyism" and ultimately forced him to withdraw the nomination, but not before it was revealed that Fortas had received $15,000 to teach a course at a local university while on the bench. The next year Life magazine revealed that Fortas had accepted and then returned $20,000 from a charitable foundation controlled by the family of an indicted stock manipulator. Although denying any wrongdoing, Fortas resigned from the Court. As a consequence, President Nixon was able to fill two vacancies early in his term, thereby helping to fulfill his campaign promise to "roll back" the Warren Court revolution. See L. Kalman, Abe Fortas: A Biography (1990); B. Murphy, Fortas: The Rise and Ruin of a Supreme Court Justice (1988).

FELIX FRANKFURTER (1882-1965): An immigrant from Austria, Felix Frankfurter grew up in poverty on New York's lower east side. Before his appointment to the Court by President Roosevelt in 1939, he taught at the Harvard Law School, helped found The New Republic, served in a variety of public positions, and provided important, informal advice to Roosevelt in formulating the New Deal. Frankfurter's scholarly writings contributed significantly to understanding of administrative law, labor law, and the relationship between federal and state courts. As a justice, Frankfurter's career was marked by a preoccupation with problems of judicial legitimacy and self-restraint. He frequently clashed with Justices Douglas and Black, also Roosevelt appointees, over the "preferred position" of the first amendment and the incorporation doctrine. His concern over the countermajoritarian aspect of judicial review led him to argue for deference to legislative judgment in such landmark cases as Dennis v. United States, 341 U.S. 494 (1951), and Baker v. Carr, 369 U.S. 186 (1962). See P. Kurland, Felix Frankfurter on the Supreme Court (1970); J. Lash, From the Diaries of Felix Frankfurter (1974).

RUTH BADER GINSBURG (1933-): When Ruth Bader Ginsburg graduated from law school, one of her mentors suggested to Justice Felix Frankfurter that he take her on as a law clerk. Despite Ginsburg's brilliant law school record (earned while caring for an infant daughter), Justice Frankfurter told her sponsor that he just was not ready to hire a woman. Thirty-three years after this rebuff, Ginsburg assumed her seat on the Supreme Court. In the intervening years, Ginsburg gained fame as the first tenured woman professor at the Columbia Law School; as the director of the Women's Rights Project of the American Civil Liberties Union, where she won many pioneering victories in the legal battle against gender discrimination; and as a judge on the U.S. Court of Appeals for the District of Columbia Circuit. She has been called "the Thurgood Marshall of gender equality law" and is said to be "as responsible as any one person for legal advances that women made under the Equal Protection Clause." As a lower court judge, however, she gained a reputation for caution and sometimes disappointed her more activist supporters. A strong defender of abortion rights, she has nonetheless criticized Roe v. Wade for rejecting a narrower approach to the abortion question that might have "served to reduce rather than to fuel controversy."

JOHN MARSHALL HARLAN (1833-1911): Although a slaveholder and a member of the southern aristocracy, John Harlan remained loyal to the Union during the Civil War and commanded a regiment of Kentucky volunteers in the Union forces. At a critical moment in the deadlocked Republican convention of 1876, Harlan threw the support of the Kentucky delegation behind Rutherford B. Hayes, who rewarded him a year later with an appointment to the Court. Before his appointment, Harlan opposed the postwar amendments ending slavery and guaranteeing equal rights for blacks. (He opposed Lincoln and supported Democrat John McClellan in the 1864 presidential election.) Once on the Court, however, he advocated a broad reading of these amendments. His famous dissenting opinions in The Civil Rights Cases, 109 U.S: 3 (1883), and Plessy v. Ferguson, 163 U.S. 537 (1896), argued for Congress's power to defend the newly freed slaves from "private" discrimination and against the constitutionality of state-mandated separation of the races. It was in *Plessy* that Harlan declared that "[o]ur Constitution is color blind" and rightly predicted that "the judgment this day rendered will, in time, prove to be quite as pernicious as the decision . . . in the *Dred Scott* case." Well known for his distinctive personal style, Harlan often delivered his opinions extemporaneously in the fashion of an oldtime Kentucky stump speed. Justice Holmes described him as "the last of the tobacco-spitting judges." See F. Latham, The Great Dissenter: John Marshall Harlan (1970).

JOHN MARSHALL HARLAN (1899-1971): The grandson of the first Justice Harlan, John Harlan was appointed to the Court by President Eisenhower in 1955. Before his appointment, Harlan spent a quarter of a century in practice with a prominent Wall Street law firm, served as chief counsel to the New York State Crime Commission, and sat briefly on the Court of Appeals for the Second Circuit. On the Court, Justice Harlan became the intellectual leader of the "conservative" wing, often dissenting from "activist" decisions during the stewardship of Chief Justice Warren. He defended the values of federalism and never accepted the incorporation of the bill of rights against the states. Nor was he ever reconciled to the Court's broad reading of the equal protection clause, especially when strict scrutiny was utilized to defend "fundamental" values. There was also a strong libertarian strain in Justice Harlan's opinions, however. His belief in federalism and rejection of "judicial activism" did not prevent him from finding, for example, that the due process clause precluded the states from restricting the use of contraceptives by married couples. He also wrote for the Court in a series of important first amendment decisions, narrowly construing federal statutes prohibiting subversive advocacy and defending the right of a Vietnam War protestor to wear a jacket inscribed with the message "Fuck the Draft." It was in the latter case that Harlan proclaimed that "one man's vulgarity is another's lyric." During his tenure, Harlan was widely respected, even by opponents of his philosophy, for his thoroughness, candor, and civility. Although he often disagreed publicly with Justice Black, they were close friends in private. They were hospitalized together during their final illnesses and died within a short period of each other. See D. Shapiro, The Evolution of a Judicial Philosophy: Selected Opinions and Papers of Justice John M. Harlan (1969).

OLIVER WENDELL HOLMES, JR. (1841-1935): Oliver Wendell Holmes, the son of a famous poet and essayist, survived three wounds in the Civil War. He had already enjoyed a distinguished career as a practitioner, author, professor, and justice on the Supreme Judicial Court of Massachusetts before his appointment to the Supreme Court by President Roosevelt in 1902. Holmes, then sixty-two years old, seemed to be at the close of his career. A life-long Republican, he was expected to be a loyal supporter of the President on the bench. Few could have anticipated that he would serve on the Court for twenty-nine years, that his tenure would be marked by a fierce independence, and that he would exercise virtually unparalleled influence over modern constitutional theory. Holmes is perhaps best remembered for his formulation of the "clear and present danger test" for subversive advocacy and his rejection of substantive due process as a limitation on state social and economic legislation. His judicial philosophy was marked by skepticism, particularism, and pragmatism. He doubted that general propositions decided particular cases or that broad value judgments could be objectively defended. He thought that the law was necessarily unconcerned with the thought processes of those it regulated, and that it had no independent existence apart from what people did in response to what judges said. For twenty-five years, he walked daily the two and one-half miles from his home to the Court, never missing a session. He finally retired at ninety years of age and died two days before his ninety-fourth birthday. See G. White, Justice Oliver Wendell Holmes: Law and the Inner Self (1993); M. Howe, Justice Oliver Wendell Holmes: The Proving Years (1963); M. Howe, Justice Oliver Wendell Holmes: The Shaping Years (1957).

CHARLES EVANS HUGHES (1862-1948): After defeating William Randolph Hearst for the governorship of New York, Charles Evans Hughes served as governor for one term and part of another until 1910, when President Taft appointed him to the Court. In 1916, Hughes resigned to run for the presidency on the Republican and Progressive tickets against Woodrow Wilson. On election eve, he went to bed thinking that he was President, but when the final returns were counted, he had lost by a scant twenty-three electoral votes. Hughes returned to New York law practice until President Harding appointed him secretary of state. In 1930, President Hoover returned Hughes to the Court, this time as chief justice. Hughes served as chief justice during the tumultuous eleven-year period when the Court blocked much of President Roosevelt's New Deal, then survived a direct attack on its independence, and finally reconciled itself to the fundamental changes wrought by Roosevelt's program. Throughout this period, Hughes occupied a centrist position. Although closely identified with the conservative New York bar, he often joined the liberals on the Court who dissented from invalidation of social and economic legislation. But he also defended the institutional independence of the Court when it was attacked by President Roosevelt. At a crucial point in the "Court-packing" controversy, Hughes sent a letter to Senator Wheeler arguing that the Court was current in its work, and that the addition of new justices would create serious inefficiencies. Upon his retirement in 1941, Justice Frankfurter likened his leadership ability to that of "Toscanini lead[ing] an orchestra." See M. Pusey, Charles Evans Hughes (1951).

ROBERT H. JACKSON (1892-1954): A skillful advocate and brilliant legal stylist, Robert Jackson rose quickly in the early Roosevelt administration, eventually becoming one of President Roosevelt's closest advisors. After serving as counsel to the Internal Revenue Bureau, where he won a $750,000 judgment against former Treasury Secretary Andrew W. Mellon, Jackson served successively as assistant attorney general, solicitor general, and attorney general. President Roosevelt named him to the Supreme Court in 1941 to fill the seat vacated by Justice Stone when Stone was appointed chief justice. Jackson is perhaps best remembered for his graceful prose and his subtle and original efforts to articulate a coherent theory of separation of powers in his opinions in such cases as Youngstown Sheet & Tube Co. v. Sawyer, 342 U.S. 579 (1952), and Korematsu v. United States, 323 U.S. 214 (1944). In 1945, while still on the Court, Jackson served as the chief U.S. prosecutor at the Nuremburg war crimes trial. This exposure to German fascism may have influenced Jackson's subsequent approach to constitutional interpretation. Many of his later first amendment opinions, for example, were preoccupied with the attempt to draw a bright line between protected freedom of conscience and unprotected speech that threatened the public peace and order. Jackson's willingness to permit government regulation of subversive or abusive advocacy in cases such as Dennis v. United States, 341 U.S. 494 (1951), and Terminiello v. Chicago, 337 U.S. 1 (1949), brought him into sharp conflict with Justices Black and Douglas — conflict that was exacerbated by deteriorating personal relationships. When Chief Justice Stone died, it was reported that several justices threatened to resign if Jackson was elevated to the chief justiceship. Jackson never became chief justice, but remained on the Court until his death in 1954. See E. Gerhart, America's Advocate: Robert H. Jackson (1958); G. White, The American Judicial Tradition ch. 11 (1976).

ANTHONY M. KENNEDY (1936-): President Reagan's effort to fill the seat vacated by the retirement of Justice Powell, who was widely viewed as a "swing vote" on a number of important issues, sparked an extraordinary controversy about the future direction of the Supreme Court. His first nominee, Robert Bork, was defeated on the Senate floor after a long and bitter debate that pitted "originalists" against those who would treat the Constitution as incorporating values not directly derived from the text. His second nominee, Douglas Ginsburg, was forced to withdraw from consideration after it was revealed that he had used marijuana. In the wake of these events, the Senate greeted with relief the nomination of Anthony Kennedy, a relatively colorless and nonideological conservative. After graduating from Harvard Law School in 1961, Kennedy worked as a lawyer and lobbyist in California until his appointment to the Ninth Circuit by President Ford in 1975. Since joining the Supreme Court, he has been a reliable conservative. He criticized his colleagues for "trivializing constitutional adjudication" by engaging in a "jurisprudence of minutiae" in its enforcement of the establishment clause and for moving "from 'separate but equal' to 'unequal but benign'" in upholding an affirmative action plan. However, he joined some of his liberal colleagues when he twice cast the deciding vote to uphold the first amendment right of protestors to burn the American flag and disappointed some of his conservative supporters when he coauthored a joint opinion with Justices Souter and O'Connor declining to overrule Roe v. Wade.

JOHN MARSHALL (1755-1835): A century and a half after his death, John Marshall remains perhaps the most important single figure in American constitutional history. Born in a log cabin on the Virginia frontier, he served in the Continental Army during the Revolutionary War. After only the briefest formal instruction, he began the practice of law, specializing in the defense of Virginians against British creditors. Before entering public life, Marshall himself was constantly hounded by creditors. He wrote his five-volume biography of George Washington in an unsuccessful effort to raise money to pay off his debts. In 1799, Marshall entered the House of Representatives, and the following year he became secretary of state in the Adams administration. During his brief tenure, he signed and sealed, but failed to deliver, the famous commission naming William Marbury justice of the peace for the District of Columbia. In 1800, Adams appointed Marshall chief justice after John Jay, the Court's first chief justice, declined reappointment to the position. Marshall served for thirty-four years, participated in more than one thousand decisions, and wrote over five hundred opinions. He is best remembered for establishing the Court's power to declare congressional statutes unconstitutional in Marbury v. Madison, 5 U.S. (1 Cranch) 137 (1803), although his contemporaries found the portion of *Marbury* asserting judicial control over presidential appointees much more controversial. But in some ways his *refusal* to invalidate a statute enacted pursuant to Congress's powers in McCulloch v. Maryland, 17 U.S. (4 Wheat.) 316 (1819), and his willingness to strike down *state* statutes interfering with federal powers or individual rights in such cases as *McCulloch*, Gibbons v. Ogden, 22 U.S. (9 Wheat.) 1 (1824), and Fletcher v. Peck, 10 U.S. (6 Cranch) 87 (1810), were even more influential on modern constitutional theory. In 1807, Marshall presided over the treason trial of former Vice President Aaron Burr. In the course of that trial, he signed the famous subpoena directing President Jefferson to produce various documents relevant to the trial — a precedent much cited over a century and a half later when Richard Nixon asserted "executive privilege" to resist a judicial subpoena. See L. Baker, John Marshall: A Life in the Law (1974); A. Beveridge, The Life of John Marshall (1916).

THURGOOD MARSHALL (1908-1993): The son of a primary school teacher and a club steward, Thurgood Marshall became the first black to serve on the Court when he was appointed by President Johnson in 1967. But Marshall had already made an enduring mark on American legal history decades before his judicial career began. After graduating first in his class from Howard Law School, Marshall began his long involvement with the National Association for the Advancement of Colored People. For two decades, he traveled across the country coordinating the NAACP's attack on segregation in housing, employment, voting, public accommodations, and especially education. His most famous victory during this period came in Brown v. Board of Education, 347 U.S.

483 (1954), where he successfully argued that segregated public education violated the equal protection clause. In 1961, President Kennedy nominated him to serve on the U.S. Court of Appeals for the Second Circuit. Although southern senators blocked his confirmation for a year, he finally assumed his seat, where he served until 1965 when President Johnson appointed him solicitor general. As a justice, Marshall was known primarily for his unstinting defense of racial and other minorities, his liberal interpretation of free speech and press guarantees, his "multi-tiered" theory of equal protection analysis, and his fervent opposition to capital punishment. See M. Tushnet, Making Civil Rights Law: Thurgood Marshall and the Supreme Court, 1931-1961 (1994).

JAMES C. McREYNOLDS (1862-1946): Although remembered today primarily as one of the "four horsemen of reaction" who helped block Franklin Roosevelt's New Deal, James McReynolds first came to public attention as a vigorous "trust buster" in the Theodore Roosevelt and Wilson administrations. In the year that he served as Wilson's attorney general, he angered many members of Congress and of the administration with his arrogance and ill-temper. President Wilson named him to the Court in 1914 largely to quiet the controversy. His judicial career was marked by an unyielding commitment to strict constructionism and conservative principles. His personal manner continued to alienate many of his colleagues. After The Gold Clause Cases were decided in 1935, he proclaimed, "Shame and humiliation are on us now. Moral and financial chaos may confidently be expected." Chief Justice Taft remarked that McReynolds "has a continual grouch" and "seems to delight in making others uncomfortable." Widely accused of antisemitism, McReynolds conspicuously failed to sign the letter of affection and regret drafted by his brethren on Justice Brandeis's retirement from the Court.

SANDRA DAY O'CONNOR (1930-): The first woman ever to serve on the Court, Sandra Day O'Connor was appointed by President Reagan in 1981. O'Connor was a classmate of Justice Rehnquist at the Stanford Law School, where she was an editor of the Stanford Law Review. Despite her outstanding academic achievements, O'Connor found it difficult to locate a job on graduation. When she applied to the firm in which future Attorney General William French Smith was a partner, she was offered the position of secretary. After briefly serving as deputy county attorney for San Mateo County in California, she worked as a civilian attorney for the army while her husband served his tour of duty. She then spent eight years as a mother, homemaker, and volunteer while her three children grew up. When she resumed her legal career, she became an assistant attorney general in Arizona. In 1970, she was elected to the Arizona senate and eventually became majority leader. She then served on the Superior Court for Maricopa County and the Arizona Court of Appeals. Although her nomination to the Supreme Court was opposed by some conservatives, Justice O'Connor frequently aligned herself with the conservative wing of the Court. However, she has shown a preference for a balancing approach to constitutional law and case-by-case particularism — a stance that has created conflict with Justice Scalia, who claims to favor a rule-based approach. She initially urged her colleagues to reconsider its analysis of the abortion question in Roe v. Wade, but later surprised many by coauthoring an important opinion preserving Roe's central holding at a time when many thought it would be overruled. She wrote for a five-to-four majority in Mississippi University for Women v. Hogan, 458 U.S. 718 (1982), to invalidate a state nursing school's single-sex admissions policy. Widely respected for her incisive and informed questioning at oral argument, O'Connor is known for her deference to the political branches of government, for her defense of federalism, and for her original approach to the problem of church-state relations. See Comment, The Emerging Jurisprudence of Justice O'Connor, 52 U. Chi. L. Rev. 389 (1985).

LEWIS F. POWELL, JR. (1907-1998): Following his graduation from Harvard Law School, Lewis Powell returned to his native Virginia, where he joined one of Richmond's most prestigious law firms. As president of the Richmond school board during a period of intense controversy concerning school desegregation, Powell gained a reputation as a racial moderate. Despite intense pressure from those advocating "massive resistance," he insisted on keeping the schools open. Powell was elected president of the American Bar Association in 1964. In that capacity, he worked to establish a legal services program within the Office of Economic Opportunity and spoke out against civil disobedience and "parental permissiveness." In 1971, President Nixon fulfilled his promise to name a southerner to the Court by selecting Powell to fill the vacancy created by the resignation of Justice Black. A few years after his appointment, Powell seemed to speak for the South in his concurring opinion in Keyes v. School District, 413 U.S. 189 (1973), in which he argued that there was no significant legal distinction between northern and southern school segregation. Over time, Powell gained the reputation as an ad hoc "balancer," often casting the critical "swing vote" in important decisions. In Regents of the University of California v. Bakke, 438 U.S. 265 (1978), Trimble v. Gordon, 430 U.S. 762 (1977), and Branzburg v. Hayes, 408 U.S. 665 (1972), for example, he controlled the disposition even though he was the only justice adopting his particular view of affirmative action, the rights of nonmarital children, and press rights, respectively. See J. Jeffries, Justice Lewis F. Powell, Jr. (1994).

WILLIAM H. REHNQUIST (1924-): After graduation from Stanford Law School, William Rehnquist came to Washington in 1952 to clerk for Associate Justice Robert Jackson. During his clerkship, he wrote a controversial memorandum for Justice Jackson supporting the constitutionality of "separate but equal" education for blacks. When the memorandum surfaced years later during Rehnquist's confirmation hearings, he explained that it represented Jackson's views and not his own. Following his clerkship, Rehnquist moved to Phoenix, Arizona, where he became involved in Republican politics. A strong supporter of Barry Goldwater, Rehnquist headed the Justice Department's Office of Legal Counsel in the Nixon administration. President Nixon named him to the Court in 1971, and President Reagan named him chief justice in 1986. Chief Justice Rehnquist is known for his commitment to judicial restraint and majoritarianism. His opinions in the areas of equal protection, due process, and free speech consistently reflect a narrow construction of constitutional rights. For example, he would limit strict scrutiny under the equal protection clause to cases involving racial discrimination. Unlike conservative justices of an earlier era, however, Rehnquist would maintain the same deferential stance when reviewing state legislation arguably interfering with private markets and the free flow of commerce. (See, e.g., his opinion for the Court in Posadas de Puerto Rico Associates v. Tourism Co. of Puerto Rico, 478 U.S. 328 (1986), and his dissenting opinion in Kassel v. Consolidated Freightways Corp., 450 U.S. 662 (1981).) Nonetheless, Rehnquist has supported judicial intervention to protect the prerogatives of the states from federal interference and to place constitutional limits on affirmative action programs arguably discriminating in favor of racial minorities. See Shapiro, Mr. Justice Rehnquist: A Preliminary View, 90 Harv. L. Rev. 293 (1976).

ANTONIN SCALIA (1936-): The son of an Italian immigrant, Antonin Scalia was the first Italian-American to be appointed to the Supreme Court. A former law professor and assistant attorney general, he earned a reputation as an intelligent, hardworking, and dedicated conservative while serving as a judge on the U.S. Court of Appeals for the District of Columbia Circuit. Since his elevation to the Supreme Court, Justice Scalia has become known for his forceful opposition to constitutional balancing tests and to reliance on nontextual sources of interpretation. This posture has most often led him to "conservative" outcomes. He is a strong defender of executive prerogatives and is perhaps the Court's most vigorous opponent of affirmative action and abortion rights. The same posture has occasionally led him to vote with the Court's "liberals," however, especially on free speech and search and seizure questions. He is widely admired for his independence and intellectual integrity and for the clarity and forcefulness of his opinions, especially when in dissent.

DAVID HACKETT SOUTER (1939-): Prior to his nomination to the Supreme Court by President Bush, David Souter was a virtual unknown. In his long career as a justice on the New Hampshire Supreme Court, a judge on the New Hampshire trial court, and New Hampshire's attorney general, he seldom had occasion to express his views on contentious constitutional issues such as abortion and affirmative action. Indeed, some critics suggested that President Bush, mindful of the searing controversy surrounding the nomination of Judge Bork, selected Souter principally because he lacked a "paper trail." But although Souter had little experience in constitutional adjudication, he came to the Court with solid intellectual credentials. A Rhodes scholar and graduate of the Harvard Law School, he was praised by liberals and conservatives alike for his intelligence and fair-mindedness. The counsel for the New Hampshire State Democratic Party and president of the New Hampshire Bar Association characterized him as "an enormous intellectual" and "about 135 pounds — and about 120 pounds of brain." Before his appointment, Justice Souter lived by himself in a ramshackle New Hampshire farmhouse laden with stacks of books. Friends said that he liked to work seven days a week, taking time out to hike and listen to classical music. As a justice, Souter is known for careful, lawyerlike opinions and his moderate, nonideological stance toward controversial constitutional issues.

JOHN PAUL STEVENS (1920-): A graduate of Northwestern Law School, John Paul Stevens clerked for Justice Wiley B. Rutledge before joining a Chicago law firm specializing in antitrust work. He taught part-time at the University of Chicago and Northwestern Law Schools until his appointment to the Seventh Circuit Court of Appeals in 1970. Although a registered Republican, Justice Stevens was never active in partisan politics. President Ford elevated him to the Supreme Court in 1975. Stevens is known for his independence and an unwillingness to be bound by rigid formulas. He rejected the position that equal protection analysis can be reduced to various "tiers" of review, for example, arguing that various factors must be weighed under the same standard in every case to ensure that the state has met its obligation to govern impartially. And in free speech cases Stevens staked out his own theory that fits comfortably within neither the traditional "liberal" nor the "conservative" ideology. See, e.g., Smith v. United States, 431 U.S. 291 (1977); Young v. American Mini Theatres, 427 U.S. 50 (1976).

POTTER STEWART (1915-1985): Son of the Republican mayor of Cincinnati, Potter Stewart became active in Ohio Republican politics at an early age. He was twice elected to the city council and served one term as vice mayor before President Eisenhower appointed him to the Sixth Circuit Court of Appeals in 1954. In 1958, Eisenhower elevated him to the Supreme Court, where he served until his retirement in 1981. Although his political background was conservative, Stewart occupied a centrist position on the Court. He frequently voted with the liberal justices on first amendment issues (an orientation perhaps influenced by his experience as editor of a student newspaper while at Yale), but with conservative justices on equal protection issues. On many questions, his position simply could not be predicted in advance, and he had little difficulty in changing his mind about views he had expressed in earlier opinions. Perhaps his most famous opinion was a concurrence in Jacobellis v. Ohio, 378 U.S. 184 (1964), in which he said of "hard core" pornography, "I shall not today attempt further to define the kinds of material I understand to be embraced within that shorthand description; and perhaps I could never succeed in intelligibly doing so. But I know it when I see it, and the motion picture involved in this case is not that." Although sometimes ridiculed, this statement in some ways summarized Stewart's judicial philosophy, which tended to be particularistic, intuitive, and pragmatic.

HARLAN FISKE STONE (1872-1946): For twenty-five years, Harlan Fiske Stone practiced law with a Wall Street law firm and served as a professor and the dean of the Columbia Law School. In 1924, President Coolidge appointed Stone, his old friend and classmate, to head a Department of Justice demoralized by the Teapot Dome scandal. A year later Coolidge appointed Stone to the Court. Although a Republican and moderate conservative, Stone sided with the wing of the Court willing to uphold New Deal programs during the great controversy that engulfed the Court in the early 1930s. In 1941, President Roosevelt elevated Stone to chief justice, an appointment that Archibald MacLeish called "the perfect word spoken at the perfect moment." Justice Stone's footnote 4 in United States v. Carolene Products, 304 U.S. 144 (1938), is doubtless the most famous footnote in constitutional law and has formed the basis of much of modern constitutional theory. During his twenty-one years on the bench, Stone occupied every seat from junior associate justice, to senior associate justice, to chief justice — a feat accomplished by no other justice. He died "with his boots on" — stricken while reading a dissenting opinion from the bench in 1946. See A. Mason, Harlan Fiske Stone: A Pillar of the Law (1956); G. White, The American Judicial Tradition ch. 10 (1976); Dunham, Mr. Chief Justice Stone, in A. Dunham and P. Kurland, Mr. Justice 229-251 (1956).

JOSEPH STORY (1779-1845): Joseph Story was only thirty-two years old and had had no judicial experience when James Madison appointed him to the Court in 1811. Although a Republican, Story had strong nationalist sympathies and sided with John Marshall throughout much of his judicial career. His opinion in Martin v. Hunter's Lessee, 14 U.S. (1 Wheat.) 304 (1816), established the finality of the Court's constitutional authority against the states. His nationalist inclinations were also reflected in Swift v. Tyson, 41 U.S. (16 Pet.) 1 (1842), which upheld the power of federal courts to create a national commercial law. As a circuit justice, Story was said to absorb "jurisdiction as a sponge took up water," and some claimed that, "if a bucket of water were brought into his court with a corn cob floating in it, he would at once extend the admiralty jurisdiction of the United States over it." A serious scholar, Story was elected to the Harvard Board of Overseers and played a key role in the founding of the Harvard Law School. His Commentaries on the Constitution, published in 1833, was a classic of its time. On Marshall's death in 1835, Story hoped to be nominated chief justice, but Andrew Jackson, who had called him "the most dangerous man in America," named Roger Taney instead. Story was frequently in dissent during the nine years he sat on the Taney Court. See, e.g., Charles River Bridge v. Warren Bridge, 36 U.S. (11 Pet.) 420 (1837). Frustrated by the direction of the Court, which he saw as undermining the Marshall Court's conception of the Constitution, he planned to resign in 1845, but fell ill and died before he could complete his unfinished business. See G. Dunne, Justice Joseph Story and the Rise of the Supreme Court (1970); K. Neumyer, Supreme Court Justice Joseph Story (1984).

GEORGE SUTHERLAND (1862-1942): A friend and close advisor to President Harding, George Sutherland was appointed to the Court in 1922. Before his appointment, he served in the U.S. Senate for twelve years, where he developed a reputation as an authority on constitutional questions and a conservative who nonetheless occasionally supported progressive causes. While on the Court, he was the intellectual leader of the conservative wing. He strongly objected to what he considered the evisceration of the contract clause and vigorously opposed the constitutionality of minimum wage laws. See Home Building & Loan Association v. Blaisdell, 290 U.S. 398 (1934); Adkins v. Children's Hospital, 261 U.S. 525 (1923). But his concern for the rights of the individual and broad reading of the due process clause also led him to write for the majority in Powell v. Alabama, 287 U.S. 45 (1932), which reversed the conviction of the "Scottsboro Boys" and began the process of applying constitutionally based rules of criminal procedure to the states. See J. Paschal, Mr. Justice Sutherland: A Man against the State (1951).

WILLIAM HOWARD TAFT (1857-1930): The only person to serve as both President and chief justice, William Howard Taft's career was marked by genial conservatism and a commitment to the institutional independence of each branch of the federal government. Taft served as secretary of war in Theodore Roosevelt's administration and became one of Roosevelt's closest advisors. With support from Roosevelt, he was elected President in 1908. Soon after his inauguration, however, he and Roosevelt split, and he lost his bid for reelection in 1912, when Roosevelt splintered the Republican vote by running as an independent. After leaving the presidency, Taft taught constitutional law at Yale University and served for a year as president of the American Bar Association. Along with several other former ABA presidents, Taft fought to block Louis Brandeis's nomination to the Court in 1916. President Harding named Taft chief justice in 1921. Taft was responsible for passage of the Judiciary Act of 1925, which gave the Supreme Court effective control over its own appellate jurisdiction and for the appropriation of funds for construction of the present Supreme Court building. See A. Mason, William Howard Taft: Chief Justice (1964).

ROGER B. TANEY (1777-1864): Prior to his appointment as chief justice by President Jackson in 1835, Roger Taney served as Jackson's attorney general and secretary of the treasury. While serving in Jackson's cabinet, he became enmeshed in the controversy surrounding the second Bank of the United States. As attorney general, Taney drafted Jackson's message vetoing the bank's recharter, and when the secretary of the treasury refused to withdraw federal funds from the Bank, Jackson named Taney to the post so that he could do so. But when Jackson submitted Taney's name to the Senate for confirmation, he was defeated and forced to resign. Senate Whigs, who feared that Taney was too radical, again blocked his nomination as associate justice in 1835. Shortly thereafter, however, he was successfully nominated to replace John Marshall as chief justice. Taney's career on the Court is overshadowed by his opinion in Scott v. Sandford, 60 U.S. (19 How.) 393 (1857), widely viewed as one of the great legal and moral blunders in the Court's history. The rest of his tenure, however, was marked by the cautious and careful use of judicial power. Contrary to the expectations of his contemporaries, he did not support the wholesale abandonment of the Marshall legacy. Instead, he steered a middle course between the extreme nationalism and extreme localism of his colleagues. But as the nation approached Civil War, the ground in the middle became increasingly unstable, and Taney's one spasmodic effort to end the nation's agony over slavery by imposing a constitutional solution in *Dred Scott* ended in a tragedy that permanently marred his reputation. See C. Swisher, Roger B. Taney (1935); G. White, The American Judicial Tradition ch. 3 (1976).

CLARENCE THOMAS (1948-): Born into grinding poverty in segregated coastal Georgia, Clarence Thomas became the second African-American and one of the youngest justices to join the Court when he was appointed by President Bush in 1991. He was confirmed by the Senate to fill the seat vacated by the retirement of Thurgood Marshall after extraordinary confirmation hearings that opened with a moving account of his personal saga and closed with charges of sexual harassment leveled against him by Anita Hill, who had worked with him at the Department of Education and the Equal Employment Opportunity Commission. A graduate of the Yale Law School, he served as assistant secretary for civil rights at the Department of Education and chair of the Equal Employment Opportunity Commission in the Reagan administration. During his controversial seven-year stewardship of the EEOC, Thomas's fierce opposition to affirmative action antagonized liberals and members of the civil rights community. In

1989, President Bush appointed Thomas to the U.S. Court of Appeals for the District of Columbia, where he served for fifteen months before his elevation to the Supreme Court. Known as a staunch conservative, Thomas's extrajudicial writings suggest an interest in natural law as a basis for constitutional adjudication. Since joining the Court, he has written a series of distinctive dissents and concurrences, often demonstrating a willingness to reject settled precedent in favor of his understanding of the constitutional text. On racial issues, he strongly opposes what he considers liberal condescension in the form of affirmative action and the assumption that majority black institutions are necessarily inferior.

WILLIS VAN DEVANTER (1859-1941): A lawyer's lawyer, William Van Devanter invariably sided with the conservative wing of the Court, but, unlike some of his colleagues, never resorted to divisive ideological rhetoric. Instead, he relied on his mastery of technical doctrine to become a "master of formulas that decided cases without creating precedents." Van Devanter, who was active in Republican politics in Wyoming, came to Washington during the McKinley administration and was named to the Eighth Circuit Court of Appeals by Theodore Roosevelt. When President Taft nominated him to serve as an associate justice, William Jennings Bryan complained that he was "the judge that held that two railroads running parallel to each other for two thousand miles were not competing lines, one of the roads being that of Union Pacific," one of Van Devanter's former clients. It has been said that Van Devanter came to the Court "fully equipped with a lawyer's understanding of federal jurisdiction, a frontiersman's knowledge of Indian affairs, and a native hostility to governmental regulation." His years on the Court were marked by a concern for technical jurisdictional questions and opposition to government intervention in all forms. His retirement in June of 1937 gave Franklin Roosevelt his first appointment and helped defuse the crisis created by the Court's opposition to the New Deal.

EARL WARREN (1891-1974): Both vilified and canonized during his tenure, Earl Warren presided as chief justice over one of the most tumultuous and portentous periods in the Court's history. The emotions that he aroused are hard to reconcile with his political stance, which was, essentially, centrist and pragmatic. As Republican governor of California, he denounced "communistic radicals" and supported the wartime order to forcibly evacuate Japanese-Americans. (The Court subsequently upheld the constitutionality of the evacuation in Korematsu v. United States, 323 U.S. 214 (1944).) In his later years as governor, however, he developed a reputation as a progressive and proposed state programs for prepaid medical insurance and liberal welfare benefits. In 1948, he ran for Vice President on the ticket headed by Thomas Dewey. In 1952, he mounted his own presidential effort. At the Republican convention, however, he threw his support behind Dwight Eisenhower. President Eisenhower repaid Warren by nominating him as chief justice in 1953 — a nomination Eisenhower later called "the biggest damn-fool mistake I ever made." Perhaps Warren's greatest accomplishment on the Court was his painstaking and successful effort to maintain a united front as the Court overturned the separate but equal doctrine in Brown v. Board of Education, 347 U.S. 873 (1954), and then confronted southern violence and intransigence. Warren himself believed that his opinion in Reynolds v. Sims, 377 U.S. 533 (1964), establishing the one person, one vote formula, was of greater significance. In the end, however, it may have been his opinions in the field of criminal procedure — especially Miranda v. Arizona, 384 U.S. 436 (1966) — that attracted the most controversy. This controversy tended to obscure the fact that there was a strong conservative and moralistic tone to many of Warren's opinions. He opposed constitutional protection for "pornographic" literature, for example, and dissented in Shapiro v. Thompson, 394 U.S. 618 (1969), when the Court invalidated durational residency requirements for welfare recipients. Warren was distrustful of complex doctrinal argument. His opinions were thus marked by a confident, intuitively grounded insistence on fair play and fundamental justice. See B. Schwartz, Superchief (1983); E. Warren, The Memoirs of Earl Warren (1977); G. White, Earl Warren (1982).

BYRON R. WHITE (1917-): An outstanding scholar-athlete, Byron "Whizzer" White was first in his class at the University of Colorado, a Rhodes scholar, and a professional football player with the Detroit Lions before beginning his legal career. White served in the navy during World War II and graduated from Yale Law School magna cum laude. After serving as law clerk to Chief Justice Fred Vinson, he returned to his native Colorado where he practiced with a prominent Denver law firm for fourteen years. A longtime friend of John Kennedy, White headed Kennedy's preconvention presidential campaign in Colorado in 1960 and subsequently became chairman of National Citizens for Kennedy. After the election, Kennedy named him deputy attorney general and in 1962 elevated him to the Court. As a justice, White was known as a strong advocate of school desegregation and a defender of the rights of minorities. Although more ready than his colleagues to find legislation lacking in a "rational basis" when challenged under "low-level" equal protection review, he also criticized his colleagues for too aggressive use of substantive due process analysis. For example, joined only by Justice Rehnquist, White dissented in Roe v. Wade, 410 U. S. 113 (1973), which held that women have a constitutionally protected liberty interest in securing abortions. White opposed many of the Warren Court decisions extending new protections to criminal defendants and in later years often voted to limit the scope of those holdings. See D. Hutchinson, The Man Who Was Whizzer White: A Portrait of Justice Byron R. White (1998).

The Supreme Court since 1789

The Supreme Court since 1789

Year	Administration	Chief Justice	2	3	4	5	6	7	8	9	Major Cases
1789	Washington	John Jay	John Rutledge	William Cushing	James Wilson	John Blair	James Iredell				
1790			Thomas Johnson William Paterson								
1795		John Rutledge Oliver Ellsworth									
	J. Adams					Samuel Chase					
					Bushrod Washington		Alfred Moore				
1800	Jefferson	John Marshall (Adams)					William Johnson				
								Thomas Todd			Marbury v. Madison (1803)
1805			H. Brockholst Livingston								
1810	Madison			Joseph Story		Gabriel Duvall					

McCulloch v. Maryland (1819)

Gibbons v. Ogden (1824)

Barron v. Baltimore (1833)

John McKinley

John Catron

Robert Trimble

John McLean

James M. Wayne

Philip P. Barbour

Peter V. Daniel (Van Buren)

Henry Baldwin

Smith Thompson

Roger B. Taney

Monroe

J. Q. Adams

Jackson

Van Buren

W. Harrison Tyler

1815

1820

1825

1830

1835

1840

Year	Administration	Chief Justice	2	3	4	5	6	7	8	9	Major Cases
1845	Polk		Samuel Nelson (Tyler)	Levi Woodbury	Robert C. Grier						
1850	Taylor / Fillmore			Benjamin R. Curtis							
1855	Pierce									John A. Campbell	Dred Scott v. Sandford (1857)
1860	Buchanan			Nathan Clifford		Samuel F. Miller		Noah H. Swayne	10 Stephen J. Field	David Davis	
1865**	Lincoln	Salmon P. Chase									
**	A. Johnson										
1870	Grant		Ward Hunt		William Strong		Joseph P. Bradley				Slaughter-House Cases (1873)

Timeline (1875–1900)

Years marked: 1875, 1880, 1885, 1890, 1895, 1900

Presidents: Hayes · Garfield / Arthur · Cleveland · B. Harrison · Cleveland · McKinley · T. Roosevelt

Justices and notable cases:

- Morrison R. Waite
- Samuel Blatchford
- Melville W. Fuller
- Edward D. White
- John M. Harlan
- Horace Gray (Arthur)
- William B. Woods
- Stanley Matthews (Garfield)
- Lucius Q. C. Lamar
- Henry B. Brown
- George Shiras
- David J. Brewer
- Howell E. Jackson (Harrison)
- Rufus W. Peckham
- Joseph McKenna

- Civil Rights Cases (1883)
- Plessy v. Ferguson (1896)

Year	Administration	Chief Justice	2	3	4	5	6	7	8	9	Major Cases
1905				Oliver W. Holmes			William R. Day				Lochner v. N.Y. (1905)
						William H. Moody					
1910	Taft	Edward D. White	Willis Van Devanter		Horace H. Lurton			Charles E. Hughes			
						Joseph R. Lamar				Mahlon Pitney	
1915	Wilson				James C. McReynolds						
						Louis D. Brandeis		John H. Clarke			
1920	Harding	William H. Taft						George Sutherland		Edward T. Sanford (Harding)	Schenk v. U.S. (1919)
	Coolidge						Pierce Butler		Harlan F. Stone		
1925											

xciv

Hoover

F. D. Roosevelt

Truman

| | 1930 | | | | 1935 | | | | 1940 | | | | 1945 | | | | 1950 | | |

Charles E. Hughes

Benjamin N. Cardozo

Hugo L. Black

Harlan F. Stone

Felix Frankfurter

James F. Byrnes

Wiley B. Rutledge

William O. Douglas

Frank Murphy

Fred M. Vinson

Sherman Minton

Tom C. Clark

Stanley F. Reed

Robert H. Jackson

Owen J. Roberts

Harold H. Burton

Schechter Poultry v. U.S. (1935)

West Coast Hotel v. Parrish (1937)

U.S. v. Carolene Prods. (1938)

Dennis v. U.S. (1951)

Youngstown Sheet v. Sawyer (1952)

This chart shows a timeline (1955–1970+) of U.S. Supreme Court Justices by administration, chief justice, seat number, and major cases.

Administration	Chief Justice	2	3	4	5	6	7	8	9	Major Cases
Eisenhower	Earl Warren									Brown v. Bd. of Ed. (1954)
				William J. Brennan				John M. Harlan		
									Potter Stewart	
Kennedy			Arthur J. Goldberg				Charles E. Whittaker			N.Y. Times v. Sullivan (1964)
L. B. Johnson			Abe Fortas				Byron R. White			
						Thurgood Marshall				
Nixon	Warren E. Burger		Harry A. Blackmun							Brandenburg v. Ohio (1969)
		Lewis F. Powell								N.Y. Times v. U.S. (1971)
								William H. Rehnquist		
Ford										Roe v. Wade (1973) U.S. v. Nixon (1974)

Timeline markings: 1955, 1960, 1965, 1970

This is a timeline chart of Supreme Court justices and cases, 1975–1995.

Year markers	Presidents	Justices	Cases

Cases (top, with dates):
- Washington v. Davis (1976)
- U. Cal. v. Bakke (1978)
- City of Richmond v. J.A. Croson Co. (1989)
- Planned Parenthood of S.E. Pa. v. Casey (1992)
- United States v. Lopez (1995); Adarand Constr. v. Pena (1995)

Justices:
- Sandra Day O'Connor
- Antonin Scalia
- Ruth Bader Ginsburg
- Clarence Thomas
- John Paul Stevens
- David H. Souter
- Stephen G. Breyer
- Anthony M. Kennedy
- William H. Rehnquist

Presidents:
- Carter
- Reagan
- Bush
- Clinton

Timeline years: 1975, 1980, 1985, 1990, 1995

Administration	Chief Justice	2	3	4	5	6	7	8	9	Major Cases
										United States v. Virginia (1996) City of Boerne v. Flores (1997)

2000

*In 1863 Congress established a tenth seat, to which Stephen J. Field was appointed.

**In 1866 Congress reduced the size of the Court to six justices. Consequently, the seats of Justices Catron and Wayne remained unfilled after their deaths in 1865 and 1867. Congress restored the Court to nine seats in 1869.

Constitutional Law

I

The Role of the Supreme Court in the Constitutional Order

This chapter deals primarily with the role of the Supreme Court in the constitutional order. What is the nature of the authority of the Supreme Court over Congress, the President, and the states? What are the sources and limits of that authority? And what devices are available to Congress and the President if they disagree with the Court?

It is important to understand, however, that American constitutional law concerns many topics other than judicial review and the role of the Supreme Court. The Constitution sets up a framework of relations that often have little or nothing to do with the federal judiciary. It binds members of Congress, the executive branch, and state government as well as Supreme Court justices. It therefore imposes on them the responsibility of obeying constitutional requirements — regardless of whether a litigated case deals with the question. Moreover, much of constitutional "law" consists of informal accommodations and historical practices among the various parts of the national government and between the federal government and the states. Consider, for example, the extent to which power over foreign affairs is shared not because of constitutional text but because of traditions that have grown up between Congress and the executive branch. Those accommodations and practices in turn play an important role in Supreme Court decisions when and if the issues are litigated.

A. INTRODUCTION: SOME NOTES ON THE HISTORY AND THEORY OF THE CONSTITUTION

The Declaration of Independence was signed in 1776. Hostilities with England substantially ceased in 1781 after the Yorktown campaign; the American Revolution was formally completed in 1783 with the signing of a final peace treaty with England. In February of 1781, the thirteen colonies ratified the Articles of Confederation, under which they lived for seven years. The Constitution was written in 1787 and ratified in 1789. Two years later the bill of rights was added.

Why did the states find it necessary to adopt a new Constitution in 1787? What were the problems for which the Constitution was supposed a remedy? Views about the Constitution and its framers span a wide range. To some, the framers were intellectual giants, equipped with extraordinary foresight, vision, and faith in democracy and self-rule, who were able to rise above the squabbles of the day in order to institute into law principles that are timeless or at least enduring. See J. Fiske, The Critical Period of American History (1888). To others, the Constitution is best understood as a series of ad hoc compromises, designed to resolve very specific issues over which the young country was divided. See M. Farrand, The Framing of the Constitution of the United States (1913). A third strand in American historical thought treats the Constitution as a product of aristocratic conservatives who, far from trusting the people and believing in self-rule, intended to protect private property, and the position of the well-to-do, from the workings of democratic politics. See C. Beard, An Economic Interpretation of the Constitution of the United States (1913). There are, of course, numerous variations on these general approaches. For discussion, see G. Wood, The Creation of the American Republic, 1776-1787 (1969); G. Wood, ed., The Confederation and the Constitution (1978); G. Wood, The Radicalism of the American Revolution (1993); R. Horwitz, ed., The Moral Foundations of the American Republic (2d ed. 1979); J. G. A. Pocock, The Machiavellian Moment (1975); Kloppenberg, The Virtues of Liberalism: Christianity, Republicanism and Ethics in Early American Political Discourse, 74 J. Am. Hist. 9 (1987).

To understand the Constitution and the surrounding debates on its purposes and effects, it is useful to have some understanding of the Articles of Confederation, which the Constitution replaced. The Articles were adopted shortly after the Revolution in order to ensure some unification of the states regarding common foreign and domestic problems, but the overriding understanding was that the states would remain sovereign. The first substantive provision of the Articles announced that "each state retains its sovereignty, freedom, and independence, and every Power, Jurisdiction, and right, which is not by this confederation expressly delegated to the United States, in Congress assembled." A number of powers were, however, conferred on "the United States in Congress assembled." These powers included "the sole and exclusive right and power of determining on peace and war"; the authority to resolve disputes between the states; the power to regulate "the alloy and value of coin struck by their own authority, or by that of the respective states"; and the authority to control dealings with Indian tribes, to establish or regulate post offices, and to appoint naval and other offices in federal service.

But at least by modern standards, there were conspicuous gaps. Two of the most important powers of the modern national government were missing altogether — the power to tax and the power to regulate commerce. Moreover, two of the three branches of the national government were absent. There was no executive authority. There was no general national judicial authority; the only relevant provision authorized Congress to establish a national appellate tribunal to decide maritime cases. Of course, there was no bill of rights (though it should be noted that the absence of a bill of rights was not in any way the impetus behind the Constitution and indeed the federalists thought, at the time of ratification, that a bill of rights did not belong in the Constitution at all).

There is considerable dispute about the nature and extent of the problems encountered by the states under the Articles. The conventional wisdom refers to Congress's inability to raise revenue to perform necessary functions; to the perceived need for executive authority to provide energy and resolution in domestic and foreign affairs; and to interstate jealousies, which produced retaliatory trade measures and inhibited the flow of interstate commerce. Consider the following account of the situation:

> Almost everything points in only one direction — toward the need of a competent central government and the necessity of finding a system of union which could maintain itself. [The] whole story is one of gradually increasing ineptitude; of a central government which could less and less function as it was supposed to function; of a general system which was creaking in every joint and beginning to hobble at every step. . . .
>
> Interstate jealousy [added] to the complexities of the situation. The contest for local rights under the old imperial system had strengthened the sense of state reality; men were conscious of their states; the states were in a sense their own creation. It was difficult, after the strain of war had gone, to feel acutely the reality of America and the dependence of its members one upon another; and as the days went by disorganization rather than integration seemed to be gathering headway, until the more serious patriots and watchers of the night feared for the safety of their country. States with commodious harbors had an advantage over their neighbors, and they did not shrink from using it. [The] experience of those years brought clearly home to thinking men the need of some general regulation of commerce.
>
> The industrial and commercial conditions after the war were in considerable confusion. [Commercial] treaties were desirable, and some steps were taken in that direction; but it was hard to do anything effectively as long as the individual states could not be relied on to fulfill their obligations. Foreign nations naturally queried whether America was one or many, or, perhaps, one today and thirteen tomorrow. . . .
>
> The pivotal problem, the immediate and unrelenting problem, was how to get revenue for the pressing needs of the Confederation. Financial affairs were in a pitiful shape and conditions daily grew worse. [The] sums due for interest on the domestic and foreign debts were piling up to staggering heights and even the principal of the debts — for, strange as it may seem, Congress had succeeded in borrowing — was increasing ominously.
>
> [Within] the individual states, paper money added to the confusion and made recovery of economic stability difficult. Some of the states refused to be drawn down into the whirlpool; but seven of the thirteen had entered upon the scheme. . . .
>
> Social unrest passed beyond the grumbling stage in Massachusetts where Shay's rebellion broke out and aroused the anxieties of the conservatives from one end of the continent to the other. [It] unquestionably had the effect of prompting men of mind as well as men of property to strengthen the union and to create self-respecting government. "There are combustibles in every State," Washington wrote in 1786, "which a spark might set fire to." . . .
>
> Men interested in public affairs were actively discussing the nature and the defects of the union. [Hamilton] in 1783 drafted resolutions "Intended to be submitted to Congress, but abandoned for want of support." He enumerated at length the defects of the Confederation, and made a severe arraignment of the system. The first defect consisted in "confining the power of the Federal Government within too

narrow limits." [He] plainly objected not only to the inconsistencies of the Articles, but to the impracticability of their effective operation. In 1785, Noah Webster [announced]: ". . . in all the affairs that respect the whole, Congress must have the same power to enact laws and compel obedience throughout the continent, as the legislatures of the several states have in their respective jurisdictions."

Of most significance, however, is the report (August, 1786) of a grand committee of Congress. [The] report proposed that Congress [should] be given the power to regulate interstate and foreign trade, with the consent of nine states, and the power of levying additional requisitions in the way of punishment upon any state not promptly complying with requisitions for men or money. If the delinquent and disobedient state should persist in its conduct, while the majority had lived up to their obligations, then Congress should have power to levy and collect taxes and in the last extremity compel the local officers in the delinquent state to do their duty; should such a step prove ineffective, then Congress might itself appoint assessors and collectors.

Nothing could more amply demonstrate the feebleness and distraction of Congress and the necessity for energetic reform, if the union was to last many days. The cumbersome methods proposed for getting money, the practical admission of a continuing and probably inescapable refusal of the states to comply with reasonable requests to defray the absolutely necessary common expenses, and above all, the more pitiful suggestion of measures which might induce members from the states to come to Congress and attend to business, were a confession of masterly incapacity.

Another source of anxiety was the light-hearted way in which treaties were regarded by the states. . . .

[In] March, 1787, resolutions were passed by Congress declaring treaties constitutionally made were "part of the law of the land"; the states were called upon to repeal acts violating the treaty with Britain and to direct the state courts to adjudge cases in accord with the treaty, "any thing in [other] . . . acts to the contrary . . . notwithstanding."

But what was the very center of the difficulty? What was the chief problem of the time? The trouble and confusion were manifestly caused by the failure of the states to abide by their obligations. The problem was to find a method, if union was to subsist at all, for overcoming the difficulty, to find therefore some arrangement, some scheme or plan of organization wherein there would be reasonable assurance that the states would fulfill their obligations and play their part under established articles of union and not make mockery of union by willing disregard or negligent delay. That was the chief problem of the day.

A. McLaughlin, A Constitutional History of the United States 137-147 (1936)

A revisionist view has it that the Articles of Confederation did not generate severe general problems. On this view, the problems were faced principally by commercial and mercantile interests who were adversely affected by the various states engaging in protectionist measures, and who needed national authority for help against states that had not fully respected rights of private property and private contract. See, e.g., M. Jensen, Articles of Confederation (1940); M. Jensen, The New Nation (1950).

However those questions may be resolved, there was by 1786 agreement on the part of many that amendments to the Articles were required. In that year, state representatives met in Annapolis to discuss problems that had arisen under the Articles; they adopted a resolution to hold a convention in Philadelphia to remedy those problems. But the nation's charge to the framers was much narrower than the ultimate product would suggest. The framers, chosen by state legislatures, were instructed "to meet at Philadelphia [to] take into consideration the situation of the United States, to devise such further provisions as shall appear to them necessary to render the constitution of the federal government adequate to the exigencies of the Union." The limited character of this charge proved a serious embarrassment to the framers, whose product reflected their view that it was necessary to provide not "further provisions" but an entirely new governing document whose character was not clearly proportionate to the weaknesses of the Articles.

There is therefore a sense in which the Constitution was itself an unlawful act. Notably, the Convention disregarded the amending procedure set out in the Articles, which required approval by all thirteen state legislatures. The Constitution was instead sent to Congress, with a request that it be sent in turn to state legislatures. The state legislatures would then send it to popularly elected state ratifying conventions.

The Constitution changed the framework set up by the Articles of Confederation in a number of ways. Among the most important changes were the creation of an executive branch; the grant to Congress of the powers to tax and to regulate commerce; and the creation of a federal judiciary, including the Supreme Court and, if Congress chose, lower federal courts. The tenth amendment, added two years later, was a pale echo of the first provisions of the Articles of Confederation, deleting the word "expressly," and it was countered by the clause granting Congress the authority to make "all laws necessary and proper" to effectuate its enumerated powers.

What was the underlying theory to which the Constitution responded? In this section we discuss some of the issues and problems with which the framers attempted to deal. We explore some of the general theoretical issues here; discussion of more particular issues and provisions is deferred until later chapters.

1. The Antifederalist Case

One of the best ways of approaching the thought of the framers is through the views of their adversaries — the so-called antifederalists, opponents of the Constitution who contended that the document amounted to a betrayal of the principles underlying the Revolution. See H. Storing, What the Antifederalists Were For (1981). Antifederalist thought derived at least in some respects from classical republicanism, a theory of government that influenced, among others, Montesquieu and Rousseau. A large part of the republican and antifederalist argument relied on civic virtue — the willingness of citizens to subordinate their private interests to the general good. Politics thus consisted of self-rule, but it was self-rule of a particular sort. Self-rule was a matter not of pursuing self-interest, or of aggregating "preferences," but instead of selecting the values that ought to control public and private life. Dialogue and discussion among the citizenry were critical features in the governmental process. Political participation should be active and frequent and not limited to voting or other similar statements of preference. Civil society was to operate as a sort of teacher, inculcating virtue, and not merely as a regulator of private conduct. The model for government was the town meeting, a metaphor that played an explicit role in the antifederalist conception of politics. Consider in this regard Thomas Jefferson's suggestion that the Constitution should be amended in every generation, partly in order to promote general attention to public affairs; this suggestion was a natural one for those who saw frequent participation and virtue as important ingredients in democratic self-government. See Letter to Samuel Kercheval, July 12, 1816, in The Portable Thomas Jefferson 557-558 (M. Peterson ed. 1975).

In the view of the antifederalists, government's first task was to ensure the flourishing of the necessary public-spiritedness. The antifederalists thus believed in decentralization, for only in small communities would it be possible to find and develop the unselfishness and devotion to the public good on which genuine freedom depends. The antifederalist "Brutus" emphasized the need for homogeneity: "In a republic, the manners, sentiments, and interests of the people should be similar. If this be not the case, there will be a constant clashing of opinions; and the representatives of one part will be continually striving against those of the other." 2 The Complete Antifederalist 369 (H. Storing ed. 1980). In these respects, the antifederalists echoed traditional republican theory.

The antifederalists were especially hostile to a dramatic expansion in the powers of the national government. In a decentralized society it would be possible to achieve the sort of homogeneity and dedication to the public good that would prevent the government from degenerating into tyranny from the center or a mere clash of private interests. A powerful national government would be inconsistent with the spirit of civic virtue, creating heterogeneity and distance from the sphere of power, both of which would undermine deliberative processes and the citizens' willingness to subordinate their private interests to the public good. Closely connected to this view was the antifederalists' desire to avoid extreme disparities in wealth, education, and power.

It should not be difficult to see why the antifederalists would have had at best an ambivalent attitude toward a system in which decisions were made by representatives of the people rather than by the people themselves. According to one strand of republican thought, all decisions should be made in small communities or even during a face-to-face process of deliberation and debate. Such a process would inculcate civic virtue in the public at large, virtue from which the process itself would simultaneously benefit.

The antifederalists acknowledged, however, that representation was necessary at both the state and the national levels. The size of both governments made it impossible to conduct political affairs on the model of the town meeting. But representation was hardly to be welcomed, and indeed it was understood as an evil made necessary only because of the impracticability of governance by the people themselves.

From this perspective, the proposed Constitution would undermine the system of decentralization on which true liberty depended. It would prevent citizens from having effective control over their representatives and deprive them of an opportunity to participate in public affairs. It would thus pose a severe threat to the underlying principle of civic virtue. Rule by remote national leaders would attenuate the scheme of representation, rupturing the alliance of interests between the rulers and the ruled. It would create a class of quasi-aristocrats, charging them with the task of directing a huge national government. The antifederalists foresaw a system in which the people would be effectively excluded from the world of public affairs and in which national leaders, only weakly accountable, would have enormous discretion to make law and policy. (Do this and other aspects of the antifederalist case reflect admirable foresight or instead a lack of realism, a nostalgia for a past that never was? This question is very much with us today.)

The antifederalists were also skeptical of the emerging interest in commercial development that played a prominent role in the decision to abandon the Articles of Confederation. In the antifederalists' view, commerce was a threat to the principles underlying the Revolution, for it gave rise to ambition and avarice and thus to the dissolution of communal bonds. Insofar as the proposed Constitution was designed to promote commerce and commercial mores, it would undermine the Revolution itself. Montesquieu, an important source for federalists and antifederalists alike, had said that "in countries where the people are actuated only by the spirit of commerce, they make a traffic of all the humane, all the moral virtues; the most trifling things, those which humanity would demand, are there done, or there given, only for money." Montesquieu, The Spirit of Laws bk. XX, ch. ii (spec. ed. 1984) (1751).

In sum, the antifederalists attacked the proposed Constitution on the ground that it was inconsistent with the underlying principles of republicanism. The removal of the people from the political process, the creation of a powerful and remote national government, and the new emphasis on commerce — all of these threatened to undermine the purposes for which the Revolution had been fought.

2.   *The Federalist Response*

The antifederalist objections to the proposed Constitution provoked a theoretical justification that amounted in many respects to a new conception of politics — in Gordon Wood's words, a "political theory worthy of a prominent place in the history of Western thought." G. Wood, The Creation of the American Republic, 1776-1787, at 615 (1969). That conception consisted of a reformulation of the principles of republicanism — a reformulation that attempted to synthesize elements of traditional republicanism with an emerging theory that welcomed rather than feared heterogeneity, and that understood the reality that self-interest would often be a motivating force for political actors.

Much of that reformulation can be found in The Federalist Papers — essays attempting to defend the proposed Constitution to the country against antifederalist attack. The Federalist Papers were published under the name "Publius," but were in fact written by James Madison, Alexander Hamilton, and John Jay. Although the papers are often consulted as a means of understanding the theory underlying the Constitution, and the "intentions" of its drafters, it is important to keep in mind that the essays were in many respects propaganda pieces, designed to persuade the ambivalent. Nonetheless, The Federalist Papers count among the classic works in the theory of democracy and constitutionalism.

The Federalist No. 10 (Madison)

(1787)

TO THE PEOPLE OF THE STATE OF NEW YORK:

Among the numerous advantages promised by a well-constructed Union, none deserves to be more accurately developed than its tendency to break and control the violence of faction. The friend of popular governments never finds himself so much alarmed for their character and fate, as when he contemplates their propensity to this dangerous vice. [The] instability, injustice, and confusion introduced into the public councils, have, in truth, been the mortal diseases under which popular governments have everywhere perished; as they continue to be the favorite and fruitful topics from which the adversaries to liberty derive their most specious declamations. [Complaints] are everywhere heard from our most considerate and virtuous citizens, equally the friends of public and private faith, and of public and personal liberty, that our governments are too unstable, that the public good is disregarded in the conflicts of rival parties, and that measures are too often decided, not according to the rules of justice and the rights of the minor party, but by the superior force of an interested and overbearing majority. However anxiously we may wish that these complaints had no foundation, the evidence of known facts will not permit us to deny that they are in some degree true. [The] distresses under which we labor [must] be chiefly, if not wholly, effects of the unsteadiness and injustice with which a factious spirit has tainted our public administrations.

By a faction, I understand a number of citizens, whether amounting to a majority or minority of the whole, who are united and actuated by some common impulse of passion, or of interest, adverse to the rights of other citizens, or to the permanent and aggregate interests of the community.

There are two methods of curing the mischiefs of faction: the one, by removing its causes; the other, by controlling its effects.

There are again two methods of removing the causes of faction: the one, by destroying the liberty which is essential to its existence; the other, by giving to every citizen the same opinions, the same passions, and the same interests.

It could never be more truly said than of the first remedy, that it was worse than the disease. Liberty is to faction what air is to fire, an aliment without which it instantly expires. But it could not be less folly to abolish liberty, which is essential to political life, because it nourishes faction, than it would be to wish the annihilation of air, which is essential to animal life, because it imparts to fire its destructive agency.

The second expedient is as impracticable as the first would be unwise. As long as the reason of man continues fallible, and he is at liberty to exercise it, different opinions will be formed. As long as the connection subsists between his reason and his self-love, his opinions and his passions will have a reciprocal influence on each other; and the former will be objects to which the latter will attach themselves. The diversity in the faculties of men, from which the rights of property originate, is not less an insuperable obstacle to a uniformity of interests. The protection of these faculties is the first object of government. From the protection of different and unequal faculties of acquiring property, the possession of different degrees and kinds of property immediately results; and from the influence of these on the sentiments and views of the respective proprietors, ensues a division of the society into different interests and parties.

The latent causes of faction are thus sown in the nature of man; and we see them everywhere brought into different degrees of activity, according to the different circumstances of civil society. A zeal for different opinions, concerning religion, concerning government, and many other points, as well of speculation as of practice; an attachment to different leaders ambitiously contending for preeminence and power; or to persons of other descriptions whose fortunes have been interesting to the human passions, have, in turn, divided mankind into parties, inflamed them with mutual animosity, and rendered them much more disposed to vex and oppress each other than to co-operate for their common good. So strong is this propensity of mankind to fall into mutual animosities, that where no substantial occasion presents itself, the most frivolous and fanciful distinctions have been sufficient to kindle their unfriendly passions and excite their most violent conflicts. But the most common and durable source of factions has been the various and unequal distribution of property. Those who hold and those who are without property have ever formed distinct interests in society. Those who are creditors, and those who are debtors, fall under a like discrimination. A landed interest, a manufacturing interest, a mercantile interest, a moneyed interest, with many lesser interests, grow up of necessity in civilized nations, and divide them into different classes, actuated by different sentiments and views. The regulation of these various and interfering interests forms the principal task of modern legislation, and involves the spirit of party and faction in the necessary and ordinary operations of the government.

No man is allowed to be a judge in his own cause, because his interest would certainly bias his judgment, and, not improbably, corrupt his integrity. With equal, nay with greater reason, a body of men are unfit to be both judges and parties at the same time; yet what are many of the most important acts of legislation, but so many judicial determinations, not indeed concerning the rights of single persons, but concerning the rights of large bodies of citizens? And what are the different classes of legislators but advocates and parties to the causes which they determine? Is a law proposed concerning private debts? It is a question to which the creditors are parties on one side and the debtors on the other. Justice ought to hold the balance between them. Yet the parties are, and must be, themselves, the judges; and the most numerous party, or, in other words, the most powerful faction must be expected to prevail. Shall domestic manufacturers be encouraged, and in what degree, by restrictions on foreign manufacturers? are questions which would be differently decided by the landed and the manufacturing classes, and probably by neither with a sole regard to justice and the public good.

It is in vain to say that enlightened statesmen will be able to adjust these clashing interests, and render them all subservient to the public good. Enlightened statesmen will not always be at the helm. . . .

The inference to which we are brought is, that the *causes* of faction cannot be removed, and that relief is only to be sought in the means of controlling its *effects*.

If a faction consists of less than a majority, relief is supplied by the republican principle, which enables the majority to defeat its sinister views by regular vote. It may clog the administration, it may convulse the society; but it will be unable to execute and mask its violence under the forms of the Constitution. When a majority is included in a faction, the form of popular government, on the other hand, enables it to sacrifice to its ruling passion or interest both the public good and the rights of other citizens. To secure the public good and private rights against the danger of such a faction, and at the same time to preserve the spirit and the form of popular government, is then the great object to which our inquiries are directed. Let me add that it is the great desideratum by which this form of government can be rescued from the opprobrium under which it has so long labored, and be recommended to the esteem and adoption of mankind.

By what means is this object attainable? Evidently by one of two only. Either the existence of the same passion or interest in a majority at the same time must be prevented, or the majority, having such coexistent passion or interest, must be rendered, by their number and local situation, unable to concert and carry into effect schemes of oppression. If the impulse and the opportunity be suffered to coincide, we well know that neither moral nor religious motives can be relied on as an adequate control. They are not found to be such on the injustice and violence of individuals, and lose their efficacy in proportion to the number combined together, that is, in proportion as their efficacy becomes needful.

From this view of the subject it may be concluded that a pure democracy, by which I mean a society consisting of a small number of citizens, who assemble and administer the government in person, can admit of no cure for the mischiefs of faction. A common passion or interest will, in almost every case, be felt by a majority of the whole; a communication and concert result from the form of government itself; and there is nothing to check the inducements to sacrifice the weaker party or an obnoxious individual. Hence it is that such democracies have ever been spectacles of turbulence and contention; have ever been found incompatible with personal security or the rights of property; and have in general been as short in their lives as they have been violent in their deaths. Theoretic politicians, who have patronized this species of government, have erroneously supposed that by reducing mankind to a perfect equality in their political rights, they would, at the same time, be perfectly equalized and assimilated in their possessions, their opinions, and their passions.

A republic, by which I mean a government in which the scheme of representation takes place, opens a different prospect, and promises the cure for which we are seeking. . . .

The two great points of difference between a democracy and a republic are: first, the delegation of the government, in the latter, to a small number of citizens elected by the rest; secondly, the greater number of citizens, and greater sphere of country, over which the latter may be extended.

The effect of the first difference is, on the one hand, to refine and enlarge the public views, by passing them through the medium of a chosen body of citizens, whose wisdom may best discern the true interest of their country, and whose patriotism and love of justice will be least likely to sacrifice it to temporary or partial considerations. Under such a regulation, it may well happen that the public voice, pronounced by the representatives of the people, will be more consonant to the public good than if pronounced by the people themselves, convened for the purpose. On the other hand, the effect may be inverted. Men of factious tempers, of local prejudices, or of sinister designs, may, by intrigue, by corruption, or by other means, first obtain the suffrages, and then betray the interests, of the people. The question resulting is, whether small or extensive republics are more favorable to the election of proper guardians of the public weal; and it is clearly decided in favor of the latter by two obvious considerations:

In the first place, it is to be remarked that, however small the republic may be, the representatives must be raised to a certain number, in order to guard against the cabals of a few; and that, however large it may be, they must be limited to a certain number, in order to guard against the confusion of a multitude. Hence, the number of representatives in the two cases not being in proportion to that of the two constituents, and being proportionally greater in the small republic, it follows that, if the proportion of fit characters be not less in the large than in the small republic, the former will present a greater option, and consequently a greater probability of a fit choice.

In the next place, as each representative will be chosen by a greater number of citizens in the large than in the small republic, it will be more difficult for unworthy candidates to practice with success the vicious arts by which elections are too often carried; and the suffrages of the people being more free, will be more likely to center in men who possess the most attractive merit and the most diffusive and established characters.

It must be confessed that in this, as in most other cases, there is a mean, on both sides of which inconveniences will be found to lie. By enlarging too much the number of electors, you render the representative too little acquainted with all their local circumstances and lesser interests as by reducing it too much, you render him unduly attached to these, and too little fit to comprehend and pursue great and national objects. The federal Constitution forms a happy combination in this respect; the great and aggregate interests being referred to the national, the local and particular to the State legislatures.

The other point of difference is, the greater number of citizens and extent of territory which may be brought within the compass of republican than of democratic government; and it is this circumstance principally which renders factious combinations less to be dreaded in the former than in the latter. The smaller the society, the fewer probably will be the distinct parties and interests composing it; the fewer the distinct parties and interests, the more frequently will a majority be found of the same party; and the smaller the number of individuals composing a majority, and the smaller the compass within which they are placed, the more easily will they concert and execute their plans of oppression. Extend the sphere, and you take in a greater variety of parties and interests; you make it less probable that a majority of the whole will have a common motive to invade the rights of other citizens; or if such a common motive exists, it will be more difficult for all who feel it to discover their own strength, and to act in unison with each other. Besides other impediments, it may be remarked that, where there is a consciousness of unjust or dishonorable purposes, communication is always checked by distrust in proportion to the number whose concurrence is necessary.

Hence, it clearly appears, that the same advantage which a republic has over a democracy, in controlling the effects of faction, is enjoyed by a large over a small republic, — is enjoyed by the Union over the States composing it. Does the advantage consist in the substitution of representatives whose enlightened views and virtuous sentiments render them superior to local prejudices and to schemes of injustice? It will not be denied that the representation of the Union will be most likely to possess these requisite endowments. Does it consist in the greater security afforded by a greater variety of parties, against the event of any one party being able to outnumber and oppress the rest? In an equal degree does the increased variety of parties comprised within the Union, increase this security. Does it, in fine, consist in the greater obstacles opposed to the concert and accomplishment of the secret wishes of an unjust and interested majority? Here, again, the extent of the Union gives it the most palpable advantage.

The influence of factious leaders may kindle a flame within their particular States, but will be unable to spread a general conflagration through the other States. A religious sect may degenerate into a political faction in a part of the

Confederacy; but the variety of sects dispersed over the entire face of it must secure the national councils against any danger from that source. A rage for paper money, for an abolition of debts, for an equal division of property, or for any other improper or wicked project, will be less apt to pervade the whole body of the Union than a particular member of it; in the same proportion as such a malady is more likely to taint a particular county or district, than an entire State.

In the extent and proper structure of the Union, therefore, we behold a republican remedy for the diseases most incident to republican government. And according to the degree of pleasure and pride we feel in being republicans, ought to be our zeal in cherishing the spirit and supporting the character of Federalists.

Publius

Note:　*Madisonian Republicanism*

The Federalist No. 10 reveals that for Madison the primary problem of governance consists in control of factions. The antifederalists rooted the problem of faction in that of corruption; their solution rested in the effort to control the factional spirit and the power of representatives. In their view, the civic virtue of the citizenry and of its representatives would work as a safeguard against factional tyranny.

The Federalist No. 10 turned the antifederalist understanding on its head. For Madison, and for many other federalists, the question of corruption was transformed into that of faction, which was itself an inevitable product of liberty, which would produce inequality in the ownership of property. Crucially, this redefinition meant that the basic problem could not be solved by the traditional republican means of education and inculcation of virtue. Moreover, the problem of faction was likely to be most, not least, severe in a small republic. It was in a small republic that a self-interested private group would be most likely to be able to seize political power in order to distribute wealth or opportunities in its favor. Indeed, in the view of the federalists, this was precisely what had happened in the years since the Revolution. In that period, factions had usurped the processes of state government, putting both liberty and property at risk. Consider in this regard Madison's rejection of Jefferson's proposal of frequent constitutional amendment on the ground that such a proposal would produce "the most violent struggle between the parties interested in reviving and those interested in reforming the antecedent state of property." M. Meyers, ed., The Mind of the Founder 232 (1969). For Jefferson, by contrast, turbulence is "productive of good. It prevents the degeneracy of government, and nourishes a general attention to the public affairs. I hold that a little rebellion now and then is a good thing." Letter to Madison, Jan. 30, 1787, in The Portable Thomas Jefferson 416-417 (M. Peterson ed. 1975). For Madison, ongoing processes of self-government produced not the promise of genuine self-determination but instead the danger of factional warfare.

Madison thought that both the experience of ancient republics and recent history furnished clear evidence that traditional conceptions of civic virtue, or public education, could not guard against factional tyranny. Such devices would be unable to overcome the natural self-interest of citizens, even in their capacity as political actors. To this point Madison added the familiar idea that "education" of that sort would carry a risk of tyranny of its own. What emerged was a theory of human nature that saw self-interest as an inevitable force in political behavior. The federalists did not, however, suppose that self-interest was all there was to human beings. "The supposition of universal venality in human nature is little less an error in political reasoning than the supposition of universal rectitude," wrote Hamilton in The Federalist No. 76. And in No. 55, Madison made the same point, claiming that "[a]s there is a degree of depravity in mankind which requires a certain degree of circumspection and distrust, so there are other qualities in human nature, which justify a certain portion of esteem and confidence."

In any case, the specter of faction was sufficient to justify rejection of the antifederalist understanding that in a small republic the problem of faction could be overcome. But it was in developing a solution that Madison was particularly original. The solution began with the insight that in a direct democracy the problem posed by factions is especially acute, for a "common passion or interest will, in almost every case, be felt by a majority of the whole" and there will be no protection for the minority. But safeguards would be found in a large republic. There, the diversity of interests would reduce the risk that a common desire would be felt by sufficient numbers of people to oppress minorities. In this respect, the likelihood of factional tyranny contained a built-in check in a large republic.

On this view, heterogeneity — Brutus's fear — was a positive good. It would work against factionalism and parochialism. At the same time "differences of opinion, and the jarrings of parties [would] . . . promote deliberation and circumspection; and serve to check the excesses of the majority." The Federalist No. 70. Differences and disagreement were not harmful to a deliberative republic. On the contrary, they were indispensable to its successful operation.

Nor were these the only virtues of size. The other feature of the large republic was that the principle of representation would serve in that setting as a substantial solution to the problem of faction. The central phrase here is Madison's suggestion that that principle would "refine and enlarge the public views, by passing them through the medium of a chosen body of citizens, whose wisdom may best discern the true interest of their country, and whose patriotism and love of justice will be least likely to sacrifice it to temporary or partial considerations." This is so in part because in a large republic the dangers produced by undue attachment to local interests would be reduced.

This conception of representation appears throughout The Federalist Papers and indeed throughout Madison's work. In No. 57, Madison urges that "the aim of every political constitution is, or ought to be, first to obtain for rulers men who possess most wisdom to discern, and most virtue to pursue, the common good of society; and in the next place, to take the most effectual precautions for keeping them virtuous while they continue to hold the public trust." Elsewhere he suggests that "wisdom" and "virtue" will characterize national representatives. Where the antifederalists accepted representation as a necessary evil, Madison regarded it as an opportunity for achieving governance by officials devoted to a public good distinct from the struggle of private interests.

Thus it is that Madison favored long length of service and large election districts — precisely what the antifederalists most feared. Thus, the federalists spoke most favorably of the presidency, highly of the Senate, and less favorably of the House — precisely the opposite of the valuations of the antifederalists. Thus, the antifederalists sought a "right to instruct" representatives as part of the bill of rights — a right successfully resisted by the federalists on the theory that deliberation required representatives to be free from commitments, undertaken in advance, to their constituents.

In the Madisonian account, representatives were to have the time and temperament to engage in a form of collective reasoning. They were not to be mere "transmission belts" for the will of the various constituencies, much less to be a mechanism for aggregating interests. The hope, in short, was for a genuinely national politics. The representatives of the people — not the people themselves — would be free to engage in the process of discussion and debate from which the common good would emerge. Consider the fact that the first Congress rejected a right to instruct, by which constituents would be authorized to give binding instructions to representatives. Those who opposed this right contended that it would be inconsistent with the point of the legislative meeting: public-spirited deliberation among people with different points of view.

This, then, is the account offered in The Federalist No. 10. But there is some evidence that Madison had a greater influence on posterity than he did on his contemporaries. On one view, the framers were generally "deaf to Madison's theory," see Kramer, Madison's Audience, 112 Harv. L. Rev. 611, 677 (1999), and "the Founding may have been a more conventional intellectual event than we have come to believe." Id. at 673. Thus, Kramer urges that in "its original context" Madison's "new theory of the extended republic was an insignificant detail, an unappreciated ingredient in the larger sweep of events," id. at 679, and to the extent that "the Constitution embodies Madison's theory, it has come to do so only in our own century, as a reflection of our present intellectual tastes." Id. On this view, Madison's quite fundamental rethinking of governmental structure was less central to the founding than "the successful distillation and application of already familiar ideas about separating and balancing power, together with some undeniably impressive political maneuvering." Id. at 673. For a contrary view, see Rakove, The Great Compromise: Ideas, Interests, and the Politics of Constitution Making, 44 Wm. & Mary Q. 424 (1987).

Even if The Federalist No. 10 is taken to set out some central themes in the new Constitution, it is far from the entire story. The Constitution embodies a set of structural provisions designed to bring about public-spirited representation, to provide safeguards in the event that it is absent, and to ensure an important measure of popular control. The various systems of representation in the different branches of the national government were designed to promote deliberation in government and to control possible abuses. Recognizing that sovereignty lay in the people, the framers designed a system in which no branch could speak authoritatively for the people themselves. On this view, the Constitution's structural provisions can be seen as a kind of bill of rights, designed to protect against tyranny.

Bicameralism — the division of Congress into the House and the Senate, with two-year and six-year terms, respectively — was intended to ensure that some representatives would be relatively isolated from the people and that others would be relatively close to them. The fact that the houses of the legislature were divided in this way would combine political accountability (on the part of the House) with a degree of independence (on the part of the Senate), enabling the Senate to serve a kind of "cooling" function. Indirect election of representatives played a far more important role at the time of ratification than it does today. Only the House of Representatives was to be directly elected, thus providing additional insulation from political pressure and factional tyranny. The electoral college is an important example; it was to be a deliberative body standing to some degree apart from constituent pressures.

Perhaps most important, the system of checks and balances was designed with the recognition that even national representatives may be prone to the influence of "interests" that is inconsistent with the public welfare. In The Federalist No. 10 itself, Madison recognizes that "[e]nlightened statesmen will not always be at the helm." The Federalist No. 51 is the most celebrated elaboration of this point.

The Federalist No. 51 (Madison)

(1788)

In order to lay a due foundation for that separate and distinct exercise of the different powers of government, which to a certain extent is admitted on all hands to be essential to the preservation of liberty, it is evident that each department should have a will of its own; and consequently should be so constituted that the members of each should have as little agency as possible in the appointment of the members of the others. Were this principle rigorously adhered to, it would require that all the appointments for the supreme executive, legislative, and judiciary magistracies should be drawn from the same fountain of authority, the people, through channels having no communication whatever with one another. [Some] difficulties, and some additional expense would attend the execution of it. Some deviations, therefore, from the principle must be admitted. In the constitution of the judiciary department in particular, it might be inexpedient to insist rigorously on the principle: first, because peculiar qualifications being essential in the members, the primary consideration ought to be to select that mode of choice which best secures these qualifications; secondly, because the permanent tenure by which the appointments are held in that department, must soon destroy all sense of dependence on the authority conferring them.

It is equally evident, that the members of each department should be as little dependent as possible on those of the others, for the emoluments annexed to their offices. Were the executive magistrate, or the judges, not independent of the legislature in this particular, their independence in every other would be merely nominal.

But the great security against a gradual concentration of the several powers in the same department, consists in giving to those who administer each department the necessary constitutional means and personal motives to resist encroachments of the others. The provision for defence must in this, as in all other cases, be made commensurate to the danger of attack. Ambition must be made to counteract ambition. The interest of the man must be connected with the constitutional rights of the place. It may be a reflection on human nature, that such devices should be necessary to control the abuses of government. But what is government itself, but the greatest of all reflections on human nature? If men were angels, no government would be necessary. If angels were to govern men, neither external nor internal controls on government would be necessary. In framing a government which is to be administered by men over men, the great difficulty lies in this: you must first enable the government to control the governed; and in the next place oblige it to control itself. A dependence on the people is, no doubt, the primary control on the government; but experience has taught mankind the necessity of auxiliary precautions.

This policy of supplying, by opposite and rival interests, the defect of better motives, might be traced through the whole system of human affairs, private as well as public. We see it particularly displayed in all the subordinate distributions of power, where the constant aim is to divide and arrange the several offices in such a manner as that each may be a check on the other — that the private interest of every individual may be a sentinel over the public rights. These inventions of prudence cannot be less requisite in the distribution of the supreme powers of the State.

But it is not possible to give to each department an equal power of self-defence. In republican government, the legislative authority necessarily predominates. The remedy for this inconveniency is to divide the legislature into different branches; and to render them, by different modes of election and different principles of action, as little connected with each other as the nature of their common functions and their common dependence on the society will admit. It may even be necessary to guard against dangerous encroachments by still further precautions. As the weight of the legislative authority requires that it should be thus divided, the weakness of the executive may require, on the other hand, that it should be fortified. An absolute negative on the legislature appears, at first view, to be the natural defence with which the executive magistrate should be armed. But perhaps it would be neither altogether safe nor alone sufficient. On ordinary occasions it might not be exerted with the requisite firmness, and on extraordinary occasions it might be perfidiously abused. May not this defect of an absolute negative be supplied by some qualified connection between this weaker department and the weaker branch of the stronger department, by which the latter may be led to support the constitutional rights of the former, without being too much detached from the rights of its own department?

There are, moreover, two considerations particularly applicable to the federal system of America, which place that system in a very interesting point of view.

First. In a single republic, all the power surrendered by the people is submitted to the administration of a single government; and the usurpations are guarded against by a division of the government into distinct and separate departments. In the compound republic of America, the power surrendered by the people is first divided between two distinct governments, and then the portion allotted to each subdivided among distinct and separate departments. Hence a double security arises to the rights of the people. The different governments will control each other, at the same time that each will be controlled by itself.

Second. It is of great importance in a republic not only to guard the society against the oppression of its rulers, but to guard one part of the society against the injustice of the other part. Different interests necessarily exist in different classes of citizens. If a majority be united by a common interest, the rights of the minority will be insecure. There are but two methods of providing against this evil: the one by creating a will in the community independent of the majority — that is, of the society itself; the other, by comprehending in the society so many separate descriptions of citizens as will render an unjust combination of a majority of the whole very improbable, if not impracticable. The first method [is] but a precarious security; because a power independent of the society may as well espouse the unjust views of the major, as the rightful interests of the minor party, and may possibly be turned against both parties. The second method will be exemplified in the federal republic of the United States. Whilst all authority in it will be derived from and dependent on the society, the society itself will be broken into so many parts, interests and classes of citizens, that the rights of individuals, or of the minority, will be in little danger from interested combinations of the majority. In a free government the security for civil rights must be the same as that for religious rights. It consists in the one case in the multiplicity of interests, and in the other in the multiplicity of sects. The degree of security in both cases will depend on the number of interests and sects; and this may be presumed to depend on the extent of country and number of people comprehended under the same government. This view of the subject must particularly recommend a proper federal system to all the sincere and considerate friends of republican government, since it shows that in exact proportion as the territory of the Union may be formed into more circumscribed Confederacies, or States, oppressive combinations of a majority will be facilitated; the best security, under the republican forms, for the rights of every class of citizens, will be diminished; and consequently the stability and independence of some member of the government, the only other security, must be proportionally increased.

[In] a society under the forms of which the stronger faction can readily unite and oppress the weaker, anarchy may as truly be said to reign as in a state of nature, where the weaker individual is not secured against the violence of the stronger; and as, in the latter state, even the stronger individuals are prompted, by the uncertainty of their condition, to submit to a government which may protect the weak as well as themselves; so, in the former state, will the more powerful factions or parties be gradually induced, by a like motive, to wish for a government which will protect all parties, the weaker as well as the more powerful. It can be little doubted that if the State of Rhode Island was separated from the Confederacy and left to itself, the insecurity of rights under the popular form of government, within such narrow limits would be displayed by such reiterated oppressions of factious majorities that some power altogether independent of the people would soon be called for by the voice of the very factions whose misrule had proved the necessity of it. In the extended republic of the United States, and among the great variety of interests, parties, and sects which it embraces, a coalition of a majority of the whole society could seldom take place on any other principles than those of justice and the general good; whilst there being thus less danger to a minor from the will of a major party, there must be less pretext, also, to provide for the security of the former, by introducing into the government a will not dependent on the latter, or, in other words, a will independent of the society itself. It is no less certain than it is important, notwithstanding the contrary opinions which have been entertained, that the larger the society, provided it lie within a practical sphere, the more duly capable it will be of self-government. And happily for the *republican cause*, the practicable sphere may be carried to a very great extent, by a judicious modification and mixture of the *federal principle*.

Publius

Note: Madisonian Republicanism and Checks and Balances

The system of checks and balances within the federal structure was thus intended to prevent both factionalism and self-interested representation. If a segment of rulers was influenced by interests that diverged from those of the people, other national officials would have both the incentive and the means to resist. The result is an additional protection against tyranny. We might also think of the system as one in which the sovereign people can pursue a strategy of divide and conquer. Rather than undemocratically limiting majority will, the distribution of national powers might be seen, at least in part, as a way of maximizing the power of the public by fragmenting the power of the governors. See, on this and related questions, Sunstein, Constitutionalism after the New Deal, 101 Harv. L. Rev. 421, 430-437 (1989). Of course, this view is controversial. The fragmentation does allow the status quo to remain undisturbed, and many have argued that this effect insulates existing practices, including distributions of wealth, from democratic control. This was a particular theme in the New Deal period, when President Franklin Delano Roosevelt succeeded in concentrating power — including lawmaking and law-interpreting power — in the executive branch. See id.; 2 B. Ackerman, We the People: Transformations (1998).

The federal system, too, would act as an important safeguard. The "different governments will control each other" and ensure stalemate rather than action at the behest of particular private interests. The jealousy of state governments, and the attachment of the citizenry to local interests, would provide additional protection against the aggrandizement of power in national institutions. The federal system would allow flexibility, experimentation, accountability, and diversity and permit a measure of self-determination through the classically republican institution of small governmental units. At the same time, the power of individual citizens to move from one state to another would operate as a check on governmental tyranny. The right of "exit" would deter local oppression, as people could vote with their feet.

The result is a complex system of checks: National representation, bicameralism, indirect election, distribution of powers, and the federal-state relationship would operate in concert to counteract the effects of faction in spite of the inevitability of the factional spirit. And the Constitution itself, enforced by disinterested judges and adopted at a moment in which that spirit had perhaps been temporarily extinguished, would prevent majorities or minorities from usurping government power to distribute wealth or opportunities in their favor.

There has been no discussion thus far of private property, freedom of contract, and the various issues raised by governmental redistribution of resources. The protection of property and contractual liberty were principal interests of the framers, and one of their principal targets was debtor-relief legislation. Some of the framers saw a close practical relationship between the desire to protect private property (along with other forms of private liberty) from governmental intrusion and devices to guard against the dangers posed by faction. For the framers, the problem of faction lay partly in the danger that a self-interested group would obtain governmental power in order to put rights of property at risk. The experience under the Articles of Confederation, in which popular majorities had operated as factions in state legislatures, confirmed the existence of this danger.

In this respect, the federalists may be contrasted with their antifederalist opponents, whose generally weaker objections to laws redistributing property coexisted easily with their preference for decentralized democracy. Indeed, many of the antifederalists approved of debtor-relief laws and saw economic equality as indispensable to a republic. As "Centinel" wrote, a "republican, or free government, can only exist where the body of the people are virtuous, and where property is pretty equally divided; in such a government the people are the sovereign and their sense or opinion is the criterion of every public measure; for when this ceases to be the case, the nature of the government is changed, and an aristocracy, monarchy, or despotism will rise on its ruin." The Antifederalist 16 (H. Storing ed., M. Dry abr. 1985). Such sentiments can rarely be found within the federalist literature.

Moreover, the federalists' hospitable view toward lengthy deliberation and government inaction may be associated with a desire to protect private property. Inaction, of course, preserves the existing distribution of wealth. For a discussion with some provocative claims about how to rethink the separation of powers and with reference to comparative materials, see Ackerman, The New Separation of Powers, 113 Harv. L. Rev. 33 (2000).

The picture that emerges is in an important sense one of a government that was intended to engage in deliberation. But politics was to be deliberative in a special sense. Representatives were to be accountable to the public; their deliberative task was not disembodied. The framers were thus careful to create political checks designed to ensure that representatives would not stray too far from the desires of their constituents. The result was a kind of hybrid conception of representation, in which legislators were neither to respond blindly to constituent pressures nor to undertake their deliberations in a vacuum. (Note also the restrictions on who would do the deliberating: The framers appeared comfortable with many limits on the franchise; women and slaves, among others, could not vote. It is interesting to ask whether these exclusions were essential to their kind of republicanism or instead a betrayal of its basic principles.)

In these respects, the federalists managed a kind of synthesis of the classical republican conception, as they understood it, and the emerging principles of pluralism, in accordance with which politics should be seen as an inevitably self-interested struggle among competing social groups. See, e.g., A. Bentley, The Process of Government (1908); R. Dahl, A Preface to Democratic Theory (1956); D. Truman, The Governmental Process (1962). For the federalists, politics rightly consisted of deliberation and discussion about the public good. But that process could not be brought about in the traditional republican fashion; such an effort, in light of human nature, would deteriorate into a struggle among warring factions. A partial solution lay in principles of representation. At the same time, the representatives would be kept accountable to the public. The mechanisms of accountability would prevent representatives from acquiring interests distinct from those of their constituents. The system of checks and balances would ensure that, if representatives became self-interested, or if a particular group acquired too much power over one set of representatives, there would be safeguards to prevent either representatives or private groups from obtaining authority over the national government in general.

Where does judicial review fit into this framework? Notice that the Constitution does not explicitly authorize judicial review, but it appears to have been widely anticipated. To a large degree, the Court was intended to enforce the lines of division set down in the Constitution, in order to ensure that the areas marked off from politics would not be subject to political revision. The boundaries set in the Constitution, and thus by "We the People," were to be unrevisable by electoral majorities — a safeguard that would buttress the other institutional checks. In this sense, judicial review would ensure the supremacy of the Constitution, embodying the will of the sovereign public, against temporary majorities. This idea responded to the distinction drawn by the framers between "law" — the realm of judgment — and "politics" — the realm of will, or personal preference. See The Federalist No. 78, infra. The existence of a realm of "law" immune from "politics" fit securely within a system intended to protect both the public good and private rights from perceived majoritarian excesses.

Note finally that this entire framework reflects a new conception of sovereignty, which lay with the people, not with any king, and not with any branch or set of rulers. One of the most important contributions of the new Constitution consisted in the rejection of the monarchical legacy in favor of this new understanding of where sovereignty could be found. See G. Wood, The Radicalism of the American Revolution (1993).

Note: Madisonian Republicanism and Contemporary Constitutionalism

The foregoing materials raise a large set of questions; we will be exploring them at many places in this book. Here are a few problems that might be kept in mind at the outset.

1. The account that we have offered — of a particular understanding of Madisonian republicanism — is an attempt to reconstruct the founders' view, but any such attempt is bound to be controversial. Some people think that an account of the kind offered here downplays the framers' belief in individual rights, operating as checks against politics — even deliberative politics. Others think that the framers offered a highly complex set of ideas not reducible to any single "account." Still others think that deliberation was a theme in the founding generation but not an entirely central one; in their view the framers were well aware of the importance of interest groups, and they did not place a great premium on political deliberation. For various discussions, see W. Bessette, The Mild Voice of Reason (1994); Flaherty, History "Lite" in Modern American Constitutionalism, 95 Colum. L. Rev. 523 (1995); Powell, Reviving Republicanism, 97 Yale L.J. 1703 (1988).

2. At least since the late 1970s there has been considerable interest — in history, political theory, and law — in "republican" theories of the Constitution. But the word "republican" is ambiguous. Sometimes the term refers to some version of classical republicanism, that is, enthusiasm for small-scale democracy, civic virtue, and participation in government. Sometimes this version of republicanism is opposed to "liberalism," which is said to be focused on rights, self-interest, and side-constraints on government rather than on civic virtue and democratic self-determination. On the asserted tension between liberalism and republicanism, see, e.g., Habermas, Three Models of Democracy, 1 Constellations 1 (1994); Horwitz, History and Theory, 96 Yale L.J. 1825, 1831-1835 (1987). For an important general discussion showing the American progression in the early period from monarchy to republicanism to democracy, see G. Wood, The Radicalism of the American Revolution (1993).

3. What does republicanism, Madisonian or otherwise, have to offer to people currently assessing American constitutional law? Republican thought might argue in favor of a deferential rather than an aggressive judicial role. After all, it was

the antifederalists who were least favorably disposed toward a powerful Supreme Court. In addition, if democratic self-determination is the end, a powerful judiciary hardly seems the means.

4. Is the deliberative conception of representation elitist or worse? The question assumes considerable importance in light of the fact that many people have argued in favor of a larger role for popular referenda, in which decisions are made on particular issues not by representatives but instead by popular vote. It might be urged that the process of referendum is far more democratic than the process of decision by representative bodies.

In recent years, popular referenda have both grown out of and produced constitutional confrontations. Consider recent proposed or actual referenda calling for an end to affirmative action; for exclusion of children of unlawful aliens from public services, including health and education; for bans on laws forbidding discrimination on the basis of sexual orientation. Discussions of "electronic town meetings" have heightened interest in more direct forms of democracy; modern technologies make direct popular input far more feasible. On referenda generally, see T. Cronin, Direct Democracy (1989); D. Magleby, Direct Legislation (1991); Charlow, Judicial Review, Equal Protection and the Problem with Plebiscites, 79 Cornell L. Rev. 527 (1994); Eule, Judicial Review of Direct Democracy, 99 Yale L.J. 1503 (1990).

5. Consider as well the view that the republican commitment to "deliberation" is unrealistic. "As a descriptive matter, there is abundant evidence that all too often politics is just the way the pluralists describe it: ceaseless compromises between competing factions, none of which would pay a nickel to advance the common good, even if they could identify it. [In] the face of this massive volume of special interest politics, how can republicanism be thought to describe the dominant patters of political discourse?" Epstein, Modern Republicanism — Or the Flight from Substance, 97 Yale L.J. 1633, 1637-1638 (1988). Might the commitment to deliberation also be empty, since it tells us nothing about what goes into deliberative processes or what might come out of them?

6. Serious questions are raised by efforts to adapt the original constitutional framework to modern government. At every stage, the original commitments have been severely qualified in the nineteenth and twentieth centuries. Thus, for example, the national government engages in many tasks originally thought to be within the province of the states — a phenomenon that can be attributed in large part to the Civil War and Franklin Roosevelt's New Deal, which saw a huge expansion in federal power. The system of checks and balances has been altered by the grant of broad adjudicatory and policymaking power to the President and regulatory agencies. The American conception of constitutional rights has come to include private property and contract — but only quite qualified forms of both of these — and also rights of political participation, of freedom of expression, of antidiscrimination on the basis of race and sex, and of "privacy" that were either unanticipated by the founders or are far broader than what they expected. On these and related issues, see T. Lowi, The Personal President (1985).

The American Constitution is often celebrated for its stability and longevity. But its real nature has changed dramatically over time, often without formal amendment. How might those in the executive, legislative, and judicial branches maintain fidelity to constitutional commitments in a time in which government does altogether different things, and does those things in altogether new ways?

See generally Lessig, Fidelity in Translation, 71 Tex. L. Rev. 1165 (1993); Lessig, Understanding Changed Readings: Fidelity and Theory, 47 Stan. L. Rev. 395 (1995). This is a large question that unites a wide range of modern controversies.

7. Has the American Constitution had just one, or two, or three, or more fundamental "constitutional moments"? 1 B. Ackerman, We the People: Foundations (1991), argues that there have been several such moments, and indeed that the founding, the Civil War, and the New Deal resulted in three different constitutional "republics." On Ackerman's account, the Constitution represents a "dualist democracy," that is, a system that distinguishes between the higher politics of constitution-making and the "normal politics" of day-to-day life. Constitutional politics has many of the features of republican self-governance; normal politics acknowledges the partial truths of pluralism. Ackerman claims that there have been three large periods of constitutional politics, setting forth the nation's basic political aspirations. In his view, much of the work of the Supreme Court can be understood as efforts to synthesize the commitments of these three different republics. Ackerman's arguments are controversial, but as we will see, both the Civil War period and the New Deal did help inaugurate major changes in constitutional law.

B.   THE BASIC FRAMEWORK

Marbury v. Madison

5 U.S. (1 Cranch) 137 (1803)

[William Marbury had been appointed a justice of the peace by the defeated incumbent Federalist President, John Adams, in the closing stages of the Adams administration. The Federalist-controlled Senate confirmed the appointments of Adams's last-minute appointees, including Marbury, on March 3, 1801. The formal commissions had not been delivered when Thomas Jefferson, the Republican President, assumed office several days later. Jefferson refused to deliver the commissions of the justices appointed by Adams. Marbury and others sought a writ of mandamus to compel Madison, Jefferson's Secretary of State (replacing John Marshall, Adams's Secretary of State), to deliver the commissions. (The underlying controversy is set out in more detail in a historical note that follows the opinion.)]

Opinion of the Court [by MARSHALL, CHIEF JUSTICE].

At the last term on the affidavits then read and filed with the clerk, a rule was granted in this case, requiring the secretary of state to show cause why a mandamus should not issue, directing him to deliver to William Marbury his commission as a justice of the peace for the county of Washington, in the district of Columbia.

No cause has been shown, and the present motion is for a mandamus. The peculiar delicacy of this case, the novelty of some of its circumstances, and the real difficulty attending the points which occur in it, require a complete exposition of the principles on which the opinion to be given by the court is founded.

In the order in which the court has viewed this subject, the following questions have been considered and decided.

1st. Has the applicant a right to the commission he demands?

2dly. If he has a right, and that right has been violated, do the laws of his country afford him a remedy?

3dly. If they do afford him a remedy, is it a mandamus issuing from this court?

The first object of inquiry is,

1st. Has the applicant a right to the commission he demands?

His right originates in an act of congress passed in February, 1801, concerning the district of Columbia. . . .

In order to determine whether he is entitled to this commission, it becomes necessary to inquire whether he has been appointed to the office. For if he has been appointed, the law continues him in office for five years, and he is entitled to the possession of those evidences of office, which, being completed, became his property.

The last act to be done by the president is the signature of the commission: he has then acted on the advice and consent of the senate to his own nomination. The time for deliberation has then passed. . . .

It is, [decidedly] the opinion of the court, that when a commission has been signed by the president, the appointment is made; and that the commission is complete, when the seal of the United States has been affixed to it by the secretary of state.

Where an officer is removable at the will of the executive, the circumstance which completes his appointment is of no concern; because the act is at any time revocable; and the commission may be arrested, if still in the office. But when the officer is not removable at the will of the executive, the appointment is not revocable, and cannot be annulled: it has conferred legal rights which cannot be resumed. [To] withhold his commission, therefore, is an act deemed by the court not warranted by law, but violative of a vested legal right.

2. This brings us to the second inquiry; which is: If he has a right, and that right has been violated, do the laws of his country afford him a remedy? The very essence of civil liberty certainly consists in the right of every individual to claim the protection of the laws, whenever he receives an injury. One of the first duties of government is to afford that protection. In Great Britain, the king himself is sued in the respectful form of a petition, and he never fails to comply with the judgment of his court.

The government of the United States has been emphatically termed a government of laws, and not of men. It will certainly cease to deserve this high appellation, if the laws furnish no remedy for the violation of a vested legal right. If this obloquy is to be cast on the jurisprudence of our country, it must arise from the peculiar character of the case.

It behooves us, then, to inquire whether there be in its composition any ingredient which shall exempt it from legal investigation, or exclude the injured party from legal redress. . . .

Is it in the nature of the transaction? Is the act of delivering or withholding a commission to be considered as a mere political act, belonging to the executive department alone, for the performance of which entire confidence is placed by our constitution in the supreme executive; and for any misconduct respecting which, the injured individual has no remedy? That there may be such cases is not to be questioned; but that every act of duty, to be performed in any of the great departments of government, constitutes such a case, is not to be admitted.

It follows, then, that the question, whether the legality of an act of the head of a department be examinable in a court of justice or not, must always depend on the nature of that act. If some acts be examinable, and others not, there must be some rule of law to guide the court in the exercise of its jurisdiction. In some instances, there may be difficulty in applying the rule to particular cases; but there cannot, it is believed, be much difficulty in laying down the rule.

By the constitution of the United States, the president is invested with certain important political powers, in the exercise of which he is to use his own discretion, and is accountable only to his country in his political character, and to his own conscience. To aid him in the performance of these duties, he is authorized to appoint certain officers, who act by his authority, and in conformity with his orders. In such cases, their acts are his acts; and whatever opinion may be entertained of the manner in which executive discretion may be used, still there exists, and can exist, no power to control that discretion. The subjects are political: they respect the nation, not individual rights, and being entrusted to the executive, the decision of the executive is conclusive. The application of this remark will be perceived, by adverting to the act of congress for establishing the department of foreign affairs. This officer, as his duties were prescribed by that act, is to conform precisely to the will of the president: he is the mere organ by whom that will is communicated. The acts of such an officer, as an officer, can never be examinable by the courts. But when the legislature proceeds to impose on that officer other duties; when he is directed peremptorily to perform certain acts; when the rights of individuals are dependent on the performance of those acts; he is so far the officer of the law; is amenable to the laws for his conduct; and cannot, at his discretion, sport away the vested rights of others.

The conclusion from this reasoning is, that where the heads of departments are the political or confidential agents of the executive, merely to execute the will of the president, or rather to act in cases in which the executive possesses a constitutional or legal discretion, nothing can be more perfectly clear, than that their acts are only politically examinable. But where a specific duty is assigned by law, and individual rights depend upon the performance of that duty, it seems equally clear, that the individual who considers himself injured, has a right to resort to the laws of his country for a remedy.

The question whether a right has vested or not, is, in its nature, judicial, and must be tried by the judicial authority. If, for example, Mr. Marbury had taken the oaths of a magistrate, and proceeded to act as one; in consequence of which, a suit has been instituted against him, in which his defence had depended on his being a magistrate, the validity of his appointment must have been determined by judicial authority. So, if he conceives that, by virtue of his appointment, he has a legal right either to the commission which has been made out for him, or to a copy of that commission, it is equally a question examinable in a court, and the decision of the court upon it must depend on the opinion entertained of his appointment. That question has been discussed, and the opinion is, that the latest point of time which can be taken as that at which the appointment was complete, and evidenced, was when, after the signature of the president, the seal of the United States was affixed to the commission.

It is, then, the opinion of the Court: 1st. That by signing the commission of Mr. Marbury, the President of the United States appointed him a justice of peace [and] that the appointment conferred on him a legal right to the office for the space of five years. 2d. That, having this legal title to the office, he has a consequent right to the commission; a refusal to deliver which is a plain violation of that right, for which the laws of his country afford him a remedy.

3. It remains to be inquired whether he is entitled to the remedy for which he applies? This depends on — 1st. The nature of the writ applied for; and 2d. The power of this court.

1st. The nature of the writ. . . .

[To] render the mandamus a proper remedy, the officer to whom it is to be directed, must be one to whom, on legal principles, such writ may be directed; and the person applying for it must be without any other specific and legal remedy.

1. With respect to the officer to whom it would be directed. The intimate political relation subsisting between the president of the United States and the heads of departments, necessarily renders any legal investigation of the acts of one of those high officers peculiarly irksome, as well as delicate; and excites some hesitation with respect to the propriety of entering into such investigation. Impressions are often received, without much reflection or examination, and it is not wonderful, that in such a case as this, the assertion, by an individual, of his legal claims in a court of justice, to which claims it is the duty of that court to attend, should at first view be considered by some, as an attempt to intrude into the cabinet, and to intermeddle with the prerogatives of the executive.

It is scarcely necessary for the court to disclaim all pretensions to such a jurisdiction. An extravagance, so absurd and excessive, could not have been entertained for a moment. The province of the court is, solely, to decide on the rights of individuals, not to inquire how the executive, or executive officers, perform duties in which they have a discretion. Questions in their nature political, or which are, by the constitution and laws, submitted to the executive, can never be made in this court.

But, if this be not such a question; if, so far from being an intrusion into the secrets of the cabinet, it respects a paper which, according to law, is upon record, and to a copy of which the law gives a right, on the payment of ten cents; if it be no intermeddling with a subject over which the executive can be considered as having exercised any control; what is there, in the exalted station of the officer, which shall bar a citizen from asserting, in a court of justice, his legal rights, or shall forbid a court to listen to the claim, or to issue a mandamus, directing the performance of a duty, not depending on executive discretion, but on particular acts of congress, and the general principles of law?

[Where the head of a department] is directed by law to do a certain act affecting the absolute rights of individuals, [it] is not perceived on what grounds the courts of the country are [excused] from the duty of giving judgment. . . .

[This,] then, is a plain case for a mandamus, either to deliver the commission, or a copy of it from the record; and it only remains to be inquired,

Whether it can issue from this court.

The act to establish the judicial courts of the United States authorizes the supreme court "to issue writs of mandamus, in cases warranted by the principles and usages of law, to any courts appointed, or persons holding, office, under the authority of the United States."*

The secretary of state, being a person holding an office under the authority of the United States, is precisely within the letter of the description; and if this court is not authorized to issue a writ of mandamus to such an officer, it must be because the law is unconstitutional, and therefore absolutely incapable of conferring the authority, and assigning the duties which its words purport to confer and assign.

The constitution vests the whole judicial power of the United States in one supreme court, and such inferior courts as congress shall, from time to time, ordain and establish. This power is expressly extended to all cases arising under the laws of the United States; and, consequently, in some form, may be exercised over the present case; because the right claimed is given by a law of the United States.

In the distribution of this power it is declared that "the supreme court shall have original jurisdiction in all cases affecting ambassadors, other public ministers and consuls, and those in which a state shall be a party. In all other cases, the supreme court shall have appellate jurisdiction."

It has been insisted, at the bar, that as the original grant of jurisdiction, to the supreme and inferior courts, is general, and the clause, assigning original jurisdiction to the supreme court, contains no negative or restrictive words, the power remains to the legislature, to assign original jurisdiction to that court in other cases than those specified in the article which has been recited; provided those cases belong to the judicial power of the United States.

If it had been intended to leave it in the discretion of the legislature to apportion the judicial power between the supreme and inferior courts according to the will of that body, it would certainly have been useless to have proceeded further than to have defined the judicial power, and the tribunals in which it should be vested. The subsequent part of the section is mere surplusage, is entirely without meaning, if such is to be the construction. If congress remains at liberty to give this court appellate jurisdiction, where the constitution has declared their jurisdiction shall be original; and original jurisdiction where the constitution has declared it shall be appellate; the distribution of jurisdiction, made in the constitution, is form without substance.

Affirmative words are often, in their operation, negative of other objects than

---

*The full text of Section 13 of the Judiciary Act of 1789, 1 Stat. 73, reads:

And be it further enacted, That the Supreme Court shall have exclusive jurisdiction of all controversies of a civil nature, where a state is a party, except between a state and its citizens; and except also between a state and citizens of other states, or aliens, in which latter case it shall have original but not exclusive jurisdiction. And shall have exclusively all such jurisdiction of suits or proceedings against ambassadors, or other public ministers, or their domestics, or domestic servants, as a court of law can have or exercise consistently with the law of nations; and original, but not exclusive jurisdiction of all suits brought by ambassadors, or other public ministers, or in which a consul, or vice consul, shall be a party. And the trial of issues of fact in the Supreme Court, in all actions at law against citizens of the United States, shall be by jury. The Supreme Court shall also have appellate jurisdiction from the circuit courts and courts of the several states, in the cases herein after specially provided for; and shall have power to issue writs of prohibition to the district courts, when proceeding as courts of admiralty and maritime jurisdiction, and writs of mandamus, in cases warranted by the principles and usages of law, to any courts appointed, or persons holding office, under the authority of the United States.

those affirmed; and in this case, a negative or exclusive sense must be given to them, or they have no operation at all.

It cannot be presumed that any clause in the constitution is intended to be without effect; and, therefore, such a construction is inadmissible, unless the words require it. . . .

When an instrument organizing fundamentally a judicial system, divides it into one supreme, and so many inferior courts as the legislature may ordain and establish; then enumerates its powers, and proceeds so far to distribute them, as to define the jurisdiction of the supreme court by declaring the cases in which it shall take original jurisdiction, and that in others it shall take appellate jurisdiction; the plain import of the words seems to be, that in one class of cases its jurisdiction is original, and not appellate; in the other it is appellate, and not original. If any other construction would render the clause inoperative, that is an additional reason for rejecting such other construction, and for adhering to their obvious meaning.

To enable this court, then, to issue a mandamus, it must be shown to be an exercise of appellate jurisdiction, or to be necessary to enable them to exercise appellate jurisdiction.

It has been stated at the bar that the appellate jurisdiction may be exercised in a variety of forms, and that if it be the will of the legislature that a mandamus should be used for that purpose, that will must be obeyed. This is true, yet the jurisdiction must be appellate, not original.

It is the essential criterion of appellate jurisdiction, that it revises and corrects the proceedings in a cause already instituted, and does not create that cause. Although, therefore, a mandamus may be directed to courts, yet to issue such a writ to an officer for the delivery of a paper, is in effect the same as to sustain an original action for that paper, and, therefore, seems not to belong to appellate, but to original jurisdiction. Neither is it necessary in such a case as this, to enable the court to exercise its appellate jurisdiction.

The authority, therefore, given to the supreme court, by the act establishing the judicial courts of the United States, to issue writs of mandamus to public officers, appears not to be warranted by the constitution; and it becomes necessary to inquire whether a jurisdiction so conferred can be exercised.

The question, whether an act, repugnant to the constitution, can become the law of the land, is a question deeply interesting to the United States; but, happily, not of an intricacy proportioned to its interest. It seems only necessary to recognize certain principles, supposed to have been long and well established, to decide it.

That the people have an original right to establish, for their future government, such principles as, in their opinion, shall most conduce to their own happiness is the basis on which the whole American fabric has been erected. The exercise of this original right is a very great exertion; nor can it, nor ought it, to be frequently repeated. The principles, therefore, so established, are deemed fundamental. And as the authority from which they proceed is supreme, and can seldom act, they are designed to be permanent.

This original and supreme will organizes the government, and assigns to different departments their respective powers. It may either stop here, or establish certain limits not to be transcended by those departments.

The government of the United States is of the latter description. The powers of the legislature are defined and limited; and that those limits may not be mistaken, or forgotten, the constitution is written. To what purpose are powers limited, and to what purpose is that limitation committed to writing, if these limits may, at any time, be passed by those intended to be restrained? The distinction between a government with limited and unlimited powers is abolished, if those limits do not confine the persons on whom they are imposed, and if acts prohibited and acts allowed, are of equal obligation. It is a proposition too plain to be contested, that the constitution controls any legislative act repugnant to it; or, that the legislature may alter the constitution by an ordinary act.

Between these alternatives there is no middle ground. The constitution is either a superior paramount law, unchangeable by ordinary means, or it is on a level with ordinary legislative acts, and, like other acts, is alterable when the legislature shall please to alter it.

If the former part of the alternative be true, then a legislative act contrary to the constitution is not law: if the latter part be true, then written constitutions are absurd attempts, on the part of the people, to limit a power in its own nature illimitable.

Certainly all those who have framed written constitutions contemplate them as forming the fundamental and paramount law of the nation, and, consequently, the theory of every such government must be, that an act of the legislature, repugnant to the constitution, is void.

This theory is essentially attached to a written constitution, and, is consequently, to be considered, by this court, as one of the fundamental principles of our society. It is not therefore to be lost sight of in the further consideration of this subject.

If an act of the legislature, repugnant to the constitution, is void, does it, notwithstanding its invalidity, bind the courts, and oblige them to give it effect? Or, in other words, though it be not law, does it constitute a rule as operative as if it was a law? This would be to overthrow in fact what was established in theory; and would seem, at first view, an absurdity too gross to be insisted on. It shall, however, receive a more attentive consideration.

It is emphatically the province and duty of the judicial department to say what the law is. Those who apply the rule to particular cases, must of necessity expound and interpret that rule. If two laws conflict with each other, the courts must decide on the operation of each.

So if a law be in opposition to the constitution; if both the law and the constitution apply to a particular case, so that the court must either decide that case conformably to the law, disregarding the constitution; or conformably to the constitution, disregarding the law; the court must determine which of these conflicting rules governs the case. This is of the very essence of judicial duty. If, then, the courts are to regard the constitution, and the constitution is superior to any ordinary act of the legislature, the constitution, and not such ordinary act, must govern the case to which they both apply.

Those, then, who controvert the principle that the constitution is to be considered, in court, as a paramount law, are reduced to the necessity of maintaining that courts must close their eyes on the constitution, and see only the law.

This doctrine would subvert the very foundation of all written constitutions. It would declare that an act which, according to the principles and theory of our government, is entirely void, is yet, in practice, completely obligatory. It would declare that if the legislature shall do what is expressly forbidden, such act, notwithstanding the express prohibition, is in reality effectual. It would be giving to the legislature a practical and real omnipotence, with the same breath which professes to restrict their powers within narrow limits. It is prescribing limits, and declaring that those limits may be passed at pleasure.

That it thus reduces to nothing what we have deemed the greatest improvement on political institutions, a written constitution, would of itself be sufficient, in America, where written constitutions have been viewed with so much reverence, for rejecting the construction. But the peculiar expressions of the constitution of the United States furnish additional arguments in favor of its rejection.

The judicial power of the United States is extended to all cases arising under the constitution.

Could it be the intention of those who gave this power, to say that in using it the constitution should not be looked into? That a case arising under the constitution should be decided without examining the instrument under which it arises?

This is too extravagant to be maintained.

In some cases, then, the constitution must be looked into by the judges. And if they can open it at all, what part of it are they forbidden to read or to obey?

There are many other parts of the constitution which serve to illustrate this subject.

It is declared that "no tax or duty shall be laid on articles exported from any state." Suppose a duty on the export of cotton, of tobacco, or of flour; and a suit instituted to recover it. Ought judgment to be rendered in such a case? Ought the judges to close their eyes on the constitution, and only see the law?

The constitution declares "that no bill of attainder or ex post facto law shall be passed."

If, however, such a bill should be passed, and a person should be prosecuted under it; must the court condemn to death those victims whom the constitution endeavors to preserve?

"No person," says the constitution, "shall be convicted of treason unless on the testimony of two witnesses to the same overt act, or on confession in open court."

Here the language of the constitution is addressed especially to the courts. It prescribes, directly for them, a rule of evidence not to be departed from. If the legislature should change that rule, and declare *one* witness, or a confession *out* of court, sufficient for conviction, must the constitutional principle yield to the legislative act?

From these, and many other selections which might be made, it is apparent, that the framers of the constitution contemplated that instrument as a rule for the government of *courts*, as well as of the legislature.

Why otherwise does it direct the judges to take an oath to support it? This oath certainly applies in an especial manner, to their conduct in their official character. How immoral to impose it on them, if they were to be used as the instruments, and the knowing instruments, for violating what they swear to support!

The oath of office, too, imposed by the legislature, is completely demonstrative of the legislative opinion on this subject. It is in these words: "I do solemnly swear that I will administer justice without respect to persons, and do equal right to the poor and to the rich; and that I will faithfully and impartially discharge all the duties incumbent on me as, according to the best of my abilities and understanding, agreeably to *the constitution* and laws of the United States."

Why does a judge swear to discharge his duties agreeably to the constitution of the United States, if that constitution forms no rule for his government? if it is closed upon him, and cannot be inspected by him? If such be the real state of things, this is worse than solemn mockery. To prescribe, or to take this oath, becomes equally a crime.

It is also not entirely unworthy of observation, that in declaring what shall be the *supreme* law of the land, the *constitution* itself is first mentioned; and not the laws of the United States generally, but those only which shall be made in *pursuance* of the constitution, have that rank.

Thus, the particular phraseology of the constitution of the United States confirms and strengthens the principle, supposed to be essential to all written constitutions, that a law repugnant to the constitution is void; and that courts, as well as other departments, are bound by that instrument.

The rule must be discharged.

Note: Marbury v. Madison

1. *Background.* The *Marbury* case was decided against a complex background and was in some respects the culmination of a lengthy political battle. The Federalist President, John Adams, had been defeated by the Republican candidate, Thomas Jefferson, who was to take office on March 4, 1801. The Federalist Congress responded by, among other things, attempting to obtain control of the federal judiciary. On February 16, 1801, that Congress enacted the Circuit Court Act, creating sixteen new circuit judges and eliminating the circuit-riding duties of the Supreme Court. Congress also decreased the size of the Supreme Court in order to deny the incoming President Jefferson the power to appoint a successor to Justice Cushing. Two weeks later Congress enacted another statute creating forty-two positions for justices of the peace in the District of Columbia. President Adams nominated the authorized judges, who were confirmed on March 2 and 3, just one day before President Jefferson was to assume office.

At this point, John Marshall, then Secretary of State under President Adams — who had appointed Marbury and the other petitioners in the *Marbury* case — became involved in the circumstances that gave rise to the case. Although Marshall took his oath of office as Chief Justice on February 4, 1801, he continued to serve as Secretary of State at least until March 3 of that year. President Adams and Acting Secretary of State Marshall had signed the commissions of the petitioners in the *Marbury* case by March 3, but the commissions had not been delivered by the time Adams and Marshall left the executive branch. Adams's successor, Thomas Jefferson, thereafter refused to deliver the commissions, claiming that they were nullities. (Should Marshall have disqualified himself from *Marbury?*)

In the next year — before *Marbury* was decided — the Circuit Court Act was repealed by the Republican Congress; the statute creating justices of the peace was left intact. But Congress also abolished the June and December terms of the Court, leaving the Court adjourned from December 1801 until February 1803 — and thus abolishing the 1802 term. The reason for Congress's actions was to avoid a constitutional challenge to the repeal of the Circuit Court Act.

A footnote: Six days after *Marbury* was decided, the Court upheld the repeal. Stuart v. Laird, 5 U.S. (1 Cranch) 299 (1803). The history is illuminatingly discussed in O'Fallon, *Marbury*, 44 Stan. L. Rev. 219 (1992).

2. *Method, antecedents.* What does the opinion in Marbury v. Madison indicate about opinion-writing method? What are the sources of the decision? What in the Constitution supports judicial review?

a. Chief Justice Marshall does not begin the opinion in *Marbury* with the question of jurisdiction, although a court's jurisdiction is usually the first problem to be examined. Why did Chief Justice Marshall fail to deal first with the jurisdictional issue?

b. The actual holding of *Marbury* is that the Supreme Court is without power to direct the President to deliver Marbury's commission. This conclusion allowed the Court to avoid the problem of ordering President Jefferson to deliver commissions to President Adams's appointees. There was, of course, no assurance that President Jefferson would have complied with such a decree. The existence of judicial review was therefore established in a case in which the Court concluded that it had no power to do anything to remedy official illegality. Consider in this regard the suggestion that the "decision is a masterwork of indirection, a brilliant example of Chief Justice Marshall's capacity to sidestep danger while seeming to court it, to advance in one direction while his opponents are looking in another." R. McCloskey, The American Supreme Court 40 (1960).

What is the basis for Chief Justice Marshall's conclusion that the Court lacked jurisdiction? Consider the following rejoinders to his reasoning: (1) The categories of original and appellate jurisdiction are not mutually exclusive. The Constitution sets up a provisional allocation, which Congress can alter if it wishes. The power to alter is recognized in the "exceptions" clause. It is therefore constitutional for Congress to grant to the Court original jurisdiction over cases over which it had appellate jurisdiction under the Constitution's provisional allocation. (2) The Constitution defines an irreducible minimum of original jurisdiction but permits Congress to expand original jurisdiction if it chooses to do so. Is either of these views less persuasive, as a textual matter, than Chief Justice Marshall's?

Note in this regard that the reasoning of *Marbury* has been rejected insofar as it suggests that Congress may not give the lower courts jurisdiction over cases falling within the original jurisdiction of the Supreme Court. See, e.g., Illinois v. Milwaukee, 406 U.S. 91 (1972).

c. Chief Justice Marshall acknowledges that, "where the heads of departments are the political or confidential agents of the executive, merely to execute the will of the president, or rather to act in cases in which the executive possesses a constitutional or legal discretion, nothing can be more perfectly clear, than that their acts are only politically examinable." This acknowledgment created the category of cases involving "political questions," which are not subject to judicial review. See Chapter 1, section E, infra. What falls in this category? In Chief Justice Marshall's view, is there any case of official illegality that is not judicially cognizable? On one view, the answer is no: Political questions, as Chief Justice Marshall understands them, are questions in which there is no constitutional obstacle to the acts in question. Note also the contrast drawn by Chief Justice Marshall between cases involving "individual rights" and cases involving "discretion." What is the relationship between those two categories of cases?

d. *Judicial review.* The most important holding in the case is that the Supreme Court has the power to declare acts of Congress unconstitutional. It is striking to many modern readers that Chief Justice Marshall's principal arguments rely not on the text of the Constitution but instead on its structure and on the consequences of a conclusion that judicial review was unavailable.

Consider the view that the

> issue of judicial review was by no means new. The Privy Council had occasionally applied the ultra vires principle to set aside legislative acts contravening municipal or colonial charters. State courts had set aside state statutes under constitutions no more explicit about judicial review than the federal. The Supreme Court itself had measured a state law against a state constitution in Cooper v. Telfair, 4 U.S. (4 Dall.) 14 (1800), and had struck down another under the supremacy clause in Ware v. Hylton, 3 U.S. (3 Dall.) 199 (1796); in both cases the power of judicial review was expressly affirmed. Even Acts of Congress had been struck down by federal circuit courts, and the Supreme Court, while purporting to reserve the question of its power to do so, had reviewed the constitutionality of a federal statute in Hylton v. United States, 3 U.S. (3 Dall.) 171 (1796). Justice James Iredell had explicitly asserted this power both in Chisholm v. Georgia, 2 U.S. (2 Dall.) 419 (1793) and in Calder v. Bull, 3 U.S. (3 Dall.) 386 (1798), and Chase had acknowledged it in [*Cooper*]. In the Convention, moreover, both proponents and opponents of the proposed Council of Revision had recognized that the courts would review the validity of congressional legislation, and Alexander Hamilton had proclaimed the same doctrine in The Federalist. Yet though Marshall's principal arguments echoed those of Hamilton, he made no mention of any of this material, writing as if the question had never arisen before.

Currie, The Constitution in the Supreme Court: The Powers of the Federal Courts, 1801-1835, 49 U. Chi. L. Rev. 646, 655-656 (1982). In what ways was the issue in *Ware* and *Cooper* different from that in *Marbury*?

3. *The justifications for judicial review.* Consider the various bases for the power of judicial review.

a. *Written Constitution.* Chief Justice Marshall's first argument is that judicial review is a necessary inference from the fact of a written Constitution. "The distinction between a government with limited and unlimited powers is abolished, if those limits do not confine the persons on whom they are imposed, and if acts prohibited and acts allowed, are of equal obligation." But this argument seems to confound two different issues. (1) Is the Constitution binding on the national government? (2) Are the courts authorized to enforce their interpretation of the Constitution against that of other branches of the national government? Everyone agreed on the first question. The dispute centered on the second. Many countries have had written constitutions without having judicial review. Would it be plausible to respond that the Constitution would be ineffective or merely hortatory if it were not subject to judicial enforcement? Consider in this regard The Federalist No. 78, infra; and note that in Eastern Europe, emerging from communism, and South Africa, emerging from apartheid, nations have chosen both a written constitution and judicial review of one sort or another. Indeed, judicial review has been seen as a central part of the new constitutional orders. Consider also Currie, supra, at 657: "Surely the Framers were reasonable people, and surely they could not have meant to appoint the fox as guardian of the henhouse." But on the facts of *Marbury*, who was the fox? Note also that in both Eastern Europe and South Africa, some constitutional provisions, such as those involving social and economic guarantees and environmental protections, are expressly made nonjusticiable in courts.

b. *Notions of judicial role.* Chief Justice Marshall claims that the ordinary role of the courts is to interpret the law. That role, he claims, requires judges to construe the Constitution in the ordinary course of conducting judicial business. But it might be responded that constitutional interpretation — when it takes the form of invalidation of the outcomes reached by the more political branches — is special because of its highly intrusive and largely final character. Should this difference mean that the ordinary interpretive task is no longer appropriate?

c. *Supremacy clause.* The supremacy clause provides that the "Constitution, and the Laws of the United States which shall be made in Pursuance thereof . . . shall be the supreme Law of the Land." Does this establish the existence of judicial review?

> Assuming that an act repugnant to the Constitution is not a law "in pursuance thereof" and thus must not be given effect as the supreme law of the land, who according to the Constitution, is to make the determination as to whether any given law is in fact repugnant to the Constitution itself? [Chief Justice Marshall] never confronts this question. His substitute question, whether a law repugnant to the Constitution still binds the courts, assumes that such repugnance has appropriately been determined by those granted such power under the Constitution. It is clear, however, that the supremacy clause itself cannot be the clear textual basis for a claim by the judiciary that this prerogative to determine repugnancy belongs to it.

Van Alstyne, A Critical Guide to Marbury v. Madison, 1969 Duke L.J. 1, 22.

Note also that Chief Justice Marshall gains rhetorical force for his position by referring to clauses that in his view have a "plain" meaning opposed to acts of Congress. But one might doubt whether constitutional provisions are likely to have such meanings in many cases on which Congress and Court will differ. In any event, consider the possibility that the use of these hypothetical cases is misleading in light of the more open-ended character of most constitutional interpretation — of which *Marbury* itself is an example.

d. *Grant of jurisdiction.* The Constitution extends the judicial power of the United States to all cases arising under the Constitution. Chief Justice Marshall argues that the grant of jurisdiction would be meaningless if the courts did not have authority to examine the constitutionality of acts of Congress. Consider A. Bickel, The Least Dangerous Branch 6 (1962):

> If it were impossible to conceive a case "arising under the Constitution" which would not require the Court to pass on the constitutionality of congressional legislation, then [Marshall might be correct, for without judicial review] this clause [would be] quite senseless. But there are such cases which may call into question the constitutional validity of judicial, administrative, or military actions without attacking legislative or even presidential acts as well, or which call upon the Court, under appropriate statutory authorization, to apply the Constitution to acts of the states. Any reading but his own was for Marshall "too extravagant to be maintained." His own, although out of line with the general scheme of Article III, may be possible; but it is optional. This is the strongest bit of textual evidence in support of Marshall's view, but it is merely a hint.

e. *Judges' oath.* Chief Justice Marshall relies on the fact that judges take an oath to uphold the Constitution. But consider the fact that the

> oath to support the Constitution is not peculiar to the judges, but is taken indiscriminately by every officer of the government, and is designed rather as a test of the political principles of the man, than to bind the officer in the discharge of his duty. [But] granting it to relate to the official conduct of the judge, as well as every other officer, and not to his political principles, still it must be understood in reference to supporting the constitution, *only as far as that may be involved in his official duty*; and consequently, if his official duty does not comprehend an inquiry into the authority of the legislature, neither does his oath.

Eakin v. Raub, 12 Serg. & Rawle 330, 353 (Pa. 1825). In short, the oath requires judges to support the Constitution; however, if the Constitution assigns ultimate interpretive power to the legislature, or to the President, then judicial review is not contemplated by the Constitution but is in violation of it. Does this suggest that the "oath" argument is a makeweight?

Perhaps these various arguments appear more forceful in combination than they appear when separated. One might claim that while none is independently decisive, the various arguments together suggest that judicial review is a part of the constitutional structure.

4. *The view of the framers.* The relevant documents at the time of the framing indicate that judicial review was generally contemplated. See also A. Bickel, supra, at 15-16:

> [It] is as clear as such matters can be that the Framers of the Constitution specifically, if tacitly, expected that the federal courts would assume a power — of whatever exact dimensions — to pass on the constitutionality of actions of the Congress and the President, as well as of the several states. Moreover, not even a colorable showing of decisive historical evidence to the contrary can be made. Nor can it be maintained that the language of the Constitution is compellingly the other way. At worst it may be said that the intentions of the Framers cannot be ascertained with finality.

Consider Hamilton's views in The Federalist No. 78:

> Some perplexity respecting the rights of the courts to pronounce legislative acts void, because contrary to the constitution, has arisen from an imagination that the doctrine would imply a superiority of the judiciary to the legislative power. It is urged that the authority which can declare the acts of another void, must necessarily be superior to the one whose acts may be declared void. . . .
>
> There is no position which depends on clearer principles, than that every act of a delegated authority, contrary to the tenor of the commission under which it is exercised, is void. No legislative act, therefore, contrary to the Constitution, can be valid. To deny this, would be to affirm, that the deputy is greater than his principal; that the servant is above his master; that the representatives of the people are superior to the people themselves; that men acting by virtue of powers, may do not only what their powers do not authorize, but what they forbid.
>
> If it be said that the legislative body are themselves the constitutional judges of their own powers, and that the construction they put upon them is conclusive upon the other departments, it may be answered, that this cannot be the natural presumption, where it is not to be collected from any particular provisions in the Constitu-

tion. It is not otherwise to be supposed, that the Constitution could intend to enable the representatives of the people to substitute their *will* to that of their constituents. It is far more rational to suppose, that the courts were designed to be an intermediate body between the people and the legislature, in order, among other things, to keep the latter within the limits assigned to their authority. The interpretation of the laws is the proper and peculiar province of the courts. A constitution is, in fact, and must be regarded by the judges, as a fundamental law. It therefore belongs to them to ascertain its meaning, as well as the meaning of any particular act proceeding from the legislative body. If there should happen to be an irreconcilable variance between the two, that which has the superior obligation and validity ought, of course, to be preferred; or, in other words, the Constitution ought to be preferred to the statute, the intention of the people to the intention of their agents.

Nor does this conclusion by any means suppose a superiority of the judicial to the legislative power. It only supposes that the power of the people is superior to both; and that where the will of the legislature, declared in its statutes, stands in opposition to that of the people, declared in the Constitution, the judges ought to be governed by the latter rather than the former. They ought to regulate their decisions by the fundamental laws, rather than by those which are not fundamental. . . .

[In] regard to the interfering acts of a superior and subordinate authority, of an original and derivative power, the nature and reason of the thing indicate the converse of that rule as proper to be followed. They teach us that the prior act of a superior ought to be preferred to the subsequent act of an inferior and subordinate authority; and that accordingly, whenever a particular statute contravenes the Constitution, it will be the duty of the judicial tribunals to adhere to the latter and disregard the former.

It can be of no weight to say that the courts, on the pretence of a repugnancy, may substitute their own pleasure to the constitutional intentions of the legislature. This might as well happen in the case of two contradictory statutes; or it might as well happen in every adjudication upon any single statute. The courts must declare the sense of the law; and if they should be disposed to exercise WILL instead of JUDGMENT, the consequence would equally be the substitution of their pleasure to that of the legislative body. The observation, if it prove any thing, would prove that there ought to be no judges distinct from that body.

How, if at all, do Hamilton's justifications for judicial review differ from Chief Justice Marshall's? Is the distinction between "will" and "judgment" a plausible one? Note that Hamilton attempts to overcome the claim that judicial review is undemocratic by claiming that through such review, courts vindicate the will of the people (as expressed in the Constitution) against the will of mere representatives. This is a long-standing, and often controversial, theme in constitutional law; it becomes most controversial where courts cannot obviously trace what that are doing to any concrete judgment of "the people."

Note: *Constitutions, Democracy, and Judicial Review*

One of the most important dilemmas in American constitutional law arises from the tension between the basic principle that the Constitution reposes sovereign authority in the people, who elect their representatives, and the (perhaps) competing principle that the Constitution itself defeats democratic efforts by the public to proceed in one or another direction. Is a constitution, in that way, an obstacle to democracy?

The dilemma seems heightened by the fact that, in interpreting the Constitution under the doctrine of judicial review, the courts have final say over the political process. Judicial review is a mechanism by which the courts may invalidate decisions of Congress and the President, subject only to the burdensome process of constitutional amendment. Because they are subject to electoral control, Congress and the President are generally regarded as more accountable to the citizenry than federal judges, who have life tenure. In these circumstances, the existence of judicial review is often said to give rise to a "countermajoritarian difficulty." See A. Bickel, The Least Dangerous Branch 16 (1962). Under what premises can the allocation of power in *Marbury* be justified? At least some answers tend to turn on particular conceptions about the process of constitutional "interpretation."

1. *Democracy, constitutions, and "mechanical" interpretation.* It is often suggested that the tension between judicial review and democracy would be eliminated, or at least sharply reduced, if judicial review were simply a mechanical process of deciding whether an act of Congress violated some decision made by the ratifiers of the Constitution. In such circumstances, the judges would not be imposing their own judgments about basic values but would instead be forcing current legislatures to conform to earlier choices made by the people. This understanding reflects Hamilton's distinction between "will" — the province of politics — and "judgment" — the province of the courts.

The understanding of judicial review as essentially mechanical is captured in United States v. Butler, 297 U.S. 1 (1936), where the Court wrote,

> It is sometimes said that the court assumes a power to overrule or control the action of the people's representatives. This is a misconception. [When] an act of Congress is appropriately challenged in the courts as not conforming to the constitutional mandate the judicial branch of the Government has only one duty — to lay the article of the Constitution which is invoked beside the statute which is challenged and to decide whether the latter squares with the former.

Consider whether this understanding of constitutional interpretation is (a) similar to the Court's understanding of the interpretive process in *Marbury* and to Hamilton's understanding in The Federalist No. 78 and (b) an accurate description of how the various constitutional questions in *Marbury* were in fact resolved.

This view, moreover, raises two different problems. First: Even if constitutional interpretation were understood in these terms, there would remain a possible tension between constitutionalism and democracy. Why should current legislators and current citizens be forced to conform to some will of the people, all of them dead, expressed many years ago? Here there is a problem with constitutional constraints even if the Constitution speaks clearly. There are several possible answers. Perhaps the Constitution can guarantee the preconditions for democracy by, for example, protecting rights of free speech and ensuring that no one may be excluded from the democratic process. Perhaps no branch of government can be said to speak at any particular time for "We the People," and perhaps the Constitution embodies deeper and more widespread public judgments. Perhaps the Constitution can be understood as a kind of "precommitment strategy," through which people bind themselves to certain institutions and constraints that make self-government work. For discussion, see J. H. Ely, Democracy and Distrust (1980); S. Holmes, Passions and Constraint (1994); Seidman, Ambivalence and

Accountability, 61 S. Cal. L. Rev. 1571 (1988); Sunstein, Constitutionalism and Secession, 58 U. Chi. L. Rev. 633, 636-643 (1991).

Second: If *Butler* does capture the nature of constitutional interpretation, is it a good thing to have such interpretation carried out by judges rather than elected officials? See M. Tushnet, Taking the Constitution Away from the Courts (1999). One view is that judges are better at interpretation precisely because of their insulation from political pressures. That insulation permits them to follow "the ways of the scholar," A. Bickel, supra, at 26, in finding the meaning of the text. Those who are subject to political pressures, by contrast, are likely to have the process of interpretation infected or distorted by prevailing political sentiments. Consider, for example, the difference between a judge and a legislator in deciding the meaning of freedom of speech in a climate of popular hostility to a particular point of view. Accountability might in such circumstances be a vice rather than a virtue. Note, on the other hand, that judges have sometimes been less than hospitable to first amendment claims in times of such hostility. There is also the problem of explaining why the comparative accountability of the legislative and executive branches should not be regarded as a virtue in giving meaning to constitutional provisions.

See, in this regard, Ackerman, Discovering the Constitution, 93 Yale L.J. 1013, 1023, 1049 (1984):

> We must reconsider the levelling opinion that indicts the Supreme Court as a "deviant institution of American democracy," doomed forever to bear the stigma of the "countermajoritarian difficulty." [Consider] the obvious sense in which it is false. When the Court invokes the Constitution, it appeals to legal enactments that *were* approved by a whole series of majorities — namely the majorities of those representative bodies that proposed and ratified the original Constitution and its subsequent amendments. Rather than a countermajoritarian difficulty, the familiar platitude identifies an intertemporal difficulty.

Ackerman adds that constitutional provisions are adopted in a time of "appeals to the common good, ratified by a mobilized mass of American citizens expressing their assent through extraordinary institutional forms." He contrasts this form of politics, termed "constitutional politics," which is "the highest kind," with "a second form of activity" in which "factions try to manipulate the constitutional forms of political life to pursue their own narrow interests." In this framework, judicial review, by preventing normal politics from overcoming constitutional politics, is a means of ensuring that "the ignorance, apathy and selfishness of normal politics" are not permitted to overcome decisions made by "the public during a period of heightened mobilization and public-spiritness." See also 1 B. Ackerman, We the People: Foundations (1991). Compare the conceptions of politics set out in The Federalist No. 10, discussed supra. Consider also the possibility that, in Madison's view at least, the system was to be structured so as to ensure that factional manipulation would not occur even in periods without "heightened mobilization." See generally Ackerman, Constitutional Politics/Constitutional Law, 99 Yale L.J. 453 (1989).

Perhaps, too, Ackerman's account romanticizes "constitutional politics." Consider Brest, Constitutional Citizenship, 34 Clev. St. L. Rev. 175, 187-188 (1986):

> Some of the Federalists, who urged ratification of the Constitution of 1787, and some of the Anti-Federalists, who opposed it, undoubtedly took the long view. The

proponents and opponents were also concerned with immediate economic problems, and the solutions provided by the new Constitution — for example, a strong central government — were widely understood to serve the interests of some groups at the expense of others. . . .

Considering issues from the moral point of view requires habits and attitudes that come from regular practice and that are not readily acquired on the spur of the moment. It is simply not plausible to expect citizens or officials to act out of self interest day to day, and adopt a very different perspective when the word "constitutional" is invoked.

See also Seidman, Public Principle and Private Choice: The Uneasy Case for a Boundary Maintenance Theory of Constitutional Law, Yale L.J. 1006, 1021, 1050 (1987). In any case a question remains: Why is judicial review legitimated by the presence of deliberative judgments by long-dead people in the distant past?

Some people have suggested that aggressive constitutional review by the courts has harmful consequences for "normal politics." Consider J. Thayer, John Marshall 103-107 (1901), suggesting that in light of the existence of judicial review, legislatures

more and more readily incline [to] shed the consideration of constitutional restraints, [turning] that subject over to the courts; and, what is worse, they insensibly fall into a habit of assuming that whatever they can constitutionally do they may do, — as if honor and fair dealing and common honesty were not relevant to their inquiries. [It] should be remembered that the exercise of judicial review, even when unavoidable, is always attended with a serious evil, namely, that the correction of legislative mistakes comes from the outside, and the people thus lose the political experience, and the moral education and stimulus that come from fighting the question out in the ordinary way, and correcting their own errors. [The] tendency of a common and easy resort to this great function [is] to dwarf the political capacity of the people, and to deaden its sense of moral responsibility. It is no light thing to do that.

The claim here is that the institution of judicial review tends to remove questions of principle from the political process. But how realistic is the idea that such review has a significant adverse impact on the public's "sense of moral responsibility"? Might review actually heighten people's sense of the extent to which political debates often involve matters of high principle? See R. Dworkin, Freedom's Law (1997).

Concerns about the perceived tension between judicial review and democracy have led to suggestions that courts should strike down statutes

only when those who have the right to make laws have not merely made a mistake, but have made a very clear one, — so clear that it is not open to rational question. [This] rule recognizes that, having regard to the great, complex, ever-unfolding exigencies of government, much which will seem unconstitutional to one man, or body of men, may reasonably not seem so to another[,] that there is often a range of choice and judgment[,] and that whatever choice is rational is constitutional.

Thayer, The Origin and Scope of the American Doctrine of Constitutional Law, 7 Harv. L. Rev. 129, 144 (1893). But might this approach undo the advantages supposed to derive from judicial independence and insulation?

Questions of this sort raise a further issue: Why is the Constitution binding at all? Usually the binding character of the Constitution is taken as an axiom, but it is always helpful to have a reason for an important stance, even one that amounts to an axiom. Consider the following possibilities: (a) The Constitution is binding because it arose out of a process in which we, or the people, agreed to it. But does it matter that the relevant people all died long ago? That the "we" excluded large numbers of people, including all women, all Indians, and all blacks? That the percentage of the people who actually ratified the Constitution was quite small? (b) The Constitution is binding because the Constitution is a good one. On this view, the binding force of a document has a lot to do with whether the substantive argument on its behalf is sound. But this cannot be the entire story. If a committee in California were to draw up a new and (let us assume) better Constitution, that new document would not be binding simply because of its high quality. (c) The Constitution is binding because it is enabling rather than constraining to treat it that way. If the Constitution were not binding, chaos would ensue. People would have to decide (for example) not simply who will be President but also how many presidents there should be. Issues of basic structure would be up for grabs — hardly a desirable state of affairs. To treat the Constitution as binding facilitates democratic self-government; it does not impede it. Does the experience of countries like the United Kingdom, which lack a written constitution, support this claim?

One might ask as well about the implications of these arguments for reliance on original intent or on the other possible sources of constitutional law.

2. Marbury *and the discretionary character of interpretation*. Many of the doubts raised about judicial review rest on a concern that in interpreting the Constitution, the judges will not be enforcing the judgments of its drafters and ratifiers but will instead be influenced by their own views about how society should be ordered. (Consider whether that is a sensible or coherent dichotomy.) Many of the Constitution's provisions are vague and ambiguous. Their interpretation calls for the exercise of discretion. It is in these circumstances that the tension between judicial review and democracy becomes more acute. Consider, for example, whether school segregation denies "equal protection of the laws," whether a law providing for prayer in the public schools is a "law respecting an establishment of religion," and whether a prohibition of second-trimester abortions is a deprivation of "life, liberty, or property, without due process of law."

Acknowledging the existence of discretion, the Court has said that

> [i]t is no answer [to] insist that what the provision of the Constitution meant to the vision of [the framers'] day it must mean to the vision of our time. If by the statement that what the Constitution meant at the time of its adoption it means today, it is intended to say that the great clauses of the Constitution must be confined to the interpretation which the framers, with the conditions and outlook of their time, would have placed upon them, the statement carries its own refutation.

Home Building & Loan Association v. Blaisdell, 290 U.S. 398, 442-443 (1934).

There have been numerous efforts to respond to or to escape the countermajoritarian difficulties produced by the discretionary character of interpretation. Most of them are rooted in the notion that it is critically important to ensure that constitutional decisions rest on something other than the value judgments, or policy preferences, of the judges. Numerous disputes in constitutional law are in fact about the adequacy of these various efforts to control judicial discretion. We deal with those efforts in more detail below. Consider at the outset the appeal and limitations of the following. Which, if any, of the following is a useful or appropriate *source* of constitutional outcomes? Which, if any, limits judicial discretion? What is the proper conception of constitutional interpretation? It may be useful to keep the school prayer, school segregation, and abortion examples in mind.

a. *The original meaning, understanding, or intent of the framers and ratifiers.* It is sometimes suggested that the meaning of a constitutional provision should be ascertained by reference to its original meaning, or the intent of the framers and ratifiers. Perhaps the original understanding can discipline the judges and diminish the democratic problems posed by judicial review; perhaps the original understanding can make interpretation more mechanical and more rule-like, and also minimize judicial discretion. In recent years, Justice Thomas has spoken on behalf of "originalism" in constitutional law, as has Justice Scalia. See A. Scalia, A Matter of Interpretation (1997). But note the following questions.

(1) *Whose understanding?* The relevant understanding might be that of the drafters of the Constitution or the people in the various states who ratified it. In either case, the problem of ascertaining the "intention" of a collective decision-making body is sometimes serious. Often there are disagreements among the various decisionmakers. Sometimes they will have no "intent" with respect to a particular question that arises in the future. How serious are these obstacles to a finding of framers' or ratifiers' understanding? Perhaps they suggest some hard questions but still allow one to say that some things clearly go beyond, or against, the original understanding. Perhaps one might respond that original meaning, rather than subjective intent, is what is controlling. And perhaps the problems in uncovering the original understanding are real but no more severe than the problems facing other approaches to constitutional law. See Scalia, Originalism: The Lesser Evil, 57 U. Cin. L. Rev. 849 (1989).

(2) *Intent or meaning at what level of generality: the problem of interpretive intent.* As noted above, many constitutional provisions are vague and ambiguous. Consider, for example, the commerce clause, the equal protection clause, the cruel and unusual punishments clause, and the freedom of speech clause. Those provisions might be read to enact either a particular "conception" fixed for all time or a general "concept" to be filled in over time. The choice between the two will have enormous consequences for constitutional interpretation. For example, the question might be whether the equal protection clause applies only to discrimination against African-Americans — the principal historical concern — or whether it sets forth a more general prohibition of unjustifiable distinctions between classes of people. How does one decide whether a provision establishes specific conceptions or general concepts?

(a) From the text of the Constitution, it might seem plausible to suggest that the framers intended to delegate to people in the future the power to make decisions about what the provision means in the particular circumstances. Some framers, in short, may have intended the provision to set forth a general concept and to delegate to others the decision about the meaning of the provision in new settings. "If the abstract statement is chosen as the appropriate mode or level of investigation into the original intention, then judges must make substantive decisions of political morality not in place of judgments made by the 'Framers' but rather in service of those judgments." Dworkin, The Forum of Principle, 56 N.Y.U. L. Rev. 469, 490 (1981). This is the problem of interpretive intent.

How does one decide whether, with respect to a particular provision, the framers intended to enact a general concept or a particular conception? Consider the following possibilities: (i) The language of the Constitution is the best evidence, and most of the important provisions read as general concepts. (ii) It is implausible to attribute to the framers a desire to set out general concepts because interpretive freedom would then be unlimited. If courts were empowered to wield general concepts against the political branches, there would be a significant risk of judicial tyranny — and it is hardly plausible to impute that to the framers. (iii) It is highly unlikely that one will be able to identify a coherent interpretive intention on the part of the framers. With respect to most provisions there was a mixture of general concepts and particular conceptions. Very few, if any, of the framers made a decision between the two. The notion that "they" had any particular position on the question is fanciful. On the framers' own view of intent, see Powell, The Original Understanding of Original Intent, 99 Harv. L. Rev. 885 (1985); see also R. Bork, The Tempting of America (1989).

(b) Suppose the framers did in fact intend to set forth conceptions, not concepts (or vice versa). It would still remain to show that their intention *on that matter* is controlling. One might believe that the constitutional text binds future decisionmakers, but that it is up to future decisionmakers, not to the framers, to decide how the document should be interpreted. "Some part of any constitutional theory must be independent of the intentions or beliefs or indeed acts of the people the theory designates as Framers. Some part must stand on its own in political or moral theory; otherwise the theory would be wholly circular." Dworkin, The Forum of Principle, supra, at 496. On this view, a decision to rely on the interpretive intent of the framers must be independently justified. Can it be? Consider here the question whether the arguments for the binding character of the Constitution show that the original meaning or the intent ought to be taken to be binding.

(c) Suppose circumstances have changed dramatically since the framers wrote. How does one understand the framers' "intent" with respect to (i) a new problem or (ii) an old problem in dramatically changed circumstances? See Tushnet, Following the Rules Laid Down: A Critique of Interpretivism and Neutral Principles, 96 Harv. L. Rev. 781 (1983); Lessig, Fidelity in Translation, 71 Tex. L. Rev. 1165 (1993); Lessig, Understanding Changed Readings: Fidelity and Theory, 47 Stan. L. Rev. 395 (1995). Consider, for example, both the vastly changed role of public education and the status of blacks in the period between the framing of the fourteenth amendment and the time of the desegregation decision, Brown v. Board of Education, in 1954. How does one apply the framers' "intent" in light of such changes? Consider the view that courts must uphold all measures that the framers did not mean to invalidate, since without a decision by the framers, the judges will be unable to trace judicial outcomes to decisions made by others. Easterbrook, Legal Interpretation and the Power of the Judiciary, 7 Harv. J.L. & Pub. Poly. 87, 94-99 (1984). But consider the view that intent cannot be mechanically transported to a new setting; to be faithful to it, one has to engage in the difficult and discretionary task of "translation" — seeing what the instructions mean in new circumstances.

While it is important at the outset to have some understanding of the role of the framers' intent or the original understanding in constitutional interpretation, one should be able to recognize as well other possible sources of constitutional rulings. Each of these sources is discussed in more detail in subsequent chapters; we outline some of the principal sources here as an aid to understanding the implications of *Marbury* and for future reference.

What constraints do the following impose on interpretation? One might ask whether they were helpful in *Marbury* itself or whether they might be useful in a case involving the constitutionality of school prayer, abortion, or school segregation.

b. *The text of the Constitution.* Courts and commentators generally agree that the text of the Constitution is binding on courts. But even here there are counterexamples. The first amendment appears to apply only to "Congress," but courts apply free speech principles to the executive and the judiciary too. See also Camera v. Municipal Court, 387 U.S. 523 (1967) (requiring use of administrative warrants on less than probable cause despite the fourth amendment's unambiguous probable cause requirement for warrants). And assuming that the text is binding, what constraints does it impose? See Schauer, Easy Cases, 58 S. Cal. L. Rev. 399, 414 (1985):

> Once we expand our notion of a case to include all legal events, it becomes clear that there *are* easy cases in constitutional law — lots of them. The parties concerned know, for example, that Ronald Reagan cannot run for a third term; [that] bills receiving less than a majority of votes in either the House or the Senate are not laws of the United States; [and] that a twenty-nine-year-old is not going to be President of the United States. [The] foregoing is only a small sample of the legal events that are "easy" constitutional cases.

But consider Perry, The Authority of Text, Tradition, and Reason: A Theory of Constitutional "Interpretation," 58 S. Cal. L. Rev. 551, 566 (1985): "[Just] about any choice a majority of the Supreme Court is likely to make would probably fall within [the] boundary [set by] accepted canons of judicial behavior, even in conjunction with the constitutional text."

c. *Tradition; precedent.* Sometimes the scope of a provision is determined in part by reference to tradition and the Court's own precedents. Under this approach, constitutional law operates as a form of common law, developing over time, but constrained by the past. On this view, the constraints on judicial power come not primarily from text and history but from the ongoing development of "common law" understandings. See Strauss, Common Law Constitutional Interpretation, 63 U. Chi. L. Rev. 877 (1996), for an extended discussion; see also Wellington, Common Law Rules and Constitutional Double Standards: Some Notes on Adjudication, 83 Yale L.J. 221 (1973). On one view, the common law prizes "tradition," which then becomes a source of law but one that is not static. Is the countermajoritarian character of judicial review a reason to reject a common law or tradition-based model of constitutional adjudication? Note the possibility that tradition should be binding only if one has a generally favorable view toward the tradition. Here, of course, there is room for much disagreement. See generally West, Progressive and Conservative Constitutionalism, 88 Mich. L. Rev. 641 (1990).

d. *Prevailing morality, or social consensus.* An open-ended constitutional provision might be given content by referring to prevailing morality or to some form of consensus. But this possibility raises two questions. First, it is hardly clear that judges are better than legislators as registers of social consensus. Second, in light of the fact that the Constitution, or at least the bill of rights, is often regarded as a shield against social consensus, it might be odd to suggest that its content derives from that consensus.

e. *Conceptions of justice; principle.* See A. Bickel, supra, at 23-28:

> Courts have certain capacities for dealing with matters of principle that legislatures and executives do not possess. Judges have, or should have, the leisure, the training, and the insulation to follow the ways of the scholar in pursuing the ends of government. This is crucial in sorting out the enduring values of a society. [Their] insulation and the marvelous mystery of time give courts the capacity to appeal to men's better natures, to call forth their aspirations, which may have been forgotten in the moment's hue and cry.

Compare with this justification Madison's conception of the role of national representatives in The Federalist No. 10, supra, who were to "refine," rather than reflect, the public view. Note also the view that the distinctive role of courts is to set out "principles," a role that is distinct from the legislative task of making "policy." See R. Dworkin, A Matter of Principle (1985); R. Dworkin, Taking Rights Seriously (1977). On this account, the term "democracy" should not be a trump card. The American system is not purely majoritarian nor even an untrammeled democracy. It contains a range of checks on what the democratic process can do, and one of these checks is discretionary judicial review, oriented to the derivation of principles by people well suited for that enterprise.

This justification differs dramatically from that offered by Hamilton and Chief Justice Marshall, who did not acknowledge this kind of role for the judges. Note the position of Thayer, Origin and Scope of the American Doctrine of Constitutional Law, supra, that the legislature should be and often is concerned with issues of principle — a view supported by Madison's form of republicanism. And consider Brest, Who Decides?, 58 S. Cal. L. Rev. 661, 664, 670 (1985):

> The mere demography of the judiciary suggests that judges, especially federal judges, are far from a representative cross section of American society. They are overwhelmingly Anglo, male, well educated, and upper or upper middle class. They are also members of the legal profession — an affiliation that by definition sets them apart from other members of society. [The] net effect [of judicial review] is to systematically exclude citizens and their representatives from the most fundamental decisions of the polity. This is completely at odds with the classical conception of citizenship held by political theorists such as Aristotle, J. S. Mill, Rousseau, and Jefferson, for whom the very concept of citizenship involved participation in those decisions.

How do these various possible sources of constitutional decision fit together? Sometimes they will, of course, point in different directions, creating what might be called a "commensurability problem." Fallon, A Constructivist Coherence Theory of Constitutional Interpretation, 100 Harv. L. Rev. 1189 (1987). And consider the possibility that judges might decide constitutional cases without converging on a single "theory" of interpretation. Much of constitutional law reflects an effort to resolve particular problems by judges who are uncertain about abstract issues and who seek, if they can, to bracket such issues. See Sunstein, Incompletely Theorized Agreements, 108 Harv. L. Rev. 1733 (1995).

3. *The countermajoritarian difficulty: escape routes.* A separate effort to respond to the countermajoritarian difficulty suggests that in reality there is no such difficulty, since the role of the court is to promote, rather than to undermine, democracy, properly understood. This effort in turn takes several forms.

Under one view, the judicial effort to impose constitutional constraints on the political process promotes democracy, since those constraints were adopted by the people in a time of heightened democratic awareness and therefore occupy a superior status to the decisions of temporary majorities. This is the position taken in Ackerman, Discovering the Constitution, supra, and it has roots in Hamilton's position in The Federalist No. 78 and in *Marbury* itself.

Under another view, the role of the courts is to protect certain rights indispensable to politics and certain groups that are for one reason or another excluded from or unable fully to participate in politics. The relative inability of such groups to participate in or to be represented by the political process is said to justify a judicial role designed to bring about better democracy. See McCulloch v. Maryland, infra, and generally J. H. Ely, Democracy and Distrust (1980), which is an extended elaboration of this theme. Cases involving free speech and voting would call for a greater role for the judiciary in order to protect the democratic process itself.

A third position would suggest that the role of the Court is indeed to improve democracy but not only by protecting the opportunity of traditionally disadvantaged groups to participate or to be represented. On this view, the Court might attempt to ensure, for example, that legislation is not merely a response to the factional pressures described in The Federalist No. 10 or that it does not reflect existing relations of power as between whites and blacks or men and women.

These various positions attempt to defuse the countermajoritarian difficulty by suggesting that in reality there is no such difficulty at all. The claim is sometimes buttressed with the suggestion that the so-called democratic process is filled with democratic infirmities. These include possible disparities in political influence, according to wealth, race, and gender; the difficulties in aggregating the different preferences of legislators, see K. Arrow, Social Choice and Individual Values (1951); the occasional unresponsiveness of the political process to the popular will and its occasional overresponsiveness to particular groups; and the fact that some groups are well organized and others not, see R. Hardin, Collective Action (1981). See generally M. Shapiro, Freedom of Speech: The Supreme Court and Judicial Review 32 (1966):

> [The] lawmaker to whom the nasty old undemocratic Supreme Court is supposed to yield so reverently because of his greater democratic virtues is the entire mass of majoritarian-antimajoritarian, elected-appointed, special interest-general interest, responsible-irresponsible elements that make up American national politics. If we are off on a democratic quest, the dragon begins to look better and better and St. George worse and worse.

See also Michelman, Foreword: Traces of Self-Government, 100 Harv. L. Rev. 4, 75 (1986):

[For] citizens of the United States, national politics are not imaginably the arena of self-government in its positive, freedom-giving sense. As a constituted nation we are, it seems, necessarily committed to the sovereign separation of rulers from ruled. [Congress] is not us. The President is not us. ["We"] are not "in" those bodies. Their determinations are not our self-government. Judges overriding those determinations do not, therefore, necessarily subtract anything from our freedom, although the judges also, obviously are not us. Their actions may augment our freedom. As usual, it all depends.

But this position of course depends on a controversial portrait of national law-making institutions, and an equally controversial understanding that the remedy for defects in those institutions might be found in judicial review instead of — for example — institutional reform through the political process itself. We return to these themes at numerous points below.

The following case raises issues similar to, but distinct from, those in *Marbury*: the authority of the Supreme Court over decisions by state courts. That question is closely related to the question of Supreme Court review of state as distinct from federal laws.

Martin v. Hunter's Lessee

14 U.S. (1 Wheat.) 304 (1816)

[This case arose out of a dispute over the ownership of land in Virginia. Hunter claimed the land pursuant to a grant from the state of Virginia in 1789, which confiscated lands owned by British subjects. Martin, a British subject, claimed that the attempted confiscation was ineffective under anticonfiscation clauses of treaties between the United States and England.

[The Virginia trial court held in favor of Martin; the Virginia Court of Appeals reversed, concluding that the state's title to the land had vested before the relevant treaties, and alternatively that Martin's claim was defeated by a 1796 Act of Compromise between the state and Martin's uncle, from whom Martin's claim derived. The Supreme Court of the United States reversed the Virginia Court of Appeals, neglecting to mention the Act of Compromise, but claiming that Virginia had not perfected its title before the relevant treaties. Fairfax's Devisee v. Hunter's Lessee, 7 Cranch 603 (1813). The Supreme Court remanded the case to the Virginia Court of Appeals with instructions to enter judgment for the appellant. But on remand the Virginia court declined. The court said that section 25 of the Judiciary Act was unconstitutional insofar as it extended the appellate jurisdiction of the Supreme Court to the Virginia court.

[In its opinion, the court emphasized that the act placed the courts of one sovereign — Virginia — under the direct control of another, an arrangement incompatible with the notion of sovereignty. "It must have been foreseen that controversies would sometimes arise as to the boundaries of the two jurisdictions. Yet the constitution has provided no umpire, has erected no tribunal by which they shall be settled. The omission proceeded, probably, from the belief, that such a tribunal would produce evils greater than those of the occasional collisions which it would be designed to remedy."

[The excerpts here deal only with the question of whether the Supreme Court has appellate jurisdiction over constitutional decisions by state courts.]

MR. JUSTICE STORY delivered the opinion of the Court. . . .

[The] appellate power is not limited by the terms of the third article to any particular courts. The words are, "the judicial power (which includes appellate power) shall extend *to all cases*," &c., and "in all other cases before mentioned the supreme court shall have appellate jurisdiction." It is the *case*, then, and not *the court*, that gives the jurisdiction. If the judicial power extends to the case, it will be in vain to search in the letter of the constitution for any qualification as to the tribunal where it depends. [If] the text be clear and distinct, no restriction upon its plain and obvious import ought to be admitted, unless the inference be irresistible.

If the constitution meant to limit the appellate jurisdiction to cases pending in the courts of the United States, it would necessarily follow that the jurisdiction of these courts would, in all the cases enumerated in the constitution, be exclusive of state tribunals. How otherwise could the jurisdiction extend to *all* cases arising under the constitution, laws, and treaties of the United States, or *to all cases* of admiralty and maritime jurisdiction? If some of these cases might be entertained by state tribunals, and no appellate jurisdiction as to them should exist, then the appellate power would not extend to *all*, but to *some*, cases. If state tribunals might exercise concurrent jurisdiction over all or some of the other classes of cases in the constitution without control, then the appellate jurisdiction of the United States might, as to such cases, have no real existence, contrary to the manifest intent of the constitution. [This] construction would abridge the jurisdiction of such court far more than has been ever contemplated in any act of congress. . . .

[It] is plain that the framers of the constitution did contemplate that cases within the judicial cognizance of the United States not only might but would arise in the state courts, in the exercise of their ordinary jurisdiction. With this view the sixth article declares, that "this constitution, and the laws of the United States, which shall be made in pursuance thereof, and all treaties made, or which shall be made, under the authority of the United States, shall be the supreme law of the land, and the judges in every state shall be bound thereby, any thing in the constitution or laws of any state to the contrary notwithstanding." It is obvious that this obligation is imperative upon the state judges in their official, and not merely in their private, capacities. From the very nature of their judicial duties they would be called upon to pronounce the law applicable to the case in judgment. They were not to decide merely according to the laws or constitution of the state, but according to the constitution, laws and treaties of the United States — "the supreme law of the land."

A moment's consideration will show us the necessity and propriety of this provision in cases where the jurisdiction of the state courts is unquestionable. Suppose a contract for the payment of money is made between citizens of the same state, and performance thereof is sought in the courts of that state; no person can doubt that the jurisdiction completely and exclusively attaches, in the first instance, to such courts. Suppose at the trial the defendant sets up in his defence a tender under a state law, making paper money a good tender, or a state law, impairing the obligation of such contract, which law, if binding, would defeat the suit. The constitution of the United States has declared that no state shall make any thing but gold or silver coin a tender in payment of debts, or pass a law impairing the obligation of contracts. If congress shall not have passed a law providing for the removal of such a suit to the courts of the United States, must not the state court proceed to hear and determine it? [Suppose] an indictment for a crime in a state court, and the defendant should allege in his defence that the crime was created by an ex post facto act of the state, must not the state court, in the exercise of a jurisdiction which has already rightfully attached, have a right to pronounce on the validity and sufficiency of the defence? It would be extremely difficult, upon any legal principles, to give a negative answer to these inquiries. Innumerable instances of the same sort might be stated, in illustration of the position; and unless the state courts could sustain jurisdiction in such cases, this clause of the sixth article would be without meaning or effect, and public mischiefs, of a most enormous magnitude, would inevitably ensue.

It must, therefore, be conceded that the constitution not only contemplated, but meant to provide for cases within the scope of the judicial power of the United States, which might yet depend before state tribunals. It was foreseen that in the exercise of their ordinary jurisdiction, state courts would incidentally take cognizance of cases arising under the constitution, the laws, and treaties of the United States. Yet to all these cases the judicial power, by the very terms of the constitution, is to extend. It cannot extend by original jurisdiction if that was already rightfully and exclusively attached in the state courts, which (as has been already shown) may occur; it must, therefore, extend by appellate jurisdiction, or not at all. It would seem to follow that the appellate power of the United States must, in such cases, extend to state tribunals; and if in such cases, there is no reason why it should not equally attach upon all others within the purview of the constitution.

It has been argued that such an appellate jurisdiction over state courts is inconsistent with the genius of our governments, and the spirit of the constitution. That the latter was never designed to act upon state sovereignties, but only upon the people, and that if the power exists, it will materially impair the sovereignty of the states, and the independence of their courts. . . .

It is a mistake that the constitution was not designed to operate upon states, in their corporate capacities. It is crowded with provisions which restrain or annul the sovereignty of the states in some of the highest branches of their prerogatives. The tenth section of the first article contains a long list of disabilities and prohibitions imposed upon the states. Surely, when such essential portions of state sovereignty are taken away, or prohibited to be exercised, it cannot be correctly asserted that the constitution does not act upon the states. The language of the constitution is also imperative upon the states as to the performance of many duties. It is imperative upon the state legislatures to make laws prescribing the time, places, and manner of holding elections for senators and representatives, and for electors of president and vice-president. And in these, as well as some other cases, congress have a right to revise, amend, or supercede the laws which may be passed by state legislatures. When, therefore, the states are stripped of some of the highest attributes of sovereignty, and the same are given to the United States; when the legislatures of the states are, in some respects, under the control of congress, and in every case are, under the constitution, bound by the paramount authority of the United States; it is certainly difficult to support the argument that the appellate power over the decisions of state courts is contrary to the genius of our institutions. The courts of the United States can, without question, revise the proceedings of the executive and legislative authorities of the states, and if they are found to be contrary to the constitution, may declare them to be of no legal validity. Surely the exercise of the same right over judicial tribunals is not a higher or more dangerous act of sovereign power.

Nor can such a right be deemed to impair the independence of state judges. It is assuming the very ground in controversy to assert that they possess an absolute independence of the United States. In respect to the powers granted to the United States, they are not independent; they are expressly bound to obedience by the letter of the constitution; and if they should unintentionally transcend their authority, or misconstrue the constitution, there is no more reason for giving their judgments an absolute and irresistible force, than for giving it to the acts of the other co-ordinate departments of state sovereignty.

The argument urged from the possibility of the abuse of the revising power, is equally unsatisfactory. It is always a doubtful course, to argue against the use or existence of a power, from the possibility of its abuse. It is still more difficult, by such an argument, to ingraft upon a general power a restriction which is not to be found in the terms in which it is given. From the very nature of things, the absolute right of decision, in the last resort, must rest somewhere — wherever it may be vested it is susceptible of abuse. In all questions of jurisdiction the inferior, or appellate court, must pronounce the final judgment; and common sense, as well as legal reasoning, has conferred it upon the latter.

It is further argued, that no great public mischief can result from a construction which shall limit the appellate power of the United States to cases in their own courts: first, because state judges are bound by an oath to support the constitution of the United States, and must be presumed to be men of learning and integrity; and, secondly, because congress must have an unquestionable right to remove all cases within the scope of the judicial power from the state courts to the courts of the United States, at any time before final judgment, though not after final judgment. As to the first reason — admitting that the judges of the state courts are, and always will be, of as much learning, integrity, and wisdom, as those of the courts of the United States, (which we very cheerfully admit,) it does not aid the argument. It is manifest that the constitution has proceeded upon a theory of its own, and given or withheld powers according to the judgment of the American people, by whom it was adopted. [The] constitution has presumed (whether rightly or wrongly we do not inquire) that state attachments, state prejudices, state jealousies, and state interests, might sometimes obstruct, or control, or be supposed to obstruct or control, the regular administration of justice. Hence, in controversies between states; between citizens of different states; between citizens claiming grants under different states; between a state and its citizens, or foreigners, and between citizens and foreigners, it enables the parties, under the authority of congress, to have the controversies heard, tried, and determined before the national tribunals. No other reason than that which has been stated can be assigned, why some, at least, of those cases should not have been left to the cognizance of the state courts. In respect to the other enumerated cases — the cases arising under the constitution, laws, and treaties of the United States, cases affecting ambassadors and other public ministers, and cases of admiralty and maritime jurisdiction — reasons of a higher and more extensive nature, touching the safety, peace, and sovereignty of the nation, might well justify a grant of exclusive jurisdiction.

This is not all. A motive of another kind, perfectly compatible with the most sincere respect for state tribunals, might induce the grant of appellate power over their decisions. That motive is the importance, and even necessity of *uniformity* of decisions throughout the whole United States, upon all subjects within the purview of the constitution. Judges of equal learning and integrity, in different states, might differently interpret a statute, or a treaty of the United States, or even the constitution itself: If there were no revising authority to control these jarring and discordant judgments, and harmonize them into uniformity, the laws, the treaties, and the constitution of the United States would be different in different states, and might, perhaps, never have precisely the same construction, obligation, or efficacy, in any two states. The public mischiefs that would attend such a state of things would be truly deplorable; and it cannot be believed that they could have escaped the enlightened convention which formed the constitution. What, indeed, might then have been only prophecy, has now become fact; and the appellate jurisdiction must continue to be the only adequate remedy for such evils.

There is an additional consideration, which is entitled to great weight. The constitution of the United States was designed for the common and equal benefit of all the people of the United States. The judicial power was granted for the same benign and salutary purposes. It was not to be exercised exclusively for the benefit of parties who might be plaintiffs, and would elect the national forum, but also for the protection of defendants who might be entitled to try their rights, or assert their privileges, before the same forum. Yet, if the construction contended for be correct, it will follow, that as the plaintiff may always elect the state court, the defendant may be deprived of all the security which the constitution intended in aid of his rights. Such a state of things can, in no respect, be considered as giving equal rights. . . .

On the whole, the court are of opinion, that the appellate power of the United States does extend to cases pending in the state courts; and that the 25th section of the judiciary act, which authorizes the exercise of this jurisdiction in the specified cases, by a writ of error, is supported by the letter and spirit of the constitution. We find no clause in that instrument which limits this power; and we dare not interpose a limitation where the people have not been disposed to create one. . . .

[Reversed.]

Note: Supreme Court Review of State Courts and State Laws

1. *Supreme Court review of state court decisions — underlying concerns.* In what ways does the issue in *Martin* differ from that in *Marbury*? Why is it important to have Supreme Court jurisdiction over the state courts? Justice Story's opinion stresses that, if there were "no revising authority," the federal system would make possible "jarring and discordant judgment." The appellate jurisdiction of the Supreme Court is, in this view, necessary to ensure the uniformity of federal law. But that raises the question why federal law must be uniform. As a general rule, legal requirements may vary from one state to another. What would be the evil in having disparate interpretations of the federal Constitution?

The Virginia judges in *Martin* made two arguments for their conclusion. First, they claimed not that the Constitution did not bind state judges, but that one sovereign could not control another; the risk of centralization thus outweighed the risk of disharmony. Second, they contended that other devices were available in order to minimize that latter risk and to bring about uniformity. Congress could, for example, allow removal to federal court of all cases involving a federal question. The position of the Virginia judges was that Congress had to take action to eliminate the risk of lack of uniformity through creating lower federal courts and expanding removal jurisdiction. The Court's view, by contrast, is that the more direct mechanism of control — appellate jurisdiction — is constitutionally permissible.

In addition to the uniformity point, note the possibility that Supreme Court review is necessary because of state hostility to, or lack of sufficient sympathy for, federal rights. The argument here is that state judges will be less likely to react sympathetically to federal claims — either because they lack the tenure and salary protections of article III, and are thus more susceptible to political influence, or because they have a natural alliance with the legislative and executive parts of state government. Perhaps, in short, state judges are insufficiently independent of the forces against which constitutional guarantees are supposed to run. Neuborne, The Myth of Parity, 90 Harv. L. Rev. 1105, 1127-1128 (1977), speaks of the difference between federal district judges and state trial judges, but the arguments are applicable to appellate judges as well:

> Federal district judges [are] as insulated from majoritarian pressures as is functionally possible, precisely to insure their ability to enforce the Constitution without fear of reprisal. State trial judges, on the other hand, generally are elected for a fixed term, rendering them vulnerable to majoritarian pressure when deciding constitutional cases. [This] insulation factor, I suggest, explains the historical preference for federal enforcement of controversial constitutional norms.

This view has often played an important role in constitutional history. But one might ask whether it might not be the federal judges who are likely to be biased.

Another justification for Supreme Court review of state court decisions stresses the comparative expertise of the federal courts in dealing with federal constitutional questions. Neuborne, supra, at 1120, suggests that "federal trial courts tend to be better equipped to analyze complex, often conflicting lines of authority and more likely to produce competently written, persuasive opinions than are state trial courts." Why should this be the case?

2. *Supreme Court review of state laws — constitutional basis. Martin* involved Supreme Court review of state court decisions, not of state laws; but elements of the Court's reasoning are applicable to the latter problem. Do the arguments, textual and otherwise, for the power of judicial review of state laws carry more force than those for judicial review of federal laws? Consider Justice Holmes's view: "I do not think the United States would come to an end if we lost our power to declare an Act of Congress void. I do think the Union would be imperiled if we could not make that declaration as to the laws of the several States." O. W. Holmes, Collected Legal Papers 295-296 (1920).

3. *Justice Story and article III.* In *Martin*, Justice Story interpreted article III to require that the whole judicial power of the United States should be at all times vested, either in an original or appellate form, in some courts created under its authority. If it were accepted, this conclusion would have dramatic practical consequences. It means that, at any time, some federal court must have the power to decide any case to which the federal judicial power extends. On what does Justice Story base his conclusion?

Consider Currie, The Constitution in the Supreme Court: The Powers of the Federal Courts, 1801-1835, 49 U. Chi. L. Rev. 646, 685-686 (1982), suggesting that Story's conclusion

> was contrary to Supreme Court precedent [as] well as to consistent congressional practice. [The] strongest argument against giving a natural reading to the ostensibly unlimited discretion of Congress to limit federal jurisdiction is *Marbury's* principle that the courts were intended to enforce constitutional limits on legislative power. Story's interpretation poorly comports with that principle, for it outlaws such minor caseload adjustments as the jurisdictional amount while allowing Congress to evade any substantial check by vesting sole power over important constitutional questions in a single lower court selected for the complaisance of its judges.

4. *Cohens v. Virginia.* In Cohens v. Virginia, 19 U.S. (6 Wheat.) 264 (1821), the Court reaffirmed *Martin* in the context of review of state criminal proceedings. The case involved defendants who had been convicted of the unlawful sale of lottery tickets in Virginia. They defended on the ground that an act of Congress authorized the local government of the District of Columbia to establish a lottery. The Court, per Chief Justice Marshall, affirmed, concluding that the congressional statute did not authorize the sale outside the territorial boundaries of the District of Columbia. But the importance of the case lies in the holding that the Supreme Court could exercise jurisdiction over decisions of the state courts in criminal cases and in cases in which the state was a party. As to the fact that the state was a party, Chief Justice Marshall noted that "the judicial power, as originally given, extends to all cases arising under the constitution or a law of the United States, whoever may be the party." The language of article III, Chief Justice Marshall claimed, referred to "all" federal question cases. The same reasoning applied to the claim that the fact that a criminal case was involved made *Cohens* different from *Martin.*

Note: *Judicial Exclusivity in Constitutional Interpretation?*

In Cooper v. Aaron, 358 U.S. 1 (1958), Arkansas had failed to comply with a district court order requiring desegregation. Its brief stated that the "legislative, executive, and judicial departments of the state government opposed the desegregation of Little Rock schools by enacting laws, calling out troops, making statements vilifying federal law and federal courts, and failing to utilize state law enforcement agencies and judicial processes to maintain public peace."

The state argued that desegregation would lead to undue violence and disorder and that those consequences justified disobedience of the decree. The Court rejected that argument on the ground that "law and order are not here to be preserved by depriving the Negro children of their constitutional rights." But the Court went on to meet the view that "the Governor and Legislature [are] not bound by our holding in the *Brown* case":

> Article VI of the Constitution makes the Constitution the "supreme Law of the Land." In 1803, Chief Justice Marshall, speaking for a unanimous Court, referring to the Constitution as "the fundamental and paramount law of the nation," de-

clared in the notable case of Marbury v. Madison [that] "It is emphatically the province and duty of the judicial department to say what the law is." This decision declared the basic principle that the federal judiciary is supreme in the exposition of the law of the Constitution, and that principle has ever since been respected by this Court and the Country as a permanent and indispensable feature of our constitutional system. It follows that the interpretation of the Fourteenth Amendment enunciated by this Court in the *Brown* case is the supreme law of the land, and Art. VI of the Constitution makes it of binding effect on the States "any Thing in the Constitution or Laws of any State to the Contrary notwithstanding." Every state legislator and executive and judicial officer is solemnly committed by oath taken pursuant to Art. VI, cl. 3, "to support this Constitution."

Cooper might well be thought to go beyond *Marbury*. *Marbury* established that in the course of deciding cases, courts must look to the Constitution as an enforceable source of law. When there is a conflict between the Constitution and a statute, and when the conflict is relevant to the resolution of a justiciable controversy, the courts must allow the Constitution, as they interpret it, to prevail. But this principle might not establish any *special* judicial authority to interpret the Constitution. On one view, *Marbury* means only that every branch of government, acting within its sphere, is authorized to interpret the Constitution.

Cooper v. Aaron suggests that the courts should see themselves as having been entrusted with a special and distinctive role as ultimate guardians of the meaning of the Constitution, and that other government officials must not interpret the Constitution for themselves but instead must look to the courts' interpretation and take it as authoritative. The result would be that judicial rulings are authoritative, even if there is no decree against the relevant officials in a litigated case. Perhaps more generally such a view would suggest that Presidents, members of Congress, and others should not think independently about what the Constitution requires, but should instead ask how the Supreme Court would be likely to decide.

If the passage from *Cooper* should be so understood, does it go too far in establishing "judicial supremacy"? What are the practical differences between *Cooper* and the narrower interpretation of *Marbury?*

1. *The view from the presidency.* Consider in this regard the responsibility of political actors, including most prominently the President, in circumstances in which (a) they believe that a statute is unconstitutional in the face of a court's conclusion that it is constitutional, or in the expectation that the court will uphold it, and (b) they believe that the statute or measure is constitutional in the face of a judicial conclusion that it is unconstitutional, or in the expectation that the court will invalidate it.

Consider the following view with respect to the first situation. Suppose that the Supreme Court has upheld or would uphold a statute that the President believes unconstitutional. (It might be a statute calling for literacy tests, attacked as racially discriminatory, or a retroactive environmental statute, attacked as a "taking" of property.) The Constitution imposes on all branches of government, not just the courts, a duty to comply with the Constitution. A necessary inference is that the President and members of Congress must make their own judgments on constitutional issues. This responsibility is especially insistent in light of the fact that moral issues frequently become constitutional issues. If the courts' duty is exclusive, politics becomes drained of morality, and political actors will be making decisions on the basis of expediency alone. Thus, for example, if the President or a member of Congress believes that a statute is unconstitutional, he or she must ignore it, even if the Court would uphold it. The Constitution plainly speaks to all public officials, and it is simply too important to be left entirely to the justices. See the veto message of Andrew Jackson, 1832, on an act to recharter the Bank of the United States, 2 Messages and Papers of the Presidents 576, 581-582 (J. Richardson ed. 1900) (vetoing on constitutional grounds a measure that had been upheld by the Court: "[The] opinion of the judges has no more authority over Congress than the opinion of Congress has over the judges, and on that point the President is independent of both").

Consider the views expressed by Jefferson, Letter to Abigail Adams, Sept. 11, 1804, in 8 The Writings of Thomas Jefferson 310 (M. Ford ed. 1897):

> You seem to think it devolved on the judges to decide on the validity of the sedition law. But nothing in the Constitution has given them a right to decide for the Executive, any more than to the Executive to decide for them. Both magistracies are equally independent in the sphere of action assigned to them. The judges, believing the law constitutional, had a right to pass a sentence of fine and imprisonment, because that power was placed in their hands by the Constitution. But the Executive, believing the law to be unconstitutional, was bound to remit the execution of it; because that power has been confided to him by the Constitution. That instrument meant that its coordinate branches should be checks on each other. But the opinion which gives to the judges the right to decide what laws are constitutional, and what not, not only for themselves in their sphere of action, but for the Legislature and Executive also, would make the judiciary a despotic branch.

With respect to the second situation, suppose the President, or some other public official, believes that the Supreme Court has wrongly invalidated a statute. Recent examples include decisions invalidating laws calling for segregation, laws restricting abortions, laws protecting flags from being burned, and laws requiring school prayer. What is the President's duty in the face of such laws? May he sign or propose legislation that would run afoul of the Court's decision? May he attempt to get the Court to overrule its decision through such acts and through repetitive and insistent litigation? May he campaign against the Court? See Lincoln's First Inaugural Address, Mar. 4, 1861, in 6 Messages and Papers of the Presidents 5 (J. Richardson ed. 1900):

> I do not forget the position assumed by some that constitutional questions are to be decided by the Supreme Court; nor do I deny that such decisions must be binding, in any case, upon the parties to a suit, as to the object of that suit, while they are also entitled to a very high respect and consideration in all parallel cases by all other departments of the government. And, while it is obviously possible that such decision may be erroneous in any given case, still the evil effect following it, being limited to that particular case, with the chance that it may be overruled and never become a precedent for other cases, can better be borne than could the evils of a different practice. At the same time, the candid citizen must confess that if the policy of the government, upon vital questions affecting the whole people, is to be irrevocably fixed by decisions of the Supreme Court, the instant they are made, in ordinary litigation between parties in personal actions, the people will have ceased to be their own rulers, having to that extent practically resigned the government into the hands of that eminent tribunal. Nor is there in this view any assault upon

the court or the judges. It is a duty from which they may not shrink to decide cases properly brought before them, and it is no fault of theirs if others seek to turn their decisions to political purposes.

Other Presidents, including Franklin Roosevelt and Richard Nixon, have expressed similar views. Can this position be distinguished from the refusal of Governor Faubus of Arkansas to comply with the decision in Brown v. Board of Education? See if you can draw a distinction that does *not* speak of the moral or legal correctness of *Brown*.

Consider the views of President Reagan's Attorney General Edwin Meese in The Law of the Constitution, 61 Tul. L. Rev. 979 (1987):

> [There] is [a] necessary distinction between the Constitution and constitutional law. The two are not synonymous. . . .
>
> Obviously [a Supreme Court decision] does have binding quality: It binds the parties in a case and also the executive branch for whatever enforcement is necessary. But such a decision does not establish a "supreme Law of the Land" that is binding on all persons and parts of government, henceforth and forevermore. . . .
>
> To confuse the Constitution with judicial pronouncements allows no standard by which to criticize and to seek the overruling of [cases] such as *Dred Scott*, and Plessy v. Ferguson. To do otherwise, as Lincoln said, is to submit to government by judiciary. But such a state could never be consistent with the principles of our Constitution. Indeed, it would be utterly inconsistent with the very idea of the rule of law to which we, as a people, have always subscribed.

2. *"Underenforced" constitutional norms.* It might be argued that the Constitution sometimes invalidates official action, even if the Supreme Court declines so to hold. There is, in this view, a difference between what the Constitution requires and what the Court says it requires. The Court might decide that, because of the need to defer to other branches of government or because of other limitations on its own competence, some measure does not violate the Constitution; but such a holding might not bind other officials in the process of deciding whether a proposed course of action is constitutional, since those officials are not constrained by principles of deference.

See Sager, Fair Measure: The Status of Underenforced Constitutional Norms, 91 Harv. L. Rev. 1212, 1220-1221, 1227 (1978):

> Conventional analysis does not distinguish between fully enforced and underenforced constitutional norms; as a general matter, the scope of a constitutional norm is considered to be coterminous with the scope of its judicial enforcement. [Where] a federal judicial construct is found not to extend to certain official behavior because of institutional concerns rather than analytical perceptions, it seems strange to regard the resulting decision as a statement about the meaning of the constitutional norm in question. After all, what the members of the federal tribunal have actually determined is that there are good reasons for stopping short of exhausting the content of the constitutional concept with which they are dealing; the limited judicial construct which they have fashioned or accepted is occasioned by this determination and does not derive from a judgment about the scope of the constitutional concept itself.
>
> [The] most direct consequence of adopting this revised view is the perception that government officials have a legal obligation to obey an underenforced consti-

tutional norm which extends beyond its interpretation by the federal judiciary to the full dimensions of the concept which the norm embodies. This obligation to obey constitutional norms at their underenforced margins requires governmental officials to fashion their own conceptions of these norms and measure their conduct by reference to these conceptions. Public officials cannot consider themselves free to act at what they perceive or ought to perceive to be peril to constitutional norms merely because the federal judiciary is unable to enforce these norms at their margins.

On this view, branches of government other than courts act properly when they interpret the Constitution more expansively than does the Court. Perhaps, then, political branches are within their rights if they conclude (for example) that the death penalty is unconstitutional, that affirmative action programs are unconstitutional, that environmental statutes violate the takings clause, or that government must fund abortions — even if the Supreme Court disagrees.

3. *Settlement.* Consider the position that the view of judicial supremacy suggested in Cooper v. Aaron can be defended simply as a way of ensuring settlement of questions that badly need to be settled. See Alexander and Schauer, On Extrajudicial Constitutional Interpretation, 110 Harv. L. Rev. 1377 (1997). In this argument, "good institutional design requires norms that compel decision-makers to defer to the judgments of others with which they disagree." Id. at 1387. But it might be asked whether it is possible, or desirable, for the Supreme Court to have the power to "settle" constitutional questions.

C. THE SOURCES OF JUDICIAL DECISIONS: TEXT, "REPRESENTATION-REINFORCEMENT," AND NATURAL LAW

This section explores three possible sources of constitutional doctrine that have, in one or another form, played an important role in constitutional adjudication: the text (often but not always understood by reference to the original understanding); "reinforcement," or improvement, of democratic processes; and natural law and natural rights, sometimes understood in the modern era as moral or philosophical argument about rights. The roots of the resulting debates can be found in early decisions by the Supreme Court.

McCulloch v. Maryland

17 U.S. (4 Wheat.) 316 (1819)

[This was an action brought by John James, for himself and the state of Maryland, against James McCulloch, cashier of a branch of the Bank of the United States. James alleged that McCulloch had failed to pay a state tax assessed against the bank. The court below held for the plaintiff. For background, see the Notes following the opinion.]

MR. CHIEF JUSTICE MARSHALL delivered the opinion of the Court.

In the case now to be determined, the defendant, a sovereign State, denies the obligation of a law enacted by the legislature of the Union, and the plaintiff, on his part, contests the validity of an act which has been passed by the legislature of that State. The constitution of our country, in its most interesting and vital parts, is to be considered; the conflicting powers of the government of the Union and of its members, as marked in that constitution, are to be discussed; and an opinion given, which may essentially influence the great operations of the government. No tribunal can approach such a question without a deep sense of its importance, and of the awful responsibility involved in its decision. But it must be decided peacefully, or remain a source of hostile legislation, perhaps of hostility of a still more serious nature; and if it is to be so decided, by this tribunal alone can the decision be made. On the Supreme Court of the United States has the constitution of our country devolved this important duty.

The first question made in the cause is, has Congress power to incorporate a bank?

It has been truly said, that this can scarcely be considered as an open question, entirely unprejudiced by the former proceedings of the nation respecting it. The principle now contested was introduced at a very early period of our history, has been recognized by many successive legislatures, and has been acted upon by the judicial department, in cases of peculiar delicacy, as a law of undoubted obligation.

It will not be denied, that a bold and daring usurpation might be resisted, after an acquiescence still longer and more complete than this. But it is conceived that a doubtful question [ought] to receive a considerable impression from that practice. An exposition of the constitution, deliberately established by legislative acts, on the faith of which an immense property has been advanced, ought not to be lightly disregarded.

The power now contested was exercised by the first Congress elected under the present constitution. The bill for incorporating the bank of the United States did not steal upon an unsuspecting legislature, and pass unobserved. Its principle was completely understood, and was opposed with equal zeal and ability. After being resisted, first in the fair and open field of debate, and afterwards in the executive cabinet, with as much persevering talent as any measure has ever experienced, and being supported by arguments which convinced minds as pure and as intelligent as this country can boast, it became a law. The original act was permitted to expire; but a short experience of the embarrassments to which the refusal to revive it exposed the government, convinced those who were most prejudiced against the measure of its necessity, and induced the passage of the present law. It would require no ordinary share of intrepidity to assert that a measure adopted under these circumstances was a bold and plain usurpation, to which the constitution gave no countenance.

These observations belong to the cause; but they are not made under the impression that, were the question entirely new, the law would be found irreconcilable with the constitution.

In discussing this question, the counsel for the State of Maryland have deemed it of some importance, in the construction of the constitution, to consider that instrument not as emanating from the people, but as the act of sovereign and independent States. The powers of the general government, it has been said, are delegated by the States, who alone are truly sovereign; and must be exercised in subordination to the States, who alone possess supreme dominion.

It would be difficult to sustain this proposition. The Convention which framed the constitution was indeed elected by the State legislatures. But the instrument, when it came from their hands, was a mere proposal, without obligation, or pretensions to it. It was reported to the then existing Congress of the United States, with a request that it might "be submitted to a Convention of Delegates, chosen in each State by the people thereof, under the recommendation of its Legislature, for their assent and ratification." This mode of proceeding was adopted; and by the Convention, by Congress, and by the State Legislatures, the instrument was submitted to the people. They acted upon it in the only manner in which they can act safely, effectively, and wisely, on such a subject, by assembling in Convention. It is true, they assembled in their several States — and where else should they have assembled? No political dreamer was ever wild enough to think of breaking down the lines which separate the States, and of compounding the American people into one common mass. Of consequence, when they act, they act in their States. But the measures they adopt do not, on that account, cease to be the measures of the people themselves, or become the measures of the State governments.

From these Conventions the constitution derives its whole authority. The government proceeds directly from the people; is "ordained and established" in the name of the people; and is declared to be ordained, "in order to form a more perfect union, establish justice, ensure domestic tranquillity, and secure the blessings of liberty to themselves and to their posterity." The assent of the States, in their sovereign capacity, is implied in calling a Convention, and thus submitting that instrument to the people. But the people were at perfect liberty to accept or reject it; and their act was final. It required not the affirmance, and could not be negatived, by the State governments. The constitution, when thus adopted, was of complete obligation, and bound the State sovereignties. . . .

The government of the Union, then, (whatever may be the influence of this fact on the case,) is emphatically, and truly, a government of the people. In form and in substance it emanates from them. Its powers are granted by them, and are to be exercised directly on them, and for their benefit.

This government is acknowledged by all to be one of enumerated powers. The principle that it can exercise only the powers granted to it [is] now universally admitted. But the question respecting the extent of the powers actually granted, is perpetually arising, and will probably continue to arise, as long as our system shall exist.

In discussing these questions, the conflicting powers of the general and State governments must be brought into view, and the supremacy of their respective laws, when they are in opposition, must be settled.

If any one proposition could command the universal assent of mankind, we might expect it would be this — that the government of the Union, though limited in its powers, is supreme within its sphere of action. This would seem to result necessarily from its nature. It is the government of all; its powers are delegated by all; it represents all, and acts for all. Though any one State may be willing to control its operations, no State is willing to allow others to control them. The nation, on those subjects on which it can act, must necessarily bind its component parts. But this question is not left to mere reason: the people have, in express terms, decided it, by saying, "this constitution, and the laws of the United States, which shall be made in pursuance thereof," "shall be the supreme law of the land," and by requiring that the members of the State legislatures, and the officers of the executive and judicial departments of the States, shall take the oath of fidelity to it. . . .

Among the enumerated powers, we do not find that of establishing a bank or creating a corporation. But there is no phrase in the instrument which, like the articles of confederation, excludes incidental or implied powers; and which requires that every thing granted shall be expressly and minutely described. Even the 10th amendment, which was framed for the purpose of quieting the excessive jealousies which had been excited, omits the word "expressly," and declares only that the powers "not delegated to the United States, nor prohibited to the States, are reserved to the States or to the people" thus leaving the question, whether the particular power which may become the subject of contest has been delegated to the one government, or prohibited to the other, to depend on a fair construction of the whole instrument. The men who drew and adopted this amendment had experienced the embarrassments resulting from the insertion of this word in the articles of confederation, and probably omitted it to avoid those embarrassments. A constitution, to contain an accurate detail of all the subdivisions of which its great powers will admit, and of all the means by which they may be carried into execution, would partake of the prolixity of a legal code, and could scarcely be embraced by the human mind. It would probably never be understood by the public. Its nature, therefore, requires, that only its great outlines should be marked, its important objects designated, and the minor ingredients which compose those objects be deduced from the nature of the objects themselves. That this idea was entertained by the framers of the American constitution, is not only to be inferred from the nature of the instrument, but from the language. Why else were some of the limitations, found in the ninth section of the 1st article, introduced? It is also, in some degree, warranted by their having omitted to use any restrictive term which might prevent its receiving a fair and just interpretation. In considering this question, then, we must never forget, that it is *a constitution* we are expounding.

Although, among the enumerated powers of government, we do not find the word "bank" or "incorporation," we find the great powers to lay and collect taxes; to borrow money; to regulate commerce; to declare and conduct a war; and to raise and support armies and navies. The sword and the purse, all the external relations, and no inconsiderable portion of the industry of the nation, are entrusted to its government. It can never be pretended that these vast powers draw after them others of inferior importance, merely because they are inferior. Such an idea can never be advanced. But it may with great reason be contended, that a government, entrusted with such ample powers, on the due execution of which the happiness and prosperity of the nation so vitally depends, must also be entrusted with ample means for their execution. The power being given, it is the interest of the nation to facilitate its execution. It can never be their interest, and cannot be presumed to have been their intention, to clog and embarrass its execution by withholding the most appropriate means. Throughout this vast republic, from the St. Croix to the Gulph of Mexico, from the Atlantic to the Pacific, revenue is to be collected and expended, armies are to be marched and supported. The exigencies of the nation may require that the treasure raised in the north should be transported to the south, that raised in the east conveyed to the west, or that this order should be reversed. Is that construction of the constitution to be preferred which would render these operations difficult, hazardous, and expensive? Can we adopt that construction, (unless the words imperiously require it,) which would impute to the framers of that instrument, when granting these powers for the public good, the intention of impeding their exercise by withholding a choice of means? . . .

It is not denied, that the powers given to the government imply the ordinary means of execution. That, for example, of raising revenue, and applying it to national purposes, is admitted to imply the power of conveying money from place to place, as the exigencies of the nation may require, and of employing the usual means of conveyance. . . .

But the constitution of the United States has not left the right of Congress to employ the necessary means, for the execution of the powers conferred on the government, to general reasoning. To its enumeration of powers is added that of making "all laws which shall be necessary and proper, for carrying into execution the foregoing powers, and all other powers vested by this constitution, in the government of the United States, or in any department thereof."

The counsel for the State of Maryland have urged various arguments, to prove that this clause, though in terms a grant of power, is not so in effect; but is really restrictive of the general right, which might otherwise be implied, of selecting means for executing the enumerated powers. . . .

[The] argument on which most reliance is placed, is drawn from the peculiar language of this clause. Congress is not empowered by it to make all laws, which may have relation to the powers conferred on the government, but such only as may be "*necessary and proper*" for carrying them into execution. The word "*necessary*," is considered as controlling the whole sentence, and as limiting the right to pass laws for the execution of the granted powers, to such as are indispensable, and without which the power would be nugatory. That it excludes the choice of means, and leaves to Congress, in each case, that only which is most direct and simple.

Is it true, that this is the sense in which the word "necessary" is always used? Does it always import an absolute physical necessity, so strong, that one thing, to which another may be termed necessary, cannot exist without that other? We think it does not. If reference be had to its use, in the common affairs of the world, or in approved authors, we find that it frequently imports no more than that one thing is convenient, or useful, or essential to another. To employ the means necessary to an end, is generally understood as employing any means calculated to produce the end, and not as being confined to those single means, without which the end would be entirely unattainable. Such is the character of human language, that no word conveys to the mind, in all situations, one single definite idea; and nothing is more common than to use words in a figurative sense. Almost all compositions contain words, which, taken in their rigorous sense, would convey a meaning different from that which is obviously intended. It is essential to just construction, that many words which import something excessive, should be understood in a more mitigated sense — in that sense which common usage justifies. The word "necessary" is of this description. It has not a fixed character peculiar to itself. It admits of all degrees of comparison; and is often connected with other words, which increase or diminish the impression the mind receives of the urgency it imports. A thing may be necessary, very necessary, absolutely or indispensably necessary. To no mind would the same idea be conveyed, by these several phrases. This comment on the word is well illustrated, by the passage cited at the bar, from the 10th section of the 1st article of the constitution. It is, we think, impossible to compare the sentence which prohibits a State from laying "imposts, or duties on imports or exports, except what may be *absolutely* necessary for executing its inspection laws," with that which authorizes Congress "to make all laws which shall be necessary and proper for carrying into execution" the powers of the general government, without feeling a conviction that the convention understood itself to change materially the meaning of the word "necessary," by prefixing the word "absolutely." This word, then, like others, is used in various senses; and, in its construction, the subject, the context, the intention of the person using them, are all to be taken into view.

Let this be done in the case under consideration. The subject is the execution of those great powers on which the welfare of a nation essentially depends. It must have been the intention of those who gave these powers, to insure, as far as human prudence could insure, their beneficial execution. This could not be done by confiding the choice of means to such narrow limits as not to leave it in the power of Congress to adopt any which might be appropriate, and which were conducive to the end. This provision is made in a constitution intended to endure for ages to come, and, consequently, to be adapted to the various *crises* of human affairs. To have prescribed the means by which government should, in all future time, execute its powers, would have been to change, entirely, the character of the instrument, and give it the properties of a legal code. It would have been an unwise attempt to provide, by immutable rules, for exigencies which, if foreseen at all, must have been seen dimly, and which can be best provided for as they occur. To have declared that the best means shall not be used, but those alone without which the power given would be nugatory, would have been to deprive the legislature of the capacity to avail itself of experience, to exercise its reason, and to accommodate its legislation to circumstances. If we apply this principle of construction to any of the powers of the government, we shall find it so pernicious in its operation that we shall be compelled to discard it. . . .

So, with respect to the whole penal code of the United States: whence arises the power to punish in cases not prescribed by the constitution? All admit that the government may, legitimately, punish any violation of its laws; and yet, this is not among the enumerated powers of Congress. The right to enforce the observance of law, by punishing its infraction, might be denied with the more plausibility, because it is expressly given in some cases. Congress is empowered "to provide for the punishment of counterfeiting the securities and current coin of the United States," and "to define and punish piracies and felonies committed on the high seas, and offenses against the law of nations." The several powers of Congress may exist, in a very imperfect state to be sure, but they may exist and be carried into execution, although no punishment should be inflicted in cases where the right to punish is not expressly given.

Take, for example, the power "to establish post offices and post roads." This power is executed by the single act of making the establishment. But, from this has been inferred the power and duty of carrying the mail along the post road, from one post office to another. And, from this implied power, has again been inferred the right to punish those who steal letters from the post office, or rob the mail. It may be said, with some plausibility, that the right to carry the mail, and to punish those who rob it, is not indispensably necessary to the establishment of a post office and post road. This right is indeed essential to the beneficial exercise of the power, but not indispensably necessary to its existence. So, of the punishment of the crimes of stealing or falsifying a record or process of a Court of the United States, or of perjury in such Court. To punish these offenses is certainly conducive to the due administration of justice. But courts may exist, and may decide the causes brought before them, though such crimes escape punishment.

The baneful influence of this narrow construction in all the operations of the government, and the absolute impracticability of maintaining it without rendering the government incompetent to its great objects, might be illustrated by numerous examples drawn from the constitution, and from our laws. . . .

In ascertaining the sense in which the word "necessary" is used in this clause of the constitution, we may derive some aid from that with which it is associated. Congress shall have power "to make all laws which shall be necessary and *proper* to carry into execution" the powers of the government. If the word "necessary" was used in that strict and rigorous sense for which the counsel for the State of Maryland contend, it would be an extraordinary departure from the usual course of the human mind, as exhibited in composition, to add a word, the only possible effect of which is to qualify that strict and rigorous meaning; to present to the mind the idea of some choice of means of legislation not straitened and compressed within the narrow limits for which gentlemen contend.

But the argument which most conclusively demonstrates the error of the construction contended for by the counsel for the State of Maryland, is founded on the intention of the Convention, as manifested in the whole clause. To waste time and argument in proving that, without it, Congress might carry its powers into execution, would be not much less idle than to hold a lighted taper to the sun. As little can it be required to prove, that in the absence of this clause, Congress would have some choice of means. That it might employ those which, in its judgment, would most advantageously effect the object to be accomplished. That any means adapted to the end, any means which tended directly to the execution of the constitutional powers of the government, were in themselves constitutional. This clause, as construed by the State of Maryland, would abridge, and almost annihilate this useful and necessary right of the legislature to select its means. That this could not be intended, is, we should think, had it not been already controverted, too apparent for controversy. We think so for the following reasons:

1st. The clause is placed among the powers of Congress, not among the limitations on those powers.

2nd. Its terms purport to enlarge, not to diminish the powers vested in the government. It purports to be an additional power, not a restriction on those already granted. No reason has been, or can be assigned for thus concealing an intention to narrow the discretion of the national legislature under words which purport to enlarge it. . . .

The result of the most careful and attentive consideration bestowed upon this clause is, that if it does not enlarge, it cannot be construed to restrain the powers of Congress, or to impair the right of the legislature to exercise its best judgment in the selection of measures to carry into execution the constitutional powers of the government. If no other motive for its insertion can be suggested, a sufficient one is found in the desire to remove all doubts respecting the right to legislate on that vast mass of incidental powers which must be involved in the constitution, if that instrument be not a splendid bauble.

We admit, as all must admit, that the powers of the government are limited, and that its limits are not to be transcended. But we think the sound construction of the constitution must allow to the national legislature that discretion, with respect to the means by which the powers it confers are to be carried into execution, which will enable that body to perform the high duties assigned to it, in the manner most beneficial to the people. Let the end be legitimate, let it be within the scope of the constitution, and all means which are appropriate, which are plainly adapted to that end, which are not prohibited, but consist with the letter and spirit of the constitution, are constitutional. . . .

If a corporation may be employed indiscriminately with other means to carry into execution the powers of the government, no particular reason can be assigned for excluding the use of a bank, if required for its fiscal operations. To use one, must be within the discretion of Congress, if it be an appropriate mode of executing the powers of government. That it is a convenient, a useful, and essential instrument in the prosecution of its fiscal operations, is not now a subject of controversy. All those who have been concerned in the administration of our finances, have concurred in representing its importance and necessity; and so strongly have they been felt, that statesmen of the first class, whose previous opinions against it had been confirmed by every circumstance which can fix the human judgment, have yielded those opinions to the exigencies of the nation. Under the confederation, Congress, justifying the measure by its necessity, transcended perhaps its powers to obtain the advantage of a bank; and our own legislation attests the universal conviction of the utility of this measure. The time has passed away when it can be necessary to enter into any discussion in order to prove the importance of this instrument, as a means to effect the legitimate objects of the government.

But, were its necessity less apparent, none can deny its being an appropriate measure; and if it is, the degree of its necessity, as has been very justly observed, is to be discussed in another place. Should Congress, in the execution of its powers, adopt measures which are prohibited by the constitution; or should Congress, under the pretext of executing its powers, pass laws for the accomplishment of objects not entrusted to the government; it would become the painful duty of this tribunal, should a case requiring such a decision come before it, to say that such an act was not the law of the land. But where the law is not prohibited, and is really calculated to effect any of the objects entrusted to the government, to undertake here to inquire into the degree of its necessity, would be to pass the line which circumscribes the judicial department, and to tread on legislative ground. This court disclaims all pretensions to such a power. . . .

It being the opinion of the Court, that the act incorporating the bank is constitutional; and that the power of establishing a branch in the State of Maryland might be properly exercised by the bank itself, we proceed to inquire —

2. Whether the State of Maryland may, without violating the constitution, tax that branch?

That the power of taxation is one of vital importance; that it is retained by the States; that it is not abridged by the grant of a similar power to the government of the Union; that it is to be concurrently exercised by the two governments: are truths which have never been denied. But, such is the paramount character of the constitution, that its capacity to withdraw any subject from the action of even this power, is admitted. The States are expressly forbidden to lay any duties on imports or exports, except what may be absolutely necessary for executing their inspection laws. If the obligation of this prohibition must be conceded — if it may restrain a State from the exercise of its taxing power on imports and exports; the same paramount character would seem, to restrain, as it certainly may restrain, a State from such other exercise of this power, as is in its nature incompatible with, and repugnant to, the constitutional laws of the Union. A law, absolutely repugnant to another, as entirely repeals that other as if express terms of repeal were used.

On this ground the counsel for the bank place its claim to be exempted from the power of a State to tax its operations. There is no express provision for the case, but the claim has been sustained on a principle which so entirely pervades the constitution, is so intermixed with the materials which compose it, so interwoven with its web, so blended with its texture, as to be incapable of being separated from it, without rendering it into shreds.

This great principle is, that the constitution and the laws made in pursuance thereof are supreme; that they control the constitution and laws of the respective States, and cannot be controlled by them. From this, which may be almost termed an axiom, other propositions are deduced as corollaries, on the truth or error of which, and on their application to this case, the cause has been supposed to depend. These are, 1st. that a power to create implies a power to preserve. 2nd. That a power to destroy, if wielded by a different hand, is hostile to, and incompatible with these powers to create and to preserve. 3d. That where this repugnancy exists, that authority which is supreme must control, not yield to that over which it is supreme. . . .

That the power of taxing it by the States may be exercised so as to destroy it, is too obvious to be denied. But taxation is said to be an absolute power, which acknowledges no other limits than those expressly prescribed in the constitution, and like sovereign power of every other description, is trusted to the discretion of those who use it. But the very terms of this argument admit that the sovereignty of the State, in the article of taxation itself, is subordinate to, and may be controlled by the constitution of the United States. How far it has been controlled by that instrument must be a question of construction. In making this construction, no principle not declared, can be admissible, which would defeat the legitimate operations of a supreme government. It is of the very essence of supremacy to remove all obstacles to its action within its own sphere, and so to modify every power vested in subordinate governments, as to exempt its own operations from their own influence. This effect need not be stated in terms. It is so involved in the declaration of supremacy, so necessarily implied in it, that the expression of it could not make it more certain. We must, therefore, keep it in view while construing the constitution.

The argument on the part of the State of Maryland, is, not that the States may directly resist a law of Congress, but that they may exercise their acknowledged powers upon it, and that the constitution leaves them this right in the confidence that they will not abuse it.

Before we proceed to examine this argument, and to subject it to the test of the constitution, we must be permitted to bestow a few considerations on the nature and extent of this original right of taxation, which is acknowledged to remain with the States. It is admitted that the power of taxing the people and their property is essential to the very existence of government, and may be legitimately exercised on the objects to which it is applicable, to the utmost extent to which the government may choose to carry it. The only security against the abuse of this power, is found in the structure of the government itself. In imposing a tax the legislature acts upon its constituents. This is in general a sufficient security against erroneous and oppressive taxation.

The people of a State, therefore, give to their government a right of taxing themselves and their property, and as the exigencies of government cannot be limited, they prescribe no limits to the exercise of this right, resting confidently on the interest of the legislator, and on the influence of the constituents over their representative, to guard them against its abuse. But the means employed by the government of the Union have no such security, nor is the right of a State to tax them sustained by the same theory. Those means are not given by the people of a particular State, not given by the constituents of the legislature, which claim the right to tax them, but by the people of all the States. They are given by all for the benefit of all — and upon theory, should be subjected to that government only which belongs to all. . . .

We find, then, on just theory, a total failure of this original right to tax the means employed by the government of the Union, for the execution of its powers. The right never existed, and the question whether it has been surrendered, cannot arise.

But, waiving this theory for the present, let us resume the inquiry, whether this power can be exercised by the respective States, consistently with a fair construction of the constitution?

That the power to tax involves the power to destroy; that the power to destroy may defeat and render useless the power to create; that there is a plain repugnance, in conferring on one government a power to control the constitutional measures of another, which other, with respect to those very measures, is declared to be supreme over that which exerts the control, are propositions not to be denied. But all inconsistencies are to be reconciled by the magic of the word CONFIDENCE. Taxation, it is said, does not necessarily and unavoidably destroy. To carry it to the excess of destruction would be an abuse, to presume which, would banish that confidence which is essential to all government.

But is this a case of confidence? Would the people of any one State trust those of another with a power to control the most insignificant operations of their State government? We know they would not. Why, then, should we suppose that the people of any one State should be willing to trust those of another with a power to control the operations of a government to which they have confided their most important and most valuable interests? In the legislature of the Union alone, are all represented. The legislature of the Union alone, therefore, can be trusted by the people with the power of controlling measures which concern all, in the confidence that it will not be abused. This, then, is not a case of confidence, and we must consider it as it really is. . . .

If we apply the principle for which the State of Maryland contends, to the constitution generally, we shall find it capable of changing totally the character of that instrument. We shall find it capable of arresting all the measures of the government, and of prostrating it at the foot of the States. [If] the states may tax one instrument, [they] may tax any and every other instrument. [The] American people [did] not design to make their government dependent on the states. . . .

It has also been insisted, that, as the power of taxation in the general and State governments is acknowledged to be concurrent, every argument which would sustain the right of the general government to tax banks chartered by the States, will equally sustain the right of the States to tax banks chartered by the general government.

But the two cases are not on the same reason. The people of all the States have created the general government, and have conferred upon it the general power of taxation. The people of all the States, and the States themselves, are represented in Congress, and, by their representatives, exercise this power. When they tax the chartered institutions of the States, they tax their constituents; and these taxes must be uniform. But, when a State taxes the operations of the government of the United States, it acts upon institutions created, not by their own constituents, but by people over whom they claim no control. It acts upon the measures of a government created by others as well as themselves, for the benefit of others in common with themselves. The difference is that which always exists, and always must exist, between the action of the whole on a part, and the action of a part on the whole — between the laws of a government declared to be supreme, and those of a government which, when in opposition to those laws, is not supreme.

But if the full application of this argument could be admitted, it might bring into question the right of Congress to tax the State banks, and could not prove the right of the States to tax the Bank of the United States. . . .

[We] conclude that the states have no power, by taxation or otherwise, to retard, impede, burden, or in any manner control, the operations of the constitutional laws enacted by Congress. . . .

This opinion does not deprive the States of any resources which they originally possessed. It does not extend to a tax paid by the real property of the bank, in common with the other real property within the State, nor to a tax imposed on the interest which the citizens of Maryland may hold in this institution, in common with other property of the same description throughout the State.

[Reversed.]

Note: *Constitutional Methodology and Constitutional Interpretation in* McCulloch

McCulloch resolves a number of important questions, relating both to the judicial role and to the allocation of powers as between the federal government and the states.

1. *Background.* The first Bank of the United States was created in 1790, shortly after ratification of the Constitution, in order to furnish loans to the federal government and to help collect taxes. The constitutional issue was sharply debated. Madison, a member of the House of Representatives, spoke against the bank, claiming that Congress had no constitutional authority to create it. Hamilton, Secretary of the Treasury, was one of its staunchest supporters and indeed drafted the plan for the bank. Jefferson also opposed the first bank on constitutional grounds, invoking the tenth amendment and venturing as well that "the Constitution allows only the means which are *necessary*, not merely 'convenient,' for effecting the enumerated powers. If such a latitude of construction be allowed to this phrase as to give any non-enumerated power [to Congress,] it would swallow

up all the delegated powers, and reduce the whole to one power." Opinion on the Constitutionality of the Bill for Establishing a National Bank, in 19 Papers of Thomas Jefferson 275, 279-280 (J. Boyd ed. 1974). Hamilton in turn offered a defense of the constitutionality of the bank that was quite close to Chief Justice Marshall's. See Opinion on the Constitutionality of an Act to Establish a Bank, 8 Papers of Alexander Hamilton 97 (H. Syrett and J. Cooke eds. 1965):

> It is essential to the being of the National government, that so erroneous a conception of the meaning of the word *necessary*, should be exploded.
>
> It is certain, that neither the grammatical, nor popular sense of the term requires that construction. According to both, *necessary* often means no more than *needful, requisite, incidental, useful, or conducive to*. . . .
>
> [This] is the true [meaning] in which it is to be understood as used in the constitution. The whole turn of the clause containing it indicates that it was the intent of the convention, by that clause to give a liberal latitude to the existence of the specified powers. . . .
>
> [Any other] interpretation would beget endless uncertainty & embarrassment. The cases must be palpable and extreme in which it could be pronounced with certainty, that a measure was absolutely necessary, or one without which the exercise of a given power would be nugatory. . . .

Hamilton went on to explain that the creation of a national bank had "a relation more or less direct to the power of collecting taxes; to that of borrowing money; to that of regulating trade between the states; and to those of raising, supporting & maintaining fleets and armies."

In 1811, the bank's charter lapsed, and Congress did not renew it. The private business and banking communities vigorously opposed renewal. In 1815, however, Congress created a second Bank of the United States, responding to a period of considerable economic turmoil following the War of 1812. At this stage, there was little discussion of the constitutional question. Jefferson himself supported the bank, partly in response to political pressures and perceived practical necessities, and Madison wrote that the issue had been settled in favor of its constitutionality. But many states objected to the creation of a second bank and imposed taxes of the sort at issue in *McCulloch*. To what extent, if any, do you think the decision in *McCulloch* was or should have been different in 1819 from what it would have been had the issue arisen in 1791?

2. *Methods of constitutional interpretation.* Note Chief Justice Marshall's remarks on the distinctive character of constitutions and of constitutional interpretation.

Chief Justice Marshall's suggestion that "it is *a constitution* we are expounding" has been called, by no less an authority than Justice Frankfurter, "the single most important utterance in the literature of constitutional law — most important because most comprehensive and most comprehending." Frankfurter, John Marshall and the Judicial Function, 69 Harv. L. Rev. 217, 219 (1955). But the statement and the interpretive strategies to which it has led are not universally admired. Compare, for example, Justice Frankfurter's suggestion that "precisely *because* 'it is a *constitution* we are expounding,' we ought not to take liberties with it." National Mutual Insurance Co. v. Tidewater Transfer Co., 337 U.S. 581, 647 (1949) (Frankfurter, J., dissenting). See also Kurland, Curia Regis: Some Comments on the Divine Right of Kings and Courts to Say What the Law Is, 23 Ariz.

L. Rev. 582, 591 (1981), suggesting that, whenever a judge quotes this passage, "you can be sure that the court will be throwing the constitutional text, its history, and its structure to the winds in reaching its conclusion."

Consider the following possible interpretations of Chief Justice Marshall's position. (a) The power-granting provisions of the Constitution should be broadly construed. Those provisions are meant to endure over time. They should be interpreted flexibly as new and unforeseen problems arise. But to say this is emphatically not to say that courts ought to have a license, often or ever, to strike down legislative action on grounds of changed circumstances. (b) All provisions of the Constitution, including those granting powers and those creating rights, should be broadly construed. Constitutions simply do not contain specific answers to all questions for all times. (c) The meaning of the Constitution changes with changing circumstances, in accordance with changing social norms and needs. Judges need not adhere to the specific "intent" of the framers or the original meaning of the text, but must interpret the document flexibly in light of contemporary necessities.

3. *Structural approaches to constitutional interpretation.* In the view of some, the approach in *McCulloch* is distinctive in large part because of Chief Justice Marshall's willingness to rely on the "structures and relationships" set up by the Constitution, and not only the text, in resolving constitutional questions.

> I am inclined to think well of the method of reasoning from structure and relation. I think well of it, above all, because to succeed it has to make sense — current, practical sense. The textual-explication method, operating on general language, [contains] within itself no guarantee that it will make sense, for a court may always present itself or even see itself as being bound by the stated intent, however nonsensical, of somebody else. [With structural approaches] we can and must begin to argue at once about the practicalities and proprieties of the thing, without getting out dictionaries whose entries will not really respond to the question we are putting. [We] will have to deal with policy and not with grammar.

C. Black, Structure and Relationship in Constitutional Law 22-23 (1969). Does Black's position mean that the Constitution should be interpreted to mean whatever the judges think it *should* mean? Consider whether it leaves more or less interpretive freedom than a textual approach. Compare Amar, Intratextualism, 112 Harv. L. Rev. 747 (1999), which argues that textualism can impose more than usual discipline if judges look at how constitutional terms are used in various contexts.

4. *The necessary and proper clause; implied powers.* a. What, if anything, does the necessary and proper clause add, in the Court's view, to the constitutional powers granted to the Congress? Note that the Court's analysis of the problem of "implied" powers depends in the first instance not on the language or history of the Constitution but on the perceived harmful consequences for American government of a contrary construction. What role should such perceptions of consequences play in constitutional interpretation?

It is not clear that the *McCulloch* decision recognizes implied powers at all. Perhaps it merely recognizes that a power naturally includes the appropriate means for achieving the intended end. What is the difference between these formulations?

b. The Court's construction of the necessary and proper clause resolved an extraordinarily important interpretive question that had divided, among others, Thomas Jefferson and Alexander Hamilton. On what does Chief Justice Marshall base his acceptance of the Hamilton position? Note the pertinence of the suggestion that that "provision is made in a constitution intended to endure for ages to come, and, consequently, to be adapted to the various *crises* of human affairs."

c. Even with the Court's interpretation of the necessary and proper clause, it remains to explain how the creation of a national bank is "necessary and proper" to the exercise of one of Congress's enumerated powers. What enumerated powers are helpful here? Consider Currie, The Constitution in the Supreme Court: State and National Powers, 1801-1835, 49 U. Chi. L. Rev. 887, 932-933 (1982), noting that Chief Justice Marshall "mentioned in passing various enumerated powers to which the creation of a bank might be incidental. [What] is striking is that he made no serious effort to demonstrate how the bank was necessary and proper, or even conducive, to any one of them." But consider the implications of Chief Justice Marshall's reference to the extended territory of the United States. Is Hamilton's explanation persuasive in this regard?

d. What limitations does Chief Justice Marshall recognize on congressional power? The key sentence here, frequently quoted by the Supreme Court throughout its history, is this: "Let the end be legitimate, let it be within the scope of the Constitution, and all means which are appropriate, which are plainly adapted to that end, which are not prohibited, but consist with the letter and spirit of the Constitution, are constitutional." The Court adds that if Congress enacts a law "for the accomplishment of objects not entrusted to the national government," and if Congress has acted under the "pretext" of using its enumerated powers, the law will be invalidated. Does this mean that the Court will scrutinize the motivations of legislators? (The benefits and disadvantages of motivation-centered inquiries are explored in Chapters 3 and 5 infra.) What else might it mean?

5. *The tenth amendment.* The second principal provision interpreted in *McCulloch* is the tenth amendment. How does Chief Justice Marshall construe this provision? Does the tenth amendment add anything of substance to the Constitution in Chief Justice Marshall's view? Perhaps it does not; but the tenth amendment might nonetheless have important civic purposes, by reminding everyone of the limited nature of the federal government. Note that in the Articles of Confederation the word "expressly" preceded the limitation analogous to the tenth amendment. How much support does the deletion of that word add to Chief Justice Marshall's construction?

6. *Representation-reinforcement.* Chief Justice Marshall finds an implicit prohibition on state taxation of the national bank. What constitutional provision does the tax violate?

Chief Justice Marshall's analysis of the problem is largely an inquiry not into the constitutional text and history but into the operations of representative government. "In imposing a tax the legislature acts upon its constituents. This is in general a sufficient security against erroneous and oppressive taxation." And in "the legislature of the Union alone, are all represented." The claim here is that the power to elect representatives will act as a safeguard against the abuse of political power by elected officials. The judicial role is defined by reference to the understanding that the political process itself will ensure against improper conduct.

Does Chief Justice Marshall overlook the possibility that constituents, or sub-groups thereof, might not have sufficient political power to prevent oppression?

Chief Justice Marshall also indicates that the ordinary presumption — that the processes of representation are an effective safeguard against abuse — disappears when a state imposes taxes on a national instrumentality because in so doing, the state is harming people who are not represented in the state legislature. Judicial intervention is justified in order to make up for the absence of political remedies for those burdened by legislative action. But if citizens generally are oppressed by state taxation of national banks, doesn't Congress have the power to enact a law to outlaw state taxation? Why is judicial intervention necessary or appropriate? Consider the possibility that the immunity is conferred by the statute creating the bank, interpreted in light of the concerns about representation.

Note, by contrast, Chief Justice Marshall's suggestion that, while the federal government has an (implicit) immunity from state taxation, states may not be immune from federal taxation. How does Chief Justice Marshall's theory of representation operate differently here? For further discussion of intergovernmental immunity, see Chapter 3 infra.

McCulloch might be understood as the foundation for the notion of "representation-reinforcement" as a justification of and guide for judicial action — an occasionally prominent theme in constitutional law. The central idea is that the judicial role is to make up for defects in the ordinary operation of representative government; the source of judicial decision is a breakdown in political processes. See generally J. H. Ely, Democracy and Distrust (1980). How does this approach differ from that in *Marbury*? The problem of representation-reinforcement is taken up in Chapters 3 and 5 infra.

CALDER v. BULL, 3 U.S. (3 Dall.) 386 (1798). The Connecticut legislature ordered a new trial in a will contest, setting aside a judicial decree. The Court unanimously held that the legislature's action was not an "ex post facto Law" forbidden the states by article I, section 10. Although Justices Chase and Iredell agreed on the "ex post facto" issue, they disagreed over the appropriate role of "natural law" in constitutional interpretation. Justice Chase wrote:

"I cannot subscribe to the omnipotence of a state legislature, or that it is absolute and without control; although its authority should not be expressly restrained by the constitution, or fundamental law of the state. The people of the United States erected their constitutions or forms of government, to establish justice, to promote the general welfare, to secure the blessings of liberty, and to protect their persons and property from violence. The purposes for which men enter into society will determine the nature and terms of the social compact; and as they are the foundation of the legislative power, they will decide what are the proper objects of it. The nature, and ends of legislative power will limit the exercise of it. This fundamental principle flows from the very nature of our free republican governments. [There] are acts which the federal, or state legislature cannot do, without exceeding their authority. There are certain vital principles in our free republican governments, which will determine and overrule an apparent and flagrant abuse of legislative power. [An] act of the legislature (for I cannot call it a law), contrary to the great first principles in the social compact, cannot be considered a rightful exercise of legislative authority. [A] law that punishes a citizen for an innocent [action;] a law that destroys or impairs the lawful private contracts of citizens; a law that makes a man a judge in his own cause; or a law that takes property from A. and gives it to B.: it is against all reason and justice, for a people to entrust a legislature with such powers; and therefore, it cannot be presumed that they have done it. The genius, the nature and the spirit of our state governments, amount to a prohibition of such acts of legislation; and the general principles of law and reason forbid them. [To] maintain that our federal, or state legislature possesses such powers, if they had not been expressly restrained, would, in my opinion, be a political heresy, altogether inadmissible in our free republican governments." (Chase upheld the legislature's action, however, on the ground that it impaired no vested right.)

Justice Iredell replied: "[Some] speculative jurists have held, that a legislative act against natural justice must, in itself, be void; but I cannot think that, under such a government any court of justice would possess a power to declare it so. [It] has been the policy of all the American states, [and] of the people of the United States, [to] define with precision the objects of the legislative power, and to restrain its exercise within marked and settled boundaries. If any act of congress, or of the legislature of a state, violates those constitutional provisions, it is unquestionably void. [If,] on the other hand, the legislature of the Union, or the legislature of any member of the Union, shall pass a law, within the general scope of their constitutional power, the court cannot pronounce it to be void, merely because it is, in their judgment, contrary to the principles of natural justice. The ideas of natural justice are regulated by no fixed standard: the ablest and the purest men have differed upon the subject; and all that the court could properly say, in such an event, would be, that the legislature (possessed of an equal right of opinion) had passed an act which, in the opinion of the judges, was inconsistent with the abstract principles of natural justice. [If] the legislature pursue the authority delegated to them, their acts are valid. [In such circumstances,] they exercise the discretion vested in them by the people, to whom alone they are responsible for the faithful discharge of their trust."

Note: Natural Law, Moral Argument, and the Supreme Court

In one form or another, the dispute between Justice Chase and Justice Iredell has proved fundamental to constitutional law.

1. *The original understanding.* Marbury v. Madison rested in part on the understanding that a written Constitution necessarily contemplated judicial enforcement of its terms. Otherwise, the restrictions imposed by the Constitution would be meaningless. We have seen that the argument is in some respects vulnerable. But Justice Chase goes further. His position is that there is an "unwritten" Constitution, consisting of principles of natural law, which is enforceable as against the states even though it cannot be found in the Constitution.

Justice Iredell's response is that the very fact of a written Constitution is authority against the position that courts may call on principles of natural justice. But does Justice Chase's position itself show that at least some of the framers believed in the existence of a natural law supplement to the Constitution's explicit prohibitions? Sherry, The Founders' Unwritten Constitution, 54 U. Chi. L. Rev. 1127 (1987), contains an extended argument for that view, with multiple references. See also Grey, Do We Have an Unwritten Constitution?, 27 Stan. L. Rev. 703 (1975); Grey, Origins of the Unwritten Constitution, 30 Stan. L. Rev. 843 (1978), suggesting that the framers believed that judges would enforce a category of natural law constraints on state and federal legislation. But see J. H. Ely, Democracy and Distrust (1980), for a skeptical view. On the ninth amendment, see Chapter 6 infra.

2. *Judges as political philosophers?* What would be the advantages and disadvantages of recognizing judicial authority of the sort claimed by Justice Chase? Consider M. Perry, The Courts, the Constitution, and Human Rights 100-101 (1982):

> In any recent generation, certain political issues have been widely perceived to be fundamental moral issues as well — issues that challenge and unsettle conventional ways of understanding the moral universe and that serve as occasions for forging alternative ways of understanding. In twentieth-century America, there have been several such issues: for example, distributive justice and the role of government, freedom of political dissent, racism and sexism, the death penalty, human sexuality. Our electorally accountable policymaking institutions are not well suited to deal with such issues in a way that is faithful to the notion of moral evolution. [Those] institutions, when finally they confront such issues at all, tend simply to rely on established moral conventions and to refuse to see in such issues occasions for moral revaluation and possible moral growth. [Executive] and especially legislative officials tend to deal with fundamental political-moral problems, at least highly controversial ones, by reflexive reference to the established moral conventions of the greater part of their particular constituencies.

See also A. Bickel, The Least Dangerous Branch (1962); R. Dworkin, Freedom's Law (1997); Dworkin, The Forum of Principle, 56 N.Y.U. L. Rev. 469 (1981); Wellington, Common Law Rules and Constitutional Double Standards: Some Notes on Adjudication, 83 Yale L.J. 221 (1973).

This view may depend on a skeptical view of the political process as consisting of a more or less mechanical reflection of constituent pressures. In its most extreme form, this view treats politics as an unprincipled power struggle among self-interested groups, or factions. This view has played a prominent role in modern political and economic theory. See Stigler, A Theory of Economic Regulation, 2 Bell. J.L. & Mgmt. Sci. 3 (1971); R. Dahl, A Preface to Democratic Theory (1956). In this view, Justice Chase's classic violation of natural law — taking from A to give to B — is a frequent occurrence. If the skeptical view is accepted, an active judicial role in deciding moral issues might seem attractive.

But consider the possibility that this view depends on an unduly pessimistic view of politics; an unwarranted belief in the possibility of "right answers" to political questions; an unduly optimistic view of judicial decisionmaking; or all three. Whether representatives in fact respond mechanically to political pressures is a sharply disputed question. A. Maass, Congress and the Common Good (1983), suggests that members of Congress often engage in some form of deliberation about what the public good requires. See also S. Kelman, Making Public Policy (1985). If representative processes embody a large measure of deliberation — as Madison anticipated — the comparative advantage claimed for courts may not exist at all. Note also that Perry's view, like Justice Chase's acceptance of natural law, depends on the existence of "right answers" to moral questions. It thus rests on a rejection of ethical or moral skepticism — the view that issues of politics or morality present problems of taste or aesthetics and are not susceptible to answer. For discussion with skeptical overtones, see R. Posner, The Problematics of Moral and Legal Argument (1998). Consider, for example, the issues of abortion, segregation, and discrimination on the basis of gender. Are there right answers to the dilemmas those issues pose?

Even if we are not skeptics about right answers, we might be skeptics about courts. Are justices likely to know what the right answers are? If not, might interest-group or deliberative politics be the best available alternative? Even if one accepts the skeptical view of politics, and even if one believes that ethical and political questions have right answers, one might respond to a natural law court in the same way as did Judge Learned Hand: "For myself it would be most irksome to be ruled by a bevy of nine Platonic Guardians, even if I knew how to choose them, which I assuredly do not." L. Hand, The Bill of Rights 73 (1958). Consider also Hand's claim that "[a] society so riven that the spirit of moderation is gone, no court can save; a society where that spirit flourishes, no court need save; and in a society which evades its responsibilities by thrusting upon the courts the nurture of that spirit, that spirit in the end will perish." L. Hand, The Contribution of an Independent Judiciary to Civilization (1944), in The Spirit of Liberty 155, 164 (I. Dilliard ed. 1960). On the danger that judges will make mistakes about morality, see C. Sunstein, One Case at a Time (1999).

See also A. Cox, The Role of the Supreme Court in American Government 116 (1976): "I should be no less irked than Judge Hand if the Supreme Court were to void an ordinance adopted in the open Town Meeting in the New England town in which I live — a meeting in which all citizens can participate — but I should have little such feeling about a statute enacted by the Massachusetts legislature in the normal political pattern, and none about a law made in that pattern by the Congress of the United States." Does this view undervalue the fact that state and federal laws are at least in some sense the product of representative processes?

D. THE POWER OF REPRISAL: POLITICAL CONTROL OF THE SUPREME COURT

This section examines ways in which the Court's authority is subject to *external* political control. A principal issue here is whether and to what extent those mechanisms of control affect the perceived tension between the power of judicial review and conventional notions of representative democracy.

Note: Amendment, Appointment, Impeachment, and the Election Returns

1. *Constitutional amendment.* The most straightforward way for the people to respond to a Supreme Court decision with which they disagree is to amend the Constitution. But an amendment is difficult to obtain. Under article V, the amending process may begin only if two-thirds of both Houses propose an amend-

ment or if the legislatures of two-thirds of the states call for a constitutional convention. No amendment may be adopted until it is ratified by three-fourths of the states. These requirements were a deliberate effort to make it difficult to amend the Constitution. Why were constitutional amendments to be discouraged?

Consider in this regard Jefferson's view that the Constitution should be rewritten by the people every generation, on the theory that without frequent constitution-making there would be too little participation in and concern for the affairs of government. See Letter to Samuel Kercheval, July 12, 1816, in The Portable Thomas Jefferson 552, 558-561 (M. Peterson ed. 1975). Note in particular the view that

> [s]ome men look at constitutions with sanctimonious reverence, and deem them like the ark of the covenant, too sacred to be touched. They ascribe to the men of the preceding age a wisdom more than human, and suppose what they did to be beyond amendment. I knew that age well. [It] was very like the present, but without the experience of the present. [Let] us [not] weakly believe that one generation is not as capable as another of taking care of itself, and of ordering its own affairs. . . . The dead have no rights.

Id. at 558-559. See generally H. Arendt, On Revolution (1965), for discussion of Jefferson's preference for citizen participation in affairs of government and for frequent constitutional revision.

Madison rejected such proposals on the ground that they would produce "the most violent struggle between the parties interested in reviving and those interested in reforming the antecedent state of property." Letter to Thomas Jefferson, Feb. 4, 1790, in The Mind of the Founder 232 (M. Meyers ed. 1969). Compare The Federalist Nos. 10 and 51, section A, supra. Jefferson's contrary view was that even turbulence "is productive of good. It prevents the degeneracy of government, and nourishes a general attention to the public affairs. I hold that a little rebellion now and then is a good thing." Letter to Madison, Jan. 30, 1787, in The Portable Thomas Jefferson, supra, at 416-417. Under this view, frequent revision of basic institutional arrangements might be welcomed. But as Madison's view suggests, the stability of the Constitution is often taken to be one of its great virtues. Consider in this regard the discussion of the separation of the realm of law and the realm of politics in The Federalist No. 78 and in *Marbury* itself. If frequent constitutional amendments were permitted, that distinction would be much less crisp; the effect of insulating certain decisions from politics would be undermined. Would that be a good or a bad thing? See generally S. Holmes, Passions and Constraint (1995); S. Levinson, ed., Responding to Imperfection (1995).

Note also that many states make it possible to amend their state constitutions through simple referendum. As a result, state constitutions are frequently altered. Thus, the Alabama Consitution has been amended over 700 times; the New York Constitution, over 200 times; the California Constitution, over 500 times; and the Texas Constitution, over 300 times.

Under such regimes, the public is frequently involved in the process of constitutional decisionmaking — in such areas as desegregation remedies, budget deficits, permissible tax levels, environmental protection, and discrimination on the basis of race and sexual orientation. Consider the fact that constitutional amendments have frequently been on the national agenda in the last two decades. Might systems that allow frequent amendment operate as a salutary check on judicial review, or do they erase the advantages of ensuring that an insulated body will decide constitutional issues? Note also that many other nations, especially those emerging from communism, make it relatively easy to amend the Constitution.

There are now over twenty amendments to the federal Constitution. Four of them represent successful efforts to overturn decisions by the Supreme Court. See U.S. Const. amends. XI (limiting jurisdiction of federal courts to hear suits brought against states); XIV (deeming Americans of African descent citizens of the United States); XVI (expanding power of Congress to tax); XXVI (setting voting age). Numerous other amendments have been offered but thus far without success. They have dealt with, for example, child labor, abortion, school desegregation, school prayer, flag burning, the line-item veto, and a balanced budget. Proposed constitutional amendments were especially popular in the 1970s, 1980s, and 1990s. Consider also the lengthy history of the proposed equal rights amendment, discussed in Chapter 5 infra, which would have provided that equality under the law may not be denied on the basis of sex. See J. Mansbridge, Why We Lost the ERA (1986). For what issues is constitutional amendment desirable?

Consider the following views. (a) For reasons hinted at by Madison, there should be a strong presumption against any constitutional amendment. The Constitution is a wise and broad charter of government with sufficient flexibility to accommodate changes in circumstances. It is a mistake to "constitutionalize" any particular set of norms in the absence of exceptional circumstances; frequent amendment is a danger to constitutionalism itself. (b) For reasons set out by Jefferson, proposed amendments should be welcomed. There is no reason to give special deference to decisions of the past, often of the long-distant past. The amendment process involves the democratic process in constitutional law, and that is a good thing. Moreover, circumstances and values change, and past generations have no monopoly on wisdom. Sometimes new conditions call for new constitutive provisions. (c) Constitutional amendments should be adopted only if they remedy serious structural defects or attempt to include groups previously excluded from the polity. The Constitution is concerned by and large with institutional design; structural provisions allow flexibility for current majorities. Under this view, a balanced budget amendment, for example, should be disfavored; it "would impose a controversial economic doctrine on the Constitution." Note, The Balanced Budget Amendment: An Inquiry into Appropriateness, 96 Harv. L. Rev. 1600, 1619 (1983).

Where does an individual rights provision fit in this framework? Consider the efforts in the wake of Texas v. Johnson, Chapter 7 infra, to amend the Constitution to protect the American flag against desecration. Many constitutional scholars argued vigorously that it would be especially risky to allow a constitutional amendment to counteract a Supreme Court decision protecting individual rights. Might there be a Jeffersonian response to this concern?

Even if efforts at amendment are unsuccessful, perhaps they should be welcomed because of the effect that they have on the public and the Court itself. Consider the possibility that amendment efforts, like political pressures generally, exercise some influence over Supreme Court decisions. The effort to amend the Constitution might be a salutary part of an ongoing conversation among the Court, other branches, and the public at large.

If a constitutional convention were called, would its authority be limited to particular issues or would it have general authority to amend the constitution as it chooses? See Special Constitutional Convention Study Committee, American Bar Association, Amendment of the Constitution by the Convention Method under Article V (1974). Should a court decide the issue? See the materials on the political question doctrine, section E infra.

On the amending process generally, see S. Levinson, ed., Responding to Imperfection (1995); C. Vose, Constitutional Change: Amendment Politics and Supreme Court Litigation since 1900 (1972); Corwin and Ramsey, The Constitutional Law of Constitutional Amendment, 26 Notre Dame Law. 165 (1951); Dellinger, The Legitimacy of Constitutional Change: Rethinking the Amendment Process, 97 Harv. L. Rev. 386 (1983); Symposium on the Article V Convention Process, 66 Mich. L. Rev. 837 (1968). For an excellent overview, see D. Kyvig, Explicit and Authentic Acts: Amending the U.S. Constitution 1776-1995 (1996). For recommendations, see Citizens for the Constitution, "Great and Extraordinary Occasions": Developing Guidelines for Constitutional Change (1999).

Note also that many nations allow constitutional amendment through a process that is far less arduous than the American one, and also that some constitutions allow legislatures to "overrule" decisions of the highest court. Consider in this regard article 33 of the Canadian Constitution Act of 1982, which allows Parliament to declare expressly that a particular statute shall stand despite its conflict with many (not all) of the enumerated rights of the citizen.

2. *The power to appoint.* Members of the Supreme Court are appointed by the President, subject to the advice and consent of the Senate. As a result, the President has an opportunity to put justices on the Court who share his views. The appointing power has been important in controlling the direction of the Supreme Court. President Roosevelt responded to the efforts of the Court to invalidate aspects of the New Deal by appointing, among others, Justices Black, Douglas, Frankfurter, and Jackson. All of them turned out to be generally sympathetic to government regulation of the economy, although there developed sharp disputes among them over the scope of judicial protection of individual rights. After election campaigns marked by an emphasis on obtaining "strict constructionists" on the Court, President Nixon appointed Chief Justice Burger and Justices Blackmun, Powell, and Rehnquist. Those appointments led to a more conservative Court and brought about some changes of direction, albeit of disputed scope. See V. Blasi, ed., The Burger Court: The Counterrevolution That Wasn't (1983). President Reagan's appointees — Chief Justice Rehnquist and Justices O'Connor, Scalia, and Kennedy — have generally moved the Court in directions favored by President Reagan.

But Presidents have sometimes been surprised to find that their appointees' performance on the bench was more "liberal" or more "conservative" than expected. President Eisenhower, for example, appointed Earl Warren as Chief Justice, relying in part on Warren's conservative, law-and-order reputation as governor of California. Eisenhower later claimed that the appointment was one of the worst mistakes he had ever made. Eisenhower also appointed Justice Brennan, whose record turned out to be quite different from what had been expected. Some of the votes of Justices O'Connor, Kennedy and Souter have been a disappointment to many supporters of Presidents Reagan and Bush; consider their failure to vote to overrule Roe v. Wade, discussed in Chapter 6 infra.

Events of this sort indicate that the appointments process is not a guarantee of political control; justices do not move in lockstep with the President who appointed them. But the record strongly suggests that presidential control can shift the Court significantly, and that the appointments process makes it unlikely that Supreme Court justices will diverge too sharply or for too long from the desires of those with political power. See generally H. Abraham, Justices and Presidents (1985); J. Schmidhauser, Judges and Justices (1979). Note, however, that ideology is far from the only consideration in the appointments process. Region, race, gender, and religion of the appointee will often play a role in the President's decision. For general discussion, see id. at 41-82.

The appointment decision is not the President's alone. Consider the view that "the role of the Senate as well as interest groups cannot be overlooked. Particularly in periods in which a president lacked party or ideological support in the Senate, the influence of senatorial confirmation assumed far-reaching importance. Approximately one-fifth of the presidential nominations for Supreme Court appointments have been dealt with negatively by the Senate." Id. at 91. The Senate's power to advise and consent may affect the composition of the Court in two ways. First, it may lead the President to avoid highly controversial appointees. Second, the Senate may refuse to confirm presidential appointees — for reasons of incompetence, venality, or ideology. In this century, however, Supreme Court nominees have been rejected on only four occasions — President Reagan's appointment of Judge Robert Bork, President Nixon's appointments of Judges Clement Haynesworth and Harold Carswell, and President Hoover's appointment of Judge John Parker. (President Reagan's nominee Judge Douglas Ginsburg withdrew after reports that he had smoked marijuana.) Earlier Senates often exercised a more active role. See generally L. Tribe, God Save This Honorable Court (1985).

Would a resumption of that earlier role be desirable? Should the Senate disapprove Supreme Court nominees who are perceived to be too "conservative" or too "liberal"?

Consider in this regard the extraordinary public debate in 1987 over President Reagan's nomination of Judge Robert Bork. Judge Bork had been known as a distinguished lawyer, professor, and judge; he was also one of the most outspoken critics of what he saw as unjustified judicial activism on the part of the Supreme Court under Chief Justices Warren and Burger. An especially controversial article, Bork, Neutral Principles and Some First Amendment Problems, 47 Ind. L.J. 1 (1971), was taken by many readers as a broadside attack on the Supreme Court's decisions in such areas as privacy, voting rights, and discrimination. This Indiana Law Journal article — and other writings by Judge Bork — provided the focus for a heated and lengthy confirmation process in which the Senate Judiciary Committee heard testimony from Judge Bork himself and from numerous lawyers and law professors. There was intense lobbying on both sides; the lobbying efforts included national advertisements, in newspapers and journals as well as on television and radio, predicting the consequences of Judge Bork's confirmation. See generally Bork's own account in The Temptation of America (1989) and The Bork Nomination: Essays and Reports, 9 Cardozo L. Rev. 1 (1987). Judge Bork's nomination was defeated by the largest margin of any Supreme Court nominee in American history. What, if any, implications does the defeat have for constitutional interpretation? It is possible to think that the nation in some sense rejected Judge Bork's views; it is also possible to think that his defeat was a result of an intense and in many ways misleading lobbying effort — producing a new word, "Borking," said to involve an all-out, often personal campaign against a public figure.

Does the experience with Judge Bork suggest that an aggressive senatorial role in the confirmation process is desirable? What does it suggest about the idea that the appointments process weakens the countermajoritarian difficulty? For varying views on these and related questions, see Essays on the Supreme Court Appointment Process, 101 Harv. L. Rev. 1146 (1988); Carter, The Confirmation Mess (1993), deploring the role of caricature and "soundbite politics." Many people believe that the defeat of the Bork nomination has contributed to general caution on the part of Presidents, ensuring that they will not appoint controversial candidates, and that they will avoid nominees with a contestable "paper trail."

3. *Impeachment.* Justices of the Supreme Court "hold their Offices during good Behavior." U.S. Const. art. III, §1. They may "be removed from Office on Impeachment for, and Conviction of, Treason, Bribery, or other high Crimes and Misdemeanors." Under what circumstances may federal judges be impeached? See, for general discussion, Chapter 4 infra; R. Berger, Impeachment (1970).

No Supreme Court justice has been removed from office in the nation's history; Justice Samuel Chase was impeached but never convicted. Members of the lower federal courts have been impeached and removed from office, and there have been efforts to impeach Supreme Court justices. See K. Hall, The Politics of Justice (1979). The most celebrated example involved Justice Douglas. A resolution calling for an investigation referred, among other things, to Justice William O. Douglas's having married four times; to the fact that one of his former wives was "a cocktail waitress"; to his votes in favor of defendants in cases involving "subversive questions"; to his traveling to Peking; and to various "left-wing" statements in his book, Points of Rebellion. See 116 Cong. Rec. H12,111-12,114 (daily ed. Apr. 16, 1970). An impeachment resolution was introduced against him in part on the basis of articles published in Playboy magazine, in which Justice Douglas, among other things, expressed some sympathy for rebellious groups in the 1960s. In the course of the proceedings, then-Representative Gerald Ford argued that the grounds for impeachment were "whatever a majority of the House of Representatives considers them to be at a given moment in history." 116 Cong. Rec. H3113-3114 (daily ed. Apr. 15, 1970).

Notwithstanding the latter suggestion, the device of impeachment has not been used as a means of obtaining political control over the Supreme Court. This phenomenon may be attributable in part to the prestige of an independent judiciary, in part to general acceptance of Marbury v. Madison, and in part to legal doubts about the wisdom and legality of using the impeachment mechanisms for this purpose. On the latter question, see Chapter 4 infra.

4. *Life tenure.* Under the Constitution federal judges are appointed for life. This provision is obviously associated with the goal of promoting judicial independence. But there are other ways to promote independence. Some states and some nations impose an age ceiling on judges, requiring retirement at age sixty-five or seventy. The "independent regulatory commissions," including the Federal Trade Commission and the Federal Communications Commission, allow members to serve for six-year terms, and they can be removed for "neglect of duty, malfeasance, or inefficiency in office." If you were starting a constitutional order from scratch — in, say, South Africa, Romania, or Poland — what sort of design would you favor?

5. *Controlling sitting judges; informal mechanisms and self-imposed limits.* To what extent is the Supreme Court subject to informal mechanisms of control? Mr. Dooley — the pen name and principal character of Finley Peter Dunne, who wrote around the turn of the twentieth century — explained in a now-celebrated statement that "[n]o matter whether th' constitution follows th' flag or not, th' supreme court follows th' ilection returns." F. P. Dunne, The Supreme Court's Decisions, in Mr. Dooley's Opinions 26 (1900). This statement is not literally true, but there can be little doubt that the Court is reluctant to make decisions that depart too sharply from what it perceives as a political consensus. As some have suggested, the Court has, or perceives itself as having, a limited amount of "political capital," and it tends to budget its expenditure of that capital in the number and kinds of controversial decisions it renders. See J. Choper, Judicial Review and the National Political Process (1981); A. Bickel, The Least Dangerous Branch (1962).

The Court's perception of its limited political capital may sometimes manifest itself in sensitivity to the views of elected officials and private citizens. Thus, for example, the end of the *Lochner* period — in which the Court struggled against government regulation of the economy, see Chapter 6 infra — may be understood in part as a response to popular pressures, though the problem of identifying "cause and effect" is formidable. See C. Vose, supra. There are few occasions in the nation's history in which the Court has persisted in a course to which the country is sharply opposed. See A. Bickel, supra. On the other hand, the Court's decisions may themselves help to shape a national consensus (is that a good or a bad thing?), and it is undoubtedly true that on occasion the Court has been willing to insist on a course of action notwithstanding considerable public disagreement. Consider in this regard the school prayer controversy, Chapter 8 infra; the problem of school desegregation, Chapter 5 infra; and the abortion controversy, Chapter 6 infra.

There is little empirical work on the effect of popular opinion on Supreme Court decisions, perhaps because of the difficulties in tracing causation. Perhaps the most that can be said is that the Court is sometimes sensitive to the perceived mood of the country, and that it is generally unwilling to continue for long periods on courses that face intense popular disagreement. A provocative, important, and controversial discussion is G. Rosenberg, The Hollow Hope (1991), which discusses what the author claims to be the surprisingly limited effectiveness of the Supreme Court in producing social change, even in the area of race relations, and which suggests that the Court's lack of political authority is connected with its lack of effectiveness.

Ex parte McCardle

74 U.S. (7 Wall.) 506 (1869)

[McCardle published articles in a newspaper in Mississippi, which was then under the control of the national army pursuant to the Reconstruction plan adopted by Congress after the Civil War. He was arrested under charges of libel; disturbing the peace; inciting insurrection, disorder, and violence; and impeding reconstruction. McCardle sought habeas corpus from a federal court in Mississippi, claiming that Congress lacked constitutional authority to establish a system of military government in the states. The case was in this sense a fundamental challenge to Congress's reconstruction power. After losing in the trial court, McCardle appealed, invoking a habeas corpus act enacted in 1867. Congress feared that the case would be a vehicle for invalidating the reconstruction plan. Congress therefore enacted — while the case was pending, and over presidential veto on constitutional grounds — a statute that repealed the provision of the 1867 habeas corpus act that McCardle had invoked.]

THE CHIEF JUSTICE delivered the opinion of the court.

The first question necessarily is that of jurisdiction; for, if the act of March, 1868, takes away the jurisdiction defined by the act of February, 1867, it is useless, if not improper, to enter into any discussion of other questions.

It is quite true, as was argued by the counsel for the petitioner, that the appellate jurisdiction of this court is not derived from acts of Congress. It is, strictly speaking, conferred by the Constitution. But it is conferred "with such exceptions and under such regulations as Congress shall make."

It is unnecessary to consider whether, if Congress had made no exceptions and no regulations, this court might not have exercised general appellate jurisdiction under rules prescribed by itself. For among the earliest acts of the first Congress, at its first session, was the act of September 24th, 1789, to establish the judicial courts of the United States. That act provided for the organization of this court, and prescribed regulations for the exercise of its jurisdiction. . . .

The principle that the affirmation of appellate jurisdiction implies the negation of all such jurisdiction not affirmed having been thus established, it was an almost necessary consequence that acts of Congress, providing for the exercise of jurisdiction, should come to be spoken of as acts granting jurisdiction, and not as acts making exceptions to the constitutional grant of it.

The exception to appellate jurisdiction in the case before us, however, is not an inference from the affirmation of other appellate jurisdiction. It is made in terms. The provision of the act of 1867, affirming the appellate jurisdiction of this court in cases of habeas corpus is expressly repealed. It is hardly possible to imagine a plainer instance of positive exception.

We are not at liberty to inquire into the motives of the legislature. We can only examine into its power under the Constitution; and the power to make exceptions to the appellate jurisdiction of this court is given by express words.

What, then, is the effect of the repealing act upon the case before us? We cannot doubt as to this. Without jurisdiction the court cannot proceed at all in any cause. Jurisdiction is power to declare the law, and when it ceases to exist, the only function remaining to the court is that of announcing the fact and dismissing the cause. And this is not less clear upon authority than upon principle.

Counsel seem to have supposed, if effect be given to the repealing act in question, that the whole appellate power of the court, in cases of habeas corpus, is denied. But this is an error. The act of 1868 does not except from that jurisdiction any cases but appeals from Circuit Courts under the act of 1867. It does not affect the jurisdiction which was previously exercised.

The appeal of the petitioner in this case must be dismissed for want of jurisdiction.

Note: Political Control over Jurisdiction of Article III Courts

Does Ex parte McCardle stand for the proposition that Congress has plenary power over the appellate jurisdiction of the Supreme Court? In Ex parte Yerger,

75 U.S. (8 Wall.) 85 (1869), the Court converted into a holding the last paragraph of the *McCardle* opinion. In *Yerger*, the Court asserted appellate jurisdiction over a habeas corpus proceeding brought by a petitioner in military detention. The source of jurisdiction was certiorari based on pre-1867 legislation. The language of Ex parte McCardle suggests that there are no constitutional constraints on Congress's power over the appellate jurisdiction of the Supreme Court; but its holding might be read more narrowly in light of the conclusion, noted in *McCardle* itself and made clear in *Yerger*, that there was an alternative means of obtaining Supreme Court review.

The question of congressional power over the appellate jurisdiction of the Supreme Court has occasionally assumed considerable importance, with proposals to prevent the Supreme Court from hearing cases involving (among other things) school prayer, reapportionment, school desegregation, and abortion. No such proposal has passed Congress. But there has been substantial debate about the constitutionality of the proposals, versions of which have been introduced at numerous stages in the history of the nation. Consider the following proposal:

> The Supreme Court shall not have jurisdiction to review, by appeal, writ of certiorari, or otherwise, any case arising out of any State statute, ordinance, rule, regulation, or any part thereof, or arising out of any act interpreting, applying, or enforcing a State statute, ordinance, rule, or regulation, which relates to voluntary prayers in public schools and public buildings.

1. *Restricting jurisdiction and the separation of powers.* If plenary power to restrict jurisdiction existed, Congress could immunize state and federal laws from Supreme Court review. Congress could, for example, enact a law and provide that the Supreme Court could not assess its constitutionality. Indeed, Congress could for all practical purposes cut the Supreme Court out of the constitutional scheme — for example, by depriving the Court of jurisdiction in all federal question cases. At first glance, such a power might seem to be a striking intrusion on the separation of powers system.

Would it be possible to argue that the power to restrict jurisdiction is not such an intrusion at all but is instead a means of making it tolerable to have judicial review in a system of representative government? See C. Black, Decision According to Law (1981). Under this view, the availability of the power to limit jurisdiction is an important check on the Supreme Court, discouraging it from straying too far from "popular will," as expressed in legislative and executive enactments, and allowing the legislature to retain ultimate control over the Court. At the same time, the existence of an unexercised, but broad, exceptions power gives reason to find public acquiescence in or ratification of Supreme Court decisions. But perhaps such arguments attribute too much to legislative inaction.

In any event, the nature and limits of the exceptions power remain shrouded in uncertainty. The remainder of this Note outlines some of the competing views.

2. *The plenary power argument.* To some, the exceptions clause grants Congress plenary power over the appellate jurisdiction of the Supreme Court. Congress may make exceptions whenever and for whatever reasons it chooses. This view draws support from the literal language of the Constitution. The text itself contains no limits on congressional power to make "exceptions" to the appellate jurisdiction of the Supreme Court. The only limits in this view are those that de-

rive from the political process. The plenary power argument obtains support from *McCardle* and from numerous dicta in early cases. See Van Alstyne, A Critical Guide to *Ex parte McCardle*, 15 Ariz. L. Rev. 229 (1973).

3. *Separation of powers constraints: the "essential functions" hypothesis.* One argument against recognition of a plenary power under the exceptions clause is based on the proposition that Congress cannot "destroy the essential role of the Supreme Court in the constitutional plan." Hart, The Power of Congress to Limit the Jurisdiction of Federal Courts: An Exercise in Dialectic, 66 Harv. L. Rev. 1362, 1365 (1953). The argument is largely a structural one. The framers, it is claimed, intended the Court to perform an important function in the separation of powers scheme: to ensure that Congress, the President, and the states are kept within constitutional limits. (Consider The Federalist No. 78 and Martin v. Hunter's Lessee.) If Congress had power to remove the Court's jurisdiction, it could insulate its own laws, or those of the states, from constitutional attack, effectively writing the Court out of the constitutional system. Such a power, it is sometimes claimed, is not consistent with the intended function of courts in the constitutional order. See Ratner, Congressional Power over the Appellate Jurisdiction of the Supreme Court, 109 U. Pa. L. Rev. 157 (1960).

Can this view be reconciled with the language of the exceptions clause? Proponents suggest that the use of the term "exceptions" itself contemplates a narrow power, one that is consistent with the general view that the Court would exercise jurisdiction in all or most federal question cases. See Ratner, supra; Sager, Foreword: Constitutional Limitations on Congress' Authority to Regulate the Jurisdiction of the Federal Courts, 95 Harv. L. Rev. 17 (1981). On this view, the extent of Congress's power may not be subject to precise limits, but it is clear that Congress cannot deprive the Court of jurisdiction in (all or some?) constitutional cases. See also R. Berger, Congress vs. the Supreme Court (1969) (suggesting that the exceptions power is limited to issues of fact).

Is this position supported or undermined by Marbury v. Madison? Consider Wechsler, The Courts and the Constitution, 65 Colum. L. Rev. 1001, 1005-1006 (1965):

> The plan of the Constitution for the courts [was] quite simply that the Congress would decide from time to time how far the federal judicial institution should be used within the limits of the federal judicial power. [Federal] courts, including the Supreme Court, do not pass on constitutional questions because there is a special function vested in them to enforce the Constitution or police the other agencies of government. They do so rather for the reason that they must decide a litigated case that is otherwise within their jurisdiction and in doing so must give effect to the supreme law of the land. That is, at least, what Marbury v. Madison was all about.

Is this a proper reading of *Marbury?* Consider the following view: *Marbury* and The Federalist No. 78 rest on the broader ground that the Supreme Court was accorded a distinctive role as the guarantor of the supremacy of the federal Constitution as against the states and the federal legislature: Recognition of an unlimited power to make exceptions would be inconsistent with the intended role of the Supreme Court in the separation of powers scheme, generating precisely the evils that led Hamilton to support the existence of judicial review. Cf. Cooper v. Aaron, supra.

Does it matter whether the exceptions power is used to insulate federal or state laws from judicial review? Would the dangers be different in the two different cases? See Sager, supra, at 55:

> To remove or permit the removal from the entire federal judiciary, including the Supreme Court, of the constitutional review of state conduct would be to alter the balance of federal authority fundamentally and dangerously. In an observation intended to defuse rather than ignite the sense of crisis that surrounded the Court in 1913, Justice Holmes uttered his famous words on the matter of Supreme Court jurisdiction: "I do not think the United States would come to an end if we lost our power to declare an Act of Congress void. I do think the Union would be imperiled if we could not make that declaration as to the laws of the several States." [The] case for regarding federal judicial supervision of the states as essential to the scheme of the Constitution is a strong one.

Even if it is accepted that there is an "essential functions" limitation on jurisdictional restrictions, the question remains whether particular provisions are inconsistent with the Court's "essential function." Would the bill reprinted above, eliminating federal court jurisdiction in school prayer cases, destroy the Supreme Court's "essential role"? Consider the fact that the Court would retain jurisdiction in all other cases raising constitutional questions.

4. *Independent constitutional barriers.* There is little doubt that other constitutional provisions, like the equal protection clause, limit Congress's power under the exceptions clause. For example, Congress could not constitutionally provide that Republicans, but no one else, may have access to the Supreme Court. Such a provision would violate the first amendment and thus would be independently unconstitutional.

How far does this rationale extend? Does it justify a conclusion that selective withdrawals of jurisdiction — for example, busing, abortion, or school prayer — are unconstitutional? See Tribe, Jurisdictional Gerrymandering: Zoning Disfavored Rights out of the Federal Courts, 16 Harv. C.R.-C.L. L. Rev. 129 (1981). Consider Bator, Congressional Power over the Jurisdiction of the Federal Courts, 27 Vill. L. Rev. 1030, 1036-1037 (1982):

> Neither the equal protection clause nor any other clause of the Constitution requires equal jurisdiction treatment for different subject-matters of litigation. [A] somewhat narrower argument is that if it is shown that Congress' motive in requiring a certain category of case to be brought in the exclusive original jurisdiction of the state courts is "hostility" to the substantive constitutional right in question, it can be struck down. I do not understand how such a rule could be administered. What would be an adequate indication of hostility? [The] state courts, equally with the federal, are charged with the task of enforcing and protecting federal constitutional rights.

5. *The relevance of United States v. Klein.* Consider in this regard United States v. Klein, 80 U.S. (13 Wall.) 128 (1872). Klein had sued for indemnification of property taken during the Civil War. It was a necessary predicate for relief that the claimant show that he' was not a supporter of the rebellion against the national government, and the courts had held that a presidential pardon was evidence that the claimant had not in fact participated.

A statute, enacted while the United States' appeal was pending from a decision awarding indemnification to Klein, provided that a presidential pardon was to be used as evidence that the person pardoned had participated in a rebellion. The statute added that courts should dismiss suits involving such claimants for want of jurisdiction. The Court invalidated the statute on the ground that dismissal would allow Congress to "prescribe rules of decision to the Judicial Department of the government in cases pending before it." According to the Court, this was inconsistent with the separation of powers. The Court added that the statute would be permissible under the exceptions clause if it were a denial of "the right to appeal in a particular class of cases." The problem here was that it was "a means to an end," that is, denial "to pardons granted by the President of the effect which this court had adjudged them to have."

Perhaps *Klein* is different from *McCardle* because it involved not merely a withdrawal of jurisdiction but also an effort "to bind the Court to decide [the] case in accordance with a rule of law [that is] independently unconstitutional." See P. Bator, P. Mishkin, D. Shapiro, and H. Wechsler, Hart & Wechsler's The Federal Courts and the Federal System 316 (2d ed. 1973).

Note also Justice Douglas's contention that "[t]here is a serious question whether the *McCardle* case could command a majority view today." Glidden Co. v. Zdanok, 370 U.S. 530, 605 (1962) (dissenting opinion).

6. *The lower federal courts.* The power of Congress over the jurisdiction of the lower federal courts raises somewhat different issues. It is generally agreed that article III imposes on Congress no obligation to create lower federal courts at all. See Sheldon v. Sill, 49 U.S. (8 How.) 441 (1850). If Congress need not create lower federal courts, a natural inference might be that Congress has plenary power over the sorts of issues that lower courts might hear. This is a classic "lesser included" argument: The authority to create the lower courts necessarily includes the power to restrict the lower courts to certain specified issues.

The argument is also, however,

> based on the fact that this reading is the only one consistent with the understanding which animated the compromise adopted by the Framers. The essence of that compromise was an agreement that the question whether access to the lower courts was necessary to assure the effectiveness of federal law [should] be left a matter of political and legislative judgment, to be made from time to time in the light of particular circumstances. It would make nonsense of that notion to hold that the only power to be exercised is the all-or-nothing power to decide whether *none* or *all* of the cases to which the federal judicial power extends need the haven of a lower court.

Bator, supra, at 1031.

Are there any limits on Congress's power over the lower federal courts? Suppose, for example, that Congress bars the lower federal courts from hearing cases involving abortion, school prayer, or desegregation — as numerous bills introduced in the late 1970s and 1980s threatened to do. Consider the following possibilities.

a. Eisenberg, in Congressional Authority to Restrict Lower Federal Court Jurisdiction, 83 Yale L.J. 498, 532-533 (1974), relies on the expansion of the caseload of the lower federal courts and their important role in protecting federal rights to argue:

> The inability of the Supreme Court to do justice in every case within the Article III grant of jurisdiction has broad implications. It means that Congress cannot deny

lower federal courts jurisdiction on the ground that Supreme Court review of state court judgments provides an adequate vindication for federal rights. [The] lower federal courts are thus indispensable if the judiciary is to be a co-equal branch and if the "judicial Power of the United States" is to remain the power to protect rights guaranteed by the Constitution and its amendments. Abolition of the lower federal courts is no longer constitutionally permissible.

b. The "independent constitutional constraints" on congressional limits on the jurisdiction of the Supreme Court apply as well to limits on the jurisdiction of the lower courts. Here, the same considerations apply as discussed above.

c. Note also the position of Justice Story in Martin v. Hunter's Lessee, supra, to the effect that at any time *some* federal court must have jurisdiction over any case to which the article III power extends. This view, however, has been rejected in modern practice. Note that diversity jurisdiction extends only to cases in which the amount in controversy is over $50,000.

For a careful elaboration on these questions of a position similar to that of Justice Story, see Amar, A Neo-Federalist View of Article III: Separating the Two Tiers of Federal Jurisdiction, 65 B.U. L. Rev. 205 (1985).

Note: The Power of Reprisal — General Thoughts

What conclusions do these various mechanisms of control — constitutional amendment, appointment, impeachment, popular opinion, and jurisdictional limits — suggest? Do Congress and the President have enough, or too much, authority over the Court? Consider the following views: (1) In light of the various mechanisms of control, the countermajoritarian difficulty said to be produced by the existence of judicial review is much less severe than it appears at first glance. The various safeguards make it much less troublesome that interpretation is often or inevitably discretionary; there is usually a political corrective, even in the short run. (2) The mechanisms of control make the courts so dependent on the political branches that justifications for *Marbury* that rely on the political insulation of the judges ultimately break down. It turns out that the judges are not insulated at all. They are emphatically political actors. (3) The various mechanisms are insufficient to allay the countermajoritarian difficulty. It remains the case that the power of judicial review permits unelected judges to have what is in effect the final say on issues of public importance. The fact that the judges are subject to some control through other means does not respond to the basic problem.

Consider, finally, the question of efficacy. Often Supreme Court decisions have less fundamental consequences for the real world than its advocates and its critics think. For example, only about 2 percent of black children in the South attended desegregated schools *ten years* after the Supreme Court's decision in Brown v. Board of Education. Especially when the Court is attempting to engage in large-scale social reform, its efforts are likely to be disappointing. Frequently lawyers and law students assume that society will simply follow Supreme Court decisions, but difficulties of implementation severely complicate this assumption. It may be that these difficulties provide an additional argument against an active judicial role in social reform. For elaborations of this theme, see G. Rosenberg, The Hollow Hope (1991); D. Horowitz, The Courts and Social Policy (1979).

E. "CASE OR CONTROVERSY" REQUIREMENTS AND THE PASSIVE VIRTUES

A number of devices require or permit federal courts not to hear certain issues. Most of these devices are, in whole or in part, an inference from article III, section 2, providing that the "Judicial Power shall extend" to enumerated "Cases" and "Controversies." This provision, it is often said, forbids the courts from invalidating legislative or executive action "merely" because it is unconstitutional. The courts may rule only in the context of a constitutional case.

This principle has a number of concrete implications. In general, it means that courts may not issue "advisory opinions"; may not decide "political questions"; must have before them someone with "standing," or with some kind of personal stake in the controversy; and may not decide issues that are either "premature" or "moot." What purposes are served by the "case or controversy" requirement? There are several candidates.

First, the requirement might serve the end of judicial restraint. By limiting the occasions for judicial intervention into legislative or executive processes, the case or controversy requirement reduces the friction between the branches produced by judicial review. This rationale is often tied to a concern with the countermajoritarian difficulty. The questions raised by this rationale are whether judicial restraint, thus understood, is desirable, and, if so, whether the case or controversy requirement is a sensible way to promote such restraint. Note in particular that judicial restraint is promoted by these devices not by requiring a deferential approach to the merits but by preventing the courts from reaching the merits at all.

Second, the case or controversy requirement might ensure that constitutional issues will be resolved only in the context of concrete disputes rather than in response to problems that may be hypothetical, abstract, or speculative. This consequence, it is sometimes said, distinguishes legislative and judicial decision-making and promotes sound constitutional conclusions.

Third, the case or controversy requirement is said to promote the ends of individual autonomy and self-determination by ensuring that constitutional decisions are rendered at the behest of those actually injured rather than at the behest of bystanders attempting to disrupt mutually advantageous accommodations or to impose their own views of public policy on government. Consider, for example, the fact that the rights of those subject to racial discrimination or environmental harm can be raised only by those subject to those injuries. Outsiders with an ideological interest are barred. This rationale is sometimes accompanied by a suggestion that case or controversy limitations ensure real adversity between the parties and thus ensure against collusive litigation. But note that sometimes the fact that a lawsuit has not resulted stems from ignorance, poverty, or alienation rather than from satisfaction with the status quo.

Consider also A. Bickel, The Least Dangerous Branch 115-116 (1965):

> One of the chief faculties of the judiciary, which is lacking in the legislature and which fits the courts for the function of evolving and applying constitutional principles, is that the judgment of courts can come later, after the hopes and prophecies expressed in legislation have been tested in the actual workings of our society; the judgment of courts may be had in concrete cases that exemplify the actual con-

sequences of legislative or executive actions. [It] may be added that the opportunity to relate a legislative policy to the flesh-and-blood facts of an actual case [to] observe and describe in being what the legislature may or may not have foreseen as probable — this opportunity as much as, or more than, anything else enables the Court to appeal to the nation's second thought. Moreover, [these requirements] create a time lag between legislation and adjudication. [Hence] it cushions the clash between the Court and any given legislative majority.

In Bickel's view, the "passive virtues" of inaction operate as a necessary means of mediating between the two (competing) ideas at work in U.S. government: electoral accountability and governance according to principle. The "passive virtues" operate to ensure that the latter idea does not swallow up the former, by permitting the Court to defer to the political process without resolving the issue either way. But see Gunther, The Subtle Vices of the Passive Virtues, 64 Colum. L. Rev. 1 (1964), objecting that an "unprincipled" approach to justiciability issues is unacceptable and will ultimately undermine the Court's role. Note also that the various justiciability doctrines are largely a creation not of the founding period but of the twentieth century — in particular, of efforts by Justices Brandeis, Frankfurter, and others seeking to immunize what they considered to be progressive government, and especially administrative agencies, from judicial review. The fact that justiciability constraints are mostly traceable to this period, rather than to the founding, might have significant implications for current approaches to those constraints.

1.   Advisory Opinions

One justiciability doctrine is unquestionably traceable to the early period. Under the first President, the Supreme Court said that it was constitutionally forbidden to issue "advisory opinions" — opinions on the constitutionality of legislative or executive actions that did not grow out of a case or controversy. President Washington, through Secretary of State Thomas Jefferson, asked the justices whether he might request their views about legal questions growing out of a war, in which the United States was neutral, between England and France. The justices responded:

> The three departments of the government [being] in certain respects checks upon each other, and our being judges of a court in the last resort, are considerations which accord strong arguments against the propriety of our extrajudicially deciding the questions alluded to, especially as the power given by the Constitution to the President, of calling on the heads of departments for opinions, seems to have been purposely as well as expressly united to the executive departments. We exceedingly regret every event that may cause embarrassment to your administration, but we derive consolation from the reflection that your judgment will discern what is right.

Is the Court's conclusion a natural or an inevitable interpretation of article III? Note that the power to issue advisory opinions would enable executive and legislative officials to obtain authoritative judgments on constitutional issues before relevant actions are taken — something that would have significant advantages. Some state supreme courts are authorized to issue advisory opinions; many nations in Eastern Europe have been given this power in the aftermath of communism. Note also that the Office of Legal Counsel of the Department of Justice has, at least for the executive branch, assumed an advice-giving role, informing the President and other members of the executive branch of its views about the constitutionality of proposed courses of action. But perhaps advisory bodies of this kind end up having close collegial relations with those to whom they give advice; perhaps there is greater independence in an institution that only decides actual cases.

Some of the gains provided by advisory opinions are furnished by the declaratory judgment procedure. Why is that procedure constitutional? See Nashville, Cincinnati & St. Louis Railway v. Wallace, 288 U.S. 249 (1933).

2.   *Standing*

Allen v. Wright

468 U.S. 737 (1984)

[This was a nationwide class action brought by parents of black school children against the Internal Revenue Service (IRS), contending that the IRS had not carried out its obligation to deny tax-exempt status to private schools that discriminated on the basis of race. The IRS generally does require, as a condition for tax-exempt status (and eligibility to receive deductible charitable contributions), that schools not discriminate on that basis. In Bob Jones University v. United States, 461 U.S. 574 (1983), the Court held that the governing statute disqualified such schools from receiving tax-exempt status as "charities."

[According to the parents — respondents in this case representing several million people — the IRS's regulations, procedures, and policies resulted in a failure to enforce the statutory mandate: The IRS had not denied tax-exempt status to many schools that in fact discriminated on the basis of race. Some schools, for example, received the exemption as a result of the tax-exempt status of "umbrella" organizations that support or operate such schools. According to the parents, the failure to carry out the statutory mandate (1) amounted to federal support for segregated schools and (2) fostered the organization and expansion of such schools, thus interfering with the efforts of federal agencies and courts to bring about desegregation in public school districts that had been segregated in the past. Respondents did not allege that they had applied to the private schools in question but claimed instead that the IRS's unlawful activities had harmed their children attending schools that were undergoing or might undergo desegregation. They claimed that by failing to deny the exemption, the IRS subsidized discriminatory private schools and thus decreased the likelihood that desegregation plans would be effective. Respondents sought declaratory and injunctive relief requiring the IRS to issue guidelines so as to deny tax exemptions to all private schools that discriminated on the basis of race. The court of appeals held in their favor.]

Justice O'Connor delivered the opinion of the Court.

[Standing] doctrine embraces several judicially self-imposed limits on the exercise of federal jurisdiction, such as the general prohibition on a litigant's raising another person's legal rights, the rule barring adjudication of generalized grievances more appropriately addressed in the representative branches, and the requirement that a plaintiff's complaint fall within the zone of interests protected by the law invoked. [The] requirement of standing, however, has a core component derived directly from the Constitution. A plaintiff must allege personal injury fairly traceable to the defendant's allegedly unlawful conduct and likely to be redressed by the requested relief.

Like the prudential component, the constitutional component of standing doctrine incorporates concepts concededly not susceptible of precise definition. The injury alleged must be, for example, "'distinct and palpable,'" [and] not "abstract" or "conjectural" or "hypothetical." [The] injury must be "fairly" traceable to the challenged action, and relief from the injury must be "likely" to follow from a favorable decision. [These] terms cannot be defined so as to make application of the constitutional standing requirement a mechanical exercise.

[More] important, the law of Art. III standing is built on a single basic idea — the idea of separation of powers. Determining standing in a particular case may be facilitated by clarifying principles or even clean rules developed in prior cases. Typically, however, the standing inquiry requires careful judicial examination of a complaint's allegations to ascertain whether the particular plaintiff is entitled to an adjudication of the particular claims asserted. Is the injury too abstract, or otherwise not appropriate, to be considered judicially cognizable? Is the line of causation between the illegal conduct and injury too attenuated? Is the prospect of obtaining relief from the injury as a result of a favorable ruling too speculative? . . .

Respondents allege two injuries in their complaint to support their standing to bring this lawsuit. First, they say that they are harmed directly by the mere fact of Government financial aid to discriminatory private schools. Second, they say that the federal tax exemptions to racially discriminatory private schools in their communities impair their ability to have their public schools desegregated.

[Respondents'] first claim of injury [might] be a claim simply to have the Government avoid the violation of law alleged in respondents' complaint. Alternatively, it might be a claim of stigmatic injury, or denigration, suffered by all members of a racial group when the Government discriminates on the basis of race. Under neither interpretation is this claim of injury judicially cognizable.

This Court has repeatedly held that an asserted right to have the Government act in accordance with law is not sufficient, standing alone, to confer jurisdiction on a federal court. [Recently,] in [Valley Forge Christian College v. Americans United for Separation of Church and State, Inc., 454 U.S. 464 (1982),] we rejected a claim of standing to challenge a Government conveyance of property to a religious institution. Insofar as the plaintiffs relied simply on "'their shared individuated right'" to a Government that made no law respecting an establishment of religion [we] held that plaintiffs had not alleged a judicially cognizable injury. . . .

Neither do they have standing to litigate their claims based on the stigmatizing injury often caused by racial discrimination. There can be no doubt that this sort of noneconomic injury is one of the most serious consequences of discriminatory government action and is sufficient in some circumstances to support standing. [Our] cases make clear, however, that such injury accords a basis for standing only to "those persons who are personally denied equal treatment" by the challenged discriminatory conduct. . . . [If] the abstract stigmatic injury were cognizable, standing would extend nationwide to all members of the particular racial groups against which the Government was alleged to be discriminating by its grant of a tax exemption to a racially discriminatory school, regardless of the location of that school. All such persons could claim the same sort of abstract stigmatic injury respondents assert in their first claim of injury. [It] is in their complaint's second claim of injury that respondents allege harm to a concrete, personal interest that can support standing in some circumstances. The injury they identify — their children's diminished ability to receive an education in a racially integrated school — is, beyond any doubt, not only judicially cognizable but, as shown by cases from Brown v. Board of Education, 347 U.S. 483 (1954), to Bob Jones University v. United States, 461 U.S. — (1983), one of the most serious injuries recognized in our legal system. Despite the constitutional importance of curing the injury alleged by respondents, however, the federal judiciary may not redress it unless standing requirements are met. In this case, respondents' second claim of injury cannot support standing because the injury alleged is not fairly traceable to the Government conduct respondents challenge as unlawful.

The illegal conduct challenged by respondents is the IRS's grant of tax exemptions to some racially discriminatory schools. The line of causation between that conduct and desegregation of respondents' schools is attenuated at best. From the perspective of the IRS, the injury to respondents is highly indirect and "results from the independent action of some third party not before the court."

The diminished ability of respondents' children to receive a desegregated education would be fairly traceable to unlawful IRS grants of tax exemptions only if there were enough racially discriminatory private schools receiving tax exemptions in respondents' communities for withdrawal of those exemptions to make an appreciable difference in public-school integration. Respondents have made no such allegation. It is, first, uncertain how many racially discriminatory private schools are in fact receiving tax exemptions. Moreover, it is entirely speculative [whether] withdrawal of a tax exemption from any particular school would lead the school to change its policies. [It] is just as speculative whether any given parent of a child attending such a private school would decide to transfer the child to public school as a result of any changes in educational or financial policy made by the private school once it was threatened with loss of tax-exempt status. It is also pure speculation whether, in a particular community, a large enough number of the numerous relevant school officials and parents would reach decisions that collectively would have a significant impact on the racial composition of the public schools.

The links in the chain of causation between the challenged Government conduct and the asserted injury are far too weak for the chain as a whole to sustain respondents' standing. In [Simon v. Eastern Kentucky Welfare Rights Organization (EKWRO), 426 U.S. 26 (1976),] the Court held that standing to challenge a Government grant of a tax exemption to hospitals could not be founded on the asserted connection between the grant of tax-exempt status and the hospitals' policy concerning the provision of medical services to indigents. The causal connection depended on the decisions hospitals would make in response to withdrawal of tax-exempt status, and those decisions were sufficiently uncertain to break the chain of causation between the plaintiff's injury and the challenged Government action. [The] chain of causation is even weaker in this case. It involves numerous third parties (officials of racially discriminatory schools receiving tax exemptions and the parents of children attending such schools) who may not even exist in respondents' communities and whose independent decisions may not collectively have a significant effect on the ability of public-school students to receive a desegregated education.

The idea of separation of powers that underlies standing doctrine explains why our cases preclude the conclusion that respondents' alleged injury "fairly can be traced to the challenged action" of the IRS. That conclusion would pave the way generally for suits challenging, not specifically identifiable Government violations of law, but the particular programs agencies establish to carry out their legal obligations. Such suits, even when premised on allegations of several instances of violations of law, are rarely if ever appropriate for federal-court adjudication.

Carried to its logical end, [respondents'] approach would have the federal courts as virtually continuing monitors of the wisdom and soundness of Executive action; such a role is appropriate for the Congress acting through its committees and the "power of the purse"; it is not the role of the judiciary, absent actual present or immediately threatened injury resulting from unlawful governmental action. . . .

[Most] relevant to this case is the principle articulated in [Rizzo v. Goode, 423 U.S. 362 (1976)]: "When a plaintiff seeks to enjoin the activity of a government agency, even within a unitary court system, his case must contend with the well-established rule that the Government has traditionally been granted the widest latitude in the dispatch of its own internal affairs." When transported into the Art. III context, that principle, grounded as it is in the idea of separation of powers, counsels against recognizing standing in a case brought, not to enforce specific legal obligations whose violation works a direct harm, but to seek a restructuring of the apparatus established by the Executive Branch to fulfill its legal duties. The Constitution, after all, assigns to the Executive Branch, and not to the Judicial Branch, the duty to "take Care that the Laws be faithfully executed." U.S. Const., Art. II, §3. We could not recognize respondents' standing in this case without running afoul of that structural principle. . . .

[The] judgment of the Court of Appeals is accordingly reversed, and the injunction issued by that court is vacated.

It is so ordered.

Justice Marshall took no part in the decision of the case.

Justice Brennan, dissenting. . . .
Viewed in light of the injuries they claim, the respondents have alleged a direct causal relationship between the government action they challenge and the injury they suffer: their inability to receive an education in a racially integrated school is directly and adversely affected by the tax-exempt status granted by the IRS to racially discriminatory schools in their respective school districts. [The] elimination of tax-exempt status for racially discriminatory private schools would serve to lessen the impact that those institutions have in defeating efforts to desegregate the public schools. . . .

More than one commentator has noted that the causation component of the Court's standing inquiry is no more than a poor disguise for the Court's view of the merits of the underlying claims. The Court today does nothing to avoid that criticism.

Justice Stevens, with whom Justice Blackmun joins, dissenting.
In final analysis, the wrong the respondents allege that the Government has committed is to subsidize the exodus of white children from schools that would otherwise be racially integrated. The critical question in this case, therefore, is whether respondents have alleged that the Government has created that kind of

subsidy. If the granting of preferential tax treatment would "encourage" private segregated schools to conduct their "charitable" activities, it must follow that the withdrawal of the treatment would "discourage" them, and hence promote the process of desegregation. [When] a subsidy makes a given activity more or less expensive, injury can be fairly traced to the subsidy for purposes of standing analysis because of the resulting increase or decrease in the ability to engage in the activity.

This causation analysis is nothing more than a restatement of elementary economics: when something becomes more expensive, less of it will be purchased. [The] process of desegregation will be advanced [since the] withdrawal of the subsidy for segregated schools means the incentive structure facing white parents who seek such schools for their children will be altered.

Considerations of tax policy, economics, and pure logic all confirm the conclusion that respondents' injury in fact is fairly traceable to the Government's allegedly wrongful conduct. The Court therefore is forced to introduce the concept of "separation of powers" into its analysis.

[The] Court could be saying that it will require a more direct causal connection when it is troubled by the separation of powers implications of the case before it. That approach confuses the standing doctrine with the justiciability of the issues that respondents seek to raise. The purpose of the standing inquiry is to measure the plaintiff's stake in the outcome, not whether a court has the authority to provide it with the outcome it seeks. . . . [The] strength of the plaintiff's interest in the outcome has nothing to do with whether the relief it seeks would intrude upon the prerogatives of other branches of government; the possibility that the relief might be inappropriate does not lessen the plaintiff's stake in obtaining that relief. If a plaintiff presents a nonjusticiable issue, or seeks relief that a court may not award, then its complaint should be dismissed for those reasons, and not because the plaintiff lacks a stake in obtaining that relief and hence has no standing. Imposing an undefined but clearly more rigorous standard for redressability for reasons unrelated to the causal nexus between the injury and the challenged conduct can only encourage undisciplined, ad hoc litigation, a result that would be avoided if the Court straightforwardly considered the justiciability of the issues respondents seek to raise, rather than using those issues to obfuscate standing analysis.

[The] Court could be saying that it will not treat as legally cognizable injuries that stem from an administrative decision concerning how enforcement resources will be allocated. [Respondents] do seek to restructure the IRS' mechanisms for enforcing the legal requirement that discriminatory institutions not receive tax-exempt status. Such restructuring would dramatically affect the way in which the IRS exercises its prosecutorial discretion. The Executive requires latitude to decide how best to enforce the law, and in general the Court may well be correct that the exercise of that discretion, especially in the tax context, is unchallengeable.

However, this principle does not apply when suit is brought "to enforce specific legal obligations whose violation works a direct harm." For example, despite the fact that they were challenging the methods used by the Executive to enforce the law, citizens were accorded standing to challenge a pattern of police misconduct that violated the constitutional constraints on law enforcement activities in Allee v. Medrano, 416 U.S. 802 (1974). Here, respondents contend that the IRS is violating a specific constitutional limitation on its enforcement discretion. [It] has been clear since [Marbury v. Madison,] that "[i]t is emphatically the province and duty of the judicial department to say what the law is." Deciding whether the Treasury has violated a specific legal limitation on its enforcement discretion does not intrude upon the prerogatives of the Executive, for in so deciding we are merely saying "what the law is."

In short, I would deal with the question of the legal limitations on the IRS' enforcement discretion on its merits, rather than by making the untenable assumption that the granting of preferential tax treatment to segregated schools does not make those schools more attractive to white students and hence does not inhibit the process of desegregation.

Lujan v. Defenders of Wildlife
504 U.S. 555 (1992)

JUSTICE SCALIA delivered the opinion of the Court with respect to Parts I, II, III-A, and IV, and an opinion with respect to Part III-B in which THE CHIEF JUSTICE, JUSTICE WHITE, and JUSTICE THOMAS join.

This case involves a challenge to a rule promulgated by the Secretary of the Interior interpreting §7 of the Endangered Species Act of 1973 (ESA), in such fashion as to render it applicable only to actions within the United States or on the high seas. The preliminary issue, and the only one we reach, is whether the respondents here, plaintiffs below, have standing to seek judicial review of the rule.

I

The ESA seeks to protect species of animals against threats to their continuing existence caused by man. The ESA instructs the Secretary of the Interior to promulgate by regulation a list of those species which are either endangered or threatened under enumerated criteria, and to define the critical habitat of these species. Section 7(a)(2) of the Act then provides, in pertinent part:

> Each Federal agency shall, in consultation with and with the assistance of the Secretary [of the Interior], insure that any action authorized, funded, or carried out by such agency . . . is not likely to jeopardize the continued existence of any endangered species or threatened species or result in the destruction or adverse modification of habitat of such species which is determined by the Secretary, after consultation as appropriate with affected States, to be critical.

In 1978, the Fish and Wildlife Service (FWS) and the National Marine Fisheries Service (NMFS), on behalf of the Secretary of the Interior and the Secretary of Commerce respectively, promulgated a joint regulation stating that the obligations imposed by §7(a)(2) extend to actions taken in foreign nations. The next year, however, the Interior Department began to reexamine its position. A revised joint regulation, reinterpreting §7(a)(2) to require consultation only for actions taken in the United States or on the high seas, was proposed in 1983, and promulgated in 1986.

Shortly thereafter, respondents, organizations dedicated to wildlife conservation and other environmental causes, filed this action against the Secretary of the

Interior, seeking a declaratory judgment that the new regulation is in error as to the geographic scope of §7(a)(2), and an injunction requiring the Secretary to promulgate a new regulation restoring the initial interpretation. . . .

II

Over the years, our cases have established that the irreducible constitutional minimum of standing contains three elements: First, the plaintiff must have suffered an "injury in fact" — an invasion of a legally-protected interest which is (a) concrete and particularized, and (b) "actual or imminent, not 'conjectural' or 'hypothetical.'" Second, there must be a causal connection between the injury and the conduct complained of — the injury has to be "fairly . . . traceable to the challenged action of the defendant, and not . . . the result [of] the independent action of some third party not before the court." Third, it must be "likely," as opposed to merely "speculative," that the injury will be "redressed by a favorable decision."

The party invoking federal jurisdiction bears the burden of establishing these elements. [At] the pleading stage, general factual allegations of injury resulting from the defendant's conduct may suffice, for on a motion to dismiss we "presume that general allegations embrace those specific facts that are necessary to support the claim." In response to a summary judgment motion, however, the plaintiff can no longer rest on such "mere allegations," but must "set forth" by affidavit or other evidence "specific facts," Fed. Rule Civ. Proc. 56(e), which for purposes of the summary judgment motion will be taken to be true. And at the final stage, those facts (if controverted) must be "supported adequately by the evidence adduced at trial."

When the suit is one challenging the legality of government action or inaction, the nature and extent of facts that must be averred (at the summary judgment stage) or proved (at the trial stage) in order to establish standing depends considerably upon whether the plaintiff is himself an object of the action (or forgone action) at issue. If he is, there is ordinarily little question that the action or inaction has caused him injury, and that a judgment preventing or requiring the action will redress it. When, however, as in this case, a plaintiff's asserted injury arises from the government's allegedly unlawful regulation (or lack of regulation) of someone else, much more is needed. In that circumstance, causation and redressability ordinarily hinge on the response of the regulated (or regulable) third party to the government action or inaction — and perhaps on the response of others as well. The existence of one or more of the essential elements of standing "depends on the unfettered choices made by independent actors not before the courts and whose exercise of broad and legitimate discretion the courts cannot presume either to control or to predict," ASARCO Inc. v. Kadish, 490 U.S. 605, 615 (1989) (opinion of Kennedy, J.); and it becomes the burden of the plaintiff to adduce facts showing that those choices have been or will be made in such manner as to produce causation and permit redressability of injury. Thus, when the plaintiff is not himself the object of the government action or inaction he challenges, standing is not precluded, but it is ordinarily "substantially more difficult" to establish. . . .

III

A

Respondents' claim to injury is that the lack of consultation with respect to certain funded activities abroad "increases the rate of extinction of endangered and threatened species." Of course, the desire to use or observe an animal species, even for purely aesthetic purposes, is undeniably a cognizable interest for purpose of standing. . . .

[With] respect to this aspect of the case, the Court of Appeals focused on the affidavits of two Defenders' members — Joyce Kelly and Amy Skilbred. Ms. Kelly stated that she traveled to Egypt in 1986 and "observed the traditional habitat of the endangered nile crocodile there and intends to do so again, and hopes to observe the crocodile directly," and that she "will suffer harm in fact as a result of [the] American . . . role . . . in overseeing the rehabilitation of the Aswan High Dam on the Nile . . . and [in] developing . . . Egypt's . . . Master Water Plan." Ms. Skilbred averred that she traveled to Sri Lanka in 1981 and "observed the habitat" of "endangered species such as the Asian elephant and the leopard" at what is now the site of the Mahaweli Project funded by the Agency for International Development (AID), although she "was unable to see any of the endangered species"; "this development project," she continued, "will seriously reduce endangered, threatened, and endemic species habitat including areas that I visited . . . [, which] may severely shorten the future of these species"; that threat, she concluded, harmed her because she "intends to return to Sri Lanka in the future and hopes to be more fortunate in spotting at least the endangered elephant and leopard." When Ms. Skilbred was asked at a subsequent deposition if and when she had any plans to return to Sri Lanka, she reiterated that "I intend to go back to Sri Lanka," but confessed that she had no current plans: "I don't know when. There is a civil war going on right now. I don't know. Not next year, I will say. In the future."

We shall assume for the sake of argument that these affidavits contain facts showing that certain agency-funded projects threaten listed species — though that is questionable. They plainly contain no facts, however, showing how damage to the species will produce "imminent" injury to Mss. Kelly and Skilbred. That the women "had visited" the areas of the projects before the projects commenced proves nothing. [Such] "some day" intentions — without any description of concrete plans, or indeed even any specification of when the some day will be — do not support a finding of the "actual or imminent" injury that our cases require.

Besides relying upon the Kelly and Skilbred affidavits, respondents propose a series of novel standing theories. The first, inelegantly styled "ecosystem nexus," proposes that any person who uses any part of a "contiguous ecosystem" adversely affected by a funded activity has standing even if the activity is located a great distance away. This approach, as the Court of Appeals correctly observed, is inconsistent with our opinion in [Lujan v. National Wildlife Federation, 497 U.S. 871, 887-889 (1990)], which held that a plaintiff claiming injury from environmental damage must use the area affected by the challenged activity and not an area roughly "in the vicinity" of it. It makes no difference that the general-purpose section of the ESA states that the Act was intended in part "to provide a means whereby the ecosystems upon which endangered species and threatened species depend may be conserved," 16 U.S.C. §1531(b). To say that the Act protects eco-systems is not to say that the Act creates (if it were possible) rights of action in per-sons who have not been injured in fact, that is, persons who use portions of an ecosystem not perceptibly affected by the unlawful action in question.

Respondents' other theories are called, alas, the "animal nexus" approach, whereby anyone who has an interest in studying or seeing the endangered ani-mals anywhere on the globe has standing; and the "vocational nexus" approach, under which anyone with a professional interest in such animals can sue. Under these theories, anyone who goes to see Asian elephants in the Bronx Zoo, and anyone who is a keeper of Asian elephants in the Bronx Zoo, has standing to sue because the Director of AID did not consult with the Secretary regarding the AID-funded project in Sri Lanka. This is beyond all reason. Standing is not "an ingenious academic exercise in the conceivable," United States v. Students Chal-lenging Regulatory Agency Procedures (SCRAP), 412 U.S. 669, 688 (1973), but as we have said requires, at the summary judgment stage, a factual showing of perceptible harm. It is clear that the person who observes or works with a partic-ular animal threatened by a federal decision is facing perceptible harm, since the very subject of his interest will no longer exist. It is even plausible — though it goes to the outermost limit of plausibility — to think that a person who observes or works with animals of a particular species in the very area of the world where that species is threatened by a federal decision is facing such harm, since some animals that might have been the subject of his interest will no longer exist, see Japan Whaling Assn. v. American Cetacean Soc., 478 U.S. 221, 231, n.4 (1986). It goes beyond the limit, however, and into pure speculation and fantasy, to say that anyone who observes or works with an endangered species, anywhere in the world, is appreciably harmed by a single project affecting some portion of that species with which he has no more specific connection. . . .

B

The most obvious problem in the present case is redressability. Since the agen-cies funding the projects were not parties to the case, the District Court could ac-cord relief only against the Secretary: He could be ordered to revise his regulation to require consultation for foreign projects. But this would not remedy respon-dents' alleged injury unless the funding agencies were bound by the Secretary's regulation, which is very much an open question. . . .

Respondents assert that this legal uncertainty did not affect redressability (and hence standing) because the District Court itself could resolve the issue of the Secretary's authority as a necessary part of its standing inquiry. Assuming that it is appropriate to resolve an issue of law such as this in connection with a thresh-old standing inquiry, resolution by the District Court would not have remedied respondents' alleged injury anyway, because it would not have been binding upon the agencies. They were not parties to the suit, and there is no reason they should be obliged to honor an incidental legal determination the suit produced. . . .

A further impediment to redressability is the fact that the agencies generally supply only a fraction of the funding for a foreign project. AID, for example, has provided less than 10% of the funding for the Mahaweli Project. Respondents have produced nothing to indicate that the projects they have named will either be suspended, or do less harm to listed species, if that fraction is eliminated. As in [Simon v. Eastern Kentucky Welfare Rights Organization, 426 U.S. 26 (1976)], it is entirely conjectural whether the nonagency activity that affects respondents will be altered or affected by the agency activity they seek to achieve. There is no standing.

IV

The Court of Appeals found that respondents had standing for an additional reason: because they had suffered a "procedural injury." The so-called "citizen-suit" provision of the ESA provides, in pertinent part, that "any person may commence a civil suit on his own behalf (A) to enjoin any person, including the United States and any other governmental instrumentality or agency . . . who is alleged to be in violation of any provision of this chapter." The court held that, because §7(a)(2) requires interagency consultation, the citizen-suit provision creates a "procedural right" to consultation in all "persons" — so that anyone can file suit in federal court to challenge the Secretary's (or presumably any other official's) failure to follow the assertedly correct consultative procedure, notwithstanding their inability to allege any discrete injury flowing from that failure. To understand the remarkable nature of this holding one must be clear about what it does not rest upon: This is not a case where plaintiffs are seeking to enforce a procedural requirement the disregard of which could impair a separate concrete interest of theirs (e.g., the procedural requirement for a hearing prior to denial of their license application, or the procedural requirement for an environmental impact statement before a federal facility is constructed next door to them).[7] Nor is it simply a case where concrete injury has been suffered by many persons, as in mass fraud or mass tort situations. Nor, finally, is it the unusual case in which Congress has created a concrete private interest in the outcome of a suit against a private party for the government's benefit, by providing a cash bounty for the victorious plaintiff. Rather, the court held that the injury-in-fact requirement had been satisfied by congressional conferral upon all persons of an abstract, self-contained, noninstrumental "right" to have the Executive observe the procedures required by law. We reject this view.

We have consistently held that a plaintiff raising only a generally available grievance about government — claiming only harm to his and every citizen's interest in proper application of the Constitution and laws, and seeking relief that no more directly and tangibly benefits him than it does the public at large — does not state an Article III case or controversy. . . .

7. There is this much truth to the assertion that "procedural rights" are special: The person who has been accorded a procedural right to protect his concrete interests can assert that right without meeting all the normal standards for redressability and immediacy. Thus, under our case law, one living adjacent to the site for proposed construction of a federally licensed dam has standing to challenge the licensing agency's failure to prepare an Environmental Impact Statement, even though he cannot establish with any certainty that the Statement will cause the license to be withheld or altered, and even though the dam will not be completed for many years. (That is why we do not rely, in the present case, upon the Government's argument that, even if the other agencies were obliged to consult with the Secretary, they might not have followed his advice.) What respondents' "procedural rights" argument seeks, however, is quite different from this: standing for persons who have no concrete interests affected — persons who live (and propose to live) at the other end of the country from the dam.

To be sure, our generalized-grievance cases have typically involved Government violation of procedures assertedly ordained by the Constitution rather than the Congress. But there is absolutely no basis for making the Article III inquiry turn on the source of the asserted right. Whether the courts were to act on their own, or at the invitation of Congress, in ignoring the concrete injury requirement described in our cases, they would be discarding a principle fundamental to the separate and distinct constitutional role of the Third Branch — one of the essential elements that identifies those "Cases" and "Controversies" that are the business of the courts rather than of the political branches. "The province of the court," as Chief Justice Marshall said in Marbury v. Madison, 1 Cranch 137, 170 (1803), "is, solely, to decide on the rights of individuals." Vindicating the public interest (including the public interest in government observance of the Constitution and laws) is the function of Congress and the Chief Executive. The question presented here is whether the public interest in proper administration of the laws (specifically, in agencies' observance of a particular, statutorily prescribed procedure) can be converted into an individual right by a statute that denominates it as such, and that permits all citizens (or, for that matter, a subclass of citizens who suffer no distinctive concrete harm) to sue. If the concrete injury requirement has the separation-of-powers significance we have always said, the answer must be obvious: To permit Congress to convert the undifferentiated public interest in executive officers' compliance with the law into an "individual right" vindicable in the courts is to permit Congress to transfer from the President to the courts the Chief Executive's most important constitutional duty, to "take Care that the Laws be faithfully executed," Art. II, §3. It would enable the courts, with the permission of Congress, "to assume a position of authority over the governmental acts of another and co-equal department," Frothingham v. Mellon, 262 U.S., at 489, and to become "'virtually continuing monitors of the wisdom and soundness of Executive action.'" [Allen v. Wright,] 468 U.S., at 760 (quoting Laird v. Tatum, 408 U.S. 1, 15 (1972)). We have always rejected that vision of our role:

> When Congress passes an Act empowering administrative agencies to carry on governmental activities, the power of those agencies is circumscribed by the authority granted. This permits the courts to participate in law enforcement entrusted to administrative bodies only to the extent necessary to protect justiciable individual rights against administrative action fairly beyond the granted powers. . . . This is very far from assuming that the courts are charged more than administrators or legislators with the protection of the rights of the people. Congress and the Executive supervise the acts of administrative agents. . . . But under Article III, Congress established courts to adjudicate cases and controversies as to claims of infringement of individual rights whether by unlawful action of private persons or by the exertion of unauthorized administrative power.

Stark v. Wickard, 321 U.S. 288, 309-310 (1944). "Individual rights," within the meaning of this passage, do not mean public rights that have been legislatively pronounced to belong to each individual who forms part of the public. See also [Sierra Club v. Morton, 405 U.S. 727, 740-741, n.16 (1972)].

Nothing in this contradicts the principle that "the . . . injury required by Art. III may exist solely by virtue of 'statutes creating legal rights, the invasion of which creates standing.'" [Warth v. Seldin, 422 U.S. 490, 500 (1975) (quoting Linda

R. S. v. Richard D., 410 U.S. 614, 617, n. 3 (1973)).] Both of the cases used by *Linda R. S.* as an illustration of that principle involved Congress's elevating to the status of legally cognizable injuries concrete, de facto injuries that were previously inadequate in law (namely, injury to an individual's personal interest in living in a racially integrated community, see Trafficante v. Metropolitan Life Ins. Co., 409 U.S. 205, 208-212 (1972), and injury to a company's interest in marketing its product free from competition, see Hardin v. Kentucky Utilities Co., 390 U.S. 1, 6 (1968)). As we said in *Sierra Club,* "[Statutory] broadening [of] the categories of injury that may be alleged in support of standing is a different matter from abandoning the requirement that the party seeking review must himself have suffered an injury." 405 U.S., at 738. Whether or not the principle set forth in *Warth* can be extended beyond that distinction, it is clear that in suits against the government, at least, the concrete injury requirement must remain.

We hold that respondents lack standing to bring this action.

JUSTICE KENNEDY, with whom JUSTICE SOUTER joins, concurring in part and concurring in the judgment. . . .

While it may seem trivial to require that Mss. Kelly and Skilbred acquire airline tickets to the project sites or announce a date certain upon which they will return, this is not a case where it is reasonable to assume that the affiants will be using the sites on a regular basis, nor do the affiants claim to have visited the sites since the projects commenced. [I] am not willing to foreclose the possibility, however, that in different circumstances a nexus theory similar to those proffered here might support a claim to standing. See Japan Whaling Assn. v. American Cetacean Soc., 478 U.S. 221, 231, n. 4 (1986) ("respondents . . . undoubtedly have alleged a sufficient 'injury in fact' in that the whale watching and studying of their members will be adversely affected by continued whale harvesting").

In light of the conclusion that respondents have not demonstrated a concrete injury here sufficient to support standing under our precedents, I would not reach the issue of redressability. . . .

I also join [the] Court's opinion with the following observations. As government programs and policies become more complex and far-reaching, we must be sensitive to the articulation of new rights of action that do not have clear analogs in our common-law tradition. [In] my view, Congress has the power to define injuries and articulate chains of causation that will give rise to a case or controversy where none existed before, and I do not read the Court's opinion to suggest a contrary view. In exercising this power, however, Congress must at the very least identify the injury it seeks to vindicate and relate the injury to the class of persons entitled to bring suit. The citizen-suit provision of the Endangered Species Act does not meet these minimal requirements, because while the statute purports to confer a right on "any person . . . to enjoin . . . the United States and any other governmental instrumentality or agency . . . who is alleged to be in violation of any provision of this chapter," it does not of its own force establish that there is an injury in "any person" by virtue of any "violation."

JUSTICE STEVENS, concurring in the judgment. . . .

In my opinion a person who has visited the critical habitat of an endangered species, has a professional interest in preserving the species and its habitat, and intends to revisit them in the future has standing to challenge agency action that threatens their destruction. [We] have no license to demean the importance of the interest that particular individuals may have in observing any species or its habitat, whether those individuals are motivated by aesthetic enjoyment, an interest in professional research, or an economic interest in preservation of the species. Indeed, this Court has often held that injuries to such interests are sufficient to confer standing, and the Court reiterates that holding today.

The Court nevertheless concludes that respondents have not suffered "injury in fact" because they have not shown that the harm to the endangered species will produce "imminent" injury to them. I disagree. An injury to an individual's interest in studying or enjoying a species and its natural habitat occurs when someone (whether it be the government or a private party) takes action that harms that species and habitat. . . .

The plurality also concludes that respondents' injuries are not redressable in this litigation for two reasons. First, respondents have sought only a declaratory judgment that the Secretary of the Interior's regulation interpreting §7(a)(2) to require consultation only for agency actions in the United States or on the high seas is invalid and an injunction requiring him to promulgate a new regulation requiring consultation for agency actions abroad as well. But, the plurality opines, even if respondents succeed and a new regulation is promulgated, there is no guarantee that federal agencies that are not parties to this case will actually consult with the Secretary. Furthermore, the plurality continues, respondents have not demonstrated that federal agencies can influence the behavior of the foreign governments where the affected projects are located. Thus, even if the agencies consult with the Secretary and terminate funding for foreign projects, the foreign governments might nonetheless pursue the projects and jeopardize the endangered species. Neither of these reasons is persuasive.

We must presume that if this Court holds that §7(a)(2) requires consultation, all affected agencies would abide by that interpretation and engage in the requisite consultations. Certainly the Executive Branch cannot be heard to argue that an authoritative construction of the governing statute by this Court may simply be ignored by any agency head. Moreover, if Congress has required consultation between agencies, we must presume that such consultation will have a serious purpose that is likely to produce tangible results. . . .

Although I believe that respondents have standing, I nevertheless concur in the judgment of reversal because I am persuaded that the Government is correct in its submission that §7(a)(2) does not apply to activities in foreign countries. . . .

JUSTICE BLACKMUN, with whom JUSTICE O'CONNOR joins, dissenting. . . .

[By] requiring a "description of concrete plans" or "specification of when the some day [for a return visit] will be," the Court, in my view, demands what is likely an empty formality. No substantial barriers prevent Kelly or Skilbred from simply purchasing plane tickets to return to the Aswan and Mahaweli projects. . . .

The Court also rejects respondents' claim of vocational or professional injury. The Court says that it is "beyond all reason" that a zoo "keeper" of Asian elephants would have standing to contest his government's participation in the eradication of all the Asian elephants in another part of the world. I am unable to see how the distant location of the destruction necessarily (for purposes of ruling at summary judgment) mitigates the harm to the elephant keeper. If there is no more access to a future supply of the animal that sustains a keeper's livelihood, surely there is harm.

I have difficulty imagining this Court applying its rigid principles of geographic formalism anywhere outside the context of environmental claims. As I understand it, environmental plaintiffs are under no special constitutional standing disabilities. . . .

I find myself unable to agree with the plurality's analysis of redressability, based as it is on its invitation of executive lawlessness, ignorance of principles of collateral estoppel, unfounded assumptions about causation, and erroneous conclusions about what the record does not say. In my view, respondents have satisfactorily shown a genuine issue of fact as to whether their injury would likely be redressed by a decision in their favor. . . .

The Court expresses concern that allowing judicial enforcement of "agencies' observance of a particular, statutorily prescribed procedure" would "transfer from the President to the courts the Chief Executive's most important constitutional duty, to 'take Care that the Laws be faithfully executed,' Art. II, sec. 3." In fact, the principal effect of foreclosing judicial enforcement of such procedures is to transfer power into the hands of the Executive at the expense — not of the courts — but of Congress, from which that power originates and emanates. . . .

[There] may be factual circumstances in which a congressionally imposed procedural requirement is so insubstantially connected to the prevention of a substantive harm that it cannot be said to work any conceivable injury to an individual litigant. But, as a general matter, the courts owe substantial deference to Congress' substantive purpose in imposing a certain procedural requirement. In all events, "our separation-of-powers analysis does not turn on the labeling of an activity as 'substantive' as opposed to 'procedural.'" There is no room for a per se rule or presumption excluding injuries labeled "procedural" in nature.

In conclusion, I cannot join the Court on what amounts to a slash-and-burn expedition through the law of environmental standing. In my view, "the very essence of civil liberty certainly consists in the right of every individual to claim the protection of the laws, whenever he receives an injury." Marbury v. Madison, 1 Cranch 137, 163 (1803).

I dissent.

Note: The "Law" of Standing

1. *Underlying concerns.* What functions are served by standing limitations? Consider the following possibilities. (a) They ensure that the courts will decide cases that are concrete rather than abstract or hypothetical. To what extent is this so? Was the dispute in *Allen* abstract or hypothetical? One might think that the question of standing has little or no connection with the question whether a dispute is abstract or hypothetical. (b) They promote judicial restraint by limiting the occasions for judicial intervention into the political process. But are standing limitations an arbitrary means of limiting such intrusions? Perhaps the fact that injuries to citizens at large are not cognizable judicially, but only politically, helps to answer that question in the negative. (c) They ensure that decisions will be made at the behest of those directly affected rather than on behalf of outsiders

with a purely ideological interest in the controversy. This factor will simultaneously promote vigorous advocacy. Was there a danger of insufficiently vigorous
advocacy in *Allen?* Note that sometimes those directly affected will fail to sue for
reasons other than contentment with the status quo. Note also that one needs a
theory with which to decide who is "directly affected" and who is an "outsider."
(d) Standing doctrines are an important part of the separation of powers system.
They ensure that courts will not hear cases simply because they want to; they require a concrete stake and thus give the executive and legislative branches a range
of breathing space. For discussion of some of these considerations, see Scalia,
The Doctrine of Standing as an Essential Element of the Separation of Powers,
17 Suffolk U.L. Rev. 881 (1983); Sunstein, Standing and the Privatization of Public Law, 88 Colum. L. Rev. 1432 (1988).

2. *Doctrinal components.* The Court has divided standing requirements into
several parts. Article IIII is now taken to require (a) an injury in fact that (b) is
due to the defendant's behavior and (c) is likely to be redressed by a decree in the
plaintiff's favor. Prudential requirements, not based on Article III and subject to
congressional override, require that the plaintiff's injury (a) be arguably within
the zone of interests protected or regulated by the statutory or constitutional provision at issue and (b) not be too generalized, that is, be particular and not shared
by all or almost all citizens. See Federal Election Commission v. Akins, 524 U.S.
11 (1998).

a. *Injury in fact.* Standing limitations, in their current form, are actually quite
new. The injury in fact requirement evolved from the earlier requirement of a
"legal injury." A "legal injury" pointed to different considerations from those embodied in the requirement of "injury in fact." To show a legal injury, one had to
show that some law entitled one to relief; this showing could be made by identifying an injury to an interest that was protected at common law, or that entitled
the plaintiff to redress under a relevant statute. On this view, the question whether
there was standing was essentially the question whether there was a cause of action. Someone would have "standing" if she had a claim to relief under a statute.
In this sense, the questions of standing, cause of action, and the merits were fused.

In the early days of standing doctrine — the first decades of the twentieth cen-
tury — a common law interest was often treated as a necessary basis for standing.
Standing limits, like other justiciability doctrines, were principally a creation of
justices allied with the progressive movement or the New Deal — most notably
Justices Brandeis and Frankfurter, defenders of the regulatory state — who sought
to develop devices immunizing government from judicial review. See, e.g., Joint
Anti-Fascist Refugee Committee v. McGrath, 341 U.S. 123, 154-155 (1951)
(Frankfurter, J., concurring); Alabama Power Co. v. Ickes, 302 U.S. 464, 479-480
(1938); Ashwander v. Tennessee Valley Authority, 297 U.S. 288, 341-345 (1936)
(Brandeis, J., concurring); Fairchild v. Hughes, 258 U.S. 126, 129-130 (1922).

Although these justices were hardly critical of government intervention into
the economy, the consequence of the new standing requirements was a body of
doctrine that was in fact rooted in a sharp split between the public and private
spheres. Usually one had to show at least a common law interest to obtain standing. Beneficiaries of government action — consumers, public interest groups,
victims of discrimination — were denied standing. Courts could be invoked by
those trying to fend off government activity but not by those trying to obtain government protection. Private property was the usual basis for obtaining review.

See generally J. Vining, Legal Identity (1978). This understanding was an amalgam of common law and statutory interpretation. For the most part it was not thought to be constitutional in nature. For a detailed discussion of the relevant history, along with an evaluation of standing limits, see Winter, The Metaphor of Standing and the Problem of Self-Governance, 40 Stan. L. Rev. 1371 (1988).

In the 1960s and 1970s, however, courts emphasized that people invoking statutory interests also suffered "legal injury." On this view, the fact that an interest protected by statute was at stake gave rise to an inference that Congress had intended to allow someone invoking that interest to bring suit. For example, listeners of the radio could challenge decisions of the Federal Communications Commission, and people who enjoyed the environment could challenge the building of a power plant near a river. See Office of Communication of the United Church of Christ v. FCC, 359 F.2d 994 (D.C. Cir. 1966); Scenic Hudson Preservation Conference v. FPC, 354 F.2d 608 (2d Cir. 1965). Notably, this broadening of standing was done under the rubric of statutory interpretation. It continued the original idea that whether someone had standing depended on whether Congress had conferred on that person a right to relief. Thus far, no "injury in fact" was required, and article III was implicated only insofar as courts treated a congressional grant of a right to relief as a necessary condition for standing.

The real roots of modern standing law can be found not in the founding period, and not even during the New Deal, but instead in Association of Data Processing Services Organizations v. Camp, 397 U.S. 150 (1970). In that case, the Court boldly altered previous law by abandoning the legal interest test altogether in favor of a new inquiry into whether there was injury in fact. Several things are notable about *Data Processing*. First, the decision purported to be an interpretation of the Administrative Procedure Act (APA), not of article III; the injury in fact test was said to be part of the APA. Second, the Court clearly intended to broaden, rather than to narrow, standing. It emphasized that the injury in fact requirement is relatively lenient. According to the Court, it may include a wide variety of economic, aesthetic, environmental, and other harms.

The consequence of *Data Processing* is that beneficiaries of government regulation, not merely those trying to fend off government action, can have standing to sue. But even under *Data Processing*, a merely ideological interest — or an interest in bringing about compliance with the law — is insufficient. But what is the line between an "injury in fact" and a "mere" ideological injury? Might not that line turn on whether Congress has created a right to relief?

Standing was denied on injury in fact grounds in Sierra Club v. Morton, 405 U.S. 727 (1972). The case involved an effort by an organization with "a special interest in the conservation and sound maintenance of the national parks" to challenge construction of a recreation area in a national forest. In the plaintiffs' view, the construction would have violated federal law. The Court denied standing, saying that the fact that an aesthetic, conservational, or recreational harm would be sufficient did not mean that the Court would abandon "the requirement that the party seeking review must have himself suffered an injury." In this case, the "Sierra Club failed to allege that it or its members" used the site in question.

What is the purpose of denying standing in *Sierra Club?* Would the Sierra Club have been an ineffective or a half-hearted advocate? Was there no case or controversy? Consider the view that the Sierra Club was litigating the rights of others who had a more direct stake in the controversy and the idea that those others, and not an intermeddling bystander, should have an exclusive right to raise the underlying legal issues.

Insofar as it involved a "stigmatic" injury, the Court treated Allen v. Wright as a variation on the *Sierra Club* case. But *Allen* was somewhat different because (1) there was no problem of litigating the rights of others and (2) a "stigmatic" injury might be different from a generalized interest in law enforcement. Compare Allen v. Wright with Heckler v. Mathews, 465 U.S. 728 (1984) (holding that stigmatic injury incurred as a result of gender discrimination in pension plans was sufficient to confer standing).

Sierra Club might be contrasted with United States v. SCRAP, 412 U.S. 669 (1973), in which the Court held that environmental groups could challenge the Interstate Commerce Commission's failure to suspend a surcharge on railroad freight rates as unlawful under the Interstate Commerce Commission Act. The plaintiffs claimed that their members "used the forests, streams, mountains, and other resources in the Washington metropolitan area for camping, hiking, fishing, and sightseeing." According to the Court, the Constitution was satisfied by the

> attenuated line of causation to the eventual injury of which the [plaintiffs] complained — a general rate increase would allegedly cause increased use of nonrecyclable commodities as compared to recyclable goods, thus resulting in the need to use more natural resources to produce such goods, some of which resources might be taken from the Washington area, and resulting in more refuse that might be discarded in national parks in the Washington area.

It is not at all clear, however, that *SCRAP* could command a majority today.

b. *Widely diffused harms*. Should the Court refuse to decide cases in which the harm caused by government action is widely diffused — in the sense that many or all citizens feel it equally? Consider in this regard Schlesinger v. Reservists to Stop the War, 418 U.S. 208 (1974), which involved a claim, made by an association of present and former members of the Reserves, that the Reserve membership of certain members of Congress violated the incompatibility clause. That clause provides that "no Person holding any Office under the United States, shall be a member of either House during his Continuance in Office." The Court said:

> The only interest [is one] shared by all citizens. [The] claimed nonobservance [of that Clause], standing alone, would adversely affect only the generalized interest of all citizens in constitutional governance, and that is an abstract injury. . . .
>
> To permit a complainant who has no concrete injury to require a court to rule on important constitutional issues in the abstract would create the potential for abuse of the judicial process, distort the role of the Judiciary in its relationship to the Executive and the Legislature and open the Judiciary to an arguable charge of "government by injunction."

The Court added that the plaintiffs did not meet the requirements of Flast v. Cohen, infra. Justices Douglas, Brennan, and Marshall dissented.

Consider also United States v. Richardson, 418 U.S. 166 (1974), an effort by a taxpayer to challenge the Central Intelligence Agency Act of 1949, which provides that Central Intelligence Agency expenditures may not be made public. According to the plaintiff, the act violated article I, section 9, clause 7 of the Constitution, which provides that "a regular statement of Account of the Receipts and

Expenditures of all public Money shall be published from time to time." The Court responded that the plaintiff's claim was only "a generalized grievance" that was "common to all members of the public. While we can hardly dispute that this respondent has a genuine interest in the use of funds and that his interest may be prompted by his status as a taxpayer, he has not alleged that, as a taxpayer, he is in danger of suffering any particular concrete injury as a result of the operation of this statute." The Court added:

> It can be argued that if respondent is not permitted to litigate this issue, no one can do so. In a very real sense, the absence of any particular individual or class to litigate these claims gives support to the argument that the subject matter is com- mitted to the surveillance of Congress, and ultimately to the political process. Any other conclusion would mean that the Founding Fathers intended to set up some- thing in the nature of an Athenian democracy or a New England town meeting to oversee the conduct of the National Government by means of lawsuits in federal courts. The Constitution created a *representative* Government with the represen- tatives directly responsible to their constituents at stated periods of two, four, and six years; that the Constitution does not afford a judicial remedy does not, of course, completely disable the citizen who is not satisfied with the "ground rules" estab- lished by the Congress for reporting expenditures of the Executive Branch. Lack of standing within the narrow confines of Art. III jurisdiction does not impair the right to assert his views in the political forum or at the polls. Slow, cumbersome, and unresponsive though the traditional electoral process may be thought at times, our system provides for changing members of the political branches when dissatisfied citizens convince a sufficient number of their fellow electors that elected repre- sentatives are delinquent in performing duties committed to them.

In an influential concurring opinion, Justice Powell added:

> The power recognized in [*Marbury*] is a potent one. Its prudent use seems to me incompatible with unlimited notions of taxpayer and citizen standing. [Due] to what many have regarded as the unresponsiveness of the Federal Government to recognized needs or serious inequities in our society, recourse to the federal courts has attained an unprecedented popularity in recent decades. Those courts have of- ten acted as a major instrument of social reform. But this has not always been the case, as experiences under the New Deal illustrate. The public reaction to the sub- stantive due process holdings of the federal courts during that period requires no elaboration, and it is not unusual for history to repeat itself.
>
> Quite apart from this possibility, we risk a progressive impairment of the effec- tiveness of the federal courts if their limited resources are diverted increasingly from their historic role to the resolution of public-interest suits brought by litigants who cannot distinguish themselves from all taxpayers or all citizens. The irreplace- able value of the power articulated by Mr. Chief Justice Marshall lies in the pro- tection it has afforded the constitutional rights and liberties of individual citizens and minority groups against oppressive or discriminatory government action. It is this role, not some amorphous general supervision of the operations of govern- ment, that has maintained public esteem for the federal courts and has permitted the peaceful coexistence of the countermajoritarian implications of judicial review and the democratic principles upon which our Federal Government in the final analysis rests.
>
> The considerations outlined above underlie, I believe, the traditional hostility of the Court to federal taxpayer or citizen standing where the plaintiff has nothing at

stake other than his interest as a taxpayer or citizen. It merits noting how often and how unequivocally the Court has expressed its antipathy to efforts to convert the Judiciary into an open forum for the resolution of political or ideological disputes about the performance of government.

The problem of widely diffused injuries is associated with that of taxpayer standing. The Court has rarely recognized such standing, but did so in Flast v. Cohen, 392 U.S. 83 (1968), which involved a taxpayer challenge to aid to religious schools. The Court said that taxpayer standing would be permitted in *Flast* because there was "a logical nexus between the status asserted and the claim thought to be adjudicated." According to the Court,

> the nexus demanded of federal taxpayers has two aspects to it. First, the taxpayer must establish a logical link between that status and the type of legislative enactment attacked. [It] will not be sufficient to allege an incidental expenditure of tax funds in the administration of an essentially regulatory measure. Secondly, the taxpayer must establish a nexus between that status and the precise nature of the constitutional infringement alleged. Under this requirement, the taxpayer must show that the challenged enactment exceeds specific constitutional limitations imposed upon the exercise of the congressional taxing and spending powers.

The Court held that the requirement was satisfied in the case of a taxpayer challenging an expenditure of public funds as violative of the establishment clause.

In two other cases, the Court has denied taxpayer standing. See Frothingham v. Mellon, 262 U.S. 447 (1923) (refusing to allow taxpayer to enjoin under the tenth amendment expenditures made to reduce maternal and infant mortality under federal statute), and Valley Forge Christian College v. Americans United, 454 U.S. 464 (1982), in which the Court refused to permit a taxpayer to challenge under the establishment clause a conveyance of property formerly used as a military hospital to the Valley Forge Christian College. In *Valley Forge*, the Court emphasized that the plaintiffs challenged a property transfer, not an expenditure of funds.

Compare to the foregoing cases the important decision in Federal Election Commission v. Akins, 524 U.S. 11 (1998). At issue there was an effort by interested citizens to require the Federal Election Commission (FEC) to classify the American Israel Public Affairs Committee (AIPAC) as a "political committee," and thus to require AIPAC to make disclosures to the public about its membership, contributions, and expenditures. The FEC contended that because the plaintiffs could not distinguish themselves from all other citizens, standing should be denied. The Court held that the ban on generalized grievances was prudential, and not rooted in article III, and hence that standing was available here because Congress had expressly given a cause of action to "any person." The Court said that the injury in fact "consists of their inability to obtain information . . . that, on respondents' view of the law, the statute requires that AIPAC make public." The Court acknowledged that it had "sometimes determined that where large numbers of Americans suffer alike, the political process, rather than the judicial process, may provide the more appropriate remedy for a widely shared grievance." In those cases, however, the injury was "not only widely shared, but . . . also of an abstract and indefinite nature." Here, the injury was "concrete, though widely shared," and hence sufficient for standing. The Court distinguished

United States v. Richardson, supra, on the ground that in *Akins* there was a statute that "does seek to protect individuals such as respondents from the kind of harm they say they have suffered." Justice Scalia dissented, joined by Justice O'Connor and Thomas.

Consider the following views. (1) *Richardson, Schlesinger,* and *Valley Forge* were rightly decided, and *Flast* and *Akins* wrongly. If a harm is shared by the plaintiff in common with all other citizens or taxpayers, the appropriate forum is the legislature, not the court. The mechanisms of political accountability are a sufficient guaranty. And if those mechanisms fail, the problem must not be severe in any event. The Constitution requires more than able litigants and a legal question. (2) Constitutional requirements are not meant to vary with popular opinion; they operate largely as constraints on outcomes, even if they accurately reflect popular opinion. *Richardson, Schlesinger,* and *Valley Forge* were incorrectly decided because they render constitutional constraints unenforceable. If the plaintiffs in those cases do not have standing, no one ever will. (3) The real standing question is whether any law creates a cause of action. When a constitutional provision benefits all citizens, courts should not infer from it a cause of action on behalf of any citizen in particular. *Flast* is a sensible exception because of the distinctive character of the establishment clause, a guarantee against the expenditure of taxpayer funds for religion.

Why, under *Akins,* is the "generalized injury" requirement prudential, rather than constitutional, in nature?

c. *Nexus.* Allen v. Wright was decided in part on "nexus" grounds. As suggested by *Allen* and by *Valley Forge,* the nexus requirement has two prongs: The plaintiff must show that (1) the allegedly unlawful conduct has caused his or her "injury in fact" and (2) the injury is likely to be redressed by a favorable decision. In practice, these two prongs almost always amount to the same thing.

The nexus requirement has been an important limitation in standing cases. One of the key cases is Linda R. S. v. Richard D., 410 U.S. 614 (1972), which involved an action by an unwed mother of an illegitimate child to enjoin discriminatory application of a Texas criminal statute that penalized any parent who failed to support his children. Plaintiff contended that judicial interpretation had excluded illegitimate fathers from prosecution and sought to require a prosecutor to initiate criminal proceedings for failure to provide child support. The Court denied standing, claiming that, because prosecution might lead only to the father's incarceration, the "prospect that prosecution will [result] in payment of support can, at best, be termed only speculative." *Linda R. S.* took place in an unusual setting, for criminal prosecutors have usually been held to have unreviewable discretion whether to bring enforcement actions. Should the decision have been based on standing grounds? Consider Easterbrook, Foreword: The Court and the Economic System, 98 Harv. L. Rev. 4, 40 (1984): "[It] is hard to take seriously the claim that enforcement of legal rules does not affect bystanders. [I] suffer an injury if the police announce that they will no longer enforce [the rule against murder] in my neighborhood. [A] plaintiff need not show a sure gain from winning in order to prove that some probability of gain is better than none, and thus he suffers injury in fact." Consider also the view that the plaintiff's claim in *Linda R. S.* was of unequal treatment, and if the injury is one of inequality under the law, there is no problem of redressability.

Another case in the same vein as *Linda R. S.* is Simon v. Eastern Kentucky Welfare Rights Organization (EKWRO), 426 U.S. 26 (1976). The action was brought by several indigents and organizations challenging an Internal Revenue Service Revenue Ruling that granted favorable tax treatment to certain nonprofit hospitals that limited aid to indigents for emergency room services. According to the plaintiffs, the ruling was unlawful because it reduced the amount of services necessary to qualify as charitable corporations. The consequence, plaintiffs claimed, was that the indigents would have less in the way of medical services available to them.

The Court, in an opinion by Justice Powell, held that there was no standing. In the Court's view, the plaintiffs' contention that the new ruling "encouraged" denial of services to indigents was inadequate.

> It is purely speculative whether the denials of service specified in the complaint fairly can be traced to the Service's "encouragement" or instead result from decisions made by hospitals without regard to their tax implications. [It] is equally speculative whether the desired exercise of the court's remedial powers in this suit would result in the availability [of] such services. So far as the complaint sheds light, it is just as plausible that the hospitals to which plaintiffs may apply for service would elect to forego favorable tax treatment to avoid the undetermined financial drain of an increase in the level of uncompensated services.

Justice Brennan, joined by Justice Marshall, dissented. Justice Brennan claimed that the relevant injury was to the "opportunity and ability" to receive free medical services, that that interest was not too diffuse to support standing, and that the further requirement imposed by the Court served no purpose. Under what circumstances should a plaintiff have standing to bring suit against the government for "encouraging" harmful activity? Should the intervening conduct of third parties — hospitals in Simon v. Eastern Kentucky Welfare Rights Organization and schools in Allen v. Wright — play a role in the standing inquiry?

Compare Duke Power Co. v. Carolina Environmental Study Group, 438 U.S. 59 (1978). In that case, the plaintiffs — consisting of forty people who lived near planned power plants, an environmental group, and a labor organization — sought a declaration to challenge the Price-Anderson Act. The act limited aggregate liability for a single nuclear power plant accident to $560 million. Plaintiffs claimed that the plant would produce environmental and aesthetic injuries. The Court found a sufficiently concrete injury: "It is enough that several of the 'immediate' impacts were found to harm appellees. Certainly the environmental and aesthetic consequences of the thermal pollution of the two lakes in the vicinity of the disputed power plants is the type of harmful effect which has been deemed adequate in prior cases to satisfy the 'injury in fact' standard."

Note also Regents of the University of California v. Bakke, 438 U.S. 265 (1978), where plaintiff challenged an affirmative action program established by the University of California at Davis without alleging that, if the program were not in place, he would have been admitted to the medical school. The Court responded:

> The constitutional element of standing is plaintiff's demonstration of any injury to himself that is likely to be redressed by favorable decision of his claim. The trial court found such an injury, apart from failure to be admitted, in the University's

decision not to permit Bakke to compete for all 100 places in the class, simply because of his race. Hence the constitutional requirements of Art. III were met. The
question of Bakke's admission vel non is merely one of relief.

If the Court is correct on this point, is *EKWRO* wrongly decided? Compare with
Lujan the striking decision in Northeastern Florida Chapter of Associated General Contractors v. Jacksonville, 508 U.S. 656 (1993). Jacksonville enacted an
ordinance requiring that 10 percent of the money spent on city contracts be "set
aside" for minority business enterprises. A contractors' association, consisting
mostly of members who would not qualify as minority enterprises, brought suit,
claiming that the set-aside violated the equal protection clause. The lower court
denied standing on the ground that no member of the association had demonstrated that, "but for the program, any AGC member would have bid successfully
for any of these contracts." There was therefore no injury in fact.

The Supreme Court responded: "When the government erects a barrier that
makes it more difficult for members of one group to obtain a benefit than it is for
members of another group, a member of the former group seeking to challenge
the barrier need not allege that he would have obtained the benefit but for the
barrier in order to establish standing. The 'injury in fact' in an equal protection
case of this variety is the denial of equal treatment resulting from the imposition
of the barrier, not the ultimate inability to obtain the benefit. And in the context
of a challenge to a set-aside program, the 'injury in fact' is the inability to compete on an equal footing in the bidding process, not the loss of a contract. To establish standing, therefore, a party challenging a set-aside program like Jacksonville's need only demonstrate that it is able and ready to bid on contracts and that
a discriminatory policy prevents it from doing so on an equal basis."

In an intriguing footnote, the Court added, "It follows from our definition of
'injury in fact' that petitioner has sufficiently alleged both that the city's ordinance is the 'cause' of its injury and that a judicial decree directly to the city to
discontinue its program would 'redress' the injury."

What is the purpose of the "nexus" or "causation" requirement? Is that requirement merely one of pleading — or does it establish a threshold requirement of
proof on the plaintiff's part? One possibility is that the requirement operates as a
safeguard against advisory opinions. If the plaintiff is unable to show that the requested relief would remedy his injury, it becomes necessary to ask why the court
should become involved at all. Is this a persuasive justification for the results in
Linda R. S. and *EKWRO*? What level of certainty should be necessary in order
to justify judicial relief?

Consider the view that whether an injury is speculative depends on how it is
characterized. If the injury in *Bakke* is characterized as a denial of admission,
standing should be denied; if it is characterized as an opportunity to compete,
standing should be available. So, too, in *EKWRO*, standing should be denied if
the injury is described as a refusal to grant medical care; but if it is described as
a denial of the opportunity to receive such care in a system undistorted by unlawful tax incentives, standing should be granted. When should an injury be treated
as a harm to an "opportunity," and when should it be treated as a narrower and
more discrete, common law-like one? For discussion, see Sunstein, What's Standing after *Lujan?* Of Citizen Suits, "Injuries," and Article III, 91 Mich. L. Rev. 163
(1992); Fallon, Of Justiciability, Remedies, and Public Law Litigation: Notes on

the Jurisprudence of *Lyons*, 59 N.Y.U. L. Rev. 1 (1984); Nichol, Causation as a Standing Requirement: The Unprincipled Use of Judicial Restraint, 69 Ky. L. Rev. 185 (1980-1981).

In this regard, it is useful to compare Steel Company v. Citizens for A Better Environment, 523 U.S. 83 (1998), with Friends of the Earth v. Laidlaw Environmental Services, 120 S. Ct. 693 (2000). In *Steel Company*, the plaintiffs, an environmental organization, sued a company that had released discharges of toxic pollutants in excess of those allowed by its permit. After the suit was filed, the company agreed to comply with its duties under its permit. The plaintiffs nonetheless continued the suit, attempting to ensure that the company would pay civil penalties to the U.S. Treasury. The Court held that standing was unavailable because the plaintiffs could not meet the redressability requirement. There was no showing that the payment of civil penalties to the Treasury would benefit the plaintiffs at all. In *Laidlaw*, the plaintiffs contended that they used certain areas for swimming and recreational activity, and that these areas had been polluted by the defendants' unlawful discharges. The plaintiffs sought civil damages, partly to "encourage defendants to discontinue current violations and deter them from committing future ones." The Court distinguished *Steel Company* on the ground that "in that case there was no allegation in the complaint of any continuing or imminent violation." Here, by contrast, the violations were "ongoing at the time of the complaint" and "could continue into the future if undeterred." See also Federal Election Commission v. Akins, supra, where the Court rejected the claim that standing should be denied on the ground that "even had the FEC agreed with respondent's view of the law, it would still have decided in the exercise of its discretion not to require AIPAC to produce the information." The Court said: "Agencies often have discretion about whether or not to take a particular action. Yet those adversely affected by a discretionary agency decision generally have standing to complain that the agency based its decision upon an improper legal ground." Consider the view that this holding is inconsistent with the views of the plurality on the issue of redressability in *Lujan*. Is there a way to reconcile the two?

d. *Injuries to third parties and "the zone of interests."* The "zone of interests" test derives from *Data Processing*, supra, which, in the course of discussing standing requirements under the Administrative Procedure Act, said that a plaintiff must show that he or she is "arguably within the zone of interests" protected or regulated by the statutory scheme. As applied in the constitutional context, the notion is that the plaintiff must be an intended beneficiary of the constitutional provision at issue. This requirement has never been the basis for denying standing in a constitutional case.

The notion that a plaintiff may not litigate the rights of third parties is closely related to the "injury in fact" requirement. The plaintiff must litigate on the basis of an injury to him or her; it is up to third parties to litigate their own rights. See, e.g., Tileston v. Ullman, 318 U.S. 44 (1943) (doctor may not challenge statute on ground that it would deprive patients of their lives without due process). See generally Monaghan, Third Party Standing, 84 Colum. L. Rev. 567 (1984); Brilmayer, The Jurisprudence of Article III: Perspectives on the "Case or Controversy" Requirement, 93 Harv. L. Rev. 297 (1979).

For the first (and thus far only) Supreme Court decision denying standing on zone of interests grounds, see Air Courier Conference v. APWU, 498 U.S. 517

(1991). The case grew out of a decision of the U.S. Postal Service partly to relinquish its monopoly of the mails by allowing private courier services to engage in the practice of "international remailing." With international remailing, such services can bypass the Postal Service and deposit in foreign postal systems letters destined for foreign addresses.

Employees of the Postal Service brought suit. The Court concluded that they were not within the zone of interests of the statutes creating a national postal monopoly. "The particular language of the statutes provides no support" for the view "that Congress intended to protect jobs with the Postal Service." Nor was that claim supported by the history and structure of these statutes. Because the employment interests were statutorily irrelevant, standing was denied.

Consider also International Primate Protection League v. Administrators, 500 U.S. 72 (1991). There, the plaintiffs brought suit to challenge the use of certain monkeys in federally funded medical experiments. The suit was filed in state court and removed to federal court; the question raised was whether, assuming that plaintiffs lacked standing to sue, they had standing to contest the removal. The Court said that "standing is gauged by the specific common law, statutory or constitutional claims that a party presents" and quoted the Fletcher article, see section 4 of this Note, infra, to the effect that standing "should be seen as a question of substantive law, answerable by reference to the statutory and constitutional provision whose protection is invoked." Here, the Court said, the right to sue in the Louisiana court was an injury traceable to the challenged action and likely to be redressed by the remedy the plaintiffs sought.

It is possible that, taken together, these two cases have started to reassert the view that standing is ultimately a question of substantive law: whether relevant statutes and constitutional provisions confer on the plaintiff a right to bring suit.

3. *Threatened injury.* The "injury in fact" requirement is usually met by those who can show a sufficient threat of future injury, as *Duke Power* and *SCRAP* make clear. This threat must, however, be real and immediate rather than "merely" speculative or hypothetical. The refusal to recognize speculative or hypothetical harms plays an important role in suits seeking injunctive relief. Consider City of Los Angeles v. Lyons, 461 U.S. 95 (1983), an action brought against the Los Angeles police department and city officials, seeking injunctive relief to prevent the use of "chokeholds" in arrests. Lyons, the plaintiff, had in fact been the victim of a chokehold; he also brought an action for damages. But the Court said that the fact that he was also seeking damages did not mean he could obtain an injunction when he was not "likely to suffer future injury from the use of chokeholds by police officers." In order to show such a likelihood, he would have "to make the incredible assertion either, (1) that *all* police officers in Los Angeles *always* choke any citizen with whom they happen to have an encounter whether for the purpose of arrest, issuing a citation or for questioning or, (2) that the City ordered or authorized police officers to act in such a manner." Assume the practice at issue in *Lyons* is unconstitutional. Would anyone have standing to enjoin it?

4. *A new (or old) question?* Consider the following view: Standing doctrine went wrong in *Data Processing*. The real question is whether Congress has created a cause of action, not whether there is an "injury in fact" or adequate causation. The existence of an injury in fact is necessary only when Congress has said that people with an injury in fact have standing — as, arguably, Congress did in

the Administrative Procedure Act. But what article III requires is a congressional grant of a right to bring suit, not an "injury in fact." It follows that there are few or perhaps no limits on Congress's power to confer standing. It also follows that the Court has both denied standing where it should be allowed and granted it where it should be denied. In any case, the Court has failed to ask the relevant question. That question is not always easy to answer, but it is the right one. It is also the one that prevailed at the time of the framing.

This view is set out in Fletcher, The Structure of Standing, 98 Yale L.J. 221, 229 (1988): "The essence of a true standing question is the following: Does the plaintiff have a legal right to judicial enforcement of an enforceable legal duty? This question should be seen as a question of substantive law, answerable by reference to the statutory or constitutional provision whose protection is invoked." Fletcher goes on to suggest that this question would call for a reexamination of all of current standing law. He also urges that, where a constitutional violation is at issue, the question is whether the constitutional provision confers on the plaintiff a right to relief. Similar views are expressed in Albert, Standing to Challenge Administrative Action: An Inadequate Surrogate for Claims for Relief, 83 Yale L.J. 425 (1974); Currie, Misunderstanding Standing, 1981 Sup. Ct. Rev. 41; Sunstein, What's Standing after *Lujan?*, supra. If Fletcher's view were to prevail, how would the cases in this section come out?

5. *Congressional power and citizens' suits.* Does *Lujan* mean that Congress is completely without constitutional power to grant standing to citizens? If so, what is the source of this conclusion in article III or the relevant history? Consider the view that citizen standing was fairly common in England and the colonies at the time of the framing. See Berger, Standing to Sue in Public Actions: Is It a Constitutional Requirement?, 78 Yale L.J. 816 (1969); Jaffe, Standing in Public Actions, 74 Harv. L. Rev. 1265, 1274 (1961); Sunstein, What's Standing after *Lujan?*, supra. Is *Lujan* an "originalist" opinion? Should it have been?

Compare the following cases to *Lujan*: (a) The plaintiffs obtain a plane ticket to go to the relevant nations. The implications of *Lujan* is that the injury in fact requirement would be met in that event — but four justices indicated that there would continue to be a problem of redressability. (b) Congress tries to grant standing to citizens to enforce the environmental law against both private defendants and government officials — but unlike in *Lujan*, it also says that every victorious plaintiff receives a $200 bounty. In Vermont Agency of Natural Resources v. United States, 120 S. Ct. 1850 (2000), the Court held that Congress has the power to create "qui tam" actions, by which citizens can sue to obtain damages on behalf of the United States, to recover damages done to the United States. In a qui tam action, the plaintiff receives money as a kind of bounty. In upholding this action, the Court emphasized the long history of support for its validity. The Court also said that the qui tam action should be understood to create an assignment from the United States to the plaintiff as "assignee," recovering money not as a stranger but as a result of the assignment.

Recall Federal Election Commission v. Akins, supra, where the Court upheld a legislative grant of standing to "any person" to bring suit to compel disclosure of information from political committees. The Court held that Congress could create an "injury in fact," in the form of deprivation of legally required information, and allow every citizen in the nation to bring suit to redress that injury. Is it sensible to say that the difference between *Akins* and *Lujan* is that in the latter case, unlike the former, there was no injury in fact? (For discussion of the tension between the two cases, see Sunstein, Informational Regulation and Informational Standing: *Akins* and Beyond, 147 U. Pa. L. Rev. 613 (1999).)

Suppose that you have answered "yes" to the question just asked. Now suppose that Congress amends the Endangered Species Act to create a "property interest," on the part of each American, in the continued existence of some or all endangered species — and that Congress then gives each American a right to bring suit against any action, or failure to act, that threatens to infringe that "property interest." Is the case more like *Lujan* or more like *Akins?*

Finally, suppose that members of Congress bring suit to object to a statute that, in their view, intrudes on their powers as representatives. How can they show injury in fact? See Raines v. Byrd, 521 U.S. 811 (1997), where six members brought suit to challenge the Line Item Veto Act, which, in their view, violated the separation of powers. (The Court subsequently agreed; see pages 358-359 infra.) The Court held that no "personal injury" had been established, a judgment informed by the suggestion that "our standing inquiry has been especially rigorous when reaching the merits of the dispute would force us to decide whether an action taken by one of the other two branches was unconstitutional." In this case, the plaintiffs "have not alleged that they voted for a specific bill, that there were sufficient votes to pass the bill, and that the bill was nonetheless deemed defeated." In this way the Court distinguished Coleman v. Miller, 307 U.S. 433 (1939), where, by a five-to-four vote, standing had been granted to twenty of Kansas's state senators, complaining that the child labor amendment had been unlawfully adopted. The *Coleman* plaintiffs claimed that with a twenty-twenty split, the amendment would not have been ratified, but that a procedural irregularity, in the form of a tie-breaking vote by the Lieutenant Governor, produced a false and unlawful claim of ratification. "There is a vast difference between the level of vote nullification at issue in *Coleman* and the abstract dilution of institutional legislative power that is alleged here." What, then, must members of Congress show in order to have standing?

3.   *Political Questions*

Baker v. Carr

369 U.S. 186 (1962)

[Voters in Tennessee brought suit challenging a state statute, passed in 1901, that apportioned the members of the state General Assembly among the state's ninety-five counties. Under the 1901 standard, representation was allocated among those counties in accordance with the number of qualified voters in those counties. But substantial growth in Tennessee and redistribution of the population between 1901 and 1961 led, in the plaintiffs' view, to a system in which apportionment was made "arbitrarily and capriciously" and "without reference to any logical or reasonable formula whatever." Claiming that their votes were diluted under the 1901 system, the plaintiffs sought an injunction prohibiting elections under that system and requiring either a reapportionment in accordance with the number of voters under federal census figures or "at-large" elections.]

MR. JUSTICE BRENNAN delivered the opinion of the Court.

[We] hold that this challenge to an apportionment presents no nonjusticiable "political question." . . .

Of course the mere fact that the suit seeks protection of a political right does not mean it presents a political question. Such an objection "is little more than a play upon words." Rather, it is argued that apportionment cases, whatever the actual wording of the complaint, can involve no federal constitutional right except one resting on the guaranty of a republican form of government, and that complaints based on that clause have been held to present political questions which are nonjusticiable.

We hold that the claim pleaded here neither rests upon nor implicates the Guaranty Clause. [To] show why we reject the argument based on the Guaranty Clause, we must examine the authorities under it. But because there appears to be some uncertainty as to why those cases did present political questions, and specifically as to whether this apportionment case is like those cases, we deem it necessary first to consider the contours of the "political question" doctrine.

Our discussion [requires] review of a number of political question cases, in order to expose the attributes of the doctrine — attributes which, in various settings, diverge, combine, appear, and disappear in seeming disorderliness.

We have said that "In determining whether a question falls within [the political question] category, the appropriateness under our system of government of attributing finality to the action of the political departments and also the lack of satisfactory criteria for a judicial determination are dominant considerations." The nonjusticiability of a political question is primarily a function of the separation of powers. Much confusion results from the capacity of the "political question" label to obscure the need for case-by-case inquiry. Deciding whether a matter has in any measure been committed by the Constitution to another branch of government, or whether the action of that branch exceeds whatever authority has been committed, is itself a delicate exercise in constitutional interpretation, and is a responsibility of this Court as ultimate interpreter of the Constitution.

Foreign relations: There are sweeping statements to the effect that all questions touching foreign relations are political questions. Not only does resolution of such issues frequently turn on standards that defy judicial application, or involve the exercise of a discretion demonstrably committed to the executive or legislature; but many such questions uniquely demand single-voiced statement of the Government's views. Yet it is error to suppose that every case or controversy which touches foreign relations lies beyond judicial cognizance. Our cases in this field seem invariably to show a discriminating analysis of the particular question posed, in terms of the history of its management by the political branches, of its susceptibility to judicial handling in the light of its nature and posture in the specific case, and of the possible consequences of judicial action.

Dates of duration of hostilities: Though it has been stated broadly that "the power which declared the necessity is the power to declare its cessation, and what the cessation requires," here too analysis reveals isolable reasons for the presence of political questions, underlying this Court's refusal to review the political departments' determination of when or whether a war has ended. Dominant is the need for finality in the political determination, for emergency's nature demands "A prompt and unhesitating obedience." . . . Further, clearly definable criteria for decision may be available. In such cases the political question barrier falls away. . . .

Validity of enactments: In Coleman v. Miller, [307 U.S. 433 (1939)], this Court held that the questions of how long a proposed amendment to the Federal Constitution remained open to ratification, and what effect a prior rejection had on a subsequent ratification, were committed to congressional resolution and involved criteria of decision that necessarily escaped the judicial grasp. Similar considerations apply to the enacting process: "The respect due to coequal and independent departments," and the need for finality and certainty about the status of a statute contribute to judicial reluctance to inquire whether, as passed, it complied with all requisite formalities. . . .

It is apparent that several formulations which vary slightly according to the settings in which the questions arise may describe a political question, although each has one or more elements which identify it as essentially a function of the separation of powers. Prominent on the surface of any case held to involve a political question is found a textually demonstrable constitutional commitment of the issue to a coordinate political department; or a lack of judicially discoverable and manageable standards for resolving it; or the impossibility of deciding without an initial policy determination of a kind clearly for nonjudicial discretion; or the impossibility of a court's undertaking independent resolution without expressing lack of the respect due coordinate branches of government; or an unusual need for unquestioning adherence to a political decision already made; or the potentiality of embarrassment from multifarious pronouncements by various departments on one question.

Unless one of these formulations is inextricable from the case at bar, there should be no dismissal for nonjusticiability on the ground of a political question's presence. The doctrine of which we treat is one of "political questions," not one of "political cases." . . .

But it is argued that this case shares the characteristics of decisions that constitute a category not yet considered, cases concerning the Constitution's guaranty [of] a republican form of government. [Guaranty] Clause claims involve those elements which define a "political question," and for that reason and no other, they are nonjusticiable. In particular, [the] nonjusticiability of such claims has nothing to do with their touching upon matters of state governmental organization.

Luther v. Borden, [7 How. 1 (1849)], though in form simply an action for damages for trespass was, as Daniel Webster said in opening the argument for the defense, "an unusual case." The defendants, admitting an otherwise tortious breaking and entering, sought to justify their action on the ground that they were agents of the established lawful government of Rhode Island, which State was then under martial law to defend itself from active insurrection; that the plaintiff was engaged in that insurrection; and that they entered under orders to arrest the plaintiff. The case arose "out of the unfortunate political differences which agitated the people of Rhode Island in 1841 and 1842," [and] which had resulted in a situation wherein two groups laid competing claims to recognition as the lawful government. The plaintiff's right to recover depended upon which of the two groups was entitled to such recognition; but the lower court's refusal to receive evidence or hear argument on that issue, its charge to the jury that the earlier established or "charter" government was lawful, and the verdict for the defendants, were affirmed upon appeal to this Court.

Chief Justice Taney's opinion for the Court reasoned as follows: (1) If a court were to hold the defendants' acts unjustified because the charter government had no legal existence during the period in question, it would follow that all of that government's actions — laws enacted, taxes collected, salaries paid, accounts settled, sentences passed — were of no effect; and that "the officers who carried their decisions into operation [were] answerable as trespassers, if not in some cases as criminals." [A] decision for the plaintiff would inevitably have produced some significant measure of chaos. . . .

(2) No state court had recognized as a judicial responsibility settlement of the issue of the locus of state governmental authority. Indeed, the courts of Rhode Island had in several cases held that "it rested with the political power to decide whether the charter government had been displaced or not," and that that department had acknowledged no change.

(3) Since "[t]he question relates, altogether, to the constitution and laws of [the] . . . State," the courts of the United States had to follow the state courts' decisions unless there was a federal constitutional ground for overturning them.

(4) No provision of the Constitution could be or had been invoked for this purpose except Art. IV, §4, the Guaranty Clause. Having already noted the absence of standards whereby the choice between governments could be made by a court acting independently, Chief Justice Taney now found further textual and practical reasons for concluding that, if any department of the United States was empowered by the Guaranty Clause to resolve the issue, it was not the judiciary:

> Under this article of the Constitution it rests with Congress to decide what government is the established one in a State. . . .
> [After] the President has acted and called out the militia, is a Circuit Court of the United States authorized to inquire whether his decision was right? . . . If the judicial power extends so far, the guarantee contained in the Constitution of the United States is a guarantee of anarchy, and not of order. . . .

Clearly, several factors were thought by the Court in *Luther* to make the question there "political": the commitment to the other branches of the decision as to which is the lawful state government; the unambiguous action by the President, in recognizing the charter government as the lawful authority; the need for finality in the executive's decision; and the lack of criteria by which a court could determine which form of government was republican.

But the only significance that *Luther* could have for our immediate purposes is in its holding that the Guaranty Clause is not a repository of judicially manageable standards which a court could utilize independently in order to identify a State's lawful government. . . .

We come, finally, to the ultimate inquiry whether our precedents as to what constitutes a nonjusticiable "political question" bring the case before us under the umbrella of that doctrine. A natural beginning is to note whether any of the common characteristics which we have been able to identify and label descriptively are present. We find none: The question here is the consistency of state action with the Federal Constitution. We have no question decided, or to be decided, by a political branch of government coequal with this Court. Nor do we risk embarrassment of our government abroad, or grave disturbance at home if we take issue with Tennessee as to the constitutionality of her action here challenged. Nor need the appellants, in order to succeed in this action, ask the Court to enter upon policy determinations for which judicially manageable standards are lacking. Judicial standards under the Equal Protection Clause are well developed and familiar, and it has been open to courts since the enactment of the

Fourteenth Amendment to determine, if on the particular facts they must, that a discrimination reflects *no* policy, but simply arbitrary and capricious action.

This case does, in one sense, involve the allocation of political power within a State, and the appellants might conceivably have added a claim under the Guaranty Clause. Of course, as we have seen, any reliance on that clause would be futile. But because any reliance on the Guaranty Clause could not have succeeded it does not follow that appellants may not be heard on the equal protection claim which in fact they tender. True, it must be clear that the Fourteenth Amendment claim is not so enmeshed with those political question elements which render Guaranty Clause claims nonjusticiable as actually to present a political question itself. But we have found that not to be the case here.

[Reversed and remanded.]

MR. JUSTICE FRANKFURTER, whom MR. JUSTICE HARLAN joins, dissenting.

The Court today reverses a uniform course of decision established by a dozen cases, including one by which the very claim now sustained was unanimously rejected only five years ago. The impressive body of rulings thus cast aside reflected the equally uniform course of our political history regarding the relationship between population and legislative representation — a wholly different matter from denial of the franchise to individuals because of race, color, religion or sex. [Disregard] of inherent limits in the effective exercise of the Court's "judicial Power" not only presages the futility of judicial intervention in the essentially political conflict of forces by which the relation between population and representation has time out of mind been and now is determined. It may well impair the Court's position as the ultimate organ of "the supreme Law of the Land" in that vast range of legal problems, often strongly entangled in popular feeling, on which this Court must pronounce. The Court's authority — possessed of neither the purse nor the sword — ultimately rests on sustained public confidence in its moral sanction. Such feeling must be nourished by the Court's complete detachment, in fact and in appearance, from political entanglements and by abstention from injecting itself into the clash of political forces in political settlements.

A hypothetical claim resting on abstract assumptions is now for the first time made the basis for affording illusory relief for a particular evil even though it foreshadows deeper and more pervasive difficulties in consequence. The claim is hypothetical and the assumptions are abstract because the Court does not vouchsafe the lower courts — state and federal — guidelines for formulating specific, definite, wholly unprecedented remedies for the inevitable litigations that today's umbrageous disposition is bound to stimulate in connection with politically motivated reapportionments in so many States. In such a setting, to promulgate jurisdiction in the abstract is meaningless. It is as devoid of reality as "a brooding omnipresence in the sky," for it conveys no intimation what relief, if any, a District Court is capable of affording that would not invite legislatures to play ducks and drakes with the judiciary. [To] charge courts with the task of accommodating the incommensurable factors of policy that underlie these mathematical puzzles is to attribute, however flatteringly, omnicompetence to judges. . . .

We were soothingly told at the bar of this Court that we need not worry about the kind of remedy a court could effectively fashion once that abstract constitutional right to have courts pass on a state-wide system of electoral districting is recognized as a matter of judicial rhetoric, because legislatures would heed the

Court's admonition. This is not only a euphoric hope. It implies a sorry confession of judicial impotence in place of a frank acknowledgment that there is not under our Constitution a judicial remedy for every political mischief, for every undesirable exercise of legislative power. [Appeal] must be to an informed, civically militant electorate. In a democratic society like ours, relief must come through an aroused popular conscience that sears the conscience of the people's representatives. In any event there is nothing judicially more unseemly nor more self-defeating than for this Court to make in terrorem pronouncements, to indulge in merely empty rhetoric, sounding a word of promise to the ear, sure to be disappointing to the hope.

[From] its earliest opinions this Court has consistently recognized a class of controversies which do not lend themselves to judicial standards and judicial remedies. . . .

1. The cases concerning war or foreign affairs, for example, are usually explained by the necessity of the country's speaking with one voice in such matters. While this concern alone undoubtedly accounts for many of the decisions, others do not fit the pattern. It would hardly embarrass the conduct of war were this Court to determine, in connection with private transactions between litigants, the date upon which war is to be deemed terminated. But the Court has refused to do so. [A] controlling factor in such cases is that [there] exists no standard ascertainable [by] reference to which a political decision affecting the question at issue between the parties can be judged. . . .

2. The Court has been particularly unwilling to intervene in matters concerning the structure and organization of the political institutions of the States. The abstention from judicial entry into such areas has been greater even than that which marks the Court's ordinary approach to issues of state power challenged under broad federal guarantees. . . .

Where, however, state law has made particular federal questions determinative of relations within the structure of state government, not in challenge of it, the Court has resolved such narrow, legally defined questions in proper proceedings. In such instances there is no conflict between state policy and the exercise of federal judicial [power.] . . .

3. The cases involving Negro disfranchisement are no exception to the principle of avoiding federal judicial intervention into matters of state government in the absence of an explicit and clear constitutional imperative. For here the controlling command of Supreme Law is plain and unequivocal. An end of discrimination against the Negro was the compelling motive of the Civil War Amendments. . . .

4. The Court has refused to exercise its jurisdiction to pass on "abstract questions of political power, of sovereignty, of government." [The] "political question" doctrine, in this aspect, reflects the policies underlying the requirement of "standing": that the litigant who would challenge official action must claim infringement of an interest particular and personal to himself, as distinguished from a cause of dissatisfaction with the general frame and functioning of government — a complaint that the political institutions are awry. [What] renders cases of this kind non-justiciable is not necessarily the nature of the parties to them, for the Court has resolved other issues between similar parties; nor is it the nature of the legal question involved, for the same type of question has been adjudicated when presented in other forms of controversy. The crux of the matter is that courts are not fit instruments of decision where what is essentially at stake is the

composition of those large contests of policy traditionally fought out in non-judicial forums, by which governments and the actions of governments are made and unmade. . . .

5. The influence of these converging considerations — the caution not to undertake decision where standards meet for judicial judgment are lacking, the reluctance to interfere with matters of state government in the absence of an unquestionable and effectively enforceable mandate, the unwillingness to make courts arbiters of the broad issues of political organization historically committed to other institutions and for whose adjustment the judicial process is ill-adapted — has been decisive of the settled line of cases, reaching back more than a century, which holds that Art. IV, §4, of the Constitution, guaranteeing to the States "a Republican Form of Government," is not enforceable through the courts. . . .

The present case involves all of the elements that have made the Guarantee Clause cases non-justiciable. It is, in effect, a Guarantee Clause claim masquerading under a different label. But it cannot make the case more fit for judicial action that appellants invoke the Fourteenth Amendment rather than Art. IV, §4, where, in fact, the gist of their complaint is the same — unless it can be found that the Fourteenth Amendment speaks with greater particularity to their situation. We have been admonished to avoid "the tyranny of labels." Art. IV, §4, is not committed by express constitutional terms to Congress. It is the nature of the controversies arising under it, nothing else, which has made it judicially unenforceable. But where judicial competence is wanting, it cannot be created by invoking one clause of the Constitution rather than another.

[Appellants] invoke the right to vote[, but] they are permitted to vote and their votes are counted. [Their] complaint is simply that the representatives are not sufficiently numerous or powerful. [It] will add a virulent source of friction and tension in Federal-state relations to embroil the Federal judiciary in [apportionment battles]. . . .

[Concurring opinions by Justices Douglas, Clark, and Stewart are omitted here. Justice Clark stressed that Tennessee's apportionment scheme was "a crazy quilt." A dissenting opinion by Justice Harlan, arguing that no federal constitutional right was at stake, is also omitted.]

DAVIS v. BANDEMER, 478 U.S. 109 (1986). This case concerned an equal protection challenge to "political gerrymandering" by the Indiana legislature. Although the legislative districts created by the Republican-controlled legislature were substantially equal in population, the Democrats claimed that the district lines were deliberately drawn so as to understate Democratic voting strength. The trial court agreed and ordered preparation of a new plan. On appeal, a majority of the Supreme Court held that "political gerrymandering" was not a nonjusticiable political question. A plurality held, however, that the trial court had erred in finding a substantive constitutional violation. (This question is covered in more detail in Chapter 7 infra.)

Justice White delivered the Court's opinion with respect to the political question issue: "Disposition of this question does not involve us in a matter more properly decided by a coequal branch of our Government. There is no risk of foreign or domestic disturbance, and in light of our cases since *Baker* we are not persuaded that there are no judicially discernible and manageable standards by which political gerrymander cases are to be decided.

"It is true that the type of claim that was presented in Baker v. Carr was subsequently resolved in this Court by the formulation of the 'one person, one vote' rule. The mere fact, however, that we may not now similarly perceive a likely arithmetic presumption in the instant context does not compel a conclusion that the claims presented here are non-justiciable. The one person, one vote principle had not yet been developed when *Baker* was decided. At that time, the Court did not rely on the potential for such a rule in finding justiciability. Instead, [the] Court contemplated simply that legislative line-drawing in the districting context would be susceptible of adjudication under the applicable constitutional criteria. . . .

"[Justice O'Connor's dissent] would transform the narrow categories of 'political questions' that Baker v. Carr carefully defined into an ad hoc litmus test of this Court's reactions to the desirability of and need for judicial application of constitutional or statutory standards to a given type of claim. [She] concludes that because political gerrymandering may be a 'self-limiting enterprise' there is no need for judicial intervention. She also expresses concern that our decision today will lead to 'political instability and judicial malaise,' because nothing will prevent members of other identifiable groups from bringing similar claims. To begin with, Justice O'Connor's factual assumptions are by no means obviously correct: It is not clear that political gerrymandering *is* a self-limiting enterprise or that other groups will have any great incentive to bring gerrymandering claims, given the requirement of a showing of discriminatory intent. At a more fundamental level, however, Justice O'Connor's analysis is flawed because it focuses on the perceived need for judicial review and on the potential practical problems with allowing such review. Validation of the consideration of such amorphous and wide-ranging factors in assessing justiciability would alter substantially the analysis the Court enunciated in Baker v. Carr, and we decline Justice O'Connor's implicit invitation to rethink that approach."

Turning to the merits, Justice White (now writing for only a four-justice plurality of the Court) held that "a group's electoral power is not unconstitutionally diminished by the simple fact of an apportionment scheme that makes winning elections more difficult, and a failure of proportional representation alone does not constitute impermissible discrimination." In order to establish a constitutional violation, the party challenging a districting scheme must show that "the electoral system is arranged in a manner that will consistently degrade a voter's or a group of voters' influence on the political process as a whole." (See Chapter 7 for a fuller discussion.)

Justice O'Connor, joined by Chief Justice Burger and Justice Rehnquist, dissented from the Court's justiciability holding: "The step taken today is a momentous one, which if followed in the future can only lead to political instability and judicial malaise. If members of the majority political parties are protected by the Equal Protection Clause from dilution of their voting strength, then members of every identifiable group that possesses distinctive interests and tends to vote on the basis of those interests should be able to bring similar claims. Federal courts will have no alternative but to attempt to recreate the complex process of legislative apportionment in the context of adversary litigation in order to reconcile the competing claims of political, religious, ethnic, racial, occupational, and socio-economic groups. [There] is simply no clear stopping point to prevent the gradual evolution of a requirement of roughly proportional representation for every cohesive political group.

"In my view, this enterprise is flawed from its inception. The Equal Protection Clause does not supply judicially manageable standards for resolving purely political gerrymandering claims, and no group right to an equal share of political power was ever intended by the Framers of the Fourteenth Amendment. . . .

"[There] is good reason to think that political gerrymandering is a self-limiting enterprise. In order to gerrymander, the legislative majority must weaken some of its safe seats, thus exposing its own incumbents to greater risks of defeat — risks they may refuse to accept past a certain point. [More] generally, each major party presumably has ample weapons at its disposal to conduct the partisan struggle that often leads to a partisan apportionment, but also often leads to a bipartisan one. There is no proof before us that political gerrymandering is an evil that cannot be checked or cured by the people or by the parties themselves. . . .

"The standard the plurality proposes exemplifies the intractable difficulties in deriving a judicially manageable standard from the Equal Protection Clause for adjudicating political gerrymandering claims. [In] my view, this standard will over time either prove unmanageable and arbitrary or else evolve towards some loose form of proportionality. . . .

"Absent [a norm of proportionality] the inquiry the plurality proposes would be so standardless as to make the adjudication of political gerrymandering claims impossible. . . .

"Of course, in one sense a requirement of proportional representation, whether loose or absolute, is judicially manageable. If this Court were to declare that the Equal Protection Clause required proportional representation within certain fixed tolerances, I have no doubt that district courts would be able to apply this edict. The flaw in such a pronouncement, however, would be the use of the Equal Protection Clause as the vehicle for making a fundamental policy choice that is contrary to the intent of its Framers and to the traditions of this republic. The political question doctrine as articulated in Baker v. Carr rightly requires that we refrain from making such policy choices in order to evade what would otherwise be a lack of judicially manageable standards."

Chief Justice Burger also wrote a short opinion arguing that the issue was nonjusticiable.

Justice Powell, joined by Justice Stevens, wrote an opinion agreeing with Justice White that this issue was justiciable, but arguing that the trial court had applied the correct substantive standard and that its judgment should be affirmed.

For criticism of *Bandemer*, see Schuck, The Thickest Thicket: Partisan Gerrymandering and Judicial Regulation of Politics, 87 Colum. L. Rev. 1325 (1987).

The Court rejected a political question claim in United States Department of Commerce v. Montana, 503 U.S. 442 (1992). Congress chose a certain apportionment method for the House of Representatives; several states objected to the choice. Significantly, the Court said that in "invoking the political question doctrine, a court acknowledges the possibility that a constitutional provision may not be judicially enforceable. Such a decision is of course very different from determining that specific congressional action does not violate the Constitution." The Court thus rejected the suggestion that a political question existed when, and only when, there was no constitutional violation. Nonetheless, the Court held that the case was indeed justiciable because it was no different from *Baker* itself.

NIXON v. UNITED STATES, 506 U.S. 224 (1993). Nixon, a former district court judge who was convicted of making false statements before a federal grand jury, sought judicial review of his subsequent removal from office by impeachment. He claimed that the Senate had failed to "try" him within the meaning of the impeachment clause of article I. Upon receiving articles of impeachment from the House, the Senate referred the matter to a committee, which reported to the full body. Although the committee presented the Senate with a transcript of the proceedings and Nixon was permitted to make a personal appeal to the Senate, the full body did not receive any of the evidence.

Chief Justice Rehnquist delivered the opinion of the Court:

"[Before] we reach the merits of such a claim, we must decide whether it is 'justiciable,' that is, whether it is a claim that may be resolved by the courts. We conclude that it is not. . . .

"A controversy is nonjusticiable — i.e., involves a political question — where there is 'a textually demonstrable constitutional commitment of the issue to a coordinate political department; or a lack of judicially discoverable and manageable standards for resolving it' [*Baker*]. But the courts must, in the first instance, interpret the text in question and determine whether and to what extent the issue is textually committed. [The] concept of a textual commitment to a coordinate political department is not completely separate from the concept of a lack of judicially discoverable and manageable standards for resolving it; the lack of judicially manageable standards may strengthen the conclusion that there is a textually demonstrable commitment to a coordinate branch. . . .

"In this case, we must examine Art. I, §3, cl. 6 [which provides that '[t]he Senate shall have the sole Power to try all Impeachments.' This provision] is a grant of authority to the Senate, and the word 'sole' indicates that this authority is reposed in the Senate, and nowhere else. . . .

"Petitioner argues that the word 'try' [requires that] the proceedings must be in the nature of a judicial trial. . . .

"The word 'try,' both in 1787 and later, has considerably broader meanings than those to which petitioner would limit it. [Based] on the variety of definitions, [we] cannot say that the Framers used the word [as] an implied limitation on the method by which the Senate might proceed in trying impeachments. . . .

"The conclusion that the use of the word 'try' [lacks] sufficient precision to afford any judicially manageable standard of review of the Senate's actions is fortified by the existence of the three very specific requirements that the Constitution does impose on the Senate when trying impeachments: the members must be under oath, a two-thirds vote is required to convict, and the Chief Justice presides when the President is tried. These limitations are quite precise, and their nature suggests that the Framers did not intend to impose additional limitations on the form of the Senate proceedings by the use of the word ['try.']

"[The] common sense meaning of the word 'sole' is that the Senate alone shall have authority to determine whether an individual should be acquitted or convicted. . . .

"[Judicial] review would be inconsistent with the Framers' insistence that our system be one of checks and balances. In our constitutional system, impeachment was designed to be the *only* check on the Judicial Branch by the Legislature. [Judicial] involvement in impeachment proceedings, even if only for purposes of judicial review, is counterintuitive because it would eviscerate the 'important constitutional check' placed on the Judiciary by the Framers. Nixon's argument would place final reviewing authority with respect to impeachments in the hands of the same body that the impeachment process is meant to regulate. . . .

"In addition to the textual commitment argument, we are persuaded that the lack of finality and the difficulty of fashioning relief counsel against justiciability. [Opening] the door of judicial review to the procedures used by the Senate in trying impeachments would 'expose the political life of the country to months, or perhaps years, of chaos.' This lack of finality would manifest itself most dramatically if the President were impeached. The legitimacy of any successor, and hence his effectiveness, would be impaired severely, not merely while the judicial process was running its course, but during any retrial that a differently constituted Senate might conduct if its first judgment of conviction were invalidated. Equally uncertain is the question of what relief a court may give other than simply setting aside the judgment of conviction. Could it order the reinstatement of a convicted federal judge, or order Congress to create an additional judgeship if the seat had been filled in the interim? . . .

"We agree with Nixon that courts possess power to review either legislative or executive action that transgresses identifiable textual limits. As we have made clear, 'whether the action of [either the Legislative or the Executive Branch] exceeds whatever authority has been committed, is itself a delicate exercise in constitutional interpretation, and is a responsibility of this Court as ultimate interpreter of the Constitution.' [*Baker.*] But we conclude, after exercising that delicate responsibility, that the word 'try' in the Impeachment Clause does not provide an identifiable textual limit on the authority which is committed to the Senate."

Justice White, joined by Justice Blackmun, concurred in the judgment:

"Petitioner contends that the method by which the Senate convicted him on two articles of impeachment violates Art. I, §3, cl. 6 of the Constitution, which mandates that the Senate 'try' impeachments. The Court is of the view that the Constitution forbids us even to consider his contention. I find no such prohibition and would therefore reach the merits of the claim. I concur in the judgment because the Senate fulfilled its constitutional obligation to 'try' petitioner. . . .

"[The] discord between the majority's position and the basic principles of checks and balances underlying the Constitution's separation of powers is clear. In essence, the majority suggests that the Framers conferred upon Congress a potential tool of legislative dominance yet at the same time rendered Congress' exercise of that power one of the very few areas of legislative authority immune from any judicial review. While the majority rejects petitioner's justiciability argument as espousing a view 'inconsistent with the Framers' insistence that our system be one of checks and balances,' it is the Court's finding of nonjusticiability that truly upsets the Framers' careful design. In a truly balanced system, impeachments tried by the Senate would serve as a means of controlling a largely unaccountable judiciary, even as judicial review would ensure that the Senate adhered to a minimal set of procedural standards in conducting impeachment trials."

Justice Souter also concurred in the judgment:

"[The] political question doctrine [derives] in large part from prudential concerns about the respect we owe the political departments. Not all interference is inappropriate or disrespectful, however, and application of the doctrine ultimately turns, as Learned Hand put it, on 'how importunately the occasion demands an answer.'

"This occasion does not demand an answer. [It] seems fair to conclude that the [Impeachment] Clause contemplates that the Senate may determine, within broad boundaries, such subsidiary issues as the procedures for receipt and consideration of evidence necessary to satisfy its duty to 'try' [impeachments].

"One can, nevertheless, envision different and unusual circumstances that might justify a more searching review of impeachment proceedings. If the Senate were to act in a manner seriously threatening the integrity of its results, convicting, say, upon a coin-toss, or upon a summary determination that an officer of the United States was simply 'a bad guy,' judicial interference might well be appropriate. In such circumstances, the Senate's action might be so far beyond the scope of its constitutional authority, and the consequent impact on the Republic so great, as to merit a judicial response despite the prudential concerns that would ordinarily counsel silence. 'The political question doctrine, a tool for maintenance of governmental order, will not be so applied as to promote only disorder.' [*Baker.*]"

Justice Stevens concurred in the decision.

Note: Political Questions

1. *In general.* Alexis de Toqueville observed that "[t]here is hardly a political question in the United States that does not sooner or later turn into a judicial one." Democracy in America 270 (J. P. Mayer ed. 1969). After Baker v. Carr and *Bandemer*, the narrowness of the political question doctrine might be thought to support the point. At least if there are genuine constitutional constraints on the executive or legislative conduct at issue, the political question doctrine is unlikely to come into play. Note that this conclusion was presaged by Marbury v. Madison, in which Chief Justice Marshall said questions would be deemed "political" if there was "legal discretion" in the circumstances. Note also that for the most part the political question doctrine became a serious one only in the twentieth century, largely as a response by certain justices to the judicial assault on the rise of the administrative state.

It is possible that standing doctrine has been altered to diminish the "friction" between the branches after (what some consider) the narrow interpretation of the political question doctrine in Baker v. Carr. Consider the possibility that Lujan v. Defenders of Wildlife, Allen v. Wright, *Richardson*, and *Schlesinger* reflect lurking "political question" concerns.

2. *Justiciable standards.* The primary — though probably not exclusive — ground on which to find a political question is that there are no "judicially cognizable standards" by which to assess the claim of unconstitutionality. This understanding means that, in order to say whether there is a political question, the court has to examine both the relevant constitutional provision and the plaintiff's

legal claim: Does the former set out criteria by which a court can assess the latter? If it does not, the question is labeled "political."

If this is the correct approach, there may be no difference between saying that a suit presents a political question and saying that there is no constitutional violation on the merits. If there is indeed no difference, one might conclude that there is no "political question doctrine" at all. Cases are deemed "political" only when there is no constitutional violation. See Henkin, Is There a Political Question Doctrine?, 85 Yale L.J. 597 (1976).

Note also that in cases in which there are no legal standards for assessing a claim of unconstitutionality, there is no tension between the political question doctrine and Marbury v. Madison. The Court retains the authority to "say what the law is." The reason the case is nonjusticiable is that the law does not say anything that is relevant to the particular dispute.

3. *Prudential concerns and* Marbury. Should the Court find nonjusticiable on political question grounds any cases or issues that do not fall within the category of "no judicially cognizable standards"? Some might think that an affirmative answer would be inconsistent with *Marbury*. But it is not hard to identify cases in which one might conclude that, even if there is a constitutional violation, courts ought not to have the authority to intervene. Consider cases in which recognition of the constitutional claim might require a change in relations with a foreign government, a cessation of a war, a substantial expenditure of federal funds, or, in the words of the Court in Allen v. Wright, a restructuring of the operations of a coordinate branch of government. In all these cases, there are political safeguards to redress the challenged action. In some or all of these cases, judicial involvement might risk usurpation of authority ordinarily thought to be that of the democratic branches. Should a court be less willing to hear such cases? Note the discussion of *Richardson* and *Schlesinger*, supra.

If the answer is affirmative, perhaps it is because the Supreme Court should act in a statesmanlike manner and not merely as a pronouncer of law. And in deciding when to pronounce law, perhaps the Court ought to be humble in assessing its own role in comparison to those of other branches, especially when the concerns identified in *Baker* are present. Is this position vulnerable to a change of lawlessness?

Exactly what sorts of standards did the Constitution supply in Davis v. Bandemer? What is the difference between saying that there was no violation on the merits and saying that the question was nonjusticiable? Consider what sorts of cases might be brought after *Bandemer* and whether those cases would place the Court in a "political thicket."

Some of the "political question" cases have been connected in some way to foreign affairs, and even when the Court does review a claim of unconstitutionality in that context, it is often quite deferential to the President and Congress. How might this phenomenon be justified? Perhaps it is because the costs of error on the part of the Court are unusually high, and because the courts' expertise and accountability are low.

Consider the following cases.

a. *Congressional power: excluding representatives, foreign affairs, and impeachment.* Powell v. McCormack, 395 U.S. 486 (1969), involved a House resolution that forbade Adam Clayton Powell from taking his seat in the House because of a finding that Powell had, among other things, "wrongfully diverted House funds for the use of others and himself" and had "made false reports on expenditures of foreign currency to the Committee on House Administration." Noting that he satisfied the age, citizenship, and residence requirements of article I, section 2, clause 2, Powell sought a declaration that his exclusion was unconstitutional.

The defendant invoked article I, section 5, clause 1, which states that "each House shall be the Judge of the . . . Qualifications of its own Members," contending that this clause revealed a textually demonstrable commitment to the House of power to set qualifications for membership and to judge whether those qualifications had been met. The Court said:

> In order to determine whether there has been a textual commitment to a co-ordinate department of the Government, we must interpret the Constitution. In other words, we must first determine what power the Constitution confers upon the House through Art. I, §5, before we can determine to what extent, if any, the exercise of that power is subject to judicial review. Respondents maintain that the House has broad power under §5, and, they argue, the House may determine which are the qualifications necessary for membership. . . .
>
> If examination of §5 disclosed that the Constitution gives the House judicially unreviewable power to set qualifications for membership and to judge whether prospective members meet those qualifications, further review of the House determination might well be barred by the political question doctrine. On the other hand, if the Constitution gives the House power to judge only whether elected members possess the three standing qualifications set forth in the Constitution, further consideration would be necessary to determine whether any of the other formulations of the political question doctrine are inextricable from the case at bar.
>
> In other words, whether there is a "textually demonstrable constitutional commitment of the issue to a coordinate political department" of government and what is the scope of such commitment are questions we must resolve for the first time in this case.
>
> In order to determine the scope of any "textual commitment" under Art. I, §5, we necessarily must determine the meaning of the phrase to "be the Judge of the Qualifications of its own Members." Petitioners argue that the records of the debates during the Constitutional Convention; available commentary from the post-Convention, pre-ratification period; and early congressional applications of Art. I, §5, support their construction of the section. Respondents insist, however, that a careful examination of the pre-Convention practices of the English Parliament and American colonial assemblies demonstrates that by 1787, a legislature's power to judge the qualifications of its members was generally understood to encompass exclusion or expulsion on the ground that an individual's character or past conduct rendered him unfit to serve. When the Constitution and the debates over its adoption are thus viewed in historical perspective, argue respondents, it becomes clear that the "qualifications" expressly set forth in the Constitution were not meant to limit the long-recognized legislative power to exclude or expel at will, but merely to establish "standing incapacities," which could be altered only by a constitutional amendment. Our examination of the relevant historical materials leads us to the conclusion that petitioners are correct and that the Constitution leaves the House without authority to *exclude* any person, duly elected by his constituents, who meets all the requirements for membership expressly prescribed in the Constitution.
>
> [Respondents'] alternate contention is that the case presents a political question because judicial resolution of petitioners' claim would produce a "potentially embarrassing confrontation between coordinate branches" of the Federal Government. But, as our interpretation of Art. I, §5, discloses, a determination of petitioner

Powell's right to sit would require no more than an interpretation of the Constitution. Such a determination falls within the traditional role accorded courts to interpret the law, and does not involve a "lack of the respect due [a] coordinate [branch] of government," nor does it involve an "initial policy determination of a kind clearly for nonjudicial discretion." [Baker v. Carr.] Our system of government requires that federal courts on occasion interpret the Constitution in a manner at variance with the construction given the document by another branch. The alleged conflict that such an adjudication may cause cannot justify the courts' avoiding their constitutional responsibility.

Nor are any of the other formulations of a political question "inextricable from the case at bar." [Baker v. Carr.] Petitioners seek a determination that the House was without power to exclude Powell from the 90th Congress, which, we have seen, requires an interpretation of the Constitution — a determination for which clearly there are "judicially . . . manageable standards." Finally, a judicial resolution of petitioners' claim will not result in "multifarious pronouncements by various departments on one question." For [it] is the responsibility of this Court to act as the ultimate interpreter of the Constitution. [*Marbury.*] Thus, we conclude that petitioners' claim is not barred by the political question doctrine, and, having determined that the claim is otherwise generally justiciable, we hold that the case is justiciable.

Compare with *Powell* the decision in Goldwater v. Carter, 444 U.S. 996 (1979), summarily reversing a court of appeals decision that the President has authority to terminate a treaty with Taiwan without congressional approval. Justice Rehnquist, in an opinion joined by the Chief Justice and Justices Stewart and Stevens, wrote an opinion concurring in the judgment:

> I am of the view that the basic question presented by the petitioners in this case is "political" and therefore nonjusticiable because it involves the authority of the President in the conduct of our country's foreign relations and the extent to which the Senate or the Congress is authorized to negate the action of the President. In Coleman v. Miller, 307 U.S. 433 (1939), a case in which members of the Kansas Legislature brought an action attacking a vote of the State Senate in favor of the ratification of the Child Labor Amendment, Mr. Chief Justice Hughes wrote in what is referred to as the "Opinion of the Court":
>
>> We think that . . . the question of the efficacy of ratifications by state legislatures, in the light of previous rejection or attempted withdrawal, should be regarded as a political question pertaining to the political departments, with the ultimate authority in the Congress in the exercise of its control over the promulgation of the adoption of the Amendment. . . .
>
> Thus, Mr. Chief Justice Hughes' opinion concluded that "Congress in controlling the promulgation of the adoption of a constitutional amendment has the final determination of the question whether by lapse of time its proposal of the amendment had lost its vitality prior to the required ratifications."
>
> I believe it follows a fortiori from *Coleman* that the controversy in the instant case is a nonjusticiable political dispute that should be left for resolution by the Executive and Legislative Branches of the Government. Here, while the Constitution is express as to the manner in which the Senate shall participate in the ratification of a treaty, it is silent as to that body's participation in the abrogation of a treaty. [In] light of the absence of any constitutional provision governing the termination of a treaty, and the fact that different termination procedures may be appropriate for different treaties the instant case in my view also "must surely be controlled by political standards."

I think that the justifications for concluding that the question here is political in nature are even more compelling than in *Coleman* because it involves foreign relations — specifically a treaty commitment to use military force in the defense of a foreign government if attacked.

The present case differs in several important respects from [Youngstown Sheet & Tube Co. v. Sawyer, Chapter 4 infra]. [Here we] are asked to settle a dispute between coequal branches of our Government, each of which has resources available to protect and assert its interests, resources not available to private litigants outside the judicial forum. Moreover, [the] effect of this action, as far as we can tell, is "entirely external to the United States, and [falls] within the category of foreign affairs." Finally, as already noted, the situation presented here is closely akin to that presented in *Coleman*, where the Constitution spoke only to the procedure for ratification of an amendment, not to its rejection.

Justice Powell wrote a separate concurring opinion:

Although I agree with the result reached by the Court, I would dismiss the complaint as not ripe for judicial review.

[No] constitutional provision explicitly confers upon the President the power to terminate treaties. Further, Art. II, §2, of the Constitution authorizes the President to make treaties with the advice and consent of the Senate. Article VI provides that treaties shall be a part of the supreme law of the land. These provisions add support to the view that the text of the Constitution does not unquestionably commit the power to terminate treaties to the President alone.

[There] is no "lack of judicially discoverable and manageable standards for resolving" this case; nor is a decision impossible "without an initial policy determination of a kind clearly for nonjudicial discretion." We are asked to decide whether the President may terminate a treaty under the Constitution without congressional approval. Resolution of the question may not be easy, but it only requires us to apply normal principles of interpretation to the constitutional provisions at issue. The present case involves neither review of the President's activities as Commander in Chief nor impermissible interference in the field of foreign affairs. [This] case "touches" foreign relations, but the question presented to us concerns only the constitutional division of power between Congress and the President.

[Interpretation] of the Constitution does not imply lack of respect for a coordinate branch. If the President and the Congress had reached irreconcilable positions, final disposition of the question presented by this case would eliminate, rather than create, multiple constitutional interpretations. The specter of the Federal Government brought to a halt because of the mutual intransigence of the President and the Congress would require this Court to provide a resolution pursuant to our duty "'to say what the law is.'"

Justice Brennan dissented:

In stating that this case presents a nonjusticiable "political question," Mr. Justice Rehnquist, in my view, profoundly misapprehends the political-question principle as it applies to matters of foreign relations. Properly understood, the political-question doctrine restrains courts from reviewing an exercise of foreign policy judgment by the coordinate political branch to which authority to make that judgment has been "constitutional[ly] commit[ted]." But the doctrine does not pertain when a court is faced with the *antecedent* question whether a particular branch has been constitutionally designated as the repository of political decisionmaking power. The issue of decisionmaking authority must be resolved as a matter of constitutional law, not political discretion; accordingly, it falls within the competence of the courts.

The constitutional question raised here is prudently answered in narrow terms. Abrogation of the defense treaty with Taiwan was a necessary incident to Executive recognition of the Peking Government, because the defense treaty was predicated upon the now-abandoned view that the Taiwan Government was the only legitimate political authority in China. Our cases firmly establish that the Constitution commits to the President alone the power to recognize, and withdraw recognition from, foreign regimes. That mandate being clear, our judicial inquiry into the treaty rupture can go no further.

Consider the following case after Powell v. McCormack and Goldwater v. Carter. The Senate impeaches the President for a "high crime and misdemeanor." The Senate's view that the presidential misconduct is a "high crime and misdemeanor" would be rejected by the Court if it were to reach the question. But the Constitution grants to the Senate the "sole power to try all impeachments." Is judicial review of impeachment foreclosed because of a textual commitment to the Senate? Because of some other concern? Cf. Roudebush v. Hartke, 405 U.S. 15 (1972) (decision as to which candidate has received more lawful votes in an election is constitutionally committed to Senate).

The twenty-seventh amendment, requiring that congressional pay raises take effect only after an election has intervened, was ratified by the Michigan legislature on May 7, 1992. The amendment had been among the first proposed by James Madison and sent to the states for ratification by the first Congress. Five states ratified the amendment in 1789-1791 and one in 1873. From 1978 on, ratifications gradually accumulated, and Michigan's was the thirty-eighth ratification.

Is the amendment now part of the Constitution? A federal statute provides that the national Archivist must certify the receipt of a sufficient number of ratifications, after which a constitutional amendment becomes "valid." If the Archivist refused to so certify on the ground that there was insufficient indication of contemporaneous consensus on the amendment, who would have standing to challenge that refusal? If the Archivist did so certify, who might have standing to challenge that decision and to make the ensuing claim that the amendment was unlawfully included in the Constitution? In any event, is certification necessary under the Constitution?

Suppose no one — member of the public or member of Congress — had standing to raise the question of whether the amendment was part of the Constitution and the Supreme Court never answers that question. Is it meaningful to say that the amendment is (or is not) part of the Constitution in the same way that the third amendment, or the guaranty clause, is? Suppose Congress adopts the practice of deferring the effective date of pay raises, consistent with the amendment. Does that strengthen or weaken the claim that the amendment is part of the Constitution?

b. *The peculiar case of the "Republican Form of Government" clause.* Section 4 of article IV of the Constitution provides that "[t]he United States shall guarantee to every State in this Union a Republican Form of Government." Several times this provision has been invoked by private litigants, but as Baker v. Carr suggests, the Supreme Court appears to have rendered it a dead letter with the political question doctrine.

The key case is Luther v. Borden, 7 How. 1 (1849), an action for trespass. *Luther* grew out of the Dohr Rebellion in Rhode Island and a conflict between various people claiming authority to act for the government of Rhode Island. The defendants claimed that the acts charged as a trespass were done under the authority of the charter government during a period of martial law in order to aid in the suppression of a revolt by supporters of an insurrectionary government. The defendants thus admitted that they had trespassed, but claimed that they were agents of the lawful government of Rhode Island, and that their acts were authorized as part of an order to arrest the plaintiffs. The plaintiffs claimed that the charter government was unlawful. They invoked the republican form of government clause, claiming that the people have the ultimate power of sovereignty, and that, if the government was to be free, they must have a right to change their constitution. The case thus turned on which of the two groups was entitled to recognition as the lawful government.

The Court responded:

[It] rests with congress to decide what government is the established one in a State. For, as the United States guarantee to each State a republican government, congress must necessarily decide what government is established in the State before it can determine whether it is republican or not. And when the senators and representatives of a State are admitted into the councils of the Union, the authority of the government under which they are appointed, as well as its republican character, is recognized by the proper constitutional authority. And its decision is binding on every other department of the government, and could not be questioned in a judicial tribunal. It is true that the contest in this case did not last long enough to bring the matter to this issue; and as no senators or representatives were elected under the authority of the government of which Mr. Dorr was the head, congress was not called upon to decide the controversy. Yet the right to decide is placed there, and not in the courts.

Recall the Court's explanation of *Luther* in Baker v. Carr. Is the explanation faithful to the opinion in *Luther?*

In Pacific Telephone Co. v. Oregon, 223 U.S. 118 (1912), plaintiffs challenged a citizen initiatives provision in the Oregon constitution, which allowed a stated number of voters to secure at any time a submission to popular vote for approval of any matter that it wished to have enacted into law. Any proposal approved in that way would become law. The law at issue in *Pacific Telephone* taxed certain telephone and telegraph companies at a certain rate. According to those companies, the initiative procedure violated the republican form of government clause.

The Court responded by referring to "the inconceivable expansion of the judicial power" that would result from an adjudication:

[However] perfect and absolute may be the establishment and dominion in fact of a state government, however complete may be its participation in and enjoyment of all its powers and rights as a member of national Government, [nevertheless] every citizen of such State [may] be heard, for the purpose of defeating the payment of such taxes or avoiding the discharge of such duty, to assail in a court of justice the rightful existence of the State.

Is *Pacific Telephone* consistent with Baker v. Carr? Note that the republican form of government clause is addressed to the "United States," not only to Congress. And one might wonder whether that clause failed to provide justiciable standards in *Luther* and *Pacific Telephone.* Suppose a state set up a monarchy. Would the guarantee clause be unavailable? For discussion, see W. Wiecek, The Guarantee Clause of the United States Constitution (1947); Bonfield, The Guarantee Clause of Article IV, Section 4: A Study in Constitutional Desuetude, 46 Minn. L. Rev. 513 (1962); Note, A Niche for the Guarantee Clause, 94 Harv. L. Rev. 681 (1981).

c. *Constitutional amendments.* Assume there is some irregularity in the process by which a constitutional amendment is ratified. Should a court declare the amendment ineffective? The principal case here is Coleman v. Miller, 307 U.S. 433 (1939), discussed supra, which involved a proposed child labor amendment to the Constitution. Of the forty senators in Kansas, twenty had voted in favor and twenty against; the Lieutenant Governor cast his vote in favor, and the amendment was eventually considered to have been adopted by the Kansas legislature. The twenty senators who had voted against ratification brought suit, contending that the Lieutenant Governor had no right to cast the tie-breaking vote, and that the proposed amendment lost its vitality because of its rejection by Kansas and other states within what they claimed to be the requisite reasonable time. The remedy sought was a writ of mandamus to compel the Kansas Secretary of State to endorse on the relevant documents that the amendment had not been passed and to restrain state officials from signing the resolution and delivering it to the Governor.

On the question whether the Lieutenant Governor was part of the legislature for article V purposes, the Court was evenly divided on the "political question" issue and therefore expressed no view. But on the "reasonable time" question, the Court concluded that the case was not justiciable:

> Where are to be found the criteria for such a judicial determination? None are to be found in the Constitution itself. In their endeavor to answer this question petitioners' counsel have suggested that at least two years should be allowed; that six years would not seem to be unreasonably long. [To] this list of variables, counsel add that "the nature and extent of publicity and the activity of the public and of legislatures of the several States in relation to any particular proposal should be taken into consideration." This statement is pertinent, but there are additional matters to be examined and weighed. [In] short, the question of a reasonable time in many cases would involve, as this case does involve, an appraisal of a great variety of relevant conditions, political, social and economic, which can hardly be said to be within the appropriate range of evidence receivable in a court of justice. [These] conditions are appropriate for the consideration of the political departments of the Government.

Several separate opinions were filed. Justice Black, joined by Justices Roberts, Frankfurter, and Douglas, expressed a somewhat broader view. He wrote that the

> Constitution grants Congress exclusive power to control submission of constitutional amendments. [In] the exercise of that power, Congress, of course, is governed by the Constitution. However, whether submission, intervening procedure, or Congressional determination of ratification conforms to the commands of the Constitution, calls for decisions by a "political department" of questions of a type which this Court has frequently designated "political."

Justice Frankfurter expressed the view that the state senators had no standing to bring suit. Justice Butler dissented. In his view, "[a]rticle V impliedly requires amendments submitted to be ratified within a reasonable time after proposal," and "more than a reasonable time had elapsed" in this case.

To what extent should *Coleman* be read to immunize the amendment process from judicial supervision? This issue arose most recently over the equal rights amendment, in the context both of efforts by some states to rescind earlier ratifications — efforts that, in the view of some, were not legally effective — and of an attempted extension by Congress of the period for ratification. Should the Court decide either or both of these questions?

Consider Dellinger, The Legitimacy of Constitutional Change: Rethinking the Amendment Process, 97 Harv. L. Rev. 386, 397-398, 411 (1983), which labels *Coleman* an "aberration" and contends that

> [t]he assumption that judicial review is precluded by the existence of the exclusive power of the promulgating Congress to determine the validity of ratifications is, in my view, wholly unwarranted. Neither the text of the Constitution nor prior congressional practice nor judicial precedent supports this bestowal of exclusive power on Congress. [Whether] or not judicial review of Article V issues would materially advance larger goals of the amendment process, such review is justified as an initial matter by the same considerations that have made judicial review an accepted part of the Constitution since Marbury v. Madison.

Professor Dellinger stresses the increased certainty that would result from some judicial supervision of the amendment process.

Compare Tribe, A Constitution We Are Amending: In Defense of a Restrained Judicial Role, 97 Harv. L. Rev. 433, 435-446 (1983), rejecting the view that

> added certainty in the application of article V is enough of a virtue to warrant the enormous vices that exclusive judicial review [would] entail. Among those vices is the danger [of] having the Supreme Court closely "oversee the very constitutional process used to reverse its decision." [The] resort to amendment — to constitutional politics as opposed to constitutional law — should be taken as a sign that the legal system has come to a point of discontinuity, a point at which something less radical than revolution but distinctly more radical than ordinary legal evolution is called for. To say that at such a moment in history we should necessarily conduct our legal business as usual, seeking certainty and harmony rather than tolerating discord, is to miss the very essence of the event at hand.

d. *Foreign affairs.* Some of the political question cases have arisen in the field of foreign affairs. Consider Goldwater v. Carter, supra, and the discussion in Baker v. Carr. What considerations support a deferential judicial posture? The high costs of error? The need for the nation to speak with one voice?

Consider Japan Whaling Association v. Baldridge, 478 U.S. 238 (1986). A federal statute requires the Secretary of Commerce to certify to the President whether a foreign country engaged in fishing operations is diminishing the effectiveness of quotas set by the International Whaling Commission (IWC). Once the certification is made, the President is required to impose economic sanctions against the offending nation. After Japan announced that it would not comply with IWC quotas, the United States and Japan entered into negotiations culminating in an executive agreement according to which Japan would cease commercial whaling by 1988 and the Secretary would not certify that Japan was in violation of the IWC quotas. This action was then filed by several conservation groups seeking to compel the Secretary to certify Japanese violations. In an opinion by Justice White, the Court rejected the contention that the political question doctrine barred adjudication of the dispute.

> The political question doctrine excludes from judicial review those controversies which revolve around policy choices and value determinations constitutionally committed for resolution to the halls of Congress or the confines of the Executive Branch. The judiciary is particularly ill-suited to make such decisions. . . .
>
> As *Baker* plainly held, however, the courts have the authority to construe treaties and executive agreements, and it goes without saying that interpreting congressional legislation is a recurring and accepted task for the federal courts. It is also evident that the challenge to the Secretary's decision not to certify Japan for harvesting whales in excess of IWC quotas presents a purely legal question of statutory interpretation.

The Court held that the Secretary's decision did not violate the statutory mandate.

Consider the following case: The President initiates a war in circumstances in which he is not constitutionally authorized to do so. (On the question of presidential warmaking authority, see Chapter 4 infra.) If a declaration or injunction is sought, is judicial review available? Some of these issues arose in the context of the Vietnam War. See Mora v. McNamara, 389 U.S. 934 (1967) (Stewart, J., dissenting from denial of certiorari in case involving legality of Vietnam War); Orlando v. Laird, 443 F.2d 1039 (2d Cir. 1971) (finding some issues raised by Vietnam War to be justiciable). See generally Tigar, The "Political Question" Doctrine and Foreign Relations, 17 UCLA L. Rev. 1135 (1970); Velvel, The War in Viet Nam: Unconstitutional, Justiciable, and Jurisdictionally Attackable, 16 Kan. L. Rev. 449 (1968). Are political safeguards sufficient in this context?

e. *Miscellaneous cases.* In many cases, of course, the Court has reached the merits of a constitutional controversy notwithstanding the implications for foreign affairs, the high stakes, or the fact of interbranch disagreement. In INS v. Chadha, 462 U.S. 919 (1983), the Court rejected a political question challenge to its power to consider the legality of the "legislative veto" — a device, opposed by every President from Woodrow Wilson to Ronald Reagan, by which one House of Congress might "veto" executive action by a majority vote. The Court observed that the controversy "may, in a sense, be termed 'political.' But the presence of constitutional issues with significant political overtones does not automatically invoke the political question doctrine. Resolution of litigation challenging the constitutional authority of one of the three branches cannot be evaded by courts because the issues have political implications in the sense urged by Congress."

See also Dames & Moore v. Regan, 453 U.S. 654 (1981) (reaching merits of dispute over legality of President Carter's executive agreement for the release of U.S. hostages in Iran); United States v. Nixon, 418 U.S. 683 (1974) (ordering President Nixon to turn over Watergate tapes); Youngstown Sheet & Tube Co. v. Sawyer, 343 U.S. 579 (1952) (invalidating President Truman's seizure of the steel mills despite President's claim that national emergency required seizure); United States v. Curtiss-Wright Export Corp., 299 U.S. 304 (1936) (reaching merits of congressional delegation of power to President to prohibit sale of arms to countries engaged in armed conflict).

4. *Concluding thoughts.* Consider Henkin, supra, at 622-624:

> The "political question doctrine," I conclude, is an unnecessary, deceptive packaging of several established doctrines that has misled lawyers and courts to find in it things that were never put there. [I] see its proper content as consisting of the following propositions: 1. The courts are bound to accept decisions by the political branches within their constitutional authority. 2. The courts will not find limitations or prohibitions on the powers of the political branches where the Constitution does not prescribe any. 3. Not all constitutional limitations or prohibitions imply rights and standing to object in favor of private parties. 4. The courts may refuse some (or all) remedies for want of equity. 5. In principle, finally, there might be constitutional provisions which can properly be interpreted as wholly or in part "self-monitoring" and not the subject of judicial review. (But the only one courts have found is the "guarantee clause" as applied to challenges to state action, and even that interpretation was not inevitable.) [These] propositions do not include any basis for refusing to consider, in a category of cases uncertain in rationale and definition, an allegation that the political branches have acted unconstitutionally.

Note that this approach would permit courts to reach issues, in both domestic and foreign realms, no matter how great the level of friction thereby created between courts and other branches of the government. And consider the fact that on perhaps rare occasions the Court seems to have found a "political question" because of the high stakes involved and the harmful consequences of judicial intrusion. Does Henkin's approach unduly limit the political question doctrine for these reasons or for any other?

Note: Questions of Timing — Ripeness and Mootness

1. *In general.* Additional justiciability barriers relate to the timing of judicial review. The doctrine of ripeness bars courts from deciding cases that are premature — too speculative or remote to warrant judicial intervention. A classic example would be a case brought to challenge a criminal statute before a prosecution is initiated, in circumstances in which the mere existence of the statute is not alleged to produce actual harm. The doctrine of mootness prevents courts from hearing cases when events subsequent to the institution of the lawsuit have deprived the plaintiff of a stake in the action. A classic example would be a case brought by a plaintiff challenging a statute prohibiting her from obtaining employment where the plaintiff has been given the job before the appeal. A case is not ripe when it is brought too soon; it is moot when it is brought too late.

2. *Ripeness.* Laird v. Tatum, 408 U.S. 1 (1972), involved a class action brought for injunctive relief against alleged "surveillance of lawful citizen political activity" by the U.S. Army. According to the plaintiffs, the army had collected information about political activities that had some potential for civil disorder; plaintiffs also claimed that they were targets of the surveillance, and that, as a result, they were "chilled" from engaging in constitutionally protected activity. The Court held that the plaintiffs did not present "a case for resolution by the courts."

According to the Court, a "chilling effect" was insufficient if it arose "merely from the individual's knowledge that a government agency was engaged in certain activities or from the individual's concomitant fear that, armed with the fruits of those activities, the agency might in the future take some *other* and additional action detrimental to that individual." The Court said that the plaintiff's "approach would have the federal courts as virtually continuing monitors of the wisdom and soundness of Executive action; such a role is appropriate for the Congress rather than the judiciary, absent actual present or immediately threatened injury resulting from unlawful governmental action." Justice Douglas, joined by Justice Marshall, dissented. What was the timing problem in *Tatum?* When might these litigants be able to challenge the surveillance?

Compare with *Tatum* the decision in Adler v. Board of Education, 342 U.S. 485 (1952), which involved a challenge to a state law disqualifying from employment in public schools anyone who was a member of assorted "subversive organizations." The plaintiffs, seeking a declaratory judgment, included parents and teachers of school children. The Court reached the merits without discussion, notwithstanding a dissent on ripeness grounds by Justice Frankfurter, who invoked United Public Workers v. Mitchell, 330 U.S. 75 (1947). In *Mitchell*, federal civil service employees sought a declaratory judgment against the Hatch Act, which prohibits federal employees from participating in the management of political campaigns. The Court said that the plaintiffs' affidavits

> declare a desire to act contrary to the rule against political activity but not that the rule has been violated. [Appellants] seem clearly to seek advisory opinions upon broad claims. [Appellants] want to engage in "political management and political campaigns," [but] such generality of objection is really an attack on the political expediency of the Hatch Act, not a presentation of legal issues. It is beyond the competence of courts to render such a decision.

Did *Mitchell* in fact involve a legal question? Why was the threat of prosecution in *Mitchell* (or *Tatum*) insufficient to justify judicial relief? Was the abstract character of the dispute a real problem?

See also Socialist Labor Party v. Gilligan, 406 U.S. 583 (1972) (refusing to hear challenge to a statute requiring party members to pledge that they were not engaged in "an attempt to overthrow the government by force"; Court notes that the pleadings did not allege that party members have ever refused in the past or will now refuse to sign the oath, which has been in existence since 1941); Poe v. Ullman, 367 U.S. 497 (1961) (refusing to hear challenge to Connecticut prohibition on use of contraceptive devices on ground that there was no allegation that state threatened prosecution).

3. *Mootness.* DeFunis v. Odegaard, 416 U.S. 312 (1974), involved a challenge to a preferential admissions program adopted by the University of Washington Law School. By the time the case reached the Court, DeFunis was in his third year of law school as a result of a decision below ordering his admission. According to the law school, his registration would not be cancelled regardless of the Supreme Court's decision. The Court noted that voluntary cessation of allegedly unlawful conduct does not make the case moot; if it did, the defendant would be "free to return to his old ways." Here, however, mootness "depends not at all upon a 'voluntary cessation' of the admissions practices that were the subject of this litigation. It depends, instead, upon the simple fact that DeFunis is now in the final

quarter of the final year of his course of study, and the settled and unchallenged policy of the Law School to permit him to complete the term for which he is now enrolled." The lower court found the case moot.

Compare Roe v. Wade, 410 U.S. 113 (1973), involving a challenge to abortion statutes. Roe herself was no longer pregnant by the time the case came to the Supreme Court. The Court nonetheless held that it was not moot, relying on the exception for cases that are "capable of repetition, yet evading review." If the termination of a pregnancy, the Court said, "makes a case moot, pregnancy litigation seldom will survive much beyond the trial stage, and appellate review will be effectively denied."

F.   THE JURISDICTION OF THE SUPREME COURT

1. *In general.* For constitutional purposes, the jurisdiction of the Supreme Court is set out in article III. But Congress has never granted litigants access to the Court in all cases for which article III provides authorization. The governing provisions are set out in 28 U.S.C. §§1251-1257.

These provisions furnished two principal routes to the Supreme Court. The first, abandoned in 1988 except for rare cases, is through an appeal; the second is through certiorari. It is generally said that the appellate jurisdiction is "mandatory." If a party who has lost below seeks review, the Court must hear any case that falls within its appellate jurisdiction. Certiorari jurisdiction, by contrast, is discretionary. The Court may deny certiorari for some reason other than its agreement with the decision below — the unimportance of the issue, the unusual character of the particular facts, the desire to see the issue "percolate" in the lower courts, the controversial character of the problem, or the wish to allow the political process time to consider the problem before an authoritative resolution is obtained.

Litigants seeking certiorari must file a petition for certiorari, setting out the reasons the case deserves plenary consideration. Supreme Court Rule 17, "while neither controlling nor fully measuring the Court's discretion, [indicates] the character of the reasons that will be considered":

(a) When a federal court of appeals has rendered a decision in conflict with the decision of another federal court of appeals on the same matter; or has decided a federal question in a way in conflict with a state court of last resort; or has so far departed from the accepted and usual course of judicial proceedings [as] to call for an exercise of this Court's power of supervision.
(b) When a state court of last resort has decided a federal question in a way in conflict with the decision of another state court of last resort or of a federal court of appeals.
(c) When a state court or a federal court of appeals has decided an important question of federal law which has not been, but should be, settled by this Court, or has decided a federal question in a way in conflict with applicable decisions of this Court.

Rules of the Supreme Court, 445 U.S. 983, 1003 (1980).

The manner of screening cases varies among the justices. Some members of the Court rely on law clerks to write brief memoranda about cases presented for certiorari; some justices read all or some of the petitions themselves; many of them participate in a "cert pool," in which one law clerk is assigned responsibility for writing a memorandum circulated to many of the chambers. Cases perceived to be of importance are placed on the "Discuss List" — the list of cases to be discussed by the justices in conference. From that list, the Court decides which cases to hear. See generally Alsup, A Policy Assessment of the National Court of Appeals, 25 Hastings L.J. 1313 (1974).

The general rule is that a denial of certiorari does not have any precedential value. Why might the Court be careful to ensure the perpetuation of that rule?

2. *Independent and adequate state grounds.* Note also that the Court does not have jurisdiction under the relevant statutes to hear a case when the decision below rests on "adequate and independent state grounds" — that is, when an issue of state law was actually decided that is sufficient to support the outcome. See Herb v. Pitcairn, 324 U.S. 117, 125 (1945); Michigan v. Long, 463 U.S. 1032 (1983). What is the reason for this rule? Can it be related to the ban on advisory opinions?

3. *The workload problem.* Considerable concern is sometimes expressed about the Supreme Court's workload, which had grown rapidly until the last few years. In recent years, the Court has faced over 4,000 annual filings; in the 1940s, the Court faced fewer than 1,500. The number of full opinions, however, has not changed dramatically. For general discussion of the caseload problem of the federal courts, see R. Posner, Federal Courts: Crisis and Reform (1985); for the caseload in the Supreme Court, see the annual Supreme Court issue of the Harvard Law Review.

4. *Not giving reasons.* In some of the areas we have discussed, the Court has, in a sense, declined to give reasons. When the Court denies certiorari, it does not explain itself. When the Court finds a case nonjusticiable, it may do so partly because it does not want to address itself to the underlying issue. Frederick Schauer, in Giving Reasons, 47 Stan. L. Rev. 633 (1995), argues that reason-giving may have some of the problems associated with rules, and that it is sometimes legitimate not to give reasons. That is, reasons may be both overinclusive and underinclusive, and an institution that gives reasons may later have cause for regret. "When juries deliver verdicts, when the Supreme Court denies certiorari, when state supreme courts refuse review, when federal courts of appeals dispose of cases from the bench or without opinion, when trial judges rule on objections and frequently when they rule on motions, when lawyers exercise peremptory challenges and sometimes when judges dismiss jurors for cause, when housing and zoning authorities refuse to grant variances from their regulations, and sometimes when judges impose sentences, the conclusion stands alone, unsupported by reasons, justifications, or explanation." Can you think of factors that would justify a failure to give reasons? Might the answer lie partly in an assessment of the burdens of doing so and the likelihood that reasons will cause problems for the future?

II

The Powers of Congress

A. INTRODUCTION

Note: A Government of Enumerated Powers

1. *The origins of enumeration.* After the Revolution, the American colonists faced the task of creating one or more governments. Their first efforts, in which self-governing states joined a loose confederation, proved unsatisfactory. The government established under the Articles of Confederation was unable to guarantee that international commitments would be honored, to assure that sufficient force could be amassed to combat threats to security originating both within and without the states, or to establish a framework within which stable economic growth might proceed unhampered by localist jealousies.

Provoked by these difficulties, a number of leading political figures gathered in a convention designed nominally to amend, but actually to replace, the Articles of Confederation. Their goals were stated in the Preamble to the Constitution. The framers regarded it as significant that, while the prior government was a federation created by the states, the new one was created by "the People." The contemporary significance of this choice was discussed in U.S. Term Limits v. Thornton, 514 U.S. 779 (1995). In arguing that states could not impose term limits on members of Congress, Justice Stevens wrote:

> Prior to the adoption of the Constitution, the States had joined together under the Articles of Confederation. In that system, "the States retained most of their sovereignty, like independent nations bound together only by treaties." Wesberry v. Sanders, 376 U.S. 1, 9 (1964). After the Constitutional Convention convened, the Framers [adopted] "[a] plan not merely to amend the Articles of Confederation but to create an entirely new National [Government]." In adopting that plan, the Framers envisioned a uniform national system, rejecting the notion that the Nation was a collection of States, and instead creating a direct link between the National Government and the people of the United States. In that National Government, representatives owe primary allegiance not to the people of a State, but to the people of the Nation. [The] Congress of the United States, therefore, is not a confed-

eration of nations in which separate sovereigns are represented by appointed delegates, but is instead a body composed of representatives of the people.

Justice Kennedy, concurring, added:

> The Framers split the atom of sovereignty. It was the genius of their idea that our citizens would have two political capacities, one state and one federal, each protected from incursion by the other. [A] distinctive character of the National Government [is] that it owes its existence to the act of the whole people who created it. [There] can be no doubt [that] there exists [a] relationship between the people of the Nation and their National Government, with which the States may not interfere.

Justice Thomas, in dissent, responded, "Our system of government rests on one overriding principle: all power stems from the consent of the people. [The] ultimate source of the Constitution's authority is the consent of the people of each individual State, not the consent of the undifferentiated people of the Nation as a whole." Do these different conceptions of the relations among individuals, states, and the nation imply different conceptions of the scope of national power? Of the scope of state power?

The background of the Constitution made it clear to the framers that the primary defect in the Articles of Confederation was the failure to give sufficient power to the national government. The framers therefore wanted to increase the power of the new government as compared to the old. But this raised two problems: (1) The framers believed that states ought to remain as significant units of government. The national government ought to exercise its power only on distinctively national subjects, while states would exercise control over most matters of general government. (2) Power granted to the national government might be improvidently used, so as to suppress liberty and choke economic development.

The framers sought to respond to those concerns by enumerating the powers granted to the national government.

2. *How enumeration limits powers: explicit limitations as an alternative.* In The Federalist No. 84, Hamilton argued that the enumeration made unnecessary a bill of rights, which would explicitly limit Congress's powers:

> It has been several times truly remarked that bills of rights are, in their origin, stipulations between kings and their subjects, abridgments of prerogative in favor of privilege, reservations of rights not surrendered to the prince. [Here,] in strictness, the people surrender nothing; and as they retain everything they have no need of particular reservations. . . .
>
> I go further and affirm that bills of rights [are] not only unnecessary in the proposed Constitution but would even be dangerous. They would contain various exceptions to powers not granted; and, on this very account, would afford a colorable pretext to claim more than were granted. For why declare that things shall not be done which there is no power to do? Why, for instance, should it be said that the liberty of the press shall not be restrained, when no power is given by which restrictions may be imposed? I will not contend that such a provision would confer a regulating power; but it is evident that it would furnish, to men disposed to usurp, a plausible pretense for claiming that power. They might urge with a semblance of reason that the Constitution ought not to be charged with the absurdity of providing against the abuse of an authority which was not given, and that the provision against restraining the liberty of the press afforded a clear implication that a power

to prescribe proper regulations concerning it was intended to be vested in the national government. . . .

On the subject of the liberty of the press, as much as has been said, I cannot forbear adding a remark or two. [What] is the liberty of the press? Who can give it any definition which would not leave the utmost latitude for evasion? I hold it to be impracticable; and from this I infer that its security, whatever fine declarations may be inserted in any constitution respecting it, must altogether depend on public opinion, and on the general spirit of the people and of the government.* And here, after all, [must] we seek for the only solid basis of all our rights.

As you study the materials that follow, consider whether Hamilton was right.

Note: The Values of Federalism

What values are served by a system that distributes governmental authority between state and nation, that is, by federalism? For an overview of contemporary issues, see D. L. Shapiro, Federalism: A Dialogue (1995).

1. *Efficiency.* Given wide variations in the circumstances obtaining in different areas of the country, it is likely that different solutions to specific problems will be appropriate in different areas. A national government can also respond to problems created for one state or region by activities elsewhere. Prichard, Securing the Canadian Economic Union: Federalism and Internal Barriers to Trade, in Federalism and the Canadian Economic Union 6 (M. Trebilcock et al. eds. 1983), argues that "economic integration" allows gains to all participants by "spreading the risk of economic instability" and by allowing "cooperation in the provision of joint services (e.g., defence, transport, communications) characterized by economies of scale."

2. *Promoting individual choice.* A national government can enforce the values shared by a majority in the nation as a whole, even against those who are a majority in one or a few states. Consider these observations by James Madison, from The Federalist No. 46:

[The] federal and State governments are in fact but different agents and trustees of the people, constituted with different powers and designed for different purposes. [The] ultimate authority, wherever the derivative may be found, resides in the people alone, and [it] will not depend merely on the comparative ambition or address of the different governments whether either, or which of them, will be able to enlarge its sphere of jurisdiction at the expense of the other. . . .

If, therefore, [the] people should in future become more partial to the federal than to the State governments, the change can only result from such manifest and

---

*To show that there is a power in the Constitution by which the liberty of the press may be affected, recourse has been had to the power of taxation. It is said that duties may be laid upon the publications so high as to amount to a prohibition. I know not by what logic it could be maintained that the declarations in the State constitutions, in favor of the freedom of the press, would be a constitutional impediment to the imposition of duties upon publications by the State legislatures. [And] if duties of any kind may be laid without a violation of that liberty, it is evident that the extent must depend on legislative discretion, regulated by public opinion; so that, after all, general declarations respecting the liberty of the press will give it no greater security than it will have without them. [It] would be quite as significant to declare that government ought to be free, that taxes ought not to be excessive, etc., as that the liberty of the press ought not to be restrained.

irresistible proofs of a better administration as will overcome all their antecedent propensities. And in that case, the people ought not surely to be precluded from giving most of their confidence where they may discover it to be most due; but even in that case the State governments could have little to apprehend, because it is only within a certain sphere that the federal power can, in the nature of things, be advantageously administered. . . .

In contrast, disabling the national government from acting on some subjects while allowing states to act in varying ways allows people to move from one area to another in order to select the kind of government policies they prefer.

Consider this example from McConnell, Federalism: Evaluating the Founders' Design, 54 U. Chi. L. Rev. 1484, 1494 (1987):

[Assume] that there are only two states, with equal populations of 100. [Assume] further that 70 percent of State A, and only 40 percent of State B, wish to outlaw smoking in public buildings. [If] a decision is made on a national basis by a majority rule, 110 people will be pleased, and 90 displeased. If a separate decision is made by majorities in each state, 130 will be pleased, and only 70 displeased. The level of satisfaction will be still greater if some smokers in State A decide to move to State B, and some anti-smokers in State B decide to move to State A.

An example pointing in the opposite direction is provided by Baker and Dinkin, The Senate: An Institution Whose Time Has Gone?, 13 J.L. & Pol. 21, 49-50 (1997):

[A] state's prohibition against the death penalty [could] be understood as its determination that the benefits of precluding a type of state action that some consider morally repugnant outweigh the costs of any foregone deterrence of crime. In the absence of a federal government, a state in which the death penalty is available would have only two ways to compete with a state that chose to prohibit the execution of individuals it convicts of crimes. It could continue to offer its current package of taxes and services, including the availability of the death penalty. [Or,] the state could make some adjustment(s) to its package, which may include adopting a [prohibition] against the death penalty. But the existence of our federal legislature gives states that favor the death penalty a third, competition-impeding option: their congressional representatives could enact legislation [requiring] all states to make the death penalty available. [Through] such homogenizing legislation, a majority of states can force an outlier state to disgorge any competitive gains that its uncommon choice previously afforded. [Such] legislation reduces the diversity among the states.

Why would the senators from State B vote for a nationwide ban rather than a local option? And what is the nature of the competition over crime control policy? If the policy in question is a ban on discrimination against people with disabilities, does a local option maximize "pleasure"?

Prichard, supra, at 17-18, suggests that the political process is likely to favor decentralization:

First, interest groups that may be minorities nationally are more likely to be majorities locally. Second, [the] greater the homogeneity of interests on a geographical basis, the more often minorities become majorities as decentralization increases. Third, decentralization of functions in a hierarchical way disaggregates policy packages and allows a citizen to cast different votes on different components of policy because they are vested in different levels of government in the jurisdictional hierarchy. Fourth, decentralization, by creating a diversity of jurisdictions, allows a better matching of preferences and policies because voters can choose that jurisdiction which offers the most preferred policy package. That is, citizens may "vote with their feet," searching out the jurisdiction offering the most attractive set of policies. Simultaneously, the threat of exit by voters from a jurisdiction forces the decentralized governments to reflect the policy preferences of their existing or potential constituents as the jurisdictions compete for voters. Fifth, given the greater homogeneity of tastes as boundaries contract, decentralization reduces the likelihood of policy compromises being adopted that create minimum winning coalitions but do not accurately reflect the interests of any particular interest group. . . .

A sixth advantage of decentralization is the reduction of "signalling" and other "transactions costs" for expressing citizen preferences [such as] participation in efforts to influence the actions of lobbies and large pressure groups [and] voting or the act of giving one's support to or withholding it from a candidate of a political party or, in very special cases, a policy.

The origin of this approach is Tiebout, A Pure Theory of Local Expenditures, 64 J. Pol. Econ. 416 (1956). Note that this view of federalism may overestimate the ease with which voters may relocate. For elaboration and critique, see A. Hirschman, Exit, Voice, and Loyalty (1970); D. Mueller, Public Choice 125-147 (1979).

3. *Encouraging experimentation.* Justice Brandeis, dissenting in New State Ice Co. v. Liebmann, 285 U.S. 262 (1932), wrote:

To stay experimentation in things social and economic is a grave responsibility. Denial of the right to experiment may be fraught with serious consequences to the Nation. It is one of the happy incidents of the federal system that a single courageous State may, if its citizens choose, serve as a laboratory; and try novel social and economic experiments without risk to the rest of the country. This Court has the power to prevent an experiment. [But] in the exercise of this high power, we must ever be on our guard, lest we erect our prejudices into legal principles. If we would guide by the light of reason, we must let our minds be bold.

The majority in *New State Ice* held that a *state* law unconstitutionally limited the operation of the national market; the case does not (directly) involve questions about national power. Note that experiments on the local level can teach the people of the whole nation that particular innovations are valuable enough to be adopted throughout the nation.

Rose-Ackerman, Risk Taking and Reelection: Does Federalism Promote Innovation?, 9 J. Legal Stud. 593 (1980), develops a formal model suggesting that Brandeis overstated his case. She assumes that politicians seek only to be reelected and that voters "have a wide range of risk preferences." Following Brandeis, she argues that innovations in one jurisdiction can be copied in other jurisdictions, which will not have to bear the costs associated with undertaking risky projects. Individual jurisdictions, however, have no incentive to take account of the benefits obtained by others. This will limit experimentation and implies that jurisdictions will not design controlled experiments capable of replication elsewhere. As she states, "[If] state and local governments are supposed to be 'laboratories,' then my model predicts that few useful experiments will be carried out in them." Rose-Ackerman explains that her assumptions impose limits on the realism of her model.

4. *Promoting democracy.* State and local governments provide the opportunity for people to participate directly in the activities of governments that have significant effects on their lives. This participation would make them the active citizens valued in one version of democratic theory rather than the passive subjects of a remote national government. Does federalism serve this value today?

Consider Rapaczynski, From Sovereignty to Process: The Jurisprudence of Federalism after *Garcia*, 1985 Sup. Ct. Rev. 341, 402-403, 407-408:

> [If] there is some genuine room for noninstrumental participation in American political life, it can realistically exist only on the local level. [The] existence of participatory politics on the state level [is] by no means a fiction. [The] most traditional American mechanism of participatory democracy — the town meeting — is very much alive in a large section of the country. [Further], throughout the country, there is significant citizen involvement in the local planning process, school boards, the budget process, and other governmental functions. [Finally], a special role of the most powerful tool of direct government on a larger scale — the referendum — must be mentioned.

A national government with plenary power might choose to exercise that power in ways that encourage experimentation, efficiency, and choice. It could divide the nation into administrative regions and give revocable grants of autonomy to the regions with respect to certain subjects. What values of federalism would be impaired by such a system? Do national lawmakers have incentives to set up such a system?

5. *Preventing tyranny.* Consider Rapaczynski, above, at 341, 385-386, 388-389:

> Many American liberals tend to look with skepticism on the states as the protectors of individual freedom and they point to a whole host of situations in which the states [have] engaged in practices violative of individual rights. [While] the states are more easily captured by relatively undifferentiated majoritarian interests intent on suppressing small minorities, the federal government may be a more likely subject of capture by a set of special minoritarian interests, precisely because the majority interest of the national constituency is so large, diffuse, and enormously difficult to organize. . . .
>
> [Should] the federal government ever be captured by an authoritarian movement [the] resulting oppression would almost certainly be much more severe and durable than that of which any state would be capable. [It] is precisely because the states are governmental bodies that break the national authorities' monopoly on coercion that they constitute the most fundamental bastion against a successful conversion of the federal government into a vehicle of the worst kind of oppression.

Consider Stacy, Whose Interests Does Federalism Protect?, 45 U. Kan. L. Rev. 1185, 1190 (1997):

> [Federalism] would not seem to promote limited government at all insofar as it diffuses authority into mutually exclusive state and national realms. [In] according state and national governments complete sovereignty within their own domains, the lines enforcing zones of exclusive authority will eliminate rather than create checks against the exercise of authority.

6. *The forms of federalism.* In considering the material in this chapter, keep in mind that there are a number of ways to distribute power in a federal system.

a. *Neither* state nor nation may have power to act. The first amendment, applicable to the states through the fourteenth amendment, exemplifies this situation: If some regulation violates the first amendment, neither state governments nor Congress may adopt it (although sometimes the substantive standards applicable to analyze the constitutional question will vary depending on whether the enacting body is a state government or Congress).

b. The *national* government may be given *exclusive* power to regulate in some area. Article I, section 10 itemizes a number of activities in which states may not engage even though Congress is given power in article I, section 8 to do so: States may not, but Congress may, "coin Money," for example.

c. *State* governments may have *exclusive* power to regulate some area. The central controversies in this chapter involve two related questions about this category: Are there *any* subjects in the category, and if so, *what* subjects may the states, but not Congress, regulate?

d. State and national governments may have *concurrent* power to regulate some area. The supremacy clause, article VI, paragraph 2, establishes that, where the nation and the states have concurrent power that Congress chooses to exercise, the national legislation prevails over conflicting state legislation. Chapter 3 examines such questions as these: Has Congress chosen to exercise its concurrent power? Does state legislation conflict with national statutes? Does Congress's failure to exercise its power authorize — or prohibit — state legislation in the area?

Note: A Comparative Perspective — U.S. Federalism as a Model?

Stepan, Federalism and Democracy: Beyond the U.S. Model, 10:4 J. Democracy 19 (1999), describes U.S. federalism as "coming-together" (the government was created by previously independent states), "*demos*-constraining" (federalism is designed to protect individuals against encroachments by the central government), and symmetrical (each state has the same constitutional status and powers). Stepan argues that federalism is particularly appropriate for multinational democracies, but that most such systems will hold a democracy together by creating institutions in which one or more subunits have greater power than others. He points out that "most democratic countries that have adopted federal systems have chosen not to follow the U.S. model." That model "is bolstered by a certain normative disinclination on the part of Americans to accept the concept of collective rights." In light of Stepan's observations, what reasons might there be for students of U.S. constitutional law to consider the constitutional systems of other democracies?

B.   THE BASIC ISSUES: FEDERALISM AND JUDICIAL REVIEW

Gibbons v. Ogden

22 U.S. (9 Wheat.) 1 (1824)

[The New York legislature enacted a statute granting Robert Fulton and Robert Livingston the exclusive right to operate steamboats in New York waters. The statute was designed to encourage investment in the development of the then-novel technology of steamboats. Fulton and Livingston licensed Ogden to operate a ferry between New York City and Elizabethtown Point in New Jersey. Gibbons began operating a competing ferry service that, because it necessarily entered New York waters, violated the grant to Fulton and Livingston and the license to Ogden. Gibbons's ferries were, however, licensed as "vessels [in] the coasting trade" under a statute enacted by Congress in 1793. Ogden obtained an injunction against Gibbons from the New York courts.]

MR. CHIEF JUSTICE MARSHALL delivered the opinion of the Court.

[The] subject to be regulated is commerce; and our constitution being [one] of enumeration, and not of definition, to ascertain the extent of the power, it becomes necessary to settle the meaning of the word. The counsel for the appellee would limit it to traffic, to buying and selling, or the interchange of commodities, and do not admit that it comprehends navigation. This would restrict a general term, applicable to many objects, to one of its significations. Commerce, undoubtedly, is traffic, but it is something more: it is intercourse. It describes the commercial intercourse between nations, and parts of nations, in all its branches, and is regulated by prescribing rules for carrying on that intercourse. . . .

[All] America understands [the] word "commerce," to comprehend navigation. [The] power over commerce, including navigation, was one of the primary objects for which the people of American adopted their government. . . .

The subject to which the power is next applied, is to commerce "among the several States." The word "among" means intermingled with. A thing which is among others, is intermingled with them. Commerce among the States, cannot stop at the external boundary line of each State, but may be introduced into the interior.

It is not intended to say that these words comprehend that commerce, which is completely internal, which is carried on between man and man in a State, or between different parts of the same State, and which does not extend to or affect other States. Such a power would be inconvenient, and is certainly unnecessary.

Comprehensive as the word "among" is, it may very properly be restricted to that commerce which concerns more States than one. The phrase is not one which would probably have been selected to indicate the completely interior traffic of a State. [The] enumeration presupposes something not enumerated; and that something, if we regard the language or the subject of the sentence, must be the exclusively internal commerce of a State. The genius and character of the whole government seem to be, that its action is to be applied to all the external concerns of the nation, and to those internal concerns which affect the States generally; but not to those which are completely within a particular State, which do not affect other States, and with which it is not necessary to interfere, for the purpose of executing some of the general powers of the government. The completely internal commerce of a State, then, may be considered as reserved for the State itself.

But, in regulating commerce with foreign nations, the power of Congress does not stop at the jurisdictional lines of the several States. It would be a very useless power, if it could not pass those lines. [The] deep streams which penetrate our country in every direction, pass through the interior of almost every State in the Union, and furnish the means of exercising this right. If Congress has the power to regulate it, that power must be exercised whenever the subject exists. . . .

[The states] either join each other, in which case they are separated by a mathematical line, or they are remote from each other, in which case other States lie between them. What is commerce "among" them; and how is it to be conducted? Can a trading expedition between two adjoining States, commence and terminate outside of each? And if the trading intercourse be between two States remote from each other, must it not commence in one, terminate in the other, and probably pass through a third? Commerce among the States must, of necessity, be commerce with the States. [The] power of Congress, then, whatever it may be, must be exercised within the territorial jurisdiction of the several States. . . .

[What] is this power?

It is the power [to] prescribe the rule by which commerce is to be governed. This power, like all others vested in Congress, is complete in itself, may be exercised to its utmost extent, and acknowledges no limitations, other than are prescribed in the constitution. [If,] as has always been understood, the sovereignty of Congress, though limited to specified objects, is plenary as to those objects, the power over commerce with foreign nations, and among the several States, is vested in Congress as absolutely as it would be in a single government, having in its constitution the same restrictions on the exercise of the power as are found in the constitution of the United States. The wisdom and the discretion of Congress, their identity with the people, and the influence which their constituents possess at elections, are, in this, as in many other instances, as that, for example, of declaring war, the sole restraints on which they have relied, to secure them from its abuse. They are the restraints on which the people must often rely solely, in all representative governments.

[Ogden argued that state laws requiring inspections of cargo demonstrated that the power to regulate commerce was not exclusively in Congress.]

That inspection laws may have a remote and considerable influence on commerce, will not be denied; but that a power to regulate commerce is the source from which the right to pass them is derived, cannot be admitted. The object of inspection laws, is to improve the quality of articles produced by the labour of a country; to fit them for exportation; or, it may be, for domestic use. They act upon the subject before it becomes an article of foreign commerce, or of commerce among the States, and prepare it for that purpose. They form a portion of that immense mass of legislation, which embraces everything within the territory of a State, not surrendered to the general government: all which can be most advantageously exercised by the States themselves. Inspection laws, quarantine laws, health laws of every description, as well as laws for regulating the internal commerce of a State, and those which respect turnpike roads, ferries, &c., are component parts of this mass.

No direct general power over these objects is granted to Congress; and, consequently, they remain subject to State legislation. If the legislative power of the Union can reach them, it must be for national purposes; it must be where the power is expressly given for a special purpose, or is clearly incidental to some power which is expressly given. . . .

Powerful and ingenious minds, taking, as postulates, that the powers expressly granted to the government of the Union, are to be contracted by construction, into the narrowest possible compass, and that the original powers of the States are retained, if any possible construction will retain them, may, by a course of well digested, but refined and metaphysical reasoning, founded on these premises, explain away the constitution of our country, and leave it, a magnificent structure, indeed, to look at, but totally unfit for use. They may so entangle and perplex the understanding, as to obscure principles, which were before thought quite plain, and induce doubts where, if the mind were to pursue its own course, none would be perceived. In such a case, it is peculiarly necessary to recur to safe and fundamental principles to sustain those principles, and when sustained, to make them the tests of the arguments to be examined.

[The Court interpreted the 1793 statute to authorize the entry of Gibbons's ferries into New York waters. The New York monopoly was therefore invalid under the supremacy clause, and the injunction was accordingly dissolved.]

Note: Gibbons v. Ogden

1. *The purposes of the commerce clause.* What were the purposes for which Congress was given the power to regulate interstate commerce? Consider the description of the problems under the Articles of Confederation from Justice Johnson's concurring opinion in *Gibbons:* "For a century the States had submitted, with murmurs, to the commercial restrictions imposed by the parent State; and now, finding themselves in the unlimited possession of those powers over their own commerce, which they had so long been deprived of, and so earnestly coveted, that selfish principle which, well controlled, is so salutary, and which, unrestricted, is so unjust and tyrannical, guided by inexperience and jealousy, began to show itself in iniquitous laws and impolitic measures, from which grew up a conflict of commercial regulations, destructive to the harmony of the States, and fatal to their commercial interests abroad." Does this history justify interpreting the commerce clause to do more than authorize Congress to override state laws obstructing the free flow of trade across state and national borders? On this view, does the commerce clause authorize Congress to enact regulations that it regards as appropriate to the development of the national economy?

2. *Limiting the commerce clause.* The commerce clause could be limited in two ways: (a) *"Internal" limits:* The clause might define a specific subject matter, such that Congress would lack power to do anything other than regulate anything other than interstate and foreign commerce. These limits are imposed to protect the values of federalism. (b) *"External" limits:* The clause might grant plenary power to Congress by allowing it to do anything reasonably regarded as regulation of anything reasonably regarded as interstate or foreign commerce, but other provisions of the Constitution, such as the first amendment, might bar the exercise of a power concededly granted. Recall here Chief Justice Marshall's statement in *McCulloch*, Chapter 1 supra:

> Let the end be legitimate, let it be within the scope of the constitution, and all means which are appropriate, which are plainly adapted to that end, which are not prohibited, but consist with the letter and spirit of the constitution, are constitutional. [Should] Congress, in the execution of its powers, adopt measures which are prohibited by the constitution; or should Congress, under the pretext of executing its powers, pass laws for the accomplishment of objects not entrusted to the government; it would become the painful duty of this tribunal, should a case requiring such a decision come before it, to say that such an act was not the law of the land. But where the law is not prohibited, and is really calculated to effect any of the objects entrusted to the government, to undertake here to inquire into the degree of

its necessity, would be to pass the line which circumscribes the judicial department, and to tread on legislative ground.

Does this imply that the courts will enforce both internal and external limits?

The distinction between internal and external limits is closely tied to resolution of questions about judicial enforcement of limits on Congress's powers: It is usually conceded that the courts can enforce external limits such as the first amendment. But judicial enforcement of federalism-based limits is more controversial. Consider the implications of the claim that, although limits such as the first amendment are relatively clear, there are no equivalently clear provisions available for the courts to rely on in enforcing federalism-based limits on Congress's power.

3. *Internal limits.* What "internal" limits might be found in the commerce clause? Chief Justice Marshall considers three:

a. *"Commerce."* Is there a plausible theory under which the operation of a ferry, or navigation, is not commerce? Note that, when discussing state inspection laws, he suggests that they act on the subject "before it becomes an article of" interstate commerce. Does this indicate a retreat from the broad definition earlier in the opinion? This phrase occurs when Chief Justice Marshall is considering whether the national power is exclusive. Does the difference in context explain or justify a difference in definition?

b. *"Among the several States."* Chief Justice Marshall says that the clause does not extend to "that commerce which is completely internal [and] which does not [affect] other States." Later he adds that Congress may lack power only if, in addition to these conditions being satisfied, it was "unnecessary" to regulate commerce. Note the conjunctive form of the statements. Was there such commerce in 1824? Can any commercial activity today satisfy all three requirements? Are the courts in a good position to determine whether congressional regulation of some (arguably or clearly) intrastate commerce is necessary? Whether that intrastate commerce affects other states? Why would giving power to Congress to regulate "completely internal" commerce be "inconvenient"?

c. *"Regulate."* How does Chief Justice Marshall define "regulation"? According to his definition, must a statute, in order to qualify as a "regulation," be directed at commercial goals?

Hammer v. Dagenhart (The Child Labor Case)
247 U.S. 251 (1918)

[In 1916, Congress responded to a decade-long lobbying effort by enacting the Child Labor Act. The act prohibited the transportation in interstate commerce of goods produced in factories employing children under age fourteen or employing fourteen- to sixteen-year-olds for more than eight hours a day, or six days a week, or at night. Two children, one under age fourteen and the other under age sixteen, were employed in a cotton mill in North Carolina. Their father secured an injunction against the enforcement of the act on grounds of its unconstitutionality.]

MR. JUSTICE DAY delivered the opinion of the Court. . . .

[The] power [to regulate interstate commerce] is one to control the means by which commerce is carried on, which is directly the contrary of the assumed right to forbid commerce from moving and thus destroy it as to particular commodities. But it is insisted that adjudged cases in this court establish the doctrine that the power to regulate given to Congress incidentally includes the authority to prohibit the movement of ordinary commodities and therefore that the subject is not open for discussion. The cases demonstrate the contrary. They rest upon the character of the particular subjects dealt with and the fact that the scope of governmental authority, state or national, possessed over them is such that the authority to prohibit is as to them but the exertion of the power to regulate. . . .

[The] thing intended to be accomplished by this statute is the denial of the facilities of interstate commerce to those manufacturers in the States who employ children within the prohibited ages. The act in its effect does not regulate transportation among the States, but aims to standardize the ages at which children may be employed in mining and manufacturing within the States. The goods shipped are of themselves harmless. [When] offered for shipment, and before transportation begins, the labor of their production is over, and the mere fact that they were intended for interstate commerce transportation does not make their production subject to federal control under the commerce power. . . .

It is further contended that the authority of Congress may be exerted to control interstate commerce in the shipment of child-made goods because of the effect of the circulation of such goods in other States where the evil of this class of labor has been recognized by local legislation, and the right to thus employ child labor has been more rigorously restrained than in the State of production. In other words, that the unfair competition, thus engendered, may be controlled by closing the channels of interstate commerce to manufacturers in those States where the local laws do not meet what Congress deems to be the more just standard of other States.

There is no power vested in Congress to require the States to exercise their police power so as to prevent possible unfair competition. Many causes may cooperate to give one State, by reason of local laws or conditions, an economic advantage over others. The Commerce Clause was not intended to give to Congress a general authority to equalize such conditions. . . .

[To] sustain this statute would not be in our judgment a recognition of the lawful exertion of congressional authority over interstate commerce, but would sanction an invasion by the federal power of the control of a matter purely local in its character, and over which no authority has been delegated to Congress in conferring the power to regulate commerce among the States. . . .

In our view the necessary effect of this act is, by means of a prohibition against the movement in interstate commerce of ordinary commercial commodities, to regulate the hours of labor of children in factories and mines within the States, a purely state authority. Thus the act in a twofold sense is repugnant to the Constitution. It not only transcends the authority delegated to Congress over commerce but also exerts a power as to a purely local matter to which the federal authority does not extend. The far reaching result of upholding the act cannot be more plainly indicated than by pointing out that if Congress can thus regulate matters entrusted to local authority by prohibition of the movement of commodities in interstate commerce, all freedom of commerce will be at an end, and the power of the States over local matters may be eliminated, and thus our system of government be practically destroyed.

Mr. Justice Holmes, dissenting. . . .

[If] an act is within the powers specifically conferred upon Congress, it seems to me that it is not made any less constitutional because of the indirect effects that it may have, however obvious it may be that it will have those effects, and that we are not at liberty upon such grounds to hold it void. . . .

[The] statute in question is within the power expressly given to Congress if considered only as to its immediate effects and [if] invalid it is so only upon some collateral ground. The statute confines itself to prohibiting the carriage of certain goods in interstate or foreign commerce. Congress is given power to regulate such commerce in unqualified terms. . . .

[The] question then is narrowed to whether the exercise of its otherwise constitutional power by Congress can be pronounced unconstitutional because of its possible reaction upon the conduct of the States in a matter upon which I have admitted that they are free from direct control. I should have thought that that matter had been disposed of so fully as to leave no room for doubt. . . .

[The] manufacture of oleomargarine is as much a matter of state regulation as the manufacture of cotton cloth. Congress levied a tax upon the compound when colored so as to resemble butter that was so great as obviously to prohibit the manufacture and sale. In a very elaborate discussion the present Chief Justice excluded any inquiry into the purpose of an act which apart from that purpose was within the power of Congress. McCray v. United States, 195 U.S. 27. . . .

The notion that prohibition is any less prohibition when applied to things now thought evil I do not understand. But if there is any matter upon which civilized countries have agreed, [it] is the evil of premature and excessive child labor. I should have thought that if we were to introduce our own moral conceptions where in my opinion they do not belong, this was preeminently a case for upholding the exercise of all its powers by the United States. . . .

The act does not meddle with anything belonging to the States. They may regulate their internal affairs and their domestic commerce as they like. But when they seek to send their products across the state line they are no longer within their rights. [The] national welfare as understood by Congress may require a different attitude within its sphere from that of some self-seeking State. It seems to me entirely constitutional for Congress to enforce its understanding by all the means at its command.

Mr. Justice McKenna, Mr. Justice Brandeis, and Mr. Justice Clarke concur in this opinion.

Wickard v. Filburn

317 U.S. 111 (1942)

[Under the Agricultural Adjustment Act, the Secretary of Agriculture set a quota for wheat production, after finding that the total supply of wheat would substantially exceed a normal year's domestic consumption and export needs. The 1941 quota was approved in a referendum of wheat growers, required by the act, by 81 to 19 percent. Under the quota, each wheat grower was given an allotment. Filburn had a dairy farm in Montgomery County, Ohio, on which he also raised small amounts of wheat for his livestock, for making flour at home, for seed purposes, and for sale. His 1941 allotment was 222 bushels, but he harvested 461 bushels. Under the act, he was penalized $117. Filburn sued the Secretary of Agriculture to enjoin enforcement of the penalty. The lower court issued the injunction.]

MR. JUSTICE JACKSON delivered the opinion of the Court. . . .

It is urged that under the Commerce Clause, [Congress] does not possess the power it has in this instance sought to exercise. The question would merit little consideration [except] for that fact that this Act extends federal regulation to pro-duction not intended in any part for commerce but wholly for consumption on the farm. [Marketing] quotas not only embrace all that may be sold without pen-alty but also what may be consumed on the premises. . . .

Appellee says that this is a regulation of production and consumption of wheat. Such activities are, he urges, [local] in character, and their effects upon interstate commerce are at most "indirect." . . .

[Questions] of the power of Congress are not to be decided by reference to any formula which would give controlling force to nomenclature such as "produc-tion" and "indirect" and foreclose consideration of the actual effects of the activ-ity in question upon interstate commerce.

At the beginning Chief Justice Marshall described the federal commerce power with a breadth never yet exceeded. [Gibbons v. Ogden.] He made em-phatic the embracing and penetrating nature of this power by warning that effec-tive restraints on its exercise must proceed from political rather than from judi-cial processes. . . .

The Court's recognition of the relevance of the economic effects in the ap-plication of the Commerce Clause [has] made the mechanical application of le-gal formulas no longer feasible. Once an economic measure of the reach of the power granted to Congress in the Commerce Clause is accepted, questions of federal power cannot be decided simply by finding the activity in question to be "production," nor can consideration of its economic effects be foreclosed by call-ing them "indirect." . . .

Whether the subject of the regulation in question was "production," "con-sumption," or "marketing" is, therefore, not material for purposes of deciding the question of federal power before us. [But] even if appellee's activity be local and though it may not be regarded as commerce, it may still, whatever its nature, be reached by Congress if it exerts a substantial economic effect on interstate com-merce, and this irrespective of whether such effect is what might at some earlier time have been defined as "direct" or "indirect."

The parties have stipulated a summary of the economics of the wheat industry. . . .

The wheat industry has been a problem industry for some years. Largely as a result of increased foreign production and import restrictions, annual exports of wheat and flour from the United States during the ten-year period ending in 1940 averaged less than 10 per cent of total production, while during the 1920's they averaged more than 25 per cent. The decline in the export trade has left a large surplus in production which, in connection with an abnormally large supply of wheat, [caused] congestion in a number of markets; tied up railroad cars; and caused elevators in some instances to turn away grains, and railroads to institute embargoes to prevent further congestion. . . .

The effect of consumption of home-grown wheat on interstate commerce is due to the fact that it constitutes the most variable factor in the disappearance of the wheat crop. Consumption on the farm where grown appears to vary in an amount greater than 20 per cent of average production. The total amount of wheat consumed as food varies but relatively little, and use as seed is relatively constant.

The maintenance by government regulation of a price for wheat undoubtedly can be accomplished as effectively by sustaining or increasing the demand as by limiting the supply. The effect of the statute before us is to restrict the amount which may be produced for market and the extent as well to which one may forestall resort to the market by producing to meet his own needs. That appellee's own contribution to the demand for wheat may be trivial by itself is not enough to remove him from the scope of federal regulation where, as here, his contribution, taken together with that of many others similarly situated, is far from trivial.

[A] factor of such volume and variability as home-consumed wheat would have a substantial influence on price and market conditions. This may arise because being in marketable condition such wheat overhangs the market and, if induced by rising prices, tends to flow into the market and check price increases. But if we assume that it is never marketed, it supplies a need of the man who grew it which would otherwise be reflected by purchases in the open market. Home-grown wheat in this sense competes with wheat in commerce. The stimulation of commerce is a use of the regulatory function quite as definitely as prohibitions or restrictions thereon. This record leaves us in no doubt that Congress may properly have considered that wheat consumed on the farm where grown, if wholly outside the scheme of regulation, would have a substantial effect in defeating and obstructing its purpose to stimulate trade therein at increased prices. . . .

[Reversed.]

Note: Political Constraints versus Judicial Enforcement

The Constitution's enumeration of congressional powers, including the power to regulate commerce among the states, allocates power between the nation and the states. Is that allocation to be enforced by the courts or through political checks on Congress? Note that both the courts and the political process are imperfect. Courts may invalidate laws that are consistent with the proper allocation, and Congress may enact laws inconsistent with the proper allocation despite the political constraints. Note also that the courts have the opportunity to review only laws Congress has enacted.

1. *Madison's argument.* In The Federalist No. 45 and No. 46, Madison suggests that members of Congress will be so imbued with respect for local governments that they will rarely exercise even broad grants of power improvidently. Do Madison's reasons seem persuasive under modern conditions?

> The State governments will have the advantage of the federal government, whether we compare them in respect to the immediate dependence of the one on the other; to the weight of personal influence which each side will possess; to the powers respectively vested in them; to the predilection and probable support of the people; to the disposition and faculty of resisting and frustrating the measures of each other.
>
> The State governments may be regarded as constituent and essential parts of the federal government; whilst the latter is nowise essential to the operation or organization of the former. Without the intervention of the State legislatures, the President of the United States cannot be elected at all. They must in all cases have a

great share in his appointment. [The] Senate will be elected absolutely and exclusively by the State legislatures. Even the House of Representatives, though drawn immediately from the people, will be chosen very much under the influence of that class of men whose influence over the people obtains for themselves an election into the State legislatures. Thus, each of the principal branches of the federal government will owe its existence more or less to the favor of the State governments, and must consequently feel a dependence, which is much more likely to beget a disposition too obsequious than too overbearing towards them. On the other side, the component parts of the State governments will in no instance be indebted for their appointment to the direct agency of the federal government, and very little, if at all, to the local influence of its members.

The number of individuals employed under the Constitution of the United States will be much smaller than the number employed under the particular States. There will consequently be less of personal influence on the side of the former than of the latter. The members of the legislative, executive, and judiciary departments of thirteen and more States, the justices of peace, officers of militia, ministerial officers of justice, with all the county, corporation, and town officers, for three millions and more of people, intermixed and having particular acquaintance with every class and circle of people must exceed, beyond all proportion, both in number and influence, those of every description who will be employed in the administration of the federal system. Compare [the] militia officers of three millions of people with the military and marine officers of any establishment which is within the compass of probability, [and] in this view alone, we may pronounce the advantage of the States to be decisive. . . .

The powers delegated by the proposed Constitution to the federal government are few and defined. Those which are to remain in the State governments are numerous and indefinite. The former will be exercised principally on external objects, as war, peace, negotiation, and foreign commerce; with which last the power of taxation will, for the most part, be connected. The powers reserved to the several States will extend to all the objects which, in the ordinary course of affairs, concern the lives, liberties, and properties of the people, and the internal order, improvement, and prosperity of the State.

The operations of the federal government will be most extensive and important in times of war and danger; those of the State governments in times of peace and security. As the former periods will probably bear a small proportion to the latter, the State governments will here enjoy another advantage over the federal government. The more adequate, indeed, the federal powers may be rendered to the national defense, the less frequent will be those scenes of danger which might favor their ascendancy over the governments of the particular States. . . .

The Federalist No. 45 (Madison) (1788).

Many considerations [seem] to place it beyond doubt that the first and most natural attachment of the people will be to the governments of their respective States. Into the administration of these a greater number of individuals will expect to rise. From the gift of these a greater number of offices and emoluments will flow. By the superintending care of these, all the more domestic and personal interests of the people will be regulated and provided for. With the affairs of these, the people will be more familiarly and minutely conversant. And with the members of these will a greater proportion of the people have the ties of personal acquaintance and friendship, and of family and party attachments; on the side of these, therefore, the popular bias may well be expected most strongly to incline. . . .

[The] prepossessions, which the members themselves will carry into the federal government, will generally be favorable to the States; whilst it will rarely happen that the members of the State governments will carry into the public councils a bias in favor of the general government. A local spirit will infallibly prevail much more in the members of Congress than a national spirit will prevail in the legislatures of the particular States. Everyone knows that a great proportion of the errors committed by the State legislatures proceeds from the disposition of the members to sacrifice the comprehensive and permanent interest of the State to the particular and separate views of the counties or districts in which they reside. And if they do not sufficiently enlarge their policy to embrace the collective welfare of their particular State, how can it be imagined that they will make the aggregate prosperity of the Union, and the dignity and respectability of its government, the objects of their affections and consultations? [Measures] will too often be decided according to their probable effect, not on the national prosperity and happiness, but on the prejudices, interests, and pursuits of the governments and people of the individual States. [The] new federal government [will] partake sufficiently of the spirit of both to be disinclined to invade the rights of the individual States, or the prerogatives of their governments. The motives on the part of the State governments to augment their prerogatives by defalcations from the federal government will be overruled by no reciprocal predispositions in the members.

Were it admitted, however, that the federal government may feel an equal disposition with the State governments to extend its power beyond the due limits, the latter would still have the advantage in the means of defeating such encroachments. If an act of a particular State, though unfriendly to the national government, be generally popular in that State, and should not too grossly violate the oaths of the State officers, it is executed [immediately]. The opposition of the federal government, or the interposition of federal officers, would but inflame the zeal of all parties on the side of the State, and the evil could not be prevented or repaired, if at all, without the employment of means which must always be resorted to with reluctance and difficulty. On the other hand, should an unwarrantable measure of the federal government be unpopular in particular States, which would seldom fail to be the case, or even a warrantable measure be so, which may sometimes be the case, the means of opposition to it are powerful and at hand. The disquietude of the people; their repugnance and, perhaps, refusal to co-operate with the officers of the Union; the frowns of the executive magistracy of the State; the embarrassments created by legislative devices, which would often be added on such occasions, would oppose, in any State, difficulties not to be despised; would form, in a large State, very serious impediments; and where the sentiments of several adjoining States happened to be in unison, would present obstructions which the federal government would hardly be willing to encounter.

But ambitious encroachments of the federal government on the authority of the State governments would not excite the opposition of a single State, or of a few States only. They would be signals of general alarm. Every government would espouse the common cause. A correspondence would be opened. Plans of resistance would be concerted. One spirit would animate and conduct the whole. . . .

The Federalist No. 46 (Madison) (1788).

2. *Wechsler's argument.* Herbert Wechsler updated Madison's argument in The Political Safeguards of Federalism, in H. Wechsler, Principles, Politics, and Fundamental Law 49-82 (1961; first published in 1954). To Wechsler, "Madison's analysis has never lost its thrust," despite "the rise of national parties [and] the shift to popular election of the Senate." Wechsler began by noting that "national

action has [always] been regarded as exceptional in our polity. [Those] who would advocate [the] exercise [of national power] must [answer] the preliminary question why the matter should not be left to the states." Wechsler augmented Madison's argument by invoking more modern political devices that led the Senate "to function as the guardian of state interests as such," including seniority and the filibuster. As to the House, he relied on "the states' control of voters' qualifications [and] of districting." Even though the President must "balance the localism and the separatism of the Congress by presenting programs that reflect the needs of the entire nation," that office is influenced by localism as well. The allocation of votes in the electoral college affects the allocation of time in presidential campaigns; party rules allocate convention votes based on some localist considerations. To build a winning coalition, a presidential candidate must appeal to groups that "approach balance-of-power status in important states"; some of these groups may promote "local values." For Wechsler, the size of the present national government is attributable "mainly to the magnitude of unavoidable responsibility under the circumstances of our time."

Wechsler drew the conclusion that judicial review was intended to maintain

national supremacy against nullification or usurpation by the individual states. [The] Court is on weakest ground when it opposes its interpretation of the Constitution to that of Congress in the interest of the states, whose representatives control the legislative process and, by hypothesis, have broadly acquiesced in sanctioning the challenged Act of Congress. Federal intervention as against the states is thus primarily a matter for congressional determination in our system as it now stands.

See also J. Choper, Judicial Review and the National Political Process 171-259 (1980).

Kramer, But When Exactly Was Judicially-Enforced Federalism "Born" in the First Place?, 22 Harv. J.L. & Pub. Poly. 123, 127-128, 136 (1998), argues that, for the framers, "Congress would be restrained by politics — not politics in the sense of the sterile structural devices described by [Wechsler] but *real* politics: state officials organizing opposition among the people, establishing committees of correspondence [or] by actively campaigning to unseat unsatisfactory representatives. [The] critical feature of [the] process [that emerged in the 1790s] was a unique system of political parties that linked the fortunes of state and federal officers, and in this way, assured respect for state officers and state sovereignty. The parties dominated intergovernmental relations at least until the New Deal, and they continue to serve this function to an unexpectedly large extent today. But [they] have been supplemented by [other] mediating institutions — the most important of which is an interlocking state-federal administrative bureaucracy."

3. *Some views from the justices.* In Garcia v. San Antonio Metropolitan Transit Authority, 469 U.S. 528 (1985), writing for a majority upholding the constitutionality of the application of federal wage and hour laws to state and local employees, Justice Blackmun wrote,

[The] principal means chosen by the Framers to ensure the role of the States in the federal system lies in the structure of the Federal Government itself. It is no novelty to observe that the composition of the Federal Government was designed in large part to protect the States from overreaching by Congress.[11] . . .

11. See, e.g., [Choper; Wechsler].

The extent to which the structure of the Federal Government itself was relied on to insulate the interests of the States is evident in the views of the Framers. [Citing The Federalist No. 46.] [The] Framers chose to rely on a federal system in which special restraints on federal power over the States inhered principally in the workings of the National Government itself, rather than in discrete limitations on the objects of federal authority. State sovereign interests [are] more properly protected by procedural safeguards inherent in the structure of the federal system than by judicially created limitations on federal power.

The effectiveness of the federal political process in preserving the States' interests is apparent even today in the course of federal legislation. . . .

[At] the same time that the States have exercised their influence to obtain federal support, they have been able to exempt themselves from a wide variety of obligations imposed by Congress under the Commerce Clause. For example, [the] National Labor Relations Act, [the] Occupational Safety and Health Act, the Employee Retirement Insurance Security Act, and the Sherman Act all contain express or implied exemptions for States and their subdivisions. The fact that some federal statutes such as the FLSA [Fair Labor Standards Act] extend general obligations to the States cannot obscure the extent to which the political position of the States in the federal system has served to minimize the burdens that the States bear under the Commerce Clause.

We realize that changes in the structure of the Federal Government have taken place since 1789, not the least of which has been the substitution of popular election of Senators by the adoption of the Seventeenth Amendment in 1913, and that these changes may work to alter the influence of the States in the federal political process. Nonetheless, against this background, we are convinced that the fundamental limitation that the constitutional scheme imposes on the Commerce Clause to protect the "States as States" is one of process rather than one of result.

Justice Powell responded,

Members of Congress are elected from the various States, but once in office they are members of the federal government.[8] Although the States participate in the Electoral College, this is hardly a reason to view the President as a representative of the States' interest against federal encroachment. We noted recently "the hydraulic pressure inherent within each of the separate Branches to exceed the outer limits of its power. . . ." Immigration and Naturalization Service v. Chadha, 462 U.S. 919, 951 (1983). The Court offers no reason to think that this pressure will not operate when Congress seeks to invoke its powers under the Commerce Clause, notwithstanding the electoral role of the States.[9]

8. One can hardly imagine this Court saying that because Congress is composed of individuals, individual rights guaranteed by the Bill of Rights are amply protected by the political process. Yet, the position adopted today is indistinguishable in principle. The Tenth Amendment also is an essential part of the Bill of Rights.

9. At one time in our history, the view that the structure of the federal government sufficed to protect the States might have had a somewhat more practical, although not a more logical, basis. Professor Wechsler, whose seminal article in 1954 proposed the view adopted by the Court today, predicated his argument on assumptions that simply do not accord with current reality. Professor Wechsler wrote: "National action has . . . always been regarded as exceptional in our polity. . . ." Not only is the premise of this view clearly at odds with the proliferation of national legislation over the past 30 years, but "a variety of structural and political changes in this century have combined to make Congress particularly *insensitive* to state and local values." Advisory Commission on Intergovernmental Relations [ACIR], Regulatory Federalism: Policy, Process, Impact and Reform 50 (1984). The adoption of the Seventeenth Amendment (providing for direct election of senators), the weakening of political parties on the local level, and the rise of national media, among other

The Court apparently thinks that the States' success at obtaining federal funds for various projects and exemptions from the obligations of some federal statutes is indicative of the "effectiveness of the federal political process in preserving the States' interests. . . ." But such political success is not relevant to the question whether the political *processes* are the proper means of enforcing constitutional limitations.[11] The fact that Congress generally does not transgress constitutional limits on its power to reach State activities does not make judicial review any less necessary to rectify the cases in which it does do so.[12] The States' role in our system of government is a matter of constitutional law, not of legislative grace. . . .

More troubling than the logical infirmities in the Court's reasoning is the result of its holding, i.e., that federal political officials, invoking the Commerce Clause, are the sole judges of the limits of their own power. This result is inconsistent with the fundamental principles of our constitutional system. At least since Marbury v. Madison it has been the settled province of the federal judiciary "to say what the law is" with respect to the constitutionality of acts of Congress. In rejecting the role of the judiciary in protecting the States from federal overreaching, the Court's opinion offers no explanation for ignoring the teaching of the most famous case in our history.[13]

Note that Justice Blackmun asserted that the political process had in fact protected state interests to a satisfactory degree. The state in *Garcia* contended that, whatever might be true about congressional protection of state interests in other contexts, here the congressional process had failed to do so. What response, if any, could Justice Blackmun offer to that argument? To Justice Powell's reliance on *Marbury*? To Justice Powell's note about individual rights?

Consider this suggestion, from Regan, How to Think About the Federal Commerce Power and Incidentally Rewrite United States v. Lopez, 94 Mich. L. Rev. 554, 557, 560-561 (1995): "[In] thinking about whether the federal government has the power to do something or other, we should ask what special reason there is for the federal government to have that power. What reason is there to think the states are incapable or untrustworthy? [Is there] any reason why the regulation

---

things, have made Congress increasingly less representative of State and local interests, and more likely to be responsive to the demands of various national constituencies. [Thus,] even if one were to ignore the numerous problems with the Court's position in terms of constitutional theory, there would remain serious questions as to its factual premises.

11. Apparently in an effort to reassure the States, the Court identifies several major statutes that thus far have not been made applicable to State governments. [The] Court does not suggest that this restraint will continue after its decision here. Indeed, it is unlikely that special interest groups will fail to accept the Court's open invitation to urge Congress to extend these and other statutes to apply to the States and their local subdivisions.

12. This Court has never before abdicated responsibility for assessing the constitutionality of challenged action on the ground that affected parties theoretically are able to look out for their own interests through the electoral process. [A] much stronger argument as to inherent structural protections could have been made in either Buckley v. Valeo, 424 U.S. 1 (1976), or Myers v. United States, 272 U.S. 52 (1926), than can be made here. In these cases, the President signed legislation that limited his authority with respect to certain appointments and thus arguably "it was no concern of this Court that the law violated the Constitution." 426 U.S., at 841-842 n.12. The Court nevertheless held the laws unconstitutional because they infringed on presidential authority, the President's consent notwithstanding. . . .

13. [The] Court does not explain how leaving the States virtually at the mercy of the federal government, without recourse to judicial review, will enhance their opportunities to experiment and serve as "laboratories."

under consideration should come from the federal government[?]" Should this be supplemented by another question: "What reason is there to think that the courts are better able than Congress to determine whether the states are incapable or untrustworthy?"

4. *Updating the argument.* Kramer, Putting the Politics Back into the Political Safeguards of Federalism, 100 Colum. L. Rev. 215 (2000), argues that, while Wechsler's argument is "flawed and unpersuasive" and has been "robbed" of force by "subsequent experience and later developments," his "core insight is still valid." Kramer agrees with Wechsler's critics that the structural safeguards he identified "(possibly) give state and local interests a greater voice in national politics, but in ways that do not necessarily protect state and local institutions." Kramer argues that federalism, understood as a system in which state governments hold significant governing power, is protected by the national political party system, an institution that the Constitution's framers did not anticipate:

> Making state and national leaders accountable to the same constituents transformed politics by making it politically advantageous to build alliances across formal institutional boundaries. [For] most of our history, the decentralized American party systems [protected] the states by making national officials politically dependent upon state and local party organizations. [The parties] fostered a mutual dependency that induced federal lawmakers to defer to the desires of state officials and state parties.

According to Kramer, this resulted from the nonprogrammatic and decentralized nature of American political parties. "Members of local, state, and national networks are encouraged [to] work for the election of candidates at every level. This [promotes] relationships and establishes obligations among officials that cut across governmental planes." Kramer acknowledges changes in party organization in the modern era but concludes that these changes, often described as ones that weaken the parties, have not eliminated the party system as a safeguard of federalism. Note the difference between Wechsler's argument, which finds safeguards of federalism in specific constitutional provisions, and Kramer's, which finds them in political arrangements induced but not required by the Constitution. Should this difference matter on the question of whether (or the degree to which) the courts should overturn congressional judgments based on the courts' assessment of the impact of national legislation on constitutionally mandated allocations of power between states and nation?

5. *A skeptical perspective.* Cross, Realism about Federalism, 74 N.Y.U. L. Rev. 1304 (1999), argues that "federalism will be selectively invoked by courts only when ideologically convenient, so that it has no authentic restraining power of its own," and treats recent decisions invoking federalism concerns to invalidate national legislation, see sections C and E infra, "as mere stalking horses for an antiregulatory ideological conservative agenda." Cross also argues that the courts are unlikely to provide sustained support for state-oriented federalism:

> For their "rights," [states] are supplicants before a group of courts that are agencies of the federal government. [Judges] ruling in federalism disputes are, like legislators, typically "members of the federal government" with human concerns for "power, prestige, and glory." If the interests of states are not sufficiently represented in the national legislature, they are represented no better in the makeup of the fed-

eral courts. [If] the political safeguards approach to federalism is erroneous due to the hegemonic interests of the legislative and executive branches, how likely is it that those branches will place individuals on the Court who will countermand those interests?

6. *The seventeenth amendment and other constitutional changes.* The seventeenth amendment replaced election of senators by state legislators with direct election. Justice Souter, dissenting in United States v. Morrison, 120 S. Ct. 1740 (2000), argued that the seventeenth amendment, along with the Reconstruction amendments, fundamentally altered the assumptions about the division of power between states and nation. Consider the following argument: In 1789 the framers believed (a) that they were creating a government of limited powers and (b) that the grant of power to Congress to regulate commerce among the several states did not give Congress the power to regulate everything. These two beliefs were compatible in 1789. Belief (b) is no longer accurate, given transformations in the economy, but it is important to maintain the compatibility between the contemporary facts and the overall Constitution. The seventeenth amendment demonstrates that the underlying theory of the Constitution has changed in a way that makes it possible to reject belief (a) and make the Constitution compatible with contemporary reality. How does this argument differ from the "political safeguards" one?

7. *The significance of unfunded mandates.* The Unfunded Mandates Reform Act of 1995, 2 U.S.C. §1501ff (1995), establishes a procedure for consideration of bills that would impose unfunded mandates on state and local governments. Such mandates prescribe rules, compliance with which is costly, but do not authorize the expenditure of federal funds to offset those costs. The act applies to mandates of $50 million or more; it exempts mandates that enforce constitutional rights or antidiscrimination statutory rights. It structures the internal procedures of the House and Senate, with the effect that each House must take a separate and recorded vote on whether to impose an unfunded mandate. Posner, Unfunded Mandate Reform: 1996 and Beyond, 27:2 Publius 53 (1997), argues that the act's primary impact occurs in deterring proposals at the drafting and early consideration stages, and in affecting the timing and structure of mandates. Does the existence of unfunded mandates demonstrate that Wechsler's argument is wrong? Does the enactment of the statute demonstrate that Wechsler's argument is correct?

8. *A procedural perspective.* Justice Breyer, dissenting in United States v. Morrison, 120 S. Ct. 1740 (2000), found it significant, and perhaps dispositive of a constitutional challenge, that Congress "followed procedures that help to protect the federalism values at stake. It provided adequate notice to the States of its intent to legislation. [In] response, attorneys general in [thirty-eight] States supported congressional legislation." Further, Congress compiled "a 'mountain of data'" supporting its legislation. The resulting statutes "focused [upon] documented deficiencies in state legal systems," and Congress "tailored the law to prevent its use in certain areas. [The] law [seems] to represent an instance, not of state/federal conflict, but of state/federal efforts to [cooperate]." The majority responded that Congress's data and findings were irrelevant because they were predicated on a theory of the commerce clause that the Court rejected. Is there a relation between Justice Breyer's procedural emphasis and the idea of political enforcement?

9. *Some objections.* Does the Madisonian argument, as updated to take account of present political practices, meet the objection that modern conditions have altered the political forces on which the argument relies? Consider the impact of increasing mobility among the population (and among people with political ambitions). Note that, in the past, service in state and local government may have been the best method to gain exposure to congressional-district and statewide constituencies, and consider the extent to which candidates may today gain similar exposure by other methods. Is the party system so strong as to overcome localist biases? The power of special interest groups? The power of single-issue lobbies? What is the impact of decisions requiring that states district strictly according to population? Consider the objection that judicial review may sometimes eliminate legislation enacted by Congress that serves the interest of several regions at the expense of the interests of another region, and in this connection consider the implications of the Civil War and its outcome.

10. *The Constitution as structure.* Arguments like Madison's rely on the incentives political actors have as the primary guarantee that legislation will respect constitutional norms. Proponents of term limits believe that altering the incentives legislators have will affect outcomes. The twenty-seventh amendment has a similar purpose. Consider (a) whether designing appropriate incentives for legislators is a more effective guarantee that the Constitution's norms will be respected than is judicial review and (b) the extent to which the Constitution relies on such incentives.

Note: A Comparative Perspective

Consider whether the choice between judicial and political enforcement of federalism limits should depend on the structure of the political system. A Canadian scholar responding to arguments against judicial enforcement of such limits in that nation argues:

> The parliamentary nature of our institutions [imposes] obstacles to the representation of regional interests nationally. [Ministers] are hampered in their ability to act as strong regional spokesmen by [Cabinet] solidarity and party discipline [which] make it impossible for them to speak independently on regional issues or to form coalitions with their counterparts in the other parties. Backbench members are also constrained from working with other parties on regional issues, for party loyalty is a requirement for those seeking party advancement.

K. Swinton, The Supreme Court and Canadian Federalism: The Laskin-Dickson Years 48 (1990).

For a similar concern in the Australian context, see Gageler, Foundations of Australian Federalism and the Role of Judicial Review, 17 Fed. L. Rev. 162, 195 (1987):

> [The] existence of responsible government and a strong party system in Australia may result in the political system affording less protection to state interests than in the United States. [The] argument assumes that the legislative outcomes of individual representatives [acting] relatively independently in the Congressional deliberative process will better reflect state concerns than will those of a cohesive Parliamentary party sensitive to regional electoral responses.

Is it appropriate to rely on analyses of the actual operations of the political system as the basis for constitutional decisions?

C.   THE EVOLUTION OF COMMERCE CLAUSE DOCTRINE: THE LESSONS (?) OF HISTORY

Until the late nineteenth century, Congress rarely exercised its power to regulate interstate commerce. It acted to promote economic growth by establishing, for part of the era, the Bank of the United States; by transferring public lands to private owners; and by securing the nation's borders and its trade against foreign attack. The slavery controversy limited the opportunities for a consensus to form in favor of extensive exercise of the commerce power.

The Civil War and its aftermath inaugurated an era in which Congress began to act more vigorously. The economy became obviously interconnected; problems were no longer localized, so that it became difficult to imagine a purely internal commerce that affected no other states. During the Reconstruction era, supporters of the Union saw that the rights of freed slaves and their friends in the South were not adequately protected by state governments. They concluded that national intervention was appropriate and developed theories of federalism that justified broad exercises of national power. Finally, the mobilization of the northern economy to fight the Civil War showed that national power could be used efficiently, rather than wastefully, and the experience of the Civil War demonstrated that national power could indeed be used to promote liberty.

These factors combined to make Congress more willing to exercise its power to regulate interstate commerce. The Interstate Commerce Act of 1887 and the Sherman Antitrust Act of 1890 illustrate the opening of the new era. Congress's earlier interventions in the economy, such as its disposal of public lands, had not created constituencies that strongly objected to the interventions. But the new regulatory mode of action automatically generated such constituencies in the groups newly burdened by regulation. When these groups objected to national legislation on the ground that only the states could regulate their activities, they could provide relatively concrete examples of how in their view the national legislation threatened liberty and impaired the incentives needed to promote economic growth.

This section opens by examining a number of doctrinal devices that the Supreme Court developed to deal with federalism-based objections to national legislation, and then turns to the abandonment and revival of such doctrines. The legislation subject to review takes two forms. Sometimes Congress imposes regulation on the industry, and sometimes it prohibits the shipment across state lines of goods that failed to meet specified conditions. Do the doctrinal tests differ depending on the form of the legislation? Should they?

Note also that congressional legislation only sometimes was designed to promote commercial goals directly. (Were those goals always the promotion of the free flow of goods?) At other times, Congress acted to promote social goals, which were viewed as valuable wholly apart from their relation to economic development. Are such uses of the power to regulate interstate commerce appropriate?

Are they constitutional? Did the doctrinal tests differ depending on the goal of the legislation? Should they? Is it possible to sustain the distinction between commercial and social goals?

The cases invoked two general approaches. Under the *formal* approach, the Court examined the statute and the regulated activity to determine whether certain objective criteria are satisfied. For example, upholding regulation triggered by the fact that goods cross state lines is a formal approach that ignores actual economic effects and actual legislative motivation. In contrast, the *realist* approach attempted to determine the actual economic impact of the regulation or the actual motivation of Congress. Both formalism and realism were used to invalidate legislation and to uphold it. Can you discern any pattern to the results? Do the availability and use of competing approaches to yield varying results illuminate the question of whether courts should enforce limits on Congress's power in the name of federalism?

UNITED STATES v. E. C. KNIGHT CO., 156 U.S. 1 (1895). The United States invoked the Sherman Act to set aside the acquisition by the American Sugar Refining Company of four competing refineries. The acquisition left only one independent refinery in operation, which produced 2 percent of the sugar refined in the country. The Supreme Court, through Chief Justice Fuller, held that the Sherman Act did not reach this monopoly because the Constitution did not allow Congress to regulate "manufacturing." The government argued "that the power to control the manufacture of refined sugar is a monopoly over a necessary of life, to the enjoyment of which by a large part of the population of the United States interstate commerce is indispensable, and that, therefore, the general government may repress such monopoly directly and set aside the instruments which have created it." Chief Justice Fuller responded, "[T]his argument cannot be confined to necessaries of life merely, and must include all articles of general consumption. Doubtless the power to control the manufacture of a given thing involves in a certain sense the control of its disposition, but this is a secondary and not the primary sense; and although the exercise of that power may result in bringing the operation of commerce into play, it does not control it, and affects it only incidentally and indirectly. Commerce succeeds to manufacture, and is not a part of it. [The] fact that an article is manufactured for export to another State does not of itself make it an article of interstate commerce, and the intent of the manufacturer does not determine the time when the article or product passes from the control of the State and belongs to commerce."

Justice Harlan dissented. Agreeing that it was important to preserve "the just authority of the States," he insisted that it was equally important to preserve national authority, whose "destruction [would] be fatal to the peace and well-being of the American people." To him, a monopoly that "obstructs freedom in buying and selling articles" to be sold out of state "affects, not incidentally, but directly, the people of all the States. [When] manufacture ends, that which has been manufactured becomes a subject of commerce; [buying] and selling succeed manufacture, come into existence after the process of manufacture is completed, precede transportation, and are as much commercial intercourse, where articles are bought *to be* carried from one State to another, as is the manual transportation of such articles after they have been so purchased. [Whatever] improperly obstructs the free course of interstate intercourse and trade, as involved in the buying and selling of articles to be carried from one State to another, may be reached by Congress. . . .

"[In] my judgment, the general government is not placed by the Constitution in such a condition of helplessness that it must fold its arms and remain inactive while capital combines, under the name of a corporation, to destroy competition, not in one State only, but throughout the entire country, in the buying and selling of articles — especially the necessaries of life — that go into commerce among the States. The doctrine of the autonomy of the States cannot properly be invoked to justify a denial of power in the national government to meet such an emergency. . . .

"[To] the general government has been committed the control of commercial intercourse among the States, to the end that it may be free at all times from any restraints except such as Congress may impose or permit for the benefit of the whole country. The common government of all the people is the only one that can adequately deal with a matter which directly and injuriously affects the entire commerce of the country, which concerns equally all the people of the Union, and which, it must be confessed, cannot be adequately controlled by any one State. Its authority should not be so weakened by construction that it cannot reach and eradicate evils that, beyond all question, tend to defeat an object which that government is entitled, by the Constitution, to accomplish."

HOUSTON, EAST & WEST TEXAS RAILWAY v. UNITED STATES (The Shreveport Rate Cases), 234 U.S. 342 (1914). The railway operated lines between Texas and Louisiana. Shipments from Dallas to Marshall, Texas, a distance of 150 miles, cost 37 cents; shipments from Shreveport, Louisiana, to Marshall (42 miles), cost 56 cents. The Interstate Commerce Commission set a maximum rate for shipments from Shreveport to Texas and ordered the railway to charge no higher rates per mile for shipments to Marshall from Shreveport or Dallas in order to eliminate the "discrimination" against Shreveport. The Supreme Court, in an opinion by Justice Hughes, held that the commission could set rates for the intrastate Dallas-to-Marshall route.

Congress's "authority, extending to these interstate carriers as instruments of interstate commerce, necessarily embraces the right to control their operations in all matters having such a close and substantial relation to interstate traffic that the control is essential or appropriate to the security of that traffic, to the efficiency of the interstate service, and to the maintenance of conditions under which interstate commerce may be conducted upon fair terms and without molestation or hindrance. [Wherever] the interstate and intrastate transactions of carriers are so related that the government of the one involves the control of the other, it is Congress, and not the State, that is entitled to prescribe the final and dominant rule, for otherwise Congress would be denied the exercise of its constitutional authority and the State, and not the Nation, would be supreme within the national field. . . .

"Congress in the exercise of its paramount power may prevent the common instrumentalities of interstate and intrastate commercial intercourse from being used in their intrastate operations to the injury of interstate commerce. This is not to say that Congress possesses the authority to regulate the internal commerce of a State, as such, but that it does possess the power to foster and protect interstate commerce, and to take all measures necessary or appropriate to that end, although intrastate transactions of interstate carriers may thereby be controlled."

Justices Lurton and Pitney dissented.

Note: Direct, Indirect, and Stream of Commerce Tests

1. *Intent and Congress's power.* Suppose the government proved that American Sugar intended by its near-monopoly to restrict interstate commerce and not merely production. On Chief Justice Fuller's analysis, would Congress then have power to regulate? Coronado Coal Co. v. United Mine Workers, 268 U.S. 295 (1925), applied the Sherman Act to a strike against mine operators. Carter v. Carter Coal Co., infra, distinguished *Coronado* from *E. C. Knight*: "The acts of the persons involved were local in character, but the intent was to restrain interstate commerce, and the means employed were calculated to carry that intent into effect. Interstate commerce was the direct object of attack; and the restraint of such commerce was the necessary consequence of the acts and the immediate end in view." Reducing the supply of a good is "ordinarily an indirect and remote obstruction" of interstate commerce, but "when the intent [is] to restrain or control the supply" in interstate commerce, the Sherman Act is violated. Is the distinction between *E. C. Knight* and *Coronado* intelligible?

2. *The formalist approach.* Chief Justice Fuller appears to have some temporal sequence in mind as the basis for his exclusion of categories of activities from the scope of the power to regulate interstate commerce: Certain activities, which are not commerce, precede it (manufacturing), and presumably other activities, which are also not commerce, succeed it (retail sales?). Does Chief Justice Fuller explain why the relevant temporal line is drawn to exclude manufacturing, rather than at an earlier point, such as acquisition of raw materials?

3. *National power where state cannot effectively act.* The monopolist in *E. C. Knight* conceded that New Jersey could prohibit locally chartered corporations from acquiring monopolies. Note that, so long as a single state is willing to allow its corporations to acquire monopolies — for example, in exchange for an annual tax that is less than the monopolistic profits — the practical consequence of American Sugar's position is to make it impossible to have effective antimonopoly legislation for manufacturing. Does the inability of any single state or group of states to control manufacturing monopolies justify finding power in Congress to do so?

4. *"Stream of commerce."* Stafford v. Wallace, 258 U.S. 495 (1922), involved the Packers and Stockyards Act of 1921, which authorized the Secretary of Commerce to regulate rates and prescribe standards for the operation of stockyards where livestock was kept for sale or shipment in interstate commerce. Chief Justice Taft's opinion for the Court upholding the act said that the "only question [is] whether the business done in the stockyards between the receipt of the live stock in the yards and the shipment of them therefrom is a part of interstate commerce. [The] stockyards are but a throat through which the current flows, and the transactions which occur therein are only incident to this current from the West to the East, and from one State to another. Such transactions can not be separated from the movement to which they contribute and necessarily take on its character." Is the metaphor of a "current" or "stream of commerce" helpful? How do you know when a stream begins and ends? Why doesn't *Stafford* involve

two streams of commerce, one ending with the arrival of the cattle at the stock-yards and the other beginning with their departure?

5. *Consistent precedents?* As Congress began to regulate the national economy more extensively, the Supreme Court generally focused on practical reality and found that Congress had exercised its power in accordance with the Constitution. In addition to the principal cases, see Southern Railway v. United States, 222 U.S. 20 (1911) (upholding Federal Safety Appliance Act as applied to railroad cars with defective couplers because, although the cars were used in intrastate traffic, the act applied to cars "used on any railroad engaged in interstate commerce"). Even *E. C. Knight* had limited effects. Swift & Co. v. United States, 196 U.S. 375 (1905), sustained the application of the Sherman Act to meat dealers, invoking the "current of commerce" metaphor and calling interstate commerce "not a technical legal conception, but a practical one."

In the next case, a version of formalism leads to upholding a statute, whereas in Hammer v. Dagenhart, supra, a version of realism led to invalidating a statute. Are these versions sufficiently similar to the ones you have already examined to justify treating "formalism" and "realism" as unifying themes?

CHAMPION v. AMES (The Lottery Case), 188 U.S. 321 (1903). The Federal Lottery Act of 1895 prohibited the interstate transportation of foreign lottery tickets. Champion was indicted for shipping a box of Paraguayan lottery tickets from Texas to California. In an opinion by Justice Harlan, the Supreme Court rejected his challenge to the constitutionality of the act. Justice Harlan's opinion stated, "[Undoubtedly,] the carrying from one State to another by independent carriers of things or commodities that are ordinary subjects of traffic, and which have in themselves a recognized value in money, constitutes interstate commerce."

Harlan continued, "[It] is said that the statute in question does not regulate the carrying of lottery tickets from State to State, but by punishing those who cause them to be so carried Congress in effect prohibits such carrying. [If] lottery traffic, *carried on through interstate commerce,* is a matter of which Congress may take cognizance and over which its power may be exerted, [may] not Congress, for the protection of the people of all the States, [devise] such means, within the scope of the Constitution, and not prohibited by it, as will drive that traffic out of commerce among the States? . . .

"[It] must not be forgotten that the power of Congress to regulate commerce among the States is plenary, is complete in itself, and is subject to no limitations except such as may be found in the Constitution. [What] clause can be cited which, in any degree, countenances the suggestion that one may, of right, carry or cause to be carried from one State to another that which will harm the public morals? [Surely] it will not be said to be a part of any one's liberty, as recognized by the supreme law of the land, that he shall be allowed to introduce into commerce among the States an element that will be confessedly injurious to the public morals."

According to Justice Harlan, "Congress [does] not assume to interfere with traffic or commerce in lottery tickets carried on exclusively within the limits of any State, but has in view only commerce of that kind among the several States. It has not assumed to interfere with the completely internal affairs of any State, and has only legislated in respect of a matter which concerns the people of the United States. As a State may, for the purpose of guarding the morals of its own people, forbid all sales of lottery tickets within its limits, so Congress, for the purpose of guarding the people of the United States against the 'widespread pestilence of lotteries' and to protect the commerce which concerns all the States, may prohibit the carrying of lottery tickets from one State to another. In legislating upon the subject of the traffic in lottery tickets, as carried on through interstate commerce, Congress only supplemented the action of those States — perhaps all of them — which, for the protection of the public morals, prohibit the drawing of lotteries, as well as the sale or circulation of lottery tickets, within their respective limits. It said, in effect, that it would not permit the declared policy of the States, which sought to protect their people against the mischiefs of the lottery business, to be overthrown or disregarded by the agency of interstate commerce."

The opinion concluded, "It is said, however, that if, in order to suppress lotteries carried on through interstate commerce, Congress may exclude lottery tickets from such commerce, that principle leads necessarily to the conclusion that Congress may arbitrarily exclude from commerce among the States any article, commodity or thing, of whatever kind or nature, or however useful or valuable, which it may choose, no matter with what motive, to declare shall not be carried from one State to another. [The] present case does not require the court to declare the full extent of the power that Congress may exercise in the regulation of commerce among the States. We may, however, repeat, in this connection, what the court has heretofore said, that the power of Congress to regulate commerce among the States, although plenary, cannot be deemed arbitrary, since it is subject to such limitations or restrictions as are prescribed by the Constitution. This power, therefore, may not be exercised so as to infringe rights secured or protected by that instrument. It would not be difficult to imagine legislation that would be justly liable to such an objection as that stated, and be hostile to the objects for the accomplishment of which Congress was invested with the general power to regulate commerce among the several States. But, as often said, the possible abuse of a power is not an argument against its existence. There is probably no governmental power that may not be exerted to the injury of the public. If what is done by Congress is manifestly in excess of the powers granted to it, then upon the courts will rest the duty of adjudging that its action is neither legal nor binding upon the people. But if what Congress does is within the limits of its power, and is simply unwise or injurious, the remedy is that suggested by Chief Justice Marshall in Gibbons v. Ogden [quoting the 'wisdom and discretion' passage]."

Chief Justice Fuller, joined by Justices Brewer, Shiras, and Peckham, dissented, arguing that the Court's analysis gave Congress a "general police power" because it amounted to saying "that everything is an article of commerce the moment it is taken to be transported from place to place, and of interstate commerce if from State to State.

"An invitation to dine, or to take a drive, or a note of introduction, all become articles of commerce under the ruling in this case, by being deposited with an express company for transportation. This in effect breaks down all the differences between that which is, and that which is not, an article of commerce, and the necessary consequence is to take from the States all jurisdiction over the subject so far as interstate communication is concerned. It is a long step in the direction of wiping out all traces of state lines, and the creation of a centralized Government."

Note: Prohibiting Interstate Transportation — Proper Regulation or Improper Pretext?

1. *Enforcement of limits again.* Does Justice Harlan define any judicially enforceable limits on Congress's power to regulate by means of prohibiting interstate shipment? Note the concluding citation to Gibbons v. Ogden. What reasons does he suggest for Congress's action? Can its reason for prohibiting the shipment of lottery tickets be distinguished from the usual reasons for exercising a general police power?

2. *Regulation or pretext?* Under the majority's holding, is there anything left to the "pretext" limitation stated by Chief Justice Marshall in *McCulloch?* Should it make a difference that *Champion* involves a regulation whose apparent purpose is not obviously "commercial"? Is there a "commercial" argument for the statute in *Champion?*

If the statute's purpose were to promote moral or social goals, would the use of the commerce power be a pretext of the sort Chief Justice Marshall disapproved in *McCulloch?* Consider that applying a "pretext" test requires a definition of the proper purposes for which a power may be exercised. Did Chief Justice Marshall in *Gibbons* say or assume that the commerce power was limited to commercial purposes? If it is not limited to commercial purposes, how might a "pretext" test be applied?

3. *Concluding remarks.* Does the Court's record from the 1880s to the 1920s on the issues considered here reflect (a) a principled effort to develop a coherent body of law in an area where determining appropriate doctrine is difficult; (b) an unprincipled effort to uphold laws that enough justices thought wise and to strike down those they thought unwise; (c) an effort to ensure that Congress attend to considerations of federalism by developing a doctrinal repertoire that allowed the Court occasionally to hold a statute unconstitutional?

Whatever the Court's intentions, by 1930 it had at hand a group of precedents that gave it substantial flexibility in assessing the constitutionality of Congress's efforts to regulate the economy. Over the following decade, those precedents were applied and then abandoned.

Note: The New Deal Crisis

As soon as Franklin D. Roosevelt took office in 1933, he proposed — and Congress quickly enacted — a series of statutes designed to ameliorate the consequences of the ongoing economic crisis and to stabilize the economy so that such a severe crisis could not recur. It was possible to find analogues in the past for each specific item of legislation, yet their sheer numbers, the swiftness with which they were enacted, and the sense of national crisis joined to make the New Deal legislation unprecedented in an important sense.

Much of the legislation interfered with what many had come to regard as the prerogatives of private property and, incidentally, the proper domain of the states. The New Deal statutes were sure to generate challenges to their constitutionality. Supporters of the statutes, and those who attacked them, could draw on a complex, well-developed, and not entirely coherent body of law regarding the extent of Congress's power to regulate interstate commerce. (In addition, a similarly complex and not entirely coherent body of law existed regarding external limits — notably the due process clause — on Congress's power.)

In 1934 and 1935, the first challenges reached the Supreme Court. A useful discussion of the overall litigation is P. Irons, The New Deal Lawyers (1982). The Court's first signals were mixed. By five-to-four votes, the Court rejected challenges to state legislation designed to alleviate the effects of the Depression in Home Building & Loan Association v. Blaisdell, 290 U.S. 398 (1934) (obligation of contracts clause), and Nebbia v. New York, 291 U.S. 502 (1934) (due process clause). It also upheld the Roosevelt administration's repudiation of contractual duties to repay debts in gold, Norman v. Baltimore & Ohio Railroad, 294 U.S. 240 (1935). But the Court invalidated a portion of the National Industrial Recovery Act of 1933, holding that the act excessively delegated power to the President, Panama Refining Co. v. Ryan, 293 U.S. 388 (1935).

Railroad Retirement Board v. Alton Railroad Co., 295 U.S. 330 (1935), foreshadowed what was to come. There, the Court invalidated the Railroad Retirement Act of 1934. Justice Roberts's opinion for a five-person majority held that, though Congress had power to regulate the safety of railroad operation, it lacked power to establish a compulsory retirement and pension plan. Such a plan was not "related to efficiency of transportation" and was too "remote from any regulation of commerce as such." Three weeks later the Court decided the *Schechter* case, invalidating the National Industrial Recovery Act of 1933, in many ways the conceptual centerpiece of the New Deal recovery program.

A. L. A. SCHECHTER POULTRY CORP. v. UNITED STATES, 295 U.S. 495 (1935). The National Industrial Recovery Act authorized the President to approve "codes of fair competition" developed by boards from various industries. President Roosevelt approved a Live Poultry Code applicable in metropolitan New York, the largest live poultry market in the country. The code established a forty-hour work week and a minimum wage of 50 cents per hour; it prohibited child labor and established the right of employees to organize and bargain collectively. The code also regulated a variety of trade practices.

Virtually all of the live poultry sold in New York was shipped by railroad from other states. After arrival, the poultry was assigned to commission sales agents, who sold the poultry to slaughterhouse operators such as the Schechters. They bought poultry for slaughter and resale. The poultry was shipped by truck from the rail terminals to the Schechters' slaughterhouse in Brooklyn and from there, within twenty-four hours, to butchers who sold directly to consumers. The Schechters were convicted of violating the wage and hour provisions of the code, as well as a trade practice requirement that purchasers buy an entire "run" of a coop, including sick poultry. The Supreme Court struck down the statute.

Chief Justice Hughes's opinion for the Court began by addressing the relation between the Constitution and "the grave national crisis with which Congress was confronted. Undoubtedly, the conditions to which power is addressed are always to be considered when the exercise of power is challenged. Extraordinary conditions may call for extraordinary remedies. But [extraordinary] conditions do not create or enlarge constitutional power. The Constitution established a national government with powers deemed to be adequate, [but] these powers of the national government are limited by the constitutional grants. Those who act under these grants are not at liberty to transcend the imposed limits because they believe that more or different power is necessary. Such assertions of extraconstitutional authority were anticipated and precluded by the explicit terms of the Tenth Amendment."

Turning to the application of the Live Poultry Code to intrastate transctions, Chief Justice Hughes first asked whether these transactions were *"in"* interstate commerce. "Much is made of the fact that almost all the poultry coming to New York is sent there from other States. But [when] defendants had made their purchases, [the] poultry was trucked to their slaughterhouses in Brooklyn for local disposition. The interstate transactions in relation to that poultry then ended. Defendants held the poultry at their slaughterhouse markets for slaughter and local sale to retail dealers and butchers who in turn sold directly to consumers. Neither the slaughtering nor the sales by defendants were transactions in interstate commerce.

"The undisputed facts thus afford no warrant for the argument that the poultry handled by defendants at their slaughterhouse markets was in a *'current'* or *'flow'* of interstate commerce and was thus subject to congressional regulation. The mere fact that there may be a constant flow of commodities into a State does not mean that the flow continues after the property has arrived and has become commingled with the mass of property within the State and is there held solely for local disposition and use. So far as the poultry here in question is concerned, the flow in interstate commerce had ceased. [Hence], decisions which deal with a stream of interstate commerce — where goods come to rest within a State temporarily and are later to go forward in interstate commerce — [are] not applicable here."

Next Chief Justice Hughes asked whether the transactions "directly *'affect'* interstate commerce. [In] determining how far the federal government may go in controlling intrastate transactions upon the ground that they 'affect' interstate commerce, there is a necessary and well-established distinction between direct and indirect effects. [Direct] effects are illustrated by [the] effect of failure to use prescribed safety appliances on railroads which are the highways of both interstate and intrastate commerce, [and] the fixing of rates for intrastate transportation which unjustly discriminate against interstate commerce. But where the effect of intrastate transactions upon interstate commerce is merely indirect, such transactions remain within the domain of state power. If the commerce clause were construed to reach all enterprises and transactions which could be said to have an indirect effect upon interstate commerce, the federal authority would embrace practically all the activities of the people and the authority of the State over its domestic concerns would exist only by sufferance of the federal government. Indeed, on such a theory, even the development of the State's commercial facilities would be subject to federal control."

The wage and hours provisions "are imposed in order to govern the details of defendants' management of their local business. The persons employed in slaughtering and selling in local trade are not employed in interstate commerce.

Their hours and wages have no direct relation to interstate commerce. [This] appears from an examination of the considerations urged by the Government with respect to conditions in the poultry trade. Thus, the Government argues that hours and wages affect prices; that slaughterhouse men sell at a small margin above operating costs; that labor represents 50 to 60 per cent. of these costs; that a slaughterhouse operator paying lower wages or reducing his cost by exacting long hours of work, translates his saving into lower prices; that this results in demands for a cheaper grade of goods; and that the cutting of prices brings about a demoralization of the price structure. [The] argument of the Government proves too much. If the federal government may determine the wages and hours of employees in the internal commerce of a State, because of their relation to cost and prices and their indirect effect upon interstate commerce, it would seem that a similar control might be exerted over other elements of cost, also affecting prices. . . ."

The opinion concluded, "It is not the province of the Court to consider the economic advantages or disadvantages of [a] centralized system. It is sufficient to say that the Federal Constitution does not provide for it. Our growth and development have called for wide use of the commerce power of the federal government in its control over the expanded activities of interstate commerce, and in protecting that commerce from burdens, interferences, and conspiracies to restrain and monopolize it. But the authority of the federal government may not be pushed to such an extreme as to destroy the distinction, which the commerce clause itself establishes, between commerce 'among the several States' and the internal concerns of a State. [Stress] is laid upon the great importance of maintaining wage distributions which would provide the necessary stimulus in starting 'the cumulative forces making for expanding commercial activity.' Without in any way disparaging this motive, it is enough to say that the recuperative efforts of the federal government must be made in a manner consistent with the authority granted by the Constitution."

Justice Cardozo, joined by Justice Stone, concurred: "[There] is a view of causation that would obliterate the distinction between what is national and what is local in the activities of commerce. Motion at the outer rim is communicated perceptibly, though minutely, to recording instruments at the center. A society such as ours 'is an elastic medium which transmits all tremors throughout its territory; the only question is of their size.' Per Learned Hand, J., in the court below. The law is not indifferent to considerations of degree. Activities local in their immediacy do not become interstate and national because of distant repercussions. What is near and what is distant may at times be uncertain. There is no penumbra of uncertainty obscuring judgment here. To find immediacy or directness here is to find it almost everywhere. If centripetal forces are to be isolated to the exclusion of the forces that oppose and counteract them, there will be an end to our federal system."

CARTER v. CARTER COAL CO., 298 U.S. 238 (1936). The Bituminous Coal Conservation Act of 1935 was intended to stabilize the industry during a period of sustained industrial crisis. The first section of the act contained a long recitation of the importance of coal to the national economy, the need for "just and rational relations" between labor and management, and the existence of inefficient practices that "directly affect[ed] interstate commerce." The act established a system of local coal boards to set minimum prices, with variations for particular mines as each board thought appropriate. The boards were to administer a code that allowed employees to bargain collectively. Once a sufficient number of collective bargaining agreements had been negotiated, their wage and hour terms would bind all mine operators in the area. A stockholder in Carter Coal sued to enjoin the company from complying with the code. The Court, in an opinion by Justice Sutherland, invalidated the statute's labor provisions. Holding that those provisions were not severable from the price-fixing provisions, the Court did not discuss the price-fixing provisions separately.

Justice Sutherland said that "the recitals contained in [the first section of] the act plainly suggest that its makers were of opinion that its constitutionality could be sustained under some general federal power, thought to exist, apart from the specific grants of the Constitution. [These] affirmations [do] not constitute an exertion of the *will* of Congress which is legislation, but a recital of considerations which in the *opinion* of that body existed and justified the expression of its will in the present act. Nevertheless, this preamble may not be disregarded. On the contrary it is important, because it makes clear, except for the pure assumption that the conditions described 'directly' affect interstate commerce, that the powers which Congress undertook to exercise are not specific but of the most general character — namely, to protect the general public interest and the health and comfort of the people, to conserve privately-owned coal, maintain just relations between producers and employees and others, and promote the general welfare, by controlling nation-wide production and distribution of coal. These, it may be conceded, are objects of great worth; but are they ends, the attainment of which has been committed by the Constitution to the federal government?"

Justice Sutherland continued, "The ruling and firmly established principle is that the powers which the general government may exercise are only those specifically enumerated in the Constitution, and such implied powers as are necessary and proper to carry into effect the enumerated powers. Whether the end sought to be attained by an act of Congress is legitimate is wholly a matter of constitutional power and not at all of legislative discretion. [The] distinction between these two things — power and discretion — is not only very plain but very important. Thus, it may be said that to a constitutional end many ways are open; but to an end not within the terms of the Constitution, all ways are closed. . . .

"[Every] journey to a forbidden end begins with the first step; and the danger of such a step by the federal government in the direction of taking over the powers of the states is that the end of the journey may find the states so despoiled of their powers, or — what may amount to the same thing — so relieved of the responsibilities which possession of the powers necessarily enjoins, as to reduce them to little more than geographical subdivisions of the national domain. It is safe to say that if, when the Constitution was under consideration, it had been thought that any such danger lurked behind its plain words, it would never have been ratified. . . ."

For Sutherland, "[the] word 'commerce' is the equivalent of the phrase 'intercourse for the purposes of trade.' Plainly, the incidents leading up to and culminating in the mining of coal do not constitute such intercourse. The employment of men, the fixing of their wages, hours of labor and working conditions, the bargaining in respect of these things — whether carried on separately or collectively — each and all constitute intercourse for the purposes of production, not of trade. [Extraction] of coal from the mine is the aim and the completed result of local activities. Commerce in the coal mined is not brought into being by force of these activities, but by negotiations, agreements, and circumstances entirely apart from production. Mining brings the subject matter of commerce into existence. Commerce disposes of it." Citing *Schechter*, Justice Sutherland continued, "Everything which moves in interstate commerce has had a local origin. Without local production somewhere, interstate commerce, as now carried on, would practically disappear. Nevertheless, the local character of mining, of manufacturing and of crop growing is a fact, and remains a fact, whatever may be done with the products."

In discussing the "direct/indirect" test, Justice Sutherland wrote, "Whether the effect of a given activity or condition is direct or indirect is not always easy to determine. The word 'direct' implies that the activity or condition invoked or blamed shall operate proximately — not mediately, remotely, or collaterally — to produce the effect. [The] distinction between a direct and an indirect effect turns, not upon the magnitude of either the cause or the effect, but entirely upon the manner in which the effect has been brought about. If the production by one man of a single ton of coal intended for interstate sale and shipment, and actually so sold and shipped, affects interstate commerce indirectly, the effect does not become direct by multiplying the tonnage, or increasing the number of men employed, or adding to the expense or complexities of the business, or by all combined. It is quite true that rules of law are sometimes qualified by considerations of degree, as the government argues. But the matter of degree has no bearing upon the question here, since that question is not — What is the *extent* of the local activity or condition, or the *extent* of the effect produced upon interstate commerce? but — What is the *relation* between the activity or condition and the effect?

"Much stress is put upon the evils which come from the struggle between employers and employees over the matter of wages, working conditions, the right of collective bargaining, etc., and the resulting strikes, curtailment and irregularity of production and effect on prices; and it is insisted that interstate commerce is *greatly* affected thereby. But, [the] conclusive answer is that the evils are all local evils over which the federal government has no legislative control. [Working] conditions are obviously local conditions. The employees are not engaged in or about commerce, but exclusively in producing a commodity. And the controversies and evils, which it is the object of the act to regulate and minimize, are local controversies and evils affecting local work undertaken to accomplish that local result. Such effect as they may have upon commerce, however extensive it may be, is secondary and indirect. An increase in the greatness of the effect adds to its importance. It does not alter its character."

Justice Sutherland argued that "[the] only perceptible difference between [*Schechter*] and this [case] is that [there] the federal power was asserted with respect to commodities which had come to rest after their interstate transportation; while here, the case deals with commodities at rest before interstate commerce has begun. That difference is without significance. The federal regulatory power ceases when interstate commercial intercourse ends; and, correlatively, the power does not attach until interstate commercial intercourse begins."

Justice Cardozo, joined by Justices Brandeis and Stone, would have upheld the price-fixing provisions, finding the labor provisions severable and the challenge to them premature. "Regulation of prices being an exercise of the commerce power in respect of interstate transactions, the question remains whether it comes within that power as applied to intrastate sales where interstate prices are directly or intimately affected. [Sometimes] it is said that the relation must be 'direct' to bring that power into play. In many circumstances such a description will be sufficiently precise to meet the needs of the occasion. But a great principle of constitutional law is not susceptible of comprehensive statement in an adjective. The underlying thought is merely this, that 'the law is not indifferent to considerations of degree.' [*Schechter*, concurring opinion.] It cannot be indifferent to them without an expansion of the commerce clause that would absorb or imperil the reserved powers of the states. At times, as in the case cited, the waves of causation will have radiated so far that their undulatory motion, if discernible at all, will be too faint or obscure, too broken by crosscurrents, to be heeded by the law. [Always] the setting of the facts is to be viewed if one would know the closeness of the tie. Perhaps, if one group of adjectives is to be chosen in preference to another, 'intimate' and 'remote' will be found to be as good as any. At all events, 'direct' and 'indirect,' even if accepted as sufficient, must not be read too narrowly. A survey of the cases shows that the words have been interpreted with suppleness of adaptation and flexibility of meaning. The power is as broad as the need that evokes it."

Justice Cardozo then discussed the distinction between direct and indirect effects on commerce, in light of the Shreveport Rate Cases. "What the cases really mean is that the causal relation in such circumstances is so close and intimate and obvious as to permit it to be called direct without subjecting the word to an unfair or excessive strain. There is a like immediacy here. Within rulings the most orthodox, the prices for intrastate sales of coal have so inescapable a relation to those for interstate sales that a system of regulation for transactions of the one class is necessary to give adequate protection to the system of regulation adopted for the other. . . ."

According to Justice Cardozo, "Overproduction was at a point where free competition had been degraded into anarchy. Prices had been cut so low that profit had become impossible for all except the lucky handful. Wages came down along with prices and with profits. There were strikes, at times nation-wide in extent, at other times spreading over broad areas and many mines, with the accompaniment of violence and bloodshed and misery and bitter feeling. [During] the twenty-three years between 1913 and 1935, there were nineteen investigations or hearings by Congress or by specially created commissions with reference to conditions in the coal mines. The hope of betterment was faint unless the industry could be subjected to the compulsion of a code. In the weeks immediately preceding the passage of this Act the country was threatened once more with a strike of ominous proportions. The plight of the industry was not merely a menace to owners and to mine workers; it was and had long been a menace to the public, deeply concerned in a steady and uniform supply of a fuel so vital to the national economy.

"Congress was not condemned to inaction in the face of price wars and wage wars so pregnant with disaster. Commerce had been choked and burdened; its normal flow had been diverted from one state to another; there had been bankruptcy and waste and ruin alike for capital and for labor. [There] is testimony [even] by the assailants of the statute [that] only through a system of regulated prices can the industry be stabilized and set upon the road of orderly and peaceful progress. [After] making every allowance for difference of opinion as to the most efficient cure, the student of the subject is confronted with the indisputable truth that there were ills to be corrected, and ills that had a direct relation to the maintenance of commerce among the states without friction or diversion. An evil existing, and also the power to correct it, the lawmakers were at liberty to use their own discretion in the selection of the means."

Chief Justice Hughes agreed that the labor provisions were unconstitutional but wrote separately to say that the price-fixing provisions were severable.

Note: New Deal Legislation and Commerce Clause Tests in the 1930s

1. Schechter's *significance*. At the start of the New Deal, the NIRA was a popular and apparently successful program, less because the codes of fair competition established a sensible regime for developing macroeconomic policy than because the evidence of concerted national action gave the public confidence that something was being done. Over the next two years, however, the regulatory apparatus became much less popular. The codes had done little to stabilize, much less restore, production, and opponents fearing congressional control of the economy obtained injunctions against some codes, which further weakened the program. The act was due to expire a few weeks after *Schechter* was decided, and there had been no effort to extend its life even before the decision. The decision in *Schechter* was thus less important for its precise holding than for the approaches it articulated toward Congress's powers.

What values of federalism are served by limiting Congress's power in *Schechter*?

2. *New Deal economics*. What were the National Industrial Recovery Act and the Bituminous Coal Conservation Act designed to do? Were their provisions well adapted to their goals? Economists usually argue that minimum price statutes promote inefficient uses of resources: The guaranteed minimums lead to excess coal production; because some people who could afford to pay the production price (which must be lower than the prescribed minimum) will not buy at the regulated price, unsold coal piles up. Is Justice Cardozo's response in *Carter* to these and similar arguments persuasive? Note also the manner in which area-wide minimum wages were set. Again, economists usually argue that such methods enhance the economic position of workers, usually in unions, who negotiate the initial agreements, at the expense of nonunionized workers (in other areas or industries) and of the consuming public. Should these arguments, if correct, affect the analysis of the statute's constitutionality?

3. *"Current of commerce."* Why were the chickens not still part of a flow of interstate commerce? Does the Court explain why the flow ended at the slaughterhouses and not, for example, at the butcher's final sale? Or even further at the disposition of the chickens' bones at the garbage dump?

4. *"Direct effects."* Justice Sutherland invokes the *E. C. Knight* approach to directness, treating it as a logical category defined in terms of a beginning and an end to interstate commerce. Justice Cardozo treats directness as he would the tort law concept of proximate cause, in which directness is determined with reference to the purposes sought to be achieved by the test. According to Justice Cardozo,

what are those purposes? Could Justice Sutherland have used Justice Cardozo's test to hold the Bituminous Coal Act unconstitutional? Is Cardozo's effort to distinguish *Schechter* and *Carter* persuasive?

5. *Alternatives to national power.* Justice Sutherland's opinion described an alternative to the use of national power:

> There are many subjects in respect of which the several states have not legislated in harmony with one another, and in which their varying laws and the failure of some of them to act at all have resulted in injurious confusion and embarrassment. The state laws with respect to marriage and divorce present a case in point; and the great necessity of national legislation on that subject has been from time to time vigorously urged. [In] many of these fields of legislation, the necessity of bringing the applicable rules of law into general harmonious relation has been so great that a Commission on Uniform State Laws, composed of commissioners from every state in the Union, has for many years been industriously and successfully working to that end by preparing and securing the passage by the several states of uniform laws. If there be an easier and constitutional way to these desirable results through congressional action, it thus far has escaped discovery.

Consider this argument: No system of government is perfect. One imperfection in the federal system of the United States is that it is sometimes difficult to solve national problems. Coordinated action by the states is possible but costly. Coordinated action by the national government is less costly, but it may threaten important values of a federal system. To Justice Sutherland, the costs of obtaining coordinated action by the states were worth bearing in order to avoid threats to the values promoted by federalism. How persuasive is that argument in general? In the circumstances of *Carter*? If its persuasiveness varies with the context, what are the implications for judicial enforcement of federalism-based limits on congressional power?

Article I, section 10 prohibits states from entering into agreements with each other unless Congress consents. Interstate compacts can be used to alleviate regional difficulties. The affected states can negotiate acceptable agreements among themselves and present them to Congress for approval. Members of Congress representing other states are less likely to tinker with such agreements than they would with a statute originating in Congress. Compacts typically involve distribution of interstate resources such as water and sewage. They have also been used to regulate the penal treatment of prisoners who have violated or are charged with violating the laws of a number of states. To what extent are compacts a satisfactory substitute for direct congressional action?

6. *The New Deal response to the Court.* Because *Schechter* dealt with an activity near the retailing end of the spectrum of economic activity, supporters of the New Deal thought that their program could survive in areas closer to the center of the economy. The Bituminous Coal Conservation Act of 1935 was enacted after *Schechter*. It was invalidated in Carter v. Carter Coal Co. The National Labor Relations Act became effective after *Schechter*, and supporters of the New Deal believed that the Court might hold it unconstitutional. See also United States v. Butler, 297 U.S. 1 (1936), section D3 infra (holding Agricultural Adjustment Act of 1933 unconstitutional as beyond the scope of the spending power); Morehead v. New York ex rel. Tipaldo, 298 U.S. 587 (1936) (invalidating state minimum wage law for women as violating due process).

These decisions, coupled with Roosevelt's massive victory in the 1936 elections, led Roosevelt to propose changes in the structure of the Supreme Court. Seizing on the fact that six justices were over seventy years old in 1937, Roosevelt proposed that one additional justice, up to a total of fifteen, be appointed for each justice over seventy who did not resign or retire. His message to Congress argued that older justices were unable to fulfill their responsibilities, thus increasing the workload of the younger justices. Yet it was widely understood that the real point of the proposal was to increase the number of justices who would find New Deal legislation constitutional, and that the workload argument was essentially a makeweight.

The proposal encountered substantial opposition: It was attacked as disingenuous and contrary to the spirit of the Constitution. (Was it the latter?) During the debate over the proposal, Justice Van Devanter retired. In addition, the Court upheld a state minimum wage statute in West Coast Hotel Co. v. Parrish, 300 U.S. 379 (1937). Justice Roberts, who had voted with the five-person majority in *Morehead*, now voted to uphold a similar statute. The Court had taken a preliminary vote in *West Coast Hotel* before Roosevelt submitted his "Court-packing" plan. A later memorandum by Justice Roberts explained that he had joined the majority in *Morehead* only because those seeking to uphold the minimum wage statute sought to distinguish prior cases, instead of urging that they be overruled. When in *West Coast Hotel* the argument for overruling was made, Justice Roberts agreed with it. Note his position in National Labor Relations Board (NLRB) v. Jones & Laughlin Steel Co., infra, decided while the Senate was debating the Court-packing plan. Roberts's position was widely characterized as "the switch in time that saved Nine." The Senate Judiciary Committee on June 14, after *Jones & Laughlin* and *West Coast Hotel*, emphatically rejected Roosevelt's proposal. The majority leader of the Senate, Joseph Robinson, exerted a great deal of personal pressure on other senators and appeared to have accumulated enough votes to secure passage of a slightly modified Court-packing bill by early July. However, Robinson died of a heart attack before the vote was taken, and the plan was rejected in the Senate in mid-July. See Leuchtenberg, The Origins of Franklin D. Roosevelt's "Court-Packing" Plan, 1966 Sup. Ct. Rev. 347.

Was the New Deal position on national powers completely vindicated by the cases that follow, and by Wickard v. Filburn, section B supra? Should *Schechter* and *Carter* be understood as aberrational deviations from well-established prior law? Should the New Deal cases be so understood? For a vigorous challenge to the post-New Deal expansion of the commerce power, see Epstein, The Proper Scope of the Commerce Power, 73 Va. L. Rev. 1387 (1987).

NLRB v. Jones & Laughlin Steel Corp.
301 U.S. 1 (1937)

[The National Labor Relations Act established a comprehensive system for regulating labor/management relations. It established the right of employees to organize and bargain collectively and created a board to supervise elections and to enforce the act's prohibition of such unfair labor practices as discrimination against union members. The act contained the following "findings":

The denial by employers of the right of employees to organize and the refusal by employers to accept the procedure of collective bargaining lead to strikes and other forms of industrial strife or unrest, which have the intent or the necessary effect of burdening or obstructing commerce by (a) impairing the efficiency, safety, or operation of the instrumentalities of commerce; (b) occurring in the current of commerce; (c) materially affecting, restraining, or controlling the flow of raw materials or manufactured or processed goods from or into the channels of commerce, or the prices of such materials or goods in commerce; or (d) causing diminution of employment and wages in such volume as substantially to impair or disrupt the market for goods flowing from or into the channels of commerce.

The inequality of bargaining power between employees who do not possess full freedom of association or actual liberty of contract, and employers who are organized in the corporate or other forms of ownership association substantially burdens and affects the flow of commerce, and tends to aggravate recurrent business depressions, by depressing wage rates and the purchasing power of wage earners in industry and by preventing the stabilization of competitive wage rates and working conditions within and between industries.

Experience has proved that protection by law of the right of employees to organize and bargain collectively safeguards commerce from injury, impairment, or interruption, and promotes the flow of commerce by removing certain recognized sources of industrial strife and unrest, by encouraging practices fundamental to the friendly adjustment of industrial disputes arising out of differences as to wages, hours, or other working conditions, and by restoring equality of bargaining power between employers and employees.

It is hereby declared to be the policy of the United States to eliminate the causes of certain substantial obstructions to the free flow of commerce and to mitigate and eliminate these obstructions when they have occurred by encouraging the practice and procedure of collective bargaining and by protecting the exercise by workers of full freedom of association, self-organization, and designation of representatives of their own choosing, for the purpose of negotiating the terms and conditions of their employment or other mutual aid or protection.

[The National Labor Relations Board charged Jones & Laughlin with the unfair labor practice of firing employees because they sought to organize a union. The court of appeals held the act unconstitutional.]

MR. CHIEF JUSTICE HUGHES delivered the opinion of the Court. . . .

[Jones & Laughlin] is engaged in the business of manufacturing iron and steel in plants situated in Pittsburgh and nearby Aliquippa, Pennsylvania. It manufactures and distributes a widely diversified line of steel and pig iron, being the fourth largest producer of steel in the United States. With its subsidiaries — nineteen in number — it is a completely integrated enterprise, owning and operating ore, coal and limestone properties, lake and river transportation facilities and terminal railroads located at its manufacturing plants. It owns or controls mines in Michigan and Minnesota. It operates four ore steamships on the Great Lakes, used in the transportation of ore to its factories. It owns coal mines in Pennsylvania. It operates towboats and steam barges used in carrying coal to its factories. It owns limestone properties in various places in Pennsylvania and West Virginia. It owns the Monongahela connecting railroad which connects the plants of the Pittsburgh works and forms an interconnection with the Pennsylvania, New York Central and Baltimore and Ohio Railroad systems. It owns the Aliquippa and Southern Railroad Company which connects the Aliquippa works with the Pittsburgh and Lake Erie part of the New York Central system. Much of its product is shipped to its warehouses in Chicago, Detroit, Cincinnati and Memphis, — to the last two places by means of its own barges and transportation equipment. In Long Island City, New York, and in New Orleans it operates structural steel fabricating shops in connection with the warehousing of semi-finished materials sent from its works. Through one of its wholly-owned subsidiaries it owns, leases and operates stores, warehouses and yards for the distribution of equipment and supplies for drilling and operating oil and gas wells and for pipe lines, refineries and pumping stations. It has sales offices in twenty cities in the United States and a wholly-owned subsidiary which is devoted exclusively to distributing its product in Canada. Approximately 75 percent. of its product is shipped out of Pennsylvania.

Summarizing these operations, the Labor Board concluded that the works in Pittsburgh and Aliquippa "might be likened to the heart of a self-contained, highly integrated body. They draw in the raw materials from Michigan, Minnesota, West Virginia, Pennsylvania in part through arteries and by means controlled by the respondent; they transform the materials and then pump them out to all parts of the nation through the vast mechanism which the respondent has elaborated." . . .

Respondent points to evidence that the Aliquippa plant, in which the discharged men were employed, contains complete facilities for the production of finished and semi-finished iron and steel products from raw materials. [The] iron ore which is procured from mines in Minnesota and Michigan and transported to respondent's plant is stored in stock piles for future use, the amount of ore in storage varying with the season but usually being enough to maintain operations from nine to ten months. . . .

First. The Scope of the Act

[It] is a familiar principle that acts which directly burden or obstruct interstate or foreign commerce, or its free flow, are within the reach of the congressional power. Acts having that effect are not rendered immune because they grow out of labor disputes. It is the effect upon commerce, not the source of the injury, which is the criterion. Whether or not particular action does affect commerce in such a close and intimate fashion as to be subject to federal control [is] left by the statute to be determined as individual cases arise. We are thus to inquire whether in the instant case the constitutional boundary has been passed.

Second. The Unfair Labor Practices in Question . . .

[In] its present application, the statute goes no further than to safeguard the right of employees to self-organization and to select representatives of their own choosing for collective bargaining or other mutual protection without restraint or coercion by their employer.

That is a fundamental right. Employees have as clear a right to organize and select their representatives for lawful purposes as the respondent has to organize its business and select its own officers and agents. Discrimination and coercion to prevent the free exercise of the right of employees to self-organization and representation is a proper subject for condemnation by competent legislative authority. . . .

THIRD. THE APPLICATION OF THE ACT TO EMPLOYEES ENGAGED IN PRODUCTION. THE PRINCIPLE INVOLVED

Respondent says that whatever may be said of employees engaged in interstate commerce, the industrial relations and activities in the manufacturing department of respondent's enterprise are not subject to federal regulation. The argument rests upon the proposition that manufacturing in itself is not commerce. [*Schechter*; Carter v. Carter Coal Co.]

The Government distinguishes these cases. The various parts of respondent's enterprise are described as interdependent. [It] is urged that these activities constitute a "stream" or "flow" of commerce, of which the Aliquippa manufacturing plant is the focal point, and that industrial strife at that point would cripple the entire movement. Reference is made to [Stafford v. Wallace]. . . .

We do not find it necessary to determine whether these features of defendant's business dispose of the asserted analogy to the "stream of commerce" cases. The instances in which that metaphor has been used are but particular, and not exclusive, illustrations of the protective power which the Government invokes in support of the present Act. The congressional authority to protect interstate commerce from burdens and obstructions is not limited to transactions which can be deemed to be an essential part of a "flow" of interstate or foreign commerce. Burdens and obstructions may be due to injurious action springing from other sources. [Although] activities may be intrastate in character when separately considered, if they have such a close and substantial relation to interstate commerce that their control is essential or appropriate to protect that commerce from burdens and obstructions, Congress cannot be denied the power to exercise that control. [*Schechter.*] Undoubtedly the scope of this power must be considered in the light of our dual system of government and may not be extended so as to embrace effects upon interstate commerce so indirect and remote that to embrace them, in view of our complex society, would effectually obliterate the distinction between what is national and what is local and create a completely centralized government. The question is necessarily one of degree. . . .

It is thus apparent that the fact that the employees here concerned were engaged in production is not determinative. The question remains as to the effect upon interstate commerce of the labor practice involved. In the *Schechter* case, we found that the effect there was so remote as to be beyond the federal power. To find "immediacy or directness" there was to find it "almost everywhere," a result inconsistent with the maintenance of our federal system. In the *Carter* case, the Court was of the opinion that the provisions of the statute relating to production were invalid upon several [grounds]. These cases are not controlling here.

FOURTH. EFFECTS OF THE UNFAIR LABOR PRACTICE IN RESPONDENT'S ENTERPRISE

Giving full weight to respondent's contention with respect to a break in the complete continuity of the "stream of commerce" by reason of respondent's manufacturing operations, the fact remains that the stoppage of those operations by industrial strife would have a most serious effect upon interstate commerce. In view of respondent's far-flung activities, it is idle to say that the effect would be indirect or remote. It is obvious that it would be immediate and might be catastrophic. We are asked to shut our eyes to the plainest facts of our national life and to deal with the question of direct and indirect effects in an intellectual vacuum. Because there may be but indirect and remote effects upon interstate commerce in connection with a host of local enterprises throughout the country, it does not follow that other industrial activities do not have such a close and intimate relation to interstate commerce as to make the presence of industrial strife a matter of the most urgent national concern. When industries organize themselves on a national scale, making their relation to interstate commerce the dominant factor in their activities, how can it be maintained that their industrial labor relations constitute a forbidden field into which Congress may not enter when it is necessary to protect interstate commerce from the paralyzing consequences of industrial war? We have often said that interstate commerce itself is a practical conception. It is equally true that interferences with that commerce must be appraised by a judgment that does not ignore actual experience.

Experience has abundantly demonstrated that the recognition of the right of employees to self-organization and to have representatives of their own choosing for the purpose of collective bargaining is often an essential condition of industrial peace. Refusal to confer and negotiate has been one of the most prolific causes of strife. . . .

[Reversed.]

[Justices McReynolds, Van Devanter, Sutherland, and Butler dissented.]

UNITED STATES v. DARBY, 312 U.S. 100 (1941). Darby was charged with violating the Fair Labor Standards Act of 1938. The act prohibited the shipment in interstate commerce of goods manufactured by employees who were paid less than a prescribed minimum wage or who worked more than a prescribed maximum number of hours and prohibited the employment of workers in production "for interstate commerce" at other than the prescribed wages and hours. The district court sustained Darby's objections to the constitutionality of the act. The Supreme Court reversed, in an opinion by Justice Stone.

The opinion said that the act's purpose was "to exclude from interstate commerce goods produced for the commerce and to prevent their production for interstate commerce, under conditions detrimental to the maintenance of the minimum standards of living necessary for health and general well-being; and to prevent the use of interstate commerce as the means of competition in the distribution of goods so produced, and as the means of spreading and perpetuating such substandard labor conditions among the workers of the several states."

Justice Stone's analysis began with this statement: "While manufacture is not of itself interstate commerce, the shipment of manufactured goods interstate is such commerce and the prohibition of such shipment by Congress is indubitably a regulation of the commerce." Responding to the argument that "while the prohibition is nominally a regulation of the commerce its motive or purpose is regulation of wages and hours of persons engaged in manufacture, the control of which has been reserved to the states and upon which Georgia and some of the states of destination have placed no restriction," Justice Stone wrote, "[Congress,] following its own conception of public policy concerning the restrictions which may appropriately be imposed on interstate commerce, is free to exclude from the commerce articles whose use in the states for which they are destined it may conceive to be injurious to the public health, morals, or welfare, even though the state has not sought to regulate their use. [Lottery Case.]

"Such regulation is not a forbidden invasion of state power merely because either its motive or its consequence is to restrict the use of articles of commerce within the states of destination; and is not prohibited unless by other Constitutional provisions. It is no objection to the assertion of the power to regulate interstate commerce that its exercise is attended by the same incidents which attend the exercise of the police power of the states."

Justice Stone continued, "The motive and purpose of the present regulation are plainly to make effective the Congressional conception of public policy that interstate commerce should not be made the instrument of competition in the distribution of goods produced under substandard labor conditions, which competition is injurious to the commerce and to the states from and to which the commerce flows. The motive and purpose of a regulation of interstate commerce are matters for the legislative judgment upon the exercise of which the Constitution places no restriction and over which the courts are given no control. [Whatever] their motive and purpose, regulations of commerce which do not infringe some constitutional prohibition are within the plenary power conferred on Congress by the Commerce Clause. Subject only to that limitation, [we] conclude that the prohibition of the shipment interstate of goods produced under the forbidden substandard labor conditions is within the constitutional authority of Congress."

According to Justice Stone, only Hammer v. Dagenhart was inconsistent with this analysis, and that case "has not been followed. [The] conclusion is inescapable that Hammer v. Dagenhart was a departure from the principles which have prevailed in the interpretation of the Commerce Clause both before and since the decision and that such vitality, as a precedent, as it then had has long since been exhausted. It should be and now is overruled."

The Court upheld the wage and hour requirements as applied to employees producing goods for interstate commerce, defining that category to include employees working on goods that the employer intends or expects to be sent to out-of-state customers. According to Justice Stone, Congress's power "extends to those activities intrastate which so affect interstate commerce [as] to make regulation of them appropriate means to the attainment of a legitimate end, the exercise of the granted power of Congress to regulate interstate commerce. [Congress], having by the present Act adopted the policy of excluding from interstate commerce all goods produced for the commerce which do not conform to the specified labor standards, it may choose the means reasonably adapted to the attainment of the permitted end, even though they involve control of intrastate activities."

According to the Court, these provisions were also "sustainable independently" of the ban on interstate shipment. "[The] evils aimed at by the Act are the spread of substandard labor conditions through the use of the facilities of interstate commerce for competition by the goods so produced with those produced under the prescribed or better labor conditions; and the consequent dislocation of the commerce itself caused by the impairment or destruction of local businesses by competition made effective through interstate commerce. The Act is thus directed at the suppression of a method or kind of competition in interstate commerce which it has in effect condemned as '[unfair.]'"

The opinion also said, "Our conclusion is unaffected by the Tenth Amendment. [The] amendment states but a truism that all is retained which has not been surrendered. There is nothing in the history of its adoption to suggest that it was more than declaratory of the relationship between the national and state governments as it had been established by the Constitution before the amendment or that its purpose was other than to allay fears that the new national government might seek to exercise powers not granted, and that the states might not be able to exercise fully their reserved powers."

Note: The New Deal Legacy

1. *The "realist" approach.* In *Jones & Laughlin* the Court chose the "economic" or "pragmatic" approach to determining whether an activity affects interstate commerce. Recall that in *Wickard v. Filburn*, the Court focused on the national market in wheat, while in *Jones & Laughlin*, it focused on Jones & Laughlin's own steel plants. Are the factual differences relevant to the doctrinal distinctions between *Schechter* and *Jones & Laughlin?* Consider whether the factual differences may have affected the majority's view of the constitutional issue. For a description of the background of *Jones & Laughlin*, see Casebeer, Aliquippa: The Company Town and Contested Power in the Construction of Law, 43 Buff. L. Rev. 617 (1995).

2. *The "formalist" approach.* *Darby* is divided into two parts. Are the analyses the same in both?

a. *Prohibiting interstate shipment.* Congress prohibited the shipment in interstate commerce of certain goods. Does this intrude on state policies in a way distinguishable from the statutes in the Lottery Case? Note that the Court refuses to use Congress's "motive and purpose" as a basis for its constitutional analysis. Can that be reconciled with the "pretext" language of *McCulloch?* Can a "pretext" test ever be applied without the courts' exercising "control" over motive and purpose?

b. *Regulating directly.* Congress directly regulated the wages and hours of employees producing goods for interstate commerce. The Court in *Darby* justifies the direct regulation as a necessary and proper means of enforcing the ban on interstate shipment. Are there any limitations to the use of this technique? Does this approach eliminate all distinctions between direct regulation and a prohibition on interstate shipment, on the theory that direct regulation will always be a necessary and proper method of ensuring that the prohibition will not be violated?

The Fair Labor Standards Act was amended in 1961 and 1966 to cover the wages and hours of every employee of "an enterprise engaged in commerce." The constitutionality of the amendment was upheld in Maryland v. Wirtz, 392 U.S. 183 (1968). Justice Harlan for the Court stated: "Neither here nor in *Wickard* has the Court declared that Congress may use a relatively trivial impact on commerce as an excuse for broad general regulation of [private] activities. The Court has said only that where a general regulatory statute bears a substantial relation to commerce, the de minimis character of individual instances arising under that statute is of no consequence." Is that a fair characterization of *Wickard*?

c. *Unfair competition.* The Court justifies the direct regulation on an "independent" ground, that of eliminating unfair competition. In what sense is the competition "unfair"? Note that, absent the federal statute, paying sub-"minimum" wages was lawful in some states. Paying such wages is "unfair" only in that some states chose to require employers located there to pay higher wages.

3. *Later developments.* Perez v. United States, 402 U.S. 146 (1971), upheld a federal criminal statute prohibiting "extortionate credit transactions" — loansharking enforced by threats of violence. Justice Douglas's opinion for the Court recited the findings Congress had made after a series of hearings, although the statute itself resulted from a floor amendment. With regard to the findings, Justice Douglas wrote, "We have mentioned in detail the economic, financial, and social setting of the problem as revealed to Congress. We do so not to infer that Congress need make particularized findings in order to legislate. We relate the history of the Act in detail to answer the impassioned plea of petitioner that all that is involved in loan sharking is a traditionally local activity." The Court relied on *Darby* to uphold the statute. There, Justice Douglas said, "*a class of activities* was held properly regulated by Congress without proof that the particular intrastate activity against which a sanction was laid had an effect on commerce. [Petitioner] is clearly *a member of the class* which engages in 'extortionate credit transactions' as defined by Congress and the description of that class has the required definiteness. [Where] the class of activities is regulated and that class is within the reach of federal power, the courts have no power 'to excise, as trivial, individual instances' of the class. Maryland v. Wirtz, 392 U.S. 183, 193." Justice Stewart dissented, saying that he could not "discern any rational distinction between loan sharking and other local crime." For him, it was "not enough to say that loan sharking is a national problem, for all crime is a national problem. It is not enough to say that some loan sharking has interstate characteristics, for any crime may have an interstate setting. And the circumstance that loan sharking has an adverse impact on interstate business is not a distinguishing attribute, for interstate business suffers from almost all criminal activity, be it shoplifting or violence in the streets."

4. *Federalism and statutory interpretation.* In *Wickard*, Justice Jackson said that considerations of federalism might affect the courts' construction of a statute: "That an activity is of local character may help in a doubtful case to determine whether Congress intended to reach it." Why? What is a "doubtful case"? In United States v. Bass, 404 U.S. 336 (1971), the Court held that, under the following statute, a defendant could not be convicted for possessing a gun without proof that the gun had been possessed "in commerce or affecting commerce": "Any person who — (1) has been convicted [of] a felony [and] who receives, possesses, or transports in commerce or affecting commerce [any] firearm shall be fined not more than $10,000 or imprisoned for not more than two years, or both." It found the statute ambiguous on the question of whether the "in commerce or affecting commerce" phrase modified "transports" only, or "receives [or] possesses" as well. If it modified "transports" only, the Court said, the statute would have the "curious" effect of criminalizing all possessions and receipts while not criminalizing some (purely intrastate) transportations that result in the criminalized possessions and receipts. Justice Blackmun disagreed: "The structure of the

vital language and its punctuation make it refer to one who receives, to one who possesses, and to one who transports in commerce. If one wished to say that he would welcome a cat, would welcome a dog, or would welcome a cow that jumps over the moon, he would likely say 'I would like to have a cat, a dog, or a cow that jumps over the moon.' So it is here."

HEART OF ATLANTA MOTEL v. UNITED STATES, 379 U.S. 241 (1964). Title II of the 1964 Civil Rights Act provides that "all persons shall be entitled to the full and equal enjoyment of the goods, services, . . . and accommodations of any place of public accommodation . . . without discrimination or segregation on the ground of race, color, religion, or national origin." The statute defines places of public accommodation as those whose "operations affect commerce." It declares that hotels and motels that provide rooms for transient guests affect commerce per se. A restaurant is covered if it serves or offers to serve interstate travelers or if "a substantial portion of the food which it serves . . . has moved in commerce." The Heart of Atlanta Motel sought a declaratory judgment that Title II was unconstitutional. The motel, located in downtown Atlanta, had 216 rooms. It advertised in national magazines and on billboards. About 75 percent of its registered guests were from out of state.

The Court upheld the statute as a valid exercise of the power to regulate interstate commerce. The Court relied on evidence elicited in congressional hearings "of the burdens that discrimination by race or color places upon interstate commerce. This testimony included the fact that our people have become increasingly mobile with millions of people of all races traveling from State to State; that Negroes in particular have been the subject of discrimination in transient accommodations, having to travel great distances to secure the same; that often they have been unable to obtain accommodations and have had to call upon friends to put them up overnight; and that these conditions had become so acute as to require the listing of available lodging for Negroes in a special guidebook which was itself 'dramatic testimony to the difficulties' Negroes encounter in travel." The evidence "indicated a qualitative as well as quantitative effect on interstate travel by Negroes. The former was the obvious impairment of the Negro traveler's pleasure and convenience that resulted when he continually was uncertain of finding lodging. As for the latter, there was evidence that this uncertainty stemming from racial discrimination had the effect of discouraging travel on the part of a substantial portion of the Negro community."

The Court acknowledged that "[in] framing Title II of this Act Congress was also dealing with what it considered a moral problem. But that fact does not detract from the overwhelming evidence of the disruptive effect that racial discrimination has had on commercial intercourse. It was this burden which empowered Congress to enact appropriate legislation, and, given this basis for the exercise of its power, Congress was not restricted by the fact that the particular obstruction to interstate commerce with which it was dealing was also deemed a moral and social wrong." Further, it did not matter that the motel was "of a purely local character" because "the power of Congress to promote interstate commerce also includes the power to regulate the local incidents thereof, including local activities in both the States of origin and destination, which might have a substantial and harmful effect upon that commerce. One need only examine the evidence [to] see that Congress may [prohibit] racial discrimination by motels serving travelers, however 'local' their operations may appear." Justice Clark's opinion for the Court concluded, "How obstructions in commerce may be removed — what means are to be employed — is within the sound and exclusive discretion of the Congress. It is subject only to one caveat — that the means chosen by it must be reasonably adapted to the end permitted by the Constitution. We cannot say that its choice here was not so adapted. The Constitution requires no more."

KATZENBACH v. MCCLUNG, 379 U.S. 294 (1964). This was a companion case to *Heart of Atlanta Motel*. It involved Ollie's Barbecue, a family-owned restaurant in Birmingham, Alabama, with a seating capacity of 220 customers. "It is located on a state highway 11 blocks from an interstate one and a somewhat greater distance from railroad and bus stations. The restaurant caters to a family and white-collar trade with a take-out service for Negroes. It employs 36 persons, two-thirds of whom are Negroes." The restaurant bought about $150,000 worth of food, of which about $70,000 worth was meat bought from a local supplier who purchased it out of state. The restaurant challenged the constitutionality of applying Title II of the 1964 Civil Rights Act to it.

Justice Clark's opinion for the Court relied on congressional testimony "that discrimination in restaurants had a direct and highly restrictive effect upon interstate travel by Negroes. This resulted, it was said, because discriminatory practices prevent Negroes from buying prepared food served on the premises while on a trip, except in isolated and unkempt restaurants and under most unsatisfactory and often unpleasant conditions. This obviously discourages travel and obstructs interstate commerce for one can hardly travel without eating. Likewise, it was said, that discrimination deterred professional, as well as skilled, people from moving into areas where such practices occurred and thereby caused industry to be reluctant to establish there."

This was sufficient to support "the conclusion that established restaurants in such areas sold less interstate goods because of the discrimination, that interstate travel was obstructed directly by it, that business in general suffered and that many new businesses refrained from establishing there as a result of it." The Court agreed that "viewed in isolation, the volume of food purchased by Ollie's Barbecue from sources supplied from out of state was insignificant when compared with the total foodstuffs moving in commerce." The restaurant argued that the Constitution required "a case-by-case determination — judicial or administrative — that racial discrimination in a particular restaurant affects commerce." The Court disagreed. "Here, as [in *Darby*], Congress has determined for itself that refusals of service to Negroes have imposed burdens both upon the interstate flow of food and upon the movement of products generally. Of course, the mere fact that Congress has said when particular activity shall be deemed to affect commerce does not preclude further examination by this Court. But where we find that the legislators, in light of the facts and testimony before them, have a rational basis for finding a chosen regulatory scheme necessary to the protection of commerce, our investigation is at an end. The only remaining question — one answered in the affirmative by the court below — is whether the particular restaurant either serves or offers to serve interstate travelers or serves food a substantial portion of which has moved in interstate commerce." Congress, the Court said, "had a rational basis for finding that racial discrimination in restaurants had a direct and adverse effect on the free flow of interstate commerce. Insofar as the sections of the Act here relevant are concerned, Congress prohibited discrimination only in those establishments having a close tie to interstate commerce, i.e., those, like the McClungs', serving food that has come from out of the State. We think in so doing that Congress acted well within its power to protect and foster commerce in extending the coverage of Title II only to those restaurants offering to serve interstate travelers or serving food, a substantial portion of which has moved in interstate commerce."

Justice Black's concurring opinion applied to both *Heart of Atlanta Motel* and *Katzenbach v. McClung.* "[I] recognize that every remote, possible, speculative effect on commerce should not be accepted as an adequate constitutional ground to uproot and throw into the discard all our traditional distinctions between what is purely local, and therefore controlled by state laws, and what affects the national interest and is therefore subject to control by federal laws. I recognize too that some isolated and remote lunchroom which sells only to local people and buys almost all its supplies in the locality may possibly be beyond the reach of the power of Congress to regulate commerce, just as such an establishment is not covered by the present Act. But in deciding the constitutional power of Congress in cases like the two before us we do not consider the effect on interstate commerce of only one isolated, individual, local event, without regard to the fact that this single local event when added to many others of a similar nature may impose a burden on interstate commerce by reducing its volume or distorting its flow. There are approximately 20,000,000 Negroes in our country. Many of them are able to, and do, travel among the States in automobiles. Certainly it would seriously discourage such travel by them if, as evidence before the Congress indicated has been true in the past, they should in the future continue to be unable to find a decent place along their way in which to lodge or eat. And the flow of interstate commerce may be impeded or distorted substantially if local sellers of interstate food are permitted to exclude all Negro consumers. Measuring, as this Court has so often held is required, by the aggregate effect of a great number of such acts of discrimination, I am of the opinion that Congress has constitutional power under the Commerce and Necessary and Proper Clauses to protect interstate commerce from the injuries bound to befall it from these discriminatory practices."

Note: Federalism and Congressional Motivation

1. *Commerce clause versus (?) fourteenth amendment motivations.* The central issues arising from these cases involve the tension between the evident motivation behind the enactment of the statute — an antidiscrimination, moral motivation — and the use of the commerce power. Those issues arose because the Civil Rights Cases, 109 U.S. 3 (1883), held unconstitutional the Civil Rights Act of 1875, which relied on section 5 of the fourteenth amendment to prohibit discrimination in "inns, public conveyances, . . . theaters, and other places of public amusement." In *Heart of Atlanta Motel,* the Court's opinion observed, "the fact that certain kinds of businesses may not in 1875 have been sufficiently involved in interstate commerce to warrant bringing them within the ambit of the commerce power is not necessarily dispositive of the same question today. Our populace had not reached its present mobility, nor were facilities, goods and services circulat-

ing as readily in interstate commerce as they are today. Although the principles which we apply today are those first formulated by Chief Justice Marshall in Gibbons v. Ogden, the conditions of transportation and commerce have changed dramatically, and we must apply those principles to the present state of commerce. The sheer increase in volume of interstate traffic alone would give discriminatory practices which inhibit travel a far larger impact upon the Nation's commerce than such practices had on the economy of another day." Justice Douglas, concurring, wrote, "A decision based on the Fourteenth Amendment would have a more settling effect, making unnecessary litigation over whether a particular restaurant or inn is within the commerce definitions of the Act or whether a particular customer is an interstate traveler."

Should Congress have relied on the fourteenth amendment instead of the commerce clause? Suppose a member of Congress believed that the 1964 Civil Rights Act actually served the equality goals of the fourteenth amendment and (a) believed that the Civil Rights Cases had been wrongly decided or (b) believed that the Supreme Court in 1964 would have overruled the Civil Rights Cases or (c) was uncertain about the Court's position in 1964. How, if at all, would these views affect the design of the statute? Should they affect the member's vote on the statute in the form actually presented?

2. *The scope of the rationale.* Must there be a connection between the activities found to "affect" commerce and the regulations Congress imposes? Consider in this connection the role played in the analysis by the food Ollie's Barbecue purchased. Do the food purchases demonstrate that the restaurant's actions "affect" interstate commerce? Could Congress require that the restaurant comply with regulations for the disposal by its carry-out customers of their trash? Regulations regarding the maintenance of its lawn and parking lot? Alternatively, is the activity that affects commerce the discrimination? Is racial discrimination in the sale of services a commercial activity?

United States v. Lopez
514 U.S. 549 (1995)

CHIEF JUSTICE REHNQUIST delivered the opinion of the Court.

In the Gun-Free School Zones Act of 1990, Congress made it a federal offense "for any individual knowingly to possess a firearm at a place that the individual knows, or has reasonable cause to believe, is a school zone." 18 U.S.C. §922(q)(1)(A). The Act neither regulates a commercial activity nor contains a requirement that the possession be connected in any way to interstate commerce. We hold that the Act exceeds the authority of Congress "to regulate Commerce . . . among the several States . . . ."

We start with first principles. The Constitution creates a Federal Government of enumerated powers. As James Madison wrote, "the powers delegated by the proposed Constitution to the federal government are few and defined. Those which are to remain in the State governments are numerous and indefinite." The Federalist No. 45. This constitutionally mandated division of authority "was adopted by the Framers to ensure protection of our fundamental liberties." Gregory v. Ashcroft, 501 U.S. 452, 458 (1991) (internal quotation marks omitted). "Just as the separation and independence of the coordinate branches of the Federal Government serves to prevent the accumulation of excessive power in any one branch, a healthy balance of power between the States and the Federal Government will reduce the risk of tyranny and abuse from either front." Ibid. . . .

[The Court reviewed its cases dealing with the scope of congressional power under the commerce clause.]

Jones & Laughlin Steel, *Darby*, and *Wickard* ushered in an era of Commerce Clause jurisprudence that greatly expanded the previously defined authority of Congress under that Clause. In part, this was a recognition of the great changes that had occurred in the way business was carried on in this country. Enterprises that had once been local or at most regional in nature had become national in scope. But the doctrinal change also reflected a view that earlier Commerce Clause cases artificially had constrained the authority of Congress to regulate interstate commerce.

But even these modern-era precedents which have expanded congressional power under the Commerce Clause confirm that this power is subject to outer limits. . . .

[We] have identified three broad categories of activity that Congress may regulate under its commerce power. First, Congress may regulate the use of the channels of interstate commerce. Second, Congress is empowered to regulate and protect the instrumentalities of interstate commerce, or persons or things in interstate commerce, even though the threat may come only from intrastate activities. Finally, Congress' commerce authority includes the power to regulate those activities having a substantial relation to interstate commerce, [*Jones & Laughlin Steel*], i.e., those activities that substantially affect interstate commerce.

Within this final category, [our] case law has not been clear whether an activity must "affect" or "substantially affect" interstate commerce in order to be within Congress' power to regulate it under the Commerce Clause. We conclude, consistent with the great weight of our case law, that the proper test requires an analysis of whether the regulated activity "substantially affects" interstate commerce. . . .

[If] §922(q) is to be sustained, it must be under the third category as a regulation of an activity that substantially affects interstate commerce.

First, we have upheld a wide variety of congressional Acts regulating intrastate economic activity where we have concluded that the activity substantially affected interstate commerce. Examples include the regulation of intrastate coal mining, intrastate extortionate credit transactions, restaurants utilizing substantial interstate supplies, inns and hotels catering to interstate guests, and production and consumption of home-grown wheat. These examples are by no means exhaustive, but the pattern is clear. Where economic activity substantially affects interstate commerce, legislation regulating that activity will be sustained.

Even *Wickard*, which is perhaps the most far reaching example of Commerce Clause authority over intrastate activity, involved economic activity in a way that the possession of a gun in a school zone does not. . . .

Section 922(q) is a criminal statute that by its terms has nothing to do with "commerce" or any sort of economic enterprise, however broadly one might define those terms. Section 922(q) is not an essential part of a larger regulation of economic activity, in which the regulatory scheme could be undercut unless the intrastate activity were regulated. It cannot [be] sustained under our cases upholding regulations of activities that arise out of or are connected with a commercial transaction, which viewed in the aggregate, substantially affects interstate commerce.

Second, §922(q) contains no jurisdictional element which would ensure, through case-by-case inquiry, that the firearm possession in question affects interstate commerce. . . .

The Government's essential contention [is] that we may determine here that §922(q) is valid because possession of a firearm in a local school zone does indeed substantially affect interstate commerce. The Government argues that possession of a firearm in a school zone may result in violent crime and that violent crime can be expected to affect the functioning of the national economy in two ways. First, the costs of violent crime are substantial, and, through the mechanism of insurance, those costs are spread throughout the population. Second, violent crime reduces the willingness of individuals to travel to areas within the country that are perceived to be unsafe. Cf. [*Heart of Atlanta Motel*]. The Government also argues that the presence of guns in schools poses a substantial threat to the educational process by threatening the learning environment. A handicapped educational process, in turn, will result in a less productive citizenry. That, in turn, would have an adverse effect on the Nation's economic well-being. As a result, the Government argues that Congress could rationally have concluded that §922(q) substantially affects interstate commerce.

We pause to consider the implications of the Government's arguments. The Government admits, under its "costs of crime" reasoning, that Congress could regulate not only all violent crime, but all activities that might lead to violent crime, regardless of how tenuously they relate to interstate commerce. Similarly, under the Government's "national productivity" reasoning, Congress could regulate any activity that it found was related to the economic productivity of individual citizens: family law (including marriage, divorce, and child custody), for example. Under the theories that the Government presents in support of §922(q), it is difficult to perceive any limitation on federal power, even in areas such as criminal law enforcement or education where States historically have been sovereign. Thus, if we were to accept the Government's arguments, we are hard-pressed to posit any activity by an individual that Congress is without power to regulate. . . .

Justice Breyer [reasons] that (1) gun-related violence is a serious problem; (2) that problem, in turn, has an adverse effect on classroom learning; and (3) that adverse effect on classroom learning, in turn, represents a substantial threat to trade and commerce. This analysis would be equally applicable, if not more so, to subjects such as family law and direct regulation of education.

For instance, if Congress can, pursuant to its Commerce Clause power, regulate activities that adversely affect the learning environment, then, a fortiori, it also can regulate the educational process directly. Congress could determine that a school's curriculum has a "significant" effect on the extent of classroom learning. As a result, Congress could mandate a federal curriculum for local elementary and secondary schools because what is taught in local schools has a significant "effect on classroom learning," and that, in turn, has a substantial effect on interstate commerce. [Justice] Breyer's rationale lacks any real limits because, depending on the level of generality, any activity can be looked upon as commercial. Under the dissent's rationale, Congress could just as easily look at child rearing as "falling on the commercial side of the line" because it provides a "valuable service — namely, to equip [children] with the skills they need to survive in life and, more specifically, in the workplace." We do not doubt that Congress has authority under the Commerce Clause to regulate numerous commercial activities that substantially affect interstate commerce and also affect the educational process. That authority, though broad, does not include the authority to regulate each and every aspect of local schools.

Admittedly, a determination whether an intrastate activity is commercial or noncommercial may in some cases result in legal uncertainty. But, so long as Congress' authority is limited to those powers enumerated in the Constitution, and so long as those enumerated powers are interpreted as having judicially enforceable outer limits, congressional legislation under the Commerce Clause always will engender "legal uncertainty." [The] Constitution mandates this uncertainty by withholding from Congress a plenary police power that would authorize enactment of every type of legislation. Congress has operated within this framework of legal uncertainty ever since this Court determined that it was the judiciary's duty "to say what the law is." [*Marbury*.] Any possible benefit from eliminating this "legal uncertainty" would be at the expense of the Constitution's system of enumerated powers.

In *Jones & Laughlin Steel*, we held that the question of congressional power under the Commerce Clause "is necessarily one of degree." . . .

These are not precise formulations, and in the nature of things they cannot be. But we think they point the way to a correct decision of this case. The possession of a gun in a local school zone is in no sense an economic activity that might, through repetition elsewhere, substantially affect any sort of interstate commerce. Respondent was a local student at a local school; there is no indication that he had recently moved in interstate commerce, and there is no requirement that his possession of the firearm have any concrete tie to interstate commerce.

To uphold the Government's contentions here, we would have to pile inference upon inference in a manner that would bid fair to convert congressional authority under the Commerce Clause to a general police power of the sort retained by the States. Admittedly, some of our prior cases have taken long steps down that road, giving great deference to congressional action. The broad language in these opinions has suggested the possibility of additional expansion, but we decline here to proceed any further. To do so would require us to conclude that the Constitution's enumeration of powers does not presuppose something not enumerated, cf. Gibbons v. Ogden, and that there never will be a distinction between what is truly national and what is truly local. This we are unwilling to do.

For the foregoing reasons the judgment of the Court of Appeals is affirmed.

JUSTICE KENNEDY, with whom JUSTICE O'CONNOR joins, concurring.

The history of the judicial struggle to interpret the Commerce Clause during the transition from the economic system the Founders knew to the single, national market still emergent in our own era counsels great restraint before the Court determines that the Clause is insufficient to support an exercise of the national power. That history gives me some pause about today's decision, but I join the Court's opinion with these observations on what I conceive to be its necessary though limited holding. . . .

The history of our Commerce Clause decisions contains at least two lessons of relevance to this case. The first [is] the imprecision of content-based boundaries used without more to define the limits of the Commerce Clause. The second, [of] even greater consequence, is that the Court as an institution and the legal system as a whole have an immense stake in the stability of our Commerce Clause jurisprudence as it has evolved to this point. [That] fundamental restraint on our power forecloses us from reverting to an understanding of commerce that would serve only an 18th-century economy, dependent then upon production and trading practices that had changed but little over the preceding centuries; it also mandates against returning to the time when congressional authority to regulate undoubted commercial activities was limited by a judicial determination that those matters had an insufficient connection to an interstate system. Congress can regulate in the commercial sphere on the assumption that we have a single market and a unified purpose to build a stable national economy. . . .

The theory that two governments accord more liberty than one requires for its realization two distinct and discernable lines of political accountability: one between the citizens and the Federal Government; the second between the citizens and the States. If, as Madison expected, the federal and state governments are to control each other, see The Federalist No. 51, and hold each other in check by competing for the affections of the people, see The Federalist No. 46, those citizens must have some means of knowing which of the two governments to hold accountable for the failure to perform a given function. [Were] the Federal Government to take over the regulation of entire areas of traditional state concern, areas having nothing to do with the regulation of commercial activities, the boundaries between the spheres of federal and state authority would blur and political responsibility would become illusory. The resultant inability to hold either branch of the government answerable to the citizens is more dangerous even than devolving too much authority to the remote central power.

To be sure, one conclusion that could be drawn from The Federalist Papers is that the balance between national and state power is entrusted in its entirety to the political process. Madison's observation that "the people ought not surely to be precluded from giving most of their confidence where they may discover it to be most due," The Federalist No. 46, can be interpreted to say that the essence of responsibility for a shift in power from the State to the Federal Government rests upon a political judgment. . . .

For these reasons, it would be mistaken and mischievous for the political branches to forget that the sworn obligation to preserve and protect the Constitution in maintaining the federal balance is their own in the first and primary instance. In the Webster-Hayne Debates and the debates over the Civil Rights Acts, some Congresses have accepted responsibility to confront the great questions of the proper federal balance in terms of lasting consequences for the constitutional design. The political branches of the Government must fulfill this grave constitutional obligation if democratic liberty and the federalism that secures it are to endure.

At the same time, the absence of structural mechanisms to require those officials to undertake this principled task, and the momentary political convenience often attendant upon their failure to do so, argue against a complete renunciation of the judicial role. Although it is the obligation of all officers of the Government to respect the constitutional design, the federal balance is too essential a part of our constitutional structure and plays too vital a role in securing freedom for us to admit inability to intervene when one or the other level of Government has tipped the scales too far. . . .

[As] the branch whose distinctive duty it is to declare "what the law is," Marbury v. Madison, we are often called upon to resolve questions of constitutional law not susceptible to the mechanical application of bright and clear lines. The substantial element of political judgment in Commerce Clause matters leaves our institutional capacity to intervene more in doubt than when we decide cases, for instance, under the Bill of Rights even though clear and bright lines are often absent in the latter class of disputes. But our cases do not teach that we have no role at all in determining the meaning of the Commerce Clause. . . .

The statute before us upsets the federal balance to a degree that renders it an unconstitutional assertion of the commerce power, and our intervention is required. [In] a sense any conduct in this interdependent world of ours has an ultimate commercial origin or consequence, but we have not yet said the commerce power may reach so far. If Congress attempts that extension, then at the least we must inquire whether the exercise of national power seeks to intrude upon an area of traditional state concern.

An interference of these dimensions occurs here, for it is well established that education is a traditional concern of the States. The proximity to schools, including of course schools owned and operated by the States or their subdivisions, is the very premise for making the conduct criminal. In these circumstances, we have a particular duty to insure that the federal-state balance is not destroyed.

While it is doubtful that any State, or indeed any reasonable person, would argue that it is wise policy to allow students to carry guns on school premises, considerable disagreement exists about how best to accomplish that goal. In this circumstance, the theory and utility of our federalism are revealed, for the States may perform their role as laboratories for experimentation to devise various solutions where the best solution is far from clear. See [New State Ice Co. v. Leibman, 285 U.S. 262 (1932)] (Brandeis, J., dissenting).

If a State or municipality determines that harsh criminal sanctions are necessary and wise to deter students from carrying guns on school premises, the reserved powers of the States are sufficient to enact those measures. Indeed, over 40 States already have criminal laws outlawing the possession of firearms on or near school grounds.

Other, more practicable means to rid the schools of guns may be thought by the citizens of some States to be preferable for the safety and welfare of the schools those States are charged with maintaining. These might include inducements to inform on violators where the information leads to arrests or confiscation of the guns, programs to encourage the voluntary surrender of guns with some provision for amnesty, penalties imposed on parents or guardians for failure to supervise the child, laws providing for suspension or expulsion of gun-toting students, or programs for expulsion with assignment to special facilities.

The statute now before us forecloses the States from experimenting and exercising their own judgment in an area to which States lay claim by right of history and expertise, and it does so by regulating an activity beyond the realm of commerce in the ordinary and usual sense of that term. The tendency of this statute to displace state regulation in areas of traditional state concern is evident from its territorial operation. There are over 100,000 elementary and secondary schools in the United States. Each of these now has an invisible federal zone extending 1,000 feet beyond the (often irregular) boundaries of the school property. In some communities no doubt it would be difficult to navigate without infringing on those zones. Yet throughout these areas, school officials would find their own programs for the prohibition of guns in danger of displacement by the federal authority unless the State chooses to enact a parallel rule.

This is not a case where the etiquette of federalism has been violated by a formal command from the National Government directing the State to enact a certain policy, cf. New York v. United States, 505 U.S. 144 (1992), or to organize its governmental functions in a certain way. While the intrusion on state sovereignty may not be as severe in this instance as in some of our recent Tenth Amendment cases, the intrusion is nonetheless significant. Absent a stronger connection or identification with commercial concerns that are central to the Commerce Clause, that interference contradicts the federal balance the Framers designed and that this Court is obliged to enforce.

For these reasons, I join in the opinion and judgment of the Court.

JUSTICE THOMAS, concurring. . . .

At the time the original Constitution was ratified, "commerce" consisted of selling, buying, and bartering, as well as transporting for these purposes. . . .

As one would expect, the term "commerce" was used in contradistinction to productive activities such as manufacturing and agriculture. Alexander Hamilton, for example, repeatedly treated commerce, agriculture, and manufacturing as three separate endeavors. See, e.g., The Federalist No. 36, at 224 (referring to "agriculture, commerce, manufactures"). . . .

[Interjecting] a modern sense of commerce into the Constitution generates significant textual and structural problems. For example, one cannot replace "commerce" with a different type of enterprise, such as manufacturing. When a manufacturer produces a car, assembly cannot take place "with a foreign nation" or "with the Indian Tribes." Parts may come from different States or other nations and hence may have been in the flow of commerce at one time, but manufacturing takes place at a discrete site. Agriculture and manufacturing involve the production of goods; commerce encompasses traffic in such articles. . . .

Put simply, much if not all of Art. I, §8 (including portions of the Commerce Clause itself) would be surplusage if Congress had been given authority over matters that substantially affect interstate commerce. An interpretation of cl. 3 that makes the rest of §8 superfluous simply cannot be correct. Yet this Court's Commerce Clause jurisprudence has endorsed just such an interpretation: the power we have accorded Congress has swallowed Art. I, §8. . . .

[The] substantial effects test suffers from the further flaw that it appears to grant Congress a police power over the Nation [because] of its "aggregation principle." Under so-called "class of activities" statutes, Congress can regulate whole categories of activities that are not themselves either "interstate" or "commerce." In applying the effects test, we ask whether the class of activities as a whole substantially affects interstate commerce, not whether any specific activity within the class has such effects when considered in isolation.

The aggregation principle is clever, but has no stopping point. Suppose all would agree that gun possession within 1,000 feet of a school does not substantially affect commerce, but that possession of weapons generally [does]. Under our substantial effects doctrine, even though Congress cannot single out gun possession, it can prohibit weapon possession generally. But one always can draw the circle broadly enough to cover an activity that, when taken in isolation, would not have substantial effects on commerce. . . .

JUSTICE STEVENS, dissenting. . . .

Guns are both articles of commerce and articles that can be used to restrain commerce. Their possession is the consequence, either directly or indirectly, of commercial activity. In my judgment, Congress' power to regulate commerce in firearms includes the power to prohibit possession of guns at any location because of their potentially harmful use; it necessarily follows that Congress may also prohibit their possession in particular markets. The market for the possession of handguns by school-age children is, distressingly, substantial. Whether or not the national interest in eliminating that market would have justified federal legislation in 1789, it surely does today.

JUSTICE SOUTER, dissenting.

In reviewing congressional legislation under the Commerce Clause, we defer to what is often a merely implicit congressional judgment that its regulation addresses a subject substantially affecting interstate commerce "if there is any rational basis for such a finding."

The practice of deferring to rationally based legislative judgments "is a paradigm of judicial restraint." FCC v. Beach Communications, Inc., 508 U.S. 307, 314 (1993). In judicial review under the Commerce Clause, it reflects our respect for the institutional competence of the Congress on a subject expressly assigned to it by the Constitution and our appreciation of the legitimacy that comes from Congress's political accountability in dealing with matters open to a wide range of possible choices. . . .

[Justice Souter reviewed the history of the Court's commerce clause doctrine.]

There is today [a] backward glance at [the] old pitfalls, as the Court treats deference under the rationality rule as subject to gradation according to the commercial or noncommercial nature of the immediate subject of the challenged regulation. The distinction between what is patently commercial and what is not looks much like the old distinction between what directly affects commerce and what touches it only indirectly. And the act of calibrating the level of deference by drawing a line between what is patently commercial and what is less purely so will probably resemble the process of deciding how much interference with contractual freedom was fatal. Thus, it seems fair to ask whether the step taken by the Court today does anything but portend a return to the untenable jurisprudence from which the Court extricated itself almost 60 years ago. The answer is not reassuring. . . .

The Court observes that the Gun-Free School Zones Act operates in two areas traditionally subject to legislation by the States, education and enforcement of criminal law. The suggestion is either that a connection between commerce and these subjects is remote, or that the commerce power is simply weaker when it touches subjects on which the States have historically been the primary legislators. Neither suggestion is tenable. As for remoteness, it may or may not be wise for the National Government to deal with education, but Justice Breyer has surely demonstrated that the commercial prospects of an illiterate State or Nation are not rosy, and no argument should be needed to show that hijacking interstate shipments of cigarettes can affect commerce substantially, even though the States have traditionally prosecuted robbery. And as for the notion that the commerce power diminishes the closer it gets to customary state concerns, that idea has been flatly rejected. [The] commerce power, we have often observed, is plenary. . . .

Because Justice Breyer's opinion demonstrates beyond any doubt that the Act in question passes the rationality review that the Court continues to espouse, to-day's decision may be seen as only a misstep, its reasoning and its suggestions not quite in gear with the prevailing standard, but hardly an epochal case. I would not argue otherwise, but I would raise a caveat. Not every epochal case has come in epochal trappings. *Jones & Laughlin* did not reject the direct-indirect standard in so many words; it just said the relation of the regulated subject matter to commerce was direct enough. But we know what happened.

I respectfully dissent.

JUSTICE BREYER, with whom JUSTICE STEVENS, JUSTICE SOUTER, and JUSTICE GINSBURG join, dissenting. . . .

I . . .

[The] Constitution requires us to judge the connection between a regulated activity and interstate commerce, not directly, but at one remove. Courts must give Congress a degree of leeway in determining the existence of a significant factual connection between the regulated activity and interstate commerce — both because the Constitution delegates the commerce power directly to Congress and because the determination requires an empirical judgment of a kind that a legislature is more likely than a court to make with accuracy. The traditional words "rational basis" capture this leeway. . . .

II . . .

[Could] Congress rationally have found that "violent crime in school zones," through its effect on the "quality of education," significantly (or substantially) affects "interstate" or "foreign commerce"? As long as one views the commerce connection, not as a "technical legal conception," but as "a practical one," Swift & Co. v. United States, 196 U.S. 375, 398 (1905) (Holmes, J.), the answer to this question must be yes. Numerous reports and studies — generated both inside and outside government — make clear that Congress could reasonably have found the empirical connection that its law, implicitly or explicitly, asserts. (See Appendix for a sample of the documentation. . . .)

For one thing, reports, hearings, and other readily available literature make clear that the problem of guns in and around schools is widespread and extremely serious. These materials report, for example, that four percent of American high school students (and six percent of inner-city high school students) carry a gun to school at least occasionally; that 12 percent of urban high school students have had guns fired at them; that 20 percent of those students have been threatened with guns; and that, in any 6-month period, several hundred thousand school-children are victims of violent crimes in or near their schools. And, they report that this widespread violence in schools throughout the Nation significantly interferes with the quality of education in those schools. Based on reports such as these, Congress obviously could have thought that guns and learning are mutually exclusive. . . .

Having found that guns in schools significantly undermine the quality of education in our Nation's classrooms, Congress could also have found, given the effect of education upon interstate and foreign commerce, that gun-related violence in and around schools is a commercial, as well as a human, problem. Education, although far more than a matter of economics, has long been inextricably intertwined with the Nation's economy. . . .

Finally, there is evidence that, today more than ever, many firms base their location decisions upon the presence, or absence, of a work force with a basic education. . . .

The economic links I have just sketched seem fairly obvious. Why then is it not equally obvious, in light of those links, that a widespread, serious, and substantial physical threat to teaching and learning also substantially threatens the commerce to which that teaching and learning is inextricably tied? That is to say, guns in the hands of six percent of inner-city high school students and gun-related violence throughout a city's schools must threaten the trade and commerce that those schools support. The only question, then, is whether the latter threat is (to use the majority's terminology) "substantial." And, the evidence of (1) the extent of the gun-related violence problem, (2) the extent of the resulting negative effect on classroom learning, and (3) the extent of the consequent negative commercial effects, when taken together, indicate a threat to trade and commerce that is "substantial." At the very least, Congress could rationally have concluded that the links are "substantial." . . .

To hold this statute constitutional is not to "obliterate" the "distinction of what is national and what is local"; nor is it to hold that the Commerce Clause permits the Federal Government to "regulate any activity that it found was related to the economic productivity of individual citizens," to regulate "marriage, divorce, and child custody," or to regulate any and all aspects of education. For one thing, this statute is aimed at curbing a particularly acute threat to the educational process — the possession (and use) of life-threatening firearms in, or near, the classroom. The empirical evidence that I have discussed above unmistakably documents the special way in which guns and education are incompatible. [For] another thing, the immediacy of the connection between education and the national economic well-being is documented by scholars and accepted by society at large in a way and to a degree that may not hold true for other social institutions. It must surely be the rare case, then, that a statute strikes at conduct that (when considered in the abstract) seems so removed from commerce, but which (practically speaking) has so significant an impact upon commerce.

In sum, a holding that the particular statute before us falls within the commerce power would not expand the scope of that Clause. Rather, it simply would apply pre-existing law to changing economic circumstances. See [*Heart of Atlanta Motel*]. It would recognize that, in today's economic world, gun-related violence near the classroom makes a significant difference to our economic, as well as our social, well-being. . . .

III

The majority's holding [creates] three serious legal problems. First, the majority's holding runs contrary to modern Supreme Court cases that have upheld congressional actions despite connections to interstate or foreign commerce that are less significant than the effect of school violence. In Perez v. United States, the Court held that the Commerce Clause authorized a federal statute that makes it a crime to engage in loan sharking ("extortionate credit transactions") at a local level. The Court said that Congress may judge that such transactions, "though purely *intra*state, . . . affect *inter*state commerce." Presumably, Congress reasoned that threatening or using force, say with a gun on a street corner, to collect a debt occurs sufficiently often so that the activity (by helping organized crime) affects commerce among the States. But, why then cannot Congress also reason that the threat or use of force — the frequent consequence of possessing a gun — in or near a school occurs sufficiently often so that such activity (by inhibiting basic education) affects commerce among the States? The negative impact upon the national economy of an inability to teach basic skills seems no smaller (nor less significant) than that of organized crime.

In Katzenbach v. McClung, this Court upheld, as within the commerce power, a statute prohibiting racial discrimination at local restaurants, in part because that discrimination discouraged travel by African Americans and in part because that discrimination affected purchases of food and restaurant supplies from other States. [The] Court understood that the specific instance of discrimination (at a local place of accommodation) was part of a general practice that, considered as a whole, caused not only the most serious human and social harm, but had nationally significant economic dimensions as well. It is difficult to distinguish the case before us, for the same critical elements are present. Businesses are less likely to locate in communities where violence plagues the classroom. Families will hesitate to move to neighborhoods where students carry guns instead of books. [And] (to look at the matter in the most narrowly commercial manner), interstate publishers therefore will sell fewer books and other firms will sell fewer school supplies where the threat of violence disrupts learning. Most importantly, like [local] racial discrimination, [the] local instances here, taken together and considered as a whole, create a problem that causes serious human and social harm, but also has nationally significant economic dimensions. . . .

The second legal problem the Court creates comes from its apparent belief that it can reconcile its holding with earlier cases by making a critical distinction between "commercial" and noncommercial "transactions." That is to say, the Court believes the Constitution would distinguish between two local activities, each of which has an identical effect upon interstate commerce, if one, but not the other, is "commercial" in nature. [The] majority's test is not consistent with what the Court saw as the point of the cases that the majority now characterizes. Although the majority today attempts to categorize *Perez*, *McClung*, and *Wickard* as involving intrastate "economic activity," the Courts that decided each of those cases did not focus upon the economic nature of the activity regulated. Rather, they focused upon whether that activity affected interstate or foreign commerce. In fact, the *Wickard* Court expressly held that Wickard's consumption of home grown wheat, *"though it may not be regarded as commerce,"* could nevertheless be regulated — *"whatever its nature"* — so long as "it exerts a substantial economic effect on interstate commerce." [*Wickard*] (emphasis added).

More importantly, if a distinction between commercial and noncommercial activities is to be made, this is not the case in which to make it. The majority clearly cannot intend such a distinction to focus narrowly on an act of gun possession standing by itself, for such a reading could not be reconciled with either the civil rights cases or *Perez* — in each of those cases the specific transaction (the race-based exclusion, the use of force) was not itself "commercial." And, if the majority instead means to distinguish generally among broad categories of activities, differentiating what is educational from what is commercial, then, as a practical matter, the line becomes almost impossible to draw. Schools that teach reading, writing, mathematics, and related basic skills serve both social and commercial purposes, and one cannot easily separate the one from the other. . . .

The third legal problem created by the Court's holding is that it threatens legal uncertainty in an area of law that, until this case, seemed reasonably well settled. Congress has enacted many statutes (more than 100 sections of the United States Code), including criminal statutes (at least 25 sections), that use the words "affecting commerce" to define their scope, see, e.g., 18 U.S.C. §844(i) (destruction of buildings used in activity affecting interstate commerce), and other statutes that contain no jurisdictional language at all, see, e.g., 18 U.S.C. §922(o)(1) (possession of machine guns). Do these, or similar, statutes regulate noncommercial activities? If so, would that alter the meaning of "affecting commerce" in a jurisdictional element? More importantly, in the absence of a jurisdictional element, are the courts nevertheless to take *Wickard* (and later similar cases) as inapplicable, and to judge the effect of a single noncommercial activity on interstate commerce without considering similar instances of the forbidden conduct? . . .

IV

In sum, to find this legislation within the scope of the Commerce Clause would [interpret] the Clause as this Court has traditionally interpreted it, with the exception of one wrong turn subsequently corrected. Upholding this legislation would do no more than simply recognize that Congress had a "rational basis" for finding a significant connection between guns in or near schools and (through their effect on education) the interstate and foreign commerce they threaten. For these reasons, I would reverse the judgment of the Court of Appeals. Respectfully, I dissent.

[The Appendix, listing over 160 sources, is omitted.]

UNITED STATES v. MORRISON, 120 S. CT. 1740 (2000). The Court held the civil remedy provision of the Violence Against Women Act unconstitutional. The statute, enacted in 1994, provided a damage remedy for the victim against any person "who commits a crime of violence motivated by gender." The statute contains detailed findings, backed up by a substantial legislative history, that "gender-motivated violence affects interstate commerce 'by deterring potential victims from traveling interstate, from engaging in employment in interstate business, and from transacting with business, and in places involved in interstate commerce. . . .'"

Chief Justice Rehnquist, writing for the same justices who formed the majority in *Lopez*, wrote that "[gender]-motivated crimes of violence are not [economic] activity. While we need not adopt a categorical rule against aggregating the effects of any noneconomic activity in order to decide these cases, thus far in our Nation's history our cases have upheld Commerce Clause regulation of intrastate activity only where that activity is economic in nature." Congress's findings "are substantially weakened by the fact that they rely so heavily on a method of reasoning that we have already rejected as unworkable if we are to maintain the Constitution's enumeration of powers. [Given] these findings, [the] concern we expressed in *Lopez* that Congress might use the Commerce Clause to completely obliterate the Constitution's distinction between national and local authority seems well-founded. The reasoning [seeks] to follow the but-for causal chain from the initial occurrence of violent crime (the suppression of which has always been the prime object of the States' police power) to every attenuated effect upon interstate commerce. If accepted, petitioners' reasoning would allow Congress to regulate any crime as long as the nationwide, aggregated impact of that crime has substantial effects on employment, production, transit, or consumption." He concluded, "The Constitution requires a distinction between what is truly national and what is truly local. In recognizing this fact we preserve one of the few principles that has been consistent since the Clause was adopted."

Justice Souter, writing for the four dissenters, observed: "If we now ask why the formalistic economic/noneconomic distinction might matter today, after its rejection in *Wickard*, the answer is not that the majority fails to see causal connections in an integrated economic world. The answer is that in the minds of the majority there is a new animating theory that makes categorical formalism seem useful again. Just as the old formalism had value in the service of an economic conception, the new one is useful in serving a conception of federalism. It is the instrument by which assertions of national power are to be limited in favor of preserving a supposedly discernible, proper sphere of state autonomy to legislate or refrain from legislating as the individual States see fit. The legitimacy of the Court's current emphasis on the noncommercial nature of regulated activity, then, does not turn on any logic serving the text of the Commerce Clause or on the realism of the majority's view of the national economy."

Justice Souter also wrote, "[In] the centuries since the framing the relative powers of the two sovereign systems have markedly changed. Nationwide economic integration is the norm, the national political power has been augmented by its vast revenues, and the power of the States has been drawn down by the Seventeenth Amendment. [Economic] growth and the burgeoning of federal revenue have not amended the Constitution, which contains no circuit breaker to preclude the political consequences of these developments. Nor is there any justification for attempts to nullify the natural political impact of the particular amendment that was adopted. [Amendments] that alter the balance of power between the National and State Governments, like the Fourteenth, or that change the way the States are represented within the Federal Government, like the Seventeenth, are not rips in the fabric of the Framers' Constitution, inviting judicial repairs. The Seventeenth Amendment may indeed have lessened the enthusiasm of the Senate to represent the States as discrete sovereignties, but the Amendment did not convert the judiciary into an alternate shield against the commerce power." His opinion concluded, "[The] practice of such ad hoc review cannot preserve the distinction between the judicial and the legislative, and this Court, in any event, lacks the institutional capacity to maintain such a regime for very long. [The] facts that cannot be ignored today are the facts of integrated national commerce and a political relationship between States and Nation much affected by their respective treasuries and constitutional modifications adopted by the people. The federalism of some earlier time is no more adequate to account for those facts today than the theory of laissez-faire was able to govern the national economy 70 years ago."

Justice Breyer also wrote a dissent. He asked, "Does the local street corner mugger engage in 'economic' activity or 'noneconomic' activity when he mugs for money? Would evidence that desire for economic domination underlies many brutal crimes against women save the present statute? [The] Court itself would permit Congress to aggregate, hence regulate, 'noneconomic' activity taking place at economic establishments. [Can] Congress simply rewrite the present law and limit its application to restaurants, hotels, perhaps universities, and other places of public accommodation? [Can] Congress save the present law by including it, or much of it, in a broader 'Safe Transport' or 'Workplace Safety' act? More important, why should we give critical constitutional importance to the economic, or noneconomic, nature of an interstate-commerce-affecting cause? If chemical emanations through indirect environmental change cause identical, severe commercial harm outside a State, why should it matter whether local factories or home fireplaces release them?" He noted, "[In] a world where most everyday products or their component parts cross interstate boundaries, Congress will frequently find it possible to redraft a statute using language that ties the regulation to the interstate movement of some relevant object, thereby regulating local criminal activity or, for that matter, family affairs. Although this possibility does not give the Federal Government the power to regulate everything, it means that any substantive limitation will apply randomly in terms of the interests the majority seeks to protect. How much would be gained, for example, were Congress to reenact the present law in the form of 'An Act Forbidding Violence Against Women Perpetrated at Public Accommodations or by Those Who Have Moved in, or through the Use of Items that Have Moved in, Interstate Commerce'? Complex Commerce Clause rules creating fine distinctions that achieve only random results do little to further the important federalist interests that called them into being."

Note: Federalism after the New Deal

1. *The values of federalism.* Which values of federalism, if any, does *Lopez* promote? Consider Justice Kennedy's discussion of alternative modes of regulation. Are any of them incompatible with the federal statute? Does the fact that forty states prohibit guns in schools demonstrate the value of states as laboratories of social experimentation? Why could not Congress conclude on the basis of those experiments that such a criminal prohibition was sound enough policy to be imposed nationwide?

Congress reenacted the Gun Free School Zones Act, modifying the statute to make it a criminal offense to possess a weapon near a school if the weapon has been transported in interstate commerce. (The statute has the same designation, 18 U.S.C. §922(q).) Is the new statute constitutional under *Lopez*? If so, what values of federalism does *Lopez* serve? If not, are the criminal statutes Justice Breyer describes unconstitutional?

Consider these observations about why some matters ought to be left exclusively to state control:

> [State] sovereignty over family law preserves the constitutional ideal of citizenship by promoting the development of civic virtue [in] maturing children. Federalism [destroys] the federal government's power to mold the moral character of future citizens in its own uniform image. [The] communitarian nature of family law requires a level of political engagement and a sense of community identity that lie beyond the reach of national politics. [As] the bonds of community thin out, the danger that shared values will degenerate into governmentally dictated values increases. By situating communitarian politics at the state level, [localism] ensures that the civic participation, political dialogue, and shared values essential to family law will develop within the states' smaller, relatively more accessible political locales. Second, state sovereignty over family law serves to diffuse governmental power over the formation of individual values and moral aspirations. [Localism] promotes diversity [in] the name of preserving citizen choice in matters of family life.

Dailey, Federalism and Families, 143 U. Pa. L. Rev. 1787, 1820, 1871-1872 (1995). To what extent can a parallel argument be made as to education? Consumer protection laws?

2. *The doctrine.* Is the following a fair description of the majority's analysis?

> The actual limiting principle [on] which Chief Justice Rehnquist can be said to rely [is] the weirdly circular proposition that there must *be* a limiting principle. [There] must be some morsel of state power, however tempting, that Congress would feel compelled, in order to avoid an attack of constitutional indigestion, to leave daintily on its plate. Otherwise nothing prevents the nation from devouring the states. [It] could only be a matter of time until the states disappeared into the blimp-like figure of a now satiated Uncle Sam: the *consolidation catastrophe.*

Weinberg, Fear and Federalism, 23 Ohio N.U. L. Rev. 1295, 1323-1324 (1997). Consider Justice Breyer's observation in *Morrison* that the Court's approach, understood in light of the exceptions the Court embraces, makes the doctrine purely formal, with no connection to any functions that federalism might serve, and Justice Souter's comments in *Morrison* about the Court's formalism. Can the Court's formalism be defended, or can *Lopez* and *Morrison* be stabilized as doctrine only if the Court rethinks its commitment to *Wickard's* approach to aggregation of commercial activity as well? Note here Justice Thomas's concurrence in *Lopez*.

Is the Court correct in saying that the dissent fails to indicate limits on congressional power? Under the dissent's theory, could Congress prescribe the curriculum to be followed in all public schools? Under the dissent's theory, could Congress require that no divorces be granted when the married couple has children under the age of ten, unless a state court finds that the divorce will have no adverse consequences for the psychological well-being of the children?

Nagle, The Commerce Clause Meets the Delhi Sands Flower-Loving Fly, 97 Mich. L. Rev. 174 (1998), examines a case in which the federal Endangered Species Act was applied to a fly whose only known habitat lies entirely within California. Applying the statute meant that construction of a public hospital could not proceed. Nagle summarizes the relevant facts: "(1) endangered species generally are substantially related to interstate commerce by virtue of the many utilitarian roles that they perform; (2) someday the fly could have a substantial effect on interstate commerce; and (3) the county hospital [would] rely upon materials, employees, and other connections to interstate commerce. [The] Fly itself does not have an actual, substantial effect on interstate commerce. [There] appear to be many species without which the ecosystem and interstate commerce would continue unaffected, but Congress apparently concluded otherwise." Id. at 190. Under what theory might Congress have the constitutional power to protect the fly? Nagle identifies three relevant questions: "[What] is the appropriate level of aggregation when comparing an activity to interstate commerce? [Can] a potential effect [ever] qualify as a substantial effect? [What] is the activity that must be connected to interstate commerce?" Id. at 191. Should we be concerned with the fly, or with all endangered species, or with some other aggregation? Does *Lopez* explain why it answers these questions as it does? If the explanation is that the answers must be such that Congress does not have power to regulate everything, do the answers in fact explain the limits, if any, of the *Lopez* doctrine?

3. *"Cuing" Congress.* Why did Congress enact the statute in *Lopez*? Consider the possibility that members of Congress were attempting primarily to claim credit for addressing a problem their constituents cared about, without concern for actually reducing crime. The existence of state statutes addressing the problem suggests little need for a national statute. Could Congress have thought that local enforcement efforts would be inadequate? Should a court be concerned about these issues?

P. Bobbitt, Constitutional Fate 191, 195 (1982), describes a "cuing" function of constitutional decisions. Such decisions remind members of Congress that they must "[judge] their own actions to see if they conform to the limits and restraints placed on them by the Constitution." Was *Lopez* an exercise of this cuing function? Was it an appropriate case for exercising it? Given *Lopez*, was *Morrison*? Can a decision justified as an exercise of the cuing function properly generate doctrine that the courts should enforce in subsequent cases?

4. *Constitutional moments?* B. Ackerman, We the People: Foundations 6 (1991), distinguishes "between two different decisions that may be made in a democracy. [Decisions] by the People occur rarely, and under special conditions. Before gaining the authority to make supreme law in the name of the People, a movement's political partisans must, first, convince an extraordinary number of their fellow citizens to take their proposed initiative with a seriousness that they do not normally accord to politics; second, they must allow their opponents a fair opportunity to organize their own forces; third, they must convince a majority of their fellow Americans to support their initiative as its merits are discussed, time and again, in the deliberative fora provided for 'higher lawmaking.' [Decisions] made by the government occur daily." Ackerman describes the conditions for decisions by the People as "constitutional moments" and contrasts them with the conditions of "ordinary politics." Do *Lopez* and *Morrison* represent the Court's response to a constitutional moment? Its participation in such a moment? If

so, do they suggest that the Court will assert the power of judicial review more frequently?

5. *Social and economic change.* What effects should social and economic change have on federalism and its judicial enforcement? Consider the argument in Ulen, Economic and Public-Choice Forces in Federalism, 6 Geo. Mason L. Rev. 921, 943 (1998):

> The efficient structure of a federation should change when the benefits and costs of federal affiliation change in response to real forces. [Suppose] that up to a certain time air and water pollution is local so that member-state governments can optimally regulate the externality-generators. But then suppose that changes in the technology of production cause new forms of pollution to appear that stray across state borders. [The] most efficient locus of regulation [would] change from the state to the federal level. [Further,] changes in the assignment of governmental responsibility would occur only when there are changes in the strength and breadth of political interest groups. If interest groups are primarily local, [then] they will probably be content with local or state regulation. [If] the concerns of interest groups cross jurisdictional borders, [they] will prefer federal regulation.

Do these concerns justify *Lopez*? Consider the argument defending *Lopez* in Clark, Translating Federalism: A Structural Approach, 66 Geo. Wash. L. Rev. 1161, 1175, 1176-1177 (1998):

> To the extent that changed circumstances have led us to expand our understanding of what constitutes "commerce among the several states," changed circumstances may also lead us to narrow our conception of which means are "necessary and proper" to regulate such commerce. [In] 1819, the constitutional structure arguably favored broad implied power to ensure that Congress would have ample means at its disposal to further the limited objects entrusted to the federal government. [Increases] in the incidence of [interstate] commerce necessarily present Congress with greater opportunities to exercise regulatory authority. [Any] ambiguities in the text of the clause [should] now be resolved in a manner that avoids finding virtually unlimited federal power.

Compare this argument to Weinberg's criticism of *Lopez* in section 2 of this Note.

6. *The New Deal legacy in light of Lopez.* Consider the argument that the text and the original understanding conflict in *Lopez*:

> There is little doubt that the scope of the powers now exercised by Congress far exceeds that imagined by the framers. They struggled over whether the commerce power included the power to build roads; they wouldn't have struggled over its power to reach the possession of guns near schools. But [the] language of the Constitution [plainly] supports this expanse of federal power. [As] commerce today seems plainly to reach practically every activity of social life, it would seem to follow that Congress has the power to reach, through regulation, practically every activity of social life.

Lessig, Translating Federalism: United States v. Lopez, 1995 Sup. Ct. Rev. 125, 129-130. Can the original balance between state and nation be restored through interpreting the commerce power?

Nagel, The Future of Federalism, 46 Case W. Res. L. Rev. 643, 649, 652 (1996), describes *Lopez* as invoking a technique of "successive validation." The technique addresses the dilemma that "our Constitution only authorizes certain enu-merated powers for the national government, but also authorizes some enumer-ated powers that are broad enough to allow congressional control over any aspect of human affairs." In "successive validation," "one horn of the dilemma is subor-dinated in the case at hand but the equivalency of the competing constitutional proposition is reasserted by a stated commitment to enforce that proposition in some future case. [By] promising future enforcement, these kinds of commitments reduce the pressure to devalue either of the competing propositions. [The] great difficulty [is] that the method is inconsistent with the legalistic ideals of consis-tency and authoritativeness." Is the technique of successive validation a legal tech-nique or an observation made by, for example, a political scientist?

D.   OTHER POWERS OF CONGRESS: ARE THEY MORE (OR LESS) PLENARY THAN THE COMMERCE POWER?

The preceding examination of the history of constitutional doctrine regarding the commerce clause explored the scope of Congress's power under that clause, the dimensions of judicially enforceable limits on that power in the name of fed-eralism, and the justifications for those limits. Many other clauses of the Consti-tution confer power on Congress. This section examines a number of those other powers. With respect to each of them, consider the following questions, versions of which will be raised throughout: Is the scope of this power broader or narrower than, or the same as, the scope of the commerce power? Do the words of the Con-stitution provide sufficient guidance to answer that question? Are the political constraints on Congress different with respect to this power, such that the courts should be more (or less) willing to enforce federalism-based limitations on con-gressional power?

1.   The Treaty and War Powers

Missouri v. Holland

252 U.S. 416 (1920)

MR. JUSTICE HOLMES delivered the opinion of the court.

This is a bill in equity brought by the State of Missouri to prevent a game war-den of the United States from attempting to enforce the Migratory Bird Treaty Act of 1918 and the regulations made by the Secretary of Agriculture in pursu-ance of the same. The ground of the bill is that the statute is an unconstitutional interference with the rights reserved to the States by the Tenth Amendment, and that the acts of the defendant done and threatened under that authority invade the sovereign right of the State and contravene its will manifested in statutes. . . .

On December 8, 1916, a treaty between the United States and Great Britain was proclaimed by the President. It recited that many species of birds in their an-nual migrations traversed certain parts of the United States and of Canada, that they were of great value as a source of food and in destroying insects injurious to vegetation, but were in danger of extermination through lack of adequate protection. It therefore provided for specified close seasons [and] agreed that the two powers would take or propose to their law-making bodies the necessary measures for carrying the treaty out. [The act] prohibited the killing, capturing or selling any of the migratory birds included in the terms of the treaty except as permitted by regulations [to] be made by the Secretary of Agriculture. . . .

[It] is not enough to refer to the Tenth Amendment, reserving the powers not delegated to the United States, because by Article II, §2, the power to make treaties is delegated expressly, and by Article VI treaties made under the authority of the United States [are] declared the supreme law of the land. If the treaty is valid there can be no dispute about the validity of the statute under Article I, §8, as a necessary and proper means to execute the powers of the Government. . . .

It is said that a treaty cannot be valid if it infringes the Constitution, that there are limits, therefore, to the treaty-making power, and that one such limit is that what an act of Congress could not do unaided, in derogation of the powers reserved to the States, a treaty cannot do. An earlier act of Congress that attempted by itself and not in pursuance of a treaty to regulate the killing of migratory birds within the States had been held bad in the District Court. . . .

Whether the [cases] were decided rightly or not they cannot be accepted as a test of the treaty power. Acts of Congress are the supreme law of the land only when made in pursuance of the Constitution, while treaties are declared to be so when made under the authority of the United States. It is open to question whether the authority of the United States means more than the formal acts prescribed to make the convention. We do not mean to imply that there are no qualifications to the treaty-making power; but they must be ascertained in a different way. It is obvious that there may be matters of the sharpest exigency for the national well being that an act of Congress could not deal with but that a treaty followed by such an act could, and it is not lightly to be assumed that, in matters requiring national action, "a power which must belong to and somewhere reside in every civilized government" is not to be found. [When] we are dealing with words that also are a constituent act, like the Constitution of the United States, we must realize that they have called into life a being the development of which could not have been foreseen completely by the most gifted of its begetters. It was enough for them to realize or to hope that they had created an organism; it has taken a century and has cost their successors much sweat and blood to prove that they created a nation. The case before us must be considered in the light of our whole experience and not merely in that of what was said a hundred years ago. The treaty in question does not contravene any prohibitory words to be found in the Constitution. The only question is whether it is forbidden by some invisible radiation from the general terms of the Tenth Amendment. We must consider what this country has become in deciding what that Amendment has reserved. . . .

Here a national interest of very nearly the first magnitude is involved. It can be protected only by national action in concert with that of another power. The subject matter is only transitorily within the State and has no permanent habitat therein. But for the treaty and the statute there soon might be no birds for any powers to deal with. We see nothing in the Constitution that compels the Government to sit by while a food supply is cut off and the protectors of our forests and our crops are destroyed. It is not sufficient to rely upon the States. The reliance is vain, and were it otherwise, the question is whether the United States is forbidden to act. We are of opinion that the treaty and statute must be upheld.

Decree affirmed.

MR. JUSTICE VAN DEVANTER and MR. JUSTICE PITNEY dissent.

Note: *Federalism and the Treaty Power*

1. *The scope of Missouri v. Holland as applied to federalism.* What is the "different way" that federalism-based limits on the treaty power are to be ascertained? Bradley, The Treaty Power and American Federalism, 97 Mich. L. Rev. 390 (1998), argues for "subject[ing] the treaty power to the same federalism restrictions that apply to Congress's legislative powers. [The] treaty power would not confer any additional regulatory powers on the federal government, just the power to bind the United States on the international plane." This appears to imply that the treaty power authorizes the national government to bind the nation to take actions that it was constitutionally barred from taking (e.g., implementing protection of religious liberty that Congress could not enact pursuant to any enumerated power). Note that the domain covered by treaties has expanded beyond relations between nations as such to include economic relations (which might be covered by Congress's power to regulate foreign commerce) and human rights. Does this development make it more necessary to devise judicial doctrines limiting the ability of the national government to enact laws under the treaty power?

Can courts determine what are "matters requiring national action" by treaty followed by legislation rather than by legislation alone? How likely is the President to negotiate and the Senate to ratify a treaty on a matter not requiring national action in Holmes's sense?

2. *Self-executing treaties.* Would different issues arise had the treaty been "self-executing," that is, not requiring as a matter of U.S. law implementing legislation in order to impose legally enforceable obligations on Americans? How would the political process differ?

3. *The scope of Missouri v. Holland as applied to separation of powers and individual rights.* Does Missouri v. Holland deal only with federalism-based limitations on national power?

a. In the early 1950s, a coalition of conservative Republicans and southern Democrats sponsored the Bricker Amendment, which would have added to the Constitution provisions stating that (1) "a provision of a treaty which conflicts with this Constitution shall not be of any force or effect" and (2) "a treaty shall become effective as internal law [only] through legislation which would be valid in the absence of treaty." Was the first provision necessary in light of Missouri v. Holland? What effects would the second provision have had? The southern Democrats who supported the Bricker Amendment did so out of concern that provisions of the United Nations Charter and associated treaties would make unlawful aspects of the existing system of race discrimination. In light of *Heart of Atlanta* and *McClung,* would the Bricker Amendment have had any effects in this area? The Bricker Amendment fell short of adoption by the Senate in 1954 by a vote of sixty in favor, thirty-one opposed.

b. Consider Reid v. Covert, 354 U.S. 1 (1957): Mrs. Covert, a civilian residing with her serviceman husband on a military base in England, was convicted by a military tribunal of killing him. The Supreme Court held that a civilian in her position could not be tried in the military courts. The plurality emphasized that all of Congress's powers, including its power to regulate the armed forces, were limited by the bill of rights, including its requirement of trial by jury. The plurality also discussed the effects of treaties and executive agreements on congressional power:

> [No] agreement with a foreign nation can confer power on the Congress, or on any other branch of Government, which is free from the restraints of the Constitution. . . .
>
> [The] reason treaties were not limited to those made in "pursuance" of the Constitution was so that agreements made by the United States under the Articles of Confederation, including the important peace treaties which concluded the Revolutionary War, would remain in effect. It would be manifestly contrary to the objectives of those who created the Constitution, as well as those who were responsible for the Bill of Rights — let alone alien to our entire constitutional history and tradition — to construe Article VI as permitting the United States to exercise power under an international agreement without observing constitutional prohibitions. In effect, such construction would permit amendment of that document in a manner not sanctioned by Article V. The prohibitions of the Constitution were designed to apply to all branches of the National Government and they cannot be nullified by the Executive or by the Executive and the Senate combined. . . .
>
> There is nothing in Missouri v. Holland which is contrary to the position taken here. There the Court carefully noted that the treaty involved was not inconsistent with any specific provision of the Constitution. The Court was concerned with the Tenth Amendment which reserves to the States or the people all power not delegated to the National Government. To the extent that the United States can validly make treaties, the people and the States have delegated their power to the National Government and the Tenth Amendment is no barrier.

Note: The "War" Power

In Woods v. Cloyd W. Miller Co., 333 U.S. 138 (1948), the Supreme Court upheld the constitutionality of the Housing and Rent Act of 1947, which froze rents at their wartime levels. It concluded that "the war power sustains this legislation." Even though the President had declared hostilities terminated on December 31, 1946, before the statute was enacted, "the war power does not necessarily end with the cessation of hostilities." When Congress acted, there was a

> deficit in housing which in considerable measure was caused by the heavy demobilization of veterans and by the cessation or reduction in residential construction during the period of hostilities due to the allocation of building materials to military projects. Since the war effort contributed heavily to that deficit, Congress has the power even after the cessation of hostilities to act to control the forces that a short supply of the needed article created. . . .
>
> We recognize the force of the argument that the effects of war under modern conditions may be felt in the economy for years and years, and that if the war power can be used in days of peace to treat all the wounds which war inflicts on our society, it may not only swallow up all other powers of Congress but largely obliterate the Ninth and Tenth Amendments as well. There are no such implications in today's decision. We deal here with the consequences of a housing deficit greatly in-

tensified during the period of hostilities by the war effort. Any power, of course, can be abused. But we cannot assume that Congress is not alert to its constitutional responsibilities. And the question whether the war power has been properly employed in cases such as this is open to judicial inquiry.

The question of the constitutionality of action taken by Congress does not depend on recitals of the power which it undertakes to exercise. Here it is plain from the legislative history that Congress was invoking its war power to cope with a current condition of which the war was a direct and immediate cause.

Justice Jackson's concurring opinion expressed "misgivings" about "this vague, undefined and indefinable 'war power'":

No one will question that this power is the most dangerous one to free government in the whole catalogue of powers. It is usually invoked in haste and excitement when calm legislative consideration of constitutional limitation is difficult. It is executed in a time of patriotic fervor that makes moderation unpopular. And, worst of all, it is interpreted by judges under the influence of the same passions and pressures. Always, [the] Government urges hasty decision to forestall some emergency or serve some purposes and pleads that paralysis will result if its claims to power are denied or their confirmation delayed.

Particularly when the war power is invoked to do things to the liberties of people, or to their property or economy that only indirectly affect conduct of the war and do not relate to the management of the war itself, the constitutional basis should be scrutinized with care.

He concluded that "the present state of war [was not] merely technical," and that the statute was constitutional.

What is "the war power" on which the Court relies? Justice Jackson suggests that the political constraints on congressional action are loosened in all areas when the war powers are invoked. Is he correct?

2. *The Taxing Power*

After Hammer v. Dagenhart, section B supra, Congress enacted the Child Labor Tax Act. The statute required that anyone who employed child labor, defined as it had been in the statute invalidated in *Hammer*, pay an excise tax equivalent to 10 percent of the entire net profits of the mine or factory. In Bailey v. Drexel Furniture Co., 259 U.S. 20 (1922), the Supreme Court held the act unconstitutional. It posed the issue in this way: "Does this law impose a tax with only that incidental restraint and regulation which a tax must inevitably involve? Or does it regulate by the use of the so-called tax as a penalty?" The "detailed and specified course of conduct in business" set out in the act demonstrated its purpose, as did provisions authorizing inspection of factories and mines by the Department of Labor, "whose normal function is the advancement and protection of the welfare of workers. In the light of these features of the act, a court must be blind not to see that the so-called tax is imposed to stop the employment of children within the age limits prescribed. Its prohibitory and regulatory effect and purpose are palpable. All others can see and understand this. How can we properly shut our minds to it?"

The Court continued:

Grant the validity of this law, and all that Congress would need to do, hereafter, in seeking to take over to its control any one of the great number of subjects of public interest, jurisdiction of which the States have never parted with, and which are reserved to them by the Tenth Amendment, would be to enact a detailed measure of complete regulation of the subject and enforce it by a so-called tax upon departures from it. To give such magic to the word "tax" would be to break down all constitutional limitation of the powers of Congress and completely wipe out the sovereignty of the States.

[Where] the sovereign enacting the law has power to impose both tax and penalty the difference between revenue production and mere regulation may be immaterial, but not so when one sovereign can impose a tax only, and the power of regulation rests in another. Taxes are occasionally imposed in the discretion of the legislature on proper subjects with the primary motive of obtaining revenue from them and with the incidental motive of discouraging them by making their continuance onerous. They do not lose their character as taxes because of the incidental motive. But there comes a time in the extension of the penalizing features of the so-called tax when it loses its character as such and becomes a mere penalty with the characteristics of regulation and punishment. Such is the case in the law before us. Although Congress does not invalidate the contract of employment or expressly declare that the employment within the mentioned ages is illegal, it does exhibit its intent practically to achieve the latter result by adopting the criteria of wrongdoing and imposing its principal consequence on those who transgress its standard.

Is the distinction between a penalty and a tax cogent? Does it turn on Congress's motive? Consider whether distinctions between the commerce power and the taxing power make it easier to determine motive with respect to the use of the taxing power. Is there any other difference between the tax and the commerce powers that makes the "pretext" analysis more cogent? Recall that a "pretext" analysis requires a prior determination of the proper purposes for which a power may be exercised. Are the purposes of the power to tax more clearly defined than those of the power to regulate interstate commerce?

Many taxes serve both revenue-raising and regulatory purposes. Is it helpful to say that taxes must raise nontrivial amounts of revenue, even if they have a substantial regulatory effect? Rejecting a challenge to the federal occupational tax levied on people in the business of accepting bets in United States v. Kahriger, 345 U.S. 22 (1953), the Court listed cases in which it had upheld taxes on colored oleomargarine, McCray v. United States, 195 U.S. 27 (1904); on narcotics, United States v. Doremus, discussed infra; and on firearms, Sonzinsky v. United States, 300 U.S. 506 (1937). A footnote added:

One of the indicia which appellee offers to support his contention that the wagering tax is not a proper revenue measure is that the tax amount collected under it was $4,371,869, as compared with an expected amount of $400,000,000 a year. The figure of $4,371,869, however, is relatively large when it is compared with the $3,501 collected under the tax on adulterated and process or renovated butter and filled cheese, the $914,910 collected under the tax on narcotics, including marihuana and special taxes, and the $28,911 collected under the tax on firearms, transfer and occupational taxes.

(The Court later held that the occupational tax violated the self-incrimination clause of the fifth amendment. Marchetti v. United States, 390 U.S. 39 (1968).)

Does the distinction between a penalty and a tax turn on "detail[ing a] speci-fied course of conduct"? Why isn't that just a description of the activity subject to tax? Does the distinction turn on the presence of a complex enforcement scheme? In *Kahriger*, the statute required the tax collector to furnish copies of a list of those who paid the wagering tax to state law enforcement officials.

Consider the discussion of United States v. Doremus, 249 U.S. 86 (1919), in Bailey v. Drexel Furniture:

> [*Doremus*] involved the validity of the Narcotic Drug Act, which imposed a special tax on the manufacture, importation and sale or gift of opium or coca leaves or their compounds or derivatives. It required every person subject to the special tax to register with the Collector of Internal Revenue his name and place of business and forbade him to sell except upon the written order of the person to whom the sale was made on a form prescribed by the Commissioner of Internal Revenue. The vendor was required to keep the order for two years, and the purchaser to keep a duplicate for the same time and both were to be subject to official inspection. Similar requirements were made as to sales upon prescriptions of a physician and as to the dispensing of such drugs directly to a patient by a physician. The validity of a special tax in the nature of an excise tax on the manufacture, importation and sale of such drugs was, of course, unquestioned. The provisions for subjecting the sale and distribution of the drugs to official supervision and inspection were held to have a reasonable relation to the enforcement of the tax and were therefore held valid.
>
> The court [in *Doremus*] said that the act could not be declared invalid just be-cause another motive than taxation, not shown on the face of the act, might have contributed to its passage. This case does not militate against the conclusion we have reached in respect of the law now before us. The court, there, made manifest its view that the provisions of the so-called taxing act must be naturally and reason-ably adapted to the collection of the tax and not solely to the achievement of some other purpose plainly within state power.

Are you persuaded that *Doremus* is distinguishable from Bailey v. Drexel Furniture?

3.   *The Spending Power*

United States v. Butler

297 U.S. 1 (1936)

[The Agricultural Adjustment Act of 1933 was designed to stabilize production in agriculture by assuring farmers that their products would be sold at a fair price. The act imposed a tax on processors of agricultural commodities such as cotton. The proceeds of the tax were to be used to subsidize farmers who agreed to re-strict their production.]

MR. JUSTICE ROBERTS delivered the opinion of the Court. . . .

There should be no misunderstanding as to the function of this court in such a case. It is sometimes said that the court assumes a power to overrule or control the action of the people's representatives. This is a misconception. The Consti-tution is the supreme law of the land ordained and established by the people. All legislation must conform to the principles it lays down. When an act of Congress is appropriately challenged in the courts as not conforming to the constitutional mandate the judicial branch of the Government has only one duty, — to lay the article of the Constitution which is invoked beside the statute which is challenged and to decide whether the latter squares with the former. All the court does, or can do, is to announce its considered judgment upon the question. The only power it has, if such it may be called, is the power of judgment. This court neither approves nor condemns any legislative policy. Its delicate and difficult office is to ascertain and declare whether the legislation is in accordance with, or in contravention of, the provisions of the Constitution; and, having done that, its duty ends.

The question is not what power the Federal Government ought to have but what powers in fact have been given by the people. [The] federal union is a government of delegated powers. It has only such as are expressly conferred upon it and such as are reasonably to be implied from those granted. . . .

The clause thought to authorize the legislation [confers] upon the Congress power "to lay and collect Taxes, Duties, Imposts and Excises, to pay the Debts and provide for the common Defence and general Welfare of the United States. . . ." It is not contended that this provision grants power to regulate agricultural production upon the theory that such legislation would promote the general welfare. The Government concedes that the phrase "to provide for the general welfare" qualifies the power "to lay and collect taxes." The view that the clause grants power to provide for the general welfare, independently of the taxing power, has never been authoritatively accepted. Mr. Justice Story points out that if it were adopted "it is obvious that under color of the generality of the words, to 'provide for the common defence and general welfare,' the government of the United States is, in reality, a government of general and unlimited powers, notwithstanding the subsequent enumeration of specific powers." The true construction undoubtedly is that the only thing granted is the power to tax for the purpose of providing funds for payment of the nation's debts and making provision for the general welfare.

Nevertheless the Government asserts that warrant is found in this clause for the adoption of the Agricultural Adjustment Act. The argument is that Congress may appropriate and authorize the spending of moneys for the "general welfare"; that the phrase should be liberally construed to cover anything conducive to national welfare; that decision as to what will promote such welfare rests with Congress alone, and the courts may not review its determination; and finally that the appropriation under attack was in fact for the general welfare of the United States. . . .

Since the foundation of the Nation sharp differences of opinion have persisted as to the true interpretation of the phrase. Madison asserted it amounted to no more than a reference to the other powers enumerated in the subsequent clauses of the same section; that, as the United States is a government of limited and enumerated powers, the grant of power to tax and spend for the general national welfare must be confined to the enumerated legislative fields committed to the Congress. In this view the phrase is mere tautology, for taxation and appropriation are or may be necessary incidents of the exercise of any of the enumerated legislative powers. Hamilton, on the other hand, maintained the clause confers a power separate and distinct from those later enumerated, is not restricted in meaning by the grant of them, and Congress consequently has a substantive power to tax and to appropriate, limited only by the requirement that it shall be exercised to provide for the general welfare of the United States. [We] conclude that the reading advocated by [Hamilton] is the correct one. While, therefore, the power to tax is not unlimited, its confines are set in the clause which confers it, and not in those of §8 which bestow and define the legislative powers of the Congress. It results that the power of Congress to authorize expenditure of public moneys for public purposes is not limited by the direct grants of legislative power found in the Constitution.

But the adoption of the broader construction leaves the power to spend subject to limitations. . . .

We are not now required to ascertain the scope of the phrase "general welfare of the United States" or to determine whether an appropriation in aid of agriculture falls within it. Wholly apart from that question, another principle embedded in our Constitution prohibits the enforcement of the Agricultural Adjustment Act. The act invades the reserved rights of the states. It is a statutory plan to regulate and control agricultural production, a matter beyond the powers delegated to the federal government. The tax, the appropriation of the funds raised, and the direction for their disbursement, are but parts of the plan. They are but means to an unconstitutional end. . . .

[If] the taxing power may not be used as the instrument to enforce a regulation of matters of state concern with respect to which the Congress has no authority to interfere, may it, as in the present case, be employed to raise the money necessary to purchase a compliance which the Congress is powerless to command? The Government asserts that whatever might be said against the validity of the plan if compulsory, it is constitutionally sound because the end is accomplished by voluntary co-operation. There are two sufficient answers to the contention. The regulation is not in fact voluntary. The farmer, of course, may refuse to comply, but the price of such refusal is the loss of benefits. The amount offered is intended to be sufficient to exert pressure on him to agree to the proposed regulation. The power to confer or withhold unlimited benefits is the power to coerce or destroy. If the cotton grower elects not to accept the benefits, he will receive less for his crops; those who receive payments will be able to undersell him. The result may well be financial ruin. . . .

But if the plan were one for purely voluntary co-operation it would stand no better so far as the federal power is concerned. At best it is a scheme for purchasing with federal funds submission to federal regulation of a subject reserved to the states. . . .

We are not here concerned with a conditional appropriation of money, nor with a provision that if certain conditions are not complied with the appropriation shall no longer be available. By the Agricultural Adjustment Act the amount of the tax is appropriated to be expended only in payment under contracts whereby the parties bind themselves to regulation by the Federal Government. There is an obvious difference between a statute stating the conditions upon which moneys shall be expended and one effective only upon assumption of a contractual obligation to submit to a regulation which otherwise could not be enforced. [We] are referred to appropriations in aid of education, and it is said that no one has doubted the power of Congress to stipulate the sort of education for which money shall be expended. But an appropriation to an educational institution which by its terms is to become available only if the beneficiary enters into a contract to teach doctrines subversive of the Constitution is clearly bad. An affirmance of the authority of Congress so to condition the expenditure of an appropriation would tend to nullify all constitutional limitations upon legislative power. . . .

Congress has no power to enforce its commands on the farmer to the ends sought by the Agricultural Adjustment Act. It must follow that it may not indirectly accomplish those ends by taxing and spending to purchase compliance. The Constitution and the entire plan of our government negative any such use of the power to tax and to spend as the act undertakes to authorize. It does not help to declare that local conditions throughout the nation have created a situation of national concern; for this is but to say that whenever there is a widespread similarity of local conditions, Congress may ignore constitutional limitations upon its own powers and usurp those reserved to the states. If, in lieu of compulsory regulation of subjects within the states' reserved jurisdiction, which is prohibited, the Congress could invoke the taxing and spending power as a means to accomplish the same end, clause 1 of §8 of Article I would become the instrument for total subversion of the governmental powers reserved to the individual states.

If the act before us is a proper exercise of the federal taxing power, evidently the regulation of all industry throughout the United States may be accomplished by similar exercises of the same power. It would be possible to exact money from one branch of an industry and pay it to another branch in every field of activity which lies within the province of the states. The mere threat of such a procedure might well induce the surrender of rights and the compliance with federal regulation as the price of continuance in business. A few instances will illustrate the thought.

Let us suppose Congress should determine that the farmer, the miner or some other producer of raw materials is receiving too much for his products, with consequent depression of the processing industry and idleness of its employes. Though, by confession, there is no power vested in Congress to compel by statute a lowering of the prices of the raw material, the same result might be accomplished, if the questioned act be valid, by taxing the producer upon his output and appropriating the proceeds to the processors, either with or without conditions imposed as the consideration for payment of the subsidy.

We have held in [*Schechter*], that Congress has no power to regulate wages and hours of labor in a local business. If the petitioner is right, this very end may be accomplished by appropriating money to be paid to employers from the federal treasury under contracts whereby they agree to comply with certain standards fixed by federal law or by contract. . . .

Suppose that there are too many garment workers in the large cities; that this results in dislocation of the economic balance. Upon the principle contended for an excise might be laid on the manufacture of all garments manufactured and the proceeds paid to those manufacturers who agree to remove their plants to cities having not more than a hundred thousand population. Thus, through the asserted power of taxation, the federal government, against the will of individual states, might completely redistribute the industrial population. . . .

These illustrations are given, not to suggest that any of the purposes mentioned are unworthy, but to demonstrate the scope of the principle for which the Government contends; to test the principle by its applications; to point out that, by the exercise of the asserted power, Congress would, in effect, under the pretext of

exercising the taxing power, in reality accomplish prohibited ends. It cannot be said that they envisage improbable legislation. The supposed cases are no more improbable than would the present act have been deemed a few years ago. . . .
    [Affirmed.]

    MR. JUSTICE STONE, dissenting. . . .
    The power of courts to declare a statute unconstitutional is subject to two guiding principles of decision which ought never to be absent from judicial consciousness. One is that courts are concerned only with the power to enact statutes, not with their wisdom. The other is that while unconstitutional exercise of power by the executive and legislative branches of the government is subject to judicial restraint, the only check upon our own exercise of power is our own sense of self-restraint. For the removal of unwise laws from the statute books appeal lies not to the courts but to the ballot and to the processes of democratic government. . . .
    [The] suggestion of coercion finds no support in the record or in any data showing the actual operation of the Act. Threat of loss, not hope of gain, is the essence of economic coercion. Members of a long depressed industry have undoubtedly been tempted to curtail acreage by the hope of resulting better prices and by the proffered opportunity to obtain needed ready money. . . .
    It is upon the contention that state power is infringed by purchased regulation of agricultural production that chief reliance is placed. It is insisted that, while the Constitution gives to Congress, in specific and unambiguous terms, the power to tax and spend, the power is subject to limitations which do not find their origin in any express provision of the Constitution and to which other expressly delegated powers are not subject.
    The Constitution requires that public funds shall be spent for a defined purpose, the promotion of the general welfare. Their expenditure usually involves payment on terms which will insure use by the selected recipients within the limits of the constitutional purpose. Expenditures would fail of their purpose and thus lose their constitutional sanction if the terms of payment were not such that by their influence on the action of the recipients the permitted end would be attained. The power of Congress to spend is inseparable from persuasion to action over which Congress has no legislative control. Congress may not command that the science of agriculture be taught in state universities. But if it would aid the teaching of that science by grants to state institutions, it is appropriate [that] the grant be on the condition [that] it be used for the intended purpose. Similarly it would seem to be compliance with the Constitution, not violation of it, for the government to take and the university to give a contract that the grant would be so used. It makes no difference that there is a promise to do an act which the condition is calculated to induce. Condition and promise are alike valid since both are in furtherance of the national purpose for which the money is appropriated. . . .
    The limitation now sanctioned must lead to absurd consequences. The government may give seeds to farmers, but may not condition the gift upon their being planted in places where they are most needed or even planted at all. The government may give money to the unemployed, but may not ask that those who get it shall give labor in return, or even use it to support their families. It may give money to sufferers from earthquake, fire, tornado, pestilence or flood, but may not impose conditions — health precautions designed to prevent the spread of

disease, or induce the movement of population to safer or more sanitary areas. All that, because it is purchased regulation infringing state powers, must be left for the states, who are unable or unwilling to supply the necessary relief. [If] the expenditure is for a national public purpose, that purpose will not be thwarted because payment is on condition which will advance that purpose. The action which Congress induces by payments of money to promote the general welfare, but which it does not command or coerce, is but an incident to a specifically granted power, but a permissible means to a legitimate end. If appropriation in aid of a program of curtailment of agricultural production is constitutional, and it is not denied that it is, payment to farmers on condition that they reduce their crop acreage is constitutional. It is not any the less so because the farmer at his own option promises to fulfill the condition.

That the governmental power of the purse is a great one is not now for the first time announced. . . .

The suggestion that it must now be curtailed by judicial fiat because it may be abused by unwise use hardly rises to the dignity of argument. [The] power to tax and spend is not without constitutional restraints. One restriction is that the purpose must be truly national. Another is that it may not be used to coerce action left to state control. Another is the conscience and patriotism of Congress and the Executive. "It must be remembered that legislators are the ultimate guardians of the liberties and welfare of the people in quite as great a degree as the courts." Justice Holmes, in Missouri, Kansas & Texas Ry. Co. v. May, 194 U.S. 267, 270.

A tortured construction of the Constitution is not to be justified by recourse to extreme examples of reckless congressional spending which might occur if courts could not prevent — expenditures which, even if they could be thought to effect any national purpose, would be possible only by action of a legislature lost to all sense of public responsibility. Such suppositions are addressed to the mind accustomed to believe that it is the business of courts to sit in judgment on the wisdom of legislative action. Courts are not the only agency of government that must be assumed to have capacity to govern. Congress and the courts both unhappily may falter or be mistaken in the performance of their constitutional duty. But interpretation of our great charter of government which proceeds on any assumption that the responsibility for the preservation of our institutions is the exclusive concern of any one of the three branches of government, or that it alone can save them from destruction is far more likely, in the long run, "to obliterate the constituent members" of "an indestructible union of indestructible states" than the frank recognition that language, even of a constitution, may mean what it says: that the power to tax and spend includes the power to relieve a nationwide economic maladjustment by conditional gifts of money.

MR. JUSTICE BRANDEIS and MR. JUSTICE CARDOZO join in this opinion.

Note: The Spending Power and Dual Federalism

1. *Dual federalism.* Having adopted the Hamiltonian position on the scope of the spending power, is the Court consistent in finding the act unconstitutional? Does Justice Roberts take the position that there are no judicially enforceable *internal* limitations on the spending power — the courts will not determine whether

an expenditure promotes the "general welfare" — but that there are judicially enforceable federalism-based *external* limitations on that power?

2. *Political restraints.* What answers does Justice Stone offer to the Court's parade of horribles? Could the courts enforce the requirement that "the purpose must be truly national" in the face of congressional action, by saying that, although action was taken, it was not for a truly national purpose? Note Justice Stone's invocation of the legislature's "sense of public responsibility." Does this provide a better answer than Justice Roberts does to the problem of federal grants to state universities on the condition that they teach agriculture? Does Justice Roberts have any answer to that problem?

Steward Machine Co. v. Davis
301 U.S. 548 (1937)

[Under the federal unemployment compensation system, an employer paid a tax to the U.S. Treasury. If the employer also made contributions to a state unemployment fund that had been certified by the Secretary of the Treasury as meeting certain "minimum criteria" designed to assure financial stability and accountability, the employer received a credit of up to 90 percent against the federal tax. This system, the Court concluded, did not "[involve] the coercion of the States in contravention of the Tenth Amendment or of restrictions implicit in our federal form of government."]

MR. JUSTICE CARDOZO delivered the opinion of the Court. . . .

[Before] the statute succumbs to an assault[, there] must be a showing [that] the tax and credit in combination are weapons of coercion, destroying or impairing the autonomy of the states. . . .

To draw the line intelligently between duress and inducement there is need to remind ourselves of facts as to the problem of unemployment that are now matters of common knowledge. [Justice Cardozo then recited facts drawn from the government's brief describing the national problem of unemployment. "The fact developed quickly that the states were unable to give the requisite relief."]

In the presence of this urgent need for some remedial expedient, the question is to be answered whether the expedient adopted has overleapt the bounds of power. The assailants of the statute say that its dominant end and aim is to drive the state legislatures under the whip of economic pressure into the enactment of unemployment compensation laws at the bidding of the central government. Supporters of the statute say that its operation is not constraint, but the creation of a larger freedom, the states and the nation joining in a cooperative endeavor to avert a common evil. Before Congress acted, unemployment compensation insurance was still, for the most part, a project and no more. Wisconsin was the pioneer. Her statute was adopted in 1931. [In] 1935, four states (California, Massachusetts, New Hampshire and New York) passed unemployment laws on the eve of the adoption of the Social Security Act, and two others did likewise after the federal act and later in the year. [In] 1936, twenty-eight other states fell in line, and eight more the present year. But if states had been holding back before the passage of the federal law, inaction was not owing, for the most part, to the lack of sympathetic interest. Many held back through alarm lest, in laying such a toll upon their industries, they would place themselves in a position of economic disadvantage as compared with neighbors or competitors. Two consequences ensued. One was that the freedom of a state to contribute its fair share to the solution of a national problem was paralyzed by fear. The other was that in so far as there was failure by the states to contribute relief according to the measure of their capacity, a disproportionate burden, and a mountainous one, was laid upon the resources of the Government of the nation.

The Social Security Act is an attempt to find a method by which all these public agencies may work together to a common end. Every dollar of the new taxes will continue in all likelihood to be used and needed by the nation as long as states are unwilling, whether through timidity or for other motives, to do what can be done at home. [On] the other hand fulfilment of the home duty will be lightened and encouraged by crediting the taxpayer upon his account with the Treasury of the nation to the extent that his contributions under the laws of the locality have simplified or diminished the problem of relief and the probable demand upon the resources of the fisc. . . .

Who then is coerced through the operation of this statute? Not the taxpayer. He pays in fulfilment of the mandate of the local legislature. Not the state. Even now she does not offer a suggestion that in passing the unemployment law she was affected by duress. For all that appears she is satisfied with her choice, and would be sorely disappointed if it were now to be annulled. The difficulty with the petitioner's contention is that it confuses motive with coercion. "Every tax is in some measure regulatory. To some extent it interposes an economic impediment to the activity taxed as compared with others not taxed." Sonzinsky v. United States. In like manner every rebate from a tax when conditioned upon conduct is in some measure a temptation. But to hold that motive or temptation is equivalent to coercion is to plunge the law in endless difficulties. The outcome of such a doctrine is the acceptance of a philosophical determinism by which choice becomes impossible. Till now the law has been guided by a robust common sense which assumes the freedom of the will as a working hypothesis in the solution of its problems. The wisdom of the hypothesis has illustration in this case. Nothing in the case suggests the exertion of a power akin to undue influence, if we assume that such a concept can ever be applied with fitness to the relations between state and nation. Even on that assumption the location of the point at which pressure turns into compulsion, and ceases to be inducement, would be a question of degree, — at times, perhaps, of fact. The point had not been reached when Alabama made her choice. We cannot say that she was acting not of her unfettered will, but under the strain of a persuasion equivalent to undue influence, when she chose to have relief administered under laws of her own making, by agents of her own selection, instead of our federal laws, administered by federal officers, with all the ensuing evils, at least to many minds, of federal patronage and power. . . .

In ruling as we do, we leave many questions open. We do not say that a tax is valid, when imposed by act of Congress, if it is laid upon the condition that a state may escape its operation through the adoption of a statute unrelated in subject matter to activities fairly within the scope of national policy and power. [In] the tender of this credit Congress does not intrude upon fields foreign to its function. The purpose of its intervention [is] to safeguard its own treasury and as an incident to that protection to place the states upon a footing of equal opportunity.

Drains upon its own resources are to be checked; obstructions to the freedom of the states are to be leveled. It is one thing to impose a tax dependent upon the conduct of the taxpayers, or of the state in which they live, where the conduct to be stimulated or discouraged is unrelated to the fiscal need subserved by the tax in its normal operation, or to any other end legitimately national. [It] is quite another thing to say that a tax will be abated upon the doing of an act that will satisfy the fiscal need, the tax and the alternative being approximate equivalents. In such circumstances, if in no others, inducement or persuasion does not go beyond the bounds of power. We do not fix the outermost line. Enough for present purposes that wherever the line may be, this statute is within it. Definition more precise must abide the wisdom of the future. . . .

[The] statute does not call for a surrender by the states of powers essential to their quasi-sovereign existence.

Argument to the contrary has its source in two sections of the act [defining] the minimum criteria to which a state compensation system is required to conform if it is to be accepted by the Board as the basis for a credit. . . .

A credit to taxpayers for payments made to a State under a state unemployment law will be manifestly futile in the absence of some assurance that the law leading to the credit is in truth what it professes to be. [What] is basic and essential may be assured by suitable conditions. The terms embodied in these sections are directed to that end. A wide range of judgment is given to the several states as to the particular type of statute to be spread upon their books. [What] they may not do, if they would earn the credit, is to depart from those standards which in the judgment of Congress are to be ranked as fundamental. Even if opinion may differ as to the fundamental quality of one or more of the conditions, the difference will not avail to vitiate the statute. In determining essentials Congress must have the benefit of a fair margin of discretion. One cannot say with reason that this margin has been exceeded, or that the basic standards have been determined in any arbitrary fashion. . . .

[Affirmed.]

[Justices McReynolds, Sutherland, Van Devanter, and Butler dissented.]

Note: Conditional Spending, Coercion, and the Political Process

1. *Distinguishing* Butler. Is *Steward Machine Co.* consistent with *Butler?* Consider the proposition that the unemployment system is more objectionable than the Agricultural Adjustment Act because the former "coerces" the states directly while the latter does so only indirectly by allowing contracts between the United States and private parties that have the effect of undermining local policy. Note that the states are "coerced" into participating by a provision that affects the taxes paid by private parties, who thus have an incentive to locate in participating states.

2. *The modern view.* As the Court adopted broader views of the power granted Congress elsewhere in article I, the differences between the Hamiltonian and the Madisonian views on the scope of the spending power diminished substantially. The revival of federalism-based limits on congressional power in *Lopez* and *Morrison* placed the issue of the scope of the spending power on the table again. South Dakota v. Dole, 483 U.S. 203 (1987), upheld a federal statute that directed the Secretary of Transportation to withhold a portion of federal highway funds

from states that do not prohibit the purchase of alcohol by people under the age of twenty-one. Congress used this technique because of uncertainty about its power to impose a national minimum drinking age directly, in light of the twenty-first amendment. Although most of Chief Justice Rehnquist's opinion for the Court discussed whether the twenty-first amendment was a limitation on Congress's power to spend, the opinion also contained some general observations about the scope of the conditional spending power:

> The spending power is of course not unlimited, but is instead subject to several general restrictions. [First,] the exercise of the spending power must be in pursuit of "the general welfare." [*Butler.*] In considering whether a particular expenditure is intended to serve general public purposes, courts should defer substantially to the judgment of Congress. Second, [if] Congress desires to condition the States' receipt of federal funds, it "must do so [unambiguously."] Third, our cases have suggested (without significant elaboration) that conditions on federal grants might be illegitimate if they are unrelated "to the federal interest in particular national projects or programs." Finally, [other] constitutional provisions may provide an independent bar to the conditional grant of federal funds.

The twenty-one-year-old drinking age condition satisfied all of these requirements. It served the general welfare because different drinking ages in different states created incentives for young people "to combine their desire to drink with their ability to drive."

The Court agreed with the suggestion in *Steward Machine Co.* that at some point "pressure turns into coercion." But here, because

> all South Dakota would lose if she adheres to her chosen course as to a suitable minimum drinking age is 5% of the funds otherwise obtainable under specified highway grant programs, the argument as to coercion is shown to be more rhetoric than fact. [Here] Congress has offered relatively mild encouragement to the States to enact higher minimum drinking ages than they would otherwise choose. [But] the enactment of such laws remains the prerogative of the States not merely in theory but in fact.

Justice O'Connor's dissenting opinion argued that the minimum drinking age "is not sufficiently related to interstate highway construction to justify" the condition placed on funds "appropriated for that purpose":

> When Congress appropriates money to build a highway, it is entitled to insist that the highway be a safe one. But it is not entitled to insist as a condition of the use of highway funds that the State impose or change regulations in other areas of the State's social and economic life because of an attenuated or tangential relationship to highway use or safety. [If] the rule were otherwise, the Congress could effectively regulate almost any area of a State's social, political, or economic life on the theory that use of the interstate transportation system is somehow enhanced.

She would have relied on an approach "hark[ing] back" to *Butler,* under which the test would be whether the condition is a regulation or a specification of "how the money should be spent." *Butler* was wrong only because of "its crabbed view of the extent of Congress' regulatory power under the Commerce Clause, not because it insisted that conditions on spending be non-regulatory."

For general discussions of the conditional spending power, see Rosenthal, Conditional Federal Spending and the Constitution, 39 Stan. L. Rev. 1103 (1987); Engdahl, The Spending Power, 44 Duke L.J. 1 (1994).

3. *Coercion and states' rights.* Why is the state not coerced into participating in the unemployment system or into raising the drinking age by fear of the flight of business to states that have qualifying unemployment systems or by fear of the fiscal consequences of attempting to maintain highways without federal aid, respectively? In *Butler*, Justice Stone said, "Threat of loss, not hope of gain, is the essence of economic coercion." Which one is operating in *Steward Machine Co.* and *Dole?* These questions raise deep conceptual issues. For an introduction, see Nozick, Coercion, in Philosophy, Science and Method (S. Morgenbesser ed. 1969); Zimmerman, Coercive Wage Offers, 10 Phil. & Pub. Aff. 121 (1981).

The difficulty of the questions turns on identifying a baseline set of "entitlements" held by states, here the set of activities in which the states and not the national government can engage. Note that Justice Cardozo argues that "the statute does not call for a surrender [of] powers essential to their quasi-sovereign existence." For a comprehensive discussion, see Kreimer, Allocational Sanctions: The Problem of Negative Rights in a Positive State, 132 U. Pa. L. Rev. 1293 (1984). For additional discussion, see Chapter 9 infra.

4. *States' rights limitations on conditional spending.* What limitations does the Court suggest? Is it helpful to say that the issues are ones of degree and fact? What sort of facts?

a. In analyzing the "surrender of essential powers" issue, Justice Cardozo finds that the conditions imposed were within the "margin of discretion" Congress has in determining what standards are "fundamental." What criteria might there be for a judicial determination that Congress had adopted arbitrary conditions? Is there a justification for different rules in connection with exercises of the commerce power and the spending power?

b. Must the conditions imposed be related to the activity receiving the federal subsidy? Note that the Court's precise formulation is "unrelated to the fiscal need [or] to any other end legitimately national." Is the latter anything more than the Hamiltonian position on the scope of the spending power? Could Congress require that state universities whose students receive federally guaranteed loans (a) not discriminate on the basis of race and gender in their admissions policies; (b) not discriminate on the basis of race and gender in faculty employment; (c) conduct research for federal agencies on the development of nuclear power? Could Congress require that states accepting federal funds for elementary and secondary education ban the possession of guns near schools? That such states suspend students who bring guns to schools?

5. *Avoiding the race to the bottom.* Consider the following argument in support of the national legislation: Every state desires to alleviate the burdens of unemployment by adopting some sort of unemployment system. But any state that does so runs the risk that a neighboring state will not, or will adopt a somewhat different system. If the neighboring state has no unemployment system, or has one financed more favorably to employers, the state that adopts the less favorable system runs the risk that employers will relocate. In order to assure that no risk of "unfair competition" of this sort — sometimes called a "race to the bottom" — can occur, coordinated action on the national level is necessary.

Note the following points about this argument: (a) Mechanisms of voluntary coordination exist, as the Court discussed in Carter v. Carter Coal Co. (b) Can we distinguish between failure of a state legislature to act because it fears unfair competition from a neighboring state and failure to act because it believes that unemployment compensation systems are unsound as a matter of policy? Is it sufficient to answer that that is the kind of judgment we leave to Congress? Suppose both senators and the majority of the representatives from some state voted against the national legislation. How confident can we be that national action was needed to avoid a universally undesired race to the bottom? And if the race is not universally undesired, does the preceding argument retain its force? Even if the senators and representatives from a state favored the legislation, might there be differences between their constituencies and the constituencies of local legislators such that we still could not be confident that the state legislature that failed to enact an unemployment compensation system did so from fear of unfair competition? (c) Note that five states, including New York and California, had adopted unemployment compensation systems before Congress acted. Does that cast doubt on the argument that states failed to act out of fear of unfair competition? Why should those states fear such competition any less than other states did?

Baker, Conditional Federal Spending After *Lopez*, 95 Colum. L. Rev. 1911 (1995), criticizes the "political constraints" theory on the ground that it fails to deal with "the ability of some states to harness the federal lawmaking power to oppress other states." Conditional funding statutes, Baker argues, divide states into two groups, one of whose members "already willingly comply with, or favor, the stated condition." Representatives of such states may support a conditional funding statute to "garner the approval of 'single issue' voters and interest groups" or the votes of constituents who believe that activities in other states impose externalities on them. Id. at 1940-1943. Why is such action properly characterized as oppression?

6. *Statutory interpretation as a limiting technique.* The questions raised above can be avoided by construing ambiguous statutes so as not to impose the problematic obligations on the states. As Justice Rehnquist wrote in South Dakota v. Dole, Congress must state "unambiguously" the conditions it imposes on states that accept federal funds. For an example, see Pennhurst State School & Hospital v. Halderman, 451 U.S. 1 (1981).

4.   The Power to Enforce the Reconstruction Amendments

Note: Congressional Power to Enforce or Interpret (?) the Constitution

1. *The text.* The fourteenth amendment provides, in its first section, that "No state shall make or enforce any law which shall abridge the privileges or immunities of citizens of the United States; nor shall any State deprive any person of life, liberty, or property, without due process of law; nor deny to any person within its jurisdiction the equal protection of the laws." The courts identify specific rights created by this section. Section 5 of the amendment provides that Congress "shall have the power to enforce, by appropriate legislation, the provi-

sions of" section 1. What power does this give Congress? Specifically, may Congress "enforce" a liberty or property right that the courts have not recognized? What about congressional "enforcement" of so-called rights that the courts have held are *not* protected by section 1? Note that these questions arise only when the sole source of Congress's power is section 5. Congress can create many statutory rights, including rights to liberty or property, when exercising other powers. For example, the Court has held that Congress creates property rights through the patent laws, an exercise of its power under Art. I, §8, cl. 8. Florida Prepaid Postsecondary Education Expense Board v. College Savings Bank, 527 U.S. 627 (1999).

2. *Possible interpretations of the section 5 power.* Section 1 alone allows citizens or persons to assert that a state action against them violates section 1 rights. Under the most modest interpretation, section 5 gives Congress the power to create a cause of action allowing those whose rights are violated to *bring* a lawsuit, rather than simply assert section 1 rights as a defense. What more might section 5 authorize?

a. *Complex remedies.* Section 5 might authorize Congress to create remedies that courts would have difficulty developing on their own in the ordinary course of case-by-case adjudication. Consider in this connection South Carolina v. Katzenbach, 383 U.S. 301 (1966): After an extensive investigation into racial discrimination in voting practices, Congress enacted the Voting Rights Act of 1965, which gave the Attorney General and the Director of the Census unreviewable authority to determine that a literacy test or other device had been used in a state or political subdivision and to determine that less than 50 percent of its voting residents were registered to vote or had voted. Once those findings were made, the use of "tests or devices" was suspended. In addition, the state or subdivision could not adopt any new standards or procedures with respect to voting without prior submission of the standards to federal authorities, who would determine whether their use would violate the fifteenth amendment. If this "preclearance" resulted in a conclusion by the federal agency that the changes were racially motivated or would have the effect of discriminating on the basis of race, the changes could not be implemented until the state or subdivision secured an appropriate ruling from a federal court. The Court upheld these provisions as permissible exercises of Congress's power under section 2 of the fifteenth amendment "to enforce . . . by appropriate legislation" the right guaranteed by section 1 of that amendment. (The cases have not distinguished between the enforcement powers granted Congress by the fourteenth amendment and those granted by the fifteenth.)

b. *Preventive or "prophylactic" remedies.* Congress might have the power to forestall the occurrence of acts that would violate rights that the courts have found or would find protected by the Constitution. Note that the "remedy" here occurs before the "violation" does. See City of Rome v. United States, 446 U.S. 156 (1980): The city challenged the application of the preclearance provisions of the Voting Rights Act on the ground, among others, that the fifteenth amendment prohibited only purposeful discrimination. The Voting Rights Act required preclearance of changes that had discriminatory effects, even if they had no discriminatory purposes. The Attorney General had found that the city's changes had the impermissible effects but not the impermissible purposes. Under those circumstances, the city argued, Congress's power to enforce the fifteenth amendment did not extend to its proposed changes. The Court, through Justice Marshall, rejected the city's argument. It assumed that the fifteenth amendment prohibited only intentional discrimination. But "Congress could rationally have concluded that, because electoral changes by jurisdictions with a demonstrable history of intentional racial discrimination in voting create the risk of purposeful discrimination, it was proper to prohibit changes that have a discriminatory impact."

Is the "risk" that at some time in the future, the city will adopt purposefully discriminatory changes? If so, why won't preclearance then, and judicial scrutiny directly under the fifteenth amendment, be enough to preclude the adoption of those — but only those — changes? Or is the "risk" that neither the Attorney General nor the courts will be able accurately to determine in every instance whether a change had a discriminatory purpose? How substantial must either of these risks be? Is it enough that Congress found them substantial, or must the Court agree, based on its independent analysis of the situation? Justice Rehnquist's dissent, joined by Justice Stewart, argued that, having established that it had no discriminatory purpose, the city would not violate the Constitution in adopting its new rules, and that Congress therefore lacked power to "remedy" a nonexistent violation by requiring preclearance of the changes. It also argued that a preventive "remedy" was constitutional only if the Court agreed that the risk of a substantive violation was substantial.

KATZENBACH v. MORGAN, 384 U.S. 641 (1966). Lassiter v. Northampton Election Board, 360 U.S. 45 (1959), held that an English-language literacy requirement did not violate the substantive guarantees of the fourteenth and fifteenth amendments. Section 4(e) of the Voting Rights Act of 1965 provides that no person who has completed sixth grade in a Puerto Rican school, where instruction was in Spanish, shall be denied the right to vote because of his or her inability to read or write English. This provision was designed to enfranchise several hundred thousand people who had migrated to New York from Puerto Rico by overriding a New York statute requiring that voters be literate in English. The Court rejected a constitutional challenge to section 4(e).

Justice Brennan, writing for the Court, rejected the state's argument that section 4(e) could not be "sustained as appropriate legislation to enforce the Equal Protection Clause unless the judiciary decides — even with the guidance of a congressional judgment — that [English-language literacy requirements violate] the Equal Protection Clause itself. [A] construction of §5 that would require a judicial determination that the enforcement of the state law precluded by Congress violated the Amendment [would] depreciate both congressional resourcefulness and congressional responsibility for implementing the Amendment. It would confine the legislative power in this context to the insignificant role of abrogating only those state laws that the judicial branch was prepared to adjudge unconstitutional, or of merely informing the judgment of the judiciary by particularizing the 'majestic generalities' of §1 of the Amendment." Section 4(e) "may be viewed as a measure to secure for the Puerto Rican community residing in New York nondiscriminatory treatment by government — both in the imposition of voting qualifications and the provision or administration of governmental services, such as public schools, public housing and law enforcement. [The] practical effect of §4(e) is to prohibit New York from denying the right to vote to large segments of its Puerto Rican community. [This] enhanced political power will be helpful in gaining nondiscriminatory treatment in public services for the entire Puerto Rican community. [It] was well within congressional authority to say that this need of the Puerto Rican minority for the vote warranted federal intrusion upon any state interests served by the English literacy requirement. It was for Congress [to] assess and weigh the various conflicting considerations — the risk or pervasiveness of the discrimination in governmental services, the effectiveness of eliminating the state restriction on the right to vote as a means of dealing with the evil, the adequacy or availability of alternative remedies, and the nature and significance of the state interests that would be affected by the nullification of the English literacy requirement. [It] is not for us to review the congressional resolution of these factors. It is enough that we be able to perceive a basis upon which the Congress might resolve the conflict as it did."

The Court then considered "whether §4(e) was merely legislation aimed at the elimination of an invidious discrimination in establishing voter qualifications. We are told that New York's English literacy requirement originated in the desire to provide an incentive for non-English speaking immigrants to learn the English language and in order to assure the intelligent exercise of the franchise. Yet Congress might well have questioned, in light of the many exemptions provided and some evidence suggesting that prejudice played a prominent role in the enactment of the requirement whether these were actually the interests being served. Congress might have also questioned whether denial of a right deemed so precious and fundamental in our society was a necessary or appropriate means of encouraging persons to learn English, or of furthering the goal of an intelligent exercise of the franchise. Finally, Congress might well have concluded that as a means of furthering the intelligent exercise of the franchise, an ability to read or understand Spanish is as effective as ability to read English for those to whom Spanish-language newspapers and Spanish-language radio and television programs are available to inform them of election issues and governmental affairs. Since Congress undertook to legislate so as to preclude the enforcement of the state law, and did so in the context of a general appraisal of literacy requirements for voting, to which it brought a specially informed legislative competence, it was Congress' prerogative to weigh these competing considerations. Here again, it is enough that we perceive a basis upon which Congress might predicate a judgment that the application of New York's English literacy requirement to deny the right to vote to a person with a sixth grade education in Puerto Rican schools in which the language of instruction was other than English constituted an invidious discrimination in violation of the Equal Protection Clause."

Justice Harlan, joined by Justice Stewart, dissented. He interpreted the decision as adopting a test of rationality: "[Was] Congress acting rationally in declaring that the New York statute is irrational?" For him, it was "a judicial question whether the condition with which Congress has thus sought to deal is in truth an infringement of the Constitution, something that is the necessary prerequisite to bringing the §5 power into play at all. [Were] the rule otherwise, Congress would be able to qualify this Court's constitutional decisions under the Fourteenth and Fifteenth Amendments [by] resorting to congressional power under the Necessary and Proper Clause. [In] effect the Court reads §5 of the Fourteenth Amendment as giving Congress the power to define the *substantive* scope of the Amendment. If that indeed be the true reach of §5, then I do not see why Congress should not be able as well to exercise its §5 'discretion' by enacting statutes so as in effect to dilute equal protection and due process decisions of this Court. In all such cases there is room for reasonable men to differ as to whether or not a denial of equal protection or due process has occurred, and the final decision is one of judgment. Until today this judgment has always been one for the judiciary to resolve." He acknowledged that "[decisions] on questions of equal protection and due process are based not on abstract logic, but on empirical foundations. To the extent 'legislative facts' are relevant to a judicial determination, Congress is well equipped to investigate them, and such determinations are of course entitled to due respect." But he found "no [factual] data" showing that "Spanish-speaking citizens are fully as capable of making informed decisions in a New York election as are English-speaking citizens. Nor was there any showing [to] support the Court's alternative argument that §4(e) should be viewed as but a remedial measure designed to cure or assure against unconstitutional discrimination of other varieties." He concluded, "To deny the effectiveness of this congressional enactment is not of course to disparage Congress' exertion of authority in the field of civil rights; it is simply to recognize that the Legislative Branch like the other branches of federal authority is subject to the governmental boundaries set by the Constitution. To hold, on this record, that §4(e) overrides the New York literacy requirement seems to me tantamount to allowing the Fourteenth Amendment to swallow the State's constitutionally ordained primary authority in this field. For if Congress by what, as here, amounts to mere *ipse dixit* can set that otherwise permissible requirement partially at naught I see no reason why it could not also substitute its judgment for that of the States in other fields of their exclusive primary competence as well."

Note: The Scope of Section 5

What interpretation of section 5 does *Morgan* adopt? The Court mentions a preventive or prophylactic rationale, but some of its language suggests broader interpretations.

1. *Remedies for arguable violations.* Perhaps Congress can provide remedies for violations of rights that *arguably* are protected by the Constitution, that is, where there are good grounds for thinking that, given what the courts have said about a problem, the courts *might* find a constitutional violation.

> Congress may scrutinize any state regime which the Court has found to be constitutionally questionable because it involves a suspect classification or a fundamental right. [Congress may] investigate the facts surrounding state action of this type and then prohibit the practice if, in Congress' judgment, it lacks the compelling basis which the Court demands to uphold it. [Under] this reading [Congress] is free to invalidate government actions that the Court has already upheld or might otherwise uphold in the future. But this would only permit Congress to "expand" on judicial conceptions [in] those very limited situations where Congress, with its special competence in the circumstances, has appraised the relevant factors and concluded that the law [is] not justified by the required state interest — a decision which differs from that which the Court, with its more limited capabilities, either has already reached or would otherwise make when the issue was presented to it. Thus, in enacting section 4(e) of the Voting Rights Act, Congress might be said to have concluded that, in its judgment, contrary to the Court's holding in [*Lassiter*],

there was no compelling basis for states' denying the franchise to persons not literate in English.

Choper, Congressional Power to Expand Judicial Definitions of the Substantive Terms of the Civil War Amendments, 67 Minn. L. Rev. 299, 308-309 (1982). The interpretations of section 5 authorizing complex or preventive remedies rest on the proposition that somewhere in the situation lurks a constitutional violation that the courts would themselves declare to be a violation. Does Choper's analysis rest on that proposition or a similar one? If not, what reason is there for adopting it?

2. *Substantive interpretations.* "Congress, in the field of state activities and except as confined by the Bill of Rights, has the power to enact any law which may be viewed as a measure for correction of any condition which Congress might believe involves a denial of equality or other fourteenth amendment rights." Cox, Constitutional Adjudication and the Promotion of Human Rights, 80 Harv. L. Rev. 91, 107 (1966). Is this consistent with the text of section 5? On what bases might we rest this independent power in Congress to interpret the Constitution in ways that the Court would (might?) not?

a. *Fact-finding ability.* Cox argues that "the Court has long been committed both to the presumption that facts exist which sustain congressional legislation and also to deference to congressional judgment about questions of degree and proportion." Id. The due process and equal protection requirements depend "to a large extent upon finding and appraisal of the practical importance of relevant facts," and "there is often room for differences of opinion in interpreting the available data." Id. at 106.

b. *Reasonable alternative interpretations of "liberty."* Consider the possibility that (1) with respect to some constitutional guarantees, there is a (broad or narrow) range of permissible interpretations; and (2) the courts are sometimes constrained by their institutional characteristics — for example, by limits on their ability to define rules with sufficient clarity — to adopt only one interpretation within that range. Congress, lacking the same kinds of institutional characteristics, might adopt another interpretation yet still remain within the range of permissible interpretations. Note that this might authorize Congress to reject Court interpretations of section 1 that in the Court's view expand liberty but that in Congress's view mistakenly identify what liberty is. Does this analysis threaten the theory of Marbury v. Madison? For a full discussion, see Monaghan, Constitutional Common Law, 89 Harv. L. Rev. 1 (1975); Burt, *Miranda* and Title II: A Morganatic Marriage, 1969 Sup. Ct. Rev. 81. Note that some "expansions" of one constitutional "right" might contract other constitutional "rights." Consider a statute barring all private employers from discriminating in hiring on the basis of gender, as applied to a church whose doctrines limit the ministry to men (or women). Is this statute an expansion or a dilution of constitutional rights?

Carter, The *Morgan* "Power" and the Forced Reconsideration of Constitutional Decisions, 53 U. Chi. L. Rev. 819, 824 (1986), argues that *Morgan* is "best understood as a tool that permits the Congress to use its power to enact ordinary legislation to engage the Court in a dialogue about our fundamental rights, thereby 'forcing' the Justices to take a fresh look at their own judgments." Compare this power with that of Congress to regulate (or restrict) the jurisdiction of the federal courts.

3. *Federalism.* Cohen, Congressional Power to Interpret Due Process and Equal Protection, 27 Stan. L. Rev. 603 (1975), argues that Katzenbach v. Morgan is defensible as an ordinary application of the general proposition that the courts will not enforce federalism-based limitations on congressional power because the political constraints on Congress are sufficient to protect against improvident national action. With respect to political constraints on Congress, are there differences between Congress's article I powers and its powers to enforce the fourteenth and fifteenth amendments? Do the differences, if any, argue in favor of or against more expansive interpretations of the latter than the former?

City of Boerne v. Flores

521 U.S. 507 (1997)

Justice Kennedy delivered the opinion of the Court.

A decision by local zoning authorities to deny a church a building permit was challenged under the Religious Freedom Restoration Act of 1993 (RFRA). The case calls into question the authority of Congress to enact RFRA. We conclude the statute exceeds Congress' power. . . .

II

Congress enacted RFRA in direct response to the Court's decision in Employment Div., Dept. of Human Resources of Ore. v. Smith, 494 U.S. 872 (1990) [Chapter 8 infra]. There we considered a Free Exercise Clause claim brought by members of the Native American Church who were denied unemployment benefits when they lost their jobs because they had used peyote. Their practice was to ingest peyote for sacramental purposes, and they challenged an Oregon statute of general applicability which made use of the drug criminal. In evaluating the claim, we declined to apply the balancing test set forth in Sherbert v. Verner, 374 U. S. 398 (1963). [We] stated:

> "Government's ability to enforce generally applicable prohibitions of socially harmful conduct . . . cannot depend on measuring the effects of a governmental action on a religious objector's spiritual development. To make an individual's obligation to obey such a law contingent upon the law's coincidence with his religious beliefs, except where the State's interest is 'compelling' . . . contradicts both constitutional tradition and common sense." . . .

[These] points of constitutional interpretation were debated by Members of Congress in hearings and floor debates. Many criticized the Court's reasoning, and this disagreement resulted in the passage of RFRA. . . .

RFRA prohibits "government" from "substantially burdening" a person's exercise of religion even if the burden results from a rule of general applicability unless the government can demonstrate the burden "(1) is in furtherance of a compelling governmental interest; and (2) is the least restrictive means of furthering that compelling governmental interest." The Act's mandate applies to any "branch, department, agency, instrumentality, and official (or other person acting under color of law) of the United States," as well as to any "State, or . . . sub-division of a State." . . .

III

A . . .

[In] defense of the Act respondent contends [that] RFRA is permissible enforce-ment legislation. Congress, it is said, is only protecting by legislation one of the liberties guaranteed by the Fourteenth Amendment's Due Process Clause, the free exercise of religion, beyond what is necessary under *Smith*. It is said the con-gressional decision to dispense with proof of deliberate or overt discrimination and instead concentrate on a law's effects accords with the settled understanding that §5 includes the power to enact legislation designed to prevent as well as rem-edy constitutional violations. It is further contended that Congress' §5 power is not limited to remedial or preventive legislation. . . .

[Legislation] which deters or remedies constitutional violations can fall within the sweep of Congress' enforcement power even if in the process it prohibits con-duct which is not itself unconstitutional and intrudes into "legislative spheres of autonomy previously reserved to the States." Fitzpatrick v. Bitzer, 427 U.S. 445, 455 (1976). . . .

[In] assessing the breadth of §5's enforcement power, we begin with its text. Congress has been given the power "to enforce" the "provisions of this article." [Congress'] power to enforce the Free Exercise Clause follows from our hold-ing in Cantwell v. Connecticut, 310 U.S. 296, 303 (1940), that the "fundamen-tal concept of liberty embodied in [the Fourteenth Amendment's Due Process Clause] embraces the liberties guaranteed by the First Amendment."

Congress' power under §5, however, extends only to "enforcing" the provisions of the Fourteenth Amendment. The Court has described this power as "reme-dial" [South Carolina v. Katzenbach]. The design of the Amendment and the text of §5 are inconsistent with the suggestion that Congress has the power to decree the substance of the Fourteenth Amendment's restrictions on the States. Legislation which alters the meaning of the Free Exercise Clause cannot be said to be enforcing the Clause. Congress does not enforce a constitutional right by changing what the right is. It has been given the power "to enforce," not the power to determine what constitutes a constitutional violation. Were it not so, what Congress would be enforcing would no longer be, in any meaningful sense, the "provisions of [the Fourteenth Amendment]."

While the line between measures that remedy or prevent unconstitutional ac-tions and measures that make a substantive change in the governing law is not easy to discern, and Congress must have wide latitude in determining where it lies, the distinction exists and must be observed. There must be a congruence and proportionality between the injury to be prevented or remedied and the means adopted to that end. Lacking such a connection, legislation may become substantive in operation and effect. . . .

Any suggestion that Congress has a substantive, non-remedial power under the Fourteenth Amendment is not supported by our case law. . . .

There is language in our opinion in Katzenbach v. Morgan which could be in-terpreted as acknowledging a power in Congress to enact legislation that expands the rights contained in §1 of the Fourteenth Amendment. This is not a necessary interpretation, however, or even the best one. . . .

If Congress could define its own powers by altering the Fourteenth Amendment's meaning, no longer would the Constitution be "superior paramount law, unchangeable by ordinary means." It would be "on a level with ordinary legislative acts, and, like other acts, . . . alterable when the legislature shall please to alter it." [*Marbury.*] Under this approach, it is difficult to conceive of a principle that would limit congressional power. Shifting legislative majorities could change the Constitution and effectively circumvent the difficult and detailed amendment process contained in Article V. . . .

B

Respondent contends that RFRA is a proper exercise of Congress' remedial or preventive power. The Act, it is said, is a reasonable means of protecting the free exercise of religion as defined by *Smith*. It prevents and remedies laws which are enacted with the unconstitutional object of targeting religious beliefs and practices. To avoid the difficulty of proving such violations, it is said, Congress can simply invalidate any law which imposes a substantial burden on a religious practice unless it is justified by a compelling interest and is the least restrictive means of accomplishing that interest. If Congress can prohibit laws with discriminatory effects in order to prevent racial discrimination in violation of the Equal Protection Clause, then it can do the same, respondent argues, to promote religious liberty.

While preventive rules are sometimes appropriate remedial measures, there must be a congruence between the means used and the ends to be achieved. The appropriateness of remedial measures must be considered in light of the evil presented. Strong measures appropriate to address one harm may be an unwarranted response to another, lesser one. . . .

[RFRA] cannot be considered remedial, preventive legislation, if those terms are to have any meaning. RFRA is so out of proportion to a supposed remedial or preventive object that it cannot be understood as responsive to, or designed to prevent, unconstitutional behavior. It appears, instead, to attempt a substantive change in constitutional protections. Preventive measures prohibiting certain types of laws may be appropriate when there is reason to believe that many of the laws affected by the congressional enactment have a significant likelihood of being unconstitutional. . . .

The substantial costs RFRA exacts, both in practical terms of imposing a heavy litigation burden on the States and in terms of curtailing their traditional general regulatory power, far exceed any pattern or practice of unconstitutional conduct under the Free Exercise Clause as interpreted in *Smith*. Simply put, RFRA is not designed to identify and counteract state laws likely to be unconstitutional because of their treatment of religion. . . .

When Congress acts within its sphere of power and responsibilities, it has not just the right but the duty to make its own informed judgment on the meaning and force of the Constitution. This has been clear from the early days of the Republic. In 1789, when a Member of the House of Representatives objected to a debate on the constitutionality of legislation based on the theory that "it would be officious" to consider the constitutionality of a measure that did not affect the

House, James Madison explained that "it is incontrovertibly of as much importance to this branch of the Government as to any other, that the constitution should be preserved entire. It is our duty." Were it otherwise, we would not afford Congress the presumption of validity its enactments now enjoy.

Our national experience teaches that the Constitution is preserved best when each part of the government respects both the Constitution and the proper actions and determinations of the other branches. When the Court has interpreted the Constitution, it has acted within the province of the Judicial Branch, which embraces the duty to say what the law is. [*Marbury.*] When the political branches of the Government act against the background of a judicial interpretation of the Constitution already issued, it must be understood that in later cases and controversies the Court will treat its precedents with the respect due them under settled principles, including stare decisis, and contrary expectations must be disappointed. RFRA was designed to control cases and controversies, such as the one before us; but as the provisions of the federal statute here invoked are beyond congressional authority, it is this Court's precedent, not RFRA, which must control.

* * *

It is for Congress in the first instance to "determine whether and what legislation is needed to secure the guarantees of the Fourteenth Amendment," and its conclusions are entitled to much deference. [Katzenbach v. Morgan]. Congress' discretion is not unlimited, however, and the courts retain the power, as they have since Marbury v. Madison, to determine if Congress has exceeded its authority under the Constitution. Broad as the power of Congress is under the Enforcement Clause of the Fourteenth Amendment, RFRA contradicts vital principles necessary to maintain separation of powers and the federal balance. The judgment of the Court of Appeals sustaining the Act's constitutionality is reversed.

[Justice Stevens concurred in the Court's opinion, and noted as well that he believed that RFRA violated the establishment clause of the first amendment. Justice O'Connor dissented, saying that in her view *Smith* was wrongly decided and should be overruled, but she agreed with the Court's analysis of Congress's power under section 5. Justice Breyer joined her discussion of *Smith* but did not "find it necessary" to consider the question of congressional power under section 5. Justice Souter also dissented, saying that the Court should have dismissed the writ of certiorari as improperly granted.]

Note: The Roles of Court and Congress

1. *"Changing" or "defining" constitutional rights.* The Court argues that "Congress does not enforce a constitutional right by changing what the right is." Consider the theory of judicial supremacy implicit in that phrase. Should Congress have the power to (conclusively) define a right in a reasonable manner inconsistent with a prior judicial determination of what the right is? Would that allow Congress to dilute constitutional protections? Can that question be answered without a broader theory of the relation between Court and Congress in defining constitutional rights? For an argument against judicial supremacy, see M. Tushnet, Taking the Constitution Away from the Courts (1999).

Is the problem in *Boerne* that Congress acted too swiftly and in direct contradiction of a recent Supreme Court decision? What would Congress have to do to establish that a more focused statute, imposing the statutory standard for zoning decisions, for example, was appropriately "congruent" and "proportional"?

2. *The congressional "sphere of power."* In light of *Boerne*, what incentives does Congress have to "make its own informed judgment" about the Constitution's meaning? (a) Does the Court mean more than that Congress can adopt constitutional views, inconsistent with the Court's, that lead it to refrain from enacting statutes that the Court would uphold? (b) Note that the issue in *Boerne* might be described as implicating the boundaries of Congress's powers, or alternatively as implicating the boundaries of the Court's power. Consider the proposition that both Congress and the Court are self-interested in resolving the issue: RFRA "expands" congressional power and "contracts" judicial power; *Boerne* "expands" judicial power and "contracts" congressional power.

Note: The Eleventh Amendment and the Constitutional Immunity of States from Certain Forms of Liability

The Supreme Court has limited congressional power not only by its construction of the Constitution's grants of substantive power but also by limiting Congress's power to create judicial remedies for enforcing federal constitutional and statutory rights. It has relied principally on the eleventh amendment, which provides, "The judicial power of the United States shall not be construed to extend to any suit in law or equity, commenced or prosecuted against one of the United States by Citizens of another State, or by Citizens or Subjects of any Foreign State." The amendment was adopted in response to the Supreme Court's ruling in Chisholm v. Georgia, 2 U.S. (2 Dall.) 419 (1793), which involved a suit by a South Carolina citizen seeking to recover a debt owed for materials supplied to Georgia during the Revolutionary War. The Supreme Court upheld federal jurisdiction by a four-to-one vote. Congress submitted the proposed eleventh amendment to the states within three weeks of the decision in *Chisholm*, and the required three-quarters of the states ratified it within a year, although the official proclamation of ratification did not occur until 1797.

The amendment's text refers only to suits against states brought by citizens of other states or foreign nations. Hans v. Louisiana, 134 U.S. 1 (1890), relied on Congress's immediate reaction to *Chisholm* to support its holding that the judicial power of the United States did not extend to suits by citizens against their own states. As the Court later explained, *Hans* adopts the view that states' immunity from suit was a presupposition of the constitutional order, not displaced by the mere adoption of the Constitution.

Does Congress have the power to eliminate the states' immunity from suit? For a period the Court held that the Constitution's grants of power to Congress, in article I, section 8 and elsewhere, gave Congress the power to displace state immunity. See, e.g., Pennsylvania v. Union Gas, 491 U.S. 1 (1989). Seminole Tribe of Florida v. Florida, 517 U.S. 44 (1996), rejected those decisions and held that state immunity could not be displaced by an exercise of the powers granted Congress in 1789. The eleventh amendment was not directly applicable, but, according to the Court, its adoption showed that those who adopted the original Constitution did not believe that they were creating a national government authorized to eliminate state immunity. Alden v. Maine, 527 U.S. 706 (1999), held that Congress could not require state courts to entertain suits by individuals seeking damages for violation of a national statute, where the state courts refused to do so on the basis of state sovereign immunity rules that did not themselves discriminate against national claims. Again, the decision cannot be explained as relying on the eleventh amendment, which refers only to the judicial power of the United States.

The Court has held, however, that section 5 of the fourteenth amendment does give Congress the power to displace state immunity when it develops remedies for violations of rights protected by section 1 of that amendment. In the Court's view, not only does the fourteenth amendment come later in time than the eleventh, but it also expresses a view of the relation between the states and the nation in which state sovereign immunity must yield to congressional judgments. Congress must declare clearly that the statute imposes liability on states, and its exercise of power under section 5 must satisfy the requirement of *Boerne* that the remedy be a proportionate and congruent response to identified constitutional violations.

The Court held unconstitutional a statute authorizing federal courts to impose monetary liability on states that violated the property rights conferred by the patent laws. Florida Prepaid Postsecondary Education Expense Board v. College Savings Bank, 527 U.S. 627 (1999). According to the Court, the only constitutional violation was the deprivation of property without due process of law, and there was insufficient evidence that states were denying due process by, for example, making it impossible for the patent holders to obtain damages in state courts. The Court also held unconstitutional the imposition of damage liability on states for violations of the Age Discrimination in Employment Act. Kimel v. Florida Board of Regents, 120 S. Ct. 645 (2000). Under the Court's equal protection holdings, age discrimination by state officials is unconstitutional only when it is irrational. See Chapter 5 infra. Again the Court found insufficient evidence that states were engaging in such widespread irrational (and therefore unconstitutional) age discrimination to justify a general remedy of damages for all acts of age discrimination.

The body of law dealing with state immunity is quite complex. Three other aspects of that law, stated broadly and without the qualifications needed for a complete understanding, are these: (1) States are not immune to actions filed by the United States, whether for damages or injunctive relief. (2) Individuals may obtain injunctions issued by the federal courts against continuing violations of national law, by naming as defendants the state officials engaging in unconstitutional action or enforcing the asserted unlawful state law. Ex parte Young, 209 U.S. 123 (1908). (3) Individuals may obtain damages from state officials who engage in unconstitutional action, but the officials may assert as a defense that their actions were not clearly unconstitutional at the time they acted.

The doctrines of state immunity taken together imply that the Constitution limits but does not eliminate Congress's ability to choose a scheme for remedying violations of national law. Congress may be required to select a remedial scheme that is less than completely effective, as judged by Congress itself. Is the Supreme Court justified in imposing such a limitation on Congress in the absence of specific constitutional text?

*Note: Congressional Power to Regulate "Private" Action for Civil
Rights Purposes*

1. *The thirteenth amendment.* In Jones v. Alfred H. Mayer Co., 392 U.S. 409
(1968), the plaintiffs alleged that Mayer, the developer of a large suburban housing complex, had refused to sell them a home solely because one of them was
black. They claimed that this violated 42 U.S.C. §1982, which provides: "All citizens [shall] have the same right, in every State and Territory, as is enjoyed by white
citizens thereof, to inherit, purchase, lease, sell, hold, and convey real and personal property." The Court, through Justice Stewart, held that the statute barred
private racial discrimination in the sale of property, and that, "thus construed, [it]
is a valid exercise of the power of Congress to enforce the Thirteenth Amendment." Citing the Civil Rights Cases, Chapter 9, section A, infra, the Court said
that the amendment is "an absolute declaration that slavery or involuntary servitude shall not exist in any part of the United States." Its second section "clothed
'Congress with power to pass *all laws necessary and proper for abolishing all
badges and incidents of slavery in the United States*' (emphasis added). [Surely]
Congress has the power [rationally] to determine what are the badges and the incidents of slavery." It was not "irrational" for Congress to conclude that private restraints on the ability of blacks to engage in otherwise normal market transactions
were such badges and incidents. Justice Harlan, joined by Justice White, would
have dismissed the writ of certiorari as improvidently granted because the Civil
Rights Act of 1968 covered essentially the same ground as that raised by Jones's
complaint.

2. *The fourteenth amendment.* The fourteenth amendment provides that "no
state shall [deny] to any person [the] equal protection of the laws." The reference
to "states" has generated a large body of doctrine regarding the so-called state
action doctrine, discussed in detail in Chapter 9 infra. For present purposes, the
doctrine means that, for the fourteenth amendment to be implicated (and therefore for Congress to have power to enforce its protections), there must be either
a sufficient degree of state involvement with the action or a failure by the state to
act in circumstances where the Constitution affirmatively requires action.

United States v. Morrison, 120 S. Ct. 1740 (2000), held that the civil remedy
provision of the Violence Against Women Act was not a constitutionally permissible exercise of Congress's power under section 5. The statute's defenders relied
on "evidence that many participants in state justice systems are perpetuating an
array of erroneous stereotypes and assumptions. Congress concluded that these
discriminatory stereotypes often result in insufficient investigation and prosecution of gender-motivated crime, inappropriate focus on the behavior and credibility of the victims of that crime, and unacceptably lenient punishments for
those who are actually convicted of gender-motivated violence." They argued
that "this bias denies victims of gender-motivated violence the equal protection
of the laws and that Congress therefore acted appropriately in enacting a private
civil remedy against the perpetrators of gender-motivated violence to both remedy
the States' bias and deter future instances of discrimination in the state courts."
The Court rejected this argument: "[The] remedy is simply not 'corrective in its
character, adapted to counteract and redress the operation of such prohibited
state laws or proceedings of state officers.' Civil Rights Cases, 109 U.S. at 18. Or,

as we have phrased it in more recent cases, prophylactic legislation under §5 must have a 'congruence and proportionality between the injury to be prevented or remedied and the means adopted to that end.' [*Boerne*]. Section 13981 is not aimed at proscribing discrimination by officials which the Fourteenth Amendment might not itself proscribe; it is directed not at any State or state actor, but at individuals who have committed criminal acts motivated by gender bias." Justice Breyer's dissent asked, "[Given] the relation between remedy and violation — the creation of a federal remedy to substitute for constitutionally inadequate state remedies — where is the lack of 'congruence'?"

3. *Problems of statutory interpretation.* The statutes discussed here are the legacy of Reconstruction, a period when concepts of civil rights and federalism were different from our own. The Court has been criticized and praised for infusing these old statutes with contemporary content. See, e.g., Casper, *Jones v. Mayer:* Clio, Bemused and Confused Muse, 1968 Sup. Ct. Rev. 89; Kohl, The Civil Rights Act of 1866, Its Hour Come Round at Last, 55 Va. L. Rev. 272 (1969). If the language of the statutes is fairly susceptible to the Court's interpretations, should it matter that its adopters had a narrower understanding of civil rights? What if their understanding was confused (on our terms or theirs)?

Modern civil rights statutes cover many of the acts also covered by the Reconstruction statutes under the Court's interpretations. The Civil Rights Act of 1968, for example, makes unlawful the activity at issue in Jones v. Mayer. The act is broader than the 1866 act in some ways, by covering other forms of discrimination and providing additional forms of remedial assistance to a complainant, and is narrower in others, by containing some exemptions. Is it appropriate to revive old statutes when Congress has recently addressed the general problem in a different way?

E.   IMPLIED LIMITS ON CONGRESS'S POWERS

With some exceptions, the cases in the preceding sections involve the constitutionality of national legislation regulating the activities of private persons or corporations. The primary question in those cases was whether the legislation fell within the scope of one of the powers granted to Congress in the Constitution. A secondary question was whether the legislation interfered with or improperly displaced the authority of state governments to regulate. Are there other limits on Congress's power to regulate, designed to protect state authority in some other way?

National League of Cities v. Usery, 426 U.S. 833 (1976), held that the commerce clause did not empower Congress to enforce the minimum wage and overtime provisions of the Fair Labor Standards Act (FLSA) against the states "in areas of traditional governmental functions." The Court agreed that the wages and hours of state employees affected interstate commerce but found the application of the statute to state and local employees unconstitutional. Over the next decade, the Court struggled to identify the contours of the protection afforded state and local governments by *National League of Cities.*

Hodel v. Virginia Surface Mining Association, 452 U.S. 264 (1981), upheld the constitutionality of a federal statute regulating the operation of strip mines. The statute required strip-mine operators to return the area to its "approximate original contour," which substantially increased the cost of operating certain strip mines. The Court held that the federal statute did not affect "State as States," and therefore did not violate a state's constitutional immunity from regulation. The lower court had held that the federal statute interfered with the "traditional governmental function" of land use regulation. From the states' point of view, why should it matter that a federal regulation affects them directly rather than by increasing the operating costs of locally important industries?

United Transportation Union v. Long Island Railroad, 455 U.S. 678 (1982), upheld the constitutionality of applying the Railway Labor Act's collective bargaining provisions to the state-owned Long Island Railroad. Consider the proposition that maintaining the railroad was as essential to the infrastructure of economic and social activities in New York as is setting wages and hours of state employees.

Federal Energy Regulatory Commission v. Mississippi, 456 U.S. 742 (1982), upheld certain provisions of the Public Utilities Regulatory Policies Act (PURPA) of 1978. PURPA requires state utilities commissions to consider a specified list of approaches to structuring rates and to consider adopting standards regarding rate disclosure and the recovery of advertising costs in rates. It requires the commissions to consider these standards at public hearings and to issue written statements if the standards are not adopted. PURPA also authorizes the Federal Energy Regulatory Commission to adopt rules encouraging small power production facilities. These rules would be enforced by the state commissions. The Court held that the state commissions could be required to enforce federal standards, relying on Testa v. Katt, 330 U.S. 386 (1947). It upheld the mandatory consideration requirement on the ground that Congress, having the power to preempt state regulation entirely, could adopt the less intrusive scheme of PURPA.

EEOC v. Wyoming, 460 U.S. 226 (1983), upheld the application of the Age Discrimination in Employment Act to state employees. The Court found that the act did not impair states' abilities to structure their integral operations to a degree making the act unconstitutional. The act allows employees to be discharged for cause and authorizes mandatory retirement policies that are shown to be bona fide occupational qualifications. The costs of eliminating mandatory retirement policies were said to be neither "direct" nor "obvious."

GARCIA v. SAN ANTONIO METROPOLITAN TRANSIT AUTHORITY, 469 U.S. 528 (1985).

The Court overruled *National League of Cities*, concluding that the "traditional governmental functions" test was "unworkable." According to Justice Blackmun's majority opinion, "[the] problem is that [no] distinction [that] purports to separate out important governmental functions can be faithful to the role of federalism in a democratic society. The essence of our federal system is that within the realm of authority left open to them under the Constitution, the States must be equally free to engage in any activity that their citizens choose for the common weal, no matter how unorthodox or unnecessary anyone else — including the judiciary — deems state involvement to be. Any rule of state immunity that looks to the 'traditional,' 'integral,' or 'necessary' nature of governmental functions inevitably invites an unelected federal judiciary to make decisions about which state policies it favors and which ones it dislikes." The

Court therefore "reject[ed], as unsound in principle and unworkable in practice, a rule of state immunity from federal regulation that turns on a judicial appraisal of whether a particular governmental function is 'integral' or 'traditional.' Any such rule leads to inconsistent results at the same time that it disserves principles of democratic self-governance, and it breeds inconsistency precisely because it is divorced from those principles."

Conceding that there are "limits on the Federal Government's power to interfere with state functions," the Court examined "the manner in which the Constitution insulates States from the reach of Congress' power under the Commerce Clause." It was unlikely "that courts ultimately can identify principled constitutional limitations on the scope of Congress' Commerce Clause powers over the States merely by relying on *a priori* definitions of state sovereignty." The states retained sovereign authority, but "only to the extent that the Constitution has not divested them of their original powers and transferred those powers to the Federal Government. [The] principal means chosen by the Framers to ensure the role of the States in the federal system lies in the structure of the Federal Government itself. [State] sovereign interests, then, are more properly protected by procedural safeguards inherent in the structure of the federal system than by judicially created limitations on federal power."

Chief Justice Burger and Justices Powell, Rehnquist, and O'Connor dissented. Justice Powell's dissent said, "The Framers recognized that the most effective democracy occurs at local levels of government, where people with first hand knowledge of local problems have more ready access to public officials responsible for dealing with them. This is as true today as it was when the Constitution was adopted. 'Participation is likely to be more frequent, and exercised at more different stages of a governmental activity at the local level, or in regional organizations, than at the state and federal levels.' [ACIR], Citizen Participation in the American Federal System 95 (1979)."

Justice Powell referred to the recent "rise of numerous special interest groups that engage in sophisticated lobbying, and make substantial campaign contributions to some members of Congress. These groups are thought to have significant influence in the shaping and enactment of certain types of legislation. Contrary to the Court's view, a 'political process' that functions in this way is unlikely to safeguard the sovereign rights of States and localities." In contrast to the Court's observation that "the standard approved in *National League of Cities* 'disserves principles of democratic self government,'" Justice Powell observed, "[T]he Court looks myopically only to persons elected to positions in the federal government. It disregards entirely the far more effective role of democratic self-government at the state and local levels. One must compare realistically the operation of the state and local governments with that of the federal government. Federal legislation is drafted primarily by the staffs of the congressional committees. In view of the hundreds of bills introduced at each session of Congress and the complexity of many of them, it is virtually impossible for even the most conscientious legislators to be truly familiar with many of the statutes enacted. Federal departments and agencies customarily are authorized to write regulations. Often these are more important than the text of the statutes. As is true of the original legislation, these are drafted largely by staff personnel. The administration and enforcement of federal laws and regulations necessarily are largely in the hands of staff and civil service employees. These employees may have little or no knowledge of the States and localities that will be affected by the statutes and regulations for which they are responsible. In any case, they hardly are as accessible and responsive as those who occupy analogous positions in State and local governments."

Justice O'Connor's dissent stated, "There is more to federalism than the nature of the constraints that can be imposed on the States in 'the realm of authority left open to them by the Constitution.' The central issue of federalism, of course, is whether any realm is left open to the States by the Constitution — whether any area remains in which a State may act free of federal interference. 'The issue . . . is whether the federal system has any *legal* substance, any core of constitutional right that courts will enforce.' C. Black, Perspectives in Constitutional Law 30 (1963). The true 'essence' of federalism is that the States *as States* have legitimate interests which the National Government is bound to respect even though its laws are supreme. If federalism so conceived and so carefully cultivated by the Framers of our Constitution is to remain meaningful, this Court cannot abdicate its constitutional responsibility to oversee the Federal Government's compliance with its duty to respect the legitimate interests of the States." She also said, "[With] the abandonment of *National League of Cities*, all that stands between the remaining essentials of state sovereignty and Congress is the latter's underdeveloped capacity for self-restraint."

Note: *From* Garcia *to* New York v. United States

1. *The aftermath in Congress.* Nine months after the Court's decision in *Garcia*, Congress enacted the Fair Labor Standards Amendments of 1985. Under the original Fair Labor Standards Act, private employers must pay overtime to employees who work more than a stated number of hours at a rate of one and one-half times their regular pay. The amendments allow public employers to substitute compensatory time off for the overtime pay, again at the rate of one and one-half hours compensatory time for each hour of overtime. Compensatory time off is limited to 480 hours for public safety employees and employees in seasonal work and to 240 hours for other public employees; after that, public employers must pay for overtime. Does the adoption of the amendments demonstrate that *Garcia* was correctly decided? Does it show that the Court unnecessarily forced Congress to act so as to maintain the proper system of federal nonregulation of state employment practices? Note that the amendments do not restore the pre-*Garcia* status quo because they define limits on the use of compensatory time off.

2. Garcia *applied.* South Carolina v. Baker, 485 U.S. 505 (1988): A 1982 tax reform statute removed the exemption from federal taxes of income from certain state bonds. The Supreme Court held that the statute was not unconstitutional. "*Garcia* holds that the limits [on Congress's power] are structural, not substantive — i.e., that States must find their protection from congressional regulation through the national political process, not through judicially defined spheres of unregulable state activity. South Carolina contends that the political process failed here because Congress had no concrete evidence quantifying the tax evasion attributable [to the affected bonds] and relied instead on anecdotal evidence. [It] also argues that Congress chose an ineffective remedy. [Although] *Garcia* left open the possibility that some extraordinary defects in the national political pro-

cess might render congressional regulation of state activities invalid, [South] Carolina has not even alleged that it was deprived of any right to participate in the national political process or that it was singled out in a way that left it politically isolated and powerless." The Court also rejected the argument that the statute "commandeered" states by "coercing [them] into enacting legislation" that would allow them to issue bonds that *would* continue to receive federal tax-exempt status. The Court said that the federal statute simply regulated state activity, and that any "commandeering" that occurred was "an inevitable consequence of regulating a state activity."

Justice O'Connor dissented, arguing that the statute was unconstitutional because the Court failed "to inquire into the substantial adverse effects on state and local governments that would follow from state taxation of the interest on state and local bonds." Chief Justice Rehnquist concurred in the result, relying on the Special Master's finding that depriving the particular bonds in question of tax-exempt status would have "no substantial effect on the abilities of States to raise debt capital."

3. *The aftermath in the Court.* In Gregory v. Ashcroft, 501 U.S. 452 (1991), the Court held that the Age Discrimination in Employment Act (ADEA) did not apply to a state's mandatory retirement provisions affecting appointed state judges. The ADEA bars employers, including state governments, from adopting mandatory retirement policies, but as to state employers, it exempts "appointees on a policymaking level." In interpreting this provision, the Court noted that the state's retirement provision "is a decision of the most fundamental sort for a sovereign entity" and required that Congress's intention to displace state decisions in this area be clearly stated.

New York v. United States

505 U.S. 144 (1992)

JUSTICE O'CONNOR delivered the opinion of the Court.

This case implicates one of our Nation's newest problems of public policy and perhaps our oldest question of constitutional law. The public policy issue involves the disposal of radioactive waste: In this case, we address the constitutionality of three provisions of the Low-Level Radioactive Waste Policy Amendments Act of 1985. The constitutional question is as old as the Constitution: It consists of discerning the proper division of authority between the Federal Government and the States. We conclude that while Congress has substantial power under the Constitution to encourage the States to provide for the disposal of the radioactive waste generated within their borders, the Constitution does not confer upon Congress the ability simply to compel the States to do so. . . .

I

We live in a world full of low level radioactive waste. Radioactive material is present in luminous watch dials, smoke alarms, [and] the protective gear and construction materials used by workers at nuclear power plants. [The] waste must be isolated from humans for long periods of time, often for hundreds of years. Millions of cubic feet of low level radioactive waste must be disposed of each year.

[In 1971, there were six waste disposal sites, but by 1979, only one remained open, in South Carolina. The state's Governor ordered a 50 percent reduction in the waste accepted there. In 1980, Congress adopted a statute declaring that each state was primarily responsible for disposing of low-level radioactive waste produced within its borders and authorizing states to enter into regional compacts for disposal facilities. In 1985, Congress enacted the provisions at issue. They were based on a proposal from the National Governors' Association and represented a compromise between states with disposal sites and those without them. From 1986 to 1992, states with disposal sites could impose surcharges for waste from elsewhere; after 1992, they could exclude waste from states not participating in their regional compacts.

[The 1985 act had three incentives to induce states to provide for disposal of waste generated within their borders. (1) *Monetary:* Part of the surcharges were transferred to the Secretary of Energy, and that money would be returned to a state that was able to dispose of its own waste by 1993. (2) *Access:* The surcharges for access to existing disposal sites escalate, and after a series of deadlines, access to those sites could be denied. (3) *The "take title" provision:* If a state was unable to provide for disposal of its own waste by 1996, it was to "take title to the waste" and would "be obligated to take possession of the waste." New York, which generates a relatively large portion of the nation's low-level radioactive waste, identified several possible local disposal sites but faced political opposition at each location. Instead of proceeding with development of a disposal site, the state challenged the constitutionality of the 1985 Act.]

II

A

[While] no one disputes the proposition that "the Constitution created a Federal Government of limited powers," Gregory v. Ashcroft, and while the Tenth Amendment makes explicit that "the powers not delegated to the United States by the Constitution, nor prohibited by it to the States, are reserved to the States respectively, or to the people," the task of ascertaining the constitutional line between federal and state power has given rise to many of the Court's most difficult and celebrated cases. . . .

[In] some cases the Court has inquired whether an Act of Congress is authorized by one of the powers delegated to Congress in Article I of the Constitution. In other cases the Court has sought to determine whether an Act of Congress invades the province of state sovereignty reserved by the Tenth Amendment. See, e.g., [Garcia]. In a case like this one, involving the division of authority between federal and state governments, the two inquiries are mirror images of each other. If a power is delegated to Congress in the Constitution, the Tenth Amendment expressly disclaims any reservation of that power to the States; if a power is an attribute of state sovereignty reserved by the Tenth Amendment, it is necessarily a power the Constitution has not conferred on Congress. . . .

Congress exercises its conferred powers subject to the limitations contained in the Constitution. Thus, for example, under the Commerce Clause Congress may regulate publishers engaged in interstate commerce, but Congress is constrained in the exercise of that power by the First Amendment. The Tenth Amendment likewise restrains the power of Congress, but this limit is not derived from the text of the Tenth Amendment itself, which [is] essentially a tautology. Instead, the Tenth Amendment confirms that the power of the Federal Government is subject to limits that may, in a given instance, reserve power to the States. The Tenth Amendment thus directs us to determine [whether] an incident of state sovereignty is protected by a limitation on an Article I power.

The benefits of this federal structure have been extensively catalogued elsewhere, but they need not concern us here. Our task would be the same even if one could prove that federalism secured no advantages to anyone. It consists not of devising our preferred system of government, but of understanding and applying the framework set forth in the Constitution. "The question is not what power the Federal Government ought to have but what powers in fact have been given by the people." [United States v. Butler].

This framework has been sufficiently flexible over the past two centuries to allow for enormous changes in the nature of government. The Federal Government undertakes activities today that would have been unimaginable to the Framers in two senses; first, because the Framers would not have conceived that any government would conduct such activities; and second, because the Framers would not have believed that the Federal Government, rather than the States, would assume such responsibilities. Yet the powers conferred upon the Federal Government by the Constitution were phrased in language broad enough to allow for the expansion of the Federal Government's role. . . .

The actual scope of the Federal Government's authority with respect to the States has changed over the years, therefore, but the constitutional structure underlying and limiting that authority has not. In the end, just as a cup may be half empty or half full, it makes no difference whether one views the question at issue in this case as one of ascertaining the limits of the power delegated to the Federal Government under the affirmative provisions of the Constitution or one of discerning the core of sovereignty retained by the States under the Tenth Amendment. Either way, we must determine whether any of the three challenged provisions [oversteps] the boundary between federal and state authority.

B

Petitioners do not contend that Congress lacks the power to regulate the disposal of low level radioactive waste. [Petitioners] likewise do not dispute that under the Supremacy Clause Congress could, if it wished, pre-empt state radioactive waste regulation. . . .

Most of our recent cases interpreting the Tenth Amendment have concerned the authority of Congress to subject state governments to generally applicable laws. This case presents no occasion to apply or revisit the holdings of any of these cases, as this is not a case in which Congress has subjected a State to the same legislation applicable to private parties.

This case instead concerns the circumstances under which Congress may use the States as implements of regulation; that is, whether Congress may direct or otherwise motivate the States to regulate in a particular field or a particular way. . . .

1

As an initial matter, Congress may not simply "commandeer the legislative processes of the States by directly compelling them to enact and enforce a federal regulatory program." [Hodel v. Virginia Surface Mining.] . . .

[While] Congress has substantial powers to govern the Nation directly, including in areas of intimate concern to the States, the Constitution has never been understood to confer upon Congress the ability to require the States to govern according to Congress' instructions. . . .

Indeed, the question whether the Constitution should permit Congress to employ state governments as regulatory agencies was a topic of lively debate among the Framers. Under the Articles of Confederation, Congress lacked the authority in most respects to govern the people directly. In practice, Congress "could not directly tax or legislate upon individuals; it had no explicit legislative or governmental power to make binding law enforceable as such." Amar, Of Sovereignty and Federalism, 96 Yale L.J. 1425, 1447 (1987).

The inadequacy of this governmental structure was responsible in part for the Constitutional Convention. Alexander Hamilton observed: "The great and radical vice in the construction of the existing Confederation is in the principle of LEGISLATION for STATES or GOVERNMENTS, in their CORPORATE or COLLECTIVE CAPACITIES, and as contradistinguished from the INDIVIDUALS of whom they consist." The Federalist No. 15. . . .

In the end, the Convention opted for a Constitution in which Congress would exercise its legislative authority directly over individuals rather than over States. [This] choice was made clear to the subsequent state ratifying conventions. Oliver Ellsworth, a member of the Connecticut delegation in Philadelphia, explained the distinction to his State's convention: "This Constitution does not attempt to coerce sovereign bodies, states, in their political capacity. . . . But this legal coercion singles out the . . . individual." 2 J. Elliot, Debates on the Federal Constitution 197 (2d ed. 1863). . . .

In providing for a stronger central government, therefore, the Framers explicitly chose a Constitution that confers upon Congress the power to regulate individuals, not States. [We] have always understood that even where Congress has the authority under the Constitution to pass laws requiring or prohibiting certain acts, it lacks the power directly to compel the States to require or prohibit those acts. The allocation of power contained in the Commerce Clause, for example, authorizes Congress to regulate interstate commerce directly; it does not authorize Congress to regulate state governments' regulation of interstate commerce.

2

This is not to say that Congress lacks the ability to encourage a State to regulate in a particular way, or that Congress may not hold out incentives to the States as a method of influencing a State's policy choices. Our cases have identified a variety of methods, short of outright coercion, by which Congress may urge a State to adopt a legislative program consistent with federal interests. Two of these methods are of particular relevance here.

First, under Congress' spending power, "Congress may attach conditions on the receipt of federal funds." [South Dakota v. Dole.] Such conditions must (among other requirements) bear some relationship to the purpose of the federal spending; otherwise, [the] spending power could render academic the Constitution's other grants and limits of federal authority. Where the recipient of federal funds is a State, as is not unusual today, the conditions attached to the funds by Congress may influence a State's legislative choices. . . .

Second, where Congress has the authority to regulate private activity under the Commerce Clause, we have recognized Congress' power to offer States the choice of regulating that activity according to federal standards or having state law pre-empted by federal regulation. This arrangement, which has been termed "a program of cooperative federalism," is replicated in numerous federal statutory schemes. . . .

By either of these two methods, [the] residents of the State retain the ultimate decision as to whether or not the State will comply. If a State's citizens view federal policy as sufficiently contrary to local interests, they may elect to decline a federal grant. If state residents would prefer their government to devote its attention and resources to problems other than those deemed important by Congress, they may choose to have the Federal Government rather than the State bear the expense of a federally mandated regulatory program, and they may continue to supplement that program to the extent state law is not pre-empted. Where Congress encourages state regulation rather than compelling it, state governments remain responsive to the local electorate's preferences; state officials remain accountable to the people.

By contrast, where the Federal Government compels States to regulate, the accountability of both state and federal officials is diminished. If the citizens of New York, for example, do not consider that making provision for the disposal of radioactive waste is in their best interest, they may elect state officials who share their view. That view can always be pre-empted under the Supremacy Clause if it is contrary to the national view, but in such a case it is the Federal Government that makes the decision in full view of the public, and it will be federal officials that suffer the consequences if the decision turns out to be detrimental or unpopular. But where the Federal Government directs the States to regulate, it may be state officials who will bear the brunt of public disapproval, while the federal officials who devised the regulatory program may remain insulated from the electoral ramifications of their decision. Accountability is thus diminished when, due to federal coercion, elected state officials cannot regulate in accordance with the views of the local electorate in matters not pre-empted by federal regulation. . . .

III . . .

A

The first set of incentives works in three steps. First, Congress has authorized States with disposal sites to impose a surcharge on radioactive waste received from other States. Second, the Secretary of Energy collects a portion of this surcharge and places the money in an escrow account. Third, States achieving a series of milestones receive portions of this fund.

The first of these steps is an unexceptionable exercise of Congress' power to authorize the States to burden interstate commerce. . . .

The second step, the Secretary's collection of a percentage of the surcharge, is no more than a federal tax on interstate commerce, which petitioners do not claim to be an invalid exercise of either Congress' commerce or taxing power.

The third step is a conditional exercise of Congress' authority under the Spending Clause: Congress has placed conditions — the achievement of the milestones — on the receipt of federal funds. [The] expenditure is for the general welfare; the States are required to use the money they receive for the purpose of assuring the safe disposal of radioactive waste. The conditions imposed are unambiguous; the Act informs the States exactly what they must do and by when they must do it in order to obtain a share of the escrow account. The conditions imposed are reasonably related to the purpose of the expenditure; both the conditions and the payments embody Congress' efforts to address the pressing problem of radioactive waste disposal. Finally, petitioners do not claim that the conditions imposed by the Act violate any independent constitutional prohibition. . . .

B

In the second set of incentives, Congress has authorized States and regional compacts with disposal sites gradually to increase the cost of access to the sites, and then to deny access altogether, to radioactive waste generated in States that do not meet federal deadlines. As a simple regulation, this provision would be within the power of Congress to authorize the States to discriminate against interstate commerce. Where federal regulation of private activity is within the scope of the Commerce Clause, we have recognized the ability of Congress to offer states the choice of regulating that activity according to federal standards or having state law pre-empted by federal regulation.

This is the choice presented to nonsited States by the Act's second set of incentives: States may either regulate the disposal of radioactive waste according to federal standards by attaining local or regional self-sufficiency, or their residents who produce radioactive waste will be subject to federal regulation authorizing sited States and regions to deny access to their disposal sites. The affected States are not compelled by Congress to regulate, because any burden caused by a State's refusal to regulate will fall on those who generate waste and find no outlet for its disposal, rather than on the State as a sovereign. A State whose citizens do not wish it to attain the Act's milestones may devote its attention and its resources to issues its citizens deem more worthy; the choice remains at all times with the residents of the State, not with Congress. The State need not expend any funds, or participate in any federal program, if local residents do not view such expenditures or participation as worthwhile. Nor must the State abandon the field if it does not accede to federal direction; the State may continue to regulate the generation and disposal of radioactive waste in any manner its citizens see fit.

The Act's second set of incentives thus represents a conditional exercise of Congress' commerce power, along the lines of those we have held to be within Congress' authority. As a result, the second set of incentives does not intrude on the sovereignty reserved to the States by the Tenth Amendment.

C

The take title provision is of a different character. This third so-called "incentive" offers States, as an alternative to regulating pursuant to Congress' direction, the option of taking title to and possession of the low level radioactive waste generated within their borders and becoming liable for all damages waste generators suffer as a result of the States' failure to do so promptly. In this provision, Congress has crossed the line distinguishing encouragement from coercion. . . .

The take title provision offers state governments a "choice" of either accepting ownership of waste or regulating according to the instructions of Congress. [On] one hand, the Constitution would not permit Congress simply to transfer radioactive waste from generators to state governments. Such a forced transfer, standing alone, would in principle be no different than a congressionally compelled subsidy from state governments to radioactive waste producers. The same is true of the provision requiring the States to become liable for the generators' damages. Standing alone, this provision would be indistinguishable from an Act of Congress directing the States to assume the liabilities of certain state residents. Either type of federal action would "commandeer" state governments into the service of federal regulatory purposes, and would for this reason be inconsistent with the Constitution's division of authority between federal and state governments. On the other hand, the second alternative held out to state governments — regulating pursuant to Congress' direction — would, standing alone, present a simple command to state governments to implement legislation enacted by Congress. As we have seen, the Constitution does not empower Congress to subject state governments to this type of instruction.

Because an instruction to state governments to take title to waste, standing alone, would be beyond the authority of Congress, and because a direct order to regulate, standing alone, would also be beyond the authority of Congress, it follows that Congress lacks the power to offer the States a choice between the two. Unlike the first two sets of incentives, the take title incentive does not represent the conditional exercise of any congressional power enumerated in the Constitution. [A] choice between two unconstitutionally coercive regulatory techniques is no choice at all. Either way, "the Act commandeers the legislative processes of the States by directly compelling them to enact and enforce a federal regulatory program," [Hodel], an outcome that has never been understood to lie within the authority conferred upon Congress by the Constitution.

Respondents emphasize the latitude given to the States to implement Congress' plan. The Act enables the States to regulate pursuant to Congress' instructions in any number of different ways. [States] that host sites may employ a wide range of designs and disposal methods, subject only to broad federal regulatory limits. This line of reasoning, however, only underscores the critical alternative a State lacks: A State may not decline to administer the federal program. No matter which path the State chooses, it must follow the direction of Congress.

The take title provision appears to be unique. No other federal statute has been cited which offers a state government no option other than that of implementing legislation enacted by Congress. . . .

IV . . .

A . . .

First, the United States argues that the Constitution's prohibition of congressional directives to state governments can be overcome where the federal interest is sufficiently important to justify state submission. This argument contains a kernel of truth: In determining whether the Tenth Amendment limits the ability of Congress to subject state governments to generally applicable laws, the Court has in some cases stated that it will evaluate the strength of federal interests in light of the degree to which such laws would prevent the State from functioning as a sovereign; that is, the extent to which such generally applicable laws would impede a state government's responsibility to represent and be accountable to the citizens of the State. . . .

[Whether] or not a particularly strong federal interest enables Congress to bring state governments within the orbit of generally applicable federal regulation, no Member of the Court has ever suggested that such a federal interest would enable Congress to command a state government to enact state regulation. No matter how powerful the federal interest involved, the Constitution simply does not give Congress the authority to require the States to regulate. The Constitution instead gives Congress the authority to regulate matters directly and to pre-empt contrary state regulation. Where a federal interest is sufficiently strong to cause Congress to legislate, it must do so directly; it may not conscript state governments as its agents.

Second, the United States argues that the Constitution does, in some circumstances, permit federal directives to state governments. Various cases are cited for this proposition, but none support it. Some of these cases discuss the well established power of Congress to pass laws enforceable in state courts. These cases involve no more than an application of the Supremacy Clause's provision that federal law "shall be the supreme Law of the Land," enforceable in every State. More to the point, all involve congressional regulation of individuals, not congressional requirements that States regulate. Federal statutes enforceable in state courts do, in a sense, direct state judges to enforce them, but this sort of federal "direction" of state judges is mandated by the text of the Supremacy Clause. No comparable constitutional provision authorizes Congress to command state legislatures to legislate. . . .

While the Framers no doubt endowed Congress with the power to regulate interstate commerce in order to avoid further instances of the interstate trade disputes that were common under the Articles of Confederation, the Framers did not intend that Congress should exercise that power through the mechanism of mandating state regulation. The Constitution established Congress as "a superintending authority over the reciprocal trade" among the States, The Federalist No. 42, by empowering Congress to regulate that trade directly, not by authorizing Congress to issue trade-related orders to state governments. As Madison and Hamilton explained, "a sovereignty over sovereigns, a government over governments, a legislation for communities, as contradistinguished from individuals, as it is a solecism in theory, so in practice it is subversive of the order and ends of civil polity." Id., No. 20.

B

The sited State respondents focus their attention on the process by which the Act was formulated. They correctly observe that public officials representing the State of New York lent their support to the Act's enactment. [Respondents] note that the Act embodies a bargain among the sited and unsited States, a compromise to which New York was a willing participant and from which New York has reaped much benefit. Respondents then pose what appears at first to be a troubling question: How can a federal statute be found an unconstitutional infringement of State sovereignty when state officials consented to the statute's enactment?

The answer follows from an understanding of the fundamental purpose served by our Government's federal structure. The Constitution does not protect the sovereignty of States for the benefit of the States or state governments as abstract political entities, or even for the benefit of the public officials governing the States. To the contrary, the Constitution divides authority between federal and state governments for the protection of individuals. State sovereignty is not just an end in itself: "Rather, federalism secures to citizens the liberties that derive from the diffusion of sovereign power." Coleman v. Thompson, 501 U.S. 722, 759 (1991) (Blackmun, J., dissenting). "Just as the separation and independence of the coordinate Branches of the Federal Government serves to prevent the accumulation of excessive power in any one Branch, a healthy balance of power between the States and the Federal Government will reduce the risk of tyranny and abuse from either front." Gregory v. Ashcroft. See The Federalist No. 51.

Where Congress exceeds its authority relative to the States, therefore, the departure from the constitutional plan cannot be ratified by the "consent" of state officials. An analogy to the separation of powers among the Branches of the Federal Government clarifies this point. The Constitution's division of power among the three Branches is violated where one Branch invades the territory of another, whether or not the encroached-upon Branch approves the encroachment [citing Buckley v. Valeo and INS v. Chadha, Chapter 4 infra]. [The] constitutional authority of Congress cannot be expanded by the "consent" of the governmental unit whose domain is thereby narrowed, whether that unit is the Executive Branch or the States.

State officials thus cannot consent to the enlargement of the powers of Congress beyond those enumerated in the Constitution. Indeed, the facts of this case raise the possibility that powerful incentives might lead both federal and state officials to view departures from the federal structure to be in their personal interests. Most citizens recognize the need for radioactive waste disposal sites, but few want sites near their homes. As a result, while it would be well within the authority of either federal or state officials to choose where the disposal sites will be, it is likely to be in the political interest of each individual official to avoid being held accountable to the voters for the choice of location. If a federal official is faced with the alternatives of choosing a location or directing the States to do it, the official may well prefer the latter, as a means of shifting responsibility for the eventual decision. If a state official is faced with the same set of alternatives — choosing a location or having Congress direct the choice of a location — the state official may also prefer the latter, as it may permit the avoidance of personal responsibility. The interests of public officials thus may not coincide with the Constitution's intergovernmental allocation of authority. Where state officials purport to submit to the direction of Congress in this manner, federalism is hardly being advanced. . . .

VII

Some truths are so basic that, like the air around us, they are easily overlooked. Much of the Constitution is concerned with setting forth the form of our government, and the courts have traditionally invalidated measures deviating from that form. The result may appear "formalistic" in a given case to partisans of the measure at issue, because such measures are typically the product of the era's perceived necessity. But the Constitution protects us from our own best intentions: It divides power among sovereigns and among branches of government precisely so that we may resist the temptation to concentrate power in one location as an expedient solution to the crisis of the day. The shortage of disposal sites for radioactive waste is a pressing national problem, but a judiciary that licensed extraconstitutional government with each issue of comparable gravity would, in the long run, be far worse.

States are not mere political subdivisions of the United States. State governments are neither regional offices nor administrative agencies of the Federal Government. The positions occupied by state officials appear nowhere on the Federal Government's most detailed organizational chart. The Constitution instead "leaves to the several States a residuary and inviolable sovereignty," The Federalist No. 39, reserved explicitly to the States by the Tenth Amendment.

Whatever the outer limits of that sovereignty may be, one thing is clear: The Federal Government may not compel the States to enact or administer a federal regulatory program. The Constitution permits both the Federal Government and the States to enact legislation regarding the disposal of low level radioactive waste. The Constitution enables the Federal Government to pre-empt state regulation contrary to federal interests, and it permits the Federal Government to hold out incentives to the States as a means of encouraging them to adopt suggested regulatory schemes. It does not, however, authorize Congress simply to direct the States to provide for the disposal of the radioactive waste generated within their borders. While there may be many constitutional methods of achieving regional self-sufficiency in radioactive waste disposal, the method Congress has chosen is not one of them. The judgment of the Court of Appeals is accordingly affirmed in part and reversed in part.

JUSTICE WHITE, with whom JUSTICE BLACKMUN and JUSTICE STEVENS join . . . dissenting [as to the "take title" holding]. . . .

I . . .

[The] Low-Level Radioactive Waste Policy Act [resulted] from the efforts of state leaders to achieve a state-based set of remedies to the waste problem. They sought not federal pre-emption or intervention, but rather congressional sanction of interstate compromises they had reached. . . .

A movement [arose] to achieve a compromise [in] which the sited States agreed to continue accepting waste in exchange for the imposition of stronger measures to guarantee compliance with the unsited States' assurances that they would develop alternate disposal facilities. [In] sum, the 1985 Act was very much the product of cooperative federalism, in which the States bargained among themselves to achieve compromises for Congress to sanction. . . .

II . . .

B

[Seen] as a term of an agreement entered into between the several States, this measure proves to be less constitutionally odious than the Court opines. First, the practical effect of New York's position is that because it is unwilling to honor its obligations to provide in-state storage facilities for its low-level radioactive waste, other States with such plants must accept New York's waste, whether they wish to or not. Otherwise, the many economically and socially-beneficial producers of such waste in the State would have to cease their operations. The Court's refusal to force New York to accept responsibility for its own problem inevitably means that some other State's sovereignty will be impinged by it being forced, for public health reasons, to accept New York's low-level radioactive waste. I do not understand the principle of federalism to impede the National Government from acting as referee among the States to prohibit one from bullying another. . . .

III . . .

The Court's distinction between a federal statute's regulation of States and private parties for general purposes, as opposed to a regulation solely on the activities of States, is unsupported by our recent Tenth Amendment cases. [The] Court makes no effort to explain why this purported distinction should affect the analysis of Congress' power under general principles of federalism and the Tenth Amendment. [An] incursion on state sovereignty hardly seems more constitutionally acceptable if the federal statute that "commands" specific action also applies to private parties. The alleged diminution in state authority over its own affairs is not any less because the federal mandate restricts the activities of private parties. . . .

[The] more appropriate analysis should flow from *Garcia*. . . .

[Where] it addresses this aspect of respondents' argument, the Court tacitly concedes that a failing of the political process cannot be shown in this case because it refuses to rebut the unassailable arguments that the States were well able to look after themselves in the legislative process that culminated in the 1985 Act's passage. [The] Court rejects this process-based argument by resorting to generalities and platitudes about the purpose of federalism being to protect individual rights.

Ultimately, I suppose, the entire structure of our federal constitutional government can be traced to an interest in establishing checks and balances to prevent the exercise of tyranny against individuals. But these fears seem extremely far distant to me in a situation such as this. We face a crisis of national proportions in the disposal of low-level radioactive waste, and Congress has acceded to the wishes of the States by permitting local decisionmaking rather than imposing a solution from Washington. [For] me, the Court's civics lecture has a decidedly hollow ring at a time when action, rather than rhetoric, is needed to solve a national problem.[3]

3. [I] do not read the majority's many invocations of history to be anything other than elaborate window-dressing. [The] majority's historical analysis has a distinctly wooden quality. One would not know from reading the majority's account, for instance, that the nature of federal-state relations changed fundamentally after the Civil War. That conflict produced in its wake a tremendous expansion in the scope of the Federal Government's law-making authority, so much so that the persons who helped to found the Republic would scarcely have recognized the many added roles the National Government assumed for itself. Moreover, the majority fails to mention the New Deal era, in which the Court recognized the enormous growth in Congress' power under the Commerce Clause. While I believe we should not be blind to history, neither should we read it so selectively as to restrict the proper scope of Congress' powers under Article I, especially when the history not mentioned by the majority fully supports a more expansive understanding of the legislature's authority than may have existed in the late 18th-century. Given the scanty textual support for the majority's position, it would be far more sensible to defer to a coordinate branch of government in its decision to devise a solution to a national problem of this kind. . . .

V

The ultimate irony of the decision today is that in its formalistically rigid obeisance to "federalism," the Court gives Congress fewer incentives to defer to the wishes of state officials in achieving local solutions to local problems. This legislation was a classic example of Congress acting as arbiter among the States in their attempts to accept responsibility for managing a problem of grave import. [By] invalidating the measure designed to ensure compliance for recalcitrant States, such as New York, the Court upsets the delicate compromise achieved among the States and forces Congress to erect several additional formalistic hurdles to clear before achieving exactly the same objective. Because the Court's justifications for undertaking this step are unpersuasive to me, I respectfully dissent.

JUSTICE STEVENS, concurring in part and dissenting in part.

Under the Articles of Confederation, the Federal Government had the power to issue commands to the States. Because that indirect exercise of federal power proved ineffective, the Framers of the Constitution empowered the Federal Government to exercise legislative authority directly over individuals within the States, even though that direct authority constituted a greater intrusion on State sovereignty. Nothing in that history suggests that the Federal Government may not also impose its will upon the several States as it did under the Articles. The Constitution enhanced, rather than diminished, the power of the Federal Government.

The notion that Congress does not have the power to issue "a simple command to state governments to implement legislation enacted by Congress" is incorrect and unsound. [To] the contrary, the Federal Government directs state governments in many realms. The Government regulates state-operated railroads, state school systems, state prisons, state elections, and a host of other state functions. [I] see no reason why Congress may not also command the States to enforce federal water and air quality standards or federal standards for the disposition of low-level radioactive wastes. . . .

With respect to the problem presented by the case at hand, if litigation should develop between States that have joined a compact, we would surely have the power to grant relief in the form of specific enforcement of the take title provision. Indeed, even if the statute had never been passed, if one State's radioactive waste created a nuisance that harmed its neighbors, it seems clear that we would have had the power to command the offending State to take remedial action. If this Court has such authority, surely Congress has similar authority. . . .

PRINTZ v. UNITED STATES, 521 U.S. 898 (1997). The Brady Act required the Attorney General to establish a national instant background check system by November 1998. Until then, gun dealers were required to send a form identifying a purchaser to the "chief law enforcement officer" (CLEO) of a prospective purchaser's residence, unless the purchaser already had a permit or unless the state already had an instant background check system. The dealer then had to wait five days to complete the sale. When the CLEO received the form, the CLEO had to "make a reasonable effort to ascertain . . . whether receipt or possession would be in violation of the law," as when the purchaser was a convicted felon. The CLEO was not required to notify the gun dealer that the purchaser was ineligible to own a gun, but if the CLEO did so, the purchaser must be notified of the reasons for that determination. Two CLEOs from Montana and

Arizona challenged the Brady Act, which the court of appeals found to be constitutional. The Supreme Court, in an opinion by Justice Scalia, reversed.

Noting that "there is no constitutional text speaking to this precise question," the Court found its answer "in historical understanding and practice, in the structure of the Constitution, and in the jurisprudence of this Court." Examining prior practice, the Court agreed with the sheriffs' contention that "compelled enlistment of state executive officers for the administration of federal programs is, until very recent years at least, unprecedented." Contrary examples, the Court found, involved state judges subject to the supremacy clause and accustomed to enforcing the law of other sovereigns, and statutes requesting states to allow their officials to enforce national law. Turning to "the structure of the Constitution," the Court observed, "The power of the Federal Government would be augmented immeasurably if it were able to impress into its service — and at no cost to itself — the police officers of the 50 States." In addition, in tension with article II's requirement that the President "take Care that the Laws be faithfully executed," the Brady Act "transfers this responsibility to thousands of CLEOs in the 50 States, who are left to implement the program without meaningful Presidential control." Relying on *New York*, the Court concluded that the Brady Act was not a "proper" method of implementing a delegated power.

Finally, the Court held that the reasons given in *New York* for denying Congress the power to commandeer state legislatures were applicable as well to attempts to commandeer state executive officials:

> Executive action that has utterly no policymaking component is rare, particularly at an executive level as high as a jurisdiction's chief law-enforcement officer. Is it really true that there is no policymaking involved in deciding, for example, what "reasonable efforts" shall be expended to conduct a background check? It may well satisfy the Act for a CLEO to direct that (a) no background checks will be conducted that divert personnel time from pending felony investigations, and (b) no background check will be permitted to consume more than one-half hour of an officer's time. But nothing in the Act *requires* a CLEO to be so parsimonious; diverting at least *some* felony-investigation time, and permitting at least *some* background checks beyond one-half hour would certainly not be *un*reasonable. Is this decision whether to devote maximum "reasonable efforts" or minimum "reasonable efforts" not preeminently a matter of policy? It is quite impossible [to] draw the Government's proposed line at "no policymaking," and we would have to fall back upon a line of "not too much policymaking." How much is too much is not likely to be answered precisely; and an imprecise barrier against federal intrusion upon state authority is not likely to be an effective one. [The] Government also maintains that requiring state officers to perform discrete, ministerial tasks specified by Congress does not violate the principle of New York because it does not diminish the accountability of state or federal officials. This argument fails even on its own terms. By forcing state governments to absorb the financial burden of implementing a federal regulatory program, Members of Congress can take credit for "solving" problems without having to ask their constituents to pay for the solutions with higher federal taxes. And even when the States are not forced to absorb the costs of implementing a federal program, they are still put in the position of taking the blame for its burdensomeness and for its defects. Under the present law, for example, it will be the CLEO and not some federal official who stands between the gun purchaser and immediate possession of his gun. And it will likely be the CLEO, not some federal official, who will be blamed for any error (even one in the designated federal database) that causes a purchaser to be mistakenly rejected.

The Court rejected the argument that the Brady Act's constitutionality should be determined by balancing its purposes against the "minimal and only temporary burden" it placed on state officials: "[Where] it is the whole object of the law to direct the functioning of the state executive, [such] a 'balancing' analysis is inappropriate. It is the very principle of separate state sovereignty that such a law offends, and no comparative assessment of the various interests can overcome that fundamental defect."

Justice Thomas concurred, suggesting that the second amendment barred Congress from regulating "purely intrastate sale or possession of firearms."

Justice Stevens, joined by Justices Souter, Ginsburg, and Breyer, dissented. "When Congress exercises the powers delegated to it by the Constitution, it may impose affirmative obligations on executive and judicial officers of state and local governments as well as ordinary citizens. This conclusion is firmly supported by the text of the Constitution, the early history of the Nation, decisions of this Court, and a correct understanding of the basic structure of the Federal Government." He argued that "[under] the Articles of Confederation the National Government had the power to issue commands to the several sovereign states, but it had no authority to govern individuals directly," but "[that] method of governing proved to be unacceptable [because] it was cumbersome and inefficient. [The] historical materials strongly suggest that the Founders intended to enhance the capacity of the federal government by empowering it — as a part of the new authority to make demands directly on individual citizens — to act through local officials. Hamilton made clear that the new Constitution, 'by extending the authority of the federal head to the individual citizens of the several States, will enable the government to employ the ordinary magistracy of each, in the execution of its laws.' The Federalist No. 27, at 180. Hamilton's meaning was unambiguous; the federal government was to have the power to demand that local officials implement national policy programs."

Justice Stevens disagreed with the Court's assessment of early practice, finding that Congress sometimes had required state officials to enforce national law. Relying on *Garcia*, he argued: "Given the fact that the Members of Congress are elected by the people of the several States, with each State receiving an equivalent number of Senators in order to ensure that even the smallest States have a powerful voice in the legislature, it is quite unrealistic to assume that they will ignore the sovereignty concerns of their constituents. It is far more reasonable to presume that their decisions to impose modest burdens on state officials from time to time reflect a considered judgment that the people in each of the States will benefit therefrom." The opinion noted, "Recent developments demonstrate that the political safeguards protecting Our Federalism are effective. The majority expresses special concern that were its rule not adopted the Federal Government would be able to avail itself of the services of state government officials 'at no cost to itself.' But this specific problem of federal actions that have the effect of imposing so-called 'unfunded mandates' on the States has been identified and meaningfully addressed by Congress in recent legislation. See Unfunded Mandates Reform Act of 1995."

A footnote argued that the "concern" about Congress requiring state officials to "'take the blame' for failed programs" was "vastly overstated [because] to the extent that a particular action proves politically unpopular, we may be confident that elected officials charged with implementing it will be quite clear to their constituents where the source of the misfortune lies. [They] will inform disgruntled constituents who have been denied permission to purchase a handgun about the origins of the Brady Act requirements. The Court's suggestion that voters will be confused over who is to 'blame' for the statute reflects a gross lack of confidence in the electorate that is at war with the basic assumptions underlying any democratic government." In addition, Justice Stevens argued, "the majority's rule seems more likely to damage than to preserve the safeguards against tyranny provided by the existence of vital state governments. By limiting the ability of the Federal Government to enlist state officials in the implementation of its programs, the Court creates incentives for the National Government to aggrandize itself. In the name of State's rights, the majority would have the Federal Government create vast national bureaucracies to implement its policies." The dissent concluded, "the Framers entrusted Congress with the task of creating a working structure of intergovernmental relationships around the framework that the Constitution authorized. Neither explicitly nor implicitly did the Framers issue any command that forbids Congress from imposing federal duties on private citizens or on local officials. As a general matter, Congress has followed the sound policy of authorizing federal agencies and federal agents to administer federal programs. That general practice, however, does not negate the existence of power to rely on state officials in occasional situations in which such reliance is in the national interest. Rather, the occasional exceptions confirm the wisdom of Justice Holmes' reminder that 'the machinery of government would not work if it were not allowed a little play in its joints.' Bain Peanut Co. of Tex. v. Pinson, 282 U.S. 499, 501 (1931)."

Justice Souter's separate dissent focused on his interpretation of several passages in The Federalist Papers.

Note: The "Anticommandeering" Principle

1. *The scope of the decisions.* Reno v. Condon, 528 U.S. 141 (2000), upheld the federal Driver's Privacy Protection Act (DPPA). The act regulates the disclosure of personal information in the records of state motor vehicles departments. Some states had received substantial income from sales of such information to commercial enterprises. The act prohibits state officials from disclosing "personal information" such as a person's photograph, name and address, and medical or disability information unless the driver consents to the disclosure. The act requires disclosure of personal information, however, in connection with "matters of motor vehicle or driver safety or threat, motor vehicle emissions," and automobile recalls, and it permits disclosure under some other circumstances. The act also regulates the resale and redisclosure of drivers' personal information by private entities that lawfully received the information from a state motor vehicles department. Writing for a unanimous Court, Chief Justice Rehnquist rejected the argument that the statute violated the anticommandeering principle even though the statute "will require time and effort on the part of state employees." "[The] DPPA does not require the States in their sovereign capacity to regulate their own citizens. The DPPA regulates the States as the owners of databases. It does not require the South Carolina Legislature to enact any laws or regulations, and it does not require state officials to assist in the enforcement of federal statutes regulating private individuals." The Court also concluded that the statute was "generally applicable" and did not regulate the states exclusively because it "reg-

ulates the universe of entities that participate as suppliers to the market for motor vehicle information — the States as initial suppliers [and] private resellers."
Does *Condon* make dispositive the distinction between states acting "in their sovereign capacities" and states acting in some other capacity? If so, why is the sale
of information to enhance state revenues (and reduce the need to rely on taxes)
not an act taken in the states' sovereign capacity? The statute compels state officials to *refrain* from taking certain actions, in the service of a federal policy. Do
the principles articulated in *New York* and *Printz* support a distinction between
compelled action and compelled inaction, both in the service of federal rather
than state policy?

2. *The scope of the decisions: judicial, legislative, and executive officials.* The
Court does not repudiate decisions like Testa v. Katt, which require state courts
to enforce national law. Why do courts fall outside the anticommandeering principle? Note that state executive and legislative officials are required to take an
oath to support the Constitution. Does the supremacy clause bind state judges in
a stronger way? Is political responsibility less diffused when state judges enforce
national law?

3. *The scope of the decisions: preemption and conditional spending statutes.* Preemption, Chapter 3 infra, is a command from Congress that states *not* regulate
some area as they otherwise would. Why is that less offensive than a command
that they affirmatively regulate?

Justice White suggested that under the Court's holding, Congress could still
"condition the payment of funds [for example, from the surcharge account] on
the State's willingness to take title if it has not already provided a waste disposal
facility" or "regulate directly the producers of the waste" by, for example, banning
the shipment of waste from New York unless the state either creates a disposal site
or takes title to the waste. Do you agree? If Justice White is correct, are his solutions more or less intrusive on state interests than the one the Court held unconstitutional? Consider the Court's discussion of the location of political responsibility for siting decisions.

4. *An originalist perspective.* Consider Powell, The Oldest Question of Constitutional Law, 79 Va. L. Rev. 633, 658 (1993):

> [Justice O'Connor's] federalism [in *New York*] is one of process, not of substance.
> [This] turns the primary Anti-Federalist criticism [upside] down. The Anti-
> Federalist concern was that the Constitution ultimately would reduce the states to
> the status of municipal corporations not by preempting their processes but by pre-
> empting their business. [O'Connor's] federalism accepts as legitimate the effective
> extension of congressional authority to all areas of major legislative interest; yet this
> extension is precisely the consequence of adopting the Constitution that the Anti-
> Federalists predicted and "new federalism" was meant to rebut.
>
> Justice O'Connor's federalism thus endorses exactly the result the Federalists
> denied that the Constitution would produce — the reduction of the states to au-
> tonomous governmental processes concerned with only those affairs left to them by
> Congress.

Does the history recited in New York v. United States establish that the framers
wanted to supplant national power to regulate the states or only that they wanted
to supplement it with power to regulate individuals directly?

5. *An "autonomy" model of federalism.* Consider Merritt, Three Faces of Fed-

eralism: Finding a Formula for the Future, 47 Vand. L. Rev. 1563, 1571, 1575, 1583 (1994):

> [Courts] should intervene in the political process to protect the independence of state governments, but only when the federal government has tampered with the independent relationship between a state government and its voters. [The] auton-omy model of federalism is useful because it recognizes [that state] governments forced to implement federal commands are unlikely to check the power of their commanding officer. Nor are such governments likely to give political newcomers the training they need to succeed in national politics. Middle managers who lack autonomy to govern their own domains never have been known for promoting di-verse living conditions or social experiments. [Through] the Guaranty Clause [ar-ticle IV, section 4], the national government pledges to maintain autonomous gov-ernments in each state — governments that are responsible to the people of that state rather than to the national government.

In response, consider Abrams, No "There" There: State Autonomy and Voting Rights Regulation, 65 U. Colo. L. Rev. 835, 838 (1994): "What does it mean for a state to be free to set the retirement age of judges, but not the kind of districts from which they may be elected? Or, for a state to be free to establish the loca-tion of its state capital, but not the basis of representation, or the shape of the dis-tricts for electing those who serve there?"

6. *Defending* Printz. Hills, The Political Economy of Cooperative Federalism: Why State Autonomy Makes Sense and "Dual Sovereignty" Doesn't, 96 Mich. L. Rev. 813, 819-821 (1998), defends the entitlement *Printz* gives states to refuse to comply with federal directives (unless they choose to do so) on functional grounds:

> The federal government should commandeer the services of nonfederal govern-ments no more than it should commandeer the services of private organizations or persons. [It] is *unnecessary* [because] the federal government can purchase the ser-vices of state and local governments whenever it is cost-effective to do so. [There] is a vigorous intergovernmental marketplace in which municipalities, countries, and states [compete] with each other for the chance to obtain federal revenue. [Whenever] the national government values such services enough to pay nonfed-eral governments the costs of providing them, the national government can obtain the cooperation of state or local governments. [When] the government conscripts specific types of private services, [it] can inefficiently discourage private persons [from] investing resources in the production of such services. [These] same consid-erations suggest that the federal government ought not to conscript services [from] nonfederal governments. [One] would expect such demands inefficiently to dis-courage involvement in state and local politics.

Compare Jackson, Federalism and the Uses and Limits of Law: *Printz* and Prin-ciple?, 111 Harv. L. Rev. 2180 (1998), which argues for a strong presumption against "commandeering" state legislative action, and a much weaker presump-tion against commandeering state executive officials.

> [Judicial] enforcement [against] collective bodies [poses] difficulties less likely to be present in the enforcement of orders against the executive or judicial officials. [There] is a close association [between voting] and speech; compelled voting by legislative representatives [bears] a disquieting similarity to governmentally com-pelled speech. [Legislatures] are more closely bound up with public understandings

of self-government than either executive officers or courts. Compelled legislation may therefore have greater potential for voter confusion than mandates directed to other branches of state government.

Id. at 2251.

[Courts] could adopt a presumption that federal directives to state legislatures are not "Necessary and Proper" if the same goal can be accomplished through other means, such as direct federal legislation. It is hard to imagine circumstances in which national purposes could be served only by requiring state legislatures to adopt federally mandated legislation. [It] is less difficult to imagine circumstances in which a national purpose could be well served only by utilizing available state or local law enforcement officers. [An] important or legitimate governmental interest test might be imposed. [Constitutional] inquiry might consider the size of the burden or amount of state time and resources needed to perform the federally mandated tasks — thereby permitting distinctions between relatively minor record-keeping [and] more substantial impositions on state resources involving matters that [come] close to the core of legislative responsibilities.

Id. at 2253-2254. Does this proposed balancing approach underestimate the benefits of the Court's clear doctrinal standard in providing guidance to Congress (and lower court judges)?

7. *The tenth amendment and state power.* Does the tenth amendment have any implications for the scope of state power? In U.S. Term Limits v. Thornton, 514 U.S. 779 (1995), Justice Stevens's opinion for the Court argued that the tenth amendment "could only 'reserve' that which existed before. As Justice Story recognized, 'the states can exercise no powers whatsoever, which exclusively spring out of the existence of the national government, which the constitution does not delegate to them. . . . No state can say, that it has reserved, what it never possessed.'" Justice Thomas's dissent, which was joined by Chief Justice Rehnquist and Justices O'Connor and Scalia, responded, "As far as the Federal Constitution is concerned, [the] States can exercise all powers that the Constitution does not withhold from them. The Federal Government and the States thus face different default rules: where the Constitution is silent about the exercise of a particular power — that is, where the Constitution does not speak either expressly or by necessary implication — the Federal Government lacks that power and the States enjoy it." Justice Thomas continued, "The majority's essential logic is that the state governments could not 'reserve' any powers that they did not control at the time the Constitution was drafted. But it was not the state governments that were doing the reserving. The Constitution derives its authority instead from the consent of the people of the States. Given the fundamental principle that all governmental powers stem from the people of the States, it would simply be incoherent to assert that the people of the States could not reserve any powers that they had not previously controlled."

8. *The role of comparative law.* Justice Breyer's separate dissent in *Printz* noted,

At least some other countries, facing the same basic problem, have found that local control is better maintained through application of a principle that is the direct opposite of the principle the majority derives from the silence of our Constitution. The federal systems of Switzerland, Germany, and the European Union [all] provide that constituent states, not federal bureaucracies, will themselves implement many of the laws, rules, regulations, or decrees enacted by the central "federal" body. They do so in part because they believe that such a system interferes less, not more, with the independent authority of the "state," member nation, or other subsidiary government, and helps to safeguard individual liberty as well.

Justice Scalia's opinion for the Court responded, "We think such comparative analysis inappropriate to the task of interpreting a constitution, though it was of course quite relevant to the task of writing one." Justice Breyer replied,

> [W]e are interpreting our own Constitution, not those of other nations, and there may be relevant political and structural differences between their systems and our own. But their experience may nonetheless cast an empirical light on the consequences of different solutions to a common legal problem — in this case the problem of reconciling central authority with the need to preserve the liberty-enhancing autonomy of a smaller constituent governmental entity. And that experience here offers empirical confirmation of the implied answer to a question Justice Stevens asks: Why, or how, would what the majority sees as a constitutional alternative — the creation of a new federal gun-law bureaucracy, or the expansion of an existing federal bureaucracy — better promote either state sovereignty or individual liberty?

Consider the following argument: In the absence of controlling constitutional text, courts appropriately make considerations of policy one factor in determining the Constitution's meaning. Examining constitutional experience elsewhere may illuminate the relevant policy considerations. Alternatively, in the absence of controlling constitutional text, courts should interpret the Constitution in a manner consistent with its basic structure. But structural considerations often fail to determine precisely which of many possible structures is most consistent with the U.S. Constitution. Examining constitutional experience elsewhere may illuminate the choice among alternative reasonable specifications of the U.S. Constitution's structure. Are the Court's and Justice Breyer's discussions of comparative constitutional law consistent with either of these arguments?

Note: *The Second Amendment*

The second amendment contains a statement of purpose as well as a guarantee of a right to bear arms. What is the connection between the right to bear arms and the purpose of maintaining a well-regulated militia? Disputes over the amendment's interpretation can be described as centering on the choice between saying that the amendment confers an individual right, held by every person without regard to his or her participation in or connection with an organized and well-regulated militia, or saying that it confers a collective right, held by the people collectively in connection with such participation.

Proponents of the competing interpretations agree that the amendment was designed to guard against the possibility that the national government would need to be checked, by military force if necessary. Proponents of the "collective right" interpretation argue that well-regulated militias were controlled by state governments. Today, statutes authorize the national government to take control of the National Guard, the modern equivalent of state militias. Critics of the "collective right" interpretation argue that the National Guard therefore cannot serve the intended function of state-organized militias, and conclude that the amendment should today be interpreted to confer an individual right because there is no contemporary analogue of state-organized militias as the Framers understood them. Is this an example of an appropriate translation into modern terms of provisions written in the 18th century?

Proponents of the "individual rights" interpretation also argue that the second amendment uses the same term — "the right of the people" — that the first amendment does and that the first amendment clearly confers an individual right. The fourth and ninth amendments use the same phrase, apparently to refer to individual rights. They also rely on the tradition of civic republicanism, Chapter 1 supra, which made a central feature of active citizenship the citizen's ability to join with others to resist government overreaching by force of arms. Their critics argue that the tradition of civic republicanism developed in a society lacking substantial democratic participation in government, through elected representatives responsive to the people. Under modern circumstances elections and free speech reduce the risk of governmental overreaching to the point where an individual right of armed resistance is unnecessary. Some argue that the conditions making civic republicanism a coherent theory of society, such as widespread equality in economic condition and widespread commitment to and action in accordance with ideas of civic virtue, are absent in today's society, making it inappropriate to rely on civic republicanism to justify an interpretation of the second amendment. Is this an example of an appropriate translation into modern terms of provisions written in the 18th century?

Suppose that the second amendment confers an individual right to bear arms. What statutes infringe the right? Should courts adopt a stringent standard, like that applied to certain forms of regulation of expression, or a loose one, like that applied to regulation of economic activities? On what basis should that choice be made?

State regulations of firearms would be subject to the second amendment only if the court held that its provisions were "incorporated" in the fourteenth amendment. If the "individual rights" interpretation rests on ideas about civic republicanism, how much weight should be placed on the fact that, by the time the fourteenth amendment was ratified, the civic republican tradition had become substantially less important in the society than it had been when the original Constitution and the Bill of Rights were ratified?

There is a substantial academic literature on the second amendment. Some of the leading works are Levinson, The Embarrassing Second Amendment, 99 Yale L. J. 637 (1989); Williams, Civic Republicanism and the Citizen Militia: The Terrifying Second Amendment, 101 Yale L. J. 551 (1991); and Powe, Guns, Words, and Constitutional Interpretation, 38 William & Mary L. Rev. 1311 (1997).

Note: *Concluding Observations on Congress's Powers*

Over its history, the Court has sporadically attempted to enforce federalism-based limitations on Congress's power. It has repeatedly abandoned those efforts after a time, only to revive them a while later. What accounts for this pattern? Consider the proposition that the Court has from time to time forgotten what the Constitution means. But did it forget during the periods of enforcement or of nonenforcement of such limits?

III

Judicial Efforts to Protect the Expansion of the Market against Assertions of Local Power

Since the early years of constitutional adjudication, the Supreme Court has asserted the authority to invalidate state and local laws that the Court finds to interfere improperly with interstate and foreign commerce. When it invalidates state laws for this reason, it says that the commerce clause has been violated (even though the commerce clause, by its terms, is only a grant of power to Congress, not a restriction on state power). This chapter deals with two major problems: (a) What is the *source* of the Court's authority in this area (the primary subject of section A), and (b) what are the *criteria* for determining when a state or local law improperly interferes with interstate commerce (the primary subject of the remainder of the chapter)? For a survey, see Eule, Laying the Dormant Commerce Clause to Rest, 91 Yale L.J. 425 (1982).

A. THE FUNDAMENTAL FRAMEWORK

Note: *The Classical View*

1. *The vices of "protectionism."* The framers were concerned that states would erect barriers to trade in order to protect the economic activities of local residents. Protectionism may impede economic development by making it more difficult for goods and capital to move to places where they are more valued. It also may impair the development of a sense of national unity. These two vices of protectionism may have different implications for the constitutional scheme. Regardless of the reasons for their creation, barriers to trade impede economic development. But they need not impair national unity if out-of-state residents understand that the barriers were created to further important local goals unrelated to the suppression of free trade.

The materials that follow address several aspects of the vices of protectionism. (a) Whatever free trade norms the Constitution embodies, which branch — Congress or the courts — should enforce them? (b) How can protectionist legislation be identified? Some statutes apply one rule to economic activity originating locally and another to activity originating elsewhere. Are all such statutes protectionist? Other statutes have a disparate impact on local and out-of-state trade. When should they be characterized as protectionist? Will the degree of the disparate impact matter? Still other statutes erect barriers to trade without regard to its origin locally or elsewhere. Should such statutes ever be considered protectionist or otherwise constitutionally suspect?

2. *A congressional veto of state laws?* At the Constitutional Convention, Madison proposed that Congress have the power to veto state laws contravening the Constitution, and that a Council of Revision composed of the President and Supreme Court justices have authority to review such vetoes. Apparently because the Council of Revision would also have had authority to review all federal legislation, and believing that the ordinary processes of judicial review would be sufficient as to federal legislation, the Convention rejected the entire proposal. 1 J. Goebel, History of the Supreme Court: Antecedents and Beginnings to 1801, at 208-210 (1971). Does the rejection shed any light on whether the Court may invalidate state laws (on the basis of the commerce clause or on the basis of any other provision in the original Constitution) in the absence of congressional action?

3. *Exclusive congressional power?* In Gibbons v. Ogden, Chapter 2 supra, Chief Justice Marshall found "great force" in an argument made in Justice Johnson's concurrence, that Congress's power to regulate interstate commerce was exclusive — that is, that the Constitution necessarily withdrew that power from the states. Under this view, the states lacked power to enact laws that regulated interstate commerce, and the courts could invalidate any such laws on the ground that they exceeded the states' authority in our federal system. (Article I, section 10 expressly disables states from certain activities that are elsewhere committed to Congress. Why should the commerce power standing alone be exclusive when these other powers require a specific provision denying state power for them to be exclusive?)

The exclusive power argument was troublesome for practical reasons because where Congress's power is exclusive, the states may not act, even if Congress, too, has failed to act. (Note that the acceptability of the "exclusive power" argument may turn on the scope one gives to the affirmative grant of power to Congress.) If *some* regulation is thought appropriate, the "exclusive power" argument may go too far in insisting that the regulation always derive from Congress.

Difficulties with the breadth of the "exclusive power" argument led the Court to develop a number of doctrines designed to limit it.

a. *Purpose.* In *Gibbons*, Justice Johnson coupled his "exclusive power" argument with the contention that Congress was granted the power to regulate interstate commerce only to achieve commercial ends. It followed that the states lacked power only insofar as they sought to achieve similar ends, such as the protection of local enterprises from out-of-state competition, but not insofar as they exercised their general "police" powers, those designed to promote the health and safety of their citizens. This limitation requires the Court to distinguish between statutes designed to serve commercial goals and those designed to serve police power ones; determining the legislature's purpose in light of the impact of its actions may be quite difficult.

In Willson v. Black-Bird Creek Marsh Co., 27 U.S. (2 Pet.) 245 (1829), a Delaware statute authorized the company to erect a dam on a stream deep enough to be used by boats in interstate commerce. The dam helped dry up a marsh in the area. Chief Justice Marshall's brief opinion for the Court held that the statute did not violate the commerce clause. "The value of the property on [the] banks [of the creek] must be enhanced [by the dam], and the health of the inhabitants probably improved. Measures calculated to produce these objects, provided they do not come into collision with the powers of the general government, are undoubtedly within those reserved to the states." Does this adopt a "purpose" limitation? Why did Marshall speak of the "powers" of the national government rather than, for example, its "statutes"?

b. *Direct/indirect.* DiSanto v. Pennsylvania, 273 U.S. 34 (1927), invalidated a licensing statute for those wishing to sell tickets for transportation to or from foreign countries. The state argued that the statute was designed to prevent exploitation of recent immigrants who wished to purchase tickets for relatives still in Europe; before the licensing scheme was adopted, some ticket agents had required the immigrants to make payments into an account with the agents, who would not purchase the tickets until full payment had been made. The majority, noting that "Congress has complete and paramount authority to regulate foreign commerce and [to] protect the public against [frauds,]" stated that a "statute which by its necessary operation directly interferes with or burdens foreign commerce is a prohibited regulation and invalid, regardless of the purpose with which it was passed. Such legislation cannot be sustained as an exertion of the police power of the State to prevent possible fraud." Justice Stone's dissent called the "direct/indirect" test "too mechanical, too uncertain in its application, and too remote from actualities to be of value." He called the terms "labels to describe a result rather than any trustworthy formula by which it is reached." For a rare modern application of the directness test, see Brown-Forman Distillers Corp. v. New York State Liquor Authority, 476 U.S. 573 (1986): New York's complex regulatory scheme for liquor pricing in effect prohibited distillers from lowering their prices in other states once they set prices for New York. The Court said that this prohibition "regulates out-of-state transactions in violation of the Commerce Clause. [Forcing] a merchant to seek regulatory approval in one State before undertaking a transaction in another directly regulates interstate commerce."

Note the rejection of "direct/indirect" and "purpose" as tests to determine the scope of Congress's affirmative power to regulate interstate commerce, Chapter 2, section C, supra. Consider the possibility (a) that the tests were rejected there and here because of their inherent flaws, or (b) that they were rejected when one overall approach to constitutional doctrine replaced another.

c. *Inherently local/national.* Cooley v. Board of Port Wardens, 53 U.S. (12 How.) 299 (1852), involved a Pennsylvania law, adopted in 1803, requiring all ships entering or leaving the port of Philadelphia to use a local pilot or pay a fine into a fund to support retired pilots and their dependents. The Court agreed that the regulation of pilots was a regulation of interstate commerce, even though pilots stayed with the ships for only brief periods. It upheld the statute:

[The] power to regulate commerce, embraces a vast field, containing not only many, but exceedingly various subjects, quite unlike in their nature; some imperatively demanding a single uniform rule, operating equally on the commerce of the United States in every port; and some, like the subject now in question, as imperatively demanding that diversity, which alone can meet the local necessities of navigation.

Either absolutely to affirm, or to deny that the nature of this power requires exclusive legislation by Congress, is to lose sight of the nature of the subjects of this power, and to assert concerning all of them, what is really applicable but to a part. Whatever subjects of this power are in their nature national, or admit only of one uniform system [may] justly be said to be of such a nature as to require exclusive legislation by Congress. That this cannot be affirmed of laws for the regulation of [pilotage] is clear.

Cooley requires that the Court determine whether a "subject" is of "a nature" requiring uniform national regulation or diverse local regulation. (1) What are the criteria for determining what is the national or local nature of the "subject" of the legislation? The Court treats *Cooley* as involving the subject of pilotage; would the analysis or result differ if the subject were retirement systems? (2) Why does the Court refuse to recognize the possibility of diverse national regulation? Congress could adopt regulations specific to each named port (or create an administrative agency charged with developing appropriate regulations for each port). Yet if uniformity does not necessarily follow from the exercise of national power, how can we decide whether a subject ought to be local or national?

As you study the modern cases, note the extent to which intuitions or express judgments about (1) the "national versus local" nature of the problem, (2) the "commercial versus police powers" purposes of the regulation, and (3) the directness of the effect on interstate commerce appear to influence outcomes and doctrinal formulations.

4. *"Exclusive power" and the slavery issue.* Before the Civil War, discussions of the exclusivity and scope of Congress's power were deeply influenced by the issue of slavery. Supporters of slavery were concerned that, if slavery were treated as involving interstate commerce in human beings, they would lose the power to regulate slavery. Mayor of New York v. Miln, 36 U.S. (11 Pet.) 102 (1837), invoked the "police powers" test to uphold a statute requiring shipmasters to report the names and residences of passengers. In the Passenger Cases, 48 U.S. (7 How.) 283 (1849), the Court, dividing five to four with each justice writing an opinion, held unconstitutional one statute imposing a tax on each incoming passenger, to be used to defray the costs of health inspections and treatment, and another requiring a bond to be posted for each immigrant likely to become a public charge.

The issue of slavery affected these discussions directly and indirectly. The Passenger Cases held that people could be objects of commerce. That raised questions about Congress's power to regulate the interstate trade in slaves. If Congress's power were exclusive, not only could it regulate the trade, but also the states could not. Southern interests were opposed to treating people as objects of commerce because that would affirm national power. But once they were so treated, the same interests opposed the "exclusive power" position because it would bar southern states from regulating the interstate slave trade, which the slave-exporting states of the upper South and the slave-importing states of the lower South both wanted to regulate.

More generally, lodging "exclusive power" in the national government meant that if people wanted action on some matter within the exclusive national power, they had to direct their attention to the national government. If states had concurrent power, people could look to their states first. After the early years of the nineteenth century, southern interests were less confident that they could retain permanent control of the national government and more devoted to enhancing local authority.

5. *The demise of the classical framework.* After the Civil War, the doctrinal tensions became less important. The slavery issue disappeared. Further, as *DiSanto* suggests, for a while it did not trouble a majority of the Court that the "exclusive power" position led to a regime in which economic activity was unregulated: The states could not act because they lacked power, and Congress did not act because it had other things to do that it regarded as more pressing. The various limitations on the "exclusive power" argument could be deployed to allow deviations from a regime of laissez-faire in practice where a majority of the Court believed that deviations were appropriate. (Consider here the extent to which the statute in *DiSanto* rested on an expansive definition of fraud.) Eventually the Court abandoned the classical framework, although it retains some vestigial force.

Note: The Modern View

1. *General theories.* The modern law of the commerce clause, in its negative or dormant aspect considered in this chapter, rests on at least three theories, which sometimes conflict in particular cases.

a. A *purely political theory.* Some state statutes are incompatible with the ideal of a unified nation. In particular, "protectionist" statutes — those that aim at (or achieve?) the promotion of in-state interests at the expense of out-of-state interests — demonstrate that the enacting state does not take seriously the proposition that all the states are partners in a single national enterprise. If the statute says expressly that local interests will be treated differently from out-of-state interests, it signals clearly the state's indifference to its national obligations. What if the statute does not draw such an express line, but the inference of indifference is strong in light of the differential impact of the statute on in-state and out-of-state interests?

b. A *purely economic theory.* Protectionist legislation, and some other laws, interfere with the efficient disposition of resources throughout the country. By excluding some commerce from a state, these statutes may lead to a lower level of economic performance than would be possible in the absence of the statutes.

c. A *mixed political and economic theory.* Protectionist legislation, and some other laws, result from the operation of a political process that can be understood as "distorted." In particular, consider this observation by Justice Stone in South Carolina State Highway Department v. Barnwell Brothers, 303 U.S. 177 (1938):

> State regulations affecting interstate commerce, whose purpose or effect is to gain for those within the state an advantage at the expense of those without, or to burden those out of the state without any corresponding advantage to those within, have been thought to impinge upon the constitutional prohibition even though Congress has not acted.
>
> Underlying the stated rule has been the thought, often expressed in judicial opinion, that when the regulation is of such a character that its burden falls principally upon those without the state, legislative action is not likely to be subjected to those political restraints which are normally exerted on legislation where it affects adversely some interests within the state. See [*Cooley*].

Consider the possibility of a fourth approach, *formalism*. One could apply the preceding approaches directly and ask whether a statute is protectionist or results from a distorted political process. A formalist may argue against directly applying the approaches, and might conclude that statutes using geographical terms should be viewed with great suspicion, not because every such statute is protectionist or expresses a state's willingness to separate itself from the rest of the nation, but because *most* such statutes do so. Legislatures directed never to use geographical terms will adopt fewer protectionist or otherwise troublesome statutes than legislatures whose actions are tested against some more complicated standards.

A summary of the theories, limited however to protectionist statutes, is Regan, The Supreme Court and State Protectionism: Making Sense of the Dormant Commerce Clause, 84 Mich. L. Rev. 1091 (1986). In analyzing the cases that follow, consider carefully which theory or theories explain each case, and notice in particular the cases in which the theories might yield conflicting results.

2. *The relevance of preemption and consent.* In Exxon Corp. v. Governor of Maryland, 437 U.S. 117 (1978), the Court rejected a commerce clause challenge to a statute prohibiting gasoline producers and refiners from operating retail gas stations in the state. Suppose the major gasoline producers such as Exxon continue to object to the burdens the statute places on them. The major producers might seek congressional action to preempt Maryland's law. Once Congress acts, its statutes prevail over conflicting state laws by reason of the supremacy clause.

Suppose the Court had held that the Maryland statute violated the commerce clause. Could the local retailers who supported the statute have it reinstated by persuading Congress to act on their behalf?

a. *Early formulations of congressional power to consent or preempt.* In 1827, the Supreme Court held that states could not exercise their power to tax items of interstate commerce so long as the items remained in their original packages. Brown v. Maryland, 25 U.S. (12 Wheat.) 419 (1827), limited in Michelin Tire Corp. v. Wages, 423 U.S. 276 (1976). In 1873, Iowa passed a statute prohibiting the sale of beer. In Leisy v. Hardin, 135 U.S. 100 (1890), the Leisys brewed beer in Illinois and shipped it to Iowa, where they sought to sell it in the original kegs. When Hardin, the town marshal, seized the kegs, the Leisys sued for their return. They argued that, although Iowa had the power to regulate liquor consumption, the original package doctrine barred it from regulating the sale of beer in its original kegs. A divided Supreme Court agreed. Chief Justice Fuller's majority opinion concluded that Iowa's prohibition statute "[inhibited], directly or indirectly, the receipt of an imported commodity" and was therefore unconstitutional. The opinion stated that "the responsibility is upon Congress [to] remove the restriction upon the State [if] in its judgment the end to be secured justifies and requires such action." If Congress has the power to displace the Court's judgment, in what sense was Iowa's statute "unconstitutional"?

Supporters of prohibition accepted the Court's suggestion that they seek congressional permission for state prohibition laws. In August 1890, a few months after *Leisy*, Congress enacted the Wilson Act, which stated that liquor imported into a state "shall upon arrival [be] subject to" local laws as if it had been locally produced, "and shall not be exempt therefrom by reason of being [in] original packages." In re Rahrer, 140 U.S. 545 (1891), held that the Wilson Act was a constitutional exercise of Congress's exclusive power to regulate interstate commerce and that Rahrer's conviction for selling liquor in its original package contrary to

Kansas law did not violate the Constitution. Chief Justice Fuller again wrote the Court's opinion, which argued that the Constitution transferred authority to regulate from the states to Congress; it did not give an "affirmative guaranty" that any activity would remain unregulated. "Congress could [in] the exercise of the discretion reposed in it, concluding that the common interests did not require entire freedom in the traffic in ardent spirits, enact the law in question. In so doing Congress [has] taken its own course and made its own regulation, applying to these subjects of interstate commerce one common rule, whose uniformity is not affected by variations in state laws in dealing with such property." For a general discussion, see Cohen, Congressional Power to Validate Unconstitutional State Laws, 35 Stan. L. Rev. 387 (1983).

b. *Congressional silence and inertia.* Taken together, the doctrines of preemption and consent mean that a judicial decision on a commerce clause challenge need not be final. If the challenge is rejected, those who oppose state regulation may secure federal legislation preempting it. If the challenge is sustained, those who support state regulation may secure federal legislation permitting it. Under these circumstances, why should the courts intervene rather than letting the burdens of regulation lie where they fall and allowing the political process to adjust the balance between burdens and benefits?

Concurring in Duckworth v. Arkansas, 314 U.S. 390 (1941), Justice Jackson said:

> [These] restraints are individually too petty, too diversified, and too local to get the attention of a Congress hard pressed with more urgent matters. [The] sluggishness of government, the multitude of matters that clamor for attention, and the relative ease with which men are persuaded to postpone troublesome decisions, all make inertia one of the most decisive powers in determining the course of our affairs and frequently gives [sic] to the established order of things a longevity and vitality much beyond its merits.

Thus, he concluded, the courts should intervene because of congressional inertia. If the restraints are indeed petty, in what sense could they unduly burden interstate commerce? Should the assumption be instead that restraints serious enough to violate the Constitution ought to be of such economic significance as to attract congressional attention? How can we distinguish congressional inaction due to inertia from inaction due to a considered judgment that on balance the state regulation does not unduly burden interstate commerce? Why should inaction with respect to statutes that *regulate* be treated differently from inaction that takes the form of *failing* to regulate? For discussions of congressional silence, see Biklé, The Silence of Congress, 41 Harv. L. Rev. 200 (1927); Tribe, Toward a Syntax of the Unsaid: Construing the Sounds of Congressional and Constitutional Silence, 57 Ind. L.J. 515 (1982).

Note that securing congressional action is costly. If the costs of mobilizing Congress to act exceed the burdens a regulation places on interstate commerce, Congress's failure to act may reflect a rational calculation of the costs and benefits of political action. Judicial intervention might be justified if it is less expensive than the burdens on interstate commerce and the cost of mobilizing Congress. Should Congress create an administrative agency to review state regulations? Note (1) that such an agency might be seen as a modern version of Madison's proposed Council of Revision; (2) that it would plainly be a body exercising the power Congress has to regulate commerce; (3) that an agency is an attractive sub-stitute for direct congressional action because it is relatively easier to bring a prob-lem to its attention than to Congress's; and (4) that the courts could be seen as the proposed agency. Is there anything wrong in taking this last step? As you study the materials in section B of this chapter, consider whether review of state regulations is a sound use of the courts' time, compared to other possible uses of that time.

c. *Allocating the burden of inertia.* Under the modern view, the fundamental issue in this area is who should bear the burden of overcoming congressional in-ertia. Note that Justice Jackson's justification for judicial intervention concludes with a reference to the "merits" of the status quo. What are the criteria for deter-mining the "merits" in this setting?

(1) *Substantive preference for free trade.* H. P. Hood & Sons v. DuMond, 336 U.S. 525 (1949) (Jackson, J.):

> While the Constitution vests in Congress the power to regulate commerce among the states, it does not say what the states may or may not do in the absence of con-gressional action. [This] Court has advanced the solidarity and prosperity of this Nation by the meaning it has given to these great silences of the Constitution. . . .
>
> [The] principle that our economic unit is the Nation, which alone has the gamut of powers necessary to control the economy, including the vital power of erecting customs barriers against foreign competition, has as its corollary that the states are not separable economic units. . . .
>
> The material success that has come to inhabitants of the states which make up this federal free trade unit has been the most impressive in the history of com-merce, but the established interdependence of the states only emphasizes the ne-cessity of protecting interstate movement of goods against local burdens and repres-sions. We need only consider the consequences if each of the few states that produce copper, lead, [cotton,] oil or gas should decree that industries located in that state shall have priority. What fantastic rivalries and dislocations and reprisals would en-sue if such practices were begun! [May] Michigan provide that automobiles can-not be taken out of the State until local dealers' demands are fully met? [Could] Ohio then pounce upon the rubber-tire industry, on which she has a substantial grip, to retaliate for Michigan's auto monopoly?
>
> Our system, fostered by the Commerce Clause, is that every farmer and every craftsman shall be encouraged to produce by the certainty that he will have free ac-cess to every market in the Nation, that no home embargoes will withhold his ex-ports, and no foreign state will by customs duties or regulations exclude them. Like-wise, every consumer may look to the free competition from every producing area in the Nation to protect him from exploitation by any. Such was the vision of the Founders; such has been the doctrine of this Court which has given it reality.

Justice Jackson's description of the political and economic benefits of free trade reflects the preconstitutional history of interstate commercial rivalries and the modern economic theory of free trade. On the latter, consider Prichard, Se-curing the Canadian Economic Union: Federalism and Internal Barriers to Trade, in Federalism and the Canadian Economic Union 1, 6 (M. Trebilcock et al. eds. 1983):

> [The] tension between political autonomy and economic integration is inescap-able in any non-unitary political system. Only by the mutual sacrifice of indepen-

dence of action can states reap the full advantages of integration, because [they] flow from the adoption of common [rather] than competing policies. [Through] integration the participants may reap the benefits of the theory of comparative advantage through specialization and exchange. These gains are maximized when the factors of production and the resulting goods and services are allowed to move freely among participants to locations where the highest value is put on them. Thus gains from trade should increase the gross national product [as] long as the free movement of factors is maintained.

Dowling, Interstate Commerce and State Power, 27 Va. L. Rev. 1, 20 (1940), proposes the following rule as a description of then-current practice: "[In] the absence of affirmative consent a Congressional negative will be presumed in the courts against state action which in its effect upon interstate commerce constitutes an unreasonable interference with national interests, the presumption being rebuttable at the pleasure of Congress." (This article and its successor, Interstate Commerce and State Power — Revised Version, 47 Colum. L. Rev. 547 (1947), remain the most useful overviews of the problems addressed in this section.) Does Dowling's rule respond equally well to the political and economic considerations discussed so far?

(2) *Minimizing costs.* Obtaining congressional preemption or consent requires interest groups to invest time and effort in the political process. If the burden of overcoming inertia is placed on the group *less* likely to succeed in that effort, it may be discouraged from the investment. If that occurs, the courts will have arrived at the outcome that Congress would have, and at a lower cost. How accurately can the courts determine who is less likely to succeed? What if the loser in the courts is not discouraged?

Consider the extent to which the distinction in *Cooley* between national and local subject matters and that in *Gibbons* between commercial and police power regulations assist in determining who should bear the burden of overcoming congressional inertia. Finally, note Powell, The Still Small Voice of the Commerce Clause, in 3 Selected Essays on Constitutional Law 932 (1938): "If congress keeps silent about the interstate commerce that is not national in character, [then] congress is silently silent, and the states may regulate. But if congress keeps silent about the kind of commerce that is national in character, [then] congress is silently vocal and says that the commerce must be free from state regulation."

3. *The availability of nonconstitutional grounds for decision.* Note in the following materials the cases in which federal statutes might have been used as the basis for decisions on preemption or consent grounds. Consider what reasons the Court might have for relying on "constitutional," rather than statutory, grounds.

4. *A preliminary overview.* It may help in understanding the material that follows to have a summary of the Court's overall doctrine in mind. Lawrence, Toward a More Coherent Dormant Commerce Clause: A Proposed Unitary Framework, 21 Harv. J.L. & Pub. Poly. 395, 416-417 (1998), proposes the following analysis: If the statute is facially discriminatory, it is "virtually *per se* invalid. The State has the heavy burden of proving that the measure is virtually certain to achieve its legitimate purpose and that the purpose cannot be served as well by available *less* discriminatory means." Statutes with discriminatory purposes are per se invalid; challengers must establish the impermissible purpose. If the statutes are applied evenhandedly to both in-state and out-of-state commerce, they are constitutional unless the challenger shows that the statute's burden on inter-

state commerce "is clearly excessive in relation to state benefits." "Where a measure imposes a burden *mostly,* although not exclusively, on out-of-state interests, the State has the burden of justifying that the measure is likely to achieve its legitimate purpose; the challenger then has the burden of either rebutting the State's justification or of showing that the purpose can be served as well by available nondiscriminatory [alternatives.] Where the measure imposes a burden *exclusively* on out-of-state interests, the State has the burden of proving that the measure is *highly* likely to achieve its legitimate purpose *and* that the purpose cannot be served as well by available nondiscriminatory alternatives." Are the decisions that follow compatible with any of the theoretical approaches described in this Note?

B.   PROTECTION AGAINST DISCRIMINATION

In Wyoming v. Oklahoma, 502 U.S. 437 (1992), the Court held unconstitutional an Oklahoma statute requiring coal-fired electric utilities in the state to burn a mixture containing at least 10 percent Oklahoma-mined coal. This "preference for coal from domestic sources cannot be characterized as anything other than protectionist." Why was the statute passed? Who benefits from it? Who bears the costs? Recall Justice Stone's observation about the imbalance in the political process where burdens fall primarily out of state and benefits flow primarily in state. Does this "thought" explain the outcome in *Wyoming?* The implications of Stone's observations provide the structure for this section.

Note: General Considerations

1. *Cost-benefit analysis.* The costs of economic regulation are not always paid by those who receive its benefits. The distribution of costs and benefits across different groups means that the mere adoption of a regulation need not establish that its benefits to the entire society exceed its costs. Further, the distribution of costs and benefits across different groups affects the political forces supporting and opposing adoption or repeal of regulations. Under what conditions might regulations be adopted when their total social costs exceed their total social benefits?

If benefits will be conferred on a relatively small group, each member can agree to finance lobbying efforts to secure the legislation (on the condition that every other member also contribute). (Why is the condition important?) Each will expect to recover his or her investment in political activity from the benefits to be gained by the legislation. If the regulation also imposes costs on a broad group, those who bear the costs will find it difficult to organize in opposition. The costs imposed on each member of the group are likely to be smaller than the amount each would have to invest in an effective lobbying effort. Further, there is a free-rider problem: Each member of the group may hang back, expecting that others will engage in lobbying that, if successful, would benefit the free rider at no cost to him or herself. This theory is developed in detail in M. Olson, The

Logic of Collective Action (1965). To what extent is it weakened by the development of "watchdog" organizations? (How and why are they funded?) Note that the theory is not confined to state legislation that affects interstate commerce. Consider, for example, how it might be applied to Lochner v. New York, Chapter 5 infra.

Consider the extent to which a theory like Olson's may underlie the discrimination cases that follow and the "undue burden" cases in section C infra.

2. *"Exporting" costs*. Regulations may be adopted when the beneficiaries within the jurisdiction adopting it outweigh in political power those within the jurisdiction who will bear (some of) its costs. They may do so because of numbers or because of the organizational factors discussed by Olson. Total social costs may still exceed total social benefits, but if the local beneficiaries can export enough costs so that the local benefits exceed the local costs, the regulation may be adopted. Is this the "thought" Stone described? Consider whether the statute in *Wyoming* involves this kind of cost-exporting.

Note that in every case some local residents — those who prefer doing business with out-of-staters — will be worse off. In the simplest case, the benefits to local residents exceed the costs to local residents. Even though some local residents (and therefore voters) will bear some costs, the "gross state product" will be greater after the regulation is adopted than before. The local beneficiaries may then use some of their new profits to subsidize the local cost-bearers, reducing the political opposition to the adoption of the regulation. Consider in this connection Dean Milk Co. v. Madison, infra.

Although Congress may not "export" costs of national regulations in the same way, note that it may distribute costs and benefits among various geographical areas. Two constitutional provisions have been interpreted to require geographical uniformity in regulation: article I, section 8, clause 4 (power "to establish [uniform] Laws [on] Bankruptcies") and article I, section 8, clause 1 (power to tax requires that "all Duties, Imposts, and Excises [be] uniform throughout the United States"). The latter clause was applied in United States v. Ptasynski, 462 U.S. 74 (1983), which found constitutional a provision of the Windfall Profit Tax of 1980 that excluded "exempt Alaskan oil" from its coverage. The Court noted that the exempt oil could have been described in nongeographical terms and, after "closely" examining the statute, concluded that the exemption was based on "neutral factors" such as climate and difficulty of extraction. Would a tax imposed only on Alaskan oil violate the uniformity clause? For a discussion of the clause's background, see Knowlton v. Moore, 178 U.S. 41 (1900). Consider Comment, The Uniformity Clause, 51 U. Chi. L. Rev. 1193, 1194 (1984): "[The] uniformity clause should be read in light of the Constitution's general preference for free markets and unrestrained economic competition." Is there such a general preference?

3. *Incidence analysis*. Under what circumstances can a state export the costs of regulation? This is the subject of a branch of economics called incidence analysis. McLure, Incidence Analysis and the Supreme Court: An Examination of Four Cases from the 1980 Term, 1 Sup. Ct. Econ. Rev. 69 (1982), provides a useful introduction to this complex subject, with illustrations taken from the matters covered in this section.

McLure identifies the following as among the "pervasive determinants of incidence": (a) "Short-term versus long-term" perspectives. In the short run, a state may be able to export the costs of regulation by imposing the regulation on an activity where fixed capital investments (in plants and equipment, for example) out of state are proportionally more significant than fixed capital in state. But over time investors will adjust their activities to take account of the regulation. (b) "Market dominance." If the state has a monopoly or near-monopoly on the regulated activity, the costs of regulation can be shifted to consumers. If the consumers are largely out of state, the costs will be exported, even if the regulated activity takes place entirely within the state. For a detailed examination of this aspect of the problem, see Levmore, Interstate Exploitation and Judicial Intervention, 69 Va. L. Rev. 563 (1983). (c) "Substitution." Costs can be exported if there are no or few substitutes for the regulated activity at almost equal prices, and (again) if consumers are largely out of state. For example, if a commodity such as coal must be shipped out of state on railroads, the costs of railroad regulation can be exported. If shippers can switch to trucks, the costs of railroad regulation cannot be exported. McLure notes that careful definition of the relevant market is essential when considering the latter two determinants.

Try to apply this analysis to the *Wyoming* case that introduced this section. Which of the cases that follow involve regulations that have the characteristic of allowing enough costs to be exported so that local benefits will exceed local costs?

4. *Possible burdens on the local economy.* In *Wyoming*, out-of-state coal producers were deprived of some opportunities to make profits on their Oklahoma operations. The regulation also diminished the competition faced by Oklahoma coal producers. Would they raise the prices they charged? Oklahoma's consumers might find it difficult to organize political opposition to a statute raising coal prices in Oklahoma. Should the courts be concerned about that problem?

5. *An alternative framework.* The materials in this chapter are organized around the theme of cost-exporting. After working through the materials, consider whether that organization is more helpful than one focused on the subject matter of the regulation (e.g., transportation, natural resources, end products of complex manufacturing processes). Be careful to note as well the varying doctrinal formulations the Court offers. Are the variations associated with relevant differences (a) in the likelihood of cost-exporting, or (b) in the subject matter, or (c) anything?

City of Philadelphia v. New Jersey

437 U.S. 617 (1978)

MR. JUSTICE STEWART delivered the opinion of the Court.

A New Jersey law prohibits the importation of most "solid or liquid waste which originated or was collected outside the territorial limits of the State." In this case we are required to decide whether this statutory prohibition violates the Commerce Clause of the United States Constitution. . . .

[Private landfill operators challenged the statute on preemption and constitutional grounds. The state supreme court found that the statute "advanced vital health and environmental objectives with no economic discrimination against, and with little burden upon, interstate commerce." It also found no preemption.]

We agree with the New Jersey court that the state law has not been pre-empted by federal legislation.[4] The dispositive question, therefore, is whether the law is constitutionally permissible in light of the Commerce Clause of the Constitution.

II

Before it addressed the merits of the appellants' claim, the New Jersey Supreme Court questioned whether the interstate movement of those wastes banned by ch. 363 is "commerce" at all within the meaning of the Commerce Clause. Any doubts on that score should be laid to rest at the outset. . . .

[All] objects of interstate trade merit Commerce Clause protection; none is excluded by definition at the outset. Hence, we reject the state court's suggestion that the banning of "valueless" out-of-state wastes by [the statute] implicates no constitutional protection. Just as Congress has power to regulate the interstate movement of these wastes, States are not free from constitutional scrutiny when they restrict that movement.

III

A

Although the Constitution gives Congress the power to regulate commerce among the States, many subjects of potential federal regulation under that power inevitably escape congressional attention "because of their local character and their number and diversity." South Carolina State Highway Dept. v. Barnwell Bros., Inc., 303 U.S. 177, 185. In the absence of federal legislation, these subjects are open to control by the States so long as they act within the restraints imposed by the Commerce Clause itself. The bounds of these restraints appear nowhere in the words of the Commerce Clause, but have emerged gradually in the decisions of this Court giving effect to its basic purpose. That broad purpose was well expressed by Mr. Justice Jackson in his opinion for the Court in H. P. Hood & Sons, Inc. v. Du Mond, [quoted supra]. . . .

The opinions of the Court through the years have reflected an alertness to the evils of "economic isolation" and protectionism, while at the same time recognizing that incidental burdens on interstate commerce may be unavoidable when a State legislates to safeguard the health and safety of its people. Thus, where simple economic protectionism is effected by state legislation, a virtually per se rule

4. [From] our review of this federal legislation, we find no "clear and manifest purpose of Congress," Rice v. Santa Fe Elevator Corp., 331 U.S. 218, 230, to pre-empt the entire field of interstate waste management or transportation, either by express statutory command, or by implicit legislative design. To the contrary, Congress expressly has provided that "the collection and disposal of solid wastes should continue to be primarily the function of State, regional, and local agencies. . . ." 42 U.S.C. §6901(a)(4) (1976 ed.). Similarly, [the statute] is not pre-empted because of a square conflict with particular provisions of federal law or because of general incompatibility with basic federal objectives. In short, [the statute] can be enforced consistently with the program goals and the respective federal-state roles intended by Congress when it enacted the federal legislation.

of invalidity has been erected. See, e.g., [*H. P. Hood & Sons*]. The clearest example of such legislation is a law that overtly blocks the flow of interstate commerce at a State's borders. But where other legislative objectives are credibly advanced and there is no patent discrimination against interstate trade, the Court has adopted a much more flexible approach, the general contours of which were outlined in Pike v. Bruce Church, Inc., 397 U.S. 137, 142:

> Where the statute regulates evenhandedly to effectuate a legitimate local public interest, and its effects on interstate commerce are only incidental, it will be upheld unless the burden imposed on such commerce is clearly excessive in relation to the putative local benefits. . . . If a legitimate local purpose is found, then the question becomes one of degree. And the extent of the burden that will be tolerated will of course depend on the nature of the local interest involved, and on whether it could be promoted as well with a lesser impact on interstate activities.

The crucial inquiry, therefore, must be directed to determining whether [the statute] is basically a protectionist measure, or whether it can fairly be viewed as a law directed to legitimate local concerns, with effects upon interstate commerce that are only incidental.

B

The purpose of [the statute] is set out [as] follows:

> The Legislature finds and determines that . . . the volume of solid and liquid waste continues to rapidly increase, that the treatment and disposal of these wastes continues to pose an even greater threat to the quality of the environment of New Jersey, that the available and appropriate land fill sites within the State are being diminished, that the environment continues to be threatened by the treatment and disposal of waste which originated or was collected outside the State, and that the public health, safety and welfare require that the treatment and disposal within this State of all wastes generated outside of the State be prohibited.

The New Jersey Supreme Court accepted this statement of the state legislature's purpose. The state court additionally found that New Jersey's existing landfill sites will be exhausted within a few years; that to go on using these sites or to develop new ones will take a heavy environmental toll, both from pollution and from loss of scarce open lands; that new techniques to divert waste from landfills to other methods of disposal and resource recovery processes are under development, but that these changes will require time; and finally, that "the extension of the lifespan of existing landfills, resulting from the exclusion of out-of-state waste, may be of crucial importance in preventing further virgin wetlands or other undeveloped lands from being devoted to landfill purposes." Based on these findings, the court concluded that [the statute] was designed to protect, not the State's economy, but its environment, and that its substantial benefits outweigh its "slight" burden on interstate commerce.

The appellants strenuously contend that [the statute], "while outwardly cloaked 'in the currently fashionable garb of environment protection,' . . . is actually no more than a legislative effort to suppress competition and stabilize the cost of solid waste disposal for New Jersey residents. . . ." They cite passages of legislative history suggesting that the problem [is] primarily financial: Stemming the flow of out-of-state waste into certain landfill sites will extend their lives, thus delaying the day when New Jersey cities must transport their waste to more distant and expensive sites.

The appellees [deny] that [the statute] was motivated by financial concerns or economic protectionism. In the words of their brief, "[n]o New Jersey commercial interests stand to gain advantage over competitors from outside the state as a result of the ban on dumping out-of-state waste." Noting that New Jersey landfill operators are among the plaintiffs, the appellee's brief argues that "[t]he complaint is not that New Jersey has forged an economic preference for its own commercial interests, but rather that it has denied a small group of its entrepreneurs an economic opportunity to traffic in waste in order to protect the health, safety and welfare of the citizenry at large."

This dispute about ultimate legislative purpose need not be resolved, because its resolution would not be relevant to the constitutional issue to be decided in this case. Contrary to the evident assumption of the state court and the parties, the evil of protectionism can reside in legislative means as well as legislative ends. Thus, it does not matter whether the ultimate aim of [the statute] is to reduce the waste disposal costs of New Jersey residents or to save remaining open lands from pollution, for we assume New Jersey has every right to protect its residents' pocketbooks as well as their environment. And it may be assumed as well that New Jersey may pursue those ends by slowing the flow of *all* waste into the State's remaining landfills, even though interstate commerce may incidentally be affected. But whatever New Jersey's ultimate purpose, it may not be accomplished by discriminating against articles of commerce from outside the State unless there is some reason, apart from their origin, to treat them differently. Both on its face and in its plain effect, [the statute] violates this principle of nondiscrimination.

The Court has consistently found parochial legislation of this kind to be constitutionally invalid. [A] presumably legitimate goal was sought to be achieved by the illegitimate means of isolating the State from the national economy.

Also relevant here are the Court's decisions holding that a State may not accord its own inhabitants a preferred right of access over consumers in other States to natural resources located within its borders. These cases stand for the basic principle that a "State is without power to prevent privately owned articles of trade from being shipped and sold in interstate commerce on the ground that they are required to satisfy local demands or because they are needed by the people of the State." Foster-Fountain Packaging Co. v. Haydel, [278 U.S. 1], at 10.

The New Jersey law at issue in this case falls squarely within the area that the Commerce Clause puts off limits to state regulation. On its face, it imposes on out-of-state commercial interests the full burden of conserving the state's remaining landfill space. It is true that in our previous cases the scarce natural resource was itself the article of commerce, whereas here the scarce resource and the article of commerce are distinct. But that difference is without consequence. In both instances, the State has overtly moved to slow or freeze the flow of commerce for protectionist reasons. It does not matter that the State has shut the article of commerce inside the State in one case and outside the State in the other. What is crucial is the attempt by one State to isolate itself from a problem common to many by erecting a barrier against the movement of interstate trade. . . .

[Certain] quarantine laws have not been considered forbidden protectionist measures, even though they were directed against out-of-state commerce. But those quarantine laws banned the importation of articles such as diseased live-stock that required destruction as soon as possible because their very movement risked contagion and other evils. Those laws thus did not discriminate against interstate commerce as such, but simply prevented traffic in noxious articles, whatever their origin.

The New Jersey statute is not such a quarantine law. There has been no claim here that the very movement of waste into or through New Jersey endangers health, or that waste must be disposed of as soon and as close to its point of generation as possible. The harms caused by waste are said to arise after its disposal in landfill sites, and at that point, as New Jersey concedes, there is no basis to distinguish out-of-state waste from domestic waste. If one is inherently harmful, so is the other. Yet New Jersey has banned the former while leaving its landfill sites open to the latter. . . .

Today, cities in Pennsylvania and New York find it expedient or necessary to send their waste into New Jersey for disposal, and New Jersey claims the right to close its borders to such traffic. Tomorrow, cities in New Jersey may find it expedient or necessary to send their waste into Pennsylvania or New York for disposal, and those States might then claim the right to close their borders. The Commerce Clause will protect New Jersey in the future, just as it protects her neighbors now, from efforts by one State to isolate itself in the stream of interstate commerce from a problem shared by all. The judgment is reversed.

MR. JUSTICE REHNQUIST, with whom [CHIEF JUSTICE BURGER] joins, dissenting.

A growing problem in our Nation is the sanitary treatment and disposal of solid waste. For many years, solid waste was incinerated. Because of the significant environmental problems attendant on incineration, however, this method of solid waste disposal has declined in use in many localities, including New Jersey. "Sanitary" landfills have replaced incineration as the principal method of disposing of solid waste. [But] landfills also present extremely serious health and safety problems. First, in New Jersey, "virtually all sanitary landfills can be expected to produce leachate, a noxious and highly polluted liquid which is seldom visible and frequently pollutes . . . ground and surface waters." [Landfills] can also generate "health hazards caused by rodents, fires and scavenger birds" and, "needless to say, do not help New Jersey's aesthetic appearance nor New Jersey's noise or water or air pollution problems."

The health and safety hazards associated with landfills present appellees with a currently unsolvable dilemma. Other, hopefully safer, methods of disposing of solid wastes are still in the development stage and cannot presently be used. But appellees obviously cannot completely stop the tide of solid waste that its citizens will produce in the interim. For the moment, therefore, appellees must continue to use sanitary landfills to dispose of New Jersey's own solid waste despite the critical environmental problems thereby created.

The question presented in this case is whether New Jersey must also continue to receive and dispose of solid waste from neighboring States, even though these will inexorably increase the health problems discussed above. The Court answers this question in the affirmative. New Jersey must either prohibit *all* landfill operations, leaving itself to cast about for a presently nonexistent solution to the serious problem of disposing of the waste generated within its own borders, or it must accept waste from every portion of the United States, thereby multiplying the health and safety problems which would result if it dealt only with such wastes generated within the State. . . .

[New] Jersey may require germ-infected rags or diseased meat to be disposed of as best as possible within the State, but at the same time prohibit the *importation* of such items for disposal at the facilities that are set up within New Jersey for disposal of such material generated *within* the State. The physical fact of life that New Jersey must somehow dispose of its own noxious items does not mean that it must serve as a depository for those of every other State. Similarly, New Jersey should be free under our past precedents to prohibit the importation of solid waste because of the health and safety problems that such waste poses to its citizens. The fact that New Jersey continues to, and indeed must continue to, dispose of its own solid waste does not mean that New Jersey may not prohibit the importation of even more solid waste into the State. I simply see no way to distinguish solid waste, on the record of this case, from germ-infected rags, diseased meat, and other noxious items.

[I] do not see why a State may ban the importation of items whose movement risks contagion, but cannot ban the importation of items which, although they may be transported into the State without undue hazard, will then simply pile up in an ever increasing danger to the public's health and safety. The Commerce Clause was not drawn with a view to having the validity of state laws turn on such pointless distinctions.

[The] Court implies that the challenged laws must be invalidated because New Jersey has left its landfills open to domestic waste. But, as the Court notes, this Court has repeatedly upheld quarantine laws "even though they appear to single out interstate commerce for special treatment." The fact that New Jersey has left its landfill sites open for domestic waste does not, of course, mean that solid waste is not innately harmful. Nor does it mean that New Jersey prohibits importation of solid waste for reasons other than the health and safety of its population. New Jersey must out of sheer necessity treat and dispose of its solid waste in some fashion, just as it must treat New Jersey cattle suffering from hoof-and-mouth disease. It does not follow that New Jersey must, under the Commerce Clause, accept solid waste or diseased cattle from outside its borders and thereby exacerbate its problems.

Note: Facial/Intentional Discrimination

1. *Winners and losers.* Who gains the benefits and who bears the costs of New Jersey's statute? There are four groups to consider: out-of-state waste producers, out-of-state landfill operators, in-state waste producers, and in-state landfill operators. (a) *Costs:* The statute reduces the supply of landfill available to out-of-state waste producers and may therefore increase the price they must pay for disposal. It reduces the demand for New Jersey landfills and may therefore decrease the profits of in-state landfill operators. (b) *Benefits:* The statute benefits in-state waste producers by reducing demand and decreasing prices and by improving their environment; it benefits out-of-state landfill operators by increasing demand and

raising profits. Out-of-state waste producers might benefit from increased costs that encourage each of them to reduce the amount of waste each produces, which might benefit them in the aggregate. Note that from the point of view of cost-exporting, New Jersey does not care whether the benefits to out-of-state land-fill operators exceed the costs to out-of-state waste producers. Its sole concern is that the decreased prices paid by New Jersey waste producers exceed the profits New Jersey operators lose by being unable to accept out-of-state waste. Is it likely that the local benefits exceed the local costs? (What is the relevance, if any, of the fact that New Jersey landfill operators are among the plaintiffs in the case?)

Heinzerling, The Commercial Constitution, 1995 Sup. Ct. Rev. 217, argues that the Court's unwillingness to assess the costs of outside commerce "on account of its outsider status" distorts its cost-benefit calculations. She argues that in-state residents believe that outside commerce imposes costs because it is "intrusive" and "forced" on the in-staters, and that these are as much costs of the outside commerce as the "statistical risk of physical harm" with which the Court's analysis is exclusively concerned: "'Dangerousness' and 'cost' do not [include] the qualitative attributes of risk." Is the perceived extra cost due to "intrusive" waste a cost the Constitution should acknowledge?

Consider the proposition that this Note's focus on a detailed analysis of economic effects is misguided because the Court (a) properly uses facial discrimination as a rough indication that out-of-state burdens exceed local benefits and (b) refrains from looking at economic effects in more detail because it lacks the expertise to do so (in contrast to Congress, which may displace the Court's judgment if it chooses). If the courts cannot do a full cost-benefit analysis, should they refrain from invalidating state laws on commerce clause grounds? Consider also the proposition that the focus on economic effects and their relation to interest-group politics is misguided because interest-group politics are irrelevant to a proper interpretation of the Constitution.

2. *Local versus overall benefits.* Suppose local benefits exceed local costs. It may nonetheless be true that the total social benefits of the regulation exceed the total social costs. Why should New Jersey be barred from enforcing its statute without the opponents showing that total costs also exceed total benefits? Reducing the supply of landfills in the Northeast may encourage the development of alternative means of waste disposal. Or waste producers in the Northeast may have refrained from making economically sound investments in local waste disposal plants because they relied on the availability of New Jersey's landfills. There may also be issues of distribution: The welfare of the Northeast might be increased by making New Jersey a little less polluted and Pennsylvania a little more. Pennsylvania's failure to regulate waste production can be considered *its* attempt to export costs to New Jersey.

Recall that the fundamental issue in this section is determining who should bear the burden of overcoming congressional inertia. Is the possibility that exporting costs will produce a situation in which total costs exceed total benefits by a large amount enough to justify placing that burden on a state that manages to export enough of the costs of regulation? ("Enough" means sufficient to make local benefits exceed local costs.) Consider in this connection the interpretation of the federal statutes in footnote 4 of *City of Philadelphia*. Should the Court have considered whether the statute gave New Jersey permission to do what it did?

How confident are you that the courts can reliably determine whether enough costs can be exported in these cases? Should the courts use the appearance of discrimination on the face of the statute, or anticommercial intent, as a rough approximation of the incidence analysis? As the basis for allocating the burden of overcoming congressional inertia? Note that the Court's insistence on a clear indication of congressional intent to authorize discriminatory state laws increases the burden of overcoming inertia.

3. *Intent.* Is it fair to say that the Court infers from a statute's use of distinctions between in-state and out-of-state economic actors an intent to benefit local interests and harm out-of-state ones? Does the use of a local/out-of-state distinction justify a presumption of intent to export costs?

4. *The relevance of retaliation.* City of Philadelphia v. New Jersey concludes by invoking fears of retaliatory responses by other states. Why should that be a matter of concern? Retaliation would increase the costs borne by local residents, thus eliminating the export of costs and reducing the incentive to adopt the regulation. Note, however, that retaliation may not be completely effective, so that it inflicts some pure economic losses on the states involved with neither an economic nor a distributive justification, and that retaliation, at least until the trade barriers are lowered, is likely to alter the patterns of investment as resources shift to take account of the costs imposed by retaliatory regulations in one sector of the economy but not in another.

Consider Sporhase v. Nebraska, 458 U.S. 941 (1982): A Nebraska statute prohibited the withdrawal of ground water from any well within Nebraska intended for use in another state that fails to grant reciprocal rights to withdraw and transport ground water to Nebraska. Colorado does not grant reciprocal rights. Owners of contiguous land on the Nebraska/Colorado border claimed that the statute unconstitutionally barred them from transferring ground water from a Nebraska well to the Colorado land. The Supreme Court agreed. It found the reciprocity requirement not "narrowly tailored" to serve conservation goals. Citing A&P Tea Co. v. Cottrell, 424 U.S. 366 (1976), it noted that the reciprocity requirement could not be justified "as a response to another State's unreasonable burden on commerce." Why not?

Cottrell defended its position that retaliation was not permitted, even if it was intended to provide an incentive to eliminate trade barriers, on the ground that the state's proper remedy for trade barriers was a challenge in court, not retaliation. (Suppose a state desires to "retaliate" against another state's *failure* to regulate.) Retaliation is common in the international sphere. It is dealt with by the negotiation of bilateral and multilateral trade agreements. Have the states already negotiated such an agreement, calling it the commerce clause rather than a trade treaty?

C & A Carbone, Inc. v. Clarkstown

511 U.S. 383 (1994)

JUSTICE KENNEDY delivered the opinion of the Court. . . .

[Clarkstown, New York, subsidized a private "waste transfer station" to collect solid waste, separate recyclable from nonrecyclable items, and dispose of the waste, by guaranteeing a minimum flow of waste to the station, which would then collect a fee that exceeded the disposal cost of unsorted solid waste in the private market. To assure the guaranteed flow, Clarkstown enacted a "flow control ordinance," requiring that all solid waste within the town be deposited at the station.

Carbone was a private recycler with a sorting facility in Clarkstown. It collected waste from elsewhere in New York and New Jersey, carried it to its facility, and sorted it into recyclable and nonrecyclable items. The flow control ordinance required Carbone to take the nonrecyclable material to the transfer station and pay the fee. Without the ordinance, Carbone would have shipped the nonrecyclable materials to out-of-state destinations at a lower cost than the fee the transfer station charged. The Supreme Court upheld Carbone's challenge to the constitutionality of the flow control ordinance.]

While the immediate effect of the ordinance is to direct local transport of solid waste to a designated site within the local jurisdiction, its economic effects are interstate in reach. The Carbone facility in Clarkstown receives and processes waste from places other than Clarkstown, including from out of State. By requiring Carbone to send the nonrecyclable portion of this waste to the [transfer] station at an additional cost, the flow control ordinance drives up the cost for out-of-state interests to dispose of their solid waste. Furthermore, even as to waste originant in Clarkstown, the ordinance prevents everyone except the favored local operator from performing the initial processing step. The ordinance thus deprives out-of-state businesses of access to a local market. These economic effects are more than enough to bring the Clarkstown ordinance within the purview of the Commerce Clause. . . .

The central rationale for the rule against discrimination is to prohibit state or municipal laws whose object is local economic protectionism, laws that would excite those jealousies and retaliatory measures the Constitution was designed to prevent. We have interpreted the Commerce Clause to invalidate local laws that impose commercial barriers or discriminate against an article of commerce by reason of its origin or destination out of State. See, e.g., Philadelphia [v. New Jersey].

Clarkstown protests that its ordinance does not discriminate because it does not differentiate solid waste on the basis of its geographic origin. All solid waste, regardless of origin, must be processed at the designated transfer station before it leaves the town. Unlike the statute in *Philadelphia*, says the town, the ordinance erects no barrier to the import or export of any solid waste but requires only that the waste be channeled through the designated facility. Our initial discussion of the effects of the ordinance on interstate commerce goes far toward refuting the town's contention that there is no discrimination in its regulatory scheme. The town's own arguments go the rest of the way. As the town itself points out, what makes garbage a profitable business is not its own worth but the fact that its possessor must pay to get rid of it. In other words, the article of commerce is not so much the solid waste itself, but rather the service of processing and disposing of it.

With respect to this stream of commerce, the flow control ordinance discriminates, for it allows only the favored operator to process waste that is within the limits of the town. The ordinance is no less discriminatory because in-state or in-town processors are also covered by the prohibition. In Dean Milk Co. v. Madison, 340 U.S. 349 (1951), we struck down a city ordinance that required all milk sold in the city to be pasteurized within five miles of the city lines. We found it "immaterial that Wisconsin milk from outside the Madison area is subjected to the same proscription as that moving in interstate commerce." Id., at 354, n.4.

In this light, the flow control ordinance is just one more instance of local processing requirements that we long have held invalid. The essential vice in laws of this sort is that they bar the import of the processing service. Out-of-state meat inspectors, or shrimp hullers, or milk pasteurizers, are deprived of access to local demand for their services. Put another way, the offending local laws hoard a local resource — be it meat, shrimp, or milk — for the benefit of local businesses that treat it.

The flow control ordinance has the same design and effect. It hoards solid waste, and the demand to get rid of it, for the benefit of the preferred processing facility. The only conceivable distinction from the cases cited above is that the flow control ordinance favors a single local proprietor. But this difference just makes the protectionist effect of the ordinance more acute. In *Dean Milk*, the local processing requirement at least permitted pasteurizers within five miles of the city to compete. An out-of-state pasteurizer who wanted access to that market might have built a pasteurizing facility within the radius. The flow control ordinance at issue here squelches competition in the waste-processing service altogether, leaving no room for investment from outside.

Discrimination against interstate commerce in favor of local business or investment is per se invalid, save in a narrow class of cases in which the municipality can demonstrate, under rigorous scrutiny, that it has no other means to advance a legitimate local interest. A number of amici contend that the flow control ordinance fits into this narrow class. They suggest that as landfill space diminishes and environmental cleanup costs escalate, measures like flow control become necessary to ensure the safe handling and proper treatment of solid waste.

The teaching of our cases is that these arguments must be rejected absent the clearest showing that the unobstructed flow of interstate commerce itself is unable to solve the local problem. . . .

The flow control ordinance does serve a central purpose that a nonprotectionist regulation would not: It ensures that the town-sponsored facility will be profitable, so that the local contractor can build it and Clarkstown can buy it back at nominal cost in five years. In other words, [the] flow control ordinance is a financing measure. By itself, of course, revenue generation is not a local interest that can justify discrimination against interstate commerce. Otherwise States could impose discriminatory taxes against solid waste originating outside the State.

Clarkstown maintains that special financing is necessary to ensure the long-term survival of the designated facility. If so, the town may subsidize the facility through general taxes or municipal bonds. New Energy Co. of Indiana v. Limbach, 486 U.S. 269, 278 (1988). But having elected to use the open market to earn revenues for its project, the town may not employ discriminatory regulation to give that project an advantage over rival businesses from out of State. . . .

State and local governments may not use their regulatory power to favor local enterprise by prohibiting patronage of out-of-state competitors or their facilities. We reverse the judgment and remand the case for proceedings not inconsistent with this decision.

JUSTICE O'CONNOR, concurring in the judgment.

Local Law 9 [lacks] an important feature common to the regulations at issue in [prior] cases — namely, discrimination on the basis of geographic origin. [In] *Dean Milk*, [the] city of Madison drew a line around its perimeter and required that all milk sold in the City be pasteurized only by dairies located inside the line. This type of geographic distinction, which confers an economic advantage on local interests in general, is common to all the local processing cases cited by the majority. And the Court has, I believe, correctly concluded that these arrangements are protectionist either in purpose or practical effect, and thus amount to virtually per se discrimination.

In my view, the majority fails to come to terms with a significant distinction between the laws in the local processing cases discussed above and Local Law 9. Unlike the regulations we have previously struck down, Local Law 9 does not give more favorable treatment to local interests as a group as compared to out-of-state or out-of-town economic interests. Rather, the garbage sorting monopoly is achieved at the expense of all competitors, be they local or nonlocal. That the ordinance does not discriminate on the basis of geographic origin is vividly illustrated by the identity of the plaintiff in this very action: petitioner is a local recycler, physically located in Clarkstown, that desires to process waste itself, and thus bypass the town's designated transfer facility. Because in-town processors — like petitioner — and out-of-town processors are treated equally, I cannot agree that Local Law 9 "discriminates" against interstate commerce. Rather, Local Law 9 "discriminates" evenhandedly against all potential participants in the waste processing business, while benefiting only the chosen operator of the transfer facility.

I believe this distinction has more doctrinal significance than the majority acknowledges. In considering state health and safety regulations such as Local Law 9, we have consistently recognized that the fact that interests within the regulating jurisdiction are equally affected by the challenged enactment counsels against a finding of discrimination. And for good reason. The existence of substantial in-state interests harmed by a regulation is "a powerful safeguard" against legislative discrimination. The Court generally defers to health and safety regulations because "their burden usually falls on local economic interests as well as other States' economic interests, thus insuring that a State's own political processes will serve as a check against unduly burdensome regulations." Raymond Motor Transportation, Inc. v. Rice, 434 U.S. 429, 444, n.18 (1978). Thus, while there is no bright line separating those enactments which are virtually per se invalid and those which are not, the fact that in-town competitors of the transfer facility are equally burdened by Local Law 9 leads me to conclude that Local Law 9 does not discriminate against interstate commerce.

[Justice O'Connor concluded that the ordinance imposed "an excessive burden on interstate trade when considered in relation to the local benefits conferred." See section C below.]

JUSTICE SOUTER, with whom [CHIEF JUSTICE REHNQUIST] and JUSTICE BLACK-MUN join, dissenting.

[The] exclusion worked by Clarkstown's Local Law 9 bestows no benefit on a class of local private actors, but instead directly aids the government in satisfying a traditional governmental responsibility. The law does not differentiate between all local and all out-of-town providers of a service, but instead between the one entity responsible for ensuring that the job gets done and all other enterprises, regardless of their location. The ordinance thus falls outside that class of tariff or protectionist measures that the Commerce Clause has traditionally been thought to bar States from enacting against each other, and when the majority subsumes the ordinance within the class of laws this Court has struck down as facially discriminatory (and so avails itself of our "virtually per se rule" against such statutes, see [Philadelphia v. New Jersey]), the majority is in fact greatly extending the Clause's dormant reach.

[There] is no indication in the record that any out-of-state trash processor has been harmed, or that the interstate movement or disposition of trash will be affected one whit. To the degree Local Law 9 affects the market for trash processing services, it does so only by subjecting Clarkstown residents and businesses to burdens far different from the burdens of local favoritism that dormant Commerce Clause jurisprudence seeks to root out. The town has found a way to finance a public improvement, not by transferring its cost to out-of-state economic interests, but by spreading it among the local generators of trash, an equitable result with tendencies that should not disturb the Commerce Clause and should not be disturbed by us. . . .

II . . .

The outstanding feature of the statutes [in] the local processing cases is their distinction between two classes of private economic actors according to location, favoring [milk] pasteurizers within five miles of the center of Madison, and so on. Since nothing in these local processing laws prevented a proliferation of local businesses within the State or town, the out-of-town processors were not excluded as part and parcel of a general exclusion of private firms from the market, but as a result of discrimination among such firms according to geography alone. It was because of that discrimination in favor of local businesses, preferred at the expense of their out-of-town or out-of-state competitors, that the Court struck down those local processing laws as classic examples of [economic] protectionism. [In] the words of one commentator summarizing our case law, it is laws "adopted for the purpose of improving the competitive position of local economic actors, just because they are local, vis-à-vis their foreign competitors" that offend the Commerce Clause. Regan, The Supreme Court and State Protectionism: Making Sense of the Dormant Commerce Clause, 84 Mich. L. Rev. 1091, 1138 (1986). The Commerce Clause does not otherwise protect access to local markets. Id., at 1128.

The majority recognizes, but discounts, this difference between laws favoring all local actors and this law favoring a single municipal one. According to the majority, "this difference just makes the protectionist effect of the ordinance more acute" because outside investors cannot even build competing facilities within Clarkstown. But of course Clarkstown investors face the same prohibition, which is to say that Local Law 9's exclusion of outside capital is part of a broader exclusion of private capital, not a discrimination against out-of-state investors as such. Thus, while these differences may underscore the ordinance's anticompetitive effect, they substantially mitigate any protectionist effect, for subjecting out-of-town investors and facilities to the same constraints as local ones is not economic protectionism. . . .

III

[The] primary burden Carbone attributes to flow control ordinances such as Local Law 9 is that they "prevent trash from being sent to the most cost-effective dis-

posal facilities, and insulate the designated facility from all price competition."
In this case, customers must pay $11 per ton more for dumping trash at the
Clarkstown transfer station than they would pay at Carbone's facility, although
this dollar figure presumably overstates the burden by disguising some differences between the two: according to its state permit, 90 percent of Carbone's
waste stream comprises recyclable cardboard, while the Clarkstown facility takes
all manner of less valuable waste, which it treats with state-of-the-art environmental technology not employed at Carbone's more rudimentary plant.

Fortunately, the dollar cost of the burden need not be pinpointed, its nature
being more significant than its economic extent. When we look to its nature, it
should be clear that the monopolistic character of Local Law 9's effects is not itself suspicious for purposes of the Commerce Clause. [The] dormant Commerce
Clause does not "protect the particular structure or methods of operation in
any . . . market." Exxon Corp. v. Governor of Md., 437 U.S. 117, 127 (1978). The
only right to compete that it protects is the right to compete on terms independent of one's location.

While the monopolistic nature of the burden may be disregarded, any geographically discriminatory elements must be assessed with care. We have already
observed that there is no geographically based selection among private firms, and
it is clear from the face of the ordinance that nothing hinges on the source of
trash that enters Clarkstown or upon the destination of the processed waste that
leaves the transfer station. There is, to be sure, an incidental local economic benefit, for the need to process Clarkstown's trash in Clarkstown will create local jobs.
But this local boon is mitigated by another feature of the ordinance, in that it finances whatever benefits it confers on the town from the pockets of the very citizens who passed it into law. On the reasonable assumption that no one can avoid
producing some trash, every resident of Clarkstown must bear a portion of the
burden Local Law 9 imposes to support the municipal monopoly, an uncharac-
teristic feature of statutes claimed to violate the Commerce Clause.

By way of contrast, most of the local processing statutes we have previously invalidated imposed requirements that made local goods more expensive as they
headed into the national market, so that out-of-state economies bore the bulk of
any burden. [In] Philadelphia v. New Jersey, the State attempted to export the
burden of conserving its scarce landfill space by barring the importation of out-
of-state waste. Courts step in through the dormant Commerce Clause to prevent such exports because legislative action imposing a burden "principally upon
those without the state . . . is not likely to be subjected to those political restraints
which are normally exerted on legislation where it affects adversely some interests within the state." [*Barnwell Brothers.*] Here, in contrast, every voter in Clarkstown pays to fund the benefits of flow control, however high the tipping fee is set.
Since, indeed, the mandate to use the town facility will only make a difference
when the tipping fee raises the cost of using the facility above what the market
would otherwise set, the Clarkstown voters are funding their benefit by assessing
themselves and paying an economic penalty. Any whiff of economic protectionism is far from obvious. . . .

This skepticism that protectionism is afoot here is confirmed again when we
examine the governmental interests apparently served by the local law. [The]
State and its municipalities need prompt, sanitary trash processing, which is imperative whether or not the private market sees fit to serve this need at an afford-

able price and to continue doing so dependably into the future. The state and local governments also have a substantial interest in the flow-control feature to minimize the risk of financing this service, for [a] "put or pay" contract of the type Clarkstown signed will be a significant inducement to accept municipal responsibility to guarantee efficiency and sanitation in trash processing. Waste disposal with minimal environmental damage requires serious capital investment, and there are limits on any municipality's ability to incur debt or to finance facilities out of tax revenues.

Moreover, flow control offers an additional benefit that could not be gained by financing through a subsidy derived from general tax revenues, in spreading the cost of the facility among all Clarkstown residents who generate trash. The ordinance does, of course, protect taxpayers, including those who already support the transfer station by patronizing it, from ending up with the tab for making provision for large-volume trash producers like Carbone, who would rely on the municipal facility when that was advantageous but opt out whenever the transfer station's price rose above the market price. In proportioning each resident's burden to the amount of trash generated, the ordinance has the added virtue of providing a direct and measurable deterrent to the generation of unnecessary waste in the first place. And in any event it is far from clear that the alternative to flow control (i.e., subsidies from general tax revenues or municipal bonds) would be less disruptive of interstate commerce than flow control, since a subsidized competitor can effectively squelch competition by underbidding it. . . .

The Commerce Clause was not passed to save the citizens of Clarkstown from themselves. It should not be wielded to prevent them from attacking their local garbage problems with an ordinance that does not discriminate between local and out-of-town participants in the private market for trash disposal services and that is not protectionist in its purpose or effect. Local Law 9 conveys a privilege on the municipal government alone, the only market participant that bears responsibility for ensuring that adequate trash processing services continue to be available to Clarkstown residents. Because the Court's decision today is neither compelled by our local processing cases nor consistent with this Court's reason for inferring a dormant or negative aspect to the Commerce Clause in the first place, I respectfully dissent.

Note: Geographic Discrimination

1. *Cost-benefit analysis.* What is the cost-benefit analysis of the ordinance in *Carbone?* Note that the economic good the city is protecting is not its waste but its "processing services." Consider Justice Souter's description of the ordinance's economic effects. Are they different from the economic effects of the statute in *City of Philadelphia?* Is the Court's concern that such statutes actually interfere with the national economic market? Would granting a monopoly over waste disposal in the city to an out-of-state company interfere less with the national market? Does the Court's opinion indicate that such a monopoly would violate the Constitution? Alternatively, is the Court's concern that such statutes signal an undesirable attitude toward out-of-state economic actors, without regard to whether the economic effects undermine the national market? The first concern is eco-

nomic, the second political. Which appears to be of more concern to the Court in *Carbone?*

2. *Reasonable alternatives and the relevance of harms to in-state producers.* Dean Milk Co. v. Madison, 340 U.S. 349 (1951), invalidated an ordinance adopted by the Madison City Council that prohibited the sale of milk in the city unless it had been bottled at an approved plant within five miles of the city. The "avowed purpose," ensuring by inspection of bottling plants that milk was bottled under sanitary conditions, was acceptable. But the "practical effect" was to prevent the sale in Madison of wholesome milk produced in Illinois and in parts of Wisconsin. "In thus erecting an economic barrier protecting a major local industry against competition from without the State, Madison plainly discriminates against interstate commerce. This it cannot do, even in the exercise of its unquestioned power to protect the health and safety of its people, if reasonable nondiscriminatory alternatives, adequate to serve legitimate local interests, are available." The Court concluded that two alternatives existed: Madison could send its inspectors to Illinois and charge the reasonable costs of inspection to the importing producers, or it could rely on inspections by federal authorities complying with the regulatory standards in the Madison ordinance, which itself adopted the provisions of a model ordinance recommended by a federal agency. "To permit Madison to adopt a regulation not essential for the protection of local health interests and placing a discriminatory burden on interstate commerce would invite a multiplication of preferential trade areas destructive of the very purpose of the Commerce Clause." Is the doctrinal formulation in *Dean Milk* the same as that in *Carbone?* Do the cases pose the same problem?

The majority opinion stated in a footnote, "It is immaterial that Wisconsin milk from outside the Madison area is subjected to the same proscription as that moving in interstate commerce." Doesn't that show that Madison is not exporting as much of the costs of regulation outside the state as would a statewide requirement? Why might legislators from other parts of Wisconsin allow Madison to adopt its ordinance?

3. *Permissible discrimination.* In Maine v. Taylor, 477 U.S. 131 (1986), the Court upheld the constitutionality of a Maine statute that prohibited the importation of live baitfish. Writing for eight justices, Justice Blackmun noted that the statute affirmatively discriminated against interstate transactions and therefore could be upheld only if it survived "the strictest scrutiny." The burden was on the state to show that the statute served a legitimate local purpose, and that the purpose could not be served as well by an available nondiscriminatory means. In this case, however, the Court held that, in light of the trial court's findings of fact, both branches of this test had been satisfied. Evidence before the trial court indicated that Maine's population of wild fish might be placed at risk by parasites prevalent in out-of-state baitfish but not common in wild fish in Maine. Moreover, nonnative species inadvertently included in shipments of live baitfish could disturb Maine's aquatic ecology to an unpredictable extent by competing with, or preying on, native species. Finally, there was no satisfactory way to inspect imported baitfish for parasites and commingled species.

The Supreme Court held that these findings were sufficient to sustain the statute. Although importation of the baitfish might not adversely affect the environment, "Maine has a legitimate interest in guarding against imperfectly understood environmental risks, despite the possibility that they may ultimately prove to be negligible." Moreover, the mere "abstract possibility" of developing an acceptable testing procedure did not constitute an available nondiscriminatory alternative. Nor was there convincing evidence that the statute was the product of a protectionist intent. The state's justification was not undermined "by the fact that other States may not have enacted similar bans" because "Maine's fisheries are unique and unusually fragile." Nor was it relevant "that fish can swim directly into Maine from New Hampshire" because "impediments to complete success [cannot] be [grounds] for preventing a state from using its best efforts to limit [an environmental] risk."

4. *The relevance of conflict.* In Bibb v. Navajo Freight Lines, 359 U.S. 520 (1959), Justice Douglas wrote the Court's opinion invalidating an Illinois law requiring that trucks in the state use curved mudguards to prevent spatter and promote safety. Straight mudflaps were legal in forty-five other states; curved mudflaps were illegal in Arkansas and were required in no other state. The trial court found that curved mudflaps have "no" safety advantages over straight ones and introduce "hazards previously unknown to those using the highways" by increasing the heat around the tires and thereby reducing the effectiveness of the trucks' brakes. However, the Court said, "If we had here only a question whether the cost of adjusting an interstate operation to these new local safety regulations [unduly] burdened interstate commerce, we would have to sustain the law. [The] same result would obtain if we had to resolve the much discussed issues of safety." The case was different, though, because of the impossibility of using a single truck whose mudflaps complied with both Illinois and Arkansas law. Further, the Illinois law "seriously [interfered] with" interlining, the practice of having one carrier bring a trailer to a depot and another take it to its destination without unloading and reloading. The case was "one of those cases — few in number — where local safety measures that are nondiscriminatory place an unconstitutional burden on interstate commerce." In what sense do the Arkansas and Illinois regulations conflict other than that complying with both would increase costs enormously by requiring unloading and reloading? Why is it a problem for Illinois, rather than for Arkansas, that a shipper could not use a single trailer that complied with both states' regulations?

Note these observations from Justice O'Connor's opinion in *Carbone*:

["The] practical effect of [Local Law 9] must be evaluated not only by considering the consequences of the statute itself, but also by considering how the challenged statute may interact with the legitimate regulatory regimes of the other States and what effect would arise if not one, but many or every, [jurisdiction] adopted similar legislation." [Wyoming v. Oklahoma]. This is not a hypothetical inquiry. Over 20 states have enacted statutes authorizing local governments to adopt flow control laws. If the localities in these States impose the type of restriction on the movement of waste that Clarkstown has adopted, the free movement of solid waste in the stream of commerce will be severely impaired. Indeed, pervasive flow control would result in the type of balkanization the Clause is primarily intended to prevent. See [H. P. Hood & Sons].

Given that many jurisdictions are contemplating or enacting flow control, the potential for conflicts is high. For example, in the State of New Jersey, just south of Clarkstown, local waste may be removed from the State for the sorting of recyclables "as long as the residual solid waste is returned to New Jersey." Under Local Law 9, however, if petitioners bring waste from New Jersey for recycling at their

Clarkstown operation, the residual waste may not be returned to New Jersey, but must be transported to Clarkstown's transfer facility. As a consequence, operations like petitioners' cannot comply with the requirements of both jurisdictions. Non-discriminatory state or local laws which actually conflict with the enactments of other States are constitutionally infirm if they burden interstate commerce. The increasing number of flow control regimes virtually ensures some inconsistency between jurisdictions, with the effect of eliminating the movement of waste between jurisdictions.

5. *Are the regulated subjects "the same"?* General Motors Corp. v. Tracy, 519 U.S. 278 (1997), discussed a question the Court said often "remained dormant" in dormant commerce clause cases: whether the subjects treated differently were "substantially similar." The question matters because "the difference in products may mean that the different entities serve different markets and would continue to do so even if the supposedly discriminatory burden were removed. If in fact that should be the case, eliminating the tax or other regulatory differential would not serve the dormant Commerce Clause's fundamental objective of preserving a national market for competition undisturbed by preferential advantages conferred by a State upon its residents or resident competitors." The Court then engaged in a detailed analysis of the market for natural gas products. Can an argument be developed in each of the cases in this section that the subjects were not substantially similar because they served different markets?

West Lynn Creamery, Inc. v. Healy
512 U.S. 186 (1994)

JUSTICE STEVENS delivered the opinion of the Court.

[Massachusetts taxed all milk sales in the state. The taxes, collected on sales of milk produced both in the state and outside it, went to a subsidy fund whose proceeds were then distributed to Massachusetts milk producers. An out-of-state producer challenged the combined nondiscriminatory-tax-plus-local-subsidy program. The Court found the program unconstitutional.]

The paradigmatic example of a law discriminating against interstate commerce is the protective tariff or customs duty, which taxes goods imported from other States, but does not tax similar products produced in-state. A tariff is an attractive measure because it simultaneously raises revenue and benefits local producers by burdening their out-of-state competitors. Nevertheless, it violates the principle of the unitary national market by handicapping out-of-state competitors, thus artificially encouraging in-state production even when the same goods could be produced at lower cost in other States. . . .

[Massachusetts'] pricing order is clearly unconstitutional. Its avowed purpose and its undisputed effect are to enable higher cost Massachusetts dairy farmers to compete with lower cost dairy farmers in other States. The "premium payments" are effectively a tax which makes milk produced out of State more expensive. Although the tax also applies to milk produced in Massachusetts, its effect on Massachusetts producers is entirely (indeed more than) offset by the subsidy provided exclusively to Massachusetts dairy farmers. Like an ordinary tariff, the tax is thus effectively imposed only on out-of-state products. The pricing order thus allows

Massachusetts dairy farmers who produce at higher cost to sell at or below the price charged by lower cost out-of-state producers. . . .

Respondent's principal argument is that, because "the milk order achieves its goals through lawful means," the order as a whole is constitutional. He argues that the payments to Massachusetts dairy farmers from the Dairy Equalization Fund are valid, because subsidies are constitutional exercises of state power, and that the order premium which provides money for the Fund is valid, because it is a nondiscriminatory tax. Therefore the pricing order is constitutional, because it is merely the combination of two independently lawful regulations. In effect, respondent argues, if the State may impose a valid tax on dealers, it is free to use the proceeds of the tax as it chooses; and if it may independently subsidize its farmers, it is free to finance the subsidy by means of any legitimate tax.

Even granting respondent's assertion that both components of the pricing order would be constitutional standing alone, the pricing order nevertheless must fall. A pure subsidy funded out of general revenue ordinarily imposes no burden on interstate commerce, but merely assists local business. The pricing order in this case, however, is funded principally from taxes on the sale of milk produced in other States. . . .

More fundamentally, respondent errs in assuming that the constitutionality of the pricing order follows logically from the constitutionality of its component parts. By conjoining a tax and a subsidy, Massachusetts has created a program more dangerous to interstate commerce than either part alone. Nondiscriminatory measures, like the evenhanded tax at issue here, are generally upheld, in spite of any adverse effects on interstate commerce, in part because "the existence of major in-state interests adversely affected . . . is a powerful safeguard against legislative abuse." Minnesota v. Clover Leaf Creamery Co., 449 U.S. 456, 473, n.17 (1981). However, when a nondiscriminatory tax is coupled with a subsidy to one of the groups hurt by the tax, a state's political processes can no longer be relied upon to prevent legislative abuse, because one of the in-state interests which would otherwise lobby against the tax has been mollified by the subsidy. So, in this case, one would ordinarily have expected at least three groups to lobby against the order premium, which, as a tax, raises the price (and hence lowers demand) for milk: dairy farmers, milk dealers, and consumers. But because the tax was coupled with a subsidy, one of the most powerful of these groups, Massachusetts dairy farmers, instead of exerting their influence against the tax, were in fact its primary supporters. . . .

[Respondent] ignores the fact that Massachusetts dairy farmers are part of an integrated interstate market. [The] purpose and effect of the pricing order are to divert market share to Massachusetts dairy farmers. This diversion necessarily injures the dairy farmers in neighboring States. [The] obvious impact of the order on out-of-state production demonstrates that it is simply wrong to assume that the pricing order burdens only Massachusetts consumers and dealers.

JUSTICE SCALIA, with whom JUSTICE THOMAS joins, concurring in the judgment. . . .

[The] Court guardedly asserts that a "pure subsidy funded out of general revenue ordinarily imposes no burden on interstate commerce, but merely assists local business," but under its analysis that must be taken to be true only because most local businesses (e.g., the local hardware store) are not competing with businesses out of State. The Court notes that, in funding this subsidy, Massachusetts has taxed milk produced in other States, and thus "not only assists local farmers, but burdens interstate commerce." But the same could be said of almost all subsidies funded from general state revenues. [Such] subsidies, particularly where they are in the form of cash or [tax] forgiveness, are often admitted to have as their purpose — indeed, are nationally advertised as having as their purpose — making it more profitable to conduct business in-state than elsewhere, i.e., distorting normal market incentives. . . .

There are at least four possible devices that would enable a State to produce the economic effect that Massachusetts has produced here: (1) a discriminatory tax upon the industry, imposing a higher liability on out-of-state members than on their in-state competitors; (2) a tax upon the industry that is nondiscriminatory in its assessment, but that has an "exemption" [for] in-state members; (3) a nondiscriminatory tax upon the industry, the revenues from which are placed into a segregated fund, which fund is disbursed as "rebates" [to] in-state members of the industry; [and] (4) [a] subsidy for the in-state members of the industry, funded from the State's general revenues. It is long settled that the first of these methodologies is unconstitutional under the negative Commerce Clause. The second of them, "exemption" from [a] "neutral" tax, is no different in principle from the first, and has likewise been held invalid. The fourth methodology, application of a state subsidy from general revenues, is so far removed from what we have hitherto held to be unconstitutional, that prohibiting it must be regarded as an extension of our negative-Commerce-Clause jurisprudence and therefore, to me, unacceptable. . . .

The issue before us in the present case is whether the third of these methodologies must fall. Although the question is close, I conclude it would not be a principled point at which to disembark from the negative-Commerce-Clause train. The only difference between methodology (2) [and] methodology (3) [is] that the money is taken and returned rather than simply left with the favored in-state taxpayer in the first place. The difference between (3) and (4), on the other hand, is the difference between assisting in-state industry through discriminatory taxation, and assisting in-state industry by other means.

I would therefore allow a State to subsidize its domestic industry so long as it does so from nondiscriminatory taxes that go into the State's general revenue fund. Perhaps [that] line comports with an important economic reality: a State is less likely to maintain a subsidy when its citizens perceive that the money (in the general fund) is available for any number of competing, non-protectionist, purposes. That is not, however, the basis for my position. [I] draw the line where I do because it is a clear, rational line at the limits of our extant negative-Commerce-Clause jurisprudence.

CHIEF JUSTICE REHNQUIST, with whom JUSTICE BLACKMUN joins, dissenting. . . .

[The] Court strikes down this method of state subsidization because the nondiscriminatory tax levied against all milk dealers is coupled with a subsidy to milk producers. The Court does this because of its view that the method of imposing the tax and subsidy distorts the State's political process: the dairy farmers, who would otherwise lobby against the tax, have been mollified by the subsidy. But as the Court itself points out, there are still at least two strong interest groups opposed to the milk order — consumers and milk dealers. More importantly, nothing in the dormant Commerce Clause suggests that the fate of state regulation should turn upon the particular lawful manner in which the state subsidy is enacted or promulgated. Analysis of interest group participation in the political process may serve many useful purposes, but serving as a basis for interpreting the dormant Commerce Clause is not one of them. . . .

[No] decided case supports the Court's conclusion that the negative Commerce Clause prohibits the State from using money that it has lawfully obtained through a neutral tax on milk dealers and distributing it as a subsidy to dairy farmers. Indeed, the case which comes closest to supporting the result the Court reaches is the ill-starred opinion in United States v. Butler, 297 U.S. 1 (1936), in which the Court held unconstitutional what would have been an otherwise valid tax on the processing of agricultural products because of the use to which the revenue raised by the tax was put. . . .

[The] wisdom of a messianic insistence on a grim sink-or-swim policy of laissez-faire economics would be debatable had Congress chosen to enact it; but Congress has done nothing of the kind. It is the Court which has imposed the policy under the dormant Commerce Clause, a policy which bodes ill for the values of federalism which have long animated our constitutional jurisprudence.

Note: The Alternative of Subsidies

1. *Tax incentives as subsidies.* Camps Newfound/Owatonna, Inc. v. Town of Harrison, 520 U.S. 564 (1997), held unconstitutional a tax statute that exempted property owned by local charitable organizations but denied the exemption to organizations operated principally for nonresidents. The Court first concluded that the statute would violate the commerce clause if it were targeted at profit-making organizations because it encouraged them "to limit their out-of-state clientele" in a way that would lead to economic balkanization. It was "functionally [an] export tariff that targets out-of-state customers by taxing the businesses that principally serve them." Relying on New Energy Co. of Indiana v. Limbach, cited in *Carbone*, the Court then rejected the argument that the tax exemption amounted to a permissible "discriminatory subsidy." Even if such subsidies were constitutional, discriminatory tax exemptions were not. Justices Scalia and Thomas and Chief Justice Rehnquist dissented.

For a discussion of the distinction between tax incentives and subsidies, see Hellerstein and Coenen, Commerce Clause Restraints on State Business Development Incentives, 81 Cornell L. Rev. 789 (1996). It argues that tax incentives are unconstitutional if they "favor in-state over out-of-state activities" and "implicate the coercive powers of the state." Although subsidies are not dramatically different in economic terms from tax incentives, there should be a presumption that subsidies are constitutional. The reason is that form matters: "[Consideration] of a subsidy forces the mind of the public body to consider most pointedly the cost and consequences of moving forward."

2. *The politics of subsidies.* Why are subsidies from general revenues permissible but ones from industry-specific taxes impermissible? Note that an annual appropriation in the form of a direct subsidy might be more visible politically than the indirect subsidy through regulation. Justice Stevens's opinion suggests that

the courts should carefully examine legislation that shifts one interest group from one side of an issue to another. Is there any economic regulation that does not have that effect? Coenen, Business Subsidies and the Dormant Commerce Clause, 107 Yale L.J. 965, 985-992 (1998), enumerates a number of functional distinctions between direct subsidies and tax breaks:

> [A] state's imposition of costs on its citizens is more visible when the state awards outright subsidies than when it doles out tax relief. [The] extent of cost [is] more readily perceptible when the state's support of local industry takes the form of a monetary subsidy [because] the total amount of subsidy payments can be determined through the easy means of tallying total payments [whereas] tax expenditures are made [passively.] [Tax] credits, exemptions, and the like are resistant to repeal because legislatures typically enact them as presumptively permanent features of state tax codes. In contrast, because subsidies involve the direct expenditure of funds, they routinely show up — and are subject to recurring reevaluation — as expense items in perennially controversial state budget bills. [Tax] breaks [have] an open-ended, unrestricted quality. [Subsidy] programs are usually more costly for the state to administer. [Cash] subsidies are less likely than discriminatory tax breaks to take hold and to persist because most people view tax structures [as] an esoteric specialty beyond their capability and willingness to understand. [Tax] breaks are more likely to gain acceptance because citizens do not perceive them as taking away that which those citizens see as already being their own or as channeling scarce state funds to competing [claimants.]

Coenen develops criteria for determining when a subsidy is closely enough linked to a discriminatory tax break to make the subsidy unconstitutional.

Are Justices Scalia and Rehnquist correct in asserting that consideration of the politics of subsidies is irrelevant to constitutional analysis? Consider this summary: Existing doctrine "create[s] the following modified process-reinforcing regime: When the costs of a potential state policy will be shared between an organized but out-of-state interest group and a diffuse group of local residents, the courts will presume that the diffuse locals will virtually represent the out-of-state interests against the policy when the policy requires an expenditure of tax dollars, but they will not so presume when the policy is implemented through regulation alone." Korobkin, The Local Politics of Acid Rain: Public Versus Private Decisionmaking and the Dormant Commerce Clause in a New Era of Environmental Law, 75 B.U. L. Rev. 689, 756 (1995). Why are the diffuse interests of taxpayers better able to represent out-of-state interests than the diffuse interests of consumers affected by higher prices due to regulation?

3. *Devising a subsidy.* Justice O'Connor's opinion in *Carbone* observed that "[the] town could finance the project by imposing taxes, by issuing municipal bonds, or even by lowering its price for processing to a level competitive with other waste processing facilities." What political and economic constraints would Clarkstown face in choosing those financing methods? Can you design a subsidy for Clarkstown that would survive constitutional scrutiny under *West Lynn Creamery?*

Note: *Other Doctrines Concerning Discrimination*

1. *The market-participant doctrine.* (a) *The contours of the doctrine.* The Supreme Court has held that states may discriminate when they act as participants

in the market, but not when they act as regulators. Hughes v. Alexandria Scrap Corp., 426 U.S. 794 (1976), upheld a Maryland program designed to reduce the number of abandoned cars in the state. It purchased junked cars, paying a "bounty" for those with Maryland license plates and imposing more stringent documentation requirements on out-of-state processors of junked cars than on in-state processors. The Court said that "nothing in the purposes animating the Commerce Clause prohibits a State [from] participating in the market and exercising the right to favor its own citizens over others." Reeves, Inc. v. Stake, 447 U.S. 429 (1980), upheld a state policy restricting the sale of cement produced in a state-owned plant to state residents, relying on "the long recognized right of trader or manufacturer, engaged in an entirely private business, freely to exercise his own independent discretion as to parties with whom he will deal."

What is the distinction between regulation and market participation? South-Central Timber Development v. Wunnicke, 467 U.S. 82 (1984), held unconstitutional Alaska's inclusion of a requirement that purchasers of state-owned timber process it within the state before it was shipped out of state. According to a plurality opinion by Justice White, Alaska could not impose "downstream" conditions in the timber-processing market as a result of its ownership of the timber itself. The opinion noted that "[if] the State directly subsidized the timber-processing industry, [the] purchaser would retain the option of taking advantage of the subsidy by processing timber in the State or forgoing the benefits of the subsidy and exporting unprocessed timber. Under the Alaska requirement, however, the choice is made for him: if he buys timber from the State he is not free to take the timber out of state prior to processing." It summarized "[the] limit of the market-participant doctrine" as "[allowing] a State to impose burdens on commerce within the market in which it is a participant, but allows it to go no further. The State may not impose conditions [that] have a substantial regulatory effect outside of that particular market. Unless the 'market' is relatively narrowly defined, the doctrine has the potential of swallowing up the rule that States may not impose substantial burdens on interstate commerce even if they act with the permissible state purpose of fostering local industry." According to Justice White, there were "sound reasons for distinguishing between a State's preferring its own residents in the initial disposition of goods when it is a market participant and a State's attachment of restrictions on dispositions subsequent to the goods coming to rest in private hands. First, simply as a matter of intuition a State market participant has a greater interest as a 'private trader' in the immediate transaction than it has in what its purchaser does with the goods after the State no longer has an interest in them." He noted that the common law and antitrust law recognized this point. "Second, downstream restrictions have a greater regulatory effect than do limitations on the immediate transaction. Instead of merely choosing its own trading partners, the State is attempting to govern the private, separate economic relationships of its trading partners; that is, it restricts the post-purchase activity of the purchaser, rather than merely the purchasing activity." Justice Marshall did not participate in the decision; Justice Powell and Chief Justice Burger would have remanded the case for further consideration. Justice Brennan concurred in the result, and Justices Rehnquist and O'Connor dissented.

(b) Is the *economic* effect of discriminatory market participation different from that of discriminatory regulation? According to Justice Blackmun's opinion for the Court in Reeves v. Stake, when states act in the marketplace, they resemble private businesses and should be free to exercise a similar discretion to choose the parties with whom they deal. Note that private businesses are constrained to some extent by competition and the profit motive to purchase from the cheapest seller and sell to the buyer willing to pay most. States in contrast may buy and sell without that constraint, using their power to tax as the mechanism to force some taxpayers to subsidize "uneconomic" transactions. See generally Wells and Hellerstein, The Governmental-Proprietary Distinction in Constitutional Law, 66 Va. L. Rev. 1073 (1980).

(c) Can the market-participant doctrine be defended as allowing states to capture the benefits of their tax expenditures? Consider L. Tribe, Constitutional Choices 145 (1985): The doctrine is justified by "the sense of fairness in allowing a community to retain the public benefits created by its own public investment. [The] broader theme that underlies each case seems to be *creation* of commerce: whatever the state's ultimate goal, the state is approaching that goal by channeling its resources into commerce rather than by placing restrictions on commerce already in existence."

In *Reeves*, the public expenditure is the outlay for cement production. How does that differ from the state's expenditures for the general provision of social order in Philadelphia v. New Jersey? The expenditures differ in the specificity with which they affect particular transactions, but is that relevant to any constitutionally significant matters?

Consider that we have now seen four types of subsidy: via regulation, via targeted tax breaks, via participation in the market, and via direct appropriations from general revenues. Only the first two are subject to close commerce clause scrutiny. Recall the suggestion that direct appropriations have more political visibility than do regulatory subsidies. Which does a market-participation subsidy more closely resemble?

Regan, The Supreme Court and State Protectionism: Making Sense of the Dormant Commerce Clause, 84 Mich. L. Rev. 1091, 1194 (1986), defends the market-participant exception as applied to cases involving "state spending as opposed to mere regulation or the positive imposition of a tax" on the following grounds: (1) "state spending programs are less coercive than regulatory programs or taxes with similar purposes"; (2) such programs "seem less hostile to other states and less inconsistent with the conception of union than discriminatory regulation or taxation"; (3) "many spending programs are positively beneficial from the point of view of the nation as a whole [but] many of these programs would not exist if the state could not channel the primary benefits to locals"; (4) "the very fact that spending programs involve spending and are therefore relatively expensive as a way of securing local benefits [means that they are] less likely to proliferate than measures like tariffs"; and (5) such measures "are less likely to produce resentment and retaliation."

(d) Can market participation be distinguished from regulation on the ground that the latter affects all actors in the market, while the former affects only those whom the state chooses as its buyers or sellers? South-Central can buy timber from other sellers; a regulation requiring local processing would affect it no matter from whom it bought. Consider, however, that this ignores the actual economic effect on South-Central of Alaska's participation in the market.

Can the argument be strengthened by considering the market power of the state as a market participant? The greater its market power, the more coercive its contractual conditions and so the more they resemble regulations. Does this in fact distinguish the cases? If the state has little market power, how can its decisions as market participant burden interstate commerce? On this view, the market-participant doctrine is a convenient shorthand for the application of ordinary dormant commerce clause tests to a set of activities that do not burden interstate commerce. Note, however, that this version requires reconsideration of the almost automatic invalidation of facially discriminatory regulations.

Reconsider *Carbone*. After ownership of the plant is transferred to Clarkstown, may the city control the flow of garbage by directing that all locally generated solid waste be deposited at the plant? Is this regulation or market participation? (If it is regulation, what is the standard by which its constitutionality will be measured?) Justice Souter's dissenting opinion contained the following observations:

> Nor is the monopolist created by Local Law 9 just another private company successfully enlisting local government to protect the jobs and profits of local citizens. [Clarkstown's] transfer station is essentially a municipal facility, built and operated under a contract with the municipality and soon to revert entirely to municipal ownership. . . .
>
> The majority ignores this distinction between public and private enterprise, equating Local Law 9's "hoarding" of solid waste for the municipal transfer station with the design and effect of ordinances that restrict access to local markets for the benefit of local private firms. But private businesses, whether local or out of State, first serve the private interests of their owners, and there is therefore only rarely a reason other than economic protectionism for favoring local businesses over their out-of-town competitors. The local government itself occupies a very different market position, however, being the one entity that enters the market to serve the public interest of local citizens quite apart from private interest in private gain. Reasons other than economic protectionism are accordingly more likely to explain the design and effect of an ordinance that favors a public facility. The facility as constructed might, for example, be one that private economic actors, left to their own devices, would not have built, but which the locality needs in order to abate (or guarantee against creating) a public nuisance. [An] ordinance that favors a municipal facility [is] one that favors the public sector, and if "we continue to recognize that the States occupy a special and specific position in our constitutional system and that the scope of Congress' authority under the Commerce Clause must reflect that position," Garcia v. San Antonio Metropolitan Transit Authority, 469 U.S. 528, 556 (1985), then surely this Court's dormant Commerce Clause jurisprudence must itself see that favoring state-sponsored facilities differs from discriminating among private economic actors, and is much less likely to be protectionist. . . .
>
> [In] a market served by a municipal facility, a law that favors that single facility over all others is a law that favors the public sector over all private-sector processors, whether local or out of State. Because the favor does not go to local private competitors of out-of-state firms, out-of-state governments will at the least lack a motive to favor their own firms in order to equalize the positions of private competitors. While a preference in favor of the government may incidentally function as local favoritism as well, a more particularized enquiry is necessary before a court can say whether such a law does in fact smack too strongly of economic protectionism.

(e) Note Justice Souter's citation to *Garcia*. Hughes v. Alexandria Scrap was decided on the same day as *National League of Cities*, Chapter 2 supra. What is the relation between the market-participant doctrine and state sovereignty? Under New York v. United States, could Congress prohibit Alaska's local processing requirement? If states may be regulated by Congress as market participants, the market-participant doctrine does not completely exempt state activities from compliance with the norms of the commerce clause. Instead, it exempts them in the absence of a congressional prohibition. This reverses the "presumption" Dowling's analysis would have established against burdensome regulations. Is it plausible to think that Congress will be more alert to burdens imposed on commerce by states as market participants than to those imposed by states as regulators?

2. *The privileges and immunities clause of Article IV.* (a) *The contours of the doctrine.* Article IV provides, "The citizens of each State shall be entitled to all the Privileges and Immunities of Citizens in the several States." United Building & Construction Trades Council v. Camden, 465 U.S. 208 (1984), involved a New Jersey statute authorizing cities to adopt affirmative action plans. Camden passed an ordinance requiring that at least 40 percent of the employees of contractors and subcontractors on city projects be Camden residents. After holding that the privilege and immunities clause was applicable even though the ordinance excluded citizens of New Jersey (those living outside of Camden) as well as citizens from Pennsylvania and other states, Justice Rehnquist's opinion for the Court described the clause's primary purpose: "to help fuse into one Nation a collection of independent, sovereign States. It was designed to insure to a citizen of State A who ventures into State B the same privileges which the citizens of State B enjoy." The clause applied when a privilege or immunity was burdened. The Court held that an out-of-state resident's interest in employment on public works contracts was "'fundamental' to the promotion of interstate harmony" and therefore protected by the clause.

Justice Rehnquist's opinion distinguished between the market-participant doctrine, which allows states to prefer their own, and the privileges and immunities clause. Congress has the power under the commerce clause to regulate state market participation, but it lacks power to authorize regulations that violate article IV. "The Privileges and Immunities Clause [imposes] a direct restraint on state action in the interests of interstate harmony. This concern with comity cuts across the market regulator-market participant distinction that is crucial under the Commerce Clause. It is discrimination against out-of-state residents on matters of fundamental concern which triggers the Clause, not regulation affecting interstate commerce." The Court remanded the case for consideration of whether the infringement of a right protected by the clause was constitutionally permissible. The clause "does not preclude discrimination against citizens of other States where there is a 'substantial reason' for the difference in treatment. '[T]he inquiry in each case must be concerned with whether such reasons do exist and whether the degree of discrimination bears a close relation to them.'" As part of any justification offered for the discriminatory law, nonresidents must somehow be shown to "constitute a peculiar source of the evil at which the statute is aimed." Preference for residents might be justified as a necessary means of counteracting "[spiralling] unemployment, a sharp decline in population, and a dramatic reduction in the number of businesses located in the city [which] have eroded property values and depleted the city's tax base."

Supreme Court of New Hampshire v. Piper, 470 U.S. 274 (1985), held that a rule limiting bar admission to local residents violated the privileges and immunities clause. Justice Powell's opinion for the Court stated that the clause "was intended to create a national economic union." The practice of law was a "privilege" because of "the lawyer's role in the national economy" and the profession's "noncommercial role [in representing] persons who raise unpopular federal claims." Applying the twofold standard discussed in *Camden*, the Court found none of the asserted justifications for the discrimination substantial: There was no evidence that nonresident lawyers would fail to keep up with developments in local law or behave unethically. Nonresidents, especially those living far from the state, might be less available for hearings and for local pro bono work, but the state could "protect its interests through less restrictive means" such as requiring that a nonresident lawyer "who resides at a great distance [retain] a local attorney." Justice Rehnquist's dissent argued that the practice of law is "fundamentally different" from other occupations because of the role lawyers play in a state's "self-governance": "[Law] is one occupation that does not readily translate across state lines." He found "less restrictive means analysis [out] of place" here; the courts should not "independently [scrutinize] each asserted state interest to see if [they] could devise a better way than the State to accomplish that goal." See also Supreme Court of Virginia v. Friedman, 487 U.S. 59 (1988). What result in *Piper* under the commerce clause tests (a) for facial discrimination, (b) for other forms of discrimination, and (c) for undue burdens? Is New Hampshire a market regulator or a market participant?

(b) *The doctrine's history.* In Corfield v. Coryell, Fed. Cas. No. 3,230 (Cir. Ct. E.D. Pa. 1823), Justice Bushrod Washington stated that the clause protected interests "which are fundamental; which belong, of right, to the citizens of all free governments. [These] may [all be] comprehended under the following general heads: Protection by the government, the enjoyment of life and liberty, with the right to acquire and possess property of every kind, and to pursue and obtain happiness and safety; subject nevertheless to such restraints as the government may prescribe for the general good of the whole." *Corfield* held that a New Jersey statute forbidding nonresidents from gathering clams from state waters did not violate the clause because the clams were the property of the state. (What result under modern commerce clause doctrine?) See generally Varat, State "Citizenship" and Interstate Equality, 48 U. Chi. L. Rev. 487 (1981).

The fourteenth amendment also contains a privileges and immunities clause, which has been held to prohibit state infringements of the privileges of national citizenship. Those privileges might also be identified as fundamental rights. See Chapter 6, section E, infra. What is the difference between a fundamental right as defined in *Corfield* and a fundamental right under the fourteenth amendment?

(c) What does article IV, section 2 add to the commerce clause? Suppose Camden had imposed the residency requirement on all businesses located in Camden or supplying goods to the city. What result under the commerce clause? In many ways, the modern function of article IV, section 2 appears to be that of carving out an exception to the market-participant exception to the commerce clause. Note, however, that corporations are not "citizens" within the meaning of the privileges and immunities clause. Paul v. Virginia, 75 U.S. (8 Wall.) 168 (1868). Is the test formulated by the Court in *Camden* different from the undue burden test under the commerce clause? Note, however, that Camden's ordinance is discriminatory. What commerce clause test would apply to it?

(d) Justice Blackmun's dissent in *Camden* argued that New Jersey residents excluded from jobs in Camden could adequately represent the interests of out-of-state citizens. Justice Rehnquist replied that the ordinance was enacted pursuant to a state law authorizing every city to adopt similar programs. This, he said, made it "hard to see how New Jersey residents living outside Camden will protect the interests of out-of-state citizens." Is this problem different from that in *Dean Milk?*

3. *The equal protection clause.* Consider Metropolitan Life Insurance Co. v. Ward, 470 U.S. 869 (1985). Paul v. Virginia, supra, held that insurance contracts were not in interstate commerce. As a result, states developed extensive and sometimes burdensome systems for regulating insurance. In 1944, the Court rejected *Paul* in United States v. South-Eastern Underwriters Association, 322 U.S. 533. Congress responded by passing the McCarran-Ferguson Act, which declared it to be national policy that "the continued regulation and taxation by the several States of the business of insurance is in the public interest, and that silence on the part of Congress shall not be construed to impose any barrier to the regulation or taxation of such business by the several States." Alabama placed a 1 percent tax on the gross receipts of local insurance companies, while requiring that out-of-state companies pay a tax of 3 to 4 percent, which could be lowered by 1 percent if the companies invested substantially in Alabama. The equal protection clause allows such discrimination if it is a rational means to accomplish a "legitimate state purpose." The Court, dividing five to four, held that the state's purpose of "encouraging the formation of new insurance companies in Alabama" was an impermissible one. It was "purely and completely discriminatory" for Alabama "to [erect] barriers to foreign companies [in] order to improve its domestic insurers' ability to compete at home." This is "the very sort of parochial discrimination that the Equal Protection Clause was intended to prevent." The state may encourage the growth of new business by granting out-of-state companies exemptions from regulations but not by imposing burdens on them that are not placed on local companies. Further, the McCarran-Ferguson Act was irrelevant because it lifted commerce clause restrictions but not equal protection ones. "Under Commerce Clause analysis, the State's interest, if legitimate, is weighed against the burden the state law would impose on interstate commerce. In the equal protection context, however, if the State's purpose is found to be legitimate, the state law stands as long as the burden it imposes is found to be rationally related to that purpose, a relationship that is not difficult to establish. The two [provisions] perform different functions — [one] protects interstate commerce, and the other protects persons from unconstitutional discrimination." The Court conceded that "the *effect* of the discrimination in this case is similar to the type of burden with which the Commerce Clause would also be concerned," but said that "acceptance of [the] contention that promotion of domestic industry is always a legitimate state purpose under equal protection analysis would eviscerate the Equal Protection Clause in this context."

Justice O'Connor's long dissent was joined by Justices Brennan, Marshall, and Rehnquist. She said that "it is obviously legitimate for a State to seek to promote local business" and described the different markets served by domestic and out-of-state insurers to point up Alabama's goals: The former served rural and less affluent purchasers, the latter urban, high-volume, and more affluent ones. Justice O'Connor criticized the Court for "collapsing the two prongs of the rational relationship test into one" by its declaration that "the ends of promoting a domestic insurance industry and attracting investments to the State *when accomplished through the means of discriminatory taxation* are not legitimate state purposes."

To the extent that the equal protection clause served a nationalizing goal, "any federalism component of equal protection is fully vindicated where Congress has explicitly validated a parochial focus," as in the McCarran-Ferguson Act.

Why is encouraging entry by exempting out-of-state companies from regulation different from doing so by differential taxation? Note that in *Metropolitan Life*, if the state's policy succeeds, local insurers will face greater competition. What result in *Metropolitan Life* under the commerce clause? Is the Court's distinction between the purposes of the two clauses persuasive where, as in *Metropolitan Life*, the commerce clause challenge rests on facial discrimination? Would the Court "weigh" the competing interests in a commerce clause challenge to Alabama's statute? What is the effect of the McCarran-Ferguson Act after *Metropolitan Life*?

Note: Concluding Observations

The various doctrines concerning discrimination are not entirely consistent. The market-participant doctrine exempts states from judicial supervision pursuant to ordinary commerce clause analysis; the privileges and immunities clause reimposes that scrutiny in cases involving individuals (perhaps under a somewhat less rigorous standard); and the equal protection clause may reimpose it in cases involving corporations (again perhaps under a somewhat less rigorous standard). Why has the Court constructed the doctrine in this complex way?

Consider the possibility that the Court finds itself caught between the implications of two intuitions. The dormant commerce clause may imply that states may never favor their own citizens. Basic ideas of federalism suggest that one of the points of having state governments is to allow state citizens control over their governors precisely in order to secure benefits to themselves that they do not have to distribute to outsiders. Does the fundamental difficulty stem from attempting to implement the "thought" that the Constitution endorses some vision of a governmental process in which the preferences of citizens are perfectly aggregated, in a federal system where, because people are simultaneously citizens of state and nation, it is always unclear whose preferences ought to be perfectly aggregated?

C. FACIALLY NEUTRAL STATUTES WITH SIGNIFICANT EFFECTS ON INTERSTATE COMMERCE

Exxon Corp. v. Governor of Maryland

437 U.S. 117 (1978)

MR. JUSTICE STEVENS delivered the opinion of the Court.

A Maryland statute provides that a producer or refiner of petroleum products [may] not operate any retail service station within the State.

The Maryland statute is an outgrowth of the 1973 shortage of petroleum. In response to complaints about inequitable distribution of gasoline among retail stations, the Governor of Maryland directed the State Comptroller to conduct a market survey. The results of that survey indicated that gasoline stations operated by producers or refiners had received preferential treatment during the period of short supply. The Comptroller therefore proposed legislation which, according to the Court of Appeals, was "designed to correct the inequities in the distribution and pricing of gasoline reflected by the survey." After legislative hearings and a "special veto hearing" before the Governor, the bill was enacted and signed into law. . . .

[All] of the gasoline sold by Exxon in Maryland is transported into the State from refineries located elsewhere. Although Exxon sells the bulk of this gas to wholesalers and independent retailers, it also sells directly to the consuming public through 36 company-operated stations. Exxon uses these stations to test innovative marketing concepts or products. . . .

[Other plaintiffs], or their subsidiaries, sell their gasoline in Maryland exclusively through company-operated stations. These refiners, using trade names such as "Red Head" and "Scot," concentrate largely on high-volume sales with prices consistently lower than those offered by independent dealer-operated major brand stations. Testimony presented by these refiners indicated that company ownership is essential to their method of private brand, low-priced competition. . . .

[Approximately] 3,800 retail service stations in Maryland sell over 20 different brands of gasoline. However, no petroleum products are produced or refined in Maryland, and the number of stations actually operated by a refiner or an affiliate is relatively small, representing about 5% of the total number of Maryland retailers.

The refiners introduced evidence indicating that their ownership of retail service stations has produced significant benefits for the consuming public. Moreover, the three refiners that now market solely through company-operated stations may elect to withdraw from the Maryland market altogether if the statute is enforced. There was, however, no evidence that the total quantity of petroleum products shipped into Maryland would be affected by the statute. . . .

Plainly, the Maryland statute does not discriminate against interstate goods, nor does it favor local producers and refiners. Since Maryland's entire gasoline supply flows in interstate commerce and since there are no local producers or refiners, such claims of disparate treatment between interstate and local commerce would be meritless. Appellants, however, focus on the retail market, arguing that the effect of the statute is to protect in-state independent dealers from out-of-state competition. They contend that the divestiture provisions "create a protected enclave for Maryland independent dealers. . . ." As support for this proposition, they rely on the fact that the burden of the divestiture requirements falls solely on interstate companies. But this fact does not lead, either logically or as a practical matter, to a conclusion that the State is discriminating against interstate commerce at the retail level.

As the record shows, there are several major interstate marketers of petroleum that own and operate their own retail gasoline stations. These interstate dealers, who compete directly with the Maryland independent dealers, are not affected by the Act because they do not refine or produce gasoline. In fact, the Act creates no barriers whatsoever against interstate independent dealers; it does not prohibit the flow of interstate goods, place added costs upon them, or distinguish between in-state and out-of-state companies in the retail market. The absence of any of these factors fully distinguishes this case from those in which a State has been found to have discriminated against interstate commerce. See, e.g., [*Dean Milk Co.*] [While] the refiners will no longer enjoy their same status in the Maryland market, in-state independent dealers will have no competitive advantage over out-of-state dealers. The fact that the burden of a state regulation falls on some interstate companies does not, by itself, establish a claim of discrimination against interstate commerce.[16]

Some refiners may choose to withdraw entirely from the Maryland market, but there is no reason to assume that their share of the entire supply will not be promptly replaced by other interstate refiners. The source of the consumers' supply may switch from company-operated stations to independent dealers, but interstate commerce is not subjected to an impermissible burden simply because an otherwise valid regulation causes some business to shift from one interstate supplier to another.

The crux of appellants' claim is that, regardless of whether the State has interfered with the movement of goods in interstate commerce, it has interfered "with the natural functioning of the interstate market either through prohibition or through burdensome regulation." Hughes v. Alexandria Scrap Corp., 426 U.S. 794, 806. Appellants then claim that the statute "will surely change the market structure by weakening the independent refiners. . . ." We cannot, however, accept appellants' underlying notion that the Commerce Clause protects the particular structure or methods of operation in a retail market. As indicated by the Court in *Hughes*, the Clause protects the interstate market, not particular interstate firms, from prohibitive or burdensome regulations. It may be true that the consuming public will be injured by the loss of the high-volume, low-priced stations operated by the independent refiners, but again that argument relates to the wisdom of the statute, not to its burden on commerce.

Finally, we cannot adopt appellants' novel suggestion that because the economic market for petroleum products is nationwide, no State has the power to regulate the retail marketing of gas. [This] Court has only rarely held that the Commerce Clause itself pre-empts an entire field from state regulation, and then only when a lack of national uniformity would impede the flow of interstate goods. [*Cooley*.] The evil that appellants perceive in this litigation is not that the several States will enact differing regulations, but rather that they will all conclude that divestiture provisions are warranted. The problem thus is not one of national uniformity. In the absence of a relevant congressional declaration of policy, or a showing of a specific discrimination against, or burdening of, interstate commerce, we cannot conclude that the States are without power to regulate in this area.

[The Court also rejected a preemption argument made by Exxon.]

The judgment is affirmed.

---

16. If the effect of a state regulation is to cause local goods to constitute a larger share, and goods with an out-of-state source to constitute a smaller share, of the total sales in the market — as in [*Dean Milk*] — the regulation may have a discriminatory effect on interstate commerce. But the Maryland statute has no impact on the relative proportions of local and out-of-state goods sold in Maryland and, indeed, no demonstrable effect whatsoever on the interstate flow of goods. The sales by independent retailers are just as much a part of the flow of interstate commerce as the sales made by the refiner-operated stations.

So ordered.

Mr. Justice Powell took no part in the consideration or decision of these cases.

Mr. Justice Blackmun, [dissenting as to the commerce clause issue].

[The] divestiture provisions preclude out-of-state competitors from retailing gasoline within Maryland. The effect is to protect in-state retail service station dealers from the competition of the out-of-state businesses. This protectionist discrimination is not justified by any legitimate state interest that cannot be vindicated by more evenhanded regulation. . . .

I

A

The Commerce Clause forbids discrimination against interstate commerce, which repeatedly has been held to mean that States and localities may not discriminate against the transactions of out-of-state actors in interstate markets. E.g., [*Dean Milk.*] The discrimination need not appear on the face of the state or local regulation. "The commerce clause forbids discrimination, whether forthright or ingenious. In each case it is our duty to determine whether the statute under attack, whatever its name may be, will in its practical operation work discrimination against interstate commerce." The state or local authority need not intend to discriminate in order to offend the policy of maintaining a free-flowing national economy. [A] statute that on its face restricts both intrastate and interstate transactions may violate the Clause by having the "practical effect" of discriminating in its operation. . . .

B

With this background, the unconstitutional discrimination in the Maryland statute becomes apparent. No facial inequality exists. [But] given the structure of the retail gasoline market in Maryland, the effect [is] to exclude a class of predominantly out-of-state gasoline retailers while providing protection from competition to a class of nonintegrated retailers that is overwhelmingly composed of local businessman. [Of] the class of stations statutorily insulated from the competition of the out-of-state integrated firms [more] than 99% were operated by local business interests. Of the class of enterprises excluded entirely from participation in the retail gasoline market, 95% were out-of-state firms, operating 98% of the stations in the class. . . .

[The] ban [will] preclude the majors from enhancing brand recognition and consumer acceptance through retail outlets with company-controlled standards. Their ability directly to monitor consumer preferences and reactions will be diminished. And their opportunity for experimentation with retail marketing techniques will be curtailed. In short, the divestiture provisions, which will require the appellant majors to cease operation of property valued at more than $10 million, will inflict significant economic hardship on Maryland's major brand companies, all of which are out-of-state firms.

Similar hardship is not imposed upon the local service station dealers by the divestiture provisions. Indeed, rather than restricting their ability to compete, the Maryland Act effectively and perhaps intentionally improves their competitive position by insulating them from competition by out-of-state integrated producers and refiners. [At] trial the State's expert said that the legislation would have the effect of protecting the local dealers against the out-of-state competition. In short, the foundation of the discrimination in this case is that the local dealers may continue to enter retail transactions and to compete for retail profits while the statute will deny similar opportunities to the class composed almost entirely of out-of-state businesses.

With discrimination proved against interstate commerce, the burden falls upon the State to justify the distinction with legitimate state interests that cannot be vindicated with more evenhanded regulation. On the record before the Court, the State fails to carry its burden. It asserts only in general terms a desire to maintain competition in gasoline retailing. [The] State [does] not even attempt to demonstrate why competition cannot be preserved without banning the out-of-state interests from the retail market.

The State's showing may be so meager because any legitimate interest in competition can be vindicated with more evenhanded regulation. First, to the extent that the State's interest in competition is nothing more than a desire to protect particular competitors — less efficient local businessmen — from the legal competition of more efficient out-of-state firms, the interest is illegitimate under the Commerce Clause. A national economy would hardly flourish if each State could effectively insist that local nonintegrated dealers handle product retailing to the exclusion of out-of-state integrated firms that would not have sufficient local political clout to challenge the influence of local businessmen with their local government leaders.[8] Each State would be encouraged to "legislate according to its estimate of its own interests, the importance of its own products, and the local advantages or disadvantages of its position in a political or commercial view." J. Story, Commentaries on the Constitution of the United States §259 (4th ed. 1873), quoted in [H. P. Hood & Sons]. The Commerce Clause simply does not countenance such parochialism.

Second, a legitimate concern of the State could be to limit the economic power of vertical integration. But nothing in the record suggests that the vertical

---

8. There is support in the record for the inference that the Maryland Legislature passed the divestiture provisions in response to the pleas of local gasoline dealers for protection against the competition of both the price marketers and the major oil companies. [The] executive director of the Greater Washington/Maryland Service Station Association [testified] before the [Maryland] Senate:

I would like to begin by telling you gentlemen that these are desperate days for service station dealers. . . .
Now beset by the critical gasoline supply situation, the squeeze by his landlord-supplier and the shrinking service [market], the dealer is now faced with an even more serious threat.
That is the sinister threat of the major oil companies to complete their takeover to the retail-marketing of gasoline, not just to be in competition with their own branded dealers, but to squeeze them out and convert their stations to company operation. . . .
Are the legislators of Maryland about to let this octopus loose and unrestricted in the state of Maryland, among our small businessmen to devour them? We sincerely hope not. . . .

integration that has already occurred in the Maryland petroleum market has inhibited competition. . . .

II . . .

To accept the argument of the Court, that is, that discrimination must be universal to offend the Commerce Clause, naively will foster protectionist discrimination against interstate commerce.[13] In the future, States will be able to insulate
in-state interests from competition by identifying the most potent segments of
out-of-state business, banning them, and permitting less effective out-of-state actors to remain. The record shows that the Court permits Maryland to effect just
such discrimination in this case. The State bans the most powerful out-of-state
firms from retailing gasoline within its boundaries. It then insulates the forced divestiture of 199 service stations from constitutional attack by permitting out-of-
state firms [to] continue to operate 34 gasoline stations. Effective out-of-state competition is thereby emasculated — no doubt, an ingenious discrimination. But as
stated at the outset, "the commerce clause forbids discrimination, whether forthright or ingenious."

[Merely] demonstrating a burden on some out-of-state actors does not prove
unconstitutional discrimination. But when the burden is significant, when it falls
on the most numerous and effective group of out-of-state competitors, when a
similar burden does not fall on the class of protected in-state businessmen, and
when the State cannot justify the resulting disparity by showing that its legislative
interests cannot be vindicated by more evenhanded regulation, unconstitutional
discrimination exists. . . .

[The state] Court of Appeals reasoned that [the statute] did not discriminate
against the class of out-of-state refiners and producers because the wholesale flow
of petroleum products into the State was not restricted. [The] Maryland statute
has not effected discrimination with regard to the wholesaling or interstate transport of petroleum. The discrimination exists with regard to retailing. The fact
that gasoline will continue to flow into the State does not permit the State to deny
out-of-state firms the opportunity to retail it once it arrives.

[The] State argues that discrimination against interstate commerce has not occurred because "[n]o nexus between interstate as opposed to local interests inheres in the production or refining of petroleum." Although this statement might
be correct in the abstract, it is incorrect in reality, given the structure of the Mary-

---

13. The Court also notes that [the statute does] not discriminate against interstate goods and
does not favor local producers and refiners. While true, the observation is irrelevant because it
does not address the discrimination inflicted upon retail marketing in the State.

Footnote 16 of the Court's opinion suggests that unconstitutional discrimination does not exist
unless there is an effect on the quantity of out-of-state goods entering a State. This is too narrow
a view of the Commerce Clause. [Interstate] commerce consists of far more than mere production of goods. It also consists of transactions — of repeated buying and selling of both goods
and services. By focusing exclusively on the quantity of goods, the Court limits the protection of
the Clause to producers and handlers of goods before they enter a discriminating State. In our
complex national economy, commercial transactions continue after the goods enter a State. The
Court today permits a State to impose protectionist discrimination upon these latter transactions
to the detriment of out-of-state participants. [Relocated footnote — Eds.]

land petroleum market. Due to geological formation as so far known, no petroleum is produced in Maryland; due to the economics of production and refining, as well as to the geology, no petroleum is refined in Maryland. As a matter of actual fact, then, an inherent nexus does exist between the out-of-state status of producers and refiners and the distribution and retailing of gasoline in Maryland. The Commerce Clause does not forbid only legislation that discriminates under all factual circumstances. It forbids discrimination in effect against interstate commerce on the specific facts of each case. If production or refining of gasoline occurred in Maryland, [the statute] might not be unconstitutional. Under those different circumstances, however, the producers and refiners would have a fair opportunity to influence their local legislators and thereby to prevent the enactment of economically disruptive legislation. Under those circumstances, the economic disruption would be felt directly in Maryland, which would tend to make the local political processes responsive to the problems thereby created. Under those circumstances, [the statute] might never have been passed. In this case, however, the economic disruption of the sections is visited upon out-of-state economic interests and not upon in-state businesses. One of the basic assumptions of the Commerce Clause is that local political systems will tend to be unresponsive to problems not felt by local constituents; instead, local political units are expected to act in their constituents' interests. One of the basic purposes of the Clause, therefore, is to prevent the vindication of such self-interest from unfairly burdening out-of-state concerns and thereby disrupting the national economy. . . .

III

The Court's decision brings to mind the well-known words of Mr. Justice Cardozo:

> To give entrance to [protectionism] would be to invite a speedy end of our national solidarity. The Constitution was framed under the dominion of a political philosophy less parochial in range. It was framed upon the theory that the peoples of the several states must sink or swim together, and that in the long run prosperity and salvation are in union and not division.

Baldwin v. G. A. F. Seelig, Inc., 294 U.S. 511, 523 (1935). Today, the Court fails to heed the Justice's admonition. The parochial political philosophy of the Maryland Legislature thereby prevails. I would reverse the judgment of the Maryland Court of Appeals.

Note: Facially Neutral Statutes with (Merely?) Disproportionate Effects for Commercial or Social Purposes

1. *Commerce — gasoline or retailing?* The Court argues that interstate commerce in gasoline will be unaffected by the statute because all it can do is force Maryland consumers to switch from cheaper brands of gasoline originating out of state to more expensive brands also originating out of state. Justice Blackmun argues that the courts should confine their attention to the subject regulated — here, retailing. Why? Consider the implications of the following argument: In a

strongly interconnected economy, local regulations can do no more than alter the patterns of interstate trade; they cannot reduce it. Isn't this the lesson of Wickard v. Filburn and Katzenbach v. McClung, Chapter 2 supra? States may succeed in protecting particular local industries, but they cannot protect their entire economies. Thus, local regulations serve only distributional goals, altering the relative wealth of in-state and out-of-state producers and of consumers. What, if anything, is there in the materials presented here that suggests that the Constitution is concerned with these goals?

2. *Cost-benefit analysis.* Who bears the costs and gains the benefits of Maryland's statutes? How substantial are the higher prices that Maryland consumers are likely to face? Consider L. Tribe, American Constitutional Law 417 (2d ed. 1988):

> Behind the Court's analysis in *Exxon* stands an important doctrinal theme: the negative implications of the commerce clause derive principally from a *political* theory of union, not from an *economic* theory of free trade. The function of the clause is to ensure national solidarity, not economic efficiency. Although the Court's commerce clause opinions have often employed the language of economics, the decisions have not interpreted the Constitution as establishing the inviolability of the free market. More particularly, the constitutional vice of economic protectionism is not implicated by a regulation which makes impossible the economies of scale that a fully open market permits.

How is national solidarity promoted other than by economic integration? By prohibiting states from enacting statutes designed to hurt other states' interests? By prohibiting states from adopting statutes whose terms indicate willingness to go it alone?

3. *The problem of sales and compensating use taxes.* Henneford v. Silas Mason Co., 300 U.S. 577 (1937), involved Washington's sales and use taxes. The state adopted a 2 percent tax. To avoid losing business to retailers in other states, it also adopted a 2 percent "compensating use tax," levied on the price of goods purchased elsewhere for the "privilege of using" them in Washington. Justice Cardozo's opinion for the Court, upholding the compensating use tax, described it as designed to promote equality. The tax's challengers relied primarily on Baldwin v. G. A. F. Seelig, Inc., 294 U.S. 511 (1935), invalidating a New York statute requiring that milk purchased from out-of-state (Vermont) producers could not be sold in New York unless the out-of-state producers had received at least the minimum price required by New York's price maintenance statute for sale of milk produced in New York. Justice Cardozo, the author of *Baldwin*, distinguished it as follows: There New York

> was attempting to project its legislation within the borders of another state by regulating the price to be paid in that state for milk acquired there. She said in effect to farmers in Vermont: your milk cannot be sold by dealers to whom you ship it in New York unless you sell it to them in Vermont at a price determined here. What Washington is saying to sellers beyond her borders is something very different. In substance what she says is this: You may ship your goods in such amounts and at such prices as you please, but the goods when used in Washington after the transit is completed, will share an equal burden with goods that have been purchased here.

Does that make economic sense? Is the underlying distinction one between taxes and regulations? Between price competition due to "natural" advantages and that due to "state-created" ones? Is either distinction coherent?

A modern discussion of compensating use taxes is Oregon Waste Systems v. Department of Environmental Quality, 511 U.S. 93 (1994). Oregon charged a fee of $0.85 per ton on the disposal of waste generated in Oregon and a fee of $2.25 on the disposal in Oregon of waste generated outside the state. The Court held that the differential was discriminatory and triggered the "virtually per se rule of invalidity." Treating the differential as a compensatory use tax, the Court, in an opinion by Justice Thomas, clarified the doctrine by stressing that the fact that a tax or fee is "compensatory" is "merely a specific way of justifying a facially discriminatory tax." Compensating use taxes must be imposed on "substantially equivalent events." This implied that the state could not justify a specific tax like the one at issue here by pointing to "general taxation, such as income taxes," that in-state generators pay, but out-of-state generators do not.

Note that compensating use taxes are not facially neutral. The Court treated Henneford v. Silas Mason as still good law because sale and use are "substantially equivalent taxable events." Chief Justice Rehnquist's dissent in *Oregon Waste Systems* claimed that out-of-state commerce gained a competitive advantage from the Court's rule that it will not consider whether general taxes in Oregon offset the difference between the higher fees charged those who dispose of out-of-state waste and those who dispose of in-state waste: Only Oregon businesses "will have to pay the 'nondisposal' fees associated with solid waste: landfill siting, landfill clean-up, insurance to cover environmental accidents, and transportation improvement costs associated with out-of-state waste being transported into the State." Could the courts administer a rule examining general taxes to see if they offset the difference?

Hunt v. Washington State Apple Advertising Commission

432 U.S. 333 (1977)

CHIEF JUSTICE BURGER delivered the opinion of the Court. . . .

[North Carolina enacted a statute requiring all closed containers of apples sold or shipped into the state to bear "no grade other than the applicable U.S. grade or standard." Washington, the country's largest producer of apples, requires that apples be tested and graded under a system of grades superior to the standards adopted by the U.S. Department of Agriculture. North Carolina agreed that the statute placed substantial financial burdens on Washington apple producers, who could comply with North Carolina law only by altering the containers used to pack apples, by repacking those that were shipped to North Carolina, or by discontinuing use of preprinted containers with the Washington grades entirely. North Carolina defended its regulation as a measure designed to protect against fraud in apple marketing. The Court held the regulation unconstitutional.]

[Not] every exercise of state authority imposing some burden on the free flow of commerce is invalid. [Our] opinions have long recognized that, "in the absence of conflicting legislation by Congress, there is a residuum of power in the state to make laws governing matters of local concern which nevertheless in some measure affect interstate commerce or even, to some extent, regulate it." Southern Pacific Co. v. Arizona ex rel. Sullivan, 325 U.S. 761, 767 (1945). Moreover, [that] "residuum" is particularly strong when the State acts to protect its citizenry in matters pertaining to the sale of foodstuffs. By the same token, however, a finding that state legislation furthers matters of legitimate local concern, even in the health and consumer protection areas, does not end the inquiry. Such a view ["would] mean that the Commerce Clause of itself imposes no limitations on state action . . . save for the rare instance where a state artlessly discloses an avowed purpose to discriminate against interstate goods." [*Dean Milk Co.*] Rather, when such state legislation comes into conflict with the Commerce Clause's overriding requirement of a national "common market," we are confronted with the task of effecting an accommodation of the competing national and local interests. . . .

[The] challenged statute has the practical effect of not only burdening interstate sales of Washington apples, but also discriminating against them. This discrimination takes various forms. The first [is] the statute's consequence of raising the costs of doing business in the North Carolina market for Washington apple growers and dealers, while leaving those of their North Carolina counterparts unaffected. [This] disparate effect results from the fact that North Carolina apple producers, unlike their Washington competitors, were not forced to alter their marketing practices in order to comply with the statute. They were still free to market their wares under the USDA grade or none at all as they had done prior to the statute's enactment. Obviously, the increased costs imposed by the statute would tend to shield the local apple industry from the competition of Washington apple growers and dealers who are already at a competitive disadvantage because of their great distance from the North Carolina market.

Second, the statute has the effect of stripping away from the Washington apple industry the competitive and economic advantages it has earned for itself through its expensive inspection and grading system. [The] Washington apple-grading system has gained nationwide acceptance in the apple trade. [Apple] brokers and dealers located both inside and outside of North Carolina [state] their preference [for] apples graded under the Washington [system] because of [its] greater consistency, its emphasis on color, and its supporting mandatory inspections. Once again, the statute had no similar impact on the North Carolina apple industry and thus operated to its benefit.

Third, by prohibiting Washington growers and dealers from marketing apples under their State's grades, the statute has a leveling effect which insidiously operates to the advantage of local apple producers. [The] Washington State grades are equal or superior to the USDA grades in all corresponding categories. Hence, with free market forces at work, Washington sellers would normally enjoy a distinct market advantage vis-à-vis local producers in those categories where the Washington grade is superior. However, because of the statute's operation, Washington apples which would otherwise qualify for and be sold under the superior Washington grades will now have to be marketed under their inferior USDA counterparts. Such "downgrading" offers the North Carolina apple industry the very sort of protection against competing out-of-state products that the Commerce Clause was designed to prohibit. At worst, it will have the effect of an embargo against those Washington apples in the superior grades as Washington dealers withhold them from the North Carolina market. At best, it will deprive

Washington sellers of the market premium that such apples would otherwise command. . . .

The several States unquestionably possess a substantial interest in protecting their citizens from confusion and deception in the marketing of foodstuffs, but the challenged statute does remarkably little to further that laudable goal at least with respect to Washington apples and grades. The statute [permits] the marketing of closed containers of apples under no grades at all. Such a result can hardly be thought to eliminate the problems of deception and confusion created by the multiplicity of differing state grades; indeed, it magnifies them by depriving purchasers of all information concerning the quality of the contents of closed apple containers. Moreover, although the statute is ostensibly a consumer protection measure, it directs its primary efforts, not at the consuming public at large, but at apple wholesalers and brokers who are the principal purchasers of closed containers of apples. And those individuals are presumably the most knowledgeable individuals in this area. Since the statute does nothing at all to purify the flow of information at the retail level, it does little to protect consumers against the problems it was designed to eliminate. Finally, we note that any potential for confusion and deception created by the Washington grades was not of the type that led to the statute's enactment. Since Washington grades are in all cases equal or superior to their USDA counterparts, they could only "deceive" or "confuse" a consumer to his benefit, hardly a harmful result.

In addition, it appears that nondiscriminatory alternatives to the outright ban of Washington State grades are readily available. For example, North Carolina could effectuate its goal by permitting out-of-state growers to utilize state grades only if they also marked their shipments with the applicable USDA label. In that case, the USDA grade would serve as a benchmark against which the consumer could evaluate the quality of the various state grades. If this alternative was for some reason inadequate to eradicate problems caused by state grades inferior to those adopted by the USDA, North Carolina might consider banning those state grades which, unlike Washington's, could not be demonstrated to be equal or superior to the corresponding USDA categories. Concededly, even in this latter instance, some potential for "confusion" might persist. However, it is the type of "confusion" that the national interest in the free flow of goods between the States demands be tolerated.

Note: Facially Neutral Statutes with Discriminatory Effects — Gerrymandering?

1. *Gerrymandering or mere facial neutrality?* In *Exxon*, Justice Blackmun's dissent argued that the case was indistinguishable from *Hunt*:

> [The] unconstitutional discrimination in *Hunt* was not against all out-of-state interests. [The] provision imposed no discrimination on growers from States that employed only the United States Department of Agriculture grading system. Despite this lack of universal discrimination, the Court declared the provision unconstitutional because it discriminated against a single segment of out-of-state marketers of apples, namely, the Washington State growers who employed the superior grading

system. In this regard, the Maryland divestiture provisions are identical to, not distinguishable from, the North Carolina statute in *Hunt*. Here, the discrimination has been imposed against a segment of the out-of-state retailers of gasoline, namely, those who also refine or produce petroleum.

Is the inference of anticommercial intent weaker in *Exxon* than in *Hunt*? Note footnote 8 in Justice Blackmun's opinion. Does *Exxon* involve anticommercial intent but no significant anticommercial impact? Consider whether the cases make a statute's use of express or strongly implied discrimination conclusive. Is such formalism justified on the grounds that form is strongly, though not perfectly, correlated with cost-exporting, and that the gains from allowing courts to look beyond form are outweighed by the costs in encouraging complex litigation? Can that be reconciled with the concern for representation expressed by Justice Stone in *Barnwell Brothers*, infra, and reiterated by Justice Blackmun's dissent in *Exxon*?

2. *Inferring intent from effect.* Should the courts infer a discriminatory or anticommercial purpose from neutral criteria that have the effect of distinguishing in-state and out-of-state producers? How precisely must the neutral criteria target out-of-state producers to justify that inference? Consider these comments in the Court's opinion in *Hunt*:

> Despite the statute's facial neutrality, the Commission suggests that its discriminatory impact on interstate commerce was not an unintended byproduct and there are some indications in the record to that effect. The most glaring is the response of the North Carolina Agriculture Commissioner to the Commission's request for an exemption following the statute's passage in which he indicated that before he could support such an exemption, he would "want to have the sentiment from our apple producers *since they were mainly responsible for this legislation being passed.* . . ." [However], we need not ascribe an economic protection motive to the North Carolina Legislature to resolve this case; we conclude that the challenged statute cannot stand insofar as it prohibits the display of Washington State grades even if enacted for the declared purpose of protecting consumers from deception and fraud in the marketplace.

How important should be the presence or absence of evidence like that taken from the state's Agriculture Commissioner?

Note: Inferring Intent

Consider Minnesota v. Clover Leaf Creamery Co., 449 U.S. 456 (1981). Minnesota prohibited the sale of milk in plastic disposable containers but allowed its sale in paper nonreturnable cartons. The Supreme Court accepted the argument that the statute served its stated purposes of promoting conservation, easing waste disposal problems, and conserving energy. The state's trial court had found that the "actual basis" of the statute "was to promote the economic interests of certain segments of the local dairy and pulpwood industries at the expense of the economic interests of other segments of the dairy industry and the plastics industry." It also had found that banning the use of plastic bottles would not in fact promote conservation or save energy because paper containers are "a more environmentally harmful product." The Supreme Court responded:

Minnesota's statute does not effect "simple protectionism," but "regulates even-handedly" by prohibiting all milk retailers from selling their products in plastic, nonreturnable milk containers, without regard to whether the milk, the containers, or the sellers are from outside the State. This statute is therefore unlike statutes discriminating against interstate commerce, which we have consistently struck down. E.g., [*Hughes*; Philadelphia v. New Jersey; *Hunt*]. . . .

[Within] Minnesota, business will presumably shift from manufacturers of plastic nonreturnable containers to producers of paperboard cartons, refillable bottles, and plastic pouches, but there is no reason to suspect that the gainers will be Minnesota firms, or the losers out-of-state firms. Indeed, two of the three dairies, the sole milk retailer, and the sole milk container producer challenging the statute in this litigation are Minnesota firms.[17]

Pulpwood producers are the only Minnesota industry likely to benefit significantly from the Act at the expense of out-of-state firms. Respondents point out that plastic resin, the raw material used for making plastic nonreturnable milk jugs, is produced entirely by non-Minnesota firms, while pulpwood, used for making paperboard, is a major Minnesota product. Nevertheless, it is clear that respondents exaggerate the degree of burden on out-of-state interests, both because plastics will continue to be used in the production of plastic pouches, plastic returnable bottles, and paperboard itself, and because out-of-state pulpwood producers will presumably absorb some of the business generated by the Act. . . .

In [*Exxon*, we] stressed that the Commerce Clause "protects the interstate market, not particular interstate firms, from prohibitive or burdensome regulations." A nondiscriminatory regulation serving substantial state purposes is not invalid simply because it causes some business to shift from a predominantly out-of-state industry to a predominantly in-state industry. Only if the burden on interstate commerce clearly outweighs the State's legitimate purposes does such a regulation violate the Commerce Clause.

Is this analysis of the issue of intent persuasive? Is the problem addressed here different from that in *Hunt?* In Philadelphia v. New Jersey?

SOUTH CAROLINA HIGHWAY DEPARTMENT v. BARNWELL BROTHERS, 303 U.S. 177 (1938). The Court upheld the constitutionality of a South Carolina statute prohibiting the use on state highways of trucks that were over ninety inches wide or over 20,000 pounds in gross weight. Approximately 85 to 90 percent of the nation's trucks exceeded these limits. The trial court found that gross weight was not an accurate measure of a truck's potential to cause damage to highways, whereas axle weight was, and that trucks weighing over 20,000 pounds in gross weight could be used without damaging the highways. Justice Stone's opinion for the Court cited *Cooley* to show that "there are matters of local concern, the regulation of which unavoidably involves some regulation of interstate commerce but which, because of their local character and their number and diversity, may never be fully dealt with by Congress. Notwithstanding the commerce clause, such regulation in the absence of Congressional action has for the most part been left to the states. . . .

"The commerce clause, by its own force, prohibits discrimination [even] when state legislation nominally of local concern is in point of fact aimed at interstate

---

17. The existence of major in-state interests adversely affected by the Act is a powerful safeguard against legislative abuse. [*Barnwell Bros.*]

commerce, or by its necessary operation is a means of gaining a local benefit by throwing the attendant burdens on those without the state. [However,] few subjects of state regulation are so peculiarly of local concern as is the use of state highways." Sometimes such regulations burdened interstate commerce, but "so long as the state action does not discriminate, the burden is one which the Constitution permits because it is an inseparable incident of the exercise of a legislative authority, which, under the Constitution, has been left to the states."

In the absence of congressional action, the test was "whether the state legislature in adopting regulations such as the present has acted within its province, and whether the means of regulation chosen are reasonably adapted to the end sought." In "resolving the second [inquiry], the courts do not sit as Legislatures [to weigh] all the conflicting interests. [Fairly] debatable questions as to [a regulation's] reasonableness, wisdom and propriety are not for the determination of courts, but for the legislative body." The court must decide "upon the whole record whether it is possible to say that the legislative choice is without rational basis." Here the state reasonably chose to use gross weight for "convenience of application and consequent lack of need for rigid supervisory enforcement." Further, many of the state's roads were old and liable to crack more frequently than newer roads. As to the width limitation, 100 miles of the state's roads were sixteen feet wide, which left no margin for passing a ninety-six-inch-wide truck.

SOUTHERN PACIFIC CO. v. ARIZONA, 325 U.S. 761 (1945). The Court, again through Chief Justice Stone, found unconstitutional a 1912 statute limiting train lengths to fourteen passenger or seventy freight cars. Citing *Gibbons*, the Court said that states may not regulate subjects "which, because of the need for national uniformity, demand that their regulation, if any, be prescribed by a single authority." At this point, a footnote said, "In applying this rule the Court has often recognized that to the extent that the burden of state regulation falls on interests outside the state, it is unlikely to be alleviated by the operation of those political restraints normally exerted when interests within the state are affected." Reviewing the Court's prior decisions, the Court concluded that "the states [have] wide scope for the regulation of matters of local state concern, even though it in some measure affects the commerce, provided it does not materially restrict the free flow of commerce across state lines, or interfere with it in matters with respect to which uniformity of regulation is of predominant national concern."

Chief Justice Stone then stated "the matters for ultimate determination": "the nature and extent of the burden which the state regulation, [adopted] as a safety measure, imposes on interstate commerce, and whether the relative weights of the state and national interests are such as to make inapplicable the rule [that] the free flow of interstate commerce [in] matters requiring uniformity of regulation" is protected by the commerce clause. The Court reviewed "detailed findings of fact" made in a long trial below. The operation of trains longer than those allowed in Arizona was "standard practice." Railroads had to operate 30 percent more trains in Arizona than they otherwise would, at a cost of over $1 million a year. Breaking up and remaking long trains at the state's borders delayed traffic. "Enforcement of the law in Arizona [must] inevitably result in an impairment of efficient railroad operation because the railroads are subjected to regulation which is not uniform in its application. [Either trains are broken up and reconstituted, or] the carrier [must] conform to the lowest train limit restriction of any of the states through which its trains pass, whose laws thus control the carriers' operations both within and without the regulating state."

The Court then turned to the safety benefits of the law: "The decisive question is whether in the circumstances the total effect of the law as a safety measure in reducing accidents and casualties is so slight or problematical as not to outweigh the national interest in keeping interstate commerce free from interferences which seriously impede it and subject it to local regulation which does not have a uniform effect on the interstate train journey which it interrupts." Longer trains cause accidents by "slack action," the movement of one car before it transmits its momentum to the next one to which it is loosely coupled. The more slack action there is, the more likely workers are to be injured, especially on freight trains. But the evidence showed that, in states leaving train lengths unregulated, the accident rate on long trains was the same as that on Arizona's shorter trains. Further, because the regulation meant that more trains had to be used, there were more grade-crossing collisions and collisions between trains in the course of switching tracks. The Court found that the regulation, "viewed as a safety measure, affords at most slight and dubious advantage, if any, over unregulated train lengths, because it results in an increase in the number of trains and train operations and the consequent increases in train accidents of a character generally more severe than those due to slack action."

The Court distinguished *Barnwell Brothers* by stressing its point about the peculiarly local nature of highway control. "The fact that [regulations of highways] affect alike shippers in interstate and intrastate commerce in great numbers, within as well as without the state, is a safeguard against regulatory abuses." It concluded, "Here examination of all the relevant factors makes it plain that the state interest is outweighed by the interest of the nation in an adequate, economical and efficient railway transportation service, which must prevail."

Justice Black's dissenting opinion described the Arizona statute as the product of a long-standing political struggle between railroads and railroad workers, conducted in state legislatures and in Congress. He called the trial in *Southern Pacific* "extraordinary" in that the issue was "whether the law was unconstitutional [because] the legislature had been guilty of misjudging the facts concerning the degree of the danger of long trains. [This] new pattern of trial procedure makes it necessary for a judge to hear all the evidence offered as to why a legislature passed a law and to make findings of fact as to the validity of those reasons. [In] this respect, [this] Court today is acting as a 'super-legislature.'"

Justice Black's examination of the record convinced him that there was evidence to justify the conclusion that the statute promoted safety to some extent. "Under those circumstances, the determination of whether it is in the interest of society for the length of trains to be governmentally regulated is a matter of public policy. Someone must fix that policy — either the Congress, or the state, or the courts. A century and a half of constitutional history and government admonishes this Court to leave that choice to the elected legislative representatives [where] it properly belongs both on democratic principles and the requirements of efficient government."

Stating that "Congress knew about the Arizona law," and that the appropriate congressional committees "keep in close and intimate touch with the affairs of railroads," he concluded that Congress has made "a deliberate choice" to "leave the state free in this field." "We are not left in doubt as to why, as against the potential peril of injuries to employees, the Court tips the scales on the side of 'uniformity.' For the evil it finds in a lack of uniformity is that it (1) delays interstate commerce, (2) increases its cost and (3) impairs its efficiency. All three of these boil down to the same thing, and that is that running shorter trains would increase the cost of railroad operations. The 'burden' on interstate commerce reduces itself to mere cost because there was no [evidence] to support a finding that by the expenditure of sufficient sums of money, the railroads could not enable themselves to carry goods and passengers just as quickly and efficiently with short trains as with long trains. Thus the conclusion that a requirement for long trains will 'burden interstate commerce' is a mere euphemism for the statement that a requirement for long trains will increase the cost of railroad operations." He criticized the Court for "requiring that money costs outweigh human values" in the name of "an 'economical national railroad system.' I cannot believe that if Congress had defined what it meant by 'economical,' it would have required money to be saved at the expense of the personal safety of railway employees."

Justice Douglas also dissented, saying that "the courts should intervene only where the state legislation discriminated against interstate commerce or was out of harmony with laws which Congress had enacted." It was "particularly appropriate" for the courts to abstain, given the ability of the "expert" Interstate Commerce Commission "to police the field." He also suggested that a state law "requiring all railroads within its borders to operate on [nonstandard] tracks" would be unconstitutional. "The question is one of degree and calls for a close appraisal of the facts." He was unpersuaded that the railroads' evidence overcame the "presumption of validity to which this train-limit law is entitled."

Kassel v. Consolidated Freightways Corp.

450 U.S. 662 (1981)

JUSTICE POWELL announced the judgment of the Court and delivered an opinion, in which JUSTICE WHITE, JUSTICE BLACKMUN, and JUSTICE STEVENS joined.

The question is whether an Iowa statute that prohibits the use of certain large trucks within the State unconstitutionally burdens interstate commerce.

I . . .

[Consolidated, one of the nation's largest common carriers, used two types of trucks: the "semi," 55 feet long, and the "double," a 65-foot-long combination of a tractor and two trailers. It operated on Interstate Routes 80 and 35, major transportation corridors through Iowa.] Unlike all other States in the West and Midwest, Iowa generally prohibits the use of 65-foot doubles within its borders. Instead, most truck combinations are restricted to 55 feet in length. Doubles, mobile homes, trucks carrying vehicles such as tractors and other farm equipment, and singles hauling livestock, are permitted to be as long as 60 feet. Notwithstanding these restrictions, Iowa's statute permits cities abutting the state line by local ordinance to adopt the length limitations of the adjoining State. Where a city has exercised this option, otherwise oversized trucks are permitted within the city limits and in nearby commercial zones.

Iowa also provides for two other relevant exemptions. An Iowa truck manufacturer may obtain a permit to ship trucks that are as large as 70 feet. Permits also are available to move oversized mobile homes, provided that the unit is to be moved from a point within Iowa or delivered for an Iowa resident.[7]

Because of Iowa's statutory scheme, Consolidated cannot use its 65-foot doubles to move commodities through the State. Instead, the company must do one of four things: (i) use 55-foot singles; (ii) use 60-foot doubles; (iii) detach the trailers of a 65-foot double and shuttle each through the State separately; or (iv) divert 65-foot doubles around Iowa.

Dissatisfied with these options, Consolidated filed this suit in the District Court averring that Iowa's statutory scheme unconstitutionally burdens interstate commerce. Iowa defended the law as a reasonable safety measure enacted pursuant to its police power. The State asserted that 65-foot doubles are more dangerous than 55-foot singles and, in any event, that the law promotes safety and reduces road wear within the State by diverting much truck traffic to other States.

In a 14-day trial, both sides adduced evidence on safety, and on the burden on interstate commerce imposed by Iowa's law. On the question of safety, the District Court found that the "evidence clearly establishes that the twin is as safe as the semi." For that reason,

> there is no valid safety reason for barring twins from Iowa's highways because of their configuration. . . .
>
> Twins and semis have different characteristics. Twins are more maneuverable, are less sensitive to wind, and create less splash and spray. However, they are more likely than semis to jackknife or upset. They can be backed only for a short distance. The negative characteristics are not such that they render the twin less safe than semis overall. Semis are more stable but are more likely to "rear end" another vehicle.

II . . .

[A] State's power to regulate commerce is never greater than in matters traditionally of local concern. For example, regulations that touch upon safety — especially highway safety — are those that "the Court has been most reluctant to invalidate." Indeed, "if safety justifications are not illusory, the Court will not second-guess legislative judgment about their importance in comparison with related burdens on interstate commerce." [Raymond Motor Transportation, Inc. v. Rice, 434 U.S. 429], at 449 (Blackmun, J., concurring). Those who would challenge such bona fide safety regulations must overcome a "strong presumption of validity." [Bibb.]

But the incantation of a purpose to promote the public health or safety does not insulate a state law from Commerce Clause attack. Regulations designed for that salutary purpose nevertheless may further the purpose so marginally, and interfere with commerce so substantially, as to be invalid under the Commerce Clause. In [Raymond], we declined to "accept the State's contention that the in-

---

7. The parochial restrictions in the mobile home provision were enacted after Governor Ray vetoed a bill that would have permitted the interstate shipment of all mobile homes through Iowa. Governor Ray commented, in his veto message: "This bill . . . would make Iowa a bridge state as these oversized units are moved into Iowa after being manufactured in another state and sold in a third. None of this activity would be of particular economic benefit to Iowa."

quiry under the Commerce Clause is ended without a weighing of the asserted safety purpose against the degree of interference with interstate commerce." This "weighing" by a court requires — and indeed the constitutionality of the state regulation depends on — "a sensitive consideration of the weight and nature of the state regulatory concern in light of the extent of the burden imposed on the course of interstate commerce."

III

Applying these general principles, we conclude that the Iowa truck-length limitations unconstitutionally burden interstate commerce. [The] State failed to present any persuasive evidence that 65-foot doubles are less safe than 55-foot singles. Moreover, Iowa's law is now out of step with the laws of all other Midwestern and Western States. Iowa thus substantially burdens the interstate flow of goods by truck. In the absence of congressional action to set uniform standards, some burdens associated with state safety regulations must be tolerated. But where, as here, the State's safety interest has been found to be illusory, and its regulations impair significantly the federal interest in efficient and safe interstate transportation, the state law cannot be harmonized with the Commerce Clause.[12]

A . . .

[The] District Court found that the "evidence clearly establishes that the twin is as safe as the semi." The record supports this finding. . . .

[The] State points to only three ways in which the 55-foot single is even arguably superior: singles take less time to be passed and to clear intersections; they may back up for longer distances; and they are somewhat less likely to jackknife.

The first two of these characteristics are of limited relevance on modern interstate highways. As the District Court found, the negligible difference in the time required to pass, and to cross intersections, is insignificant on 4-lane divided highways because passing does not require crossing into oncoming traffic lanes, and interstates have few, if any, intersections. The concern over backing capability also is insignificant because it seldom is necessary to back up on an interstate.[15] In any event, no evidence suggested any difference in backing capability between the 60-foot doubles that Iowa permits and the 65-foot doubles that it bans. Similarly, although doubles tend to jackknife somewhat more than singles, 65-foot doubles actually are less likely to jackknife than 60-foot doubles.

Statistical studies supported the view that 65-foot doubles are at least as safe overall as 55-foot singles and 60-foot doubles. . . .

B

Consolidated, meanwhile, demonstrated that Iowa's law substantially burdens interstate commerce. Trucking companies that wish to continue to use 65-foot dou-

---

12. It is highly relevant that [the] state statute contains exemptions that weaken the deference traditionally accorded to a state safety regulation.

15. Evidence at trial did show that doubles could back up far enough to move around an accident.

bles must route them around Iowa or detach the trailers of the doubles and ship them through separately. Alternatively, trucking companies must use the smaller 55-foot singles or 60-foot doubles permitted under Iowa law. Each of these options engenders inefficiency and added expense. The record shows that Iowa's law added about $12.6 million each year to the costs of trucking companies. Consolidated alone incurred about $2 million per year in increased costs.

In addition to increasing the costs of the trucking companies (and, indirectly, of the service to consumers), Iowa's law may aggravate, rather than ameliorate, the problem of highway accidents. Fifty-five foot singles carry less freight than 65-foot doubles. Either more small trucks must be used to carry the same quantity of goods through Iowa, or the same number of larger trucks must drive longer distances to bypass Iowa. In either case, [the] restriction requires more highway miles to be driven to transport the same quantity of goods. Other things being equal, accidents are proportional to distance traveled. Thus, if 65-foot doubles are as safe as 55-foot singles, Iowa's law tends to *increase* the number of accidents, and to shift the incidence of them from Iowa to other States.[18]

IV

Perhaps recognizing the weakness of the evidence supporting its safety argument, and the substantial burden on commerce that its regulations create, Iowa urges the Court simply to "defer" to the safety judgment of the State. It argues that the length of trucks is generally, although perhaps imprecisely, related to safety. The task of drawing a line is one that Iowa contends should be left to its legislature.

The Court normally does accord "special deference" to state highway safety regulations. [*Raymond.*] This traditional deference "derives in part from the assumption that where such regulations do not discriminate on their face against interstate commerce, their burden usually falls on local economic interests as well as other States' economic interests, thus insuring that a State's own political processes will serve as a check against unduly burdensome regulations." Less deference to the legislative judgment is due, however, where the local regulation bears disproportionately on out-of-state residents and businesses. Such a disproportionate burden is apparent here. Iowa's scheme, although generally banning large doubles from the State, nevertheless has several exemptions that secure to Iowans many of the benefits of large trucks while shunting to neighboring States many of the costs associated with their use.

At the time of trial there were two particularly significant exemptions. First, singles hauling livestock or farm vehicles were permitted to be as long as 60 feet. [This] provision undoubtedly was helpful to local interests. Second, cities abutting other States were permitted to enact local ordinances adopting the larger length limitation of the neighboring State. This exemption offered the benefits of longer trucks to individuals and businesses in important border cities without burdening Iowa's highways with interstate through traffic.

18. The District Court [noted] that Iowa's law causes "more accidents, more injuries, more fatalities and more fuel consumption." Appellant Kassel conceded as much at trial. Kassel explained, however, that most of these additional accidents occur in States other than Iowa because truck traffic is deflected around the State. He noted: "Our primary concern is the citizens of Iowa and our own highway system we operate in this state."

The origin of the "border cities exemption" also suggests that Iowa's statute may not have been designed to ban dangerous trucks, but rather to discourage interstate truck traffic. In 1974, the legislature passed a bill that would have permitted 65-foot doubles in the State. Governor Ray vetoed the bill. He said:

> I find sympathy with those who are doing business in our state and whose enterprises could gain from increased cargo carrying ability by trucks. However, with this bill, the Legislature has pursued a course that would benefit only a few Iowa-based companies while providing a great advantage for out-of-state trucking firms and competitors at the expense of our Iowa citizens.

After the veto, the "border cities exemption" was immediately enacted and signed by the Governor.

It is thus far from clear that Iowa was motivated primarily by a judgment that 65-foot doubles are less safe than 55-foot singles. Rather, Iowa seems to have hoped to limit the use of its highways by deflecting some through traffic. In the District Court and Court of Appeals, the State explicitly attempted to justify the law by its claimed interest in keeping trucks out of Iowa. [A] State cannot constitutionally promote its own parochial interests by requiring safe vehicles to detour around it.

V . . .

Because Iowa has imposed this burden without any significant countervailing safety interest, its statute violates the Commerce Clause. The judgment of the Court of Appeals is affirmed.

It is so ordered.

JUSTICE BRENNAN, with whom JUSTICE MARSHALL joins, concurring in the judgment. . . .

For me, analysis of Commerce Clause challenges to state regulations must take into account three principles: (1) The courts are not empowered to second-guess the empirical judgments of lawmakers concerning the utility of legislation. (2) The burdens imposed on commerce must be balanced against the local benefits actually sought to be achieved by the State's lawmakers, and not against those suggested after the fact by counsel. (3) Protectionist legislation is unconstitutional under the Commerce Clause, even if the burdens and benefits are related to safety rather than economics.

I

Both the opinion of my Brother Powell and the opinion of my Brother Rehnquist are predicated upon the supposition that the constitutionality of a state regulation is determined by the factual record created by the State's lawyers in trial court. But that supposition cannot be correct, for it would make the constitutionality of state laws and regulations depend on the vagaries of litigation rather than on the judgments made by the State's lawmakers.

In considering a Commerce Clause challenge to a state regulation, the judicial task is to balance the burden imposed on commerce against the local benefits sought to be achieved by the State's *lawmakers*. In determining those benefits, a court should focus ultimately on the regulatory purposes identified by the lawmakers and on the evidence before or available to them that might have supported their judgment. See generally [*Clover Leaf*]. [It] is not the function of the court to decide whether *in fact* the regulation promotes its intended purpose, so long as an examination of the evidence before or available to the lawmaker indicates that the regulation is not wholly irrational in light of its purposes. See [*Clover Leaf*].[1]

II . . .

[Although] Iowa's lawyers in this litigation have defended the truck-length regulation on the basis of the safety advantages of 55-foot singles and 60-foot doubles over 65-foot doubles, Iowa's actual rationale for maintaining the regulation had nothing to do with these purported differences. Rather, Iowa sought to discourage interstate truck traffic on Iowa's highways. Thus, the safety advantages and disadvantages of the types and lengths of trucks involved in this case are irrelevant to the decision.

III

Though my Brother Powell recognizes that the State's actual purpose in maintaining the truck-length regulation was "to limit the use of its highways by deflecting some through traffic," he fails to recognize that this purpose, being *protectionist* in nature, is *impermissible* under the Commerce Clause. . . .

Iowa may not shunt off its fair share of the burden of maintaining interstate truck routes, nor may it create increased hazards on the highways of neighboring States in order to decrease the hazards on Iowa highways. Such an attempt has all the hallmarks of the "simple . . . protectionism" this Court has condemned in the economic area. [Philadelphia v. New Jersey.] Just as a State's attempt to avoid interstate competition in economic goods may damage the prosperity of the Nation as a whole, so Iowa's attempt to deflect interstate truck traffic has been found to make the Nation's highways as a whole more hazardous. That attempt should therefore be subject to "a virtually per se rule of invalidity." . . .

---

1. Moreover, I would emphasize that in the field of safety — and perhaps in other fields where the decisions of state lawmakers are deserving of a heightened degree of deference — the role of the courts is not to balance asserted burdens against intended benefits as it is in other fields. Compare [*Raymond*] (Blackmun, J., concurring) (safety regulation) with Pike v. Bruce Church, Inc., 397 U.S. 137, 143 (1970) (regulation intended "to protect and enhance the reputation of growers within the State"). In the field of safety, once the court has established that the intended safety benefit is not illusory, insubstantial, or nonexistent, it must defer to the State's lawmakers on the appropriate balance to be struck against other interests. I therefore disagree with my Brother Powell when he asserts that the degree of interference with interstate commerce may in the first instance be "weighed" against the State's safety interests. . . .

[Here], the decision of Iowa's lawmakers to promote *Iowa's* safety and other interests at the direct expense of the safety and other interests of neighboring States merits no such deference. No special judicial acuity is demanded to perceive that this sort of parochial legislation violates the Commerce Clause. As Justice Cardozo has written, the Commerce Clause "was framed upon the theory that the peoples of the several states must sink or swim together, and that in the long run prosperity and salvation are in union and not division." [Baldwin v. G. A. F. Seelig.]

I therefore concur in the judgment.

JUSTICE REHNQUIST, with whom THE CHIEF JUSTICE and JUSTICE STEWART join, dissenting. . . .

I . . .

[Iowa's] action in limiting the length of trucks which may travel on its highway is in no sense unusual. Every State in the Union regulates the length of vehicles permitted to use the public roads. Nor is Iowa a renegade in having the length limits which operate to exclude the 65-foot doubles favored by Consolidated. These trucks are prohibited in other areas of the country as well, some 17 States and the District of Columbia, including all of New England and most of the Southeast. . . .

II . . .

A determination that a state law is a rational safety measure does not end the Commerce Clause inquiry. A "sensitive consideration" of the safety purpose in relation to the burden on commerce is required. [*Raymond.*] When engaging in such a consideration the Court does not directly compare safety benefits to commerce costs and strike down the legislation if the latter can be said in some vague sense to "outweigh" the former. Such an approach would make an empty gesture of the strong presumption of validity accorded state safety measures, particularly those governing highways. It would also arrogate to this Court functions of forming public policy, functions which, in the absence of congressional action, were left by the Framers of the Constitution to state legislatures. . . .

The purpose of the "sensitive consideration" referred to above is rather to determine if the asserted safety justification, although rational, is merely a pretext for discrimination against interstate commerce. We will conclude that it is if the safety benefits from the regulation are demonstrably trivial while the burden on commerce is great. . . .

III

Iowa defends its statute as a highway safety regulation. There can be no doubt that the challenged statute is a valid highway safety regulation and thus entitled to the strongest presumption of validity against Commerce Clause challenges.

As noted, all 50 States regulate the length of trucks which may use their highways. The American Association of State Highway and Transportation Officials (AASHTO) has consistently recommended length as well as other limits on vehicles. [There] can also be no question that the particular limit chosen by Iowa — 60 feet — is rationally related to Iowa's safety objective. Most truck limits are between 55 and 65 feet, and Iowa's choice is thus well within the widely accepted range.

Iowa adduced evidence supporting the relation between vehicle length and highway safety. The evidence indicated that longer vehicles take greater time to pass, thereby increasing the risks of accidents, particularly during the inclement weather not uncommon in Iowa. The 65-foot vehicle exposes a passing driver to visibility-impairing splash and spray during bad weather for a longer period than do the shorter trucks permitted in Iowa. Longer trucks are more likely to clog intersections, and although there are no intersections on the Interstate Highways, the order below went beyond the highways themselves and the concerns about greater length at intersections would arise "[a]t every trip origin, every trip destination, every intermediate stop for picking up trailers, reconfiguring loads, change of drivers, eating, refueling — every intermediate stop would generate this type of situation." . . .

The District Court approached the case as if the question were whether Consolidated's 65-foot trucks were as safe as others permitted on Iowa highways. [The] question, however, is whether the Iowa Legislature has acted rationally in regulating vehicle lengths and whether the safety benefits from this regulation are more than slight or problematical. "[Since] the adoption of one weight or width regulation, rather than another, is a legislative and not a judicial choice, its constitutionality is not to be determined by weighing in the judicial scales the merits of the legislative choice and rejecting it if the weight of evidence presented in court appears to favor a different standard." [Barnwell Brothers.]

The answering of the relevant question is not appreciably advanced by comparing trucks slightly over the length limit with those at the length limit. It is emphatically not our task to balance any incremental safety benefits from prohibiting 65-foot doubles as opposed to 60-foot doubles against the burden on interstate commerce. Lines drawn for safety purposes will rarely pass muster if the question is whether a slight increment can be permitted without sacrificing safety. [The] question is rather whether it can be said that the benefits flowing to Iowa from a rational truck-length limitation are "slight or problematical." See [Bibb.] The particular line chosen by Iowa — 60 feet — is relevant only to the question whether the limit is a rational one. Once a court determines that it is, it considers the overall safety benefits *from the regulation* against burdens on interstate commerce, and not any marginal benefits from the scheme the State established as opposed to that the plaintiffs desire.

The difficulties with the contrary approach are patent. While it may be clear that there are substantial safety benefits from a 55-foot truck as compared to a 105-foot truck, these benefits may not be discernible in 5-foot jumps. Appellee's approach would permit what could not be accomplished in one lawsuit to be done in 10 separate suits, each challenging an additional five feet. . . .

[Striking] down Iowa's law because Consolidated has made a voluntary business decision to employ 65-foot doubles, a decision based on the actions of other state legislatures, would essentially be compelling Iowa to yield to the policy choices of neighboring States. Under our constitutional scheme, however, there is only one legislative body which can pre-empt the rational policy determination of the Iowa Legislature and that is Congress. Forcing Iowa to yield to the policy choices of neighboring States perverts the primary purpose of the Commerce Clause, that of vesting power to regulate interstate commerce in Congress, where all the States are represented. . . .

Both the plurality and concurring opinions attach great significance to the Governor's veto of a bill passed by the Iowa Legislature permitting 65-foot doubles. [The] law which the Court strikes down today was not passed to achieve the protectionist goals the plurality and the concurrence ascribe to the Governor. Iowa's 60-foot length limit was established in 1963, at a time when very few States permitted 65-foot doubles. Striking down legislation on the basis of asserted legislative motives is dubious enough, but the plurality and concurrence strike down the legislation involved in this case because of asserted impermissible motives for *not* enacting *other* legislation, motives which could not possibly have been present when the legislation under challenge here was considered and passed. Such action is, so far as I am aware, unprecedented in this Court's history.

Furthermore, the effort in both the plurality and concurring opinions to portray the legislation involved here as protectionist is in error. Whenever a State enacts more stringent safety measures than its neighbors, in an area which affects commerce, the safety law will have the incidental effect of deflecting interstate commerce to the neighboring States. Indeed, the safety and protectionist motives cannot be separated: The whole purpose of safety regulation of vehicles is to *protect* the State from unsafe vehicles. If a neighboring State chooses *not* to protect its citizens from the danger discerned by the enacting State, that is its business, but the enacting State should not be penalized when the vehicles it considers unsafe travel through the neighboring State. . . .

Note: *Facially Neutral Statutes with (Merely?) Disproportionate Effects for Police Power Purposes*

1. *Cost-benefit analysis — the benefits.* In *Southern Pacific,* who gains the benefits of Arizona's statute? Consider these two lines of analysis.

a. The net safety benefits are positive: The reduction in slack-action accidents (slightly) offsets the increase in grade-crossing and other accidents. Should this alone establish that the balance between benefits and burdens on interstate commerce favors the statute no matter what the burdens are? Consider in this connection Justice Black's observations in his opinion for the Court in Brotherhood of Locomotive Firemen & Engineers v. Chicago, Rock Island & Pacific Railroad, 393 U.S. 129 (1968). The lower court had found that requiring trains to carry a stipulated number of crew members imposed "substantial financial burdens" on railroads in light of technological changes that reduced the need for crews as large as had been needed in the past and had "no substantial effect on safety." Applying the *Southern Pacific* balancing test, it found the statute unconstitutional. The Supreme Court reversed. Justice Black wrote:

[The District Court should not have placed] a value on the additional safety in terms of dollars and cents, in order to see whether this value, as calculated by the court, exceeded the financial cost to the railroads. [It] is difficult at best to say that financial losses should be balanced against the loss of lives and limbs of workers and people using the highways.

On the assumption that the net safety benefits in *Southern Pacific* are positive, are the cases distinguishable? How can burdens on interstate commerce be balanced against the accomplishment of police power goals unless some sort of monetary value can be placed on both?

b. The net safety benefits are negative: The increase in grade-crossing accidents exceeds the reduction in slack-action accidents. Railroad employees gain at the expense of road users and others injured in grade-crossing accidents. If both groups are largely composed of Arizonans, the statute redistributes wealth from one group of Arizonans to another. Should the courts be concerned about that? How can the distributive impact be balanced against the cost imposed on interstate commerce?

Which of these lines of analysis did the Court pursue?

2. *Cost-benefit analysis — the costs*. Does the Arizona statute discriminate against interstate commerce, either in terms or in effect? If not, why should the Court intervene? Who bears the costs of Arizona's statute? Does the cost of complying with the regulation measure the burden on interstate commerce? Suppose railroads have a slight cost advantage over trucks in transporting goods through Arizona to California. By complying with the statute, the railroads face cost increases that they must either absorb or pass on to their customers. If they pass the costs on, they lose business to trucks. In either event, how exactly is interstate commerce burdened? To what extent?

Ultimately someone has to pay for Arizona's regulation, either in increased prices for goods shipped to California on railroads or in increased prices for goods shipped on the more expensive trucks. Is this what the Court meant by the footnote reiterating the "thought" from *Barnwell Brothers* describing the political process? Does *Southern Pacific* persuasively distinguish *Barnwell*? What prevents the railroads from raising the prices they charge for delivering goods to Arizona?

3. *Kassel versus* Exxon. What are the grounds on which *Exxon* and *Kassel* can be distinguished? Is the evidence of discriminatory intent more persuasive in *Kassel*? Is the social purpose of the statute in *Exxon*, to preserve corner gas stations from absorption into the major oil producers, more substantial than the social purpose of the statute in *Kassel*? Is the statute in *Exxon* more likely to accomplish its purposes than the statute in *Kassel*? Regan, The Supreme Court and State Protectionism: Making Sense of the Dormant Commerce Clause, 84 Mich. L. Rev. 1091, 1185 (1986), argues that the Supreme Court should protect the national transportation network from state legislation that places excessive burdens on it because in such cases "there is a national interest in the existence of an effective transportation network linking the states." Should *Kassel* be treated as a transportation case in this sense? Should *Exxon*?

4. *Discrimination*. Did Iowa discriminate against interstate commerce? Are any of the in-staters who benefit from the statute competitors of out-of-staters who bear its costs? Are there nondiscriminatory explanations for the exceptions in the statute? (Is the "farm vehicles" exemption relevant at all?)

Justice Rehnquist argues that the existence of an undue burden triggers inquiry into whether the regulation is a pretext for discrimination but does not in itself establish a commerce clause violation. Is that an accurate characterization of *Southern Pacific* and *Bibb*?

5. *Economic isolationism?* If Iowa's statute is treated as nondiscriminatory, what benefits does it provide? Does it enhance safety in Iowa? In the region? Justice Brennan says that Iowa must bear its "fair share" of safety problems in the region. Suppose Iowa provides so little maintenance on its highways that shippers choose to send their trucks on routes through Missouri. Would Iowa's policy violate the commerce clause? If not, how might Justice Brennan distinguish that policy from the prohibition on sixty-five-foot trucks?

6. *"Obstructing" commerce.* In Buck v. Kuykendall, 267 U.S. 307 (1925), Buck, a citizen of Washington, wished to operate an "auto stage" line between Portland, Oregon, and Seattle, Washington. After obtaining a license from Oregon, he applied to the Washington authorities for a certificate that would allow him to begin operations. The certificate was denied on the ground that the route was already adequately served by railroads and four other auto stage lines. The Court held that the denial violated the commerce clause. The purpose was "the prohibition of competition." Its effect was "not merely to burden [interstate commerce], but to obstruct it." The Court also noted that the prohibition "[defeated] the purpose of Congress" in legislation providing federal aid for highway construction.

Aside from preemption, why should Washington be barred from limiting competition in transportation? Who bears the burdens and gains the benefits of Washington's statute? Assuming that the statute protects existing carriers from competition, is it protectionist in the sense of promoting local carriers at the expense of out-of-state ones? Does the case rest on the proposition that the Constitution embodies a substantive preference for free trade sufficient to place the burden of overcoming congressional inertia on those who support regulations that have significant, though nondiscriminatory, effects on interstate commerce?

7. *Judicial capacity.* During the late 1940s, Justice Black was concerned about the propriety of balancing as a technique of adjudication in other areas as well. Are Black's criticisms of the nature of the trial in *Southern Pacific* well taken? Why are legislators better, in Justice Black's view, than courts in balancing the probabilities that increased safety to workers will be offset by greater danger of grade-crossing accidents? Is this a factual or a normative issue? Are the considerations the same when the statute is discriminatory?

How apt were Justice Black's concerns in his *Southern Pacific* dissent over the capacity of trial and appellate courts to base their decisions on the results of such factual inquiries? Should a sound body of constitutional law include a rule that allows one state to maintain a policy that another may not, simply because the lawyers for the former were better than those for the latter? Note Justice Brennan's concern in *Kassel* that the Court rely on a legislature's actual purposes, not those asserted by the state's lawyers in litigation.

In balancing costs and benefits, should (can) the courts take into account broader social effects, such as the strengthening of the union movement by its ability to show potential members that it is a powerful force in politics? If they cannot, is the balance they strike an accurate one? Consider Justice Scalia's observation in his concurring opinion in CTS Corp. v. Dynamics Corp., 481 U.S. 69 (1987), where the Court rejected a commerce clause challenge to a state anti-takeover statute:

I do not know what qualifies us to make [the] ultimate (and most ineffable) judgment as to whether, given the importance-level x, and effectiveness-level y, the worth of the statute is "outweighed" by impact-on-commerce z. One commentator has suggested that, at least much of the time, we do not in fact mean what we say when we declare that statutes which neither discriminate against commerce nor present a threat of multiple and inconsistent burdens might nonetheless be unconstitutional under a "balancing" test. [Regan, supra.] If he is not correct, he ought to be. As long as a State's [law does] not discriminate against out-of-state interests, it should survive this Court's scrutiny. [Beyond] that, it is for Congress to prescribe its invalidity.

8. *Congress intervenes.* Do *Southern Pacific* and *Kassel* turn on implicit decisions that, under *Cooley*, the regulation of train and truck lengths is an inherently national subject? Who should bear the burden of persuading Congress that length regulation is desirable or undesirable?

In 1981, Congress enacted the Economic Recovery Tax Act, which substantially reduced individual income tax rates. In 1982, it enacted the Surface Transportation Act. One provision of the act recaptured some of the revenue lost in 1981 by increasing the excise tax on trucks and the tax on gasoline and diesel fuel. Trucking interests opposed these increased taxes but withdrew their opposition in exchange for another provision in the act eliminating the restrictions states placed on the use of doubles on interstate highways, to take effect in 1984. Although the increased tax on gasoline went into effect relatively quickly, collection of the excise tax on trucks was deferred until 1985 because of technical difficulties in defining truck weights. A 1984 amendment to the act allows the Secretary of Transportation, rather than the states, to invoke safety reasons for excluding doubles from some portions of the interstate system. Governors may petition the Secretary for such an exclusion and must demonstrate that the safety reasons are genuine. In addition, the Secretary may, with the permission of a state's Governor, open primary noninterstate highways to doubles. Is this congressional action relevant to the constitutional issues discussed in the cases?

Note: A Comparative Perspective

The 1991 General Agreement on Tariffs and Trade (GATT) bars "contracting parties" (including the United States) from imposing quantitative restrictions (quotas or embargoes) on the importation of goods. It allows parties to impose internal regulations on imports if the regulations do not discriminate among imports from different nations, do not protect domestic producers, and treat imported goods no less favorably than domestic ones. It also allows parties to adopt trade restrictions if they are necessary to protect human or animal life or health. Finally, parties may adopt trade measures that are necessary to conserve exhaustible natural resources; such measures must not be arbitrary and must be made in conjunction with restrictions on domestic production or consumption.

The U.S. Marine Mammal Protection Act (MMPA) was enacted in response to concern that too many dolphins were being taken along with tuna because fishers used a technique that caught dolphins in their nets along with the tuna. It specifies a permissible rate for incidental dolphin injuries from U.S. activities. It bans the importation of tuna from any nation that exceeds the U.S. rate. Mexico challenged the MMPA before a GATT panel. The panel found that the embargo violated the GATT. It held that exceptions from the ban on embargoes are to be narrowly construed. The embargo was not an internal regulation of trade because it regulated the production process (the manner by which tuna were caught) rather than the product (sales of tuna). It was not justified as necessary to protect human or animal life. That provision applied primarily to measures to safeguard life or health within the nation's territorial jurisdiction. The panel also found that the United States had not shown that an embargo was necessary to protect life or health, in light of other methods — such as negotiating international cooperative agreements — that could reduce the incidental taking of dolphins. The "exhaustible natural resources" provision was inapplicable because it, too, applied primarily to matters within the nation's territory, and because the MMPA was an arbitrary method of conserving dolphin, using the unpredictable factor of the U.S. taking rate rather than an objective limit on dolphin deaths as its standard. United States — Restrictions on Imports of Tuna (GATT Dispute Settlement Panel), 30 I.L.M. 1594 (1991).

What result in this dispute under commerce clause standards? For a discussion of the panel decision, see Note, International Trade v. Environmental Protection: The Case of the U.S. Embargo on Mexican Tuna, 24 Law & Poly. in Intl. Bus. 123 (1992).

Note: Taxation of Interstate Commerce

Consider Commonwealth Edison Co. v. Montana, 453 U.S. 609 (1981). In 1975, Montana imposed a tax on the severance of coal. The rate of 30 percent of the contract sales price was substantially higher than the rate in similar severance taxes in most other states. The proceeds of the tax were to be put into a permanent trust fund from which appropriations of principal could be made only by a three-fourths vote of both houses of the state legislature. The tax produced almost 20 percent of the state's revenue. Montana has 25 percent of the nation's coal reserves and over 50 percent of its low-sulfur coal reserves. Low-sulfur coal can be burned to produce electricity while complying with environmental regulations in plants that do not require extensive modification. Approximately 90 percent of the coal is shipped out of state.

The Court rejected a commerce clause challenge to the tax. It applied a four-part test as stated in Complete Auto Transit v. Brady, 430 U.S. 274 (1977): The tax must be "applied to an activity with a substantial nexus with the taxing State, [must be] fairly apportioned, [must] not discriminate against interstate commerce, and [must be] fairly related to services provided by the State." On the discrimination issue, the Court said:

> [The] Montana tax is computed at the same rate regardless of the final destination of the coal, and there is no suggestion here that tax is administered in a manner that departs from this evenhanded formula. We are not, therefore, confronted here with the type of differential tax treatment of interstate and intrastate commerce that the Court has found in other "discrimination" cases. [Philadelphia v. New Jersey.]
>
> Instead, the gravamen of appellants' claim is that a state tax must be considered discriminatory for purposes of the Commerce Clause if the tax burden is borne primarily by out-of-state consumers. . . .

[Appellants'] assertion that Montana may not "exploit" its "monopoly" position by exporting tax burdens to other States cannot rest on a claim that there is need to protect the out-of-state consumers of Montana coal from discriminatory tax treatment. [There] is no real discrimination in this case; the tax burden is borne according to the amount of coal consumed and not according to any distinction between in-state and out-of-state consumers. Rather, appellants assume that the Commerce Clause gives residents of one State a right of access at reasonable prices to resources located in another State that is richly endowed with such resources, without regard to whether and on what terms residents of the resource-rich State have access to resources. We are not convinced that the Commerce Clause, of its own force, gives the residents of one State the right to control in this fashion the terms of resource development and depletion in a sister State. Cf. [Philadelphia v. New Jersey.][8]

The Montana Supreme Court held that the coal severance tax is "imposed for the general support of the government" and we have no reason to question this characterization of the Montana tax as a general revenue tax.

[In] essence, appellants ask this Court to prescribe a test for the validity of state taxes that would require state and federal courts, as a matter of federal constitutional law, to calculate acceptable rates or levels of taxation of activities that are conceded to be legitimate subjects of taxation. This we decline to do.

In the first place, it is doubtful whether any legal test could adequately reflect the numerous and competing economic, geographic, demographic, social, and political considerations that must inform a decision about an acceptable rate or level of state taxation, and yet be reasonably capable of application in a wide variety of individual cases. [Under] our federal system, the determination is to be made by state legislatures in the first instance and, if necessary, by Congress, when particular state taxes are thought to be contrary to federal interests.[18]

The Court also rejected a preemption argument. Justice White began his concurring opinion by calling the case "very troublesome," but concluded:

Congress has the power to protect interstate commerce from intolerable or even undesirable burdens. It is also very much aware of the Nation's energy needs, of the Montana tax, and of the trend in the energy-rich States to aggrandize their position and perhaps lessen the tax burdens on their own citizens by imposing unusually high taxes on mineral extraction. But Congress is so far content to let the matter rest. [The] constitutional authority and the machinery to thwart efforts such as those of Montana, if thought unacceptable, are available to Congress, and surely Montana and other similarly situated States do not have the political power to impose their will on the rest of the country. As I presently see it, therefore, the better

8. Nor do we share appellants' apparent view that the Commerce Clause injects principles of antitrust law into the relations between the States by reference to such imprecise standards as whether one State is "exploiting" its "monopoly" position with respect to a natural resource when the flow of commerce among them is not otherwise impeded. The threshold questions whether a State enjoys a "monopoly" position and whether the tax burden is shifted out of state, rather than borne by in-state producers and consumers, would require complex factual inquiries about such issues as elasticity of demand for the product and alternative sources of supply. Moreover, under this approach, the constitutionality of a state tax could well turn on whether the in-state producer is able, through sales contracts or otherwise, to shift the burden of the tax forward to its out-of-state customers. . . .

18. The controversy over the Montana tax has not escaped the attention of the Congress. Several bills were introduced during the 96th Congress to limit the rate of state severance taxes. Similar bills have been introduced in the 97th Congress.

part of both wisdom and valor is to respect the judgment of the other branches of the Government.

Complete Auto Transit shows that the stated tests in cases challenging taxes as undue burdens on interstate commerce differ from the stated tests in cases challenging regulations. Should they? The doctrines applying the commerce clause to state taxes are extremely complex, but *Complete Auto Transit* and *Commonwealth Edison* suggest that doctrines regarding taxes and regulations are in the process of converging. Did Justice White properly allocate the burden of securing congressional action?

In connection with inferences from Congress's failure to act, consider the implications of the following sequence of cases. National Bellas Hess, Inc. v. Department of Revenue, 386 U.S. 753 (1967), held unconstitutional attempts by states to collect use taxes not from purchasers but from out-of-state mail-order sellers who had neither outlets nor sales representatives in the state. The Court held that the states violated the due process clause of the fourteenth amendment in attempting to tax entities that had insufficient connections with them. It also held that requiring the sellers to collect the use taxes imposed an unconstitutional burden on interstate commerce. Note that the due process holding probably (why only probably?) barred Congress from enacting a statute allowing states to require mail-order sellers to collect use taxes.

In Quill Corp. v. North Dakota, 504 U.S. 298 (1992), the Supreme Court revisited this issue. It overruled the due process holding of *National Bellas Hess* but reaffirmed the commerce clause holding. Five justices joined an opinion by Justice Stevens that justified the result on the ground that it developed a "bright-line rule" to

> demarcat[e] a discrete realm of commercial activity that is free from interstate taxation. [Like] other bright-line tests, the *Bellas Hess* rule appears artificial at the edges. [This] artificiality, however, is more than offset by the benefits of a clear rule. Such a rule firmly establishes the boundaries of legitimate state authority to impose a duty to collect sales and use taxes and reduces litigation concerning those taxes.

Justice Scalia, joined by Justices Kennedy and Thomas, concurred in the result, relying entirely on stare decisis considerations regarding the commerce clause holding.

Justice Stevens's opinion concluded by pointing out that the issue was "not only one that Congress may be better qualified to resolve, but also one that Congress has the ultimate power to resolve." It also noted that congressional action might have been "dictated" by the due process holding in *National Bellas Hess*, "but today we have put that problem to rest. Accordingly, Congress is now free to decide whether, when, and to what extent the States may burden interstate mail-order concerns with a duty to collect use taxes."

Note: Preemption

Should Congress alone deal with state regulations that assertedly interfere with interstate commerce? Congress may preempt state regulation. According to the Court, ["The] question whether a certain state action is pre-empted by federal law is one of congressional intent. 'The purpose of Congress is the ultimate touchstone.'" Gade v. National Solid Wastes Management Association, 505 U.S. 88 (1992), citing Allis-Chalmers Corp. v. Lueck, 471 U.S. 202, 206 (1985). Preemption decisions are often tied closely to the language and purposes of particular statutes, but there are some general themes in the law of preemption. Sometimes questions quite similar to those that arise under the Court's dormant commerce clause doctrine arise in connection with the interpretation of federal statutes.

The Court has distinguished three types of preemption. (1) Express preemption: Here a statute contains a provision specifically referring to preemption and indicating which state laws the national statute supplants. Note, however, that the courts will often be called on to interpret the precise scope of the express preemption provision, and that in doing so they may invoke more general concerns. (2) Field preemption: Here the scheme of federal regulation is "so pervasive as to make reasonable the inference that Congress left no room for the States to supplement it," Rice v. Santa Fe Elevator Corp., 331 U.S. 218, 230 (1947). (3) Conflict preemption: Here "compliance with both federal and state regulations is a physical impossibility," Florida Lime & Avocado Growers, Inc. v. Paul, 373 U.S. 132, 142-143 (1963), or state law "stands as an obstacle to the accomplishment and execution of the full purposes and objectives of Congress." Hines v. Davidowitz, 312 U.S. 52, 67 (1941).

Each method raises questions of characterization, in two directions: (a) What subjects did Congress expressly preempt, or what is the field that Congress has occupied? (b) Is the state regulation in question one that falls within the domain that Congress expressly preempted or occupied? What concerns influence the Court's approach to the characterization questions? Frequently the concerns that underlie dormant commerce clause analysis — national uniformity, interference with interstate commerce, preservation of a proper sphere for local regulation — affect the Court's decisions. For an overview of contemporary issues in preemption law, see Nelson, Preemption, 86 Va. L. Rev. 225 (2000).

The following cases illustrate some persistent themes and problems, but they are by no means comprehensive.

1. *Conflict and express preemption.* Consider *Gade,* supra. Illinois enacted two laws dealing with the licensing of workers who handle solid waste, for the stated purpose of "promot[ing] job safety" and "protect[ing] life, limb, and property." The laws required workers to take forty hours of approved training in Illinois, pass a written examination, and complete an annual refresher course. Federal regulations under the Occupational Safety and Health Act required that the workers receive a minimum of forty hours of instruction off-site and a minimum of three days of field experience under the supervision of a trained supervisor. A sharply divided Court held that the federal regulations preempted the state laws. Justice O'Connor's opinion for the Court found the state laws impliedly preempted "as in conflict with the full purposes and objectives of the OSH Act," which indicated that "Congress intended to subject employers and employees to only one set of regulations." Justice Kennedy, in an opinion concurring in the judgment, would have found express preemption because Congress intended to displace state regulations even when, as he believed was true in *Gade,* there was no actual conflict between the state laws and the federal regulations. Justice Souter, joined

by Justices Blackmun, Stevens, and Thomas, dissented. He relied on the "rule" that "traditional police powers of the State survive until Congress has made a purpose to pre-empt them clear."

Is the purpose of the state regulation in *Gade* workplace safety or safety of state citizens, including but not limited to workers? On what basis might the Court select the former characterization over the latter? Would the choice affect the result of the preemption analysis? Consider the proposition that dormant commerce clause concerns strongly influence the choice: National uniformity in workplace safety regulation is extremely important, whereas the varying social policies states might choose to pursue justify refraining from the broader characterization of the field.

2. *Field preemption.* Note the consequences of finding field preemption: There is no federal regulation with which the state law conflicts (otherwise preemption by conflict would occur); finding preemption therefore means that the matter is left unregulated by both federal and state law. Does that justify a strong presumption against preemption of this sort? What if a system of nonregulation makes social or economic sense? See Farmers Educational & Cooperative Union v. WDAY, Inc., 360 U.S. 525 (1959), holding that the Federal Communications Act, which required broadcasters to carry some political speeches without censoring them, occupied the field and therefore immunized broadcasters from liability under state libel laws.

3. *Preemption in the service of other interests.* Consider Perez v. Campbell, 402 U.S. 637 (1971): Arizona suspends the driver's license of people who have not satisfied judgments against them in accident cases. A discharge in a federal bankruptcy proceeding, which relieves the debtor of the duty to satisfy the judgment, does not lift the suspension, which thus remains as an inducement to satisfy the judgment. Adolfo Perez was in an accident in 1965. Judgment was entered against him on November 8, 1967. Two days earlier he had filed a petition in bankruptcy, and he received a discharge from all debts, including the accident judgment, on July 8, 1968. The Court held that Arizona's use of license suspension as a means of inducing financial responsibility conflicted with and so was preempted by the federal bankruptcy law. Four justices dissented, arguing that Arizona's purpose was to "assure driving competence" and therefore its statute did not conflict with federal law.

Perez may reflect the Court's view on the relative wisdom of the state and federal laws. In addition to *Perez*, consider Pennsylvania v. Nelson, 350 U.S. 497 (1956), which held that the federal Smith Act, prohibiting the knowing advocacy of the overthrow of the national government by force and violence, preempted the Pennsylvania Sedition Act. Nelson, a leader in the Communist Party, had been sentenced to twenty years in prison for violating the Pennsylvania act. In contemporaneous decisions, the Court was influenced by first amendment concerns to construe the Smith Act fairly narrowly.

Preemption may be used to avoid other constitutional issues. In addition to *Nelson*, consider that the Court's decision in *Perez* also involved Mrs. Perez, against whom the liability judgment had been entered because Arizona was a community property state. The Court unanimously found Arizona's statute preempted as to her. Might there be due process or equal protection problems in depriving her of her license "solely because she is the impecunious wife of an impecunious, negligent driver in a community property state," as Justice Blackmun put it? See also Note, Pre-emption as a Preferential Ground: A New Canon of Construction, 12 Stan. L. Rev. 208 (1959).

See also Crosby v. National Foreign Trade Council, 120 S. Ct. 2288 (2000), which relied on a statute delegating broad power to the President to devise a strategy for imposing economic sanctions on Burma to induce it to improve its human rights performance as the basis for finding preempted a Massachusetts statute barring the state government's departments from buying goods or services from companies doing business with Burma. The state statute, the Court held, stood as an obstacle to the accomplishment of the federal statute's purposes, and was inconsistent with Congress's purpose of ensuring that the President would have flexibility in devising strategies for inducing Burma to improve its performance.

4. *Federalism and preemption.* Individual justices' general attitudes about federalism may influence their decisions. See Note, The Preemption Doctrine: Shifting Perspectives on Federalism and the Burger Court, 75 Colum. L. Rev. 623 (1975), which surveys the changing doctrinal presumptions favoring and disfavoring findings of preemption. Preemption decisions may be influenced by the same considerations that enter into dormant commerce clause decisions. For example, finding that federal statutes "occupy the field" in some area may not be significantly different from finding that the area is inherently national under *Cooley*. Consider in this connection the history of Florida Lime & Avocado Growers v. Paul, supra. The Court decided by a five-to-four vote that federal marketing regulations did not preempt California's statute prohibiting the sale in California of avocados containing less than 8 percent of oil. The oil content is one measure of an avocado's maturity, and its maturity when picked affects its appearance and taste. Immature avocados may be indistinguishable in appearance on the grocer's shelf from mature ones, but they may become unpalatable after purchase. The federal marketing regulations for Florida avocados, developed by a committee of Florida growers, determined maturity based on a schedule of picking dates, sizes, and weights. As a result, some mature Florida avocados do not satisfy California's oil-content test. The majority held that California's statute did not conflict with the federal marketing system. Florida avocados could be left on their trees until they met the 8 percent oil requirement. "The maturity of avocados seems to be an inherently unlikely candidate for exclusive federal regulation. [The] supervision of the readying of foodstuffs for market has always been deemed a matter of peculiarly local concern."

Finding the record inadequate to determine whether California's statute unduly burdened or discriminated against interstate commerce, the Court remanded for a trial. It noted that "the Florida industry was well-developed when the California industry was in its infancy," that "the passage of the California statute was immediately and vigorously protested by Florida producers," and that there was "contemporaneous recognition that [the] statute severely restricted the access of Florida growers to [some California] markets." However, California growers have had "difficulty meeting the oil content requirement, and sizable shipments must be destroyed." Ten years later a federal district court in California held the California statute unconstitutional on commerce clause grounds.

The cases are discussed in Deutsch, Precedent and Adjudication, 83 Yale L.J. 1553 (1974), a profound and difficult work that ranges deeply into important matters of constitutional theory in general. What result in *Gade* under the commerce clause?

5. *An overview.* Consider the following argument: The courts will consider issues about the scope of preemption only when there are reasonable arguments supporting competing characterizations of what Congress sought to accomplish in expressly preempting, occupying the field, or enacting regulations with which the state laws are said to conflict. No matter how detailed the statutory scheme, it will be applied (or at least litigated) in situations that Congress did not anticipate. The courts will therefore be called on to fill gaps. In dormant commerce clause cases, the courts may say, "Leave the problem to Congress." In preemption cases, however, Congress has acted, and saying "Leave it to Congress" amounts to imposing on Congress a requirement of explicitness, usually in cases where it is relatively easy to find that Congress had not acted explicitly enough to displace state regulation.

Note: Concluding Observations

Consider Justice Scalia's assessment of the law in this area, as expressed in his opinion dissenting in relevant part in Tyler Pipe Industries, Inc. v. Washington State Department of Revenue, 483 U.S. 232 (1987), where the Court held unconstitutional some provisions of Washington's system of taxing goods in interstate commerce. Justice Scalia argued that

> to the extent that we have gone beyond guarding against rank discrimination against citizens of other States — which is regulated not by the Commerce Clause but by the Privileges and Immunities Clause — the Court for over a century has engaged in an enterprise that it has been unable to justify by textual support or even coherent nontextual theory, that it was almost certainly not intended to undertake, and that it has not undertaken very well.

He noted that "pre-emption of state legislation would automatically follow [if] the grant of power to Congress to regulate interstate commerce were exclusive," but added that

> the language of the Commerce Clause gives no indication of exclusivity. Nor can one assume generally that Congress' Article I powers are exclusive. [Furthermore], there is no correlative denial of power over commerce to the States [as] there is [with] the power to coin money or make treaties. [The] exclusivity rationale is infinitely less attractive today than it was in 1847. Now that we know interstate commerce embraces such activities as growing wheat for home consumption [*Wickard*] and local loan sharking [Perez v. United States, Chapter 2, section C, supra], it is more difficult to imagine what state activity would survive an exclusive Commerce Clause than to imagine what would be precluded.

Justice Scalia argued that the Court could not distinguish, as *Cooley* attempted to, among the subjects of the commerce power because the Constitution treats commerce "as a unitary subject," or between preempting state laws "*intended* to regulate commerce (as opposed to those intended, for example, to promote health)," because the distinction was "metaphysical, [not] useful as a practical technique for marking out the powers of separate sovereigns." He called "least plausible" the theory that in enforcing the negative Commerce Clause the Court is not applying a constitutional command at all, but is merely interpreting the will of Congress, whose silence in certain fields of interstate commerce (but not in others) is to be taken as a prohibition of regulation. There is no conceivable reason why congressional inaction under the Commerce Clause should be deemed to have the same pre-emptive effect elsewhere accorded only to congressional action. There, as elsewhere, "Congress' silence is just that — silence."

Are there plausible answers to this criticism? Consider whether the law in this area might be justified as articulating a series of canons of construction to be applied to whatever federal legislation there is that regulates the subject matter of the state laws at issue.

IV

The Distribution of
National Powers

A. INTRODUCTION

The Constitution distributes power horizontally as well as vertically. Dispersion of authority is a product not only of the separation between the national government and the states but also of the allocation of power among the legislative, executive, and judicial branches. This chapter explores the purposes and effects of that allocation.

The Federalist No. 47 (Madison)
(1787)

One of the principal objections inculcated by the more respectable adversaries to the Constitution is its supposed violation of the political maxim that the legislative, executive, and judiciary departments ought to be separate and distinct. . . .

The oracle who is always consulted and cited on this subject, is the celebrated Montesquieu.

The British constitution was to Montesquieu, [the] standard, or to use his own expression, [the] mirror of political liberty.

On the slightest view of the British Constitution, we must perceive that the legislative, executive, and judiciary departments are by no means totally separate and distinct from each other. . . .

[Thus, Montesquieu] did not mean that these departments ought to have no partial agency in, or no *control* over, the acts of each other. His meaning, [can] amount to no more than this, that where the *whole* power of one department is exercised by the same hands which possess the *whole* power of another department, the fundamental principles of a free constitution are subverted. . . .

The reasons on which Montesquieu grounds his maxim are a further demonstration of his meaning. "When the legislative and executive powers are united in the same person or body," says he, "there can be no liberty, because apprehensions may arise lest *the same* monarch or senate should *enact* tyrannical laws to execute them in a tyrannical manner." Again: "Were the power of judging joined with the legislative, the life and liberty of the subject would be exposed to arbitrary control, for *the judge* would then be *the legislator.* Were it joined to the executive power, *the judge* might behave with all the violence of *an oppressor.*" . . .

If we look into the constitutions of the several States we find that, notwithstanding the emphatical and, in some instances, the unqualified terms in which this axiom has been laid down, there is not a single instance in which the several departments of power have been kept absolutely separate and distinct. . . .

[The] charge brought against the proposed Constitution of violating the sacred maxim of free government is warranted neither by the real meaning annexed to that maxim by its author, nor by the sense in which it has hitherto been understood in America.

The Federalist No. 48 (Madison)
(1787)

It was shown in the last paper that the political apothegm there examined does not require that the legislative, executive, and judiciary departments should be wholly unconnected with each other. I shall undertake, in the next place, to show that unless these departments be so far connected and blended as to give to each a constitutional control over the others, the degree of separation which the maxim requires, as essential to a free government, can never in practice be duly maintained.

It is agreed on all sides that the powers properly belonging to one of the departments ought not to be directly and completely administered by either of the other departments. [After] discriminating, therefore, in theory, the several classes of power, as they may in their nature be legislative, executive or judiciary, the next and most difficult task is to provide some practical security for each, against the invasion of the others. What this security ought to be is the great problem to be solved.

Will it be sufficient to mark, with precision, the boundaries of these departments in the constitution of the government, and to trust to these parchment barriers against the encroaching spirit of power? This is the security which appears to have been principally relied on by the compilers of most of the American constitutions. But experience assures us that the efficacy of the provision has been greatly overrated; and that some more adequate defense is indispensably necessary for the more feeble against the more powerful members of the government. The legislative department is everywhere extending the sphere of its activity and drawing all power into its impetuous vortex. . . .

In a government where numerous and extensive prerogatives are placed in the hands of an hereditary monarch, the executive department is very justly regarded as the source of danger, and watched with all the jealousy which a zeal for liberty ought to inspire. In a democracy, where a multitude of people exercise in person the legislative functions and are continually exposed, by their incapacity for regular deliberation and concerted measures, to the ambitious intrigues of their executive magistrates, tyranny may well be apprehended, on some favorable emergency, to start up in the same quarter. But in a representative republic where the executive magistracy is carefully limited, both in the extent and the duration of its power; and where the legislative power is exercised by an assembly, which is inspired by a supposed influence over the people with an intrepid confidence in its own strength; which is sufficiently numerous to feel all the passions which actuate a multitude, yet not so numerous as to be incapable of pursuing the objects of its passions by means which reason prescribes; it is against the enterprising ambition of this department that the people ought to indulge all their jealousy and exhaust all their precautions.

Note: The Theory of Separation and Checks and Balances

1. *In general.* The Constitution distributes national power among the legislative, executive, and judicial branches of the national government. The resulting scheme is usually described as one of either "separation of powers" or "checks and balances." The former description captures the constitutional effort to allocate different sorts of power among three governmental entities that are constituted in different ways. The latter description, in some ways more accurate, focuses on the constitutional effort to ensure that the system will be able to guard against usurpation of authority by any one branch.

The two descriptions emphasize different aspects of the distribution of national powers. Indeed, to some extent the two work against each other. The principle of separation suggests three autonomous entities working independently. The principle of checks and balances suggests overlapping functions in which each branch is able to intrude on and thereby to check the power of the others. The constitutional framework is best understood as a scheme that embodies a partial, rather than complete, separation of powers, and that supplements the separation by creating devices by which one branch can monitor and check the others. In order to provide the important checking function, the Constitution had to allow some of the branches to play a role in functions assigned to the others.

The Constitution does not separate rigidly the powers of the three branches. For example, the President is expressly given a role in legislation: No law may be enacted without allowing him an opportunity to veto. On the other hand, the Senate is required to consent to presidential appointments, and the power to withhold consent has sometimes been important in permitting Congress to impose its views on the executive branch.

The roles of the respective branches are especially blurred in the area of foreign affairs. Congress is authorized to declare war, but the President is made commander-in-chief of the armed services. "The foreign relations powers appear not so much 'separated' as fissured, along jagged lines indifferent to classical categories of governmental power. [Irregular], uncertain division renders claims of usurpation more difficult to establish." L. Henkin, Foreign Affairs and the Constitution 32 (1965).

2. *The purposes of separation and checks.* Throughout American history the distribution of national powers has been said to serve two distinct purposes. The first is efficiency. In this view, a division of labor among the various branches makes government more efficient, especially because of the concentration of executive power in the President, who can act with dispatch. The second purpose is the prevention of tyranny. The separation of powers diffuses governmental

power, diminishing the likelihood that any one branch will be able to use its power against the citizenry.

3. *The constitutional distribution of powers: contemporary criticism.* The constitutional distribution of national powers has come under sharp attack in the late twentieth century. See, e.g., T. Lowi, The End of Liberalism (2d ed. 1980); Cutler and Johnson, Regulation and the Political Process, 84 Yale L.J. 1395 (1975). Part of the attack is based on the perceived inefficiency of the system. The concern is that in light of the existence of powerful checks, it is difficult for the federal government to accomplish anything. Instead, it is reduced to a series of stalemates. Sometimes this critique is attached to a belief that the separation of powers interferes with democratic processes by preventing popular majorities from bringing about change. This belief in turn raises the question whether insulation from dramatic change is a good or a bad thing.

A related attack is that the separation of powers scheme, instead of solving the problem of factions, aggravates it by allowing well-organized private groups to block necessary regulation. In these circumstances, it is sometimes urged that constitutional doctrine should be altered to recognize a greater role for the President.

A different attack is that power is now concentrated in the executive branch and that it is thus necessary to restore Congress to its original status of preeminence. Finally, it is sometimes suggested that the growth of an enormous national bureaucracy, operating for the most part within the executive branch, has fundamentally altered the original constitutional framework and requires some sort of response if the original constitutional concerns are to be satisfied. We return to these issues below.

4. *The judicial role.* What role should the courts play in preserving the barriers against combination of powers and the maintenance of checks and balances? Should the judicial role differ from that in cases involving (1) civil rights and liberties or (2) federalism disputes?

Consider J. Choper, Judicial Review and the National Political Process 263, 269, 275 (1982):

> The federal judiciary should not decide constitutional questions concerning the respective powers of Congress and the President vis-à-vis one another; rather, the ultimate constitutional issues [should] be held nonjusticiable, their final resolution to be remitted to the interplay of the national political process. [The] important message [to] be gleaned from [the] founders' thinking is that the checks on legislative autocracy that they contemplated exist independently of judicial supervision of the constitutionally mandated separation of powers between the President and Congress.

Does this argument disregard the possibility that a judicial role is necessary to prevent a stalemate between the branches and potential constitutional crises? Does it overemphasize the usefulness of nonjudicial techniques in reaching accommodation? Although the Court has not considered separation of powers cases to be nonjusticiable, it has had relatively few occasions in which to set out the governing constitutional principles. It is for this reason that there is perhaps less guidance here than in other areas of constitutional law. What principles there are derive from a relatively few "great cases" involving conflicts between two branches of the federal government. Much of the "law" in the area therefore amounts to historical practices, informal and formal, of the various branches and to understandings that take the Constitution as their starting point, but that derive in large part from perceived practical necessities.

Note: A Comparative Perspective

In light of these criticisms, would American government be improved by abandoning the separation of powers model and adopting a parliamentary system? Under such a system, the chief executive is chosen by, and responsible to, the majority party in the legislature. Although the chief executive can be deposed by a vote of no confidence, he or she is typically not constrained by the "gridlock" that has dominated modern American politics. Over a century ago, Woodrow Wilson, in his classic study, Congressional Government (1885), praised the virtues of parliamentary systems:

> In both England and France a ministry composed of the chief officers of the executive departments are constituted at once the leaders of legislation and the responsible heads of administration, — a binding link between the legislative and executive branches of the government. In this regard these two systems present a strong contrast to our own. They recognize and support simple, straightforward, inartificial party government, under a standing committee of responsible party leaders, bringing legislature and executive side by side in intimate but open cooperation; whilst we, preferring to keep Congress and the departments at arm's length, permit only a less direct government by party majorities, checking party action by a complex legislative machinery of [legislative committees].

Id at 128-129.

For more recent arguments in favor of parliamentarianism, see C. Hardin, Presidential Power and Accountability: Toward a New Constitution (1974); J. M. Burns, The Power to Lead: The Crisis of the American Presidency (1984). Consider whether these approaches overlook the value of conflict between the branches as a method of formulating public policy that takes into account a variety of perspectives. See Sargentich, The Limits of the Parliamentary Critique of the Separation of Powers, 34 Wm. & Mary L. Rev. 679, 730 (1993):

> The parliamentary critique's leading image of government is of an efficient machine of centralized decisionmaking that sets its goals clearly, accomplishes them smoothly, and does not engage in wrangling about ends or means. . . .
>
> [In] the end the President's success becomes the definition of success in general. It matters not at all what Congress proposes. The underlying notion is that the government's manager — the President in our system, the Prime Minister in the British system — needs to be able to manage. This view removes from consideration the possibility that another branch of government might have something usefully different to say about public policy. . . .
>
> Managerialists may be frustrated because Congress does not speak their language, but that is precisely the point: Congress speaks the language not of managers, but of democratic process, messy though it is.

For an argument in favor of "constrained parliamentarianism," which combines the British model of a unified legislative and executive branch with various constraints on parliamentary supremacy, see Ackerman, The New Separation of Powers, 113 Harv. L. Rev. 634 (2000).

B.   A CASE STUDY: PRESIDENTIAL SEIZURE

Youngstown Sheet & Tube Co. v. Sawyer (The Steel Seizure Case)

343 U.S. 579 (1952)

MR. JUSTICE BLACK delivered the opinion of the Court.

We are asked to decide whether President Truman was acting within his constitutional power when he issued an order directing the Secretary of Commerce to take possession of and operate most of the Nation's steel mills. The mill owners argue that the President's order amounts to lawmaking, a legislative function which the Constitution has expressly confided to the Congress and not to the President. The Government's position is that the order was made on findings of the President that his action was necessary to avert a national catastrophe which would inevitably result from a stoppage of steel production, and that in meeting this grave emergency the President was acting within the aggregate of his constitutional powers as the Nation's Chief Executive and the Commander in Chief of the Armed Forces of the United States. The issue emerges here from the following series of events:

In the latter part of 1951, a dispute arose between the steel companies and their employees over terms and conditions that should be included in new collective bargaining agreements. [On] April 4, 1952, the Union gave notice of a nation-wide strike called to begin at 12:01 A.M. April 9. The indispensability of steel as a component of substantially all weapons and other war materials led the President to believe that the proposed work stoppage would immediately jeopardize our national defense and that governmental seizure of the steel mills was necessary in order to assure the continued availability of steel. Reciting these considerations for his action, the President, a few hours before the strike was to begin, issued Executive Order 10340. [The] order directed the Secretary of Commerce to take possession of most of the steel mills and keep them running. [The] next morning the President sent a message to Congress reporting his action.

[Twelve] days later he sent a second message. [Congress] has taken no action. . . .

[The Court noted that the companies had obeyed the order under protest and brought suit against the Secretary of Commerce in district court. On April 30, that court issued a temporary restraining order prohibiting the Secretary from continuing the seizure and possession of the plants. On the same day, the district court's order was stayed by the court of appeals. The Supreme Court granted certiorari on May 3 and heard argument on May 12; the decision was announced on June 2.]

The President's power, if any, to issue the order must stem either from an act of Congress or from the Constitution itself. There is no statute that expressly authorizes the President to take possession of property as he did here. Nor is there any act of Congress to which our attention has been directed from which such a power can fairly be implied. [There] are two statutes which do authorize the President to take both personal and real property under certain conditions. However, the Government admits that these conditions were not met and that the President's order was not rooted in either of the statutes. The Government refers to the seizure provisions of one of these statutes as "much too cumbersome, involved, and time-consuming for the crisis which was at hand."

Moreover, the use of the seizure technique to solve labor disputes in order to prevent work stoppages was not only unauthorized by any congressional enactment; prior to this controversy, Congress had refused to adopt that method of settling labor disputes. When the Taft-Hartley Act was under consideration in 1947, Congress rejected an amendment which would have authorized such governmental seizures in cases of emergency. . . .

It is clear that if the President had authority to issue the order he did, it must be found in some provision of the Constitution. And it is not claimed that express constitutional language grants this power to the President. The contention is that presidential power should be implied from the aggregate of his powers under the Constitution. Particular reliance is placed on provisions in Article II which say that "The executive Power shall be vested in a President . . ."; that "he shall take Care that the Laws be faithfully executed"; and that he "shall be Commander in Chief of the Army and Navy of the United States."

The order cannot properly be sustained as an exercise of the President's military power as Commander in Chief of the Armed Forces. The Government attempts to do so by citing a number of cases upholding broad powers in military commanders engaged in day-to-day fighting in a theater of war. Such cases need not concern us here. Even though "theater of war" be an expanding concept, we cannot with faithfulness to our constitutional system hold that the Commander in Chief of the Armed Forces has the ultimate power as such to take possession of private property in order to keep labor disputes from stopping production. This is a job for the Nation's lawmakers, not for its military authorities.

Nor can the seizure order be sustained because of the several constitutional provisions that grant executive power to the President. In the framework of our Constitution, the President's power to see that the laws are faithfully executed refutes the idea that he is to be a lawmaker. The Constitution limits his functions in the lawmaking process to the recommending of laws he thinks wise and the vetoing of laws he thinks bad. And the Constitution is neither silent nor equivocal about who shall make laws which the President is to execute. The first section of the first article says that "All legislative Powers herein granted shall be vested in a Congress of the United States. . . ." After granting many powers to the Congress, Article I goes on to provide that Congress may "make all Laws which shall be necessary and proper for carrying into Execution the foregoing Powers, and all other Powers vested by this Constitution in the Government of the United States, or in any Department or Officer thereof."

The President's order does not direct that a congressional policy be executed in a manner prescribed by Congress — it directs that a presidential policy be executed in a manner prescribed by the President. The preamble of the order itself, like that of many statutes, sets out reasons why the President believes certain policies should be adopted, proclaims these policies as rules of conduct to be followed, and again, like a statute, authorizes a government official to promulgate additional rules and regulations consistent with the policy proclaimed and needed to carry that policy into execution. The power of Congress to adopt such public policies as those proclaimed by the order is beyond question. [The] Constitution does not subject this lawmaking power of Congress to presidential or military supervision or control.

It is said that other Presidents without congressional authority have taken possession of private business enterprises in order to settle labor disputes. But even if this be true, Congress has not thereby lost its exclusive constitutional authority to make laws necessary and proper to carry out the powers vested by the Constitution "in the Government of the United States, or any Department or Officer thereof."

The Founders of this Nation entrusted the lawmaking power to the Congress alone in both good and bad times. It would do no good to recall the historical events, the fears of power and the hopes for freedom that lay behind their choice. Such a review would but confirm our holding that this seizure order cannot stand.

The judgment of the District Court is affirmed.

MR. JUSTICE FRANKFURTER, concurring.

[We] must [put] to one side consideration of what powers the President would have had if there had been no legislation whatever bearing on the authority asserted by the seizure, or if the seizure had been only for a short, explicitly temporary period, to be terminated automatically unless Congressional approval were given. . . .

The question before the Court comes in this setting. Congress has frequently — at least 16 times since 1916 — specifically provided for executive seizure of production, transportation, communications, or storage facilities. In every case it has qualified this grant of power with limitations and safeguards. This body of enactments demonstrates that Congress deemed seizure so drastic a power as to require that it be carefully circumscribed whenever the President was vested with this extraordinary authority. . . .

In any event, nothing can be plainer than that Congress made a conscious choice of policy in a field full of perplexity and peculiarly within legislative responsibility for choice. In formulating legislation for dealing with industrial conflicts, Congress could not more clearly and emphatically have withheld authority than it did in [the Taft-Hartley Act of] 1947. . . .

It cannot be contended that the President would have had power to issue this order had Congress explicitly negated such authority in formal legislation. Congress has expressed its will to withhold this power from the President as though it had said so in so many words. . . .

To be sure, the content of the three authorities of government is not to be derived from an abstract analysis. The areas are partly interacting, not wholly disjointed. The Constitution is a framework for government. Therefore the way the framework has consistently operated fairly establishes that it has operated according to its true nature. Deeply embedded traditional ways of conducting government cannot supplant the Constitution or legislation, but they give meaning to the words of a text or supply them. It is an inadmissibly narrow conception of American constitutional law to confine it to the words of the Constitution and to disregard the gloss which life has written upon them. In short, a systematic, unbroken, executive practice, long pursued to the knowledge of the Congress and never before questioned, engaged in by Presidents who have also sworn to uphold the Constitution, making as it were such exercise of power part of the structure of our government, may be treated as a gloss on "executive Power" vested in the President by §1 of Art. II. . . .

Down to the World War II period, [the] record is barren of instances comparable to the one before us. [In] this case, reliance on the powers that flow from declared war has been commendably disclaimed by the Solicitor General. Thus the list of executive assertions of the power of seizure in circumstances comparable to the present reduces to three in the six-month period from June to December of 1941. [Without] passing on their validity, as we are not called upon to do, it suffices to say that these three isolated instances do not add up, either in number, scope, duration or contemporaneous legal justification, to the necessary kind of executive construction of the Constitution. [Nor] do they come to us sanctioned by long-continued acquiescence of Congress giving decisive weight to a construction by the Executive of its powers. [No] doubt a government with distributed authority, subject to be challenged in the courts of law, at least long enough to consider and adjudicate the challenge, labors under restrictions from which other governments are free. It has not been our tradition to envy such governments. In any event our government was designed to have such restrictions. The price was deemed not too high in view of the safeguards which these restrictions afford. . . .

[Justice Frankfurter added a lengthy historical appendix to his opinion.]

MR. JUSTICE JACKSON, concurring in the judgment and opinion of the Court.

[A] judge, like an executive adviser, may be surprised at the poverty of really useful and unambiguous authority applicable to concrete problems of executive power as they actually present themselves. Just what our forefathers did envision, or would have envisioned had they foreseen modern conditions, must be divined from materials almost as enigmatic as the dreams Joseph was called upon to interpret for Pharaoh. A century and a half of partisan debate and scholarly speculation yields no net result but only supplies more or less apt quotations from respected sources on each side of any question. They largely cancel each other. And court decisions are indecisive because of the judicial practice of dealing with the largest questions in the most narrow way.

The actual art of governing under our Constitution does not and cannot conform to judicial definitions of the power of any of its branches based on isolated clauses or even single Articles torn from context. While the Constitution diffuses power the better to secure liberty, it also contemplates that practice will integrate the dispersed powers into a workable government. It enjoins upon its branches separateness but interdependence, autonomy but reciprocity. Presidential powers are not fixed but fluctuate, depending upon their disjunction or conjunction with those of Congress. We may well begin by a somewhat over-simplified grouping of practical situations in which a President may doubt, or others may challenge, his powers, and by distinguishing roughly the legal consequences of this factor of relativity.

1. When the President acts pursuant to an express or implied authorization of Congress, his authority is at its maximum, for it includes all that he possesses in his own right plus all that Congress can delegate. In these circumstances, and in these only, may he be said (for what it may be worth) to personify the federal sovereignty. If his act is held unconstitutional under these circumstances, it usually

means that the Federal Government as an undivided whole lacks power. A seizure executed by the President pursuant to an Act of Congress would be supported by the strongest of presumptions and the widest latitude of judicial interpretation, and the burden of persuasion would rest heavily upon any who might attack it.

2. When the President acts in absence of either a congressional grant or denial of authority, he can only rely upon his own independent powers, but there is a zone of twilight in which he and Congress may have concurrent authority, or in which its distribution is uncertain. Therefore, congressional inertia, indifference or quiescence may sometimes, at least as a practical matter, enable, if not invite, measures on independent presidential responsibility. In this area, any actual test of power is likely to depend on the imperatives of events and contemporary imponderables rather than on abstract theories of law.

3. When the President takes measures incompatible with the expressed or implied will of Congress, his power is at its lowest ebb, for then he can rely only upon his own constitutional powers minus any constitutional powers of Congress over the matter. Courts can sustain exclusive presidential control in such a case only by disabling the Congress from acting upon the subject. Presidential claim to a power at once so conclusive and preclusive must be scrutinized with caution, for what is at stake is the equilibrium established by our constitutional system.

Into which of these classifications does this executive seizure of the steel industry fit? It is eliminated from the first by admission, for it is conceded that no congressional authorization exists for this seizure. . . .

Can it then be defended under flexible tests available to the second category? It seems clearly eliminated from that class because Congress has not left seizure of private property an open field but has covered it by three statutory policies inconsistent with this seizure. . . .

This leaves the current seizure to be justified only by the severe tests under the third grouping, where it can be supported only by any remainder of executive power after subtraction of such powers as Congress may have over the subject. In short, we can sustain the President only by holding that seizure of such strike-bound industries is within his domain and beyond control by Congress. . . .

The Solicitor General seeks the power of seizure in three clauses of the Executive Article, the first reading, "The executive Power shall be vested in a President of the United States of America." [I] quote the interpretation which his brief puts upon it: "In our view, this clause constitutes a grant of all the executive powers of which the Government is capable." If that be true, it is difficult to see why the forefathers bothered to add several specific items, including some trifling ones.

The example of such unlimited executive power that must have most impressed the forefathers was the prerogative exercised by George III, and the description of its evils in the Declaration of Independence leads me to doubt that they were creating their new Executive in his image. [And] if we seek instruction from our own times, we can match it only from the executive powers in those governments we disparagingly describe as totalitarian. I cannot accept the view that this clause is a grant in bulk of all conceivable executive power but regard it as an allocation to the presidential office of the generic powers thereafter stated.

The clause on which the Government next relies is that "The President shall be Commander in Chief of the Army and Navy of the United States. . . ." These cryptic words [imply] something more than an empty title. But just what authority goes with the name has plagued presidential advisers who would not waive or narrow it by nonassertion yet cannot say where it begins or ends. It undoubtedly puts the Nation's armed forces under presidential command. Hence, this loose appellation is sometimes advanced as support for any presidential action, internal or external, involving use of force, the idea being that it vests power to do anything, anywhere, that can be done with an army or navy.

That seems to be the logic of an argument tendered at our bar — that the President having, on his own responsibility, sent American troops abroad derives from that act "affirmative power" to seize the means of producing a supply of steel for them. . . .

I cannot foresee all that it might entail if the Court should indorse this argument. Nothing in our Constitution is plainer than that declaration of a war is entrusted only to Congress. Of course, a state of war may in fact exist without a formal declaration. But no doctrine that the Court could promulgate would seem to me more sinister and alarming than that a President whose conduct of foreign affairs is so largely uncontrolled, and often even is unknown, can vastly enlarge his mastery over the internal affairs of the country by his own commitment of the Nation's armed forces to some foreign venture. I do not, however, find it necessary or appropriate to consider the legal status of the Korean enterprise to discountenance argument based on it.

Assuming that we are in a war *de facto*, whether it is or is not a war *de jure*, does that empower the Commander in Chief to seize industries he thinks necessary to supply our army? The Constitution expressly places in Congress power "to raise and *support* Armies" and "to *provide* and *maintain* a Navy." (Emphasis supplied.) This certainly lays upon Congress primary responsibility for supplying the armed forces. Congress alone controls the raising of revenues and their appropriation and may determine in what manner and by what means they shall be spent for military and naval procurement. . . .

There are indications that the Constitution did not contemplate that the title Commander in Chief *of the Army and Navy* will constitute him also Commander in Chief of the country, its industries and its inhabitants. He has no monopoly of "war powers," whatever they are. . . .

The third clause in which the Solicitor General finds seizure powers is that "he shall take Care that the Laws be faithfully executed. . . ." That authority must be matched against words of the Fifth Amendment that "No person shall be . . . deprived of life, liberty or property, without due process of law. . . ." One gives a governmental authority that reaches so far as there is law, the other gives a private right that authority shall go no farther. These signify about all there is of the principle that ours is a government of laws, not of men, and that we submit ourselves to rulers only if under rules.

The Solicitor General lastly grounds support of the seizure upon nebulous, inherent powers never expressly granted but said to have accrued to the office from the customs and claims of preceding administrations. The plea is for a resulting power to deal with a crisis or an emergency according to the necessities of the case, the unarticulated assumption being that necessity knows no law.

Loose and irresponsible use of adjectives colors all nonlegal and much legal discussion of presidential powers. "Inherent" powers, "implied" powers, "incidental" powers, "plenary" powers, "war" powers and "emergency" powers are used, often interchangeably and without fixed or ascertainable meanings.

The vagueness and generality of the clauses that set forth presidential powers afford a plausible basis for pressures within and without an administration for presidential action beyond that supported by those whose responsibility it is to defend his actions in court. The claim of inherent and unrestricted presidential powers has long been a persuasive dialectical weapon in political controversy. While it is not surprising that counsel should grasp support from such unadjudicated claims of power, a judge cannot accept self-serving press statements of the attorney for one of the interested parties as authority in answering a constitutional question, even if the advocate was himself. But prudence has counseled that actual reliance on such nebulous claims stop short of provoking a judicial test. . . .

The appeal, however, that we declare the existence of inherent powers ex necessitate to meet an emergency asks us to do what many think would be wise, although it is something the forefathers omitted. They knew what emergencies were, knew the pressures they engender for authoritative action, knew, too, how they afford a ready pretext for usurpation. We may also suspect that they suspected that emergency powers would tend to kindle emergencies. Aside from suspension of the privilege of the writ of habeas corpus in time of rebellion or invasion, when the public safety may require it, they made no express provision for exercise of extraordinary authority because of a crisis. I do not think we rightfully may so amend their work. . . .

In view of the ease, expedition and safety with which Congress can grant and has granted large emergency powers, certainly ample to embrace this crisis, I am quite unimpressed with the argument that we should affirm possession of them without statute. Such power either has no beginning or it has no end. If it exists, it need submit to no legal restraint. I am not alarmed that it would plunge us straightway into dictatorship, but it is at least a step in that wrong direction.

As to whether there is imperative necessity for such powers, it is relevant to note the gap that exists between the President's paper powers and his real powers. The Constitution does not disclose the measure of the actual controls wielded by the modern presidential office. That instrument must be understood as an Eighteenth-Century sketch of a government hoped for, not as a blueprint of the Government that is. Vast accretions of federal power, eroded from that reserved by the States, have magnified the scope of presidential activity. Subtle shifts take place in the centers of real power that do not show in the face of the Constitution.

Executive power has the advantage of concentration in a single head in whose choice the whole Nation has a part, making him the focus of public hopes and expectations. In drama, magnitude and finality his decisions so far overshadow any others that almost alone he fills the public eye and ear. No other personality in public life can begin to compete with him in access to the public mind through modern methods of communications. By his prestige as head of state and his influence upon public opinion he exerts a leverage upon those who are supposed to check and balance his power which often cancels their effectiveness.

Moreover, rise of the party system has made a significant extraconstitutional supplement to real executive power. No appraisal of his necessities is realistic which overlooks that he heads a political system as well as a legal system. Party loyalties and interests, sometimes more binding than law, extend his effective control into branches of government other than his own and he often may win, as a political leader, what he cannot command under the Constitution. . . .

But I have no illusion that any decision by this Court can keep power in the hands of Congress if it is not wise and timely in meeting its problems. A crisis that challenges the President equally, or perhaps primarily, challenges Congress. If not good law, there was worldly wisdom in the maxim attributed to Napoleon that "The tools belong to the man who can use them." We may say that power to legislate for emergencies belongs in the hands of Congress, but only Congress itself can prevent power from slipping through its fingers.

The essence of our free Government is "leave to live by no man's leave, underneath the law" — to be governed by those impersonal forces which we call law. Our Government is fashioned to fulfill this concept so far as humanly possible. [The] executive action we have here originates in the individual will of the President and represents an exercise of authority without law. No one, perhaps not even the President, knows the limits of the power he may seek to exert in this instance and the parties affected cannot learn the limit of their rights. We do not know today what powers over labor or property would be claimed to flow from Government possession if we should legalize it, what rights to compensation would be claimed or recognized, or on what contingency it would end. With all its defects, delays and inconveniences, men have discovered no technique for long preserving free government except that the Executive be under the law, and that the law be made by parliamentary deliberations.

Such institutions may be destined to pass away. But it is the duty of the Court to be last, not first, to give them up.

[The concurring opinions of Justices Burton and Clark are omitted.]

MR. JUSTICE DOUGLAS, concurring. . . .

The legislative nature of the action taken by the President seems to me to be clear. . . .

[The] President might seize and the Congress by subsequent action might ratify the seizure. But until and unless Congress acted, no condemnation would be lawful. The branch of government that has the power to pay compensation for a seizure is the only one able to authorize a seizure or make lawful one that the President has effected. That seems to me to be the necessary result of the condemnation provision in the Fifth Amendment. It squares with the theory of checks and balances expounded by Mr. Justice Black in the opinion of the Court in which I join.

If we sanctioned the present exercise of power by the President, we would be expanding Article II of the Constitution and rewriting it to suit the political conveniences of the present emergency. . . .

We pay a price for our system of checks and balances, for the distribution of power among the three branches of government. It is a price that today may seem exorbitant to many. Today a kindly President uses the seizure power to effect a wage increase and to keep the steel furnaces in production. Yet tomorrow another President might use the same power to prevent a wage increase, to curb trade-unionists, to regiment labor as oppressively as industry thinks it has been regimented by this seizure.

MR. CHIEF JUSTICE VINSON, with whom MR. JUSTICE REED and MR. JUSTICE MINTON join, dissenting.

The President of the United States directed the Secretary of Commerce to take temporary possession of the Nation's steel mills during the existing emergency because "a work stoppage would immediately jeopardize and imperil our national defense and the defense of those joined with us in resisting aggression, and would add to the continuing danger of our soldiers, sailors, and airmen engaged in combat in the field." . . .

In passing upon the question of Presidential powers in this case, we must first consider the context in which those powers were exercised. . . .

The President has the duty to execute [legislative programs.] Their successful execution depends upon continued production of steel and stabilized prices for steel. Accordingly, when the collective bargaining agreements between the Nation's steel producers and their employees, represented by the United Steel Workers, were due to expire on December 31, 1951, and a strike shutting down the entire basic steel industry was threatened, the President acted to avert a complete shutdown of steel production. . . .

One is not here called upon even to consider the possibility of executive seizure of a farm, a corner grocery store or even a single industrial plant. Such considerations arise only when one ignores the central fact of this case — that the Nation's entire basic steel production would have shut down completely if there had been no Government seizure. Even ignoring for the moment whatever confidential information the President may possess as "the Nation's organ for foreign affairs," the uncontroverted affidavits in this record amply support the finding that "a work stoppage would immediately jeopardize and imperil our national defense."

Plaintiffs do not remotely suggest any basis for rejecting the President's finding that any stoppage of steel production would immediately place the Nation in peril. [Under the plaintiffs'] view, the President is left powerless at the very moment when the need for action may be most pressing and when no one, other than he, is immediately capable of action. Under this view, he is left powerless because a power not expressly given to Congress is nevertheless found to rest exclusively with Congress. [But the] whole of the "executive Power" is vested in the President. . . .

This comprehensive grant of the executive power to a single person was bestowed soon after the country had thrown the yoke of monarchy. Only by instilling initiative and vigor in all of the three departments of Government, declared Madison, could tyranny in any form be avoided. [It] is thus apparent that the Presidency was deliberately fashioned as an office of power and independence. Of course, the Framers created no autocrat capable of arrogating any power unto himself at any time. But neither did they create an automaton impotent to exercise the powers of Government at a time when the survival of the Republic itself may be at stake. . . .

A review of executive action demonstrates that our Presidents have on many occasions exhibited the leadership contemplated by the Framers when they made the President Commander in Chief, and imposed upon him the trust to "take Care that the Laws be faithfully executed." With or without explicit statutory authorization, Presidents have at such times dealt with national emergencies by acting promptly and resolutely to enforce legislative programs, at least to save those programs until Congress could act. Congress and the courts have responded to such executive initiative with consistent approval. . . .

[Chief Justice Vinson discussed historical practices, including:]

In an action furnishing a most apt precedent for this case, President Lincoln without statutory authority directed the seizure of rail and telegraph lines leading to Washington. [In] his autobiography, President [Theodore] Roosevelt expounded the "Stewardship Theory" of Presidential power, stating that "the executive is subject only to the people, and, under the Constitution, bound to serve the people affirmatively in cases where the Constitution does not explicitly forbid him to render the service." . . .

[During] World War I, President Wilson established a War Labor Board without awaiting specific direction by Congress. [Twenty years later] the President directed seizure of the Nation's coal mines to remove an obstruction to the effective prosecution of the war. . . .

[This] is but a cursory summary of executive leadership. But it amply demonstrates that Presidents have taken prompt action to enforce the laws and protect the country whether or not Congress happened to provide in advance for the particular method of execution. [The] fact that Congress and the courts have consistently recognized and given their support to such executive action indicates that such a power of seizure has been accepted throughout our history. . . .

Much of the argument in this case has been directed at straw men. We do not now have before us the case of a President acting solely on the basis of his own notions of the public welfare. Nor is there any question of unlimited executive power in this case. The President himself closed the door to any such claim when he sent his Message to Congress stating his purpose to abide by any action of Congress, whether approving or disapproving his seizure action. Here, the President immediately made sure that Congress was fully informed of the temporary action he had taken only to preserve the legislative programs from destruction until Congress could act.

The absence of a specific statute authorizing seizure of the steel mills as a mode of executing the laws — both the military procurement program and the anti-inflation program — has not until today been thought to prevent the President from executing the laws. Unlike an administrative commission confined to the enforcement of the statute under which it was created, or the head of a department when administering a particular statute, the President is a constitutional officer charged with taking care that a "mass of legislation" be executed. Flexibility as to mode of execution to meet critical situations is a matter of practical necessity. . . .

The broad executive power granted by Article II to an officer on duty 365 days a year cannot, it is said, be invoked to avert disaster. Instead, the President must confine himself to sending a message to Congress recommending action. Under this messenger-boy concept of the Office, the President cannot even act to preserve legislative programs from destruction so that Congress will have something left to act upon. There is no judicial finding that the executive action was unwarranted because there was in fact no basis for the President's finding of the existence of an emergency for, under this view, the gravity of the emergency and the immediacy of the threatened disaster are considered irrelevant as a matter of law. . . .

Note: Youngstown *and the Power of the President*

1. *Background.* The Steel Seizure Case was decided against a complex background. At the end of 1950, U.S. steel producers and the steelworkers union had agreed on a wage increase. Shortly thereafter, however, the Economic Stabiliza-

tion Agency effectively froze all price and wage increases, thus preventing implementation of the agreement. In these circumstances, the labor force threatened a strike in December 1951. Because the President feared that a strike would endanger the Korean effort, he prevailed on the union to postpone the strike while his Wage Stabilization Board — made up of representatives of steel producers, workers, and the general public — could study the problem. The board recommended certain staggered wage increases and union benefits, but the proposals were rejected by the industry. The steelworkers union set a strike date for April 9, 1952.

At this time, President Truman's popularity, which had soared at the start of the Korean War, had fallen drastically. Disillusionment over the war effort, fear of economic deterioration, charges that the administration was riddled with Communism and corruption, and numerous political defeats in Congress had contributed to Truman's announcement that he would not run for reelection that year. Despite the decline in his popularity, Truman refused to waver on his plans in Korea or — more particularly — in his refusal to impose any labor injunctions that might be available to him through the Taft-Hartley Act (a measure that had been enacted over his veto). Truman had had a long and close political alliance with organized labor. In order to preserve steel production, Truman set out an executive order transferring control over the industries to the government.

The *Youngstown* decision was reached only two months after Truman seized the industries — a rapid timetable for which the Court has been criticized, especially in light of the importance of the issues. Consider the implications of the following events, as related by a historian of the dispute:

> By midafternoon [shortly before public announcement that the Supreme Court had granted certiorari in the case, the parties] apparently arrived at a satisfactory settlement, and all that remained to be done was for [the negotiators] to check with other members of their respective groups. The bargaining session recessed to allow them time to do so. During the recess, however, word of the Supreme Court's [decision granting certiorari and prohibiting the government from changing wages or working conditions during the pendency of the suit] flashed across the White House news ticker, and when the bargaining session reconvened, the attitudes of the negotiators had changed dramatically. . . .
>
> Unquestionably, the Supreme Court's [order] radically affected the collective bargaining at the White House. [No] longer under pressure to resolve the dispute, for the threat of a government-imposed wage increase had been removed, the industry saw no reason to make concessions in order to arrive at a settlement when it had nothing to lose by waiting for the Supreme Court to decide the case.

M. Marcus, Truman and the Steel Seizure Case: The Limits of Presidential Power 147-148 (1977).

Although Supreme Court intervention may have caused a problem that would not otherwise have existed, it is also clear in hindsight that the Truman administration greatly exaggerated the seriousness of the problem. After the Court's ruling on June 2, the union struck for fifty-three days. In fact, no steel shortage materialized, and the strike had no discernible impact on the war effort. Industry owners eventually negotiated an agreement similar to the Wage Stabilization Board's recommendations. For discussion, see M. Marcus, supra; A. Westin, The Anatomy of a Constitutional Case (1958); Corwin, The Steel Seizure Case: A Ju-

dicial Brick without Straw, 53 Colum. L. Rev. 53 (1953); Kauper, The Steel Seizure Case: Congress, the President, and the Supreme Court, 51 Mich. L. Rev.
141 (1952).

2. *The problem of methodology.* There are significant differences between the
views expressed in the majority opinion by Justice Black and those expressed by
other members of the Court both in dissent and in concurrence. Justice Black's
approach is rigidly textual and largely one of classification: Does the asserted
power fall within the category of "legislation" or that of "execution," as those
terms are conventionally understood? (Note the commonality between Justice
Black's approach here and his approach in other areas of the law, most notably
the first amendment and incorporation.) By contrast, Justice Jackson (and to
some extent Justice Frankfurter) examines (a) whether Congress has granted or
refused to grant the relevant power, (b) whether historical practices support the
assertion of power, and (c) whether "contemporary imponderables," or "the imperatives of events," argue in favor of or against the asserted power. Note also Justice Jackson's "tripartite" approach.

Does Justice Black oversimplify a complicated problem? Consider the view
that separation of powers questions cannot be resolved through a mechanical
process of classification. The terms "legislation" and "execution" are too loaded
with ambiguity to support the Court's rationale; it was by no means clear that the
seizure of the steel mills was a "legislative" act. Does Justice Douglas's approach
meet these criticisms?

On the other hand, does Justice Jackson's alternative position involve an unduly open-ended, discretionary inquiry — and allow irrelevant factors to influence the analysis? Precisely how does one resolve cases within Justice Jackson's
"twilight zone"?

Note that Justices Frankfurter and Jackson agree that the text of the Constitution is not conclusive. Both believe that "history" is relevant as a "gloss" on the
text. Does this view permit the Constitution to be amended through historical
practices, amounting to a kind of adverse possession rule for constitutional interpretation? Would such a mechanism of "amendment" be legitimate? Compare
Ackerman and Golove, Is NAFTA Constitutional?, 198 Harv. L. Rev. 799 (1995)
(arguing that the Constitution can be amended without resort to an article V procedure) with Tribe, Taking Text and Structure Seriously: Reflection on Free-
Form Method of Constitutional Interpretation, 108 Harv. L. Rev. 1221 (1995)
(the Ackerman and Golove position forsakes genuine interpretation of the Constitution). Exactly why and to what extent are historical considerations relevant?

Why should it matter whether Congress remains silent (Justice Jackson's second category) or disapproves of a presidential initiative (his third category)? If the
President's conduct is not within his article II authority, how does congressional
silence add to his powers? Conversely, if the President's conduct is within his article II authority, how can mere congressional disapproval deprive him of powers
granted by the Constitution? Consider the possibility that Justice Jackson's approach implicitly assumes that the meaning of article II should be resolved by political, rather than legal, processes. Is this approach justified? Does it help explain
the relevance of historical practice?

3. *Implied and emergency powers.* Does the President have any implied or
emergency powers after *Youngstown?* The existence of implied or emergency
presidential powers has been sharply disputed throughout the nation's history.

Note that article I refers to "legislative powers herein granted," while article II refers to "executive power" without a "herein granted" qualification. In Alexander Hamilton's view, the "different modes of expression in regard to the two powers confirm the inference that the authority vested in the President is not limited to the specific cases of executive power delineated in Article II." 7 Works of Alexander Hamilton 80 (1851).

This line of reasoning led to the conclusion, reached by Theodore Roosevelt and adhered to by many subsequent Presidents, that the President "was a steward of the people bound actively and affirmatively to do all he could for the people [unless] such action was forbidden by the Constitution or by the law." T. Roosevelt, Autobiography 372 (1914). Contrast with this the view, of President Taft and others, that the President may exercise only those powers traceable to a constitutional grant of authority. Does *Youngstown* resolve this dispute?

For a detailed historical analysis of implied presidential power, see Monaghan, The Protective Power of the Presidency, 93 Colum. L. Rev. 1 (1993).

Dames & Moore v. Regan
453 U.S. 654 (1981)

JUSTICE REHNQUIST delivered the opinion of the Court.

[In 1979, American embassy personnel were seized and held hostage in revolutionary Iran. In response to the resulting crisis, President Carter, acting pursuant to the International Emergency Economic Powers Act, declared a national emergency and blocked the removal or transfer of all property belonging to Iran. Shortly thereafter, the Treasury Department issued a regulation nullifying "any attachment, judgment, decree, lien, execution, garnishment, or other judicial process" with respect to Iranian property.

[After these orders had gone into effect, Dames & Moore filed a suit in United States District Court against the Government of Iran, alleging breach of contract. The district court issued orders of attachment directed against property of the defendant.

[On January 20, 1981, the Americans held hostage were released pursuant to an executive agreement that provided, inter alia, that all litigation "between the Government of each party and the nationals of the other" would be resolved through binding arbitration. The agreement called for the establishment of an Iran-United States Claims Tribunal, which would arbitrate any claims not settled within six months. Awards of the tribunal were to be "final and binding." Moreover, the United States agreed to terminate all legal proceedings in American courts involving such claims and to "bring about the transfer" of all Iranian assets held in the United States by American banks to a security account in the Bank of England, to the account of the Algerian Central Bank, and to use these sums to satisfy awards rendered against Iran by the Claims Tribunal.

[After taking office, President Reagan issued an executive order ratifying the terms of the agreement, suspending all "claims which may be presented to the . . . Tribunal," and providing that these claims "shall have no legal effect in any action now pending in any court of the United States." The lower court upheld the executive actions at issue.]

The parties and the lower courts [have] all agreed that much relevant analysis is contained in [*Youngstown*]. . . .

Although we have in the past found and do today find Justice Jackson's classification of executive actions into three general categories analytically useful, [Justice] Jackson himself recognized that his three categories represented "a somewhat over-simplified grouping," and it is doubtless the case that executive action in any particular instance falls, not neatly in one of three pigeonholes, but rather at some point along a spectrum running from explicit congressional authorization to explicit congressional prohibition. This is particularly true as respects cases such as the one before us, involving responses to international crises the nature of which Congress can hardly have been expected to anticipate in any detail.

[The] Government has principally relied on §203 of the [International Emergency Economic Powers Act, or IEEPA] [as] authorization for these actions. [That section] provides in part:

> [The] President may [nullify,] void, prevent or prohibit, any acquisition, holding, withholding, use, transfer, withdrawal, transportation, importation or exportation of, or dealing in, or exercising any right, power, or privilege with respect to, or transactions involving, any property in which any foreign country or a national thereof has any interest; by any person, or with respect to any property, subject to the jurisdiction of the United States.

The Government contends that the acts of "nullifying" the attachments and ordering the "transfer" of the frozen assets are specifically authorized by the plain language of the above statute. . . .

Because the President's action in nullifying the attachments and ordering the transfer of the assets was taken pursuant to specific congressional authorization, it is "supported by the strongest of presumptions and the widest latitude of judicial interpretation, and the burden of persuasion would rest heavily upon any who might attack it." *Youngstown*, 343 U.S., at 637 (Jackson, J., concurring). Under the circumstances of this case, we cannot say that petitioner has sustained that heavy burden. A contrary ruling would mean that the Federal Government as a whole lacked the power exercised by the President, and that we are not prepared to say.

Although we have concluded that the IEEPA constitutes specific congressional authorization to the President to nullify the attachments and order the transfer of Iranian assets, there remains the question of the President's authority to suspend claims pending in American courts. Such claims have, of course, an existence apart from the attachments which accompanied them. In terminating these claims [the] President purported to act under authority of both the IEEPA and [the] so-called "Hostage Act." We conclude that neither the IEEPA nor the Hostage Act constitutes specific authorization of the President's action suspending claims. This is not to say[, however,] that these statutory provisions are entirely irrelevant to the question of the validity of the President's action. We think both statutes highly relevant in the looser sense of indicating congressional acceptance of a broad scope for executive action in circumstances such as those presented in this case. [The] IEEPA delegates broad authority to the President to act in times of national emergency with respect to property of a foreign country.

The Hostage Act similarly indicates congressional willingness that the President have broad discretion when responding to the hostile acts of foreign sovereigns....

[We] cannot ignore the general tenor of Congress' legislation in this area in trying to determine whether the President is acting alone or at least with the acceptance of Congress. [Congress] cannot anticipate and legislate with regard to every possible action the President may find it necessary to take or every possible situation in which he might act. Such failure of Congress specifically to delegate authority does not, "especially . . . in the areas of foreign policy and national security," imply "congressional disapproval" of action taken by the Executive. On the contrary, the enactment of legislation closely related to the question of the President's authority in a particular case which evinces legislative intent to accord the President broad discretion may be considered to "invite" "measures on independent presidential responsibility." *Youngstown* (Jackson, J., concurring). At least this is so where there is no contrary indication of legislative intent and when, as here, there is a history of congressional acquiescence in conduct of the sort engaged in by the President. It is to that history which we now turn.

Not infrequently in affairs between nations, outstanding claims by Nationals of one country against the government of another country are "sources of friction" between the two sovereigns. To resolve these difficulties, nations have often entered into agreements settling the claims of their respective nations. [Under] such agreements, the President has agreed to renounce or extinguish claims of United States nationals against foreign governments in return for lump-sum payments or the establishment of arbitration procedures. . . .

Crucial to our decision today is the conclusion that Congress has implicitly approved the practice of claim settlement by executive agreement. This is best demonstrated by Congress' enactment of the International Claims Settlement Act of 1949. . . .

Over the years Congress has frequently amended the International Claims Settlement Act to provide for particular problems arising out of settlement agreements, thus demonstrating Congress' continuing acceptance of the President's claim settlement authority. . . .

In light of all of the foregoing — the inferences to be drawn from the character of the legislation Congress has enacted in the area such as the IEEPA and the Hostage Act, and from the history of acquiescence in executive claims settlement — we conclude that the President was authorized to suspend pending claims. [As] Justice Frankfurter pointed out in *Youngstown*, "a systematic, unbroken, executive practice, long pursued to the knowledge of the Congress and never before questioned . . . may be treated as a gloss on 'Executive Power' vested in the President by §1 of Art. II." Past practice does not, by itself, create power, but "long-continued practice, known to and acquiesced in by Congress, would raise a presumption that the [action] had been [taken] in pursuance of its consent. . . ." United States v. Midwest Oil Co., 236 U.S. 459, 474 (1915). . . .

Our conclusion is buttressed by the fact that the means chosen by the President to settle the claims of American nationals provided an alternative forum, the Claims Tribunal, which is capable of providing meaningful relief. . . .

Just as importantly, Congress has not disapproved of the action taken here. Though Congress has held hearings on the Iranian Agreement itself, Congress has not enacted legislation, or even passed a resolution, indicating its displeasure with the Agreement. Quite the contrary, the relevant Senate Committee has stated that the establishment of the Tribunal is "of vital importance to the United States." We are thus clearly not confronted with a situation in which Congress has in some way resisted the exercise of Presidential authority.

Finally, we re-emphasize the narrowness of our decision. We do not decide that the President possesses plenary power to settle claims, even as against foreign governmental entities. [But] where, as here, the settlement of claims has been determined to be a necessary incident to the resolution of a major foreign policy dispute between our country and another, and where, as here, we can conclude that Congress acquiesced in the President's action, we are not prepared to say that the President lacks the power to settle such claims.

[Affirmed.]

[A concurring opinion by Justice Powell is omitted.]

Note: Iranian Claims and Executive Power

1. *The setting. Dames & Moore* must be understood as a late stage of the crisis growing out of the holding of U.S. citizens as hostages by Iranian terrorists. President Carter was able to secure the release of the hostages in return for the various agreements at issue in the Court's opinion. In these circumstances, there was considerable pressure for the Court to decide the case as it did.

See in this regard Miller, *Dames & Moore v. Regan:* A Political Decision by a Political Court, 29 UCLA L. Rev. 1104, 1105, 1127 (1982):

> Although crafted in familiar lawyers' language, Justice Rehnquist's opinion for the Court reeks with the odor of compromise forced by necessity. Principle, as usual, gave way to *realpolitik.* The Justices had, in the last analysis, no choice save to sustain the validity of President Carter's hurried deal for the release of the hostages. Invalidation of the executive agreement would have placed the prospective conduct of American policy in an intolerable position. [I] do not suggest that the Constitution, as written, is irrelevant in such cases as *Dames & Moore.* Of course it has pertinence, but only as a point of departure for political decisions politically made.

Do you agree? Compare H. Koh, The National Security Constitution: Sharing Power after the Iran-Contra Affair 139-140 (1990):

> It is hard to fault the result in *Dames & Moore,* given the crisis atmosphere that surrounded its decision and the national mood of support for the hostage accord. Yet [the] Court should have demanded more specific legislative approval for the president's far-reaching measures. The hostages had returned home months earlier and the hostage accord had given the United States government six months before the frozen Iranian assets were to be transferred — plenty of time for the president to ask a supportive Congress for a swift joint resolution of approval.

2. Dames & Moore *versus* Youngstown. Does the Court's opinion resolve the question of methodology raised by *Youngstown?* Consider the possibility that it represents a rejection of the approach taken by Justice Black, at least in cases involving foreign affairs, in favor of an approach that borrows from Justices Frankfurter and Jackson.

Questions of methodology to one side, can the result in *Dames & Moore* be reconciled with that in *Youngstown?* See H. Koh, supra, at 140:

[By] finding legislative "approval" when Congress had given none, [the *Dames & Moore* Court] not only inverted the *Steel Seizure* holding — which construed statutory nonapproval of the president's act to mean legislative disapproval — but also condoned legislative inactivity at a time that demanded interbranch dialogue and bipartisan consensus.

Is the Court's reliance on congressional silence consistent with the constitutional requirement that statutes be enacted by both Houses of Congress and subject to a presidential veto? Consider the implications of INS v. Chadha, page 370, infra, striking down the one-House "legislative veto" on the ground that it violated the presentment and bicameralism clauses of the Constitution.

C.   DOMESTIC AFFAIRS

1.   *Executive Authority*

Article II, section 1 of the Constitution vests "the executive power" in the President of the United States, and article II, section 3 provides that the President "shall take Care that the Laws be faithfully executed." To what extent does this power free the President from legislative and judicial control when he purports to be executing the laws?

United States v. Nixon

418 U.S. 683 (1974)

Mr. Chief Justice Burger delivered the opinion of the Court.

[Employees of the reelection committee for President Nixon broke into the Democratic National Committee headquarters at the Watergate Hotel in Washington, D.C., on June 17, 1972. In February of the next year, a Senate Select Committee on the Watergate affair was set up by a unanimous vote of the Senate. The committee was charged with investigating the alleged illegal break-in and the question of White House involvement. In late May, under considerable public pressure, President Nixon appointed Archibald Cox as special prosecutor to investigate, among other things, any participation by the White House in the Watergate affair. The President was himself implicated by former White House counsel John Dean in testimony before the Senate in June, and in July one member of the House introduced an impeachment resolution. On February 6, 1974, the House formally authorized the Judiciary Committee to begin impeachment hearings. The hearings were ongoing at the time that the following decision was rendered.]

This litigation presents for review the denial of a motion, filed in the District Court on behalf of [President Nixon] in the case of United States v. Mitchell, to quash a third-party subpoena duces tecum issued by the [District Court] pursuant to Fed. Rule Crim. Proc. 17(c). The subpoena directed the President to produce certain tape recordings and documents relating to his conversations with aides and advisers.

On March 1, 1974, a grand jury of the United States District Court for the District of Columbia returned an indictment charging seven named individuals with various offenses, including conspiracy to defraud the United States and to obstruct justice. Although he was not designated as such in the indictment, the grand jury named the President, among others, as an unindicted coconspirator. On April 18, 1974, upon motion of the Special Prosecutor, [a] subpoena duces tecum was issued [to] the President by the United States District Court [requiring] the production, in advance of the September 9 trial date, of certain tapes, memoranda, papers, transcripts, or other writings relating to certain precisely identified meetings between the President and others. [On] April 30, the President publicly released edited transcripts of 43 conversations; portions of 20 conversations subject to subpoena in the present case were included. On May 1, 1974, the President's counsel filed a "special appearance" and a motion to quash the subpoena [on grounds] of privilege.

On May 20, 1974, the District Court denied the motion to quash and [ordered the] "President or any subordinate officer, official, or employee with custody or control of the documents or objects subpoenaed," [to] deliver to the District Court, on or before May 31, 1974, the originals of all subpoenaed items. [The President sought review in the court of appeals, but the Supreme Court granted review before judgment.]

In the District Court, the President's counsel argued that the Court lacked jurisdiction to issue the subpoena because the matter was an intra-branch dispute between a subordinate and superior officer of the Executive Branch and hence not subject to judicial resolution. [Since] the Executive Branch has exclusive authority and absolute discretion to decide whether to prosecute a case, [it] is contended that a President's decision is final in determining what evidence is to be used in a given criminal case. . . .

Under the authority of Article II, §2, Congress has vested in the Attorney General the power to conduct the criminal litigation of the United States Government. It has also vested in him the power to appoint subordinate officers to assist him in the discharge of his duties. [Acting] pursuant to those statutes, the Attorney General has delegated the authority to represent the United States in these particular matters to a Special Prosecutor with unique authority and tenure. The regulation gives the Special Prosecutor explicit power to contest the invocation of executive privilege in the process of seeking evidence deemed relevant to the performance of these specially delegated duties. . . .

[It] is theoretically possible for the Attorney General to amend or revoke the regulation defining the Special Prosecutor's authority. But he has not done so. So long as this regulation remains in force the Executive Branch is bound by it, and indeed the United States as the sovereign composed of the three branches is bound to respect and to enforce it. . . .

In light of the uniqueness of the setting in which the conflict arises, the fact that both parties are officers of the Executive Branch cannot be viewed as a barrier to justiciability. It would be inconsistent with the applicable law and regulation, and the unique facts of this case to conclude other than that the Special Prosecutor has standing to bring this action and that a justiciable controversy is presented for decision. . . .

[The Court held that the subpoena met the requirements of Fed. R. Crim. Proc. 17(c), including relevance, specificity, and admissibility.]

[W]e turn to the claim that the subpoena should be quashed because it demands "confidential conversations between a President and his close advisors that it would be inconsistent with the public interest to produce." [The] first contention is a broad claim that the separation of powers doctrine precludes judicial review of a President's claim of privilege. The second contention is that if he does not prevail on the claim of absolute privilege, the court should hold as a matter of constitutional law that the privilege prevails over the subpoena duces tecum.

In the performance of assigned constitutional duties each branch of the Government must initially interpret the Constitution, and the interpretation of its powers by any branch is due great respect from the others. The President's counsel [reads] the Constitution as providing an absolute privilege of confidentiality for all Presidential communications. Many decisions of this Court, however, have unequivocally reaffirmed the holding of [*Marbury*, that] "[i]t is emphatically the province and duty of the judicial department to say what the law is." . . .

No holding of the Court has defined the scope of judicial power specifically relating to the enforcement of a subpoena for confidential Presidential communications for use in a criminal prosecution, but other exercises of power by the Executive Branch and the Legislative Branch have been found invalid as in conflict with the Constitution. Powell v. McCormack, 395 U.S. 486 (1969); [*Youngstown*]. [In] a series of cases, the Court interpreted the explicit immunity conferred by express provisions of the Constitution on Members of the House and Senate by the Speech or Debate Clause. Since this Court has consistently exercised the power to construe and delineate claims arising under express powers, it must follow that the Court has authority to interpret claims with respect to powers alleged to derive from enumerated powers.

Our system of government "requires that federal courts on occasion interpret the Constitution in a manner at variance with the construction given the document by another branch." [Notwithstanding] the deference each branch must accord the others, the "judicial Power of the United States" vested in the federal courts [can] no more be shared with the Executive Branch than the Chief Executive, for example, can share with the Judiciary the veto power. [Any] other conclusion would be contrary to the basic concept of separation of powers and the checks and balances that flow from the scheme of a tripartite government. [We] therefore reaffirm that it is the province and duty of this Court "to say what the law is" with respect to the claim of privilege presented in this case.

[In support of his claim of privilege, the President argued that there was a valid need to protect the confidentiality of communications between high government officials, and that the privilege was implicit in the doctrine of separation of powers. The Court recognized the legitimacy of the President's interest in confidentiality.]

However, neither the doctrine of separation of powers, nor the need for confidentiality of high-level communications, without more, can sustain an absolute, unqualified Presidential privilege of immunity from judicial process under all circumstances. The President's need for complete candor and objectivity from advisers calls for great deference from the courts. However, when the privilege depends solely on the broad, undifferentiated claim of public interest in the confidentiality of such conversations, a confrontation with other values arises. Absent a claim of need to protect military, diplomatic, or sensitive national security secrets, we find it difficult to accept the argument that even the very important interest in confidentiality of Presidential communications is significantly diminished by production of such material for in camera inspection with all the protection that a district court will be obliged to provide.

The impediment that an absolute, unqualified privilege would place in the way of the primary constitutional duty of the Judicial Branch to do justice in criminal prosecutions would plainly conflict with the function of the courts under Art. III. In designing the structure of our Government and dividing and allocating the sovereign power among three co-equal branches, the Framers of the Constitution sought to provide a comprehensive system, but the separate powers were not intended to operate with absolute independence. . . .

The expectation of a President to the confidentiality of his conversations and correspondence, like the claim of confidentiality of judicial deliberations, for example, has all the values to which we accord deference for the privacy of all citizens and, added to those values, is the necessity for protection of the public interest in candid, objective, and even blunt or harsh opinions in Presidential decisionmaking. [The] privilege is fundamental to the operation of Government and inextricably rooted in the separation of powers under the Constitution. . . .

But this presumptive privilege must be considered in light of our historic commitment to the rule of law. This is nowhere more profoundly manifest than in our view that "the twofold aim [of criminal justice] is that guilt shall not escape or innocence suffer." We have elected to employ an adversary system of criminal justice in which the parties contest all issues before a court of law. The need to develop all relevant facts in the adversary system is both fundamental and comprehensive. . . .

[Evidentiary privileges] are designed to protect weighty and legitimate competing interests. Thus, the Fifth Amendment to the Constitution provides that no man "shall be compelled in any criminal case to be a witness against himself." And, generally, an attorney or a priest may not be required to disclose what has been revealed in professional confidence. These and other interests are recognized in law by privileges against forced disclosure. [Whatever] their origins, these exceptions to the demand for every man's evidence are not lightly created nor expansively construed, for they are in derogation of the search for truth.

In this case the President challenges a subpoena served on him as a third party requiring the production of materials for use in a criminal prosecution; he does so on the claim that he has a privilege against disclosure of confidential communications. He does not place his claim of privilege on the ground they are military or diplomatic secrets. As to these areas of Art. II duties the courts have traditionally shown the utmost deference to Presidential responsibilities.

[No] case of the Court, however, has extended this high degree of deference to a President's generalized interest in confidentiality. Nowhere in the Constitution [is] there any explicit reference to a privilege of confidentiality, yet to the extent this interest relates to the effective discharge of a President's powers, it is constitutionally based.

The right to the production of all evidence at a criminal trial similarly has constitutional dimensions. The Sixth Amendment explicitly confers upon every defendant in a criminal trial the right "to be confronted with the witnesses against him" and "to have compulsory process for obtaining witnesses in his favor." Moreover, the Fifth Amendment also guarantees that no person shall be deprived of liberty without due process of law. . . .

In this case we must weigh the importance of the general privilege of confidentiality of Presidential communications in performance of the President's responsibilities against the inroads of such a privilege on the fair administration of criminal justice.[19] The interest in preserving confidentiality is weighty indeed and entitled to great respect. However, we cannot conclude that advisers will be moved to temper the candor of their remarks by the infrequent occasions of disclosure because of the possibility that such conversations will be called for in the context of a criminal prosecution.

On the other hand, the allowance of the privilege to withhold evidence that is demonstrably relevant in a criminal trial would cut deeply into the guarantee of due process of law and gravely impair the basic function of the courts. A President's acknowledged need for confidentiality in the communications of his office is general in nature, whereas the constitutional need for production of relevant evidence in a criminal proceeding is specific and central to the fair adjudication of a particular criminal case in the administration of justice. Without access to specific facts a criminal prosecution may be totally frustrated. The President's broad interest in confidentiality of communications will not be vitiated by disclosure of a limited number of conversations preliminarily shown to have some bearing on the pending criminal cases. . . .

[If] a President concludes that compliance with a subpoena would be injurious to the public interest he may properly, as was done here, invoke a claim of privilege on the return of the subpoena. Upon receiving a claim of privilege from the Chief Executive, it became the further duty of the District Court to treat the subpoenaed material as presumptively privileged and to require the Special Prosecutor to demonstrate that the Presidential material was "essential to the justice of the [pending criminal] case." [We] are unable to conclude that the District Court erred in ordering the inspection. Accordingly we affirm the order of the District Court that subpoenaed materials be transmitted to that court. We now turn to the important question of the District Court's responsibilities in conducting the in camera examination of Presidential materials or communications delivered under the compulsion of the subpoena duces tecum. . . .

[Statements] that meet the test of admissibility and relevance must be isolated; all other material must be excised. At this stage the District Court is not limited to representations of the Special Prosecutor as to the evidence sought by the subpoena; the material will be available to the District Court. It is elementary that in camera inspection of evidence is always a procedure calling for scrupulous protection against any release or publication of material not found by the court, at that stage, probably admissible in evidence and relevant to the issues of the trial for which it is sought. That being true of an ordinary situation, it is obvious that the District Court has a very heavy responsibility to see to it that Presidential con-

19. We are not here concerned with the balance between the President's generalized interest in confidentiality and the need for relevant evidence in civil litigation, nor with that between the confidentiality interest and congressional demands for information, nor with the President's interest in preserving state secrets. We address only the conflict between the President's assertion of a generalized privilege of confidentiality and the constitutional need for relevant evidence in criminal trials.

versations, which are either not relevant or not admissible, are accorded that high degree of respect due the President of the United States. . . .

Affirmed.

MR. JUSTICE REHNQUIST took no part in the consideration or decision of these cases.

Note: Presidential Immunity

Among the claims made by President Nixon and rejected by the Court was the assertion that he was immune from judicial process while in office. (This argument should be distinguished from arguments, which Nixon also made, that he alone should determine the scope of executive privilege, and that, even if the scope should be determined by the Court, his invocation of the privilege was appropriate.) Consider the extent to which the immunity argument has force in the following settings.

1. *Immunity from injunctive relief.* In Mississippi v. Johnson, 71 U.S. (4 Wall.) 475 (1867), the Court refused to hear a suit attempting to enjoin the President's enforcement of the Reconstruction laws. The Court concluded that courts did not have power to issue an injunction against the President. The Court referred in particular to the difficulties of enforcement and to the alternative route of impeachment. Does *Johnson* survive United States v. Nixon? Note also that, while President Truman was not the named defendant in *Youngstown*, his order was in fact the subject of the Court's injunction.

2. *Damages for misconduct while in office.* In Nixon v. Fitzgerald, 457 U.S. 731 (1982), Fitzgerald brought an action against President Nixon on the ground that he had been discharged from a government position because he had exercised his right to freedom of speech. The Court held, by a five-to-four vote, that the President was immune from an action for damages. The opinion was written by Justice Powell. According to the Court, "[T]he President occupies a unique position in the constitutional scheme. [Because] of the singular importance of the President's duties, diversion of his energies by concern with private lawsuits would raise unique risks to the effective functioning of government." The Court referred to "the sheer prominence of the President's office," which would make him "an easily identifiable target for suits for civil damages. Cognizance of this personal vulnerability frequently could distract a President from his public duties, to the detriment not only of the President and his office but also the Nation that the Presidency was designed to serve."

The Court also responded to the suggestion that absolute immunity would "leave the Nation without sufficient protection against misconduct on the part of the Chief Executive." A number of safeguards were already in place: The remedy of impeachment, "constant scrutiny by the press," "vigilant oversight by Congress," "a desire to earn re-election, the need to maintain prestige as an element of Presidential influence, and a President's traditional concern for his historical stature" would all play a role. The Court left open, however, the question whether Congress might constitutionally subject the President to liability for damages.

In Harlow v. Fitzgerald, 457 U.S. 800 (1982), the Court declined to extend presidential immunity to presidential aides. Notice that Nixon v. Fitzgerald was not brought until after President Nixon had left office. Given its timing, how could such a suit have "[risked] the effective function of government" or "[distracted] a President from his public duties"?

3. *Damages for claims unrelated to service in office.* Compare Nixon v. Fitzgerald with Clinton v. Jones, 520 U.S. 681 (1997). *Jones* differed from *Fitzgerald* in two respects. First, it arose out of alleged misconduct occurring before the President's term began and unrelated to his conduct while in office. Second, the suit was brought during the President's term of office.

Jones alleged that in 1991, while Clinton was Governor of Arkansas, he enticed her to a hotel room where he made "abhorrent" sexual advances toward her. She claimed that this conduct violated federal and state law and sought monetary damages. In response, President Clinton did not claim immunity from suit but did argue that the litigation should be delayed until the conclusion of his presidential term. In a unanimous decision, the Supreme Court, per Justice Stevens, rejected this claim. The Court held that *Fitzgerald* was distinguishable because it had involved official conduct. Such immunity "serves the public interest in enabling [officials] to perform their designated functions effectively without fear that a particular decision may give rise to personal liability. . . . But we have never suggested that the President, or any other official, has an immunity that extends beyond the scope of any action taken in an official capacity."

The Court also rejected Clinton's contention that permitting the suit would risk violation of separation of powers principles:

> Respondent is merely asking the courts to exercise their core Article III jurisdiction to decide cases and controversies. Whatever the outcome of this case, there is no possibility that the decision will curtail the scope of the official powers of the Executive Branch. The litigation of questions that relate entirely to the unofficial conduct of the individual who happens to be the President poses no perceptible risk of misallocation of either judicial power or executive power.

President Clinton claimed that defense of civil litigation would impose an unacceptable burden on his time and energy, thereby impairing his effective performance in office. In the Court's view, however, "if properly managed by the District Court, [it is highly unlikely that defense of the suit would] occupy any substantial amount of petitioner's time." Moreover, "[the] fact that a federal court's exercise of its traditional Article III jurisdiction may significantly burden the time and attention of the Chief Executive is not sufficient to establish a violation of the Constitution." The Court relied on *Youngstown* and United States v. Nixon in support of this proposition, pointing out that in both cases sitting presidents were required to respond to judicial process despite the "serious impact" of the litigation on the president's ability to perform his functions.

The Court also rejected the argument that permitting such litigation would generate a large volume of "politically motivated harassing and frivolous litigation":

> Most frivolous and vexatious litigation is terminated at the pleading stage or on summary judgment, with little if any personal involvement by the defendant. Moreover, the availability of sanctions provides a significant deterrent to litigation directed at the President in his unofficial capacity for purposes of political gain or harassment. History indicates that the likelihood that a significant number of such cases will be filed is remote. Although scheduling problems may arise, there is no

reason to assume that the District Courts will be either unable to accommodate the President's needs or unfaithful to the tradition — especially in matters involving national security — of giving "the utmost deference to Presidential responsibilities."

Note: The Politics of Impeachment

Both the *Nixon* and *Clinton* cases generated a political response that threatened each President's ability to remain in office. In reviewing the material set out below, consider whether the Court played a constructive role in framing the political issues, or whether the issues might better have been left entirely to the political process.

1. *The Nixon resignation.* On July 27, 1974, two days after the Supreme Court handed down its decision in *Nixon*, the House Judiciary Committee adopted an article of impeachment, charging the President with obstruction of justice with respect to the Watergate break-in and other activities. On July 29, it adopted a second article involving abuse of power by misusing executive agencies and violating constitutional rights of the citizenry. On July 30, it adopted a third article, charging the President with willful disobedience of subpoenas issued by the Judiciary Committee. On August 6, twelve days after the Supreme Court decision, President Nixon decided to make the transcript of the tapes available to the public. Three days thereafter, on August 9, he resigned. On August 20, the Judiciary Committee filed its impeachment report with the House, which took no further action.

In light of the ongoing impeachment investigation, did the *Nixon* decision improperly substitute a legal for a political judgment? Consider Gunther, Judicial Hegemony and Legislative Autonomy: The *Nixon* Case and the Impeachment Process, 22 UCLA L. Rev. 30, 31 (1974):

> [T]he most admirable feature of our recent constitutional history lies in the demonstration that the House of Representatives is capable of taking its impeachment responsibilities seriously. [To] a regrettable extent, the triumph of the legislative branch was diminished by the Supreme Court's performance. For most of the first half of 1974, the Judiciary Committee proceedings were at center stage. That is where they belonged. The impeachment route is the most appropriate one in our Constitution for the pursuit of problems such as those raised by Watergate.

Note in this regard the implications of the Court's observations concerning the justiciability of the suit. If President Nixon had ordered the Attorney General to rescind the regulations governing the special prosecutor and then ordered the prosecutor not to seek production of the tapes, what result would have followed? What reasons might President Nixon have had for not pursuing this course?

2. *The Clinton impeachment.* After the Supreme Court rejected President Clinton's argument that the *Jones* suit should be postponed until he left office, the plaintiff commenced pretrial discovery. In deposition testimony, on January 17, 1998, President Clinton denied having a "sexual affair," a "sexual relationship," or "sexual relations" with former White House intern Monica Lewinsky. At the time of his testimony, Clinton was unaware that a day earlier, the Special Division of the United States Court of Appeals for the District of Columbia Circuit had expanded the jurisdiction of Independent Counsel Kenneth Starr to investi-

gate "whether Monica Lewinsky or others suborned perjury, obstructed justice, intimidated witnesses, or otherwise violated federal law" in conjunction with an affidavit prepared for the *Jones* litigation. On January 27, 1998, the Office of Independent Counsel opened a grand jury inquiry into the Lewinsky affair. Six months later, Lewinsky entered an immunity agreement with the Independent Counsel. On the next day, President Clinton testified before the grand jury via closed circuit television. Although insisting that his testimony at the Jones deposition was accurate, he acknowledged "inappropriate contact" with Lewinsky.

On September 9, 1998, Independent Counsel Starr, acting pursuant to the Independent Counsel Act, notified the House of Representatives that he had "substantial and credible information . . . that may constitute grounds for impeachment." After hearings marked by rancorous argument and partisan division, the House Judiciary Committee approved four articles of impeachment, alleging that Clinton had perjured himself before the grand jury, that he obstructed justice by inducing others to lie in order to conceal his affair with Lewinsky, that he perjured himself in his Jones deposition, and that he abused his power by providing legalistic answers to questions put to him by the House Judiciary Committee. Three months later, the House approved two of the articles alleging perjury before the grand jury and obstruction of justice. On February 12, 1999, the Senate voted by margins of 55-45 and 50-50 to acquit Clinton of both charges. All of the relevant votes were highly partisan, with Democrats overwhelmingly voting against impeachment and conviction, and Republicans voting overwhelmingly in favor.

In light of these events, reconsider the Court's conclusion in *Jones* that "if properly managed by the District Court, it appears to us highly unlikely [that the suit would] occupy any substantial amount of petitioner's time." Do subsequent events demonstrate that the burden of defending civil lawsuits inevitably hampers the President in the performance of his duties and that such lawsuits are bound to be politicized, or instead that President Clinton's response to this lawsuit led to an appropriate inquiry into his fitness for office and that the inquiry did no serious harm to the country?

Note: The "Law" of Impeachment

Article II, section 4 of the Constitution provides that "[the] President, Vice President and all civil Officers of the United States, shall be removed from Office on Impeachment for, and Conviction of, Treason, Bribery, or other high Crimes and Misdemeanors." Article I, section 2 provides that "The House of Representatives shall [have] the sole Power of Impeachment." Article I, section 3 provides as follows:

> The Senate shall have the sole Power to try all Impeachments. When sitting for that Purpose, they shall be on Oath or Affirmation. When the President of the United States is tried, the Chief Justice shall preside: And no Person shall be convicted without the Concurrence of two thirds of the Members present.
>
> Judgment in Cases of Impeachment shall not extend further than to remove from Office, and disqualification to hold and enjoy any Office of honor, Trust or Profit under the United States: but the Party convicted shall nevertheless be liable and subject to Indictment, Trial, Judgment and Punishment, according to Law.

In light of these provisions, consider the following legal issues raised by the Nixon and Clinton affairs.

1. *"High Crimes and Misdemeanors."* What kinds of offenses are encompassed by the phrase "high Crimes and Misdemeanors"? For example, was President Clinton's allegedly false testimony in a civil lawsuit unrelated to his official duties covered? Was President Nixon's alleged malfeasance an impeachable offense even if it did not violate the criminal law?

Early proposals at the Constitutional Convention limited the grounds for impeachment to neglect of duty or misuse of official power. At a later point, it was proposed that the grounds for impeachment of the President be limited to "treason or bribery." George Mason opposed this limitation and moved to add "maladministration" to the list. James Madison responded that "[so] vague a term will be equivalent to a tenure during the pleasure of the Senate." Mason thereupon withdrew his motion, and substituted "bribery and other high crimes or misdemeanors against the State." This motion carried. At a later point, the Convention agreed to replace the word "State" with the words "United States." The Committee of Style and Arrangement thereupon eliminated the words "against the United States," apparently because it thought the phrase redundant.

In light of this history consider the following views:

a. Dwight, Trial by Impeachment, 6 Am. L. Reg. (N.S.) 257, 264 (1867):

> The decided weight of authority is, that no impeachment will lie except for a true crime [or] a breach of the common or statute law, which [would] be the subject of indictment.

b. R. Berger, Impeachment 62-63, 67, 90 (1973):

> "[High] crimes and misdemeanors" appear to be words of art confined to impeachments, without roots in the ordinary criminal law and which, so far as I could discover, had no relation to whether an indictment would lie in the particular circumstances. . . . [But the framers intended] to preclude resort to impeachment of the President for petty misconduct.

c. Testimony of Professor Laurence Tribe before the Subcommittee on the Constitution of the House Judiciary Committee investigating the impeachment of President Clinton:

> What distinguishes certain offenses as "high Crimes and Misdemeanors" must be *not* the fact that serious crimes are involved but the fact that those offenses are similar [to] treason and bribery. But that in turn means that [high] crimes and misdemeanors [must] refer to major offenses against our very system of government, or serious abuses of the governmental power with which a public official has been entrusted [or] grave wrongs in pursuit of governmental [power]. . . .
>
> [It] apparently did not occur to the framers or ratifiers that some sufficiently monstrous but purely private crimes against individuals might require impeachment and removal from office in order to safeguard the government and the people it serves.

d. Testimony of Professor Richard Parker before the same body:

> [It] is not clear why substantial presidential misconduct should be *presumed* nonimpeachable just because it "arose from" a realm of "private" life. . . .

[In] terms of constitutional principle, [this claim makes] no sense. The reason is that the phrase, "other high Crimes and Misdemeanors," must be understood in light of "Bribery," one of its referents. Acts of bribery — as is well known — tend to arise from the "private" lives of actors. The fact that bribery may arise from private greed (or need) does not presumptively immunize it from impeachment. Why, then, should public acts be presumptively immunized solely on the ground that they arose from private lust?

e. Remarks of then Congressman Gerald Ford, proposing the impeachment of Justice William O. Douglas in a speech on the House floor in 1970:

What, then, is an impeachable offense? The only honest answer is that an impeachable offense is whatever a majority of the House of Representatives considers it to be at a given moment in history; conviction results from whatever offense or offenses two-thirds of the other body considers to be sufficiently serious to require removal of the accused from office.

2. *Punishment other than impeachment.* Can a sitting President be indicted for criminal offenses? Although Article II makes clear that criminal penalties do not attach to a judgment of impeachment and that such a judgment does not bar subsequent prosecution, the Constitution is silent as to whether such a prosecution can be undertaken while the President is in office. Consider what, if any, bearing *Jones* has on this question. Independent Counsel serving during the Nixon and Clinton administrations actively considered indicting the President, but in both cases they rejected this course (although President Nixon was named as an unindicted coconspirator by the Watergate grand jury).

Throughout the proceedings against President Clinton, some impeachment opponents argued that the President should be censured rather than impeached. Is censure a constitutionally permissible alternative to impeachment? The Constitution makes no reference to censure, but both the House and the Senate regularly adopt resolutions without the force of law expressing opinions about various matters, and there are several historical precedents for the censure of Presidents and federal judges. Consider the views of Professor and former Congressman Robert Drinan, who served on the House Judiciary Committee that voted articles of impeachment against Richard Nixon:

The Constitution states clearly that the House may impeach or not impeach. The separation of powers guarantees the president immunity from any other penalty.

To encourage or allow the House to "censure" the President for misconduct bypasses the only process set forth in the Constitution to penalize a president. A vote to censure a president by one or both bodies of Congress would establish a dangerous precedent which would weaken the institution of the presidency. It would invite the erosion of the separation of powers in ways which the framers sought carefully to prevent.

3. *The role of Independent Counsel.* Independent Counsel, not directly responsible to the President, played a significant role in both the Nixon and Clinton affairs. A provision in effect at the time of the Clinton impeachment required the Independent Counsel to "advise the House of Representatives of any substantial and credible information which such independent counsel receives, in carrying out the independent counsel's responsibilities [that] may constitute grounds for

impeachment." Are there serious constitutional issues raised by this provision? Consider Gormley, Impeachment and the Independent Counsel: A Dysfunctional Union, 51 Stan. L. Rev. 309, 313 (1999):

> [Even] if the independent counsel can prosecute a sitting President (a dubious proposition at best), the impeachment referral provision [obliterates] the prosecutor's ability to function as a prosecutor. [The provision] not only allows but mandates that the independent counsel wear two incompatible hats: one as a detached criminal prosecutor hired to conduct a neutral criminal investigation on behalf of the executive branch, and the other as a pre-impeachment deputy for the House of Representatives, gathering evidence that may be relevant to Congress' impeachment work. The latter job inevitably clashes with the prosecutor's ability to handle his or her criminal case in a responsible fashion. It also disrupts the work of the grand jury, which (in effect) is forced to accuse public officials of wrongdoing without indicting — something that is generally disfavored in American jurisprudence.

Recall that the statute requires only that the Independent Counsel "advise" the House if he discovers evidence of an impeachable offense. Would it be constitutionally troubling if an Independent Counsel happened across such evidence and so informed Congress on his own initiative? If not, why is it constitutionally objectionable for Congress to direct the Independent Counsel to so inform Congress? Compare O'Sullivan, The Interaction between Impeachment and the Independent Counsel Statute, 86 Geo. L.J. 2193 (1998):

> As a practical matter, the referral provision may permit an [independent counsel] to control the timing, scope, and content of impeachment inquiries. To the extent that an [independent counsel's] referral significantly alters the impeachment dynamic and lends the [independent counsel] credibility as the apolitical investigator of executive misconduct to impeachment inquiries, thus diminishing congressional responsibility for such inquiries, [independent counsel] referral [threatens] to disrupt the traditional balance of power between the executive and the legislative branches.

Consider whether the outcome of the Clinton impeachment proceedings tends to support, or to alleviate, these worries. After the Clinton impeachment, Congress allowed the Independent Counsel statute to expire. For a more detailed discussion of its constitutionality, see section C2, infra.

4. *Law versus politics.* During the latter stages of the Watergate episode, President Nixon's popularity rating approached historic lows. In contrast, throughout the impeachment proceedings against President Clinton, his personal popularity was extraordinarily high, and large majorities of those polled opposed impeachment. Should a conscientious member of Congress take these facts into account? Should it matter to such a member whether the impeachment resolutions achieved bipartisan support? Whether the President is, or is perceived to be, doing a good job? Are questions about presidential impeachment appropriately resolved as a matter of constitutional principle, as a matter of ordinary politics, or as some mixture of the two?

Consider in this regard Klarman, Constitutional Fetishism and the Clinton Impeachment Debate, 85 Va. L. Rev. 631, 631, 656-657 (1999):

> One striking feature of the impeachment debate was the certitude with which politicians and academics espoused a wide variety of constitutional interpretations,

notwithstanding the thinness of the constitutional law governing impeachment. Extraordinary claims were made on both sides of the aisle about what the United States Constitution requires and prohibits regarding various impeachment issues about which the traditional sources of constitutional law — text, original intent, and precedent — rather plainly have little to say. . . .

In the face of legal indeterminacy, it seems natural that political factors will determine constitutional interpretations. . . .

[The] use of constitutional rhetoric simply masks political preferences rather than substituting the preferences of one set of actors for those of another. Since the constitutional rhetoric is transparent to most participants, it is not obvious that constitutionalizing a political debate like impeachment alters it in any significant way. Only when Republican Members of Congress came to believe their own constitutional rhetoric and concluded that their constituents' preferences were irrelevant to the question of whether the President should have been removed from office did constitutionalizing the impeachment debate become pernicious.

For comprehensive discussions of the law of impeachment, see M. Gerhardt, The Federal Impeachment Process: A Constitutional and Historic Analysis (1996); R. Berger, Impeachment: The Constitutional Problems (1973). For general discussions of the legal issues raised by the Clinton impeachment, compare Sunstein, Impeaching the President, 147 U. Pa. L. Rev. 279 (1998) (concluding that impeachment was unconstitutional) with R. Posner, The Trial and Impeachment of William Jefferson Clinton (1999) (concluding that impeachment was constitutionally permissible).

2.   *Legislative Authority*

Much of the debate about legislative authority centers around disagreement concerning "formal," as opposed to "functional," theories of constitutional interpretation. See generally Strauss, Formal and Functional Approaches to Separation-of-Powers Questions: A Foolish Inconsistency?, 72 Cornell L. Rev. 488 (1972). Formalists believe that separation of powers doctrine is governed by relatively clear rules that demarcate separate spheres of governmental authority. In contrast, functionalists believe in a more fluid approach that prohibits "aggrandizement of power" or "undue mingling of functions," but that allows some overlap and is more receptive to changing the boundaries so as to deal with changing situations.

The underlying dispute has both a historical and an interpretive dimension. Some formalists defend their position on originalist grounds, see, e.g., Calabresi and Prakash, The President's Power to Execute the Law, 104 Yale L.J. 541 (1994), while some functionalists have used originalism to criticize formalism. See, e.g., Casper, An Essay on Separation of Powers: Some Early Versions and Practices, 30 Wm. & Mary L. Rev. 211 (1989). Other functionalists concede that formalism may be defensible on originalist grounds but defend functionalist decisions as the best way to make sense of the constitutional structure under modern circumstances, in which the President's power threatens to undermine the constitutional structure. See, e.g., Justice White's dissenting opinions in INS v. Chadha and Bowsher v. Synar, pages 370 and 381; Greene, Checks and Balances in an Era of Presidential Lawmaking, 61 U. Chi. L. Rev. 123 (1994). And some defenders of formalism have argued that the Court has a good reason to proceed in a formalist way so as to ensure against various problems presented by modern legislative initatives, even if formalism is not defensible historically. See Lessig and Sunstein, The President and the Administration, 94 Colum. L. Rev. 1 (1994).

As you read the material that follows, consider which approach makes the best sense of the cases.

Note: The Nondelegation Doctrine and "Quasi-Constitutional" Statutes

1. *Introduction.* Conventionally, Congress affects public policy by passing statutes that the executive is bound to administer. Justice Black's opinion for the Court in *Youngstown*, for example, reflects the view that only Congress can pass laws.

But the conventional understanding — that the legislature is the exclusive lawmaker — no longer reflects reality. In every industrialized nation, administrative agencies, which are generally part of the executive branch, have been granted considerable lawmaking power. Congress has given such agencies regulatory authority, but often it offers them little guidance for the task. It has, for example, told agencies to regulate "unreasonable risks" to consumers and to promote "the public interest" in broadcasting regulation. The process of giving content to these vague standards — a process undertaken by the executive — can be understood only as one of lawmaking.

Under current doctrine, there are very few, if any, constitutional restraints on Congress's power to delegate. But it was not always so. Early on the Court made clear that article I, by vesting legislative power in Congress, imposed constraints on the national legislature's authority to delegate that power to others. For example, the Court stated that the applicable test was whether Congress has laid "down by legislative act an intelligible principle to which the person or body authorized to take action is directed to conform." J. W. Hampton, Jr. & Co. v. United States, 276 U.S. 394, 409 (1928).

2. *Panama Refining and Schechter.* The issues raised by the nondelegation doctrine came to a head in two cases involving legislation designed to ease the Depression during President Roosevelt's famous first "100 days." The National Industrial Recovery Act of 1933 (NIRA) attempted to permit representatives of labor and management in each industry to meet and to design codes of "fair competition." The goal was to help stabilize wages and prices in order to stop the precipitous decline of both, thus restoring the confidence of industry and stabilizing the economy.

The act's declaration of policy referred to Congress's desire to promote cooperative action among trade groups, to maintain united action on the part of management and labor, to eliminate unfair competitive practices, to increase purchasing power and thus consumption of industrial and agricultural products, and to avoid undue restriction of production (except as may be temporarily required). The President was supposed to approve such codes if he made several findings, including (a) that there were "no inequitable restrictions on admission to membership" and (b) that the codes were not designed to promote monopoly or to oppress small enterprises.

In the first case decided under the NIRA, Panama Refining Co. v. Ryan, 293 U.S. 388 (1935), the Court invalidated a provision of the NIRA authorizing the President to prohibit, as part of a petroleum code, the transportation in interstate commerce of oil produced in violation of state-imposed production quotas. The Court emphasized that the statute did not supply standards that would tell the President when to exercise that power. In the Court's view, the NIRA authorized the President to prohibit transportation of "hot oil" whenever he chose.

The second case, Schechter Poultry Corp. v. United States, 295 U.S. 495 (1935), involved the "live poultry code," which contained maximum hour and minimum wage provisions and prohibited various practices said to be "unfair methods of competition." The code identified such practices in provisions that, among other things, (a) barred the sale of unfit chickens and (b) stated that buyers could not be allowed to select particular chickens, but instead must "accept the run of any half coop, coop, or coops." Schechter Poultry was prosecuted for violating both of these provisions. It sought to invalidate the statute authorizing creation of the code on the ground that it was an impermissible delegation of legislative authority. The Court, unanimous on the point, said:

> [The] Constitution has never been regarded as denying to Congress the necessary resources of flexibility and practicality, which will enable it to perform its function in laying down policies and establishing standards, while leaving to selected instrumentalities the making of subordinate rules within prescribed limits and the determination of facts to which the policy as declared by the legislature is to apply. But we said that the constant recognition of the necessity and validity of such provisions, and the wide range of administrative authority which has been developed by means of them cannot be allowed to obscure the limitations of the authority to delegate, if our constitutional system is to be maintained. . . .
>
> What is meant by "fair competition" as the term is used in the Act? . . .
>
> The Government urges that the codes will "consist of rules of competition deemed fair for each industry by representative members of that industry — by the persons most vitally concerned and most familiar with its problems." [But] would it be seriously contended that Congress could delegate its legislative authority to trade or industrial associations or groups so as to empower them to enact the laws they deem to be wise and beneficent for the rehabilitation and expansion of their trade or industries? Could trade or industrial associations or groups be constituted legislative bodies for that purpose because such associations or groups are familiar with the problem of their enterprises? [Such] a delegation of legislative power is unknown to our law and is utterly inconsistent with the constitutional prerogatives and duties of Congress. . . .

3. *The purported demise of the nondelegation doctrine.* The nondelegation doctrine has all but disappeared as a constraint on the delegation of authority to administrative agencies. Indeed, *Panama Refining* and *Schechter* are the only two decisions that have invalidated federal statutes on nondelegation grounds in the nation's history. Statutes authorizing regulation of "unreasonable risks" or administrative action "in the public interest" appear immune from attack. See, for an example of the modern approach, Amalgamated Meat Cutters v. Connally, 337 F. Supp. 737 (D.D.C. 1971). In that case, the court upheld a statute authorizing the President to impose wage and price controls on the ground that implicit standards of "broad fairness and avoidance of gross inequity" were sufficient. The court referred in particular to the temporary character of the delegation, to the

fact that the President could not discriminate unreasonably among industries, and to an implicit requirement that the President come up with standards to limit his own discretion. See also Loving v. United States, 517 U.S. 748 (1996) (rejecting a nondelegation challenge to presidential regulations defining the aggrevating and mitigating circumstances determining whether a court martial can impose the death penalty); Touby v. United States, 500 U.S. 160 (1991) (rejecting a nondelegation challenge to certain aspects of the Controlled Substances Act).

4. *Nondelegation redux?* Note, however, that *Schechter* itself has never been formally overruled. In recent years, a variety of academics, with some support from the Court, have suggested that a revival of the nondelegation doctrine may be desirable. Consider, for example, the following:

a. D. Schoenbrod, Power without Responsibility 10, 21 (1993):

Congress and the president delegate for much the same reason that they continue to run budget deficits. With deficit spending, they can claim credit for benefits of their expenditures yet escape blame for the costs. . . .

Likewise, delegation allows legislators to claim credit for benefits which a regulatory statute promises yet escape the blame for the burdens it will impose, because they do not issue the laws needed to achieve those benefits. The public inevitably must suffer regulatory burdens to realize regulatory benefits, but the laws will come from an agency that legislators can then criticize for imposing excessive burdens on their constituents. . . .

It is the Supreme Court that should take the lead in bringing delegation to an end. Although the Constitution does not prohibit deficit spending, it does prohibit delegation of legislative power. Yet since the New Deal, the Court has left the decision of whether to delegate largely up to Congress and the president, in part out of a belief that legislators' concern for their own power will keep Congress from delegating too much. This belief is simplistic. Legislators enhance their power by delegating: they retain the ability to influence events by pressuring agencies, while they shed responsibility for the exercise of power by avoiding public votes on hard choices.

Compare Lovell, That Sick Chicken Won't Hunt: The Limits of a Judicially Enforced Non-Delegation Doctrine, 17 Con. Comm. 79, 89-90 (2000) (arguing that "even if the courts deprive Congress of the power to delegate rule-making authority to executive branch agencies, Congress would retain numerous substitute strategies that circumvent democratic controls just as capably as current forms of legislative delegation"); Bell, Dead Again: The Nondelegation Doctrine, the Rules/Standards Dilemma and the Line Item Veto, 44 Vill. L. Rev. 189 (1999) (arguing that "courts cannot be expected to set forth the proper scope of delegation or specificity of statutes because courts cannot be expected to craft a judicially administrable resolution of the rules/standards debate").

b. On rare occasions, the doctrine has been invoked as an aid to statutory construction: The fear of a broad delegation is a reason to construe administrative authority narrowly. See Industrial Union Department v. American Petroleum Institute, 448 U.S. 607 (1980) (plurality opinion) (narrowing authority of OSHA to regulate toxic substances in the workplace); National Cable Television Association v. United States, 415 U.S. 336 (1974) (narrowly construing fee-setting authority of federal agencies). For an argument in favor of "nondelegation canons" pursuant to which courts interpret statutes so as to bar delegations in certain, specified areas in the absence of a clear statement from Congress, see Sunstein, Nondelegation Canons, 67 U. Chi. L. Rev. 315 (2000).

c. Justice Rehnquist attempted to use the doctrine in *Industrial Union*, which involved the interpretation of the Occupational Safety and Health Act. Two provisions were relevant. The first defined occupational safety and health standards as those "reasonably necessary or appropriate to provide safe or healthful employment." The second required the Secretary of Labor to "set the standard which most adequately assures, to the extent feasible, on the basis of the best available evidence, that no employee will suffer material impairment of health." The plurality concluded that the "reasonably necessary or appropriate" language required the Secretary to show a "significant risk" before undertaking to regulate. But Justice Rehnquist would have decided the case on nondelegation grounds:

> It is difficult to imagine a more obvious example of Congress simply avoiding a choice which was both fundamental for purposes of the statute and yet so politically divisive that the necessary decision or compromise was difficult, if not impossible, to hammer out in the legislative forge. [If] Congress wishes to legislate in an area which it has not previously sought to enter, it will in today's political world undoubtedly run into opposition no matter how the legislation is formulated. But that is the very essence of legislative authority under our system. It is the hard choices, and not the filling in of the blanks, which must be made by the elected representatives of the people. When fundamental policy decisions underlying important legislation about to be enacted are to be made, the buck stops with Congress and the President insofar as he exercises his constitutional role in the legislative process.

See also American Textile Manufacturers Institute v. Donovan, 452 U.S. 490, 543-548 (1981) (Rehnquist, J., joined by Burger, C.J., dissenting). Notice that, to the extent that Congress is put to such "hard choices," its ability to enact legislation declines and more activity is left unregulated within the private sphere.

d. Consider the implications of Clinton v. City of New York, 547 U.S. 417 (1998). In a six-to-three decision, the Court, per Justice Stevens, invalidated the "Line Item Veto Act," which authorized the President to "cancel in whole" any items of new spending or any "limited tax benefit." A so-called "lock-box" provision required that savings resulting from cancelled items be used to reduce the budget deficit. In identifying items for cancellation, the President was directed to consider the legislative history, purposes, and other relevant information about the cancelled items. In addition, before cancelling an item, the statute required the President to find that the cancellation will reduce the budget deficit, not impair essential government functions, and not harm the national interest.

Writing for the Court, Justice Stevens reasoned that the statute authorized the president to amend previously enacted legislation by repealing a portion of it, and that there was "no provision in the Constitution that authorizes the President to enact, to amend, or to repeal statutes." Toward the end of its opinion, the Court noted that

> [w]e have been favored with extensive debate about the scope of Congress' power to delegate law-making authority, or its functional equivalent, to the President. The excellent briefs filed by the parties and their amici curiae have provided us with valuable historical information that illuminates the delegation issue but does not really bear on the narrow issue that is dispositive of these cases. Thus, because we conclude that the Act's cancellation provisions violate Article I, §7, of the Consti-

tution [specifying how a bill becomes a law], we find it unnecessary to consider the District Court's alternative holding that the Act "impermissibly disrupts the balance of powers among the three branches of government."

Was the "line item veto" functionally distinguishable from a delegation of lawmaking authority to the President? Despite the Court's disclaimer, how can the result in the case be understood absent a prohibition on such delegations? Consider in this connection Justice Breyer's dissenting opinion:

> Literally speaking, the President has not "repealed" or "amended" anything. He has simply executed a power conferred upon him by Congress, which power is contained in laws that were enacted in compliance with the exclusive method set forth in the Constitution.

Justice Scalia, in another dissent, added the following:

> [Had] the Line Item Veto Act authorized the President to "decline to spend" any item of spending contained in the Balanced Budget Act of 1997, there is not the slightest doubt that authorization would have been constitutional. What the Line Item Veto Act does instead — authorizing the President to "cancel" an item of spending — is technically different. But the technical difference does not relate to the technicalities of the Presentment Clause, which have been fully complied with; and the doctrine of unconstitutional delegation, which is at issue here, is preeminently not a doctrine of technicalities. The title of the Line Item Veto Act [has] succeeded in faking out the Supreme Court.

Does Clinton v. City of New York presage a revival of the nondelegation doctrine? Alternatively, does the Court's explicit refusal to rely on nondelegation analysis suggest that there are significant obstacles to such a revival?

5. *Structural statutes.* If the nondelegation doctrine is not revived, and if it proves impossible for Congress to set forth clear standards to govern decisions by administrative agencies, are there alternative means by which Congress might establish its original position as lawmaker?

Congress has sporadically attempted to reassert its authority by enacting structural or "quasi-constitutional" statutes. Although consisting of ordinary legislation, these measures attempt to structure future legislative and executive decisions in much the way that a constitution would. For example, Congress has attempted to control administrative agencies by creating a legislative veto, which would allow one or both Houses of Congress to invalidate decisions made by administrative agencies. It has structured prosecutorial decisions when wrongdoing is alleged against high executive officials by mandating the appointment of Independent Counsel. It has attempted to control future spending decisions by enacting various balanced budget provisions, by structuring executive decisions regarding spending of appropriated funds, and by limiting its own ability to foist unfunded mandates on the states. And it has attempted to control the President's use of the armed forces by enacting a War Powers Resolution.

How should the Supreme Court respond to these experiments in governance? On one view, structural statutes unconstitutionally expand Congress's powers. Advocates of this view insist that the framers bound us to a particular structure of government, and that Congress cannot bind us to a new structure without amending the Constitution. On the other view, structural statutes do no more than reestablish Congress's original powers in a modern environment that the framers could not have imagined. Advocates of this view maintain that structural statutes preserve the original balance between Congress and the President in a regulatory context where broad delegations to the executive are a fact of life. As you read the cases that follow, consider which view is more persuasive.

INS v. Chadha

462 U.S. 919 (1983)

CHIEF JUSTICE BURGER delivered the opinion of the Court.

Chadha is an East Indian who was born in Kenya and holds a British passport. He was lawfully admitted to the United States in 1966 on a nonimmigrant student visa. His visa expired on June 30, 1972. On October 11, 1973, the District Director of the Immigration and Naturalization Service ordered Chadha to show cause why he should not be deported for having "remained in the United States for a longer time than permitted." [After a hearing, an immigration judge ordered] that Chadha's deportation be suspended. The immigration judge found that Chadha met the requirements of [the statute]: he had resided continuously in the United States for over seven years, was of good moral character, and would suffer "extreme hardship" if deported.

Pursuant to [the statute the] immigration judge suspended Chadha's deportation and a report of the suspension was transmitted to Congress.

Once the Attorney General's recommendation for suspension of Chadha's deportation was conveyed to Congress, Congress had the power under [the statute to] veto the Attorney General's determination that Chadha should not be deported. . . .

On December 12, 1975, Representative Eilberg, Chairman of the Judiciary Subcommittee on Immigration, Citizenship, and International Law, introduced a resolution opposing "the granting of permanent residence in the United States to [six] aliens," including Chadha. [The] resolution was passed without debate or recorded vote. Since the House action was pursuant to [the statute] the resolution was not treated as an Article I legislative act; it was not submitted to the Senate or presented to the President for his action.

After the House veto of the Attorney General's decision to allow Chadha to remain in the United States, the immigration judge reopened the deportation proceedings and [Chadha] was ordered deported pursuant to the House action. . . .

We turn now to the question whether action of one House of Congress under [the statute] violates strictures of the Constitution. [The] fact that a given law or procedure is efficient, convenient, and useful in facilitating functions of the government, standing alone, will not save it if it is contrary to the Constitution. Convenience and efficiency are not the primary objectives — or the hallmarks — of democratic government and our inquiry is sharpened rather than blunted by the fact that Congressional veto provisions are appearing with increasing frequency in statutes which delegate authority to executive and independent agencies:

> Since 1932, when the first veto provision was enacted into law, 295 congressional veto-type procedures have been inserted in 196 different statutes as follows: from 1932 to 1939, five statutes were affected; from 1940-49, nineteen statutes; between 1950-59, thirty-four statutes; and from 1960-69, forty-nine. From the year 1970

through 1975, at least one hundred sixty-three such provisions were included in eighty-nine laws.

Justice White undertakes to make a case for the proposition that the one-House veto is a useful "political invention." [But] policy arguments supporting even useful "political inventions" are subject to the demands of the Constitution which defines powers and, with respect to this subject, sets out just how those powers are to be exercised.

Explicit and unambiguous provisions of the Constitution prescribe and define the respective functions of the Congress and of the Executive in the legislative process. [Article] I provides:

> All legislative Powers herein granted shall be vested in a Congress of the United States, which shall consist of a Senate *and* a House of Representatives.

Art. I, §1. (Emphasis added).

> Every Bill which shall have passed the House of Representatives and the Senate, *shall*, before it becomes a Law, be presented to the President of the United States; . . .

Art. I, §7, cl. 2. (Emphasis added).

> Every Order, Resolution, or Vote to which the Concurrence of the Senate and House of Representatives may be necessary (except on a question of Adjournment) *shall be* presented to the President of the United States; and before the Same shall take Effect, *shall be* approved by him, or being disapproved by him, *shall be* re-passed by two thirds of the Senate and House of Representatives, according to the Rules and Limitations prescribed in the Case of a Bill.

Art. I, §7, cl. 3. (Emphasis added).

These provisions of Art. I are integral parts of the constitutional design for the separation of powers. . . .

[When] the Executive acts, it presumptively acts in an executive or administrative capacity as defined in Art. II. And when, as here, one House of Congress purports to act, it is presumptively acting within its assigned sphere. Beginning with this presumption, we must nevertheless establish that the challenged action under [the statute] is of the kind to which the procedural requirements of Art. I, §7 apply. Not every action taken by either House is subject to the bicameralism and presentment requirements of Art. I. [Whether] actions taken by either House are, in law and fact, an exercise of legislative power depends not on their form but upon "whether they contain matter which is properly to be regarded as legislative in its character and effect." . . .

Examination of the action taken here by one House [reveals] that it was essentially legislative in purpose and effect. In purporting to exercise power defined in Art. I, §8, cl. 4 to "establish an uniform Rule of Naturalization," the House took action that had the purpose and effect of altering the legal rights, duties and relations of persons, including the Attorney General, Executive Branch officials and Chadha, all outside the legislative branch. [The] one-House veto operated in this case to overrule the Attorney General and mandate Chadha's deportation; absent the House action, Chadha would remain in the United States. Congress has *acted* and its action has altered Chadha's status.

The legislative character of the one-House veto in this case is confirmed by the character of the Congressional action it supplants. Neither the House of Representatives nor the Senate contends that, absent the veto provision, [either] of them, or both of them acting together, could effectively require the Attorney General to deport an alien once the Attorney General, in the exercise of legislatively delegated authority, had determined the alien should remain in the United States. Without the challenged provision, [this] could have been achieved, if at all, only by legislation requiring deportation. . . .

The nature of the decision implemented by the one-House veto in this case further manifests its legislative character. After long experience with the clumsy, time consuming private bill procedure, Congress made a deliberate choice to delegate to the Executive Branch, [the] authority to allow deportable aliens to remain in this country in certain specified circumstances. It is not disputed that this choice to delegate authority is precisely the kind of decision that can be implemented only in accordance with the procedures set out in Art. I. Disagreement with the Attorney General's decision on Chadha's deportation — that is, Congress' decision to deport Chadha — no less than Congress' original choice to delegate to the Attorney General the authority to make that decision, involves determinations of policy that Congress can implement in only one way, bicameral passage followed by presentment to the President. Congress must abide by its delegation of authority until that delegation is legislatively altered or revoked.

Finally, we see that when the Framers intended to authorize either House of Congress to act alone and outside of its prescribed bicameral legislative role, they narrowly and precisely defined the procedure for such action. There are but four provisions in the Constitution, explicit and unambiguous, by which one House may act alone with the unreviewable force of law, not subject to the President's veto.

[The Court referred to the House's power to initiate impeachments, the Senate's power to conduct trials following impeachment, the Senate's power over presidential appointments, and the Senate's power to ratify treaties.[21]]

[These provisions give] further support for the conclusion that Congressional authority is not to be implied. . . .[22]

---

21. Justice Powell's position is that the one-House veto in this case is a *judicial* act, and therefore unconstitutional as beyond the authority vested in Congress by the Constitution. We agree that there is a sense in which one-House action pursuant to [the statute] has a judicial cast, since it purports to "review" Executive action. [But] the attempted analogy between judicial action and the one-House veto is less than perfect. Federal courts do not enjoy a roving mandate to correct alleged excesses of administrative agencies; we are limited by Art. III to hearing cases and controversies and no justiciable case or controversy was presented by the Attorney General's decision to allow Chadha to remain in this country. We are aware of no decision [where] a federal court has reviewed a decision of the Attorney General suspending deportation of an alien pursuant to the standards set out in [the statute.] This is not surprising, given that no party to such action has either the motivation or the right to appeal from it. As Justice White correctly notes, "the courts have not been given the authority to review whether an alien should be given permanent status; review is limited to whether the Attorney General has properly applied the statutory standards for" *denying* a request for suspension of deportation. [Thus,] Justice Powell's statement that the one-House veto in this case is "clearly adjudicatory," simply is not supported by his accompanying assertion that the House has "assumed a function ordinarily entrusted to the federal courts." We are satisfied that the one-House veto is legislative in purpose and effect and subject to the procedures set out in Art. I.

22. [Justice] White suggests that the Attorney General's action suspending deportation is equivalent to a *proposal* for legislation and that because Congressional approval is indicated "by failure

The choices we discern as having been made in the Constitutional Convention impose burdens on governmental processes that often seem clumsy, inefficient, even unworkable, but those hard choices were consciously made by men who had lived under a form of government that permitted arbitrary governmental acts to go unchecked. There is no support in the Constitution or decisions of this Court for the proposition that the cumbersomeness and delays often encountered in complying with explicit Constitutional standards may be avoided, either by the Congress or by the President. See [*Youngstown*]. With all the obvious flaws of delay, untidiness, and potential for abuse, we have not yet found a better way to preserve freedom than by making the exercise of power subject to the carefully crafted restraints spelled out in the Constitution.

We hold that the Congressional veto provision [is unconstitutional]. Accordingly, the judgment of the Court of Appeals is affirmed.

JUSTICE POWELL, concurring in the judgment.

On its face, the House's action appears clearly adjudicatory. The House did not enact a general rule; rather it made its own determination that six specific persons did not comply with certain statutory criteria. It thus undertook the type of decision that traditionally has been left to other branches.

The impropriety of the House's assumption of this function is confirmed by the fact that its action raises the very danger the Framers sought to avoid — the exercise of unchecked power. In deciding whether Chadha deserves to be deported, Congress is not subject to any internal constraints that prevent it from arbitrarily depriving him of the right to remain in this country. Unlike the judiciary or an administrative agency, Congress is not bound by established substantive rules. Nor is it subject to the procedural safeguards, such as the right to counsel and a hearing before an impartial tribunal, that are present when a court or an agency adjudicates individual rights. The only effective constraint on Congress' power is political, but Congress is most accountable politically when it prescribes rules of general applicability. When it decides rights of specific persons, those rights are subject to "the tyranny of a shifting majority."

[In] my view, when Congress undertook to apply its rules to Chadha, it exceeded the scope of its constitutionally prescribed authority. I would not reach the broader question whether legislative vetoes are invalid under the Presentment Clauses.

JUSTICE WHITE, dissenting.

Today the Court not only invalidates §244(c)(2) of the Immigration and Nationality Act, but also sounds the death knell for nearly 200 other statutory provisions in which Congress has reserved a "legislative veto." For this reason, the Court's decision is of surpassing importance. And it is for this reason that the

---

to veto, the one-House veto satisfies the requirement of bicameral approval." [However,] as the Court of Appeals noted, that approach "would analogize the effect of the one house disapproval to the failure of one house to vote affirmatively on a private bill." Even if it were clear that Congress entertained such an arcane theory when it enacted [the statute] which Justice White does not suggest, this would amount to nothing less than an amending of Art. I. The legislative steps outlined in Art. I are not empty formalities; they were designed to assure that both Houses of Congress and the President participate in the exercise of lawmaking authority.

Court would have been well-advised to decide the case, if possible, on the narrower grounds of separation of powers, leaving for full consideration the constitutionality of other congressional review statutes operating on such varied matters as war powers and agency rulemaking, some of which concern the independent regulatory agencies.

The prominence of the legislative veto mechanism in our contemporary political system and its importance to Congress can hardly be overstated. It has become a central means by which Congress secures the accountability of executive and independent agencies. Without the legislative veto, Congress is faced with a Hobson's choice: either to refrain from delegating the necessary authority, leaving itself with a hopeless task of writing laws with the requisite specificity to cover endless special circumstances across the entire policy landscape, or in the alternative, to abdicate its lawmaking function to the executive branch and independent agencies. To choose the former leaves major national problems unresolved; to opt for the latter risks unaccountable policymaking by those not elected to fill that role. . . .

[Justice White summarized the history of the legislative veto, noting that it was a response to "the sprawling government structure" created after the Depression; that it "balanced delegations of statutory authority in new areas"; and that it played an important role in disputes in the 1970s over impoundment, war, and national emergency powers.]

Even this brief review suffices to demonstrate that the legislative veto [is an] important if not indispensable political invention that allows the President and Congress to resolve major constitutional and policy differences, assures the accountability of independent regulatory agencies, and preserves Congress' control over lawmaking. . . .

The history of the legislative veto also makes clear that it has not been a sword with which Congress has struck out to aggrandize itself at the expense of the other branches — the concerns of Madison and Hamilton. Rather, the veto has been a means of defense, a reservation of ultimate authority necessary if Congress is to fulfill its designated role under Article I as the nation's lawmaker. While the President has often objected to particular legislative vetoes, generally those left in the hands of congressional committees, the Executive has more often agreed to legislative review as the price for a broad delegation of authority. To be sure, the President may have preferred unrestricted power, but that could be precisely why Congress thought it essential to retain a check on the exercise of delegated authority. . . .

[The] Constitution does not directly authorize or prohibit the legislative veto. Thus, our task should be to determine whether the legislative veto is consistent with the purposes of Art. I and the principles of Separation of Powers. [We] should not find the lack of a specific constitutional authorization for the legislative veto surprising, and I would not infer disapproval of the mechanism from its absence. From the summer of 1787 to the present the government of the United States has become an endeavor far beyond the contemplation of the Framers. Only within the last half century has the complexity and size of the Federal Government's responsibilities grown so greatly that the Congress must rely on the legislative veto as the most effective if not the only means to insure their role as the nation's lawmakers. But the wisdom of the Framers was to anticipate that the nation would grow and new problems of governance would require different solutions. Accordingly, our Federal Government was intentionally chartered with the flexibility to respond to contemporary needs without losing sight of fundamental democratic principles. . . .

[The presentment and bicameralism requirements do] not [answer] the constitutional question before us. The power to exercise a legislative veto is not the power to write new law without bicameral approval or presidential consideration. The veto must be authorized by statute and may only negative what an Executive department or independent agency has proposed. On its face, the legislative veto no more allows one House of Congress to make law than does the presidential veto confer such power upon the President. Accordingly, the Court properly recognizes that it "must establish that the challenged action [is] of the kind to which the procedural requirements of Art. I, §7 apply." . . .

The terms of the Presentment Clauses suggest only that bills and their equivalent are subject to the requirements of bicameral passage and presentment to the President.

Although the Clause does not specify the actions for which the concurrence of both Houses is "necessary," the proceedings at the Philadelphia Convention suggest its purpose was to prevent Congress from circumventing the presentation requirement in the making of new legislation. . . .

When the Convention did turn its attention to the scope of Congress' lawmaking power, the Framers were expansive. The Necessary and Proper Clause, Art. I, §8, cl. 18, vests Congress with the power "to make all laws which shall be necessary and proper for carrying into Execution the foregoing Powers [the enumerated powers of §8], and all other Powers vested by this Constitution in the government of the United States, or in any Department or Officer thereof." It is long-settled that Congress may "exercise its best judgment in the selection of measures, to carry into execution the constitutional powers of the government," and "avail itself of experience, to exercise its reason, and to accommodate its legislation to circumstances." [*McCulloch*.]

The Court heeded this counsel in approving the modern administrative state. The Court's holding today that all legislative type action must be enacted through the lawmaking process ignores that legislative authority is routinely delegated to the Executive Branch, to the independent regulatory agencies, and to private individuals and groups. . . .

This Court's decisions sanctioning such delegations make clear that Article I does not require all action with the effect of legislation to be passed as a law. . . .

If Congress may delegate lawmaking power to independent and executive agencies, it is most difficult to understand Article I as forbidding Congress from also reserving a check on Legislative power for itself. Absent the veto, the agencies receiving delegations of legislative or quasi-legislative power may issue regulations having the force of law without bicameral approval and without the President's signature. It is thus not apparent why the reservation of a veto over the exercise of that legislative power must be subject to a more exacting test. In both cases, it is enough that the initial statutory authorizations comply with the Article I requirements. . . .

Nor are there strict limits on the agents that may receive such delegations of legislative authority so that it might be said that the legislature can delegate authority to others but not to itself. While most authority to issue rules and regulations is given to the executive branch and the independent regulatory agencies, statutory delegations to private persons have also passed this Court's scrutiny. [More] fundamentally, even if the Court correctly characterizes the Attorney General's authority under [the statute] as an Article II Executive power, the Court concedes that certain administrative agency action, such as rulemaking, "may resemble lawmaking" and recognizes that "[t]his Court has referred to agency activity as being 'quasi-legislative' in character." [Such] rules and adjudications by the agencies meet the Court's own definition of legislative action for they "alter[ ] the legal rights, duties, and relations of persons . . . outside the legislative branch," and involve "determinations of policy." Under the Court's analysis, the Executive Branch and the independent agencies may make rules with the effect of law while Congress, in whom the Framers confided the legislative power, Art. I, §1, may not exercise a veto which precludes such rules from having operative force. If the effective functioning of a complex modern government requires the delegation of vast authority which, by virtue of its breadth, is legislative or "quasi-legislative" in character, I cannot accept that Article I — which is, after all, the source of the non-delegation doctrine — should forbid Congress from qualifying that grant with a legislative veto.

The Court also takes no account of perhaps the most relevant consideration: However resolutions of disapproval under [the statute] are formally characterized, in reality, a departure from the status quo occurs only upon the concurrence of opinion among the House, Senate, and President. Reservations of legislative authority to be exercised by Congress should be upheld if the exercise of such reserved authority is consistent with the distribution of and limits upon legislative power that Article I provides. . . .

[Justice White argued that the veto "did not alter the division of actual authority between Congress and the executive," since a change in the alien's legal status could occur only with the concurrence of the President and both Houses. Thus, the purposes of the presentment and bicameralism requirements were satisfied.]

[The] history of the separation of powers doctrine is also a history of accommodation and practicality. Apprehensions of an overly powerful branch have not led to undue prophylactic measures that handicap the effective working of the national government as a whole. The Constitution does not contemplate total separation of the three branches of Government.

[The] legislative veto provision does not "prevent the Executive Branch from accomplishing its constitutionally assigned functions." First, it is clear that the Executive Branch has no "constitutionally assigned" function of suspending the deportation of aliens. "'Over no conceivable subject is the legislative power of Congress more complete than it is over' the admission of aliens." . . .

Moreover, the Court believes that the legislative veto [is] best characterized as an exercise of legislative or quasi-legislative authority. Under this characterization, the practice does not, even on the surface, constitute an infringement of executive or judicial prerogative. The Attorney General's suspension of deportation is equivalent to a proposal for legislation. . . .

Nor does [the statute] infringe on the judicial power, as Justice Powell would hold. [The statute] makes clear that Congress has reserved its own judgment as part of the statutory process. Congressional action does not substitute for judicial review of the Attorney General's decisions. . . .

I do not suggest that all legislative vetoes are necessarily consistent with separation of powers principles. A legislative check on an inherently executive function, for example that of initiating prosecutions, poses an entirely different question. But the legislative veto device here — and in many other settings — is far from an instance of legislative tyranny over the Executive. It is a necessary check on the unavoidably expanding power of the agencies, both executive and independent, as they engage in exercising authority delegated by Congress.

[The court's decision] reflects a profoundly different conception of the Constitution than that held by the Courts which sanctioned the modern administrative state. Today's decision strikes down in one fell swoop provisions in more laws enacted by Congress than the Court has cumulatively invalidated in its history. I fear it will now be more difficult "to insure that the fundamental policy decisions in our society will be made not by an appointed official but by the body immediately responsible to the people," Arizona v. California, 373 U.S. 546, 625 (1963) (Harlan, J., dissenting). I must dissent.

[Justice Rehnquist dissented on the ground that the legislative veto provision was not severable.]

Note: The Legislative Veto

1. Chadha *in context: legislative control of the bureaucracy.* The legislative veto is one of a number of means by which Congress has attempted to control administrative agencies to which Congress has delegated substantial discretionary authority. For example, congressional committees or subcommittees might hold oversight hearings, in which they call executive officials before them and question the officials about past and future conduct. Such hearings may produce considerable publicity and lead to pressure for changes in executive policy. A more formal mechanism is the appropriations rider — an attachment to an authorization of expenditure of federal funds that prohibits the agency from engaging in certain courses of conduct. Similarly, Congress may decrease or increase an agency's budget, in the annual appropriations process, in order to express its views on the mission of the agency and on whether more or less enforcement is desirable. Alternatively, Congress might enact "sunset" legislation, providing that agency authority will terminate after a certain period unless Congress reenacts the substantive statute. Of course, Congress may also enact a measure repealing the agency's authority or rewrite the statute so as to limit authority. In light of all these clearly constitutional alternatives to the legislative veto mechanism, does the Court's decision accomplish anything of significance? Consider the view that easy circumvention is a necessary cost of respect for formal rules. The very rigidity that formalism prizes means that the rules lack the suppleness necessary to respond to evasive maneuvers. Yet without this rigidity, constitutional commands are reduced to nothing more than shifting and controversial policy judgments that cannot be separated from appropriately contestable views about the merits of political disputes.

2. *The reach of* Chadha. Should the *Chadha* decision apply to *all* legislative vetoes? The case itself involved, as Justice Powell emphasized, an "adjudicatory" proceeding involving a single person. But in Process Gas Consumers Group v. Consumers Energy Council of America, 463 U.S. 1216 (1983), the Court summarily affirmed, on the authority of *Chadha*, a decision invalidating a legislative veto as applied to certain Federal Energy Regulatory Commission regulations of

natural gas pricing. See also United States Senate v. FTC, 463 U.S. 1216 (1983) (summarily affirming decision invalidating legislative veto as applied to rule-making by FTC). Both of these summary affirmances also involved independent agencies; the FTC case involved a "two-House veto," in which both Houses of Congress must agree before the veto may become effective. The summary affirmances thus confirm Justice White's suggestion that the reach of the decision is quite broad.

3. *The Court's approach.* Many commentators have been critical of the reasoning in *Chadha.* See, e.g., Elliott, *INS v. Chadha:* The Administrative Constitution, the Constitution, and the Legislative Veto, 1983 Sup. Ct. Rev. 125; Spann, Deconstructing the Legislative Veto, 68 Minn. L. Rev. 473 (1984); Strauss, Was There a Baby in the Bathwater? A Comment on the Supreme Court's Legislative Veto Decision, 1983 Duke L.J. 789; Tribe, The Legislative Veto Decision: A Law by Any Other Name?, 21 Harv. J. on Legis. 1 (1984). In their view, there is no doubt that the bicameralism and presentation requirements are applicable to the enactment of a law. But the question in *Chadha* was whether the legislative veto was the sort of action to which those requirements were applicable. Congress does many things without being bound by the formal requirements for legislation: It holds hearings, engages in investigations, confirms presidential appointments, and passes resolutions sending proposed constitutional amendments to the states. Consider Strauss, supra, at 794: "The Chief Justice essentially overcomes this problem by assertion." Does anything in the Court's opinion help to solve the problem?

Note: *Where Do Administrative Agencies "Fit" in the Separation of Powers Scheme?*

1. *Introduction.* Article II vests the executive power in the President, not in subordinate officials. This decision was based on a rejection of the notion of a "plural executive." See The Federalist No. 70; E. Corwin, The President — Office and Powers 3-30 (1957).

But the Constitution does not explicitly resolve the question whether Congress may immunize subordinate officials from presidential control. Suppose, for example, Congress provides that the Environmental Protection Agency, or the Civil Rights Commission, should do its work free from interference by the President. Would such a statute be constitutional under the necessary and proper clause? Would such a statute be inconsistent with the framers' decision to create a unitary executive and to vest all of the executive power in one person — the President? Compare Calabresi and Rhodes, The Structural Constitution: Unitary Executive, Plural Judiciary, 105 Harv. L. Rev. 1153 (1992) and Calabresi and Prakash, The President's Power to Execute the Law, 104 Yale L.J. 541 (1994) with Lessig and Sunstein, The President and the Administration, 94 Colum. L. Rev. 1 (1994) and Froomkin, The Imperial Presidency's New Vestments, 88 Nw. U.L. Rev. 1346 (1994). See generally Strauss, The Place of Agencies in Government: Separation of Powers and the Fourth Branch, 84 Colum. L. Rev. 452 (1984). The question is important, especially in an era in which lawmaking authority has been concentrated in executive officials.

2. Myers *and presidential supremacy.* Myers v. United States, 272 U.S. 52 (1926), involved a statute that provided that postmasters "shall be appointed and may be removed by the President and with the advice and consent of the Senate." President Wilson attempted to remove Myers, a postmaster appointed for a four-year term in Portland, Oregon, before the expiration of his term. The Court, in an opinion by Chief Justice (and former President) Taft, held that the removal was lawful because the attempted limitation on the President's removal power was unconstitutional under article II. The Court relied on several conclusions: (a) The act of removal is itself executive in nature and must therefore be performed by the President; (b) under the "take Care" clause, it is the President, not his subordinates, who must take care that the laws be faithfully executed; and (c) article II vests executive power in the President, not subordinate officials.

Justices Holmes, joined by Justices Brandeis and McReynolds, dissented: "We have to deal with an office that owes its existence to Congress and that Congress may abolish tomorrow. [With] such power over its own creation, I have no more trouble in believing that Congress has power to prescribe a term of life for it free from any interference than I have in accepting the undoubted power of Congress to decree its end."

Under *Myers*, are the civil services statutes — immunizing lower-level federal officials from power to discharge "at will" — constitutionally acceptable? If so, is it because such officials are not "Officers of the United States," see Buckley v. Valeo, infra? Consider the view that *Myers* is satisfied so long as the official who is in charge of the basic chain of command is subject to presidential control.

Myers derives considerable support from the vesting of executive power in the President and from the basic decision to have a unitary, rather than plural, executive branch. But the historical support for the decision is far from unambiguous. There is evidence that at least some of the founders distinguished between "executive" and "administrative" authority, and that they believed that Congress should share in the power to remove some of what we now treat as executive officials. See Lessig and Sunstein, supra; Casper, The American Constitutional Tradition of Shared and Separated Powers: An Essay in Separation of Powers, 30 Wm. & Mary L. Rev. 211 (1989); Grundstein, Presidential Power, Administration and Administrative Law, 18 Geo. Wash. L. Rev. 285 (1950).

3. Humphrey's Executor, Wiener, *and the rise of "independent" agencies.* Humphrey's Executor v. United States, 295 U.S. 602 (1935), involved a statute providing that members of the Federal Trade Commission could be "removed by the President for inefficiency, neglect of duty, or malfeasance in office." The history of the statute indicated that the legislative goal was to entrust regulatory decisions to a body of nonpartisan "experts," insulated from political pressures. President Roosevelt removed Humphrey from office, contending not that removal was justified by one of the statutory conditions, but that the limitation of the removal power was unconstitutional under *Myers.* In short, President Roosevelt urged that any subordinate official served, by virtue of article II as interpreted in *Myers*, at the pleasure of the President. A unanimous Court disagreed, distinguishing and confining the reach of *Myers:*

The office of a postmaster is so essentially unlike the office now involved that the decision in the *Myers* case cannot be accepted as controlling our decision here. A postmaster is an executive officer restricted to the performance of executive functions. He is charged with no duty at all related to either the legislative or judicial power. The actual decision in the *Myers* case finds support in the theory that such an officer is merely one of the units in the executive department and, hence, inherently subject to the exclusive and illimitable power of removal by the Chief Executive, whose subordinate and aid he is. [The] necessary reach of the decision goes far enough to include all purely executive officers. It goes no farther; much less does it include an officer who occupies no place in the executive department and who exercises no part of the executive power vested by the Constitution in the President.

The Federal Trade Commission is an administrative body created by Congress to carry into effect legislative policies embodied in the statute in accordance with the legislative standard therein prescribed, and to perform other specified duties as a legislative or as a judicial aid. Such a body cannot in any proper sense be characterized as an arm or an eye of the executive. Its duties are performed without executive leave and, in the contemplation of the statute, must be free from executive control. [The] Commission acts in part quasi-legislatively and in part quasi-judicially. . . .

See also Wiener v. United States, 357 U.S. 349 (1958) (concluding that, even though the statute creating the War Claims Commission was silent on the question of removal, the commission's adjudicatory nature implied a limitation on the President's power to remove).

Humphrey's Executor and *Wiener* recognize a congressional power to create "independent" agencies — governmental entities that are free from presidential removal power and, to some uncertain degree, presidential power to supervise and control the decisions of their officers. The Federal Trade Commission, the Federal Energy Regulatory Commission, and the Federal Communications Commission are examples of independent agencies.

4. *Buckley v. Valeo.* The Federal Election Campaign Act created an eight-member Federal Election Commission to oversee federal elections. Two members of the commission were appointed by the President pro tempore of the Senate, two by the Speaker of the House, and two by the President. The Secretary of the Senate and the Clerk of the House also served as ex-officio, nonvoting members. The commission was authorized to investigate, to maintain records, to make rules governing federal elections, and to impose sanctions on those who violated the act and its own regulations. In Buckley v. Valeo, 424 U.S. 1 (1976), the Court unanimously held that vesting a commission whose members were appointed in this manner with some of these functions violated the appointments clause of article II of the Constitution. The clause provides:

[The President] shall nominate, and by and with the Advice and Consent of the Senate, shall appoint Ambassadors, other public Ministers and Consuls, Judges of the supreme Court, and all other Officers of the United States, whose Appointments are not herein otherwise provided for, and which shall be established by Law: but the Congress may by Law vest the Appointment of such inferior Officers, as they think proper, in the President alone, in the Courts of Law, or in the Heads of Departments.

The Court began its analysis by holding that "any appointee exercising significant authority pursuant to the laws of the United States is an 'Officer of the United States' and must, therefore, be appointed in the manner prescribed by [the appointments clause]." Four of the six members of the commission were not appointed by the President, and, although the Constitution permitted appointments by "Heads of Departments," this phrase, "used as it is in conjunction with the phrase 'Courts of Law,' suggests that the Departments referred to are themselves in the Executive Branch or at least have some connection with that branch."

It did not follow from this conclusion that the commission was entirely powerless. "Insofar as the powers confided in the Commission are essentially of an investigative and informative nature, falling in the same general category as those powers which Congress might delegate to one of its own committees, there can be no question that the Commission as presently constituted may exercise them."

However, with regard to the more substantial powers exercised by the commission, the Court reached a different conclusion:

> The Commission's enforcement power, exemplified by its discretionary power to seek judicial relief, is authority that cannot possibly be regarded as merely in aid of the legislative function of Congress. [It] is to the President, and not to the Congress, that the Constitution entrusts the responsibility to "take Care that the Laws be faithfully executed."

Similarly, it was unconstitutional to vest in a commission so appointed rulemaking power and power to render advisory opinions or to determine the eligibility for funds:

> These functions, exercised free from day-to-day supervision of either Congress or the Executive Branch [are] of kinds usually performed by independent regulatory agencies or by some department in the Executive Branch under the direction of an Act of Congress. [While] the President may not insist that such functions be delegated to an appointee of his removable at will [*Humphrey's Executor*], none of them operates merely in aid of congressional authority to legislate or is sufficiently removed from the administration and enforcement of public law to allow it to be performed by the present Commission.

5. *Limiting executive discretion.* What implications do *Chadha, Myers, Humphrey's Executor,* and *Buckley* hold for other techniques designed to limit executive discretion? Should it matter whether Congress attempts to arrogate to itself control of executive agencies or whether it merely attempts to make the agencies independent of presidential control? Consider the following.

Bowsher v. Synar

478 U.S. 714 (1986)

CHIEF JUSTICE BURGER delivered the opinion of the Court.

The question presented by these appeals is whether the assignment by Congress to the Comptroller General of the United States of certain functions under the Balanced Budget and Emergency Deficit Control Act of 1985 [the Gramm-Rudman-Hollings Act] violates the doctrine of separation of powers.

[The Comptroller General is the head of the General Accounting Office. His office was created by the Budget and Accounting Act of 1921, which vested him with the duty, inter alia, of investigating all matters relating to the receipt and disbursement of public funds and of reporting to Congress and the President about these matters. Although the Comptroller General is nominated by the President from a list of three individuals recommended by the Speaker of the House of Representatives and the President pro tempore of the Senate, he is removable only at the initiative of Congress. He may be removed by impeachment or by a joint resolution of Congress (subject to presidential veto) on the basis of permanent disability, inefficiency, neglect of duty, malfeasance, commission of a felony, or conduct involving moral turpitude.

[The issue in this case concerned the Comptroller General's role in effectuating "automatic," across-the-board spending reductions mandated in certain circumstances by the Gramm-Rudman-Hollings Act. Passed during a period of mounting concern about the size of the federal budget deficit, this act established declining maximum deficit amounts for each fiscal year beginning in 1986, until the deficit was to have been reduced to zero in fiscal year 1991. Each year the directors of the Office of Management and Budget (OMB) and the Congressional Budget Office (CBO) were required to estimate independently the amount of the federal budget deficit for the next fiscal year. If the deficit exceeded the target, the directors were required to calculate independently, on a program-by-program basis, the budget reductions necessary to meet the target and to report the results to the Comptroller General. The Comptroller General was thereupon directed to prepare a report to the President. Although he was obligated to have "due regard" for the estimates and reductions set forth in the joint report submitted to him by the directors of CBO and OMB, the act required that he exercise independent judgment in evaluating those estimates. Upon receipt of the Comptroller General's report, the President was required to issue a sequestration order, mandating any spending reductions specified by the Comptroller General, which after a specified period became final unless Congress legislated other spending reductions to obviate the need for the order.

[A "fallback" provision in the act provided that, if these procedures were declared unconstitutional, Congress would consider a joint resolution (subject to presidential veto) embodying the reports of OMB and CBO. Upon its enactment, the joint resolution would then be treated as the equivalent of the Comptroller General's report.

[This action was brought by Congressman Synar, who had voted against the act, and by the National Treasury Employees Union, which claimed that its members were injured because the automatic spending reduction provisions suspended certain cost-of-living benefit increases. A three-judge district court held that the act was unconstitutional on the ground that the Comptroller General exercised executive functions under the act — functions that could not constitutionally be exercised by an officer removable by Congress.]

The Constitution does not contemplate an active role for Congress in the supervision of officers charged with the execution of the laws it enacts. The President appoints "Officers of the United States" with the "Advice and Consent of the Senate. . . ." Article II, §2. Once the appointment has been made and confirmed, however, the Constitution explicitly provides for removal of Officers of the United States by Congress only upon impeachment by the House of Representatives and conviction by the Senate. . . .

In light of [*Myers* and *Humphrey's Executor*] we conclude that Congress cannot reserve for itself the power of removal of an officer charged with the execution of the laws except by impeachment. To permit the execution of the laws to be vested in an officer answerable only to Congress would, in practical terms, reserve in Congress control over the execution of the laws.[4] [The] structure of the Constitution does not permit Congress to execute the laws; it follows that Congress cannot grant to an officer under its control what it does not possess. . . .

To permit an officer controlled by Congress to execute the laws would be, in essence, to permit a congressional veto. Congress could simply remove, or threaten to remove, an officer for executing the laws in any fashion found to be unsatisfactory to Congress. This kind of congressional control over the execution of the laws, *Chadha* makes clear, is constitutionally impermissible. . . .

Appellants urge that the Comptroller General performs his duties independently and is not subservient to Congress. We agree with the District Court that this contention does not bear close scrutiny. . . .

The [Budget and Accounting Act of 1921] permits removal for "inefficiency," "neglect of duty," or "malfeasance." These terms are very broad and, as interpreted by Congress, could sustain removal of a Comptroller General for any number of actual or perceived transgressions of the legislative will. The Constitutional Convention chose to permit impeachment of executive officers only for "Treason, Bribery, or other high Crimes and Misdemeanors." It rejected language that would have permitted impeachment for "maladministration," arguing that "[s]o vague a term will be equivalent to a tenure during pleasure of the Senate." . . .

It is clear that Congress has consistently viewed the Comptroller General as an officer of the Legislative Branch. The Reorganization Acts of 1945 and 1949, for example, both stated that the Comptroller General and the GAO are "a part of the legislative branch of the Government." Similarly, in the Accounting and Auditing Act of 1950, Congress required the Comptroller General to conduct audits "as an agent of the Congress."

Over the years, the Comptrollers General have also viewed themselves as part of the Legislative Branch. . . .

Against this background, we see no escape from the conclusion that, because Congress had retained removal authority over the Comptroller General, he may not be entrusted with executive powers. The remaining question is whether the Comptroller General has been assigned such powers in the [Gramm-Rudman-Hollings] Act. . . .

Appellants suggest that the duties assigned to the Comptroller General in the Act are essentially ministerial and mechanical so that their performance does not constitute "execution of the law" in a meaningful sense. On the contrary, we view these functions as plainly entailing execution of the law in constitutional terms. Interpreting a law enacted by Congress to implement the legislative mandate is

---

4. Appellants [are] wide of the mark in arguing that an affirmance in this case requires casting doubt on the status of "independent" agencies because no issues involving such agencies are presented here. [This] case involves [a] statute that provides for direct Congressional involvement over the decision to remove the Comptroller General. Appellants have referred us to no independent agency whose members are removable by the Congress for certain causes short of impeachable offenses, as is the Comptroller General. [Relocated footnote — EDS.]

the very essence of "execution" of the law. Under [the statute], the Comptroller General must exercise judgment concerning facts that affect the application of the Act. He must also interpret the provisions of the Act to determine precisely what budgetary calculations are required. Decisions of that kind are typically made by officers charged with executing a statute.

The executive nature of the Comptroller General's functions under the Act is revealed in §252(a)(3) which gives the Comptroller General the ultimate authority to determine the budget cuts to be made. Indeed, the Comptroller General commands the President himself to carry out, without the slightest variation (with exceptions not relevant to the constitutional issues presented), the directive of the Comptroller General as to the budget reductions....

[As] *Chadha* makes clear, once Congress makes its choice in enacting legislation, its participation ends. Congress can thereafter control the execution of its enactment only indirectly — by passing new legislation. By placing the responsibility for execution of the Balanced Budget and Emergency Deficit Control Act in the hands of an officer who is subject to removal only by itself, Congress in effect has retained control over the execution of the Act and has intruded into the executive function. The Constitution does not permit such intrusion....[10]

[The] judgment and order of the District Court are affirmed....

JUSTICE STEVENS, with whom JUSTICE MARSHALL joins, concurring in the judgment.

[I] agree with the Court that the "Gramm-Rudman-Hollings" Act contains a constitutional infirmity so severe that the flawed provision may not stand. I disagree with the Court, however, on the reasons why the Constitution prohibits the Comptroller General from exercising the powers assigned to him by [the] Act. It is not the dormant, carefully circumscribed congressional removal power that represents the primary constitutional evil. Nor do I agree with the conclusion of both the majority and the dissent that the analysis depends on a labeling of the functions assigned to the Comptroller General as "executive powers." Rather, I am convinced that the Comptroller General must be characterized as an agent of Congress because of his longstanding statutory responsibilities; that the powers assigned to him under the Gramm-Rudman-Hollings Act require him to make policy that will bind the Nation; and that, when Congress, or a component or an agent of Congress, seeks to make policy that will bind the Nation, it must follow the procedures mandated by Article I of the Constitution — through passage by both Houses and presentment to the President....

The Court concludes that the Gramm-Rudman-Hollings Act impermissibly assigns the Comptroller General "executive powers." The dissent agrees that "the powers exercised by the Comptroller under the Act may be characterized as 'executive' in that they involve the interpretation and carrying out of the Act's mandate." This conclusion is not only far from obvious but also rests on the unstated

---

10. Because we conclude that the Comptroller General, as an officer removable by Congress, may not exercise the powers conferred upon him by the Act, we have no occasion for considering appellees' other challenges to the Act, including their argument that the assignment of powers to the Comptroller General in [the Act] violates the delegation doctrine. [Relocated footnote — EDS.]

and unsound premise that there is a definite line that distinguishes executive power from legislative power. . . .

The powers delegated to the Comptroller General by [the] Act before us today have a [chameleon-like] quality. The District Court persuasively explained why they may be appropriately characterized as executive powers. But, when that delegation is held invalid, the "fallback provision" provides that the report that would otherwise be issued by the Comptroller General shall be issued by Congress itself. In the event that the resolution is enacted, the congressional report will have the same legal consequences as if it had been issued by the Comptroller General. . . .

Under [the] analysis adopted by the majority today, it would therefore appear that the function at issue is "executive" if performed by the Comptroller General but "legislative" if performed by the Congress. In my view, however, the function may appropriately be labeled "legislative" even if performed by the Comptroller General or by an executive agency.

Despite the statement in Article I of the Constitution that "All legislative Powers herein granted shall be vested in a Congress of the United States," it is far from novel to acknowledge that independent agencies do indeed exercise legislative powers. . . .

Thus, I do not agree that the Comptroller General's responsibilities under the Gramm-Rudman-Hollings Act must be termed "executive powers," or even that our inquiry is much advanced by using that term. For, whatever the label given the functions to be performed by the Comptroller General under [the reporting provision] — or by the Congress under [the fallback provision] — the District Court had no difficulty in concluding that Congress could delegate the performance of those functions to another branch of the Government. If the delegation to a stranger is permissible, why may not Congress delegate the same responsibilities to one of its own agents? That is the central question before us today. . . .

The Gramm-Rudman-Hollings Act assigns to the Comptroller General the duty to make policy decisions that have the force of law. . . .

Article I of the Constitution specifies the procedures that Congress must follow when it makes policy that binds the Nation: its legislation must be approved by both Houses of Congress and presented to the President. . . .

In short, even though it is well settled that Congress may delegate legislative power to independent agencies or to the Executive, and thereby divest itself of a portion of its lawmaking power, when it elects to exercise such power itself, it may not authorize a lesser representative of the Legislative Branch to act on its behalf. It is for this reason that I believe [the reporting provisions] of the Act are unconstitutional. . . .

JUSTICE WHITE, dissenting.

The Court, acting in the name of separation of powers, takes upon itself to strike down the Gramm-Rudman-Hollings Act, one of the most novel and far-reaching legislative responses to a national crisis since the New Deal. The basis of the Court's action is a solitary provision of another statute that was passed over sixty years ago and has lain dormant since that time. I cannot concur in the Court's action. Like the Court, I will not purport to speak to the wisdom of the policies incorporated in the legislation the Court invalidates; that is a matter for the Congress and the Executive, *both* of which expressed their assent to the statute barely half a year ago. I will, however, address the wisdom of the Court's willingness to interpose its distressingly formalistic view of separation of powers as a bar to the attainment of governmental objectives through the means chosen by the Congress and the President in the legislative process established by the Constitution. . . .

[The] Court's decision rests on a feature of the legislative scheme that is of minimal practical significance and that presents no substantial threat to the basic scheme of separation of powers. . . .

Before examining the merits of the Court's argument, I wish to emphasize what it is that the Court quite pointedly and correctly does *not* hold: namely, that "executive" powers of the sort granted the Comptroller by the Act may only be exercised by officers removable at will by the President. [There] are undoubtedly executive functions that, regardless of the enactments of Congress, must be performed by officers subject to removal at will by the President. Whether a particular function falls within this class or within the far larger class that may be relegated to independent officers "will depend upon the character of the office." [*Humphrey's Executor.*] . . .

It is evident (and nothing in the Court's opinion is to the contrary) that the powers exercised by the Comptroller General under the Gramm-Rudman Act are not such that vesting them in an officer not subject to removal at will by the President would in itself improperly interfere with Presidential powers. Determining the level of spending by the Federal Government is not by nature a function central either to the exercise of the President's enumerated powers or to his general duty to ensure execution of the laws; rather, appropriating funds is a peculiarly legislative function. . . .

[The] question remains whether, as the Court concludes, the fact that the officer to whom Congress has delegated the authority to implement the Act is removable by a joint resolution of Congress should require invalidation of the Act. . . .

I have no quarrel with the proposition that the powers exercised by the Comptroller under the Act may be characterized as "executive" in that they involve the interpretation and carrying out of the Act's mandate. I can also accept the general proposition that although Congress has considerable authority in designating the officers who are to execute legislation, the constitutional scheme of separated powers does prevent Congress from reserving an executive role for itself or for its "agents." [*Buckley* (White, J., concurring in part and dissenting in part).] I cannot accept, however, that the exercise of authority by an officer removable for cause by a joint resolution of Congress is analogous to the impermissible execution of the law by Congress itself, nor would I hold that the congressional role in the removal process renders the Comptroller an "agent" of the Congress, incapable of receiving "executive" power. . . .

[The] Court baldly mischaracterizes the removal provision when it suggests that it allows Congress to remove the Comptroller for "executing the laws in any fashion found to be unsatisfactory"; in fact, Congress may remove the Comptroller only for one or more of five specified reasons, which "although not so narrow as to deny Congress any leeway, circumscribe Congress' power to some extent by providing a basis for judicial review of congressional removal." Ameron, Inc. v. United States Army Corps of Engineers, 787 F.2d 875, 895 (3d Cir. 1986)

(Becker, J., concurring in part). [More] to the point, the Court overlooks or deliberately ignores the decisive difference between the congressional removal provision and the legislative veto struck down in *Chadha*: under the Budget and Accounting Act, Congress may remove the Comptroller only through a joint resolution, which by definition must be passed by both Houses and signed by the President. In other words, a removal of the Comptroller under the statute *satisfies the requirements of bicameralism and presentment laid down in* Chadha.[7]. . .

That such action may represent a more or less successful attempt by Congress to "control" the actions of an officer of the United States surely does not in itself indicate that it is unconstitutional, for no one would dispute that Congress has the power to "control" administration through legislation imposing duties or substantive restraints on executive officers, through legislation increasing or decreasing the funds made available to such officers, or through legislation actually abolishing a particular office. . . .

The practical result of the removal provision is not to render the Comptroller unduly dependent upon or subservient to Congress, but to render him one of the most independent officers in the entire federal establishment. Those who have studied the office agree that the procedural and substantive limits on the power of Congress and the President to remove the Comptroller make dislodging him against his will practically impossible. . . .

[The] role of this Court should be limited to determining whether the Act so alters the balance of authority among the branches of government as to pose a genuine threat to the basic division between the lawmaking power and the power to execute the law. Because I see no such threat, I cannot join the Court in striking down the Act.

I dissent.

[A dissenting opinion by Justice Blackmun has been omitted.]

Morrison v. Olson

487 U.S. 654 (1988)

CHIEF JUSTICE REHNQUIST delivered the opinion of the Court.

This case presents us with a challenge to the independent counsel provisions of the Ethics in Government Act of 1978. We hold today that these provisions of the Act do not violate the Appointments Clause of the Constitution, Art. II, §2,

7. Because a joint resolution passed by both Houses of Congress and signed by the President (or repassed over the President's veto) is legislation having the same force as any other Act of Congress, it is somewhat mysterious why the Court focuses on the Budget and Accounting Act's authorization of removal of the Comptroller through such a resolution as an indicator that the Comptroller may not be vested with executive powers. After all, even without such prior statutory authorization, Congress could pass, and the President sign, a joint resolution purporting to remove the Comptroller, and the validity of such legislation would seem in no way dependent on previous legislation contemplating it. [A] joint resolution purporting to remove the Comptroller, or any other executive officer, might be constitutionally infirm, but Congress' advance assertion of the power to enact such legislation seems irrelevant to the question whether exercise of authority by an officer who might in the future be subject to such a possibly valid and possibly invalid resolution is permissible, since the provision contemplating a resolution of removal obviously cannot in any way add to Congress' power to enact such a resolution. . . . [Relocated footnote — EDS.]

cl. 2, or the limitations of Article III, nor do they impermissibly interfere with the President's authority under Article II in violation of the constitutional principle of separation of powers.

I

Briefly stated, Title VI of the Ethics of Government Act allows for the appointment of an "independent counsel" to investigate and, if appropriate, prosecute certain high ranking government officials for violations of federal criminal laws. The Act requires the Attorney General, upon receipt of information that he determines is "sufficient to constitute grounds to investigate whether any person [covered by the Act] may have violated any Federal criminal law," to conduct a preliminary investigation of the matter. When the Attorney General has completed this investigation, or 90 days has elapsed, he is required to report to a special court (the Special Division) created by the Act "for the purpose of appointing independent counsels." If the Attorney General determines that "there are no reasonable grounds to believe that further investigation is warranted," then he must notify the Special Division of this result. In such a case, "the division of the court shall have no power to appoint an independent counsel." If, however, the Attorney General has determined that there are "reasonable grounds to believe that further investigation or prosecution is warranted," then he "shall apply to the division of the court for the appointment of an independent counsel." The Attorney General's application to the court "shall contain sufficient information to assist the [court] in selecting an independent counsel and in defining that independent counsel's prosecutorial jurisdiction." Upon receiving this application, the Special Division "shall appoint an appropriate independent counsel and shall define that independent counsel's prosecutorial jurisdiction." . . .

[The act provides that the independent counsel can be removed from office only by impeachment or by personal action of the Attorney General for good cause, physical disability, mental incapacity, "or any other condition that substantially impairs the performance of such independent counsel's duties." It also provides that the counsel can be "terminated" if the Special Division finds that "the investigation of all matters within the prosecutorial jurisdiction of such independent counsel . . . have been completed or so substantially completed that it would be appropriate for the Department of Justice to complete such investigations and prosecutions."]

A divided Court of Appeals [invalidated the act]. We now reverse. . . .

III

[The Court quotes the appointments clause of article II, reproduced on page 380, supra.]

The line between "inferior" and "principal" officers is one that is far from clear, and the Framers provided little guidance into where it should be drawn. . . .

We need not attempt here to decide exactly where the line falls between the two types of officers, because in our view appellant clearly falls on the "inferior officer" side of that line. Several factors lead to this conclusion.

[The Court relies on the fact that the special prosecutor could be removed by the Attorney General, that she was authorized to perform only certain limited duties, and that her office was limited in jurisdiction and tenure.]

This does not, however, end our inquiry under the Appointments Clause. Appellees argue that even if appellant is an "inferior" officer, the Clause does not empower Congress to place the power to appoint such an officer outside the Executive Branch. They contend that the Clause does not contemplate congressional authorization of "interbranch appointments," in which an officer of one branch is appointed by officers of another branch. The relevant language of the Appointments Clause is worth repeating. It reads: ". . . but the Congress may by Law vest the Appointment of such inferior Officers, as they think proper, in the President alone, in the courts of Law, or in the Heads of Departments." On its face, the language of this "excepting clause" admits of no limitation on interbranch appointments. Indeed, the inclusion of "as they think proper" seems clearly to give Congress significant discretion to determine whether it is "proper" to vest the appointment of, for example, executive officials in the "courts of Law." . . .

We do not mean to say that Congress' power to provide for interbranch appointments of "inferior officers" is unlimited. In addition to separation of powers concerns, which would arise if such provisions for appointment had the potential to impair the constitutional functions assigned to one of the branches, [Congress'] decision to vest the appointment power in the courts would be improper if there was some "incongruity" between the functions normally performed by the courts and the performance of their duty to appoint. [In] this case, however, we do not think it impermissible for Congress to vest the power to appoint independent counsels in a specially created federal court. We thus disagree with the Court of Appeals' conclusion that there is an inherent incongruity about a court having the power to appoint prosecutorial officers.[12] We have recognized that courts may appoint private attorneys to act as prosecutor for judicial contempt judgments. . . .

Congress of course was concerned when it created the office of independent counsel with the conflicts of interest that could arise in situations when the Executive Branch is called upon to investigate its own high-ranking officers. If it were to remove the appointing authority from the Executive Branch, the most logical place to put it was in the Judicial Branch. In the light of the Act's provision making the judges of the Special Division ineligible to participate in any matters relating to an independent counsel they have appointed, we do not think that appointment of the independent counsels by the court runs afoul of the constitutional limitation on "incongruous" interbranch appointments.

---

12. Indeed, in light of judicial experience with prosecutors in criminal cases, it could be said that courts are especially well qualified to appoint prosecutors. This is not a case in which judges are given power to appoint an officer in an area in which they have no special knowledge or expertise, as in, for example, a statute authorizing the courts to appoint officials in the Department of Agriculture or the Federal Energy Regulatory Commission.

IV

Appellees next contend that the powers vested in the Special Division by the Act conflict with Article III of the Constitution. . . .

[The Court concludes that miscellaneous powers granted to the Special Division are mostly either "passive" or "ministerial" in nature and therefore pose no serious Article III difficulty. Although the provision authorizing the Special Division to terminate the office of independent counsel was more troubling, the Court interprets the provision as no more than "a device for removing from the public payroll an independent counsel who has served her purpose, but is unwilling to acknowledge the fact." As so construed, the termination power did not "pose a sufficient threat of judicial intrusion into matters that are more properly within the Executive's authority to require that the Act be invalidated as inconsistent with Article III."]

V

We now turn to consider whether the Act is invalid under the constitutional principle of separation of powers. Two related issues must be addressed: The first is whether the provision of the Act restricting the Attorney General's power to remove the independent counsel to only those instances in which he can show "good cause," taken by itself, impermissibly interferes with the President's exercise of his constitutionally appointed functions. The second is whether, taken as a whole, the Act violates the separation of powers by reducing the President's ability to control the prosecutorial powers wielded by the independent counsel.

A

We held in *Bowsher* that "Congress cannot reserve for itself the power of removal of an officer charged with the execution of the laws except by impeachment." A primary antecedent for this ruling was our 1925 decision in [*Myers*] . . . .

Unlike both *Bowsher* and *Myers*, this case does not involve an attempt by Congress itself to gain a role in the removal of executive officials other than its established powers of impeachment and conviction. The Act instead puts the removal power squarely in the hands of the Executive Branch; an independent counsel may be removed from office, "only by the personal action of the Attorney General, and only for good cause." There is no requirement of congressional approval of the Attorney General's removal decision, though the decision is subject to judicial review. In our view, the removal provisions of the Act make this case more analogous to Humphrey's Executor v. United States, and Weiner v. United States, than to *Myers* or *Bowsher*. . . .

Appellees contend that *Humphrey's Executor* and *Wiener* are distinguishable from this case because they did not involve officials who performed a "core executive function." They argue that our decision in *Humphrey's Executor* rests on a distinction between "purely executive" officials and officials who exercise "quasi-legislative" and "quasi-judicial" powers. . . .

We undoubtedly did rely on the terms "quasi-legislative" and "quasi-judicial" to distinguish the officials involved in *Humphrey's Executor* and *Wiener* from those in *Myers,* but our present considered view is that the determination of whether the Constitution allows Congress to impose a "good cause"-type restriction on the President's power to remove an official cannot be made to turn on whether or not that official is classified as "purely executive." The analysis contained in our removal cases is designed not to define rigid categories of those officials who may or may not be removed at will by the President, but to ensure that Congress does not interfere with the President's exercise of the "executive power" and his constitutionally appointed duty to "take care that the laws be faithfully executed" under Article II. . . .

We do not mean to suggest that an analysis of the functions served by the officials at issue is irrelevant. But the real question is whether the removal restrictions are of such a nature that they impede the President's ability to perform his constitutional duty, and the functions of the officials in question must be analyzed in that light.

Considering for the moment the "good cause" removal provision in isolation from the other parts of the Act at issue in this case, we cannot say that the imposition of a "good cause" standard for removal by itself unduly trammels on executive authority. . . .

Although the counsel exercises no small amount of discretion and judgment in deciding how to carry out her duties under the Act, we simply do not see how the President's need to control the exercise of that discretion is so central to the functioning of the Executive Branch as to require as a matter of constitutional law that the counsel be terminable at will by the President.

Nor do we think that the "good cause" removal provision at issue here impermissibly burdens the President's power to control or supervise the independent counsel, as an executive official, in the execution of her duties under the Act. This is not a case in which the power to remove an executive official has been completely stripped from the President, thus providing no means for the President to ensure the "faithful execution" of the laws. Rather, because the independent counsel may be terminated for "good cause," the Executive, through the Attorney General, retains ample authority to assure that the counsel is competently performing her statutory responsibilities in a manner that comports with the provisions of the Act. Although we need not decide in this case exactly what is encompassed with the term "good cause" under the Act, the legislative history of the removal provision also makes clear that the Attorney General may remove an independent counsel for "misconduct." . . .

We do not think that this limitation as it presently stands sufficiently deprives the President of control over the independent counsel to interfere impermissibly with his constitutional obligation to ensure the faithful execution of the laws.

B

The final question to be addressed is whether the Act, taken as a whole, violates the principle of separation of powers by unduly interfering with the role of the Executive Branch. . . .

[We] have never held that the Constitution requires that the three Branches of Government "operate with absolute independence." . . .

We observe first that this case does not involve an attempt by Congress to increase its own powers at the expense of the Executive Branch. Unlike some of our previous cases, most recently Bowsher v. Synar, this case simply does not pose a "dange[r] of congressional usurpation of Executive Branch functions," [See] also [*Chadha*]. . . .

Similarly, we do not think that the Act works any *judicial* usurpation of properly executive functions. . . .

Finally, we do not think that the Act "impermissibly undermine[s]" the powers of the Executive Branch, or "disrupts the proper balance between the coordinate branches [by] prevent[ing] the Executive Branch from accomplishing its constitutionally assigned functions." It is undeniable that the Act reduces the amount of control or supervision that the Attorney General and, through him, the President exercises over the investigation and prosecution of a certain class of alleged criminal activity. . . .

Nonetheless, the Act does give the Attorney General several means of supervising or controlling the prosecutorial powers that may be wielded by an independent counsel. . . .

The decision of the Court of Appeals is therefore reversed. . . .

JUSTICE SCALIA, dissenting. . . .

II

If to describe this case is not to decide it, the concept of a government of separate and coordinate powers no longer has meaning. The Court devotes most of its attention to such relatively technical details as the Appointments Clause and the removal power, addressing briefly and only at the end of its opinion the separation of powers. [I] think that has it backwards. Our opinions are full of the recognition that it is the principle of separation of powers, and the inseparable corollary that each department's "defense must . . . be made commensurate to the danger of attack," Federalist No. 51, p. 322 (J. Madison), which gives comprehensible content to the appointments clause, and determines the appropriate scope of the removal power. . . .

Art. II, §1, cl. 1 of the Constitution provides: "The executive Power shall be vested in a President of the United States." [T]his does not mean *some of* the executive power, but *all of* the executive power. It seems to me, therefore, that the decision of the Court of Appeals invalidating the present statute must be upheld on fundamental separation-of-powers principles if the following two questions are answered affirmatively: (1) Is the conduct of a criminal prosecution (and of an investigation to decide whether to prosecute) the exercise of purely executive power? (2) Does the statute deprive the President of the United States of exclusive control over the exercise of that power? Surprising to say, the Court appears to concede an affirmative answer to both questions, but seeks to avoid the inevitable conclusion that since the statute vests some purely executive power in a person who is not the President of the United States it is void.

The Court concedes that "[t]here is no real dispute that the functions performed by the independent counsel are 'executive,'" though it qualifies that concession by adding "in the sense that they are 'law enforcement' functions that typically have been undertaken by officials within the Executive Branch." The qualifier adds nothing but atmosphere. In what *other* sense can one identify "the executive Power" that is supposed to be vested in the President (unless it includes everything the Executive Branch is given to do) *except* by reference to what has always and everywhere — if conducted by Government at all — been conducted never by the legislature, never by the courts, and always by the executive. There is no possible doubt that the independent counsel's functions fit this description. . . .

As for the second question, whether the statute before us deprives the President of exclusive control over that quintessentially executive activity, the Court does not, and could not possibly, assert that it does not. That is indeed the whole object of the statute. Instead, the Court points out that the President, through his Attorney General, has at least *some* control. That concession is alone enough to invalidate the statute, but I cannot refrain from pointing out that the Court greatly exaggerates the extent of that "some" presidential control. . . .

The utter incompatibility of the Court's approach with our constitutional traditions can be made more clear, perhaps, by applying it to the powers of the other two Branches. Is it conceivable that if Congress passed a statute depriving itself of less than full and entire control over some insignificant area of legislation, we would inquire whether the matter was "*so central* to the functioning of the Legislative Branch" as really to require complete control, or whether the statute gives Congress "*sufficient* control over the surrogate legislator to ensure that Congress is able to perform its constitutionally assigned duties"? Of course we would have none of that. Once we determined that a purely legislative power was at issue we would require it to be exercised, wholly and entirely, by Congress. Or to bring the point closer to home, consider a statute giving to non-Article III judges just a tiny bit of purely judicial power in a relatively insignificant field, with substantial control, though not total control, in the courts — perhaps "clear error" review, which would be a fair judicial equivalent of the Attorney General's "for cause" removal power here. Is there any doubt that we would not pause to inquire whether the matter was "*so central* to the functioning of the Judicial Branch" as really to require complete control, or whether we retained "*sufficient* control over the matters to be decided that we are able to perform our constitutionally assigned duties"? We would say that our "constitutionally assigned duties" include *complete* control over all exercises of the judicial power — or, as the plurality opinion said in Northern Pipeline Construction Co. v. Marathon Pipe Line Co. [458 U.S. 50, 58-59 (1982)], that "[t]he inexorable command of [article III] is clear and definite: The judicial power of the United States must be exercised by courts having the attributes prescribed in Art. III." We should say here that the President's constitutionally assigned duties include *complete* control over investigation and prosecution of violations of the law, and that the inexorable command of Article II is clear and definite: the executive power must be vested in the President of the United States.

Is it unthinkable that the President should have such exclusive power, even when alleged crimes by him or his close associates are at issue? No more so than that Congress should have the exclusive power of legislation, even when what is at issue is its own exemption from the burdens of certain laws. No more so than that this Court should have the exclusive power to pronounce the final decision on justiciable cases and controversies, even those pertaining to the constitutionality of a statute reducing the salaries of the Justices. A system of separate and coordinate powers necessarily involves an acceptance of exclusive power that can theoretically be abused. . . .

The Court has, nonetheless, replaced the clear constitutional prescription that the executive power belongs to the President with a "balancing test." What are the standards to determine how the balance is to be struck, that is, how much removal of presidential power is too much? Many countries of the world get along with an Executive that is much weaker than ours — in fact, entirely dependent upon the continued support of the legislature. Once we depart from the text of the Constitution, just where short of that do we stop? The most amazing feature of the Court's opinion is that it does not even purport to give an answer. It simply *announces*, with no analysis, that the ability to control the decision whether to investigate and prosecute the President's closest advisors, and indeed the President himself, is not "so central to the functioning of the Executive Branch" as to be constitutionally required to be within the President's control. . . .

Besides weakening the Presidency by reducing the zeal of his staff, it must also be obvious that the institution of the independent counsel enfeebles him more directly in his constant confrontations with Congress, by eroding his public support. Nothing is so politically effective as the ability to charge that one's opponent and his associates are not merely wrong-headed, naive, ineffective, but, in all probability, "crooks." And nothing so effectively gives an appearance of validity to such charges as a Justice Department investigation and, even better, prosecution. The present statute provides ample means for that sort of attack, assuring that massive and lengthy investigations will occur, not merely when the Justice Department in the application of its usual standards believes they are called for, but whenever it cannot be said that there are "no reasonable grounds to believe" they are called for. . . .

[The] Court does not attempt to "decide exactly" what establishes the line between principal and "inferior" officers, but is confident that, whatever the line may be, appellant "clearly falls on the 'inferior officer' side" of it. . . .

[Justice Scalia points out that most principal officers are removable at will and not simply for cause and argues that the majority understates the scope of the independent counsel's powers.] I think it preferable to look to the text of the Constitution and the division of power that it establishes. These demonstrate, I think, that the independent counsel is not an inferior officer because she is not *subordinate* to any officer in the Executive Branch (indeed, not even to the President). Dictionaries in use at the time of the Constitutional Convention gave the word "inferiour" two meanings which it still bears today: (1) "[l]ower in place, . . . station, . . . rank of life, . . . value or excellency," and (2) "[s]ubordinate." S. Johnson, Dictionary of the English Language (6th ed. 1785). In a document dealing with the structure (the constitution) of a government, one would naturally expect the word to bear the latter meaning — indeed, in such a context it would be unpardonably careless to use the word *unless* a relationship of subordination was intended. . . .

IV . . .

There is of course no provision in the Constitution stating who may remove executive officers, except the provisions for removal by impeachment. Before the present decision it was established, however, (1) that the President's power to remove principal officers who exercise purely executive powers could not be restricted, see [*Myers*], and (2) that his power to remove inferior officers who exercise purely executive powers, and whose appointment Congress had removed from the usual procedure of presidential appointment with Senate consent, could be restricted, at least where the appointment had been made by an officer of the Executive Branch. . . .

Since our 1935 decision in [*Humphrey's Executor*] — which was considered by many at the time the product of an activist, anti-New Deal court bent on reducing the power of President Franklin Roosevelt — it has been established that the line of permissible restriction upon removal of principal officers lies at the point at which the powers exercised by those officers are no longer purely executive. . . .

What *Humphrey's Executor* (and presumably *Myers*) really means, we are now told, is not that there are any "rigid categories of those officials who may or may not be removed at will by the President," but simply that Congress cannot "interfere with the President's exercise of the 'executive power' and his constitutionally appointed duty to 'take care that the laws be faithfully executed.'" . . .

Humphrey's Executor at least had the decency formally to observe the constitutional principle that the President had to be the repository of *all* executive power, which, as *Myers* carefully explained, necessarily means that he must be able to discharge those who do not perform executive functions according to his liking. . . .

By contrast, "our present considered view" is simply that *any* Executive officer's removal can be restricted, so long as the President remains "able to accomplish his constitutional role." There are now no lines. If the removal of a prosecutor, the virtual embodiment of the power to "take care that the laws be faithfully executed," can be restricted, what officer's removal cannot? This is an open invitation for Congress to experiment. What about a special Assistant Secretary of State, with responsibility for one very narrow area of foreign policy, who would not only have to be confirmed by the Senate but could also be removed only pursuant to certain carefully designed restrictions? Could this possibly render the President "[un]able to accomplish his constitutional role"? Or a special Assistant Secretary of Defense for Procurement? The possibilities are endless, and the Court does not understand what the separation of powers, what "[a]mbition . . . counteract[ing] ambition," Federalist No. 51, p. 322 (Madison), is all about, if it does not expect Congress to try them. As far as I can discern from the Court's opinion, it is now open season upon the President's removal power for all executive officers, with not even the superficially principled restriction of *Humphrey's Executor* as cover. The Court essentially says to the President "Trust us. We will make sure that you are able to accomplish your constitutional role." I think the Constitution gives the President — and the people — more protection than that.

V

The purpose of the separation and equilibration of powers in general, and of the unitary Executive in particular, was not merely to assure effective government but to preserve individual freedom. Those who hold or have held offices covered by the Ethics in Government Act are entitled to that protection as much as the rest of us, and I conclude my discussion by considering the effect of the Act upon the fairness of the process they receive.

Only someone who has worked in the field of law enforcement can fully appreciate the vast power and the immense discretion that are placed in the hands of a prosecutor with respect to the objects of his investigation. . . .

Under our system of government, the primary check against prosecutorial abuse is a political one. The prosecutors who exercise this awesome discretion are selected and can be removed by a President, whom the people have trusted enough to elect. Moreover, when crimes are not investigated and prosecuted fairly, nonselectively, with a reasonable sense of proportion, the President pays the cost in political damage to his administration. . . .

That is the system of justice the rest of us are entitled to, but what of that select class consisting of present or former high-level executive-branch officials? If an allegation is made against them of any violation of any federal criminal law (except Class B or C misdemeanors or infractions) the Attorney General must give it his attention. That in itself is not objectionable. But if, after a 90-day investigation without the benefit of normal investigatory tools, the Attorney General is unable to say that there are "no reasonable grounds to believe" that further investigation is warranted, a process is set in motion that is *not* in the full control of persons "dependent on the people," and whose flaws cannot be blamed on the President. An independent counsel is selected, and the scope of her authority prescribed, by a panel of judges. What if they are politically partisan, as judges have been known to be, and select a prosecutor antagonistic to the administration, or even to the particular individual who has been selected for this special treatment? There is no remedy for that, not even a political one. . . .

It is, in other words, an additional advantage of the unitary Executive that it can achieve a more uniform application of the law. Perhaps that is not always achieved, but the mechanism to achieve it is there. The mini-Executive that is the independent counsel, however, operating in an area where so little is law and so much is discretion, is intentionally cut off from the unifying influence of the Justice Department, and from the perspective that multiple responsibilities provide. What would normally be regarded as a technical violation (there are no rules defining such things), may in her small world assume the proportions of an indictable offense. . . .

The ad hoc approach to constitutional adjudication has real attraction, even apart from its work-saving potential. It is guaranteed to produce a result, in every case, that will make a majority of the Court happy with the law. The law is, by definition, precisely what the majority thinks, taking all things into account, it *ought* to be. I prefer to rely upon the judgment of the wise men who constructed our system, and of the people who approved it, and of two centuries of history that have shown it to be sound. Like it or not, that judgment says, quite plainly, that "[t]he executive Power shall be vested in a President of the United States."

Note: Congressional Control over Administrative Officials

1. Chadha *and* Bowsher. Although both *Chadha* and *Bowsher* invalidated innovative schemes designed to preserve congressional control of delegated authority, the two decisions utilize different approaches. In *Chadha*, the Court treats Congress's decision regarding Chadha's immigration status as an exercise of legislative authority and finds it invalid because it failed to comport with the present-

ment and bicameral requirements for the enactment of statutes. A difficulty with this approach is that in the absence of the legislative veto, Chadha's immigration status would be determined by the Immigration and Naturalization Service. Yet the service's decision also fails to comport with the bicameralism requirement.

Bowsher avoids this difficulty by reversing the analysis. The constitutional defect in the Gramm-Rudman-Hollings law was not that Congress was legislating, but that it was *not* legislating. The Court treats the Comptroller General's budget-cutting authority as an exercise of *executive* power and holds that Congress had unconstitutionally trenched on executive authority by vesting this authority in an officer under legislative control. Is this approach more satisfactory? If the Comptroller General's budget-cutting authority is executive, why is the "fallback" provision, under which Congress itself would enact the budget cuts, constitutional?

2. Morrison *and* Bowsher. Can *Bowsher* and *Morrison* be reconciled? The Court appears to distinguish between statutory schemes designed to assert congressional control over administrative officials (prohibited in *Myers, Chadha,* and *Bowsher*) and statutory schemes designed to protect administrative officials from executive control (permitted in *Humphrey's Executor* and *Morrison*). On this view, Congress may make some executive officers independent, but it may not itself control them. Notice that this distinction privileges arrangements that shield administrative officers from accountability to either of the popularly elected branches of government. Doesn't this turn the traditional concern about delegated power on its head?

3. *Mistretta.* Consider in this connection the implications of Mistretta v. United States, 488 U.S. 361 (1989). The United States Sentencing Commission has seven members appointed by the President, of whom three must be federal judges; the statute creating the commission states that it is "an independent commission located in the judicial branch." The commission was created in response to concern that sentences for similar offenses and of similar offenders in the federal system varied too substantially to promote the goals of sentencing. Its role is to create mandatory sentencing guidelines specifying rather narrow ranges of permissible sentences for different offenses, taking some account of the different circumstances under which different people commit crimes.

The Court, in an opinion by Justice Blackmun, rejected a variety of separation of powers challenges to the commission. Relying on the "intelligible principle" test derived from prior nondelegation cases, the Court found that the Congress had given the commission sufficiently detailed guidance as to the purposes its guidelines were to serve and the considerations the commission was to take into account. Addressing more general separation of powers concerns, the Court cited Justice Jackson's opinion in *Youngstown* for "the pragmatic, flexible view of differentiated governmental power to which we are heir." In particular, the Court acknowledged a "twilight" area in which the functions of the various branches merged. Thus, although courts may not generally exercise executive and administrative duties of a nonjudicial nature, some forms of judicial rule-making are permissible. "[Consistent] with separation of powers, Congress may delegate nonadjudicatory functions that do not trench upon the prerogatives of another branch and that are appropriate to the central mission of the Judiciary." For example, Congress had appropriately delegated to the courts the power to develop rules of procedure. In the Court's view, the development of sentencing guidelines also came within this category.

In a dissenting opinion, Justice Scalia argued that "[the] decisions made by the Commission are far from technical, but are heavily laden [with] value judgments and policy assessments." He therefore expressed some sympathy for the position that the commission's mandate violated the nondelegation doctrine, but acknowledged that the doctrine "is not [readily] enforceable by the courts." However,

> [precisely] because the scope of delegation is largely uncontrollable by the courts, we must be particularly rigorous in preserving the Constitution's structural restrictions that deter excessive delegation. The major one [is] that the power to make law cannot be exercised by anyone other than Congress, except in conjunction with the lawful exercise of executive or judicial power. [Until Morrison v. Olsen,] it could have been said that Congress could delegate lawmaking authority only at the expense of increasing the power of either the President or the courts. [Thus,] the need for delegation would have to be important enough to induce Congress to aggrandize its primary competitor for political power, and the recipient of the policymaking authority, while not Congress itself, would at least be politically accountable. . . .
>
> [I] anticipate that Congress will find delegation of its lawmaking powers much more attractive in the future. If rulemaking can be entirely unrelated to the exercise of judicial or executive powers, I foresee all manner of "expert" bodies, insulated from the political process, to which Congress will delegate various portions of its lawmaking responsibility. . . .
>
> I think the Court errs [not] so much because it mistakes the degree of commingling [of the branches of government], but because it fails to recognize that this case is not about commingling, but about the creation of a new branch altogether, a sort of junior-varsity Congress. It may well be that in some circumstances such a branch would be desirable. [But] there are many desirable dispositions that do not accord with the constitutional structure we live under. And in the long run the improvisation of a constitutional structure on the basis of currently perceived utility will be disastrous.

4. *Nonpresidential appointments.* Exactly when can cross-branch appointments be made? Could Congress vest in the Secretary of State the power to appoint law clerks? In the courts the power to appoint lower-level officials in the Occupational Safety and Health Administration?

Since *Morrison,* the Court has rejected three additional constitutional challenges to nonpresidential appointments. See Freytag v. Commissioner of Internal Revenue, 501 U.S. 868 (1991) (upholding the power of the chief judge of the Tax Court to appoint "special trial judges" on the ground that the Tax Court was a "Court of Law" within the meaning of the appointments clause); Weiss v. United States, 510 U.S. 163 (1994) (upholding the power of the Judge Advocate General to appoint military judges serving on special and general courts martial on the ground that although the officers received judicial assignments from the Judge Advocate General, they had already been appointed as commissioned officers by the President); Edmond v. United States, 520 U.S. 651 (1997) (upholding power of the Secretary of Transportation to appoint civilian members of the Coast Guard Court of Appeals on the ground that these judges were "inferior officers" who could be appointed by a head of department).

5. *Justice Scalia's position.* Consider Justice Scalia's concern, expressed at the conclusion of his *Morrison* dissent, about the possibility of "a [special] prosecutor antagonistic to the administration" who might treat a "technical violation"

as an indictable offense. Justice Scalia expressed these views before the Clinton impeachment . Do the events surrounding the impeachment prove that he was right? (For a brief chronology of the events surrounding the impeachment, see pages 359-360, supra.) Can Justice Scalia's overt invocation of policy concerns be reconciled with the insistence of obedience to formal, textual constraints expressed in the rest of the opinion? Following the Clinton impeachment, Congress permitted the Independent Counsel Act to expire. Does this fact support the view that the Court should have invalidated the act, or does it demonstrate that ordinary democratic processes were sufficient to correct any problems produced by it? In his *Morrison* and *Mistretta* dissents, Justice Scalia objects to the results reached by the Court because they permit Congress to establish arrangements that minimize political accountability. Is this position consistent with his willingness to use the courts to police separation of powers decisions made by the politically accountable branches?

6. Congressional control over administrative agencies after Chadha *and* Bowsher. Recall that in Buckley v. Valeo, page 380, supra, the Court upheld the Federal Campaign Act insofar as the powers that it delegated to the Federal Election Commission were "essentially of an investigative and informative nature, falling in the same general category as those which Congress might delegate to one of its own committees." Does this holding survive *Chadha?* Would it survive the approach outlined in Justice Stevens's concurring opinion in *Bowsher?* Does *Bowsher* raise nontrivial questions about direct congressional control over the policies adopted by administrative agencies through the passage of ordinary legislation contravening those policies? Consider the following.

METROPOLITAN WASHINGTON AIRPORTS AUTHORITY v. CITIZENS FOR THE ABATEMENT OF AIRCRAFT NOISE, 501 U.S. 252 (1991). Before 1986, National and Dulles Airports, outside of Washington, D.C., were operated by the federal government. In that year, Congress enacted the Transfer Act, which authorized the transfer of the airports to the Metropolitan Washington Airports Authority, an entity created by statutes enacted by Virginia and the District of Columbia. However, Congress conditioned the transfer on the creation of a Board of Review with the power to veto major decisions made by the directors of the authority. The Transfer Act provided that the Board of Review would consist of nine members of Congress, who would serve "in their individual capacities, as representatives of users of the [airports]." Eight of the nine were to be members of various committees with jurisdiction over transportation issues. All nine were to be appointed by the authority's board of directors from lists provided by the Speaker of the House and the President pro tempore of the Senate. Virginia and the District of Columbia thereupon amended their statutes to authorize creation of the Board of Review, and its members were appointed by the directors pursuant to the statutory procedure.

Respondents, representing citizens who resided under the flight paths of aircraft using National Airport, sought a declaration that the power of the Board of Review to veto actions of the authority violated separation of powers principles. In a six-to-three decision, the Court, per Justice Stevens, held that the statute was unconstitutional.

The Court began its analysis by rejecting arguments that separation of powers principles were inapplicable because the Board of Review was created by state statutes: "We [confront] an entity created at the initiative of Congress, the powers of which Congress has delineated, the purpose of which is to protect an acknowledged federal interest, and membership in which is restricted to congressional officials. Such an entity necessarily exercises sufficient federal power as an agent of Congress to mandate separation-of-powers scrutiny."

Having established that the Board of Review was subject to scrutiny under separation of powers principles, the Court then held that those principles had been violated: "The abuses by the monarch recounted in the Declaration of Independence provided dramatic evidence of the threat to liberty posed by a too powerful executive. But, as James Madison recognized, the representatives of the majority in a democratic society, if unconstrained, may pose a similar threat. [The Court here quoted from The Federalist No. 48, section A, supra.] . . .

"To forestall the danger of encroachment 'beyond the legislative sphere,' the Constitution imposes two basic and related constraints on Congress. It may not 'invest itself or its Members with either executive power or judicial power.' And, when it exercises its legislative power, it must follow the 'single, finely wrought and exhaustively considered procedures' specified in Article I.

"The first constraint is illustrated by the Court's holding in [Bowsher]. . . .

"The second constraint is illustrated by our decision in Chadha. . . .

"The Court of Appeals found it unnecessary to discuss the second constraint because the court was satisfied that the power exercised by the Board of Review over 'key operational decisions is quintessentially executive.' We need not agree or disagree with this characterization [to] conclude that the Board of Review's power is constitutionally impermissible. If the power is executive, the Constitution does not permit an agent of Congress to exercise it. If the power is legislative, Congress must exercise it in conformity with the bicameralism and presentment requirements of Art I, §7. [See Chadha]."

In a footnote at the end of its opinion, the Court noted that it need not address the claim that the Transfer Act violated the ineligibility clause of article I, section 6, which prohibits members of Congress from holding any "Office under the United States," or the claim that it violated the appointments clause of article II, section 2, clause 2.

Justice White, joined by Chief Justice Rehnquist and Justice Marshall, dissented. He argued that separation of powers principles were inapplicable because the authority and the board were creatures of state law: "As an initial matter, the Board may not have existed but for Congress, but it does not follow that Congress created the Board or even that Congress' role is a 'factor' mandating separation-of-powers scrutiny. [The] majority's conclusion ignores the entire series of voluntary and intervening actions, agreements, and enactments on the part of the Federal Executive, Virginia, the District and the Authority, without which the Transfer Act would have been a nullity and the Board of Review would not have existed."

Turning to the merits of respondents' separation of powers claim, Justice White began by challenging the majority's attempt "to clear the path for its decision by stressing the Framers' fear of overweening legislative authority. It cannot be seriously maintained . . . that the basis for fearing legislative encroachment has increased or even persisted rather than substantially diminished. At one point Congress may have reigned as the preeminent Branch, much as the Framers predicted. It does so no longer. This century has witnessed a vast increase in the power that Congress has transferred to the Executive. Given this shift in the constitutional balance, the Framers' fears of legislative tyranny ring hollow when invoked to portray a body like the Board as a serious encroachment on the powers of the Executive."

If the board really was exercising federal executive power, White maintained, the majority had inexplicably failed to rely on the ineligibility clause, which was directly on point. "If the Board did exercise executive authority that is federal in nature, the Court would have no need to say anything other than that congressional membership on the Board violated [this] express constitutional [limitation]. The majority's failure is either unaccountable or suggests that it harbors a certain discomfort with its own position that the Board in fact exercises significant federal power. Whichever is the case, the Court instead relies on expanding nontextual principles as articulated in [*Bowsher*]. . . .

"As *Bowsher* made clear, a 'critical factor' in determining whether an official is 'subservient to Congress' is the degree to which Congress maintains the power of removal. [Here,] Congress exercises no such power. Unlike the statutes struck down in *Bowsher* and *Myers*, the Transfer Act contains no provision authorizing Congress to discharge anyone from the board. . . .

"Nor has Congress improperly influenced the appointment process, which is ordinarily a less important factor in separation-of-powers analysis in any event. . . .

"Twice in recent Terms the Court has considered [appointment] mechanisms [similar to the Transfer Act] without suggesting that they raised any constitutional concern. In *Bowsher*, the Court voiced no qualms concerning Presidential appointment of the Comptroller General from a list of three individuals suggested by the House Speaker and the President pro tempore. Likewise, in *Mistretta*, the Court upheld Congress' authority to require the President to appoint three federal judges to the Sentencing Commission after considering a list of six judges recommended by the Judicial Conference of the United States. . . .

"The majority alternatively suggests that the Board wields an unconstitutional legislative veto contrary to *Chadha*. [The] problem with this theory is that if the Board is exercising federal power, its power is not legislative. . . .

"Before their transfer to the Airports Authority, National and Dulles were managed by the Federal Aviation Administration, which in turn succeeded the Civil Aeronautics Agency. There is no question that these two agencies exercised paradigmatic executive power or that the transfer of the airports in no way altered that power, which is now in the hands of the Authority. [*Chadha*] is therefore inapposite."

Note: Metropolitan Washington Airports Authority *and Congressional Control over Executive Agencies*

The Court held that the Transfer Act was unconstitutional regardless of whether the Board of Review was exercising executive or legislative authority. Assume, first, it was exercising executive authority. What then explains the Court's decision to eschew reliance on the relatively clear requirements of the appointments and ineligibility clauses in favor of the more amorphous, arguably nontextual *Bowsher* principle? Recall Chief Justice Burger's forceful invocation of textualism in *Chadha*. Does *Metropolitan Washington Airports Authority* suggest an abandonment of this approach in separation of powers cases?

It seems to follow from the Court's failure to reach the appointments and ineligibility clause arguments that the act is unconstitutional simply because congressional control over the Board of Review turned it into an "agent of Congress," and that the particular technique by which the control was exercised was relatively unimportant. Suppose Congress chose to exercise control over airport decisions by

a. refusing to enact legislation transferring authority over the airports unless the Board of Review established certain substantive policies favored by Congress;

b. refusing to enact legislation transferring authority over the airports unless the President promised to appoint certain named individuals to the Board of Review;

c. enacting legislation requiring the Board of Review to establish certain substantive policies regarding airport use; or

d. refusing to enact legislation transferring authority over the airports and enacting all airport rules in the form of federal statutes subject to presidential veto.

Would any of these techniques be unconstitutional? If not, how are they distinguishable from what Congress in fact did? Are alternatives *a* and *c* distinguishable because they involve congressional control over discrete questions rather than generalized, pervasive congressional control? Is alternative *b* distinguishable because the President could always break his promise? Are alternatives *c* and *d* distinguishable because they preserve presidential involvement in policy decisions through the veto power? Do any of these distinctions have a basis in the constitutional text?

Alternatively, assume the Board of Review is exercising legislative authority. Is there then any explanation for why it was constitutional for the Federal Aviation Administration to run the airport prior to the transfer?

D.   FOREIGN AFFAIRS

In the domestic sphere, the Supreme Court has at least sporadically asserted that separation of powers questions can be guided by the textual division of authority among the executive, legislative, and judicial branches. That division is ambiguous, with hard intermediate cases.

The foreign sphere is different. There the allocation of authority

is not determined by any "natural" division. As they have evolved, the foreign relations powers appear [fissured]: [some] powers and functions belong to the President, some to Congress, some to the President-and-Senate; some can be exercised by either the President or the Congress, some require the joint authority of both.

Irregular, uncertain division renders claims of usurpation more difficult to establish and the courts have not been available to adjudicate them.

L. Henkin, Foreign Affairs and the Constitution 32 (1972).

In these circumstances, much of the "law" is the product of historical practice and practical accommodations, formal and informal, between the executive and legislative branches.

1. Executive Authority

United States v. Curtiss-Wright Corp.

299 U.S. 304 (1936)

MR. JUSTICE SUTHERLAND delivered the opinion of the Court.

[An] indictment was returned in the court below, the first count of which charges that appellees [conspired] to sell in the United States certain arms of war, namely fifteen machine guns, to Bolivia, a country then engaged in armed conflict in the Chaco, in violation of the Joint Resolution of Congress approved May 28, 1934, and the provisions of a proclamation issued on the same day by the President [pursuant] to authority conferred by §1 of the resolution. [The joint resolution authorized the President to prohibit the sale of arms if he found that such a prohibition would contribute to establishment of peace in the region. The lower court held that the joint resolution was an unconstitutional delegation of legislative power to the President.]

Whether, if the Joint Resolution had related solely to internal affairs it would be open to the challenge that it constituted an unlawful delegation of legislative power to the Executive, we find it unnecessary to determine. [Curtiss-Wright was decided one year after the Court invalidated the National Industrial Recovery Act on the ground that it impermissibly delegated a legislative function to the President. See Schecter Poultry Corp. v. United States, section C2, supra.] The whole aim of the resolution is to affect a situation entirely external to the United States, and falling within the category of foreign affairs. [Assuming] (but not deciding) that the challenged delegation, if it were confined to internal affairs, would be invalid, may it nevertheless be sustained on the ground that its exclusive aim is to afford a remedy for a hurtful condition within foreign territory?

It will contribute to the elucidation of the question if we first consider the differences between the powers of the federal government in respect of foreign or external affairs and those in respect of domestic or internal affairs. . . .

The two classes of powers are different, both in respect of their origin and their nature. The broad statement that the federal government can exercise no powers except those specifically enumerated in the Constitution, and such implied powers as are necessary and proper to carry into effect the enumerated powers, is categorically true only in respect of our internal affairs. In that field, the primary purpose of the Constitution was to carve from the general mass of legislative powers *then possessed by the states* such portions as it was thought desirable to vest in the federal government, leaving those not included in the enumeration still in the states. [That] this doctrine applies only to powers which the states had, is self evident. And since the states severally never possessed international powers, such powers could not have been carved from the mass of state powers but obviously were transmitted to the United States from some other source. . . .

As a result of the separation from Great Britain by the colonies acting as a unit, the powers of external sovereignty passed from the Crown not to the colonies severally, but to the colonies in their collective and corporate capacity as the United States of America. [Rulers] come and go; governments end and forms of government change; but sovereignty survives. A political society cannot endure without a supreme will somewhere. Sovereignty is never held in suspense. When, therefore, the external sovereignty of Great Britain in respect of the colonies ceased, it immediately passed to the Union. . . .

It results that the investment of the federal government with the powers of external sovereignty did not depend upon the affirmative grants of the Constitution. The powers to declare and wage war, to conclude peace, to make treaties, to maintain diplomatic relations with other sovereignties, if they had never been mentioned in the Constitution, would have vested in the federal government as necessary concomitants of nationality. . . .

Not only, as we have shown, is the federal power over external affairs in origin and essential character different from that over internal affairs, but participation in the exercise of the power is significantly limited. In this vast external realm, with its important, complicated, delicate and manifold problems, the President alone has the power to speak or listen as a representative of the nation. He *makes* treaties with the advice and consent of the Senate; but he alone negotiates. Into the field of negotiation the Senate cannot intrude; and Congress itself is powerless to invade it. As Marshall said [in] the House of Representatives, "The President is the sole organ of the nation in its external relations, and its sole representative with foreign nations." . . .

It is important to bear in mind that we are here dealing not alone with an authority vested in the President by an exertion of legislative power, but with such an authority plus the very delicate, plenary and exclusive power of the President as the sole organ of the federal government in the field of international relations — a power which does not require as a basis for its exercise an act of Congress. [It] is quite apparent that if, in the maintenance of our international relations, embarrassment — perhaps serious embarrassment — is to be avoided and success for our aims achieved, congressional legislation [must] often accord to the President a degree of discretion and freedom from statutory restriction which would not be admissible were domestic affairs alone involved. Moreover, he, not Congress, has the better opportunity of knowing the conditions which prevail in foreign countries, and especially is this true in time of war. He has his confidential sources of information. He has his agents in the form of diplomatic, consular and other officials. Secrecy in respect of information gathered by them may be highly necessary, and the premature disclosure of it productive of harmful results. . . .

In the light of the foregoing observations, it is evident that this court should not be in haste to apply a general rule which will have the effect of condemning legislation like that under review as constituting an unlawful delegation of legislative power. The principles which justify such legislation find overwhelming support in the unbroken legislative practice which has prevailed almost from the inception of the national government to the present day. . . .

[Reversed.]
MR. JUSTICE MCREYNOLDS dissented without opinion.

Note: The President and Foreign Affairs

1. *Text, history, and presidential power. Curtiss-Wright* involved a delegation from Congress to the President. Were the Court's broad pronouncements about presidential power therefore unnecessary to the decision? Why does the Court believe that the President is "the sole organ of the federal government in the field of international relations"?

Consider, first, arguments from text and historical practice. Notice that the Constitution's text does not make the President the sole organ of the federal government. It vests in Congress a number of foreign affairs powers, including the power to declare war; the power to regulate commerce with foreign nations; the power to raise and support armies; the power to provide and maintain a navy; the power to provide for organizing, arming, and disciplining the militia; and the power to make rules for calling forth the militia to repel invasions. The President, to be sure, is commander-in-chief of the armed forces and the militia; and he is given other authority as well. But the text hardly provides unambiguous support for the Court's broad statements.

The history is also uncertain. From the first, it was clear that the President would have to assume a special role of leadership and initiative in the realm of foreign policy. Many Presidents assumed such a role, concluding that the necessities of international relations prevented Congress, with its many members, from acting expeditiously. Consider in this regard the framers' desire to ensure an energetic executive. But that raises two questions. First, does the somewhat ambiguous history in fact support the Court's conclusion? Second, what role should historical practices have in interpreting the relevant constitutional provisions? Why should those practices not be considered a usurpation of the original allocation of constitutional authority?

2. *Functionalism and the autonomy of constitutional interpretation.* The *Curtiss-Wright* Court makes reference to both text and history, but it relies as well on arguments from function. Only the President, the Court asserts, can "[know] the conditions which prevail in foreign countries," has "confidential sources of information," and can maintain secrecy. Exclusive presidential authority is essential if "embarrassment — perhaps serious embarrassment — is to be avoided and success for our aims achieved."

Notice that this argument parallels the argument for delegation of legislative power to the executive in domestic affairs: Only the administrative state, it is argued, can regulate the economy in an efficient and effective fashion. Do arguments of this sort have any role in constitutional interpretation? Are these arguments independent from controversial political judgments about the appropriate role of the federal government? Advocates of free markets at home and of isolationism abroad will hardly be persuaded to support executive authority on the ground that it promotes interventionism in both spheres. Isn't constitutional law supposed to be independent of these contested political judgments? Is there a good reason for supporting a particular allocation of power that is not grounded in the belief that, over the range of cases, the allocation is likely to produce sound policy? If not, won't constitutional judgments in this field inevitably be grounded in the political positions of the people making the judgments?

Note: The Allocation of Warmaking Authority

The Constitution is notoriously ambiguous on the allocation of warmaking power as between the President and the Congress. The President is made commander-in-chief of the armed forces, and there is no doubt that the framers intended the President to play the principal role as the representative of the United States in relations with other nations. On the other hand, Congress is expressly empowered to "declare war." How should these provisions be reconciled?

1. *The original understanding.* Some guidance was provided during the Constitutional Convention:

"To make war."

Mr. Pinkney opposed the vesting this power in the Legislature. Its proceedings were too slow. It wd. meet but once a year. The Hs. of Reps. would be too numerous for such deliberations. The Senate would be the best depository, being more acquainted with foreign affairs, and most capable of proper resolutions. If the States are equally represented in Senate, so as to give no advantage to large States, the power will notwithstanding be safe, as the small have their all at stake in such cases as well as the large States. It would be singular for one authority to make war, and another peace.

Mr. Butler. The Objections agst the Legislature lie in a great degree agst the Senate. He was for vesting the power in the President, who will have all the requisite qualities, and will not make war but when the Nation will support it.

Mr. M[adison] and Mr. Gerry moved to insert "*declare*," striking out "*make*" war; leaving to the Executive the power to repel sudden attacks.

Mr. Sharman thought it stood very well. The Executive shd. be able to repel and not to commence war. "Make" better than "declare" the latter narrowing the power too much.

Mr. Gerry never expected to hear in a republic a motion to empower the Executive alone to declare war.

Mr. Elseworth. There is a material difference between the cases of making *war*, and making *peace*. It shd. be more easy to get out of war, than into it. War also is a simple and overt declaration, peace attended with intricate & secret negotiations.

Mr. Mason was agst giving the power of war to the Executive, because not [safely] to be trusted with it; or to the Senate, because not so constructed as to be entitled to it. He was for clogging rather than facilitating war; but for facilitating peace. He preferred "*declare*" to "*make.*"

On the Motion to insert *declare* — in place of *Make*, [it was agreed to.]

2. *The meaning of "war" and of "sudden attack."* This colloquy seems to indicate a constitutional judgment that the President should be able to act to "repel sudden attacks." But in other contexts, he could not initiate "war" without a congressional declaration. How much weight should such a colloquy have? Note that, even if it is accorded considerable authority, the colloquy leaves open a number of questions: (1) Is the power to "repel sudden attacks" a part of the Constitution as well as its drafting history? (2) Exactly what does that power include?

Does it extend beyond purely defensive measures? (3) May the President do anything other than repel sudden attacks without a congressional declaration? Note also the changes in the nature of the international context since the Constitution was drafted. Might "repel sudden attack" and "war" mean something different today from what they meant in that era?

3. *Judicial construction.* Although the existence and scope of the President's power to use the armed forces have been controversial throughout our history, the courts have rarely addressed the issue. The Supreme Court's most extensive discussion appears in The Prize Cases, 67 U.S. (2 Black) 635 (1863). At issue was the lawfulness of President Lincoln's proclamation establishing a blockade of southern ports after the secession of the southern states. The Court, in an opinion by Justice Grier, upheld the blockade. Justice Grier began his analysis by arguing that a state of war existed between the northern and southern states. "As a civil war is never publicly proclaimed, [its] actual existence is a fact in our domestic history which the Court is bound to notice and to know." Although Congress had the exclusive power to declare a national or foreign war, it could not

> declare war against a State, or any number of States, by virtue of any clause in the Constitution. The Constitution confers on the President the whole Executive power. [He] has no power to initiate or declare a war either against a foreign nation or a domestic State. But by [Acts] of Congress, [he] is authorized to [call] out the militia and use the military and naval forces of the United States in case of invasion by foreign nations, and to suppress insurrection against the government of a State or of the United States.
> If a war be made by invasion of a foreign nation, the President is not only authorized but bound to resist force by force. He does not initiate the war, but is bound to accept the challenge without waiting for any special legislative authority. And whether the hostile party be a foreign invader, or States organized in rebellion, it is none the less a war, although the declaration of it be "*unilateral.*"

Justice Nelson, joined by Chief Justice Taney and Justices Castrom and Clifford, dissented:

> By our Constitution [the] war power is lodged in Congress. . . .
> [It] has [been] argued that [the President's commander-in-chief power] from necessity should be construed as vesting him with the war power, or the Republic might greatly suffer or be in danger from the attacks of the hostile party before the assembling of Congress. But we have seen that the whole military and naval force are in his hands under the municipal laws of the country. He can meet the adversary upon land and water with all the forces of the Government. The truth is, this idea of the existence of any necessity for clothing the President with the war power [is] simply a monstrous exaggeration; for besides having the command of the whole of the army and navy, Congress can be assembled within thirty days, if the safety of the country requires that the war power shall be brought into operation.

4. *Three case studies.* In the absence of authoritative judicial pronouncements, most of the "law" of warmaking power has been made by the actual practice of Congress and the President. The case studies that follow illustrate this interaction in three contemporary contexts. With respect to each of them, consider whether the results would have been superior if the courts had played a larger role.

a. *The Persian Gulf War.* On August 8, 1990, six days after Iraq invaded Kuwait, President Bush deployed the largest American combat force since the Vietnam War to protect Saudi Arabia from an Iraqi attack. Throughout the fall, soldiers and reservists from around the nation were sent to the Persian Gulf region. In October, both the House and the Senate passed resolutions that supported the defensive operations but stopped short of declaring war. On November 8, notwithstanding the limited congressional authorization, President Bush doubled the existing 230,000 American troops in the Gulf in order to provide the United States with "an adequate *offensive* military operation." On November 29, at the behest of the Bush administration, the United Nations Security Council passed a resolution demanding that Iraq unconditionally withdraw from Kuwait by January 15, 1991, and authorizing member nations to "use necessary means" to free Kuwait and force Iraqi compliance.

Tensions escalated throughout the next month, and on January 8 the President formally requested Congress to pass a joint resolution supporting "the use of all necessary means" to achieve the goals of the United Nations resolution. Four days later, Congress complied. House Joint Resolution 77, 105 Stat. 3 (1991), approved the use of American military force against Iraq after January 15, provided that the President determined and reported to Congress that all diplomatic efforts had been exhausted. Five days later, on January 17, the United States and its allies unleashed Operation Desert Storm, flying over 1,400 air sorties against Iraqi targets. On February 24, the allies launched a land invasion of Kuwait. Three days later, President Bush asserted that Kuwait had been liberated and ordered a cease-fire. Iraq immediately announced that it would comply with all United Nations Security Council resolutions passed during the crisis.

Did the President have the constitutional authority to approve the buildup in Saudi Arabia without congressional approval? Would it have been constitutional for him to have launched Operation Desert Storm in the absence of House Joint Resolution 77? After President Bush's November 8 announcement of an intent to gain an offensive capability, fifty-four members of Congress filed suit to enjoin the President from ordering American forces into war "absent meaningful consultation with and genuine approval by Congress." In Dellums v. Bush, 752 F. Supp. 1141 (D.D.C. 1990), the district court rejected the plaintiffs' motion for a preliminary injunction for lack of ripeness. In the course of so holding, however, the court said that it had "no hesitation in concluding that an offensive entry into Iraq by several hundred thousand United States servicemen [could] be described as a 'war' within the meaning of [the Constitution]," and that, "in principle, an injunction may issue at the request of members of Congress to prevent the conduct of war which is about to be carried on without congressional authorization."

Was House Joint Resolution 77 constitutionally adequate to authorize Operation Desert Storm? During debate on the floor, both sponsors and opponents of the resolution spoke of it as equivalent to a declaration of war. But consider Sidak, To Declare War, 41 Duke L.J. 29, 33, 68 (1991):

> To commence warfare on the scale witnessed against Iraq, the President needed to receive a formal declaration of war. He did not. [Although] politically significant, [the joint resolution] was a legal nullity, a merely precatory or hortatory gesture.

For an opposing point of view, see Koh, The Coase Theorem and the War Power: A Response, 41 Duke L.J. 122, 127 (1991):

[Members] of Congress were painfully aware not only that they were voting on the functional equivalent of a declaration of war, but also that their votes would be intensely scrutinized. Pre-vote speeches were nationally televised, and the roll-call votes were published in every newspaper. [Given] these indicia of public accountability, it is difficult to see what additional accountability would have been gained had the resolution been styled as a declaration of war.

b. *The War in Kosovo.* On March 24, 1999, the United States commenced its largest military operation since the Gulf War. Americans joined a NATO air operation designed to deter and, subsequently, to reverse the "ethnic cleansing" of Kosovo, a province of Yugoslavia. Once again, the operation was undertaken without benefit of a formal congressional declaration of war.

The air strikes began after Yugoslavia's rejection of NATO demands designed to ensure Kosovo's autonomy. On March 26, 1999, the President submitted a formal report to Congress that, he said, was "part of my efforts to keep Congress fully informed consistent with the War Powers Resolution." (The War Powers Resolution is discussed at pages 410-415, infra.) In the report, he asserted that he was undertaking the action "pursuant to my constitutional authority to conduct U.S. foreign relations and as Commander-in-Chief and Chief Executive."

Congress took a number of seemingly inconsistent actions with regard to the war. On March 23, 1999, the Senate passed a resolution authorizing the President to conduct military air operations in Yugoslavia, but the House rejected a similar measure in a tie vote on April 28, 1999. On the same day, the House defeated a measure declaring a state of war between the United States and Yugoslavia and a measure directing the President to remove all U.S. armed forces from the operations against Yugoslavia, but adopted a measure prohibiting the use of funds for the deployment of ground troops. On May 6, 1999, the House passed a measure providing emergency funding for the war.

On April 30, 1999, several members of Congress filed suit in United States District Court seeking a declaratory judgment that the Kosovo action was unconstitutional without a congressional declaration of war and that under section 1544(b) of the War Powers Resolution, the President was obligated to terminate hostilities within sixty calendar days of his report to Congress. In Campbell v. Clinton, 203 F.3d 19 (D.C. Cir. 2000), decided after hostilities had ended, the court held that the plaintiffs lacked standing to maintain the action. Should the court have considered the claim? If so, how should it have ruled on the merits?

c. *United Nations "peacekeeping" and "peace enforcement."* In recent years, the President has authorized use of American forces in United Nations-sponsored military actions in Bosnia, Haiti, and Somalia. In each of these cases, the President did not seek prior congressional approval before troops were committed. Does the Constitution require congressional action before troops are sent as "peacekeepers" or "peace enforcers"? Consider Stromseth, Collective Force and Constitutional Responsibility: War Powers in the Post-Cold War Era, 50 Miami L. Rev. 145, 165, 166 (1995):

[Given] the spectrum of U.N.-authorized military actions, the authority of the President to commit American forces without congressional approval will vary depending on the nature and risks of each operation. At one end of the spectrum are actions that clearly have the character and risks of "war" and are best understood as requiring prior authorization from Congress. At the other end of the spectrum are [peacekeeping] operations that enjoy the consent of all of the parties and are deployed in situations posing little risk of hostilities. Although Congress may limit American involvement in such peacekeeping operations, the President has a strong argument that sending American forces to these operations falls within well-established historical patterns of presidential peacetime troop deployments. Many if not most of the U.N.-authorized operations in which the United States is likely to participate, however, will fall into the more ambiguous middle ground. These include ["peace] enforcement" operations involving hostilities, but on a limited scale. Strong constitutional arguments in favor of congressional authorization can be made in many such cases, but grey areas and room for disagreement admittedly will exist.

2.   *Legislative Authority*

As already noted, in the absence of judicial decisions, the constitutional division of foreign affairs authority has been resolved primarily by the political branches themselves. Sometimes the political resolution has taken the form of structural or "quasi-constitutional" statutes, analogous to the measures governing the domestic sphere discussed at pages 365-370, supra. As noted above, the Supreme Court has suggested that executive power has special significance in the realm of foreign affairs. Do these suggestions mean that framework statutes governing foreign affairs are especially problematic? Consider the following.

The War Powers Resolution

50 U.S.C. §§1541-1548 (1973)

§1541. PURPOSE AND POLICY

(A) CONGRESSIONAL DELEGATION

It is the purpose of this joint resolution to fulfill the intent of the framers of the Constitution of the United States and insure that the collective judgment of both the Congress and the President will apply to the introduction of United States Armed Forces into hostilities, or into situations where imminent involvement in hostilities is clearly indicated by the circumstances, and to the continued use of such forces in hostilities or in such situations.

(B) CONGRESSIONAL LEGISLATIVE POWER UNDER NECESSARY AND PROPER CLAUSE

Under article I, section 8, of the Constitution, it is specifically provided that the Congress shall have the power to make all laws necessary and proper for carrying into execution, not only its own powers but also all other powers vested by the Constitution in the Government of the United States, or in any department or officer thereof.

(C) PRESIDENTIAL EXECUTIVE POWER AS COMMANDER-IN-CHIEF; LIMITATION

The constitutional powers of the President as Commander-in-Chief to introduce United States Armed Forces into hostilities, or into situations where imminent involvement in hostilities is clearly indicated by the circumstances, are exercised only pursuant to (1) a declaration of war, (2) specific statutory authorization, or (3) a national emergency created by attack upon the United States, its territories or possessions, or its armed forces.

§1542. CONSULTATION; INITIAL AND REGULAR CONSULTATIONS

The President in every possible instance shall consult with Congress before introducing United States Armed Forces into hostilities or into situations where imminent involvement in hostilities is clearly indicated by the circumstances, and after every such introduction shall consult regularly with the Congress until United States Armed Forces are no longer engaged in hostilities or have been removed from such situations.

§1543. REPORTING REQUIREMENT

(A) WRITTEN REPORT; TIME OF SUBMISSION; CIRCUMSTANCES NECESSITATING SUBMISSION; INFORMATION REPORTED

In the absence of a declaration of war, in any case in which United States Armed Forces are introduced —

> (1) into hostilities or into situations where imminent involvement in hostilities is clearly indicated by the circumstances;
> (2) into the territory, airspace or waters of a foreign nation, while equipped for combat, except for deployments which relate solely to supply, replacement, repair, or training of such forces; or
> (3) in numbers which substantially enlarge United States Armed Forces equipped for combat already located in a foreign nation;

the President shall submit within 48 hours to the Speaker of the House of Representatives and to the President pro tempore of the Senate a report, in writing [setting forth "the circumstances necessitating the introduction of armed forces," "the constitutional and legislative authority" under which it occurred, "the estimated scope and duration of the hostilities," and "such other information as the Congress may request"].

§1544. CONGRESSIONAL ACTION . . .

(B) TERMINATION OF USE OF UNITED STATES ARMED FORCES; EXCEPTIONS; EXTENTION PERIOD

Within sixty calendar days after a report is submitted or is required to be submitted pursuant to section 1543(a)(1) of this Title, whichever is earlier, the President shall terminate any use of United States Armed Forces with respect to which such report was submitted (or required to be submitted), unless the Congress (1) has declared war or has enacted a specific authorization for such use of United States Armed Forces, (2) has extended by law such sixty-day period, or (3) is physically unable to meet as a result of an armed attack upon the United States. Such sixty-day period shall be extended for not more than an additional thirty days if the President determines and certifies to the Congress in writing that unavoidable military necessity respecting the safety of United States Armed Forces requires the continued use of such armed forces in the course of bringing about a prompt removal of such forces.

(C) CONCURRENT RESOLUTION FOR REMOVAL BY PRESIDENT OF UNITED STATES ARMED FORCES

Notwithstanding subsection (b) of this Section, at any time that United States Armed Forces are engaged in hostilities outside the territory of the United States, its possessions and territories without a declaration of war or specific statutory authorization, such forces shall be removed by the President if the Congress so directs by concurrent resolution. . . .

§1547. INTERPRETATION OF JOINT RESOLUTION

(A) INFERENCES FROM ANY LAW OR TREATY

Authority to introduce United States Armed Forces into hostilities or into situations wherein involvement in hostilities is clearly indicated by the circumstances shall not be inferred—

(1) from any provision of law (whether or not in effect before [the date of the enactment of this joint resolution]), including any provision contained in any appropriation Act, unless such provision specifically authorizes the introduction of United States Armed Forces into hostilities or into such situations and states that it is intended to constitute specific statutory authorization within the meaning of this chapter; or

(2) from any treaty heretofore or hereafter ratified unless such treaty is implemented by legislation specifically authorizing the introduction of United States Armed Forces into hostilities or into such situations and stating that it is intended to constitute specific statutory authorization within the meaning of this chapter.

(B) JOINT HEADQUARTERS OPERATIONS OF HIGH-LEVEL MILITARY COMMAND

Nothing in this chapter shall be construed to require any further specific statutory authorization to permit members of United States Armed Forces to participate jointly with members of the armed forces of one or more foreign countries in the headquarters operations of high-level military commands which were established prior to the date of enactment of this chapter and pursuant to the United Nations Charter or any treaty ratified by the United States prior to such date.

(C) INTRODUCTION OF UNITED STATES ARMED FORCES

For purposes of this chapter the term "introduction of United States Armed Forces" includes the assignment of members of such armed forces to command, coordinate, participate in the movement of, or accompany the regular or irregular military forces of any foreign country or government when such military forces are engaged, or there exists an imminent threat that such forces will become engaged, in hostilities.

(D) CONSTITUTIONAL AUTHORITY OR EXISTING TREATIES
      UNAFFECTED; CONSTRUCTION AGAINST GRANT OF
      PRESIDENTIAL AUTHORITY RESPECTING USE OF UNITED
      STATES ARMED FORCES

Nothing in this chapter —

(1) is intended to alter the constitutional authority of the Congress or of the President, or the provisions of existing treaties; or

(2) shall be construed as granting any authority to the President with respect to the introduction of United States Armed Forces into hostilities or into situations wherein involvement in hostilities is clearly indicated by the circumstances which authority he would not have had in the absence of this chapter. . . .

Note: The War Powers Resolution

1. *Some questions of interpretation.* What does the act mean by "introduction" of U.S. armed forces "into hostilities"? When is "imminent involvement in hostilities" clearly indicated by the circumstances? Suppose the President (a) attempts a military action to rescue U.S. citizens held hostage overseas or (b) orders the Marines into a foreign country, as a show of force, in order to prevent revolutionary acts. Must he inform Congress? If it is assumed that he need not do so, should he? Should the President construe the resolution broadly or narrowly? Consider also the possible need for secrecy in such operations.

Note that the War Powers Resolution contains a legislative veto. Is the veto constitutional after *Chadha?* Compare M. Glennon, Constitutional Diplomacy 98 (1990) (legislative veto in section 1544(c) "clearly invalid") with Ely, Suppose Congress Wanted a War Powers Act That Worked, 88 Colum. L. Rev. 1379, 1395 (1988) ("section [1544(c)] does not appear to be unconstitutional"). Consider also M. Glennon, supra, at 99:

[Whereas] a concurrent resolution adopted under section [1544(c)] can have no mandatory effect in requiring presidential withdrawal of the armed forces, such a resolution could nonetheless suffice under Justice Jackson's analysis [in *Youngstown*] to place the President's power at its lowest ebb.

2. *The constitutional issue.* Consider, in the light of the preceding materials, the constitutionality of the War Powers Resolution. Which provisions are most troublesome? Consider also the following views:

a. *The War Powers Resolution is an unconstitutional infringement on the powers of the President.* The Constitution gives the President the authority to introduce armed forces into hostilities without a congressional declaration of war. Moreover, at least in cases of an effort to "repel sudden attacks" on the United States and its allies, the resolution is far too broad. It allows a congressional role in areas in which such a role is constitutionally proscribed.

b. *The War Powers Resolution is constitutional.* It merely restores the constitutional balance that had been upset by a long period of congressional inactivity before its passage. In essence, the resolution allows Congress to ensure that
there is no undeclared war. Indeed, to the extent that it suffers from any constitutional defect, it is in yielding undue power to the President — for the resolution
seems to allow the President to wage war without a declaration in far too many
circumstances.

c. *Section 1547(d)(1) makes the preceding provisions of the resolution effectively
meaningless.* It restores the constitutional status quo and remits individuals deciding on the distribution of the war powers — in the executive, legislative, and judicial branches — to the Constitution itself. Why was this section included?

3. *Practice under the resolution.* Most commentators have agreed that the War
Powers Resolution has been ineffective in constraining executive discretion.
Congress has never formally enacted a resolution pursuant to the War Powers Resolution, and Presidents have regularly ignored it. Consider the following summary of actual practice under the resolution:

Congress passed the War Powers Resolution to prevent future Vietnams, undeclared
creeping wars that start and build before Congress or the public are fully aware. Yet
Congress markedly undercut the resolution's effectiveness by failing to address two
new types of military action that soon came to dominate the 1980s. First, the resolution did not address covert wars, in which intelligence operatives acting under
civilian supervision conduct paramilitary activities against foreign governments.
By its own terms, the resolution regulates only "United States Armed Forces" and
did not reach the allegedly private activities of former [CIA] operatives such as Eugene Hasenfus, who later worked during the Iran-contra affair for the "Enterprise"
supervised by Oliver North. Second, Congress said nothing about short-term military strikes that could be completed well within the resolution's sixty-day time limit.
Congress's silence has freed the executive branch to treat that statutory limit as de
facto congressional permission to commit troops abroad for a time period of up to
sixty days. Thus, in 1975 President Ford sent troops briefly to Vietnam to evacuate
American citizens and to Cambodia to free the *Mayaguez,* an American merchant
ship. President Carter attempted an abortive military rescue of American hostages
in Iran in April 1980. President Reagan dispatched forces to Grenada in October
1983, authorized a "surgical" strike against Libya in April 1986, and ordered attacks
on Iranian oil platforms in the Persian Gulf in October 1987 and April 1988. During his first year as president, George Bush sent U.S. troops to El Salvador, the Philippines, and Panama, in each case avoiding full compliance with the resolution's
consultation and reporting requirements.

   Ironically, the resolution has also demonstrably failed to prevent even the type of
creeping escalation that it was expressly enacted to control. For example, President
Reagan sent U.S. troops to Lebanon in August 1982 without prior consultation with
Congress and kept them there until February 1984. When Congress finally sought
to force the removal of those troops after more than two hundred combat fatalities,
the president successfully bargained for a joint resolution extending the time deadlines of the War Powers Resolution from sixty days to eighteen months, without ever
articulating what policy the United States military presence was meant to serve.

   Similarly, while the Iran-Contra furor raged, American ships continued to patrol
the Persian Gulf, convoying reflagged Kuwaiti tankers. Fearing Iranian attacks on
United States ships, which might have prompted President Reagan to ask Congress
for another joint resolution of support, the Senate passed a bill in the fall of 1987
that imposed a new sixty-day reporting requirement on the president and that

contemplated a future resolution setting durational limits on the commitment of troops in the Persian Gulf without express congressional authorization. The House took no action on this de facto proposal to reenact the War Powers Resolution because more than one hundred of its members had filed suit in federal court to force the president to acknowledge the applicability of the existing War Powers Resolution to his Persian Gulf activities. But as the 100th Congress concluded, no new law had been passed, the congressional suit had been dismissed as a nonjusticiable political question, and an American navy ship acting out of perceived self-defense had shot down an Iranian jetliner in the Gulf. Thus, more than fifteen years after the War Powers Resolution first became law, scholars and legislators continued to debate whether Congress should reenact a variant of it in order to enforce the resolution's original purpose. Years of congressional-executive struggle over the war powers had brought us from the Tonkin Gulf only so far as the Persian Gulf.

H. Koh, The National Security Constitution 39-40 (1990).

Could a revised, more carefully drafted War Powers Resolution more effectively ensure a congressional role in warmaking? Consider Ely, supra, at 1419-1420:

> In large measure the tale of the War Powers Resolution of 1973 has been a tale of congressional spinelessness. [However], the general idea — that Congress, like Ulysses binding himself to the mast, might take steps to bind itself to accountability for future wars — is by no means unthinkable. That, in fact, is precisely what Congress attempted to do in 1973. Unfortunately it did not sufficiently plan for presidential defiance. However, [that] defect can be repaired, if Congress still has the will to be held accountable.

Compare M. Glennon, supra, at 123:

> No modification of the Resolution will in itself "insure that the collective judgment of both the Congress and the President will apply to the introduction of United States Armed Forces into hostilities. . . ." [The] most that a statute can do, however artfully drawn, is to facilitate the efforts of individual members of Congress to carry out their responsibilities under the Constitution. To do that requires understanding, and it also requires courage; it demands an insight into the delicacy with which our separated powers are balanced and the fortitude to stand up to those who equate criticism with lack of patriotism. For a Congress composed of such members, no War Powers Resolution would be necessary; for a Congress without them, no War Powers Resolution would be sufficient.

Note: The Boland Amendments and the Iran-Contra Affair

Is Congress more likely to be effective if it attempts to influence the President's policy with regard to individual controversies rather than utilizing structural statutes that attempt to channel executive discretion over the range of cases? Is individual action by Congress less constitutionally troublesome?

Consider the controversy generated by the disagreement between Congress and President Reagan concerning support for rebel forces operating in Nicaragua.

1. *Background.* Beginning in late 1982, the American press began to carry reports concerning the administration's "secret war" in Nicaragua. Concerned about American support for the Contras, Congress attached a series of restric-

tions on American involvement in Nicaragua to annual appropriations bills enacted between 1982 and 1986 (the Boland Amendments). The restrictions took different forms in different years, but in general they barred any "agency or entity of the United States involved in intelligence activities" from spending funds "to support military or paramilitary operations in Nicaragua."

While these restrictions were in effect, members of the National Security Council staff assisted in raising funds from third countries and private individuals to aid the Contras. In addition, administration officials helped run a resupply operation for Contra troops in the field and recruited other individuals to assist in logistical operations. These operations created a major scandal when it came to light that profits from secret arms sales to Iran had been used to help finance the Contras.

2. *The constitutional issue.* While the Boland Amendments were in effect, administration officials claimed that they were complying with their letter and spirit. Later, however, some officials insisted that they were entitled to ignore at least some of the restrictions contained in the amendments because they unconstitutionally invaded executive authority. Are there nonfrivolous arguments that the amendments were unconstitutional? Consider Report of the Congressional Committees Investigating the Iran-Contra Affair, S. Rep. No. 100-216, H. Rep. No. 100-433 (1987) (minority views) at 473, 476:

> [The] Constitution gives the President some power to act on his own in foreign affairs. What kinds of activities are set aside for him? The most obvious — other than the Commander-in-Chief power and others explicitly listed in Article II — is the one named in *Curtiss-Wright:* the President is the "sole organ" of the government in foreign affairs. . . .
>
> [Congress] may not use its control over appropriations, including salaries, to prevent the executive or judiciary from fulfilling Constitutionally mandated obligations. The implication for the Boland amendments is obvious. If any part of the amendments would have used Congress's control over salaries to prevent executive actions that Congress may not prohibit directly, the amendments would be just as unconstitutional as if they had dealt with the subject directly. . . .

Compare id. at 406 (majority views):

> [One] does not have to be a proponent of an imperial Congress to see that [*Curtiss-Wright*] has little application to the situation here. We are not confronted with a situation where the President is claiming inherent constitutional authority in the absence of an Act of Congress. Instead, to succeed on this argument the Administration must claim it retains authority to proceed in derogation of an Act of Congress — and not just any act, at that. Here, Congress relied on its traditional authority over appropriations, the "power of the purse," to specify that no funds were to be expended by certain entities in a certain fashion. . . .
>
> While each branch of our Government undoubtedly has primacy in certain spheres, none can function in secret disregard of the others in any sphere. That, in essence, was the Administration's attempt here.

3. *The Constitution without courts.* Note that both the War Powers Resolution and the Boland Amendments represent efforts by Congress to utilize self-help in enforcing constitutional boundaries. Does our recent experience with these ef-

forts suggest that judicial review is essential to the preservation of constitutional government in this area?

Consider the following conclusions that might be drawn from our recent experience:

a. Because the Court usually "rubber stamps" executive foreign policy decisions when it adjudicates cases involving foreign affairs, judicial review is not the solution to the inadequate enforcement of constitutional limitations on executive power. Rather, constitutional requirements are best enforced through the give and take of the political process.

b. Constitutional limitations have been inadequately enforced precisely because the Supreme Court has mistakenly remitted these questions to the political process.

c. Constitutional limitations have not been inadequately enforced. Although neither the Court nor Congress has been successful in restraining executive power, the framers deliberately created a strong executive and in any event wrote a document flexible enough to accommodate the changed circumstances that have caused our political system to tilt toward a powerful President.

Note: *Congressional Control over Agreements with Foreign States — Treaties, Executive Agreements, and Congressional-Executive Agreements*

What role should Congress play when the question is the making of peace rather than war?

1. *Treaties.* Article II, section 2 of the Constitution grants to the President the power "by and with the Advice and Consent of the Senate, to make Treaties, provided two thirds of the Senators present concur," and article VI, section 6 makes "all Treaties made, or which shall be made, under the Authority of the United States" the supreme law of the land. Do these provisions authorize the President, acting with the acquiescence of two-thirds of the Senate and the agreement of a foreign country, to countermand otherwise applicable statutes? See, e.g., Whitney v. Robertson, 124 U.S. 190 (1888):

> By the Constitution, a treaty is placed on the same footing, and made of like obligation, with an act of legislation. Both are declared by that instrument to be the supreme law of the land, and no supreme efficacy is given to either over the other. [If] the two are inconsistent, the one last in date will control the other, provided always the stipulation of the treaty on the subject is self-executing.

Notice, however, that, at least with regard to domestic law, a later act of Congress can also repeal a treaty, although the repeal may violate international law. See, e.g., The Head Money Cases, 112 U.S. 580, 599 (1884). Consider also L. Henkin, Foreign Affairs and the Constitution 143 (1972):

> A treaty [must] be a *bona fide* agreement between states, not a "mock marriage," nor a unilateral act by the United States to which a foreign government lends itself as an accommodation in order to bring it within the United States Treaty Power. So if, to circumvent the House of Representatives and the States, a uniform divorce law for the United States alone were written into "a treaty" and Canada cooperated

in the scheme by signing its name to it, it would not be a treaty under international law, and therefore not a treaty under the Constitution.

For a discussion of the impact of treaties on state law, see pages 203-206.

2. *Executive agreements.* If a President lacks the support of two-thirds of the Senate, may he make domestic law without the acquiescence of either House by entering into an executive agreement with another country? Since the beginning of the country, Presidents have entered into thousands of such agreements. Although there is no express constitutional authority for this practice, the Constitution seems indirectly to recognize the possibility of nontreaty international agreements in article I, section 10, which prohibits states from entering treaties but authorizes them to enter an "Agreement or Compact with [a] foreign Power" with the consent of Congress.

Are there constitutional limits on the scope of such ageements when entered into by the President? Recall that in Dames & Moore v. Regan, section B, supra, the Court upheld the constitutionality of presidential action taken pursuant to an executive agreement with Iran. Notice, however, that the Court did so only after finding congressional authorization for (or at least acquiescence in) the President's decision. In United States v. Belmont, 301 U.S. 324 (1937), the Court upheld the terms of an executive agreement surrounding the United States' recognition of the Soviet Union, even though the agreement was reached without prior congressional authorization. In doing so, the Court relied heavily on the President's express constitutional authority to "receive Ambassadors." Could the President act unilaterally in cases where he lacks express constitutional authority? Consider L. Henkin, supra, at 179:

> There have [been] suggestions, claiming support in *Belmont*, that the President is constitutionally free to make any agreement on any matter involving our relations with another country, although for political reasons — especially if he will later require Congressional implementation — he will often seek Senate consent. As a matter of constitutional construction, however, that view is unacceptable, for it would wholly remove the "check" of Senate consent which the Framers struggled and compromised to write into the Constitution. One is compelled to conclude that there are agreements which the President can make on his sole authority and others which he can make only with the consent of the Senate, but neither Justice Sutherland [the author of *Belmont*] nor any one else has told us which are which.

Consider the possibility that the constitutional "check" consists of no more than the Senate's ability to use this sort of constitutional rhetoric in a political struggle to force the President to seek its acquiescence.

3. *Congressional-executive agreements.* In recent years, the President has often eschewed reliance on either treaties or executive agreements. Instead, he has resorted to congressional-executive agreements, which are approved by simple majorities of both Houses of Congress. For example, both the North American Free Trade Agreement (NAFTA) and the General Agreement on Tariffs and Trade (GATT) were approved by simple majorities of the House and Senate rather than by a two-thirds majority of the Senate. These agreements have the potential to effect broad changes in domestic law. Would they be constitutional in the absence of approval by two-thirds of the Senate? Consider Tribe, Taking Text and Struc-

ture Seriously: Reflections on Free-Form Method in Constitutional Interpretation, 108 Harv. L. Rev. 1221, 1268-1269 (1995):

> If [the] unenumerated power to enter non-treaty agreements exists within the federal government, it seems clear that it is the President, not Congress, who has the authority to exercise this power on behalf of the nation. [Because] of the broad delegation in Article II, the President is understood to have inherent power to perform all executive acts, subject, of course, to the specific limitations in Articles I and II and other constitutional provisions. The authority to make international agreements that do not rise to the level of treaties has long been correctly recognized as one such inherent executive power. The only role that Congress may play is to delegate still further authority to the President, pursuant to an enumerated power of Congress, that the President may in turn combine with his inherent power to enter non-treaty agreements with foreign nations. [Nothing] in this analysis, however, suggests that Congress may play an ex post role in *approving* agreements with foreign nations on behalf of the United States.

Compare Ackerman and Golove, Is NAFTA Constitutional?, 108 Harv. L. Rev. 799, 919-920 (1995):

> In approving the [World Trade Organization provided for in GATT], Congress is enacting a "law" that is formally identical to all others passed under Article I. . . .
>
> This is by no means the only case in which the text creates multiple legislative procedures for accomplishing the same end. The text provides no fewer than four ways of passing a constitutional amendment. And there are, of course, two ways of passing a statute — one with, and one without, the cooperation of the President.
>
> Similarly, Articles I and II set up alternative systems through which the nation can commit itself internationally — one with, and one without, the cooperation of the House.

Note: *Distribution of National Powers — Final Thoughts*

Do the preceding materials suggest that the distribution of national powers has served its intended function? Has it limited factional control over governmental processes? Has it served as an important safeguard of liberty? Or has it created so many "checks" that (1) democratic processes are unable to bring about substantial reform or (2) the government is prevented from taking necessary action?

The preceding materials raise institutional issues as well. To what extent has judicial review contributed to the development of the present distribution of national powers? What has been the effect of structural legislation such as the War Powers Resolution? Consider the possibility that the written Constitution has played a surprisingly small role. Do the materials support the suggestion that the process of bargaining between Congress and the executive branch is a sufficient safeguard against abuse? What is abuse in this context?

V

Equality
and the Constitution

This chapter explores the Court's struggle to define and apply the Constitution's requirement of equal treatment. Section A is devoted to a historical case study. It examines the ways in which the Court has interacted with other social forces in dealing with issues of racial equality. The remaining sections focus more directly on constitutional doctrine. Section B explores the meaning of "equality" in the context of "rational basis" review of "ordinary" social or economic classifications. Section C returns to racial classifications as the prime example of "suspect" classifications subject to "heightened scrutiny." Sections D and E discuss the problems of classifications based on gender and sexual orientation. Finally, Section F explores the claims of other "disadvantaged" groups, such as aliens and the poor, to special scrutiny of laws arguably discriminating against them.

A. RACE AND THE CONSTITUTION

This section traces the evolution of constitutional doctrine concerning discrimination against African-Americans. There are several reasons for beginning the study of constitutionally protected individual rights with this issue.

First, in one form or another the controversy about the legal status of African-Americans has been central to U.S. politics since the founding of the Republic. As you read through this material, consider the extent to which judicial decisions have shaped that controversy and the extent to which they have been shaped by it. At each stage, could the Court have acted differently? Was its power meaningfully constrained by the language and history of the Constitution? By the constellation of social and political forces at the time? By widely held ethical norms?

Second, the Court's analysis of discrimination against African-Americans has served as a prototype for the development of other constitutional doctrines. In the nineteenth century, the argument over slavery provoked a fundamental realignment of federal and state power and gave birth to a new strategy for the protection of individual rights. In our own time, controversies over school segregation, racial discrimination in access to political power, and "affirmative action" have shaped attitudes toward the proper scope of constitutional protection for minorities generally. To what extent is our experience with discrimination against African-Americans generalizable?

Finally, a chronological examination of this issue provides insight into the influence of broader historical forces on constitutional adjudication. What factors are most important in determining the course of judicial decisions? The strategy of individual litigants? The Court's formulation of the issues? The reactions of the other branches of government? Does the Supreme Court ultimately have the power to impose its own version of racial justice? Or are its decisions merely the product of broad historical forces over which it exercises little control?

1.   Slavery and the Constitution

Although the word "slavery" nowhere appears in the original Constitution, three provisions recognize and arguably legitimate the practice. Article I, section 9 prohibits Congress from outlawing the slave trade until 1808. Article I, section 2 requires apportionment of legislators on the basis of the "whole number of free persons" in each state and "three fifths of all other persons." Article IV, section 2, clause 3 requires states to "[deliver] up" escaped slaves and prohibits states from discharging them.

Do these provisions make the Constitution a pro-slavery document? Consider D. Robinson, Slavery in the Structure of American Politics 1765-1820, at 209, 210, 244-246 (1971):

> In the drama that produced the Constitution, Southern delegates were unmistakably prominent players. James Madison, the man whose leadership during the Convention earned him the title "Father of the Constitution," was a Southerner, a slave-owning Virginian. [John] Rutledge, certainly a leading nationalist and chairman of the important Committee of Detail, which provided the first definition of legislative powers under the Constitution, was one of the wealthiest and best-established planters at the Convention, and deliberately represented the most candid slave owners. [George] Washington [was] an exceedingly rich man, whose fortune arose largely from the labor of slaves in and around Mount Vernon, Virginia. In fact, of the fifteen delegates whom Clinton Rossiter has termed either "principals" or "influentials," seven were planters. . . .
>
> The South's enthusiastic participation in the nationalizing thrust of 1787 carried one portentous qualification: the national government could be as powerful as the vision of a great national empire demanded, *provided that it keep its hands off slavery.* . . .
>
> The framers [dealt] with slavery by seeking, so far as possible, to take it out of the national political arena. They were unable in 1787 to settle the issue, one way or the other. They could not establish straightforward Constitutional guarantees against emancipation, as the South Carolinians desired, because many Northerners, and perhaps some Southerners, would not permit it. Nor could they give Congress power to regulate slavery in any way, much less abolish it, because Southerners refused to yield control over the institution. Realizing that it was utterly beyond their power to fashion a national consensus on slavery, or to "govern" the issue in the absence of one, they had contented themselves with measures aimed at preventing friction over slavery between the states and sections. . . .

There is no evidence that any framer thought the Constitution contained power to abolish slavery. They all knew how the Deep Southerners felt, and however much some of them may have regretted the hold that slavery had on the South, they were all fully sympathetic with the determination of the Deep Southerners to resist abolition in the present circumstances. . . .

But there was no guarantee that powers of emancipation were forever denied to the federal government.

The evidence there is permits the conclusion that the future, with respect to possible public action against slavery, was left open on purpose. [The] framers, as of 1787, agreed unanimously to place the institution of slavery, as it existed within the South, not "on the course of ultimate extinction," as Lincoln argued, but beyond national regulation.

In light of the provisions in the Constitution protecting slavery, should it have been ratified? Consider the views of Justice Thurgood Marshall:

I [do not] find the wisdom, foresight, and sense of justice exhibited by the framers particularly profound. To the contrary, the government they devised was defective from the start, requiring several amendments, a civil war, and momentous social transformation to attain the system of constitutional government, and its respect for the individual freedoms and human rights we hold as fundamental today.

Marshall, Commentary: Reflections on the Bicentennial of the United States Constitution, 101 Harv. L. Rev. 1, 2 (1987).

Compare Levinson, 1787: The Constitution in Perspective — Pledging Faith in the Civil Religion; Or, Would You Sign the Constitution?, 29 Wm. & Mary L. Rev. 113, 133 (1987):

[The] central problem with "disunionist" thinking [is] that it focuses more on the immorality of collaboration with slavery [than] on the question of how one most quickly can bring slavery to an end. We know that with ratification chattel slavery ended by 1865. Is there good reason to believe that it would have ended earlier had the Constitution not been ratified and balkanization followed? I suspect not. But the important point is surely this: Can one who believes that the ratification of the Constitution *did* enhance the prospects (and actuality) of chattel slavery sign the Constitution? What precisely is the value of the Constitution and of the concomitant nation that would justify even an extra week's slavery? What precisely is the omelet that justified breaking those particular eggs?

State v. Post

20 N.J.L. 368 (1845)

NEVIUS, J.

This proceeding is designed to present for our adjudication the question, whether slavery can exist within the limits of this state under its present constitution and laws; and it derives signal and solemn importance from its bearing upon a class of human beings, still claimed to be lawfully held in slavery, and upon the interest of those communities where most of that class are still found. I have listened with great pleasure and deep interest to the arguments and remarks and the pathetic appeals, which have been urged before us, in support of this demurrer, and in behalf of the colored race; and whilst I most sincerely respect the zeal and humane spirit by which they were dictated, and the ingenuity, talents and research of the counsel, I am nevertheless constrained to say, that much of the argument seemed rather addressed to the feelings than to the legal intelligence of the court. . . .

In 1804, the legislature adopted a plan for the gradual abolition of slavery, and passed an act declaring, "That every child born of a slave, after the 4th of July of that year, should be free, but remain the servant of the owner of the mother [until] he or she should arrive at a specified age." [Under] the operation of [the statute] and the benign spirit of the age, which inclined men to manumit their slaves, slavery has become nearly extinct in this state and must soon pass entirely away. [According] to the last census [the number of slaves] was reduced to 674; of whom [349 were] over the age of fifty-five years. Those who yet survive and have not been manumitted, remain still the slaves of their masters; but have a legal claim upon the latter for maintenance, in the case of their inability to support themselves, unless by the provisions of the new constitution, framed and adopted in 1844, slavery is abolished. If such be the case, it will follow as a legal consequence, that masters too, are absolved from the obligation of maintenance. [These] consequences, while they can have no legitimate influence upon the decision of the question, nevertheless give it more than ordinary importance, and call for our most serious and anxious consideration.

[Abolitionists argued that slavery was made illegal in New Jersey by a provision in the state's 1844 constitution declaring that "all men are by nature free and independent, and have certain natural and unalienable rights, among which are those of enjoying and defending life and liberty, acquiring, possessing and protecting property, and of pursuing and obtaining safety and happiness."]

If the [New Jersey constitutional] convention intended to say that all men, in a state of civil or political society, were free and independent and entitled to the exercise and enjoyment of the rights mentioned, the expression must be understood in a modified sense according to the nature, the condition and laws of the society to which they belong. For man, under no form of government, can be said to be absolutely free and independent, and have the absolute and uncontrollable right over his own actions, according to his own free will, unrestrained by the rights of others and the laws of the government, under which he lives. Authority and subordination are essential under every form of civil society, and one of its leading principles is that the citizen yields to it a portion of his natural rights, for the better protection of the remainder. In such a state, man's right to freedom and independence, to enjoy and defend life and liberty, to acquire, possess and protect property, and to pursue and obtain safety and happiness, are ever subject to, and regulated by, laws fundamental or otherwise, which the majority of the people in a republic, have established for their government. . . .

[Had] the convention intended to abolish slavery and domestic relations, well known to exist in this state and to be established by law, and to divest the master of his right of property in his slave and the slave of his right to protection and support from the master, no one can doubt but that it would have adopted some clear and definite provision to effect it, and not have left so important and grave a question, involving such extensive consequences, to depend upon the doubtful construction of an indefinite abstract political proposition. . . .

The declaration of independence, the basis of our free government, declares that all men are created free and equal, and the constitution of the United States proclaims that the people have formed it to secure the blessings of liberty to themselves and their posterity; yet by the express language of the latter instrument, the relation of master and slave is recognized; showing that the framers of that constitution did not deem their general declaration in favor of liberty, incompatible with its other provisions; and it has never been judicially determined that slavery, in the United States, was thereby abrogated. On the contrary it has been often adjudged, both by the State and Federal courts, that slavery still exists; that the master's right of property in the slave has not been affected either by the declaration of independence, or the constitution of the United States. [It] was argued before us, that, under the declaration of rights in the constitution of Massachusetts, which contains the same language, it has been judicially held, that slavery was no more. And we are referred to [Commonwealth v. Aves], 18 Pick. R. 193. [In *Aves*], Chief Justice Shaw declares "that slavery is contrary to natural right, to the principles of justice and humanity, and repugnant to the constitution." I am unwilling to yield to any one, in high respect for the supreme judicial tribunal of that enlightened state; but [I] do not find the reason or argument, which satisfies my mind of the soundness of its conclusion. [How] far the humane spirit of abolitionism, which prevailed in that state, the fewness or worthlessness of that species of property, the feebleness of the defence made by masters, or the collateral mode in which the question was presented, or the fact that slavery had only been tolerated, but never actually established by law, may have influenced the opinion of the court, [I] will not undertake to determine. By this remark I mean to cast no imputation upon the judicial intelligence or integrity of that court; but judges must be more than men, if they can always escape the influence of a strong popular opinion of society upon great questions of state policy and human benevolence, which have been long agitated and much discussed; and it is no matter of surprise that Chief Justice Shaw, entertaining the opinions he did upon this question of slavery, should have found it repugnant to the spirit of their constitution. . . .

Note: The Constitutionality of Slavery

1. Post *and the problem of judicial power.* For 150 years, U.S. courts have vacillated between attempts to impose a judicial solution to the problem of racial justice and attempts to leave the matter to the political process. In *Post*, the Court chose the latter course. Is the decision an example of moral cowardice or of fidelity to law?

Was the Court bound to reach the result it did by the words of the provision in question? By the intent of the framers? Where else might it have looked for guidance? See Chapter 1, section C, supra.

Justice Nevius says judges must be "more than men" to ignore "strong popular opinion." Does this susceptibility to public pressure suggest that he should have used his power more confidently? How likely is it that a court would construe the Constitution in a manner most people violently opposed? That it would succeed in enforcing such a construction in the long run?

Is the 1804 statute, providing for gradual manumission and welfare protection for the remaining slaves, relevant to the Court's decision? For a discussion, see R. Cover, Justice Accused 54-55 (1975).

Of course, in a southern state in 1845 a judicial decision abolishing slavery would have been revolutionary. If a southern judge had written such a decision, what do you suppose the result would have been?

2. *Constitutional attacks on slavery. Post* typifies judicial analysis of slavery prior to the Civil War. Although abolitionist lawyers won isolated victories, even judges strongly opposed to slavery usually ruled against them. See generally R. Cover, supra; L. Levy, The Law of the Commonwealth and Chief Justice Shaw (1957).

Although *Post* dealt exclusively with *state* constitutional issues, Alvan Stewart, the abolitionist lawyer who argued *Post*, relied on the federal Constitution as well. See J. TenBroek, The Antislavery Origins of the Fourteenth Amendment 43-45 (1951). See also E. Foner, Free Soil, Free Labor, Free Men: The Ideology of the Republican Party before the Civil War 76-77 (1970). Stewart claimed that slavery deprived slaves of life, liberty, and property in violation of the due process clause of the fifth amendment, that it deprived New Jersey of a republican form of government in violation of article IV, that it violated the preamble of the Constitution, and that it violated the Treaty of Ghent, which outlawed the slave trade. See Ernst, Legal Positivism, Abolitionist Litigation, and the New Jersey Slave Case of 1845, 4 Law & Hist. Rev. 337, 350-351 (1986). The Court apparently thought these arguments too flimsy to merit a response. Are the arguments tenable?

3. *Judicial support for slavery.* From the perspective of the present, it may seem that courts should have done more to combat the evils of slavery. In fact, however, when the courts did intervene in the pre-Civil War period, it was more often to invalidate political arrangements that tended to *limit* slavery.

Most of the federal litigation centered on the fugitive slave clause, article IV, section 2, which required the return of escaped slaves. In Prigg v. Pennsylvania, 41 U.S. (16 Pet.) 539 (1842), the Court, in an opinion by Justice Story, held unconstitutional a Pennsylvania statute prohibiting any person from removing blacks from the state by force or violence with the intention of detaining them as slaves. The Court explained that article IV, section 2 "contemplates the existence of a positive, unqualified right on the part of the owner of the slave, which no state law or regulation can in any way qualify, regulate, control, or restrain." The Court therefore held the statute invalid as applied to an escaped slave because "any state law or state regulation, which interrupts, limits, delays, or postpones the right of the owner to the immediate possession of the slave, and the immediate command of his service and labor, operates, pro tanto, a discharge of the slave therefrom." The Court further held that article IV, section 2 implicitly vested Congress with the power to assist owners in securing the return of escaped slaves, that Congress had exercised that power by enacting the Fugitive Slave Act of 1793, that this national power was exclusive, and that any state laws regulating the means by which slaves were to be delivered up were unconstitutional.

Superficially *Prigg* seemed a pro-slavery decision, but its legacy was ambiguous. The decision left intact the power of both free states and the national government to limit the growth of slavery by freeing slaves brought into free areas. Moreover, by nationalizing the rendition question the Court relieved free states of this distasteful obligation and intensified the political struggle over the future of slavery on a national level. See 5 C. Swisher, History of the Supreme Court of the United States: The Taney Period 1836-64, at 546 (1974). For an argument that Justice Story's antislavery reputation is overblown, see Holden-Smith, Lords of Lash, Loom, and Law: Justice Story, Slavery, and Prigg v. Pennsylvania, 78 Cornell L. Rev. 1086 (1993). Fifteen years after *Prigg* the Court attempted to cut off the political struggle in an opinion that presaged the Civil War.

Dred Scott v. Sandford
60 U.S. (19 How.) 393 (1857)

Mr. Chief Justice Taney delivered the opinion of the Court. . . .

[Dred Scott, admittedly once a slave but claiming now to be a citizen of Missouri, brought an action for trespass in the Circuit Court of the United States for the District of Missouri against John F. A. Sandford, a citizen of New York. Federal jurisdiction was premised on diversity of citizenship. In 1834, Scott's former owner had taken him from Missouri to Illinois, where they resided for two years before moving to Minnesota, then part of the Louisiana Territory. In 1838, they returned to Missouri, and Scott was sold as a slave to Sandford. Although slavery was legal in Missouri, it was prohibited in Illinois by the state constitution and in the Louisiana Territory by the federal statute embodying the Missouri Compromise — the Act of March 6, 1820, 3 Stat. 545. Scott argued that these provisions made him a free man. In response, Sandford contended that, even if Scott were free, he was not a citizen of Missouri, and that the court therefore lacked jurisdiction under the diversity of citizenship provisions of article III. Moreover, Scott was not free, since his presence in Illinois and the Louisiana Territory could not deprive his former owner of his property interest in Scott when he returned to Missouri.]

I

[The Court first addressed the question whether Scott was a citizen of Missouri for diversity purposes.]

The words "people of the United States" and "citizens" are synonymous terms, and mean the same thing. They both describe the political body who, according to our republican institutions, form the sovereignty, and who hold the power and conduct the Government through their representatives. They are what we familiarly call the "sovereign people," and every citizen is one of this people, and a constituent member of this sovereignty. The question before us is, whether the class of persons described in the plea in abatement compose a portion of this people, and are constituent members of this sovereignty? We think they are not, and that they are not included, and were not intended to be included, under the word "citizens" in the Constitution, and can therefore claim none of the rights and privileges which that instrument provides for and secures to citizens of the United States. On the contrary, they were at that time considered as a subordinate and inferior class of beings, who had been subjugated by the dominant race, and, whether emancipated or not, yet remained subject to their authority, and had no rights or privileges but such as those who held the power and the Government might choose to grant them.

It is not the province of the court to decide upon the justice or injustice, the policy or impolicy, of these laws. The decision of that question belonged to the political or law-making power; to those who formed the sovereignty and framed the Constitution. The duty of the court is, to interpret the instrument they have framed, with the best lights we can obtain on the subject, and to administer it as we find it, according to its true intent and meaning when it was adopted. . . .

In the opinion of the court, the legislation and histories of the times, and the language used in the Declaration of Independence, show, that neither the class of persons who had been imported as slaves, nor their descendants, whether they had become free or not, were then acknowledged as a part of the people, nor intended to be included in the general words used in that memorable instrument.

It is difficult at this day to realize the state of public opinion in relation to that unfortunate race, which prevailed in the civilized and enlightened portions of the world at the time of the Declaration of Independence, and when the Constitution of the United States was framed and adopted. But the public history of every European nation displays it in a manner too plain to be mistaken.

They had for more than a century before been regarded as beings of an inferior order, and altogether unfit to associate with the white race, either in social or political relations; and so far inferior, that they had no rights which the white man was bound to respect; and that the negro might justly and lawfully be reduced to slavery for his benefit. He was bought and sold, and treated as an ordinary article of merchandise and traffic, whenever a profit could be made by it. This opinion was at that time fixed and universal in the civilized portion of the white race. It was regarded as an axiom in morals as well as in politics, which no one thought of disputing, or supposed to be open to dispute; and men in every grade and position in society daily and habitually acted upon it in their private pursuits, as well as in matters of public concern, without doubting for a moment the correctness of this opinion. . . .

[Upon] a full and careful consideration of the subject, the court is of opinion, that, upon the facts stated in the plea in abatement, Dred Scott was not a citizen of Missouri within the meaning of the Constitution of the United States, and not entitled as such to sue in its courts; and, consequently, that the Circuit Court had no jurisdiction of the case, and that the judgment on the plea in abatement is erroneous. . . .

II . . .

[The Court then discussed whether Scott remained a slave after his sojourn in the Louisiana Territory and Illinois.]

The act of Congress, upon which the plaintiff relies, declares that slavery and involuntary servitude, except as a punishment for crime, shall be forever prohibited in all that part of the territory ceded by France, under the name of Louisiana, which lies north of thirty-six degrees thirty minutes north latitude, and not included within the limits of Missouri. And the difficulty which meets us at the threshold of this part of the inquiry is, whether Congress was authorized to pass this law under any of the powers granted to it by the Constitution; for if the authority is not given by that instrument, it is the duty of this court to declare it void and inoperative, and incapable of conferring freedom upon any one who is held as a slave under the laws of any one of the States. . . .

[The] power of Congress over the person or property of a citizen can never be a mere discretionary power under our Constitution and form of Government. The powers of the Government and the rights and privileges of the citizen are regulated and plainly defined by the Constitution itself. [An] act of Congress which deprives a citizen of the United States of his liberty or property, merely because he came himself or brought his property into a particular Territory of the United States, and who had committed no offence against the laws, could hardly be dignified with the name of due process of law. . . .

[The] right of property in a slave is distinctly and expressly affirmed in the Constitution. The right to traffic in it, like an ordinary article of merchandise and property, was guarantied to the citizens of the United States, in every State that might desire it, for twenty years. And the Government in express terms is pledged to protect it in all future time, if the slave escapes from his owner. This is done in plain words — too plain to be misunderstood. And no word can be found in the Constitution which gives Congress a greater power over slave property, or which entitles property of that kind to less protection than property of any other description. The only power conferred is the power coupled with the duty of guarding and protecting the owner in his rights.

Upon these considerations, it is the opinion of the court that the act of Congress which prohibited a citizen from holding and owning property of this kind in the territory of the United States north of the line therein mentioned, is not warranted by the Constitution, and is therefore void; and that neither Dred Scott himself, nor any of his family, were made free by being carried into this territory; even if they had been carried there by the owner, with the intention of becoming a permanent resident.

[Finally, the Court addressed Scott's contention that he had been made free by his visit to Illinois, a free state. The Court held that his status on his return to Missouri was to be determined by Missouri law, rather than Illinois law, and that under that law he remained a slave.

[Justices Wayne, Daniel, Campbell, Grier, Nelson, and Catron each wrote separate concurring opinions. Justices McLean and Curtis dissented.]

Note: Dred Scott *and the Power of Judicial Review*

1. *The meaning of* Dred Scott. *After Dred Scott,* were free blacks in northern states citizens of those states for federal constitutional purposes? Short of amending the Constitution, was there anything that either those states or the federal government could do to make them citizens? If Scott and his owner had remained in the Louisiana Territory, could Congress have prohibited the owner from holding Scott as a slave?

2. *Chief Justice Taney's opinion and the problem of judicial review.* It is frequently noted that the Supreme Court first asserted the power to invalidate acts of Congress in Marbury v. Madison. Less often mentioned is the fact that the Court's second assertion of this power came fifty-four years later in Scott v. Sandford. What lessons does *Dred Scott* teach about judicial review?

It is generally acknowledged that *Dred Scott* is one of the great disasters in the history of the Supreme Court. But what precisely is wrong with Chief Justice Taney's opinion? Consider the following possibilities:

a. *The Court's decision is racist in its premises and morally obtuse in its result.* Is this fair? Notice that Chief Justice Taney does not claim that blacks are "a subordinate and inferior class of beings," but only that they were so viewed by the authors of the Constitution. See 2 C. Warren, The Supreme Court in United States History 303 (1922). If they were so viewed, does that fact establish that the framers wished to exclude free blacks from ever becoming citizens? Even if the framers' attitude toward free blacks was ambiguous, can it be doubted that they viewed slaves as a form of property? Is the problem with *Dred Scott* that the Court was too "passive" in rigidly saddling the country with outdated moral attitudes, or that it was too "active" in reading the contemporary moral attitudes of the justices into the constitutional text?

b. *The Court unnecessarily and unwisely reached out to decide an issue not properly presented.* The first part of Chief Justice Taney's opinion held that Scott was not a citizen of Missouri, and that the court below therefore lacked jurisdiction. Was it proper for the Court to decide the questions addressed in the second part of the opinion? Why was it necessary to determine Scott's status outside Missouri? Even if Scott was free when he lived outside Missouri, did the Constitution preclude Missouri from enslaving him when he returned?

Did Chief Justice Taney have to read the diversity clause as establishing federal standards for state citizenship? Why wasn't it sufficient to hold that Scott, even if free, was not a citizen under Missouri law?

c. *The Court unwisely assumed that it could finally resolve a divisive political issue by taking it "out of politics."* Consider R. Burt, The Constitution in Conflict 193 (1992):

> [*Dred Scott* inflamed] northern fears and [emboldened] southern leaders to escalate their demands for national legitimation of slavery. The Court had already set this course in *Prigg*; by shutting off all possible meliorist interventions in the fugitive slave rendition process, [the] Court drove the abolitionist lawyers out of public institutions [and] into the streets. The Court gave them virtually no option but to join [William Lloyd] Garrison there, as he burned a copy of the Constitution, describing it as a "compact with the devil" and proclaiming that only destruction of the Union could abate the evils of slavery.
>
> *Dred Scott* continued the course. [It drove] each side to more desperate or provocative claims which, in turn, increased the apparent need, if public order were to be preserved, for some single sovereign authority to exert command over the warring parties. [These] inflated expectations, paradoxically enough, had led the Court to issue blustering commands that only provoked heightened disobedience and ignited more violence.

Modern constitutional doctrines are sometimes justified on the ground that they remove highly divisive questions from the political process. For example, the abortion decisions and expansive readings of the first amendment religion clauses are sometimes defended on the ground that the underlying questions are inappropriate for political resolution. What are the characteristics of such questions? Was the future and spread of slavery such a question?

d. *The problem was not that the Court attempted to impose a solution to the slavery problem, but that it attempted to impose the wrong solution.* The decision failed to solve the problem and exacerbated sectional tensions. Should Supreme Court decisions be judged by whether they "work" in this sense? Should justices consider whether their decisions will be "accepted"? Whether they will produce "wise" social policy?

2.   *Reconstruction and Retreat*

A central paradox in constitutional law is that, in order to enforce limitations on government power, it is necessary to create some countervailing government power. A constitutional provision may, by its terms, prohibit certain forms of government action. That limitation might be obeyed simply because actors in the system recognize a moral obligation not to transgress it. But if the prohibition is to be legally enforceable, then some other branch of government must be invested with the power to enforce it. The risk, of course, is that this power will be misused and will serve to undermine the very rights it was created to protect. Does it follow that the real choice for the framers of a constitution is not between individual rights and government power, but between different distributions of government power providing more or less effective enforcement of individual rights with more or less risk of abuse?

Before the Civil War, there were few constitutional constraints on the power of state governments. Although the first eight amendments to the Constitution protected individual rights against federal intrusion, the Supreme Court held in 1833 that they did not limit state power. See Barron v. Mayor & City Council of Baltimore, 32 U.S. (7 Pet.) 243 (1833), Chapter 6, section C, infra. The failure of the framers to protect individual rights from state governments was a product of neither indifference nor oversight. It stemmed instead from the view that the most serious threat to individual liberty came from the federal government, and that the states could be relied on to "afford complete security against invasions of the public liberty by the national authorities." The Federalist No. 28 (Hamilton). A federal bill of rights applicable to the states would have enhanced federal power at the expense of the states and thus increased the risk of federal domination.

By the close of the Civil War, it was clear that this strategy required some modification. The southern states could not be depended on to protect the rights of the newly freed slaves, and it could hardly be maintained that the main threat to those rights came from the federal government. Under the pressure of this reality, a shift occurred: Instead of viewing the Constitution as a protection from federal power and the states as a bulwark against federal interference, at least some people came to see constitutional rights as a basis for the *assertion* of federal power to protect individuals against *state* interference.

Note: *The Work of the Reconstruction Congress*

The Reconstruction Congress laid the groundwork for the expansion of federal authority by enacting three constitutional amendments, each of which conferred additional substantive power on Congress. On December 31, 1865, the thirteenth amendment became part of the Constitution. The amendment ratified and extended President Lincoln's Emancipation Proclamation by prohibiting slavery and involuntary servitude throughout the United States. In addition, section 2 of the amendment granted Congress the power "to enforce this article by appropriate legislation."

The formal eradication of slavery was insufficient to change the real status of southern blacks. The bonds of slavery were quickly replaced by "Black Codes" in many southern states, which prohibited African-Americans from exercising basic civil rights like owning property, pursuing ordinary occupations, or giving testimony in court.

Congress attempted to make the thirteenth amendment effective against the challenge posed by the Black Codes through enactment of the Civil Rights Act of 1866. Passed over President Johnson's veto, the act declared that "all persons born in the United States and not subject to any foreign power, excluding Indians not taxed," were citizens of the United States. Such citizens were granted the same right to make and enforce contracts, sue, give evidence, acquire property, and "to full and equal benefit of all laws and proceedings for the security of person and property as is enjoyed by white citizens." Moreover, all citizens were to be "subject to like punishment, pains, and penalties, and to none other, any law, statute, ordinance, regulation or custom to the contrary notwithstanding."

Even before the civil rights bill was passed, doubt arouse about Congress's power to enact such a law. Thus, on February 13 and 26, 1866, Congressman Bingham introduced the first version of what was to become the fourteenth amendment. It stated that "[t]he Congress shall have the power to make all laws which shall be necessary and proper to secure to the citizens of each State all privileges and immunities of citizens in the several States, and to all persons in the several States equal protection in the rights of life, liberty, and property." Cong. Globe, 39th Cong., 1st Sess. 813, 1034 (1866).

On April 30, 1866, after extensive debate, the Joint Committee on Reconstruction reported a new proposal that provided that "[n]o state shall make or enforce any law which shall abridge the privileges or immunities of citizens of the United States, nor shall any State deprive any person of life, liberty, or property without due process of law; nor deny any person within its jurisdiction the equal protection of the laws." These substantive prohibitions were coupled with another grant of power to Congress to enforce them "by appropriate legislation." The amendment was adopted by the House in this form. When the amendment reached the Senate, the first sentence of section 1 — making all persons born or naturalized in the United States and subject to the jurisdiction thereof citizens of the United States and of the state wherein they reside — was added. The amendment was ratified on July 28, 1868.

Two years later, on March 30, 1870, Congress added the last of the Reconstruction amendments, which prohibited both the United States and any state from denying or abridging the right to vote on account of race, color, or previous condition of servitude. The amendment granted Congress the power to enforce this provision by appropriate legislation.

Invoking this new constitutional authority, the Reconstruction Congress enacted an extensive legislative program. In 1870, Congress reenacted the 1866 Civil Rights Act and added criminal penalties for deprivation of rights under the law. In the same year, Congress passed the Enforcement Act, which attached crimi-

nal penalties to interference with the right to vote and made it a felony to con-
spire to injure, oppress, threaten, or intimidate any citizen with the intent to prevent or hinder the free exercise of any right granted by the Constitution or laws
of the United States. One year later Congress enacted the Ku Klux Klan Act,
which criminally punished conspiracies to deprive a class of persons of equal protection of the laws and created civil liability for state officials who deprived persons
of federal rights under the color of state laws. Finally, in 1875 Congress enacted
a sweeping public accommodations law requiring all inns, public conveyances,
theaters, and other places of public amusement to admit all persons regardless of
race, color, or previous condition of servitude.

Did this flurry of legislative activity fundamentally alter the constitutional
structure that existed before the Civil War? This question has two dimensions.
First, how did the Reconstruction Congress alter the power balance between the
federal and state governments? No doubt the Reconstruction amendments were
intended to provide a new source of federal power to protect the newly freed
slaves. But were they also a more general rejection of the traditional theory that
state governments would serve to protect individual liberties? Or was the federal
government to intervene only interstitially when the states were unwilling or unable to provide protection? Second, how did the amendments alter the balance
of power between the judiciary and the political branches? As noted above, the
primary impetus for passage of the fourteenth amendment was the need to provide a basis for federal *legislative* action against the states. But was the amendment intended as well to be a basis for federal *judicial* power?

Note: The Judicial Reaction

1. *The Slaughter-House Cases and the reassertion of federalism constraints.* The
Supreme Court's first opportunity to assess the impact of the Reconstruction
amendments came in The Slaughter-House Cases, 83 U.S. (16 Wall.) 36 (1873),
in which the Court rejected a thirteenth and fourteenth amendment attack on a
Louisiana statute granting to a single company the right to engage in the slaughterhouse business within an area including the city of New Orleans. (These cases
are dealt with at greater length at Chapter 6, section B, infra.) Justice Miller's
analysis in his opinion for the Court begins with a ringing declaration that "the
one pervading purpose" of the amendments was "[t]he freedom of the slave race,
the security and firm establishment of that freedom, and the protection of the
newly-made freeman and citizen from the oppressions of those who had formerly
exercised unlimited dominion over him." The Court emphasized that it did not
follow from this purpose that the framers of the amendments intended to transfer general responsibility for protection of civil rights from the states to the federal government. Such a broad reading of the amendments would "degrade the
State governments by subjecting them to the control of Congress, in the exercise
of powers heretofore universally conceded to them of the most ordinary and fundamental character" and "radically [change] the whole theory of the relations of
the State and Federal governments to each other and both of these governments
to the people." Thus, the privileges and immunities clause of the fourteenth
amendment did not provide general federal protection for citizens. Rather, it pro-

tected only a few rights, "which owe their existence to the Federal government, its National character, its Constitution, or its laws." Nor was the due process clause implicated by the Louisiana statute. As for petitioners' equal protection clause arguments, the Court "[doubted] very much whether any action of a State not directed by way of discrimination against the negroes as a class, or on account of their race, will ever be held to come within the purview of this provision."

2. *Federalism and protection of the newly freed slaves.* The Slaughter-House Cases suggest a two-tier approach to the fourteenth amendment: When the rights of newly freed slaves are at stake, the amendment must be read expansively to provide comprehensive federal protection. But when racial discrimination is not at issue, the protections of federal citizenship are narrower, and a state resident's primary recourse for protection of his rights remains to his own state government.

This approach is consistent with the history of the fourteenth amendment, which was unquestionably written primarily to protect the newly freed slaves. Note, however, that the language of the amendment provides no support for the distinction. Was the Court correct in emphasizing the history rather than the language?

In some measure, the Court's treatment of the fourteenth amendment in the wake of *Slaughter-House* conformed to the two-tier approach and, indeed, remnants of it remain today. Thus, on the one hand, the Court has continued to be quite deferrential to political outcomes when "ordinary social and economic legislation" is challenged under the fourteenth amendment. On the other hand, the Court quickly established that federal protection was available when the states singled out blacks for discriminatory treatment. In Strauder v. West Virginia, 100 U.S. 303 (1879), for example, the Court relied on the fourteenth amendment to reverse the murder conviction of a black tried before a jury from which members of his race were excluded by law. See also Ex parte Virginia, 100 U.S. 339 (1880).

3. *Judicial invalidation of civil rights legislation.* The result in *Strauder* seems to follow logically from the Court's opinion in *Slaughter-House.* What was less predictable, however, was that the Court's narrow interpretation of the Reconstruction amendments would eventually obstruct federal efforts to protect newly freed slaves.

The first intimations of difficulty came in United States v. Reese, 92 U.S. 214 (1875), which involved a federal criminal prosecution against two Kentucky municipal elections inspectors who were charged with refusing to permit a black to vote. The defendants were charged with violating two of the voting rights sections of the 1870 Enforcement Act. Because the relevant sections of the act were not expressly limited to actions that were racially motivated, the Court held that they exceeded Congress's power under the fifteenth amendment, and that the prosecution therefore could not proceed. See also Virginia v. Rives, 100 U.S. 313 (1879).

The Court further restricted the scope of Reconstruction legislation in United States v. Cruikshank, 92 U.S. 542 (1875). The case grew out of the Grant Parish massacre, which has been called "perhaps the bloodiest racial conflict in Louisiana history." R. Kaczorowski, The Politics of Judicial Interpretation: The Federal Courts, Department of Justice and Civil Rights, 1866-1876, at 175 (1985). Following the state election of 1872 both the conservatives and the Republicans claimed victory. The Republicans succeeded in gaining control of the parish courthouse and were attacked by a "veritable army" of "old time Ku Klux Klan." According to federal investigators sent to the scene, "[At] least 60 freedmen were killed after they had surrendered, and their bodies were mutilated and left to rot in the parching sun." Id. Although ninety-seven defendants were indicted under the Enforcement Act of 1870, only nine defendants were brought to trial, and three were convicted. When the case reached the Supreme Court, it reversed these convictions. The Court rejected the government's argument that the criminal conspiracy section of the 1870 act was applicable to the lynching of two blacks because it had interfered with their right of peaceable assembly. Since there was no claim that the blacks had assembled to petition the federal government, the prosecution had not alleged that the rights of national citizenship were violated, and punishment of the killings therefore exceeded Congress's power under the fourteenth amendment. Nor could the prosecution proceed on the theory that the due process rights of blacks were violated, since "the fourteenth amendment prohibits a State from depriving any person of life, liberty, or property, without due process of law; but this adds nothing to the rights of one citizen as against another."

In United States v. Harris, 106 U.S. 629 (1882), the Court reached a similar result with respect to the criminal conspiracy sections of the Ku Klux Klan Act of 1871. The Court held that, because the fourteenth amendment did not reach purely private conduct, Congress lacked the power to punish members of a lynch mob who had seized prisoners held by a state deputy sheriff.

But the most damaging judicial attack on Reconstruction legislation came in The Civil Rights Cases, 109 U.S. 3 (1883), where the Court invalidated the public accommodation sections of the 1875 Civil Rights Act. (The Civil Rights Cases are excerpted more fully in Chapter 9, section A1, infra.) The Court, in an opinion by Justice Bradley, denied that either the thirteenth or the fourteenth amendment conferred on Congress the power to prohibit private discrimination in public accommodations. The Court's discussion of the fourteenth amendment is usually treated as establishing the requirement of "state action" for a fourteenth amendment violation — a requirement examined in greater detail in Chapter 9. The Court held that "[t]he first section of the Fourteenth Amendment [is] prohibitory in its character, and prohibitory upon the States. [It] is State action of a particular character that is prohibited. Individual invasion of individual rights is not the subject matter of the amendment."

Note, however, that this reading of the fourteenth amendment grew out of the same view of the states as the primary protector of individual rights that the Court expressed in Slaughter-House. The Court in The Civil Rights Cases found the statute constitutionally offensive in part because "[i]t applies equally to cases arising in States which have the justest laws respecting the personal rights of citizens, and whose authorities are ever ready to enforce such laws, as to those which arise in States that may have violated the prohibition of the amendment." In the Court's view, "An individual cannot deprive a man of his [rights]; he may, by force or fraud, interfere with the enjoyment of the right in a particular case; [but] unless protected in these wrongful acts by some shield of State law or State authority, he cannot destroy or injure the right; he will only render himself amenable to satisfaction or punishment." It followed that, "in all those cases where the Constitution seeks to protect the rights of the citizen against discriminative and unjust laws of the State, [it] is not individual offences, but abrogation and denial of rights which it denounces, and for which it clothes the Congress with power to provide a remedy."

Would the result in The Civil Rights Cases have been different if the prosecution had alleged that state law permitted owners of public accommodations to discriminate? If the Civil Rights Act of 1875 applied only in states that provided no remedy for such discrimination?

Turning to the thirteenth amendment, the Court agreed that laws enacted under this head of authority "may be primary and direct in [character]; for the thirteenth amendment is not a mere prohibition of State laws establishing or upholding slavery, but an absolute declaration that slavery or involuntary servitude shall not exist in any part of the United States." The Court also agreed that Congress was empowered under the amendment "to pass all laws necessary and proper for abolishing all badges and incidents of slavery in the United States." But the crucial question was whether the discriminatory refusal to serve a black in a public accommodation was such a badge or incident. The Court thought that accepting this position "would be running the slavery argument into the ground." A refusal of service "has nothing to do with slavery or involuntary servitude. [If] it is violative of any right of the party, his redress is to be sought under the laws of the State; or if those laws are adverse to his rights and do not protect him, his remedy will be found in the corrective legislation which Congress has adopted, or may adopt, for counteracting the effect of State laws, or State action, prohibited by the Fourteenth Amendment."

Was the Reconstruction Court concerned primarily with what the rights of blacks should be, with the source of interference with those rights, or with which organ of government should have the power to vindicate them? In cases where racial discrimination affected federal rights, the Court upheld Reconstruction legislation. Thus, in Ex parte Yarbrough, 110 U.S. 651 (1884), the Court sustained a conviction of a private individual under the Ku Klux Klan Act of 1871 for using violence against blacks voting in a *congressional* election. See also Ex parte Siebold, 100 U.S. 371 (1879). Similarly, in Logan v. United States, 144 U.S. 263 (1892), the Court held that Congress had the power to punish conspiracies to injure persons in custody of a U.S. marshal. It is at least possible to argue from these cases that the justices were authentically concerned about the expansion of federal power. But what about the expansion of federal *judicial* power that The Civil Rights Cases represented? Was that expansion consistent with the approach of The Slaughter-House Cases? With the intent of the framers of the Reconstruction amendments? In the context of the 1880s, was it meaningful to speak of the rights of blacks without an expansion of federal power?

At the same time that the Court was dismantling much of the Reconstruction legislation, the political coalition behind Reconstruction was also collapsing. The turning point is usually said to have come with the disputed election of 1876. In return for accepting Hayes's election, Democratic leaders were promised the withdrawal of federal troops from the South and the inclusion of southern Democrats in the cabinet. The post-Reconstruction status of blacks was not, however, a foregone conclusion. As C. Vann Woodward writes in his classic study, "Southern white people themselves [were not] so united on that subject at first as has been generally assumed. The determination of the Negro's 'place' took shape gradually under the influence of economic and political conflicts among divided white people — conflicts that were eventually resolved in part at the expense of the Negro." The Strange Career of Jim Crow 6-7 (1957).

Consider also J. Williamson, The Crucible of Race 109-111, 116-117, 224-225 (1984):

[Southern] Racial Conservatives, ruling again in the 1880s, built their power, in part, upon the assumption that the Negro would remain in the South and that he would be willingly and harmoniously subordinate. They resisted strenuously both attempts in the 1880s to raise blacks substantially higher in the scale of white civilization and efforts in the 1890s to exclude them altogether. [In] the late 1880s and on through the 1890s, caught in a depression in which opportunities for everyone diminished with sickening rapidity, racial Conservatives found themselves losing power and fighting for survival. . . .

Radicalism appeared in strength in 1889 and spread rapidly through the South. The core of the Radical mentality was the concept that Negroes, freed from the restraining influences of slavery, were rapidly "retrogressing" toward their natural state of bestiality. [Ultimately], Radicals believed, there would be no place for blacks in the South or in America. . . .

The assault upon idealized Southern womanhood by the "nigger beast" was the keen cutting edge of Radicalism. Let Benjamin Ryan Tillman of South Carolina catch the scene for us, as he did for his colleagues on the floor of the United States Senate in 1907. As he drew the picture, white women in the rural South were virtually besieged by Negro brutes who roamed almost without restraint, their "breasts pulsating with the desire to sate their passions upon white maidens and wives." . . .

Rapes and the lynchings that followed became the special studies of the Radicals, and provided the most vital of their statistics. It is vastly significant that the lynching of black men for the rape of white women was not the subject of intense observation and comment in the South before 1889. [In] and after 1889, however, that crime and its punishment commanded a new and tremendously magnified attention. . . .

Violence and the great threat of violence was one way in which Radicals sought to lower the self-esteem of blacks and thus render them more controllable on the way to their demise. But there were other, more subtle means to effect that end. . . .

Two of the tools used to reduce and, hence, to manage blacks were disfranchisement and segregation. . . .

Radicalism had a special motive in its effort to pass laws to disfranchise black men and to separate the races in public places, one that was distinctly different from the special motive of Conservatism in the same process. The Radical motive was to depress the expectations of blacks, especially black men, to make them less secure and ultimately less aggressive, to lead them to follow with minimal resistance the inevitable path to racial extinction. Radicals readily recognized [that] blacks were already practically disfranchised and segregated, but to Radicals the laws were useful in showing explicitly and blatantly the power of whites. They were tokens of hard and present truths and signs of things to come — of the surety of white supremacy and the futility of black resistance.

Plessy v. Ferguson

163 U.S. 537 (1896)

MR. JUSTICE BROWN [delivered] the opinion of the court.

[A Louisiana statute enacted in 1890 required railroad companies to provide "equal but separate accommodations for the white and colored races," with the provision that "nothing in this act shall be construed as applying to nurses attending children of the other race." A passenger using facilities intended for a different race was made criminally liable. Plessy, who claimed to be seven-eighths Caucasian, was prosecuted under the statute when he failed to leave the coach reserved for whites. The state supreme court upheld the constitutionality of the statute.]

The object of the [fourteenth] amendment was undoubtedly to enforce the absolute equality of the two races before the law, but, in the nature of things, it could not have been intended to abolish distinctions based upon color, or to enforce social, as distinguished from political, equality, or a commingling of the two races upon terms unsatisfactory to either. Laws permitting, and even requiring, their separation, in places where they are liable to be brought into contact, do not necessarily imply the inferiority of either race to the other, and have been generally, if not universally, recognized as within the competency of the state legislatures in the exercise of their police power. The most common instance of this is connected with the establishment of separate schools for white and colored children, which have been held to be a valid exercise of the legislative power even by courts of states where the political rights of the colored race have been longest and most earnestly enforced. . . .

[Counsel for Plessy suggests] that the same argument that will justify the state legislature in requiring railways to provide separate accommodations for the two races will also authorize them to require separate cars to be provided for people whose hair is of a certain color, or who are aliens, or who belong to certain nationalities, or to enact laws requiring colored people to walk upon one side of the street, and white people upon the other, or requiring white men's houses to be painted white, and colored men's black, or their vehicles or business signs to be of different colors, upon the theory that one side of the street is as good as the other, or that a house or vehicle of one color is as good as one of another color. The reply to all this is that every exercise of the police power must be reasonable, and extend only to such laws as are enacted in good faith for the promotion of the public good, and not for the annoyance or oppression of a particular class. . . .

So far, then, as a conflict with the fourteenth amendment is concerned, the case reduces itself to the question whether the statute of Louisiana is a reasonable regulation, and with respect to this there must necessarily be a large discretion on the part of the legislature. In determining the question of reasonableness, it is at liberty to act with reference to the established usages, customs, and traditions of the people, and with a view to the promotion of their comfort, and the preservation of the public peace and good order. Gauged by this standard, we cannot say that a law which authorizes or even requires the separation of the two races in public conveyances is unreasonable, or more obnoxious to the fourteenth amendment than the acts of congress requiring separate schools for colored children in the District of Columbia, the constitutionality of which does not seem to have been questioned, or the corresponding acts of state legislatures.

We consider the underlying fallacy of the plaintiff's argument to consist in the assumption that the enforced separation of the two races stamps the colored race with a badge of inferiority. If this be so, it is not by reason of anything found in the act, but solely because the colored race chooses to put that construction upon it. The argument necessarily assumes that if, as has been more than once the case, and is not unlikely to be so again, the colored race should become the dominant power in the state legislature, and should enact a law in precisely similar terms, it would thereby relegate the white race to an inferior position. We imagine that the white race, at least, would not acquiesce in this assumption. The argument also assumes that social prejudices may be overcome by legislation, and that equal rights cannot be secured to the negro except by an enforced commingling of the two races. We cannot accept this proposition. If the two races are to meet upon terms of social equality, it must be the result of natural affinities, a mutual appreciation of each other's merits, and a voluntary consent of individuals. [Legislation] is powerless to eradicate racial instincts, or to abolish distinctions based upon physical differences, and the attempt to do so can only result in accentuating the difficulties of the present situation. If the civil and political rights of both races be equal, one cannot be inferior to the other civilly or politically. If one race be inferior to the other socially, the constitution of the United States cannot put them upon the same plane. . . .

Mr. Justice Harlan, dissenting. . . .

In respect of civil rights, common to all citizens, the constitution of the United States does not, I think, permit any public authority to know the race of those entitled to be protected in the enjoyment of such rights. Every true man has pride of race, and under appropriate circumstances, when the rights of others, his equals before the law, are not to be affected, it is his privilege to express such pride and to take such action based upon it as to him seems proper. But I deny that any legislative body or judicial tribunal may have regard to the race of citizens when the civil rights of those citizens are involved. Indeed, such legislation as that here in question is inconsistent not only with that equality of rights which pertains to citizenship, national and state, but with the personal liberty enjoyed by every one within the United States. . . .

It was said in argument that the statute of Louisiana does not discriminate against either race, but prescribes a rule applicable alike to white and colored citizens. But this argument does not meet the difficulty. Every one knows that the statute in question had its origin in the purpose, not so much to exclude white persons from railroad cars occupied by blacks, as to exclude colored people from coaches occupied by or assigned to white persons. . . .

[If] a state can prescribe, as a rule of civil conduct, that whites and blacks shall not travel as passengers in the same railroad coach, why may it not so regulate the use of the streets of its cities and towns as to compel white citizens to keep on one side of a street and black citizens to keep on the other? Why may it not, upon like grounds, punish whites and blacks who ride together in street cars or in open vehicles on a public road or street? . . .

The answer given at the argument to these questions was that regulations of the kind they suggest would be unreasonable, and could not, therefore, stand before the law. Is it meant that the determination of questions of legislative power depends upon the inquiry whether the statute whose validity is questioned is, in the judgment of the courts, a reasonable one, taking all the circumstances into consideration? A statute may be unreasonable merely because a sound public policy forbade its enactment. But I do not understand that the courts have anything to do with the policy or expediency of legislation. . . .

The white race deems itself to be the dominant race in this country. And so it is, in prestige, in achievements, in education, in wealth, and in power. So, I doubt not, it will continue to be for all time, if it remains true to its great heritage, and holds fast to the principles of constitutional liberty. But in view of the constitution, in the eye of the law, there is in this country no superior, dominant, ruling class of citizens. There is no caste here. Our constitution is color-blind, and neither knows nor tolerates classes among citizens. In respect of civil rights, all citizens are equal before the law. The humblest is the peer of the most powerful. The law regards man as man, and takes no account of his surroundings or of his color when his civil rights as guaranteed by the supreme law of the land are involved. . . .

In my opinion, the judgment this day rendered will, in time, prove to be quite as pernicious as the decision made by this tribunal in the *Dred Scott Case*. [The] present decision, it may well be apprehended, will not only stimulate aggressions, more or less brutal and irritating, upon the admitted rights of colored citizens, but will encourage the belief that it is possible, by means of state enactments, to defeat the beneficent purposes which the people of the United States had in view when they adopted the recent amendments of the constitution. [Sixty] millions of whites are in no danger from the presence here of eight millions of blacks. The destinies of the two races, in this country, are indissolubly linked together, and the interests of both require that the common government of all shall not permit the seeds of race hate to be planted under the sanction of law. What can more certainly arouse race hate, what more certainly create and perpetuate a feeling of distrust between these races, than state enactments which, in fact, proceed on the ground that colored citizens are so inferior and degraded that they cannot be allowed to sit in public coaches occupied by white citizens? That, as all will admit, is the real meaning of such legislation as was enacted in Louisiana.

There is a race so different from our own that we do not permit those belonging to it to become citizens of the United States. [I] allude to the Chinese race. But by the statute in question, a Chinaman can ride in the same passenger coach with white citizens of the United States, while citizens of the black race in Louisiana, many of whom, perhaps, risked their lives for the preservation of the Union, who are entitled by law, to participate in the political control of the State and nation, who are not excluded, by law or by reason of their race, from public stations of any kind, and who have all the legal rights that belong to white citizens, are yet declared to be criminals, liable to imprisonment, if they ride in a public coach occupied by citizens of the white race. It is scarcely just to say that a colored citizen should not object to occupying a public coach assigned to his own race. [He] ought never to cease objecting to the proposition, that citizens of the white and black races can be adjudged criminals because they sit [in] the same public coach on a public highway.

Note: *Separate but Equal*

1. *Equality of separate facilities.* Although Plessy v. Ferguson is often said to have inaugurated the "separate but equal" doctrine, notice that *Plessy* itself does not require the equality of separate facilities. Why not? If one reads *Plessy* together with The Civil Rights Cases, was the railroad constitutionally obligated to provide equal facilities? Was a state that required private entities to maintain separate facilities constitutionally obligated to enforce an equality requirement as well?

Three years after *Plessy* the Court squarely addressed the equality problem for the first time in Cumming v. Board of Education, 175 U.S. 528 (1899). Petitioners, black taxpayers and parents, challenged their tax assessment on the ground that the money was utilized to support a high school open only to white students. The school board had initially operated a separate black high school, but the facility had been closed to free funds for the education of black primary school students. In an opinion by Justice Harlan, who had dissented in *Plessy* and The Civil Rights Cases, the Court rejected the challenge. The basis for and scope of the Court's holding are not altogether clear. The Court thought it significant that

the substantial relief asked is an injunction that would either impair the efficiency of the high school provided for white children or compel the Board to close it. But if that were done, the result would only be to take from white children educational privileges enjoyed by them, without giving to colored children additional opportunities for the education furnished in high schools. [If,] in some appropriate proceeding instituted directly for that purpose, the plaintiffs had sought to compel the Board of Education, out of funds in its hands or under its control, to establish and maintain a high school for colored children, and if it appeared that the Board's refusal to maintain such a school was in fact an abuse of its discretion and in hostility to the colored population because of their race, different questions might have arisen in the state court.

The Court made clear, however, that local authorities were to be accorded substantial discretion in allocating funds between white and black facilities, and that "any interference on the part of Federal authority with the management of such schools cannot be justified except in the case of a clear and unmistakable disregard of rights secured by the supreme law of the land."

Compare *Plessy* and *Cumming* with McCabe v. Atchison, Topeka & Santa Fe Railway, 235 U.S. 151 (1914). An Oklahoma statute required railroads to provide separate but equal coach facilities. The statute also authorized railroads to haul sleeping cars, dining cars, and chair cars to be used exclusively by one race but not the other. The state justified this latter provision on the ground that the minimal black demand for sleeping and dining facilities made it impractical to haul separate cars for this purpose. The Court found this argument "without merit" because

[it] makes the constitutional right depend upon the number of persons who may be discriminated against, whereas the essence of the constitutional right is that it is a personal one. Whether or not particular facilities shall be provided may doubtless be conditioned upon there being a reasonable demand therefor, but if facilities are provided, substantial equality of treatment of persons traveling under like conditions cannot be refused. It is the individual who is entitled to the equal protection of the laws, and if he is denied by a common carrier, acting in the matter under the authority of a state law, a facility of convenience in the course of his journey which under substantially the same circumstances is furnished to another traveler, he may properly complain that his constitutional privilege has been invaded.

Can *McCabe* be reconciled with *Cumming*? With *Plessy*? After *McCabe*, suppose a black student sought admission to a white public school on the ground that it was closer to his home than the nearest black school? Cf. Gong Lum v. Rice, 275 U.S. 78 (1927).

2. *The state interest in separate facilities.* Note that *Plessy* does not approve all statutes mandating separate treatment. Only those that are "reasonable" are permissible. What state interest made racial separation "reasonable" in *Plessy*? Justice Brown's majority opinion disapproves of the "enforced commingling of the two races" and states that, "[i]f the two races are to meet upon terms of social equality, it must be the result of [a] voluntary consent of individuals." Do these observations support the result reached by the Court? What might have led the Court to suppose that a statute prohibiting blacks and whites who wanted to sit together from doing so was supported by the "voluntary consent of individuals"? Suppose it were true that a majority of the population would prefer segregated facilities. Is respect for majority preferences alone a sufficient justification for separation? How would Justice Brown have answered this question?

Compare *Plessy* with Berea College v. Kentucky, 211 U.S. 45 (1908). The college, a private institution, was convicted under a statute making it a crime to operate a school "where persons of the white and negro races are both received as pupils for instruction." The Court affirmed the conviction, but on the ground that the college was a corporation that did not have all the rights of individuals. In light of *Plessy*, why did the Court think it necessary to qualify its holding in this way? If an individual had been prosecuted under the same statute, what result?

In Buchanan v. Warley, 245 U.S. 60 (1917), the Court held that a statute prohibiting whites from occupying a residence in a block where the majority of houses were occupied by blacks, and vice versa, violated the fourteenth amendment. The challenge to the statute arose in the context of a suit by a white seller to enforce specifically a contract with a black purchaser, who claimed that the law barred him from occupying the residence. The Court acknowledged that "there exists a serious and difficult problem arising from a feeling of race hostility which the law is powerless to control, and to which it must give a measure of consideration." But the Court believed that "such legislation must have its limitations," and that these legitimate objectives could not "be accomplished by laws or ordinances which deny rights created or protected by the Federal Constitution." The Court distinguished *Plessy* and *Berea College*: "In each instance the complaining person was afforded the opportunity to ride, or to attend institutions of learning, or afforded the thing of whatever nature to which in the particular case he was entitled. The most that was done was to require him as a member of a class to conform with reasonable rules in regard to separation of races. In none of them was he denied the right to use, control, or dispose of his property, as in this case."

Does this distinction make sense? Is there a general principle that explains the results in *Plessy, Cumming, McCabe, Berea College,* and *Buchanan*?

3.   *The Attack on Jim Crow*

As the previous section indicates, the framers of the Reconstruction amendments almost certainly intended that the rights of newly freed slaves would be protected by federal *legislative* action authorized by the new sources of congressional power contained in those amendments. This intent was frustrated by the Court's adherence to an older version of federalism and by the collapse of the political consensus supporting civil rights legislation.

One ironic consequence of the Court's invalidation of Reconstruction legislation was that, when meaningful reform finally came, it was the courts, rather than Congress, that provided the impetus for change. From 1938, when the NAACP won its first Supreme Court victory in a school desegregation case, until the 1960s, when a political consensus favoring civil rights again emerged, the courts stood virtually alone in articulating and enforcing the law of race discrimination. What difference might it make that the protection of blacks was left to judicial interpretations of the Constitution rather than to legislative action?

Note: The NAACP's Legal Strategy

1. *The Garland Fund.* Consider R. Kluger, Simple Justice 132-133 (1976):

In 1922, a twenty-one-year-old Harvard undergraduate named Charles Garland had chosen not to accept his share of the estate left by his father, a Boston millionaire. Believing that it was wrong for anyone to be handed a fortune he had done nothing to create, young Garland announced, "I am placing my life on a Christian basis," and gave some $800,000 to establish a foundation for the support of liberal and radical causes. He tarried long enough to see it christened the American Fund for Public Service before he himself took up a farmer's life.

[A committee formed to administer the Garland Fund] recommended that [it] finance a large-scale, widespread dramatic campaign to give the Southern Negro his constitutional rights, his political and civil equality, and therewith a self-consciousness and self-respect which would inevitably tend to effect a revolution in the economic life of the country. [A] grant of $100,000 to the NAACP to carry out such a legal campaign was suggested, along with a memorandum of proposed legal strategy, especially in the education area. Taxpayers' suits were urged, to assure equal as well as separate public schools in the seven states that most flagrantly discriminated against Negroes in their school allocations. . . .

Not everyone at the Garland Fund was enthusiastic about the idea. Indeed, the man who had most experience in such undertakings — Roger Baldwin of the ACLU — was the most skeptical. He was convinced that the legal approach would misfire "because the forces that keep the Negro under subjection will find some way of accomplishing their purposes, law or no law." [Baldwin] favored "the union of white and black workers against their common exploiters." But the committee report carried anyway, the $100,000 was earmarked for the effort, and the first $8,000 transferred to the NAACP for drawing up a detailed blueprint of the legal campaign.

2. *Strategy.* Suppose you were a member of the NAACP's governing board. What use of the Garland Fund money would you favor? Consider the following possibilities:

a. Contributing to scholarship funds for needy black students;
b. Contributing to the political campaigns of candidates sympathetic to the plight of black Americans;
c. Financing litigation demanding the equalization of separate black facilities;
d. Financing litigation demanding the admission of blacks to white facilities on the ground that parallel black facilities were unequal;
e. Financing litigation that frontally attacked *Plessy* and demanded integrated facilities.

In fact, the NAACP did not unwaveringly pursue any single strategy to end discrimination. Rather, it "attacked what might be called targets of opportunity. [If] the military metaphor referring to a litigation campaign is helpful, the campaign was conducted on a terrain that repeatedly required changes in maneuvers." M. Tushnet, Segregated Schools and Legal Strategy: The NAACP's Campaign against Segregated Education, 1925-1950, at 145-146 (1987).

Although the NAACP's campaign was neither systematic nor invariably successful, it slowly remade the law.

Note: *The Road to* Brown

1. *Gaines.* Missouri law required separate education for whites and blacks. Although the University of Missouri operated a law school, the parallel black institution, Lincoln University, did not. A Missouri statute, however, authorized the board of curators to arrange for attendance of black residents at institutions in neighboring states and to pay reasonable tuition rates for such attendance when no black in-state facility was available. In Missouri ex rel. Gaines v. Canada, 305 U.S. 337 (1938), the Supreme Court, in a seven-to-two decision, held that this practice denied a black applicant to the University of Missouri Law School equal protection. Writing for the Court, Chief Justice Hughes stated that

> [the] basic consideration is not as to what sort of opportunities other States provide, or whether they are as good as those in Missouri, but as to what opportunities Missouri itself furnishes to white students and denies to negroes solely upon the ground of color. [The] white resident is afforded legal education within the State; the negro resident having the same qualification is refused it there and must go outside the State to obtain it. That is a denial of the equality of legal right to the enjoyment of the privilege which the state has set up, and the provision for the payment of tuition fees in another State does not remove the discrimination.

2. Gaines *and the meaning of equal treatment.* Why was the out-of-state education Missouri provided to blacks unequal to the in-state education it provided to whites? If Missouri had established a special in-state law school for blacks attended by one student (Gaines), would such a facility have satisfied the Constitution?

Note that there are two questions at issue in cases like *Gaines:* Which institution of government should determine whether the facilities are equal, and how should that determination be made? Cumming v. Board of Education was preoccupied with the first question. The Court argued that state officials should be left free to make their own determinations of equality as long as they acted in good faith and their determinations were reasonable. The *Gaines* majority, however, assumed without discussion that it must make a de novo determination of equality. What is the justification for this change? Would the *Cumming* approach necessarily have made the equality requirement meaningless?

Because of the way it answered the first question, the *Gaines* Court was forced to confront the second. This is a problem of considerable complexity. Presumably the equality requirement does not mean that parallel facilities must be identical. If classrooms in the University of Missouri are painted green and those in Lincoln University yellow, this fact alone would not violate the equal protection clause. How is the Court to evaluate which differences in facilities are relevant for equality purposes? Suppose, for example, Missouri has an outstanding mathematics department, but a weak history department, while Lincoln excels in history, but does poorly in mathematics. Can a court evaluate the equality of the two institutions without deciding a priori on the relative worth of education in mathematics and history? How is a court to do that?

The *McCabe* principle complicates matters further. Under *McCabe*, which held that the constitutional right is an individual one, the state could not defend Lincoln's weak mathematics department on the ground that the vast majority of its students valued history more highly. How can one determine the worth of an entity apart from the value that most people place on it? Suppose a single student at Lincoln attached extraordinary value to attending an institution with green walls. Might yellow walls violate the equality principle after all?

3. *From* Gaines *to* Brown. The analysis above suggests that, at least as a doctrinal matter, the way the Court answered the first question in *Gaines* led inevitably to the ultimate abandonment of the effort to answer the second. This was true not only because there were difficulties in finding a principled way for courts to evaluate the equality of different facilities, but also because the task of performing the evaluation, in the context of thousands of separate facilities each of which had countless different variables to compare, was unmanageable.

Thus, as a matter of legal analysis, it is possible to draw a fairly straight line from *Gaines* to the ultimate abandonment of the separate but equal formula sixteen years later. Consider the extent to which external events, rather than the internal logic of the legal doctrine, explain subsequent developments. Between 1938 and 1954, the United States fought and won a world war against an overtly racist regime in Germany; African-Americans moved into northern cities in increasing numbers, where they became a much more potent political interest group; America became embroiled in a "cold war" in which racist policies in the South were used to discredit the United States in the underdeveloped world; and the first African-American baseball player joined the Brooklyn Dodgers.

During the same period, the Supreme Court decided three school desegregation cases.

a. In Sipuel v. Board of Regents, 332 U.S. 631 (1948), petitioner applied to the only state law school and was denied admission because of her race. In a unanimous, four-paragraph per curiam opinion issued only four days after oral argument, the Court reaffirmed *Gaines* and held that the state was constitutionally obligated to provide the petitioner with an equal legal education. On remand, the trial court gave the state the option of either admitting Sipuel or immediately establishing a separate black law school. Sipuel thereupon sought mandamus in the Supreme Court, claiming that this disposition was inconsistent with the Court's mandate, since the hastily established black school could not possibly provide an equal education. In Fisher v. Hurst, 333 U.S. 147 (1948), the Court, over two dissents, denied relief. The Court noted that "the petition for certiorari in [*Sipuel*] did not present the issue whether a state might not satisfy the equal protection clause of the Fourteenth Amendment by establishing a separate school for Negroes." For an account of the Court's deliberations over *Sipuel* and *Fisher*, see Hutchinson, Unanimity and Desegregation: Decisionmaking in the Supreme Court, 1948-1958, 68 Geo. L.J. 1, 6-9 (1979).

b. In Sweatt v. Painter, 339 U.S. 629 (1950), the Court did what it had declined to do in *Fisher* — order the admission of a black student to a white school. Sweatt was denied admission to the University of Texas Law School on the ground that a parallel black school, opened after the litigation commenced, was a substantially equal facility. The Court held that the facility was not in fact equal, and that Sweatt therefore could not be denied admission to the white school. In reaching this conclusion, the Court was aided by the obvious inequality between the two schools in objectively measurable factors like size of library and number of full-time faculty. But the Court did not limit its examination to these factors:

> What is more important, the University of Texas Law School possesses to a far greater degree those qualities which are incapable of objective measurement but which make for greatness in a law school. Such qualities, to name but a few, include reputation of the faculty, experience of the administration, position and influence of the alumni, standing in the community, traditions and prestige. It is difficult to believe that one who had a free choice between these law schools would consider the question close.
>
> Moreover, although the law is a highly learned profession, we are well aware that it is an intensely practical one. The law school, the proving ground for legal learning and practice, cannot be effective in isolation from the individuals and institutions with which the law interacts. Few students and no one who has practiced law would choose to study in an academic vacuum, removed from the interplay of ideas and the exchange of views with which the law is concerned. The law school to which Texas is willing to admit petitioner excludes from its student body members of the racial groups which number 85% of the population of the State and include most of the lawyers, witnesses, jurors, judges and other officials with whom petitioner will inevitably be dealing when he becomes a member of the Texas Bar. With such a substantial and significant segment of society excluded, we cannot conclude that the education offered petitioner is substantially equal to that which he would receive if admitted to the University of Texas Law School.

c. The Court further elaborated on this theme in McLaurin v. Oklahoma State Regents, 339 U.S. 637 (1950), decided the same day as *Sweatt*. In *McLaurin*, the state, under the pressure of litigation, admitted petitioner to the previously all-white University of Oklahoma Department of Education. However, McLaurin was made to sit in a special seat in the classroom reserved for blacks, could not eat with other students in the cafeteria, and was given a special table in the library. Although McLaurin could not claim that the physical facilities provided him were unequal, the Court held the restrictions unconstitutional because they "[impaired] and [inhibited] his ability to study, to engage in discussions and exchange views with other students, and, in general, to learn his profession."

After *Sweatt* and *McLaurin*, was there anything left for the Court to decide in *Brown*?

Brown v. Board of Education of Topeka (*Brown I*)
347 U.S. 483 (1954)

MR. CHIEF JUSTICE WARREN delivered the opinion of the Court. . . .

In each of [these] cases, minors of the Negro race, through their legal representatives, seek the aid of the courts in obtaining admission to the public schools of their community on a nonsegregated basis. In each instance, they had been denied admission to schools attended by white children under laws requiring or permitting segregation according to race. This segregation was alleged to deprive the plaintiffs of the equal protection of the laws under the Fourteenth Amendment. . . .

Reargument was largely devoted to the circumstances surrounding the adoption of the Fourteenth Amendment in 1868. It covered exhaustively consideration of the Amendment in Congress, ratification by the states, then existing practices in racial segregation, and the views of proponents and opponents of the Amendment. This discussion and our own investigation convince us that, although these sources cast some light, it is not enough to resolve the problem with which we are faced. At best, they are inconclusive. The most avid proponents of the post-War Amendments undoubtedly intended them to remove all legal distinctions among "all persons born or naturalized in the United States." Their opponents, just as certainly, were antagonistic to both the letter and the spirit of the Amendments and wished them to have the most limited effect. What others in Congress and the state legislatures had in mind cannot be determined with any degree of certainty.

An additional reason for the inconclusive nature of the Amendment's history, with respect to segregated schools, is the status of public education at that time. In the South, the movement toward free common schools, supported by general taxation, had not yet taken hold. Education of white children was largely in the hands of private groups. Education of Negroes was almost nonexistent, and practically all of the race were illiterate. In fact, any education of Negroes was forbidden by law in some states. Today, in contrast, many Negroes have achieved outstanding success in the arts and sciences as well as in the business and professional world. It is true that public school education at the time of the Amendment had advanced further in the North, but the effect of the Amendment on Northern States was generally ignored in the congressional debates. Even in the North, the conditions of public education did not approximate those existing today. The curriculum was usually rudimentary; ungraded schools were common in rural areas; the school term was but three months a year in many states; and compulsory school attendance was virtually unknown. As a consequence, it is not surprising that there should be so little in the history of the Fourteenth Amendment relating to its intended effect on public education. . . .

In approaching this problem, we cannot turn the clock back to 1868 when the Amendment was adopted, or even to 1896 when [Plessy] was written. We must consider public education in the light of its full development and its present place in American life throughout the Nation. Only in this way can it be determined if segregation in public schools deprives these plaintiffs of the equal protection of the laws.

Today, education is perhaps the most important function of state and local governments. Compulsory school attendance laws and the great expenditures for education both demonstrate our recognition of the importance of education to our democratic society. It is required in the performance of our most basic public responsibilities, even service in the armed forces. It is the very foundation of good citizenship. Today it is a principal instrument in awakening the child to cultural values, in preparing him for later professional training, and in helping him to adjust normally to his environment. In these days, it is doubtful that any child may reasonably be expected to succeed in life if he is denied the opportunity of an education. Such an opportunity, where the state has undertaken to provide it, is a right which must be made available to all on equal terms.

We come then to the question presented: Does segregation of children in public schools solely on the basis of race, even though the physical facilities and other "tangible" factors may be equal, deprive the children of the minority group of equal educational opportunities? We believe that it does.

In [*Sweatt*], in finding that a segregated law school for Negroes could not provide them equal educational opportunities, this Court relied in large part on "those qualities which are incapable of objective measurement but which make for greatness in a law school." In [*McLaurin*], the Court, in requiring that a Negro admitted to a white graduate school be treated like all other students, again resorted to intangible considerations: ". . . his ability to study, to engage in discussions and exchange views with other students, and, in general, to learn his profession." Such considerations apply with added force to children in grade and high schools. To separate them from others of similar age and qualifications solely because of their race generates a feeling of inferiority as to their status in the community that may affect their hearts and minds in a way unlikely ever to be undone. The effect of this separation on their educational opportunities was well stated by a finding in the Kansas case by a court which nevertheless felt compelled to rule against the Negro plaintiffs:

> Segregation of white and colored children in public schools has a detrimental effect upon the colored children. The impact is greater when it has the sanction of the law; for the policy of separating the races is usually interpreted as denoting the inferiority of the negro group. A sense of inferiority affects the motivation of a child to learn. Segregation with the sanction of law, therefore, has a tendency to [retard] the educational and mental development of negro children and to deprive them of some of the benefits they would receive in a racial[ly] integrated school system.

Whatever may have been the extent of psychological knowledge at the time of [*Plessy*], this finding is amply supported by modern authority.[11] Any language in [*Plessy*] contrary to this finding is rejected.

We conclude that in the field of public education the doctrine of "separate but equal" has no place. Separate educational facilities are inherently unequal. Therefore, we hold that the plaintiffs and others similarly situated for whom the actions have been brought are, by reason of the segregation complained of, deprived of the equal protection of the laws guaranteed by the Fourteenth Amendment.

Note: *Justifications and Explanations for* Brown

1. *The Court's justifications.* Did *Brown* adequately explain why segregation denied minority students equal educational opportunity even when "tangible" factors were equalized? Consider the following arguments:

11. K. B. Clark, Effect of Prejudice and Discrimination on Personality Development (Mid-century White House Conference on Children and Youth, 1950); Witmer & Kotinsky, Personality in the Making (1952), c. VI; Deutscher & Chein, The Psychological Effects of Enforced Segregation: A Survey of Social Science Opinion, 26 J. Psychol. 259 (1948); Chein, What Are the Psychological Effects of Segregation under Conditions of Equal Facilities?, 3 Int. J. Opinion & Attitude Res. 229 (1949); Brameld, Educational Costs, in Discrimination and National Welfare (MacIver, ed., 1949), 44-48; Frazier, The Negro in the United States (1949), 674-681. And see generally Myrdal, An American Dilemma (1944).

a. *The legislative history of the equal protection clause is consistent with the position that segregated education is unconstitutional.* Note that the Court does not assert that the framers of the fourteenth amendment specifically intended to outlaw segregated education. Is such an assertion plausible? In 1868, eight northern states permitted segregated schools, and five additional northern states excluded black children entirely from public education. See R. Kluger, Simple Justice 633-634 (1976). The Reconstruction Congress itself permitted the District of Columbia schools to remain segregated, see Frank and Munro, The Original Understanding of "Equal Protection of the Laws," 1972 Wash. U.L.Q. 421, 460-462, and even the spectators in the gallery listening to the senators debate the fourteenth amendment were segregated by race. See R. Berger, Government by Judiciary: The Transformation of the Fourteenth Amendment 123-125 (1977). Moreover, the sponsors of the Civil Rights Act of 1866, which the fourteenth amendment was intended to constitutionalize, specifically disclaimed any intent to interfere with segregated education. See Statement of James Wilson, Cong. Globe, 39th Cong., 1st Sess. 1117-1118 (1866). See generally Bickel, The Original Understanding and the Segregation Decision, 69 Harv. L. Rev. 1, 11-40 (1955).

For an unusual dissenting view of the original understanding, see McConnell, Originalism and the Desegregation Decisions, 81 Va. L. Rev. 947 (1995). Professor McConnell relies heavily on the ultimately unsuccessful efforts of Republicans in the Reconstruction Congress to include schools within the scope of the 1875 Civil Rights Act, which broadly prohibited segregation in public accommodations, to argue that the framers intended to prohibit school segregation.

Even if McConnell is wrong about the framers' specific intent, might it nonetheless be argued that the equal protection clause represented "a compromise permitting [Moderates and Radicals] to go to the country with language which they could, where necessary, defend against damaging alarms raised by the opposition, but which at the same time was sufficiently elastic to permit reasonable future advances"? Bickel, supra, at 61. If, as Bickel maintains, the legislative history "left the way open to, in fact invited, a decision based on the moral and material state of the nation in 1954, not 1866," id. at 65, does not the burden remain on the defenders of *Brown* to explain why segregation in 1954 denied equality?

In Bolling v. Sharpe, 347 U.S. 497 (1954), decided on the same day as *Brown*, the Court unanimously held school segregation in the District of Columbia unconstitutional. Since the fourteenth amendment applies only to the states, the Court could not rely on the equal protection clause. But although equal protection and due process are not "interchangeable phrases," the Court held that "discrimination may be so unjustifiable as to be violative of [the due process clause of the fifth amendment]." Moreover, "[i]n view of our decision that the Constitution prohibits the States from maintaining racially segregated public schools, it would be unthinkable that the same Constitution would impose a lesser duty on the Federal Government."

Does the legislative history of the fifth and fourteenth amendments really make this result "unthinkable"? When the fifth amendment was adopted, most blacks in the United States were slaves, and the Constitution itself implicitly acknowledged that fact. Does *Bolling* suggest that the fourteenth amendment somehow modified the fifth amendment? The framers of the fourteenth amendment chose to make the equal protection guarantee applicable solely to the states. This decision presumably reflected the view that institutional safeguards on the federal level made a constitutional guarantee of equality unnecessary. Does the Court care what those who wrote the fifth and fourteenth amendments meant by them? Should it?

See also the discussion of original intent in constitutional interpretation in Chapter 1, section B, supra, and in Chapter 6, section A, infra.

b. *"Today, education is perhaps the most important function of state and local governments."* Does this observation, even if correct, in any way advance the argument that segregated education is per se discriminatory? Is *Brown* supported by the deep-seated view of U.S. public schools as a "secular, nationalizing, assimilationist agent [charged] with the task of Americanization, of melding backgrounds, and creating one nation"? A. Bickel, The Supreme Court and the Idea of Progress 121-122 (1970). Does the Constitution require this view of education, or does it permit (compel?) recognition of competing values, such as cultural diversity, parental control, and freedom of association? See Board of Education, Island Trees Union Free School District v. Pico, Chapter 7, section E2d, infra.

In a series of terse per curiam opinions handed down in the years immediately after *Brown*, the Court held unconstitutional segregation in a wide variety of other public facilities. See, e.g., Gayle v. Browder, 352 U.S. 903 (1956) (buses); Holmes v. City of Atlanta, 350 U.S. 879 (1955) (municipal golf courses); Mayor of Baltimore v. Dawson, 350 U.S. 877 (1955) (public beaches and bathhouses). In light of these decisions, is it possible to maintain that *Brown* rested on the special status of public education?

c. *"To separate [minority children] from others of similar age and qualifications solely because of their race generates a feeling of inferiority as to their status in the community that may affect their hearts and minds in a way unlikely ever to be undone."* Is stigma alone a sufficient injury to constitute a denial of equal protection? Is the perception of stigma sufficient to invalidate a law that is supported by a valid, neutral purpose? In *Bolling*, the Court observed that "[s]egregation in public education is not reasonably related to any proper governmental objective, and thus it imposes on Negro children [a] burden that constitutes an arbitrary deprivation of their liberty."

Consider Black, The Lawfulness of the Segregation Decisions, 69 Yale L.J. 421, 424-426 (1960): "[Segregation was] set up and continued for the very purpose of keeping [blacks] in an inferior station. [This purpose was a] matter of common notoriety [not] so much for judicial notice as for background knowledge of educated men who live in the world." Would segregated education have achieved this purpose if all tangible facilities were really equalized in black and white schools? Suppose segregation was imposed for the purpose of disadvantaging blacks, but that overwhelmingly persuasive data demonstrated that blacks in fact benefited from a segregated, but truly equal, environment?

d. *"Segregation with the sanction of law [has] a tendency to [retard] the educational and mental development of Negro children."* *Brown's* reliance on empirical social science data to support this conclusion has been the subject of continuing controversy. See, e.g., Cahn, Jurisprudence, 30 N.Y.U. L. Rev. 150 (1955); Van den Haag, Social Science Testimony in the Desegregation Cases — A Reply to Professor Kenneth Clark, 6 Vill. L. Rev. 69 (1960). See generally Symposium, The Courts, Social Science and School Desegregation, 39 Law & Contemp. Probs. 1 (Winter/Spring 1975). Indeed, it appears that "[v]irtually everyone who has examined the question now agrees that the Court erred [in relying upon the social science data]. The proffered evidence was methodologically unsound." Yudof, School Desegregation: Legal Realism, Reasoned Elaboration, and Social Science Research in the Supreme Court, 42 Law & Contemp. Probs. 57, 70 (1978).

The conflict over the reliability of the data has tended to obscure more fundamental questions. Even if it could be demonstrated unambiguously that blacks perform better in an integrated than a segregated environment, why should that fact be constitutionally determinative? Does the Constitution require the arrangement that maximizes the achievement of black students?

If whites in an integrated classroom receive better test scores than blacks, does *Brown* suggest that the class must be *segregated* so that blacks can be given a different curriculum that will produce equal test scores? Is the *Brown* Court's reliance on social science data consistent with *McCabe's* holding that the fourteenth amendment protects *individual* rights?

Consider Justice Thomas's comments on the social science arguments for *Brown* in his concurring opinion in Missouri v. Jenkins, 515 U.S. 70 (1995):

Segregation was not unconstitutional because it might have caused psychological feelings of inferiority. Public school systems that separated blacks and provided them with superior education resources — making blacks "feel" superior to whites sent to lesser schools — would violate the Fourteenth Amendment, whether or not the white students felt stigmatized, just as do school systems in which the positions of the races are reversed. Psychological injury or benefit is irrelevant to the question whether state actors have engaged in intentional discrimination — the critical inquiry for ascertaining violations of the Equal Protection Clause. The judiciary is fully competent to make independent determinations concerning the existence of state action without the unnecessary and misleading assistance of the social sciences.

Regardless of the relative quality of the schools, segregation violated the Constitution because the State classified students based on their race. . . .

Given that desegregation has not produced the predicted leaps forward in black educational achievement, there is no reason to think that black students cannot learn as well when surrounded by members of their own race as when they are in an integrated environment. . . .

"Racial isolation" itself is not a harm; only state-enforced segregation is. After all, if separation itself is a harm, and if integration therefore is the only way that blacks can receive a proper education, then there must be something inferior about blacks. Under this theory, segregation injures blacks because blacks, when left on their own, cannot achieve. To my way of thinking, that conclusion is the result of a jurisprudence based on a theory of black inferiority.

2. *Alternative rationales and explanations.* If the Court's reasoning in *Brown* is less than satisfactory, are there better justifications for the result? Even if it cannot be justified legally, are there plausible explanations for the Court's decision? Consider the following possibilities:

a. Wechsler, Toward Neutral Principles of Constitutional Law, 73 Harv. L. Rev. 1, 34 (1959):

Assuming equal facilities, the question posed by state-enforced segregation is not one of discrimination at all. Its human and its constitutional dimensions lie entirely elsewhere, in the denial by the state of freedom to associate, a denial that impinges in the same way on any groups or races that may be involved.

Wechsler goes on to ask whether in

> a situation where the state must practically choose between denying the association
> to those individuals who wish it or imposing it on those who would avoid it, [there
> is] a basis in neutral principles for holding that the Constitution demands that the
> claims for association should prevail.

Is *Brown* premised on the assumption that in a white-dominated society, segregation harms blacks more severely than whites? That blacks are harmed more severely by forced separation than whites are harmed by forced association? Does it matter to the freedom of association argument that in the school context, it is generally parents who have the freedom but children who do the associating?

b. Bell, Brown v. Board of Education and the Interest-Convergence Dilemma, 93 Harv. L. Rev. 518, 524-525 (1980):

> [The] decision in *Brown* to break with the Court's long-held position on these is-
> sues cannot be understood without some consideration of the decision's value to
> whites [able] to see the economic and political advantages at home and abroad that
> would follow the abandonment of segregation. [*Brown* provided] immediate credi-
> bility to America's struggle with Communist countries to win the hearts and minds
> of emerging third world people [and] offered much needed reassurance to Ameri-
> can blacks. [Moreover,] there were whites who realized that the South could make
> the transition from a rural, plantation society to the sunbelt with all its poten-
> tial and profit only when it ended its struggle to remain divided by state-sponsored
> segregation.

If desegregation was really in the interest of the white majority, why did it have to be judicially imposed? Was the campaign to overrule *Plessy* ultimately successful because "the dominant elites in the South, even if they controlled public opin-ion there, [were] only a fragment of the national ruling class, and [the] interests of the ruling class as a whole [differed] from those of its southern fragment"? M. Tushnet, Segregated Schools and Legal Strategy: The NAACP's Campaign against Segregated Education, 1925-1950, at 12 (1987). If the result in *Brown* was in the interest of the white majority, does that support the decision by answering those who claimed that the Court had unjustifiably imposed its own social views on the country?

c. Consider the following argument: Most critics of *Brown* have treated the de-cision as an unjustified assertion of judicial power. But *Brown* can be viewed in-stead as a product of the institutional *weakness* of the judiciary. Prior to *Brown*, the Court had committed itself to the position that separate educational facili-ties had to be equalized, and that the courts were duty bound to decide de novo whether such equality actually existed. Might such a doctrine, by requiring the courts to evaluate the level of "equality" in thousands of segregated school sys-tems throughout the country, have produced an even more serious judicial in-trusion on the political branches than *Brown*? Note that, even if you believe that segregated schools as they existed in the southern states in 1954 violated the equal protection clause, it does not follow that *Brown* was correctly decided. The hard question is why desegregation was the constitutionally required alternative to a judicially mandated regime of real equality.

Consider the following argument, made by Geneva Crenshaw, the fictional heroine in D. Bell, And We Are Not Saved 111-113 (1987):

> We civil rights lawyers attacked segregation in the public schools because it was the weak link in the "separate but equal" chain. Our attack worked. But to equate integration with the effective education black children need — well, that was a mistake. . . .
>
> [I] don't agree that a better desegregation policy was beyond the reach of intelligent people whose minds were not clogged with integrationist dreams. [Suppose] the Court had issued the following orders:
>
> 1. Even though we encourage voluntary desegregation, we will not order racially integrated assignments of students or staff for ten years.
>
> 2. Even though "separate but equal" no longer meets the constitutional equal-protection standard, we will require immediate equalization of all facilities and resources.
>
> 3. Blacks must be represented on school boards and other policy-making bodies in proportions equal to those of black students in each school district.
>
> [Rather] than beat our heads against the wall seeking pupil-desegregation orders the courts were unwilling to enter or enforce, we could have organized parents and communities to ensure effective implementation for the equal-funding and equal-representation mandates.

Did the *Brown* Court abandon a truly serious effort to achieve racial justice for a slogan? Could it have done otherwise?

3. *The meaning of* Brown. What precisely did *Brown* require southern school systems to do? Could that question be answered before the ambiguity as to *Brown's* reasoning was resolved? For example, if *Brown* was premised on the stigma associated with state-enforced segregation, then presumably a simple declaration that race would no longer be considered in school assignments would be sufficient. But if *Brown* meant that educational equality could be achieved only if blacks and whites attended school together, something more might be required.

The initial *Brown* opinion did not answer the remedy question. Instead, the Court restored the case to the docket for reargument. As you read the opinion that follows, think about whether the Court answered or avoided the substantive questions that remained after *Brown I*.

Brown v. Board of Education of Topeka (*Brown II*)
349 U.S. 294 (1955)

MR. CHIEF JUSTICE WARREN delivered the opinion of the Court.

These cases were decided on May 17, 1954. The opinions of that date, declaring the fundamental principle that racial discrimination in public education is unconstitutional, are incorporated herein by reference. All provisions of federal, state, or local law requiring or permitting such discrimination must yield to this principle. There remains for consideration the manner in which relief is to be accorded.

Because these cases arose under different local conditions and their disposition will involve a variety of local problems, we requested further argument on the question of relief. In view of the nationwide importance of the decision, we invited the Attorney General of the United States, and the Attorneys General of all states requiring or permitting racial discrimination in public education to present their views on that question. . . .

Full implementation of these constitutional principles may require solution of varied local school problems. School authorities have the primary responsibility for elucidating, assessing, and solving these problems; courts will have to consider whether the action of school authorities constitutes good faith implementation of the governing constitutional principles. Because of their proximity to local conditions and the possible need for further hearings, the courts which originally heard these cases can best perform this judicial appraisal. Accordingly, we believe it appropriate to remand the cases to those courts.

In fashioning and effectuating the decrees, the courts will be guided by equitable principles. Traditionally equity has been characterized by a practical flexibility in shaping its remedies and by a facility for adjusting and reconciling public and private needs. These cases call for the exercise of these traditional attributes of equity power. At stake is the personal interest of the plaintiffs in admission to public schools as soon as practicable on a nondiscriminatory basis. To effectuate this interest may call for elimination of a variety of obstacles in making the transition to school systems operated in accordance with the constitutional principles set forth in our May 17, 1954, decision. Courts of equity may properly take into account the public interest in the elimination of such obstacles in a systematic and effective manner. But it should go without saying that the vitality of these constitutional principles cannot be allowed to yield simply because of disagreement with them.

While giving weight to these public and private considerations, the courts will require that the defendants make a prompt and reasonable start toward full compliance with our May 17, 1954, ruling. Once such a start has been made, the courts may find that additional time is necessary to carry out the ruling in an effective manner. The burden rests upon the defendants to establish that such time is necessary in the public interest and is consistent with good faith compliance at the earliest practicable date. To that end, the courts may consider problems related to administration, arising from the physical condition of the school plant, the school transportation system, personnel, revision of school districts and attendance areas into compact units to achieve a system of determining admission to the public schools on a nonracial basis, and revision of local laws and regulations which may be necessary in solving the foregoing problems. They will also consider the adequacy of any plans the defendants may propose to meet these problems and to effectuate a transition to a racially nondiscriminatory school system. During this period of transition, the courts will retain jurisdiction of these cases.

The judgments below, except that in the Delaware case, are accordingly reversed and the cases are remanded to the District Courts to take such proceedings and enter such orders and decrees consistent with this opinion as are necessary and proper to admit to public schools on a racially nondiscriminatory basis with all deliberate speed the parties to these cases. The judgment in the Delaware case — ordering the immediate admission of the plaintiffs to schools previously attended only by white children — is affirmed on the basis of the principles stated in our May 17, 1954, opinion, but the case is remanded to the Supreme

Court of Delaware for such further proceedings as that Court may deem necessary in light of this opinion.

Note: "All Deliberate Speed"

Brown II's "all deliberate speed" formulation has been widely criticized. Consider the following arguments against the approach:

1. *If segregation is unconstitutional, the Court cannot legitimately tolerate continued segregation while jurisdictions make "a prompt and reasonable start toward" desegregation.* Was *Brown II* premised on the notion that "Negroes (unlike whites) possess rights as a race rather than as individuals, so that a particular Negro can rightly be delayed in the enjoyment of his established rights if progress is being made in improving the legal status of Negroes generally"? Lusky, The Stereotype: Hard Core of Racism, 13 Buffalo L. Rev. 450, 457 (1963). See also Carter, The Warren Court and Desegregation, 67 Mich. L. Rev. 237, 243-244 (1968). Did *Brown I* involve the rights of individual black students? For example, after *Brown I*, could a school board argue that a particular black child in a particular district would receive a better education in a segregated, rather than an integrated, school? If *Brown I* was designed to protect the rights of blacks *as a group*, is it fair to attack *Brown II* for providing group-oriented remedies?

2. Brown II *needlessly encouraged white resistance to desegregation by failing to demand an immediate remedy.* See, e.g., Black, The Unfinished Business of the Warren Court, 46 Wash. L. Rev. 3, 22 (1970). *Brown II* was followed by an extended period of "massive resistance" during which there was virtually no actual desegregation in the South. See pages 456-460 infra. But the causal link between *Brown II* and the slow pace of desegregation is uncertain, and some have defended the decision on the ground that "any head-on challenge to the segregated South in 1955 would have produced civil strife sufficient to make Little Rock and Birmingham seem gatherings of good will." J. Wilkinson, From *Brown* to *Bakke* 68 (1979). See also Bickel, The Decade of School Desegregation: Progress and Prospects, 64 Colum. L. Rev. 193, 201-202 (1964). What could the Court have done if an order for immediate desegregation had simply been defied? Note that in 1955 it was uncertain whether either the President or the Congress would support the Court if such an order were disobeyed.

Does *Brown II* prove that the Court "was a white court which would protect the interests of White America in the maintenance of stable institutions"? Steel, Nine Men in Black Who Think White, N.Y. Times Magazine, Oct. 13, 1968, at 112, col. 4. Or does the decision merely reflect the inherent limits of judicial power — limits that arguably influenced the formulation of the *Brown I* standard in the first place?

3. Brown II *overstated the administrative difficulties of desegregation.* What precisely were the "varied local school problems" that might justify delay? Does the answer to that question depend in part on what *Brown I* required? If *Brown I* required no more than the repeal of laws prohibiting blacks from attending white schools, it is hard to see why this could not be accomplished instantly. But if *Brown I* required school boards to take affirmative steps to dismantle dual school systems and produce actual integration, the process might be more complex. Did

the Court act responsibly in authorizing a period of delay without specifying what was to be accomplished during that period?

4. *The Court acted unwisely in remitting the task of enforcement and elucidation of* Brown I *to the lower federal courts.* To the extent that the remaining difficulties were solely remedial and technical, it was perhaps appropriate to remand the cases to local federal judges familiar with local conditions. But could these courts be expected to devise appropriate remedies when the content of the right to be vindicated remained so vague? As the next Note indicates, *Brown II* was followed by an extended period during which the lower courts wrestled with the question of remedy in the face of intransigence and subterfuge. When, some fifteen years after *Brown II*, the Court finally returned to the question of rights, its views were crucially influenced by this remedial struggle.

4.   *Fulfilling* Brown's *Promise*

Note: *The Response to* Brown

1. *Tokenism and massive resistance.* Suppose you were a southern governor in 1955 determined to minimize the impact of *Brown*. What policies would you pursue? In retrospect, it seems at least possible that the immediate, good faith dismantling of the formal structure of segregation might have satisfied the courts while producing only minor disruption. Instead, *Brown* was greeted throughout the South with defiance and evasion. In the short term, this approach stymied judicial enforcement efforts. But in the longer term, the strategy had two unanticipated consequences. First, it helped mobilize political support for desegregation. Second, the long struggle to impose meaningful remedies in the face of "massive resistance" subtly influenced the way in which the fourteenth amendment was interpreted.

Southern resistance took several different forms. In part, it was rhetorical. For example, most southern members of Congress signed the "Southern Manifesto" asserting the illegitimacy of *Brown* and the right of the states to ignore the decision. See 102 Cong. Rec. H3948, 4004 (daily ed. Mar. 12, 1956). Other southern politicians advanced their careers by vowing never to permit integration. In some communities, this verbal resistance was supplemented by intimidation and violence. And throughout the South, school districts devised a bewildering variety of legal strategies designed to slow or stop desegregation. A few communities took the extreme measure of closing their public schools altogether to avoid desegregation. Others adopted complex pupil placement laws giving local officials discretion to place students in different schools on the basis of supposedly nonracial criteria. Still others utilized "freedom of choice" plans whereby students were assigned to their old schools unless they applied for transfer. The common feature of all these plans was that they produced virtually no actual integration. For accounts of early efforts to circumvent *Brown*, see McKay, "With All Deliberate Speed," 31 N.Y.U. L. Rev. 991 (1956); Powe, The Road to *Swann*: Mobile County Crawls to the Bus, 51 Tex. L. Rev. 505 (1973). Some of the rhetoric from the period is collected in J. Wilkinson, From *Brown* to *Bakke* 69-74 (1979).

2. *The early judicial response.* The judicial response to these strategems varied. Pupil placement, freedom of choice, and grade-per-year plans were all both in-

validated and upheld by various lower courts. In the face of massive community opposition, a few district court judges insisted on far-reaching and effective desegregation plans. See generally J. Peltason, Fifty-Eight Lonely Men (1971). But the more common judicial attitude toward *Brown* ranged from caution to outright hostility. In one widely quoted opinion written shortly after *Brown*, a district court held that *Brown* did not require "the states [to] mix persons of different races in the schools. [What] it has decided [is] that a state may not deny any person on account of race the right to attend any school that it maintains. [The] Constitution, in other words, does not require integration. [It] merely forbids the use of governmental power to enforce segregation." Briggs v. Elliott, 132 F. Supp. 776, 777 (E.D.S.C. 1955). Other judges read *Brown* even more narrowly. For example, one judge announced at the conclusion of a suit to desegregate the Dallas schools that "the white man has a right to maintain his racial integrity and it can't be done so easily in integrated schools. [We] will not name any date or issue any order. [The] School Board should further study this question and perhaps take further action, maybe an election." J. Peltason, supra, at 118-119. Overall, the pace of desegregation was painfully slow. By 1964, ten years after *Brown I*, only 2.3 percent of the black children in the South were attending desegregated schools. See Dunn, Title VI, the Guidelines, and School Desegregation in the South, 53 Va. L. Rev. 42, 44 n.9 (1967).

Despite the lack of uniformity and absence of progress, the Supreme Court remained almost entirely silent during this early period. It intervened only once — and then only in the face of outright defiance. Cooper v. Aaron, 358 U.S. 1 (1958), grew out of efforts to desegregate the Little Rock public school system. Pursuant to a plan developed by the Little Rock School Board, nine black children were scheduled to enroll in all-white Central High School at the start of the 1957 term. These plans were stymied by Arkansas Governor Orval Faubus, who ordered the Arkansas National Guard to block the entry of the children. The students were admitted only after President Eisenhower dispatched troops to enforce federal law. Under the protection of these troops and the federalized National Guard, the black students remained in Central High School through February 1958. The school board then sought permission from the federal district court to terminate the desegregation program because of the extreme public hostility. The district court granted the board's request, but the court of appeals reversed. In an extraordinary opinion, signed by all nine justices, the Supreme Court affirmed the court of appeals and ordered desegregation to proceed. The Court held that "the constitutional rights of respondents are not to be sacrificed or yielded to the violence and disorder which have followed upon the actions of the Governor and Legislature. [Law] and order are not here to be preserved by depriving the Negro children of their constitutional rights." In response to the Governor's assertion that he was not bound by *Brown*, the Court declared that "the federal judiciary is supreme in the exposition of the law of the Constitution," and that "the interpretation of the Fourteenth Amendment enunciated by this Court in the *Brown* case is the supreme law of the land."

3. *The end of deliberate speed.* Cooper v. Aaron was a powerful statement of judicial supremacy and an attack on outright defiance of *Brown*. It did little, however, to clarify the confusion concerning what *Brown* required. It was not until the early 1960s that the Court began to intervene more effectively and systematically to oversee the desegregation process. See Watson v. Memphis, 373 U.S. 526

(1963) (holding the "all deliberate speed" formulation inapplicable to segregated municipal recreation facilities and ordering immediate desegregation); Goss v. Board of Education, 373 U.S. 683 (1963) (invalidating "one-way transfer" plans permitting students to transfer from schools where they were in the racial minority to schools where they were in the majority); Griffin v. County School Board, 377 U.S. 218 (1964) (holding unconstitutional the closing of county schools to avoid desegregation).

The Court's renewed interest in the pace of school desegregation coincided with the reemergence of an effective political coalition supporting black equality for the first time since Reconstruction. The changed political atmosphere resulted in part from extralegal events — in particular, "direct action" campaigns against southern segregation led by Martin Luther King and other civil rights activists. These campaigns, and the sometimes violent and brutal response that they engendered, helped to mobilize northern public opinion against segregation.

An important turning point was passage of the Civil Rights Act of 1964, 42 U.S.C. §2000a et seq. Although the most widely debated sections of the act prohibited racial discrimination in places of public accommodation, the act also had important provisions dealing with school desegregation. Title IV authorized the Attorney General to institute desegregation suits in the name of the United States, thereby ending the need to rely on individual lawsuits by private plaintiffs. More significantly, title VI established a parallel desegregation mechanism that avoided the necessity of lawsuits altogether. Racial discrimination was prohibited in any program receiving federal financial assistance, and federal agencies were authorized to issue regulations enforcing this prohibition and to terminate funding upon noncompliance. Pursuant to this authority, the Department of Health, Education, and Welfare promulgated desegregation guidelines in 1965. The first guidelines did not require substantially more than was already mandated by contemporary case law, but revised guidelines, issued in March 1966, were considerably stiffer. They provided, inter alia, that attendance zones could not be drawn to "maintain what is essentially a dual school structure," and that freedom of choice plans would be "[scrutinized] with special care" and judged by whether "minority group students have in fact transferred from segregated schools."

The guidelines were important not only because the threatened fund cutoff provided an impetus for desegregation but also because they allowed courts to escape from the morass of case-by-case litigation over individual desegregation plans. In a series of landmark decisions, the Fifth Circuit Court of Appeals used the guidelines to formulate model decrees, applicable throughout the circuit, which regulated every detail of the desegregation process. See, e.g., United States v. Jefferson County Board of Education, 380 F.2d 385 (5th Cir.), cert. denied, 389 U.S. 840 (1967). The effect was dramatic. The percentage of southern black children attending desegregated schools jumped from 2.3 percent in 1964, to 7.5 percent in 1965, to 12.5 percent in 1966. See Dunn, supra, at 43 n.8. For a discussion of the effect of the guidelines, see Note, The Courts, HEW, and Southern School Desegregation, 77 Yale L.J. 321 (1967).

What does this history suggest about the relative importance of legal and political forces in effecting social change? Consider Klarman, The Puzzling Resistance to Political Process Theory, 77 Va. L. Rev. 747, 813 (1991):

[To] the extent that post-*Brown* Supreme Court decisions deserve even partial credit for the demise of southern school segregation, it is crucial to note that those decisions *post*-dated the emergence of a national political coalition committed to eliminating racial segregation and discrimination. [A] great deal of the school desegregation that ultimately flowed from *Brown* appears to have been more directly attributable to the intervention of a racially-enlightened national political process than to the Supreme Court.

Compare J. Greenberg, Crusaders in the Courts: How a Dedicated Band of Lawyers Fought for the Civil Rights Revolution 12 (1994) (arguing that *Brown* triggered the civil rights movement, which in turn produced civil rights legislation).

Four years after passage of the 1964 Civil Rights Act, the Court began dismantling the last barriers to desegregation in the rural South by questioning the "freedom of choice" plans widely used throughout the region. In Green v. County School Board, 391 U.S. 430 (1968), the Court invalidated a "freedom of choice" plan that the district had adopted to avoid loss of federal funds. The district had only two schools, one of which had been all-black and the other all-white prior to *Brown*. Since there was little residential segregation, a plan utilizing geographical districts would have created integrated schools. Instead, each pupil was required to choose between the two schools on entering first and eighth grades. Children in other grades were permitted to choose but were assigned to the school last attended if they made no choice. After the plan had been in effect for three years, 85 percent of the black children and none of the white children were attending the black school.

A unanimous Court held that this freedom of choice plan could not "be accepted as a sufficient step to 'effectuate a transition' to a unitary school system." Justice Brennan's opinion emphasized the Court's impatience at the pace of desegregation: "In determining whether [the board satisfied *Brown*] by adopting its 'freedom-of-choice' plan, it is relevant that this first step did not come until some 11 years after *Brown I* was decided and 10 years after *Brown II* directed the making of a 'prompt and reasonable start.' [The] burden on a school board today is to come forward with a plan that promises realistically to work, and promises realistically to work *now*."

Moreover, the Court rejected the argument that the institution of "freedom of choice" itself satisfied the board's constitutional obligation. Rather, freedom of choice had to be judged by its effectiveness as a means to achieve a unitary school system. The ultimate test was whether "the plan [promises] realistically to convert promptly to a system without a 'white' school and a 'Negro' school, but just schools."

Like most of the Court's pronouncements on school desegregation since *Brown II*, *Green* focused on the adequacy of remedy. Did the Court explain what *substantive* deprivation the board had failed to remedy? What made the *Green* school system nonunitary? As a practical matter, a network of formal and informal sanctions made black freedom wholly illusory under many freedom of choice plans. But *Green* did not rely on the illusory nature of the choice in invalidating the plan. Rather, the Court suggested that a system is not unitary even if truly free choice fails to produce integration. In a system where each child freely chooses his school, how has the *state* erected racial barriers violative of equal protection? Does the state violate the Constitution when it fails affirmatively to encourage racial mixing in the schools? If so, can *Green* be confined to districts with a prior history of legally imposed segregation? The *Green* Court hinted that on the facts of the case, a plan for neighborhood schools would have made the system "unitary." In *Green,* and in much of the rural South, neighborhood schools would have produced substantial integration. Would a neighborhood school system be "unitary" in urban areas, where residential segregation patterns would be mirrored in school populations? If free choice failing to produce integration is unconstitutional, does it follow a fortiori that *Brown* is violated when children are *compelled* to attend one-race schools in their neighborhoods?

4. *Busing and the problem of race-conscious remedies.* The Court provided some answers to these questions in Swann v. Charlotte-Mecklenburg Board of Education, 402 U.S. 1 (1971). The case arose in a school district that had been segregated by law prior to 1954. Although geographic zoning and free transfers were introduced in 1965, by 1968 over half the black students were still attending schools that were at least 99 percent black. In order to deal with this problem, the district court adopted a new plan involving gerrymandering of school districts and busing of students between inner-city and outlying schools. In a unanimous opinion by Chief Justice Burger, the Supreme Court affirmed this order. Emphasizing the scope and flexibility of equitable remedies, the Court held that mathematical ratios and racial assignments could be a useful starting point in fashioning relief. It also endorsed the busing of students outside their neighborhoods as "one tool of school desegregation." On the other hand, the Court emphasized that "[the] constitutional command to desegregate schools does not mean that every school in every community must always reflect the racial composition of the school system as a whole."And it warned that

> [absent] a constitutional violation there would be no basis for judicially ordering assignment of students on a racial basis. . . .
>
> At some point, these school authorities and others like them should have achieved full compliance with the Court's decision in *Brown I.* The systems will then be "unitary" in the sense required by our decisions. . . .
>
> Neither school authorities nor district courts are constitutionally required to make year-by-year adjustments of the racial composition of student bodies once the affirmative duty to desegregate has been [accomplished]. This does not mean that federal courts are without power to deal with future problems; but in the absence of a showing that either the school authorities or some other agency of the State has deliberately attempted to fix or alter demographic patterns to affect the racial composition of the schools, further intervention by a district court should not be necessary.

Note: Swann *and the Collapse of Southern Resistance*

Swann was the last major desegregation decision that was entirely "southern" in its orientation. It thus ended an era begun with *Brown II.* In one sense, the Court's efforts to desegregate the South were stunningly successful. The Court's studied ambiguity concerning the scope of *Brown I* provided it with the flexibility to respond to each of the subterfuges advanced to defeat desegregation. Moreover, the "all deliberate speed" formulation allowed the Court to avoid defeat when significant progress was not politically feasible and then to push ahead when a coalition for change finally emerged. The results of this strategy speak for themselves: By 1971, 44 percent of the black students in the South attended majority white schools, compared to only 28 percent in the North and West. See 18 Cong. Rec. S564 (daily ed. Jan. 20, 1972) (remarks of Sen. Stennis).

Yet in another sense the strategy carried with it serious weaknesses. Southern intransigence forced the Court to adopt broader and broader statements of what *Brown* required. But in the long term the gradual expansion of *Brown* helped to undermine the political support that made progress possible. To avoid endless litigation with school boards operating in bad faith, the Court moved toward result-oriented, bright-line remedies. This made the promise of *Brown* a reality in hundreds of school districts. But the Court paid for these advances by sacrificing the claim that it was merely announcing principles of "simple justice" directly commanded by the Constitution. And by conceding that judges had discretion in the remedy they imposed, the Court lost the political insulation that came with the argument that the constitutional text left the judiciary with no choice. Moreover, the Court's preoccupation with empirical results made it vulnerable to empirical attack. So long as *Brown* prohibited only decisions made on racist grounds, the decision could be defended as a matter of principle. But if the constitutionality of a particular plan turned on the results it produced, then it became relevant to ask what tangible results in terms of educational quality integration actually achieved.

Finally, the expansion of *Brown* — and, indeed, the Court's very success in enforcing the decision — helped erode the distinction between North and South. To be sure, *Swann* clung to the position that judicial intervention was permissible only to correct deliberate segregative acts. But the result-oriented remedies *Swann* approved, and the fact that the South had become the most integrated area of the country, made it increasingly difficult to defend the proposition that judicial intervention was permissible only below the Mason-Dixon line. The Court was therefore faced with a dilemma. If *Brown* remained applicable only to the South, southerners could, with some justice, complain of hypocrisy and a double standard. Yet if the fight for integrated education was pressed in the North and West, the collapse of political support was inevitable.

KEYES v. SCHOOL DISTRICT NO. 1, DENVER, COLO., 413 U.S. 189 (1973). This was the first case in which the Supreme Court considered the lawfulness of school segregation in a northern city that had never mandated segregated education by statute. The district court found that the Denver School Board had for a period of ten years maintained deliberately segregated schools in the Park Hill section of the city through use of gerrymandered attendance zones and similar devices. Although the district court ordered desegregation of the Park Hill schools, it held that the finding of purposeful segregation in this area did not require the board to remedy racial imbalance in other areas of the city. The court of appeals affirmed this portion of the district court's order, but the Supreme Court, in an opinion by Justice Brennan, reversed and held that systemwide relief might be appropriate.

The Court assumed that plaintiffs bore the burden of establishing that segregated schools had been brought about or maintained by intentional state action. However, once such a showing had been made with regard to a substantial portion of the system, plaintiffs need not bear the additional burden of showing deliberate segregation as to each school within the school system.

"[Common] sense dictates the conclusion that racially inspired school board actions have an impact beyond the particular schools that are subject to those actions." Although there might be "rare" cases where the effect of discriminatory conduct was isolated, in the more usual case proof of unlawful segregation in a substantial portion of a district was sufficient to support a finding of the existence of a dual school system.

Moreover, even if the effect of discriminatory action in a part of the system was isolated, it might still serve as the evidentiary predicate for systemwide relief. This was so because "a finding of intentionally segregative school board actions in a meaningful portion of a school system, creates [a] prima facie case of unlawful segregative design on the part of school authorities, and shifts to those authorities the burden of proving that other segregated schools within the system are not also the result of intentionally segregative actions. This is true even if it is determined that different areas of the school district should be viewed independently of each other because, even in that situation, there is high probability that where school authorities have effectuated an intentionally segregative policy in a meaningful portion of the school system, similar impermissible considerations have motivated their actions in other areas of the system. . . ."

Justice Powell concurred in part and dissented in part:

"The situation in Denver is generally comparable to that in other large cities across the country in which there is a substantial minority population and where desegregation has not been ordered by the federal courts. There is segregation in the schools of many of these cities fully as pervasive as that in southern cities prior to the desegregation decrees of the past decade and a half. The focus of the school desegregation problem has now shifted from the South to the country as a whole. Unwilling and footdragging as the process was in most places, substantial progress toward achieving integration has been made in Southern States. No comparable progress has been made in many nonsouthern cities with large minority populations primarily because of the de facto/de jure distinction nurtured by the courts and accepted complacently by many of the same voices which denounced the evils of segregated schools in the South. But if our national concern is for those who attend such schools, rather than for perpetuating a legalism rooted in history rather than present reality, we must recognize that the evil of operating separate schools is no less in Denver than in Atlanta. . . .

"In my view we should abandon a distinction which long since has outlived its time, and formulate constitutional principles of national rather than merely regional application. . . .

"Whereas *Brown I* rightly decreed the elimination of state-imposed segregation in that particular section of the country where it did exist, *Swann* imposed obligations on southern school districts to eliminate conditions which are not regionally unique but are similar both in origin and effect to conditions in the rest of the country. [I] would hold, quite simply, that where segregated public schools exist within a school district to a substantial degree, there is a prima facie case that the duly constituted public authorities [are] sufficiently responsible to warrant imposing upon them a nationally applicable burden to demonstrate they nevertheless are operating a genuinely integrated school system. [This] means that school authorities, consistent with the generally accepted educational goal of attaining quality education for all pupils, must make and implement their customary decisions with a view toward enhancing integrated school opportunities. . . .

"An integrated school system does not mean — and indeed could not mean in view of the residential patterns of most of our major metropolitan areas — that *every school* must in fact be an integrated unit. A school which happens to be all or predominantly white or all or predominantly black is not a 'segregated' school in an unconstitutional sense if the system itself is a genuinely integrated one.

"Public schools are creatures of the State, and whether the segregation is state-created or state-assisted or merely state-perpetuated should be irrelevant to constitutional principle. The school board exercises pervasive and continuing responsibility over the long-range planning as well as the daily operations of the public school system. [School] board decisions obviously are not the sole cause of segregated school conditions. But if, after such detailed and complete public supervision, substantial school segregation still persists, the presumption is strong that the school board, by its acts or omissions, is in some part responsible. . . .

"Where school authorities have defaulted in their duty to operate an integrated school system, district courts must insure that affirmative desegregative steps ensue. Many of these can be taken effectively without damaging state and parental interests in having children attend schools within a reasonable vicinity of home. Where desegregative steps are possible within the framework of a system of "neighborhood education," school authorities must pursue them. . . .

"A *constitutional requirement* of extensive student transportation solely to achieve integration presents a vastly more complex problem. It promises, on the one hand, a greater degree of actual desegregation, while it infringes on what may fairly be regarded as other important community aspirations and personal rights. Such a requirement is also likely to divert attention and resources from the foremost goal of any school system: the best quality education for all pupils. The Equal Protection Clause does, indeed, command that racial discrimination not be tolerated in the decisions of public school authorities. But it does not require that school authorities undertake widespread student transportation solely for the sake of maximizing integration.

"This obviously does not mean that bus transportation has no place in public school systems or is not a permissible means in the desegregative process. [The] crucial issue is when, under what circumstances, and to what extent such transportation may appropriately be ordered. The answer to this turns — as it does so often in the law — upon a sound exercise of discretion under the circumstances. . . .

"[This] would [require] that the legitimate community interests in neighborhood school systems be accorded far greater respect. [As] a minimum, this Court should not require school boards to engage in the unnecessary transportation away from their neighborhoods of elementary-age children. . . ."

Justice Rehnquist dissented: "Underlying the Court's entire opinion is its apparent thesis that a district judge is at least permitted to find that if a single attendance zone between two individual schools in the large metropolitan district is found by him to have been 'gerrymandered,' the school district is guilty of operating a 'dual' school system, and is apparently a candidate for what is in practice a federal receivership. [It] would therefore presumably be open to the District Court to require, inter alia, that pupils be transported great distances throughout the district to and from schools whose attendance zones have not been gerrymandered. Yet, unless the Equal Protection Clause of the Fourteenth Amendment now be held to embody a principle of 'taint,' found in some primitive legal systems but discarded centuries ago in ours, such a result can only be described as the product of judicial fiat. . . .

"The Court has taken a long leap in this area of constitutional law in equating the district-wide consequences of gerrymandering individual attendance zones in a district where separation of the races was never required by law with statutes or ordinances in other jurisdictions which did so require. It then adds to this potpourri a confusing enunciation of evidentiary rules in order to make it more likely that the trial court will on remand reach the result which the Court apparently wants it to reach. Since I believe neither of these steps is justified by prior decisions of this Court, I dissent."

5.   The End of an Era

In recent years, the Court has turned away from the ambitious and sweeping desegregation decrees that marked the 1960s and 1970s. Instead, modern school desegregation cases have primarily concerned the limits on the equitable power of district courts and the evidentiary predicate necessary for formerly segregated systems to establish "unitary" status. At the same time, the modern Court has used the rhetoric of *Brown* to attack race-specific "affirmative action" programs allegedly designed to enhance the education, employment prospects, and political power of African-Americans. (These cases are considered in more detail in section C4 infra.)

Do these modern cases bring into question the efficacy or legitimacy of the Court's twenty-year experiment in desegregation?

Note: Modern Limits on the Duty to Desegregate

1. *The political environment.* Recall the manner in which progress toward southern desegregation coincided with the emergence of the political branches as effective allies of the courts. As the desegregation effort spread north, and as the southern problem began to look like the northern one, some of this support dissipated. In 1968, Richard Nixon, while seeking the presidential nomination, told southern Republican leaders that he thought "all deliberate speed" required reinterpretation, and that he opposed compulsory busing of students. See T. White, The Making of the President: 1968, at 137-138 (1969). When President Nixon assumed office, the Justice Department for the first time since 1954 intervened on behalf of a southern school board to seek additional time for desegregation. Although the Supreme Court emphatically rejected the request, see Alexander v. Holmes County Board of Education, 396 U.S. 19 (1969), the episode nonetheless marked a significant turning point away from the alliance that produced change in the 1960s.

After *Swann*, Congress enacted legislation purporting to limit the use of busing as a remedy for desegregation. The Education Amendments of 1972, 20 U.S.C. §§1651-1656, prohibited the appropriation of federal funds for transportation of students to achieve racial balance. Moreover, federal agencies were prohibited from requiring states to use funds for this purpose unless constitutionally required. See 20 U.S.C. §1652. In 1974, Congress went further and prohibited any "court, department, or agency of the United States [from ordering] transportation of any student to a school other than the school closest or next closest to his place of residence which provides the appropriate grade level, and type of education for such student." Equal Education Opportunities Act of 1974, 20

U.S.C. §1714. This legislation had little direct effect on judicial conduct. Relying on another provision of the 1972 act stating that it is "not intended to modify or diminish the authority of the courts of the United States to enforce fully the fifth and fourteenth amendments to the Constitution of the United States," courts interpreted the 1972 legislation as applicable only to efforts to remedy de facto segregation. See, e.g., Drummond v. Acree, 409 U.S. 1228 (1972) (Powell, J.); United States v. Texas Education Agency, 532 F.2d 380, 394 n.18 (5th Cir.), vacated on other grounds sub nom. Austin Independent School District v. United States, 429 U.S. 990 (1976).

Far more sweeping measures were proposed in Congress, however, including constitutional amendments prohibiting any court from requiring the assignment or exclusion of any person from any school on the basis of race (see H.R.J. Res. 56, 97th Cong., 2d Sess. (1982)) and statutes purporting to deprive the Supreme Court and lower courts of jurisdiction in cases where transportation orders are requested or to otherwise limit the remedies available to lower courts in desegregation cases. See S. 37, 99th Cong., 1st Sess. (1985); H.R. 81, 99th Cong., 1st Sess. (1985); H.R. 1211, 99th Cong., 1st Sess. (1985); H.R. 527, 99th Cong., 1st Sess. (1985).

2. "*White flight.*" This upsurge in political opposition to desegregation coincided with renewed doubts about the ability of courts to bring about integrated schools. In many jurisdictions, large numbers of white students abandoned public education, leaving the schools as segregated as ever.

The extent to which court-ordered desegregation in fact caused whites to abandon urban public schools has been hotly debated in the social science literature. Compare, e.g., J. Coleman, S. Kelly, and J. Moore, Trends in School Segregation 1968-73 (1975) with Pettigrew and Green, School Desegregation in Large Cities: A Critique of the Coleman "White Flight" Thesis, 46 Harv. Educ. Rev. 1 (1976). See also G. Orfield, The Growth of Segregation in American Schools: Changing Patterns of Separation and Poverty since 1968, at 6 (1994) (concluding that "[the] great increase in the proportion of non-white students has not been a consequence of 'white flight' [but] the product of huge changes in birth rates and immigration patterns," and that "there has been no significant redistribution between the sectors of American education"). It is beyond dispute, however, that for whatever reason, the percentage of whites in many urban public schools has declined.

3. *The Court's response.* How should the Court have responded to these new challenges to desegregation? In the 1960s, the Court had bravely announced that political opposition and "white flight" were no excuse for avoiding constitutional requirements. For example, in Monroe v. Board of Commissioners, 391 U.S. 450 (1968), a companion case to *Green*, the school board defended its "free transfer" plan on the ground that it was necessary to prevent whites from leaving the system altogether. A unanimous Court rejected the argument, citing *Brown II* for the proposition that "[t]he vitality of these constitutional principles cannot be allowed to yield simply because of disagreement with them." See also United States v. Scotland Neck City Board of Education, 407 U.S. 484, 490-491 (1972).

Some critics argued that this approach was simply unrealistic. Consider L. Graglia, Disaster by Decree 82 (1976): "Insistence on principle and legality in the face of threatened lawlessness can be justified even where great immediate costs are involved, but to ignore the existence of perfectly legal means of avoiding a requirement is to bury one's head in the sand." Compare Gewirtz, Remedies and Resistance, 92 Yale L.J. 585, 661 (1983): "[Realism] can be a dangerous aspiration for people, such as judges or law professors, who are often accused of not being realistic enough. Newly initiated into the jurisprudence of limitation, judges may become too realistic, taking reality to be more resistant than it is."

Whether justified or not, the Court (newly reconstituted with nine appointments by Republican Presidents, and none by Democratic Presidents, between 1969 and 1992) began to restrict the scope of constitutionally mandated desegregation.

a. *Interdistrict relief.* In Milliken v. Bradley, 418 U.S. 717 (1974) (*Milliken I*), the Court held that federal courts lack the power to impose interdistrict remedies for school segregation absent an interdistrict violation or interdistrict effects. After a lengthy trial, the district court found that the Detroit schools had been deliberately segregated, and that any Detroit-only remedy "would make the Detroit school system more identifiably black [thereby] increasing the flight of whites from the city and the system." Consequently, the court ordered a desegregation plan encompassing fifty-three suburban school districts surrounding Detroit. The court of appeals affirmed after noting that "any less comprehensive [solution would] result in an all black school system immediately surrounded by practically all white suburban school systems, with an overwhelmingly white majority population in the local metropolitan area."

The Court, in an opinion by Chief Justice Burger, reversed. The Court rejected the "notion that school district lines may be casually ignored or treated as a mere administrative convenience. [No] single tradition in public education is more deeply rooted than local control over the operation of schools." To be sure, in cases where school district lines violate constitutional rights, a federal court can order an appropriate remedy. But no such violation occurs simply because the racial composition of schools within a district fails to reflect the racial composition of the metropolitan area as a whole. To justify interdistrict relief,

> it must be shown that racially discriminatory acts of the state or local school districts, or of a single school district have been a substantial cause of interdistrict segregation. Thus, an interdistrict remedy might be in order where the racially discriminatory acts of one or more school districts caused racial segregation in an adjacent district, or where district lines have been deliberately drawn on the basis of race. [But] without an interdistrict violation and interdistrict effect, there is no constitutional wrong calling for an interdistrict remedy.

These conclusions were unaffected by the fact that the state of Michigan had exercised substantial control over the activity of local school districts, and that state agencies had participated in the deliberate segregation of the Detroit schools. Despite this state activity, "[d]isparate treatment of white and Negro students occurred within the Detroit school system, and not elsewhere, and on this record the remedy must be limited to that system."

In a dissenting opinion that was joined by Justices Douglas, Brennan, and White, Justice Marshall complained that the Court had rendered the district judge

> powerless to require the State to remedy its constitutional violation in any meaningful fashion. Ironically purporting to base its result on the principle that the scope of the remedy in a desegregation case should be determined by the nature and ex-

tent of the constitutional violation, the Court's answer is to provide no remedy at all for the violation proved in this case, thereby guaranteeing that Negro children in Detroit will receive the same separate and inherently unequal education in the future as they have been unconstitutionally afforded in the past.

b. *Intradistrict remediation.* After remand in *Milliken I*, the district court confronted the task of attempting to desegregate a school system that was approximately 70 percent black. The court rejected a plan establishing schools reflecting Detroit's racial balance — a plan that, inter alia, would have required the busing of large numbers of minority students from one majority-black school to another. Instead, the court ordered a plan requiring extensive educational reform, including remedial education, counseling, and career guidance. In Milliken v. Bradley, 433 U.S. 267 (1977) (*Milliken II*), the Supreme Court affirmed. The Court rejected the notion that desegregation remedies were limited to pupil assignment and held that a district judge could order the expenditure of state funds for remedial education as part of an effort to return victims of unconstitutional conduct to the position they would have enjoyed but for the violation. Taken together, do *Milliken I* and *II* represent a turning away from *Brown* and a return to the "separate but equal" philosophy? Has the Court resolved the difficulties with that philosophy that caused its abandonment in the first place?

In Missouri v. Jenkins, 495 U.S. 33 (1990) (*Jenkins I*), the Court addressed potential limits on the ability of district courts to order intradistrict remediation. After finding that the Kansas City, Missouri, public schools were unconstitutionally segregated, a district judge ordered a sweeping remedy designed to create "magnet schools" that would attract white children into the district. In order to fund the program, the court ordered that the property tax levy within the school district be raised by almost 100 percent for the next fiscal year. On certiorari, the Supreme Court limited its review to the legitimacy of the judicially imposed tax increase and assumed without deciding that the underlying remedy was within the district court's powers. In a five-to-four decision, the Court, in an opinion by Justice White, held that the district judge had abused his discretion by ordering the tax increase. The Court went on to hold, however, that the district judge could order a local government body to raise its own taxes, even in excess of the limit set by state law.

The Court again considered Kansas City desegregation efforts in Jenkins v. Missouri, 515 U.S. 70 (1995) (*Jenkins II*), and on this occasion it substantially restricted the power of district courts to order *Milliken II*-type remedies. At issue was a district court order mandating salary increases for instructional and noninstructional staff within the school district. The state argued that this order exceeded the district court's remedial authority because it was designed to serve the interdistrict goal of attracting white students from surrounding school districts. In a five-to-four decision, the Court, in an opinion by Chief Justice Rehnquist, agreed:

We previously have approved of intradistrict desegregation remedies involving magnet schools. See, e.g. *Milliken II.* . . .

The District Court's remedial plan in this case, however, is not designed solely to redistribute the students within the [Kansas City school district]. Instead, its purpose is to attract nonminority students from outside the [district]. But this *interdis*trict goal is beyond the scope of the *intra*district violation identified by the District

Court. In effect, the District Court has devised a remedy to accomplish indirectly what it admittedly lacks the remedial authority to mandate directly: the interdistrict transfer of students.

In a strongly worded concurrence, Justice Thomas expressed amazement

that the courts are so willing to assume that anything that is predominantly black must be inferior. Instead of focusing on remedying the harm done to those black school children injured by segregation, the District Court here sought to convert the Kansas City, Missouri, School District into a "magnet district" that would reverse the "white flight" caused by *desegregation.* . . .

Two threads in our jurisprudence have produced this unfortunate situation, in which a District Court has taken it upon itself to experiment with the education of the [district's] black youth. First, the court has read our cases to support the theory that black students suffer an unspecified psychological harm from segregation that retards their mental and educational development. This approach not only relies upon questionable social science research rather than constitutional principle, but it also rests on an assumption of black inferiority. Second, we have permitted the federal courts to exercise virtually unlimited equitable powers to remedy this alleged constitutional violation. The exercise of this authority has trampled upon principles of federalism and the separation of powers and has freed courts to pursue other agendas unrelated to the narrow purpose of precisely remedying a constitutional harm.

c. *Resegregation and "unitary" status.* In a series of cases decided since the mid-1970s, the Court has disapproved efforts by the lower courts to prevent resegregation and suggested guidelines for districts attempting to achieve unitary status. See Pasadena Board of Education v. Spangler, 427 U.S. 424 (1976) (disapproving lower court order requiring annual readjustment of school boundaries); Board of Education of Oklahoma City Public Schools v. Dowell, 498 U.S. 237 (1991) (holding that a district would achieve unitary status upon a showing that it was "[operating] in compliance with the commands of the Equal Protection Clause [and] that it was unlikely that [it] would return to its former ways"); Freeman v. Pitts, 503 U.S. 467 (1992) (holding that "federal courts have the authority to relinquish supervision and control of school districts in incremental stages, before full compliance has been achieved in every area of school operations").

d. *Modern "freedom of choice."* Do the *Green* and *Swann* standards apply in a context where individuals are not compelled to utilize the facility in question? Consider Bazemore v. Friday, 478 U.S. 385 (1986). Prior to 1965, the North Carolina Agricultural Extension Service operated racially segregated 4-H and Homemaker Clubs. In response to the 1964 Civil Rights Act, the service discontinued its segregated club policy and opened any club to any otherwise eligible person regardless of race. Despite this change of policy, many clubs remained racially segregated, and petitioners brought this action seeking to compel the service to take affirmative measures designed to integrate the clubs. The district court denied relief after finding that any racial imbalance was the result of a wholly voluntary choice by private individuals, and the Supreme Court affirmed. The Court, in an opinion by Justice White, distinguished *Green* as follows:

While school children must go to school, there is no compulsion to join 4-H or Homemaker Clubs, and while School Boards customarily have the power to create school attendance areas and otherwise designate the school that particular students may attend, there is no statutory or regulatory authority to deny a young person the right to join any Club he or she wishes to join.

What implications does *Bazemore* hold for a court's remedial powers concerning state universities formerly segregated by law? Consider United States v. Fordice, 505 U.S. 717 (1992). For years, Mississippi's public university system was segregated by law. Although the state eventually ended its system of formal racial exclusion, various colleges in the system retained their racial identities. By the mid-1980s, more than 99 percent of the state's white students were enrolled at four of the universities, which were overwhelmingly white. Seventy-one percent of the black students attended three other universities, where the racial composition ranged from 92 to 99 percent black. Despite these statistics, a district court refused to order relief. Relying on *Bazemore*, the court found that in the context of higher education, "the affirmative duty to desegregate does not contemplate either restricting choice or the achievement of any degree of racial balance."

The Supreme Court, in an opinion by Justice White, reversed. The Court held that the fact that "college attendance is by choice and not by assignment does not mean that a race-neutral admissions policy cures the constitutional violation of a dual system."

The Court distinguished *Bazemore* as follows:

[In *Bazemore*], the District Court found that the policy of segregation had been completely abandoned and that no evidence existed of any lingering [discrimination]; any racial imbalance resulted from the wholly voluntary and unfettered choice of private individuals. In this context, we held inapplicable the *Green* Court's judgment that a voluntary choice program was insufficient to dismantle a *de jure* system in public primary and secondary schools, but only after satisfying ourselves that the State had not fostered segregation by playing a part in the decision of which club an individual chose to join.

Bazemore plainly does not excuse inquiry into whether Mississippi has left in place certain aspects of its prior dual system that perpetuate the racially segregated education system.

The Court focused on four "suspect" aspects of the state's system: differing admission standards for various state universities, program duplication, institutional mission assignments for the various universities, and the continued operation of all eight universities within the system. It held that, although the fact that "an institution is predominantly white or black does not in itself make out a constitutional violation," the state could not "leave in place policies rooted in its prior officially-segregated system that serve to maintain the racial identifiability of its universities if those policies can practicably be eliminated without eroding sound educational policies."

The Court rejected the suggestion that it order the upgrading of the historically black institutions "so that they may be publicly financed, exclusively black enclaves of private choice. [The] State provides these facilities for *all* its citizens, and it has not met its burden under *Brown* to take affirmative steps to dismantle its prior *de jure* system when it perpetuates a separate, but 'more equal' one." It left open the "different question" whether "an increase in funding is necessary to achieve a full dismantlement under the standards we have outlined."

Justice Thomas filed a concurring opinion:

I write separately to emphasize that [the Court's] standard is far different from the one adopted to govern the grade-school context in [*Green*]. In particular, because it does not compel the elimination of all observed racial imbalance, it portends neither the destruction of historically black colleges nor the severing of those institutions from their distinctive histories and traditions. . . .

[We] do not foreclose the possibility that there exists "sound educational justification" for maintaining historically black colleges *as such*. Despite the shameful history of state-enforced segregation, these institutions have survived and flourished. . . .

Obviously, a State cannot maintain such traditions by closing particular institutions, historically white or historically black, to particular racial groups. Nonetheless, it hardly follows that a State cannot operate a diverse assortment of institutions — including historically black institutions — open to all on a race-neutral basis, but with established traditions and programs that might disproportionately appeal to one race or another. [It] would be ironic, to say the least, if the institutions that sustained blacks during segregation were themselves destroyed in an effort to combat its vestiges.

Justice Scalia filed an opinion concurring in the judgment in part and dissenting in part:

Ironically enough, [today's] decision seems to prevent adoption of a policy of [equal funding for historically black universities]. [Equal] funding, like program duplication, facilitates continued segregation — enabling students to attend schools where their own race predominates without paying a penalty in the quality of education. Nor could such an equal-funding policy be saved on the basis that it serves what the Court calls a "sound educational justification." The only conceivable *educational* value it furthers is that of fostering schools in which blacks receive their education in a "majority" setting; but to acknowledge that as a "value" would contradict the compulsory-integration philosophy that underlies *Green*. Just as vulnerable, of course, would be all other programs that have the effect of facilitating the continued existence of predominantly black institutions. . . .

What the Court's test is designed to achieve is the elimination of predominantly black institutions. [In] a perverse way, [the] insistence [that] such institutions not be permitted to endure perpetuates the very stigma of black inferiority that *Brown I* sought to destroy. . . .

I [predict that this decision will result in] a number of years of litigation-driven confusion and destabilization in the university systems of all the formerly *de jure* States, that will benefit neither blacks nor [whites]. Nothing good will come of this judicially ordained turmoil, except the public recognition that any Court that would knowingly impose it must hate segregation. We must find some other way of making that point.

For a careful and detailed discussion of *Fordice*, see Davis, The Quest for Equal Education in Mississippi: The Implications of *United States v. Fordice*, 62 U. Miss. L. Rev. 405 (1993).

e. *"Affirmative action" and remediation outside the educational context*. If, as the *Brown* Court asserted, segregated education is unconstitutional because of its long-term effect on the life chances of minority children, may a court remedy the effects of segregation by attempting to improve those life chances? In recent years, the Court has answered this question with a resounding "no." For example, in Washington v. Davis, 426 U.S. 229 (1976), the Court rejected a challenge to a qualifying test administered to applicants for positions as District of Columbia police officers. Black applicants claimed that the test was unconstitutional because a disproportionate percentage of blacks failed the test. In rejecting the challenge, the Court ignored the possibility that some blacks may have performed badly on the test because they received segregated educations. Instead, it read *Brown* and its progeny as supporting the view "that the invidious quality of a law claimed to be racially discriminatory must ultimately be traced to a racially discriminatory purpose. That there are both predominantly black and predominantly white schools in a community is not alone violative of the Equal Protection Clause." (*Washington* is discussed in greater detail at page 514 infra.)

Washington suggests that the government is not constitutionally *required* to engage in race-conscious remediation outside the context of education. More recently the Court has held that such race-conscious remediation may not be constitutionally *permitted*. For example, in City of Richmond v. J. A. Croson Co., 488 U.S. 469 (1989), the Court rejected the claim that a program setting aside 30 percent of city subcontracts for "Minority Business Enterprises" was justified as a means to remedy prior school segregation:

> While there is no doubt that the sorry history of both private and public discrimination in this country has contributed to a lack of opportunities for black entrepreneurs, this observation, standing alone, cannot justify a rigid racial quota in the awarding of public [contracts]. Like the claim that discrimination in primary and secondary schooling justifies a rigid racial preference in medical school admissions, an amorphous claim that there has been past discrimination in a particular industry cannot justify the use of an unyielding racial quota. . . .
>
> To accept Richmond's claim that past societal discrimination alone can serve as the basis for rigid racial preferences would be to open the door to competing claims for "remedial relief" for every disadvantaged group. The dream of a Nation of equal citizens in a society where race is irrelevant to personal opportunity and achievement would be lost in a mosaic of shifting preferences based on inherently unmeasurable claims of past wrongs. [We] think such a result would be contrary to both the letter and spirit of a constitutional provision whose central command is equality.

(*Croson* and the affirmative action problem are discussed at greater length at pages 553-596 infra.)

Note: *Final Thoughts on School Desegregation and the Efficacy of Judicial Review*

What does the Court's long struggle to define and implement the principle of racial equality reveal about the efficacy of judicial review? Has the Court been able to achieve the objectives it established in *Brown*?

These questions raise difficult issues about the extent to which the Court can control social, historical, and political forces and the extent to which it is controlled by them. Many scholars have concluded that *Brown* was instrumental in sparking the civil rights movement. See, e.g., Gill, The Shaping of Race Relations by the Federal Judiciary in Court Decisions, 11 Negro Educ. Rev. 15, 15-16

(1960) ("It is clear that official action to improve the condition of the Negro minority probably would never have been taken in many instances had it not been for the Federal Courts"). See generally sources collected in Klarman, Civil Rights Law: Who Made It and How Much Did It Matter?, 83 Geo. L.J. 433, 452 n.91 (1994).

Much of the recent literature has been more skeptical, however. For example, in The Hollow Hope: Can Courts Bring About Social Change? 157 (1991), Gerald Rosenberg concludes that there is "little evidence that the judicial system [produced] much of the massive change in civil rights that swept the United States in the 1960s. [While] we can never know what would have happened if the Court had not acted as it did [the] existence and strength of pro-civil-rights forces at least suggest that change would have occurred [without judicial intervention], albeit at a pace unknown." Compare Klarman, *Brown*, Racial Change, and the Civil Rights Movement, 80 Va. L. Rev. 7, 11 (1994) (arguing that *Brown* helped create a climate "conducive to the brutal suppression of civil rights demonstrations" that, in turn, led to northern white support for civil rights legislation).

Is there a plausible argument that *Brown* actually *weakened* the civil rights movement? Rosenberg suggests that civil rights litigation "siphon[ed] off crucial resources and talent [thereby] weakening political efforts":

> A further danger of litigation as a strategy for significant social reform is that symbolic victories may be mistaken for substantive ones, covering a reality that is distasteful. Rather than working to change that reality, reformers relying on a litigation strategy for reform may be misled (or content?) to celebrate the illusion of change.

Rosenberg, supra, at 340. See also Seidman, *Brown* and *Miranda*, 80 Cal. L. Rev. 673, 717 (1992):

> It came to be seen that the *Brown* Court offered the country a kind of deal, and, from the perspective of defenders of the status quo, not a bad one at that. Prior to *Brown* [contradictions] in the ideology of the separate-but-equal doctrine were permanently destabilizing and threatened any equilibrium.
>
> By purporting to resolve those contradictions, *Brown* also served to end their destabilizing potential. The Court resolved the contradictions by definitional fiat: separate facilities were now simply proclaimed to be inherently unequal. But the flip side of this aphorism was that once white society was willing to make facilities legally nonseparate, the demand for equality had been satisfied and blacks no longer had just cause for complaint. The mere existence of *Brown* thus served [to] legitimate current arrangements. True, many blacks remained poor and disempowered. But their status was now no longer a result of the denial of equality. Instead, it marked a personal failure to take advantage of one's definitionally equal status.

There is similar controversy about how much change was actually achieved, whatever its cause. The Court has been overwhelmingly successful in removing legally mandated segregation. The results in terms of actual integration are more mixed, however. A study published in 1999 shows that two-thirds of all African-American students attend predominantly minority schools. See Kemerer, School Choice Accountability, in S. Sugarman and F. Kemerer, School Choice and Social Controversy 181-191 (1999). Progress was substantial in the South during the 1960s and 1970s, but in 1988 the trend reversed itself, and since then segregation has risen substantially. Segregation remains most intense in large northern cities, where desegregation was never accomplished. As of 1994, 73 percent of African-Americans in metropolitan New York City, 77 percent of African-Americans in Chicago, and 58 percent of African-Americans in Los Angeles attended schools that were at least 90 percent African-American. C. Clotfelter, Public School Segregation in Metropolitan Areas at table 2 (National Bureau of Economic Research Working Paper Series 1998). Finally, even in schools that are formally integrated, the interracial contact envisioned by *Brown* has frequently not materialized. Thus, a significant percentage of blacks attending integrated schools are assigned to segregated, or substantially segregated, classrooms. See Fulfilling the Letter and Spirit of the Law: Desegregation of the Nation's Public Schools 233-234 (U.S. Commission on Civil Rights 1976). Indeed, "tracking" schemes and assignment of black children to special education programs in disproportionate numbers may have aggravated the sense of inferiority *Brown* was designed to combat. See G. Orfield, How to Make Desegregation Work: The Adaptation of Schools to Their Newly Integrated Bodies 327-328 (1976). See generally D. Bell, Race, Racism and American Law 424-428 (2d ed. 1980).

If one asks whether integration, where it has occurred, has produced equal educational opportunity, the evidence is even more mixed. While there is no proof that integration has reduced white achievement levels, neither is there proof that it has aided blacks in any demonstrable fashion. See, e.g., St. John, The Effects of Desegregation on Children, in Yarmolinsky, Liebman, and Schelling, Race and Schooling in the City 85-102 (1981); Armor, The Evidence on Busing, Pub. Interest 90 (Summer 1972). Recent studies show that the gap between black and white school achievement levels is large and growing. See Stedman, An Assessment of the Contemporary Debate over U.S. Achievement, in Brookings Papers on Education Policy (D. Ravitch ed. 1998).

What if one asks, more broadly still, whether the Court has succeeded in implementing the great aims of the Reconstruction amendments — eliminating the wounds of slavery and integrating blacks into the mainstream of U.S. life?

Consider the following argument: *Brown* was a great success. Before *Brown*, it was constitutionally legitimate in our society for government to legislate the separation of the races. *Brown* put an end to the most degrading and most humiliating form of discrimination — state-mandated, legally enforced racial separation. Moreover, *Brown* opened the door to the civil rights movement. In so doing, the Court took a critical first step toward forming the political coalition that produced the civil rights legislation of the 1960s.

Compare with this optimistic view the following summary, which Derrick Bell puts into the mouth of his fictional heroine Geneva Crenshaw:

[Because] the Supreme Court is unable or unwilling to recognize and remedy the real losses resulting from long-held, race-based, subordinated status, the relief the Court has been willing to grant, while welcome, proves of less value than expected and exacts the exorbitant price of dividing the black community along economic lines. . . .

[There] seems little doubt that abandonment of overtly discriminatory policies has lowered racial barriers for some talented and skilled blacks seeking access to opportunity and advancement. Even their upward movement is, however, pointed to by much of the society as the final proof that racism is dead — a too hasty pronouncement which dilutes the achievement of those who have moved ahead and denies even society's sympathy to those less fortunate blacks whose opportunities and life fortunes are less promising today than they were twenty-five years ago.

D. Bell, And We Are Not Saved 48-49 (1987).

Which of these views is most consistent with statistics concerning the current status of blacks in U.S. society? Blacks have made great strides in educational achievement since *Brown*. See H. Levin, Education and Earnings of Blacks and the *"Brown"* Decision 12 (1981). As recently as 1965, only 27.2 percent of African Americans who were at least twenty-five years old had completed four years of high school, as compared to 51.3 percent of white adults. By 1998, 76 percent of blacks and over 83 percent of whites had completed high school. See Statistical Abstract of the United States: The National Data Book, table no. 263, at 169 (1999).

However, statistics concerning school attendance may mask a more disturbing underlying reality concerning what actually happens within the school. Black children are three times more likely than white children to be placed in classes for the educable mentally retarded and only one-half as likely to be in classes for the gifted and talented. In high schools, black students are suspended about three times more often than whites. See Committee on Policy for Racial Justice, Visions of a Better Way 14 (1989). A 1996 study shows that twelfth-grade African-American students are performing at the level of white eighth-graders. See Stedman, supra, at 72-73.

Moreover, educational gains have not been uniformly translated into economic progress. In 1998, the total U.S. unemployment rate was 4.5 percent, while the black unemployment rate was 8.9 percent. Statistical Abstract, supra, table no. 680, at 430. Black median income stayed at approximately 59 percent of white median income between 1970 and 1997, and the difference in constant dollars has marginally increased during this period. See Statistical Abstract, supra, table nos. 742, 743, at 474. The median income of young black families fell from $27, 838 to $25,165 in constant dollars between 1973 and 1998. See Table F-11B, Age of Householder — Black Familes by Median and Mean Income: 1967 to 1998 at www.census.gov/hhes/income/histinc/f011b.html. And while the gap in the poverty rate between whites and blacks has been narrowing, the black poverty rate is still more than double that for whites. See Statistical Abstract, supra, table no. 760, at 483.

Do these statistics provide appropriate criteria by which to judge the Court's work? If not, what criteria would you suggest? In reviewing the Court's performance from before the Civil War through the modern desegregation controversies, think about the extent to which the Court has been able to function as an effective alternative power center for dealing with the race question. Has the Court's effectiveness been hampered (augmented?) by the necessity of formulating public policy through the litigation process? By the obligation to write opinions tying its conclusions to the constitutional text?

When the Court has opposed the political branches, has it done so effectively? Has it been right?

B.   EQUAL PROTECTION METHODOLOGY: RATIONAL BASIS REVIEW

The preceding section examined the development of equal protection principles in the context of race. Standing alone, however, this material provides an incomplete picture of the equal protection clause in two respects: First, although the impetus for passage of the equal protection clause was the problem of the newly freed slaves, its language is more general. It is therefore not surprising that the Court has applied the clause to controversies unrelated to race. Second, while historical circumstances undoubtedly influenced the development of equal protection doctrine, it is also true that the doctrine has taken on a life of its own, and that it shapes the way lawyers think about equal protection problems. One therefore cannot understand the equal protection clause without first understanding the general methodology courts use to resolve equal protection disputes.

This section and those following it examine that methodology in both racial and nonracial contexts. In recent years, the Court's approach has involved creation of various "tiers" of review. Classifications based on race and a few other suspect characteristics are subject to varying degrees of heightened review and are frequently, although not invariably, invalidated. In contrast, classifications not drawn on a "suspect basis" are subject to "low-level" or "rational basis" review and are frequently, although not invariably, upheld. The remainder of this chapter examines the characteristics of each form of review and the bases on which the Court has placed various types of classifications in each tier.

New York City Transit Authority v. Beazer
440 U.S. 568 (1979)

MR. JUSTICE STEVENS delivered the opinion of the Court.

The New York City Transit Authority refuses to employ persons who use methadone. The District Court found that this policy violates the Equal Protection Clause of the Fourteenth Amendment. [The] Court of Appeals affirmed. [We] now reverse.

[A New York City Transit Authority (TA) rule prohibited employment of persons who use narcotic drugs. TA applied the rule to persons receiving methadone — a synthetic narcotic that, when taken orally, blocks the effect of heroin. The drug is widely used in the treatment of heroin addiction.]

The trial record contains extensive evidence concerning the success of methadone maintenance programs, the employability of persons taking methadone, and the ability of prospective employers to detect drug abuse or other undesirable characteristics of methadone users. In general, the District Court concluded that there are substantial numbers of methadone users who are just as employable as other members of the general population and that normal personnel-screening procedures — at least if augmented by some method of obtaining information from the staffs of methadone programs — would enable TA to identify the unqualified applicants on an individual basis. On the other hand, the District Court recognized that at least one-third of the persons receiving methadone treatment — and probably a good many more — would unquestionably be classified as unemployable.

[The District Court concluded that because] it is clear that substantial numbers of methadone users are capable of performing many of the jobs at TA, [the] Constitution will not tolerate a blanket exclusion of all users from all jobs.

The District Court enjoined TA from denying employment to any person solely because of participation in a methadone maintenance program. Recognizing, however, the special responsibility for public safety borne by certain TA employees and the correlation between longevity in a methadone maintenance program and performance capability, the injunction authorized TA to exclude methadone users from specific categories of safety-sensitive positions and also to condition eligibility on satisfactory performance in a methadone program for at least a year. In other words, the court held that TA could lawfully adopt general rules excluding all methadone users from some jobs and a large number of methadone users from all jobs. . . .

At its simplest, the District Court's conclusion was that TA's rule is broader than necessary to exclude those methadone users who are not actually qualified to work for TA. We may assume not only that this conclusion is correct but also that it is probably unwise for a large employer like TA to rely on a general rule instead of individualized consideration of every job applicant. But these assumptions concern matters of personnel policy that do not implicate the principle safeguarded by the Equal Protection Clause. As the District Court recognized, the special classification created by TA's rule serves the general objectives of safety and efficiency.[39] Moreover, the exclusionary line challenged by respondents "is not one which is directed 'against' any individual or category of persons, but rather it represents a policy choice . . . made by that branch of Government vested with the power to make such choices." Marshall v. United States, 414 U.S. 417, 428. Because it does not circumscribe a class of persons characterized by some unpopular trait or affiliation, it does not create or reflect any special likelihood of bias on the part of the ruling majority. Under these circumstances, it is of no constitutional significance that the degree of rationality is not as great with respect to certain ill-defined subparts of the classification as it is with respect to the classification as a whole.

No matter how unwise it may be for TA to refuse employment to individual car cleaners, track repairmen, or busdrivers simply because they are receiving methadone treatment, the Constitution does not authorize a federal court to interfere in that policy decision. The judgment of the Court of Appeals is reversed.

[Justice Powell's opinion, concurring in part and dissenting in part, and Justice Brennan's dissenting statement are omitted.]

MR. JUSTICE WHITE, with whom MR. JUSTICE MARSHALL joins, dissenting. . . .
    The question before us is the rationality of placing successfully maintained or recently cured persons in the same category as those just attempting to escape heroin addiction or who have failed to escape it, rather than in with the general population. The asserted justification for the challenged classification is the objective of a capable and reliable work force, and thus the characteristic in question is employability. "Employability," in this regard, does not mean that any particular applicant, much less every member of a given group of applicants, will turn out to be a model worker. Nor does it mean that no such applicant will ever become or be discovered to be a malingerer, thief, alcoholic, or even heroin ad-

---

39. "[L]egislative classifications are valid unless they bear no rational relationship to the State's objectives. Massachusetts Bd. of Retirement v. Murgia, [427 U.S. 307, 314]. State legislation 'does not violate the Equal Protection Clause merely because the classifications [it makes] are imperfect.' Dandridge v. Williams, 397 U.S. 471, 485." Washington v. Yakima Indian Nation, 439 U.S. 463, 501-502. . . .

dict. All employers take such risks. Employability, as the District Court used it in reference to successfully maintained methadone users, means only that the employer is no more likely to find a member of that group to be an unsatisfactory employee than he would an employee chosen from the general population.

Petitioners had every opportunity, but presented nothing to negative the employability of successfully maintained methadone users as distinguished from those who were unsuccessful. [That] 20% to 30% are unsuccessful after one year in a methadone program tells us nothing about the employability of the successful group, and it is the latter category of applicants that the District Court and the Court of Appeals held to be unconstitutionally burdened by the blanket rule disqualifying them from employment. . . .

Of course, the District Court's order permitting total exclusion of all methadone users maintained for less than one year, whether successfully or not, would still exclude some employables and would to this extent be overinclusive. "Overinclusiveness" as to the primary objective of employability is accepted for less successful methadone users because it fulfills a secondary purpose and thus is not "overinclusive" at all. Although many of those who have not been successfully maintained for a year are employable, as a class they, unlike the protected group, are not as employable as the general population. Thus, even assuming the bad risks could be identified, serving the end of employability would require unusual efforts to determine those more likely to revert. But that legitimate secondary goal is not fulfilled by excluding the protected class: The District Court found that the fact of successful participation for one year could be discovered through petitioners' normal screening process without additional effort and, I repeat, that those who meet that criterion are no more likely than the average applicant to turn out to be poor employees. Accordingly, the rule's classification of successfully maintained persons as dispositively different from the general population is left without any justification and, with its irrationality and invidiousness thus uncovered, must fall before the Equal Protection Clause.[15]

Finally, even were the District Court wrong, and even were successfully maintained persons marginally less employable than the average applicant, the blan-

---

15. [Heroin] addiction is a special problem of the poor, and the addict population is composed largely of racial minorities that the Court has previously recognized as politically powerless and historical subjects of majoritarian neglect. Persons on methadone maintenance have few interests in common with members of the majority, and thus are unlikely to have their interests protected, or even considered, in governmental decisionmaking. Indeed, petitioners stipulated that "[o]ne of the reasons for the . . . drug policy is the fact that [petitioners] fee[l] an adverse public reaction would result if it were generally known that [petitioners] employed persons with a prior history of drug abuse, including persons participating in methadone maintenance programs." It is hard for me to reconcile that stipulation of animus against former addicts with our past holdings that "a bare . . . desire to harm a politically unpopular group cannot constitute a legitimate governmental interest." United States Dept. of Agriculture v. Moreno, 413 U.S. 528, 534 (1973). On the other hand, the afflictions to which petitioners are more sympathetic, such as alcoholism and mental illness, are shared by both white and black, rich and poor.

Some weight should also be given to the history of the rule. Petitioners admit that it was not the result of a reasoned policy decision and stipulated that they had never studied the ability of those on methadone maintenance to perform petitioners' jobs. Petitioners are not directly accountable to the public, are not the type of official body that normally makes legislative judgments of fact such as those relied upon by the majority today, and are by nature more concerned with business efficiency than with other public policies for which they have no direct responsibility. . . .

ket exclusion of only these people, when but a few are actually unemployable and when many other groups have varying numbers of unemployable members, is arbitrary and unconstitutional. Many persons now suffer from or may again suffer from some handicap related to employability. But petitioners have singled out respondents — unlike ex-offenders, former alcoholics and mental patients, diabetics, epileptics, and those currently using tranquilizers, for example — for sacrifice to this at best ethereal and likely nonexistent risk of increased unemployability. Such an arbitrary assignment of burdens among classes that are similarly situated with respect to the proffered objectives is the type of invidious choice forbidden by the Equal Protection Clause.

Note: The Structure of Equal Protection Review

1. *The nature of equality.* What does it mean to treat two people, or two groups of people, "equally" for purposes of the equal protection clause? Consider, for example, whether any of the following hypothetical employment rules for the New York City Transit Authority provide for equal treatment:

a. No position shall be filled by a woman.
b. No position shall be filled by a person weighing less than 175 pounds.
c. No position shall be filled by a person without a high school diploma.
d. All positions shall be filled by lot.
e. All persons applying for any position shall be hired.

In a trivial sense, each of these rules provides for equal treatment. Under each of them, every applicant is equally subject to the same criteria. Thus, under rule *c*, all applicants are equally subject to the requirement of a high school diploma, and under rule *a*, all applicants are equally subject to the requirement that they be male. Indeed, *all* rules provide for equality in this sense.

In a similarly trivial sense, each of the hypothetical employment rules denies equal treatment. Under each of them, some people are denied a benefit that is granted to others. Inequality in this sense is also inescapable. Even rule *e*, which requires hiring all people who apply for the position, discriminates against the class of people who have not applied.

These examples illustrate another difficulty with the concept of equality: Providing similar treatment to two groups will not result in equal treatment if the groups are not similarly situated. Rule *b*, for example, provides similar treatment to all applicants: They cannot weigh less than 175 pounds. But in one obvious sense, the rule does not provide equal treatment because applicants are not similarly situated with respect to the rule. Similarly, rule *d* gives everyone an equal chance to win a job in a lottery. But even if the lottery is "fairly" conducted, the rule denies equal treatment, for the winner may be less qualified for the job or less in need of it or less "deserving" of it than the loser.

2. *The "relevant difference" requirement.* One might therefore say that the principle of equal treatment requires that all individuals be treated similarly to the extent that they are the same and treated differently to the extent that they are different. But individuals are both the same and different in an infinite variety of respects. For example, although competing applicants under rule *a* are different

in that some are men and some are women, they are all persons wishing to work for the Transit Authority.

Thus, the equality principle must be modified to provide that differences in treatment can be justified only by *relevant* differences between individuals. A difference is relevant if, but only if, it bears an empirical relationship to the purpose of the rule. This is presumably what the Court means in *Beazer* when it says that "legislative classifications are valid unless they bear no rational relationship to the State's objectives." Even though the Transit Authority's no-methadone rule treated methadone users and nonusers differently, the Court thought that the rule did not violate the equality principle because there was a difference between the two classes relevant to the state's objective of a safe and efficient transit system.

3. *Relevant differences and efficiency.* Is there a sound reason why we should insist that legislative classifications be based on relevant distinctions in this sense? This rule seems to turn the equality requirement into no more than a mandate for economic efficiency. Note, for example, that the requirement of a relevant distinction provides no guidance as to how the social costs of achieving the state's objective are to be distributed when different distributions are equally efficacious in achieving the state's goal. Nor does it provide any protection against the concentration of extreme costs on a small group when a "fairer" distribution of the costs over a larger group might be slightly less "efficient."

Another problem with this version of the "relevant difference" requirement is that it becomes meaningless unless some restriction is placed on the kinds of purposes the legislature may pursue. For example, if one supposes a Transit Authority uninterested in operating a safe subway, but determined to provide enhanced employment opportunities for men, then rule *a* satisfies the equality principle. Indeed, without a limit on the kinds of purposes that may be pursued, one can formulate a purpose for every possible rule, for every rule may be said to have the purpose of doing what it does.

Do these difficulties make the equality principle "empty"? Consider Westen, The Empty Idea of Equality, 95 Harv. L. Rev. 537, 548, 551 (1982):

> To say that two persons are the same in a certain respect is to presuppose a rule — a prescribed standard for treating them — that both fully satisfy. Before such a rule is established, no standard of comparison exists. After such a rule is established, equality between them is a "logical consequence" of the established rule. [It] is true that rules should be applied equally [if] by "equally," [one] means the tautological proposition that the rule should be applied in all cases to which the terms of the rule dictate that it be applied. [To] say that a rule should be applied "equally" [means] simply that the rule should be applied to the cases to which it applies.

Compare Simons, Equality as a Comparative Right, 65 B.U. L. Rev. 387, 389 (1985) (arguing that the equality principle need not be tautological if it is treats equality as a comparative claim to receive treatment because another person receives that treatment).

4. *Relevant differences and a "class of one."* Suppose that the Transit Authority requires its employees to have a high school diploma but "irrationally" concludes that a particular employee lacks such a diploma. Would this decision deprive the employee of equal protection? Would the case be meaningfully different if the Transit Authority intentionally required one employee to have a high school diploma when it required this of no one else?

Consider in this connection Village of Willowbrook v. Olech, 120 S. Ct. 1073 (2000). Plaintiffs asked the Village to connect their property to the municipal water supply, but the Village refused to do so unless plaintiffs provided it with a thirty-three-foot easement. Plaintiffs alleged that the village required only a fifteen-foot easement from other property owners, that this difference of treatment was "irrational and wholly arbitrary," and that it was motivated by ill will resulting from a previous unrelated law suit, which plaintiffs had successfully brought against the Village.

In a per curiam opinion, the Court held that the plaintiffs had stated a valid equal protection claim. According to the Court, a plaintiff belonging to a "class of one" can maintain such a claim "where [she] alleges that she has been intentionally treated differently from others similarly situated and that there is no rational basis for the difference in treatment." The majority held that these allegations were sufficient "quite apart from the Village's subjective motivation" and that it was therefore unnecessary to reach plaintiffs' alternative theory of subjective ill will.

In a concurring opinion, Justice Breyer expressed sympathy for the view that this holding might "transform many ordinary violations of city or state law into violations of the Constitution. [Zoning] decisions, for example, will often, perhaps almost always treat one landowner differently from another, and one might claim that, when a city's zoning authority takes an action that fails to conform to a city zoning regulation, it lacks a 'rational basis' for its [action]." Justice Breyer nonetheless concurred in the result on the ground that plaintiffs had also alleged "vindictive action."

Why does the majority limit its holding to plaintiffs who allege that they are *intentionally* treated differently? What does "intentionally" mean in this context?

5. *The normative appeal of equality.* Even if we could give substantive content to the equality requirement, it is not clear why it has any normative appeal. Although the demands of the equal protection clause can be satisfied by extending the contested benefit to a broader group, the government need not respond in this fashion. It may also fully satisfy the demand of equality by denying *both* groups the contested benefit. Suppose both A and B deserve a benefit, but B does not receive it. If A is also denied the benefit, does this make the outcome more or less just? How is A made better off by B's misfortune? Consider in this regard the problem posed by Heckler v. Mathews, 465 U.S. 728 (1984). Congress amended the Social Security Act to extend certain benefits to women but not to men. Concerned that the courts might invalidate the law on equal protection grounds, Congress also included a provision stating that, if the law were invalidated, neither men nor women would get the benefit. The Court upheld the right of a man to challenge the provision. Should it have?

6. *Relevant differences and the public interest.* Can problems with a normatively attractive, nontautological definition of equality be avoided if rationality review is understood not as a requirement of efficiency but rather as a guarantor of a political process that is public-regarding and not merely the product of self-serving activity? On this view, differential treatment violates the equality principle when its purpose is to advance the interests of politically powerful individuals but is permissible when it serves the public welfare. The requirement that the government show a connection between the means chosen and a public end might then be understood as a method of seeing whether the public end in fact

accounts for the classification. If there is a close connection between the classification and a public end, the court may be persuaded that the legitimate end is in fact at work. If there is no such connection, there is reason to suspect that the legitimate end is a fraud. See J. Ely, Democracy and Distrust 145-148 (1980); Sunstein, Naked Preferences and the Constitution, 84 Colum. L. Rev. 1689, 1713 (1984).

Does this "public interest" requirement adequately capture the equality principle? Does it provide adequate protection against the infliction of very severe deprivations on small groups when those deprivations serve the public interest?

Note: The Means/Ends Nexus

To survive equal protection attack, the different treatment of two classes of persons must be justified by a relevant difference between them. But when is a difference relevant, and what constitutes an adequate justification? Suppose, first, every member of the disadvantaged class has a trait that every member of the advantaged class lacks, and that the trait is related in some way to achievement of the state's goal. Suppose, for example, every methadone user is an unsafe worker, while every nonuser is a safe worker. Would this showing be sufficient to satisfy the equality requirement? Arguably the difference between users and nonusers would still not justify the difference in treatment unless the benefit derived, for example, from a safer transit system outweighed the cost imposed on users denied employment.

As complex as this analysis is, it vastly oversimplifies the problems encountered in the real world. For in almost all cases, the classification will not be perfectly efficient but will be either "overinclusive" or "underinclusive" or both. A classification is "overinclusive" if it disadvantages some people who do not in fact threaten the state's interest. It is "underinclusive" if some people are not disadvantaged even though they threaten the state's interest.

1. *Overinclusion.* Consider, first, the problem of overinclusion in *Beazer.* If every methadone user were a safe and efficient worker, the exclusion of the class would not advance the state's purpose at all and hence would be unconstitutional. Both the majority and the dissent seem to agree, however, that at least *some* methadone users were unsuited for transit work. Is it sufficient to uphold the classification to show that it advances the state's purpose to some extent — if, for example, the transit system would be somewhat safer without methadone users than with them? Such a test would permit the state to impose severe deprivations in exchange for trivial benefits.

A rule requiring the state to demonstrate that every member of the disadvantaged class possesses the trait relevant to the state's objective is no more satisfactory. This test would make legislation virtually impossible, for almost all laws group people together based on generalizations that do not universally hold. It may be that there is somewhere a ten-year-old who would make a perfectly safe transit worker. Yet the Transit Authority is surely justified in imposing a minimum age requirement on the individuals it employs.

It seems clear therefore that the permissibility of a legislative generalization must turn on the cost of the generalization as compared to the cost of a more individualized judgment. Making this comparison involves a complex process. In

Beazer, for example, a no-methadone rule eliminates some unsafe workers but at the cost of denying jobs to some safe ones. A more individualized judgment would permit more safe workers to be employed but arguably at the cost of employing more unsafe workers who might go undetected. To strike the balance, one must first weigh the importance of safety against the importance of employment and then discount each side of the equation by the risk of error. Moreover, even if one concludes that the cost imposed on safe methadone users wrongly denied employment under the no-methadone rule outweighs the cost imposed by unsafe methadone users wrongly employed under a more individualized approach, it does not follow that the no-methadone rule is invalid. The administrative costs associated with a more individualized assessment might still justify use of a prophylactic rule. For example, if the Transit Authority must conduct lengthy interviews with each methadone user to assure his or her safety, it might reasonably conclude that the cost of such interviews outweighs the cost of denying employment to those users who would be safe workers.

2. *Underinclusion.* A similarly complex weighing process is required when it is alleged that a classification is underinclusive. Is the Transit Authority's rule unconstitutional because it applies only to methadone users, and not to ex-offenders, former alcoholics and mental patients, people with diabetes or epilepsy, and others who arguably pose an equal or greater safety risk? The Court has sometimes said that the equal protection clause permits the legislature to deal with one problem at a time or to proceed step by step. See, e.g., Williamson v. Lee Optical Co., 348 U.S. 483, 489 (1955). One cannot, however, take these statements literally. If the legislature were completely free to select which part of a problem to attack, the equal protection clause would be meaningless. For example, such a rule would permit the state to deny driver's licenses to all people with green eyes on the theory that such people cause traffic accidents (albeit not a disproportionate number), and that their exclusion therefore advances the state's goal of traffic safety. If the legislature may disqualify a group posing a lesser risk while leaving untouched another group posing an equal or greater risk, then it could arbitrarily disadvantage virtually any group.

One might therefore conclude that the equal protection clause prohibits any law that denies a benefit to a group but grants the benefit to other groups imposing equal or greater costs. Such a rule once again oversimplifies the analysis, however. Suppose, for example, 25 percent of persons with epilepsy would make unsafe transit workers, while only 10 percent of methadone users pose an unacceptable risk. But suppose further only a small number of persons with epilepsy apply for employment, while large numbers of methadone users seek transit jobs. May the Transit Authority disqualify methadone users, but not persons with epilepsy, on the theory that by doing so, it is dealing with a larger share of the total problem? May it disqualify persons with epilepsy, but not methadone users, on the theory that a given person with epilepsy is more likely to cause safety problems than a given methadone user?

Closely associated with this problem is the difficulty of relative administrative costs. It may be, for example, that methadone users are easier to identify than persons with epilepsy, or that unsafe persons with epilepsy are easier to identify than unsafe methadone users. In either event, the state might be justified in excluding users of methadone, even though they cause less of the problem, because the cost of exclusion is less.

Moreover, the cost calculation must include the cost of not achieving ancillary goals that may qualify the purpose of achieving a safe transit system. Suppose, for example, persons with epilepsy impose greater safety costs than methadone users. The Transit Authority might nonetheless employ persons with epilepsy, but not methadone users, if it believes that drug addicts, but not victims of epilepsy, are responsible for their plight.

Finally, the underinclusion analysis is affected by the manner in which the advantaged class is characterized. In *Beazer*, for example, it may seem quite sensible to disadvantage methadone users, but not persons with epilepsy, if methadone users pose more of a problem. There is no reason in principle, however, to compare methadone users to the class of persons with epilepsy as opposed to, for example, the class of persons with epilepsy, former offenders, and former mental patients, who, taken together, may pose more of a problem than methadone users alone. Indeed, one could characterize the advantaged class still more broadly. The methadone users might ask why the state is worried about the social cost of their unsafe conduct when it does nothing to control the arguably greater social cost imposed by automobile drivers who do not wear seat belts or cigarette smokers who pollute the air around them or parents who abuse their children.

Note: *The Problem of Judicial Review*

The preceding material demonstrates that a serious effort to evaluate the nexus between means and ends is extraordinarily complex. In fact, however, courts rarely rigorously pursue this analysis when assessing the validity of statutes subject to equal protection attack.

The Supreme Court has not been altogether consistent in formulating a standard against which to measure statutes subject to "low-level" scrutiny. In F. S. Royster Guano Co. v. Virginia, 253 U.S. 412 (1920), the Court said that "the classification must be reasonable, not arbitrary, and must rest upon some ground of difference having a fair and substantial relation to the object of the legislation, so that all persons similarly circumstanced shall be treated alike." Other cases suggest a more lenient standard of review. In New Orleans v. Dukes, 427 U.S. 297 (1976), for example, the Court held that the equal protection clause is satisfied so long as the classification is "rationally related to a legitimate state interest." Other cases purport to follow an even more deferential standard. In McGowan v. Maryland, 366 U.S. 420 (1961), for example, the Court said that "[t]he constitutional safeguard is offended only if the classification rests on grounds wholly irrelevant to the achievement of the State's objective. State legislatures are presumed to have acted within their constitutional power despite the fact that, in practice, their laws result in some inequality. A statutory discrimination will not be set aside if any state of facts reasonably may be conceived to justify it."

Compare these formulations with the methods of analyzing the means/ends nexus outlined above. Can you state precisely what relationship between the classification and the legislative purpose must be shown to satisfy the Court? Must proponents of the law demonstrate that the classification advances the legislative purpose to some extent? That a rational person would so believe? That a rational person would so believe if the facts were as the legislature supposed them to be?

Or must the proponents demonstrate that the various trade-offs outlined above between the costs of narrower and broader classifications are "rational"?

Regardless of the verbal distinctions, in practice the application of any of the standards has usually led to validation of the legislative scheme. Three examples illustrate the Court's approach.

RAILWAY EXPRESS AGENCY v. NEW YORK, 336 U.S. 106 (1949). A New York traffic regulation prohibited the operation of "advertising vehicles," but permitted placing "business notices upon business delivery vehicles, so long as such vehicles are engaged in the usual business or regular work of the owner and not used merely or mainly for advertising." Justice Douglas delivered the Court's opinion:

"[The] regulation draws the line between advertisements of products sold by the owner of the truck and general advertisements. It is argued that unequal treatment on the basis of such a distinction is not justified by the aim and purpose of the regulation. It is said, for example, that one of appellant's trucks carrying the advertisement of a commercial house would not cause any greater distraction of pedestrians and vehicle drivers than if the commercial house carried the same advertisement on its own truck. . . .

"That, however, is a superficial way of analyzing the problem. [The] local authorities may well have concluded that those who advertise their own wares on their trucks do not present the same traffic problem in view of the nature or extent of the advertising which they use. [And] the fact that New York City sees fit to eliminate from traffic this kind of distraction but does not touch what may be even greater ones in a different category, such as the vivid displays on Times Square, is immaterial. It is no requirement of equal protection that all evils of the same genus be eradicated or none at all."

Justice Jackson wrote a concurring opinion: "There are two clauses of the Fourteenth Amendment which this Court may invoke to invalidate ordinances by which municipal governments seek to solve their local problems [— the due process clause and the equal protection clause]. . . .

"The burden should rest heavily upon one who would persuade us to use the due process clause to strike down a substantive law or ordinance. [Invalidation] of a statute [on] due process grounds leaves ungoverned and ungovernable conduct which many people find objectionable.

"Invocation of the equal protection clause, on the other hand, does not disable any governmental body from dealing with the subject at hand. It merely means that the prohibition or regulation must have a broader impact. I regard it as a salutary doctrine that [governments] must exercise their powers so as not to discriminate between their inhabitants except upon some reasonable differentiation fairly related to the object of regulation. [There] is no more effective practical guaranty against arbitrary and unreasonable government than to require that the principles of law which officials would impose upon a minority must be imposed generally. Conversely, nothing opens the door to arbitrary action so effectively as to allow those officials to pick and choose only a few to whom they will apply legislation and thus to escape the political retribution that might be visited upon them if larger numbers were affected. . . .

"This case affords an illustration. Even casual observations from the sidewalks of New York will show that an ordinance which would forbid all advertising on vehicles would run into conflict with many interests, including some, if not all, of the great metropolitan newspapers, which use that advertising extensively. [But] any regulation applicable to all such advertising would require much clearer justification in local conditions to enable its enactment than does some regulation applicable to a few. . . .

"There is not even a pretense here that the traffic hazard created by the advertising which is forbidden is in any manner or degree more hazardous than that which is permitted. It is urged with considerable force that this local regulation does not comply with the equal protection clause because it applies unequally upon classes whose differentiation is in no way relevant to the objects of the regulation. . . .

"The question in my mind comes to this. Where individuals contribute to an evil or danger in the same way and to the same degree, may those who do so for hire be prohibited, while those who do so for their own commercial ends but not for hire be allowed to continue? I think the answer has to be that the hireling may be put in a class by himself and may be dealt with differently than those who act on their own. But this is not merely because such a discrimination will enable the lawmaker to diminish the evil. That might be done by many classifications, which I should think wholly unsustainable. It is rather because there is a real difference between doing in self-interest and doing for hire, so that it is one thing to tolerate action from those who act on their own and it is another thing to permit the same action to be promoted for a price."

WILLIAMSON v. LEE OPTICAL, 348 U.S. 483 (1955). An Oklahoma statute made it unlawful for any person not a licensed optometrist or ophthalmologist to fit lenses to a face or to duplicate or replace lenses into frames except on a written prescription of an ophthalmologist or optometrist. In practical effect the statute prevented opticians from fitting old glasses into new frames or supplying new or duplicate lenses without a prescription. However, the statute specifically exempted sellers of ready-to-wear glasses. The district court held that this discrimination against opticians violated the equal protection clause. In a unanimous opinion written by Justice Douglas, the Supreme Court reversed:

"The problem of legislative classification is a perennial one, admitting of no doctrinaire definition. Evils in the same field may be of different dimensions and proportions, requiring different remedies. Or so the legislature may think. Or the reform may take one step at a time, addressing itself to the phase of the problem which seems most acute to the legislative mind. The legislature may select one phase of one field and apply a remedy there, neglecting the others. The prohibition of the Equal Protection Clause goes no further than the invidious discrimination. We cannot say that the point has been reached here. For all this record shows, the ready-to-wear branch of this business may not loom large in Oklahoma or may present problems of regulation distinct from the other branch."

MINNESOTA v. CLOVER LEAF CREAMERY CO., 449 U.S. 456 (1981). This case concerned the constitutionality of a Minnesota law that banned the retail sale of milk in plastic nonreturnable, nonrefillable containers but permitted such sale in nonreturnable paperboard milk cartons. A state trial court held the law violative of the equal protection clause in part because the "actual basis" for the law was to promote the economic interests of local dairy and pulpwood industries rather than to serve the environmental objectives that supporters of the law advanced for it. On appeal, the Minnesota Supreme Court concluded that the law was indeed designed to serve environmental purposes. Nonetheless, it affirmed the trial court on the ground that the ban on plastic containers was not rationally related to these purposes. The Supreme Court reversed. Justice Brennan wrote the Court's opinion:

"The parties agree that the standard of review applicable to this case under the Equal Protection Clause is the familiar 'rational basis' test. Moreover, they agree that the purposes of the Act cited by the legislature — promoting resource conservation, easing solid waste disposal problems, and conserving energy — are legitimate state purposes.[7]

"[Respondents] apparently have not challenged the *theoretical* connection between a ban on plastic nonreturnables and the purposes articulated by the legislature; instead, they have argued that there is no *empirical* connection between the two. They produced impressive supporting evidence at trial to prove that the probable consequences of the ban on plastic nonreturnable milk containers will be to deplete natural resources, exacerbate solid waste disposal problems, and waste energy, because consumers unable to purchase milk in plastic containers will turn to paperboard milk cartons, allegedly a more environmentally harmful product.

"But States are not required to convince the courts of the correctness of their legislative judgments. . . .

"Although parties challenging legislation under the Equal Protection Clause may introduce evidence supporting their claim that it is irrational, they cannot prevail so long as 'it is evident from all the considerations presented to [the legislature], and those of which we may take judicial notice, that the question is at least debatable.' [United States v. Carolene Products Co., 304 U.S. 144, 154 (1938).] Where there was evidence before the legislature reasonably supporting the classification, litigants may not procure invalidation of the legislation merely by tendering evidence in court that the legislature was mistaken."

Note: Deferential Review — Abdication or Self-Restraint?

1. *Evaluating the means/ends nexus: the problem of fact.* Whether a particular means is "rationally related" to the legislature's ends frequently turns on the answers to antecedent questions of fact — for example, will the prohibition of plastic milk containers in fact make for a cleaner environment, or how much expertise is necessary to fit lenses into an eyeglass frame? How should these answers be ascertained? Has the Court gone too far in curtailing the right of litigants to prove that the facts are not as the legislature supposed them to be? A court faced with a factual dispute generally resolves it pursuant to detailed procedural rules designed to give both parties a fair opportunity to bring to the factfinder's attention

7. [In] equal protection analysis, this Court will assume that the objectives articulated by the legislature are actual purposes of the statute, unless an examination of the circumstances forces us to conclude that they "could not have been a goal of the legislation." [Weinberger v. Wiesenfeld, 420 U.S. 636, 648 n.16 (1975).] Here, a review of the legislative history supports the Minnesota Supreme Court's conclusion that the principal purposes of the Act were [environmental]. The contrary evidence cited by respondents [is] easily understood, in context, as economic defense of an Act genuinely proposed for environmental reasons. We will not invalidate a state statute under the Equal Protection Clause merely because some legislators sought to obtain votes for the measure on the basis of its beneficial side effects on state industry.

all relevant evidence. Although legislatures frequently hold hearings before enacting statutes, their procedures tend to be far less careful and structured. Indeed,
there is no requirement that a legislator hear any of the evidence or know anything about the subject before voting on a bill. If the court, after a full trial, determines that the legislature is factually mistaken, why should the statute nonetheless be upheld?

2. *Evaluating the means/ends nexus: the problem of value.* If we assume agreement about the underlying facts, should the Court be more aggressive in evaluating legislative means? Or are there sound institutional reasons for deference to
the legislative judgment? Consider Gunther, Foreword: In Search of Evolving
Doctrine on a Changing Court — A Model for a Newer Equal Protection, 86
Harv. L. Rev. 1, 21 (1972):

> [I]nvigorated [equal] protection scrutiny would not involve adjudication on the ba-
> sis of fundamental interests with shaky constitutional roots. Nor would it require a
> critical evaluation of the relative weights of asserted state purposes. Rather, it would
> permit the state to achieve a wide range of objectives. The yard-stick for the accept-
> ability of the means would be the purpose chosen by the legislatures, not "consti-
> tutional" interests drawn from the value perception of the Justices.

Is it really possible to balance the environmental benefits associated with the
prohibition of plastic milk containers against the burden imposed on consumers
without "[evaluating] the relative weights of asserted state purposes"? Could the
Court decide whether persons hired to advertise should be distinguished from
those advertising their own products without reference to the "value perception
of the Justices"?

Even if there is no problem with the judicial value judgments arguably inherent in rationality review, might there not still be a risk that the sporadic nature of
judicial review will cause the Court to overlook the overall political context that
makes a legislative judgment rational? For example, one might believe that requiring prescriptions from optometrists before opticians can replace lenses imposes costs that cannot be justified in terms of the marginal improvement in public safety. But suppose consumer groups agreed not to oppose the law in exchange
for passage of measures that regulated the price that optometrists could charge
their customers? Can a state defend an otherwise irrational classification on the
ground that it is the product of compromise? Consider Bowen v. Owens, 476 U.S.
1137 (1986), where the Court defended deferential review of classifications contained in the Social Security law as follows:

> Congress' adjustments of this complex system of entitlements necessarily create
> distinctions among categories of beneficiaries, a result that could be avoided only
> by making sweeping changes in the Act instead of incremental ones. A constitu-
> tional rule that would invalidate Congress' attempts to proceed cautiously in award-
> ing increased benefits might deter Congress from making any increases at all.

Compare the views of Justice Marshall expressed in a dissenting opinion:

> [I] suspect that the Court is right to characterize the distinction drawn by [the act
> in question] as the product of Congress' decision to "take one step at a time." How-
> ever under [equal protection principles] even legislative classifications that result

from compromise must bear at least a rational relationship to a legitimate state purpose. Had Congress accommodated the House's reform goals with the Senate's more conservative outlook in this area by passing a law giving benefits to only those [born] on odd-numbered days of the calendar, we would surely have to strike the provision down as irrational.

Is a court competent to make judgments concerning the kinds of trade-offs between groups that are permissible?

3. *The underenforcement thesis.* Even if problems inherent in judicial review preclude vigorous judicial enforcement of the rationality requirement, might not that requirement still retain significance for other actors in the system? Consider the following view: Pure interest-group deals, justified by nothing other than the political strength of the beneficiaries, are prohibited by the equal protection clause. This prohibition is not subject to principled judicial enforcement because inquiries into the legislative process would prove unmanageable and strain judicial competence and authority. But although this prohibition is "underenforced," it nonetheless remains binding on legislators and administrators who have an obligation to obey the Constitution. See generally Sager, Fair Measure: The Status of Underenforced Constitutional Norms, 91 Harv. L. Rev. 122 (1978).

4. *The controversy over nondeferential low-level review.* The Court has generally been extremely deferential to legislative judgments when utilizing low-level scrutiny. It would be a mistake, however, to assume that such scrutiny inevitably leads to validation of the legislative scheme. Consider the following decision.

City of Cleburne v. Cleburne Living Center
473 U.S. 432 (1985)

JUSTICE WHITE delivered the opinion of the Court.

A Texas city denied a special use permit for the operation of a group home for the mentally retarded, acting pursuant to a municipal zoning ordinance requiring permits for such homes. The Court of Appeals [held that] the ordinance violated the Equal Protection Clause. [We affirm.]

[Respondent purchased a building with the intention of converting it into a group home for thirteen mentally retarded men and women who would reside there under the constant supervision of staff members. A city zoning ordinance permitted a wide variety of structures on the proposed site, including "[h]ospitals, sanitariums, nursing homes or homes for convalescents or aged." However, the ordinance specifically excepted "homes for [the] insane or feeble-minded or alcoholics or drug addicts."

[In the first part of the opinion, the Court held that the lower court erred in treating the mentally retarded as a "quasi-suspect class" and subjecting the law to "middle level scrutiny." This portion of the opinion is discussed at section F3, infra.]

Our refusal to recognize the retarded as a quasi-suspect class does not leave them entirely unprotected from invidious discrimination. To withstand equal protection review, legislation that distinguishes between the mentally retarded and others must be rationally related to a legitimate governmental purpose. . . .

[The] mentally retarded as a group are indeed different from others not sharing their misfortune, and in this respect they may be different from those who would occupy other facilities that would be [permitted.] But this difference is largely irrelevant unless the [home] and those who would occupy it would threaten legitimate interests of the city in a way that other permitted uses such as boarding houses and hospitals would not. . . .

The District Court found that the City Council's insistence on the permit rested on several factors. [The] Council was concerned with the negative attitude of the majority of property owners located within 200 feet of the [facility], as well as with the fears of elderly residents of the neighborhood. But mere negative attitudes, or fear, unsubstantiated by factors which are properly cognizable in a zoning proceeding, are not permissible bases for treating a home for the mentally retarded differently from apartment houses, multiple dwellings, and the like. It is plain that the electorate as a whole [could] not order city action violative of the Equal Protection Clause, and the City may not avoid the strictures of that Clause by deferring to the wishes or objections of some fraction of the body politic. . . .

[The] Council had two objections to the location of the facility. It was concerned that the facility was across the street from a junior high school, and it feared that the students might harass the occupants of the [home]. But the school itself is attended by about 30 mentally retarded students, and denying a permit based on such vague, undifferentiated fears is again permitting some portion of the community to validate what would otherwise be an equal protection violation. The other objection to the home's location was that it was located on "a five hundred year flood plain." This concern with the possibility of a flood, however, can hardly be based on a distinction between the [home] and, for example, nursing homes, homes for convalescents or the aged, or sanitariums or hospitals, any of which could be located on the [site] without obtaining a special use permit. The same may be said of another concern of the Council — doubts about the legal responsibility for actions which the mentally retarded might take. If there is no concern about legal responsibility with respect to other uses that would be permitted in the area, such as boarding and fraternity houses, it is difficult to believe that the groups of mildly or moderately mentally retarded individuals who would live at [the home] would present any different or special hazard. . . .

The short of it is that requiring the permit in this case appears to us to rest on an irrational prejudice against the mentally retarded, including those who would occupy the [facility] and who would live under the closely supervised and highly regulated conditions expressly provided for by state and federal law. . . .

JUSTICE STEVENS, with whom [CHIEF JUSTICE BURGER] joins, concurring.

[Our] cases reflect a continuum of judgmental responses to differing classifications which have been explained in opinions by terms ranging from "strict scrutiny" at one extreme to "rational basis" at the other. I have never been persuaded that these so called "standards" adequately explain the decisional process. [In] my own approach to these cases, I have always asked myself whether I could find a "rational basis" for the classification at issue. The term "rational," of course, includes a requirement that an impartial lawmaker could logically believe that the classification would serve a legitimate public purpose that transcends the harm to the members of the disadvantaged class. Thus, the word "rational" — for me at least — includes elements of legitimacy and neutrality that must always characterize the performance of the sovereign's duty to govern impartially. . . .

[The] Court of Appeals correctly observed that through ignorance and prejudice the mentally retarded "have been subjected to a history of unfair and often grotesque mistreatment." The discrimination against the mentally retarded that is at issue in this case is the city's decision to require an annual special use permit before property in an apartment house district may be used as a group home for persons who are mildly retarded. The record convinces me that this permit was required because of the irrational fears of neighboring property owners, rather than for the protection of the mentally retarded persons who would reside in [the] home.

JUSTICE MARSHALL, with whom JUSTICE BRENNAN and JUSTICE BLACKMUN join, concurring in the judgment in part and dissenting in part. . . .

[The] Court holds the ordinance invalid on rational-basis grounds and disclaims that anything special, in the form of heightened scrutiny, is taking place. Yet Cleburne's ordinance surely would be valid under the traditional rational-basis test applicable to economic and commercial regulation. . . .

The Court, for example, concludes that legitimate concerns for fire hazards or the serenity of the neighborhood do not justify singling out respondents to bear the burdens of these concerns, for analogous permitted uses appear to pose similar threats. Yet under the traditional and most minimal version of the rational-basis test, "reform may take one step at a time, addressing itself to the phase of the problem which seems most acute to the legislative mind." [*Williamson*.] The "record" is said not to support the ordinance's classifications, but under the traditional standard we do not sift through the record to determine whether policy decisions are squarely supported by a firm factual foundation. Finally, the Court further finds it "difficult to believe" that the retarded present different or special hazards than other groups. In normal circumstances, the burden is not on the legislature to convince the Court that the lines it has drawn are sensible; legislation is presumptively constitutional, and a State "is not required to resort to close distinctions or to maintain a precise, scientific uniformity with reference" to its goals. Allied Stores of Ohio, Inc. v. Bowers, 358 U.S. 522, 527 (1959).

I share the Court's criticisms of the overly broad lines that Cleburne's zoning ordinance has drawn. But if the ordinance is to be invalidated for its imprecise classifications, it must be pursuant to more powerful scrutiny than the minimal rational-basis test used to review classifications affecting only economic and commercial matters. The same imprecision in a similar ordinance that required opticians but not optometrists to be licensed to practice, see [*Williamson*], [would] hardly be fatal to the statutory scheme.

Note: *Equal Protection as a Tautology*

1. *Mental retardation and the rational basis test.* Did the Court in *Cleburne* in fact apply the rational basis test? If you agree with Justice Marshall that the Court was actually using some form of heightened scrutiny, what was it about the case that triggered this more careful review?

Compare *City of Cleburne* with Heller v. Doe, 509 U.S. 312 (1993), where the Court in a five-to-four decision rejected an equal protection attack against Kentucky statutes that allowed for involuntary commitment for the mentally retarded on the basis of clear and convincing evidence, while mandating a "beyond a reasonable doubt" standard for involuntary commitment based on mental illness. In an opinion by Justice Kennedy, the Court held that Kentucky might rationally conclude that a higher standard of proof was necessary for mental illness because it was more difficult to diagnose. A higher burden of proof therefore tended "to equalize the risks of an erroneous determination that the subject of a commitment proceeding has the condition in question." A higher standard might also be justified because "[the] prevailing methods of treatment for the mentally retarded, as a general rule, are much less invasive than are those given the mentally ill."

The Court also upheld Kentucky's decision to allow close relatives of the mentally retarded, but not of the mentally ill, to participate as parties in the commitment proceedings. The Court reasoned that because mental retardation manifested itself early in the developmental process, Kentucky might reasonably conclude that close relatives had a valuable contribution to make to the proceedings. Mental illness, in contrast, might manifest itself suddenly only after minority. "In addition, adults previously of sound mental health who are diagnosed as mentally ill may have a need for privacy that justifies the State in confining a commitment proceeding to the smallest group compatible with due process."

Is the *Heller* Court's willingness to accept generalizations about the mentally retarded consistent with its approach in *City of Cleburne?* Is it relevant that in *Heller*, the Court was measuring the rights of the mentally retarded against those of another relatively disadvantaged group?

2. City of Cleburne *and the "rationality" of attitudinal preferences.* Should the Court have ignored the attitudinal preferences of property owners living near the Cleburne Living Center? The Court is surely correct when it argues that it would render the equal protection clause meaningless if the legislature could "avoid the strictures of that Clause by deferring to the wishes or objections of some fraction of the body politic." But how can a court evaluate the "rationality" of these wishes and objections when they are premised on noninstrumental considerations? Is it "irrational," for example, for the legislature to conclude that factories, prisons, homeless shelters, or buildings over a certain height are inappropriate in residential neighborhoods? Would "mere negative attitudes" be an insufficient basis for a zoning ordinance excluding such structures?

3. *The tautological equal protection clause.* Consider Note, Legislative Purpose, Rationality, and Equal Protection, 82 Yale L.J. 123, 128 (1972):

> It is always possible to define the legislative purpose of a statute in such a way that the statutory classification is rationally related to it. When a statute names a class, that class must share some common characteristic for that is the definitional attribute of a "class." The nature of the burdens or benefits created by a statute and the nature of the chosen class's commonality will always suggest a statutory purpose — to so burden or benefit the common trait shared by members of the identified class. A statute's classification will be rationally related to such a purpose because the reach of the purpose has been derived from the classifications themselves.

Is there an escape from this tautology? Two possibilities suggest themselves. First, some statutes might be invalidated on the theory that, even though they promote the purpose the legislature actually had, that purpose is illegitimate. In *Cleburne*, for example, the Court assumes arguendo that the ordinance was based in part on the desire to vindicate the preferences of surrounding property owners. While there is no doubt that the ordinance was "rationally related" to this purpose, this relationship does not save the statute because "mere negative attitudes [are] not permissible bases" for differential treatment of a home for the mentally retarded.

Second, even if the legislature's purpose is legitimate, statutes might nonetheless be invalidated if they are judged on the basis of that actual purpose rather than on the basis of post hoc justifications. One might then say that the law fails because there is no reasonable nexus between the classification and what the legislature *actually* wished to achieve, even though one might hypothesize a *possible* purpose advanced by the statute.

On occasion, the Court has relied on both of these techniques to invalidate statutes as "irrational," although both remain controversial. The controversy is explored below.

U.S. DEPARTMENT OF AGRICULTURE v. MORENO, 413 U.S. 528 (1973). Section 3(e) of the Food Stamp Act of 1964 (as amended in 1971) excluded from participation in the food stamp program any household containing an individual who is unrelated to any other member of the household. Appellees in this case consisted of several groups of individuals who alleged that, although they satisfied the income eligibility requirements for the program, they were excluded solely because persons in each group were not related to each other. For example, one appellee had a daughter with an acute hearing deficiency who required special instruction in a school for the deaf. Because the school was located in an area in which appellee could not afford to live, she agreed to share an apartment near the school with another woman on public assistance. Since she was not related to the woman, she was threatened with termination of food stamp assistance. Appellees claimed that the "unrelated persons" provision created an irrational classification in violation of the equal protection component of the due process clause of the fifth amendment. Justice Brennan delivered the Court's opinion:

"Under traditional equal protection analysis, a legislative classification must be sustained if the classification itself is rationally related to a legitimate governmental interest. [The act stated that it was the policy of Congress to 'raise levels of nutrition among low-income households' and increase utilization of food so as to 'strengthen our agricultural economy.'] The challenged statutory classification [is] clearly irrelevant to [these purposes]. . . .

"Thus, if it is to be sustained, the challenged classification must rationally further some legitimate governmental interest other than those specifically stated in [the act]. Regrettably, there is little legislative history to illuminate the purposes of the [act]. The legislative history that does exist, however, indicates that that amendment was intended to prevent so-called 'hippies' and 'hippie communes' from participating in the food stamp program. The challenged classification clearly cannot be sustained by reference to this congressional purpose. For if the constitutional conception of 'equal protection of the laws' means anything, it must at the very least mean that a bare congressional desire to harm a politically unpopular group cannot constitute a *legitimate* governmental interest."

Justice Douglas wrote a separate concurring opinion.

Justice Rehnquist, with whom Chief Justice Burger joined, dissented: "I do not think it is unreasonable for Congress to conclude that the basic unit which it was willing to support with federal funding [is] some variation on the family as we know it — a household consisting of related individuals. This unit provides a guarantee which is not provided by households containing unrelated individuals that the household exists for some purpose other than to collect federal food stamps."

ROMER v. EVANS, 517 U.S. 620 (1996). By statewide initiative, Colorado enacted a constitutional amendment prohibiting local governments from enacting antidiscrimination measures protecting "homosexual, lesbian, or bisexual orientation, conduct, practices or relationships." In a six-to-three decision, the Court, per Justice Kennedy, invalidated the amendment:

"Amendment 2 fails, indeed defies, [conventional rational basis] inquiry. First, the amendment has the peculiar property of imposing a broad and undifferentiated disability on a single named group, an exceptional and [invalid] form of legislation. Second, its sheer breadth is so discontinuous with the reasons offered for it that the amendment seems inexplicable by anything but animus toward the class that it affects; it lacks a rational relationship to legitimate state interests. . . .

"[Laws] of the kind now before us raise the inevitable inference that the disadvantage imposed is born of animosity toward the class of persons affected. 'If the constitutional conception of "equal protection of the laws" means anything, it must at the very least mean that a bare . . . desire to harm a politically unpopular group cannot constitute a legitimate governmental interest.' [*Moreno.*] Even laws enacted for broad and ambitious purposes often can be explained by reference to legitimate public policies which justify the incidental disadvantages they impose on certain persons. Amendment 2, however, in making a general announcement that gays and lesbians shall not have any particular protections from the law, inflicts on them immediate, continuing, and real injuries that outrun and belie any legitimate justifications that may be claimed for it."

Compare Justice Scalia's dissenting opinion, joined by Chief Justice Rehnquist and Justice Thomas:

"The Court's opinion contains grim, disapproving hints that Coloradans have been guilty of 'animus' or 'animosity' toward homosexuality, as though that has been established as Unamerican. Of course it is our moral heritage that one should not hate any human being or class of human beings. But I had thought that one could consider certain conduct reprehensible — murder, for example, or polygamy, or cruelty to animals — and could exhibit even 'animus' toward such conduct. Surely that is the only sort of 'animus' at issue here: moral disapproval of homosexual conduct, the same sort of moral disapproval that produced the centuries-old criminal laws [prohibiting sodomy] that we held constitutional in [Bowers v. Hardwick, 478 U.S. 186 (1986)]."

Romer is considered in greater detail in section E infra.

Note: *Equality as a Limitation on Permissible Governmental Purposes*

What makes a legislative purpose invalid under the equal protection clause? Of course, if the legislature is pursuing a goal that is independently unconstitutional, a classification designed to accomplish that goal is presumably unconstitutional as well. But one could then rely on the substantive constitutional provision to invalidate the law, and reference to the equal protection clause would be superfluous. Does the equal protection clause of its own force prohibit the government from pursuing certain ends that are otherwise constitutionally permissible? If so, what ends does it prohibit? Consider the following possibilities:

1. *Expressions of animosity.* Do you agree that the "desire to harm a politically unpopular group cannot constitute a *legitimate* governmental interest"? If the unadorned desire to harm a group disadvantaged by a statute could shield the statute from equal protection attack, wouldn't the clause be a nullity? On the other hand, the disadvantaged group is always defined in the statute by some trait shared by its members. Why, then, can't such statutes be justified by the legislature's desire to discourage or disapprove of that trait? For example, even if the *Moreno* statute was aimed at disadvantaging hippies, persons harmed by it could nonetheless escape its force if they adopted a more conventional lifestyle. Is it really unconstitutional for the legislature to determine that one lifestyle is preferable to another and therefore more worthy of support? Would it be unconstitutional, for example, for the legislature to subsidize small family farms, but not large-scale industry, on the theory that farm life is "wholesome"?

Does this suggest that laws should be subject to special scrutiny when they disadvantage groups based on immutable traits, since the immutability eliminates the possibility that the legislature is attempting to change behavior? See section C1 infra. For example, although the *Moreno* statute could be justified as an attempt to discourage certain lifestyles, the zoning ordinance in *Cleburne* could not sensibly be defended as a measure designed to deter mental retardation. On which side of this line does the measure invalidated by *Romer* fall?

On the other hand, the "immutability" of the classifying trait might be viewed as a kind of protection because it ensures that the legislature is not attempting to change behavior in an impermissible way. For example, in Metropolitan Life Insurance Co. v. Ward, 470 U.S. 869 (1985), the court utilized impermissible purpose review to invalidate an Alabama statute imposing a substantially lower gross premiums tax on domestic insurance companies than out-of-state companies doing business in Alabama. The Court reasoned that "Alabama's aim to promote domestic industry is purely and completely discriminatory, designed only to favor domestic industry within the State, no matter what the cost to foreign corporations also seeking to do business there." In this context, the very fact that foreign insurance companies could change their behavior by establishing an Alabama domicile might suggest that the legislature is pursuing an impermissible purpose. In any event, aren't some traits relevant to legitimate governmental objectives even if a person is powerless to change them?

2. *"External" preferences.* Is the equal protection clause violated when the legislature pursues a purpose that is not derived from the aggregation of the personal preferences of its constituents? Consider R. Dworkin, Taking Rights Seriously 275 (1978):

> Utilitarian arguments fix on the fact that a particular constraint on liberty will make more people happier, or satisfy more of their preferences. [But] people's overall preference for one policy rather than another may be seen to include, on further analysis, both preferences that are *personal*, because they state a preference for

the assignment of one set of goods or opportunities to him and preferences that are *external*, because they state a preference for one assignment of goods or opportunities to others. But a utilitarian argument that assigns critical weight to the external preferences of members of the community will not be egalitarian. [It] will not respect the right of everyone to be treated with equal concern and respect.

Suppose, for example, that a number of individuals in the community hold racist rather than utilitarian political theories. They believe, not that each man is to count for one and no more than one in the distribution of goods, but rather that a black man is to count for less and a white man therefore to count for more than one. [If] this preference or pleasure is given the normal weight in a utilitarian calculation and blacks suffer accordingly, then their own assignment of goods and opportunities will depend, not simply on the competition among personal preferences that abstract statements of utilitarianism suggest, but precisely on the fact that they are thought less worthy of concern and respect than others are.

Does the equal protection clause prohibit a classification designed to vindicate "external preferences"? Consider Hart, Between Utility and Rights, 79 Colum. L. Rev. 828, 843 (1979):

What is fundamentally wrong [with Dworkin's argument] is the suggested interpretation of denials of freedom as denials of equal concern or respect. This surely is mistaken. It is indeed least credible where the denial of a liberty is the upshot of a utilitarian decision procedure or majority vote in which the defeated minority's preferences or votes for the liberty were weighed equally with others and outweighed by numbers. Then the message need not be, as Dworkin interprets it, "You and your views are inferior, not entitled to equal consideration concern or respect," but "You and your supporters are too few. You, like everyone else, are counted as one but no more than one. Increase your numbers and then your views may win out."

3. *Public values.* Might it be argued that Dworkin's theory is precisely backwards — that the equal protection clause prohibits vindication of *personal* preferences and requires that the state purpose be based on *external* preferences? Consider Sunstein, Public Values, Private Interests, and the Equal Protection Clause, 1982 Sup. Ct. Rev. 127, 134:

When the government operates to benefit A and burden B, it can do so only if it is prepared to justify its decision by reference to a public value. [Legislation] may not be merely the adjustment of private interests, or the transfer of wealth or opportunity from one person to another; it must be in some sense public-serving. [Nor] is political strength a legitimate justification. [The] institution that made the discrimination must be attempting to remedy a perceived public evil, and must not be responding only to the interests or preferences of some of its constituents.

Can the distinction between public and private interests, on which this theory rests, be maintained? What is the public interest if not the aggregation of the private preferences of individual participants in the political process?

Note: "Actual Purpose" Review

1. *Justifications for "actual purpose" review.* Even if one does not believe that the equal protection clause places substantive limits on the purposes that the state

may pursue, rationality review might still be possible if defenders of a statute are permitted to justify it only in terms of the legislature's actual purpose rather than in terms of any conceivable purpose. Is this limitation appropriate? Does it make sense to invalidate a law that advances a legitimate state purpose simply because the legislators were not thinking of that purpose when they enacted it? Once such a law is struck down, could the legislature reenact it if it thinks of that purpose while doing so? What if the legislature enacted the law for irrational reasons but fails to repeal it because it turns out to advance important goals? On the other hand, why should deference to the legislature require upholding a statute that advances a policy that the legislature had no interest in pursuing? Even if a law turns out to advance legitimate purposes, we do not know that it would have been enacted if the legislature had not believed that it advanced other goals that in fact it does not achieve.

2. *The state of the law.* Neither the Court nor individual justices have been altogether consistent on the issue of review based on actual purpose. For example, in U.S. Railroad Retirement Board v. Fritz, 449 U.S. 166 (1980), Justice Rehnquist's opinion for the Court states that "[where], as here, there are plausible reasons for Congress' action, our inquiry is at an end. It is, of course, 'constitutionally irrelevant whether this reasoning in fact underlay the legislative decision,' [quoting Flemming v. Nestor, 363 U.S. 603, 612 (1960)] because this Court has never insisted that a legislative body articulate its reasons for enacting a statute." Yet Justice Rehnquist has also insisted that the Court should not strictly scrutinize a facially neutral statute that has the effect of disadvantaging a racial minority unless the challenger can prove that the legislature intended to produce this effect. See, e.g., Jefferson v. Hackney, 406 U.S. 535 (1972) (Rehnquist, J.). See generally section C2 infra. Can these positions be reconciled?

Consider Minnesota v. Clover Leaf Creamery Co., supra, decided the same term as *Fritz*. In his opinion for the Court, Justice Brennan (who dissented in *Fritz* on the ground that the statute did not achieve Congress' articulated purpose) makes the following observations regarding review based on actual purpose:

> In equal protection analysis, the Court will assume that the objectives articulated by the legislature are actual purposes of the statute, unless an examination of the circumstances forces us to conclude that they "could not have been the goal of the legislation." [Weinberger v. Wiesenfeld, 420 U.S. 636, 648 n.16 (1975).] Here, review of the legislative history supports the Minnesota Supreme Court's conclusion that the principal purposes of the Act were to promote conservation and ease solid waste disposal problems.

Does this formulation treat as "constitutionally irrelevant" the reasons that "in fact underlay the legislative decision" as *Fritz* requires?

The Court's most recent discussions of "actual purpose" review have done little to clarify the issue. In Nordlinger v. Hahn, 505 U.S. 1 (1992), the Court suggested that, at least in some circumstances, it was receptive to measuring a statute against the legislature's actual purpose. The case concerned a portion of the California Constitution, as amended by Proposition 13, which capped property taxes for current owners at 1 percent of the property's assessed value as of the 1975-1976 year, with small annual adjustments for inflation. In contrast, newly purchased property was assessed at its value at the time of purchase. This scheme meant that new owners were required to pay dramatically higher taxes, even though their land might be less valuable than land owned by pre-1975 purchasers.

In an opinion by Justice Blackmun, the Court rejected an equal protection challenge to these disparities. Applying rational basis review, the Court held that the scheme rationally furthered the state's interest in preserving the continuity and stability of local neighborhoods and in protecting the reliance interests of existing owners.

In their challenge to the California scheme, plaintiffs relied on the Court's earlier decision in Allegheny Pittsburgh Coal Co. v. Webster County, 488 U.S. 226 (1989). In *Allegheny Pittsburgh*, the Court held that the equal protection clause invalidated the practice of a county tax assessor who assessed recently purchased property on the basis of its purchase price, while making only minor modifications in the assessments of property that had not been recently sold.

The *Nordlinger* Court distinguished *Allegheny Pittsburgh* because in that case, state law provided for assessments of property at its true current value and there was no indication that the policies underlying California's acquisition value scheme could conceivably have been the purpose for the *Allegheny Pittsburgh* tax assessor's unequal valuations:

> To be sure, the Equal Protection Clause does not demand for purposes of rational-basis review that a legislature or governing decisionmaker actually articulate at any time the purpose or rationale supporting its classification. Nevertheless, this Court's review does require that a purpose may conceivably or "may reasonably have been the purpose and policy" of the relevant governmental decisionmaker. Allied Stores of Ohio, Inc. v. Bowers, 358 U.S. 522, 528-529 (1959). *Allegheny Pittsburgh* was the rare case where the facts precluded any plausible inference that the reason for the unequal assessment practice was to achieve the benefits of an acquisition-value tax scheme. By contrast, [Proposition 13] was enacted precisely to achieve the benefits of an acquisition-value system.

Compare *Nordlinger* with Federal Communications Commission v. Beach Communications, Inc., 508 U.S. 307 (1993), decided the following term. In the Communications Policy Act of 1984, Congress exempted from otherwise applicable regulation cable facilities that served buildings under common ownership or management, so long as they provided services without using public rights-of-way. Respondents, who provided a satellite master antenna service to a complex of buildings that were not under common ownership, claimed that there was no rational basis for the distinction, and that it therefore violated the equal protection component of the fifth amendment's due process clause.

In an opinion by Justice Thomas, the Court emphatically rejected this challenge:

> In areas of social and economic policy, a statutory classification that neither proceeds along suspect lines nor infringes fundamental constitutional rights must be upheld against equal protection challenge if there is any reasonably conceivable state of facts that could provide rational basis for the classification. . . .
>
> [Because] we never require a legislature to articulate its reasons for enacting a statute, it is entirely irrelevant for constitutional purposes whether the conceived reason for the challenged distinction actually motivated the legislature.

3. *The epistemological problem.* Does the difficulty in discovering the legislature's "actual purpose" counsel against utilizing this standard of review? Consider
Kassel v. Consolidated Freightways Corp., 450 U.S. 662 (1981) (Rehnquist, J.,
dissenting):

> [Actual purpose review] assumes that individual legislators are motivated by one
> discernible "actual" purpose, and ignores the fact that different legislators may vote
> for a single piece of legislation for widely different reasons. [How], for example,
> would a court adhering to [actual purpose review] approach a statute, the legis-
> lative history of which indicated that 10 votes were based on [permissible consid-
> erations], 10 votes were based on [impermissible considerations] and the statute
> passed by a vote of 40-20?

Justice Rehnquist has also pointed out that under actual purpose review, "litigants who wish to succeed in invalidating a law [must] have a certain schizophre-
nia if they are to be successful in their advocacy: They must first convince this
Court that the legislature had a particular purpose in mind in enacting the law,
and then convince it that the law was not at all suited to the accomplishment of
that purpose." Trimble v. Gordon, 430 U.S. 762, 783 (1977) (dissenting opinion).
    Are these problems insurmountable? Need an advocate be "schizophrenic" in
a case where the statute itself or its legislative history makes plain that the legislature intended to accomplish results that fail to validate the statute?
    4. *Requirement of statement of purpose.* Do these epistemological difficulties
suggest that the Court should require or encourage the legislature to state explicitly the purposes it wishes a statute to achieve? Lawyers for the state would
then be limited to these purposes in defending the constitutionality of the statute. Consider, for example, Justice Powell's dissenting opinion in Schweiker v.
Wilson, 450 U.S. 221 (1981):

> The deference to which legislative accommodation of conflicting interests is en-
> titled rests in part upon the principle that the political process of our majoritarian
> democracy responds to the wishes of the people. Accordingly, an important touch-
> stone for equal protection review of statutes is how readily a policy can be discerned
> which the legislature intended to serve. When a legitimate purpose for a statute ap-
> pears in the legislative history or is implicit in the statutory scheme itself, a court
> has some assurance that the legislature made a conscious policy choice. Our dem-
> ocratic system requires that legislation intended to serve a discernible purpose re-
> ceive the most respectful deference. . . .
>   In my view, the Court should receive with some skepticism post hoc hypotheses
> about legislative purpose, unsupported by the legislative history. When no indica-
> tion of legislative purpose appears other than the current position of [an executive
> officer,] the Court should require that the classification bear a "fair and substantial
> relation" to the asserted purpose. . . . This marginally more demanding scrutiny
> indirectly would test the plausibility of the tendered purpose and preserve equal
> protection review as something more than "a mere tautological recognition of the
> fact that Congress did what it intended to do." [*Fritz* (Stevens, J., concurring in the
> judgment).]

Presumably the heightened scrutiny Justice Powell would impose in the absence
of a clearly discernible legislative purpose would provide incentives for the legislature to state its purpose explicitly. Might not the result of this requirement be

no more than "boilerplate" statements of worthwhile purposes that fail to state the legislature's true objectives? Doesn't Justice Powell's position turn actual purpose review on its head by according "the most respectful deference" in precisely those cases where the legislative purpose is clear, and where rigorous judicial review is therefore possible?

Compare Justice Powell's views in *Schweiker* with Justice Brennan's *Fritz* dissent. Justice Brennan argued that "[w]here Congress has expressly stated the purpose of a piece of legislation, but where the challenged classification is either irrelevant to or counter to that purpose, we must view any post hoc justifications proffered by Government attorneys with skepticism." Doesn't this suggest that legislative classifications may be subject to *more* rigorous review when the legislature articulates its purpose? Wouldn't such enhanced review discourage the legislators from candidly stating why they enacted the statute?

In any event, is there a legitimate constitutional basis for the Court skewing review in an effort to force legislative articulation of purpose?

C.   EQUAL PROTECTION METHODOLOGY: HEIGHTENED SCRUTINY AND THE PROBLEM OF RACE

This section, and those that follow it, explore the circumstances under which the Court has subjected classifications to some form of review more rigorous than the "rational relationship" test. When is such review appropriate? What must be shown to satisfy the more demanding standard?

The best established case for heightened review is for classifications based on race. This section explores four different varieties of classifications arguably discriminating on the basis of race and the Court's response to each.

1.   Race-Specific Classifications That Expressly Disadvantage Racial Minorities

Strauder v. West Virginia

100 U.S. (10 Otto) 303 (1880)

MR. JUSTICE STRONG delivered the opinion of the court.

[Strauder, a black man, was convicted of murder before an all-white jury in a West Virginia trial court. A West Virginia statute limited jury service to "white male persons who are twenty-one years of age and who are citizens of this State." Strauder claimed that his conviction by a jury chosen pursuant to this provision violated the fourteenth amendment.]

[The] controlling [question is] whether by the Constitution and laws of the United States, every citizen of the United States has a right to a trial of an indictment against him by a jury selected and impanelled without discrimination against his race or color. . . .

It is to be observed that the [question] is not whether a colored man, when an indictment has been preferred against him, has a right to a grand or a petit jury composed in whole or in part of persons of his own race or color, but it is whether, in the composition or selection of jurors by whom he is to be indicted or tried, all persons of his race or color may be excluded by law, solely because of their race or color, so that by no possibility can any colored man sit upon the jury. . . .

[The fourteenth amendment] is one of a series of constitutional provisions having a common purpose; namely, securing to a race recently emancipated, a race that through many generations had been held in slavery, all the civil rights that the superior race enjoy. [At] the time when they were incorporated into the Constitution, it required little knowledge of human nature to anticipate that those who had long been regarded as an inferior and subject race would, when suddenly raised to the rank of citizenship, be looked upon with jealousy and positive dislike, and that State laws might be enacted or enforced to perpetuate the distinctions that had before existed. [The] colored race, as a race, was abject and ignorant, and in that condition was unfitted to command the respect of those who had superior intelligence. Their training had left them mere children, and as such they needed the protection which a wise government extends to those who are unable to protect themselves. They especially needed protection against unfriendly action in the States where they were resident. It was in view of these considerations the Fourteenth Amendment was framed and adopted. It was designed to assure to the colored race the enjoyment of all the civil rights that under the law are enjoyed by white persons, and to give to that race the protection of the general government, in that enjoyment, whenever it should be denied by the States. It not only gave citizenship and the privileges of citizenship to persons of color, but it denied to any State the power to withhold from them the equal protection of the laws, and authorized Congress to enforce its provisions by appropriate legislation. . . .

[What] is this but declaring that the law in the States shall be the same for the black as for the white; that all persons, whether colored or white, shall stand equal before the laws of the States, and, in regard to the colored race, for whose protection the amendment was primarily designed, that no discrimination shall be made against them by law because of their color? The words of the amendment, it is true, are prohibitory, but they contain a necessary implication of a positive immunity, or right, most valuable to the colored race, — the right to exemption from unfriendly legislation against them distinctively as colored, — exemption from legal discriminations, implying inferiority in civil society, lessening the security of their enjoyment of the rights which others enjoy, and discriminations which are steps towards reducing them to the condition of a subject race.

That the West Virginia statute respecting juries [is] such a discrimination ought not to be doubted. [The] very fact that colored people are singled out and expressly denied by a statute all right to participate in the administration of the law, as jurors, because of their color, though they are citizens, and may be in other respects fully qualified, is practically a brand upon them, affixed by the law, an assertion of their inferiority, and a stimulant to that race prejudice which is an impediment to securing to individuals of the race that equal justice which the law aims to secure to all others. . . .

[It] is well known that prejudices often exist against particular classes in the community, which sway the judgment of jurors, and which, therefore, operate in some cases to deny to persons of those classes the full enjoyment of that protection which others enjoy. . . .

In view of these considerations, it is hard to see why the statute of West Virginia should not be regarded as discriminating against a colored man when he is put upon trial for an alleged criminal offence against the State. It is not easy to comprehend how it can be said that while every white man is entitled to a trial by a jury selected from persons of his own race or color, or, rather, selected without discrimination against his color, and a negro is not, the latter is equally protected by the law with the former. . . .

We do not say that within the limits from which it is not excluded by the amendment a State may not prescribe the qualifications of its jurors, and in so doing make discriminations. It may confine the selection to males, to freeholders, to citizens, to persons within certain ages, or to persons having educational qualifications. We do not believe the Fourteenth Amendment was ever intended to prohibit this. Looking at its history, it is clear it had no such purpose. Its aim was against discrimination because of race or color. . . .

The judgment of the Supreme Court of West Virginia will be reversed, and the case remitted with instructions to reverse the judgment of the Circuit Court of Ohio county; and it is *so ordered*.

[Justice Field and Justice Clifford dissented.]

Korematsu v. United States

323 U.S. 214 (1944)

MR. JUSTICE BLACK delivered the opinion of the Court.

[On February 19, 1942, some two months after the United States declared war against Japan, President Roosevelt issued Executive Order No. 9066, which authorized military commanders to "prescribe military areas [from] which any or all persons may be excluded, and with respect to which, the right of any person to enter, remain in, or leave shall be subject to whatever restrictions [the Military] Commander may impose in his discretion." On March 21, 1942, Congress enacted legislation making it a crime to violate an order issued by a military commander pursuant to this authority. Three days later, the military commander of the western defense command ordered imposition of a curfew on all persons of Japanese ancestry living on the West Coast. The Supreme Court upheld the constitutionality of this order in Hirabayashi v. United States, 320 U.S. 81 (1943).

[On May 3, 1942, the same military commander issued one of a series of exclusion orders, requiring persons of Japanese descent, whether or not they were U.S. citizens, to leave their homes on the West Coast. Persons so ordered were required to report to "Assembly Centers." While some detainees were released from these centers on condition that they remain outside the prohibited zone, others were shipped to "Relocation Centers," which they were prohibited from leaving without permission of the military commander.

[Korematsu, a U.S. citizen of unchallenged loyalty, but of Japanese descent, was tried and convicted for remaining in his home contrary to the exclusion order.]

It should be noted, to begin with, that all legal restrictions which curtail the civil rights of a single racial group are immediately suspect. That is not to say that all such restrictions are unconstitutional. It is to say that courts must subject them to the most rigid scrutiny. Pressing public necessity may sometimes justify the existence of such restrictions; racial antagonism never can. . . .

In the light of the principles we announced in the *Hirabayashi* case, we are unable to conclude that it was beyond the war power of Congress and the Executive to exclude those of Japanese ancestry from the West Coast war area at the time they did. True, exclusion from the area in which one's home is located is a far greater deprivation than constant confinement to the home from 8 P.M. to 6 A.M. Nothing short of apprehension by the proper military authorities of the gravest imminent danger to the public safety can constitutionally justify either. But exclusion from a threatened area, no less than curfew, has a definite and close relationship to the prevention of espionage and sabotage. The military authorities, charged with the primary responsibility of defending our shores, concluded that curfew provided inadequate protection and ordered exclusion. . . .

Here, as in the *Hirabayashi* case,

> . . . we cannot reject as unfounded the judgment of the military authorities and of Congress that there were disloyal members of that population, whose number and strength could not be precisely and quickly ascertained. We cannot say that the war-making branches of the Government did not have ground for believing that in a critical hour such persons could not readily be isolated and separately dealt with, and constituted a menace to the national defense and safety, which demanded that prompt and adequate measures be taken to guard against it.

Like curfew, exclusion of those of Japanese origin was deemed necessary because of the presence of an unascertained number of disloyal members of the group, most of whom we have no doubt were loyal to this country. It was because we could not reject the finding of the military authorities that it was impossible to bring about an immediate segregation of the disloyal from the loyal that we sustained the validity of the curfew order as applying to the whole group. In the instant case, temporary exclusion of the entire group was rested by the military on the same ground. The judgment that exclusion of the whole group was for the same reason a military imperative answers the contention that the exclusion was in the nature of group punishment based on antagonism to those of Japanese origin. That there were members of the group who retained loyalties to Japan has been confirmed by investigations made subsequent to the exclusion. Approximately five thousand American citizens of Japanese ancestry refused to swear unqualified allegiance to the United States and to renounce allegiance to the Japanese Emperor, and several thousand evacuees requested repatriation to Japan.

We uphold the exclusion order as of the time it was made and when the petitioner violated it. [In] doing so, we are not unmindful of the hardships imposed by it upon a large group of American citizens. But hardships are part of war, and war is an aggregation of hardships. All citizens alike, both in and out of uniform, feel the impact of war in greater or lesser measure. Citizenship has its responsibilities as well as its privileges, and in time of war the burden is always heavier. Compulsory exclusion of large groups of citizens from their homes, except under circumstances of direst emergency and peril, is inconsistent with our basic governmental institutions. But when under conditions of modern warfare our shores are threatened by hostile forces, the power to protect must be commensurate with the threatened danger. . . .

It is said that we are dealing here with the case of imprisonment of a citizen in a concentration camp solely because of his ancestry, without evidence or inquiry concerning his loyalty and good disposition towards the United States. Our task would be simple, our duty clear, were this a case involving the imprisonment of a loyal citizen in a concentration camp because of racial prejudice. Regardless of the true nature of the assembly and relocation centers — and we deem it unjustifiable to call them concentration camps with all the ugly connotations that term implies — we are dealing specifically with nothing but an exclusion order. To cast this case into outlines of racial prejudice, without reference to the real military dangers which were presented, merely confuses the issue. Korematsu was not excluded from the Military Area because of hostility to him or his race. He *was* excluded because we are at war with the Japanese Empire, because the properly constituted military authorities feared an invasion of our West Coast and felt constrained to take proper security measures, because they decided that the military urgency of the situation demanded that all citizens of Japanese ancestry be segregated from the West Coast temporarily, and finally, because Congress, reposing its confidence in this time of war in our military leaders — as inevitably it must — determined that they should have the power to do just this. There was evidence of disloyalty on the part of some, the military authorities considered that the need for action was great, and time was short. We cannot — by availing ourselves of the calm perspective of hindsight — now say that at that time these actions were unjustified.

Affirmed.

[A concurring opinion by Justice Frankfurter and a dissenting opinion by Justice Roberts have been omitted.]

MR. JUSTICE MURPHY, dissenting.

This exclusion of "all persons of Japanese ancestry, both alien and non-alien," from the Pacific Coast area on a plea of military necessity in the absence of martial law ought not to be approved. Such exclusion goes over "the very brink of constitutional power" and falls into the ugly abyss of racism.

In dealing with matters relating to the prosecution and progress of a war, we must accord great respect and consideration to the judgments of the military authorities who are on the scene and who have full knowledge of the military facts. . . .

At the same time, however, it is essential that there be definite limits to military discretion, especially where martial law has not been declared. Individuals must not be left impoverished of their constitutional rights on a plea of military necessity that has neither substance nor support. Thus, like other claims conflicting with the asserted constitutional rights of the individual, the military claim must subject itself to the judicial process of having its reasonableness determined and its conflicts with other interests reconciled. . . .

It must be conceded that the military and naval situation in the spring of 1942 was such as to generate a very real fear of invasion of the Pacific Coast, accompanied by fears of sabotage and espionage in that area. The military command was therefore justified in adopting all reasonable means necessary to combat these dangers. In adjudging the military action taken in light of the then apparent dangers, we must not erect too high or too meticulous standards; it is necessary only that the action have some reasonable relation to the removal of the dangers of invasion, sabotage and espionage. But the exclusion, either temporarily or permanently, of all persons with Japanese blood in their veins has no such reasonable relation. And that relation is lacking because the exclusion order necessarily must rely for its reasonableness upon the assumption that *all* persons of Japanese ancestry may have a dangerous tendency to commit sabotage and espionage and to aid our Japanese enemy in other ways. It is difficult to believe that reason, logic or experience could be marshalled in support of such an assumption. . . .

The main reasons relied upon by those responsible for the forced evacuation, therefore, do not prove a reasonable relation between the group characteristics of Japanese Americans and the dangers of invasion, sabotage and espionage. The reasons appear, instead, to be largely an accumulation of much of the misinformation, half-truths and insinuations that for years have been directed against Japanese Americans by people with racial and economic prejudices — the same people who have been among the foremost advocates of the evacuation. A military judgment based upon such racial and sociological considerations is not entitled to the great weight ordinarily given the judgments based upon strictly military considerations. Especially is this so when every charge relative to race, religion, culture, geographical location, and legal and economic status has been substantially discredited by independent studies made by experts in these matters. . . .

[No] one denies, of course, that there were some disloyal persons of Japanese descent on the Pacific Coast who did all in their power to aid their ancestral land. Similar disloyal activities have been engaged in by many persons of German, Italian and even more pioneer stock in our country. But to infer that examples of individual disloyalty prove group disloyalty and justify discriminatory action against the entire group is to deny that under our system of law individual guilt is the sole basis for deprivation of rights. . . .

MR. JUSTICE JACKSON, dissenting. . . .

It would be impracticable and dangerous idealism to expect or insist that each specific military command in an area of probable operations will conform to conventional tests of constitutionality. When an area is so beset that it must be put under military control at all, the paramount consideration is that its measures be successful, rather than legal. . . .

But if we cannot confine military expedients by the Constitution, neither would I distort the Constitution to approve all that the military may deem expedient. That is what the Court appears to be doing, whether consciously or not. . . .

The [limitations] under which courts always will labor in examining the necessity for a military order are illustrated by this case. How does the Court know that these orders have a reasonable basis in necessity? No evidence whatever on that subject has been taken by this or any other court. . . .

Much is said of the danger to liberty from the Army program for deporting and detaining these citizens of Japanese extraction. But a judicial construction of the due process clause that will sustain this order is a far more subtle blow to liberty than the promulgation of the order itself. A military order, however unconstitutional, is not apt to last longer than the military emergency. Even during that period a succeeding commander may revoke it all. But once a judicial opinion rationalizes such an order to show that it conforms to the Constitution, or rather rationalizes the Constitution to show that the Constitution sanctions such an order, the Court for all time has validated the principle of racial discrimination in criminal procedure and of transplanting American citizens. The principle then lies about like a loaded weapon ready for the hand of any authority that can bring forward a plausible claim of an urgent need. Every repetition imbeds that principle more deeply in our law and thinking and expands it to new purposes. . . .

I should hold that a civil court cannot be made to enforce an order which violates constitutional limitations even if it is a reasonable exercise of military authority. The courts can exercise only the judicial power, can apply only law, and must abide by the Constitution, or they cease to be civil courts and become instruments of military policy.

Of course the existence of a military power resting on force, so vagrant, so centralized, so necessarily heedless of the individual, is an inherent threat to liberty. But I would not lead people to rely on this Court for a review that seems to me wholly delusive. The military reasonableness of these orders can only be determined by military superiors. If the people ever let command of the war power fall into irresponsible and unscrupulous hands, the courts wield no power equal to its restraint. The chief restraint upon those who command the physical forces of the country, in the future as in the past, must be their responsibility to the political judgments of their contemporaries and to the moral judgments of history.

My duties as a justice as I see them do not require me to make a military judgment as to whether General DeWitt's evacuation and detention program was a reasonable military necessity. I do not suggest that the courts should have attempted to interfere with the Army in carrying out its task. But I do not think they may be asked to execute a military expedient that has no place in law under the Constitution. I would reverse the judgment and discharge the prisoner.

Note: *Justifications for Special Scrutiny of Racial Classifications*

Korematsu is frequently said to mark the last occasion on which the Supreme Court has upheld a race-specific statute disadvantaging a racial minority. It has been widely and severely criticized. See, e.g., P. Irons, Justice at War (1983); R. Daniels, Concentration Camps: North America — Japanese in the United States and Canada during World War II (rev. ed. 1981); J. TenBroek, E. Barnhart, and F. Matson, Prejudice, War and the Constitution (1954). In 1984, a federal district court overturned Korematsu's conviction on the ground that the government had "knowingly withheld information from the courts when they were considering the critical question of military necessity." See Korematsu v. United States, 584 F. Supp. 1406 (N.D. Cal. 1984). Four years later, Congress enacted legislation acknowledging "the fundamental injustice" of the evacuation and providing for restitution for individuals forced to leave their homes. See Pub. L. No. 100-338, 102 Stat. 903 (1988).

Thus, despite its specific holding, *Korematsu* today can be taken to "stand" for the proposition that statutes that facially discriminate against racial minorities are almost always unjust and unconstitutional. (Notice how this subsequent history reverses the fears expressed in Justice Jackson's dissenting opinion.) Does this generalization necessarily flow from the particular abuses that led to *Korematsu*? What specifically makes racial classifications especially problematic? Consider the following possibilities.

1. *The framers of the fourteenth amendment intended to protect African-Americans from "unfriendly" actions in the states where they were resident.* Even if this is a correct account of the framers' intent, why does it require special scrutiny for race-specific classifications? Suppose Strauder were tried by a "fairly" selected jury that happened to be all-white. If race prejudice is as prevalent as the *Strauder* Court believed, why isn't this an "unfriendly action"? If a randomly selected jury were all African-American, would it be an "unfriendly action" for the judge to insist on some white representation?

The argument from the framers' intent also fails to explain the special scrutiny accorded statutes directed against Japanese or other racial or ethnic minorities. Note that the words of the fourteenth amendment provide no support for special treatment of race cases. Moreover, it is far from clear that the Reconstruction Congress meant to invalidate all statutory classifications based on race. Consider R. Berger, Government by Judiciary 10, 15 (1977):

> The key to an understanding of the Fourteenth Amendment is that the North was shot through with Negrophobia, that the Republicans, except for a minority of extremists, were swayed by the racism that gripped their constituents rather than by abolitionist ideology. [While] most men were united in a desire to protect the freedmen from outrage and oppression in the South by prohibiting discrimination with respect to "fundamental rights," without which freedom was illusory, to go beyond this with a campaign for political and social equality was, as Senator James R. Doolittle of Wisconsin confessed, "frightening" to the Republicans who "represented States containing the despised and feared negroes."

2. *Race is rarely, if ever, relevant to any legitimate governmental purpose.* This argument is subject to two objections. First, it may not be empirically correct. Some would maintain that in our culture, race *does* matter. Racial identification correlates (albeit imperfectly) with other attributes that might be relevant to a variety of governmental policy objectives. Notice that the *Strauder* Court itself seems to acknowledge this fact. If race were really irrelevant to the way jurors voted, it is hard to see how Strauder was harmed when he stood trial before an all-white jury.

Second, even if it were true that race is rarely relevant to legitimate government objectives, this would mean only that most race classifications would not survive rational basis review. Why should we require stricter scrutiny of racial classifications that are rational?

3. *The prohibition against racial classifications reflects a fundamental moral norm.* Consider Brest, Foreword: In Defense of the Antidiscrimination Principle, 90 Harv. L. Rev. 1, 5-6 (1976):

> The antidiscrimination principle rests on fundamental moral values that are widely shared in our society. [The] text and history of the [equal protection] clause are vague and ambiguous and cannot, in any event, infuse the antidiscrimination principle with moral force or justify its extension to novel circumstances and new beneficiaries. Therefore, the argument [against racial classifications] does not ultimately turn on authority, but on whether it comports with the reader's reflective understanding of the antidiscrimination principle.

If the antidiscrimination principle really "rests on fundamental moral values widely shared in our society," why is special judicial scrutiny required when it is violated? Doesn't the very fact that the principle is widely shared and deeply ingrained provide a built-in guarantee that, when it is overridden, there is a very good reason for doing so? Does this argument lead to the conclusion that courts properly invalidate race-specific statutes adopted in only a few states, but not laws more widely adopted? On the other hand, if the principle is not widely shared, and if it is not required by the text or history of the Constitution, what justification is there for judicial enforcement of it?

If one individual is unfairly denied a benefit on racial grounds, and if another is unfairly denied precisely the same benefit on some other grounds, why are the costs incurred by one different from those incurred by the other?

4. *Stigma.* The *Strauder* Court thought the exclusion of blacks from juries was "practically a brand upon them" and "an assertion of inferiority." Does infliction of this additional injury justify enhanced review? Consider Brest, supra, at 10:

> Generalizations based on immutable personal traits such as race [are] especially frustrating because we can do nothing to escape their operation. These generalizations are still more pernicious, for they are often premised on the supposed correlation between the inherited characteristic and the undesirable voluntary behavior of those who possess the characteristic. [Because] the behavior is voluntary, and hence the proper object of moral condemnation, individuals as to whom the generalization is inaccurate may justifiably feel that the decisionmaker has passed moral judgment on them.

5. *Defects in the political process make it especially likely that racial classifications will be based on "hostility" or inaccurate stereotypes.* In United States v. Carolene Products, 304 U.S. 144 (1938), page 729 infra, the Court used rational basis review to uphold a federal statute prohibiting interstate shipment of filled milk, which the statute defined as a milk product to which "any fat or oil other than milk fat" had been added. Today the case is less significant for its holding than for its famous footnote 4, in which Justice Stone, writing for the Court, intimated that a more stringent standard of review might apply to statutes "directed at particular religious or national or racial minorities." Justice Stone argued that stricter review might be appropriate in such cases because "prejudice against discrete and insular minorities may be a special condition, which tends seriously to curtail the operation of those political processes ordinarily to be relied upon to protect minorities." It followed that "correspondingly more searching judicial inquiry" was appropriate.

The *Carolene Products* footnote has been called "the most celebrated footnote in constitutional law." Powell, *Carolene Products* Revisited, 82 Colum. L. Rev. 1087, 1087 (1982). See also Fiss, The Supreme Court, 1978 Term — Foreword: The Forms of Justice, 93 Harv. L. Rev. 1, 6 (1979) (*Carolene Products* footnote "[the] great and modern charter for ordering the relations between judges and other agencies of government"). It has been the subject of extensive scholarly commentary. See, e.g., Ackerman, Beyond *Carolene Products*, 98 Harv. L. Rev. 713 (1985); Ball, Judicial Protection of Powerless Minorities, 59 Iowa L. Rev. 1059 (1974); Cover, The Origins of Judicial Activism in the Protection of Minorities, 91 Yale L.J. 1287 (1982). For an interesting exposition of the history of the footnote, see Lusky, Footnote Redux: A *Carolene Products* Reminiscence, 82 Colum. L. Rev. 1093 (1982).

Does the *Carolene Products* footnote provide a principled basis for judicial intervention to protect minorities? Why does the "discreteness" and "insularity" of these minorities interfere with their ability to protect themselves in the political process? Consider Ackerman, supra, at 728:

In fact, for all our *Carolene* talk about the powerlessness of insular groups, we are perfectly aware of the enormous power such voting blocs have in American politics. The story of the protective tariff is [the] classic illustration of insularity's power in American history. Over the past half-century, we have been treated to an enormous number of welfare-state variations on the theme of insularity by the farm bloc, the steel lobby, the auto lobby, and others too numerous to mention. In this standard scenario of pluralistic politics, it is precisely the diffuse character of the majority forced to pay the bill for tariffs, agricultural subsidies, and the like, that allows strategically located Congressmen to deliver the goods to their well-organized constituents. Given these familiar stories, it is really quite remarkable to hear lawyers profess concern that insular interests have too little influence in Congress.

Is it the "prejudice" directed against discrete and insular minorities that justifies judicial intervention? The concept of prejudice lies at the heart of the most comprehensive and careful modern elaboration of the theory behind footnote 4 — J. Ely, Democracy and Distrust (1980). Ely begins with the premise that "the Constitution [cannot] coherently be interpreted as outlining some 'appropriate' distributional pattern against which actual allocations of hurts and benefits can be traced to see if they are constitutional. The constitutionality of most distributions thus cannot be determined simply by looking to see who ended up with what, but rather can be approached intelligibly only by attending to the process that brought about the distribution in question." Generally the Constitution prescribes a process of representative democracy to allocate costs and benefits. This process includes "the sort of pluralist wheeling and dealing by which the various minorities that make up our society typically interact to protect their interests."

This process sometimes breaks down. Prejudice directed at certain minorities may obstruct their ability to form coalitions, so that "a system of 'mutual defense pacts' will prove recurrently unavailing."

Is this an adequate defense of enhanced judicial review of racial classifications? Do you agree that the equal protection clause speaks only to the process by which decisions are made, and not to the results of those decisions? Is strict scrutiny of racial classifications really designed to eliminate inaccurate generalizations? Consider Strauss, The Myth of Colorblindness, 1986 Sup. Ct. Rev. 99, 119:

[The argument that] racial generalizations are unacceptable because there is too great a danger that they will be factually inaccurate — for example, because they are based on inaccurate stereotypes — [misses] the point of the prohibition against discrimination. If the prohibition against discrimination were based on the danger that racial generalizations tend to be overgeneralizations, states would be allowed to defend racial generalizations by showing that they are in fact accurate and are not overgeneralizations.

[It] is quite clear, however, that this is not the way the prohibition against discrimination operates.

Does Ely's analysis adequately distinguish between groups that are unfairly treated in the political process and groups that are simply outvoted? Consider the views of Justice Powell in *Carolene Products* Revisited, supra, at 1090:

[In] one sense, any group that loses a legislative battle can be regarded as both "discrete" and "insular." It is discrete because it supported or opposed legislation not supported or opposed by the majority. It is insular because it was unable to form coalitions with other groups that would have enabled it to achieve its desired ends through the political process. On this view the drug cult — or for that matter public utilities — could be considered discrete and insular.

Ely would limit judicial intervention to cases where a group suffers political losses because of generalizations about its members that are more inaccurate than the legislature realizes. Is judicial review of racial classifications justified because racial prejudice is likely to be unconscious? Consider Lawrence, The Id, the Ego, and Equal Protection: Reckoning with Unconscious Racism, 39 Stan. L. Rev. 317, 330, 349 (1987):

Racism is irrational in the sense that we are not fully aware of the meanings we attach to race or why we have made race significant. It is also arguably dysfunctional to the extent that its irrationality prevents the optimal use of human resources. [But] unlike other forms of irrational and dysfunctional behavior, which we think of as deviant or abnormal, racism is "normal." It is a malady that we all share, because we have all been scarred by a common history. . . .
    [Unconscious] prejudice presents [a problem] in that it is not subject to self-correction within the political process. When racism operates at a conscious level, opposing forces can attempt to prevail upon the rationality and moral sensibility of racism's proponents. [But] when the discriminator is not aware of his prejudice and is convinced that he already walks in the path of righteousness, neither reason nor moral persuasion is likely to succeed. The process defect is all the more intractable, and judicial scrutiny becomes imperative.

Why should we assume that courts are more sensitive than legislatures to unconscious racism and inaccurate generalizations? Consider Ackerman, supra, at 739:

It is simply self-congratulatory to suppose that members of our own persuasion have reached their convictions in a deeply reflective way, whereas those espousing opinions we hate are superficial. [Given] the complexity of the human comedy, a judge is bound on a fool's errand if he imagines that the good guys and bad guys of American politics can be neatly classified according to the seriousness with which they have considered opposing points of view. Processual prejudice is a pervasive problem in the American political system.

6. *The equal protection clause prohibits the subordination of any group.* The arguments discussed above are premised on the assumption that the equal protection clause protects individuals from being unfairly pigeonholed in disfavored groups. Might special review of racial classifications be defended on the alternative theory that the equal protection clause protects the rights of particular social groups as such? Consider Colker, Anti-Subordination above All: Sex, Race, and Equal Protection, 61 N.Y.U. L. Rev. 1003, 1005, 1007 (1986):

Under the anti-differentiation perspective, it is inappropriate to treat individuals differently on the basis of a particular normative view about [race]. . . .

[In contrast, under] the anti-subordination perspective, it is inappropriate for certain groups in society to have subordinated status because of their lack of power in society as a whole.

Consider also Fiss, Groups and the Equal Protection Clause, 5 J. Phil. & Pub. Aff. 107, 150-151 (1976):

We must [realize that blacks] are a very special type of social group. [They] are very badly off, probably our worst-off class (in terms of material well-being second only to the American Indians), and in addition they have occupied the lowest rung for several centuries. In a sense, they are America's perpetual underclass. It is both of these characteristics — the relative position of the group and the duration of the position — that makes efforts to improve the status of the group defensible. This redistribution may be rooted in a theory of compensation — blacks as a group were *put* in that position by others and the redistributive means are *owed* to the group as a form of compensation. . . .

[But] a redistributive strategy need not rest on this idea of compensation. [The] redistributive strategy could give expression to an ethical view against caste, one that would make it undesirable for any social group to occupy a position of subordination for any extended period of time.

Is Fiss's view of the equal protection clause too narrow because "it is unjust for society to attach negative significance to a morally irrelevant factor even when doing so does not eventuate in a specially disadvantaged group, but only in harm to, and suffering on the part of, the particular individual affected"? Perry, The Principle of Equal Protection, 32 Hastings L. Rev. 1133, 1146 (1981). Is Fiss's view too broad because it confers special rights on members of a subjugated group, even if an individual member enjoying these rights is not himself subjugated? Consider also Brest, supra, at 49-50:

If a society can be said to have an underlying political theory, ours has not been a theory of organic groups but of liberalism, focusing on the rights of individuals including rights of distributive justice. . . .

[Although] the practices of nations — including our own — often fall short of their aspirations, most societies in which power is formally allocated among racial and national groups are strikingly oppressive, unequal and unstable. In view of all this, it seems reasonable to place the burden on proponents of a theory of group racial justice to show that it is morally tenable and consistent with other values we cherish.

7. *Economic models of the political process justify strict scrutiny.* Consider Stout, Strict Scrutiny and Social Choice: An Economic Inquiry into Fundamental Rights and Suspect Classifications, 80 Geo. L.J. 1787, 1814-1817 (1992):

[Social] choice theory suggests that strict judicial scrutiny of statutes employing suspect classifications may [serve] an important economic function. If statutes employing suspect classifications are inordinately likely to be wealth transferring rather than wealth creating, strict judicial scrutiny that discourages such legislation reduces the deadweight losses associated with competing for and enacting it. . . .

If legislatures can dole out resources or impose burdens according to race, racial interest groups have tremendous incentive to seek purely redistributive legislation. . . .

A classification based on an immutable trait is both less likely to serve a welfare-increasing function, and more likely to provide opportunities to exploit others without risk to oneself. . . .

Social choice theory thus supports the notion that classifications based on immutable traits such as race or gender deserve stricter scrutiny under the Equal Protection Clause than classifications based on characteristics that are changeable, such as age, health, or wealth.

Can the concept of racial equality really be reduced to the avoidance of deadweight losses associated with political bargaining? Compare Ackerman, supra, at 743:

Although the bargaining model captures an important aspect of American politics, it does not do justice to the most fundamental episodes of our constitutional history. We make a mistake, for example, to view the enactment of the Bill of Rights and the Civil War Amendments as if they were outcomes of ordinary pluralist bargaining. Instead, these constitutional achievements represent the highest legal expression of a different kind of politics — one characterized by mass mobilization and struggle that [yielded] fundamental principles transcending the normal processes of interest group accommodation.

Can strict scrutiny of racial classifications be understood as an effort to ensure that public deliberation involves something more than a power struggle between competing interest groups? Consider Sunstein, Interest Groups in American Public Law, 38 Stan. L. Rev. 29, 57 (1985):

Underlying the Court's approach is a perception that classifications in [certain contexts] are likely to reflect private power, even if it is possible to come up with a public value that the relevant classification can be said to serve. . . .

This understanding is in important respects classically republican. The role of the representative is to deliberate on the public good, not to respond mechanically to existing social conceptions. Under the Court's framework, such conceptions must themselves be subjected to critical review. They cannot be automatically translated into law. The result is to apply the deliberative task to social practices that had previously been accepted as natural and inviolate.

Note that this view does not take individual private preferences as the starting point for analysis. Instead, it assumes that "politics properly has, as one of its central functions, the selection, evaluation, and shaping of preferences. [There] is, in short, something like a 'common good' or 'public interest' that in some contexts amounts to something other than the aggregation of private preferences or utilities." Id. at 82.

Why should we assume that authentic deliberation about public issues will not produce racial discrimination? How can one know that racial classifications merely reflect "existing social conceptions" and are not in fact in the "public interest"? How likely is it that courts will be able to stand above existing power relationships and determine what is truly in the "common good"? If the "public interest" is in fact different from the aggregation of our private preferences, why does it follow that our private desires should be subordinated to those that emerge from public processes?

Note: The Nature of Special Scrutiny

Korematsu held that racial classifications should be subject to "rigid scrutiny." If some sort of enhanced review is in fact appropriate, what should it consist of? Can the scrutiny be structured to avoid the problem of judicial value judgments encountered in connection with rational relationship review? Consider the following possibilities:

1. *Ends scrutiny. Korematsu* held that a racial classification must be supported by a "pressing public necessity." Presumably this language means that the end purportedly advanced by the classification must be unusually important. But how should a court rank the importance of various constitutionally permissible ends?

If the evil to be avoided is race prejudice and stereotyping, why should the importance of the end matter? Ends scrutiny is sometimes defended as a mechanism for filtering out statutes motivated by prejudice. On this theory, if the legitimate ends advanced to justify the statute are relatively unimportant, the claim that the statute was motivated by these ends becomes correspondingly less plausible. A court is therefore more justified in concluding that the real purpose of the law is to harm an unpopular group.

Are you persuaded? One can hardly doubt that winning World War II counts as a "pressing public necessity." Does it follow that the decision to advance that goal by interning Japanese-Americans was not infected by race prejudice? Conversely, a publicly financed production of *Othello* presumably ranks as something less than a necessity. Yet a race-based classification in casting the lead might well be uninfluenced by race prejudice. If, alternatively, the reason for ends scrutiny is to avoid making powerless minorities bear disproportionate social costs, should not the test require consideration not only of the importance of the state's end but also the gravity of the injury inflicted to achieve it? Suppose, for example, the state's goal is legitimate, albeit relatively unimportant, but the deprivation required to achieve it is more trivial still?

2. *Means scrutiny.* It is possible to read the *Korematsu* test as focusing not only on ends but also on means. Thus, even if winning World War II was a "pressing public necessity," it is hard to see how that necessity justified a racial classification that only marginally contributed to achieving the end. In other cases, the Court has been more explicit in requiring a tight fit between means and ends when reviewing racial classifications. In McLaughlin v. Florida, 379 U.S. 184, 196 (1964), for example, the Court said that racial classifications "[bear] a heavy burden of justification [and] will be upheld only if [necessary] and not merely rationally related, to the accomplishment of a permissible state policy." See also In re Griffiths, 413 U.S. 717, 721-722 (1973).

Does means-oriented strict scrutiny escape the problem of judicial value judgments? If the scrutiny is so strict that the existence of *any* alternative means, regardless of cost, is sufficient to invalidate a racial classification, then presumably the Court would be freed from the necessity of balancing. But could any racial classification survive this test? If, alternatively, a balance must be struck between the cost of the classification and the cost of forgoing it, must not the Court some-how attach values to these factors so that they can be weighed against each other?

Note how fact dependent means-oriented scrutiny is. In *Korematsu*, for exam-ple, the necessity of a racial classification turned on questions such as how seri-ous the threat of sabotage was, how many Japanese-Americans were disloyal, and how hard it would have been to separate the loyal from the disloyal. Did the *Ko-rematsu* Court "rigidly scrutinize" the military commander's judgment? Would it be tolerable for nine justices in Washington to substitute their judgment for that of the military on questions such as these? Does "rigid scrutiny" amount to anything more than a rubber stamp if the Court is unwilling to look behind the factual judgments made by other branches?

3. *Absolute prohibition.* In light of the difficulties posed by both means and ends scrutiny, would it be preferable for the Court to adopt a bright-line rule prohib-iting all racial classifications that burden racial minorities? See, e.g., A. Bickel, The Morality of Consent 133 (1975) ("discrimination on the basis of race is illegal, immoral, unconstitutional, inherently wrong, and destructive of demo-cratic society"). But see Greenawalt, Judicial Scrutiny of "Benign" Racial Pref-erence in Law School Admissions, 75 Colum. L. Rev. 559, 568 (1975) (nighttime curfew on all Japanese-Americans might have been reasonable if hard evidence that a substantial percentage of them were training to commit sabotage in aid of much more probable and imminent invasion).

Consider Palmore v. Sidoti, 466 U.S. 429 (1984). The case arose from a cus-tody battle between Palmore and Sidoti (who were both white) following their di-vorce. Originally the trial court awarded custody of the couple's three-year-old daughter to the mother. When the mother remarried an African-American, how-ever, the court determined that the best interests of the child required that the fa-ther be awarded custody. The trial court ruled that, "despite the strides that have been made in bettering relations between the races in this country, it is inevitable that [the child] will, if allowed to remain in her present situation [suffer] from the social stigmatization that is sure to come."

A unanimous Supreme Court reversed. Chief Justice Burger's opinion for the Court acknowledged that the state had "a duty of the highest order to protect the interests of minor children," and that "[there] is a risk that a child living with a step-parent of a different race may be subject to a variety of pressures and stresses not present if the child were living with parents of the same racial or ethnic ori-gin." But the Court nonetheless held that the "reality of private biases and the possible injury they might inflict" were not "permissible considerations. [Private] biases may be outside the reach of the law, but the law cannot, directly or indi-rectly, give them effect."

Would the result in *Sidoti* have been the same if detailed empirical study demonstrated that children in mixed-race homes suffered psychological damage? Would a statute giving preference to prospective adoptive parents who are the same race as the child to be adopted be constitutional? Compare Bartholet, Where Do Black Children Belong? The Politics of Race Matching in Adoption, 139 U. Pa. L. Rev. 1163 (1991) (attacking preference) with In the Matter of the Petition of RMG & EMG, No. 79-747 (D.C. 1982) (striking down absolute pro-hibition of cross-racial adoptions, but holding that preference for same-race adoptions survives strict scrutiny). Is it constitutional to allow prospective parents to specify the race of their adopted child in state-sponsored adoptions? Compare

Banks, The Color of Desire: Fullfilling Adoptive Parents' Racial Preferences through Discriminatory State Action, 107 Yale L.J. 875 (1998) (no) with Bartholet, Private Race Preferences in Family Formation, 107 Yale L. J. 2351 (1998) (yes).

Would a statute be constitutional that required blacks, but not whites, contemplating marriage to be tested for sickle-cell anemia and to undergo genetic counseling if they have it? See J. Ely, Democracy and Distrust 247-248 n.46 (1980). Is it unconstitutional for immigration officials to take ethnic appearance into account when investigating immigration violations? See United States v. Martinez-Fuerte, 428 U.S. 543, 563 (1976) (upholding selective referral of motorists at immigration checkpoints to secondary inspection areas based largely on "apparent Mexican ancestry").

2.   Non-Race-Specific Classifications That Disadvantage Racial Minorities

Washington v. Davis

426 U.S. 229 (1976)

MR. JUSTICE WHITE delivered the opinion of the Court.

This case involves the validity of a qualifying test administered to applicants for positions as police officers in the District of Columbia Metropolitan Police Department. The test was sustained by the District Court but invalidated by the Court of Appeals. We are in agreement with the District Court and hence reverse the judgment of the Court of Appeals. . . .

[Respondents, unsuccessful black applicants for positions on the police force, claimed that a test measuring verbal ability, vocabulary, and reading comprehension unconstitutionally discriminated against them. According to the district court, respondents' evidence supported the conclusion that a higher percentage of blacks than whites failed the test, and that the test had not been validated to establish its reliability for measuring subsequent job performance. Respondents made no claim that administration of the test constituted an "intentional" or "purposeful" act of discrimination.]

The central purpose of the Equal Protection Clause of the Fourteenth Amendment is the prevention of official conduct discriminating on the basis of race. [But] our cases have not embraced the proposition that a law or other official act, without regard to whether it reflects a racially discriminatory purpose, is unconstitutional *solely* because it has a racially disproportionate impact.

Almost 100 years ago, Strauder v. West Virginia established that the exclusion of Negroes from grand and petit juries in criminal proceedings violated the Equal Protection Clause, but the fact that a particular jury or a series of juries does not statistically reflect the racial composition of the community does not in itself make out an invidious discrimination forbidden by the Clause. . . .

The rule is the same in other contexts. Wright v. Rockefeller, 376 U.S. 52 (1964), upheld a New York congressional apportionment statute against claims that district lines had been racially gerrymandered. The challenged districts were made up predominantly of whites or of minority races, and their boundaries were irregularly drawn. The challengers did not prevail because they failed to prove that [the] statute "was the product of a state contrivance to segregate on the basis of race or place of origin." . . .

The school desegregation cases have also adhered to the basic equal protection principle that the invidious quality of a law claimed to be racially discriminatory must ultimately be traced to a racially discriminatory purpose. That there are both predominantly black and predominantly white schools in a community is not alone violative of the Equal Protection Clause. The essential element of de jure segregation is "a current condition of segregation resulting from intentional state action." Keyes v. School Dist. No. 1.

[The] Court has also recently rejected allegations of racial discrimination based solely on the statistically disproportionate racial impact of various provisions of the Social Security Act because "[t]he acceptance of appellants' constitutional theory would render suspect each difference in treatment among the grant classes, however lacking in racial motivation and however otherwise rational the treatment might be." Jefferson v. Hackney, 406 U.S. 535, 548 (1972).

This is not to say that the necessary discriminatory racial purpose must be express or appear on the face of the statute, or that a law's disproportionate impact is irrelevant in cases involving Constitution-based claims of racial discrimination. A statute, otherwise neutral on its face, must not be applied so as invidiously to discriminate on the basis of race. . . .

Necessarily, an invidious discriminatory purpose may often be inferred from the totality of the relevant facts, including the fact, if it is true, that the law bears more heavily on one race than another. It is also not infrequently true that the discriminatory impact — in the jury cases for example, the total or seriously disproportionate exclusion of Negroes from jury venires — may for all practical purposes demonstrate unconstitutionality because in various circumstances the discrimination is very difficult to explain on nonracial grounds. Nevertheless, we have not held that a law, neutral on its face and serving ends otherwise within the power of government to pursue, is invalid under the Equal Protection Clause simply because it may affect a greater proportion of one race than of another. Disproportionate impact is not irrelevant, but it is not the sole touchstone of an invidious racial discrimination forbidden by the Constitution. Standing alone, it does not trigger the rule, that racial classifications are to be subjected to the strictest scrutiny and are justifiable only by the weightiest of considerations. . . .

[We] have difficulty understanding how a law establishing a racially neutral qualification for employment is nevertheless racially discriminatory and denies "any person . . . equal protection of the laws" simply because a greater proportion of Negroes fail to qualify than members of other racial or ethnic groups. Had respondents, along with all others who had failed [the test], whether white or black, brought an action claiming that [it] denied each of them equal protection of the laws as compared with those who had passed with high enough scores to qualify them as police recruits, it is most unlikely that their challenge would have been sustained. [The test], which is administered generally to prospective Government employees, concededly seeks to ascertain whether those who take it have acquired a particular level of verbal skill; and it is untenable that the Constitution prevents the Government from seeking modestly to upgrade the communicative abilities of its employees rather than to be satisfied with some lower level of competence, particularly where the job requires special ability to communicate orally and in writing. Respondents, as Negroes, could no more successfully claim that the test denied them equal protection than could white applicants who also failed. The conclusion would not be different in the face of proof that more Negroes than whites had been disqualified by [the test]. That other Negroes also failed to score well would, alone, not demonstrate that respondents individually were being denied equal protection of the laws by the application of an otherwise valid qualifying test being administered to prospective police recruits.

Nor on the facts of the case before us would the disproportionate impact of [the test] warrant the conclusion that it is a purposeful device to discriminate against Negroes and hence an infringement of the constitutional rights of respondents as well as other black applicants. As we have said, the test is neutral on its face and rationally may be said to serve a purpose the Government is constitutionally empowered to pursue. Even agreeing with the District Court that the differential racial effect of [the test] called for further inquiry, we think the District Court correctly held that the affirmative efforts of the Metropolitan Police Department to recruit black officers, the changing racial composition of the recruit classes and of the force in general, and the relationship of the test to the training program negated any inference that the Department discriminated on the basis of race or that "a police officer qualifies on the color of his skin rather than ability." . . .

A rule that a statute designed to serve neutral ends is nevertheless invalid, absent compelling justification, if in practice it benefits or burdens one race more than another would be far reaching and would raise serious questions about, and perhaps invalidate, a whole range of tax, welfare, public service, regulatory, and licensing statutes that may be more burdensome to the poor and to the average black than to the more affluent white. . . .

Mr. Justice Stevens, concurring. . . .

The requirement of purposeful discrimination is a common thread running through the cases summarized in [the majority's opinion]. These cases include criminal convictions which were set aside because blacks were excluded from the grand jury, a reapportionment case in which political boundaries were obviously influenced to some extent by racial considerations, a school desegregation case, and a case involving the unequal administration of an ordinance purporting to prohibit the operation of laundries in frame buildings. Although it may be proper to use the same language to describe the constitutional claim in each of these contexts, the burden of proving a prima facie case may well involve differing evidentiary considerations. The extent of deference that one pays to the trial court's determination of the factual issue, and indeed, the extent to which one characterizes the intent issue as a question of fact or a question of law, will vary in different contexts.

Frequently the most probative evidence of intent will be objective evidence of what actually happened rather than evidence describing the subjective state of mind of the actor. For normally the actor is presumed to have intended the natural consequences of his deeds. This is particularly true in the case of governmental action which is frequently the product of compromise, of collective decisionmaking, and of mixed motivation. It is unrealistic, on the one hand, to require the victim of alleged discrimination to uncover the actual subjective intent of the decisionmaker or, conversely, to invalidate otherwise legitimate action simply because an improper motive affected the deliberation of a participant in the decisional process. A law conscripting clerics should not be invalidated because an atheist voted for it.

My point in making this observation is to suggest that the line between discriminatory purpose and discriminatory impact is not nearly as bright, and perhaps not quite as critical, as the reader of the Court's opinion might assume. I agree, of course, that a constitutional issue does not arise every time some disproportionate impact is shown. On the other hand, when the disproportion is dramatic, [it] really does not matter whether the standard is phrased in terms of purpose or effect. Therefore, although I accept the statement of the general rule in the Court's opinion, I am not yet prepared to indicate how that standard should be applied in the many cases which have formulated the governing standard in different language. . . .

[A dissenting opinion by Justice Brennan is omitted.]

Note: *Rational Basis Review of Non-Race-Specific Classifications*

1. *Some preliminary questions.* After Washington v. Davis, a court confronted with a classification that disadvantages a racial minority must first determine whether it is race-specific. If it is, either because it explicitly draws racial lines or because it is motivated by a racial purpose, the court will use strict scrutiny and probably invalidate it. If the classification is non-race-specific, the court will use rational basis review despite its disproportionate impact on the minority group. Has the Supreme Court given an adequate account of why non-race-specific classifications that harm racial minorities should not be strictly scrutinized in the absence of a discriminatory purpose? Is it because such classifications are less likely to stigmatize? Because they are less likely to perpetuate stereotypes? Because it would be impractical to invalidate all the "tax, welfare, public service, regulatory, and licensing statutes that may be more burdensome to [the] average black than to the [average] white"? Even if strict scrutiny and virtual per se invalidation are inappropriate for non-race-specific classifications, why shouldn't the fact that they disproportionately impact on racial minorities trigger some form of intermediate review more rigorous than the rational relationship test?

2. *Effects tests and the problem of preferential treatment.* Would heightened review of non-race-specific classifications that disadvantage racial minorities turn the equal protection clause on its head by constitutionally requiring legislatures to be race-conscious as to outcomes rather than race-neutral as to the legal rules producing those outcomes? Consider Ely, Legislative and Administrative Motivation in Constitutional Law, 79 Yale L.J. 1205, 1255, 1260 (1970):

> A number of commentators have asserted that government officials may, if they wish, go out of their way to favor the members of minority races without violating the Constitution. But none of whom I am aware, and certainly not the Court, has argued that such favoritism is constitutionally required. . . .
> [So] long as the Court remains unwilling to order states to take race into account [judicial] review must await proof of racial motivation and cannot be triggered by disproportion per se. To undertake automatically to invalidate [state actions] because of racial disproportion would obviously be to order that balance be intentionally achieved.

3. *The problem of remedy.* These arguments against an effects test assume that, so long as a disproportionate impact is unintended, it is merely a matter of chance. Is this assumption warranted? Would an effects test require preferential treatment for blacks if blacks and whites are differently situated with respect to the law because of *prior* unequal treatment by government? Consider Perry, The Disproportionate Impact Theory of Racial Discrimination, 125 U. Pa. L. Rev. 540, 558 (1977):

> Laws having a disproportionate racial impact burden blacks *because* of their especially disadvantaged position in American society. A failure to require government to take account of that especially disadvantaged social position by selecting and fine-tuning laws to avoid the unnecessary or thoughtless aggravation of the situation would effectively ignore American society's responsibility for that social position. Furthermore, the failure would compound the responsibility.

Compare Alexander, What Makes Wrongful Discrimination Wrong? Biases, Preferences, Stereotypes, and Proxies, 141 U. Pa. L. Rev. 149, 213 (1992):

> If one lacks a preferred trait that one would have possessed were one not the victim of wrongful discrimination, may one demand in addition to compensation from one's victimizers that others overlook the absence of the trait? Surely not. If I was a promising neurosurgeon before my hands were mangled by a drunk driver, I cannot ask others to ignore my lack of dexterity in their choice of neurosurgeons. [Preferences] for scarce traits do not become immoral merely because the scarcity is in part due to the immoralities of others, even when just reparations have not been fully paid.

4. *Disproportionate impact and the theory of passive government.* Even if the government is not responsible for the fact that blacks are differently situated with respect to a non-race-specific classification, why should that fact matter? Doesn't treating people the same when they are relevantly different deny equality just as effectively as treating them differently when they are relevantly the same? Compare, for example, the following two hypothetical admissions policies followed by a state university:

a. No blind applicants will be admitted.
b. All applicants, whether sighted or blind, must take a written examination, and those receiving the highest scores will be admitted.

The first treats blind and sighted applicants differently, although they are (arguably) relevantly the same. The second treats blind and sighted applicants the same, although they are (arguably) relevantly different. Does either satisfy the equality principle?

Recall the suggestion that race-specific classifications are strictly scrutinized in order to deal with problems of legislative purpose. When the classification is race-specific, the purpose question is not whether the legislature intended to treat blacks and whites differently. The classification itself establishes that purpose. Rather, the question is whether the legislature intended to disadvantage a racial minority simply for the sake of harming it rather than for the sake of achieving some permissible goal. The strict scrutiny doctrine holds that only a showing of a close fit and an overriding governmental interest can overcome the inference that the classification was motivated by a desire to harm the minority. See section C1 supra. See also Personnel Administrator of Massachusetts v. Feeney, 442 U.S. 256, 272 (1979). But why shouldn't the same inference be drawn, and the same strict scrutiny required, when a non-race-specific classification disproportionately disadvantages a racial minority? Isn't treating blacks and whites the same despite the fact that they are differently situated just as effective a strategy for disadvantaging blacks as treating them differently despite the fact that they are similarly situated?

Note: Heightened Scrutiny for Improperly Motivated Classifications

Washington v. Davis makes clear that a facially neutral classification is not race-specific and hence not subject to strict scrutiny merely because of its disproportionate racial impact. Does such a classification become race-specific if the disproportionate racial impact was intentional?

1. *Discriminatory administration.* In Yick Wo v. Hopkins, 118 U.S. 351 (1886), petitioner was convicted of violating a local ordinance prohibiting operation of a laundry not located in a brick or stone building without the consent of the board of supervisors. He alleged that he and more than 200 other Chinese nationals had petitioned the board of supervisors for consent, but that all of the petitions were denied, whereas all but one of the petitions filed by non-Chinese were granted. The Court unanimously reversed Yick Wo's conviction. The Court held that "the facts shown establish an administration directed so exclusively against a particular class of persons as to warrant and require the conclusion, that, whatever may have been the intent of the ordinances as adopted, they are applied by the public authorities charged with their administration, and thus representing the State itself, with a mind so unequal and oppressive as to amount to a practical denial by the State of [equal] protection of the laws."

There is a well-developed line of authority reversing convictions where it is shown that facially neutral jury selection statutes are administered in discriminatory fashion. See, e.g., Castaneda v. Partida, 430 U.S. 482 (1977); Carter v. Jury Commission, 396 U.S. 320 (1970); Avery v. Georgia, 345 U.S. 559 (1953). Moreover, in the jury context, reversal is required even in the absence of a showing that any prejudice resulted from the discriminatory policy. See Vasquez v. Hillery, 474 U.S. 254 (1986); Rose v. Mitchell, 443 U.S. 545 (1979).

In Batson v. Kentucky, 476 U.S. 79 (1986), the Court extended these cases to the use of peremptory challenges by prosecutors to remove individual jurors on the basis of race. In an opinion by Justice Powell, the Court held that

[although] a prosecutor ordinarily is entitled to exercise permitted peremptory challenges "for any reason at all, as long as that reason is related to his view concerning the outcome" of the case to be tried, the Equal Protection Clause forbids the prosecutor to challenge potential jurors solely on account of their race or on the assumption that black jurors as a group will be unable impartially to consider the State's case against a black defendant.

In a dissenting opinion, Chief Justice Burger, joined by Justice Rehnquist, argued that

> peremptory challenges are often lodged, of necessity, for reasons "normally thought irrelevant to legal proceedings or official actions, namely, the race, religion, nationality, occupation or affiliation of people summoned for jury duty." Moreover, in making peremptory challenges, both the prosecutor and defense attorney necessarily act on only limited information or hunch. The process can not be indicted on the sole basis that such decisions are made on the basis of "assumption" or "intuitive judgment." As a result, unadulterated equal protection analysis is simply inapplicable to peremptory challenges exercised in any particular case.

Justice Rehnquist, joined by Chief Justice Burger, also wrote a dissenting opinion:

> [There] is simply nothing "unequal" about the State using its peremptory challenges to strike blacks from the jury in cases involving black defendants so long as such challenges are also used to exclude whites in cases involving white defendants, Hispanics in cases involving Hispanic defendants, Asians in cases involving Asian defendants, and so on. This case-specific use of peremptory challenges by the State does not single out blacks, or members of any other race for that matter, for discriminatory treatment. Such use of peremptories is at best based upon seat-of-the-pants instincts, which are undoubtedly crudely stereotypical and may in many cases be hopelessly mistaken. But as long as they are applied across the board to jurors of all races and nationalities, I do not see [how] their use violates the Equal Protection Clause.

See also Powers v. Ohio, 499 U.S. 400 (1991) (holding that *Batson* applied when the defendant and the excluded juror do not "share the same race"); Edmonson v. Leesville Concrete Co., 500 U.S. 614 (1991) (holding that race-based peremptory challenges by private litigants in civil litigation violated the Constitution); Georgia v. McCollum, 505 U.S. 42 (1992) (holding that *Batson* applied to defense, as well as prosecutorial, challenges).

Consider Justice Thomas's attack on *Batson* in his opinion concurring in the judgment in *McCollum:*

> [I] am certain that black criminal defendants will rue the day that this court ventured down this road that inexorably will lead to the elimination of peremptory strikes.
>
> In *Strauder* [we] invalidated a state law that prohibited blacks from serving on juries. In the course of the decision, we observed that the racial composition of a jury may affect the outcome of a criminal case. . . .
>
> I do not think that this basic premise of *Strauder* has become obsolete. . . .
>
> In *Batson,* however, this Court began to depart from *Strauder* by holding that, without some actual showing, suppositions about the possibility that jurors may harbor prejudice have no legitimacy. We said, in particular, that a prosecutor could not justify peremptory strikes "by stating merely that he challenged jurors of the defendant's race on the assumption — or his intuitive judgment — that they would be partial to the defendant because of their shared race." [Our] decision in *Strauder,* [however,] rested on precisely such an "assumption" or "intuition." We reasonably surmised, without direct evidence in any particular case, that all-white juries might judge black defendants unfairly.

2. *Statutes enacted for discriminatory purposes*. Is discriminatory purpose review less troublesome when a statute contains a classification that is deliberately "gerrymandered" to produce a disproportionate impact on racial minorities? Compare *Yick Wo* with Gomillion v. Lightfoot, 364 U.S. 339 (1960). An Alabama statute altered the shape of the city of Tuskegee from a square to an "uncouth twenty-eight sided figure." Petitioners alleged that the new boundary lines removed from the city all but four or five of the 400 black voters, while not removing a single white voter. The Court held that, if these allegations were proved, the statute infringed on the right of blacks to vote in violation of the fifteenth amendment:

> If these allegations upon a trial remained uncontradicted or unqualified, the conclusion would be irresistible, tantamount for all practical purposes to a mathematical demonstration, that the legislation is solely concerned with segregating white and colored voters by fencing Negro citizens out of town so as to deprive them of their pre-existing municipal vote. It is difficult to appreciate what stands in the way of adjudging a statute having this inevitable effect invalid.

Compare *Gomillion* to Hunter v. Underwood, 421 U.S. 222 (1985). A provision of the Alabama Constitution, adopted in 1901, disfranchised all persons convicted of crimes of moral turpitude. A unanimous Court, in an opinion by Justice Rehnquist, invalidated the provision because it was partially motivated by the desire to disfranchise blacks. Why should the motivation of the 1901 legislature determine the validity of the provision in 1985?

3. *Racially motivated classifications that are not strictly scrutinized*. Does it follow from *Yick Wo* and *Gomillion* that racially motivated classifications should always be subject to strict scrutiny? The Court has demonstrated some reluctance to strictly scrutinize such classifications in three situations:

a. Palmer *and the problem of racially motivated classifications with neutral effects*. Compare *Gomillion* with Palmer v. Thompson, 403 U.S. 217 (1971), in which a city council closed municipal swimming pools following court-ordered integration. In a five-to-four decision, the Court held that the closing did not violate the equal protection clause. After observing that "no case in this Court has held that a legislative act may violate equal protection solely because of the motivations of the men who voted for it," the Court advanced several reasons why investigation of purpose was improper:

> First, it is extremely difficult for a court to ascertain the motivation, or collection of different motivations, that lie behind a legislative enactment. [Furthermore], there is an element of futility in a judicial attempt to invalidate a law because of the bad motives of its supporters. If the law is struck down for this reason, rather than because of its facial content or effect, it would presumably be valid as soon as the legislature or relevant governing body repassed it for different reasons.

The Court distinguished *Gomillion* as a case resting "on the actual effect of the [enactment], not upon the motivation which led the [State] to behave as [it] did."

Is this explanation of *Gomillion* consistent with Washington v. Davis? The *Washington* Court attempted to explain *Palmer* on the ground that the pool closing extended "identical treatment to both whites and Negroes." Taken together, *Palmer* and *Washington* suggest that a facially neutral statute is subject to enhanced review only when it has *both* a discriminatory purpose *and* a disproportionate impact. However, it is difficult to see how a holding that the closing of integrated pools does not produce a disproportionate racial impact is consistent with Brown v. Board of Education. See Brest, Palmer v. Thompson: An Approach to the Problem of Unconstitutional Legislative Motive, 1971 Sup. Ct. Rev. 95, 132. Is it conceivable that the Court would uphold a statute that by its terms required the closing of any municipal facility ordered desegregated? Cf. Bush v. Orleans Parish School Board, 187 F. Supp. 42 (E.D. La. 1960), aff'd, 365 U.S. 569 (1961) (statute providing for closing of all integrated schools unconstitutional).

b. *"Discretionary" decisions.* Should there be a class of "discretionary" governmental decisions not subject to improper purpose review? Suppose, for example, that the President chooses a nominee for the Supreme Court or for a cabinet post partially on the basis of racial or ethnic considerations. Compare Mayor of Philadelphia v. Educational Equality League, 415 U.S. 605 (1974) (expressing concern that "judicial oversight of discretionary appointments may interfere with the ability of an elected official to respond to the mandate of his constituency") with Davis v. Passman, 442 U.S. 228 (1979) (holding that an employee of a congressman had asserted violation of a constitutionally protected right when she alleged that she had been fired because she was a woman).

c. *The causation requirement.* Should an improperly motivated classification be subject to strict scrutiny if the state is able to show that the same classification would have been utilized even in the absence of the improper motive? Consider Mt. Healthy City School District Board of Education v. Doyle, 429 U.S. 274 (1977). The district court found that Doyle was not rehired as a teacher because he had engaged in conduct protected by the first amendment. Although accepting these findings of fact, the Supreme Court held that it did not necessarily follow that he was entitled to reinstatement and back pay. Writing for a unanimous court, Justice Rehnquist observed that

> [a] rule of causation which focuses solely on whether protected conduct played a part, "substantial" or otherwise, in a decision not to rehire could place an employee in a better position as a result of the exercise of constitutionally protected conduct than he would have occupied had he done nothing. . . .
>
> Initially, in this case, the burden was properly placed upon [Doyle] to show that his conduct was constitutionally protected, and that this conduct was a "substantial factor" [in] the Board's decision not to rehire him. [Doyle] having carried that burden, however, the District Court should have gone on to determine whether the Board had shown by a preponderance of the evidence that it would have reached the same decision as to [Doyle's] reemployment even in the absence of the protected conduct.

Is the Court's approach in *Mt. Healthy* consistent with its treatment of statutes that facially discriminate against racial minorities? The Court has never suggested that such statutes can be saved from strict scrutiny by a showing that the same classification would have been utilized in the absence of racial animus. Indeed, on one view the reason why the Court requires a compelling government interest and a tight fit between means and ends is to ascertain whether the same law would have been adopted if the legislature were not "prejudiced." Does it follow that strict scrutiny is also the appropriate technique for investigating the causation question when facially neutral statutes are infected by a discriminatory purpose?

VILLAGE OF ARLINGTON HEIGHTS v. METROPOLITAN HOUS-ING DEVELOPMENT CORP., 429 U.S. 252 (1977). Respondent applied to the Village of Arlington Heights for rezoning of a fifteen-acre parcel so as to permit construction of low- and moderate-income housing. When the request was denied, respondent brought this suit claiming that the denial was racially discriminatory and violated the equal protection clause. Justice Powell wrote the Court's opinion:

"Determining whether invidious discriminatory purpose was a motivating factor demands a sensitive inquiry into such circumstantial and direct evidence of intent as may be available. The impact of the official action [may] provide an important starting point. Sometimes a clear pattern, unexplainable on grounds other than race, emerges from the effect of the state action even when the governing legislation appears neutral on its face. The evidentiary inquiry is then relatively easy. But such cases are rare. Absent a pattern as stark as that in *Gomillion* or *Yick Wo*, impact alone is not determinative, and the Court must look to other evidence.

"The historical background of the decision is one evidentiary source, particularly if it reveals a series of official actions taken for invidious purposes. The specific sequence of events leading up to the challenged decision also may shed some light on the decisionmaker's purposes. [Departures] from the normal procedural sequence also might afford evidence that improper purposes are playing a role. Substantive departures too may be relevant, particularly if the factors usually considered important by the decisionmaker strongly favor a decision contrary to the one reached.

"The legislative or administrative history may be highly relevant, especially where there are contemporary statements by members of the decisionmaking body, minutes of its meetings, or reports. In some extraordinary instances the members might be called to the stand at trial to testify concerning the purpose of the official action, although even then such testimony frequently will be barred by privilege. . . .

"[Here, respondents] simply failed to carry their burden of proving that discriminatory purpose was a motivating factor in the Village's decision."

McCleskey v. Kemp

481 U.S. 279 (1987)

JUSTICE POWELL delivered the opinion of the Court.

[McCleskey, an African-American, was convicted in a Georgia state court of murdering a white and sentenced to death. On habeas corpus, he alleged that the Georgia capital sentencing scheme was administered in a racially discriminatory manner in violation of the equal protection clause.

[In support of this claim, he proffered a statistical study prepared by Professor David Baldus (the "Baldus study"), which examined over 2,000 murder cases occurring in Georgia in the 1970s. The raw numbers collected by Baldus indicated that the death penalty was assessed in 22 percent of the cases involving black defendants and white victims; 8 percent of the cases involving white defendants and white victims; 1 percent of the cases involving black defendants and black victims; and 3 percent of the cases involving white defendants and black victims.

[Baldus then subjected his data to statistical analysis that attempted to account for other variables that might have explained these differences on nonracial grounds. After taking into account a variety of nonracial variables, he concluded that defendants charged with killing whites were 4.3 times as likely to receive a death sentence as defendants charged with killing blacks. The study further indicated that black defendants who killed white victims had the greatest likelihood of receiving a death sentence.

[The district court found the Baldus study flawed in several respects, held that it "[failed] to contribute anything of value" to McCleskey's claim, and dismissed the petition. The court of appeals affirmed. Although it assumed arguendo that the study was valid, the court held that the statistics were "insufficient to demonstrate discriminatory intent."]

Our analysis begins with the basic principle that a defendant who alleges an equal protection violation has the burden of proving "the existence of purposeful discrimination."[7] Thus, to prevail under the Equal Protection Clause, McCleskey must prove that the decisionmakers in *his* case acted with discriminatory purpose. He offers no evidence specific to his own case that would support an inference that racial considerations played a part in his sentence. . . .

The Court has accepted statistics as proof of intent to discriminate in certain limited contexts [such as jury discrimination cases and job discrimination cases brought under Title VII of the 1964 Civil Rights Act].

But the nature of the capital sentencing decision, and the relationship of the statistics to that decision, are fundamentally different from the corresponding elements in the venire-selection or Title VII cases. Most importantly, each particular decision to impose the death penalty is made by a petit jury selected from a properly constituted venire. Each jury is unique in its composition, and the Constitution requires that its decision rest on consideration of innumerable factors that vary according to the characteristics of the individual defendant and the facts of the particular capital offense. Thus, the application of an inference drawn from the general statistics to a specific decision in a trial and sentencing simply is not comparable to the application of an inference drawn from general statistics to a specific venire-selection or Title VII case. In those cases, the statistics relate to fewer entities, and fewer variables are relevant to the challenged decisions.

Another important difference [is] that, in the venire-selection and Title VII contexts, the decisionmaker has an opportunity to explain the statistical disparity. Here, the State has no practical opportunity to rebut the Baldus study. [The] policy considerations behind a prosecutor's traditionally "wide discretion" sug-

7. [As] did the Court of Appeals, we assume the study is valid statistically without reviewing the factual findings of the District Court. Our assumption that the Baldus study is statistically valid does not include the assumption that the study shows that racial considerations actually enter into any sentencing decisions in Georgia. Even a sophisticated multiple regression analysis such as the Baldus study can only demonstrate a *risk* that the factor of race entered into some capital sentencing decisions and a necessarily lesser risk that race entered into any particular sentencing decision. [Relocated footnote — EDS.]

gest the impropriety of our requiring prosecutors to defend their decisions to seek death penalties, "often years after they were made."[17] Moreover, absent far stronger proof, it is unnecessary to seek such a rebuttal, because a legitimate and unchallenged explanation for the decision is apparent from the record: McCleskey committed an act for which the United States Constitution and Georgia laws permit imposition of the death penalty.

Finally, McCleskey's statistical proffer must be viewed in the context of his challenge. McCleskey challenges decisions at the heart of the State's criminal justice system. [Because] discretion is essential to the criminal justice process, we would demand exceptionally clear proof before we would infer that the discretion has been abused. . . .

McCleskey also suggests that the Baldus study proves that the State as a whole has acted with a discriminatory purpose. He appears to argue that the State has violated the Equal Protection Clause by adopting the capital punishment statute and allowing it to remain in force despite its allegedly discriminatory application. But "'[d]iscriminatory purpose' . . . implies more than intent as volition or intent as awareness of consequences. It implies that the decisionmaker, in this case a state legislature, selected or reaffirmed a particular course of action at least in part 'because of,' not merely 'in spite of,' its adverse effects upon an identifiable group." [Personnel Administrator v. Feeney, 442 U.S. 256 (1979).] For this claim to prevail, McCleskey would have to prove that the Georgia Legislature enacted or maintained the death penalty statute *because of* an anticipated racially discriminatory effect. [There is] no evidence [that] the Georgia Legislature enacted the capital punishment statute to further a racially discriminatory purpose. . . .

There is, of course, some risk of racial prejudice influencing a jury's decision in a criminal case. [The] question "is at what point that risk becomes constitutionally unacceptable," Turner v. Murray, 476 U.S. 28, 36, n.8 (1986). McCleskey asks us to accept the likelihood allegedly shown by the Baldus study as the constitutional measure of an unacceptable risk of racial prejudice influencing capital sentencing decisions. This we decline to do. . . .

[The] capital sentencing decision requires the individual jurors to focus their collective judgment on the unique characteristics of a particular criminal defendant. It is not surprising that such collective judgments often are difficult to explain. But the inherent lack of predictability of jury decisions does not justify their condemnation. On the contrary, it is the jury's function to make the difficult and uniquely human judgments that defy codification and that "buil[d] discretion, equity, and flexibility into a legal system." H. Kalven & H. Zeisel, The American Jury 498 (1966).

McCleskey's argument that the Constitution condemns the discretion allowed decisionmakers in the Georgia capital sentencing system is antithetical to the fundamental role of discretion in our criminal justice system. [Of] course, "the power to be lenient [also] is the power to discriminate," K. Davis, Discretionary Justice 170 (1973), but a capital-punishment system that did not allow for discretionary acts of leniency "would be totally alien to our notions of criminal justice." Gregg v. Georgia, 428 U.S. 153, 200, n.50 (1976).

17. Requiring a prosecutor to rebut a study that analyzes the past conduct of scores of prosecutors is quite different from requiring a prosecutor to rebut a contemporaneous challenge to his own acts. See Batson v. Kentucky, 476 U.S. 79 (1986).

[Where] the discretion that is fundamental to our criminal process is involved, we decline to assume that what is unexplained is invidious. In light of the safeguards designed to minimize racial bias in the process, the fundamental value of jury trial in our criminal justice system, and the benefits that discretion provides to criminal defendants, we hold that the Baldus study does not demonstrate a constitutionally significant risk of racial bias affecting the Georgia capital sentencing process.

Two additional concerns inform our decision in this case. First, McCleskey's claim, taken to its logical conclusion, throws into serious question the principles that underlie our entire criminal justice system. [If] we accepted McCleskey's claim that racial bias has impermissibly tainted the capital sentencing decision, we could soon be faced with similar claims as to other types of penalty. Moreover, the claim that his sentence rests on the irrelevant factor of race easily could be extended to apply to claims based on unexplained discrepancies that correlate to membership in other minority groups, and even to gender. [The] Constitution does not require that a State eliminate any demonstrable disparity that correlates with a potentially irrelevant factor in order to operate a criminal justice system that includes capital punishment. . . .

Second, McCleskey's arguments are best presented to the legislative bodies. It is not the responsibility — or indeed even the right — of this Court to determine the appropriate punishment for particular crimes. [Legislatures are] better qualified to weigh and "evaluate the results of statistical studies in terms of their own local conditions and with a flexibility of approach that is not available to the courts." Capital punishment is now the law in more than two thirds of our States. It is the ultimate duty of courts to determine on a case-by-case basis whether these laws are applied consistently with the Constitution. Despite McCleskey's wide ranging arguments that basically challenge the validity of capital punishment in our multi-racial society, the only question before us is whether in his case the law of Georgia was properly applied. We agree with the District Court and the Court of Appeals [that] this was carefully and correctly done in this case.

[Affirmed.]

JUSTICE BRENNAN, with whom JUSTICE MARSHALL, [JUSTICE BLACKMUN, and JUSTICE STEVENS] join, dissenting. . . .

At some point in this case, Warren McCleskey doubtless asked his lawyer whether a jury was likely to sentence him to die. A candid reply to this question would have been disturbing. [The] story could be told in a variety of ways, but McCleskey could not fail to grasp its essential narrative line: there was a significant chance that race would play a prominent role in determining if he lived or died. . . .

The Baldus study indicates that, after taking into account some 230 nonracial factors that might legitimately influence a sentencer, the jury *more likely than not* would have spared McCleskey's life had his victim been black. . . .

Evaluation of McCleskey's evidence cannot rest solely on the numbers themselves. We must also ask whether the conclusion suggested by those numbers is consonant with our understanding of history and human experience. Georgia's legacy of a race-conscious criminal justice system, as well as this Court's own recognition of the persistent danger that racial attitudes may affect criminal proceedings, indicate that McCleskey's claim is not a fanciful product of mere statistical artifice.

For many years, Georgia operated openly and formally precisely the type of dual system the evidence shows is still effectively in place. The criminal law expressly differentiated between crimes committed by and against blacks and whites, distinctions whose lineage traced back to the time of slavery. . . .

This historical review of Georgia criminal law is not intended as a bill of indictment calling the State to account for past transgressions. Citation of past practices does not justify the automatic condemnation of current ones. But it would be unrealistic to ignore the influence of history in assessing the plausible implications of McCleskey's evidence. "[A]mericans share a historical experience that has resulted in individuals within the culture ubiquitously attaching a significance to race that is irrational and often outside their awareness." Lawrence, The Id, The Ego, and Equal Protection: Reckoning with Unconscious Racism, 39 Stan. L. Rev. 327 (1987). . . .

It is true that every nuance of decision cannot be statistically captured, nor can any individual judgment be plumbed with absolute certainty. Yet the fact that we must always act without the illumination of complete knowledge cannot induce paralysis when we confront what is literally an issue of life and death. Sentencing data, history, and experience all counsel that Georgia has provided insufficient assurance of the heightened rationality we have required in order to take a human life. . . .

The Court maintains that petitioner's claim "is antithetical to the fundamental role of discretion in our criminal justice system." . . .

Reliance on race in imposing capital punishment, however, is antithetical to the very rationale for granting sentencing discretion. Discretion is a means, not an end. . . .

Considering the race of a defendant or victim in deciding if the death penalty should be imposed is completely at odds with [the] concern that an individual be evaluated as a unique human being. Decisions influenced by race rest in part on a categorical assessment of the worth of human beings according to color, insensitive to whatever qualities the individuals in question may possess. . . .

The Court next states that its unwillingness to regard the petitioner's evidence as sufficient is based in part on the fear that recognition of McCleskey's claim would open the door to widespread challenges to all aspects of criminal sentencing. Taken on its face, such a statement seems to suggest a fear of too much justice. Yet surely the majority would acknowledge that if striking evidence indicated that other minority groups, or women, or even persons with blond hair, were disproportionately sentenced to death, such a state of affairs would be repugnant to deeply rooted conceptions of fairness. The prospect that there may be more widespread abuse than McCleskey documents may be dismaying, but it does not justify complete abdication of our judicial role. . . .

Finally, the Court justifies its rejection of McCleskey's claim by cautioning against usurpation of the legislatures' role in devising and monitoring criminal punishment. . . .

Those whom we would banish from society or from the human community itself often speak in too faint a voice to be heard above society's demand for punishment. It is the particular role of courts to hear these voices, for the Constitution declares that the majoritarian chorus may not alone dictate the conditions of social life. The Court thus fulfills, rather than disrupts, the scheme of separation of powers by closely scrutinizing the imposition of the death [penalty]. . . .

It is tempting to pretend that minorities on death row share a fate in no way connected to our own, that our treatment of them sounds no echoes beyond the chambers in which they die. Such an illusion is ultimately corrosive, for the reverberations of injustice are not so easily confined. "The destinies of the two races in this country are indissolubly linked together," [Plessy v. Ferguson (Harlan, J., dissenting)], and the way in which we choose those who will die reveals the depth of moral commitment among the living.

The Court's decision today will not change what attorneys in Georgia tell other Warren McCleskeys about their chances of execution. Nothing will soften the harsh message they must convey, nor alter the prospect that race undoubtedly will continue to be a topic of discussion. McCleskey's evidence will not have obtained judicial acceptance, but that will not affect what is said on death row. However many criticisms of today's decision may be rendered, these painful conversations will serve as the most eloquent dissents of all.

[A dissenting opinion by Justice Blackmun, joined by Justices Marshall and Stevens and, in part, by Justice Brennan, and a dissenting opinion by Justice Stevens, joined by Justice Blackmun, are omitted.]

Note: The Definition of Discriminatory Purpose

1. *The problem of selective insensitivity.* Does the Court's formulation of the intent requirement in *McCleskey* adequately heed the risk that legislatures will be selectively indifferent to the welfare of politically powerless groups? Consider the following argument: Of course, the equal protection clause prohibits governmental action deliberately undertaken to harm racial and other minorities. But few laws are passed because legislators have a sadistic desire to inflict disabilities on these groups. The more common problem arises when the legislature is pursuing a neutral aim but, in doing so, is selectively indifferent to the welfare of certain groups. Thus, the question the *McCleskey* Court should have asked is not whether Georgia's capital punishment scheme was designed to harm African-Americans, but rather whether the legislature would have been as willing to inflict the death penalty if most of the law's victims had been white. Cf. Brest, Foreword: In Defense of the Antidiscrimination Principle, 90 Harv. L. Rev. 1, 6-8 (1976).

Compare *McCleskey* to Personnel Administrator of Massachusetts v. Feeney, 442 U.S. 256 (1977), a gender discrimination case relied on by the *McCleskey* Court. Under Massachusetts law, all veterans who qualified for state civil service positions had to be considered for appointment ahead of any qualifying nonveterans. The preference operated overwhelmingly to the advantage of males. In an opinion by Justice Stewart, the Court upheld the preference against equal protection attack. It conceded that it would be "disingenuous" to say that the legislation's effect on women was unintended "in the sense that [it] was not volitional or in the sense that [it] was not foreseeable." But

"discriminatory purpose" [implies] more than intent as volition or intent as awareness of consequences. It implies that the decisionmaker [selected] or reaffirmed a
particular course of action at least in part "because of," not merely "in spite of" its
adverse effects upon an identifiable group. Yet nothing in the record demonstrates
that this preference for veterans was originally devised or subsequently re-enacted
because it would accomplish the collateral goal of keeping women in a stereotypic
or predefined place in the Massachusetts Civil Service.

Should the *Feeney* Court have focused on whether the Massachusetts legislature would have enacted the same preference if most veterans had been women?
For a discussion of some problems with this approach, see Seidman, Public Principle and Private Choice: The Uneasy Case for a Boundary Maintenance Theory of Constitutional Law, 96 Yale L.J. 1006, 1038-1039 (1987).

2. *Selective insensitivity and the criminal justice system.* The Court returned
to the problem of defining discriminatory purpose in a criminal justice context
in United States v. Armstrong, 517 U.S. 456 (1996). Armstrong, an African-
American, had been charged with conspiring to possess with intent to distribute
"crack" cocaine. He sought discovery from the prosecution to gather evidence supporting his claim that the government was not prosecuting similarly situated sus-
pects of other races. The court of appeals upheld an order granting this request.
In an eight-to-one decision the Supreme Court, per Chief Justice Rehnquist, reversed, holding that the defendant had failed to make a threshold showing:

> To establish a discriminatory effect in a race case, the claimant must show that sim-
> ilarly situated individuals of a different race were not prosecuted. . . .
> [If] the claim of selective prosecution were well founded, it should not have
> been an insuperable task to prove that persons of other races were being treated dif-
> ferently than respondents. . . . [We] think the required threshold — a credible show-
> ing of different treatment of similarly situated persons — adequately balances the
> Government's interest in vigorous prosecution and the defendant's interest in avoid-
> ing selective prosecution. . . .
> The Court of Appeals reached its decision in part because it started "with the
> presumption that people of *all* races commit *all types of crimes* — not with the prem-
> ise that any type of crime is the exclusive province of any particular racial or eth-
> nic group." It cited no authority for this proposition, which seems contradicted by
> the most recent statistics of the United States Sentencing Commission. Those sta-
> tistics show that: More than 90% of the persons sentenced in 1994 for crack cocaine
> trafficking were black; 93.4% of convicted LSD dealers were white; and 91% of
> those convicted for pornography or prostitution were white. Presumptions at war
> with presumably reliable statistics have no proper place in the analysis of this issue.

Do statistics about racial differentials in sentencing and conviction refute
claims of racial discrimination in prosecution? Assuming that they do, how can
the Court's position in *Armstrong* be reconciled with *Batson* and other cases holding that the constitutional prohibition against race discrimination prevents the
state from relying on even accurate racial generalizations?

Note that Armstrong did not allege that the statutory penalties for possession
and distribution of "crack" were influenced by the racial composition of the class
charged with violating the statute. How should such a claim be evaluated?

3. *Classifications that describe racial minorities.* Should a statute be subject to strict scrutiny even if it does not use race per se as a classifying principle if it disadvantages individuals based on characteristics that effectively describe members of a minority race?

Suppose, for example, it could be shown that, as a statistical matter, African-Americans default on loans more frequently than other groups. Obviously a law requiring a state lender to charge higher interest rates to African-Americans would be subject to strict scrutiny. But suppose further there is a high degree of residential segregation in the state. It is therefore also possible to show a correlation between default rates and the zip code of the borrower — a correlation that is entirely the product of the fact that African-Americans live in the neighborhoods with high default rates. How should a court treat a statute requiring higher interest rates for borrowers with certain zip codes? Is such a statute subject only to low-level review because the purpose of its drafters was to avoid defaults rather than to harm African-Americans? Or is it subject to strict scrutiny because, whatever their purpose, the drafters of the statute are using zip codes as a proxy for race? Would the case be different if there was a high correlation between zip code and race, but the correlation between zip code and default rate was unrelated to race?

Consider Hernandez v. New York, 500 U.S. 352 (1991). Hernandez claimed that the prosecutor at his criminal trial had used peremptory challenges to exclude Latinos from the jury. The prosecutor told the trial judge that the challenges were based on his fear that the challenged bilingual jurors would have difficulty following only the official interpreter for Spanish-speaking witnesses rather than their own understanding of the testimony. The trial court rejected the defendant's claim, and the Supreme Court, in an opinion by Justice Kennedy, affirmed. According to the Court, this was a disparate impact case and therefore governed by Washington v. Davis:

> As explained by the prosecutor, the challenges rested neither on the intention to exclude Latino or bilingual jurors, nor on stereotypical assumptions about Latinos or bilinguals. The prosecutor's articulated basis for these challenges divided potential jurors into two classes: those whose conduct during the *voir dire* would persuade him they might have difficulty in accepting the translator's rendition of Spanish-language testimony and those potential jurors who gave no such reason for doubt. Each category would include both Latinos and non-Latinos. While the prosecutor's criterion might well result in the disproportionate removal of prospective Latino jurors, that disproportionate impact does not turn the prosecutor's actions into a *per se* violation of the Equal Protection Clause.

The Court went on to note, however, that it was not resolving the "more difficult question" of how the concept of racial classification should be defined:

> We would face a quite different case if the prosecutor had justified his peremptory challenges with the explanation that he did not want Spanish-speaking jurors. It may well be, for certain ethnic groups and in some communities, that proficiency in a particular language, like skin color, should be treated as a surrogate for race under equal protection analysis. And [a] policy of striking all who speak a given language, without regard to the particular circumstances of the trial or the individual responses of the jurors, may be found by the trial judge to be a pretext for racial discrimination. But that case is not before us.

Justice O'Connor, joined by Justice Scalia, concurred in the judgment:

> [I] believe that the plurality opinion goes farther than it needs to in assessing the constitutionality of the prosecutor's asserted justification for his peremptory strikes. . . .
>
> In this case, the prosecutor's asserted justification for striking certain Hispanic jurors was his uncertainty about the jurors' ability to accept the official translation of trial testimony. If this truly was the purpose of the strikes, they were not strikes because of race, and therefore did not violate the Equal Protection Clause. [They] may have acted like strikes based on race, but they were *not* based on race. No matter how closely tied or significantly correlated to race the explanation for a peremptory strike may be, the strike does not implicate the Equal Protection Clause unless it is based on race.

Compare *Hernandez* with Rice v. Cayetano, 120 S. Ct. 1044 (2000). The Hawaiian constitution establishes the Office of Hawaiian Affairs (OHA), which is vested with authority to administer revenue from land held in trust for the betterment of the conditions of the descendants of the indigenous people who inhabited the island in 1778, the date when England's Captain Cook made landfall in Hawaii. (The constitutionality of this arrangement was not before the Court, and the Court expressed no opinion on this subject.) The right to vote for the nine trustees composing the governing body of the OHA was limited to descendants of people inhabiting Hawaii in 1778. Petitioner challenged this limitation on the ground that it violated the fifteenth amendment prohibition against racial restrictions on the right to vote. In a seven-to-two decision, the Supreme Court, per Justice Kennedy, held that the restriction amounted to racial discrimination and, therefore, violated the amendment:

> Ancestry can be a proxy for race. It is that proxy here. Even if the residents of Hawaii in 1778 had been of more diverse ethnic backgrounds and cultures, it is far from clear that a voting test favoring their descendants would not be a race-based qualification. But that is not this case. For centuries Hawaii was isolated from migration. The inhabitants shared common physical characteristics, and by 1778 they had a common culture [The] provisions before us reflect the State's effort to preserve that commonality of people to the present day. . . .
>
> Simply because a class defined by ancestry does not include all members of the race does not suffice to make the classification race neutral. Here, the State's argument is undermined by its express racial purpose and by its actual effects.

Justice Stevens, in an opinion joined by Justice Ginsburg, dissented:

> The OHA voter qualification speaks in terms of ancestry and current residence, not of race or color. . . .
>
> Ancestry surely can be a proxy for race, or a pretext for invidious racial discrimination. But it is simply neither proxy nor pretext here. All of the persons who are eligible to vote for the trustees of OHA share two qualifications that no other person old enough to vote possesses: They are beneficiaries of the public trust created by the State and administered by OHA, and they have at least one ancestor who was a resident of Hawaii in 1778. A trust whose terms provide that the trustees shall be elected by a class including the beneficiaries is hardly a novel concept. . . .
>
> [The] OHA election provision excludes all full-blooded Polynesians currently residing in Hawaii who are not descended from a 1778 resident of Hawaii. Conversely, [the] OHA scheme excludes no descendant of a 1778 resident because he

or she is also part European, Asian, or African as a matter of race. The classification here is thus both too inclusive and not inclusive enough to fall strictly along racial lines.

Are *Hernandez* and *Cayetano* consistent?

Note: The Problem of Proof

Stated abstractly, there appears to be a sharp distinction between a "purpose" and an "effects" test for the constitutionality of facially neutral statutes that disproportionately disadvantage racial minorities. In practical effect, however, the importance of the distinction turns on the willingness of courts to infer discriminatory purpose from either discriminatory effect or the absence of other plausible purposes. The more willing the courts are to infer purpose from effect or to insist on proof of important nondiscriminatory purposes, the less important the distinction is. In *Arlington Heights* and *McCleskey*, the Court maintained a fairly sharp distinction between the treatment of race-specific classifications on the one hand, and facially neutral classifications with a disproportionate racial impact on the other. In other contexts, however, the Court has been more willing to infer purpose from effect and to evaluate the strength of a putative permissible purpose in deciding whether the actual purpose of a facially neutral statute is discriminatory.

1. *The jury cases.* When jury selection procedures are challenged as racially discriminatory, the Court has been receptive to arguments based on effect alone, at least as a device for shifting the burden of proof to the state. Castaneda v. Partida, 430 U.S. 482 (1977), sets out the standard method of proof:

> [In] order to show that an equal protection violation has occurred [the] defendant must show that the procedure employed resulted in substantial underrepresentation of his race or of the identifiable groups to which he belongs. The first step is to establish that the group is one that is a recognizable, distinct class, singled out for different treatment under the laws, as written or as applied. [Next,] the degree of underrepresentation must be proved, by comparing the proportion of the group in the total population to the proportion called to serve as [jurors], over a significant period of time. [Finally, a] selection procedure that is susceptible of abuse or is not racially neutral supports the presumption of discrimination raised by the statistical showing. [Once] the defendant has shown substantial underrepresentation of his group, he has made out a prima facie case of discriminatory purpose, and the burden then shifts to the State to rebut that case.

What explains the Court's greater willingness to infer purpose from effect in the jury context?

2. *The school desegregation cases.* Review pages 446-474 supra. Swann v. Charlotte-Mecklenburg Board of Education, section A4 supra, establishes that important inferences about the constitutional adequacy of a school desegregation plan can be drawn from its effect. Thus, there is a presumption against plans providing for one-race schools, and mathematical ratios can serve as "a starting point in the process of shaping a remedy." Moreover, the state interests in avoiding student transportation and maintaining compact attendance zones, although rational, are not sufficiently weighty to establish the constitutionality of neighborhood schools. Can *Swann* be distinguished from *Arlington Heights* and *McCles-*

key on the ground that it speaks to the remedies for constitutional violations rather than to the proof necessary to establish the violation? Is this distinction consistent with the assertions in *Swann* that "judicial powers may be exercised only on the basis of a constitutional violation," and that "the nature of the violation determines the scope of the remedy"? Why couldn't an effects test be justified in cases such as Washington v. Davis and Personnel Administrator of Massachusetts v. Feeney on a remedial theory?

3. *The vote-dilution cases.* What sort of proof of discriminatory purpose suffices when a particular electoral system is challenged on the ground that it results in inadequate representation of minority groups? Rogers v. Lodge, 458 U.S. 613 (1982), concerned an equal protection attack on an at-large voting system that effectively submerged the black minority of voters. Although blacks composed 53.6 percent of the population and 38 percent of the registered voters in Burke County, Georgia, no black had ever been elected to the county's Board of Commissioners. The district court struck down the system of at-large elections, holding that the system had a racially neutral purpose when adopted but was maintained for the purpose of diluting black voting strength. The Court affirmed in an opinion written by Justice White, which seemed to demonstrate much more willingness to infer purpose from effect than *Arlington Heights* standing alone would suggest. Thus, the Court held that the fact that no black had ever been elected to the board was "important evidence of purposeful exclusion." While this evidence alone was insufficient to establish discriminatory purpose, the district court's conclusion was also supported by findings of past discrimination in voting and schooling that limited black participation in the political process, the unresponsiveness of elected officials to black concerns, and the depressed socioeconomic status of blacks. Moreover, the size of the district made it difficult for blacks to get to polling places, and the absence of residency requirements meant that all candidates could reside in "lily-white" neighborhoods.

What explains the Court's reliance on effect in this context? For a discussion of the role of purpose and effect in evaluating the constitutionality of districts drawn so as to avoid subsuming minorities in majority districts, see pages 543-553 infra.

3. *Race-Specific Classifications That Are Facially Neutral*

Loving v. Virginia

388 U.S. 1 (1967)

MR. CHIEF JUSTICE WARREN delivered the opinion of the Court.

This case presents a constitutional question never addressed by this Court: whether a statutory scheme adopted by the State of Virginia to prevent marriages between persons solely on the basis of racial classifications violates the Equal Protection and Due Process Clauses of the Fourteenth Amendment. For reasons which seem to us to reflect the central meaning of those constitutional commands, we conclude that these statutes cannot stand consistently with the Fourteenth Amendment. . . .

[The Lovings challenged their conviction under a Virginia statute making it a felony for "any white person [to] intermarry with a colored person, or any colored person [to] intermarry with a white person." The Supreme Court of Appeals of Virginia upheld the statute's constitutionality. The state court relied on its own earlier decision holding that the statute served the legitimate state purposes of preserving the "racial integrity" of its citizens and preventing "corruption of blood," the creation of "a mongrel breed of citizens," and "the obliteration of racial pride."]

[The] State argues that the meaning of the Equal Protection Clause, as illuminated by the statements of the Framers, is only that state penal laws containing an interracial element as part of the definition of the offense must apply equally to whites and Negroes in the sense that members of each race are punished to the same degree. Thus, the State contends that, because its miscegenation statutes punish equally both the white and the Negro participants in an interracial marriage, these statutes, despite their reliance on racial classifications, do not constitute an invidious discrimination based upon race. . . .

Because we reject the notion that the mere "equal application" of a statute containing racial classifications is enough to remove the classifications from the Fourteenth Amendment's proscription of all invidious racial discriminations, we do not accept the State's contention that these statutes should be upheld if there is any possible basis for concluding that they serve a rational purpose. The mere fact of equal application does not mean that our analysis of these statutes should follow the approach we have taken in cases involving no racial discrimination. . . .

[T]he Equal Protection Clause requires the consideration of whether the classifications drawn by any statute constitute an arbitrary and invidious discrimination. The clear and central purpose of the Fourteenth Amendment was to eliminate all official state sources of invidious racial discrimination in the States.

There can be no question but that Virginia's miscegenation statutes rest solely upon distinctions drawn according to race. The statutes proscribe generally accepted conduct if engaged in by members of different races. [At] the very least, the Equal Protection Clause demands that racial classifications, especially suspect in criminal statutes, be subjected to the "most rigid scrutiny," [*Korematsu*], and, if they are ever to be upheld, they must be shown to be necessary to the accomplishment of some permissible state objective, independent of the racial discrimination which it was the object of the Fourteenth Amendment to eliminate. . . .

There is patently no legitimate overriding purpose independent of invidious racial discrimination which justifies this classification. The fact that Virginia prohibits only interracial marriages involving white persons demonstrates that the racial classifications must stand on their own justification, as measures designed to maintain White Supremacy.[11] We have consistently denied the constitutionality of measures which restrict the rights of citizens on account of race. There can be no doubt that restricting the freedom to marry solely because of racial classifications violates the central meaning of the Equal Protection Clause. . . .

---

11. Appellants point out that the State's concern in these statutes, as expressed in the words of the 1924 Act's title, "An Act to Preserve Racial Integrity," extends only to the integrity of the white race. While Virginia prohibits whites from marrying any nonwhite, [Negroes], Orientals, and any other racial class may intermarry without statutory interference. Appellants contend that this distinction renders Virginia's miscegenation statutes arbitrary and unreasonable even assuming the constitutional validity of an official purpose to preserve "racial integrity." We need not reach this contention because we find the racial classifications in these statutes repugnant to the Fourteenth Amendment, even assuming an even-handed state purpose to protect the "integrity" of all races.

These convictions must be reversed.
It is so ordered.

MR. JUSTICE STEWART, concurring.

I have previously expressed the belief that "it is simply not possible for a state law to be valid under our Constitution which makes the criminality of an act depend upon the race of the actor." McLaughlin v. Florida, 379 U.S. 184, 198 (concurring opinion). Because I adhere to that belief, I concur in the judgment of the Court.

Washington v. Seattle School District No. 1

458 U.S. 457 (1982)

JUSTICE BLACKMUN delivered the opinion of the Court.

We are presented here with an extraordinary question: whether an elected local school board may use the Fourteenth Amendment to *defend* its program of busing for integration from attack by the State.

[In 1978, the Seattle School Board voluntarily adopted a plan to alleviate racial isolation in the schools. The plan made extensive use of busing and mandatory reassignment. Opponents of the plan responded by drafting a statewide initiative designed to terminate use of mandatory busing for purposes of racial integration. The proposal, known as Initiative 350, prohibited school boards from requiring students to attend schools not nearest or next nearest to their place of residence. The initiative included a series of exceptions, however, which permitted such assignments for a variety of nonracial reasons, such as overcrowding or special education needs. It also permitted racial reassignments when a court found that they were constitutionally required.

[The initiative was adopted by a substantial statewide majority, including a majority of Seattle voters. The Seattle School Board thereupon initiated this litigation challenging the constitutionality of the initiative under the equal protection clause of the fourteenth amendment. The district court held that the initiative was unconstitutional, and the court of appeals affirmed.]

II

The Equal Protection Clause of the Fourteenth Amendment guarantees racial minorities the right to full participation in the political life of the community. It is beyond dispute, of course, that given racial or ethnic groups may not be denied the franchise, or precluded from entering into the political process in a reliable and meaningful manner. But the Fourteenth Amendment also reaches "a political structure that treats all individuals as equals," Mobile v. Bolden, 446 U.S. 55, 84 (1980) (Stevens, J., concurring in the judgment), yet more subtly distorts governmental processes in such a way as to place special burdens on the ability of minority groups to achieve beneficial legislation.

This principle received its clearest expression in Hunter v. Erickson, [393 U.S. 385 (1969)], a case that involved attempts to overturn antidiscrimination legislation in Akron, Ohio. The Akron city council, pursuant to its ordinary legislative processes, had enacted a fair housing ordinance. In response, the local citizenry, using an established referendum procedure, amended the city charter to provide that ordinances regulating real estate transactions "on the basis of race, color, religion, national origin or ancestry must first be approved by a majority of the electors voting on the question at a regular or general election before said ordinance shall be effective." This action "not only suspended the operation of the existing ordinance forbidding housing discrimination, but also required the approval of the electors before any future [fair housing] ordinance could take effect." In essence, the amendment changed the requirements for the adoption of one type of local legislation: to enact an ordinance barring housing discrimination on the basis of race or religion, proponents had to obtain the approval of the city council *and* of a majority of the voters citywide. To enact an ordinance preventing housing discrimination on other grounds, or to enact any other type of housing ordinance, proponents needed the support of only the city council.

In striking down the charter amendment, the *Hunter* Court recognized that, on its face, the provision "draws no distinctions among racial and religious groups." But it did differentiate "between those groups who sought the law's protection against racial . . . discriminations in the sale and rental of real estate and those who sought to regulate real property transactions in the pursuit of other ends," thus "disadvantag[ing] those who would benefit from laws barring racial . . . discriminations as against those who would bar other discriminations or who would otherwise regulate the real estate market in their favor." In "reality," the burden imposed by such an arrangement necessarily "falls on the minority. The majority needs no protection against discrimination and if it did, a referendum might be bothersome but no more than that." In effect, then, the charter amendment served as an "explicitly racial classification treating racial housing matters differently from other racial and housing matters." This made the amendment constitutionally suspect: "the State may no more disadvantage any *particular* group by making it more difficult to enact legislation in its behalf than it may dilute any person's vote or give any group a smaller representation than another of comparable size." . . .

[This case yields] a simple but central principle. [The] political majority may generally restructure the political process to place obstacles in the path of everyone seeking to secure the benefits of governmental action. But a different analysis is required when the State allocates governmental power non-neutrally, by explicitly using the *racial* nature of a decision to determine the decisionmaking process. State action of this kind, the Court said, "places *special* burdens on racial minorities within the governmental process. . . ."

III

In our view, Initiative 350 must fall because it does "not attemp[t] to allocate governmental power on the basis of any general principle." Hunter v. Erickson. Instead, it uses the racial nature of an issue to define the governmental decisionmaking structure, and thus imposes substantial and unique burdens on racial minorities.

A

Noting that Initiative 350 nowhere mentions "race" or "integration," appellants suggest that the legislation has no racial overtones; they maintain that *Hunter* is inapposite because the initiative simply permits busing for certain enumerated purposes while neutrally forbidding it for all other reasons. We find it difficult to believe that appellants' analysis is seriously advanced, however, for despite its facial neutrality there is little doubt that the initiative was effectively drawn for racial purposes. [It] is beyond reasonable dispute, then, that the initiative was enacted "'because of,' not merely 'in spite of,' its adverse effects upon" busing for integration. Personnel Administrator of Massachusetts v. Feeney. . . .

[It] undoubtedly is true, as the United States suggests, that the proponents of mandatory integration cannot be classified by race: Negroes and whites may be counted among both the supporters and the opponents of Initiative 350. And it should be equally clear that white as well as Negro children benefit from exposure to "ethnic and racial diversity in the classroom." Columbus Board of Education v. Penick, 443 U.S. 449 (1979) (Powell, J., dissenting). But neither of these factors serves to distinguish *Hunter*, for we may fairly assume that members of the racial majority both favored and benefited from Akron's fair housing ordinance.

In any event, our cases suggest that desegregation of the public schools, like the Akron open housing ordinance, at bottom inures primarily to the benefit of the minority, and is designed for that purpose. . . .

B

We are also satisfied that the practical effect of Initiative 350 is to work a reallocation of power of the kind condemned in *Hunter*. The initiative removes the authority to address a racial problem — and only a racial problem — from the existing decisionmaking body, in such a way as to burden minority interests. . . .

The state appellants and the United States, in response to this line of analysis, argue that Initiative 350 has not worked *any* reallocation of power. They note that the State necessarily retains plenary authority over Washington's system of education, and therefore they suggest that the initiative amounts to nothing more than an unexceptional example of a State's intervention in its own school system. . . .

But "insisting that a State may distribute legislative power as it desires . . . furnish[es] no justification for a legislative structure which otherwise would violate the Fourteenth Amendment." [It] is irrelevant that the State might have vested all decisionmaking authority in itself, so long as the political structure it in fact erected imposes comparative burdens on minority interests; that much is settled by *Hunter*. And until the passage of Initiative 350, Washington law in fact had established the local school board, rather than the State, as the entity charged with making decisions of the type at issue here. . . .

[Before] adoption of the initiative, the power to determine what programs would most appropriately fill a school district's educational needs — including programs involving student assignment and desegregation — was firmly committed to the local board's discretion. The question whether to provide an integrated learning environment rather than a system of neighborhood schools surely involved a decision of that sort. After passage of Initiative 350, authority over all but one of those areas remained in the hands of the local board. By placing power over desegregative busing at the state level, then, Initiative 350 plainly "differentiates between the treatment of problems involving racial matters and that afforded other problems in the same area."[23] . . .

C

To be sure, "the simple repeal or modification of desegregation or antidiscrimination laws, without more, never has been viewed as embodying a presumptively invalid racial classification."

Initiative 350, however, works something more than the "mere repeal" of a desegregation law by the political entity that created it. It burdens all future attempts to integrate Washington schools in districts throughout the State, by lodging decisionmaking authority over the question at a new and remote level of government. Indeed, the initiative, like the charter amendment at issue in *Hunter*, has its most pernicious effect on integration programs that do "*not* arouse extraordinary controversy." In such situations the initiative makes the enactment of racially beneficial legislation difficult, though the particular program involved might not have inspired opposition had it been promulgated through the usual legislative processes used for comparable legislation. . . .

IV

In the end, appellants are reduced to suggesting that *Hunter* has been effectively overruled by more recent decisions of this Court. As they read it, *Hunter* applied a simple "disparate impact" analysis: it invalidated a facially neutral ordinance because of the law's adverse effects upon racial minorities. Appellants therefore contend that *Hunter* was swept away, along with the disparate impact approach to equal protection, in [Washington v. Davis]. . . .

There is one immediate and crucial difference between *Hunter* and the cases cited by appellants. While decisions such as [Washington v. Davis] considered classifications facially unrelated to race, the charter amendment at issue in *Hunter* dealt in explicitly racial terms with legislation designed to benefit minorities "as minorities," not legislation intended to benefit some larger group of underprivileged citizens among whom minorities were disproportionately represented. This does not mean, of course, that every attempt to address a racial issue

23. Throughout his dissent, Justice Powell insists that the Court has created a "vested constitutional right to local decisionmaking," that under our holding "the people of the State of Washington apparently are forever barred from developing a different policy on mandatory busing where a School District previously has adopted one of its own," and that today's decision somehow raises doubts about "the authority of a State to abolish school boards altogether." These statements evidence a basic misunderstanding of our decision. Our analysis vests no rights, and has nothing to do with whether school board action predates that taken by the State. Instead, what we find objectionable about Initiative 350 is the comparative burden it imposes on minority participation in the political process — that is, the racial nature of the way in which it structures the *process* of decisionmaking. It is evident, then, that the horribles paraded by the dissent — which have nothing to do with the ability of minorities to participate in the process of self-government — are entirely unrelated to this case. It is equally clear, as we have noted at several points in our opinion, that the State remains free to vest all decisionmaking power in state officials, or to remove authority from local school boards in a race-neutral manner.

gives rise to an impermissible racial classification. But when the political process or the decisionmaking mechanism used to *address* racially conscious legislation — and only such legislation — is singled out for peculiar and disadvantageous treatment, the governmental action plainly "rests on 'distinctions based on
race.'"[29] And when the State's allocation of power places unusual burdens on the
ability of racial groups to enact legislation specifically designed to overcome the
"special condition" of prejudice, the governmental action seriously "curtail[s]
the operation of those political processes ordinarily to be relied upon to protect
minorities." [*Carolene Products.*] In a most direct sense, this implicates the judiciary's special role in safeguarding the interests of those groups that are "relegated
to such a position of political powerlessness as to command extraordinary protection from the majoritarian political process." . . .

Accordingly, the judgment of the Court of Appeals is affirmed.

JUSTICE POWELL, with whom [CHIEF JUSTICE BURGER], JUSTICE REHNQUIST,
and JUSTICE O'CONNOR join, dissenting. . . .

[In] the absence of a prior constitutional violation, the States are under no constitutional duty to adopt integration programs in their schools, and certainly they
are under no duty to establish a regime of mandatory busing. Nor does the Federal Constitution require that particular decisions concerning the schools or any
other matter be made on the local as opposed to the State level. . . .

Application of these settled principles demonstrates the serious error of today's
decision — an error that cuts deeply into the heretofore unquestioned right of a
State to structure the decisionmaking authority of its government. In this case, by
Initiative 350, the State has adopted a policy of racial neutrality in student assignments. The policy in no way interferes with the power of State or Federal
Courts to remedy constitutional violations. And if such a policy had been adopted
by any of the school districts in this litigation there could have been no question
that the policy was constitutional.

The issue here arises only because the Seattle School District — in the absence of a then established State policy — chose to adopt race specific school assignments with extensive busing. It is not questioned that the District itself, at any
time thereafter, could have changed its mind and cancelled its integration program without violating the Federal Constitution. Yet this Court holds that neither
the legislature nor the people of the State of Washington could alter what the District had decided.

The Court argues that the people of Washington by Initiative 350 created a racial classification, and yet must agree that identical action by the Seattle School
District itself would have created no such classification. This is not an easy argument to answer because it seems to make no sense. School boards are the creation
of supreme State authority, whether in a State Constitution or by legislative enactment. Until today's decision no one would have questioned the authority of a
State to abolish school boards altogether, or to require that they conform to any
lawful State policy. And in the State of Washington, a neighborhood school policy would have been lawful.

29. Thus we do not hold, as the dissent implies, that the State's attempt to repeal a desegregation program creates a racial classification, while "identical action" by the Seattle School Board
does not. It is the State's race-conscious restructuring of its decisionmaking process that is impermissible, not the simple repeal of the Seattle Plan.

Under today's decision this heretofore undoubted supreme authority of a State's electorate is to be curtailed whenever a school board — or indeed any other state board or local instrumentality — adopts a race specific program that arguably benefits racial minorities. Once such a program is adopted, *only* the local or subordinate entity that approved it will have authority to change it. The Court offers no authority or relevant explanation for this extraordinary subordination of the ultimate sovereign power of a State to act with respect to racial matters by subordinate bodies. It is a strange notion — alien to our system — that local governmental bodies can forever preempt the ability of a State — the sovereign power — to address a matter of compelling concern to the State. The Constitution of the United States does not require such a bizarre result. . . .

[Initiative] 350 places no "special burdens on racial minorities within the governmental process," [*Hunter*], such that interference with the State's distribution of authority is justified. Initiative 350 is simply a reflection of the State's political process at work. It does not alter that process in any respect. It does not require, for example, that all matters dealing with race — or with integration in the schools — must henceforth be submitted to a referendum of the people. Cf. Hunter v. Erickson, supra. The State has done no more than precisely what the Court has said that it should do: It has "resolved through the political process" the "desirability and efficacy of [mandatory] school desegregation" where there has been no unlawful segregation.

The political process in Washington, as in other States, permits persons who are dissatisfied at a local level to appeal to the State legislature or the people of the State for redress. It permits the people of a State to preempt local policies, and to formulate new programs and regulations. Such a process is inherent in the continued sovereignty of the States. This is our system. Any time a State chooses to address a major issue some persons or groups may be disadvantaged. In a democratic system there are winners and losers. But there is no inherent unfairness in this and certainly no Constitutional violation. . . .

Nothing in *Hunter* supports the Court's extraordinary invasion into the State's distribution of authority. [In] this case, unlike in *Hunter*, the political system has *not* been redrawn or altered. The authority of the State over the public school system, acting through Initiative or the legislature, is plenary. Thus, the State's political system is not altered when it adopts for the first time a policy, concededly within the area of its authority, for the regulation of local school [districts.]

Hunter, therefore, is simply irrelevant. It is the *Court* that by its decision today disrupts the normal course of State government. Under its unprecedented theory of a vested constitutional right to local decisionmaking, the State apparently is now forever barred from addressing the perplexing problems of how best to educate fairly *all* children in a multi-racial society where, as in this case, the local school board has acted first.[16] . . .

16. Responding to this dissent, the Court denies that its opinion limits the authority of the people of the State of Washington and the Legislature to control or regulate school boards. It further states that "the State remains free to vest all decisionmaking power in state officials, or to remove authority from local school boards in a race-neutral manner." These are puzzling statements that seem entirely at odds with much of the text of the Court's opinion. It will be surprising if officials of the State of Washington — with the one exception mentioned below — will have any clear idea as to what the State now lawfully may do.

The Court does say that "[i]t is the State's race-conscious restructuring of its decisionmaking process that is impermissible, not the simple repeal of the Seattle plan." Apparently the Court is

Note: Strict Scrutiny for "Neutral" Race-Specific Classifications

1. *Why strict scrutiny?* Compare Chief Justice Warren's opinion in *Loving* with his opinion in Brown v. Board of Education (*Brown I*), page 446 supra. Does *Loving* provide a more satisfactory account of why neutral race-specific laws are strictly scrutinized?

What class of people was disadvantaged by the statute invalidated in *Loving*? Since the class necessarily includes an equal number of blacks and whites (for every black/white marriage, there must be one black and one white who wish to marry each other), how can the Court say that the statute constitutes "invidious racial discrimination"? Is the point that in a culture dominated by whites, blacks are harmed more than whites by laws separating the races or suggesting that race is a relevant factor in decisionmaking? That because there are fewer blacks than whites, a higher percentage of the total black community will be prospective partners in mixed-race marriages? Why should these disproportionate impact arguments trigger strict scrutiny when the disproportionate impact shown in Washington v. Davis did not?

Is the point that race-specific classifications, even when facially neutral, are particularly likely to be motivated by race prejudice? See Palmore v. Sidoti, page 513 supra: "Classifying persons according to their race is more likely to reflect racial prejudice than legitimate public concerns; the race, not the person, dictates the category."

Compare Justice Scalia's dissenting opinion in Powers v. Ohio, 499 U.S. 400 (1991), criticizing the Court's invalidation of racially based peremptory challenges:

> [When a] group, like all others, has been made subject to peremptory challenge on the basis of its group characteristic, its members have been treated not differently but the same. In fact, it would constitute discrimination to exempt them from the peremptory-strike exposure to which all others are subject. . . .
>
> Unlike the categorical exclusion of a group from jury service, which implies that all its members are incompetent or untrustworthy, a peremptory strike on the basis of group membership implies nothing more than the undeniable reality [that] all groups tend to have particular sympathies and hostilities. [Since] that reality is acknowledged as to all groups, and forms the basis for peremptory strikes as to all of them, there is no implied criticism or dishonor to a strike.

In his opinion for the Court, Justice Kennedy responded as follows:

> We reject [the] view that race-based peremptory challenges survive equal protection scrutiny because members of all races are subject to like treatment, which is to say that white jurors are subject to the same risk of peremptory challenges based on race as are all other jurors. The suggestion that racial classifications may survive when visited upon all persons is no more authoritative today than the case which

---

saying that, despite what else may be said in its opinion, the people of the State — or the State legislature — may repeal the *Seattle plan*, even though neither the people nor the legislature validly may prescribe statewide standards. I perceive no logic in — and certainly no constitutional basis for — a distinction between repealing the Seattle plan of mandatory busing and establishing a statewide policy to the same effect. The people of a State have far greater interest in the general problems associated with compelled busing for purpose of integration than in the plan of a single school board.

advanced the theorem, Plessy v. Ferguson. This idea has no place in our modern equal protection jurisprudence. It is axiomatic that racial classifications do not become legitimate on the assumption that all persons suffer them in equal degree. Loving v. Virginia.

2. *What makes a neutral statute race-specific?* The antimiscegenation statute invalidated in *Loving* was race-specific in the sense that the legal consequence of a marriage turned on the races of the married couple. But the statute invalidated in *Seattle* nowhere mentioned race. What made it race-specific and therefore subject to strict scrutiny?

Compare *Seattle* with James v. Valtierra, 402 U.S. 137 (1971), where the Court upheld a provision of the California Constitution prohibiting state entities from constructing low-rent housing projects unless approved by a majority of those voting in a community election. The Court held that the provision was not a racial classification, since it "[required] referendum approval for any low-rent public housing project, not only for projects which will be occupied by a racial minority. And the record here would not support any claim that a law seemingly neutral on its face is in fact aimed at a racial minority." Can this language be reconciled with the *Seattle* Court's holding that Initiative 350 was race-specific because school desegregation "inures primarily to the benefit of the minority," and because, "[i]n 'reality,' the burden imposed by [the Initiative] necessarily 'falls on the minority'" (quoting from Hunter v. Erickson). Is *Seattle* consistent with Washington v. Davis, where the Court treated state actions disproportionately burdening blacks as facially neutral? Note that the Court in *Seattle* distinguishes *Davis* on the ground that it "considered classifications facially unrelated to race." Does this distinction beg the very question the Court is attempting to answer?

3. Seattle *and* Crawford. In Crawford v. Board of Education, 458 U.S. 527 (1982), decided on the same day as *Seattle*, the Court upheld an amendment to the California Constitution prohibiting state courts from ordering mandatory pupil assignment or transportation unless a federal court would do so to remedy a violation of the federal equal protection clause. The amendment followed a decision by the California Supreme Court interpreting the state constitution as prohibiting de facto segregation and ordering "reasonable steps" to alleviate it. Can the results in *Seattle* and *Crawford* be reconciled? (In fact, five of the nine justices thought that the cases were indistinguishable; the Court reached different results only because this majority was divided between four justices who thought that both measures were constitutional and one justice who thought that both were unconstitutional.) The majority opinion in *Crawford* was written by Justice Powell, a *Seattle* dissenter. He argued that the California measure did not embody a racial classification:

> It neither says nor implies that persons are to be treated differently on account of their race. It simply forbids state courts to order pupil school assignment or transportation in the absence of a Fourteenth Amendment violation. The benefit it seeks to confer — neighborhood schooling — is made available regardless of race in the discretion of school [boards].

Nor did the provision distort the political process: "[Having] gone beyond the requirements of the Federal Constitution, the State was free to return in part to the standard prevailing generally throughout the United States."

Justice Blackmun, the author of *Seattle*, concurred, emphasizing the "critical distinctions" between the two cases:

> State courts do not create the rights they enforce; those rights originate elsewhere — in the state legislature, in the States' political subdivisions, or in the state constitution itself. When one of those rights is repealed, and therefore is rendered unenforceable in the courts, that action hardly can be said to restructure the State's decisionmaking mechanism. While the California electorate may have made it more difficult to achieve desegregation when it enacted [the amendment], it did so not by working a structural change in the political *process* so much as by simply repealing the right to invoke a judicial busing remedy.

Does this distinction make sense?

4. *The source of the difficulty.* Consider the possibility that *Seattle* and *Crawford* are hard cases because they force the court to reconcile two lines of authority that are ultimately inconsistent. On the one hand, Washington v. Davis and its progeny suggest an approach to the race problem that eschews an effort to guarantee any substantive position for blacks in U.S. society. Rather than focusing on the substantive content of statutes affecting blacks, it directs attention to the process by which the statutes are enacted. Thus, facially neutral statutes that have an adverse impact on blacks are subject only to rational basis review, so long as the process by which they are enacted is not infected by an illegitimate purpose. These precedents inevitably channeled the Court's *Seattle* and *Crawford* opinions into a discussion of whether the political process had been unfairly restructured. On the other hand, *Loving*, as well as its lineal antecedent Brown v. Board of Education, are fundamentally inconsistent with this process approach. These cases can be read as outlawing certain outcomes of even a "fair" process when those outcomes disadvantage blacks in certain ways. They suggest that race-specific classifications are evil because their effect, at least in our culture, is to leave blacks in a permanently subservient position. In *Seattle* and *Crawford*, the analogy to *Brown* and *Loving* was too close for the Court to ignore. Yet it is hardly surprising that the Court failed to pursue the logic of these precedents. To do so would require the justices to articulate and justify a substantive theory about the distribution of resources among groups in our society, and the Court is simply not prepared to undertake that task.

Note: The Special Problem of Facially Neutral but Race-Specific Voting Districts

1. *The problem.* Should *Brown*, *Loving*, and *Washington* apply when racial criteria influence electoral districting decisions? Gomillion v. Lightfoot, page 521 supra, and Rogers v. Lodge, page 533 supra, establish that when districts are purposely "gerrymandered" so as to reduce the voting power of minorities, or when minority representation is purposely diluted, the districting is subject to strict scrutiny even when the lines are drawn in a facially neutral fashion. This is so because the lines have both the purpose and the effect of harming a racial minority. In contrast, if districting lines are drawn so as to magnify minority voting strength, they would presumably be judged according to standards developed to

deal with "affirmative action" programs. (These standards are discussed in section C4 infra.)

The problem is more complex when a legislature draws district lines in a fashion designed accurately to *reflect*, rather than to reduce or to enhance, overall minority voting strength. Suppose, for example, that 30 percent of a state's population is African-American, but African-Americans are spread widely throughout the state. If district lines are drawn according to "traditional" districting criteria (e.g., geographically compact districts) and if there is racial bloc voting, the result may be that African-American votes are "diluted" by forming only an insubstantial minority in each district. Is it permissible for the state to counteract this effect by deliberately drawing district lines so as to ensure that 30 percent of the districts have African-American majorities? On the one hand, state efforts to ensure that groups are represented in proportion to their numbers might be thought desirable and, perhaps, even constitutionally mandatory. Yet on the other hand, deliberately placing individuals within districts based on race might be thought to run afoul of the prohibition on even facially neutral race-specific classifications.

2. *Shaw.* In Shaw v. Reno, 509 U.S. 630 (1993), plaintiffs challenged the constitutionality of a state reapportionment plan that included one "majority-minority" district with what the Court characterized as a "dramatically irregular" shape. In a five-to-four decision, the Court, per Justice O'Connor, held that the plaintiffs had stated a cognizable claim. The Court explained that

> [Appellants] did not claim that the General Assembly's reapportionment plan unconstitutionally "diluted" white voting strength. They did not even claim to be white. Rather, appellants' complaint alleged that the deliberate segregation of voters into separate districts on the basis of race violated their constitutional right to participate in a "color-blind" electoral process.

In the course of evaluating this claim, the Court made clear that it was not suggesting that race-conscious districting was impermissible in all circumstances. Instead, it held that districting was unconstitutional when "though race-neutral on its face, [it] rationally cannot be understood as anything other than an effort to separate voters into different districts on the basis of race, and that the separation lacks sufficient justification." This might be the case, for example, when a state "concentrated a dispersed minority population in a single district by disregarding traditional districting principles such as compactness, contiguity, and respect for political subdivisions." As the Court explained:

> [We] believe that reapportionment is one area in which appearances do matter. A reapportionment plan that includes in one district individuals who belong to the same race, but who are otherwise widely separated by geographical and political boundaries, and who may have little in common with one another but the color of their skin, bears an uncomfortable resemblance to political apartheid. It reinforces the perception that members of the same racial group — regardless of their age, education, economic status, or the community in which they live — think alike, share the same political interests, and will prefer the same candidates at the polls. We have rejected such perceptions elsewhere as impermissible racial stereotypes. By perpetuating such notions, a racial gerrymander may exacerbate the very patterns of racial bloc voting the majority-minority districting is sometimes said to counteract.

3. *Remaining questions.* The *Shaw* Court decided only that plaintiffs had presented a cognizable claim. The opinion left many questions unanswered, including whether "bizarreness" of shape was a necessary part of the claim itself or whether it was relevant only as evidence of a racial purpose; when might a compelling state interest justify racially based districting; and what to do about "mixed motive" cases when bizarrely shaped districts result from the intersection of ordinary political considerations and racial criteria. Consider whether the Court's subsequent decisions provide adequate answers to these questions.

Miller v. Johnson

515 U.S. 90 (1995)

JUSTICE KENNEDY delivered the opinion of the Court. . . .

In Shaw v. Reno, we held that a plaintiff states a claim under the Equal Protection Clause by alleging that a state redistricting plan, on its face, has no rational explanation save as an effort to separate voters on the basis of race. The question we now decide is whether Georgia's new Eleventh District gives rise to a valid equal protection claim under the principles announced in *Shaw*, and, if so, whether it can be sustained nonetheless as narrowly tailored to serve a compelling governmental interest.

I . . .

Between 1980 and 1990, one of Georgia's 10 congressional districts was a majority-black district, that is, a majority of the district's voters were black. The 1990 Decennial Census indicated that Georgia's population of 6,478,216 persons, 27% of whom are black, entitled it to an additional eleventh congressional seat, prompting Georgia's General Assembly to redraw the State's congressional districts. Both the House and the Senate adopted redistricting guidelines which, among other things, required single-member districts of equal population, contiguous geography, nondilution of minority voting strength, fidelity to precinct lines where possible, and compliance with [the Voting Rights Act of 1965]. . . .

[The Voting Rights Act prohibits any practice or procedure that "results in the denial or abridgement of the right of any citizen [to] vote on account of race or color." A practice or procedure has such a result if "based on the totality of circumstances, it is shown that the political processes leading to nomination or election in the State or political subdivision are not equally open to participation by members of the [protected] class of citizens [in] that members have less opportunity than other members of the electorate to participate in the political process and to elect representatives of their choice." In addition, certain covered jurisdictions are required to "preclear" with the Attorney General or with the United States District Court of the District of Columbia any change in a "standard, practice, or procedure with respect to voting." Preclearance is granted if the change does "not have the purpose and will not have the effect of denying or abridging the right to vote on account of race or color." The act is discussed in greater detail at pages 221-222 supra.]

A special session opened in August 1991, and the General Assembly submitted a congressional redistricting plan to the Attorney General for preclearance on October 1, 1991. [The Attorney General rejected the plan, which provided for two majority-minority districts, as well as a second plan, which also provided for only two such districts. In doing so, the Attorney General relied] on alternative plans proposing three majority-minority districts. One of the alternative schemes relied on by the Department was the so-called "max-black" plan, drafted by the American Civil Liberties Union (ACLU) for the General Assembly's black caucus. [Twice] spurned, the General Assembly set out to create three majority-minority districts to gain preclearance. Using the ACLU's "max-black" plan as its benchmark, the General Assembly enacted a plan that "bore all the signs of [the Justice Department's] involvement." [The] Eleventh District lost the black population of Macon, but picked up Savannah, thereby connecting the black neighborhoods of metropolitan Atlanta and the poor black populace of coastal Chatham County, though 260 miles apart in distance and worlds apart in culture. In short, the social, political and economic makeup of the Eleventh District tells a tale of disparity, not community. . . .

The Almanac of American Politics has this to say about the Eleventh District: "Geographically, it is a monstrosity, stretching from Atlanta to Savannah. Its core is the plantation country in the center of the state, lightly populated, but heavily black. It links by narrow corridors the black neighborhoods in Augusta, Savannah and southern DeKalb County." M. Barone & G. Ujifusa, Almanac of American Politics 356 (1994). Georgia's plan included three majority-black districts, though, and received Justice Department preclearance on April 2, 1992. . . .

II

A

Finding that the "evidence of the General Assembly's intent to racially gerrymander the Eleventh District is overwhelming, and practically stipulated by the parties involved," the District Court held that race was the predominant, overriding factor in drawing the Eleventh District. Appellants do not take issue with the court's factual finding of this racial motivation. Rather, they contend that evidence of a legislature's deliberate classification of voters on the basis of race cannot alone suffice to state a claim under *Shaw*. They argue that, regardless of the legislature's purposes, a plaintiff must demonstrate that a district's shape is so bizarre that it is unexplainable other than on the basis of race, and that appellees failed to make that showing here. Appellants' conception of the constitutional violation misapprehends our holding in *Shaw* and the Equal Protection precedent upon which *Shaw* relied.

[Just] as the State may not, absent extraordinary justification, segregate citizens on the basis of race in its public parks, buses, golf courses, beaches, and schools, so did we recognize in *Shaw* that it may not separate its citizens into different voting districts on the basis of race. . . .

Our observation in *Shaw* of the consequences of racial stereotyping was not meant to suggest that a district must be bizarre on its face before there is a constitutional violation. [Shape] is relevant not because bizarreness is a necessary element of the constitutional wrong or a threshold requirement of proof, but because it may be persuasive circumstantial evidence that race for its own sake, and not other districting principles, was the legislature's dominant and controlling rationale in drawing its district lines. The logical implication, as courts applying *Shaw* have recognized, is that parties may rely on evidence other than bizarreness to establish race-based districting. . . .

[Appellants] and some of their amici argue that the Equal Protection Clause's general proscription on race-based decisionmaking does not obtain in the districting context because redistricting by definition involves racial considerations. Underlying their argument are the very stereotypical assumptions the Equal Protection Clause forbids. . . .

B

Federal court review of districting legislation represents a serious intrusion on the most vital of local functions. [The] distinction between being aware of racial considerations and being motivated by them may be difficult to make. This evidentiary difficulty, together with the sensitive nature of redistricting and the presumption of good faith that must be accorded legislative enactments, requires courts to exercise extraordinary caution in adjudicating claims that a state has drawn district lines on the basis of race. The plaintiff's burden is to show, either through circumstantial evidence of a district's shape and demographics or more direct evidence going to legislative purpose, that race was the predominant factor motivating the legislature's decision to place a significant number of voters within or without a particular district. To make this showing, a plaintiff must prove that the legislature subordinated traditional race-neutral districting principles, including but not limited to compactness, contiguity, respect for political subdivisions or communities defined by actual shared interests, to racial considerations. Where these or other race-neutral considerations are the basis for redistricting legislation, and are not subordinated to race, a state can "defeat a claim that a district has been gerrymandered on racial lines." . . .

In our view, the District Court applied the correct analysis, and its finding that race was the predominant factor motivating the drawing of the Eleventh District was not clearly erroneous. The court found it was "exceedingly obvious" from the shape of the Eleventh District, together with the relevant racial demographics, that the drawing of narrow land bridges to incorporate within the District outlying appendages containing nearly 80% of the district's total black population was a deliberate attempt to bring black populations into the district. Although by comparison with other districts the geometric shape of the Eleventh District may not seem bizarre on its face, when its shape is considered in conjunction with its racial and population densities, the story of racial gerrymandering seen by the District Court becomes much clearer. Although this evidence is quite compelling, we need not determine whether it was, standing alone, sufficient to establish a *Shaw* claim that the Eleventh District is unexplainable other than by race. The District Court had before it considerable additional evidence showing that the General Assembly was motivated by a predominant, overriding desire to assign black populations to the Eleventh District and thereby permit the creation of a third majority-black district in the Second.

The court found that "it became obvious," both from the Justice Department's objection letters and the three preclearance rounds in general, "that [the Justice Department] would accept nothing less than abject surrender to its maximization agenda." It further found that the General Assembly acquiesced and as a consequence was driven by its overriding desire to comply with the Department's maximization demands. . . .

III . . .

We do not accept the contention that the State has a compelling interest in complying with whatever preclearance mandates the Justice Department issues. When a state governmental entity seeks to justify race-based remedies to cure the effects of past discrimination, we do not accept the government's mere assertion that the remedial action is required. . . .

Georgia's drawing of the Eleventh District was not required under the Act because there was no reasonable basis to believe that Georgia's earlier enacted plans violated [the Act]. Wherever a plan is "ameliorative," a term we have used to describe plans increasing the number of majority-minority districts, it "cannot violate [the Act] unless the new apportionment itself so discriminates on the basis of race or color as to violate the Constitution." Georgia's first and second proposed plans increased the number of majority-black districts from 1 out of 10 (10%) to 2 out of 11 (18.18%). These plans were "ameliorative" and could not have violated [the Act]. . . .

Instead of grounding its objections on evidence of a discriminatory purpose, it would appear the Government was driven by its policy of maximizing majority-black districts. [In] utilizing [the Act] to require States to create majority-minority districts wherever possible, the Department of Justice expanded its authority under the statute beyond what Congress intended and we have upheld. . . .

JUSTICE O'CONNOR, concurring.

[To] invoke strict scrutiny, a plaintiff must show that the State has relied on race in substantial disregard of customary and traditional districting practices. Those practices provide a crucial frame of reference and therefore constitute a significant governing principle in cases of this kind. The standard would be no different if a legislature had drawn the boundaries to favor some other ethnic group; certainly the standard does not treat efforts to create majority-minority districts less favorably than similar efforts on behalf of other groups. Indeed, the driving force behind the adoption of the Fourteenth Amendment was the desire to end legal discrimination against blacks.

Application of the Court's standard does not throw into doubt the vast majority of the Nation's 435 congressional districts, where presumably the States have drawn the boundaries in accordance with their customary districting principles. That is so even though race may well have been considered in the redistricting process. But application of the Court's standard helps achieve Shaw's basic objective of making extreme instances of gerrymandering subject to meaningful judicial review. I therefore join the Court's opinion.

JUSTICE GINSBURG, with whom JUSTICES STEVENS and BREYER join, and with whom JUSTICE SOUTER joins except as to Part III-B, dissenting. . . .

II

A . . .

The problem in *Shaw* was not the plan architects' consideration of race as relevant in redistricting. Rather, in the Court's estimation, it was the virtual exclusion of other factors from the calculus. Traditional districting practices were cast aside, the Court concluded, with race alone steering placement of district lines.

B

The record before us does not show that race similarly overwhelmed traditional districting practices in Georgia. Although the Georgia General Assembly prominently considered race in shaping the Eleventh District, race did not crowd out all other factors, as the Court found it did in North Carolina's delineation of the *Shaw* district.

In contrast to the snake-like North Carolina district inspected in *Shaw*, Georgia's Eleventh District is hardly "bizarre," "extremely irregular," or "irrational on its face." Instead, the Eleventh District's design reflects significant consideration of "traditional districting factors (such as keeping political subdivisions intact) and the usual political process of compromise and trades for a variety of nonracial reasons." . . .

Nor does the Eleventh District disrespect the boundaries of political subdivisions. Of the 22 counties in the District, 14 are intact and 8 are divided. That puts the Eleventh District at about the state average in divided counties. . . .

Evidence at trial similarly shows that considerations other than race went into determining the Eleventh District's boundaries. For a "political reason" — to accommodate the request of an incumbent State Senator regarding the placement of the precinct in which his son lived — the DeKalb County portion of the Eleventh District was drawn to include a particular (largely white) precinct. The corridor through Effingham County was substantially narrowed at the request of a (white) State Representative. In Chatham County, the District was trimmed to exclude a heavily black community in Garden City because a State Representative wanted to keep the city intact inside the neighboring First District. The Savannah extension was configured by "the narrowest means possible" to avoid splitting the city of Port Wentworth.

Georgia's Eleventh District, in sum, is not an outlier district shaped without reference to familiar districting techniques. Tellingly, the District that the Court's decision today unsettles is not among those on a statistically calculated list of the 28 most bizarre districts in the United States, a study prepared in the wake of our decision in *Shaw*. . . .

D

Along with attention to size, shape, and political subdivisions, the Court recognizes as an appropriate districting principle, "respect for . . . communities defined by actual shared interests." The Court finds no community here, however, because a report in the record showed "fractured political, social, and economic interests within the Eleventh District's black population."

But ethnicity itself can tie people together, as volumes of social science litera- ture have documented — even people with divergent economic interests. . . .

[To] accommodate the reality of ethnic bonds, legislatures have long drawn voting districts along ethnic lines. Our Nation's cities are full of districts identi- fied by their ethnic character — Chinese, Irish, Italian, Jewish, Polish, Russian, for example. The creation of ethnic districts reflecting felt identity is not ordinar- ily viewed as offensive or demeaning to those included in the delineation.

III

To separate permissible and impermissible use of race in legislative apportion- ment, the Court orders strict scrutiny for districting plans "predominantly moti- vated" by race. No longer can a State avoid judicial oversight by giving — as in this case — genuine and measurable consideration to traditional districting prac- tices. Instead, a federal case can be mounted whenever plaintiffs plausibly allege that other factors carried less weight than race. This invitation to litigate against the State seems to me neither necessary nor proper.

A . . .

[In] adopting districting plans, [States] do not treat people as individuals. Appor- tionment schemes, by their very nature, assemble people in groups. States do not assign voters to districts based on merit or achievement, standards States might use in hiring employees or engaging contractors. . . .

[That] ethnicity defines some of these groups is a political reality. Until now, no constitutional infirmity has been seen in districting Irish or Italian voters together, for example, so long as the delineation does not abandon familiar ap- portionment practices. If Chinese-Americans and Russian-Americans may seek and secure group recognition in the delineation of voting districts, then African- Americans should not be dissimilarly treated. Otherwise, in the name of equal protection, we would shut out "the very minority group whose history in the United States gave birth to the Equal Protection Clause." . . .

C

The Court's disposition renders redistricting perilous work for state legislatures. Statutory mandates and political realities may require States to consider race when drawing district lines. . . .

Only after litigation — under either the Voting Rights Act, the Court's new *Miller* standard, or both — will States now be assured that plans conscious of race are safe. Federal judges in large numbers may be drawn into the fray. This en- largement of the judicial role is unwarranted. The reapportionment plan that re- sulted from Georgia's political process merited this Court's approbation, not its condemnation. Accordingly, I dissent.

[A dissenting opinion by Justice Stevens is omitted.]

Note: *Strict Scrutiny for Race-Specific Districting*

1. *The problem of injury.* Who is harmed by race-specific districting? In *Brown*, the Court thought that racial segregation generated "a feeling of inferiority as to [the] status [of black children] in the community that may affect their hearts and minds in a way unlikely ever to be undone." In *Loving* the Court found that the ban on interracial marriages was "designed to maintain White Supremacy." In affirmative action cases, the Court has held that plaintiffs denied the possibility of competing for a benefit or position on equal terms are harmed by that denial. See Northeastern Florida Chapter of Associated General Contractors v. Jacksonville, 508 U.S. 656 (1993); see also section C4 infra. Is it plausible that race-specific districting equalizing statewide representation has any of these effects?

In United States v. Hays, 515 U.S. 737 (1995), the Court held that plaintiffs living within a district subject to a racial gerrymander have standing to contest the districting, but that plaintiffs outside the district lack standing unless they can show that they have personally been subject to a racial classification:

> Where a plaintiff resides in a racially gerrymandered district [the] plaintiff has been denied equal treatment because of the legislature's reliance on racial [criteria]. Voters in such districts may suffer the special representational harms racial classifications can cause in the voting context. On the other hand, where a plaintiff does not live in such a district, he or she does not suffer those special harms.

Why doesn't the recognition of "representational harms" implicate the very stereotypes about correlations between race and voting behavior that the Court rejects? Consider Justice Stevens's discussion of the standing issue in his dissenting opinion in Shaw v. Hunt, 517 U.S. 899 (1996):

> [Counsel for plaintiffs suggests] that the plaintiffs objected to the use of race [not] because of any adverse consequence that these plaintiffs, on account of their race, had suffered more than other persons, but rather because the States' failure to obey the constitutional command to legislate in a color-blind manner conveyed a message to voters across the state that "there are two black districts and ten white districts."
>
> [But the] supposedly insidious messages that [*Shaw*] contends will follow from extremely irregular race-based districting will presumably be received in equal measure by all State residents. For that reason, the claimed violation of a shared right to a color-blind districting process would not seem to implicate the Equal Protection Clause at all precisely because it rests neither on a challenge to the State's decision to distribute burdens and benefits unequally, nor on a claim that the State's formally equal treatment of its citizens in fact stamps persons of one race with a badge of inferiority in a context that results in no race-based unequal treatment.

2. *Triggering strict scrutiny.* Both *Shaw* and *Miller* make plain that districts are not unconstitutional merely because those who drew them took race into account. In her plurality opinion in Bush v. Vera, 517 U.S. 952 (1996), Justice O'Connor sought to clarify the relevant criteria:

> Strict scrutiny does not apply merely because redistricting is performed with consciousness of race. Nor does it apply to all cases of intentional creation of majority-minority districts. [For] strict scrutiny to apply, the plaintiffs must prove that other,

legitimate districting principles were "subordinated" to race. By that, we mean that race must be "the predominant factor motivating the legislature's [redistricting] decision."

Compare Justice Thomas's concurring opinion, joined by Justice Scalia:

I cannot agree with Justice O'Connor's assertion that strict scrutiny is not invoked by the intentional creation of majority-minority districts. . . .
Strict scrutiny applies to all governmental classifications based on race, and we have expressly held that there is no exception for race-based redistricting.

Recall that in other contexts the Court has held that strict scrutiny is appropriate when racial considerations are the "but for" cause of government action. See pages 522-523 supra. Why should there be a different standard in this context?

3. *Compelling state interests.* Once strict scrutiny is triggered, what sort of government interest is sufficiently weighty to justify race-specific districting?

a. *Compliance with the Voting Rights Act.* Recall that the Voting Rights Act, unlike the Constitution, does more than merely prohibit districting that has the purpose of reducing minority representation. To some indeterminate extent, it also requires jurisdictions to avoid districting that has the "result" of understating such representation. Of course, to the extent that jurisdictions attempt to avoid this result, they run the risk of violating the *Miller* and *Shaw* restrictions on race-specific districting. This dilemma might be avoided if the Court treated compliance with the act as a compelling state interest sufficient to justify race-specific districting. In Bush v. Vera, supra, Justice O'Connor, writing for a plurality of the Court, assumed, without deciding, that compliance with the act was such an interest. The Court found, however, that the act did not require "a State to create, on predominantly racial lines, a district that is not 'reasonably compact.'" Since Texas had created such a district, the Court did not have to reach the question whether the need to obey the act would provide a compelling government interest. A majority of the Court reached a similar conclusion in Shaw v. Hunt, supra. However, in an unusual concurrence to her own plurality opinion in *Bush,* Justice O'Connor stated her view that compliance with the "results" test mandated by the act was a compelling interest.

b. *Remedying the effects of prior discrimination.* In Bush v. Vera, Justice O'Connor's plurality opinion addressed the argument that remedying the effects of racially polarized voting, produced by prior discrimination, was a compelling governmental interest. Drawing from the Court's affirmative action jurisprudence, see section C4 infra, she concluded that the state has a compelling interest in remedying prior discrimination only when there is "specific, identified discrimination" and when the state has a "strong basis in evidence" to conclude that the remedial action is necessary. The Court returned to this issue in *Shaw.* Writing for the majority, Chief Justice Rehnquist acknowledged that "[a] State's interest in remedying the effects of past or present racial discrimination may in the proper case justify a government's use of racial distinctions." However, on the facts of this case, "the District Court found that an interest in ameliorating past discrimination did not actually precipitate the use of race in the redistricting plan." Compare Justice Stevens's dissenting opinion:

[Some] legislators felt that the sorry history of race relations in North Carolina [was] sufficient reason for making it easier for more black leaders to participate in the legislative [process]. Even if that history does not provide the kind of precise guidance that will justify certain specific affirmative action programs in particular industries, it surely provides an adequate basis for a decision to facilitate the election of representatives of the previously disadvantaged minority.

4. *Two hypotheticals.* Consider the following two hypothetical cases:

a. In a jurisdiction characterized by racial bloc voting, a nonpartisan commission draws district lines utilizing a computer program that takes into account only "traditional" districting concerns. By happenstance, the districts it creates substantially understate minority voting strength. However, if the lines were drawn slightly differently, the districting would accurately reflect the voting strength of all ethnic and racial groups without doing serious injury to "traditional" districting concerns. The jurisdiction chooses the second plan.

b. In order to ensure "fair" representation in a jurisdiction characterized by racial bloc voting, the legislature establishes a "race election." Under the plan, separate, jurisdiction-wide elections are conducted for each racial group, with voters assigned to the various elections according to race. Representation is then determined by giving each group the number of representatives that corresponds to its percentage of the population.

Under current law, plan *a* is almost certainly constitutional, while plan *b* is almost certainly unconstitutional. Is there a dispositive difference between the two plans? If so, how should a court determine the point at which constitutionally permissible racial "adjustments" to district lines turn into unconstitutional "race elections." If not, which of the two results should be changed?

4.   Race-Specific Classifications That Benefit Racial Minorities

What standard of review should a court use to evaluate so-called benign racial classifications that purportedly benefit racial minorities? What kinds of justifications are constitutionally adequate to support such classifications? If "benign" classifications should be judged by some test less rigorous than strict scrutiny, how should a court determine whether a classification is in fact benign?

Note: The Pre-*Croson* Cases

For over a decade, beginning in the late 1970s, the Court struggled inconclusively with these issues. Throughout this period, the justices repeatedly divided over both the permissible goals for "affirmative action" programs and the appropriate standard of review without ever succeeding in formulating a single approach that attracted the votes of a majority of the Court.

1. *Bakke.* The Court's first sustained encounter with "affirmative action" came in Regents of the University of California v. Bakke, 438 U.S. 265 (1978), a case concerning the constitutionality of a program designed to increase minority enrollment at the University of California at Davis medical school. Under the pro-

gram, sixteen of the school's 100 seats were set aside each year for members of minority groups found by a special committee to have suffered from economic or educational deprivation.

Four justices (Brennan, White, Marshall, and Blackmun) would have upheld the program. They would have utilized an "intermediate" level of scrutiny somewhere between the rational basis test used for "ordinary" legislation and the strict scrutiny used for race-specific statutes that disadvantage minorities. As Justice Brennan explained:

> [Because] of the significant risk that racial classifications established for ostensibly benign purposes can be misused, causing effects not unlike those created by invidious classifications, it is inappropriate to inquire only whether there is any conceivable basis that might sustain such a classification. Instead, to justify such a classification an important and articulated purpose for its use must be shown. In addition, any statute must be stricken that stigmatizes any group or that singles out those least well represented in the political process to bear the brunt of a benign program.

For this group of justices, the purpose of remedying prior discrimination was legitimate and sufficiently important to satisfy this test. Since the use of race was reasonable in light of the program's objectives, and since there was no evidence that the program stigmatized any individual or group, these justices would have upheld it.

Four other justices (Burger, Stewart, Rehnquist, and Stevens) thought that the program violated title VI of the 1964 Civil Rights Act and therefore would not have reached its constitutionality. (Title VI prohibits racial discrimination in programs receiving federal financial assistance.)

The Court's judgment was controlled by Justice Powell, although in some respects he disagreed with all eight of his colleagues. Justice Powell argued that all racial classifications — including those supposedly benefiting racial minorities — were suspect and should be subject to the same heightened review. Although the state had a "legitimate and substantial" interest in remedying prior discrimination, that interest did not justify the Davis program because there had been no prior judicial, administrative, or legislative findings of prior discrimination. Although the university's interest in a diverse student body did justify some use of racial criteria in admission decisions, it did not justify Davis's rigid, two-track system under which nonminority applicants were precluded from competing for certain seats. Hence, Justice Powell joined Justices Burger, Stewart, Rehnquist, and Stevens to hold that Bakke had been unconstitutionally denied admission under the existing Davis plan. However, he also joined Justices Brennan, Marshall, White, and Blackmun in refusing to enjoin all use of race in the future. Instead, he would have permitted an admissions program under which "race [was] deemed a 'plus' in a particular applicant's file," but did not

> insulate the individual from comparison with all other candidates for the available seats. [An] admissions program operated in this way is flexible enough to consider all pertinent elements of diversity in light of the particular qualifications of each applicant, and to place them on the same footing for consideration, although not necessarily according them the same weight.

2. *Fullilove.* Two years after *Bakke*, in Fullilove v. Klutznick, 448 U.S. 448 (1980), the Court considered an affirmative action program created on the fed-

eral level in the context of public contracting. The results were again inconclusive. At issue was a provision of the Public Works Employment Act of 1977, which provided federal financial assistance to state and local governments to build public facilities. The act required that, absent an administrative waiver, 10 percent of the funds granted for the projects had to be used to procure services or supplies from "minority business enterprises" (MBEs) — defined as businesses owned or controlled by "citizens of the United States who are Negroes, Spanish-speaking, Orientals, Indians, Eskimos, and Aleuts." On this occasion, the Court upheld the program but, once again, no opinion attracted the votes of a majority of the justices.

In an opinion announcing the Court's judgment and joined by Justices White and Powell, Chief Justice Burger emphasized the narrowness of the holding. Although rejecting the claim that in a remedial context Congress must act "in a wholly 'color-blind' fashion," the plurality noted that "a program that employs racial or ethnic criteria, even in a remedial context, calls for close examination." Here, the program was constitutional, albeit reaching the outer limits of congressional authority. In reaching this conclusion, the plurality relied in part on the limited duration of the program, on Congress's unique authority to devise remedial measures for racial discrimination, on the fact that no nonminority contractor was severely injured by the program, and on the fact that a waiver provision permitted deviation from the 10 percent requirement in cases where the increased costs of nonminority contractors could be shown not to be caused by prior discrimination.

In a concurring opinion, Justice Powell repeated his view that "[racial] classifications must be assessed under the most stringent level of review because immutable characteristics, which bear no relation to individual merit or need, are irrelevant to almost every governmental decision." In this case, however, he agreed with the plurality that the statute was "justified as a remedy that serves the compelling governmental interest in eradicating the continuing effects of past discrimination identified by Congress."

Justice Marshall, joined by Justices Brennan and Blackmun, also concurred. He argued that Congress had a sound basis for finding that minority firms were hampered by the continuing effects of past discrimination, and that the means chosen by Congress were substantially related to the achievement of this remedial purpose.

In a dissenting opinion joined by Justice Rehnquist, Justice Stewart asserted that "[under] our Constitution, the government may never act to the detriment of a person solely because of that person's race." Justice Stevens also dissented in an opinion that emphasized the absence of congressional deliberation over the measure:

> Rather than take the substantive position expressed in [Justice Stewart's dissent], I would hold this statute unconstitutional on a narrower ground. It cannot fairly be characterized as a "narrowly tailored" racial classification because it simply raises too many serious questions that Congress failed to answer or even to address in a responsible way.

3. *The pre-Croson compromise.* Between 1980, when the Court decided *Fullilove,* and its 1989 decision in City of Richmond v. J. A. Croson Co., infra, the

Court decided a series of cases in which affirmative action measures were utilized to remedy employment discrimination. See United States v. Paradise, 480 U.S. 149 (1987) (upholding district court order requiring 50 percent of promotions to go to qualified black candidates, if available, as remedy for persistent and egregious employment discrimination by Alabama Department of Public Safety); Local 28, Sheet Metal Workers International Association v. EEOC, 478 U.S. 421 (1986) (upholding "narrowly tailored" racial goals for union membership as remedy for egregious title VII violation); Wygant v. Jackson Board of Education, 476 U.S. 267 (1986) (invalidating racial preference employed by school district in laying off teachers previously hired under affirmative action plan designed to remedy prior discrimination). See also Local No. 93, International Association of Firefighters v. Cleveland, 478 U.S. 501 (1986) (upholding judicially imposed affirmative action plan against nonconstitutional attack); Johnson v. Transportation Agency, 480 U.S. 616 (1987) (upholding voluntarily adopted affirmative action plan for women against nonconstitutional attack).

Throughout this period, the Court remained closely divided on the issues posed by these programs and continued to disagree concerning the appropriate goals and standard of review for them. Nevertheless, a few clear principles seemed to emerge. The Court appeared to steer a middle course between the extremes of completely outlawing affirmative action programs and granting them automatic approval.

On the one hand, the Court made plain that the voluntary use by government employers of race-conscious "goals" or "timetables" designed to remedy prior discrimination was not per se unconstitutional. It was also permissible for these race-conscious measures to provide for "class-wide" relief, and there was no requirement that they be limited to "making whole" the actual victims of prior discriminatory acts. Moreover, court-ordered affirmative action plans (directed at either public or private entities) to remedy violations of the Constitution or of the statutory mandate against employment discrimination were also not per se unconstitutional. (Whether such orders are within the power granted to federal courts under title VII of the 1964 Civil Rights Act poses difficult issues of statutory construction that are beyond the scope of this Note.)

On the other hand, the Court repeatedly recognized that race-conscious remedies pose potentially serious constitutional problems and must therefore be carefully scrutinized. During this period, the Court failed to agree on a verbal formulation describing either the appropriate standard of review for such remedies or the characteristics a plan must have to survive review. The cases seemed to indicate, however, that the Court was unwilling to accept race-conscious measures as the norm. It was therefore important that affirmative action plans be bounded in some fashion. The Court made clear that it was unlikely to approve loosely drafted race-conscious measures not closely tied to remediation of prior violations. Moreover, the Court was sensitive to the claims of the "innocent victims" of race-conscious measures. The fact that there were such "victims" was not necessarily fatal to a race-conscious plan. But a plan was more likely to survive constitutional attack if its costs were broadly diffused, and, in particular, if it did not interfere with the seniority-based expectations of present employees.

4. *Unraveling of the compromise?* In 1987, Justice Powell retired. After his first nominee for the vacant seat failed to secure Senate confirmation and the second nominee withdrew, President Reagan nominated, and the Senate confirmed, An-

thony Kennedy to replace Justice Powell. The appointment was widely viewed as creating a solid "conservative" majority on many constitutional issues. During Justice Kennedy's first term, the Court revisited the affirmative action problem — this time in the context of government contract "set-asides" — and for the first time a majority was able to agree on an appropriate standard of review. Consider how much of the pre-*Croson* approach survives its decision.

City of Richmond v. J. A. Croson Co.
488 U.S. 469 (1989)

JUSTICE O'CONNOR announced the judgment of the Court and delivered the opinion of the Court with respect to Parts I, III-B, and IV, an opinion with respect to Part II, in which the CHIEF JUSTICE and JUSTICE WHITE join, and an opinion with respect to Parts III-A and V, in which the CHIEF JUSTICE, JUSTICE WHITE and JUSTICE KENNEDY join.

I

[The City of Richmond adopted a set-aside program, modeled on the one upheld in *Fullilove*, requiring prime contractors on city projects to subcontract at least 30 percent of the amount of the contract to minority business enterprises (MBEs). Adopting the definition used by Congress in *Fullilove*, the Richmond City Council defined minority group members as "Blacks, Spanish-speaking, Orientals, Indians, Eskimos, or Aleuts." Regulations under the plan provided that no waivers would be granted except under exceptional circumstances, when "every feasible attempt has been made to comply, and it has been demonstrated that sufficient, relevant, qualified Minority Business Enterprises . . . are unavailable or unwilling to participate in the contract."]

The Plan was adopted by the Richmond City Council after a public hearing. Seven members of the public spoke to the merits of the ordinance: five were in opposition, two in favor. Proponents of the set-aside provision relied on a study which indicated that, while the general population of Richmond was 50% black, only .67% of the city's prime construction contracts had been awarded to minority businesses in the 5-year period from 1978 to 1983. It was also established that a variety of contractors' associations, whose representatives appeared in opposition to the ordinance, had virtually no minority businesses within their membership. The city's legal counsel indicated his view that the ordinance was constitutional under this Court's decision in Fullilove v. Klutznick. Councilperson Marsh, a proponent of the ordinance, made the following statement:

> There is some information, however, that I want to make sure that we put in the record. I have been practicing law in this community since 1961, and I am familiar with the practices in the construction industry in this area, in the State, and around the nation. And I can say without equivocation, that the general conduct of the construction industry in this area, and the State, and around the nation, is one in which race discrimination and exclusion on the basis of race is widespread.

There was no direct evidence of race discrimination on the part of the city in letting contracts or any evidence that the city's prime contractors had discriminated against minority-owned subcontractors. . . .

II

[Appellant] and its supporting amici rely heavily on *Fullilove* for the proposition that a city council, like Congress, need not make specific findings of discrimination to engage in race-conscious relief. Thus, appellant argues "[i]t would be a perversion of federalism to hold that the federal government has a compelling interest in remedying the effects of racial discrimination in its own public works program, but a city government does not."

What appellant ignores is that Congress, unlike any State or political subdivision, has a specific constitutional mandate to enforce the dictates of the Fourteenth Amendment. The power to "enforce" may at times also include the power to define situations which *Congress* determines threaten principles of equality and to adopt prophylactic rules to deal with those situations. See Katzenbach v. Morgan [Chapter 2, section D4, supra]. . . .

That Congress may identify and redress the effects of society-wide discrimination does not mean that, a fortiori, the States and their political subdivisions are free to decide that such remedies are appropriate. Section 1 of the Fourteenth Amendment is an explicit *constraint* on state power, and the States must undertake any remedial efforts in accordance with that provision. To hold otherwise would be to cede control over the content of the Equal Protection Clause to the 50 state legislatures and their myriad political subdivisions. . . .

[Thus,] our treatment of an exercise of congressional power in *Fullilove* cannot be dispositive here. . . .

It would seem equally clear, however, that a state or local subdivision (if delegated the authority from the State) has the authority to eradicate the effects of private discrimination within its own legislative jurisdiction. This authority must, of course, be exercised within the constraints of §1 of the Fourteenth Amendment. [As] a matter of state law, the city of Richmond has legislative authority over its procurement policies, and can use its spending powers to remedy private discrimination, if it identifies that discrimination with the particularity required by the Fourteenth Amendment. . . .

Thus, if the city could show that it had essentially become a "passive participant" in a system of racial exclusion practiced by elements of the local construction industry, we think it clear that the city could take affirmative steps to dismantle such a system. It is beyond dispute that any public entity, state or federal, has a compelling interest in assuring that public dollars, drawn from the tax contributions of all citizens, do not serve to finance the evil of private prejudice.

III

A

The Equal Protection Clause of the Fourteenth Amendment provides that "[N]o State shall . . . deny to *any person* within its jurisdiction the equal protection of the laws" (emphasis added). [The] Richmond Plan denies certain citizens the opportunity to compete for a fixed percentage of public contracts based solely upon their race. To whatever racial group these citizens belong, their "personal rights" to be treated with equal dignity and respect are implicated by a rigid rule erecting race as the sole criterion in an aspect of public decisionmaking.

Absent searching judicial inquiry into the justification for such race-based measures, there is simply no way of determining what classifications are "benign" or "remedial" and what classifications are in fact motivated by illegitimate notions of racial inferiority or simple racial politics. Indeed, the purpose of strict scrutiny is to "smoke out" illegitimate uses of race by assuring that the legislative body is pursuing a goal important enough to warrant use of a highly suspect tool. The test also ensures that the means chosen "fit" this compelling goal so closely that there is little or no possibility that the motive for the classification was illegitimate racial prejudice or stereotype.

Classifications based on race carry a danger of stigmatic harm. Unless they are strictly reserved for remedial settings, they may in fact promote notions of racial inferiority and lead to a politics of racial hostility. [The] standard of review under the Equal Protection Clause is not dependent on the race of those burdened or benefited by a particular classification.

Our [adherence] to the standard of review [does] not, as Justice Marshall's dissent suggests, indicate that we view "racial discrimination as largely a phenomenon of the past" or that "government bodies need no longer preoccupy themselves with rectifying racial injustice." As we indicate below, States and their local subdivisions have many legislative weapons at their disposal both to punish and prevent present discrimination and to remove arbitrary barriers to minority advancement. Rather, our interpretation of §1 stems from our agreement with the view expressed by Justice Powell in *Bakke*, that "[t]he guarantee of equal protection cannot mean one thing when applied to one individual and something else when applied to a person of another color."

Under the standard proposed by Justice Marshall's dissent, "[r]ace-conscious classifications designed to further remedial goals," are forthwith subject to a relaxed standard of review. How the dissent arrives at the legal conclusion that a racial classification is "designed to further remedial goals," without first engaging in an examination of the factual basis for its enactment and the nexus between its scope and that factual basis we are not told. However, once the "remedial" conclusion is reached, the dissent's standard is singularly deferential, and bears little resemblance to the close examination of legislative purpose we have engaged in when reviewing classifications based on [race]. The dissent's watered-down version of equal protection review effectively assures that race will always be relevant in American [life].

Even were we to accept a reading of the guarantee of equal protection under which the level of scrutiny varies according to the ability of different groups to defend their interests in the representative process, heightened scrutiny would still be appropriate in the circumstances of this case. One of the central arguments for applying a less exacting standard to "benign" racial classifications is that such measures essentially involve a choice made by dominant racial groups to disadvantage [themselves].

In this case, blacks comprise approximately 50% of the population of the city of Richmond. Five of the nine seats on the city council are held by blacks. The concern that a political majority will more easily act to the disadvantage of a minority based on unwarranted assumptions or incomplete facts would seem to militate for, not against, the application of heightened judicial scrutiny in this case. . . .

B

The District Court found the city council's "findings sufficient to ensure that, in adopting the Plan, it was remedying the present effects of past discrimination in the *construction industry*." [A] generalized assertion that there has been past discrimination in an entire industry provides no guidance for a legislative body to determine the precise scope of the injury it seeks to remedy. It "has no logical stopping point." *Wygant*, at 275 (plurality opinion). "Relief" for such an ill-defined wrong could extend until the percentage of public contracts awarded to MBEs in Richmond mirrored the percentage of minorities in the population as a whole.

Appellant argues that it is attempting to remedy various forms of past discrimination that are alleged to be responsible for the small number of minority businesses in the local contracting industry. Among these the city cites the exclusion of blacks from skilled construction trade unions and training programs. This past discrimination has prevented them "from following the traditional path from laborer to entrepreneur." The city also lists a host of nonracial factors which would seem to face a member of any racial group attempting to establish a new business enterprise, such as deficiencies in working capital, inability to meet bonding requirements, unfamiliarity with bidding procedures, and disability caused by an inadequate track record.

While there is no doubt that the sorry history of both private and public discrimination in this country has contributed to a lack of opportunities for black entrepreneurs, this observation, standing alone, cannot justify a rigid racial quota in the awarding of public contracts in Richmond, Virginia. Like the claim that discrimination in primary and secondary schooling justifies a rigid racial preference in medical school admissions, an amorphous claim that there has been past discrimination in a particular industry cannot justify the use of an unyielding racial quota.

It is sheer speculation how many minority firms there would be in Richmond absent past societal discrimination, just as it was sheer speculation how many minority medical students would have been admitted to the medical school at Davis absent past discrimination in educational opportunities. Defining these sorts of injuries as "identified discrimination" would give local governments license to create a patchwork of racial preferences based on statistical generalizations about any particular field of endeavor.

These defects are readily apparent in this case. The 30% quota cannot in any realistic sense be tied to any injury suffered by anyone. The District Court relied upon five predicate "facts" in reaching its conclusion that there was an adequate basis for the 30% quota: (1) the ordinance declares itself to be remedial; (2) several proponents of the measure stated their views that there had been past discrimination in the construction industry; (3) minority businesses received .67% of prime contracts from the city while minorities constituted 50% of the city's population; (4) there were very few minority contractors in local and state contractors' associations; and (5) in 1977, Congress made a determination that the effects of past discrimination had stifled minority participation in the construction industry nationally.

None of these "findings," singly or together, provide the city of Richmond with a "strong basis in evidence for its conclusion that remedial action was necessary." *Wygant*, 476 U.S., at 277 (plurality opinion). There is nothing approaching a prima facie case of a constitutional or statutory violation by *anyone* in the Richmond construction industry.

The District Court accorded great weight to the fact that the city council designated the Plan as "remedial." But the mere recitation of a "benign" or legitimate purpose for a racial classification, is entitled to little or no weight. Racial classifications are suspect, and that means that simple legislative assurances of good intention cannot suffice.

The District Court also relied on the highly conclusionary statement of a proponent of the Plan that there was racial discrimination in the construction industry "in this area, and the State, and around the nation." It also noted that the city manager had related his view that racial discrimination still plagued the construction industry in his home city of Pittsburgh. These statements are of little probative value in establishing identified discrimination in the Richmond construction industry. . . .

Reliance on the disparity between the number of prime contracts awarded to minority firms and the minority population of the city of Richmond is similarly misplaced. . . .

In this case, the city does not even know how many MBEs in the relevant market are qualified to undertake prime or subcontracting work in public construction projects. Nor does the city know what percentage of total city construction dollars minority firms now receive as subcontractors on prime contracts let by the city.

To a large extent, the set-aside of subcontracting dollars seems to rest on the unsupported assumption that white prime contractors simply will not hire minority firms. [Without] any information on minority participation in subcontracting, it is quite simply impossible to evaluate overall minority representation in the city's construction expenditures.

The city and the District Court also relied on evidence that MBE membership in local contractors' associations was extremely low. Again, standing alone this evidence is not probative of any discrimination in the local construction industry. There are numerous explanations for this dearth of minority participation, including past societal discrimination in education and economic opportunities as well as both black and white career and entrepreneurial choices. Blacks may be disproportionately attracted to industries other than [construction].

For low minority membership in these associations to be relevant, the city would have to link it to the number of local MBEs eligible for membership. If the statistical disparity between eligible MBEs and MBE membership were great enough, an inference of discriminatory exclusion could arise. In such a case, the city would have a compelling interest in preventing its tax dollars from assisting these organizations in maintaining a racially segregated construction market.

Finally, the city and the District Court relied on Congress' finding in connection with the set-aside approved in *Fullilove* that there had been nationwide discrimination in the construction industry. The probative value of these findings for demonstrating the existence of discrimination in Richmond is extremely limited. By its inclusion of a waiver procedure in the national program addressed in

Fullilove, Congress explicitly recognized that the scope of the problem would vary from market area to market area. . . .

Justice Marshall apparently views the requirement that Richmond identify the discrimination it seeks to remedy in its own jurisdiction as a mere administrative headache, an "onerous documentary obligatio[n]." We cannot agree. . . . The "evidence" relied upon by the dissent, the history of school desegregation in Richmond and numerous congressional reports, does little to define the scope of any injury to minority contractors in Richmond or the necessary remedy. The factors relied upon by the dissent could justify a preference of any size or duration.

Moreover, Justice Marshall's suggestion that findings of discrimination may be "shared" from jurisdiction to jurisdiction in the same manner as information concerning zoning and property values is unprecedented. [See] Renton v. Playtime Theatres, Inc., 475 U.S. 41, 51-52 (1986). We have never approved the extrapolation of discrimination in one jurisdiction from the experience of another. . . .

To accept Richmond's claim that past societal discrimination alone can serve as the basis for rigid racial preferences would be to open the door to competing claims for "remedial relief" for every disadvantaged group. The dream of a Nation of equal citizens in a society where race is irrelevant to personal opportunity and achievement would be lost in a mosaic of shifting preferences based on inherently unmeasurable claims of past wrongs. [We] think such a result would be contrary to both the letter and spirit of a constitutional provision whose central command is equality.

The foregoing analysis applies only to the inclusion of blacks within the Richmond set-aside program. There is *absolutely no evidence* of past discrimination against Spanish-speaking, Oriental, Indian, Eskimo, or Aleut persons in any aspect of the Richmond construction industry. The District Court took judicial notice of the fact that the vast majority of "minority" persons in Richmond were black. It may well be that Richmond has never had an Aleut or Eskimo citizen. The random inclusion of racial groups that, as a practical matter, may never have suffered from discrimination in the construction industry in Richmond, suggests that perhaps the city's purpose was not in fact to remedy past discrimination. . . .

IV

As noted by the court below, it is almost impossible to assess whether the Richmond Plan is narrowly tailored to remedy prior discrimination since it is not linked to identified discrimination in any way. We limit ourselves to two observations in this regard.

First, there does not appear to have been any consideration of the use of race-neutral means to increase minority business participation in city contracting. Many of the barriers to minority participation in the construction industry relied upon by the city to justify a racial classification appear to be race neutral. If MBEs disproportionately lack capital or cannot meet bonding requirements, a race-neutral program of city financing for small firms would, a fortiori, lead to greater minority participation. . . .

Second, the 30% quota cannot be said to be narrowly tailored to any goal, except perhaps outright racial balancing. It rests upon the "completely unrealistic" assumption that minorities will choose a particular trade in lockstep proportion to their representation in the local population.

Since the city must already consider bids and waivers on a case-by-case basis, it is difficult to see the need for a rigid numerical quota. As noted above, the congressional scheme upheld in *Fullilove* allowed for a waiver of the set-aside provision where an MBE's higher price was not attributable to the effects of past discrimination. Based upon proper findings, such programs are less problematic from an equal protection standpoint because they treat all candidates individually, rather than making the color of an applicant's skin the sole relevant consideration. Unlike the program upheld in *Fullilove*, the Richmond Plan's waiver system focuses solely on the availability of MBEs; there is no inquiry into whether or not the particular MBE seeking a racial preference has suffered from the effects of past discrimination by the city or prime contractors.

Given the existence of an individualized procedure, the city's only interest in maintaining a quota system rather than investigating the need for remedial action in particular cases would seem to be simple administrative convenience. But the interest in avoiding the bureaucratic effort necessary to tailor remedial relief to those who truly have suffered the effects of prior discrimination cannot justify a rigid line drawn on the basis of a suspect classification. Under Richmond's scheme, a successful black, Hispanic, or Oriental entrepreneur from anywhere in the country enjoys an absolute preference over other citizens based solely on their race. We think it obvious that such a program is not narrowly tailored to remedy the effects of prior discrimination.

V

Nothing we say today precludes a state or local entity from taking action to rectify the effects of identified discrimination within its jurisdiction. If the city of Richmond had evidence before it that non-minority contractors were systematically excluding minority businesses from subcontracting opportunities it could take action to end the discriminatory exclusion. Where there is a significant statistical disparity between the number of qualified minority contractors willing and able to perform a particular service and the number of such contractors actually engaged by the locality or the locality's prime contractors, an inference of discriminatory exclusion could arise. Under such circumstances, the city could act to dismantle the closed business system by taking appropriate measures against those who discriminate on the basis of race or other illegitimate criteria. In the extreme case, some form of narrowly tailored racial preference might be necessary to break down patterns of deliberate exclusion.

Nor is local government powerless to deal with individual instances of racially motivated refusals to employ minority contractors. Where such discrimination occurs, a city would be justified in penalizing the discriminator and providing appropriate relief to the victim of such discrimination. Moreover, evidence of a pattern of individual discriminatory acts can, if supported by appropriate statistical proof, lend support to a local government's determination that broader remedial relief is justified.

Even in the absence of evidence of discrimination, the city has at its disposal a whole array of race-neutral devices to increase the accessibility of city contracting opportunities to small entrepreneurs of all races. [Business] as usual should not mean business pursuant to the unthinking exclusion of certain members of our society from its rewards.

In the case at hand, the city has not ascertained how many minority enterprises are present in the local construction market nor the level of their participation in city construction projects. The city points to no evidence that qualified minority contractors have been passed over for city contracts or subcontracts, either as a group or in any individual [case].

Proper findings in this regard are necessary to define both the scope of the injury and the extent of the remedy necessary to cure its effects. Such findings also serve to assure all citizens that the deviation from the norm of equal treatment of all racial and ethnic groups is a temporary matter, a measure taken in the service of the goal of equality itself. [Because] the city of Richmond has failed to identify the need for remedial action in the awarding of its public construction contracts, its treatment of its citizens on a racial basis violates the dictates of the Equal Protection Clause. Accordingly, the judgment of the Court of Appeals for the Fourth Circuit is

Affirmed.

[Separate opinions by Justice Stevens and Justice Kennedy, concurring in part and concurring in the judgment, have been omitted].

JUSTICE SCALIA, concurring in the judgment.

I agree with much of the Court's opinion, and, in particular, with Justice O'Connor's conclusion that strict scrutiny must be applied to all governmental classifications by race, whether or not its asserted purpose is "remedial" or "benign." I do not agree [with] the Court's dicta suggesting that, despite the Fourteenth Amendment, state and local governments may in some circumstances discriminate on the basis of race in order (in a broad sense) "to ameliorate the effects of past discrimination." The benign purpose of compensating for social disadvantages, whether they have been acquired by reason of prior discrimination or otherwise, can no more be pursued by the illegitimate means of racial discrimination than can other assertedly benign purposes we have repeatedly rejected. The difficulty of overcoming the effects of past discrimination is as nothing compared with the difficulty of eradicating from our society the source of those effects, which is the tendency — fatal to a nation such as ours — to classify and judge men and women on the basis of their country of origin or the color of their skin. A solution to the first problem that aggravates the second is no solution at [all]. At least where state or local action is at issue, only a social emergency rising to the level of imminent danger to life and limb — for example, a prison race riot, requiring temporary segregation of inmates — can justify an exception to the principle embodied in the Fourteenth Amendment that "[o]ur Constitution is color-blind, and neither knows nor tolerates classes among citizens," [Plessy v. Ferguson (Harlan, J., dissenting)]. . . .

A sound distinction between federal and state (or local) action based on race rests not only upon the substance of the Civil War Amendments, but upon social reality and governmental theory. It is a simple fact that what Justice Stewart described in *Fullilove* as "the dispassionate objectivity [and] the flexibility that are needed to mold a race-conscious remedy around the single objective of eliminating the effects of past or present discrimination" — political qualities already to be doubted in a national legislature, *Fullilove*, at 527, (Stewart, J., with whom Rehnquist, J., joined, dissenting) — are substantially less likely to exist at the state or local level. The struggle for racial justice has historically been a struggle by the national society against oppression in the individual States. And the struggle retains that character in modern times. Not all of that struggle has involved discrimination against blacks, and not all of it has been in the Old South. What the record shows, in other words, is that racial discrimination against any group finds a more ready expression at the state and local than at the federal level. To the children of the Founding Fathers, this should come as no surprise. An acute awareness of the heightened danger of oppression from political factions in small, rather than large, political units dates to the very beginning of our national history. As James Madison observed in support of the proposed Constitution's enhancement of national powers:

> The smaller the society, the fewer probably will be the distinct parties and interests composing it; the fewer the distinct parties and interests, the more frequently will a majority be found of the same party; and the smaller the number of individuals composing a majority, and the smaller the compass within which they are placed, the more easily will they concert and execute their plan of oppression. Extend the sphere and you take in a greater variety of parties and interests; you make it less probable that a majority of the whole will have a common motive to invade the rights of other citizens; or if such a common motive exists, it will be more difficult for all who feel it to discover their own strength and to act in unison with each other.

The Federalist No. 10, pp. 82-84 (C. Rossiter ed. 1961).

The prophesy of these words came to fruition in Richmond in the enactment of a set-aside clearly and directly beneficial to the dominant political group, which happens also to be the dominant racial group. The same thing has no doubt happened before in other cities (though the racial basis of the preference has rarely been made textually explicit) — and blacks have often been on the receiving end of the injustice. Where injustice is the game, however, turn-about is not fair play.

In my view there is only one circumstance in which the States may act *by race* to "undo the effects of past discrimination": where that is necessary to eliminate their own maintenance of a system of unlawful racial classification. If, for example, a state agency has a discriminatory pay scale compensating black employees in all positions at 20% less than their nonblack counterparts, it may assuredly promulgate an order raising the salaries of "all black employees" by 20%. This distinction explains our school desegregation cases, in which we have made plain that States and localities sometimes have an obligation to adopt race-conscious remedies. . . .

I agree with the Court's dictum that a fundamental distinction must be drawn between the effects of "societal" discrimination and the effects of "identified" discrimination, and that the situation would be different if Richmond's plan were "tailored" to identify those particular bidders who "suffered from the effects of past discrimination by the city or prime contractors." In my view, however, the reason that would make a difference is not, as the Court states, that it would justify race-conscious action, but rather that it would enable race-neutral remediation. Nothing prevents Richmond from according a contracting preference to identified victims of discrimination. While most of the beneficiaries might be black, neither the beneficiaries nor those disadvantaged by the preference would be identified *on the basis of their race*. In other words, far from justifying racial classification, identification of actual victims of discrimination makes it less supportable than ever, because more obviously unneeded. . . .

It is plainly true that in our society blacks have suffered discrimination immeasurably greater than any directed at other racial groups. But those who believe that racial preferences can help to "even the score" display, and reinforce, a manner of thinking by race that was the source of the injustice and that will, if it endures within our society, be the source of more injustice still. The relevant proposition is not that it was blacks, or Jews, or Irish who were discriminated against, but that it was individual men and women, "created equal," who were discriminated against. And the relevant resolve is that that should never happen again. Racial preferences appear to "even the score" (in some small degree) only if one embraces the proposition that our society is appropriately viewed as divided into races, making it right that an injustice rendered in the past to a black man should be compensated for by discriminating against a white. Nothing is worth that embrace. Since blacks have been disproportionately disadvantaged by racial discrimination, any race-neutral remedial program aimed at the disadvantaged *as such* will have a disproportionately beneficial impact on blacks. Only such a program, and not one that operates on the basis of race, is in accord with the letter and the spirit of our Constitution.

Since I believe that the appellee here had a constitutional right to have its bid succeed or fail under a decisionmaking process uninfected with racial bias, I concur in the judgment of the Court.

Justice Marshall, with whom Justice Brennan and Justice Blackmun join, dissenting.

It is a welcome symbol of racial progress when the former capital of the Confederacy acts forthrightly to confront the effects of racial discrimination in its midst. In my view, nothing in the Constitution can be construed to prevent Richmond, Virginia, from allocating a portion of its contracting dollars for businesses owned or controlled by members of minority groups. Indeed, Richmond's set-aside program is indistinguishable in all meaningful respects from — and in fact was patterned upon — the federal set-aside plan which this Court upheld in Fullilove v. Klutznick.

A majority of this Court holds today, however, that the Equal Protection Clause of the Fourteenth Amendment blocks Richmond's initiative. The essence of the majority's position is that Richmond has failed to catalogue adequate findings to prove that past discrimination has impeded minorities from joining or participating fully in Richmond's construction contracting industry. I find deep irony in second-guessing Richmond's judgment on this point. As much as any municipality in the United States, Richmond knows what racial discrimination is; a century of decisions by this and other federal courts has richly documented the city's disgraceful history of public and private racial discrimination. In any event, the Richmond City Council *has* supported its determination that minorities have been wrongly excluded from local construction contracting. Its proof includes statistics showing that minority-owned businesses have received virtually no city contracting dollars and rarely if ever belonged to area trade associations; testimony by municipal officials that discrimination has been widespread in the local construction industry; and the same exhaustive and widely publicized federal studies relied on in *Fullilove*, studies which showed that pervasive discrimination in the Nation's tight-knit construction industry had operated to exclude minorities from public contracting. These are precisely the types of statistical and testimonial evidence which, until today, this Court had credited in cases approving of race-conscious measures designed to remedy past discrimination.

More fundamentally, today's decision marks a deliberate and giant step backward in this Court's affirmative action jurisprudence. Cynical of one municipality's attempt to redress the effects of past racial discrimination in a particular industry, the majority launches a grapeshot attack on race-conscious remedies in general. The majority's unnecessary pronouncements will inevitably discourage or prevent governmental entities, particularly States and localities, from acting to rectify the scourge of past discrimination. This is the harsh reality of the majority's decision, but it is not the Constitution's command.

I

As an initial matter, the majority takes an exceedingly myopic view of the factual predicate on which the Richmond City Council relied when it passed the Minority Business Utilization Plan. The majority analyzes Richmond's initiative as if it were based solely upon the facts about local construction and contracting practices adduced during the City Council session at which the measure was enacted. In so doing, the majority down-plays the fact that the City Council had before it a rich trove of evidence that discrimination in the Nation's construction industry had seriously impaired the competitive position of businesses owned or controlled by members of minority groups. It is only against this backdrop of documented national discrimination, however, that the local evidence adduced by Richmond can be properly understood. The majority's refusal to recognize that Richmond has proven itself no exception to the dismaying pattern of national exclusion which Congress so painstakingly identified infects its entire analysis of this case. . . .

[As] of 1977, there was "abundant evidence" in the public domain "that minority businesses ha[d] been denied effective participation in public contracting opportunities by procurement practices that perpetuated the effects of prior discrimination." *Fullilove*, at 477-478. Significantly, this evidence demonstrated that discrimination had prevented existing or nascent minority-owned businesses from obtaining not only federal contracting assignments, but state and local ones as well.

The members of the Richmond City Council were well aware of these exhaustive congressional findings, a point the majority, tellingly, elides. The transcript of the session at which the Council enacted the local set-aside initiative contains numerous references to the 6-year-old congressional set-aside program, to the evidence of nationwide discrimination barriers described above, and to the *Fullilove* decision itself. . . .

II

A

1

[Richmond] has two powerful interests in setting aside a portion of public contracting funds for minority-owned enterprises. The first is the city's interest in eradicating the effects of past racial discrimination. It is far too late in the day to doubt that remedying such discrimination is a compelling, let alone an important, interest. . . .

Richmond has a second compelling interest in setting aside, where possible, a portion of its contracting dollars. That interest is the prospective one of preventing the city's own spending decisions from reinforcing and perpetuating the exclusionary effects of past discrimination. . . .

The majority is wrong to trivialize the continuing impact of government acceptance or use of private institutions or structures once wrought by discrimination. When government channels all its contracting funds to a white-dominated community of established contractors whose racial homogeneity is the product of private discrimination, it does more than place its imprimatur on the practices which forged and which continue to define that community. It also provides a measurable boost to those economic entities that have thrived within it, while denying important economic benefits to those entities which, but for prior discrimination, might well be better qualified to receive valuable government contracts. . . .

2

The remaining question with respect to the "governmental interest" prong of equal protection analysis is whether Richmond has proffered satisfactory proof of past racial discrimination to support its twin interests in remediation and in governmental [nonperpetuation].

The varied body of evidence on which Richmond relied provides a "strong," "firm," and "unquestionably legitimate" basis upon which the City Council could determine that the effects of past racial discrimination warranted a remedial and prophylactic governmental response. [Richmond] acted against a backdrop of congressional and Executive Branch studies which demonstrated with such force the nationwide pervasiveness of prior discrimination that Congress presumed that "present economic inequities" in construction contracting resulted from "past discriminatory systems." The city's local evidence confirmed that Richmond's construction industry did not deviate from this pernicious national pattern. The fact that just .67% of public construction expenditures over the previous five years had gone to minority-owned prime contractors, despite the city's racially mixed population, strongly suggests that construction contracting in the area was rife with "present economic inequities." To the extent this enormous disparity did not itself demonstrate that discrimination had occurred, the descriptive testimony of Richmond's elected and appointed leaders drew the necessary link between the pitifully small presence of minorities in construction contracting and past exclusionary practices. That *no one* who testified challenged this depiction of widespread racial discrimination in area construction contracting lent significant weight to these accounts. The fact that area trade associations had virtually no minority members dramatized the extent of present inequities and suggested the lasting power of past discriminatory systems. In sum, to suggest that the facts on which Richmond has relied do not provide a sound basis for its finding of past racial discrimination simply blinks credibility. . . .

The majority states [that] reliance on the disparity between the share of city contracts awarded to minority firms (.67%) and the minority population of Richmond (approximately 50%) is "misplaced." It is true that, when the factual predicate needed to be proved is one of *present* discrimination, we have generally credited statistical contrasts between the racial composition of a work force and the general population as proving discrimination only where this contrast revealed "gross statistical disparities." But this principle does not impugn Richmond's statistical contrast, for two reasons. First, considering how minuscule the share of Richmond public construction contracting dollars received by minority-owned businesses is, it is hardly unreasonable to conclude that this case involves a "gross statistical disparit[y]." There are roughly equal numbers of minorities and nonminorities in Richmond — yet minority-owned businesses receive *one-seventy-fifth* the public contracting funds that other businesses receive.

Second, and more fundamentally, where the issue is not present discrimination but rather whether *past* discrimination has resulted in the *continuing exclusion* of minorities from an historically tight-knit industry, a contrast between population and work force is entirely appropriate to help gauge the degree of the exclusion. In Johnson v. Transportation Agency, Justice O'Connor specifically observed that, when it is alleged that discrimination has prevented blacks from "obtaining th[e] experience" needed to qualify for a position, the "relevant comparison" is not to the percentage of blacks in the pool of qualified candidates, but to "the total percentage of blacks in the labor force." 480 U.S., at 651. This contrast is especially illuminating in cases like this, where a main avenue of introduction into the work force — here, membership in the trade associations whose members presumably train apprentices and help them procure subcontracting assignments — is itself grossly dominated by nonminorities. The majority's assertion that the city "does not even know how many MBE's in the relevant market are qualified," is thus entirely beside the point. . . .

The majority's perfunctory dismissal of the testimony of Richmond's appointed and elected leaders is also deeply disturbing. . . .

Had the majority paused for a moment on the facts of the Richmond experience, it would have discovered that the city's leadership is deeply familiar with what racial discrimination is. The members of the Richmond City Council have spent long years witnessing multifarious acts of discrimination, including, but not limited to, the deliberate diminution of black residents' voting rights, resistance to school desegregation, and publicly sanctioned housing discrimination. Numerous decisions of federal courts chronicle this disgraceful recent history.

When the legislatures and leaders of cities with histories of pervasive discrimination testify that past discrimination has infected one of their industries, armchair cynicism like that exercised by the majority has no place. . . .

Finally, I vehemently disagree with the majority's dismissal of the congressional and Executive Branch findings noted in *Fullilove* as having "extremely limited" probative value in this case. The majority concedes that Congress established nothing less than a "presumption" that minority contracting firms have been disadvantaged by prior discrimination. The majority, inexplicably, would forbid Richmond to "share" in this information, and permit only Congress to take note of these ample findings. In thus requiring that Richmond's local evidence be severed from the context in which it was prepared, the majority would require cities seeking to eradicate the effects of past discrimination within their borders to reinvent the evidentiary wheel and engage in unnecessarily duplicative, costly, and time-consuming factfinding.

No principle of federalism or of federal power, however, forbids a state or local government from drawing upon a nationally relevant historical record prepared by the Federal Government. See Renton v. Playtime Theatres, Inc., 475 U.S. 41, 51-52 (1986). . . .

B

In my judgment, Richmond's set-aside plan also comports with the second prong of the equal protection inquiry, for it is substantially related to the interests it seeks to serve in remedying past discrimination and in ensuring that municipal contract procurement does not perpetuate that discrimination. . . .

[The] majority takes issue [with] two aspects of Richmond's tailoring: the city's refusal to explore the use of race-neutral measures to increase minority business participation in contracting, and the selection of a 30% set-aside figure. The majority's first criticism is flawed in two respects. First, the majority overlooks the fact that since 1975, Richmond has barred both discrimination by the city in awarding public contracts and discrimination by public contractors. The virtual absence of minority businesses from the city's contracting rolls, indicated by the fact that such businesses have received less than 1% of public contracting dollars, strongly suggests that this ban has not succeeded in redressing the impact of past discrimination or in preventing city contract procurement from reinforcing racial homogeneity. Second, the majority's suggestion that Richmond should have first undertaken such race-neutral measures as a program of city financing for small firms, ignores the fact that such measures, while theoretically appealing, have been discredited by Congress as ineffectual in eradicating the effects of past discrimination in this very industry. For this reason, this Court in *Fullilove* refused to fault Congress for not undertaking race-neutral measures as precursors to its race-conscious [set-aside].[11]

As for Richmond's 30% target, the majority states that this figure "cannot be said to be narrowly tailored to any goal, except perhaps outright racial balancing." The majority ignores two important facts. First, the set-aside measure affects only 3% of overall city contracting; thus, any imprecision in tailoring has far less impact than the majority suggests. But more important, the majority ignores the fact that Richmond's 30% figure was patterned directly on the *Fullilove* precedent. Congress' 10% figure fell "roughly halfway between the present percentage

11. The majority also faults Richmond's ordinance for including within its definition of "minority group members" not only black citizens, but also citizens who are "Spanish-speaking, Oriental, Indian, Eskimo, or Aleut persons." This is, of course, precisely the same definition Congress adopted in its set-aside legislation. Even accepting the majority's view that Richmond's ordinance is overbroad because it includes groups, such as Eskimos or Aleuts, about whom no evidence of local discrimination has been proffered, it does not necessarily follow that the balance of Richmond's ordinance should be invalidated. [Relocated footnote — EDS.]

of minority contractors and the percentage of minority group members in the Nation." *Fullilove*, 448 U.S., at 513-514 (Powell, J., concurring). The Richmond City Council's 30% figure similarly falls roughly halfway between the present percentage of Richmond-based minority contractors (almost zero) and the percentage of minorities in Richmond (50%). . . .

III

I would ordinarily end my analysis at this point and conclude that Richmond's ordinance satisfies both the governmental interest and substantial relationship prongs of our Equal Protection Clause analysis. However, I am compelled to add more, for the majority has gone beyond the facts of this case to announce a set of principles which unnecessarily restrict the power of governmental entities to take race-conscious measures to redress the effects of prior discrimination.

A

Today, for the first time, a majority of this Court has adopted strict scrutiny as its standard of Equal Protection Clause review of race-conscious remedial measures. This is an unwelcome development. A profound difference separates governmental actions that themselves are racist, and governmental actions that seek to remedy the effects of prior racism or to prevent neutral governmental activity from perpetuating the effects of such racism.

Racial classifications "drawn on the presumption that one race is inferior to another or because they put the weight of government behind racial hatred and separatism" warrant the strictest judicial scrutiny because of the very irrelevance of these rationales. By contrast, racial classifications drawn for the purpose of remedying the effects of discrimination that itself was race-based have a highly pertinent basis: the tragic and indelible fact that discrimination against blacks and other racial minorities in this Nation has pervaded our Nation's history and continues to scar our society. . . .

In concluding that remedial classifications warrant no different standard of review under the Constitution than the most brute and repugnant forms of state-sponsored racism, a majority of this Court signals that it regards racial discrimination as largely a phenomenon of the past, and that government bodies need no longer preoccupy themselves with rectifying racial injustice. I, however, do not believe this Nation is anywhere close to eradicating racial discrimination or its vestiges. In constitutionalizing its wishful thinking, the majority today does a grave disservice not only to those victims of past and present racial discrimination in this Nation whom government has sought to assist, but also to this Court's long tradition of approaching issues of race with the utmost sensitivity.

B

I am also troubled by the majority's assertion that, even if it did not believe generally in strict scrutiny of race-based remedial measures, "the circumstances of this case" require this Court to look upon the Richmond City Council's measure with the strictest scrutiny. The sole such circumstance which the majority cites, however, is the fact that blacks in Richmond are a "dominant racial grou[p]" in the city. In support of this characterization of dominance, the majority observes that "blacks comprise approximately 50% of the population of the city of Richmond" and that "[f]ive of the nine seats on the City Council are held by blacks."

While I agree that the numerical and political supremacy of a given racial group is a factor bearing upon the level of scrutiny to be applied, this Court has never held that numerical inferiority, standing alone, makes a racial group "suspect" and thus entitled to strict scrutiny review. Rather, we have identified *other* "traditional indicia of suspectness": whether a group has been "saddled with such disabilities, or subjected to such a history of purposeful unequal treatment, or relegated to such a position of political powerlessness as to command extraordinary protection from the majoritarian political process." San Antonio Independent School District v. Rodriguez, 411 U.S. 1, 28 (1973).

It cannot seriously be suggested that nonminorities in Richmond have any "history of purposeful unequal treatment." Nor is there any indication that they have any of the disabilities that have characteristically afflicted those groups this Court has deemed suspect. Indeed, the numerical and political dominance of nonminorities within the State of Virginia and the Nation as a whole provide an enormous political check against the "simple racial politics" at the municipal level which the majority fears. If the majority really believes that groups like Richmond's nonminorities, which comprise approximately half the population but which are outnumbered even marginally in political fora, are deserving of suspect class status for these reasons alone, this Court's decisions denying suspect status to women, and to persons with below-average incomes, stand on extremely shaky ground.

In my view, the "circumstances of this case," underscore the importance of *not* subjecting to a strict scrutiny straitjacket the increasing number of cities which have recently come under minority leadership and are eager to rectify, or at least prevent the perpetuation of, past racial discrimination. In many cases, these cities will be the ones with the most in the way of prior discrimination to rectify. . . .

Richmond's own recent political history underscores the facile nature of the majority's assumption that elected officials' voting decisions are based on the color of their skins. In recent years, white and black councilmembers in Richmond have increasingly joined hands on controversial matters. When the Richmond City Council elected a black man Mayor in 1982, for example, his victory was won with the support of the City Council's four white members. The vote on the set-aside plan a year later also was not purely along racial lines. Of the four white councilmembers, one voted for the measure and another abstained. The majority's view that remedial measures undertaken by municipalities with black leadership must face a stiffer test of Equal Protection Clause scrutiny than remedial measures undertaken by municipalities with white leadership implies a lack of political maturity on the part of this Nation's elected minority officials that is totally unwarranted. Such insulting judgments have no place in constitutional jurisprudence.

C

Today's decision, finally, is particularly noteworthy for the daunting standard it imposes upon States and localities contemplating the use of race-conscious measures to eradicate the present effects of prior discrimination and prevent its perpetuation. The majority restricts the use of such measures to situations in which a State or locality can put forth "a prima facie case of a constitutional or statutory violation." . . .

[If] Congress tomorrow dramatically expanded Title VII of the Civil Rights Act of 1964 — or alternatively, if it repealed that legislation altogether — the meaning of equal protection would change precipitously along with it. Whatever the Framers of the Fourteenth Amendment had in mind in 1868, it certainly was not that the content of their Amendment would turn on the amendments to or the evolving interpretations of a federal statute passed nearly a century later.

To the degree that this parsimonious standard is grounded on a view that either §1 or §5 of the Fourteenth Amendment substantially disempowered States and localities from remedying past racial discrimination, the majority is seriously mistaken. With respect, first, to §5, our precedents have never suggested that this provision — or, for that matter, its companion federal-empowerment provisions in the Thirteenth and Fifteenth Amendments — was meant to pre-empt or limit state police power to undertake race-conscious remedial measures. . . .

As for §1, it is too late in the day to assert seriously that the Equal Protection Clause prohibits States — or for that matter, the Federal Government, to whom the equal protection guarantee has largely been applied — from enacting race-conscious remedies. Our cases in the areas of school desegregation, voting rights, and affirmative action have demonstrated time and again that race is constitutionally germane, precisely because race remains dismayingly relevant in American life.

In adopting its prima facie standard for States and localities, the majority closes its eyes to this constitutional history and social reality. So, too, does Justice Scalia. He would further limit consideration of race to those cases in which States find it "necessary to eliminate their own maintenance of a system of unlawful racial classification" — a "distinction" which, he states, "explains our school desegregation cases." But this Court's remedy-stage school desegregation decisions cannot so conveniently be cordoned off. These decisions (like those involving voting rights and affirmative action) stand for the same broad principles of equal protection which Richmond seeks to vindicate in this case: all persons have equal worth, and it is permissible, given a sufficient factual predicate and appropriate tailoring, for government to take account of race to eradicate the present effects of race-based subjugation denying that basic equality. Justice Scalia's artful distinction allows him to avoid having to repudiate "our school desegregation cases," but, like the arbitrary limitation on race-conscious relief adopted by the majority, his approach "would freeze the status quo that is the very target" of the remedial actions of States and localities.

The fact is that Congress' concern in passing the Reconstruction Amendments, and particularly their congressional authorization provisions, was that States would *not* adequately respond to racial violence or discrimination against newly freed slaves. To interpret any aspect of these Amendments as proscribing state remedial responses to these very problems turns the Amendments on their heads. . . .

[Nothing] in the Amendments themselves, or in our long history of interpreting or applying those momentous charters, suggests that States, exercising their police power, are in any way constitutionally inhibited from working alongside the Federal Government in the fight against discrimination and its effects. . . .

[Justice Blackmun's dissenting opinion, joined by Justice Brennan, has been omitted].

Adarand Constructors, Inc. v. Pena

515 U.S. 200 (1995)

JUSTICE O'CONNOR announced the judgment of the Court and delivered an opinion with respect to Parts I, II, III-A, III-B, III-D, and IV, which is for the Court except insofar as it might be inconsistent with the views expressed in Justice Scalia's concurrence, and an opinion with respect to Part III-C in which JUSTICE KENNEDY joins.

Petitioner Adarand Constructors, Inc., claims that the Federal Government's practice of giving general contractors on government projects a financial incentive to hire subcontractors controlled by "socially and economically disadvantaged individuals," and in particular, the Government's use of race-based presumptions in identifying such individuals, violates the equal protection component of the Fifth Amendment's Due Process Clause. The Court of Appeals rejected Adarand's claim. We conclude, however, that courts should analyze cases of this kind under a different standard of review than the one the Court of Appeals applied. We therefore vacate the Court of Appeals' judgment and remand the case for further proceedings.

I

In 1989, the Central Federal Lands Highway Division (CFLHD), which is part of the United States Department of Transportation (DOT), awarded the prime contract for a highway construction project in Colorado to Mountain Gravel & Construction Company. Mountain Gravel then solicited bids from subcontractors for the guardrail portion of the contract. Adarand, a Colorado-based highway construction company specializing in guardrail work, submitted the low bid. Gonzales Construction Company also submitted a bid.

The prime contract's terms provide that Mountain Gravel would receive additional compensation if it hired subcontractors certified as small businesses controlled by "socially and economically disadvantaged individuals." Gonzales is certified as such a business; Adarand is not. Mountain Gravel awarded the subcontract to Gonzales, despite Adarand's low bid, and Mountain Gravel's Chief Estimator has submitted an affidavit stating that Mountain Gravel would have accepted Adarand's bid, had it not been for the additional payment it received by hiring Gonzales instead. Federal law requires that a subcontracting clause similar to the one used here must appear in most federal agency contracts, and it also requires the clause to state that "the contractor shall presume that socially and economically disadvantaged individuals include Black Americans, Hispanic Americans, Native Americans, Asian Pacific Americans, and other minorities, or any other individual found to be disadvantaged by the [Small Business] Administration pursuant to section 8(a) of the Small Business Act." Adarand claims that the presumption set forth in that statute discriminates on the basis of race in violation of the Federal Government's Fifth Amendment obligation not to deny anyone equal protection of the laws. . . .

II

[In this section, the Court holds that Adarand had standing to seek injunctive relief against further use of the subcontractor compensation clause.]

III

The Government urges that "the Subcontracting Compensation Clause program is . . . a program based on disadvantage, not on race," and thus that it is subject only to "the most relaxed judicial scrutiny." To the extent that the statutes and regulations involved in this case are race neutral, we agree. The Government concedes, however, that "the race-based rebuttable presumption used in some certification determinations under the Subcontracting Compensation Clause" is subject to some heightened level of scrutiny. The parties disagree as to what that level should be. (We note, incidentally, that this case concerns only classifications based explicitly on race, and presents none of the additional difficulties posed by laws that, although facially race neutral, result in racially disproportionate impact and are motivated by a racially discriminatory purpose. . . .)

Adarand's claim arises under the Fifth Amendment to the Constitution, which provides that "No person shall . . . be deprived of life, liberty, or property, without due process of law." Although this Court has always understood that Clause to provide some measure of protection against arbitrary treatment by the Federal Government, it is not as explicit a guarantee of equal treatment as the Fourteenth Amendment, which provides that "No State shall . . . deny to any person within its jurisdiction the equal protection of the laws." Our cases have accorded varying degrees of significance to the difference in the language of those two Clauses. We think it necessary to revisit the issue here.

A

[After a review of the cases, the Court concludes that there is no distinction between claims brought under the fourteenth amendment's equal protection clause and those brought under the "equal protection component" of the fifth amendment's due process clause.]

B

With *Croson*, the Court finally agreed that the Fourteenth Amendment requires strict scrutiny of all race-based action by state and local governments. But *Croson* of course had no occasion to declare what standard of review the Fifth Amendment requires for such action taken by the Federal Government. *Croson* observed simply that the Court's "treatment of an exercise of congressional power in *Fullilove* cannot be dispositive here," because *Croson's* facts did not implicate Congress' broad power under §5 of the Fourteenth Amendment. . . .

Despite lingering uncertainty in the details, however, the Court's cases through *Croson* had established three general propositions with respect to governmental racial classifications. First, skepticism: "any preference based on racial or ethnic criteria must necessarily receive a most searching examination." [*Wygant.*] Second, consistency: "the standard of review under the Equal Protection Clause is not dependent on the race of those burdened or benefited by a particular classification," [*Croson*]. And third, congruence: "equal protection analysis in the Fifth Amendment area is the same as that under the Fourteenth Amendment," [Buckley v. Valeo, 424 U.S. 1 (1976)]. Taken together, these three propositions lead to the conclusion that any person, of whatever race, has the right to demand that any governmental actor subject to the Constitution justify any racial classification subjecting that person to unequal treatment under the strictest judicial scrutiny. . . .

A year later, however, the Court took a surprising turn.

[The Court describes Metro Broadcasting, Inc. v. Federal Communications Commission, 497 U.S. 547 (1990), which concerned two FCC policies favoring minority firms. Under one policy, the commission considered minority ownership as a "plus" to be weighed with other factors in a comparative hearing designed to determine which applicant should be awarded a license. The other policy created an exception favoring minorities in cases where a licensee's qualifications to hold a license come into question. Normally, such a licensee may not transfer the license until the FCC has resolved the matter. However, the FCC policy permitted such a licensee to assign the license to an FCC-approved minority enterprise. Both policies were justified on the ground that minorities were inadequately represented in the broadcast media, and that greater minority representation would enhance the diversification of programming.

[In a five-to-four decision written by Justice Brennan, the Court upheld the constitutionality of both policies. The Court distinguished *Croson* on the ground that both policies had been "specifically approved — indeed, mandated — by Congress." It held that "benign race-conscious measures mandated by Congress — even if those measures are not 'remedial' in the sense of being designed to compensate victims of past governmental or society discrimination — are constitutionally permissible to the extent that they serve important governmental objectives within the power of Congress and are substantially related to the achievement of those objectives."]

In *Metro Broadcasting*, the Court repudiated the long-held notion that "it would be unthinkable that the same Constitution would impose a lesser duty on the Federal Government" than it does on a State to afford equal protection of the laws, [Bolling v. Sharpe, 347 U.S. 497 (1954)]. It did so by holding that "benign" federal racial classifications need only satisfy intermediate scrutiny, even though *Croson* had recently concluded that such classifications enacted by a State must satisfy strict scrutiny. [The] Court did not explain how to tell whether a racial classification should be deemed "benign," other than to express "confidence that an 'examination of the legislative scheme and its history' will separate benign measures from other types of racial classifications." . . .

By adopting intermediate scrutiny as the standard of review for congressionally mandated "benign" racial classifications, *Metro Broadcasting* departed from prior cases in two significant respects. First, it turned its back on *Croson's* explanation of why strict scrutiny of all governmental racial classifications is essential:

> Absent searching judicial inquiry into the justification for such race-based measures, there is simply no way of determining what classifications are "benign" or "remedial" and what classifications are in fact motivated by illegitimate notions of racial inferiority or simple racial politics. Indeed, the purpose of strict scrutiny is to "smoke out" illegitimate uses of race by assuring that the legislative body is pursuing a goal important enough to warrant use of a highly suspect tool. The test also ensures that the means chosen "fit" this compelling goal so closely that there is little or no possibility that the motive for the classification was illegitimate racial prejudice or stereotype. *Croson* (plurality opinion of O'Connor, J.).

We adhere to that view today, despite the surface appeal of holding "benign" racial classifications to a lower standard, because "it may not always be clear that a so-called preference is in fact benign," *Bakke* (opinion of Powell, J.). . . .

Second, *Metro Broadcasting* squarely rejected one of the three propositions established by the Court's earlier equal protection cases, namely, congruence between the standards applicable to federal and state racial classifications, and in so doing also undermined the other two — skepticism of all racial classifications, and consistency of treatment irrespective of the race of the burdened or benefited group. . . .

The three propositions undermined by *Metro Broadcasting* all derive from the basic principle that the Fifth and Fourteenth Amendments to the Constitution protect persons, not groups. It follows from that principle that all governmental action based on race — a group classification long recognized as "in most circumstances irrelevant and therefore prohibited," [Hirabayashi v. United States, 320 U.S. 81 (1943)] — be subjected to detailed judicial inquiry to ensure that the personal right to equal protection of the laws has not been infringed. [Accordingly,] we hold today that all racial classifications, imposed by whatever federal, state, or local governmental actor, must be analyzed by a reviewing court under strict scrutiny. In other words, such classifications are constitutional only if they are narrowly tailored measures that further compelling governmental interests. To the extent that *Metro Broadcasting* is inconsistent with that holding, it is overruled.

[In dissent,] Justice Stevens concurs in our view that courts should take a skeptical view of all governmental racial classifications. He also allows that "nothing is inherently wrong with applying a single standard to fundamentally different situations, as long as that standard takes relevant differences into account." What he fails to recognize is that strict scrutiny does take "relevant differences" into account — indeed, that is its fundamental purpose. The point of carefully examining the interest asserted by the government in support of a racial classification, and the evidence offered to show that the classification is needed, is precisely to distinguish legitimate from illegitimate uses of race in governmental decision-making. And Justice Stevens concedes that "some cases may be difficult to classify"; all the more reason, in our view, to examine all racial classifications carefully. Strict scrutiny does not "treat dissimilar race-based decisions as though they were equally objectionable"; to the contrary, it evaluates carefully all governmental race-based decisions in order to decide which are constitutionally objectionable and which are not. By requiring strict scrutiny of racial classifications, we require courts to make sure that a governmental classification based on race, which "so seldom provides a relevant basis for disparate treatment," *Fullilove* (Stevens, J., dissenting), is legitimate, before permitting unequal treatment based on race to proceed.

Justice Stevens chides us for our "supposed inability to differentiate between 'invidious' and 'benign' discrimination," because it is in his view sufficient that "people understand the difference between good intentions and bad." But, [the] point of strict scrutiny is to "differentiate between" permissible and impermissible governmental use of race. And Justice Stevens himself has already explained in his dissent in *Fullilove* why "good intentions" alone are not enough to sustain a supposedly "benign" racial classification: "Even though it is not the actual predicate for this legislation, a statute of this kind inevitably is perceived by many as resting on an assumption that those who are granted this special preference are less qualified in some respect that is identified purely by their race. Because that perception — especially when fostered by the Congress of the United States — can only exacerbate rather than reduce racial prejudice, it will delay the time when race will become a truly irrelevant, or at least insignificant, factor. Unless Congress clearly articulates the need and basis for a racial classification, and also tailors the classification to its justification, the Court should not uphold this kind of statute." *Fullilove* (dissenting opinion). . . .

Perhaps it is not the standard of strict scrutiny itself, but our use of the concepts of "consistency" and "congruence" in conjunction with it, that leads Justice Stevens to dissent. According to Justice Stevens, our view of consistency "equates remedial preferences with invidious discrimination," and ignores the difference between "an engine of oppression" and an effort "to foster equality in society," or, more colorfully, "between a 'No Trespassing' sign and a welcome mat." It does nothing of the kind. The principle of consistency simply means that whenever the government treats any person unequally because of his or her race, that person has suffered an injury that falls squarely within the language and spirit of the Constitution's guarantee of equal protection. It says nothing about the ultimate validity of any particular law; that determination is the job of the court applying strict scrutiny. The principle of consistency explains the circumstances in which the injury requiring strict scrutiny occurs. The application of strict scrutiny, in turn, determines whether a compelling governmental interest justifies the infliction of that injury. . . .

Justice Stevens also claims that we have ignored any difference between federal and state legislatures. But requiring that Congress, like the States, enact racial classifications only when doing so is necessary to further a "compelling interest" does not contravene any principle of appropriate respect for a co-equal Branch of the Government. . . .

C

[In this section of the opinion, joined only by Justice Kennedy, Justice O'Connor explains why stare decisis does not mandate adherence to *Metro Broadcasting*.]

D

Our action today makes explicit what Justice Powell thought implicit in the *Fullilove* lead opinion: federal racial classifications, like those of a State, must serve a compelling governmental interest, and must be narrowly tailored to further that interest. [Of] course, it follows that to the extent (if any) that *Fullilove* held federal racial classifications to be subject to a less rigorous standard, it is no longer controlling. But we need not decide today whether the program upheld in *Fullilove* would survive strict scrutiny as our more recent cases have defined it. . . .

Finally, we wish to dispel the notion that strict scrutiny is "strict in theory, but fatal in fact." *Fullilove* (Marshall, J., concurring in judgment). The unhappy persistence of both the practice and the lingering effects of racial discrimination against minority groups in this country is an unfortunate reality, and government is not disqualified from acting in response to it. When race-based action is necessary to further a compelling interest, such action is within constitutional constraints if it satisfies the "narrow tailoring" test this Court has set out in previous cases.

IV

Because our decision today alters the playing field in some important respects, we think it best to remand the case to the lower courts for further consideration in light of the principles we have announced. The Court of Appeals, following *Metro Broadcasting* and *Fullilove*, analyzed the case in terms of intermediate scrutiny. It upheld the challenged statutes and regulations because it found them to be "narrowly tailored to achieve [their] significant governmental purpose of providing subcontracting opportunities for small disadvantaged business enterprises." The Court of Appeals did not decide the question whether the interests served by the use of subcontractor compensation clauses are properly described as "compelling." It also did not address the question of narrow tailoring in terms of our strict scrutiny cases, by asking, for example, whether there was "any consideration of the use of race-neutral means to increase minority business participation" in government contracting, *Croson*, or whether the program was appropriately limited such that it "will not last longer than the discriminatory effects it is designed to eliminate," *Fullilove* (Powell, J., concurring). . . .

Accordingly, the judgment of the Court of Appeals is vacated, and the case is remanded for further proceedings consistent with this opinion.

It is so ordered.

JUSTICE SCALIA, concurring in part and concurring in the judgment.

I join the opinion of the Court, except Part III-C, and except insofar as it may be inconsistent with the following: In my view, government can never have a "compelling interest" in discriminating on the basis of race in order to "make up" for past racial discrimination in the opposite direction. Individuals who have been wronged by unlawful racial discrimination should be made whole; but under our Constitution there can be no such thing as either a creditor or a debtor race. That concept is alien to the Constitution's focus upon the individual, [and] its rejection of dispositions based on [race]. To pursue the concept of racial entitlement — even for the most admirable and benign of purposes — is to reinforce and preserve for future mischief the way of thinking that produced race slavery, race privilege and race hatred. In the eyes of government, we are just one race here. It is American.

It is unlikely, if not impossible, that the challenged program would survive under this understanding of strict scrutiny, but I am content to leave that to be decided on remand.

JUSTICE THOMAS, concurring in part and concurring in the judgment.

I agree with the majority's conclusion that strict scrutiny applies to all government classifications based on race. I write separately, however, to express my disagreement with the premise underlying Justice Stevens' and Justice Ginsburg's dissents: that there is a racial paternalism exception to the principle of equal protection. I believe that there is a "moral [and] constitutional equivalence," (Stevens, J., dissenting), between laws designed to subjugate a race and those that distribute benefits on the basis of race in order to foster some current notion of equality. Government cannot make us equal; it can only recognize, respect, and protect us as equal before the law.

That these programs may have been motivated, in part, by good intentions cannot provide refuge from the principle that under our Constitution, the government may not make distinctions on the basis of race. As far as the Constitution is concerned, it is irrelevant whether a government's racial classifications are drawn by those who wish to oppress a race or by those who have a sincere desire to help those thought to be disadvantaged. There can be no doubt that the paternalism that appears to lie at the heart of this program is at war with the principle of inherent equality that underlies and infuses our Constitution. See Declaration of Independence ("We hold these truths to be self-evident, that all men are created equal, that they are endowed by their Creator with certain unalienable Rights, that among these are Life, Liberty, and the pursuit of Happiness").

These programs not only raise grave constitutional questions, they also undermine the moral basis of the equal protection principle. Purchased at the price of immeasurable human suffering, the equal protection principle reflects our Nation's understanding that such classifications ultimately have a destructive impact on the individual and our society. Unquestionably, "invidious [racial] discrimination is an engine of oppression." It is also true that "remedial" racial preferences may reflect "a desire to foster equality in society." But there can be no doubt that racial paternalism and its unintended consequences can be as poisonous and pernicious as any other form of discrimination. So-called "benign" discrimination teaches many that because of chronic and apparently immutable handicaps, minorities cannot compete with them without their patronizing indulgence. Inevitably, such programs engender attitudes of superiority or, alternatively, provoke resentment among those who believe that they have been wronged by the government's use of race. These programs stamp minorities with a badge of inferiority and may cause them to develop dependencies or to adopt an attitude that they are "entitled" to preferences. . . .

In my mind, government-sponsored racial discrimination based on benign prejudice is just as noxious as discrimination inspired by malicious prejudice. In each instance, it is racial discrimination, plain and simple.

JUSTICE STEVENS, with whom JUSTICE GINSBURG joins, dissenting.

Instead of deciding this case in accordance with controlling precedent, the Court today delivers a disconcerting lecture about the evils of governmental racial classifications. For its text the Court has selected three propositions, represented by the bywords "skepticism," "consistency," and "congruence." . . .

I

The Court's concept of skepticism is, at least in principle, a good statement of law and of common sense. Undoubtedly, a court should be wary of a governmental decision that relies upon a racial classification. [But], as the opinions in *Fullilove* demonstrate, substantial agreement on the standard to be applied in deciding difficult cases does not necessarily lead to agreement on how those cases actually should or will be resolved. In my judgment, because uniform standards are often anything but uniform, we should evaluate the Court's comments on "consistency," "congruence," and stare decisis with the same type of skepticism that the Court advocates for the underlying issue.

II

The Court's concept of "consistency" assumes that there is no significant difference between a decision by the majority to impose a special burden on the members of a minority race and a decision by the majority to provide a benefit to certain members of that minority notwithstanding its incidental burden on some members of the majority. In my opinion that assumption is untenable. There is no moral or constitutional equivalence between a policy that is designed to perpetuate a caste system and one that seeks to eradicate racial subordination. Invidious discrimination is an engine of oppression, subjugating a disfavored group to enhance or maintain the power of the majority. Remedial race-based preferences reflect the opposite impulse: a desire to foster equality in society. No sensible conception of the Government's constitutional obligation to "govern impartially," should ignore this distinction.

To illustrate the point, consider our cases addressing the Federal Government's discrimination against Japanese Americans during World War II, Hirabayashi v. United States, and Korematsu v. United States. The discrimination at issue in those cases was invidious because the Government imposed special burdens — a curfew and exclusion from certain areas on the West Coast — on the members of a minority class defined by racial and ethnic characteristics. Members of the same racially defined class exhibited exceptional heroism in the service of our country during that War. Now suppose Congress decided to reward that service with a federal program that gave all Japanese-American veterans an extraordinary preference in Government employment. Cf. Personnel Administrator of Mass. v. Feeney. If Congress had done so, the same racial characteristics that motivated the discriminatory burdens in Hirabayashi and Korematsu would have defined the preferred class of veterans. Nevertheless, "consistency" surely would not require us to describe the incidental burden on everyone else in the country as "odious" or "invidious" as those terms were used in those cases. We should reject a concept of "consistency" that would view the special preferences that the National Government has provided to Native Americans since 1834 as comparable to the official discrimination against African Americans that was prevalent for much of our history.

The consistency that the Court espouses would disregard the difference between a "No Trespassing" sign and a welcome mat. It would treat a Dixiecrat Senator's decision to vote against Thurgood Marshall's confirmation in order to keep African Americans off the Supreme Court as on a par with President Johnson's evaluation of his nominee's race as a positive factor. It would equate a law that made black citizens ineligible for military service with a program aimed at recruiting black soldiers. An attempt by the majority to exclude members of a minority race from a regulated market is fundamentally different from a subsidy that enables a relatively small group of newcomers to enter that market. An interest in "consistency" does not justify treating differences as though they were similarities.

The Court's explanation for treating dissimilar race-based decisions as though they were equally objectionable is a supposed inability to differentiate between "invidious" and "benign" discrimination. But the term "affirmative action" is common and well understood. Its presence in everyday parlance shows that people understand the difference between good intentions and bad. As with any legal concept, some cases may be difficult to classify, but our equal protection jurisprudence has identified a critical difference between state action that imposes burdens on a disfavored few and state action that benefits the few "in spite of" its adverse effects on the many. *Feeney*.

Indeed, our jurisprudence has made the standard to be applied in cases of invidious discrimination turn on whether the discrimination is "intentional," or whether, by contrast, it merely has a discriminatory "effect." Washington v. Davis. Surely this distinction is at least as subtle, and at least as difficult to apply, as the usually obvious distinction between a measure intended to benefit members of a particular minority race and a measure intended to burden a minority race. A state actor inclined to subvert the Constitution might easily hide bad intentions in the guise of unintended "effects"; but I should think it far more difficult to enact a law intending to preserve the majority's hegemony while casting it plausibly in the guise of affirmative action for minorities.

Nothing is inherently wrong with applying a single standard to fundamentally different situations, as long as that standard takes relevant differences into account. For example, if the Court in all equal protection cases were to insist that differential treatment be justified by relevant characteristics of the members of the favored and disfavored classes that provide a legitimate basis for disparate treatment, such a standard would treat dissimilar cases differently while still recognizing that there is, after all, only one Equal Protection Clause. Under such a standard, subsidies for disadvantaged businesses may be constitutional though special taxes on such businesses would be invalid. But a single standard that purports to equate remedial preferences with invidious discrimination cannot be defended in the name of "equal protection."

Moreover, the Court may find that its new "consistency" approach to race-based classifications is difficult to square with its insistence upon rigidly separate categories for discrimination against different classes of individuals. For example, as the law currently stands, the Court will apply "intermediate scrutiny" to cases of invidious gender discrimination and "strict scrutiny" to cases of invidious race discrimination, while applying the same standard for benign classifications as for invidious ones. [The Court's articulation of an "intermediate" standard of review in cases of gender discrimination is discussed at pages 602-610 infra.] If this remains the law, then today's lecture about "consistency" will produce the anomalous result that the Government can more easily enact affirmative-action programs to remedy discrimination against women than it can enact affirmative-action programs to remedy discrimination against African Americans — even though the primary purpose of the Equal Protection Clause was to end discrimination against the former slaves. When a court becomes preoccupied with abstract standards, it risks sacrificing common sense at the altar of formal consistency.

As a matter of constitutional and democratic principle, a decision by representatives of the majority to discriminate against the members of a minority race is fundamentally different from those same representatives' decision to impose incidental costs on the majority of their constituents in order to provide a benefit to a disadvantaged minority. Indeed, as I have previously argued, the former is virtually always repugnant to the principles of a free and democratic society, whereas the latter is, in some circumstances, entirely consistent with the ideal of equality. By insisting on a doctrinaire notion of "consistency" in the standard applicable to all race-based governmental actions, the Court obscures this essential dichotomy.

III

The Court's concept of "congruence" assumes that there is no significant difference between a decision by the Congress of the United States to adopt an affirmative-action program and such a decision by a State or a municipality. In my opinion that assumption is untenable. It ignores important practical and legal differences between federal and state or local decisionmakers. . . .

[Federal] affirmative-action programs represent the will of our entire Nation's elected representatives, whereas a state or local program may have an impact on nonresident entities who played no part in the decision to enact it. Thus, in the state or local context, individuals who were unable to vote for the local representatives who enacted a race-conscious program may nonetheless feel the effects of that program. This difference recalls the goals of the Commerce Clause, which permits Congress to legislate on certain matters of national importance while denying power to the States in this area for fear of undue impact upon out-of-state residents. . . .

Presumably, the majority is now satisfied that its theory of "congruence" between the substantive rights provided by the Fifth and Fourteenth Amendments disposes of the objection based upon divided constitutional powers. But it is one thing to say (as no one seems to dispute) that the Fifth Amendment encompasses a general guarantee of equal protection as broad as that contained within the Fourteenth Amendment. It is another thing entirely to say that Congress' institutional competence and constitutional authority entitles it to no greater deference when it enacts a program designed to foster equality than the deference due a State legislature. . . .

[A dissenting opinion by Justice Souter, with whom Justice Ginsburg and Justice Breyer join, is omitted.]

JUSTICE GINSBURG, with whom JUSTICE BREYER joins, dissenting.

[I] write separately to underscore not the differences the several opinions in this case display, but the considerable field of agreement — the common understandings and concerns — revealed in opinions that together speak for a majority of the Court.

I

The statutes and regulations at issue, as the Court indicates, were adopted by the political branches in response to an "unfortunate reality": "the unhappy persistence of both the practice and the lingering effects of racial discrimination against minority groups in this country." The United States suffers from those lingering effects because, for most of our Nation's history, the idea that "we are just one race," (Scalia, J., concurring in part and concurring in judgment), was not embraced. For generations, our lawmakers and judges were unprepared to say that there is in this land no superior race, no race inferior to any other. . . .

The divisions in this difficult case should not obscure the Court's recognition of the persistence of racial inequality and a majority's acknowledgement of Congress' authority to act affirmatively, not only to end discrimination, but also to counteract discrimination's lingering effects. Those effects, reflective of a system of racial caste only recently ended, are evident in our workplaces, markets, and neighborhoods. Job applicants with identical resumes, qualifications, and interview styles still experience different receptions, depending on their race. White and African-American consumers still encounter different deals. People of color looking for housing still face discriminatory treatment by landlords, real estate agents, and mortgage lenders. Minority entrepreneurs sometimes fail to gain contracts though they are the low bidders, and they are sometimes refused work even after winning contracts. Bias both conscious and unconscious, reflecting traditional and unexamined habits of thought, keeps up barriers that must come down if equal opportunity and nondiscrimination are ever genuinely to become this country's law and practice.

Given this history and its practical consequences, Congress surely can conclude that a carefully designed affirmative action program may help to realize, finally, the "equal protection of the laws" the Fourteenth Amendment has promised since 1868.

II

The lead opinion uses one term, "strict scrutiny," to describe the standard of judicial review for all governmental classifications by race. But that opinion's elaboration strongly suggests that the strict standard announced is indeed "fatal" for classifications burdening groups that have suffered discrimination in our society. That seems to me, and, I believe, to the Court, the enduring lesson one should draw from Korematsu v. United States, for in that case, scrutiny the Court described as "most rigid," nonetheless yielded a pass for an odious, gravely injurious racial classification. A Korematsu-type classification, as I read the opinions in this case, will never again survive scrutiny: such a classification, history and precedent instruct, properly ranks as prohibited.

For a classification made to hasten the day when "we are just one race," (Scalia, J., concurring in part and concurring in judgment), however, the lead opinion has dispelled the notion that "strict scrutiny" is "'fatal in fact.'" Properly, a majority of the Court calls for review that is searching, in order to ferret out classifications in reality malign, but masquerading as benign. The Court's once lax review of sex-based classifications demonstrates the need for such suspicion. Today's decision thus usefully reiterates that the purpose of strict scrutiny "is precisely to distinguish legitimate from illegitimate uses of race in governmental decisionmaking," "to 'differentiate between' permissible and impermissible governmental use of race," to distinguish "'between a "No Trespassing" sign and a welcome mat.'"

Close review also is in order for this further reason. [As] this very case shows, some members of the historically favored race can be hurt by catch-up mechanisms designed to cope with the lingering effects of entrenched racial subjugation. Court review can ensure that preferences are not so large as to trammel unduly upon the opportunities of others or interfere too harshly with legitimate expectations of persons in once-preferred groups. . . .

While I would not disturb the programs challenged in this case, and would leave their improvement to the political branches, I see today's decision as one that allows our precedent to evolve, still to be informed by and responsive to changing conditions.

Note: The Constitutionality of "Benign" Racial Classifications

Adarand and *Croson* establish that "benign" racial classifications, like those that harm racial minorities, are subject to strict scrutiny. The decisions leave uncertain, however, the exact nature of this scrutiny, as well as the kinds of justifications that will count as "compelling" government interests.

1. *The level of scrutiny for classifications that benefit racial minorities.* Recall the justifications for strict scrutiny for race-based classifications that harm racial minorities, discussed at pages 505-512 supra. Which, if any, of these arguments apply to affirmative action measures?

a. *Text and original intent.* By its terms, the fourteenth amendment says nothing about heightened review for racial classifications contained in affirmative action measures. As noted above, see page 432, the original impetus for passage of the amendment was a desire to expand the scope of congressional power to enact the nineteenth-century analogue of affirmative action measures. For a discussion, see Schnapper, Affirmative Action and the Legislative History of the Fourteenth Amendment, 71 Va. L. Rev. 753 (1985). Congress wished to lay a firm constitutional grounding for Reconstruction statutes that had the specific purpose of benefiting and protecting the newly freed slaves. There is also a sense in which the amendment was designed to *restrict* judicial power. Members of the Reconstruction Congress feared that the Supreme Court would invalidate the 1866 Civil Rights Act and adopted the fourteenth amendment so as to avoid that result. In light of this history, is there an originalist justification for strict scrutiny of affirmative action measures? Might such scrutiny be defended as the most appropriate conception of equality in a changed environment, much as the *Brown*

Court defended desegregation in a modern context despite the framers' specific intent to the contrary?

b. *Race consciousness.* Do affirmative action measures merit strict scrutiny because of "the basic principle that the Fifth and Fourteenth Amendments to the Constitution protect persons, not groups"? *Adarand,* supra. The Court's statement cannot be taken literally in light of its regular application of low-level scrutiny to statutes that use group characteristics to categorize people in nonracial contexts. See pages 475-488 supra. Perhaps, though, there are special dangers associated with group generalizations based on race. Consider, for example, the proposition that the very act of categorizing people according to their race, necessary for any affirmative action plan, is offensive and serves to reenforce simplistic and invidious racial categories. See Ford, Administering Identity: The Determination of "Race" in Race-Conscious Law, 82 Cal. L. Rev. 1231, 1239 (1994):

> While different species cannot breed with each other, humans invariably do — and the phenotypical characteristics we traditionally associate with particular "races" are not quanta of racial identity but infinitely modulated characteristics which further shade into each other with each successive union. [However] strongly racial and ethnic differences may be perceived, and however "real" they may be insofar as they powerfully affect the lives people lead, can they be pinned down with the conceptual coherence and replicability that group-oriented benefit allocation requires?

Compare Aleinikoff, A Case for Race-Consciousness, 91 Colum. L. Rev. 1061, 1087-1088, 1109-1110 (1991):

> [Recognizing] race validates the lives and experiences of those who have been burdened because of their race. White racism has made "blackness" a relevant category in our society. Yet colorblindness seeks to deny the continued social significance of the category, to tell blacks that they are no different from whites, even though blacks as blacks are persistently made to feel that difference.

See also Gotanda, A Critique of "Our Constitution Is Color-Blind," 44 Stan. L. Rev. 1, 18-19 (1991):

> In everyday American life, [color-blind] nonrecognition is self-contradictory because it is impossible to not think about a subject without having first thought about it at least a little. Nonrecognition differs from nonperception. Compare color-blind nonrecognition with medical color-blindness. A medically color-blind person is someone who cannot see what others can. [To] be racially color-blind, on the other hand, is to ignore what one has already noticed. [This] is not just a semantic distinction. The characteristics of race that are noticed (before being ignored) are situated within an already existing understanding of race. That is, race carries with it a complex social meaning. . . .
>
> This pre-existing race consciousness makes it impossible for an individual to be truly nonconscious of race. To argue that one did not *really* consider the race of an African-American is to concede that there was an identification of Blackness. Suppressing the recognition of a racial classification in order to act as if a person were not of some cognizable racial class is inherently racially premised.

c. *History.* Does the fact that whites as a group have not suffered from a history of discrimination justify a lower standard of review for statutes disadvantaging them? Consider Lempert, The Force of Irony: On the Morality of Affirmative Action and United Steelworkers v. Weber, 95 Ethics 86, 89 (1984):

> Why does racial discrimination excite us when so many other kinds of discrimination do not? It is because of the way we interpret history, associating racial discrimination with practices that now appear self-evidently evil: forcing blacks from their homeland, enslaving blacks, lynching blacks for actions that among whites would not be criminal, intimidating blacks who sought to exercise their rights — in sum, systematically disadvantaging a people in almost every way that mattered because of the color of their skin. [A] claim made by a white person as a member of the dominant majority draws its moral force largely from our collective horror at centuries of oppressing black people. It would be ironic indeed if evils visited on blacks had lent enough force to the moral claims of whites to prevent what appears to many at this point to be the most effective means of eliminating the legacy of those evils.

Might not the same history be characterized as demonstrating the evils of racial discrimination regardless of the race against which it is directed?

d. *Political process.* Does the fact that whites have "adequate" political power justify a lower level of scrutiny when laws disadvantage them? Consider Ely, The Constitutionality of Reverse Racial Discrimination, 41 U. Chi. L. Rev. 723, 735-736 (1974):

> When the group that controls the decision making process classifies so as to advantage a minority and disadvantage itself, the reasons for being unusually suspicious, and, consequently, employing a stringent brand of review are lacking. A White majority is unlikely to disadvantage itself for reasons of racial prejudice; nor is it likely to be tempted either to underestimate the needs and deserts of Whites relative to those of others, or to overestimate the cost of devising an alternative classification that would extend to certain Whites the advantages generally extended to Blacks. . . .
>
> [Whether] or not it is more blessed to give than to receive, it is surely less suspicious.

Is it a necessary implication of this view that a race-conscious program might be constitutional if adopted by a city council dominated by whites but unconstitutional if adopted by a city council like Richmond's with a black majority? If the arguments for affirmative action are ultimately persuasive, why should it matter who is persuaded by them?

Does Ely's argument unrealistically assume that affirmative action disadvantages a monolithic white majority capable of protecting itself politically?

e. *"Innocent victims."* It is sometimes argued that "benign" discrimination should be strictly scrutinized because it disadvantages individuals on the basis of immutable characteristics when those individuals are not themselves responsible for the evil to be corrected. Note, however, that in a remedial context, innocent victims will be disadvantaged by their race whether or not an affirmative action program is adopted. In any event, is it tenable to insist on a general rule that the government should not disadvantage "innocent" individuals when doing so promotes the general welfare? Would a meritocratic system for dispensing scarce resources satisfy this requirement? Consider Karst and Horowitz, Affirmative Action and Equal Protection, 60 Va. L. Rev. 955, 962 (1974):

Whether "merit" be defined in terms of demonstrated achievement or of potential achievement, it includes a large and hard-to-isolate ingredient of native talents. These talents resemble race in that they are beyond the control of the individual whose "merit" is being evaluated. If racial classifications are "suspect" partly for this reason, then it may be appropriate to insist that public rewards for native talents be justified by a showing of compelling necessity.

Is the "innocent victims" argument merely an artifact of an unduly narrow conception of the purposes of affirmative action programs? Consider Sullivan, Sins of Discrimination: Last Term's Affirmative Action Cases, 100 Harv. L. Rev. 78, 80-81, 96 (1986):

[The] Court has approved affirmative action only as precise penance for the specific sins of racism a government, union, or employer has committed in the past. Not surprisingly, this approach has invited claims [that] nonsinners — white workers "innocent" of their bosses' or union leadership's past discrimination — should not pay for "the sins of others of their own race," [*Fullilove*], nor should nonvictims benefit from their sacrifice. . . .

But public and private employers often adopt affirmative action less to purge their past than to build their future. In so doing, they are not "engineering" racial balance as an end in itself but are promoting a variety of goals dependent on racial balance, from securing workplace peace to eliminating workplace caste. . . .

If such aspirations for the future rather than past sin were the basis for affirmative action, would white claims of "innocence" count for less? They should, for it is easier to show that displacing "innocent" whites is narrowly tailored to goals that turn on integrating institutions now than it is to show that doing so is narrowly tailored to purging past sins of discrimination that the displaced whites did not themselves "commit."

Compare Delgado, Affirmative Action as a Majoritarian Device: Or, Do You Really Want to Be a Role Model?, 89 Mich. L. Rev. 1222, 1223-1224 (1991):

Affirmative action [generally] frames the question of minority representation in an interesting way: Should we as a society admit, hire, appoint, or promote some designated number of people of color in order to promote certain policy goals, such as social stability, an expanded labor force, and an integrated society? [Minorities] are hired or promoted not because we have been unfairly treated, denied jobs, deprived of our lands, or beaten and brought here in chains. [The] system thus bases inclusion of people of color on principles of social utility, not reparations or *rights*. When those in power decide the goal has been accomplished, or is incapable of being reached, what logically happens? Naturally, the program stops. At best, then, affirmative action serves as a homeostatic device, assuring that only a small number of women and people of color are hired or promoted. Not too many, for that would be terrifying, nor too few, for that would be destabilizing. Just the right small number, generally those of us who need it least, are moved ahead.

f. *Identifying "affirmative action."* Is strict scrutiny for affirmative action programs necessary because, without such scrutiny, "there is simply no way of determining what classifications are 'benign' or 'remedial'"? *Croson*, supra.

If race-based classifications were subject to a lower standard of review because they were "affirmative action" measures, courts would have to determine what "counts" as affirmative action. How should such a determination be made?

2. *Justifications for affirmative action.* Under the strict scrutiny that *Adarand* and *Croson* require, "benign" classifications will be upheld only if they are narrowly tailored to achieve a compelling governmental interest. What interests are compelling?

a. *Remedying prior discrimination.* Under limited circumstances, the remedying of prior discrimination can serve as a compelling governmental interest. In Shaw v. Hunt, discussed at greater length at page 551 supra, Chief Justice Rehnquist summarized the requirements:

> For [the State's interest in remedying the effects of past or present racial discrimination] to rise to the level of a compelling state interest, it must satisfy two conditions. First, the discrimination must be "identified discrimination." "While the States and their subdivisions may take remedial action when they possess evidence" of past or present discrimination, "they must identify that discrimination, public or private, with some specificity before they may use race-conscious relief." A generalized assertion of past discrimination in a particular industry or region is not adequate because it "provides no guidance for a legislative body to determine the precise scope of the injury it seeks to remedy." Accordingly, an effort to alleviate the effects of societal discrimination is not a compelling interest. Second, the institution that makes the racial distinction must have had a "strong basis in evidence" to conclude that remedial action was necessary, "before it embarks on an affirmative-action program."

Even if the state interest is compelling, the remedy must be "narrowly tailored" in order to achieve it. As the *Adarand* Court explained, narrow tailoring requires a demonstration that race-neutral techniques will not achieve the remedial ends. It also draws into question rigid, nonindividualized quotas.

Do these requirements make sense? Why doesn't the government have a compelling interest in remedying pervasive, generalized discrimination? Consider Fishkin, Justice, Equal Opportunity and the Family 117 (1983):

> If we were to embark upon the admittedly difficult task of imagining the alternative world (or worlds) that might have occurred had injustices to blacks not been committed, it is arguable that we might find a society in which race functioned somewhat the way eye color does now. In a racially neutral society, blacks would not constitute a social group or natural class. Their status, identity, and welfare would not be tied to their group membership. Therefore, but for the injustices for which compensation is being advocated, the group to be compensated would not exist as a social group. [The] group cannot be returned to the level of well-being it would have enjoyed, had the injustices not occurred, because had the injustices not occurred, it would not have been a group, at least in the same strict sense.

Why are the facially race-neutral remedial techniques that narrow tailoring requires preferable to overtly race-specific techniques? If Washington v. Davis applies to affirmative action measures, then facially neutral laws with a racial purpose are also suspect. Does *Adarand*'s endorsement of these measures suggest that *Washington* is inapplicable in this context? Compare Miller v. Johnson, 515 U.S. 900 (1995), where the Court strictly scrutinized congressional district lines that were facially race-neutral but drawn to achieve a racial purpose:

> Laws classifying citizens on the basis of race cannot be upheld unless they are narrowly tailored to achieving a compelling state interest. . . .

This prohibition extends not just to explicit racial classifications, but also to laws neutral on their face but "unexplainable on grounds other than race." [*Arlington Heights.*]

Suppose a government employer hires employees on the basis of an examination that has only a marginal relationship to job performance, but that disproportionately excludes minority applicants. If the employer discontinues the test because of this disproportionate impact, is this decision subject to strict scrutiny?

b. *Diversity.* In *Metro Broadcasting,* the Court upheld an FCC policy favoring minority broadcast licensees on the ground that this preference encouraged programing diversity. *Adarand* overruled *Metro Broadcasting* insofar as it utilized intermediate scrutiny to reach this result, but it leaves uncertain the status of diversity as a compelling government interest that might satisfy strict scrutiny.

Should universities be permitted to pursue affirmative action policies because of "the social significance of race, quite apart from its statistical correlation with other attributes"? Sandalow, Racial Preferences in Higher Education: Political Responsibility and the Judicial Role, 42 U. Chi. L. Rev. 653, 685-686 (1975). Sandalow argues in the preferential admissions context that "[precisely] because race itself is socially significant, students need knowledge of the attitudes, views, and background of racial minorities." Compare McCormack, Race and Politics in the Supreme Court: *Bakke* to Basics, 1979 Utah L. Rev. 491, 530: "Most educators would agree that some element of diversity in a student body is healthy, but few would assert that this factor is the primary motivation behind minority preferences or that it is sufficiently important to justify a practice that would otherwise be illegal or unconstitutional. Thus, one problem with this approach is that it is simply not the most honest statement of the objectives of the program."

c. *The role model theory.* Can affirmative action be justified as providing a role model for other members of minority groups? In Wygant v. Jackson Board of Education, 476 U.S. 267 (1986), a plurality of the Court held that the goal of providing "minority role models" for African-American students was not sufficiently "compelling" to justify race-based layoffs of white teachers:

> The role model theory allows the Board to engage in discriminatory hiring and layoff practices long past the point required by any legitimate remedial purpose. . . .
> Moreover, because the role model theory does not necessarily bear a relationship to the harm caused by prior discriminatory hiring practices, it actually could be used to escape the obligation to remedy such practices by justifying the small percentage of black teachers by reference to the small percentage of black students.

Compare Justice Stevens's dissenting opinion:

> In the context of public education, it is quite obvious that a school board may reasonably conclude that an integrated faculty will be able to provide benefits to the student body that could not be provided by an all white, or nearly all white, faculty. For one of the most important lessons that the American public schools teach is that the diverse ethnic, cultural, and national backgrounds that have been brought together in our famous "melting pot" do not identify essential differences among the human beings that inhabit our land. It is one thing for a white child to be taught by a white teacher that color, like beauty, is only "skin deep"; it is far more convincing to experience that truth on a day to day basis during the routine, ongoing learning process.

Consider Delgado, supra, at 1228:

> The job of role model requires that you *lie* — that you tell not little, but big, whop-ping lies, and that is bad for your soul. Suppose I am sent to an inner city school to talk to kids and serve as role model of the month. I am *expected* to tell the kids that if they study hard and stay out of trouble, they can become a law professor like me. That, however, is a very big lie: a whopper.

d. *The "special" case of American Indians.* Are the many statutes providing spe-cial treatment for American Indians consistent with the strict scrutiny supposedly accorded race-specific statutes? In his dissenting opinion in Rice v. Cayetano, 120 S. Ct. 1044 (2000), Justice Stevens summarized the current state of the law:

> Throughout our Nation's history, this Court has recognized both the plenary power of Congress over the affairs of native Americans and the fiduciary character of the special federal relationship with descendants of those once sovereign peoples. . . . As our cases have consistently recognized, Congress' plenary power over these peo-ples has been exercised time and again to implement a federal duty to provide na-tive peoples with special "care and protection." [Today], the Federal Bureau of In-dian Affairs [administers] countless modern programs responding to [pragmatic] concerns, including health, education, housing, and impoverishment. Federal reg-ulation in this area is not limited to the strictly practical but has encompassed as well the protection of cultural values. . . .
>   [This] Court has taken account of the "numerous occasions" on which "legisla-tion that singles out Indians for particular and special treatment" has been upheld, and has concluded that as "long as the special treatment can be tied rationally to fulfillment of Congress' unique obligations towards the Indians, such legislative judgments will not be disturbed."

Can this body of law be reconciled with the Court's treatment of race-based af-firmative action in other contexts? What is it about sovereignty — as distinct from individual liberty — that justifies placing unique obligations on Congress with respect to Native Americans but not with respect to African-Americans?

Consider in this regard the Court's treatment in *Rice* of a statute restricting the franchise in certain elections to descendants of native Hawaiians. Hawaii's con-stitution charges the Office of Hawaiian Affairs (OHA) with the task of managing huge plots of land held in trust for the descendants of the Polynesians who occu-pied the Hawaiian Islands before the 1778 arrival of Captain Cook. Among its other tasks, OHA is charged with carrying out the duties of the trust relation-ship between the Islands' indigenous peoples and the Government of the United States, compensating for past wrongs to the ancestors of those people, and help-ing to preserve the indigenous culture that existed before 1778.

In a seven-to-two decision, the Court assumed, without deciding, that the sub-stantive activities of OHA were constitutional. It found, however, that the method by which the trustees who administered OHA were elected violated the fifteenth amendment because the franchise was limited to descendants of people inhabiting the Islands in 1778. Writing for the Court, Justice Kennedy rejected the analogy to statutes dealing specially with American Indians:

> The decisions of this Court, interpreting the effect of treaties and congressional en-actments on the subject, have held that various tribes retained some elements of

quasi-sovereign authority, even after cession of their lands to the United States. In reliance on that theory the Court has sustained a federal provision giving employment preferences to persons of tribal ancestry. [Morton v. Mancari, 417 U.S. 535 (1974).] . . .

It does not follow from *Mancari*, however, that Congress may authorize a State to establish a voting scheme that limits the electorate for its public officials to a class of tribal Indians, to the exclusion of all non-Indian citizens.

[If] a non-Indian lacks the right to vote in tribal elections, it is for the reason that such elections are the internal affair of a quasi-sovereign. The OHA elections, by contrast, are the affair of the State of Hawaii. . . .

To extend *Mancari* to this context would be to permit a State, by racial classification, to fence out whole classes of its citizens from decisionmaking in critical state affairs.

Justice Stevens, joined by Justice Ginsburg, dissented:

The descendants of the native Hawaiians share with the descendants of the Native Americans on the mainland or in the Aleutian islands not only a history of subjugation at the hands of colonial forces, but also a purposefully created and specialized "guardian-ward" relationship with the Government of the United States. It follows that legislation targeting the native Hawaiians must be evaluated according to the same understanding of equal protection that this Court has long applied to the Indians on the continental United States: that "special treatment . . . be tied rationally to the fulfillment of Congress' unique obligation" toward the native peoples. . . .

[The] Federal Government [has] not been limited in its special dealings with the native peoples to laws affecting tribes or tribal Indians alone. In light of this precedent, it is a painful irony indeed to conclude that native Hawaiians are not entitled to special benefits designed to restore a measure of native self-governance because they currently lack any vestigial native government — a possibility of which history and the actions of this Nation have deprived them.

Consider the extent to which the last paragraph of Justice Stevens's opinion might apply to African-Americans as well.

3. *Affirmative action as an analytic category.* The previous discussion assumes that it is possible to distinguish between affirmative action on the one hand and race-neutral measures on the other. Is this assumption justified? Consider, first, the possibility that race neutrality in certain contexts constitutes a kind of affirmative action. See Strauss, The Myth of Colorblindness, 1986 Sup. Ct. Rev. 99, 100, 105-106:

The prohibition against discrimination established by *Brown* is not rooted in colorblindness at all. Instead, it is, like affirmative action, deeply race-conscious; like affirmative action, the prohibition against discrimination reflects a deliberate decision to treat blacks differently from other groups, even at the expense of innocent whites. It follows that affirmative action is not at odds with the principle of nondiscrimination established by *Brown* but is instead logically continuous with that principle. It also follows that the interesting question is not whether the Constitution permits affirmative action but why the Constitution does not require affirmative action.

Second, consider the possibility that in some contexts the failure to pursue "affirmative action" is not race-neutral. Suppose a state university uses special admission standards for applicants disadvantaged on a variety of nonracial grounds, such as physical disability and poverty. If the university recognizes all other forms of disadvantage, but not disadvantage produced by generalized societal discrimination against African-Americans, isn't it discriminating against racial minorities?

4. *The empirical dimension.* To what extent does the dispute about affirmative action turn on disagreement about empirical questions? For example, opponents and proponents of affirmative action may disagree about whether affirmative action helps or hurts its intended beneficiaries, about whether it increases or decreases racial antagonism, and about whether a "colorblind" regime eliminates or perpetuates discrimination.

For an excellent summary of the social psychological literature bearing on these and other questions, see Krieger, Civil Rights Perestroika: Intergroup Relations after Affirmative Action, 86 Cal. L. Rev. 1251, 1264, 1267-1268, 1294, 1331 (1998). According to Krieger, there is reason for concern that at least certain types of affirmative action may harm intended beneficiaries. The evidence that affirmative action produces self-derogating effects is mixed and largely depends on how the program is described and implemented. The effects of such programs on nonbeneficiaries is more troublesome. For example:

> In one group of studies, experimenters asked subjects to evaluate the qualifications of people supposedly selected for employment or admission to programs of higher education. Researchers indirectly informed subjects in one condition that the selecting institution had an affirmative action program. In a second condition, researchers made no mention of affirmative action. Subjects in the "affirmative action" condition consistently rated the files of selected women and minorities as reflecting lower levels of competence, qualification, and accomplishment than did subjects evaluating identical files in the "non-affirmative action" condition.

Researchers have also found that

> there are serious bases for concern that preferential forms of affirmative action might reinforce subtle negative expectancies relating to members of beneficiary groups. For example, using overt preferences in selection decision making can increase the salience of race or gender in those institutions. As many social cognition researchers have demonstrated, the more salient a particular characteristic in the mind of the observer, the more likely that observer will use it in making causal attributions. . . .
>
> Absent some explanatory theory, the presence of women or minorities [in positions] [indicating] high levels of ability and accomplishment would disconfirm a variety of inconsistent, negative racial or gender stereotypes. [Preferential] selection, however, provides a plausible situational attribution for the stereotype-inconsistent information. Once female or minority presence in "high places" is attributed to preferential selection rather than to merit-related factors, pre-existing negative stereotypes are insulated from the potentially disconfirming effect of the otherwise stereotype disconfirming data.

To some degree these negative effects can be mitigated by programs that take into account both "merit" and group membership, by emphasizing a pattern of discrimination against the group in describing the programs, and by avoiding numerical quotas. Moreover, Krieger claims, that a "colorblind" approach is unlikely to eliminate discrimination:

[Research] strongly suggests that cognitive biases in social judgment operate automatically, without intention or awareness, and can be controlled only through subsequent, deliberate "mental correction" that takes group status squarely into account. . . .

When we encounter a person in our social environment, we automatically place that person into pre-existing categorical structures. [Admonitions] to refrain from categorizing the social environment in a particular way will prove ineffective if those categories reflect patterns made salient by history, culture, or observable patterns of economic, demographic, or political distribution. Whether we like it or not, it is highly implausible to assume that an American of one race encountering an American of another race would not notice racial attributes or use those attributes in initially categorizing the person perceived. [Nothing] in the colorblindness approach to nondiscrimination provides social decision makers with the tools required to recognize or to correct for biases of this sort. . . .

[Only] the application of deliberate, controlled, corrective processes can prevent stereotypes and subtle ingroup priming valences from biasing interpersonal judgment.

According to Krieger, this problem is aggravated by subtle biases in the construction of "merit":

Social identity research [has] shown that we undervalue the product of an outgroup in relation to our own group's products. Accordingly, if those who control the definition of merit in a particular social context belong to the same social reference group, and if members of that group tend to excel on one of the relevant performance dimensions in relation to the others, social identity theory predicts that those who determine merit will tend to overvalue performance in the domain where they collectively excel.

Krieger concludes that

[f]or better or for worse, the application of insights from social cognition and social identity theory complicates rather than simplifies the affirmative action debate. On the one hand, there is reason to fear that preferential forms of affirmative action, at least in some contexts, may indeed exacerbate intergroup tensions and perpetuate rather than reduce subtle forms of intergroup bias. [On] the other hand, insights derived from these fields suggest that we are not yet ready to abandon preferential forms of affirmative action for the simple reason that we have nothing adequate with which to replace them.

For a detailed and mostly positive empirical study of the effects of affirmative action in higher education, see William Bowen and Derek Bok, The Shape of the River (1998). How, if at all, do you think that such studies should affect the constitutional issue?

Note: A Comparative Perspective

Should the Constitution be amended to explicitly define the allowable scope of affirmative action (if any)? Does the inclusion of a specific provision dealing with affirmative action mean that the general equality provision would otherwise bar this practice?

Like the United States, India is a multicultural democracy with a history of class and religious divisions. Before independence in 1948, the British frequently distributed benefits based on membership in ethnic or communal groups. The original India Constitution sharply restricted these practices. The drafters rejected proposals to reserve legislative seats, cabinet posts, and public positions for minorities and included a broad provision prohibiting the state from discriminating "against any citizen on grounds only of religion, race, caste, sex, place of birth, or any of them." However, another, nonjusticiable provision provides that "[t]he State shall promote with special care the educational and economic interests of the weaker sections of the people, and, in particular, of the Scheduled Castes and the Scheduled Tribes, and shall protect them from social injustice and all forms of exploitation."

In 1951, the India Supreme Court invalidated a state program that allocated seats in medical and engineering colleges on the basis of caste and religion. See State of Madras v. Champakam Dorairajan, A.I.R. 1951 S.C. 226, 1951 S.C.J. 313. Within two months of the decision, it had been reversed by a series of constitutional amendments. Among the amendments adopted was one providing that nothing in the constitution "shall prevent the State from making any special provision for the advancement of any socially and educationally backward classes of citizens or for the Scheduled Castes and Scheduled Tribes."

There has been considerable controversy about how to reconcile this and other amendments apparently authorizing affirmative action with the broader guarantee of equality. Some cases have treated the two sets of provisions as in conflict with each other and have therefore read the authorization for affirmative action narrowly. See, e.g., State of Andhra Pradesh v. Sagar, A.I.R. 1968 S.C. 1379, 1382 (broad reading would effectively eviscerate guarantee of equality). However, in a path-breaking decision in 1975, the India Supreme Court held that in some contexts affirmative action was *required* by the equality requirement rather than being in tension with it. See State of Kerala v. N. M. Thomas, A.I.R. 1976 S.C. 490. This decision has granted the government greater discretion as to its choice of means in pursuing compensatory measures, and today there are widespread "reservations" of positions in employment and education based on caste and minority status. For an account, see M. Galanter, Competing Equalities 363-395 (1985).

These reservations have produced considerable resentment and even violence. See, e.g., India College, Job Quotas Reignite Old Caste Hatred, Los Angeles Times, Apr. 28, 1985, at 1, col. 1. For conflicting accounts of their success in reducing inequality, compare M. Galanter, Law and Society in Modern India 185-197 (1989) (a costly success) with T. Sowell, Preferential Policies 90-103 (1990) (a failure). Galanter argues that compensatory discrimination has produced substantial redistribution, contributed to the growth of a middle class, and diminished stereotypes concerning ignorance and incompetence among the lower castes. Sowell argues that reserved seats in universities are often unused because they require supplemental assistance to take advantage of them, that they have led to a lowering of standards, that the most prosperous members of the benefited groups receive a disproportionate share of the benefits, and that resentment against preferential policies has led to a violent backlash.

Consider also Cunningham and Menon, Race, Class, Caste . . . ? Rethinking Affirmative Action, 97 Mich. L. Rev. 1296 (1999). The authors argue that if the

United States followed the Indian model of directing affirmative action against caste-like structures, it would result in

> [a reduction in] the absolute number of persons eligible for affirmative action [even] if the number of identified groups was expanded somewhat beyond the four commonly listed: black, Hispanic, Native American and Asian. [The] Indian approach has been to create artificial groups [that] use intersecting cultural, social and economic factors to narrow, not expand the number of potentially eligible persons. The first limiting principle is that [a] group that intermarries freely with other groups, although identifiable in other way, would not be eligible. The second limitation would be that the [group] be significantly below average levels of educational [attainment]. The third factor would consist of a mix of socioeconomic factors indicative of continuing effects of past discrimination. It is likely that such heterogenous categories as "Asian" and "Hispanic" would break into much more discrete units, some of which would present more compelling cases for affirmative action than others; such a process might even take place within the group now called African-American, which [might] also be quite heterogenous.

Would this approach to affirmative action be preferable to methods used in the United States? Under current doctrine, would it be constitutionally permissible? Consider more generally the extent to which the Indian experience has relevance to the United States in light of the arguably unique history of race relations in this country.

D. EQUAL PROTECTION METHODOLOGY: HEIGHTENED SCRUTINY AND THE PROBLEM OF GENDER

Does the Constitution impose a special burden of justification when government action discriminates on the basis of gender? Does it matter whether the government action disadvantages men or women? Is it ever proper for a legislature to recognize "inherent" differences between the sexes?

1. The Early Cases

Until the 1970s, the Court applied only minimal scrutiny to gender classifications and consistently rejected constitutional attacks on statutes disadvantaging women. In Bradwell v. Illinois, 83 U.S. (16 Wall.) 130 (1873), for example, decided the day after The Slaughter-House Cases, page 433 supra, the Court rejected an attack on Illinois' refusal to license a woman to practice law. In an opinion by Justice Miller, the author of The Slaughter-House Cases, the Court held that the right to practice law was not a privilege or immunity of national citizenship and therefore was not protected by the fourteenth amendment.

Justice Bradley, who had dissented in The Slaughter-House Cases, added a much-quoted concurring opinion. In The Slaughter-House Cases, Justice Bradley had written that "a law which prohibits a large class of citizens from adopting a lawful [employment deprives] them of liberty as well as property without due process of law." In *Bradwell*, however, he asserted that

> [the] natural and proper timidity and delicacy which belongs to the female sex evidently unfits it for many of the occupations of civil life. The constitution of the family organization, which is founded in the divine ordinance, as well as in the nature of things, indicates the domestic sphere as that which properly belongs to the domain and functions of womanhood. The harmony, not to say identity, of interests and views which belong or should belong to the family institution, is repugnant to the idea of a woman adopting a distinct and independent career from that of her husband. . . .
>
> It is true that many women are unmarried and not affected by any of the duties, complications, and incapacities arising out of the married state but these are exceptions to the general rule. The paramount destiny and mission of woman are to fulfill the noble and benign offices of wife and mother. This is the law of the Creator. And the rules of civil society must be adapted to the general constitution of things, and cannot be based upon exceptional cases.

See also In re Lockwood, 154 U.S. 116 (1894).

Two years later, in Minor v. Happersett, 88 U.S. (21 Wall.) 162 (1875), the Court acknowledged that women were "persons" and "citizens" within the meaning of the fourteenth amendment, but held that the right to vote was not a privilege of U.S. citizenship and that women could therefore be denied the franchise.

These early cases were decided against the backdrop of The Slaughter-House Cases, which had given an extremely narrow reading to the fourteenth amendment's due process and equal protection clauses. They therefore paid little attention to claims that gender discrimination violated these provisions. But even when the Court began to invalidate other legislation on due process and equal protection grounds, it resisted application of these clauses to gender discrimination.

In Muller v. Oregon, 208 U.S. 412 (1908), for example, the Court upheld an Oregon statute prohibiting the employment of women in factories for more than ten hours per day. In doing so, it distinguished its earlier decision in Lochner v. New York, 198 U.S. 45 (1905), in which it had held that the liberty of contract implicit in the due process clause prohibited a similar restriction on the working hours of bakers. See Chapter 6, section D, infra. In *Muller*, the Court maintained that "the inherent difference between the two sexes" justified limitations on a woman's right to contract. But see Adkins v. Children's Hospital, 261 U.S. 525 (1923) (invalidating minimum wage legislation for women on substantive due process grounds). *Adkins* was overruled in West Coast Hotel Co. v. Parrish, 300 U.S. 379 (1937). See generally Chapter 6, section D, infra.

The Court was similarly unsympathetic to equal protection claims. In Goesaert v. Cleary, 335 U.S. 464 (1948), for example, the Court, in an opinion by Justice Frankfurter, held that a Michigan statute prohibiting a woman from working as a bartender unless she was the wife or daughter of a male owner did not violate the equal protection clause. See also Quong Wing v. Kirkendall, 223 U.S. 59 (1912). As late as 1961, the Court, in Hoyt v. Florida, 368 U.S. 57 (1961), upheld as "rational" a jury selection system excluding women who did not affirmatively indicate a desire to serve.

2. *The Road to Intermediate Scrutiny*

In the early 1970s, the Court became more receptive to constitutional attacks on gender classifications.

REED v. REED, 404 U.S. 71 (1971). This was the first Supreme Court decision to invalidate a gender classification under the equal protection clause. An Idaho statute established a hierarchy of persons entitled to administer the estate of a decedent who died intestate (e.g., (1) parent, (2) child, (3) sibling, etc.). The statute provided further that, when two or more persons were of the same entitlement class, preference should be given to the male. The state justified this preference on the ground that it eliminated an area of controversy when two or more persons, otherwise equally entitled, sought to administer an estate.

In a terse opinion, a unanimous Court held that this preference violated the equal protection clause. Chief Justice Burger, writing for the Court, characterized the issue as "whether a difference in the sex of competing applicants [bears] a rational relationship to a state objective that is sought to be advanced by the operation of [the statute]." Although recognizing that the objective of reducing the workload of probate courts by eliminating one class of contests was legitimate, the Court maintained that the means used to achieve that objective — that is, a gender classification — was "the very kind of arbitrary legislative choice forbidden by the Equal Protection Clause."

FRONTIERO v. RICHARDSON, 411 U.S. 677 (1973). Under federal law, a male member of the uniformed services could automatically claim his spouse as a dependent, thereby receiving greater quarters allowance and medical benefits. However, a female member of the uniformed services could claim comparable benefits only if she demonstrated that her spouse was in fact dependent on her for over half his support. Although divided as to the appropriate standard of review, eight members of the Court agreed that this distinction violated the equal protection component of the fifth amendment's due process clause.

Writing for four justices, Justice Brennan argued that classifications based on gender are inherently suspect and, like racial classifications, should be subject to close scrutiny. Justice Brennan found "at least implicit support for such an approach" in *Reed*, since there the Court had "implicitly rejected appellee's apparently rational explanation of the statutory scheme." Moreover, this departure from "'traditional' rational-basis analysis" was "clearly justified" in Justice Brennan's opinion:

"There can be no doubt that our Nation has had a long and unfortunate history of sex discrimination. Traditionally, such discrimination was rationalized by an attitude of 'romantic paternalism' which, in practical effect, put women, not on a pedestal, but in a cage. . . .

"As a result of notions such as these, our statute books gradually became laden with gross, stereotyped distinctions between the sexes and, indeed, throughout much of the 19th century the position of women in our society was, in many respects, comparable to that of blacks under the pre-Civil War slave codes. Neither slaves nor women could hold office, serve on juries, or bring suit in their own names, and married women traditionally were denied the legal capacity to hold or convey property or to serve as legal guardians of their own children. And although blacks were guaranteed the right to vote in 1870, women were denied even that right [until] adoption of the Nineteenth Amendment half a century later.

"It is true, of course, that the position of women in America has improved markedly in recent decades. Nevertheless, it can hardly be doubted that, in part because of the high visibility of the sex characteristic, women still face pervasive, although at times more subtle, discrimination in our educational institutions, in the job market and, perhaps most conspicuously in the political arena.

"Moreover, since sex, like race and national origin, is an immutable characteristic determined solely by the accident of birth, the imposition of special disabilities upon the members of a particular sex because of their sex would seem to violate 'the basic concept of our system that legal burdens should bear some relationship to individual responsibility.' And what differentiates sex from such nonsuspect statutes as intelligence or physical disability, and aligns it with the recognized suspect criteria, is that the sex characteristic frequently bears no relation to ability to perform or contribute to society."

Finally, relying on title VII of the 1964 Civil Rights Act, which prohibited employment discrimination based on gender, and congressional approval of the equal rights amendment to the Constitution, Justice Brennan argued that "Congress itself has concluded that classifications based upon sex are inherently invidious, and this conclusion of a coequal branch of Government is not without significance." [At the time Justice Brennan wrote, the equal rights amendment had been submitted to the states for ratification. In 1982, the time period for ratification expired. See section D5 infra.]

Turning to the classification at issue, Justice Brennan concluded that it could not survive strict scrutiny. The government argued that differential treatment of men and women served the purpose of administrative convenience, since, as an empirical matter, wives in our society are usually dependent on their husbands for at least half their support, whereas husbands are rarely so dependent upon their wives. "The Government offers no concrete evidence [tending] to support its view that such differential treatment in fact saves the Government any money. [In] any case, [when] we enter the realm of 'strict judicial scrutiny,' there can be no doubt that 'administrative convenience' is not a shibboleth, the mere recitation of which dictates constitutionality. On the contrary, any statutory scheme which draws a sharp line between the sexes, *solely* for the purpose of achieving administrative convenience, necessarily commands 'dissimilar treatment for men and women who are [similarly] situated,' and, therefore, involves the 'very kind of arbitrary legislative choice forbidden by the [Constitution]' [*Reed*]."

In a separate opinion joined by Chief Justice Burger and Justice Blackmun, Justice Powell concurred in the judgment but expressly disassociated himself from Justice Brennan's assertion that classifications based on sex are suspect. Justice Powell thought that in light of *Reed* it was unnecessary to reach this question in order to invalidate the statute. Moreover, he noted that the equal rights amendment, which had been passed by Congress and was then pending ratification by the states, would, if adopted, resolve the issue. "If this Amendment is duly adopted, it will represent the will of the people accomplished in the manner prescribed by the Constitution. By acting prematurely and unnecessarily, [the] Court has assumed a decisional responsibility at the very time when state legislatures, functioning within the traditional democratic processes, are debating the proposed Amendment."

Justice Stewart also concurred solely in the judgment with the notation that he believed "the statutes before us work an invidious discrimination in violation of the Constitution. [*Reed*]." Justice Rehnquist dissented without opinion.

Note: *From* Reed *to* Craig — *Evolution and Doctrinal Confusion*

Reed inaugurated a period of intense judicial interest in gender classifications, and the Court began to utilize a variety of techniques to invalidate laws embodying distinctions based on sex.

1. *Due process and conclusive presumptions.* A few months after *Reed*, a divided Court in Stanley v. Illinois, 405 U.S. 645 (1972), struck down an Illinois statute that automatically made children of unwed fathers wards of the state on the death of their mothers. In contrast, unwed mothers could be deprived of their children only on a showing that they were unfit parents. The Court held that this scheme deprived fathers of due process of law by erecting a "conclusive presumption" of unfitness. In Cleveland Board of Education v. LaFleur, 414 U.S. 632 (1974), the Court used a similar technique to invalidate regulations requiring a school teacher to take maternity leave well before the expected birth date of her child. The Court held that the due process clause did not permit a "conclusive presumption" that such women were medically unfit to teach. (In Weinberger v. Salfi, 422 U.S. 749 (1975), the Court sharply restricted use of the "conclusive presumption" technique for attacking statutory classifications. For a more detailed discussion of the problem, see Chapter 6, section G2, infra.)

2. *Fair and impartial juries.* In Taylor v. Louisiana, 419 U.S. 522 (1975), the Court distinguished Hoyt v. Florida, section D1 supra, and held that the exclusion of women from jury service deprived the defendant of his sixth amendment right to a fair and impartial jury. The Court explained that "*Hoyt* did not involve a defendant's Sixth Amendment right to a jury drawn from a fair cross section of the community. [The] right to a proper jury cannot be overcome on merely rational grounds."

3. *Equal protection.* In Weinberger v. Wiesenfeld, 420 U.S. 636 (1975), the Court used equal protection analysis to strike down a section of the Social Security Act entitling a widowed mother, but not a widowed father, to benefits based on the earnings of the deceased spouse. The Court characterized *Frontiero* as standing for the proposition that gender classifications based on "archaic and overbroad [generalizations]" were unconstitutional. The statutory distinction between widows and widowers ran afoul of this principle by assuming "that male workers' earnings are vital to the support of their families, while the earnings of female wage earners do not significantly contribute to their families' support."

Less than a month after *Wiesenfeld*, the Court renewed its attack on "old notions" regarding sex roles as a sufficient justification for gender classifications. A Utah statute required parents to support their male children until age twenty-one, but required support of female children only until age eighteen. In Stanton v. Stanton, 421 U.S. 7 (1975), the Court held that this distinction violated the equal protection clause. The state argued that it was generally the responsibility of men to provide a home, and that they therefore needed a good education before undertaking this task. Women, in contrast, "tend generally to mature physically, emotionally and mentally before boys" and "tend to marry earlier." The Court categorically rejected this justification. "Notwithstanding the 'old notions' to which the [state refers], we perceive nothing rational in the distinction drawn by [the statute]. [No] longer is the female destined solely for the home and the rearing of the family, and only the male for the marketplace and the world of ideas. Women's activities and responsibilities are increasing and expanding."

4. *Unsuccessful challenges to gender classifications.* Although the post-*Reed* period was marked by dramatic advances for opponents of gender classifications, not all of their attacks were successful.

In Kahn v. Shevin, 416 U.S. 351 (1974), for example, the Court sustained a Florida statute providing a property tax exemption for widows but not widowers. The Court held that the distinction was justified by the greater financial difficulties confronting a lone woman: "Whether from overt discrimination or from the socialization process of a male-dominated culture, the job market is inhospitable to the woman seeking any but the lowest paid jobs." (The problem of affirmative action in the gender context is discussed more fully in section D4 infra.)

In Geduldig v. Aiello, 417 U.S. 484 (1974), the Court rejected an attack on California's disability insurance program that excluded pregnancy-related disabilities from coverage. The Court held that California's insurance limitation was justified by the state's "legitimate interest in maintaining the self-supporting nature of its insurance program." In a footnote, the Court added that the case was "a far cry from cases like [*Reed*] and [*Frontiero*], involving discrimination based on gender as such. The California insurance program does not exclude anyone from benefit eligibility because of gender but merely removes one physical condition — pregnancy — from the list of compensable disabilities."

Finally, in Schlesinger v. Ballard, 419 U.S. 498 (1975), the Court sustained a federal statute granting women in the navy a longer period in which to achieve mandatory promotion than men. The Court reasoned that this distinction, unlike those disapproved in *Frontiero* and *Reed*, was not based on "archaic and overbroad generalizations." Rather, it reflected the "demonstrable fact that male and female line officers in the Navy are not similarly situated with respect to opportunities for professional service." Since women were precluded from participating in combat and most sea duty, they would "not generally have compiled records of seagoing service comparable to those of male lieutenants."

5. *The legacy of* Reed. These mixed results in the period immediately following *Reed* sent confused signals. On the one hand, it was indisputable that the Court had become far more receptive to claims of sex discrimination. It seemed clear as well that, whatever it said in its opinions, the Court was subjecting gender classifications to some form of heightened scrutiny. Yet, on the other hand, the justices went to extraordinary lengths to leave intact prior equal protection doctrine that had supported the old approach. Thus, in *Taylor, Stanley,* and *LaFleur,* the Court managed to overturn gender classifications without any substantial reliance on equal protection analysis. While the Court did resort to equal protection principles in *Reed, Stanton,* and *Wiesenfeld,* it purported to utilize only low-level, rational basis review to invalidate the challenged statutes. And when confronted with an express invitation to afford heightened scrutiny for gender classifications in *Frontiero,* five justices declined to accept. In the case that follows, the Court for the first time applied heightened review to a gender classification.

Craig v. Boren

429 U.S. 190 (1976)

MR. JUSTICE BRENNAN delivered the opinion of the Court.

The interaction of two sections of an Oklahoma statute prohibits the sale of "nonintoxicating" 3.2% beer to males under the age of 21 and to females under the age of 18. The question to be decided is whether such a gender-based differential constitutes a denial to males 18-20 years of age of the equal protection of the laws in violation of the Fourteenth Amendment. . . .

[Analysis] may appropriately begin with the reminder that *Reed* emphasized that statutory classifications that distinguish between males and females are "subject to scrutiny under the Equal Protection Clause." To withstand constitutional challenge, previous cases establish that classifications by gender must serve important governmental objectives and must be substantially related to achievement of those objectives. Thus, in *Reed*, the objectives of "reducing the workload on probate courts," and "avoiding intrafamily controversy," were deemed of insufficient importance to sustain use of an overt gender criterion in the appointment of administrators of intestate decedents' estates. Decisions following *Reed* similarly have rejected administrative ease and convenience as sufficiently important objectives to justify gender-based classifications.[6]

Reed v. Reed has also provided the underpinning for decisions that have invalidated statutes employing gender as an inaccurate proxy for other, more germane bases of classification. . . .

In this case, too, "*Reed*, we feel, is controlling . . . ," [*Stanton*]. We turn then to the question whether, under *Reed*, the difference between males and females with respect to the purchase of 3.2% beer warrants the differential in age drawn by the Oklahoma statute. We conclude that it does not. . . .

We accept for purposes of discussion the District Court's identification of the objective underlying [the statute] as the enhancement of traffic safety. Clearly, the protection of public health and safety represents an important function of state and local governments. However, appellees' statistics in our view cannot support the conclusion that the gender-based distinction closely serves to achieve that objective and therefore the distinction cannot under *Reed* withstand equal protection challenge. The appellees introduced a variety of statistical surveys. . . .

Even were this statistical evidence accepted as accurate, it nevertheless offers only a weak answer to the equal protection question presented here. The most focused and relevant of the statistical surveys, arrests of 18-20-year-olds for alcohol-related driving offenses, exemplifies the ultimate unpersuasiveness of this evidentiary record. Viewed in terms of the correlation between sex and the actual activity that Oklahoma seeks to regulate — driving while under the influence of alcohol — the statistics broadly establish that .18% of females and 2% of males in that age group were arrested for that offense. While such a disparity is not trivial

---

6. [*Kahn*] and [*Ballard*], upholding the use of gender-based classifications, rested upon the Court's perception of the laudatory purposes of those laws as remedying disadvantageous conditions suffered by women in economic and military life. Needless to say, in this case Oklahoma does not suggest that the age-sex differential was enacted to ensure the availability of 3.2% beer for women as compensation for previous deprivations.

in a statistical sense, it hardly can form the basis for employment of a gender line as a classifying device. Certainly if maleness is to serve as a proxy for drinking and driving, a correlation of 2% must be considered an unduly tenuous "fit."[12] Indeed, prior cases have consistently rejected the use of sex as a decisionmaking factor even though the statutes in question certainly rested on far more predictive empirical relationships than this.[13]

Moreover, the statistics exhibit a variety of other shortcomings that seriously impugn their value to equal protection analysis. Setting aside the obvious methodological problems,[14] the surveys do not adequately justify the salient features of Oklahoma's gender-based traffic-safety law. None purports to measure the use and dangerousness of 3.2% beer as opposed to alcohol generally, a detail that is of particular importance since, in light of its low alcohol level, Oklahoma apparently considers the 3.2% beverage to be "nonintoxicating."

There is no reason to belabor this line of analysis. It is unrealistic to expect either members of the judiciary or state officials to be well versed in the rigors of experimental or statistical technique. But this merely illustrates that proving broad sociological propositions by statistics is a dubious business, and one that inevitably is in tension with the normative philosophy that underlies the Equal Protection Clause. Suffice to say that the showing offered by the appellees does not satisfy us that sex represents a legitimate, accurate proxy for the regulation of drinking and driving. In fact, when it is further recognized that Oklahoma's statute prohibits only the selling of 3.2% beer to young males and not their drinking the beverage once acquired (even after purchase by their 18-20-year-old female companions), the relationship between gender and traffic safety becomes far too tenuous to satisfy *Reed's* requirement that the gender-based difference be substantially related to achievement of the statutory objective.

We hold, therefore, that under *Reed*, Oklahoma's 3.2% beer statute invidiously discriminates against males 18-20 years of age. . . .

MR. JUSTICE POWELL, concurring.

I join the opinion of the Court as I am in general agreement with it. I do have reservations as to some of the discussion concerning the appropriate standard for equal protection analysis and the relevance of the statistical evidence.

Reed and subsequent cases involving gender-based classifications make clear that the Court subjects such classifications to a more critical examination than is

---

12. Obviously, arrest statistics do not embrace all individuals who drink and drive. But for purposes of analysis, this "underinclusiveness" must be discounted somewhat by the shortcomings inherent in this statistical sample. In any event, we decide this case in light of the evidence offered by Oklahoma and know of no way of extrapolating these arrest statistics to take into account the driving and drinking population at large, including those who avoided arrest.

13. For example, we can conjecture that in *Reed*, Idaho's apparent premise that women lacked experience in formal business matters (particularly compared to men) would have proved to be accurate in substantially more than 2% of all cases. And in both *Frontiero* and *Wiesenfeld*, we expressly found appellees' empirical defense of mandatory dependency tests for men but not women to be unsatisfactory, even though we recognized that husbands are still far less likely to be dependent on their wives than vice versa.

14. The very social stereotypes that find reflection in age-differential laws, see [*Stanton*], are likely substantially to distort the accuracy of these comparative statistics. Hence "reckless" young men who drink and drive are transformed into arrest statistics, whereas their female counterparts are chivalrously escorted home. . . .

normally applied when "fundamental" constitutional rights and "suspect classes" are not present.*

I view this as a relatively easy case. No one questions the legitimacy or importance of the asserted governmental objective: the promotion of highway safety. The decision of the case turns on whether the state legislature, by the classification it has chosen, has adopted a means that bears a "fair and substantial relation" to this objective.

It seems to me that the statistics offered by appellees and relied upon by the District Court do tend generally to support the view that young men drive more, possibly are inclined to drink more, and — for various reasons — are involved in more accidents than young women. Even so, I am not persuaded that these facts and the inferences fairly drawn from them justify this classification based on a three-year age differential between the sexes, and especially one that is so easily circumvented as to be virtually meaningless. Putting it differently, this gender-based classification does not bear a fair and substantial relation to the object of the legislation.

MR. JUSTICE STEVENS, concurring.

There is only one Equal Protection Clause. It requires every State to govern impartially. It does not direct the courts to apply one standard of review in some cases and a different standard in other cases. Whatever criticism may be leveled at a judicial opinion implying that there are at least three such standards applies with the same force to a double standard.

I am inclined to believe that what has become known as the two-tiered analysis of equal protection claims does not describe a completely logical method of deciding cases, but rather is a method the Court has employed to explain decisions that actually apply a single standard in a reasonably consistent fashion. I also suspect that a careful explanation of the reasons motivating particular decisions may contribute more to an identification of that standard than an attempt to articulate it in all-encompassing terms. It may therefore be appropriate for me to state the principal reasons which persuaded me to join the Court's opinion.

In this case, the classification is not as obnoxious as some the Court has condemned, nor as inoffensive as some the Court has accepted. It is objectionable because it is based on an accident of birth, because it is a mere remnant of the now almost universally rejected tradition of discriminating against males in this age bracket, and because, to the extent it reflects any physical difference between males and females, it is actually perverse.[4] The question then is whether the traf-

---

*As is evident from our opinions, the Court has had difficulty in agreeing upon a standard of equal protection analysis that can be applied consistently to the wide variety of legislative classifications. There are valid reasons for dissatisfaction with the "two-tier" approach that has been prominent in the Court's decisions in the past decade. Although viewed by many as a result-oriented substitute for more critical analysis, that approach — with its narrowly limited "upper-tier" — now has substantial precedential support. As has been true of *Reed* and its progeny, our decision today will be viewed by some as a "middle-tier" approach. While I would not endorse that characterization and would not welcome a further subdividing of equal protection analysis, candor compels the recognition that the relatively deferential "rational basis" standard of review normally applied takes on a sharper focus when we address a gender-based classification. So much is clear from our recent cases. . . .

4. Because males are generally heavier than females, they have a greater capacity to consume alcohol without impairing their driving ability than do females.

fic safety justification put forward by the State is sufficient to make an otherwise offensive classification acceptable.

The classification is not totally irrational. For the evidence does indicate that there are more males than females in this age bracket who drive and also more who drink. Nevertheless, there are several reasons why I regard the justification as unacceptable. It is difficult to believe that the statute was actually intended to cope with the problem of traffic safety, since it has only a minimal effect on access to a not very intoxicating beverage and does not prohibit its consumption. Moreover, the empirical data submitted by the State accentuate the unfairness of treating all 18-20-year-old males as inferior to their female counterparts. The legislation imposes a restraint on 100% of the males in the class allegedly because about 2% of them have probably violated one or more laws relating to the consumption of alcoholic beverages. It is unlikely that this law will have a significant deterrent effect either on that 2% or on the law-abiding 98%. But even assuming some such slight benefit, it does not seem to me that an insult to all of the young men of the State can be justified by visiting the sins of the 2% on the 98%.

[Concurring opinions by Justices Stewart and Blackmun and a dissenting opinion by Chief Justice Burger are omitted.]

MR. JUSTICE REHNQUIST, dissenting.

The Court's disposition of this case is objectionable on two grounds. First is its conclusion that *men* challenging a gender-based statute which treats them less favorably than women may invoke a more stringent standard of judicial review than pertains to most other types of classifications. Second is the Court's enunciation of this standard, without citation to any source, as being that "classifications by gender must serve *important* governmental objectives and must be *substantially* related to achievement of those objectives." The only redeeming feature of the Court's opinion, to my mind, is that it apparently signals a retreat by those who joined the plurality opinion in [*Frontiero*] from their view that sex is a "suspect" classification for purposes of equal protection analysis. I think the Oklahoma statute challenged here need pass only the "rational basis" equal protection analysis. . . .

Most obviously unavailable to support any kind of special scrutiny in this case, is a history or pattern of past discrimination, such as was relied on by the plurality in *Frontiero* to support its invocation of strict scrutiny. There is no suggestion in the Court's opinion that males in this age group are in any way peculiarly disadvantaged, subject to systematic discriminatory treatment, or otherwise in need of special solicitude from the courts. . . .

The Court's conclusion that a law which treats males less favorably than females "must serve important governmental objectives and must be substantially related to achievement of those objectives" apparently comes out of thin air. The Equal Protection Clause contains no such language, and none of our previous cases adopt that standard. I would think we have had enough difficulty with the two standards of review which our cases have recognized — the norm of "rational basis," and the "compelling state interest" required where a "suspect classification" is involved — so as to counsel weightily against the insertion of still another "standard" between those two. How is this Court to divine what objectives are important? How is it to determine whether a particular law is "substantially" related to the achievement of such objective, rather than related in some other way to its achievement? Both of the phrases used are so diaphanous and elastic as to invite subjective judicial preferences or prejudices relating to particular types of legislation, masquerading as judgments whether such legislation is directed at "important" objectives or, whether the relationship to those objectives is "substantial" enough. . . .

The Court "accept[s] for purposes of discussion" the District Court's finding that the purpose of the provisions in question was traffic safety, and proceeds to examine the statistical evidence in the record in order to decide if "the gender-based distinction *closely* serves to achieve that objective." [One] need not immerse oneself in the fine points of statistical analysis, however, in order to see the weaknesses in the Court's attempted denigration of the evidence at hand.

One survey of arrest statistics assembled in 1973 indicated that males in the 18-20 age group were arrested for "driving under the influence" almost 18 times as often as their female counterparts, and for "drunkenness" in a ratio of almost 10 to 1. Accepting, as the Court does, appellants' comparison of the total figures with 1973 Oklahoma census data, this survey indicates a 2% arrest rate among males in the age group, as compared to a .18% rate among females. . . .

The Court's criticism of the statistics relied on by the District Court conveys the impression that a legislature in enacting a new law is to be subjected to the judicial equivalent of a doctoral examination in statistics. Legislatures are not held to any rules of evidence such as those which may govern courts or other administrative bodies, and are entitled to draw factual conclusions on the basis of the determination of probable cause which an arrest by a police officer normally represents. In this situation, they could reasonably infer that the incidence of drunk driving is a good deal higher than the incidence of arrest.

And while, [such] statistics may be distorted as a result of stereotyping, the legislature is not required to prove before a court that its statistics are perfect. In any event, if stereotypes are as pervasive as the Court suggests, they may in turn influence the conduct of the men and women in question, and cause the young men to conform to the wild and reckless image which is their stereotype. . . .

[The] Court notes that only 2% of males (as against .18% of females) in the age group were arrested for drunk driving, and that this very low figure establishes "an unduly tenuous 'fit'" between maleness and drunk driving in the 18-20-year-old group. On this point the Court misconceives the nature of the equal protection inquiry. . . .

[The] clearest demonstration of this is the fact that the precise argument made by the Court would be equally applicable to a flat bar on such purchases by *anyone*, male or female, in the 18-20 age group; in fact it would apply a fortiori in that case given the even more "tenuous 'fit'" between drunk-driving arrests and femaleness. The statistics indicate that about 1% of the age group population as a whole is arrested. What the Court's argument is relevant to is not equal protection, but due process — whether there are enough persons in the category who drive while drunk to justify a bar against purchases by all members of the group. . . .

This is not a case where the classification can only be justified on grounds of administrative convenience. There being no apparent way to single out persons likely to drink and drive, it seems plain that the legislature was faced here with the not atypical legislative problem of legislating in terms of broad categories with regard to the purchase and consumption of alcohol. I trust [that] there would be no due process violation if no one in this age group were allowed to purchase 3.2% beer. Since males drink and drive at a higher rate than the age group as a whole, I fail to see how a statutory bar with regard only to them can create any due process problem.

Note: Heightened Scrutiny for Gender Classifications?

1. *The relevance of heightened scrutiny.* Since *Craig* the Court has not been altogether consistent in its articulation of the appropriate standard of review in gender discrimination cases. For example, in Michael M. v. Sonoma County Superior Court, page 621 infra, Justice Rehnquist, writing for the Court, propounded a seemingly less stringent test: "[This] Court has consistently upheld statutes where the gender classification is not invidious, but rather realistically reflects the fact that the sexes are not similarly situated in certain circumstances." On the other hand, in United States v. Virginia, page 611 infra, Justice Ginsburg, writing for the Court, announced a seemingly more stringent test: "[The] reviewing court must determine whether the proffered justification is 'exceedingly persuasive.' The burden of justification is demanding and it rests entirely on the State." As you read the material that follows, consider the extent to which the standard of review makes a difference. Is the Court evaluating fact situations under a predetermined standard of review, or is it manipulating the standard of review so as to justify a predetermined result?

2. *Arguments for heightened scrutiny.* Assuming that racial classifications require heightened scrutiny, are there persuasive reasons to accord gender classifications similar treatment? Consider the following possibilities:

a. *History.* In The Slaughter-House Cases, Justice Miller began his consideration of the fourteenth amendment by observing that its "one pervading purpose" was "the freedom of the slave race, the security and firm establishment of that freedom, and the protection of the newly-made freeman and citizen from the oppressions of those who had formerly exercised unlimited dominion over him." Is there anything in the history of the fourteenth amendment that provides analogous support for heightened scrutiny of gender classifications?

Ironically, the second section of the fourteenth amendment for the first time introduced explicit gender discrimination into the Constitution. The section, which required reduction of representation in the House of Representatives for states that "denied [the right to vote] to any of the male inhabitants of such State, being twenty-one years of age, and citizens of the United States," infuriated feminists, such as Susan B. Anthony and Elizabeth Cady Stanton, who worked tirelessly, but unsuccessfully, for defeat of the amendment. See E. Flexner, Century of Struggle 146-148 (1975).

Even apart from the history surrounding section 2 of the amendment, it is hard to make the case that the framers had any intention of bringing into question laws that discriminated on the basis of gender. As Justice Ginsburg wrote in an article published before her appointment to the Court:

Boldly dynamic interpretation, departing radically from the original understanding, is required to tie to the fourteenth amendment's equal protection clause a command that government treat men and women as individuals equal in rights, responsibilities, and opportunities. . . .

> When the post-Civil War amendments were added to the Constitution, women were not accorded the vote. [Married] women in many states could not contract, hold property, litigate on their own behalf, or even control their own earnings. The fourteenth amendment left all that untouched.

Ginsburg, Sexual Equality under the Fourteenth and Equal Rights Amendments, 1979 Wash. U. L.Q. 161, 161-163.

b. *Arguments by analogy.* Even if the framers of the equal protection clause did not specifically intend to ban gender discrimination, might the clause be read to require a special burden of justification for classifications that are relevantly similar to racial classifications? Does gender discrimination satisfy this test? For example, should gender discrimination be treated like racial discrimination because it is based on "a trait that is immutable and highly visible" and therefore "lends itself to a system of thought dominated by stereotype, which automatically consigns an individual to a general category [often] implying the inferiority of the person so categorized"? Karst, Foreword: Equal Citizenship under the Fourteenth Amendment, 91 Harv. L. Rev. 1, 23 (1977). Because the pervasive nature of sexual stereotypes and the historical subjugation of women make gender "like" race for purposes of the equal protection clause? Because women, like blacks, are effectively excluded from the political process?

c. *"Archaic" gender distinctions.* Should gender distinctions be subject to heightened scrutiny when they are "archaic"? Consider J. Ely, Democracy and Distrust (1980) 167: "[Most] laws classifying by sex weren't passed this morning or even the day before yesterday: in fact, it is rare to see a gender-based classification enacted since the New Deal. In general, women couldn't even *vote* until the Nineteenth Amendment was ratified in 1920, and most of these laws probably predate even that: they should be invalidated." Compare *Michael M.*, in which the Court upheld California's statutory rape law making men, but not women, criminally liable for acts of sexual intercourse involving a female under age eighteen. In a footnote to his plurality opinion, Justice Rehnquist noted that the California legislature had recently rejected a proposal to make the statute sex-neutral. "That is enough to answer petitioner's contention that the statute was the 'accidental byproduct of a traditional way of thinking about females.' Certainly this decision of the California Legislature is as good a source as is this Court in deciding what is 'current' and what is 'outmoded' in the perception of women."

d. *The problem of overgeneralization.* Can heightened scrutiny of even modern statutes be defended on the ground that gender classifications pose a peculiar risk of unthinking overgeneralization? Consider the suggestion in Mississippi University for Women v. Hogan, 458 U.S. 718 (1982), that a skeptical attitude toward gender classifications is designed to ensure that government action is "determined through reasoned analysis rather than through the mechanical application of traditional, often inaccurate assertions about the proper roles of men and women." Under this view, judicial inspection of the means/ends connection and the substantiality of the state's interest is intended to ensure that such "reasoned analysis" is in fact at work.

3. *Gender segregation.* As the preceding discussion suggests, gender classifications are like racial classifications in some respects but different in others. Does the intermediate scrutiny announced in *Craig* therefore represent a sensible

compromise, recognizing that the analogy has force in some contexts but not in others? In what contexts is the analogy inappropriate?

Consider in this connection the problem of gender segregation. In some situations, gender segregation is relatively uncontroversial:

[The] primary evil of [racial segregation] was that [it] designedly and effectively marked off all black persons as degraded, dirty, less than fully developed persons who were unfit for full membership in the political, social, and moral community. [It] is worth observing that the social realities of sexually segregated bathrooms appear to be different. [There] is no notion of the possibility of contamination from use; or [of] inferiority or superiority. What seems to be involved — at least in part — is the importance of inculcating and preserving a sense of secrecy concerning the genitalia of the opposite sex.

R. Wasserstrom, Philosophy and Social Issues 21 (1980).

Is the analogy between gender and racial segregation more persuasive in other settings? Recall Loving v. Virginia, in which the Court invalidated a Virginia statute prohibiting cross-racial marriages. Do laws prohibiting same-sex marriages raise nontrivial constitutional questions? See generally W. Eskridge, The Case for Same-Sex Marriage: From Sexual Liberty to Civilized Commitment (1996). For a further discussion, see section E infra.

For an example of the Court's treatment of gender segregation in a somewhat different context, consider Mississippi University for Women v. Hogan, supra. Hogan, a man, claimed that his exclusion from the Mississippi University for Women school of nursing solely on the basis of gender violated the equal protection clause. In a five-to-four decision, the Supreme Court agreed. In an opinion by Justice O'Connor, the Court recognized that Hogan could have attended classes in one of Mississippi's state-supported coeducational nursing programs. But since these programs were a considerable distance from his home, and since many students at the school of nursing were able to hold full-time jobs, "[the] policy of denying males the right to obtain credit toward a baccalaureate degree [imposed] upon Hogan 'a burden he would not bear were he female.' Orr v. Orr, 440 U.S. 268, 273 (1979)." This burden was unconstitutional because "excluding males from admission to the School of Nursing tends to perpetuate the stereotyped view of nursing as an exclusively woman's job. By assuring that Mississippi allots more openings in its state-supported nursing schools to women than it does to men [petitioner's] admissions policy lends credibility to the old view that women, not men, should become nurses, and makes the assumption that nursing is a field for women a self-fulfilling prophecy." The Court was careful to note, however, that it was not ruling on the constitutionality of the exclusion of males from other schools in the Mississippi University for Women or on the permissibility of a general policy of "separate but equal" education for men and women.

After Hogan, must the Mississippi University for Women admit male applicants who live close to coeducational nursing programs? Could the university deny Hogan admission if it established an all-male nursing school? If the all-male program were farther from Hogan's home than the all-female program?

The Court threw some light on these questions in United States v. Virginia, a case considered in more detail in the following section, where the Court held that Virginia's policy of prohibiting women from enrolling in the state-run Virginia Military Institute (VMI) violated the equal protection clause. In the course of her opinion for the Court, Justice Ginsburg acknowledged the argument that

> diversity in educational opportunities is an altogether appropriate governmental pursuit and that single-sex schools can contribute importantly to such diversity. Indeed, it is the mission of some single-sex schools "to dissipate, rather than perpetuate, traditional gender classifications." We do not question the State's prerogative evenhandedly to support diverse educational opportunities.

Nonetheless, Virginia could not rely on putative benefits of single-sex education to justify the exclusion of women from VMI because there was no showing of a state policy

> evenhandedly to advance diverse educational options. . . . A purpose genuinely to advance an array of educational options [is] not served by VMI's historic and consistent plan — a plan to "afford a unique educational benefit only to males." However "liberally" this plan serves the State's sons, it makes no provision whatever for her daughters. That is not equal protection.

In light of *Hogan* and *Virginia*, are state-supported, sexually segregated athletic programs unconstitutional because they reinforce stereotypes concerning women's athletic ability? Would integrated programs be unconstitutional because they fail to take account of differences between men and women and therefore deny women an equal chance to participate?

4. *The remaining questions. Craig* establishes that heightened scrutiny is required for at least some forms of gender discrimination. However, the case raises two additional questions of considerable complexity. First, what sort of showing is necessary to satisfy the Court's test? The next section explores this question.

Second, as Justice Rehnquist noted in his dissent, the statute invalidated in *Craig* disadvantaged men rather than women. Section D4 explores the problem of "benign" gender discrimination and discrimination against men. A final section briefly discusses the equal rights amendment and the effect its passage might have on current doctrine.

3. Archaic and Overbroad Generalizations versus "Real" Differences

In the cases decided since *Craig,* the Court has attempted to assimilate the analysis of gender discrimination into its basic equal protection methodology. Thus, it has looked (albeit with heightened scrutiny) to see whether a law or policy treats men and women differently. If it does, it has asked whether the difference in treatment corresponds to a relevant difference between the genders.

As applied to gender discrimination, this methodology has been criticized on a number of grounds. Some critics have complained that the differences between men and women that the Court has relied on to justify different treatment are not "natural" or inevitable. Instead, they are "constructed" by the very legal regime that they are used to defend. Others have argued that the Court's insistence on "facial" or "formal" equality has harmed women by ignoring important differences between the genders. Requiring formal equality is said to hold women to an implicitly male standard. Still others have complained that the pre-occupation with "sameness" and "difference" is diversionary and that the Court should instead focus on fundamental power imbalances between the genders. On this view, constitutional doctrine should be reformulated so as to end male domination.

As you read the material below, consider which, if any, of these criticisms is valid. Has the Court responded to the most serious obstacles to gender equality? Is such a response possible from within standard constitutional methodology?

United States v. Virginia
518 U.S. 515 (1996)

JUSTICE GINSBURG delivered the opinion of the Court.

Virginia's public institutions of higher learning include an incomparable military college, Virginia Military Institute (VMI). The United States maintains that the Constitution's equal protection guarantee precludes Virginia from reserving exclusively to men the unique educational opportunities VMI affords. We agree.

I

Founded in 1839, VMI is today the sole single-sex school among Virginia's 15 public institutions of higher learning. VMI's distinctive mission is to produce "citizen-soldiers," men prepared for leadership in civilian life and in military service. VMI pursues this mission through pervasive training of a kind not available anywhere else in Virginia. Assigning prime place to character development, VMI uses an "adversative method" modeled on English public schools and once characteristic of military instruction. . . .

VMI has notably succeeded in its mission to produce leaders; among its alumni are military generals, Members of Congress, and business executives. The school's alumni overwhelmingly perceive that their VMI training helped them to realize their personal goals. VMI's endowment reflects the loyalty of its graduates; VMI has the largest per-student endowment of all undergraduate institutions in the Nation. . . .

II

A . . .

VMI produces its "citizen-soldiers" through "an adversative, or doubting, model of education" which features "physical rigor, mental stress, absolute equality of treatment, absence of privacy, minute regulation of behavior, and indoctrination in desirable values.". . .

VMI cadets live in spartan barracks where surveillance is constant and privacy nonexistent; they wear uniforms, eat together in the mess hall, and regularly participate in drills. Entering students are incessantly exposed to the rat line, "an extreme form of the adversative model," comparable in intensity to Marine Corps boot camp. Tormenting and punishing, the rat line bonds new cadets to their fellow sufferers and, when they have completed the 7-month experience, to their former tormentors. . . .

B

[In 1990, the United States sued Virginia and VMI, alleging that VMI's admission policy violated the equal protection clause. At the conclusion of a trial, the district court found that "some women, at least" would want to attend VMI and were capable of all the activities required of VMI cadets. The district court nonetheless ruled in favor of VMI. The court acknowledged that women were denied a unique education opportunity available only at VMI, but held that if women were admitted, "some aspects of the [school's] distinctive method would be altered." Specifically, allowance for personal privacy would have to be made, physical education requirements would have to be altered, and the adversative environment could not survive unmodified. The court found that these changes would impinge on the state interest in diversity in public education.

[The court of appeals reversed, holding that "neither the goal of producing citizen soldiers nor VMI's implementing methodology is inherently unsuitable to women." It remanded the case to the district court for purposes of selecting a remedy.]

C

In response to the Fourth Circuit's ruling, Virginia proposed a parallel program for women: Virginia Women's Institute for Leadership (VWIL). The 4-year, state-sponsored undergraduate program would be located at Mary Baldwin College, a private liberal arts school for women, and would be open, initially, to about 25 to 30 students. Although VWIL would share VMI's mission — to produce "citizen-soldiers" — the VWIL program would differ, as does Mary Baldwin College, from VMI in academic offerings, methods of education, and financial resources.

The average combined SAT score of entrants at Mary Baldwin is about 100 points lower than the score for VMI freshmen. Mary Baldwin's faculty holds "significantly fewer Ph.D.'s than the faculty at VMI," and receives significantly lower salaries, While VMI offers degrees in liberal arts, the sciences, and engineering, Mary Baldwin, at the time of trial, offered only bachelor of arts degrees. A VWIL student seeking to earn an engineering degree could gain one, without public support, by attending Washington University in St. Louis, Missouri, for two years, paying the required private tuition.

Experts in educating women at the college level composed the Task Force charged with designing the VWIL program; Task Force members were drawn from Mary Baldwin's own faculty and staff. Training its attention on methods of instruction appropriate for "most women," the Task Force determined that a military model would be "wholly inappropriate" for VWIL. . . .

In lieu of VMI's adversative method, the VWIL Task Force favored "a cooperative method which reinforces self-esteem." In addition to the standard bachelor of arts program offered at Mary Baldwin, VWIL students would take courses in leadership, complete an off-campus leadership externship, participate in community service projects, and assist in arranging a speaker series.

Virginia represented that it will provide equal financial support for in-state VWIL students and VMI cadets, and the VMI Foundation agreed to supply a $5.4625 million endowment for the VWIL program. Mary Baldwin's own endowment is about $19 million; VMI's is $131 million. Mary Baldwin will add $35 million to its endowment based on future commitments; VMI will add $220 million. The VMI Alumni Association has developed a network of employers interested in hiring VMI graduates. The Association has agreed to open its network to VWIL graduates, but those graduates will not have the advantage afforded by a VMI degree. . . .

D

[The district court approved this remedial plan, and the court of appeals affirmed.] . . .

IV

[Parties] who seek to defend gender-based government action must demonstrate an "exceedingly persuasive justification" for that action. . . .

[The] burden of justification is demanding and it rests entirely on the State. The State must show "at least that the [challenged] classification serves 'important governmental objectives and that the discriminatory means employed' are 'substantially related to the achievement of those objectives.'" The justification must be genuine, not hypothesized or invented post hoc in response to litigation. And it must not rely on overbroad generalizations about the different talents, capacities, or preferences of males and females.

The heightened review standard our precedent establishes does not make sex a proscribed classification. Supposed "inherent differences" are no longer accepted as a ground for race or national origin classifications. See Loving v. Virginia. Physical differences between men and women, however, are enduring. . . .

"Inherent differences" between men and women, we have come to appreciate, remain cause for celebration, but not for denigration of the members of either sex or for artificial constraints on an individual's opportunity. Sex classifications may be used to compensate women "for particular economic disabilities [they have] suffered," to "promote equal employment opportunity," to advance full development of the talent and capacities of our Nation's people. But such classifications may not be used, as they once were, to create or perpetuate the legal, social, and economic inferiority of women.

Measuring the record in this case against the review standard just described, we conclude that Virginia has shown no "exceedingly persuasive justification" for excluding all women from the citizen-soldier training afforded by VMI. We therefore affirm the Fourth Circuit's initial judgment, which held that Virginia had violated the Fourteenth Amendment's Equal Protection Clause. Because the remedy proffered by Virginia — the Mary Baldwin VWIL program — does not cure the constitutional violation, i.e., it does not provide equal opportunity, we reverse the Fourth Circuit's final judgment in this case.

V

[Virginia] asserts two justifications in defense of VMI's exclusion of women. First, the Commonwealth contends, "single-sex education provides important educational benefits," and the option of single-sex education contributes to "diversity in educational approaches." Second, the Commonwealth argues, "the unique VMI method of character development and leadership training," the school's adversative approach, would have to be modified were VMI to admit women. We consider these two justifications in turn.

A

Single-sex education affords pedagogical benefits to at least some students, Virginia emphasizes, and that reality is uncontested in this litigation. Similarly, it is not disputed that diversity among public educational institutions can serve the public good. But Virginia has not shown that VMI was established, or has been maintained, with a view to diversifying, by its categorical exclusion of women, educational opportunities within the State. In cases of this genre, our precedent instructs that "benign" justifications proffered in defense of categorical exclusions will not be accepted automatically; a tenable justification must describe actual state purposes, not rationalizations for actions in fact differently grounded. . . .

B

Virginia next argues that VMI's adversative method of training provides educational benefits that cannot be made available, unmodified, to women. Alterations to accommodate women would necessarily be "radical," so "drastic," Virginia asserts, as to transform, indeed "destroy," VMI's program. . . .

[It] is uncontested that women's admission would require accommodations, primarily in arranging housing assignments and physical training programs for female cadets. It is also undisputed, however, that "the VMI methodology could be used to educate women." ["Some] women," the expert testimony established, "are capable of all of the individual activities required of VMI cadets." The parties, furthermore, agree that "some women can meet the physical standards [VMI] now imposes on men." . . .

It may be assumed, for purposes of this decision, that most women would not choose VMI's adversative method. As Fourth Circuit Judge Motz observed, however, in her dissent from the Court of Appeals' denial of rehearing en banc, it is also probable that "many men would not want to be educated in such an environment." (On that point, even our dissenting colleague might agree.) Education, to be sure, is not a "one size fits all" business. The issue, however, is not whether "women — or men — should be forced to attend VMI"; rather, the question is whether the State can constitutionally deny to women who have the will and capacity, the training and attendant opportunities that VMI uniquely affords.

The notion that admission of women would downgrade VMI's stature, destroy the adversative system and, with it, even the school, is a judgment hardly proved, a prediction hardly different from other "self-fulfilling prophecies," once routinely used to deny rights or opportunities. When women first sought admission to the bar and access to legal education, concerns of the same order were expressed. For example, in 1876, the Court of Common Pleas of Hennepin County, Minnesota, explained why women were thought ineligible for the practice of law. Women train and educate the young, the court said, which "forbids that they shall bestow that time (early and late) and labor, so essential in attaining to the eminence to which the true lawyer should ever aspire. It cannot therefore be said that the opposition of courts to the admission of females to practice . . . is to any extent the outgrowth of . . . 'old fogyism[.]' . . . It arises rather from a comprehension of the magnitude of the responsibilities connected with the successful practice of law, and a desire to grade up the profession." A like fear, according to a 1925 report, accounted for Columbia Law School's resistance to women's admission, although

> "the faculty . . . never maintained that women could not master legal learning. . . . No, its argument has been . . . more practical. If women were admitted to the Columbia Law School, [the faculty] said, then the choicer, more manly and red-blooded graduates of our great universities would go to the Harvard Law School!" The Nation, Feb. 18, 1925, p.173. . . .

Women's successful entry into the federal military academies, and their participation in the Nation's military forces, indicate that Virginia's fears for the future of VMI may not be solidly grounded. The State's justification for excluding all women from "citizen-soldier" training for which some are qualified, in any event, cannot rank as "exceedingly persuasive," as we have explained and applied that standard.

Virginia and VMI trained their argument on "means" rather than "end," and thus misperceived our precedent. Single-sex education at VMI serves an "important governmental objective," they maintained, and exclusion of women is not only "substantially related," it is essential to that objective. By this notably circular argument, the "straightforward" test *Mississippi Univ. for Women* described was bent and bowed.

The State's misunderstanding and, in turn, the District Court's, is apparent from VMI's mission: to produce "citizen-soldiers," individuals "imbued with love of learning, confident in the functions and attitudes of leadership, possessing a high sense of public service, advocates of the American democracy and free enterprise system, and ready . . . to defend their country in time of national peril."

Surely that goal is great enough to accommodate women, who today count as citizens in our American democracy equal in stature to men. Just as surely, the State's great goal is not substantially advanced by women's categorical exclusion, in total disregard of their individual merit, from the State's premier "citizen-soldier" corps. Virginia, in sum, "has fallen far short of establishing the 'exceedingly persuasive justification,'" that must be the solid base for any gender-defined classification.

VI . . .

A . . .

Virginia chose not to eliminate, but to leave untouched, VMI's exclusionary policy. For women only, however, Virginia proposed a separate program, different in kind from VMI and unequal in tangible and intangible facilities. Having violated the Constitution's equal protection requirement, Virginia was obliged to show that its remedial proposal "directly addressed and related to" the violation, i.e., the equal protection denied to women ready, willing, and able to benefit from educational opportunities of the kind VMI offers. . . .

VWIL affords women no opportunity to experience the rigorous military training for which VMI is famed. Instead, the VWIL program "deemphasizes" military education, and uses a "cooperative method" of education "which reinforces self-esteem." . . .

Virginia maintains that these methodological differences are "justified pedagogically," based on "important differences between men and women in learning and developmental needs," "psychological and sociological differences" Virginia describes as "real" and "not stereotypes." . . .

As earlier stated, generalizations about "the way women are," estimates of what is appropriate for most women, no longer justify denying opportunity to women whose talent and capacity place them outside the average description. Notably, Virginia never asserted that VMI's method of education suits most men. It is also revealing that Virginia accounted for its failure to make the VWIL experience "the entirely militaristic experience of VMI" on the ground that VWIL "is planned for women who do not necessarily expect to pursue military careers." By that reasoning, VMI's "entirely militaristic" program would be inappropriate for men in general or as a group, for "only about 15% of VMI cadets enter career military service."[19] . . .

B

In myriad respects other than military training, VWIL does not qualify as VMI's equal. VWIL's student body, faculty, course offerings, and facilities hardly match VMI's. Nor can the VWIL graduate anticipate the benefits associated with VMI's 157-year history, the school's prestige, and its influential alumni network. . . .

Virginia, in sum, while maintaining VMI for men only, has failed to provide any "comparable single-gender women's institution." Instead, the Commonwealth has created a VWIL program fairly appraised as a "pale shadow" of VMI in terms of the range of curricular choices and faculty stature, funding, prestige, alumni support and influence.

Virginia's VWIL solution is reminiscent of the remedy Texas proposed 50 years ago, in response to a state trial court's 1946 ruling that, given the equal protection guarantee, African Americans could not be denied a legal education at a state facility. See Sweatt v. Painter. Reluctant to admit African Americans to its flagship Univesity of Texas Law School, the State set up a separate school for Herman Sweatt and other black law students. . . .

More important than the tangible features, the [Sweatt] Court emphasized, are "those qualities which are incapable of objective measurement but which make for greatness" in a school, including "reputation of the faculty, experience of the administration, position and influence of the alumni, standing in the community, traditions and prestige." Facing the marked differences reported in the Sweatt opinion, the Court unanimously ruled that Texas had not shown "substan-

---

19. Admitting women to VMI would undoubtedly require alterations necessary to afford members of each sex privacy from the other sex in living arrangements, and to adjust aspects of the physical training programs. [Experience] shows such adjustments are manageable. [Relocated footnote — EDS.]

tial equality in the [separate] educational opportunities" the State offered. Accordingly, the Court held, the Equal Protection Clause required Texas to admit African Americans to the University of Texas Law School. In line with *Sweatt*, we rule here that Virginia has not shown substantial equality in the separate educational opportunities the State supports at VWIL and VMI. . . .

Justice Thomas took no part in the consideration or decision of this case.

CHIEF JUSTICE REHNQUIST, concurring in judgment.

The Court holds first that Virginia violates the Equal Protection Clause by maintaining [VMI's] all-male admissions policy, and second that establishing the [VWIL] program does not remedy that violation. While I agree with these conclusions, I disagree with the Court's analysis and so I write separately.

I

Two decades ago in Craig v. Boren, we announced that "to withstand constitutional challenge, . . . classifications by gender must serve important governmental objectives and must be substantially related to achievement of those objectives." We have adhered to that standard of scrutiny ever since. While the majority adheres to this test today, it also says that the State must demonstrate an "exceedingly persuasive justification" to support a gender-based classification. It is unfortunate that the Court thereby introduces an element of uncertainty respecting the appropriate test.

While terms like "important governmental objective" and "substantially related" are hardly models of precision, they have more content and specificity than does the phrase "exceedingly persuasive justification." That phrase is best confined, as it was first used, as an observation on the difficulty of meeting the applicable test, not as a formulation of the test itself. See, e.g., [Personnel Administrator of Massachusetts v. Feeney, 442 U.S. 256 (1979)] ("These precedents dictate that any state law overtly or covertly designed to prefer males over females in public employment require an exceedingly persuasive justification"). . . .

II

An adequate remedy in my opinion might be a demonstration by Virginia that its interest in educating men in a single-sex environment is matched by its interest in educating women in a single-sex institution. To demonstrate such, the State does not need to create two institutions with the same number of faculty PhD's, similar SAT scores, or comparable athletic fields. Nor would it necessarily require that the women's institution offer the same curriculum as the men's; one could be strong in computer science, the other could be strong in liberal arts. It would be a sufficient remedy, I think, if the two institutions offered the same quality of education and were of the same overall calibre.

If a state decides to create single-sex programs, the state would, I expect, consider the public's interest and demand in designing curricula. And rightfully so. But the state should avoid assuming demand based on stereotypes; it must not assume a priori, without evidence, that there would be no interest in a women's school of civil engineering, or in a men's school of nursing.

In the end, the women's institution Virginia proposes, VWIL, fails as a remedy, because it is distinctly inferior to the existing men's institution and will continue to be for the foreseeable future. VWIL simply is not, in any sense, the institution that VMI is. In particular, VWIL is a program appended to a private college, not a self-standing institution; and VWIL is substantially underfunded as compared to VMI. I therefore ultimately agree with the Court that Virginia has not provided an adequate remedy.

JUSTICE SCALIA, dissenting.

Today the Court shuts down an institution that has served the people of the Commonwealth of Virginia with pride and distinction for over a century and a half. To achieve that desired result, it rejects (contrary to our established practice) the factual findings of two courts below, sweeps aside the precedents of this Court, and ignores the history of our people. As to facts: it explicitly rejects the finding that there exist "gender-based developmental differences" supporting Virginia's restriction of the "adversative" method to only a men's institution, and the finding that the all-male composition of the Virginia Military Institute (VMI) is essential to that institution's character. As to precedent: it drastically revises our established standards for reviewing sex-based classifications. And as to history: it counts for nothing the long tradition, enduring down to the present, of men's military colleges supported by both States and the Federal Government.

Much of the Court's opinion is devoted to deprecating the closed-mindedness of our forebears with regard to women's education, and even with regard to the treatment of women in areas that have nothing to do with education. Closed-minded they were — as every age is, including our own, with regard to matters it cannot guess, because it simply does not consider them debatable. The virtue of a democratic system with a First Amendment is that it readily enables the people, over time, to be persuaded that what they took for granted is not so, and to change their laws accordingly. That system is destroyed if the smug assurances of each age are removed from the democratic process and written into the Constitution. So to counterbalance the Court's criticism of our ancestors, let me say a word in their praise: they left us free to change. The same cannot be said of this most illiberal Court, which has embarked on a course of inscribing one after another of the current preferences of the society (and in some cases only the counter-majoritarian preferences of the society's law-trained elite) into our Basic Law. Today it enshrines the notion that no substantial educational value is to be served by an all-men's military academy — so that the decision by the people of Virginia to maintain such an institution denies equal protection to women who cannot attend that institution but can attend others. Since it is entirely clear that the Constitution of the United States — the old one — takes no sides in this educational debate, I dissent. . . .

Note: "Real Differences" and Formal Equality

1. *Integration or "separate but equal"?* As the *Virginia* Court acknowledges, only a small number of women are likely to benefit from the education VMI provides. Is the cause of gender equality significantly advanced by giving an opportunity to these women? Would the "separate but equal" approach suggested by Chief Justice Rehnquist's opinion do more or less to benefit women?

Virginia raises difficult questions about the extent to which the cause of gender equality is advanced by insisting on formally equal treatment. On the one hand, *Virginia* vindicates the right of individual women to be judged by the same standard used to judge men. It does so by refusing to permit the state to generalize about men and women as a group. On the other, to the extent that these generalizations are accurate, the decision leaves women as a group vulnerable to standards created for men. Notice in this regard that *Virginia* does not cast constitutional doubt on the "adversative" model itself.

In contrast to the majority's approach, Chief Justice Rehnquist would use VMI's policy as a lever to extract from the state resources that might provide a better education to a larger group of women. In doing so, however, he would provide no remedy for individual women who might benefit from adversative training. Moreover, his approach arguably leaves intact gender stereotypes that reenforce existing gender roles. Which approach better promotes gender equality?

2. *In a different "voice"?* Consider, in this connection, whether it is ever constitutional for the government to recognize that men and women speak with a different "voice" on some questions. Is there a plausible argument that the government might be constitutionally *compelled* to recognize these differences?

For an unusually candid debate among the justices on this topic, see J.E.B. v. Alabama ex rel. T.B., 511 U.S. 127 (1994). The case concerned the constitutionality of the state's use of gender-based peremptory challenges in a trial to determine whether the defendant was the father of a child and the extent of his child support obligations. (For a discussion of the constitutionality of race-based peremptory challenges, see pages 519-520 supra.) After the court excused three jurors for cause, only ten of the remaining thirty-three jurors were male. The state then used nine of its ten peremptory strikes to remove male jurors. The defendant used all but one of his strikes to remove female jurors. As a result, all the selected jurors were female.

In an opinion by Justice Blackmun, the Court held that gender-based peremptory challenges were unconstitutional:

> Far from proffering an exceptionally persuasive justification for its gender-based peremptory challenges, respondent maintains that its decision to strike virtually all the males from the jury in this case "may reasonably have been based upon the perception, supported by history, that men otherwise totally qualified to serve upon a jury might be more sympathetic and receptive to the arguments of a man alleged in a paternity action to be the father of an out-of-wedlock child, while women equally qualified to serve upon a jury might be more sympathetic and receptive to the arguments of the complaining witness who bore the child."
>
> We shall not accept as a defense to gender-based peremptory challenges "the very stereotype the law condemns." [Respondent] offers virtually no support for the conclusion that gender alone is an accurate predictor of juror's attitudes; yet it urges this Court to condone the same stereotypes that justified the wholesale exclusion of women from juries and the ballot box. Respondent seems to assume that gross generalizations that would be deemed impermissible if made on the basis of race are somehow permissible when made on the basis of gender.

In a footnote, Justice Blackmun added that, even if "a measure of truth can be found in some of the gender stereotypes used to justify gender-based peremptory challenges," that fact was irrelevant. "[A] shred of truth may be contained in some stereotypes, but [the equal protection clause] requires that state actors look be-

yond the surface before making judgments about people that are likely to stigmatize as well as to perpetuate historical patterns of discrimination."

Consider Justice O'Connor's concurring opinion:

> We know that like race, gender matters. A plethora of studies make clear that in
> rape cases, for example, female jurors are somewhat more likely to vote to convict
> than male jurors. Moreover, though there have been no similarly definitive studies
> regarding, for example, sexual harassment, child custody, or spousal or child abuse,
> one need not be a sexist to share the intuition that in certain cases a person's gen-
> der and resulting life experience will be relevant to his or her view of the case.
>
> Today's decision severely limits a litigant's ability to act on this intuition. [But] to
> say that gender makes no difference as a matter of law is not to say that gender
> makes no difference as a matter of fact. [Today's] decision is a statement that, in an
> effort to eliminate the potential discriminatory use of the peremptory, gender is
> now governed by the special rule of relevance formerly reserved for race. Though
> we gain much from this statement, we cannot ignore what we lose.

Justice Kennedy also wrote a concurring opinion:

> We do not prohibit racial and gender bias in jury selection only to encourage it in
> jury deliberations. Once seated, a juror should not give free rein to some racial or
> gender bias of his or her own. [A] juror who allows racial or gender bias to influence
> assessment of the case [renounces] his or her oath.
>
> In this regard, it is important to recognize that a juror sits not as a representative
> of a racial or sexual group but as an individual citizen. Nothing would be more per-
> nicious to the jury system than for society to presume that persons of different back-
> grounds go to the jury room to voice prejudice. [Thus], the Constitution guaran-
> tees a right only to an impartial jury, not to a jury composed of members of a
> particular race or gender.

Is gender discrimination in jury selection unconstitutional because the law recognizes that the genders speak with different "voices" and that both require representation, or because it insists that they speak with the same "voice" and that
distinctions between them are therefore irrational?

3. *The cases.* In other cases, mostly decided before *Virginia*, the Court has
shown some willingness to allow accommodation for the supposed "real differences" between men and women. In considering the cases discussed below, think
about whether the Court itself has escaped the gender stereotypes it purports to
be policing. How many of these decisions survive *Virginia*?

a. *Women in the military.* In light of *Virginia*, is there an "exceedingly persuasive" justification for the exclusion of all women from combat positions in the
military? In Rostker v. Goldberg, 453 U.S. 57 (1981), the Court upheld a statute
requiring men, but not women, to register for the draft. In an opinion by Justice
Rehnquist, the Court explained that the congressional decision to exclude
women must be understood in light of the fact that registration was intended

> as a prelude to a draft in a time of national emergency. [Congress] determined that
> any future draft, which would be facilitated by the registration scheme, would be
> characterized by a need for combat troops. [Women] as a group, however, unlike
> men as a group, are not eligible for combat [and the] President expressed his intent
> to continue the current military policy of precluding women for combat.

Rostker was decided fifteen years before *Virginia*, and the *Rostker* plaintiffs did not challenge the combat exclusion itself. Would the exclusion survive the *Virginia* test?

b. *Statutory rape.* In Michael M. v. Sonoma County Superior Court, 450 U.S. 464 (1981), the Court upheld a statute defining statutory rape as "an act of sexual intercourse accomplished with a female not the wife of the perpetrator, where the female is under the age of 18 years." Petitioner, a seventeen-year-old male, was convicted under the statute for having intercourse with a sixteen-year-old female. In an opinion for a plurality of the Court, Justice Rehnquist found that the purpose of the statute was to prevent illegitimate pregnancies and that the state had a strong interest in preventing such pregnancies:

> Because virtually all of the significant harmful and inescapably identifiable consequences of teenage pregnancy fall on the young female, a legislature acts well within its authority when it elects to punish only the participant who, by nature, suffers few of the consequences of his conduct. [Moreover], the risk of pregnancy itself constitutes a substantial deterrence to young females. No similar natural sanctions deter males. A criminal sanction imposed solely on males thus serves to roughly "equalize" the deterrents on the sexes.

Is it relevant, even if true, that more women than men are deterred by the risk of pregnancy from engaging in sexual intercourse? Since the California statute prohibits *consensual* intercourse, it presently applies only in cases where the woman partner is *undeterred* by the risk of pregnancy (else the intercourse would not be consensual). What difference does it make, then, that there is another class of women, to whom the statute has no application in any event, who are deterred by this risk?

Might the result in *Michael M.* be justified on the ground that many rape laws fail to deal adequately with acts of intercourse that do not involve overt force, yet are also not fully consensual? See, e.g., S. Estrich, Real Rape 29-41 (1987); Olsen, Statutory Rape: A Feminist Critique of Rights Analysis, 63 Tex. L. Rev. 387, 427-428 (1984). Does this problem amount to the kind of "exceedingly persuasive" justification that *Virginia* requires?

c. *Family rights.* In a variety of settings involving family relations, the Court has drawn an uncertain line between "real differences" separating the genders on the one hand and "archaic overgeneralizations" on the other. See Parham v. Hughes, 441 U.S. 347 (1979) (upholding the constitutionality of a Georgia statute permitting the mother, but not the father, of an illegitimate child to sue for wrongful death of the child when the father had not formally legitimated the child); Kirchberg v. Feenstra, 450 U.S. 455 (1981) (striking down a statute giving a husband unilateral authority to dispose of jointly owned property without a wife's consent); Caban v. Mohammed, 441 U.S. 380 (1979) (striking down a statute that required the consent of the mother, but not the father, for the adoption of a child born out of wedlock); Lehr v. Robertson, 463 U.S. 248 (1983) (upholding a New York statute permitting adoption of a nonmarital child without notice to the biological father unless the father registered his intent to claim paternity with a "putative father's registry" or had met certain other statutory criteria such as living openly with the child).

The Court's most recent decision on this subject arose in the context of federal naturalization law. A federal statute provides that an out-of-wedlock child born outside the United States to a citizen mother and noncitizen father is a U.S. citizen if the mother has previously been physically present in the United States for one year. In contrast, an out-of-wedlock child born to a citizen father and noncitizen mother is a U.S. citizen only if the child obtains formal proof of paternity before the age of eighteen, either through legitimation, written acknowledgment by the father under oath, or adjudication by a competent court.

In Miller v. Albright, 523 U.S. 420 (1998), petitioner was born in the Philippines to a Filipino mother. The government conceded that her father was an American citizen and, indeed, a "Voluntary Paternity Decree" entered by a Texas court established that he was the biological father. The government nonetheless refused to recognize her citizenship because she had not been legitimated before the age of eighteen as required by the statute. Petitioner claimed that the statutory distinctions based on the gender of her parents violated equal protection principles. Although the Supreme Court ultimately ruled against her, only Justice Stevens, who announced the Court's judgment, and Chief Justice Rehnquist, who joined Justice Stevens's opinion, specifically rejected her gender discrimination claim.

Justice Stevens argued that unmarried fathers and mothers were differently situated:

> If the citizen is the unmarried female, she must first choose to carry the pregnancy to term and reject the alternative of abortion. [She] must actually give birth to the child. [The statute] rewards that choice and that labor by conferring citizenship on her child.
>
> If the citizen is the unmarried male, he need not participate in the decision to give birth rather than to choose an abortion; he need not be present at the birth; and for at least 17 years thereafter he need not provide any parental support, either moral or financial to either the mother or the child, in order to preserve his right to confer citizenship on the child.
>
> [There] is thus a vast difference between the burdens imposed on the respective parents of potential citizens born out of wedlock in a foreign land. It seems obvious that the burdens imposed on the female citizen are more severe than those imposed on the male citizen.

In Justice Stevens's view, the statutory requirement for male citizens served the purpose of "ensur[ing] that a person born out of wedlock who claims citizenship by birth actually shares a blood relationship with an American citizen":

> [It cannot] be denied that the male and female parents are differently situated in this respect. The blood relationship to the birth mother is immediately obvious and is typically established by hospital records and birth certificates; the relationship to the unmarried father may often be undisclosed and unrecorded in any contemporary public record. Thus, the requirement that the father make a timely written acknowledgment under oath, or that the child obtain a court adjudication of paternity, produces the rough equivalent of the documentation that is already available to evidence the blood relationship [between] the mother and the child.

Moreover, two other interests, unrelated to the determination of paternity, were also served by the statute: the interest in encouraging the development of a healthy relationship between the citizen parent and the child while the child is a minor, and the related interest in fostering ties between the foreign-born child and the United States.

The remaining votes necessary to support the Court's judgment were supplied by Justice O'Connor, in an opinion joined by Justice Kennedy, and Justice Scalia, in an opinion joined by Justice Thomas.

Justice O'Connor would have held that the petitioner lacked standing to raise the gender discrimination claim that might have been brought by her father. (She took this position even though, at an earlier stage in the litigation, the petitioner's father, on the government's motion, had been dismissed from the suit for lack of standing.) As applied to petitioner, the statute was gender-neutral, since the standards for citizenship were the same for male and female out-of-wedlock children:

> Given that petitioner cannot raise a claim of discrimination triggering heightened scrutiny, she can argue only that [the statute] irrationally discriminates between illegitimate children of citizen fathers and citizen mothers. Although I do not share Justice Stevens' assessment that the provision withstands heightened scrutiny, I believe it passes rational scrutiny for the reasons he gives for sustaining it under the higher standard. It is unlikely, in my opinion, that any gender classification based on stereotypes can survive heightened scrutiny, but under rational scrutiny, a statute may be defended based on generalized classifications unsupported by empirical evidence.

Justice Scalia also concurred in the judgment but argued that "it makes no difference whether or not [the statute] passes 'heightened scrutiny' or any other test members of this Court may choose to apply." Instead, in his judgment,

> the complaint must be dismissed because the Court has no power to provide the relief requested: conferral of citizenship on a basis other than that prescribed by Congress. . . .
>
> [Because] only Congress has the power to set the requirements for acquisition of citizenship by persons not born within the territory of the United States, federal courts cannot exercise that power under the guise of their remedial authority. . . .
>
> I know of no instance [in] which this Court has severed an unconstitutional restriction upon the grant of immigration or citizenship. It is in my view incompatible with the plenary power of Congress over those fields for judges to speculate as to what Congress would have enacted if it had not enacted what it did — whether it would, for example have preferred to extend the requirements of [the statute] to mothers instead of eliminating them for fathers, or even to deny citizenship to illegitimate children entirely.

Justice Breyer, in an opinion joined by Justices Souter and Ginsburg, dissented:

> Distinctions of this kind — based upon gender — are subject to a "strong presumption" of constitutional invalidity. [United States v. Virginia.] The Equal Protection Clause permits them only if the Government meets the "demanding" burden of showing an "exceedingly persuasive" justification for the distinction. [Virginia.] . . .
>
> The statutory distinctions here violate these standards. They depend for their validity upon the generalization that mothers are significantly more likely than fathers to care for their children, or to develop caring relationships with their children. But consider how the statutes work once one abandons that generalization as the illegitimate basis for legislative linedrawing we have held it to be. First, assume

that the American citizen is also the Caretaker Parent. The statute would then require a Male Caretaker Parent to acknowledge his child prior to the child's 18th birthday. [It] would not require a Female Caretaker Parent to do [so]. The gender-based distinction that would impose added burdens only upon the Male Caretaker Parent would serve no purpose at all. Second, assume that the American citizen is the Non-caretaker Parent. In that circumstance, the statute would forgive a Female Non-caretaker Parent from complying with the requirements [that] it would impose upon a Male Non-caretaker Parent. Again, the gender based distinction that would impose lesser burdens only upon the Female Non-caretaker Parent would serve no purpose.

Justice Ginsburg also filed a dissenting opinion that was joined by Justices Souter and Breyer.

Given *Miller*, what result should a lower court reach in a suit brought by a citizen-father challenging the statute?

Note: The Relevance of "Real Differences"

1. *What makes a difference real?* In light of the cases discussed above, consider what makes a difference between the genders "real" for constitutional purposes. Must it be linked to some purely physiological distinction between the sexes? Which, if any, of the statutes considered above can be justified on this basis alone? Are demonstrated differences in behavior sufficient? It is at least conceivable that some such differences are a product of cultural expectations reinforced by the very statutes under attack. To the extent that this is true, the statutes become self-validating. Recall, for example, Justice O'Connor's concern in Mississippi University for Women v. Hogan that Mississippi's policy "makes the assumption that nursing is a field for women a self-fulfilling prophecy." Is it this phenomenon that concerned Justice Brennan in *Craig* when he wrote that statistical demonstrations are "in tension with the normative philosophy that underlies the Equal Protection Clause"?

Consider the argument that differences between the genders not only are socially constructed but also serve to reenforce male domination. See C. MacKinnon, Feminism Unmodified: Discourses on Life and Law 3, 8-9 (1987):

[The] social relation between the sexes is organized so that men may dominate and women must submit and this relation is sexual — in fact, is sex. Men in particular, if not men alone, sexualize inequality, especially the inequality of the sexes. [To] treat gender as a difference (with or without a French accent) means to treat it as a bipolar distinction, each pole of which is defined in contrast to the other by opposed intrinsic attributes. Beloved of left and right alike, construing gender as a difference [obscures] and legitimizes the way gender is imposed by force. It hides that force behind a static description of gender as a biological or social or mythic or semantic partition, engraved or inscribed or inculcated by god, nature, society (agents unspecified), the unconscious, or the cosmos. The idea of gender difference helps keep the reality of male dominance in place. . . .

Difference is the velvet glove on the iron fist of domination. This is as true when differences are affirmed as when they are denied, when their substance is applauded or when it is disparaged, when women are punished or [when] they are protected in their name. A sex inequality is not a difference gone wrong, a lesson the law of sex discrimination has yet to learn. One of the most deceptive antifeminisms in society, scholarship, politics, and law is the persistent treatment of gender as if it truly is a question of difference, rather than treating the gender difference as a construct of the difference gender makes.

If many gender differences are socially constructed, is the right question, what, if any, gender differences would exist in a "state of nature" before cultural forces have taken hold? Recall Justice Bradley's assertion over a century ago that a woman's duty "to fulfill the noble and benign offices of wife and mother" was "the law of the Creator." Is the current Court's search for "real differences" a modern-day analogue to this sort of reasoning? How likely is it that the justices can escape their own culture in deciding which differences are culturally determined?

Consider Case, Of Richard Epstein and Other Radical Feminists, 18 Harv. J.L. & Pub. Poly. 369, 375 (1995):

> Law is precisely that which fights against nature. If something were all that natural, a law would not be needed to bring it about. This is clear in almost every area of legal scholarship other than those pertaining to sex and gender. [The] evidence for natural human aggression is far stronger than any of the evidence [in] favor of difference between the sexes. No one [would], however, suggest that just because human beings are naturally aggressive there should be no laws of murder and assault.

2. *Difference and domination.* The arguments above criticize a focus on "difference" because the difference itself may be socially constructed. A second sort of critique takes the opposite tack. It argues that there *are* significant differences between men and women, and that the law's insistence on formal equality in the face of these differences leads to male domination. This might be true because a focus on differences tends to treat male traits as the norm and to marginalize females. Alternatively, it might be true because traditional equal protection analysis focuses solely on legislative means (i.e., on whether a difference between men and women is relevant to a given legislative end), even though legislative ends, which are treated as outside of the analysis, may themselves be the product of male domination.

With regard to the weaknesses of formal equality as a method of attacking male domination, consider Becker, Prince Charming: Abstract Equality, 1988 Sup. Ct. Rev. 201, 247:

> Formal equality [can] effect only limited change. It cannot, for example, ensure that jobs are structured so that female workers and male workers are equally able to combine wage work and parenthood. Nor can it ensure that social security, unemployment compensation, and other safety nets are structured so as to provide for women's financial security as well as they provide for men's. Moreover, women, especially ordinary mothers and wives, have been harmed by the changes effected to date by the movement towards formal equality. Further movement in that direction could bring additional harm. Any other satisfactory and workable general standard to be applied by judges is as yet unimagined and likely to be so for the foreseeable future.

A different view is presented in Littleton, Reconstructing Sexual Equality, 75 Cal. L. Rev. 1279 (1987), urging a model of "equality as acceptance" that would make social or biological differences "costless." See also Minow, Foreword: Justice Engendered, 101 Harv. L. Rev. 4 (1987)

How would constitutional doctrine have to be constructed to respond to these observations by Becker, Obscuring the Struggle: Sex Discrimination, Social Security, and Stone, Seidman, Sunstein & Tushnet's Constitutional Law, 89 Colum. L. Rev. 264, 283 (1989):

> [The] social security system fails to afford women as reliable an old-age security system as that afforded men. [Women] who lead ordinary lives are less likely to be well protected by the social security system than men who live ordinary lives because the system prefers those who have successfully fulfilled men's traditional breadwinner role over those who fulfilled women's traditional roles. Social security discriminates against women because it is designed so that women are at a much greater risk of poverty than are men. It exerts pressure on homemakers to depend economically on men in old age, despite the riskiness of such dependence.

To these observations by Z. Eisenstein, The Female Body and the Law 42-43 (1988):

> [Because] law is [structured] through the multiple oppositional layerings embedded in the dualism of man/woman, it is not able to move beyond the male referent as the standard for sex equality. [This] establishes men and women as opposites while privileging men. [The] legal notion of sex equality resulting from this stance is contradictory. It is progressive to the degree that it assumes men and women to be the same, and reactionary to the extent that its notion of what is "the same" derives from the phallus. It is progressive to the degree that it recognizes sex difference(s) as potentially creative and productive, and reactionary to the extent that it differentiates women according to their gender.

3. *Real differences and substantive values.* If we cannot rely on actual differences in behavior between men and women, and if we also cannot rely on suppositions about differences that would exist in the absence of cultural forces, what test should we utilize to evaluate gender discrimination claims? Is there in the end any way to judge the appropriateness of gender classifications without a substantive vision of the role gender would play in a just society? Consider Freedman, Sex Equality, Sex Differences, and the Supreme Court, 92 Yale L.J. 913, 961 (1983): "The choice to pursue sex equality rather than other social goals [can] be justified only on the basis of an explicitly normative theory of sex equality that identifies with some particularity the dynamics and harmful consequences of sexism." But what is the source of this normative vision?

4. *Beyond real differences.* Do the difficulties associated with the identification of "real differences" suggest that we might be better off, after all, with a virtual per se rule prohibiting gender classifications? Consider Brown, Emerson, Falk, and Freedman, The Equal Rights Amendment: A Constitutional Basis for Equal Rights for Women, 80 Yale L.J. 871, 873-874 (1971):

> Many of the efforts to create a separate legal status for women stem from a good faith attempt to advance the interests of women. Nevertheless, the preponderant effect has been to buttress the social and economic subordination of women. [Whatever] the motivation for different treatment, the result is to create a dual system of rights and responsibilities in which the rights of each group are governed by

a different set of values. History and experience have taught us that in such a dual system one group is always dominant and the other subordinate. As long as woman's place is defined as separate, a male-dominated society will define her place as inferior.

Is the cause of equality advanced by insisting on gender-neutral laws that disproportionately affect women because they are differently situated with respect to the laws? Consider Law, Rethinking Sex and the Constitution, 132 U. Pa. L. Rev. 955, 1007 (1984): "[Pregnancy,] abortion, reproduction, and creation of another human being *are* special — very special. Women have these experiences. Men do not. An equality doctrine that ignores the unique quality of these experiences implicitly says that women can claim equality only insofar as they are like men. Such doctrine demands that women deny an important aspect of who they are."

4.   *"Benign" Gender Classifications and Discrimination against Men*

Califano v. Goldfarb

430 U.S. 199 (1977)

MR. JUSTICE BRENNAN announced the judgment of the Court and delivered an opinion in which MR. JUSTICE WHITE, MR. JUSTICE MARSHALL, and MR. JUSTICE POWELL joined.

Under the Federal Old-Age, Survivors, and Disability Insurance Benefits (OASDI) program, survivors' benefits based on the earnings of a deceased husband covered by the Act are payable to his widow. Such benefits on the basis of the earnings of a deceased wife covered by the Act are payable to the widower, however, only if he "was receiving at least one-half of his support" from his deceased wife. The question in this case is whether this gender-based distinction violates the Due Process Clause of the Fifth Amendment.

I

[Hannah Goldfarb worked as a secretary for the New York City public schools for almost twenty-five years until her death. Although she had paid her Social Security taxes in full during this period, her husband was denied a widower's benefit on her death because he could not show that he had been receiving one-half of his support from his wife when she died. Relying on Weinberger v. Wiesenfeld, the district court held that this requirement was unconstitutional.]

II

The gender-based distinction drawn by [the statute] — burdening a widower but not a widow with the task of proving dependency upon the deceased spouse — presents an equal protection question indistinguishable from that decided in

[*Wiesenfeld*]. That decision and the decision in [*Frontiero*] plainly require affirmance of the judgment of the District Court.

[The reasoning in *Wiesenfeld*] condemns the gender-based distinction made by [the statute] in this case. For that distinction [like the distinction in *Wiesenfeld*] operates "to deprive women of protection for their families which men receive as a result of their employment": social security taxes were deducted from Hannah Goldfarb's salary during the quarter century she worked as a secretary, yet, in consequence of [the statute], she also "not only failed to receive for her [spouse] the same protection which a similarly situated male worker would have received [for his spouse] but she also was deprived of a portion of her own earnings in order to contribute to the fund out of which benefits would be paid to others." *Wiesenfeld* thus inescapably compels the conclusion reached by the District Court that the gender-based differentiation created by [the statute] — that results in the efforts of female workers required to pay social security taxes producing less protection for their spouses than is produced by the efforts of men — is forbidden by the Constitution, at least when supported by no more substantial justification than "archaic and overbroad" generalizations, [*Ballard*], or "old notions," [*Stanton*], such as "assumptions as to dependency," [*Wiesenfeld*], that are more consistent with "the role-typing society has long imposed," [*Stanton*], than with contemporary reality. . . .

III

Appellant, however, would focus equal protection analysis, not upon the discrimination against the covered wage earning female, but rather upon whether her surviving widower was unconstitutionally discriminated against by burdening him but not a surviving widow with proof of dependency. The gist of the argument is that, analyzed from the perspective of the widower, "the denial of benefits reflected the congressional judgment that aged widowers as a class were sufficiently likely not to be dependent upon their wives that it was appropriate to deny them benefits unless they were in fact dependent."

But [*Wiesenfeld*] rejected the virtually identical argument when appellant's predecessor argued that the statutory classification there attacked should be regarded from the perspective of the prospective beneficiary and not from that of the covered wage earner. . . .

From its inception, the social security system has been a program of social insurance. Covered employees and their employers pay taxes into a fund administered distinct from the general federal revenues to purchase protection against the economic consequences of old age, disability, and death. But under [this statute] female insureds received less protection for their spouses solely because of their sex. Mrs. Goldfarb worked and paid social security taxes for 25 years at the same rate as her male colleagues, but because of [the statute] the insurance protection received by the males was broader than hers. Plainly then [the statute] disadvantages women contributors to the social security system as compared to similarly situated men. . . .

[In] a sense, of course, both the female wage earner and her surviving spouse are disadvantaged by operation of the statute, but this is because "Social Security is designed . . . for the protection of the *family*" [quoting from Justice Powell's concurring opinion in *Wiesenfeld*] and the section discriminates against one particular category of family — that in which the female spouse is a wage earner covered by social security. Therefore decision of the equal protection challenge in this case cannot focus solely on the distinction drawn between widowers and widows but, as *Wiesenfeld* held, upon the gender-based discrimination against covered female wage earners as well.[8]. . .

IV . . .

B

Appellant next argues that *Frontiero* and *Wiesenfeld* should be distinguished as involving statutes with different objectives from [this one]. Rather than merely enacting presumptions designed to save the expense and trouble of determining which spouses are really dependent, providing benefits to all widows, but only to such widowers as prove dependency, [this statute], it is argued, rationally defines different standards of eligibility because of the differing social welfare needs of widowers and widows. That is, the argument runs, Congress may reasonably have presumed that nondependent widows, who receive benefits, are needier than nondependent widowers, who do not, because of job discrimination against women (particularly older women), and because they are more likely to have been more dependent on their spouses.

But "inquiry into the actual purposes" of the discrimination, [*Wiesenfeld*], proves the contrary. First, [the statute] itself is phrased in terms of *dependency*, not *need*. Congress chose to award benefits, not to widowers who could prove that they are needy, but to those who could prove that they had been dependent on their wives for more than one-half of their support. On the face of the statute, dependency, not need, is the criterion for inclusion.

Moreover, the general scheme of OASDI shows that dependence on the covered wage earner is the critical factor in determining beneficiary categories. . . .

[Nothing] whatever suggests a reasoned congressional judgment that nondependent widows should receive benefits because they are more likely to be needy than nondependent widowers. . . .

We conclude, therefore, that the differential treatment of nondependent widows and widowers results not, as appellant asserts, from a deliberate congressional intention to remedy the arguably greater needs of the former, but rather from an

---

8. In any event, gender-based discriminations against men have been invalidated when they do not "serve important governmental objectives and [are not] substantially related to the achievement of those objectives." [*Craig*.] Neither [*Kahn*], nor [*Ballard*], relied on by appellant, supports a contrary conclusion. The gender-based distinctions in the statutes involved in *Kahn* and *Ballard* were justified because the only discernible purpose of each was the permissible one of redressing our society's longstanding disparate treatment of women.

But "the mere recitation of a benign, compensatory purpose is not an automatic shield which protects against any inquiry into the actual purposes underlying a statutory scheme." [*Wiesenfeld*.] That inquiry in this case demonstrates that [this statute] has no such remedial purpose. Moreover, the classifications challenged in *Wiesenfeld* and in this case rather than advantaging women to compensate for past wrongs compounds those wrongs by penalizing women "who do work and whose earnings contribute significantly to their families' support."

intention to aid the dependent spouses of deceased wage earners, coupled with a presumption that wives are usually dependent. [We] held in *Frontiero*, and again in *Wiesenfeld*, and therefore hold again here, that such assumptions do not suffice to justify a gender-based discrimination in the distribution of employment-related benefits.

Affirmed.

MR. JUSTICE STEVENS, concurring in the judgment.

Although my conclusion is the same, my appraisal of the relevant discrimination and my reasons for concluding that it is unjustified, are somewhat different from those expressed by Mr. Justice Brennan.

First, I agree with Mr. Justice Rehnquist that the constitutional question raised by this plaintiff requires us to focus on his claim for benefits rather than his deceased wife's tax obligation. She had no contractual right to receive benefits or to control their payment; moreover, the payments are not a form of compensation for her services. . . .

Second, I also agree with Mr. Justice Rehnquist that a classification which treats certain aged widows more favorably than their male counterparts is not "invidious." Such a classification does not imply that males are inferior to females; does not condemn a large class on the basis of the misconduct of an unrepresentative few; and does not add to the burdens of an already disadvantaged discrete minority.

It is also clear that the disparate treatment of widows and widowers is not the product of a conscious purpose to redress the "legacy of economic discrimination" against females. [*Kahn* (Brennan, J., dissenting).] The widows who benefit from the disparate treatment are those who were sufficiently successful in the job market to become nondependent on their husbands. Such a widow is the least likely to need special benefits. . . .

[The] history of the statute is entirely consistent with the view that Congress simply assumed that all widows should be regarded as "dependents" in some general sense, even though they could not satisfy the statutory support test later imposed on men. It is fair to infer that habit, rather than analysis or actual reflection, made it seem acceptable to equate the terms "widow" and "dependent surviving spouse." . . .

I am therefore persuaded that this discrimination against a group of males is merely the accidental byproduct of a traditional way of thinking about females. I am also persuaded that a rule which effects an unequal distribution of economic benefits solely on the basis of sex is sufficiently questionable that "due process requires that there be a legitimate basis for presuming that the rule was actually intended to serve [the] interest" put forward by the Government as its justification. . . .

MR. JUSTICE REHNQUIST, with whom [CHIEF JUSTICE BURGER], MR. JUSTICE STEWART, and MR. JUSTICE BLACKMUN join, dissenting.

In light of this Court's recent decisions beginning with [*Reed*], one cannot say that there is no support in our cases for the result reached by the Court. One can, however, believe as I do that careful consideration of these cases affords more support for the opposite result than it does for that reached by the Court. . . .

[The] effect of the statutory scheme is to make it easier for widows to obtain benefits than it is for widowers, since the former qualify automatically while the latter must show proof of need. Such a requirement in no way perpetuates or exacerbates the economic disadvantage which has led the Court to conclude that gender-based discrimination must meet a different test from other types of classifications. . . .

Perhaps because the reasons asserted for "heightened scrutiny" of gender-based distinctions are rooted in the fact that *women* have in the past been victims of unfair treatment, see [*Frontiero*], the plurality says that the difference in treatment here is not only between a widow and a widower, but between the respective deceased spouses of the two. It concludes that wage-earning wives are deprived "of protection for their families which men receive as a result of their employment."

But this is a questionable tool of analysis which can be used to prove virtually anything. It might just as well have been urged in [*Kahn*], where we upheld a Florida property tax exemption redounding to the benefit of widows but not widowers, that the real discrimination was between the deceased spouses of the respective widow and widower, who had doubtless by their contributions to the family or marital community helped make possible the acquisition of the property which was now being disparately taxed.

Since the claim to social security benefits is noncontractual in nature, the contributions of the deceased spouse cannot be regarded as creating any sort of contractual entitlement on the part of either the deceased wife or the surviving husband. Here the female wage earner has gotten the degree of protection for her family which Congress was concerned to extend to all. Neither she nor her surviving husband has any constitutional claim to more, simply because Congress has chosen, for administrative reasons, to give benefits to widows without requiring proof of dependency. . . .

[The] present statutory treatment of widows and widowers would seem to reflect a pair of legislative judgments about the needs of those two groups. The first is that the persons qualifying for spousal benefits are likely to have even more substantial needs after the passing of their spouse. . . .

The second legislative judgment implicit in the widow's and widower's provisions is that widows, as a practical matter, are much more likely to be without adequate means of support than are widowers. The plurality opinion makes much of establishing this point, that the absence of any dependency prerequisite to the award of widow's benefits reflects a judgment, resting on "administrative convenience," that dependence among aged widows is frequent enough to justify waiving the requirement entirely. I differ not with the recognition of this administrative convenience purpose but with the conclusion that such a purpose *necessarily* invalidates the resulting classification. Our decisions dealing with social welfare legislation indicate that our inquiry must go further. For rational classifications aimed at distributing funds to beneficiaries under social insurance legislation weigh a good deal more heavily on the governmental interest side of the equal protection balance than they may in other legislative contexts. The "administrative convenience" which is afforded by such classifications in choosing the administrator of a decedent's estate, see [*Reed*], is significantly less important to the effectiveness of the legislative scheme than is the "convenience" afforded by classifications in administering an Act designed to provide benefits to millions upon millions of beneficiaries with promptness and certainty. . . .

[Whatever] his actual needs, Goldfarb would, of course, have no complaint if Congress had chosen to require proof of dependency by widows as well as widowers, or if it had simply refrained from making any provision whatever for benefits to surviving spouses. [Any] claim which he has must therefore turn upon the alleged impropriety of giving benefits to widows without requiring them to make the same proof of dependency required of widowers. Yet, in the context of the legislative purpose, this amounts not to exclusion but to overinclusiveness for reasons of administrative convenience which, if reasonably supported by the underlying facts, is not offensive to the Equal Protection Clause in social welfare cases.[7]

This case is also distinguishable from [Frontiero], in the sense that social insurance differs from compensation for work done. While there is no basis for assessing the propriety of a given allocation of funds within a social insurance program apart from an identifiable legislative purpose, a compensatory scheme may be evaluated under the principle of equal pay for equal work done. This case is therefore unlike Frontiero, where the Court invalidated sex discrimination among military personnel in their entitlement to increased quarters allowances on account of marriage, and in the eligibility of their spouses for dental and medical care. These compensatory fringe benefits were available to male employees as a matter of course, but were unavailable to females except on proof that their husbands depended on them for over one-half of their support. . . .

[The] very most that can be squeezed out of the facts of this case in the way of cognizable "discrimination" is a classification which favors aged widows. Quite apart from any considerations of legislative purpose and "administrative convenience" which may be advanced to support the classification, this is scarcely an invidious discrimination. [The] differentiation in no way perpetuates the economic discrimination which has been the basis for heightened scrutiny of gender-based classifications, and is, in fact, explainable as a measure to ameliorate the characteristically depressed condition of aged widows. [Kahn] is therefore also authority for upholding it. For both of these reasons, I would reverse the judgment of the District Court.

CALIFANO v. WEBSTER, 430 U.S. 313 (1977). In this case, decided less than three weeks after Goldfarb, the Court unanimously sustained the constitutionality of a provision of the Social Security Act that had the effect of granting to retired female workers higher monthly old-age benefits than those received by

7. There is substantial statistical evidence indicating that the differential treatment of widows and widowers is economically justifiable on the basis of administrative convenience. . . .

[The] number of married women over 55 who would satisfy the dependency test is something like 88.5% — the 77% who do not work, plus half of the remaining 23% who do. This nine-tenths correlation appears sufficiently high to justify extension of benefits to the other one-tenth for reasons of administrative convenience.

On the side of widower's benefits, the incidence of dependent husbands is certainly low enough to justify any administrative expense incurred in screening out those who are not dependent. In 1970, only 2.5% of *working* wives contributed more than 75% of the family income which renders the husband dependent. Since only 43% of all wives work, the incidence of dependent husbands among all married couples is approximately 1%. . . .

similarly situated retired male workers. The act provided that benefits were to be computed based on the average monthly wage of the worker during certain statutorily defined "benefit computation years." Until its amendment in 1972, the statutory formula permitted women to exclude more lower earning years from this average than men could exclude. A district judge held that this gender-based distinction violated the equal protection component of the fifth amendment due process clause, but the Court, in a per curiam opinion, reversed.

The Court began its analysis by reciting the familiar *Craig* test for classifications based on gender — the classification "must serve important governmental objectives and must be substantially related to achievement of those objectives." It then noted that "[reduction] of the disparity in economic condition between men and women caused by the long history of discrimination against women has been recognized as such an important governmental objective [*Ballard*; *Kahn*]." Of course, the mere recitation of a compensatory purpose did not automatically shield a statute from inquiry into its actual purpose. "Accordingly, we have rejected attempts to justify gender classifications as compensatory for past discrimination against women when the classifications in fact penalized women wage earners, or when the statutory structure and its legislative history revealed that the classification was not enacted as compensation for past discrimination [*Goldfarb*; *Wiesenfeld*]."

In the Court's opinion, however, this provision was more analogous to those upheld in *Kahn* and *Ballard* than to those struck down in *Wiesenfeld* and *Goldfarb*. "The more favorable treatment of the female wage earner enacted here was not a result of 'archaic and overbroad generalizations' about women [*Ballard*] or of 'the role-typing society has long imposed' upon women [*Stanton*], such as casual assumptions that women are 'the weaker sex' or are more likely to be child rearers or dependents." Rather, "[t]he challenged statute operated directly to compensate women for past economic discrimination. Retirement benefits under the Act are based on past earnings. But as we have recognized: 'Whether from overt discrimination or from the socialization process of a male-dominated culture, the job market is inhospitable to the woman seeking any but the lowest paid jobs' [*Kahn*]. Thus, allowing women, who as such have been unfairly hindered from earning as much as men, to eliminate additional low-earning years from the calculation of their retirement benefits works directly to remedy some part of the effect of past discrimination."

Moreover, after canvassing the legislative history of the provision, the Court concluded that "the differing treatment of men and women [was] not 'the accidental byproduct of a traditional way of thinking about females,' [*Goldfarb* (Stevens, J., concurring)], but rather was deliberately enacted to compensate for particular economic disabilities suffered by women."

Chief Justice Burger, with whom Justices Stewart, Blackmun, and Rehnquist joined, concurred in the judgment: "While I am happy to concur in the Court's judgment, I find it somewhat difficult to distinguish the Social Security provision upheld here from that struck down so recently in [*Goldfarb*]. Although the distinction drawn by the Court between this case and *Goldfarb* is not totally lacking in substance, I question whether certainty in the law is promoted by hinging the validity of important statutory schemes on whether five Justices view them to be more akin to the 'offensive' provisions struck down in [*Wiesenfeld*] and [*Frontiero*], or more like the 'benign' provisions upheld in [*Ballard*] and [*Kahn*]."

Note: The Problem of "Benign" Gender Classifications

1. *Discrimination against men.* In what sense did the statute invalidated in *Goldfarb* discriminate against women? Consider Becker, Obscuring the Struggle: Sex Discrimination, Social Security, and Stone, Seidman, Sunstein & Tushnet's Constitutional Law, 89 Colum. L. Rev. 264, 274-276 (1989):

> Relative to the changes necessary to achieve equality between the sexes, [*Goldfarb*] is trivial. [It] is trivial in another sense: it involves a challenge to the award of benefits to a man. [One] would expect the case to have had only the most limited effect on the status of women in the real world during their lives and marriages. True, after *Goldfarb*, a very few working women and retired women workers [could] sleep more soundly knowing that in the event of their deaths, their widowers would receive more money. But these women tend to be relatively powerful. [It] surely would be relevant to note that the Court developed its constitutional standard for sex equality in trivial cases. It seems likely that development in such a context might affect the effectiveness of a substantive standard.

Would the *Goldfarb* statute have discriminated against women if the benefits to widows and widowers were funded from general revenues? Compare *Goldfarb* with Wengler v. Druggists Mutual Insurance Co., 446 U.S. 142 (1980), in which the Court invalidated a portion of Missouri's workers' compensation statute under which a widower of a deceased worker was entitled to death benefits only if he was mentally or physically incapacitated from wage earning or proved actual dependence on his wife's earnings. In contrast, a widow was automatically entitled to death benefits without having to demonstrate dependence. Appellees attempted to distinguish *Goldfarb* on the ground that, unlike the Social Security program, workers' compensation was not based on mandatory contributions from wage earnings of the employee. Therefore, women workers could not complain that they were being deprived of a portion of their earnings to contribute to a fund from which their husbands would receive no benefits. In a footnote, the Court responded as follows: "We have before rejected the proposition that 'the Constitution is indifferent to a statute that conditions the availability of noncontributory welfare benefits on the basis of gender' [Califano v. Westcott, 443 U.S. 76, 85 (1979)], and we refuse to part ways with our earlier decisions by applying a different standard of review in this case simply because the system is funded by employer rather than employee contributions."

In the body of the opinion, the Court argued that the challenged statute discriminated against both men and women. Women were harmed because "[the] benefits [that] the working woman can expect to be paid to her spouse in the case of her work-related death are less than those payable to the spouse of the deceased male wage earner." Men were also discriminated against because "the surviving male spouse must prove his incapacity or dependency [while the] widow of a deceased wage earner [is] presumed dependent and is guaranteed a weekly benefit for life or until remarriage." However the discrimination was characterized, the Court wrote, "our precedents require that gender-based discrimination [meet the *Craig* test]." Here, the state's "claimed justification of administrative convenience fails, just as it has in our prior cases."

If, as the Court asserts, the Missouri statute discriminated against women simply because their spouses were deprived of a benefit, don't virtually all laws that discriminate against men also discriminate against women? In *Webster*, for example, might it not be argued that the wives of retired male workers were harmed by granting such workers lower old-age benefits than those accorded to retired female workers?

If, as the Court asserts, the Missouri statute discriminates against both men and women, in what sense does it involve *gender* discrimination? What argument is there for heightened scrutiny of statutes that classify on the basis of gender if neither men nor women as a class are disadvantaged by them?

Assuming arguendo that the Missouri statute discriminated against men, but not women, should it be subjected to heightened scrutiny? Note that in *Craig* and *Mississippi University for Women*, the Court utilized heightened scrutiny in cases where men were the disadvantaged class. But under a representation-reinforcement theory, doesn't the justification for such scrutiny disappear if the discrimination operates to disadvantage a powerful group?

Consider Kanowitz, "Benign" Sex Discrimination: Its Troubles and Their Cure, 31 Hastings L.J. 1379, 1394 (1980):

> [A] casual glance at the treatment males have received at the hands of the law solely because they are males suggests that they have paid an awesome price for other advantages they have presumably enjoyed over females in our society. Whether one talks of the male's unique obligation of compulsory military service, his primary duty for spousal and child support, his lack of the same kinds of protective labor legislation that have traditionally been enjoyed by women, or the statutory or judicial preference in child custody disputes that has long been accorded to mothers vis-à-vis fathers of minor children, sex discrimination against males in statutes and judicial decisions has been widespread and severe.

But if it is *men* as a class who have been historically disadvantaged, why should laws discriminating against *women* be subject to heightened scrutiny? It is, of course, possible that both men and women have been harmed in different ways by gender stereotyping. But if both sexes are harmed equally, what is the basis for judicial intervention? Kanowitz argues:

> Centuries of sex-role allocations, based on "habit, rather than analysis," simply disabled Americans of either sex from restructuring the duties of military service, family support, and protections in the work place so as to permit men and women to share the burdens and benefits of social existence more equitably. Viewed in this light, the apparent power of men to change their sex-based roles in the past can be seen as being more theoretical than real. In this respect, men were as powerless as any other discrete, insular minority.

Can *both* men and women be discrete and insular minorities? Under this expansive version of the political process argument, is there any group that cannot claim judicial protection?

Is the real point of *Goldfarb* and *Wengler* that, even though the laws invalidated in those cases superficially benefited women, they "really" discriminated against them by reinforcing stereotypes of dependence and passivity that make women the losers in the long run? Consider C. MacKinnon, Sexual Harassment of Working Women 116-117 (1979):

[Sex] discrimination is a system that defines women as inferior from men, that cumulatively disadvantages women for their differences from men, as well as ignores their similarities. [The] only question for litigation is whether the policy or practice in question integrally contributes to the maintenance of an underclass or a deprived position because of gender status. The disadvantage which constitutes the injury of discrimination is not the failure to be treated "without regard to" one's sex; that is the injury of arbitrary differentiation. The unfairness lies in being deprived *because of* being a woman or a man, a deprivation given meaning in the social context of the dominance or preference of one sex over the other.

Is this approach consistent with *Michael M.* and *Rostker?* Is it one that the justices who wrote those opinions could possibly administer? Compare Law, Rethinking Sex and the Constitution, 132 U. Pa. L. Rev. 955, 1005 (1984):

Professor MacKinnon's approach is ambitious, but it adds unnecessary complexity to the application of sex equality doctrine in a large number of cases. The determination of what reinforces or undermines a sex-based underclass is exceedingly difficult. Professor MacKinnon may overestimate judges' capacities to identify and avoid socially imposed constraints on equality. She disregards our history in which laws justified as protecting women have been a central means of oppressing them. Most fundamentally, her proposed standard may incorporate and perpetuate a false belief that a judicially enforced constitutional standard can, by itself, dismantle the deep structures that "integrally contribute" to sex-based deprivation.

2. *Affirmative action for women.* The Court seems to have taken the view that affirmative action measures disadvantaging men are subject to intermediate scrutiny, and that remedying disparities between men and women, at least if caused by prior discrimination, qualifies as an "important government objective" for purposes of that test. However, the Court's pronouncements on this matter occurred at a time when the appropriate standard for *racial* affirmative action was still confused. The Court now insists that in the racial context, affirmative action statutes are subject to the same strict scrutiny as statutes disadvantaging racial minorities. See section C4 supra. What impact does this change have on the gender cases? Given the history of the equal protection clause, it seems implausible that efforts to remedy racial discrimination must satisfy a stricter test than efforts to remedy gender discrimination. Perhaps, then, gender affirmative action measures should also be subject to strict scrutiny. But this result is also deeply problematic, since it would leave laws disadvantaging women subject to a lower level of review than laws benefiting them.

3. *Affirmative action and the nature of equality.* In light of the difficulties posed by gender classifications allegedly designed to remedy prior discrimination, should such laws be treated as per se invalid? Consider, e.g., Olsen, The Family and the Market: A Study of Ideology and Legal Reform, 96 Harv. L. Rev. 1497, 1555 (1983):

Although the doctrine of affirmative action presupposes prior discrimination against women, affirmative action policies pretend to have ended such discrimination. Affirmative action thus creates another reason for women to blame themselves when they fail in the marketplace. Moreover, although affirmative action may expand women's social roles, it also tends to reenforce the ideology of inequality and to reintroduce problems of paternalism.

Is the goal of equality better served by insisting on laws that are facially gender-neutral, but that in fact affect women unequally because they are differently situated with respect to the laws? Recall Justice Stewart's assertion in *Geduldig*, page 601 supra, that the exclusion of pregnancy benefits from an insurance program was not gender discrimination because it did "not exclude anyone from benefit eligibility because of gender but merely [removed] one physical condition — pregnancy — from the list of compensable disabilities." Is that the sort of analysis that helps undercut "the ideology of inequality"?

5.   *The Irrelevant Constitution?*

1. *The equal rights amendment.* In 1972, Congress approved and submitted to the states for ratification the following constitutional amendment:

> Section 1. Equality of rights under the law shall not be denied or abridged by the United States or by any State on account of sex.
> Section 2. The Congress shall have the power to enforce, by appropriate legislation, the provisions of this article.
> Section 3. This amendment shall take effect two years after the date of ratification.

Although about half of the required three-fourths of the states ratified the amendment within a few months of its submission, progress then became stalled. In 1978, Congress extended the period for ratification until June 30, 1982, but the second deadline expired with only thirty-five of the necessary thirty-eight states having approved the amendment.

What advantages does a constitutional amendment have over specific statutory measures designed to correct the problems that exist? Over continued case-by-case litigation under the equal protection clause? If the Court's interpretation of the fourteenth amendment in the gender context has been less than fully satisfactory, is a constitutional amendment necessary to refocus its decisions? Do the vagueness and sweep of the proposed amendment constitute a virtual invitation to the Supreme Court to "solve" our gender problem in the manner it thinks best? Does the Court's performance to date justify confidence in the kind of solution it is likely to formulate?

2. *The declining importance of constitutional law.* Proponents of the equal rights amendment hoped to constitutionalize a wide variety of issues relating to gender discrimination. In recent years, however, the Court seems to have lost interest in the constitutional status of gender. Since 1983, it has decided only a handful of case involving an equal protection challenge to a gender classification. During the same period, many of the issues that might have been resolved on a constitutional basis in an earlier era have instead been treated as matters of statutory construction.

Does this recent history suggest that the remaining issues concerning gender equality are particularly resistant to constitutional analysis? If so, why? Note that many of the statutory cases involve private parties, whose conduct would not be controlled by the Constitution. See Chapter 9 infra. Consider also Becker, The Politics of Women's Wrongs and the Bill of "Rights": A Bicentennial Perspective, 59 U. Chi. L. Rev. 453, 456 (1992):

The Bill of Rights incorporates a private-public split with only negative rights under a limited government. As a result, women's activities and concerns — from economic rights to religion — seem beyond the proper scope of government. That women are poorer than, and subordinate to, men appears "natural" and pre-political. . . .

Any [written set of cryptic, abstract, and negative rights enforced by judges] will better protect the powerful against government action harmful to their interests than the less powerful, who need protection against the powerful as well as against the government. [The] less powerful need many concrete, positive rights. These rights require detailed implementation schemes and the expenditure of funds. Judges are not likely to order either when enforcing abstract clauses.

E.   EQUAL PROTECTION METHODOLOGY: THE PROBLEM OF SEXUAL ORIENTATION

Should laws and policies that discriminate on the basis of sexual orientation be strictly scrutinized? If so, how should the protected class be defined?

In Bowers v. Hardwick, 478 U.S. 186 (1986), the Court rejected a substantive due process attack on a Georgia sodomy statute brought by an adult male who had been criminally charged for a sexual act performed in his own bedroom with another adult male. (This aspect of *Bowers* is discussed at greater length at page 896 infra.) On its face, the statute did not distinguish between heterosexual and homosexual sodomy, and the Court purported not to reach any equal protection questions raised by it. However, the Court also limited its holding to the question of homosexual sodomy posed by the facts before it and explicitly refused to decide whether the statute's application to heterosexuals would be constitutional. Does the Court's willingness to uphold the statute as applied to homosexuals, while reserving the possibility that it might be unconstitutional as applied to heterosexuals, implicitly settle the equal protection question? Consider the following.

Romer v. Evans
517 U.S. 620 (1996)

JUSTICE KENNEDY delivered the opinion of the Court.

One century ago, the first Justice Harlan admonished this Court that the Constitution "neither knows nor tolerates classes among citizens." Plessy v. Ferguson (dissenting opinion). Unheeded then, those words now are understood to state a commitment to the law's neutrality where the rights of persons are at stake. The Equal Protection Clause enforces this principle and today requires us to hold invalid a provision of Colorado's Constitution.

I

["Amendment 2" was added to the state constitution by a statewide referendum held in 1992. It was enacted after a number of Colorado municipalities had adopted ordinances prohibiting discrimination on the basis of sexual orientation in many transactions and activities such as housing, employment, education, public accommodations, and health and welfare services. It provided:

> NO PROTECTED STATUS BASED ON HOMOSEXUAL, LESBIAN, OR
> BISEXUAL ORIENTATION
> Neither the State of Colorado, through any of its branches or departments, nor any of its agencies, political subdivisions, municipalities or school districts, shall enact, adopt or enforce any statute, regulation, ordinance or policy whereby homosexual, lesbian or bisexual orientation, conduct, practices or relationships shall constitute or otherwise be the basis of or entitle any person or class of persons to have or claim any minority status, quota preferences, protected status or claim of discrimination. This Section of the Constitution shall be in all respects self-executing.

[The Colorado Supreme Court held that Amendment 2 was subject to strict scrutiny under the equal protection clause on the ground that it impinged on the right of homosexuals to participate in the political process.] On remand, the State advanced various arguments in an effort to show that Amendment 2 was narrowly tailored to serve compelling interests, but the trial court found none sufficient. It enjoined enforcement of Amendment 2, and the Supreme Court of Colorado, in a second opinion, affirmed the ruling. We granted certiorari and now affirm the judgment, but on a rationale different from that adopted by the State Supreme Court.

II

The State's principal argument in defense of Amendment 2 is that it puts gays and lesbians in the same position as all other persons. So, the State says, the measure does no more than deny homosexuals special rights. This reading of the amendment's language is implausible. We rely not upon our own interpretation of the amendment but upon the authoritative construction of Colorado's Supreme Court. The state court, deeming it unnecessary to determine the full extent of the amendment's reach, found it invalid even on a modest reading of its implications. The critical discussion of the amendment [is] as follows:

> The immediate objective of Amendment 2 is, at a minimum, to repeal existing statutes, regulations, ordinances, and policies of state and local entities that barred discrimination based on sexual orientation.
> The "ultimate effect" of Amendment 2 is to prohibit any governmental entity from adopting similar, or more protective statutes, regulations, ordinances, or policies in the future unless the state constitution is first amended to permit such measures.

Sweeping and comprehensive is the change in legal status effected by this law. So much is evident from the ordinances that the Colorado Supreme Court declared would be void by operation of Amendment 2. Homosexuals, by state decree, are put in a solitary class with respect to transactions and relations in both the private and governmental spheres. The amendment withdraws from homosexuals, but no others, specific legal protection from the injuries caused by discrimination, and it forbids reinstatement of these laws and policies.

The change that Amendment 2 works in the legal status of gays and lesbians in the private sphere is far-reaching, both on its own terms and when considered in light of the structure and operation of modern anti-discrimination laws. That structure is well illustrated by contemporary statutes and ordinances prohibiting discrimination by providers of public accommodations. "At common law, innkeepers, smiths, and others who 'made profession of a public employment,' were prohibited from refusing, without good reason, to serve a customer." Hurley v. Irish-American Gay, Lesbian and Bisexual Group of Boston, Inc., 515 U.S. 557 (1995). The duty was a general one and did not specify protection for particular groups. The common law rules, however, proved insufficient in many instances, and it was settled early that the Fourteenth Amendment did not give Congress a general power to prohibit discrimination in public accommodations. In consequence, most States have chosen to counter discrimination by enacting detailed statutory schemes.

Colorado's state and municipal laws typify this emerging tradition of statutory protection and follow a consistent pattern. The laws first enumerate the persons or entities subject to a duty not to discriminate. The list goes well beyond the entities covered by the common law. The Boulder ordinance, for example, has a comprehensive definition of entities deemed places of "public accommodation." They include "any place of business engaged in any sales to the general public and any place that offers services, facilities, privileges, or advantages to the general public or that receives financial support through solicitation of the general public or through governmental subsidy of any kind." . . .

These statutes and ordinances also depart from the common law by enumerating the groups or persons within their ambit of protection. Enumeration is the essential device used to make the duty not to discriminate concrete and to provide guidance for those who must comply. In following this approach, Colorado's state and local governments have not limited anti-discrimination laws to groups that have so far been given the protection of heightened equal protection scrutiny under our cases. Rather, they set forth an extensive catalogue of traits which cannot be the basis for discrimination, including age, military status, marital status, pregnancy, parenthood, custody of a minor child, political affiliation, physical or mental disability of an individual or of his or her associates and, in recent times, sexual orientation.

Amendment 2 bars homosexuals from securing protection against the injuries that these public-accommodations laws address. That in itself is a severe consequence, but there is more. Amendment 2, in addition, nullifies specific legal protections for this targeted class in all transactions in housing, sale of real estate, insurance, health and welfare services, private education, and employment.

Not confined to the private sphere, Amendment 2 also operates to repeal and forbid all laws or policies providing specific protection for gays or lesbians from discrimination by every level of Colorado government. The State Supreme Court cited two examples of protections in the governmental sphere that are now rescinded and may not be reintroduced. The first is Colorado Executive Order D0035 (1990), which forbids employment discrimination against "'all state employees, classified and exempt' on the basis of sexual orientation." Also repealed, and now forbidden, are "various provisions prohibiting discrimination based on sexual orientation at state colleges." The repeal of these measures and the prohibition against their future reenactment demonstrates that Amendment 2 has the same force and effect in Colorado's governmental sector as it does elsewhere and that it applies to policies as well as ordinary legislation.

Amendment 2's reach may not be limited to specific laws passed for the benefit of gays and lesbians. It is a fair, if not necessary, inference from the broad language of the amendment that it deprives gays and lesbians even of the protection of general laws and policies that prohibit arbitrary discrimination in governmental and private settings. At some point in the systematic administration of these laws, an official must determine whether homosexuality is an arbitrary and thus forbidden basis for decision. Yet a decision to that effect would itself amount to a policy prohibiting discrimination on the basis of homosexuality, and so would appear to be no more valid under Amendment 2 than the specific prohibitions against discrimination the state court held invalid.

If this consequence follows from Amendment 2, as its broad language suggests, it would compound the constitutional difficulties the law creates. The state court did not decide whether the amendment has this effect, however, and neither need we. In the course of rejecting the argument that Amendment 2 is intended to conserve resources to fight discrimination against suspect classes, the Colorado Supreme Court made the limited observation that the amendment is not intended to affect many anti-discrimination laws protecting non-suspect classes. In our view that does not resolve the issue. In any event, even if, as we doubt, homosexuals could find some safe harbor in laws of general application, we cannot accept the view that Amendment 2's prohibition on specific legal protections does no more than deprive homosexuals of special rights. To the contrary, the amendment imposes a special disability upon those persons alone. Homosexuals are forbidden the safeguards that others enjoy or may seek without constraint. They can obtain specific protection against discrimination only by enlisting the citizenry of Colorado to amend the state constitution or perhaps, on the State's view, by trying to pass helpful laws of general applicability. This is so no matter how local or discrete the harm, no matter how public and widespread the injury. We find nothing special in the protections Amendment 2 withholds. These are protections taken for granted by most people either because they already have them or do not need them; these are protections against exclusion from an almost limitless number of transactions and endeavors that constitute ordinary civic life in a free society.

III

The Fourteenth Amendment's promise that no person shall be denied the equal protection of the laws must co-exist with the practical necessity that most legislation classifies for one purpose or another, with resulting disadvantage to various groups or persons. We have attempted to reconcile the principle with the reality by stating that, if a law neither burdens a fundamental right nor targets a suspect class, we will uphold the legislative classification so long as it bears a rational relation to some legitimate end.

Amendment 2 fails, indeed defies, even this conventional inquiry. First, the amendment has the peculiar property of imposing a broad and undifferentiated disability on a single named group, an exceptional and, as we shall explain, invalid form of legislation. Second, its sheer breadth is so discontinuous with the reasons offered for it that the amendment seems inexplicable by anything but animus toward the class that it affects; it lacks a rational relationship to legitimate state interests.

Taking the first point, even in the ordinary equal protection case calling for the most deferential of standards, we insist on knowing the relation between the classification adopted and the object to be attained. The search for the link between classification and objective gives substance to the Equal Protection Clause; it provides guidance and discipline for the legislature, which is entitled to know what sorts of laws it can pass; and it marks the limits of our own authority. In the ordinary case, a law will be sustained if it can be said to advance a legitimate government interest, even if the law seems unwise or works to the disadvantage of a particular group, or if the rationale for it seems tenuous. [The Court cites cases using rational basis review to uphold various statutes.] [The] laws challenged in the cases just cited were narrow enough in scope and grounded in a sufficient factual context for us to ascertain that there existed some relation between the classification and the purpose it served. By requiring that the classification bear a rational relationship to an independent and legitimate legislative end, we ensure that classifications are not drawn for the purpose of disadvantaging the group burdened by the law.

Amendment 2 confounds this normal process of judicial review. It is at once too narrow and too broad. It identifies persons by a single trait and then denies them protection across the board. The resulting disqualification of a class of persons from the right to seek specific protection from the law is unprecedented in our jurisprudence. The absence of precedent for Amendment 2 is itself instructive; "discriminations of an unusual character especially suggest careful consideration to determine whether they are obnoxious to the constitutional provision." Louisville Gas & Elec. Co. v. Coleman, 277 U.S. 32, 37-38 (1928).

It is not within our constitutional tradition to enact laws of this sort. Central both to the idea of the rule of law and to our own Constitution's guarantee of equal protection is the principle that government and each of its parts remain open on impartial terms to all who seek its assistance. "'Equal protection of the laws is not achieved through indiscriminate imposition of inequalities.'" Sweatt v. Painter (quoting Shelley v. Kraemer [334 U.S. 1 (1948)]). Respect for this principle explains why laws singling out a certain class of citizens for disfavored legal status or general hardships are rare. A law declaring that in general it shall be more difficult for one group of citizens than for all others to seek aid from the government is itself a denial of equal protection of the laws in the most literal sense. "The guaranty of 'equal protection of the laws is a pledge of the protection of equal laws.'" Skinner v. Oklahoma ex rel. Williamson, [316 U.S. 535 (1942) quoting Yick Wo v. Hopkins].

Davis v. Beason, 133 U.S. 333 (1890), not cited by the parties but relied upon by the dissent, is not evidence that Amendment 2 is within our constitutional tradition, and any reliance upon it as authority for sustaining the amendment is misplaced. In Davis, the Court approved an Idaho territorial statute denying Mormons, polygamists, and advocates of polygamy the right to vote and to hold office because, as the Court construed the statute, it "simply excludes from the privilege of voting, or of holding any office of honor, trust or profit, those who have been convicted of certain offences, and those who advocate a practical resistance to the laws of the Territory and justify and approve the commission of crimes forbidden by it." To the extent *Davis* held that persons advocating a certain practice may be denied the right to vote, it is no longer good law. Brandenburg v. Ohio, 395 U.S. 444 (1969) (per curiam). To the extent it held that the groups designated in the statute may be deprived of the right to vote because of their status, its ruling could not stand without surviving strict scrutiny, a most doubtful outcome. Dunn v. Blumstein, 405 U.S. 330, 337 (1972). To the extent Davis held that a convicted felon may be denied the right to vote, its holding is not implicated by our decision and is unexceptionable. See Richardson v. Ramirez, 418 U.S. 24 (1974).

A second and related point is that laws of the kind now before us raise the inevitable inference that the disadvantage imposed is born of animosity toward the class of persons affected. "If the constitutional conception of 'equal protection of the laws' means anything, it must at the very least mean that a bare . . . desire to harm a politically unpopular group cannot constitute a legitimate governmental interest." Department of Agriculture v. Moreno. Even laws enacted for broad and ambitious purposes often can be explained by reference to legitimate public policies which justify the incidental disadvantages they impose on certain persons. Amendment 2, however, in making a general announcement that gays and lesbians shall not have any particular protections from the law, inflicts on them immediate, continuing, and real injuries that outrun and belie any legitimate justifications that may be claimed for it. We conclude that, in addition to the far-reaching deficiencies of Amendment 2 that we have noted, the principles it offends, in another sense, are conventional and venerable; a law must bear a rational relationship to a legitimate governmental purpose, and Amendment 2 does not.

The primary rationale the State offers for Amendment 2 is respect for other citizens' freedom of association, and in particular the liberties of landlords or employers who have personal or religious objections to homosexuality. Colorado also cites its interest in conserving resources to fight discrimination against other groups. The breadth of the Amendment is so far removed from these particular justifications that we find it impossible to credit them. We cannot say that Amendment 2 is directed to any identifiable legitimate purpose or discrete objective. It is a status-based enactment divorced from any factual context from which we could discern a relationship to legitimate state interests; it is a classification of persons undertaken for its own sake, something the Equal Protection Clause does not permit. "Class legislation . . . [is] obnoxious to the prohibitions of the Fourteenth Amendment. . . ." Civil Rights Cases, 109 U.S. at 24.

We must conclude that Amendment 2 classifies homosexuals not to further a proper legislative end but to make them unequal to everyone else. This Colorado cannot do. A State cannot so deem a class of persons a stranger to its laws. Amendment 2 violates the Equal Protection Clause, and the judgment of the Supreme Court of Colorado is affirmed.

JUSTICE SCALIA, with whom [CHIEF JUSTICE REHNQUIST] and JUSTICE THOMAS join, dissenting.

The Court has mistaken a Kulturkampf for a fit of spite. The constitutional amendment before us here is not the manifestation of a "bare . . . desire to harm" homosexuals, but is rather a modest attempt by seemingly tolerant Colo-

radans to preserve traditional sexual mores against the efforts of a politically powerful minority to revise those mores through use of the laws. That objective, and
the means chosen to achieve it, are not only unimpeachable under any constitutional doctrine hitherto pronounced (hence the opinion's heavy reliance upon
principles of righteousness rather than judicial holdings); they have been specifically approved by the Congress of the United States and by this Court.

In holding that homosexuality cannot be singled out for disfavorable treatment,
the Court contradicts a decision, unchallenged here, pronounced only 10 years
ago, see Bowers v. Hardwick, and places the prestige of this institution behind the
proposition that opposition to homosexuality is as reprehensible as racial or religious bias. Whether it is or not is precisely the cultural debate that gave rise to the
Colorado constitutional amendment (and to the preferential laws against which
the amendment was directed). Since the Constitution of the United States says
nothing about this subject, it is left to be resolved by normal democratic means,
including the democratic adoption of provisions in state constitutions. This
Court has no business imposing upon all Americans the resolution favored by the
elite class from which the Members of this institution are selected, pronouncing
that "animosity" toward homosexuality, is evil. I vigorously dissent.

I

Let me first discuss Part II of the Court's opinion, its longest section, which is devoted to rejecting the State's arguments that Amendment 2 "puts gays and lesbians in the same position as all other persons," and "does no more than deny
homosexuals special rights." The Court concludes that this reading of Amendment 2's language is "implausible" under the "authoritative construction" given
Amendment 2 by the Supreme Court of Colorado.

In reaching this conclusion, the Court considers it unnecessary to decide the
validity of the State's argument that Amendment 2 does not deprive homosexuals of the "protection [afforded by] general laws and policies that prohibit arbitrary discrimination in governmental and private settings." I agree that we need
not resolve that dispute, because the Supreme Court of Colorado has resolved it
for us. [The] Colorado court stated:

> It is significant to note that Colorado law currently proscribes discrimination
> against persons who are not suspect classes, including discrimination based on age,
> marital or family status, veterans' status, and for any legal, off-duty conduct such as
> smoking tobacco. Of course Amendment 2 is not intended to have any effect on
> this legislation, but seeks only to prevent the adoption of anti-discrimination laws
> intended to protect gays, lesbians, and bisexuals.

The Court utterly fails to distinguish this portion of the Colorado court's opinion. [The] clear import of the Colorado court's conclusion [is] that "general laws
and policies that prohibit arbitrary discrimination" would continue to prohibit
discrimination on the basis of homosexual conduct as well. This analysis, which
is fully in accord with (indeed, follows inescapably from) the text of the constitutional provision, lays to rest such horribles, raised in the course of oral argument,

as the prospect that assaults upon homosexuals could not be prosecuted. The amendment prohibits special treatment of homosexuals, and nothing more. It would not affect, for example, a requirement of state law that pensions be paid to all retiring state employees with a certain length of service; homosexual employees, as well as others, would be entitled to that benefit. But it would prevent the State or any municipality from making death-benefit payments to the "life partner" of a homosexual when it does not make such payments to the long-time roommate of a nonhomosexual employee. . . .

Despite all of its hand-wringing about the potential effect of Amendment 2 on general antidiscrimination laws, the Court's opinion ultimately does not dispute all this, but assumes it to be true. The only denial of equal treatment it contends homosexuals have suffered is this: They may not obtain preferential treatment without amending the state constitution. That is to say, the principle underlying the Court's opinion is that one who is accorded equal treatment under the laws, but cannot as readily as others obtain preferential treatment under the laws, has been denied equal protection of the laws. If merely stating this alleged "equal protection" violation does not suffice to refute it, our constitutional jurisprudence has achieved terminal silliness.

The central thesis of the Court's reasoning is that any group is denied equal protection when, to obtain advantage (or, presumably, to avoid disadvantage), it must have recourse to a more general and hence more difficult level of political decisionmaking than others. The world has never heard of such a principle, which is why the Court's opinion is so long on emotive utterance and so short on relevant legal citation. And it seems to me most unlikely that any multilevel democracy can function under such a principle. For whenever a disadvantage is imposed, or conferral of a benefit is prohibited, at one of the higher levels of democratic decisionmaking (i.e., by the state legislature rather than local government, or by the people at large in the state constitution rather than the legislature), the affected group has (under this theory) been denied equal protection. To take the simplest of examples, consider a state law prohibiting the award of municipal contracts to relatives of mayors or city councilmen. Once such a law is passed, the group composed of such relatives must, in order to get the benefit of city contracts, persuade the state legislature — unlike all other citizens, who need only persuade the municipality. It is ridiculous to consider this a denial of equal protection, which is why the Court's theory is unheard-of.

The Court might reply that the example I have given is not a denial of equal protection only because the same "rational basis" (avoidance of corruption) which renders constitutional the substantive discrimination against relatives (i.e., the fact that they alone cannot obtain city contracts) also automatically suffices to sustain what might be called the electoral-procedural discrimination against them (i.e., the fact that they must go to the state level to get this changed). This is of course a perfectly reasonable response, and would explain why "electoral-procedural discrimination" has not hitherto been heard of: a law that is valid in its substance is automatically valid in its level of enactment. But the Court cannot afford to make this argument, for as I shall discuss next, there is no doubt of a rational basis for the substance of the prohibition at issue here. The Court's entire novel theory rests upon the proposition that there is something special — something that cannot be justified by normal "rational basis" analysis — in making a disadvantaged group (or a nonpreferred group) resort to a higher decision-making level. That proposition finds no support in law or logic.

II

I turn next to whether there was a legitimate rational basis for the substance of the constitutional amendment — for the prohibition of special protection for homosexuals. It is unsurprising that the Court avoids discussion of this question, since the answer is so obviously yes. The case most relevant to the issue before us today is not even mentioned in the Court's opinion: In Bowers v. Hardwick, we held that the Constitution does not prohibit what virtually all States had done from the founding of the Republic until very recent years — making homosexual conduct a crime. That holding is unassailable, except by those who think that the Constitution changes to suit current fashions. But in any event it is a given in the present case: Respondents' briefs did not urge overruling Bowers, and at oral argument respondents' counsel expressly disavowed any intent to seek such overruling. If it is constitutionally permissible for a State to make homosexual conduct criminal, surely it is constitutionally permissible for a State to enact other laws merely disfavoring homosexual conduct. [And] a fortiori it is constitutionally permissible for a State to adopt a provision not even disfavoring homosexual conduct, but merely prohibiting all levels of state government from bestowing special protections upon homosexual conduct. Respondents (who, unlike the Court, cannot afford the luxury of ignoring inconvenient precedent) counter Bowers with the argument that a greater-includes-the-lesser rationale cannot justify Amendment 2's application to individuals who do not engage in homosexual acts, but are merely of homosexual "orientation." . . .

But assuming that, in Amendment 2, a person of homosexual "orientation" is someone who does not engage in homosexual conduct but merely has a tendency or desire to do so, Bowers still suffices to establish a rational basis for the provision. If it is rational to criminalize the conduct, surely it is rational to deny special favor and protection to those with a self-avowed tendency or desire to engage in the conduct. Indeed, where criminal sanctions are not involved, homosexual "orientation" is an acceptable stand-in for homosexual conduct. A State "does not violate the Equal Protection Clause merely because the classifications made by its laws are imperfect," Dandridge v. Williams [397 U.S. 471, 485 (1970)]. Just as a policy barring the hiring of methadone users as transit employees does not violate equal protection simply because some methadone users pose no threat to passenger safety, see New York City Transit Authority v. Beazer, and just as a mandatory retirement age of 50 for police officers does not violate equal protection even though it prematurely ends the careers of many policemen over 50 who still have the capacity to do the job, see Massachusetts Bd. of Retirement v. Murgia [427 U.S. 307 (1976)], Amendment 2 is not constitutionally invalid simply because it could have been drawn more precisely so as to withdraw special antidiscrimination protections only from those of homosexual "orientation" who actually engage in homosexual conduct. As Justice Kennedy wrote, when he was on the Court of Appeals, in a case involving discharge of homosexuals from the Navy: "Nearly any statute which classifies people may be irrational as applied in particular cases. Discharge of the particular plaintiffs before us would be rational, under minimal scrutiny, not because their particular cases present the dangers which justify Navy policy, but instead because the general policy of discharging all homosexuals is rational." Beller v. Middendorf, 632 F.2d 788, 808-809, n.20 (CA9 1980) (citation omitted). . . .

III

The foregoing suffices to establish what the Court's failure to cite any case remotely in point would lead one to suspect: No principle set forth in the Constitution, nor even any imagined by this Court in the past 200 years, prohibits what Colorado has done here. But the case for Colorado is much stronger than that. What it has done is not only unprohibited, but eminently reasonable, with close, congressionally approved precedent in earlier constitutional practice.

First, as to its eminent reasonableness. The Court's opinion contains grim, disapproving hints that Coloradans have been guilty of "animus" or "animosity" toward homosexuality, as though that has been established as Unamerican. Of course it is our moral heritage that one should not hate any human being or class of human beings. But I had thought that one could consider certain conduct reprehensible — murder, for example, or polygamy, or cruelty to animals — and could exhibit even "animus" toward such conduct. Surely that is the only sort of "animus" at issue here: moral disapproval of homosexual conduct, the same sort of moral disapproval that produced the centuries-old criminal laws that we held constitutional in *Bowers*. The Colorado amendment does not, to speak entirely precisely, prohibit giving favored status to people who are homosexuals; they can be favored for many reasons — for example, because they are senior citizens or members of racial minorities. But it prohibits giving them favored status because of their homosexual conduct — that is, it prohibits favored status for homosexuality.

But though Coloradans are, as I say, entitled to be hostile toward homosexual conduct, the fact is that the degree of hostility reflected by Amendment 2 is the smallest conceivable. The Court's portrayal of Coloradans as a society fallen victim to pointless, hate-filled "gay-bashing" is so false as to be comical. Colorado not only is one of the 25 States that have repealed their antisodomy laws, but was among the first to do so. But the society that eliminates criminal punishment for homosexual acts does not necessarily abandon the view that homosexuality is morally wrong and socially harmful; often, abolition simply reflects the view that enforcement of such criminal laws involves unseemly intrusion into the intimate lives of citizens.

There is a problem, however, which arises when criminal sanction of homosexuality is eliminated but moral and social disapprobation of homosexuality is meant to be retained. The Court cannot be unaware of that problem; it is evident in many cities of the country, and occasionally bubbles to the surface of the news, in heated political disputes over such matters as the introduction into local schools of books teaching that homosexuality is an optional and fully acceptable "alternate life style." The problem (a problem, that is, for those who wish to retain social disapprobation of homosexuality) is that, because those who engage in homosexual conduct tend to reside in disproportionate numbers in certain communities, have high disposable income, and of course care about homosexual-rights issues much more ardently than the public at large, they possess political power much greater than their numbers, both locally and statewide. Quite understandably, they devote this political power to achieving not merely a grudging social toleration, but full social acceptance, of homosexuality.

By the time Coloradans were asked to vote on Amendment 2, their exposure to homosexuals' quest for social endorsement was not limited to newspaper accounts of happenings in places such as New York, Los Angeles, San Francisco, and Key West. Three Colorado cities — Aspen, Boulder, and Denver — had enacted ordinances that listed "sexual orientation" as an impermissible ground for discrimination, equating the moral disapproval of homosexual conduct with racial and religious bigotry. The phenomenon had even appeared statewide: the Governor of Colorado had signed an executive order pronouncing that "in the State of Colorado we recognize the diversity in our pluralistic society and strive to bring an end to discrimination in any form," and directing state agency-heads to "ensure non-discrimination" in hiring and promotion based on, among other things, "sexual orientation." I do not mean to be critical of these legislative successes; homosexuals are as entitled to use the legal system for reinforcement of their moral sentiments as are the rest of society. But they are subject to being countered by lawful, democratic countermeasures as well.

That is where Amendment 2 came in. It sought to counter both the geographic concentration and the disproportionate political power of homosexuals by (1) resolving the controversy at the statewide level, and (2) making the election a single-issue contest for both sides. It put directly, to all the citizens of the State, the question: Should homosexuality be given special protection? They answered no. The Court today asserts that this most democratic of procedures is unconstitutional. Lacking any cases to establish that facially absurd proposition, it simply asserts that it must be unconstitutional, because it has never happened before. . . .

[The constitutions] of the States of Arizona, Idaho, New Mexico, Oklahoma, and Utah to this day contain provisions stating that polygamy is "forever prohibited." Polygamists, and those who have a polygamous "orientation," have been "singled out" by these provisions for much more severe treatment than merely denial of favored status; and that treatment can only be changed by achieving amendment of the state constitutions. The Court's disposition today suggests that these provisions are unconstitutional, and that polygamy must be permitted in these States on a state-legislated, or perhaps even local-option, basis — unless, of course, polygamists for some reason have fewer constitutional rights than homosexuals.

The United States Congress, by the way, required the inclusion of these anti-polygamy provisions in the constitutions of Arizona, New Mexico, Oklahoma, and Utah, as a condition of their admission to statehood. (For Arizona, New Mexico, and Utah, moreover, the Enabling Acts required that the antipolygamy provisions be "irrevocable without the consent of the United States and the people of said State" — so that not only were "each of [the] parts" of these States not "open on impartial terms" to polygamists, but even the States as a whole were not; polygamists would have to persuade the whole country to their way of thinking.) [Thus], this "singling out" of the sexual practices of a single group for statewide, democratic vote — so utterly alien to our constitutional system, the Court would have us believe — has not only happened, but has received the explicit approval of the United States Congress.

I cannot say that this Court has explicitly approved any of these state constitutional provisions; but it has approved a territorial statutory provision that went even further, depriving polygamists of the ability even to achieve a constitutional amendment, by depriving them of the power to vote. In Davis v. Beason, 133 U.S. 333 (1890), Justice Field wrote for a unanimous Court:

> In our judgment, §501 of the Revised Statutes of Idaho Territory, which provides that "no person . . . who is a bigamist or polygamist or who teaches, advises, counsels, or encourages any person or persons to become bigamists or polygamists, or to commit any other crime defined by law, or to enter into what is known as plural or celestial marriage, or who is a member of any order, organization or association which teaches, advises, counsels, or encourages its members or devotees or any other persons to commit the crime of bigamy or polygamy, or any other crime defined by law . . . is permitted to vote at any election, or to hold any position or office of honor, trust, or profit within this Territory," is not open to any constitutional or legal objection.

To the extent, if any, that this opinion permits the imposition of adverse consequences upon mere abstract advocacy of polygamy, it has of course been overruled by later cases. See Brandenburg v. Ohio, 395 U.S. 444 (1969) (per curiam). But the proposition that polygamy can be criminalized, and those engaging in that crime deprived of the vote, remains good law. See Richardson v. Ramirez, 418 U.S. 24, 53 (1974). Beason rejected the argument that "such discrimination is a denial of the equal protection of the laws." Among the Justices joining in that rejection were the two whose views in other cases the Court today treats as equal-protection lodestars — Justice Harlan, who was to proclaim in Plessy v. Ferguson (dissenting opinion), that the Constitution "neither knows nor tolerates classes among citizens," and Justice Bradley, who had earlier declared that "class legislation . . . [is] obnoxious to the prohibitions of the Fourteenth Amendment," Civil Rights Cases.

This Court cited Beason with approval as recently as 1993, in an opinion authored by the same Justice who writes for the Court today. That opinion said: "Adverse impact will not always lead to a finding of impermissible targeting. For example, a social harm may have been a legitimate concern of government for reasons quite apart from discrimination. . . . See, e.g., . . . Davis v. Beason." Church of Lukumi Babalu Aye, Inc. v. Hialeah, 508 U.S. 520, 535 (1993). It remains to be explained how §501 of the Idaho Revised Statutes was not an "impermissible targeting" of polygamists, but (the much more mild) Amendment 2 is an "impermissible targeting" of homosexuals. Has the Court concluded that the perceived social harm of polygamy is a "legitimate concern of government," and the perceived social harm of homosexuality is not?

IV

I strongly suspect that the answer to the last question is yes, which leads me to the last point I wish to make: The Court today, announcing that Amendment 2 "defies . . . conventional [constitutional] inquiry," and "confounds [the] normal process of judicial review," employs a constitutional theory heretofore unknown to frustrate Colorado's reasonable effort to preserve traditional American moral values. The Court's stern disapproval of "animosity" towards homosexuality might be compared with what an earlier Court (including the revered Justices Harlan and Bradley) said in Murphy v. Ramsey, 114 U.S. 15 (1885), rejecting a constitutional challenge to a United States statute that denied the franchise in federal territories to those who engaged in polygamous cohabitation:

> Certainly no legislation can be supposed more wholesome and necessary in the founding of a free, self-governing commonwealth, fit to take rank as one of the coordinate States of the Union, than that which seeks to establish it on the basis of the idea of the family, as consisting in and springing from the union for life of one man and one woman in the holy estate of matrimony; the sure foundation of all that is stable and noble in our civilization; the best guaranty of that reverent morality which is the source of all beneficent progress in social and political improvement.

I would not myself indulge in such official praise for heterosexual monogamy, because I think it no business of the courts (as opposed to the political branches) to take sides in this culture war.

But the Court today has done so, not only by inventing a novel and extravagant constitutional doctrine to take the victory away from traditional forces, but even by verbally disparaging as bigotry adherence to traditional attitudes. To suggest, for example, that this constitutional amendment springs from nothing more than "a bare . . . desire to harm a politically unpopular group" is nothing short of insulting. (It is also nothing short of preposterous to call "politically unpopular" a group which enjoys enormous influence in American media and politics, and which, as the trial court here noted, though composing no more than 4% of the population had the support of 46% of the voters on Amendment 2.)

When the Court takes sides in the culture wars, it tends to be with the knights rather than the villeins — and more specifically with the Templars, reflecting the views and values of the lawyer class from which the Court's Members are drawn. How that class feels about homosexuality will be evident to anyone who wishes to interview job applicants at virtually any of the Nation's law schools. The interviewer may refuse to offer a job because the applicant is a Republican; because he is an adulterer; because he went to the wrong prep school or belongs to the wrong country club; because he eats snails; because he is a womanizer; because she wears real-animal fur; or even because he hates the Chicago Cubs. But if the interviewer should wish not to be an associate or partner of an applicant because he disapproves of the applicant's homosexuality, then he will have violated the pledge which the Association of American Law Schools requires all its member-schools to exact from job interviewers: "assurance of the employer's willingness" to hire homosexuals. This law-school view of what "prejudices" must be stamped out may be contrasted with the more plebeian attitudes that apparently still prevail in the United States Congress, which has been unresponsive to repeated attempts to extend to homosexuals the protections of federal civil rights laws, and which took the pains to exclude them specifically from the Americans With Disabilities Act of 1990.

Today's opinion has no foundation in American constitutional law, and barely pretends to. The people of Colorado have adopted an entirely reasonable provision which does not even disfavor homosexuals in any substantive sense, but merely denies them preferential treatment. Amendment 2 is designed to prevent piecemeal deterioration of the sexual morality favored by a majority of Coloradans, and is not only an appropriate means to that legitimate end, but a means that Americans have employed before. Striking it down is an act, not of judicial judgment, but of political will. I dissent.

Note: *The Meaning of* Romer

1. *Baselines again.* The Court claims that its decision guarantees for homosexuals only "equal" and not "special" protection. This is so, the Court asserts, because under modern conditions the baseline is a general right to be free from discrimination. Protections against discrimination are "taken for granted by most people either because they already have them or do not need them; these are protections against exclusion from an almost limitless number of transactions and endeavors that constitute ordinary civic life in a free society." Suppose Colorado had never enacted Amendment 2 but had simply failed to enact measures protecting homosexuals from discrimination. Does it follow from the Court's analysis that a state acts "irrationally" and therefore violates the Constitution if it provides general protection against discrimination for a wide range of groups but fails to provide such protection for gays? Is this position consistent with Washington v. Davis?

2. *Justice Scalia's dissent.* What is the meaning of the first sentence of Justice Scalia's opinion? "Kulturkampf" is the German word for "culture war." The term refers to the effort by the German government in the late nineteenth century, under the leadership of Count Bismarck, to reduce the influence of the Roman Catholic Church. Among other things, Bismarck insisted that the state train and license priests and imprisoned priests and bishops who disobeyed his orders. Consider the possibility that our Constitution outlaws state-supported "Kulturkampfs" and that Amendment 2 violated the Constitution precisely because it formed part of an official "culture war" against a particular subsection of the population. Note that the majority and dissenting opinions each accuse the other of departing from a position of state neutrality in this conflict. The majority disclaims any effort to give homosexuals "special" rights and claims that Colorado has failed to treat them "equally." The dissent, in turn, accuses the majority of siding with homosexuals against their adversaries. What does state neutrality mean in this context? Is neutrality a desirable or constitutionally required objective? For a discussion of the equal rights/special rights distinction, see Rubin, Equal Rights, Special Rights, and the Nature of Antidiscrimination Law, 97 Mich. L. Rev. 564 (1998).

3. *Romer's implications.* What, if any, implications does *Romer* have for other laws and government policies that discriminate against gay people?

a. *Sodomy laws.* The *Romer* Court asserts that Amendment 2 raises "the inevitable inference that the disadvantage imposed is born of animosity toward the class of persons affected" and relies on *Moreno* for the proposition that "[if] the constitutional conception of 'equal protection of the laws' means anything, it must at the very least mean that a bare . . . desire to harm a politically unpopular group cannot constitute a legitimate governmental interest." Can this argument against Amendment 2 be squared with the Court's holding in *Bowers* that moral opposition to homosexuality is a sufficiently strong government interest to justify criminalization of homosexual sodomy? Note that the Court fails to cite *Bowers*, although the decision is surely at least tangentially relevant to the Court's analysis. What message does this failure send?

Does it follow from the government's hypothetical and unexercised ability to criminalize certain activity that any other disadvantage the government imposes on those who engage in it is automatically permissible under the equal protection clause? Could the government deny a driver's license to a person caught smoking cigarettes?

b. *Don't ask, don't tell.* Shortly after assuming office, President Clinton indicated that he might soon change military policy concerning service by homosexuals. A political uproar ensued, which culminated in a new policy directive issued by the Secretary of Defense. Under the new policy, no one applying to the armed services "will be asked about his or her sexual orientation," and while "homosexual acts" would be a basis for rejection, "sexual orientation" would not be. On the other hand, statements that "reflect an intent or propensity to engage in such acts" might lead to disqualification. Under the new policy, a member who makes a statement that he is a homosexual will be separated unless he demonstrates that he does not engage in, intend to engage in, or have a "propensity" to engage in such acts. Congress also responded by codifying the new standards. See Pub. L. No. 103-160, 107 Stat. 1679 (1993). After *Romer,* is the new policy vulnerable to constitutional challenge? If homosexual "orientation" is no longer a grounds for disqualification, what is the relevance of statements reflecting that orientation?

c. *Same-sex marriage.* Courts in both Hawaii and Vermont have invalidated laws restricting the benefits of marriage to different-sex couples.

In Baehr v. Lewin, 74 Haw. 645, 852 P.2d 44 (1993), the Hawaii Supreme Court held that the existing restriction on marriage violated the equal protection clause of the state constitution unless it could be shown that excluding same-sex couples served a compelling state interest. It remanded the case to the trial court to determine whether there was such an interest. In Baehr v. Miike, 65 U.S.L.W. 2399 (1996), the court held that no such interest existed and enjoined the state from banning same-sex marriages. However, the decision was effectively overruled by a state constitutional amendment providing that "[t]he legislature shall have the power to reserve marriage to opposite-sex couples." Is the amendment vulnerable to federal constitutional challenge under *Romer?*

In Baker v. Vermont, 744 A.2d 864 (Vt. 1999), the plaintiffs challenged restrictions on the right of same-sex couples to the benefits of marriage under a state constitutional provision stating:

> The government is, or ought to be, instituted for the common benefit, protection, and security of the people, nation, or community, and not by the particular emolument or advantage of any single person, family, or set of persons, who are part only of that community.

The Vermont Supreme Court held that the restrictions were inconsistent with this provision. However, the court declined to require same-sex marriages. Instead, it left to the legislature the choice of either legalizing such marriages or devising another institution that gave same-sex couples the benefits of marriage. The legislature responded by creating "civil unions" that, while not technically "marriages," provide for virtually all the rights and privileges of marriage. Does the Vermont solution resolve any constitutional questions about same-sex marriages? Since civil unions and marriages have identical legal consequences, what state interest justifies reserving the term "marriage" for different-sex couples?

While the same-sex marriage question was being litigated in Hawaii, Congress responded by enacting the Defense of Marriage Act, Pub. L. No. 104-199, 110 Stat. 2419 (1996). The act provides that in determining the meaning of any act of Congress the word "marriage" means only a legal union between one man and one woman as husband and wife, and that "[no] State [shall] be required to give effect to any public act, record, or judicial proceeding of any other State [respecting] a relationship between persons of the same-sex that is treated as a marriage under the laws of such state. . . ." Does *Romer* raise nontrivial questions about the constitutionality of this provision? What, if any, impact does it have on the federal and interstate status of Vermont's civil unions?

d. *The commentators react.* Commentators have offered a variety of different opinions concerning the meaning and scope of *Romer.* On the decision's reach, compare Sunstein, Foreword: Leaving Things Undecided, 110 Harv. L. Rev. 4 (1996) (defending a "minimalist" interpretation) with Seidman, *Romer's* Radicalism: The Unexpected Revival of Warren Court Activism, 1996 Sup. Ct. Rev. 67 (defending a "radical" interpretation). On its meaning, see, e.g., Jeffries and Levinson, The Non-Retrogression Principle in Constitutional Law, 86 Cal. L. Rev. 1211 (1998) (analyzing and criticizing *Romer* as embodying a nonretrogression principle); Amar, Attainder and Amendment 2: *Romer's* Rightness, 95 Mich. L. Rev. 203 (1996) (analyzing *Romer* under the bill of attainder clause); Farber and Sherry, The Pariah Principle, 13 Con. Comm. 257 (1996) (analyzing *Romer* under the principle that "forbids government from designating any societal group as untouchable, regardless of whether the group in question is generally entitled to some special degree of judicial protection"); Alexander, Sometimes Better Boring and Correct: Romer v. Evans as an Exercise of Ordinary Equal Protection Analysis, 68 U. Col . L. Rev. 335 (1996) (analyzing *Romer* in terms of "ordinary" equal protection principles). See generally Symposium, Gay Rights and the Courts: The Amendment 2 Controversy, 68 U. Colo. L. Rev. 285 (1996).

Note: Strict Scrutiny for Discrimination Based on Sexual Orientation?

1. Romer *and rational basis review.* The *Romer* Court asserts that it is utilizing rational basis review to invalidate Amendment 2. Is this claim plausible? Recall Reed v. Reed, page 598 supra, where the Court inaugurated its modern encounter with gender discrimination by purporting to utilize rational basis review to invalidate gender-specific laws. Only later did the Court acknowledge that it was utilizing heightened scrutiny. See Craig v. Boren, page 602 supra. Does *Romer* mark the beginning of an analogous transformation of the Court's jurisprudence regarding sexual orientation? If so, what institutional interests are served by insisting on rational basis review at the beginning of this process?

Note that Amendment 2 was unusually broad in scope. Unlike state constitutional provisions that simply outlaw certain practices, such as polygamy, or the "don't ask/don't tell" policy, which disadvantages homosexuals in a particular context, this provision deprived a class of citizens of access to any protection against discrimination, regardless of context, on the basis of a single trait. Even if the denial of protection to homosexuals is rational in some contexts, might not the general denial of such protection regardless of context be irrational?

2. *Strict scrutiny — defining the suspect class.* The arguments for and against strict scrutiny depend to some extent on how the putatively suspect class is defined. Is the relevant group individuals who engage in homosexual acts (however defined) or individuals who have a desire or propensity to engage in such acts? Consider the alternative possibilities.

a. *Acts.* Given the Court's holding in *Bowers* that individuals have no constitutional right to engage in homosexual sodomy, does it make sense to say that laws discriminating against individuals who engage in this conduct should be strictly scrutinized? The Court has rejected the claim that illegal aliens constitute a suspect class in part because, "[unlike] most of the classifications that we have recognized as suspect, entry into this class, by virtue of entry into this country, is the product of voluntary action." See Plyler v. Doe, 457 U.S. 202 (1982). Does this argument apply to homosexual acts as well?

Is there a plausible argument that, even if there is no substantive right to engage in homosexual conduct, the distinction between permitted and prohibited conduct should nonetheless be strictly scrutinized? Can this argument be disentangled from views about the morality of homosexual conduct? Consider Richards, Sexual Preference as a Suspect (Religious) Classification: An Alternative Perspective on the Unconstitutionality of Anti-Lesbian/Gay Initiatives, 55 Ohio St. L.J. 491, 532 (1994):

> Homosexual relations are and foreseeably will remain the preference of small minorities of the population, who are as committed to principles of social cooperation and contribution as any other group in society at large. The issue, as with all suspect classes, is [whether] we should treat such a minority justly with respect as persons or unjustly with contempt as unspeakably heretical outcasts. Indeed, the very accusation of heresy or treason illustrates an important feature of the traditional moral condemnation in its contemporary vestments. It no longer rests on generally acceptable arguments of necessary protections of the rights of persons to general goods. [Today], such condemnation appeals to arguments internal to highly personal, often sectarian religious decisions about acceptable ways of belief and lifestyle. When a moral tradition [abandons] certain of its essential grounds in general goods, [it] no longer expresses nonsectarian ethical arguments that may be imposed fairly on all persons but rather perspectives reasonably authoritative only for those who adhere to the tradition.

Consider whether this argument itself reflects a controversial moral view located within a particular tradition concerning "acceptable ways of belief and lifestyle."

b. *Desires.* Suppose the suspect class is defined in terms of "orientation" or "desires" rather than in terms of acts. Is the state ever justified in discriminating against an individual because of a wholly mental event? Might not mental states be relevant in some context because they demonstrate a propensity to commit certain acts? Consider in this regard Equality Foundation of Greater Cincinnati v. Cincinnati, 54 F.3d 261 (6th Cir. 1995), vacated and remanded for reconsideration, 518 U.S. 1001 (1996), reaffirmed, 128 F.3d 289 (6th Cir. 1997):

[No] law can successfully be drafted that is calculated to burden or penalize [an] unidentifiable group or class of individuals whose identity is defined by subjective and unapparent characteristics such as innate desires, drives, and thoughts. Those persons having a homosexual "orientation" simply do not, as such comprise an identifiable class. Many homosexuals successfully conceal their orientation. Because homosexuals generally are not identifiable "on sight," unless they elect to be so identifiable by conduct, [they] cannot constitute a suspect [class].

Does this argument overlook the relevance of Washington v. Davis? Even if it is technically impossible to legislate against wholly internal mental states, laws prohibiting conduct might be enacted "because of," rather than "in spite of," their disproportionate impact on people who have those mental states. See Personnel Administrator of Massachusetts v. Feeney, page 528 supra. On this view, laws regulating various acts would be subject to strict scrutiny if, but only if, they were enacted because of antipathy toward people with a particular mental state.

3. *Strict scrutiny — indicia of suspectness.* However the class is defined, does the long history of hatred directed against homosexuals and disabilities imposed on them justify strict scrutiny? Doesn't the relevance of this history turn, once again, on contested judgments about the morality of the acts in question? Consider Duncan, Who Wants to Stop the Church?: Homosexual Rights Legislation, Public Policy, and Religious Freedom, 69 Notre Dame Law. 393, 406 (1994):

Civil rights laws were enacted against a background of devastating and widespread discrimination that relegated blacks in particular to only the most menial occupations and the least attractive housing opportunities. . . .

Have gay rights proponents proven their case that homosexuals have been economically impoverished by discrimination in employment, housing, and public [accommodations]? No. Not only have they failed to prove that homosexuals have been impoverished by discrimination, but the data support the opposite conclusion — homosexuals are an economically advantaged group in our society. . . .

Like racial minorities and in contrast to homosexuals, women have a proven history of economic disadvantage. People with disabilities likewise have a proven and compelling need for governmental assistance in employment and housing. Also, like race and unlike sexual orientation and behavior, both gender and disability are morally neutral characteristics.

Consider the possibility that homosexuals have avoided discrimination that has plagued other groups only to the extent that they have remained "in the closet," and that the "closet" phenomenon is itself the result of systemic prejudice.

Do homosexuals suffer from disabilities that prevent them from achieving a "fair" amount of political power? Consider J. Ely, Democracy and Distrust 162-163 (1980): "Homosexuals for years have been victims of [prejudice]. Our stereotypes — whether to the effect that male homosexuals are effeminate, females 'butch'; that they are untrustworthy, unusually menacing to children, or whatever — are likely to remain fixed given our obliviousness to the fact that the people around us may well be counterexamples." See also Sunstein, Homosexuality and the Constitution, 70 Ind. L.J. 1, 8 (1994):

Homosexuals may well be politically powerless in the constitutionally relevant sense. [Precisely] because they are often anonymous [and] diffuse [they] face large barriers to exerting adequate political influence. [The] ability to conceal can actually make things worse from the standpoint of exercising political power. This problem, severe in itself, is heightened by the fact that people who challenge discrimination on the basis of sexual orientation are often "accused" of being homosexuals [themselves]. The existence of widespread hostility against homosexuals can thus make it difficult for homosexuals and heterosexuals alike to speak out against this form of discrimination.

Compare Duncan, supra, at 409:

Not only are homosexuals an affluent and a highly educated class, they are also politically powerful. Homosexuals are far more likely than average to vote, and one of the fastest-growing political action organizations in Washington is the Human Rights Campaign, a pro-gay group that raised $4.5 million in 1992. During the Democratic primaries in [1992], all five of the leading Democratic candidates for president "actively courted the gay vote." And, of course, President Clinton is a strong supporter of the gay political agenda.

4. *Strict scrutiny — gender discrimination?* Should laws that discriminate against homosexuals be subject to heightened scrutiny on the ground that they are a form of gender discrimination? Consider the problem of same-sex marriages. In Baehr v. Lewin, supra, the Hawaii Supreme Court relied in part on the fact that laws against same-sex unions embodied gender discrimination to subject such laws to strict scrutiny (i.e., women but not men are prohibited from marrying women). Compare State v. Walsh, 713 S.W.2d 508, 510 (Mo. 1986) (en banc):

The State concedes that the statute prohibits men from doing what women may do, namely, engage in sexual activity with men. However, the State argues that it likewise prohibits women from doing something which men can do: engage in sexual activity with women. We believe it applies equally to men and women because it prohibits both classes from engaging in sexual activity with members of their own sex. Thus, there is no denial of equal protection on that basis.

Does this argument successfully distinguish the statute invalidated in Loving v. Virginia, page 533 supra, which, the Court held, embodied race discrimination even though it prohibited blacks and whites alike from intermarrying? *Loving* rested in part on the Court's view that the facially neutral prohibition against miscegenation supported a system of white supremacy. Is it distinguishable on the ground that the facially neutral prohibition against homosexual conduct has nothing to do with male supremacy? Consider Koppelman, Why Discrimination against Lesbians and Gay Men Is Sex Discrimination, 69 N.Y.U. L. Rev. 197, 235 (1994) (emphasis omitted):

Most Americans learn no later than high school that one of the nastier sanctions that one will suffer if one deviates from the behavior traditionally deemed appropriate for one's sex is the imputation of homosexuality. . . .
[The] central outrage of male sodomy is that a man is reduced to the status of a woman, which is understood to be degrading. Just as miscegenation was threatening because it called into question the distinctive and superior status of being white, homosexuality is threatening because it calls into question the distinctive and superior status of being male. Male homosexuals and lesbians, respectively, are understood to be guilty of one aspect of the dual crime of the miscegenating white woman: self-degradation and insubordination. As with miscegenation, a mem-

ber of the superior caste who allows his body to be penetrated is thereby polluted and degraded, and he assumes the status of the subordinate caste: he becomes woman-like.

5. *The Court's role.* Even if some or all of the arguments for treating homosexuals as a suspect class are valid, are there nonetheless sound reasons why the Court should avoid involvement in this area? Consider Sunstein, supra, at 26:

> [The] argument [that] same-sex relations and even same-sex marriages may not be banned consistently with the Equal Protection Clause [is], to say the least, quite adventurous. If the Supreme Court of the United States accepted the argument [soon], it might cause a constitutional crisis, a weakening of the legitimacy of the Court, an intensifying of homophobia, a constitutional amendment overturning the Court's decision, and much more. Any Court, even one committed to the basic principle, should hesitate in the face of such prospects. It would be far better for the Court to start cautiously and to proceed incrementally.

Does this overtly "political" approach to constitutional adjudication squander the Court's moral authority? Does it take into account the interests of individual litigants? See Fajer, With All Deliberate Speed? A Reply to Professor Sunstein, 79 Ind. L.J. 39, 43 (1994) (arguing that Sunstein's position necessarily implies sacrificing individual litigants to benefit the movement for gay and lesbian rights in the long run). What, if any, lessons can be drawn from the Court's previous efforts to stimulate social change in cases like Brown v. Board of Education and Roe v. Wade? Consider in this regard Massaro, Gay Rights, Thick and Thin, 49 Stan. L. Rev. 45 (1996):

> Legal categories [tend] to repress or problematize nuances. [The] very nature of legal reasoning, especially its reliance on analogical reasoning, demands that lawyers hew to heterosexual norms when arguing for gay rights. However, this strategy, in flattening crucial nuances, produces marginality instead of equality.

For Massaro, however, these and other arguments against a litigation strategy are beside the point:

> The problem [is] that litigation continues despite the many good reasons not to pursue it. . . .
> [The] pertinent question is neither whether to pursue litigation at all, nor whether change ever happens. The important question is how advocates who do pursue litigation can make the best of a legal structure that is [shaped] by "an implicit, trans-individual Western project or fantasy of eradicating [gay] identity," but that is also evolving. How might theories and advocates best mitigate the harsh effects of what may be unavoidable double-binds? What legal cord should they attempt to cut first, and with what tools?

F.   EQUAL PROTECTION METHODOLOGY: OTHER CANDIDATES FOR HEIGHTENED SCRUTINY

What, if any, other classifications should be regarded as "suspect"? What criteria should the Court utilize in assessing the claims of other "disadvantaged" groups for heightened scrutiny? Is the analogy to race and gender useful? If so, which characteristics of blacks and women must other candidates for heightened scrutiny share? Might heightened scrutiny for some classifications be justified even though the problems of the group are entirely different from those facing racial minorities and women? If so, what sorts of problems should trigger judicial intervention?

1. Alienage

One way to think about heightened scrutiny for suspect classifications is that it is the appropriate judicial response to efforts by the majority to exclude certain groups from the political community. Yet many people would agree that our political institutions need not show equal concern and respect for the well-being of everyone. The U.S. government does not show the same concern for people living in Mexico as it does for people living in Texas. See, e.g., United States v. Verdugo-Urquidez, 494 U.S. 259 (1990) (fourth amendment protection against unreasonable search and seizures does not apply to search of property in foreign country owned by nonresident alien). Indeed, membership in our political community derives much of its value from the fact that it is not universal.

There is also general agreement that the government has some power to define the boundaries of the political community within our territorial limits. For example, most (although not all) people would agree that our political institutions need not show the same concern and respect for animals that they show for people. Others would exclude fetuses from the political community.

The moral and legal legitimacy of this power to define boundaries for the political community is intensely controversial. At one time, many viewed black slaves in the way that many view animals and fetuses today. Powerful arguments have been advanced that our preference for Americans over Mexicans, for the born over fetuses, or for people over animals represents no more than chauvinism. See, e.g., J. Noonan, The Morality of Abortion: Legal and Historical Perspectives 51-58 (1970) (moral obligation to fetuses); T. Regan and P. Singer, Animal Rights and Human Obligations (1976) (moral obligation to animals); Lopez, Undocumented Mexican Migration: In Search of a Just Immigration Law and Policy, 28 UCLA L. Rev. 615 (1981) (moral obligation to Mexicans).

And yet at some point lines must be drawn. For example, some who claim that the U.S. government owes a duty to citizens of Mexico base the claim on physical proximity and are prepared to acknowledge that it may not owe the same duty to citizens of Pakistan. See Lopez, supra, at 698-700. And presumably even the most ardent advocates of animal rights are prepared to acknowledge the lesser status of plants.

Are these boundaries justified by the innate limits on the ability to communicate across cultural and a fortiori species lines? Consider J. Dunn, Western Political Theory in the Face of the Future 76-77 (1979):

> Because both what man makes himself and a large part of what he is caused to become are mediated by human speech, the potential community of those with whom men can in practice communicate, to whom they can in practice render themselves lucidly intelligible, can be a human community in an altogether deeper

sense than practical aggregations of human beings of any scale who are unable to address each other or comprehend each other with such directness. [Herder], it seems, sensed this when he wrote [that] "The savage who loves himself, his wife and his child [and] works for the good of his tribe as for his own [is] in my view more genuine than that human ghost, the [citizen] of the world, who, burning with love for all his fellow ghosts, loves a chimera. The savage in his hut has room for any stranger. [The] saturated heart of the idle cosmopolitan is a home for no one."

Do these observations cast doubt as well on the characterization of the United States as a single political community? If we are willing to concede that some groups outside the political community need not receive the same attention as those within the community, what are the implications of the existence of subnational political communities? Consider whether the materials on federalism shed light on these issues.

Can the need to draw some boundaries around the political community be reconciled with heightened scrutiny for classifications disadvantaging some groups outside those boundaries? Are there principled limits on the way in which the boundaries can be defined? The Supreme Court's treatment of statutes disadvantaging aliens raises these questions.

Sugarman v. Dougall

413 U.S. 634 (1973)

MR. JUSTICE BLACKMUN delivered the opinion of the Court. . . .

[Appellees challenged the constitutionality of a New York statute that excluded aliens from all government civil service positions filled by competitive examination. Such positions included the "full range of work tasks [all] the way from the menial to the policy making." However, the exclusion did not apply to higher offices in the state executive departments and to elected officers and offices filled by the Governor or by legislative appointment.]

As is so often the case, it is important at the outset to define the precise and narrow issue that is here presented. The Court is faced only with the question whether New York's flat statutory prohibition against the employment of aliens in the competitive classified civil service is constitutionally valid. The Court is not asked to decide whether a particular alien, any more than a particular citizen, may be refused employment or discharged on an individual basis for whatever legitimate reason the State might possess.

Neither is the Court reviewing a legislative scheme that bars some or all aliens from closely defined and limited classes of public employment on a uniform and consistent basis. The New York scheme, instead, is indiscriminate. . . .

It is established, of course, that an alien is entitled to the shelter of the Equal Protection Clause. [Appellants] argue, however, that [the statute] does not violate the equal protection guarantee of the Fourteenth Amendment because [it] "establishes a generic classification reflecting the special requirements of public employment in the career civil service." The distinction drawn between the citizen and the alien, it is said, "rests on the fundamental concept of identity between a government and the members, or citizens, of the state." The civil servant "participates directly in the formulation and execution of government policy," and thus must be free of competing obligations to another power. The State's interest in having an employee of undivided loyalty is substantial, for obligations attendant upon foreign citizenship "might impair the exercise of his judgment or jeopardize public confidence in his objectivity." [It] is at once apparent, however, that appellants' asserted justification proves both too much and too little. [The] State's broad prohibition of the employment of aliens applies to many positions with respect to which the State's proffered justification has little, if any, relationship. At the same time, the prohibition has no application at all to positions that would seem naturally to fall within the State's asserted purpose. Our standard of review of statutes that treat aliens differently from citizens requires a greater degree of precision.

In Graham v. Richardson, 403 U.S. 365, 372 (1971), we observed that aliens as a class "are a prime example of a 'discrete and insular' minority (see United States v. Carolene Products Co., 304 U.S. 144, 152-153, n.4 (1938))," and that classifications based on alienage are "subject to close judicial scrutiny."

[Graham concerned a constitutional challenge to state statutes disqualifying aliens from receipt of various forms of welfare assistance. Justice Blackmun's opinion for the Court held that "classifications based on alienage, like those based on nationality or race, are inherently suspect." Applying strict scrutiny to the challenged statutes, the Court found that the "State's desire to preserve limited welfare benefits for its own citizens is inadequate to justify [making] noncitizens ineligible for public assistance."]

Applying this standard to New York's purpose in confining civil servants in the competitive class to those persons who have no ties of citizenship elsewhere, [the statute] does not withstand the necessary close scrutiny. We recognize a State's interest in establishing its own form of government, and in limiting participation in that government to those who are within "the basic conception of a political community." Dunn v. Blumstein, 405 U.S. 330, 344 (1972). We recognize, too, the State's broad power to define its political community. But in seeking to achieve this substantial purpose, with discrimination against aliens, the means the State employs must be precisely drawn in light of the acknowledged purpose.

[The statute] is neither narrowly confined nor precise in its application. Its imposed ineligibility may apply to the "sanitation man, class B," to the typist, and to the office worker, as well as to the person who directly participates in the formulation and execution of important state policy. . . .

While we rule that [the statute] is unconstitutional, we do not hold that, on the basis of an individualized determination, an alien may not be refused, or discharged from, public employment, even on the basis of noncitizenship, if the refusal to hire, or the discharge, rests on legitimate state interests that relate to qualifications for a particular position or to the characteristics of the employee. We hold only that a flat ban on the employment of aliens in positions that have little, if any, relation to a State's legitimate interest, cannot withstand scrutiny under the Fourteenth Amendment.

Neither do we hold that a State may not, in an appropriately defined class of positions, require citizenship as a qualification for office. Just as "the Framers of the Constitution intended the States to keep for themselves, as provided in the Tenth Amendment, the power to regulate elections," "[e]ach State has the power to prescribe the qualifications of its officers and the manner in which they shall be chosen." Such power inheres in the State by virtue of its obligation, already noted above, "to preserve the basic conception of a political community." And this power and responsibility of the State applies, not only to the qualifications of voters, but also to persons holding state elective or important nonelective executive, legislative, and judicial positions, for officers who participate directly in the formulation, execution, or review of broad public policy perform functions that go to the heart of representative government. . . .

We have held, of course, that such state action, particularly with respect to voter qualifications, is not wholly immune from scrutiny under the Equal Protection Clause. But our scrutiny will not be so demanding where we deal with matters resting firmly within a State's constitutional prerogatives. This is no more than a recognition of a State's historical power to exclude aliens from participation in its democratic political institutions, and a recognition of a State's constitutional responsibility for the establishment and operation of its own government, as well as the qualifications of an appropriately designated class of public office holders. This Court has never held that aliens have a constitutional right to vote or to hold high public office under the Equal Protection Clause. Indeed implicit in many of this Court's voting rights decisions is the notion that citizenship is a permissible criterion for limiting such rights. A restriction on the employment of noncitizens, narrowly confined, could have particular relevance to this important state responsibility, for alienage itself is a factor that reasonably could be employed in defining "political community."

The judgment of the District Court is affirmed.

MR. JUSTICE REHNQUIST, dissenting.

The Court [holds] that an alien is not really different from a citizen, and that any legislative classification on the basis of alienage is "inherently suspect." The Fourteenth Amendment, the Equal Protection Clause of which the Court interprets as invalidating the state legislation here involved, contains no language concerning "inherently suspect classifications," or for that matter, merely "suspect classifications." The principal purpose of those who drafted and adopted the Amendment was to prohibit the States from invidiously discriminating by reason of race, Slaughter-House Cases, and, because of this plainly manifested intent, classifications based on race have rightly been held "suspect" under the Amendment. But there is no language used in the Amendment, or any historical evidence as to the intent of the Framers, which would suggest to the slightest degree that it was intended to render alienage a "suspect" classification, that it was designed in any way to protect "discrete and insular minorities" other than racial minorities, or that it would in any way justify the result reached by the Court in these two cases. . . .

[The record contains] no indication that the aliens suffered any disability that precluded them, either as a group or individually, from applying for and being granted the status of naturalized citizens. [The] "status" of these individuals was not, therefore, one with which they were forever encumbered; they could take steps to alter it when and if they chose.[1] . . .

---

1. Although some of the members of the class had not been residents of the United States for five years at the time the complaint was filed, and therefore were ineligible to apply immediately for citizenship, there is no indication that these members, assuming that they are in the same "class" as the named appellees, would be prohibited from seeking citizenship status after they had

The Court, by holding in these cases and in Graham v. Richardson that a citizen-alien classification is "suspect" in the eyes of our Constitution, fails to mention, let alone rationalize, the fact that the Constitution itself recognizes a basic difference between citizens and aliens. That distinction is constitutionally important in no less than 11 instances in a political document noted for its brevity. . . .

Our society, consisting of over 200 million individuals of multitudinous origins, customs, tongues, beliefs, and cultures is, to say the least, diverse. It would hardly take extraordinary ingenuity for a lawyer to find "insular and discrete" minorities at every turn in the road. Yet, unless the Court can precisely define and constitutionally justify both the terms and analysis it uses, these decisions today stand for the proposition that the Court can choose a "minority" it "feels" deserves "solicitude" and thereafter prohibit the States from classifying that "minority" differently from the "majority." I cannot find, and the Court does not cite, any constitutional authority for such a "ward of the Court" approach to equal protection. . . .

It is not irrational to assume that aliens as a class are not familiar with how we as individuals treat others and how we expect "government" to treat us. An alien who grew up in a country in which political mores do not reject bribery or self-dealing to the same extent that our culture does; in which an imperious bureaucracy historically adopted a complacent or contemptuous attitude toward those it was supposed to serve; in which fewer if any checks existed on administrative abuses; in which "low-level" civil servants serve at the will of their superiors — could rationally be thought not to be able to deal with the public and with citizen civil servants with the same rapport that one familiar with our political and social mores would, or to approach his duties with the attitude that such positions exist for service, not personal sinecures of either the civil servant or his or her superior.

Note: Strict Scrutiny for Aliens — Defining the Political Community

Is there an adequate justification for subjecting alienage classifications to special scrutiny? Consider the following arguments.

1. *History of discrimination.* Is strict scrutiny for alienage classifications required because aliens, like blacks and women, have suffered a history of discrimination in the United States? Historically, different states at different times have denied aliens the right to vote, prohibited them from engaging in a wide range of occupations, discriminated against them in taxation, and restricted their ownership of property. Moreover, a general sense of xenophobia has affected American attitudes and policies at various times in our history. In the Alien Act of 1798 and during the "Red Scare" after World War I, for example, the federal government

---

resided in this country for the required period. In any event, this circumstance only underscores the fact that it is not unreasonable to assume that they have not learned about and adapted to our mores and institutions to the same extent as one who had lived here for five years would have through social contact.

adopted especially severe measures to deal with suspected subversion by aliens. See generally W. Gibson, Aliens and the Law (1940); M. Konvitz, The Alien and the Asiatic in American Law (1946); J. Smith, Freedom's Fetters (1956). See also Takahashi v. Fish & Game Commission, 334 U.S. 410 (1948) (invalidating a California law restricting the right of aliens to fish); Oyama v. California, 332 U.S. 633 (1948) (invalidating a California law restricting the right of aliens to own land); Truax v. Raich, 239 U.S. 33 (1915) (invalidating an Arizona law prohibiting any business employing five or more persons to employ more than 20 percent aliens).

2. *Alienage as an immutable characteristic.* Is strict scrutiny for alienage classifications required because it is an immutable characteristic over which the disadvantaged individual can exercise no control? Consider Nyquist v. Mauclet, 432 U.S. 1 (1977). Under New York law, an applicant for state higher education financial assistance must be a U.S. citizen, must have made application for citizenship, or, if not qualified for citizenship, must submit a statement affirming an intent to apply for U.S. citizenship as soon as qualified to do so. The state argued that this statute need not be strictly scrutinized because it did not discriminate against aliens as such but only against those aliens unwilling to apply for citizenship. In a five-to-four decision, the Court rejected this argument and invalidated the law. Justice Blackmun delivered the opinion of the Court: "The important points are that [the statute] is directed at aliens and that only aliens are harmed by it. The fact that the statute is not an absolute bar does not mean that it does not discriminate against the class." Nor was it relevant that aliens could voluntarily withdraw from the disfavored status. By this logic, "the suspect class for alienage would be defined to include at most only those who have resided in this country for less than five years, since after that time, if not before, resident aliens are generally eligible to become citizens. The Court has never suggested, however, that the suspect class is to be defined so narrowly."

In a dissenting opinion, Justice Rehnquist, joined by Chief Justice Burger, complained of the Court's

> somewhat mechanical application [of] equal protection jurisprudence. [Here,] unlike the other cases, the resident alien is not a member of a discrete and insular minority for purposes of the classification, even during the period that he must remain an alien, because he has at all times the means to remove himself immediately from the disfavored classification. [The] alien is not, therefore, for any period of time, forced into a position as a discrete and insular minority.

Chief Justice Burger and Justice Powell also filed separate dissenting opinions.

Does the Court adequately answer Justice Rehnquist's objection? If aliens are free to change their status at will, why aren't classifications disadvantaging this group justified as a means of encouraging naturalization? Compare Plyler v. Doe, 457 U.S. 202 (1982), where the Court invalidated a Texas policy of refusing to provide free public education to *illegally present* alien children. The Court rejected the assertion that illegal aliens are a suspect class. "Unlike most of the classifications that we have recognized as suspect, entry into this class, by virtue of entry into this country, is the product of voluntary action. Indeed, entry into the class is itself a crime." But, although "[p]ersuasive arguments support the view that a State may withhold its beneficence from those whose very presence within the United States is the product of their own unlawful conduct," these arguments

> do not apply with the same force to classifications imposing disabilities on the minor *children* of such illegal entrants. [The] "parents have the ability to conform their conduct to societal norms," and presumably the ability to remove themselves from the State's jurisdiction; but the children who are plaintiffs in these cases "can affect neither their parents' conduct nor their own status" [quoting Trimble v. Gordon, 430 U.S. 762 (1977)]. Even if the State found it expedient to control the conduct of adults by acting against their children, legislation directing the onus of a parent's misconduct against his children does not comport with fundamental conceptions of justice.

Because Texas's policy "[imposed] a lifetime hardship on a discrete class of children not accountable for their disabling status," the Court concluded that the discrimination "can hardly be considered rational unless it furthers some substantial goal of the State." Chief Justice Burger filed a dissenting opinion, in which Justices White, Rehnquist, and O'Connor joined.

Illegal aliens are subject to deportation and, if deported, these aliens would be denied an education in the Texas public schools. Does it make sense, then, to say that their rights are violated when they are denied such an education while illegally residing in Texas? *Plyler* is examined more fully in Chapter 6, section E5, *infra*.

3. *Aliens as a "discrete" and "insular" minority.* Are aliens members of a "discrete and insular [minority]" hampered by the kind of prejudice "which tends seriously to curtail the operation of those political processes ordinarily to be relied upon to protect minorities"? United States v. Carolene Products, page 507 supra. Consider Lusky, Footnote Redux: A *Carolene Products* Reminiscence, 82 Colum. L. Rev. 1087, 1093 n.72 (1982):

> As a matter of language, "discrete" means separate or distinct and "insular" means isolated or detached. The words do not describe aliens as such; many of them, who are anglophones, pass unnoticed, and many if not most others fit into the social scene with little difficulty. Of course, there are sizeable ethnic groups, *and they include citizens as well as aliens*, who are held at arm's length — Chicanos, Orientals, and so on — but that is quite another matter.

But compare Rosberg, The Protection of Aliens from Discriminatory Treatment by the National Government, 1977 Sup. Ct. Rev. 275, 309-310:

> Given the exclusion of aliens from the political process, it is [reasonable] for the Court to demand a special showing from the state if it is to classify on the basis of alienage. The state has presumably weighed its interest in giving a preference to the members of its polity against the aliens' interest in enjoying the benefits at issue. But aliens have had no opportunity to participate in the process of measuring the relative weight of these two interests. Since the legislature has denied aliens any chance to assert their own interests in the political forum, it cannot expect the courts to maintain their usual deference to the legislature's balancing of the interests.

Does basing strict scrutiny on the political disabilities that the law itself imposes on aliens involve circular reasoning? In the second paragraph of the *Caro-*

lene Products footnote, Justice Stone suggested that strict scrutiny might be appropriate for laws that "[restrict] those political processes which can ordinarily be expected to bring about repeal of undesirable legislation." If aliens are politically vulnerable because they lack the franchise, why isn't the appropriate solution to scrutinize strictly the laws denying them the right to vote? See generally Rosberg, Aliens and Equal Protection: Why Not the Right to Vote?, 75 Mich. L. Rev. 1092 (1977). Note that the Court in *Sugarman* affirms the states' right to restrict the franchise and policymaking positions to citizens. Is there a justification for these restrictions that would survive strict scrutiny?

Presumably the justification relates to historical considerations, perceptions of the framers' "intent," and the general interest of the state in limiting political rights to members of the political community. The citizenship clause of the fourteenth amendment itself seems to recognize the legitimacy of this interest. But if fundamental political rights like the franchise may be limited to citizens, why may not the state restrict less basic benefits like public employment to members of the political community as well?

4. *Alienage and the political community.* In In re Griffiths, 413 U.S. 717 (1973), a case decided on the same day as *Sugarman*, the Court held that a state could not constitutionally exclude aliens from membership in the bar. However, in a series of subsequent cases the Court has upheld a number of state restrictions on employment of aliens on the theory that the positions involve the formulation or execution of broad public policy and may therefore be limited to members of the political community. See Foley v. Connelie, 435 U.S. 291 (1978) (upholding prohibition on aliens serving on state police force); Ambach v. Norwick, 441 U.S. 68 (1979) (upholding citizenship requirement for public school teachers); Cabell v. Chavez-Salido, 454 U.S. 432 (1982) (upholding citizenship requirement for probation officers). In Bernal v. Fainter, 467 U.S. 216 (1984), however, a unanimous Court invalidated a citizenship requirement for notaries public.

Can the results in these cases be reconciled? In Cabell v. Chavez-Salido, the Court acknowledged that the alienage decisions "have not formed an unwavering line over the years. [But] to say that the decisions do not fall into a neat pattern is not to say that they fall into no pattern." According to the Court,

> [t]he cases through *Graham* dealt for the most part with attempts by the States to retain certain economic benefits exclusively for citizens. Since *Graham*, the Court has confronted claims distinguishing between the economic and sovereign functions of government. This distinction has been supported by the argument that although citizenship is not a relevant ground for the distribution of economic benefits, it is a relevant ground for determining membership in the political community.

Is this distinction sound? Note that the Court has relied on a similar distinction under the dormant commerce clause where it has been willing to uphold state actions as a "market participant" that would be invalidated if the state were acting as a "market regulator." See Chapter 3, pages 288-292 supra.

How does one separate the "economic" and "sovereign" functions of government? In *Cabell*, the Court set out a two-pronged test:

> First, the specificity of the classification will be examined: a classification that is substantially overinclusive or underinclusive tends to undercut the governmental claim that the classification serves legitimate political ends. [Second], even if the

classification is sufficiently tailored, it may be applied in the particular case only to "persons holding state elective or important nonelective executive, legislative, and judicial positions," those officers who "participate directly in the formulation, execution, or review of broad public policy" and hence "perform functions that go to the heart of representative government." [*Sugarman.*]

Is this test workable? How can one determine whether a classification is over- or underinclusive without first settling on the level of review under which the fit is to be measured?

What is the justification for separating the "economic" and "sovereign" functions of government? Doesn't this distinction turn the *Carolene Products* theory on its head? That theory suggests that strict scrutiny is appropriate precisely when political, rather than economic, rights are at stake.

If "representation-reinforcement" for politically disadvantaged minorities is not the basis for the Court's intervention in this area, what is? Consider the possibility that the decisions reflect a concern that classifications in this area are peculiarly likely to reflect hostility or prejudice and not to respond to a legitimate effort by the state to promote the public interest. Is that a plausible distinction? How does it differ from an approach based on representation-reinforcement?

Note: *Alienage and Federal Preemption*

Can the alienage cases be explained on the ground that the states have only a narrow role to play when dealing with problems of immigration and naturalization? On this view, many state alienage classifications are invalid not simply because they discriminate against aliens, or because the policies they advance are inherently illegitimate, but rather because those policies are best pursued in a unified way on the national level. See Note, The Equal Treatment of Aliens: Preemption or Equal Protection?, 31 Stan. L. Rev. 1069 (1979).

In *Graham* itself, which first announced that alienage classifications were suspect for equal protection purposes, the Court also relied on federalism grounds as an alternative basis for invalidating the state law. State restrictions on the eligibility of aliens for welfare benefits, in the Court's view, conflicted with "overriding national policies in an area constitutionally entrusted to the Federal Government." Since *Graham*, federalism and preemption concerns have become an increasingly important theme in alienage cases.

1. *The federal cases.* In Mathews v. Diaz, 426 U.S. 67 (1976), a unanimous Court upheld a federal statute limiting participation in a federal medical insurance program to citizens and aliens who had continuously resided in the United States for five years and had been admitted for permanent residence. Writing for the Court, Justice Stevens explained:

In the exercise of its broad power over naturalization and immigration, Congress regularly makes rules that would be unacceptable if applied to citizens. [In] particular, the fact that Congress has provided some welfare benefits for citizens does not require it to provide like benefits for *all aliens.* Neither the overnight visitor, the unfriendly agent of a hostile foreign power, the resident diplomat, nor the illegal entrant, can advance even a colorable constitutional claim to a share in the bounty that a conscientious sovereign makes available to its own citizens and *some* of its guests. The decision to share that bounty with our guests may take into account the character of the relationship between the alien and this country: Congress may decide that as the alien's tie grows stronger, so does the strength of his claim to an equal share of that munificence.

Graham v. Richardson, in the Court's view, was fully consistent with this analysis. Indeed, the federalism prong of the *Graham* holding "actually supports our holding today that it is the business of the political branches of the Federal Government, rather than that of either the States or the Federal Judiciary, to regulate the conditions of entry and residence of aliens." Moreover, the equal protection analysis in *Graham* involved "significantly different considerations." Whereas the states had

little, if any, basis for treating persons who are citizens of another State differently from persons who are citizens of another country, [a] comparable classification by the Federal Government is a routine and normally legitimate part of its business. Furthermore, whereas the Constitution inhibits every State's power to restrict travel across its own borders, Congress is explicitly empowered to exercise that type of control over travel across the borders of the United States.

After *Mathews*, do any limits remain on the federal government's power to impose special rules governing the conduct of aliens? Could Congress prohibit resident aliens from having abortions? From working as lawyers? Could it insist that an alien doctor admitted to this country to practice medicine continue to do so while she or he remains here? See Reno v. American-Arab Anti-Discrimination Committee, 525 U.S. 936 (1999) (holding that in general aliens cannot challenge their deportations on the ground that they are being selectively prosecuted).

Can federal power over aliens be justified on the ground that the federal government could exclude aliens altogether, and that it therefore may condition their admission on the waiver of certain rights? Consider Rosberg, The Protection of Aliens from Discriminatory Treatment by the National Government, 1977 Sup. Ct. Rev. 275, 334-336:

To resolve the equal protection issue presented in [*Mathews*] the Court did not have to explore the ultimate limits of federal power to reshape the fundamental precepts of the nation's immigration policy. . . .

Some conditions on admission — for example, the restrictions against foreign students' working in the United States — are open and notorious. [The] restriction is plainly an integral part of the immigration scheme, and it is debated in terms of its impact on immigration policy: How many aliens can the country reasonably admit?

Unlike the rules that prevent nonimmigrants from accepting employment, the great majority of the statutory provisions discriminating against resident aliens, certainly including the provision at issue in [*Mathews*], have no explicit connection with immigration. They are not codified in the immigration laws. For the most part they did not originate in immigration legislation and were not acted upon by the congressional committees primarily concerned with immigration. [Aliens] are subject to discriminatory treatment because Congress, in the course of deciding who should receive the benefits of a particular program, decides to leave them out. [There] may, to be sure, be good reasons for excluding aliens from the program. [But the] point of treating alienage as a suspect classification is to make clear that the legislature must have more than just a good reason for treating them differently from citizens, because resident aliens cannot protect their own interests.

Compare *Mathews* with Hampton v. Mow Sun Wong, 426 U.S. 88 (1976), decided on the same day. In *Hampton*, the Court invalidated a Civil Service Commission policy excluding aliens from most civil service jobs. The Court, in an opinion by Justice Stevens, acknowledged that "there may be overriding national interests which justify selective federal legislation that would be unacceptable for an individual State. [The] paramount federal power over immigration and naturalization [forecloses] a simple extension of the holding in *Sugarman*." Nonetheless, the Court held that imposition of a citizenship requirement *by the Civil Service Commission* violated due process:

> We may assume [that] if the Congress or the President had expressly imposed the citizenship requirement, it would be justified by the national interest in providing an incentive for aliens to become naturalized, or possibly even as providing the President with an expendable token for treaty negotiating purposes; but we are not willing to presume that the Chairman of the Civil Service Commission [was] deliberately fostering an interest so far removed from his normal responsibilities. [By] broadly denying this class substantial opportunities for employment, the Civil Service Commission rule deprives its members of an aspect of liberty. Since these residents were admitted as a result of decisions made by the Congress and the President, [due process] requires that the decision to impose that deprivation of an important liberty be made either at a comparable level of government or, if it is to be permitted to be made by the Civil Service Commission, that it be justified by reasons which are properly the concern of that agency.

Justice Rehnquist wrote a dissenting opinion that was joined by Chief Justice Burger and Justices White and Blackmun.

If Congress could exclude aliens from civil service jobs, why is there a constitutional obstacle to congressional delegation of this power to the Civil Service Commission? Does *Hampton* suggest a revitalization of the nondelegation doctrine? See Chapter 4, section C2, supra.

2. *The state cases.* Can the state cases also be read as resting on a concern that the proper unit of government make a judgment about the status of aliens rather than on a concern about the merits of the judgment itself? On occasion, the Court has expressly relied on preemption grounds to invalidate state citizenship requirements. In Toll v. Moreno, 458 U.S. 1 (1982), for example, the Court considered a state policy denying in-state status to nonimmigrant aliens for purposes of qualifying for tuition reductions at state universities. Without reaching the equal protection question, the Court held the state policy unconstitutional under the supremacy clause. In light of the "long recognized [preeminent] role of the Federal Government with respect to the regulation of aliens within our borders," the Court held that "'state regulation not congressionally sanctioned that discriminates against aliens lawfully admitted to the country is impermissible if it imposes additional burdens not contemplated by Congress'" (quoting De Canas v. Bica, 424 U.S. 351 (1976)).

In other cases, however, federalism concerns have played a more indirect role in the Court's reasoning. Instead of relying directly on the supremacy clause, the Court has referred to the federal government's "preeminent role" regarding aliens when it assesses the legitimacy of state concerns that might otherwise justify the classification under the equal protection clause. In Nyquist v. Mauclet, supra, for example, the state sought to justify its citizenship requirement for higher education financial assistance on the ground that it encouraged naturalization and ensured a "degree of national affinity." But the Court rejected this goal as "not a permissible one for a State. Control over immigration and naturalization is entrusted exclusively to the Federal Government, and a State has no power to interfere." Similarly, in Plyler v. Doe, supra, the Court was unimpressed by the state's claim that its refusal to enroll illegal aliens in public schools supported the federal policy against illegal immigration:

> To be sure, like all persons who have entered the United States unlawfully, these children are subject to deportation. But there is no assurance that a child subject to deportation will ever be deported. An illegal entrant might be granted federal permission to continue to reside in this country, or even to become a citizen. In light of the discretionary federal power to grant relief from deportation, a State cannot realistically determine that any particular undocumented child will in fact be deported until after deportation proceedings have been completed. It would of course be most difficult for the State to justify a denial of education to a child enjoying an inchoate federal permission to remain.

2. Wealth Classifications

Are the poor entitled to special judicial protection under the equal protection clause? In the late 1950s and 1960s, the Court repeatedly suggested that classifications based on indigency were suspect. See, e.g., Griffin v. Illinois, 351 U.S. 12 (1956) ("In criminal trials a State can no more discriminate on account of poverty than on account of religion, race, or color"); Harper v. Virginia Board of Elections, 383 U.S. 663 (1966) ("Lines drawn on the basis of wealth or property, like those of race, are traditionally disfavored"). More recently, however, the Court has shown increasing reluctance to strictly scrutinize state practices withholding benefits because of inability to pay for them. As the Court in Maher v. Roe, 432 U.S. 464 (1977), summarized the current state of the law in the context of state refusals to fund abortions for indigents:

> An indigent woman desiring an abortion does not come within the limited category of disadvantaged classes so recognized by our cases. Nor does the fact that the impact of the regulation falls upon those who cannot pay lead to a different conclusion. In a sense, every denial of welfare to an indigent creates a wealth classification as compared to nonindigents who are able to pay for the desired goods or services. But this Court has never held that financial need alone identifies a suspect class for purposes of equal protection analysis.

Note: Uncertain Protection for the Poor

1. *Facial discrimination.* As early as 1941, the Court suggested that there were serious constitutional obstacles to laws that expressly discriminated against indigents. In Edwards v. California, 314 U.S. 160 (1941), the Court invalidated a

California statute barring the bringing of indigents into the state. Although the Court relied solely on the commerce clause to invalidate the statute, it suggested in passing that it would not accept stereotypical judgments about the poor as justifications for laws disadvantaging them: "Whatever may have been the [previously prevailing] notion, we do not think that it will now be seriously contended that because a person is without employment and without funds he constitutes a 'moral pestilence.' Poverty and immorality are not synonymous." Justice Jackson's concurring opinion went further. He urged the Court to "say now, and in no uncertain terms, that a man's mere property status, without more, cannot be used by a state to test, qualify, or limit his rights as a citizen of the United States. 'Indigence' in itself is neither a source of rights nor a basis for denying them. The mere state of being without funds is a neutral fact — constitutionally an irrelevance, like race, creed or color."

2. *Heightened scrutiny for "de facto" wealth classifications.* Statutes that facially discriminate against the poor, such as the one invalidated in *Edwards*, are relatively rare. Far more common are statutes that create de facto wealth classifications either by charging money for some governmental service or benefit (e.g., a poll tax or tuition charge at a state university) or by failing to subsidize some activity that can be engaged in only if one has the money to purchase it in private markets (e.g., the exclusion of abortions from Medicaid coverage). Note that Justice Jackson's insistence that wealth be treated as a "neutral fact" does little to assist the poor when they are denied benefits on this basis.

Beginning in the late 1950s, however, a series of decisions suggested that such de facto wealth classifications were constitutionally suspect. (This line of cases is discussed more fully in conjunction with the "implied fundamental rights" strand of equal protection, Chapter 6, section E, infra.) See, e.g., Griffin v. Illinois, 351 U.S. 12 (1956) (holding that the equal protection clause requires states to provide trial transcripts or their equivalent to indigents appealing their criminal convictions); Douglas v. California, 372 U.S. 353 (1963) (holding that states must provide indigents with counsel on a first appeal of right to challenge a criminal conviction); Harper v. Virginia Board of Elections, 383 U.S. 663 (1966) (holding a state law conditioning the vote on payment of a $1.50 poll tax denied equal protection); Cipriano v. City of Houma, 395 U.S. 701 (1969) (holding invalid a state statute restricting the franchise to property owners in a state election to approve issuance of revenue bonds by a municipal utility).

During the same period, the Court also hinted that strict judicial scrutiny might be appropriate when the state failed to provide the poor with "necessities." See, e.g., Shapiro v. Thompson, 394 U.S. 618 (1969) (classification "[denies] welfare aid upon which may depend the ability of the families to obtain the very means to subsist — food, shelter, and other necessities of life"); Goldberg v. Kelly, 397 U.S. 254 (1970) ("Welfare, by meeting the basic demands of subsistence, can help bring within the reach of the poor the same opportunities that are available to others to participate meaningfully in the life of the community. [Public] assistance, then, is not mere charity, but a means to 'promote the general Welfare, and secure the Blessings of Liberty to ourselves and our Posterity'").

But although some of the Court's rhetoric was sweeping, its actual holdings were far narrower. Those wealth classifications that were invalidated were all associated with access to "fundamental" rights, such as the franchise and the ability to challenge criminal convictions. No holding during this period established that it was unconstitutional as a general matter for the state to deny services or benefits to those who could not pay for them. Moreover, even with regard to fundamental rights, the Court never suggested that absolute equality was required so long as the poor were not denied minimal benefits (e.g., although the poor were entitled to representation on a first appeal of right, the Court never suggested that they had a constitutional right to the best lawyer that money could buy). Finally, despite some suggestive dicta, no holding during this period established that the state had an affirmative constitutional obligation to guarantee subsistence to those in need.

3. *The Court's retreat from heightened scrutiny.* In the 1970s, the Court veered sharply away from its earlier suggestions that wealth classifications should be strictly scrutinized. Although none of the earlier holdings were overturned, the Court was, in general, unwilling to extend these holdings. See, e.g., Ross v. Moffitt, 417 U.S. 600 (1974) (refusing to extend the *Douglas* principle to require counsel in discretionary appeals beyond a first appeal of right); United States v. Kras, 409 U.S. 434 (1973) (holding that there is no general equal protection principle barring the imposition of filing fees in ordinary civil litigation, even when they prevent the indigent from securing access to the courts).

At about the same time, the Court ended speculation that it might read the equal protection clause to impose an affirmative obligation on government to provide the poor with necessities. In Dandridge v. Williams, 397 U.S. 471 (1970), for example, the Court turned aside an equal protection challenge to Maryland's practice of imposing an upper limit on the size of grants under its Aid to Families with Dependent Children Program regardless of the size of the family. Similarly, in Lindsey v. Normet, 405 U.S. 56 (1972), the Court rejected a constitutional challenge to Oregon's summary eviction procedures. Writing for the Court, Justice White rejected appellants' argument that

> the "need for decent shelter" and the "right to retain peaceful possession of one's home" are fundamental interests which are particularly important to the poor and which may be trenched upon only after the State demonstrates some superior interest. [The] Constitution does not provide judicial remedies for every social and economic ill. We are unable to perceive in that document any constitutional guarantee of access to dwellings of a particular quality. [Absent] constitutional mandate, the assurance of adequate housing and the definition of landlord-tenant relationships are legislative, not judicial, functions.

The Court's most detailed treatment of a wealth discrimination claim during this period came in San Antonio School District v. Rodriguez, 411 U.S. 1 (1973). The decision grew out of a constitutional challenge to the manner in which Texas, and many other states, financed public education. Much of the revenues needed for public schools were raised locally by an ad valorem property tax on the property located within each district. The result of this system was that children located in districts with more valuable property benefited from higher expenditures than children in districts with less valuable property, even though both districts made the same tax effort. Appellees claimed that this method of financing education should be strictly scrutinized under the equal protection clause because, inter alia, it discriminated against the poor. (Appellees also argued that it impinged on their fundamental right to education. This aspect of the case is discussed in greater detail in Chapter 6, section E5, infra.)

In a five-to-four decision, the Court rejected this claim and, applying low-level scrutiny, upheld the system. In its discussion of the wealth discrimination claim, the Court, in an opinion by Justice Powell, said that in prior cases,

> [the] individuals, or groups of individuals, who constituted the class discriminated against [shared] two distinguishing characteristics; because of their impecunity they were completely unable to pay for some desired benefit, and as a consequence, they sustained an absolute deprivation of a meaningful opportunity to enjoy that benefit. [Even] a cursory examination, however, demonstrates that neither of the two distinguishing characteristics of wealth classifications can be found here. First, in support of their charge that the system discriminates against the "poor," appellees have made no effort to demonstrate that it operates to the peculiar disadvantage of any class fairly definable as indigent. [There] is no basis on the record in this case for assuming that the poorest people — defined by reference to any level of absolute impecunity — are concentrated in the poorest districts.
>
> Second, [lack] of personal resources has not occasioned an absolute deprivation of the desired benefit. [Apart] from the unsettled and disputed question whether the quality of education may be determined by the amount of money expended for it, a sufficient answer to appellees' argument is that, at least where wealth is involved, the Equal Protection Clause does not require absolute equality or precisely equal advantages.

Similarly, in Kadrmas v. Dickinson Public Schools, 487 U.S. 450 (1988), the Court rejected an equal protection attack against the decision of a public school system to charge a fee for bus service to and from the schools.

4. *Continued protection for the poor?* The Court's retreat from strict scrutiny for wealth classifications, like its initial endorsement of the concept, has been ambiguous, however. For example, analysis in *Rodriguez* was complicated by the fact that the statute disadvantaged poor *districts* but not necessarily poor *people*. A district with valuable commercial or industrial property (and hence a relatively large tax base) might also contain large numbers of poor people. It was therefore unclear that the method of school finance at issue worked to the disadvantage of the poor.

In a few other areas, the Court has built on some of its earlier cases strictly scrutinizing laws disadvantaging the poor. With regard to the criminal process, for example, the Court has held that a criminal defendant cannot be imprisoned for a period beyond the statutory maximum for the offense for failure to pay a fine. See Williams v. Illinois, 399 U.S. 235 (1970); Tate v. Short, 401 U.S. 395 (1971). Similarly, the Court has extended the scope of the franchise cases to invalidate filing fee requirements for candidates that effectively excluded the poor. See Bullock v. Carter, 405 U.S. 134 (1972); Lubin v. Panish, 415 U.S. 709 (1974).

Finally, although the Court has shown increasing reluctance to treat the poor as a "suspect" class for equal protection purposes, it has sometimes reached the same result through other doctrinal routes. Recall, for example, United States Department of Agriculture v. Moreno, section B supra, where the Court utilized rational basis review to invalidate a law disqualifying from the federal food stamp program unrelated individuals who lived together. Similarly, some cases have extended rights to the poor through due process analysis. See, e.g., M.L.B. v. S.L.J., 519 U.S. 102 (1996) (using both due process and equal protection analysis to hold that the state may not condition appeals from decrees terminating parental rights on the parent's ability to pay record preparation fees); Ake v. Oklahoma, 470 U.S. 68 (1985) (due process requires the state to pay for psychiatric assistance for indigent defendant where there is preliminary showing that sanity is likely to be significant factor at trial); Evitts v. Lucey, 469 U.S. 387 (1985) (holding that due process requires effective assistance of counsel on first appeal of right, and suggesting that *Griffin-Douglas* line of cases rests in part on due process principles); Little v. Streater, 452 U.S. 1 (1981) (due process requires state to pay for blood test of indigent defendant in paternity action); Boddie v. Connecticut, 401 U.S. 371 (1971) (holding unconstitutional on due process grounds the imposition of court fees preventing an indigent from securing a divorce).

Do these cases suggest that the Court in fact uses heightened scrutiny for classifications that deny "necessities" to the poor? Consider Michelman, Welfare Rights in a Constitutional Democracy, 1979 Wash U.L.Q. 659, 664: "These cases could be cited in support of welfare rights should the Court eventually come to see them as a correct conclusion from accepted forms of legal argument. [The] cases alone do not establish the welfare-rights thesis, but they do go far to answer [two] objections against it — that it is purely fanciful and that it thrusts inappropriate tasks on the courts." For an effort to build a case for the constitutional protection of welfare rights from strands in existing doctrine, see Edelman, Essay: The Next Century of Our Constitution: Rethinking Our Duty to the Poor, 39 Hastings L.J. 1 (1987).

Note: Wealth Discrimination and the Problem of Affirmative Rights

1. *Facial discrimination.* Should laws that expressly classify on the basis of wealth be strictly scrutinized? In many respects, the poor would seem to be a prime example of a discrete and insular minority. Consider Michelman, Foreword: On Protecting the Poor through the Fourteenth Amendment, 83 Harv. L. Rev. 7, 21 (1969):

> If money is power, then a class deliberately defined so as to include everyone who has less wealth or income than any person outside it may certainly be deemed, as racial minorities are by many observers deemed, to be especially susceptible to abuse by majoritarian process; and classifications of "the poor" as such may, like classification of racial minorities as such, be popularly understood as a badge of inferiority. Especially is this so in light of the extreme difficulty of imagining proper governmental objectives which require for their achievement the explicit carving out, for relatively disadvantageous treatment, of a class defined by relative paucity of wealth or income.

But compare Bork, The Impossibility of Finding Welfare Rights in the Constitution, 1979 Wash. U.L.Q. 695, 701:

> The premise that the poor [are] underrepresented politically is quite dubious. In the past two decades we have witnessed an explosion of welfare legislation, massive income redistributions, and civil rights laws of all kinds. The poor and the minorities have had access to the political process and have done very well through it. In addition to its other defects, then, the welfare-rights theory rests less on demonstrated fact than on a liberal shibboleth.

If "the poor" are a suspect class, how should the class be defined? The concept of "poverty," unlike gender and alienage, is inherently relative and is usually associated with particular goods to which the "poor" are denied access. Cases such as *Griffin* and *Douglas* seem to define the class with reference to these goods. Does this approach make sense? Doesn't defining the class in this fashion amount to saying that there is a constitutional right to the good in question? For example, if a government hospital charges for the full cost of a heart transplant and if a "middle-class" person is unable to pay the cost, does the hospital's policy discriminate against the poor? Alternatively, suppose a "poor" person were able to pay the $1.50 poll tax at issue in *Harper*. Would such a person therefore not be "poor" for equal protection purposes? (Note that in *Harper*, unlike *Griffin* and *Douglas*, the Court invalidated the tax, even as applied to those who could afford to pay it. Under what theory does it violate the equality principle to require a rich person to pay $1.50 before voting?)

If the class is defined with reference to the good in question, what should be done about the individual who can barely afford the good, but will be left with less money after purchasing it than the "poor" person who is not charged for it? Consider in this connection Fuller v. Oregon, 417 U.S. 40 (1974), in which the Court sustained an Oregon statute requiring convicted defendants who escaped indigency to repay the state for the cost of their defense:

> The fact that an indigent who accepts state-appointed legal representation knows that he might someday be required to repay the costs of these services in no way affects his eligibility to obtain counsel. [We] live in a society where the distribution of legal assistance, like the distribution of all goods and services, is generally regulated by the dynamics of private enterprise. A defendant in a criminal case who is just above the line separating the indigent from the nonindigent must borrow money, sell off his meager assets, or call upon his family or friends in order to hire a lawyer. We cannot say that the Constitution requires that those only slightly poorer must remain forever immune from any obligation to shoulder the expenses of their legal defense, even when they are able to pay without hardship.

But see James v. Strange, 407 U.S. 128 (1972) (recoupment provision violates equal protection when none of exemptions provided generally for other judgment debtors available to indigent defendants); Rinaldi v. Yeager, 384 U.S. 305 (1966) (recoupment provision violates equal protection when limited to defendants confined to state institutions).

2. *"De facto" wealth classifications and the Washington v. Davis problem.* It would be possible, of course, to define the protected class in terms of some absolute level of destitution rather than with reference to the particular good at issue. But if the class is defined in this fashion, do laws that require payment of the price for goods like counsel or a transcript in a criminal case discriminate facially against the poor? Can *Griffin* and *Douglas* be reconciled with the Court's refusal in Washington v. Davis to scrutinize statutes strictly because of the disproportionate impact they have on a suspect group? Consider in this connection M.L.B. v. S.L.J., 519 U.S. 102 (1996), where the state relied on Washington v. Davis to defend its requirement that litigants pay record preparation fees before appealing from decisions terminating parental rights. The state reasoned that this requirement, like the practice at issue in *Washington*, had no more than a dispropor-

tionate impact on the affected class. In a six-to-three decision, the Court rejected this argument:

> Sanctions of [this] genre [are] not merely *disproportionate* in impact. Rather, they are wholly contingent on one's ability to pay, and thus "visit different consequences on two categories of persons" [citing Williams v. Illinois]; they apply to all indigents and do not reach anyone outside that class.

As a facial matter, doesn't the requirement that litigants pay the record preparation fee disadvantage everyone who, for whatever reason, does not pay the fee? If so, in what sense does the requirement apply only to indigents?

Compare *M.L.B.* to James v. Valtierra, 402 U.S. 137 (1971). An amendment to the state's constitution provided that no low-rent housing project should be developed, constructed, or acquired in any manner by a state public body until the project was approved by a majority of those voting at a community election. Plaintiffs argued that this amendment violated the equal protection clause because other public programs were not subject to the mandatory referendum provision. They relied on Hunter v. Erickson, section C3 supra, where the Court invalidated a city charter provision requiring referendum approval for statutes prohibiting racial discrimination in housing. In rejecting plaintiffs' argument and upholding the statute, the Court distinguished *Hunter*:

> Unlike the [*Hunter*] referendum provision, it cannot be said that California's Article XXXIV rests on "distinctions based on race." The Article requires referendum approval for any low-rent public housing project, not only for projects which will be occupied by a racial minority. [Plaintiffs] suggest that the mandatory nature of the Article XXXIV referendum constitutes unconstitutional discrimination because it hampers persons desiring public housing from achieving their objective when no such roadblock faces other groups seeking to influence other public decisions to their advantage. But of course a lawmaking procedure that "disadvantages" a particular group does not always deny equal protection. Under any such holding, presumably a State would not be able to require referendums on any subject unless referendums were required on all, because they would always disadvantage some group.

Consider the possibility that, given Washington v. Davis, both *M.L.B.* and *James* are wrongly decided: Unlike the statute invalidated in *M.L.B.*, the provision upheld in *James* really does facially discriminate against the indigent.

3. *"De facto" wealth discrimination and the efficient allocation of scarce resources.* Even if charging a price for a government service discriminates in some sense against the poor, might not the differential treatment be justified by the state's desire to allocate scarce resources in an efficient manner? Consider, for example, Michelman, Foreword: On Protecting the Poor through the Fourteenth Amendment, supra, at 27-28:

> Unlike a de facto racial classification which usually must seek its justifications in purposes completely distinct from its race-related impacts, a de facto pecuniary classification typically carries a highly persuasive justification inseparable from the very effect which excites antipathy — i.e., the hard choices it forces upon the financially straitened. [A] de facto pecuniary classification [is] usually nothing more or less than the making of a market (e.g., in trial transcripts) or the failure to relieve

someone of the vicissitudes of market pricing (e.g., for appellate legal services). But the risk of exposure to markets and their "decisions" is not normally deemed objectionable, to say the least, in our society. Not only do we not inveigh generally against unequal distribution of income or full-cost pricing for most goods. We usually regard it as both the fairest and most efficient arrangement to require each consumer to pay the full market price of what he consumes, limiting his consumption to what his income permits.

Is this argument persuasive when the government charges for "public goods" where the consumption of the goods by some does not interfere with their consumption by others? Is it constitutional, for example, for the government to charge an admission fee to cover the cost of running a municipal swimming pool when the cost remains constant regardless of the number of users?

Is the argument persuasive when the government charges for goods in circumstances where the demand declines relatively little, even when the price rises? For example, could a government hospital refuse to perform life-saving surgery on a person too poor to pay the cost?

Is it constitutional for the state to substitute government regulation for the constraint normally exercised by the market when providing benefits to poor people? Would it be constitutional, for example, to provide appellate counsel for the poor only in cases where a preliminary review of the record demonstrated that there were nonfrivolous issues to be raised on appeal? Consider Draper v. Washington, 372 U.S. 487 (1963):

> The State [argues] that in practical effect there is no difference at all between the rights it affords indigents and nonindigents, because a moneyed defendant, motivated by a "sense of thrift," will choose not to appeal in exactly the same circumstances that an indigent will be denied a transcript. We reject this contention as untenable. It defies common sense to think that a moneyed defendant faced with long-term imprisonment and advised by counsel that he has substantial grounds for appeal, as petitioners were here, will choose not to appeal merely to save the cost of a transcript.

But see Smith v. Robbins, 120 S. Ct. 746 (2000), upholding a procedure under which appellate counsel who believes that there are no nonfrivolous issues to appeal files a brief summarizing the procedural and factual history of the case and attesting that he has reviewed the record, explained his evaluation of the case to his client, provided the client with a copy of the brief, and informed the client of his right to file a pro se supplemental brief. Counsel then requests that the court independently examine the record for arguable issues.

Might the allocative distortions produced by government subsidization of particular goods be avoided if the Constitution were read to provide the poor with a minimum income, to be spent as they saw fit? Is the desire to maintain the incentive to work a sufficiently weighty state interest to justify the failure to enact such a program? Could the courts articulate and enforce a constitutional right to basic subsistence while staying within the bounds of their appropriate role?

Consider Bork, The Impossibility of Finding Welfare Rights in the Constitution, supra, at 699:

> The effort to apply [the representation-reinforcement value to create a right to welfare] would completely transform the nature and role of courts. [Advocates of the

right] apparently [conclude] that a claimant cannot go into a court and demand a welfare program as a constitutional right, but if a welfare program already exists, he can demand that it be broadened. The right to broadening rests upon the premise that there is a basic right to the program. If so, why cannot the Court order a program to start up from scratch?

But compare L. Tribe, American Constitutional Law 1337 (2d ed. 1988):

[If] the state and federal governments were to wash their hands altogether of the sick, hungry, and poor, none of the interstitial doctrines sketched here could provide a remedy. But that is simply a reminder of the basic point suggested as long ago as 1827 by Chief Justice Marshall [dissenting in Ogden v. Saunders, 25 U.S. (12 Wheat.) 213 (1827)] — that a government which wholly failed to discharge its duty to protect its citizens would be answerable primarily in the streets and at the polling booth, and only secondarily if at all in the courts. To say this is not to deny that government has affirmative duties to its citizens arising out of the basic necessities of bodily survival, but only to deny that all such duties are perfectly enforceable in the courts of law.

4. *The Constitution and affirmative rights.* Are the wealth cases explicable in terms of a more general principle of constitutional construction under which the Constitution is seen primarily as a limitation on governmental power and not as an affirmative guarantee against conditions for which government is not responsible? Consider, for example, Justice Harlan's dissenting opinions in *Griffin* and *Douglas*, the cases establishing the equal protection right of the poor to a counsel and a trial transcript in order to pursue an appeal of right in a criminal case. In *Griffin*, Justice Harlan wrote that "[all] that Illinois has done is to fail to alleviate the consequences of differences in economic circumstances that exist wholly apart from any state action. [The] issue here is not the typical equal protection question of the reasonableness of a 'classification' on the basis of which the State has imposed legal disabilities, but rather the reasonableness of the State's failure to remove natural disabilities." In *Douglas*, he added that

every financial exaction which the State imposes on a uniform basis is more easily satisfied by the well-to-do than by the indigent. Yet I take it that no one would dispute the constitutional power of the State to levy a uniform sales tax, to charge tuition at a state university, to fix rates for the purchase of water from a municipal corporation, to impose a standard fine for criminal violations, or to establish minimum bail for various categories of offenses. Laws such as these do not deny equal protection to the less fortunate for one essential reason: the Equal Protection Clause does not impose on the States "an affirmative duty to lift the handicaps flowing from differences in economic circumstances" [quoting from his *Griffin* dissent]. To so construe it would be to read into the Constitution a philosophy of leveling that would be foreign to many of our basic concepts of the proper relations between government and society.

Note the affinity between this argument and the Washington v. Davis principle. One way to state that principle is that the equal protection clause does not impose on the states an affirmative obligation to compensate for unequal outcomes produced by a facially neutral governmental policy. The argument is also closely related to the "state action" doctrine. Under that doctrine, the Constitution in general protects individuals from state invasions of their rights and does not confer a right to affirmative governmental intervention to remedy privately imposed deprivations. (The state action doctrine is discussed in greater detail in Chapter 9 infra.) Finally, the argument is related to the more general orientation toward the equal protection clause pursuant to which different treatment of individuals similarly situated is viewed as more problematical than similar treatment of individuals differently situated.

Is Justice Harlan's argument persuasive? In what sense are the disabilities under which the poor labor "natural"? Why is the state not responsible for them? Consider L. Tribe, supra, at 1335-1336:

> [The] demise of the *Lochner* era [during which the Supreme Court read the due process clause to protect liberty of contract and thereby invalidated much social legislation] reflected the view that [the] system of governmental decisions — some statutory and some made by common-law judges — bore an active responsibility for the plight of those who could not earn a decent living. [It] should be stressed that this perspective does *not* entail a judicially cognizable remedy against government for every instance of substandard wages or unmet needs. [But] at least sometimes, the person who is forced to work too hard for too little, or can find no work at all, must be regarded as the victim of the system of contract and property rights rather than the author of his own plight.

Is it sensible to suppose that a court could ever ascertain the extent to which the condition of the poor is the product of government action? Even if it were possible to do so in principle, why should the answer to this question matter? Why is the equality principle satisfied by government inaction that leaves the disadvantaged at the mercy of private forces?

In connection with these issues, consider Harris v. McRae, 448 U.S. 297 (1980), wherein the Court upheld the constitutionality of the so-called Hyde Amendment prohibiting virtually all federal funding for abortions under the Medicaid program. The Court acknowledged that the Constitution protected a woman's freedom of choice regarding abortions. But in its view

> it simply [did] not follow that a woman's freedom of choice carries with it a constitutional entitlement to financial resources to avail herself of the full range of protected choices. [Although] government may not place obstacles in the path of a woman's exercise of her freedom of choice, it need not remove those not of its own creation. Indigency falls in the latter category. [Although] Congress has opted to subsidize medically necessary services generally, but not certain medically necessary abortions, the fact remains that the Hyde Amendment leaves an indigent woman with at least the same range of choice in deciding whether to obtain a medically necessary abortion as she would have had if Congress had chosen to subsidize no health care costs at all.

In a footnote, the Court rejected the argument that the Hyde Amendment unconstitutionally "penalized" a woman's choice to abort the fetus because funding was available for live births. It noted, however:

> A substantial constitutional question would arise if Congress had attempted to withhold all Medicaid benefits from an otherwise eligible candidate simply because that candidate had exercised her constitutionally protected freedom to terminate

her pregnancy by abortion. [But] the Hyde Amendment [does] not provide for such a broad disqualification from receipt of public benefits. Rather, the Hyde Amendment [represents] simply a refusal to subsidize certain protected conduct. A refusal to fund protected activity, without more, cannot be equated with the imposition of a "penalty" on that activity.

Is the Court's distinction between penalization and refusal to subsidize convincing? If one begins with the premise that it is important for women to have the abortion option, is there a sensible theory under which it is possible to distinguish between interference with that option by state action and interference by private action that the state fails to prevent? *Harris* is examined further in Chapter 6, section F2, infra.

3. *Other Disadvantaged Groups*

Are there other "discrete and insular minorities" entitled to special judicial protection from the political process?

CITY OF CLEBURNE v. CLEBURNE LIVING CENTER, 473 U.S. 432 (1985). This case concerned an equal protection challenge to a zoning ordinance that prevented construction of a group home for the mentally retarded in a residential neighborhood. Although it affirmed the decision below insofar as it invalidated the ordinance as applied, the Supreme Court held that the lower court had erred in utilizing heightened scrutiny. The Court, in an opinion by Justice White, advanced several reasons for rejecting heightened scrutiny:

"First, it is undeniable [that] those who are mentally retarded have a reduced ability to cope with and function in the everyday world. [They] are thus different, immutably so, in relevant respects, and the states' interest in dealing with and providing for them is plainly a legitimate one. How this large and diversified group is to be treated under the law is a difficult and often technical matter, very much a task for legislators guided by qualified professionals and not by the perhaps ill-informed opinions of the judiciary.

"Second, the distinctive legislative response, both national and state, to the plight of those who are mentally retarded demonstrates not only that they have unique problems, but also that the lawmakers have been addressing their difficulties in a manner that belies a continuing antipathy or prejudice and a corresponding need for more intrusive oversight by the judiciary. Thus, the federal government has not only outlawed discrimination against the mentally retarded in federally funded programs, but it has also provided the retarded with the right to receive 'appropriate treatment services and habilitation' in a setting that is 'least restrictive of [their] personal liberty.' . . .

"Such legislation thus singling out the retarded for special treatment reflects the real and undeniable differences between the retarded and others. That a civilized and decent society expects and approves such legislation indicates that governmental consideration of those differences in the vast majority of situations is not only legitimate but desirable. [Even] assuming that many of these laws could be shown to be substantially related to an important governmental purpose, merely requiring the legislature to justify its efforts in these terms may lead it to refrain from acting at all. [Especially] given the wide variation in the abilities and needs of the retarded themselves, governmental bodies must have a certain amount of flexibility and freedom from judicial oversight in shaping and limiting their remedial efforts.

"Third, the legislative response, which could hardly have occurred and survived without public support, negates any claim that the mentally retarded are politically powerless in the sense that they have no ability to attract the attention of lawmakers. . . .

"Fourth, if the large and amorphous class of the mentally retarded were deemed quasi-suspect [it] would be difficult to find a principled way to distinguish a variety of other groups who have perhaps immutable disabilities setting them off from others, who cannot themselves mandate the desired legislative responses, and who can claim some degree of prejudice from at least part of the public at large. One need mention in this respect only the aging, the disabled, the mentally ill, and the infirm. We are reluctant to set out on that course, and we decline to do so.

"Doubtless, there have been and there will continue to be instances of discrimination against the retarded that are in fact [invidious]. But the appropriate method of reaching such instances is not to create a new quasi-suspect classification and subject all governmental action based on that classification to more searching evaluation."

The Court thereupon held that the refusal to permit construction of the home could not survive low-level review and was therefore unconstitutional. This portion of the Court's opinion is examined at section B supra. Justice Marshall, joined by Justices Brennan and Blackmun, wrote an opinion concurring in the judgment in part and dissenting in part:

"[The] mentally retarded have been subject to a 'lengthy and tragic history' of segregation and discrimination that can only be called grotesque. [By] the latter part of the [nineteenth] century and during the first decades of the new one, [social] views of the retarded underwent a radical transformation. Fueled by the rising tide of Social Darwinism, the 'science' of eugenics, and the extreme xenophobia of those years, leading medical authorities and others began to portray the 'feebleminded' as a 'menace to society and civilization [responsible] in a large degree for many, if not all, our social problems.' A regime of state-mandated segregation and degradation soon emerged that in its virulence and bigotry rivaled, and indeed paralleled, the worst excesses of Jim Crow. . . .

"Prejudice, once let loose, is not easily cabined. As of 1979, most states still categorically disqualified 'idiots' from voting, without regard to individual capacity and with discretion to exclude left in the hands of low-level officials. Not until Congress enacted the Education of the Handicapped Act were 'the door[s] of public education' opened wide to handicapped children. But most important, lengthy and continuing isolation of the retarded has perpetuated the ignorance, irrational fears, and stereotyping that long have plagued them.

"In light of the importance of the interest at stake and the history of discrimination the retarded have suffered, the Equal Protection Clause requires us to do more than review the distinctions drawn by Cleburne's zoning ordinance as if they appeared in a taxing statute or in economic or commercial legislation. The searching scrutiny I would give to restrictions on the ability of the retarded to establish community group homes leads me to conclude that Cleburne's vague generalizations for classifying the 'feeble minded' with drug addicts, alcoholics, and the insane, and excluding them where the elderly, the ill, the boarder, and the transient are allowed, are not substantial or important enough to overcome the suspicion that the ordinance rests on impermissible assumptions or outmoded and perhaps invidious stereotypes."

Justice Stevens, joined by Chief Justice Burger, also wrote a concurring opinion.

Note: Evaluating the Claims of Other Disadvantaged Groups

1. *The mentally retarded as a suspect class.* Does the *Cleburne* Court adequately explain why classifications disadvantaging the mentally retarded need only survive low-level review? Why is the judiciary less equipped to deal with "technical" questions concerning the mentally retarded than with the problems of gender and race? Do you think that federal judges are likely to be more poorly informed about these questions than the Cleburne City Council? Why does legislative protection for the mentally retarded, but not for blacks and women, argue against heightened review? Are the problems of affirmative action and the need for flexibility really more compelling in this context? Even if "the real and undeniable differences between the retarded and others" make strict scrutiny inappropriate, why didn't the Court opt for intermediate review?

2. *Other potentially suspect classifications.* In light of *Cleburne*, are there any other groups that can plausibly claim suspect status? In a series of cases beginning in 1968, the Court has invalidated a number of statutes disadvantaging nonmarital children. Although the Court has refused formally to elevate discrimination against this group to "suspect" status, it has at least on occasion subjected them to something more than conventional rational basis review. See, e.g., Levy v. Louisiana, 391 U.S. 68 (1968) (invalidating statute that excluded nonmarital children from coverage of wrongful death statute); Glona v. American Guarantee & Liability Insurance Co., 391 U.S. 73 (1968) (same); Weber v. Aetna Casualty & Surety Co., 406 U.S. 164 (1972) (exclusion from workers' compensation invalidated); Gomez v. Perez, 409 U.S. 535 (1973) (failure to provide support rights for nonmarital children violates equal protection). But see Mathews v. Lucas, 427 U.S. 495 (1976) (upholding section of Social Security Act depriving certain nonmarital children of survivors' benefits); Lalli v. Lalli, 439 U.S. 259 (1978) (upholding statute providing that nonmarital children could inherit intestate from father only if court declared paternity during lifetime of father). In general, the Court has rejected the argument that statutes disadvantaging nonmarital children can be justified as a means of deterring or punishing their parents for illicit sexual activity. It has been somewhat more sympathetic to the argument that special problems concerning proof of paternity when parents are not married may justify different treatment.

In Massachusetts Board of Retirement v. Murgia, 427 U.S. 307 (1976), the Court rejected the argument that the aged were entitled to special judicial solicitude:

> While the treatment of the aged in this Nation has not been wholly free of discrimination, such persons, unlike, say, those who have been discriminated against on

the basis of race or national origin, have not experienced a "history of purposeful unequal treatment" or been subjected to unique disabilities on the basis of stereotyped characteristics not truly indicative of their abilities. [Old] age does not define a "discrete and insular" group in need of "extraordinary protection from the majoritarian political process." Instead, it marks a stage that each of us will reach if we live out our normal span.

See also Vance v. Bradley, 440 U.S. 93 (1979) (utilizing rational basis review to uphold federal law requiring Foreign Service personnel to retire at age sixty). Cf. Schweiker v. Wilson, 450 U.S. 221 (1981) (avoiding the question whether mentally ill are a discrete and insular minority).

For a discussion of whether and to what extent suspect categories should be expanded, see Scales-Trent, Black Women and the Constitution: Finding Our Place, Asserting Our Rights, 24 Harv. C.R.-C.L. L. Rev. 9 (1989).

Consider whether statutes disadvantaging any of the following groups should be strictly scrutinized: ethnic minorities; children; families with children; families without children; future generations; the physically disabled; "ugly" persons; obese persons; residents of the District of Columbia; incarcerated individuals.

Do the Court's decisions provide reasonably clear standards under which the claims of these groups can be evaluated? Some of the Court's decisions indicate that heightened scrutiny is applied when there is a likelihood of impermissible motivation. But what is the motivation made impermissible by the equal protection clause? Can one distinguish between hostility or prejudice and good faith moral beliefs? Is the notion that legislation must be based on "reasoned analysis" and reflect something other than power subject to judicial enforcement? Consider in this regard the approach suggested in Minow, When Difference Has Its Home: Group Homes for the Mentally Retarded, Equal Protection and Legal Treatment of Difference, 22 Harv. C.R.-C.L. L. Rev. 111 (1987). Minow develops a "social relations" theory for evaluating discriminatory treatment of "deviant" groups such as the mentally retarded. This approach

> challenges the categories and differences used to define and describe people on a group basis. Such suspicion stems [from] a view that attribution itself hides the power of those who classify as well as those defined as different. A focus on social relations casts suspicion on the very claim to knowledge manifested by the labeling of any group as different, because that claim disguises the act of power by which the namers simultaneously assign names and deny their relationships with, and power over, the named.

Under such an approach, "[attributions] of difference should be sustained only if they do not express or confirm the distribution of power in ways that harm the less powerful and benefit the more powerful." Id. at 128. Does such an approach take adequate account of the possibility that differences in power might themselves be a product of real differences that are not merely social constructs? Is it unduly optimistic about the ability of judges using the approach to transcend their own social position?

Do you agree with Justice Rehnquist that "[i]t would hardly take extraordinary ingenuity for a lawyer to find 'insular and discrete' minorities at every turn in the road"? Sugarman v. Dougall (dissenting opinion), supra. Or do you think, alternatively, that the Court's approach is flawed because it assumes that in general the political system operates fairly? Has the Court not gone far enough to correct pervasive malfunctioning? Consider Parker, The Past of Constitutional Theory — and Its Future, 42 Ohio St. L.J. 223, 253 (1981):

> [The] central problem is not *whether* a majority of citizens (actually) rules, but *that* a majority of citizens (supposedly) rules. Thus, the primary worry of [political process] theorists — the concern around which their theory pivots — is that "majorities" may disregard or undervalue the interests of "minorities." If they even acknowledge the opposite concern — that powerful minorities can get the state to act in ways that disregard or undervalue interests of nonmobilized majorities and that, in any event, legislative majorities often fail to champion the interests of passive popular majorities — they tend abruptly to dismiss it.

3. *The relevance of suspectness.* In *Cleburne*, the Court insisted that it was not subjecting the statute to heightened scrutiny. Nonetheless, it looked closely enough at the purported justifications for the law to invalidate it. In this respect, the decision is reminiscent of the early gender discrimination cases in which the Court struck down a number of statutes disadvantaging women, while insisting that it was engaged in low-level review. Only in retrospect did the Court acknowledge that these cases in fact involved heightened scrutiny. See section D2 supra.

On the other hand, the Court has upheld a number of gender-based statutes, racial affirmative action measures, and laws disadvantaging aliens despite the supposedly heightened review to which these laws were subjected. These cases raise questions concerning the significance of the Court's categorization of levels of review. Is the Court really following a two-step process pursuant to which it first decides how closely to scrutinize a classification and then applies that level of scrutiny? Is it possible (desirable) to insulate the two steps of this process from each other? Might the Court's decisions more accurately be described as a series of ad hoc, intuitive judgments concerning the appropriateness of various classifications?

Is the effort to single out particular groups entitled to special judicial protection from majoritarian processes a useful way to think about constitutional law? Is there a better alternative?

VI

Implied Fundamental Rights

A. INTRODUCTION

This chapter examines whether and in what sense the Constitution creates "implied" rights, especially under the fourteenth amendment.

An important caveat: The line between express and implied rights is hardly a clear one, and we offer it for purposes of exposition and without insisting on it. The right to equal protection of the laws is an express right. But what about the right to be free from racial segregation? The right to free speech is express. But what about the right to spend large sums of money on political campaigns? In disputed cases, the general express right does not answer the question whether the particular right at issue is entitled to protection. For this reason, no sharp distinction can be drawn between the implied rights discussed in this chapter and other rights. We deal here with particular rights whose inference from general constitutional guarantees has been especially controversial.

The debate over implied fundamental rights goes back to the very beginning of constitutional interpretation. Recall Calder v. Bull, 3 U.S. (3 Dall.) 386 (1798), Chapter 1, section C, supra.

Note: Theories of Constitutional Interpretation — "Originalism" and Its Critics

1. *The terms of the debate.* Originalism embodies the view that judges deciding constitutional issues should confine themselves to enforcing norms that were stated or clearly implicit in the Constitution *as it was understood by those who ratified it.* Critics of originalism argue that the task of interpretation authorizes courts to make particular judgments not foreseen by, or even contrary to, those of the Constitution's ratifiers.

2. *The nature and stakes of the debate.* Whether the original understanding is binding and, if so, how the original understanding should be characterized are questions of considerable importance. There is reasonable doubt, for example,

685

whether the "intent of the framers" or the text as originally understood — at least if narrowly construed — supports the Supreme Court's decisions outlawing racial segregation; recognizing a constitutional right of privacy; affording women protection against discrimination; protecting commercial, libelous, and sexually explicit speech; and applying the bill of rights to the states. (We do not say that none of these results could be justified in originalist terms — only that the question, on those terms, is a disputed one.) It is useful to distinguish here between two forms of originalism — what we might call "hard" and "soft." Hard originalists believe that the meaning of the Constitution should be settled by asking the framers and ratifiers some very particular questions: Does the due process clause include the right to choose abortion? Does it protect consensual sexual activity? Does the equal protection clause ban school segregation? Does it ban discrimination against women in the armed forces? Does it allow state governments to dismiss homosexuals? Soft originalists believe that the original understanding is important not for particular answers to particular questions but in order to get a general sense of purposes and aspirations.

Most justices are, at least some of the time, soft originalists; hard originalism is more controversial. Of recent members of the Court, Justices Thomas and Scalia have been the most consistent advocates of hard originalism. See Antonin Scalia, A Matter of Interpretation (1997), for an argument on behalf of hard originalism. Originalists of both stripes tend to argue that originalism promotes democratic values, because it ensures that judicial judgments can be traced to democratic judgments, and also that it promotes values associated with the rule of law, because it ensures what Justice Scalia describes as a "rock-hard, unchanging" Constitution. See id.

In considering the various arguments below, and the possible sources of constitutional decisionmaking, it is useful also to consider whether those arguments and sources provide justifications or critiques of the Court's decisions on such issues as segregation, abortion, privacy, gender discrimination, and incorporation. We now provide an outline of the debate; we use the terms "originalism" and "hard originalism" interchangeably, though the outline bears on soft originalism as well.

3. *Arguments for originalism.* Consider A. Scalia, A Matter of Interpretation 45-47 (1997):

> [T]he originalist at least knows what he is looking for: the original meaning of the text. Often — indeed, I dare say usually — that is easy to discern and simple to apply. . . . [T]he difficulties and uncertainties of determining original meaning and applying it to modern circumstances are negligible compared with the difficulties and uncertainties of the philosophy which says that the Constitution changes; that the very act which it once prohibited it now permits, and which it once permitted it now forbids; and that the key to that change is unknown and unknowable. . . . The American people have been converted to belief in The Living Constitution, a "morphing" document that means, from age to age, which it ought to mean. . . . [If] the courts are free to write the Constitution anew, they will, by God, write it the way the majority wants; the appointment and confirmation process will see to that. This, of course, is the end of the Bill of Rights, whose meaning will be committed to the very body it was meant to protect against: the majority. By trying to make the Constituton do everything that needs doing from age to age, we shall have caused it to do nothing at all.

Consider also R. Bork, The Tempting of America 264-265 (1989):

[L]egal reasoning is an intellectual exercise essential to the preservation of freedom and democracy. When a court strikes down a statute, it always denies the freedom of the people who voted for the representatives who enacted the law. We accept that more readily when the decision is based upon a fair reading of a constitutional provision. . . . But when the Court, without warrant in the Constitution, strikes down a democratically produced statute, that act substitutes the will of a majority of nine lawyers for the will of the people. That is what is always involved when constitutional adjudication proceeds by a concern for results rather than by concern for reasoning from original understanding. . . .

Legal reasoning, which is rooted in a concern for legitimate process rather than preferred results, is an instrument designed to restrict judges to their proper role in a constitutional democracy. That style of analysis marks off the line between judicial power and legislative power, which is to say that it preserves the constitutional separation of powers, which is to say that it preserves both democratic freedom and individual freedom. Yet legal reasoning must begin with a body of rules or principles or major premises that are independent of the judge's preferences. That [is] impossible under any philosophy of judging other than the view that the original understanding of the Constitution is the exclusive source for those exterior principles. . . .

The man who prefers results to processes has no reason to say that the Court is more legitimate than any other institution capable of wielding power. If the Court will not agree with him, why not argue his case to some other group, say the Joint Chiefs of Staff, a body with rather better means for enforcing its decisions? No answer exists.

See also Monaghan, Our Perfect Constitution, 56 N.Y.U. L. Rev. 353 (1981); Rehnquist, The Notion of a Living Constitution, 54 Tex. L. Rev. 693 (1976); Scalia, Originalism: The Lesser Evil, 57 U. Cin. L. Rev. 849 (1989) (acknowledging the weaknesses of originalism but concluding that it is superior to any other judicial method).

4. *Problems with originalism.* a. Consider the following problems: (1) In deciding on the original understanding, who counts? Do we consider only the intentions of those who drafted the provision? Those who voted for it in Congress? Those who voted against it? Those who voted in the ratification process? (2) What is the relevant psychological state? Are we interested in what a legislator expected the provision to do? What he feared it would do? What he hoped it would do? (3) What combination of individual intentions is controlling? Must we find that a majority of the relevant persons held the same "understanding"? (4) Are we interested in abstract or concrete intentions? Are we interested, for example, in the framers' view of equality generally or in their view of racial segregation in the schools? Do we care how they would have liked us to resolve the conflict? See Powell, The Original Understanding of the Original Understanding, 98 Harv. L. Rev. 885 (1985). For the view that the framers themselves did not believe the original understanding to be binding, see id. But consider the view that the difficulties stressed thus far, albeit real, are something that the judge should seriously grapple with rather than take as a license to abandon originalism altogether.

b. Tushnet, Following the Rules Laid Down: A Critique of Interpretivism and Neutral Principles, 96 Harv. L. Rev. 781, 784-785, 800, 802 (1983):

Interpretivism [is] designed to remedy a central problem of liberal theory by constraining the judiciary sufficiently to prevent judicial tyranny. [It] attempts to implement the rule of law by assuming that the meanings of words and rules are stable over extended [periods]. But [in] imaginatively entering the world of the past, we not only reconstruct it, [we] also creatively construct it. For such creativity is the only way to bridge the gaps between that world and ours. The past, particularly the aspects that the interpretivists care about, is in its essence indeterminate; the interpretivist project cannot be carried to its conclusion. [The] hermeneutic tradition tells us that we cannot understand the acts of those in the past without entering into their mental world. [The] imagination that we have used to adjust and readjust our understandings makes it impossible to claim that any one reconstruction is uniquely correct. The past shapes the materials on which we use our imaginations; our interests, concerns, and preconceptions shape our imaginations themselves.

For an analysis of the limits of historical inquiry, see Powell, Rules for Originalists, 73 Va. L. Rev. 659 (1987).

5. *Nonoriginalist approaches.* Even if the attacks on originalism have some force, the arguments from history and democracy still have to be met. To meet those arguments, one must identify and explain the appropriate sources of constitutional decisions if the original understanding is abandoned. Consider the following possibilities:

a. *Natural law.* Grey, Do We Have an Unwritten Constitution?, 27 Stan. L. Rev. 703, 715-716 (1975):

For the generation that framed the Constitution, the concept of a "higher law," protecting "natural rights," and taking precedence over ordinary positive law as a matter of political obligation, was widely shared and deeply felt. An essential element of American constitutionalism was the reduction to written form — and hence to positive law — of some of the principles of natural rights. But at the same time, it was generally recognized that written constitutions could not completely codify the higher law. Thus in the framing of the original American constitutions it was widely accepted that there remained unwritten but still binding principles of higher law. [And as] it came to be accepted that the judiciary had the power to enforce the commands of the written Constitution when these conflicted with ordinary law, it was also widely assumed that judges would enforce as constitutional restraints the unwritten natural rights as well.

For a comprehensive historical discussion of the framers' intent, concluding that the "founding generation . . . expected the judiciary to keep legislatures from transgressing the natural rights of mankind, whether or not those rights found their way into the written Constitution," see Sherry, The Founders' Unwritten Constitution, 54 U. Chi. L. Rev. 1127, 1177 (1987). See also Grey, Origins of the Unwritten Constitution: Fundamental Law in American Revolutionary Thought, 30 Stan. L. Rev. 843 (1978); Corwin, The "Higher Law" Background of American Constitutional Law, 42 Harv. L. Rev. 149, 365 (1928-1929).

b. *Moral arguments and the search for "intergrity."* A. Bickel, The Least Dangerous Branch 24-26 (1962):

[Government] should serve not only what we conceive from time to time to be our immediate material needs but also certain enduring values. [But] such values do not present themselves ready-made. They [must] be continually derived, enunciated, and seen in relevant application. [Courts] have certain capacities for dealing with matters of principle that legislatures and executives do not possess. Judges have, or should have, the leisure, the training, and the insulation to follow the ways of the scholar in pursuing the ends of government. This is crucial in sorting out the enduring values of a society.

See also R. Dworkin, Freedom's Law (1997). Dworkin's theory of interpretation — to simplify a complex account — asks judges to provide the "best constructive account" of existing legal materials by putting constitutional text, and constitutional precedents, in the best possible light. On this view, judges have two obligations: to "fit" the existing legal materials and to "justify" them by making them sensible and good rather than senseless and bad. Judges therefore have obligations to constitutional text and history, but they also have an obligation to make the system fair and just rather than the opposite. See generally R. Dworkin, Law's Empire (1985). Moral philosophy plays a role in this account, not on the ground that judges should do what philosophy tells them to do, but on the ground that when the legal materials leave gaps and uncertainties, judges should try to put them in the best light, and here philosophical arguments, of one kind or another, are inevitable. Consider the view that these claims show, at a minimum, that originalism has to be justified as making sense of our constitutional tradition. Consider the more ambitious claim that originalism must be rejected, first because it does not "fit" our tradition, and second because it does not "justify" it, for a system of constitutional law based on originalism would offer an absurdly truncated set of constitutional rights. How might an originalist respond to these claims?

c. *Tradition.* Sandalow, Constitutional Interpretation, 79 Mich. L. Rev. 1033, 1036, 1068-1069, 1071 (1971):

[There is a] need to accommodate the Constitution to changing circumstances and values. [Constitutional] law thus emerges not as exegesis, but as a process by which each generation gives formal expression to the values it holds [fundamental]. Judges [who] wish to appeal to the Constitution must demonstrate that the principles upon which they propose to confer constitutional status express values that [are] rooted in history. [The] relevant past for purposes of constitutional law, thus, is to be found not only in the intentions of those who drafted and ratified the document but in the entirety of our history.

d. *The common law and consensus.* Perhaps constitutional law is a common law process in which judgments emerge from particular cases rather than from text or history. See Strauss, Common Law Constitutional Interpretation, 63 U. Chi. L. Rev. 977 (1996), for a detailed treatment. Perhaps those judgments reflect social consensus of some sort. See Wellington, Common Law Rules and Constitutional Double Standards: Some Notes on Adjudication, 83 Yale L.J. 221, 244, 284 (1973):

[When] dealing with legal principles a court must take a moral point of view. Yet I doubt one would want to say that a court is entitled or required to assert *its* moral point of view. Unlike the moral philosopher, the court is required to assert *ours.* [The] Court's task is to ascertain [the] conventional morality and to convert [moral] principle[s] into [legal ones] by connecting [them] with the body of constitutional law.

e. *Representation-reinforcement.* J. Ely, Democracy and Distrust 7-8, 87-88 (1980):

[Rule] in accord with the consent of a majority [is] the core of the American governmental system. [But] that cannot be the whole story, since a majority with untrammeled power [is] in a position to deal itself benefits at the expense of the [minority]. The tricky task [is to devise] a way [of] protecting minorities from majority tyranny that is not a flagrant contradiction of the principle of majority [rule]. [To accomplish this task,] the Constitution [is] overwhelmingly concerned [with] procedural fairness [and] with ensuring broad participation in the processes [of] government. [Thus,] a representation-reinforcing approach to judicial review, [which focuses on "clearing the channels of political change" and "facilitating the representation of minorities," is] supportive of [the] underlying premises of the American system of representative democracy. [Moreover,] such an approach [involves] tasks that courts, as experts on process and [as] political outsiders, can sensibly claim to be better qualified [to] perform than political officials.

Under this view, decisions that depart from the original understanding or that look outside the four corners of the document are justifiable when they promote representation, but not if they recognize or create fundamental rights unrelated to representation. This position would support decisions protecting minorities and rights of access to the political process. It would not readily support decisions recognizing rights of privacy or economic liberty. C. Sunstein, The Partial Constitution (1993), argues that the constitutional commitment to "deliberative democracy" should be the source of interpretative principles; this approach has a clear connection to Ely's.

6. *Rebuttals.* Do the sources outlined above meet the objections from history and democracy? Consider the following objections:

a. *Natural law.* Ely, supra, at 48-50:

At the time the original Constitution was ratified, [a] number of people espoused the existence of a system of natural law principles. [But the] historical record [is] not so uncomplicated as it is sometimes made to appear. [In any event, the] idea is a discredited one in our society, [and] for good reason. "[A]ll theories of natural law have a singular vagueness which is both an advantage and disadvantage in the application of the theories." The advantage [is] that you can invoke natural law to support anything you want. The disadvantage is that everybody understands that.

b. *Moral arguments.* Ely, supra, at 56-58:

[The view] that judges, in seeking constitutional value judgments, should [employ] "the method of reason familiar to the discourse of moral philosophy" [assumes] that moral philosophy is what constitutional law is properly about, that there exists a correct way of doing such philosophy, and that judges are better than others at identifying and engaging in it. [But] surely the claim here cannot be that lawyers and judges are the best imaginable people to tell good moral philosophy from bad. [Moreover, this view assumes] that something exists called "the method of moral philosophy" whose contours sensitive experts will agree on. [That] is not the way things are. [There] simply does not exist a method of moral philosophy.

Consider the following response: The existence of competing methods of moral philosophy no more disqualifies moral philosophy as a source of constitutional interpretation than the existence of competing methods of ascertaining the original understanding disqualifies originalism as a source of constitutional interpretation. The critical issue is not whether there are unitary or uncontroversial answers to moral questions, but whether it is possible to engage in rational discourse about such questions — whether moral philosophy is ultimately about anything more than a wholly subjective and inevitably relativist choice of competing value preferences. But might we be nervous about moral reasoning by judges even if we are not nervous about moral reasoning in general? See R. Posner, The Problematics of Moral and Legal Theory (1998); C. Sunstein, Legal Reasoning and Political Conflict (1997), both emphasizing the problems with judge-made assessments of political philosophy.

c. *Tradition.* Ely, supra, at 60, 62:

Tradition is an obvious place to seek fundamental values, but one whose problems are also obvious. [Tradition] can be invoked in support of almost any cause. [Moreover, tradition's] overtly backward-looking character highlights its undemocratic nature: it is hard to square with the theory of our government that yesterday's majority [should not] control today's. [And] "[i]f the Constitution protects only interests which comport with traditional values, the persons most likely to be penalized for their way of life will be those least likely to receive judicial protection," and that flips the point of the [Constitution] exactly upside down.

d. *Consensus.* See Ely, supra, at 63-64, 67:

[The problem with the] idea that society's "widely shared values" should give content to the [Constitution is] that that consensus is not reliably discoverable, at least not by the courts. [In] any event the comparative judgment is devastating: as between courts and legislatures, it is clear that the latter are better suited to reflect consensus. [We] may grant until we're blue in the face that legislatures aren't wholly democratic, but that isn't going to make courts more democratic than legislatures.

e. *Representation-reinforcement.* Brest, The Substance of Process, 42 Ohio St. L.J. 131, 140, 142 (1981):

[Most] instances of representation-reinforcing review demand value judgments not different in kind or scope from the fundamental values sort. [Indeed, the] representation-reinforcing enterprise is shot full of value choices, starting with the decision of just *how* representative our various systems of government ought to be and who ought to be included in the political community, and ending with (covert) choices about who is justifiably the object of prejudice and whether legislative goals are sufficiently important to warrant the burdens they impose on some members of society. [In his] attempt to establish a value-free mode of constitutional adjudication, [Ely] has come as close as anyone could to proving that it can't be done.

7. *Concluding thoughts.* In reading the materials, you might consider the following tentative thoughts:

a. There is an ambiguous relation between originalism and judicial restraint. At least some versions of originalism are perfectly comfortable with relatively frequent judicial invalidation of democratic decisions; they insist only that such invalidation must follow from the original understanding. When it does, originalist judges let the chips fall where they may. Originalists are concerned to limit judicial discretion but not necessarily to restrict the number of invalidations. Some originalists believe in an active judicial role in invalidating statutes; others do not.

b. Any system of interpretation has to be supported by reasons, or "values," and these will inevitably involve contestable claims about what a well-functioning constitutional democracy would look like. Those who defend an active judicial role in (for example) protecting minorities will have to resort to something other than history. So, too, with those who defend originalism. In these respects, some kind of choice about values is inescapable — originalists themselves must defend their choices in terms of political theory — even though people often try to escape it.

c. The line between originalism and nonoriginalism should not be overdrawn. Nonoriginalists rarely believe that judges should entirely abandon the original understanding, and they almost always believe that the text is controlling. Often they merely characterize the original understanding broadly (as containing general concepts rather than particular conceptions) or emphasize the existence of new or unforeseen circumstances. Originalists often treat interpretation as a complex matter and acknowledge (for example) that changed circumstances are relevant to interpretation. For this reason, originalists are often comfortable with Brown v. Board of Education and with a relatively broad approach to the first amendment. Nonoriginalism that is responsible and sensitive to the risks of judicial overreaching is not altogether different from originalism that is sensitive to the difficulties of transplanting constitutional provisions to new periods and new problems.

d. Notwithstanding item c, a pervasive issue has to do with how one assesses the risks of judicial discretion, subjectivity, and overreaching on the one hand, and the dangers of majoritarian tyranny (how and by whom defined?) on the other. Consider how these risks have played themselves out in the context of implied fundamental rights.

e. The Court has not selected any particular "theory" of interpretation; it has not settled on any particular "method." Instead, it decides cases, sometimes bracketing theoretical issues. See Cass R. Sunstein, One Case at a Time (1999); Sunstein, Incompletely Theorized Agreements, 108 Harv. L. Rev. 1733 (1995). Would it be better if the Court made a decision in favor of a single method of interpretation?

B.   THE PRIVILEGES OR IMMUNITIES CLAUSE

Section 1 of the fourteenth amendment provides that "[n]o State shall make or enforce any law which shall abridge the privileges or immunities of citizens of the United States." The enactment of the fourteenth amendment is examined in Chapter 5, section A, supra. Of the considerable body of literature concerning the adoption of the Civil War amendments, useful works are A. Amar, The Bill of Rights (1999); R. Berger, Government by Judiciary (1977); C. Fairman, Reconstruction and Reunion, 1864-1888, pt. 1, ch. 20 (1971); H. Flack, The Adoption of the Fourteenth Amendment (1908); J. James, The Framing of the Fourteenth

Amendment (1956); Fairman, Does the Fourteenth Amendment Incorporate the Bill of Rights? The Original Understanding, 2 Stan. L. Rev. 5 (1949); Frank and Munro, The Original Understanding of "Equal Protection of the Laws," 1972 Wash. U.L.Q. 421.

What are the "privileges or immunities of citizens of the United States"?

The Slaughter-House Cases

83 U.S. (16 Wall.) 36 (1873)

MR. JUSTICE MILLER delivered the opinion of the Court.

[A statute passed by the Louisiana legislature granted to the Crescent City Live-Stock Landing and Slaughter-House Company the exclusive right to engage in the livestock landing and slaughterhouse business within an area including the City of New Orleans. The company was required to permit any person to slaughter animals in its slaughterhouse at charges fixed by law. Plaintiffs in error, several butchers whose businesses were restricted by the statute, sued to invalidate the monopoly.]

The plaintiffs in error [allege] that the statute is a violation of the Constitution of the United States in these several particulars:

That it creates an involuntary servitude forbidden by the thirteenth article of amendment;

That it abridges the privileges and immunities of citizens of the United States;

That it denies to the plaintiffs the equal protection of the laws; and,

That it deprives them of their property without due process of law; contrary to the provisions of the first section of the fourteenth article of amendment.

This court is thus called upon for the first time to give construction to these articles. . . .

The most cursory glance at these articles discloses a unity of purpose, when taken in connection with the history of the times, which cannot fail to have an important bearing on any question of doubt concerning their true meaning. [For] in the light of [events,] almost too recent to be called history, but which are familiar to us all; and on the most casual examination of the language of these amendments, no one can fail to be impressed with the one pervading purpose found in them all, lying at the foundation of each, and without which none of them would have been even suggested; we mean the freedom of the slave race, the security and firm establishment of that freedom, and the protection of the newly-made freeman and citizen from the oppressions of those who had formerly exercised unlimited dominion over him. . . .

We do not say that no one else but the negro can share in this protection. [But] what we do say, and what we wish to be understood is, that in any fair and just construction of any section or phrase of these amendments, it is necessary to look to the purpose which we have said was the pervading spirit of them all. . . .

The first section of the fourteenth article, to which our attention is more specially invited, opens with a definition of citizenship — not only citizenship of the United States, but citizenship of the States. . . .

"All persons born or naturalized in the United States, and subject to the jurisdiction thereof, are citizens of the United States and of the State wherein they reside."

The first observation we have to make on this clause is, that it [overturns] the *Dred Scott* decision by making *all persons* born within the United States and subject to its jurisdiction citizens of the United States. . . .

The next observation is more important in view of the arguments of counsel in the present case. It is, that the distinction between citizenship of the United States and citizenship of a State is clearly recognized and established. [There] is a citizenship of the United States, and a citizenship of a State, which are distinct from each other, and which depend upon different characteristics or circumstances in the individual.

We think this distinction and its explicit recognition in this amendment of great weight in this argument, because the next paragraph of this same section, which is the one mainly relied on by the plaintiffs in error, speaks only of privileges and immunities of citizens of the United States, and does not speak of those of citizens of the several States. . . .

The language is, "No State shall make or enforce any law which shall abridge the privileges or immunities of citizens of *the United States.*" It is a little remarkable, if this clause was intended as a protection to the citizen of a State against the legislative power of his own State, that the word citizen of the State should be left out when it is so carefully used, and used in contradistinction to citizens of the United States, in the very sentence which precedes it. It is too clear for argument that the change in phraseology was adopted understandingly and with a purpose.

Of the privileges and immunities of the citizen of the United States, and of the privileges and immunities of the citizen of the State, and what they respectively are, we will presently consider; but we wish to state here that it is only the former which are placed by this clause under the protection of the Federal Constitution, and that the latter, whatever they may be, are not intended to have any additional protection by this paragraph of the amendment.

If, then, there is a difference between the privileges and immunities belonging to a citizen of the United States as such, and those belonging to the citizen of the State as such, the latter must rest for their security and protection where they have heretofore rested; for they are not embraced by this paragraph of the amendment.

The first occurrence of the words "privileges and immunities" in our [Constitution] is to be found in [article IV, section 2, which provides that] "The citizens of each State shall be entitled to all the privileges and immunities of citizens of the several States." [The] first and the leading case on [this clause] is that of Corfield v. Coryell, decided by Mr. Justice Washington in the Circuit Court for the District of Pennsylvania in 1823.

"The inquiry," he says,

> is, what are the privileges and immunities of citizens of the several States? We feel no hesitation in confining these expressions to those privileges and immunities which are *fundamental*; which belong of right to the citizens of all free governments, and which have at all times been enjoyed by citizens of the several States which compose this Union, from the time of their becoming free, independent, and sovereign. What these fundamental principles are, it would be more tedious than difficult to enumerate. They may all, however, be comprehended under the following general heads: protection by the government, with the right to acquire and possess property of every kind, and to pursue and obtain happiness and safety,

subject, nevertheless, to such restraints as the government may prescribe for the general good of the whole. . . .

[Article IV, section 2] did not create those rights, which it called privileges and immunities of citizens of the States. [Its] sole purpose was to declare to the several States, that whatever those rights, as you grant or establish them to your own citizens, or as you limit or qualify, or impose restrictions on their exercise, the same, neither more nor less, shall be the measure of the rights of citizens of other States within your jurisdiction.

[Thus,] up to the adoption of the recent amendments, no claim or pretence was set up that those rights depended on the Federal government for their existence or protection. [Was] it the purpose of the fourteenth amendment, by the simple declaration that no State should make or enforce any law which shall abridge the privileges and immunities of *citizens of the United States*, to transfer the security and protection of all the civil rights which we have mentioned, from the States to the Federal government? And where it is declared that Congress shall have the power to enforce that article, was it intended to bring within the power of Congress the entire domain of civil rights heretofore belonging exclusively to the States?

All this and more must follow, if the proposition of the plaintiffs in error be sound. For not only are these rights subject to the control of Congress whenever in its discretion any of them are supposed to be abridged by State legislation, but that body may also pass laws in advance, limiting and restricting the exercise of legislative power by the States, in their most ordinary and usual functions, as in its judgment it may think proper on all such subjects. And still further, such a construction [would] constitute this court a perpetual censor upon all legislation of the States, on the civil rights of their own citizens, with authority to nullify such as it did not approve as consistent with those rights, as they existed at the time of the adoption of this amendment. The argument we admit is not always the most conclusive which is drawn from the consequences urged against the adoption of a particular construction of an instrument. But when, as in the case before us, these consequences are so serious, so far-reaching and pervading, so great a departure from the structure and spirit of our institutions; when the effect is to fetter and degrade the State governments by subjecting them to the control of Congress, in the exercise of powers heretofore universally conceded to them of the most ordinary and fundamental character; when in fact it radically changes the whole theory of the relations of the State and Federal governments to each other and of both these governments to the people; the argument has a force that is irresistible, in the absence of language which expresses such a purpose too clearly to admit of doubt.

We are convinced that no such results were intended by the Congress which proposed these amendments, nor by the legislatures of the States which ratified them.

Having shown that the privileges and immunities relied on in the argument are those which belong to citizens of the States as such, and that they are left to the State governments for security and protection, and not by this article placed under the special care of the Federal government, we may hold ourselves excused from defining the privileges and immunities of citizens of the United States which no State can abridge, until some case involving those privileges may make it necessary to do so.

But lest it should be said that no such privileges and immunities are to be found if those we have been considering are excluded, we venture to suggest some which owe their existence to the Federal government, its National character, its Constitution, or its laws.

One of these is well described in the case of Crandall v. Nevada. [73 U.S. (6 Wall.) 35 (1867).] It is said to be the right of the citizen of this great country, protected by implied guarantees of its Constitution, "to come to the seat of government to assert any claim he may have upon that government, to transact any business he may have with it, to seek its protection, to share its offices, to engage in administering its functions. He has the right of free access to its seaports, through which all operations of foreign commerce are conducted, to the subtreasuries, land offices, and courts of justice in the several States."

Another privilege of a citizen of the United States is to demand the care and protection of the Federal government over his life, liberty, and property when on the high seas or within the jurisdiction of a foreign government. [The] right to peaceably assemble and petition for redress of grievances, the privilege of the writ of habeas corpus, are rights of the citizen guaranteed by the Federal Constitution. The right to use the navigable waters of the United States, however they may penetrate the territory of the several States, all rights secured to our citizens by treaties with foreign nations, are dependent upon citizenship of the United States, and not citizenship of a State. [To] these may be added the rights secured by the thirteenth and fifteenth articles of amendment, and by the other clause[s] of the fourteenth. . . .

But it is useless to pursue this branch of the inquiry, since we are of opinion that the rights claimed by these plaintiffs in error, if they have any existence, are not privileges and immunities of citizens of the United States within the meaning of the clause of the fourteenth amendment under consideration.

[The Court also rejected claims that the statute violated the thirteenth amendment and the equal protection and due process clauses of the fourteenth amendment.]

The judgments of the Supreme Court of Louisiana in these cases are affirmed.

MR. JUSTICE FIELD, dissenting. . . .

The act of Louisiana presents the naked case [where] a right to pursue a lawful and necessary calling, previously enjoyed by every citizen, [is] taken away and vested exclusively [in] a single corporation. . . .

The question presented is, therefore, one of the gravest importance, not merely to the parties here, but to the whole country. It is nothing less than the question whether the recent amendments to the Federal Constitution protect the citizens of the United States against the deprivation of their common rights by State legislation. In my judgment the fourteenth amendment does afford such protection, and was so intended by the Congress which framed and the States which adopted it. . . .

If [the privileges and immunities clause] only refers, as held by the majority of the court in their opinion, to such privileges and immunities as were before its adoption specially designated in the Constitution or necessarily implied as belonging to citizens of the United States, it was a vain and idle enactment, which accomplished nothing, and most unnecessarily excited Congress and the people on its passage. With privileges and immunities thus designated or implied no State could ever have interfered by its laws, and no new constitutional provision was required to inhibit such interference. The supremacy of the Constitution and the laws of the United States always controlled any State legislation of that character. But if the amendment refers to the natural and inalienable rights which belong to all citizens, the inhibition has a profound significance and consequence.

What, then, are the privileges and immunities which are secured against abridgment by State legislation?

[Justice Washington's interpretation of the "privileges and immunities" protected by article IV, section 2] appears to me to be a sound construction of the clause in question. The privileges and immunities designated are those *which of right belong to the citizens of all free governments*. Clearly among these must be placed the right to pursue a lawful employment in a lawful manner, without other restraint than such as equally affects all persons. . . .

What [article IV, section 2] did for the protection of the citizens of one State against hostile and discriminating legislation of other States, the fourteenth amendment does for the protection of every citizen of the United States against hostile and discriminating legislation against him in favor of others, whether they reside in the same or in different States. . . .

It will not be pretended that under the fourth article of the Constitution any State could create a monopoly in any known trade or manufacture in favor of her own citizens [which] would exclude an equal participation [by] citizens of other States. [And] what [article IV, section 2] does for the protection of citizens of one State against the creation of monopolies in favor of citizens of other States, the fourteenth amendment does for the protection of every citizen of the United States against the creation of any monopoly whatever. The privileges and immunities of citizens of the United States, of every one of them, is secured against abridgment in any form by any State. The fourteenth amendment places them under the guardianship of the National authority. All monopolies in any known trade or manufacture are an invasion of these privileges, for they encroach upon the liberty of citizens to acquire property and pursue happiness. . . .

This equality of right, with exemption from all disparaging and partial enactments, in the lawful pursuits of life, throughout the whole country, is the distinguishing privilege of citizens of the United States. To them, everywhere, all pursuits, all professions, all avocations are open without other restrictions than such as are imposed equally upon all others of the same age, sex, and condition. The State may prescribe such regulations for every pursuit and calling of life as will promote the public health, secure the good order and advance the general prosperity of society, but when once prescribed, the pursuit or calling must be free to be followed by every citizen who is within the conditions designated, and will conform to the regulations. This is the fundamental idea upon which our institutions rest. . . .*

---

* "The property which every man has in his own labor," says Adam Smith,

as it is the original foundation of all other property, so it is the most sacred and inviolable. The patrimony of the poor man lies in the strength and dexterity of his own hands; and to hinder him from employing this strength and dexterity in what manner he thinks proper, without injury to his neighbor, is a plain violation of this most sacred property. It is a manifest encroachment upon the just liberty both of the workman and of those who might be disposed to employ him. As it hinders the one from working at what he thinks proper, so it hinders the others from employing whom they think proper. (Smith's Wealth of Nations, b. 1, ch. 10, part 2.) . . . [Relocated footnote — EDS.]

I am authorized by THE CHIEF JUSTICE, MR. JUSTICE SWAYNE, and MR. JUS-TICE BRADLEY, to state that they concur with me in this dissenting opinion.

MR. JUSTICE BRADLEY, also dissenting. . . .

The right of a State to regulate the conduct of its citizens is undoubtedly a very broad and extensive one, and not to be lightly restricted. But there are certain fundamental rights which this right of regulation cannot infringe. It may pre-scribe the manner of their exercise, but it cannot subvert the rights themselves. [In] this free country, the people of which inherited certain traditionary rights and privileges from their ancestors, citizenship means something. . . .

The people of this country brought with them to its shores the rights of Eng-lishmen; the rights which had been wrested from English sovereigns at various periods of the nation's history. [Blackstone] classifies these fundamental rights un-der three heads, as the absolute rights of individuals, to wit: the right of personal security, the right of personal liberty, and the right of private property. [These] are the fundamental rights which can only be [interfered with] by lawful regula-tions necessary or proper for the mutual good of all. . . . [And among the privi-leges and immunities of citizens,] none is more essential and fundamental than the right to follow such profession or employment as each one may choose, sub-ject only to uniform regulations equally applicable to all. . . .

The keeping of a slaughter-house is part of, and incidental to, the trade of a butcher — one of the ordinary occupations of human life. To compel a butcher [to] slaughter [his] cattle in another person's slaughter-house and pay him a toll therefor, is such a restriction upon the trade as materially to interfere with its pros-ecution. It is onerous, unreasonable, arbitrary, and unjust. It has none of the qual-ities of a police regulation. If it were really a police regulation, it would undoubt-edly be within the power of the legislature. [But the] granting of monopolies, or exclusive privileges to individuals or corporations, is an invasion of the right of others to choose a lawful calling, and an infringement of personal liberty. . . .

[Great] fears are expressed that this construction of the amendment will lead to enactments by Congress interfering with the internal affairs of the States, and [that] it will lead the Federal courts to draw to their cognizance the supervision of State tribunals on every subject of judicial inquiry, on the plea of ascertaining whether the privileges and immunities of citizens have not been abridged.

In my judgment no such practical inconveniences would arise. Very little, if any, legislation on the part of Congress would be required to carry the amend-ment into effect. [And as] the privileges and immunities protected are only those fundamental ones which belong to every citizen, they would soon become so far defined as to cause but a slight accumulation of business in the Federal courts. [In any event, the] argument from inconvenience ought not to have a very con-trolling influence in questions of this sort. The National will and National inter-est are of far greater importance. . . . [A dissenting opinion by Justice Swayne is omitted.]

Note: The Demise of the Privileges or Immunities Clause

1. *The Slaughter-House Cases.* Consider the following criticisms of Justice Mil-ler's interpretation of the privileges or immunities clause:

a. "Unique among constitutional provisions, the privileges and immunities clause of the Fourteenth Amendment enjoys the distinction of having been rendered a 'practical nullity' by a single decision of the Supreme Court within five years after its ratification." E. Corwin, The Constitution of the United States of America 965 (1953). See Currie, The Constitution in the Supreme Court: Limitations on State Power, 1865-1873, 51 U. Chi. L. Rev. 329, 348 (1983):

[As Justice Field observed in dissent, the difficulty] was with Miller's apparent conclusion that the sole office of the clause was to protect rights already given by some other federal law. Apart from the amendment's less than conclusive reference to dual citizenship, his sole justification was that a broader holding would "radically [change] the whole theory of the relations of the State and Federal governments to each other and of both these governments to the people" — which quite arguably was precisely what the authors of the amendment had in mind.

b. Graham, Our "Declaratory" Fourteenth Amendment, 7 Stan. L. Rev. 3, 23, 25 (1954):

A single change was made in Section One after it had been reported by the Joint Committee. This was the addition of the first sentence defining citizenship. [Significantly,] no one observed that while citizenship was made dual in this first sentence, only the privileges or immunities of "citizens of the United States" were specifically protected in the second sentence against abridgment by the states. The reason for this apparent oversight is that [opponents] of slavery had regarded all the important "natural" and constitutional rights as being privileges or immunities of *citizens of the United States*. This had been the cardinal premise of antislavery theory. [The] real purpose of adding this citizenship definition was to [overrule *Dred Scott*]. [To] reach the conclusion of Justice Miller and the majority, one must disregard not only all antislavery from 1834 on, but one must ignore virtually every word said in the debates of 1865-66.

For a defense of Justice Miller's opinion, see Palmer, The Parameters of Constitutional Reconstruction: *Slaughter-House, Cruikshank*, and the Fourteenth Amendment, 1984 U. Ill. L. Rev. 739.

c. Kaczorowski, The Politics of Judicial Interpretation: The Federal Courts, Department of Justice and Civil Rights, 1866-1876, at 154-155, 161 (1985):

Theoretical rationalizations of legal doctrine are also means to achieve political objectives. [*Slaughter-House*] may thus be explained in terms of its political goals. Miller was quite explicit about the majority's desire to resist the nationalizing impact of the Civil War by redefining American federalism as a states rights-centered dual federalism. [Although the Court may not have] shared the political objectives and values of Democratic Conservatives of the South, [it clearly was] more concerned about preserving the states' regulatory functions [than] in establishing national authority to protect the civil rights of black Americans. [Moreover, the] revitalization of states rights was crucial to the success of Northern states in their struggle to cope with the stresses of industrialization, [for] it endorsed the state police power necessary to control the growing concentrations of monopolistic power of rising business.

2. *The* Slaughter-House *dissents*. The dissenters maintained that the "right to pursue a lawful employment in a lawful manner" is a "fundamental" right that

belongs "to the citizens of all free governments." But perhaps this formulation is "question begging, because [the] question how lawfulness is to be determined is unresolved." Kurland, The Privileges or Immunities Clause: "Its Hour Come Round at Last"?, 1972 Wash. U.L.Q. 405, 409. If the *Slaughter-House* dissenters had prevailed, what *other* rights would constitute "privileges or immunities of citizens"?

3. *Alternative interpretations.* a. "My study of the historical events that culminated in the Fourteenth Amendment [persuades] me that one of the chief objects that [the] Amendment's first section [was] intended to accomplish was to make the Bill of Rights applicable to the states." Adamson v. California, 332 U.S. 46, 71-72 (1947) (Black, J., dissenting). "[The] words 'No State shall make or enforce any law which shall abridge the privileges or immunities of citizens of the United States' seem to me an eminently reasonable way of expressing the idea that henceforth the Bill of Rights shall apply to the States. What more precious 'privilege' of American citizenship could there be than that privilege to claim the protection of our great Bill of Rights?" Duncan v. Louisiana, 391 U.S. 145, 166 (1968) (Black, J., concurring). In support of this view, note that Representative Bingham, the framer of the provision, stated that "the privileges and immunities of citizens of the United States [are] chiefly defined in the first eight amendments to the Constitution." Cong. Globe, 42d Cong., 1st Sess., app. 85 (1871). See also Kaczorowski, Revolutionary Constitutionalism in the Era of the Civil War and Reconstruction, 61 N.Y.U. L. Rev. 863 (1986). But note also that the privileges and immunities of the original Constitution referred to something altogether different from the original bill of rights; and note also that the due process clause is included in the fourteenth amendment, an inclusion that would create redundancy if the bill of rights was already comprehended within the privileges and immunities clause.

b. Fairman, Does the Fourteenth Amendment Incorporate the Bill of Rights? The Original Understanding, 2 Stan. L. Rev. 5, 132, 137-139 (1949):

> [Apart from a few isolated references, the theory that the] privileges and immunities clause incorporated Amendments I to VIII found no recognition in the practice of Congress, or the action of state legislatures, constitutional conventions, or courts. [The] freedom that the states traditionally [had] exercised to develop their own systems for administering justice repels any thought that the [Bill of Rights] provisions on grand jury, criminal jury, and civil jury were fastened upon them in 1868. Congress would not have attempted such a thing, the country would not have stood for it, the legislatures would not have ratified. . . .
>
> If the founders of the Fourteenth Amendment did not intend the privileges and immunities clause to impose Amendments I to VIII, then what, it may be asked, did they mean? [If] one seeks some inclusive and exclusive definition, such that one could say, this is precisely what they had in mind — pretty clearly there never was any such clear conception. [The opponents of the measure magnified] the proposal to render it odious. [The advocates] offered illustrations of particular evils that would be repressed; [but] stayed away from any explanation of a fundamental principle. [Brooding] over the matter [has] slowly brought [me to] the conclusion that [the protection of those rights that are] "implicit in the concept of ordered liberty" [comes] as close as one can to catching the vague aspirations that were hung upon the privileges and immunities clause.

In support of this view, note that Senator Howard, who presented the amendment to the Senate on behalf of the Joint Committee on Reconstruction, explained that the clause protects all "fundamental rights lying at the basis of all society," and that the precise scope of the rights incorporated in the clause would be left "to be discussed and adjudicated when they should happen practically to arise." Cong. Globe, 39th Cong., 1st Sess. 2765-2766 (1866).

c. R. Berger, Government by Judiciary 18, 20 (1977):

The "privileges or immunities" clause was the central provision of the Amendment's §1, and the key to its meaning is furnished by the immediately preceding Civil Rights Act of 1866, which, all are agreed, it was the purpose of the Amendment to embody and protect. The objectives of the [Civil Rights] Act were quite limited. [The Act provided that "there shall be no discrimination in civil rights or immunities on account of race [but] the inhabitants of every race [shall] have the same right to make and enforce contracts, to sue, be parties, and give evidence; to inherit, purchase, lease, sell, hold and convey real and personal property, and to full and equal benefit of all laws and proceedings for the security of person and property, and shall be subject to like punishment [and] no other."] The three clauses of §1 [of the fourteenth amendment] were [thus] three facets of one and the same concern: to insure that there would be no discrimination against [blacks] in respect of "fundamental rights," which had a clearly understood and narrow compass [as exemplified by the Civil Rights Act].

In support of this view, note Representative Garfield's comment that the proposed amendment will "lift [the Civil Rights Act] above the reach of political strife, [where] no storm of passion can shake it." Cong. Globe, 39th Cong., 1st Sess. 2462 (1866).

d. Amar, The Bill of Rights and the Fourteenth Amendment, 101 Yale L.J. 1193 (1992), argues for "refined incorporation":

[A]*ll* of the privileges and immunities of citizens recognized in the Bill of Rights became applicable against states by dint of the Fourteenth Amendment. But not all of the provisions of the original Bill of Rights were indeed rights of citizens. Some instead were at least in part rights of states, and as such, awkward to incorporate fully *against* states. . . . The right question is whether the provision really guarantees a privilege or immunity of individual citizens rather than a right of states or the public at large.

Amar's basic conclusion is that when a privilege or immunity of individual citizens is at issue, incorporation is appropriate. See also A. Amar, The Bill of Rights (1998).

4. *Subsequent developments.* The Court has generally adhered to the *Slaughter-House* interpretation of the privileges or immunities clause, thus rendering the clause essentially "superfluous." L. Tribe, American Constitutional Law 423 (1978). Although the Court invoked the clause in Colgate v. Harvey, 296 U.S. 404 (1935), to invalidate a state income tax levied against in-state residents exclusively on dividends and interest earned outside the state, *Colgate* was expressly overruled only five years later in Madden v. Kentucky, 309 U.S. 83 (1940). But a majority invoked the clause more recently in Saenz v. Roe, 526 U.S. 489 (1999) (right to travel), discussed in more detail in section E3 infra.

In several instances, a minority of the Court has relied on the clause. See, e.g., Hague v. CIO, 307 U.S. 496 (1939) (opinion of Roberts, J.) (right to assemble and discuss national issues is a privilege of national citizenship); Edwards v. California, 314 U.S. 160 (1941) (Douglas, J., concurring) (right of interstate travel is a privilege of national citizenship); Duncan v. Louisiana, 391 U.S. 145 (1968) (Black, J., concurring) (right to jury trial is a privilege of national citizenship).

C.   THE INCORPORATION CONTROVERSY

In Barron v. Baltimore, 32 U.S. (7 Pet.) 243 (1833), infra, the Court held that the rights guaranteed in the first eight amendments do not apply to the states. In *Slaughter-House*, the Court held that the rights guaranteed in the first eight amendments are not "privileges or immunities of citizens of the United States" and thus are not applicable to the states via the privileges or immunities clause of the fourteenth amendment. The fourteenth amendment also provides, however, that "[n]o State shall [deprive] any person of life, liberty, or property, without due process of law." To what extent, if any, does the fourteenth amendment due process clause "incorporate" the specific guarantees of the bill of rights?

This section traces the process by which the Court, since *Slaughter-House*, has gradually held most of the rights guaranteed in the first eight amendments applicable to the states via the due process clause of the fourteenth amendment. The incorporation controversy is important not only because of the questions it raises about the identification of fundamental values but also because of the questions it raises about the nature and structure of the federal system.

BARRON v. MAYOR & CITY COUNCIL OF BALTIMORE, 32 U.S. (7 Pet.) 243 (1833). Barron sued the City for ruining his wharf in Baltimore harbor. Barron claimed that municipal street construction had diverted the flow of streams so that they deposited silt in front of his wharf, and that this made the water too shallow for most vessels. Barron maintained that this action violated the fifth amendment, which provides that private property shall not be "taken for public use, without just compensation." The Court rejected Barron's contention that the fifth amendment, "being in favour of the liberty of the citizens, ought to be so construed as to restrain the legislative power of a state, as well as that of the United States." Chief Justice Marshall delivered the opinion:

"The question [is] of great importance, but not of much difficulty. The constitution was ordained and established by the people of the United States for themselves, for their own government, and not for the government of the individual states. Each state established a constitution for itself, and in that constitution, provided such limitations and restrictions on the powers of its particular government, as its judgment dictated. The people of the United States framed such a government for the United States as they supposed best adapted to their situation and best calculated to promote their interests. The powers they conferred on this government were to be exercised by itself; and the limitations on power, if expressed in general terms, are naturally, and, we think, necessarily, applicable to the government created by the instrument. . . .

"[Article I, section 10, of the original constitution expressly enumerates those limitations] which were to operate on the state legislatures. [Had] the framers of [the] amendments intended them to be limitations on the powers of the state governments, they would have imitated the framers of the original constitution, and have expressed that intention. Had congress engaged in the extraordinary occupation of improving the constitutions of the several states, by affording the people additional protection from the exercise of power by their own governments, in matters which concerned themselves alone, they would have declared this purpose in plain and intelligible language.

"But it is universally understood, it is a part of the history of the day, that the great revolution which established the constitution of the United States, was not effected without immense opposition. Serious fears were extensively entertained, that those powers which the patriot statesmen, who then watched over the interests of our country, deemed essential to union, and to the attainment of those invaluable objects for which union was sought, might be exercised in a manner dangerous to liberty. In almost every convention by which the constitution was adopted, amendments to guard against the abuse of power were recommended. These amendments demanded security against the apprehended encroachments of the general government — not against those of the local governments. In compliance with a sentiment thus generally expressed, to quiet fears thus extensively entertained, amendments were proposed by the required majority in congress, and adopted by the states. These amendments contain no expression indicating an intention to apply them to the state governments. This court cannot so apply them.

"We are of opinion, that the [just compensation] provision in the fifth amendment [is] intended solely as a limitation on the exercise of power by the government of the United States, and is not applicable to legislation of the states."

"In terms of the original understanding, *Barron* was almost certainly correctly decided." J. Ely, Democracy and Distrust 196 n.58 (1980). In the framers' view, citizen control over state government — embodied in state constitutions and the power to elect representatives — would apparently serve as an adequate safeguard of individual liberty. The enactment of the bill of rights was above all associated with special concerns about the power of the remote federal government. See Chapter 5, section A, supra.

The Civil War, however, and the Civil War amendments fundamentally realigned federal-state relations. And although the Court rejected the application of the bill of rights to the states through the privileges or immunities clause in The Slaughter-House Cases, that did not end the matter. The *Murray* case, which follows, offers a pre-fourteenth amendment perspective on "due process." The remaining cases address the issue of incorporation.

MURRAY v. HOBOKEN LAND & IMPROVEMENT CO., 59 U.S. (18 How.) 272 (1856). In *Murray,* several years before the adoption of the fourteenth amendment, Justice Curtis described the origin and scope of the due process clause of the fifth amendment: "The words, 'due process of law,' were undoubtedly intended to convey the same meaning as the words, 'by the law of the land,' in Magna Charta. [The] constitution contains no description of those processes which it was intended to allow or forbid. It does not even declare what principles are to be applied to ascertain whether it be due process. [To] what principles, then, are we to resort to ascertain whether [a particular process] is due process? [We] must look to those settled usages and modes of proceeding existing in the common and statute law of England, before the emigration of our ancestors, and which are shown not to have been unsuited to their civil and political condition by having been acted on by them after the settlement of this country."

TWINING v. NEW JERSEY, 211 U.S. 78 (1908). In a state court prosecution, the jury was instructed that it might draw an unfavorable inference against the defendants from their failure to testify. The Court rejected the defendants' contention that this instruction violated their rights under the federal Constitution:

"[It] is possible that some of the personal rights safeguarded by the first eight amendments against National action may also be safeguarded against state action, because a denial of them would be a denial of due process of law. [If] this is so, it is not because those rights are enumerated in the first eight Amendments, but because they are of such a nature that they are included in the conception of due process of law. . . .

"[We] prefer to rest our decision on broader grounds, and inquire whether the exemption from self-incrimination is [a] fundamental principle of liberty and justice which inheres in the very idea of free government and is the inalienable right of a citizen of such a government. [None] of the great instruments in which we are accustomed to look for the declaration of the fundamental rights [such as Magna Charta and the Petition of Right] made reference to [the exemption from self-incrimination]. [Moreover, of the thirteen states which ratified the original Constitution, only four proposed amendments to incorporate] the privilege in the Constitution, [and] Congress, in submitting the amendments to [the] States, treated [due process of law and the privilege against self-incrimination] as exclusive of each other. [Thus, the] inference is irresistible that it has been the opinion of constitution makers that the privilege, if fundamental in any sense, is not fundamental in due process of law, nor an essential part of it. . . .

"Even if the historical meaning of due process of law [did] not exclude the privilege from it, it would be going far to rate it as an immutable principle of [justice]. [There is no reason] for straining the meaning of due process of law to include this privilege within it."

Justice Harlan dissented.

PALKO v. CONNECTICUT, 302 U.S. 319 (1937). *Palko* concerned the constitutionality of a Connecticut statute permitting the state to appeal in criminal cases. Although the Court "assumed for the purpose of the case" that such a statute, if enacted by the United States, would violate the double jeopardy clause of the fifth amendment, it rejected appellant's contention that the challenged statute violated the due process clause of the fourteenth amendment. Noting that the Court had incorporated such rights as freedom of speech, press, assembly, and religion and the right to counsel, but not the fifth amendment right to be free from self-incrimination or the right to trial by jury, Justice Cardozo delivered the opinion of the Court:

"The line of division may seem to be wavering and broken if there is a hasty catalogue of the cases on the one side and the other. [But] there emerges the perception of a rationalizing principle which gives to discrete instances a proper order and coherence. The right to trial by jury and the immunity from prosecution except as the result of an indictment may have value and importance. Even so, they are not of the very essence of a scheme of ordered liberty. To abolish them is not to violate a 'principle of justice so rooted in the tradition and conscience of our people as to be ranked as fundamental.' [Few] would be so narrow or provincial as to maintain that a fair and enlightened system of justice would be impossible without them. What is true of jury trials and indictments is true also [of] the immunity from compulsory self-incrimination. This too might be lost, and justice still be done.

"We reach a different plane of social and moral values when we pass to the privileges and immunities that have been taken over from the earlier articles of the federal bill of rights and brought within the Fourteenth Amendment by a process of absorption. [The] process of absorption has had its source in the belief that neither liberty nor justice would exist if they were sacrificed. [This] is true, for illustration, of freedom of thought and speech. Of that freedom one may say that it is the matrix, and indispensable condition, of nearly every other form of freedom. [Fundamental] too in the concept of due process, and so in that of liberty, is the thought that condemnation shall be rendered only after trial.

"[Is] that kind of double jeopardy to which the statute has subjected him a hardship so acute and shocking that our polity will not endure it? Does it violate those 'fundamental principles of liberty and justice which lie at the base of all our civil and political institutions'? [The] answer must surely be 'no.'"

Justice Butler dissented.

Note that by 1937 there was no longer any doubt that "due process" could embrace not only procedural rights but also substantive rights such as freedom of speech and religion. Is this consistent with the textual guarantee of "due process"?

ADAMSON v. CALIFORNIA, 332 U.S. 46 (1947). In a state court prosecution, the prosecution was permitted to comment on the defendant's failure to take the stand. The Court assumed that such comment "would infringe defendant's privilege against self-incrimination [if] this were a trial in a court of the United States." The Court, in a five-to-four decision, held that the fourteenth amendment did not incorporate the privilege. In a lengthy dissenting opinion, Justice Black, joined by Justice Douglas, set forth his theory of "total" incorporation:

"This decision reasserts a constitutional theory spelled out in [*Twining*], that this Court is endowed by the Constitution with boundless power under 'natural law' periodically to expand and contract constitutional standards to conform to the Court's conception of what at a particular time constitutes 'civilized decency' and 'fundamental liberty and justice.' [I] would not reaffirm the *Twining* decision. I think that decision and the 'natural law' theory of the Constitution upon which it relies degrade the constitutional safeguards of the Bill of Rights and simultaneously appropriate for this Court a broad power which we are not authorized by the Constitution to exercise. . . .

"My study of the historical events that culminated in the Fourteenth Amendment, and the expressions of those who sponsored and favored, as well as those who opposed its submission and passage, persuades me that one of the chief objects that the provisions of the Amendment's first section, separately, and as a whole, were intended to accomplish was to make the Bill of Rights applicable to the states. With full knowledge of the import of the *Barron* decision, the framers

and backers of the Fourteenth Amendment proclaimed its purpose to be to overturn the constitutional rule that case had announced. . . .

"[I] fear to see the consequences of the Court's practice of substituting its
own concepts of decency and fundamental justice for the language of the Bill
of Rights as its point of departure in interpreting and enforcing that Bill of Rights.
[I] would follow what I believe was the original purpose of the Fourteenth Amendment — to extend to all the people of the nation the complete protection of the
Bill of Rights. . . ."

In a concurring opinion, Justice Frankfurter attacked Justice Black's theory of
"total" incorporation: "For historical reasons a limited immunity from the common duty to testify was written into the Federal Bill of Rights, and I am prepared
to agree that, as part of that immunity, comment on failure of an accused to take
the witness stand is forbidden in federal prosecutions. [But] to suggest that such
a limitation can be drawn out of 'due process' in its protection of ultimate decency in a civilized society is to suggest that the Due Process Clause fastened fetters of unreason upon the States. . . .

"The short answer to the suggestion that the [due process clause of the fourteenth amendment] was a way of saying that every State must thereafter initiate
prosecutions through indictment by a grand jury, must have a trial by a jury of
twelve in criminal cases, and must have trial by such a jury in common law suits
where the amount in controversy exceeds twenty dollars, is that it is a strange way
of saying it. [Those] reading the English language with the meaning which it ordinarily conveys [would] hardly recognize the Fourteenth Amendment as a cover
for the various explicit provisions of the first eight Amendments. . . .

"Judicial review of th[e due process] guaranty [inescapably] imposes upon this
Court an exercise of judgment upon the whole course of the proceedings in order to ascertain whether they offend those canons of decency and fairness which
express the notions of justice of English-speaking peoples. [These] standards
[are] not authoritatively formulated anywhere as though they were prescriptions
in a pharmacopoeia. But neither does the application of the Due Process Clause
imply that judges are wholly at large. The judicial judgment in applying the Due
Process Clause must move within the limits of accepted notions of justice and is
not to be based upon the idiosyncrasies of a merely personal judgment. [An] important safeguard against such merely individual judgment is an alert deference
to the judgment of the State court under review."

Note: The Black/Frankfurter Debate

1. *"Total" incorporation.* Justice Black's "total" incorporation theory has never
commanded a majority of the Court. The historical record is ambiguous, and
there is no clear consensus on the actual intentions of the framers and ratifiers
of the fourteenth amendment. For analysis of the historical issue, see generally
A. Amar, The Bill of Rights (1998); R. Berger, Government by Judiciary (1977);
J. Ely, Democracy and Distrust (1980); H. Flack, The Adoption of the Fourteenth
Amendment (1908); W. Guthrie, The Fourteenth Article of Amendment to the
Constitution of the United States (1898); TenBroek, The Antislavery Origins of
the Fourteenth Amendment (1951); Amar, The Bill of Rights and the Fourteenth
Amendment, 101 Yale L.J. 1193 (1992); Crosskey, "Legislative History" and the

Constitutional Limitations on State Authority, 22 U. Chi. L. Rev. 1 (1954); Fairman, Does the Fourteenth Amendment Incorporate the Bill of Rights? The Original Understanding, 2 Stan. L. Rev. 5 (1949);

2. *"Fundamental fairness."* For about fifteen years after *Adamson,* the Court continued to employ the "fundamental fairness" approach to due process. In applying this approach, the Court struggled to avoid decisions based on what Justice Frankfurter termed "the idiosyncrasies of a merely personal judgment." Consider Kadish, Methodology and Criteria in Due Process Adjudication — A Survey and Criticism, 66 Yale L.J. 319, 327-328 (1957):

> The effort to eliminate the purely personal preference from flexible due process decision making has taken two main forms. One has been a respectful deference to the judgment of the state court or the act of the legislature under review. The other had been an attempt to rest conclusions upon external and objective evidence in such fashion that as far as possible it can be said that the Court is not so much itself creating its own policy determinations as it is interpreting and reading determinations that have already been made. [The] most significant kind of such objective data has consisted of the moral judgments already made on the point at issue, sought for in the express or implicit view of important segments of our society, past or present. [The Court has thus looked to four primary sources]: (1) the opinions of the progenitors and architects of American institutions; (2) the implicit opinions of the policymaking organs of state governments; (3) the explicit opinions of other American courts that have evaluated the fundamentality of [the asserted right]; or, (4) the opinions of other countries in the Anglo-American tradition "not less civilized than our own" as reflected in their statutes, decisions and practices.

3. *The "demise" of "fundamental fairness."* In the early 1960s, the Warren Court, without expressly abandoning "fundamental fairness," began to modify incorporation methodology. As the Court looked increasingly to the bill of rights for guidance, it "selectively" incorporated more and more of the specific guarantees of the bill of rights into the due process clause of the fourteenth amendment. These developments are traced in *Duncan.*

DUNCAN v. LOUISIANA, 391 U.S. 145 (1968). In *Duncan,* the Court held the sixth amendment right to jury trial applicable to the states via the fourteenth amendment due process clause. Justice White delivered the opinion of the Court: "[Many] of the rights guaranteed by the first eight Amendments [have] been held to be protected against state action by the Due Process Clause of the Fourteenth Amendment. That clause now protects the right to compensation for property taken by the State [Chicago, Burlington & Quincy Railroad v. Chicago, 166 U.S. 226 (1897)]; the rights of speech, press, and religion covered by the First Amendment [Fiske v. Kansas, 274 U.S. 380 (1927)]; the Fourth Amendment rights to be free from unreasonable searches and seizures and to have excluded from criminal trials any evidence illegally seized [Mapp v. Ohio, 367 U.S. 643 (1961)]; the right guaranteed by the Fifth Amendment to be free of compelled self-incrimination [Malloy v. Hogan, 378 U.S. 1 (1964), overruling *Twining* and *Adamson*]; and the Sixth Amendment rights to counsel [Gideon v. Wainwright, 372 U.S. 335 (1963)], to a speedy and public trial [Klopfer v. North Carolina, 386 U.S. 213 (1967); In re Oliver, 333 U.S. 257 (1948)], to confrontation of opposing witnesses

[Pointer v. Texas, 380 U.S. 400 (1965)], and to compulsory process for obtaining witnesses [Washington v. Texas, 388 U.S. 14 (1967)].

"The test for determining whether a right extended by the Fifth and Sixth Amendments with respect to federal criminal proceedings is also protected against state action by the Fourteenth Amendment has been phrased in a variety of ways in opinions of this Court. The question has been asked whether a right is among those 'fundamental principles of liberty and justice which lie at the base of all our civil and political institutions,' [whether] it is 'basic in our system of jurisprudence,' [and] whether it is a 'fundamental right, essential to a fair trial.' . . .

"[In] one sense recent cases applying provisions of the first eight Amendments to the States represent a new approach to the 'incorporation' debate. Earlier the Court can be seen as having asked [if] a civilized system could be imagined that would not accord the particular protection. [Citing *Palko*.] The recent cases, on the other hand, have proceeded upon the valid assumption that state criminal processes are not imaginary and theoretical schemes but actual systems bearing virtually every characteristic of the common-law system that has been developing contemporaneously in England and in this country. The question thus is whether given this kind of system a particular procedure is fundamental — whether, that is, a procedure is necessary to an Anglo-American regime of ordered liberty. . . .

"When the inquiry is approached in this way the question whether the State can impose criminal punishment without granting a jury trial appears quite different from the way it appeared in the older [cases]. A criminal process which was fair and equitable but used no juries is easy to imagine. It would make use of alternative guarantees and protections which would serve the purposes that the jury serves in the English and American systems. Yet no American State has undertaken to construct such a system. [In] every State [the] structure and style of the criminal process [are] the sort that naturally complement jury trial, and have developed in connection with and in reliance upon jury trial. . . .

"Because we believe that trial by jury in criminal cases is fundamental to the American scheme of justice, we hold that the Fourteenth Amendment guarantees a right of jury trial in all criminal cases which — were they to be tried in a federal court — would come within the Sixth Amendment's guarantee. . . ."

Justice Black, joined by Justice Douglas, filed a concurring opinion; Justice Fortas also filed a concurring opinion; Justice Harlan, joined by Justice Stewart, dissented.

Note: Incorporation since Duncan

1. *The current scope of incorporation.* Although the Court has never embraced Justice Black's total incorporation theory, it has used selective incorporation to make almost all the specific guarantees of the bill of rights applicable to the states. To the enumeration set out in *Duncan*, the Court has added the fifth amendment prohibition on "double jeopardy," Benton v. Maryland, 395 U.S. 784 (1969), overruling *Palko*; the eighth amendment prohibition on "cruel and unusual punishment," Robinson v. California, 370 U.S. 660 (1962); and the eighth amendment prohibition on "excessive" bail, Schilb v. Kuebel, 404 U.S. 357 (1971). The only provisions of the first eight amendments that have not been

incorporated are the second and third amendments, the fifth amendment's requirement of grand jury indictment, and the seventh amendment.

Within the American public, if not now within American courts, there is much controversy over whether the second amendment is or should be incorporated. Is the individual right to bear arms fundamental? In what sense? Is it an individual right at all? Recall Amar's view that the incorporation question is whether an individual right or right of the public as a whole is at stake. What is the answer for the second amendment? See A. Amar, The Bill of Rights (1998), for discussion.

2. *Incorporation "jot-for-jot."* Prior to the 1960s, there were frequent suggestions that, even if a specific guarantee of the bill of rights was incorporated in the due process clause of the fourteenth amendment, it did not necessarily apply to the states in the same manner as it applied to the federal government. In Wolf v. Colorado, 338 U.S. 25 (1949), for example, the Court held that the "security of one's privacy against arbitrary intrusion by the police — which is at the core of the fourth amendment — is basic to a free society" and "is therefore implicit in 'the concept of ordered liberty' and as such enforceable against the States through the Due Process Clause." Nonetheless, the Court refused to apply the exclusionary rule, which was applicable to the federal government, to the states. Similarly, in Roth v. United States, 354 U.S. 476 (1957), Justice Harlan argued that the first amendment imposed fewer limits on state regulation of obscenity than it did on federal regulation.

As illustrated by *Duncan*, however, by the 1960s the Court had reached the conclusion that the guarantees of the bill of rights that were "selectively" incorporated in the due process clause of the fourteenth amendment should apply to the states in *precisely* the same manner as they applied to the federal government. See also Malloy v. Hogan, 378 U.S. 1 (1964) (self-incrimination); Pointer v. Texas, 380 U.S. 400 (1965) (confrontation); Benton v. Maryland, 395 U.S. 784 (1969) (double jeopardy). See also Williams v. Florida, 399 U.S. 78 (1970) ("the twelve-man panel is not a necessary ingredient of 'trial by jury'"); Apodaca v. Oregon, 406 U.S. 404 (1972) (upholding the constitutionality of less-than-unanimous jury verdicts in state criminal cases); Crist v. Bretz, 437 U.S. 28, 52-53 (1978) (Powell, J., joined by Burger, C.J., and Rehnquist, J., dissenting) (arguing that the fourteenth amendment does not "necessarily" impose on the states particular aspects of the fifth amendment's prohibition on "double jeopardy").

3. *Evaluation.* Consider Israel, Selective Incorporation Revisited, 71 Geo. L.J. 253, 336-338 (1982):

Over the years [the Court's incorporation] opinions [have] referred largely to five concerns: (1) adhering to the language of the amendment and the intent of its framers; (2) avoiding vague standards that invite the Justices to apply their own subjective and idiosyncratic views of basic justice; (3) providing broad protection of individual liberties against state systems too often willing to sacrifice those [liberties]; (4) giving appropriate recognition to the principles of federalism; and (5) providing sufficient direction to state courts to gain consistent enforcement of federal constitutional [standards]. Perhaps no concern has been mentioned more frequently than the first, [but] neither the language nor the history has proven especially [confining]. [In] the end, the fifth concern [may] have proven the most significant, [for selective incorporation's relative clarity] may do more to promote a vital federalist system than [an approach that] gives the state slightly greater leeway at the fringes.

D.   SUBSTANTIVE DUE PROCESS: THE PROTECTION OF ECONOMIC INTERESTS AND THE PROBLEM OF "REDISTRIBUTION"

The Constitution contains several provisions that expressly restrict government's power to interfere with market ordering and the private economic interests of individuals. The fifth and fourteenth amendments, for example, provide that "[n]o person shall [be] deprived of [property,] without due process of law." Article I, section 10 provides that "[n]o State shall [pass] any [Law] impairing the Obligation of Contracts." And the fifth amendment provides that "private property" shall not "be taken for public use, without just compensation." Although these provisions reflect the importance of private property, they have usually been understood to protect private economic interests only against certain narrowly defined forms of government interference. See section H infra. Is there a more general constitutional limitation on the power of government to interfere with private economic decisions?

In its 1905 decision in Lochner v. New York, infra, the Court held that the due process clauses of the fifth and fourteenth amendments protect liberty of contract and private property against unwarranted government interference. The *Lochner* period has played a major role in defining the appropriate place of the Court in American government. This section traces the rise — and fall — of this exceptionally important doctrine.

Note: *The Road to* Lochner

1. *Early intimations.* Although the doctrine of economic substantive process did not come into full flower until the Court's 1905 decision in *Lochner*, several pre-*Lochner* decisions flirted with analogous doctrines. In Calder v. Bull, Chapter 1, section C, supra, more than a century before *Lochner*, Justice Chase's "natural law" theory clearly reflected a concern with property rights, and in Fletcher v. Peck, 10 U.S. (6 Cranch) 87 (1810), in which the Court held that a state legislature could not constitutionally rescind land grants to individuals who had purchased the land in good faith, Chief Justice Marshall explained that the result was justified both by the contract clause and "by general principles which are common to our free institutions." In Wynehamer v. People, 13 N.Y. 378 (1856), the New York Court of Appeals relied expressly on the state due process clause in invalidating a liquor prohibition statute that prohibited the use or possession even of liquor owned prior to the enactment of the statute. The New York court explained that, when "a law annihilates the value of property, [the] owner is deprived of it [within] the spirit of a constitutional provision intended expressly to shield private rights from the exercise of arbitrary power." A year after *Wynehamer*, in Dred Scott v. Sanford, 60 U.S. (19 How.) 393 (1857), the Court held that Congress could not prohibit slavery in the territories. The Court observed, without explanation, that an "act of Congress which deprives a citizen of the United States of his liberty or property, merely because he came himself or brought his property into a particular [Territory,] could hardly be dignified with the name of due process of law."

These intermittent intimations of economic substantive due process did not seriously challenge the prevailing view that the due process guarantee was essentially *procedural* in nature. See Den ex dem. Murray v. Hoboken Land & Improvement Co., 59 U.S. (18 How.) 272 (1856). Moreover, in The Slaughter-House Cases, the Court held not only that the Louisiana statute did not violate the privileges or immunities clause of the fourteenth amendment but also that it did not violate the fourteenth amendment due process clause. The Court explained that "under no construction of that provision we have ever seen, or any that we deem admissible, can the restraint imposed by the State of Louisiana upon the exercise of their trade by the butchers of New Orleans be held to be a deprivation of property within the meaning of that provision."

The (ambiguous) sentence in *Slaughter-House* did not end the matter, however. As Professor Corwin, a leading commentator on the era, observed: "In less than twenty years from the time of its rendition, the crucial ruling in *Wynehamer* [was] far on the way to being assimilated into the accepted constitutional law of the country. The 'due process' clause, which had been intended originally to consecrate a mode of procedure, had become a constitutional test of ever increasing reach of the substantive content of legislation." E. Corwin, Liberty against Government 114 (1948). See Corwin, The Doctrine of Due Process before the Civil War, 24 Harv. L. Rev. 366, 460 (1911); Corwin, The Basic Doctrine of American Constitutional Law, 12 Mich. L. Rev. 247 (1914); Corwin, The "Higher Law" Background of American Constitutional Law, 42 Harv. L. Rev. 149, 365 (1928-1929).

2. *Lochner's antecedents.* The shift identified by Professor Corwin was directed, in part, by economic and social developments. The rise of industrial organization in the late nineteenth century transformed American society. As ownership of productive property became increasingly concentrated, inequalities in private economic power grew sharper, and the number of persons without significant productive property and dependent on industrial employment increased. As the twentieth century approached, state legislatures began to address the conditions accompanying the concentration of private power in business. Opponents of the new regulatory laws maintained that "fundamental" rights of property were not being respected by the popularly controlled state legislatures. See, e.g., C. Tiedeman, A Treatise on the Limitations of the Police Power in the United States (1886). They also claimed that such laws would in the end help well-organized interest groups, like unions, without helping workers as a whole. Thus, for example, the minimum wage was said to be a way of increasing unemployment, thus harming some of the most vulnerable members of society, at the same time that it was said to invade the fundamental right of workers and employers to reach agreements on whatever terms they freely chose.

Armed with the laissez-faire doctrines of the eighteenth-century economist Adam Smith and the nineteenth-century social darwinist Herbert Spencer, and supported by the leading constitutional law text of the period, Thomas M. Cooley's Constitutional Limitations (1868), legal representatives of the regulated industries increasingly urged the courts to invalidate the new legislation.

In Munn v. Illinois, 94 U.S. 113 (1877), the Court held that an Illinois law fixing the maximum charges for grain-storage warehouses did not violate the due process clause of the fourteenth amendment. The Court noted, however, that "under some circumstances," such statutes may violate due process. The critical inquiry was whether the "private property is 'affected with a public interest,' [for when] one devotes his property to a use in which the public has an interest, he, in effect, grants to the public an interest in that use, and must submit to be controlled by the public for the common good." The Court held that the businesses regulated in *Munn* were clearly "affected with a public interest," for they had a "virtual monopoly" on the storage of grain bound from the Midwest to national and international markets. In such circumstances, the Court would not consider the "reasonableness" of the rates.

By the late 1880s, a decade after *Munn* and some fifteen years after *Slaughter-House*, the make-up of the Court had changed almost completely, and the new appointees were increasingly inclined to use the due process clause to protect substantive rights of property. Whether this shift was due to the justices' conservative economic policies, see A. Paul, Conservative Crisis and the Rule of Law (1969), their hostility to labor regulations, see L. Beth, The Development of the American Constitution 1877-1917, at 138-168 (1971), or their acceptance of the liberty-based, antigovernment, "free labor" jurisprudence of the antislavery movement, see Nelson, The Impact of the Antislavery Movement upon Styles of Judicial Reasoning in Nineteenth Century America, 87 Harv. L. Rev. 513, 547-566 (1974), the shift in judicial attitude was evident.

In the Railroad Commission Cases, 116 U.S. 307 (1886), the Court sustained state regulation of railroad rates but emphasized that there was a limit to judicial deference: "[The] power to regulate is not a power to [destroy]. Under pretence of regulating fares and freights, the State cannot require a railroad corporation to carry persons or property without reward; neither can it do that which in law amounts to a taking of private property for public use without just compensation, or without due process of law."

Later that same year, in Santa Clara County v. Southern Pacific Railroad, 116 U.S. 394 (1886), the Court held, without argument, that corporations were "persons" within the meaning of the due process clause of the fourteenth amendment, thus opening the door for direct challenges to regulations by corporations. See Graham, The "Conspiracy Theory" of the Fourteenth Amendment, 47 Yale L.J. 371 (1938). The following year, in Mugler v. Kansas, 123 U.S. 623 (1887), the Court upheld a state law prohibiting the sale of alcoholic beverages but again cautioned that not every regulatory measure "is to be accepted as a legitimate exertion of the police powers of the State." In The Minnesota Rate Case (Chicago, Milwaukee & St. Paul Railway v. Minnesota), 134 U.S. 418 (1890), the Court held unconstitutional a state statute authorizing a commission to set final and unreviewable railroad rates, thus marking the first time that the Court relied directly on the due process clause to invalidate a state economic regulation. The Court explained that "[t]he question of reasonableness of a rate of charge for transportation by a railroad company [is] eminently a question for judicial investigation, requiring due process of law for its determination." By the end of the decade, the Court was actively in the business of reviewing the reasonableness of rates. See Smith v. Ames, 169 U.S. 466 (1898) (establishing the rule that rates must yield a fair return on a fair present value); Federal Power Commission v. Hope Natural Gas Co., 320 U.S. 591 (1944) (tracing the evolution and eventual repudiation of the rule of Smith v. Ames); Siegel, Understanding the *Lochner* Era: Lessons from the Controversy over Railroad and Utility Rate Regulation, 70 Va. L. Rev. 187 (1984).

In Allgeyer v. Louisiana, 165 U.S. 578 (1897), the Court took the final step toward *Lochner*. In *Allgeyer*, the Court invalidated a state statute that prohibited any person from issuing insurance on property in the state with companies that had not been admitted to do business in the state. Although Justice Peckham, writing for a unanimous Court, focused primarily on state power over foreign corporations, he also offered a comprehensive articulation of the "liberty of contract":

> The liberty mentioned in [the due process clause] means not only the right of the citizen to be free from the mere physical restraint of his person, as by incarceration, but the term is deemed to embrace the right of the citizen to be free in the enjoyment of all his faculties; to be free to use them in all lawful ways; to live and work where he will; to earn his livelihood by any lawful calling; to pursue any livelihood or avocation, and for that purpose to enter into all contracts which may be proper, necessary and essential to his carrying out to a successful conclusion the purposes mentioned above. [In] the privilege of pursuing an ordinary calling or trade and of acquiring, holding and selling property must be embraced the right to make all proper contracts in relation thereto, and although it may be conceded that this right to contract [or] to do business within the jurisdiction of the State may be regulated and sometimes prohibited when the contracts or business conflict with the policy of the State as contained in its statutes, yet the power does not and cannot extend to prohibiting a citizen from making contracts of the nature involved in this case outside of the limits and jurisdiction of the State, and which are also to be performed outside of such jurisdiction.

Lochner v. New York

198 U.S. 45 (1905)

MR. JUSTICE PECKHAM [delivered] the opinion of the Court.

[The Court held unconstitutional a New York statute providing that no employee shall "work in a biscuit, bread or cake bakery or confectionary establishment more than sixty hours in any one week, or more than ten hours in any one day."]

The statute necessarily interferes with the right of contract between the employer and employes, concerning the number of hours in which the latter may labor in the bakery of the employer. The general right to make a contract in relation to his business is part of the liberty of the individual protected by the Fourteenth Amendment of the Federal Constitution. [*Allgeyer*.] Under that provision no State can deprive any person of life, liberty or property without due process of law. The right to purchase or to sell labor is part of the liberty protected by this amendment, unless there are circumstances which exclude the right. There are, however, certain powers, existing in the sovereignty of each State in the Union, somewhat vaguely termed police powers, the exact description and limitation of which have not been attempted by the courts. Those powers [relate] to the safety, health, morals and general welfare of the public. Both property and liberty are held on such reasonable conditions as may be imposed by the governing power of the State in the exercise of those powers, and with such conditions the Fourteenth Amendment was not designed to interfere. [*Mugler*.]

This court has recognized the existence and upheld the exercise of the police powers of the States in many cases. [Among] the [cases] where the state law has been upheld by this court is that of Holden v. Hardy, 169 U.S. 366 [1898]. A provision in the act of the legislature of Utah was there under consideration, the act limiting the employment of workmen in all underground mines or workings, to eight hours per day, "except in cases of emergency, where life or property is in imminent danger." [The] act was held to be a valid exercise of the police powers of the State. [It] was held that the kind of employment [and] the character of the employes [were] such as to make it reasonable and proper for the State to interfere to prevent the employes from being constrained by the rules laid down by the proprietors in regard to labor. [There] is nothing in Holden v. Hardy which covers the case now before us. . . .

It must, of course, be conceded that there is a limit to the valid exercise of the police power by the State. There is no dispute concerning this general proposition. Otherwise the Fourteenth Amendment would have no efficacy and the legislatures of the States would have unbounded power. [In] every case that comes before this court, therefore, where legislation of this character is concerned and where the protection of the Federal Constitution is sought, the question necessarily arises: Is this a fair, reasonable and appropriate exercise of the police power of the State, or is it an unreasonable, unnecessary and arbitrary interference with the right of the individual to his personal liberty or to enter into those contracts in relation to labor which may seem to him appropriate or necessary for the support of himself and his family? Of course the liberty of contract relating to labor includes both parties to it. The one has as much right to purchase as the other to sell labor.

This is not a question of substituting the judgment of the court for that of the legislature. If the act be within the power of the State it is valid, although the judgment of the court might be totally opposed to the enactment of such a law. But the question would still remain: Is it within the police power of the State? and that question must be answered by the court.

The question whether this act is valid as a labor law, pure and simple, may be dismissed in a few words. There is no reasonable ground for interfering with the liberty of person or the right of free contract, by determining the hours of labor, in the occupation of a baker. There is no contention that bakers as a class are not equal in intelligence and capacity to men in other trades or manual occupations, or that they are not able to assert their rights and care for themselves without the protecting arm of the State, interfering with their independence of judgment and of action. They are in no sense wards of the State. Viewed in the light of a purely labor law, with no reference whatever to the question of health, we think that a law like the one before us involves neither the safety, the morals nor the welfare of the public, and that the interest of the public is not in the slightest degree affected by such an act. The law must be upheld, if at all, as a law pertaining to the health of the individual engaged in the occupation of a baker. It does not affect any other portion of the public than those who are engaged in that occupation. Clean and wholesome bread does not depend upon whether the baker works but ten hours per day or only sixty hours a week. . . .

It is a question of which of two powers or rights shall prevail — the power of the State to legislate or the right of the individual to liberty of person and freedom of contract. The mere assertion that the subject relates though but in a remote degree to the public health does not necessarily render the enactment valid. The act must have a more direct relation, as a means to an end, and the end itself must be appropriate and legitimate, before an act can be held to be valid which interferes with the general right of an individual to be free in his person and in his power to contract in relation to his own labor. . . .

We think the limit of the police power has been reached and passed in this case. There is, in our judgment, no reasonable foundation for holding this to be necessary or appropriate as a health law to safeguard the public health or the health of the individuals who are following the trade of a baker. If this statute be valid, [there] would seem to be no length to which legislation of this nature might not go. . . .

We think that there can be no fair doubt that the trade of a baker, in and of it-self, is not an unhealthy one to that degree which would authorize the legislature to interfere with the right to labor, and with the right of free contract on the part of the individual, either as employer or employé. In looking through statistics re-garding all trades and occupations, it may be true that the trade of a baker does not appear to be as healthy as some other trades, and is also vastly more healthy than still others. To the common understanding the trade of a baker has never been regarded as an unhealthy one. [It] might be safely affirmed that almost all occupations more or less affect the health. There must be more than the mere fact of the possible existence of some small amount of unhealthiness to warrant legislative interference with liberty. It is unfortunately true that labor, even in any department, may possibly carry with it the seeds of unhealthiness. But are we all, on that account, at the mercy of legislative majorities? . . .

It is also urged, pursuing the same line of argument, that it is to the interest of the State that its population should be strong and robust, and therefore any leg-islation which may be said to tend to make people healthy must be valid as health laws, enacted under the police power. If this be a valid argument and a justifi-cation for this kind of legislation, it follows that the protection of the Federal Con-stitution from undue interference with liberty of person and freedom of contract is visionary, wherever the law is sought to be justified as a valid exercise of the po-lice power. Scarcely any law but might find shelter under such assumptions. . . . Not only the hours of employes, but the hours of employers, could be regulated, and doctors, lawyers, scientists, all professional men, as well as athletes and arti-sans, could be forbidden to fatigue their brains and bodies by prolonged hours of exercise, lest the fighting strength of the State be impaired. We mention these ex-treme cases because the contention is extreme. We do not believe in the sound-ness of the views which uphold this law. [The] act is not, within any fair meaning of the term, a health law, but is an illegal interference with the rights of individ-uals, both employers and employes, to make contracts regarding labor upon such terms as they may think best, or which they may agree upon with the other parties to such contracts. Statutes of the nature of that under review, limiting the hours in which grown and intelligent men may labor to earn their living, are mere med-dlesome interferences with the rights of the individual, and they are not saved from condemnation by the claim that they are passed in the exercise of the po-lice power and upon the subject of the health of the individual whose rights are interfered with, unless there be some fair ground, reasonable in and of itself, to say that there is material danger to the public health or to the health of the employ-ees, if the hours of labor are not curtailed. [All that the State] could properly do has been done by it with regard to the conduct of bakeries, as provided for in the other sections of the act, [which] provide for the inspection of the premises where the bakery is carried on, with regard to furnishing proper wash-rooms and water-closets, [with] regard to providing proper drainage, plumbing and painting [and] for other things of that nature. . . .

It was further urged [that] restricting the hours of labor in the case of bakers was valid because it tended to cleanliness on the part of the workers, as a man was more apt to be cleanly when not overworked, and if cleanly then his "output" was also more likely to be so. [In] our judgment it is not possible in fact to discover the connection between the number of hours a baker may work in the bakery and the healthful quality of the bread made by the workman. The connection, if any exists, is too shadowy and thin to build any argument for the interference of the legislature. [When] assertions such as we have adverted to become necessary in order to give, if possible, a plausible foundation for the contention that the law is a "health law," it gives rise to at least a suspicion that there was some other motive dominating the legislature than the purpose to subserve the public health or welfare.

This interference on the part of the legislatures of the several States with the ordinary trades and occupations of the people seems to be on the increase. . . .

It is impossible for us to shut our eyes to the fact that many of the laws of this character, while passed under what is claimed to be the police power for the purpose of protecting the public health or welfare, are, in reality, passed from other motives. We are justified in saying so when, from the character of the law and the subject upon which it legislates, it is apparent that the public health or welfare bears but the most remote relation to the law. The purpose of a statute must be determined from the natural and legal effect of the language employed; and whether it is or is not repugnant to the Constitution of the United States must be determined from the natural effect of such statutes when put into operation, and not from their proclaimed purpose. [The] court looks beyond the mere letter of the law in such cases. Yick Wo v. Hopkins, 118 U.S. 356.

It is manifest to us that the [law here] has no such direct relation to and no such substantial effect upon the health of the employe, as to justify us in regarding the section as really a health law. It seems to us that the real object and purpose were simply to regulate the hours of labor between the master and his employes (all being men, sui juris), in a private business, not dangerous in any degree to morals or in any real and substantial degree, to the health of the employes. Under such circumstances the freedom of master and employe to contract with each other in relation to their employment [cannot] be prohibited or interfered with, without violating the Federal Constitution. . . .

Reversed.

MR. JUSTICE HARLAN, with whom MR. JUSTICE WHITE and MR. JUSTICE DAY concurred, dissenting. . . .

[The] statute must be taken as expressing the belief of the people of New York that, as a general rule, and in the case of the average man, labor in excess of sixty hours during a week in such establishments may endanger the health of those who thus labor. Whether or not this be wise legislation it is not the province of the court to inquire. Under our systems of government the courts are not concerned with the wisdom or policy of legislation. So that in determining the question of power to interfere with liberty of contract, the court may inquire whether the means devised by the State are germane to an end which may be lawfully accomplished and have a real or substantial relation to the protection of health, as involved in the daily work of the persons, male and female, engaged in bakery and confectionery establishments. But when this inquiry is entered upon I find it impossible, in view of common experience, to say that there is here no real or substantial relation between the means employed by the State and the end sought to be accomplished by its legislation. . . .

Professor Hirt in his treatise on the "Diseases of the Workers" has said:

The labor of the bakers is among the hardest and most laborious imaginable, because it has to be performed under conditions injurious to the health of those engaged in it. It is hard, very hard work, not only because it requires a great deal of physical exertion in an overheated workshop and during unreasonably long hours, but more so because of the erratic demands of the public, compelling the baker to perform the greater part of his work at night, thus depriving him of an opportunity to enjoy the necessary rest and sleep, a fact which is highly injurious to his health.

Another writer says:

The constant inhaling of flour dust causes inflammation of the lungs and of the bronchial tubes. The eyes also suffer through this dust. . . . The long hours of toil to which all bakers are subjected produce rheumatism, cramps and swollen legs. The intense heat in the workshops [is] another source of a number of diseases of various organs. [The] average age of a baker is below that of other workmen; they seldom live over their fiftieth year, most of them dying between the ages of forty and fifty. . . .

We judicially know that the question of the number of hours during which a workman should continuously labor has been, for a long period, and is yet, a subject of serious consideration among civilized peoples, and by those having special knowledge of the laws of health. . . .

We also judicially know that the number of hours that should constitute a day's labor in particular occupations involving the physical strength and safety of workmen has been the subject of enactments by Congress and by nearly all of the States. Many, if not most, of those enactments fix eight hours as the proper basis of a day's labor.

I do not stop to consider whether any particular view of this economic question presents the sounder theory. What the precise facts are it may be difficult to say. It is enough for the determination of this case, and it is enough for this court to know, that the question is one about which there is room for debate and for an honest difference of opinion. There are many reasons of a weighty, substantial character, based upon the experience of mankind, in support of the theory that, all things considered, more than ten hours' steady work each day, from week to week, in a bakery or confectionery establishment, may endanger the health, and shorten the lives of the workmen, thereby diminishing their physical and mental capacity to serve the State, and to provide for those dependent upon them.

If such reasons exist that ought to be the end of this case, for the State is not amenable to the judiciary, in respect of its legislative enactments, unless such enactments are plainly, palpably, beyond all question inconsistent with the Constitution of the United States. . . .

MR. JUSTICE HOLMES dissenting. . . .

This case is decided upon an economic theory which a large part of the country does not entertain. If it were a question whether I agreed with that theory,

I should desire to study it further and long before making up my mind. But I do not conceive that to be my duty, because I strongly believe that my agreement or disagreement has nothing to do with the right of a majority to embody their opinions in law. It is settled by various decisions of this court that state constitutions and state laws may regulate life in many ways which we as legislators might think as injudicious or if you like as tyrannical as this, and which equally with this interfere with the liberty to contract. Sunday laws and usury laws are ancient examples. A more modern one is the prohibition of lotteries. The liberty of the citizen to do as he likes so long as he does not interfere with the liberty of others to do the same, which has been a shibboleth for some well-known writers, is interfered with by school laws, by the Post Office, by every state or municipal institution which takes his money for purposes thought desirable, whether he likes it or not. The Fourteenth Amendment does not enact Mr. Herbert Spencer's Social Statics. The other day we sustained the Massachusetts vaccination law. Jacobson v. Massachusetts, 197 U.S. 11. United States and state statutes and decisions cutting down the liberty to contract by way of combination are familiar to this court. [The] decision sustaining an eight hour law for miners is still recent. [Holden v. Hardy.] Some of these laws embody convictions or prejudices which judges are likely to share. Some may not. But a constitution is not intended to embody a particular economic theory, whether of paternalism and the organic relation of the citizen to the State or of laissez faire. It is made for people of fundamentally differing views, and the accident of our finding certain opinions natural and familiar or novel and even shocking ought not to conclude our judgment upon the question whether statutes embodying them conflict with the Constitution of the United States.

General propositions do not decide concrete cases. The decision will depend on a judgment or intuition more subtle than any articulate major premise. But I think that the proposition just stated, if it is accepted, will carry us far toward the end. Every opinion tends to become a law. I think that the word liberty in the Fourteenth Amendment is perverted when it is held to prevent the natural outcome of a dominant opinion, unless it can be said that a rational and fair man necessarily would admit that the statute proposed would infringe fundamental principles as they have been understood by the traditions of our people and our law. It does not need research to show that no such sweeping condemnation can be passed upon the statute before us. A reasonable man might think it a proper measure on the score of health. Men whom I certainly could not pronounce unreasonable would uphold it as a first instalment of a general regulation of the hours of work. . . .

Note: The (Alleged?) Vices of Lochner

Lochner "is one of the most condemned cases in United States history and has been used to symbolize judicial dereliction and abuse." B. Siegan, Economic Liberties and the Constitution 23 (1980). But people have differed in their explanation of *why* the decision should be condemned; not everyone is sure that it should be condemned; and in the different reactions to Lochner can be found the most important positions on the largest questions of constitutional law and theory.

Consider the following criticisms:

1. *The "liberty of contract" protected in* Lochner *is not within the "liberty" protected by the due process clause.* In *Allgeyer,* the Court announced that the "'liberty' mentioned in [the due process clause] is deemed to embrace the right [to] make all proper contracts." This view has been disputed. Consider Warren, The New "Liberty" under the Fourteenth Amendment, 39 Harv. L. Rev. 431, 440 (1926):

> The phrase, "life, liberty or property without due process of law" came to us from the English common law; and there seems to be little question that, under the common law, the word "liberty" meant simply "liberty of the person," or, in other words, "the right to have one's person free from physical restraint." [It] is unquestionable that when the First Congress adopted the Fifth Amendment and inserted the Due Process Clause, they took it with the meaning it then bore.

Perhaps Warren's conception of "liberty" is too narrow. It would exclude all rights except the right not to be locked up, and if the Civil Rights Act of 1866 was the provision whose constitutionality the fourteenth amendment was designed to make secure, a wide range of rights, including the right to make contracts, should be comprehended within the category of "liberty." Should the "liberty of contract" protected in *Lochner* be based not in the "liberty" component of the due process clause but in its "property" component? See Coppage v. Kansas, 236 U.S. 1 (1915) ("included in the right [of] personal property [is] the right to make contracts").

2. *Even if the "liberty of contract" is a "liberty" or "property" protected by the due process clause, that clause does not accord "substantive" protection to the "liberty of contract."* First, one might argue (naturally enough) that the due process clause is concerned exclusively with "procedure," and thus has no relevance to the statute at issue in *Lochner.* "Substantive due process," it has been argued, "is a contradiction in terms — sort of like 'green pastel redness.'" J. Ely, Democracy and Distrust 18 (1980). Note, however, that "the words that follow 'due process' are 'of law,' and the word 'law' seems to have been the textual point of departure for substantive due process." Tribe, The Puzzling Persistence of Process-Based Constitutional Theories, 89 Yale L.J. 1063, 1066 n.9 (1980).

Second, one might argue that the due process clause accords substantive protection to all "fundamental" rights, but that the "liberty of contract" is not "fundamental." Under this view, "the error of [*Lochner*] lay not in judicial intervention to protect 'liberty' but in a misguided understanding of what liberty actually required." L. Tribe, American Constitutional Law 564 (1978).

Is the "liberty of contract" a "fundamental" right? Consider Siegan, supra, at 83:

> A free society cannot exist unless government is prohibited from confiscating private property. If government can seize something owned by a private citizen, it can exert enormous power over people. One would be reluctant to speak, write, pray, or petition in a manner displeasing to the authorities lest he lose what he has already earned and possesses. As [Alexander] Hamilton stated, a power over a man's subsistence amounts to a power over his will.

The historical commitment to the "liberty of contract" and to rights of property runs deep: "[In the view of the Framers,] a major function of government was protecting and preserving property rights. [The] Framers probably subscribed to

Blackstone's definition that the right of property is 'absolute . . . [and] consists in the free use, enjoyment and disposal [by man] of all his acquisitions, without any control or diminution, save only by the laws of the land.'" Siegan, supra, at 30-31. See also R. Epstein, Takings (1985). Moreover, in Calder v. Bull, Justice Chase maintained that "natural law" prohibits "a law that destroys or impairs the lawful private contracts of citizens [or] that takes property from A. and gives it to B." In Corfield v. Coryell, 6 F. Cas. 546 (1823), a decision recognized by all of the justices participating in *Slaughter-House* as defining the "fundamental" rights of individuals, Justice Washington declared that the "fundamental" privileges and immunities of individuals include the "right [to] take, hold and dispose of property." The Civil Rights Act of 1866, which provided the impetus for the fourteenth amendment, expressly protected the right of blacks "to make and enforce contracts [and to] purchase, lease, sell, hold and convey real and personal property."

3. *The means/ends connection: Even if the "liberty of contract" is entitled to "substantive" protection under the due process clause, the statute at issue in Loch-ner was justified by the state's interest in protecting the health of bakery employees.* In his opinion for the Court, Justice Peckham declared that, for the statute to be "saved from condemnation," there must "be some fair ground, reasonable in and of itself, to say that there is material danger to the public health or to the health of the employes, if the hours of labor are not curtailed." But perhaps this standard is too stringent. Perhaps the Court should have sustained the law because, as Justice Harlan observed, "the question is one about which there is room for debate and for an honest difference of opinion." Even if one assumes that Justice Peckham stated the appropriate standard, why weren't the data offered by Justice Harlan sufficient to satisfy that standard?

The Court's careful examination of the means/ends connection might be criticized on two grounds. The first is that judges do not have the fact-finding competence to engage in such inquiries; the second is that judges are unelected and therefore lack the accountability that would support such a role. Note, however, that careful examination of the means/ends connection is a common feature of modern constitutional law. Recall, for example, the Court's analysis of "suspect" classifications under the equal protection clause. See Chapter 5 supra.

Note that in Muller v. Oregon, 208 U.S. 412 (1908), the Court sustained against due process attack an Oregon statute forbidding the employment of women "in any mechanical establishment, or factory, or laundry" for more than ten hours in any one day because the extensive evidence marshaled by Louis D. Brandeis in his "factual" brief convinced the Court that there was ample justification for the "widespread belief that woman's physical structure, and the functions she performs in consequence thereof, justify special legislation restricting or qualifying the conditions under which she should be permitted to toil." On the "Brandeis brief," see P. Freund, On Understanding the Supreme Court 86-91 (1949); Bikle, Judicial Determination of Questions of Fact Affecting the Constitutional Validity of Legislative Action, 38 Harv. L. Rev. 6 (1924); Karst, Legislative Facts in Constitutional Litigation, 1960 Sup. Ct. Rev. 75. Is *Muller* explainable on the ground that the Court regarded women as a dependent class analogous to children or workers in mining camps? Recall the discussion of gender discrimination in Chapter 5, section D, supra.

4. *The problem of ends: Even if the "liberty of contract" is entitled to "substantive" protection under the due process clause, the statute at issue in* Lochner *was*

justified as a "labor law, pure and simple." Why wasn't the New York statute justified as a means of compensating for the unequal bargaining position of bakery workers? Here, the Court seems to have ruled redistributive regulation off limits. There are indeed problems with "unequal bargaining power" as an argument for government regulation; such regulation may make workers even worse off; the minimum wage, for example, may increase unemployment. What is especially notable is that the Court dismissed the "labor law" justification, unlike the health justification, as an effort to further an illegitimate end. What made this purpose illegitimate? Consider the following observations.

a. Coppage v. Kansas, 236 U.S. 1, 17-18 (1915):

[It] is said [that] "employees, as a rule, are not financially able to be as independent in making contracts for the sale of their labor as are employers in making contracts of purchase thereof." No doubt, wherever the right of private property exists, there must and will be inequalities of fortune. [Thus, it is] impossible to uphold freedom of contract and the right of private property without at the same time recognizing as legitimate those inequalities of fortune that are the necessary result of the exercise of those rights. [And] since a State may not strike [those rights] down directly it is clear that it may not do so indirectly, as by declaring in effect that the public good requires the removal of those inequalities that are but the normal and inevitable result of their [exercise]. The police power is broad, [but] it cannot be given the wide scope that is here asserted for it, without in effect nullifying the constitutional guaranty.

b. Sunstein, Naked Preferences and the Constitution, 84 Colum. L. Rev. 1689, 1697, 1718 (1984):

In the *Lochner* era, the Court attempted to create a separate category of impermissible ends, using the libertarian framework of the common law as a theoretical basis. Under that framework, the government's police power was sharply limited, and modern social legislation [appeared] not as an effort to promote a public value, but instead as a raw exercise of political power by the beneficiaries of the legislation. But the theoretical basis of the *Lochner* era [is undermined once one recognizes] that the market status quo [is] itself the product of government choices. [Once it becomes] clear that harms produced by the marketplace [are themselves] the products of public choices, efforts to alleviate those harms [must] be regarded as permissible exercises of government power.

c. Siegan, supra, at 123-124:

[Judges] who had received their education [during] the Civil War era viewed labor [in light of the antislavery tradition]. Freedom of contract for both employer and employee was strongly espoused by the antislavery movement. It was accepted that the right of the individual to bestow his labor as he pleased was among the rights for which the Civil War had been fought. [Accordingly, the Court's] contention [that] government has no legitimate interest in [protecting labor] was far less controversial than contemporary generations might suppose. The Court believed that the labor market itself would operate to support the welfare of both workers and employers.

For evaluations of this "belief," compare Kennedy, Distributive and Paternalistic Motives in Contract and Tort Law, with Special Reference to Compulsory

Terms and Unequal Bargaining Power, 41 Md. L. Rev. 563 (1982) with Epstein, A Common Law for Labor Relations: A Critique of the New Deal Labor Legislation, 92 Yale L.J. 1357 (1983). Note that redistributive regulation will not in fact simply transfer resources from employers to employees. A minimum wage law might at least to some extent increase unemployment, thus hurting especially vulnerable members of society; and a maximum hour law will hurt at least some workers who would much prefer to continue to work rather than to have increased leisure.

5. Lochner *and the political process.* Consider the following arguments.

a. *Lochner* is defensible in terms of "representation-reinforcement." There are circumstances in which statutes owe their existence primarily to the organized power of special interest groups and are enacted even though the majority does not approve of them and even though the majority may be harmed by their operation. Indeed, the theory of "public choice" postulates certain conditions in which even a properly functioning democratic process will frequently thwart majority values. See Stigler, The Theory of Economic Regulation, 2 Bell J. Econ. & Mgmt. Sci. 3 (1971). The theory of "public choice" is examined in more detail in the context of the dormant commerce clause. See Chapter 3, section A, supra.

In *Lochner* itself, the New York statute was at least arguably the product of a political process in which labor unions had an organizational advantage (1) over consumers, who would ultimately pay for the regulation through higher prices for bread, and (2) over nonunionized, frequently immigrant workers who were willing or even eager to accept long-hour jobs in unregulated transactions with employers. Moreover, large employers and those already engaged in collective bargaining with unions had little incentive to oppose the legislation, for it simply imposed on all bakers regulations that had already been extracted in collective bargaining from some. In such circumstances, the unions were able, through maximum hour laws, to capture the legislative process to the disadvantage of the majority and to the disadvantage of otherwise competitive immigrant labor as well. The Court acted appropriately to rectify this defect in the operation of the representative process. For description of the political circumstances surrounding the adoption of the New York legislation, see Siegan, supra, at 116-118; Tarrow, Lochner versus New York: A Political Analysis, 5 Lab. Hist. 277 (1964).

b. *Lochner* was wrongly decided because, as Justice Holmes recognized, the political process is inevitably a process of unprincipled compromises among competing social groups. Indeed, most "public policies are better explained as the outcome of a pure power struggle — clothed in a rhetoric of public interest that is a mere figleaf — among narrow interest or pressure groups." Posner, The *DeFunis* Case and the Constitutionality of Preferential Treatment of Racial Minorities, 1974 Sup. Ct. Rev. 1, 27. The due process clause cannot logically prohibit legislatures from passing laws merely because powerful groups want and press for them. Such an approach would ultimately prove counterproductive, for, if the courts prevent powerful groups from having their way in the legislative process, the political pressures will be bottled up and eventually emerge in even more destructive forms elsewhere.

Consider the view that Justice Holmes's position in *Lochner* was closely tied to his general acceptance of social darwinism: "What proximate test of excellence can be found except correspondence to the actual equilibrium of force in the community — that is, conformity to the wishes of the dominant power. Of course, such conformity may lead to destruction, and it is desirable that the dominant power be wise. But wise or not, the proximate test of a good government is that the dominant power has its way." Justice Oliver Wendell Holmes: His Book Notices and Uncollected Letters and Papers 250 (H. C. Shriver ed. 1936). See generally Rogat, Mr. Justice Holmes: Some Modern Views — The Judge as Spectator, 31 U. Chi. L. Rev. 213 (1964).

6. *Summary.* Objections to the *Lochner* decision generally fall into two camps. Some are *institutional* and emphasize that the Court overstepped its bounds in relation to the legislature. These objections focus on the Court's careful scrutiny of the means/ends connection and on its willingness to declare certain legislative ends impermissible. The problem here is that the Court interfered in a realm of policymaking; it does not matter what the basis for the interference was.

Other objections are *substantive*, in the sense that they have less to do with the role of the Court and more to do with the particular ideas at work in *Lochner* about the appropriate role of government. Here the problem is that the Court attempted to vindicate, as a matter of constitutional law, a laissez-faire conception of the role of government that could not be sustained. Under this view, *Lochner* saw the market status quo — market wages and prices — as a part of the state of nature rather than as a product of a set of legal choices defined in terms of common law categories. *Lochner* thus relied on a bad "baseline" from which to see whether there was impermissible redistribution. It took the existing distribution of rights and entitlements as a neutral or natural standpoint from which to see whether government had been impermissibly partisan.

Note that these two types of objections have very different implications. The institutional view suggests that courts should take a deferential approach to legislation — particularly in the realm of social and economic affairs. The substantive view leaves open the possibility that judicial deference might not be required if the Court acts in the service of some end other than laissez-faire.

For a description of the substantive view, see Sunstein, *Lochner*'s Legacy, 87 Colum. L. Rev. 873, 874-875 (1987):

> The received wisdom is that *Lochner* was wrong because it involved "judicial activism." . . .
>
> [But it is possible] to understand *Lochner* from a different point of view. For the *Lochner* Court, neutrality, understood in a particular way, was a constitutional requirement. The key concepts here are threefold: governmental inaction, the existing distribution of wealth and entitlements, and the baseline set by the common law. Governmental intervention was constitutionally troublesome, whereas inaction was not; and both neutrality and inaction were defined as respect for the behavior of private actors pursuant to the common law, in light of the existing distribution of wealth and entitlements. . . .
>
> [If] *Lochner* is understood in these terms, its heirs are not Roe v. Wade and Miranda v. Arizona, but instead such decisions as Washington v. Davis, Buckley v. Valeo, Regents of California v. Bakke, and various cases immunizing those who are thought not to be "state actors" from constitutional constraints.

See C. Sunstein, The Partial Constitution (1993), for a general elaboration of this view and for many applications.

Note: The Lochner *Era — 1905-1934*

From the decision in *Lochner* in 1905 to the mid-1930s, the Court invalidated approximately 200 economic regulations, usually under the due process clause of the fourteenth amendment. These decisions centered primarily, although not exclusively, on labor legislation, the regulation of prices, and restrictions on entry into business. Although the Court employed substantive due process on many occasions, it sustained as many regulations as it struck down. Moreover, as reflected in *Lochner*, the Court was often divided. Justices Holmes, Brandeis, Stone, and Cardozo and Chief Justice Hughes dissented regularly from the Court's invalidation of economic regulations. This Note describes some of the more significant decisions. For comprehensive surveys, see F. Strong, Substantive Due Process of Law: A Dichotomy of Sense and Nonsense (1986); The Constitution of the United States 1602-1612, 1643-1709 (Government Printing Office 1973 ed.); B. Wright, The Growth of American Constitutional Law 153-168 (1942); Jacobson, Federalism and Property Rights, 15 N.Y.U. L.Q. Rev. 319 (1938).

1. *Maximum hour legislation.* Although the Court invalidated maximum hour legislation in *Lochner*, three years later, in Muller v. Oregon, 208 U.S. 412 (1908), the Court upheld a statute prohibiting the employment of women in laundries for more than ten hours per day. The Court distinguished *Lochner* on the ground that "woman's physical structure" placed her at a disadvantage in the "struggle for subsistence" and legislation to protect women was thus "necessary to secure a real equality of right." In Bunting v. Oregon, 243 U.S. 426 (1917), the Court, in a rather cryptic opinion, upheld a statute establishing a maximum ten-hour day for factory workers of both sexes. Although *Bunting* overruled the specific holding of *Lochner* sub silentio, the constitutional theory on which *Lochner* was based continued to be enforced. Consider whether the validation of maximum hour laws for women might be thought to naturalize sex differences, just as *Lochner* itself naturalized the common law; both of these might be thought to be products of law rather than, as the Court then saw it, part of the state of nature.

2. *"Yellow-dog" contracts.* In Adair v. United States, 208 U.S. 161 (1908), and Coppage v. Kansas, 236 U.S. 1 (1915), the Court invalidated federal and state legislation forbidding employers to require employees to agree not to join a union. The Court observed in *Adair* that "it is not within the functions of government [to] compel any person in the course of his business [to] retain the personal services of another." In *Coppage*, the Court emphasized that efforts to compensate for "unequal" bargaining power were beyond the legitimate scope of the police power and maintained that, although the individual has a right "to join the union, he has no inherent right to do this and still remain in the employ of one who is unwilling to employ a union man, any more than the same individual has a right to join the union without the consent of that organization."

3. *Minimum wages.* Although *Muller* upheld a law establishing maximum working hours for women, the Court invalidated a law establishing minimum wages for women in Adkins v. Children's Hospital, 261 U.S. 525 (1923). In distinguishing *Muller*, the Court observed:

But the ancient inequality of the sexes, otherwise than physical, [has] continued "with diminishing intensity." In view of the great [changes] which have taken place since [*Muller*], in the contractual, political and civil status of women, culminating in the Nineteenth Amendment, it is not unreasonable to say that these differences have now come almost, if not quite, to the vanishing point. [Thus], while the physical differences must be recognized in appropriate cases, and legislation fixing hours or conditions of work may properly take them into account, we cannot accept the doctrine that women of mature age, sui juris, require or may be subjected to restrictions upon their liberty of contract which could not lawfully be imposed in the case of men under similar circumstances.

4. *Price regulation.* In a line of cases after Munn v. Illinois, the Court initially adopted a broad definition of "affected with a public interest" and thus upheld a wide range of laws regulating prices. See, e.g., German Alliance Insurance Co. v. Lewis, 233 U.S. 389 (1914) (fire insurance); Block v. Hirsh, 256 U.S. 135 (1921) (rental housing). Thereafter, the Court increasingly narrowed the *Munn* standard and thus invalidated laws regulating prices with regard to such matters as gasoline, Williams v. Standard Oil Co., 278 U.S. 235 (1929); employment agencies, Ribnik v. McBride, 277 U.S. 350 (1928); and theater tickets, Tyson & Brother v. Banton, 273 U.S. 418 (1927).

5. *Business entry.* On several occasions, the Court invalidated laws restricting entry into particular lines of business. In New State Ice Co. v. Liebmann, 285 U.S. 262 (1932), for example, the Court invalidated a law prohibiting any person to manufacture ice without first obtaining a certificate of convenience and necessity. The Court explained that, as in the context of price regulation, the critical issue was "whether the business is [charged] with a public use," for "a regulation which has the effect of denying [the] common right to engage in a lawful private business, such as that under review, cannot be upheld." See also Louis K. Liggett Co. v. Baldridge, 278 U.S. 105 (1928) (invalidating a law limiting entry into the pharmacy business to pharmacists).

6. *The demise of* Lochner. As these decisions indicate, the Court's decisions in the *Lochner* era were often inconsistent. The unifying theme seemed to be the Court's perception of the "real" reason for the regulation. If the Court believed the regulation was truly designed to protect the health, safety, or morals of the general public, it was apt to uphold the law. But if the Court perceived the law to be an effort to readjust the market in favor of one party to the contract, it was likely to hold the regulation invalid.

By the mid-1930s, the Court was prepared to abandon *Lochner*. This was due to changes in the composition of the Court, internal tensions in the doctrine, an attack on market ordering as a product of law and as sometimes inefficient and unjust, increasing judicial and academic criticism, and, perhaps most important, the economic realities of the Depression, which seemed to undermine *Lochner's* central premises.

NEBBIA v. NEW YORK, 291 U.S. 502 (1934). During 1932, the prices received by farmers for milk fell much below the cost of production, and the situation of the families of dairy producers in New York grew "desperate." A legislative committee, established to investigate the matter, concluded that milk "is an essential item of diet," and that the failure "of producers to receive a reasonable return for their labor and investment over an extended period threatens a relaxation of vigilance against contamination." The committee further found that the "production and distribution of milk is a paramount industry of the state" and that the "milk industry is affected by factors of [price] instability [which] call for special methods of control." The legislature thus established the Milk Control Board, which was authorized to fix minimum and maximum retail prices for milk. Nebbia, the owner of a grocery store in Rochester, was convicted of selling milk below the minimum price fixed by the board. The Court, in a five-to-four decision, upheld the law. Justice Roberts delivered the opinion of the Court:

"The legislature adopted [the law] as a method of correcting the evils, which the report of the committee showed could not be expected to right themselves through the ordinary play of the forces of supply and demand, owing to the peculiar and uncontrollable factors affecting the industry. [Under] our form of government the use of property and the making of contracts are normally matters of private and not of public concern. The general rule is that both shall be free of governmental interference. But neither property rights nor contract rights are absolute; for government cannot exist if the citizen may at will use his property to the detriment of his fellows, or exercise his freedom of contract to work them harm. [Thus] has this court from the early days affirmed that the power to promote the general welfare is inherent in government. [These] correlative rights, that of the citizen to exercise exclusive dominion over property and freely to contract about his affairs, and that of the state to regulate the use of property and the conduct of business, are always in collision. [But] subject only to constitutional restraint the private right must yield to the public need.

"The Fifth Amendment, in the field of federal activity, and the Fourteenth, as respects state action, do not prohibit governmental regulation for the public welfare. They merely condition the exertion of the admitted power, by securing that the end shall be accomplished by methods consistent with due process. And the guaranty of due process, as has often been held, demands only that the law shall not be unreasonable, arbitrary or capricious, and that the means selected shall have a real and substantial relation to the object sought to be attained. [The] Constitution does not guarantee the unrestricted privilege to engage in a business or to conduct it as one pleases. . . .

"But we are told that because the law essays to control prices it denies due process. Notwithstanding the admitted power to correct existing economic ills by appropriate regulation of business, [the] appellant urges that direct fixation of prices [is] per se unreasonable and unconstitutional, save as applied to businesses affected with a public interest; [and that no] business is so affected [unless it is in the nature of a public utility or a monopoly]. But this is a misconception. [There] is no closed class or category of businesses affected with a public interest, and the function of courts in the application of the Fifth and Fourteenth Amendments is to determine in each case whether circumstances vindicate the challenged regulation as a reasonable exertion of governmental authority or condemn it as arbitrary or discriminatory. [The] phrase 'affected with a public interest' can, in the nature of things, mean no more than that an industry, for adequate reason, is subject to control for the public good. . . .

"So far as the requirement of due process is concerned, [a] state is free to adopt whatever economic policy may reasonably be deemed to promote public welfare, and to enforce that policy by legislation adapted to its purpose. The courts are without authority either to declare such policy, or, when it is declared by the legislature, to override it. [If] the legislative policy be to curb unrestrained and harmful competition [it] does not lie with the courts to determine that the rule is unwise. [Times] without number we have said that the legislature is primarily the judge of the necessity of such an enactment, that every possible presumption is in favor of its validity, and that though the court may hold views inconsistent with the wisdom of the law, it may not be annulled unless palpably in excess of legislative power. [Price] control, like any other form of regulation, is unconstitutional only if arbitrary, discriminatory, or demonstrably irrelevant to the policy the legislature is free to adopt, and hence an unnecessary and unwarranted interference with individual liberty."

Justice McReynolds, joined by Justices Van Devanter, Sutherland, and Butler, dissented: "This is not regulation, but management, control, dictation — it amounts to the deprivation of the fundamental right which one has to conduct his own affairs honestly and along customary lines. [It is the duty of this Court to inquire] whether the means proposed have reasonable relation to something within legislative power. [Here,] we find direct interference with guaranteed rights defended upon the ground that the purpose was to promote the public welfare by increasing milk prices at the farm. [But it is unclear] how higher charges at stores to impoverished customers when the output is excessive [can] possibly increase receipts at the farm. [I]t appears to me wholly unreasonable to expect this legislation to accomplish the proposed end."

WEST COAST HOTEL CO. v. PARRISH, 300 U.S. 379 (1937). In a five-to-four decision, the Court explicitly overruled Adkins v. Children's Hospital and upheld a state law establishing a minimum wage for women. Chief Justice Hughes delivered the opinion of the Court:

"[The] violation alleged by those attacking minimum wage regulation for women is deprivation of freedom of contract. What is this freedom of contract? The Constitution does not speak of freedom of contract. It speaks of liberty and prohibits the deprivation of liberty without due process of law. [Regulation] which is reasonable in relation to its subject and is adopted in the interests of the community is due process. . . .

"What can be closer to the public interest than the health of women and their protection from unscrupulous and overreaching employers? And if the protection of women is a legitimate end of the exercise of state power, how can it be said that the requirement of the payment of a minimum wage fairly fixed in order to meet the very necessities of existence is not an admissible means to that end? The legislature of the State was clearly entitled to consider the situation of women in employment, the fact that they are in the class receiving the least pay, that their bargaining power is relatively weak, and that they are the ready victims of those who would take advantage of their necessitous circumstances. The legislature was entitled to adopt measures to reduce the evils of the 'sweating system,' the exploiting of workers at wages so low as to be insufficient to meet the bare cost of living, thus making their very helplessness the occasion of a most injurious competition. The legislature had the right to consider that its minimum wage requirements would be an important aid in carrying out its policy of protection. The adoption of similar requirements by many States evidences a deep-seated conviction both as to the presence of the evil and as to the means adapted to check it. Legislative response to that conviction cannot be regarded as arbitrary or capricious, and that is all we have to decide. Even if the wisdom of the policy be regarded as debatable and its effects uncertain, still the legislature is entitled to its judgment. . . .

"There is an additional and compelling consideration which recent economic experience has brought into a strong light. The exploitation of a class of workers who are in an unequal position with respect to bargaining power and are thus relatively defenseless against the denial of a living wage is not only detrimental to their health and well being but casts a direct burden for their support upon the community. What these workers lose in wages the taxpayers are called upon to pay. The bare cost of living must be met. We may take judicial notice of the unparalleled demands for relief which arose during the recent period of depression. [The] community is not bound to provide what is in effect a subsidy for unconscionable employers. The community may direct its law-making power to correct the abuse which springs from their selfish disregard of the public interest. [*Adkins*] should be, and it is, overruled."

Justice Sutherland, joined by Justices Van Devanter, McReynolds, and Butler, dissented.

For discussion of the political context of *West Coast Hotel*, and the possible significance of President Roosevelt's "Court-packing plan," see Chapter 2, section C, supra.

Note the suggestion in *West Coast Hotel* that the "community is not bound to provide what is in effect a subsidy for unconscionable employers." Consider the possibility that in *West Coast Hotel* the Court largely abandoned the *Lochner*-era understanding that private ordering, within the common law framework, was natural and not the result of governmental choice. On this view, *West Coast Hotel* suggests that governmental "inaction" is itself a constitutionally significant decision. This theme is echoed in other decisions of the era. See, e.g., Miller v. Schoene, section H2 infra. The issue of governmental inaction as governmental action is explored more fully in Chapter 9 infra.

Note: The End of an Era

Since 1937, the Court's abandonment of *Lochner*-style substantive due process review of economic regulation has been unequivocal. In the years after *West Coast Hotel*, the Court overruled prior decisions and consistently rejected challenges to legislation based on assertions of a constitutional preference for laissez-faire economics.

In United States v. Darby, 312 U.S. 100 (1941), for example, the Court unanimously rejected a substantive due process challenge to the provisions of the Fair Labor Standards Act establishing maximum hours and minimum wages for all covered employees. Later that term, in Phelps Dodge Corp. v. National Labor Relations Board, 313 U.S. 177 (1941), the Court upheld a provision of the National Labor Relations Act declaring it an unfair labor practice for an employer to encourage or discourage union membership. That same day, in Olsen v. Nebraska, 313 U.S. 236 (1941), the Court unanimously upheld a state statute fixing the maximum fee that an employment agency could collect from employees, thus overruling Ribnik v. McBride, 277 U.S. 350 (1928). The Court observed that "the only constitutional prohibitions or restraints which respondents have suggested for invalidation of this legislation are those notions of public policy embodied in earlier decisions of this Court but which, as Mr. Justice Holmes long admonished, should not be read into the Constitution." In Lincoln Federal Union v. Northwestern Iron & Metal Co., 335 U.S. 525 (1949), the Court upheld a state right-to-work law that prohibited closed shops. The Court explained that it had abandoned "the *Allgeyer-Lochner-Adair-Coppage* constitutional doctrine" and returned "to the earlier constitutional principle that states have power to legislate against what are found to be injurious practices in their internal commercial and business affairs, so long as their laws do not run afoul of some specific federal constitutional prohibition." And in Day-Brite Lighting, Inc. v. Missouri, 342 U.S. 421 (1952), the Court upheld a law authorizing employees to take four hours' leave with full pay on election day, noting that, "if our recent cases mean anything, they leave debatable issues as respects business, economic, and social affairs to legislative decision."

Consider the following three decisions.

UNITED STATES v. CAROLENE PRODUCTS CO., 304 U.S. 144 (1938). After extensive hearings, two congressional committees made the following findings:

There is an extensive commerce in milk compounds made of condensed milk from which the butter fat has been extracted and an equivalent amount of vegetable oil [has been] substituted. [By] reason of the extraction of the natural milk fat the compounded product [known as "filled milk"] can be manufactured and sold at a lower cost than pure milk. Butter fat [is] rich in vitamins [that] are wanting in vegetable oils. The use of filled milk as a dietary substitute for pure milk results [in] undernourishment. [Despite] compliance with the branding and labeling requirements of the Pure Food and Drugs Act, there is widespread use of filled milk as a substitute for pure milk. This is aided by their identical taste and appearance, by the similarity of the containers in which they are sold, by the practice of dealers in offering the inferior product to customers as being as good as or better than pure condensed milk sold at a higher price, by customers' ignorance of the respective food values of the two products, and in many sections of the country by their inability to read the labels.

Based on these findings, Congress enacted the Filled Milk Act of 1923, which declared that "filled milk" is an "adulterated article of food, injurious to the public health," and that "its sale constitutes a fraud upon the public." The act therefore prohibited any person to ship filled milk in interstate commerce. In *Carolene Products*, the Court upheld the act. Justice Stone delivered the opinion of the Court:

"We may assume for present purposes that no pronouncement of a legislature can forestall attack upon the constitutionality of [a prohibition] by applying opprobrious epithets to the prohibited act, and that a statute would deny due process which precluded the disproof in judicial proceedings of all facts which would show or tend to show that a statute depriving the suitor of life, liberty or property had a rational basis.

"But such we think is not the purpose [of] the statutory characterization of filled milk as injurious to health and as a fraud upon the public. There is no need to consider it here as more than a declaration of the legislative findings deemed to support and justify the action taken, [aiding] informed judicial review, as do the reports of legislative committees, by revealing the rationale of the legislation. Even in the absence of such aids the existence of facts supporting the legislative judgment is to be presumed, for regulatory legislation affecting ordinary commercial transactions is not to be pronounced unconstitutional unless in the light of the facts made known or generally assumed it is of such a character as to preclude the assumption that it rests upon some rational basis. . . .

"Where the existence of a rational basis for legislation [depends] upon facts beyond the sphere of judicial notice, such facts may properly be made the subject of judicial inquiry, [and] the constitutionality of a statute predicated upon the existence of a particular state of facts may be challenged by showing to the court that those facts have ceased to exist. [Similarly] we recognize that the constitutionality of a statute, valid on its face, may be assailed by proof of facts tending to show that the statute as applied to a particular article is without support in reason because the article, although within the prohibited class, is so different from others of the class as to be without the reason for the prohibition, [though] the effect of such proof depends on the relevant circumstances of each case, as for example the administrative difficulty of excluding the article from the regulated class. [But] by their very nature such inquiries, where the legislative judgment is drawn in question, must be restricted to the issue whether any state of facts either known or which could reasonably be assumed affords support for it. Here the [appellee] challenges the validity of the statute on its face and it is evident from all the considerations presented to Congress, and those of which we may take judicial notice, that the question is at least debatable whether commerce in filled milk should be left unregulated, or in some measure restricted, or wholly prohibited. As that decision was for Congress, neither the finding of a court arrived at by weighing the evidence, nor the verdict of a jury can be substituted for it. [The Act is] constitutional."

Does *Carolene Products* accord too much deference to legislative judgment? Consider the following variations:

1. At trial, appellee presents expert witnesses who testify that filled milk is just as nourishing as pure milk. No one contradicts this testimony.

2. At trial, appellee presents expert witnesses who testify that *his* filled milk is just as nourishing as pure milk. No one contradicts this testimony.

3. At trial, appellee demonstrates that his product is packaged in a container that conspicuously states: "Filled Milk. Not as Nourishing as Pure Milk. But Cheaper."

4. Suppose Congress had enacted the measure without the express legislative findings, and that at trial appellee presents expert witnesses who testify that filled milk is just as nourishing as pure milk.

For a detailed study of the problem in *Carolene Products*, see Miller, The True Story of *Carolene Products*, 1988 Sup. Ct. Rev. 397, 398-399, claiming that the

statute upheld in the case was an utterly unprincipled "example of special interest legislation." The purported "public interest" justifications so credulously reported by Justice Stone were patently bogus. . . . The consequence of the decision was to expropriate the property of a lawful and beneficial industry; to deprive working and poor people of a healthful, nutritious, and low-cost food; and to impair the health of the nation's children by encouraging the use as baby food of a sweetened condensed milk product that was 42 percent sugar.

Suppose it is clear that Professor Miller's account is accurate. Was the case wrongly decided?

WILLIAMSON v. LEE OPTICAL OF OKLAHOMA, 348 U.S. 483 (1955). An ophthalmologist is a licensed physician who specializes in the care of the eyes. An optometrist examines for refractive error, recognizes diseases of the eye, and fills prescriptions for eyeglasses. An optician is an artisan qualified to grind lenses, fill prescriptions, and fit frames. In *Lee Optical*, the Court considered the constitutionality of an Oklahoma statute that made it unlawful for an optician to fit or duplicate lenses without a prescription from an ophthalmologist or optometrist. The district court held that through "ordinary skills the optician could take a broken lens or a fragment thereof, measure its power, and reduce it to prescriptive terms," that the requirement of a prescription from an ophthalmologist or optometrist was thus not "reasonably and rationally related to the health and welfare of the people," and that the law therefore "violated the Due Process Clause by arbitrarily interfering with the optician's right to do business." The Supreme Court reversed. Justice Douglas delivered the opinion of the Court:

"The Oklahoma law may exact a needless, wasteful requirement in many cases. But it is for the legislature, not the courts, to balance the advantages and disadvantages of the new requirement. It appears that in many cases the optician can easily supply the new frames or new lenses without reference to the old written prescription. [But] in some cases the directions contained in the prescription are essential. [The] legislature might have concluded that the frequency of occasions when a prescription is necessary was sufficient to justify this regulation of the fitting of eyeglasses. [Or] the legislature may have concluded that eye examinations were so critical, not only for correction of vision but also for detection of latent ailments or diseases, that every change in frames and every duplication of a lens should be accompanied by a prescription from a medical expert. To be sure, the present law does not require a new examination of the eyes every time the frames are changed or the lenses duplicated. [But] the law need not be in every respect logically consistent with its aims to be constitutional. It is enough that there is an evil at hand for correction, and that it might be thought that the particular legislative measure was a rational way to correct it. [The] day is gone when this Court uses the Due Process Clause [to] strike down state laws, regulatory of business and industrial conditions, because they may be unwise, improvident, or out of harmony with a particular school of thought."

FERGUSON v. SKRUPA, 372 U.S. 726 (1963). A Kansas statute declared it unlawful for any person to engage in the business of debt adjusting except as incident to "the lawful practice of law." The statute defined "debt adjusting" as the making of a contract with a debtor whereby the debtor pays money periodically to the adjuster who then distributes it to the debtor's creditors in accordance with an agreed-on plan. Skrupa, a debt adjustor who was put out of business by the statute, filed this action. The district court held that the statute was an unreasonable regulation of a "lawful business" and thus violative of due process. The Supreme Court reversed. Justice Black delivered the opinion of the Court:

"Under the system of government created by our Constitution, it is up to legislatures, not courts, to decide on the wisdom and utility of legislation. There was a time when the Due Process Clause was used by this Court to strike down laws which were thought unreasonable, that is, unwise or incompatible with some particular economic or social philosophy. [That doctrine] has long since been discarded. [It] is now settled that States 'have power to legislate against what are found to be injurious practices in their internal commercial and business affairs, so long as their laws do not run afoul of some specific federal constitutional prohibition. . . .' [The] Kansas legislature was free to decide for itself that legislation was needed to deal with the business of debt adjusting. Unquestionably, there are arguments showing that the business of debt adjusting has social utility, but such arguments are properly addressed to the legislature, not to us. [The] Kansas debt adjusting statute may be wise or unwise. But relief, if any be needed, lies not with us but with the body constituted to pass laws for the State of Kansas."

Justice Harlan concurred in the judgment "on the ground that this state measure bears a rational relation to a constitutionally permissible objective. See [*Lee Optical*]."

Note: *Pluralism, Naked Wealth Transfers, and the Courts*

1. *Economic substantive due process today.* In *Carolene Products*, the Court indicated that it would uphold economic legislation if any state of facts either known or reasonably inferable could support the legislative judgment. In *Lee Optical*, however, the Court went even further and resorted to wholly hypothetical facts and reasons to sustain the legislation. And in *Ferguson*, the Court appeared to uphold the legislation without any inquiry into the rationality of the means/ends connection.

It has been argued that economic substantive due process review has become so deferential in the post-*Lochner* era in part because "a wide range of justifications count as exercises of the police power and are not treated as naked wealth transfers." Sunstein, Naked Preferences and the Constitution, 84 Colum. L. Rev. 1689, 1718 (1984). Thus, almost all legislation — even that which reflects the untrammeled play of private self-interested groups, with the thinnest veil of public-regarding justifications — is upheld. In the post-*Lochner* era, what, if anything, constitutes an "impermissible" end? Are governmental actions based only on raw power and unsupported by *any* public value "impermissible"? Would *Carolene Products*, *Lee Optical*, and *Ferguson* pass muster under such a standard? Consider Komesar, Taking Institutions Seriously: Introduction to a Strategy for Constitutional Analysis, 51 U. Chi. L. Rev. 366, 416 (1984):

> It does not take much scrutiny to see the dairy lobby at work behind the passage [of] the "filled milk" act. Indeed, [it] is not too uncharitable, perhaps, to suggest that concern for the dairies' pocketbooks rather than for the consumer's health best explains the dairy lobby's efforts. In fact, though [the] legislation seemed to be aimed at helping consumers, it may have harmed them. They were "saved" from "adulterated" products, but only at the cost of higher prices, while the dairy industry benefited from reduced competition.

In any event, after decisions like *Carolene Products, Lee Optical,* and *Ferguson,* "there could be little doubt as to the practical result: no claim of substantive economic rights would now be sustained by the Supreme Court. The judiciary had abdicated the field." McCloskey, Economic Due Process and the Supreme Court: An Exhumation and Reburial, 1962 Sup. Ct. Rev. 34, 38. Indeed, the Court has not invalidated an economic regulation on substantive due process grounds since 1937. For decisions rejecting substantive due process challenges to economic regulation, see, e.g., Texaco v. Short, 454 U.S. 516 (1982); PruneYard Shopping Center v. Robins, 447 U.S. 74 (1980); Duke Power Co. v. Carolina Environmental Study Group, Inc., 438 U.S. 59 (1978); Exxon Corp. v. Governor of Maryland, 437 U.S. 117 (1978). Due process review has persisted with some vitality in state adjudication, however. See Hetherington, State Economic Regulation and Substantive Due Process of Law, 53 Nw. U.L. Rev. 13, 226 (1958); Note, State Economic Substantive Due Process: A Proposed Approach, 88 Yale L.J. 1487 (1979).

2. *Alternatives to abdication?* Perhaps the Court has gone too far in its withdrawal from the substantive review of economic legislation. Should it continue to ask whether there was a substantial relationship between the statute at issue and legitimate statutory ends? Consider B. Siegan, Economic Liberties and the Constitution 260, 262, 284, 302-303 (1980):

> The low esteem in which economic due process is held suggests to many that judicial review of economic matters is undesirable and harmful and that the judiciary should accept without reservation almost all legislative and administrative solutions to social and economic problems. Society was worse off, the proponents of this approach contend, as a result of the interventions of the "laissez-faire" Court. [But] studies effectively disclose the error in [the] New Deal emphasis on government intervention to solve existing economic problems. The studies demonstrate that the very people who [most] require the regulators' assistance — those at the lower end of the economic spectrum — actually suffer greatly from regulation. [The studies] are proving the wisdom of the Old Court's guiding principle, that freedom of contract is the rule and restraint the exception. [The] conclusion is warranted that the Old Court's policy of review is [preferable] to the contemporary Supreme Court's abdication.

But see Elhauge, Does Interest Group Theory Justify More Intrusive Judicial Review?, 101 Yale L.J. 31 (1991). Elhauge offers a number of arguments in favor of a negative answer to the conclusion posed in his title. He argues:

> What interest group theory does identify are the factors that make certain groups more willing than others to expend resources on petitioning for governmental action. However, identifying those factors cannot alone demonstrate which groups' petitioning efforts are *normatively* disproportionate. Such a normative conclusion is only possible if we have some baseline for determining what level of petitioning activity is normatively proportional to each group's interest. Interest group theory does not itself provide such a normative baseline. Rather, implicit normative baselines are adopted, usually without any discussion, when analysis draws normative implications from the degree of political influence predicted by interest group theory.

Elhauge also claims that "interest group theory does not establish . . . that the litigation process is, overall, less defective than the political process," and that "more intrusive judicial review would have several adverse effects on the transaction costs of legal change."

3. *The implications of abdication: the decline of* Lochner *and the doctrine of governmental action.* Consider the following view: The position suggested in *West Coast Hotel* and other decisions marking the decline of *Lochner* — that government's apparent failure to act may in some circumstances amount to governmental action — does not justify judicial abdication as a general rule. To the contrary, the understanding that the "private" sphere is itself a governmental creation suggests that a wide range of practices might be vulnerable to constitutional attack. Perhaps most dramatically, the existence of poverty itself may be understood as in part the product of governmental "action." Alternatively: Some redistributions are in fact unprincipled and in fact hurt only the vulnerable members of society — including those nominally designed to help the disadvantaged. The wholesale exclusion of debt adjusters from the marketplace might well be an example; so, too, with the burdens placed on opticians. Is it so clear that the courts should do nothing about this? Recall the discussion of Madisonian republicanism in Chapter 1. In this connection, consider the following:

> The demise of the laissez-faire jurisprudence of the *Lochner* era [came] at a most inopportune time for black Americans. Federal labor law and policy of the 1930s cartelized the labor market on behalf of racist labor unions, while black workers remained unprotected by civil rights legislation. Lochnerian judicial intervention to protect free labor markets could have saved hundreds of thousands [of] blacks from being permanently deprived of their livelihoods. [It] is possible to imagine that but for the interruption of the Great Depression and the New Deal, entirely different forms of civil rights protections would have arisen — a laissez-faire combination of equal protection of the law, liberty of contract, and freedom of association, instead of the more statist combination of interest group liberalism, the welfare state, and government enforcement of nondiscrimination norms against private parties.

Bernstein, Roots of the "Underclass": The Decline of Laissez-Faire Jurisprudence and the Rise of Racist Labor Legislation, 43 Am. U.L. Rev. 85, 86-87, 135 (1993).

4. *The implications of abdication: the decline of* Lochner *and the rise of the "double standard."* Why is there a "presumption of constitutionality" when the Court reviews economic legislation? Does this presumption govern all constitutional review? All substantive due process review? All substantive due process review except where the right at issue is expressly guaranteed in the bill of rights? All substantive due process review except where the right at issue is "fundamental"? Consider Justice Stone's famous footnote 4 in *Carolene Products:*

> There may be narrower scope for operation of the presumption of constitutionality when legislation appears on its face to be within a specific prohibition of the Constitution, such as those of the first ten amendments, which are deemed equally specific when held to be embraced within the Fourteenth. . . .
>
> It is unnecessary to consider now whether legislation which restricts those political processes [such as voting, expression, and political association] which can ordinarily be expected to bring about repeal of undesirable legislation, is to be subjected to more exacting judicial scrutiny under the general prohibitions of the Fourteenth Amendment than are most other types of legislation. . . .
>
> Nor need we enquire whether similar considerations enter into the review of statutes directed at particular religious, [or] national, [or] racial minorities[;] whether prejudice against discrete and insular minorities may be a special condition, which

tends seriously to curtail the operation of those political processes ordinarily to be relied upon to protect minorities, and which may call for a correspondingly more searching judicial inquiry.

For an interesting account of the origins of footnote 4, see Lusky, Footnote Redux: A *Carolene Products* Reminiscence, 82 Colum. L. Rev. 1093 (1982).

5. *The framers*, Lochner, *and* Carolene Products. Consider W. Nelson, The Fourteenth Amendment: From Political Principle to Judicial Doctrine 8-10, 197-200 (1988):

> [Those who wrote the Fourteenth Amendment] had a political agenda and a historical past that kept them from experiencing as clearly as we do the conflict between the protection of individual rights and the preservation of state legislative freedom. [Conflict] between these principles, though foreseeable, was not thought to be inevitable. [Indeed, the framers explained to their critics that no serious conflict was likely because] the amendment did not remove fundamental individual rights from the sphere of state control; [rather, it prohibited only] arbitrary and unreasonable lawmaking on the part of the States. [Although] this explanation remained at a vague level of rhetorical abstraction, [the framers left] the business of giving precise content to the Fourteenth Amendment [to] the Supreme Court. . . .
>
> Once the amendment had been adopted, the Supreme Court confronted the same two values, often in tension with one another. [Faithful] to the compromises that had taken place during the framing and ratification of the amendment, the late nineteenth-century Court [avoided] extreme positions and usually deferred to legislative judgments. Only when the Court found that legislative acts were plainly arbitrary would it declare them unconstitutional. [In *Lochner* and its progeny, however, the Court read the Fourteenth Amendment as authorizing] the federal courts to immunize fundamental rights from all legislative regulation; it thereby transformed the Fourteenth Amendment from a bar to arbitrary and unequal state action into a charter identifying fundamental rights and immunizing them from all legislative regulation. [This view] ignored the original understanding of the framers that "[t]he preservation of the just powers of the states is quite as vital as the preservation of the powers of the general government," and thereby "enlarg[ed] the scope of the [Fourteenth] Amendment far beyond its original purpose." . . .
>
> For reasons that the proponents of the Fourteenth Amendment had fully appreciated, [this] broad reading had to be rejected. But by the time it rejected the broad reading, the [Court] appears to have forgotten the line that the proponents of the Fourteenth Amendment and the late nineteenth-century judges had drawn in order to prevent the amendment from overwhelming the states. [For] whatever reason, the Court did not cut back on *Lochner* by distinguishing between reasonable and arbitrary state regulations, permitting the former and prohibiting the latter; instead, it distinguished in the *Carolene Products* case between economic and non-economic rights, giving government plenary power to regulate the former and little power over the latter. A half century after *Carolene Products*, the nineteenth century's approach to limiting the reach of the Fourteenth Amendment had been largely forgotten.

E. FUNDAMENTAL INTERESTS AND THE EQUAL PROTECTION CLAUSE

This section explores the intersection of equal protection and implied fundamental rights jurisprudence. Chapter 5, supra, examined two basic models of equal protection analysis. The first model focuses on classification based on race or other "suspect" criteria. As we saw, the Court tests such classifications by varying forms of "strict" scrutiny. The second model focuses on classifications in the economic and social realm that do not involve "suspect" criteria. As we also saw, the Court tests such classifications by a highly deferential form of "rational basis" review, similar to the standard that the Court currently employs in considering substantive due process challenges to economic regulation.

This section asks whether there is a third model of equal protection analysis. That is: Should the degree of scrutiny vary not only with the "suspectness" of the criterion on which the classification is based but also with the "importance" or "fundamentality" of the interest that is distributed or affected "unequally"? Should inequalities involving "fundamental" interests be analyzed differently from inequalities involving "nonfundamental" interests?

Several years before *Skinner*, infra, in Buck v. Bell, 274 U.S. 200 (1927), the Court upheld a Virginia statute authorizing the sterilization of inmates of state institutions who were found, after a hearing, to be afflicted with a hereditary form of insanity or imbecility. Justice Holmes, writing for the Court, observed: "It is better for all the world, if instead of waiting to execute degenerate offspring for crime, or to let them starve for their imbecility, society can prevent those who are manifestly unfit from continuing their kind. [Three] generations of imbeciles are enough."

Skinner v. Oklahoma

316 U.S. 535 (1942)

MR. JUSTICE DOUGLAS delivered the opinion of the Court.

This case touches a sensitive and important area of human rights. Oklahoma deprives certain individuals of a right which is basic to the perpetuation of a race — the right to have offspring. . . .

The statute involved is Oklahoma's Habitual Criminal Sterilization Act. That Act defines an "habitual criminal" as a person who [has been convicted three] or more times for crimes "amounting to felonies involving moral turpitude." [Machinery] is provided for the institution by the Attorney General of a proceeding against such a person in the Oklahoma courts for a judgment that such person shall be rendered sexually sterile. [If] the court or jury finds that the defendant is an "habitual criminal" and that he "may be rendered sexually sterile without detriment to his or her general health," then the court "shall render judgment to the effect that said defendant be rendered sexually sterile" by the operation of vasectomy in case of a male, and of salpingectomy in case of a female. Only one other provision of the Act is material here, and that provides that "offenses arising out of the violation of the prohibitory laws, revenue acts, embezzlement, or political offenses, shall not come or be considered within the terms of this Act."

Petitioner was convicted in 1926 of the crime of stealing chickens, [and in 1929 and 1934] he was convicted of robbery with firearms. . . . In 1936 the Attorney General instituted proceedings against him. [A] judgment directing that the operation of vasectomy be performed on petitioner was affirmed by the Supreme Court of Oklahoma. . . .

Several objections to the constitutionality of the Act have been pressed upon us. It is urged that the Act cannot be sustained as an exercise of the police power, in view of the state of scientific authorities respecting inheritability of criminal traits. It is argued that due process is lacking because, under this Act, unlike the Act upheld in Buck v. Bell, 274 U.S. 200, the defendant is given no opportunity to be heard on the issue as to whether he is the probable potential parent of socially undesirable offspring. [It] is also suggested that the Act is penal in character and that the sterilization provided for is cruel and unusual punishment and violative of the Fourteenth Amendment. [We] pass those points without intimating an opinion on them, for there is a feature of the Act which clearly condemns it. That is, its failure to meet the requirements of the equal protection clause of the Fourteenth Amendment.

We do not stop to point out all of the inequalities in this Act. A few examples will suffice. In Oklahoma, grand larceny is a felony. Larceny is grand larceny when the property taken exceeds $20 in value. Embezzlement is punishable "in the manner prescribed for feloniously stealing property of the value of that embezzled." Hence, he who embezzles property worth more than $20 is guilty of a felony. A clerk who appropriates over $20 from his employer's till and a stranger who steals the same amount are thus both guilty of felonies. If the latter repeats his act and is convicted three times, he may be sterilized. But the clerk is not subject to the pains and penalties of the Act no matter how large his embezzlements nor how frequent his convictions. A person who enters a chicken coop and steals chickens commits a felony and he may be sterilized if he is thrice convicted. If, however, he is a bailee of the property and fraudulently appropriates it, he is an embezzler. Hence, no matter how habitual his proclivities for embezzlement are and no matter how often his conviction, he may not be sterilized. Thus, the nature of the two crimes is intrinsically the same and they are punishable in the same manner. . . .

It was stated in [Buck v. Bell] that the claim that state legislation violates the equal protection clause of the Fourteenth Amendment is "the usual last resort of constitutional arguments." Under our constitutional system the States in determining the reach and scope of particular legislation need not provide "abstract symmetry." They may mark and set apart the classes and types of problems according to the needs and as dictated or suggested by experience. [Thus,] if we had here only a question as to a State's classification of crimes, such as embezzlement or larceny, no substantial federal question would be raised. [For] a State is not constrained in the exercise of its police power to ignore experience which marks a class of offenders or a family of offenses for special treatment. Nor is it prevented by the equal protection clause from confining "its restrictions to those classes of cases where the need is deemed to be clearest." . . .

But the instant legislation runs afoul of the equal protection clause, though we give Oklahoma that large deference which the rule of the foregoing cases requires. We are dealing here with legislation which involves one of the basic civil rights of man. Marriage and procreation are fundamental to the very existence and survival of the race. The power to sterilize, if exercised, may have subtle, far-reaching and devastating effects. In evil or reckless hands it can cause races or types which are inimical to the dominant group to wither and disappear. There is no redemption for the individual whom the law touches. Any experiment which the State conducts is to his irreparable injury. He is forever deprived of a basic liberty. We mention these matters not to reexamine the scope of the police power of the States. We advert to them merely in emphasis of our view that strict scrutiny of the classification which a State makes in a sterilization law is essential, lest unwittingly, or otherwise, invidious discriminations are made against groups or types of individuals in violation of the constitutional guaranty of just and equal laws. The guaranty of "equal protection of the laws is a pledge of the protection of equal laws." When the law lays an unequal hand on those who have committed intrinsically the same quality of offense and sterilizes one and not the other, it has made as invidious a discrimination as if it had selected a particular race or nationality for oppressive treatment. Sterilization of those who have thrice committed grand larceny, with immunity for those who are embezzlers, is a clear, pointed, unmistakable discrimination. Oklahoma makes no attempt to say that he who commits larceny by trespass or trick or fraud has biologically inheritable traits which he who commits embezzlement lacks. [We] have not the slightest basis for inferring that that line has any significance in eugenics, nor that the inheritability of criminal traits follows the neat legal distinctions which the law has marked between those two offenses. In terms of fines and imprisonment, the crimes of larceny and embezzlement rate the same under the Oklahoma code. Only when it comes to sterilization are the pains and penalties of the law different. The equal protection clause would indeed be a formula of empty words if such conspicuously artificial lines could be drawn. . . .

Reversed.

MR. CHIEF JUSTICE STONE, concurring.

I concur in the result, but I am not persuaded that we are aided in reaching it by recourse to the equal protection clause.

If Oklahoma may resort generally to the sterilization of criminals on the assumption that their propensities are transmissible to future generations by inheritance, I seriously doubt that the equal protection clause requires it to apply the measure to all criminals in the first instance, or to none.

Moreover, if we must presume that the legislature knows — what science has been unable to ascertain — that the criminal tendencies of any class of habitual offenders are transmissible regardless of the varying mental characteristics of its individuals, I should suppose that we must likewise presume that the legislature, in its wisdom, knows that the criminal tendencies of some classes of offenders are more likely to be transmitted than those of others. And so I think the real question we have to consider is not one of equal protection, but whether the wholesale condemnation of a class to such an invasion of personal liberty, without opportunity to any individual to show that his is not the type of case which would justify resort to it, satisfies the demands of due process.

There are limits to the extent to which the presumption of constitutionality can be pressed, especially where the liberty of the person is concerned (see United States v. Carolene Products Co., 304 U.S. 144, 152, n.4) and where the presumption is resorted to only to dispense with a procedure which the ordinary dictates of prudence would seem to demand for the protection of the individual from arbitrary action. Although petitioner here was given a hearing to ascertain whether sterilization would be detrimental to his health, he was given none to discover whether his criminal tendencies are of an inheritable type. . . .

[A] law which condemns, without hearing, all the individuals of a class to so harsh a measure as the present because some or even many merit condemnation, is lacking in the first principles of due process. [The] state is called on to sacrifice no permissible end when it is required to reach its objective by a reasonable and just procedure adequate to safeguard rights of the individual which concededly the Constitution protects.

[A concurring opinion of Justice Jackson is omitted.]

Note: The Fundamental "Right to Have Offspring"

1. *Alternative bases of resolution.* The Court in *Skinner* found it unnecessary to address three "objections to the constitutionality of the Act" that did not involve the equal protection clause. First, it was argued that "the Act cannot be sustained as an exercise of the police power, in view of the state of scientific authorities respecting inheritability of criminal traits." At the time of *Skinner*, the scientific evidence was inconclusive. Second, it was argued "that due process is lacking because, under this Act, unlike the Act upheld in Buck v. Bell, the defendant is given no opportunity to be heard on the issue as to whether he is the probable potential parent of socially undesirable offspring." Third, it was argued that "the Act is penal in character and that the sterilization provided for is cruel and unusual punishment."

2. *Equal protection: rational basis review.* Could the Court have invalidated the act on the ground that the distinction between embezzlers and larceners was irrational? Note Justice Douglas's observation that "a classification of crimes, such as embezzlement or larceny," would raise "no substantial federal question." If the classification is rational for those purposes, one might doubt that it is any less rational when it is drawn for purposes of sterilization.

3. *"Fundamental" interests and the equal protection clause.* *Skinner* might be thought inconsistent with the Court's essentially contemporaneous renunciation of economic substantive due process. Can the right to have offspring, unlike the liberty of contract, be thought to be a true "fundamental" right? Or is fundamental interest analysis more appropriate in equal protection jurisprudence than in due process jurisprudence?

Consider the following arguments: (a) Inequality with respect to a trivial interest is not as significant as inequality with respect to an important interest. (b) Inequality with respect to a fundamental interest is inherently irrational unless there are very good reasons for the inequality. (c) Inequality with respect to a fundamental interest suggests a possible improper motivation, for it is unlikely that those who framed the classification would have deprived themselves of the fundamental interest in the absence of extraordinary necessity. (d) The 1866 Civil Rights Act, on which the fourteenth amendment was based, protected blacks against inequality only with respect to certain specified interests, thus suggesting that the importance of the interest affected is central to the constitutionality of a classification.

4. *Is the "right to have offspring" a "fundamental" interest?* Is the right to have offspring more "fundamental" than the "liberty of contract"? Consider the following views:

a. "[The] Court in *Skinner* was moved to recognize the fundamental personal character of a right to reproductive autonomy in part because of fear about the invidious and potentially genocidal way in which governmental control over reproductive matters might be exercised if the choice of whether or when to beget a child were to be transferred from the individual to the state." L. Tribe, American Constitutional Law 923 (1978). Note in this regard that the statutory distinction in *Skinner* was itself at least arguably class-based. White-collar crimes, and others likely to be committed by those relatively better off, would not be punished with sterilization. Should this bear on the equal protection issue?

b. "[The] right of procreation [rests] most securely on the interest in status and dignity. [The] choice to be [a] parent is, among other things, a choice of social role and of self-concept. For the state to deny such a choice is for the organized society to deny the individual [the] presumptive right to be treated as a person, one of equal worth among citizens." Karst, Foreword: Equal Citizenship under the Fourteenth Amendment, 91 Harv. L. Rev. 1, 32 (1977).

c. *Skinner* was simply wrong. The case is an example of the proposition that hard cases make bad law. Lacking a secure constitutional foundation for invalidating an oppressive law, the Court just made it up.

5. *A right not to have offspring?* In *Skinner*, the Court held that the right to have offspring is "fundamental." Is there also a fundamental right *not* to have offspring? See section F infra.

1.   Voting

In footnote 4 of *Carolene Products*, Chief Justice Stone suggested that there "may be a narrower scope for operation of the presumption of constitutionality when [legislation] restricts those political processes which can ordinarily be expected to bring about repeal of undesirable legislation." He then offered "restrictions upon the right to vote" as a specific example. This section examines three aspects of the right to vote: denial of the right to vote, dilution of the right to vote, and denial of access to the ballot.

a.   Denial of the "Right to Vote"

The original Constitution left it entirely to the states to determine the qualifications of voters for both national and state elections. See U.S. Const. art. I, §2, cl. 1; art. II, §1. The fourteenth amendment, enacted in 1868, did not directly prohibit discrimination in voting. Section 2 of the amendment, however, provided for a reduction in representation in the House of Representatives in proportion to the number of "male inhabitants of [the] State, being twenty-one years of age, and citizens of the United States," who were not permitted to vote. The fifteenth amendment, adopted in 1870, provided that the right of citizens to vote "shall not be denied or abridged [on] account of race, color or previous condition of servitude." The nineteenth amendment, enacted in 1920, provided that the right of citizens to vote "shall not be denied or abridged [on] account of sex." The twenty-fourth amendment, adopted in 1964, provided that the right of any citizen to vote in any election for president, vice-president, or members of Congress "shall not be denied or abridged [by] reason of failure to pay any poll tax or other tax." And the twenty-sixth amendment, enacted in 1971, provided that the right of any citizen eighteen years or older to vote "shall not be denied or abridged [on] account of age."

Except where a particular qualification was expressly prohibited by a specific amendment, the Court, until the 1960s, generally deferred to the states in determining the qualifications to vote. In Breedlove v. Suttles, 302 U.S. 277 (1937), for example, the Court unanimously upheld a Georgia statute requiring the payment of a $1 poll tax as a precondition for voting. Similarly, in Lassiter v. Northampton County Board of Elections, 360 U.S. 45 (1959), the Court unanimously upheld a North Carolina statute providing that to be eligible to vote an individual must "be able to read and write any section of the [state constitution] in the English language." The Court said that "in our society where newspapers, periodicals, books, and other printed matter canvass and debate campaign issues, a State might conclude that only those who are literate should exercise the franchise."

In 1964, however, in Reynolds v. Sims, section E1b infra, a decision involving dilution of the right to vote, the Court observed: "[The] right of suffrage is a fundamental matter in a free and democratic society. Especially since the right to exercise the franchise in a free and unimpaired manner is preservative of other basic civil and political rights, any alleged infringement of the right of citizens to vote must be carefully and meticulously scrutinized." Reynolds opened the door to a more active judicial scrutiny of voter qualifications.

Harper v. Virginia State Board of Elections

383 U.S. 663 (1966)

[The Court, overruling Breedlove v. Suttles, invalidated a Virginia law requiring the payment of a poll tax not to exceed $1.50 as a precondition for voting. The Court held that "a State violates the Equal Protection Clause [whenever] it makes the affluence of the voter or payment of any fee an electoral standard."]

MR. JUSTICE DOUGLAS delivered the opinion of the Court. . . .

[The] right to vote in state elections is nowhere expressly mentioned [in the Constitution]. It is argued that the right to vote in state elections is implicit, particularly by reason of the First Amendment. [We] do not stop to canvass the relation between voting and political expression. For it is enough to say that once the franchise is granted to the electorate, lines may not be drawn which are inconsistent with the Equal Protection Clause of the Fourteenth Amendment. . . .

[The] Lassiter case does not govern the result here, because, unlike a poll tax, the "ability to read and write . . . has some relation to standards designed to promote intelligent use of the ballot." [Voter] qualifications have no relation to wealth nor to paying or not paying this or any other tax. . . .

It is argued that a State may exact fees from citizens for many different kinds of licenses; that if it can demand from all an equal fee for a driver's license, it can demand from all an equal poll tax for voting. But we must remember that the interest of the State, when it comes to voting, is limited to the power to fix qualifications. Wealth, like race, creed, or color, is not germane to one's ability to participate intelligently in the electoral process. Lines drawn on the basis of wealth or property, like those of race [are] traditionally disfavored. See [Griffin v. Illinois and Douglas v. California, section E2 infra]. To introduce wealth or payment of a fee as a measure of a voter's qualifications is to introduce a capricious or irrelevant factor. . . .

We agree, of course, with Mr. Justice Holmes that the Due Process Clause of the Fourteenth Amendment "does not enact Mr. Herbert Spencer's Social Statics." [*Lochner.*] Likewise, the Equal Protection Clause is not shackled to the political theory of a particular era. In determining what lines are unconstitutionally discriminatory, we have never been confined to historic notions of [equality]. Notions of what constitutes equal treatment for purposes of the Equal Protection Clause *do* change. [Comparing Plessy v. Ferguson with Brown v. Board of Education.]

[We] have long been mindful that where fundamental rights and liberties are asserted under the Equal Protection Clause, classifications which might invade or restrain them must be closely scrutinized and carefully confined. See, e.g., [*Skinner*].

Those principles apply here. For to repeat, wealth or fee paying has, in our view, no relation to voting qualifications; the right to vote is too precious, too fundamental to be so burdened or conditioned.

Reversed.

Mr. Justice Black, dissenting. . . .

[Under] a proper interpretation of the Equal Protection Clause States are to have the broadest kind of leeway in areas where they have a general constitutional competence to act. [State] poll tax legislation can "reasonably," "rationally" and without an "invidious" or evil purpose to injure anyone be found to rest on a number of state policies including (1) the State's desire to collect its revenue, and (2) its belief that voters who pay a poll tax will be interested in furthering the State's welfare when they vote. [And] history is on the side of "rationality" of the State's poll tax policy. Property qualifications existed in the Colonies and were continued by many States after the Constitution was adopted. . . .

Another reason for my dissent [is that the Court] seems to be using the old "natural-law-due-process formula" to justify striking down state laws as violations of the Equal Protection Clause. . . .

Mr. Justice Harlan, whom Mr. Justice Stewart joins, dissenting. . . .

[The Court uses] captivating phrases, but they are wholly inadequate to satisfy the standard governing adjudication of the equal protection issue: Is there a rational basis for Virginia's poll tax as a voting qualification? I think the answer to that question is undoubtedly "yes."

Property qualifications and poll taxes have been a traditional part of our political structure. In the Colonies the franchise was generally a restricted one. [It] is certainly a rational argument that payment of some minimal poll tax promotes civic responsibility, weeding out those who do not care enough about public affairs to pay $1.50 or thereabouts a year for the exercise of the franchise. It is also arguable, indeed it was probably accepted as sound political theory by a large percentage of Americans through most of our history, that people with some property have a deeper stake in community affairs, and are consequently more responsible, more educated, more knowledgeable, more worthy of confidence, than those without means, and that the community and Nation would be better managed if the franchise were restricted to such citizens. . . .

[It] was not too long ago that Mr. Justice Holmes felt impelled to remind the Court that the Due Process Clause of the Fourteenth Amendment does not enact the laissez-faire theory of society, [*Lochner*]. The times have changed, and perhaps it is appropriate to observe that neither does the Equal Protection Clause of that Amendment rigidly impose upon America an ideology of unrestrained egalitarianism. . . .

Note: Is the Right to Vote "Fundamental"?

1. *The equal protection clause, voting, and the intent of the framers.* In his dissenting opinion in Reynolds v. Sims, 377 U.S. 533 (1964), section E1b infra, Justice Harlan argued that the equal protection clause was "never intended" to inhibit the states in setting the qualifications for voting. Justice Harlan emphasized several factors: (a) Section 2 of the fourteenth amendment "expressly recognizes" the power of the states to deny the right to vote and expressly provides a remedy for such denial — a proportionate reduction in their representation in Congress. (b) The debates on the amendment reflected "the understanding of those who proposed and ratified it" that it would not affect the "power of a State to withhold the right to vote." (c) The adoption of the fifteenth amendment, which guaranteed the right to vote to blacks, only two years after the adoption of the fourteenth amendment, demonstrates that the framers of the fourteenth amendment did not intend it to guarantee the right to vote. For further elaboration of this view, see Oregon v. Mitchell, 400 U.S. 112, 152 (1970) (Harlan, J.); R. Berger, Government by Judiciary ch. 4 (1977). For a contrary view, see Oregon v. Mitchell, 400 U.S. 112, 229 (1970) (Brennan, J.); Van Alstyne, The Fourteenth Amendment, the "Right" to Vote, and the Understanding of the Thirty-Ninth Congress, 1965 Sup. Ct. Rev. 33.

2. *The basis of* Harper: *wealth as a "suspect classification."* The Court relied in *Harper* on both the "suspect classification" and the "fundamental interest" aspects of equal protection analysis. To what extent, if any, can *Harper* be explained on the ground that "lines drawn on the basis of wealth [are] traditionally disfavored"? Consider that (a) the poll tax does not expressly classify on the basis of wealth; (b) like ordinary license fees, and indeed any system that requires an expenditure, it might be seen to have a differential effect on the poor; and (c) the Court invalidated the poll tax in its entirety, not only as applied to the poor.

3. *The basis of* Harper: *voting as a fundamental interest.* The Court conceded in *Harper* that there is no constitutional right to vote in state elections. How, then, does it justify its conclusion that the right to vote is "fundamental"? Consider J. Ely, Democracy and Distrust 77, 101-103 (1980):

Carolene Products [focused, in part,] on whether the opportunity to participate [in] the political [process] has been unduly constricted. [The framers of the Constitution created a representative democracy in which] the people in their self-interest would choose representatives whose interests intertwined with [theirs]. The Constitution has [proceeded] from the quite sensible assumption that an effective majority will not inordinately threaten its own rights, and has sought to assure that such a majority will not systematically treat others less well than it treats [itself]. Malfunction occurs when [the] ins are choking off the channels of political change to ensure that they will stay in and the outs will stay out. [Unblocking] stoppages in the democratic process is what judicial review ought preeminently to be about, and denial of the vote seems the quintessential stoppage. [We] cannot trust the ins to decide who stays out, and it is therefore incumbent on the courts to ensure not only that no one is denied the vote for no reason, but also that where there is a reason [it] had better be a very convincing one.

Kramer v. Union Free School District

395 U.S. 621 (1969)

MR. CHIEF JUSTICE WARREN delivered the opinion of the Court.

[Section 2012] of the New York Education Law [provides] that in certain New York school districts residents [may] vote in the school district election only if they (1) own (or lease) taxable real property within the district, or (2) are parents (or have custody of) children enrolled in the local public schools. Appellant, a bachelor who neither owns nor leases taxable real property, [claims] that §2012 denied him equal protection of the laws. . . .

In determining whether or not [this] law violates the Equal Protection Clause, [we] must give the statute a close and exacting examination. [This] careful examination is necessary because statutes distributing the franchise constitute the foundation of our representative society.

[Statutes] granting the franchise to residents on a selective basis always pose the danger of denying some citizens any effective voice in the governmental affairs which substantially affect their lives. Therefore, if a challenged state statute grants the right to vote to some bona fide residents of requisite age and citizenship and denies the franchise to others, the Court must determine whether the exclusions are necessary to promote a compelling state interest.

[The] presumption of constitutionality and the approval given "rational" classifications in other types of enactments are based on an assumption that the institutions of state government are structured so as to represent fairly all the people. However, when the challenge to the statute is in effect a challenge of this basic assumption, the assumption can no longer serve as the basis for presuming constitutionality. And, the assumption is no less under attack because the legislature which decides who may participate at the various levels of political choice is fairly elected. Legislation which delegates decision making to bodies elected by only a portion of those eligible to vote for the legislature can cause unfair representation. . . .

[We] turn therefore to question whether the exclusion is necessary to promote a compelling state interest. [Appellees] argue that the State has a legitimate interest in limiting the franchise in school district elections [to] those "primarily interested in such elections" [and] that the State may reasonably and permissibly conclude that "property taxpayers" (including lessees of taxable property who share the tax burden through rent payments) and parents of the children enrolled in the district's schools are those "primarily interested" in school affairs. . . .

We need express no opinion as to whether the State in some circumstances might limit the exercise of the franchise to those "primarily interested" or "primarily affected." [For,] assuming, arguendo, that New York legitimately might limit the franchise in these school district elections to those "primarily interested in school affairs," close scrutiny of the §2012 classifications demonstrates that they do not accomplish this purpose with sufficient precision to justify denying appellant the franchise.

[The] requirements of §2012 are not sufficiently tailored to limiting the franchise to those "primarily interested" in school affairs to justify the denial of the franchise to appellant and members of his class. . . .

MR. JUSTICE STEWART, with whom MR. JUSTICE BLACK and MR. JUSTICE HARLAN join, dissenting. . . .

Clearly a State may reasonably assume that its residents have a greater stake in the outcome of elections held within its boundaries than do other persons. Likewise, it is entirely rational for a state legislature to suppose that residents, being generally better informed regarding state affairs than are nonresidents, will be more likely than nonresidents to vote responsibly. And the same may be said of legislative assumptions regarding the electoral competence of adults and literate persons on the one hand, and of minors and illiterates on the other. It is clear, of course, that lines thus drawn cannot infallibly perform their intended legislative function. Just as "[i]lliterate people may be intelligent voters," nonresidents or minors might also in some instances be interested, informed, and intelligent participants in the electoral process.

[Nor] is there any other justification for imposing the Court's "exacting" equal protection test. This case does not involve racial classifications [and] this statute is not one that impinges upon a constitutionally protected right, [for] "the Constitution of the United States does not confer the right of suffrage upon any one." . . .

Note: Kramer *and Its Progeny*

In examining the Court's decisions since *Kramer*, consider what the Court means in this context by "strict scrutiny."

1. *Property requirements: special purpose elections.* In Cipriano v. City of Houma, 395 U.S. 701 (1969), decided on the same day as *Kramer*, the Court invalidated a Louisiana law permitting only property-owning taxpayers to vote whether to issue municipal utility bonds. The Court emphasized that the revenue bonds were to be paid entirely from the operation of the utilities, and that they therefore did not especially burden the owners of real property.

The following year, in Phoenix v. Kolodziejski, 399 U.S. 204 (1970), the Court invalidated an Arizona law permitting only property-owning taxpayers to vote whether to issue general obligation bonds. Although the bonds in *Kolodziejski*, unlike those in *Cipriano*, were to be paid substantially from property taxes, the Court observed that nonproperty owners had a substantial interest in the services and facilities financed by the bonds, and that the differences between the interests of property owners and nonproperty owners were therefore "not sufficiently substantial to justify excluding the latter from the franchise." Justice Stewart, joined by Chief Justice Burger and Justice Harlan, dissented.

2. *Property requirements: limited purpose government units.* In Salyer Land Co. v. Tulare Lake Basin Water Storage District, 410 U.S. 719 (1973), the Court up-

held a California statute permitting only landowners to vote in water storage district elections and allocating votes in proportion to the assessed valuation of the land. The main purpose of the districts was to provide water for farming. The districts' project costs were assessed against the land in proportion to the benefits received. Emphasizing that the district does "not exercise what might be thought of as 'normal governmental' authority," the Court held that the "strict scrutiny" demanded by *Kramer, Cipriano,* and *Kolodziejski* was inapplicable to the district "by reason of its special limited purpose and of the disproportionate effect of its activities on landowners as a group." It then concluded that the franchise restriction was constitutional because it was not "wholly irrelevant to achievement" of a legitimate objective. Justice Douglas, joined by Justices Brennan and Marshall, dissented.

In Ball v. James, 451 U.S. 355 (1981), the Court extended *Salyer* and upheld a "one acre-one vote" scheme for voting for directors of a large water reclamation district in Arizona. Unlike the water district in *Salyer,* which covered only a sparsely populated agricultural area, the water reclamation district in *Ball* financed most of its water operations by selling electricity to several hundred thousand residents. Nonetheless, the Court found *Salyer,* rather than *Kramer,* controlling. The Court explained that the district "cannot enact any laws governing the conduct of citizens, nor does it administer such normal functions of government as the maintenance of streets, the operation of schools, or sanitation, health, and welfare services." Moreover, the Court rejected the argument that "the sheer size of the power operations and the great number of people they affect serve to transform the [district] into an entity of general governmental power." Rather, the relationship between nonvoting residents and the district was "essentially that between consumers and a business enterprise from which they buy." Justice White, joined by Justices Brennan, Marshall, and Blackmun, dissented.

3. *Durational residency requirements.* In Dunn v. Blumstein, 405 U.S. 330 (1972), the Court expressly reaffirmed the states' power to limit the franchise to bona fide residents but invalidated a Tennessee statute conditioning eligibility to vote on one year's residence in the state and three months' residence in the county. The Court explained that because durational residence requirements curtail the "fundamental interest" in voting, they are unconstitutional "unless the State can demonstrate that [they] 'are *necessary* to promote a *compelling* governmental interest.'" Tennessee offered two such purposes: to "insure purity of the ballot box" by protecting against fraud and to assure a "knowledgeable voter." The Court conceded that prevention of fraud was a legitimate interest but concluded that "30 days appears to be an ample period of time [to] complete whatever administrative tasks are necessary to prevent fraud." And, although also conceding the legitimacy of the state's interest in having "knowledgeable" voters, the Court concluded that "the conclusive presumptions of durational residence requirements are much too crude." In Marston v. Lewis, 410 U.S. 679 (1973), and Burns v. Fortson, 410 U.S. 686 (1973), the Court upheld fifty-day durational residence requirements, noting that the fifty-day period was "necessary" to serve the states' "important interest in accurate voter lists."

4. *Absentee ballots.* In McDonald v. Board of Election Commissioners, 394 U.S. 802 (1969), decided after *Harper,* but shortly before *Kramer,* the Court upheld an Illinois statute that granted absentee ballots to some classes of persons but not to "unsentenced inmates awaiting trial." The Court noted that "there is nothing in the record to indicate [that] Illinois has in fact precluded appellants from

voting," for "the record is barren of any indication that the State might not [furnish] the jails with special polling booths [or] provide guarded transportation to the polls." It thus concluded that it "is [not] the right to vote that is at stake here but a claimed right to receive absentee ballots." It therefore applied the "traditional standards" of equal protection review and sustained the statute. In O'Brien v. Skinner, 414 U.S. 524 (1974), the Court invalidated a New York statute that did not provide absentee ballots to persons in jail awaiting trial. The Court explained that, since the statute provided absentee ballots to persons absent from their home county, those held in jail in a county other than their residence could vote, but "persons confined for the same reason in the county of their residence are completely denied the ballot." The Court concluded that this distinction was "wholly arbitrary." Justice Blackmun, joined by Justice Rehnquist, dissented.

5. *Disenfranchising felons.* In Richardson v. Ramirez, 418 U.S. 24 (1974), the Court upheld a California law that denied the vote to convicted felons, even if they had completed their sentences and paroles. The Court, in an opinion by Justice Rehnquist, adopted an "intent of the framers" approach. The Court observed that many state constitutions in effect when the fourteenth amendment was adopted denied the vote to convicted felons, and that section 2 of the amendment expressly reduced the representation in the House to the extent a state denied the vote to adult male citizens, "except for participation in rebellion, or other crime." It then concluded that "the exclusion of felons from the vote has an affirmative sanction [that] was not present in the case of the other restrictions on the franchise" invalidated in the *Harper/Kramer* line of cases.

Justice Marshall, joined by Justice Brennan, dissented on the ground that "§2 was not intended and should not be construed to be a limitation on the other sections of the Fourteenth Amendment," and that under "strict scrutiny" "the blanket disenfranchisement of ex-felons cannot stand." Justice Douglas dissented on other grounds.

6. *Enrollment requirements for voting in primaries.* In Rosario v. Rockefeller, 410 U.S. 752 (1973), the Court upheld a New York statute requiring voters to register their party affiliation at least thirty days before a general election in order to be eligible to vote in the next party primary, which might be as many as eleven months later. The Court distinguished Dunn v. Blumstein and held that the law did not violate the right of petitioners to vote in the primary "of their choice" because the law "did not absolutely disenfranchise" petitioners but "merely imposed a time deadline," and that petitioners' inability to vote in the primary of their choice was caused "by their own failure to take timely steps to effect their enrollment." The Court maintained that the law furthered the "important state goal" of inhibiting party raiding, "whereby voters in sympathy with one party designate themselves as voters of another party [to] influence [the] results of the other party's primary." Justice Powell, joined by Justices Douglas, Brennan, and Marshall, dissented.

Several months later, in Kusper v. Pontikes, 414 U.S. 51 (1973), the Court distinguished *Rosario* and invalidated an Illinois statute that prohibited any person "from voting in the primary election of a political party if he has voted in the primary of any other party within the preceding 23 months." The Court explained that "[t]he Illinois law, unlike [the law in *Rosario*,] 'locks' voters into a pre-existing party affiliation from one primary to the next, and the only way to break the 'lock' is to forgo voting in *any* primary for a period of almost two years." It concluded that such a scheme "substantially restricts an Illinois voter's freedom to change his political party affiliation" and is not the least drastic means of attaining the state's objectives. Justices Blackmun and Rehnquist dissented.

b. Dilution of the "Right to Vote"

Until 1962, the Court held that legislative districting controversies were non-justiciable. In Colegrove v. Green, 328 U.S. 549 (1946), for example, the Court declined to consider a claim that an Illinois law unconstitutionally prescribed congressional districts that were not approximately equal in population. Justice Frankfurter, writing for a plurality, explained that "this controversy concerns matters that bring courts into immediate and active relations with party contests. [It] is hostile to a democratic system to involve the judiciary in the politics of the people. [Courts] ought not to enter this political thicket."

In Baker v. Carr, 369 U.S. 186 (1962), however, which involved a claim that the apportionment of the Tennessee General Assembly violated the appellants' rights under the equal protection clause "by virtue of the debasement of their votes," the Court held "that a justiciable cause of action is stated upon which appellants would be entitled to appropriate relief." *Baker* is examined more fully in Chapter 1, section E3, supra.

Reynolds v. Sims
377 U.S. 533 (1964)

[In *Reynolds* and five companion cases, the Court held that in six states the system of apportionment of one or both houses of the legislature was unconstitutional. *Reynolds* involved Alabama; the other cases involved Colorado, Delaware, Maryland, New York, and Virginia. The Court observed: "Legislative apportionment in Alabama is signally illustrative and symptomatic of the seriousness of this problem in a number of States. [There has] been no reapportionment of seats in the Alabama Legislature for over 60 years. [This has resulted] in the perpetuated scheme becoming little more than an irrational anachronism [enabling] a minority stranglehold on the State Legislature."]

MR. CHIEF JUSTICE WARREN delivered the opinion of the Court. . . .

A predominant consideration in determining whether a State's legislative apportionment scheme constitutes an invidious discrimination violative of rights asserted under the Equal Protection Clause is that the rights allegedly impaired are individual and personal in nature. [Since] the right of suffrage is a fundamental matter in a free and democratic society [and] is preservative of other basic civil and political rights, any alleged infringement of the right of citizens to vote must be carefully and meticulously scrutinized. . . .

Legislators represent people, not trees or acres. Legislators are elected by voters, not farms or cities or economic interests. As long as ours is a representative form of government, [the] right to elect legislators in a free and unimpaired fashion is a bedrock of our political system. It could hardly be gainsaid that a constitutional claim had been asserted by an allegation that certain otherwise qualified voters had been entirely prohibited from voting for members of their state legislature. And, if a State should provide that the votes of citizens in one part of the

State should be given two times, or five times, or 10 times the weight of votes of citizens in another part of the State, it could hardly be contended that the right to vote of those residing in the disfavored areas had not been effectively diluted. [Of] course, the effect of state legislative districting schemes which give the same number of representatives to unequal numbers of constituents is identical. . . .

Logically, in a society ostensibly grounded on representative government, it would seem reasonable that a majority of the people of a State could elect a majority of that State's legislators. [To] sanction minority control of state legislative bodies, would appear to deny majority rights in a way that far surpasses any possible denial of minority rights that might otherwise be thought to result. [The] concept of equal protection has been traditionally viewed as requiring the uniform treatment of persons standing in the same relation to the governmental action questioned or challenged. With respect to the allocation of legislative representation, all voters, as citizens of a State, stand in the same relation regardless of where they live. Any suggested criteria for the differentiation of citizens are insufficient to justify any discrimination, as to the weight of their votes, unless relevant to the permissible purposes of legislative apportionment. Since the achieving of fair and effective representation for all citizens is concededly the basic aim of legislative apportionment, we conclude that the Equal Protection Clause guarantees the opportunity for equal participation by all voters in the election of state legislators. Diluting the weight of votes because of place of residence impairs basic constitutional rights under the Fourteenth Amendment. [Our] constitutional system amply provides for the protection of minorities by means other than giving them majority control of state legislatures. . . .

We are told that the matter of apportioning representation in a state legislature is a complex and many-faceted one. We are advised that States can rationally consider factors other than population in apportioning legislative representation. We are admonished not to restrict the power of the States to impose differing views as to political philosophy on their citizens. We are cautioned about the dangers of entering into political thickets and mathematical quagmires. Our answer is this: a denial of constitutionally protected rights demands judicial protection; our oath and our office require no less of us. [To] the extent that a citizen's right to vote is debased, he is that much less a citizen. [The] weight of a citizen's vote cannot be made to depend on where he lives. Population is, of necessity, the starting point for consideration and the controlling criterion for judgment in legislative apportionment controversies. A citizen, a qualified voter, is no more nor no less so because he lives in the city or on the farm. This is the clear and strong command of our Constitution's Equal Protection Clause. . . .

We hold that, as a basic constitutional standard, the Equal Protection Clause requires that the seats in both houses of a bicameral state legislature must be apportioned on a population basis. Simply stated, an individual's right to vote for state legislators is unconstitutionally impaired when its weight is in a substantial fashion diluted when compared with votes of citizens living in other parts of the State. . . .

[We] find the federal analogy inapposite and irrelevant to state legislative districting schemes. . . .

The system of representation in the two Houses of the Federal Congress is one ingrained in our Constitution [and] is based on the consideration that in establishing our type of federalism a group of formerly independent States bound themselves together under one national government. [A] compromise between the larger and smaller States on this matter averted a deadlock in the Constitutional Convention which had threatened to abort the birth of our Nation. . . .

Political subdivisions of States — counties, cities, or whatever — never were and never have been considered as sovereign entities. . . .

By holding that as a federal constitutional requisite both houses of a state legislature must be apportioned on a population basis, we mean that the Equal Protection Clause requires that a State make an honest and good faith effort to construct districts, in both houses of its legislature, as nearly of equal population as is practicable. We realize that it is a practical impossibility to arrange legislative districts so that each one has an identical number of residents, or citizens, or voters. [So] long as the divergences from a strict population standard are based on legitimate considerations incident to the effectuation of a rational state policy, some deviations from the equal-population principle are constitutionally permissible [but] neither history alone, nor economic or other sorts of group interests, are permissible factors in attempting to justify disparities from population-based representation. Citizens, not history or economic interests, cast votes. Considerations of area alone provide an insufficient justification for deviations from the equal-population principle. Again, people, not land or trees or pastures, vote. . . .

A consideration that appears to be of more substance in justifying some deviations from population-based representation in state legislatures is that of insuring some voice to political subdivisions, as political subdivisions. [In] many States much of the legislature's activity involves the enactment of so-called local legislation, directed only to the concerns of particular political subdivisions. [But] if, even as a result of a clearly rational state policy of according some legislative representation to political subdivisions, population is submerged as the controlling consideration in the apportionment of seats in the particular legislative body, then the right of all of the State's citizens to cast an effective and adequately weighted vote would be unconstitutionally impaired. . . .

[Affirmed and remanded.]

MR. JUSTICE HARLAN, dissenting [in all six cases]. . . .

[The] history of the adoption of the Fourteenth Amendment provides conclusive evidence that neither those who proposed nor those who ratified the Amendment believed that the Equal Protection Clause limited the power of the States to apportion their legislatures as they saw fit. Moreover, the history demonstrates that the intention to leave this power undisturbed was deliberate and was widely believed to be essential to the adoption of the Amendment. [Justice Harlan's extensive historical analysis is omitted.]

It is difficult to imagine a more intolerable and inappropriate interference by the judiciary with the independent legislatures of the States. . . .

Although the Court — necessarily, as I believe — provides only generalities in elaboration of its main thesis, its opinion nevertheless fully demonstrates how far removed these problems are from fields of judicial competence. [In] one or another of today's opinions, the Court declares it unconstitutional for a State to give effective consideration to any of the following in establishing legislative districts:

(1) history;
(2) "economic or other sorts of group interests";
(3) area;

    (4) geographical considerations;
    (5) a desire "to insure effective representation for sparsely settled areas";
    (6) "availability of access of citizens to their representatives";
    (7) theories of bicameralism (except those approved by the Court);
    (8) occupation;
    (9) "an attempt to balance urban and rural power";
  (10) the preference of a majority of voters in the State.

So far as presently appears, the *only* factor which a State may consider, apart from numbers, is political subdivisions. But even "a clearly rational state policy" recognizing this factor is unconstitutional if "population is submerged as the controlling consideration. . . ."

I know of no principle of logic or practical or theoretical politics, still less any constitutional principle, which establishes all or any of these exclusions. [The] Court says [only] that "legislators represent people, not trees or acres." [This] may be conceded. But it is surely equally obvious, and, in the context of elections, more meaningful to note that people are not ciphers and that legislators can represent their electors only by speaking for their interests — economic, social, political — many of which do reflect the place where the electors live. . . .

MR. JUSTICE STEWART, whom MR. JUSTICE CLARK joins, dissenting [in the Colorado and New York cases]. . . .

[My] own understanding of the various theories of representative government is that no one theory has ever commanded unanimous assent. [But] even if it were thought that the rule announced today by the Court is, as a matter of political theory, the most desirable general rule which can be devised, [I] could not join in the fabrication of a constitutional mandate which imports and forever freezes one theory of political thought into our Constitution. . . .

Representative government is a process of accommodating group interests through democratic institutional arrangements. [Appropriate] legislative apportionment, therefore, should ideally be designed to insure effective representation in the State's legislature, in cooperation with other organs of political power, of the various groups and interests making up the electorate. [Population] factors must often to some degree be subordinated in devising a legislative apportionment plan which is to achieve the important goal of ensuring a fair, effective, and balanced representation of the regional, social, and economic interests within a State. [What] constitutes a rational plan reasonably designed to achieve this objective will vary from State to State, since each State is unique, in terms of topography, geography, demography, history, heterogeneity and concentration of population, variety of social and economic interests, and in the operation and interrelation of its political institutions. But so long as a State's apportionment plan reasonably achieves, in the light of the State's own characteristics, effective and balanced representation of all substantial interests, without sacrificing the principle of effective majority rule, that plan cannot be considered irrational.

[The] Equal Protection Clause demands but two basic attributes of any plan of state legislative apportionment. First, it demands that, in the light of the State's own characteristics and needs, the plan must be a rational one. Secondly, it demands that the plan must be such as not to permit the systematic frustration of the will of a majority of the electorate of the State. [But,] beyond this, I think there is nothing in the Federal Constitution to prevent a State from choosing any electoral legislative structure it thinks best suited to the interests, temper, and customs of its people.

[Applying these standards, Justice Stewart voted to uphold the Colorado and New York plans of legislative apportionment. The Colorado House was apportioned on a population basis, but rural areas were significantly "overrepresented" in the Senate. Stewart maintained that this departure from a population-based apportionment was permissible because it had been adopted in a statewide referendum and because it accommodated the distinct interests and characteristics of the state's various regions. Stewart thought that smaller population districts were reasonable in sparsely populated areas, for example, to enable senators "to maintain close contact with [constituents]," and he thought they were reasonable in certain agricultural areas to prevent the grouping of this portion of the electorate "in districts with larger numbers of voters with wholly different interests." Moreover, Stewart noted, because of the strength of the urban areas, "no possible combination of Colorado senators from rural districts [could] control the Senate." Stewart thus concluded that the Colorado scheme represented a reasonable "choice to protect the minority's interests." The New York plan assured smaller counties greater representation in the Assembly than would be warranted under a population-based apportionment and limited representation of the largest counties. Justice Stewart argued that this was justified as a counterweight to New York City's "concentration of population, homogeneity of interest, and political cohesiveness."]

Note: Reynolds *and Its Progeny*

1. *"One person, one vote."* Note that Kramer was denied the right to vote, whereas no one in *Reynolds* was denied that right. This makes it necessary to question whether "one person, one vote" follows in any way from the equality principle or from the conclusion that the "right to vote" is "fundamental." Does Justice Stewart's emphasis on "systematic frustration of the majority" provide a preferable focus for judical inquiry? Consider the following views.

a. R. Bork, The Tempting of America 86-87 (1989):

The Warren majority's new constitutional doctrine was supported by nothing. . . . Madison's writing on the republican form of government specified by the guarantee clause suggests that state governments, which were structured as representative democracies, could take many forms, so long as those forms do not become "aristocratic or monarchical." That is not easily translated into a rigid requirement of equal weight for every vote. It translates far more readily into Justice Stewart's position. . . .

b. Auerbach, The Reapportionment Cases: One Person, One Vote — One Vote, One Value, 1964 Sup. Ct. Rev. 1, 2:

It is paradoxical for the judicial activists, who extol the Court as the protector of minorities, to praise it for helping to erase the power of minorities to curb majority rule in our state legislatures. But it is also paradoxical for the advocates of judicial self-limitation to criticize the Court for helping to make majority rule effective, because the case for self-restraint rests on the assumption that the Court is reviewing the leg-islative acts of representatives who are put in office [by] a majority of the people. Since malapportionment destroys this assumption, judicial intervention to remove this obstacle to majority rule may be less intolerable than the self-perpetuation of minority rule.

c. J. Ely, Democracy and Distrust 124 (1980):

[There] were two ways to avoid the unadministrability thicket. One was to stay out of the area altogether. That would have meant, however, that the ins would simply have gone on maintaining their positions by valuing one person's vote at a sixth of another's. Everyone [agreed] that that was no more compatible with the underlying theory of our Constitution than taking away some people's votes altogether. So the Court entered, and *precisely because of considerations of administrability*, soon found itself with no perceived alternative but to move to a one person, one vote standard.

2. *Reapportionment: a "success story"?* Consider McKay, Reapportionment: Success Story of the Warren Court, 67 Mich. L. Rev. 223, 226-229 (1968):

By 1960 malapportionment in the United States had attained such proportions that the integrity of representative government was in many instances endangered. [*Reynolds*, however, was viewed by some] as an abuse of judicial power. [Oppo-nents] of reapportionment swiftly mounted an attack [that included] efforts to limit the jurisdiction of the federal courts [and to amend the Constitution. These] efforts were unsuccessful [for] the simple reason that the public did not oppose the deci-sions. [Moreover, while] there was some footdragging, and judicial proceedings were often necessary, [within four years of *Reynolds* congressional and state leg-islative district lines had been redrawn in almost every state].

For more skeptical views, see A. Bickel, The Supreme Court and the Idea of Progress (1970); Bork, supra, at 88-90. For a discussion of the circumstances un-der which courts can produce social reform — labeling reapportionment a case in point — see G. Rosenberg, The Hollow Hope (1993).

3. *Popularly mandated malapportionment. Reynolds* was designed, in part, to protect majoritarianism and to prevent "minority control of state legislative bod-ies." But malapportionment has been held unconstitutional even if it is approved by a majority of the state's voters. In Lucas v. Forty-Fourth General Assembly, 377 U.S. 713 (1964), a companion case to *Reynolds*, the Colorado scheme, which ap-portioned only one of the two Houses on the basis of population, had been ap-proved in 1962 by a statewide referendum in which the voters specifically re-jected a plan to apportion both Houses on the basis of population. Nonetheless, the Court held the scheme invalid: "An individual's constitutionally protected right to cast an equally weighted vote cannot be denied even by a vote of a ma-jority of a State's electorate, if the apportionment scheme [fails] to measure up to the requirements of the Equal Protection Clause. [A] citizen's constitutional rights can hardly be infringed simply because a majority of the people choose that it be."

4. *Supermajorities.* If *Reynolds* was designed in part to protect majoritarian-ism and to prevent minority control of government, may a state constitutionally require the assent of a "supermajority" to enact legislation or take other action? In Gordon v. Lance, 403 U.S. 1 (1971), the Court upheld a West Virginia law

prohibiting political subdivisions from incurring bonded indebtedness without the approval of 60 percent of the voters in a referendum election. The Court explained:

> [Any] departure from strict majority rule gives disproportionate power to the minority. But there is nothing in the language of the Constitution, our history or our cases that requires that a majority always prevail on every issue. [The] Constitution itself provides that a simple majority vote is insufficient on some issues. [We] conclude that so long as such provisions do not discriminate against or authorize discrimination against any identifiable class they do not violate the Equal Protection Clause.

The Court added in a footnote: "We intimate no view on the constitutionality of a provision requiring unanimity or giving a veto power to a very small group. Nor do we decide whether a State may [require] extraordinary majorities for the election of public officers."

After *Lance*, may a state require a 60 percent majority in the legislature to increase taxes? May it require a 60 percent majority to unseat an incumbent? May it prohibit a new county charter from being adopted unless it is approved by "majorities of the voters who live in the cities within the county, and of those who live outside the cities"? See Lockport v. Citizens for Community Action, 430 U.S. 259 (1977), in which the Court upheld such a scheme. The Court reasoned that "[t]he equal protection principles applicable in gauging the fairness of an election involving the choice of legislative representatives are of limited relevance [in] analyzing the propriety of recognizing distinctive voter interests in a 'single-shot' referendum." The Court concluded that the "differing interests of city and noncity voters in the adoption of a new county charter" were sufficient to justify the scheme.

5. *Local government units.* In Avery v. Midland County, 390 U.S. 474 (1968), the Court extended *Reynolds* to subunits of state government. The Midland County Commissioners Court, which had "general responsibility and power for local affairs," consisted of five commissioners, one elected at large and one elected from each of four districts. One of these districts had 67,000 residents; the other three had fewer than 1,000 each. Noting that the commissioners had jurisdiction over tax rates and adoption of the county budget, the Court rejected an argument that the commissioners' responsibilities were "insufficiently legislative" to require their election to conform to the principle of one person, one vote.

In Hadley v. Junior College District, 397 U.S. 50 (1970), the Court extended *Avery* to a junior college district consisting of eight districts, where one district with 60 percent of the population was authorized to elect only 50 percent of the junior college district's trustees. The Court explained that the district's powers to run the schools, levy taxes, and issue bonds were "general enough and [had] sufficient impact throughout the district" to require equal apportionment. It noted, however, "that there might be some cases in which a State elects certain functionaries whose duties are so far removed from normal governmental activities and so disproportionately affect different groups that a popular election in compliance with *Reynolds* [might] not be required." Chief Justice Burger and Justices Harlan and Stewart dissented.

6. *Permissible deviations from "one person, one vote."* The courts have developed a number of statistical indices to measure malapportionment. The most

prominent index is the "maximum percentage deviation." For example, if a state with a population of 10 million is allotted ten congressmen, the ideal district will have a population of 1 million. If the largest district has a population of 1.1 million (10 percent above the ideal) and the smallest has 0.9 million (10 percent below the ideal), the maximum percentage deviation is 20 percent. What is the maximum percentage deviation that should satisfy *Reynolds?* How should one measure "population" — eligible voters, registered voters, total population?

a. *Congressional districting.* In Wesberry v. Sanders, 376 U.S. 1 (1964), the Court held that the provision of article I, section 2 that United States representatives "be chosen 'by the People of the several States' means that as nearly as is practicable one man's vote in a congressional election is to be worth as much as another's." The Court thus invalidated a Georgia congressional districting scheme with a maximum percentage deviation of more than 140 percent. The Court has relied on *Wesberry* to invalidate congressional districting plans with much smaller deviations. See Kirkpatrick v. Preisler, 394 U.S. 526 (1969) (5.97 percent); Wells v. Rockefeller, 394 U.S. 542 (1969) (13.1 percent); White v. Weiser, 412 U.S. 783 (1973) (4.13 percent); Karcher v. Daggett, 462 U.S. 725 (1983) (0.7 percent).

In *Kirkpatrick,* the Court held that no variance from absolute equality could be justified as de minimis. In *Karcher,* the Court reaffirmed *Kirkpatrick.* It again explained that states must "come as nearly as practicable to population equality." Justice White, joined by Chief Justice Burger and Justices Powell and Rehnquist, dissented, concluding that if *Kirkpatrick* required the invalidation of a districting plan with a maximum percentage deviation of only 0.7 percent, then it was time to reconsider *Kirkpatrick.*

b. *State districting.* Under the equal protection clause, the Court has tolerated significant deviations from the mathematical ideal in its review of districting plans for state and local offices. In Mahan v. Howell, 410 U.S. 315 (1973), the Court upheld a Virginia legislative districting plan with a maximum percentage deviation of 16.4 percent. The Court distinguished *Kirkpatrick* and explained that "more flexibility was constitutionally permissible with respect to state legislative reapportionment" because of the interest in "the normal functioning of state and local governments." It held that the deviations in the Virginia plan satisfied *Reynold's* goal of "substantial equality of population" and were justified by "the State's policy of maintaining the integrity of political subdivision lines."

Later that term, in Gaffney v. Cummings, 412 U.S. 735 (1973), and White v. Regester, 412 U.S. 755 (1973), the Court recognized a category of "minor" deviations that require no justification at all. In opinions by Justice White, the Court upheld state legislative districting plans with maximum percentage deviations of 9.9 and 7.8 percent. The Court observed that these "relatively minor" deviations were insufficient to meet the "threshold requirement of proving a prima facie case of invidious discrimination" and thus required no justification. It distinguished these cases from cases like *Reynolds,* which involved "enormous" and unjustifiable deviations, and cases like *Mahan,* which involved deviations "sufficiently large to require justification," but which were justifiable. It concluded that *Reynolds'* goal of "substantial equality" did "not in any commonsense way depend upon eliminating the insignificant population variation [in these cases]." In subsequent decisions, the Court has "established that, as a general matter, an apportionment plan with a maximum population deviation of under 10 percent falls within [the] category of minor deviations." Brown v. Thompson, 462 U.S. 835 (1983).

7. *Political gerrymandering.* In Gaffney v. Cummings, supra, the challengers of the districting plan maintained that, even if the plan satisfied the one person, one vote requirement of *Reynolds,* it was nonetheless "invidiously discriminatory" because it was admittedly drawn to "achieve a rough approximation of statewide political strengths of the Democratic and Republican Parties." The Court held that the "political fairness principle" was not unconstitutional:

> Politics and political considerations are inseparable from districting and apportionment. [It] may be suggested that those who redistrict and reapportion should work with census, not political, data and achieve population equality without regard for political impact. But this politically mindless approach may produce, whether intended or not, the most grossly gerrymandered results. [Districting schemes may be invalid] if racial or political groups [are] fenced out of the political process and their voting strength invidiously minimized, [but there is no] constitutional warrant to invalidate a state plan, otherwise within tolerable population limits, because it undertakes, not to minimize or eliminate the political strength of any group or party, but to recognize it and, through districting, provide a rough sort of proportional representation in the legislative halls of the State.

Suppose a districting scheme adversely affects the relative political power of an identifiable political or racial group?

City of Mobile v. Bolden
446 U.S. 55 (1980)

[Since 1911, the city of Mobile, Alabama, has been governed by a City Commission consisting of three commissioners who jointly exercise all legislative, executive, and administrative power. The commissioners are elected not by the residents of three distinct districts but by the residents of the city at large. This electoral system "is followed by literally thousands of municipalities." Although Mobile has a substantial black population, no black has ever been elected to the commission. In *Bolden,* the Court rejected a claim that the retention of the at-large electoral system in such circumstances unconstitutionally diluted the voting strength of blacks.]

MR. JUSTICE STEWART announced the judgment of the Court and delivered an opinion, in which THE CHIEF JUSTICE, MR. JUSTICE POWELL, and MR. JUSTICE REHNQUIST joined.

[At the outset, Justice Stewart observed that the "claim that at-large electoral schemes" violate the equal protection clause "is rooted in their winner-take-all aspects, their tendency to submerge minorities." Stewart noted that, despite this feature, multimember legislative districts "are not unconstitutional per se." Rather, he maintained, they are invalid only if their purpose is "invidiously to minimize or cancel out the voting potential of racial or ethnic minorities." "A plaintiff," in other words, "must prove that the disputed plan was 'conceived or operated' as [a] purposeful devic[e] to further [racial] discrimination." Justice Stewart explained that this "burden of proof is simply one aspect of the basic principle that only if there is purposeful discrimination can there be a violation of the Equal Protection Clause." To illustrate, Justice Stewart pointed to Gomillion v. Lightfoot, 364 U.S. 339 (1960), in which the Court had invalidated a "racially motivated gerrymander of municipal boundaries"; White v. Regester, 412 U.S. 755 (1973), in which the Court had invalidated a multimember district plan that minimized the voting strength of blacks and Mexican-Americans where it was proved that "the political processes [were] not equally open to participation by the group[s] in question"; and Wright v. Rockefeller, 376 U.S. 52 (1964), in which the Court had sustained a state congressional reapportionment statute against claims that the district lines had been racially gerrymandered because the plaintiffs had failed to prove that the legislature had been "motivated by racial considerations." Applying the intent standard, Justice Stewart concluded that "the evidence [falls] far short of showing that the appellants 'conceived or operated [a] purposeful devic[e] to further racial [discrimination].'" (This aspect of *Bolden* is addressed in Chapter 5, section C2, supra.)]

We turn finally to the arguments advanced in [Mr.] Justice Marshall's dissenting opinion. The theory [appears] to be that every "political group," or at least every such group that is in the minority, has a federal constitutional right to elect candidates in proportion to its numbers.[22] Moreover, a political group's "right" to have its candidates elected is said to be a "fundamental interest," the infringement of which may be established without proof that a State has acted with the purpose of impairing anybody's access to the political process. This dissenting opinion finds the "right" infringed in the present case because no Negro has been elected to the Mobile City Commission.

Whatever appeal the dissenting opinion's view may have as a matter of political theory, it is not the law. The Equal Protection Clause [does] not require proportional representation as an imperative of political organization. The entitlement that the dissenting opinion assumes to exist simply is not to be found in the Constitution of the United States.

It is of course true that a law that impinges upon a fundamental right [is] presumptively unconstitutional. [And it is true] that the Equal Protection Clause confers a substantive right to participate in elections on an equal basis with other qualified voters. See [Dunn v. Blumstein; Reynolds v. Sims]. But this right to equal participation in the electoral process does not protect any "political group," however defined, from electoral defeat.

The dissenting opinion erroneously discovers the asserted entitlement to group representation within the "one person, one vote" principle of Reynolds v. Sims, supra, and its progeny. [The] Court [there] recognized that a voter's right to "have an equally effective voice" in the election of representatives is impaired where representation is not apportioned substantially on a population basis. [There] can be, of course, no claim that the "one person, one vote" principle has been violated in this case, because the city of Mobile is a unitary electoral district and the Commission elections are conducted at large. It is therefore obvious that

22. The dissenting opinion seeks to disclaim this description of its theory by suggesting that a claim of vote dilution may require, in addition to proof of electoral defeat, some evidence of "historical and social factors" indicating that the group in question is without political influence. [Putting] to the side the evident fact that these gauzy sociological considerations have no constitutional basis, it remains far from certain that they could, in any principled manner, exclude the claims of any discrete political group that happens, for whatever reason, to elect fewer of its candidates than arithmetic indicates it might. Indeed, the putative limits are bound to prove illusory if the express purpose informing their application would be, as the dissent assumes, to redress the "inequitable distribution of political influence."

nobody's vote has been "diluted" in the sense in which that word was used in the *Reynolds* case. [It] is, of course, true that the right of a person to vote on an equal basis with other voters draws much of its significance from the political associations that its exercise reflects, but it is an altogether different matter to conclude that political groups themselves have an independent constitutional claim to representation.[26]

[Reversed and remanded.]

MR. JUSTICE BLACKMUN, concurring in the result.

[I] am inclined to agree with Mr. Justice White that, in this case, "the findings of the District Court amply support an inference of purposeful discrimination." I concur in the Court's judgment of reversal, however, because I believe that the relief afforded appellees by the District Court, [changing the form of the city's government to a mayor-council system], was not commensurate with the sound exercise of judicial discretion. . . .

MR. JUSTICE STEVENS, concurring in the judgment. . . .

In my view, there is a fundamental distinction between state action that inhibits an individual's right to vote and state action that affects the political strength of various groups that compete for leadership in a democratically governed community. That distinction divides so-called vote dilution practices into two different categories "governed by entirely different constitutional considerations."

In the first category are practices such as poll taxes or literacy tests that deny individuals access to the ballot. Districting practices that make an individual's vote in a heavily populated district less significant than an individual's vote in a smaller district also belong in that category. [Such] practices must be tested by the strictest of constitutional standards. . . .

This case does not fit within the first category. [Rather,] this case draws into question a political structure that treats all individuals as equals but adversely affects the political strength of a racially identifiable group. . . .

In my view [a challenged scheme should be invalidated if three objective factors are present]: (1) [it] was manifestly not the product of a routine or a traditional political decision; (2) it [has] a significant adverse impact on a minority group; and (3) it [is] unsupported by any neutral justification and thus [is] either

---

26. It is difficult to perceive how the implications of the dissenting opinion's theory of group representation could rationally be cabined. Indeed, certain preliminary practical questions immediately come to mind: Can only members of a minority of the voting population in a particular municipality be members of a "political group"? How large must a "group" be to be a "political group"? Can any "group" call itself a "political group"? If not, who is to say which "groups" are "political groups"? Can a qualified voter belong to more than one "political group"? Can there be more than one "political group" among white voters (e.g., Irish-American, Italian-American, Polish-American, Jews, Catholics, Protestants)? Can there be more than one "political group" among nonwhite voters? Do the answers to any of these questions depend upon the particular demographic composition of a given city? Upon the total size of its voting population? Upon the size of its governing body? Upon its form of government? Upon its history? Its geographic location? The fact that even these preliminary questions may be largely unanswerable suggests some of the conceptual and practical fallacies in the constitutional theory espoused by the dissenting opinion, putting to one side the total absence of support for that theory in the Constitution itself.

totally irrational or entirely motivated by a desire to curtail the political strength of the minority. . . .

[In] this case, if the commission form of government in Mobile were extraordinary, or if it were nothing more than a vestige of history, with no [rational] justification, it would surely violate the Constitution [because of] its adverse impact on black voters plus the absence of any legitimate justification for the system. [And this would be so] without reference to the subjective intent of the political body that has refused to alter it.

Conversely, I [am] persuaded that a political decision that affects group voting rights may be valid even if it can be proved that irrational or invidious factors have played some part in its enactment or retention. The [process of] drawing political boundaries [inevitably] involves a series of compromises among different group interests. If the process is to work, it must reflect an awareness of group interests and it must tolerate some attempts to advantage or to disadvantage particular segments of the voting populace. [The] standard cannot, therefore, be so strict that any evidence of a purpose to disadvantage a bloc of voters will justify a finding of "invidious discrimination"; otherwise, the facts of political life would deny legislatures the right to perform the districting function. Accordingly, a political decision that is supported by valid and articulable justifications cannot be invalid simply because some participants in the decisionmaking process were motivated by a purpose to disadvantage a minority group.

The decision to retain the commission form of government in Mobile, Ala., is such a decision. [The] fact that these at-large systems characteristically place one or more minority groups at a significant disadvantage in the struggle for political power cannot invalidate all such systems. Nor can it be the law that such systems are valid when there is no evidence that they were instituted or maintained for discriminatory reasons, but that they may be selectively condemned on the basis of the subjective motivation of some of their supporters. A contrary view "would spawn endless litigation" [and] would entangle the judiciary in a voracious political thicket.

In sum, I believe we must accept the choice to retain Mobile's commission form of government as constitutionally permissible even though that choice may well be the product of mixed motivation, some of which is invidious. . . .

MR. JUSTICE BRENNAN, dissenting.

I dissent because I agree with Mr. Justice Marshall that proof of discriminatory impact is sufficient in these cases. I also dissent because, even accepting the plurality's premise that discriminatory purpose must be shown, I agree with Mr. Justice Marshall and Mr. Justice White that the appellees have clearly met that burden.

MR. JUSTICE WHITE, dissenting.

[In a lengthy opinion, Justice White maintained] that the findings of the District Court amply support an inference of purposeful discrimination. . . .

MR. JUSTICE MARSHALL, dissenting. . . .

[The] equal protection problem attacked by the "one person, one vote" principle is [one] of vote dilution: under *Reynolds*, each citizen must have an "equally effective voice" in the election of representatives. In the present cases, the alleged vote dilution, though caused by the combined effects of the electoral structure and social and historical factors rather than by unequal population distribution, is analytically the same concept: the unjustified abridgment of a fundamental right. . . .

The plurality's response is that my approach amounts to nothing less than a constitutional requirement of proportional representation for groups. [I] explicitly reject the notion that the Constitution contains any such requirement. The constitutional protection against vote dilution [does] not extend to those situations in which a group has merely failed to elect representatives in proportion to its share of the population. To prove unconstitutional vote dilution, the group is also required to carry the far more onerous burden of demonstrating that it has been effectively fenced out of the political process. Typical of the plurality's mischaracterization of my position is its assertion that I would provide protection against vote dilution for "every 'political group,' or at least every such group that is in the minority." The vote-dilution doctrine can logically apply only to groups whose electoral discreteness and insularity allow dominant political factions to ignore them.

The plaintiffs [proved] that no Negro had ever been elected to the Mobile City Commission, despite the fact that Negroes constitute about one-third of the electorate, and that the persistence of severe racial bloc voting made it highly unlikely that any Negro could be elected at large in the foreseeable future. [The] plaintiffs convinced the District Court that Mobile Negroes were unable to use alternative avenues of political influence. They showed that Mobile Negroes still suffered pervasive present effects of massive historical official and private discrimination, and that the City Commission had been quite unresponsive to the needs of the minority community. [Negroes] are grossly underrepresented on city boards and committees. [The] city's distribution of public services is racially discriminatory. . . .

[Even if] it is assumed that proof of discriminatory intent is necessary to support the vote-dilution claims in these cases, the question becomes what evidence will satisfy this requirement. . . .

I would apply the common-law foreseeability presumption to the present cases. [Because] the foreseeable disproportionate impact was so severe, the burden of proof should have shifted to the defendants, and they should have been required to show that they refused to modify the districting schemes in spite of, not because of, their severe discriminatory effect. Reallocation of the burden of proof is especially appropriate in these cases, where the challenged state action infringes the exercise of a fundamental right. The defendants would carry their burden of proof only if they showed that they considered submergence of the Negro vote a detriment, not a benefit, of the multimember systems, that they accorded minority citizens the same respect given to whites, and that they nevertheless decided to maintain the systems for legitimate reasons. . . .

The plurality [fails] to recognize that the maintenance of multimember districts in the face of foreseeable discriminatory consequences strongly suggests that officials are blinded by "racially selective sympathy and indifference." Like outright racial hostility, selective racial indifference reflects a belief that the concerns of the minority are not worthy of the same degree of attention paid to problems perceived by whites. When an interest as fundamental as voting is diminished along racial lines, a requirement that discriminatory purpose must be proved should be satisfied by a showing that official action was produced by this type of pervasive bias. . . .

Note: Vote Dilution and the Interests of Groups

1. A *"fundamental interest" in "proportional" representation?* Do you agree with Justice Stewart that there is no constitutional right to proportional representation? How would you distinguish between "one person, one vote" and "one group, one representative"? Consider Note, The Constitutional Imperative of Proportional Representation, 94 Yale L.J. 163, 172-173, 175-176, 182 (1984):

Two fundamental values underlie the Supreme Court's debate about constitutional rights in voting: majority rule and minority representation. The debate has taken the traditional system of winner-take-all single-member districts as a given. [But this] system contains a strong majoritarian bias. If the supporters of two parties were distributed uniformly throughout the area of the elections, the party winning the most votes would win every seat in the legislature. The votes for the minority candidate would in effect be wasted. [Under the Court's analysis, majority] rule is conceptualized [as] an individual right deserving the strongest protection, whereas minority representation is conceptualized [as] a group right that will not be vindicated without proof of invidious discrimination. But the opposition of individual and group rights is logically [untenable]: The rights labeled as group rights are also individual rights and vice versa. [The] real distinction [is] not between individual and group rights but between the right to an equally weighted vote and the right to an equally powerful or equally meaningful vote. [The relevant] constitutional values [can] be fully guaranteed only by [proportional representation, for] proportional representation [is the only system that both achieves] majority rule [and] simultaneously guarantee[s] the individual and group right to both an equally weighted vote and an equally meaningful vote.

It is not so clear, though, that proportional representation is always in the interest of an electoral minority. Sometimes a minority is better off with a number of representatives at least partly beholden to it than with one or two representatives wholly within their control. Consider the view that in the 1980s southern Democrats in the House and Senate were particularly attuned to the interests of black voters, and that, if there had been a system of proportional representation — with two or three representatives who were themselves black, and all other representatives without much of a need or desire to listen to blacks — the influence of blacks would actually have diminished. Consider also the view that it is false and pernicious to refer to something called "the interest of blacks" and "the interest of whites," as if these were unitary things rather than to emphasize overlapping interests among racial and other groups.

But perhaps there are systematic patterns of racial bloc voting, and perhaps it is unacceptable if one group finds itself in the situation of permanent loser. See generally L. Guinier, The Tyranny of the Majority (1993). Guinier argues, in particular, for a system designed to ensure that all groups are permitted to select representatives of their choice. She argues that cumulative voting can bring about this result. She suggests: "[A] system is procedurally fair only to the extent that it gives each participant an equal opportunity to influence outcomes. I call this principle one-vote, one-value. . . . Race-conscious districting is simply one expression of a larger reality: winner-take-all districting. Both justify wasting votes." Id. at 156. In Guinier's view, constitutional and statutory schemes have suffered to the extent that they have not allowed voters, whatever their group, to have a realistic chance of electing someone of their choice. "Interest representation . . . [fulfills] the dual vision [that] minority groups should enjoy equal voting weight *and* equal power. Instead of emphasizing arbitrary territorial boundaries, which waste the votes of both minority and majority groups, interest representation favors allowing voters of the same interests to join together in voting for candidates of their choice, regardless of where voters live in the jurisdiction." Id. at 117. Guinier's complex and controversial argument deserves careful attention.

2. A *"fundamental" interest in "fair" representation?* How does Justice Marshall's argument differ from a right to proportional representation? For a comprehensive discussion of the problem, see Symposium: Gerrymandering and the Courts, 22 UCLA L. Rev. 1 (1985).

3. *Discriminatory purpose.* As is evident in *Bolden*, the Court will invalidate a gerrymander or multimember district plan if it is adopted or retained for the *purpose* of minimizing the relative voting strength of blacks. See Rogers v. Lodge, 458 U.S. 613 (1982) (invalidating an at-large system because it was maintained for a racially discriminatory purpose); Gomillion v. Lightfoot, 364 U.S. 339 (1960) (invalidating a districting plan because the lines were drawn with a racially discriminatory purpose). The issue of discriminatory purpose is examined more fully in Chapter 5, section C2, supra. But perhaps the standard for proving discriminatory purpose should be relaxed when the challenged law involves a "fundamental interest," or when, as in *Bolden*, it involves the structure of political representation. Consider, on the other hand, Justice Stevens's argument that the Court should not invalidate a gerrymander or multimember district plan because "irrational or invidious factors [played] some part in its enactment or retention." In his view, the process of drawing "political boundaries [must] reflect an awareness of group interests and [must] tolerate some attempts to advantage or to disadvantage particular segments of the voting populace."

If racially motivated gerrymanders are impermissible, what about gerrymanders designed to minimize the relative voting strength of particular political parties, ethnic groups, or economic factions? Suppose, for example, a state draws district lines in order to minimize the relative voting strength of farmers. May a state draw district lines in order to assure at least proportional representation for particular groups? In *Gaffney*, the Court upheld the "fairness principle" as applied to political parties. Consider United Jewish Organizations v. Carey, 430 U.S. 144 (1979), in which New York redrew district lines in Brooklyn in order to maintain black representation in the state legislature. To achieve this result, the redistrict divided the local Hasidic community into several districts, thus assuring that each district had a substantial nonwhite majority. The Court upheld the plan. Justice White, joined by Justices Brennan, Blackmun, and Stevens, concluded that the Constitution did not prohibit the use of race in this manner where the redistricting was authorized by the Voting Rights Act and the percentage of districts in the county with substantial nonwhite majorities did not exceed the percentage of the population of the county that was nonwhite. In a separate part of his opinion, Justice White, joined by Justices Stevens and Rehnquist, concluded that, wholly apart from the Voting Rights Act, this use of race was permissible because it "represented no racial slur or stigma with respect to whites or any other race" and did not "minimize or unfairly cancel out white voting strength." Justice White observed that racial voting is a common, if "unfortunate," practice and stated that it is "permissible for a State, employing sound districting principles [to] attempt to prevent racial minorities from being repeatedly outvoted." Justice Stewart, joined by Justice Powell, concluded that there had been no showing of racial discrimination, and that racial awareness in legislative reapportionment is not per se unconstitutional. Chief Justice Burger dissented on the ground that the Constitution mandates reapportionment along racially neutral lines.

May a state, as a form of "affirmative action," draw district lines in order to give blacks *greater* than proportional representation? The issue of "affirmative action" is examined more fully in Chapter 5, section C4, supra.

4. *Beyond discriminatory purpose: Justice Stevens's view.* Do you agree with Justice Stevens that the appropriate test should focus on objective factors rather than on the "subjective intent" of the decisionmakers? One might ask whether Justice Stevens's approach is an effort to balance the interest in fair representation against competing state interests or is instead merely an objective means of ascertaining intent.

Justice Stevens elaborated on his *Bolden* concurrence in Karcher v. Daggett, 462 U.S. 725 (1983) (Stevens, J., concurring):

> [Judicial] preoccupation with the goal of perfect population equality is an inadequate method of judging the constitutionality of an apportionment plan. [Although numerical equality] directly protects individuals, it protects groups only indirectly at best, [for] a standard "of absolute equality is perfectly compatible with 'gerrymandering' of the worst sort." [In] evaluating equal protection challenges to districting plans, [I] would consider whether the plan has a significant adverse impact on an identifiable political group, whether the plan has objective indicia of irregularity, and then, whether the State is able to produce convincing evidence that the plan nevertheless serves neutral, legitimate interests of the community as a whole. [To demonstrate that there are "objective indicia of irregularity," the plaintiffs might prove that the districts have "dramatically irregular shapes," or that they deviate extensively "from established political boundaries," or that "the process for formulating and adopting a plan excluded divergent viewpoints, openly reflected the use of partisan criteria, and provided no explanation of the reasons for selecting one plan over another."] Although a scheme in fact worsens the voting position of a particular group, and though its geographic configuration or genesis is sufficiently irregular to violate one or more of the criteria just [mentioned], it will nevertheless be constitutionally valid if the State can demonstrate that the plan as a whole [advances] "legitimate considerations incident to the effectuation of a rational state policy." [But] if a State is unable to respond to a plaintiff's prima facie case by showing that its plan is supported by adequate neutral criteria, I believe a court could properly conclude that the challenged scheme is either totally irrational or entirely motivated by a desire to curtail the political strength of the affected group.

See also Rogers v. Lodge, 458 U.S. 613 (1982) (Stevens, J., dissenting). What exactly is the difference between Justice Stevens's approach and that of the plurality?

Davis v. Bandemer

478 U.S. 109 (1986)

JUSTICE WHITE announced the judgment of the Court and delivered the opinion of the Court as to Part II and an opinion in which JUSTICE BRENNAN, JUSTICE MARSHALL, and JUSTICE BLACKMUN joined as to Parts I, III, and IV.

In this case, we review a judgment [which] sustained an equal protection challenge to Indiana's 1981 state apportionment on the basis that the law unconstitutionally diluted the votes of Indiana Democrats. Although we find such political gerrymandering to be justiciable, we conclude that the District Court applied an insufficiently demanding standard in finding unconstitutional vote dilution. Consequently, we reverse.

I

[The challenged apportionment plan, adopted by the Republican-controlled state legislature in 1981, provided for state senate and house districts of substantially equal population. The Democrats nonetheless claimed that, by using a mix of single and multimembered districts and gerrymandering district lines, the plan substantially understated Democratic voting strength. In elections held under the plan in 1982, the Democrats received 51.9 percent of the total house vote and 53.1 percent of the total senate vote, yet won only forty-three of 100 house seats and only thirteen of twenty-five senate seats.

[According to facts contained in Justice Powell's dissenting opinion, the districting plan was written by a conference committee of the state legislature with the aid of a private computer firm. All members of the conference committee were Republicans, and the information fed into the computer primarily concerned the political complexion of the state's precincts. The redistricting process was conducted in secret, and the plan was not revealed until two days before the conclusion of the legislative session. On the last day of the session, it was adopted by party line votes in both houses.]

II

[In this section of his opinion, Justice White, writing for the Court, holds that the political question doctrine does not prevent the Court from reaching the merits. This portion of the opinion is discussed in Chapter 1 supra.]

III

[Parts III and IV of the opinion are joined only by Justices Brennan, Marshall, and Blackmun.]

[We agree] with the District Court that in order to succeed the [plaintiffs] were required to prove both intentional discrimination against an identifiable political group and an actual discriminatory effect on that group. Further, we are confident that if the law challenged here had discriminatory effects on Democrats, this record would support a finding that the discrimination was intentional. Thus, we decline to overturn the District Court's finding of discriminatory intent as clearly erroneous.

Indeed, quite aside from the anecdotal evidence, the shape of the House and Senate Districts, and the alleged disregard for political boundaries, we think it most likely that whenever a legislature redistricts, those responsible for the legislation will know the likely political composition of the new districts and will have a prediction as to whether a particular district is a safe one for a Democratic or Republican candidate or is a competitive district that either candidate might win. . . .

As long as redistricting is done by a legislature, it should not be very difficult to prove that the likely political consequences of the reapportionment were intended.

We do not accept, however, the District Court's legal and factual bases for concluding that the 1981 Act visited a sufficiently adverse effect on the appellees' constitutionally protected rights to make out a violation of the Equal Protection Clause. The District Court held that because any apportionment scheme that purposely prevents proportional representation is unconstitutional, Democratic voters need only show that their proportionate voting influence has been adversely affected. Our cases, however, clearly foreclose any claim that the Constitution requires proportional representation or that legislatures in reapportioning must draw district lines to come as near as possible to allocating seats to the contending parties in proportion to what their anticipated statewide vote will be.

The typical election for legislative seats in the United States is conducted in described geographical districts, with the candidate receiving the most votes in each district winning the seat allocated to that district. If all or most of the districts are competitive — defined by the District Court in this case as districts in which the anticipated split in the party vote is within the range of 45% to 55% — even a narrow statewide preference for either party would produce an overwhelming majority for the winning party in the state legislature. This consequence, however, is inherent in winner-take-all, district-based elections, and we cannot hold that such a reapportionment law would violate the Equal Protection Clause because the voters in the losing party do not have representation in the legislature in proportion to the statewide vote received by their party candidates. . . .

To draw district lines to maximize the representation of each major party would require creating as many safe seats for each party as the demographic and predicted political characteristics of the State would permit. This in turn would leave the minority in each safe district without a representative of its choice. We upheld this "political fairness" approach in Gaffney v. Cummings, despite its tendency to deny safe district minorities any realistic chance to elect their own representatives. But *Gaffney* in no way suggested that the Constitution requires the approach that Connecticut had adopted in that case. . . .

[The] mere fact that a particular apportionment scheme makes it more difficult for a particular group in a particular district to elect the representatives of its choice does not render that scheme constitutionally infirm. [The] power to influence the political process is not limited to winning elections. An individual or a group of individuals who votes for a losing candidate is usually deemed to be adequately represented by the winning candidate and to have as much opportunity to influence that candidate as other voters in the district. We cannot presume in such a situation, without actual proof to the contrary, that the candidate elected will entirely ignore the interests of those voters. This is true even in a safe district where the losing group loses election after election. Thus, a group's electoral power is not unconstitutionally diminished by the simple fact of an apportionment scheme that makes winning elections more difficult, and a failure of proportional representation alone does not constitute impermissible discrimination under the Equal Protection Clause.

As with individual districts, where unconstitutional vote dilution is alleged in the form of statewide political gerrymandering, the mere lack of proportional representation will not be sufficient to prove unconstitutional discrimination. [Unconstitutional] discrimination occurs only when the electoral system is arranged in a manner that will consistently degrade a voter's or a group of voters' influence on the political process as a whole. . . .

[An] equal protection violation may be found only where the electoral system substantially disadvantages certain voters in their opportunity to influence the political process effectively. In this context, such a finding of unconstitutionality must be supported by evidence of continued frustration of the will of a majority of the voters or effective denial to a minority of voters of a fair chance to influence the political process.

Based on these views, we would reject the District Court's apparent holding that *any* interference with an opportunity to elect a representative of one's choice would be sufficient to allege or make out an equal protection violation, unless justified by some acceptable state interest that the State would be required to demonstrate. In addition to being contrary to the above-described conception of an unconstitutional political gerrymander, such a low threshold for legal action would invite attack on all or almost all reapportionment statutes.[14]

The District Court's findings do not satisfy this threshold condition to stating and proving a cause of action. . . .

Relying on a single election to prove unconstitutional discrimination is unsatisfactory. The District Court observed, and the parties do not disagree, that Indiana is a swing State. Voters sometimes prefer Democratic candidates, and sometimes Republican. The District Court did not find that because of the 1981 Act the Democrats could not in one of the next few elections secure a sufficient vote to take control of the assembly. Indeed, the District Court declined to hold that the 1982 election results were the predictable consequences of the 1981 Act and expressly refused to hold that those results were a reliable prediction of future ones. . . .

We recognize that our own view may be difficult of application. Determining when an electoral system has been "arranged in a manner that will consistently degrade a voter's or a group of voters' influence on the political process as a whole," is of necessity a difficult inquiry. Nevertheless, we believe that it recognizes the delicacy of intruding on this most political of legislative functions and is at the same time consistent with our prior cases regarding individual multi-member districts, which have formulated a parallel standard.

---

14. The requirement of a threshold showing is derived from the peculiar characteristics of these political gerrymandering claims. We do not contemplate that a similar requirement would apply to our Equal Protection cases outside of this particular context. [Relocated footnote — EDS.]

IV

In sum, we hold that political gerrymandering cases are properly justiciable under the Equal Protection Clause. We also conclude, however, that a threshold showing of discriminatory vote dilution is required for a prima facie case of an equal protection violation. In this case, the findings made by the District Court of an adverse effect on the appellees do not surmount the threshold requirement. Consequently, the judgment of the District Court is reversed.

[Chief Justice Burger's opinion concurring in the judgment is omitted.]

[Justice O'Connor's opinion, joined by Chief Justice Burger and Justice Rehnquist, arguing that political gerrymandering poses a nonjusticiable political question, is discussed in Chapter 1 supra. In the course of arguing that there are no judicially manageable standards to resolve the controversy, she accused the plurality of moving toward a constitutionally mandated system of proportional representation for political parties:

> To be sure, the plurality has qualified its use of a *standard* of proportional representation in a variety of ways so as to avoid a *requirement* of proportional representation. The question is whether these qualifications are likely to be enduring in the face of the tremendous political pressures that courts will confront when called on to decide political gerrymandering claims. Because the most easily measured indicia of political power relate solely to winning and losing elections, there is a grave risk that the plurality's various attempts to qualify and condition the group right the Court has created will gradually pale in importance. What is likely to remain is a loose form of proportionality, under which *some* deviations from proportionality are permissible, but any significant, persistent deviations from proportionality are suspect.]

Justice Powell, with whom Justice Stevens joins, concurring in Part II, and dissenting.

[The] plurality argues [that] appellees failed to establish that their voting strength was diluted statewide despite uncontradicted proof that certain key districts were grotesquely gerrymandered to enhance the election prospects of Republican candidates. This argument appears to rest solely on the ground that the legislature accomplished its gerrymander consistent with "one person, one vote," in the sense that the legislature designed voting districts of approximately equal population and erected no direct barriers to Democratic voters' exercise of the franchise. Since the essence of a gerrymandering claim is that the members of a political party as a group have been denied their right to "fair and effective representation," [*Reynolds*], I believe that the claim cannot be tested solely by reference to "one person, one vote." Rather, a number of other relevant neutral factors must be considered. . . .

Gerrymandering is "the deliberate and arbitrary distortion of district boundaries and populations for partisan or personal political purposes." [The] term "gerrymandering," however, is also used loosely to describe the common practice of the party in power to choose the redistricting plan that gives it an advantage at the polls. An intent to discriminate in this sense may be present whenever redistricting occurs. . . .

Consequently, only a sensitive and searching inquiry can distinguish gerrymandering in the "loose" sense from gerrymandering that amounts to unconstitutional discrimination. Because it is difficult to develop and apply standards that will identify the unconstitutional gerrymander, courts may seek to avoid their responsibility to enforce the Equal Protection Clause by finding that a claim of gerrymandering is nonjusticiable. I agree with the plurality that such a course is mistaken. . . .

Moreover, I am convinced that appropriate judicial standards can and should be developed. [The proper] definition of unconstitutional gerrymandering properly focuses on whether the boundaries of the voting districts have been distorted deliberately and arbitrarily to achieve illegitimate ends. Under this definition, the merits of a gerrymandering claim must be determined by reference to the configurations of the districts, the observance of political subdivision lines, and other criteria that have independent relevance to the fairness of redistricting. . . .

The most important [factors in determining the constitutionality of redistricting plans] are the shapes of voting districts and adherence to established political subdivision boundaries. Other relevant considerations include the nature of the legislative procedures by which the apportionment law was adopted and legislative history reflecting contemporaneous legislative goals. To make out a case of unconstitutional partisan gerrymandering, the plaintiff should be required to offer proof concerning these factors, which bear directly on the fairness of a redistricting plan, as well as evidence concerning population disparities and statistics tending to show vote dilution. No one factor should be dispositive.[13]

[Accordingly,] I would affirm the judgment of the District Court.

c.   Denial of "Access to the Ballot"

WILLIAMS v. RHODES, 393 U.S. 23 (1968). Under Ohio law, political parties that had received 10 percent of the vote in the prior gubernatorial election automatically qualified for the next presidential election ballot. Other political parties, however, could earn a place on the ballot only if they had an elaborate party structure, held "a primary election conforming to detailed and rigorous standards," and filed a petition nine months before the election signed "by qualified electors totaling 15 percent of the number of ballots cast in the last preceding gubernatorial election." Noting that the law had "made it virtually impossible for a new political party [to] be placed on [the] ballot," the Court invalidated the Ohio scheme. Justice Black delivered the opinion of the Court:

"In determining whether or not a state law violates the Equal Protection Clause, we must consider the facts and circumstances behind the law, the interests which the State claims to be protecting, and the interests of those who are disadvantaged by the classification. [Here] the state laws [burden] two different, although overlapping, kinds of rights — the right of individuals to associate for the advancement of political beliefs, and the right of qualified voters [to] cast their votes effectively. [The challenged laws] give the two old, established parties a de-

13. Groups may consistently fail to elect representatives under a perfectly neutral election scheme. Thus, a test that turns only on election results, as the plurality's standard apparently does, likely would identify an unconstitutional gerrymander where none existed. . . .

cided advantage [and] thus place substantially unequal burdens on both the right to vote and the right to associate. [In] determining whether the State has power to place such unequal burdens on minority groups where rights of this kind are at stake, [we] have consistently held that 'only a compelling interest [can] justify limiting [such] freedoms.' . . .

"The State asserts that [it] may validly promote a two-party system in order to encourage compromise and political stability. [But] the Ohio system does not merely favor a 'two-party system'; it favors two particular parties — the Republicans and the Democrats — and in effect [gives] them a complete monopoly. [Ohio argues further] that its highly restrictive provisions are justified because without them a large number of parties might qualify for the ballot, and the voters would then be confronted with a choice so confusing that the popular will could be frustrated. But [experience] demonstrates that no more than a handful of parties attempts to qualify for ballot positions even when a very low number of signatures, such as 1% of the electorate, is required. [Thus,] at the present time this danger [is] no more than 'theoretically imaginable.' No such remote danger can justify the immediate and crippling impact on the basic constitutional rights involved in this case."

Justice Harlan concurred in the result on the ground "that Ohio's statutory scheme violates the basic right of political association assured by the First Amendment." Chief Justice Warren and Justices Stewart and White dissented.

Note: Williams *and Its Progeny*

1. *Access to the ballot.* If there is a fundamental interest in gaining access to the franchise, is there necessarily also a fundamental interest in gaining access to the ballot? Whose right is the Court protecting? The candidate's? The party member's? The potential voter's?

2. *Petition requirements.* In *Williams*, the Court invalidated the requirement that, to gain access to the presidential election ballot, a new or minor party must file a petition nine months before the election "signed by qualified electors totaling 15% of the number of ballots cast in the last preceding gubernatorial election." In Jenness v. Forston, 403 U.S. 431 (1971), the Court unanimously upheld a Georgia law providing that any political organization whose candidate received 20 percent of the vote at the most recent gubernatorial or presidential election automatically qualified for the ballot, but that a nominee of any other political organization must file a petition five months before the election signed by at least 5 percent of those eligible to vote at the last election for the office he is seeking. The Court explained:

> Unlike Ohio, Georgia freely provides for write-in votes, [it] does not require every candidate to be the nominee of a political party, [it] does not fix an unreasonably early filing deadline, [and it] does not impose upon a small party or a new party [the] requirement of establishing elaborate primary election [machinery]. In a word, Georgia in no way freezes the status [quo].

Similarly, in American Party of Texas v. White, 415 U.S. 767 (1974), the Court upheld a Texas law providing that candidates of "major" parties could gain access to the ballot by being nominated in a primary election, but that "minor" parties could obtain ballot access only by holding nominating conventions and obtaining signatures totaling at least 1 percent of the persons voting in the last preceding gubernatorial election. See also Illinois State Board of Elections v. Socialist Workers Party, 440 U.S. 173 (1979) (invalidating a state statute that had the effect of requiring more signatures to qualify for access to the ballot in Chicago elections than in statewide elections). The Court relied on *Jenness* and *White* in Munro v. Socialist Workers Party, 479 U.S. 189 (1986), to uphold a state law that prevented minor party candidates from appearing on the general election ballot unless they received at least 1 percent of the votes cast in a "blanket primary" at which registered voters could vote for any candidate, irrespective of the candidate's political party affiliation.

3. *Filing fees.* In Lubin v. Panish, 415 U.S. 709 (1974), the Court invalidated as applied to indigents a California law requiring payment of a filing fee of 2 percent of the annual salary for the office sought. The Court explained:

> [The] State's interest in keeping its ballots within manageable, understandable limits is of the highest order [but it] must be achieved by a means that does not unfairly or unnecessarily burden either a minority party's or an individual candidate's equally important interest in the continued availability of political opportunity. [The] process of qualifying candidates [may] not constitutionally be measured solely in dollars. [A] wealthy candidate with not the remotest chance of election may secure a place on the ballot by writing a check [while] impecunious but serious candidates may be prevented from running. [A] State may [not] require from an indigent candidate filing fees he cannot pay.

4. *Party loyalty requirements.* In Storer v. Brown, 415 U.S. 724 (1974), the Court upheld a California statute forbidding a ballot position to an independent candidate who "had a registered affiliation with [a] political party at any time within one year prior to the immediately preceding primary election." The Court explained:

> [The challenged provision] involves no discrimination against independents. [Just as] the independent candidate must be clear of political party affiliations for a year before the primary, the party candidate must not have been registered with another party for a year before he files his [declaration]. [The challenged provision] protects the direct primary process by refusing to recognize independent candidates who do not make early plans to leave a [party]. It works against independent candidacies prompted by short-range political goals, pique, or personal quarrel. [It thus] furthers the State's [compelling] interest in the stability of its political system.

Justices Douglas, Brennan, and Marshall dissented.

In Tashjian v. Republican Party, 479 U.S. 208 (1986), the Court distinguished *Storer* and invalidated a Connecticut statute requiring the voters in any party primary to be registered members of that party. The Republican Party, which had adopted a party rule permitting independents to vote in its primary, challenged the provision. Writing for the Court, Justice Marshall distinguished *Storer* as follows:

> The statute in *Storer* was designed to protect the parties and the party system against the disorganizing effect of independent candidacies launched by unsuc-

cessful putative party nominees. This protection [was] undertaken to prevent the disruption of the political parties from without, and not, as in this case, to prevent the parties from taking internal steps affecting their own process for the selection of candidates. . . .

The Party's determination of the boundaries of its own association, and of the structure which best allows it to pursue its political goals, is protected by the Constitution.

Justice Stevens, joined by Justice Scalia, dissented. Justice Scalia also wrote a separate dissenting opinion, joined by Chief Justice Rehnquist and Justice O'Connor.

5. *Disqualification of public officials.* In Clements v. Fashing, 457 U.S. 957 (1982), the Court upheld two provisions of the Texas Constitution. Section 19 provides that certain public officials shall not "be eligible to the Legislature" until the expiration of their current term of office. Section 65 provides that certain public officials who run for any other state or federal office must automatically resign their current position.

In a plurality opinion, Justice Rehnquist, joined by Chief Justice Burger and Justices Powell and O'Connor, reasoned:

[We have never held that] candidacy [is] a "fundamental right." [Rather, our] ballot access cases [focus] on the degree to which the challenged restrictions operate as a mechanism to exclude certain classes of candidates from the electoral process. The inquiry is whether the challenged restriction unfairly or unnecessarily burdens the "availability of political opportunity." [The] Court has departed from traditional equal protection analysis [in] two [lines] of ballot access cases. One line [involves] classifications based on wealth. [E.g., *Lubin.*] The second [involves] classification schemes that impose burdens on new or small political parties or independent candidates. [E.g., *Williams; White; Storer.*] The provisions [challenged] in this case do not [fall within either of these lines]. [It is thus] necessary to examine the provisions in question in terms of the extent of the burdens that they place on the candidacy of current holders of public office. [Section 19] merely prohibits officeholders from cutting short their current term of office in order to serve in the Legislature. [As applied to appellee, a Justice of the Peace, section 19 establishes] a maximum "waiting period" of two [years]. A "waiting period" is hardly a significant barrier to candidacy. [Citing *Storer.*] We conclude that this sort of insignificant interference with access to the ballot need only rest on a rational predicate in order to [survive]. Section 19 clearly rests on a rational predicate [for] Texas has a legitimate interest in discouraging its Justices of the Peace from vacating their current terms of office. [The] burdens that §65 imposes on candidacy are even less substantial than those imposed by §19 [and the] two provisions [serve] essentially the same state interests.

Justice Stevens concurred in the judgment; Justice Brennan, joined by Justices Marshall, Blackmun, and White, dissented.

6. *A different approach?* In Anderson v. Celebrezze, 460 U.S. 780 (1983), the Court invalidated an Ohio law requiring independent candidates to file their nominating petitions in mid-March in order to qualify for the ballot in the November election. Interestingly, Justice Stevens's majority opinion relied on the first amendment rather than the equal protection clause:

[We] base our conclusions directly on the First [Amendment] and do not engage in a separate Equal Protection Clause analysis. We rely, however, on the analysis in a number of our prior election cases resting on the Equal Protection Clause. [These] cases, applying the "fundamental rights" strand of equal protection analysis, have identified the First [Amendment] rights implicated by restrictions on the eligibility of voters and [candidates]. Constitutional challenges to specific provisions of a State's election laws [cannot] be resolved by any "litmus-paper test" that will separate valid from invalid restrictions. Instead, a court [must] first consider the character and magnitude of the asserted injury to [First Amendment rights]. It then must identify and evaluate the precise interests put forward by the State as justifications for the burden imposed. [The] Court must not only determine the legitimacy and strength of each of those interests; it also must consider the extent to which those interests make it necessary to burden [First Amendment] rights. Only after weighing all these factors is the reviewing court in a position to decide whether the challenged provision is unconstitutional.

The Court concluded that Ohio's interests in "voter education, equal treatment for partisan and independent candidates, and political stability" were either illegitimate or too remotely related to the early filing deadline to justify such a substantial barrier to independent candidates. Justice Rehnquist, joined by Justices White, Powell, and O'Connor, dissented.

2. Access to the Judicial Process

If there is a fundamental interest in equal access to the franchise, is there also a fundamental interest in equal access to the judicial process? Consider Michelman, The Supreme Court and Litigation Access Fees: The Right to Protect One's Rights — Part II, 1974 Duke L.J. 527, 534-540:

There are a number of striking resemblances between the interests in voting and in litigating. [Both] the voting and litigating interests base a claim to "fundamentality" on the idea that they are "preservative of all rights"; of both it can be said that "in social compact terms, in exchange for this legal and orderly method of resolving disputes, one restricts his power to satisfy his claims by force"; [and that] "ability to litigate just claims, like availability of the franchise, gives legitimacy to the state's coercive power." [Indeed,] litigation and legislation [are] bound up with one another in an entire, political-legal order in which the court's part is no less critical than the [legislature's]. Access to courts and access to legislatures are [thus] claims that merge into one another, [and you] cannot, without confusion, call a person a citizen and at the same time sanction [his] exclusion [from] that process.

GRIFFIN v. ILLINOIS, 351 U.S. 12 (1956). The Court held in *Griffin* that a state must furnish an indigent criminal defendant with a free trial transcript if such a transcript is necessary for "adequate and effective appellate review" of his conviction. In a plurality opinion, Justice Black, joined by Chief Justice Warren and Justices Douglas and Clark, explained: "[Our] constitutional guaranties of due process and equal protection both call for procedures in criminal trials which allow no invidious discriminations between persons and different groups of persons. [Plainly] the ability to pay costs in advance bears no rational relationship to a defendant's guilt or innocence and could not be used as an excuse to deprive a defendant of a fair trial. [It] is true that a State is not required by the Federal Constitution to provide appellate courts or a right to appellate review at all. See, e.g., McKane v. Durston, 153 U.S. 684 [1894]. But that is not to say that a State that does grant appellate review can do so in a way that discriminates against some convicted defendants on account of their poverty. . . .

"All of the States now provide some method of appeal from criminal convictions, recognizing the importance of appellate review to a correct adjudication of guilt or innocence. Statistics show that a substantial proportion of criminal convictions are reversed by state appellate courts. Thus to deny adequate appellate review to the poor means that many of them may lose their life, liberty or property because of unjust convictions which appellate courts would set aside. Many States have recognized this and provided aid for convicted defendants who have a right to appeal and need a transcript but are unable to pay for it. A few have not. Such a denial is a misfit in a country dedicated to affording equal justice to all and special privileges to none in the administration of its criminal law. There can be no equal justice where the kind of trial a man gets depends on the amount of money he has. Destitute defendants must be afforded as adequate appellate review as defendants who have money enough to buy transcripts."

Justice Frankfurter concurred in the judgment. Justices Burton, Minton, Reed, and Harlan dissented.

DOUGLAS v. CALIFORNIA, 372 U.S. 353 (1963). In a six-to-three decision, the Court held unconstitutional a California rule requiring state appellate courts, on the request of an indigent criminal defendant for counsel on appeal, to make "an independent investigation of the record" and to "appoint counsel [only] if in their opinion it would be helpful to the defendant or the court." Justice Douglas delivered the opinion of the Court:

"[The denial] 'of counsel on appeal [to an indigent] would seem to be at least as invidious [a discrimination] as that condemned in [*Griffin*].' [Under the California rule,] the type of an appeal a person is afforded [hinges] upon whether or not he can pay for the assistance of counsel. . . .

"When an indigent is forced to run this gauntlet of a preliminary showing of merit, the right to appeal does not comport with fair procedure. [The] discrimination is not between 'possibly good and obviously bad cases,' but between cases where the rich man can require the court to listen to argument of counsel before deciding on the merits, but a poor man cannot. There is lacking that equality demanded by the Fourteenth Amendment where the rich man, who appeals as of right, enjoys the benefit of counsel's examination into the record, research of the law, and marshalling of arguments on his behalf, while the indigent, already burdened by a preliminary determination that his case is without merit, is forced to shift for himself. The indigent, where the record is unclear or the errors are hidden, has only the right to a meaningless ritual, while the rich man has a meaningful appeal."

Justice Harlan, joined by Justice Stewart, dissented: "[To] approach the present problem in terms of the Equal Protection Clause is, I submit, but to substitute resounding phrases for analysis. [The] States, of course, are prohibited by the Equal Protection Clause from discriminating between 'rich' and 'poor' as such in the formulation and application of their laws. But it is a far different thing to suggest that this provision prevents the State from adopting a law of general applicability that may affect the poor more harshly than it does the [rich]. Every financial exaction which the State imposes on a uniform basis is more easily satisfied by the well-to-do than by the indigent. [The] State may have a moral obligation to eliminate the evils of poverty, but it is not required by the Equal Protection Clause to give to some whatever others can afford. . . ."

Note: Fundamental Interests and the Criminal Justice System

1. *The basis of* Griffin *and* Douglas: *wealth as a "suspect" classification.* As in *Harper,* section E1a supra, the Court in *Griffin* and *Douglas* relied on both the "suspect" classification and the "fundamental" interest aspects of equal protection analysis. To what extent, if any, can *Griffin* and *Douglas* be explained on the ground that "a State can no more discriminate on account of poverty than on account of religion, race, or color"? Consider that the rules invalidated in *Douglas* and *Griffin* (a) do not expressly classify on the basis of wealth but instead involved a fee of the sort that is charged in the private market and often by the state as it provides services; (b) like ordinary license fees, have a differential effect on the poor; and (c) unlike the poll tax, were invalidated not in their entirety but only as applied to the poor.

2. *The basis of* Griffin *and* Douglas: *equal access to appeal as a fundamental interest.* Justice Black conceded in *Griffin* that there is no constitutional right "to appellate review." How, then, does he justify his implicit conclusion that the right "to appellate review" is fundamental? In *Harper,* the Court suggested that the right to vote is fundamental because it is "preservative of all rights." Perhaps the "right to sue and defend in the courts" is similarly fundamental because "it is the right conservative of all other rights, and lies at the foundation of orderly government." Chambers v. Baltimore & Ohio Railroad, 207 U.S. 142, 148 (1907). Consider Note, The Supreme Court — 1972 Term, 87 Harv. L. Rev. 57, 66 (1973): "The right to vote and the right to hold office are means of participation in the democratic process which are fundamental to the protection of other interests. A function of similar importance is performed by the judiciary. If the election of the public officials who make and administer the laws is so fundamental as to require access, it would make little sense to deny indigents access to the only forum in which rights arising under those laws may be enforced."

3. *Equal protection or due process?* What is the real concern in *Griffin* and *Douglas* — the inequality or the lack of an effective opportunity to appeal? Consider Clune, The Supreme Court's Treatment of Wealth Discriminations under the Fourteenth Amendment, 1975 Sup. Ct. Rev. 289, 298: "Harlan thought the equal protection model was quite wrong. [The defendants] were asking to be treated differently rather than similarly, asking in fact, for a specific entitlement. Because they could not be entitled constitutionally to every resource needed or wanted for an appeal, Harlan argued that the particular necessity of this resource was the true issue, a traditional due process inquiry."

Consider the following response: Justice Harlan suggests that the equal protection clause cannot require people who are different — in this case, the indigent — to be treated differently in the interest of equality. But he does not support this suggestion; he simply asserts it. It is fully plausible, if not logically necessary, to think that an equality principle might sometimes require the differently situated to be treated differently. To put it another way: The equality question is not whether the similarly situated are treated similarly, but instead whether a difference — here poverty — has been turned, without sufficient justification, into a legal disability. Justice Harlan never squarely confronts this claim, which relates closely to some of the most sharply controversial issues in current equal protection law, including affirmative action, sex discrimination, and race discrimination generally.

As for due process: If the due process clause guarantees a right to appeal, *Griffin* and *Douglas* would pose a coherent due process issue. But everyone seems to agree that the due process clause does not require the states to create an appeals system, and that there is thus no due process right to appeal. That being so, can one sensibly argue that the restrictions at issue in *Griffin* and *Douglas* violate due process because they limit the opportunity to appeal? Consider the following argument: Even if the due process clause does not require a state to create an appeals system, it does require a state that decides voluntarily to create such a system to permit access to the system unless its restrictions are justified by important government interests.

If there is no due process right to appeal, can one nonetheless argue that the interest in equal access to appeal is "fundamental" for purposes of the equal protection clause?

4. *The limits of* Griffin *and* Douglas: Ross v. Moffitt. In Ross v. Moffitt, 417 U.S. 600 (1974), the Court held that the Constitution does not require states to provide counsel for indigent defendants petitioning for discretionary state appellate review or for review in the U.S. Supreme Court. Justice Rehnquist delivered the opinion of the Court:

> The precise rationale for the *Griffin* and *Douglas* lines of cases has never been explicitly stated, some support being derived from the Equal Protection Clause [and] some from the Due Process [Clause]. Neither clause by itself provides an entirely satisfactory basis for the result reached, each depending on a different inquiry which emphasizes different factors. . . .
>
> We do not believe that the Due Process Clause requires North Carolina to provide [counsel in this situation]. [T]he State need not provide any appeal at all. [The] fact that an appeal *has* been provided does not automatically mean that a State then acts unfairly by refusing to provide counsel to indigent defendants at every stage of the way. [Unfairness] results only if indigents are singled out by the State and denied meaningful access to the appellate system because of their poverty. That question is more profitably considered under an equal protection analysis. . . .
>
> The [equal protection clause] "does not require absolute equality or precisely equal advantages," nor does it require the State to "equalize economic conditions." It does require that the state appellate system be "free of unreasoned distinctions," and that indigents have an adequate opportunity to present their claims fairly within the adversary system. The State cannot adopt procedures which leave an indigent defendant "entirely cut off from any appeal at all," by virtue of his indigency, or extend to such indigent defendants merely a "meaningless ritual" while others in better economic circumstances have a "meaningful appeal." That question is not one of absolutes, but one of degrees. . . .
>
> North Carolina has followed the mandate of Douglas v. California [and] authorized appointment of counsel for a convicted defendant appealing to the intermediate Court of Appeals, but has not gone beyond *Douglas* to provide for appointment of counsel for a defendant who seeks [review] in the Supreme Court of North

Carolina or a writ of certiorari here. We do not believe that [a] defendant in respondent's circumstances is denied meaningful access to the [state] Supreme Court [or to this Court] simply because the State does not appoint counsel to aid him in seeking [review]. At that stage he will have, at the very least, a transcript or other record of trial proceedings, a brief on his behalf in the Court of Appeals setting forth his claims of error, and in many cases an opinion by the Court of Appeals disposing of his case. These materials [would] appear to provide [an] adequate basis for [the] decision to grant or deny review. [This] is not to say, of course, that a skilled lawyer [would] not prove helpful to any litigant able to employ him. [But] the fact that a particular service might be of benefit to an indigent defendant does not mean that the service is constitutionally required. The duty of the State [is] not to duplicate the legal arsenal that may be privately [retained,] but only to assure the indigent defendant an adequate opportunity to present his claims fairly in the context of the State's appellate process. We think respondent was given that opportunity under the existing North Carolina system.

Justice Douglas, joined by Justices Brennan and Marshall, dissented. See also United States v. MacCollom, 426 U.S. 317 (1976), in which the Court, relying on *Ross*, held in a five-to-four decision that an indigent criminal defendant does not have a constitutional right to a free trial transcript for use in a collateral attack on a federal conviction if a federal judge finds that the claim is "frivolous," and that the transcript is not "needed to decide the issue."

5. *The limits of* Griffin *and* Douglas: *Fuller v. Oregon.* When a state assists an indigent in the criminal process, may it claim reimbursement for its expenditures on his behalf? In Fuller v. Oregon, 417 U.S. 40 (1974), the Court held that a state may recoup legal expenses paid on behalf of a convicted defendant to the extent that he later becomes able to pay. The Court rejected the argument that "a defendant's knowledge that he may remain under an obligation to repay the expenses incurred in providing him legal representation might impel him to decline the services of an appointed attorney and thus 'chill' his constitutional right to counsel." The Court explained:

We live in a society where the distribution of legal assistance, like the distribution of all goods and services, is generally regulated by the dynamics of private enterprise. A defendant in a criminal case who is just above the line separating the indigent from the nonindigent must borrow money, sell off his meager assets, or call upon his family or friends in order to hire a lawyer. We cannot say that the Constitution requires that those only slightly poorer must remain forever immune from any obligation to shoulder the expenses of their legal defense.

See also James v. Strange, 407 U.S. 128 (1972) (invalidating a statute providing for the recoupment of all state expenditures for indigent defendants because the statute deprived such defendants of all the exemptions and restrictions ordinarily afforded civil judgment debtors and thus failed to accord "even treatment of indigent criminal defendants with other classes of debtors"); Rinaldi v. Yeager, 384 U.S. 305 (1966) (invalidating on similar grounds a statute requiring unsuccessful appellants confined to prison, but not those receiving suspended sentences, placed on probation, or penalized only by a fine, to repay the state for the cost of transcripts).

6. *The reach of* Griffin *and* Douglas: *Williams v. Illinois.* In Williams v. Illinois, 399 U.S. 235 (1970), appellant, who had been convicted of petty theft, received

the maximum authorized sentence of one year in prison and a $500 fine. A state statute provided that defendants in default of payment of a fine must remain in jail to "work off" their obligations at a rate of $5 per day. "Applying the teaching [of] *Griffin*," the Court held the statute unconstitutional as applied to an indigent defendant insofar as it authorized imprisonment beyond the maximum statutory term. The Court reasoned that "when the aggregate imprisonment exceeds the maximum period fixed by the statute and results directly from an involuntary nonpayment of a fine or court costs we are confronted with an impermissible discrimination that rests on ability to pay." The Court concluded that no substantial state interest justified the discriminatory impact, for the state had "numerous alternatives," including the use of installment plans, for recouping the monetary penalties from indigents.

See also Tate v. Short, 401 U.S. 395 (1971), in which the Court held that a state could not constitutionally imprison an indigent defendant for failure to pay traffic fines not otherwise punishable by imprisonment, but added that *Williams* did not necessarily preclude imprisonment "as an enforcement method when alternative means are unsuccessful despite the defendant's reasonable efforts to satisfy the fines by those means"; Bearden v. Georgia, 461 U.S. 660 (1983), in which the Court, relying on *Williams* and *Tate*, held that probation may be revoked for nonpayment of a fine only if the probationer made no bona fide effort to pay or there are no "adequate alternative forms of punishment."

7. *The reach of* Griffin *and* Douglas: *noneconomic classifications.* In the voting context, the Court in *Harper* invalidated the poll tax, which involved both the "fundamental" interest in voting and a disproportionate impact on the poor but then extended the doctrine to all restrictions on voting, whether or not they implicated the poor. Do *Griffin* and *Douglas* invite a similar extension? Suppose, for example, a state authorizes appeal only by those convicted of capital offenses. Suppose it permits appeal by embezzlers but not other larceners? Should a court subject such classifications to heightened scrutiny because they implicate the "fundamental" interest in equal access to appeal?

The Court has generally required only a rational basis for non-wealth-related classifications in the criminal justice context. In McGinnis v. Royster, 410 U.S. 263 (1973), for example, the Court upheld a New York law granting "good time" credit toward parole eligibility for time spent in a state prison after sentencing but not for time spent in a county jail before sentencing. The Court, applying a rational basis standard, rejected a claim that the law discriminated against defendants who did not make bail before trial. It explained that "good time" was designed to reflect a prisoner's rehabilitation, and that the state reasonably offered rehabilitative programs only in its prisons.

Similarly, in Marshall v. United States, 414 U.S. 417 (1974), the Court, applying a rational basis standard, upheld a provision of the Narcotic Addict Rehabilitation Act excluding convicted addicts with two or more prior felony convictions from participation in a drug rehabilitation program in lieu of penal incarceration. The Court explained that Congress "could rationally have assumed that a person who has committed two or more prior felonies [is] less likely to be susceptible of rehabilitation [and would pose] a greater threat to society upon release."

BODDIE v. CONNECTICUT, 401 U.S. 371 (1971). In *Boddie*, the Court held unconstitutional as applied to indigents a state requirement that individuals pay court fees and costs of about $60 in order to sue for divorce. Justice Harlan delivered the opinion of the Court: "American society [bottoms] its systematic definition of individual rights and duties [on] the common-law model. It is to courts [that] we ultimately look for the implementation of a regularized, orderly process of dispute settlement. [It] is upon this premise that this Court has [put] flesh upon the due process principle. [Past] litigation has, however, typically involved rights of defendants — not, as here, persons seeking access to the judicial process in the first instance. This is because our society has been so structured that resort to the courts is not usually the only available, legitimate means of resolving private disputes. Indeed, private structuring of individual relationships [is] largely encouraged in American life, [and] this Court has [thus] seldom been asked to view access to the courts as an element of due process. . . .

"As this Court [has] recognized, marriage involves interests of basic importance in our society. See, e.g., Loving v. Virginia [Chapter 5, section C3, supra]; Skinner v. Oklahoma [section E supra]; Meyer v. Nebraska [section F infra]. It is not surprising, then, that the States have seen fit to oversee many aspects of that institution. Without a prior judicial imprimatur, individuals may freely enter into and rescind commercial contracts, for example, but we are unaware of any jurisdiction where private citizens may covenant for or dissolve marriages without state approval. [The] State's refusal to admit these appellants to its courts, the sole means in Connecticut for obtaining a divorce, must be regarded as the equivalent of denying them an opportunity to be heard upon their claimed right to a dissolution of their marriages, and, in the absence of a sufficient countervailing [justification,] a denial of due process."

The Court emphasized that "[w]e do not decide that access for all individuals to the courts is a right that is, in all circumstances, guaranteed by the Due Process Clause," but only that, "given the basic position of the marriage relationship in this society's hierarchy of values and the concomitant state monopolization of the means for legally dissolving this relationship, due process does prohibit a State from denying, solely because of inability to pay, access to its courts to individuals who seek judicial dissolution of their marriages."

Justice Douglas and Justice Brennan concurred.

Justice Black dissented: "[*Griffin* is distinguishable.] Civil lawsuits [are] not like government prosecutions for crime. [In] such cases the government is not usually involved as a party, and there is no deprivation of life, liberty, or property as punishment for crime. [There] is consequently no necessity [why] government should in civil trials be hampered [by the strict] due process rules the Constitution has provided to protect people charged with crime. [The] Court's opinion appears to rest solely on a philosophy that any law violates due process if it is unreasonable, arbitrary, indecent, deviates from the fundamental, is shocking to the conscience, or fails to meet other tests [equally] lacking in any possible constitutional precision. [The] Due Process and Equal Protection Clauses [do not justify] judges in trying [to] hold laws constitutional or not on the basis of a judge's sense of fairness."

Note: Access to the Judicial Process in Civil Cases

1. *The rationale of* Boddie. Note the three distinct positions on the constitutionality of filing fees that preclude indigents from initiating civil litigation: (a) con-

stitutional (Black); (b) unconstitutional; (c) unconstitutional only if the litigation involves "interests of basic importance in our society" and there is "state monopolization of the means" for protecting such interests (Harlan). Which position is most consistent with the *Griffin/Douglas* principle? Does *Boddie* implicitly reject the voting analogy and the proposition that there is a "fundamental" interest in equal access to the judicial process?

2. *Monopolization.* Why the "monopolization" requirement? Consider Michelman, The Supreme Court and Litigation Access Fees: The Right to Protect One's Rights — Part I, 1973 Duke L.J. 1153, 1178-1180:

> The monopoly notion is disarmingly simple. Divorce [is] different from most other kinds of affirmative relief [in] that it is absolutely unavailable except in the form of a judicial decree. It takes judicial action to dissolve a marriage, but not to release a creditor's claim. [In practical effect, however, the court] has a monopoly on lawful deployment of remedial force; and this monopoly applies to plaintiffs across the board. [Consider] the case of an impoverished person who objects to emission of poisonous gases near his residence. [Although] out-of-court settlement [is theoretically available, it is in fact unlikely if] the complaining party lacks [the money even to file a] lawsuit. [Moreover, the monopolization notion] is unpersuasive [for another reason as well]. The notion appears to have been conceived by Justice Harlan [to assimilate] the predicament of the *Boddie* petitioners to the plight common to civil defendants. [Just] as a person once married cannot become unmarried without gaining access to a court, so a person once haled into court cannot avoid an adverse judgment without making an appearance. But is the latter proposition true? Quite plainly it is not, [for it assumes] that the defendant will fail in any attempt to gain [a settlement]. [Thus, monopoly] fails to distinguish [civil plaintiffs] from civil defendants.

3. *Due process or equal protection?* Note Justice Harlan's reliance on due process rather than equal protection. Does Justice Harlan's analysis invalidate *every* limitation on the filing of divorce actions or only those that exclude the poor? Consider Clune, The Supreme Court's Treatment of Wealth Discriminations under the Fourteenth Amendment, 1975 Sup. Ct. Rev. 289, 309-310: "Harlan's effort to forge due process into a tool that bridges the civil and criminal processes and also operates solely for the benefit of the poor is impressive. [T]o limit the holding to the poor, [Harlan recognized] that poor people have a unique claim [because they] have an acceptable excuse for not paying; poverty is important [because] it removes the ordinary interpretation put on nonpayment, that is, waiver or default."

4. *The limits of* Boddie: Kras. In United States v. Kras, 409 U.S. 434 (1973), the Court upheld a provision of the Bankruptcy Act requiring individuals seeking voluntary discharge to pay costs and fees of about $50. Justice Blackmun delivered the opinion of the Court:

> The denial of access to the judicial forum in *Boddie* touched directly [on] the marital relationship and on the associational interests that surround the establishment and dissolution of that relationship. On many occasions we have recognized the fundamental importance of these interests under our Constitution. [Kras's] alleged interest in the elimination of his debt burden [does] not rise to the same constitutional level. If Kras is not discharged in bankruptcy, his position will not be materially altered in any constitutional sense. . . .

Nor is the government's control over the establishment, enforcement, or dissolution of debts nearly so exclusive as [its] control over the marriage relationship. [In] contrast with divorce, bankruptcy is not the only method available to a debtor for the adjustment of his legal relationship with his creditors. . . .

We are also of the opinion that the filing fee requirement does not deny Kras the equal protection of the laws. Bankruptcy is hardly akin to free speech or marriage or to those other rights [that] the Court has come to regard as fundamental and that demand the lofty requirement of a compelling governmental interest before they may be significantly regulated.

Justice Stewart, joined by Justices Douglas, Brennan, and Marshall, dissented:

The violation of due process seems to me [as] clear in the present case [as in *Boddie*]. [The] bankrupt is bankrupt precisely for the reason that the State stands ready to exact all of his debts through [the] panoply of [creditor] remedies. [In] the unique situation of the indigent bankrupt, the Government provides the only effective means of his ever being free of these Government-imposed obligations. [Unless] the Government provides him access to the bankruptcy court, Kras will remain in the totally hopeless situation he now finds himself. [The] Court today holds that Congress may say that some of the poor are too poor even to go bankrupt. I cannot agree.

Justice Marshall filed a separate dissent: "The majority says that '[t]he denial of access to the judicial forum in *Boddie* touched directly . . . on the marital relationship.' It sees 'no fundamental interest that is gained or lost depending on the availability of a discharge in bankruptcy.' [But] I view the case as involving the right of access to the courts, the opportunity to be heard when one claims a legal right."

5. *The limits of* Boddie: Ortwein. In Ortwein v. Schwab, 410 U.S. 656 (1973), the Court, in a per curiam opinion, upheld a $25 appellate court filing fee as applied to indigents who sought to appeal administrative decisions reducing their welfare benefits:

[The] interest [in increased welfare payments], like [the interest at issue in] *Kras*, has far less constitutional significance than the interest of the *Boddie* appellants. [Moreover, each] of the present appellants has received an agency [hearing, and this] Court has long recognized that, even in criminal cases, due process does not require a State to provide an appellate system. [Under] the facts of this case, appellants were not denied due process. [Nor does the filing fee violate equal protection on the ground that it discriminates] against the poor. As in *Kras*, this [litigation] "is in the area of economics and social welfare" [and the] applicable standard is [thus] that of rational justification.

Justices Douglas, Stewart, Brennan, and Marshall dissented. On welfare as a "fundamental" interest, see section E4 infra.

6. *Variations.* Consider the following: (a) A state law authorizes state courts to grant a divorce only if both parties reside in the state. Cf. Sosna v. Iowa, 419 U.S. 393 (1975) (upholding a requirement that an individual reside in the state for one year before suing a nonresident for divorce and distinguishing *Boddie* on the ground that the one-year residency requirement involves "not total deprivation, as in *Boddie*, but only delay"). (b) A state law imposes a filing fee for all civil ac-

tions, as applied to an indigent seeking to sue for a claimed violation of first amendment rights. (c) A state law requires the party moving for blood grouping tests in a paternity action to pay for the tests, as applied to an indigent party. Cf. *Little v. Streater*, 452 U.S. 1 (1981) (invalidating such a statute). (d) A state law requires all civil parties to pay an appearance fee, as applied to an indigent who is sued for repossession of his furniture.

M.L.B. v. S.L.J., 519 U.S 102 (1996). In this case, the Court held that a state may not, under the due process and equal protection clauses, condition appeals from trial court decrees terminating parental rights on the affected party's payment of fees for preparing a record. Mississippi had done exactly that, in a case in which M.L.B.'s parental rights to two minor children were permanently terminated. The Court stressed that the principle in *Griffin* "has not been confined to cases in which imprisonment is at stake. . . . [A]s *Ortwein* underscored, this Court has not extended *Griffin* to the broad array of civil cases. But tellingly, the Court has consistently set apart from the main run of cases those involving state controls or intrusions on family relationships. In that domain, to guard against undue official intruson, the Court has examined closely and contextually the importance of the governmental interest advanced in defense of the intrusion. . . . M.L.B.'s case, involving the State's authority to severe permanently a parent-child bond, demands the close consideration the Court has long required when a family association so undeniably important is at stake." The Court found the state unable to justify the record payment requirement, since the interest was so substantial, and since the termination order "describes no evidence" and does not detail reasons for finding M.L.B. clearly and convincingly unfit to be a parent. Nor were financial reasons sufficient to justify the payment requirement. "[I]n the tightly circumscribed category of parental status termination cases, appeals are few, and not likely to impose an undue burden on the state." Joined by Chief Justice Rehnquist and Justice Scalia, Justice Thomas dissented, fearing that the "new-found constitutional right to free transcripts in civil appeals can be effectively restricted to this case." Justice Thomas contended "that the equal protection theory underlying the *Griffin* line of cases" does not "remain viable." He "would be inclinded to overrule *Griffin* and its progency" and in any case would not extend them to the civil context.

Question: Why didn't the Court choose between a due process and equal protection rationale in *M.L.B.?*

3. Travel

Shapiro v. Thompson

394 U.S. 618 (1969)

MR. JUSTICE BRENNAN delivered the opinion of the Court.

[Each of these three appeals is] from a decision [holding] unconstitutional a State or District of Columbia statutory provision which denies welfare assistance to residents [who] have not resided within their jurisdictions for at least one year immediately preceding their applications for such assistance. We affirm. . . .

There is no dispute that the effect of the waiting-period requirement [is] to create two classes of needy resident families indistinguishable from each other except that one is composed of residents who have resided a year or more, and the second of residents who have resided less than a year, in the jurisdiction. [The] second class is denied welfare aid upon which may depend the ability of the families to obtain the very means to subsist — food, shelter, and other necessities of life. [This scheme] constitutes an invidious discrimination [denying] equal protection of the laws. [The] interests which appellants assert are promoted by the classification either may not constitutionally be promoted by government or are not compelling governmental interests.

Primarily, appellants justify the waiting-period requirement as a protective device to preserve the fiscal integrity of state public assistance programs. It is asserted that people who require welfare assistance during their first year of residence in a State are likely to become continuing burdens on state welfare programs. Therefore, the argument runs, if such people can be deterred from entering the jurisdiction by denying them welfare benefits during the first year, state programs to assist long-time residents will not be impaired by a substantial influx of indigent newcomers. . . .

We do not doubt that the one-year waiting-period device is well suited to discourage the influx of poor families in need of assistance. An indigent who desires to migrate, resettle, find a new job, and start a new life will doubtless hesitate if he knows that he must risk making the move without the possibility of falling back on state welfare assistance during his first year of residence, when his need may be most acute. But the purpose of inhibiting migration by needy persons into the State is constitutionally impermissible.

This Court long ago recognized that the nature of our Federal Union and our constitutional concepts of personal liberty unite to require that all citizens be free to travel throughout the length and breadth of our land uninhibited by statutes, rules, or regulations which unreasonably burden or restrict this movement. . . .

We have no occasion to ascribe the source of this right to travel interstate to a particular constitutional provision. It suffices that, as Mr. Justice Stewart said for the Court in United States v. Guest, 383 U.S. 745, 757-758 (1966): "The constitutional right to travel from one State to another . . . occupies a position fundamental to the concept of our Federal Union. It is a right that has been firmly established and repeatedly recognized. . . ."

Thus, the purpose of deterring the in-migration of indigents cannot serve as justification for the classification created by the one-year waiting period, since that purpose is constitutionally impermissible. If a law has "no other purpose . . . than to chill the assertion of constitutional rights by penalizing those who choose to exercise them, then it [is] patently unconstitutional."

Alternatively, appellants argue that even if it is impermissible for a State to attempt to deter the entry of all indigents, the challenged classification may be justified as a permissible state attempt to discourage those indigents who would enter the State solely to obtain larger benefits. [But] a State may no more try to fence out those indigents who seek higher welfare benefits than it may try to fence out indigents generally. [We] do not perceive why a mother who is seeking to make a new life for herself and her children should be regarded as less deserving because she considers, among other factors, the level of a State's public assistance. Surely such a mother is no less deserving than a mother who moves into a particular State in order to take advantage of its better educational facilities.

Appellants argue further that the challenged classification may be sustained as an attempt to distinguish between new and old residents on the basis of the contribution they have made to the community through the payment of taxes. [But this] would logically permit the State to bar new residents from schools, parks, and libraries or deprive them of police and fire protection. Indeed it would permit the State to apportion all benefits and services according to the past tax contributions of its citizens. The Equal Protection Clause prohibits such an apportionment of state services.[10]

We recognize that a State [may] legitimately attempt to limit its expenditures, whether for public assistance, public education, or any other program. But a State may not accomplish such a purpose by invidious distinctions between classes of its citizens. It could not, for example, reduce expenditures for education by barring indigent children from its schools. Similarly, [appellants] must do more than show that denying welfare benefits to new residents saves money. The saving of welfare costs cannot justify an otherwise invidious classification. . . .

Appellants next advance as justification certain administrative and related governmental objectives allegedly served by the waiting-period requirement. They argue that the requirement (1) facilitates the planning of the welfare budget; (2) provides an objective test of residency; (3) minimizes the opportunity for recipients fraudulently to receive payments from more than one jurisdiction; and (4) encourages early entry of new residents into the labor force.

At the outset, we reject appellants' argument that a mere showing of a rational relationship between the waiting period and these four admittedly permissible state objectives will suffice to justify the classification, [for] in moving from State to State or to the District of Columbia appellees were exercising a constitutional right, and any classification which serves to penalize the exercise of that right, unless shown to be necessary to promote a *compelling* governmental interest, is unconstitutional. Cf. [*Skinner*].

The argument that the waiting-period requirement facilitates budget predictability is wholly unfounded. The records [are] utterly devoid of evidence that either State or the District of Columbia in fact uses the one-year requirement as a means to predict the number of people who will require assistance in the budget year. . . .

The argument that the waiting period serves as an administratively efficient rule of thumb for determining residency similarly will not withstand scrutiny. [Before] granting an application, the welfare authorities investigate the applicant [and] in the course of the inquiry necessarily learn the facts upon which to determine whether the applicant is a resident.

Similarly, there is no need for a State to use the one-year waiting period as a safeguard against fraudulent receipt of benefits; for less drastic means are available, and are employed, to minimize that hazard. . . .

[Finally, a] state purpose to encourage employment provides no rational basis for imposing a one-year waiting-period restriction on new residents only [for there is no reason not to require a similar waiting period for this reason for long-term residents].

We conclude therefore that appellants [have] no need to use the one-year requirement for the governmental purposes suggested. Thus, even under traditional equal protection tests a classification of welfare applicants according to

---

10. We are not dealing here with state insurance programs which may legitimately tie the amount of benefits to the individual's contributions.

whether they have lived in the State for one year would seem irrational and unconstitutional. But, of course, the traditional criteria do not apply in these cases.
Since the classification here touches on the fundamental right of interstate movement, its constitutionality must be judged by the stricter standard of whether it
promotes a *compelling* state interest. Under this standard, the waiting-period requirement clearly violates the Equal Protection Clause.[21]

[The Court also rejected the states' argument that Congress had expressly authorized the one-year waiting period and added that, "even if . . . Congress did
approve the imposition of a . . . waiting period," such an approval "would be unconstitutional," for "Congress may not authorize the States to violate the Equal
Protection Clause."]

MR. JUSTICE STEWART, concurring.

The Court today does *not* "pick out particular human activities, characterize
them as 'fundamental,' and give them added protection. . . ." To the contrary, the
Court simply recognizes, as it must, an established constitutional right, and gives
to that right no less protection than the Constitution itself demands. [As] Mr. Justice Harlan wrote for the Court more than a decade ago, "[T]o justify the deterrent effect . . . on the free exercise . . . of their constitutionally protected right . . .
a '. . . subordinating interest of the State must be compelling.'" [NAACP v. Alabama, 357 U.S. 449 (1958).] . . .

MR. CHIEF JUSTICE WARREN, with whom MR. JUSTICE BLACK joins,
dissenting. . . .

Congress has imposed a residence requirement in the District of Columbia
and authorized the States to impose similar requirements. The issue before us
must therefore be framed in terms of whether Congress may create minimal residence requirements, not whether the States, acting alone, may do so. . . .

Congress, pursuant to its commerce power, has enacted a variety of restrictions
upon interstate travel. It has taxed air and rail fares and the gasoline needed to
power cars and trucks which move interstate. Many of the federal safety regulations of common carriers which cross state lines burden the right to travel. And
Congress has prohibited by criminal statute interstate travel for certain purposes.
Although these restrictions operate as a limitation upon free interstate movement
of persons, their constitutionality appears well settled. . . .

The Court's right-to-travel cases lend little support to the view that congressional action is invalid merely because it burdens the right to travel. Most of our
cases fall into two categories: those in which *state*-imposed restrictions were involved, see, e.g., Edwards v. California, 314 U.S. 160 (1941); Crandall v. Nevada,
6 Wall. 35 (1868), and those concerning congressional decisions to remove impediments to interstate movement, see, e.g., United States v. Guest, 383 U.S. 745
(1966). [Here,] travel itself is not prohibited. Any burden inheres solely in the fact
that a potential welfare recipient might take into consideration the loss of welfare
benefits for a limited period of time if he changes his residence. . . .

---

21. We imply no view of the validity of waiting-period *or* residence requirements determining
eligibility to vote, eligibility for tuition-free education, to obtain a license to practice a profession,
to hunt or fish, and so forth. Such requirements may promote compelling state interests on the
one hand, or, on the other, may not be penalties upon the exercise of the constitutional right of
interstate travel.

[Our] cases require only that Congress have a rational basis for finding that a chosen regulatory scheme is necessary to the furtherance of interstate commerce. Certainly, a congressional finding that residence requirements allowed each State to concentrate its resources upon new and increased programs of rehabilitation ultimately resulting in an enhanced flow of commerce as the economic condition of welfare recipients progressively improved is rational and would justify imposition of residence requirements under the Commerce Clause.

Mr. Justice Harlan, dissenting.

In upholding the equal protection argument, the Court has applied an equal protection doctrine of relatively recent vintage: the rule that statutory classifications which [affect] "fundamental rights" will be held to deny equal protection unless justified by a "compelling" governmental interest.

[I] think this [doctrine] particularly unfortunate [because] it creates an exception which threatens to swallow the standard equal protection rule. Virtually every state statute affects important rights. [The] doctrine is also unnecessary. When the right affected is one assured by the Federal Constitution, any infringement can be dealt with under the Due Process Clause. But when a statute affects only matters not mentioned in the Federal Constitution and is not arbitrary or irrational, I must reiterate that I know of nothing which entitles this Court to pick out particular human activities, characterize them as "fundamental," and give them added protection under an unusually stringent equal protection test. . . .

[If] the issue is regarded purely as one of equal protection, [this] classification should be judged by ordinary equal protection standards. [And in] light of [the] undeniable relation of residence requirements to valid legislative aims, [I] can find no objection to these residence requirements under the Equal Protection Clause. . . .

The next issue [is] whether a one-year welfare residence requirement amounts to an undue burden upon the right of interstate travel [which I conclude] is a "fundamental" right [which] should be regarded as having its source in the Due Process Clause of the Fifth Amendment. . . .

[The decisive question is] whether the governmental interests served by residence requirements outweigh the burden imposed upon the right to travel. [Taking] all of [the] competing considerations into account, I believe that the balance definitely favors constitutionality. In reaching that conclusion, I do not minimize the importance of the right to travel interstate. However, the impact of residence conditions upon that right is indirect and apparently quite insubstantial. On the other hand, the governmental purposes served by the requirements are legitimate and real, and the residence requirements are clearly suited to their accomplishment. To abolish residence requirements might well discourage highly worthwhile experimentation in the welfare field. The statutes come to us clothed with the authority of Congress and attended by a correspondingly heavy presumption of constitutionality. Moreover, although [it is argued] that the same objectives could have been achieved by less restrictive means, this is an area in which the judiciary should be especially slow to fetter [legislative] judgment. . . . Residence requirements have advantages, such as administrative simplicity and relative certainty, which are not shared by the alternative solutions. . . . In these circumstances, I cannot find that the burden imposed by residence requirements upon ability to travel outweighs the governmental interests in their continued employment. . . .

SAENZ v. ROE, 119 S. CT. 1518 (1999). Here the Court reaffirmed Shapiro v. Thompson, though on new grounds, and invalidated a California law imposing durational residence requirements by limiting welfare benefits during the recipient's first year of residence. More particularly, California amended its welfare program by limiting new residents to the benefits they would have received in the state of their prior residence — a change approved by the Secretary of Health and Human Services and subsequently by Congress. The Court held that the change violated the privileges or immunities clause of the fourteenth amendment.

The Court began by distinguishing three components of the right to travel: (1) the right to enter and leave another state, an inference from the federal structure without explicit textual support; (2) the right to be treated as "a welcome visitor rather than an unfriendly alien when temporarily present" in a second state, a right rooted in article IV, section 2; and (3) "for those travellers who elect to become permanent residents," the right to be treated like other citizens of that state. It was the third component of the right that was at issue in *Saenz*, and the Court squarely rooted that right on the fourteenth amendment ban on "any law which shall abridge the privileges or immunities of citizens of the United States." The discrimination at issue here, against those "who have completed their interstate travel," was clearly a "penalty" on the exercise of the right to travel.

Adhering to *Shapiro*, the Court said that it was illegitimate to defend the classifications "by a purpose to deter welfare applicants from migrating to California"; this was an impermissible purpose. Nor was the prospect of saving $10.9 million annually sufficient. The question is "whether the state may accomplish that end by the discriminatory means it has chosen." The citizenship clause of the fourteenth amendment "does not tolerate a hierarchy of 45 subclasses of similarly situated citizens based on the location of their prior residence." Nor was federal approval sufficient to save the law, since "Congress may not authorize the States to violate the Fourteenth Amendent," and since "the protection afforded to the citizen by the Citizenship Clause of that Amendment is a limitation on the powers of the National Government as well as the States."

Chief Justice Rehnquist, joined by Justice Thomas, dissented. He urged that here the right to travel was not implicated, for anyone who has finished his journey is "no longer 'travelling.'" He also objected to what he saw as a new reading of the privileges or immunities clause, contending that the California provision was a reasonable and "bona fide residence requirement," akin to durational residence requirements for college eligibility and for divorce. Thus, this was a legitimate effort to ensure that services provided for state residents are enjoyed only by state residents. Justice Thomas, joined by Justice Rehnquist, urged the Court to investigate the original meaning of the privileges or immunities clause, which, he said, was quite limited. Thus the "privileges or immunities of citizens" were understood as "fundamental rights, rather than every public benefit established by positive law."

Note: *The Right to Travel as a "Fundamental Interest"*

1. *The right to travel.* As noted in *Shapiro*, the Court has long recognized a constitutional right to travel, even though the precise source of the right remains somewhat obscure. In Crandall v. Nevada, 73 U.S. (6 Wall.) 35 (1868), for exam-

ple, the Court invalidated a state law imposing a capitation tax of one dollar on "every person leaving the State by any [vehicle engaged] in the business of transporting passengers for hire." The Court explained that "[f]or all the great purposes for which the Federal Government was formed we are one people, with one common country [and] as members of the same community must have the right to pass and repass through every part of it without interruption." Similarly, in Edwards v. California, 314 U.S. 160 (1941), the Court, relying on the commerce clause, invalidated a state statute prohibiting any person from "bringing into the State any indigent person who is not a resident of the State." Four justices concurred on the ground that the statute violated the privileges or immunities clause of the fourteenth amendment. Recall The Slaughter-House Cases, section B supra, and the Court's emphasis on the privileges or immunities clause in *Saenz*.

2. *The right to travel versus equal protection.* Given the Court's view that there is an independent constitutional right to travel, it is not clear why the Court relied in *Shapiro* on the equal protection clause, and perhaps the alternative view in *Saenz* is more straightforward. Do the durational residence requirements at issue in *Shapiro* violate the right to travel by itself? Abolition of a welfare program would *not* have violated the Constitution; perhaps this point makes reliance on the equal protection clause necessary for the *Shapiro* outcome. But if the abolition of a welfare program would be constitutional, and if the program at issue in *Shapiro* interfered with the right to travel less than that (admittedly permissible) outcome, consider whether reliance on the right to travel might not be misleading and the *Shapiro* outcome therefore incorrect. Does the rationale is *Saenz*, emphasizing equal treatment of new permanent residents, clear up the confusion?

3. *The right to travel and the "necessities of life."* Note the Court's reference in *Shapiro* to the "necessities of life." To what extent does *Shapiro* turn on this aspect of the case? Do laws that unequally distribute the "necessities of life" infringe a "fundamental" interest? This issue is examined in section E4 infra.

Note: "Penalizing" the Right to Travel

1. *Impermissible purposes.* The Court in *Shapiro* distinguished between two types of state purposes — those that are "constitutionally impermissible" and those that are permissible but insufficient to satisfy the "compelling" interest standard. One might ask whether it is "constitutionally impermissible" for a state (a) to attempt to deter "the in-migration of indigents"; (b) to "attempt to discourage those indigents who would enter the State solely to obtain larger benefits"; and (c) to "attempt to distinguish between new and old residents on the basis of the contribution they have made to the community through the payment of taxes."

In Zobel v. Williams, 457 U.S. 55 (1982), the Court held that an Alaska statute distributing the income derived from its natural resources to adult citizens in varying amounts depending on length of residence in the state violated the equal protection clause. Citing *Shapiro*, the Court dismissed the state's objective of rewarding "citizens for past contributions" as "not a legitimate state purpose."

Consider Justice O'Connor's observations in a concurring opinion:

[The] Court misdirects its criticism when it labels Alaska's objective illegitimate. A desire to compensate citizens for their prior contributions is neither inherently invidious nor irrational. [The] difficulty is that plans enacted to further this objective necessarily treat new residents of a State less favorably than the longer-term residents who have past contributions to "reward." This inequality [conflicts] with the constitutional purpose of maintaining a Union rather than a mere "league of States." [The] Court's task, therefore, should be (1) to articulate this constitutional principle, explaining its textual sources, and (2) to test the strength of Alaska's objective against the constitutional imperative. [The] Privileges and Immunities Clause of Article IV [addresses] just this type of discrimination. [In this case, the statute is invalid, not because the objective is illegitimate, but because] Alaska has not shown that its new residents are the "peculiar source" of any evil [or that there is] a "substantial relationship" between the evil and the discrimination practiced against the noncitizens.

Consider also the views expressed by Justice Brennan in a separate concurring opinion, joined by Justices Marshall, Blackmun, and Powell:

[The] illegitimacy of [the] state purpose [reflects] not the structure of the Federal Union but the idea of constitutionally protected equality. [Even if] the Alaska plan [did not] apply to migrants from sister States [the discrimination would] be constitutionally suspect. [Length] of residence has only the most tenuous relation to the actual service of individuals to the State. Thus, the past contribution rationale proves much too little to provide a rational predicate for discrimination on the basis of length of residence. But it also proves far too much, for "it would permit the State to apportion all benefits and services according to the [past] contributions of its citizens." [*Shapiro.*] In my view, it is difficult to escape from the recognition that underlying any scheme of classification on the basis of duration of residence, we shall almost invariably find the unstated premise that "some citizens are more equal than others." We rejected that premise [when] we adopted the Equal Protection Clause.

In Hooper v. Bernalillo County Assessor, 472 U.S. 612 (1985), the Court held that a New Mexico statute granting a special tax exemption to Vietnam veterans who were New Mexico residents before May 8, 1976, violated the equal protection clause. The Court distinguished *Shapiro* and Dunn v. Blumstein, Memorial Hospital v. Maricopa County, and Sosna v. Iowa, all discussed infra, on the ground that they involved waiting periods, whereas the New Mexico statute, like the Alaska law invalidated in *Zobel*, "creates 'fixed, permanent distinctions between . . . classes of concededly bona fide residents' based on when they arrived in the State." The Court held that, "stripped of its asserted justifications, the New Mexico statute suffers from the same constitutional flaw as the Alaska statute in *Zobel*." The Court explained:

The New Mexico statute, by singling out previous residents for the tax exemption, rewards only those citizens for their "past contributions" toward our nation's military effort in Vietnam. *Zobel* teaches that such an objective is "not a legitimate state purpose." The State may not favor established residents over new residents based on the view that the State may take care of "its own," if such is defined by prior residence. Newcomers, by establishing bona fide residence in the State, become the State's "own" and may not be discriminated against solely on the basis of their arrival in the State after May 8, 1976. [The] Constitution will not tolerate a state benefit program that creates "fixed, permanent distinctions . . . between . . . classes of concededly bona fide residents," based on how long they have been in the State.

Justice Stevens, joined by Justices Rehnquist and O'Connor, dissented.

In Attorney General of New York v. Soto-Lopez, 476 U.S. 898 (1986), the Court invalidated on "right to travel" grounds a New York statute granting an employment preference to resident veterans who resided in New York at the time that they entered military service. Although appellees were long-time New York residents, they were nonetheless denied the preference under the statute because they were not residents at the time they joined the military. Writing for a plurality of the Court, Justice Brennan explained that "the right to migrate protects residents of a State from being disadvantaged, or from being treated differently, simply because of the timing of their migration, from other similarly situated residents." In separate concurring opinions, Chief Justice Burger and Justice White argued that the statute should be invalidated under the rational basis test. Justices O'Connor, Stevens, and Rehnquist dissented.

2. *Penalties and objectives.* In what circumstances may a state burden the right to travel in order to further a constitutionally *permissible* objective? In *Shapiro*, the Court invoked strict scrutiny because the durational residence requirements "penalized" the right to travel. Do you accept the "penalty" characterization? Consider the following arguments:

a. In the usual "penalty" case, the existence of a condition on eligibility for a state's program makes a person worse off with respect to the constitutional right in question than if there were no program at all. For example, if a state grants welfare benefits only to persons who agree not to vote, the right to vote is pressured in a way it would not be if there were no welfare program at all. The situation is different, however, in *Shapiro*. If state X has a durational residence requirement for the receipt of welfare benefits, a person contemplating a move to state X is no worse off with respect to the right to travel than if state X had no welfare system at all.

b. In the usual "penalty" case, a state withholds an otherwise available benefit from an individual unless she forgoes a constitutional right. For example, if a state grants welfare benefits only to persons who agree not to vote, an individual who exercises her constitutional right to vote will lose a benefit she would otherwise receive. The benefit program thus "penalizes" the exercise of her right. The situation is different, however, in *Shapiro*. If state X has a durational residence requirement for the receipt of welfare benefits, a person contemplating a move to state X will not receive benefits from state X even if she decides not to travel. If she exercises her right to travel, she does not lose a benefit she would otherwise have received from state X. Thus, insofar as state X is concerned, the individual is no worse off if she moves than if she stays put. State X's residence requirement therefore does not "penalize" her right to travel.

3. *Other penalties on the right to travel.* Are all durational residence requirements unconstitutional "penalties" on the right to travel? Note footnote 21 in *Shapiro*, and consider the following cases:

a. *Voting.* In Dunn v. Blumstein, 405 U.S. 330 (1972), the Court, in a six-to-one decision, held that Tennessee's one-year residence requirement for voting violated the equal protection clause. The Court employed strict equal protection scrutiny both because the requirement interfered with the "fundamental" right to vote, see section E1 supra, and because it "penalized" the "fundamental" right to travel. On the latter issue, the Court explained:

> Tennessee seeks to avoid the clear command of *Shapiro* by arguing that durational residence requirements for voting neither seek to nor actually do deter [travel]. This view represents a fundamental misunderstanding of the law. It is irrelevant whether disenfranchisement or denial of welfare is the more potent deterrent to travel. *Shapiro* did not rest upon a finding that denial of welfare actually deterred travel. [In] *Shapiro* we explicitly stated that the compelling-state-interest test would be triggered by "any classification which serves to *penalize* the exercise of that right. . . ." [Durational] residence laws impermissibly condition and penalize the right to travel by imposing their prohibitions on only those persons who have recently exercised that right. In the present case, such laws force a person [to] choose between travel and the basic right to vote. [Absent] a compelling state interest, a State may not burden the right to travel in this way.

Chief Justice Burger dissented.

b. *Nonemergency medical care.* In Memorial Hospital v. Maricopa County, 415 U.S. 250 (1974), the Court held that an Arizona statute requiring a year's residence in a county as a condition to receiving nonemergency medical care at county expense violated the equal protection clause. The Court explained:

> Although any durational residence requirement imposes a potential cost on migration, [*Shapiro*] cautioned that some "waiting-period[s] . . . may not be penalties." [In *Dunn*], the Court found that the denial of the franchise, "a fundamental political right," [was] a penalty requiring application of the compelling-state-interest test. In *Shapiro*, the Court found denial of the basic "necessities of life" to be a penalty. [Whatever] the ultimate parameters of the *Shapiro* penalty analysis, it is at least clear that medical care is as much "a basic necessity of life" to an indigent as welfare assistance. [It] would be odd, indeed, to find that [Arizona] was required to afford [appellant] welfare assistance to keep him from the discomfort of inadequate housing or the pangs of hunger but could deny him the medical care necessary to relieve him from the wheezing and gasping for breath that attend his illness. [Thus, the challenged requirement] penalizes indigents for exercising their right to migrate [and], "unless shown to be necessary to promote a compelling governmental interest, is unconstitutional."

The Court held that the state's justifications for the requirement were not "compelling." Chief Justice Burger and Justice Blackmun concurred in the result. Justice Douglas concurred in a separate opinion. Justice Rehnquist was the lone dissenter.

c. *Divorce.* In Sosna v. Iowa, 419 U.S. 393 (1975), the Court upheld a one-year residence requirement for bringing a divorce action against a nonresident. The Court, in an opinion by Justice Rehnquist, explained:

> Appellant was not irretrievably foreclosed from obtaining some part of what she sought, as was the case with the welfare recipients in *Shapiro*, the voters in *Dunn*, or the indigent patient in *Maricopa County*. [Iowa's] requirement delayed her access to the courts, but, by fulfilling it, she could ultimately have obtained the same opportunity for adjudication which she asserts ought to have been hers at an earlier point in time. [Moreover, unlike the residency requirements invalidated in *Shapiro*, *Dunn*, and *Maricopa County*,] Iowa's residency requirement may reason-

ably be justified on grounds other than purely budgetary considerations or administrative convenience. [A] decree of divorce [may affect the parties' marital status, their property rights, and their children]. With consequences of such moment riding on a divorce decree [Iowa] may insist that one seeking to initiate such a proceeding have the modicum of attachment to the State required here. Such a requirement additionally furthers the State's parallel interests both in avoiding officious intermeddling in matters in which another State has a paramount interest, and in minimizing the susceptibility of its own divorce decrees to collateral attack. [Iowa] may quite reasonably decide that it does not wish to become a divorce mill.

Justice Marshall, joined by Justice Brennan, dissented.

d. *Variations.* In the light of *Shapiro, Dunn, Maricopa County,* and *Sosna,* consider the following: (1) a one-year residency requirement for admittance to the bar, cf. Supreme Court of New Hampshire v. Piper, 470 U.S. 274 (1985) (holding that a bona fide residency requirement for admission to the bar violates the privileges and immunities clause of article IV, section 2); (2) a one-year residency requirement for reduced tuition at a state university, cf. Vlandis v. Kline, 412 U.S. 441 (1973) (invalidating such a requirement under the due process clause as an unconstitutional "irrebuttable presumption"); (3) a state statute making it a misdemeanor for a parent to abandon a dependent child and a felony for the parent to leave the state after the abandonment, see Jones v. Helms, 452 U.S. 412 (1981) (upholding such a statute).

4. *Bona fide residency requirements. Shapiro* dealt with the right to travel in the sense of changing one's residence from one state to another. After *Shapiro,* could a state constitutionally deny welfare benefits to nonresidents who are in the state temporarily? Is such a law permissible because it does not implicate the right to travel?

Shapiro dealt with a classification between two groups of residents. After *Shapiro,* could a state constitutionally deny welfare benefits to former residents who had moved to another state? Consider McCarthy v. Philadelphia Civil Service Commission, 424 U.S. 645 (1976), in which the Court upheld the dismissal of an employee of the fire department who was terminated because he moved to New Jersey in violation of a requirement that city employees be residents of Philadelphia. In a summary per curiam disposition, the Court explained that *Shapiro* dealt only with durational residence requirements and "did not question 'the validity [of] bona fide residence requirements.'" Consider also Martinez v. Bynum, 461 U.S. 321 (1983), in which the Court upheld a bona fide residence requirement for attending a state's public schools. The Court explained: "A bona fide residence requirement [furthers] the substantial state interest in assuring that services provided for its residents are enjoyed only by residents. Such a requirement with respect to attendance in public free schools does not violate the Equal Protection Clause. [It] does not burden or penalize the constitutional right of interstate travel, for any person is free to move to a State and to establish residence there."

Is the issue in *McCarthy* and *Martinez* more sensibly analyzed under the privileges and immunities clause of article IV, section 2? See Supreme Court of New Hampshire v. Piper, supra (bona fide residence requirement for admission to the bar violates article IV, section 2); Supreme Court of Virginia v. Friedman, 487 U.S. 59 (1988) (same); United Building & Construction Trades Council v. Mayor of Camden, 465 U.S. 208 (1984) (ordinance requiring at least 40 percent of employees of contractors working on city projects to be city residents may violate article IV, section 2); Hicklin v. Orbeck, 437 U.S. 518 (1978) (Alaska statute requiring private employers to grant hiring preferences to Alaska residents violates article IV, section 2); Baldwin v. Fish & Game Commission, 436 U.S. 371 (1978) (upholding against article IV, section 2 and equal protection attack a requirement that nonresidents pay higher fees than residents for hunting licenses). The privileges and immunities clause of article IV, section 2 is examined more fully in Chapter 3, section B, supra.

4. Welfare

In *Harper, Griffin,* and *Douglas,* the Court emphasized the impact of certain forms of inequality on the poor. In *Shapiro,* the Court observed that durational residence requirements for welfare affect "the ability [of] families to obtain the very means to subsist — food, shelter, and other necessities of life." After *Shapiro,* a number of courts and commentators maintained that welfare constituted a "fundamental" interest for purposes of equal protection review.

Some people have suggested that welfare, like voting and access to the judicial process, is a "fundamental" interest because it is "preservative of all rights." Consider Michelman, Welfare Rights in a Constitutional Democracy, 1979 Wash. U.L.Q. 659, 677:

> [What] hope is there of effective participation in [the] political system [without] health and vigor, presentable attire, and shelter not only from the elements but from the physical and psychological onslaughts of social debilitation? Are not these interests the universal, rock-bottom prerequisites of effective participation in democratic representation — even paramount in importance to [the] niceties of apportionment, districting, and ballot access on which so much judicial and scholarly labor has been lavished? How can there be those sophisticated rights to a formally unbiased majoritarian system, but no rights to the indispensable means of effective participation in that system?

See also Michelman, Foreword: On Protecting the Poor through the Fourteenth Amendment, 83 Harv. L. Rev. 7, 9, 14-19 (1969). Many nations, including South Africa, have constitutionalized welfare rights in one or another form. Note, however, that such rights are often not subject to judicial enforcement; they amount to judicially unenforceable obligations placed on the legislature.

DANDRIDGE v. WILLIAMS, 397 U.S. 471 (1970). The Court upheld a provision of Maryland's Aid to Families with Dependent Children (AFDC) program that granted most eligible families their computed "standard of need," but imposed a maximum monthly grant of $250 per family regardless of family size or computed need. Justice Stewart delivered the opinion of the Court: "[Here] we deal with state regulation in the social and economic field, not affecting freedoms guaranteed by the Bill of Rights, and claimed to violate the Fourteenth Amendment only because the regulation results in some disparity in grants of welfare payments to the largest AFDC families. For this Court to approve the invalidation of state economic or social regulation [here] would be far too reminiscent of an era when the Court thought the Fourteenth Amendment gave it power to strike down state laws 'because they may be unwise, improvident, or out of harmony with a particular school of thought' [Williamson v. Lee Optical Co.].

"In the area of economics and social welfare, a State does not violate the Equal Protection Clause merely because the classifications made by its laws are imperfect. If the classification has some 'reasonable basis,' it does not offend the [Constitution]. To be sure, the cases [enunciating] this [standard] have in the main involved state regulation of business or industry. The administration of public welfare assistance, by contrast, involves the most basic economic needs of impoverished human beings. We recognize the dramatically real factual difference between the [business] cases and this one, but we can find no basis for applying a different constitutional standard. . . .

"[The] maximum grant regulation is constitutionally valid. [By] keying the maximum family AFDC grants to the minimum wage a steadily employed head of a household receives, [the regulation encourages employment and avoids discrimination between welfare families and the families of the working poor]. [Although the regulation may be both over- and underinclusive,] the Equal Protection Clause does not require that a State must choose between attacking every aspect of a problem or not attacking the problem at all. [It] is enough that the State's action be rationally based and free from invidious discrimination. The regulation before us meets that test."

Justice Marshall, joined by Justice Brennan, dissented: "The cases [that used] a 'mere rationality' test [involved] the regulation of business interests. [But this] case, involving the literally vital interests of a powerless minority — poor families without breadwinners — is far removed from the area of business regulation. [On the other hand, in] my view, equal protection analysis of this case is not appreciably advanced by the a priori definition of a 'right,' fundamental or otherwise. Rather, concentration must be placed upon the character of the classification in question, the relative importance to individuals in the class discriminated against of the governmental benefits that they do not receive, and the asserted state interests in support of the classification. . . .

"It is the individual interests here at stake [that] most clearly distinguish this case from the 'business regulation' equal protection cases. AFDC support to needy dependent children provides the stuff that sustains those children's lives: food, clothing, shelter. And this Court has already recognized [that] when a benefit [is] necessary to sustain life, stricter constitutional standards, both procedural and substantive, are applied to the deprivation of that benefit. [Citing, e.g., Shapiro v. Thompson, section E3 supra; Goldberg v. Kelly, section G1 infra.] . . .

"Appellees are not a gas company or an optical dispenser, they are needy dependent children and families who are discriminated against by the State. The basis of that discrimination [is] too arbitrary, [the] impact on those discriminated against [too] great, and the supposed interests served [too] attenuated to meet the requirements of the Constitution."

Note: Dandridge *and the Judicial Role in the* Welfare *Context*

1. *Dandridge.* Note that in the welfare context the claimant is not asking the government to leave him alone but is asking it to *give* him something. The Constitution is ordinarily thought of as creating limitations on government rather

than as establishing affirmative rights. In this sense, constitutional doctrine has a powerful libertarian dimension. Recall the discussion of *Lochner* in section D supra. Does this fact distinguish welfare from other interests that have been declared "fundamental"? Note that the eminent domain and contracts clauses also have a positive dimension, since private property rights depend on the state's willingness to have and to enforce trespass laws, and since courts have to be available to vindicate contractual rights.

Note also that spending decisions have a "polycentric" character. If the Court expands the class of beneficiaries, the state may simply reduce the benefits for all recipients. Thus, the effect of declaring welfare to be a fundamental interest may be not to benefit the poor as a class but to benefit some poor persons at the expense of others. On the relevance of this point, see S. Holmes and C. Sunstein, The Cost of Rights (1999).

2. *Procreation.* Should the Court have subjected the regulation at issue in *Dandridge* to strict scrutiny because it imposed a penalty on the "fundamental" interest in procreation?

3. *The reach of* Dandridge: *welfare.* Since *Dandridge*, the Court has generally adhered to the view that rational basis review is the appropriate standard for the evaluation of welfare classifications. See, e.g., Califano v. Boles, 443 U.S. 282 (1979) (upholding a provision of the Social Security Act restricting "mothers' insurance benefits" to widows and divorced wives of wage earners); Jefferson v. Hackney, 406 U.S. 535 (1972) (upholding a provision of a state welfare program authorizing payment of a lower percentage of need to recipients of AFDC than to recipients of other forms of categorical welfare assistance); Richardson v. Belcher, 404 U.S. 78 (1971) (upholding a provision of the Social Security Act reducing disability benefits for amounts received from workers' compensation but not for amounts received from private insurance).

4. *The reach of* Dandridge: *housing and health.* In Lindsey v. Normet, 405 U.S. 56 (1972), the Court upheld a state's summary "forcible entry and wrongful detainer" procedures for the eviction of tenants after alleged nonpayment of rent. The Court rejected a claim that "the 'need for decent shelter' and the 'right to retain peaceful possession of one's home' are fundamental interests which are particularly important to the poor and which may be trenched upon only after the State demonstrates some superior interest." Applying rational basis review, the Court found no constitutional defect in the fact that eviction actions are more summary than "other litigation," for the "unique factual and legal characteristics of the landlord-tenant relationship [justify] special statutory treatment." Justices Douglas and Brennan dissented.

The Court rejected a claim to governmental protection in Collins v. Texas, 484 U.S. 924 (1992). Larry Collins, a municipal employee, died of asphyxia after entering a manhole to unstop a sewer line. His widow brought suit, claiming that her husband had a constitutional right to be free from unreasonable risks of harm or at least to be protected from deliberate official indifference to employee safety. The Court concluded that the Constitution had not been violated, at least in the absence of an allegation of deliberate harm or of willful violation of rights.

"Neither the text nor the history of the Due Process Clause supports petitioner's claim that the governmental employer's duty to provide its employees with a safe working environment is a substantive component of the Due Process Clause." Relying on the *DeShaney* case (see page 1507) and the action/inaction distinction, the Court found "unprecedented" the suggestion that there is "a federal constitutional obligation to provide . . . employees with certain minimal levels of safety and security." Nor was a duty of training or warning implied by the Constitution. "Decisions concerning the allocation of resources to individual programs, such as sewer maintenance, and to particular aspects of those programs, such as the training and compensation of employees, involve a host of policy choices that must be made by locally elected representatives."

The *Collins* Court acknowledged that there might be a constitutional claim if the state had coerced a citizen by placing him in hazardous conditions — for example, if a citizen confined in a facility for mental illness is not provided with "minimal custodial standards." What is the difference between such a case and *Collins* itself?

5. *The limits of* Dandridge: Moreno. In U.S. Department of Agriculture v. Moreno, 413 U.S. 528 (1973), the Court, in a seven-to-two decision, invalidated a provision of the Food Stamp Act excluding from participation in the program any household containing an individual who is unrelated to any other household member. The government argued that the challenged classification was rationally related to the legitimate government interest in minimizing fraud because "Congress might rationally have thought [that] households with one or more unrelated members are more likely than 'fully related' households to contain individuals who abuse the program by fraudulently failing to report sources of income." In rejecting this argument, the Court maintained that "the challenged classification [does] not operate so as rationally to further the prevention of fraud," for, "even if we were to accept as rational the Government's [assumptions] concerning the differences between 'related' and 'unrelated' households, we still could not agree" that the challenged provision "constitutes a rational effort to deal with" this concern, for "in practical operation," it "excludes from participation in [the] program, *not* those persons who are 'likely to abuse the program' but, rather, *only* those persons who are so desperately in need of aid that they cannot even afford to alter their living arrangements so as to retain their eligibility."

Does *Moreno* suggest that, despite *Dandridge*, the Court may apply a more stringent standard where a law involves not a mere *relative* deprivation of welfare benefits, as in *Dandridge*, but an *absolute* deprivation, as in *Moreno*?

5.   *Education*

San Antonio Independent School District v. Rodriguez

411 U.S. 1 (1973)

[Public school education has long been financed largely by means of property taxes imposed by local school districts. This suit challenged the constitutionality of Texas's use of this financing system on the ground that it produced substantial interdistrict disparities in per-pupil expenditures. For example, the Edgewood Independent School District, the least affluent of the seven school districts in metropolitan San Antonio, had an assessed property value of $5,960 per student. By imposing a property tax of $1.05 per $100 of assessed property value — the highest rate in the metropolitan area — the district raised $26 per student in local funds. In contrast, the Alamo Heights Independent School District, the most affluent in the area, had an assessed property value per student of more than $49,000 and with a tax rate of only $.85 per $100 was able to raise $333 per student. Although contributions from a state-funded "foundation program" tended to reduce interdistrict disparities, the inclusion of such funds still left a substantial difference — $248 per pupil in Edgewood as compared to $558 in Alamo Heights. A federal district court, applying strict scrutiny, held that the Texas scheme violated the equal protection clause. The Supreme Court reversed.]

MR. JUSTICE POWELL delivered the opinion of the Court. . . .

I

[We] must decide, first, whether the Texas system of financing public education operates to the disadvantage of some suspect class or impinges upon a fundamental right explicitly or implicitly protected by the Constitution, thereby requiring strict judicial scrutiny. If so, the judgment of the District Court should be affirmed. If not, the Texas scheme must still be examined to determine whether it rationally furthers some legitimate, articulated state purpose and therefore does not constitute an invidious discrimination in violation of the Equal Protection Clause of the Fourteenth Amendment.

II

[We] find neither the suspect-classification nor the fundamental-interest analysis persuasive.

A

[The Court rejected the claim that strict scrutiny was appropriate because the Texas system discriminated against the "poor." The Court explained that in prior cases, like *Griffin* and *Douglas*, the "individuals, or groups of individuals, who constituted the class discriminated against [shared] two distinguishing characteristics: because of their impecunity they were completely unable to pay for some desired benefit, and as a consequence, they sustained an absolute deprivation of a meaningful opportunity to enjoy that benefit." The Court maintained here that "neither of the two distinguishing characteristics of wealth classifications" is present. First, "appellees have made no effort to demonstrate that [the Texas system] operates to the peculiar disadvantage" of the poor. To the contrary, "there is reason to believe that the poorest families are not necessarily clustered in the poorest property districts," for the poor are often "clustered around commercial and industrial areas," which produce a relatively high property tax income. Second, the Texas system "has not occasioned an absolute deprivation of the desired benefit." Rather, the sole claim is that appellees "are receiving a poorer quality education [than] children" in other districts,[56] and "at least where wealth is involved,

56. Each of appellees' possible theories of wealth discrimination is founded on the assumption that the quality of education varies directly with the amount of funds expended on it and that, therefore, the difference in quality between two schools can be determined simplistically by look-

the Equal Protection Clause does not [require] precisely equal advantages." The Court thus concluded that the "disadvantaged class is not susceptible of identification in traditional terms."[60] The issue of wealth discrimination in *Rodriguez* is addressed more fully in Chapter 5 supra.]

B

In Brown v. Board of Education, a unanimous Court recognized that "education is perhaps the most important function of state and local governments." . . .

Nothing this Court holds today in any way detracts from our historic dedication to public education. [But] the importance of a service performed by the State does not determine whether it must be regarded as fundamental for purposes of examination under the Equal Protection Clause.

[It] is not the province of this Court to create substantive constitutional rights in the name of guaranteeing equal protection of the laws. Thus, the key to discovering whether education is "fundamental" is not to be found in comparisons of the relative societal significance of education as opposed to subsistence or housing. Nor is it to be found by weighing whether education is as important as the right to travel. Rather, the answer lies in assessing whether there is a right to education explicitly or implicitly guaranteed by the Constitution.[76]

Education, of course, is not among the rights afforded explicit protection under our Federal Constitution. Nor do we find any basis for saying it is implicitly so protected. [It] is appellees' contention, however, that education is distinguishable from other services and benefits provided by the State because it bears a peculiarly close relationship to other rights and liberties accorded protection under the Constitution. Specifically, they insist that education is itself a fundamental personal right because it is essential to the effective exercise of First Amendment freedoms and to intelligent utilization of the right to vote. In asserting a nexus between speech and education, appellees urge that the right to speak is meaningless unless the speaker is capable of articulating his thoughts intelligently and persuasively. . . .

A similar line of reasoning is pursued with respect to the right to vote.[78] Exercise of the franchise, it is contended, cannot be divorced from the educational foundation of the voter. . . .

---

ing at the difference in per-pupil expenditures. This is a matter of considerable dispute among educators and commentators.

60. An educational financing system might be hypothesized, however, in which the analogy to the wealth discrimination cases would be considerably closer. If elementary and secondary education were made available by the State only to those able to pay a tuition assessed against each pupil, there would be a clearly defined class of "poor" people — definable in terms of their inability to pay the prescribed sum — who would be absolutely precluded from receiving an education. That case would present a far more compelling set of circumstances for judicial assistance than the case before us today. After all, Texas has undertaken to do a good deal more than provide an education to those who can afford it. It has provided what it considers to be an adequate base education for all children and has attempted, though imperfectly, to ameliorate by state funding and by the local assessment program the disparities in local tax resources.

76. [*Skinner,* for example,] applied the standard of close scrutiny to a state law permitting forced sterilization of "habitual criminals." Implicit in the Court's opinion is the recognition that the right of procreation is among the rights of personal privacy protected under the Constitution. See Roe v. Wade, 410 U.S. 113, 152 (1973). [Relocated footnote — EDS.]

78. Since the right to vote, per se, is not a constitutionally protected right, we assume that appellees' references to that right are simply shorthand references to the protected right, implicit in

We need not dispute any of these propositions. The Court has long afforded zealous protection against unjustifiable governmental interference with the individual's rights to speak and to vote. Yet we have never presumed to possess either the ability or the authority to guarantee to the citizenry the most *effective* speech or the most *informed* electoral choice. That these may be desirable goals [is] not to be doubted. [But] they are not values to be implemented by judicial intrusion into otherwise legitimate state activities.

[Whatever] merit appellees' argument might have if a State's financing system occasioned an absolute denial of educational opportunities to any of its children, that argument provides no basis for finding an interference with fundamental rights where only relative differences in spending levels are involved and where — as is true in the present case — no charge fairly could be made that the system fails to provide each child with an opportunity to acquire the basic minimal skills necessary for the enjoyment of the rights of speech and of full participation in the political process.

Furthermore, the logical limitations on appellees' nexus theory are difficult to perceive. How, for instance, is education to be distinguished from the significant personal interests in the basics of decent food and shelter? Empirical examination might well buttress an assumption that the ill-fed, ill-clothed, and ill-housed are among the most ineffective participants in the political process, and that they derive the least enjoyment from the benefits of the First Amendment. If so, appellees' thesis would cast serious doubt on the authority of Dandridge v. Williams and Lindsey v. Normet [405 U.S. 56 (1972)]. . . .

C

[We] have here nothing less than a direct attack on the way in which Texas has chosen to raise and disburse state and local tax revenues. [A]ppellees would have the Court intrude in an area in which it has traditionally deferred to state legislatures. [No] scheme of taxation, whether the tax is imposed on property, income, or purchases of goods and services, has yet been devised which is free of all discriminatory impact. In such a complex arena in which no perfect alternatives exist, the Court does well not to impose too rigorous a standard of scrutiny lest all local fiscal schemes become subjects of criticism under the Equal Protection Clause.

[Moreover], this case also involves the most persistent and difficult questions of educational policy, another area in which this Court's lack of specialized knowledge and experience counsels against premature interference with the informed judgments made at the state and local levels. Education, perhaps even more than welfare assistance, presents a myriad of "intractable economic, social, and even philosophical problems." . . .

III

[While] assuring a basic education for every child in the State, [the Texas system of school financing] permits and encourages a large measure of participation in

---

our constitutional system, to participate in state elections on an equal basis with other qualified voters whenever the State has adopted an elective process for determining who will represent any segment of the State's population.

and control of each district's schools at the local level. In an era that has witnessed a consistent trend toward centralization of the functions of government, local sharing of responsibility for public education has survived. [In] part, local control means [the] freedom to devote more money to the education of one's children. Equally important, however, is the opportunity it offers for participation in the decisionmaking process that determines how those local tax dollars will be spent. Each locality is free to tailor local programs to local needs. Pluralism also affords some opportunity for experimentation, innovation, and a healthy competition for educational [excellence]. Appellees suggest that local control could be preserved and promoted under other financing systems that resulted in more equality in educational expenditures. While it is no doubt true that reliance on local property taxation for school revenues provides less freedom of choice with respect to expenditures for some districts than for others, the existence of "some inequality" in the manner in which the State's rationale is achieved is not alone a sufficient basis for striking down the entire system. [Nor] must the financing system fail because, as appellees suggest, other methods of satisfying the State's interest, which occasion "less drastic" disparities in expenditures, might be conceived. Only where state action impinges on the exercise of fundamental constitutional rights or liberties must it be found to have chosen the least restrictive alternative. [It] is also well to remember that even those districts that have reduced ability to make free decisions with respect to how much they spend on education still retain under the present system a large measure of authority as to how available funds will be allocated. They further enjoy the power to make numerous other decisions with respect to the operation of the schools. The people of Texas may be justified in believing that other systems of school financing, which place more of the financial responsibility in the hands of the State, will result in a comparable lessening of desired local autonomy. . . .

Appellees further urge that the Texas system is unconstitutionally arbitrary because it allows the [quality] of education to fluctuate on the basis of the fortuitous positioning of the boundary lines of political subdivisions. [But] any scheme of local taxation — indeed the very existence of identifiable local governmental units — requires the establishment of jurisdictional boundaries that are inevitably arbitrary. [And] if local taxation for local expenditures were an unconstitutional method of providing for education then it might be an equally impermissible means of providing other necessary services customarily financed largely from local property taxes, including local police and fire protection, public health and hospitals, and public utility facilities of various kinds. We perceive no justification for such a severe denigration of local property taxation and control. . . .

[The] constitutional standard under the Equal Protection Clause is whether the challenged state action rationally furthers a legitimate state purpose or interest. We hold that the Texas plan abundantly satisfies this standard. . . .

Reversed.

[The concurring opinion of Justice Stewart and the dissenting opinion of Justice Brennan are omitted.]

Mr. Justice White, with whom Mr. Justice Douglas and Mr. Justice Brennan join, dissenting.

[This] case would be quite different if it were true that the Texas system, while insuring minimum educational expenditures in every district through state funding, extended a meaningful option to all local districts to increase their per-pupil [expenditures. But for] districts with a low per-pupil real estate tax base [the] Texas system utterly fails to extend a realistic choice to parents because the property tax, which is the only revenue-raising mechanism extended to school districts, is practically and legally unavailable. . . .

In order to equal the highest yield in any other Bexar County district, [Edgewood] would be required to tax at the prohibitive rate of $5.76 per $100. But state law places a $1.50 per $100 ceiling on the maintenance tax rate. [Edgewood] is thus precluded in law, as well as in fact, from achieving a yield even close to that of some other districts. [Requiring] the State to establish only that unequal treatment is in furtherance of a permissible goal, without also requiring the State to show that the means chosen to effectuate that goal are rationally related to its achievement, makes equal protection analysis no more than an empty gesture. . . .

MR. JUSTICE MARSHALL, with whom MR. JUSTICE DOUGLAS concurs, dissenting.

[The] Court apparently seeks to establish today that equal protection cases fall into one of two neat categories which dictate the appropriate standard of review — strict scrutiny or mere rationality. But this Court's decisions in the field of equal protection defy such easy categorization. A principled reading of what this Court has done reveals that it has applied a spectrum of standards in reviewing discrimination allegedly violative of the Equal Protection Clause. This spectrum clearly comprehends variations in the degree of care with which the Court will scrutinize particular classifications, depending, I believe, on the constitutional and societal importance of the interest adversely affected and the recognized invidiousness of the basis upon which the particular classification is drawn. . . .

[I] would like to know where the Constitution guarantees the right to procreate [Skinner v. Oklahoma], or the right to vote in state elections [Reynolds v. Sims],[60] or the right to an appeal from a criminal conviction [Griffin].[61] These are instances in which, due to the importance of the interests at stake, the Court has displayed a strong concern with the existence of discriminatory state treatment. But the Court has never said or indicated that these are interests which independently enjoy full-blown constitutional protection. . . .

The majority is, of course, correct when it suggests that the process of determining which interests are fundamental is a difficult one. But I do not think the problem is insurmountable. [The] determination of which interests are fundamental should be firmly rooted in the text of the Constitution. The task in every case should be to determine the extent to which constitutionally guaranteed rights are dependent on interests not mentioned in the Constitution. As the

60. It is interesting that in its effort to reconcile the state voting rights cases with its theory of fundamentality the majority can muster nothing more than the contention that "[t]he constitutional underpinnings of the *right to equal treatment in the voting process* can no longer be doubted. . . ." If, by this, the Court intends to recognize a substantive constitutional "right to equal teatment in the voting process" independent of the Equal Protection Clause, the source of such a right is certainly a mystery to me.

61. It is true that *Griffin* [also] involved discrimination against indigents, that is, wealth discrimination. But, as the majority points out, the Court has never deemed wealth discrimination alone to be sufficient to require strict judicial scrutiny; rather, such review of wealth classifications has been applied only where the discrimination affects an important individual interest, see, e.g., [*Harper*]. Thus, I believe *Griffin* [can] only be understood as premised on a recognition of the fundamental importance of the criminal appellate process.

nexus between the specific constitutional guarantee and the nonconstitutional interest draws closer, the nonconstitutional interest becomes more fundamental and the degree of judicial scrutiny applied when the interest is infringed on a discriminatory basis must be adjusted accordingly. Thus, it cannot be denied that interests such as procreation, the exercise of the state franchise, and access to criminal appellate processes are not fully guaranteed to the citizen by our Constitution. But these interests have nonetheless been afforded special judicial consideration in the face of discrimination because they are, to some extent, interrelated with constitutional guarantees. Procreation is now understood to be important because of its interaction with the established constitutional right of privacy. The exercise of the state franchise is closely tied to basic civil and political rights inherent in the First Amendment. And access to criminal appellate processes enhances the integrity of the range of rights implicit in the [guarantee] of due process of law. Only if we closely protect the related interests from state discrimination do we ultimately ensure the integrity of the constitutional guarantee itself. This is the real lesson that must be taken from our previous decisions involving interests deemed to be fundamental. . . .

[It] is true that this Court has never deemed the provision of free public education to be required by the Constitution. [Nevertheless] the fundamental importance of education is amply indicated by the prior decisions of this Court, by the unique status accorded public education by our society, and by the close relationship between education and some of our most basic constitutional values. . . .

Education directly affects the ability of a child to exercise his First Amendment rights, both as a source and as a receiver of information and ideas. [Of] particular importance is the relationship between education and the political process [and] the demonstrated effect of education on the exercise of the franchise by the electorate. [It] is this very sort of intimate relationship between a particular personal interest and specific constitutional guarantees that has heretofore caused the Court to attach special significance, for purposes of equal protection analysis, to individual interests such as procreation and the exercise of the state franchise.[74] [These factors] compel us to recognize the fundamentality of education and to scrutinize with appropriate care the bases for state discrimination affecting equality of educational opportunity in Texas' school districts — a conclusion which is only strengthened when we consider the character of the classification in this case.

74. I believe that the close nexus between education and our established constitutional values with respect to freedom of speech and participation in the political process makes this a different case from our prior decisions concerning discrimination affecting public welfare, see, e.g., [Dandridge] or housing, see, e.g., [Lindsey v. Normet]. There can be no question that, as the majority suggests, constitutional rights may be less meaningful for someone without enough to eat or without decent housing. But the crucial difference lies in the closeness of the relationship. Whatever the severity of the impact of insufficient food or inadequate housing on a person's life, they have never been considered to bear the same direct and immediate relationship to constitutional concerns for free speech and for our political processes as education has long been recognized to bear. Perhaps, the best evidence of this fact is the unique status which has been accorded public education as the single public service nearly unanimously guaranteed in the constitutions of our States. Education, in terms of constitutional values, is much more analogous, in my judgment, to the right to vote in state elections than to public welfare or public housing. Indeed, it is not without significance that we have long recognized education as an essential step in providing the disadvantaged with the tools necessary to achieve economic self-sufficiency.

[On the "wealth" issue, Justice Marshall maintained that *Harper, Griffin,* and *Douglas* refuted the Court's contention "that we have in the past required an absolute deprivation before subjecting wealth classifications to strict scrutiny." Justice Marshall conceded, however, that "the form of wealth classification in this case" differs "from those recognized [in] previous decisions," for "the children of the disadvantaged Texas school districts are being discriminated against not necessarily because of their personal wealth, [but] because of the taxable property wealth of the residents of the district in which they happen to live." Nonetheless, Justice Marshall concluded that "discrimination on the basis of group wealth in this case likewise calls for careful judicial scrutiny," for "it bears no relationship whatsoever to the interest of Texas schoolchildren in the educational opportunity afforded them," it "involves wealth over which the disadvantaged individual has no significant control," and it was the State, not the operation of the market, "that has [tied] educational funding [to] local district wealth."]

[The] only justification offered [to] sustain the discrimination in educational opportunity caused by the Texas financing scheme is local educational control. [But] on this record, it is apparent that the State's purported concern with local control is offered primarily as an excuse rather than as a justification for interdistrict inequality.

In Texas, statewide laws regulate [the] most minute details of local public education. [But] even if we accept Texas' general dedication to local control in educational matters, it is difficult to find any evidence of such dedication with respect to fiscal matters. [If] Texas had a system truly dedicated to local fiscal control, one would expect the quality of the educational opportunity provided in each district to vary with the decision of the voters in that district as to the level of sacrifice they wish to make for public education. In fact, the Texas scheme produces precisely the opposite result. Local school districts cannot choose to have the best education in the State by imposing the highest tax rate. Instead, the quality of the educational opportunity offered by any particular district is largely determined by the amount of taxable property located in the district — a factor over which local voters can exercise no control. . . .

In my judgment, any substantial degree of scrutiny of the operation of the Texas financing scheme reveals that the State has selected means wholly inappropriate to secure its purported interest in assuring its school districts local fiscal control. [Appellees] have pointed out a variety of alternative financing schemes which may serve the State's purported interest in local control as well as, if not better than, the present scheme without the current impairment of the educational opportunity of vast numbers of Texas schoolchildren.

I see no need, however, to explore the practical or constitutional merits of those suggested alternatives at this time for, whatever their positive or negative features, experience with the present financing scheme impugns any suggestion that it constitutes a serious effort to provide local fiscal control. . . .

Note: The Rodriguez Formulation

1. *The competing views.* There are two critical points of disagreement in *Rodriguez:* (a) The Court confined "fundamental" interests to only those rights that are "explicitly or implicitly protected by the Constitution," whereas Justice Mar-

shall offered a "nexus" approach, focusing on the "extent to which constitutionally protected rights are dependent on interests not mentioned in the Constitution." (b) The Court adhered to the two-tier theory of equal protection review, whereas Justice Marshall, as in *Dandridge*, offered his sliding-scale approach.

2. *Education as a fundamental interest.* To what extent, if any, does footnote 60 impeach the Court's conclusion that education is not a "fundamental" interest? To what extent does the Court's reiteration that the Texas system did not involve an "absolute deprivation" of education impeach this conclusion? And if the state is under no obligation to provide police services to protect life (as *DeShaney*, Chapter 9 infra, seems to suggest), how can it be under an obligation to provide some level of educational services?

If education *were* a "fundamental" interest, note that there would be serious problems in judicial assessment of what kind of education, and how much education, a person is entitled to receive. Would public schools be required to adopt standardized curricula? Would state universities be required to pay the tuition costs of indigents?

3. *Territorial discrimination.* The school financing scheme upheld in *Rodriguez* treats individuals differently depending on where they live in the state. How should the Court analyze such inequalities? Can a state constitutionally provide more money for the education of students who live in the northern part of the state? For discussion, see Neuman, Territorial Discrimination, Equal Protection, and Self-Determination, 135 U. Pa. L. Rev. 261 (1987).

Compare *Rodriguez* to Papasan v. Allain, 478 U.S. 265 (1986). While Mississippi was still a territory, Congress reserved certain plots of land within each township for support of public schools. However, Congress failed to reserve such lands in northern Mississippi, which was then held by the Chickasaw Indian Nation. In 1836, Congress sought to remedy this oversight by vesting certain lands in the state for the use of schools within the Chickasaw Cession, but the state (with the permission of Congress) sold these lands and invested the proceeds in railroads that were destroyed during the Civil War. The result is that today school districts in most of the state receive an average income of $75.34 per pupil from reserved lands located within their borders, while Chickasaw Cession schools receive annual appropriations, designed to compensate for the lost lands, of only $.63 per pupil.

Petitioners filed an action claiming, inter alia, that the disparity in funding violated the equal protection clause. The court of appeals held that in light of *Rodriguez*, the trial court correctly granted respondent's motion to dismiss; but the Supreme Court, in an opinion by Justice White, reversed. Because petitioners had not alleged any facts supporting the contention that they were denied a minimally adequate education, the Court found it unnecessary to determine whether such a denial would infringe on a fundamental right and trigger strict scrutiny. Nonetheless, the Court ruled that the lower court had erred in holding that *Rodriguez* compelled dismissal of the suit:

> As we read their complaint, the petitioners do not challenge the overall organization of the Mississippi public school financing program. Instead, their challenge is restricted to one aspect of that program. . . .
> This case is [very] different from *Rodriguez*, where the differential financing available to school districts was traceable to school district funds available from lo-

cal real estate taxation, not to a state decision to divide state resources unequally among school districts. The rationality of the disparity in *Rodriguez*, therefore, which rested on the fact that funding disparities based on differing local wealth were a necessary adjunct of allowing meaningful local control over school funding, does not settle the constitutionality of disparities alleged in this case.

The Court remanded the case so that the lower court could consider in the first instance whether, given state title to the lands, the equal protection clause permitted the state to distribute income from them unequally among school districts.

Justice Powell, joined by Chief Justice Burger and Justice Rehnquist, dissented. He pointed out that income from the lands accounted for only 1.5 percent of overall funding for the schools and argued that such de minimis variations in funding were insufficient to establish an equal protection clause violation.

4. *The impact of* Rodriguez. The Court attempted in *Rodriguez* to add a measure of certainty to equal protection jurisprudence and to withdraw from the arguably "subjective" enterprise of selecting "fundamental" interests. Since 1973, the Court has generally adhered to the *Rodriguez* reformulation. That is, although the Court has continued to enforce "fundamental" interest analysis in the areas of procreation, voting, access to the courts, and travel, it has essentially frozen the list of "fundamental" interests and maintained its two-tier approach. But not entirely. Consider Plyler v. Doe.

Plyler v. Doe
457 U.S. 202 (1982)

JUSTICE BRENNAN delivered the opinion of the Court. . . .

[The Court held unconstitutional a Texas statute that authorized local school districts to deny free public education to children who had not been "legally admitted" into the United States. Pursuant to this statute, the Tyler Independent School District required "undocumented" children to pay a "tuition fee" in order to enroll.]

[In] applying the Equal Protection Clause to most forms of state action, we [seek] only the assurance that the classification at issue bears some fair relationship to a legitimate public purpose.

But we would not be faithful to our obligations under the Fourteenth Amendment if we applied so deferential a standard to every classification. [With] respect to [some] classifications, it is appropriate to enforce the mandate of equal protection by requiring the State to demonstrate that its classification has been precisely tailored to serve a compelling governmental interest. In addition, we have recognized that certain forms of legislative classification, while not facially invidious, nonetheless give rise to recurring constitutional difficulties; in these limited circumstances we have sought the assurance that the classification reflects a reasoned judgment consistent with the ideal of equal protection by inquiring whether it may fairly be viewed as furthering a substantial interest of the State. We turn to a consideration of the standard appropriate for the evaluation of [the challenged law].

Sheer incapability or lax enforcement of the laws barring entry into this country, [has] resulted in the creation of a substantial "shadow population" of illegal migrants — numbering in the millions — within our borders. This situation raises the specter of a permanent caste of undocumented resident aliens, encouraged by some to remain here as a source of cheap labor, but nevertheless denied the benefits that our society makes available to citizens and lawful residents. [The Court rejected the claim that "illegal aliens" are a suspect class on the ground that illegal status is at least partly voluntary and that that status is not irrelevant to legitimate government purposes.]

The children who are plaintiffs in these cases are special members of this underclass. [Adults] who elect to enter our territory by stealth and in violation of our law should be prepared to bear the consequences, including, but not limited to, deportation. But the children [of] illegal entrants are not comparably situated. [They] "can affect neither their parents' conduct nor their own status." [Trimble v. Gordon, 430 U.S. 762 (1977).]

[Of] course, undocumented status is not irrelevant to any proper legislative goal. Nor is undocumented status an absolutely immutable characteristic since it is the product of conscious, indeed unlawful, action. But [the challenged law] is directed against children, and imposes its discriminatory burden on the basis of a legal characteristic over which children can have little control. It is thus difficult to conceive of a rational justification for penalizing these children for their presence within the United States. Yet that appears to be precisely the effect of [the law].

Public education is not a "right" granted to individuals by the Constitution. [*Rodriguez.*] But neither is it merely some governmental "benefit" indistinguishable from other forms of social welfare legislation. Both the importance of education in maintaining our basic institutions, and the lasting impact of its deprivation on the life of the child, mark the distinction. ["Some] degree of education is necessary to prepare citizens to participate effectively and intelligently in our open political system if we are to preserve freedom and independence." [In] addition, education provides the basic tools by which individuals might lead economically productive lives to the benefit of us all. In sum, education has a fundamental role in maintaining the fabric of our society. We cannot ignore the significant social costs borne by our Nation when select groups are denied the means to absorb the values and skills upon which our social order rests.

In addition to the pivotal role of education in sustaining our political and cultural heritage, denial of education to some isolated group of children poses an affront to one of the goals of the Equal Protection Clause: the abolition of governmental barriers presenting unreasonable obstacles to advancement on the basis of individual merit. [Illiteracy] is an enduring disability. The inability to read and write will handicap the individual deprived of a basic education each and every day of his life. The inestimable toll of that deprivation on the social, economic, intellectual, and psychological well-being of the individual, and the obstacle it poses to individual achievement, make it most difficult to reconcile [a] status-based denial of basic education with the framework of equality embodied in the Equal Protection Clause.

These well-settled principles allow us to determine the proper level of deference to be afforded [the Texas statute]. Undocumented aliens [are not] a suspect class [and] education [is not] a fundamental [right]. But more is involved in [this case] than the abstract question whether [the Texas statute] discriminates against a suspect class, or whether education is a fundamental right. [The statute] imposes a lifetime hardship on a discrete class of children not accountable for their disabling status. [In] determining the rationality of [the challenged statute], we may appropriately take into account its costs to the Nation and to the innocent children who are its victims. In light of these countervailing costs, the discrimination contained in [the statute] can hardly be considered rational unless it furthers some substantial goal of the State.

It is the State's principal argument [that] the undocumented status of these children vel non establishes a sufficient rational basis for denying them benefits that a State might choose to afford other residents. The State notes that while other aliens are admitted "on an equality of legal privileges with all citizens under non-discriminatory laws," the asserted right of these children to an education can claim no implicit congressional imprimatur. Indeed, in the State's view, Congress' apparent disapproval of the presence of these children within the United States [provides] authority for its decision to impose upon them special disabilities. Faced with an equal protection challenge respecting the treatment of aliens, we agree that the courts must be attentive to congressional policy; [but] we are unable to find in the congressional immigration scheme any statement of policy that might weigh significantly in arriving at an equal protection balance concerning the State's authority to deprive these children of an education.

Congress has developed a complex scheme governing admission to our Nation and status within our borders. The obvious need for delicate policy judgments has counseled the Judicial Branch to avoid intrusion into this field. But this traditional caution does not persuade us that unusual deference must be shown the [challenged classification]. The States enjoy no power with respect to the classification of aliens. This power is "committed to the political branches of the Federal Government." [And although] the States do have some authority to act with respect to illegal aliens, at least where such action mirrors federal objectives and furthers a legitimate state [goal], there is no indication that the disability imposed by [the challenged law] corresponds to any identifiable congressional policy. . . .

To be sure, like all persons who have entered the United States unlawfully, these children are subject to deportation. But there is no assurance that a child subject to deportation will ever be deported. [We] are reluctant to impute to Congress the intention to withhold from these children, for so long as they are present in this country through no fault of their own, access to a basic education. In other contexts, undocumented status, coupled with some articulable federal policy, might enhance state authority with respect to the treatment of undocumented aliens. But in the area of special constitutional sensitivity presented by these cases, and in the absence of any contrary indication fairly discernible in the present legislative record, we perceive no national policy that supports the State in denying these children an elementary education. . . .

[The State argues further] that the classification at issue furthers an interest in the "preservation of the state's limited resources for the education of its lawful residents." [But the] State must do more than justify its classification with a concise expression of an intention to discriminate. [We] discern three colorable state interests that might support [the classification].

First, [the State suggests that it may] protect itself from an influx of illegal immigrants. [But there] is no evidence in the record suggesting that illegal entrants impose any significant burden on the State's economy. To the contrary, the available evidence suggests that illegal aliens underutilize public services, while contributing their labor to the local economy and tax money to the state fisc.

[Second,] the State suggests that undocumented children are appropriately singled out for exclusion because of the special burdens they impose on the State's ability to provide high-quality public education. But the record in no way supports the claim that exclusion of undocumented children is likely to improve the overall quality of education in the State. [Moreover], even if improvement in the quality of education were a likely result of barring some *number* of children from the schools of the State, the State must support its selection of *this* group as the appropriate target for exclusion. In terms of educational cost and need, however, undocumented children are "basically indistinguishable" from legally resident alien children.

Finally, [the State suggests] that undocumented children are appropriately singled out because their unlawful presence within the United States renders them less likely than other children to remain within the [State], and to put their education to productive social or political use within the State. Even assuming that such an interest is legitimate, it is an interest that is most difficult to quantify. The State has no assurance that any child, citizen or not, will employ the education provided by the State within the confines of the State's borders. In any event, the record is clear that many of the undocumented children disabled by this classification will remain in this country indefinitely, and that some will become lawful residents or citizens of the United States. It is difficult to understand precisely what the State hopes to achieve by promoting the creation and perpetuation of a subclass of illiterates within our boundaries, surely adding to the problems and costs of unemployment, welfare, and crime. It is thus clear that whatever savings might be achieved by denying these children an education, they are wholly insubstantial in light of the costs involved to these children, the State, and the Nation.

If the State is to deny a discrete group of innocent children the free public education that it offers to other children residing within its borders, that denial must be justified by a showing that it furthers some substantial state interest. No such showing was made here. . . .

Affirmed.

JUSTICE MARSHALL, concurring.

While I join the Court opinion, I do so without in any way retreating from my opinion in [*Rodriguez*].

JUSTICE BLACKMUN, concurring.

[This] conclusion is fully consistent with *Rodriguez*, [for the] Court there reserved judgment on the constitutionality of a state system that "occasioned an absolute denial of educational opportunities to any of its children." . . .

JUSTICE POWELL, concurring.

I join the opinion of the Court, and write separately to emphasize the unique character of the [case] before us. . . .

Although the analogy is not perfect, our holding today does find support in decisions of this Court with respect to the status of illegitimates. [In this case], Texas effectively denies to the school-age children of illegal aliens the opportunity to attend the free public schools that the State makes available to all residents. They are excluded only because of a status resulting from the violation by parents or guardians of our immigration laws and the fact that they remain in our country unlawfully. The appellee children are innocent in this respect.

[A] legislative classification that threatens the creation of an underclass of future citizens and residents cannot be reconciled with one of the fundamental purposes of the Fourteenth Amendment. In these unique circumstances, the Court properly may require that the State's interests be substantial and that the means bear a "fair and substantial relation" to these interests.[3] . . .

CHIEF JUSTICE BURGER, with whom JUSTICE WHITE, JUSTICE REHNQUIST, and JUSTICE O'CONNOR join, dissenting.

[The] Court expressly — and correctly — rejects any suggestion that illegal aliens are a suspect class, or that education is a fundamental right. Yet by patching together bits and pieces of what might be termed quasi-suspect-class and quasi-fundamental-rights analysis, the Court spins out a theory custom-tailored to the facts of [this case]. If ever a court was guilty of an unabashedly result-oriented approach, this case is a prime example.

The Court first suggests that these illegal alien children, although not a suspect class, are entitled to special solicitude under the Equal Protection Clause because they lack "control" over or "responsibility" for their unlawful entry into this country. Similarly, the Court appears to take the position that [the law] is presumptively "irrational" because it has the effect of imposing "penalties" on "innocent" children. However, the Equal Protection Clause does not preclude legislators from classifying among persons on the basis of factors and characteristics over which individuals may be said to lack "control." [A] state legislature is not barred from considering, for example, relevant differences between the mentally healthy and the mentally ill, or between the residents of different counties, simply because these may be factors unrelated to individual choice or to any "wrongdoing."

[The] Court's analogy to cases involving discrimination against illegitimate children is grossly misleading. The State has not thrust any disabilities upon appellees due to their "status of birth." Rather, appellees' status is predicated upon the circumstances of their concededly illegal presence in this country. . . .

The second strand of the Court's analysis rests on the premise that, although public education is not a constitutionally guaranteed right, "neither is it merely some governmental 'benefit' indistinguishable from other forms of social welfare legislation." [This] opaque observation [has] no bearing on the issues at hand. [The] importance of education is beyond dispute. Yet we have held repeatedly that the importance of a governmental service does not elevate it to the status of a "fundamental right" for purposes of equal protection analysis. Moreover, the Court points to no meaningful way to distinguish between education and other governmental benefits in this context. Is the Court suggesting that educa-

---

3. The Chief Justice argues [that] this heightened standard of review is inconsistent with [*Rodriguez*]. But in *Rodriguez* no group of children was singled out by the State and then penalized because of their parents' status. Rather, funding for education varied across the State because of the tradition of local control. Nor, in that case, was any group of children totally deprived of all education as in these cases.

tion is more "fundamental" than food, shelter, or medical care? [The] Equal Protection Clause [does] not mandate a constitutional hierarchy of governmental services. . . .

Once it is conceded [that] illegal aliens are not a suspect class, and that education is not a fundamental right, our inquiry should focus on and be limited to whether the legislative classification at issue bears a rational relationship to a legitimate state purpose. [*Dandridge.*] [It] simply is not "irrational" for a state to conclude that it does not have the same responsibility to provide benefits for persons whose very presence in the state and this country is illegal as it does to provide for persons lawfully present. [The] Federal Government has seen fit to exclude illegal aliens from numerous social welfare programs, such as the food stamp program, the old-age assistance, aid to families with dependent children, aid to the blind, aid to the permanently and totally disabled, and supplemental security income [programs]. [These] exclusions [support] the rationality of [the challenged statute]. . . .

Note: Plyler *and the Equal Protection Clause*

1. *The rationale and limits of* Plyler. What is the rationale of *Plyler?* Consider the view that the Court has cobbled together a set of disparate doctrines in a way that creates a kind of one-way ticket. Does the Court invoke ideas of semi-suspect classes and semi-fundamental rights in a way that fits poorly with the rest of the fabric of the law? In Martinez v. Bynum, 461 U.S. 321 (1983), the Court upheld a Texas statute that authorized local school districts to deny tuition-free admission to public schools to minors who live apart from their parents or guardians and whose presence in the district is "for the primary purpose of attending the public free schools." Justice Powell wrote the opinion of the Court:

[The challenged bona fide residence] requirement implicates no "suspect" classification; [it] does not burden or penalize the constitutional right of interstate travel, for any person is free to move to [the] State and to establish residence there; [and] the "service" [denied] to nonresidents is not a fundamental right protected by the Constitution. [Citing *Plyler.*] [Moreover, as a bona fide residence requirement, the challenged statute furthers] the substantial state interest in assuring that [educational] services provided for its residents are enjoyed only by residents. [The requirement thus] satisfies constitutional standards.

Justice Marshall dissented. Is *Martinez* consistent with *Plyler?*

2. *More limits of* Plyler: Kadrmas. In Kadrmas v. Dickinson Public Schools, 487 U.S. 450 (1988), the Court, in a five-to-four decision, upheld a program whereby North Dakota permitted local school boards to assess a user fee for transporting students to and from public schools. Relying primarily on *Plyler,* appellants contended that the user fee, which could not exceed the estimated cost to the school district of providing the service, unconstitutionally deprived those who could not "afford to pay it of 'minimum access to education.'" The Court explained that it had not extended *Plyler* beyond its "unique circumstances." Moreover, *Plyler* did not govern this case, for the children in this case "had not been penalized by the government for illegal conduct by [their] parents," and the Court saw no "reason to suppose that this user fee will 'promot[e] the creation

and perpetuation of a sub-class of illiterates.'" The Court emphasized that, because the Constitution does not require the state to provide bus service at all, it surely does not require the state to provide free bus service to anyone.

Justice Marshall, joined by Justice Brennan, dissented:

> This case involves state action that places a special burden on poor families in their pursuit of education. [The] intent of the Fourteenth Amendment was to abolish class legislation. When state action has the predictable tendency to entrap the poor and create a permanent underclass, that intent is frustrated. Thus, to the extent that a law places discriminatory barriers between indigents and the basic tools and opportunities that might enable them to rise, exacting scrutiny should be applied.

Justice Stevens, joined by Justice Blackmun, also dissented.

3. *"Fundamental" interests and the equal protection clause: concluding thoughts.* What is the justification for special scrutiny of classifications affecting fundamental interests under the equal protection clause? Consider these ideas, which seem to run through the cases. (a) Sometimes the Constitution recognizes that the state need not provide certain things, but it constrains the distribution of those things once the state has provided them. (b) Sometimes the government's justification for an inequality must become more persuasive as the interest being treated unequally becomes more important. (c) Sometimes there are constitutional constraints on the use of *wealth*, even the de facto use of wealth, in allocating interests that go to one's status as a citizen in a democratic nation.

But consider this evaluation:

> The relationship of [the] "fundamental personal right" analysis to the constitutional guarantee of equal protection of the law is approximately the same as that of "freedom of contract" to the constitutional guarantee that no person shall be deprived of life, liberty, or property without due process of law. It is an invitation for judicial exegesis over and above the commands of the Constitution, in which values that cannot possibly have their source in that instrument are invoked to either validate or condemn the countless laws enacted by the various States.

Weber v. Aetna Casualty & Surety Co., 406 U.S. 164, 182 (1972) (Rehnquist, J., dissenting).

F.   MODERN SUBSTANTIVE DUE PROCESS: PRIVACY, PERSONHOOD, AND FAMILY

Although the Court employed substantive due process in the *Lochner* era primarily in the realm of economic regulation and the liberty of contract, not all of its decisions were so limited. In Meyer v. Nebraska, 262 U.S. 390 (1923), for example, the Court invalidated a state law prohibiting the teaching of any modern language other than English in any public or private grammar school. The Court explained:

> [The "liberty" guaranteed by the due process clause of the fourteenth amendment] denotes not merely freedom from bodily restraint but also the right of the individ-

ual to contract, to engage in any of the common occupations of life, to acquire useful knowledge, to marry, establish a home and bring up children, to worship God according to the dictates of his own conscience, and generally to enjoy those privileges long recognized at common law as essential to the orderly pursuit of happiness by free men. [This] liberty may not be interfered with [by] legislative action which is arbitrary or without reasonable relation to some purpose within the competency of the state to effect. [That] the State may do much [to] improve the quality of its citizens [is] clear; but the individual has certain fundamental rights which must be respected. [Here, no] emergency has arisen which renders knowledge of a child of some language other than English so clearly harmful as to justify [its] infringement of the right long freely enjoyed.

Justice Holmes, joined by Justice Sutherland, dissented. Similarly, in Pierce v. Society of Sisters, 268 U.S. 510 (1925), the Court invalidated a state statute requiring students to attend public rather than private schools. The Court held that the statute "unreasonably [interfered] with the liberty of parents and guardians to direct the upbringing and education of children under their control."

1.   The Right of Privacy

Griswold v. Connecticut

381 U.S. 479 (1965)

MR. JUSTICE DOUGLAS delivered the opinion of the Court.

Appellant Griswold is Executive Director of the Planned Parenthood League of Connecticut. Appellant Buxton is a licensed physician and a professor at the Yale Medical School who served as Medical Director for the League. . . .

They gave information, instruction, and medical advice to *married persons* as to the means of preventing conception. [Fees] were usually charged, although some couples were serviced free.

[A Connecticut statute prohibits any person to use "any drug, medicinal article or instrument for the purpose of preventing conception."]

The appellants were found guilty as accessories and fined $100 each, against the claim that the accessory statute as so applied violated the Fourteenth Amendment. . . .

We think that appellants have standing to raise the constitutional rights of the married people with whom they had a professional relationship. [Certainly] the accessory should have standing to assert that the offense which he is charged with assisting is not, or cannot constitutionally be, a crime. . . .

Coming to the merits, we are met with a wide range of questions that implicate the Due Process Clause of the Fourteenth Amendment. Overtones of some arguments suggest that [*Lochner*] should be our guide. But we decline that invitation as we did in [West Coast Hotel Co. v. Parrish and Williamson v. Lee Optical, section D supra]. We do not sit as a super-legislature to determine the wisdom, need, and propriety of laws that touch economic problems, business affairs, or social conditions. This law, however, operates directly on an intimate relation of husband and wife and their physician's role in one aspect of that relation.

The association of people is not mentioned in the Constitution nor in the Bill of Rights. The right to educate a child in a school of the parents' choice —

whether public or private or parochial — is also not mentioned. Nor is the right to study any particular subject or any foreign language. Yet the First Amendment has been construed to include certain of those rights. [As Pierce v. Society of Sisters, Meyer v. Nebraska, and other decisions suggest, the] right of freedom of speech and press includes not only the right to utter or to print, but the right to distribute, the right to receive, the right to read and freedom of inquiry, freedom of thought, and freedom to teach — indeed the freedom of the entire university community. Without those peripheral rights the specific rights would be less secure. And so we reaffirm the principle of the *Pierce* and the *Meyer* cases.

In NAACP v. Alabama, [Chapter 7, section E1, infra], we protected the "freedom to associate and privacy in one's associations," noting that freedom of association was a peripheral First Amendment right. Disclosure of membership lists of a constitutionally valid association, we held, was invalid. [In] other words, the First Amendment has a penumbra where privacy is protected from governmental intrusion. In like context, we have protected forms of "association" that are not political in the customary sense but pertain to the social, legal, and economic benefit of the members. NAACP v. Button, [Chapter 7, section E5, infra]. [While association] is not expressly included in the First Amendment its existence is necessary in making the express guarantees fully meaningful.

The foregoing cases suggest that specific guarantees in the Bill of Rights have penumbras, formed by emanations from those guarantees that help give them life and substance. See Poe v. Ullman, 367 U.S. 497, 516-522 [Douglas, J., dissenting]. Various guarantees create zones of privacy. The right of association contained in the penumbra of the First Amendment is one, as we have seen. The Third Amendment in its prohibition against the quartering of soldiers "in any house" in time of peace without the consent of the owner is another facet of that privacy. The Fourth Amendment explicitly affirms the "right of the people to be secure in their persons, houses, papers, and effects, against unreasonable searches and seizures." The Fifth Amendment in its Self-Incrimination Clause enables the citizen to create a zone of privacy which government may not force him to surrender to his detriment. The Ninth Amendment provides: "The enumeration in the Constitution, of certain rights, shall not be construed to deny or disparage others retained by the people."

The Fourth and Fifth Amendments were described in Boyd v. United States, 116 U.S. 616, 630, as protection against all governmental invasions "of the sanctity of a man's home and the privacies of life." We recently referred in Mapp v. Ohio, 367 U.S. 643, 656, to the Fourth Amendment as creating a "right to privacy, no less important than any other right carefully and particularly reserved to the people."

We have had many controversies over these penumbral rights of "privacy and repose." [Skinner v. Oklahoma and other] cases bear witness that the right of privacy which presses for recognition here is a legitimate one.

The present case, then, concerns a relationship lying within the zone of privacy created by several fundamental constitutional guarantees. And it concerns a law which, in forbidding the *use* of contraceptives rather than regulating their manufacture or sale, seeks to achieve its goals by means having a maximum destructive impact upon that relationship. Such a law cannot stand in light of the familiar principle, so often applied by this Court, that a "governmental purpose to control or prevent activities constitutionally subject to state regulation may not be achieved by means which sweep unnecessarily broadly and thereby invade the area of protected freedoms." [NAACP v. Alabama.] Would we allow the police to search the sacred precincts of marital bedrooms for telltale signs of the use of contraceptives? The very idea is repulsive to the notions of privacy surrounding the marriage relationship.

We deal with a right of privacy older than the Bill of Rights. [Marriage] is a coming together for better or for worse, hopefully enduring, and intimate to the degree of being sacred. It is an association that promotes a way of life, not causes; a harmony in living, not political faiths; a bilateral loyalty, not commercial or social projects. Yet it is an association for as noble a purpose as any involved in our prior decisions.

Reversed.

MR. JUSTICE GOLDBERG, whom THE CHIEF JUSTICE and MR. JUSTICE BRENNAN join, concurring.

[My] conclusion that the concept of liberty [embraces] the right of marital privacy though that right is not mentioned explicitly in the Constitution is supported both by numerous decisions of this Court, referred to in the Court's opinion, and by the language and history of the Ninth Amendment [which] reveal that the Framers of the Constitution believed that there are additional fundamental rights, protected from governmental infringement. . . .

The Ninth Amendment [was] proffered to quiet expressed fears that a bill of specifically enumerated rights could not be sufficiently broad to cover all essential rights and that the specific mention of certain rights would be interpreted as a denial that others were protected. . . .

While this Court has had little occasion to interpret the Ninth Amendment, "[i]t cannot be presumed that any clause in the constitution is intended to be without effect." [To] hold that a right so basic and fundamental and so deep-rooted in our society as the right of privacy in marriage may be infringed because that right is not guaranteed in so many words by the first eight amendments to the Constitution is to ignore the Ninth Amendment and to give it no effect whatsoever. . . .

I do not mean to imply that the Ninth Amendment is applied against the States by the Fourteenth. [Rather,] the Ninth Amendment [simply] lends strong support to the view that the "liberty" protected by the Fifth and Fourteenth Amendments from infringement by the Federal Government or the States is not restricted to rights specifically mentioned in the first eight amendments. . . .

In determining which rights are fundamental, judges are not left at large to decide cases in light of their personal and private notions. Rather, they must look to the "traditions and [collective] conscience of our people" to determine whether a principle is "so rooted [there] . . . as to be ranked as fundamental." The inquiry is whether a right involved "is of such a character that it cannot be denied without violating those 'fundamental principles of liberty and justice which lie at the base of all our civil and political institutions.' . . ."

The entire fabric of the Constitution and the purposes that clearly underlie its specific guarantees demonstrate that the rights to marital privacy and to marry and raise a family are of similar order and magnitude as the fundamental rights specifically protected.

Although the Constitution does not speak in so many words of the right of privacy in marriage, I cannot believe that it offers these fundamental rights no protection. The fact that no particular provision of the Constitution explicitly forbids the State from disrupting the traditional relation of the family — a relation as old and as fundamental as our entire civilization — surely does not show that the Government was meant to have the power to do so. . . .

The logic of the dissents would sanction federal or state legislation that seems to me even more plainly unconstitutional than the statute before us. Surely the Government, absent a showing of a compelling subordinating state interest, could not decree that all husbands and wives must be sterilized after two children have been born to them. Yet by their reasoning such an invasion of marital privacy would not be subject to constitutional challenge because, while it might be "silly," no provision of the Constitution specifically prevents the Government from curtailing the marital right to bear children and raise a family. . . .

[The] State, at most, argues that there is some rational relation between this statute and what is admittedly a legitimate subject of state concern — the discouraging of extra-marital relations. It says that preventing the use of birth-control devices by married persons helps prevent the indulgence by some in such extramarital relations. The rationality of this justification is dubious, particularly in light of the admitted widespread availability to all persons [in] Connecticut, unmarried as well as married, of birth-control devices for the prevention of disease, as distinguished from the prevention of conception. But, in any event, it is clear that the state interest in safeguarding marital fidelity can be served by a more discriminately tailored statute, which does not, like the present one, sweep unnecessarily broadly, reaching far beyond the evil sought to be dealt with and intruding upon the privacy of all married couples. [Connecticut] does have statutes, the constitutionality of which is beyond doubt, which prohibit adultery and fornication. . . .

MR. JUSTICE HARLAN, concurring in the judgment.

[I] fully agree with the judgment of reversal, but [cannot] join the Court's opinion [because it evinces the view that] the Due Process Clause of the Fourteenth Amendment does not touch this Connecticut statute unless the enactment is found to violate some right assured by the letter or penumbra of the Bill of Rights. . . .

In my view, the proper constitutional inquiry in this case is whether this Connecticut statute infringes the Due Process Clause of the Fourteenth Amendment because the enactment violates basic values "implicit in the concept of ordered liberty," [Palko v. Connecticut, section C supra]. For reasons stated at length in my dissenting opinion in Poe v. Ullman, [367 U.S. 497 (1961)], I believe that it does. While the relevant inquiry may be aided by resort to one or more of the provisions of the Bill of Rights, it is not dependent on them or any of their radiations. The Due Process Clause of the Fourteenth Amendment stands, in my opinion, on its own bottom. . . .

While I could not more heartily agree that judicial "self restraint" is an indispensable ingredient of sound constitutional adjudication, I do submit that the formula suggested [by the dissenters] for achieving it is more hollow than real. "Specific" provisions of the Constitution, no less than "due process," lend themselves as readily to "personal" interpretations by judges whose constitutional outlook is simply to keep the Constitution in supposed "tune with the times." . . .

Judicial self-restraint will not, I suggest, be brought about in the "due process" area by the historically unfounded incorporation formula long advanced by my

Brother Black. It will be achieved in this area, as in other constitutional areas, only by continual insistence upon respect for the teachings of history, solid recognition of the basic values that underlie our society, and wise appreciation of the great roles that the doctrines of federalism and separation of powers have played in establishing and preserving American freedoms. . . .

[Justice Harlan dissented in Poe v. Ullman, in which the Court dismissed on justiciability grounds a challenge to the Connecticut statute invalidated in *Griswold*. Harlan argued:]

[I] believe that a statute making it a criminal offense for *married couples* to use contraceptives is an intolerable and unjustifiable invasion of privacy in the conduct of the most intimate concerns of an individual's personal life. [Since this contention draws its] basis from no explicit language of the Constitution, [I] feel it desirable [to] state the framework of Constitutional principles in which I think the issue must be judged.

[Because] it is the Constitution alone which warrants judicial interference in sovereign operations of the State, the basis of judgment as to the Constitutionality of state action must be a rational one, approaching the text [not] in a literalistic way, as if we had a tax statute before us, but as the basic charter of our society, setting out in spare but meaningful terms the principles of government. . . .

It is but a truism to say that [the Due Process Clause] is not self-explanatory. [It] is important to note, however, that two views of the [Fourteenth] Amendment have not been accepted. . . . One view [sought] to limit the provision to a guarantee of procedural fairness. [The] other [would] have it that the Fourteenth Amendment, whether by way of the Privileges and Immunities Clause or the Due Process Clause, applied against the States only and precisely those restraints which [are embodied in the Bill of Rights]. However, "due process" in the consistent view of this Court has ever been a broader concept than the first view and more flexible than the second. . . .

[It] is not the particular enumeration of rights in the first eight Amendments which spells out the reach of Fourteenth Amendment due process, but rather, as was suggested in another context long before the adoption of that Amendment, those concepts which are considered to embrace those rights "which are . . . *fundamental*; which belong . . . to the citizens of all free governments," [Corfield v. Coryell], for "the purposes [of securing] which men enter into society," [Calder v. Bull]. . . .

Due process has not been reduced to any formula; its content cannot be determined by reference to any code. The best that can be said is that through the course of this Court's decisions it has represented the balance which our Nation, built upon postulates of respect for the liberty of the individual, has struck between that liberty and the demands of organized society. If the supplying of content to this Constitutional concept has of necessity been a rational process, it certainly has not been one where judges have felt free to roam where unguided speculation might take them. The balance of which I speak is the balance struck by this country, having regard to what history teaches are the traditions from which it developed as well as the traditions from which it broke. That tradition is a living thing. . . .

[The] liberty guaranteed by the Due Process Clause [is] not a series of isolated points [represented by the Bill of Rights]. It is a rational continuum which, broadly speaking, includes a freedom from all substantial arbitrary impositions and purposeless restraints, [citing, e.g., Allgeyer v. Louisiana, Skinner v. Oklahoma], and which also recognizes, what a reasonable and sensitive judgment must, that certain interests require particularly careful scrutiny of the state needs asserted to justify their abridgment. . . .

The State [asserts] that it is acting to protect the moral welfare of its citizenry. [Society] has traditionally concerned itself with the moral soundness of its people. [Certainly,] Connecticut's judgment [here] is no more demonstrably correct or incorrect than are the varieties of judgment, expressed in law, on marriage and divorce, on adult consensual homosexuality, abortion, and sterilization, or euthanasia and suicide. If we had a case before us which required us to decide simply, and in abstraction, whether the moral judgment implicit in the [present statute] was a sound one, the very controversial nature of these questions would, I think, require us to hesitate long before concluding that the Constitution precluded Connecticut from choosing as it has. . . .

But, as might be expected, we are not presented simply with this moral judgment to be passed on as an abstract proposition. The secular state [must] operate in the realm of behavior, [and] where it does so operate, not only the underlying, moral purpose of its operations, but also the *choice of means* becomes relevant to any Constitutional judgment on what is done. . . .

Precisely what is involved here is this: the State is asserting the right to enforce its moral judgment by intruding upon the most intimate details of the marital relation with the full power of the criminal law. Potentially, this could allow the deployment of all the incidental machinery of the criminal law, arrests, searches and seizures; inevitably, it must mean at the very least the lodging of criminal charges, a public trial, and testimony as the corpus delicti. [The] statute allows the State to enquire into, prove and punish married people for the private use of their marital intimacy.

[This] enactment involves what, by common understanding throughout the English-speaking world, must be granted to be a most fundamental aspect of "liberty," the privacy of the home in its most basic sense, and it is this which requires that the statute be subjected to "strict scrutiny." [Skinner v. Oklahoma.]

That aspect of liberty which embraces the concept of the privacy of the home receives explicit Constitutional protection at two places only. These are the Third [and Fourth Amendments]. . . .

It is clear, of course, that this Connecticut statute does not invade the privacy of the home in the usual sense, since the invasion involved here may [be] accomplished without any physical intrusion [into] the home. [But it] would surely be an extreme instance of sacrificing substance to form were it to be held that the Constitutional principle of privacy against arbitrary official intrusion comprehends only physical invasions by the police. [If] the physical curtilage of the home is protected, it is surely as a result of solicitude to protect the privacies of the life within. Certainly the safeguarding of the home does not follow merely from the sanctity of property rights. The home derives its pre-eminence as the seat of family life. [Of the] whole "private realm of family life" it is difficult to imagine what is more private or more intimate than a husband and wife's marital relations. . . .

Of course, [there] are countervailing considerations. "[T]he family . . . is not beyond regulation," and it would be an absurdity to suggest either that offenses may not be committed in the bosom of the family or that the home can be made a sanctuary for crime. The right of privacy [is] not an absolute. Thus, I would not suggest that adultery, homosexuality, fornication and incest are immune from criminal enquiry, however privately practiced. [But] not to discriminate between what is involved in this case and either the traditional offenses against good morals or crimes which, though they may be committed anywhere, happen to have been committed or concealed in the home, would entirely misconceive the argument that is being made.

[The] intimacy of husband and wife is necessarily an essential and accepted feature of the institution of marriage, an institution which the State not only must allow, but which always and in every age it has fostered and protected. It is one thing when the State exerts its power either to forbid extra-marital sexuality altogether, or to say who may marry, but it is quite another when, having acknowledged a marriage and the intimacies inherent in it, it undertakes to regulate by means of the criminal law the details of that intimacy. . . .

[Since,] as it appears to me, the statute marks an abridgment of important fundamental liberties protected by the Fourteenth Amendment, it will not do to urge [that it] is rationally related to the effectuation of a proper state purpose. A closer scrutiny and stronger justification than that are required.

[Though] the State has argued the Constitutional permissibility of the moral judgment underlying this statute, [it does not] even remotely [suggest] a justification for the obnoxiously intrusive means it has chosen to effectuate that policy. To me the very circumstance that Connecticut has not chosen to press the enforcement of this statute against individual users [conduces] to the inference either that it does not consider the policy of the statute a very important one, or that it does not regard the means it has chosen for its effectuation as appropriate or necessary.

But conclusive, in my view, is the utter novelty of this enactment. Although the Federal Government and many States have at one time or other had on their books statutes forbidding or regulating the distribution of contraceptives, none, so far as I can find, has made the *use* of contraceptives a crime. . . .

Mr. Justice White, concurring in the judgment.

[The] State claims [that] its anti-use statute [serves its] policy against all forms of promiscuous or illicit sexual relationships, be they premarital or extramarital, concededly a permissible and legitimate legislative goal. [But I] fail to see how the ban on the use of contraceptives by married couples in any way reinforces the State's ban on illicit sexual relationships. [Perhaps] the theory is that the flat ban on use prevents married people from possessing contraceptives and without the ready availability of such devices for use in the marital relationship, there will be no or less temptation to use them in extramarital ones. This reasoning rests on the premise that married people will comply with the ban in regard to their marital relationship, notwithstanding total nonenforcement in this context and apparent nonenforcibility, but will not comply with criminal statutes prohibiting extramarital affairs and the anti-use statute in respect to illicit sexual relationships, a premise whose validity has not been demonstrated and whose intrinsic validity is not very evident. [I] find nothing in this record justifying the sweeping scope of this statute. . . .

Mr. Justice Black, with whom Mr. Justice Stewart joins, dissenting. . . .

The Court talks about a constitutional "right of privacy" as though there is some constitutional [provision] forbidding any law ever to be passed which might abridge the "privacy" of individuals. But there is not. There are, of course, guarantees in certain specific constitutional provisions which are designed in part to protect privacy at certain times and places with respect to certain activities. Such, for example, is the Fourth Amendment's guarantee against "unreasonable searches and seizures." But I think it belittles that Amendment to talk about it as though it protects nothing but "privacy." [The] average man would very likely not have his feelings soothed any more by having his property seized openly than by having it seized privately and by stealth. [I] get nowhere in this case by talk about a constitutional "right of privacy" as an emanation from one or more constitutional provisions.[1] I like my privacy as well as the next one, but I am nevertheless compelled to admit that government has a right to invade it unless prohibited by some specific constitutional provision. . . .

[Of] the cases on which my Brothers White and Goldberg rely so heavily, undoubtedly the reasoning of two of them supports their result here — as would that of a number of others which they do not bother to name, e.g., [Lochner]. The two they do cite and quote from, [Meyer and Pierce], elaborated the same natural law due process philosophy found in [Lochner]. [That was a] philosophy which many later opinions repudiated, and which I cannot accept. . . .

My Brother Goldberg has adopted the recent discovery that the Ninth Amendment as well as the Due Process Clause can be used by this Court as authority to strike down all state legislation which this Court thinks violates "fundamental principles of liberty and justice," or is contrary to the "traditions and [collective] conscience of our people." He also states [that] in making decisions on this basis judges will not consider "their personal and private notions." One may ask how they can avoid considering them. Our Court certainly has no machinery with which to take a Gallup Poll. And the scientific miracles of this age have not yet produced a gadget which the Court can use to determine what traditions are rooted in the "[collective] conscience of our people." Moreover, one would certainly have to look far beyond the language of the Ninth Amendment to find that the Framers vested in this Court any such awesome veto powers over lawmaking, either by the States or by the Congress. [That] Amendment was passed [to] assure the people that the Constitution in all its provisions was intended to limit the Federal Government to the powers granted expressly or by necessary implication. [This] fact is perhaps responsible for the peculiar phenomenon that for a period of a century and a half no serious suggestion was ever made that the Ninth Amendment [could] be used as a weapon of federal power to prevent state legislatures from passing laws they consider appropriate to govern local affairs. . . .

I realize that many good and able men have eloquently spoken and written [about] the duty of this Court to keep the Constitution in tune with the times.

1. The phrase "right to privacy" appears first to have gained currency from an article written by Messrs. Warren and (later Mr. Justice) Brandeis in 1890 which urged that States should give some form of tort relief to persons whose private affairs were exploited by others. The Right to Privacy, 4 Harv. L. Rev. 193. [Today] this Court, which I did not understand to have power to sit as a court of common law, now appears to be exalting a phrase which Warren and Brandeis used in discussing grounds for tort relief, to the level of a constitutional rule which prevents state legislatures from passing any law deemed by this Court to interfere with "privacy."

[For] myself, I must with all deference reject that philosophy. The Constitution makers knew the need for change and provided for it. [The] Due Process Clause with an "arbitrary and capricious" or "shocking to the conscience" formula was liberally used by this Court to strike down economic legislation in the early decades of this century, threatening, many people thought, the tranquility and stability of the Nation. That formula, based on subjective considerations of "natural justice," is no less dangerous when used to enforce this Court's views about personal rights than those about economic rights. . . .

MR. JUSTICE STEWART, whom MR. JUSTICE BLACK joins, dissenting. . . .

I think this is an uncommonly silly law. [But] we are not asked in this case to say whether we think this law is unwise, or even asinine. We are asked to hold that it violates the United States Constitution. And that I cannot do.

In the course of its opinion the Court refers to no less than six Amendments to the Constitution: the First, the Third, the Fourth, the Fifth, the Ninth, and the Fourteenth. But the Court does not say which of these Amendments, if any, it thinks is infringed by this Connecticut law.

[What] provision of the Constitution, then, does make this state law invalid? The Court says it is the right of privacy "created by several fundamental constitutional guarantees." With all deference, I can find no such general right of privacy in the Bill of Rights, in any other part of the Constitution, or in any case ever before decided by this Court. . . .

Note: Griswold *and the Right of Privacy*

1. *Griswold.* There is no explicit general right to privacy in the Constitution. The Court's use of privacy was at least partly an effort to overcome the specter of *Lochner,* which of course relied on the due process clause. Consider the following evaluations:

a. Henkin, Privacy and Autonomy, 74 Colum. L. Rev. 1410, 1421-1422 (1974):

> Justice Douglas's argument seems to go something like this: since the Constitution, in various "specifics" of the Bill of Rights and in their penumbra, protects rights which partake of privacy, it protects other aspects of privacy as well, indeed it recognizes a general, complete right of privacy. [A] legal draftsman [might] suggest the opposite: when the Constitution sought to protect private rights it specified them; that it explicitly protects some elements of privacy, but not others, suggests that it did not mean to protect those not mentioned.

b. Kauper, Penumbras, Peripheries, Emanations, Things Fundamental and Things Forgotten: The *Griswold* Case, 64 Mich. L. Rev. 235, 252-253 (1965):

> I have no difficulty with [a] theory of implied rights. For example, the right to associate [seems] fairly to be implied from the first amendment. It is another thing, however, to [convert] a freedom from unreasonable police searches into a fundamental substantive right restricting legislative action in formulating social policy. [The] accordion-like qualities of the emanations-and-penumbra theory [become] evident when one considers its application to [other areas. For example], since the body of the Constitution protects against the impairment of the obligations of con-

tracts, it does not require a far-fetched application of [the] theory to suggest that implicit in the contracts clause (or at least radiating from it) is a constitutional right to enter into contracts. [In] extending the specifics to the periphery, [the] Court is [essentially engaging in substantive due process], but dignifying it with a different name and thereby creating the illusion of greater objectivity.

Similarly, one might challenge the Court's analysis on the ground that the Court separated the values underlying the relevant clauses from the means set out in the Constitution for promoting those values. But the values and the means cannot be separated; if the values are taken independently, and used as a basis for prohibiting additional "means," the Constitution is infinitely expandable and means nothing at all. The problem, in short, is that there is no constitutional basis for a privacy right — unless privacy is thought part of "liberty," a theory that raises problems of its own.

c. Rubenfeld, The Right to Privacy, 102 Harv. L. Rev. 737, 784 (1989):

The distinctive and singular characteristic of the laws against which the right of privacy has been applied lies in their *productive* or *affirmative* consequences. [Such laws] all involve the forcing of lives into well-defined and highly confined institutional layers. At the simplest [level], such laws tend to *take over* the lives of the persons involved; they occupy and preoccupy. . . . These laws do not simply proscribe one act or remove one liberty; they inform the totality of a person's life. The principle of the right to privacy is not the freedom to do certain, particular acts determined to be fundamental through some ever-progressing normative lens. It is the fundamental freedom not to have one's life too totally determined by a progressively more normalizing state.

2. *The ninth amendment.* Consider the following views:
a. J. Ely, Democracy and Distrust 34-38 (1980):

The received account of the Ninth Amendment, [offered by Justice Black in *Griswold*, goes] like this. There was fear that the inclusion of a bill of rights [would] be taken to imply that federal power was [not] limited to the authorities enumerated in Article I, Section 8, [but] extended all the way up to the edge of the rights stated in the first eight amendments. [The] Ninth Amendment, the received version goes, was attached to the Bill of Rights [to] negate that inference. [But the] Tenth Amendment, submitted and ratified at the same time, completely fulfills [that] function. [Moreover, the legislative history of the Ninth Amendment is consistent with Justice Goldberg's view, and] the conclusion that the Ninth Amendment was intended to signal the existence of federal constitutional rights beyond those specifically enumerated in the Constitution is the only conclusion its language seems comfortably able to support.

If the ninth amendment has this meaning, why was it never invoked by even a single Supreme Court justice until the 1960s? (Note, however, that nontextual constraints on government do have support in the founding period. See Chapter 1 supra.)

b. Berger, The Ninth Amendment, 66 Cornell L. Rev. 1, 2-3, 20, 14 (1980):

[The ninth and tenth amendments] are complementary: the ninth deals with *rights* "retained by the people," the tenth with *powers* "reserved" to the states or the people. [Madison] made clear that the retained rights [constitute] an area in which the "Government ought not to act." This means, in my judgment, that the courts have not been empowered to enforce the retained rights. [Rather, in] "retaining" the un-enumerated rights, the people reserved to themselves power to add to or subtract from the rights enumerated in the Constitution by the process of amendment. [If] this be deemed supererogatory, be it remembered that according to Madison the ninth amendment itself was "inserted merely for greater caution."

c. Caplan, The History and Meaning of the Ninth Amendment, 69 Va. L. Rev. 223, 264-265, 227-228 (1983):

[The] ninth amendment was drafted in order to allay concern that the Consti-tution might abolish rights traditionally guaranteed by state law. [These] "other" rights were understood to refer to the common law, along with the state constitu-tions and statutes engrafted onto it. [But the] ninth amendment [did] not transform these unenumerated rights into constitutional [rights]. Instead, it simply provides that the individual rights contained in state law are to continue in force under the Constitution until modified or eliminated by state enactment, by federal preemp-tion, or by a judicial determination of unconstitutionality.

Since *Griswold*, various justices have alluded to the ninth amendment but without offering a comprehensive theory of precisely what unenumerated rights it protects. See, e.g., Richmond Newspapers v. Virginia, 448 U.S. 555, 579 n.15 (1980) (opinion of Burger, C.J.) (concerning the right of the people to attend criminal trials). For a broad range of views on the ninth amendment, see the Sym-posium on Interpreting the Ninth Amendment, 64 Chi.-Kent L. Rev. 37 (1988).

3. *Outdated norms.* Was the real problem in *Griswold* one of desuetude? Con-sider the view that the law at issue could not be enforced directly against married couples because the Connecticut citizenry would be aghast at any such enforce-ment action. In this sense, the law was out of step with democratic convictions. Perhaps a law should not be usable at all if the public would not permit it to be enforced in the way that it reads. This view, perhaps involving a genuinely pro-cedural due process claim, would read the so-called privacy cases as involving a judicial insistence that, if laws cannot be enforced directly — through the crimi-nal law prohibiting certain activities — they cannot be enforced through indirect, sporadic, discriminatory routes that escape the same degree of public account-ability. How would this argument apply to Bowers v. Hardwick, section F3 infra? Would it result in a narrower or broader role for the Court? Would it be a better reading of the cases? See C. Sunstein, One Case at a Time (1999), for a defense of this approach to *Griswold*.

4. *The right of "privacy."* What is the nature of the right of "privacy" protected in *Griswold*? Is *Griswold* about the privacy of the home? The privacy of informa-tion concerning intimate matters? The integrity of the marriage relationship? Sexual freedom? Autonomy over decisions relating to childbearing? Autonomy generally?

5. *The reach of* Griswold: *the unmarried.* In Eisenstadt v. Baird, 405 U.S. 438 (1972), the Court, in a six-to-one decision, held that a Massachusetts statute pro-hibiting the distribution of any drug or device to unmarried persons for the pre-vention of conception violated the equal protection clause because it provided dissimilar treatment for married and unmarried persons.

Purporting to apply traditional rational basis review, the Court, in an opinion by Justice Brennan, held that none of the interests asserted in defense of the statute was sufficient to justify the challenged classification. First, the Court concluded that the deterrence of premarital sex could not reasonably be regarded as the purpose of the law. This was so because (a) the statute did not prohibit the distribution of contraceptives to prevent the "spread of disease," and thus was "so riddled with exceptions" that its effect "has at best a marginal relation to the proffered objective"; and (b) in any event, it "would be plainly unreasonable to assume that Massachusetts has prescribed pregnancy and the birth of an unwanted child as punishment for fornication, which is a misdemeanor under Massachusetts [law]."

Second, the Court rejected the contention that the classification was designed to "serve the health needs of the community by regulating the distribution of potentially harmful articles." This was so because (a) "not all contraceptives are potentially dangerous" and (b) this rationale does not serve to distinguish between married and unmarried persons.

Finally, the Court rejected the argument that the statute could be sustained on moral grounds "as a prohibition on contraception." The Court explained:

> [Whatever] the rights of the individual to access to contraceptives may be, the rights must be the same for the unmarried and the married alike. If under *Griswold* the distribution of contraceptives to married persons cannot be prohibited, a ban on distribution to unmarried persons would be equally impermissible. It is true that in *Griswold* the right of privacy in question inhered in the marital relationship. Yet the marital couple is not an independent entity with a mind and heart of its own, but an association of two individuals each with a separate intellectual and emotional makeup. If the right of privacy means anything, it is the right of the *individual*, married or single, to be free from unwarranted governmental intrusion into matters so fundamentally affecting a person as the decision whether to bear or beget a child. [On] the other hand, if *Griswold* is no bar to a prohibition on the distribution of contraceptives, the State could not, consistently with the Equal Protection Clause, outlaw distribution to unmarried but not to married persons. In each case the evil, as perceived by the State, would be identical, and the underinclusion would be invidious.

Chief Justice Burger dissented.

Note that the Massachusetts statute would easily satisfy the traditional rational basis review. What, then, really explains the outcome here?

6. *The reach of* Griswold: *access to contraceptives.* In Carey v. Population Services International, 431 U.S. 678 (1977), the Court, in a seven-to-two decision, invalidated a New York law prohibiting any person other than a licensed pharmacist to distribute contraceptives. The Court, in an opinion by Justice Brennan, explained:

> *Griswold* may no longer be read as holding only that a State may not prohibit a married couple's use of contraceptives. Read in light of its progeny, the teaching of *Griswold* is that the Constitution protects individual decisions in matters of childbearing from unjustified intrusion by the State. Restrictions on the distribution of contraceptives clearly burden the freedom to make such decisions. [Limiting] the distribution of nonprescription contraceptives to licensed pharmacists clearly imposes a significant burden on the right of individuals to use contraceptives if they choose

to do so. [Accordingly, the challenged law] "may be justified only by a 'compelling state interest' [and] must be narrowly drawn to express only the legitimate state interests at stake." [None of the interests asserted in defense of this statute is] compelling.

Chief Justice Burger and Justice Rehnquist dissented.

2.   *Abortion*

Roe v. Wade

410 U.S. 113 (1973)

MR. JUSTICE BLACKMUN delivered the opinion of the Court.

This [appeal presents] constitutional challenges to state criminal abortion legislation. The Texas statutes under attack here [make procuring an abortion a crime except "by medical advice for the purpose of saving the life of the mother." These statutes] are typical of those that have been in effect in many States for approximately a century. . . .

We forthwith acknowledge our awareness of the sensitive and emotional nature of the abortion controversy, of the vigorous opposing views, even among physicians, and of the deep and seemingly absolute convictions that the subject inspires. . . .

Our task, of course, is to resolve the issue by constitutional measurement, free of emotion and of predilection. We seek earnestly to do this, and, because we do, we have inquired into, and in this opinion place some emphasis upon, medical and medical-legal history and what that history reveals about man's attitudes toward the abortion procedure over the centuries. . . .

[The] restrictive criminal abortion laws in effect in a majority of States today are of relatively recent vintage. [They] derive from statutory changes effected, for the most part, in the latter half of the 19th century.

[Abortion] was practiced in Greek times as well as in the Roman Era. [Most] Greek thinkers [commended] abortion, at least prior to viability. [At] common law, abortion performed *before* "quickening" — the first recognizable movement of the fetus in utero, appearing usually from the 16th to the 18th week of pregnancy — was not an indictable offense. [It] was not until [the] middle and late 19th century [that] the quickening distinction [was abandoned] and the degree of the offense [increased]. [Thus,] at common law, at the time of the adoption of our Constitution, and throughout the major portion of the 19th century, [a] woman enjoyed a substantially broader right to terminate a pregnancy than she does in most States today. . . .

Three reasons have been advanced to explain historically the enactment of criminal abortion laws in the 19th century and to justify their continued existence.

It has been argued occasionally that these laws were [designed] to discourage illicit sexual conduct. Texas, however, does not advance this justification in the present case. . . .

A second reason is concerned with abortion as a medical procedure. When most criminal abortion laws were first enacted, the procedure was [hazardous]. [Thus,] it has been argued that a State's real concern in enacting a criminal abortion law was to protect the pregnant woman. [Modern] medical techniques have altered this situation. [Mortality] rates for women undergoing early abortions [appear] to be as low as or lower than the rates for normal childbirth. [Of] course, important state interests in the areas of health and medical standards do remain. The State has a legitimate interest in seeing to it that abortion, like any other medical procedure, is performed under circumstances that insure maximum safety for the patient [and] the State retains a definite interest in protecting the woman's own health and safety when an abortion is proposed at a late stage of pregnancy.

The third reason is the State's interest [in] protecting prenatal life. Some of the argument for this justification rests on the theory that a new human life is present from the moment of conception. [But in] assessing the State's interest, recognition may [also] be given to the less rigid claim that [at] least *potential* life is involved. . . .

The Constitution does not explicitly mention any right of privacy. [But] the Court has recognized that a right of personal privacy, or a guarantee of certain areas or zones of privacy, does exist under the Constitution. In varying contexts, the Court or individual Justices have, indeed, found at least the roots of that right in the First Amendment, Stanley v. Georgia, [Chapter 7, section D4, infra]; in the Fourth and Fifth Amendments; in the penumbras of the Bill of Rights, [*Griswold*]; in the Ninth Amendment, id., (Goldberg, J., concurring); or in the concept of liberty guaranteed by the first section of the Fourteenth Amendment, see Meyer v. Nebraska. These decisions make it clear that only personal rights that can be deemed "fundamental" or "implicit in the concept of ordered liberty," are included in this guarantee of personal privacy. They also make it clear that the right has some extension to activities relating to marriage, Loving v. Virginia, [Chapter 5, section C3, supra]; procreation, [*Skinner*]; contraception, [*Eisenstadt*]; family relationships, Prince v. Massachusetts, 321 U.S. 158 (1944); and child rearing and education, [*Pierce; Meyer*].

This right of privacy, whether it be founded in the Fourteenth Amendment's concept of personal liberty [as] we feel it is, or [in] the Ninth [Amendment], is broad enough to encompass a woman's decision whether or not to terminate her pregnancy. The detriment that the State would impose upon the pregnant woman by denying this choice altogether is apparent. Specific and direct harm medically diagnosable even in early pregnancy may be involved. Maternity, or additional offspring, may force upon the woman a distressful life and future. Psychological harm may be imminent. Mental and physical health may be taxed by child care. There is also the distress, for all concerned, associated with the unwanted child, and there is the problem of bringing a child into a family already unable, psychologically and otherwise, to care for it. In other cases, [the] additional difficulties and continuing stigma of unwed motherhood may be involved. All these are factors the woman and her responsible physician necessarily will consider in consultation.

On the basis of elements such as these, appellant [argues] that the woman's right is absolute and that she is entitled to terminate her pregnancy at whatever time, in whatever way, and for whatever reason she alone chooses. With this we do not agree. [The] Court's decisions recognizing a right of privacy also acknowledge that some state regulation in areas protected by that right is appropriate. . . .

Where certain "fundamental rights" are involved, the Court has held that regulation limiting these rights may be justified only by a "compelling state interest," and that legislative enactments must be narrowly drawn to express only the legitimate state interests at stake. . . .

The appellee [argues] that the fetus is a "person" within the language and meaning of the Fourteenth Amendment. [If] this suggestion of personhood is established, the appellant's case, of course, collapses, for the fetus' right to life would then be guaranteed specifically by the Amendment. . . .

The Constitution does not define "person" in so many words. Section 1 of the Fourteenth Amendment contains three references to "person." ["Person"] is used in other places in the Constitution: in the listing of qualifications for Representatives and Senators, Art. I, §2, cl. 2, and §3, cl. 3; in the Apportionment Clause, Art. I, §2, cl. 3;[53] in the Migration and Importation provision, Art. I, §9, cl. 1; in the Emolument Clause, Art. I, §9, cl. 8; in the Electors provisions, Art. II, §1, cl. 2, and the superseded cl. 3; in the provision outlining qualifications for the office of President, Art. II, §1, cl. 5; in the Extradition provisions, Art. IV, §2, cl. 2, and the superseded Fugitive Slave Clause 3; and in the Fifth, Twelfth, and Twenty-second Amendments, as well as in §§2 and 3 of the Fourteenth Amendment. But in nearly all these instances, the use of the word is such that it has application only postnatally. None indicates, with any assurance, that it has any possible pre-natal application.

All this, together with our observation that throughout the major portion of the 19th century prevailing legal abortion practices were far freer than they are today, persuades us that the word "person," as used in the Fourteenth Amendment, does not include the unborn. [Thus,] we pass on to other considerations. The pregnant woman cannot be isolated in her privacy. She carries an embryo and, later, a fetus. [The] situation therefore is inherently different from marital intimacy, or bedroom possession of obscene material, or marriage, or procreation, or education, with which *Eisenstadt* and *Griswold, Stanley, Loving, Skinner,* and *Pierce* and *Meyer* were respectively concerned. [It] is reasonable and appropriate for a State to decide that at some point in time another interest, that of health of the mother or that of potential human life, becomes significantly involved. . . .

Texas urges that, apart from the Fourteenth Amendment, life begins at conception and is present throughout pregnancy, and that, therefore, the State has a compelling interest in protecting that life from and after conception. We need not resolve the difficult question of when life begins. When those trained [in] medicine, philosophy, and theology are unable to arrive at any consensus, the judiciary, at this point in the development of man's knowledge, is not in a position to speculate as to the answer.

It should be sufficient to note briefly the wide divergence of thinking on [this] question. There has always been strong support for the view that life does not begin until live birth. This was the belief of the Stoics. It appears to be the predominant, though not the unanimous, attitude of the Jewish faith. It may be taken to represent also the position of a large segment of the Protestant community. [The]

---

53. We are not aware that in the taking of any census under this clause, a fetus has ever been counted.

common law found greater significance in quickening. Physicians and their scientific colleagues have [tended] to focus either upon conception, upon live birth, or upon the interim point at which the fetus becomes "viable," that is, potentially able to live outside the mother's womb, albeit with artificial aid. Viability is usually placed at about seven months (28 weeks) but may occur earlier, even at 24 weeks. [The Catholic church recognizes] the existence of life from the moment of conception. . . .

In areas other than criminal abortion [such as torts and inheritance], the law has been reluctant to endorse any theory that life, as we recognize it, begins before live birth or to accord legal rights to the unborn except in narrowly defined situations and except when the rights are contingent upon live birth. . . .

In view of all this, we do not agree that, by adopting one theory of life, Texas may override the rights of the pregnant woman that are at stake. We repeat, however, that the State does have an important and legitimate interest in preserving and protecting the health of the pregnant woman [and] that it has still *another* important and legitimate interest in protecting the potentiality of human life. These interests are separate and distinct. Each grows in substantiality as the woman approaches term and, at a point during pregnancy, each becomes "compelling."

With respect to [the] interest in the health of the mother, the "compelling" point, in the light of present medical knowledge, is at approximately the end of the first trimester. This is so because of the now-established medical fact [that] until the end of the first trimester mortality in abortion may be less than mortality in normal childbirth. It follows that, from and after this point, a State may regulate the abortion procedure to the extent that the regulation reasonably relates to the preservation and protection of maternal health. Examples of permissible state regulation in this area are requirements as to the qualifications of the person who is to perform the abortion; [as] to the facility in which the procedure is to be performed; [and] the like.

This means, on the other hand, that, for the period of pregnancy prior to this "compelling" point, the attending physician, in consultation with his patient, is free to determine, without regulation by the State, that, in his medical judgment, the patient's pregnancy should be terminated. If that decision is reached, the judgment may be effectuated by an abortion free of interference by the State.

With respect to [the] interest in potential life, the "compelling" point is at viability. This is so because the fetus then presumably has the capability of meaningful life outside the mother's womb. State regulation protective of fetal life after viability thus has both logical and biological justifications. If the State is interested in protecting fetal life during that period, it may go so far as to proscribe abortion during that period, except when it is necessary to preserve the life or health of the mother.

Measured against these standards, [the Texas statute] sweeps too broadly [and] therefore, cannot survive the constitutional attack made upon it here. . . .

To summarize and to repeat: . . .

(a) For the stage prior to approximately the end of the first trimester, the abortion decision and its effectuation must be left to the medical judgment of the pregnant woman's attending physician.

(b) For the stage subsequent to approximately the end of the first trimester, the State, in promoting its interest in the health of the mother, may, if it chooses, regulate the abortion procedure in ways that are reasonably related to maternal health.

(c) For the stage subsequent to viability, the State in promoting its interest in the potentiality of human life may, if it chooses, regulate, and even proscribe, abortion except where it is necessary, in appropriate medical judgment, for the preservation of the life or health of the mother. . . .

This holding, we feel, is consistent with the relative weights of the respective interests involved, with the lessons and examples of medical and legal history, with the lenity of the common law, and with the demands of the profound problems of the present day. . . .

MR. JUSTICE STEWART, concurring.

[The] Constitution nowhere mentions a specific right of personal choice in matters of marriage and family life, but the "liberty" protected by the Due Process Clause of the Fourteenth Amendment covers more than those freedoms explicitly named in the Bill of Rights. [In *Eisenstadt*], we recognized "the right of the *individual*, married or single, to be free from unwarranted governmental intrusion into matters so fundamentally affecting a person as the decision whether to bear or beget a child." That right necessarily includes the right of a woman to decide whether or not to terminate her pregnancy. . . .

It is evident that the Texas abortion statute infringes that right directly. [The] question then becomes whether the state interests advanced to justify this abridgment can survive the "particularly careful scrutiny" that the Fourteenth Amendment here requires.

The asserted state interests are protection of the health and safety of the pregnant woman, and protection of the potential future human life within her. These are legitimate objectives, [but as] the Court today has thoroughly demonstrated, [these] state interests cannot constitutionally support the broad abridgment of personal liberty worked by the existing Texas law. . . .

MR. JUSTICE DOUGLAS, concurring.

[The] Ninth Amendment [does] not create federally enforceable rights. [But] a catalogue of [the rights "retained by the people"] includes customary, traditional, and time-honored rights, amenities, privileges, and immunities that come within the sweep of "the Blessings of Liberty" mentioned in the preamble to the Constitution. Many of them, in my view, come within the meaning of the term "liberty" as used in the Fourteenth Amendment.

First is the autonomous control over the development and expression of one's intellect, interests, tastes, and personality.

Second is freedom of choice in the basic decisions of one's life respecting marriage, divorce, procreation, contraception, and the education and upbringing of children.

Third is the freedom to care for one's health and person, freedom from bodily restraint or compulsion, freedom to walk, stroll, or loaf.

[While] childbirth endangers the lives of some women, voluntary abortion at any time and place regardless of medical standards would impinge on a rightful concern of society. The woman's health is part of that concern; as is the life of the fetus after quickening. These concerns justify the State in treating the procedure as a medical one. . . .

[A concurring opinion of Chief Justice Burger, noting that "the Court today rejects any claim that the Constitution requires abortion on demand," is omitted.]

MR. JUSTICE WHITE, with whom MR. JUSTICE REHNQUIST joins, dissenting.

[I] find nothing in the language or history of the Constitution to support the Court's judgment. The Court simply fashions and announces a new constitutional right for pregnant mothers and, with scarcely any reason or authority for its action, invests that right with sufficient substance to override most existing state abortion statutes. The upshot is that the people and the legislatures of the 50 States are constitutionally disentitled to weigh the relative importance of the continued existence and development of the fetus, on the one hand, against a spectrum of possible impacts on the mother, on the other hand. As an exercise of raw judicial power, the Court perhaps has authority to do what it does today; but in my view its judgment is an improvident and extravagant exercise of the power of judicial review that the Constitution extends to this Court. . . .

MR. JUSTICE REHNQUIST, dissenting. . . .

I have difficulty in concluding [that] the right of "privacy" is involved in this case. Texas [bars] the performance of a medical abortion by a licensed physician on a plaintiff such as Roe. A transaction resulting in an operation such as this is not "private" in the ordinary usage of that word. Nor is the "privacy" that the Court finds here even a distant relative of the freedom from searches and seizures protected by the Fourth Amendment. . . .

If the Court means by the term "privacy" no more than that the claim of a person to be free from unwanted state regulation of consensual transactions may be a form of "liberty" protected by the Fourteenth Amendment, there is no doubt that similar claims have been upheld in our earlier decisions on the basis of that liberty. [The] test traditionally applied in the area of social and economic legislation is whether or not a law such as that challenged has a rational relation to a valid state objective. The Due Process Clause of the Fourteenth Amendment undoubtedly does place a limit, albeit a broad one, on legislative power to enact laws such as this. If the Texas statute were to prohibit an abortion even where the mother's life is in jeopardy, I have little doubt that such a statute would lack a rational relation to a valid state objective. But the Court's sweeping invalidation of any restrictions on abortion during the first trimester is impossible to justify under that standard, and the conscious weighing of competing factors that the Court's opinion apparently substitutes for the established test is far more appropriate to a legislative judgment than to a judicial one. While the Court's opinion quotes from the dissent of Mr. Justice Holmes in [Lochner], the result it reaches is more closely attuned to the majority opinion of Mr. Justice Peckham in that case. . . .

The fact that a majority of the States reflecting, after all, the majority sentiment in those States, have had restrictions on abortions for at least a century is a strong indication, it seems to me, that the asserted right to an abortion is not "so rooted in the traditions and conscience of our people as to be ranked as fundamental." Even today, when society's views on abortion are changing, the very existence of the debate is evidence that the "right" to an abortion is not so universally accepted as the appellant would have us believe.

To reach its result, the Court necessarily has had to find within the scope of the Fourteenth Amendment a right that was apparently completely unknown to the drafters of the Amendment. [By] the time of the adoption of the Fourteenth Amendment in 1868, there were at least 36 laws enacted by state or territorial legislatures limiting abortion. [The] only conclusion possible from this history is that the drafters did not intend to have the Fourteenth Amendment withdraw from the States the power to legislate with respect to this matter. . . .

Note: *The Abortion Decision*

1. Griswold *to* Eisenstadt *to* Roe. A central issue in *Roe* was whether there was a constitutional basis for the woman's right of "privacy." The Court relied heavily on precedent to establish this right, but critics argue that the precedents did not establish a general right of privacy, let alone a right broad enough to reach abortion. Consider, for example, Ely, The Wages of Crying Wolf: A Comment on Roe v. Wade, 82 Yale L.J. 920, 930 (1973):

> [The] Court in *Griswold* stressed that it was invalidating only that portion of the Connecticut law that proscribed the *use,* as opposed to the manufacture, sale, or other distribution of contraceptives. That distinction [makes] sense [only] if the case is rationalized on the ground that [enforcement of the challenged provision] *would have been virtually impossible without* the most outrageous sort of governmental prying into the privacy of the home. [No] such rationalization is [possible in *Roe*], for whatever else may be involved, it is not a case about governmental snooping.

Defenders of *Roe,* on the other hand, argue that, taken together, the *Meyer/ Pierce/Griswold/Eisenstadt* line of cases delineates a sphere of interests — which the Court now groups and denominates "privacy" — implicit in the "liberty" protected by the fourteenth amendment:

> At the core of this sphere is the right of the individual to make for himself [the] fundamental decisions that shape family life: whom to marry; whether and when to have children; and with what values to rear those children. [Plainly] the right [to an abortion] falls within [this] class of [interests]. The question of constitutionality [in *Roe*] is a more difficult one than that involved in *Griswold* and *Eisenstadt* only because the asserted state interest is more important, not because of any difference in the individual interests involved.

Heymann and Barzelay, The Forest and the Trees: Roe v. Wade and Its Critics, 53 B.U. L. Rev. 765, 772, 775 (1973).

2. *The right of privacy.* The Court concluded in *Roe* that there is a constitutional right of privacy, that the right is based in the due process clause, and that it is "broad enough to encompass a woman's decision whether or not to terminate her pregnancy." We might distinguish between two questions here. (a) Does *Roe* involve a right that the government may invade only with special justification? (b) Even if the question in (a) is answered affirmatively, does the interest in protecting fetal life qualify as a special justification?

On the first question, consider Ely, supra, at 935-936, 947:

What is frightening about *Roe* is that [its] super-protected right is not inferable from the language of the Constitution, the framers' thinking respecting the specific problem in issue, any general value derivable from the provisions they included, or the nation's governmental structure. Nor is it explainable in terms of the unusual political impotence of the group judicially protected vis-à-vis the interest that legislatively prevailed over it. [*Roe*] is bad because it is bad constitutional law, or rather because it is *not* constitutional law and gives almost no sense of an obligation to try to be.

Does Ely's list exhaust the legitimate bases for the recognition of constitutional rights? Recall the originalism/nonoriginalism debate in section A supra.

3. *In defense of* Roe: *the question of a prima facie right to reproductive autonomy.* Consider the following arguments:

a. Heymann and Barzelay, supra, at 772-773:

[The] family unit [is] an integral part of [our constitutional system]. In democratic theory as well as in practice, it is in the family that children are expected to learn the values and beliefs that democratic institutions later draw on. [The] immensely important power of deciding about matters of early socialization has been allocated to the family, not to the government. [If] a state government decided that all children would be reared [from] birth under [complete] control of a state [official], the effect on our present notions of democratic government would be immense. [The] long line of precedent in this area [is] entirely principled. For the Court to have declined strict review of state legislation that limits the private right to choose whom to marry and whether to raise a family, or to decide within wide bounds how to rear one's children, would have been to leave the most basic substructure of our society and government [to] political whim.

b. Unlike any of the other privacy cases, *Roe* involved the interest to control over one's own body, or bodily integrity. This interest is far more tightly connected to the original or core concerns of the due process clause — and the common law itself — than the "privacy" right at issue in *Griswold*. Whether or not the government's justification is sufficient, surely the interest at issue is one that can be invaded only with special justification — unless the government can compel sterilization or involuntary medical treatment of multiple kinds.

c. The problem of abortion raises questions not of privacy, or not mostly of privacy, but instead, or in addition, of sex discrimination. The first point here is that only women become pregnant, and only women need abortions. Because laws prohibiting abortion are targeted at a class consisting exclusively of women, they should be understood as embodying a form of discrimination. On this view, the Court's decisions in *Griswold, Eisenstadt,* and *Roe,* and its decisions granting special protection to women under the equal protection clause (see Chapter 5, section D, supra), "present various faces of a single issue: the roles women are to play in our society." It "is simply inconceivable that the majority Justices in *Roe* were indifferent to this question." Karst, Book Review, 89 Harv. L. Rev. 1028, 1036-1037 (1976).

Consider L. Tribe, Constitutional Choices 243 (1985):

[Although] current law nowhere forces *men* to sacrifice their bodies and restructure their lives even in those tragic situations (of needed organ transplants, for example) where nothing less will permit their children to survive, those who would outlaw abortion [would] rely [on] physiological circumstances — the supposed dictates of the natural — to conscript women [as] involuntary incubators and thus to usurp a control over sexual activity and its consequences that men [take] for granted. To one who regards this outcome as unjust, a right to end pregnancy might be seen more plausibly as a matter of resisting sexual [domination] than as a matter of shielding from public control "private" transactions.

On this view, the problem with laws forbidding abortion is that they turn a biological difference with no necessary social consequences — women's capacity to bear children — into a social disadvantage. Such laws do not simply let nature run its course; instead, they compel women to be involuntary incubators. See also Regan, Rewriting Roe v. Wade, 77 Mich. L. Rev. 1569 (1979). This view has the advantage of making it unnecessary, or arguably unnecessary, to decide on the moral status of the fetus. A selective cooptation of human bodies for the protection of third parties would be unconstitutional, even if those third parties are human beings. To this it might be added that laws forbidding abortion exist only because of traditional (and constitutionally barred) notions about the naturalness of women's roles as first and foremost childbearers. (In fact, restrictions on abortion rights have often been sought by people also enthusiastic about women's traditional role.) If men could get pregnant, it might be urged, abortion restrictions would not exist.

But do laws that discriminate against persons who are pregnant in fact discriminate against women? See Geduldig v. Aiello, Chapter 5, section D, supra. Perhaps they do; but the point is not obvious. Even if they do, it does not necessarily follow that abortion restrictions are a form of sex discrimination. Consider Ely, supra, at 933-935:

> In his famous *Carolene Products* footnote, Justice Stone suggested that the interests to which the Court can responsibly give extraordinary constitutional protection include not only those expressed in the Constitution but also those that are unlikely to receive adequate consideration in the political process, specifically the interests of "discrete and insular minorities" unable to form effective political alliances. [But] *Roe* is not an appropriate case for [the] invocation [of this theory]. Compared with men, very few women sit in our legislatures. [But] no fetuses sit [there]. [Footnote 4] should be reserved for those interests which, *as compared with the interests to which they have been subordinated*, constitute minorities unusually incapable of protecting themselves. Compared with men, women may constitute such a "minority"; compared with the unborn, they do not.

For discussion of the abortion problem as one of sex discrimination, see Ginsburg, Some Thoughts on Autonomy and Equality in Relation to Roe v. Wade, 63 N.C. L. Rev. 375 (1985); Law, Rethinking Sex and the Constitution, 132 U. Pa. L. Rev. 955 (1984). For the view that the conception of the abortion right as one of "privacy" is fundamentally wrong, see MacKinnon, Roe v. Wade: A Study in Male Ideology in Abortion — Moral and Legal Perspectives 45, 49, 51 (J. Garfield ed. 1985):

> In feminist terms, [*Roe*] translates the ideology of the private sphere into the individual woman's legal right to privacy as a means of subordinating women's collective needs to the imperatives of male supremacy. [Under] conditions of gender inequality, [*Roe*] does not free women, it frees male sexual aggression. The avail-

ability of abortion [removes] the one remaining legitimized reason that women have had for refusing sex besides the headache.

On this account, the problem with the privacy notion is that it suggests that the realm of family, sex, and reproduction is essentially voluntary and free from power and politics. Notions of privacy in these arenas tend to confirm, rather than to undermine, the power of men over women.

For additional arguments to the effect that abortion restrictions should be seen as a form of sex discrimination, see MacKinnon, Reflections on Sex Equality under Law, 100 Yale L.J. 1281, 1308-1324 (1991); Sunstein, Neutrality in Constitutional Law (with Special Reference to Pornography, Abortion, and Surrogacy), 92 Colum. L. Rev. 1 (1992). For a detailed historical examination of abortion restrictions, with special reference to sex equality and equal protection, see Siegel, Reasoning from the Body: A Historical Perspective on Abortion Regulation and Questions of Equal Protection, 44 Stan. L. Rev. 261 (1992).

4. *"Compelling state interest."* Even if (a) laws forbidding abortion are a form of sex discrimination or (b) there is a constitutional "right of privacy" and that right is "broad enough to encompass a woman's decision whether or not to terminate her pregnancy," the question remains whether the prohibition of abortion serves a "compelling state interest." The Court in *Roe* identified two such interests — protecting the health of the pregnant woman and protecting the "potentiality of human life" of the fetus. The Court held that at various points these interests become "compelling." But why isn't the interest in protection of fetal life sufficient at every stage of pregnancy? At first glance, the protection of life — even if unborn — seems far stronger a justification than anything found in the previous privacy cases.

Consider Epstein, Substantive Due Process by Any Other Name: The Abortion Cases, 1973 Sup. Ct. Rev. 159, 172, 176, 182:

> [The] preference for individual choice [cannot] be accepted where the very question raised concerns the appropriate social limits to be placed upon individual choice. [It] makes no sense to hold in conclusionary terms that "by adopting one theory of life, Texas may [not] override the rights of the pregnant [woman]." [We] could as well claim that the Court, by adopting another theory of life, has decided to override the rights of the unborn child.

See also Tribe, Foreword: Toward a Model of Roles in the Due Process of Life and Law, 87 Harv. L. Rev. 1, 11, 15, 22 (1973):

> [The Court in *Roe* was choosing not] between the alternatives of abortion and continued pregnancy, [but] among alternative allocations of decisionmaking authority. [The] Court [transferred] the role of decisionmaker from the government to the woman herself. [In] the role-allocation model, the due process clause is violated whenever the state [assumes] a role the Constitution entrusts to another. [The] highly charged and distinctly sectarian religious controversy [at the center of the abortion issue] strongly supports the basic allocation of roles mandated by *Roe*. For [the] "first and most immediate purpose" of the establishment clause was to prevent "a union of government and religion."

Several years later Tribe changed his view: "[On] reflection, [my former] view appears to give too little weight to the value of allowing religious groups freely to express their convictions in the political process, underestimates the power of moral convictions unattached to religious beliefs on this issue, and makes the unrealistic assumption that a constitutional ruling could somehow disentangle religion from future public debate on the question." L. Tribe, American Constitutional Law 1350 (2d ed. 1988); see also L. Tribe, Abortion: A Conflict of Absolutes (1990).

5. *The fetus as "person."* Do you agree with the Court that, to decide *Roe*, it need not "resolve the difficult question of when life begins"? Perhaps the inability of those trained in "medicine, philosophy, and theology [to] arrive at [a] consensus" means that the Court should simply have deferred to the legislative judgment.

6. *The fetus as "person" or as otherwise providing a sufficient end for government restrictions: a "dispositive" issue?* It is often assumed that, if the fetus is a "person," or if the interest in protecting it is "compelling," *Roe* is necessarily wrong. But consider the following views.

a. L. Tribe, American Constitutional Law 931 (1978):

> [Prior to *Roe*, antiabortion laws] were not consistently enforced [either] against the affluent, who could evade them by obtaining lawful abortions outside their own restrictive jurisdictions, or against the poor, untold numbers of whom would unavoidably "subject themselves to the notorious backstreet abortion . . . fraught with the myriad possibilities of mutilation, infection, sterility and death." Thus, [in] view of the realities too commonplace to be ignored, the Court might understandably have viewed restrictive abortion laws less as meaningful protections for unborn life than as relatively pointless and economically skewed expressions of outdated worry about the health of the women involved coupled with disapproval of their moral choices.

Consider in this regard these (contestable but frequently agreed-upon) facts: (1) When abortion was unlawful, several thousand women died per year as a result of illegal abortions; (2) several more thousands of women faced serious health impairment, including emergency hospital admissions, as a result of illegal abortions; (3) the abortion rate before *Roe* was somewhere between 20 percent and 25 percent, whereas after *Roe* it is somewhere around 27 percent; (4) it is hard to demonstrate that there was a large increase in abortions as a result of *Roe*. Are any or all of these facts relevant? Consider the view that these contestable claims should play absolutely no role in constitutional law.

b. Thomson, A Defense of Abortion, 1 Phil. & Pub. Aff. 47, 48-49, 55-59 (1971):

> I propose [that] we grant [for the sake of argument] that the fetus is a person from the moment of conception. How does the [antiabortion] argument go from here? Something like this, I take it. Every person has a right to life. So the fetus has a right to life. No doubt the mother has a right to decide what shall happen in and to her body; [but] surely a person's right to life is stronger [than] the mother's right to decide what happens in and to her body, and so outweighs it. So the fetus may not be killed; an abortion may not be performed.
>
> It sounds plausible. But now let me ask you to imagine this. You wake up in the morning and find yourself back to back in bed with an unconscious violinist. [He] has been found to have a fatal kidney ailment, and the Society of Music Lovers has canvassed all the available medical records and found that you alone have the right

blood type to help. They have therefore kidnapped you [and] plugged [the violinist's circulatory system] into yours. [To] unplug you would be to kill him. But never
mind, it's only for nine months. By then he will have recovered [and] can safely be
unplugged. [Is] it morally incumbent on you to accede to this situation? . . .

The emendation which may be made at this point is this: the right to life consists not in the right not to be killed, but rather in the right not to be killed unjustly.
[This enables] us to square the fact that the violinist has a right to life with the fact
that you do not act unjustly toward him in unplugging yourself, thereby killing
him. For if you do not kill him unjustly, you do not violate his right to life. [But] if
this emendation is accepted, the gap in the argument against abortion stares us
plainly in the face: it is by no means enough to show that the fetus is a person, and
to remind us that all persons have a right to life — we need to be shown also that
killing the fetus violates its right to life, i.e., that abortion is unjust killing. And is it?

I suppose we may take it as a datum that in the case of pregnancy due to rape the
mother has not given the unborn person a right to the use of her body for food and
shelter. [But suppose] a woman voluntarily indulges in intercourse, knowing of the
chance it will issue in pregnancy, and then she does become pregnant; is she not
in part responsible for the presence, in fact the very existence, of the unborn person inside her? No doubt she did not invite it in. But doesn't her partial responsibility for its being there itself give it a right to the use of her body? If so, then her
aborting it [would] be depriving it of what it does have a right to, and thus would
be doing it an injustice. . . .

[But] it is not at all plain that this argument really [goes as] far as it purports to.
[Suppose] it were like this: people-seeds drift about in the air like pollen, and if you
open your windows, one may drift in and take root in your carpets or upholstery.
You don't want children, so you fix up your windows with fine mesh screens, the
very best you can buy. As can happen, however, [one] of the screens is defective;
and a seed drifts in and takes root. Does the person-plant who now develops have a
right to the use of your house? Surely [not]. Someone may argue that you are responsible for its rooting, that it does have a right to your house, because after all you
could have lived out your life with bare floors and furniture, or with sealed windows
and doors. But this won't do — for by the same token anyone can avoid a pregnancy
due to rape by having a hysterectomy, or anyway by never leaving home without a
(reliable!) army.

For elaboration of a similar view, see Regan, supra.

For criticism of this view, consider M. Tooley, Abortion and Infanticide 45-49
(1983):

[There] is a possibly crucial difference between the situation of the violinist and
that of the foetus. Both need the use of a certain person's body if they are to survive.
But in the case of the violinist, the relevant person is in no way responsible for the
violinist's being in need of assistance, whereas in the case of the foetus it can be said
that the woman is among those who are at least partially responsible [for] the foetus's being in need of a life-support system — assuming that the pregnancy did not
result from rape. . . .

Thomson raises this objection herself [but concludes] it is not convincing. [But]
consider the structure of [her] argument. First, she has offered an argument that
lends support to the view that abortion is justified at least in the case of rape. Second, she has pointed out that one cannot drive a wedge between rape and other
cases simply by appealing to the fact that in other cases the woman is responsible
for there being a foetus that needs assistance, since the woman is also to some ex-

tent responsible in cases of rape. [She therefore concludes] that abortion is morally permissible in at least some cases where intercourse is voluntary. . . .

[But there is] the following disanalogy between the people-seed case and that of pregnancy resulting from voluntary intercourse. In the people-seed case, there are only two sorts of alternatives. Either one exposes oneself to the danger of people-seeds taking root in one's house, or one reconciles oneself to a somewhat dreary existence in rooms that are stuffy and uncarpeted. In contrast, it does not seem that one is thus limited in the real life case; the choice is not confined to chastity on the one hand, and the risk of pregnancy on the other.

Consider the view that this position disregards the circumstances (including rape, pressure of various kinds, and ignorance about contraception) under which many or most women become pregnant.

7. *Viability.* The court held that, with "respect to [the] interest in potential life, the 'compelling' point is at viability [because] the fetus then presumably has the capability of meaningful life outside the mother's womb." Does this conclusion "mistake a definition for a syllogism"? Ely, supra, at 924. Consider Tribe, Foreword, supra, at 27-28: "Once the fetus can be severed from the woman by a process which enables it to survive, leaving the abortion decision to private choice would confer not only a right to remove an unwanted fetus from one's body, but also an entirely separate right to ensure its death. [Viability] thus marks a point after which [the] state could properly conclude that permitting abortion would be tantamount to permitting murder."

The viability principle poses several potential problems.

a. *Shifting viability.* Viability is not biologically fixed. It will arrive earlier in gestation as better techniques are developed for sustaining existence outside the womb. Is this a problem? One might see this as a built-in social safety valve. If society really cares about fetal life, it can do something about it by advancing technology. See Tribe, Structural Due Process, 10 Harv. C.R.-C.L. L. Rev. 269 (1975).

Is the right of privacy recognized in *Roe* about the right not to continue an unwanted pregnancy, or is it about the right not to have unwanted children? If *Roe* is about the right not to be a mother, shifting viability should not matter. But the viability line itself suggests that *Roe* is about the right not to be pregnant, not the right not to be a mother.

b. *Uncertain viability.* The point of viability varies from fetus to fetus, and it is extremely difficult to determine the precise point of viability for any particular fetus. How, then, should viability be defined? At the point at which the average fetus is viable? At the earliest point at which a fetus has been found viable?

8. *The attack on* Roe. *Roe* has been subject to strong attacks from a wide variety of quarters. Indeed, the decision helped mobilize the Moral Majority, which played a role in the election of President Reagan, who made the *Roe* decision a major campaign issue and whose administration sought to persuade the Court to overrule its decision.

9. *Regulating abortion.* Although the Court held in *Roe* that a state may not prohibit abortion entirely, it left many subsidiary questions unanswered. The following discussion deals with these and related issues.

MAHER v. ROE, 432 U.S. 464 (1977). In a six-to-three decision, the Court upheld a state regulation granting Medicaid benefits for childbirth but denying such benefits for nontherapeutic abortions (i.e., abortions that are not "medically necessary"). Justice Powell delivered the opinion of the Court:

"The Constitution imposes no obligation on the States to pay the pregnancy-related medical expenses of indigent women, or indeed to pay any of the medical expenses of indigents. But when a State decides to alleviate some of the hardships of poverty by providing medical care, the manner in which it dispenses benefits is subject to constitutional limitations. Appellees' claim is that [the State] must accord equal treatment to both abortion and childbirth, and may not evidence a policy preference by funding only the medical expenses incident to childbirth. This [presents] a question [under] the Equal Protection Clause. . . .

"This case involves no discrimination against a suspect class. An indigent woman desiring an abortion does not come within the limited category of [suspect classes]. Nor does the fact that the impact of the regulation falls upon those who cannot pay lead to a different conclusion. In a sense, every denial of welfare to an indigent creates a wealth classification as compared to nonindigents who are able to pay for the desired goods or services. But this Court has never held that financial need alone identifies a suspect [class]. [Cases such as *Griffin* and *Douglas* are distinguishable. Such cases] are grounded in the criminal justice system, a governmental monopoly in which participation is compelled. Our subsequent decisions have made it clear that the principles underlying *Griffin* and *Douglas* do not extend to legislative classifications generally.

"[Accordingly], the central question in this case is whether a regulation 'impinges upon a fundamental right explicitly or implicitly protected by the Constitution.' [Quoting San Antonio Independent School District v. Rodriguez.] The District Court read [*Roe*] as establishing a fundamental right to abortion and therefore concluded that nothing less than a compelling state interest would justify [the] different treatment of abortion and childbirth. [This misconceives] the nature and scope of the fundamental right recognized in *Roe*.

"[*Roe* involved] a Texas law [prohibiting] abortion, except [to save] the life of the mother. [We] held that only a compelling state interest would justify such a sweeping restriction on a constitutionally protected [interest]. [Although] a state-created obstacle [to abortion] need not be absolute to be impermissible, see Doe v. Bolton, 410 U.S. 179 (1973) [invalidating a law requiring that all first-trimester abortions be performed in a hospital], [*Roe*] did not declare an unqualified 'constitutional right to an abortion.' [Rather], the right protects the woman [only] from unduly burdensome interference with her freedom to decide whether to terminate her pregnancy. It implies no limitation on the authority of a State to make a value judgment favoring childbirth over abortion, and to implement that judgment by the allocation of public funds.

"The [regulation] before us is different in kind from the laws invalidated in our previous [decisions. It] places no obstacles — absolute or otherwise — in the pregnant woman's path to an abortion. An indigent woman who desires an abortion suffers no disadvantage as a consequence of [the State's] decision to fund childbirth; she continues as before to be dependent on private sources for the service she desires. The State may have made childbirth a more attractive alternative, thereby influencing the woman's decision, but it has imposed no restriction on access to abortions that was not already there. The indigency that may make it difficult — and in some cases, perhaps, impossible — for some women to have abortions is neither created nor in any way affected by [the] regulation.

[The challenged] regulation does not impinge upon the fundamental right recognized in *Roe*.

"[*Shapiro*] and *Maricopa County* [section E3 supra] recognized that denial of welfare to one who had recently exercised the right to travel [was] sufficiently analogous to a criminal fine to justify strict judicial scrutiny. If [the State] denied general welfare benefits to all women who had obtained abortions and who were otherwise entitled to the benefits, we would have a close analogy [to] *Shapiro*, and strict scrutiny might be [appropriate]. But the claim here is that the State 'penalizes' the woman's decision to have an abortion by refusing to pay for it. *Shapiro* and *Maricopa County* did not hold that States would penalize the right to travel [by] refusing to pay the bus fares of the indigent [travelers]. Sherbert v. Verner [see Justice Brennan's dissenting opinion] similarly is inapplicable here. . . .

"Our conclusion signals no retreat from [*Roe*]. There is a basic difference between direct state interference with a protected activity and state encouragement of an alternative [activity]. Constitutional concerns are greatest when the State attempts to impose its will by force of law; the State's power to encourage actions deemed to be in the public interest is necessarily far broader. . . .

"The question remains whether [the challenged] regulation can be sustained under the less demanding test of [rationality]. [*Roe*] itself explicitly acknowledged the State's strong interest in protecting the potential life of the fetus. [The] State unquestionably has a 'strong and legitimate interest in encouraging normal childbirth.' [There can be no] question that the [regulation] rationally furthers that interest. . . . [We] certainly are not unsympathetic to the plight of an indigent woman who desires an abortion, but 'the Constitution does not provide judicial remedies for every social and economic ill.' . . ."

Justice Brennan, joined by Justices Marshall and Blackmun, dissented: "[A] distressing insensitivity to the plight of impoverished pregnant women is inherent in the Court's analysis. The stark reality for too many, not just 'some,' indigent pregnant women is that indigency makes access to competent licensed physicians not merely 'difficult' but 'impossible.' As a practical matter, many indigent women will feel they have no choice but to carry their pregnancies to term because the State will pay for the associated medical services, even though they would have chosen to have abortions if the State had also provided funds for that procedure, or indeed if the State had provided funds for neither procedure. This disparity in funding [clearly] operates to coerce indigent pregnant women to bear children they would not otherwise choose to have. . . .

"[The] regulation unconstitutionally impinges upon [the right] of privacy by bringing financial pressures on indigent women that force them to bear children they would not otherwise have. [The] fact that the [challenged] scheme may not operate as an absolute bar preventing all indigent women from having abortions is not critical. What is critical is that the State has inhibited their fundamental right to make that choice free from state interference. [Citing, e.g., Doe v. Bolton; Carey v. Population Services International, section F1 supra.]

"Nor does the manner in which [the State] has burdened the right [save its] program. The [challenged] scheme cannot be distinguished from other grants and withholdings of financial benefits that we have held unconstitutionally burdened a fundamental right. Sherbert v. Verner, [374 U.S. 398 (1963),] struck down [a] statute that denied unemployment compensation to a woman who for religious reasons could not work on Saturday. [*Sherbert*] held that 'the pressure upon her to forgo [her religious] practice [was] unmistakable,' [and that] the effect was the same as a fine imposed for Saturday worship. Here, though the burden is upon the right to privacy [and] not upon freedom of religion, [the] governing principle is the same. . . .

"[The] Court [says] that a state requirement is unconstitutional [only] if it 'unduly burdens the right to seek an abortion.' [The challenged regulation] has 'unduly' burdened the fundamental right of pregnant women to be free to choose to have an abortion because the State has advanced no compelling state interest to justify its interference in that choice. . . ."

Justice Marshall also filed a dissenting opinion: "It is all too obvious that the [challenged regulation], ostensibly [adopted] to 'encourage' women to carry pregnancies to term, [is] in reality intended to impose a moral viewpoint that no State may constitutionally enforce. Since efforts to overturn [*Roe*] have been unsuccessful, the opponents of abortion have attempted every imaginable means to circumvent the commands of the Constitution and impose their moral choices upon the rest of society. [The] present [case involves] the most vicious [attack] yet devised. [I] am appalled at the ethical bankruptcy of those who preach a 'right to life' that means, under present social policies, a bare existence in utter misery for so many poor women and their children. [Today's decision] will be an invitation to public officials [to] approve more such restrictions. [When] elected leaders cower before public pressure, this Court, more than ever, must not shirk its duty to enforce the Constitution for the benefit of the poor and powerless."

HARRIS v. MCRAE, 448 U.S. 297 (1980). In a five-to-four decision, the Court upheld the "Hyde Amendment," which prohibited the use of federal Medicaid funds "to perform abortions except where the life of the mother would be endangered if the fetus were carried to term; or except for such medical procedures necessary for the victims of rape or incest." Justice Stewart delivered the opinion of the Court:

"The present case [differs] factually from *Maher* insofar as that case involved a failure to fund nontherapeutic abortions, whereas the Hyde Amendment withholds funding of certain medically necessary abortions. [Appellees] argue that because the Hyde Amendment affects a significant interest not present [in] *Maher* — the interest of a woman in protecting her health during pregnancy — and because that interest lies at the core of the personal constitutional freedom recognized in [*Roe*], the present case is constitutionally different from *Maher*. [It] is evident that a woman's interest in protecting her health was an important theme in [*Roe*]. [But], regardless of whether the freedom of a woman to choose to terminate her pregnancy for health reasons lies at the core or the periphery of the due process liberty recognized in [*Roe*], it simply does not follow that a woman's freedom of choice carries with it a constitutional entitlement to the financial resources to avail herself of the full range of protected choices. The reason why was explained in *Maher*: although government may not place obstacles in the path of a woman's exercise of her freedom of choice, it need not remove those not of its own creation. Indigency falls in the latter category. [The] Hyde Amendment leaves an indigent woman with at least the same range of choice in deciding whether to obtain a medically necessary abortion as she would have had if Congress had chosen to subsidize no health care costs at all. [To invalidate the Hyde Amendment] would mark a drastic change in our understanding of the Constitution. It cannot be that because government may not prohibit the use of contraceptives, [*Griswold*], or prevent parents from sending their child to a private school, [*Pierce*], government, therefore, has an affirmative constitutional obligation to ensure that all persons have the financial resources to obtain contraceptives or send their children to private schools. [Nothing] in the Due Process Clause supports such an extraordinary result."

Justice Stewart rejected the equal protection challenge for reasons similar to those stated in *Maher*: "[Because Congress] has neither invaded a substantive constitutional right [nor] enacted legislation [that] operates to the detriment of a suspect class, [strict scrutiny is inappropriate. And it is not] irrational that Congress has authorized federal reimbursement for medically necessary services generally, but not [for] medically necessary abortions, [for] no other [medical] procedure involves the purposeful termination of a potential life."

Justice Brennan, joined by Justices Marshall and Blackmun, dissented for essentially the reasons stated in his *Maher* dissent: "The proposition for which [*Roe* stands] is not that the State is under an affirmative obligation to ensure access to abortions for all who may desire them; it is that the State must refrain from wielding its enormous power and influence in a manner that might burden the pregnant woman's freedom to choose whether to have an abortion. [What] the Court fails to appreciate is that it is not simply the woman's indigency that interferes with her freedom of choice, but the combination of her own poverty and the Government's unequal subsidization of abortion and childbirth."

Justice Stevens was the only member of the *Maher* majority to dissent in *Harris*: "[This case involves women] who, by definition, are confronted with a choice [between] serious health damage to themselves [and abortion]. [In *Roe*, the Court held that, even after viability, a State cannot constitutionally prohibit an abortion that is necessary to preserve the "health of the mother." Thus, *Roe*] squarely held that state interference is unreasonable if it attaches a greater importance to the interest in potential life than to the interest in protecting the mother's health. [Having] decided to alleviate some of the hardships of poverty by providing necessary medical care, the government must use neutral criteria in distributing benefits. [It] may not create exceptions for the sole purpose of furthering a governmental interest that is constitutionally subordinate to the individual interest that the entire program was designed to protect."

Note: The Abortion-Funding Cases

Consider the following views:

1. Perry, Why the Supreme Court Was Plainly Wrong in the Hyde Amendment Case: A Brief Comment on Harris v. McRae, 32 Stan. L. Rev. 1113, 1115-1116, 1125 (1980):

In *Roe* the Court held [that] in the previability period a woman's interest in terminating her pregnancy [is] weightier, as a constitutional matter, than government's interest in preventing the taking of fetal life, *where preventing the taking of fetal life is government's ultimate interest.* [This reasoning] necessarily entails the proposition that *no* governmental action can be predicated on the view that in the previability period abortion is per se morally objectionable. [*Harris* was wrong because the] view, constitutionally illicit under *Roe*, that in and of itself abortion is morally objectionable indisputably played a determinative role in the passage of the Hyde Amendment.

For a contrary view, consider Westen, Correspondence, 33 Stan. L. Rev. 1187 (1981): "No one can deny that Professor Perry's conclusion follows from his premises. As with most syllogisms, however, the real issue is the validity of the major premise — that *Roe* necessarily prohibited the state from taking *any* action premised on moral objections to abortion."

2. L. Tribe, Constitutional Choices 243-244 (1985):

> The Court's willingness to uphold laws whose apparent injustice is thought simply to reflect the world's own cruelty [seems] most vivid in a case like [*Harris*]. [In *Roe*], abortion was not perceived as involving the intensely [public] question of the subordination of the poor to the rich through the instrument of coerced childbirth for those unable to afford medical procedures placed by the state on an ability-to-pay basis. [If the issue had been seen in this light], then even the state's use of selective funding to encourage the birth of unwanted children might resemble a program to foster involuntary servitude more closely than an exercise of government's prerogative to set its own priorities.

Should *Maher* and *Harris* be treated as unconstitutional conditions cases? Under the unconstitutional conditions doctrine, it is sometimes said that government may not "penalize" people for exercising constitutional rights or do indirectly what it cannot do directly. The unconstitutional conditions doctrine raises a number of puzzles, not least in the selection of the baseline from which to decide whether there has been an impermissible penalty or a permissible refusal to subsidize. See generally Sullivan, Unconstitutional Conditions, 102 Harv. L. Rev. 1413 (1989); see also Chapter 9 infra.

The Court extended *Maher* and *Harris* in Rust v. Sullivan, 500 U.S. 173 (1991). In that case, the government refused to fund speech that involved abortion; the refusal was challenged on both first and fifth amendment grounds. On the fifth amendment issue, the Court said:

> We recently reaffirmed the long-recognized principle that "the Due Process Clauses generally confer no affirmative right to governmental aid, even where such aid may be necessary to secure life, liberty, or property interests of which the government itself may not deprive the individual." [Webster v. Reproductive Health Services, infra], quoting DeShaney v. Winnebago County Dept. of Social Services, 489 U.S. 189, 196 (1989). The Government has no constitutional duty to subsidize an activity merely because the activity is constitutionally protected and may validly choose to fund childbirth over abortion and "implement that judgment by the allocation of public funds" for medical services relating to childbirth but not to those relating to abortion. The Government has no affirmative duty to "commit any resources to facilitating abortions," *Webster*, and its decision to fund childbirth but not abortion "places no governmental obstacle in the path of a woman who chooses to terminate her pregnancy, but rather, by means of unequal subsidization of abortion and other medical services, encourages alternative activity deemed in the public interest."
>
> That the regulations do not impermissibly burden a woman's Fifth Amendment rights is evident from the line of cases beginning with *Maher* and *McRae* and culminating in our most recent decision in *Webster*. Just as Congress' refusal to fund

abortions in *McRae* left "an indigent woman with at least the same range of choice in deciding whether to obtain a medically necessary abortion as she would have had if Congress had chosen to subsidize no health care costs at all," 448 U.S., at 317, and "Missouri's refusal to allow public employees to perform abortions in public hospitals leaves a pregnant woman with the same choices as if the State had chosen not to operate any public hospitals," Congress' refusal to fund abortion counseling and advocacy leaves a pregnant woman with the same choices as if the government had chosen not to fund family-planning services at all. The difficulty that a woman encounters when a Title X project does not provide abortion counseling or referral leaves her in no different position than she would have been if the government had not enacted Title X.

In *Webster* we stated that "[h]aving held that the State's refusal [in *Maher*] to fund abortions does not violate *Roe v. Wade*, it strains logic to reach a contrary result for the use of public facilities and employees." It similarly would strain logic, in light of the more extreme restrictions in those cases, to find that the mere decision to exclude abortion-related services from a federally funded pre-conceptual family planning program, is unconstitutional.

Petitioners also argue that by impermissibly infringing on the doctor/patient relationship and depriving a Title X client of information concerning abortion as a method of family planning, the regulations violate a woman's Fifth Amendment right to medical self-determination and to make informed medical decisions free of government-imposed harm. They argue that under our decisions in Akron v. Akron Center for Reproductive Health, Inc., 462 U.S. 416 (1983), and Thornburgh v. American College of Obstetricians and Gynecologists, 476 U.S. 747 (1986), the government cannot interfere with a woman's right to make an informed and voluntary choice by placing restrictions on the patient/doctor dialogue. [It] would undoubtedly be easier for a woman seeking an abortion if she could receive information about abortion from a Title X project, but the Constitution does not require that the Government distort the scope of its mandated program in order to provide that information.

Petitioners contend, however, that most Title X clients are effectively precluded by indigency and poverty from seeing a health care provider who will provide abortion-related services. But once again, even these Title X clients are in no worse position than if Congress had never enacted Title X. "The financial constraints that restrict an indigent woman's ability to enjoy the full range of constitutionally protected freedom of choice are the product not of governmental restrictions on access to abortion, but rather of her indigency." *McRae*, at 316.

The current Court has been increasingly insistent on the proposition that the Constitution only protects "negative" rights. Indeed, this insistence is a hallmark of contemporary doctrine. But is the basic claim right? Consider the following view.

The Constitution creates several positive rights. The contracts clause protects a "positive" right — the right to available courts, to enforce contractual agreements. The eminent domain clause protects a positive right — the right to governmental help to protect private property from invasions by others, including private persons. Consider whether it would be unconstitutional for a state to repeal its trespass laws. If it would, the fifth amendment creates a right to affirmative protection. Even the due process clause creates a right to governmental assistance against public and private invasions. It is thus false to say that the Constitution is only about negative rights.

On this view, the current Court, in *Rust* and elsewhere, is simply relying on a common law baseline (the common law interests in property and contract), or on existing distributions of assets, in deciding what counts as positive and what as negative. It is not truly distinguishing between positive and negative rights at all. A right is characterized as negative if it is the sort of right recognized at common law, or if it is a right that someone enjoys in the world before the welfare state; it is otherwise characterized as positive. And this view in turn replicates the errors of the *Lochner* era; indeed, it is the precise modern analogue to *Lochner*; and it is poorly adapted to constitutionalism in the world of the welfare state. On this and related questions, see Strauss, Due Process, Government Inaction, and Private Wrongs, 1989 Sup. Ct. Rev. 53; Sunstein, Neutrality in Constitutional Law (with Special Reference to Pornography, Abortion, and Surrogacy), 92 Colum. L. Rev. 1 (1992).

CITY OF AKRON v. AKRON CENTER FOR REPRODUCTIVE HEALTH, INC., 462 U.S. 416 (1983). In *City of Akron*, the Court considered the constitutionality of "several provisions of an ordinance" designed "to regulate the performance of abortions." Justice Powell delivered the opinion of the Court:

"Section 1870.03 of the Akron ordinance requires that any [second-trimester abortion] must be 'performed in a hospital.' [There] can be no doubt that [the] second-trimester hospitalization requirement places a significant obstacle in the path of women seeking an abortion. A primary burden created by the requirement is additional cost to the woman. [Moreover, experience since *Roe*] indicates that [at least during the early weeks of the second trimester, certain types of abortion procedures] may be performed safely on an outpatient basis in appropriate nonhospital facilities. [We] conclude, therefore, that 'present medical knowledge' [convincingly] undercuts Akron's justification for requiring that *all* second-trimester abortions be performed in a hospital.

"[Section 1870.06(A) of the Akron ordinance] provides that no abortion shall be performed except 'with the informed written consent of the pregnant woman [given] freely and without coercion.' [Section 1870.06(B) provides that], 'in order to insure that the consent for an abortion is truly informed consent,' the woman must be 'orally informed by her attending physician' of the status of her pregnancy, the development of her fetus, the date of possible viability, the physical and emotional complications that may result from an abortion, and the availability of agencies to provide her with assistance and information with respect to birth control, adoption, and childbirth. [In Planned Parenthood of Central Missouri v. Danforth, infra,] we upheld a Missouri law requiring a pregnant woman to 'certif[y]' in writing her consent to the [abortion].'

"[We] believe that §1870.06(B) attempts to extend the State's interest in ensuring 'informed consent' beyond permissible limits. [Much] of the information required is designed not to inform the woman's consent but rather to persuade her to withhold it altogether. Subsection (3) requires the physician to inform his patient that 'the unborn child is a human life from the moment of conception,' a requirement inconsistent with the Court's holding in [*Roe*] that a State may not adopt one theory of when life begins to justify its regulation of abortions. [And] subsection (5) [begins] with the dubious statement that 'abortion is a major surgical procedure' and proceeds to describe numerous [possible] complications [in] a 'parade of horribles' intended to suggest that abortion [is] particularly dangerous. . . .

"Section 1870.06(C) [provides that] the 'attending physician' must inform the woman 'of the particular risks associated with her own pregnancy [and provide] her with at least a general description of the medical instructions to be followed subsequent to the [abortion].' The information required clearly is related to maternal health and to the State's legitimate purpose in requiring informed consent. [But requiring] physicians personally to discuss the abortion decision [with] each patient may in some cases add to the [cost]. [We] are not convinced [that] there is as vital a state need for insisting that [a physician] counsel the patient. [The] critical factor is whether [the woman] obtains the necessary information and counseling from a qualified person, not the identity of the person from whom she obtains it. [Section 1870.06(C) is thus unreasonable and] invalid. . . .

"[Section 1870.07] prohibits a physician from performing an abortion until 24 hours after the pregnant woman signs a consent form. [This] increases the cost of obtaining an abortion by requiring the woman to make two separate trips to the abortion facility. [Akron] has failed to demonstrate that any legitimate state interest is furthered by an arbitrary and inflexible waiting period."

Justice O'Connor, joined by Justices White and Rehnquist, dissented.

Note: *Regulating Abortion*

The following decisions have been thrown into doubt by Webster v. Reproductive Health Services and Planned Parenthood of Southeastern Pennsylvania v. Casey, discussed infra; we outline them briefly here.

1. *Spousal consent.* In Planned Parenthood of Central Missouri v. Danforth, 428 U.S. 52 (1976), the Court invalidated a Missouri statute requiring the prior written consent of the spouse of the woman seeking an abortion unless "the abortion is certified by a licensed physician to be necessary in order to preserve the life of the mother." The Court explained:

> [We] recognize that the decision whether to undergo or to forgo an abortion may have profound effects on the future of any marriage, effects that are both physical and mental, and possibly deleterious. [Ideally], the decision to terminate a pregnancy should be one concurred in by both the wife and her husband. [But] it is difficult to believe that the goal of fostering mutuality and trust in a marriage [will] be achieved by giving the husband a veto [power]. We recognize, of course, that when a woman, [without] the approval of her husband, decides to terminate her pregnancy, it could be said that she is acting unilaterally. The obvious fact is that when the wife and the husband disagree on this decision, the view of only [one] can prevail. Inasmuch as it is the woman who physically bears the child and who is the more directly and immediately affected by the pregnancy, as between the two, the balance weighs in her favor.

Justice White, joined by Chief Justice Burger and Justice Rehnquist, dissented:

> A father's interest in having a child — perhaps his only child — may be unmatched by any other interest in his life. [It] is truly surprising that the majority finds in the [Constitution] a rule that the State must assign a greater value to a mother's decision to cut off a potential human life by abortion than to a father's decision to let it mature into a live child. [These] are matters which a State should be able to decide free from the suffocating power of the federal judge.

2. *Parental consent.* In *Danforth*, supra, the Court, in a five-to-four decision, also invalidated a Missouri statute prohibiting an unmarried woman under

age eighteen from obtaining an abortion without the written consent of a parent or person in loco parentis unless "the abortion is certified by a licensed physician as necessary in order to preserve the life of the mother." Justice White, joined by the Chief Justice and Justice Rehnquist, dissented; Justice Stevens dissented separately.

In Bellotti v. Baird, 443 U.S. 622 (1979) (*Bellotti II*), the Court invalidated a Massachusetts statute prohibiting an unmarried woman under age eighteen from obtaining an abortion unless both of her parents consent or a court orders the abortion "for good cause shown." In Planned Parenthood Association of Kansas City v. Ashcroft, 462 U.S. 476 (1983), the Court upheld a parental consent requirement that contained an "alternative procedure" sufficient to meet the standards established in Justice Powell's plurality opinion in *Bellotti II*. Justice Powell, joined by Chief Justice Burger, sustained the statute on the basis of his opinion in *Bellotti II*. Justice O'Connor, joined by Justices White and Rehnquist, sustained the statute on the ground that "it imposes no undue burden on any right that a minor may have to undergo an abortion." Justice Blackmun, joined by Justices Brennan, Marshall, and Stevens, dissented.

3. *Parental notification.* In his plurality opinion in *Bellotti II*, supra, Justice Powell discussed the extent to which a minor employing the "alternative procedure" has a constitutional right "to obtain judicial consent to an abortion" without parental consultation:

> [Many] parents hold strong views on the subject of abortion, and young pregnant minors, especially those living at home, are particularly vulnerable to their parents' efforts to obstruct both an abortion and their access to court. [We] conclude, therefore, that [every] minor must have the opportunity [to] go directly to a court without first consulting or notifying her parents. If she satisfies the court that she is mature and well enough informed to make intelligently the abortion decision on her own, the court must authorize her to act without parental consultation or consent. If she fails to satisfy the court that she is competent to make this decision independently, she must be permitted to show that an abortion nevertheless would be in her best interests. [In making this determination, the court may consider whether] her best interests would be served [by parental consultation]. But this is the full extent to which parental involvement may be required.

Justice White stated in dissent that "I would have thought inconceivable a holding that the [Constitution] forbids even notice to parents when their minor child who seeks surgery objects to such notice and is able to convince a judge that the parents should be denied participation in the decision." Justices Brennan, Marshall, Blackmun, and Stevens did not address the issue.

H.L. v. Matheson, 450 U.S. 398 (1981), concerned a Utah statute requiring a physician to notify, if possible, the parents or guardian of any minor woman on whom an abortion is to be performed. The Court held that the plaintiff lacked standing to challenge the statute "on its face." In a narrow decision, the Court upheld the statute as applied to minor women who are "living with and dependent upon [their] parents," who are "not emancipated by marriage or otherwise," and who have "made no claim or showing as to [their] maturity." The Court explained that, as "applied to immature and dependent minors, the statute plainly serves the important considerations of family integrity and protecting adolescents" and provides "an opportunity for parents to supply essential medical and other information to a physician." Although conceding that "the requirement of notice to parents may inhibit some minors from seeking abortions," the Court maintained that this is "not a valid basis to void the statute as applied [to] the class [before] us." The Court thus concluded that, although "a state may not constitutionally legislate a blanket, unreviewable power of parents to veto their daughter's abortion, a statute setting out a 'mere requirement of parental notice' does not violate the constitutional rights of an immature, dependent minor."

For the Court's more recent pronouncements on these questions, see the discussion of the cases following *Webster*, infra.

4. *Minors and contraceptives.* If minors have a right to an abortion, do they also have a right to contraceptives? In what circumstances, and to what extent, may a state regulate a minor's access to contraceptives? In Carey v. Population Services International, 431 U.S. 678 (1977), the Court invalidated a New York statute prohibiting the distribution of contraceptives to persons under age sixteen. In a plurality opinion, Justice Brennan, joined by Justices Stewart, Marshall, and Blackmun, reasoned:

> [The] right to privacy in connection with decisions affecting procreation extends to minors as well as adults. [Citing *Danforth*.] [The State argues], however, that significant state interests are served by restricting minors' access to contraceptives, because free availability to minors of contraceptives would lead to increased sexual activity among the [young]. The same argument, however, would support a ban on abortions for [minors]. [As we said in *Eisenstadt*]: "It would be plainly unreasonable to assume that [the State] has prescribed pregnancy [as] punishment for fornication." [Moreover], there is substantial reason for doubt whether limiting access to contraceptives will in fact substantially discourage early sexual behavior. [When] a State, as here, burdens the exercise of a fundamental right, its attempt to justify that burden as a rational means for the accomplishment of some significant state policy requires more than a bare assertion [that] the burden is connected to such a policy.

Justice White concurred in the result. He emphasized that "the legality of state laws forbidding premarital intercourse is not at issue here." Justice White concurred because "the State has not demonstrated that the prohibition against distribution of contraceptives to minors measurably contributes to the deterrent purposes which the State advances." Justice Powell also concurred in the result. In Justice Powell's view, the challenged statute was "defective" because it "prohibits parents from distributing contraceptives to their children, a restriction that unjustifiably interferes with parental interests in rearing their children."

5. *Protecting the viable fetus.* In *Danforth*, supra, the Court upheld a statute that defined "viability" as "that stage of fetal development when the life of the unborn child may be continued indefinitely outside the womb by natural or artificial life-supportive systems." The Court rejected the contention "that a specified number of weeks in pregnancy must be fixed by statute as the point of viability": "[I]t is not the proper function of the legislature or the courts to place viability, which essentially is a medical concept, at a specific point in the gestation period. The time when viability is achieved may vary with each pregnancy, and the determination of whether a particular fetus is viable is, and must be, a matter for the judgment of the responsible attending physician."

In Colautti v. Franklin, 439 U.S. 379 (1979), the Court invalidated a Pennsylvania statute that requires every person who performs an abortion first to determine, "based on his experience, judgment or professional competence," that the fetus is not viable. If the person performing the abortion determines that the fetus "is viable," or "if there is sufficient reason to believe that the fetus may be viable," the statute requires the person performing the abortion to exercise the same care to preserve the life and health of the fetus as would be required if the fetus were intended to be born alive, and to use the abortion technique providing the best opportunity for the fetus to be born alive, so long as a different technique is not necessary to preserve the life or health of the mother. The Court held the provision "void-for-vagueness" because (a) the "distinction between the phrases 'is viable' and 'may be viable' [is] elusive," (b) the standard-of-care provision is "uncertain" as to whether the physician may "consider his duty to the patient to be paramount [or] whether it requires the physician to make a 'trade-off' between the woman's health and additional percentage points of fetal survival," and (c) the provision "subjects the physician to potential criminal liability without regard to fault," thus compounding the problem of vagueness. Justice White, joined by Chief Justice Burger and Justice Rehnquist, dissented.

In Planned Parenthood Association of Kansas City v. Ashcroft, 462 U.S. 476 (1983), the Court upheld a Missouri statute requiring the attendance of a second physician at all postviability abortions.

6. *Miscellaneous regulations.* For the Court's analysis of other regulations of abortion, see *Danforth,* supra (upholding a recordkeeping requirement even as applied to first-trimester abortions); *Ashcroft,* supra (upholding a requirement that, when an abortion is performed, a tissue sample be submitted to a certified pathologist for a report); *Danforth,* supra (invalidating a prohibition on the use of saline amniocentesis abortions); *City of Akron,* supra (invalidating on vagueness grounds a requirement that physicians dispose of "the remains of the unborn child [in] a humane and sanitary manner").

In Thornburgh v. American College of Obstetricians and Gynecologists, 476 U.S. 747 (1986) — a pre-*Webster* decision — the Court exhibited some impatience with state efforts to regulate the abortion decision. The case concerned a Pennsylvania statute that, inter alia, required physicians to provide women seeking abortions with information allegedly designed to secure informed consent, required detailed recordkeeping concerning abortions, required use of the abortion technique that would provide the most protection for the life of the fetus in postviability abortions unless the technique posed "significantly greater" medical risks to the pregnant mother, and required the presence of a second physician for postviability abortions. In a five-to-four decision, the Court, in an opinion by Justice Blackmun, held each of these provisions unconstitutional.

Note: *The* Webster *Case*

In Webster v. Reproductive Health Services, 452 U.S. 450 (1989), the Court upheld several provisions of a Missouri statute regulating abortions. Much more important, a plurality endorsed a significant reformulation of *Roe's* trimester scheme. In *Webster,* the Court found, first, that a statement in the abortion statute's preamble that "the life of each human being begins at conception" was not in conflict with the statement in *Roe* that "a State may not adopt one theory of when life begins to justify its regulation of abortions." The preamble simply "express[ed] . . . [a] value judgment" in the abstract.

Relying on Harris v. McRae and related cases, the Court also upheld a bar on state employees performing abortions and a ban on the use of public facilities for performing abortions — even when the patient paid for the abortion herself. "Missouri's refusal to allow public employees to perform abortions in public hospitals leaves a pregnant woman with the same choices as if the State had chosen not to operate any hospitals at all." According to the Court, "[I]f the State does recoup all of its costs in performing abortions, and no state subsidy, direct or indirect, is available, it is difficult to see how any procreational choice is burdened by the State's ban on the use of its facilities or employees for performing abortions."

The Court noted that "a different analysis might apply if a particular State had socialized medicine and all of its hospitals and physicians were publicly funded. This case also might be different if the State barred doctors who performed abortions in private facilities from the use of public facilities for any purpose." (Justice O'Connor's concurring opinion also stated that "there may be conceivable applications of the ban on the use of public facilities that would be unconstitutional," citing the suggestion by appellees that "the State could try to enforce the ban against private hospitals using public water and sewage lines." But she found it unnecessary to decide whether these applications of the ban would be unconstitutional.)

The final provision at issue in Webster, as interpreted by the Court, required a physician, prior to performing an abortion "on a woman he has reason to believe is carrying an unborn child of twenty or more weeks gestational age," to perform tests that, in the physician's reasonable professional judgment, would be useful in determining the viability of the fetus. The plurality, in an opinion by Chief Justice Rehnquist, said that this statute, which regulated the performance of abortions in the second trimester in the interest not of maternal health, but in the interest of protecting potential human life, conflicted with the trimester system articulated in Roe and applied in Colautti. "It undoubtedly does superimpose state regulation on the medical determination of whether a particular fetus is viable." In addition, the plurality said that, "to the extent that the viability tests increase the cost of what are in fact second-trimester abortions" — in cases where the tests show that the fetus was not viable — "their validity may also be questioned under Akron."

With respect to this issue, the plurality acknowledged that "[s]tare decisis is a cornerstone of our legal system, but it has less power in constitutional cases, where, save for constitutional amendments, this Court is the only body able to make needed changes." In a key passage, the plurality argued that Roe's trimester system should be abandoned. "The rigid Roe framework is hardly consistent with the notion of a Constitution cast in general terms, as ours is, and usually speaking in general principles, as ours does."

Note: Abortion after Webster

There was a remarkable public reaction to Webster. The decision served to galvanize pro-choice (and feminist) forces in a way that seemed to have a significant impact on elections in many parts of the country.

Consider in this light the following (highly controversial) assessment. Ironically, Roe helped create the Moral Majority, demobilized the feminist movement, helped defeat the equal rights amendment, harmed the judiciary, and had serious harmful long-term consequences for civil rights, at the executive and legislative levels, in the areas of both race and sex. *Webster* has had the opposite consequences, with perhaps more favorable long-term results for the cause of sexual equality than a liberal Court could ever have achieved. At least for advocates of sexual equality, *Roe* thus gives extremely serious pause to those who believe in an aggressive role for the Supreme Court in promoting social change. It suggests that nonjudicial institutions are far preferable. On these and related issues, see generally G. Rosenberg, The Hollow Hope (1991).

In Hodgson v. Minnesota, 457 U.S. 417 (1990), and Ohio v. Akron Center for Reproductive Health, 457 U.S. 502 (1990), the Court was confronted with two statutes regulating minors' access to abortion. In *Hodgson*, the Court invalidated a provision of a Minnesota statute that prohibited the performance of abortions on women under the age of eighteen unless at least forty-eight hours had elapsed since the time when both parents were notified. In an opinion written by Justice Stevens and joined in principal part by Justices Brennan, Marshall, Blackmun, and O'Connor, the Court said that the two-parent requirement was "not reasonably related to legitimate state interests."

The Court emphasized extensive testimony at trial to the effect that parents of minors seeking abortion were frequently divorced or separated, and that in these circumstances the two-parent notification requirement could have severe adverse effects on both the minor and the custodial parent. These adverse effects included the possibility of violence from fathers. The Court stessed that the trial court found that "many minors in Minnesota 'live in fear of violence by family members' and 'are, in fact, victims of rape, incest, neglect, and violence.'"

In a part of his opinion joined only by Justice O'Connor, Justice Stevens suggested that the state interests in the welfare of the pregnant minor and her parents, and in the family unit, could be served by single-parent notification accompanied by the brief forty-eight-hour delay. (The opinions in both *Hodgson* and *Akron* reveal that a majority of the Court supports this position and would therefore uphold such a requirement. Justice Marshall, in a partial dissent joined by Justices Brennan and Blackmun, argued that such a provision would also be unconstitutional; he cited the increased health risks and costs of the delay.) The Court said that the two-parent notification requirement fails "to serve any state interest with respect to functioning families" and "disserves the state interest in protecting and assisting the minor with respect to dysfunctional families."

In a brief concurring opinion, Justice O'Connor reiterated the "undue burdens" test that she had first outlined earlier in *City of Akron* and said that here there was no sufficient justification for two-parent notification, especially in light of the fact that only half of the minors in Minnesota live with both biological parents. She argued that the statute's exception to notification for minors who are victims of neglect and abuse serves in practice as a means of contacting the parent and therefore does not protect minors from neglectful or abusive parents at all. Justice Kennedy, in an opinion joined by the Chief Justice and Justices White and Scalia, dissented on this point. He emphasized that "it was reasonable for the legislature to conclude that in most cases notice to both parents will work to the minor's benefit."

In *Hodgson*, a different majority of the Court upheld a part of the Minnesota statute to the effect that, if the two-parent requirement is found unconstitutional, the same notice requirement is effective *unless* the pregnant woman obtains a court order permitting the abortion to proceed. On this proposition, there was no opinion for the Court. The key vote came from Justice O'Connor, who said simply that "the interference with the internal operation of the family . . . simply does not exist where the minor can avoid notifying one or both parents by use of the bypass procedure." On this point, Justice Stevens dissented, saying that a "judicial bypass that is designed to handle exceptions from a reasonable general rule . . . is quite different from a requirement that a minor . . . must apply to a court for permission to avoid the application of a rule that is not reasonably related to legitimate state goals. . . . Where the parents are living together and have joint custody over the child, the State has no legitimate interests in the communication between father and mother about the child." And when there is a divorce, Justice Stevens argued, the question of notification is for the minor and the custodial parent rather than the state.

In *Akron*, the Court upheld an Ohio statute that, with certain exceptions, prohibited any person from performing an abortion on an unmarried, unemancipated minor without giving notice to one of her parents or receiving a court order of approval. Twenty-four hours after notice, an abortion would be permitted. No notice would be required, moreover, if the minor and another relative filed an affidavit stating that the minor fears physical, sexual, or severe emotional abuse from the parent. The notice provisions could also be bypassed entirely if the minor could file a complaint showing that notice is not in her best interests, or that she has sufficient maturity and information to make an intelligent decision without notice, or that one of her parents has engaged in a pattern of physical, sexual, or emotional abuse.

In an opinion by Justice Kennedy, the Court said that it did not have to decide whether notice statutes must provide bypass procedures at all. In this case, the procedures were adequate. They allowed the minor to prove maturity and information; they contained a general "best interests" exception; they guaranteed anonymity to the minor; and they ensured that the procedure would be conducted expeditiously (here, within twenty-two days as a "worst case," and in all likelihood significantly less time).

Justice Blackmun, joined by Justices Brennan and Marshall, dissented.

Would the case for abortion rights be weakened if the United States provided stronger social supports for women with small children? Has abortion turned out to be the United States' odd response to the problem of unwanted pregnancy? Might compromise on this matter be possible if social supports were offered as a kind of quid pro quo for social or legal limits on abortion? For an intriguing comparative discussion, see M. Glendon, Abortion and Divorce in American Law 2-3, 15-17, 18-19, 40, 52, 54 (1987):

> When American abortion law is viewed in comparative perspective, it presents several unique features. Not only do we have less regulation of abortion in the interest of the fetus than any other Western nation, but we provide less public support for maternity and child raising. And, to a greater extent than in any other country, our courts have shut down the legislative process of bargaining, education, and persuasion on the abortion issue. [The] roots of these differences can be traced in part to [the] realm of ideas. [In] France since 1975 abortion has been available, up to the end of the tenth week of pregnancy, to any woman "whose condition places her in a situation of distress." "Distress" is not defined, and the statute makes the woman herself the sole judge of whether she is in it. [Thus,] if all one is interested

in is how easily an abortion can be obtained, [in] fact there is abortion on demand in France. [But there] is a considerable difference between saying that the decision whether or not to abort is up to the woman, and saying that the state recognizes this option only in the case of women who are in "distress." [The] "distress" requirement [does] communicate a message. [The] physician who receives the woman's initial request for termination of her pregnancy must furnish her with a brochure (supplied by the government) informing her that the law limits abortion to cases of distress. [The] pregnant woman is required to have a private interview [with] a government-approved counseling service which [is] supposed to furnish the woman with assistance and advice, "especially with a view toward enabling her to keep her child." [At] least one week must elapse from the time of her initial request for an abortion, and at least two days from the time of the mandatory consultation, before the abortion can be performed. [The] present French abortion law [is] a humane, democratic compromise. [The] legislation as a whole is pervaded by compassion for pregnant women, by concern for fetal life, and by expression of the commitment of society as a whole to help minimize occasions for tragic choices between them. This commitment is carried out by provision of birth control assistance, and by comparatively generous financial support for married as well as unwed mothers. [It] is worth noting that the French statute "names" the underlying problem as one involving human life, not as a conflict involving a woman's individual liberty or privacy and a non-person. While showing great concern for the pregnant woman, it tries [to] make her aware of alternatives without either frightening or unduly burdening her. [The] European countries have been able to live relatively peacefully with these laws without experiencing the violence born of complete frustration and without foreclosing re-examination and renegotiation of the issues. [A] decision leaving abortion regulation basically up to state legislatures would have encouraged constructive activity by partisans of both sides. [The] voice we hear in the Supreme Court's abortion narrative — presenting us with the image of the pregnant woman as autonomous, separate, and distinct from the father of the unborn child (and from her parents if she is a minor), and insulated from the larger society [— is] more distinctively American than it is masculine in its lonely individualism and libertarianism. [A] Martian trying to infer our culture's attitude toward children from our abortion and social welfare laws might think we had deliberately decided to solve the problem of children in poverty by choosing to abort them rather than to support them with tax dollars. [European] abortion law has been heavily influenced by notions of what is reasonable to require from a pregnant woman, and European child support law by notions of what it is reasonable to require from an absent father. American abortion law and, at least until recently, child support law has expected little from either men or women.

For a discussion of some of the facts relating to the abortion problem, see R. Posner, Sex and Reason 272-290 (1992).

Planned Parenthood of Southeastern Pennsylvania v. Casey

505 U.S. 833 (1992)

JUSTICE O'CONNOR, JUSTICE KENNEDY, and JUSTICE SOUTER announced the judgment of the Court and delivered the opinion of the Court with respect to Parts I, II, III, V-A, V-C, and VI, an opinion with respect to Part V-E, in which Justice Stevens joins, and an opinion with respect to Parts IV, V-B, and V-D.

I

Liberty finds no refuge in a jurisprudence of doubt. Yet 19 years after our holding that the Constitution protects a woman's right to terminate her pregnancy in its early stages, that definition of liberty is still questioned. Joining the respondents as amicus curiae, the United States, as it has done in five other cases in the last decade, again asks us to overrule *Roe*.

At issue in these cases are five provisions of the Pennsylvania Abortion Control Act of 1982 as amended in 1988 and 1989. [The] Act requires that a woman seeking an abortion give her informed consent prior to the abortion procedure, and specifies that she be provided with certain information at least 24 hours before the abortion is performed. For a minor to obtain an abortion, the Act requires the informed consent of one of her parents, but provides for a judicial bypass option if the minor does not wish to or cannot obtain a parent's consent. Another provision of the Act requires that, unless certain exceptions apply, a married woman seeking an abortion must sign a statement indicating that she has notified her husband of her intended abortion. The Act exempts compliance with these three requirements in the event of a "medical emergency." [In] addition to the above provisions regulating the performance of abortions, the Act imposes certain reporting requirements on facilities that provide abortion services.

[After] considering the fundamental constitutional questions resolved by *Roe*, principles of institutional integrity, and the rule of stare decisis, we are led to conclude this: the essential holding of Roe v. Wade should be retained and once again reaffirmed.

It must be stated at the outset and with clarity that *Roe*'s essential holding, the holding we reaffirm, has three parts. First is a recognition of the right of the woman to choose to have an abortion before viability and to obtain it without undue interference from the State. Before viability, the State's interests are not strong enough to support a prohibition of abortion or the imposition of a substantial obstacle to the woman's effective right to elect the procedure. Second is a confirmation of the State's power to restrict abortions after fetal viability, if the law contains exceptions for pregnancies which endanger a woman's life or health. And third is the principle that the State has legitimate interests from the outset of the pregnancy in protecting the health of the woman and the life of the fetus that may become a child.

II

Constitutional protection of the woman's decision to terminate her pregnancy derives from the Due Process Clause of the Fourteenth Amendment. [A]lthough a literal reading of the Clause might suggest that it governs only the procedures by which a State may deprive persons of liberty, for at least 105 years, [t]he Clause has been understood to contain a substantive component as well.

[I]t is also tempting [t]o suppose that the Due Process Clause protects only those practices, defined at the most specific level, that were protected against government interference by other rules of law when the Fourteenth Amendment was ratified. See Michael H. v. Gerald D., 491 U.S. 110, 127-128, n.6 (1989) (opinion of Scalia, J.). But such a view would be inconsistent with our law. It is a promise of the Constitution that there is a realm of personal liberty which the government may not enter. We have vindicated this principle before. Marriage is mentioned nowhere in the Bill of Rights and interracial marriage was illegal in most States in the 19th century, but the Court was no doubt correct in finding it to be an aspect of liberty protected against state interference by the substantive component of the Due Process Clause in Loving v. Virginia. [N]either the Bill of Rights nor the specific practices of States at the time of the adoption of the Fourteenth Amendment marks the outer limits of the substantive sphere of liberty which the Fourteenth Amendment protects. See U.S. Const., Amend. 9.

[Abortion] is a unique act. It is an act fraught with consequences for others: for the woman who must live with the implications of her decision; for the persons who perform and assist in the procedure; for the spouse, family, and society which must confront the knowledge that these procedures exist, procedures some deem nothing short of an act of violence against innocent human life; and, depending on one's beliefs, for the life or potential life that is aborted. [The] mother who carries a child to full term is subject to anxieties, to physical constraints, to pain that only she must bear. That these sacrifices have from the beginning of the human race been endured by woman with a pride that ennobles her in the eyes of others and gives to the infant a bond of love cannot alone be grounds for the State to insist she make the sacrifice. Her suffering is too intimate and personal for the State to insist, without more, upon its own vision of the woman's role, however dominant that vision has been in the course of our history and our culture. The destiny of the woman must be shaped to a large extent on her own conception of her spiritual imperatives and her place in society.

It should be recognized, moreover, that in some critical respects the abortion decision is of the same character as the decision to use contraception, to which Griswold v. Connecticut, Eisenstadt v. Baird, and Carey v. Population Services International afford constitutional protection. We have no doubt as to the correctness of those decisions. They support the reasoning in Roe relating to the woman's liberty because they involve personal decisions concerning not only the meaning of procreation but also human responsibility and respect for it. . . .

III

A

[In] this case we may inquire whether Roe's central rule has been found unworkable; whether the rule's limitation on state power could be removed without serious inequity to those who have relied upon it or significant damage to the stability of the society governed by the rule in question; whether the law's growth in the intervening years has left Roe's central rule a doctrinal anachronism discounted by society; and whether Roe's premises of fact have so far changed in the ensuing two decades as to render its central holding somehow irrelevant or unjustifiable in dealing with the issue it addressed.

1

Although Roe has engendered opposition, it has in no sense proven "unworkable," representing as it does a simple limitation beyond which a state law is unenforceable. While Roe has, of course, required judicial assessment of state laws affecting the exercise of the choice guaranteed against government infringement, and although the need for such review will remain as a consequence of today's decision, the required determinations fall within judicial competence.

2

The inquiry into reliance counts the cost of a rule's repudiation as it would fall on those who have relied reasonably on the rule's continued application. . . .

While neither respondents nor their amici in so many words deny that the abortion right invites some reliance prior to its actual exercise, one can readily imagine an argument stressing the dissimilarity of this case to one involving property or contract. Abortion is customarily chosen as an unplanned response to the consequence of unplanned activity or to the failure of conventional birth control, and except on the assumption that no intercourse would have occurred but for *Roe*'s holding, such behavior may appear to justify no reliance claim.

[To] eliminate the issue of reliance that easily, however, one would need to limit cognizable reliance to specific instances of sexual activity. But to do this would be simply to refuse to face the fact that for two decades of economic and social developments, people have organized intimate relationships and made choices that define their views of themselves and their places in society, in reliance on the availability of abortion in the event that contraception should fail. The ability of women to participate equally in the economic and social life of the Nation has been facilitated by their ability to control their reproductive lives. See, e.g., R. Petchesky, Abortion and Woman's Choice 109, 133, n.7 (rev. ed. 1990). The Constitution serves human values, and while the effect of reliance on *Roe* cannot be exactly measured, neither can the certain cost of overruling *Roe* for people who have ordered their thinking and living around that case be dismissed.

3

No evolution of legal principle has left *Roe*'s doctrinal footings weaker than they were in 1973. No development of constitutional law since the case was decided has implicitly or explicitly left *Roe* behind as a mere survivor of obsolete constitutional thinking.

It will be recognized, of course, that *Roe* stands at an intersection of two lines of decisions, but in whichever doctrinal category one reads the case, the result for present purposes will be the same. The *Roe* Court itself placed its holding in the succession of cases most prominently exemplified by Griswold v. Connecticut, 381 U.S. 479 (1965), see *Roe*, 410 U.S., at 152-153. [*Roe*,] however, may be seen not only as an exemplar of *Griswold* liberty but as a rule (whether or not mistaken) of personal autonomy and bodily integrity, with doctrinal affinity to cases recognizing limits on governmental power to mandate medical treatment or to bar its rejection. If so, our cases since *Roe* accord with *Roe*'s view that a State's interest in the protection of life falls short of justifying any plenary override of individual liberty claims. Cruzan v. Director, Missouri Dept. of Health [section F4 infra]. Finally, one could classify *Roe* as sui generis. If the case is so viewed, then there clearly has been no erosion of its central determination.

[The] soundness of this prong of the *Roe* analysis is apparent from a consideration of the alternative. If indeed the woman's interest in deciding whether to bear and beget a child had not been recognized as in *Roe*, the State might as readily restrict a woman's right to choose to carry a pregnancy to term as to terminate it, to further asserted state interests in population control, or eugenics, for example. Yet *Roe* has been sensibly relied upon to counter any such suggestions. E.g., Arnold v. Board of Education of Escambia County, Ala., 880 F.2d 305, 311 (CA11 1989) (relying upon *Roe* and concluding that government officials violate the Constitution by coercing a minor to have an abortion); Avery v. County of Burke, 660 F.2d 111, 115 (CA4 1981) (county agency inducing teenage girl to undergo unwanted sterilization on the basis of misrepresentation that she had sickle cell trait); see also In re Quinlan, 70 N.J. 10, 355 A.2d 647, cert. denied sub nom. Garger v. New Jersey, 429 U.S. 922 (1976) (relying on *Roe* in finding a right to terminate medical treatment).

4

[Time] has overtaken some of *Roe's* factual assumptions: advances in maternal health care allow for abortions safe to the mother later in pregnancy than was true in 1973. But these facts go only to the scheme of time limits on the realization of competing interests, and the divergences from the factual premises of 1973 have no bearing on the validity of *Roe's* central holding, that viability marks the earliest point at which the State's interest in fetal life is constitutionally adequate to justify a legislative ban on nontherapeutic abortions.

5

The sum of the precedential inquiry to this point shows *Roe's* underpinnings unweakened in any way affecting its central holding. . . .

B

In a less significant case, stare decisis analysis could, and would, stop at the point we have reached. But the sustained and widespread debate *Roe* has provoked calls for some comparison between that case and others of comparable dimension that have responded to national controversies and taken on the impress of the controversies addressed. Only two such decisional lines from the past century present themselves for examination, and in each instance the result reached by the Court accorded with the principles we apply today.

The first example is that line of cases identified with Lochner v. New York. [West] Coast Hotel Co. v. Parrish signalled the demise of *Lochner* by overruling *Adkins.* In the meantime, the Depression had come and, with it, the lesson that seemed unmistakable to most people by 1937, that the interpretation of contractual freedom protected in *Adkins* rested on fundamentally false factual assumptions about the capacity of a relatively unregulated market to satisfy minimal levels of human welfare. As Justice Jackson wrote of the constitutional crisis of 1937 shortly before he came on the bench, "The older world of laissez faire was recognized everywhere outside the Court to be dead." R. Jackson, The Struggle for Judicial Supremacy 85 (1941). The facts upon which the earlier case had premised a constitutional resolution of social controversy had proved to be untrue, and history's demonstration of their untruth not only justified but required the new choice of constitutional principle that *West Coast Hotel* announced. Of course, it was true that the Court lost something by its misperception, or its lack of prescience, and the Court-packing crisis only magnified the loss; but the clear demonstration that the facts of economic life were different from those previously assumed warranted the repudiation of the old law.

The second comparison that 20th century history invites is with the cases employing the separate-but-equal rule for applying the Fourteenth Amendment's equal protection guarantee. They began with Plessy v. Ferguson. [The] *Plessy* Court considered "the underlying fallacy of the plaintiff's argument to consist in the assumption that the enforced separation of the two races stamps the colored race with a badge of inferiority. If this be so, it is not by reason of anything found in the act, but solely because the colored race chooses to put that construction upon it." [But] this understanding of the facts and the rule it was stated to justify were repudiated in *Brown*. As one commentator observed, the question before the Court in *Brown* was "whether discrimination inheres in that segregation which is imposed by law in the twentieth century in certain specific states in the American Union. And that question has meaning and can find an answer only on the ground of history and of common knowledge about the facts of life in the times and places aforesaid." Black, The Lawfulness of the Segregation Decisions, 69 Yale L.J. 421, 427 (1960).

The Court in *Brown* addressed these facts of life by observing that whatever may have been the understanding in *Plessy*'s time of the power of segregation to stigmatize those who were segregated with a "badge of inferiority," it was clear by 1954 that legally sanctioned segregation had just such an effect, to the point that racially separate public educational facilities were deemed inherently unequal. Society's understanding of the facts upon which a constitutional ruling was sought in 1954 was thus fundamentally different from the basis claimed for the decision in 1896. While we think *Plessy* was wrong the day it was decided, see *Plessy* (Harlan, J., dissenting), we must also recognize that the *Plessy* Court's explanation for its decision was so clearly at odds with the facts apparent to the Court in 1954 that the decision to reexamine *Plessy* was on this ground alone not only justified but required.

West Coast Hotel and *Brown* each rested on facts, or an understanding of facts, changed from those which furnished the claimed justifications for the earlier constitutional resolutions. Each case was comprehensible as the Court's response to facts that the country could understand, or had come to understand already, but which the Court of an earlier day, as its own declarations disclosed, had not been able to perceive. As the decisions were thus comprehensible they were also defensible, not merely as the victories of one doctrinal school over another by dint of numbers (victories though they were), but as applications of constitutional principle to facts as they had not been seen by the Court before. In constitutional adjudication as elsewhere in life, changed circumstances may impose new obligations, and the thoughtful part of the Nation could accept each decision to overrule a prior case as a response to the Court's constitutional duty.

Because the case before us presents no such occasion it could be seen as no such response. Because neither the factual underpinnings of *Roe*'s central holding nor our understanding of it has changed (and because no other indication of weakened precedent has been shown) the Court could not pretend to be reexamining the prior law with any justification beyond a present doctrinal disposition to come out differently from the Court of 1973. To overrule prior law for no other reason than that would run counter to the view repeated in our cases, that a decision to overrule should rest on some special reason over and above the belief that a prior case was wrongly decided. . . .

C

The examination of the conditions justifying the repudiation of *Adkins* by *West Coast Hotel* and *Plessy* by *Brown* is enough to suggest the terrible price that would have been paid if the Court had not overruled as it did. In the present case, however, as our analysis to this point makes clear, the terrible price would be paid for overruling. Our analysis would not be complete, however, without explaining why overruling *Roe*'s central holding would not only reach an unjustifiable result under principles of stare decisis, but would seriously weaken the Court's capacity to exercise the judicial power and to function as the Supreme Court of a Nation dedicated to the rule of law.

[The] need for principled action to be perceived as such is implicated to some degree whenever this, or any other appellate court, overrules a prior case. [In] two circumstances, however, the Court would almost certainly fail to receive the benefit of the doubt in overruling prior cases. There is, first, a point beyond which frequent overruling would overtax the country's belief in the Court's good faith. [That] first circumstance can be described as hypothetical; the second is to the point here and now. Where, in the performance of its judicial duties, the Court decides a case in such a way as to resolve the sort of intensely divisive controversy reflected in *Roe* and those rare, comparable cases, its decision has a dimension that the resolution of the normal case does not carry. It is the dimension present whenever the Court's interpretation of the Constitution calls the contending sides of a national controversy to end their national division by accepting a common mandate rooted in the Constitution. [To] overrule under fire in the absence of the most compelling reason to reexamine a watershed decision would subvert the Court's legitimacy beyond any serious question. [A] decision to overrule *Roe*'s essential holding under the existing circumstances would address error, if error there was, at the cost of both profound and unnecessary damage to the Court's legitimacy, and to the Nation's commitment to the rule of law. It is therefore imperative to adhere to the essence of *Roe*'s original decision, and we do so today.

IV

[The] woman's liberty is not so unlimited, however, that from the outset the State cannot show its concern for the life of the unborn, and at a later point in fetal development the State's interest in life has sufficient force so that the right of the woman to terminate the pregnancy can be restricted.

[We] conclude the line should be drawn at viability, so that before that time the woman has a right to choose to terminate her pregnancy. We adhere to this principle for two reasons. First, as we have said, is the doctrine of stare decisis. [The] second reason is that the concept of viability, as we noted in *Roe*, is the time at which there is a realistic possibility of maintaining and nourishing a life outside the womb, so that the independent existence of the second life can in reason and all fairness be the object of state protection that now overrides the rights of the woman. . . .

On the other side of the equation is the interest of the State in the protection of potential life. [It] must be remembered that Roe v. Wade speaks with clarity in establishing not only the woman's liberty but also the State's "important and legitimate interest in potential life." That portion of the decision in *Roe* has been given too little acknowledgement and implementation by the Court in its subsequent cases. [We] reject the trimester framework, which we do not consider to be part of the essential holding of *Roe*. [The] trimester framework suffers from these basic flaws: in its formulation it misconceives the nature of the pregnant woman's interest; and in practice it undervalues the State's interest in potential life, as recognized in *Roe*. . . .

[These] considerations of the nature of the abortion right illustrate that it is an overstatement to describe it as a right to decide whether to have an abortion "without interference from the State." [Not] all governmental intrusion is of necessity unwarranted; and that brings us to the other basic flaw in the trimester framework: even in *Roe's* terms, in practice it undervalues the State's interest in the potential life within the woman. . . .

[Not] all burdens on the right to decide whether to terminate a pregnancy will be undue. In our view, the undue burden standard is the appropriate means of reconciling the State's interest with the woman's constitutionally protected liberty. . . .

A finding of an undue burden is a shorthand for the conclusion that a state regulation has the purpose or effect of placing a substantial obstacle in the path of a woman seeking an abortion of a nonviable fetus. A statute with this purpose is invalid because the means chosen by the State to further the interest in potential life must be calculated to inform the woman's free choice, not hinder it. And a statute which, while furthering the interest in potential life or some other valid state interest, has the effect of placing a substantial obstacle in the path of a woman's choice cannot be considered a permissible means of serving its legitimate ends. [Understood] another way, we answer the question, left open in previous opinions discussing the undue burden formulation, whether a law designed to further the State's interest in fetal life which imposes an undue burden on the woman's decision before fetal viability could be constitutional. The answer is no.

Some guiding principles should emerge. What is at stake is the woman's right to make the ultimate decision, not a right to be insulated from all others in doing so. Regulations which do no more than create a structural mechanism by which the State, or the parent or guardian of a minor, may express profound respect for the life of the unborn are permitted, if they are not a substantial obstacle to the woman's exercise of the right to choose. Unless it has that effect on her right of choice, a state measure designed to persuade her to choose childbirth over abortion will be upheld if reasonably related to that goal. Regulations designed to foster the health of a woman seeking an abortion are valid if they do not constitute an undue burden.

[We] give this summary:

(a) To protect the central right recognized by Roe v. Wade while at the same time accommodating the State's profound interest in potential life, we will employ the undue burden analysis as explained in this opinion. An undue burden exists, and therefore a provision of law is invalid, if its purpose or effect is to place a substantial obstacle in the path of a woman seeking an abortion before the fetus attains viability.

(b) We reject the rigid trimester framework of Roe v. Wade. To promote the State's profound interest in potential life, throughout pregnancy the State may take measures to ensure that the woman's choice is informed, and measures designed to advance this interest will not be invalidated as long as their purpose is to persuade the woman to choose childbirth over abortion. These measures must not be an undue burden on the right.

(c) As with any medical procedure, the State may enact regulations to further the health or safety of a woman seeking an abortion. Unnecessary health regulations that have the purpose or effect of presenting a substantial obstacle to a woman seeking an abortion impose an undue burden on the right.

(d) Our adoption of the undue burden analysis does not disturb the central holding of Roe v. Wade, and we reaffirm that holding. Regardless of whether exceptions are made for particular circumstances, a State may not prohibit any woman from making the ultimate decision to terminate her pregnancy before viability.

(e) We also reaffirm *Roe*'s holding that "subsequent to viability, the State in promoting its interest in the potentiality of human life may, if it chooses, regulate, and even proscribe, abortion except where it is necessary, in appropriate medical judgment, for the preservation of the life or health of the mother."

V

A

Because it is central to the operation of various other requirements, we begin with the statute's definition of medical emergency. Under the statute, a medical emergency is

> that condition which, on the basis of the physician's good faith clinical judgment, so complicates the medical condition of a pregnant woman as to necessitate the immediate abortion of her pregnancy to avert her death or for which a delay will create serious risk of substantial and irreversible impairment of a major bodily function.

[The] District Court found that there were three serious conditions which would not be covered by the statute: preeclampsia, inevitable abortion, and premature ruptured membrane. Yet, as the Court of Appeals observed, it is undisputed that under some circumstances each of these conditions could lead to an illness with substantial and irreversible consequences. While the definition could be interpreted in an unconstitutional manner, the Court of Appeals construed the phrase "serious risk" to include those circumstances. [We] conclude that, as construed by the Court of Appeals, the medical emergency definition imposes no undue burden on a woman's abortion right.

B

[Except] in a medical emergency, the statute requires that at least 24 hours before performing an abortion a physician inform the woman of the nature of the procedure, the health risks of the abortion and of childbirth, and the "probable gestational age of the unborn child." The physician or a qualified nonphysician must inform the woman of the availability of printed materials published by the State describing the fetus and providing information about medical assistance for childbirth, information about child support from the father, and a list of agencies which provide adoption and other services as alternatives to abortion. An abortion may not be performed unless the woman certifies in writing that she has been informed of the availability of these printed materials and has been provided them if she chooses to view them. . . .

To the extent *Akron I* [i.e., *City of Akron*] and *Thornburgh* find a constitutional violation when the government requires, as it does here, the giving of truthful, nonmisleading information about the nature of the procedure, the attendant health risks and those of childbirth, and the "probable gestational age" of the fetus, those cases go too far, are inconsistent with *Roe*'s acknowledgment of an important interest in potential life, and are overruled. [In] attempting to ensure that a woman apprehend the full consequences of her decision, the State furthers the legitimate purpose of reducing the risk that a woman may elect an abortion, only to discover later, with devastating psychological consequences, that her decision was not fully informed. If the information the State requires to be made available to the woman is truthful and not misleading, the requirement may be permissible.

We also see no reason why the State may not require doctors to inform a woman seeking an abortion of the availability of materials relating to the consequences to the fetus, even when those consequences have no direct relation to her health. . . .

All that is left of petitioners' argument is an asserted First Amendment right of a physician not to provide information about the risks of abortion, and childbirth, in a manner mandated by the State. To be sure, the physician's First Amendment rights not to speak are implicated, but only as part of the practice of medicine, subject to reasonable licensing and regulation by the State. We see no constitutional infirmity in the requirement that the physician provide the information mandated by the State here.

The Pennsylvania statute also requires us to reconsider the holding in *Akron I* that the State may not require that a physician, as opposed to a qualified assistant, provide information relevant to a woman's informed consent. Since there is no evidence on this record that requiring a doctor to give the information as provided by the statute would amount in practical terms to a substantial obstacle to a woman seeking an abortion, we conclude that it is not an undue burden. . . .

[In] *Akron I* we said: "Nor are we convinced that the State's legitimate concern that the woman's decision be informed is reasonably served by requiring a 24-hour delay as a matter of course." We consider that conclusion to be wrong. The idea that important decisions will be more informed and deliberate if they follow some period of reflection does not strike us as unreasonable, particularly where the statute directs that important information become part of the background of the decision. . . .

Whether the mandatory 24-hour waiting period is nonetheless invalid because in practice it is a substantial obstacle to a woman's choice to terminate her pregnancy is a closer question. The findings of fact by the District Court indicate that because of the distances many women must travel to reach an abortion provider, the practical effect will often be a delay of much more than a day because the waiting period requires that a woman seeking an abortion make at least two visits to the doctor. The District Court also found that in many instances this will increase the exposure of women seeking abortions to "the harassment and hostility of anti-abortion protestors demonstrating outside a clinic." As a result, the District Court found that for those women who have the fewest financial resources, those who must travel long distances, and those who have difficulty explaining their whereabouts to husbands, employers, or others, the 24-hour waiting period will be "particularly burdensome."

These findings are troubling in some respects, but they do not demonstrate that the waiting period constitutes an undue burden. [As] we have stated, under the undue burden standard a State is permitted to enact persuasive measures which favor childbirth over abortion, even if those measures do not further a health interest. And while the waiting period does limit a physician's discretion, that is not, standing alone, a reason to invalidate it.

We also disagree with the District Court's conclusion that the "particularly burdensome" effects of the waiting period on some women require its invalidation....

We are left with the argument that the various aspects of the informed consent requirement are unconstitutional because they place barriers in the way of abortion on demand. Even the broadest reading of Roe, however, has not suggested that there is a constitutional right to abortion on demand. Rather, the right protected by Roe is a right to decide to terminate a pregnancy free of undue interference by the State. Because the informed consent requirement facilitates the wise exercise of that right it cannot be classified as an interference with the right Roe protects. The informed consent requirement is not an undue burden on that right.

C

Section 3209 of Pennsylvania's abortion law provides, except in cases of medical emergency, that no physician shall perform an abortion on a married woman without receiving a signed statement from the woman that she has notified her spouse that she is about to undergo an abortion. The woman has the option of providing an alternative signed statement certifying that her husband is not the man who impregnated her; that her husband could not be located; that the pregnancy is the result of spousal sexual assault which she has reported; or that the woman believes that notifying her husband will cause him or someone else to inflict bodily injury upon her. A physician who performs an abortion on a married woman without receiving the appropriate signed statement will have his or her license revoked, and is liable to the husband for damages.

The District Court heard the testimony of numerous expert witnesses, and made detailed findings of fact regarding the effect of this statute. These included:

> [279.] The "bodily injury" exception could not be invoked by a married woman whose husband, if notified, would, in her reasonable belief, threaten to (a) publicize her intent to have an abortion to family, friends or acquaintances; (b) retaliate against her in future child custody or divorce proceedings; (c) inflict psychological intimidation or emotional harm upon her, her children or other persons; (d) inflict bodily harm on other persons such as children, family members or other loved ones; or (e) use his control over finances to deprive of necessary monies for herself or her children....
>
> 281. Studies reveal that family violence occurs in two million families in the United States. This figure, however, is a conservative one that substantially under-

states (because battering is usually not reported until it reaches life-threatening proportions) the actual number of families affected by domestic violence. In fact, researchers estimate that one of every two women will be battered at some time in their life. . . .

282. A wife may not elect to notify her husband of her intention to have an abortion for a variety of reasons, including the husband's illness, concern about her own health, the imminent failure of the marriage, or the husband's absolute opposition to the abortion. . . .

[286.] Married women, victims of battering, have been killed in Pennsylvania and throughout the United States. . . .

[289.] Mere notification of pregnancy is frequently a flashpoint for battering and violence within the family. The number of battering incidents is high during the pregnancy and often the worst abuse can be associated with pregnancy. . . . The battering husband may deny parentage and use the pregnancy as an excuse for abuse. . . .

290. Secrecy typically shrouds abusive families. Family members are instructed not to tell anyone, especially police or doctors, about the abuse and violence. Battering husbands often threaten their wives or her children with further abuse if she tells an outsider of the violence and tells her that nobody will believe her. A battered woman, therefore, is highly unlikely to disclose the violence against her for fear of retaliation by the abuser. . . .

[298.] Because of the nature of the battering relationship, battered women are unlikely to avail themselves of the exceptions to section 3209 of the Act, regardless of whether the section applies to them.

These findings are supported by studies of domestic violence. [There] are millions of women in this country who are the victims of regular physical and psychological abuse at the hands of their husbands. Should these women become pregnant, they may have very good reasons for not wishing to inform their husbands of their decision to obtain an abortion. . . .

[Respondents] attempt to avoid the conclusion that §3209 is invalid by pointing out that [the] effects of §3209 are felt by only one percent of the women who obtain abortions. [We] disagree with respondents' basic method of analysis.

The analysis does not end with one percent of women upon whom the statute operates; it begins there. Legislation is measured for consistency with the Constitution by its impact on those whose conduct it affects. [The] unfortunate yet persisting conditions we document above will mean that in a large fraction of the cases in which §3209 is relevant, it will operate as a substantial obstacle to a woman's choice to undergo an abortion. It is an undue burden, and therefore invalid.

This conclusion is in no way inconsistent with our decisions upholding parental notification or consent requirements. Those enactments, and our judgment that they are constitutional, are based on the quite reasonable assumption that minors will benefit from consultation with their parents and that children will often not realize that their parents have their best interests at heart. We cannot adopt a parallel assumption about adult women. . . .

Before birth, however, the issue takes on a very different cast. It is an inescapable biological fact that state regulation with respect to the child a woman is carrying will have a far greater impact on the mother's liberty than on the father's. The effect of state regulation on a woman's protected liberty is doubly deserving of scrutiny in such a case, as the State has touched not only upon the private sphere of the family but upon the very bodily integrity of the pregnant woman. The Court has held that "when the wife and the husband disagree on this decision, the view of only one of the two marriage partners can prevail. Inasmuch as it is the woman who physically bears the child and who is the more directly and immediately affected by the pregnancy, as between the two, the balance weighs in her favor." *Danforth*. This conclusion rests upon the basic nature of marriage and the nature of our Constitution: "The marital couple is not an independent entity with a mind and heart of its own, but an association of two individuals each with a separate intellectual and emotional makeup. If the right of privacy means anything, it is the right of the individual, married or single, to be free from unwarranted governmental intrusion into matters so fundamentally affecting a person as the decision whether to bear or beget a child." Eisenstadt v. Baird[, 405 U.S. 438 (1972)]. The Constitution protects individuals, men and women alike, from unjustified state interference, even when that interference is enacted into law for the benefit of their spouses.

[The] husband's interest in the life of the child his wife is carrying does not permit the State to empower him with this troubling degree of authority over his wife. The contrary view leads to consequences reminiscent of the common law. A husband has no enforceable right to require a wife to advise him before she exercises her personal choices. [A] State may not give to a man the kind of dominion over his wife that parents exercise over their children.

Section 3209 embodies a view of marriage consonant with the common-law status of married women but repugnant to our present understanding of marriage and of the nature of the rights secured by the Constitution. Women do not lose their constitutionally protected liberty when they marry. . . .

D

We next consider the parental consent provision. Except in a medical emergency, an unemancipated young woman under 18 may not obtain an abortion unless she and one of her parents (or guardian) provides informed consent as defined above. If neither a parent nor a guardian provides consent, a court may authorize the performance of an abortion upon a determination that the young woman is mature and capable of giving informed consent and has in fact given her informed consent, or that an abortion would be in her best interests. . . .

The only argument made by petitioners respecting this provision and to which our prior decisions do not speak is the contention that the parental consent requirement is invalid because it requires informed parental consent. For the most part, petitioners' argument is a reprise of their argument with respect to the informed consent requirement in general, and we reject it for the reasons given above. . . .

E

Under the recordkeeping and reporting requirements of the statute, every facility which performs abortions is required to file a report stating its name and address as well as the name and address of any related entity, such as a controlling or subsidiary organization. In the case of state-funded institutions, the information becomes public. . . .

In *Danforth*, we held that recordkeeping and reporting provisions "that are reasonably directed to the preservation of maternal health and that properly respect a patient's confidentiality and privacy are permissible." We think that under this standard, all the provisions at issue here except that relating to spousal notice are constitutional. Although they do not relate to the State's interest in informing the woman's choice, they do relate to health. The collection of information with respect to actual patients is a vital element of medical research, and so it cannot be said that the requirements serve no purpose other than to make abortions more difficult. Nor do we find that the requirements impose a substantial obstacle to a woman's choice. At most they might increase the cost of some abortions by a slight amount. While at some point increased cost could become a substantial obstacle, there is no such showing on the record before us. . . .

VI

Our Constitution is a covenant running from the first generation of Americans to us and then to future generations. It is a coherent succession. Each generation must learn anew that the Constitution's written terms embody ideas and aspirations that must survive more ages than one. We accept our responsibility not to retreat from interpreting the full meaning of the covenant in light of all of our precedents. We invoke it once again to define the freedom guaranteed by the Constitution's own promise, the promise of liberty.

JUSTICE BLACKMUN, concurring in part, concurring in the judgment in part, and dissenting in part. . . .

State restrictions on abortion violate a woman's right of privacy in two ways. First, compelled continuation of a pregnancy infringes upon a woman's right to bodily integrity by imposing substantial physical intrusions and significant risks of physical harm. During pregnancy, women experience dramatic physical changes and a wide range of health consequences. Labor and delivery pose additional health risks and physical demands. In short, restrictive abortion laws force women to endure physical invasions far more substantial than those this Court has held to violate the constitutional principle of bodily integrity in other contexts. See, e.g., Winston v. Lee, 470 U.S. 753 (1985) (invalidating surgical removal of bullet from murder suspect); Rochin v. California, 342 U.S. 165 (1952) (invalidating stomach-pumping).

Further, when the State restricts a woman's right to terminate her pregnancy, it deprives a woman of the right to make her own decision about reproduction and family planning — critical life choices that this Court long has deemed central to the right to privacy. . . .

A State's restrictions on a woman's right to terminate her pregnancy also implicate constitutional guarantees of gender equality. State restrictions on abortion compel women to continue pregnancies they otherwise might terminate. By restricting the right to terminate pregnancies, the State conscripts women's bodies into its service, forcing women to continue their pregnancies, suffer the pains of childbirth, and in most instances, provide years of maternal care. The State does not compensate women for their services; instead, it assumes that they owe this duty as a matter of course. This assumption — that women can simply be forced to accept the "natural" status and incidents of motherhood — appears to rest upon a conception of women's role that has triggered the protection of the Equal

Protection Clause. The joint opinion recognizes that these assumptions about women's place in society "are no longer consistent with our understanding of the family, the individual, or the Constitution." . . .

The 24-hour waiting period following the provision of the foregoing information is [clearly] unconstitutional. [The] Pennsylvania statute requires every facility performing abortions to report its activities to the Commonwealth. [The] Commonwealth attempts to justify its required reports on the ground that the public has a right to know how its tax dollars are spent. A regulation designed to inform the public about public expenditures does not further the Commonwealth's interest in protecting maternal health. Accordingly, such a regulation cannot justify a legally significant burden on a woman's right to obtain an abortion. . . .

JUSTICE STEVENS, concurring in part and dissenting in part. . . .

[The] societal costs of overruling *Roe* at this late date would be enormous. *Roe* is an integral part of a correct understanding of both the concept of liberty and the basic equality of men and women. . . .

My disagreement with the joint opinion begins with its understanding of the trimester framework established in *Roe*. [It] is not a "contradiction" to recognize that the State may have a legitimate interest in potential human life and, at the same time, to conclude that that interest does not justify the regulation of abortion before viability (although other interests, such as maternal health, may). The fact that the State's interest is legitimate does not tell us when, if ever, that interest outweighs the pregnant woman's interest in personal liberty. It is appropriate, therefore, to consider more carefully the nature of the interests at stake.

First, it is clear that, in order to be legitimate, the State's interest must be secular; consistent with the First Amendment the State may not promote a theological or sectarian interest. . . .

Identifying the State's interests — which the States rarely articulate with any precision — makes clear that the interest in protecting potential life is not grounded in the Constitution. It is, instead, an indirect interest supported by both humanitarian and pragmatic concerns. Many of our citizens believe that any abortion reflects an unacceptable disrespect for potential human life and that the performance of more than a million abortions each year is intolerable; many find third-trimester abortions performed when the fetus is approaching personhood particularly offensive. The State has a legitimate interest in minimizing such offense. The State may also have a broader interest in expanding the population, believing society would benefit from the services of additional productive citizens — or that the potential human lives might include the occasional Mozart or Curie.

[Under] these principles, §§3205(a)(2)(i)-(iii) of the Pennsylvania statute are unconstitutional. Those sections require a physician or counselor to provide the woman with a range of materials clearly designed to persuade her to choose not to undergo the abortion. While the State is free, pursuant to §3208 of the Pennsylvania law, to produce and disseminate such material, the State may not inject such information into the woman's deliberations just as she is weighing such an important choice.

Under this same analysis, §§3205(a)(1)(i) and (iii) of the Pennsylvania statute are constitutional. Those sections, which require the physician to inform a woman of the nature and risks of the abortion procedure and the medical risks of carrying to term, are neutral requirements comparable to those imposed in other medical procedures. Those sections indicate no effort by the State to influence the woman's choice in any way. If anything, such requirements enhance, rather than skew, the woman's decisionmaking.

The 24-hour waiting period required by §§3205(a)(1)-(2) of the Pennsylvania statute raises even more serious concerns. Such a requirement arguably furthers the State's interests in two ways, neither of which is constitutionally permissible.

In my opinion, a correct application of the "undue burden" standard leads to the same conclusion concerning the constitutionality of these requirements. A state-imposed burden on the exercise of a constitutional right is measured both by its effects and by its character: A burden may be "undue" either because the burden is too severe or because it lacks a legitimate, rational justification.

The 24-hour delay requirement fails both parts of this test. . . . The counseling provisions are similarly infirm. Whenever government commands private citizens to speak or to listen, careful review of the justification for that command is particularly appropriate. In this case, the Pennsylvania statute directs that counselors provide women seeking abortions with information concerning alternatives to abortion, the availability of medical assistance benefits, and the possibility of child-support payments. The statute requires that this information be given to all women seeking abortions, including those for whom such information is clearly useless, such as those who are married, those who have undergone the procedure in the past and are fully aware of the options, and those who are fully convinced that abortion is their only reasonable option. Moreover, the statute requires physicians to inform all of their patients of "the probable gestational age of the unborn child." This information is of little decisional value in most cases, because 90% of all abortions are performed during the first trimester when fetal age has less relevance than when the fetus nears viability. . . .

CHIEF JUSTICE REHNQUIST, with whom JUSTICE WHITE, JUSTICE SCALIA, and JUSTICE THOMAS join, concurring in the judgment in part and dissenting in part.

The joint opinion, following its newly-minted variation on stare decisis, retains the outer shell of Roe v. Wade, but beats a wholesale retreat from the substance of that case. We believe that Roe was wrongly decided, and that it can and should be overruled consistently with our traditional approach to stare decisis in constitutional cases. We would adopt the approach of the plurality in Webster v. Reproductive Health Services, and uphold the challenged provisions of the Pennsylvania statute in their entirety.

I

[Unlike] marriage, procreation and contraception, abortion "involves the purposeful termination of potential life." Harris v. McRae, 448 U.S. 297, 325 (1980). [One] cannot ignore the fact that a woman is not isolated in her pregnancy, and that the decision to abort necessarily involves the destruction of a fetus.

Nor do the historical traditions of the American people support the view that the right to terminate one's pregnancy is "fundamental." The common law which we inherited from England made abortion after "quickening" an offense. At the time of the adoption of the Fourteenth Amendment, statutory prohibitions or restrictions on abortion were commonplace; in 1868, at least 28 of the then-37

States and 8 Territories had statutes banning or limiting abortion. By the turn
of the century virtually every State had a law prohibiting or restricting abortion
on its books. By the middle of the present century, a liberalization trend had set
in. But 21 of the restrictive abortion laws in effect in 1868 were still in effect in
1973 when *Roe* was decided, and an overwhelming majority of the States prohibited abortion unless necessary to preserve the life or health of the mother.

[We] think, therefore, both in view of this history and of our decided cases dealing with substantive liberty under the Due Process Clause, that the Court was
mistaken in *Roe* when it classified a woman's decision to terminate her pregnancy
as a "fundamental right" that could be abridged only in a manner which with-
stood "strict scrutiny."

II

[The] joint opinion [cannot] bring itself to say that *Roe* was correct as an original
matter, but the authors are of the view that "the immediate question is not the
soundness of *Roe's* resolution of the issue, but the precedential force that must
be accorded to its holding." Instead of claiming that *Roe* was correct as a matter
of original constitutional interpretation, the opinion therefore contains an elaborate discussion of stare decisis. This discussion of the principle of stare decisis
appears to be almost entirely dicta, because the joint opinion does not apply that
principle in dealing with *Roe*. *Roe* decided that a woman had a fundamental
right to an abortion. The joint opinion rejects that view. *Roe* decided that abortion regulations were to be subjected to "strict scrutiny" and could be justified
only in the light of "compelling state interests." The joint opinion rejects that
view. *Roe* analyzed abortion regulation under a rigid trimester framework, a
framework which has guided this Court's decisionmaking for 19 years. The joint
opinion rejects that framework.

[In] our view, authentic principles of stare decisis do not require that any portion of the reasoning in *Roe* be kept intact. [Erroneous] decisions in such constitutional cases are uniquely durable, because correction through legislative action, save for constitutional amendment, is impossible. . . .

The joint opinion discusses several stare decisis factors which, it asserts, point
toward retaining a portion of *Roe*. Two of these factors are that the main "factual
underpinning" of *Roe* has remained the same, and that its doctrinal foundation
is no weaker now than it was in 1973. Of course, what might be called the basic
facts which gave rise to *Roe* have remained the same — women become pregnant,
there is a point somewhere, depending on medical technology, where a fetus becomes viable, and women give birth to children. But this is only to say that the
same facts which gave rise to *Roe* will continue to give rise to similar cases. It is
not a reason, in and of itself, why those cases must be decided in the same incorrect manner as was the first case to deal with the question. . . .

The joint opinion also points to the reliance interests involved in this context
in its effort to explain why precedent must be followed for precedent's sake. Certainly it is true that where reliance is truly at issue, as in the case of judicial decisions that have formed the basis for private decisions, "considerations in favor of
stare decisis are at their acme." But, as the joint opinion apparently agrees, ante,
any traditional notion of reliance is not applicable here.

[Apparently] realizing that conventional stare decisis principles do not support its position, the joint opinion advances a belief that retaining a portion of *Roe* is necessary to protect the "legitimacy" of this Court. Because the Court must take care to render decisions "grounded truly in principle," and not simply as political and social compromises, the joint opinion properly declares it to be this Court's duty to ignore the public criticism and protest that may arise as a result of a decision.

[But] the joint opinion goes on to state that when the Court "resolves the sort of intensely divisive controversy reflected in *Roe* and those rare, comparable cases," its decision is exempt from reconsideration under established principles of stare decisis in constitutional cases. [The] first difficulty with this principle lies in its assumption that cases which are "intensely divisive" can be readily distinguished from those that are not. The question of whether a particular issue is "intensely divisive" enough to qualify for special protection is entirely subjective and dependent on the individual assumptions of the members of this Court.

[The] joint opinion picks out and discusses two prior Court rulings that it believes are of the "intensely divisive" variety, and concludes that they are of comparable dimension to *Roe*. It appears to us very odd indeed that the joint opinion chooses as benchmarks two cases in which the Court chose not to adhere to erroneous constitutional precedent, but instead enhanced its stature by acknowledging and correcting its error, apparently in violation of the joint opinion's "legitimacy" principle. . . .

The joint opinion agrees that the Court's stature would have been seriously damaged if in *Brown* and *West Coast Hotel* it had dug in its heels and refused to apply normal principles of stare decisis to the earlier decisions. But the opinion contends that the Court was entitled to overrule *Plessy* and *Lochner* in those cases, despite the existence of opposition to the original decisions, only because both the Nation and the Court had learned new lessons in the interim. This is at best a feebly supported, post hoc rationalization for those decisions.

For example, the opinion asserts that the Court could justifiably overrule its decision in *Lochner* only because the Depression had convinced "most people" that constitutional protection of contractual freedom contributed to an economy that failed to protect the welfare of all. Surely the joint opinion does not mean to suggest that people saw this Court's failure to uphold minimum wage statutes as the cause of the Great Depression! In any event, the *Lochner* Court did not base its rule upon the policy judgment that an unregulated market was fundamental to a stable economy; it simply believed, erroneously, that "liberty" under the Due Process Clause protected the "right to make a contract." Lochner v. New York, 198 U.S., at 53. Nor is it the case that the people of this Nation only discovered the dangers of extreme laissez faire economics because of the Depression. . . .

When the Court finally recognized its error in *West Coast Hotel*, it did not engage in the post hoc rationalization that the joint opinion attributes to it today; it did not state that *Lochner* had been based on an economic view that had fallen into disfavor, and that it therefore should be overruled. Chief Justice Hughes in his opinion for the Court simply recognized what Justice Holmes had previously recognized in his *Lochner* dissent, that "the Constitution does not speak of freedom of contract."

[The] Court in *Brown* simply recognized, as Justice Harlan had recognized beforehand, that the Fourteenth Amendment does not permit racial segregation.

The rule of *Brown* is not tied to popular opinion about the evils of segregation; it is a judgment that the Equal Protection Clause does not permit racial segregation, no matter whether the public might come to believe that it is beneficial. . . .

[A] woman's interest in having an abortion is a form of liberty protected by the Due Process Clause, but States may regulate abortion procedures in ways rationally related to a legitimate state interest. With this rule in mind, we examine each of the challenged provisions. . . .

The question before us is therefore whether the spousal notification requirement rationally furthers any legitimate state interests. We conclude that it does. First, a husband's interests in procreation within marriage and in the potential life of his unborn child are certainly substantial ones. [By] providing that a husband will usually know of his spouse's intent to have an abortion, the provision makes it more likely that the husband will participate in deciding the fate of his unborn child, a possibility that might otherwise have been denied him. This participation might in some cases result in a decision to proceed with the pregnancy.

[The] State also has a legitimate interest in promoting "the integrity of the marital relationship." [In] our view, the spousal notice requirement is a rational attempt by the State to improve truthful communication between spouses and encourage collaborative decisionmaking, and thereby fosters marital integrity.

[We would] hold that each of the challenged provisions of the Pennsylvania statute is consistent with the Constitution. It bears emphasis that our conclusion in this regard does not carry with it any necessary approval of these regulations. Our task is, as always, to decide only whether the challenged provisions of a law comport with the United States Constitution. If, as we believe, these do, their wisdom as a matter of public policy is for the people of Pennsylvania to decide.

JUSTICE SCALIA, with whom THE CHIEF JUSTICE, JUSTICE WHITE, and JUSTICE THOMAS join, concurring in the judgment in part and dissenting in part. . . .

[The] issue in this case: not whether the power of a woman to abort her unborn child is a "liberty" in the absolute sense; or even whether it is a liberty of great importance to many women. Of course it is both. The issue is whether it is a liberty protected by the Constitution of the United States. I am sure it is not. I reach that conclusion [for] the same reason I reach the conclusion that bigamy is not constitutionally protected — because of two simple facts: (1) the Constitution says absolutely nothing about it, and (2) the longstanding traditions of American society have permitted it to be legally proscribed.

[Applying] the rational basis test, I would uphold the Pennsylvania statute in its entirety. I must, however, respond to a few of the more outrageous arguments in today's opinion, which it is beyond human nature to leave unanswered.

[The] Court's description of the place of *Roe* in the social history of the United States is unrecognizable. Not only did *Roe* not, as the Court suggests, resolve the deeply divisive issue of abortion; it did more than anything else to nourish it, by elevating it to the national level where it is infinitely more difficult to resolve. National politics were not plagued by abortion protests, national abortion lobbying, or abortion marches on Congress, before Roe v. Wade was decided. Profound disagreement existed among our citizens over the issue — as it does over other issues, such as the death penalty — but that disagreement was being worked out at the state level. As with many other issues, the division of sentiment within each State was not as closely balanced as it was among the population of the Nation as a whole, meaning not only that more people would be satisfied with the results of state-by-state resolution, but also that those results would be more stable. Pre-*Roe*, moreover, political compromise was possible.

Roe's mandate for abortion-on-demand destroyed the compromises of the past, rendered compromise impossible for the future, and required the entire issue to be resolved uniformly, at the national level. At the same time, *Roe* created a vast new class of abortion consumers and abortion proponents by eliminating the moral opprobrium that had attached to the act. ("If the Constitution guarantees abortion, how can it be bad?" — not an accurate line of thought, but a natural one.) Many favor all of those developments, and it is not for me to say that they are wrong. But to portray *Roe* as the statesmanlike "settlement" of a divisive issue, a jurisprudential Peace of Westphalia that is worth preserving, is nothing less than Orwellian. *Roe* fanned into life an issue that has inflamed our national politics in general, and has obscured with its smoke the selection of Justices to this Court in particular, ever since.

[What] makes all this relevant to the bothersome application of "political pressure" against the Court are the twin facts that the American people love democracy and the American people are not fools. As long as this Court thought (and the people thought) that we Justices were doing essentially lawyers' work up here — reading text and discerning our society's traditional understanding of that text — the public pretty much left us alone. Texts and traditions are facts to study, not convictions to demonstrate about.

[There] is a poignant aspect to the Court's opinion. Its length, and what might be called its epic tone, suggest that its authors believe they are bringing to an end a troublesome era in the history of our Nation and of our Court. "It is the dimension" of authority, they say, to "call the contending sides of national controversy to end their national division by accepting a common mandate rooted in the Constitution."

There comes vividly to mind a portrait by Emanuel Leutze that hangs in the Harvard Law School: Roger Brooke Taney, painted in 1859, the 82d year of his life, the 24th of his Chief Justiceship, the second after his opinion in *Dred Scott*. He is all in black, sitting in a shadowed red armchair, left hand resting upon a pad of paper in his lap, right hand hanging limply, almost lifelessly, beside the inner arm of the chair. He sits facing the viewer, and staring straight out. There seems to be on his face, and in his deep-set eyes, an expression of profound sadness and disillusionment. Perhaps he always looked that way, even when dwelling upon the happiest of thoughts. But those of us who know how the lustre of his great Chief Justiceship came to be eclipsed by *Dred Scott* cannot help believing that he had that case — its already apparent consequences for the Court, and its soon-to-be-played-out consequences for the Nation — burning on his mind. I expect that two years earlier he, too, had thought himself "calling the contending sides of national controversy to end their national division by accepting a common mandate rooted in the Constitution."

It is no more realistic for us in this case, than it was for him in that, to think that an issue of the sort they both involved — an issue involving life and death, freedom and subjugation — can be "speedily and finally settled" by the Supreme Court, as President James Buchanan in his inaugural address said the issue of slavery in the territories would be. Quite to the contrary, by foreclosing all democratic outlet for the deep passions this issue arouses, by banishing the issue from the political forum that gives all participants, even the losers, the satisfaction of a fair hearing and an honest fight, by continuing the imposition of a rigid national rule instead of allowing for regional differences, the Court merely prolongs and intensifies the anguish.

We should get out of this area, where we have no right to be, and where we do neither ourselves nor the country any good by remaining.

Note: Casey *and the Role of the Court*

1. *Politics and judicial independence. Casey* raises a number of important issues about stare decisis, liberty, equality, and the role of the Court in general. Note first that five of the justices on the *Casey* Court were appointed by Presidents Reagan and Bush, both sharp critics of *Roe*. Does the decision contain lessons about the power of the President to remake the Court? Does it suggest that law does indeed operate in a way that is independent of politics?

2. *Stare decisis and constitutional history.* Consider the discussion in the lead opinion of what happened between *Lochner* and *West Coast Hotel,* and between *Plessy* and *Brown.* Exactly what, in the authors' opinions, changed in the relevant period? Much, in their view, appears to have turned on some change in "the facts," or in social understanding of "the facts." What is the difference between a change in "facts" and a change in "understanding of facts"? Perhaps what really changed was simply values; changes in values often produce changes in understandings of facts.

Consider the following views:

a. The justices are really saying something deeply true: that *Lochner* was wrong because the system of laissez-faire disserved human liberty, and that *Plessy* was wrong because the social stigma of segregation was misattributed to black people when it should have been attributed to the law. Both of the cases thus depended on judgments that could not long be supported. *West Coast Hotel* and *Brown* were important corrections here. They saw that regulatory improvements on laissez-faire could serve human liberty, and that segregation was a system of second-class citizenship for blacks.

b. In discussing *Lochner* and *Plessy,* the justices are not thinking enough about whether the specific constitutional provision justified these decisions. The problem with *Lochner* was the Court's creation of aggressive substantive due process (the same problem as in *Roe*). The problem with *Plessy* was that the Court wrongly allowed racial segregation under the equal protection clause. None of this has to do with changes or with new facts. See in this regard the views on *Lochner* and *Plessy* in the dissenting opinions.

3. *Abortion and gender equality.* Note that Justice Blackmun, Justice Stevens, and the joint opinion all refer to equality on the basis of gender and to the relationship between the *Roe* right and gender equality. Is there now an argument that restrictions on abortion implicate the equal protection clause? What is it, and what implications might it have for other areas of constitutional law? See in this regard Strauss, Abortion, Toleration, and Moral Uncertainty, 1993 Sup. Ct. Rev. 1, 27: "The Court in *Casey* addressed, essentially for the first time, the issues that ought to be central to the legal debate over abortion: not whether there are 'unenumerated rights' in the Constitution, but how to deal with fetal life, on the

one hand, and the effect of abortion laws on the status of women, on the other. [T]he Court adopted [a] plausible and coherent justification for a regime of toleration in the area of abortion. That justification is premised on, first, fundamental moral uncertainty about the status of fetal life; and, second, the danger that the political process will subordinate women, a danger that is the basis of the well-established constitutional principles governing gender discrimination." Strauss grounds this argument on a claim for tolerance in the face of moral uncertainty — a claim that, on his view, is analogous to the claim for tolerance in the religious setting. The question of the role of religion in this setting is taken up in detail in R. Dworkin, Life's Dominion (1993), which argues on behalf of the abortion right on the basis of the "essentially religious" nature of the key question, which is the sanctity of human life.

4. *Roe and the democratic process.* Has the experience with *Roe* really been healthy for the country, for democracy, or for women? Is it appropriate for the confirmation hearings to focus a great deal on likely votes on *Roe?* Is it appropriate for presidential elections to turn a great deal on the likely votes of Supreme Court nominees? Might social fragmentation have been produced, not alleviated, by *Roe* and (now) *Casey?*

Stenberg v. Carhart

120 S. Ct. 2597 (2000)

JUSTICE BREYER delivered the opinion of the Court.

Three established principles determine the issue before us. We shall set them forth in the language of the joint opinion in *Casey.* First, before "viability . . . the woman has a right to choose to terminate her pregnancy." 505 U.S. at 870 (joint opinion of O'Connor, Kennedy, and Souter, JJ.).

Second, "a law designed to further the State's interest in fetal life which imposes an undue burden on the woman's decision before fetal viability" is unconstitutional. An "undue burden is . . . shorthand for the conclusion that a state regulation has the purpose or effect of placing a substantial obstacle in the path of a woman seeking an abortion of a nonviable fetus."

Third, "'subsequent to viability, the State in promoting its interest in the potentiality of human life may, if it chooses, regulate, and even proscribe, abortion except where it is necessary, in appropriate medical judgment, for the preservation of the life or health of the mother.'" 505 U.S. at 879 (quoting Roe v. Wade, 410 U.S. at 164-165).

We apply these principles to a Nebraska law banning "partial birth abortion." The statute reads as follows: "No partial birth abortion shall be performed in this state, unless such procedure is necessary to save the life of the mother whose life is endangered by a physical disorder, physical illness, or physical injury, including a life-endangering physical condition caused by or arising from the pregnancy itself."

The statute defines "partial birth abortion" as: "an abortion procedure in which the person performing the abortion partially delivers vaginally a living unborn child before killing the unborn child and completing the delivery."

It further defines "partially delivers vaginally a living unborn child before killing the unborn child" to mean "deliberately and intentionally delivering into the vagina a living unborn child, or a substantial portion thereof, for the purpose of performing a procedure that the person performing such procedure knows will kill the unborn child and does kill the unborn child."

The law classifies violation of the statute as a "Class III felony" carrying a prison term of up to 20 years, and a fine of up to $25,000. It also provides for the automatic revocation of a doctor's license to practice medicine in Nebraska.

We hold that this statute violates the Constitution.

I

[Because] Nebraska law seeks to ban one method of aborting a pregnancy, we must describe and then discuss several different abortion procedures. Considering the fact that those procedures seek to terminate a potential human life, our discussion may seem clinically cold or callous to some, perhaps horrifying to others. There is no alternative way, however, to acquaint the reader with the technical distinctions among different abortion methods and related factual matters, upon which the outcome of this case depends.

The evidence before the trial court, as supported or supplemented in the literature, indicates the following:

[1. About] 90% of all abortions performed in the United States take place during the first trimester of pregnancy, before 12 weeks of gestational age. Centers for Disease Control and Prevention, Abortion Surveillance — United States, 1996, p. 41 (July 30, 1999) (hereinafter Abortion Surveillance). During the first trimester, the predominant abortion method is "vacuum aspiration," which involves insertion of a vacuum tube (cannula) into the uterus to evacuate the contents. Such an abortion is typically performed on an outpatient basis under local anesthesia. 11 F. Supp. 2d at 1102; Obstetrics: Normal & Problem Pregnancies 1253-1254 (S. Gabbe, J. Niebyl, & J. Simpson eds. 3d ed. 1996). Vacuum aspiration is considered particularly safe. The procedure's mortality rates for first trimester abortion are, for example, 5 to 10 times lower than those associated with carrying the fetus to term. Complication rates are also low. Id. at 1251; Lawson et al., Abortion Mortality, United States, 1972 through 1987, 171 Am. J. Obstet. Gynecol. 1365, 1368 (1994); M. Paul, et al., A Clinicians Guide to Medical and Surgical Abortion 108-109 (1999) (hereinafter Medical and Surgical Abortion). As the fetus grows in size, however, the vacuum aspiration method becomes increasingly difficult to use.

2. Approximately 10% of all abortions are performed during the second trimester of pregnancy (12 to 24 weeks). [The] most commonly used procedure is called "dilation and evacuation" (D&E). That procedure (together with a modified form of vacuum aspiration used in the early second trimester) accounts for about 95% of all abortions performed from 12 to 20 weeks of gestational age. Abortion Surveillance 41.

3. D&E "refers generically to transcervical procedures performed at 13 weeks gestation or later." American Medical Association, Report of Board of Trustees on Late-Term Abortion, App. 490 (hereinafter AMA Report). The AMA Report, adopted by the District Court, describes the process as follows.

Between 13 and 15 weeks of gestation: "D&E is similar to vacuum aspiration except that the cervix must be dilated more widely because surgical instruments are used to remove larger pieces of tissue. Osmotic dilators are usually used. Intravenous fluids and an analgesic or sedative may be administered. A local anesthetic such as a paracervical block may be administered; dilating agents, if used, are removed and instruments are inserted through the cervix into the uterus to removal fetal and placental tissue. Because fetal tissue is friable and easily broken, the fetus may not be removed intact. The walls of the uterus are scraped with a curette to ensure that no tissue remains." Id. at 490-491.

After 15 weeks: "Because the fetus is larger at this stage of gestation (particularly the head), and because bones are more rigid, dismemberment or other destructive procedures are more likely to be required than at earlier gestational ages to remove fetal and placental tissue." Id. at 491.

After 20 weeks: "Some physicians use intrafetal potassium chloride or digoxin to induce fetal demise prior to a late D&E (after 20 weeks), to facilitate evacuation." Id. at 491-492.

There are variations in D&E operative strategy; compare ibid. with W. Hern, Abortion Practice 146-156 (1984), and Medical and Surgical Abortion 133-135. However, the common points are that D&E involves (1) dilation of the cervix; (2) removal of at least some fetal tissue using nonvacuum instruments; and (3) (after the 15th week) the potential need for instrumental disarticulation or dismemberment of the fetus or the collapse of fetal parts to facilitate evacuation from the uterus.

4. When instrumental disarticulation incident to D&E is necessary, it typically occurs as the doctor pulls a portion of the fetus through the cervix into the birth canal. Dr. Carhart testified at trial as follows:

> Dr. Carhart: . . . "The dismemberment occurs between the traction of . . . my instrument and the counter-traction of the internal os of the cervix. . . ."
> Counsel: "So the dismemberment occurs after you pulled a part of the fetus through the cervix, is that correct?"
> Dr. Carhart: "Exactly. Because you're using — The cervix has two strictures or two rings, the internal os and the external os . . . that's what's actually doing the dismembering. . . ."
> Counsel: "When we talked before or talked before about a D&E, that is not — where there is not intention to do it intact, do you, in that situation, dismember the fetus in utero first, then remove portions?"
> Dr. Carhart: "I don't think so. . . . I don't know of any way that one could go in and intentionally dismember the fetus in the uterus. . . . It takes something that restricts the motion of the fetus against what you're doing before you're going to get dismemberment."

11 F. Supp. 2d at 1104.

[5. The] D&E procedure carries certain risks. The use of instruments within the uterus creates a danger of accidental perforation and damage to neighboring organs. Sharp fetal bone fragments create similar dangers. And fetal tissue accidentally left behind can cause infection and various other complications. Nonetheless studies show that the risks of mortality and complication that accompany the D&E procedure between the 12th and 20th weeks of gestation are significantly lower than those accompanying induced labor procedures (the next safest midsecond trimester procedures).

6. At trial, Dr. Carhart and Dr. Stubblefield described a variation of the D&E procedure, which they referred to as an "intact D&E." See 11 F. Supp. 2d at 1105, 1111. Like other versions of the D&E technique, it begins with induced dilation of the cervix. The procedure then involves removing the fetus from the uterus through the cervix "intact," i.e., in one pass, rather than in several passes. Ibid. It is used after 16 weeks at the earliest, as vacuum aspiration becomes ineffective and the fetal skull becomes too large to pass through the cervix. 11 F. Supp. 2d at 1105. The intact D&E proceeds in one of two ways, depending on the presentation of the fetus. If the fetus presents head first (a vertex presentation), the doctor collapses the skull; and the doctor then extracts the entire fetus through the cervix. If the fetus presents feet first (a breech presentation), the doctor pulls the fetal body through the cervix, collapses the skull, and extracts the fetus through the cervix. Ibid. The breech extraction version of the intact D&E is also known commonly as "dilation and extraction," or D&X. 11 F. Supp. 2d at 1112. In the late second trimester, vertex, breech, and traverse/compound (sideways) presentations occur in roughly similar proportions. Medical and Surgical Abortion 135; 11 F. Supp. 2d at 1108.

7. The intact D&E procedure can also be found described in certain obstetric and abortion clinical textbooks, where two variations are recognized. The first, as just described, calls for the physician to adapt his method for extracting the intact fetus depending on fetal presentation. A slightly different version of the intact D&E procedure, associated with Dr. Martin Haskell, calls for conversion to a breech presentation in all cases.

8. The American College of Obstetricians and Gynecologists describes the D&X procedure in a manner corresponding to a breech-conversion intact D&E, including the following steps:

1. deliberate dilatation of the cervix, usually over a sequence of days;
2. instrumental conversion of the fetus to a footling breech;
3. breech extraction of the body excepting the head; and
4. partial evacuation of the intracranial contents of a living fetus to effect vaginal delivery of a dead but otherwise intact fetus.

American College of Obstetricians and Gynecologists Executive Board, Statement on Intact Dilation and Extraction (Jan. 12, 1997) (hereinafter ACOG Statement), App. 599-560.

Despite the technical differences we have just described, intact D&E and D&X are sufficiently similar for us to use the terms interchangeably. . . .

10. [The] materials presented at trial referred to the potential benefits of the D&X procedure in circumstances involving nonviable fetuses, such as fetuses with abnormal fluid accumulation in the brain (hydrocephaly). Others have emphasized its potential for women with prior uterine scars, or for women for whom induction of labor would be particularly dangerous.

11. There are no reliable data on the number of D&X abortions performed annually.

II

The question before us is whether Nebraska's statute, making criminal the performance of a "partial birth abortion," violates the Federal Constitution, as interpreted in Planned Parenthood of Southeastern Pa. v. Casey, and Roe v. Wade. We conclude that it does for at least two independent reasons. First, the law lacks any exception "'for the preservation of the . . . health of the mother.'" *Casey*, 505 U.S. at 879 (joint opinion of O'Connor, Kennedy, and Souter, JJ.). Second, it "imposes an undue burden on a woman's ability" to choose a D&E abortion, thereby unduly burdening the right to choose abortion itself. We shall discuss each of these reasons in turn.

A

[The] fact that Nebraska's law applies both pre- and postviability aggravates the constitutional problem presented. The State's interest in regulating abortion previability is considerably weaker than postviability. See *Casey*, supra, at 870. Since the law requires a health exception in order to validate even a postviability abortion regulation, it at a minimum requires the same in respect to previability regulation. [The] Nebraska law, of course, does not directly further an interest "in the potentiality of human life" by saving the fetus in question from destruction, as it regulates only a method of performing abortion. Nebraska describes its interests differently. It says the law "'shows concern for the life of the unborn,'" "prevents cruelty to partially born children," and "preserves the integrity of the medical profession." Brief for Petitioners 48. But we cannot see how the interest-related differences could make any difference to the question at hand, namely, the application of the "health" requirement.

Consequently, the governing standard requires an exception "where it is necessary, in appropriate medical judgment for the preservation of the life or health of the mother," *Casey*, supra, at 879, for this Court has made clear that a State may promote but not endanger a woman's health when it regulates the methods of abortion.

Justice Thomas says that the cases just cited limit this principle to situations where the pregnancy itself creates a threat to health. He is wrong. The cited cases, reaffirmed in *Casey*, recognize that a State cannot subject women's health to significant risks both in that context, AND ALSO where state regulations force women to use riskier methods of abortion. Our cases have repeatedly invalidated statutes that in the process of regulating the methods of abortion, imposed significant health risks. They make clear that a risk to a women's health is the same whether it happens to arise from regulating a particular method of abortion, or from barring abortion entirely.

[Nebraska] responds that the law does not require a health exception unless there is a need for such an exception. And here there is no such need, it says. It argues that "safe alternatives remain available" and "a ban on partial-birth abortion/D&X would create no risk to the health of women." Brief for Petitioners 29, 40. The problem for Nebraska is that the parties strongly contested this factual question in the trial court below; and the findings and evidence support Dr. Carhart. The State fails to demonstrate that banning D&X without a health exception may not create significant health risks for women, because the record shows that significant medical authority supports the proposition that in some circumstances, D&X would be the safest procedure.

The upshot is a District Court finding that D&X significantly obviates health risks in certain circumstances, a highly plausible record-based explanation of why that might be so, a division of opinion among some medical experts over whether D&X is generally safer, and an absence of controlled medical studies that would help answer these medical questions. Given these medically related evidentiary circumstances, we believe the law requires a health exception.

[The] Eighth Circuit found the Nebraska statute unconstitutional because, in *Casey*'s words, it has the "effect of placing a substantial obstacle in the path of a woman seeking an abortion of a nonviable fetus." 505 U.S. at 877. It thereby places an "undue burden" upon a woman's right to terminate her pregnancy before viability. Nebraska does not deny that the statute imposes an "undue burden" if it applies to the more commonly used D&E procedure as well as to D&X. And we agree with the Eighth Circuit that it does so apply.

Our earlier discussion of the D&E procedure shows that it falls within the statutory prohibition. The statute forbids "deliberately and intentionally delivering into the vagina a living unborn child, or a substantial portion thereof, for the purpose of performing a procedure that the person performing such procedure knows will kill the unborn child." We do not understand how one could distinguish, using this language, between D&E (where a foot or arm is drawn through the cervix) and D&X (where the body up to the head is drawn through the cervix).

[Even] if the statute's basic aim is to ban D&X, its language makes clear that it also covers a much broader category of procedures. The language does not track the medical differences between D&E and D&X — though it would have been a simple matter, for example, to provide an exception for the performance of D&E and other abortion procedures. Nor does the statute anywhere suggest that its application turns on whether a portion of the fetus' body is drawn into the vagina as part of a process to extract an intact fetus after collapsing the head as opposed to a process that would dismember the fetus. Thus, the dissenters' argument that the law was generally intended to bar D&X can be both correct and irrelevant. The relevant question is not whether the legislature wanted to ban D&X; it is whether the law was intended to apply only to D&X. The plain language covers both procedures.

[The] Nebraska State Attorney General argues that the statute does differentiate between the two procedures. He says that the statutory words "substantial portion" mean "the child up to the head." He consequently denies the statute's application where the physician introduces into the birth canal a fetal arm or leg or anything less than the entire fetal body.

[We] cannot accept the Attorney General's narrowing interpretation of the Nebraska statute. This Court's case law makes clear that we are not to give the Attorney General's interpretative views controlling weight. [Even] were we to grant the Attorney General's views "substantial weight," we still have to reject his interpretation, for it conflicts with the statutory language.

[We] are aware that adopting the Attorney General's interpretation might avoid the constitutional problem discussed in this section. But we are "without power to adopt a narrowing construction of a state statute unless such a construction is reasonable and readily apparent."

In sum, using this law some present prosecutors and future Attorneys General may choose to pursue physicians who use D&E procedures, the most commonly used method for performing previability second trimester abortions. All those who perform abortion procedures using that method must fear prosecution, conviction, and imprisonment. The result is an undue burden upon a woman's right to make an abortion decision. We must consequently find the statute unconstitutional.

The judgment of the Court of Appeals is
Affirmed.

JUSTICE STEVENS, with whom JUSTICE GINSBURG joins, concurring.
Although much ink is spilled today describing the gruesome nature of late-term abortion procedures, that rhetoric does not provide me a reason to believe that the procedure Nebraska here claims it seeks to ban is more brutal, more gruesome, or less respectful of "potential life" than the equally gruesome procedure Nebraska claims it still allows. [The] notion that either of these two equally gruesome procedures performed at this late stage of gestation is more akin to infanticide than the other, or that the State furthers any legitimate interest by banning one but not the other, is simply irrational.

JUSTICE O'CONNOR, concurring.
[First,] the Nebraska statute is inconsistent with *Casey* because it lacks an exception for those instances when the banned procedure is necessary to preserve the health of the mother. [Second,] Nebraska's statute is unconstitutional on the alternative and independent ground that it imposes an undue burden on a woman's right to choose to terminate her pregnancy before viability. Nebraska's ban covers not just the dilation and extraction (D&X) procedure, but also the dilation and evacuation (D&E) procedure, "the most commonly used method for performing previability second trimester abortions." [It] is important to note that, unlike Nebraska, some other States have enacted statutes more narrowly tailored to proscribing the D&X procedure alone. [If] Nebraska's statute limited its application to the D&X procedure and included an exception for the life and health of the mother, the question presented would be quite different than the one we face today. . . .

JUSTICE GINSBURG, with whom JUSTICE STEVENS joins, concurring.
[A] state regulation that "has the purpose or effect of placing a substantial obstacle in the path of a woman seeking an abortion of a nonviable fetus" violates the Constitution. Such an obstacle exists if the State stops a woman from choosing the procedure her doctor "reasonably believes will best protect the woman in [the] exercise of [her] constitutional liberty." [As] stated by Chief Judge Posner, "if a statute burdens constitutional rights and all that can be said on its behalf is that it is the vehicle that legislators have chosen for expressing their hostility to those rights, the burden is undue."

CHIEF JUSTICE REHNQUIST, dissenting.
[I] believe Justice Kennedy and Justice Thomas have correctly applied *Casey*'s principles and join their dissenting opinions.

JUSTICE SCALIA, dissenting.
I am optimistic enough to believe that, one day, Stenberg v. Carhart will be assigned its rightful place in the history of this Court's jurisprudence beside *Korematsu* and *Dred Scott*.
[I] never put much stock in *Casey*'s explication of the inexplicable. In the last analysis, my judgment that *Casey* does not support today's tragic result can be traced to the fact that what I consider to be an "undue burden" is different from what the majority considers to be an "undue burden" — a conclusion that can not

be demonstrated true or false by factual inquiry or legal reasoning. It is a value judgment, dependent upon how much one respects (or believes society ought to respect) the life of a partially delivered fetus, and how much one respects (or believes society ought to respect) the freedom of the woman who gave it life to kill it. Evidently, the five Justices in today's majority value the former less, or the latter more, (or both), than the four of us in dissent. Case closed. There is no cause for anyone who believes in *Casey* to feel betrayed by this outcome. It has been arrived at by precisely the process *Casey* promised — a democratic vote by nine lawyers, not on the question whether the text of the Constitution has anything to say about this subject (it obviously does not); nor even on the question (also appropriate for lawyers) whether the legal traditions of the American people would have sustained such a limitation upon abortion (they obviously would); but upon the pure policy question whether this limitation upon abortion is "undue" — i.e., goes too far.

[I] must recall my bemusement, in *Casey*, at the joint opinion's expressed belief that Roe v. Wade had "called the contending sides of a national controversy to end their national division by accepting a common mandate rooted in the Constitution," and that the decision in *Casey* would ratify that happy truce. [If] only for the sake of its own preservation, the Court should return this matter to the people — where the Constitution, by its silence on the subject, left it — and let them decide, State by State, whether this practice should be allowed. *Casey* must be overruled.

JUSTICE KENNEDY, with whom THE CHIEF JUSTICE joins, dissenting.

[The] Court's failure to accord any weight to Nebraska's interest in prohibiting partial-birth abortion is erroneous and undermines its discussion and holding. The Court's approach in this regard is revealed by its description of the abortion methods at issue, which the Court is correct to describe as "clinically cold or callous." The majority views the procedures from the perspective of the abortionist, rather than from the perspective of a society shocked when confronted with a new method of ending human life. Words invoked by the majority, such as "transcervical procedures," "osmotic dilators," "instrumental disarticulation," and "paracervical block," may be accurate and are to some extent necessary, but for citizens who seek to know why laws on this subject have been enacted across the Nation, the words are insufficient. Repeated references to sources understandable only to a trained physician may obscure matters for persons not trained in medical terminology. Thus it seems necessary at the outset to set forth what may happen during an abortion.

[As] described by Dr. Carhart, the D&E procedure requires the abortionist to use instruments to grasp a portion (such as a foot or hand) of a developed and living fetus and drag the grasped portion out of the uterus into the vagina. Dr. Carhart uses the traction created by the opening between the uterus and vagina to dismember the fetus, tearing the grasped portion away from the remainder of the body. The traction between the uterus and vagina is essential to the procedure because attempting to abort a fetus without using that traction is described by Dr. Carhart as "pulling the cat's tail" or "dragging a string across the floor, you'll just keep dragging it. It's not until something grabs the other end that you are going to develop traction." The fetus, in many cases, dies just as a human adult or child would: It bleeds to death as it is torn limb from limb. The fetus can be alive at the beginning of the dismemberment process and can survive for a time while its limbs are being torn off. Dr. Carhart agreed that "when you pull out a piece of the fetus, let's say, an arm or a leg and remove that, at the time just prior to removal of the portion of the fetus, . . . the fetus [is] alive." Dr. Carhart has observed fetal heartbeat via ultrasound with "extensive parts of the fetus removed," and testified that mere dismemberment of a limb does not always cause death because he knows of a physician who removed the arm of a fetus only to have the fetus go on to be born "as a living child with one arm." At the conclusion of a D&E abortion no intact fetus remains. In Dr. Carhart's words, the abortionist is left with "a tray full of pieces."

The other procedure implicated today is called "partial-birth abortion" or the D&X. The D&X can be used, as a general matter, after 19 weeks gestation because the fetus has become so developed that it may survive intact partial delivery from the uterus into the vagina. In the D&X, the abortionist initiates the woman's natural delivery process by causing the cervix of the woman to be dilated, sometimes over a sequence of days. The fetus' arms and legs are delivered outside the uterus while the fetus is alive; witnesses to the procedure report seeing the body of the fetus moving outside the woman's body. At this point, the abortion procedure has the appearance of a live birth. As stated by one group of physicians, "as the physician manually performs breech extraction of the body of a live fetus, excepting the head, she continues in the apparent role of an obstetrician delivering a child." Brief for Association of American Physicians and Surgeons et al. as Amici Curiae 27. With only the head of the fetus remaining in utero, the abortionist tears open the skull. According to Dr. Martin Haskell, a leading proponent of the procedure, the appropriate instrument to be used at this stage of the abortion is a pair of scissors. M. Haskell, Dilation and Extraction for Late Second Trimester Abortion (1992), in 139 Cong. Rec. 8605 (1993). Witnesses report observing the portion of the fetus outside the woman react to the skull penetration. Brief for Petitioners 4. The abortionist then inserts a suction tube and vacuums out the developing brain and other matter found within the skull. The process of making the size of the fetus' head smaller is given the clinically neutral term "reduction procedure." 11 F. Supp. 2d 1099, 1106 (Neb. 1998). Brain death does not occur until after the skull invasion, and, according to Dr. Carhart, the heart of the fetus may continue to beat for minutes after the contents of the skull are vacuumed out. The abortionist next completes the delivery of a dead fetus, intact except for the damage to the head and the missing contents of the skull.

Of the two described procedures, Nebraska seeks only to ban the D&X. In light of the description of the D&X procedure, it should go without saying that Nebraska's ban on partial-birth abortion furthers purposes States are entitled to pursue.

[States have] an interest in forbidding medical procedures which, in the State's reasonable determination, might cause the medical profession or society as a whole to become insensitive, even disdainful, to life, including life in the human fetus. [It] is argued, however, that a ban on the D&X does not further these interests. This is because, the reasoning continues, the D&E method, which Nebraska claims to be beyond its intent to regulate, can still be used to abort a fetus and is no less dehumanizing than the D&X method. While not adopting the argument in express terms, the Court indicates tacit approval of it by refusing to reject it in a forthright manner. Rendering express what is only implicit in the majority opinion, Justice Stevens and Justice Ginsburg are forthright in declaring that the two procedures are indistinguishable and that Nebraska has acted both irrationally and without a proper purpose in enacting the law. The issue is not whether members of the judiciary can see a difference between the two procedures. It is whether Nebraska can. The Court's refusal to recognize Nebraska's right to declare a moral difference between the procedure is a dispiriting disclosure of the illogic and illegitimacy of the Court's approach to the entire case.

Nebraska was entitled to find the existence of a consequential moral difference between the procedures. We are referred to substantial medical authority that D&X perverts the natural birth process to a greater degree than D&E, commandeering the live birth process until the skull is pierced. American Medical Association (AMA) publications describe the D&X abortion method as "ethically wrong." AMA Board of Trustees Factsheet on HR 1122 (June 1997), in App. to Brief for Association of American Physicians and Surgeons et al. as Amici Curiae 1 (AMA Factsheet). The D&X differs from the D&E because in the D&X the fetus is "killed outside of the womb" where the fetus has "an autonomy which separates it from the right of the woman to choose treatments for her own body." Ibid. Witnesses to the procedure relate that the fingers and feet of the fetus are moving prior to the piercing of the skull; when the scissors are inserted in the back of the head, the fetus' body, wholly outside the woman's body and alive, reacts as though startled and goes limp. D&X's stronger resemblance to infanticide means Nebraska could conclude the procedure presents a greater risk of disrespect for life and a consequent greater risk to the profession and society, which depend for their sustenance upon reciprocal recognition of dignity and respect. The Court is without authority to second-guess this conclusion.

[Demonstrating] a further and basic misunderstanding of *Casey,* the Court holds the ban on the D&X procedure fails because it does not include an exception permitting an abortionist to perform a D&X whenever he believes it will best preserve the health of the woman. Casting aside the views of distinguished physicians and the statements of leading medical organizations, the Court awards each physician a veto power over the State's judgment that the procedures should not be performed. Dr. Carhart has made the medical judgment to use the D&X procedure in every case, regardless of indications, after 15 weeks gestation. Requiring Nebraska to defer to Dr. Carhart's judgment is no different than forbidding Nebraska from enacting a ban at all; for it is now Dr. Leroy Carhart who sets abortion policy for the State of Nebraska, not the legislature or the people. *Casey* does not give precedence to the views of a single physician or a group of physicians regarding the relative safety of a particular procedure.

[Substantial] evidence supports Nebraska's conclusion that its law denies no woman a safe abortion. The most to be said for the D&X is it may present an unquantified lower risk of complication for a particular patient but that other proven safe procedures remain available even for this patient. Under these circumstances, the Court is wrong to limit its inquiry to the relative physical safety of the two procedures, with the slightest potential difference requiring the invalidation of the law. [It] is also important to recognize that the D&X is effective only when the fetus is close to viable or, in fact, viable; thus the State is regulating the process at the point where its interest in life is nearing its peak.

Courts are ill-equipped to evaluate the relative worth of particular surgical procedures. The legislatures of the several States have superior factfinding capabilities in this regard.

[The] Court's next holding is that Nebraska's ban forbids both the D&X procedure and the more common D&E procedure. In so ruling the Court misapplies settled doctrines of statutory construction and contradicts *Casey's* premise that the States have a vital constitutional position in the abortion debate. [Like] the ruling requiring a physician veto, requiring a State to meet unattainable standards of statutory draftsmanship in order to have its voice heard on this grave and difficult subject is no different from foreclosing state participation altogether. [In] light of the statutory text, the commonsense understanding must be that the statute covers only the D&X.

[Ignoring] substantial medical and ethical opinion, the Court substitutes its own judgment for the judgment of Nebraska and some 30 other States and sweeps the law away. [From] the decision, the reasoning, and the judgment, I dissent.

JUSTICE THOMAS, with whom THE CHIEF JUSTICE and JUSTICE SCALIA join, dissenting.

[The] standard set forth in the *Casey* joint opinion has no historical or doctrinal pedigree. The standard is a product of its authors' own philosophical views about abortion, and it should go without saying that it has no origins in or relationship to the Constitution and is, consequently, as illegitimate as the standard it purported to replace. Even assuming, however, as I will for the remainder of this dissent, that *Casey's* fabricated undue-burden standard merits adherence (which it does not), today's decision is extraordinary. Today, the Court inexplicably holds that the States cannot constitutionally prohibit a method of abortion that millions find hard to distinguish from infanticide and that the Court hesitates even to describe.

[To] reach its decision, the majority must take a series of indefensible steps. The majority must first disregard the principles that this Court follows in every context but abortion: We interpret statutes according to their plain meaning and we do not strike down statutes susceptible of a narrowing construction. The majority also must disregard the very constitutional standard it purports to employ, and then displace the considered judgment of the people of Nebraska and 29 other States. The majority's decision is lamentable, because of the result the majority reaches, the illogical steps the majority takes to reach it, and because it portends a return to an era I had thought we had at last abandoned.

[Starting] with the statutory definition of "partial birth abortion," I think it highly doubtful that the statute could be applied to ordinary D&E. [Having] resolved that Nebraska's partial birth abortion statute permits doctors to perform D&E abortions, the question remains whether a State can constitutionally prohibit the partial birth abortion procedure without a health exception. Although the majority and Justice O'Connor purport to rely on the standard articulated in the *Casey* joint opinion in concluding that a State may not, they in fact disregard it entirely.

[There] is no question that the State of Nebraska has a valid interest — one not designed to strike at the right itself — in prohibiting partial birth abortion. *Casey* itself noted that States may "express profound respect for the life of the unborn." States may, without a doubt, express this profound respect by prohibiting a procedure that approaches infanticide, and thereby dehumanizes the fetus and trivializes human life. The AMA has recognized that this procedure is "ethically different from other destructive abortion techniques because the fetus, normally twenty weeks or longer in gestation, is killed outside the womb. The 'partial birth' gives the fetus an autonomy which separates it from the right of the woman to choose treatments for her own body." Thirty States have concurred with this view.

[The] testimony of one nurse who observed a partial birth abortion procedure makes the point even more vividly:

"The baby's little fingers were clasping and unclasping, and his little feet were kicking. Then the doctor stuck the scissors in the back of his head, and the baby's arms jerked out, like a startle reaction, like a flinch, like a baby does when he thinks he is going to fall.

"The doctor opened up the scissors, stuck a high-powered suction tube into the opening, and sucked the baby's brains out. Now the baby went completely limp." H. R. 1833 Hearing 18 (statement of Brenda Pratt Shafer).

The question whether States have a legitimate interest in banning the procedure does not require additional authority.

[The] next question, therefore, is whether the Nebraska statute is unconstitutional because it does not contain an exception that would allow use of the procedure whenever "necessary in appropriate medical judgment, for the preservation of the . . . health of the mother." According to the majority, such a health exception is required here because there is a "division of opinion among some medical experts over whether D&X is generally safer [than D&E], and an absence of controlled medical studies that would help answer these medical questions." In other words, unless a State can conclusively establish that an abortion procedure is no safer than other procedures, the State cannot regulate that procedure without including a health exception.

It is clear that the Court's understanding of when a health exception is required is not mandated by our prior cases. [The] majority assiduously avoids addressing the actual standard articulated in *Casey*—whether prohibiting partial birth abortion without a health exception poses a substantial obstacle to obtaining an abortion. And for good reason: Such an obstacle does not exist. There are two essential reasons why the Court cannot identify a substantial obstacle. First, the Court cannot identify any real, much less substantial, barrier to any woman's ability to obtain an abortion. And second, the Court cannot demonstrate that any such obstacle would affect a sufficient number of women to justify invalidating the statute on its face. [Like] the *Casey* 24-hour waiting period, and in contrast to the situation in *Danforth*, any increased health risk to women imposed by the partial birth abortion ban is minimal at most. Of the 5.5% of abortions that occur after 15 weeks (the time after which a partial birth abortion would be possible), the vast majority are performed with a D&E or induction procedure. And, for any woman with a vertex presentation fetus, the vertex presentation form of intact D&E, which presumably shares some of the health benefits of the partial birth abortion procedure but is not covered by the Nebraska statute, is available. Of the remaining women — that is, those women for whom a partial birth abortion procedure would be considered and who have a breech presentation fetus — there is no showing that any one faces a significant health risk from the partial birth abortion ban. [In] fact, there was evidence before the Nebraska Legislature that partial birth abortion increases health risks relative to other procedures.

[The] majority justifies its result by asserting that a "significant body of medical opinion" supports the view that partial birth abortion may be a safer abortion procedure. I find this assertion puzzling. If there is a "significant body of medical opinion" supporting this procedure, no one in the majority has identified it.

[Moreover,] even if I were to assume credible evidence on both sides of the debate, that fact should resolve the undue-burden question in favor of allowing Nebraska to legislate. Where no one knows whether a regulation of abortion poses any burden at all, the burden surely does not amount to a "substantial obstacle."

[Even] if I were willing to assume that the partial birth method of abortion is safer for some small set of women, such a conclusion would not require invalidating the Act, because this case comes to us on a facial challenge.

[We] were reassured repeatedly in *Casey* that not all regulations of abortion are unwarranted and that the States may express profound respect for fetal life. Under *Casey*, the regulation before us today should easily pass constitutional muster. But the Court's abortion jurisprudence is a particularly virulent strain of constitutional exegesis. And so today we are told that 30 States are prohibited from banning one rarely used form of abortion that they believe to border on infanticide. It is clear that the Constitution does not compel this result.

I respectfully dissent.

3.   Family and Other "Privacy" Interests

The modern substantive due process decisions we have examined thus far — *Griswold, Eisenstadt, Roe,* and so on — have all involved the freedom to decide "whether to bear or beget a child." Is modern substantive due process so limited?

MOORE v. CITY OF EAST CLEVELAND, 431 U.S. 494 (1977). In *Moore*, the Court invalidated a city ordinance limiting occupancy of any dwelling unit to members of the same "family," where the ordinance narrowly defined "family" as including only "a few categories of related individuals." Appellant lived with her son, Dale, and her two grandsons, Dale, Jr., and John. Under the ordinance, John could not live in the home because he was not "sufficiently related" to his uncle, Dale, and his cousin, Dale, Jr., to constitute a "family" within the meaning of the ordinance. In a plurality opinion, Justice Powell, joined by Justices Brennan, Marshall, and Blackmun, concluded that the ordinance violated the due process clause of the fourteenth amendment:

"The city argues that our decision in Village of Belle Terre v. Boraas, 416 U.S. 1 (1974), requires us to sustain the ordinance attacked here. Belle Terre, like East Cleveland, imposed limits on the types of groups that could occupy a single dwelling unit. [We] sustained the Belle Terre ordinance on the ground that it bore a rational relationship to permissible state objectives. But one overriding factor sets this case apart from *Belle Terre*. The ordinance there affected only *unrelated* individuals. It expressly allowed all who were related by 'blood, adoption, or marriage' to live [together]. East Cleveland, in contrast, has chosen to regulate the occupancy of its housing by slicing deeply into the family itself. [The ordinance] selects certain categories of relatives who may live together and declares that others may not. In particular, it makes a crime of a grandmother's choice to live with her grandson in circumstances like those presented here.

"When a city undertakes such intrusive regulation of the family, [*Belle Terre* does not govern, and] the usual judicial deference to the legislature is inappropriate. This Court has long recognized that freedom of personal choice in matters of marriage and family life is one of the liberties protected by the Due Process Clause of the Fourteenth Amendment.' [Citing, e.g., *Meyer; Pierce; Roe; Griswold; Skinner.*] [When] government intrudes on choices concerning family living arrangements, this Court must examine carefully the importance of the governmental interests advanced and the extent to which they are served by the challenged regulation. When thus examined, this ordinance cannot survive. The city seeks to justify it as a means of preventing overcrowding, minimizing traffic and parking congestion, and avoiding an undue financial burden on [the] school system. Although these are legitimate goals, the ordinance [serves] them marginally, at best. . . .

"Substantive due process has at times been a treacherous field for this Court. There *are* risks when the judicial branch gives enhanced protection to certain substantive liberties without the guidance of the more specific provisions of the Bill of Rights. As the history of the *Lochner* era demonstrates, there is reason for concern lest the only limits to such judicial intervention become the predilections of those who happen at the time to be Members of this Court. That history counsels caution and restraint. But it does not counsel abandonment. . . .

"Appropriate limits on substantive due process come [from] careful 'respect for the teachings of history [and] solid recognition of the basic values that underlie our society.' [*Griswold* (Harlan, J., concurring).] Our decisions establish that the Constitution protects the sanctity of the family precisely because the institution of the family is deeply rooted in this Nation's history and tradition. It is through the family that we inculcate and pass down many of our most cherished values, moral and cultural. [And ours] is by no means a tradition limited to respect for [the] nuclear family. The tradition of uncles, aunts, cousins, and especially grandparents sharing a household along with parents has roots equally venerable and equally deserving of constitutional recognition. [Out] of choice, necessity, or a sense of family responsibility, it has been common for close relatives to draw [together]. Especially in times of adversity [the] broader family has tended to come together for mutual [sustenance]. [The] choice of relatives in this degree of kinship to live together may not lightly be denied by the State. [The] Constitution prevents East Cleveland from standardizing its children — and its adults — by forcing all to live in certain narrowly defined family patterns."

Justice Stevens concurred in the result on the ground that the challenged ordinance "constitutes a taking of property without due process and without just compensation."

Justice Stewart, joined by Justice Rehnquist, dissented:

"To suggest [that] related persons [have] constitutional rights of association superior to those of unrelated persons is to misunderstand the nature of the associational freedoms that the Constitution has been understood to protect. Freedom of association has been constitutionally recognized because it is often indispensable to effectuation of explicit First Amendment guarantees. [Citing, e.g., NAACP v. Alabama, 357 U.S. 449 (1958).] [The] 'association' in this case is not for any purpose relating to the promotion of speech, assembly, the press, or religion.

"[Appellant] is considerably closer to the constitutional mark in asserting that [the] ordinance intrudes upon 'the private realm of family life which the state cannot enter.' [But] appellant's desire to share a single-dwelling unit [can] hardly be equated with any of the interests protected in [our prior decisions]."

Justice White also dissented: "[Although] the Due Process Clause extends substantial protection to various phases of family life, [the challenged] ordinance [merely] denies appellant the opportunity to live with all her grandchildren in this particular [suburb]."

Chief Justice Burger dissented on procedural grounds.

Note: Family and Association

1. Consider whether *Belle Terre* is distinguishable from *Moore* because the ordinance upheld in *Belle Terre* "allowed all who were related by 'blood, adoption, or marriage' to live [together]." If this distinction holds, it must be because the constitutionally mandated definition of "family" has reference to tradition. But is tradition an appropriate basis for the definition and limitation of constitutional rights? Is there any other basis for a constitutional definition of family?

See Note, Developments in the Law — The Constitution and the Family, 93 Harv. L. Rev. 1156, 1177, 1186-1187, 1190-1192 (1980):

> In the family cases, the Court has consistently turned to tradition as a source of previously unrecognized aspects of the liberty protected by the due process clauses. [Recourse] to traditional values enables the Court to afford constitutional protection to rights Americans traditionally have assumed to be part of our nation's scheme of liberty. [The] use of tradition [appeals] to the Court's need for a sense of impartiality in the application of substantive due process. [Reference] to tradition does not involve the Court in the ambitious task of developing its own unified theory of political liberty; rather, the initial appeal is to a relatively objective history.
>
> [Once] a traditional value has been accepted as an aspect of constitutional liberty, the Court must give that value a consistent and principled interpretation. Otherwise, the actual contours tradition supplies may reflect the same prejudice and insensitivity that necessitate judicial protection of unenumerated rights in the first place. [Justice] Powell stated this clearly in *Moore*, refusing to confine constitutional protection to the nuclear [family]. Because a functional approach extends the scope of a traditional right beyond its historical contours, it may be criticized as manipulation of the level of generality of the relevant tradition so that rights not historically regarded as important liberties are brought within the scope of protection. This criticism misses the point. A court which extends the right of procreative autonomy from a marital to a nonmarital context is not contending that the procreative rights of the unmarried are traditional. It is merely claiming that, given a longstanding cultural consensus that procreative activities [are special], there must be some principled basis for treating the unmarried and married differently.

2. What was actually at issue in *Moore*? Consider the possibility that the case involved an effort by a middle-class (mostly black) neighborhood to define itself as different, in social and economic respects, from lower-class (and sometimes black) neighborhoods. The limit on family size might well be closely connected with this effort at self-definition. See Burt, The Constitution of the Family, 1979 Sup. Ct. Rev. 329, 391:

> [Victory] for Mrs. Moore was total defeat for the other residents of East Cleveland, while victory for them was not total defeat for her, except insofar as she wished to remain in their community while transforming [it] to her taste. If Mrs. Moore were shut out from many different [communities] — if, that is, the city ordinance was not [unusual] — then the Court might properly have seen some role for itself in

protecting her interests. [But] the very oddity of [the] ordinance suggests [that] the city residents are more the vulnerable, isolated dissenters than [she]. The Court in *Moore* myopically saw the case as a dispute between "a family" and "the state" rather than as a dispute among citizens about the meaning of "family."

If this is how we understand the *Moore* problem, does the result in the case seem more sensible or less so?

3. After *Belle Terre* and *Moore*, could a city constitutionally prohibit "significant others" from living together?

4. Compare *Moore* with Lyng v. Castillo, 477 U.S. 635 (1986). In *Lyng*, the Court, in an opinion by Justice Stevens, upheld a provision of the federal Food Stamp Act that treated parents, children, and siblings living together as a single household whether or not they purchased food and prepared meals together. In contrast, unrelated individuals who lived together could establish separate "households" and thereby qualify for enhanced benefits so long as they did not buy and prepare food together. The Court rejected the argument that the classification should be subjected to heightened scrutiny because it interfered with family living arrangements, thereby burdening a fundamental right:

The "household" definition does not order or prevent any group of persons from dining together. Indeed, in the overwhelming majority of cases it probably has no effect at all. It is exceedingly unlikely that close relatives would choose to live apart simply to increase their allotment of food stamps, for the cost of separate housing would almost certainly exceed the incremental value of the additional stamps.

Justice Marshall dissented:

The food stamp benefits at issue are necessary for the affected families' very survival, and the Federal Government denies that benefit to families who do not, by preparing their meals together, structure themselves in a manner that the Government believes will minimize unnecessary expenditures. [The] Government has thus chosen to intrude into the family dining room — a place where I would have thought the right to privacy exists in its strongest form. What possible interest can the Government have in preventing members of a family from dining as they choose? It is simply none of the Government's business.

Consider also Bowen v. Gilliard, 483 U.S. 587 (1987). An amendment to the Aid to Families with Dependent Children program required recipient families to include within the family unit all children living within the household, including children receiving child support payments from noncustodial parents. The family's benefit level was then reduced by the amount of these payments. The Court, in an opinion by Justice Stevens, rejected appellee's argument that these requirements should be subject to heightened scrutiny because they interfered with family living arrangements:

That some families may decide to modify their living arrangements in order to avoid the effect of the amendment, does not transform the amendment into an act whose design and direct effect is to "intrud[e] on choices concerning family living arrangements." [*Moore*.]

Justice Brennan, joined by Justice Marshall, dissented:

The Government has told a child who lives with a mother receiving public assistance that it cannot both live with its mother and be supported by its father. The child must either leave the care and custody of the mother, or forgo the support of the father and become a Government client. The child is put to this choice not because it seeks Government benefits for itself, but because of a fact over which it has no control: the need of other household members for public assistance.

Justice Blackmun also filed a short dissent.

ZABLOCKI v. REDHAIL, 434 U.S. 374 (1978). In *Zablocki*, the Court invalidated a Wisconsin statute providing that any resident "having minor issue not in his custody and which he is under an obligation to support by court order" may not marry without a prior judicial determination that the support obligation has been met, and that the children "are not then and are not likely thereafter to become public charges." The Court, in an opinion by Justice Marshall, held that the statute violated the equal protection clause:

"[The] decisions of this Court confirm that the right to marry is of fundamental importance for all individuals. [Citing, e.g., Loving v. Virginia, 388 U.S. 1 (1967) (invalidating state miscegenation laws); *Griswold; Skinner; Meyer.*] It is not surprising that the decision to marry has been placed on the same level of importance as decisions relating to procreation, childbirth, child rearing, and family relationships. [It] would make little sense to recognize a right of privacy with respect to other matters of family life and not with respect to the decision to enter the relationship that is the foundation of the family in our society. [If the] right to procreate means anything at all, it must imply some right to enter the only relationship in which the [State] allows sexual relations legally to take place. [We] do not mean to suggest that every state regulation which relates in any way to the incidents of or prerequisites for marriage must be subjected to rigorous scrutiny. To the contrary, reasonable regulations that do not significantly interfere with decisions to enter into the marital relationship may legitimately be imposed. [Citing, e.g., Califano v. Jobst, infra.]

"The statutory classification at issue here, however, [interferes] directly and substantially with the right to marry. Under the challenged statute, [some persons] will never be able to obtain the necessary court order, because they either lack the financial means to meet their support obligations or cannot prove that their children will not become public charges. These persons are absolutely prevented from getting married. Many others, able in theory to satisfy the statute's requirements, will be sufficiently burdened by having to do so that they will [forgo] their right to marry. And even those who can [meet] the statute's requirements suffer a serious intrusion into their freedom of choice in an area in which we have held such freedom to be fundamental.

"When a statutory classification significantly interferes with the exercise of a fundamental right, it cannot be upheld unless it is supported by sufficiently important state interests and is closely tailored to effectuate only those interests. [The State argues that the statute protects the welfare of the out-of-custody children, but this] 'collection device' rationale cannot justify the statute's broad infringement on the right to marry. First, with respect to individuals who are unable to [pay], the statute merely prevents the applicant from getting married, without delivering any money at all into the hands of [the] children. More importantly, [the] State already has numerous other means for exacting compliance with support obligations [that] do not impinge upon the right to marry."

Justice Stewart concurred in the judgment: "To hold [that] the Wisconsin statute violates the Equal Protection Clause [misconceives] the meaning of that constitutional guarantee. [The] problem in this case is not one of discriminatory classifications, but of unwarranted encroachment upon a constitutionally protected freedom. [The] statute is unconstitutional because it exceeds the bounds of permissible state regulation of marriage, and invades the sphere of liberty protected by the Due Process Clause of the Fourteenth Amendment. [On] several occasions this Court has held that a person's inability to pay [does] not justify the total deprivation of a constitutionally protected liberty. [Citing *Boddie*.] The principle of [*Boddie*] applies [here]. We [may] assume that [the law is permissible] as applied to those who can afford to [pay] but choose not to do [so]. [But] some people simply cannot afford to [pay]. To deny these people permission to marry penalizes them for failing to do that which they cannot do. Insofar as it applies to indigents, the [law] is [irrational]."

Justice Powell also concurred in the judgment: "The Court apparently would subject all state regulation which 'directly and substantially' interferes with the decision to marry in a traditional family setting [to] 'compelling state interest' analysis. [We must recognize, however, that] domestic relations [is] 'an area that has long been regarded as a virtually exclusive province of the States.' [The] State, representing the collective expression of moral aspirations, has an undeniable interest in ensuring that its rules of domestic relations reflect the widely held values of its people. [State] regulation has included bans on incest, bigamy, and homosexuality, as well as various preconditions to marriage, such as blood tests. Likewise, a showing of fault [traditionally] has been a prerequisite to [divorce]. A 'compelling state purpose' inquiry would cast doubt on [such restrictions]." Justice Powell then argued for a more flexible approach: "The Due Process Clause requires a showing of justification 'when the government intrudes on choices concerning family living arrangements' in a manner which is contrary to deeply rooted traditions. [Quoting his plurality opinion in *Moore*.] Furthermore, under the Equal Protection Clause the means chosen by the State in this case must bear 'a fair and substantial relation' to the object of the legislation. [Quoting Reed v. Reed, 404 U.S. 71 (1971).] The [challenged statute] does not pass muster under either due process or equal protection standards. [I] do not agree with the [Court] that a State may never condition the right to marry on satisfaction of existing support obligations [where] the [person is] able to make the required support payments but simply wish[es] to shirk [his] moral and legal [obligation]. The vice inheres, not in the collection concept, but in the failure to [exempt] those without the means to [pay]. [Citing *Boddie*.]"

Justice Stevens also concurred in the judgment: "The individual's interest in making the marriage decision independently is sufficiently important to merit special constitutional protection. It is not, however, an interest which is constitutionally immune from evenhanded regulation. Thus, laws prohibiting marriage to a child, a close relative, or a person afflicted with venereal disease, are unchallenged even though they 'interfere directly and substantially with the right to marry.' [The challenged] statute has a different character. Under this statute, a person's economic status may determine his eligibility to [marry]. This type of statutory discrimination [is] inconsistent with our tradition of administering justice equally to the rich and to the poor. [Neither] the fact that the appellee's interest is constitutionally protected, nor the fact that the classification is based on economic status is sufficient to justify a 'level of scrutiny' so strict that a holding of unconstitutionality is virtually foreordained. [But] the presence of these factors precludes a holding that [rational explanation] is [sufficient]. [Here, the] discrimination between the rich and the poor is irrational in so many ways that it cannot withstand scrutiny under the Equal Protection Clause."

Justice Rehnquist was the lone dissenter: "I would view this [statute] in the light of the traditional presumption of validity. [The] statute so viewed is a permissible exercise of the State's power to regulate family life and to assure the support of minor children."

Note: Families and Traditions

1. Why did the Court rely on due process in *Moore* but on equal protection in *Zablocki?* Consider Lupu, Untangling the Strands of the Fourteenth Amendment, 77 Mich. L. Rev. 981, 982-985 (1979):

> [The] judicial selection of values for special protection against the majoritarian processes has wavered [between] a liberty base and an equality base. [This] doctrinal imprecision has bred unpredictability, disrespect, and charges of outcome-orientation. [The] equal protection clause and the due process clause are complementary — not interchangeable — [safeguards]. [Judicial] discovery of fundamental [values] outside the constitutional text [should] be grounded in the due process clause. [The] equality strand [should] not bear a substantive content — [equal] protection [should] remain substantially rooted in the pure anti-discrimination concerns that sparked the [clause].

2. In Califano v. Jobst, 434 U.S. 47 (1977), the Court unanimously upheld a section of the Social Security Act providing that benefits received by a disabled dependent child of a covered wage earner shall terminate when the child marries an individual who is not independently entitled to benefits under the act, even though that individual is also disabled. The Court applied the rational basis standard:

> Both tradition and common experience support the conclusion that marriage is an event which normally marks an important change in economic status. [Frequently], of course, financial independence and marriage do not go hand in hand. [But] there can be no question about the validity of the assumption that a married person is less likely to be dependent on his parents for support than one who is unmarried. [The challenged provision thus satisfies] the constitutional test normally applied in cases like this. That general rule is not rendered invalid simply because some persons who might otherwise have married were deterred by the rule or because some who did marry were burdened thereby. For the [challenged] rule cannot be criticized as merely [an] attempt to interfere with the individual's freedom to make a decision as important as marriage [or] to foist orthodoxy on the unwilling by banning, or criminally prosecuting, nonconforming marriages.

Consider these efforts to reconcile *Jobst* with *Zablocki*: (a) In *Zablocki*, the Court maintained that "[t]he directness and substantiality of the interference with the freedom to marry distinguish the instant case from [*Jobst*]. [The provision challenged in *Jobst*] placed no direct legal obstacle in the path of persons desiring to get married, [and] there was no evidence that the [law] significantly discouraged [or] made 'practically impossible' any marriages." (b) The provisions challenged in *Jobst* did not disadvantage the poor. (c) As Justice Stevens argued in *Zablocki*, "A classification based on marital status [e.g., *Jobst*] is fundamentally different from a classification which determines who may lawfully enter into the marriage relationship [e.g., *Zablocki*]."

3. If there is a constitutional right to marry, is there a correlative right to divorce? Recall Boddie v. Connecticut, section E2 supra. Consider Karst, The Freedom of Intimate Association, 89 Yale L.J. 624, 671 (1980): "To condition divorce on a showing of fault is to place an insuperable burden on some spouses [and] to interfere very significantly with such a spouse's decision to associate with another person in marriage. [Thus,] no-fault divorce seems implied [unless] the state can demonstrate some very strong interest in the fault requirement."

4. In Turner v. Safley, 482 U.S. 78 (1987), a unanimous Court relied on *Zablocki* to invalidate a prison regulation that permitted inmates to marry only when the superintendent found compelling reasons to grant permission. In practice, such reasons were found only in cases of pregnancy or the birth of a non-marital child. The Court, in an opinion by Justice O'Connor, held that "the right to marry, like many other rights, is subject to substantial restrictions as a result of incarceration. Many important attributes of marriage remain, however, after taking into account the limitations imposed by prison life." Although "legitimate security concerns" might require "reasonable restrictions" on the exercise of the right to marry and might "justify requiring the approval of the superintendent," this regulation represented "an exaggerated response to [security] objectives" and was therefore invalid.

5. One of the central issues in these cases is the identification, at the appropriate level of abstraction, of the "tradition" that will define the content of liberty under the due process clause: If the tradition is defined very narrowly, the legislation at issue will almost always simply illustrate the tradition, thereby depriving the appeal to tradition of any power to check legislative action. But if the tradition is defined very broadly, judges will be able to appeal to it to invalidate whatever legislation they choose to characterize as inconsistent with tradition.

This problem was the subject of an important exchange between Justices Scalia and Brennan in Michael H. v. Gerald D., 491 U.S. 505 (1989). A California statute provided that a child born to a married woman living with her husband is conclusively presumed to be a child of the marriage; this presumption has consequences for the visitation rights of the genetic father of such a child. A majority of the Court held that this statute did not violate the Constitution.

A plurality opinion by Justice Scalia said that, for the genetic father to have a liberty interest in establishing his paternity, that interest had to be both "fundamental" and "an interest traditionally protected by our society." To the plurality, the relevant tradition involved "the historic respect — indeed, sanctity would not be too strong a term — traditionally accorded to the relationships that develop within the unitary family." Because Michael H. was not part of such a unitary family, he had no interest of the necessary sort.

In a long footnote, Justice Scalia defended his reliance on "historical traditions specifically relating to the rights of an adulterous natural father, rather than [as

Justice Brennan urged] inquiring more generally 'whether parenthood is an interest that historically has received our attention and protection.'" He asked,

> Why should the relevant category not be even more general — perhaps "family relationships"; or "personal relationships"; or even "emotional attachments in general"? Though [Justice Brennan] has no basis for the level of generality [he] would select, we do: We refer to the most specific level at which a relevant tradition protecting, or denying protection to, the asserted right can be identified. If [there] were no societal tradition, either way, regarding the rights of the natural father or a child adulterously conceived, we would have to consult and if possible reason from, the traditions regarding natural fathers in general. But there is such a more specific tradition, and it unqualifiedly denies protection to such a parent. . . . Because [general] traditions provide such imprecise guidance, they permit judges to dictate rather than discern the society's views. [Although] assuredly having the virtue (if it be that) of leaving judges free to decide as they think best when the unanticipated occurs, a rule of law that binds neither by text nor by any particular, identifiable tradition, is no rule of law at all.

Although Justices O'Connor and Kennedy joined most of the plurality opinion, they specifically declined to join this footnote.
Justice Brennan responded:

> If we had looked to tradition with such specificity in past cases, many a decision would have reached a different result. [*Eisenstadt; Griswold;* Stanley v. Illinois, infra.] [The] plurality's interpretative method [ignores] the good reasons for limiting the role of "tradition" in interpreting the Constitution's deliberately capacious language. [By] suggesting that our sole function is to "*discern* the society's views," the plurality acts as if the only purpose of the Due Process Clause is to confirm the importance of interests already protected by a majority of the States. [In] construing the Fourteenth Amendment to offer shelter only to those interests specifically protected by historical practice, [the] plurality ignores the kind of society in which our Constitution exists. We are not an assimilative, homogeneous society, but a facilitative, pluralistic one, in which we must be willing to abide someone else's unfamiliar or even repellant practice because the same tolerant impulse protects our own idiosyncracies. Even if we can agree [that] "family" and "parenthood" are part of the good life, it is absurd to assume that we can agree on the content of those terms and destructive to pretend that we do. In a community such as ours, "liberty" must include the freedom not to conform. The plurality today squashes this freedom by requiring specific approval from history before protecting anything in the name of liberty.

To Justice Brennan, the case merely involved the protection of "the interest of a parent and child in their relationship with each other."
Justice Stevens, who contributed the fifth vote to support the constitutionality of the California statute, agreed that Michael H. had a liberty interest but argued that the California statutes recognized that interest to the extent required by the due process clause. For an attack on Justice Scalia's footnote, see L. Tribe and M. Dorf, On Reading the Constitution 98 (1991):

> [W]e argue that Justice Scalia's claim is false on several grounds; first, . . . the extraction of fundamental rights from societal traditions is no more value-neutral than is the extraction of fundamental rights from legal precedent; second, . . . there

is no universal metric of specificity against which to measure an asserted right; and third, [e]ven if Justice Scalia's program were workable, it would achieve a semblance of judicial neutrality only at the unacceptably high cost of near-complete abdication of the judicial responsibility to protect individual rights.

See also Balkin, Tradition, Betrayal, and the Politics of Deconstruction, 11 Cardozo L. Rev. 1613, 1615-1616 (1994):

[Justice Scalia's] test assumes that [for] each asserted right there either is or is not a specific tradition associated with its protection. Yet there are many ways of describing a liberty, and many different ways of characterizing a tradition. [There] has been no established tradition in California for protecting Justice Scalia's own rights to visit his children, since there is no tradition of affording protection to fathers who are children of Italian immigrants and who graduated from Ivy League law schools before 1965, were appointed to the United States Supreme Court by former governors of the state of California and have more than two children but less than thirteen. Indeed, the question has hardly ever come up. [To] be sure, Justice Scalia has a plausible response. When Justice Scalia claims parental rights to his children, the liberty he claims is the parental rights of fathers with respect to biological children born while the father was married to the child's mother. This has been traditionally protected. The rights of adulterous fathers, however, have not been traditionally protected. But this answer reveals that Justice Scalia's theory is not simply a preference for narrower traditions over broader traditions. It rests upon an important metaphysical set of assumptions — that traditions or (more importantly) the absences of traditions, come in discrete units with discrete boundaries. [Like] glass bottles, traditions and liberties come in premade sizes. [Thus,] there is a tradition of protecting marital privacy but not a tradition of protecting the marital privacy of a narrower class — for example, middle class persons, and certainly not a tradition of protecting the privacy of a broader class of persons that would include unmarried couples. Yet, under this logic, it is also historically clear that there is a tradition of protecting married couples' privacy, but not a historical tradition of protecting married couples' right to purchase contraceptives. Griswold v. Connecticut is thus a potential embarrassment for Justice Scalia.

6. In the context of family relations, substantive due process received a firm endorsement in Troxel v. Granville, 120 S. Ct. 2054 (2000). The case involved a Washington statute that allowed any person to petition a court for visitation rights "at any time," and authorized the court to grant visitation rights whenever "visitation may serve the best interest of the child." The Troxels had petitioned a court for the right to visit their grandchildren; the mother, a single parent, sought a limitation on visitation rights, which the court overrode, ordering significantly more visitation than the mother wanted. The Supreme Court held that the statute was unconstitutional as applied. The Court reaffirmed Meyer and Pierce, suggesting that the due process clause has a substantive component encompassing "the fundamental right of parents to make decisions concerning the care, custody, and control of their children." The law at issue here infringed on this right, partly because it "is breathtakingly broad." There is "no requirement that a court accord a parent's decision that visitation would not be in the child's best interest a presumption of validity or any weight whatever." The decision to reject the mother's judgment here "was based on precisely the type of mere disagreement we have just described and nothing more." There was no finding that the parent was unfit,

and thus the court's framework "directly contravened the traditional presumption that a fit parent will act in the best interest of his or her child." The Constitution required "at least some special weight to the parent's own determination." Nor did the mother ever seek "to cut off visitation entirely." Justice Thomas concurred on the ground that neither party had argued "that our substantive due process cases were wrongly decided and that the original understanding of the Due Process Clause precludes judicial enforcement of unenumerated rights under that constitutional provision."

Justice Stevens dissented on the ground that the statute was constitutional on its face. He emphasized that "there may be circumstances in which a child has a stronger interest at stake than mere protection from serious harm caused by the termination of visitation by a 'person' other than a parent." Justice Scalia dissented on the ground that the Constitution does not protect the "unenumerated right" at issue in the case. Justice Kennedy also dissented, objecting to the Court's "concept that the conventional nuclear family ought to establish the visitation standard for every domestic relations case."

7. In Reno v. Flores, 507 U.S. 292 (1993), the Court upheld against substantive due process challenge an Immigration and Naturalization Service (INS) regulation authorizing the arrest and holding of alien juveniles unaccompanied by parents or other related adults. The juveniles claimed a right to be released to "responsible adults," even if they were not family members. The Court doubted that "a child has a constitutional right not to be placed in a decent and humane custodial institution if there is available a responsible person unwilling to become the child's legal guardian but willing to undertake temporary legal custody." Because no fundamental right was involved — merely "the lesser" interest in being released into the custody of strangers — the Court required only a reasonable fit between the government purposes and the restriction in question. The Court said that the purpose of protecting juveniles was adequately advanced by the regulation in question, especially in light of the INS's lack of child-placement expertise and the fact that aliens were involved.

Justice O'Connor, joined by Justice Souter, wrote a lengthy concurring opinion, stressing that children have a "core liberty interest in remaining free from institutional confinement," that this freedom "is no narrower than an adult's," but that in this case "normal forms of custody," such as parents, close relatives, or legal guardians, have been unavailable, and therefore the INS program survives constitutional scrutiny. Justice Stevens, joined by Justice Blackmun, dissented on the ground that the "interest in minimizing administrative costs is a patently inadequate justification for the detention of harmless children."

In Stanley v. Illinois, 405 U.S. 645 (1972), the Court described the facts in this way: "Joan Stanley lived with Peter Stanley intermittently for 18 years, during which time they had three children. [Then Joan Stanley died.] Under Illinois law, the children of unwed fathers [automatically] become wards of the State upon the death of the mother. [Stanley maintained] that he had never been shown to be an unfit parent and that since married fathers [could] not be deprived of their children without such a showing, he had been deprived of the equal protection of the laws." The Court agreed. Justice White wrote:

[The] interest of a parent in the companionship, care, custody, and management of his or her children "come[s] to this Court with a momentum for respect lacking when appeal is made to liberties which derive merely from shifting economic arrangements." The Court has frequently emphasized the importance of the family. [Nor] has the law refused to recognize those family relationships unlegitimized by a marriage ceremony. ["To] say that the test of equal protection should be the 'legal' rather than the biological relationship is to avoid the issue. For the Equal Protection Clause necessarily limits the authority of a State to draw such 'legal' lines as it chooses." . . .

It may be [that] most unmarried fathers are unsuitable and neglectful parents. [But] all unmarried fathers are not in this category. [Given] the opportunity to make his case, Stanley may have been seen to be deserving of custody of his offspring. [Procedure] by presumption is always cheaper and easier than individualized determination. But when, as here, the procedure [needlessly] risks running roughshod over the important interests of both parent and child [it] cannot stand.

Justices Powell and Rehnquist did not participate.

8. By legitimating relationships that do not fit within the "traditional" family structure, it can be argued that *Stanley* undermines the very values that *Moore* sought to protect. Consider also in this regard Eisenstadt v. Baird, section F1 supra (unmarried persons have a constitutional right to use contraceptives); Planned Parenthood v. Danforth, section F2 supra (minors in some circumstances have a constitutional right to an abortion without parental consent); Mathews v. Lucas, 427 U.S. 495 (1976) (laws disadvantaging illegitimate children must be tested by intermediate scrutiny); Parham v. J.R., 442 U.S. 584 (1979) (due process requires at least an inquiry before a "neutral factfinder," although not a full-scale adversary hearing, before a parent may commit a minor child to a state mental hospital). See generally Burt, The Constitution of the Family, 1979 Sup. Ct. Rev. 329.

If an unwed father may have a constitutional right to custody of his illegitimate children when the mother dies, does he also have a constitutional right to veto the adoption of his illegitimate children by the mother's husband? In Quilloin v. Walcott, 434 U.S. 246 (1978), the Court unanimously held that a state could constitutionally deny such a veto to an unwed father, even though granting it to married and divorced fathers, where the unwed father had "never exercised actual or legal custody" over the child and there had been a determination that the adoption was in the "best interests of the child." In *Quilloin*, the Court also observed: "We have little doubt that the Due Process Clause would be offended '[i]f a State were to attempt to force the breakup of a natural family, over the objections of the parents and their children, without some showing of unfitness and for the sole reason that to do so was thought to be in the children's best interest.'" When *may* a state "break up" a "natural family"? May a state remove a child from his parents because they engage in criminal, adulterous, or otherwise immoral activity? See also Palmore v. Sidoti, 466 U.S. 429 (1984) (the equal protection clause prohibits a state from divesting a divorced mother of custody of her child, on petition of the child's natural father, because of the mother's remarriage to a man of a different race).

9. Does the criminal prosecution of drug-addicted mothers, for harms to their fetuses, violate the Constitution? For an affirmative answer, drawing on principles of due process and equal protection, see Roberts, Punishing Drug Addicts Who Have Babies: Women of Color, Equality, and the Right of Privacy, 104 Harv. L. Rev. 1419 (1991). Consider in particular the suggestion that the appropriate "concept of privacy includes not only the negative prosecution against govern-

ment coercion, but also the affirmative duty of government to protect the individual's personhood from degradation and to facilitate the processes of choice and self-determination. This approach shifts the focus of privacy theory from state nonintervention to an affirmative guarantee of personhood and autonomy. Under this post-liberal doctrine, the government is not only prohibited from punishing crack-addicted women for choosing to bear children; it is also required to provide drug treatment and prenatal care." Id. at 1479. Might Professor Roberts's use of the words "coercion" and "affirmative" be building on a theory that she is attempting to repudiate? And is it plausible to think that provision of these things should be a judicially enforceable right?

Note: The Limits of Privacy

1. *Freedom of intimate association.* In Roberts v. U.S. Jaycees, 468 U.S. 609 (1984), the Court upheld as applied to the Jaycees a Minnesota statute prohibiting discrimination on the basis of sex in "places of public accommodation." In the course of its opinion, the Court explained that there are two facets to the constitutionally protected freedom of association — one concerned with the exercise of first amendment rights, see Chapter 7, section E5, infra, and the other concerned with "intimate human relationships." The Court offered the following view on the freedom of "intimate" association:

> The Court has long recognized that, because the Bill of Rights is designed to secure individual liberty, it must afford the formation and preservation of certain kinds of highly personal relationships a substantial measure of sanctuary from unjustified interference by the State. [We] have noted that certain kinds of personal bonds have played a critical role in the culture and traditions of the Nation by cultivating and transmitting shared ideals and beliefs; they thereby foster diversity and act as critical buffers between the individual and the power of the State. Moreover, the constitutional shelter afforded such relationships reflects the realization that individuals draw much of their emotional enrichment from close ties with others. Protecting these relationships from unwarranted state interference therefore safeguards the ability independently to define one's identity that is central to any concept of liberty.
>
> The personal affiliations that exemplify these considerations, and that therefore suggest some relevant limitations on the relationships that might be entitled to this sort of constitutional protection, are those that attend the creations and sustenance of a family — marriage; childbirth; the raising and education of children; and cohabitation with one's relatives. Family relationships, by their nature, involve deep attachments and commitments to the necessarily few other individuals with whom one shares not only a special community of thoughts, experiences, and beliefs but also distinctively personal aspects of one's life. Among other things, therefore, they are distinguished by such attributes as relative smallness, a high degree of selectivity in decisions to begin and maintain the affiliation, and seclusion from others in critical aspects of the relationship. As a general matter, only relationships with these sorts of qualities are likely to reflect the considerations that have led to an understanding of freedom of association as an intrinsic element of personal liberty. Conversely, an association lacking these qualities — such as a large business enterprise — seems remote from the concerns giving rise to this constitutional protection. [Between] these poles, of course, lies a broad range of human relationships that may make greater or lesser claims to constitutional protection.

The Court held that, because "the local chapters of the Jaycees are large and basically unselective groups," they are "clearly [outside] the category of relationships worthy of this kind of constitutional protection." The first amendment aspects of *Roberts* are explored in Chapter 7, section E5, infra.

2. *Freedom of cultural association.* Can the state constitutionally require an organization dedicated to maintaining Irish traditions and celebrating Irish heritage to admit Italians or blacks? For a discussion of this issue, see Marshall, Discrimination and the Right of Association, 81 Nw. U.L. Rev. 68 (1986); Karst, Paths to Belonging: The Constitution and Cultural Identity, 64 N.C.L. Rev. 303 (1986). See also the questions raised by Massachusetts's effort to open the St. Patrick's Day Parade to homosexuals, discussed in Chapter 7, section E5, infra.

3. *Sexual autonomy in general.* Consider the following case.

Bowers v. Hardwick

478 U.S. 186 (1986)

JUSTICE WHITE delivered the opinion of the Court.

[Respondent, an adult male, was criminally charged for violating Georgia's sodomy statute by committing a sexual act with another adult male in his own bedroom. The statute defined sodomy as committing or submitting to "any sexual act involving the sex organs of one person and the mouth or anus of another." After the prosecutor elected not to present the case to the grand jury, respondent brought this suit in federal court challenging the constitutionality of the statute. The district court upheld the statute, but the court of appeals reversed.]

We agree with the State that the Court of Appeals erred, and hence reverse its judgment. . . .

We first register our disagreement with the Court of Appeals and with respondent that the Court's prior cases have construed the Constitution to confer a right of privacy that extends to homosexual sodomy[2] and for all intents and purposes have decided this case. . . .

[We] think it evident that none of the rights announced in [such cases as *Pierce, Skinner, Griswold,* and *Roe*] bears any resemblance to the claimed constitutional right of homosexuals to engage in acts of sodomy that is asserted in this case. No connection between family, marriage, or procreation on the one hand and homosexual activity on the other has been demonstrated, either by the Court of Appeals or by respondent. Moreover, any claim that these cases nevertheless stand for the proposition that any kind of private sexual conduct between consenting adults is constitutionally insulated from state proscription is unsupportable. . . .

Precedent aside, however, respondent would have us announce, as the Court of Appeals did, a fundamental right to engage in homosexual sodomy. This we are quite unwilling to do. . . .

Striving to assure itself and the public that announcing rights not readily identifiable in the Constitution's text involves much more than the imposition of the

---

2. The only claim properly before the Court [is] Hardwick's challenge to the Georgia statute as applied to consensual homosexual sodomy. We express no opinion on the constitutionality of the Georgia statute as applied to other acts of sodomy. [Relocated footnote — EDS.]

Justices' own choice of values on the States and the Federal Government, the Court has sought to identify the nature of the rights qualifying for heightened judicial protection. In [*Palko*] it was said that this category includes those fundamental liberties that are "implicit in the concept of ordered liberty," such that "neither liberty nor justice would exist if [they] were sacrificed." A different description of fundamental liberties appeared in [*Moore*] (opinion of Powell, J.), where they are characterized as those liberties that are "deeply rooted in this Nation's history and tradition." See also [*Griswold*].

It is obvious to us that neither of these formulations would extend a fundamental right to homosexuals to engage in acts of consensual sodomy. Proscriptions against that conduct have ancient roots. Sodomy was a criminal offense at common law and was forbidden by the laws of the original thirteen states when they ratified the Bill of Rights. In 1868, when the Fourteenth Amendment was ratified, all but 5 of the 37 States of the Union had criminal sodomy laws. In fact, until 1961, all 50 States outlawed sodomy, and today, 24 States and the District of Columbia continue to provide criminal penalties for sodomy performed in private and between consenting adults. Against this background, to claim that a right to engage in such conduct is "deeply rooted in this Nation's history and tradition" or "implicit in the concept of ordered liberty" is, at best, facetious.

Nor are we inclined to take a more expansive view of our authority to discover new fundamental rights imbedded in the Due Process Clause. The Court is most vulnerable and comes nearest to illegitimacy when it deals with judge-made constitutional law having little or no cognizable roots in the language or design of the Constitution. That this is so was painfully demonstrated by the face-off between the Executive and the Court in the 1930's, which resulted in the repudiation on much of the substantive gloss that the Court had placed on the Due Process Clause of the Fifth and Fourteenth Amendments. There should be, therefore, great resistance to expand the substantive reach of those Clauses, particularly if it requires redefining the category of rights deemed to be fundamental. Otherwise, the Judiciary necessarily takes to itself further authority to govern the country without express constitutional authority. The claimed right pressed on us today falls far short of overcoming this resistance.

Respondent, however, asserts that the result should be different where the homosexual conduct occurs in the privacy of the home. He relies on Stanley v. Georgia [394 U.S. 557 (1969)], where the Court held that the First Amendment prevents conviction for possessing and reading obscene material in the privacy of the home. . . .

Stanley did protect conduct that would not have been protected outside the home, and it partially prevented the enforcement of state obscenity laws; but the decision was firmly grounded in the First Amendment. The right pressed upon us here has no similar support in the text of the Constitution, and it does not qualify for recognition under the prevailing principles for construing the Fourteenth Amendment. Its limits are also difficult to discern. Plainly enough, otherwise illegal conduct is not always immunized whenever it occurs in the home. Victimless crimes, such as the possession and use of illegal drugs, do not escape the law where they are committed at home. *Stanley* itself recognized that its holdings offered no protection for the possession in the home of drugs, firearms, or stolen goods. And if respondent's submission is limited to the voluntary sexual conduct between consenting adults, it would be difficult, except by fiat, to limit the claimed right to homosexual conduct while leaving exposed to prosecution adultery, incest, and other sexual crimes even though they are committed in the home. We are unwilling to start down that road.

Even if the conduct at issue here is not a fundamental right, respondent asserts that there must be a rational basis for the law and that there is none in this case other than the presumed belief of a majority of the electorate in Georgia that homosexual sodomy is immoral and unacceptable. This is said to be an inadequate rationale to support the law. The law, however, is constantly based on notions of morality, and if all laws representing essentially moral choices are to be invalidated under the Due Process Clause, the courts will be very busy indeed. Even respondent makes no such claim, but insists that majority sentiments about the morality of homosexuality should be declared inadequate. We do not agree, and are unpersuaded that the sodomy laws of some 25 States should be invalidated on this basis.[8]

Accordingly, the judgment of the Court of Appeals is reversed.

CHIEF JUSTICE BURGER, concurring.

As the Court notes, the proscriptions against sodomy have very "ancient roots." Decisions of individuals relating to homosexual conduct have been subject to state intervention throughout the history of Western Civilization. Condemnation of those practices is firmly rooted in Judeo-Christian moral and ethical standards. [Blackstone] described "the infamous crime against nature" as an offense of "deeper malignity" than rape, an heinous act "the very mention of which is a disgrace to human nature," and "a crime not fit to be named."

[To] hold that the act of homosexual sodomy is somehow protected as a fundamental right would be to cast aside millennia of moral teaching.

[I] find nothing in the Constitution depriving a State of the power to enact the statute challenged here.

JUSTICE POWELL, concurring.

[The] Georgia statute at issue in this case, authorizes a court to imprison a person for up to 20 years for a single private, consensual act of sodomy. In my view, a prison sentence for such conduct — certainly a sentence of long duration — would create a serious Eighth Amendment issue. . . .

JUSTICE BLACKMUN, with whom JUSTICE BRENNAN, JUSTICE MARSHALL, and JUSTICE STEVENS join, dissenting.

This case is no more about "a fundamental right to engage in homosexual sodomy," as the Court purports to declare, than Stanley v. Georgia was about a fundamental right to watch obscene movies, or Katz v. United States, 389 U.S. 347 (1967), was about a fundamental right to place interstate bets from a telephone booth. Rather, this case is about "the most comprehensive of rights and the right most valued by civilized men," namely, "the right to be let alone." Olmstead v. United States, 277 U.S. 438, 478 (1928) (Brandeis, J., dissenting).

The statute at issue denies individuals the right to decide for themselves whether to engage in particular forms of private, consensual sexual activity. The

---

8. Respondent does not defend the judgment below based on the Ninth Amendment, the Equal Protection Clause or the Eighth Amendment.

Court concludes that [the statute] is valid essentially because "the laws of . . . many States . . . still make such conduct illegal and have done so for a very long time." But the fact that the moral judgments expressed by statutes like [this one] may be "natural and familiar . . . ought not to conclude our judgment upon the question whether statutes embodying them conflict with the Constitution of the United States." [*Roe*, quoting *Lochner* (Holmes, J., dissenting).]

The Court concludes today that none of our prior cases dealing with various decisions that individuals are entitled to make free of governmental interference "bears any resemblance to the claimed constitutional right of homosexuals to engage in acts of sodomy that is asserted in this case." While it is true that these cases may be characterized by their connection to protection of the family, see Roberts v. United States Jaycees, the Court's conclusion that they extend no further than this boundary ignores the warning in [*Moore*] against "clos[ing] our eyes to the basic reasons why certain rights associated with the family have been accorded shelter under the Fourteenth Amendment's Due Process Clause." We protect those rights not because they contribute, in some direct and material way, to the general public welfare, but because they form so central a part of an individual's life. . . .

Only the most willful blindness could obscure the fact that sexual intimacy is "a sensitive, key relationship of human existence, central to family life, community welfare, and the development of human personality," Paris Adult Theatre I v. Slaton, 413 U.S. 49, 63 (1973).

[The] fact that individuals define themselves in a significant way through their intimate sexual relationships with others suggests, in a Nation as diverse as ours, that there may be many "right" ways of conducting those relationships, and that much of the richness of a relationship will come from the freedom an individual has to *choose* the form and nature of these intensely personal bonds. . . .

The Court claims that its decision today merely refuses to recognize a fundamental right to engage in homosexual sodomy; what the Court really has refused to recognize is the fundamental interest all individuals have in controlling the nature of their intimate associations with others.

The behavior for which Hardwick faces prosecution occurred in his own home, a place to which the Fourth Amendment attaches special significance. . . .

The Court's failure to comprehend the magnitude of the liberty interests at stake in this case leads it to slight the question whether petitioner, on behalf of the State, has justified Georgia's infringement on these interests. I believe that neither of the two general justifications for [the statute] that petitioner has advanced warrants dismissing respondent's challenge for failure to state a claim.

First, petitioner asserts that the acts made criminal by the statute may have serious adverse consequences for "the general public health and welfare," such as spreading communicable diseases or fostering other criminal activity. Inasmuch as this case was dismissed by the District Court on the pleadings, it is not surprising that the record before us is barren of any evidence to support petitioner's claim. In light of the state of the record, I see no justification for the Court's attempt to equate the private, consensual sexual activity at issue here with the "possession in the home of drugs, firearms, or stolen goods," to which *Stanley* refused to extend its protection. . . .

[The] assertion that "traditional Judeo-Christian values proscribe" the conduct involved cannot provide an adequate justification for [the statute]. That certain, but by no means all, religious groups condemn the behavior at issue gives the State no license to impose their judgments on the entire citizenry. The legitimacy of secular legislation depends instead on whether the State can advance some justification for its law beyond its conformity to religious doctrine. . . .

Certainly, some private behavior can affect the fabric of society as a whole. [Statutes] banning public sexual activity are entirely consistent with protecting the individual's liberty interest in decisions concerning sexual relations: the same recognition that those decisions are intensely private which justifies protecting them from governmental interference can justify protecting individuals from unwilling exposure to the sexual activities of others. But the mere fact that intimate behavior may be punished when it takes place in public cannot dictate how States can regulate intimate behavior that occurs in intimate places. . . .

I can only hope that [the] Court soon will reconsider its analysis and conclude that depriving individuals of the right to choose for themselves how to conduct their intimate relationships poses a far greater threat to the values most deeply rooted in our Nation's history than tolerance of nonconformity could ever do. Because I think the Court today betrays those values, I dissent.

JUSTICE STEVENS, with whom JUSTICE BRENNAN and JUSTICE MARSHALL join, dissenting.

Like the statute that is challenged in this case, the rationale of the Court's opinion applies equally to the prohibited conduct regardless of whether the parties who engage in it are married or unmarried, or are of the same or different sexes. Sodomy was condemned as an odious and sinful type of behavior during the formative period of the common law. That condemnation was equally damning for heterosexual and homosexual sodomy. Moreover, it provided no special exemption for married couples. . . .

Because the Georgia statute expresses the traditional view that sodomy is an immoral kind of conduct regardless of the identity of the persons who engage in it, I believe that a proper analysis of its constitutionality requires consideration of two questions: First, may a State totally prohibit the described conduct by means of a neutral law applying without exception to all persons subject to its jurisdiction? If not, may the State save the statute by announcing that it will only enforce the law against homosexuals? . . .

[Individual] decisions by married persons, concerning the intimacies of their physical relationship, even when not intended to produce offspring, are a form of "liberty" protected by the Due Process Clause of the Fourteenth Amendment. [Griswold.] Moreover, this protection extends to intimate choices by unmarried as well as married persons. [Carey; Eisenstadt.] . . .

Society has every right to encourage its individual members to follow particular traditions in expressing affection for one another and in gratifying their personal desires. It, of course, may prohibit an individual from imposing his will on another to satisfy his own selfish interests. It also may prevent an individual from interfering with, or violating, a legally sanctioned and protected relationship, such as marriage. And it may explain the relative advantages and disadvantages of different forms of intimate expression. But when individual married couples are isolated from observation by others, the way in which they voluntarily choose to conduct their intimate relations is a matter for them — not the State — to decide. The essential "liberty" that animated the development of the law in cases like Griswold, Eisenstadt, and Carey surely embraces the right to engage in nonreproductive, sexual conduct that others may consider offensive or immoral.

Paradoxical as it may seem, our prior cases thus establish that a State may not prohibit sodomy within "the sacred precincts of marital bedrooms," *Griswold,* or indeed, between unmarried heterosexual adults. *Eisenstadt.* . . .

If the Georgia statute cannot be enforced as it is written — if the conduct it seeks to prohibit is a protected form of liberty for the vast majority of Georgia's citizens — the State must assume the burden of justifying a selective application of its law. Either the persons to whom Georgia seeks to apply its statute do not have the same interest in "liberty" that others have, or there must be a reason why the State may be permitted to apply a generally applicable law to certain persons that it does not apply to others.

The first possibility is plainly unacceptable. Although the meaning of the principle that "all men are created equal" is not always clear, it surely must mean that every free citizen has the same interest in "liberty" that the members of the majority share. From the standpoint of the individual, the homosexual and the heterosexual have the same interest in deciding how he will live his own life, and, more narrowly, how he will conduct himself in his personal and voluntary associations with his companions.

[The] second possibility is similarly unacceptable. A policy of selective application must be supported by a neutral and legitimate interest — something more substantial than a habitual dislike for, or ignorance about, the disfavored group. Neither the State nor the Court has identified any such interest in this case. The Court has posited as a justification for the Georgia statute "the presumed belief of a majority of the electorate in Georgia that homosexual sodomy is immoral and unacceptable." But the Georgia electorate has expressed no such belief — instead, its representatives enacted a law that presumably reflects the belief that *all sodomy* is immoral and unacceptable. Unless the Court is prepared to conclude that such a law is constitutional, it may not rely on the work product of the Georgia Legislature to support its holding. For the Georgia statute does not single out homosexuals as a separate class meriting special disfavored treatment. . . .

Both the Georgia statute and the Georgia prosecutor thus completely fail to provide the Court with any support for the conclusion that homosexual sodomy, *simpliciter,* is considered unacceptable conduct in that State, and that the burden of justifying a selective application of the generally applicable law has been met. . . .

I respectfully dissent.

Note: Homosexuality and Substantive Due Process

In light of the majority's framework, should a court hold unconstitutional a statute making it an offense for married heterosexuals to engage in sodomy? A statute making heterosexual sodomy between unmarried people an offense? In light of Justice Blackmun's framework, should a court hold unconstitutional a statute defining as criminal incest sexual relations between first cousins?

Consider the following views on *Hardwick:*

1. Conkle, The Second Death of Substantive Due Process, 62 Ind. L.J. 215, 232-233, 235, 242 (1987):

Under [*Eisenstadt* and *Roe*], an individual, whether married or single, has the right [to] practice birth control through the use of contraceptives [or] abortion. As a result, *Eisenstadt* and *Roe* necessarily protect [the] right of heterosexuals to engage in nonprocreative sexual relations, even outside the traditional setting of marriage. [It] is difficult to imagine how the individual interest presented in *Bowers* was less important than the interest protected in [the] earlier decisions. [Moreover,] the countervailing governmental interests asserted in *Bowers* were far less substantial than the interests asserted in *Roe*. [*Roe*] and *Bowers* are [thus] inconsistent and irreconcilable. [Viewed in this light, *Bowers*] represents the death of substantive due process as a principled doctrine of law.

2. Rubenfeld, The Right of Privacy, 102 Harv. L. Rev. 737, 770, 782, 799-800 (1989):

[Laws] against homosexual sex have an effect that most laws do not. They forcibly channel certain individuals [into] a network of social institutions and relations that will occupy their lives to a substantial degree. [The] prohibition against homosexual sex channels individuals' sexual desires into *reproductive* outlets. Although the prohibition does not, like the law against abortions, produce as an imminent consequence compulsory child-bearing, it nonetheless forcibly directs individuals into the pathways of reproductive sexuality.

3. Consider the view that *Hardwick* was correctly decided because the privacy cases have always made a bow in the direction of tradition, and because tradition was simply not implicated in that case. (Keep in mind, though, the problem of deciding the level of generality at which the tradition should be described.) In this light, perhaps the preferable route in *Hardwick* would have been to invoke principles of equal protection, which are self-consciously directed *against* tradition. On this account, *Hardwick* has no implications for an equal protection attack on laws discriminating on the basis of sexual orientation. See Sunstein, Sexual Orientation and the Constitution: A Note on the Relationship between Due Process and Equal Protection, 55 U. Chi. L. Rev. 1161 (1988).

Would *Hardwick* have been better conceived as a genuinely procedural due process case, in which police officers relied on an outmoded law no longer supported by popular convictions, as reflected in the fact that successful prosecutions for consensual homosexual sodomy were never brought? See C. Sunstein, One Case at a Time (1999). Consider the view that this narrow understanding of the *Hardwick* problem connects *Hardwick* with *Griswold*.

4. Perhaps the majority's approach could have been strengthened with the suggestion that the previous cases involved not the right to engage in sexual activity but more narrowly the right to avoid certain government *methods* for intruding on sexual liberty. On this view, the problem in the earlier cases consisted of the government's effort to stop sexual activity not through the criminal law — which the public would not allow anyway — but instead through regulation of procreation. But the earlier cases preserved the possibility that the state might use the criminal law directly if the public would permit it — as, for example, through laws forbidding fornication or adultery. On this view, the earlier cases had nothing to do with *Hardwick*.

5. Recall Chief Justice Burger's willingness to quote Blackstone's suggestion that consensual adult homosexual conduct is "an offense of 'deeper malignity' than rape." Might it be urged that this statement suggests that discrimination on the basis of sexual orientation is actually a form of discrimination on the basis of sex? Consider the view that discrimination on the former basis is (a) at least on

its face, a form of sex discrimination because it distinguishes between sexual relations with men and sexual relations with women, cf. Loving v. Virginia, 388 U.S. 1 (1967) (invalidating miscegenation law notwithstanding a claim that it was neutral as between blacks and whites); (b) part of a system of sex-role stereotyping by drawing sharp lines between men and women and their social/sexual roles; or (c) a method of subordinating women by (1) forbidding sexual alliances between women and (2) defining men as people who have sexual alliances only with women, and thus defining men under present conditions as socially superior to women. Consider whether the impetus for laws forbidding homosexual relations might be closely connected to efforts to retain male supremacy. See Koppelman, Why Discrimination against Lesbians and Gay Men Is Sex Discrimination, 69 N.Y.U. L. Rev. 197 (1994); Law, Homosexuality and the Social Meaning of Gender, 1988 Wis. L. Rev. 187.

6. *Personal appearance: hair style.* Would a state law dictating a uniform hair style for all persons infringe the "right of privacy"? In Kelley v. Johnson, 425 U.S. 238 (1976), the Court upheld a regulation limiting the length of policemen's hair. The Court explained that the "'liberty' interest" claimed in *Kelley* was "distinguishable" from those protected in *Roe, Eisenstadt, Stanley, Griswold*, and *Meyer*, for each "of those cases involved a substantial claim of infringement on the individual's freedom of choice with respect to certain basic matters of procreation, marriage, and family life." The Court thus held that the regulation was constitutional because it was "not irrational." Justice Marshall, joined by Justice Brennan, dissented on the ground that an "individual's personal appearance may reflect, sustain, and nourish his personality and may well be used as a means of expressing his attitude and lifestyle. In taking control over a citizen's personal appearance, the government forces him to sacrifice substantial elements of his integrity and identity as well."

7. *The reach of "privacy."* Consider the following assertions:

a. People v. Fries, 42 Ill. 2d 446, 250 N.E.2d 149 (1969):

> The [question] presented is whether the [State may require motorcyclists to wear] protective headgear. [The] manifest function of [the] requirement [is] to safeguard the person wearing it [from] head injuries [in the event of an accident]. Such a laudable purpose, however, cannot justify the regulation of what is essentially a matter of personal safety. [The statute violates] the fourteenth amendment.

b. Whalen v. Roe, 429 U.S. 589, 606 (1977) (Brennan, J., concurring):

> The [statute] under attack requires doctors to disclose to the State information about prescriptions for certain drugs with a high potential for abuse, and provides for the storage of that information in a central computer file. [This] information [is] made available only to a small number of public health officials with a legitimate interest in the information. [Broad] dissemination by state officials of such information, however, would clearly implicate constitutionally protected privacy rights, and would presumably be justified only by compelling state interests. See [*Roe*].

The Court in *Whalen* found it unnecessary to decide whether the right of privacy reached this far, for in light of the safeguards of the challenged statutory scheme, "the program does [not] pose a sufficiently grievous threat to [the asserted privacy] interest to establish a constitutional violation."

4. The Right to Die

Cruzan v. Director, Missouri Department of Health
457 U.S. 261 (1990)

CHIEF JUSTICE REHNQUIST delivered the opinion of the Court.

On the night of January 11, 1983, Nancy Cruzan lost control of her car as she traveled down Elm Road in Jasper County, Missouri. The vehicle overturned, and Cruzan was discovered lying face down in a ditch without detectable respiratory or cardiac function. [She] remained in a coma for approximately three weeks and then progressed to an unconscious state in which she was able to orally ingest some nutrition. In order to ease feeding and further the recovery, surgeons implanted a gastrostomy feeding and hydration tube in Cruzan with the consent of her then husband. Subsequent rehabilitative efforts proved unavailing. She now lies in a Missouri state hospital in what is commonly referred to as a persistent vegetative state: generally, a condition in which a person exhibits motor reflexes but evinces no indications of significant cognitive function. The State of Missouri is bearing the cost of her care.

After it had become apparent that Nancy Cruzan has virtually no chance of regaining her mental faculties her parents asked hospital employees to terminate the artificial nutrition and hydration procedures. All agree that such a removal would cause her death. The employees refused to honor the request without court approval.

[We] granted certiorari to consider the question of whether Cruzan has a right under the United States Constitution which would require the hospital to withdraw life-sustaining treatment from her under these circumstances.

At common law, even the touching of one person by another without consent and without legal justification was a battery. [The] logical corollary of the doctrine of informed consent is that the patient generally possesses the right not to consent, that is, to refuse treatment. Until about 15 years ago and the seminal decision in In re Quinlan, 70 N.J. 10, 355 A.2d 647, cert. denied sub nom., Garger v. New Jersey, 429 U.S. 922 (1976), the number of right-to-refuse-treatment decisions were relatively few. Most of the earlier cases involved patients who refused medical treatment forbidden by their religious beliefs, thus implicating First Amendment rights as well as common law rights of self-determination. More recently, however, with the advance of medical technology capable of sustaining life well past the point where natural forces would have brought certain death in earlier times, cases involving the right to refuse life-sustaining treatment have burgeoned. [The] common-law doctrine of informed consent is viewed as generally encompassing the right of a competent individual to refuse medical treatment.

[In] this Court, the question is simply and starkly whether the United States Constitution prohibits Missouri from choosing the rule of decision which it did. [The] principle that a competent person has a constitutionally protected liberty interest in refusing unwanted medical treatment may be inferred from our prior decisions. In Jacobson v. Massachusetts, 197 U.S. 11, 24-30 (1905), for in-

stance the Court balanced an individual's liberty interest in declining an unwanted smallpox vaccine against the State's interest in preventing disease. [Just]
this Term, in the course of holding that a State's procedures for administering
antipsychotic medication to prisoners were sufficient to satisfy due process concerns, we recognized that prisoners possess "a significant liberty interest in avoiding the unwanted administration of antipsychotic drugs under the Due Process
Clause of the Fourteenth Amendment." [Washington v. Harper, infra.]

[Petitioners] insist that under the general holdings of our cases, the forced administration of life-sustaining medical treatment, and even of artificially-delivered
food and water essential to life, would implicate a competent person's liberty interest. Although we think the logic of the cases discussed above would embrace
such a liberty interest, the dramatic consequences involved in refusal of such
treatment would inform the inquiry as to whether the deprivation of that interest
is constitutionally permissible. But for purposes of this case, we assume that the
United States Constitution would grant a competent person a constitutionally
protected right to refuse lifesaving hydration and nutrition.

Petitioners go on to assert that an incompetent person should possess the same
right in this respect as is possessed by a competent person. [The] difficulty with
petitioners' claim is that in a sense it begs the question: an incompetent person
is not able to make an informed and voluntary choice to exercise a hypothetical
right to refuse treatment or any other right. Such a "right" must be exercised for
her, if at all, by some sort of surrogate. Here, Missouri has in effect recognized
that under certain circumstances a surrogate may act for the patient in electing
to have hydration and nutrition withdrawn in such a way as to cause death, but it
has established a procedural safeguard to assure that the action of the surrogate
conforms as best it may to the wishes expressed by the patient while competent.
Missouri requires that evidence of the incompetent's wishes as to the withdrawal
of treatment be proved by clear and convincing evidence. The question, then, is
whether the United States Constitution forbids the establishment of this procedural requirement by the State. We hold that it does not.

[Missouri] relies on its interest in the protection and preservation of human
life, and there can be no gainsaying this interest. [The] majority of States in this
country have laws imposing criminal penalties on one who assists another to commit suicide. We do not think a State is required to remain neutral in the face of
an informed and voluntary decision by a physically-able adult to starve to death.

But in the context presented here, a State has more particular interests at stake.
The choice between life and death is a deeply personal decision of obvious and
overwhelming finality. We believe Missouri may legitimately seek to safeguard
the personal element of this choice through the imposition of heightened evidentiary requirements. It cannot be disputed that the Due Process Clause protects an
interest in life as well as an interest in refusing life-sustaining medical treatment.
Not all incompetent patients will have loved ones available to serve as surrogate
decisionmakers. And even where family members are present, "[t]here will, of
course, be some unfortunate situations in which family members will not act to
protect a patient." In re Jobes, 108 N.J. 394, 419, 529 A.2d 434, 477 (1987). A
State is entitled to guard against potential abuses in such situations. Similarly a
State is entitled to consider that a judicial proceeding to make a determination
regarding an incompetent's wishes may very well not be an adversarial one, with
the added guarantee of accurate factfinding that the adversary process brings with

it. Finally, we think a State may properly decline to make judgments about the "quality" of life that a particular individual may enjoy, and simply assert an unqualified interest in the preservation of human life to be weighed against the constitutionally protected interests of the individual.

In our view, Missouri has permissibly sought to advance these interests through the adoption of a "clear and convincing" standard of proof to govern such proceedings. [We] think it self-evident that the interests at stake in the instant proceedings are more substantial, both on an individual and societal level, than those in a run-of-the-mine civil dispute.

[The] Supreme Court of Missouri held that in this case the testimony adduced at trial did not amount to clear and convincing proof of the patient's desire to have hydration and nutrition withdrawn. In so doing, it reversed a decision of the Missouri trial court which had found that the evidence "suggest[ed]" Nancy Cruzan would not have desired to continue such measures, but which had not adopted the standard of "clear and convincing evidence" enunciated by the Supreme Court. The testimony adduced at trial consisted primarily of Nancy Cruzan's statement made to a housemate about a year before her accident that she would not want to live should she face life as a "vegetable," and other observations to the same effect. The observations did not deal in terms with withdrawal of medical treatment or hydration and nutrition. We cannot say that the Supreme Court of Missouri commited constitutional error in reaching the conclusion that it did.

Petitioners alternatively contend that Missouri must accept the "substituted judgment" of close family members even in the absence of substantial proof that their views reflect the views of the patient. They rely primarily upon our decisions in Michael H. v. Gerald D., 491 U.S. 505 (1989), and Parham v. J.R., 442 U.S. 584 (1979). But we do not think these cases support their claim. In *Michael H.*, we *upheld* the constitutionality of California's favored treatment of traditional family relationships; such a holding may not be turned around into a constitutional requirement that a State *must* recognize the primacy of those relationships in a situation like this. And in *Parham*, where the patient was a minor, we also *upheld* the constitutionality of a state scheme in which parents made certain decisions for mentally ill minors. Here again petitioners would seek to turn a discussion which allowed a State to rely on family decisionmaking into a constitutional requirement that the State recognize such decisionmaking. But constitutional law does not work that way.

No doubt is engendered by anything in this record but that Nancy Cruzan's mother and father are loving and caring parents. If the State were required by the United States Constitution to repose a right of "substituted judgment" with anyone, the Cruzans would surely qualify. But we do not think the Due Process Clause requires the State to repose judgment on these matters with anyone but the patient herself. Close family members may have a strong feeling — a feeling not at all ignoble or unworthy, but not entirely disinterested, either — that they do not wish to witness the continuation of the life of a loved one which they regard as hopeless, meaningless, and even degrading. But there is no automatic assurance that the view of close family members will necessarily be the same as the patient's would have been had she been confronted with the prospect of her situation while competent. All of the reasons previously discussed for allowing Missouri to require clear and convincing evidence of the patient's wishes lead us to conclude that the State may choose to defer only to those wishes, rather than confide the decision to close family members.[12]

The judgment of the Supreme Court of Missouri is affirmed.

JUSTICE O'CONNOR, concurring.

[As] the Court notes, the liberty interest in refusing medical treatment flows from decisions involving the State's invasions into the body. Because our notions of liberty are inextricably entwined with our idea of physical freedom and self-determination, the Court has often deemed state incursions into the body repugnant to the interests protected by the Due Process Clause.

[The] State's imposition of medical treatment on an unwilling competent adult necessarily involves some form of restraint and intrusion. [Artificial] feeding cannot readily be distinguished from other forms of medical treatment.

[I] also write separately to emphasize that the Court does not today decide the issue whether a State must also give effect to the decisions of a surrogate decision-maker. In my view, such a duty may well be constitutionally required to protect the patient's liberty interest in refusing medical treatment. Few individuals provide explicit oral or written instructions regarding their intent to refuse medical treatment should they become incompetent.

JUSTICE SCALIA, concurring.

[I] would have preferred that we announce, clearly and promptly, that the federal courts have no business in this field; that American law has always accorded the State the power to prevent, by force if necessary, suicide — including suicide by refusing to take appropriate measures necessary to preserve one's life; that the point at which life becomes "worthless," and the point at which the means necessary to preserve it become "extraordinary" or "inappropriate," are neither set forth in the Constitution nor known to the nine Justices of this Court any better than they are known to nine people picked at random from the Kansas City telephone directory; and hence, that even when it *is* demonstrated by clear and convincing evidence that a patient no longer wishes certain measures to be taken to preserve her life, it is up to the citizens of Missouri to decide, through their elected representatives, whether that wish will be honored.

[The] text of the Due Process Clause does not protect individuals against deprivations of liberty *simpliciter.* It protects them against deprivations of liberty "without due process of law." To determine that such a deprivation would not occur if Nancy Cruzan were forced to take nourishment against her will, it is unnecessary to reopen the historically recurrent debate over whether "due process" includes substantive restrictions.

[It] is at least true that no "substantive due process" claim can be maintained unless the claimant demonstrates that the State has deprived him of a right historically and traditionally protected against State interference. That cannot possibly be established here.

---

12. We are not faced in this case with the question of whether a State might be required to defer to the decision of a surrogate if competent and probative evidence established that the patient herself has expressed a desire that the decision to terminate life-sustaining treatment be made for her by that individual. ...

At common law in England, a suicide — defined as one who "deliberately puts an end to his own existence, or commits any unlawful malicious act, the consequence of which is his own death," 4 W. Blackstone, Commentaries *189 — was criminally liable. [And] most States that did not explicitly prohibit assisted suicide in 1868 recognized, when the issue arose in the 50 years following the Fourteenth Amendment's ratification, that assisted and (in some cases) attempted suicide were unlawful.

[Petitioners] rely on three distinctions to separate Nancy Cruzan's case from ordinary suicide: (1) that she is permanently incapacited and in pain; (2) that she would bring on her death not by any affirmative act but by merely declining treatment that provides nourishment; and (3) that preventing her from effectuating her presumed wish to die requires violation of her bodily integrity. None of these suffices. . . .

[Are] there, then, no reasonable and humane limits that ought not to be exceeded in requiring an individual to preserve his own life? There obviously are, but they are not set forth in the Due Process Clause. What assures us that those limits will not be exceeded is the same constitutional guarantee that is the source of most of our protection — what protects us, for example, from being assessed a tax of 100% of our income above the subsistence level, from being forbidden to drive cars, or from being required to send our children to school for 10 hours a day, none of which horribles is categorically prohibited by the Constitution. Our salvation is the Equal Protection Clause, which requires the democratic majority to accept for themselves and their loved ones what they impose on you and me. This Court need not, and has no authority to, inject itself into every field of human activity where irrationality and oppression may theoretically occur, and if it tries to do so it will destroy itself.

Justice Brennan, with whom Justice Marshall and Justice Blackmun join, dissenting.

[Although] the right to be free of unwanted medical intervention, like other constitutionally protected interests, may not be absolute, no State interest could outweigh the rights of an individual in Nancy Cruzan's position. Whatever a State's possible interests in mandating life-support treatment under other circumstances, there is no good to be obtained here by Missouri's insistence that Nancy Cruzan remain on life-support systems if it is indeed her wish not to do so. Missouri does not claim, nor could it, that society as a whole will be benefited by Nancy's receiving medical treatment. No third party's situation will be improved and no harm to others will be averted.

The only state interest asserted here is a general interest in the preservation of life. But the State has no legitimate general interest in someone's life, completely abstracted from the interest of the person living that life, that could outweigh the person's choice to avoid medical treatment.

[This] is not to say that the State has no legitimate interests to assert here. As the majority recognizes Missouri has a *parens patriae* interest in providing Nancy Cruzan, now incompetent, with as accurate as possible a determination of how she would exercise her rights under these circumstances. Second, if and when it is determined that Nancy Cruzan would want to continue treatment, the State may legitimately assert an interest in providing that treatment. But *until* Nancy's wishes have been determined, the only state interest that may be asserted is an interest in safeguarding the accuracy of that determination.

Accuracy, therefore, must be our touchstone. Missouri may constitutionally impose only those procedural requirements that serve to enhance the accuracy of a determination of Nancy Cruzan's wishes or are at least consistent with an accurate determination. The Missouri "safeguard" that the Court upholds today does not meet that standard. [Missouri's] rule of decision imposes a markedly asymmetrical evidentiary burden. Only evidence of specific statements of treatment choice made by the patient when competent is admissible to support a finding that the patient, now in a persistent vegetative state, would wish to avoid further medical treatment. Moreover, this evidence must be clear and convincing. No proof is required to support a finding that the incompetent person would wish to continue treatment.

[To] be constitutionally permissible, Missouri's intrusion upon these fundamental liberties must, at a minimum, bear a reasonable relationship to a legitimate state end. Missouri asserts that its policy is related to a state interest in the protection of life. In my view, however, it is an effort to define life, rather than to protect it, that is the heart of Missouri's policy. Missouri insists, without regard to Nancy Cruzan's own interests, upon equating her life with the biological persistence of her bodily functions. Nancy Cruzan, it must be remembered, is not now simply incompetent. She is in a persistent vegetative state, and has been so for seven years. The trial court found, and no party contested, that Nancy has no possibility of recovery and no consciousness.

[In] short, there is no reasonable ground for believing that Nancy Beth Cruzan has any *personal* interest in the perpetuation of what the State has decided is her life. As I have already suggested, it would be possible to hypothesize such an interest on the basis of theological or philosophical conjecture. But even to posit such a basis for the State's action is to condemn it. It is not within the province of secular government to circumscribe the liberties of the people by regulations designed wholly for the purposes of establishing a sectarian definition of life. . . .

Note: The Right to Die

1. To what extent does *Cruzan* recognize a right to die? Note that the Court recognizes a "liberty interest," but it does not say whether that interest is fundamental or not, and it does not explain whether and when the state has sufficient reasons to intrude on that interest. For this reason, the decision appears exceedingly narrow.

2. One might ask about the relationship between the right to die (said by the Court to represent liberty rather than privacy) and the previous privacy cases. After Bowers v. Hardwick, it seemed that a tradition of recognition would be a necessary condition for constitutional protection. Moreover, the *Hardwick* Court appeared to characterize the relevant tradition narrowly rather than broadly. (See also Michael H. v. Gerald D., section F3 supra, in which Justice Scalia, speaking for a plurality, made precisely this point.) One might doubt whether there is a tradition of recognition of a right to die in cases like Cruzan's; indeed, one might doubt whether there has been sufficient time to build up any such tradition. Does

the tone of the opinions in *Cruzan* suggest a greater willingness to characterize a tradition broadly than is suggested by the other recent cases? How does one explain the differences (if there are differences) between *Hardwick* and *Cruzan?*

Consider, Seidman, Confusion at the Border: *Cruzan,* "The Right to Die," and the Public/Private Distinction, 1992 Sup. Ct. Rev. 47, 68-70:

> [Justice Scalia] may be correct when he asserts that there is little support for the claim that a right to suicide is rooted in our traditions, but, as Justice Brennan forcefully argued, there is considerable support for a traditional right to avoid unwanted medical treatment. Whether the Constitution speaks to Ms. Cruzan's predicament therefore depends upon which tradition one chooses to emphasize. . . .
>
> Unfortunately, in *Cruzan,* it is far from clear which tradition is more specific and which more general. If one looks at the matter from a certain angle, one might say that Ms. Cruzan is not asserting a generalized right to end her life in all circumstances, but only a narrow, specific right to do so in circumstances where death results from abstinence from medical treatment. [On] the other hand, an opponent of such a right might plausibly respond that the narrow prohibition against suicide is more specific than a generalized right to determine medical treatment in all circumstances, including those not involving death. . . .
>
> The analysis is further complicated by the fact that some traditions are permissive, while others are restrictive. Thus, there is a tradition permitting state regulation of suicide in tension with a tradition restricting state interference with private decisions to refuse treatment. . . .
>
> Some of Justice Scalia's writing suggests that [when] a permissive and restrictive tradition conflict, the permissive tradition should prevail, whether or not it is more specific. Thus, because the state has traditionally been permitted to regulate suicide, there cannot be a constitutional right to refuse medical treatment even if the nonrecognition of this right would interfere with a restrictive tradition concerning state imposed medical treatment.
>
> But this explanation for the *Cruzan* result only begs the central question. Justice Scalia never explains why permissive traditions are favored over restrictive traditions. This preference amounts to a privileging of the domain of collective public policy over the domain of private individual rights. We are still left with the need to explain or justify the decision to place the decision in one sphere rather than the other.

3. Evaluate the following argument: The state has no legitimate interest in interfering with the parents' decision in cases like *Cruzan.* The only possible interests are religious in nature or are patently absurd. The compulsion to keep Cruzan alive in her then-current state is therefore without the secular justification necessary to survive rationality review.

4. Compare with *Cruzan* the decision in Washington v. Harper, 494 U.S. 210 (1990). There, the Court held that a mentally ill prisoner has a "significant liberty interest in avoiding the unwanted administration of antipsychotic drugs." At the same time, the Court said that this interest could be countered by the state's "interests in prison safety and security . . . even when the constitutional right claimed to have been infringed is fundamental, and the State under other circumstances would have been required to satisfy a more rigorous standard of review." Strongly emphasizing the prison setting, the Court upheld the application of these drugs, for purposes of treatment only and by a licensed psychiatrist, "to inmates who are mentally ill and who, as a result of their illness, are gravely dis-

abled or represent a significant danger to themselves or others." Justice Stevens, joined by Justices Brennan and Marshall, dissented.

5. In Foucha v. Louisiana, 504 U.S. 71 (1992), the Court invalidated a state law allowing someone acquitted of crime by reason of insanity to be confined indefinitely to a mental institution unless he is able to demonstrate that he is not dangerous to himself or to others. The Court concluded that under the due process clause, someone deprived of liberty in this way must have procedural safeguards requiring the state to show mental illness and dangerousness by clear and convincing evidence. Justice Thomas dissented, joined by the Chief Justice and Justice Scalia.

6. *Civil confinement.* An unusual substantive due process case is Kansas v. Hendricks, 521 U.S. 346 (1997). The relevant statute established procedures for civil commitment of people who, because of a "mental abnormality" or a "personality disorder," are likely to engage in "predatory acts of sexual violence." Hendricks was civilly committed after a long history of sexually molesting children. The Court upheld the statute on the ground that the state had a sufficient ground to overcome the interest in avoiding physical restraint. According to the Court, the required finding of dangerousness to self or others, in the form of evidence of past sexually violent behavior and a present mental condition making future such conduct likely, was an adequate ground for civil confinement. On the substantive due process issue, the Court was unanimous.

Washington v. Glucksberg

521 U.S. 707 (1997)

CHIEF JUSTICE REHNQUIST delivered the opinion of the Court.

The question presented in this case is whether Washington's prohibition against "caus[ing]" or "aid[ing]" a suicide offends the Fourteenth Amendment to the United States Constitution. We hold that it does not.

It has always been a crime to assist a suicide in the State of Washington. In 1854, Washington's first Territorial Legislature outlawed "assisting another in the commission of self-murder." Today, Washington law provides: "A person is guilty of promoting a suicide attempt when he knowingly causes or aids another person to attempt suicide." [At] the same time, Washington's Natural Death Act, enacted in 1979, states that the "withholding or withdrawal of life-sustaining treatment" at a patient's direction "shall not, for any purpose, constitute a suicide." . . .

I

We begin, as we do in all due-process cases, by examining our Nation's history, legal traditions, and practices. In almost every State — indeed, in almost every western democracy — it is a crime to assist a suicide. The States' assisted-suicide bans are not innovations. Rather, they are longstanding expressions of the States' commitment to the protection and preservation of all human life. [Indeed], opposition to and condemnation of suicide — and, therefore, of assisting suicide — are consistent and enduring themes of our philosophical, legal, and cultural heritages. . . .

More specifically, for over 700 years, the Anglo-American common-law tradition has punished or otherwise disapproved of both suicide and assisting suicide. . . . In the 13th century, Henry de Bracton, one of the first legal-treatise writers, observed that "[j]ust as a man may commit felony by slaying another so may he do so by slaying himself." 2 Bracton on Laws and Customs of England 423 (f.150) (G. Woodbine ed., S. Thorne transl., 1968). The real and personal property of one who killed himself to avoid conviction and punishment for a crime were forfeit to the king; however, thought Bracton, "if a man slays himself in weariness of life or because he is unwilling to endure further bodily pain . . . [only] his movable goods [were] confiscated." Id., at 423-424 (f.150). Thus, "[t]he principle that suicide of a sane person, for whatever reason, was a punishable felony was . . . introduced into English common law." Centuries later, Sir William Blackstone, whose Commentaries on the Laws of England not only provided a definitive summary of the common law but was also a primary legal authority for 18th and 19th century American lawyers, referred to suicide as "self-murder" and "the pretended heroism, but real cowardice, of the Stoic philosophers, who destroyed themselves to avoid those ills which they had not the fortitude to endure. . . ." . . .

For the most part, the early American colonies adopted the common-law approach. [Over] time, however, the American colonies abolished these harsh common-law penalties. [The] movement away from the common law's harsh sanctions did not represent an acceptance of suicide; rather, as Chief Justice Swift observed, this change reflected the growing consensus that it was unfair to punish the suicide's family for his wrongdoing. [That] suicide remained a grievous, though nonfelonious, wrong is confirmed by the fact that colonial and early state legislatures and courts did not retreat from prohibiting assisting suicide. . . .

Though deeply rooted, the States' assisted-suicide bans have in recent years been reexamined and, generally, reaffirmed. Because of advances in medicine and technology, Americans today are increasingly likely to die in institutions, from chronic illnesses. Public concern and democratic action are therefore sharply focused on how best to protect dignity and independence at the end of life, with the result that there have been many significant changes in state laws and in the attitudes these laws reflect. Many States, for example, now permit "living wills," surrogate health-care decisionmaking, and the withdrawal or refusal of life-sustaining medical treatment. [At] the same time, however, voters and legislators continue for the most part to reaffirm their States' prohibitions on assisting suicide. . . .

Thus, the States are currently engaged in serious, thoughtful examinations of physician-assisted suicide and other similar issues. . . .

II

[Our] established method of substantive-due-process analysis has two primary features: First, we have regularly observed that the Due Process Clause specially protects those fundamental rights and liberties which are, objectively, "deeply rooted in this Nation's history and tradition," and "implicit in the concept of ordered liberty," such that "neither liberty nor justice would exist if they were sacrificed," Palko v. Connecticut, 302 U.S. 319, 325, 326 (1937). Second, we have required in substantive-due-process cases a "careful description" of the asserted fundamental liberty interest. Our Nation's history, legal traditions, and practices thus provide the crucial "guideposts for responsible decisionmaking," that direct and restrain our exposition of the Due Process Clause. . . .

Justice Souter, relying on Justice Harlan's dissenting opinion in Poe v. Ullman [367 U.S. 497 (1961)], would largely abandon this restrained methodology, and instead ask "whether [Washington's] statute sets up one of those 'arbitrary impositions' or 'purposeless restraints' at odds with the Due Process Clause of the Fourteenth Amendment." In our view, however, the development of this Court's substantive-due-process jurisprudence, has been a process whereby the outlines of the "liberty" specially protected by the Fourteenth Amendment — never fully clarified, to be sure, and perhaps not capable of being fully clarified — have at least been carefully refined by concrete examples involving fundamental rights found to be deeply rooted in our legal tradition. This approach tends to rein in the subjective elements that are necessarily present in due-process judicial review. In addition, by establishing a threshold requirement — that a challenged state action implicate a fundamental right — before requiring more than a reasonable relation to a legitimate state interest to justify the action, it avoids the need for complex balancing of competing interests in every case.

[We] now inquire whether this asserted right has any place in our Nation's traditions. Here, as discussed above, we are confronted with a consistent and almost universal tradition that has long rejected the asserted right, and continues explicitly to reject it today, even for terminally ill, mentally competent adults. To hold for respondents, we would have to reverse centuries of legal doctrine and practice, and strike down the considered policy choice of almost every State. [Respondents] contend, however, that the liberty interest they assert is consistent with this Court's substantive-due-process line of cases, if not with this Nation's history and practice. Pointing to *Casey* and *Cruzan*, respondents read our jurisprudence in this area as reflecting a general tradition of "self-sovereignty," and as teaching that the "liberty" protected by the Due Process Clause includes "basic and intimate exercises of personal autonomy." According to respondents, our liberty jurisprudence, and the broad, individualistic principles it reflects, protects the "liberty of competent, terminally ill adults to make end-of-life decisions free of undue government interference." . . .

[The] right assumed in *Cruzan* [was] not simply deduced from abstract concepts of personal autonomy. Given the common-law rule that forced medication was a battery, and the long legal tradition protecting the decision to refuse unwanted medical treatment, our assumption was entirely consistent with this Nation's history and constitutional traditions. The decision to commit suicide with the assistance of another may be just as personal and profound as the decision to refuse unwanted medical treatment, but it has never enjoyed similar legal protection. Indeed, the two acts are widely and reasonably regarded as quite distinct.

[Respondents] also rely on *Casey*. [The] opinion moved from the recognition that liberty necessarily includes freedom of conscience and belief about ultimate considerations to the observation that "though the abortion decision may originate within the zone of conscience and belief, it is more than a philosophic exercise." That many of the rights and liberties protected by the Due Process Clause sound in personal autonomy does not warrant the sweeping conclusion that any and all important, intimate, and personal decisions are so protected.

[The] history of the law's treatment of assisted suicide in this country has been and continues to be one of the rejection of nearly all efforts to permit it. That being the case, our decisions lead us to conclude that the asserted "right" to assistance in committing suicide is not a fundamental liberty interest protected by the Due Process Clause. The Constitution also requires, however, that Washington's assisted-suicide ban be rationally related to legitimate government interests This requirement is unquestionably met here.

[First,] Washington has an "unqualified interest in the preservation of human life." [*Cruzan.*] The State's prohibition on assisted suicide, like all homicide laws, both reflects and advances its commitment to this interest. [This] interest is symbolic and aspirational as well as practical: "While suicide is no longer prohibited or penalized, the ban against assisted suicide and euthanasia shores up the notion of limits in human relationships. It reflects the gravity with which we view the decision to take one's own life or the life of another, and our reluctance to encourage or promote these decisions."

[Relatedly,] all admit that suicide is a serious public-health problem, especially among persons in otherwise vulnerable groups. [Those] who attempt suicide — terminally ill or not — often suffer from depression or other mental disorders. [Research] indicates, however, that many people who request physician-assisted suicide withdraw that request if their depression and pain are treated.

[The] State also has an interest in protecting the integrity and ethics of the medical profession. [And] physician-assisted suicide could, it is argued, undermine the trust that is essential to the doctor-patient relationship by blurring the time-honored line between healing and harming.

[Next,] the State has an interest in protecting vulnerable groups — including the poor, the elderly, and disabled persons — from abuse, neglect, and mistakes. The Court of Appeals dismissed the State's concern that disadvantaged persons might be pressured into physician-assisted suicide as "ludicrous on its face." We have recognized, however, the real risk of subtle coercion and undue influence in end-of-life situations. [*Cruzan.*] Similarly, the New York Task Force warned that "[l]egalizing physician-assisted suicide would pose profound risks to many individuals who are ill and vulnerable. . . . The risk of harm is greatest for the many individuals in our society whose autonomy and well-being are already compromised by poverty, lack of access to good medical care, advanced age, or membership in a stigmatized social group." New York Task Force 120; see Compassion in Dying, 49 F.3d at 593 ("[A]n insidious bias against the handicapped — again coupled with a cost-saving mentality — makes them especially in need of Washington's statutory protection"). If physician-assisted suicide were permitted, many might resort to it to spare their families the substantial financial burden of end-of-life health-care costs.

The State's interest here goes beyond protecting the vulnerable from coercion; it extends to protecting disabled and terminally ill people from prejudice, negative and inaccurate stereotypes, and "societal indifference." 49 F.3d, at 592. The State's assisted-suicide ban reflects and reinforces its policy that the lives of terminally ill, disabled, and elderly people must be no less valued than the lives of the young and healthy, and that a seriously disabled person's suicidal impulses should be interpreted and treated the same way as anyone else's. See New York Task Force 101-102; Physician-Assisted Suicide and Euthanasia in the Netherlands: A Report of Chairman Charles T. Canady, at 9, 20 (discussing prejudice toward the disabled and the negative messages euthanasia and assisted suicide send to handi-capped patients).

Finally, the State may fear that permitting assisted suicide will start it down the path to voluntary and perhaps even involuntary euthanasia. [This] concern is fur-ther supported by evidence about the practice of euthanasia in the Netherlands. The Dutch government's own study revealed that in 1990, there were 2,300 cases of voluntary euthanasia (defined as "the deliberate termination of another's life at his request"), 400 cases of assisted suicide, and more than 1,000 cases of eutha-nasia without an explicit request. In addition to these latter 1,000 cases, the study found an additional 4,941 cases where physicians administered lethal morphine overdoses without the patients' explicit consent. Physician-Assisted Suicide and Euthanasia in the Netherlands: A Report of Chairman Charles T. Canady, at 12-13 (citing Dutch study). This study suggests that, despite the existence of various reporting procedures, euthanasia in the Netherlands has not been limited to competent, terminally ill adults who are enduring physical suffering, and that regulation of the practice may not have prevented abuses in cases involving vul-nerable persons, including severely disabled neonates and elderly persons suffer-ing from dementia.

[We] need not weigh exactly the relative strengths of these various inter-ests. They are unquestionably important and legitimate, and Washington's ban on assisted suicide is at least reasonably related to their promotion and protection. We therefore hold that [the challenged law] does not violate the Fourteenth Amendment, either on its face or "as applied to competent, terminally ill adults who wish to hasten their deaths by obtaining medication prescribed by their doctors." . . .

JUSTICE O'CONNOR, concurring.

[I] join the Court's opinions because I agree that there is no generalized right to "commit suicide." But respondents urge us to address the narrower question whether a mentally competent person who is experiencing great suffering has a constitutionally cognizable interest in controlling the circumstances of his or her imminent death. I see no need to reach that question in the context of the facial challenges to the New York and Washington laws at issue here. [There] is no dis-pute that dying patients in Washington and New York can obtain palliative care, even when doing so would hasten their deaths. The difficulty in defining termi-nal illness and the risk that a dying patient's request for assistance in ending his or her life might not be truly voluntary justifies the prohibitions on assisted sui-cide we uphold here.

JUSTICE STEVENS, concurring in the judgments.

[Today], the Court decides that Washington's statute prohibiting assisted sui-cide is not invalid "on its face," that is to say, in all or most cases in which it might be applied. That holding, however, does not foreclose the possibility that some applications of the statute might well be invalid.

[The] state interests supporting a general rule banning the practice of physician-assisted suicide do not have the same force in all cases. First and fore-most of these interests is the "unqualified interest in the preservation of human life," which is equated with "the sanctity of life." That interest not only justi-fies — it commands — maximum protection of every individual's interest in remaining alive, which in turn commands the same protection for decisions about whether to commence or to terminate life-support systems or to administer pain medication that may hasten death. Properly viewed, however, this interest is not a collective interest that should always outweigh the interests of a person who because of pain, incapacity, or sedation finds her life intolerable, but rather, an aspect of individual freedom.

Many terminally ill people find their lives meaningful even if filled with pain or dependence on others. Some find value in living through suffering; some have an abiding desire to witness particular events in their families' lives; many believe it a sin to hasten death. Individuals of different religious faiths make different judgments and choices about whether to live on under such circumstances. There are those who will want to continue aggressive treatment; those who would prefer terminal sedation; and those who will seek withdrawal from life-support systems and death by gradual starvation and dehydration. Although as a general matter the State's interest in the contributions each person may make to society outweighs the person's interest in ending her life, this interest does not have the same force for a terminally ill patient faced not with the choice of whether to live, only of how to die. Allowing the individual, rather than the State, to make judgments "about the 'quality' of life that a particular individual may enjoy" does not mean that the lives of terminally-ill, disabled people have less value than the lives of those who are healthy. Rather, it gives proper recognition to the individual's interest in choosing a final chapter that accords with her life story, rather than one that demeans her values and poisons memories of her.

[Similarly,] the State's legitimate interests in preventing suicide, protecting the vulnerable from coercion and abuse, and preventing euthanasia are less significant in this context. I agree that the State has a compelling interest in preventing persons from committing suicide because of depression, or coercion by third parties. But the State's legitimate interest in preventing abuse does not apply to an individual who is not victimized by abuse, who is not suffering from depression, and who makes a rational and voluntary decision to seek assistance in dying.

[There] remains room for vigorous debate about the outcome of particular cases that are not necessarily resolved by the opinions announced today. How such cases may be decided will depend on their specific facts. . . .

JUSTICE SOUTER, concurring in the judgment.

[Just] as results in substantive due process cases are tied to the selections of statements of the competing interests, the acceptability of the results is a function of the good reasons for the selections made. It is here that the value of common-law method becomes apparent, for the usual thinking of the common law is suspicious of the all-or-nothing analysis that tends to produce legal petrification instead of an evolving boundary between the domains of old principles. Common-law method tends to pay respect instead to detail, seeking to understand old principles afresh by new examples and new counterexamples. . . .

[The] liberty interest in bodily integrity was phrased in a general way by then-Judge Cardozo when he said, "[e]very human being of adult years and sound mind has a right to determine what shall be done with his own body" in relation to his medical needs. Schloendorff v. Society of New York Hospital, 211 N.Y. 125, 129, 105 N.E. 92, 93 (1914). The familiar examples of this right derive from the common law of battery and include the right to be free from medical invasions into the body [*Cruzan*], as well as a right generally to resist enforced medication, see Washington v. Harper, 494 U.S. 210, 221-222, 229 (1990).

[The] analogies between the abortion cases and this one are several. Even though the State has a legitimate interest in discouraging abortion, see [*Casey*; *Roe*], the Court recognized a woman's right to a physician's counsel and care. Like the decision to commit suicide, the decision to abort potential life can be made irresponsibly and under the influence of others, and yet the Court has held in the abortion cases that physicians are fit assistants. Without physician assistance in abortion, the woman's right would have too often amounted to nothing more than a right to self-mutilation, and without a physician to assist in the suicide of the dying, the patient's right will often be confined to crude methods of causing death, most shocking and painful to the decedent's survivors.

[The] State has put forward several interests to justify the Washington law as applied to physicians treating terminally ill patients, even those competent to make responsible choices: protecting life generally, discouraging suicide even if knowing and voluntary, and protecting terminally ill patients from involuntary suicide and euthanasia, both voluntary and nonvoluntary.

It is not necessary to discuss the exact strengths of the first two claims of justification in the present circumstances, for the third is dispositive for me. That third justification is different from the first two, for it addresses specific features of respondents' claim, and it opposes that claim not with a moral judgment contrary to respondents', but with a recognized state interest in the protection of nonresponsible individuals and those who do not stand in relation either to death or to their physicians as do the patients whom respondents describe. The State claims interests in protecting patients from mistakenly and involuntarily deciding to end their lives, and in guarding against both voluntary and involuntary euthanasia. Leaving aside any difficulties in coming to a clear concept of imminent death, mistaken decisions may result from inadequate palliative care or a terminal prognosis that turns out to be error; coercion and abuse may stem from the large medical bills that family members cannot bear or unreimbursed hospitals decline to shoulder. Voluntary and involuntary euthanasia may result once doctors are authorized to prescribe lethal medication in the first instance, for they might find it pointless to distinguish between patients who administer their own fatal drugs and those who wish not to, and their compassion for those who suffer may obscure the distinction between those who ask for death and those who may be unable to request it. The argument is that a progression would occur, obscuring the line between the ill and the dying, and between the responsible and the unduly influenced, until ultimately doctors and perhaps others would abuse a limited freedom to aid suicides by yielding to the impulse to end another's suffering under conditions going beyond the narrow limits the respondents propose. The State thus argues, essentially, that respondents' claim is not as narrow as it sounds, simply because no recognition of the interest they assert could be limited to vindicating those interests and affecting no others. The State says that the claim, in practical effect, would entail consequences that the State could, without doubt, legitimately act to prevent.

The mere assertion that the terminally sick might be pressured into suicide decisions by close friends and family members would not alone be very telling. Of course that is possible, not only because the costs of care might be more than family members could bear but simply because they might naturally wish to see an end of suffering for someone they love. But one of the points of restricting any right of assistance to physicians, would be to condition the right on an exercise of judgment by someone qualified to assess the patient's responsible capacity and detect the influence of those outside the medical relationship.

The State, however, goes further, to argue that dependence on the vigilance of physicians will not be enough. First, the lines proposed here (particularly the requirement of a knowing and voluntary decision by the patient) would be more difficult to draw than the lines that have limited other recently recognized due process rights. Limiting a state from prosecuting use of artificial contraceptives by married couples posed no practical threat to the State's capacity to regulate contraceptives in other ways that were assumed at the time of [Poe v. Ullman] to be legitimate; the trimester measurements of *Roe* and the viability determination of *Casey* were easy to make with a real degree of certainty. But the knowing and responsible mind is harder to assess. Second, this difficulty could become the greater by combining with another fact within the realm of plausibility, that physicians simply would not be assiduous to preserve the line. They have compassion, and those who would be willing to assist in suicide at all might be the most susceptible to the wishes of a patient, whether the patient were technically quite responsible or not. Physicians, and their hospitals, have their own financial incentives, too, in this new age of managed care. Whether acting from compassion or under some other influence, a physician who would provide a drug for a patient to administer might well go the further step of administering the drug himself; so, the barrier between assisted suicide and euthanasia could become porous, and the line between voluntary and involuntary euthanasia as well. The case for the slippery slope is fairly made out here, not because recognizing one due process right would leave a court with no principled basis to avoid recognizing another, but because there is a plausible case that the right claimed would not be readily containable by reference to facts about the mind that are matters of difficult judgment, or by gatekeepers who are subject to temptation, noble or not.

Respondents propose an answer to all this, the answer of state regulation with teeth. Legislation proposed in several States, for example, would authorize physician-assisted suicide but require two qualified physicians to confirm the patient's diagnosis, prognosis, and competence; and would mandate that the patient make repeated requests witnessed by at least two others over a specified time span; and would impose reporting requirements and criminal penalties for various acts of coercion.

But at least at this moment there are reasons for caution in predicting the effectiveness of the teeth proposed. Respondents' proposals, as it turns out, sound much like the guidelines now in place in the Netherlands, the only place where experience with physician-assisted suicide and euthanasia has yielded empirical evidence about how such regulations might affect actual practice. Dutch physicians must engage in consultation before proceeding, and must decide whether the patient's decision is voluntary, well considered, and stable, whether the request to die is enduring and made more than once, and whether the patient's future will involve unacceptable suffering. See C. Gomez, Regulating Death 40-43 (1991). There is, however, a substantial dispute today about what the Dutch experience shows. Some commentators marshall evidence that the Dutch guidelines have in practice failed to protect patients from involuntary euthanasia and have been violated with impunity. See, e.g., H. Hendin, Seduced By Death 75-84

(1997) (noting many cases in which decisions intended to end the life of a fully competent patient were made without a request from the patient and without consulting the patient); Keown, Euthanasia in the Netherlands: Sliding Down the Slippery Slope?, in Euthanasia Examined 261, 289 (J. Keown ed. 1995) (guidelines have "proved signally ineffectual; non-voluntary euthanasia is now widely practised and increasingly condoned in the Netherlands"); Gomez, supra, at 104-113. This evidence is contested. [The] day may come when we can say with some assurance which side is right, but for now it is the substantiality of the factual disagreement, and the alternatives for resolving it, that matter. They are, for me, dispositive of the due process claim at this time.

[The] experimentation that should be out of the question in constitutional adjudication displacing legislative judgments is entirely proper, as well as highly desirable, when the legislative power addresses an emerging issue like assisted suicide. The Court should accordingly stay its hand to allow reasonable legislative consideration. While I do not decide for all time that respondents' claim should not be recognized, I acknowledge the legislative institutional competence as the better one to deal with that claim at this time.

JUSTICE GINSBURG, concurring in the judgments.

I concur in the Court's judgments in these cases substantially for the reasons stated by Justice O'Connor in her concurring opinion.

JUSTICE BREYER, concurring in the judgments.

[I] would not reject the respondents' claim without considering a different formulation, for which our legal tradition may provide greater support. That formulation would use words roughly like a "right to die with dignity." But irrespective of the exact words used, at its core would lie personal control over the manner of death, professional medical assistance, and the avoidance of unnecessary and severe physical suffering — combined.

[I] do not believe, however, that this Court need or now should decide whether or a not such a right is "fundamental." That is because, in my view, the avoidance of severe physical pain (connected with death) would have to comprise an essential part of any successful claim and because, as Justice O'Connor points out, the laws before us do not force a dying person to undergo that kind of pain.

[Were] the legal circumstances different — for example, were state law to prevent the provision of palliative care, including the administration of drugs as needed to avoid pain at the end of life — then the law's impact upon serious and otherwise unavoidable physical pain (accompanying death) would be more directly at issue. And as Justice O'Connor suggests, the Court might have to revisit its conclusions in these cases.

Note: *Assisted Suicide*

1. What is the precise holding of *Glucksberg?* Note that Justice O'Connor joins the majority opinion (indeed, her vote is necessary to make it a majority opinion) but also writes separately. Does her opinion suggest that there may be a right to physician-assisted suicide in cases involving both intense pain and imminent death? Do five justices so suggest? If so, what is the status of the majority opinion?

2. Probably the major theoretical dispute is between the majority, stressing the need to anchor substantive due process in history, and Justice Souter, emphasizing Justice Harlan's belief that the tradition of liberty grows over time. Is this a repeat of the debate between two wings of the Court in *Casey*? Has the plurality opinion in *Casey* been rejected by a majority of the Court?

3. Is *Glucksberg* a return to the majority opinion in Bowers v. Hardwick? What room, if any, remains for substantive due process?

G.   PROCEDURAL DUE PROCESS

The text of the due process clause — "nor shall any State deprive any person of life, liberty, or property, without due process of law" — suggests that the clause is concerned above all with procedure. This section explores the question when the clause requires procedural safeguards to accompany substantive choices. That question is an important aspect of the problem of identifying "implied" fundamental rights. As the preceding materials suggest, the terms "liberty" and "property" are not self-defining. In exploring the materials that follow, consider how and why the procedural and substantive contexts might differ. Note that this section does not deal with questions of procedural due process in conventional criminal and civil contexts — for example, burden of proof rules for criminal or civil defendants and the role of the exclusionary rule. Nor are we concerned here with the problem of incorporation, dealt with in section C supra.

1.   *Liberty and Property Interests*

Before Goldberg v. Kelly, 397 U.S. 254 (1970), the Court defined liberty and property interests by reference to the common law. If government took someone's property, or invaded his bodily integrity, the due process clause would require some kind of hearing. But the clause was inapplicable if government denied an individual some public benefit — employment, welfare, or some other advantageous opportunity. See, e.g., Bailey v. Richardson, 182 F.2d 46 (D.C. Cir. 1950), aff'd by an equally divided Court, 341 U.S. 918 (1951) (no hearing required for dismissal from government employment). This conclusion was a form of the traditional right/privilege distinction. "[Advantageous] relations with the government were mere 'privileges' or 'gratuities,' not legally protected rights. [But] with the expansion of the governmental role, it became less and less tolerable that the government should wield the degree of potentially arbitrary power over the lives of individuals implied by this doctrine." Stewart, The Reformation of American Administrative Law, 88 Harv. L. Rev. 1667, 1717-1718 (1975).

Reich, The New Property, 73 Yale L.J. 733 (1963), was an important critique of the original framework. According to Reich, that framework was anachronistic in a period in which individual security frequently depended on advantageous relationships with the government — insurance, Social Security benefits, employment, licenses, welfare, and so forth. In Reich's view, it was necessary to create a "new property" that would attach the traditional procedural safeguards to these benefits in order to furnish in the modern era the same kind of security promoted by "old property" under a common law regime. The idea was that without such safeguards, those dependent on governmental benefits would be subject to the arbitrary will of public officials.

The Supreme Court accepted Reich's approach in Goldberg v. Kelly, supra. In *Goldberg,* the Court held that a welfare recipient's interest in continued receipt of welfare benefits was a "statutory entitlement" that amounted to "property" within the meaning of the due process clause. The Court referred to the "brutal need" of welfare recipients and held that a fairly elaborate hearing was required before benefits could be terminated. But what interests amount to "liberty" or "property" once it is concluded that at least some statutory benefits amount to rights?

BOARD OF REGENTS OF STATE COLLEGES v. ROTH, 408 U.S. 564 (1972). Roth was hired for a one-year term as assistant professor at Wisconsin State University. Under state law, he did not have tenure. The president of the university informed Roth that he would not be rehired; no explanation was given for the decision, and there was no opportunity to challenge it. Roth alleged that the failure to hold a hearing violated the due process clause. In an opinion by Justice Stewart, the Court rejected Roth's claim:

"The requirements of procedural due process apply only to the deprivation of interests encompassed by the Fourteenth Amendment's protection of liberty and property. [The] range of interests protected by procedural due process is not infinite.

"The District Court decided that procedural due process guarantees apply in this case by assessing and balancing the weights of the particular interests involved. [Undeniably,] the respondent's re-employment prospects were of major concern to him — concern that we surely cannot say was insignificant. And a weighing process has long been a part of any determination of the *form* of hearing required in particular situations by procedural due process. But, to determine whether due process requirements apply in the first place, we must look not to the weight, but to the *nature* of the interest at stake.

"'Liberty' and 'property' are broad and majestic terms. They are among the '[g]reat [constitutional] concepts . . . purposely left to gather meaning from experience. . . . [T]hey relate to the whole domain of social and economic fact, and the statesmen who founded this Nation knew too well that only a stagnant society remains unchanged.' For that reason, the Court has fully and finally rejected the wooden distinction between 'rights' and 'privileges' that once seemed to govern the applicability of procedural due process rights. The Court has also made clear that the property interests protected by procedural due process extend well beyond actual ownership of real estate, chattels, or money. . . .

"While this Court has not attempted to define with exactness the liberty . . . guaranteed [by the Fourteenth Amendment], the term [denotes] not merely freedom from bodily restraint but also the right of the individual to contract, to engage in any of the common occupations of life, to acquire useful knowledge, to marry, establish a home and bring up children, to worship God according to the dictates of his own conscience, and generally to enjoy those privileges long recognized . . . as essential to the orderly pursuit of happiness by free men. In a Constitution for a free people, there can be no doubt that the meaning of 'liberty' must be broad indeed.

"The Fourteenth Amendment's procedural protection of property is a safeguard of the security of interests that a person has already acquired in specific benefits. These interests — property interests — may take many forms.

"Thus, the Court has held that a person receiving welfare benefits under statutory and administrative standards defining eligibility for them has an interest in continued receipt of those benefits that is safeguarded by procedural due process. [*Goldberg*.] [To] have a property interest in a benefit, a person clearly must have more than an abstract need or desire for it. He must have more than a unilateral expectation of it. He must, instead, have a legitimate claim of entitlement to it. It is a purpose of the ancient institution of property to protect those claims upon which people rely in their daily lives, reliance that must not be arbitrarily undermined. It is a purpose of the constitutional right to a hearing to provide an opportunity for a person to vindicate those claims.

"Property interests, of course, are not created by the Constitution. Rather, they are created and their dimensions are defined by existing rules or understandings that stem from an independent source such as state law — rules or understandings that secure certain benefits and that support claims of entitlement to those benefits.

"Just as [in *Goldberg*] the welfare recipient's 'property' interest in welfare payments was created and defined by statutory terms, so the respondent's 'property' interest in employment at Wisconsin State University–Oshkosh was created and defined by the terms of his appointment. [The] important fact in this case is that they specifically provided that the respondent's employment was to terminate on June 30. They did not provide for contract renewal absent 'sufficient cause.' Indeed, they made no provision for renewal whatsoever.

"Thus, the terms of the respondent's appointment secured absolutely no interest in re-employment for the next year. They supported absolutely no possible claim of entitlement to re-employment. Nor, significantly, was there any state statute or University rule or policy that secured his interest in re-employment or that created any legitimate claim to it. In these circumstances, the respondent surely had an abstract concern in being rehired, but he did not have a *property* interest sufficient to require the University authorities to give him a hearing when they declined to renew his contract of employment."

Justice Marshall, dissented: "In my view, every citizen who applies for a government job is entitled to it unless the government can establish some reason for denying the employment. This is the 'property' right that I believe is protected by the Fourteenth Amendment and that cannot be denied 'without due process of law.' And it is also liberty — liberty to work — which is the 'very essence of the personal freedom and opportunity' secured by the Fourteenth Amendment. . . .

"[It] may be argued that to provide procedural due process to all public employees or prospective employees would place an intolerable burden on the machinery of government. The short answer to that argument is that it is not burdensome to give reasons when reasons exist. . . ."

PERRY v. SINDERMANN, 408 U.S. 593 (1972). This was a companion case to *Roth*. Sindermann was a professor at Odessa Junior College whose contract, like Roth's, was not renewed. Sindermann claimed that Odessa had a de facto tenure program. The college had stated in a faculty guide that, despite the absence of an actual tenure system, it "wishes each faculty member to feel that he has permanent tenure so long as his teaching services are satisfactory and as long as he displays a cooperative attitude."According to Sindermann, there was a mutual expectation that he would be renewed each year. Justice Stewart wrote the opinion of the Court:

"The respondent's lack of formal contractual or tenure security in continued employment at Odessa Junior College [may] not be entirely dispositive.

"[The] respondent's allegations [raise] a genuine issue as to his interest in continued employment at Odessa Junior College. He alleged that this interest, though not secured by a formal contractual tenure provision, was secured by a no less binding understanding fostered by the college administration. . . .

"[A] written contract with an explicit tenure provision clearly is evidence of a formal understanding that supports a teacher's claim of entitlement to continued employment unless sufficient 'cause' is shown. Yet absence of such an explicit contractual provision may not always foreclose the possibility that a teacher has a 'property' interest in re-employment. . . .

"A teacher, like the respondent, who has held his position for a number of years, might be able to show from the circumstances of this service — and from other relevant facts — that he has a legitimate claim of entitlement to job tenure."

Cleveland Board of Education v. Loudermill

470 U.S. 532 (1985)

JUSTICE WHITE delivered the opinion of the Court.

In these cases we consider what pretermination process must be accorded a public employee who can be discharged only for cause.

In 1979 the Cleveland Board of Education [hired] respondent James Loudermill as a security guard. On his job application, Loudermill stated that he had never been convicted of a felony. Eleven months later, as part of a routine examination of his employment records, the Board discovered that in fact Loudermill had been convicted of grand larceny in 1968. By letter dated November 3, 1980, the Board's Business Manager informed Loudermill that he had been dismissed because of his dishonesty in filling out the employment application. Loudermill was not afforded an opportunity to respond to the charge of dishonesty or to challenge his dismissal. On November 13, the Board adopted a resolution officially approving the discharge.

Under Ohio law, Loudermill was a "classified civil servant." [Such] employees can be terminated only for cause, and may obtain administrative review if discharged. [Plaintiff's] federal constitutional claim depends on his having had a property right in continued employment. [If he did,] the State could not deprive [him] of this property without due process.

Property interests are not created by the Constitution, "they are created and their dimensions are defined by existing rules or understandings that stem from an independent source such as state law. . . ." [Roth.] [The] Ohio statute plainly creates such an interest. Respondents were "classified civil service employees," Ohio Rev. Code Ann. §124.11 (1984), entitled to retain their positions "during good behavior and efficient service," who could not be dismissed "except . . . for . . . misfeasance, malfeasance, or nonfeasance in office." The statute plainly supports the conclusion, reached by both lower courts, that respondents possessed property rights in continued employment. [The lower court thus required a hearing.]

The [Board] argues, however, that the property right is defined by, and conditioned on, the legislature's choice of procedures for its deprivation. [The] Board stresses that in addition to specifying the grounds for termination, the statute sets out procedures by which termination may take place. The procedures were adhered to in these cases. According to petitioner, "[t]o require additional procedures would in effect expand the scope of the property interest itself."

This argument, which was accepted by the District Court, has its genesis in the plurality opinion in Arnett v. Kennedy, 416 U.S. 134 (1974). Arnett involved a challenge by a former federal employee to the procedures by which he was dismissed. The plurality reasoned that where the legislation conferring the substantive right also sets out the procedural mechanism for enforcing that right, the two cannot be separated:

> The employee's statutorily defined right is not a guarantee against removal without cause in the abstract, but such a guarantee as enforced by the procedures which Congress has designated for the determination of cause.
> . . . [W]here the grant of a substantive right is inextricably intertwined with the limitations on the procedures which are to be employed in determining that right, a litigant in the position of appellee must take the bitter with the sweet.

This view garnered three votes in Arnett, but was specifically rejected by the other six Justices. [It] is [now] settled that the "bitter with the sweet" approach misconceives the constitutional guarantee. [The] point is straightforward: the Due Process Clause provides that certain substantive rights — life, liberty, and property — cannot be deprived except pursuant to constitutionally adequate procedures. The categories of substance and procedure are distinct. Were the rule otherwise, the Clause would be reduced to a mere tautology. "Property" cannot be defined by the procedures provided for its deprivation any more than can life or liberty. The right to due process "is conferred, not by legislative grace, but by constitutional guarantee. While the legislature may elect not to confer a property interest in [public] employment, it may not constitutionally authorize the deprivation of such an interest, once conferred, without appropriate procedural safeguards."

[Affirmed.]

[Justice Powell concurred in part and concurred in the result in part.]

JUSTICE REHNQUIST, dissenting.

In [Arnett] six Members of this Court agreed that a public employee could be dismissed for misconduct without a full hearing prior to termination. A plurality of Justices agreed that the employee was entitled to exactly what Congress gave him, and no more. The Chief Justice, Justice Stewart, and I said:

> Here appellee did have a statutory expectancy that he not be removed other than for "such cause as will promote the efficiency of [the] service." But the very section of the statute which granted him that right, a right which had previously existed, only by virtue of administrative regulation, expressly provided also for the procedure by which "cause" was to be determined, and expressly omitted the procedural guarantees which appellee insists are mandated by the Constitution. Only by bifur-

cating the very sentence of the Act of Congress which conferred upon appellee the right not to be removed save for cause could it be said that he had an expectancy of that substantive right without the procedural limitations which Congress attached to it. In the area of federal regulation of government employees, where in the absence of statutory limitation the governmental employer has had virtually uncontrolled latitude in decisions as to hiring and firing, we do not believe that a statutory enactment such as the Lloyd-La Follette Act may be parsed as discretely as appellee urges. Congress was obviously intent on according a measure of statutory job security to governmental employees which they had not previously enjoyed, but was likewise intent on excluding more elaborate procedural requirements which it felt would make the operation of the new scheme unnecessarily burdensome in practice. Where the focus of legislation was thus strongly on the procedural mechanism for enforcing the substantive right which was simultaneously conferred, we decline to conclude that the substantive right may be viewed wholly apart from the procedure provided for its enforcement. The employee's statutorily defined right is not a guarantee against removal without cause in the abstract, but such a guarantee as enforced by the procedures which Congress has designated for the determination of cause.

In this case, the relevant Ohio statute provides in its first paragraph that "[t]he tenure of every officer or employee in the classified service [shall] be during good behavior and efficient service." The very next paragraph of this section [provides] that in the event of suspension of more than three days or removal the appointing authority shall furnish the employee with the stated reasons for his removal. The next paragraph provides that within ten days following the receipt of such a statement, the employee may appeal in writing to the State Personnel Board of Review or the Commission, such appeal shall be heard within 30 days from the time of its filing, and the Board may affirm, disaffirm, or modify the judgment of the appointing authority.

[Here,] as in *Arnett*, "[t]he employee's statutorily defined right is not a guarantee against removal without cause in the abstract, but such a guarantee as enforced by the procedures which [the Ohio legislature] has designated for the determination of cause." (Opinion of Rehnquist, J.) We ought to recognize the totality of the State's definition of the property right in question, and not merely seize upon one of several paragraphs in a unitary statute. . . . I dissent.

Note: Defining "Liberty" and "Property"

1. *The purposes of hearings.* What goals are promoted by requiring a hearing before government deprives someone of a liberty or property interest?

a. *Obtaining more accurate factual determinations.* Suppose a welfare agency seeks to take away welfare benefits because the recipient's relatively high earnings disqualify her under the governing statute, but she disputes the government's claim that her earnings do in fact disqualify her. A hearing before an impartial arbiter might produce a more accurate resolution of the disputed factual issue than a unilateral decision by the administrator. (Note that the issue here is a dispute over the facts; hearings are generally not required on questions of law. Why?)

b. *Recognizing and promoting the dignity of those whose interests are at stake by allowing them to participate in the decision.* Consider Michelman, Formal and

Associational Aims in Procedural Due Process, in NOMOS: Due Process 126, 127-128 (J. R. Pennock and J. Chapman eds. 1977):

> Such procedures seem responsive to demands for revelation and participation. They attach value to an individual's being told why the agent is treating him unfavorably and to his having a part in the decision. [The] information may also be wanted for introspective reasons — because, for example, it fulfills a potentially destructive gap in the individual's conception of himself. Similarly, the individual may have various reasons for wanting an opportunity to discuss the decision with the agent. Some pertain to external consequences: the individual might succeed in persuading the agent away from the harmful action. But again participatory opportunity may also be psychologically important to the individual: to have played a part in, to have made one's apt contribution to, decisions which are about oneself may be counted important even though the decision, as it turns out, is the most unfavorable one imaginable and one's efforts have not proved influential.

Hearings have costs as well. If government must spend money on procedural safeguards, it will have fewer resources at its command, and the result may be that welfare benefits or salaries are correspondingly diminished. Hearing requirements may therefore not prove beneficial for the class of intended beneficiaries as a whole. Fewer employees may be hired, fewer people may be allowed on the welfare rolls, and benefit levels and salaries may be decreased. What is the relevance of these possibilities?

2. *Statutory entitlements.* Under *Roth*, interests are defined by reference to positive law. The test for deciding whether a "property" interest has been created is to examine positive law to see whether the government's discretion has been confined by existing "rules or understandings." In *Perry*, the tenure system, if there was one, meant that professors could be discharged only "for cause." In *Roth*, there was no such "for cause" limitation of the discretion of the administrator as to renewal. We might term this approach one of "statutory entitlement" or, following Reich, supra, "new property."

But why should the due process clause be read to say that a "for cause" provision creates a property interest that is not defined by reference to the procedural provisions of the same statute? If the due process clause does not require government to create a "for cause" system at all, why does it bar the government from taking the intermediate step of providing a "for cause" system without procedural safeguards? Consider Easterbrook, Substance and Due Process, 1982 Sup. Ct. Rev. 85, 112-113:

> Substance and process are intimately related. The procedures one uses determine how much substance is achieved, and by whom. Procedural rules are just a measure of how much the substantive entitlements are worth, of what we are willing to sacrifice to see a given goal attained. The body that creates a substantive rule is the logical judge of how much should be spent to avoid errors in the process of disposing of claims to that right. The substantive rule is itself best seen as a promised benefit coupled with a promised rate of mistake: the legislature sets up an X% probability that a person will receive a certain boon. The Court cannot logically be reticent about revising the substantive rules but unabashed about rewriting the procedures to be followed in administering those rules.

3. *Property and liberty interests apart from positive law.* The Supreme Court has generally been reluctant to define "property" or "liberty" interests by refer-

ence to the importance of the interest at issue; even a "grievous loss" may not be enough. In some cases, however, the Court has concluded that a "liberty" interest is at issue even though there is no positive protection of the sort required in *Roth*. See Ingraham v. Wright, 430 U.S. 651 (1977) (child's interest in bodily integrity, at stake because of practice of paddling children, is a liberty interest); Vitek v. Jones, 445 U.S. 480 (1980) (inmates' interest in preventing transfer from prison to mental institution is a liberty interest); Owen v. City of Independence, 445 U.S. 662 (1980) (the right to reputation when combined with dismissal from at-will employment is a liberty interest). Note that all of these cases involve variations on "old property" — government infringements on private autonomy as understood at common law.

Why has the Court generally been unwilling to hold that all important interests are protected by the due process clause? Why has the Court been unwilling to hold that freedom from arbitrary adjudicative procedures is itself a part of the "liberty" protected by due process? Consider the following views:

a. A determination of which statutory benefits are sufficiently important to merit protection would involve an unduly open-ended and subjective inquiry. The requirement of a statutory entitlement limits the judicial inquiry without requiring comparisons among, for example, welfare benefits, employment, and parole revocation.

b. If courts were to hold that all important interests are protected by the due process clause, they would be driven to give such interests substantive as well as procedural protection. Such a revival of substantive due process is properly resisted. Consider, for example, a probationary employee fired from a government job; assume there is no statute providing that the employee may not be discharged without "cause." If a court held that, because of the "grievous loss," there is a constitutional right to a hearing, what would the hearing be about? Unless courts implied a "for cause" provision, it is hard to see what the participants in the hearing would discuss; there would be nothing to adjudicate. Procedural safeguards make little sense without substantive rights to adjudicate; in cases with "at will" provisions, like *Roth*, there is no state-created substantive right, and there is no constitutional right to be discharged from employment only with cause.

Note: *Statutory Entitlements and Natural Liberty*

The Court has decided many cases raising the question of when there is a "statutory entitlement" or "grievous loss" amounting to a property or liberty interest.

1. *Property: state-created rights.* In Goss v. Lopez, 419 U.S. 565 (1975), the plaintiffs were sixth-grade students suspended temporarily — for periods of up to ten days — from public school. The Court found a property interest because state law provided that students may be suspended only for "misconduct." In the Court's view, this provision created "legitimate claims of entitlement to a public education. [Having] chosen to extend the right to an education to people of appellees' class generally, Ohio may not withdraw that right on grounds of misconduct, absent fundamentally fair procedures to determine whether the misconduct has occurred."

Logan v. Zimmerman Brush Co., 455 U.S. 422 (1982), involved a state statute prohibiting discrimination on the basis of handicap and providing that within

120 days of the filing of a charge of unlawful discrimination, the state fair employment practices commission "shall convene a factfinding conference." In the *Logan* case, the commission failed through negligence to hold the hearing within the requisite time, and the plaintiff's claim was extinguished by state law. The Court held that the state-created right to redress of unlawful discrimination amounted to a property interest, and that under state law, that right was to be "assessed under what is, in essence, a 'for cause' standard, based upon the substantiality of the evidence." The plaintiff was therefore entitled to a hearing.

2. *Liberty.* Paul v. Davis, 424 U.S. 693 (1976), involved a person arrested on a charge of shoplifting; Davis's name was placed on a flyer sent to 800 merchants in Louisville, designating him as an active shoplifter. The charges were dismissed, and Davis brought suit, claiming that the action had deprived him of his constitutional interest in reputation. The Court concluded that reputation, standing alone, was not a constitutionally protected liberty interest. The Court acknowledged that in conjunction with some other injury — such as a failure to rehire or a deprivation of a right to purchase liquor, see Wisconsin v. Constantineau, 400 U.S. 433 (1971) (injury to reputation by "posting" is a liberty interest when accompanied by ban on purchase of liquor) — an injury to reputation would trigger the due process clause. The Court expressed concern that a contrary holding would allow the Constitution to swallow up state tort law, making it enforceable in the federal courts. Is it odd that under Paul v. Davis, zero (discharge of a probationary employee) plus zero (injury to reputation) equals one? For a sharply critical view of the decision, see Monaghan, Of "Liberty" and "Property," 62 Cornell L. Rev. 405 (1977).

Compare with *Paul* the decision in Goss v. Lopez, supra, where the Court found a liberty interest, as well as a property interest, in freedom from arbitrary discharges. "School authorities here suspended appellees from school for periods of up to 10 days based on charges of misconduct. If sustained and recorded, those charges could seriously damage the students' standing with their fellow students and their teachers as well as interfere with later opportunities for higher education and employment."

Meachum v. Fano, 427 U.S. 215 (1976), found no constitutionally protected interest in a transfer of prisoners from a medium-security prison to a maximum-security prison on the basis of the prisoners' alleged responsibility for committing arson. The Court said:

> We reject at the outset the suggestion that *any* grievous loss visited upon a person by the State is sufficient to invoke the procedural protections of the Due Process Clause. [The] determining factor is the nature of the interest involved rather than its weight. [Given] a valid conviction, the criminal defendant has been constitutionally deprived of his liberty, to the extent that the State may confine him and subject him to the rules of its prison system so long as the conditions of confinement do not otherwise violate the Constitution. [Confinement] in any of the State's institutions is within the normal limits or range of custody which the conviction has authorized the State to impose. That life in one prison is much more disagreeable than in another does not in itself signify that a Fourteenth Amendment liberty interest is implicated.

Justice Stevens, joined by Justices Brennan and Marshall, dissented on the ground that the Court's conception of liberty was fundamentally incorrect. [If] a man were a creature of the state, the analysis would be correct. But neither the Bill of Rights nor the laws of sovereign states create the liberty which the Due Process Clause protects. [I] had thought it self-evident that all men were endowed by their Creator with liberty, as one of the cardinal unalienable rights. It is that basic freedom which the Due Process Clause protects, rather than the particular rights or privileges conferred by specific laws or regulations.

Compare Vitek v. Jones, 445 U.S. 480 (1980), which involved a transfer of a prisoner to a state mental hospital for treatment. The Court held that the due process clause was triggered, distinguishing *Meachum* in two ways. First, the state statute at issue allowed transfer only upon a finding by a designated physician or psychologist that the prisoner "suffers from a mental disease or defect" and "cannot be given treatment in that facility." The prisoner therefore had a liberty interest under Arnett v. Kennedy. Second, the Court held that the prisoner "retained a residuum of liberty that would be infringed by a transfer to a mental hospital." The Court pointed to the stigmatic consequences of involuntary commitment to a mental hospital, the possibility of compelled treatment in the form of mandatory behavior modification programs, and the increased limitations on freedom of action. Assume there was no statutory entitlement in *Vitek*. If there is a constitutionally protected liberty interest, does it follow that there is a substantive constitutional right not to be transferred to a mental institution without just cause?

Greenholtz v. Inmates, 442 U.S. 1 (1979), held that without a statutory entitlement, there is no constitutionally protected interest in a denial of parole. The Court acknowledged that a revocation of parole would trigger the due process clause but found a distinction between rescinding a benefit already conferred and refusing to grant a benefit in the first instance. In Board of Pardons v. Allen, 482 U.S. 369 (1987), the Court held that Montana's parole statute established a sufficient expectancy of release to create a liberty interest. Although acknowledging the subjective nature of the parole board's decision and the broad discretion vested in it, the Court held that the mandatory language of the parole statute created an expectancy of release. Justice O'Connor, joined by Chief Justice Rehnquist and Justice Scalia, dissented.

In Sandin v. Conner, 515 U.S. 472 (1995), the Court held that there was no due process violation when a prisoner was not permitted to present witnesses during a disciplinary hearing in which he was sentenced to disciplinary segregation for misconduct. The Court emphasized that judges should avoid involvement in "the ordinary incidents of prison life." It concluded that even if discipline was punitive, and even if state law appeared to create a statutory entitlement not to be disciplined except for "high misconduct," the due process clause would not be triggered unless it presented "a dramatic departure from the basic conditions" of the sentence. In the Court's view, the shift to segregated confinement was not such a dramatic departure, since disciplinary segregation involved conditions similar to those faced by inmates in administrative segregation and protective custody.

3. *Concluding thoughts.* In defining liberty and property interests, the Court has had three principal options. First, it could have continued to define protected interests by reference to the common law. Such an approach would deny procedural protection for all statutory interests by adhering to the preexisting framework; at the same time, it would have denied "new property" any constitutional

protection by allowing statutes to condition the interests they grant. Second, the Court could have defined protected interests in a functional way, by looking to their importance. For example, it could have assessed whether the interests in question have as much importance in the modern era as common law rights seemed to have in a very different time. Third, it could have chosen, as it did, the current course — offering procedural protection only to statutes that create "entitlements." In which direction, if any, should the Court move?

2. What Process Is Due

Mathews v. Eldridge
424 U.S. 319 (1976)

[Eldridge had received disability benefits since 1968. After considering Eldridge's response to a questionnaire about his condition, reports from Eldridge's physician and a psychiatric consultant, and Eldridge's files, the relevant state agency made a tentative determination that Eldridge's disability had ceased. Eldridge was so informed, given a statement of reasons, and offered an opportunity to submit a written response. He did so, disputing the agency's decision, but benefits were nonetheless terminated. Eldridge claimed that this procedure violated the due process clause. The court below agreed.]

MR. JUSTICE POWELL delivered the opinion of the Court.

[Procedural] due process imposes constraints on governmental decisions which deprive individuals of "liberty" or "property" interests within the meaning of the Due Process Clause of the Fifth or Fourteenth Amendment. The Secretary does not contend that procedural due process is inapplicable to terminations of Social Security disability benefits. He recognizes [that] the interest of an individual in continued receipt of these benefits is a statutorily created "property" interest protected by the Fifth Amendment. [Rather,] the Secretary contends that the existing administrative procedures [provide] all the process that is constitutionally due before a recipient can be deprived of that interest. This Court consistently has held that some form of hearing is required before an individual is finally deprived of a property interest. [The] "right to be heard before being condemned to suffer grievous loss of any kind, even though it may not involve the stigma and hardships of a criminal conviction, is a principle basic to our society." Joint Anti-Fascist Comm. v. McGrath, 341 U.S. 123, 168 (Frankfurter, J., concurring). The fundamental requirement of due process is the opportunity to be heard "at a meaningful time and in a meaningful manner." [Eldridge] agrees that the review procedures available to a claimant before the initial determination of ineligibility becomes final would be adequate if disability benefits were not terminated until after the evidentiary hearing stage of the administrative process. The dispute centers upon what process is due prior to the initial termination of benefits, pending review.

In recent years this Court increasingly has had occasion to consider the extent to which due process requires an evidentiary hearing prior to the deprivation of some type of property interest even if such a hearing is provided thereafter. In only one case, [Goldberg], has the Court held that a hearing closely approximating a judicial trial is necessary. In other cases requiring some type of pretermination hearing as a matter of constitutional right the Court has spoken sparingly about the requisite procedures. . . .

[Our] decisions underscore the truism that "'[d]ue process,' unlike some legal rules, is not a technical conception with a fixed content unrelated to time, place and circumstances." "[D]ue process is flexible and calls for such procedural protections as the particular situation demands." [Accordingly,] resolution of the issue whether the administrative procedures provided here are constitutionally sufficient requires analysis of the governmental and private interests that are affected. [*Arnett.*] More precisely, our prior decisions indicate that identification of the specific dictates of due process generally requires consideration of three distinct factors: First, the private interest that will be affected by the official action; second, the risk of an erroneous deprivation of such interest through the procedures used, and the probable value, if any, of additional or substitute procedural safeguards; and finally, the Government's interest, including the function involved and the fiscal and administrative burdens that the additional or substitute procedural requirement would entail.

[The Court described the relevant procedures. It noted that the worker bears a continuing burden of showing that he suffers from a medically determinable physical or mental impairment; that a state agency conducts continuing eligibility investigations, in which there is communication with the disabled worker; that when an agency's tentative assessment differs from the worker's, the worker is informed that benefits may be terminated and is offered an opportunity to respond in writing and to furnish new evidence; that there is review by a federal official of any state decision to terminate; that after termination, there is a right to an evidentiary hearing, in which the claimant may be represented by counsel; and that the worker may recover retroactive payments if the termination is later found erroneous.]

[Despite] the elaborate character of the administrative procedures provided by the Secretary, the courts below held them to be constitutionally inadequate, concluding that due process requires an evidentiary hearing prior to termination. In light of the private and governmental interests at stake here and the nature of the existing procedures, we think this was error.

Since a recipient whose benefits are terminated is awarded full retroactive relief if he ultimately prevails, his sole interest is in the uninterrupted receipt of this source of income pending final administrative decision on his claim.

[Only] in *Goldberg* has the Court held that due process requires an evidentiary hearing prior to a temporary deprivation. It was emphasized there that welfare assistance is given to persons on the very margin of [subsistence. Eligibility] for disability benefits, in contrast, is not based upon financial need. Indeed, it is wholly unrelated to the worker's income or support from many other sources, such as earnings of other family members, workmen's compensation awards, tort claims awards, savings, private insurance, public or private pensions, veterans' benefits, food stamps, public assistance, or the "many other important programs, both public and private, which contain provisions for disability payments affecting a substantial portion of the work force. . . ."

As *Goldberg* illustrates, the degree of potential deprivation that may be created by a particular decision is a factor to be considered in assessing the validity of any administrative decisionmaking process. The potential deprivation here is generally likely to be less than in *Goldberg*, although the degree of difference can be overstated. As the District Court emphasized, to remain eligible for benefits a recipient must be "unable to engage in substantial gainful activity." Thus, in contrast to the discharged federal employee in *Arnett*, there is little possibility that the terminated recipient will be able to find even temporary employment to ameliorate the interim loss. [Further,] "the possible length of wrongful deprivation of . . . benefits [also] is an important factor in assessing the impact of official action on the private interests." The Secretary concedes that the delay between a request for a hearing before an administrative law judge and a decision on the claim is currently between 10 and 11 months. Since a terminated recipient must first obtain a reconsideration decision as a prerequisite to invoking his right to an evidentiary hearing, the delay between the actual cutoff of benefits and final decision after a hearing exceeds one year.

In view of the torpidity of this administrative review process, and the typically modest resources of the family unit of the physically disabled worker,[26] the hardship imposed upon the erroneously terminated disability recipient may be significant. Still, the disabled worker's need is likely to be less than that of a welfare recipient. In addition to the possibility of access to private resources, other forms of government assistance will become available where the termination of disability benefits places a worker or his family below the subsistence level.

In view of these potential sources of temporary income, there is less reason here than in *Goldberg* to depart from the ordinary principle, [that] something less than an evidentiary hearing is sufficient prior to adverse administrative action.

An additional factor to be considered here is the fairness and reliability of the existing pretermination procedures, and the probable value, if any, of additional procedural safeguards. Central to the evaluation of any administrative process is the nature of the relevant inquiry. In order to remain eligible for benefits the disabled worker must demonstrate by means of "medically acceptable clinical and laboratory diagnostic techniques," that he is unable "to engage in any substantial gainful activity by reason of any *medically determinable* physical or mental impairment. . . ."

In short, a medical assessment of the worker's physical or mental condition is required. This is a more sharply focused and easily documented decision than the typical determination of welfare entitlement. [The] decision whether to discontinue disability benefits will turn, in most cases, upon "routine, standard, and unbiased medical reports by physician specialists," [concerning] a subject whom they have personally examined. [To] be sure, credibility and veracity may be a factor in the ultimate disability assessment in some cases. But procedural due process rules are shaped by the risk of error inherent in the truthfinding process as applied to the generality of cases, not the rare exceptions. The potential value of an evidentiary hearing, or even oral presentation to the decisionmaker, is substantially less in this context than in *Goldberg*.

The decision in *Goldberg* also was based on the Court's conclusion that written submissions were an inadequate substitute for oral presentation because they did not provide an effective means for the recipient to communicate his case

---

26. Amici cite statistics compiled by the Secretary which indicate that in 1965 the mean income of the family unit of a disabled worker was $3,803, while the median income for the unit was $2,836. The mean liquid assets — i.e., cash, stocks, bonds — of these family units was $4,862; the median was $940. These statistics do not take into account the family unit's nonliquid assets — i.e., automobile, real estate, and the like.

to the decisionmaker. Written submissions were viewed as an unrealistic option, for most recipients lacked the "educational attainment necessary to write effectively" and could not afford professional assistance. In addition, such submissions would not provide the "flexibility of oral presentations" or "permit the recipient to mold his argument to the issues the decision maker appears to regard as important." [In] the context of the disability-benefits-entitlement assessment the administrative procedures under review here fully answer these objections.

[A] further safeguard against mistake is the policy of allowing the disability recipient's representative full access to all information relied upon by the state agency. In addition, prior to the cutoff of benefits the agency informs the recipient of its tentative assessment, the reasons therefor, and provides a summary of the evidence that it considers most relevant. Opportunity is then afforded the recipient to submit additional evidence or arguments, enabling him to challenge directly the accuracy of information in his file as well as the correctness of the agency's tentative conclusions.

Despite these carefully structured procedures, amici point to the significant reversal rate for appealed cases as clear evidence that the current process is inadequate. Depending upon the base selected and the line of analysis followed, the relevant reversal rates urged by the contending parties vary from a high of 58.6% for appealed reconsideration decisions to an overall reversal rate of only 3.3%. Bare statistics rarely provide a satisfactory measure of the fairness of a decision-making process. Their adequacy is especially suspect here since the administrative review system is operated on an open-file basis. A recipient may always submit new evidence, and such submissions may result in additional medical examinations. . . .

In striking the appropriate due process balance the final factor to be assessed is the public interest. This includes the administrative burden and other societal costs that would be associated with requiring, as a matter of constitutional right, an evidentiary hearing upon demand in all cases prior to the termination of disability benefits. The most visible burden would be the incremental cost resulting from the increased number of hearings and the expense of providing benefits to ineligible recipients pending decision. No one can predict the extent of the increase, but the fact that full benefits would continue until after such hearings would assure the exhaustion in most cases of this attractive option. [The] parties submit widely varying estimates of the probable additional financial cost. We only need say that experience with the constitutionalizing of government procedures suggests that the ultimate additional cost in terms of money and administrative burden would not be insubstantial.

Financial cost alone is not a controlling weight in determining whether due process requires a particular procedural safeguard prior to some administrative decision. But the Government's interest, and hence that of the public, in conserving scarce fiscal and administrative resources is a factor that must be weighed. At some point the benefit of an additional safeguard to the individual affected by the administrative action and to society in terms of increased assurance that the action is just, may be outweighed by the cost. Significantly, the cost of protecting those whom the preliminary administrative process has identified as likely to be found undeserving may in the end come out of the pockets of the deserving since resources available for any particular program of social welfare are not unlimited. . . .

[But] more is implicated in cases of this type than ad hoc weighing of fiscal and administrative burdens against the interests of a particular category of claimants. The ultimate balance involves a determination as to when, under our constitutional system, judicial-type procedures must be imposed upon administrative action to assure fairness. [In] assessing what process is due in this case, substantial weight must be given to the good-faith judgments of the individuals charged by Congress with the administration of social welfare programs that the procedures they have provided assure fair consideration of the entitlement claims of individuals. . . .

We conclude that an evidentiary hearing is not required prior to the termination of disability benefits and that the present administrative procedures fully comport with due process.

The judgment of the Court of Appeals is reversed.

Mr. Justice Stevens took no part in the consideration or decision of this case.

MR. JUSTICE BRENNAN, with whom MR. JUSTICE MARSHALL concurs, dissenting.

[The] Court's consideration that a discontinuance of disability benefits may cause the recipient to suffer only a limited deprivation is no argument. It is speculative. Moreover, the very legislative determination to provide disability benefits, without any prerequisite determination of need in fact, presumes a need by the recipient which is not this Court's function to denigrate. Indeed, in the present case, [because] disability benefits were terminated there was a foreclosure upon the Eldridge home and the family's furniture was repossessed, forcing Eldridge, his wife, and their children to sleep in one bed. Finally, it is also no argument that a worker, who has been placed in the untenable position of having been denied disability benefits, may still seek other forms of public assistance.

Note: Balancing Tests and the Due Process Clause

1. *The* Mathews *test in general.* In *Mathews*, the Court adopted a three-part "test," sometimes called one of balancing or "cost-benefit" analysis, that has played an important role in constitutional law. In almost all cases raising questions of procedural regularity, the Court refers to the *Mathews* test. On what grounds might the test be criticized?

· a. *Ignoring nonutilitarian variables.* Perhaps the *Mathews* approach ignores participatory and dignitary concerns. Consider Mashaw, The Supreme Court's Due Process Calculus for Administrative Adjudication in Mathews v. Eldridge: Three Factors in Search of a Theory of Value, 44 U. Chi. L. Rev. 28, 49-51 (1976):

> The Supreme Court's analysis in *Eldridge* is not informed by systematic attention to any theory of the values underlying due process review. The approach is implicitly utilitarian but incomplete, and the Court overlooks alternative theories that might have yielded fruitful inquiry. [The] increasingly secular, scientific, and collectivist character of the modern American state reinforces our propensity to define fairness in the formal, and apparently neutral language of social utility. [Yet] the popular moral presupposition of individual dignity, and its political counterpart, self-determination, persist. State coercion must be legitimized, not only by accept-

able substantive policies, but also by political processes that respond to a demo-cratic morality's demand for participation in decisions affecting individual and group interests. [A] dignitary theory of due process might have contributed signifi-cantly to the *Eldridge* analysis. [A] disability decision is a judgment of considerable social significance, and one that the claimant should rightly perceive as having a substantive moral content.

See also J. Mashaw, Due Process in the Administrative State (1985).

b. *Vagueness.* Perhaps the three-part analysis is not useful, or perhaps it fails to constrain judicial discretion in a helpful way. Note that in economics, cost-benefit analysis is usually based on the criterion of private willingness to pay. The benefit is measured by how much people would be willing to pay for the good in question; the cost is measured similarly. But how does one assess the benefits and costs in a case like *Mathews?* Might the various factors be thought incom-mensurable, in the sense that there is no metric along which they could be aligned? See Sunstein, Incommensurability and Valuation in Law, 92 Mich. L. Rev. 779 (1994).

c. *Susceptibility to misapplication.* Perhaps a utilitarian assessment of the three factors requires courts to duplicate legislative processes. That assessment, calling for ad hoc judgments of policy, may not be readily within judicial competence. What in the text of the due process clause or in acceptable conceptions of the ju-dicial role authorizes such an approach?

This critique might be buttressed by reference to *Mathews* itself. Mashaw, The Supreme Court's Due Process Calculus for Administrative Adjudication, supra, argues that the Court misconceived the character of the disability determination. According to Mashaw, that determination is based much less on purely medical factors and much more on subjective impressions raising issues of credibility than the Court suggested. In these circumstances, oral rather than written testi-mony becomes more valuable. Note also the Court's confessed inability to eval-uate the costs of additional safeguards, captured in its statement that it could not say that they would be "insubstantial."

But is there an alternative to the *Mathews* approach that would avoid these var-ious critiques and at the same time provide a sensible approach for making deci-sions about the extent of procedural safeguards? Would bright-line rules — re-quiring, for example, trial-type hearings absent a special governmental showing or deference to the legislative determination absent special individual circum-stances — be preferable? Consider also that (1) it is possible that detailed pro-cedures may be requested only by the most educated and aggressive claimants, (2) the costs of such procedures may be taken out of the claimants' benefits else-where, and (3) formal procedures may increase the adversarial quality of relations that should be conducted in a more informal way.

See in this connection Walters v. National Association of Radiation Survivors, 473 U.S. 305 (1985), where the Court cited *Mathews* in upholding a statute pro-viding that $10 is the maximum fee that may be paid to an attorney who repre-sents a veteran seeking Veterans Administration benefits for service-related inju-ries. In a concurring opinion, Justice O'Connor, joined by Justice Blackmun, suggested that under the due process clause, courts should look at the individual claim to evaluate whether the statutory maximum is unconstitutional in particu-lar applications. Justice Stevens, joined by Justices Brennan and Marshall, dis-sented, arguing in favor of a bright-line rule in favor of counsel.

Justice Stevens renewed his call for a bright-line rule in a dissenting opinion in Brock v. Roadway Express, Inc., 481 U.S. 252 (1987):

> The Court's willingness to sacrifice due process to the Government's obscure suggestion of necessity reveals the serious flaws in its due process analysis. It is wrong to approach the due process analysis in each case by asking anew what procedures seem worthwhile and not too costly. Unless a case falls within a recognized exception, we should adhere to the strongest presumption that the Government may not take away life, liberty, or property before making a meaningful hearing available.

2. *The problem of timing.* Must hearings be held before or after adverse action is taken? The traditional rule has been that a postdeprivation remedy is insufficient. In general, government must afford procedural safeguards *before* it harms someone. But in North American Cold Storage Co. v. Chicago, 211 U.S. 306 (1908), the Court held that a prior hearing was not required before state officers destroyed stored food deemed by health officials to be unfit for human consumption. The Court noted that the existence of the food posed a threat to public health, and that a subsequent tort action would provide sufficient protection to the owner. Would the *Mathews* approach support this outcome?

How far should the *North American Cold Storage* reasoning be taken? Consider whether it should apply to cases of termination of welfare benefits or of employment. Note that in Arnett v. Kennedy, section G1 supra, a majority of the Court held that a trial-type hearing was not required before termination of a federal employee accused of bribery. Justice Powell, undertaking a balancing approach, contended that the government "must have wide discretion and control over the management of its personnel and internal affairs. This includes the prerogative to remove employees whose conduct hinders efficient operation and to do so with dispatch. [The employee's] actual injury would consist of a temporary interruption of his income during the interim. [The] possible deprivation is considerably less severe than that involved in *Goldberg*." Note, however, that in *Arnett*, there was some predeprivation procedure as well.

In *Loudermill*, supra, the Court held that the Constitution did not permit discharge of state employees without any prior procedural safeguards. The Court said: "In *Arnett* six Justices found constitutional minima satisfied where the employee had access to the material upon which the charge was based and could respond orally or in writing and present rebuttal affidavits. [The] need for some form of pretermination hearing [is] evident from a balancing of the competing interests at stake." The Court emphasized that the "private interest in retaining employment" was significant; that "some opportunity for the employee to present his side of the case is recurringly of obvious value in reaching an accurate decision," especially in light of the fact the discharge may involve a factual dispute; and that "affording the employee an opportunity to respond would impose neither a significant administrative burden nor intolerable delays."

The Court added that, even when the dispute was not factual, a hearing might allow an examination of the appropriateness or necessity of discharge, and that a hearing could serve governmental interests in retaining qualified employees. The Court said, however, that an employee's pretermination hearing need not be elaborate and could consist of "oral or written notice of the charges against him, an explanation of the employer's evidence, and an opportunity to present his side of the story."

In Brock v. Roadway Express, Inc., supra, the Court considered the converse of the problem posed by *Arnett* and *Loudermill* — that is, the kind of process that is due before an employer can be forced to reinstate a discharged worker. A federal statute protects employees in the transportation industry from discharge in retaliation for refusing to operate a motor vehicle that does not comply with state and federal safety regulations. The statute provides that, if the Secretary of Labor finds reasonable cause to believe that an employee has been discharged in violation of the act, he can issue an order reinstating the employee. An employer is entitled to a full evidentiary hearing only after the reinstatement.

In an opinion written by Justice Marshall, a plurality of the Court held that the Constitution did not require an evidentiary hearing and an opportunity to cross-examine witnesses before the government ordered temporary reinstatement. Although acknowledging the employer's substantial interest in controlling the make-up of its workforce, the plurality emphasized the government's countervailing interest in promoting highway safety and the employee's interest in retaining his job.

The plurality went on to hold, however, that the procedures would satisfy this reliability standard only if the employer received notice of the employee's allegations, notice of the substance of the relevant supporting evidence, an opportunity to submit a written response, and an opportunity to meet with the investigator and present statements from rebuttal witnesses.

In separate opinions, Justices Brennan and Stevens each argued that the due process clause required a full evidentiary hearing prior to a reinstatement order. Justice White, in an opinion joined by Chief Justice Rehnquist and Justice Scalia, argued that due process did not require that the employer be provided with information on which the reinstatement order is based, including names of witnesses, prior to reinstatement.

3. *How formal?* Goldberg v. Kelly required a trial-type hearing before termination of welfare benefits, including a number of features: a right to present oral evidence, a right to confront and cross-examine witnesses, a right to counsel, a statement by the arbiter of reasons and of the evidence relied on, and a right to an impartial decisionmaker. In recent cases, however, the Court has shown some reluctance to formalize the administrative process with such requirements.

At the opposite pole from *Goldberg*, for example, is Goss v. Lopez, section G1 supra, in which the Court found that due process required only a conversation before temporary suspension of students. This included oral or written notice of the charges against them, an explanation of the evidence the authorities have, and a chance to provide the students' side of the story. The Court said:

> Even truncated trial-type procedures might well overwhelm administrative facilities in many places and, in diverting resources, cost more than it would save in educational effectiveness. Moreover, further formalizing the suspension process and escalating its formality and adversary nature may not only make it too costly as a regular disciplinary tool but also destroy its effectiveness as part of the teaching process. On the other hand, requiring effective notice and informal hearing permitting the student to give his version of the events will provide a meaningful hedge against erroneous action.

See also Board of Curators of University of Missouri v. Horowitz, 435 U.S. 78 (1978), declining to require elaborate procedures for discharge of a woman from medical school in part because of reluctance to "formalize the academic dismissal process." And note the various conclusions on the issue of formality in *Mathews, Arnett,* and *Loudermill.*

Consider finally Greenholtz v. Inmates, 442 U.S. 1 (1979), in which the Court held that in parole decisions, based on a subjective assessment of the whole person, an oral hearing was not required. A review of the prisoner's files, the Court said, was sufficient to satisfy due process.

4. *State remedies as due process.* Sometimes the Court has held that state tort remedies may sometimes provide all the process that is constitutionally "due." Ingraham v. Wright, 430 U.S. 651 (1977), involved a claim that the due process clause required some sort of procedural safeguard before teachers "paddled" students for asserted misconduct. The Court held that the interest in avoiding "paddling" was a constitutionally protected liberty but concluded that an after-the-fact state tort remedy provided sufficient procedural safeguards. "Because paddlings are usually inflicted in response to conduct directly observed by teachers in their presence, the risk that a child will be paddled without cause is typically insignificant. [In] those cases where severe punishment is contemplated, the available civil and criminal sanctions for abuse — considered in light of the openness of the school environment — afford significant protection against unjustified corporal punishment." Justice White, in a dissent joined by Justices Brennan, Marshall, and Stevens, complained that state law was inadequate in cases of a good faith mistake in school discipline, and that the "infliction of physical pain is final and irreparable."

Compare Memphis Light, Gas, & Water Division v. Craft, 436 U.S. 1 (1978), requiring a hearing in advance of termination of electricity service for nonpayment of a disputed bill. "The factors that have justified exceptions to the requirements of some prior process are not present here. Although utility service may be restored ultimately, the cessation of essential services for any appreciable time works a uniquely final deprivation. [Moreover], the probability of error in utility cut-off decisions is not so insubstantial as to warrant dispensing with all process prior to termination."

Ingraham was extended in Parratt v. Taylor, 451 U.S. 527 (1981), which involved a negligent loss of a prisoner's hobby kit. The Court held that state tort law provided a constitutionally adequate remedy. The Court noted that the case involved a "tortious loss of [property] as a result of a random and unauthorized act by a state employee[, not] as a result of some established state procedure." A state tort remedy was therefore sufficient "process." See also Hudson v. Palmer, 468 U.S. 517 (1984), extending *Parratt* to intentional deprivations of property in the context of destruction of a prisoner's property during the search of his cell. Should it matter that property, rather than liberty, was at stake? That a prior hearing would seem impracticable?

In Logan v. Zimmerman Brush Co., section G1 supra, it was argued that *Parratt* was controlling, and that the state tort remedy provided sufficient procedural protection for the state's failure to hold a hearing on the plaintiff's claim of discrimination. The Court rejected that argument, reasserting the general principle requiring predeprivation hearings. Unlike in *Parratt,* moreover, "it is the state system itself that destroys a complainant's property interests, by operation of law, whenever the Commission fails to convene a timely conference."

In Daniels v. Williams, 474 U.S. 327 (1986), the Court overruled *Parratt* insofar as that case had suggested that a negligently inflicted loss could amount to a deprivation of due process in the absence of a state tort remedy. Although all nine justices joined the result in *Daniels*, a second case, also involving negligence by a state official and decided on the same day, evoked more controversy. In Davidson v. Cannon, 474 U.S. 344 (1986), the Court rejected the due process claim of a state prisoner who alleged that he was seriously injured when prison officials negligently failed to protect him from another inmate. Chief Justice Rehnquist again wrote the Court's opinion: "[Where] a government official is merely negligent in causing the injury, no procedure for compensation is constitutionally required. [The] guarantee of due process has never been understood to mean that the State must guarantee due care on the part of its officials."

Justice Stevens wrote an opinion concurring in the results in both *Daniels* and *Davidson*, but solely on the ground that in neither case were state remedies for the deprivations constitutionally inadequate. In an extended opinion, Justice Blackmun, joined by Justice Marshall, dissented. Justice Brennan dissented separately.

5. *Concluding note.* In exploring issues of timing, formality, and adequacy of state tort remedies, the Court has firmly relied on the tripartite test of *Mathews*. Do the outcomes suggest that the test is vulnerable to the three criticisms set out at the introduction of this Note? Or, taken as a whole, can one conclude that the test furnishes a sensible method of accommodating the various concerns at stake?

Note: The (Dead) Irrebuttable Presumption Doctrine

For a period, the Court combined principles of procedural due process and equal protection in the "irrebuttable presumption doctrine," in accordance with which decisions according to rule were sometimes unconstitutional. Cleveland Board of Education v. LaFleur, 414 U.S. 632 (1974), was the leading case. At issue was a school board regulation requiring pregnant school teachers to take an unpaid maternity leave four to five months before the expected birth. The Court invalidated the regulation on the ground that it created "a conclusive presumption that every pregnant teacher who teaches the fifth or sixth month of pregnancy is physically incapable of continuing. There is no individualized determination [as] to any particular teacher's ability to continue at her job." See also Vlandis v. Kline, 412 U.S. 441 (1973), invalidating a Connecticut statute creating an irrebuttable presumption that students transferring to a state university from out of state were nonresidents and thus not entitled to reduced tuition fees.

The doctrine has been subject to sharp criticism. Decisions made in accordance with clear rules are sometimes taken to be the model of compliance with the principle of procedural regularity. Moreover, most statutes amount to conclusive presumptions; surely the Court did not mean to invalidate them all.

See Note, Irrebuttable Presumptions: An Illusory Analysis, 27 Stan. L. Rev. 449 (1975), contending that

> [conclusive] presumption claims are correctly analyzed by determining the actual relationship between the criterion of basic fact and the consequences established by the challenged provision, the importance of the individual interest impaired by

that relationship, and the extent of overlap between the relationship established and the governmental interest sought to be effected. [The] nearly automatic application of a close scrutiny test to what are essentially equal protection claims engages the Court in the type of review that it abandoned in the 1930's and from which it has assiduously sought to abstain.

To the same effect, see Note, The Irrebuttable Presumption Doctrine in the Supreme Court, 87 Harv. L. Rev. 1534 (1974).

Weinberger v. Salfi, 422 U.S. 749 (1975), seems to have marked the demise of the doctrine. The case involved a constitutional attack on a requirement of the Social Security Act that, in order to receive benefits as a spouse of a wage earner, one must have been married to the wage earner for at least nine months prior to his death. The requirement was attacked on the ground that it did not permit individualized proof on the question whether the marriage was entered into for purposes of qualifying for Social Security benefits. The Court distinguished *LaFleur* and *Vlandis* on the ground that they did not involve "a noncontractual claim to receive funds from the public treasury." Extension of the doctrine here, the Court said,

> would turn the doctrine of those cases into a virtual engine of destruction for countless legislative judgments which have heretofore been thought wholly consistent with the [Constitution]. The question raised is not whether a statutory provision precisely filters out those, and only those, who are in the factual position which generated the congressional concern reflected in the statute. Such a rule would ban all prophylactic provisions.

The Court added that there were substantial benefits to an across-the-board rule in terms of saving the costs of individuation. Applying traditional rationality review, the Court upheld the rule. Justice Brennan, joined by Justice Marshall, dissented. For a post-*Salfi* refusal either to overrule or to reaffirm Vlandis v. Kline, see Elkins v. Moreno, 435 U.S. 647 (1978). See also Usery v. Turner Elkhorne Mining Co., 428 U.S. 1 (1976) (upholding a broad "conclusive presumption").

Is any function performed by invalidation of irrebuttable presumptions that is not performed by procedural due process, as understood in *Roth* and successor cases, or by equal protection doctrine? Note that ordinary principles of procedural due process entitle a person to a hearing to determine whether the applicable rule has been violated. Such principles are by definition inapplicable to a conclusive presumption, where there is no doubt that the government "followed the rules." Note also that ordinary principles of equal protection require a merely rational connection between the conclusive presumption and the harm sought to be avoided. Under this framework, most conclusive presumptions — like most rules — will be upheld.

But the irrebuttable presumption doctrine has been defended on the ground that procedural due process and equal protection, ordinarily conceived, neglect the possibility that procedural irregularity may consist precisely in the failure to allow individualized treatment. Under this view, the rule of law — adherence to clear principles set down in advance — can sometimes produce arbitrariness and is not (always or inevitably? generally?) a guarantee against it. Consider the following view:

There are circumstances in which individualized judgments, unbounded by rules, should not be viewed as ways of concealing arbitrary, unequal, or substantively impermissible bases for decision. The persistence of courts of equity, the emergence of concepts like "unconscionability," and, in another sphere, the vitality of successful families and other intimate communities, all belie any automatic equating of the informal with the suspect. [Is] it possible to argue that individualized and informal judgments are in some circumstances not only more "enlightened" but indeed constitutionally propelled — no less so than judgments by determinate rules are in other circumstances?

Tribe, Structural Due Process, 10 Harv. C.R.-C.L. L. Rev. 269 (1975). Tribe goes on to defend *LaFleur* on the ground that "the important interest involved in parenthood, cast in a context of social and moral flux about unmarried sex, made rulebound determination inappropriate for the issue." For extended discussion of the premises underlying preferences for rules, on the one hand, and individualized decision, on the other, see generally M. Nussbaum, The Fragility of Goodness ch. 10 (1986); Kennedy, Form and Substance in Private Law Adjudication, 89 Harv. L. Rev. 1685, 1710-1722, 1767-1774 (1976). For a treatment of male and female differences in moral reasoning, suggesting that boys tend to value rights and rules and girls care and context, see the now-classic C. Gilligan, In a Different Voice (1982).

Note: Procedural Due Process and "Legislative" Determinations

Congress and state legislatures may pass laws without affording procedural safeguards beyond those specifically required by the Constitution. The due process clause does not mean that, before passing laws, Congress must hear those who will be affected. Congress may, for example, reduce the welfare benefits of a class of people without offering anything in the way of procedure. Why? Does the same reasoning apply when administrative agencies make rules governing private conduct?

Some answers were spelled out in Bi-Metallic Investment Co. v. State Board of Equalization, 239 U.S. 441 (1915). *Bi-Metallic* involved an attempt to prevent the Denver Board of Equalization and the Colorado Tax Commission from increasing the valuation of all taxable property in Denver without affording a hearing. The Court held that no hearing was required:

Where a rule of conduct applies to more than a few people it is impracticable that every one should have a direct voice in its adoption. The Constitution does not require all public acts to be done in town meeting or an assembly of the whole. General statutes within the state power are passed that affect the person or property of individuals, sometimes to the point of ruin, without giving them a chance to be heard. Their rights are protected in the only way that they can be in a complex society, by their power, immediate or remote, over those who make the rule.

This reasoning contains two points: Processes of representation are a sufficient guarantee of legitimacy, thus serving the same ends as a hearing; and it would be impracticable to require a hearing for determinations that affect large numbers of people. Kenneth Culp Davis has added that trial-type processes are best suited for "adjudicative" facts — facts "about the parties and their activities, business, and properties. Adjudicative facts usually answer the questions of who said what, where, when, how, why, with what motive or intent." K. Davis, Administrative Law Treatise §7.02 (1958). "Legislative" facts, by contrast, raise questions of policy that are better suited to a legislative forum.

How might one challenge these claims? We might be skeptical about the idea that representative processes are a reliable safeguard when administrative agencies are making rules; they also reflect a view that judicially enforced procedures, giving a right to participate, are useful even when the issue at stake is one of policy rather than "adjudicative facts." How far should such rulings be taken? Consider the relevance of the discussion of the purposes of procedural safeguards, supra.

H.   THE CONTRACTS AND TAKINGS CLAUSES

This section explores the contracts clause and the eminent domain clause. The two clauses do not create "implied fundamental rights" in the sense that we have been discussing thus far, but they have a close association with decisions under the due process clause, and they therefore deserve treatment here.

The two clauses have been united by a single, quite general idea: Government ought not to be permitted to redistribute resources by "taking" resources from one person for the benefit of another. The contracts clause bars state government from disrupting voluntary agreements simply because government wants to help one or another side. The eminent domain clause bars the federal government (and, after incorporation, the states as well) from taking property from one person and giving it to someone else. Both clauses require the public as a whole, rather than distinct groups, to pay out funds to benefit people perceived to be in need of protection. Both clauses are in this sense allied by a fear of the power of "factions" — powerful private interests — over government and an associated belief that at least certain forms of redistribution should be banned.

Redistribution, particularly to the disadvantaged, has become an important part of the activity of the national and state governments in the aftermath of the New Deal. There has therefore been considerable pressure to limit the force of the contracts and the takings clauses. And when redistribution, to the disadvantaged or to anyone else, is perceived as inefficient or unjust, it should be unsurprising to see efforts to reinvigorate both clauses.

1.   The Contracts Clause

The contracts clause provides, "No State shall [pass] any [Law] impairing the Obligation of Contracts." U.S. Const. art. I, §10, cl. 1.

Note: Early Interpretive Problems

The contracts clause is one of the few "rights-protecting" provisions in the original Constitution. It is also one of the few such provisions that was directly applicable to the states before the adoption of the fourteenth amendment. Moreover, for a long period the contracts clause was among the most important provisions in the Constitution, at least if the structural provisions are excluded. Indeed, in the nineteenth century the clause "was the constitutional justification for more cases involving the validity of state law than all of the other clauses of the Constitution together." B. Wright, The Contract Clause of the Constitution 1 (1938). Some also highly valued the clause for its protection of a form of liberty. Sir Henry Maine claimed that the clause "is the bulwark of American individualism against democratic impatience and socialistic fantasy." H. Maine, Popular Government 247-248 (1885). Why did the framers of the Constitution single out contractual freedom as one of the only rights entitled to protection against abridgment by state governments?

A partial answer lies in the history. Between the Revolution and the drafting of the Constitution, many states had enacted "debtor relief" laws — provisions that, among other things, postponed the time for payment of private debts, allowed for issuance and required acceptance of paper money, and allowed for payments in installments or at some percentage of the appraised value of commodities. Creditors, well-to-do or otherwise, regarded these measures as an indefensible intrusion on private ordering. Many debtors found such measures to be an indispensable protection against surprise or unfair dealing. Many observers, including some of the framers, saw such measures as general, long-term obstacles to trade and commercial development — obstacles that would ultimately harm everyone, including possible debtors themselves, by discouraging contractual arrangements.

Recall here that the contracts clause was applicable only to the states, and not to the federal government — unlike the eminent domain clause, which was at its inception applicable only to the federal government. Is this an accident of history, or might it reflect a broader set of structural concerns? See McConnell, Contract Rights and Property Rights: A Case Study in the Relationship between Individual Liberties and the Constitutional Structure, 76 Cal. L. Rev. 267 (1988).

The contracts clause was designed above all to prevent states from enacting debtor relief and similar laws. See, for early cases, Sturges v. Crowninshield, 17 U.S. (4 Wheat.) 122 (1819) (invalidating a New York law discharging debtors of their obligations upon surrender of their property); Green v. Biddle, 21 U.S. (8 Wheat.) 1 (1823) (invalidating a Kentucky law designed to make it harder for landowners to eject good faith squatters). The first controversies over the clause involved three principal issues.

1. *Prospective or retrospective only?* What if a state does not reallocate rights under an existing contract but merely prohibits people from entering into certain sorts of contracts? In Ogden v. Saunders, 25 U.S. (12 Wheat.) 213 (1827), the Court was confronted with the critical question whether the prohibition of contractual impairments applies only to contracts made before the passage of the allegedly "impairing" law. The case involved a state bankruptcy law passed before the parties had entered into the relevant contract. According to the Court, the law in effect at the time a contract is formed is "the law of the contract," or a part of the contract, and therefore not an impairment at all within the meaning of the clause.

Justice Johnson, writing one of four separate opinions upholding the statute, said that the contract clause was in this respect analogous to the prohibition of bills of attainder and of ex post facto laws. All three were provisions "against arbitrary and tyrannical legislation over existing rights, whether of person or property." Statutory boundaries to contractual freedom, set in advance, were no less defensible here than "in the instances of gaming debts, usurious contracts, marriage, brokage bonds, and various others." The underlying idea is that positive law creates the background against which private parties contract, and there is no vested right to any particular background.

Chief Justice Marshall was in the minority — for the only time, in constitutional cases, during his thirty-four-year tenure as Chief Justice. He emphasized two points. First, in his view the text of the clause did not allow for a distinction between prospective and retrospective impairments. Second, Chief Justice Marshall stressed that the right to contractual freedom was a product of natural law. He said that the Court had forgotten that point by allowing positive law to dictate in advance the conditions under which contracts could go forward. The right to contractual freedom was, in his view, prepolitical: "Individuals do not derive from government their right to contract, but bring that right with them into society." Note the correspondence between Chief Justice Marshall's view and that of Justice Chase in Calder v. Bull, Chapter 1 supra.

2. *Interference with contracts under the police power.* What if a state declares unenforceable existing contractual obligations through the exercise of its police power — as, for example, by prohibiting agreements calling for the sale of heroin, or for murder, or for a certain level of pollution? To what extent does the state's reserved authority operate as an implicit qualification of the contracts clause?

In early cases, the Court ruled that the clause does not prohibit even retroactive contractual impairments if the state is operating pursuant to the police power. In Manigault v. Springs, 199 U.S. 473 (1905), neighboring landowners quarreled over a dam that one of them had built. After negotiations, the landowners agreed that the obstruction might continue for four more months, after which it would be removed, so that there would be a clear passage through the creek. The dam was accordingly removed. Several years later a statute was enacted that authorized one of the landowners to build a dam on the same creek. The statute, of course, destroyed the contractual obligation not to build a dam on the creek.

The Court upheld the statute, stating that the police power "is an exercise of the sovereign right of the government to protect the lives, health, morals, comfort, and general welfare of the people, and is paramount to any rights under contracts between individuals." Thus, "parties by entering into contracts may not estop the legislature from enacting laws intended for the public good." See also Stone v. Mississippi, 101 U.S. 814 (1880), where the Court said that no "legislature can bargain away the public health or the public morals." (Should the state be required to give compensation in cases like *Manigault* and *Stone*? This question is explored in section H2 infra.)

A police power "exception" might swallow the contract clause. If any effort that might be described as an attempt to protect the "general welfare" can justify a retroactive interference with rights acquired by contract, the clause furnishes little or no barrier to contractual impairments. Even debtor-relief legislation would be upheld, so long as the police power were understood to be sufficiently broad. For many years after *Manigault*, however, this risk did not materialize. The reason is that the police power comprehended a relatively narrow category of permissible government ends and certainly did not include the various forms of redistributive regulation characteristic of modern government.

3. *Regulation versus impairment.* In a number of early cases, the Court struggled with the issue of whether particular measures were "regulations" interfering

with remedies or genuine impairments of contractual obligations. In this view, delays in time for performance might not interfere with "substantial rights"; they merely affected the remedy. But the distinction between rights and remedies might well be thought artificial. The line here was an "obscure" one, Worthen Co. v. Kavanaugh, 295 U.S. 56 (1935), but it did allow for some flexibility on the part of the legislature. See, e.g., Honeyman v. Jacobs, 306 U.S. 539 (1939) (upholding statute designed to prevent creditor from getting more by remedy than he would have obtained had contract been performed); Richmond Mortgage & Loan Corp. v. Wachovia Bank & Trust Co., 300 U.S. 124 (1937) (same); Curtis v. Whitney, 13 Wall. 68 (1872) (upholding statute providing that a deed may not issue unless a written notice had been served on any previous owner or occupant at least three months before; statute interfered with rights received by plaintiff who had received certificate entitling her to deed before statute had been passed); Bronson v. Kinzie, 1 How. 311 (1843) (noting that state may shorten the statute of limitations period or provide what articles may be liable to execution on judgment). See generally Hale, The Supreme Court and the Contract Clause, 57 Harv. L. Rev. 512, 621, 852 (1944); B. Wright, supra.

The following case is the starting point of modern law under the contracts clause.

Home Building & Loan Association v. Blaisdell
290 U.S. 398 (1934)

[In the midst of the Depression, Minnesota passed a mortgage moratorium law to provide relief for homeowners threatened with foreclosure. The law, passed in 1933, declared an emergency and said that during the emergency period, courts could postpone mortgage sales and periods of redemption. Its provisions were to apply "only during the continuance of the emergency and in no event beyond May 1, 1935." Pursuant to the statute, Blaisdell's period of redemption was extended to May 1, 1935, subject in general to the payment by Blaisdell of $40 a month through the extended period. There was no dispute that the extension modified the lenders' contractual rights of foreclosure. The lower court upheld the statute.]

MR. CHIEF JUSTICE HUGHES delivered the opinion of the Court.

In determining whether the provision for this temporary and conditional relief exceeds the power of the State by reason of the clause in the Federal Constitution prohibiting impairment of the obligations of contracts, we must consider the relation of emergency to constitutional power, the historical setting of the contract clause, the development of the jurisprudence of this Court in the construction of that clause, and the principles of construction which we may consider to be established.

Emergency does not create power. Emergency does not increase granted power or remove or diminish the restrictions imposed upon power granted or reserved. The Constitution was adopted in a period of grave emergency. Its grants of power to the Federal Government and its limitations of the power of the States were determined in the light of emergency and they are not altered by emergency. . . .

[In] the construction of the contract clause, the debates in the Constitutional Convention are of little aid. But the reasons which led to the adoption of that clause [are] not left in doubt. [The] widespread distress following the revolution-

ary period, and the plight of debtors, had called forth in the States an ignoble array of legislative schemes for the defeat of creditors and the invasion of contractual obligations. Legislative interferences had been so numerous and extreme
that the confidence essential to prosperous trade had been undermined and the
utter destruction of credit was threatened. "The sober people of America" were
convinced that some "thorough reform" was needed which would "inspire a general prudence and industry, and give a regular course to the business of society."
The Federalist, No. 44. It was necessary to interpose the restraining power of a
central authority in order to secure the foundations even of "private faith." The
occasion and general purpose of the contract clause are summed up in the terse
statement of Chief Justice Marshall in [*Ogden*]:

> The power of changing the relative situation of debtor and creditor, of interfering
> with contracts, a power which comes home to every man, touches the interest of
> all, and controls the conduct of every individual in those things which he supposes
> to be proper for his own exclusive management, had been used to such an excess
> by the state legislatures, as to break in upon the ordinary intercourse of society, and
> destroy all confidence between man and man. This mischief had become so great,
> so alarming, as not only to impair commercial intercourse, and threaten the exis-
> tence of credit, but to sap the morals of the people, and destroy the sanctity of pri-
> vate faith. To guard against the continuance of the evil was an object of deep in-
> terest with all the truly wise, as well as the virtuous, of this great community, and
> was one of the important benefits expected from a reform of the government. . . .

[The] constitutional provision [is] qualified by the measure of control which
the State [retains] to safeguard the vital interests of its people. [Not] only are existing laws read into contracts in order to fix obligations as between the parties,
but the reservation of essential attributes of sovereign power is also read into contracts as a postulate of the legal order. The policy of protecting contracts against
impairment presupposes the maintenance of a government by virtue of which
contractual relations are worth while, — a government which retains adequate
authority to secure the peace and good order of society. This principle of harmo-
nizing the constitutional prohibition with the necessary residuum of state power
has had progressive recognition in the decisions of this Court. . . .

The legislature cannot "bargain away the public health or the public morals."
[The] question is not whether the legislative action affects contracts incidentally,
or directly or indirectly, but whether the legislation is addressed to a legitimate
end and the measures taken are reasonable and appropriate to that end. [It is ar-
gued] that the state power may be addressed directly to the prevention of the enforcement of contracts only when these are of a sort which the legislature in its
discretion may denounce as being in themselves hostile to public morals, or public health, safety or welfare, or where the prohibition is merely of injurious practices; that interference with the enforcement of other and valid contracts according to appropriate legal procedure, although the interference is temporary and
for a public purpose, is not permissible. . . .

Undoubtedly, whatever is reserved of state power must be consistent with the
fair intent of the constitutional limitation of that power. The reserved power cannot be construed so as to destroy the limitation, nor is the limitation to be construed
to destroy the reserved power in its essential aspects. They must be construed in
harmony with each other. This principle precludes a construction which would

permit the State to adopt as its policy the repudiation of debts or the destruction of contracts or the denial of means to enforce them. But it does not follow that conditions may not arise in which a temporary restraint of enforcement may be [constitutional]. . . .

[There] has been a growing appreciation of public needs and of the necessity of finding ground for a rational compromise between individual rights and public welfare. The settlement and consequent contraction of the public domain, the pressure of a constantly increasing density of population, the interrelation of the activities of our people and the complexity of our economic interests, have inevitably led to an increased use of the organization of society in order to protect the very bases of individual opportunity. Where, in earlier days, it was thought that only the concerns of individuals or of classes were involved, and that those of the State itself were touched only remotely, it has later been found that the fundamental interests of the State are directly affected; and that the question is no longer merely that of one party to a contract as against another, but of the use of reasonable means to safeguard the economic structure upon which the good of all depends.

It is no answer to say that this public need was not apprehended a century ago, or to insist that what the provision of the Constitution meant to the vision of that day it must mean to the vision of our time. If by the statement that what the Constitution meant at the time of its adoption it means to-day, it is intended to say that the great clauses of the Constitution must be confined to the interpretation which the framers, with the conditions and outlook of their time, would have placed upon them, the statement carries its own refutation. It was to guard against such a narrow conception that Chief Justice Marshall uttered the memorable warning — "We must never forget that it is *a constitution* we are expounding" [McCulloch v. Maryland] — "a constitution intended to endure for ages to come, and consequently, to be adapted to the various *crises* of human affairs." When we are dealing with the words of the Constitution, "we must realize that they have called into life a being the development of which could not have been foreseen completely by the most gifted of its begetters. . . . The case before us must be considered in the light of our whole experience and not merely in that of what was said a hundred years ago."

Nor is it helpful to attempt to draw a fine distinction between the intended meaning of the words of the Constitution and their intended application. When we consider the contract clause and the decisions which have expounded it in harmony with the essential reserved power of the States to protect the security of their peoples, we find no warrant for the conclusion that the clause has been warped by these decisions from its proper significance or that the founders of our Government would have interpreted the clause differently had they had occasion to assume that responsibility in the conditions of the later day. The vast body of law which has been developed was unknown to the fathers, but it is believed to have preserved the essential content and the spirit of the Constitution. With a growing recognition of public needs and the relation of individual right to public security, the court has sought to prevent the perversion of the clause through its use as an instrument to throttle the capacity of the States to protect their fundamental interests. This development is a growth from the seeds which the fathers planted. [The] principle of this development is, as we have seen, that the reservation of the reasonable exercise of the protective power of the State is read into all contracts. . . .

Applying the criteria established by our decisions we conclude:

1. An emergency existed in Minnesota which furnished a proper occasion for the exercise of the reserved power of the State to protect the vital interests of the community. [The] finding of the legislature and state court has support in the facts of which we take judicial notice. . . .

2. The legislation was addressed to a legitimate end, that is, the legislation was not for the mere advantage of particular individuals but for the protection of a basic interest of society.

3. In view of the nature of the contracts in question — mortgages of unquestionable validity — the relief afforded and justified by the emergency, in order not to contravene the constitutional provision, could only be of a character appropriate to that emergency and could be granted only upon reasonable conditions.

4. The conditions upon which the period of redemption is extended do not appear to be unreasonable. . . .

5. The legislation is temporary in operation. It is limited to the exigency which called it forth.

We are of the opinion that the Minnesota statute as here applied does not violate the contract clause of the Federal Constitution. Whether the legislation is wise or unwise as a matter of policy is a question with which we are not concerned. . . .

The judgment of the Supreme Court of Minnesota is affirmed.

MR. JUSTICE SUTHERLAND, dissenting.

[A] provision of the Constitution, it is hardly necessary to say, does not admit of two distinctly opposite interpretations. It does not mean one thing at one time and an entirely different thing at another time. If the contract impairment clause, when framed and adopted, meant that the terms of a contract for the payment of money could not be altered [by] a state statute enacted for the relief of hardly pressed debtors to the end and with the effect of postponing payment or enforcement during and because of an economic or financial emergency, it is but to state the obvious to say that it means the same now. . . .

Following the Revolution, and prior to the adoption of the Constitution, the American people found themselves in a greatly impoverished condition. Their commerce had been well-nigh annihilated. They were not only without luxuries, but in great degree were destitute of the ordinary comforts and necessities of life. In these circumstances they incurred indebtedness in the purchase of imported goods and otherwise, far beyond their capacity to pay. From this situation there arose a divided sentiment. On the one hand, an exact observance of public and private engagements was insistently urged. A violation of the faith of the nation or the pledges of the private individual, it was insisted, was equally forbidden by the principles of moral justice and of sound policy. [On] the other hand, it was insisted that the case of the debtor should be viewed with tenderness; and efforts were constantly directed toward relieving him from an exact compliance with his contract. [Debtors,] instead of seeking to meet their obligations by painful effort, by industry and economy, began to rest their hopes entirely upon legislative interference. The impossibility of payment of public or private debts was widely asserted, and in some instances threats were made of suspending the administration of justice by violence. The circulation of depreciated currency became common. [This] state of things alarmed all thoughtful men, and led them to seek some effective remedy. . . .

The defense of the Minnesota law is made upon grounds which were discountenanced by the makers of the Constitution. [That] defense should not now succeed, because it constitutes an effort to overthrow the constitutional provision by an appeal to facts and circumstances identical with those which brought it into existence. With due regard for the processes of logical thinking, it legitimately cannot be urged that conditions which produced the rule may now be invoked to destroy it. . . .

It is quite true also that [general] statutes to put an end to lotteries, the sale or manufacture of intoxicating liquors, the maintenance of nuisances, to protect the public safety, etc., although they have the indirect effect of absolutely destroying private contracts previously made in contemplation of a continuance of the state of affairs then in existence but subsequently prohibited, have been uniformly upheld as not violating the contract impairment clause. The distinction between legislation of that character and the Minnesota statute, however, is readily observable. . . . [The Minnesota] statute denies appellant for a period of two years the ownership and possession of the property — an asset which [is] of substantial character, and which possibly may turn out to be of great value. The statute, therefore, is not merely a modification of the remedy; it effects a material and injurious change in the obligation. . . . If the provisions of the Constitution be not upheld when they pinch as well as when they comfort, they may as well be abandoned. Being unable to reach any other conclusion than that the Minnesota statute infringes the constitutional restriction under review, I have no choice but to say so.

[Justices Van Devanter, McReynolds, and Butler joined in this dissent.]

Note: Market Ordering and Constitutional Interpretation

1. *The changing scope of the police power.* The Court had long held that the contracts clause did not forbid states from impairing the obligations of contract if the impairment resulted from an exercise of the "police power," the state's traditional authority to protect its citizens from public harms. Thus, for example, the clause did not prevent states from outlawing contracts for murder or for the sale of heroin, even if the impairing law applied retroactively. See, e.g., Manigault v. Springs, 199 U.S. 473 (1905). See generally Hale, The Supreme Court and the Contract Clause, 57 Harv. L. Rev. 621 (1944).

Why, then, was *Blaisdell* such an important case? The real shift came in the novel understanding of what the police power allowed, an understanding that resulted in a dramatic expansion of the permissible ends of government that would support a contractual impairment. That shift was part of the New Deal reformulation of the constitutional structure; it contemplated a large role for government in readjusting the benefits and burdens of social life. Was the Court correct to broaden the police power? One might criticize the decision on the ground that, if the state might impair a contract in order to protect mortgagors, and in so doing be considered to have operated within its police power, it might also be allowed to impair a contract in order to protect creditors or debtors, or any other group, as a class. This might be said to be precisely the evil at which the clause was originally aimed.

Some people say that the Court has interpreted the first amendment expansively in an effort to create a relatively broad constitutional guarantee of free expression, see Chapter 7 infra, but that in the case of the contracts clause — a similarly "express" constitutional safeguard — the Court has generally taken an opposite tack. Is the Court justified in using the contracts clause to invalidate far less than its drafters intended, while using the first amendment to invalidate far more? Note in particular that the state's "police power" may be used only in very narrow circumstances to justify infringements on freedom of expression.

2. Blaisdell *and constitutional interpretation.* The Court suggests that the framers' own interpretation of the contracts clause is not controlling. Indeed, it says that the notion that "what the Constitution meant at the time of its adoption it means to-day [carries] its own refutation." This is one of the most candid statements by the Court that a constitutional decision is not based on the framers' original intent. Is this merely another way of saying that "it is a Constitution we are expounding," or might it go far beyond what Chief Justice Marshall had in mind?

Consider Epstein, Toward a Revitalization of the Contracts Clause, 51 U. Chi. L. Rev. 703, 735-736 (1984):

> The passage contains some of the most misguided thinking on constitutional interpretation imaginable. The operative assumption seems to be that questions of constitutional law are to be answered according to whether or not we like the Constitution as it was originally drafted. If we do not, we are then free to introduce into the document those provisions that we think more congenial to our time. [By] this standard a court can invest itself with the power of a standing constitutional convention. The importance of a fixed constitutional framework and stable institutional arrangements is necessarily lost once the framework that was designed to place a limit upon politics becomes the central subject of the politics it was designed to limit.

3. *The contracts clause after* Blaisdell. After *Blaisdell,* what does the contracts clause prohibit? The answer appears to be very little. Consider, for example, El Paso v. Simmons, 379 U.S. 497 (1965). The case grew out of a 1910 sale, by contract, from the state of Texas of public land. State law provided for the termination of the contract and forfeiture of the land for nonpayment of interest, and in such a case, the purchaser could reinstate his claim on request and with payment of delinquent interest. In 1941, the state amended the law, limiting reinstatement rights to claims asserted five years from the date of forfeiture. The 1941 law operated to impair rights acquired under the 1910 contract.

The Court upheld the law, referring to its purpose "to restore confidence in the stability and integrity of land titles" and to end "the imbroglio over land titles in Texas." Justice Black, in dissent, compared the Court's decision to "balancing away the First Amendment's unequivocally guaranteed rights." See also East New York Bank v. Hahn, 326 U.S. 230 (1945) (upholding an extension of mortgage moratorium legislation); Veix v. Sixth Ward, 310 U.S. 32 (1940) (upholding right of states to restrict right of certificate holders to withdraw or recover amounts of certificates).

4. *Legislative continuity and the problem of precommitment.* The contracts clause might be understood as an effort to deal with problems of legislative continuity and discontinuity, at least when a legislature attempts to modify a bargain made by its predecessors. See the discussion in Sterk, The Continuity of Legislatures: Of Contracts and the Contracts Clause, 88 Colum. L. Rev. 647 (1988):

[W]hatever deficiencies legislatures have as agents and as deliberative bodies may be magnified when decisions of future impact are at stake. . . . [I]n its contracts clause decisions, the Supreme Court has rejected a model of strong legislative continuity. . . . Judicial intervention in contracts clause [cases] has long reflected a view of legislatures as discontinuous bodies incapable of adequately accounting for the interests of future constituents.

Should the Court be more aggressive in ensuring legislative continuity by protecting citizens against changes resulting from new legislatures? Consider how this idea might bear on *Blaisdell* itself.

Along similar lines, the contracts clause might be seen as an effort to ensure governmental power to precommit the state to a certain course of action. Without the clause, people might be insecure because they would know that contracts could be breached, and that the government cannot be bound not to breach. With the clause, government can precommit itself, and in a way that facilitates both public and private action. The power to precommit — consider marriage as well as contract — is facilitating as well as constraining. See generally S. Holmes, Passions and Constraint (1995).

UNITED STATES TRUST CO. v. NEW JERSEY, 431 U.S. 1 (1977). A New Jersey statute, in conjunction with a parallel New York provision, repealed a statutory covenant, made by the two states in 1962, that limited the ability of the Port Authority of New Jersey and New York to subsidize rail passenger transportation from revenues and reserves. The covenant had been adopted in order to provide special security for the bondholders against competition from rail transportation. But New Jersey and New York later concluded that subsidization was necessary to improve conservation and to advance rail transit. The Court, in an opinion by Justice Blackmun, invalidated the repeal of the covenant:

"The trial court concluded that repeal of the 1962 covenant was a valid exercise of New Jersey's police power because repeal served important public interests in mass transportation, energy conservation, and environmental protection. [Yet] the Contract Clause limits otherwise legitimate exercises of state legislative authority, and the existence of an important public interest is now always sufficient to overcome that limitation. . . .

"[In] applying this standard, [complete] deference to a legislative assessment of reasonableness and necessity is not appropriate [when] the State's self-interest is at stake. A governmental entity can always find a use for extra money, especially when taxes do not have to be raised. If a State could reduce its financial obligations whenever it wanted to spend the money for what it regarded as an important public purpose, the Contract Clause would provide no protection at all. . . .

"Mass transportation, energy conservation, and environmental protection are goals that are important and of legitimate public concern. Appellees contend that these goals are so important that any harm to bondholders from repeal of the 1962 covenant is greatly outweighed by the public benefit. We do not accept this invitation to engage in a utilitarian comparison of public benefit and private loss. Contrary to Mr. Justice Black's fear, expressed in sole dissent in [*El Paso*], the Court has not 'balanced away' the limitation on state action imposed by the Contract Clause. Thus a State cannot refuse to meet its legitimate financial obligations simply because it would prefer to spend the money to promote the public good rather than the private welfare of its creditors. We can only sustain the repeal of the 1962 covenant if that impairment was both reasonable and necessary to serve the admittedly important purposes claimed by the State.

"The more specific justification offered for the repeal of the 1962 covenant was the States' plan for encouraging users of private automobiles to shift to public transportation. The States intended to discourage private automobile use by raising bridge and tunnel tolls and to use the extra revenue from those tolls to subsidize improved commuter railroad service. Appellees contend that repeal of the 1962 covenant was necessary to implement this plan because the new mass transit facilities could not possibly be self-supporting and the covenant's 'permitted deficits' level had already been exceeded. We reject this justification because the repeal was neither necessary to achievement of the plan nor reasonable in light of the circumstances.

"The determination of necessity can be considered on two levels. First, it cannot be said that total repeal of the covenant was essential; a less drastic modification would have permitted the contemplated plan without entirely removing the covenant's limitations on the use of Port Authority revenues and reserves to subsidize commuter railroads. Second, without modifying the covenant at all, the States could have adopted alternative means of achieving their twin goals of discouraging automobile use and improving mass transit.

"In the instant case the need for mass transportation in the New York metropolitan area was not a new development, and the likelihood that publicly owned commuter railroads would produce substantial deficits was well known. [It] was with full knowledge of these concerns that the 1962 covenant was adopted. . . .

"During the 12-year period between adoption of the covenant and its repeal, public perception of the importance of mass transit undoubtedly grew because of increased general concern with environmental protection and energy conservation. But these concerns were not unknown in 1962, and the subsequent changes were of degree and not of kind. We cannot say that these changes caused the covenant to have a substantially different impact in 1974 than when it was adopted in 1962. And we cannot conclude that the repeal was reasonable in the light of changed circumstances."

Justice Brennan, joined by Justices White and Marshall, dissented:

"One of the fundamental premises of our popular democracy is that each generation of representatives can and will remain responsive to the needs and desires of those whom they represent. Crucial to this end is the assurance that new legislators will not automatically be bound by the policies and undertakings of earlier days. In accordance with this philosophy, the Framers of our Constitution conceived of the Contract Clause primarily as protection for economic transactions entered into by purely private parties, rather than obligations involving the State itself. The Framers fully recognized that nothing would so jeopardize the legitimacy of a system of government that relies upon the ebbs and flows of politics to 'clean out the rascals' than the possibility that those same rascals might perpetuate their policies simply by locking them into binding contracts. [But Contract] Clause challenges [are] to be resolved by according unusual deference to the lawmaking authority of state and local governments. . . .

"I would not want to be read as suggesting that the States should blithely proceed down the path of repudiating their obligations, financial or otherwise. Their credibility in the credit market obviously is highly dependent on exercising their vast lawmaking powers with self-restraint and [discipline]. [But the] role to be played by the Constitution is at most a limited one. [For] this Court should have learned long ago that the Constitution — be it through the Contract or Due Process Clause — can actively intrude into such economic and policy matters only if my Brethren are prepared to bear enormous institutional and social costs. Because I consider the potential dangers of such judicial interference to be intolerable, I dissent."

ALLIED STRUCTURAL STEEL CO. v. SPANNAUS, 438 U.S. 234 (1978). Allied Structural Steel Co. maintained an office in Illinois with thirty employees. The company operated a general pension plan under which it retained unrestricted rights (1) to amend the plan in whole or in part and (2) to terminate the plan and to distribute the assets at any time and for any reason. Employees were thus entitled to benefits if they worked until reaching age sixty-five and if the company remained in business and elected to continue the plan. The Minnesota legislature enacted a Private Pension Benefits Protection Act, under which employers would be subject to a "pension funding charge" if they terminated the plan or closed a Minnesota office. The charge was assessed if pension funds did not cover full pensions for at least ten years. Under the act, employers must satisfy the deficiency by purchasing deferred annuities, payable to employees at their normal retirement age. Periods of employment prior to the effective date of the act were to be included in the ten-year employment criterion. Allied Structural Steel attempted to terminate its operation in Minnesota; the state informed the company that it owed a pension funding charge of $185,000; and the company brought suit, claiming that the act unconstitutionally impaired its contractual obligations.

The Court, in an opinion by Justice Stewart, responded:

"There can be no question of the impact of the Minnesota Private Pension Benefits Protection Act upon the company's contractual relationships with its employees. [The] Contract Clause remains part of the Constitution. It is not a dead letter. . . . [If] the Contract Clause is to retain any meaning at all, [it] must be understood to impose *some* limits upon the power of a State to abridge existing contractual relationships, even in the exercise of its otherwise legitimate police power. . . .

"In applying these principles to the present case, the first inquiry must be whether the state law has, in fact, operated as a substantial impairment of a contractual relationship. [Minimal] alteration of contractual obligations may end the inquiry at its first stage. Severe impairment, on the other hand, will push the inquiry to a careful examination of the nature and purpose of the state legislation. . . .

"Here, the company's contracts of employment with its employees included as a fringe benefit or additional form of compensation, the pension plan. The company's maximum obligation was to set aside each year an amount based on the plan's requirements for vesting. [The] company [had] no reason to anticipate that its employees' pension rights could become vested except in accordance with the terms of the plan. It relied heavily, and reasonably, on this legitimate contractual expectation in calculating its annual contributions to the pension fund.

"The effect of Minnesota's Private Pension Benefits Protection Act on this contractual obligation was severe. The company was required in 1974 to have made its contributions throughout the pre-1974 life of its plan as if employees' pension rights had vested after 10 years, instead of vesting in accord with the terms of the plan. Thus a basic term of the pension contract — one on which the company had relied for 10 years — was substantially modified. [The] Act thus forced a current recalculation of the past 10 years' contributions based on the new, unanticipated 10-year vesting requirement.

"[Moreover,] the retroactive state-imposed vesting requirement was applied only to those employers who terminated their pension plans or who, like the company, closed their Minnesota offices. The company was thus forced to make all the retroactive changes in its contractual obligations at one time. By simply proceeding to close its office in Minnesota, a move that had been planned before the passage of the Act, the company was assessed an immediate pension funding charge of approximately $185,000.

"[Yet] there is no showing in the record before us that this severe disruption of contractual expectations was necessary to meet an important general social problem. . . .

"[The statute] clearly has an extremely narrow focus. It applies only to private employers who have at least 100 employees, at least one of whom works in Minnesota, and who have established voluntary private pension plans, qualified under §401 of the Internal Revenue Code. And it applies only when such an employer closes his Minnesota office or terminates his pension plan. Thus, this law can hardly be characterized, like the law at issue in the *Blaisdell* case, as one enacted to protect a broad societal interest rather than a narrow class. [This] legislation, imposing a sudden, totally unanticipated, and substantial retroactive obligation upon the company to its employees, was not enacted to deal with a situation remotely approaching the broad and desperate emergency economic conditions of the early 1930's — conditions of which the Court in *Blaisdell* took judicial notice.

"[If] the Contract Clause means anything at all, it means that Minnesota could not constitutionally do what it tried to do to the company in this case."

Justice Brennan, joined by Justices White and Marshall, dissented:

"The Act does not relieve either the employer or his employees of any existing contract obligation. Rather, the Act simply creates an additional, supplemental duty of the employer, no different in kind from myriad duties created by a wide variety of legislative measures which defeat settled expectations but which have nonetheless been sustained by this Court. For this reason, the Minnesota Act, in my view, does not implicate the Contract Clause in any way. . . .

"[Under] the Court's opinion, any law that may be characterized as 'superimposing' new obligations on those provided for by contract is to be regarded as creating 'sudden, substantial, and unanticipated burdens' and then to be subjected to the most exacting scrutiny. The validity of such a law will turn upon whether judges see it as a law that deals with a generalized social problem, whether it is temporary (as few will be) or permanent, whether it operates in an area previously subject to regulation, and, finally, whether its duties apply to a broad class of persons. [The] necessary consequence of the extreme malleability of these rather vague criteria is to vest judges with broad subjective discretion to protect property interests that happen to appeal to them.

"To permit this level of scrutiny of laws that interfere with contract-based expectations is an anomaly. There is nothing sacrosanct about expectations rooted in contract that justify according them a constitutional immunity denied other property rights."

Note: United States Trust, Spannaus, *and the Nonrevival of the Contracts Clause*

1. *"Heightened scrutiny" for a state's abrogation of its own contracts.* Two features of *United States Trust* are noteworthy: first, the willingness to adopt "heightened scrutiny" for a state's abrogation of its own contracts; second, the willingness to invalidate a state law under the contracts clause. The first element is in one sense familiar in constitutional law. The Court frequently adopts "heightened scrutiny" — in the form of a careful examination of means/ends connections and a search for less restrictive alternatives — when there is special reason for suspicion that an impermissible motivation is at work.

Perhaps there was such a special reason in *United States Trust*. One might think that the fact that a state abrogates a contract to which it is a party gives reason to believe that a state's self-interest, rather than some public good, is at stake. But is there a difference between a state's interest and some public good? If so, what is the impermissible end that the Court thought might be at work when a state abrogates its own contract? Note also the possibility that the Court was concerned with effects as well as purpose — the special obligation of government not to break its own promises.

2. *The police power and means/ends connections under the contracts clause.* In *United States Trust*, why did the Court conclude that the means/ends connection was too weak? Was *Spannaus* a stronger or weaker case in this regard? Construct an argument that *Spannaus* is inconsistent with the views expressed in *Blaisdell*.

3. *Subsequent developments. United States Trust* and *Spannaus* suggested that the Court might revive the contracts clause as a substantive constraint on legislation. But shortly thereafter the Court returned to its previous, more deferential approach. Consider in this regard Energy Reserves Group v. Kansas Power & Light, 459 U.S. 400 (1983). The contract at issue contained a price escalator clause that provided that, if a governmental authority fixes a price for natural gas that is higher than the price specified in the contract, the contract price would be increased to that level. A Kansas statute provided that the increase produced by a federal statute could not be taken into account in determining the contract price. The Energy Reserves Group attacked the statute on the ground that it impaired the contractual obligation by allowing for an increase in the price. In an opinion by Justice Blackmun, the Court responded:

> The threshold inquiry is "whether the state law has, in fact, operated as a substantial impairment of contractual relationship." The severity of the impairment is said to increase the level of scrutiny to which the legislation will be subjected. [In] determining the extent of the impairment, we are to consider whether the industry the complaining party has entered has been regulated in the past. . . .
>
> If the state regulation constitutes a substantial impairment, the State, in justification, must have a significant and legitimate public purpose behind the regulation, such as the remedying of a broad and general social or economic problem. Furthermore, since *Blaisdell*, the Court has indicated that the public purpose need not be addressed to an emergency or temporary situation. One legitimate state in-

terest is the elimination of unforeseen windfall profits. The requirement of a legitimate public purpose guarantees that the State is exercising its police power, rather than providing a benefit to special interests.

Once a legitimate public purpose has been identified, the next inquiry is whether the adjustment of the rights and responsibilities of contracting parties is based upon reasonable conditions and is of a character appropriate to the public purpose justifying the legislation's adoption. Unless the state is itself a contracting party, "as is customary in reviewing economic and social regulation," [courts] properly defer to legislative judgment as to the necessity and reasonableness of a particular measure.

The Court upheld the statute. First, it suggested that there was no substantial impairment: "Significant here is the fact that the parties are operating in a heavily regulated industry." Thus, "ERG knew its contractual rights were subject to alteration by state price regulation. Price regulation existed and was foreseeable as the type of law that would alter contract obligations."

The Court also concluded that any contractual impairment "rests on, and is prompted by, significant and legitimate state interests." The Court referred to two such interests. The first was the protection of consumers from the escalation of prices caused by deregulation. "The State could reasonably find that higher gas prices have caused and will cause hardship among those who use gas heat but must exist on limited fixed incomes." The second interest was "correcting the imbalance between the interstate and intrastate markets by permitting intrastate prices to rise only to the [interstate] level." Justice Powell, joined by the Chief Justice and Justice Rehnquist, concurred, agreeing that there had been no substantial impairment but refusing to reach the question whether any impairment had in the circumstances been justified.

Consider also Exxon Corp. v. Eagerton, 462 U.S. 176 (1983), which involved a state statute prohibiting producers of oil and gas from passing on to consumers the costs of any increase in a state's severance tax. The Court replied that the contracts clause did not prohibit "a generally applicable rule of conduct designed to advance 'broad social interest,' protecting consumers from excessive prices." Do *Energy Reserves* and *Exxon* implicitly overrule *Spannaus?*

The Court adopted a similarly deferential stance in the face of a contract clause claim in Keystone Bituminous Coal Association v. DeBenedictis, 480 U.S. 470 (1987). A Pennsylvania statute had the effect of voiding damage waivers that coal companies had obtained from surface owners for damage to surface property caused by mining. The Court, in an opinion by Justice Stevens, upheld the statute. In the Court's view, the state had a strong public interest in preventing the environmental harm caused by the mining. Moreover, in cases where the state itself is not a contracting party, courts should defer to the legislative judgment as to the necessity and reasonableness of the contractual abrogation.

In General Motors Corp. v. Romein, 503 U.S. 181 (1992), the Court upheld a substantial change in a workers' compensation program. In 1980, Michigan had raised the level of maximum benefits; in 1981, it allowed employers to decrease the level of the relevant benefits to disabled employees who could receive compensation from other employer-funded sources. The Michigan Supreme Court ruled that under the 1981 law employers could reduce benefits to all workers, including those injured before the statute's effective date. In 1987, the legislature repudiated this ruling and said that employers must make refunds to the previously disabled workers. According to the Supreme Court, there was no problem under the contracts clause because the allegedly impaired contracts contained "no contractual agreement regarding the specific workers' compensation terms allegedly at issue." The Court rejected the claim that their statutory right to rely on past payment periods as "closed" was incorporated by law into employment contracts. "[W]e have not held that all state regulations are implied terms of every contract entered into while they are effective. . . ."

The Court added:

> The 1987 statute did not change the legal enforceability of the employment contracts here. . . . Moreover, petitioners' suggestion that we should read every workplace regulation into the private arrangements of employers and employees would expand the definition of contract so far that the constitutional provision would lose its anchoring purpose, i.e., "enabl[ing] individuals to order their personal and business affairs according to their particular needs and interests." Instead, the Clause would protect against all changes in legislation.

4. *Concluding thoughts.* Consider the following evaluation: Modern review under the contract clause is substantially identical to modern rationality review under the due process and equal protection clauses. In all three contexts, the Court engages in the same inquiry, identifying the legitimate state interests and requiring a rough relation between the legitimate state interests and the measure under review. But the class of legitimate state interests is extremely broad; the Court has permitted any justification other than raw political power (the "special interest" problem referred to in the *Energy Reserves* case). This idea seems to follow from an understanding, prominent in the post-New Deal period, that existing distributions are never prepolitical and often unjust, and therefore a matter for democratic control. Moreover, the fit between the legitimate interest and the measure under review need not be close.

Is it troublesome that the Court has adopted the same test in all three areas — even though the contracts clause looks like an explicit limitation on contractual impairments?

2. The Eminent Domain Clause

The eminent domain clause provides, "[N]or shall private property be taken for public use, without just compensation." The clause has two requirements: (1) All takings must be for public use, and (2) even takings that are for public use must be accompanied by compensation. Consider here, as with the contracts clause, whether and how interpretation of the eminent domain clause differs from interpretation of the first amendment on the one hand, and treatment of "implied" fundamental rights on the other. Consider also how the clause interacts with competing notions about the role of government in redistributing wealth.

What is the evil at which the eminent domain clause is aimed? The history of the eminent domain clause is quite sparse, but the answer involves at least some sorts of redistribution of resources. The clause reflects a judgment that, if government is seeking to produce some public benefit (the public use requirement), it is appropriate that the payment come from the public at large — taxpayers — rather than from identifiable individuals. The compensation requirement operates as insurance to that effect. Note, in addition, that compensation tends to reduce the likelihood that a transfer has occurred merely to benefit A at the expense of B. Public willingness to pay for the transfer suggests that some general public good is at work. We begin with the logically prior public use requirement.

HAWAII HOUSING AUTHORITY v. MIDKIFF, 465 U.S. 1097 (1984). This case involved an effort to transfer ownership of property in Hawaii. Justice O'Connor, in her opinion for a unanimous Court, noted that land in Hawaii had traditionally been concentrated in the hands of few people and then summarized the facts as follows:

"[The] Land Reform Act of 1967 (Act) [created] a mechanism for condemning residential tracts and for transferring ownership of the condemned fees simple to existing lessees. By condemning the land in question, the Hawaii Legislature intended to make the land sales involuntary, thereby making the federal tax consequences less severe while still facilitating the redistribution of fees simple.

"Under the Act's condemnation scheme, tenants living on single-family residential lots [are] entitled to ask the Hawaii Housing Authority (HHA) to condemn the property on which they live.

"When 25 eligible tenants, or tenants on half the lots in the tract, whichever is less, file appropriate applications, the Act authorizes HHA to hold a public hearing to determine whether acquisition by the State [will] 'effectuate the public purposes' of the Act. If HHA finds that these public purposes will be served, it is authorized to [acquire], at prices set either by condemnation trial or by negotiation between lessors and lessees, the former fee owners' full 'right, title, and interest' in the land. . . .

"After compensation has been set, HHA may sell the land titles to tenants who have applied for fee simple [ownership]. HHA does not sell [or] lease the lot or sell it to someone else, provided that public notice has been given."

The Court upheld the statute against a claim that no "public use" was involved:

"The starting point for our analysis of the Act's constitutionality is the Court's decision in Berman v. Parker, 348 U.S. 26 (1954). In *Berman*, the Court held constitutional the District of Columbia Redevelopment Act of 1945. That Act provided both for the comprehensive use of the eminent domain power to redevelop slum areas and for the possible sale or lease of the condemned lands to private interests. In discussing whether the takings authorized by that Act were for a 'public use,' [the] Court stated 'We deal [with] what traditionally has been known as the police power. An attempt to define its reach or trace its outer limits is fruitless, for each case must turn on its own facts. The definition is essentially the product of legislative determinations addressed to the purposes of government, purposes neither abstractly nor historically capable of complete definition. Subject to specific constitutional limitations, when the legislature has spoken, the public interest has been declared in terms well-nigh conclusive. In such cases the legislature, not the judiciary, is the main guardian of the public needs to be served by social legislation.' . . .

"There is, of course, a role for courts to play in reviewing a legislature's judgment of what constitutes a public use, even when the eminent domain power is equated with the police power. But the Court in *Berman* made clear that it is 'an extremely narrow' one. . . .

"To be sure, the Court's cases have repeatedly stated that 'one person's property may not be taken for the benefit of another private person without a justifying public purpose, even though compensation be paid.' [But] where the exercise of the eminent domain power is rationally related to a conceivable public purpose, the Court has never held a compensated taking to be proscribed by the [clause]. . . .

"On this basis, we have no trouble concluding that the Hawaii Act is constitutional. The people of Hawaii have attempted [to] reduce the perceived social and economic evils of a land [oligopoly]. The land oligopoly has, according to the Hawaii Legislature, created artificial deterrents to the normal functioning of the State's residential land market and forced thousands of individual homeowners to lease, rather than buy, the land underneath their homes. Regulating oligopoly and the evils associated with it is a classic exercise of a State's police powers. [We] cannot disapprove of Hawaii's exercise of this power.

"Nor can we condemn as irrational the Act's approach to correcting the land oligopoly problem. The Act presumes that when a sufficiently large number of persons declare that they are willing but unable to buy lots at fair prices the land market is malfunctioning. When such a malfunction is signalled, the Act authorizes HHA to condemn lots in the relevant tract. The Act limits the number of lots any one tenant can purchase and authorizes HHA to use public funds to ensure that the market dilution goals will be achieved. This is a comprehensive and rational approach to identifying and correcting market failure. [When] the legislature's purpose is legitimate and its means are not irrational, our cases make clear that empirical debates over the wisdom of takings — no less than debates over the wisdom of other kinds of socioeconomic legislation — are not to be carried out in the federal courts. Redistribution of fees simple to correct deficiencies in the market determined by the state legislature to be attributable to land oligopoly is a rational exercise of the eminent domain power. Therefore, the Hawaii statute must pass the scrutiny of the Public Use Clause. . . .

"[The] mere fact that property taken outright by eminent domain is transferred in the first instance to private beneficiaries does not condemn that taking as having only a private purpose. The Court long ago rejected any literal requirement that condemned property be put into use for the general public. [A] purely private taking could not withstand the scrutiny of the public use requirement; it would serve no legitimate purpose of government and would thus be void. But no purely private taking is involved in this case."

Note: The Public Use Requirement and the Takings Clause

1. *In general.* The "public use" requirement originally operated as a serious independent constraint on government action. For a long period, the requirement was understood to mean that, if property was to be taken, it was necessary that it be used by the public; the fact that the taking was "beneficial" was not enough. Eventually, however, courts concluded that a wide range of uses could serve the public even if the public did not in fact have possession. Important examples here are the Mill Acts, which permitted riparian owners to erect and maintain dams that flooded neighboring property. For discussion, see M. Horwitz, The Transformation of American Law, 1780-1860, at 47-53 (1977). Thereafter, so many exceptions were built into the general rule of "use by the public" that the rule itself was abandoned. For discussion, see Dunham, Griggs v. Allegheny

County in Perspective: Thirty Years of Supreme Court Expropriation Law, 1962 Sup. Ct. Rev. 63, 65-71; Note, The Public Use Limitation on Eminent Domain: An Advance Requiem, 58 Yale L.J. 599 (1949).

But even if use by the public is not a prerequisite, perhaps the notion of "public use" could be defined relatively narrowly so as to impose some substantive constraints on the subject of "publicness." *Midkiff* largely abandons any such effort. For discussion and a proposal of substantive limits, see R. Epstein, Takings: Private Property and the Law of Eminent Domain (1985).

2. *Public use after* Midkiff. The public use requirement is designed to ensure against what might be called "naked" wealth transfers — takings from A in order to benefit B, supported by no "public" end, and only by a preference for B, or by B's political power. Cf. Justice Chase's position in Calder v. Bull, Chapter 1 supra, also complaining about a taking from A to benefit B.

In the *Midkiff* case, the Court uses two devices to produce a deferential judicial posture in guarding against such transfers. The first involves scrutiny of ends. The Court's broad understanding of public use means that many ends of government will be "public" and thus satisfy constitutional requirements. The second involves scrutiny of means. Here, the Court demands very little, requiring only a loose means/ends connection. Consider the possibility that, in concert, these devices mean that the public use requirement operates as no limitation on government action.

Consider also Epstein, supra, at 181:

> The rational basis test again uses false arguments to negate explicit constitutional guarantees. No antitrust expert thinks "oligopoly" because there are "only" seventy or twenty-two or eighteen landowners in a given market. Why then allow the legislature to so find? [The] case therefore is straightforward. The statute allows tenants as a class to take the reversion from the landlord. These takings do not become something else simply because a large number of tenants is involved. In no individual case is the property used for a pure public good, and in none is there universal right of access. [Land] reform thus runs afoul of the public use limitation, which deserves more respectful treatment than it receives today.

Evaluate, after *Midkiff*, Poletown Neighborhood Council v. City of Detroit, 410 Mich. 616, 304 N.W.2d 455 (1981), in which the city of Detroit condemned a neighborhood in order to permit General Motors to build a plant on the land. Was the taking for public use? Suppose the plant would employ a large number of people now on welfare or without jobs. If a General Motors plant was condemned and transferred for use by the community, would there also be a public use? Is it troublesome if the answer to both questions is yes? See also Rubenfeld, Usings, 102 Yale L.J. 1077 (1993), which argues that the takings clause is directed only against governmental "usings" of private property, that is, against situations in which government officials actually use the property that has been taken.

Pennsylvania Coal Co. v. Mahon

260 U.S. 393 (1922)

MR. JUSTICE HOLMES delivered the opinion of the Court.

This is a bill in equity brought by the [plaintiffs] to prevent the Pennsylvania Coal Company from mining under their property in such way as to remove the supports and cause a subsidence of the surface and of their house. The bill sets out a deed executed by the Coal Company in 1878, under which the plaintiffs claim. The deed conveys the surface, but in express terms reserves the right to remove all the coal under the same, and the grantee takes the premises with the risk, and waives all claim for damages that may arise from mining out the coal. But the plaintiffs say that whatever may have been the Coal Company's rights, they were taken away by an Act of Pennsylvania, [commonly] known there as the Kohler Act. . . .

The statute forbids the mining of anthracite coal in such way as to cause the subsidence of, among other things, any structure used as a human habitation, with certain exceptions, including among them land where the surface is owned by the owner of the underlying coal and is distant more than one hundred and fifty feet from any improved property belonging to any other person. As applied to this case the statute is admitted to destroy previously existing rights of property and contract. The question is whether the police power can be stretched so far.

Government hardly could go on if to some extent values incident to property could not be diminished without paying for every such change in the general law. As long recognized, some values are enjoyed under an implied limitation and must yield to the police power. But obviously the implied limitation must have its limits, or the contract and due process clauses are gone. One fact for consideration in determining such limits is the extent of the diminution. When it reaches a certain magnitude, in most if not in all cases there must be an exercise of eminent domain and compensation to sustain the act. So the question depends upon the particular facts. The greatest weight is given to the judgment of the legislature, but it always is open to interested parties to contend that the legislature has gone beyond its constitutional power. . . .

[It] is our opinion that the act cannot be sustained as an exercise of the police power, so far as it affects the mining of coal under streets or cities in places where the right to mine such coal has been reserved. [What] makes the right to mine coal valuable is that it can be exercised with profit. To make it commercially impracticable to mine certain coal has very nearly the same effect for constitutional purposes as appropriating or destroying it. This we think that we are warranted in assuming that the statute does. . . .

The rights of the public in a street purchased or laid out by eminent domain are those that it has paid for. If in any case its representatives have been so short sighted as to acquire only surface rights without the right of support, we see no more authority for supplying the latter without compensation than there was for taking the right of way in the first place and refusing to pay for it because the public wanted it very much. The protection of private property in the Fifth Amendment presupposes that it is wanted for public use, but provides that it shall not be taken for such use without compensation. [When] this seemingly absolute protection is found to be qualified by the police power, the natural tendency of human nature is to extend the qualification more and more until at last private property disappears. But that cannot be accomplished in this way under the Constitution of the United States.

The general rule at least is, that while property may be regulated to a certain extent, if regulation goes too far it will be recognized as a taking. [In] general it is not plain that a man's misfortunes or necessities will justify his shifting the damages to his neighbor's shoulders. We are in danger of forgetting that a strong public desire to improve the public condition is not enough to warrant achieving the desire by a shorter cut than the constitutional way of paying for the change. As we already have said, this is a question of degree — and therefore cannot be disposed of by general propositions.

[We] assume, of course, that the statute was passed upon the conviction that an exigency existed that would warrant it, and we assume that an exigency exists that would warrant the exercise of eminent domain. But the question at bottom is upon whom the loss of the changes desired should fall. So far as private persons or communities have seen fit to take the risk of acquiring only surface rights, we cannot see that the fact that their risk has become a danger warrants the giving to them greater rights than they bought. . . .

Decree reversed.

MR. JUSTICE BRANDEIS, dissenting. . . .

[Coal] in place is land; and the right of the owner to use his land is not absolute. He may not so use it as to create a public nuisance; and uses, once harmless, may, owing to changed conditions, seriously threaten the public welfare. Whenever they do, the legislature has power to prohibit such uses without paying compensation; and the power to prohibit extends alike to the manner, the character and the purpose of the use. Are we justified in declaring that the Legislature of Pennsylvania has, in restricting the right to mine anthracite, exercised this power so arbitrarily as to violate the Fourteenth Amendment?

Every restriction upon the use of property imposed in the exercise of the police power deprives the owner of some right theretofore enjoyed, and is, in that sense, an abridgment by the State of rights in property without making compensation. But restriction imposed to protect the public health, safety or morals from dangers threatened is not a taking. The restriction here in question is merely the prohibition of a noxious use. The property so restricted remains in the possession of its owner. The state does not appropriate it or make any use of it. The State merely prevents the owner from making a use which interferes with paramount rights of the public. Whenever the use prohibited ceases to be noxious, — as it may because of further change in local or social conditions, — the restriction will have to be removed and the owner will again be free to enjoy his property as heretofore.

The restriction upon the use of this property cannot, of course, be lawfully imposed, unless its purpose is to protect the public. But the purpose of a restriction does not cease to be public, because incidentally some private persons may thereby receive gratuitously valuable special benefits. [Restriction] upon use does not become inappropriate as a means, merely because it deprives the owner of the only use to which the property can then be profitably put. [Nor] is a restriction imposed through exercise of the police power inappropriate as a means, merely because the same end might be effected through exercise of the power of eminent domain, or otherwise at public expense. Every restriction upon the height of buildings might be secured through acquiring by eminent domain the right of each owner to build above the limiting height; but it is settled that the State need not resort to that power. . . .

[If] by mining anthracite coal the owner would necessarily unloose poisonous gasses, I suppose no one would doubt the power of the State to prevent the mining, without buying his coal fields. And why may not the State, likewise, without paying compensation, prohibit one from digging so deep or excavating so near the surface, as to expose the community to like dangers? . . .

It is said that one fact for consideration in determining whether the limits of the police power have been exceeded is the extent of the resulting diminution in value; and that here the restriction destroys existing rights of property and contract. But values are relative. [For] aught that appears the value of the coal kept in place by the restriction may be negligible as compared with the value of the whole property, or even as compared with that part of it which is represented by the coal remaining in place and which may be extracted despite the statute.

[A] prohibition of mining which causes subsidence of [structures] and facilities is obviously enacted for a public purpose. [Yet] it is said that these provisions of the act cannot be sustained as an exercise of the police power where the right to mine such coal has been reserved. The conclusion seems to rest upon the assumption that in order to justify such exercise of the police power there must be "an average reciprocity of advantage" as between the owner of the property restricted and the rest of the community; and that here such reciprocity is absent. Reciprocity of advantage is an important consideration, and may even be an essential, where the State's power is exercised for the purpose of conferring benefits upon the property of a neighborhood. [But] where the police power is exercised, not to confer benefits upon property owners, but to protect the public from detriment and danger, there is, in my opinion, no room for considering reciprocity of advantage.

Miller v. Schoene

276 U.S. 272 (1928)

MR. JUSTICE STONE delivered the opinion of the Court.

Acting under the Cedar Rust Act of Virginia, [the] state entomologist ordered the plaintiffs in error to cut down a large number of ornamental red cedar trees growing on their property, as a means of preventing the communication of a rust or plant disease with which they were infected to the apple orchards in the vicinity. The plaintiffs in error [were required to pay] $100 to cover the expense of removal of the cedars. Neither the judgment of the court nor the statute as interpreted allows compensation for the value of the standing cedars or the decrease in the market value of the realty caused by their destruction whether considered as ornamental trees or otherwise. . . .

[Cedar] rust is an infectious plant disease in the form of a fungoid organism which is destructive of the fruit and foliage of the apple, but without effect on the value of the cedar. Its life cycle has two phases which are passed alternately as a growth on red cedar and on apple trees. It is communicated by spores from one to the other over a radius of at least two miles. It appears not to be communicable between trees of the same species but only from one species to the other, and other plants seem not to be appreciably affected by it. The only practicable method of controlling the disease and protecting apple trees from its ravages is the destruction of all red cedar trees, subject to the infection, located within two miles of apple orchards.

The red cedar, aside from its ornamental use, has occasional use and value as lumber. It is indigenous to Virginia, is not cultivated or dealt in commercially on any substantial scale, and its value throughout the state is shown to be small as compared with that of the apple orchards of the state. Apple growing is one of the principal agricultural pursuits in Virginia. The apple is used there and exported in large quantities. Many millions of dollars are invested in the orchards, which furnish employment for a large portion of the population, and have induced the development of attendant railroad and cold storage facilities.

On the evidence we may accept the conclusion of the Supreme Court of Appeals that the state was under the necessity of making a choice between the preservation of one class of property and that of the other wherever both existed in dangerous proximity. It would have been none the less a choice if, instead of enacting the present statute, the state, by doing nothing, had permitted serious injury to the apple orchards within its borders to go on unchecked. When forced to such a choice the state does not exceed its constitutional powers by deciding upon the destruction of one class of property in order to save another which, in the judgment of the legislature, is of greater value to the public. It will not do to say that the case is merely one of a conflict of two private interests and that the misfortune of apple growers may not be shifted to cedar owners by ordering the destruction of their property; for it is obvious that there may be, and that here there is, a preponderant public concern in the preservation of the one interest over the other. [Where] the public interest is involved preferment of that interest over the property interest of the individual, to the extent even of its destruction, is one of the distinguishing characteristics of every exercise of the police power which affects property. . . .

We need not weigh with nicety the question whether the infected cedars constitute a nuisance according to the common law; or whether they may be so declared by statute. For where, as here, the choice is unavoidable, we cannot say that its exercise, controlled by considerations of social policy which are not unreasonable, involves any denial of due process.

[Reversed.]

Penn Central Transportation Co. v. New York City

438 U.S. 104 (1978)

MR. JUSTICE BRENNAN delivered the opinion of the Court.

The question presented is whether a city may, as part of a comprehensive program to preserve historical landmarks and historic districts, place restrictions on the development of individual historic landmarks — in addition to those imposed by applicable zoning ordinances — without effecting a "taking" requiring the payment of "just compensation." Specifically, we must decide whether the application of New York City's Landmarks Preservation Law to the parcel of land occupied by Grand Central Terminal has "taken" its owners' property in violation of the Fifth and Fourteenth Amendments.

Over the past 50 years, all 50 States and over 500 municipalities have enacted laws to encourage or require the preservation of buildings and areas with historic or aesthetic importance. These nationwide legislative efforts have been precipitated by two concerns. The first is recognition that, in recent years, large numbers of historic structures, landmarks, and areas have been destroyed without adequate consideration of either the values represented therein or the possibility of preserving the destroyed properties for use in economically productive ways. The second is a widely shared belief that structures with special historic, cultural, or architectural significance enhance the quality of life for all. Not only do these buildings and their workmanship represent the lessons of the past and embody precious features of our heritage, they serve as examples of quality for today. . . .

New York City [adopted] its Landmarks Preservation Law in 1965. The city acted from the conviction that "the standing of [New York City] as a world-wide tourist center and world capital of business, culture and government" would be threatened if legislation were not enacted to protect historic landmarks and neighborhoods from precipitate decisions to destroy or fundamentally alter their character. . . .

The New York City law is typical of many urban landmark laws in that its primary method of achieving its goals is not by acquisitions of historical properties, but rather by involving public entities in land-use decisions affecting these properties and providing services, standards, controls, and incentives that will encourage preservation by private owners and users. While the law does place special restrictions on landmark properties as a necessary feature to the attainment of its larger objectives, the major theme of the law is to ensure the owners of any such properties both a "reasonable return" on their investments and maximum latitude to use their parcels for purposes not inconsistent with the preservation goals.

[The Court noted that the law was administered by the Landmarks Preservation Commission, which identified specially important properties as designated "landmarks" and "historic districts."] [Final] designation as a landmark results in restrictions upon the property owner's options concerning use of the landmark site. First, the law imposes a duty upon the owner to keep the exterior features of the building "in good repair" to assure that the law's objectives not be defeated by the landmark's falling into a state of irremediable disrepair. [Second,] the Commission must approve in advance any proposal to alter the exterior architectural features of the landmark or to construct any exterior improvement on the landmark site, thus ensuring that decisions concerning construction on the landmark site are made with due consideration of both the public interest in the maintenance of the structure and the landowner's interest in use of the property. . . .

In the event an owner wishes to alter a landmark site, [procedures] are available through which administrative approval may be obtained. . . .

Although the designation of a landmark and landmark site restricts the owner's control over the parcel, designation also enhances the economic position of the landmark owner in one significant respect. Under New York City's zoning laws, owners of real property who have not developed their property to the full extent permitted by the applicable zoning laws are allowed to transfer development rights to contiguous parcels on the same city block. . . .

This case involves the application of New York City's Landmarks Preservation Law to Grand Central Terminal (Terminal). [The Court noted that the terminal is one of New York City's most famous buildings and that it had been designated as occupying a landmark site. Penn Central submitted two plans to the Commission for construction of an office building atop the terminal. One plan called for a fifty-five-story office building; another called for tearing down some of its facade and constructing a fifty-three-story office building. The Commission denied permission to go forward with the plans. With respect to the second plan, the Commission observed, "To protect a Landmark, one does not tear it down." With respect to the first plan, the Commission referred primarily to the adverse effect of the proposed tower on the dramatic view of the terminal from Park Avenue South. "To balance a 55-story office tower above a flamboyant Beaux-Arts facade seems nothing more than an aesthetic joke. Quite simply, the tower would over-whelm the Terminal by its sheer mass."]

The [issue is whether] the restrictions imposed by New York City's law upon appellants' exploitation of the Terminal site effect a "taking" of appellants' prop-erty for a public use within the meaning of the Fifth Amendment. While this Court has recognized that the "Fifth Amendment's guarantee . . . [is] designed to bar Government from forcing some people alone to bear public burdens which, in all fairness and justice, should be borne by the public as a whole," Armstrong v. United States, 364 U.S. 40, 49 (1960), this Court, quite simply, has been un-able to develop any "set formula" for determining when "justice and fairness" re-quire that economic injuries caused by public action be compensated by the gov-ernment, rather than remain disproportionately concentrated on a few persons.

In engaging in [essentially] ad hoc, factual inquiries, the Court's decisions have identified several factors that have particular significance. The economic impact of the regulation on the claimant and, particularly, the extent to which the regulation has interfered with distinct investment-backed expectations are, of course, relevant considerations. [So,] too, is the character of the governmental action. A "taking" may more readily be found when the interference with prop-erty can be characterized as a physical invasion by government, see, e.g., United States v. Causby, 328 U.S. 256 (1946), than when interference arises from some public program adjusting the benefits and burdens of economic life to promote the common good.

"Government hardly could go on if to some extent values incident to prop-erty could not be diminished without paying for every such change in the gen-eral law," [Mahon], and this Court has accordingly recognized, in a wide variety of contexts, that government may execute laws or programs that adversely affect recognized economic values. Exercises of the taxing power are one obvious ex-ample. A second are the decisions in which this Court has dismissed "taking" challenges on the ground that, while the challenged government action caused economic harm, it did not interfere with interests that were sufficiently bound up with the reasonable expectations of the claimant to constitute "property" for Fifth Amendment purposes. . . .

More importantly for the present case, in instances in which a state tribunal reasonably concluded that "the health, safety, morals, or general welfare" would be promoted by prohibiting particular contemplated uses of land, this Court has upheld land-use regulations that destroyed or adversely affected recognized real property interests. [Zoning] laws are, of course, the classic example, see Euclid v. Ambler Realty Co., 272 U.S. 365 (1926) (prohibition of industrial use). . . . Zon-ing laws generally do not affect existing uses of real property, but "taking" chal-lenges have also been held to be without merit in a wide variety of situations when the challenged governmental actions prohibited a beneficial use to which individual parcels had previously been devoted and thus caused substantial indi-vidualized harm. . . .

[We] emphasize what is not in dispute. Because this Court has recognized, in a number of settings, that States and cities may enact land-use restrictions or con-trols to enhance the quality of life by preserving the character and desirable aes-thetic features of a city, [appellants] do not contest that [the] restrictions imposed on its parcel are appropriate means of securing the purposes of the New York City law. [Appellants also] accept for present purposes both that the parcel of land occupied by Grand Central Terminal must, in its present state, be regarded as capable of earning a reasonable return, and that the transferable development rights [TDRs] afforded appellants by virtue of the Terminal's designation as a landmark are valuable, even if not as valuable as the rights to construct above the Terminal. . . .

[Appellants] first observe that the airspace above the Terminal is a valuable property interest. [They] urge that the Landmarks Law has deprived them of any gainful use of their "air rights" above the Terminal and that, irrespective of the value of the remainder of their parcel, the city has "taken" their right to this superjacent airspace, thus entitling them to "just compensation" measured by the fair market value of these air rights.

[The] submission that appellants may establish a "taking" simply by showing that they have been denied the ability to exploit a property interest that they heretofore had believed was available for development is quite simply untenable. [Our] jurisprudence does not divide a single parcel into discrete segments and attempt to determine whether rights in a particular segment have been entirely abrogated. In deciding whether a particular governmental action has effected a taking, this Court focuses rather both on the character of the action and on the nature and extent of the interference with rights in the parcel as a whole — here, the city tax block designated as the "landmark site."

Secondly, appellants [argue] that [the law] effects a "taking" because its operation has significantly diminished the value of the Terminal site. [Appellants] argue that New York City's regulation of individual landmarks is fundamentally different from zoning or from historic-district legislation because the controls imposed by New York City's law apply only to individuals who own selected properties.

Stated baldly, appellants' position appears to be that the only means of ensuring that selected owners are not singled out to endure financial hardship for no reason is to hold that any restriction imposed on individual landmarks pursuant to the New York City scheme is a "taking" requiring the payment of "just compensation." [Contrary] to appellants' suggestions, landmark laws are not like discriminatory [zoning:] that is, a land-use decision which arbitrarily singles out a particular parcel for different, less favorable treatment than the neighboring ones. [In] contrast to discriminatory zoning, [the] New York City law embodies a comprehensive plan to preserve structures of historic or aesthetic interest wherever they might be found in the city, and [over] 400 landmarks and 31 historic districts have been designated pursuant to this plan.

Equally without merit is the related argument that the decision to designate a structure as a landmark "is inevitably arbitrary or at least subjective, because it is basically a matter of taste," [thus] unavoidably singling out individual landowners for disparate and unfair treatment. [A] landmark owner has a right to judicial review of any Commission decision, and, [there] is no basis whatsoever for a conclusion that courts will have any greater difficulty identifying arbitrary or discriminatory action in the context of landmark regulation than in the context of classic zoning or indeed in any other context.

Next, appellants observe that New York City's law differs from zoning laws and historic-district ordinances in that the Landmarks Law does not impose identical or similar restrictions on all structures located in particular physical communities. It follows, they argue, that New York City's law is inherently incapable of producing the fair and equitable distribution of benefits and burdens of governmental action [which] they maintain is a constitutional requirement if "just compensation" is not to be afforded. It is, of course, true that the Landmarks Law has a more severe impact on some landowners than on others, but that in itself does not mean that the law effects a "taking." Legislation designed to promote the general welfare commonly burdens some more than others.

In any event, appellants' repeated suggestions that they are solely burdened and unbenefited is factually inaccurate. This contention overlooks the fact that the New York City law applies to vast numbers of structures in the city in addition to the Terminal — all the structures contained in the 31 historic districts and over 400 individual landmarks, many of which are close to the Terminal. . . .

Appellants' final broad-based attack would have us treat the law as an instance, like that in United States v. Causby, in which government, acting in an enterprise capacity, has appropriated part of their property for some strictly governmental purpose. [But the] Landmarks Law neither exploits appellants' parcel for city purposes nor facilitates nor arises from any entrepreneurial operations of the city.

[The] Landmarks Law's effect is simply to prohibit appellants or anyone else from occupying portions of the airspace above the Terminal, while permitting appellants to use the remainder of the parcel in a gainful fashion. . . .

[We] now must consider whether the interference with appellants' property is of such a magnitude that "there must be an exercise of eminent domain and compensation to sustain [it]." [*Mahon.*] [That] inquiry may be narrowed to the question of the severity of the impact of the law on appellants' parcel, and its resolution in turn requires a careful assessment of the impact of the regulation on the Terminal site. [The] New York City law does not interfere in any way with the present uses of the Terminal. Its designation as a landmark [contemplates] that appellants may continue to use the property precisely as it has been used for the past 65 years; as a railroad terminal containing office space and concessions. So the law does not interfere with what must be regarded as Penn Central's primary expectation concerning the use of the parcel [or its ability] to obtain a "reasonable return" on its investment.

Appellants, moreover, exaggerate the effect of the law on their ability to make use of the air rights above the Terminal. [First, nothing] the Commission has said or done suggests an intention to prohibit *any* construction above the Terminal.

[Second,] it is not literally accurate to say that they have been denied *all* use of even [pre-existing] air rights. [The] New York courts here supportably found that [the transferable development] rights afforded are valuable. While these rights may well not have constituted "just compensation" if a "taking" had occurred, the rights nevertheless undoubtedly mitigate whatever financial burdens the law has imposed on appellants and, for that reason, are to be taken into account in considering the impact of regulation.

On this record, we conclude that the application of New York City's Landmarks Law has not effected a "taking" of appellants' property. The restrictions imposed are substantially related to the promotion of the general welfare and not only permit reasonable beneficial use of the landmark site but also afford appellants opportunities further to enhance not only the Terminal site proper but also other properties.

Affirmed.

Mr. Justice Rehnquist, with whom The Chief Justice and Mr. Justice Stevens join, dissenting.

Only in the most superficial sense of the word can this case be said to involve "zoning." Typical zoning restrictions may, it is true, so limit the prospective uses of a piece of property as to diminish the value of that property in the abstract because it may not be used for the forbidden purposes. But any such abstract decrease in value will more than likely be at least partially offset by an increase in value which flows from similar restrictions as to use on neighboring properties. All property owners in a designated area are placed under the same restrictions, not only for the benefit of the municipality as a whole but also for the common benefit of one another. In the words of Mr. Justice Holmes, speaking for the Court in [*Mahon,*] there is "an average reciprocity of advantage."

Where a relatively few individual buildings, all separated from one another, are singled out and treated differently from surrounding buildings, no such reciprocity exists. [And] the cost associated with landmark legislation is likely to be of a completely different order of magnitude than that which results from the imposition of normal zoning restrictions. [Under] the historic-landmark preservation scheme adopted by New York, the property owner is under an affirmative duty to *preserve* his property *as a landmark* at his own expense. . . .

[Before] the city of New York declared Grand Central Terminal to be a landmark, Penn Central could have used its "air rights" over the Terminal to build a multistory office building, at an apparent value of several million dollars per year. Today, the Terminal cannot be modified in *any* form, including the erection of additional stories, without the permission of the Landmark Preservation Commission, a permission which appellants, despite good-faith attempts, have so far been unable to obtain. . . .

The nuisance exception to the taking guarantee is not coterminous with the police power itself. The question is whether the forbidden use is dangerous to the safety, health, or welfare of others. . . .

Appellees are not prohibiting a nuisance. The record is clear that the proposed addition to the Grand Central Terminal would be in full compliance with zoning, height limitations, and other health and safety requirements. Instead, appellees are seeking to preserve what they believe to be an outstanding example of beaux arts architecture. [The] city of New York, because of its unadorned admiration for the design, has decided that the owners of the building must preserve it unchanged for the benefit of sightseeing New Yorkers and tourists.

[Even] where the government prohibits a noninjurious use, the Court has ruled that a taking does not take place if the prohibition applies over a broad cross section of land and thereby "secure[s] an average reciprocity of advantage." [*Mahon.*] [While] zoning at times reduces *individual* property values, the burden is shared relatively evenly and it is reasonable to conclude that on the whole an individual who is harmed by one aspect of the zoning will be benefited by another.

Here, however, a multimillion dollar loss has been imposed on appellants; it is uniquely felt and is not offset by any benefits flowing from the preservation of some 400 other "landmarks" in New York City. Appellees have imposed a substantial cost on less than one one-tenth of one percent of the buildings in New York City for the general benefit of all its people. It is exactly this imposition of general costs on a few individuals at which the "taking" protection is directed. . . .

[A] taking does not become a noncompensable exercise of police power simply because the government in its grace allows the owner to make some "reasonable" use of his property. [Appellees] contend that, even if they have "taken" appellants' property, TDR's constitute "just compensation." [Because] the record on appeal is relatively slim. I would remand to the Court of Appeals for a determination of whether TDR's constitute a "full and perfect equivalent for the property taken."

KEYSTONE BITUMINOUS COAL ASSOCIATION v. DeBENEDICTIS, 480 U.S. 470 1987). In this case, the Court upheld a modern-day analogue of the Kohler Act, invalidated in Pennsylvania Coal Co. v. Mahon. A Pennsylvania statute enacted in 1966 prohibited mining that caused subsidence damage to public buildings, dwellings used for human habitation, and cemeteries. The administrative agency charged with enforcing the statute generally required 50 percent of the coal beneath such structures to be kept in place as a means of providing surface support. Moreover, the agency was authorized to revoke mining permits if removal of coal caused damage to such structures and the operator had not repaired or paid for the damage.

Justice Stevens delivered the Court's opinion: "Petitioners assert that disposition of their takings claim calls for no more than a straightforward application of the Court's decision in [*Pennsylvania Coal*]. Although there are some obvious similarities between the cases, we agree with the [court below] that the similarities are far less significant than the [differences]. . . .

"The two factors that the [*Pennsylvania Coal*] Court considered relevant have become integral parts of our takings analysis. We have held that land use regulation can effect a taking if it 'does not substantially advance legitimate state interests, . . . or denies an owner economically viable use of his land.' Agins v. Tiburon, 447 U.S. 255, 260 (1980).

"Application of these tests to petitioners' challenge demonstrates that they have not satisfied their burden of showing that the Subsidence Act constitutes a taking. First, unlike the Kohler Act, the character of the governmental action involved here leans heavily against finding a taking; the [state] has acted to arrest what it perceives to be a significant threat to the common welfare. Second, there is no record in this case to support a finding, similar to the one the Court made in *Pennsylvania Coal*, that the Subsidence Act makes it impossible for petitioners to profitably engage in their business, or that there has been undue interference with their investment-backed expectations. . . .

"Unlike the Kohler Act, [the] Subsidence Act does not merely involve a balancing of the private economic interests of coal companies against the private interests of the surface owners. The Pennsylvania Legislature specifically found that important public interests are served by enforcing a policy that is designed to minimize subsidence in certain areas. . . .

"The second factor that distinguishes this case from *Pennsylvania Coal* is the finding in that case that the Kohler Act made mining of 'certain coal' commercially impracticable. In this case, by contrast, petitioners have not shown any deprivation significant enough to satisfy the heavy burden placed upon one alleging a regulatory taking. . . .

"The parties have stipulated that enforcement of the [50%] rule will require petitioners to leave approximately 27 million tons of coal in place. Because they own that coal but cannot mine it, they contend that Pennsylvania has appropriated it for the public purposes described in the Subsidence Act.

"[But the] 27 million tons of coal do not constitute a separate segment of property for takings law purposes. . . .

"We do not consider Justice Holmes' statement that the Kohler Act made mining of 'certain coal' commercially impracticable as requiring us to focus on the individual pillars of coal that must be left in place. . . .

"When the coal that must remain beneath the ground is viewed in the context of any reasonable unit of petitioners' coal mining operations and financial-backed expectations, it is plain that the petitioners have not come close to satisfying their burden of proving that they have been denied the economically viable use of that property."

Chief Justice Rehnquist, in an opinion joined by Justices Powell, O'Connor, and Scalia, dissented.

Note: "Takings" and the Police Power

1. *In general.* To what does one look to decide whether there has been a "taking" of private property? Consider Michelman, Property, Utility, and Fairness: Comments on the Ethical Foundations of "Just Compensation" Law, 80 Harv. L. Rev. 1165, 1225 (1967), referring to the

> capacity of some collective actions to imply that someone may be subjected to immediately disadvantageous or painful treatment for no other apparent reason, and in accordance with no other apparent principle, than that someone else's claim to satisfaction has been ranked as intrinsically superior to his own. [Avoidance] of this evil is not the same thing as avoidance of all social action having capricious redistributive effects. The reasons begin with the universal acknowledgement that some collective constraint on individual free choice is necessary in order to [lead] to fuller achievement by each of his own ends. [It] is true that collective action which depends for its legitimacy on such understandings must look ultimately to the furtherance of *everyone's* attainment of his own ends, without "discrimination," and that this latter requirement would most obviously be met if a way were found to distribute the benefits and costs associated with each collective measure so that each person would share equally in the net benefits. But such perfection is plainly unattainable. [In] the face of this difficulty, it seems we are pleased to believe that we can arrive at an acceptable level of assurance that *over time* the burdens associated with collectively determined improvements will have been distributed "evenly" enough so that everyone will be a net gainer. The function of a compensation practice, as here viewed, is to fulfill a stronger felt need to maintain that assurance at an "acceptable" level — to justify the general expectations of long-run "evenness."

With some such general understanding, the central problem in *Mahon, Miller,* and *Keystone* remains: how to distinguish between a "taking" and "regulation." Almost all government action — to take familiar examples: zoning, minimum wage and maximum hour legislation, the relocation of a highway, or other land use regulation — diminishes the value of some people's property and increases the value of the property of other people. Redistribution in this sense is almost always the result, and often the purpose, of government action. If compensation was required in all such cases, there would, of course, be far less redistribution. The need to calculate and hand out compensation (costs independent of compensation "itself") would often prevent its occurrence. There is an additional problem: Many people are "winners" from regulation, and they are not taxed accordingly; if government must compensate, but does not tax, its own incentives may be skewed against beneficial activities. Where one sets the line between taking and regulation will to a large degree determine how much redistribution (some of it perhaps efficient and just, some of it perhaps neither) will be permitted through the regulatory process.

2. *Distinguishing takings from regulation.* How does one tell whether there has been regulation or a taking? Some candidates for a test include the following.

a. *The extent of the intrusion.* Under this view, compensation will be required if, in Justice Holmes's words, regulation "goes too far." The compensation requirement is triggered by a significant invasion. But this approach raises the issue why the extent of the intrusion is relevant to the question whether compensation need be paid at all rather than to the question of the extent of compensation.

b. *The nature of the intrusion.* Under this approach, a court could take the notion of "taking" literally by examining whether property has "actually" been taken. Has there been, for example, a physical invasion? In fact, the Court has come close to holding that a physical invasion is a sufficient condition to find a taking. But compensation may not be required if the diminution in value produced by a regulatory measure does not actually "touch" the property in question — for example, occupational safety and health regulation, relocation of a highway, minimum wage legislation, or a zoning ordinance. Also relevant may be whether government has actually appropriated the property for its own or another's use rather than simply destroyed it.

Under this view, physical invasions present a stronger case for requiring compensation than government action that diminishes value without such an invasion. The theme of physical invasion is a prominent one in the law of eminent domain. But it is not easy to expain why government action that actually "invades" in a physical sense should be treated differently from government action that in some other way diminishes value. One response is that, where there has been a physical invasion, it is easy to identify those adversely affected, and one need not worry that the costs of identifying those people entitled to compensation will prevent necessary measures from going forward. Consider the zoning example, where the number of properties adversely affected may be extremely large and the costs of identifying them, calculating their losses, and compensating them may deter socially desirable measures. Cf. R. Posner, Economic Analysis of Law 40-48 (2d ed. 1977). Note, too, that there is no "givings" clause in the Constitution, allowing government to receive resources for the benefits that it grants to property owners.

c. *Balancing.* One might approach the takings versus regulation issue by asking: How important is the state's interest? How does it compare with the private interest? But consider, with respect to this approach, the view that "use of the balancing test for such a purpose seems to be a mistake, at best reflecting a careless confusion of two quite distinct questions. These are, first, whether a given measure would be in order assuming it were accompanied by compensation payments; and, second, whether the same measure, conceding that it would be proper under conditions of full compensation, ought to be enforced without payment of any compensation. The balancing test may have something to do with the first question, but cannot have anything to do with the second." Michelman, supra, at 1193-1194. But note also a possible defense of a balancing approach as a means of testing whether the measure in question is "so obviously efficient as

to quiet the potential outrage of persons 'unavoidably' sacrificed in its interest."
Id. at 1235.

d. *The legitimacy of the state's interest: restraining harmful conduct, "mere" redistribution, and public benefit.* One might decide the takings question by asking,
like the *Keystone* Court, whether the state is attempting "merely" to redistribute
property from one person to another or attempting instead to promote a more
general good. This question is another way of asking whether the action in question falls within the police power. A more particularized version of this approach
asks whether the state is preventing the property owner from committing some
public harm or instead demanding some contribution to the public good. Perhaps the government need not compensate people when they are prevented from
harming, but compensation is necessary when government is demanding that a
private person benefit the public.

One of the principal purposes of the eminent domain clause, it is commonly
thought, is to ensure that public burdens are paid for by the public generally, not
by particular individuals. The compensation requirement promotes that goal. By
requiring compensation, the clause promotes both efficiency (by forcing government to internalize the costs of its actions) and fairness (by making the burdens
general rather than selective). But if an individual is committing some kind of
harm, the redress or prevention of the harm is something for which the individual, rather than the public, must pay. Someone who is committing a tort can be
prevented from doing so, and the state need not furnish compensation. More
broadly, if someone has no right to the property in the first place, it is hardly unfair to require him to give it up for the public good.

But how does one know in which category — prevention of tort or forced contribution to the public good — a particular measure falls? To answer that question, or to decide whether someone is being forced to give up something that belongs to him, one has to have a background understanding that specifies what is
a normal or defensible status quo — and that requires a normative theory.

Note, for example, the difficulty in *Miller* and *Mahon* of deciding whether
there is private fault or public benefit. For a long period, the common law furnished the benchmark, but in *Miller* the Court abandoned that approach, finding a harm that might be prevented without compensation, even though the conduct may not have been tortious at common law. See in this regard *Lucas*, infra.

3. *Action and inaction.* In *Miller*, the Court also stated that, if government had
failed to act, "it would have been none the less a choice. [When] forced to such
a choice the state does not exceed its constitutional powers by deciding upon the
destruction of one class of property in order to save another." The implication is
that government inaction is itself a form of regulation.

What consequences does this insight have for the eminent domain clause and
the underlying principle of private property? Consider Sunstein, Naked Preferences and the Constitution, 84 Colum. L. Rev. 1689, 1776 (1984):

> The new conception of the market status quo as neither natural nor inviolate led
> the way toward a dramatically expanded understanding of the police power. [In-
> deed], the seeds of a destruction of the eminent domain clause may lie within the
> *Miller* Court's statement. If government inaction can be understood as government
> action — if a decision not to act is understood as an intrusion in the same way as

"affirmative" regulation — then the traditional notion of private property [loses] much of its coherence.

4. *"Ordinary observing."* Note finally the approach in B. Ackerman, Private Property and the Constitution (1977). Ackerman distinguishes between two approaches to the issue of takings versus regulation: The first is that of a "scientific policymaker"; the second is that of an "ordinary observer." The former judges the issues by looking at the effects of government action on the property in question. Did it, for example, diminish in value? The latter makes a determination on the basis of a commonsense inquiry. Was there a physical invasion on the part of the government? This approach judges takings by reference to common conceptions of whether property has been "taken"; it does not rely on lawyers' references to property as a "bundle of rights," or economists' understanding of property by reference to valuable uses. Ackerman contends that current law reflects the perspective of an ordinary observer.

Note: Penn Central, Keystone, *Takings, and Related Problems*

1. *The Court's approach.* Note the frank concession by the *Penn Central* Court that the issue of whether there has been a "taking" is resolved by an "essentially ad hoc, factual" inquiry. What are the elements that go into the inquiry? Would an alternative approach be preferable? In this regard, does *Keystone* overrule *Mahon?*

2. *Assorted cases.* Probably the best way to get a sense of eminent domain doctrine is to compare the holdings in different factual settings. In reading these cases, it will be useful to examine the relative weight of the various possible tests referred to on pages 972-973.

a. Andrus v. Allard, 444 U.S. 51 (1979). The Eagle Protection Act banned the sale of bald or golden eagle parts taken before the effective date of the statute. The act did not ban the possession or transportation of such parts. The Court upheld the statute, saying that government regulation often

> curtails some potential for the use or economic exploitation of private property. To require compensation in all such circumstances would effectively compel the government to regulate by *purchase.* [The] regulations challenged here do not compel the surrender of the artifacts, and there is no physical invasion or restraint upon them. Rather, a significant restriction has been imposed on one means of disposing of the artifacts. But the denial of one traditional property right does not always amount to a taking. At least where an owner possesses a full "bundle" of property rights, the destruction of one "strand" of the bundle is not a taking, because the aggregation must be viewed in its entirety. [It] is, to be sure, undeniable that the regulations here prevent the most profitable use of appellees' property. Again, however, that is not dispositive. When we review regulation, a reduction in the value of the property is not necessarily equated with a taking.

b. Compare *Andrus* to Hodel v. Irving, 481 U.S. 704 (1987). In the nineteenth century, Congress enacted a law that divided the communal property on the reservation of the Sioux Nation into individual allotments. The allotted lands were held in trust for the Indians by the United States, and after 1910 the allottees were permitted to dispose of their interests by will in accordance with regulations promulgated by the Secretary of the Interior. As successive generations came to hold the allotted lands, ownership became fractionated into extremely small, undivided interests, with the result that it became impractical to make productive use of the lands. In order to deal with this problem, Congress enacted the Indian Land Consolidation Act in 1983, which provided that undivided, fractional interests in trust land could not be devised, but instead would escheat to the tribe if the interest represented 2 percent or less of the total acreage of the tract and had earned its owner less than $100 in the previous year.

The Court, in an opinion by Justice O'Connor, held this escheat provision unconstitutional. "[The] regulation here amounts to virtually the abrogation of the right to pass on a certain type of property [to] one's heirs. In one form or another, the right to pass on property — to one's family in particular — has been part of the Anglo-American legal system since feudal times." The Court noted, however, that it would "surely" be permissible for the government to prevent owners from further subdividing the land among future heirs on pain of escheat and to abolish descent of such interest by rules of intestacy.

Justice Scalia, in a concurring opinion joined by Chief Justice Rehnquist and Justice Powell, noted that "the present statute, insofar as concerns the balance between rights taken and rights left untouched[, is] indistinguishable from the statute that was at issue in [Allard]," and that "in finding a taking today our decision effectively limits Allard to its facts." In another concurring opinion, Justice Brennan, joined by Justices Marshall and Blackmun, found "nothing in today's opinion that would limit [Allard]. Indeed, [I] am of the view that the unique negotiations giving rise to the property rights and expectations at issue here make this case the unusual one."

c. Euclid v. Ambler Realty Co., 272 U.S. 365 (1926), involved a zoning ordinance. The tract at issue had been vacant and was held for purpose of sale and development for industrial uses; for such uses, it had a market value of about $10,000 per acre. The zoning ordinance would limit it to residential purposes, thus reducing its market value to $2,500 per acre.

The Court upheld the ordinance. It acknowledged that

the exclusion is in general terms of all industrial establishments, and it may thereby happen that not only offensive or dangerous industries will be excluded, but those which are neither offensive nor dangerous will share the same fate. But this is no more than happens in respect of many practice-forbidding laws which this Court has upheld although drawn in general terms so as to include individual cases that may turn out to be innocuous in themselves.

The Court went on to point to the various benefits of the zoning ordinance:

the segregation of residential, business, and industrial buildings will make it easier to provide fire apparatus suitable for the character and intensity of the development in each section; that it will increase the safety and security of home life; greatly tend to prevent street accidents, especially to children, by reducing the traffic and resulting confusion in residential sections; decrease noise and other conditions which produce or intensify nervous disorders; preserve a more favorable environment in which to rear children, etc.

In the Court's view, these factors were "sufficiently cogent to preclude us from saying, as it must be said before the ordinance can be declared unconstitutional, that such provisions are clearly arbitrary and unreasonable, having no substantial relation to the public health, safety, morals, or general welfare."

Note that the deferential approach of *Euclid* is inapplicable to cases of physical invasion; see, in this regard, the discussion of "ordinary observing," supra.

d. Compare Kaiser Aetna v. United States, 444 U.S. 164 (1979) to United States v. Riverside Bayview Homes, 474 U.S. 121 (1985), and PruneYard Shopping Center v. Robins, 447 U.S. 74 (1980). In *Kaiser Aetna*, the Army Corps of Engineers attempted to grant public access to Kuapa Pond, a lagoon in Hawaii that was contiguous to a navigable bay. Kaiser Aetna had obtained rights to use the lagoon and had dredged and filled parts of it, erected retaining walls, and built bridges. It also created accommodations for pleasure boats. Eventually there were about 1,500 marina waterfront lot lessees. Kaiser Aetna controlled access to and use of the marina and generally did not permit commercial use. The Army Corps of Engineers contended that Kaiser Aetna was required to allow public access to the lagoon, and that no compensation need be paid, since there was a federal navigational servitude on the property.

The Court concluded that "the Government's attempt to create a public right to access [goes] so far beyond ordinary regulation or improvement for navigation as to amount to a taking." The Court emphasized that (1) before Kaiser Aetna's improvements, the pond could not be used for navigation in interstate commerce; (2) the body of water was private property under Hawaiian law; (3) the intrusion at issue was on the right to exclude, "universally held to be a fundamental element of the property right"; and (4) there was an actual physical invasion.

In *Riverside Bayview Homes*, the Army Corps of Engineers issued regulations requiring landowners to secure permits before discharging fill material into wetlands adjacent to navigable bodies of water and their tributaries. The corps then brought this action against a landowner to enjoin respondents from placing fill material in adjacent wetlands. The district court granted the injunction, but the court of appeals reversed, holding that a narrow construction of the regulations was necessary in order to avoid a taking of private property without just compensation. The Court, in an opinion by Justice White, reversed the court of appeals. Although acknowledging that governmental land-use regulation may "under extreme circumstances" constitute a taking, the Court held that the mere assertion of regulatory jurisdiction does not amount to a taking: "A requirement that a person obtain a permit before engaging in a certain use of his or her property does not itself 'take' the property in any sense: after all, the very existence of a permit system implies that permission may be granted, leaving the landowner free to use the property as desired. Moreover, even if the permit is denied, there may be other viable uses available to the owner. Only when a permit is denied and the effect of the denial is to prevent 'economically viable' use of the land in question can it be said that a taking has occurred."

In *PruneYard*, the California Supreme Court had held that the state constitutional right of free speech compelled shopping center owners to allow protesters to exercise rights of free speech on shopping center property. The owners contended that there was a "taking" of their property. The Court said:

Here the requirement that appellants permit appellees to exercise state-protected rights of free expression and petition on shopping center property clearly does not amount to an unconstitutional infringement of appellant's property rights under the Takings Clause. There is nothing to suggest that preventing appellants from prohibiting this sort of activity will unreasonably impair the value or use of their property as a shopping center. [The] decision of the California Supreme Court makes it clear that the PruneYard may restrict expressive activity by adopting time, place, and manner regulations. [Appellees] were orderly, and they limited their activity to the common areas of the shopping center.

What is the relevance of the last two sentences in this passage?

e. In Loretto v. Teleprompter Manhattan CATV Corp, 458 U.S. 419 (1982), the issue was the constitutionality of a New York law providing that a landlord must permit a cable television company to install cable facilities on her property. The cable installation in the relevant case occupied portions of the plaintiff's roof and the side of her building. The Court concluded that the "permanent physical occupation authorized by government is a taking without regard to the public interests that it may serve." The Court added: "An owner suffers a special kind of injury when a stranger directly invades and occupies the owner's property. [The] traditional rule also avoids otherwise difficult line-drawing problems. [Whether] a permanent physical occupation has occurred presents relatively few problems of proof."

The Court distinguished Loretto in FCC v. Florida Power Corp., 480 U.S. 245 (1987), and upheld a federal statute authorizing the Federal Communications Commission to regulate the rates utility companies charge cable operators for the use of utility poles. In a unanimous opinion written by Justice Marshall, the Court held that Loretto was inapplicable to these facts:

> [While] the statute we considered in Loretto specifically *required* landlords to permit permanent occupation of their property by cable companies, nothing in [this act gives] cable companies any right to occupy space on utility poles, or prohibits utility companies from refusing to enter into attachment agreements with cable operators. The Act authorizes the FCC [to] review the rents charged by public utility landlords who have voluntarily entered into leases with cable company tenants renting space on utility poles.

Compare Connolly v. Pension Benefit Guaranty Corp., 475 U.S. 211 (1986), upholding a statute requiring an employer withdrawing from a multiemployer pension plan to pay its proportionate share of the plan's unfunded vested benefits.

f. United States v. Causby, 328 U.S. 256 (1946), raised the question whether frequent flights immediately above a landowner's property constituted a taking. The Court concluded that it did: "If, by reason of the frequency and altitude of the flights, respondents could not use this land for any purpose, their loss would be complete. It would be as complete as if the United States had entered upon the surface of the land and taken exclusive possession of it." See also Griggs v. Allegheny County, 369 U.S. 84 (1962).

g. Is the takings clause violated when the government conditions the grant of a discretionary benefit on the recipient's willingness to give up property rights that could not be taken from him without compensation?

In Bowen v. Gilliard, 483 U.S. 587 (1987), the Court considered a takings clause attack on an amendment to the Aid to Families with Dependent Children (AFDC) program that required recipient families to assign to the government child support payments received from a noncustodial parent for a child living in the covered household. The effect of the assignment was to reduce the level of support payments received by the household. Appellees argued that this reduction constituted a taking from the child because the child support payments could be legally used only for the individual child, while the compensating AFDC payments were available for the entire family. The Court, in an opinion by Justice Stevens, rejected the argument:

> Congress is not, by virtue of having instituted a social welfare program, bound to continue it at all, much less at the same benefit level. Thus, notwithstanding the technical legal arguments that have been advanced, it is imperative to recognize that the amendments at issue merely incorporate a definitional element into an entitlement program. It would be quite strange indeed if, by virtue of an offer to *provide* benefits to needy families through the entirely voluntary AFDC program, Congress or the States were deemed to have *taken* some of those very family members' property.

Compare the analysis in *Gilliard* with the following.

NOLLAN v. CALIFORNIA COASTAL COMMISSION, 483 U.S. 825 (1987). The California Coastal Commission conditioned the grant of a permit to rebuild appellants' house on their transfer to the public of an easement across their beachfront property. The Court, in an opinion by Justice Scalia, held that the attempt to impose this condition was a taking:

"Had California simply required the [appellants] to make an easement across their beachfront available to the public on a permanent [basis] we have no doubt there would have been a taking. [We] think a 'permanent physical occupation' has occurred, for purposes of [*Loretto*], where individuals are given a permanent and continuous right to pass to and fro, so that the real property may continuously be traversed, even though no particular individual is permitted to station himself permanently upon the premises. . . .[2]

"Given, then, that requiring uncompensated conveyance of the easement outright would violate the Fourteenth Amendment, the question becomes whether requiring it to be conveyed as a condition for issuing a land use permit alters the outcome. . . .

"[If] the Commission attached to the permit some condition that would have protected the public's ability to see the beach notwithstanding construction of the new house — for example, a height limitation, a width restriction, or a ban on fences — so long as the Commission could have exercised its police power (as we [assume] it could) to forbid construction of the house altogether, imposition of the condition would also be constitutional. Moreover, [the] condition would be

2. Justice Brennan [suggests] that the Commission's public announcement of its intention to condition the rebuilding of houses on the transfer of easements of access caused the Nollans to have "no reasonable claim to any expectation of being able to exclude members of the public" from walking across their beach. . . . But the right to build on one's own property — even though its exercise can be subjected to legitimate permitting requirements — cannot remotely be described as a "government benefit." [Nor] are the Nollans' rights altered because they acquired the land well after the Commission had begun to implement its policy. So long as the Commission could not have deprived the prior owners of the easement without compensating them, the prior owners must be understood to have transferred their full property rights in conveying the lot. [Relocated footnote — EDS.]

constitutional even if it consisted of the requirement that the [appellants] provide a viewing spot on their property for passersby with whose sighting of the ocean their new house would interfere. Although such a requirement [would] have to be considered a taking if it were not attached to a development permit, the Commission's assumed power to forbid construction of the house in order to protect the public's view of the beach must surely include the power to condition construction upon some concession by the owner, even a concession of property rights, that serves the same end. . . .

"The evident constitutional propriety disappears, however, if the condition substituted for the prohibition utterly fails to further the end advanced as the justification for the prohibition. When that essential nexus is eliminated, the situation becomes the same as if California law forbade shouting fire in a crowded theater, but granted dispensations to those willing to contribute $100 to the state treasury. [In] short, unless the permit condition serves the same governmental purpose as the development ban, the building restriction is not a valid regulation of land use but 'an out-and-out plan of extortion.' . . .

"Justice Brennan argues that imposition of the access requirement is not irrational. In his version of the Commission's argument, the reason for the requirement is that in its absence, a person looking toward the beach from the road will see a street of residential structures including the Nollans' new home and conclude that there is no public beach nearby. If, however, that person sees people passing and repassing along the dry sand behind the Nollans' home, he will realize that there is a public beach somewhere in the vicinity. The Commission's action, however, was based on the opposite factual finding that the wall of houses completely blocked the view of the beach and that a person looking from the road would not be able to see it at all.

"Even if the Commission had made the finding that Justice Brennan proposes, however, it is not certain that it would suffice. [We] view the Fifth Amendment's property clause to be more than a pleading requirement, and compliance with it to be more than an exercise of cleverness and imagination. [Our] cases describe the condition for abridgement of property rights through the police power as '*substantially* advanc[ing]' a legitimate State interest. We are inclined to be particularly careful about the adjective where the actual conveyance of property is made a condition to the lifting of a land use restriction, since in that context there is heightened risk that the purpose is avoidance of the compensation requirement, rather than the stated police power objective."

Justice Brennan, joined by Justice Marshall, wrote a dissenting opinion:

"[The] Court imposes a standard of precision for the exercise of a State's police power that has been discredited for the better part of this century. . . .

"It is [by] now commonplace that this Court's review of the rationality of a State's exercise of its police power demands only that the State '*could rationally have decided*' that the measure adopted might achieve the State's objective. [Minnesota v. Clover Leaf Creamery Co.]

"The Court finds fault with [the Commission's conduct] because it regards the condition as insufficiently tailored to address the precise type of reduction in access produced by the new development. The Nollans' development blocks visual access, the Court tells us, while the Commission seeks to preserve lateral access along the coastline. Such a narrow conception of rationality, however, has long since been discredited as a judicial arrogation of legislative authority. . . .

"Even if we accept the Court's unusual demand for a precise match between the condition imposed and the specific type of burden on access created by the appellants, the State's action easily satisfies this requirement. First, the lateral access condition serves to dissipate the impression that the beach that lies behind the wall of homes along the shore is for private use only. It requires no exceptional imaginative powers to find plausible the Commission's point that the average person passing along the road in front of a phalanx of imposing permanent residences [is] likely to conclude that this particular portion of the shore is not open to the public. If, however, that person can see that numerous people are passing and repassing along the dry sand, this conveys the message that the beach is in fact open for use by the public. . . .

"The second flaw in the Court's analysis [is] more fundamental. The Court assumes that the only burden with which the Coastal Commission was concerned was blockage of visual access to the beach. This is incorrect. The Commission specifically stated in its report [that] '[t]he Commission finds that the applicants' proposed development would present an increase in view blockage, *an increase in private use of the shorefront*, and that this impact would burden the public's ability to traverse to and along the shorefront.'

"[Moreover,] appellants were clearly on notice when requesting a new development permit that a condition of approval would be a provision ensuring [the easement]. [In] this respect, this case is quite similar to Ruckelshaus v. Monsanto Co., 467 U.S. 986 (1984). In *Monsanto*, the respondent had submitted trade data to the Environmental Protection Agency for the purpose of obtaining registration of certain pesticides. [The] Court conceded that the data in question constituted property under state law. It also found, however, that certain of the data had been submitted to the agency after Congress had made clear that only limited confidentiality would be given data submitted for registration purposes. [The] Court rejected respondent's argument that the requirement that it relinquish some confidentiality imposed an unconstitutional condition upon receipt of a Government benefit."[10]

Justices Blackmun and Stevens also filed dissenting opinions.

Nollan might well be seen as an unconstitutional conditions case. On this view, *Nollan* raises the question whether government might condition the receipt of a benefit — here, permission to build — on the grant of an easement. *Nollan* treats this condition as impermissible partly on the theory that the right to build on

---

10. The Court suggests that [*Monsanto*] is distinguishable, because government regulation of property in that case was a condition on receipt of a "government benefit," while here regulation takes the form of a restriction on "the right to build on one's own property." This proffered distinction is not persuasive. Both Monsanto and the Nollans hold property whose use is subject to regulation; Monsanto may not sell its property without obtaining government approval and the Nollans may not build a new development on their property without government approval. Obtaining such approval is as much a "government benefit" for the Nollans as it is for Monsanto. If the Court is somehow suggesting that "the right to build on one's own property" has some privileged natural rights status, the argument is a curious one. By any traditional labor theory of value justification for property rights, for instance, see, e.g., J. Locke, The Second Treatise of Civil Government, Monsanto would have a superior claim, for the chemical formulae which constitute its property only came into being by virtue of Monsanto's efforts. [Relocated footnote — EDS.]

one's own property is not a government "benefit," like welfare. But what is the difference between the two kinds of interests? Is one more "natural" than the others?

The Court also emphasized that the condition imposed by the state had no relation to the state's legitimate interest in preserving the view. The Court implied that a concession of property rights that involved a viewing spot rather than an easement might have been upheld. Here, however, the easement had no connection to the aesthetic goals at stake. As the Court had it, the problem was thus one of "extortion." See Epstein, Foreword: Unconstitutional Conditions, State Power, and the Limits of Consent, 102 Harv. L. Rev. 1, 62-63 (1988): "The doctrine of unconstitutional conditions limits the abuse of government discretion by severing the denial of the construction permit from the taking of the lateral easement. [The] 'relatedness' requirement [has] powerful functional roots, for it [reduces] the state's ability to extract concessions from individual owners by coordinating separate types of government initiatives."

But see Sullivan, Unconstitutional Conditions, 102 Harv. L. Rev. 1413, 1474 (1989): "Germaneness to the purpose of a benefit depends crucially on how broadly or how narrowly that purpose is defined. [The] condition invalidated in *Nollan* may be interpreted either as nongermane to the provision of visual access to the sea [or] as germane to a more general state interest in facilitating public use and enjoyment of the beach." How might a court resolve this problem?

For general discussion of this and related issues, see Symposium, The Jurisprudence of Takings, 88 Colum. L. Rev. 1581 (1988).

In Pennell v. City of San Jose, 485 U.S. 1 (1988), the Supreme Court upheld an unusual rent control ordinance. The ordinance contained a mechanism for automatically increasing annual rents by as much as 8 percent. If a tenant objects to an increase greater than 8 percent, a hearing is provided, in which a mediation hearing officer decides whether the proposed increase is "reasonable under the circumstances." The decision about reasonableness is to include consideration of

the economic and financial hardship imposed on the present tenant or tenants of the unit or units to which such increases apply. If, on balance, the Hearing Officer determinates that the proposed increase constitutes an unreasonably severe financial or economic hardship on a particular tenant, he may order that the excess of the increase . . . be disallowed. Any tenant whose household income and monthly housing expense meets [certain income requirements] shall be deemed to be suffering under financial and economic hardship which must be weighed.

The Court responded:

We think it would be premature to consider this contention on the present record. As things stand, there simply is no evidence that the "tenant hardship clause" has in fact ever been relied upon by a Hearing Officer to reduce a rent below the figure it would have been set at on the basis of the other factors set forth in the Ordinance. In addition, there is nothing in the Ordinance requiring that a Hearing Officer in fact reduce a proposed rent increase on grounds of tenant hardship. . . . Given the "essentially ad hoc, factual inquir[y]" involved in the takings analysis, Kaiser Aetna v. United States, we have found it particularly important in takings cases to adhere to our admonition that "the constitutionality of statutes ought not be decided except in an actual factual setting that makes such a decision necessary." . . .

Petitioners argue, however, that it is "arbitrary, discriminatory, or demonstrably irrelevant," for appellees to attempt to accomplish the additional goal of reducing the burden of housing costs on low-income tenants by requiring that "hardship to a tenant" be considered in determining the amount of excess rent increase that is "reasonable under the circumstances." As appellants put it, "The objective of alleviating individual tenant hardship is . . . not a 'policy the legislature is free to adopt' in a rent control ordinance."

[But] the Ordinance establishes a scheme in which a Hearing Officer considers a number of factors in determining the reasonableness of a proposed rent increase which exceeds eight percent *and* which exceeds the amount deemed reasonable. . . . The first six factors . . . focus on the individual landlord — the Hearing Officer examines the history of the premises, the landlord's costs, and the market for comparable housing. Section 5703.28(c)(5) also allows the landlord to bring forth any other financial evidence — including presumably evidence regarding his own financial status — to be taken into account by the Hearing Officer. It is in only this context that the Ordinance allows tenant hardship to be considered and . . . "balance[d]" with the other factors. . . . Within this scheme, [the Ordinance] represents a rational attempt to accommodate the conflicting interests of protecting tenants from burdensome rent increases while at the same time ensuring that landlords are guaranteed a fair return on their investment. . . .

We accordingly find that the Ordinance, which so carefully considers both the individual circumstances of the landlord and the tenant before determining whether to allow an *additional* increase in rent over and above certain amounts that are deemed reasonable, does not on its face violate the Fourteenth Amendment's Due Process Clause. . . .

In a dissenting opinion, Justice Scalia, joined by Justice O'Connor, wrote:

The "hardship" provision is invoked to meet a [distinct] social problem: the existence of some renters who are too poor to afford even reasonably priced housing. But *that* problem is no more caused or exploited by landlords than it is by the grocers who sell needy renters their food, or the department stores that sell them their clothes, or the employers who pay them their wages, or the citizens of San Jose holding the higher-paying jobs from which they are excluded. And even if the neediness of renters could be regarded as a problem distinctively attributable to landlords in general, it is not remotely attributable to the *particular* landlords that the ordinance singles out — namely, those who happen to have a "hardship" tenant at the present time, or who may happen to rent to a "hardship" tenant in the future, or whose current or future affluent tenants may happen to decline into the "hardship" category.

The traditional manner in which American government has met the problem of those who cannot pay reasonable prices for privately sold necessities — a problem caused by the society at large — has been the distribution to such persons of funds raised from the public at large through taxes, either in cash (welfare payments) or in goods (public housing, publicly subsidized housing, and food stamps). Unless we are to abandon the guiding principle of the Takings Clause that "public burdens . . . should be borne by the public as a whole," this is the only manner that our Constitution permits. . . .

The politically attractive feature of regulation is not that it permits wealth transfers to be achieved that could not be achieved otherwise; but rather that it permits them to be achieved "off budget," with relative invisibility and thus relative immunity from normal democratic processes. San Jose might, for example, have accomplished something like the result here by simply raising the real estate tax upon rental properties and using the additional revenues thus acquired to pay part of the rents of "hardship" tenants. It seems to me doubtful, however, whether the citizens of San Jose would allow funds in the municipal treasury, from wherever derived, to be distributed to a family of four with income as high as $32,400 a year — the generous maximum necessary to qualify automatically as a "hardship" tenant under the rental ordinance. The voters might well see other, more pressing, social priorities. And of course what $32,400-a-year renters can acquire through spurious "regulation," other groups can acquire as well. Once the door is opened it is not unreasonable to expect price regulations requiring private businesses to give special discounts to senior citizens (no matter how affluent), or to students, the handicapped, or war veterans. Subsidies for these groups may well be a good idea, but because of the operation of the Takings Clause our governmental system has required them to be applied, in general, through the process of taxing and spending, where both economic effects and competing priorities are more evident.

That fostering of an intelligent democratic process is one of the happy effects of the constitutional prescription — perhaps accidental, perhaps not. Its essence, however, is simply the unfairness of making one citizen pay, in some fashion other than taxes, to remedy a social problem that is none of his creation. . . . I would hold that the seventh factor in §5703.28(c) of the San Jose Ordinance effects a taking of property without just compensation.

When government regulation is sufficiently intrusive to constitute a taking, what remedy does the Constitution require? In First English Evangelical Lutheran Church of Glendale v. County of Los Angeles, 482 U.S. 304 (1987), the Court, in an opinion by Justice Rehnquist, held that the mere invalidation of the ordinance restricting use of the property in question was constitutionally insufficient. Although the state was free to end the taking by not enforcing the ordinance, it was also required to pay damages for the temporary taking effected during the period before the ordinance was invalidated. Justice Stevens, joined by Justices Blackmun and O'Connor, filed a dissenting opinion.

The Court continued to emphasize the issue of physical invasion in Yee v. Escondido, 503 U.S. 519 (1992). At issue was a local rent control ordinance, applied to mobile home owners and in particular to owners of mobile home "parks." The ordinance set rents at a 1986 level, prohibited unapproved rent increases, and specified the factors that must be considered for any increases. Mobile home park owners contended that under this system they could no longer set rents or decide who their tenants would be, and that as a result the mobile home owner became an effective perpetual tenant of the park, indefinitely enabled to occupy the home's "pad." Thus, an interest in land — the right to occupy it at submarket rent — has been transferred from the park owner to the mobile home owner. According to the park owners, there was in this sense a physical invasion of their property.

The Court disagreed. It said that "government effects a physical taking only where it requires the landowner to submit to the physical occupation of the land." Here, however, "[p]etitioners voluntarily rented their land to mobile home owners. . . . [N]either the City nor the State compels petitioners, once they have rented their property to tenants, to continue doing so." In the Court's view, "[N]o government has required any physical invasions of petitioners' property. Petitioners' tenants were invited by petitioners, not forced upon them by the government." Thus, the laws at issue "merely regulate petitioners' use of their land by regulating the relationship between landlord and tenant."

The fact that there was a transfer of wealth from park owners to incumbent mobile home owners was not decisive, since many forms of land use regulation "can also be said to transfer wealth from the one who is regulated to another." But the Court noted that a "different case would be presented" if the statute compelled "a landowner over objection to rent his property or to refrain in perpetuity from terminating a tenancy."

In the first-year course in property, it is often emphasized that property is a bundle of rights — not a "thing," and not merely a brute fact called physical possession. Has the Court disregarded this insight? If the Constitution incorporated the understandings of the first-year property course, would rent control laws generally be in jeopardy?

There is a great deal of controversy over laws that diminish property values in the process of protecting the environment. Consider, for example, laws making it unlawful to develop property in the most profitable way or making it a crime to kill animals on one's property. The most vivid example involves a law that renders land valueless. Consider the following.

Lucas v. South Carolina Coastal Council

505 U.S. 1003 (1992)

JUSTICE SCALIA delivered the opinion of the Court.

In 1986, petitioner David H. Lucas paid $975,000 for two residential lots on the Isle of Palms in Charleston County, South Carolina, on which he intended to build single-family homes. In 1988, however, the South Carolina Legislature enacted the Beachfront Management Act, which had the direct effect of barring petitioner from erecting any permanent habitable structures on his two parcels. A state trial court found that this prohibition rendered Lucas's parcels "valueless." This case requires us to decide whether the Act's dramatic effect on the economic value of Lucas's lots accomplished a taking of private property under the Fifth and Fourteenth Amendments requiring the payment of "just compensation."

I

A

South Carolina's expressed interest in intensively managing development activities in the so-called "coastal zone" dates from 1977 when, in the aftermath of Congress's passage of the federal Coastal Zone Management Act of 1972, the legislature enacted a Coastal Zone Management Act of its own. . . .

In the late 1970's, Lucas and others began extensive residential development of the Isle of Palms, a barrier island situated eastward of the City of Charleston. Toward the close of the development cycle for one residential subdivision known as "Beachwood East," Lucas in 1986 purchased the two lots at issue in this litigation for his own account. [At] the time Lucas acquired these parcels, he was not legally obliged to obtain a permit from the Council in advance of any development activity. His intention with respect to the lots was to do what the owners of the immediately adjacent parcels had already done: erect single-family residences. He commissioned architectural drawings for this purpose.

The Beachfront Management Act brought Lucas's plans to an abrupt end. Under that 1988 legislation, the Council was directed to establish a "baseline" connecting the landward-most "points of erosion . . . during the past forty years" in the region of the Isle of Palms that includes Lucas's lots. In action not challenged here, the Council fixed this baseline landward of Lucas's parcels. That was significant, for under the Act construction of occupiable improvements was flatly prohibited seaward of a line drawn 20 feet landward of, and parallel to, the baseline. The Act provided no exceptions.

Lucas promptly filed suit in the South Carolina Court of Common Pleas, contending that the Beachfront Management Act's construction bar effected a taking of his property without just compensation. Lucas did not take issue with the validity of the Act as a lawful exercise of South Carolina's police power, but contended that the Act's complete extinguishment of his property's value entitled him to compensation regardless of whether the legislature had acted in furtherance of legitimate police power objectives. Following a bench trial, the court agreed. Among its factual determinations was the finding that "at the time Lucas purchased the two lots, both were zoned for single-family residential construction and . . . there were no restrictions imposed upon such use of the property by either the State of South Carolina, the County of Charleston, or the Town of the Isle of Palms." The trial court further found that the Beachfront Management Act decreed a permanent ban on construction insofar as Lucas's lots were concerned, and that this prohibition "deprived Lucas of any reasonable economic use of the lots, . . . eliminated the unrestricted right of use, and rendered them valueless." The court thus concluded that Lucas's properties had been "taken" by operation of the Act, and it ordered respondent to pay "just compensation" in the amount of $1,232,387.50. . . .

Prior to Justice Holmes' exposition in Pennsylvania Coal Co. v. Mahon, 260 U.S. 393 (1922), it was generally thought that the Takings Clause reached only a "direct appropriation" of property, Legal Tender Cases, 12 Wall. 457, 551 (1871), or the functional equivalent of a "practical ouster of [the owner's] possession." Transportation Co. v. Chicago, 99 U.S. 635, 642 (1879). Justice Holmes recognized in *Mahon*, however, that if the protection against physical appropriations of private property was to be meaningfully enforced, the government's power to redefine the range of interests included in the ownership of property was necessarily constrained by constitutional limits. If, instead, the uses of private property were subject to unbridled, uncompensated qualification under the police power, "the natural tendency of human nature [would be] to extend the qualification more and more until at last private property disappeared." These considerations gave birth in that case to the oft-cited maxim that, "while property may be regulated to a certain extent, if regulation goes too far it will be recognized as a taking."

Nevertheless, our decision in *Mahon* offered little insight into when, and under what circumstances, a given regulation would be seen as going "too far" for purposes of the Fifth Amendment. In 70-odd years of succeeding "regulatory takings" jurisprudence, we have generally eschewed any "set formula" for determining how far is too far, preferring to "engage in . . . essentially ad hoc, factual inquiries," Penn Central Transportation Co. v. New York City, 438 U.S. 104, 124 (1978) (quoting Goldblatt v. Hempstead, 369 U.S. 590, 594 (1962)). See Epstein, Takings: Descent and Resurrection, 1987 Sup. Ct. Rev. 1, 4. We have, however, described at least two discrete categories of regulatory action as compensable without case-specific inquiry into the public interest advanced in support of the restraint. The first encompasses regulations that compel the property owner to suffer a physical "invasion" of his property. In general (at least with regard to permanent invasions), no matter how minute the intrusion, and no matter how weighty the public purpose behind it, we have required compensation. . . .

The second situation in which we have found categorical treatment appropriate is where regulation denies all economically beneficial or productive use of land. . . .[7]

We have never set forth the justification for this rule. Perhaps it is simply, as Justice Brennan suggested, that total deprivation of beneficial use is, from the landowner's point of view, the equivalent of a physical appropriation. See San Diego Gas & Electric Co. v. San Diego, 450 U.S., at 652 (Brennan, J., dissenting). "For what is the land but the profits thereof?" 1 E. Coke, Institutes ch. 1, §1 (1st Am. ed. 1812). Surely, at least, in the extraordinary circumstance when no productive or economically beneficial use of land is permitted, it is less realistic to indulge our usual assumption that the legislature is simply "adjusting the benefits and burdens of economic life," *Penn Central Transportation Co.*, in a manner that secures an "average reciprocity of advantage" to everyone concerned. *Mahon.* And the functional basis for permitting the government, by regulation, to affect property values without compensation — that "Government hardly could go on if to some extent values incident to property could not be diminished without paying for every such change in the general law" — does not apply to the relatively rare situations where the government has deprived a landowner of all economically beneficial uses.

On the other side of the balance, affirmatively supporting a compensation requirement, is the fact that regulations that leave the owner of land without economically beneficial or productive options for its use — typically, as here, by requiring land to be left substantially in its natural state — carry with them a heightened risk that private property is being pressed into some form of public service under the guise of mitigating serious public harm. As Justice Brennan explained: "From the government's point of view, the benefits flowing to the public from preservation of open space through regulation may be equally great as from creating a wildlife refuge through formal condemnation or increasing electricity

---

7. Regrettably, the rhetorical force of our "deprivation of all economically feasible use" rule is greater than its precision, since the rule does not make clear the "property interest" against which the loss of value is to be measured. When, for example, a regulation requires a developer to leave 90% of a rural tract in its natural state, it is unclear whether we would analyze the situation as one in which the owner has been deprived of all economically beneficial use of the burdened portion of the tract, or as one in which the owner has suffered a mere diminution in value of the tract as a whole. [Unsurprisingly,] this uncertainty regarding the composition of the denominator in our "deprivation" fraction has produced inconsistent pronouncements by the Court. The answer to this difficult question may lie in how the owner's reasonable expectations have been shaped by the State's law of property — i.e., whether and to what degree the State's law has accorded legal recognition and protection to the particular interest in land with respect to which the takings claimant alleges a diminution in (or elimination of) value. In any event, we avoid this difficulty in the present case, since the "interest in land" that Lucas has pleaded (a fee simple interest) is an estate with a rich tradition of protection at common law, and since the South Carolina Court of Common Pleas found that the Beachfront Management Act left each of Lucas's beachfront lots without economic value. [Relocated footnote — EDS.]

production through a dam project that floods private property." *San Diego Gas & Elec. Co.*, (Brennan, J., dissenting)....

We think, in short, that there are good reasons for our frequently expressed belief that when the owner of real property has been called upon to sacrifice all economically beneficial uses in the name of the common good, that is, to leave his property economically idle, he has suffered a taking.[8]

The trial court found Lucas's two beachfront lots to have been rendered valueless by respondent's enforcement of the coastal-zone construction ban....

It is correct that many of our prior opinions have suggested that "harmful or noxious uses" of property may be proscribed by government regulation without the requirement of compensation. For a number of reasons, however, we think the South Carolina Supreme Court was too quick to conclude that that principle decides the present case....

When it is understood that "prevention of harmful use" was merely our early formulation of the police power justification necessary to sustain (without compensation) any regulatory diminution in value; and that the distinction between regulation that "prevents harmful use" and that which "confers benefits" is difficult, if not impossible, to discern on an objective, value-free basis; it becomes self-evident that noxious-use logic cannot serve as a touchstone to distinguish regulatory "takings" — which require compensation — from regulatory deprivations that do not require compensation. A fortiori the legislature's recitation of a noxious-use justification cannot be the basis for departing from our categorical rule that total regulatory takings must be compensated. If it were, departure would virtually always be allowed. The South Carolina Supreme Court's approach would essentially nullify *Mahon's* affirmation of limits to the noncompensable exercise of the police power....

Where the State seeks to sustain regulation that deprives land of all economically beneficial use, we think it may resist compensation only if the logically antecedent inquiry into the nature of the owner's estate shows that the proscribed use interests were not part of his title to begin with. This accords, we think, with our "takings" jurisprudence, which has traditionally been guided by the understandings of our citizens regarding the content of, and the State's power over, the "bundle of rights" that they acquire when they obtain title to property. [We] think the notion pressed by the Council that title is somehow held subject to the "implied limitation" that the State may subsequently eliminate all economically valuable use is inconsistent with the historical compact recorded in the Takings Clause that has become part of our constitutional culture.

Where "permanent physical occupation" of land is concerned, we have refused to allow the government to decree it anew (without compensation), no matter how weighty the asserted "public interests" involved, though we assuredly

---

8. Justice Stevens criticizes the "deprivation of all economically beneficial use" rule as "wholly arbitrary," in that "[the] landowner whose property is diminished in value 95% recovers nothing," while the landowner who suffers a complete elimination of value "recovers the land's full value." This analysis errs in its assumption that the landowner whose deprivation is one step short of complete is not entitled to compensation. Such an owner might not be able to claim the benefit of our categorical formulation, but, as we have acknowledged time and again, "the economic impact of the regulation on the claimant and . . . the extent to which the regulation has interfered with distinct investment-backed expectations" are keenly relevant to takings analysis generally. Penn Central Transportation Co. v. New York City, 438 U.S. 104, 124 (1978)....

would permit the government to assert a permanent easement that was a pre-existing limitation upon the landowner's title. We believe similar treatment must be accorded confiscatory regulations, i.e., regulations that prohibit all economically beneficial use of land: Any limitation so severe cannot be newly legislated or decreed (without compensation), but must inhere in the title itself, in the restrictions that background principles of the State's law of property and nuisance already place upon land ownership. A law or decree with such an effect must, in other words, do no more than duplicate the result that could have been achieved in the courts — by adjacent landowners (or other uniquely affected persons) under the State's law of private nuisance, or by the State under its complementary power to abate nuisances that affect the public generally, or otherwise.

On this analysis, the owner of a lake bed, for example, would not be entitled to compensation when he is denied the requisite permit to engage in a landfilling operation that would have the effect of flooding others' land. Nor the corporate owner of a nuclear generating plant, when it is directed to remove all improvements from its land upon discovery that the plant sits astride an earthquake fault. Such regulatory action may well have the effect of eliminating the land's only economically productive use, but it does not proscribe a productive use that was previously permissible under relevant property and nuisance principles. The use of these properties for what are now expressly prohibited purposes was always unlawful, and (subject to other constitutional limitations) it was open to the State at any point to make the implication of those background principles of nuisance and property law explicit. . . .

The "total taking" inquiry we require today will ordinarily entail (as the application of state nuisance law ordinarily entails) analysis of, among other things, the degree of harm to public lands and resources, or adjacent private property, posed by the claimant's proposed activities, the social value of the claimant's activities and their suitability to the locality in question, and the relative ease with which the alleged harm can be avoided through measures taken by the claimant and the government (or adjacent private landowners) alike. The fact that a particular use has long been engaged in by similarly situated owners ordinarily imports a lack of any common-law prohibition (though changed circumstances or new knowledge may make what was previously permissible no longer so). So also does the fact that other landowners, similarly situated, are permitted to continue the use denied to the claimant.

It seems unlikely that common-law principles would have prevented the erection of any habitable or productive improvements on petitioner's land; they rarely support prohibition of the "essential use" of land, Curtin v. Benson, 222 U.S. 78, 86 (1911). The question, however, is one of state law to be dealt with on remand. We emphasize that to win its case South Carolina must do more than proffer the legislature's declaration that the uses Lucas desires are inconsistent with the public interest, or the conclusory assertion that they violate a common-law maxim such as sic utere tuo ut alienum non laedas. As we have said, a "State, by ipse dixit, may not transform private property into public property without compensation. . . ." Webb's Fabulous Pharmacies, Inc. v. Beckwith, 449 U.S. 155, 164 (1980). Instead, as it would be required to do if it sought to restrain Lucas in a common-law action for public nuisance, South Carolina must identify background principles of nuisance and property law that prohibit the uses he now intends in the circumstances in which the property is presently found. Only on this showing can the State fairly claim that, in proscribing all such beneficial uses, the Beachfront Management Act is taking nothing. . . .

The judgment is reversed and the cause remanded for proceedings not inconsistent with this opinion.

So ordered.

[Justice Souter would dismiss the writ of certiorari in this case as having been granted improvidently.]

JUSTICE KENNEDY, concurring in the judgment. . . .

In my view, reasonable expectations must be understood in light of the whole of our legal tradition. The common law of nuisance is too narrow a confine for the exercise of regulatory power in a complex and interdependent society. The State should not be prevented from enacting new regulatory initiatives in response to changing conditions, and courts must consider all reasonable expectations whatever their source. The Takings Clause does not require a static body of state property law; it protects private expectations to ensure private investment. I agree with the Court that nuisance prevention accords with the most common expectations of property owners who face regulation, but I do not believe this can be the sole source of state authority to impose severe restrictions. Coastal property may present such unique concerns for a fragile land system that the State can go further in regulating its development and use than the common law of nuisance might otherwise permit.

The Supreme Court of South Carolina erred, in my view, by reciting the general purposes for which the state regulations were enacted without a determination that they were in accord with the owner's reasonable expectations and therefore sufficient to support a severe restriction on specific parcels of property. The promotion of tourism, for instance, ought not to suffice to deprive specific property of all value without a corresponding duty to compensate. Furthermore, the means as well as the ends of regulation must accord with the owner's reasonable expectations. Here, the State did not act until after the property had been zoned for individual lot development and most other parcels had been improved, throwing the whole burden of the regulation on the remaining lots. This too must be measured in the balance.

With these observations, I concur in the judgment of the Court.

JUSTICE BLACKMUN, dissenting. . . .

I first question the Court's rationale in creating a category that obviates a "case-specific inquiry into the public interest advanced," if all economic value has been lost. If one fact about the Court's taking jurisprudence can be stated without contradiction, it is that "the particular circumstances of each case" determine whether a specific restriction will be rendered invalid by the government's failure to pay compensation. . . .

This Court repeatedly has recognized the ability of government, in certain circumstances, to regulate property without compensation no matter how adverse the financial effect on the owner may be. . . .

These cases rest on the principle that the State has full power to prohibit an owner's use of property if it is harmful to the public. "Since no individual has a right to use his property so as to create a nuisance or otherwise harm others, the State has not 'taken' anything when it asserts its power to enjoin the nuisance-like activity." *Keystone Bituminous Coal*. . . .

Ultimately even the Court cannot embrace the full implications of its per se rule: it eventually agrees that there cannot be a categorical rule for a taking based on economic value that wholly disregards the public need asserted. Instead, the Court decides that it will permit a State to regulate all economic value only if the State prohibits uses that would not be permitted under "background principles of nuisance and property law."

Until today, the Court explicitly had rejected the contention that the government's power to act without paying compensation turns on whether the prohibited activity is a common-law nuisance. . . .

[Common-law] public and private nuisance law is simply a determination whether a particular use causes harm. There is nothing magical in the reasoning of judges long dead. They determined a harm in the same way as state judges and legislatures do today. If judges in the 18th and 19th centuries can distinguish a harm from a benefit, why not judges in the 20th century, and if judges can, why not legislators? There simply is no reason to believe that new interpretations of the hoary common law nuisance doctrine will be particularly "objective" or "value-free." . . .

The Court makes sweeping and, in my view, misguided and unsupported changes in our taking doctrine. While it limits these changes to the most narrow subset of government regulation — those that eliminate all economic value from land — these changes go far beyond what is necessary to secure petitioner Lucas' private benefit. One hopes they do not go beyond the narrow confines the Court assigns them to today.

I dissent.

JUSTICE STEVENS, dissenting. . . .

In addition to lacking support in past decisions, the Court's new rule is wholly arbitrary. A landowner whose property is diminished in value 95% recovers nothing, while an owner whose property is diminished 100% recovers the land's full value. . . .

Moreover, because of the elastic nature of property rights, the Court's new rule will also prove unsound in practice. In response to the rule, courts may define "property" broadly and only rarely find regulations to effect total takings. . . .

The Court's holding today effectively freezes the State's common law, denying the legislature much of its traditional power to revise the law governing the rights and uses of property. Until today, I had thought that we had long abandoned this approach to constitutional law. More than a century ago we recognized that "the great office of statutes is to remedy defects in the common law as they are developed, and to adapt it to the changes of time and circumstances." Munn v. Illinois, 94 U.S. 113, 134 (1877). As Justice Marshall observed about a position similar to that adopted by the Court today: "If accepted, that claim would represent a return to the era of Lochner v. New York, 198 U.S. 45 (1905), when common-law rights were also found immune from revision by State or Federal Government. Such an approach would freeze the common law as it has been constructed by the courts, perhaps at its 19th-century state of development. It would allow no room for change in response to changes in circumstance. The Due Process

Clause does not require such a result." PruneYard Shopping Center v. Robins, 447 U.S. 74, 93 (1980) (concurring opinion).

Arresting the development of the common law is not only a departure from our prior decisions; it is also profoundly unwise. The human condition is one of constant learning and evolution — both moral and practical. Legislatures implement that new learning; in doing so they must often revise the definition of property and the rights of property owners. Thus, when the Nation came to understand that slavery was morally wrong and mandated the emancipation of all slaves, it, in effect, redefined "property." On a lesser scale, our ongoing self-education produces similar changes in the rights of property owners: New appreciation of the significance of endangered species, the importance of wetlands, and the vulnerability of coastal lands, shapes our evolving understandings of property rights.

Of course, some legislative redefinitions of property will effect a taking and must be compensated — but it certainly cannot be the case that every movement away from common law does so. There is no reason, and less sense, in such an absolute rule. We live in a world in which changes in the economy and the environment occur with increasing frequency and importance. If it was wise a century ago to allow Government "the largest legislative discretion" to deal with "the special exigencies of the moment," it is imperative to do so today. The rule that should govern a decision in a case of this kind should focus on the future, not the past. . . .

The Court's categorical approach rule will, I fear, greatly hamper the efforts of local officials and planners who must deal with increasingly complex problems in land-use and environmental regulation. . . .

[Even] assuming that petitioner's property was rendered valueless, the risk inherent in investments of the sort made by petitioner, the generality of the Act, and the compelling purpose motivating the South Carolina Legislature persuade me that the Act did not effect a taking of petitioner's property.

Accordingly, I respectfully dissent.

Note: Lucas, *the Environment, and Regulatory Takings*

1. Lucas's *importance. Lucas* appears to be one of the most important recent cases in the law of takings. But how could anyone object to the idea that compensation is due when government has rendered property completely "valueless"?

Suppose Lucas had owned an additional, contiguous parcel of land that was not controlled by the regulation, so that the regulation did not render his property (consisting of both parcels) completely valueless. What result? What result if the second parcel was not contiguous?

2. *Takings and the common law.* Does the *Lucas* test depend on the common law background or instead on the legal background in general? Suppose the state had said by statute, *before* Lucas purchased the property, that certain lands must not be developed in order to promote tourism and protect flora and fauna. Would the result be different? If it would be different, has the takings clause allowed the government to do basically whatever it wants through the simple redefinition of property rights?

3. *Defining the property taken.* How can we tell if property has been rendered valueless? In footnote 7, the Court suggests that the answer depends on how one defines the property; hence, it might be sufficient if 90 percent of the property is rendered valueless. But if this is right, does it follow that *Lucas* is not really limited to cases of complete valuelessness? Does footnote 7 adequately deal with the questions raised by contemporary understandings of property not as a "thing," but as a bundle of rights?

4. *Sources of property rights.* There is a large question in the background: Where do property rights come from? Sometimes it is said that property rights come from "the state," which defines them; people who say this say that government can define property rights however it wishes. Such people might acknowledge that the takings clause requires compensation, but only if the state has changed the law after the time of purchase. Other people think that there are limits on how the state can define property rights, and that states cannot, for example, limit ownership in ways that go very far beyond the law of nuisance. How would this debate be resolved?

5. *Governmental responsibilities and takings theory.* The Court has yet to supply a full response to the underlying question: Why shouldn't the government pay compensation whenever its acts have diminished the value of property? By now we should have the ingredients of a possible three-part answer: (1) Government does not tax people for the gains, in the form of (for example) safer water or increased property values, that are brought about by government action. (2) A requirement of compensation for losses would require large administrative expense, in the form not just of payouts but also of costs in identifying losers and deciding how much they have lost. (3) Because of (1) and (2), a requirement of universal compensation for losses could stop the government from doing things that it really should do. With a compensation requirement, government might not, for example, issue desirable clean air and clean water regulations because it would have to pay a lot of money to the losers, because the administrative costs would be high, and because it could not recoup from the many gainers. If this argument is persuasive, we might see the Court as struggling with this basic question: When are considerations (1), (2), and (3) relatively weak so as to justify a compensation requirement? Aren't those considerations indeed weak in *Lucas*?

It should be clear that the Supreme Court is not terribly well equipped to make case-by-case inquiries into the underlying questions, which turn on complex factual assessments. If so, perhaps the Court has underenforced the takings clause just because it knows so little. But perhaps government generally faces a larger responsibility. Consider in this regard legislative proposals, in Congress and the states, providing for compensation whenever government action has reduced the value of property by 10 percent, or 20 percent, or some such figure. Why aren't such measures an excellent response to government's judicially underenforced responsibilities? What good arguments are available to environmentalists concerned about such proposals? Consider the following argument: (a) it may be costly to identify and compensate the losers under the relevant regulations; (b) government does not capture the external benefits of such] regulations, since it imposes no tax on those whose values increase as a result; (c) because of (a) and (b), the consequence of a compensation requirement may be to lead the government not to engage in desirable regulation.

VII

Freedom of Expression

A. INTRODUCTION

The first amendment provides that "Congress shall make no law [abridging] the freedom of speech, or of the press; or the right of the people peaceably to assemble, and to petition the Government for a redress of grievances." Consider Justice Black's position: "The phrase 'Congress shall make no law' is composed of plain words, easily understood. [The] language [is] absolute. [Of] course the decision to provide a constitutional safeguard for [free speech] involves a balancing of conflicting interests. [But] the Framers themselves did this balancing when they wrote the [Constitution]. Courts have neither the right nor the power [to] make a different [evaluation]." Black, The Bill of Rights, 35 N.Y.U. L. Rev. 865, 874, 879 (1960).

The Court has never accepted Black's view. Rather, it has consistently held that "abridging" and "the freedom of speech" require interpretation, and that restraints on free expression may be "permitted for appropriate reasons." Elrod v. Burns, 427 U.S. 347, 360 (1976). This section examines two sources that might aid interpretation: the history and philosophy underlying the first amendment.

Note: The History of Free Expression

1. *The English background.* The notion that government "shall make no law [abridging] the freedom of speech, or of the press" received only gradual acceptance in Anglo-American law. Indeed, throughout much of English history the crown and Parliament attempted vigorously to suppress opinions deemed pernicious. Three forms of restraint were most commonly employed: the licensing of the press; the doctrine of constructive treason; and the law of seditious libel.

a. *Licensing.* The invention of printing greatly magnified the danger posed by "undesirable" opinions, and shortly after the first book was printed in England in 1476, the crown claimed an authority to control printing presses as a right of prerogative. The manuscript of any work intended for publication had to be submitted to crown officials empowered to censor objectionable passages and to approve or deny a license for the printing of the work. Anything published without an imprimatur was criminal. This system of "prior restraint" remained in effect until 1694, when the authorizing legislation expired and was not renewed. The decision not to renew licensing resulted not from any commitment to free expression but rather from considerations of expediency, for licensing had proved ineffective, difficult to enforce, and conducive to bribery. See generally L. Levy, Emergence of a Free Press ch. 1 (1985); F. Siebert, Freedom of the Press in England, 1476-1776 chs. 2-3, 6-12 (1952).

b. *Constructive treason.* The law of treason in England derived from the statute 25 Edward III (1352), which defined the crime as (1) compassing or imagining the king's death, (2) levying war against the king, or (3) adhering to his enemies. During the latter part of the seventeenth century, the English judges ruled that mere written or printed matter, as well as overt acts, could constitute treason. John Twyn was the first printer to suffer under this extension of the law of treason. Government officers searched Twyn's home and seized the proofs of a book suggesting that the king was accountable to the people, and that the people were entitled to self-governance. Twyn was convicted of constructive treason, hanged, drawn, and quartered.

Although constructive treason was invoked in only a few cases, the doctrine posed a serious threat to freedom of expression, for the few instances in which conviction and execution occurred served to remind potential publishers of the fate that awaited those who violated the law. The doctrine was abandoned after 1720 because juries were often reluctant to convict, the death penalty was in many cases considered too drastic, and the procedure was too detailed. See generally Siebert, supra, at 265-269.

c. *Seditious libel.* The doctrine of seditious libel first entered Anglo-American jurisprudence in a 1275 statute outlawing "any false news or tales whereby discord or occasion of discord or slander may grow between the king and his people or the great men of the realm." Violations were punished by the king's council sitting in the "starred chamber." The point of departure for the modern law of seditious libel was Sir Edward Coke's report of a Star Chamber case of 1606, which stated three central propositions: (1) A libel against a private person may be punished criminally because it may provoke revenge and thus cause a breach of the peace. (2) A libel against a government official is an even greater offense, "for it concerns not only the breach of the peace, but also the scandal of government." (3) Although the essence of the crime as fixed by the statute of 1275 was the falsity of the libel, even a true libel may be criminally punished.

The theory underlying seditious libel was explained by Chief Justice Holt in 1704: "If people should not be called to account for possessing the people with an ill opinion of the government, no government can subsist. For it is very necessary for all governments that the people should have a good opinion of it." Rex v. Tutchin, 14 Howell's State Trials 1095, 1128 (1704). Thus, a true libel is especially dangerous, for unlike a false libel, the dangers of truthful criticism cannot be defused by disproof. It was thus an oft-quoted maxim after 1606 that "the greater the truth the greater the libel."

In practice, then, seventeenth-century judges punished as seditious libel any "written censure upon any public man whatever for any conduct whatever, or upon any law or institution whatever." 2 J. Stephen, A History of the Criminal

Law of England 350 (1883). As one commentator has observed, "no single method of restricting the press was as effective as the law of seditious libel as it was developed and applied by the common-law courts in the latter part of the seventeenth century." Siebert, supra, at 269. For general discussion, see Hamburger, The Development of the Law of Seditious Libel and the Control of the Press, 37 Stan. L. Rev. 661 (1985).

In 1769, Blackstone summarized the law as follows:

> The liberty of the press [consists] in laying no *previous* restraints upon publications, and not in freedom from censure for criminal matter when published. [To] subject the press to the restrictive power of a licenser [is] to subject all freedom of sentiment to the prejudices of one man, and make him the arbitrary and infallible judge of all controverted points in learning, religion, and government. But to punish (as the law does at present) any dangerous or offensive writings, which, when published, shall on a fair and impartial trial be adjudged of a pernicious tendency, is necessary for the preservation of peace and good order, of government and religion, the only solid foundations of civil liberty.

4 W. Blackstone, Commentaries on the Laws of England *151-152.

2. *The colonial background.* The image of colonial America as a society in which freedom of expression was cherished seems largely inaccurate. Although colonial America was the scene of extraordinary diversity of opinion on religion, politics, social structure, and other subjects, each community "tended to be a tight little island clutching its own respective orthodoxy and [eager] to banish or extralegally punish unwelcome dissidents." Levy, supra, at 16.

Formal legal restraints on expression, however, were relatively rare. Licensing expired in 1725, and although there were hundreds of trials for seditious libel in England during the seventeenth and eighteenth centuries, there were not more than half a dozen such cases in colonial America. The most famous of these trials involved the prosecution of John Peter Zenger in New York in 1735. Zenger, publisher of the New York Weekly Journal, was charged with seditious libel by the Governor General of New York, whom he had criticized. Zenger argued unsuccessfully to the judge that the truth of the libel should be an absolute defense. The jury, responding to the popularity of Zenger's cause, disregarded the judge's instructions and returned a verdict of not guilty.

Although common law prosecutions for seditious libel were rare, the popularly elected colonial assemblies, imitating Parliament, assumed and vigorously exercised the power to summarily punish "seditious" expression. Any criticism of an assembly or its members was likely to be regarded as a seditious scandal against the government punishable as a "breach of privilege." Levy, supra, at 14. To cite just one example, James Franklin, the older brother of Ben, ran a brief notice in his New England Courant that the government was preparing a ship to pursue coastal pirates "sometime this month, wind and weather permitting." The insinuation that the government was not dealing effectively with the pirates angered Massachusetts's popularly elected assembly. Franklin was arrested, and after a pro forma hearing, the assembly resolved that he had committed "a High affront to this Government." Franklin was imprisoned for the remainder of the session.

3. *The first amendment.* Scholars have long puzzled over the actual intentions of the framers of the first amendment. The primary dispute is over whether the framers intended to adopt the Blackstonian view — that freedom of speech con-

sists entirely in the freedom from prior restraints — or whether they intended some broader meaning. Consider the following views.

a. Z. Chafee, Free Speech in the United States 18-20 (1941):

If we [consider] what mischief in the existing law the [framers] wished to [remedy], we can be sure that it was not [licensing]. This had expired in England in 1695, and in the colonies by 1725. [There] was no need to go to all the trouble of pushing through a constitutional amendment just to settle an issue that had been dead for decades. What the framers did have plenty of reason to fear was an entirely different danger to political writers and speakers. For years the government here and in England had substituted for [licensing] rigorous and repeated prosecutions for seditious libel [and] for years these prosecutions were opposed by liberal opinion and popular agitation. [Two] different views of the relation of rulers and people were in conflict. According to one view, the rulers were the superiors of the people, and therefore must not be subjected to any censure that would tend to diminish their authority. [According] to the other view, the rulers were agents and servants of the people, who might therefore find fault with their servants and discuss questions of their punishment or dismissal, and of governmental policy. [In] the United States the people and not the government possess the absolute sovereignty, and [government is thus not free to punish seditious libel. Indeed, one] "of the objects of the Revolution was to get rid of the English common law on liberty of speech and of the press."

b. Levy, supra, at xii-xv:

[The proposition has been conventionally accepted] that it was the intent of the American Revolution or the Framers of the First Amendment to abolish the common law of seditious libel. [The] evidence suggests that the proposition is suppositious and unprovable. [We] may even have to confront the possibility that the intentions of the Framers were not the most [libertarian]. But this should be expected because the Framers were nurtured on the crabbed historicism of Coke and the narrow conservatism of Blackstone, as well as Zenger's case. The ways of thought of a lifetime are not easily broken. The Declaration of Independence severed the political connection with England but the American states continued the English common-law system except as explicitly rejected by statute. If the Revolution produced any radical libertarians on the meaning of freedom of speech and press, they were not present at the Constitutional Convention or the First Congress, which drafted the Bill of Rights. Scholars and judges have betrayed a penchant for what John P. Roche called "retrospective symmetry," by giving to present convictions a patriotic lineage and tradition — in this case, the fatherhood of the "Framers."

For critical analyses of this view, see D. Rabban, Free Speech in Its Forgotten Years (1997); Rabban, An Ahistorical Historian: Leonard Levy on Freedom of Expression in Early American History, 37 Stan. L. Rev. 795 (1985); Mayton, From a Legacy of Suppression to the "Metaphor of the Fourth Estate," 39 Stan. L. Rev. 139 (1986).

4. *The relevance of history.* To what extent, if any, is the preceding history relevant to interpretation of the first amendment? Is the English common law important because it was what the framers rejected or because it was what they accepted? Is it plausible that states that themselves punished seditious libel intended to prohibit Congress from punishing it? And given the enormous changes in the media and politics since the adoption of the first amendment, to what ex-

tent, if any, should the intent of the framers control the contemporary resolution of first amendment issues?

5. *The Sedition Act of 1798.* The first serious challenge to freedom of expression in the United States came with the Sedition Act of 1798. Act of July 14, 1798, 1 Stat. 596. The United States was on the verge of war with France, and many of the ideas generated by the French Revolution aroused fear and hostility in segments of the U.S. population. A bitter political and philosophical debate raged between the Federalists, then in power, and the Republicans.

Against this backdrop, the Federalists enacted the Sedition Act of 1798. The act prohibited the publication of

> false, scandalous, and malicious writing or writings against the government of the United States, or either house of the Congress of the United States, or the President of the United States, with intent to defame [them]; or to bring them [into] contempt or disrepute; or to excite against them [the] hatred of the good people of the United States, or to stir up sedition within the United States, or to excite any unlawful combinations therein, for opposing or resisting any law of the United States, or any [lawful] act of the President of the United States.

The act provided further that truth would be a good defense and that malicious intent was an element of the crime. Thus, as the Federalists emphasized, the act eliminated those particular aspects of the English common law that had been the focus of attack on both sides of the Atlantic during the eighteenth century. See Levy, supra, at xi.

The Sedition Act was vigorously enforced but only against members or supporters of the Republican Party. Prosecutions were brought against the four leading Republican newspapers. The cases, often tried before openly hostile Federalist judges, resulted in ten convictions and no acquittals. Moreover, in the hands of these judges, the procedural reforms of the act proved largely illusory.

Consider, for example, the plight of Matthew Lyon, a Republican congressman from Vermont. During his reelection campaign, Lyon published an article in which he attacked the Adams administration, asserting that under President Adams "every consideration of the public welfare [was] swallowed up in a continual grasp for power, in an unbounded thirst for ridiculous pomp, foolish adulation, and selfish avarice." At Lyon's trial, the judge instructed the jury to find malicious intent unless the statement "could have been uttered with any other intent than that of making odious or contemptible the President and the government, and bringing them both into disrepute." And although Lyon was technically free to prove the "truth" of his statement in his defense, this was hardly possible, given the nature of the statement. Lyon was convicted and sentenced to a fine of $1,000 and four months in prison. The Federalist press rejoiced, but Lyon became an instant martyr and was reelected while in jail. See Trial of Matthew Lyon, in F. Wharton, State Trials 333 (1849).

The Supreme Court did not rule on the constitutionality of the Sedition Act at the time. It was upheld without dissent, however, by the lower federal courts and by three Supreme Court justices sitting on circuit. The act expired of its own force on March 3, 1801. President Jefferson thereafter pardoned all those who had been convicted under the act, and Congress eventually repaid most of the fines. It is generally agreed that the act was a factor in the defeat of the Federalists in the election of 1800. Significant cases under the Sedition Act are printed in Wharton, supra. The story of the enforcement of the act is told briefly and with liveliness in J. Miller, Crisis in Freedom (1951). A more detailed account is given in J. M. Smith, Freedom's Fetters (1956). What is the significance of the fact that the Sedition Act was approved by many of the same people who had earlier approved the first amendment?

6. *From the Sedition Act of 1798 to the Espionage Act of 1917.* The Supreme Court did not directly consider the first amendment's guarantee of free expression until Congress enacted the Espionage Act of 1917 at the outset of World War I. See section B1 infra. This is not to say, however, that controversies over free speech did not arise in the 120 years between the Sedition Act of 1798 and the Espionage Act of 1917. See generally R. Nye, Fettered Freedom (1949) (examining the efforts of southern states to suppress abolitionist literature); J. Randall, Constitutional Problems under Lincoln (1926); Curtis, The Curious History of Attempts to Suppress Antislavery Speech, Press, and Petition in 1835-37, 89 Nw. U.L. Rev. 785 (1995); Curtis, The 1837 Killing of Elijah Lovejoy by an Anti-Abolition Mob: Free Speech, Mobs, Republican Government, and the Privileges of American Citizens, 44 UCLA L. Rev. 1109 (1997); Rabban, The First Amendment in Its Forgotten Years, 90 Yale L.J. 514 (1981) (examining academic and judicial thought about free expression prior to 1919); Rabban, The IWW Free Speech Fights and Popular Conceptions of Free Expression before World War I, 80 Va. L. Rev. 1055 (1994).

Note: The Philosophy of Free Expression

"Intuition at first may suggest that an individual ought to have more freedom to speak than he has liberty in other areas. There would seem to be some truth in the adage, 'sticks and stones can break my bones, but words will never hurt me.' Yet speech often hurts. It can offend, injure reputation, fan prejudice or passion, and ignite the world. Moreover, a great deal of other conduct that the state regulates has less harmful potential." Wellington, On Freedom of Expression, 88 Yale L.J. 1105, 1106-1107 (1979). Why, then, should expression have greater immunity from government regulation than most other forms of human conduct? Why should society prohibit the making of any law "abridging the freedom of speech"?

1. *Search for truth: the "marketplace of ideas."* The search for truth rationale for the protection of free expression rests on the premise that "when men have realized that time has upset many fighting faiths, they may come to believe even more than they believe the very foundations of their own conduct that the ultimate good desired is better reached by free trade in ideas — that the best test of truth is the power of the thought to get itself accepted in the competition of the market, and that truth is the only ground upon which their wishes safely can be carried out." Abrams v. United States, 250 U.S. 616, 630 (1919) (Holmes, J., dissenting).

The search for truth rationale was first fully enunciated by John Stuart Mill in On Liberty (1859):

[The] peculiar evil of silencing the expression of an opinion is, that it is robbing the human race; posterity as well as the existing generation; those who dissent from the opinion, still more than those who hold it. . . .

First: the opinion which it is attempted to suppress [may] be true. Those who desire to suppress it [are] not infallible. They have no authority to decide the question for all mankind, and exclude every other person from the means of judging. [Of course, it is not the case] that truth always triumphs over persecution. [But the] real advantage which truth has [is] that when an opinion is true, it may be extinguished once, twice, or many times, but in the course of ages there will generally be found persons to rediscover it, until [eventually] it has made such head as to withstand all subsequent attempts to suppress it. . . .

[Second: the received opinion may be true. But however true an opinion] may be, if it is not fully, frequently, and fearlessly discussed, it will be held as a dead dogma, not a living truth. [He] who knows only his own side of the case, knows little of that. [Even if] the received opinion [is] true, a conflict with the opposite error is essential to a clear apprehension and deep feeling of its truth. . . .

[Finally,] the conflicting doctrines, instead of being one true and the other false, [may] share the truth between them; and the nonconforming opinion [may be] needed to supply the remainder of the truth, of which the received doctrine embodies only a part. [Every] opinion which embodies somewhat of the portion of truth which the common opinion omits, ought to be considered precious.

Consider the following observations.
a. Baker, Scope of the First Amendment Freedom of Speech, 25 UCLA L. Rev. 964, 974-978 (1978):

[The] hope that the marketplace leads to truth, or even to the best or most desirable decision, [is] implausible. [First, experience as well as discussion contributes to understanding. Thus,] restrictions on experience-generating conduct are as likely as restrictions on [debate] to stunt the progressive development of understanding, [but the marketplace theory gives no] constitutional protection [to] experience-producing conduct. [Second, the marketplace theory assumes] that people [use] their rational capacities to eliminate distortion caused by the form and frequency of message presentation. [This] assumption cannot be accepted. Emotional or "irrational" appeals have great [impact]. [Finally, in practice,] the marketplace of ideas appears improperly biased in favor of presently dominant groups.

b. Greenawalt, Free Speech Justifications, 89 Colum. L. Rev. 119, 135-136 (1989):

The critical question is not how well truth will advance absolutely in conditions of freedom, but how well it will advance in conditions of freedom as compared with some alternative set of conditions. Suppose one were highly pessimistic about the capacity of people to ascertain important kinds of truths, but believed that governments that suppress ideas almost always manage to promote [falsehoods]. One might then support freedom of speech as less damaging to truth than an alternative social practice. One's overall judgment on this subject must depend on a delicate judgment about people's responses to claimed truth, about the effects of inequality of private power over what is communicated, and about the soundness of government determinations about valid ideas.

c. Wellington, supra, at 1130-1132:

In the long run, true ideas do tend to drive out false ones. The problem is that the short run may be very long, that one short run follows hard upon another, and that we may become overwhelmed by the inexhaustible supply of freshly minted, often very seductive, false ideas. [Moreover,] most of us do believe that the book is closed on some issues. Genocide is an example. [Truth] may win, and in the long run it may almost always win, but millions of Jews were deliberately and systematically murdered in a very short period of time. [Before] those murders occurred, many individuals must have come "to have false beliefs."

2. *Self-governance.* The self-governance rationale is most closely identified with the work of Alexander Meiklejohn:

[The] Constitution [ordains] that all authority to exercise control, to determine common action, belongs to "We, the People." [Under this system, free men are governed] by themselves. [What,] then, does the First Amendment forbid? [The] town meeting suggests an answer. That meeting is called to discuss and, on the basis of such discussion, to decide matters of public policy. [The] voters, therefore, must be made as wise as possible. [And] this, in turn, requires that so far as time allows, all facts and interests relevant to the problem shall be fully and fairly presented to the meeting [so] that all the alternative lines of action can be wisely measured in relation to one another. . . .

The First Amendment, then, is not the guardian of unregulated talkativeness. It does not require that, on every occasion, every citizen shall take part in public debate. [Rather,] the vital point, as stated negatively, is that no suggestion of policy shall be denied a hearing because it is on one side of the issue rather than another. [Citizens] may not be barred [from speaking] because their views are thought to be false or dangerous. [The] reason for this equality of status in the field of ideas lies deep in the very foundation of the self-governing process. When men govern themselves, it is they — and no one else — who must pass judgment upon unwisdom and unfairness and danger. [Just] so far as, at any point, the citizens who are to decide an issue are denied acquaintance with information or opinion [which] is relevant to that issue, just so far the result must be ill-considered. [It] is that mutilation of the thinking process of the community against which the First Amendment [is] directed. The principle of the freedom of speech [is] not a Law of Nature or of Reason in the abstract. It is a deduction from the basic American agreement that public issues shall be decided by universal suffrage. [Thus,] the unlimited guarantee of the freedom of public discussion, which is given by the First Amendment, [protects the speech] of a citizen who is planning for the general welfare.

A. Meiklejohn, Free Speech and Its Relation to Self-Government 15-16, 24-27, 39 (1948).
Consider the following observations.
a. Chafee, Book Review, 62 Harv. L. Rev. 891, 899-900 (1949):

The most serious weakness in Mr. Meiklejohn's argument is that it rests on his supposed boundary between public speech and private speech. That line is extremely blurred. [The] truth is that there are public aspects to practically every subject. [Moreover, if Mr. Meiklejohn's public speech excludes scholarship,] art and literature, it is shocking to deprive these vital matters of the protection of [the] First Amendment. [Valuable] as self-government is, it is in itself only a small part of our lives. That a philosopher should subordinate all other activities to it is indeed surprising.

b. Meiklejohn's response:

The First Amendment [protects] the freedom of those activities of thought and communication by which we "govern." [But] voting is merely the external expression of a wide and diverse number of activities by means of which citizens attempt to meet the responsibilities of making judgments, which that freedom to govern lays upon them. [Self-government] can exist only insofar as the voters acquire the intelligence, integrity, sensitivity, and generous devotion to the general welfare that, in theory, casting a ballot is assumed to express. [Thus,] there are many forms of thought and expression within the range of human communications from which the voter derives the [necessary] knowledge, intelligence, [and] sensitivity to human values. [These], too, must suffer no abridgment of their freedom. [These include:] 1. Education, in all its phases. [2.] The achievements of philosophy and the sciences. [3.] Literature and the arts. [4.] Public discussions of public issues.

Meiklejohn, The First Amendment Is an Absolute, 1961 Sup. Ct. Rev. 245, 255-257.
    c. Bork, Neutral Principles and Some First Amendment Problems, 47 Ind. L.J. 1, 26-28 (1971):

Professor Alexander Meiklejohn seems correct when he says: "The First Amendment [protects] the freedom of those activities of thought and communication by which we 'govern.'" [But Meiklejohn goes] further and would extend the protection of the first amendment beyond speech that is explicitly political. [I disagree.] [There is, of course,] an analogy between criticism of official behavior and the publication of a novel like Ulysses, for the latter may form attitudes that ultimately affect politics. But it is an analogy, not an identity. Other human activities and experiences also form personality, teach and create attitudes just as much as does the novel, but no one would on that account [suggest] that the first amendment strikes down regulations of economic activity, control of entry into trade, laws about sexual behavior, marriage and the like. Yet these activities, in their capacity to create attitudes that ultimately impinge upon the political process, are more like literature and science than literature and science are like political speech. If the dialectical progression is not to become an analogical stampede, the protection of the first amendment must be cut off when it reaches the outer limits of political speech. [The] notion that all valuable types of speech must be protected by the first amendment confuses the constitutionality of laws with their wisdom. Freedom of nonpolitical speech rests, as does freedom for other valuable forms of behavior, upon the enlightenment of society and its elected representatives.

See also C. Sunstein, Democracy and the Problem of Free Speech (1993); Sunstein, Free Speech Now, 59 U. Chi. L. Rev. 255 (1992) ("the First Amendment is principally about political deliberation").
    d. Redish, The Value of Free Speech, 130 U. Pa. L. Rev. 591, 601, 604 (1982):

Bork and Meiklejohn [never] attempt to ascertain what basic value or values the democratic process was designed to serve. [Our nation adopted] a democratic system [because of] an implicit belief in the worth of the individual. [Political] democracy is merely a means to — or, in another sense, a logical outgrowth of — the much broader value of individual self-realization. [Bork] and Meiklejohn [have] confused one means of obtaining the ultimate value with the value itself. [The] appropriate scope of the first amendment protection is [thus] much broader than

Bork or Meiklejohn would have it. Free speech aids all life-affecting decisionmaking, no matter how personally limited, in much the same manner in which it aids the political process. [There] thus is no logical basis for distinguishing the role speech plays in the political process.

3. *Self-fulfillment and autonomy.* There are several versions of the self-fulfillment and autonomy rationales.

a. Richards, Free Speech and Obscenity Law: Toward a Moral Theory of the First Amendment, 123 U. Pa. L. Rev. 45, 62 (1974):

[People] are not to be constrained to communicate or not to communicate, to believe or not to believe, to associate or not to associate. The value placed on this cluster of ideas derives from the notion of self-respect that comes from a mature person's full and untrammelled exercise of capacities central to human rationality. Thus, the significance of free expression rests on the central human capacity to create and express symbolic systems, such as speech, writing, pictures, and [music]. Freedom of expression permits and encourages the exercise of these [capacities]. In so doing, it nurtures and sustains the self-respect of the mature person. [The] value of free expression, in this view, rests on its deep relation to self-respect arising from autonomous self-determination without which the life of the spirit is meager and slavish.

b. Scanlon, A Theory of Freedom of Expression, 1 Phil. & Pub. Aff. 204, 213-218 (1972):

[T]he powers of a state are limited to those that citizens could recognize while still regarding themselves as equal, autonomous, rational agents. [To] regard himself as autonomous [a] person must see himself as sovereign in deciding what to believe and in weighing competing reasons for action. [An] autonomous person cannot accept without independent consideration the judgment of others as to what he should believe or what he should do. [Thus,] autonomous citizens [could] not regard themselves as being under an "obligation" to believe the decrees of the state to be correct, nor could they concede to the state the right to have its decrees obeyed without deliberation, [and the] harm of coming to have false beliefs is not one that an autonomous man could allow the state to protect him against through restrictions on expression. For [if] a [person] authorized the state to protect him in this [way, he would necessarily have to bind] himself to accept the state's judgment about which views were false.

Consider the following observations:
c. Bork, supra, at 25:

[The self-fulfillment/autonomy rationale does] not distinguish speech from any other human activity. An individual may develop his faculties or derive pleasure from trading on the stock market, [working] as a barmaid, engaging in sexual activity, [or] in any of thousands of other endeavors. Speech [can] be preferred to other activities [on the basis of this rationale] only by ranking forms of personal gratification. [One] cannot, on neutral grounds, choose to protect speech [on this basis] more than [one] protects any other claimed freedom.

d. Scanlon, Freedom of Expression and Categories of Expression, 40 U. Pitt. L. Rev. 519, 532-533 (1979):

[Is my original theory] correct? I now think that it is not. To begin with, [my theory] has what seem to be implausible consequences in some cases. For example, it is hard to see how laws against deceptive advertising [could] be squared with this principle. [My theory embodies] a rejection of paternalism that is too strong and too sweeping to be plausible. [Moreover], the problems of the [theory] are not limited to cases of justified paternalism. The [theory] is appealing because it protects important [interests] in deciding for one's self what to believe and what reasons to act on. [But these] interests depend not only on freedom of expression, but also on other forms of access to [information]. Why should we be willing to bear unlimited costs to allow expression to flourish [when we are unwilling to extend this immunity to other sources of information — such as experience — that "enhance our decision-making capacity"]?

4. *Other rationales.* Although courts and commentators have focused primarily on the search for truth, self-governance, and self-fulfillment/autonomy rationales for the protection of free expression, two further rationales merit note.

a. *The checking value.* Consider Blasi, The Checking Value in First Amendment Theory, 1977 Am. B. Found. Res. J. 521, 527-542:

[Another rationale for the protection of free expression] is the value that free speech [can] serve in checking the abuse of power by public officials. [The] central premise of the checking value is that the abuse of official power is an especially serious evil [because of government's unique] capacity to employ legitimized violence. [The] government's monopoly of legitimized violence means [that the] check on government must come from the power of public opinion. [Thus,] the checking value grows out of democratic theory, but it is the democratic theory of John Locke [and] not that of Alexander Meiklejohn. Under [this] view of democracy, the role of the ordinary citizen is not so much to contribute on a continuing basis to the formation of public policy as to retain a veto power to be employed when the decisions of officials pass certain bounds.

b. *The tolerant society.* Consider L. Bollinger, The Tolerant Society: Freedom of Speech and Extremist Speech in America 9-10, 107 (1986):

[While] free speech theory has traditionally focused on the value of the protected activity (speech), [the theory offered here] seeks a justification by looking at the disvalue of the [frequently intolerant] response to that activity. [The] rationality and wisdom of choosing the course of tolerance can be derived from a neglected insight — namely, that the problematic feelings evoked [by] speech activity are precisely the same kinds of feelings evoked by a myriad of interactions in the society, not the least of which are the reactions we take toward nonspeech behavior. [The free speech principle] involves a special act of carving out one area of social interaction for extraordinary self-restraint, the purpose of which is to develop and demonstrate a social capacity to control feelings evoked by a host of social encounters. [The free speech principle is thus] concerned with nothing less than helping to shape the intellectual character of the society.

For a further elaboration of this view, see Bollinger, The Tolerant Society: A Response to Critics, 90 Colum. L. Rev. 979 (1990).

5. *Philosophy and the first amendment.* To what extent, if any, are these rationales for the protection of free expression relevant to interpretation of the first amendment? Consider Bloustein, The Origin, Validity, and Interrelationships of

the Political Values Served by Freedom of Expression, 33 Rutgers L. Rev. 372, 381 (1981): "[There] is no evidence [that these rationales were] discussed or debated during the period of the drafting and adoption of the [first] amendment [and we may thus conclude] that whatever validity and authority they may have do *not* derive directly from the intentions of the drafters." Whence, then, do the validity and authority of these rationales derive? Is it sufficient that they flow "readily" from "general advocacy, descriptions, and discussions of political individualism and democracy"?

To what extent do these rationales, if relevant to interpretation of the first amendment, provide a coherent and workable basis for the decision of actual cases? Note that in some instances it may be necessary to choose among the competing rationales. For example, the self-fulfillment/autonomy rationale does not support a distinction between political and nonpolitical expression, whereas the self-governance theory seems to compel that distinction. Despite such potential conflicts, most commentators agree that any "adequate conception of freedom of speech must [draw] upon several strands of theory in order to protect a rich variety of expressional modes." L. Tribe, American Constitutional Law 789 (2d ed. 1988). As one commentator has observed, in the "democratic state," which "is founded on a tradition of free inquiry," the "attainment of knowledge," the "consensual participation in government," and the "dignity of self-expression" are "so interdependent that they really represent three aspects [of] a single value; their relationships define a kind of culture, embracing the individual, the state, and the system of knowledge, art and other such values that we call liberal." Bloustein, supra, at 395.

Note: Organization

The remaining sections in this chapter explore the Supreme Court's interpretation of the first amendment's guarantee of free speech, press, assembly, and petition. These sections are structured in accord with two distinctions that have played a central role in the Court's analysis. First, there is the distinction between content-based and content-neutral restrictions. Content-based restrictions restrict communication because of the message conveyed. Laws prohibiting the publication of "confidential" information, forbidding the hiring of teachers who advocate the violent overthrow of government, or banning the display of the swastika in certain neighborhoods illustrate this type of restriction. Content-neutral restrictions, on the other hand, restrict communication without regard to the message conveyed. Laws prohibiting noisy speeches near a hospital, banning the erection of billboards in residential communities, or requiring the disclosure of the names of all leafleteers are examples. The Court has generally employed different standards to test the constitutionality of these two types of restrictions.

Second, there is the distinction within the realm of content-based restrictions between "high" and "low" value expression. The Court has long adhered to the view that there are certain categories of expression that do not appreciably further the values underlying the first amendment. Examples are obscenity, commercial advertising, and false statements of fact. The Court has traditionally held that such categories of expression are either unprotected or only marginally protected by the first amendment.

In line with these distinctions, sections B and C focus primarily on government efforts to suppress "high" value speech; section D explores "low" value expression; section E examines content-neutral restrictions and the problem of content-neutrality generally; and section F explores the "freedom of the press." The point of this structure is not to insulate these distinctions from challenge. It is rather to illuminate the Court's jurisprudence while at the same time facilitating critical scrutiny of the Court's analysis.

B.   CONTENT-BASED RESTRICTIONS: DANGEROUS IDEAS AND INFORMATION

In what circumstances, if any, may government, consonant with the first amendment, restrict speech because the expression of particular ideas or items of information might cause some harm to government, to private individuals, or to society in general? In addressing this question, this section examines four separate, but related, problems: expression that may induce hearers or listeners to engage in unlawful conduct; expression that "threatens" harm to others; expression that provokes a hostile audience response; and expression that discloses confidential information. In its effort to deal with these problems, the Court has struggled to identify the relevant considerations. The task is not easy. How serious must the harm be before speech may be suppressed? How likely must the harm be? How imminent must it be? Should it matter whether the speaker intended to cause the harm? Can these and other considerations be integrated into a single, coherent standard?

1.   *Expression That Induces Unlawful Conduct*

The question whether government may constitutionally restrict expression because it might persuade, incite, or otherwise "cause" readers or listeners to engage in unlawful conduct has long absorbed the Court's attention. This was the first issue of first amendment interpretation to capture the Court's sustained interest, and the debate within the Court over this question has produced some of the most powerful and most eloquent opinions in the Court's history. That the question has played so central a role in the evolution of first amendment theory is not surprising, for it focuses on government efforts to restrict advocacy in many respects similar to the traditional concept of seditious libel and thus implicates values at the very core of the first amendment.

The Supreme Court first confronted this issue in a series of cases concerning agitation against the war and the draft during World War I. Such agitation was not uncommon:

> [When] the U.S. first entered the war, [many] influential groups of people were apathetic if not actually hostile to fighting. [Organizations] which identified themselves as against the war, [such as the Socialist Party of America], made strong gains during 1917 [and] over three hundred thirty thousand draft evaders or delinquents were reported during the war. [Antiwar] sentiment did not pose a threat of revolu-

tion or violence, but it did pose a threat of spreading disaffection which could paralyze the war effort. [Attorney] General Thomas Gregory, referring to war opponents in November, 1917, stated, "May God have mercy on them, for they need expect none from an outraged people and an avenging government."

R. Goldstein, Political Repression in Modern America 105-108 (1978).

Two months after our entry into the First World War, Congress enacted the Espionage Act of 1917. Although the act was directed primarily toward such matters as actual espionage and the protection of military secrets, the third section of title I of the act made it a crime when the nation is at war for any person (1) willfully to "make or convey false reports or false statements with intent to interfere" with the military success of the United States or "to promote the success of its enemies"; (2) willfully to "cause or attempt to cause insubordination, disloyalty, mutiny, or refusal of duty, in the military or naval forces of the United States"; or (3) willfully to "obstruct the recruiting or enlistment service of the United States." Violations were punishable by fines of up to $10,000, prison sentences of up to twenty years, or both. Act of June 15, 1917, ch. 30, tit. I, §3, 40 Stat. 219.

Eleven months later, Congress enacted the Sedition Act of 1918. The 1918 act, which was repealed in 1921, made it criminal, among other things, for any person to say anything with intent to obstruct the sale of war bonds; to utter, print, write, or publish any disloyal, profane, scurrilous, or abusive language intended to cause contempt or scorn for the form of government of the United States, the Constitution, or the flag; to urge the curtailment of production of war materials with the intent of hindering the war effort; or to utter any words supporting the cause of any country at war with the United States or opposing the cause of the United States. Act of May 16, 1918, ch. 75, §1, 40 Stat. 553.

During the war years, federal authorities initiated approximately 2,000 prosecutions under these acts. Most of these prosecutions were brought under the 1917 statute. The opinions that follow represent three distinct analyses of the issue.

SHAFFER v. UNITED STATES, 255 F. 886 (9th Cir. 1919). Shaffer was convicted of violating the Espionage Act of 1917. The indictment alleged that Shaffer had mailed a book, The Finished Mystery, which contained several "treasonable, disloyal, and seditious utterances," specifying the following passages in particular:

> Standing opposite to these Satan has placed [a] certain delusion which is best described by the word patriotism, but which in reality is murder, the spirit of the very devil. [If] you say it is a war of defense against wanton and intolerable aggression, I must reply that [it] has yet to be proved that Germany has any intention or desire of attacking us. [The] war itself is wrong. Its prosecution will be a crime. There is not a question raised, an issue involved, a cause at stake, which is worth the life of one blue-jacket on the sea or one khaki-coat in the trenches.

The Court of Appeals affirmed the conviction:

"It is true that disapproval of war and the advocacy of peace are not crimes under the Espionage Act; but the question here [is] whether the natural and probable tendency and effect of [the publication] are such as are calculated to produce the result condemned by the statute. [It cannot] be said, as a matter of law, that the reasonable and natural effect of [the] publication was not to obstruct

[the] recruiting or enlistment service, and thus to injure the service of the United States. Printed matter may tend to obstruct [the] service, even if it contains no mention of recruiting or enlistment, and no reference to the military service of the United States. [The] service may be obstructed by attacking the justice of the cause for which the war is waged, and by undermining the spirit of loyalty which inspires men to enlist or to register for conscription in the service of their country. [To] teach that patriotism is murder and the spirit of the devil, and that the war against Germany was wrong and its prosecution a crime, is to weaken patriotism and the purpose to enlist or to render military service in the war. . . .

"It is argued that the evidence fails to show that [Shaffer] committed the act willfully and intentionally. But there is enough in the evidence to show the hostile attitude of his mind against the prosecution of the war by the United States, and that the books were intentionally concealed on his premises. He must be presumed to have intended the natural and probable consequences of what he knowingly did."

Masses Publishing Co. v. Patten

244 F. 535 (S.D.N.Y. 1917)

[In July 1917, the postmaster of New York, acting on the direction of the Postmaster General, advised the plaintiff, a publishing company engaged in the production of a monthly revolutionary journal called The Masses, that the August issue of the journal would be denied access to the mails under the Espionage Act of 1917. Plaintiff applied for a preliminary injunction to forbid the postmaster to refuse to accept the August issue for mailing. While objecting generally that the whole purport of the issue was in violation of the law, on the ground that it tended to produce a violation of the law, to encourage the enemies of the United States, and to hamper the government in the conduct of the war, the postmaster specified four cartoons and four pieces of text as especially falling within the act.]

LEARNED HAND, DISTRICT JUDGE [after stating the facts as above]. . . .

It must be remembered at the outset, and the distinction is of critical consequence throughout, that no question arises touching the war powers of Congress. It may be that Congress may forbid the mails to any matter which tends to discourage the successful prosecution of the war. It may be that the fundamental personal rights of the individual must stand in abeyance, even including the right of the freedom of the press, though that is not here in question. . . .

[The postmaster's] position is that to arouse discontent and disaffection among the people with the prosecution of the war and with the draft tends to promote a mutinous and insubordinate temper among the troops. This [is] true; men who become satisfied that they are engaged in an enterprise dictated by the unconscionable selfishness of the rich, and effectuated by a tyrannous disregard for the will of those who must suffer and die, will be more prone to insubordination than those who have faith in the cause and acquiesce in the means. Yet to interpret the word "cause" so broadly would [involve] necessarily as a consequence the suppression of all hostile criticism, and of all opinion except what encouraged and supported the existing policies, or which fell within the range of temperate argument. It would contradict the normal assumption of democratic government that the suppression of hostile criticism does not turn upon the justice of its substance or the decency and propriety of its temper. Assuming that the power to repress such opinion may rest in Congress in the throes of a struggle for the very existence of the state, its exercise is so contrary to the use and wont of our people that only the clearest expression of such a power justifies the conclusion that it was intended.

The [postmaster's] position, therefore, in so far as it involves the suppression of the free utterance of abuse and criticism of the existing law, or of the policies of the war, is not, in my judgment, supported by the language of the statute. Yet there has always been a recognized limit to such expressions. [One] may not counsel or advise others to violate the law as it stands. Words are not only the keys of persuasion, but the triggers of action, and those which have no purport but to counsel the violation of law cannot by any latitude of interpretation be a part of that public opinion which is the final source of government in a democratic state. [To] counsel or advise a man to an act is to urge upon him either that it is his interest or his duty to do it. While, of course, this may be accomplished as well by indirection as expressly, since words carry the meaning that they impart, the definition is exhaustive, I think, and I shall use it. Political agitation, by the passions it arouses or the convictions it engenders, may in fact stimulate men to the violation of law. Detestation of existing policies is easily transformed into forcible resistance of the authority which puts them in execution, and it would be folly to disregard the causal relation between the two. Yet to assimilate agitation, legitimate as such, with direct incitement to violent resistance, is to disregard the tolerance of all methods of political agitation which in normal times is a safeguard of free government. The distinction is not a scholastic subterfuge, but a hard-bought acquisition in the fight for freedom, and the purpose to disregard it must be evident when the power exists. If one stops short of urging upon others that it is their duty or their interest to resist the law, it seems to me one should not be held to have attempted to cause its violation. If that be not the test, I can see no escape from the conclusion that under this section every political agitation which can be shown to be apt to create a seditious temper is illegal. I am confident that by such language Congress had no such revolutionary purpose in view.

It seems to me, however, quite plain that none of the language and none of the cartoons in this paper can be thought directly to counsel or advise insubordination or mutiny, without a violation of their meaning quite beyond any tolerable understanding. I come, therefore, to the third phrase of the section, which forbids any one from willfully obstructing the recruiting or enlistment service of the United States. I am not prepared to assent to the plaintiff's position that this only refers to acts other than words, nor that the act thus defined must be shown to have been successful. One may obstruct without preventing, and the mere obstruction is an injury to the service; for it throws impediments in its way. Here again, however, since the question is of the expression of opinion, I construe the sentence, so far as it restrains public utterance, as [limited] to the direct advocacy of resistance to the recruiting and enlistment service. If so, the inquiry is narrowed to the question whether any of the challenged matter may be said to advocate resistance to the draft, taking the meaning of the words with the utmost latitude which they can bear.

As to the cartoons it seems to me quite clear that they do not fall within such a test. Certainly the nearest is that entitled "Conscription," and the most that can be said of that is that it may breed such animosity to the draft as will promote resistance and strengthen the determination of those disposed to be recalcitrant. There is no intimation that, however hateful the draft may be, one is in duty bound to resist it, certainly none that such resistance is to one's interest. I cannot, therefore, [assent] to the assertion that any of the cartoons violate the act.

The text offers more embarrassment. The poem to Emma Goldman and Alexander Berkman,* at most, goes no further than to say that they are martyrs in the cause of love among nations. Such a sentiment holds them up to admiration, and hence their conduct to possible emulation. The paragraph in which the editor offers to receive funds for their appeal also expresses admiration for them, but goes no further. The paragraphs upon conscientious objectors are of the same kind. They go no further than to express high admiration for those who have held and are holding out for their convictions even to the extent of resisting the law. [That] such comments have a tendency to arouse emulation in others is clear enough, but that they counsel others to follow these examples is not so plain. Literally at least they do not, and while, as I have said, the words are to be taken, not literally, but according to their full import, the literal meaning is the starting point for interpretation. One may admire and approve the course of a hero without feeling any duty to follow him. There is not the least implied intimation in these words that others are under a duty to follow. The most that can be said is that, if others do follow, they will get the same admiration and the same approval. Now, there is surely an appreciable distance between esteem and emulation; and unless there is here some advocacy of such emulation, I cannot see how the passages can be said to fall within the law. [The] question before me is quite the same as what would arise upon a motion to dismiss an indictment at the close of the proof: Could any reasonable man say, not that the indirect result of the language might be to arouse a seditious disposition, for that would not be enough, but that the language directly advocated resistance to the draft? I cannot think that upon such language any verdict would stand. . . .

It follows that the plaintiff is entitled to the usual preliminary injunction.

Schenck v. United States

249 U.S. 47 (1919)

MR. JUSTICE HOLMES delivered the opinion of the court. . . .

[The defendants were convicted of conspiracy to violate section 3 of the Espionage Act of 1917 by circulating "to men who had been called and accepted for

---

[*   "A TRIBUTE"
                      JOSEPHINE BELL

. . .
Emma Goldman and Alexander Berkman
Are in prison tonight,
But they have made themselves elemental forces
Like the water that climbs down the rocks:
Like the wind in the leaves:
Like the gentle night that holds us:
They are working on our destinies:
They are forging the love of the nations: . . .
Tonight they lie in prison. — EDS.]

military service" a document "alleged to be calculated" to obstruct the recruiting and enlistment service.]

The document in question, upon its first printed side, recited the 1st section of the Thirteenth Amendment, said that the idea embodied in it was violated by the Conscription Act, and that a conscript is little better than a convict. In impassioned language it intimated that conscription was despotism in its worst form and a monstrous wrong against humanity, in the interest of Wall Street's chosen few. It said: "Do not submit to intimidation"; but in form at least confined itself to peaceful measures, such as a petition for the repeal of the act. The other and later printed side of the sheet was headed, "Assert Your Rights." It stated reasons for alleging that anyone violated the Constitution when he refused to recognize "your right to assert your opposition to the draft," and went on: "If you do not assert and support your rights, you are helping to deny or disparage rights which it is the solemn duty of all citizens and residents of the United States to retain." It described the arguments on the other side as coming from cunning politicians and a mercenary capitalist press, and even silent consent to the Conscription Law as helping to support an infamous conspiracy. It denied the power to send our citizens away to foreign shores to shoot up the people of other lands, and added that words could not express the condemnation such cold-blooded ruthlessness deserves, etc., etc., winding up, "You must do your share to maintain, support, and uphold the rights of the people of this country." Of course the document would not have been sent unless it had been intended to have some effect, and we do not see what effect it could be expected to have upon persons subject to the draft except to influence them to obstruct the carrying of it out. The defendants do not deny that the jury might find against them on this point.

But it is said, suppose that that was the tendency of this circular, it is protected by the First Amendment to the Constitution. Two of the strongest expressions are said to be quoted respectively from well-known public men. It well may be that the prohibition of laws abridging the freedom of speech is not confined to previous restraints, although to prevent them may have been the main purpose, as intimated in Patterson v. Colorado, 205 U.S. 454, 462. We admit that in many places and in ordinary times the defendants, in saying all that was said in the circular, would have been within their constitutional rights. But the character of every act depends upon the circumstances in which it is done. The most stringent protection of free speech would not protect a man in falsely shouting fire in a theater, and causing a panic. It does not even protect a man from an injunction against uttering words that may have all the effect of force. The question in every case is whether the words used are used in such circumstances and are of such a nature as to create a clear and present danger that they will bring about the substantive evils that Congress has a right to prevent. It is a question of proximity and degree. When a nation is at war many things that might be said in time of peace are such a hindrance to its effort that their utterance will not be endured so long as men fight, and that no Court could regard them as protected by any constitutional right. It seems to be admitted that if an actual obstruction of the recruiting service were proved, liability for words that produced that effect might be enforced. The Statute of 1917, in §4, punishes conspiracies to obstruct as well as actual obstruction. If the act, (speaking, or circulating a paper,) its tendency and the intent with which it is done, are the same, we perceive no ground for saying that success alone warrants making the act a crime. Goldman v. United States, 245 U.S. 474, 477. Indeed, that case might be said to dispose of the present contention if the precedent covers all media concludendi. But as the right to free speech was not referred to specially we have thought fit to add a few words. . . .

Judgments affirmed.

Note: Shaffer, Masses, *and* Schenck

1. *Bad tendency. Shaffer* reflects the then-prevailing view of the lower federal courts — that speech could constitutionally be punished as an attempt to cause some forbidden or otherwise undesirable conduct if the natural and reasonable tendency of the expression might be to bring about the conduct, and if the speaker intended such a result. Under this view, intent could be inferred from the tendency of the speech itself, on the theory that one intends the natural and foreseeable consequences of one's acts. Through the twin doctrines of bad tendency and constructive intent, decisions like *Shaffer* routinely converted criticism of the war and the draft into criminal attempts to cause insubordination or obstruct recruiting. The relatively modest provisions of the 1917 act were thus converted into essentially open-ended restrictions on seditious expression. For detailed accounts of this era, see Z. Chafee, Free Speech in the United States 36-108 (1941); Rabban, The Emergence of Modern First Amendment Theory, 50 U. Chi. L. Rev. 1205 (1983). On criminal solicitation generally, see Greenawalt, Speech and Crime, 1980 Am. B. Found. Res. J. 645, 653-670.

2. *Express incitement.* Although Judge Hand technically limited himself in *Masses* to a mere interpretation of the Espionage Act, the opinion has clear constitutional overtones, and, as Hand himself made clear in private correspondence, *Masses* was "a distinctive, carefully considered alternative to the prevalent analyses of free speech issues." Gunther, Learned Hand and the Origins of Modern First Amendment Doctrine: Some Fragments of History, 27 Stan. L. Rev. 719, 720 (1975). In effect, Hand attempted in *Masses* to articulate a categorical, per se rule that would be "hard, conventional, difficult to evade." Id. at 749. Unlike the *Shaffer* and *Schenck* analyses, Judge Hand focused on the content of the speech rather than on the intent of the speaker or the consequences of the communication. Under Judge Hand's formula, the dispositive factor was whether the speaker employed express words of incitement. As Judge Hand intimated in his opinion and made explicit in correspondence, if the effect of such speech "upon the hearers is only to counsel them to violate the law, it is unconditionally illegal." Id. at 765. But if the speaker refrains from such incitement, the speech may not be restrained. For a similar analysis, predating Hand's, see E. Freund, Police Power 509-512 (1904). Consider the following propositions.

a. *Hand's analysis of express incitement is underprotective of free speech.* Judge Hand's analysis accords little, if any, constitutional protection to express advocacy of criminal conduct. Is this defensible on the ground, urged by Judge Hand, that "words [which] have no purport but to counsel the violation of law cannot by any latitude of interpretation be a part of that public opinion which is the final source of government in a democratic state"? Consider Bork, Neutral Principles and Some First Amendment Problems, 47 Ind. L. Rev. 1, 31 (1971):

Advocacy of law violation is a call to set aside the results that political speech has produced. The process of the "discovery and spread of political truth" is damaged or destroyed if the outcome is defeated by a minority that makes law enforcement, and hence the putting of political truth into practice, impossible or less effective. There should, therefore, be no constitutional protection for any speech advocating the violation of the law.

See also Stromberg v. California, 283 U.S. 359 (1931) ("The maintenance of the opportunity for free political discussion to the end that government may be responsible to the will of the people and that changes may be obtained *by lawful means* is a fundamental principle of our constitutional system.").

Even if express incitement is constitutionally "valueless," might there nonetheless be practical or institutional reasons to protect it? Consider T. Emerson, The System of Freedom of Expression 51-53 (1970): "Groups which [would] abolish democratic institutions [do] not operate in a political vacuum. They advance other ideas that may be valid [and] groups [expressing] the prohibited views usually represent real grievances, which should be heard. [Moreover, suppression] of any group in a society destroys the atmosphere of freedom essential to the life and progress of a healthy community." See also BeVier, The First Amendment and Political Speech: An Inquiry into the Substance and Limits of Principle, 30 Stan. L. Rev. 299 (1978). Should the rhetorical or hyperbolic use of express incitement ("Kill the umpire!") be constitutionally protected?

b. *The Hand formula is overprotective of the "clever" inciter.* Judge Hand's theory distinguishes between the speaker who uses express words of incitement and the speaker who specifically intends to incite but is clever enough to avoid the use of such language. Is this sensible? Consider the following arguments:

(1) The express inciter is more dangerous because he is more likely to be effective.

(2) Case-by-case inquiries into actual subjective intent are too slippery to provide adequate protection to innocent speakers. As Chafee observed, "It is only in times of popular panic and indignation that freedom of speech becomes important as an institution, and it is precisely in those times that the protection of the jury proves [illusory]. 'Men believed during [the period of the Espionage Act prosecutions] that the only verdict in a war case, which could show loyalty, was a verdict of guilty.'" Chafee, supra, at 70. See also Monaghan, First Amendment Due Process, 83 Harv. L. Rev. 518, 526-532 (1970). Thus, to avoid the dangers of "erroneous" fact-finding, and protect the rights of innocent dissenters, it is necessary to focus on more objective considerations than intent.

(3) What really matters under the first amendment is not the intent of the speaker but the value of the expression. Since the clever inciter has not used "words [which] have no purport but to counsel the violation of law," the value of his speech is indistinguishable from that of the speaker who utters the same words with a more honorable intent.

c. *The Hand formula is overprotective of the dangerous speaker.* Suppose during a famine that a speaker angrily asserts "to an excited mob assembled before the house of a corn-dealer" that "corn-dealers are starvers of the poor," thus inflaming the mob to burn down the corn-dealer's house. J. S. Mill, On Liberty ch. 3 (1859). Is it sensible to accord absolute protection to such a speaker, without regard to the potential dangers of his speech, merely because he does not use express language of incitement? Consider the following arguments: (1) It is the actor, and not the speaker, who ultimately brings about the harm. Government should thus direct its punishment and deterrence toward actors, not speakers. (2) A central premise of the first amendment is that government may not restrict expression because it does not trust citizens to make wise decisions if they are exposed to the expression. Such "paternalism" is fundamentally at odds with the very notion of free expression. (3) As Judge Hand argued, "If that be not the test, I can see no escape from the conclusion that [every] political agitation which can be shown to be apt to create a seditious temper is illegal."

3. *The fate of* Masses. Judge Hand's opinion was reversed on appeal. Masses Publishing Co. v. Patten, 246 F. 24 (2d Cir. 1917). The court of appeals flatly rejected Judge Hand's construction of the act: "If the natural and reasonable effect of what is said is to encourage resistance to a law, and the words are used in an endeavor to persuade to resistance, it is immaterial that the duty to resist is not mentioned, or the interest of the persons addressed in resistance is not suggested." Other reactions to Judge Hand's formulation were equally unsupportive, and after 1921 Judge Hand himself abandoned his advocacy of the *Masses* approach. Parts of the formula, however, have reappeared in contemporary tests of subversive advocacy. See *Yates* and *Brandenburg,* infra this section.

4. *Clear and present danger.* Whence does Justice Holmes derive the clear and present danger standard? Is Justice Holmes's famous reference to the false shout of fire helpful? Such speech, Justice Holmes implies, may be restricted because it creates a clear and present danger of panic. But suppose the shout is *true.* Would that change the analysis? Perhaps the most satisfactory explanation of Justice Holmes's use of clear and present danger in *Schenck* is that he was simply transferring his view of criminal attempts into the first amendment. See Rogat, Mr. Justice Holmes: Some Modern Views — The Judge as Spectator, 31 U. Chi. L. Rev. 213, 215 (1964); Rabban, supra, at 1267-1283.

Was there a clear and present danger in *Schenck?* Of what? That the war effort would be jeopardized? That the recruiting and enlistment service would grind to a halt? That a single person might be influenced to refuse induction or not enlist? How should we deal with the possibility that there may be many Schencks?

Was Holmes's clear and present danger standard designed to supplant the prevailing bad tendency/constructive intent test? Note that the jury instructions in *Schenck* could not have embodied the clear and present danger standard. Why, then, didn't the Court remand for a new trial?

Consider the Court's decisions in *Frohwerk* and *Debs,* handed down on the same day in the spring of 1919, exactly one week after *Schenck.* Consider also the Court's decision, and Justice Holmes's dissent, in *Abrams,* handed down the following fall.

FROHWERK v. UNITED STATES, 249 U.S. 204 (1919). As a result of his participation in the preparation and publication of a series of articles in the Missouri Staats Zeitung, a German language newspaper, Frohwerk was convicted under the Espionage Act of 1917 of conspiring to cause disloyalty, mutiny, and refusal of duty in the military and naval forces of the United States. Frohwerk was sentenced to a fine and to ten years' imprisonment. The Court, speaking through Justice Holmes, unanimously rejected Frohwerk's contention that his conviction violated the first amendment. Illustrative of the articles was one that declared "it a monumental and inexcusable mistake to send our soldiers to France" and described our participation in the war as "outright murder."

Justice Holmes began his analysis by observing that the first amendment "cannot have been, and obviously was not, intended to give immunity for every possible use of language. Neither Hamilton nor Madison, nor any other competent person then or later ever supposed that to make criminal the counseling of murder within the jurisdiction of Congress would be an unconstitutional interference with free speech." Justice Holmes then turned to the crux of the issue: "It may be that all this may be said or written even in time of war in circumstances that would not make it a crime. [But] we must take the case on the record as it is, and on the record it is impossible to say that it might not have been found that the circulation of the paper was in quarters where a little breath would be enough to kindle a flame [and that that] fact was known and relied upon by those who sent the paper out." Justice Holmes therefore concluded that "we find ourselves unable to say that the articles could not furnish a basis for a conviction."

DEBS v. UNITED STATES, 249 U.S. 211 (1919). As a result of a speech delivered to a public assembly in Canton, Ohio, in July of 1918, Eugene V. Debs, national leader of the Socialist Party, was convicted under the Espionage Act of 1917 of attempting to obstruct the recruiting and enlistment service of the United States. Debs was sentenced to a prison term of ten years. The Supreme Court, speaking once again through Justice Holmes, unanimously rejected Debs's claim that the conviction violated the first amendment. Justice Holmes noted at the outset that "[t]he main theme of the speech was socialism, its growth, and a prophecy of its ultimate success. With that we have nothing to do, but [if] one purpose of the speech, whether incidental or not does not matter, was to oppose [the] war, and if, in all the circumstances, that would be its probable effect, it would not be protected."

Turning to the speech itself, Justice Holmes observed that Debs had specifically praised several persons who previously had been convicted of aiding or encouraging others to refuse induction, and that toward the end of his address Debs had told his audience that "you need to know that you are fit for something better than slavery and cannon fodder." In such circumstances, Justice Holmes concluded that Debs's first amendment claim had in practical effect been "disposed of in [*Schenck*]." Justice Holmes emphasized that the jury in *Debs* had been "most carefully instructed that they could not find the defendant guilty for advocacy of any of his opinions unless the words used had as their natural tendency and reasonably probable effect to obstruct the recruiting service [and] unless the defendant had the specific intent to do so in his mind." As in *Frohwerk*, Justice Holmes made no reference in *Debs* to "clear and present danger."

Abrams v. United States

250 U.S. 616 (1919)

[Although Czarist Russia, like the United States, had declared war on Germany, the Bolsheviks, on seizing power, signed a peace treaty with Germany. In the summer of 1918, the United States sent a contingent of marines to Vladivostok and Murmansk. The defendants in *Abrams*, a group of Russian immigrants who were self-proclaimed socialists and anarchists, perceived the expedition as an attempt to "crush the Russian Revolution." In protest, they distributed several thousand copies of each of two leaflets, one of which was written in English, the other in Yiddish. The leaflets, which were thrown from a window and circulated secretly, called for a general strike. The defendants were arrested by the military police, and after a controversial trial, they were convicted of conspiring to violate various provisions of the 1918 amendments to the Espionage Act of 1917. The overall flavor of the trial is captured in the trial judge's remarks just prior to sentencing:

> These defendants took the stand. They talked about capitalists and producers, and I tried to figure out what a capitalist and what a producer is as contemplated by them. After listening carefully to all they had to say, I came to the conclusion that a capitalist is a man with a decent set of clothes, a minimum of $1.25 in his pocket, and a good character. And when I tried to find out what the prisoners had produced, I was unable to find out anything at all. So far as I can learn, not one of them ever produced so much as a single potato. The only thing they know how to raise is hell, and to direct it against the government of the United States. [But] we are not going to help carry out the plans mapped out by the Imperial German Government, and which are being carried out by Lenin and Trotsky. I have heard of the reported fate of the poor little daughters of the Czar, but I won't talk about that now. I might get mad. I will now sentence the prisoners.

The defendants were sentenced to prison terms ranging from three to twenty years. The Supreme Court affirmed the convictions on two counts: one charging a violation of the provision prohibiting conspiracy "to incite, provoke or encourage resistance to the United States" (count 3); the other charging a violation of the provision prohibiting conspiracy to urge curtailment of the production of war materials "with intent [to] cripple or hinder the United States in the prosecution of the war" (count 4). Speaking for the Court, Justice Clarke summarily rejected the defendants' first amendment argument, noting simply that "[t]his contention is sufficiently discussed and is definitely negatived in [*Schenck*] and [*Frohwerk*]."]

MR. JUSTICE HOLMES dissenting. . . .

The first of these leaflets says that the President's cowardly silence about the intervention in Russia reveals the hypocrisy of the plutocratic gang in Washington. It intimates that "German militarism combined with allied capitalism to crush the Russian revolution." [It] says that there is only one enemy of the workers of the world and that is capitalism; that it is a crime for workers of America, &c., to fight the workers' republic of Russia, and ends "Awake! Awake, you Workers of the World! Revolutionists." A note adds "It is absurd to call us pro-German. We hate and despise German militarism more than do you hypocritical tyrants. We have more reasons for denouncing German militarism than has the coward of the White House."

The other leaflet, headed "Workers — Wake Up," with abusive language says that [the] hypocrites shall not fool the Russian emigrants and friends of Russia in America. It tells the Russian emigrants that they now must spit in the face of the false military propaganda by which their sympathy and help to the prosecution of the war have been called forth and says that with the money they have lent or are going to lend "they will make bullets not only for the Germans but also for the Workers Soviets of Russia," and further, "Workers in the ammunition factories, you are producing bullets, bayonets, cannon, to murder not only the Germans, but also your dearest, best, who are in Russia and are fighting for freedom." It then appeals to the same Russian emigrants at some length not to consent to the "inquisitionary expedition to Russia," and says that the destruction of the Russian revolution is "the politics of the march to Russia." The leaflet winds up by saying "Workers, our reply to this barbarous intervention has to be a general strike!," and after a few words on the spirit of revolution, exhortations not to be afraid, and some usual tall talk ends "Woe unto those who will be in the way of progress. Let solidarity live! The Rebels."

[After describing the leaflets, Justice Holmes argued that the conviction under the fourth count was invalid because the defendants did not have the intent, required by the act, "to cripple or hinder the United States in the prosecution of the war." The defendants' specific intent, Justice Holmes maintained, was to help Russia, with whom we were not at war. Although conceding that "the word *intent* as vaguely used in ordinary legal discussion means no more than knowledge at the time of the act that the consequences said to be intended will ensue," Justice Holmes insisted that "this statute must be taken to use its words in a strict and accurate sense." Otherwise, Justice Holmes reasoned, the act would "be absurd," for it would make it criminal for one who thought "we were wasting money on aeroplanes" successfully to advocate curtailment if such curtailment later turned out "to hinder the United States in the prosecution of the war." Justice Holmes then passed to what he referred to as "a more important aspect of the case" — the first amendment.]

I never have seen any reason to doubt that the questions of law that alone were before this Court in the cases of *Schenck*, *Frohwerk* and *Debs* were rightly decided. I do not doubt for a moment that by the same reasoning that would justify punishing persuasion to murder, the United States constitutionally may punish speech that produces or is intended to produce a clear and imminent danger that it will bring about forthwith certain substantive evils that the United States constitutionally may seek to prevent. The power undoubtedly is greater in time of war than in time of peace because war opens dangers that do not exist at other times.

But as against dangers peculiar to war, as against others, the principle of the right to free speech is always the same. It is only the present danger of immediate evil or an intent to bring it about that warrants Congress in setting a limit to the expression of opinion where private rights are not concerned. Congress certainly cannot forbid all effort to change the mind of the country. Now nobody can suppose that the surreptitious publishing of a silly leaflet by an unknown man, without more, would present any immediate danger that its opinions would hinder the success of the government arms or have any appreciable tendency to do so. Publishing those opinions for the very purpose of obstructing, however, might indicate a greater danger and at any rate would have the quality of an attempt. So I assume that the second leaflet if published for the purposes alleged in the fourth count might be punishable. But [I] do not see how anyone can find the intent required by the statute in any of the defendants' words. The second leaflet is the only one that affords even a foundation for the charge, and there, without invoking the hatred of German militarism expressed in the former one, it is evident from the beginning to the end that the only object of the paper is to help Russia and stop American intervention there against the popular government — not to impede the United States in the war that it was carrying on. To say that two phrases taken literally might import a suggestion of conduct that would have interference with the war as an indirect and probably undesired effect seems to me by no means enough to show an attempt to produce that effect.

In this case sentences of twenty years imprisonment have been imposed for the publishing of two leaflets that I believe the defendants had as much right to publish as the Government has to publish the Constitution of the United States now vainly invoked by them. Even if I am technically wrong and enough can be squeezed from these poor and puny anonymities to turn the color of legal litmus paper; I will add, even if what I think the necessary intent were shown; the most nominal punishment seems to me all that possibly could be inflicted, unless the defendants are to be made to suffer not for what the indictment alleges but for the creed that they avow — a creed that I believe to be the creed of ignorance and immaturity when honestly held, as I see no reason to doubt that it was held here, but which, although made the subject of examination at the trial, no one has a right even to consider in dealing with the charges before the Court.

Persecution for the expression of opinions seems to me perfectly logical. If you have no doubt of your premises or your power and want a certain result with all your heart you naturally express your wishes in law and sweep away all opposition. To allow opposition by speech seems to indicate that you think the speech impotent, as when a man says that he has squared the circle, or that you do not care whole-heartedly for the result, or that you doubt either your power or your premises. But when men have realized that time has upset many fighting faiths, they may come to believe even more than they believe the very foundations of their own conduct that the ultimate good desired is better reached by free trade in ideas — that the best test of truth is the power of the thought to get itself accepted in the competition of the market, and that truth is the only ground upon which their wishes safely can be carried out. That at any rate is the theory of our Constitution. It is an experiment, as all life is an experiment. Every year if not every day we have to wager our salvation upon some prophecy based upon imperfect knowledge. While that experiment is part of our system I think that we should be eternally vigilant against attempts to check the expression of opinions that we loathe and believe to be fraught with death, unless they so imminently threaten immediate interference with the lawful and pressing purposes of the law that an immediate check is required to save the country. I wholly disagree with the argument of the Government that the First Amendment left the common law as to seditious libel in force. History seems to me against the notion. I had conceived that the United States through many years had shown its repentance for the Sedition Act of 1798, by repaying fines that it imposed. Only the emergency that makes it immediately dangerous to leave the correction of evil counsels to time warrants making any exception to the sweeping command, "Congress shall make no law . . . abridging the freedom of speech." Of course I am speaking only of expressions of opinion and exhortations, which were all that were uttered here, but I regret that I cannot put into more impressive words my belief that in their conviction upon this indictment the defendants were deprived of their rights under the Constitution of the United States.

MR. JUSTICE BRANDEIS concurs with the foregoing opinion.

Note: Abrams *and the Emergence of the Holmes/Brandeis Tradition*

1. *Historical context.* For a lively telling of the full story of the *Abrams* case, see R. Polenberg, Fighting Faiths (1987).

2. *The Holmes transformation.* Most commentators have concluded that "Justice Holmes moved from a restrictive construction of the first amendment [in] *Schenck, Frohwerk,* and *Debs* [to] a libertarian position in his dissent in *Abrams.*" Rabban, The Emergence of Modern First Amendment Doctrine, 50 U. Chi. L. Rev. 1207, 1208-1209 (1983). For an analysis of this apparent transformation, see id. at 1311-1317. For an especially critical view of Justice Holmes in this period, see Ragan, Justice Oliver Wendell Holmes, Jr., Zechariah Chafee, Jr., and the Clear and Present Danger Test for Free Speech: The First Year, 1919, 58 J. Am. Hist. 24 (1971). For a rebuttal of the transformation theory, see Novick, The Unrevised Holmes and Freedom of Expression, 1991 Sup. Ct. Rev. 303.

3. *The administrability of clear and present danger.* Is Justice Holmes's formulation of clear and present danger in *Abrams* administratively workable? Judge Hand was largely unimpressed with Justice Holmes's effort. As he wrote to Chafee,

> I am not wholly in love with Holmesey's test, [for once] you admit that the matter is one of degree, [you] give to Tomdickandharry, D.J., so much latitude that the jig is at once up. Besides [the] Nine Elder Statesmen have not shown themselves wholly immune from the "herd instinct" and what seems "immediate and direct" to-day may seem very remote next year even though the circumstances surrounding the utterance be unchanged. I own I should prefer a qualitative formula, hard, conventional, difficult to evade.

In short, Judge Hand preferred "a test based upon the nature of the utterance itself." Gunther, Learned Hand and the Origins of Modern First Amendment Doctrine: Some Fragments of History, 27 Stan. L. Rev. 719, 749 (1975).

4. *Was there a clear and present danger in* Abrams? Consider Wigmore's criticism:

> [The *Abrams* dissent] is dallying with the facts and the law. [If] these five men could, without the law's restraint, urge munition workers to a general strike and armed violence, then others could lawfully do so; and a thousand disaffected undesirables, aliens and natives alike, were ready and waiting to do so. [If] such urgings were lawful, every munitions factory in the country could be stopped by them. The relevant amount of harm that one criminal act can effect is no measure of its criminality, and no measure of the danger of its criminality.

Wigmore, Abrams v. United States: Freedom of Speech and Freedom of Thuggery in War-Time and Peace-Time, 14 Ill. L. Rev. 539, 549-550 (1920).

5. *The rationale of clear and present danger.* Does the clear and present danger standard derive from Justice Holmes's elaboration of the marketplace of ideas theory of the first amendment? Would the self-fulfillment or self-governance theory provide a sounder foundation for clear and present danger?

Consider the following rationales for the clear and present danger standard: (a) The test balances competing speech and societal interests — speech is important, so government can restrict it only when there is an "emergency"; an "emergency" exists only if the danger is "clear" and "present." (b) The test marks off a broad area of protected expression to avoid Judge Hand's concern in *Masses* that government not be permitted to render unlawful "every political agitation which can be shown to be apt to create a seditious temper." (c) The test is designed to reduce the risk that government, in the guise of preventing "danger," will in fact suppress expression because it disapproves of the substantive message.

Note that Holmes denigrates both the speakers and the speech in *Abrams*, characterizing the leaflet as "silly" and the defendants as "poor and puny anonymities." If the expression is this ineffectual, how does it make a significant contribution to the free trade in ideas? Does the asserted ineffectualness of the expression make the case for its protection stronger or weaker?

6. *Other Espionage Act decisions.* In several post-*Abrams* decisions, the Court, over the dissents of Justices Holmes and Brandeis, upheld further convictions under the Espionage Act. See Pierce v. United States, 252 U.S. 239 (1920); Schaefer v. United States, 251 U.S. 466 (1920). See also Gilbert v. Minnesota, 254 U.S. 325 (1920).

7. *The "Red Scare."* After World War I and the Russian Revolution, the United States entered a period of intense antiradicalism. In the years 1919 and 1920, an era known as the "Red Scare," two-thirds of the states enacted laws prohibiting the advocacy of criminal syndicalism and criminal anarchy. In addition, two-thirds of the states adopted "red flag" laws, which made it a crime to display a red flag with a seditious intent. See Z. Chafee, Free Speech in the United States 141-168 (1941). It was not long before the Court had to rule on the constitutionality of such legislation.

Gitlow v. New York

268 U.S. 652 (1925)

Mr. Justice Sanford delivered the opinion of the Court.

Benjamin Gitlow was indicted in the Supreme Court of New York, with three others, for the statutory crime of criminal anarchy. [He] was separately tried, convicted, and sentenced to imprisonment. . . .

The contention here is that the statute, by its terms and as applied in this case, is repugnant to the due process clause of the Fourteenth Amendment. Its material provisions are: . . .

§161. *Advocacy of criminal anarchy.* Any person [who] advocates, advises, or teaches the duty, necessity or propriety of overthrowing [organized] government by force or violence, or by assassination of [any] of the executive officials of government, or by any unlawful means; [is] guilty of a felony. . . .

[The] defendant is a member of the Left Wing Section of the Socialist Party, a dissenting branch or faction of that party formed in opposition to its dominant policy of "moderate Socialism." [The] Left Wing Section was organized nationally at a conference in New York City in June, 1919, attended by ninety delegates from twenty different States. The conference elected a National Council, of which the defendant was a member, and left to it the adoption of a "manifesto." This was published in The Revolutionary Age, the official organ of the Left

Wing. The defendant [arranged] for the printing [and publication of the first issue of the paper, which contained the Left Wing Manifesto].

[The indictment charged that, as a result of his involvement in the publication of the manifesto, he "had advocated, advised and taught the duty, necessity and propriety of overthrowing and overturning organized government by force, violence and unlawful means."]

There was no evidence of any effect resulting from the publication and circulation of the Manifesto. [The Manifesto] condemned the dominant "moderate Socialism" for its recognition of the necessity of the democratic parliamentary state; repudiated its policy of introducing Socialism by legislative measures; and advocated, in plain and unequivocal language, the necessity of accomplishing the "Communist Revolution" by a militant and "revolutionary Socialism," based on "the class struggle" and mobilizing the "power of the proletariat in action," through mass industrial revolts developing into mass political strikes and "revolutionary mass action," for the purpose of conquering and destroying the parliamentary state and establishing in its place, through a "revolutionary dictatorship of the proletariat," the system of Communist Socialism. . . .

The statute does not penalize the utterance or publication of abstract "doctrine" or academic discussion having no quality of incitement to any concrete action. It is not aimed against mere historical or philosophical essays. It does not restrain the advocacy of changes in the form of government by constitutional and lawful means. What it prohibits is language advocating, advising or teaching the overthrow of organized government by unlawful means. These words imply urging to action. . . .

The Manifesto, plainly, is neither the statement of abstract doctrine nor, as suggested by counsel, mere prediction that industrial disturbances and revolutionary mass strikes will result spontaneously in an inevitable process of evolution in the economic system. It advocates and urges in fervent language mass action which shall progressively foment industrial disturbances and through political mass strikes and revolutionary mass action overthrow and destroy organized parliamentary government. It concludes with a call to action in these words: "The proletariat revolution and the Communist reconstruction of society — *the struggle for these* — is now indispensable. . . . The Communist International calls the proletariat of the world to the final struggle!" This [is] the language of direct incitement. [That] the jury were warranted in finding that the Manifesto advocated not merely the abstract doctrine of overthrowing organized government by force, violence and unlawful means, but action to that end, is clear.

For present purposes we may and do assume that freedom of speech and of the press — which are protected by the First Amendment from abridgment by Congress — are among the fundamental personal rights and "liberties" protected by the due process clause of the Fourteenth Amendment from impairment by the States. . . .

It is a fundamental principle, long established, that the freedom of speech and of the press which is secured by the Constitution, does not confer an absolute right to speak or publish, without responsibility, whatever one may choose, or an unrestricted and unbridled license that gives immunity for every possible use of language and prevents the punishment of those who abuse this freedom. [A] State may punish utterances endangering the foundations of organized government and threatening its overthrow by unlawful means. These imperil its own existence as a constitutional State. Freedom of speech and press [does] not deprive a State of the primary and essential right of self preservation. . . .

By enacting the present statute the State has determined, through its legislative body, that utterances advocating the overthrow of organized government by force, violence and unlawful means, are so inimical to the general welfare and involve such danger of substantive evil that they may be penalized in the exercise of its police power. That determination must be given great weight. Every presumption is to be indulged in favor of the validity of the statute. Mulger v. Kansas, 123 U.S. 623, 661. And the case is to be considered "in the light of the principle that the State is primarily the judge of regulations required in the interest of public safety and welfare;" and that its police "statutes may only be declared unconstitutional where they are arbitrary or unreasonable attempts to exercise authority vested in the State in the public interest." Great Northern Ry. v. Clara City, 246 U.S. 434, 439. That utterances inciting to the overthrow of organized government by unlawful means, present a sufficient danger of substantive evil to bring their punishment within the range of legislative discretion, is clear. Such utterances, by their very nature, involve danger to the public peace and to the security of the State. They threaten breaches of the peace and ultimate revolution. And the immediate danger is none the less real and substantial, because the effect of a given utterance cannot be accurately foreseen. The State cannot reasonably be required to measure the danger from every such utterance in the nice balance of a jeweler's scale. A single revolutionary spark may kindle a fire that, smouldering for a time, may burst into a sweeping and destructive conflagration. It cannot be said that the State is acting arbitrarily or unreasonably when in the exercise of its judgment as to the measures necessary to protect the public peace and safety, it seeks to extinguish the spark without waiting until it has enkindled the flame or blazed into the conflagration. It cannot reasonably be required to defer the adoption of measures for its own peace and safety until the revolutionary utterances lead to actual disturbances of the public peace or imminent and immediate danger of its own destruction; but it may, in the exercise of its judgment, suppress the threatened danger in its incipiency. . . .

We cannot hold that the present statute is an arbitrary or unreasonable exercise of the police power of the State unwarrantably infringing the freedom of speech or press; and we must and do sustain its constitutionality.

This being so it may be applied to every utterance — not too trivial to be beneath the notice of the law — which is of such a character and used with such intent and purpose as to bring it within the prohibition of the statute. [In] other words, when the legislative body has determined generally, in the constitutional exercise of its discretion, that utterances of a certain kind involve such danger of substantive evil that they may be punished, the question whether any specific utterance coming within the prohibited class is likely, in and of itself, to bring about the substantive evil, is not open to consideration. It is sufficient that the statute itself be constitutional and that the use of the language comes within its prohibition.

It is clear that the question in such cases is entirely different from that involved in those cases where the statute merely prohibits certain acts involving the danger of substantive evil, without any reference to language itself, and it is sought to apply its provisions to language used by the defendant for the purpose of bringing about the prohibited results. There, if it be contended that the statute cannot be applied to the language used by the defendant because of its protection by the freedom of speech or press, it must necessarily be found, as an original question, without any previous determination by the legislative body, whether the specific language used involved such likelihood of bringing about the substantive evil as to deprive it of the constitutional protection. In such cases it has been held that the general provisions of the statute may be constitutionally applied to the specific utterance of the defendant if its natural tendency and probable effect was to bring about the substantive evil which the legislative body might prevent. [*Schenck*; *Debs.*] And the general statement in [*Schenck*] that the "question in every case is whether the words are used in such circumstances and are of such a nature as to create a clear and present danger that they will bring about the substantive evils," — upon which great reliance is placed in the defendant's argument — was manifestly intended, as shown by the context, to apply only in cases of this class, and has no application to those like the present, where the legislative body itself has previously determined the danger of substantive evil arising from utterances of a specified character. . . .

Affirmed.

MR. JUSTICE HOLMES dissenting.

Mr. Justice Brandeis and I are of opinion that this judgment should be reversed. The general principle of free speech, it seems to me, must be taken to be included in the Fourteenth Amendment, in view of the scope that has been given to the word "liberty" as there used, although perhaps it may be accepted with a somewhat larger latitude of interpretation than is allowed to Congress by the sweeping language that governs, or ought to govern, the laws of the United States. If I am right, then I think that the criterion sanctioned by the full court in [*Schenck*] applies: "The question in every case is whether the words used are used in such circumstances and are of such a nature as to create a clear and present danger that they will bring about the substantive evils that [the state] has a right to prevent." It is true that in my opinion this criterion was departed from in [*Abrams*], but the convictions that I expressed in that case are too deep for it to be possible for me as yet to believe that it [has] settled the law. If what I think the correct test is applied, it is manifest that there was no present danger of an attempt to overthrow the government by force on the part of the admittedly small minority who shared the defendant's views. It is said that this Manifesto was more than a theory, that it was an incitement. Every idea is an incitement. It offers itself for belief, and, if believed, it is acted on unless some other belief outweighs it, or some failure of energy stifles the movement at its birth. The only difference between the expression of an opinion and an incitement in the narrower sense is the speaker's enthusiasm for the result. Eloquence may set fire to reason. But whatever may be thought of the redundant discourse before us, it had no chance of starting a present conflagration. If, in the long run, the beliefs expressed in proletarian dictatorship are destined to be accepted by the dominant forces of the community, the only meaning of free speech is that they should be given their chance and have their way.

If the publication of this document had been laid as an attempt to induce an uprising against government at once, and not at some indefinite time in the future, it would have presented a different question. The object would have been one with which the law might deal, subject to the doubt whether there was any danger that the publication could produce any result; or, in other words, whether it was not futile and too remote from possible consequences. But the indictment alleges the publication and nothing more.

Note: Gitlow *and the Question of Deference*

1. *Incitement.* Justice Sanford emphasized repeatedly in *Gitlow* that the New York statute was not directed against "abstract doctrine," "academic discussion," "historical or philosophical essays," or "advocacy of changes in the form of government by constitutional and lawful means." Rather, it restricted only "urging to action," "incitement to [concrete] action," and "the language of direct incitement." Justice Sanford thus seemed to be suggesting an analysis reminiscent of that of Judge Hand in *Masses*, arguing implicitly that whatever protection might be appropriate for "abstract doctrine" or for general political discussion, express "incitement" of unlawful conduct is an entirely different matter. Is Justice Holmes's reply to this argument that "every idea is an incitement" a satisfactory response?

2. *The problem of deference.* Justice Sanford drew a sharp distinction in *Gitlow* between cases like *Schenck*, in which "the statute merely prohibits certain acts involving the danger of substantive evil, without any reference to language itself," and cases like *Gitlow*, in which the "legislative body has determined [that] utterances of a certain kind involve such danger of substantive evil that they may be punished." Is Justice Sanford right that the problems posed by these two types of cases are "entirely different"? Did Justice Sanford defer in *Gitlow* to the legislature's interpretation of the first amendment? To its factual assessment of the dangers of certain types of utterances?

Justice Holmes refused in *Gitlow* to defer to the legislative judgment, insisting instead that it is for the judiciary to determine in each and every instance whether the expression creates a "clear and present danger." Was Justice Holmes's disregard of the legislative judgment warranted? Can Justice Holmes's advocacy of judicial deference in the substantive due process context, see, e.g., Lochner v. New York (Holmes, J., dissenting), Chapter 6, section D, supra, be reconciled with his position in *Gitlow*?

3. *The marketplace of ideas.* In *Abrams*, Justice Holmes maintained that as an "experiment" our Constitution embraced the "theory" that "the best test of truth is the power of the thought to get itself accepted in the competition of the market." The market, however, is not perfect and in *Gitlow* Justice Holmes conceded that, "if, in the long run, the beliefs expressed in proletarian dictatorship are destined to be accepted by the dominant forces of the community, the only meaning of free speech is that they should be given their chance and have their way." What about ideas that, if accepted, would refuse to permit other ideas to compete in the "market"? Are some evils so grave that we cannot afford to "experiment"?

Consider Stone, Reflections on the First Amendment: The Evolution of the American Jurisprudence of Free Expression, 131 Proc. of the J. Am. Phil. Socy. 251, 253 (1987):

[The central principle of first amendment jurisprudence is that] the Government may *never* restrict the expression of particular ideas because it fears that citizens may adopt those ideas in the political process. As Alexander Meiklejohn explained, this principle is rooted "in the very foundations of the self-governing process," for when individuals "govern themselves it is they — and no one else — who must pass judgment upon unwisdom, unfairness and danger." Under this view, "no suggestion of policy" may be denied a hearing "because someone in control thinks it unwise."

Now, there is an anomaly in this principle, [for] if the essential goal is to preserve self-governance, why can't citizens, acting in their capacity as self-governors, decide that certain policies are simply out-of-bounds and thus prohibit further debate on such issues? Under this view, it is not the Government, as some independent entity, that is closing off debate, but citizens themselves, and they are doing so through the very self-governing process that the First Amendment is designed to promote.

The answer, I think, is that the First Amendment [places] out of bounds any law that attempts to freeze public debate at a particular moment in time. Under this view, a majority at any moment has the power to decide an issue of policy for itself, but it has no power irrevocably to decide that issue for future citizens by preventing them from continuing to debate the issue. This is [what] Justice Holmes described as the great First Amendment "experiment."

Is there a difference under the marketplace theory between advocacy of change through political processes and advocacy of change through criminal conduct? Must those who seek to implement their ideas by the use of force or violence "be given their chance" to "have their way"?

Whitney v. California

274 U.S. 357 (1927)

MR. JUSTICE SANFORD delivered the opinion of the Court.

[In 1919, Anita Whitney attended the national convention of the Socialist Party in Chicago as a delegate of the local Oakland branch of the party. At this convention, the party split between the "radicals" and the old-line Socialists. The radicals, supported by the Oakland branch delegates, formed the Communist Labor Party and promulgated a platform similar in style and substance to the Left Wing Manifesto at issue in *Gitlow*. Shortly thereafter, Whitney attended a convention held in Oakland for the purpose of organizing a California branch of the Communist Labor Party. At this convention, she sponsored a moderate resolution calling for the achievement of the party's goals through the political process. This resolution was defeated, however, and the convention adopted the more militant national platform. Whitney remained at the convention until it adjourned and remained a member of the party. As a result of her activities at the Oakland convention, she was charged with violating the California Criminal Syndicalism Act, which prohibited any person to knowingly become a member of any organization that advocates "the commission of crime, sabotage, or unlawful acts of force and violence or unlawful methods of terrorism as a means of accomplishing a change in industrial ownership or control, or effecting any political change." For an excellent account of Ms. Whitney's life and of the trial and appellate proceedings in the case, see Blasi, The First Amendment and the Ideal of Civic

Courage: The Brandeis Opinion in Whitney v. California, 29 Wm. & Mary L. Rev. 653 (1988).]

The first count of the information, on which the conviction was had, charged that [at the Oakland convention] the defendant, in violation of the Criminal Syndicalism Act, "did then and there [knowingly] became a member of [a group] organized [to advocate] criminal syndicalism." . . .

[At her trial, Whitney] testified that it was not her intention that the Communist Labor Party of California should be an instrument of terrorism or violence. [But by] enacting the provisions of the Syndicalism Act the State has declared, [for an individual] to knowingly be or become a member of [an organization that advocates criminal syndicalism] involves such danger to the public peace and the security of the State [that] these acts should be penalized in the exercise of its police power. That determination must be given great weight. . . .

The essence of the offense denounced by the Act [partakes] of the nature of a criminal conspiracy. [That] such united and joint action involves even greater danger to the public peace and security than the isolated utterances and acts of individuals, is clear. We cannot hold that, as here applied, the Act is an unreasonable or arbitrary exercise of the police power of the State. . . .

Affirmed.

MR. JUSTICE BRANDEIS, concurring. . . .

The felony which the statute created is a crime very unlike the old felony of conspiracy or the old misdemeanor of unlawful assembly. The mere act of assisting in forming a society for teaching syndicalism, of becoming a member of it, or of assembling with others for that purpose is given the dynamic quality of crime. [The] novelty in the prohibition introduced is that the statute aims, not at the practice of criminal syndicalism, nor even directly at the preaching of it, but at association with those who propose to preach it. . . .

[Although] the rights of free speech and assembly are fundamental, they are not in their nature absolute. Their exercise is subject to restriction, if the particular restriction proposed is required in order to protect the state from destruction or from serious injury, political, economic or moral. That the necessity which is essential to a valid restriction does not exist unless speech would produce, or is intended to produce, a clear and imminent danger of some substantive evil which the state constitutionally may seek to prevent has been settled. See [Schenck].

It is said to be the function of the legislature to determine whether at a particular time and under the particular circumstances the formation of, or assembly with, a society organized to advocate criminal syndicalism constitutes a clear and present danger of substantive evil; and that by enacting the law here in question the legislature of California determined that question in the affirmative. Compare [Gitlow]. The legislature must obviously decide, in the first instance, whether a danger exists which calls for a particular protective measure. But where a statute is valid only in case certain conditions exist, the enactment of the statute cannot alone establish the facts which are essential to its validity. Prohibitory legislation has repeatedly been held invalid, because unnecessary, where the denial of liberty involved was that of engaging in a particular business. The power of the courts to strike down an offending law is no less when the interests involved are not property rights, but the fundamental personal rights of free speech and assembly.

This court has not yet fixed the standard by which to determine when a danger shall be deemed clear; how remote the danger may be and yet be deemed present; and what degree of evil shall be deemed sufficiently substantial to justify resort to abridgment of free speech and assembly as the means of protection. To reach sound conclusions on these matters, we must bear in mind why a state is, ordinarily, denied the power to prohibit dissemination of social, economic and political doctrine which a vast majority of its citizens believes to be false and fraught with evil consequence.

Those who won our independence believed that the final end of the state was to make men free to develop their faculties; and that in its government the deliberative forces should prevail over the arbitrary. They valued liberty both as an end and as a means. They believed liberty to be the secret of happiness and courage to be the secret of liberty. They believed that freedom to think as you will and to speak as you think are means indispensable to the discovery and spread of political truth; that without free speech and assembly discussion would be futile; that with them, discussion affords ordinarily adequate protection against the dissemination of noxious doctrine; that the greatest menace to freedom is an inert people; that public discussion is a political duty; and that this should be a fundamental principle of the American government. They recognized the risks to which all human institutions are subject. But they knew that order cannot be secured merely through fear of punishment for its infraction; that it is hazardous to discourage thought, hope and imagination; that fear breeds repression; that repression breeds hate; that hate menaces stable government; that the path of safety lies in the opportunity to discuss freely supposed grievances and proposed remedies; and that the fitting remedy for evil counsels is good ones. Believing in the power of reason as applied through public discussion, they eschewed silence coerced by law — the argument of force in its worst form. Recognizing the occasional tyrannies of governing majorities, they amended the Constitution so that free speech and assembly should be guaranteed.

Fear of serious injury cannot alone justify suppression of free speech and assembly. Men feared witches and burned women. It is the function of speech to free men from the bondage of irrational fears. To justify suppression of free speech there must be reasonable ground to fear that serious evil will result if free speech is practiced. There must be reasonable ground to believe that the danger apprehended is imminent. There must be reasonable ground to believe that the evil to be prevented is a serious one. Every denunciation of existing law tends in some measure to increase the probability that there will be violation of it. Condonation of a breach enhances the probability. Expressions of approval add to the probability. Propagation of the criminal state of mind by teaching syndicalism increases it. Advocacy of lawbreaking heightens it still further. But even advocacy of violation, however reprehensible morally, is not a justification for denying free speech where the advocacy falls short of incitement and there is nothing to indicate that the advocacy would be immediately acted on. The wide difference between advocacy and incitement, between preparation and attempt, between assembling and conspiracy, must be borne in mind. In order to support a finding of clear and present danger it must be shown either that immediate serious violence was to be expected or was advocated, or that the past conduct furnished reason to believe that such advocacy was then contemplated.

Those who won our independence by revolution were not cowards. They did not fear political change. They did not exalt order at the cost of liberty. To courageous, self-reliant men, with confidence in the power of free and fearless reasoning applied through the processes of popular government, no danger flowing from speech can be deemed clear and present, unless the incidence of the evil apprehended is so imminent that it may befall before there is opportunity for full discussion. If there be time to expose through discussion the falsehood and fallacies, to avert the evil by the processes of education, the remedy to be applied is more speech, not enforced silence. Only an emergency can justify repression. Such must be the rule if authority is to be reconciled with freedom. Such, in my opinion, is the command of the Constitution. It is, therefore, always open to Americans to challenge a law abridging free speech and assembly by showing that there was no emergency justifying it.

Moreover, even imminent danger cannot justify resort to prohibition of these functions essential to effective democracy, unless the evil apprehended is relatively serious. Prohibition of free speech and assembly is a measure so stringent that it would be inappropriate as the means for averting a relatively trivial harm to society. A police measure may be unconstitutional merely because the remedy, although effective as means of protection, is unduly harsh or oppressive. Thus, a state might, in the exercise of its police power, make any trespass upon the land of another a crime, regardless of the results or of the intent or purpose of the trespasser. It might, also, punish an attempt, a conspiracy, or an incitement to commit the trespass. But it is hardly conceivable that this court would hold constitutional a statute which punished as a felony the mere voluntary assembly with a society formed to teach that pedestrians had the moral right to cross unenclosed, unposted, waste lands and to advocate their doing so, even if there was imminent danger that advocacy would lead to a trespass. The fact that speech is likely to result in some violence or in destruction of property is not enough to justify its suppression. There must be the probability of serious injury to the state. Among freemen, the deterrents ordinarily to be applied to prevent crime are education and punishment for violations of the law, not abridgment of the rights of free speech and assembly.

The California Syndicalism Act recites, in §4:

[This] act concerns and is necessary to the immediate preservation of the public peace and safety, for the reason that at the present time large numbers of persons are going from place to place in this state advocating, teaching and practicing criminal syndicalism. . . .

This legislative declaration satisfies the requirement of the Constitution of the state concerning emergency legislation. [But] it does not preclude inquiry into the question whether, at the time and under the circumstances, the conditions existed which are essential to validity under the Federal Constitution. As a statute, even if not void on its face, may be challenged because invalid as applied, [the] result of such an inquiry may depend upon the specific facts of the particular case. Whenever the fundamental rights of free speech and assembly are alleged to have been invaded, it must remain open to a defendant to present the issue whether there actually did exist at the time a clear danger; whether the danger, if any, was imminent; and whether the evil apprehended was one so substantial as to justify the stringent restriction interposed by the legislature. The legislative declaration, like the fact that the statute was passed and was sustained by the highest court of the state, creates merely a rebuttable presumption that these conditions have been satisfied.

Whether, in 1919, when Miss Whitney did the things complained of, there was in California such clear and present danger of serious evil, might have been made the important issue in the case. She might have required that the issue be determined either by the court or the jury. She claimed below that the statute as applied to her violated the Federal Constitution; but she did not claim that it was void because there was no clear and present danger of serious evil, nor did she request that the existence of these conditions of a valid measure thus restricting the rights of free speech and assembly be passed upon by the court or a jury. On the other hand, there was evidence on which the court or jury might have found that such danger existed. I am unable to assent to the suggestion in the opinion of the court that assembling with a political party, formed to advocate the desirability of a proletarian revolution by mass action at some date necessarily far in the future, is not a right within the protection of the Fourteenth Amendment. In the present case, however, there was other testimony which tended to establish the existence of a conspiracy, on the part of members of the International Workers of the World, to commit present serious crimes; and likewise to show that such a conspiracy would be furthered by the activity of the society of which Miss Whitney was a member. Under these circumstances the judgment of the state court cannot be disturbed. [We] lack here the power occasionally exercised on review of judgments of lower federal courts to correct in criminal cases vital errors, although the objection was not taken in the trial court. [This] is a writ of error to a state court. Because we may not inquire into the errors now alleged, I concur in affirming the judgment of the state court.

MR. JUSTICE HOLMES joins in this opinion.

Note: The Brandeis Concurrence, the Right of Association, and the Road to Dennis

1. *Clear and present danger.* Justice Brandeis attempted in *Whitney* to explicate the underlying rationale of the clear and present danger standard. Was his reliance on the intent of the framers historically sound? Note that Justice Brandeis's conception of the function of free speech differs markedly from that of Justice Holmes. Whereas Justice Holmes speaks of "free trade in ideas," Justice Brandeis emphasizes the "development of the faculties" and the "deliberative" process, and suggests that "public discussion is a political duty" and that "the greatest menace to freedom is an inert people." See Blasi, The First Amendment and the Ideal of Civic Courage: The Brandeis Opinion in Whitney v. California, 29 Wm. & Mary L. Rev. 653 (1988). The differences between Justices Holmes and Brandeis become important in connection with contemporary efforts to "improve" the quality of public debate by government regulation. See section E4 infra.

2. *The persuasion principle.* Justice Brandeis emphasized that, if the danger is not imminent, "the remedy to be applied is more speech, not enforced silence." Is the opportunity for counterspeech an adequate explanation of the imminence

requirement? Consider Strauss, Persuasion, Autonomy, and Freedom of Expression, 91 Colum. L. Rev. 334-336, 346-347, 353-356 (1991):

> The government may not suppress speech on the ground that it is too persuasive. Except, perhaps, in extraordinary circumstances, the government may not restrict speech because it fears, however justifiably, that the speech will persuade those who hear it to do something of which the government disapproves. [This] principle [unifies] much of first amendment law.
>
> [T]he persuasion principle can[not] be justified on consequentialist grounds. [Justice Brandeis's] opinion in *Whitney* [argues that "good counsels"] are a "remedy" for "evil counsels." [The] suggestion is that "more" speech can accomplish practically everything that suppression could accomplish. [If] this were true, the persuasion principle would be easy to justify. [But] there will be many occasions on which this optimistic view is an illusion. The problem with the "more speech" approach is that it is not unusual for people to be persuaded to do bad things, and it will not always be possible to talk them out of it. . . .
>
> Brandeis's opinion in *Whitney*, in addition to suggesting a consequentialist argument, uses terms that we would today say reflect a conception of human autonomy: "the final end of the State" is to make people "free to develop their faculties," and liberty is valuable "both as an end and as a means." [T]he persuasion principle can be defended on autonomy grounds in the following way: Violations of the persuasion principle are similar in kind [to] lies that are told for the purpose of influencing behavior. Violating the persuasion principle is wrong for some of the same reasons that lies of this kind are wrong: both involve a denial of autonomy in the sense that they interfere with a person's control over her own reasoning processes. [When] the government violates the persuasion principle, it has determined that people [will] pursue [the government's] objectives, instead of their own.

3. *The limits of judicial dissent.* Consider H. Kalven, A Worthy Tradition: Freedom of Speech in America 158 (1988):

> Although *Whitney* marks the sixth consecutive decision in which the majority has either ignored the clear and present danger test or found it inapplicable, Justice Brandeis [continues to assert that it "has been settled" that clear and present danger is the test for restrictions of speech]. The stamina and tactics of these classic dissents are remarkable. In professional lawyering terms, the performance of Justices Holmes and Brandeis is outrageous. They keep insisting that they are adhering to the Court's true rule adopted in *Schenck* [even though they] have been told [repeatedly] by the majority that clear and present danger is not now and never was the general [test]. Yet we are all deeply in their debt for their outrageous behavior. They have kept alive a counter-tension in the tradition, and their towering prestige has invested the slogan with almost mesmerizing force. Like twin Moses come down from Mount Sinai bearing the true Commandment, they see little need to argue that the formula is rightly derived from the First Amendment, merely that it is.

4. *Deference and the preferred freedom.* Did Justice Brandeis answer Justice Sanford's contention, arguably evaded by Justice Holmes in *Gitlow*, that the Court should defer to reasonable legislative judgments in this context? Note that, in the substantive due process decisions of the same era, Justice Brandeis argued consistently for a deferential standard of review. See Chapter 6, section D, supra. See also F. Strong, Substantive Due Process of Law: A Dichotomy of Sense and Nonsense (1986). Would Justice Brandeis have been more convincing in *Whit-*

ney had he argued that such deference is inappropriate "where legislation has undermined the reasons for deference by eroding the very processes of communication and opinion-formation on which one can ordinarily rely to cause the political branches to change course"? L. Tribe, American Constitutional Law 845 n.30 (2d ed. 1988). Under this view, a well-functioning democracy is one in which government permits free speech; when speech is suppressed, the ordinary processes of representation are no longer reliable safeguards, and the government becomes self-insulating. This view is part of the general theme of representation-reinforcement in constitutional law. See Chapter 1, section C, and Chapter 6, section A; United States v. Carolene Products Co., 304 U.S. 144, 152-153 n.4 (1938); see generally J. Ely, Democracy and Distrust (1980). Does this argument overlook the possibility that a political community may freely decide to insulate itself from the deleterious aspects of free speech? Cf. Bork, The Impossibility of Finding Welfare Rights in the Constitution, 1979 Wash. U.L.Q. 695 (arguing that the theory of representation-reinforcement is self-contradictory).

5. *Association.* In the pre-*Whitney* cases, the various defendants were prosecuted for engaging personally in prohibited expression. The California Criminal Syndicalism Act, however, declared it unlawful for any person knowingly to be a *member* of any organization that engages in unlawful advocacy. *Whitney* thus posed, but did not necessarily answer, three new questions: First, is the act of associating with others for expression-related purposes in itself protected by the first amendment? Second, assuming association is a protected first amendment activity, in what circumstances, if any, can the state constitutionally punish membership in an organization that engages in unlawful advocacy? The Court in *Whitney* held "knowing" membership unprotected. Is that the appropriate line? Third, how does the Holmes-Brandeis conception of clear and present danger apply to association? Recall the argument of Wigmore that the legislature should be permitted to consider the cumulative danger posed by many individually harmless speakers in deciding whether there is sufficient danger to warrant the suppression of speech.

6. *A new direction?* In the decade following *Whitney*, the Court handed down three decisions concerning subversive advocacy and the right of association. Although the Court did not expressly reconsider its earlier decisions in these cases, in each case the Court found a technical way to invalidate the conviction. Thus, after an era of nine consecutive affirmances of convictions for subversive advocacy, the Court in the next decade offered three consecutive reversals. See Fiske v. Kansas, 274 U.S. 380 (1927); De Jonge v. Oregon, 299 U.S. 353 (1937); Herndon v. Lowry, 301 U.S. 242 (1937).

7. *Clear and present danger from* Whitney *to* Dennis. In the quarter-century between *Whitney* and *Dennis*, the Court embraced clear and present danger as the appropriate test for a wide range of first amendment issues. See, e.g., Schneider v. State, section E1 infra (leafleting); Cantwell v. Connecticut, section B3 infra (hostile audience); Bridges v. California, section B2 infra (contempt by publication); Terminiello v. Chicago, section B3 infra (breach of peace). See also Strong, Fifty Years of "Clear and Present Danger": From *Schenck* to *Brandenburg* — and Beyond, 1969 Sup. Ct. Rev. 41.

8. *The war on communism.* With its 1951 decision in *Dennis*, the Court continued its quest for a satisfactory solution to the problem of subversive advocacy. During the post-World War II "cold war" era, fears over national security once

again generated wide-ranging federal and state restrictions on "radical" speech. These restrictions included extensive loyalty programs, emergency detention plans, attempts to "outlaw" the Communist Party, requirements that all so-called communist-front and communist-action organizations register with the government, and extensive legislative investigations of suspected "subversives." *Dennis*, which involved the prosecution under the Smith Act of the national leaders of the Communist Party of the United States, represents but one facet of this era.

Dennis v. United States

341 U.S. 494 (1951)

MR. CHIEF JUSTICE VINSON announced the judgment of the Court and an opinion in which MR. JUSTICE REED, MR. JUSTICE BURTON and MR. JUSTICE MINTON join.

Petitioners were indicted for violation of the conspiracy provisions of the Smith Act during the period of April 1945, to July, 1948. [A] verdict of guilty as to all the petitioners was returned by the jury. [The] Court of Appeals affirmed. . . .

Sections 2 and 3 of the Smith Act provide as follows:

> Sec. 2.
> (a) It shall be unlawful for any person —
>   (1) to knowingly or willfully advocate, abet, advise, or teach the duty, necessity, desirability, or propriety of overthrowing or destroying any government in the United States by force or violence, or by the assassination of any officer of such government. . . .
> Sec. 3. It shall be unlawful for any person to attempt to commit, or to conspire to commit, any of the acts prohibited by the provisions of . . . this title.

The indictment charged the petitioners with willfully and knowingly conspiring (1) to organize as the Communist Party of the United States of America a society, group and assembly of persons who teach and advocate the overthrow and destruction of the Government of the United States by force and violence, and (2) knowingly and willfully conspiring to advocate and teach the duty and necessity of overthrowing and destroying the Government of the United States by force and violence. . . .

The trial of the case extended over nine months, six of which were devoted to the taking of evidence, resulting in a record of 16,000 pages. Our limited grant of the writ of certiorari has removed from our consideration any question as to the sufficiency of the [evidence]. Whether on this record petitioners did in fact advocate the overthrow of the Government by force and violence is not before us, and we must base any discussion of this point upon the conclusion [of] the Court of Appeals, which [held] that the record in this case amply supports the necessary finding of the jury that petitioners, the leaders of the Communist Party in this country, [intended] to initiate a violent revolution whenever the propitious occasion appeared. . . .

[The petitioners attack] the statute on the grounds that by its terms it prohibits academic discussion of the merits of Marxism-Leninism, that it stifles ideas and is contrary to all concepts of a free speech and a free press. [But the] very language of the Smith Act [demonstrates that it] is directed at advocacy, not discussion. Thus, the trial judge properly charged the jury that they could not convict if they found that petitioners did "no more than pursue peaceful studies and discussions or teaching and advocacy in the realm of ideas." . . .

The rule we deduce from [the Espionage Act] cases is that where an offense is specified by a statute in nonspeech or nonpress terms, a conviction relying upon speech or press as evidence of violation may be sustained only when the speech or publication created a "clear and present danger" of attempting or accomplishing the prohibited crime. . . .

[In *Gitlow* and *Whitney*, the] legislature had found that a certain kind of speech was, itself, harmful and unlawful. [In such circumstances, the Court held that the test was] whether the statute was "reasonable." [Although] no case subsequent to *Whitney* and *Gitlow* has expressly overruled the majority opinions in those cases, there is little doubt that subsequent opinions have inclined toward the Holmes-Brandeis rationale. . . .

In this case we are [thus] squarely presented with the application of the "clear and present danger" test, and must decide what that phrase imports. We first note that [overthrow] of the Government by force and violence is certainly a substantial enough interest for the Government to limit speech. [If], then, this interest may be protected, the literal problem which is presented is what has been meant by the use of the phrase "clear and present danger." . . .

Obviously, the words cannot mean that before the Government may act, it must wait until the putsch is about to be executed, the plans have been laid and the signal is awaited. If Government is aware that a group aiming at its overthrow is attempting to indoctrinate its members and to commit them to a course whereby they will strike when the leaders feel the circumstances permit, action by the Government is required. The argument that there is no need for Government to concern itself, for Government is strong, it possesses ample powers to put down a rebellion, it may defeat the revolution with ease needs no answer. For that is not the question. Certainly an attempt to overthrow the Government by force, even though doomed from the outset because of inadequate numbers or power of the revolutionists, is a sufficient evil for Congress to prevent. The damage which such attempts create both physically and politically to a nation makes it impossible to measure the validity in terms of the probability of success, or the immediacy of a successful attempt. . . .

Chief Judge Learned Hand, writing for the majority below, interpreted the phrase as follows: "In each case [courts] must ask whether the gravity of the 'evil,' discounted by its improbability, justifies such invasion of free speech as is necessary to avoid the danger." [We] adopt this statement of the rule. As articulated by Chief Judge Hand, it is as succinct and inclusive as any other we might devise at this time. It takes into consideration those factors which we deem relevant, and relates their significances. More we cannot expect from words.

Likewise, we are in accord with the court below, which affirmed the trial court's finding that the requisite danger existed. The mere fact that from the period 1945 to 1948 petitioners' activities did not result in an attempt to overthrow the Government by force and violence is of course no answer to the fact that there was a group that was ready to make the attempt. The formation by petitioners of such a highly organized conspiracy, with rigidly disciplined members subject to call when the leaders, these petitioners, felt that the time had come for action, coupled with the inflammable nature of world conditions, similar uprisings in other countries, and the touch-and-go nature of our relations with countries with whom petitioners were in the very least ideologically attuned, convince us that their convictions were justified on this score. And this analysis disposes of the contention that a conspiracy to advocate, as distinguished from the advocacy itself, cannot be constitutionally restrained, because it comprises only the preparation. It is the existence of the conspiracy which creates the danger. . . .

[Affirmed.]

MR. Justice Clark took no part in the consideration or decision of this case.

MR. JUSTICE FRANKFURTER, concurring. . . .

Primary responsibility for adjusting the interests which compete in the situation before us of necessity belongs to the Congress. [We] are to set aside the judgment of those whose duty it is to legislate only if there is no reasonable basis for it. [After canvassing the entire corpus of the Court's first amendment jurisprudence, Justice Frankfurter set forth the following conclusions.]

First. Free-speech cases are not an exception to the principle that we are not legislators, that direct policy-making is not our province. [Second.] A survey of the relevant decisions indicates that the results which we have reached are on the whole those that would ensue from careful weighing of conflicting interests. [Third.] Not every type of speech occupies the same position on the scale of values. [On] any scale of values, [speech advocating the overthrow of the government by force and violence] ranks low. Throughout our decisions there has recurred a distinction between the statement of an idea which may prompt its hearers to take unlawful action, and advocacy that such action be taken. . . .

These general considerations underlie decision of the case before us. On the one hand is the interest in security. [In] determining whether application of the statute to the defendants is within the constitutional powers of Congress, we [must consider] whatever is relevant to a legislative judgment. [We] may take account of evidence brought forward at this trial and elsewhere, much of which has long been common knowledge, [that] would amply justify a legislature in concluding that recruitment of additional members of the Party would create a substantial danger to national security.

On the other hand is the interest in free speech. The right to exert all governmental powers in aid of maintaining our institutions and resisting their physical overthrow does not include intolerance of opinions and speech that cannot do harm although opposed and perhaps alien to dominant, traditional opinion. [Moreover, a] public interest is not wanting in granting freedom to speak their minds even to those who advocate the overthrow of the Government by force. For, as the evidence in this case abundantly illustrates, coupled with such advocacy is criticism of defects in our society. [We must also recognize that suppressing] advocates of overthrow inevitably will also silence critics who do not advocate overthrow but fear that their criticism may be so construed. [It] is self-delusion to think that we can punish [the defendants] for their advocacy without adding to the risks run by loyal citizens who honestly believe in some of the reforms these defendants advance. It is a sobering fact that in sustaining the convictions before us we can hardly escape restriction on the interchange of ideas. . . .

It is not for us to decide how we would adjust the clash of interests which this case presents were the primary responsibility for reconciling it ours. Congress has determined that the danger created by advocacy of overthrow justifies the ensu-ing restriction on freedom of speech. [To] make validity of legislation depend on judicial reading of events still in the womb of time [is] to charge the judiciary with duties beyond its equipment. . . .

MR. JUSTICE JACKSON, concurring. . . .

I would save [the clear and present danger standard], unmodified, for appli-cation as a "rule of reason" in the kind of case for which it was devised. When the issue is criminality of a hot-headed speech on a street corner, or circulation of a few incendiary pamphlets, or parading by some zealots behind a red flag, [it] is not beyond the capacity of the judicial process to gather, comprehend, and weigh the necessary materials for decision whether it is a clear and present danger of substantive evil or a harmless letting off of steam. [But] unless we are to hold our government captive in a judge-made verbal trap, we must approach the problem of a well-organized, nation-wide conspiracy [as] realistically as our predecessors faced the trivialities that were being prosecuted until they were checked with a rule of reason. . . .

The highest degree of constitutional protection is due to the [individual]. But even an individual cannot claim that the Constitution protects him in advocat-ing or teaching overthrow of government by force or violence. [I] think direct in-citement by speech or writing can be made a crime, and I think there can be a conviction without also proving that the odds favored its success by 99 to 1, or some other extremely high ratio. . . .

MR. JUSTICE BLACK, dissenting. . . .

[The] other opinions in this case show that the only way to affirm these con-victions is to repudiate directly or indirectly the established "clear and present danger" rule. This the Court does in a way which greatly restricts the protections afforded by the First Amendment. The opinions for affirmance indicate that the chief reason for jettisoning the rule is the expressed fear that advocacy of Com-munist doctrine endangers the safety of the Republic. Undoubtedly, a govern-mental policy of unfettered communication of ideas does entail dangers. To the Founders of this Nation, however, the benefits derived from free expression were worth the risk. . . .

Public opinion being what it now is, few will protest the conviction of these Communist petitioners. There is hope, however, that in calmer times, when present pressures, passions and fears subside, this or some later Court will restore the First Amendment liberties to the high preferred place where they belong in a free society.

MR. JUSTICE DOUGLAS, dissenting.

If this were a case where those who claimed protection under the First Amend-ment were teaching the techniques of sabotage, the assassination of the Presi-dent, the filching of documents from public files, the planting of bombs, the art of street warfare, and the like, I would have no doubts. The freedom to speak is not absolute; the teaching of methods of terror and other seditious conduct should be beyond the pale. [This] case was argued as if those were the facts. [But] the fact is that no such evidence was introduced at the trial. . . .

So far as the present record is concerned, what petitioners did was to organize people to teach and themselves teach the Marxist-Leninist doctrine contained chiefly in four books: Stalin, Foundations of Leninism (1924); Marx and Engels, Manifesto of the Communist Party (1848); Lenin, The State and Revolution (1917); History of the Communist Party of the Soviet Union (B.) (1939). . . .

The opinion of the Court does not outlaw these texts nor condemn them to the fire, as the Communists do literature offensive to their creed. But if the books themselves are not outlawed, if they can lawfully remain on library shelves, by what reasoning does their [use] become a crime? [The] Act, as construed, requires the element of intent — that those who teach the creed believe in it. The crime then depends not on what is taught but on who the teacher is. That is to make freedom of speech turn not on *what is said*, but on the *intent* with which it is said. Once we start down that road we enter territory dangerous to the liberties of every citizen. . . .

There comes a time when even speech loses its constitutional immunity. Speech innocuous one year may at another time fan such destructive flames that it must be halted in the interests of the safety of the Republic. That is the meaning of the clear and present danger test. When conditions are so critical that there will be no time to avoid the evil that the speech threatens, it is time to call a halt. . . .

[If] we are to take judicial notice of the threat of Communists within the nation, it should not be difficult to conclude that *as a political party* they are of little consequence. [Communism] in the world scene is no bogeyman; but Communism as a political faction or party in this country plainly is. Communism has been so thoroughly exposed in this country that it has been crippled as a political force. Free speech has destroyed it as an effective political party. . . .

How it can be said that there is a clear and present danger that this advocacy will succeed is, therefore, a mystery. [In] America, [the Communists] are miserable merchants of unwanted ideas; their wares remain unsold. The fact that their ideas are abhorrent does not make them powerful. [Thus], if we are to proceed on the basis of judicial notice, it is impossible for me to say that the Communists in this country are so potent or so strategically deployed that they must be suppressed for their speech. . . .

Note: Dennis *and the Communist "Conspiracy"*

1. *Clear and present danger: the Holmes/Brandeis formulation.* Could the Holmes/Brandeis formulation of clear and present danger sensibly be applied in *Dennis?* What "substantive evil" must be clear and present? Actual overthrow? Attempted overthrow? Conspiracy to overthrow? Conspiracy to advocate overthrow?

2. *Clear and present danger: the* Dennis *formulation.* Note that Judge Learned Hand, the author of *Masses,* also wrote the opinion for the court of appeals in *Dennis.* By the time of *Dennis,* Judge Hand had come to accept that *Masses* had found "little professional support." As he put it, he had "bid a long farewell to my little toy ship which set out quite bravely on the shortest voyage ever made." As a lower court judge "who took seriously his obligation to follow Supreme Court

precedents," Judge Hand did his best to make sense of "an array of rulings on 'clear and present danger' — a standard he disliked from the outset." Although upholding the convictions under his reformulated version of the standard, Judge Hand "insisted repeatedly" that the prosecution was "a mistake." As he wrote a friend shortly after the decision, "Personally I should never have prosecuted those birds. . . . So far as all this will do anything, it will encourage the faithful and maybe help the [Party's] Committee on Propaganda." G. Gunther, Learned Hand: The Man and the Judge 600-603 (1994).

Is the *Dennis* version of clear and present danger "simply the remote bad tendency test dressed up in modern style"? M. Shapiro, Freedom of Speech: The Supreme Court and Judicial Review 65 (1966). In his concurring opinion in *Whitney*, Justice Brandeis first introduced the "seriousness" element as a means of intensifying the clear and present danger standard. The *Dennis* formulation, however, uses "gravity" to dilute the standard. Is this dilution unreasonable? If government may restrict speech that creates an immediate 70 percent chance of a relatively modest evil (such as persuading a few persons to refuse induction), shouldn't it also be permitted to restrict speech that creates a less immediate 30 percent chance of a very serious evil (such as attempted overthrow of government)? See J. Ely, Democracy and Distrust 108 (1980); Greenawalt, Speech and Crime, 1980 Am. B. Found. Res. J. 645, 717; Posner, Free Speech in an Economic Perspective, 20 Suffolk U.L. Rev. 1 (1986).

3. *Deference.* The Court's present position on the deference issue is set out in Landmark Communications, Inc. v. Virginia, 435 U.S. 829 (1978):

> Deference to a legislative finding cannot limit judicial inquiry when First Amendment rights are at stake. "[A legislative declaration] does not preclude enquiry into the question whether, at the time and under the circumstances, the conditions existed which are essential to validity under the Federal Constitution." [A] legislature appropriately inquires into and may declare the reasons impelling legislative action but the judicial function commands analysis of whether the specific conduct charged falls within the reach of the statute and if so whether the legislation is consonant with the Constitution. Were it otherwise, the scope of freedom of speech and of the press would be subject to legislative definition and the function of the First Amendment as a check on legislative power would be nullified.

4. *The Smith Act in context — other anticommunist activity.* As noted earlier, in the post-World War II "cold war" era the federal government launched an intensive campaign against the Communist Party and its adherents that reached far beyond the Smith Act. Consider the following:

a. Because of a fear that communist officers of labor organizations might misuse their influence by calling strikes as a means of disrupting commerce and industry, section 9(h) of the Labor-Management Relations Act of 1947 prohibited the enforcement of employee representation rights of any labor union whose officers failed to execute affidavits that they were not members of the Communist Party. See American Communications Association v. Douds, 339 U.S. 382 (1950) (upholding section 9(h)).

b. The Subversive Activities Act of 1950 created a complex regulatory scheme requiring all "Communist-action organizations" to register with the Attorney General and to disclose a wide range of information, including membership lists. The act also established the Subversive Activities Control Board to administer the scheme and provided that, once a board order to register became final, various sanctions would automatically be imposed on the organization and its members. See Communist Party v. Subversive Activities Control Board, 367 U.S. 1 (1961) (upholding the registration requirement).

c. Both the state and federal governments created extensive loyalty programs for government employees, and at both the state and federal levels legislative committees were used extensively to investigate communist "infiltration." See Barenblatt v. United States, 360 U.S. 109 (1959) (upholding a contempt citation of a witness before a congressional investigating committee who refused to answer questions about his past and present membership in the Communist Party); Gibson v. Florida Legislative Investigating Committee, 372 U.S. 539 (1963) (invalidating a contempt citation of a witness before a state legislative investigating committee who refused to answer questions about whether certain identified members of the Communist Party were members of the NAACP).

d. There were also efforts during this era to prevent the importation of communist doctrine from abroad. See Lamont v. Postmaster General, 381 U.S. 301 (1965) (invalidating restrictions on the mailing of foreign "communist political propaganda"); Kleindienst v. Mandel, 408 U.S. 753 (1972) (upholding a law declaring foreign communists ineligible to visit the United States).

e. During this period, the FBI launched a wide-ranging campaign of anti-communist activities, including a program designed extralegally to "expose, disrupt, and otherwise neutralize" the domestic communist movement. Consider the 1976 findings of a Senate committee:

> The Government has often undertaken the secret surveillance of citizens of the basis of their political beliefs, even when those beliefs posed no threat of violence or illegal acts. [The] Government, operating primarily through secret informants, [has] swept in vast amounts of information about the personal lives, views, and associations of American citizens. Investigations of groups deemed potentially dangerous — and even of groups suspected of associating with potentially dangerous organizations — have continued for decades, despite the fact that those groups did not engage in unlawful activity. [FBI] headquarters alone has developed over 500,000 domestic intelligence files. [The] targets of intelligence activity have included political adherents of the right and the left, ranging from activists to casual supporters.

Senate Select Committee to Study Governmental Operations with Respect to Intelligence Activities, Final Report, Intelligence Activities and the Rights of Americans, Book II, S. Doc. No. 13133-4, 94th Cong., 2d Sess. 5-9 (1976). See also F. Donner, The Age of Surveillance (1980); A. Theoharis, Spying on Americans (1978).

Note: The Road to Brandenburg

1. *Revising the* Dennis *approach: advocacy of doctrine versus advocacy of action.* Following *Dennis*, federal authorities initiated Smith Act prosecutions against more than 120 individuals constituting the secondary leadership of the Communist Party. By 1957, the government had secured convictions in almost all of these prosecutions. In Yates v. United States, 354 U.S. 298 (1957), however,

the Court, in a six-to-one decision, adopted a narrow interpretation of the Smith Act to avoid constitutional doubts and overturned the convictions of several members of the Communist Party for conspiracy to violate the act. Justice Harlan delivered the opinion:

> [We are] faced with the question whether the Smith Act prohibits advocacy [of] forcible overthrow as an abstract principle, divorced from any effort to instigate action to that end, so long as such advocacy [is] engaged in with evil intent. We hold that it does not.
>
> The distinction between advocacy of abstract doctrine and advocacy directed at promoting unlawful action is one that has been consistently recognized in the opinions of this Court, [and] was heavily underscored in [*Gitlow*]. [We] need not, however, decide the issue before us in terms of constitutional compulsion, for our first duty is to construe this statute. In doing so we should not assume that Congress chose to disregard a constitutional danger zone so clearly marked. . . .
>
> [We reject the proposition] that mere doctrinal justification of forcible overthrow, if engaged in with the intent to accomplish overthrow, is punishable [under] the Smith Act. That sort of advocacy, even though uttered with the hope that it may ultimately lead to violent revolution, is too remote from concrete action to be regarded as the kind of indoctrination preparatory to action which was condemned in *Dennis*. [The] essential distinction is that those to whom the advocacy is addressed must be urged to *do* something, now or in the future, rather than merely to *believe* in something.

What is the basis of Justice Harlan's distinction between advocacy of action and advocacy of belief? Is it premised on the relative dangerousness of the expression? On the relative "value" of the speech?

Consider Gunther, Learned Hand and the Origins of Modern First Amendment Doctrine: Some Fragments of History, 27 Stan. L. Rev. 719, 753 (1975):

> Harlan found a way to curtail prosecutions under the Smith Act even though the constitutionality of the Act had been sustained in *Dennis*. He did it by [reading] the statute in terms of constitutional presuppositions; and he strove to find standards "manageable" by judges and capable of curbing jury discretion. He insisted on strict statutory standards of proof emphasizing the actual speech of the [defendants]. Harlan claimed to be interpreting *Dennis*. In fact, [*Yates*] represented doctrinal evolution in a new direction.

2. *Understanding* Yates. A dominant theme of Justice Harlan's opinion in *Yates* was that the Court had historically recognized an "essential distinction" between express advocacy of unlawful action on the one hand, and advocacy of "abstract doctrine" or general discussion of policies and ideas on the other. If the Court tests restrictions on express advocacy of unlawful action with the *Dennis* version of clear and present danger, what standard should it use to test restrictions on general discussion of policies and ideas? In reflecting on *Yates*, consider the Court's post-*Yates* decisions in *Kingsley Pictures* and *Bond*.

3. *Advocacy of immorality.* In Kingsley International Pictures Corp. v. Regents of New York, 360 U.S. 684 (1959), the Court held unconstitutional a New York statute prohibiting the issuance of a license to exhibit nonobscene motion pictures that "portray 'acts of sexual immorality [as] desirable, acceptable, or proper patterns of behavior.'" The state applied the statute to deny a license to the

film Lady Chatterley's Lover because its "theme" was that adultery was "proper behavior."

The Court observed that the state was attempting "to prevent the exhibition of a motion picture because that picture advocates an idea — that adultery under certain circumstances may be proper behavior. Yet the First Amendment's basic guarantee is of freedom to advocate ideas. The state, quite simply, has thus struck at the heart of constitutionally protected liberty." In response to the state's argument that its "action was justified because the motion picture attractively portrays a relationship which is contrary to [the] legal code of its citizenry," the Court maintained that the state "misconceives what it is that the Constitution protects." The first amendment, the Court declared, "protects advocacy of the opinion that adultery may sometimes be proper, no less than advocacy of socialism or the single tax." Indeed, quoting Justice Brandeis's opinion in *Whitney*, the Court explained that "advocacy of conduct proscribed by law is [not] 'a justification for denying free speech where the advocacy falls short of incitement and there is nothing to indicate that the advocacy would be immediately acted on.'"

4. *Support for war resisters.* In Bond v. Floyd, 385 U.S. 116 (1966), the Court held that the Georgia House of Representatives could not constitutionally refuse to seat Julian Bond, a duly elected representative, because of his statements, and statements to which he subscribed, criticizing the policy of the federal government in Vietnam and the operation of the selective service system. Four days before Bond was scheduled to be sworn in, the Student Nonviolent Coordinating Committee (SNCC), a civil rights organization of which Bond was the communications director, issued a statement declaring its "opposition to United States' involvement in Viet Nam." The statement concluded by announcing: "We are in sympathy with, and support, the men in this country who are unwilling to respond to a military draft."

In a unanimous opinion, the Court observed that "Bond could not have been constitutionally convicted under [the federal statute] which punishes any person who 'counsels, aids, or abets another to refuse or evade registration.'" The Court explained that, although the SNCC statement expressed sympathy with, and support for, those who refused to respond to a military draft, that statement "alone cannot be interpreted as a call to unlawful refusal to be drafted." The Court thus concluded that "Bond could not have been convicted for these statements consistently with the First Amendment. [Citing *Yates*.]"

5. *Association.* In Scales v. United States, 367 U.S. 203 (1961), the Court revisited the constitutional status of membership in "subversive" organizations. In *Whitney*, the Court had concluded that mere "knowing" membership was sufficient to remove constitutional protection. In *Scales*, however, following up on *Yates*, the Court maintained that a "blanket prohibition" of knowing membership in organizations "having both legal and illegal aims" might pose "a real danger that legitimate political expression or association would be impaired." To avoid this danger, the Court interpreted the Smith Act as making membership unlawful only if the individual was an "active" member and not merely a "nominal, passive, inactive or purely technical" member, with knowledge of the organization's illegal advocacy, and with the "specific intent" to further the organization's illegal ends. Thus, a member could be punished under the act only if he was an "active" member who specifically intended "to bring about the overthrow of government as speedily as circumstances would permit."

Brandenburg v. Ohio

395 U.S. 444 (1969)

PER CURIAM.

The appellant, a leader of a Ku Klux Klan group, was convicted under the Ohio Criminal Syndicalism statute of "advocat[ing] . . . the duty, necessity, or propriety of crime, sabotage, violence, or unlawful methods of terrorism as a means of accomplishing industrial or political reform" and of "voluntarily assembl[ing] with any society, group or assemblage of persons formed to teach or advocate the doctrines of criminal syndicalism." He was fined $1,000 and sentenced to one to 10 years' imprisonment. . . .

The record shows that a man, identified at trial as the appellant, telephoned an announcer-reporter on the staff of a Cincinnati television station and invited him to come to a Ku Klux Klan "rally" to be held at a farm in Hamilton County. With the cooperation of the organizers, the reporter and a cameraman attended the meeting and filmed the events. Portions of the films were later broadcast on the local station and on a national network.

The prosecution's case rested on the films and on testimony identifying the appellant as the person who communicated with the reporter and who spoke at the rally. The State also introduced into evidence several articles appearing in the film, including a pistol, a rifle, a shotgun, ammunition, a Bible, and a red hood worn by the speaker in the films.

One film showed 12 hooded figures, some of whom carried firearms. They were gathered around a large wooden cross, which they burned. No one was present other than the participants and the newsman who made the film. Most of the words uttered during the scene were incomprehensible when the film was projected, but scattered phrases could be understood that were derogatory of Negroes and, in one instance, of Jews. Another scene on the same film showed the appellant, in Klan regalia, making a speech. The speech, in full, was as follows:

> This is an organizers' meeting. We have had quite a few members here today which are — we have hundreds, hundreds of members throughout the State of Ohio. I can quote from a newspaper clipping from the Columbus Ohio Dispatch, five weeks ago Sunday morning. The Klan has more members in the State of Ohio than does any other organization. We're not a revengent organization, but if our President, our Congress, our Supreme Court, continues to suppress the white, Caucasian race, it's possible that there might have to be some revengence taken.
>
> We are marching on Congress July the Fourth, four hundred thousand strong. From there we are dividing into two groups, one group to march on St. Augustine, Florida, the other group to march into Mississippi. Thank you.

The second film showed six hooded figures one of whom, later identified as the appellant, repeated a speech very similar to that recorded on the first film. The reference to the possibility of "revengence" was omitted, and one sentence was added: "Personally, I believe the nigger should be returned to Africa, the Jew returned to Israel." Though some of the figures in the films carried weapons, the speaker did not.

The Ohio Criminal Syndicalism Statute was enacted in 1919. From 1917 to 1920, identical or quite similar laws were adopted by 20 States and two territories. . . . In 1927, this Court sustained the constitutionality of California's Criminal Syndicalism Act, [the] text of which is quite similar to that of the laws of Ohio. [*Whitney.*] The Court upheld the statute on the ground that, without more, "advocating violent means to effect political and economic change involves such danger to the security of the State that the State may outlaw it." [But] *Whitney* has been thoroughly discredited by later decisions. See [*Dennis*]. These later decisions have fashioned the principle that the constitutional guarantees of free speech and free press do not permit a State to forbid or proscribe advocacy of the use of force or of law violation except where such advocacy is directed to inciting or producing imminent lawless action and is likely to incite or produce such action.[1] As we [have said], "the mere abstract teaching [of] the moral propriety or even moral necessity for a resort to force and violence, is not the same as preparing a group for violent action and steeling it to such action." See also [*Bond*]. A statute which fails to draw this distinction impermissibly intrudes upon the freedoms guaranteed by the First and Fourteenth Amendments. It sweeps within its condemnation speech which our Constitution has immunized from governmental control. Cf. [*Yates*]. . . .

Measured by this test, Ohio's Criminal Syndicalism Act cannot be sustained. [Neither] the indictment nor the trial judge's instructions to the jury in any way refined the statute's bald definition of the crime in terms of mere advocacy not distinguished from incitement to imminent lawless action.

Accordingly, we are here confronted with a statute which, by its own words and as applied, purports to punish mere advocacy and to forbid, on pain of criminal punishment, assembly with others merely to advocate the described type of action. Such a statute falls within the condemnation of the First and Fourteenth Amendments. The contrary teaching of [*Whitney*] cannot be supported, and that decision is therefore overruled.

Reversed.

MR. JUSTICE BLACK, concurring.

I agree with the views expressed by Mr. Justice Douglas in his concurring opinion in this case that the "clear and present danger" doctrine should have no place in the interpretation of the First Amendment. I join the Court's opinion, which, as I understand it, simply cites [*Dennis*] but does not indicate any agreement on the Court's part with the "clear and present danger" doctrine on which *Dennis* purported to rely.

MR. JUSTICE DOUGLAS, concurring. . . .

I see no place in the regime of the First Amendment for any "clear and present danger" test, whether strict and tight as some would make it, or free-wheeling as the Court in *Dennis* rephrased it. When one reads the opinions closely and sees when and how the "clear and present danger" test has been applied, great

---

1. It was on the theory that the Smith Act [embodied] such a principle and that it had been applied only in conformity with it that this Court sustained the Act's constitutionality. [*Dennis.*] That this was the basis for *Dennis* was emphasized in [*Yates*], in which the Court overturned convictions for advocacy of the forcible overthrow of the Government under the Smith Act, because the trial judge's instructions had allowed convictions for mere advocacy, unrelated to its tendency to produce forcible action.

misgivings are aroused. First, the threats were often loud but always puny and made serious only by judges so wedded to the status quo that critical analysis made them nervous. Second, the test was so twisted and perverted in *Dennis* as to make the trial of those teachers of Marxism an all-out political trial which was part and parcel of the cold war that has eroded substantial parts of the First Amendment. . . .

The line between what is permissible and not subject to control and what may be made impermissible and subject to regulation is the line between ideas and overt acts. The example usually given by those who would punish speech is the case of one who falsely shouts fire in a crowded theatre. This is, however, a classic case where speech is brigaded with action. [They] are indeed inseparable and a prosecution can be launched for the overt acts actually caused. Apart from rare instances of that kind, speech is, I think, immune from prosecution. . . .

Note: *The* Brandenburg *Formulation*

1. *The meaning of* Brandenburg. Although the Court maintained that the pre-*Brandenburg* "decisions [fashioned] the principle" adopted in *Brandenburg*, *Brandenburg* seems to have gone far beyond settled law. Indeed, it has been said that the *Brandenburg* formulation would "have demanded the contrary result in [both] the early Espionage Act cases and the later Communist cases," J. Ely, Democracy and Distrust 115 (1980), and that *Brandenburg* combined "the most [speech] protective ingredients of the *Masses* emphasis with the most useful elements of the clear and present danger heritage" to produce "the most speech-protective standard yet evolved by the Supreme Court." Gunther, Learned Hand and the Origins of Modern First Amendment Doctrine: Some Fragments of History, 27 Stan. L. Rev. 719, 754, 755 (1975). More specifically, *Brandenburg* has been interpreted as requiring "three things: (1) express advocacy of law violation; (2) the advocacy must call for *immediate* law violation; and (3) the immediate law violation must be *likely* to occur." Schwartz, Holmes versus Hand: Clear and Present Danger or Advocacy of Unlawful Action?, 1994 Sup. Ct. Rev. 209, 240-241.

Thus interpreted, and particularly when viewed in the light of *Yates* and *Bond*, *Brandenburg* appears by implication to accord absolute protection to the speaker so long as he does not use express words of incitement. If this is so, does *Brandenburg* suggest that, as a general first amendment principle, expression should be absolutely protected against direct criminal prohibition, regardless of dangerousness and intent, so long as it is not of "low" first amendment value?

2. *Is* Brandenburg *overprotective of free speech?* Consider Blasi, The Pathological Perspective and the First Amendment, 85 Colum. L. Rev. 449, 449-500 (1985):

> [In] fashioning first amendment doctrines, courts ought to adopt what might be termed the pathological perspective. That is, the overriding objective at all times should be to equip the first amendment to do maximum service in those historical periods when intolerance of unorthodox ideas is most prevalent and when governments are most able and most likely to stifle dissent systematically. The first amendment, in other words, should be targeted for the worst of times.

How would you assess the Court's performance in general, and *Brandenburg* in particular, from this perspective? For critical analyses of the "pathological perspective," see Redish, The Role of Pathology in First Amendment Theory: A Skeptical Examination, 38 Case W. Res. L. Rev. 618 (1988); Christie, Why the First Amendment Should Not Be Interpreted from the Pathological Perspective, 1986 Duke L.J. 683.

3. *Subsequent decisions.* The Court has adhered to *Brandenburg*. In Hess v. Indiana, 414 U.S. 105 (1973), for example, the Court reversed the conviction for disorderly conduct of an individual who shouted, "We'll take the fucking street later [or again]," during an antiwar demonstration. The Court explained that "[a]t best, [the] statement could be taken as counsel for present moderation; at worst, it amounted to nothing more than advocacy of illegal action at some indefinite future time." Since there was no evidence that the "words were intended to produce, and likely to produce, *imminent* disorder," they could not constitutionally be punished "on the ground that they had 'a "tendency to lead to violence."'"

In NAACP v. Claiborne Hardware Co., 458 U.S. 886 (1982), the Court considered an NAACP-sponsored boycott of white merchants in Claiborne County, Mississippi. The boycott was designed to secure compliance by civic and business leaders with a list of demands for equality and racial justice. During the course of the boycott, Charles Evers, an NAACP official, stated in a public speech to several hundred people that "[i]f we catch any of you going in any of them racist stores, we're gonna break your damn neck." On the basis of this and similar statements, a state court found that fear of reprisals had caused some black citizens to withhold their patronage from the boycotted businesses. In an action brought by the white merchants, the state court declared the boycott unlawful and held the organizers liable for all damages resulting therefrom. The Supreme Court reversed:

> In the passionate atmosphere in which the speeches were delivered, they might have been understood as inviting an unlawful form of discipline or, at least, as intending to create a fear of violence whether or not improper discipline was specifically intended. [This] Court has made clear, however, that mere *advocacy* of the use of force or violence does not remove speech from the protection of the First Amendment. [The] emotionally charged rhetoric of Charles Evers' speeches did not transcend the bounds of protected speech set forth in *Brandenburg*. The lengthy addresses generally contained an impassioned plea for black citizens to unify, to support and respect each other, and to realize the political and economic power available to them. In the course of those pleas, strong language was used. If that language had been followed by acts of violence, a substantial question would be presented whether Evers could be held liable for the consequences of that unlawful conduct. In this case, however, [the] acts of violence occurred weeks or months after [the] speech. Strong and effective extemporaneous rhetoric cannot be nicely channeled in purely dulcet phrases. An advocate must be free to stimulate his audience with spontaneous and emotional appeals for unity and action in a common cause. When such appeals do not incite lawless action, they must be regarded as protected speech. To rule otherwise would ignore the "profound national commitment" that "debate on public issues should be uninhibited, robust, and wide-open."

See also Carey v. Population Services International, 431 U.S. 678 (1977) (invalidating a law prohibiting the advertisement or display of contraceptives); Communist Party of Indiana v. Whitcomb, 414 U.S. 441 (1974) (invalidating a state statute that denied a place on the ballot to any new party that failed to file "an affidavit, by its officers, under oath, that it does not advocate the overthrow of local, state or national government by force or violence").

4. *Additional variations.* Consider the following:

a. In Herceg v. Hustler Magazine, Inc., 814 F.2d 1017 (5th Cir. 1987), a fourteen-year-old boy was found hanging in his closet with a copy of Hustler on the floor beneath his feet, opened to an article entitled "Orgasms of Death," which detailed the procedures for autoerotic asphyxiation. The court invalidated a civil jury verdict against Hustler because *Brandenburg* was not satisfied.

b. In Olivia N. v. National Broadcasting Co., 178 Cal. Rptr. 888 (Ct. App. 1981), the court held that, even though the television movie Born Innocent, which described a rape using a "plumber's helper," had caused just such a rape of a nine-year-old girl by a group of teenage boys who had just seen Born Innocent shortly before, the rule in *Brandenburg* immunized NBC because no intent to injure could be shown.

c. In Rice v. The Paladin Enterprises, 128 F.3d 233 (4th Cir. 1997), a publisher distributed a book, entitled Hit Man, that extolled the lifestyle of contract murderers and offered detailed instructions on how to commit a contract murder. Following these instructions precisely, X killed Y in a contract murder, and Y's survivors thereafter sued the publisher for damages. The court held that *Brandenburg* does not control this situation and that the publisher could be held liable because the publisher "had intended . . . that the publication would be used by criminals to execute the crime of murder for hire."

Note: Abridgments of Free Expression Other Than by Direct Criminal Prohibition — Disclosure, Public Employment, and the Rights of Students and Soldiers

1. *Legislative investigation and the problem of disclosure.* Up to now, we have focused on direct criminal prohibitions of speech or association. But there are other forms of regulation that may "abridge" the freedom of expression. In some circumstances, for example, government may "chill" the exercise of free expression merely by disclosing it. This is especially likely where the individual's speech or association is unpopular. Should such an "indirect" abridgment of speech trigger the same standards of constitutional review as direct criminal prohibition? Consider the following decisions:

a. In Barenblatt v. United States, 360 U.S. 109 (1959), an instructor at Vassar College was subpoenaed to appear as a witness before a subcommittee of the House Committee on Un-American Activities during an inquiry into alleged Communist infiltration into the field of education. He was held in contempt of Congress for refusing to answer questions about his past and present membership in the Communist Party. The Court, in a five-to-four decision, held that this did not violate the first amendment:

> Where First Amendment rights are asserted to bar governmental interrogation resolution of the issue [involves] a balancing [of] the competing private and public interests. [Petitioner argues] that this particular investigation was aimed not at the revolutionary aspects [of Communist activity] but at the theoretical classroom

discussion of communism. [This] position rests on too constricted a view of the investigatory process. [The] strict requirements of a [criminal] prosecution [are] not the measure of the permissible scope of a congressional investigation into "overthrow," for of necessity the investigatory process must proceed step by step.

Justice Black, joined by Chief Justice Warren and Justice Douglas, dissented: "[The Court's balancing] completely leaves out the real interest in Barenblatt's silence, the interest of the people as a whole in being able to join organizations, advocate causes and make political 'mistakes' without later being subjected to governmental penalties for having dared to think for themselves." Black also questioned the tactics of the House Committee: "[T]he chief aim, purpose and practice of the House Un-American Activities Committee [is to punish witnesses] because they are or have been [Communists]. The punishment imposed is generally punishment by humiliation and public shame. [I] do not question the Committee's patriotism and sincerity in doing all this. I merely feel that it cannot be done by Congress under our Constitution." Justice Brennan also dissented.

b. In Gibson v. Florida Legislative Investigating Committee, 372 U.S. 539 (1963), the Florida legislature created a committee to investigate the infiltration of Communists into various organizations. Gibson, who was president of the Miami branch of the NAACP, was adjudged in contempt for refusing to disclose whether fourteen individuals previously identified as Communists were members of the NAACP. The Court, in an opinion by Justice Goldberg, distinguished Barenblatt and held that Gibson's conviction violated the first amendment:

> In Barenblatt, [it] was a refusal to answer [questions] concerning [membership] in the Communist Party which supported [the] conviction. [Here, however,] the entire thrust of the demands on the petitioner was that he disclose whether [certain] persons were members of the NAACP, itself a concededly legitimate and nonsubversive organization. [Such organizations do not] automatically forfeit their rights to privacy of association simply because the general subject matter of the legislative inquiry is Communist subversion or infiltration. [The] record in this case is insufficient to show a substantial connection between the Miami branch of the NAACP and Communist activities which [is] an essential prerequisite to demonstrating the immediate, substantial, and subordinating state interest necessary to sustain [the committee's] right of inquiry into the membership lists of the association.

Justice Harlan, joined by Justices Clark, Stewart and White, dissented: "The Court's reasoning is difficult to grasp. [The announced rule would apparently require] an investigating agency to prove in advance the very things it is trying to find out." Consider H. Kalven, The Negro and the First Amendment 114-115 (1965): "What of Justice Harlan's apparently deadly quip? Is it a proper answer [to] say that the same point might be made about requiring the government to arrest only people it 'knows' are guilty or only seek evidence it 'knows' is there? Can the Fourth Amendment be imported in this fashion into the First?"

After Brandenburg and Scales, what showing must a legislative investigating committee make before requiring a witness to dislose whether she is a member of a "subversive" organization? What showing, if any, must the government make before "infiltrating" such an organization with informers?

2. The rights of public employees. Does firing a public employee for her speech pose the same constitutional issue as criminally punishing a citizen for his

speech? Suppose the government refuses to hire an applicant for a position with the police department because she was once a member of an organization that advocates the violent overthrow of the government. Do *Brandenburg* and *Scales* govern these situations? Consider the following views:

a. McAuliffe v. Mayor of New Bedford, 155 Mass. 216, 29 N.E. 517 (1892) (in which Justice Holmes, speaking for the Supreme Judicial Court of Massachusetts, upheld a rule prohibiting police officers to "solicit money [for] any political purpose whatever"):

> The petitioner may have a constitutional right to talk politics, but he has no constitutional right to be a policeman. There are few employments for hire in which the servant does not agree to suspend his constitutional rights of free speech, as well as of idleness, by the implied terms of his contract. The servant cannot complain, as he takes the employment on the terms which are offered him.

b. Frost & Frost Trucking Co. v. Railroad Commission, 271 U.S. 583, 593-594 (1926):

> It would be a palpable incongruity to strike down an act of state legislation which [strips] the citizen of rights guaranteed by the federal Constitution, but to uphold an act by which the same result is accomplished under the guise of a surrender of a right in exchange for a valuable privilege which the State threatens otherwise to withhold. [It] is inconceivable that guarantees embedded in the Constitution [may] thus be manipulated out of existence.

The Court has generally followed *Frost* rather than *McAuliffe*. In Perry v. Sindermann, 408 U.S. 593, 597 (1972), for example, the Court announced that, "even though a person has no 'right' to a valuable government benefit and even though the government may deny him the benefit for any number of reasons, [it may not do so] on a basis that infringes his constitutionally protected interests — especially, his interest in freedom of speech." See Van Alstyne, The Demise of the Right-Privilege Distinction in Constitutional Law, 81 Harv. L. Rev. 1439 (1968); Kreimer, Allocational Sanctions: The Problem of Negative Rights in a Positive State, 132 U. Pa. L. Rev. 1293 (1984).

Does the rejection of *McAuliffe* suggest that the first amendment rights of government employees are coextensive with those of private individuals? Consider Pickering v. Board of Education, 391 U.S. 563, 568 (1968): "[The] State has interests as an employer in regulating the speech of its employees that differ significantly from those it possesses in [regulating] the speech of the citizenry in general. The problem in any case is to arrive at a balance between the interests of the [employee], as a citizen, in commenting upon matters of public concern, and the interests of the State, as an employer, in promoting the efficiency of the public services it performs through its employees."

3. *Subversive advocacy and the rights of public employees.* At the height of the post-World War II Communist scare, more than one-sixth of the total civilian labor force was subject to some sort of loyalty qualification, and the federal government and most of the states excluded from many areas of public employment individuals who had either advocated the violent overthrow of government or been members of a "subversive" organization. See Note, Developments in the Law — The National Security Interest and Civil Liberties, 85 Harv. L. Rev. 1130, 1160-

1165 (1972). What interests are served by the government's refusal to employ such individuals? Consider Israel, Elfbrandt v. Russell: The Demise of the Oath?, 1966 Sup. Ct. Rev. 193, 219:

> [At] least three different state interests are commonly advanced to justify disqualification of individuals from public employment on the basis of membership in organizations advocating the violent overthrow of government: (1) The elimination of persons who present a potential for sabotage, espionage, or other activities directly injurious to national security. (2) The elimination of persons who are likely to be either incompetent or untrustworthy in the performance of their duties. (3) The elimination of persons who, aside from any question of danger or fitness, simply are not considered deserving of a government position because they oppose the basic principles on which the government is founded.

In what circumstances, if any, are these interests sufficient to justify a restriction on the subversive advocacy or associations of public employees?

4. A *first answer*: Adler. In Adler v. Board of Education, 342 U.S. 485 (1952), the Court upheld a New York law providing that no person who becomes a member of any organization that advocates the violent overthrow of government, with knowledge of the organization's proscribed advocacy, "shall be appointed to any [position] in a public school":

> A teacher works in a sensitive area in a schoolroom. There he shapes the attitude of young minds towards the society in which they live. [That] the school authorities have the right and the duty to screen [teachers] as to their fitness to maintain the integrity of the schools [cannot] be doubted. One's associates, past and present, as well as one's conduct, may properly be considered in determining [fitness]. If, under [the] New York law, a person is found to be unfit and is disqualified from employment in the public school system because of membership in a [subversive] organization, he is not thereby denied the right of free speech and assembly. His freedom of choice between membership in the organization and employment in the school system might be limited, but [such] limitation is not one the State may not make in the exercise of its police power to protect the schools from pollution and thereby to defend its own existence.

See also Garner v. Board of Public Works, 341 U.S. 716 (1951) (upholding a requirement that every public employee swear that he does not advocate the overthrow of government by force, violence, or other unlawful means or belong to any organization that advocates such overthrow); Wieman v. Updegraff, 344 U.S. 183 (1952) (invalidating an oath requirement because, unlike the loyalty schemes upheld in *Adler* and *Garner*, "under the [challenged] Act, the fact of association alone determines disloyalty and disqualification," even if the individual lacked knowledge of the organization's proscribed advocacy).

5. A *second answer*: Elfbrandt. In Elfbrandt v. Russell, 384 U.S. 11 (1966), the Court invalidated an Arizona statute requiring all state employees to take an oath that they are not "knowingly" a member of the Communist Party or of "any other organization" having for "one of its purposes" the overthrow of the government of Arizona:

> We recognized in *Scales* that [a] "blanket prohibition of association with a group having both legal and illegal aims" would pose "a real danger that legitimate politi-

cal expression or association would be impaired." The statute with which we dealt in *Scales*, [the] "membership clause" of the Smith Act, was found not to suffer from this constitutional infirmity because, as the Court construed it, the statute reached only "active" membership [with] the "specific intent" of assisting in achieving the unlawful ends of the organization. Those who join an organization but do not share its unlawful purposes and who do not participate in its unlawful activities surely pose no threat, either as citizens or as public employees. [A] law which applies to membership without the "specific intent" to further the illegal aims of the organization infringes unnecessarily on protected freedoms. It rests on the doctrine of "guilt by association" which has no place here. [Such] a law cannot stand.

Is *Elfbrandt's* extension of *Scales* to the public employment context warranted? Does *Elfbrandt* suggest that the government may not refuse to employ an individual because of her advocacy or associations unless such advocacy or associations could constitutionally be declared unlawful? See also Keyishian v. Board of Regents, 385 U.S. 589 (1967) (overruling *Adler*).

6. *The reach of* Elfbrandt: Robel. In United States v. Robel, 389 U.S. 258 (1967), appellee, a member of the Communist Party who had worked at a shipyard for ten years "without incident," was charged with violating section 5(a)(1)(D) of the Subversive Activities Control Act of 1950, which prohibited any "knowing" member of a Communist-action organization "to engage in any employment in any defense facility." The Court held that section 5(a)(1)(D) was an "unconstitutional abridgment of the right of association protected by the First Amendment":

The Government [emphasizes] that the purpose of §5(a)(1)(D) is to reduce the threat of sabotage and espionage in the Nation's defense plants. The Government's interest in such a prophylactic measure is not insubstantial. But [the] means chosen to implement that governmental purpose in this instance cut deeply into the right of association. Section 5(a)(1)(D) [casts] its net across a broad range of associational activities, indiscriminately trapping membership which can be constitutionally punished [see *Scales*] and membership which cannot be so proscribed. [See *Elfbrandt*.] It is made irrelevant to the statute's operation that an individual may be a passive or inactive [member], that he may be unaware of the organization's unlawful aims, or that he may disagree with those unlawful aims. It is also made irrelevant that [the individual] may occupy a nonsensitive position in a defense facility. Thus, §5(a)(1)(D) contains the fatal defect of overbreadth because it seeks to bar employment both for association which may be proscribed and for association which may not be proscribed. [This] the Constitution will not tolerate.

After *Robel*, in what circumstances, if any, may the government refuse to employ an individual in a defense facility because of that individual's membership in a "subversive" organization, where the individual's membership does not meet the requirements of *Scales*?

7. Brandenburg *and public employees.* Suppose a public school teacher publicly advocates the use of cocaine. Can she be fired even though such advocacy would not meet the requirements of *Brandenburg*? Does it matter whether the expression occurs on school premises? During class? For a more comprehensive treatment of the first amendment rights of public employees, see G. Stone, L. Seidman, C. Sunstein and M. Tushnet, The First Amendment 408-433 (1999). For a comparative perspective, see Attis v. Board of School Trustees, 35

C.R.R.2d 1 (1996) (Canadian court upholding a rule prohibiting a public school teacher from making anti-Semitic statements and distributing anti-Semitic materials even during off-duty hours). For more on the general problem of "unconstitutional conditions," see Chapter 9, section E, infra.

8. *Compelled disclosure and the rights of public employees.* In what circumstances may government compel present or prospective public employees to disclose information about their advocacy, their beliefs, or their associations in order to assess their qualifications? May government compel the disclosure of only that information that would independently justify a finding of disqualification? May it compel the disclosure of any information that might reasonably lead to further inquiry? Consider the following decisions:

a. In Shelton v. Tucker, 364 U.S. 479 (1960), the Court, in a five-to-four decision, invalidated an Arkansas statute that compelled "every teacher, as a condition of employment in a state-supported school or college, to file annually an affidavit listing without limitation every organization to which he has belonged or regularly contributed within the preceding five years":

> [To] compel a teacher to disclose his every associational tie is to impair that teacher's right of free association. [Even] if there were no disclosure to the general public, the pressure upon a teacher to avoid any ties which might displease those who control his professional destiny would be constant and heavy. [Many] such relationships could have no possible bearing upon the teacher's occupational competence or fitness. [Even] though the governmental purpose be legitimate and substantial, that purpose cannot be pursued by means that broadly stifle fundamental personal liberties when the end can be more narrowly achieved.

b. In Konigsberg v. State Bar, 366 U.S. 36 (1961), the Court, in a five-to-four decision, upheld the decision of the Committee of Bar Examiners of California to reject Konigsberg's application for admission to the bar because he refused to answer questions concerning membership in the Communist Party. The Court explained that his refusal to answer obstructed a full investigation into his qualifications:

> We regard as untenable petitioner's contentions that the questions as to Communist Party membership were made irrelevant either by the fact that bare, innocent membership is not a ground of disqualification or by petitioner's willingness to answer such ultimate questions as whether he himself believed in violent overthrow or knowingly belonged to an organization advocating violent overthrow. "[If petitioner] had answered the question[s] that he refused to answer, an entirely new area of investigation might [have] opened up, and [the] Committee might [have discovered] that he does advocate the overthrow of government by force and violence. [The Committee does not] have to take any witness' testimony as [conclusive]." [We] regard the State's interest [in] having lawyers who are devoted to the law in its broadest sense, including [its] procedures for orderly change, as clearly sufficient to outweigh the minimal effect upon free association occasioned by compulsory disclosure in the circumstances here presented.

See also In re Anastoplo, 366 U.S. 82 (1961) (similar result). *Konigsberg* and *Anastoplo* preceded the Court's decisions in *Elfbrandt* and *Brandenburg*. What is the effect, if any, of those decisions? In three bar admissions decisions handed down on the same day in 1971, the Court reexamined *Koningsberg* and *Anasto-*

plo. Those decisions, however, produced no clear consensus. Although the Court held that the state could not constitutionally demand blanket disclosure of all organizational memberships, it appeared to uphold inquiry into Communist Party membership and inquiry into *knowing* membership in other "subversive" organizations. See Baird v. State Bar, 401 U.S. 1 (1971); In re Stolar, 401 U.S. 23 (1971); Law Students Civil Rights Research Council v. Wadmond, 401 U.S. 154 (1974).

9. *The first amendment rights of students.* May a public university deny official recognition to a student group because it advocates the use of violence to effect change? Consider Healy v. James, 408 U.S. 169 (1972):

> [In] 1969-70, [a] climate of unrest prevailed on many college campuses in this country. There had been widespread civil disobedience on some college campuses, accompanied by the seizure of buildings, vandalism, and arson. Some colleges had been shut down altogether, while at others files were looted and manuscripts destroyed. SDS chapters on some of those campuses had been a catalytic force during this period. . . .
>
> [The College argues that its denial of recognition was justified because SDS adheres to] a philosophy of violence and disruption. [But as] repugnant as these views may [be], the mere expression of them would not justify the denial of First Amendment rights. Whether petitioners did in fact advocate a philosophy of "destruction" thus becomes immaterial. The College, acting here as the instrumentality of the State, may not restrict speech or association simply because it finds the views expressed by any group to be abhorrent. [The] critical line [is] the line between mere advocacy and advocacy "directed to inciting or producing imminent lawless action and . . . likely to incite or produce such action." [*Brandenburg.*]

See also Papish v. Board of Curators of the University of Missouri, 410 U.S. 667 (1973) (a state university may not expel a student for distributing on campus a newspaper containing a political cartoon depicting policemen raping the Statue of Liberty); Tinker v. Des Moines School District, 393 U.S. 503 (1969) (a public school may not discipline students for wearing black armbands to school to publicize their objections to the war in Vietnam in the absence of a showing that the "forbidden conduct would 'materially and substantially interfere with the requirements of appropriate discipline in the operation of the school'").

10. *The first amendment rights of soldiers.* Does a soldier have a constitutional right to attempt to persuade other soldiers not to obey orders? Should *Brandenburg* govern? Consider Parker v. Levy, 417 U.S. 733 (1974), in which a captain in the army told enlisted personnel that "[t]he United States is wrong in being involved in the Viet Nam War. I would refuse to go to Viet Nam if ordered to do so. I don't see why any colored soldier would go to Viet Nam; they should refuse to go [and] if sent should refuse to fight because they are discriminated against [in] the United States, and they are sacrificed and discriminated against in Viet Nam by being given all the hazardous duty." As a consequence of such statements, appellee was court-martialed for "conduct unbecoming an officer and gentleman." The Court, in a five-to-three decision, upheld the conviction:

> [The] military is, by necessity, a specialized society separate from civilian society. [It has] developed laws and traditions of its [own]. "An army is not a deliberative body. [No] question can be left open as to the right to command in the officer, or the duty of obedience in the soldier." [While] members of the military are not ex-

cluded from the protection granted by the First Amendment, the different character of the military community and of the military mission requires a different application of those protections. The fundamental necessity for obedience [may] render permissible within the military that which would be constitutionally impermissible outside it. [Appellee's] conduct, that of a commissioned officer publicly urging enlisted personnel to refuse to obey orders which might send them into combat, was unprotected under the most expansive notions of the First Amendment.

See also Imwinkelreid and Zillman, An Evolution in the First Amendment: Overbreadth Analysis and Free Speech within the Military Community, 54 Tex. L. Rev. 42 (1975).

2.   *Criticism of the Judicial Process and Speech That "Threatens"*

The problem of subversive advocacy, though central to the first amendment, is but one example of a governmental effort to suppress speech because it conflicts with competing social, individual, or governmental interests. To what extent should the principles that emerged in the subversive advocacy context govern other situations as well?

Bridges v. California

314 U.S. 252 (1941)

[*Bridges* arose out of litigation between two rival unions. While a motion for new trial was pending, Bridges, president of the union against whom the trial judge had ruled, published a copy of a telegram he had sent to the Secretary of Labor describing the judge's decision as "outrageous" and suggesting that, if the decision were enforced, his union would call a strike that would tie up the port of Los Angeles and involve the entire Pacific Coast. As a result of this publication, Bridges was found guilty of contempt of court. In Times-Mirror Co. v. Superior Court, a companion case, the publisher of the Los Angeles Times was found guilty of contempt for publishing a series of editorials concerning the pending sentencing of two members of a labor union who had previously been convicted of assaulting nonunion truck drivers. The key editorial, entitled Probation for Gorillas?, described the defendants as "thugs" and "gorillas," called on the trial judge to sentence them to San Quentin, and concluded that the judge would "make a serious mistake if he grants probation to [them]." Bridges and the Times-Mirror Company maintained that the contempt convictions violated their rights of free speech and free press.]

MR. JUSTICE BLACK delivered the opinion of the Court. . . .

[The] "clear and present danger" language of the *Schenck* case has afforded practical guidance in a great variety of cases in which the scope of constitutional protections of freedom of expression was in issue. [What] finally emerges from the "clear and present danger" cases is a working principle that the substantive evil must be extremely serious and the degree of imminence extremely high before utterances can be punished.

We may appropriately begin our discussion of the judgments below by considering how much, as a practical matter, they would affect liberty of expression. [Public] interest is much more likely to be kindled by a controversial event of the day than by a generalization [of] the historian or scientist. Since [the judgments below] punish utterances made during the pendency of a case, [they] produce their restrictive results at the precise time when public interest in the matters discussed would naturally be at its height. . . .

This [threat] is, to be sure, limited in time, terminating as it does upon final disposition of the case. But this does not change its censorial quality. An endless series of moratoria on public discussion, even if each were very short, could hardly be dismissed as an insignificant abridgment of freedom of expression. [We] are [thus] convinced that the judgments below result in a curtailment of expression that cannot be dismissed as insignificant. If they can be justified at all, it must be in terms of some serious substantive evil which they are designed to avert. The substantive evil here [appears] to be double: disrespect for the judiciary; and disorderly and unfair administration of justice. The assumption that respect for the judiciary can be won by shielding judges from published criticism wrongly appraises the character of American public opinion. For [an] enforced silence, however limited, solely in the name of preserving the dignity of the bench, would probably engender resentment, suspicion, and contempt much more than it would enhance respect.

The other evil feared, disorderly and unfair administration of justice, is more plausibly associated with restricting publications which touch upon pending litigation. [Legal] trials are not like elections, to be won through the use of the meeting-hall, the radio, and the newspaper. But we cannot start with the assumption that publications of the kind here involved actually do threaten to change the nature of legal [trials]. [We] must therefore turn to the particular utterances here in question [to] determine to what extent the substantive evil of unfair administration of justice was a likely consequence, and whether the degree of likelihood was sufficient to justify summary punishment. . . .

[Turning first to the Times-Mirror Company, from] the indications in the record of the position taken by the Los Angeles Times on labor controversies in the past, there could have been little doubt of its attitude toward the probation of Shannon and Holmes. [It] is inconceivable that any judge in Los Angeles would expect anything but adverse criticism from it in the event probation were granted. [Hence], this editorial [did] no more than threaten future adverse criticism which was reasonably to be expected anyway in the event of a lenient disposition of the pending case. To regard it [as] in itself of substantial influence upon the course of justice would be to impute to judges a lack of firmness, wisdom, or honor — which we cannot accept as a major premise.

[With respect to the Bridges situation, let] us assume that the telegram could be construed as an announcement of Bridges' intention to call a strike, something which [neither] the general law of California nor the court's decree prohibited. With an eye on the realities of the situation, we cannot assume that Judge Schmidt was unaware of the possibility of a strike as a consequence of his decision. If he was not intimidated by the facts themselves, we do not believe that the most explicit statement of them could have sidetracked the course of justice. . . .

Reversed.

MR. JUSTICE FRANKFURTER, with whom concurred the CHIEF JUSTICE, MR. JUSTICE ROBERTS and MR. JUSTICE BYRNES, dissenting. . . .

Free speech is not so absolute or irrational a conception as to imply paralysis of the means for effective protection of all the freedoms secured by the Bill of Rights. [In] the cases before us, the claims on behalf of freedom of speech and of the press encounter claims on behalf of liberties no less precious. . . .

A trial is not a "free trade in ideas," nor is the best test of truth in a courtroom "the power of the thought to get itself accepted in the competition of the market." [A] court is a forum with strictly defined limits for discussion. It is circumscribed in the range of its inquiry and in its methods by the Constitution, by laws, and by age-old traditions. . . .

Of course freedom of speech and of the press [should] be employed in comment upon the work of [courts]. But [freedom] of expression can hardly carry implications that nullify the guarantees of impartial trials. . . .

Comment however forthright is one thing. Intimidation with respect to specific matters still in judicial suspense, quite another. [To be punishable, a publication] must refer to a matter under consideration and constitute in effect a threat to its impartial disposition. It must be calculated to create an atmospheric pressure incompatible with rational, impartial adjudication. But to interfere with justice it need not succeed. As with other offenses, the state should be able to proscribe attempts that fail because of the danger that attempts may succeed. [This case thus] tenders precisely the same kind of issues as that to which the "clear and present danger" test gives rise. "It is a question of proximity and degree." [*Schenck.*] . . .

[In the Times-Mirror case], a powerful newspaper admonished a judge, who within a year would have to secure popular approval if he desired continuance in office, that failure to comply with its demands would be "a serious mistake." Clearly, the state court was justified in treating this as a threat to impartial adjudication. [California] should not be denied the right [to] assure its citizens of their constitutional right of a fair trial. Here there was a real and substantial manifestation of an endeavor to exert outside influence. A powerful newspaper brought its full coercive power to bear in demanding a particular sentence. It cannot be denied that even a judge may be affected. . . .

[With respect to Bridges, the] publication of the telegram was regarded by the state supreme court as "a threat that if an attempt was made to enforce the decision, the ports of the entire Pacific Coast would be tied up." [This] occurred immediately after counsel had moved to set aside the judgment which was criticized, so unquestionably there was a threat to litigation obviously alive. It would be inadmissible dogmatism for us to say that in the context of the immediate case [this] could not have dominated the mind of the judge before whom the matter was pending. . . .

Note: Contempt by Publication and the Problem of "Threats"

1. *Clear and present danger.* Is clear and present danger a workable standard in a case like *Bridges?* What factors are relevant? Consider the following: (a) whether the judge must seek reelection; (b) whether the newspaper or speaker

is a powerful voice in the community; (c) whether the litigation is still pending; (d) the seriousness of the consequences threatened or predicted by the publication; (e) whether the judge should have anticipated these consequences, even in the absence of the publication; and (f) the courage and fortitude of the particular judge.

It has been said that "if Bridges' threat to cripple the economy of the entire West Coast did not present danger enough, the lesson of [*Bridges*] must be that almost nothing said outside the courtroom is punishable as contempt." L. Tribe, American Constitutional Law 857 n.1 (2d ed. 1988). Do you agree? In subsequent decisions, the Court, following *Bridges*, has consistently overturned convictions for contempt by publication, rejecting arguments that the expression created a clear and present danger of actual or apparent improper influence on judicial behavior. See Pennekamp v. Florida, 328 U.S. 331 (1946); Craig v. Harney, 331 U.S. 367 (1947). See also Landmark Communications, Inc. v. Virginia, 435 U.S. 829 (1978); Wood v. Georgia, 370 U.S. 375 (1962). But cf. Cox v. Louisiana, 379 U.S. 59 (1965) (suggesting that a state may constitutionally prohibit any person "with the intent of influencing any judge, juror, witness, or court officer, in the discharge of his duty, [to picket or parade] in or near a building housing a court of the State of Louisiana").

2. *Threats.* Consider Justice Frankfurter's assertion that Bridges and the Times-Mirror Co. "threatened" the judges. What is a "threat"? When may a "threat" be punished consistent with the first amendment? Is a threat "outside the scope of First Amendment protection because it operates more like a physical action than [a] communication of ideas or emotions"? Gey, The Nuremberg Files and the First Amendment Value of Threats, 78 Tex. L. Rev. 541, 591-593 (2000). See E. Baker, Human Liberty and Freedom of Speech 59-60 (1989) (the first amendment does not protect "speech designed to disrespect and distort the integrity of another's mental processes or autonomy"); K. Greenawalt, Speech, Crime and the Uses of Language 94 (1989) (the first amendment does not protect speech that "involves the creation of prospective harmful consequences in order to achieve one's objective").

Consider the following situations: (a) X threatens to kill Judge Y unless she acquits Z. (b) X threatens to disclose that Judge Y is having a lesbian relationship unless she acquits Z. (c) X threatens to oppose Judge Y's reelection unless she acquits Z. (d) X threatens to call a general strike unless Judge Y acquits Z. If a "threat" is subject to regulation because it affects behavior by coercion rather than by persuasion, does that rationale support any distinction among situations (a), (b), (c), and (d)?

What does "danger" mean in this context? Is it the danger that the threat actually will be carried out or is it the harm caused by the very fact of the threat itself? Consider R.A.V. v. City of St. Paul, 505 U.S. 377 (1992), section D6 infra, in which the Court observed that "threats of violence are outside the First Amendment" because of the need to protect individuals "from the fear of violence, from the disruption that fear engenders, and from the possibility that the threatened violence will occur." Does a threat have to be a threat "of violence" to be "outside the First Amendment"?

In Watts v. United States, 394 U.S. 705 (1969), petitioner, during a public rally at the Washington Monument, stated to a small group of persons: "I have already received my draft classification as 1-A and I have got to go for my physical this Monday coming. I am not going. If they ever make me carry a rifle the first man I want to get in my sights is L.B.J." For this remark, petitioner was convicted of violating a federal statute prohibiting any person "knowingly and willfully [to make] any threat to take the life of or to inflict bodily harm upon the President of the United States." Although conceding that the statute was constitutional "on its face," the Court reversed the conviction on the ground that "the kind of polit-ical hyperbole indulged in by petitioner" did not constitute a "threat" within the meaning of the statute. Petitioner's "only offense," the Court concluded, "was 'a kind of very crude offensive method of stating a political opposition to the Presi-dent.'" Do you agree that the statute is constitutional "on its face"? Is a threat to kill the President of "low" first amendment value?

3. *The Nuremberg Files.* Suppose defendant establishes a Website (called the "Nuremberg Files") that states that its purpose is to "collect dossiers on abor-tionists in anticipation that one day we may be able to hold them on trial for crimes against humanity," lists the names and addresses of abortion providers and their families, includes photographs of abortion providers in Wild-West-style "Wanted" posters, and crosses out the names of abortion providers who have been murdered. Can this expression be restricted on the ground that the Website con-stitutes "incitement"? On the ground that it constitutes a "threat"? See Planned Parenthood v. ACLA, 23 F. Supp. 2d 1182 (D. Or. 1998).

Consider the following jury instruction in the *ACLA* case: "A statement is [ac-tionable as a threat] when a reasonable person making the statement would fore-see that the statement would be interpreted by those to whom it is communicated as a serious expression of an intent to bodily harm or assault." Does the Nurem-berg Files Website satisfy this definition? Does this instruction satisfy the first amendment? See Gey, supra (this Website cannot constitutionally be restricted because all "three elements of *Brandenburg* — intent, immediate danger, and [expressly threatening] language" — must be present in order for the government to punish a public threat); Rothchild, Menacing Speech and the First Amend-ment: A Functional Approach to Incitement and Threats, 8 Tex. J. Women & L. 207 (1999) (this Website can be restricted because it combines the low value of express incitement with the harms usually associated with threats). Consider also United States v. Baker, 890 F. Supp. 1375 (E.D. Mich. 1995) (government can-not constitutionally punish as a "threat" defendant's e-mail messages to a third party that in fictional terms describe a "fantasy" rape of a named individual). Suppose the e-mails had been sent to the named individual herself?

3.   *Expression That Provokes a Hostile Audience Reaction*

This section examines the circumstances, if any, in which government may re-strict speech because the ideas expressed might provoke a hostile audience re-sponse. To what extent does the first amendment protect the speaker whose ex-pression provokes a "breach of the peace"? Must society tolerate speech that leads to fistfights, riots, or even mob violence? Is there a danger that, in attempting to maintain order, we may invite a "heckler's veto"?

TERMINIELLO v. CHICAGO, 337 U.S. 1 (1949). Terminiello was convicted of disorderly conduct based on a speech he delivered under the following circumstances: "The auditorium was filled to capacity with over eight hundred persons present. [Outside] a crowd of about one thousand persons gathered to protest against the meeting. A cordon of policemen was assigned to maintain order; but they were not able to prevent several disturbances. The crowd outside was angry and turbulent." Members of the crowd threw stink bombs and broke windows. Terminiello goaded his opponents, referring to them as "slimy scum," "snakes," and "bedbugs." In his condemnation of various political and racial groups, Terminiello "followed, with fidelity that [was] more than coincidental, the pattern of European fascist leaders." The Court found it unnecessary to decide the case on its facts. At Terminiello's trial, the jury was instructed that it could convict if it found that his speech included expression that "stirs the public to anger, invites dispute, brings about a condition of unrest, or creates a disturbance." The Court held that this instruction violated the first amendment:

"A function of free speech under our system of government is to invite dispute. It may indeed best serve its high purpose when it induces a condition of unrest, creates dissatisfaction with conditions as they are, or even stirs people to anger. [That] is why freedom of speech, though not absolute, [is] nevertheless protected against censorship or punishment, unless shown likely to produce a clear and present danger of a serious substantive evil that rises far above public inconvenience, annoyance, or unrest."

Terminiello stands for the proposition that speech may not be restricted because the ideas expressed offend the audience. Is that defensible? Because there is no clear and present danger? Because the harm is too insubstantial? Because the justification for suppression is fundamentally at odds with basic first amendment principles? Are no ideas sufficiently offensive to justify suppression on this basis?

Cantwell v. Connecticut

310 U.S. 296 (1940)

MR. JUSTICE ROBERTS delivered the opinion of the Court.

[In an effort to proselytize and solicit contributions, Jesse Cantwell, a Jehovah's Witness, played a phonograph record that sharply attacked the Roman Catholic religion to persons he encountered on the street. As a result of these activities, Cantwell was charged by information with various statutory and common law offenses. The fifth count, of concern here, charged commission of the common law offense of inciting a breach of the peace.]

Conviction on the fifth count was not pursuant to a statute evincing a legislative judgment that street discussion of religious affairs, because of its tendency to provoke disorder, should be regulated, or a judgment that the playing of a phonograph on the streets should in the interest of comfort or privacy be limited or prevented. Violation of an Act exhibiting such a legislative judgment and narrowly drawn to prevent the supposed evil, would pose a question differing from that we must here answer.[9] Such a declaration of the State's policy would weigh heavily in any challenge of the law as infringing constitutional limitations. Here, however, the judgment is based on a common law concept of the most general and undefined nature. . . .

The offense known as breach of the peace embraces a great variety of conduct destroying or menacing public order and tranquility. It includes not only violent acts but acts and words likely to produce violence in others. No one would have the hardihood to suggest that the principle of freedom of speech sanctions incitement to riot or that religious liberty connotes the privilege to exhort others to physical attack upon those belonging to another sect. When clear and present danger of riot, disorder, interference with traffic upon the public streets, or other immediate threat to public safety, peace, or order, appears, the power of the State to prevent or punish is obvious. Equally obvious is it that a State may not unduly suppress free communication of views, religious or other, under the guise of conserving desirable conditions. . . .

Having these considerations in mind, we note that Jesse Cantwell, on April 26, 1938, was upon a public street, where he had a right to be, and where he had a right peacefully to impart his views to others. There is no showing that his deportment was noisy, truculent, overbearing or offensive. He requested of two pedestrians permission to play to them a phonograph record. The permission was granted. It is not claimed that he intended to insult or affront the hearers by playing the record. It is plain that he wished only to interest them in his propaganda. The sound of the phonograph is not shown to have disturbed residents of the street, to have drawn a crowd, or to have impeded traffic. Thus far he had invaded no right or interest of the public or of the men accosted.

The record [embodies] a general attack on all organized religious systems as instruments of Satan and injurious to man; it then singles out the Roman Catholic Church for strictures couched in terms which naturally would offend not only persons of that persuasion, but all others who respect the honestly held religious faith of their fellows. The hearers were in fact highly offended. One of them said he felt like hitting Cantwell and the other that he was tempted to throw Cantwell off the street. The one who testified he felt like hitting Cantwell said, in answer to the question "Did you do anything else or have any other reaction?" "No, sir, because he said he would take the victrola and he went." . . .

Cantwell's conduct, in the view of the court below, considered apart from the effect of his communication upon his hearers, did not amount to a breach of the peace. One may, however, be guilty of the offense if he commit acts or make statements likely to provoke violence and disturbance of good order, even though no such eventuality be intended. Decisions to this effect are many, but examination discloses that, in practically all, the provocative language which was held to amount to a breach of the peace consisted of profane, indecent, or abusive remarks directed to the person of the hearer.

We find in the instant case no assault or threatening of bodily harm, no truculent bearing, no intentional discourtesy, no personal abuse. On the contrary, we find only an effort to persuade a willing listener to buy a book or to contribute

9. Compare [*Gitlow*].

money in the interest of what Cantwell, however misguided others may think him, conceived to be true religion.

In the realm of religious faith, and in that of political belief, sharp differences arise. In both fields the tenets of one man may seem the rankest error to his neighbor. To persuade others to his own point of view, the pleader, as we know, at times, resorts to exaggeration, to vilification of men who have been, or are, prominent in church or state, and even to false statement. But the people of this nation have ordained in the light of history, that, in spite of the probability of excesses and abuses, these liberties are, in the long view, essential to enlightened opinion and right conduct on the part of the citizens of a democracy. . . .

Although the contents of the record not unnaturally aroused animosity, we think that, in the absence of a statute narrowly drawn to define and punish specific conduct as constituting a clear and present danger to a substantial interest of the State, the petitioner's communication, considered in the light of the constitutional guarantees, raised no such clear and present menace to public peace and order as to render him liable to conviction of the common law offense in question. . . .

Reversed.

Note: Cantwell, *the Hostile Audience, and the Subversive Advocacy Analogy*

1. *Cantwell.* Note Justice Roberts's citation of *Gitlow* and his observation that the case would have posed a different question had Cantwell been convicted "pursuant to a statute evincing a legislative judgment that street discussion of religious affairs, because of its tendency to provoke disorder, should be regulated." How would the Court in 1940 have analyzed the constitutionality of Cantwell's conviction had he been convicted under a statute prohibiting the criticism of Roman Catholicism in any public place?

As Justice Roberts observed, Cantwell was not charged with violating a statute prohibiting the playing of phonographs "on the streets" or with disturbing the peace because the "sound of the phonograph [disturbed] residents of the street." Which law is "worse" from the standpoint of the first amendment — one that bans *all* use of phonographs on the streets or one that bans the use of phonographs *only* when used to criticize Roman Catholicism? Which is "worse" — a law that bans the use of phonographs when the *sound* disturbs residents of the street or one that bans phonographs when the *ideas* communicated disturb residents of the street?

Justice Roberts also observed that Cantwell did not intend "to insult or affront the hearers" and did not direct "profane, indecent, or abusive remarks" to them. Could Cantwell have been punished if he had directed "abusive remarks" to the hearers or intended "to insult" them?

Finally, Justice Roberts observed that there was no clear and present danger in *Cantwell*. But isn't it clear that Cantwell would eventually have instigated a fight? Could Cantwell have been punished if he had in fact provoked a fight?

2. *The subversive advocacy analogy.* In the subversive advocacy situation, the government seeks to suppress speech because it may successfully *persuade* the audience to act in an undesirable manner, whereas in the hostile audience context the government seeks to suppress speech because the audience may react *against*

the speaker. Which, if either, is more troublesome from the perspective of the first amendment? Is it especially inappropriate to restrict expression because its ideas are persuasive to others? Consider Strauss, Persuasion, Autonomy, and Freedom of Expression, 91 Colum. L. Rev. 334-336 (1991): "The government may not suppress speech [because] it fears, however justifiably, that the speech will persuade those who hear it to do something of which the government disapproves. [This] principle [unifies] much of first amendment law." See also Scanlon, A Theory of Freedom of Expression, 1 Phil. & Pub. Aff. 204 (1972).

Is it especially inappropriate to restrict expression because its ideas are offensive to others? Consider Texas v. Johnson, 491 U.S. 397 (1989), section E3 infra, in which the Court invalidated a state flag desecration statute as applied to an individual who burned an American flag as an expression of political protest: "If there is a bedrock principle underlying the First Amendment, it is that the Government may not prohibit the expression of an idea simply because society finds the idea itself offensive or disagreeable." See H. Kalven, The Negro and the First Amendment 140-145 (1965); Stone, Content Regulation and the First Amendment, 25 Wm. & Mary L. Rev. 189, 207-217 (1983); Kagan, Private Speech, Public Purpose: The Role of Governmental Motive in First Amendment Doctrine, 63 U. Chi. L. Rev. 415, 431-432 (1996) ("the government may not limit speech because other citizens deem the ideas offered to be wrong or offensive [because] the First Amendment protects no less against majority oppression than against runaway government").

Feiner v. New York

340 U.S. 315 (1951)

MR. CHIEF JUSTICE VINSON delivered the opinion of the Court.

Petitioner was convicted of the offense of disorderly conduct. . . .

On the evening of March 8, 1949, petitioner [was] addressing [a street-corner] meeting [in] the City of Syracuse. [The] police received a telephone complaint concerning the meeting, and two officers were detailed to investigate. [They] found a crowd of about seventy-five or eighty people, both Negro and white, filling the sidewalk and spreading out into the street. Petitioner, standing on a large wooden box on the sidewalk, was addressing the crowd through a loud-speaker system attached to an automobile. Although the purpose of his speech was to urge his listeners to attend a meeting to be held that night in the Syracuse Hotel, in its course he was making derogatory remarks concerning President Truman, the American Legion, the Mayor of Syracuse, and other local political officials. [Feiner referred to Truman as a "bum," to the mayor as a "champagne-sipping bum" who "does not speak for the Negro people," and to the American Legion as "a Nazi Gestapo."]

The police officers made no effort to interfere with petitioner's speech, but were first concerned with the effect of the crowd on both pedestrian and vehicular traffic. [The] crowd was restless and there was some pushing, shoving and milling around. . . .

At this time, petitioner was speaking in a "loud, high-pitched voice." He gave the impression that he was endeavoring to arouse the Negro people against the whites, urging that they rise up in arms and fight for equal rights. The statements before such a mixed audience "stirred up a little excitement." Some of the onlookers made remarks to the police about their inability to handle the crowd and at least one threatened violence if the police did not act. There were others who appeared to be favoring petitioner's arguments. Because of the feeling that existed in the crowd both for and against the speaker, the officers finally "stepped in to prevent it from resulting in a fight." One of the officers approached the petitioner, not for the purpose of arresting him, but to get him to break up the crowd. He asked petitioner to get down off the box, but the latter refused to accede to his request and continued talking. The officer waited for a minute and then demanded that he cease talking. Although the officer had thus twice requested petitioner to stop over the course of several minutes, petitioner not only ignored him but continued talking. During all this time, the crowd was pressing closer around petitioner and the officer. Finally, the officer told petitioner he was under arrest and ordered him to get down from the box, reaching up to grab him. Petitioner stepped down, announcing over the microphone that "the law has arrived, and I suppose they will take over now." In all, the officer had asked petitioner to get down off the box three times over a space of four or five minutes. Petitioner had been speaking for over a half hour.

On these facts, petitioner was specifically charged with violation of §722 of the Penal Law of New York, the pertinent part of which is set out in the margin.[1] . . .

We are not faced here with blind condonation by a state court of arbitrary police action. [The] courts below recognized petitioner's right to hold a street meeting at this locality, to make use of loud-speaking equipment in giving his speech, and to make derogatory remarks concerning public officials and the American Legion. They found that the officers in making the arrest were motivated solely by a proper concern for the preservation of order and protection of the general welfare, and that there was no evidence which could lend color to a claim that the acts of the police were a cover for suppression of petitioner's views and opinions. Petitioner was thus neither arrested nor convicted for the making or the content of his speech. Rather, it was the reaction which it actually engendered.

The language of Cantwell v. Connecticut, 310 U.S. 296 (1940), is appropriate here. ". . . When clear and present danger of riot, disorder, interference with traffic upon the public streets, or other immediate threat to public safety, peace, or order, appears, the power of the State to prevent or punish is obvious." . . .

We are well aware that the ordinary murmurings and objections of a hostile audience cannot be allowed to silence a speaker, and also mindful of the possible danger of giving overzealous police officials complete discretion to break up otherwise lawful public meetings. [But] we are not faced here with such a situation.

---

1. "Section 722. Any person who with intent to provoke a breach of the peace, or whereby a breach of the peace may be occasioned, commits any of the following acts shall be deemed to have committed the offense of disorderly conduct:

"1. Uses offensive, disorderly, threatening, abusive or insulting language, conduct or behavior;

"2. Acts in such a manner as to annoy, disturb, interfere with, obstruct, or be offensive to others;

"3. Congregates with others on a public street and refuses to move on when ordered by the police. . . ."

It is one thing to say that the police cannot be used as an instrument for the suppression of unpopular views, and another to say that, when as here the speaker passes the bounds of argument or persuasion and undertakes incitement to riot, they are powerless to prevent a breach of the peace. . . .

Affirmed.

[A concurring opinion of Justice Frankfurter and a dissenting opinion of Justice Douglas, in which Justice Minton concurred, are omitted.]

MR. JUSTICE BLACK, dissenting.

The record before us convinces me that petitioner, a young college student, has been sentenced to the penitentiary for the unpopular views he expressed on matters of public interest while lawfully making a street-corner speech. . . .

The Court's opinion apparently rests on this reasoning: The policeman, under the circumstances detailed, could reasonably conclude that serious fighting or even riot was imminent; therefore he could stop petitioner's speech to prevent a breach of peace; accordingly, it was "disorderly conduct" for petitioner to continue speaking in disobedience of the officer's request. As to the existence of a dangerous situation on the street corner, it seems far-fetched to suggest that the "facts" show any imminent threat of riot or uncontrollable disorder. It is neither unusual nor unexpected that some people at public street meetings mutter, mill about, push, shove, or disagree, even violently, with the speaker. Indeed, it is rare where controversial topics are discussed that an outdoor crowd does not do some or all of these things. Nor does one isolated threat to assault the speaker forebode disorder. Especially should the danger be discounted where, as here, the person threatening was a man whose wife and two small children accompanied him and who, so far as the record shows, was never close enough to petitioner to carry out the threat.

Moreover, assuming that the "facts" did indicate a critical situation, I reject the implication of the Court's opinion that the police had no obligation to protect petitioner's constitutional right to talk. The police of course have power to prevent breaches of the peace. But if, in the name of preserving order, they ever can interfere with a lawful public speaker, they first must make all reasonable efforts to protect him. Here the policeman did not even pretend to try to protect petitioner. According to the officers' testimony, the crowd was restless but there is no showing of any attempt to quiet it; pedestrians were forced to walk into the street, but there was no effort to clear a path on the sidewalk; one person threatened to assault petitioner but the officers did nothing to discourage this when even a word might have sufficed. Their duty was to protect petitioner's right to talk, even to the extent of arresting the man who threatened to interfere. Instead, they shirked that duty and acted only to suppress the right to speak.

Finally, I cannot agree with the Court's statement that petitioner's disregard of the policeman's unexplained request amounted to such "deliberate defiance" as would justify an arrest or conviction for disorderly conduct. On the contrary, I think that the policeman's action was a "deliberate defiance" of ordinary official duty as well as of the constitutional right of free speech. For at least where time allows, courtesy and explanation of commands are basic elements of good official conduct in a democratic society. Here petitioner was "asked" then "told" then "commanded" to stop speaking, but a man making a lawful address is certainly not required to be silent merely because an officer directs it. Petitioner was entitled to know why he should cease doing a lawful act. Not once was he told. I understand that people in authoritarian countries must obey arbitrary orders. I had hoped that there was no such duty in the United States. . . .

Note: Feiner, Kunz, *and the Search for Mechanisms of Control*

1. *Feiner.* Is *Feiner* consistent with *Cantwell* because Feiner triggered a clear and present danger? Because he passed "the bounds of argument or persuasion" and undertook "incitement to riot"? In what sense did Feiner "incite to riot"? Does "incitement" mean the same thing here as in the subversive advocacy context?

2. *Police orders.* Note that Feiner, unlike Cantwell, disobeyed a specific police order to stop speaking. What is the appropriate role of the police? Does the first amendment require the police to arrest the hostile members of the audience rather than to stop the speaker? Suppose the officers on the scene need support. Must they call in additional officers rather than stop the speaker? May an individual who is prosecuted for refusing to obey a police order to stop speaking assert the unconstitutionality of the order in his defense?

3. *Licensing.* Kunz v. New York, 340 U.S. 290 (1951), decided on the same day as *Feiner,* concerned the constitutionality of a city ordinance declaring it unlawful to hold public worship meetings on the streets without first obtaining a permit from the police commissioner. Kunz, an ordained Baptist minister, was issued a permit in 1946, but the permit was revoked after a hearing at which it was determined that Kunz had ridiculed and denounced other religious beliefs in such a way as to cause disorder. Thereafter, the city denied Kunz's permit applications, and in 1948 he was convicted for holding a meeting without a permit in violation of the ordinance. The Court did not decide whether a permit could constitutionally be denied on the ground that the speaker had previously caused disorder, holding instead that the permit scheme was invalid on its face because it failed to provide clear standards to guide the discretion of the official charged with administering the scheme. On standardless licensing, see section C2 infra.

Is a permit system preferable to the mechanism of control approved in *Feiner*? Dissenting in *Kunz*, Justice Jackson compared the two procedures: "Feiner was stopped," he noted, by "the order of patrolmen, put into immediate effect without hearing." Kunz, however, "was advised of charges, given a hearing, confronted by witnesses, and afforded a chance to deny the charges or to confess them and offer to amend his ways. The decision of revocation was made by a detached and responsible administrative official and Kunz could have had the decision reviewed in court." Justice Jackson concluded that "this procedure better protects freedom of speech" than the procedure approved in *Feiner.*

Consider Blasi, Prior Restraints on Demonstrations, 68 Mich. L. Rev. 1481, 1514 (1970):

[However one deals with an ongoing hostile audience], the problem is not so perplexing in the permit application context. Then, the hostile audience is not an actuality but merely a threat. The threat may be largely imagined or imagined by paranoid or hostile city officials; it almost certainly will be exaggerated. Even if accurately gauged, the threat may never materialize, especially if the municipality makes it clear that it will support the demonstrators. [Moreover, the] advance notice gives the city an adequate opportunity to protect the demonstrators — if necessary by requesting the governor to call out the National Guard. [In] contrast to the on-the-spot, uncontrollable emergency, it would seem to be a greater spur to vigilantism and a greater symbolic defeat for free speech if the legal system were to give in to a threat that *could* be contained, albeit by drastic action.

Consider also T. Emerson, The System of Freedom of Expression 342 (1970): "The ease with which the expression may be curtailed, the pressures to play safe, the speculative basis of the restriction, are all abundantly present when the standard of possible violence is used as grounds for denying a permit."

4. *Permit fees and the hostile audience.* In Forsythe County, Georgia v. The Nationalist Movement, 505 U.S. 123 (1992), the Court invalidated a municipal ordinance that authorized permit fees for parades, demonstrations, marches, and similar activities, up to a maximum of $1,000, based in part on the anticipated expense necessary to maintain the public order. The Court, in an opinion by Justice Blackmun, explained:

> The county envisions that the administrator [will] assess a fee to cover "the cost of necessary and reasonable protection of persons participating or observing [said] activity." [To perform this function, the administrator] "must necessarily examine the content of the message that is conveyed," [estimate] the response of others to that content, and judge the number of police necessary to meet that response. The fee assessed will depend on the administrator's measure of the amount of hostility likely to be created by the speech based on its content. Those wishing to express views unpopular with bottle throwers, for example, may have to pay more for their permit. [Speech] cannot be financially burdened, any more than it can be punished or banned, simply because it might offend a hostile mob. ["Regulations] which permit the Government to discriminate on the basis of the content of the message cannot be tolerated under the First Amendment." [The county] contends that the $1,000 cap on the fee [saves] its constitutionality. [But neither] the $1,000 cap [nor] even some lower nominal cap [could] save the ordinance because in this context the level of the fee is irrelevant. A tax based on the content of speech does not become more constitutional because it is a small tax.

Note: *Revising the* Feiner *Approach*

1. A *"far cry" from* Feiner. In Edwards v. South Carolina, 372 U.S. 229 (1963), petitioners, 187 black high school and college students, walked to the South Carolina State House grounds, an area open to the general public, to protest discrimination. About thirty law enforcement officers, who had advance knowledge of the demonstration, were present. Petitioners walked in an orderly manner through the grounds carrying placards bearing such messages as "I am proud to be a Negro" and "Down with segregation." A crowd of about 200 to 300 onlookers gathered; although some were identified as "possible trouble makers," there were no threatening remarks, hostile gestures, or offensive comments. There was no significant interference with either vehicular or pedestrian traffic. After thirty to forty-five minutes, police authorities informed petitioners that they would be arrested if they did not disperse within fifteen minutes. One of the demonstrators then delivered a "religious harangue," inspiring petitioners to sing several patri-

otic songs while loudly clapping their hands and stamping their feet. After fifteen minutes, petitioners were arrested. They were convicted of the common law
crime of breach of the peace.

The Court, in an opinion by Justice Stewart, held that the convictions "infringed the petitioners' constitutionally protected rights of free speech, free assembly, and freedom to petition for redress of their grievances." *Edwards*, the
Court explained, "was a far cry" from *Feiner*. Here, "there was no violence or
threat of violence on [the part of the petitioners], or on the part of any member
of the crowd watching them." Moreover, "police protection at the scene was at
all times sufficient to meet any foreseeable possibility of disorder." In the Court's
view, then, petitioners had been convicted because "the opinions which they
were peaceably expressing were sufficiently opposed to the views of the majority
of the community to attract a crowd and necessitate police protection." The Constitution, however, "does not permit a State to make criminal the peaceful expression of unpopular views." The Court thus concluded that, "as in [*Terminiello*],
the Courts of South Carolina have defined a criminal offense so as to permit conviction of the petitioners if their speech 'stirred people to anger, invited public
dispute, or brought about a condition of unrest. A conviction resting on any of
those grounds may not stand.'"

Justice Clark, the lone dissenter, rejected the Court's distinction of *Feiner*, insisting that the demonstration in *Edwards* "created a much greater danger of riot
and disorder." Indeed, in Justice Clark's view "anyone conversant with the almost
spontaneous combustion in some Southern communities in such a situation will
agree that the [town officials'] action may well have averted a major catastrophe.
[To] say that the police may not intervene until the riot has occurred is like keeping out the doctor until the patient dies." Finally, Justice Clark observed that,
even if the police were "honestly mistaken as to the imminence of danger, this
was certainly a reasonable request [in] an effort to avoid a public brawl. But the
response of petitioners and their leaders was defiance rather than cooperation."

2. A *"far cry"* from Feiner *II*. In Cox v. Louisiana, 379 U.S. 536 (1965), Cox, an
ordained minister, led a demonstration of approximately 2,000 black students to
protest the arrest the previous day of twenty-three black students who had picketed stores that maintained segregated lunch counters. The demonstration was
to take place at the local courthouse, which contained the parish jail in which
the twenty-three students were confined. The demonstrators walked to the courthouse in an orderly manner, two or three abreast. As they neared the courthouse,
the police chief stopped the procession and inquired as to their purpose. Cox
stated that they would sing the national anthem and a freedom song and recite
the Lord's Prayer and the pledge of allegiance, and that he would deliver a short
speech. The police chief instructed Cox to confine the demonstration to the west
side of the street, across the street from the courthouse. The demonstrators lined
up on the west sidewalk about five deep, spread along almost the entire length
of the block. A group of about 100 to 300 whites, mostly courthouse personnel,
gathered across the street on the steps of the courthouse. Seventy-five to eighty
policemen, several members of the fire department, and a fire truck were sta-
tioned in the street between the two groups.

The demonstration proceeded according to plan until Cox, in the course of his
speech, said: "It's lunch time. Let's go eat. There are twelve stores we are protesting. [These stores won't accept your money at one of their counters.] This is an

act of racial discrimination. These stores are open to the public. You are members of the public." These remarks caused some "muttering" and "grumbling" among the white onlookers. The sheriff, deeming Cox's appeal to the students to sit in at the lunch counters to be "inflammatory," ordered the demonstrators to disperse. When Cox and the students ignored the sheriff, the police fired tear gas, causing the demonstrators to flee. The following day, Cox was arrested. He was thereafter convicted of breach of the peace.

In a unanimous decision, the Court overturned Cox's conviction. Justice Goldberg, speaking for the Court, found "no conduct which the State had a right to prohibit as a breach of the peace." Cox's call to the students to sit in "obviously did not deprive the demonstration of its protected character." Moreover, the Court rejected the state's contention that the conviction could be sustained because "violence was about to erupt." The demonstrators themselves "were not violent and threatened no violence." Indeed, there was "no indication that the mood of the students was ever hostile, aggressive, or unfriendly." The fear of violence was thus "based upon the reaction of the group of white citizens looking on from across the street." Although there were some "mutterings," there was no evidence "that any member of the white group threatened violence." In any event, the police and other personnel present "could have handled the crowd." The Court thus concluded that the facts of *Cox* "are strikingly similar" to *Edwards* and, like *Edwards*, "a far cry" from *Feiner*.

Justices Black, Clark, and White filed separate opinions concurring in the Court's disposition of the breach of the peace conviction.

3. A *"far cry"* from Feiner III. In Gregory v. City of Chicago, 394 U.S. 111 (1969), Gregory led a march of about eighty-five protesters to the home of Chicago Mayor Richard Daley to protest segregation in the city's public schools. The protesters, accompanied by about 100 police, arrived at the mayor's home at 8:00 P.M. and began marching continuously around the block. For the first thirty minutes, they sang civil rights songs and chanted slogans criticizing the mayor and referring to him as a "snake." After 8:30, the protesters marched quietly but continued to carry sharply critical placards. In the next hour, the crowd of white onlookers grew rapidly to more than 1,000, and, as the evening wore on, they became increasingly unruly. In several instances, spectators attempted physically to block the march. There were threatening shouts such as "Get out of here niggers — go back where you belong or we will get you out of here," and rocks and eggs were thrown at the marchers. At about 9:30, the police officer in charge informed Gregory that "the situation was dangerous and becoming riotous" and asked Gregory to lead the marchers out of the area. When Gregory refused, he and the other protesters were arrested. They were thereafter convicted under Chicago's disorderly conduct ordinance, which declared it unlawful for any person to make "any improper noise, riot, disturbance, breach of the peace, or diversion tending to a breach of the peace."

The Court, in an opinion by Chief Justice Warren, unanimously overturned the convictions. The Court announced that "this is a simple case." Noting that "there is no evidence in this record that petitioners' conduct was disorderly," the Court concluded that "convictions so totally devoid of evidentiary support violate due process."

4. *Evaluation.* Why were these cases "a far cry" from *Feiner*? Consider the following possibilities: (a) The demonstrators in these cases did not pass "the bounds

of argument or persuasion and undertake incitement to riot"; (b) there was less likelihood in these cases of an imminent violent response; (c) the police were better able to handle the situation in *Edwards, Cox,* and *Gregory.*

Were these cases really "a far cry" from *Feiner,* or do they implicitly limit its precedential force? Do the results in *Edwards, Cox,* and *Gregory* suggest that the Court has implicitly embraced a set of principles for dealing with the hostile audience problem analogous to those articulated at approximately the same time for dealing with the problem of subversive advocacy?

What is "low" value speech in this context? The difficulties of defining "incitement" in cases like *Cantwell, Feiner, Edwards,* and *Cox* have already been noted. Consider also *Chaplinsky* and the "fighting words" doctrine.

Chaplinsky v. New Hampshire
315 U.S. 568 (1942)

Mr. Justice Murphy delivered the opinion of the Court.

Appellant, a member of the sect known as Jehovah's Witnesses, was convicted in the municipal court of Rochester, New Hampshire, for violation of Chapter 378, §2, of the Public Laws of New Hampshire:

> No person shall address any offensive, derisive or annoying word to any other person who is lawfully in any street or other public place, nor call him by an offensive or derisive name, nor make any noise or exclamation in his presence and hearing with intent to deride, offend or annoy him, or to prevent him from pursuing his lawful business or occupation.

The complaint charged that appellant,

> with force and arms, in a certain public place in said city of Rochester, to wit, on the public sidewalk on the easterly side of Wakefield Street, near unto the entrance of the City Hall, did unlawfully repeat, the words following, addressed to the complainant, that is to say, "You are a God damned racketeer" and "a damned Fascist and the whole government of Rochester are Fascists or agents of Fascists," the same being offensive, derisive and annoying words and names. . . .

There is no substantial dispute over the facts. Chaplinsky was distributing the literature of his sect on the streets of Rochester on a busy Saturday afternoon. Members of the local citizenry complained to the City Marshal, Bowering, that Chaplinsky was denouncing all religion as a "racket." Bowering told them that Chaplinsky was lawfully engaged, and then warned Chaplinsky that the crowd was getting restless. Some time later, a disturbance occurred and the traffic officer on duty at the busy intersection started with Chaplinsky for the police station, but did not inform him that he was under arrest or that he was going to be arrested. On the way, they encountered Marshal Bowering, who had been advised that a riot was under way and was therefore hurrying to the scene. Bowering repeated his earlier warning to Chaplinsky, who then addressed to Bowering the words set forth in the complaint.

Chaplinsky's version of the affair was slightly different. He testified that, when he met Bowering, he asked him to arrest the ones responsible for the disturbance.

In reply, Bowering cursed him and told him to come along. Appellant admitted that he said the words charged in the complaint, with the exception of the name of the Deity.

Over appellant's objection the trial court excluded, as immaterial, testimony relating to appellant's mission "to preach the true facts of the Bible," his treatment at the hands of the crowd, and the alleged neglect of duty on the part of the police. This action was approved by the court below, which held that neither provocation nor the truth of the utterance would constitute a defense to the charge. . . .

Allowing the broadest scope to the language and purpose of the Fourteenth Amendment, it is well understood that the right of free speech is not absolute at all times and under all circumstances. There are certain well-defined and narrowly limited classes of speech, the prevention and punishment of which have never been thought to raise any Constitutional problem. These include the lewd and obscene, the profane, the libelous, and the insulting or "fighting" words — those which by their very utterance inflict injury or tend to incite an immediate breach of the peace. It has been well observed that such utterances are no essential part of any exposition of ideas, and are of such slight social value as a step to truth that any benefit that may be derived from them is clearly outweighed by the social interest in order and morality. "Resort to epithets or personal abuse is not in any proper sense communication of information or opinion safeguarded by the Constitution, and its punishment as a criminal act would raise no question under that instrument." [*Cantwell*.] . . .

On the authority of its earlier decisions, the state court declared that the statute's purpose was to preserve the public peace, no words being "forbidden except such as have a direct tendency to cause acts of violence by the persons to whom, individually, the remark is addressed." It was further said:

> The word "offensive" is not to be defined in terms of what a particular addressee thinks. . . . The test is what men of common intelligence would understand would be words likely to cause an average addressee to fight. . . . The English language has a number of words and expressions which by general consent are "fighting words" when said without a disarming smile. . . . Such words, as ordinary men know, are likely to cause a fight. So are threatening, profane or obscene revilings. Derisive and annoying words can be taken as coming within the purview of the statute as heretofore interpreted only when they have this characteristic of plainly tending to excite the addressee to a breach of the peace. . . . The statute, as construed, does no more than prohibit the face-to-face words plainly likely to cause a breach of the peace by the addressee, words whose speaking constitutes a breach of the peace by the speaker — including "classical fighting words," words in current use less "classical" but equally likely to cause violence, and other disorderly words, including profanity, obscenity and threats.

We are unable to say that the limited scope of the statute as thus construed contravenes the Constitutional right of free expression. It is a statute narrowly drawn and limited to define and punish specific conduct lying within the domain of state power, the use in a public place of words likely to cause a breach of the peace. . . .

Nor can we say that the application of the statute to the facts disclosed by the record substantially or unreasonably impinges upon the privilege of free speech. Argument is unnecessary to demonstrate that the appellations "damned racketeer" and "damned Fascist" are epithets likely to provoke the average person to retaliation, and thereby cause a breach of the peace.

The refusal of the state court to admit evidence of provocation and evidence bearing on the truth or falsity of the utterances, is open to no Constitutional objection. Whether the facts sought to be proved by such evidence constitute a defense to the charge, or may be shown in mitigation, are questions for the state court to determine. Our function is fulfilled by a determination that the challenged statute, on its face and as applied, does not contravene the Fourteenth Amendment.

Affirmed.

Note: Fighting Words

1. *The two-level theory.* Building on dictum in *Cantwell*, the Court in *Chaplinsky* first fully enunciated what Professor Kalven later termed the "two-level" theory of speech, under which speech is either "protected" or "unprotected" by the first amendment according to the Court's assessment of its relative "value." Kalven, The Metaphysics of the Law of Obscenity, 1960 Sup. Ct. Rev. 1, 10. The analytical underpinnings and historical evolution of this theory, and the other varieties of "unprotected" speech mentioned in *Chaplinsky,* such as the "lewd," the "obscene," the "profane," and the "libelous," are examined more fully in section D infra.

2. *Fighting words as "low" value speech.* Why was Chaplinsky's expression unprotected by the first amendment? Because it consisted of "epithets or personal abuse"? What distinguishes an "epithet" from bona fide criticism? The following arguments might be advanced for the proposition that fighting words are of "low" first amendment value and therefore unprotected:

a. Fighting words are unprotected because, as "epithets or personal abuse," they are intended to inflict harm, rather than to communicate ideas, and thus are not really "speech" at all. They are "verbal assaults," more akin to a "punch in the mouth" than to constitutionally protected expression of opinion. See Greenawalt, Insults and Epithets: Are They Protected Speech?, 42 Rutgers L. Rev. 287, 291-298 (1990). If Chaplinsky had actually punched Bowering, could he successfully claim that this was merely a constitutionally protected expression of his accurate evaluation of Bowering's performance of his duties? It has been argued that fighting words, even if intended to hurt, are different from actual physical assaults, and that "Chaplinsky's statement was well within the category of criticism of government policy and personnel known as seditious libel." Gard, Fighting Words as Free Speech, 58 Wash. U.L.Q. 531, 542 (1980). Do you agree? Should Chaplinsky have been permitted to prove the "truth" of his remarks?

b. Fighting words are unprotected because they are "likely to provoke the average person to retaliation, and thereby cause a breach of the peace." The doctrine is thus merely a straightforward application of the Holmes/Brandeis version of clear and present danger. But is name-calling really likely to cause the *average* addressee to fight? Is the focus on the *average*, rather than the *actual*, addressee consistent with the Holmes/Brandeis formulation? How should we deal with the possibility that men may be more prone than women to respond with violence?

Even if the speaker creates a clear and present danger, one might argue that the state should punish the violent addressee rather than the speaker. The attractiveness of that alternative may depend on whether one thinks that the addressee's violent response is reasonable. Should that question ever be answered in the affirmative?

Should the fighting words doctrine have any application where the addressee, as in *Chaplinsky*, is an officer of the law, "trained to exercise a higher degree of restraint than the average citizen"? Lewis v. City of New Orleans, 408 U.S. 913 (1972) (Powell, J., concurring).

c. Fighting words are unprotected because they are "no essential part of any exposition of ideas." Does the Court undervalue the use of personal insults to dramatize one's point? Is the emotive impact worth protecting? Even if fighting words are not "essential" to the exposition of ideas, is this in itself a basis for holding them unprotected? Is it, in conjunction with other factors, a relevant consideration?

3. *Fighting words?* Consider whether the following constitute "fighting words": (1) Cantwell's phonograph record, which charged that Roman Catholicism "has by means of fraud and deception brought untold sorrow and suffering upon the people" and "operates the greatest racket ever employed amongst men and robs the people of their money," when played, as it was, to Roman Catholics. (2) Terminiello's speech, in which he called his opponents, who were outside the hall, "slimy scum," "snakes," and "bedbugs." (3) Kunz's public prayer meetings, in which he labeled Catholicism "a religion of the devil," declared that the Pope is "the anti-Christ," and described Jews as "Christ-killers" and "garbage that [should] have been burnt in the incinerators [of Nazi Germany]." (4) Gregory's repeated references to Mayor Daley as a "snake." Consider also the Court's post-*Chaplinsky* decisions:

a. In Street v. New York, 394 U.S. 576 (1969), Street, a black, on learning that James Meredith, a civil rights leader, had been shot, burned an American flag in public. A small crowd gathered, and Street said, "We don't need no damn flag. [If] they let that happen to Meredith we don't need an American flag." The state argued, among other things, that Street could constitutionally be convicted for this speech because of "the possible tendency of [his] words to provoke violent retaliation." The Court disagreed: "Though it is conceivable that some listeners might have been moved to retaliate upon hearing [Street's] disrespectful words, we cannot say that [his] remarks were so inherently inflammatory as to come within that small class of 'fighting words' which are 'likely to provoke the average person to retaliation, and thereby cause a breach of the peace.' [Citing *Chaplinsky*.]"

b. In Cohen v. California, 403 U.S. 15 (1971), Cohen wore a jacket bearing the words "Fuck the Draft" in a corridor of a courthouse. As a consequence, he was convicted under a California statute prohibiting any person "maliciously and willfully [to disturb] the peace or quiet of any neighborhood or person [by] offensive conduct." The state courts interpreted the phrase "offensive conduct" as "behavior which has a tendency to provoke *others* to acts of violence." In overturning the conviction, the Court rejected the state's argument that Cohen's speech constituted fighting words: "While the four-letter word displayed by Cohen in relation to the draft is not uncommonly employed in a personally provocative fashion, in this instance it was clearly not 'directed to the person of the hearer.' [Citing *Cantwell*.] No individual actually or likely to be present could reasonably have regarded the words on appellant's jacket as a direct personal insult."

c. In Gooding v. Wilson, 405 U.S. 518 (1972), Gooding said to a police officer attempting to restore access to an army induction center during an antiwar demonstration, "White son of a bitch, I'll kill you" and "You son of a bitch, I'll choke you to death." He was thereafter convicted under a Georgia statute prohibiting any person to "use to or of another, and in his [presence] opprobrious words or abusive language, tending to cause a breach of the peace." The Court found it unnecessary to decide whether Gooding's speech could constitutionally be punished under a properly drawn statute, holding instead that the Georgia law was overbroad and hence unconstitutional on its face because the state courts had repeatedly interpreted it as reaching clearly protected expression. As examples of this overbreadth, the Court noted that the state courts had failed to construe the statute as "limited in application, as in *Chaplinsky*, to words that 'have a direct tendency to cause acts of violence by the person to whom, individually, the remark is addressed,'" and further that the state courts had previously interpreted the statute as authorizing conviction even if, because of surrounding circumstances, the addressee might "'not be able at the time [of the remark] to assault and beat another,'" so long as "'it might still tend to cause a breach of the peace at some future time.'" The Court emphasized that this went beyond the fighting words doctrine, which reached only utterances tending "to incite an immediate breach of the peace." On the overbreadth doctrine, see section C1 infra.

d. Rosenfeld v. New Jersey, 408 U.S. 901 (1972); Lewis v. New Orleans, 408 U.S. 913 (1972); and Brown v. Oklahoma, 408 U.S. 914 (1972), were decided as companion cases. In *Rosenfeld*, the appellant, in the course of a public school board meeting attended by approximately 150 people, about 40 of whom were children, used the noun "mother-fucker" on four occasions to describe the teachers, the school board, the town, and the country. In *Lewis*, while the police were engaged in arresting appellant's son, she called them "god-damn-mother-fucker police." In *Brown*, appellant, a member of the Black Panthers, spoke by invitation to a large audience at the University of Tulsa's chapel. During the question-and-answer period, he referred to some police officers as "mother-fucking fascist pig cops" and to one officer in particular as a "black mother-fucking pig." Each appellant was convicted under a state law prohibiting, in varying forms, the use of profanity in public. In each case, the Court summarily vacated the judgment and reversed for reconsideration in light of *Gooding*.

Chief Justice Burger and Justices Blackmun and Rehnquist dissented in all three cases. Chief Justice Burger observed:

> It is barely a century since men in parts of this country carried guns constantly because the law did not afford protection. In that setting, the words used in these cases, if directed toward such an armed civilian, could well have led to death or serious bodily injury. When we undermine the general belief that the law will give protection against fighting words and profane and abusive language such as the utterances involved in these cases, we take steps to return to the law of the jungle.

See also Norwell v. Cincinnati, 414 U.S. 14 (1973) ("fighting words" conviction held unconstitutional); Hess v. Indiana, 414 U.S. 105 (1973) (same); City of Houston v. Hill, 482 U.S. 451 (1987) (same).

e. In Texas v. Johnson, 491 U.S. 397 (1989), the Court invalidated a Texas statute that prohibited any person to "desecrate" the American flag "in a way that the actor knows will seriously offend [others] likely to observe or discover his action," as applied to an individual who publicly burned the flag in symbolic protest of national policy. The Court held that this "expressive conduct" did not fall within the fighting words doctrine because "no reasonable onlooker would have regarded [the defendant's] generalized expression of dissatisfaction with the policies of the Federal Government as a direct personal insult or an invitation to exchange fisticuffs."

4. *Fighting words reconsidered.* It has been suggested that the post-*Chaplinsky* decisions establish that the doctrine applies only to the use of insulting and provocative epithets that describe a particular individual and are addressed specifically to that individual in a face-to-face encounter. See Gard, supra. Are these limitations defensible? Should the doctrine apply when an insult descriptive of a group is directed to an individual member of that group? Are insults descriptive of a group less likely to provoke a violent response? Are they, because of their generality, more likely to be of "high" first amendment value?

The Court has not upheld a conviction on the basis of the fighting words doctrine since *Chaplinsky.* It has been argued that the Court's post-*Chaplinsky* decisions have so narrowed the doctrine as to render it meaningless, and that the doctrine is "nothing more than a quaint remnant of an earlier morality that has no place in a democratic society dedicated to the principle of free expression." Gard, supra, at 536. Do you agree? Or is Chief Justice Burger right that "when we undermine the general belief that the law will give protection against fighting words [we] take steps to return to the law of the jungle"?

5. *The problem of underinclusion.* Suppose a law restricts only a subset of fighting words, such as (a) fighting words directed against blacks, (b) fighting words concerning religion, or (c) fighting words uttered in bars. Are such restrictions necessarily constitutional because the category of fighting words is itself "unprotected" by the first amendment? Are such restrictions subject to scrutiny, even though the category is "unprotected," because of the inequalities created by the decision to restrict less than the entire category? This issue is addressed in R.A.V. v. City of St. Paul, section D6 infra.

Note: The Skokie Controversy

In 1977, the Village of Skokie, a northern Chicago suburb, had a population of about 70,000 persons, 40,000 of whom were Jewish. Approximately 5,000 of the Jewish residents were survivors of Nazi concentration camps during World War II. In March 1977, Frank Collin, leader of the National Socialist Party of America, informed village officials that the party intended to hold a peaceable public assembly in Skokie on May 1 to protest the village's requirement that a $350,000 insurance bond be posted before the village's parks could be used for purposes of assembly. Collin explained that the demonstration would last twenty to thirty minutes and would consist of thirty to fifty demonstrators marching in single file in front of the village hall. The marchers would wear uniforms reminiscent of those worn by members of the Nazi Party in Germany under Hitler, and they would wear swastika emblems or armbands. The marchers would carry a party banner containing a swastika emblem and signs bearing such messages as "White Free Speech" and "Free Speech for the White Man."

Village officials filed suit, seeking to enjoin the marchers from wearing their uniforms, displaying the swastika, or distributing or displaying any materials "which incite or promote hatred against persons of Jewish faith or ancestry." The complaint alleged that the march, as planned, was a "deliberate and willful attempt to exacerbate the sensitivities of the Jewish population in Skokie and to incite racial and religious hatred" and that the display of the swastika in Skokie "constitutes a symbolic assault against large numbers of the residents of the plaintiff village and an incitation to violence and retaliation."

At a hearing before the trial court, the village presented evidence that some fifteen to eighteen Jewish organizations, along with various other anti-Nazi organizations, planned to hold a counterdemonstration to protest the march. Between 12,000 and 15,000 persons were expected to participate in the counterdemonstration. The village also presented evidence that there had already been many threats of violence, and that, if the party was permitted to demonstrate, "an uncontrollably violent situation would develop" and "bloodshed would occur." Finally, the village presented the testimony of a survivor of a Nazi concentration camp to the effect that for him and other survivors, "the swastika is a symbol that his closest family was killed by the Nazis, and that the lives of him and his children are not presently safe." The village maintained that the display of the swastika in such circumstances amounted to the intentional infliction of emotional harm. The witness testified further that, although he did not "intend to use violence against" the marchers, he did "not know if he [could] control himself." On April 29, the trial judge granted the injunction. The National Socialist Party appealed.

After the issuance of the injunction, the Illinois appellate courts refused to stay the injunction pending appeal, and the Illinois Supreme Court denied a petition for direct, expedited appeal. The party then sought a stay in the Supreme Court of the United States, which treated the petition as a petition for certiorari, granted the writ, and summarily reversed the state court's denial of the stay. In a five-to-four decision, the Court characterized the denial of the stay as a "final judgment for purposes of our jurisdiction" because it

> finally determined the merits of petitioners' claim that the outstanding injunction will deprive them of rights protected by the First Amendment during the period of appellate review which, in the normal course, may take a year or more to complete. If a State seeks to impose a restraint of this kind, it must provide strict procedural safeguards, [including] immediate appellate review. [Absent] such review, the State [must] allow a stay.

On remand, the Illinois appellate court in July modified the injunction, so as to enjoin the party only from displaying the swastika. Skokie v. Nationalist Socialist Party of America, 366 N.E.2d 347 (1977). The following January the Illinois Supreme Court held the entire injunction invalid. Skokie v. National Socialist Party of America, 373 N.E.2d 21 (1978).

During the course of the injunction litigation, Skokie enacted a series of ordinances designed to block the march. These ordinances (1) required applicants for parade permits to procure $300,000 in public liability insurance and $50,000 in property damage insurance; (2) prohibited the "dissemination of any material [including signs and clothing of symbolic significance] which promotes and incites hatred against persons by reason of their race, national origin, or religion, and is intended to do so"; and (3) prohibited anyone to demonstrate "on behalf of any political party while wearing a military-style uniform." All three ordinances were held to violate the first amendment. Collin v. Smith, 578 F.2d 1197 (7th Cir.), aff'g 477 F. Supp. 676 (N.D. Ill. 1978). With the march scheduled for June 25, 1978, the village requested the Supreme Court to stay the ruling of the court of appeals. The Court denied the stay, Justices Blackmun and Rehnquist dissenting. Smith v. Collin, 436 U.S. 953 (1978).

On June 22, Collin cancelled the march. He explained that he had used the threat of a march in Skokie as a means to win the right to demonstrate in Chicago, a right he had won while the Skokie litigation was proceeding. On July 9, 1978, the party held an hour-long rally in Chicago at which 400 riot-helmeted policemen protected the twenty-five Nazi demonstrators. There were seventy-two arrests and some rock and bottle throwing, but no serious violence.

Consider Douglas-Scott, The Hatefulness of Protected Speech: A Comparison of the American and European Approaches, 7 Wm. & Mary Bill Rts. J. 305, 309, 317, 343-345 (1999):

> [Controls] on free speech long have been permitted in many European countries to curb incitement to race hatred. [For] example, in the United Kingdom, Part III of the Public Order Act of 1986 prohibits behavior intended to or likely to have the result of stirring up racial hatred. [The European approach to free speech emphasizes] particular values — dignity, protection of personal identity, and equality. [This] approach recognizes a different sort of harm caused by the abuse of freedom than the danger of imminent lawless action required under American law. The *Brandenburg* requirement that violence be imminent before hateful speech may be proscribed is objectionable. . . .
>
> European case law looks not only to the harm caused by such expression, but also proceeds from a particular conception of individual personality and psychology. [European] case law rejects a conception of individuals as beings who merely should be left to their own devices to make up their own minds about the value of expression in the public domain, to be free to ignore it, or to counter it with more speech. Such an approach isolates human beings by forcing them to take the consequences of painful conduct and ignores the particular susceptibility of certain groups to injury, especially when the offense of the speech seems to be targeted at such groups because of their identity. [Surely] it is not enough for societies that claim to be committed to the ideals of social and political equality and respect for individual dignity to remain neutral and passive when threats to these values exist. Sometimes the state must act to show its solidarity with vulnerable minority groups and its commitment to equality.

Consider also Bollinger, The Skokie Legacy: Reflections on an "Easy Case" and Free Speech Theory, 80 Mich. L. Rev. 617, 629-631 (1982):

> [The] free speech principle is grounded as much in a desire to avoid being the slaves of our own intolerant impulses as it is in a desire to preserve an unshackled freedom to speak one's mind as one wishes. [From] this perspective upholding a right of free speech in a case like the Skokie case seems to make the most sense. [One] can understand [the] choice to protect the free speech activities of Nazis, but not because people should value their message in the slightest or believe it should

be seriously entertained, not because a commitment to self-government or rationality logically demands that such ideas be presented for consideration, not because a line could not be drawn that would exclude this ideology without inevitably encroaching on ideas that one likes — not for any of these reasons nor others related to them that are a part of the traditional baggage of the free speech argumentation; but rather because the danger of intolerance towards ideas is so pervasive an issue in our social lives, the process of mastering a capacity for tolerance so difficult, that it makes sense somewhere in the system to attempt to confront that problem and exercise more self-restraint than may be otherwise required. [On] this basis, then, tolerance becomes [a] symbolic act indicating an awareness of the risks and dangers of intolerance and a commitment to developing a certain attitude toward the ideas and beliefs of others.

May a police officer be fired for being a member of the Nazi Party? The Communist Party? The National Rifle Association?

4.   Expression That Discloses Confidential Information

This section examines government efforts to restrict the publication of factual information it would prefer to keep secret. The interests potentially furthered by such secrecy range from the individual's interest in privacy, to the right to a fair trial, to the rehabilitation of juvenile offenders, to the national security. The clash between the "right to know" and the need to "keep secret" is central to the first amendment. See DuVal, The Occasions of Secrecy, 47 U. Pitt. L. Rev. 579 (1986).

LANDMARK COMMUNICATIONS, INC. v. VIRGINIA, 435 U.S. 829 (1978). The Virginian Pilot, a Landmark newspaper, accurately reported that the Virginia Judicial Inquiry and Review Commission was contemplating an investigation of a particular state court judge. As a result of this disclosure, Landmark was convicted of violating a state statute prohibiting any person to divulge information regarding confidential matters pending before the commission. The Court, in an opinion by Chief Justice Burger, held the statute unconstitutional as applied.

The state argued that disclosure of confidential information about pending investigations would create a clear and present danger to the effective operation of the commission by chilling the willingness of individuals to file complaints and by subjecting judges and the judicial system generally to unfavorable publicity arising out of possibly unwarranted charges. Although assuming "for purposes of decision that confidentiality of Commission proceedings serves legitimate state interests," the Court emphasized that the question "is whether these interests are sufficient to justify the encroachment on First Amendment guarantees which the imposition of criminal sanctions entails." At the outset, the Court questioned "the relevance of [the clear and present danger] standard here," noting that "Mr. Justice Holmes' test was never intended" to serve as a doctrine of "mechanical application." Rather, "properly applied, the test requires a court to make its own inquiry into the imminence and magnitude of the danger said to flow from the particular utterances and then to balance the character of the evil, as well as its likelihood, against the need for free and unfettered expression. The possibility that other measures will serve the State's interests should also be weighed."

Applying that standard to the facts of *Landmark*, the Court noted that "the Commission has offered little more than assertion and conjecture to support its claim that without criminal sanctions the objectives of the statutory scheme would be seriously undermined." Moreover, "much of the risk [here] can be eliminated through careful internal procedures," such as prohibiting participants in commission proceedings from divulging confidential information.

Note: Landmark *and the Problem of Confidentiality*

Note that the Court in *Landmark* "[questioned] the relevance" of the clear and present danger standard. Should clear and present danger apply in this context? Note that Brandeis's "counterspeech" theory loses some of its force when the harm derives from the disclosure of truthful information. Does this suggest that "imminence" no longer matters? Note also that the Court paid special attention in *Landmark* to the gravity of the state's interests. Indeed, in a series of decisions since *Landmark*, the Court has consistently held that a state may not restrict the publication of truthful confidential information absent "a state interest of the highest order." See, e.g., Cox Broadcasting Corp. v. Cohn, 420 U.S. 469 (1975) (broadcaster cannot be held liable in damages for publishing a rape victim's name where the name was lawfully obtained by examining a copy of the indictment); The Florida Star v. B.J.F., 491 U.S. 524 (1989) (newspaper cannot be held liable in damages for publishing a rape victim's name where the name was obtained from a publicly released police report); Oklahoma Publishing Co. v. District Court, 430 U.S. 308 (1977) (reporter cannot be prohibited from disclosing the name of a juvenile offender where the name was obtained at court proceedings that were open to the public); Smith v. Daily Mail Publishing Co., 443 U.S. 97 (1979) (newspaper cannot be punished for publishing the name and photograph of a juvenile offender where the newspaper had learned the suspect's name from several witnesses to the shooting and from police and prosecutors at the scene); Butterworth v. Smith, 494 U.S. 624 (1990) (grand jury witnesses cannot generally be prohibited from publicly disclosing their own testimony). Finally, it is noteworthy that the Court in *Landmark* emphasized that there are other means, such as "internal procedures," to deal with the risk. Should that affect the analysis? Would such "internal procedures" eliminate *entirely* the need for restrictions of the publication of confidential information?

NEBRASKA PRESS ASSOCIATION v. STUART, 427 U.S. 539 (1976). In anticipation of a trial for a multiple murder that had attracted widespread news coverage, respondent, a Nebraska state trial court judge, entered an order that restrained petitioner newspapers and broadcasters from publishing or broadcasting accounts of confessions made by the accused or any other facts "strongly implicative" of the accused. The Court, in a unanimous decision, held the order unconstitutional. Chief Justice Burger delivered the opinion.

At the outset, the Court observed that the sixth amendment guarantees trial "by an impartial jury" in federal criminal prosecutions, and that the due process clause of the fourteenth amendment guarantees the same right in state criminal prosecutions. After reviewing its decisions concerning the relationship between pretrial publicity and the right of the defendant in a criminal case to a fair and impartial jury, the Court noted that, although in most cases the pretrial publicity had not been a problem, in others the Court had found the publicity so extensive as to render the conviction violative of due process. Compare Sheppard v. Maxwell, 384 U.S. 333 (1966) with Murphy v. Florida, 421 U.S. 794 (1975). The Court explained that in such circumstances the trial judge "has a major responsibility" to protect the rights of the defendant. The Court emphasized that the issue in this case, however, was not only whether the trial court had "erred in seeing the possibility of real danger to the defendant's rights," but also whether the "means employed were foreclosed by another provision of the Constitution."

The Court then noted that the first amendment "provides [special] protection against orders [that] impose [a] 'prior' restraint on speech." Indeed, such restraints "are the most serious and the least tolerable infringement on First Amendment rights," for unlike a criminal penalty, a prior restraint has "an immediate and irreversible sanction." Moreover, the "damage can be particularly great when the prior restraint falls upon the communication of news and commentary on current events," for "the element of time is not unimportant if press coverage is to fulfill its traditional function of bringing news to the public promptly," and the burden on government is therefore "not reduced by the temporary nature of a restraint."

The Court next turned to the question whether, on the facts of this case, "the gravity of the 'evil,' discounted by its improbability, justifies such invasion of free speech as is necessary to avoid the danger." [*Dennis.*] The Court explained that three considerations guide this inquiry. First, the Court found that the "trial judge was justified in concluding that there would be intense and pervasive pretrial publicity concerning this case," and that this "publicity might impair the defendant's right to a fair trial." Second, after mentioning several alternatives to prior restraint that should have been considered by the state court — including "change of trial venue to a place less exposed to the intense publicity"; "postponement of the trial to allow public attention to subside"; "searching questioning of prospective jurors [to] screen out those with fixed opinions as to guilt or innocence"; the "use of emphatic and clear instructions on the sworn duty of each juror to decide the issues only on evidence presented in open court"; sequestration of jurors during trial to enhance "the likelihood of dissipating the impact of pretrial publicity"; restricting what the lawyers, the police, and the witnesses may "say to anyone"; and closure "of pretrial proceedings with the consent of the defendant" — the Court found that the trial judge had not adequately considered whether such "alternative measures" would sufficiently have protected the defendant's rights to avoid the need for a prior restraint. Third, noting that the "territorial jurisdiction" of the trial court "is limited," and that "the events disclosed in the record took place in a community of [only] 850 people," the Court expressed doubt that "prior restraint on publication would [in fact] have protected [the defendant's] rights" in this case.

In invalidating the order, the Court concluded: "Of necessity our holding is confined to the record before us. But our conclusion is not simply a result of assessing the adequacy of the showing made in this case; it results in part from the problems inherent in meeting the heavy burden of demonstrating, in advance of trial, that without prior restraint a fair trial will be denied. The practical problems of managing and enforcing restrictive orders will always be present. In this sense, the record now before us is illustrative rather than exceptional. [But] we need not rule out the possibility of showing the kind of threat to fair trial rights that would possess the requisite degree of certainty to justify restraint."

Justice Brennan, joined by Justices Stewart and Marshall, concurred in the judgment: "The right to a fair trial by a jury of one's peers is unquestionably one of the most precious and sacred safeguards enshrined in the Bill of Rights. I would hold, however, that resort to prior restraints [is] a constitutionally impermissible method for enforcing that right; judges have at their disposal a broad spectrum of devices for ensuring that fundamental fairness is accorded the accused without necessitating so drastic an incursion on the equally fundamental and salutary constitutional mandate that discussion of public affairs in a free society cannot depend on the preliminary grace of judicial censors. [There] is, beyond peradventure, a clear and substantial damage to freedom of the press whenever even a temporary restraint is imposed on reporting of material concerning the operations of the criminal justice [system]. The press may be arrogant, tyrannical, abusive, and sensationalist, just as it may be incisive, probing, and informative. But at least in the context of prior restraints on publication, the decision of what, when, and how to publish is for editors, not judges."

New York Times Co. v. United States; United States v. Washington Post Co.

403 U.S. 713 (1971)

[On June 12-14, 1971, the New York Times and, on June 18, the Washington Post published excerpts from a top secret Defense Department study of the Vietnam War. The study, which was commissioned by Robert McNamara in 1967, filled forty-seven volumes and reviewed in great detail the formulation of U.S. policy toward Indochina, including military operations and secret diplomatic negotiations. The newspapers obtained the study, known popularly as the Pentagon Papers, from Daniel Ellsberg, a former Pentagon official. The government filed suit in federal district courts in New York and Washington, D.C., seeking to enjoin further publication of the materials, claiming that such publication would interfere with national security and would lead to the death of soldiers, the undermining of our alliances, the inability of our diplomats to negotiate, and the prolongation of the war. Between June 15 and June 23, the cases worked their way through the federal courts, and on June 26, the Supreme Court heard argument. On June 30, the Court issued its decision. Restraining orders remained in effect throughout the Court's deliberations.]

PER CURIAM.

We granted certiorari in these cases in which the United States seeks to enjoin the New York Times and the Washington Post from publishing the contents of a classified study entitled "History of U.S. Decision-Making Process on Viet Nam Policy."

"Any system of prior restraints of expression comes to this Court bearing a heavy presumption against its constitutional validity." [The] Government "thus carries a heavy burden of showing justification for the imposition of such a restraint." [The] District Court for the Southern District of New York in the New York Times case and the District Court for the District of Columbia and the Court of Appeals for the District of Columbia Circuit in the Washington Post case held that the Government had not met that burden. We agree.

The judgment of the Court of Appeals for the District of Columbia Circuit is therefore affirmed. The order of the Court of Appeals for the Second Circuit is reversed and the case is remanded with directions to enter a judgment affirming the judgment of the District Court for the Southern District of New York. The stays entered June 25, 1971, by the Court are vacated. The judgments shall issue forthwith.

So ordered.

MR. JUSTICE BLACK, with whom MR. JUSTICE DOUGLAS joins, concurring. . . .

[Every] moment's continuance of the injunctions against these newspapers amounts to a flagrant, indefensible, and continuing violation of the First Amendment. [For] the first time in the 182 years since the founding of the Republic, the federal courts are asked to hold that the First Amendment does not mean what it says, but rather means that the Government can halt the publication of current news of vital importance to the people of this country. . . .

In the First Amendment the Founding Fathers gave the free press the protection it must have to fulfill its essential role in our democracy. The press was to serve the governed, not the governors. The Government's power to censor the press was abolished so that the press would remain forever free to censure the Government. The press was protected so that it could bare the secrets of government and inform the people. Only a free and unrestrained press can effectively expose deception in government. . . .

[We] are asked to hold that despite the First Amendment's emphatic command, the Executive Branch, the Congress, and the Judiciary can make laws enjoining publication of current news and abridging freedom of the press in the name of "national security." . . .

The word "security" is a broad, vague generality whose contours should not be invoked to abrogate the fundamental law embodied in the First Amendment. The guarding of military and diplomatic secrets at the expense of informed representative government provides no real security for our Republic.

MR. JUSTICE DOUGLAS, with whom MR. JUSTICE BLACK joins, concurring. . . .

These disclosures may have a serious impact. But that is no basis for sanctioning a previous restraint on the press. [The] dominant purpose of the First Amendment was to prohibit the widespread practice of governmental suppression of embarrassing information. It is common knowledge that the First Amendment was adopted against the widespread use of the common law of seditious libel to punish the dissemination of material that is embarrassing to the powers-that-be. [A] debate of large proportions goes on in the Nation over our posture in Vietnam. That debate antedated the disclosure of the contents of the present documents. The latter are highly relevant to the debate in progress.

Secrecy in government is fundamentally anti-democratic, perpetuating bureaucratic errors. Open debate and discussion of public issues are vital to our national health. On public questions there should be "uninhibited, robust, and wide-open" debate. . . .

The stays in these cases that have been in effect for more than a week constitute a flouting of the principles of the First Amendment. . . .

MR. JUSTICE BRENNAN, concurring.

The error that has pervaded these cases from the outset was the granting of any injunctive relief whatsoever, interim or otherwise. The entire thrust of the Government's claim throughout these cases has been that publication of the material sought to be enjoined "could," or "might," or "may" prejudice the national interest in various ways. But the First Amendment tolerates absolutely no prior judicial restraints of the press predicated upon surmise or conjecture that untoward consequences may result.* Our cases, it is true, have indicated that there is a single, extremely narrow class of cases in which the First Amendment's ban on prior judicial restraint may be overridden. Our cases have thus far indicated that such cases may arise only when the Nation "is at war," [Schenck], during which times "[n]o one would question but that a government might prevent actual obstruction to its recruiting service or the publication of the sailing dates of transports or the number and location of troops." Near v. Minnesota, [section C2 infra]. Even if the present world situation were assumed to be tantamount to a time of war, or if the power of presently available armaments would justify even in peacetime the suppression of information that would set in motion a nuclear holocaust, in neither of these actions has the Government presented or even alleged that publication of items from or based upon the material at issue would cause the happening of an event of that nature. "[T]he chief purpose of [the First Amendment's] guaranty [is] to prevent previous restraints upon publication." [Near.] Thus, only governmental allegation and proof that publication must inevitably, directly, and immediately cause the occurrence of an event kindred to imperiling the safety of a transport already at sea can support even the issuance of an interim restraining order. [Every] restraint issued in this case, whatever its form, has violated the First Amendment — and not less so because that restraint was justified as necessary to afford the courts an opportunity to examine the claim more thoroughly. Unless and until the Government has clearly made out its case, the First Amendment commands that no injunction may issue.

MR. JUSTICE STEWART, with whom MR. JUSTICE WHITE joins, concurring.

In the governmental structure created by our Constitution, the Executive is endowed with enormous power in the two related areas of national defense and international relations. This power, largely unchecked by the Legislative and Judicial branches, has been pressed to the very hilt since the advent of the nuclear missile age. . . .

---

*Freedman v. Maryland, 380 U.S. 51 (1965), and similar cases regarding temporary restraints of allegedly obscene materials are not in point. For those cases rest upon the proposition that "obscenity is not protected by the freedoms of speech and press." [Here] there is no question but that the material sought to be suppressed is within the protection of the First Amendment; the only question is whether, notwithstanding that fact, its publication may be enjoined for a time because of the presence of an overwhelming national interest.

In the absence of the governmental checks and balances present in other areas of our national life, the only effective restraint upon executive policy and power in the areas of national defense and international affairs may lie in an enlightened citizenry — in an informed and critical public opinion which alone can here protect the values of democratic government. . . .

Yet it is elementary that the successful conduct of international diplomacy and the maintenance of an effective national defense require both confidentiality and secrecy. Other nations can hardly deal with this Nation in an atmosphere of mutual trust unless they can be assured that their confidences will be kept. And within our own executive departments, the development of considered and intelligent international policies would be impossible if those charged with their formulation could not communicate with each other freely, frankly, and in confidence. In the area of basic national defense the frequent need for absolute secrecy is, of course, self-evident.

I think there can be but one answer to this dilemma, if dilemma it be. The responsibility must be where the power is. If the Constitution gives the Executive a large degree of unshared power in the conduct of foreign affairs and the maintenance of our national defense, then under the Constitution the Executive must have the largely unshared duty to determine and preserve the degree of internal security necessary to exercise that power successfully. [It] is clear to me that it is the constitutional duty of the Executive — as a matter of sovereign prerogative and not as a matter of law as the courts know law — through the promulgation and enforcement of executive regulations, to protect the confidentiality necessary to carry out its responsibilities in the fields of international relations and national defense.

This is not to say that Congress and the courts have no role to play. Undoubtedly Congress has the power to enact specific and appropriate criminal laws to protect government property and preserve government secrets. . . .

But in the cases before us we are asked neither to construe specific regulations nor to apply specific laws. We are asked, instead, to perform a function that the Constitution gave to the Executive, not the Judiciary. We are asked, quite simply, to prevent the publication by two newspapers of material that the Executive Branch insists should not, in the national interest, be published. I am convinced that the Executive is correct with respect to some of the documents involved. But I cannot say that disclosure of any of them will surely result in direct, immediate, and irreparable damage to our Nation or its people. That being so, there can under the First Amendment be but one judicial resolution of the issues before us. I join the judgments of the Court.

MR. JUSTICE WHITE, with whom MR. JUSTICE STEWART joins, concurring.

I concur in today's judgments, but only because of the concededly extraordinary protection against prior restraints enjoyed by the press under our constitutional system. I do not say that in no circumstances would the First Amendment permit an injunction against publishing information about government plans or operations. Nor, after examining the materials the Government characterizes as the most sensitive and destructive, can I deny that revelation of these documents will do substantial damage to public interests. Indeed, I am confident that their disclosure will have that result. But I nevertheless agree that the United States has not satisfied the very heavy burden that it must meet to warrant an injunction against publication in these cases, at least in the absence of express and appropriately limited congressional authorization for prior restraints in circumstances such as these.

The Government's position is simply stated: The responsibility of the Executive for the conduct of the foreign affairs and for the security of the Nation is so basic that the President is entitled to an injunction against publication of a newspaper story whenever he can convince a court that the information to be revealed threatens "grave and irreparable" injury to the public interest; and the injunction should issue whether or not the material to be published is classified, whether or not publication would be lawful under relevant criminal statutes enacted by Congress, and regardless of the circumstances by which the newspaper came into possession of the information.

At least in the absence of legislation by Congress, based on its own investigations and findings, I am quite unable to agree that the inherent powers of the Executive and the courts reach so far as to authorize remedies having such sweeping potential for inhibiting publications by the press. . . .

[Prior] restraints require an unusually heavy justification under the First Amendment; but failure by the Government to justify prior restraints does not measure its constitutional entitlement to a conviction for criminal publication. That the Government mistakenly chose to proceed by injunction does not mean that it could not successfully proceed in another way. . . .

The Criminal Code contains numerous provisions potentially relevant to these cases. [Section] 793(e)[8] makes it a criminal act for any unauthorized possessor of a document "relating to the national defense" either (1) willfully to communicate or cause to be communicated that document to any person not entitled to receive it or (2) willfully to retain the document and fail to deliver it to an officer of the United States entitled to receive it. . . .

It is thus clear that Congress has addressed itself to the problems of protecting the security of the country and the national defense from unauthorized disclosure of potentially damaging information. [It] has not, however, authorized the injunctive remedy against threatened publication. It has apparently been satisfied to rely on criminal sanctions and their deterrent effect on the responsible as well as the irresponsible press. I am not, of course, saying that either of these newspapers has yet committed a crime or that either would commit a crime if it published all the material now in its possession. That matter must await resolution in the context of a criminal proceeding if one is instituted by the United States. . . .

---

8. Section 793(e) of 18 U.S.C. provides that:

(e) Whoever having unauthorized possession of, access to, or control over any document, writing, code book, signal book, sketch, photograph, photographic negative, blueprint, plan, map, model, instrument, appliance, or note relating to the national defense, or information relating to the national defense which information the possessor has reason to believe could be used to the injury of the United States or to the advantage of any foreign nation, willfully communicates, delivers, transmits or causes to be communicated, delivered, or transmitted, or attempts to communicate, deliver, transmit or cause to be communicated, delivered, or transmitted the same to any person not entitled to receive it, or willfully retains the same and fails to deliver it to the officer or employee of the United States entitled to receive it; is guilty of an offense punishable by 10 years in prison, a $10,000 fine, or both.

MR. JUSTICE MARSHALL, concurring.

I believe the ultimate issue in these cases [is] whether this Court or the Congress has the power to make law. . . .

The problem here is whether in these particular cases the Executive Branch has authority to invoke the equity jurisdiction of the courts to protect what it believes to be the national interest. [I]n some situations it may be that under whatever inherent powers the Government may have, as well as the implicit authority derived from the President's mandate to conduct foreign affairs and to act as Commander in Chief, there is a basis for the invocation of the equity jurisdiction of this Court as an aid to prevent the publication of material damaging to "national security," however that term may be defined.

It would, however, be utterly inconsistent with the concept of separation of powers for this Court to use its power of contempt to prevent behavior that Congress has specifically declined to prohibit. [The] Constitution provides that Congress shall make laws, the President execute laws, and courts interpret laws. [It] did not provide for government by injunction in which the courts and the Executive Branch can "make law" without regard to the action of Congress. [It] is clear that Congress has specifically rejected passing legislation that would have clearly given the President the power he seeks here and made the current activity of the newspapers unlawful. When Congress specifically declines to make conduct unlawful it is not for this Court to redecide those issues — to overrule Congress. . . .

MR. CHIEF JUSTICE BURGER, dissenting.

[In] these cases, the imperative of a free and unfettered press comes into collision with another imperative, the effective functioning of a complex modern government and specifically the effective exercise of certain constitutional powers of the Executive. Only those who view the First Amendment as an absolute in all circumstances — a view I respect, but reject — can find such cases as these to be simple or easy.

These cases are not simple for another and more immediate reason. We do not know the facts of the cases. No District Judge knew all the facts. No Court of Appeals judge knew all the facts. No member of this Court knows all the facts. . . .

I suggest we are in this posture because these cases have been conducted in unseemly haste. [It] seems reasonably clear now that the haste precluded reasonable and deliberate judicial treatment of these cases and was not warranted. The precipitate action of this Court aborting trials not yet completed is not the kind of judicial conduct that ought to attend the disposition of a great issue. . . .

It is not disputed that the Times has had unauthorized possession of the documents for three to four months, during which it has had its expert analysts studying them, presumably digesting them and preparing the material for publication. During all of this time, the Times, presumably in its capacity as trustee of the public's "right to know," has held up publication for purposes it considered proper and thus public knowledge was delayed. No doubt this was for a good reason; the analysis of 7,000 pages of complex material drawn from a vastly greater volume of material would inevitably take time and the writing of good news stories takes time. But why should the United States Government, from whom this information was illegally acquired by someone, along with all the counsel, trial judges, and appellate judges be placed under needless pressure? After these months of deferral, the alleged "right to know" has somehow and suddenly become a right that must be vindicated instanter. . . .

I would affirm the Court of Appeals for the Second Circuit and allow the District Court to complete the trial aborted by our grant of certiorari, meanwhile preserving the status quo in the Post case. I would direct that the District Court on remand give priority to the Times case to the exclusion of all other business of that court but I would not set arbitrary deadlines. . . .

We all crave speedier judicial processes but when judges are pressured as in these cases the result is a parody of the judicial function.

MR. JUSTICE HARLAN, with whom THE CHIEF JUSTICE and MR. JUSTICE BLACKMUN join, dissenting. . . .

With all respect, I consider that the Court has been almost irresponsibly feverish in dealing with these cases.

Both the Court of Appeals for the Second Circuit and the Court of Appeals for the District of Columbia Circuit rendered judgment on June 23. The New York Times' petition for certiorari, its motion for accelerated consideration thereof, and its application for interim relief were filed in this Court on June 24 at about 11 A.M. The application of the United States for interim relief in the Post case was also filed here on June 24 at about 7:15 P.M. This Court's order setting a hearing before us on June 26 at 11 A.M., a course which I joined only to avoid the possibility of even more peremptory action by the Court, was issued less than 24 hours before. The record in the Post case was filed with the Clerk shortly before 1 P.M. on June 25; the record in the Times case did not arrive until 7 or 8 o'clock that same night. The briefs of the parties were received less than two hours before argument on June 26.

This frenzied train of events took place in the name of the presumption against prior restraints created by the First Amendment. Due regard for the extraordinarily important and difficult questions involved in these litigations should have led the Court to shun such a precipitate timetable. . . .

Forced as I am to reach the merits of these cases, I dissent from the opinion and judgments of the Court. [It] is plain to me that the scope of the judicial function in passing upon the activities of the Executive Branch of the Government in the field of foreign affairs is very narrowly restricted. This view is, I think, dictated by the concept of separation of powers upon which our constitutional system rests. . . .

The power to evaluate the "pernicious influence" of premature disclosure is not, however, lodged in the Executive alone. I agree that, in performance of its duty to protect the values of the First Amendment against political pressures, the judiciary must review the initial Executive determination to the point of satisfying itself that the subject matter of the dispute does lie within the proper compass of the President's foreign relations power. Constitutional considerations forbid "a complete abandonment of judicial control." [Moreover], the judiciary may properly insist that the determination that disclosure of the subject matter would irreparably impair the national security be made by the head of the Executive Department concerned — here the Secretary of State or the Secretary of Defense — after actual personal consideration by that officer. . . .

But in my judgment the judiciary may not properly go beyond these two inquiries and redetermine for itself the probable impact of disclosure on the national security.

> [T]he very nature of executive decisions as to foreign policy is political, not judicial. Such decisions are wholly confided by our Constitution to the political departments of the government, Executive and Legislative. They are delicate, complex, and involve large elements of prophecy. They are and should be undertaken only by those directly responsible to the people whose welfare they advance or imperil. They are decisions of a kind for which the Judiciary has neither aptitude, facilities nor responsibility and which has long been held to belong in the domain of political power not subject to judicial intrusion or inquiry.

Chicago & Southern Air Lines v. Waterman Steamship Corp., 333 U.S. 103, 111 (1948) (Jackson, J.).

Even if there is some room for the judiciary to override the executive determination, it is plain that the scope of review must be exceedingly narrow. I can see no indication in the opinions of either the District Court or the Court of Appeals in the Post litigation that the conclusions of the Executive were given even the deference owing to an administrative agency, much less that owing to a coequal branch of the Government operating within the field of its constitutional prerogative. . . .

Pending further hearings in each case conducted under the appropriate ground rules, I would continue the restraints on publication. I cannot believe that the doctrine prohibiting prior restraints reaches to the point of preventing courts from maintaining the status quo long enough to act responsibly in matters of such national importance as those involved here.

MR. JUSTICE BLACKMUN, dissenting.

The First Amendment, after all, is only one part of an entire Constitution. Article II of the great document vests in the Executive Branch primary power over the conduct of foreign affairs and places in that branch the responsibility for the Nation's safety. Each provision of the Constitution is important, and I cannot subscribe to a doctrine of unlimited absolutism for the First Amendment at the cost of downgrading other provisions. First Amendment absolutism has never commanded a majority of this Court. [What] is needed here is a weighing, upon properly developed standards, of the broad right of the press to print and of the very narrow right of the Government to prevent. Such standards are not yet developed. The parties here are in disagreement as to what those standards should be. But even the newspapers concede that there are situations where restraint is in order and is constitutional. . . .

I therefore would remand these cases to be developed expeditiously, of course, but on a schedule permitting the orderly presentation of evidence from both sides. . . .

The Court, however, decides the cases today the other way. I therefore add one final comment.

I strongly urge, and sincerely hope, that these two newspapers will be fully aware of their ultimate responsibilities to the United States of America. Judge Wilkey, dissenting in the District of Columbia case [concluded] that there were a number of examples of documents that, if in the possession of the Post, and if published, "could clearly result in great harm to the nation," and he defined "harm" to mean "the death of soldiers, the destruction of alliances, the greatly increased difficulty of negotiation with our enemies, the inability of our diplomats to negotiate. . . ." I, for one, have now been able to give at least some cursory study not only to the affidavits, but to the material itself. I regret to say that from this examination I fear that Judge Wilkey's statements have possible foundation. I therefore share his concern. I hope that damage has not already been done. If, however, damage has been done, and if, with the Court's action today, these newspapers proceed to publish the critical documents and there results therefrom "the death of soldiers, the destruction of alliances, the greatly increased difficulty of negotiations with our enemies, the inability of our diplomats to negotiate," to which list I might add the factors of prolongation of the war and of further delay in the freeing of United States prisoners, then the Nation's people will know where the responsibility for these sad consequences rests.

Note: Nebraska Press, *the Pentagon Papers, and* Snepp

1. *Prior restraint.* In these decisions, the Court emphasized repeatedly that the "gag order" in *Nebraska Press* and the injunction in *New York Times* were "prior restraints," and that a prior restraint bears a special "presumption against its constitutional validity." Why is an injunction more threatening to the values underlying the first amendment than a criminal prosecution for publication of the same material? For analysis of the doctrine of prior restraint, see section C2 infra.

2. *Nebraska Press.* It has been suggested that, despite its disclaimers, the Court in *Nebraska Press* "announced a virtual bar to prior restraints on reporting of news about crime." L. Tribe, American Constitutional Law 858-859 (2d ed. 1988). Is an absolute bar on such prior restraints warranted? Draft a statute that exhausts a state's constitutional power to punish criminally the "reporting of news about crime."

3. *The Pentagon Papers: too much haste?* Publication of the Pentagon Papers offered the public rare and valuable insights into the processes of decisionmaking in government. Moreover, by disclosing, for example, that the Eisenhower administration's attempt to undermine the new communist regime in North Vietnam directly involved the United States in the breakdown of the 1954 Geneva settlement, that the Johnson administration took steps toward waging an overt war against North Vietnam a full year before it disclosed the depth of its involvement to the American public, and that the infiltration of men and arms from North Vietnam into South Vietnam was more important as a means of publicly justifying our involvement than for its military effects, publication of the Papers sharpened the public's understanding of the war and altered public attitudes toward a central issue of American policy. At the same time, however, one must ask whether, as the dissenters charged, the Court acted with "unseemly haste" in permitting publication of the documents. In light of the extraordinary seriousness of the government's contentions and the almost overwhelming length of the study, should the Court have permitted the injunctions to remain in effect pending a more thorough judicial determination of the risks? Was the Court, in other words, playing fast and loose with the national security? Consider in this regard Justice Brennan's argument that the very notion of an injunction against expres-

sion pending final resolution of the controversy is inherently incompatible with the first amendment.

4. *The Pentagon Papers: injunctions and the national security.* Note that the per curiam opinion did not define the precise circumstances in which a court may enjoin the publication of information relating to the national security. Does the standard enunciated by Justice Stewart, that there must be proof that the disclosure will "surely result in direct, immediate, and irreparable damage to our Nation or its people," come closest to representing the view of the Court? Why was that standard not satisfied in the Pentagon Papers case?

5. *The Pentagon Papers: criminal prosecution?* Suppose the New York Times and the Washington Post had been criminally prosecuted for their publication of the Pentagon Papers. What standard should govern? Is section 793(e) of the Federal Code, reproduced in footnote 8 of Justice White's opinion, constitutional? Should disclosure of historical information be absolutely protected? For such an argument, see Volokh, Freedom of Speech, Permissible Tailoring and Transcending Strict Scrutiny, 144 U. Pa. L. Rev. 2417, 2425-2431 (1996).

Suppose, in this hypothetical criminal prosecution, the government claimed that the newspapers' disclosure of some of the historical information weakened our alliances, increased the difficulty of negotiating with other nations, prolonged the war, and delayed the release of American prisoners of war. Could the newspapers constitutionally be convicted? Are these sorts of issues, as Justice Harlan suggested, beyond the competence of courts? Consider the following arguments: (a) The executive may consciously or unconsciously err on the side of suppression in order to prevent the revelation of potentially embarrassing information. See generally Blasi, The Checking Value in First Amendment Theory, 1977 Am. B. Found. Res. J. 521. (b) Newspapers, eager to boost sales, may undervalue the interest in national security.

In considering the Pentagon Papers controversy, recall the problem of the *true* cry of "fire." Even though the true cry may create a clear and present danger that some persons will be injured in the dash for the exit, the benefits of the speech may outweigh the harm. Do the decisions examined in this section, taken together, "leave little doubt that, except in cases involving imminent national military catastrophe, the Court will not permit previous restraints upon, or subsequent punishment for, publication in a mass medium of accurate information that the publisher has lawfully acquired"? Cox, Foreword: Freedom of Expression in the Burger Court, 94 Harv. L. Rev. 1, 17 (1980).

6. *Public employees.* The Court suggested in both *Nebraska Press* and *Pentagon Papers* that the state may keep information from the press by prohibiting government employees from disclosing that information. Suppose that the government had prosecuted Daniel Ellsberg for releasing the Pentagon Papers? Should government have greater authority to prohibit its employees from disclosing confidential information to the press than to prohibit the press from publishing such information once it comes into its hands? If an ultimate concern of the first amendment is the "public's right to know," isn't that right undermined just as much by restrictions on the press's ability to obtain information as by restrictions on its ability to publish?

Consider Snepp v. United States, 444 U.S. 507 (1980), in which Snepp, a former CIA agent, published a book about certain CIA activities in South Vietnam in violation of an express condition of his employment contract with the CIA in which he promised not to publish "any information or material relating to the Agency, its activities or intelligence activities generally, either during or after the term of [his] employment, [without] specific prior approval by the Agency." The Court, in a six-to-three decision, held that Snepp "breached a fiduciary obligation and that the proceeds of his breach are impressed with a constructive trust." The Court explained that the "Government has a compelling interest in protecting both the secrecy of information important to our national security and the apprearance of confidentiality so essential to the effective operation of our foreign intelligence service." The Court concluded that the "agreement that Snepp signed is a reasonable means for protecting this vital interest."

Consider the following views:

a. The public employee gains access to confidential government information only by virtue of her employment. Thus, for government to prohibit her disclosure of such information does not limit any first amendment right the employee would have but for such employment.

b. Easterbrook, Insider Trading, Secret Agents, Evidentiary Privileges, and the Production of Information, 1981 Sup. Ct. Rev. 309, 345-347:

> Snepp [struck] a bargain. He learned of the CIA's activities by agreeing to limit his speech about them. [So] long as he enters into the agreement without fraud or coercion, he has made a judgment that he is better off with the agreement (and off its restraints) than without; he can hardly complain that his rights have been reduced. [Constitutional] rights are waived every day. [One] aspect of the value of a right [is] that it can be sold and both parties to the bargain made better off.

c. Sunstein, Government Control of Information, 74 Cal. L. Rev. 889, 915 (1986):

> [The] first amendment is largely a structural provision. [Its] purpose is not only to protect private autonomy, but also to preserve a certain form of government. Citizens may often find it in their interest to give up rights of free speech in exchange for benefits from government. For many, these rights are not extremely valuable as individual possessions. But if government is permitted to obtain enforceable waivers, the aggregate effect may be considerable, and the deliberative processes of the public will be skewed. [Waivers] of first amendment rights thus affect people other than government employees, and effects on third parties are a classic reason to proscribe waivers. The analogy [is] to government purchases of voting rights, which are impermissible even if voters willingly assent.

d. A. Bickel, The Morality of Consent 79-82 (1975):

> The government is entitled to keep things private and will attain as much privacy as it can get away with politically by guarding its privacy internally; but with few exceptions involving the highest probability of very grave consequences, it may not do so effectively. It is severely limited as to means, being restricted, by and large, to enforcing security at the source. [Yet] the power to arrange security at the source, looked at in itself, is great, and if it were nowhere countervailed it would be quite frightening. [But] there *is* countervailing power. The press, by which is meant anybody, not only the institutionalized print and electronic press, can be prevented from publishing only in extreme and quite dire circumstances. [It] is a disorderly situation surely. But if we ordered it we would have to sacrifice one of two contend-

ing values — privacy or public discourse — which are ultimately irreconcilable. If we should let the government censor as well as withhold, that would be too much dangerous power, and too much privacy. If we should allow the government neither to censor nor to withhold, that would provide for too little privacy of decision-making and too much power in the press.

e. Sunstein, supra, at 901-902, 904:

> [Bickel's] equilibrium theory is vulnerable because it does not address three critical matters: the actual incentives of the press and the government; the respective power of the countervailing forces; and what the proper baseline for evaluating outcomes should be. [The] equilibrium theory [is] impressionistic and relies on premises that are both unsupported and unlikely. The sharp distinction between rights of access and rights of publication thus rests on unstable foundations.

In deciding whether government may constitutionally prohibit an employee's disclosure of particular "confidential" information, should courts consider not only the potential danger but also the potential value of the disclosure? For example, may an employee disclose "classified" information if it reveals a substantial abuse of power? Can a public school teacher be fired for disclosing the grade differentials between African-American and white students in an effort to protest the school's affirmative action policy? For further discussion of the issue of "unconstitutional conditions," see Chapter 9, section E, infra.

7. *Attorneys.* Should the state have greater power to restrict extrajudicial speech by attorneys in pending cases than it has to restrict speech by the press about such cases? In Gentile v. State Bar of Nevada, 501 U.S. 1030 (1991), the Court held that, although the state may not restrict speech by the press about pending criminal cases without meeting the clear and present danger standard, it may restrict speech by an attorney about pending cases if the attorney knows or reasonably should know that the speech will have a "substantial likelihood of materially prejudicing" the proceeding. Thus, in some circumstances, an attorney could be disciplined for commenting to the press about a pending case, but the press could not be restricted from publishing the attorney's comments. Is this sensible?

8. *"Technical" information.* Suppose, in addition to general historical information, the Pentagon Papers had disclosed blueprints of secret military weapons, the identity of covert agents abroad, or secret codes? Is the disclosure of such information more readily subject to restriction? See Symposium, National Security and the First Amendment, 26 Wm. & Mary L. Rev. 715 (1985). Do you agree that "the law need not treat differently the crime of one man who sells a bomb to terrorists and that of another who publishes an instructional manual for terrorists on how to build their own bombs out of old Volkswagen parts"? Tribe, supra, at 837. For analysis of the constitutional status of technical data, see Sunstein, supra, at 905-912.

Note: The Progressive Controversy

In February 1979, Howard Morland, a freelance writer, completed an article for The Progressive magazine, entitled The H-Bomb Secret — How We Got It,

Why We're Telling It. The article, which was based on information contained in publicly available literature and Morland's interviews of various scientists and government officials, was designed to demonstrate the ineffectiveness and undesirability of a government system of classification and secrecy. Uncertain of the potential legal consequences of publication, The Progressive delivered a copy of the manuscript to the Department of Energy (DOE), requesting verification of its "technical accuracy." Officials in the DOE determined that, although Morland had relied on no classified documents, the article nonetheless contained information that the Atomic Energy Act required to be classified as "restricted data." They therefore requested The Progressive not to publish the article without first permitting government officials to work with the magazine to recast the manuscript to eliminate the restricted data. The Progressive informed the DOE that it intended to publish the article without alteration.

The following day, March 8, the United States filed suit in federal district court, seeking to enjoin publication of the restricted data. The United States maintained that the suit was authorized by the Atomic Energy Act, which authorized injunctive relief to prohibit any person from disclosing restricted data, defined in the act as including any data concerning "design, manufacture, or utilization of atomic weapons," "with reason to believe such data will be utilized to injure the United States or to secure an advantage to any foreign nation." On March 9, the court issued a temporary restraining order against publication of the article. On March 26, the court held a hearing on the issuance of a preliminary injunction.

After considering several complex affidavits submitted by experts on both sides, the court found that at least some of the information in the article may not have been in the public domain. More important, "the article provides a more comprehensive, accurate, and detailed analysis of the overall construction and operation of a thermonuclear weapon than any publication to date in the public literature." The court found further that the article does not "provide a 'do-it-yourself' guide for the hydrogen bomb," but "could possibly provide sufficient information to allow a medium size nation to move faster in developing a hydrogen weapon" and "could provide a ticket to by-pass blind alleys."

The court granted the preliminary injunction. United States v. The Progressive, Inc., 467 F. Supp. 990 (W.D. Wis. 1979). The court noted that, although the purpose of the article was to "alert the people of this country to the false illusion of security created by the government's futile efforts at secrecy" and to "provide the people with needed information to make informed decisions on an urgent issue of public concern," it could "find no plausible reason why the public needs to know the technical details about hydrogen bomb construction to carry on an informed debate on this issue." Moreover, the information at issue, the court observed, deals "with the most destructive weapon in the history of mankind," and an erroneous decision against the government could "involve human life itself and on such an awesome scale." In light of this "disparity of risk," the court held that the injunction was warranted. The court distinguished the Pentagon Papers decision on the grounds that (1) the information disclosed in that case involved "historical data relating to events that occurred some three to twenty years previously"; (2) "no cogent arguments were advanced by the government" in that case "as to why the article affected national security except that publication might cause some embarrassment to the United States"; and (3) there was no specific statutory authorization of the injunction in that case.

The government's suit against The Progressive was dismissed on October 1, 1979, while pending in the U.S. Court of Appeals for the Seventh Circuit, because similar information concerning the construction of the hydrogen bomb was published independently by others. See generally Powe, The H-Bomb Injunction, 61 U. Colo. L. Rev. 55 (1990).

Suppose a terrorist posts on the Internet instructions on how to make out of common household materials a bomb that is sufficiently powerful to destroy a large building. Can this be prohibited?

Consider also Haig v. Agee, 453 U.S. 280 (1981), in which the Court upheld the revocation of Agee's passport because he engaged in activities abroad that caused "serious damage to the national security." Specifically, Agee, a former employee of the Central Intelligence Agency (CIA), engaged in a campaign "to expose CIA officers and agents and to take the measures necessary to drive them out of the countries where they are operating." Although Agee did not expressly incite "anyone to commit murder," there was evidence that his disclosures resulted in "episodes of violence against the persons and organizations identified." The Court rejected Agee's claim that the passport revocation violated his rights under the first amendment: "Long ago, [this] Court recognized that 'No one would question but that a government might prevent actual obstruction to its recruiting service or the publication of the sailing dates of transports or the number and location of troops.' [Near, section C2 infra.] Agee's disclosures [have] the declared purpose of obstructing intelligence operations and the recruiting of personnel. They are clearly not protected by the Constitution."

Is Agee consistent with the Pentagon Papers decision? Are Agee's disclosures "not protected" because they consisted of "technical," rather than "historical," information? Because they were designed to effect change not through the political process but by directly obstructing the operations of government? Consider the constitutionality of the Intelligence Identities Protection Act, 50 U.S.C. §421 (1982), which prohibits any person "with reason to believe that such activities would impair or impede the foreign intelligence activities of the United States, [to disclose] any information that identifies an individual as a covert agent, [if the disclosure is part of a] pattern of activities intended to identify or expose covert action."

Consider also the Arms Export Control Act, 22 U.S.C. §2778 (1982), which authorizes compilation of a list of items that may not be exported without a license from the State Department. This list includes not only physical objects but also information "that can be used or adapted for use" in the production, operation, or maintenance of the armaments listed and "any technology which advances the state of the art or establishes a new art in any area of significant military applicability." Export of technical data is defined to apply to disclosure to foreign nationals in the United States, including disclosure through participation in symposia.

Note: Dangerous Ideas and Information — Final Thoughts

In what circumstances, if any, may government, consonant with the first amendment, restrict speech of "high" first amendment value because, if left unchecked, it might cause some harm to government, private individuals, or society in general? As the foregoing materials illustrate, the Court's efforts to defi the perimeters of government power in this regard have focused primarily on the clear and present danger standard. Has that standard served well? In a different context, Justice Holmes, the author of the clear and present danger standard, warned of "the need of scrutinizing the reasons for the rules which we follow, and of not being contented with hollow forms of words merely because they have been used very [often]. We must think things not words, or at least we must constantly translate our words into the facts for which they stand, if we are to keep to the real and the true." O. Holmes, Collected Legal Papers 238 (1920). Has the Court been sensitive to this admonition, or has it "tended to seek [solutions] for problems of freedom of speech by invocation of magic phrases rather than hard rationalizations, if not by way of resolving the issues then by way of covering them up"? Kurland, The Irrelevance of the Constitution: The First Amendment's Freedom of Speech and Freedom of Press Clauses, 29 Drake L. Rev. 1, 5 (1979-1980).

Has the Court, in its results, been underprotective of free speech? Has it been overprotective? A canvass of what the Court has done may be more illuminating than an emphasis on what it has said. The Court has not upheld a direct prohibition of speech because it might induce readers or listeners to engage in criminal activity since *Dennis* (1951), and it has not upheld a direct prohibition of speech for this reason in the absence of express advocacy of crime since the Espionage Act cases following World War I. The Court has not upheld a restriction on speech because it might provoke a hostile audience response since *Feiner* (1951). It has never upheld a restriction on speech because the ideas expressed might have an improper influence on the judicial process. With the exception of *Agee*, it has never upheld a restriction on the publication of truthful information because the government would prefer to keep it confidential. Has clear and present danger come to mean essentially absolute protection?

On the other hand, does it really matter what the Court says or does? Consider Nagel, How Useful Is Judicial Review in Free Speech Cases?, 69 Cornell L. Rev. 302, 304-305 (1984):

> [It] is not self-evident [that] the legal rules adopted by the Court [have] had any useful systemic consequences. [A] wide range of factors coalesce to determine the amount of tolerance [in a society], including: educational levels, [economic] conditions, international politics, institutional rivalries [and] insecurities caused by flux in social [status]. Adjudication is an unlikely mechanism for controlling such large and complex factors. [The] causes of intolerance and censorship — as well as the cures — lie far beyond the sound and fury of particular cases.

C. OVERBREADTH, VAGUENESS, AND PRIOR RESTRAINT

This section represents a brief interlude in our analysis of content-based restrictions. It focuses not on what speech government may restrict but rather on how government may restrict speech. The doctrines examined in this section may be explored either as a distinct unit or as they naturally arise in the course of the preceding and succeeding material.

In interpreting the first amendment, courts have often focused not only on what speech is "protected," but also on what means of restriction are constitutionally permissible. Indeed, "courts have [come] to realize that procedural guarantees play [a] large role in protecting freedom of speech; [for like] the substantive rules themselves, insensitive procedures can 'chill' the right of free expression. Accordingly, wherever first amendment claims are involved, sensitive procedural devices are necessary." Monaghan, First Amendment "Due Process," 83 Harv. L. Rev. 518, 518-519 (1970).

The overbreadth, vagueness, and prior restraint doctrines have played an especially important role in this aspect of first amendment jurisprudence. Under each of these doctrines, courts may invalidate restrictions on expression because the means of suppression are impermissible, even though the particular speech at issue might constitutionally be restricted by some other means.

1.　Overbreadth and Vagueness

Gooding v. Wilson

405 U.S. 518 (1972)

[During an antiwar demonstration at an army induction center, police attempted to move appellee and his companions away from the door of the center. A scuffle ensued, and appellee said to several of the officers, "You son of a bitch, I'll choke you to death"; "White son of a bitch, I'll kill you"; and "You son of a bitch, if you ever put your hands on me again, I'll cut you all to pieces." Appellee was thereafter convicted of using opprobrious words and abusive language in violation of Georgia Code Ann. §26-6303, which provided: "Any person who shall, without provocation, use to or of another, and in his presence [opprobrious] words or abusive language, tending to cause a breach of the peace [shall] be guilty of a misdemeanor." The Supreme Court affirmed a decision of the U.S. Court of Appeals granting appellee's petition for federal habeas corpus relief.]

MR. JUSTICE BRENNAN delivered the opinion of the Court. . . .

Section 26-6303 punishes only spoken words. It can therefore withstand appellee's attack upon its facial constitutionality only if, as authoritatively construed by the Georgia courts, it is not susceptible of application to speech, although vulgar or offensive, that is protected by the First and Fourteenth Amendments. [Only] the Georgia courts can supply the requisite construction, since of course "we lack jurisdiction authoritatively to construe state legislation." [It] matters not that the words appellee used might have been constitutionally prohibited under a narrowly and precisely drawn statute. At least when statutes regulate or proscribe speech and when "no readily apparent construction suggests itself as a vehicle for rehabilitating the statutes in a single prosecution," [the] transcendent value to all society of constitutionally protected expression is deemed to justify allowing "attacks on overly broad statutes with no requirement that the person making the attack demonstrate that his own conduct could not be regulated by a statute drawn with the requisite narrow specificity." [This] is deemed necessary because persons whose expression is constitutionally protected may well refrain from exercising their rights for fear of criminal sanctions provided by a statute susceptible of application to protected expression. . . .

The constitutional guarantees of freedom of speech forbid the States to punish the use of words or language not within "narrowly limited classes of speech." [*Chaplinsky.*] [Statutes] must be carefully drawn or be authoritatively construed to punish only unprotected speech and not be susceptible of application to protected expression. "Because First Amendment freedoms need breathing space to survive, government may regulate in the area only with narrow specificity." . . .

Appellant does not challenge these principles but contends that the Georgia statute is narrowly drawn to apply only to a constitutionally unprotected class of words — "fighting" words — "those which by their very utterance inflict injury or tend to incite an immediate breach of the peace." [*Chaplinsky.*] In *Chaplinsky*, we sustained a conviction under [a statute] which provided: "No person shall address any offensive, derisive or annoying word to any other person who is lawfully in any street or other public place, nor call him by any offensive or derisive name. . . ." Chaplinsky was convicted for addressing to another on a public sidewalk the words, "You are a God damned racketeer," and "a damned Fascist and the whole government of Rochester are Fascists or agents of Fascists." Chaplinsky challenged the constitutionality of the statute as inhibiting freedom of expression because it was vague and indefinite. The Supreme Court of New Hampshire, however, "long before the words for which Chaplinsky was convicted," sharply limited the statutory language "offensive, derisive or annoying word" to "fighting" words. . . .

In view of that authoritative construction, this Court held: "We are unable to say that the limited scope of the statute as thus construed contravenes the Constitutional right of free expression. It is a statute narrowly drawn and limited to define and punish specific conduct lying within the domain of state power, the use in a public place of words likely to cause a breach of the peace." . . .

Appellant argues that the Georgia appellate courts have by construction limited the prescription of §26-6303 to "fighting" words, as the New Hampshire Supreme Court limited the New Hampshire statute. [We] have, however, made our own examination of the Georgia cases, both those cited and others discovered in research. That examination brings us to the conclusion, in agreement with the courts below, that the Georgia appellate decisions have not construed §26-6303 to be limited in application, as in *Chaplinsky*, to words that "have a direct tendency to cause acts of violence by the person to whom, individually, the remark is addressed."

The dictionary definitions of "opprobrious" and "abusive" give them greater reach than "fighting" words. Webster's Third New International Dictionary (1961) defined "opprobrious" as "conveying or intended to convey disgrace," and "abusive" as including "harsh insulting language." Georgia appellate decisions have construed §26-6303 to apply to utterances that, although within these definitions, are not "fighting" words as *Chaplinsky* defines them. In Lyons v. State, 94 Ga. App. 570, 95 S.E.2d 478 (1956), a conviction under the statute was sustained for [appellee's] awakening 10 women scout leaders on a camp-out by shouting, "Boys, this is where we are going to spend the night." "Get the G — d — bed rolls out . . . let's see how close we can come to the G — d — tents." Again, in Fish v. State, 124 Ga. 416, 52 S.E. 737 (1905), the Georgia Supreme Court held that a jury question was presented by the remark, "You swore a lie." Again, Jackson v. State, 14 Ga. App. 19, 80 S.E. 20 (1913), held that a jury question was presented by the words addressed to another, "God damn you, why don't you get out of the road?" Plainly, although "conveying . . . disgrace" or "harsh insulting language," these were not words "which by their very utterance . . . tend to incite an immediate breach of the peace." [*Chaplinsky.*] Indeed, the Georgia Court of Appeals in Elmore v. State, 15 Ga. App. 461, 83 S.E. 799 (1914), construed "tending to cause a breach of the peace" as [including the possibility that the addressee might retaliate at some time in the future].

Moreover, in Samuels v. State, 103 Ga. App. 66, 67, 118 S.E.2d 231, 232 (1961), the Court of Appeals, in applying another statute, adopted from a textbook the common-law definition of "breach of the peace" [that] makes it a "breach of peace" merely to speak words offensive to some who hear them. [Because] earlier appellate decisions applied §26-6303 to utterances where there was no likelihood that the person addressed would make an immediate violent response, it is clear that the standard allowing juries to determine guilt "measured by common understanding and practice" does not limit the application of §26-6303 to "fighting" words defined by *Chaplinsky.* [Unlike] the construction of the New Hampshire statute by the New Hampshire Supreme Court, the Georgia appellate courts have not construed §26-6303 "so as to avoid all constitutional difficulties." . . .

Affirmed.

MR. Justice Powell and Mr. Justice Rehnquist took no part in the consideration or decision of this case.

MR. CHIEF JUSTICE BURGER, dissenting.

I fully join in Mr. Justice Blackmun's dissent against the bizarre result reached by the Court. It is not merely odd, it is nothing less than remarkable that a court can find a state statute void on its face, not because of its language — which is the traditional test — but because of the way courts of that State have applied the statute in a few isolated cases, decided as long ago as 1905 and generally long before this Court's decision in [*Chaplinsky*]. Even if all of those cases had been decided yesterday, they do nothing to demonstrate that the narrow language of the Georgia statute has any significant potential for sweeping application to suppress or deter important protected speech. . . .

The Court apparently acknowledges that the conduct of the defendant in this case is not protected by the First Amendment, and does not contend that the Georgia statute is so ambiguous that he did not have fair notice that his conduct was prohibited. Nor does the Court deny that under normal principles of constitutional adjudication, appellee would not be permitted to attack his own conviction on the ground that the statute in question might in some hypothetical situation be unconstitutionally applied to the conduct of some party not before the Court. . . .

As the Court itself recognizes, if the First Amendment overbreadth doctrine serves any legitimate purpose, it is to allow the Court to invalidate statutes because their language demonstrates their potential for sweeping improper applications posing a significant likelihood of deterring important First Amendment speech — not because of some insubstantial or imagined potential for occasional and isolated applications that go beyond constitutional bounds. [The] actual and apparent danger to free expression [in] the case at hand is at best strained and remote.* . . .

MR. JUSTICE BLACKMUN, with whom The Chief Justice joins, dissenting. . . .

The Court would justify its conclusion by unearthing a 66-year-old decision [of] the Supreme Court of Georgia, and two intermediate appellate court cases over 55 years old, [broadly] applying the statute in those less permissive days, and by additional reference to (a) a 1956 Georgia intermediate appellate court decision, [which], were it the first and only Georgia case, would surely not support today's decision, and (b) another intermediate appellate court decision [relating], not to §26-6303, but to another statute. . . .

I wonder, now that §26-6303 is voided, just what Georgia can do if it seeks to proscribe what the Court says it still may constitutionally proscribe. The natural thing would be to enact a new statute reading just as §26-6303 reads. But it, too, presumably would be overbroad unless the legislature would add words to the effect that it means only what this Court says it may mean and no more. . . .

Note: Overbreadth

1. *The nature of overbreadth.* The traditional "as applied" mode of judicial review tests the constitutionality of legislation as it is applied to particular facts on a case-by-case basis. Suppose, for example, a state law prohibits any person to "advocate criminal conduct." Under "as applied" review, this law could constitutionally be applied to any expression that satisfies the requirements of *Brandenburg*. That the law fails "on its face" to comport with the strictures of *Brandenburg* is, under this approach, irrelevant.

The first amendment overbreadth doctrine, on the other hand, tests the constitutionality of legislation in terms of its *potential* applications. Under this approach, a state law prohibiting any person to "advocate unlawful conduct" is unconstitutional "on its face" because the law purports to forbid expression that the state may not constitutionally prohibit. That an individual defendant's own speech could constitutionally be restricted under a more narrowly drawn statute is irrelevant.

In effect, then, the overbreadth doctrine is an exception both to the traditional "as applied" mode of judicial review and to the general rule that an individual has no standing to litigate the rights of third persons. See United States v. Raines, 362 U.S. 17 (1960); Barrows v. Jackson, 346 U.S. 249 (1953); see also Note, Standing to Assert Constitutional Jus Tertii, 88 Harv. L. Rev. 423 (1974).

---

*Even assuming that the statute, on its face, were impermissibly overbroad, the Court does not satisfactorily explain why it must be invalidated in its entirety. To be sure, the Court notes that "we lack jurisdiction authoritatively to construe state legislation." But that cryptic statement hardly resolves the matter. The State of Georgia argues that the statute applies only to fighting words that *Chaplinsky* holds may be prohibited, and the Court apparently agrees that the statute would be valid if so limited. The Court should not assume that the Georgia courts, and Georgia prosecutors and police, would ignore a decision of this Court sustaining appellee's conviction narrowly and on the explicit premise that the statute may be validly applied only to "fighting words" as defined in *Chaplinsky*. . . .

2. *Justifications and criticisms of overbreadth.* The overbreadth doctrine is "highly protective of first amendment interests, not only because it sometimes prescribes invalidation of an entire provision but also because of the alacrity with which it can accomplish that result." Note, The First Amendment Overbreadth Doctrine, 83 Harv. L. Rev. 844, 846 (1970). Are you persuaded by Justice Brennan's explanation in *Gooding* that this exception to ordinary standing rules is "necessary because persons whose expression is constitutionally protected may well refrain from exercising their rights for fear of criminal sanctions provided by a statute susceptible of application to protected expression"? For an elaboration of the "chilling effect" rationale, see id. at 852-858. Are you persuaded that "one of the evils of an overly broad statute is its potential for selective enforcement," and that the doctrine is thus justified because "it can minimize [this] danger by restricting the occasions for enforcement"? Karst, Equality as a Central Principle in the First Amendment, 43 U. Chi. L. Rev. 20, 38 (1975).

What are the costs of the overbreadth doctrine? Consider the following objections: (a) Because the doctrine permits an individual whose own rights have *not* been violated to "go free" or to otherwise benefit because the statute might conceivably interfere with the rights of others, it unjustifiably frustrates legitimate state interests. (b) The doctrine enables the Court to act "as if it had a roving commission" to find and to cure unconstitutionality and is thus inconsistent with a fundamental premise of judicial review — that judicial resolution of constitutional controversies is warranted only when unavoidable. A. Cox, The Warren Court 18 (1968). (c) The doctrine necessarily requires the decision of questions not actually presented by the record and thus results in the resolution of important constitutional issues in a "sterile," abstract context, without the depth and texture ordinarily provided by a concrete factual setting. A. Bickel, The Least Dangerous Branch 115-116 (1962). (d) The doctrine may promote judicial disingenuousness, for it invites the Court to escape possibly difficult decisions concerning the constitutionality of the statute "as applied" so long as it can hypothesize potentially unconstitutional applications not actually before the Court. (e) Because the Court may invalidate a statute for overbreadth without explaining precisely how the statute should have been drafted to pass constitutional muster, invocation of the doctrine "lacks intellectual coherence" and may leave legislatures with little or no guidance on how to avoid the Court's objections in the future. Id. at 53.

3. *The problem of narrowing construction.* As noted in *Gooding*, the statute at issue in *Chaplinsky* was clearly overbroad on its face but was saved by the state court's narrowing construction. When may a court narrowly construe a facially overbroad statute to save it from invalidation? In affirming the conviction of Gooding, could the Georgia Supreme Court have limited the statute to "fighting words" and thus avoided overbreadth invalidation? Was the legislative intent too clear in *Gooding* to permit a narrowing interpretation? Would a narrowing construction by the Georgia Supreme Court have come too late to affect Gooding?

Consider Osborne v. Ohio, 495 U.S. 103 (1990), in which the Court upheld a child pornography statute as construed by the state supreme court on appeal in the same case. Although the statute, as written, was unconstitutionally overbroad, the Court held that it was saved from invalidation by the state supreme court's narrowing construction, and that the statute, as construed, could "'be applied to conduct occurring prior to the construction, provided such application affords fair warning to the defendant.'" In *Osborne*, the Court concluded that the statute afforded "fair warning" because the defendant "would not [have been] surprised to learn that his possession of [the] photographs at issue [constituted] a crime."

Note that the Supreme Court of the United States had no authority to adopt a narrowing construction in *Gooding*. Is that sensible? Wouldn't a narrowing construction have involved a less drastic exercise of federal power than invalidation? Consider Virginia v. American Booksellers Association, Inc., 484 U.S. 383 (1988), in which the Court, rather than speculate on the reach of an ambiguous state statute, certified to the Virginia Supreme Court the question whether the challenged statute actually covered those acts of expression that gave rise to the overbreadth challenge. Is this a sensible approach?

Suppose that, while a criminal prosecution is on appeal, the state legislature amends the challenged statute to eliminate the unconstitutional overbreadth. May the defendant still take advantage of the fact that the statute was overbroad at the time he violated it? See Massachusetts v. Oakes, 491 U.S. 576 (1989) (defendant may still assert overbreadth).

4. Broadrick: *requiring "substantial" overbreadth*. Chief Justice Burger maintained in *Gooding* that the overbreadth doctrine should be invoked only when there is "a significant likelihood of deterring important First Amendment speech." In Broadrick v. Oklahoma, 413 U.S. 601 (1973), the Court, in a five-to-four decision, expressly adopted such a limitation. *Broadrick* involved a state law restricting the political activities of civil servants. The plaintiffs conceded that the state could constitutionally prohibit civil servants from doing what they had done — solicit funds for political candidates. They argued, however, that the law was unconstitutionally overbroad because it attempted also to prohibit civil servants from engaging in such relatively innocuous and thus constitutionally protected activities as displaying political bumper stickers and buttons.

The Court, in an opinion by Justice White, observed that under the overbreadth doctrine, litigants "are permitted to challenge a statute not because their own rights of free expression are violated, but because of a judicial prediction or assumption that the statute's very existence may cause others not before the court to refrain from constitutionally protected speech or expression." Terming the doctrine "strong medicine," the Court argued that, although laws, "if too broadly worded, may deter protected speech to some unknown extent, there comes a point where that effect — at best a prediction — cannot, with confidence, justify invalidating a statute on its face and so prohibiting a State from enforcing the statute against conduct that is admittedly within its power to proscribe." Thus, the Court concluded, "we believe that the overbreadth of a statute must not only be real, but substantial as well, judged in relation to the statute's plainly legitimate sweep." Applying that standard to the statute in *Broadrick*, the Court concluded that, because the statute "regulates a substantial spectrum of conduct that [is] manifestly subject to state regulation," it "is not substantially overbroad [and] whatever overbreadth may exist should [thus] be cured through case-by-case analysis of the fact situations to which its sanctions, assertedly, may not be applied."

In dissent, Justice Brennan described *Broadrick* "as a wholly unjustified retreat from fundamental and previously well-established [principles]." Although conceding that the Court had "never held that a statute should be held invalid on its face merely because it is possible to conceive of a single impermissible application," and that "in that sense a requirement of substantial overbreadth is already implicit in the doctrine," Justice Brennan faulted the Court for leaving "obscure" the contours of its arguably new conception of overbreadth. The Court, Justice Brennan noted, "makes no effort to define what it means by 'substantial overbreadth'" and "no effort to explain why the overbreadth of the Oklahoma Act, while real, is somehow not quite substantial." Indeed, "no more guidance is provided" on that question "than the Court's conclusory assertion that appellants' showing here falls below the line."

5. *The impact of* Broadrick. In Los Angeles City Council v. Taxpayers for Vincent, 466 U.S. 789 (1984), the Court offered the following elaboration:

> The concept of "substantial overbreadth" is not readily reduced to an exact definition. It is clear, however, that the mere fact that one can conceive of some impermissible applications of a statute is not sufficient to render it susceptible to an overbreadth challenge. On the contrary, [there] must be a realistic danger that the statute itself will significantly compromise recognized First Amendment protections of parties not before the Court for it to be facially challenged on overbreadth grounds.

How should "substantiality" be measured: By the total number of unconstitutional applications? By the ratio of possible constitutional to possible unconstitutional applications? Should the state have to justify even an "insubstantial" overbreadth? See Redish, The Warren Court, the Burger Court and the First Amendment Overbreadth Doctrine, 78 Nw. U.L. Rev. 1031, 1067 (1983) (the "logical question [is] whether [a] more narrowly drawn [law] would inadequately achieve the state's goal"); Fallon, Making Sense of Overbreadth, 100 Yale L.J. 853, 894 (1991) (in deciding when overbreadth is "intolerably substantial," courts should weigh the state's substantive interest in being able to "employ a standard that is broader than less restrictive substitutes" against "the First Amendment interest in avoiding [the] chilling effect on constitutionally protected conduct" — the "farther [the] chilled conduct lies from the central concerns of the First Amendment [the] more [a] court should hesitate about declaring a [statute] void for overbreadth").

The ultimate impact of *Broadrick* remains obscure. See New York v. Ferber, 458 U.S. 747 (1982), section D4 infra (upholding as not substantially overbroad a child pornography statute prohibiting any person to produce, exhibit, or sell any material depicting any "performance" by a child under the age of sixteen that includes "actual or simulated sexual intercourse, deviate sexual intercourse, sexual bestiality, masturbation, sado-masochistic abuse, or lewd exhibition of the genitals"); Houston v. Hill, 482 U.S. 451 (1987) (invalidating as substantially overbroad an ordinance prohibiting any person to "assault, strike or in any manner oppose, molest, abuse or interrupt any policeman in the execution of his duty"); Board of Airport Commissioners of Los Angeles v. Jews for Jesus, Inc., 482 U.S. 569 (1987) (invalidating as substantially overbroad a regulation prohibiting any person "to engage in First Amendment activities within the Central Terminal Area at Los Angeles International Airport"); National Endowment for the Arts v. Finley, 524 U.S. 569 (1998), section E2d infra (upholding as not substantially overbroad a federal statute directing the NEA, in establishing procedures to judge the artistic merit of grant applications, to "tak[e] into consideration general standards of decency and respect for the diverse beliefs and values of the American public").

6. *Partial invalidation.* May an individual whose own rights are violated by a statute challenge the statute not only "as applied" to him but also "on its face"? In Brockett v. Spokane Arcades, Inc., 472 U.S. 491 (1985), the Court held a Washington obscenity statute unconstitutional because its definition of obscenity was too broad. Without deciding whether the statute was substantially overbroad, however, the Court declined to invalidate the law on its face:

> [An] individual whose own speech [may] validly be prohibited [is] permitted to challenge a statute on its face because it also threatens others not before the court, [and if] the overbreadth is "substantial," the law may not be enforced against anyone [until] it is narrowed to reach only unprotected activity. [But where, as here,] the parties challenging the statute are those who desire to engage in protected speech that the overbroad statute purports to punish, [there is] no want of a proper party to challenge the statute [and it] may forthwith be declared invalid to the extent it reaches too far, but otherwise left intact.

The Court emphasized that such cases are "governed by the normal rule that partial, rather than facial, invalidation is the required course."

7. *Overbreadth and access to government information.* In Los Angeles Police Department v. United Reporting Publishing Corp., 528 U.S. 32 (1999), the respondent, a private publishing company that sells the names and addresses of recently arrested individuals to attorneys, insurance companies, and drug counselors, challenged the constitutionality of a California statute authorizing public access to information about the addresses of arrestees for "scholarly, journalistic, political or governmental" purposes but prohibiting such access for commercial purposes. The Court held that the respondent could not invoke the overbreadth doctrine to challenge this statute because "this is not a case in which the government is prohibiting a speaker from conveying information that the speaker already possesses." Rather, "what we have before us is nothing more than a governmental denial of access to information in its possession. California could decide not to give out arrestee information at all without violating the First Amendment." In this situation, and where "no threat of prosecution [or] cutoff of funds" hangs over respondent's head, "resort to a facial challenge [is] not warranted because there 'is no possibility that protected speech will be muted.'"

Note: Vagueness

1. *The danger of vagueness.* Although not all overbroad laws are vague (e.g., "No person may expressly advocate criminal conduct"), and not all vague laws are overbroad (e.g., "No person may engage in any speech that the state may constitutionally restrict"), there is in most circumstances a close relation between the two doctrines. As a matter of due process, a law is void on its face if it is so vague that persons "of common intelligence must necessarily guess at its meaning and differ as to its application." Connally v. General Construction Co., 269 U.S. 385, 391 (1926). A law that fails to define clearly the conduct it proscribes "may trap the innocent by not providing fair warning" and may in practical effect impermissibly delegate "basic policy matters to policemen, judges and juries for resolution

on an ad hoc and subjective basis, with the attendant dangers of arbitrary and discriminatory application." Grayned v. Rockford, 408 U.S. 104, 108-109 (1972).

These concerns are present whenever a law is vague, whether or not it touches on expression. The vagueness doctrine has special bite in the first amendment context, however, for "where First Amendment interests are affected, a precise statute 'evincing a legislative judgment that certain specific conduct [be] proscribed,' assures us that the legislature has focused on the First Amendment interests and determined that other governmental policies compel regulation." Moreover, "where a vague statute '[abuts] upon sensitive areas of basic First Amendment freedoms,' it 'operates to inhibit the exercise of [those] freedoms.'" Uncertain meanings inevitably lead citizens to "'steer far wider of the unlawful zone' [than] if the boundaries of the forbidden areas were clearly marked." Id. at 109 & n.5; see also Smith v. Goguen, 415 U.S. 566, 572-573 (1974). In at least some instances, in other words, it may be difficult to determine whether a vague law proscribes — or purports to proscribe — constitutionally protected expression. In such circumstances, vague laws, like overbroad laws, may have a significant chilling effect and may invite selective enforcement. See Amsterdam, The Void-for-Vagueness Doctrine in the Supreme Court, 109 U. Pa. L. Rev. 67 (1960).

2. *How "vague" is "too vague"?* The degree of constitutionally tolerable vagueness "is not calculable with precision; in any particular area, the legislature confronts a dilemma: to draft with narrow particularity is to risk nullification by easy evasion of the legislative purpose; to draft with great generality is to risk ensnarement of the innocent in a net designed for others." L. Tribe, American Constitutional Law 1033 (2d ed. 1988). How vague must a law be for it to be held void on its face? Should it matter whether the vagueness is "avoidable"? Whether it is "substantial"? Consider the following:

a. A city ordinance provides that "no person, while on public or private grounds adjacent to any building in which a school [is] in session, shall willfully make [any] noise or diversion which disturbs or tends to disturb the peace or good order of such school." In Grayned v. City of Rockford, 408 U.S. 104 (1972), the Court, in the expectation that the state courts would interpret the ordinance "to prohibit only actual or imminent interference with the 'peace or good order' of the school," rejected a vagueness challenge because "we think it is clear what the ordinance as a whole prohibits."

b. A Massachusetts statute provides that any person who "publicly mutilates, tramples upon, defaces or treats contemptuously the flag of the United States" shall be guilty of a misdemeanor. In Smith v. Goguen, 415 U.S. 566 (1974), the Court invalidated the statute because nonceremonial use of the flag "for adornment or [to] attract attention" has become common, and the statutory prohibition on treating the flag "contemptuously" failed "to draw reasonably clear lines between the kinds of nonceremonial treatment that are criminal and those that are not."

3. *Vagueness and overbreadth.* The close relation between vagueness and overbreadth is apparent when one recognizes not only that many vague laws are potentially overbroad, but also that many seemingly unambiguous overbroad laws are in fact potentially vague. Although the express terms of an overbroad law may not be vague, "the clarity of its language is delusive," for if the validity of the law is determined in an "as applied" manner, "it will have to be recast in order to separate the constitutional from the unconstitutional applications." When, as is of-

ten the case, the precise definition of constitutionally protected expression is unclear, the very vagueness of the constitutional doctrine is in effect integrated into the law, thus uncovering "the vagueness that is latent in its terms." P. Freund, The Supreme Court of the United States 67-68 (1961). By declaring overbroad laws unconstitutional on their face, the overbreadth doctrine avoids the vagueness that ordinarily would result from permitting such laws to be enforced up to the limits of their constitutionality. See Fallon, Making Sense of Overbreadth, 100 Yale L.J. 853 (1991).

4. *Vagueness and standing.* When a law is overbroad, or at least substantially overbroad, an individual may assert its unconstitutionality, even if his own expression is unprotected. Is a similar waiver of traditional standing rules warranted in the vagueness context? If the law is vague as to its coverage of the individual's own expression, the problem does not arise, for the vagueness in such circumstances violates the individual's own right to due process. Suppose, however, the individual's own expression is so clearly within the statutory prohibition that he could not reasonably have been misled. See Smith v. Goguen, supra (invalidating as unconstitutionally vague on its face a statute prohibiting any person to treat the flag of the United States "contemptuously" because the statute is so vague that "no standard of conduct is specified at all"); Young v. American Mini Theatres, 427 U.S. 50 (1976) (declining to invalidate as unconstitutionally vague on its face an ordinance restricting the exhibition of sexually explicit movies where the ordinance is "unquestionably applicable" to the claimants' speech and the Court was "not persuaded" that the "ordinance [would] have a significant [chilling] effect on the exhibition of films protected by the First Amendment").

2. Prior Restraint

The doctrine of prior restraint has its roots in the sixteenth- and seventeenth-century English licensing systems under which all printing presses and printers were licensed by the state and no book or pamphlet could lawfully be published without the prior approval of a government censor. With the expiration of this system in England in 1695, the right of the press to be free from licensing gradually assumed the status of a common law right. Blackstone's definition of freedom of the press illustrates the importance of the doctrine of prior restraint in eighteenth-century thought: "The liberty of the press is indeed essential to the nature of a free state; but this consists in laying no *previous* restraints upon publications, and not in freedom from censure for criminal matter when published." 4 W. Blackstone, Commentaries *151-152.

Even after adoption of the first amendment, Justice Story and other early American commentators accepted the view that liberty of the press was limited to "the right to publish without any previous restraint or license." J. Story, Commentaries on the Constitution of the United States §1879 (1833); see also 2 J. Kent, Commentaries on American Law 23 (2d ed. 1832). Moreover, in its 1907 decision in Patterson v. Colorado, 205 U.S. 454, 462 (1907), the Court, speaking through Justice Holmes, announced that the Constitution prohibited "all such *previous restraints* upon publications as had been practiced by other governments," but not "the subsequent punishment of such as may be deemed contrary to the public welfare." And, although the Court, speaking again through Justice

Holmes, recognized a dozen years later in *Schenck* that "the prohibition of laws abridging the freedom of speech is not confined to previous restraints," the doctrine of prior restraint has continued to play a central role in the jurisprudence of the first amendment. As indicated in the *Pentagon Papers* and *Nebraska Press* decisions, section B4 supra, the Court has steadfastly held that there is a special presumption under the first amendment against the use of prior restraints.

Like the vagueness and overbreadth concepts, the doctrine of prior restraint is concerned with the permissible means of restricting speech. A prior restraint may thus be invalid even if the particular expression at issue could constitutionally be restricted by some other means, such as subsequent criminal prosecution. Although the historical origins of the doctrine are clear, its analytical and functional underpinnings are often puzzling, at best. Apart from historical considerations, why are prior restraints special? After all, "whether the sanction be fine or imprisonment for criminal violation or fine or imprisonment for violation of [a prior restraint], the judicial sanction takes its bite after the [expression.]" Freund, The Supreme Court and Civil Liberties, 4 Vand. L. Rev. 533, 537-538 (1951).

Lovell v. Griffin

303 U.S. 444 (1938)

Mr. Chief Justice Hughes delivered the opinion of the Court.

Appellant, Alma Lovell, was convicted in the Recorder's Court of the City of Griffin, Georgia, of the violation of a city ordinance and was sentenced to imprisonment for fifty days in default of the payment of a fine of fifty dollars. . . .

The ordinance in question is as follows:

> Section 1. That the practice of distributing, either by hand or otherwise, circulars, handbooks, advertising, or literature of any kind, whether said articles are being delivered free, or whether same are being sold, within the limits of the City of Griffin, without first obtaining written permission from the City Manager of the City of Griffin, such practice shall be deemed a nuisance, and punishable as an offense against the City of Griffin. . . .

The violation, which is not denied, consisted of the distribution without the required permission of a pamphlet and magazine in the nature of religious tracts, setting forth the gospel of the "Kingdom of Jehovah." Appellant did not apply for a permit. . . .

The ordinance in its broad sweep prohibits the distribution of "circulars, handbooks, advertising, or literature of any kind." [The] ordinance is not limited to "literature" that is obscene or offensive to public morals or that advocates unlawful conduct. [The] ordinance embraces "literature" in the widest sense.

The ordinance is comprehensive with respect to the method of distribution. It covers every sort of circulation "either by hand or otherwise." There is thus no restriction in its application with respect to time or place. It is not limited to ways which might be regarded as inconsistent with the maintenance of public order or as involving disorderly conduct, the molestation of the inhabitants, or the misuse or littering of the streets. The ordinance prohibits the distribution of literature of any kind at any time, at any place, and in any manner without a permit from the City Manager.

We think that the ordinance is invalid on its face. Whatever the motive which induced its adoption, its character is such that it strikes at the very foundation of the freedom of the press by subjecting it to license and censorship. The struggle for the freedom of the press was primarily directed against the power of the licensor. It was against that power that John Milton directed his assault by his "Appeal for the Liberty of Unlicensed Printing." And the liberty of the press became initially a right to publish "*without* a license what formerly could be published only *with* one." While this freedom from previous restraint upon publication cannot be regarded as exhausting the guaranty of liberty, the prevention of that restraint was a leading purpose in the adoption of the constitutional provision. . . .

Legislation of the type of the ordinance in question would restore the system of license and censorship in its baldest form. . . .

As the ordinance is void on its face, it was not necessary for appellant to seek a permit under it. She was entitled to contest its validity in answer to the charge against her. . . .

Reversed.

Mr. Justice Cardozo took no part in the consideration and decision of this case.

Note: Licensing as Prior Restraint

1. *Standardless licensing*. What is the special vice of the licensing scheme in *Lovell*? Why not simply uphold the scheme on its face but permit any person whose application for a license is unconstitutionally denied to challenge that denial in court? Is the Court's primary concern in *Lovell* the absence of standards to guide the city manager's discretion? See Kagan, Private Speech, Public Purpose: The Role of Governmental Motive in First Amendment Doctrine, 63 U. Chi. L. Rev. 415, 459-463 (1996) ("the rule against standardless licensing [serves the] function of flushing out bad motives by establishing a safeguard against administrative action based on the content of expression").

In City of Lakewood v. Plain Dealer Publishing Co., 486 U.S. 750 (1988), the Court applied the *Lovell* principle to invalidate an ordinance that gave a mayor standardless discretion to grant or deny permits to place newsracks on public property. The Court explained that the evils of standardless licensing "can be effectively alleviated only through a facial challenge":

First, the mere existence of the licensor's unfettered discretion [intimidates] parties into censoring their own speech, even if the discretion and power are never actually abused. [Self-censorship] is immune to an "as applied" challenge, for it derives from the individual's own actions, not an abuse of government power. [Only] standards limiting the licensor's discretion will eliminate this danger by adding an element of certainty to fatal self-censorship. And only a facial challenge can effectively test the statute for these standards.

Second, the absence of express standards makes it difficult to distinguish, "as applied," between a licensor's legitimate denial of a permit and its illegitimate abuse of censorial power. Standards provide the guideposts that check the licensor and allow courts quickly and easily to determine whether the licensor is discriminating against disfavored speech. Without these guideposts, post hoc rationalizations by the licensing official and the use of shifting or illegitimate criteria are far too easy, making it difficult for courts to determine in any particular case whether the licensor is permitting favorable, and suppressing unfavorable, expression.

Following *Lovell*, the Court has repeatedly held that a state "cannot vest restraining control over the right to speak [in] an administrative official where there are no appropriate standards to guide his action." Kunz v. New York, 340 U.S. 290, 295 (1951) (permit required for religious meetings); see also Shuttlesworth v. City of Birmingham, 394 U.S. 147 (1969) (permit required for parades); Staub v. City of Baxley, 355 U.S. 313 (1958) (permit required to solicit members for dues-paying organization); Saia v. New York, 334 U.S. 558 (1948) (permit required to operate sound amplifiers in public); Forsyth County, Georgia v. The Nationalist Movement, 505 U.S. 123 (1992) (even nominal permit fees for marches, demonstrations, and parades cannot be imposed in the absence of clear standards governing the setting of fees).

2. *Licensing with standards.* Suppose the authority of licensing officials to deny a permit is explicitly limited to only those circumstances in which the proposed expression could constitutionally be punished in a subsequent criminal prosecution. Would such a scheme, like that in *Lovell*, be unconstitutional on its face? Assume, for example, a state may constitutionally prohibit any person to participate in a parade that would physically interfere with another, ongoing parade. To prevent such conflicts from occurring, could the state constitutionally prohibit any person to participate in a parade without first obtaining a permit, where the licensing officials are authorized to deny a permit only on a finding that the proposed parade would physically interfere with another, previously authorized parade? Cf. Cox v. New Hampshire, 312 U.S. 569 (1941), section E2a infra. Or assume a state may constitutionally make criminal the exhibition of "obscene" motion pictures. May the state constitutionally create a licensing board to which all movies must be submitted prior to public exhibition, where the board is authorized to deny a license only on a finding that a movie is "obscene"? So long as the standards are clear, precise, and in conformity with the standards employed in subsequent criminal prosecutions, is there any reason to erect a special presumption against such "prior" restraints?

3. *The objections to licensing.* Consider Emerson, The Doctrine of Prior Restraint, 20 Law & Contemp. Probs. 648, 656-660 (1955):

[(1)] A system of prior restraint normally brings within the complex of government machinery a far greater amount of communication than a system of subsequent punishment. [The] pall of government control is, thus, likely to hang more pervasively over the area of communication.

[(2)] Under a system of subsequent punishment, the communication has already been made before the government takes action. [Under] a system of prior restraint, the communication, if banned, never reaches the market place at all. Or the communication may be withheld until the issue of its release is finally settled, at which time it may have become obsolete.

[(3)] A system of prior restraint is so constructed as to make it easier, and hence more likely, that in any particular case the government will rule adversely to free expression. [A] government official thinks longer and harder before deciding to undertake the serious task of subsequent punishment. [Under] a system of prior restraint, he can reach the result by a simple stroke of the pen.

[(4)] Under a system of prior restraint, the issue of whether a communication is to be suppressed or not is determined by an administrative rather than a criminal procedure. This means that the procedural protections built around the criminal prosecution [are] not applicable to a prior restraint.

[(5)] A system of prior restraint usually operates behind a screen of informality and partial concealment that seriously curtails opportunity for public appraisal and increases the chances of discrimination and other abuse.

[(6)] [As] common experience [shows, the] attitudes, drives, emotions, and impulses [of licensers] all tend to carry them to excesses. [The] function of the censor is to censor. He has a professional interest in finding things to suppress. [These factors combine to produce] unintelligent, overzealous, and usually absurd administration.

[(7)] A system of prior restraint is, in general, more readily and effectively enforced than a system of subsequent punishment. [A] penal proceeding to enforce a prior restraint normally involves only a limited and relatively simple issue — whether or not the communication was made without prior approval. The objection to the content or manner of the communication need not be demonstrated. And furthermore, the violation of a censorship order strikes sharply at the status of the licenser, whose prestige thus becomes involved and whose power must be vindicated.

How weighty are these concerns? In light of these concerns, should licensing ever be permitted?

4. *The* Freedman *case: procedural safeguards.* In Freedman v. Maryland, 380 U.S. 51 (1965), appellant, in violation of a state motion picture censorship statute, exhibited a film, conceded by the state not to be obscene or otherwise violative of the statutory standards, without first submitting it to the State Board of Censors for review. In a unanimous decision, the Court, speaking through Justice Brennan, held the statute invalid. At the outset, the Court emphasized that the statute was unconstitutional not because it might "prevent even the first showing of a film whose exhibition may legitimately be the subject of an obscenity prosecution," but rather because the administration of the censorship system "presents peculiar dangers to constitutionally protected speech." The Court explained that

unlike a prosecution for obscenity, a censorship proceeding puts the initial burden on the exhibitor or distributor. Because the censor's business is to censor, there inheres the danger that he may well be less responsive than a court — part of an independent branch of government — to the constitutionally protected interests in free expression. And if it is made unduly onerous, by reason of delay or otherwise, to seek judicial review, the censor's determination may in practice be final.

The Court thus concluded that "a noncriminal process which requires the prior submission of a film to a censor avoids constitutional infirmity only if it takes place under procedural safeguards designed to obviate the dangers of a censorship system."

The Court then identified and explained several constitutionally required safeguards:

First, the burden of proving that the film is unprotected expression must rest on the [censor]. Second, while the State may require advance submission of all films, in order to proceed effectively to bar all showings of unprotected films, the requirement cannot be administered in a manner which would lend an effect of finality to the censor's determination whether a film constitutes protected expression. [Because] only a judicial determination in an adversary proceeding ensures the necessary sensitivity to freedom of expression, only a procedure requiring a judicial determination suffices to impose a valid final restraint. [To] this end, the exhibitor must be assured, by statute or authoritative judicial construction, that the censor will, within a specified brief period, either issue a license or go to court to restrain showing the film. Any restraint imposed in advance of a final judicial determination on the merits must similarly be limited to preservation of the status quo for the shortest fixed period compatible with sound judicial resolution. Moreover, [the] procedure must also assure a prompt final judicial decision, to minimize the deterrent effect of an interim and possibly erroneous denial of a license. Without these safeguards, it may prove too burdensome to seek review of the censor's determination.

Because the Maryland scheme did not contain these procedural safeguards, the Court held it unconstitutional on its face. Justices Douglas and Black concurred on the ground that no "form of censorship — no matter how speedy or prolonged it may be — is permissible."

5. *The* Freedman *safeguards.* Should the *Freedman* safeguards be deemed a minimum requirement before *any* licensing scheme may pass constitutional muster? What about the parade permit scheme, noted earlier? See Blasi, Prior Restraints on Demonstrations, 68 Mich. L. Rev. 1481, 1536-1552 (1970); Monaghan, First Amendment "Due Process," 83 Harv. L. Rev. 518, 541-543 (1970). See also Southeastern Promotions, Ltd. v. Conrad, 420 U.S. 546 (1975) (*Freedman* applicable to decision of publicly appointed board not to permit performance of musical "Hair" in public auditorium); Blount v. Rizzi, 400 U.S. 410 (1971) (*Freedman* applicable to postal stop orders).

To what extent do the *Freedman* safeguards mitigate the dangers of licensing? Does it follow from *Freedman* that a licensing scheme is always constitutional so long as (a) the licenser's authority to deny a permit is limited to only those circumstances in which the expression could constitutionally be subjected to subsequent criminal prosecution and (b) the *Freedman* safeguards are employed? *Freedman* involved the licensing of motion pictures. Can government constitutionally require that all *books* be submitted to a board of censors prior to publication in order to screen out those that are obscene or include libelous statements? Can government constitutionally use licensing to deal with the problem of the hostile audience if the licensing scheme incorporates the *Freedman* safeguards? Recall Kunz v. New York, section B3 supra.

Near v. Minnesota

283 U.S. 697 (1931)

[A Minnesota statute provided for the abatement, as a public nuisance, of a "malicious, scandalous and defamatory newspaper, magazine or other periodical." The statute provided further that there "shall be available the defense that the truth was published with good motives and for justifiable ends." In November 1927, a county attorney sought to invoke this statute against The Saturday Press, which had run a series of articles charging "in substance that a Jewish gangster was in control of gambling, bootlegging and racketeering in Minneapolis, and that law enforcing officers and agencies were not energetically performing their duties." The Saturday Press was especially critical of the Chief of Police, who was charged "with gross neglect of duty, illicit relations with gangsters, and with participation in graft." Pursuant to the statute, a state trial court perpetually enjoined The Saturday Press and its owners from publishing or circulating "any publication whatsoever which is a malicious, scandalous or defamatory newspaper." The Supreme Court reversed.]

MR. CHIEF JUSTICE HUGHES delivered the opinion of the Court. . . .

[The] object of the statute is not punishment, in the ordinary sense, but suppression of the offending newspaper or periodical. The reason for the enactment, as the state court has said, is that prosecutions to enforce penal statutes for libel do not result in "efficient repression or suppression of the evils of scandal." . . .

[The statute provides] that public authorities may bring [the] publisher of a newspaper or periodical before a judge upon a charge of conducting a business of publishing scandalous and defamatory matter [and] unless [the] publisher is able [to prove] that the charges are true and are published with good motives and for justifiable ends, his newspaper or periodical is suppressed and further publication is made punishable as a contempt. This is of the essence of censorship.

The question is whether a statute authorizing such proceedings [is] consistent with the conception of the liberty of the press as historically conceived and guaranteed. In determining the extent of the constitutional protection, it has been generally, if not universally, considered that it is the chief purpose of the guaranty to prevent previous restraints upon publication. [T]he protection even as to previous restraint is not absolutely unlimited. But the limitation has been recognized only in exceptional cases. [No] one would question but that a government might prevent actual obstruction to its recruiting service or the publication of the sailing dates of transports or the number and location of troops. On similar grounds, the primary requirements of decency may be enforced against obscene publications. The security of the community life may be protected against incitements to acts of violence and the overthrow by force of orderly government. [These] limitations are not applicable here. . . .

The fact that for approximately one hundred and fifty years there has been almost an entire absence of attempts to impose previous restraints upon publications relating to the malfeasance of public officers is significant of the deep-seated conviction that such restraints would violate constitutional right. Public officers, whose character and conduct remain open to debate and free discussion in the press, find their remedies for false accusations in actions under libel laws providing for redress and punishment, and not in proceedings to restrain the publication of newspapers and periodicals. [The] fact that the liberty of the press may be abused by miscreant purveyors of scandal does not make any the less necessary the immunity of the press from previous restraint in dealing with official misconduct. Subsequent punishment for such abuses as may exist is the appropriate remedy, consistent with constitutional privilege. . . .

The statute in question cannot be justified by reason of the fact that the publisher is permitted to show, before injunction issues, that the matter published is true and is published with good motives and for justifiable ends. If such a statute, authorizing suppression and injunction on such a basis, is constitutionally valid, it would be equally permissible for the legislature to provide that at any time the publisher of any newspaper could be brought before a court, or even an administrative officer (as the constitutional protection may not be regarded as resting on mere procedural details) and required to produce proof of the truth of his publication, or of what he intended to publish, and of his motives, or stand enjoined. If this can be done, the legislature may provide machinery for determining in the complete exercise of its discretion what are justifiable ends and restrain publication accordingly. And it would be but a step to a complete system of censorship. The recognition of authority to impose previous restraint upon publication in order to protect the community against the circulation of charges of misconduct, and especially of official misconduct, necessarily would carry with it the admission of the authority of the censor against which the constitutional barrier was erected. . . .

For these reasons we hold the statute, so far as it authorized the proceedings in this action [to] be an infringement of the liberty of the press guaranteed by the Fourteenth Amendment. . . .

Judgment reversed.

MR. JUSTICE BUTLER, dissenting. . . .

The Minnesota statute does not operate as a *previous* restraint on publication within the proper meaning of that phrase. It does not authorize administrative control in advance such as was formerly exercised by the licensers and censors but prescribes a remedy to be enforced by a suit in equity. In this case there was previous publication made in the course of the business of regularly producing malicious, scandalous and defamatory periodicals. [There] is no question of the power of the State to denounce such transgressions. The restraint authorized is only in respect of continuing to do what has been duly adjudged to constitute a nuisance. [It] is fanciful to suggest similarity between the granting or enforcement of the decree authorized by this statute to prevent *further* publication of malicious, scandalous and defamatory articles and the *previous restraint* upon the press by licensers as referred to by Blackstone and described in the history of the times to which he alludes. . . .

It is well known, as found by the state supreme court, that existing libel laws are inadequate effectively to suppress evils resulting from the kind of business and publications that are shown in this case. The doctrine that measures such as the one before us are invalid because they operate as previous restraints [exposes] [every individual] to [the] false and malicious assaults of any insolvent publisher who [may] put into effect program[s] for oppression, blackmail or extortion.

The judgment should be affirmed.

MR. JUSTICE VAN DEVANTER, MR. JUSTICE MCREYNOLDS, and MR. JUSTICE SUTHERLAND concur in this opinion.

Note: *Injunction as Prior Restraint*

1. *Injunctions, criminal prosecutions, and licensing.* Assuming arguendo, as the Court apparently did in *Near,* that the speech prohibited by the injunction could constitutionally be punished in a subsequent criminal prosecution, why is the injunction invalid? Why isn't the injunction a *preferable* means of restraint? After all, unlike a criminal statute, an injunction is directed to a specific individual and is thus less likely to have a broad chilling effect. See Mayton, Toward a Theory of First Amendment Process: Injunctions of Speech, Subsequent Punishment, and

the Costs of the Prior Restraint Doctrine, 67 Cornell L. Rev. 245 (1982). More-over, unlike the licensing schemes in *Lovell* and *Freedman*, the injunctions in *Near*, the *Pentagon Papers* case, and *Nebraska Press* did not require prepublication submission to a censor for review. And, unlike licensing schemes, injunctions are issued and administered by judges rather than by censors whose "business is to censor." In what sense, then, is the injunction a prior restraint?

2. *Injunctions: are they too effective?* It has been suggested that injunctions are especially threatening to free speech because they are more likely than criminal statutes to be obeyed. Does this make sense? If an injunction prohibits only speech that could constitutionally be punished in a subsequent criminal prosecution, is the greater effectiveness of the injunction a bad thing?

Suppose an injunction prohibits speech that could not constitutionally be punished in a subsequent criminal prosecution. Is the greater effectiveness of the injunction now a bad thing?

Are injunctions in fact more likely than criminal statutes to be obeyed? It has been argued that injunctions have a special "mystique," causing individuals to accord them an unusually high degree of respect, and that injunctions are more likely to be obeyed because they are more likely to be enforced. Injunctions, after all, are directed at specific individuals, thus increasing the probability that violations will be detected, and violations may be viewed as a direct affront to the issuing judge's authority, thus increasing the likelihood that violations will be punished. On the other hand, punishments imposed for violations of injunctions are typically less severe than those for violations of criminal statutes, thus reducing the potential costs of violation. For analyses of these issues, see O. Fiss, The Civil Rights Injunction 71-73 (1978); Barnett, The Puzzle of Prior Restraint, 29 Stan. L. Rev. 539, 551-552 (1977); Blasi, Toward a Theory of Prior Restraint: The Central Linkage, 66 Minn. L. Rev. 11, 24-49 (1981).

3. *The collateral bar rule.* It has been suggested that the critical feature of injunctions, making them far more likely to be obeyed than criminal statutes, and thus appropriately rendering them prior restraints, is the rule, applicable to injunctions generally, that an injunction "must be obeyed until it is set aside, and that persons subject to the [injunction] who disobey it may not defend against the ensuing charge of criminal contempt on the ground that the order was erroneous or even unconstitutional." Barnett, supra, at 552. In the ordinary criminal prosecution, the defendant may assert the unconstitutionality of the statute as a defense. Thus, an individual whose planned expression is prohibited by a statute he believes to be invalid may elect to gamble and speak in defiance of the statute on the assumption that, if prosecuted, he will be able to persuade a court of the statute's unconstitutionality. An individual confronted with an injunction, however, has no such option, for under the "collateral bar" rule, "persons subject to an injunctive order issued by a court with jurisdiction are expected to obey that decree until it is modified or reversed, even if they have proper grounds to object to the order." GTE Sylvania v. Consumers Union, 445 U.S. 375, 386 (1980). This rule, which derives from the notion that "respect for judicial process is a small price to pay for the civilizing hand of law," has been held applicable even to injunctions directed against expression. In Walker v. City of Birmingham, 388 U.S. 307, 321 (1967), for example, a state trial court convicted eight black ministers of criminal contempt for leading mass street parades in violation of a temporary restraining order enjoining them from participating in such parades without first obtaining

a permit as required by a city ordinance. The Court, invoking the collateral bar rule, upheld the contempt convictions without passing on the constitutionality of the injunction.

The collateral bar rule may have a significant impact on an individual's willingness to disobey even a patently unconstitutional order, for if the individual violates the injunction, he is subject to punishment even if the injunction is invalid. Consider Barnett, supra, at 553:

> [The rule places the individual] in a trilemma of chilling effects unique to a prior restraint situation. [He] can comply with the order and take no legal steps, thereby accepting the suppression. [He] can appeal the order directly, [but] must obey the interim restraint while [he] does so. [Or he] can [speak] in the face of [the] order, but only at the price of forfeiting [his] legal and constitutional objections to the order and thus, in all probability, embracing a contempt conviction.

With the collateral bar rule in force, the state in effect orders the enjoined individual to delay his speech unless and until a court lifts the injunction, whether or not the injunction itself is constitutionally permissible. The rule is thus strong medicine. In *Near*, for example, The Saturday Press was silenced for four years while courts debated the constitutionality of the injunction. In the *Progressive* controversy, section B4 supra, the injunction remained in force for seven months, and in the *Skokie* controversy, section B3 supra, the injunction prohibited the Nazis from marching for more than eight months before it was set aside.

Does the existence of the collateral bar rule justify the observation that, whereas a "criminal statute chills," an injunction "freezes"? A. Bickel, The Morality of Consent 61 (1975). Does it justify the characterization of injunctions as prior restraints? See Jeffries, Rethinking Prior Restraint, 92 Yale L.J. 409 (1983).

4. *When is an injunction not a prior restraint?* Consider the following:

a. Suppose state law provides that the collateral bar rule is inapplicable to injunctions against expression. See cases cited in Rendleman, Free Press — Fair Trial: Review of Silence Orders, 52 N.C.L. Rev. 127, 153 n.181, 154 nn.182-185 (1973). Should injunctions in such a jurisdiction be treated as prior restraints? Consider Blasi, supra, at 87-91:

> [1] [A] major element in the case for a presumption against prior restraint is the undesirably abstract quality of any adjudication that occurs prior to the time the communication at issue is initially disseminated to the public. If the collateral bar rule were no longer to govern injunctions, adjudication of the first amendment claims of enjoined speakers would [still be] somewhat problematic in this regard. [The] issue in a prosecution for violating an injunction is whether the restraint on speaking was unconstitutional at the time it was imposed. That reasonable apprehensions which induced and justified the restraint in the first place failed to materialize does not impeach the state's case for the regulation.
>
> [2] Another major component of the case for linking injunctions with licensing systems is the tendency of both methods of regulation to be used more readily than methods that rely on subsequent punishment. Virtually every argument relating to overuse [would] remain applicable were the collateral bar rule no longer to govern injunctions. A stroke of the pen by a single judge would still be sufficient to create the legal prohibition. [Moreover, disobedience] of such a personalized prohibition would still be highly visible, and would often be viewed as a test of the judicial sys-

tem's will. The prospect of expeditious conviction of offenders would continue to spur prosecutorial authorities into action.

[3] An important reason for disfavoring injunctions and licensing systems as methods of speech regulation is that they rest on [the objectionable premise that] the act of speaking is an abnormally hazardous activity that warrants special regulation. [Even with abandonment of the collateral bar rule,] the choice of the injunctive method of regulation represents a judgment that the activity in question requires special, personalized, swift control. The mobilization of judicial authority at the anticipatory stage has symbolic overtones.

b. Suppose a court enjoins an individual from exhibiting any obscene motion picture, expressly defining obscenity according to the Supreme Court's definition. Do you agree that, even with the collateral bar rule in effect, such an injunction should not be treated as a prior restraint because it is "phrased in terms of a constitutionally adequate definition of obscenity" and any particular "motion picture's nonobscenity would [thus] clearly defeat any contempt proceeding [since] if the film were not obscene, there would be no violation of the injunction"? Vance v. Universal Amusement Co., 445 U.S. 308, 322 (1980) (White, J., dissenting).

c. In Pittsburgh Press Co. v. Pittsburgh Commission on Human Relations, 413 U.S. 376 (1973), the commission, after a hearing, found that the Pittsburgh Press had violated a city ordinance by displaying "help wanted" advertisements in its daily newspaper under headings designating job preference by sex. The commission therefore issued an order prohibiting the newspaper from carrying sex-designated ads in the future. In upholding the order, the Court explained that a criminal statute cast in such terms would be constitutionally permissible and then observed:

> [We have] never held that all injunctions are impermissible. [The] special vice of a prior restraint is that communication will be suppressed, either directly or by inducing excessive caution in the speaker, before an adequate determination that it is unprotected by the First Amendment. The present order does not endanger arguably protected speech. Because the order is based on a continuing course of repetitive conduct, this is not a case in which the Court is asked to speculate as to the effect of publication. Cf. [*Pentagon Papers* case]. Moreover, [because] no interim relief was granted, the order will not have gone into effect before our final determination that the actions of Pittsburgh Press were unprotected.

Consider Redish, The Proper Role of the Prior Restraint Doctrine in First Amendment Theory, 70 Va. L. Rev. 53, 55, 58 (1984):

> [Injunctions, like licensing schemes,] are appropriately disfavored [because] of the coincidental harm to fully protected expression that results [when] a *preliminary* restraint [is] imposed prior to a decision on the merits of a *final* restraint. [Such] interim restraints present a threat to first amendment rights not found in subsequent punishment schemes — the threat that expression will be abridged, if only for a short time, prior to a full and fair hearing before an independent judicial forum to determine the scope of the speaker's constitutional right. [Thus,] the doctrine should strike down [injunctions only if they are] imposed *prior* to a full and fair judicial hearing.

d. Should it matter whether an injunction is directed at the content of the restricted speech? Consider Madsen v. Women's Health Centers, Inc., 512 U.S. 753 (1994), in which the Court held that an injunction prohibiting particular named individuals from demonstrating within thirty-six feet of an abortion clinic was not a "prior restraint" because the injunction was issued "not because of the content of petitioners' expression," but "because of their prior unlawful conduct" in earlier demonstrations. Consider also an injunction prohibiting the use of loudspeakers in demonstrations within 100 feet of a hospital, school, or abortion clinic. In *Madsen*, the Court suggested that content-neutral injunctions are not "prior restraints," but that they nonetheless should be tested by more "rigorous" standards than other forms of content-neutral restrictions because injunctions "carry greater risks of censorship and discriminatory application than do general ordinances."

5. *Prior restraint revisited.* Consider Freund, The Supreme Court and Civil Liberties, 4 Vand. L. Rev. 533, 539 (1951): "In sum, it will hardly do to place 'prior restraint' in a special category for condemnation. What is needed is a pragmatic assessment of its operation in the particular circumstances. The generalization that prior restraint is particularly obnoxious in civil liberties cases must yield to more particularistic analysis." Consider also Scordato, Distinction without a Difference: A Reappraisal of the Doctrine of Prior Restraint, 68 N.C.L. Rev. 1, 34 (1989), suggesting that the "definition of prior restraint [should] be changed to include only those government actions that result in the [actual] *physical* interception and suppression of speech prior to its public expression."

D.   CONTENT-BASED RESTRICTIONS: "LOW" VALUE SPEECH

As is evident from the analysis in section B, the Court has adhered generally to a two-level theory of free expression in its interpretation of the first amendment. Some speech, in other words, is said to possess only "low" first amendment value and is thus accorded less than full constitutional protection. The two-level theory has its roots in the famous dictum of Chaplinsky v. New Hampshire, section B3 supra:

> There are certain well-defined and narrowly limited classes of speech, the prevention and punishment of which have never been thought to raise any Constitutional problem. These include the lewd and obscene, the profane, the libelous, and the insulting or "fighting" words — those which by their very utterance inflict injury or tend to incite an immediate breach of the peace. It has been well observed that such utterances are no essential part of any exposition of ideas, and are of such slight social value as a step to truth that any benefit that may be derived from them is clearly outweighed by the social interest in order and morality.

This section examines the "low" value theory in depth. In so doing, it poses a number of central first amendment questions: Is the very concept of low value speech inherently incompatible with the guarantee of free expression? That is, does the determination that certain types of speech are of "slight social value as a step to truth" compel the Court to make "value judgments concerned with the content of expression, a role foreclosed to it by the basic theory of the First Amendment"? T. Emerson, The System of Freedom of Expression 326 (1970). Is the Court's exercise of this power tolerable so long as it confines itself to defining low value speech in terms of discrete categories of expression rather than in terms of particular "good" or "bad" ideas? How is the Court to determine what speech is of low first amendment value? What follows from a determination that a certain category of expression is of low first amendment value? Is such expression wholly outside the protection of the first amendment, as suggested by *Chaplinsky*, or does such a determination trigger a form of "categorical balancing," according such speech some, but less than "full," first amendment protection?

It has been argued that the two-level theory is essential to "any well-functioning system of free expression" because without it one of two "unacceptable" results would follow — either (1) "the burden of justification imposed on government" when it regulates high value speech, such as pure political expression, "would have to be lowered," or (2) "the properly stringent standards applied to efforts to regulate" high value speech would have to be applied to low value speech, with the result that government would not be able to regulate speech "that in all probability should be regulated." C. Sunstein, The Partial Constitution 233-234 (1993). Is there any answer to this argument?

This section examines several categories of arguably "low" value expression — false statements of fact; nonnewsworthy disclosures of "private" facts; commercial advertising; obscenity; lewd, profane, and indecent speech; and hate speech and pornography.

1.   False Statements of Fact

The Supreme Court has long maintained that "[under] the First Amendment there is no such thing as a false idea. However pernicious an opinion may seem, we depend for its correction not on the conscience of judges and juries but on the competition of other ideas." Gertz v. Robert Welch, Inc., infra this section. Government, in other words, may not restrict the expression of an idea or opinion because of *its* determination that the idea or opinion is "false." What, though, of false statements of *fact*? Recall Justice Holmes's example of the "false cry of fire."

The problem of false statements of fact arises most often in the context of defamation. At the time of adoption of the first amendment, civil and criminal actions for defamation were commonplace, and in *Chaplinsky* the Court expressly included libel within the class of utterances that "are no essential part of any exposition of ideas, and are of such slight social value as a step to truth that any benefit that may be derived from them is clearly outweighed by the social interest in order and morality." A decade later, in Beauharnais v. Illinois, section D6 infra, the Court announced that libelous utterances are not "within the area of constitutionally protected speech," and, accordingly, that "no one would contend that [they] may be punished only upon a showing" of clear and present danger.

New York Times v. Sullivan

376 U.S. 254 (1964)

MR. JUSTICE BRENNAN delivered the opinion of the Court.

We are required in this case to determine for the first time the extent to which the constitutional protections for speech and press limit a State's power to award damages in a libel action brought by a public official against critics of his official conduct.

Respondent L. B. Sullivan is one of the three elected Commissioners of the City of Montgomery, Alabama. [He] brought this civil libel action against the four individual petitioners, who are Negroes and Alabama clergymen, and against petitioner the New York Times. . . .

Respondent's complaint alleged that he had been libeled by statements in a full-page advertisement that was carried in the New York Times on March 29, 1960. Entitled "Heed Their Rising Voices," the advertisement [described the civil rights movement in the South and concluded with an appeal for funds].

Of the 10 paragraphs of text in the advertisement, the third and a portion of the sixth were the basis of respondent's claim of libel. They read as follows:

Third paragraph:

In Montgomery, Alabama, after students sang "My Country, 'Tis of Thee" on the State Capital steps, their leaders were expelled from school, and truckloads of police armed with shotguns and tear-gas ringed the Alabama State College campus. When the entire student body protested to state authorities by refusing to re-register, their dining hall was padlocked in an attempt to starve them into submission.

Sixth Paragraph:

Again and again the Southern violators have answered Dr. King's peaceful protests with intimidation and violence. They have bombed his home almost killing his wife and child. They have assaulted his person. They have arrested him seven times — for "speeding," "loitering" and similar "offenses." And now they have charged him with "perjury" — a *felony* under which they could imprison him for *ten years*. . . .

Although neither of these statements mentions respondent by name, he contended that the word "police" in the third paragraph referred to him as the Montgomery Commissioner who supervised the Police Department, so that he was being accused of "ringing" the campus with police. He further claimed that the paragraph would be read as imputing to the police, and hence to him, the padlocking of the dining hall in order to starve the students into submission. As to the sixth paragraph, he contended that since arrests are ordinarily made by the police, the statement "They have arrested [Dr. King] seven times" would be read as referring to him. . . .

It is uncontroverted that some of the statements contained in the two paragraphs were not accurate descriptions of events which occurred in Montgomery. Although Negro students staged a demonstration on the State Capitol steps, they sang the National Anthem and not "My Country, 'Tis of Thee." Although nine students were expelled by the State Board of Education, this was not for leading the demonstration at the Capitol, but for demanding service at a lunch counter in the Montgomery County Courthouse on another day. Not the entire student body, but most of it, had protested the expulsion. [The] campus dining hall was not padlocked on any occasion. [Although] the police were deployed near the campus in large numbers on three occasions, they did not at any time "ring" the campus. [Dr.] King had not been arrested seven times, but only four. . . .

Respondent made no effort to prove that he suffered actual pecuniary loss as a result of the alleged libel.[3]

The trial judge submitted the case to the jury under instructions that the statements in the advertisement were "libelous per se" and were not privileged, so that petitioners might be held liable if the jury found that they had published the advertisement and that the statements were made "of and concerning" respondent. The jury was instructed that, because the statements were libelous per se, "the law . . . implies legal injury from the bare fact of publication itself," "falsity and malice are presumed," "general damages need not be alleged or proved but are presumed," and "punitive damages may be awarded by the jury even though the amount of actual damages is neither found nor shown." [The jury returned a judgment for respondent in the amount of $500,000.]

We reverse the judgment. We hold that the rule of law applied by the Alabama courts is constitutionally deficient for failure to provide the safeguards for freedom of speech and of the press that are required by the First and Fourteenth Amendments in a libel action brought by a public official against critics of his official conduct. We further hold that under the proper safeguards the evidence presented in this case is constitutionally insufficient to support the judgment for respondent.

I

We may dispose at the outset of [respondent's argument that the judgment of the state court is insulated from constitutional scrutiny because] "The Fourteenth Amendment is directed against State action and not private action." That proposition has no application to this case. Although this is a civil lawsuit between private parties, the Alabama courts have applied a state rule of law which petitioners claim to impose invalid restrictions on their constitutional freedoms of speech and press. It matters not that that law has been applied in a civil action and that it is common law only. [The] test is not the form in which state power has been applied but, whatever the form, whether such power has in fact been exercised. . . .

II . . .

Respondent relies heavily, as did the Alabama courts, on statements of this Court to the effect that the Constitution does not protect libelous publications. Those statements do not foreclose our inquiry here. None of the cases sustained the use of libel laws to impose sanctions upon expression critical of the official conduct

---

3. Approximately 394 copies of the edition of the Times containing the advertisement were circulated in Alabama. Of these, about 35 copies were distributed in Montgomery County. The total circulation of the Times for that day was approximately 650,000 copies. . . .

of public officials. [In] deciding the question now, we are compelled by neither precedent nor policy to give any more weight to the epithet "libel" than we have to other "mere labels" of state law. [Like] insurrection, contempt, advocacy of unlawful acts, breach of the peace, obscenity, solicitation of legal business, and the various other formulae for the repression of expression that have been challenged in this Court, libel can claim no talismanic immunity from constitutional limitations. It must be measured by standards that satisfy the First Amendment.

[We] consider this case against the background of a profound national commitment to the principle that debate on public issues should be uninhibited, robust, and wide-open, and that it may well include vehement, caustic, and sometimes unpleasantly sharp attacks on government and public officials. See [*Terminiello*]. The present advertisement, as an expression of grievance and protest on one of the major public issues of our time, would seem clearly to qualify for the constitutional protection. The question is whether it forfeits that protection by the falsity of some of its factual statements and by its alleged defamation of respondent.

Authoritative interpretations of the First Amendment guarantees have consistently refused to recognize an exception for any test of truth — whether administered by judges, juries, or administrative officials — and especially one that puts the burden of proving truth on the speaker. [Erroneous] statement is inevitable in free debate, [and] it must be protected if the freedoms of expression are to have the "breathing space" that they "need . . . to survive." . . .

Injury to official reputation affords no more warrant for repressing speech that would otherwise be free than does factual error. Where judicial officers are involved, this Court has held that concern for the dignity and reputation of the courts does not justify the punishment as criminal contempt of criticism of the judge or his decision. [*Bridges.*] If judges are to be treated as "men of fortitude, able to thrive in a hardy climate," [surely] the same must be true of other government officials, such as elected city commissioners. Criticism of their official conduct does not lose its constitutional protection merely because it is effective criticism and hence diminishes their official reputations.

If neither factual error nor defamatory content suffices to remove the constitutional shield from criticism of official conduct, the combination of the two elements is no less inadequate. This is the lesson to be drawn from the great controversy over the Sedition Act of 1798, which first crystallized a national awareness of the central meaning of the First Amendment. . . .

Although the Sedition Act was never tested in this Court, the attack upon its validity has carried the day in the court of history. Fines levied in its prosecution were repaid by Act of Congress on the ground that it was unconstitutional. [Jefferson], as President, pardoned those who had been convicted and sentenced under the Act and remitted their fines. [These] views reflect a broad consensus that the Act, because of the restraint it imposed upon criticism of government and public officials, was inconsistent with the First Amendment. . . .

What a State may not constitutionally bring about by means of a criminal statute is likewise beyond the reach of its civil law of libel. The fear of damage awards under a rule such as that invoked by the Alabama courts here may be markedly more inhibiting than the fear of prosecution under a criminal statute. [Alabama], for example, has a criminal libel law [which] allows as punishment upon conviction a fine not exceeding $500 and a prison sentence of six months. [The] judgment awarded in this case — without the need for any proof of actual pecuniary loss — was one thousand times greater than the maximum fine provided by the Alabama criminal statute, and one hundred times greater than that provided by the Sedition Act. [Whether] or not a newspaper can survive a succession of such judgments, the pall of fear and timidity imposed upon those who would give voice to public criticism is an atmosphere in which the First Amendment freedoms cannot survive. . . .

The state rule of law is not saved by its allowance of the defense of truth. [A] rule compelling the critic of official conduct to guarantee the truth of all his factual assertions — and to do so on pain of libel judgments virtually unlimited in amount — leads to a comparable "self-censorship." Allowance of the defense of truth, with the burden of proving it on the defendant, does not mean that only false speech will be deterred.[10] [Under] such a rule, would-be critics of official conduct may be deterred from voicing their criticism, even though it is believed to be true and even though it is in fact true, because of doubt whether it can be proved in court or fear of the expense of having to do so. They tend to make only statements which "steer far wider of the unlawful zone." [The] rule thus dampens the vigor and limits the variety of public debate. It is inconsistent with the First and Fourteenth Amendments.

The constitutional guarantees require, we think, a federal rule that prohibits a public official from recovering damages for a defamatory falsehood relating to his official conduct unless he proves that the statement was made with "actual malice" — that is, with knowledge that it was false or with reckless disregard of whether it was false or not. . . .

Such a privilege for criticism of official conduct is appropriately analogous to the protection accorded a public official when *he* is sued for libel by a private citizen. In Barr v. Matteo, 360 U.S. 564, 575, this Court held the utterance of a federal official to be absolutely privileged if made "within the outer perimeter" of his duties. The States accord the same immunity to statements of their highest officers. [The] reason for the official privilege is said to be that the threat of damage suits would otherwise "inhibit the fearless, vigorous, and effective administration of policies of government" and "dampen the ardor of all but the most resolute, or the most irresponsible, in the unflinching discharge of their duties." [Analogous] considerations support the privilege for the citizen-critic of government. It is as much his duty to criticize as it is the official's duty to administer. [As] Madison [said,] "the censorial power is in the people over the Government, and not in the Government over the people." . . .

III

We hold today that the Constitution delimits a State's power to award damages for libel in actions brought by public officials against critics of their official con-

---

10. Even a false statement may be deemed to make a valuable contribution to public debate, since it brings about "the clearer perception and livelier impression of truth, produced by its collision with error." Mill, On Liberty (Oxford: Blackwell, 1947), at 15; see also Milton, Areopagitica in Prose Works (Yale, 1959), Vol. II, at 561.

duct. Since this is such an action,[23] the rule requiring proof of actual malice is applicable. . . .

Since respondent may seek a new trial, we deem that considerations of effective judicial administration require us to review the evidence in the present record to determine whether it could constitutionally support a judgment for respondent. [The] proof presented to show actual malice lacks the convincing clarity which the constitutional standard demands. [Although] there is evidence that the Times published the advertisement without checking its accuracy against the news stories in the Times' own files, [we] think the evidence against the Times supports at most a finding of negligence in failing to discover the misstatements, and is constitutionally insufficient to show the recklessness that is required for a finding of actual malice. . . .

We also think the evidence was constitutionally defective in another respect: it was incapable of supporting the jury's finding that the allegedly libelous statements were made "of and concerning" respondent. [The state courts embraced the proposition that criticism of government action could be treated as criticism of the officials responsible for that action for purposes of a libel suit.]

This proposition has disquieting implications for criticism of government conduct. [It would transmute] criticism of government, however impersonal it may seem on its face, into personal criticism, and hence potential libel, of the officials of whom the government is composed. [We] hold that such a proposition may not constitutionally be utilized to establish that an otherwise impersonal attack on governmental operations was a libel of an official responsible for those operations. . . .

Reversed and remanded.

MR. JUSTICE BLACK, with whom MR. JUSTICE DOUGLAS joins, concurring. . . .

"Malice," even as defined by the Court, is an elusive, abstract concept, hard to prove and hard to disprove. The requirement that malice be proved provides at best an evanescent protection for the right critically to discuss public affairs and certainly does not measure up to the sturdy safeguard embodied in the First Amendment. . . .

The half-million-dollar verdict [gives] dramatic proof [that] state libel laws threaten the very existence of an American press virile enough to publish unpopular views on public affairs and bold enough to criticize the conduct of public officials. [There] is no reason to believe that there are not more such huge verdicts lurking just around the corner for the Times or any other newspaper or broadcaster which might dare to criticize public officials. In fact, briefs before us show that in Alabama there are now pending eleven libel suits by local and state officials against the Times seeking $5,600,000, and five such suits against the Columbia Broadcasting System seeking $1,700,000.

---

23. We have no occasion here to determine how far down into the lower ranks of government employees the "public official" designation would extend for purposes of this rule, or otherwise to specify categories of persons who would or would not be included. Nor need we here determine the boundaries of the "official conduct" concept. It is enough for the present case that respondent's position as an elected city commissioner clearly made him a public official, and that the allegations in the advertisement concerned what was allegedly his official conduct as Commissioner in charge of the Police Department. . . .

In my opinion the Federal Constitution has dealt with this deadly danger to the press in the only way possible without leaving the free press open to destruction — by granting the press an absolute immunity for criticism of the way public officials do their public duty. Compare Barr v. Matteo, 360 U.S. 564. Stopgap measures like those the Court adopts are in my judgment not enough. . . .

[In a separate concurring opinion, Justice Goldberg, joined by Justice Douglas, maintained that the first amendment affords "an absolute, unconditional privilege to criticize official conduct," but noted that "defamatory statements directed against the private conduct of a public official or private citizen" may be different, for "purely private defamation has little to do with the political ends of a self-governing society."]

Note: "The Central Meaning" of New York Times v. Sullivan

1. *The central meaning of the first amendment.* Professors Meiklejohn and Kalven maintained that the *New York Times* decision "is [an] occasion for dancing in the streets." Kalven, The *New York Times* Case: A Note on "The Central Meaning of the First Amendment," 1964 Sup. Ct. Rev. 191, 221 n.125. Consider id. at 208-209:

The Court did not simply, in the face of an awkward history, definitively put to rest the status of the Sedition Act. More important, it found in the controversy over seditious libel the clue to "the central meaning of the First Amendment." The choice of language was unusually apt. The Amendment has a "central meaning" — a core of protection of speech without which democracy cannot function, without which, in Madison's phrase, "the censorial power" would be in the Government over the people and not "in the people over the Government." This is not the whole meaning of the Amendment. There are other freedoms protected by it. But at the center there is no doubt what speech is being protected and no doubt why it is being protected. The theory of the freedom of speech clause was put right side up for the first time. [The] central meaning of the Amendment is that seditious libel cannot be made the subject of government sanction.

2. *Low value?* Does *New York Times* reject the view of *Chaplinsky* and *Beauharnais* (section D6 infra) that false statements of fact are of "slight social value" and hence not "within the area of constitutionally protected speech"? Consider footnote 10. Is the Court's primary concern with the protection of false statements of fact or with the risk that libel laws might generate a self-censorship that invades the zone of "high" value speech?

3. *Definitional balancing.* Consider Nimmer, The Right to Speak from *Times* to *Time*: First Amendment Theory Applied to Libel and Misapplied to Privacy, 56 Cal. L. Rev. 935, 942-943 (1968):

[*New York Times*] points the way to the employment of the balancing process on the definitional [level]. That is, the Court employs balancing [for] the purpose of defining which forms of speech are to be regarded as "speech" within the meaning of the first amendment. [By] in effect holding that knowingly and recklessly false speech was not "speech" within the meaning of the first amendment, the Court implicitly [balanced] certain competing policy considerations.

Is such "definitional balancing" an appropriate way to formulate first amend-ment doctrine? Contrast the "definitional balancing" in *New York Times* with that in *Brandenburg*. How does each treat the issue of intent? For a critique of defini-tional balancing, see Aleinikoff, Constitutional Law in the Age of Balancing, 96 Yale L.J. 943, 979-981 (1987).

4. *Is* New York Times *overprotective of false speech?* Consider the follow-ing views:

a. Even if the first amendment protects libel in the sense that government may not criminally punish such expression, it does not necessarily follow that news-papers should not have to pay for the costs of their speech. The first amendment does not require government — or public officials — to *subsidize* newspapers.

b. *New York Times* rests on the assumption that the marketplace of ideas will function better with the Court's rule than without it. But the opposite assump-tion seems at least equally plausible. First, self-censorship is not intrinsically a bad thing. It all depends on what speech is discouraged. Although traditional libel law may "chill" more valuable speech than the *New York Times* rule, it also "chills" more false speech. It is by no means clear that the effect of *New York Times* will be to improve the overall quality of public debate. Second, *New York Times* may actually reduce "the quality of information [available to the public by eliminating jury judgments] as to the truth or falsity of some accusations." Nagel, How Useful Is Judicial Review in Free Speech Cases?, 69 Cornell L. Rev. 302, 323 (1984). Finally, *New York Times* may so expose public officials to journalistic abuse that it will drive capable persons away from government service, thus frus-trating, rather than furthering, the political process.

c. Dun & Bradstreet v. Greenmoss Builders, 472 U.S. 749 (1985) (White, J., concurring):

> Instead of escalating the plaintiff's burden of proof to an almost impossible level, [the Court] could have achieved [its] goal by limiting the recoverable damages to a level that would not unduly threaten the press. Punitive [and presumed damages] might have been prohibited, or limited. Had that course been taken and the common-law standard of liability been retained, the defamed public official, upon proving falsity, could at least have had a judgment to that effect. His reputation would then be vin-dicated; and to the extent possible, the misinformation circulated would have been countered. He might also have recovered a modest amount, enough perhaps to pay his litigation expenses. [In] this way, both First Amendment and reputational in-terests would have been far better served.

d. Epstein, Was New York Times v. Sullivan Wrong?, 53 U. Chi. L. Rev. 782, 797, 804 (1986):

> The general tendency in defamation cases has always been for a powerful rule of strict liability. [In] strict liability the probability of recovery is relatively large and the damages can be kept relatively small. With actual malice the probability of re-covery is relatively small and damages are relatively large. It takes little mathemati-cal sophistication to realize that if success is more likely with strict liability, and damages are more generous with actual malice, it becomes uncertain whether the total liabilities [are] greater under the strict liability rule or the actual malice rule.

Epstein concludes that, once one takes into account "litigation costs" and "repu-tational effects," the common law rule of strict liability is preferable to the actual malice rule of New York Times v. Sullivan.

5. *Is* New York Times *underprotective of false speech?* Consider the following views:

a. Anderson, Libel and Press Self-Censorship, 53 Tex. L. Rev. 422, 424-425, 436 (1975):

[*New York Times* will not prevent self-censorship because] it does little to reduce the cost of defending against libel claims. Instead, it perpetuates a system of censorship [in] which the relevant question is not whether a story is libelous, but whether the subject is likely to sue, and if so, how much it will cost to defend. [The decision] has failed to alleviate this problem primarily because it usually has no effect until a case reaches the trial stage.

For analysis of the use of summary judgment in this context, see Louis, Summary Judgment and the Actual Malice Controversy in Constitutional Defamation Cases, 57 S. Cal. L. Rev. 707 (1984) (observing that 75 percent of all motions for summary judgment by defendants on the issue of actual malice are granted).

b. Smolla, Let the Author Beware: The Rejuvenation of the American Law of Libel, 132 U. Pa. L. Rev. 1, 4-7, 12, 91-93 (1984):

The data show a trend toward more generous jury awards, and a corresponding trend toward the media settling suits at a substantial cost. [One] study showed that thirty out of forty-seven damage awards included punitive damages, and seven of those punitive damage awards were for $1 million or more. [The] prospect of such lucrative awards is likely to entice more potential defamation plaintiffs to bring [suit]. A failure to adjust defamation doctrine [can] be expected to have a severe impact on the media. [Many] media outlets [defend] libel actions under the peril of shutdown if they lose. [One] alternative to current law is to allow punitive damages only when the plaintiff, in addition to proving actual malice, proves common law ill-will malice. [Preferably,] punitive damages should be [abolished altogether].

c. LeBel, Reforming the Tort of Defamation: An Accommodation of the Competing Interests within the Current Constitutional Framework, 66 Neb. L. Rev. 249, 293 (1987):

If one is to take seriously the image of the marketplace of ideas, one is entitled to be extremely skeptical about the claims of the judiciary to be competent to act as some sort of Consumer Product Safety Commission for that marketplace. This skepticism is particularly well placed when it is a branch of that same government that is putting itself into a definitive position to label as false a statement about government. [The] only truly adequate protection for criticism of government is an absolute privilege to say whatever one wishes about government without being called to account in any governmental forum.

6. *The limits of* New York Times. What does the Court mean by "reckless disregard"? Does *New York Times* implicitly prohibit criminal prosecutions for libel of public officials? Are all public employees "public officials" within the meaning of *New York Times?*

Consider the following decisions, which shed light on these and related issues: Masson v. New Yorker Magazine, 501 U.S. 496 (1991) (in an action for libel based on the publication of altered quotations of the plaintiff, the first amendment precludes liability even for deliberate alteration unless the plaintiff proves that the alteration "results in a material change in the meaning" and has a defamatory character); Milkovich v. Lorain Journal Co., 497 U.S. 1 (1990) (a statement "must be provable as false before there can be liability"); Harte-Hanks Communications v. Connaughton, 491 U.S. 657 (1989) (neither failure to comply with "professional standards" nor publication of falsehood in order to increase profits is in itself sufficient to establish "actual malice," but "purposeful avoidance of the truth" may be sufficient); Philadelphia Newspapers, Inc. v. Hepps, 475 U.S. 767 (1986) (the "plaintiff must bear the burden of proving that the statements at issue are false"); Herbert v. Lando, 441 U.S. 153 (1979) (a libel plaintiff may inquire into the state of mind of publishers and reporters in pretrial discovery in order to make out a case of reckless disregard); Monitor Patriot Co. v. Roy, 401 U.S. 265 (1971) ("a charge of criminal conduct, no matter how remote in time or place, can never be irrelevant to an official's or a candidate's fitness for office for purposes of application of" New York Times); St. Amant v. Thompson, 390 U.S. 727 (1968) (failure to investigate or otherwise seek corroboration prior to publication is not reckless disregard for the truth unless the publisher acts with a "high degree of awareness of [probable] falsity"); Garrison v. Louisiana, 379 U.S. 64 (1964) (first amendment does not absolutely prohibit criminal prosecution for libel even of public officials, but New York Times standard applies).

Perhaps the most important question remaining after New York Times was whether the privilege it recognized governed only libel of public officials or whether it extended to libel of other persons as well. Shortly after the decision, Professor Kalven maintained that the theory of the first amendment expounded in New York Times constituted an implicit "invitation to follow a dialectic progression from public official to government policy to public policy to matters in the public domain." Kalven, supra.

CURTIS PUBLISHING CO. v. BUTTS; ASSOCIATED PRESS v. WALKER, 388 U.S. 130 (1967). In these companion cases, the Court examined the question whether a libel action brought by an individual who is a "public figure," but not a "public official," must also be governed by the New York Times standard. Butts brought an action for libel, alleging that the defendant had published an article falsely accusing him of conspiring to "fix" a football game between the University of Georgia and the University of Alabama. At the time of the article, Butts was the athletic director of the University of Georgia, a state university, but was employed by the Georgia Athletic Association, a private corporation. Butts had served previously as head football coach at the university and had an established national reputation. In the companion case, Walker sued the Associated Press for libel, claiming that it had distributed a news dispatch falsely reporting that, when a riot erupted on the campus of the University of Mississippi because of federal efforts to enforce court-ordered desegregation, Walker had taken command of the crowd, encouraged it to use violence, and personally led a charge against the federal marshals. Walker, a private citizen at the time of the riot and publication, had pursued a distinguished military career and was a figure of national prominence. In each case, the jury found the defendant liable under state law, the trial judge approved a damage award of about $500,000, and the defendant maintained that New York Times should govern and that it thus could not be held liable without proof that it had published the story either knowing it to be false or with reckless disregard for the truth.

In a sharply divided set of opinions, the Court held the New York Times standard applicable to "public figures" as well as to "public officials," and, further, that both Butts and Walker constituted "public figures" for purposes of the rule. Chief Justice Warren, joined by Justices Brennan and White, observed that "increasingly in this country, the distinctions between governmental and private sectors are blurred," and that many individuals "who do not hold public office at the moment are nevertheless intimately involved in the resolution of important public questions or, by reason of their fame, shape events in areas of concern to society at large." Moreover, Chief Justice Warren argued, "as a class these 'public figures' have as ready access as 'public officials' to mass media of communication, both to influence policy and to counter criticism of their views and activities." Thus, Chief Justice Warren concluded, "differentiation between 'public figures' and 'public officials' and adoption of separate standards of proof for each have no basis in law, logic, or First Amendment policy." Justice Black, joined by Justice Douglas, maintained that "the First Amendment was intended to leave the press [absolutely] free from the harassment of libel judgments," but accepted the narrower rationale of Chief Justice Warren "'in order for the Court to be able at this time to agree on [a disposition of] this important case.'" Justice Harlan, joined by Justices Clark, Stewart, and Fortas, concurred in the result.

Is the extension of *New York Times* to "public figures" mandated by "the central meaning of the first amendment"? For a careful analysis of *Butts* and *Walker*, see Kalven, The Reasonable Man and the First Amendment: *Hill, Butts,* and *Walker,* 1967 Sup. Ct. Rev. 267. How should "public figure" be defined?

Gertz v. Robert Welch, Inc.
418 U.S. 323 (1974)

[In 1968, a Chicago policeman named Nuccio shot and killed a youth named Nelson. The state prosecuted Nuccio and obtained a conviction for murder. The Nelson family retained Gertz, a Chicago attorney, to represent them in civil litigation against Nuccio. In 1969, respondent, publisher of American Opinion, a monthly outlet for the views of the John Birch Society, ran an article in which it accused Gertz of being the architect of a "frame-up" of Nuccio and stated that Gertz had a criminal record and long-standing communist affiliations. Gertz filed this action for libel. After the jury returned a $50,000 verdict for Gertz, the trial court entered judgment n.o.v., concluding that the *New York Times* standard applied to any discussion of a "public issue." The court of appeals affirmed. The Supreme Court reversed.]

MR. JUSTICE POWELL delivered the opinion of the Court. . . .

II

The principal issue in this case is whether a newspaper or broadcaster that publishes defamatory falsehoods about an individual who is neither a public official nor a public figure may claim a constitutional privilege against liability for the injury inflicted by those statements. The Court considered this question on the rather different set of facts presented in Rosenbloom v. Metromedia, Inc., 403 U.S. 29 (1971), [but] no majority could agree on a controlling rationale. . . .

III

We begin with the common ground. Under the First Amendment there is no such thing as a false idea. However pernicious an opinion may seem, we depend for its correction not on the conscience of judges and juries but on the competition of other ideas. But there is no constitutional value in false statements of fact. Neither the intentional lie nor the careless error materially advances society's interest in "uninhibited, robust, and wide-open" debate on public issues. [New York Times Co. v. Sullivan.] They belong to that category of utterances which "are no essential part of any exposition of ideas, and are of such slight social value as a step to truth that any benefit that may be derived from them is clearly outweighed by the social interest in order and morality." [*Chaplinsky.*]

Although the erroneous statement of fact is not worthy of constitutional protection, it is nevertheless inevitable in free debate. [And] punishment of error runs the risk of inducing a cautious and restrictive exercise of the constitutionally guaranteed freedoms of speech and press. Our decisions recognize that a rule of strict liability that compels a publisher or broadcaster to guarantee the accuracy of his factual assertions may lead to intolerable self-censorship. [The] First Amendment requires that we protect some falsehood in order to protect speech that matters.

The need to avoid self-censorship by the news media is, however, not the only societal value at issue. If it were, this Court would have embraced long ago the view that publishers and broadcasters enjoy an unconditional and indefeasible immunity from liability for defamation. . . .

The legitimate state interest underlying the law of libel is the compensation of individuals for the harm inflicted on them by defamatory falsehood. We would not lightly require the State to abandon this purpose, for [the] individual's right to the protection of his own good name "reflects [our] basic concept of the essential dignity and worth of every human being — a concept at the root of any decent system of ordered [liberty]." Rosenblatt v. Baer, 383 U.S. 75, 92 (1966) (concurring opinion). . . .

The *New York Times* standard defines the level of constitutional protection appropriate to the context of defamation of a public person. [For] the reasons stated below, we conclude that the state interest in compensating injury to the reputation of private individuals requires that a different rule should obtain with respect to them. . . .

[We] have no difficulty in distinguishing among defamation plaintiffs. The first remedy of any victim of defamation is self-help — using available opportunities to contradict the lie or correct the error and thereby to minimize its adverse impact on reputation. Public officials and public figures usually enjoy significantly greater access to the channels of effective communication and hence have a more realistic opportunity to counteract false statements than private individuals normally enjoy.[9] Private individuals are therefore more vulnerable to injury, and the state interest in protecting them is correspondingly greater.

---

9. Of course, an opportunity for rebuttal seldom suffices to undo harm of defamatory falsehood. Indeed, the law of defamation is rooted in our experience that the truth rarely catches up with a lie. But the fact that the self-help remedy of rebuttal, standing alone, is inadequate to its task does not mean that it is irrelevant to our inquiry.

More important than the likelihood that private individuals will lack effective opportunities for rebuttal, there is a compelling normative consideration underlying the distinction between public and private defamation plaintiffs. An individual who decides to seek governmental office must accept certain necessary consequences of that involvement in public affairs. He runs the risk of closer public scrutiny than might otherwise be the case. And society's interest in the officers of government is not strictly limited to the formal discharge of official duties. . . .

Those classed as public figures stand in a similar position. Hypothetically, it may be possible for someone to become a public figure through no purposeful action of his own, but the instances of truly involuntary public figures must be exceedingly rare. For the most part those who attain this status have assumed roles of especial prominence in the affairs of society. Some occupy positions of such persuasive power and influence that they are deemed public figures for all purposes. More commonly, those classed as public figures have thrust themselves to the forefront of particular public controversies in order to influence the resolution of the issues involved. In either event, they invite attention and comment.

Even if the foregoing generalities do not obtain in every instance, the communications media are entitled to act on the assumption that public officials and public figures have voluntarily exposed themselves to increased risk of injury from defamatory falsehood concerning them. No such assumption is justified with respect to a private individual. He has not accepted public office or assumed an "influential role in ordering society." [He] has relinquished no part of his interest in the protection of his own good name, and consequently he has a more compelling call on the courts for redress of injury inflicted by defamatory falsehood. Thus, private individuals are not only more vulnerable to injury than public officials and public figures; they are also more deserving of recovery.

For these reasons we conclude that the States should retain substantial latitude in their efforts to enforce a legal remedy for defamatory falsehood injurious to the reputation of a private individual. The extension of the *New York Times* test [to defamatory falsehoods relating to private persons if the statements concerned matters of general or public interest] would abridge this legitimate state interest to a degree that we find unacceptable. And it would occasion the additional difficulty of forcing state and federal judges to decide on an ad hoc basis which publications address issues of "general or public interest" and which do not — to determine, in the words of Mr. Justice Marshall, "what information is relevant to self-government." [*Rosenbloom.*]

We doubt the wisdom of committing this task to the conscience of judges. . . .

We hold that, so long as they do not impose liability without fault, the States may define for themselves the appropriate standard of liability for a publisher or broadcaster of defamatory falsehood injurious to a private individual. . . .

IV

[We] endorse this approach in recognition of the strong and legitimate state interest in compensating private individuals for injury to reputation. But this countervailing state interest extends no further than compensation for actual injury. For the reasons stated below, we hold that the States may not permit recovery of presumed or punitive damages, at least when liability is not based on a showing of knowledge of falsity or reckless disregard for the truth.

The common law of defamation is an oddity of tort law, for it allows recovery of purportedly compensatory damages without evidence of actual loss. Under the traditional rules pertaining to actions for libel, the existence of injury is presumed from the fact of publication. Juries may award substantial sums as compensation for supposed damage to reputation without any proof that such harm actually occurred. The largely uncontrolled discretion of juries to award damages where there is no loss unnecessarily compounds the potential of any system of liability for defamatory falsehood to inhibit the vigorous exercise of First Amendment freedoms. Additionally, the doctrine of presumed damages invites juries to punish unpopular opinion rather than to compensate individuals for injury sustained by the publication of a false fact. More to the point, the States have no substantial interest in securing for plaintiffs such as this petitioner gratuitous awards of money damages far in excess of any actual injury. [It is therefore] necessary to restrict defamation plaintiffs who do not prove knowledge of falsity or reckless disregard for the truth to compensation for actual injury. . . .

We also find no justification for allowing awards of punitive damages against publishers and broadcasters held liable under state-defined standards of liability for defamation. In most jurisdictions jury discretion over the amounts awarded is limited only by the gentle rule that they not be excessive. Consequently, juries assess punitive damages in wholly unpredictable amounts bearing no necessary relation to the actual harm caused. And they remain free to use their discretion selectively to punish expressions of unpopular views. Like the doctrine of presumed damages, jury discretion to award punitive damages unnecessarily exacerbates the danger of media self-censorship, but, unlike the former rule, punitive damages are wholly irrelevant to the state interest that justifies a negligence standard for private defamation actions. They are not compensation for injury. Instead, they are private fines levied by civil juries to punish reprehensible conduct and to deter its future occurrence. In short, the private defamation plaintiff who establishes liability under a less demanding standard than that stated by *New York Times* may recover only such damages as are sufficient to compensate him for actual injury.

V

Notwithstanding our refusal to extend the *New York Times* privilege to defamation of private individuals, respondent contends that we should affirm the judgment below on the ground that petitioner is [a] public figure. [The public figure] designation may rest on either of two alternative bases. In some instances an individual may achieve such pervasive fame or notoriety that he becomes a public figure for all purposes and in all contexts. More commonly, an individual voluntarily injects himself or is drawn into a particular public controversy and thereby becomes a public figure for a limited range of issues. In either case such persons assume special prominence in the resolution of public questions.

Petitioner has long been active in community and professional affairs. He has served as an officer of local civic groups and of various professional organizations, and he has published several books and articles on legal subjects. Although petitioner was consequently well known in some circles, he had achieved no general fame or notoriety in the community. [Absent] clear evidence of general fame or notoriety in the community, and pervasive involvement in the affairs of society, an individual should not be deemed a public personality for all aspects of his life. It is preferable to reduce the public-figure question to a more meaningful context by looking to the nature and extent of an individual's participation in the particular controversy giving rise to the defamation.

In this context it is plain that petitioner was not a public figure. He played a minimal role at the coroner's inquest, and his participation related solely to his representation of a private client. He took no part in the criminal prosecution of Officer Nuccio. Moreover, he never discussed either the criminal or civil litigation with the press and was never quoted as having done so. He plainly did not thrust himself into the vortex of this public issue, nor did he engage the public's attention in an attempt to influence its outcome. We are persuaded that the trial court did not err in refusing to characterize petitioner as a public figure for the purpose of this litigation.

We therefore conclude that the *New York Times* standard is inapplicable to this case and that the trial court erred in entering judgment for respondent. Because the jury was allowed to impose liability without fault and was permitted to presume damages without proof of injury, a new trial is necessary. We reverse and remand for further proceedings in accord with this opinion.

It is so ordered.

[A concurring opinion of Justice Blackmun is omitted.]

MR. JUSTICE DOUGLAS, dissenting.

The Court describes this case as a return to the struggle of "defin[ing] the proper accommodation between the law of defamation and the freedoms of speech and press protected by the First Amendment." [I] would suggest that the struggle is a quite hopeless one, for, in light of the command of the First Amendment, no "accommodation" of its freedoms can be "proper" except those made by the Framers themselves. . . .

MR. JUSTICE BRENNAN, dissenting. . . .

I adhere to my view expressed in [*Rosenbloom*] that we strike the proper accommodation between avoidance of media self-censorship and protection of individual reputations only when we require States to apply the [*New York Times*] knowing-or-reckless-falsity standard in civil libel actions concerning media reports of the involvement of private individuals in events of public or general interest. . . .

While [the Court's] arguments are forcefully and eloquently presented, I cannot accept them, for the reasons I stated in *Rosenbloom*:

> While the argument that public figures need less protection because they can command media attention to counter criticism may be true for some very prominent people, even then it is the rare case where the denial overtakes the original charge. Denials, retractions, and corrections are not "hot" news, and rarely receive the prominence of the original story. When the public official or public figure is a minor functionary, or has left the position that put him in the public eye . . . , the argument loses all of its force. [The] unproved, and highly improbable, generaliza-

tion that an as yet [not fully defined] class of "public figures" involved in matters of public concern will be better able to respond through the media than private individuals also involved in such matters seems too insubstantial a reed on which to rest a constitutional distinction. . . .

Moreover, the argument that private persons should not be required to prove *New York Times* knowing-or-reckless falsity because they do not assume the risk of defamation by freely entering the public arena "bears little relationship either to the values protected by the First Amendment or to the nature of our society." [Social] interaction exposes all of us to some degree of public view. "[Thus,] the idea that certain 'public' figures have voluntarily exposed their entire lives to public inspection, while private individuals have kept theirs carefully shrouded from public view is, at best, a legal fiction." [*Rosenbloom.*]

MR. JUSTICE WHITE, dissenting. . . .

Scant, if any, evidence exists that the First Amendment was intended to abolish the common law of libel, at least to the extent of depriving ordinary citizens of meaningful redress against their defamers. . . . [The] law has heretofore put the risk of falsehood on the publisher where the victim is a private citizen and no grounds of special privilege are invoked. The Court would now shift this risk to the victim, even though he has done nothing to invite the calumny, is wholly innocent of fault, and is helpless to avoid his injury. [The] press today is vigorous and robust. To me, it is quite incredible to suggest that threats of libel suits from private citizens are causing the press to refrain from publishing the truth. I know of no hard facts to support that proposition, and the Court furnishes none. . . .

In any event, if the Court's principal concern is to protect the communications industry from large libel judgments, it would appear that its new requirements with respect to general and punitive damages would be ample protection. Why it also feels compelled to escalate the threshold standard of liability I cannot fathom, particularly when this will eliminate in many instances the plaintiff's possibility of securing a judicial determination that the damaging publication was indeed false, whether or not he is entitled to recover money damages. Under the Court's new rules, the plaintiff must prove not only the defamatory statement but also some degree of fault accompanying it. The publication may be wholly false and the wrong to him unjustified, but his case will nevertheless be dismissed for failure to prove negligence or other fault on the part of the publisher. I find it unacceptable to distribute the risk in this manner and force the wholly innocent victim to bear the injury; for, as between the two, the defamer is the only culpable party. It is he who circulated a falsehood that he was not required to publish. . . .

[Chief Justice Burger also filed a dissenting opinion.]

Note: *Public and Private Figures, Public and Private Speech*

1. *Public figures.* Do you agree that Gertz was not a "public figure"? Consider the following:

a. Plaintiff was divorced by Russell Firestone, the scion of one of America's wealthiest families. Time magazine erroneously reported that the divorce was granted on the ground of adultery. Plaintiff sued Time for libel. In Time, Inc. v. Firestone, 424 U.S. 448 (1976), the Court rejected Time's claim that Mrs. Firestone was a public figure: "[She] did not assume any role of especial prominence in the affairs of society, other than perhaps Palm Beach society, and she did not thrust herself to the forefront of any particular public controversy in order to influence the resolution of the issues involved in it."

b. In the late 1950s, in a widely publicized case, plaintiff was convicted of contempt for his refusal to appear before a grand jury investigating Soviet espionage. Sixteen years later, defendant published a book erroneously identifying plaintiff as a Soviet agent. Plaintiff sued for libel. In Wolston v. Reader's Digest Association, 443 U.S. 157 (1979), the Court rejected the publisher's claim that plaintiff was a "limited-purpose public figure." The Court emphasized that plaintiff had not "engaged the attention of the public in an attempt to influence the resolution of the issues involved" and explained that one who commits a crime does not become a public figure, even for the purpose "of comment on a limited range of issues relating to his conviction," for "[to] hold otherwise would create an 'open season' for all who sought to defame persons convicted of a crime."

c. Over the course of several years, various federal agencies spent almost half a million dollars funding plaintiff's research into aggressive monkey behavior. Senator Proxmire awarded the federal agencies his Golden Fleece of the Month Award, an award designed to publicize what Proxmire believed to be the most egregious examples of wasteful government spending. Claiming Proxmire's description of his research to be inaccurate, plaintiff sued for libel. In Hutchinson v. Proxmire, 443 U.S. 111 (1979), the Court rejected Proxmire's argument that plaintiff was a "limited-purpose public figure" for the "purpose of comment on his receipt of federal funds for research projects." The Court concluded that plaintiff "at no time assumed any role of public prominence in the broad question of concern about expenditures," and that "neither his applications for federal grants nor his publications in professional journals can be said to have invited that degree of public attention and comment on his receipt of federal grants essential to meet the public figure level."

2. *The need for vindication.* Justice White expressed concern in *Gertz* that the Court's decision would eliminate the private plaintiff's opportunity to vindicate himself by obtaining a judicial declaration of falsity. Is there any way to deal with this concern after *Gertz*? Consider Freund, Political Libel and Obscenity, 42 F.R.D. 491, 497 (1966): "Plaintiffs [should] be permitted to request a special verdict, so that if there is a verdict for the defendant based solely and simply on [the *New York Times* or *Gertz* privileges, the jury could nevertheless find] that the utterances were untrue." Consider also Justice Brennan's suggestion in *Gertz* that states could enact statutes "not requiring proof of fault, which provide for an action for retraction or for publication of a court's determination of falsity if the plaintiff is able to demonstrate that false statements have been published concerning his activities." Would such a statute violate the first amendment "right" of newspapers not to publish information against their will? See Miami Herald Publishing Co. v. Tornillo, 418 U.S. 241 (1974), section F4 infra.

3. *The limits of* Gertz. Does *Gertz's* "fault" standard govern all libelous statements not involving public officials or public figures, whether or not such statements concern matters of "general or public interest"? Is the *Gertz* privilege available only to media defendants? Note Justice Powell's consistent references to the

media. Can denial of the privilege to nonmedia defendants be justified on the ground that the "press" is entitled to special constitutional protection? See section F infra.

DUN & BRADSTREET v. GREENMOSS BUILDERS, 472 U.S. 749 (1985). Petitioner, a credit reporting agency, provides subscribers with financial information about businesses. All the information is confidential; under the terms of the subscription agreement, the subscribers may not reveal it to anyone else. Petitioner sent a report to five subscribers indicating that respondent, a construction contractor, had filed a voluntary petition for bankruptcy. This report was false. In respondent's defamation action against petitioner, the trial judge instructed the jury that it could award presumed and punitive damages without a showing of "actual malice." The jury returned a verdict in favor of respondent and awarded $50,000 in compensatory or presumed damages and $300,000 in punitive damages. The state supreme court upheld the award on the ground that the protections "outlined in *Gertz* are inapplicable to nonmedia defamation defendants." The Supreme Court, in a five-to-four decision, affirmed the judgment.

Justice Powell's plurality opinion was joined by Justices Rehnquist and O'Connor. Although upholding the state court judgment, Justice Powell did not address the nonmedia defendant issue: "In [*Gertz*] we held that [when] a private individual [sues] a publisher for a libel that [involves] a matter of public concern, [the] First Amendment [prohibits] awards of presumed and punitive damages [unless] the plaintiff shows 'actual malice.' [We] have never considered whether the *Gertz* balance obtains when the defamatory statements involve no issue of public concern. To make this determination, we must employ the approach approved in *Gertz* and balance the State's interest in compensating private individuals for injury to their reputation against the First Amendment interest in protecting this type of expression. [The] state interest [here] is identical to the one weighed in *Gertz*. [The] First Amendment interest, on the other hand, is less important than the one weighed in *Gertz*. We have long recognized that not all speech is of equal First Amendment importance. It is speech on '"matters of public concern"' that is 'at the heart of the First Amendment's protection.' In contrast, speech on matters of purely private concern is of less First Amendment concern. [When the state regulates such expression], 'There is no threat to the free and robust debate of public issues, [and] there is no potential interference with a meaningful dialogue of ideas concerning self-government.' [While] such speech is not totally unprotected by the First Amendment, its protections are less stringent. [In] light of the reduced constitutional value of speech involving no matters of public concern, we hold that the state interest adequately supports awards of presumed and punitive damages — even absent a showing of 'actual malice.'

"The only remaining issue is whether petitioner's credit report involved a matter of public concern. [The report] was speech solely in the individual interest of the speaker and its specific business audience. This particular interest warrants no special protection when [the] speech is wholly false and clearly damaging to the victim's business reputation. Moreover, since the credit report was made available to only five subscribers, who, under the terms of the subscription agreement, could not disseminate it further, it cannot be said that the report involves any 'strong interest in the free flow of commercial information.' [In] addition, the speech here, like advertising, is hardy, [objectively verifiable,] and unlikely to be deterred by incidental state regulation. [Citing Virginia State Board of Pharmacy v. Virginia Citizens Consumer Council, section D3 infra.]" Justice Powell thus concluded that, in light of the "content, form, and context" of the speech, it concerned "no public issue."

Chief Justice Burger concurred in the judgment: "I [agree with the plurality opinion that *Gertz* should be] limited to circumstances in which the alleged defamatory expression concerns a matter of general public importance, and that the expression at issue here relates to a matter of essentially private concern." Chief Justice Burger added that "*Gertz* should be overruled."

Justice White also concurred in the judgment: "For either of two reasons, I believe that [*Gertz* should not be applied in this case]. First, I [believe *Gertz*] should be overruled. Second, as Justice Powell indicates, the defamatory publication in this case does not deal with a matter of public importance. [Wisely], Justice Powell does not rest his application of a different rule here on a distinction drawn between media and non-media defendants. On that issue, I agree with [the four dissenting justices] that the First Amendment gives no more protection to the press in defamation suits than it does to others exercising their freedom of speech."

Justice Brennan, joined by Justices Marshall, Blackmun, and Stevens, dissented. At the outset, Justice Brennan, like Justice White, rejected the media/nonmedia distinction: "The free speech guarantee gives each citizen an equal right to self-expression and to participation in self-government. [Accordingly, a majority of the] Members of this Court agree today that, in the context of defamation law, the rights of the institutional media are no greater and no less than those enjoyed by other individuals or organizations engaged in the same activities."

Justice Brennan then turned to the "public interest" question: "One searches *Gertz* in vain for a single word to support the proposition that limits on presumed and punitive damages obtained only when speech involved matters of public interest. *Gertz* could not have been grounded in such a premise. Distrust of placing in the courts the power to decide what speech was of public concern was precisely the rationale *Gertz* offered for rejecting the *Rosenbloom* plurality approach. . . .

"Even accepting the notion that a distinction can and should be drawn between matters of public concern and matters of purely private concern, however, the [five members of the Court voting to affirm the damage award in this case] propose an impoverished definition of 'matters of public concern' that is irreconcilable with First Amendment principles. [Speech] about commercial or economic matters, even if not directly implicating 'the central meaning of the First Amendment,' is an important part of our public discourse. [The] choices we make when we step into the voting booth may well be the product of what we have learned from the myriad of daily economic and social phenomenon that surround us. [Moreover, our] economic system is predicated on the assumption that human welfare will be improved through informed decisionmaking. [Thus, even] if not at 'the essence of self-government,' the expression at issue in this case is important to both our public discourse and our private welfare. That its motivation might be the economic interest of the speaker or listeners does not diminish its First Amendment value." Justice Brennan concluded that under *Gertz* respondent "should be required to show actual malice to receive presumed or punitive damages."

Note: *Other False Statements of Fact*

In *Gertz*, the Court again made explicit its conclusion that "there is no constitutional value in false statements of fact." Nonetheless, in its *New York Times/Gertz* line of authority, the Court granted substantial first amendment protection to false statements of fact in the libel context to avoid "self-censorship" and "to protect speech that matters." How should false statements of fact be dealt with in other contexts? Consider the following:

a. Suppose an individual falsely asserts that a particular law was enacted because a majority of the legislators had been "paid off." In what circumstances, if any, may government criminally punish an individual for factually false utterances that defame government itself?

b. Recall section 3 of the Espionage Act of 1917, section B1 supra: "Whoever, when the United States is at war, shall willfully make or convey false reports [with] intent to interfere with [the] success of the military [forces] of the United States [shall be guilty of a felony]." Is the act constitutional in light of the *New York Times/Gertz* line of authority? If not, how might it be redrafted to satisfy the first amendment?

c. In Bridges v. California, section B2 supra, the Court held that an individual who criticized judges or the judicial process could not constitutionally be held in contempt absent a showing that such criticism created a clear and present danger to the fair administration of justice. What, though, if the criticism includes false statements of fact? See Pennekamp v. Florida, 328 U.S. 331 (1946); Craig v. Harney, 331 U.S. 367 (1947).

d. The problem of false statements of fact arises often in the context of political campaigns. Suppose, for example, a supporter of a candidate's opponent falsely accuses the candidate of some impropriety. So long as the candidate can meet the demands of *New York Times*, he can, of course, sue for libel. That may be small consolation, however, if he loses the election. To avoid that result, can the candidate obtain an injunction against further dissemination of the falsehood? Can a state electoral commission prohibit distribution of any campaign literature containing the falsehood? Suppose, instead of defaming an opponent, a candidate or his supporters falsely inflate the candidate's own qualifications. In what circumstances, and by what means, may such speech be restricted? See Pestrak v. Ohio Elections Commission, 926 F.2d 573 (6th Cir. 1991) (upholding state election commission's restriction on the dissemination of false statements in the context of political campaigns); Tomei v. Finley, 512 F. Supp. 695 (N.D. Ill. 1981) (granting a preliminary injunction against a candidate's use of a misleading campaign slogan); Stone, The Rules of Evidence and the Rules of Public Debate, 1993 U. Chi. Legal F. 127, 137-141 (arguing that such restrictions are invalid because of the "great danger" inherent in permitting "government to involve itself in the political process in this manner").

HUSTLER MAGAZINE v. FALWELL, 485 U.S. 46 (1988). Hustler magazine published a "parody" of an advertisement concerning the nationally known minister Jerry Falwell. The relevant item contained the name and picture of Reverend Falwell and an "interview" in which Falwell says that his "first time" was during a drunken incestuous rendezvous with his mother in an outhouse. Small print at the bottom of the page noted "ad parody — not to be taken seriously." Falwell brought suit for libel and intentional infliction of emotional distress. The jury found against Falwell on the libel claim because the ad parody could not "reasonably be understood as describing actual facts" about Falwell. The jury found in favor of Falwell on the intentional infliction of emotional distress claim, however, and awarded $100,000 in compensatory damages and $50,000 in punitive damages. The court of appeals affirmed. The Supreme Court, in a unanimous decision, reversed.

Chief Justice Rehnquist wrote the opinion: "The sort of robust political debate encouraged by the First Amendment is bound to produce speech that is critical of [public officials and public figures]. Such criticism, inevitably, will not always be reasoned or moderate; public figures as well as public officials will be subject to 'vehement, caustic, and sometimes unpleasantly sharp attacks.' [New York Times.]

"Of course, this does not mean that any speech about a public figure is immune from sanction in the form of damages. [To the contrary, because] false statements of fact are particularly valueless, [we have consistently held since New York Times] that a public figure may hold a speaker liable for the damage to reputation caused by publication of a defamatory falsehood, but only if the statement was made 'with knowledge that it was false or with reckless disregard of whether it was false or not.' . . .

"Respondent argues [that] a different standard should apply in this case because here the State seeks to prevent not reputational damage, but the severe emotional distress suffered by the person who is the subject of an offensive publication. In respondent's view, [so] long as the utterance was intended to inflict emotional distress, was outrageous, and did in fact inflict serious emotional distress, it is of no constitutional import whether the statement was a fact or an opinion, or whether it was true or false. It is the intent to cause injury that is the gravamen of the tort, and the State's interest in preventing emotional harm simply outweighs whatever interest a speaker may have in speech of this type.

"Generally speaking the law does not regard the intent to inflict emotional distress as one which should receive much [solicitude]. But [while a] bad motive may be deemed controlling for purposes of tort liability in other areas of the law, we think the First Amendment prohibits such a result in the area of public debate about public figures. Were we to hold otherwise, there can be little doubt that political cartoonists and satirists would be subjected to damage awards without any showing that their work falsely defamed its subject. [The] appeal of the political cartoon or caricature is often based on exploration of unfortunate physical traits or politically embarrassing events — an exploration often calculated to injure the feelings of the subject of the portrayal. The art of the cartoonist is often not reasoned or evenhanded, but slashing and one-sided. . . .

"Respondent contends, however, that the caricature in question was so 'outrageous' as to distinguish it from more traditional political cartoons. [If] it were possible by laying down a principled standard to separate the one from the other, public discourse would probably suffer little or no harm. But we doubt that there is any such standard, and we are quite sure that the pejorative description 'outrageous' does not supply one. 'Outrageousness' in the area of political and social discourse has an inherent subjectiveness about it which would allow a jury to impose liability on the basis of the jurors' tastes or views, or perhaps on the basis of the dislike of a particular expression. An 'outrageousness' standard thus runs afoul of our longstanding refusal to allow damages to be awarded because the speech in question may have an adverse emotional impact on the audience. . . .

"Admittedly, these oft-repeated First Amendment principles [are] subject to limitations. We recognized in *Pacifica Foundation* [section D5 infra] that [profanity] is 'not entitled to absolute constitutional protection under all circumstances.' In [*Chaplinsky*] we held that a state could lawfully punish an individual for the use of insulting or 'fighting [words].' These limitations are but recognition of the observation in [*Dun & Bradstreet*] that this Court has 'long recognized that not all speech is of equal First Amendment importance.' But the sort of expression involved in this case does not seem to us to be governed by any exception to the general First Amendment principles stated above.

"We conclude that public figures and public officials may not recover for the tort of intentional infliction of emotional distress by reason of publications such as the one here at issue without showing in addition that the publication contains a false statement of fact which was made with 'actual malice,' i.e., with knowledge that the statement was false or with reckless disregard as to whether or not it was true. . . ."

Consider Post, The Constitutional Concept of Public Discourse: Outrageous Opinion, Democratic Deliberation and Hustler Magazine v. Falwell, 103 Harv. L. Rev. 601, 624-625, 631-632 (1990):

[The] Court stated that "in the area of political and social discourse" the distinction between outrageous and non-outrageous [opinion] "has an inherent subjectiveness about it." [This] reasoning seems deeply misplaced. [To] claim that speech is outrageous is to assert much more than that it is personally unpleasant or disagreeable; it is to claim that [it is] inconsistent with common canons of decency. Such a claim may be controversial, but it need be neither arbitrary nor subjective. [The] "outrageousness" standard [can] have meaning [within] the commonly accepted norms of a particular community.

But the constitutional concept of public discourse forbids the state from enforcing such a standard [because] to do so would privilege [one community over others]. [An] "outrageousness" standard is unacceptable not because it [is subjective, but] because it would enable a single community to use the authority of the state to confine speech within its own notions of propriety. [We might say] that the concept of public discourse requires the state to remain neutral in the "marketplace of communities."

2. "Nonnewsworthy" Disclosures of "Private" Information

Cox Broadcasting Corp. v. Cohn

420 U.S. 469 (1975)

MR. JUSTICE WHITE delivered the opinion of the Court.

The issue before us in this case is whether, consistently with the First and Fourteenth Amendments, a State may extend a cause of action for damages for invasion of privacy caused by the publication of the name of a deceased rape victim which was publicly revealed in connection with the prosecution of the crime.

In August 1971, appellee's 17-year-old daughter was the victim of a rape and did not survive the incident. Six youths were soon indicted for murder and rape. Although there was substantial press coverage of the crime and of subsequent developments, the identity of the victim was not disclosed pending trial, perhaps because of Ga. Code Ann. §26-9901 (1972), which makes it a misdemeanor to publish or broadcast the name or identity of a rape victim. In April 1972, some eight months later, the six defendants appeared in court. . . .

In the course of the proceedings that day, appellant Wassell, a reporter covering the incident for his employer, learned the name of the victim from an examination of the indictments which were made available for his inspection in the courtroom. That the name of the victim appears in the indictments and that the indictments were public records available for inspection are not disputed. Later that day, Wassell broadcast over the facilities of station WSB-TV, a television station owned by appellant Cox Broadcasting Corp., a news report concerning the court proceedings. The report named the victim of the crime and was repeated the following day.

In May 1972, appellee brought an action for money damages against appellants, relying on §26-9901 and claiming that his right to privacy had been invaded by the television broadcasts giving the name of his deceased daughter. Appellants admitted the broadcasts but claimed that they were privileged under both state law and the First and Fourteenth Amendments.

[The trial court rejected appellants' constitutional claims and granted summary judgment to appellee as to liability, with the determination of damages to await trial by jury. The Georgia Supreme Court reversed the grant of summary judgment. In so doing, the court observed that the first amendment did not, as a matter of law, require judgment for appellants. Moreover, the court rejected appellants' contention that the victim's name was a matter of public interest and could thus be published with impunity, noting that it could discern "no public interest or general concern about the identity of the victim of such a crime as will make the right to disclose the identity of the victim rise to the level of First Amendment protection." At the same time, however, the court remanded to enable the jury to determine whether the public disclosure of the daughter's name actually invaded appellee's "zone of privacy" and whether appellants had invaded appellee's privacy "with willful or negligent disregard for the fact that reasonable men would find the invasion highly offensive."]

We [reverse].

Georgia stoutly defends both §26-9901 and the State's common-law privacy action challenged here. Its claims are not without force, for powerful arguments can be made, and have been made, that however it may be ultimately defined, there *is* a zone of privacy surrounding every individual, a zone within which the State may protect him from intrusion by the press, with all its attendant publicity. Indeed, the central thesis of the root article by Warren and Brandeis, The Right to Privacy, 4 Harv. L. Rev. 193, 196 (1890), was that the press was overstepping its prerogatives by publishing essentially private information and that there should be a remedy for the alleged abuses.[16]

16. "Of the desirability — indeed of the necessity — of some such protection [of the right of privacy], there can, it is believed, be no doubt. The press is overstepping in every direction the obvious bounds of propriety and of decency. Gossip is no longer the resource of the idle and of the vicious, but has become a trade, which is pursued with industry as well as effrontery. To satisfy a

More compellingly, the century has experienced a strong tide running in favor of the so-called right of privacy. "[I]n one form or another, the right of privacy is by this time recognized and accepted in all but a very few jurisdictions." W. Prosser, Law of Torts 804 (4th ed.). . . .

These are impressive credentials for a right of privacy. [The] version of the privacy tort now before us — termed in Georgia "the tort of public disclosure," [is] that in which the plaintiff claims the right to be free from unwanted publicity about his private affairs, which, although wholly true, would be offensive to a person of ordinary sensibilities. [In] this sphere of collision between claims of privacy and those of the free press, the interests on both sides are plainly rooted in the traditions and significant concerns of our society. Rather than address the broader question whether truthful publications may ever be subjected to civil or criminal liability, [it] is appropriate to focus on the narrower interface between press and privacy that this case presents, namely, whether the State may impose sanctions on the accurate publication of the name of a rape victim obtained from public records — more specifically, from judicial records which are maintained in connection with a public prosecution and which themselves are open to public inspection. We are convinced that the State may not do so.

[In] a society in which each individual has but limited time and resources with which to observe at first hand the operations of his government, he relies necessarily upon the press to bring to him in convenient form the facts of those operations. [With] respect to judicial proceedings in particular, the function of the press serves to guarantee the fairness of trials and to bring to bear the beneficial effects of public scrutiny upon the administration of justice. [The] commission of crime, prosecutions resulting from it, and judicial proceedings arising from the prosecutions [are] without question events of legitimate concern to the public and consequently fall within the responsibility of the press to report the operations of government. . . .

[Moreover, the] interests in privacy fade when the information involved already appears on the public record. [The] publication of truthful information available on the public record contains none of the indicia of those limited categories of expression, such as "fighting" words, which "are no essential part of any exposition of ideas, and are of such slight social value as a step to truth that any benefit that may be derived from them is clearly outweighed by the social interest in order and morality." [*Chaplinsky.*]

By placing the information in the public domain on official court records, the State must be presumed to have concluded that the public interest was thereby being served. Public records by their very nature are of interest to those concerned with the administration of government, and a public benefit is performed by the reporting of the true contents of the records by the media. . . .

---

prurient taste the details of sexual relations are spread broadcast in the columns of the daily papers. To occupy the indolent, column upon column is filled with idle gossip, which can only be procured by intrusion upon the domestic circle. The intensity and complexity of life, attendant upon advancing civilization, have rendered necessary some retreat from the world, and man, under the refining influence of culture, has become more sensitive to publicity, so that solitude and privacy have become more essential to the individual; but modern enterprise and invention have, through invasions upon his privacy, subjected him to mental pain and distress, far greater than could be inflicted by mere bodily injury. . . ."

We are reluctant to embark on a course that would make public records generally available to the media but forbid their publication if offensive to the sensibilities of the supposed reasonable man. Such a rule would make it very difficult for the media to inform citizens about the public business and yet stay within the law. The rule would invite timidity and self-censorship and very likely lead to the suppression of many items that would otherwise be published and that should be made available to the public. At the very least, the First and Fourteenth Amendments will not allow exposing the press to liability for truthfully publishing information released to the public in official court records. If there are privacy interests to be protected in judicial proceedings, the States must respond by means which avoid public documentation or other exposure of private information. Their political institutions must weigh the interests in privacy with the interests of the public to know and of the press to publish. Once true information is disclosed in public court documents open to public inspection, the press cannot be sanctioned for publishing it. In this instance as in others reliance must rest upon the judgment of those who decide what to publish or broadcast. . . .

Reversed.

[Concurring opinions of Chief Justice Burger and Justices Powell and Douglas are omitted, as is Justice Rehnquist's dissenting opinion, which argues that there is a "want of jurisdiction."]

Note: Invasion of Privacy and the First Amendment

1. *The reach of* Cox Broadcasting. Suppose a reporter learns the name of a rape victim from a witness rather than from a public document or proceeding? Consider also the following:

a. William Sidis was a famous child prodigy in 1910. His name and prowess were well known to newspaper readers of the period. At the age of eleven, he lectured to distinguished mathematicians on the subject of four-dimensional bodies, and at the age of sixteen, he graduated from Harvard College amid considerable public attention. Thereafter, Sidis sought to live as unobtrusively as possible, and his name disappeared from public view. In 1937, however, The New Yorker ran a biographical sketch of Sidis in its Where Are They Now? section. The article described Sidis's early achievements, his general breakdown, and his attempts to conceal his identity through his chosen career as an insignificant clerk. The article further described in intimate detail Sidis's enthusiasm for collecting streetcar transfers, his interest in the lore of the Okamakammessett Indians, and his personal lifestyle and habits. Sidis sued for invasion of privacy. Sidis v. F-R Publishing Corp., 113 F.2d 806 (2d Cir. 1940).

b. Dorothy Barber suffered from a rare condition that caused her to lose weight, even though she ate often. In its Medicine section, Time magazine reported on Barber's condition, disclosing her name and publishing a photograph that showed "her face, head and arms, with bedclothes over her chest." The article was titled Starving Glutton. Barber sued for invasion of privacy. Barber v. Time, Inc., 348 Mo. 1199, 159 S.W.2d 291 (1942).

c. In 1956, Marvin Briscoe and another man hijacked a truck. After paying his debt to society, Briscoe abandoned his life of crime, led an exemplary life, and made many friends who were unaware of the incident in his earlier life. In 1967,

Reader's Digest published an article on The Big Business of Hijacking, which reported: "Typical of many beginners, Marvin Briscoe and [another man] stole a 'valuable-looking' truck in Danville, Ky., and then fought a gun battle with the local police only to learn that they had hijacked four bowling-pin spotters." Briscoe sued for invasion of privacy. Briscoe v. Reader's Digest Association, 4 Cal. 3d 529, 93 Cal. Rptr. 866, 483 P.2d 34 (1971).

2. *Nonnewsworthiness and "low" value.* As Justice White suggested in *Cox Broadcasting,* in most states the truthful disclosure of "private" facts concerning an individual constitutes a tort if the disclosure would be "highly offensive" to a reasonable person and is not in itself newsworthy. Is the tort of public disclosure compatible with the first amendment? Should it matter that the harm caused by such speech cannot be corrected by counterspeech? That there is no significant "risk that government will [use the tort to] insulate itself from the critical views of its enemies"? L. Tribe, American Constitutional Law 889 (2d ed. 1988).

Is "nonnewsworthy" information of "low" first amendment value? Consider Bloustein, The First Amendment and Privacy: The Supreme Court Justice and the Philosopher, 28 Rutgers L. Rev. 41, 56-57 (1974): "[The] weight to be given 'the public interest in obtaining information' should depend on whether or not the information is relevant to the public's governing purposes. 'Public interest,' taken to mean curiosity, must be distinguished from 'public interest,' taken to mean value to the public of receiving information of governing importance. There is [no first amendment] right to satisfy public curiosity and publish lurid gossip about private lives."

On the other hand, consider Zimmerman, Requiem for a Heavyweight: A Farewell to Warren and Brandeis's Privacy Tort, 68 Cornell L. Rev. 291, 332-334 (1983):

> [Contemporary] society [uses] knowledge about the private lives of individual members [to] preserve and enforce social norms. [By] providing people with a way to learn about social groups to which they do not belong, gossip increases intimacy and a sense of community among disparate groups and individuals. [It] is a basic form of information exchange that teaches about other lifestyles and attitudes, and through which community values are changed or reinforced. [Perceived] in this way, gossip contributes directly to the first amendment "marketplace of ideas."

Even if "nonnewsworthy" information has only "low" first amendment value, might there nonetheless be sound reasons to reject such a standard? Recall that in *Gertz* the Court expressed "doubt" as to "the wisdom of committing [the task of deciding what information is relevant to self-government] to the conscience of judges." Is the "nonnewsworthiness" concept simply too vague to protect first amendment rights? Consider Kalven, Privacy in Tort Law — Were Warren and Brandeis Wrong?, 31 Law & Contemp. Probs. 326, 336 (1966): "What is at issue [is] whether the claim of privilege is not so overpowering as virtually to swallow the tort. [Surely] there is force to the simple contention that whatever is in the news media is by definition newsworthy, that the press must in the nature of things be the final arbiter of newsworthiness." But recall *Dun & Bradstreet.*

3. *The interest in "privacy."* Are the interests protected by the public disclosure tort of sufficient importance to justify a restriction of even "low" value expression? How would you compare the gravity of the harm caused by speech that "invades privacy" with the gravity of the harm in the incitement, fighting words, and

libel contexts? Consider Bloustein, supra, at 54: "In [public disclosure] cases the individual has been profaned by laying a private life open to public view. The intimacy and private space necessary to sustain individuality and human dignity has been impaired by turning a private life into a public spectacle. The innermost region of being [has] been bruised by exposure to the world." See also Edelman, Free Press v. Privacy: Haunted by the Ghost of Justice Black, 68 Tex. L. Rev. 1195 (1990). On the other hand, consider Posner, The Right of Privacy, 12 Ga. L. Rev. 393, 419 (1978): "If what is revealed is something the individual has concealed for purposes of misrepresenting himself to others, the fact that disclosure is offensive to him and of limited interest to the public at large is no better reason for protecting his privacy than if a seller advanced such arguments for being allowed to continue to engage in false advertising of his goods."

3. Commercial Advertising

Although the *Chaplinsky* dictum made no reference to commercial advertising, only a month after *Chaplinsky* the Court added commercial advertising to its list of "unprotected" expression in Valentine v. Chrestensen, 316 U.S. 52 (1942). In *Chrestensen*, the Court upheld a prohibition on the distribution of any "handbill [or] other advertising matter [in] or upon any street." Although conceding that a similar prohibition on noncommercial expression would violate the first amendment, the Court announced, without explanation or analysis, that the amendment imposed "no such restraint on government as respects purely commercial advertising." See also Breard v. Alexandria, 341 U.S. 622 (1951) (upholding a prohibition on door-to-door solicitation of magazine subscriptions).

Despite *Chrestensen*, the precise contours and rationale of the commercial advertising doctrine remained obscure. The mere presence of a commercial motive, for example, was not deemed dispositive, as evidenced by the Court's continued protection of books, movies, newspapers, and other forms of expression produced and sold for profit. Moreover, in New York Times v. Sullivan, section D1 supra, the Court rejected an argument that the paid "political" advertisement there at issue was unprotected commercial expression:

> The publication here was not a "commercial" advertisement in the sense in which the word was used in *Chrestensen*. It communicated information, expressed opinion, recited grievances, [and] protested claimed abuses. [That] the Times was paid for publishing the advertisement is as immaterial in this connection as is the fact that newspapers and books are sold. [Any] other conclusion would discourage newspapers from carrying "editorial advertisements" of this type, and so might shut off an important outlet for the promulgation of information and ideas by persons who do not themselves have access to publishing facilities.

In the 1970s, the Court began to narrow the scope of the commercial speech doctrine. In Bigelow v. Virginia, 421 U.S. 809 (1975), for example, the Court reversed the conviction of an individual who, prior to the Court's decision in Roe v. Wade, 410 U.S. 113 (1973), and in violation of Virginia law, published in his newspaper an advertisement announcing the availability of legal abortions in New York. The Court distinguished *Chrestensen* on the ground that the advertisement in *Bigelow* "did more than simply propose a commercial transaction. It contained factual material of clear 'public interest.'" The Court emphasized that *Chrestensen's* holding was "distinctly a limited one."

Virginia State Board of Pharmacy v. Virginia Citizens Consumer Council

425 U.S. 748 (1976)

[An organization of prescription drug consumers challenged as violative of the first and fourteenth amendments a Virginia statute providing that a pharmacist licensed in Virginia is guilty of unprofessional conduct if he "publishes, advertises, or promotes, directly or indirectly, in any manner whatsoever, any amount, price, fee, premium, discount, rebate or credit terms [for] any drugs which may be dispensed only by prescription." Although drug prices varied strikingly throughout the state and even within the same locality, the challenged law effectively prevented the dissemination of any prescription drug price information, since only licensed pharmacists were authorized to dispense such drugs. A three-judge district court held the law invalid. The Supreme Court affirmed.]

MR. JUSTICE BLACKMUN delivered the opinion of the Court. . . .*

IV

The appellants contend that the advertisement of prescription drug prices is outside the protection of the First Amendment because it is "commercial speech." There can be no question that in past decisions the Court has given some indication that commercial speech is unprotected. [Discussing *Chrestensen, Breard,* and *Bigelow.*] . . .

[The] question whether there is a First Amendment exception for "commercial speech" is squarely before us. Our pharmacist does not wish to editorialize on any subject, cultural, philosophical, or political. He does not wish to report any particularly newsworthy fact, or to make generalized observations even about commercial matters. The "idea" he wishes to communicate is simply this: "I will sell you the X prescription drug at the Y price." Our question, then, is whether this communication is wholly outside the protection of the First Amendment.

V

We begin with several propositions that already are settled or beyond serious dispute. It is clear, for example, that speech does not lose its First Amendment protection because money is spent to project it, as in a paid advertisement of one form

---

*[At the outset, Justice Blackmun rejected a claim that, even if first amendment protection attached to the flow of drug price information, it is a protection enjoyed only by advertisers and not by the appellees, who were mere recipients of such information. Justice Blackmun reasoned that, "where a speaker exists[, the] protection afforded is to the communication, to its source and to its recipients both." Thus, "if there is a right to advertise, there is a reciprocal [first amendment] right to receive the advertising." — EDS.]

or another. [Citing New York Times v. Sullivan.] Speech likewise is protected even though it is carried in a form that is "sold" for profit, [and] even though it may involve a solicitation to purchase or otherwise pay or contribute money. . . .

If there is a kind of commercial speech that lacks all First Amendment protection, therefore, it must be distinguished by its content. Yet the speech whose content deprives it of protection cannot simply be speech on a commercial subject. No one would contend that our pharmacist may be prevented from being heard on the subject of whether, in general, pharmaceutical prices should be regulated, or their advertisement forbidden. Nor can it be dispositive that a commercial advertisement is noneditorial, and merely reports a fact. Purely factual matter of public interest may claim protection. . . .

Our question is whether speech which does "no more than propose a commercial transaction" is so removed from any "exposition of ideas," [*Chaplinsky*], and from "'truth, science, morality, and arts in general, in its diffusion of liberal sentiments on the administration of Government,'" that it lacks all protection. Our answer is that it is not.

Focusing first on the individual parties to the transaction that is proposed in the commercial advertisement, we may assume that the advertiser's interest is a purely economic one. That hardly disqualifies him from protection under the First Amendment. The interests of the contestants in a labor dispute are primarily economic, but it has long been settled that both the employee and the employer are protected by the First Amendment when they express themselves on the merits of the dispute in order to influence its outcome. [We] know of no requirement that, in order to avail themselves of First Amendment protection, the parties to a labor dispute need address themselves to the merits of unionism in general or to any subject beyond their immediate dispute. . . .

As to the particular consumer's interest in the free flow of commercial information, that interest may be as keen, if not keener by far, than his interest in the day's most urgent political debate. Appellees' case in this respect is a convincing one. Those whom the suppression of prescription drug price information hits the hardest are the poor, the sick, and particularly the aged. A disproportionate amount of their income tends to be spent on prescription drugs; yet they are the least able to learn, by shopping from pharmacist to pharmacist, where their scarce dollars are best spent. When drug prices vary as strikingly as they do, information as to who is charging what becomes more than a convenience. It could mean the alleviation of physical pain or the enjoyment of basic necessities.

Generalizing, society also may have a strong interest in the free flow of commercial information. Even an individual advertisement, though entirely "commercial," may be of general public interest. The facts of decided cases furnish illustrations: advertisements stating that referral services for legal abortions are available, [*Bigelow*]; that a manufacturer of artificial furs promotes his product as an alternative to the extinction by his competitors of fur-bearing mammals, see Fur Information & Fashion Council, Inc. v. E. F. Timme & Son, 364 F. Supp. 16 (S.D.N.Y. 1973); and that a domestic producer advertises his product as an alternative to imports that tend to deprive American residents of their jobs, cf. Chicago Joint Board v. Chicago Tribune Co., 435 F.2d 470 (C.A.7 1970). [Obviously,] not all commercial messages contain the same or even a very great public interest element. There are few to which such an element, however, could not be added. Our pharmacist, for example, could cast himself as a commentator on store-to-store disparities in drug prices, giving his own and those of a competitor as proof. We see little point in requiring him to do so, and little difference if he does not.

Moreover, there is another consideration that suggests that no line between publicly "interesting" or "important" commercial advertising and the opposite kind could ever be drawn. Advertising, however tasteless and excessive it sometimes may seem, is nonetheless dissemination of information as to who is producing and selling what product, for what reason, and at what price. So long as we preserve a predominantly free enterprise economy, the allocation of our resources in large measure will be made through numerous private economic decisions. It is a matter of public interest that those decisions, in the aggregate, be intelligent and well informed. To this end, the free flow of commercial information is indispensable. [And] if it is indispensable to the proper allocation of resources in a free enterprise system, it is also indispensable to the formation of intelligent opinions as to how that system ought to be regulated or altered. Therefore, even if the First Amendment were thought to be primarily an instrument to enlighten public decisionmaking in a democracy, we could not say that the free flow of information does not serve that goal.

Arrayed against these substantial individual and societal interests are a number of justifications for the advertising ban. These have to do principally with maintaining a high degree of professionalism on the part of licensed pharmacists. Indisputably, the State has a strong interest in maintaining that professionalism. . . .

Price advertising, it is argued, will place in jeopardy the pharmacist's expertise and, with it, the customer's health. It is claimed that the aggressive price competition that will result from unlimited advertising will make it impossible for the pharmacist to supply professional services in the compounding, handling, and dispensing of prescription drugs. Such services are time consuming and expensive; if competitors who economize by eliminating them are permitted to advertise their resulting lower prices, the more painstaking and conscientious pharmacist will be forced either to follow suit or to go out of business. It is also claimed that prices might not necessarily fall as a result of advertising. If one pharmacist advertises, others must, and the resulting expense will inflate the cost of drugs. [Finally] it is argued that damage will be done to the professional image of the pharmacist. This image, that of a skilled and specialized craftsman, attracts talent to the profession and reinforces the better habits of those who are in it. Price advertising, it is said, will reduce the pharmacist's status to that of a mere retailer.

The strength of these proffered justifications is greatly undermined by the fact that high professional standards, to a substantial extent, are guaranteed by the close regulation to which pharmacists in Virginia are subject. [At] the same time, we cannot discount the Board's justifications entirely. The Court regarded justifications of this type sufficient to sustain the advertising bans challenged on due process and equal protection grounds. [Citing, e.g., Williamson v. Lee Optical of Oklahoma, 348 U.S. 483 (1955).]

The challenge now made, however, is based on the First Amendment. This casts the Board's justifications in a different light, for on close inspection it is seen that the State's protectiveness of its citizens rests in large measure on the advantages of their being kept in ignorance. The advertising ban does not directly affect professional standards one way or the other. It affects them only through the reactions it is assumed people will have to the free flow of drug price information. . . .

It appears to be feared that if the pharmacist who wishes to provide low cost, and assertedly low quality, services is permitted to advertise, he will be taken up on his offer by too many unwitting customers. They will choose the low-cost, low-quality service and drive the "professional" pharmacist out of business. They will respond only to costly and excessive advertising, and end up paying the price. They will go from one pharmacist to another, following the discount, and destroy the pharmacist-customer relationship. They will lose respect for the profession because it advertises. All this is not in their best interests, and all this can be avoided if they are not permitted to know who is charging what.

There is, of course, an alternative to this highly paternalistic approach. That alternative is to assume that this information is not in itself harmful, that people will perceive their own best interests if only they are well enough informed, and that the best means to that end is to open the channels of communication rather than to close them. If they are truly open, nothing prevents the "professional" pharmacist from marketing his own assertedly superior product, and contrasting it with that of the low-cost, high-volume prescription drug retailer. But the choice among these alternative approaches is not ours to make or the Virginia General Assembly's. It is precisely this kind of choice, between the dangers of suppressing information, and the dangers of its misuse if it is freely available, that the First Amendment makes for us. . . .

VI

In concluding that commercial speech, like other varieties, is protected, we of course do not hold that it can never be regulated in any way. Some forms of commercial speech regulation are surely permissible. We mention a few only to make clear that they are not before us and therefore are not foreclosed by this case.

There is no claim, for example, that the prohibition on prescription drug price advertising is a mere time, place, and manner restriction. We have often approved restrictions of that kind provided that they are justified without reference to the content of the regulated speech, that they serve a significant governmental interest, and that in so doing they leave open ample alternative channels for communication of the information. [Whatever] may be the proper bounds of time, place, and manner restrictions on commercial speech, they are plainly exceeded by this Virginia statute, which singles out speech of a particular content and seeks to prevent its dissemination completely.

Nor is there any claim that prescription drug price advertisements are forbidden because they are false or misleading in any way. Untruthful speech, commercial or otherwise, has never been protected for its own sake. [*Gertz.*] Obviously, much commercial speech is not provably false, or even wholly false, but only deceptive or misleading. We foresee no obstacle to a State's dealing effectively with this problem.[24] The First Amendment, as we construe it today, does not prohibit

24. In concluding that commercial speech enjoys First Amendment protection, we have not held that it is wholly undifferentiable from other forms. There are commonsense differences be-

the State from insuring that the stream of commercial information flows cleanly as well as freely. . . .

Also, there is no claim that the transactions proposed in the forbidden advertisements are themselves illegal in any way. [Finally,] the special problems of the electronic broadcast media are likewise not in this case. . . .

What is at issue is whether a State may completely suppress the dissemination of concededly truthful information about entirely lawful activity, fearful of that information's effect upon its disseminators and its recipients. Reserving other questions,[25] we conclude that the answer to this one is in the negative.

The judgment of the District Court is affirmed.

[Justice Stevens did not participate. Chief Justice Burger concurred in an opinion emphasizing the reservations set out in footnote 25. Justice Stewart concurred in an opinion emphasizing that government still should be free to regulate false or misleading commercial advertising.]

MR. JUSTICE REHNQUIST, dissenting.

The logical consequences of the Court's decision in this case, a decision which elevates commercial intercourse between a seller hawking his wares and a buyer seeking to strike a bargain to the same plane as has been previously reserved for the free marketplace of ideas, are far reaching indeed. Under the Court's opinion the way will be open not only for dissemination of price information but for active promotion of prescription drugs, liquor, cigarettes, and other products the use of which it has previously been thought desirable to discourage. Now, however, such promotion is protected by the First Amendment so long as it is not misleading or does not promote an illegal product or enterprise. . . .

The Court speaks of the consumer's interest in the free flow of commercial information, particularly in the case of the poor, the sick, and the aged. It goes on to observe that "society also may have a strong interest in the free flow of com-

---

tween speech that does "no more than propose a commercial transaction," and other varieties. Even if the differences do not justify the conclusion that commercial speech is valueless, and thus subject to complete suppression by the State, they nonetheless suggest that a different degree of protection is necessary to insure that the flow of truthful and legitimate commercial information is unimpaired. The truth of commercial speech, for example, may be more easily verifiable by its disseminator than, let us say, news reporting or political commentary, in that ordinarily the advertiser seeks to disseminate information about a specific product or service that he himself provides and presumably knows more about than anyone else. Also, commercial speech may be more durable than other kinds. Since advertising is the sine qua non of commercial profits, there is little likelihood of its being chilled by proper regulation and forgone entirely.

Attributes such as these, the greater objectivity and hardiness of commercial speech, may make it less necessary to tolerate inaccurate statements for fear of silencing the speaker. [They] may also make it appropriate to require that a commercial message appear in such a form, or include such additional information, warnings, and disclaimers, as are necessary to prevent its being deceptive. [They] may also make inapplicable the prohibition against prior restraints. . . .

25. We stress that we have considered in this case the regulation of commercial advertising by pharmacists. Although we express no opinion as to other professions, the distinctions, historical and functional, between professions may require consideration of quite different factors. Physicians and lawyers, for example, do not dispense standardized products; they render professional *services* of almost infinite variety and nature, with the consequent enhanced possibility for confusion and deception if they were to undertake certain kinds of advertising.

mercial information." [One] need not disagree with either of these statements in order to feel that they should presumptively be the concern of the Virginia Legislature, which sits to balance these and other claims in the process of making laws such as the one here under attack. The Court speaks of the importance in a "predominantly free enterprise economy" of intelligent and well-informed decisions as to allocation of resources. While there is again much to be said for the Court's observation as a matter of desirable public policy, there is certainly nothing in the United States Constitution which requires the Virginia Legislature to hew to the teachings of Adam Smith in its legislative decisions regulating the pharmacy profession. E.g., Nebbia v. New York, 291 U.S. 502 (1934); Olsen v. Nebraska, 313 U.S. 236 (1941). . . .

The Court insists that the rule it lays down is consistent even with the view that the First Amendment is "primarily an instrument to enlighten public decision-making in a democracy." I had understood this view to relate to public decision-making as to political, social, and other public issues, rather than the decision of a particular individual as to whether to purchase one or another kind of shampoo. It is undoubtedly arguable that many people in the country regard the choice of shampoo as just as important as who may be elected to local, state, or national political office, but that does not automatically bring information about competing shampoos within the protection of the First Amendment. . . .

In the case of "our" hypothetical pharmacist, he may now presumably advertise not only the prices of prescription drugs, but may attempt to energetically promote their sale so long as he does so truthfully. Quite consistently with Virginia law requiring prescription drugs to be available only through a physician, "our" pharmacist might run any of the following representative advertisements in a local newspaper:

> Pain getting you down? Insist that your physician prescribe Demerol. You pay a little more than for aspirin, but you get a lot more relief.

> Can't shake the flu? Get a prescription for Tetracycline from your doctor today.

> Don't spend another sleepless night. Ask your doctor to prescribe Seconal without delay.

Unless the State can show that these advertisements are either actually untruthful or misleading, it presumably is not free to restrict in any way commercial efforts on the part of those who profit from the sale of prescription drugs to put them in the widest possible circulation. But such a line simply makes no allowance whatever for what appears to have been a considered legislative judgment in most States that while prescription drugs are a necessary and vital part of medical care and treatment, there are sufficient dangers attending their widespread use that they simply may not be promoted in the same manner as hair creams, deodorants, and toothpaste. The very real dangers that general advertising for such drugs might create in terms of encouraging, even though not sanctioning, illicit use of them by individuals for whom they have not been prescribed, or by generating patient pressure upon physicians to prescribe them, are simply not dealt with in the Court's opinion. . . .

Note: Virginia Pharmacy *and "the Free Flow
of Commercial Information"*

1. *Is commercial speech of "low" first amendment value?* Consider the following:
   a. Jackson and Jeffries, Commercial Speech: Economic Due Process and the
First Amendment, 65 Va. L. Rev. 1, 17-18, 30-31 (1979):

> [The Court's conclusion in *Virginia Pharmacy* that commercial speech is relevant
> to self-government is] a non sequitur. It apparently rests on the assertion that be-
> cause regulation of the free enterprise system is a matter of political choice, com-
> mercial advertising that plays a part in the functioning of the free enterprise system
> is *for that reason* politically significant speech. But in terms of relevance to politi-
> cal decisionmaking, advertising is neither more nor less significant than a host of
> other market activities that legislatures concededly may regulate. [The] decisive
> point is the absence of any principled distinction between commercial soliciting
> and other aspects of economic activity. [In *Virginia Pharmacy,*] economic due pro-
> cess is resurrected, clothed in the ill-fitting garb of the first amendment.

For a thoughtful critique of this argument, see Shiffrin, The First Amendment
and Economic Regulation: Away from a General Theory of the First Amendment, 78 Nw. U.L. Rev. 1212, 1225-1239 (1983).
   b. Redish, The First Amendment in the Marketplace: Commercial Speech
and the Values of Free Expression, 39 Geo. Wash. L. Rev. 429, 433, 441-444
(1971):

> If the individual is to achieve the maximum degree of material satisfaction permit-
> ted by his resources, he must be presented with as much information as possible
> concerning the relative merits of competing products. After receiving the com-
> peting information, the individual will then be in a position [to] rationally de-
> cide which combination of features best satisfies his personal needs. [Moreover,]
> the theory of political self-government derives to a large extent from the belief
> in the intelligent free will of the individual, who is capable [of] making his per-
> sonal decision as to how he should be governed. [Development] of the mind is
> [thus] an important goal in itself. [Viewed in this light,] informational commer-
> cial speech furthers legitimate first amendment purposes. When the individual is
> presented with rational grounds for preferring one product or brand over another,
> he is encouraged to consider the competing information [and to] exercise his abil-
> ities to reason and think; this aids him towards the intangible goal of rational self-
> fulfillment.

Compare R. Collins and D. Skover, The Death of Discourse 77, 80, 105, 114
(1996):

> On the eve of the twenty-first century, America's marketplace of ideas has largely
> become a junkyard of commodity ideology. [Today's] mass advertising often has
> less to do with products than lifestyles, less to do with facts than image, and less to
> do with reason than romance. [In modern mass advertising, entire] categories of
> commercial communication are essentially bereft of any real informational con-
> tent. [If] commercial communication is safe [in the free speech marketplace], it is
> not because it *actually* furthers the First Amendment's traditional values of rational
> decisionmaking and self-realization. [The] real reason for constitutional protection
> of modern mass advertising is less ennobling: It is speech in the service of selling.

c. Coase, Advertising and Free Speech, 6 J. Legal Stud. 1, 2, 14 (1977):

It seems to be believed that [if the government intervened in the market for ideas, it] would be inefficient and wrongly motivated. [How] different is the government assumed to be when we come to economic regulation. In this area government is considered to be competent in action and pure in motivation. [Since] we are concerned with [the] same government, why is it that it is regarded as incompetent and untrustworthy in the one market and efficient and reliable in the other? [It] seems to me that the arguments [used] to support freedom in the market for ideas are equally applicable in the market for goods.

Compare Scanlon, Freedom of Expression and Categories of Expression, 40 U. Pitt. L. Rev. 519, 541 (1979): "[Commercial speech deserves less than full first amendment protection because] we regard the government as much less partisan in the competition between commercial firms than in the struggle between religious or political views." For a defense of the Court's overall commercial speech jurisprudence from a "collective choice" perspective, see Cass, Commercial Speech, Constitutionalism, Collective Choice, 56 U. Cin. L. Rev. 1317 (1988).

d. Blasi, The Pathological Perspective and the First Amendment, 85 Colum. L. Rev. 449, 486, 488 (1985):

Commercial advertising was never a concern in any of the historical political struggles over freedom of expression. The first amendment claimants in disputes over commercial advertising often are sophisticated and driven by the profit motive. The speech in question is brief and intended to evoke a reflexive, even if somewhat delayed, response from listeners. There is a strong tradition of government regulation of [advertising]. [Perhaps] most important, [the] spectacle of voluminous litigation over [product] advertising, conducted in the name of the first amendment, [would] undercut [society's] belief that first amendment freedoms represent a noble commitment well worth preserving even in the face of serious anxieties, risks, and costs. [Thus, we should] exclude commercial advertising from the protection of the first amendment.

e. Justice Powell's opinion for the Court in Ohralik v. Ohio State Bar, 436 U.S. 447 (1978):

In rejecting the notion [that expression concerning purely commercial transactions] "is wholly outside the protection of the First Amendment," [we] were careful [in Virginia Pharmacy not to discard] the "commonsense distinction between speech proposing a commercial transaction [and] other varieties of speech. [Indeed,] to require a parity of constitutional protection for commercial and noncommercial speech alike could invite dilution, simply by a leveling process, of the force of the Amendment's guarantee with respect to the latter kind of speech. Rather than subject the First Amendment to such a devitalization, we have instead afforded commercial speech a limited measure of protection, commensurate with its subordinate position in the scale of First Amendment values. . . .

2. What is "commercial" speech? In Virginia Pharmacy, the Court reaffirmed that the content of the speech, rather than the speaker's commercial or profit motivation, is determinative. What matters, in other words, is not whether the speaker is out to make money, but whether the expression does "no more than

propose a commercial transaction." Is this definition satisfactory? Does a billboard displaying a cigarette package in a pastoral setting constitute "commercial" speech under this definition? What about corporate issue advertising that describes the corporation, its activities, or its policies without explicitly identifying any of the corporation's products or services? Consider Comment, First Amendment Protection for Commercial Advertising: The New Constitutional Doctrine, 44 U. Chi. L. Rev. 205, 236 (1976): "[Commercial speech should be defined as] (1) speech that refers to a specific brand name product or service, (2) made by a speaker with a financial interest in the sale of the advertised product or service, in the sale of a competing product or service, or in the distribution of the speech, (3) that does not advertise an activity itself protected by the first amendment."

In Bolger v. Youngs Drug Products Corp., 463 U.S. 60 (1983), the Court held that various "informational pamphlets" dealing with contraceptives constituted "commercial" speech. "One of [the] pamphlets, 'Condoms and Human Sexuality,' specifically [referred] to a number of Trojan-brand condoms manufactured by [Youngs] and [described] the advantages of each type. [Another], 'Plain Talk about Venereal Disease,' [discussed] condoms without any specific reference to those manufactured by [Youngs]." The Court explained:

> The mere fact that these pamphlets are conceded to be advertisements clearly does not compel the conclusion that they are commercial speech. [Citing New York Times v. Sullivan.] Similarly, the reference to a specific product does not by itself render the pamphlets commercial speech. Finally, the fact that Youngs has an economic motivation for mailing the pamphlets would clearly be insufficient by itself to turn the materials into commercial speech. [The] combination of *all* these characteristics, however, provides strong support for [the] conclusion that the informational pamphlets [are] commercial speech. [Moreover, the pamphlets] constitute commercial speech notwithstanding the fact that they contain discussions of important public issues such as venereal disease and family planning. [Advertising] which "links a product to a current public debate" is not thereby entitled to the constitutional protection afforded noncommercial speech. [Finally, that] a product is referred to generically [and not by brand name] does not [remove] it from the realm of commercial speech. [For] a company with sufficient control of the market for a product may be able to promote the product without reference to specific brand names. [Indeed, in] this case, Youngs describes itself as "the leader in the manufacture and sale" of contraceptives.

Note: *Truthful, Nondeceptive Commercial Advertising after Virginia Pharmacy*

In the years immediately after *Virginia Pharmacy*, the Court reaffirmed and expanded its protection of truthful, nondeceptive commercial speech:

1. *Lawyer advertising.* In Bates v. State Bar of Arizona, 433 U.S. 350 (1977), the Court invalidated a state court rule prohibiting attorney advertising, as applied to a newspaper advertisement stating "DO YOU NEED A LAWYER? Legal Services at Very Reasonable Fees" and listing fees for a variety of services, such as uncontested divorce, uncontested adoption, uncontested nonbusiness bankruptcy, and name change. The Court rejected the state's argument that attorney advertising of routine services would adversely affect professionalism and the quality

of legal services, stir up unnecessary litigation, increase the overhead costs of law-yers, cause increased fees, and create difficulties in enforcing the line between protected and unprotected advertisements. Without specifying precisely what standard it was applying, the Court concluded that none "of the proffered justifi-cations [rises] to the level of an acceptable reason for the suppression of all adver-tising by attorneys."

See also Peel v. Attorney Registration and Disciplinary Commission of Illinois, 496 U.S. 91 (1990) (invalidating a rule prohibiting lawyers from truthfully hold-ing themselves out as "certified" or as "specialists" in particular fields); Shapero v. Kentucky Bar Association, 486 U.S. 466 (1988) (invalidating a rule that categor-ically prohibited lawyers from soliciting business for pecuniary gain by mailing truthful letters to potential clients known to face specific legal problems); Zaud-erer v. Office of Disciplinary Counsel, 471 U.S. 626 (1985) (invalidating disci-plinary rules prohibiting the use of illustrations in lawyer advertising and forbid-ding lawyers to solicit clients through advertisements containing information or advice regarding specific legal problems); In the Matter of R.M.J., 455 U.S. 191 (1982) (invalidating restrictions of lawyer advertising where the restrictions were not the "least restrictive" means of achieving "substantial" state interests); Ohra-lik v. Ohio State Bar, 436 U.S. 447 (1978) (upholding a disciplinary rule prohib-iting any "lawyer who has given unsolicited advice to a layman that he should obtain legal counsel or take legal action" from accepting "employment result-ing from that advice," as applied to a lawyer who personally contacted two young women who had been injured in an automobile accident and arranged to repre-sent them in subsequent litigation). Cf. Edenfield v. Fane, 507 U.S. 761 (1993) (distinguishing lawyers from accountants and therefore invalidating a state rule providing that certified public accountants "shall not by any direct, in-person, uninvited solicitation solicit an engagement to perform public accounting services").

2. *"For sale" signs.* In Linmark Associates v. Township of Willingboro, 431 U.S. 85 (1977), the Court invalidated an ordinance prohibiting the display of "For Sale" or "Sold" signs on all but model homes. The ordinance was designed to prevent "panic selling" in a racially integrated residential community that had re-cently experienced "white flight" in response to a sharp increase in the nonwhite proportion of the population. The Court recognized that the goal of "promoting stable, racially integrated housing" is "vital," but nonetheless held that the town-ship had failed to establish that the ordinance "was necessary to achieve this ob-jective." In any event, "the constitutional defect in this ordinance [is] far more basic," for the township "has sought to restrict the free flow of these data because it fears that otherwise homeowners will make decisions inimical to what the [town council] views as the homeowners' self-interest and the corporate interest of the township: they will choose to leave the town. [If] dissemination of this in-formation can be restricted, then every locality in the country can suppress any facts that reflect poorly on the locality, so long as a plausible claim can be made that disclosure would cause the recipients of the information to act 'irrationally.' [*Virginia Pharmacy*] denies government such sweeping powers."

3. *Contraceptive advertising.* In Carey v. Population Services International, 431 U.S. 678 (1977), the Court invalidated a prohibition on the advertising of contraceptives because the state's concerns "that advertisements of contraceptive products would be offensive and embarrassing to those exposed to them, and that

permitting them would legitimate sexual activity of young people" are "classically not justifications validating the suppression of expression protected by the First Amendment." See also Bolger v. Youngs Drug Products Corp., 463 U.S. 60 (1983) (invalidating a federal statute prohibiting the mailing of unsolicited advertisements for contraceptives because the interest in shielding "recipients of mail from materials that they are likely to find offensive" is not sufficiently substantial to justify the suppression of "protected speech").

4. *Spam.* Commercial advertisers often send unsolicited, bulk e-mails to thousands of recipients. This has the potential to overwhelm individuals' electronic mailboxes and thus to discourage the use of e-mail generally. Could Congress constitutionally prohibit any person to send an unsolicited commercial advertisement via e-mail? Could it constitutionally prohibit any person to send an unsolicited commercial advertisement via regular mail?

5. *Retreat?* Although *Virginia Pharmacy, Bates, Linmark,* and *Carey* afforded substantial protection to truthful, nondeceptive commercial advertising, some subsequent decisions have arguably been less solicitous of such expression. Consider *Central Hudson.*

CENTRAL HUDSON GAS v. PUBLIC SERVICE COMMISSION OF NEW YORK, 447 U.S. 557 (1980). The commission permitted electric utilities to engage in institutional and informational advertising, but, to further the conservation of energy, prohibited such utilities to engage in promotional advertising designed to stimulate the use of electricity. The Court, in an opinion by Justice Powell, held the order invalid. After observing that the "Constitution [accords] a lesser protection to commercial speech than to other constitutionally guaranteed expression," the Court maintained that in its prior decisions, it had implicitly "developed" a "four-part analysis" for commercial speech cases:

"[First], we must determine whether the expression is protected by the First Amendment. For commercial speech to come within that provision, it at least must concern lawful activity and not be misleading. [Second], we ask whether the asserted governmental interest is substantial. [Third, if] both inquiries yield positive answers, we must determine whether the regulation directly advances the governmental interest. [And fourth], if the governmental interest could be served as well by a more limited restriction on commercial speech, the excessive restrictions cannot survive."

Applying this analysis to the ban on promotional advertising, the Court noted that the "Commission does not claim that the expression at issue is either inaccurate or relates to unlawful activity." Moreover, "in view of our country's dependence on energy resources beyond our control, no one can doubt the importance of energy conservation. Plainly, therefore, the state interest asserted is substantial." Further, "the State's interest in energy conservation is directly advanced by the Commission order." Thus, "the critical inquiry" is whether the commission's complete suppression of speech ordinarily protected by the first amendment is "no more extensive than necessary to further the State's interest." The Court found the complete ban on promotional advertising to be too "extensive" for two reasons. First, no exception was made for promotional advertising of specific electric products and "services that would [increase the use of electricity, but reduce total] energy use by diverting demand from less efficient sources." And, second, the commission "has not demonstrated that its interest in conservation cannot be protected adequately by more limited regulation of [the] format and content of Central Hudson's advertising. It might, for example, require that the advertisements include information about the relative efficiency and expense of the offered service." The Court thus concluded that, "in the absence of a showing that more limited speech regulation would be ineffective, we cannot approve the complete suppression of Central Hudson's advertising."

Justice Blackmun, joined by Justice Brennan, concurred. Justice Blackmun maintained that "the test now evolved and applied by the Court is not consistent with our prior cases and does not provide adequate protection for truthful, nonmisleading, noncoercive speech." "Even though 'commercial' speech is involved," the commission's order "strikes at the heart of the First Amendment," for "it is a covert attempt by the State to manipulate the choices of its citizens, not by persuasion or direct regulation, but by depriving the public of the information needed to make a free choice." Justice Blackmun concluded that "no differences between commercial speech and other protected speech justify suppression of commercial speech in order to influence public conduct through manipulation of the availability of information."

Justice Rehnquist dissented. He argued that New York's order is essentially "an economic regulation to which virtually complete deference should be accorded by this Court," for "in terms of constitutional values," the ban on promotional advertising is "virtually indistinguishable" from a decision of the commission to raise the price of electricity in order to conserve energy.

Note: Truthful, Nondeceptive Commercial Advertising after Central Hudson

1. *Retreat?* To what extent does *Central Hudson* retreat from the Court's prior understanding of the first amendment's protection of truthful, nondeceptive commercial advertising?

The Court clarified the final part of the *Central Hudson* standard in Board of Trustees of SUNY v. Fox, 492 U.S. 469 (1989), which involved a university regulation that prohibited commercial enterprises from operating in student dormitories. Although conceding that *Central Hudson* had stated that "government restrictions upon commercial speech may be no more broad or no more expansive than 'necessary' to serve its substantial interests," the Court in *Fox*, in an opinion by Justice Scalia, held that this did not mean that the regulation must be the least restrictive measure that could effectively protect the government's interest: "What our decisions require is a '"fit" between the legislature's ends and the means chosen to accomplish those ends,' — a fit that is not necessarily perfect, but reasonable; that represents not necessarily the single best disposition but one whose scope is 'in proportion to the interest served'; that employs not necessarily the least restrictive means but [a] means narrowly tailored to achieve the desired objective. Within those bounds we leave it to governmental decisionmakers to judge what manner of regulation may best be employed."

2. *The limits of retreat.* Even if *Central Hudson* does mark a retreat from *Virginia Pharmacy*, the retreat has been far from complete. Consider the following decisions, the first two of which invalidate restrictions on commercial advertising, the second two of which uphold them:

a. In Rubin v. Coors Brewing Co., 514 U.S. 476 (1995), the Court invalidated section 205(3)(2) of the Federal Alcohol Administration Act, which prohibited beer labels from displaying alcohol content. The government argued that the labeling ban was necessary to prevent "strength wars" among brewers who, without regulation, would seek to compete in the marketplace based on the potency of their beer. Although conceding that the government has "a significant interest in protecting the health, safety, and welfare of its citizens by preventing brewers from competing on the basis of alcohol strength," the Court nonetheless concluded that "§205(e)(2) cannot directly and materially advance its asserted interest because of the overall irrationality of the Government's regulatory scheme." The Court noted, for example, that although federal law restricts beer labeling, it does not restrict "statements of alcohol content in [beer] advertising," and that the "failure to prohibit the disclosure of alcohol content in advertising, which would seem to constitute a much more influential weapon in any strength war than labels, makes no sense if the government's true aim is to suppress strength wars."

b. In Greater New Orleans Broadcasting Association, Inc. v. United States, 119 S. Ct. 1923 (1999), the Court unanimously invalidated 18 U.S.C. §1304, which prohibited radio and television broadcasters from carrying advertisements about privately operated commercial casino gambling, as applied to broadcast stations located in states where such gambling is legal. The Court concluded that, even if the federal government has "substantial" interests in "reducing the social costs associated with 'gambling'" and in "assisting States that 'restrict gambling' . . . within their own borders," the challenged legislation was nonetheless unconstitutional because it did not "directly and materially advance the asserted government interest" and it was "more extensive than necessary to serve the interests that [assertedly] support it." Citing Rubin, the Court explained that because the federal legislation exempted advertising for legal tribal casino gambling and state-operated lotteries and parimutuel gambling, it was "so pierced by exemptions and inconsistencies that the Government cannot hope to exonerate it."

c. In United States v. Edge Broadcasting Co., 509 U.S. 418 (1993), the Court considered the constitutionality of federal legislation prohibiting the broadcast of lottery advertisements, but exempting the broadcast of advertisements for state-run lotteries by stations licensed to a state that conducts such a lottery. Edge Broadcasting operates a radio station that is located in and licensed to North Carolina but that broadcasts primarily in Virginia. Because North Carolina is a nonlottery state, the effect of the federal legislation was to prohibit Edge from broadcasting advertisements for the Virginia state lottery. The Court held that this did not violate the first amendment. The Court reasoned that "instead of favoring either the lottery or the nonlottery State," Congress had "opted to support the antigambling policy of a State like North Carolina by forbidding stations in such a State from airing lottery advertising." But "at the same time it sought not to unduly interfere with the policy of a lottery sponsoring State such as Virginia," because "Virginia could advertise its lottery through radio and television stations licensed to Virginia locations, even if their signals reached deep into North Carolina." The Court concluded that "this congressional policy of balancing the interests of lottery and nonlottery States is the substantial governmental interest that satisfies Central Hudson."

d. In Florida Bar v. Went for It, 515 U.S. 618 (1995), the Court upheld a rule of the Florida bar prohibiting any lawyer to send "a written communication to a prospective client for the purpose of obtaining professional employment if [the] communication concerns an action for personal injury [arising out of] an accident [involving] the person to whom the communication is addressed or a relative of that person, unless the accident [occurred] more than 30 days prior to the mailing of the communication." The Court explained that the challenged rule advances "in a direct and material way" two substantial interests. First, it protects "the privacy and tranquility of personal injury victims [against] intrusive, unsolicited contact by lawyers," and, second, it protects "the flagging reputations of Florida lawyers by preventing them from engaging in conduct that, the Bar maintains, 'is universally regarded as deplorable [because] of its intrusion upon the special vulnerability and private grief of victims or their families.'"

3. *A ban on all cigarette advertising?* In light of *Central Hudson* and its progeny, how would you expect the Court to rule on the constitutionality of a law banning all cigarette advertising? Consider *Posadas* and *44 Liquormart.*

POSADAS DE PUERTO RICO ASSOCIATES v. TOURISM CO. OF PUERTO RICO, 478 U.S. 328 (1986). The Court upheld a Puerto Rican statute that legalized certain forms of casino gambling, but prohibited any advertising of casino gambling aimed at the residents of Puerto Rico.

Justice Rehnquist delivered the opinion of the Court: "The particular kind of commercial speech at issue here [concerns] a lawful activity and is not misleading or [fraudulent]. We must therefore proceed to the three remaining steps of the *Central Hudson* [analysis]. The first of these three steps involves an assessment of the strength of the government's interest in restricting the speech. The interest at stake in this case [is] the reduction of demand for casino gambling by the residents of Puerto Rico. [The Puerto Rico legislature apparently believed] that '[e]xcessive casino gambling among local residents [would] produce serious harmful effects,' [such as those that] have motivated the vast majority of the 50 States to prohibit casino gambling. We have no difficulty in concluding that the Puerto Rico Legislature's interest in the health, safety, and welfare of its citizens constitutes a 'substantial' governmental interest. . . .

"Step three asks the question whether the challenged restrictions on commercial speech 'directly advance' the government's asserted interest. [The] Puerto Rico Legislature obviously believed [that] advertising of casino gambling aimed at residents of Puerto Rico would serve to increase the demand for the product advertised. We think the legislature's belief is a reasonable one. . . .

"We also think it clear [that] the challenged statute [satisfies] the fourth [step] of the *Central Hudson* analysis, namely, whether the restrictions on commercial speech are no more extensive than necessary to serve the government's interest. [Appellant contends] that the First Amendment requires the Puerto Rico Legislature to reduce demand for casino gambling among the residents of Puerto Rico not by suppressing commercial speech that might *encourage* such gambling, but by promulgating additional speech designed to *discourage* it. We reject this contention. We think it is up to the legislature to decide whether or not such a 'counterspeech' policy would be as effective in reducing the demand for casino gambling as a restriction on advertising. . . .

"Appellant argues further, however, that the challenged [restrictions] are constitutionally defective under [*Carey* and *Bigelow*]. [But in] *Carey* and *Bigelow*, [which involved advertising for abortion and contraception], the underlying conduct that was the subject of the advertising restrictions was constitutionally protected and could not have been prohibited by the State. Here, on the other hand, the Puerto Rico Legislature surely could have prohibited casino gambling by the residents of Puerto Rico altogether. In our view, the greater power to completely ban casino gambling necessarily includes the lesser power to ban advertising of casino gambling, and *Carey* and *Bigelow* are hence inapposite. . . .

"[Finally, appellant argues] that, having chosen to legalize casino gambling for residents of Puerto Rico, the First Amendment prohibits the legislature from using restrictions on advertising to accomplish its goal of reducing demand for such gambling. We disagree. In our view, appellant has the argument backwards. [It] is precisely *because* the government could have enacted a wholesale prohibition of the underlying conduct that it is permissible for the government to take the less intrusive step of allowing the conduct, but reducing the demand through restrictions on advertising. [It] would [surely] be a strange constitutional doctrine which would concede to the legislature the authority to totally ban a product or activity, but deny to the legislature the authority to forbid the stimulation of demand for the product or activity through advertising. . . ."

Justice Brennan, joined by Justices Marshall and Blackmun, dissented: "I see no reason why commercial speech should be afforded less protection than other types of speech where, as here, the government seeks to suppress commercial speech in order to deprive consumers of accurate information concerning lawful activity. [Indeed, such restrictions] should be subject to strict judicial scrutiny. [Moreover, while] tipping its hat to [the *Central Hudson* standards,] the Court does little more than defer to what it perceives to be the determination by Puerto Pico's legislature that a ban on casino advertising aimed at residents is reasonable. [But] in light of the legislature's determination that serious harm will *not* result if residents are permitted [to] gamble, I do not see how Puerto Rico's interest in discouraging its residents from engaging in casino gambling can be characterized as 'substantial.' [Moreover,] I do not agree that a ban on casino advertising is 'less intrusive' than an outright prohibition of such activity. [The] 'strange constitutional doctrine' which bans Puerto Rico from banning advertisements concerning lawful casino gambling is not so strange a restraint — it is called the First Amendment."

Justice Stevens, joined by Justices Marshall and Blackmun, dissented on the ground that the challenged regulation unconstitutionally discriminated against the residents of Puerto Rico.

44 LIQUORMART, INC. v. RHODE ISLAND, 517 U.S. 484 (1996). In a divided set of opinions, the Court invalidated a Rhode Island statute prohibiting "advertising in any manner whatsoever" of the price of any alcoholic beverage offered for sale in the state, except for price tags or signs displayed within licensed premises and not visible from the street.

Justice Stevens delivered a plurality opinion joined by Justices Kennedy and Ginsburg, and joined in different parts by Justices Souter and Thomas: "As [a] review of our case law reveals, [not] all commercial speech regulations are subject to a similar form of constitutional [review]. When a State regulates commercial messages to protect consumers from misleading, deceptive, or aggressive sales practices, or requires the disclosure of beneficial consumer information, the purpose of its regulation is consistent with the reasons for according constitutional protection to commercial speech and therefore justifies less than strict review.

"However, when a State entirely prohibits the dissemination of truthful, nonmisleading commercial messages for reasons unrelated to the preservation of a fair bargaining process, there is far less reason to depart from the rigorous review that the First Amendment generally demands. [Citing *Linmark*; *Virginia Pharmacy*; and *Went for It*.] The special dangers that attend complete bans on truthful, nonmisleading commercial speech cannot be explained away by appeals to the 'commonsense distinctions' that exist between commercial and noncommercial speech. [Neither] the 'greater objectivity' nor the 'greater hardiness' of truthful, nonmisleading commercial speech justifies reviewing its complete suppression with added deference. [Bans] against truthful, nonmisleading commercial speech [usually] rest solely on the offensive assumption that the public will respond 'irrationally' to the truth. The First Amendment directs us to be especially skeptical of regulations that seek to keep people in the dark for what the government perceives to be their own good. That teaching applies equally to state attempts to deprive consumers of accurate information about their chosen products. . . .

"The State argues that the price advertising prohibition should [be] upheld because it directly advances the State's substantial interest in promoting temperance, and because it is no more extensive than necessary. [We] can agree that common sense supports the conclusion that a prohibition against price advertising [will] tend to [maintain] prices at a higher level than would prevail in a completely free market [and that] consumption [is likely to be] somewhat lower whenever a higher, noncompetitive price level prevails. However, without any [evidentiary] support [we] cannot agree with the assertion that the price advertising ban will significantly advance the State's interest. . . . [Speculation about such matters] does not suffice when the State takes aim at accurate commercial information for paternalistic ends. . . .

"The State also cannot satisfy the requirement that its restriction on speech be no more extensive than necessary. It is perfectly obvious that alternative forms of regulation that would not involve any restriction on speech would be more likely to achieve the State's goal of promoting temperance. [Higher] prices can be maintained either by direct regulation or by increased taxation. Per capita purchases could be limited as is the case with prescription drugs. Even educational campaigns focused on the problems [of] drinking might prove to be more effective. As a result, even under the less than strict standard that generally applies in commercial speech cases, the State has failed to establish a 'reasonable fit' between its abridgment of speech and its temperance goal. [It] necessarily follows that the price advertising ban cannot survive the more stringent constitutional review that *Central Hudson* itself concluded was appropriate for the complete suppression of truthful, nonmisleading commercial speech. . . .

"Relying on *Posadas* and *Edge Broadcasting*, Rhode Island [argues] that, because expert opinions as to the effectiveness of the price advertising ban 'go both ways,' [the legislation should be upheld as] a 'reasonable choice' by the legislature. The State next contends that *Posadas* requires us to give particular deference to that legislative choice because the State could, if it chose, ban the sale of alcoholic beverages outright. Finally, the State argues that deference is appropriate because alcoholic beverages are so-called 'vice' products. We consider each of these arguments in turn.

"The State's first argument fails [because the State] errs in concluding that *Edge* and *Posadas* establish the degree of deference that [is appropriate in this case.] In *Edge*, [the] statute [regulated] advertising about an activity that [was] illegal in the jurisdiction in which the broadcaster was located. Here, by contrast, the commercial speech ban targets information about entirely lawful behavior. *Posadas* is more directly relevant. [But] we are now persuaded that [*Posadas*] clearly erred in concluding that it was 'up to the legislature' to choose suppression over a less speech-restrictive policy. [In] keeping with [our pre-*Posadas*] holdings, we conclude that a state legislature does not [have] broad discretion to suppress truthful, nonmisleading information for paternalistic purposes. . . .

"We also cannot accept the State's second contention, which is premised [on] the 'greater-includes-the-lesser' reasoning endorsed [in] *Posadas*. [This reasoning] is inconsistent with both logic and well-settled doctrine. [Contrary] to the assumption made in *Posadas*, [the] Constitution presumes that attempts to regulate speech are more dangerous than attempts to regulate conduct. [As] the entire Court apparently now agrees, the statements in [*Posadas*] on which Rhode Island relies are no longer persuasive.

"Finally, we [reject] the State's contention that [the] price advertising ban should be upheld because it targets commercial speech that pertains to a 'vice' activity. [The] scope of any 'vice' exception to the protection afforded by the First Amendment would be difficult, if not impossible, to define. . . .

"Because Rhode Island has failed to carry its heavy burden of justifying its complete ban on price advertising, we conclude that [the challenged legislation is unconstitutional]."

Justice Scalia concurred in the judgment. Scalia observed that, "where the core offense of suppressing particular political ideas is not at issue," the Court should interpret the first amendment in light of "the long accepted practices of the American people," with particular reference to "the state legislative practices prevalent at the time" the first and fourteenth amendments were adopted. Because the parties in this case provided "no evidence on these points," however, Scalia concluded that the legislation was invalid under the Court's "existing jurisprudence."

Justice Thomas also filed a concurring opinion: "In cases such as this, in which the government's asserted interest is to keep legal users of a product or service ignorant in order to manipulate their choices in the marketplace, the balancing test adopted in *Central Hudson* should not be applied. [Such] an 'interest' is per se illegitimate and can no more justify regulation of 'commercial' speech than it can justify regulation of 'noncommercial' speech. [Both] Justice Stevens and Justice O'Connor appear to adopt a stricter [interpretation] of *Central Hudson* than that suggested in some of our other opinions, one that could [go] a long way toward the position I take. [But] rather than 'applying' [*Central Hudson*] to reach the inevitable result [in this case], I would [hold that] all attempts to dissuade legal choices by citizens by keeping them ignorant are impermissible."

Justice O'Connor, joined by Chief Justice Rehnquist and Justices Souter and Breyer, filed an opinion concurring in the judgment: "[This legislation] fails the final prong [of *Central Hudson*]; that is, its ban is more extensive than necessary to serve the State's interest. [The] fit between Rhode Island's method and [its] goal is not reasonable. [As demonstrated by Justice Stevens, the] State has other methods at its disposal — methods that would more directly accomplish [its] goal without intruding on sellers' ability to provide truthful, nonmisleading information to customers. [The State points] for support to *Posadas*. Since *Posadas*, however, this Court has examined more searchingly the State's professed goal, and the speech restriction put into place to further it, before accepting a State's claim that the speech restriction satisfies First Amendment scrutiny. [Citing, e.g., *Went for It* and *Coors Brewing*.] [Because the challenged legislation] fails even [the] standard set out in *Central Hudson*, nothing here requires the adoption of a new analysis for the evaluation of commercial speech regulation."

Note: Liquormart *and Additional Limitations on the Protection of Commercial Speech*

1. *The implications of* Liquormart. After *Liquormart*, how would you assess the constitutionality of a law banning all cigarette advertising? For a comparative perspective, see RJR MacDonald, Inc. v. Attorney General, 100 C.C.C.3d 449 (1995) (Supreme Court of Canada invalidates legislation prohibiting all advertising of tobacco products because the government had adduced insufficient "evidence to show that less intrusive regulation would not achieve its goal as effectively as an outright ban").

Consider also Sullivan, Cheap Spirits, Cigarettes, and Free Speech: The Implications of 44 Liquormart, 1996 Sup. Ct. Rev. 123, 126-128, 148-149, 152, 157:

> Since *Virginia Pharmacy*, the Court has treated commercial speech as protected speech, but not as fully protected speech. The principal differences are (1) that regulation of false and misleading commercial speech is subject to no First Amendment scrutiny, (2) that advertisements of illegal transactions may be banned even if they fall short of proscribable incitement, and (3) that all [other] commercial speech regulations are subject to a form of intermediate rather than strict scrutiny. . . .
>
> After *Liquormart*, it [would] appear [that the Court now views] suppressing commercial speech by reason of [its] communicative impact as suspicious, [and will test such regulations by the same standards it uses to test similar regulations of noncommercial speech]. [Having gone this far,] why does the Court not simply dissolve the category of commercial speech and assimilate advertising to the general run of First Amendment law?
>
> [What] are the possible downsides, or perceived bad consequences, of assimilating commercial speech to the Court's existing approaches to fully protected speech? There are three areas of current law [that might be especially affected by such a change: "advertisement of an illegal product or transaction"; "false or misleading commercial speech"; and content-based commercial speech regulations that, unlike the regulation at issue in *Liquormart*, are not "motivated by paternalistic concern that the listener will act wrongly on true factual information," such as "regulations designed to prevent advertisers from conveying particular images that they seek to associate with their product or service" (e.g., Joe Camel)].

How would assimilating these three types of commercial advertising "to the Court's existing approaches to fully protected speech" affect the extent to which they can be regulated? Would these changes, if any, be "bad consequences"? See Sullivan, supra.

2. *Discrimination against all commercial advertising.* All of the cases considered above involved restrictions on the advertising of particular services or products. Suppose, however, the government restricts *all* commercial advertising, as a class. How might that affect the analysis? Consider City of Cincinnati v. Discovery Network, 507 U.S. 410 (1993). In 1989, Cincinnati authorized respondent companies to place sixty-two freestanding newsracks on public property for the purpose of distributing free magazines that consisted primarily of advertisements for respondents' services. In 1990, motivated by its interest in the safety and attractive appearance of its streets and sidewalks, Cincinnati revoked respondents' permits on the ground that the magazines were "commercial handbills" whose distribution on public property could be prohibited. The Court, in an opinion by Justice Stevens, invalidated the restriction:

> [R]espondents do [not] question the substantiality of the city's interest in safety and esthetics. [The critical issue is whether the city has met its burden under *Central Hudson* and *Fox*] to establish a "reasonable fit" between its legitimate interests [and] its [ban] on newsracks dispensing "commercial handbills." . . .
>
> The city argues that there is a close fit [because] every decrease in the number of such dispensing devices necessarily effects an increase in safety and an improvement in the attractiveness of the cityscape. [This is] an insufficient justification for the discrimination against respondents' use of newsracks that are no more harmful than the [1,500 to 2,000 noncommercial newsracks that the city permits]. The major premise supporting the city's argument is the proposition that commercial speech has only a low value. Based on that premise, the city contends that the fact that assertedly more valuable publications are allowed to use newsracks does not undermine its judgment that its esthetic and safety interests are stronger than the interest in allowing commercial speakers to have similar access to the reading public.
>
> We cannot agree. [In] this case, the distinction [between commercial and noncommercial speech] bears no relationship whatsoever to the particular interests that the city has asserted. It is therefore an impermissible means of responding to the city's admittedly legitimate interests. [Respondents'] newsracks are no greater an eyesore than the newsracks permitted to remain on Cincinnati's sidewalks. [In] the absence of some basis for distinguishing between "newspapers" and "commercial handbills" that is relevant to an interest asserted by the city, we are unwilling to recognize Cincinnati's bare assertion that the "low value" of commercial speech is a sufficient justification for its selective and categorical ban on newsracks dispensing "commercial handbills."

Chief Justice Rehnquist, joined by Justices White and Thomas, dissented, arguing that one "would have thought that the city [could] have decided to place the burden of its regulatory scheme on less protected speech [without] running afoul of the First Amendment."

3. *Regulating commercial billboards.* In light of *Discovery Network*, how would you expect the Court to rule on the constitutionality of a city ordinance banning all commercial (but not political or public service) billboards? Consider Metromedia, Inc. v. San Diego, 435 U.S. 490 (1981), which involved the constitutionality of a San Diego ordinance prohibiting virtually all outdoor advertising display signs. The ordinance was designed to eliminate hazards to pedestrians and motorists and to preserve and improve the appearance of the city. Although the

Court invalidated the ordinance as applied to *noncommercial* advertising, it sustained the ordinance as applied to *commercial* messages. The Court explained that the "critical" question concerned "the third of the *Central Hudson* criteria: Does the ordinance 'directly advance' governmental interests in traffic safety and in the appearance of the city?" Although noting that there was no direct evidence in the record "to show any connection between billboards and traffic safety," the Court was reluctant "to disagree with the accumulated, common-sense judgments of local lawmakers [that] billboards are real and substantial hazards to traffic safety. There is nothing here to suggest that these judgments are unreasonable." Similarly, although noting that "esthetic judgments are necessarily subjective," the Court concluded that the city's esthetic judgment was reasonable. Can *Metromedia* be squared with *Discovery Network?*

4. *Advertisements for unlawful transactions.* The Court has repeatedly stated that commercial advertisements offering to enter into unlawful transactions are not protected by the Constitution. See, e.g., Hoffman Estates v. Flipside, 455 U.S. 489 (1982) ("government may regulate or ban entirely" commercial "speech proposing an illegal transaction"). Recall that under *Brandenburg* express advocacy of unlawful conduct may be prohibited only if it is likely imminently to bring about such conduct. Should a similar standard govern commercial advertising?

5. *Overbreadth.* In *Bates,* the Court announced in dictum that "the justification for the application of overbreadth analysis applies weakly, if at all, in the ordinary commercial context," and that the Court therefore would not apply the doctrine to commercial advertising. The Court explained that

> there are "commonsense differences" between commercial speech and other varieties. [Since] advertising is linked to commercial well-being, it seems unlikely that such speech is particularly susceptible to being crushed by overbroad regulation. [Moreover], concerns for uncertainty in determining the scope of protection are reduced; the advertiser seeks to disseminate information about a product or service that he provides, and presumably he can determine more readily than others whether his speech is truthful and protected.

6. *Factually false commercial advertising.* In footnote 24 of *Virginia Pharmacy,* the Court offered several arguments as to why factually false commercial speech may constitutionally be regulated more extensively than other forms of factually false expression. Consider the following criticisms: (a) "Commercial speech is not necessarily more verifiable than other speech. There may well be uncertainty about some quality of a product, such as the health effect of eggs. [On] the other hand, political speech is often quite verifiable by the speakers. A political candidate knows the truth about his own past and present intentions, yet misrepresentations on these subjects are immune from state regulation." Farber, Commercial Speech and First Amendment Theory, 74 Nw. U.L. Rev. 372, 385-386 (1979). (b) "[It] is also incorrect to distinguish commercial from political expression on the ground that the former is somehow hardier because of the inherent profit motive. It could just as easily be said that we need not fear that commercial magazines and newspapers will cease publication for fear of government regulation, because they are in business for profit." Redish, The Value of Free Speech, 130 U. Pa. L. Rev. 591, 633 (1982).

7. *Deceptive or misleading commercial advertising. Virginia Pharmacy* suggests that commercial advertising may be regulated or prohibited, even if it is not fac-

tually false, if it is deceptive or misleading. Is this defensible? The Court observed in *Gertz*, section D1 supra, that "there is no constitutional value in false statements of fact." Can the same be said of misleading or deceptive expression? Do you agree with the Court in *Central Hudson* that, since "the First Amendment's concern for commercial speech is based on the informational function of advertising, [there] can be no constitutional objection to the suppression of commercial messages that [are] more likely to deceive the public than to inform it"?

In *Bates*, the Court rejected a claim that price advertising of routine legal services was sufficiently "inherently misleading" to justify its prohibition. In Friedman v. Rogers, 440 U.S. 1 (1979), however, the Court upheld a Texas statute prohibiting the practice of optometry under "any trade name" as a permissible restriction of misleading advertising. The Court explained that there is "a significant possibility that trade names [could] be used to mislead the public." For example, "the public may be attracted by a trade name that reflects the reputation of an optometrist no longer associated with the practice," or a trade name may free "an optometrist from dependence on his personal reputation [and thus enable] him to assume a new trade name if negligence or misconduct casts a shadow over the old one."

In light of *Bates* and *Friedman*, to what extent may a state constitutionally restrict lawyer advertising concerning the *quality* of legal services? See Peel v. Attorney Registration & Disciplinary Commission of Illinois, 496 U.S. 91 (1990), in which the Court, in invalidating a disciplinary rule prohibiting lawyers from holding themselves out as "certified" or as "specialists" in particular fields, rejected the argument that such descriptions are "inherently misleading." See also Ibanez v. Florida Department of Business and Professional Regulation, 512 U.S. 136 (1994) (rejecting the state's claim that it is "inherently misleading" for an attorney truthfully to advertise that she is also a certified public accountant).

8. *Compelled disclosure.* In Zauderer v. Office of Disciplinary Counsel, 471 U.S. 626 (1985), an attorney advertised in a certain type of case, "if there is no recovery, no legal fees are owed by our clients." The Court upheld a disciplinary rule requiring the attorney to disclose in the advertisement that clients would have to pay "costs" even if the lawsuits were unsuccessful. The Court explained that "because the extension of First Amendment protection to commercial speech is justified principally by the value to consumers of the information such speech provides," the state may constitutionally require advertisers to disclose specific information in their advertisements if that requirement is "reasonably related to the State's interest in preventing deception of consumers."

Note: Labor Disputes and the First Amendment

Does expression concerning the merits of an ongoing labor controversy warrant full first amendment protection? Does such expression, like commercial advertising, hold only "a subordinate position" in the scale of first amendment values?

1. *Labor picketing.* Consider NLRB v. Retail Store Employees Local 1001, 447 U.S. 607 (1980), decided on the same day as *Central Hudson*. During a labor dispute with Safeco, an underwriter of real estate title insurance, Local 1001 picketed the premises of five local title companies that searched titles, performed escrow

services, and sold only Safeco insurance. The pickets carried signs declaring that Safeco had no contract with the union and distributed handbills asking consumers to support the strike by cancelling their Safeco policies. The board held that the secondary consumer picketing constituted an unfair labor practice. The board reasoned that, since the local companies sold only Safeco insurance, the union's action was "reasonably calculated to induce customers not to patronize the neutral parties at all," thus effectively coercing them to pressure Safeco into yielding to the union's demands. The union maintained that this determination violated its rights under the first amendment.

The Court upheld the board's determination on the ground that the union's activity was in furtherance of "unlawful objectives" — that is, inducing customers not to patronize the local companies in order to induce them to join in putting economic pressure on Safeco. Would a similar restriction be constitutional in the context of a political, rather than a labor, dispute? Consider Cox, Foreword: Freedom of Expression in the Burger Court, 94 Harv. L. Rev. 1, 36-37 (1980):

> The objectives were "unlawful" only in a Pickwickian sense. The customers violate no law by ceasing to do business with the [local companies]. The [local companies] violate no law by ceasing to do business with [Safeco]. [Safeco] violates no law by settling the dispute upon the union's terms. Congress deemed these consequences undesirable because they extend economic warfare by involving neutrals, but it did not proscribe anything but the appeal to the customers.

Compare NAACP v. Claiborne Hardware, section B1 supra, in which the Court held that an NAACP boycott of white businesses is constitutionally protected activity, with International Longshoremen's Association v. Allied International, 456 U.S. 212 (1982), in which the Court held that a union's refusal to unload cargoes arriving from the Soviet Union as a protest against the Soviet invasion of Afghanistan is a secondary boycott in violation of the National Labor Relations Act and thus unprotected by the first amendment.

2. *Representation elections.* In NLRB v. Gissel Packing Co., 395 U.S. 575 (1969), the International Brotherhood of Teamsters attempted to organize petitioner's employees. On learning of the union's efforts, petitioner's president attempted both in conversation and in writing to dissuade the employees from joining the union. He reminded the employees that a strike some twelve years earlier had shut down the company for three months and described the union as "strike happy." He emphasized that the company was on "thin ice" financially, that the union's "only weapon is to strike," and that a strike "could lead to the closing of the plant." He also pointed out to the employees that, because of their age and the limited usefulness of their skills outside their craft, they might not be able to find jobs elsewhere if the company went out of business. Finally, he provided the employees with a long list of firms in the town that had recently gone out of business, impliedly as a result of union demands. The union lost the representation election by a vote of seven to six, but the board set aside the election on the ground that the president's communications with the employees constituted an "unfair labor practice." Petitioner argued that this finding violated the first amendment.

In a unanimous decision, the Court upheld the board. The Court explained that, although the NLRA permits an employer to "make a prediction as to the precise effects he believes unionization will have on his company, [the] prediction must be carefully phrased on the basis of objective fact to convey [the] employer's belief as to demonstrably probable consequences beyond his control." Here, "the Board could reasonably conclude that the intended and understood import of [the president's] message was not to predict that unionization would inevitably cause the plant to close but to threaten to throw employees out of work regardless of the economic realities," for the president "had no support for [his] assumption that the union" would have to strike, he "had no basis for attributing other plant closings in the area to unionism," and the board had "often found that employees, who are particularly sensitive to rumors of plant closings, take such hints as coercive threats rather than honest forecasts." In such circumstances, the president's statement could be deemed "a threat of retaliation based on misrepresentation and coercion, and as such without the protection of the First Amendment."

Could expression analogous to that at issue in *Gissel* be restricted in the context of an ordinary political election? If not, what explains *Gissel*? Is the speech of "low" first amendment value because it concerns a private economic dispute? Is *Gissel* explicable on the ground, suggested by the Court, that the law "must take into account the economic dependence of the employees on their employers, and the necessary tendency of the former, because of that relationship, to pick up intended implications of the latter that might be more readily dismissed by a more disinterested ear"?

4. Obscenity

In the first reported obscenity case in the United States, a Pennsylvania court declared it an offense at common law to exhibit for profit a picture of a nude couple. Commonwealth v. Sharpless, 2 Serg. & Rawle 91 (1815). Despite *Sharpless*, there were few serious efforts to restrict "obscene" expression prior to the Civil War. In the late 1860s, however, Anthony Comstock, a grocer, initiated a campaign to suppress obscenity. Comstock's efforts resulted in the enactment of antiobscenity legislation in virtually every state. In applying this legislation, most courts adopted the *Hicklin* definition of obscenity: The "test of obscenity" is "whether the tendency of the matter [is] to deprave and corrupt those whose minds are open to such immoral influences." Regina v. Hicklin, 3 L.R-Q.B. 360, 371 (1868). Under this test, which resulted in the suppression of such works as Theodore Dreiser's An American Tragedy and D. H. Lawrence's Lady Chatterley's Lover, a work could be deemed obscene because of the potential effect of even isolated passages on the most susceptible readers or viewers. See Commonwealth v. Friede, 271 Mass. 318, 171 N.E. 472 (1930) (An American Tragedy); Commonwealth v. DeLacey, 271 Mass. 327, 171 N.E. 455 (1930) (Lady Chatterley's Lover). In an influential decision reviewing the suppression of James Joyce's Ulysses in the early 1930s, a federal court rejected the *Hicklin* test and adopted instead a standard focusing on the effect on the average person of the dominant theme of the work as a whole. United States v. One Book Called "Ulysses," 5 F. Supp. 182 (S.D.N.Y. 1933), aff'd, 72 F.2d 705 (2d Cir. 1934).

Throughout this era, it was generally assumed that the first amendment posed no barrier to the suppression of obscenity. Indeed, the *Chaplinsky* dictum prominently featured the "obscene" in its catalogue of "unprotected" utterances. The Supreme Court first considered the obscenity issue in a 1948 case arising out of New York's attempt to suppress Memoirs of Hecate County, a highly regarded book written by Edmund Wilson, one of America's foremost literary critics. The Court divided equally on the issue, however, and thus affirmed the conviction without opinion. Doubleday & Co. v. New York, 335 U.S. 848 (1948). Nine years later, in Roth v. United States, infra, the Court finally addressed the obscenity question. There have been two distinct periods in the Court's efforts to come to grips with obscenity. The first period, which lasted from the 1957 decision in Roth until 1973, was dominated by the Warren Court's frustrating and largely unsuccessful efforts to define "obscenity." The second period, which began with the Court's 1973 decisions in Miller v. California and Paris Adult Theatre I v. Slaton, infra, has been dominated by the Court's subsequent efforts to reformulate the doctrine. This section focuses on three questions: Is obscenity "low" value speech? What is "obscenity"? What interests justify the suppression of obscenity?

ROTH v. UNITED STATES; ALBERTS v. CALIFORNIA, 354 U.S. 476 (1957). Roth was convicted of violating a federal statute prohibiting any person to mail any "obscene" publication. Alberts was convicted of violating a California statute prohibiting any person to write, print, or sell any "obscene" writing. The Supreme Court affirmed the convictions. Justice Brennan delivered the opinion of the Court:

"The dispositive question is whether obscenity is utterance within the area of protected speech and press. [All] ideas having even the slightest redeeming social importance — unorthodox ideas, controversial ideas, even ideas hateful to the prevailing climate of opinion — have the full protection of the guarantees, unless excludable because they encroach upon the limited area of more important interests. But implicit in the history of the First Amendment is the rejection of obscenity as utterly without redeeming social importance. [Thirteen] of the 14 States which by 1792 had ratified the Constitution [provided] for the prosecution of libel, and all of those States made either blasphemy or profanity, or both, statutory crimes. [In] light of this history, it is apparent [that] obscenity, [like] libel, [was] outside the protection intended for speech and press. [We therefore] hold that obscenity is not within the area of constitutionally protected speech or press. [Accordingly,] obscene material [may be suppressed] without proof [that it will] create a clear and present danger of antisocial conduct.

"However, sex and obscenity are not synonymous. Obscene material is material which deals with sex in a manner appealing to prurient interest. The portrayal of sex, e.g., in art, literature, and scientific works, is not itself sufficient reason to deny material the constitutional protection of freedom of speech and press. Sex, a great and mysterious motive in human life, has indisputably been a subject of absorbing interest to mankind through the ages; it is one of the vital problems of human interest and public concern. [It] is therefore vital that the standards for judging obscenity safeguard the protection of freedom of speech and press for material which does not treat sex in a manner appealing to prurient interest. [The proper test is] whether to the average person, applying contemporary community standards, the dominant theme of the material taken as a whole appeals to the prurient interest."

Chief Justice Warren concurred in the result: "It is not the book that is on trial; it is a person. [The] defendants [in] these cases [were] plainly engaged in the commercial exploitation of the morbid and shameful craving for materials with prurient effect. [State] and Federal Governments can constitutionally punish such conduct. That is all that [we] need to decide."

Justice Harlan concurred in the result in *Alberts*, but dissented in *Roth* on the ground that the states have broader authority to regulate obscene expression than the federal government, which may restrict only "hard-core pornography."

Justice Douglas, joined by Justice Black, dissented: "I do not think that the problem can be resolved by the Court's statement that 'obscenity is not expression protected by the First Amendment.' [There] is no special historical evidence that literature dealing with sex was intended to be treated in a special manner by those who drafted the First Amendment. [Moreover,] I reject [the] implication that problems of freedom of speech [are] to be resolved by weighing against the values of free expression, the judgment of the Court that a particular form of expression has 'no redeeming social importance.' The First Amendment [was] designed to preclude courts as well as legislatures from weighing the values of speech against silence. [I] have the same confidence in the ability of our people to reject noxious literature as I have in their capacity to sort out the true from the false in theology, economics, politics, or any other field."

Note: Obscenity and Free Expression

1. *Entertainment, art, literature, and the first amendment.* Does the first amendment protect not only speech that expressly addresses "public" issues but also "speech" in the form of entertainment, art, and literature? Does the latter form of "speech" have a "subordinate position" in the scale of first amendment values? Consider Kalven, The Metaphysics of the Law of Obscenity, 1960 Sup. Ct. Rev. 1, 15-16:

The classic defense of John Stuart Mill and the modern defense of Alexander Meiklejohn do not help much when the question is why the novel, the poem, the painting, the drama, or the piece of sculpture falls within the protection of the First Amendment. Nor do the famous opinions of Hand, Holmes, and Brandeis. The emphasis is all on truth winning out in a fair fight between competing ideas [and on the] argument that free speech is indispensable to the informed citizenry required to make self-government work. The people need free speech because they vote. [But not] all communications are relevant to the political process. The people do not need novels or dramas or paintings or poems because they will be called upon to vote. Art and belles-lettres do not deal in such ideas — at least not good art or belles-lettres. [Thus] there seems to be a hiatus in our basic free-speech theory.

Consider Meiklejohn's response:

[There] are many forms of thought and expression within the range of human communications from which the voter derives the knowledge, intelligence, sensitivity to human values: the capacity for sane and objective judgment which, so far as possible, a ballot should express. [The] people do need novels and dramas and paintings and poems, "because they will be called upon to vote." The primary social fact which blocks and hinders the success of our experiment in self-government is that our citizens are not educated for self-government.

Meiklejohn, The First Amendment Is an Absolute, 1961 Sup. Ct. Rev. 245, 256, 263. Does the "self-fulfillment" defense of free expression fill Kalven's "hiatus" and offer a more persuasive rationale for the protection of art, literature, and entertainment?

The Court has generally assumed that nonobscene literature and entertainment are entitled to "full" first amendment protection. In Winters v. New York, 333 U.S. 507, 510 (1948), for example, the Court explained that "[t]he line between the informing and the entertaining is too elusive for the protection of the basic right. Everyone is familiar with instances of propaganda through fiction. What is one man's amusement, teaches another's doctrine." See also Schad v. Borough of Mount Ephraim, 452 U.S. 61 (1981) (holding unconstitutional a prohibition on all live entertainment in the borough). For a more thorough explication of the values of aesthetic expression, see Nahmod, Artistic Expression and Aesthetic Theory: The Beautiful, The Sublime and The First Amendment, 1987 Wis. L. Rev. 221; Hamilton, Art Speech, 49 Vand. L. Rev. 73 (1996).

2. *Is obscenity of only "low" first amendment value?* Does obscenity further any of the values underlying the protection of free expression? Consider the following arguments:

a. As the Court demonstrated in *Roth*, the historical evidence shows that obscenity "was outside the protection intended for speech and press." But consider Kalven, supra, at 9: "[The] Court's use of history was so casual as to be [alarming]. Is it clear, for example, that blasphemy can constitutionally be made a crime today? And what would the Court say to an argument along the same lines appealing to the Sedition Act of 1798 as justification for the truly liberty-defeating crime of seditious libel?"

b. Schauer, Speech and "Speech" — Obscenity and "Obscenity": An Exercise in the Interpretation of Constitutional Language, 67 Geo. L.J. 899, 906, 922, 923, 926 (1979):

> Certain uses of words, although speech in the ordinary sense, clearly are not speech in the constitutional sense. ["Speech" for first amendment purposes is defined by] the idea of cognitive content, of mental effect, of a communication designed to appeal to the intellectual process. This [includes] the artistic and the emotive as well as the propositional. [But] hardcore pornography is [by definition] designed to produce a purely physical effect. [It is] essentially a physical rather than a mental stimulus. [A] pornographic item is in a real sense a sexual surrogate. [Consider] rubber, plastic, or leather sex aids. It is hard to find any free speech aspects in their sale or use. [The] mere fact that in pornography the stimulating experience is initiated by visual rather than tactile means is irrelevant. [Neither] means constitutes communication in the cognitive sense. [Thus,] hardcore pornography *is* sex, [not "speech"].

Is this what the Court meant in *Roth* when it defined obscenity as "material which deals with sex in a manner appealing to prurient interest"? For a critique of Schauer's view, see Gey, The Apologetics of Suppression: The Regulation of Pornography as Act and Idea, 86 Mich. L. Rev. 1564 (1988).

c. As the Court observed in *Chaplinsky*, obscenity is "of such slight social value as a step to truth that any benefit that may be derived from [it] is clearly outweighed by the social interest in order and morality." Or as the Court observed in *Roth*, such expression is "utterly without redeeming social importance." But consider Richards, Free Speech and Obscenity Law: Toward a Moral Theory of the First Amendment, 123 U. Pa. L. Rev. 45, 82 (1974):

[The] First Amendment rests [fundamentally] on the moral liberties of expression, conscience and thought; these liberties are fundamental conditions of the integrity and competence of a person in mastering his life and expressing this mastery to others. [There] is no reason whatsoever to believe that the freedom to determine the sexual contents of one's communications or to be an audience to such communications is not as fundamental to this self-mastery as the freedom to decide upon any other communicative contents. [The] consequence of [laws directed against obscenity] is not only a denial of a reasonable understanding of the varieties of pleasurable sexual function, but also a crippling debasement of the human capacity to master one's sexual life in the light of independent judgment.

d. Laws directed against obscenity are not restrictions on ideas as such, for they limit the *means* of expression rather than the *ideas* expressed. As the Court said in *Chaplinsky*, obscene "utterances are no essential part of any exposition of ideas." Moreover, to the extent that obscenity is associated with a particular ideological message, such as "sexual freedom," it is an especially problematic *means* of expression, for it alters "one's tastes and preferences" not by direct persuasion or rational argument but by "a process that is, like subliminal advertising, both outside of one's rational control and quite independent of the relevant grounds for preference." Scanlon, Freedom of Expression and Categories of Expression, 40 U. Pitt. L. Rev. 519, 547 (1979). On the other hand, might it be said that the very concept of "obscenity" embodies a forbidden "viewpoint-based restriction" because "it is justified by moral objections to the ideas or messages that sexual speech is said to convey"? Heins, Viewpoint Discrimination, 24 Hast. Const. L.Q. 99, 103 (1996).

3. *The interests furthered by the suppression of obscenity.* Because the Court in *Roth* accepted the underlying premise of the *Chaplinsky* dictum — that obscene utterances are wholly "unprotected" by the first amendment — the Court found it unnecessary to inquire into the nature or substantiality of the state interests said to justify the suppression of obscene expression. The gradual breakdown of the "two-level" theory and the increased use of "definitional" balancing in such areas as libel and commercial speech, however, may raise doubts about this approach. Do the decisions to "balance" conflicting state and speech interests in the libel and commercial speech contexts suggest a need for similar balancing in the obscenity context? If so, what state interests are sufficiently important to justify restrictions on obscene expression? Consider the following:

a. The state may suppress obscenity because it may cause violent antisocial conduct. Must the state "prove" causation? What must be the nature of the correlation — clear and present danger? Bad tendency? For analysis of the "correlation," see The Report of the Commission on Obscenity and Pornography 26-27 (1970) (finding "no evidence to date that exposure to explicit sexual materials plays a significant role in the causation of delinquent or criminal behavior"). For criticism of the report, see L. Sunderland, Obscenity: The Court, the Congress and the President's Commission (1975); Clor, Science, Eros and the Law: A Critique of the Obscenity Commission Report, 10 Duq. L. Rev. 63 (1971).

Sixteen years after publication of the Commission on Obscenity and Pornography's report, a new government commission — The Attorney General's Commission on Pornography — determined that at least certain forms of obscenity could cause violent antisocial conduct. After reviewing available social science evidence, the Attorney General's commission concluded that there was a causal relationship between exposure to sexually violent material and aggressive behavior toward women. With respect to nonviolent, but "degrading," sexually explicit material, the commission found the evidence "more tentative," but nonetheless concluded that "substantial exposure to material of this type will increase acceptance of the proposition that women like to be forced into sexual practices." Although finding less evidence linking this material to sexual aggression, the commission reasoned that "[over] a large enough sample a population that believes that many women like to be raped [will] commit more acts of sexual violence [than] would a population holding these beliefs to a lesser extent." Moreover, the commission found that "substantial exposure to materials of this type bears some causal relationship to the incidence of various non-violent forms of discrimination against or subordination of women in our society." With regard to nonviolent, "nondegrading" material, the commission concluded that there was no currently available evidence supporting a causal relationship between exposure to it and acts of sexual violence.

The commission's report stirred immediate controversy, and some of the social scientists whose work the commission relied on insisted that their studies did not support the conclusions the commission drew from them. For criticism of the report, see G. Hawkins and F. Zimring, Pornography in a Free Society (1988). For further discussion of the causation issue, see Schauer, Causation Theory and the Causes of Sexual Violence, 1987 Am. B. Found. Res. J. 737.

The issue of pornography, defined expressly in terms of the subordination of women, as distinct from the more traditional concept of obscenity, is examined in section D6 infra.

b. The state may suppress obscenity because it "corrupts character," impairs "mental health," and "has a deleterious effect on the individual from which the community should protect him." Henkin, Morals and the Constitution: The Sin of Obscenity, 63 Colum. L. Rev. 391, 394 (1963).

c. The state may suppress obscenity to prevent the erosion of moral standards. Consider Lockhart and McClure, Literature, the Law of Obscenity, and the Constitution, 38 Minn. L. Rev. 295, 374-375 (1954):

The view that literature may be proscribed because [it] may [change] accepted moral standards [flies] squarely in the face of the [guarantee of free] expression. Back of this fundamental freedom lies the basic conviction that our democratic society must be free to perfect its own standards of conduct and belief [through] the heat of unrepressed controversy and debate. The remedy against those who attack currently accepted standards is [defense] of those standards, not censorship.

d. The state may suppress obscenity because it erodes moral standards not by rational persuasion but by indirect degradation of values. Consider H. Clor, Obscenity and Public Morality 121, 170-171 (1969):

[Obscene materials] do not make arguments which are to be met by intelligent defense. While they attack moral values, they do not [do so] in any sense relevant to [public debate]. [Rather,] they have an [effect] upon feeling, upon motivations — ultimately upon character and the basic attitudes which arise from character. [Constant] exposure to [obscene] materials which overemphasize sensuality and brutality, reduce love to sex, and blatantly expose to public view intimacies which have been thought [private] must eventually [erode] moral standards. [The] ethical convictions of man do not rest simply upon his explicit opinions. They rest also upon a delicate network of moral and aesthetic feelings, sensibilities, [and] tastes. [These] "finer feelings" [may be eroded] by a steady stream of [obscenity]. Men whose sensibilities are frequently assaulted by prurient and lurid impressions may become desensitized. [This] is what is meant by "an erosion of the moral fabric."

e. The state may restrict obscenity to protect individuals against the "shock effect" of unwanted exposure to such expression because "a communication of this nature, imposed upon a person contrary to his wishes, has all the characteristics of a physical assault." T. Emerson, The System of Freedom of Expression 496 (1970). May the state suppress obscenity to protect individuals against the "shock" of knowing that others are reading or viewing it?

f. The state may suppress the dissemination of obscenity to minors because they are especially vulnerable to its "harmful" effects.

Note: Developments in the Law of "Obscenity" — 1957-1973

1. *The definition of obscenity: the breakdown of consensus.* In *Roth*, the Court embraced the view that material is "obscene" if, "to the average person, applying contemporary community standards, the dominant theme of the material taken as a whole appeals to prurient interest." But agreement on the definition of obscenity was short-lived. Only a decade after *Roth*, Justice Harlan aptly observed that "[t]he subject of obscenity has produced a variety of views among the members of the Court unmatched in any other course of constitutional adjudication." As evidence, Justice Harlan noted that in the thirteen obscenity cases decided in the decade after *Roth*, there were "a total of 55 separate opinions among the Justices." Interstate Circuit, Inc. v. Dallas, 390 U.S. 676, 704-705, 705 n.1 (1968) (Harlan, J., dissenting).

By 1968, the following views had emerged:

a. Justices Clark and White adhered to the initial *Roth* formulation. See Memoirs v. Massachusetts, 383 U.S. 413, 441 (1966) (Clark, J., dissenting); id. at 460-462 (White, J., dissenting).

b. Justices Black and Douglas adhered to their view, expressed in *Roth*, that government is wholly powerless to regulate sexually oriented expression on the ground of its obscenity. See Jacobellis v. Ohio, 378 U.S. 184, 196-197 (1964) (Black, J., joined by Douglas, J., concurring).

c. Justice Harlan adhered to the view he expressed in *Roth*. See Jacobellis v. Ohio, 378 U.S. at 204 (Harlan, J., dissenting).

d. Justice Stewart "reached the conclusion [that] under the First and Fourteenth Amendments criminal laws in this area are constitutionally limited to hard-core pornography." Justice Stewart continued: "I shall not today attempt further to define the kinds of material I understand to be embraced within that shorthand description; and perhaps I could never succeed in intelligibly doing so. But I know it when I see it, and the motion picture involved in this case is not that." Jacobellis v. Ohio, id. at 197 (Stewart, J., concurring).

e. Justice Brennan, Chief Justice Warren, and Justice Fortas adopted the view that, for material to be deemed obscene, "three elements must coalesce: it must be established that (a) the dominant theme of the material taken as a whole appeals to a prurient interest in sex; (b) the material is patently offensive because it affronts contemporary community standards relating to the description or representation of sexual matters; and (c) the material is utterly without redeeming social value." Memoirs v. Massachusetts, 383 U.S. at 418 (Brennan, J., joined by Warren, C.J., and Fortas, J.). Although this formulation represented the view of only three justices, it was the formulation most often followed by state and federal courts from 1966 until the Court's 1973 decision in *Miller,* infra. Note the addition of elements (b) and (c) to the initial *Roth* formulation.

2. *The definition of obscenity: pandering and variable obscenity.* To complicate matters further, there was substantial disagreement within the Court over the extent to which factors extrinsic to the material should be considered in the obscenity determination. Two such factors were especially troublesome — "pandering" and "special" audiences:

a. In Ginzburg v. United States, 383 U.S. 463 (1966), the Court held that "the question of obscenity may include consideration of the setting in which the publications were presented." Here, the publisher had "sought mailing privileges from the postmasters of Intercourse and Blue Ball, Pennsylvania" in order to sell the "publications on the basis of salacious appeal." The Court held that such "commercial exploitation of erotica solely for the sake of their prurient appeal [may] support the determination that the material is obscene even though in other contexts the material would escape such condemnation."

b. Ginsberg v. New York, 390 U.S. 629 (1968), another "variable obscenity" case, involved the problem of children. The Court had previously addressed the problem of obscenity and children in Butler v. Michigan, 352 U.S. 380 (1957). In *Butler,* the Court held invalid a law prohibiting the sale of "lewd" material that might have a deleterious influence on youth. Justice Frankfurter, speaking for a unanimous Court, explained that the state may not "reduce the adult population of Michigan to reading only what is fit for children." In *Ginsberg,* the Court held that a state can constitutionally prohibit "the sale to minors under seventeen years of age of material defined to be obscene on the basis of its appeal to them whether or not it would be obscene to adults."

3. *The definition of obscenity:* Redrup. The inability of the Court to articulate a definition of obscenity that could command the allegiance of a majority, compounded by the potential relevance of factors extrinsic to the material itself, led to an era of chaos. In Redrup v. New York, 386 U.S. 767 (1967), the Court began the practice of per curiam reversals of convictions for the sale or exhibition of materials that at least five members of the Court, applying their separate tests, deemed not to be obscene. From 1967 to 1973, some thirty-one cases were disposed of in this fashion. The full opinion of the Court in Walker v. Ohio, 398 U.S. 434 (1970), is typical: "The judgment of the Supreme Court of Ohio is reversed. [*Redrup.*]" As Justice Brennan later commented: "[The *Redrup* approach] resolves cases as between the parties, but offers only the most obscure guidance to legislation, adjudication by other courts, and primary conduct. [It]

comes as no surprise that judicial attempts to follow our lead conscientiously have often ended in hopeless confusion." Paris Adult Theatre I v. Slaton, 413 U.S. 49, 83 (1973) (Brennan, J., dissenting).

4. *The interests furthered by the suppression of obscenity*: Stanley v. Georgia. Although debating the definitional issue endlessly, the justices in this era said almost nothing about the nature of the interests that assertedly justified the suppression of obscene expression. As noted earlier, this was due largely to *Roth's* acceptance of the underlying premise of the *Chaplinsky* dictum — obscene utterances are wholly "unprotected" by the first amendment and their restriction thus does not necessitate an inquiry into the nature or substantiality of the state interests.

There was, however, one notable exception to the Court's silence on this issue. In Stanley v. Georgia, 394 U.S. 557 (1969), the Court, speaking through Justice Marshall, held that "the mere private possession of obscene matter cannot constitutionally be made a crime." In reaching this result, the Court announced that the "right to receive information and ideas, regardless of their social worth, [is] fundamental to our free society," and that "in the context of this case — a prosecution for mere possession of printed or filmed matter in the privacy of a person's own home — that right takes on an added dimension," for "also fundamental is the right to be free, except in very limited circumstances, from unwanted governmental intrusions into one's privacy." In light of these interests, "mere categorization of these films as 'obscene' is insufficient justification for such a drastic invasion of personal liberties," for "if the First Amendment means anything, it means that a State has no business telling a man, sitting alone in his own house, what books he may read or what films he may watch."

In defense of its law, Georgia asserted "the right to protect the individual's mind from the effects of obscenity." Treating this as an "assertion that the State has the right to control the moral content of a person's thoughts," the Court declared that, although "to some, this may be a noble purpose, [it] is wholly inconsistent with the philosophy of the First Amendment." Thus, "whatever the power of the state to control public dissemination of ideas inimical to the public morality, it cannot constitutionally premise legislation on the desirability of controlling a person's private thoughts." Moreover, the law could not be defended on the ground that "exposure to obscene materials may lead to deviant sexual behavior or crimes of sexual violence," for, "given the present state of knowledge, the State may no more prohibit mere possession of obscene matter on the ground that it may lead to antisocial conduct than it may prohibit possession of chemistry books on the ground that they may lead to the manufacture of homemade spirits." Finally, the Court explained that *Roth* and the Court's other obscenity decisions were clearly distinguishable, for they "dealt with public distribution of obscene materials and such distribution is subject to different objections," such as, for example, "the danger that obscene material might fall into the hands of children," or "that it might intrude upon the sensibilities or privacy of the general public." Thus, although "the States retain broad power to regulate obscenity, that power simply does not extend to mere possession by the individual in the privacy of his own home."

5. *The implications of* Stanley: Reidel. In United States v. Reidel, 402 U.S. 351 (1971), a federal district court, relying on *Stanley*, held a federal statute prohibiting the knowing use of the mails for the delivery of obscene matter uncon-

stitutional as applied to the distribution of such matter to willing recipients who state that they are adults. The district court reasoned that, "if a person has the right to receive and possess this material, then someone must have the right to deliver it to him." The Supreme Court reversed. The Court explained that the "focus of [*Stanley*] [was] on freedom of mind and thought and on the privacy of one's home." "Reidel," however, "is in a wholly different position," for "he has no complaints about governmental violations of his private thoughts or fantasies, but stands squarely on a claimed First Amendment right to do business in obscenity and use the mails in the process. [*Stanley*] did not overrule *Roth* and we decline to do so now." To the same effect, see United States v. Thirty-Seven Photographs, 402 U.S. 363 (1971); United States v. 12 200 Ft. Reels, 413 U.S. 123 (1973); United States v. Orito, 413 U.S. 139 (1973). See also Osborne v. Ohio, 495 U.S. 103 (1990) (holding *Stanley* inapplicable to the possession of child pornography).

6. *Reformulation.* By 1973, then, the law of obscenity was in a state of considerable confusion. Two questions were especially troublesome: How should obscenity be defined? When may it be restricted? In its 1973 decisions in *Miller* and *Paris Adult Theatre*, the Court attempted to reformulate and clarify the law.

Miller v. California
413 U.S. 15 (1973)

MR. CHIEF JUSTICE BURGER delivered the opinion of the Court.

This is one of a group of "obscenity-pornography" cases being reviewed by the Court in a re-examination of [the standards] which must be used to identify obscene material that a State may regulate. . . .

[In this case, appellant] conducted a mass mailing campaign to advertise the sale of illustrated books, euphemistically called "adult" material. [Appellant's] conviction was specifically based on his conduct in causing five unsolicited advertising brochures to be sent through the mail. [The] brochures [consist primarily] of pictures and drawings very explicitly depicting men and women in groups of two or more engaging in a variety of sexual activities, with genitals often prominently displayed. [This] case [thus] involves the application of a State's criminal obscenity statute to a situation in which sexually explicit materials have been thrust by aggressive sales action upon unwilling recipients. . . .

II

[Obscene] material is unprotected by the First Amendment. [*Roth*.] [However,] State statutes designed to regulate obscene materials must be carefully limited. [Thus,] we now confine the permissible scope of such regulation to works which depict or describe sexual conduct. That conduct must be specifically defined by the applicable state law, as written or authoritatively construed. . . .

The basic guidelines for the trier of fact must be: (a) whether "the average person, applying contemporary community standards" would find that the work, taken as a whole, appeals to the prurient interest; (b) whether the work depicts or describes, in a patently offensive way, sexual conduct specifically defined by the applicable state law; and (c) whether the work, taken as a whole, lacks serious literary, artistic, political, or scientific value. We do not adopt as a constitutional standard the *"utterly* without redeeming social value" test of [*Memoirs*]. . . .

We emphasize that it is not our function to propose regulatory schemes for the States. [It] is possible, however, to give a few plain examples of what a state statute could define for regulation under part (b) of the standard announced in this opinion, supra:

(a) Patently offensive representations or descriptions of ultimate sexual acts, normal or perverted, actual or simulated.

(b) Patently offensive representations or descriptions of masturbation, excretory functions, and lewd exhibition of the genitals.

Sex and nudity may not be exploited without limit by films or pictures exhibited or sold in places of public accommodation any more than live sex and nudity can be exhibited or sold without limit in such public places. At a minimum, prurient, patently offensive depiction or description of sexual conduct must have serious literary, artistic, political, or scientific value to merit First Amendment protection. [In] resolving the inevitably sensitive questions of fact and law, we must continue to rely on the jury system, accompanied by the safeguards that judges, rules of evidence, presumption of innocence, and other protective features provide, as we do with [other] offenses against society and its individual members.

Mr. Justice Brennan [now] maintains that no formulation of this Court, the Congress, or the States can adequately distinguish obscene material unprotected by the First Amendment from protected expression, [*Paris Adult Theatre*, infra]. (Brennan J., dissenting.) [But under] the holdings announced today, no one will be subject to prosecution for the sale or exposure of obscene materials unless these materials depict or describe patently offensive "hard core" sexual conduct specifically defined by the regulating state law, as written or construed. We are satisfied that these specific prerequisites will provide fair notice to a dealer in such materials that his public and commercial activities may bring prosecution. See [*Roth*]. . . .

Mr. Justice Brennan also emphasizes "institutional stress" in justification of his change of view. [It] is certainly true that the absence, since *Roth*, of a single majority view of this Court as to proper standards for testing obscenity has placed a strain on both state and federal courts. But today, for the first time since *Roth* was decided in 1957, a majority of this Court has agreed on concrete guidelines to isolate "hard core" pornography from expression protected by the First Amendment. Now we may abandon the casual practice of [*Redrup*] and attempt to provide positive guidance to federal and state courts alike.

This may not be an easy road, free from difficulty. But no amount of "fatigue" should lead us to adopt a convenient "institutional" rationale — an absolutist, "anything goes" view of the First Amendment — because it will lighten our burdens. . . .

III

Under a National Constitution, fundamental First Amendment limitations on the powers of the States do not vary from community to community, but this does not mean that there are, or should or can be, fixed, uniform national standards of precisely what appeals to the "prurient interest" or is "patently offensive." These are essentially questions of fact, and our Nation is simply too big and too diverse for this Court to reasonably expect that such standards could be articulated for all 50 States in a single formulation, even assuming the prerequisite consensus exists. [It] is neither realistic nor constitutionally sound to read the First Amendment as requiring that the people of Maine or Mississippi accept public depiction of conduct found tolerable in Las Vegas, or New York City.[13] [People] in different States vary in their tastes and attitudes, and this diversity is not to be strangled by the absolutism of imposed uniformity. We hold that the requirement that the jury evaluate the materials with reference to "contemporary standards of the State of California" [is] constitutionally adequate.

IV

The dissenting Justices sound the alarm of repression. But, in our view, to equate the free and robust exchange of ideas and political debate with commercial exploitation of obscene material demeans the grand conception of the First Amendment. [The] First Amendment protects works which, taken as a whole, have serious literary, artistic, political, or scientific value, regardless of whether the government or a majority of the people approve of the ideas these works represent. [But] the public portrayal of hard-core sexual conduct for its own sake, and for the ensuing commercial gain, is a different matter. [There] is no evidence, empirical or historical, that the stern 19th century American censorship of public distribution and display of material relating to sex [in] any way limited or affected expression of serious literary, artistic, political, or scientific ideas. . . .

In sum, we (a) reaffirm the *Roth* holding that obscene material is not protected by the First Amendment; (b) hold that such material can be regulated by the States, subject to the specific safeguards enunciated above, without a showing that the material is "*utterly* without redeeming social value"; and (c) hold that obscenity is to be determined by applying "contemporary community standards." . . .

Vacated and remanded.

Mr. Justice Douglas, dissenting. . . .

[The] idea that the First Amendment permits punishment for ideas that are "offensive" to the particular judge or jury sitting in judgment is astounding. No greater leveler of speech or literature has ever been designed. . . .

I do not think we, the judges, were ever given the constitutional power to make definitions of obscenity. If it is to be defined, let the people [decide] by a constitutional amendment what they want to ban as [obscene]. Whatever the choice,

---

13. In [*Jacobellis*] two Justices argued that application of "local" community standards would run the risk of preventing dissemination of materials in some places because sellers would be unwilling to risk criminal conviction by testing variations in standards from place to place. [The] use of "national" standards, however, necessarily implies that materials found tolerable in some places, but not under the "national" criteria, will nevertheless be unavailable where they are acceptable. Thus, in terms of danger to free expression, the potential for suppression seems at least as great in the application of a single nationwide standard as in allowing distribution in accordance with local tastes. . . .

the courts will have some guidelines. Now we have none except our own predilections.

MR. JUSTICE BRENNAN, with whom MR. JUSTICE STEWART and MR. JUSTICE MARSHALL join, dissenting.

In my dissent in [Paris Adult Theatre, infra], I noted that I had no occasion to consider the extent of state power to regulate the distribution of sexually oriented material [to] unconsenting adults. [I] need not now decide [that question, for] it is clear that under my dissent in Paris Adult Theatre the statute under which the prosecution was brought is unconstitutionally overbroad, and therefore invalid on its face. . . .

Paris Adult Theatre I v. Slaton

413 U.S. 49 (1973)

MR. CHIEF JUSTICE BURGER delivered the opinion of the Court.

[Petitioners are two Atlanta, Georgia, movie theaters and their owners and managers, operating in the style of "adult" theaters. The theaters have a conventional, inoffensive entrance, without any pictures, but with signs indicating that the theaters exhibit "Atlanta's Finest Mature Feature Films." On the door is a sign saying "Adult Theater — You must be 21 and able to prove it. If viewing the nude body offends you, Please Do Not Enter." The local state district attorney filed civil complaints alleging that petitioners were exhibiting to the public for paid admission two allegedly obscene films, Magic Mirror and It All Comes Out in the End, which depict scenes of simulated fellatio, cunnilingus, and group sex intercourse. Respondent's complaints demanded that the two films be declared obscene, and that petitioners be enjoined from exhibiting the films. The trial judge found the films obscene, but dismissed the complaints on the ground that "the display of these films in a commercial theatre, when surrounded by requisite notice to the public of their nature and by reasonable protection against the exposure of these films to minors, is constitutionally permissible." The Georgia Supreme Court reversed and held that exhibition of the films should be enjoined. The U.S. Supreme Court vacated and remanded for reconsideration in light of Miller.]

We categorically disapprove the theory [that] obscene, pornographic films acquire constitutional immunity from state regulation simply because they are exhibited for consenting adults only. [Although] we have often pointedly recognized the high importance of the state interest in regulating the exposure of obscene materials to juveniles and unconsenting adults, [this] Court has never declared these to be the only legitimate state interests permitting regulation of obscene material. . . .

In particular, we hold that there are legitimate state interests at stake in stemming the tide of commercialized obscenity, even assuming it is feasible to enforce effective safeguards against exposure to juveniles and to passersby.[7] Rights

7. It is conceivable that an "adult" theater can — if it really insists — prevent the exposure of its obscene wares to juveniles. An "adult" bookstore, dealing in obscene books, magazines, and pictures, cannot realistically make this claim. The legitimate interest in preventing exposure of juveniles to obscene material cannot be fully served by simply barring juveniles from the imme-

and interests "other than those of the advocates are involved." [These] include the interest of the public in the quality of life and the total community environment, the tone of commerce in the great city centers, and, possibly, the public safety itself. The Hill-Link Minority Report of the Commission on Obscenity and Pornography indicates that there is at least an arguable correlation between obscene material and crime. Quite apart from sex crimes, however, there remains one problem of large proportions aptly described by Professor Bickel:

> It concerns the tone of the society, the mode, or to use terms that have perhaps greater currency, the style and quality of life, now and in the future. A man may be entitled to read an obscene book in his room, or expose himself indecently there. . . . We should protect his privacy. But if he demands a right to obtain the books and pictures he wants in the market, and to foregather in public places — discreet, if you will, but accessible to all — with others who share his tastes, *then to grant him his right is to affect the world about the rest of us, and to impinge on other privacies.* Even supposing that each of us can, if he wishes, effectively avert the eye and stop the ear (which, in truth, we cannot), what is commonly read and seen and heard and done intrudes upon us all, want it or not.

22 The Public Interest 25-26 (Winter 1971). (Emphasis added.) As Mr. Chief Justice Warren stated, there is a "right of the Nation and of the States to maintain a decent society . . ." [*Jacobellis*] (dissenting opinion). . . .

But, it is argued, there are no scientific data which conclusively demonstrate that exposure to obscene material adversely affects men and women or their society. It is urged on behalf of the petitioners that, absent such a demonstration, any kind of state regulation is "impermissible." We reject this argument. It is not for us to resolve empirical uncertainties underlying state legislation, save in the exceptional case where that legislation plainly impinges upon rights protected by the Constitution itself. [Although] there is no conclusive proof of a connection between antisocial behavior and obscene material, the legislature of Georgia could quite reasonably determine that such a connection does or might exist. In deciding *Roth*, this Court implicitly accepted that a legislature could legitimately act on such a conclusion to protect *"the social interest in order and morality."* . . .

If we accept the unprovable assumption that a complete education requires the reading of certain books, [and] the well nigh universal belief that good books, plays, and art lift the spirit, improve the mind, enrich the human personality, and develop character, can we then say that a state legislature may not act on the corollary assumption that commerce in obscene books, or public exhibitions focused on obscene conduct, have a tendency to exert a corrupting and debasing impact leading to antisocial behavior? [The] sum of experience, including that of the past two decades, affords an ample basis for legislatures to conclude that a sensitive, key relationship of human existence, central to family life, community welfare, and the development of human personality, can be debased and distorted by crass commercial exploitation of sex. Nothing in the Constitution prohibits a State from reaching such a conclusion and acting on it legislatively simply because there is no conclusive evidence or empirical data. . . .

---

diate physical premises of "adult" bookstores, when there is a flourishing "outside business" in these materials.

It is asserted, however, [that] state regulation of access by consenting adults to obscene material violates the constitutionally protected right to privacy enjoyed by petitioners' customers. [Nothing,] however, in this Court's decisions intimates that there is any "fundamental" privacy right "implicit in the concept of ordered liberty" to watch obscene movies in places of public accommodation. [Indeed], we have declined to equate the privacy of the home relied on in *Stanley* with a "zone of privacy" that follows a distributor or a consumer of obscene materials wherever he goes. [The] idea of a "privacy" right and a place of public accommodation are, in this context, mutually exclusive. . . .

It is also argued that the State has no legitimate interest in "control [of] the moral content of a person's thoughts," [*Stanley*], and we need not quarrel with this. But we reject the claim that the State of Georgia is here attempting to control the minds or thoughts of those who patronize theaters. Preventing unlimited display or distribution of obscene material, which by definition lacks any serious literary, artistic, political, or scientific value as communication, [is] distinct from a control of reason and the intellect. [The] fantasies of a drug addict are his own and beyond the reach of government, but government regulation of drug sales is not prohibited by the Constitution. . . .

Finally, petitioners argue that conduct which directly involves "consenting adults" only has, for that sole reason, a special claim to constitutional protection. Our Constitution establishes a broad range of conditions on the exercise of power by the States, but for us to say that our Constitution incorporates the proposition that conduct involving consenting adults only is always beyond state regulation, is a step we are unable to take.[15] [The] issue in this context goes beyond whether someone, or even the majority, considers the conduct depicted as "wrong" or "sinful." The States have the power to make a morally neutral judgment that public exhibition of obscene material, or commerce in such material, has a tendency to injure the community as a whole, to endanger the public safety, or to jeopardize [the] States'"right [to] maintain a decent society." . . .

Vacated and remanded.

MR. JUSTICE BRENNAN, with whom MR. JUSTICE STEWART and MR. JUSTICE MARSHALL join, dissenting. [A dissenting opinion of Justice Douglas is omitted.]

[I] am convinced that the approach initiated 16 years ago in [*Roth*], and culminating in the Court's decision today, cannot bring stability to this area of the law without jeopardizing fundamental First Amendment [values]. The vagueness of the standards in the obscenity area produces a number of separate problems, [including a] lack of fair notice, [a] chill on protected expression, and [a severe] stress [on the] judicial machinery. [These concerns] persuade me that a significant change in direction is urgently required. I turn, therefore, to the alternatives that are now open.

1. [One] approach [would] be to draw a new line between protected and unprotected [speech] that resolves all doubt in favor of state [power]. We could

---

15. The state statute books are replete with constitutionally unchallenged laws against prostitution, suicide, voluntary self-mutilation, brutalizing "bare fist" prize fights, and duels, although these crimes may only directly involve "consenting adults." Statutes making bigamy a crime surely cut into an individual's freedom to associate, but few today seriously claim such statutes violate the First Amendment or any other constitutional provision. . . .

hold, for example, that any depiction [of] human sexual organs [is] outside the protection of the First [Amendment]. That formula would [reduce the problems of vagueness]. But [it] would be appallingly [overbroad]. . . .

2. The alternative adopted by the Court [today] adopts a restatement of the *Roth-Memoirs* definition of obscenity. [This] restatement leaves unresolved the very difficulties that compel our rejection of the underlying *Roth* approach, while at the same time contributing substantial difficulties of its own. [The] Court today permits suppression if the government can prove that the materials lack "*serious* literary, artistic, political or scientific value." But [*Roth*] held that certain expression is obscene, and thus outside the protection of the First Amendment, precisely *because* it lacks even the slightest redeeming social value. [The] Court's approach [is thus] nothing less than a rejection of the fundamental First Amendment premises [of *Roth*] and an invitation to widespread suppression of sexually oriented speech. . . .

In any case, [the Court's approach] can have no ameliorative impact on [the] problems that grow out of the vagueness of our current standards. [Although] the Court's [test] does limit the definition of obscenity to depictions of physical conduct and explicit sexual acts, [even] a confirmed optimist could find little realistic comfort in the adoption of such a test. Indeed, the valiant attempt of one lower federal court to draw the constitutional line at depictions of explicit sexual conduct seems to belie any suggestion that this approach marks the road to clarity.[16] . . .

3. I have also considered the possibility of reducing our own role, and the role of appellate courts generally, in determining whether particular matter is obscene. Thus, we might conclude that juries are best suited to determine obscenity vel non and that jury verdicts in this area should not be set aside except in cases of extreme departure from prevailing standards. [But the] First Amendment requires an independent review by appellate courts of the constitutional fact of obscenity. [In] any event, even if [such an approach] would mitigate the institutional stress produced by the *Roth* approach, it would [lead] to even greater uncertainty and the consequent due process problems of fair notice. . . .

4. Finally, I have considered the view, urged so forcefully since 1957 by our Brothers Black and Douglas, that the First Amendment bars the suppression of any sexually oriented expression. That position would [strip] the States of power to an extent that cannot be justified by the commands of the Constitution, at least so long as there is available an alternative approach that strikes a better balance between the guarantee of free expression and the States' legitimate interests. . . .

[Given the] inevitable side effects of state efforts to suppress [obscenity], we must scrutinize with care the state interest that is asserted to justify the suppression. For in the absence of some very substantial interest in suppressing such speech, we can hardly condone the ill effects that seem to flow inevitably from the effort. . . .

[The] state interests in protecting children and in protecting unconsenting adults [stand] on a different footing from the other asserted state interests. [But] whatever the strength of [those] interests, [they] cannot be asserted [where, as]

---

16. Huffman v. United States, 152 U.S. App. D.C. 238, 470 F.2d 386 (1971). The test apparently requires an effort to distinguish between "singles" and "duals," between "erect penises" and "semi-erect penises," and between "ongoing sexual activity" and "imminent sexual activity."

in this case, [the] films [were] exhibited only to persons over the age of 21 who viewed them willingly and with prior knowledge of the nature of their contents. [The] justification for the suppression must be found, therefore, in some independent interest in regulating the reading and viewing habits of consenting adults. . . .

In *Stanley* we pointed out that "[t]here appears to be little empirical basis for" the assertion that "exposure to obscene materials may lead to deviant sexual behavior or crimes of sexual violence."[26] [In] any event, we added that "if the State is only concerned about printed or filmed materials inducing antisocial conduct, we believe that in the context of private consumption of ideas and information we should adhere to the view that '[a]mong free men, the deterrents ordinarily to be applied to prevent crime are education and punishment for violations of the law. . . .'"

Moreover, in *Stanley* we rejected as "wholly inconsistent with the philosophy of the First Amendment" [the] notion that there is a legitimate state concern in the "control [of] the moral content of a person's thoughts." [That] is not to say, of course, that a State must remain utterly indifferent to — and take no action bearing on — the morality of the community. The traditional description of state police power does embrace the regulation of morals as well as the health, safety, and general welfare of the citizenry. [But] the State's interest in regulating morality by suppressing obscenity, while often asserted, remains essentially unfocused and ill defined. And, since the attempt to curtail unprotected speech necessarily spills over into the area of protected speech, the effort to serve this speculative interest through the suppression of obscene material must tread heavily on rights protected by the First Amendment. . . .

In short, while I cannot say that the interests of the State — apart from the question of juveniles and unconsenting adults — are trivial or nonexistent, I am compelled to conclude that these interests cannot justify the substantial damage to constitutional rights and to this Nation's judicial machinery that inevitably results from state efforts to bar the distribution even of unprotected material to consenting adults. [I] would hold, therefore, that at least in the absence of distribution to juveniles or obtrusive exposure to unconsenting adults, the First and Fourteenth Amendments prohibit the State and Federal Governments from attempting wholly to suppress sexually oriented materials on the basis of their allegedly "obscene" contents. Nothing in this approach precludes those governments from taking action to serve what may be strong and legitimate interests through regulation of the manner of distribution of sexually oriented material. . . .

Difficult questions must still be faced, notably in the areas of distribution to juveniles and offensive exposure to unconsenting adults. Whatever the extent of state power to regulate in those areas, it should be clear that the view I espouse today would introduce a large measure of clarity to this troubled area, would reduce the institutional pressure on [the] Judiciary, and would guarantee fuller

---

26. Indeed, since *Stanley* was decided, [the] President's Commission on Obscenity and Pornography has concluded:

In sum, empirical research designed to clarify the question has found no evidence to date that exposure to explicit sexual materials plays a significant role in the causation of delinquent or criminal behavior among youth or adults. The Commission cannot conclude that exposure to erotic materials is a factor in the causation of sex crime or sex delinquency. . . .

freedom of expression while leaving room for the protection of legitimate governmental interests. . . .

Note: The 1973 Reformulation and Its Aftermath

1. Miller *and* Roth. Does the *Miller* reformulation constitute a "rejection of the fundamental first amendment premises" of *Roth*? Does its elimination of the "utterly without redeeming social value" criterion fatally undermine the notion that obscenity is of only "low" first amendment value?

2. Miller *and vagueness.* Is the *Miller* reformulation likely significantly to reduce the problems generated by the prior vagueness of the definition of obscenity? It is noteworthy that since *Miller* the Court has made clear that the two "plain examples" offered in *Miller* of the sorts of "sexual conduct" that might constitutionally be deemed "patently offensive" are not exhaustive. See Splawn v. California, 431 U.S. 595 (1977) (reaffirming the holding in *Ginzburg* that "evidence of pandering to prurient interests [is] relevant in determining whether the material is obscene").

Are there any limits on the sorts of "sexual conduct" that might constitutionally be deemed "patently offensive"? In Jenkins v. Georgia, 418 U.S. 153 (1974), the Court, in an opinion by Justice Rehnquist, overturned a state court determination that the highly acclaimed movie Carnal Knowledge was obscene. The Court explained that *Miller* "intended to fix substantive constitutional limitations, deriving from the First Amendment, on the type of material subject to [a determination of patent offensiveness]." As an example, the Court observed that "it would be wholly at odds with this aspect of *Miller* to uphold an obscenity conviction based upon a defendant's depiction of a woman with a bare midriff." As for Carnal Knowledge, the Court noted that "our own viewing of the film satisfies us that [it] could not be found under the *Miller* standards to depict sexual conduct in a patently offensive way." The Court explained that, "while the subject of the picture is, in a broader sense, sex, and there are scenes in which sexual conduct including 'ultimate sexual acts' is to be understood to be taking place, the camera does not focus on the bodies of the actors at such times. There is no exhibition of the actor's genitals, lewd or otherwise, during these scenes. There are occasional scenes of nudity, but nudity alone is not enough to make material legally obscene under the *Miller* standards." Thus, "the film could not, as a matter of constitutional law, be found to depict sexual conduct in a patently offensive way, [and] is therefore not outside the protection of the First and Fourteenth Amendments because it is obscene."

3. *Local versus national standards.* What interests are furthered by the Court's conclusion in *Miller* that "appeal to prurient interest" and "patent offensiveness" may be determined according to local rather than national standards? Consider the following objections to local standards:

a. Smith v. United States, 431 U.S. 291, 313-315 (1977) (Stevens, J., dissenting):

The geographic boundaries of [a local] community are not easily defined. They are [thus] subject to elastic adjustment to suit the needs of the prosecutor. Moreover, although a substantial body of evidence and decisional law concerning the content of a national standard could have evolved through its consistent use, the derivation of the relevant community standard for each of our countless communities is necessarily dependent on the perceptions of the individuals who happen to compose the jury in a given case.

b. Hamling v. United States, 418 U.S. 87, 144-145 (1974) (Brennan, J., dissenting):

Under [a local standards approach national] distributors [will] be forced to cope with the community standards of every hamlet into which their goods may wander. [Because] these variegated standards are impossible to discern, national distributors, fearful of risking the expense and difficulty of defending against prosecution in any of several remote communities, must inevitably [retreat] to debilitating self-censorship. [As a result], the people of many communities will be "protected" far beyond government's constitutional power to deny them access to sexually oriented materials.

c. Note, Community Standards, Class Actions, and Obscenity under Miller v. California, 88 Harv. L. Rev. 1838, 1844 (1975):

The trier of fact discretion *Miller* permits, in effect, reverses *Redrup's* institutional distortion. Direct appellate review of findings of prurient appeal and patent offensiveness becomes impossible. If the trier of fact is free to identify and apply [local] community standards, [an] appellate court is left without benchmarks by which to judge the validity of a finding of prurient appeal and patent offensiveness.

4. *Local standards: post-*Miller *decisions.* The Court has handed down several post-*Miller* rulings concerning local standards. See *Jenkins,* supra (in a state obscenity prosecution, jurors need not "apply the standards of a hypothetical statewide community," but may "rely on their understanding of community from which they come"); Hamling v. United States, 418 U.S. 87 (1974) (in a federal obscenity prosecution, jurors need not rely on national standards, but may rely on their "knowledge of the community or vicinage" from which they come); *Paris Adult Theatre,* supra (the first amendment does not "require 'expert' affirmative evidence that the materials [are] obscene when the materials themselves [are] actually placed in evidence"); Pope v. Illinois, 481 U.S. 497 (1987) (a trial court may not use community standards to decide whether a work lacks serious literary, artistic, political, or scientific value, for "the value of a work does not vary from community to community").

5. *Intent.* What state of mind must the seller or distributor have in an obscenity prosecution? As the incitement and libel cases make clear, intent can play a central role in "definitional" balancing and can do much to reduce problems caused by the vagueness of the underlying concepts.

In Smith v. California, 361 U.S. 147 (1959), appellant was convicted of violating a city ordinance construed by the state courts as imposing strict liability on the proprietor of any bookstore who possessed in his store any book later judicially determined to be obscene — even if the proprietor had no personal knowledge of the contents of the book. The Court held the imposition of strict liability invalid. This feature of the ordinance, the Court noted, "tends to impose a severe limitation on the public's access to constitutionally protected matter. For if the bookseller is criminally liable without knowledge of the contents [he] will tend to restrict the books he sells to those he has inspected." Such a state of affairs would generate a "self-censorship [affecting] the whole public."

In Hamling v. United States, supra, the Court approved a jury instruction to the effect that, in order to satisfy its burden on intent, the prosecution need only prove that the defendants "knew that [the] packages containing the subject materials were mailed [and] that they had knowledge of the character of the materials." The Court explained that the prosecution did not need to prove that the defendants knew that the materials were obscene because to "require proof of a defendant's knowledge of the legal status of the materials would permit the defendant to avoid prosecution by simply claiming that he had not brushed up on the law." Is this reconcilable with the Court's analysis of intent in the libel context? Consider Lockhart, Escape from the Chill of Uncertainty: Explicit Sex and the First Amendment, 9 Ga. L. Rev. 533, 563 (1975): "My suggestion is that [the first amendment establishes] as a defense to a criminal obscenity prosecution that the defendant *reasonably believed* that the material involved was not obscene." See also United States v. X-Citement Video, Inc., 513 U.S. 64 (1994) (interpreting the federal Protection of Children against Sexual Exploitation Act as requiring the government to prove that the defendant "knew" of the minority status of the performers and of the sexually explicit nature of the material in order to avoid "serious constitutional doubts").

6. *The regulation of obscenity.* The procedural issues involved in the regulation of obscenity have proved especially difficult. See, e.g., Times Film Corp. v. Chicago, 365 U.S. 43 (1961) (licensing); Bantam Books v. Sullivan, 372 U.S. 58 (1963) (blacklisting); *Paris Adult Theatre,* supra (injunction); Heller v. New York, 413 U.S. 483 (1973) (search and seizure); Alexander v. United States, 509 U.S. 544 (1993) (forfeiture).

NEW YORK v. FERBER, 458 U.S. 747 (1982). Ferber, the proprietor of a Manhattan bookstore specializing in sexually oriented products, was prosecuted for selling two films to an undercover police officer. The films were devoted almost entirely to depicting young boys masturbating. A jury held that the films were not obscene, but convicted Ferber of violating a New York statute prohibiting any person knowingly to produce, promote, direct, exhibit, or sell any material depicting a "sexual performance" by a child under the age of sixteen. The statute defined "sexual performance" as any performance that includes "actual or simulated sexual intercourse, deviate sexual intercourse, sexual bestiality, masturbation, sado-masochistic abuse, or lewd exhibition of the genitals." The Court unanimously upheld the conviction. Justice White delivered the opinion:

"In [the *Chaplinsky* dictum], the Court laid the foundation for the excision of obscenity from the realm of constitutionally protected expression. [For the following reasons, we are persuaded that pornographic depiction of children, like obscenity, is unprotected by the first amendment.]

"First. It is evident beyond the need for elaboration that a state's interest in 'safeguarding the physical and psychological well being of a minor' is 'compelling.' [The] use of children as subjects of pornographic materials is harmful to the physiological, emotional, and mental health of the child.

"Second. The distribution of photographs and films depicting sexual activity by juveniles is intrinsically related to the sexual abuse of children in at least two ways. First, the materials produced are a permanent record of the children's participation and the harm to the child is exacerbated by their circulation. Second, the distribution network for child pornography must be closed if the production of material which requires the sexual exploitation of children is to be effectively controlled. . . .

"Third. The advertising and selling of child pornography provides an economic motive for and is thus an integral part of the production of such materials, an activity illegal throughout the nation. [Were] the statutes outlawing the employment of children in these films and photographs fully effective, and the constitutionality of these laws have not been questioned, the First Amendment implications would be no greater than that presented by laws against distribution: enforceable production laws would leave no child pornography to be marketed.

"Fourth. The value of permitting live performances and photographic reproductions of children engaged in lewd sexual conduct is exceedingly modest, if not de minimis. We consider it unlikely that visual depictions of children performing sexual acts or lewdly exhibiting their genitals would often constitute an important and necessary part of a literary performance or scientific or educational work. [If] it were necessary for literary or artistic value, a person over the statutory age who perhaps looked younger could be utilized. Simulation outside of the prohibition of the statute could provide another alternative. Nor is there any question here of censoring a particular literary theme or portrayal of sexual activity. The First Amendment interest is limited to that of rendering the portrayal somewhat more 'realistic' by utilizing or photographing children.

"Fifth. Recognizing and classifying child pornography as a category of material outside the protection of the First Amendment is not incompatible with our earlier decisions. [It] is not rare that a content-based classification of speech has been accepted because it may be appropriately generalized that within the confines of the given classification, the evil to be restricted so overwhelmingly outweighs the expressive interests, if any, at stake, that no process of case-by-case adjudication is required. . . .

"There are, of course, limits on the category of child pornography which, like obscenity, is unprotected by the First Amendment. As with all legislation in this sensitive area, the conduct to be prohibited must be adequately defined by the applicable state law, as written or authoritatively construed. [The] test for child pornography is separate from the obscenity standard enunciated in *Miller*, but may be compared to it for purpose of clarity. The *Miller* formulation is adjusted in the following respects: A trier of fact need not find that the material appeals to the prurient interest of the average person; it is not required that sexual conduct portrayed be done so in a patently offensive manner; and the material at issue need not be considered as a whole. . . .

"It remains to address the claim that the New York statute is unconstitutionally overbroad because it would forbid the distribution of material with serious literary, scientific, or educational value or material which does not threaten the harms sought to be combated by the State. [The New York Court of Appeals, which invalidated the statute,] was understandably concerned that some protected expression, ranging from medical textbooks to pictorials in National Geographic would fall prey to the statute. [Yet] we seriously doubt, and it has not been suggested, that these arguably impermissible applications of the statute amount to more than a tiny fraction of the materials within the statute's reach. [Under] these circumstances, [the statute] is 'not substantially overbroad and whatever overbreadth exists should be cured through case-by-case analysis of the fact situations to which its sanctions, assertedly, may not be applied.' [Broadrick v. Oklahoma, section C1 supra]. As applied to [Ferber] and to others who distribute similar material, the statute does not violate the First Amendment. . . ."

Justice O'Connor filed a concurring opinion: "Although I join the Court's opinion, I write separately to stress that the Court does not hold that New York must except 'material with serious literary, scientific or educational value' from its statute. [The] compelling interests identified in today's opinion suggest that the Constitution might in fact permit New York to ban knowing distribution of works depicting minors engaged in explicit sexual conduct, regardless of the social value of the depictions."

Justice Brennan, joined by Justice Marshall, concurred in the judgment: "I agree with much of what is said in the Court's opinion. [I would make clear, however, that] application of [the New York statute] to depictions of children that in themselves do have serious literary, artistic, scientific, or medical value [would] violate the First Amendment. As the Court recognizes, the limited classes of speech, the suppression of which does not raise serious First Amendment concerns, have two attributes. They are of exceedingly 'slight social value,' and the State has a compelling interest in their regulation. See [Chaplinsky]. The First Amendment value of depictions of children that are in themselves serious contributions to art, literature or science, is, by definition, simply not de minimis. At the same time, the State's interest in suppression of such materials is likely to be far less compelling. For the Court's assumption of harm to the child resulting from the 'permanent record' and 'circulation' of the child's 'participation' [lacks] much of its force where the depiction is a serious contribution to art or science."

Justice Stevens filed an opinion concurring in the judgment. Justice Blackmun concurred in the result.

Should the Court have analyzed the New York statute not as a content-based restriction of "unprotected" speech but as a content-neutral restriction of the "means" of expression? Consider the following propositions: (1) There is no first amendment right to violate an otherwise valid criminal law that is unrelated to the suppression of free expression merely because the violation would render one's speech more effective. Cf. United States v. O'Brien, section E3 infra. Recall the *Pentagon Papers* case, section B4 supra. Could the government have punished Daniel Ellsberg for "stealing" the Pentagon Papers? (2) There is no first amendment right to depict the commission of a criminal act where the crime was committed solely to produce the depiction.

Suppose a film depicts *simulated* sex between an adult and a child but was made entirely with adult actors. Can it be prohibited after *Ferber* on the ground that its exhibition will encourage pederasty? What about an animated film?

In Osborne v. Ohio, 495 U.S. 103 (1990), the Court held that Stanley v. Georgia does not extend to the private possession of child pornography. The Court, in an opinion by Justice White, explained: "[T]he interests underlying child pornography prohibitions far exceed the interests justifying [the] law at issue in *Stanley*. [In] *Stanley*, Georgia primarily sought to proscribe the private possession of obscenity because it was concerned that obscenity will poison the mind of its viewers. [The] difference here is obvious: the State does not rely on a paternalistic interest in regulating [the defendant's] mind. Rather, [the law is designed] to protect the victims of child pornography; it hopes to destroy a national market for the exploitative use of children." Justices Brennan, Marshall, and Stevens dissented.

5.   The Lewd, the Profane, and the Indecent

In what circumstances, if any, may government restrict the public use of profane or sexually oriented, but nonobscene, expression because of its highly offensive character? Recall that in *Chaplinsky* the Court's list of utterances ("the prevention and punishment of which have never been thought to raise any Constitutional problem") expressly included not only "fighting words," the "libelous," and the "obscene," but also the "lewd" and the "profane." Moreover, in explaining why such utterances are "unprotected," the Court noted not only that they might "tend to incite an immediate breach of the peace," but also that they might "by their very utterance inflict injury."

Cohen v. California
403 U.S. 15 (1971)

MR. JUSTICE HARLAN delivered the opinion of the Court.

This case may seem at first blush too inconsequential to find its way into our books, but the issue it presents is of no small constitutional significance.

Appellant Paul Robert Cohen was convicted in the Los Angeles Municipal Court of violating that part of California Penal Code §415 which prohibits "maliciously and willfully disturb[ing] the peace or quiet of any neighborhood or person . . . by . . . offensive conduct. . . ." He was given 30 days' imprisonment. The facts upon which his conviction rests are detailed in the opinion of the [state court]:

> On April 26, 1968, the defendant was observed in the Los Angeles County Courthouse in the corridor outside [of] the municipal court wearing a jacket bearing the words "Fuck the Draft." There were women and children present in the corridor. The defendant was arrested. The defendant testified that he wore the jacket [as] a means of informing the public of the depth of his feelings against the Vietnam War and the draft.
>
> The defendant did not engage in, nor threaten to engage in, nor did anyone as the result of his conduct in fact commit or threaten to commit any act of violence. The defendant did not make any loud or unusual noise, nor was there any evidence that he uttered any sound prior to his arrest. . . .

[We reverse.]

I

In order to lay hands on the precise issue which this case involves, it is useful first to canvass various matters which this record does *not* present.

The conviction quite clearly rests upon the asserted offensiveness of the *words* Cohen used, [for] the State certainly lacks power to punish Cohen for [the] message the inscription conveyed. [Moreover], this is not [an] obscenity case. Whatever else may be necessary to give rise to the States' broader power to prohibit obscene expression, such expression must be, in some significant way, erotic. [*Roth.*] It cannot plausibly be maintained that this vulgar allusion to the Selective Service System would conjure up such psychic stimulation in anyone likely to be confronted with Cohen's crudely defaced jacket.

This Court has [held] that the States are free to [ban] so-called "fighting words," those personally abusive epithets which, when addressed to the ordinary citizen, [are] inherently likely to provoke violent reaction. [*Chaplinsky.*] While the four-letter word displayed by Cohen in relation to the draft is not uncommonly employed in a personally provocative fashion, in this instance it was clearly not "directed to the person of the hearer." [No] individual actually or likely to be present could reasonably have regarded the words on appellant's jacket as a direct personal insult. Nor do we have here an instance of the exercise of the State's police power to prevent a speaker from intentionally provoking a given group to hostile reaction. Cf. [*Feiner*]. There [is] no showing that anyone who saw Cohen was in fact violently aroused or that appellant intended such a result.

Finally, in arguments before this Court much has been made of the claim that Cohen's distasteful mode of expression was thrust upon unwilling or unsuspecting viewers, and that the State might therefore legitimately act as it did in order to protect the sensitive from otherwise unavoidable exposure to appellant's crude form of protest. Of course, the mere presumed presence of unwitting listeners or viewers does not serve automatically to justify curtailing all speech capable of giving offense. [While] this Court has recognized that government may properly act in many situations to prohibit intrusion into the privacy of the home of unwelcome views and ideas which cannot be totally banned from the public dialogue, e.g., Rowan v. Post Office Dept., 397 U.S. 728 (1970), we have at the same time consistently stressed that "we are often 'captives' outside the sanctuary of the home and subject to objectionable speech." [The] ability of government, consonant with the Constitution, to shut off discourse solely to protect others from hearing it is, in other words, dependent upon a showing that substantial privacy interests are being invaded in an essentially intolerable manner. Any broader view of this authority would effectively empower a majority to silence dissidents simply as a matter of personal predilections.

In this regard, persons confronted with Cohen's jacket were in a quite different posture than, say, those subjected to the raucous emissions of sound trucks blaring outside their residences. Those in the Los Angeles courthouse could effectively avoid further bombardment of their sensibilities simply by averting their eyes. And, while it may be that one has a more substantial claim to a recognizable privacy interest when walking through a courthouse corridor than, for example, strolling through Central Park, surely it is nothing like the interest in being free from unwanted expression in the confines of one's own home. . . .

II

Against this background, the issue flushed by this case stands out in bold relief. It is whether California can excise, as "offensive conduct," one particular scurrilous epithet from the public discourse, either upon the theory [that] its use is inherently likely to cause violent reaction or upon a more general assertion that the States, acting as guardians of public morality, may properly remove this offensive word from the public vocabulary.

The [first rationale] is plainly untenable. At most it reflects an "undifferentiated fear or apprehension of disturbance [which] is not enough to overcome the right to freedom of expression." [We] have been shown no evidence that substantial numbers of citizens are standing ready to strike out physically at whoever may assault their sensibilities with execrations like that uttered by Cohen. There may be some persons about with such lawless and violent proclivities, but that is an insufficient base upon which to erect, consistently with constitutional values, a governmental power to force persons who wish to ventilate their dissident views into avoiding particular forms of expression. The argument amounts to little more than the self-defeating proposition that to avoid physical censorship of one who has not sought to provoke such a response by a hypothetical coterie of the violent and lawless, the States may more appropriately effectuate that censorship themselves. . . .

Admittedly, it is not so obvious that the First and Fourteenth Amendments must be taken to disable the States from punishing public utterance of this unseemly expletive in order to maintain what they regard as a suitable level of discourse within the body politic. We think, however, that examination and reflection will reveal the shortcomings of a contrary viewpoint.

At the outset, we cannot overemphasize that, in our judgment, most situations where the State has a justifiable interest in regulating speech will fall within one or more of the various established exceptions, discussed above but not applicable here, to the usual rule that governmental bodies may not prescribe the form or content of individual expression. Equally important to our conclusion is the constitutional backdrop against which our decision must be made. The constitutional right of free expression is powerful medicine in a society as diverse and populous as ours. It is designed and intended to remove governmental restraints from the arena of public discussion, putting the decision as to what views shall be voiced largely into the hands of each of us, in the hope that use of such freedom will ultimately produce a more capable citizenry and more perfect polity and in the belief that no other approach would comport with the premise of individual dignity and choice upon which our political system rests. See [*Whitney* (Brandeis, J., concurring)].

To many, the immediate consequence of this freedom may often appear to be only verbal tumult, discord, and even offensive utterance. These are, however, within established limits, in truth necessary side effects of the broader enduring values which the process of open debate permits us to achieve. That the air may at times seem filled with verbal cacophony is, in this sense not a sign of weakness but of strength. We cannot lose sight of the fact that, in what otherwise might seem a trifling and annoying instance of individual distasteful abuse of a privilege, these fundamental societal values are truly implicated. . . .

Against this perception of the constitutional policies involved, we discern certain more particularized considerations that peculiarly call for reversal of this conviction. First, the principle contended for by the State seems inherently boundless. How is one to distinguish this from any other offensive word? Surely the State has no right to cleanse public debate to the point where it is grammatically palatable to the most squeamish among us. Yet no readily ascertainable general principle exists for stopping short of that result were we to affirm the judgment below. For, while the particular four-letter word being litigated here is perhaps more distasteful than most others of its genre, it is nevertheless often true that one man's vulgarity is another's lyric. Indeed, we think it is largely because governmental officials cannot make principled distinctions in this area that the Constitution leaves matters of taste and style so largely to the individual.

Additionally, we cannot overlook the fact, because it is well illustrated by the episode involved here, that much linguistic expression serves a dual communicative function: it conveys not only ideas capable of relatively precise, detached explication, but otherwise inexpressible emotions as well. In fact, words are often chosen as much for their emotive as their cognitive force. We cannot sanction the view that the Constitution, while solicitous of the cognitive content of individual speech, has little or no regard for that emotive function which, practically speaking, may often be the more important element of the overall message sought to be communicated. . . .

Finally, and in the same vein, we cannot indulge the facile assumption that one can forbid particular words without also running a substantial risk of suppressing ideas in the process. Indeed, governments might soon seize upon the censorship of particular words as a convenient guise for banning the expression of unpopular views. We have been able, as noted above, to discern little social benefit that might result from running the risk of opening the door to such grave results.

It is, in sum, our judgment that, absent a more particularized and compelling reason for its actions, the State may not, consistently with the First and Fourteenth Amendments, make the simple public display here involved of this single four-letter expletive a criminal offense. . . .

Reversed.

MR. JUSTICE BLACKMUN, with whom THE CHIEF JUSTICE and MR. JUSTICE BLACK join.

I dissent. . . .

Cohen's absurd and immature antic, in my view, was mainly conduct and little speech. [Further,] the case appears to me to be well within the sphere of [*Chaplinsky*], where Mr. Justice Murphy, a known champion of First Amendment freedoms, wrote for a unanimous bench. As a consequence, this Court's agonizing over First Amendment values seems misplaced and unnecessary.

[Justice White dissented on other grounds.]

Note: *Profanity*, Cohen, *and the Captive Audience*

1. *Profanity as "low" value speech.* Does *Cohen* repudiate *Chaplinsky's* assumption that profanity is of only "low" first amendment value? If obscenity has "no redeeming social value," why isn't the same true of profanity? Consider the following proposition: Profanity has "high" first amendment value because (a) its use may be necessary to convey "otherwise inexpressible emotions," (b) its suppression creates "a substantial risk of suppressing ideas in the process," and (c) there exists "no readily ascertainable general principle" for distinguishing between prohibitable and nonprohibitable offensive language.

Consider W. Berns, The First Amendment and the Future of American Democracy 200 (1976):

> This country managed to live most of its years under rules, conventional and legal, that forbade the public use of profanity [and] it would be an abuse of language to say that its freedom was thereby restricted in any important respect. Now, suddenly, and for reasons that ought to persuade no one, we are told that it is a violation of the First Amendment for the law to enforce these rules; that however desirable it might be to see them preserved, there is no way for the law to do this except by threatening the freedom of all speech. [Do] we really live in a world so incapable of communication that it can be said that "one man's vulgarity is another's lyric"?

2. *Profanity and fighting words.* As evident in *Chaplinsky*, the problems of fighting words and profanity are closely related. In *Cohen*, however, the Court "made clear that [the phrase 'fighting words'] was no longer to be understood as a euphemism for controversial or dirty talk but was to require instead a quite unambiguous invitation to a brawl." J. Ely, Democracy and Distrust 114 (1980). The Court thus recognized in *Cohen* that the fighting words and profanity problems are analytically distinct — although fighting words typically involve the use of profanity, this is not essential; although fighting words usually involve insults directed personally to the addressee, the problem of profanity is not so limited; and although the fighting words doctrine is designed primarily to forestall an addressee's violent response, government efforts to suppress offensive language are designed primarily to raise the level of public discourse and to protect the sensibilities of an unconsenting audience. The fighting words doctrine is examined in section B3 supra.

3. *Profanity: manner or content?* Is a law restricting the use of profanity in public more akin to a law restricting the public expression of an "offensive" idea or to a law restricting the use of an "offensive" means of expression? Compare, for example, a law prohibiting the expression of "offensive ideas" in a public park, a law prohibiting the use of profanity in a public park, and a law prohibiting the use of loudspeakers in a public park. Is the prohibition on profanity more akin to the prohibition on loudspeakers because both are directed against "consequences unrelated" to the particular ideas expressed? Cox, Foreword: Freedom of Expression in the Burger Court, 94 Harv. L. Rev. 1, 40 (1980). Is it more akin to the prohibition on "offensive ideas" because the "harms of shock and offense [flow] entirely from the communicative content of [the] message"? Ely, supra, at 114.

Consider the following views:

a. Haiman, Speech v. Privacy: Is There a Right Not to Be Spoken To?, 67 Nw. U.L. Rev. 153, 189 (1972):

> The problem with the position [that prohibitions on the use of profanity are merely restrictions on the manner of expression] is that the form and content of communications are so inextricably tied that to control the former is, in fact, to modify the latter. [For] example, it can hardly be maintained that phrases like, "Repeal the Draft," "Resist the Draft," or "The Draft Must Go" convey essentially the same message as "Fuck the Draft." Clearly something is lost in the translation.

b. Stone, Content Regulation and the First Amendment, 25 Wm. & Mary L. Rev. 189, 243-244 (1983):

Governmental efforts to limit speech because it is offensively *noisy* [do] not implicate the same kind of censorial or heckler's veto concerns as governmental efforts
to limit speech because the *ideas* are offensive. Analytically, offense at language is
more like offense at noise than offense at ideas. [Moreover, although] restrictions
on the use of profanity may affect some speakers more than others, [this] is also true
of most content-neutral restrictions.

4. *The captive audience.* Does Justice Harlan undervalue the interests of the
"audience" in *Cohen?* Consider A. Bickel, The Morality of Consent 72 (1975):
"There is such a thing as verbal violence, a kind of cursing, assaultive speech that
amounts to almost physical aggression. [The sort of speech at issue in *Cohen*]
constitutes an assault." As noted in *Chaplinsky,* such profanities "by their very utterance inflict injury." Why, then, can't such expression be suppressed? Is the interest in protecting the sensibilities of unconsenting individuals against such "assaults" simply too insubstantial to justify restrictions on "offensive" expression?
Note Justice Harlan's conclusion in *Cohen* that "[t]he ability of government [to]
shut off discourse solely to protect others from hearing it is [dependent] upon a
showing that substantial privacy interests are being invaded in an essentially intolerable manner." For analysis of the *Cohen* standard, see Stone, Fora Americana: Speech in Public Places, 1974 Sup. Ct. Rev. 233, 262-272.
   Consider the following:
   a. Suppose Congress enacts a law authorizing any homeowner who no longer
wishes to receive mail from a particular person or organization to instruct the
Postmaster General to direct that person or organization to refrain from further
mailings to the homeowner. Consider Rowan v. Post Office Department, 397
U.S. 728 (1970):

In today's complex society we are inescapably captive audiences for many purposes,
but a sufficient measure of individual autonomy must survive to permit every
householder to exercise control over unwanted mail. To make the householder the
exclusive and final judge of what will cross his threshold undoubtedly has the effect
of impeding the flow of ideas, information, and arguments that, ideally, he should
receive and consider. [But] nothing in the Constitution compels us to listen to or
view any unwanted communication, whatever its merit. [The] ancient concept
that "a man's home is his castle" into which "not even the king may enter" has lost
none of its vitality, [and we] therefore categorically reject the argument that [an in-
dividual] has a right under the Constitution [to] send unwanted material into the
home of another.

   b. Suppose Congress enacts a law prohibiting any person to mail to another
any materials containing profanity or photographs revealing bare human pubic
areas without the recipient's prior written consent. In Bolger v. Youngs Drug
Products Corp., 463 U.S. 60 (1983), the Court invalidated a federal statute prohibiting the mailing of unsolicited advertisements for contraceptives. The Court
explained:

We [have] recognized the important interest in allowing addressees to give notice
to a mailer that they wish no further mailings [citing *Rowan*]. But we have never
held that the government itself can shut off the flow of mailings to protect those
recipients who might potentially be offended. The First Amendment "does not
permit the government to prohibit speech as intrusive unless the 'captive' audi-

ence cannot avoid objectionable speech." [The] "short, regular, journey from mail box to trash can [is] an acceptable burden, at least so far as the Constitution is concerned."

See also Consolidated Edison v. Public Service Commission, 447 U.S. 530 (1980) (invalidating a rule prohibiting public utility companies from including in their monthly bills inserts discussing controversial issues).

In light of *Rowan* and *Bolger,* could Congress constitutionally require all televisions to have a chip that enables the owner to block out unwanted channels or shows? Could it constitutionally require all televisions to have a chip that enables the owner to block out only unwanted channels or shows that are rated as especially violent? Consider Balkin, Media Filters, the V-Chip, and the Foundations of Broadcast Regulation, 45 Duke L.J. 1131, 1165, 1168 (1996):

[The] development of a ratings system poses a [significant] constitutional problem. [The] regulatory apparatus surrounding the V-chip will work an enormous new delegation of information filtering to a centralized bureaucracy, whether one operated by the federal government or [by] private industry. [While] overt expressions of homophobia are likely to remain uncoded, overt homosexual expressions of affection will probably be among the first to be coded as inappropriate for children, [and the] very assumption that exposure to racist messages is less harmful to our children [than] exposure to violence [or indecency] already carries considerable political freight. [And the] more the [government] becomes involved in the ratings system, the more heavily that system will become politicized.

c. Suppose a city operates a public bus system and each bus contains twenty interior advertising spaces available for lease by private persons. May the city, to protect the sensibilities of "captive" commuters, exclude such "highly offensive" messages as "Welfare Is Black Theft," "God Is Dead," and "Abortion Is Murder"? Is this a situation in which, as in *Cohen,* the audience "could effectively avoid further bombardment of their sensibilities simply by averting their eyes"? Suppose the city excludes ads that contain profanity? Nudity? Cf. Lehman v. City of Shaker Heights, 418 U.S. 298 (1974) (plurality opinion upholding city policy permitting the display of commercial but not generally more "controversial" political or public issue advertisements in the interior of city buses), section E2c infra. Note that in the bus situation, unlike the situation in *Cohen,* the city could protect the "captive" audience by adopting a content-neutral restriction banning *all* speech. Is a content-neutral restriction preferable to a "narrower" restriction based on content? Consider Stone, supra, at 280: "If a 'true' captive audience exists, the state may protect the sensibilities of unwilling listeners by banning all speech, regardless of content. It should never, however, be permitted to use the captive audience as a lever for censorship." Should that conclusion, however justified as applied to offensive ideas, apply also to the use of profanity and to the display of "lewd" pictures?

ERZNOZNIK v. JACKSONVILLE, 422 U.S. 205 (1975). In *Erznoznik,* the Court invalidated a Jacksonville, Florida, ordinance that declared it a public nuisance for any drive-in movie theater to exhibit any motion picture "in which the human male or female bare buttocks, human female bare breasts, or human bare pubic areas are shown, if such motion picture [is] visible from any public street or place." Justice Powell delivered the opinion of the Court:

"[The city] concedes that its ordinance sweeps far beyond the permissible restraints on obscenity [and] thus applies to films that are protected by the First Amendment. [Nevertheless], it maintains that any movie containing nudity which is visible from a public place may be suppressed as a nuisance. . . .

"[The city's] primary argument is that it may protect its citizens against unwilling exposure to materials that may be offensive. Jacksonville's ordinance, however, does not protect citizens from all movies that might offend; rather it singles out films containing nudity, presumably because the lawmakers considered them especially offensive to passersby. [A] State or municipality may protect individual privacy by enacting reasonable time, place, and manner regulations applicable to all speech irrespective of content. [But] when government [undertakes] selectively to shield the public from some kinds of speech on the ground that they are more offensive than others, the First Amendment strictly limits its power. [Such] selective exclusions have been upheld only when the speaker intrudes on the privacy of the home, see [Rowan], or the degree of captivity makes it impractical for the unwilling viewer or auditor to avoid exposure. See [Lehman]. [Absent such circumstances, however], the burden normally falls upon the viewer to 'avoid further bombardment of [his] sensibilities simply by averting [his] eyes.'[Cohen.] [The] limited privacy interest of persons on the public streets cannot justify this censorship of otherwise protected speech on the basis of its content. . . .

"[The city] also attempts to support the ordinance as an exercise of the city's undoubted police power to protect children. [But] the ordinance is not directed [only] against sexually explicit [nudity]. Rather, it sweepingly forbids display of all films containing *any* uncovered buttocks or breasts, irrespective of context or pervasiveness. [Clearly] all nudity cannot be deemed obscene even as to minors. [Thus], if Jacksonville's ordinance is intended to regulate expression accessible to minors it is overbroad in its proscription. . . .

"[Finally, the city attempts] to justify the ordinance [on the ground] that nudity on a drive-in movie screen distracts passing motorists, thus slowing the flow of traffic and increasing the likelihood of accidents. [But] the legislative classification is strikingly underinclusive. There is no reason to think that a wide variety of other scenes in the customary screen diet, ranging from soap opera to violence, would be any less distracting to the passing motorist."

Justice Douglas filed a concurring opinion.

Chief Justice Burger, joined by Justice Rehnquist, dissented: "Whatever validity the notion that passersby may protect their sensibilities by averting their eyes may have when applied to words printed on an individual's jacket, see [Cohen], it distorts reality to apply that notion to the outsize screen of a drive-in movie theater. Such screens [are] designed to [attract and hold] the attention of all observers. [It] is not unreasonable for lawmakers to believe that public nudity on a giant screen, visible at night to hundreds of [drivers], may have a tendency to divert attention from their task and cause accidents. [Moreover], those persons who legitimately desire to [view such films] are not foreclosed from doing so. [Such films may be] exhibited [in] indoor theaters [and in any] drive-in movie theater [whose] screen [is shielded] from public view. Thus, [the challenged] ordinance

[is] not a restriction of any 'message.' [The] First Amendment interests involved in this case are trivial at best."

Justice White also dissented.

FCC v. Pacifica Foundation

438 U.S. 726 (1978)

MR. JUSTICE STEVENS delivered the opinion of the Court [all but Part IVB] and an opinion in which THE CHIEF JUSTICE and MR. JUSTICE REHNQUIST joined [Part IVB].

This case requires that we decide whether the Federal Communications Commission has any power to regulate a radio broadcast that is indecent but not obscene.

A satiric humorist named George Carlin recorded a 12-minute monologue entitled "Filthy Words" before a live audience in a California theater. He began by referring to his thoughts about "the words you couldn't say on the public, ah, airwaves, um, the ones you definitely wouldn't say, ever." He proceeded to list those words and repeat them over and over again in a variety of colloquialisms.* The transcript of the recording [indicates] frequent laughter from the audience.

At about 2 o'clock in the afternoon on Tuesday, October 30, 1973, a New York radio station, owned by respondent Pacifica Foundation, broadcast the "Filthy Words" monologue. A few weeks later a man, who stated that he had heard the broadcast while driving with his young son, wrote a letter complaining to the Commission. . . .

The complaint was forwarded to the station for comment. In its response, Pacifica explained that the monologue had been played during a program about contemporary society's attitude toward language and that, immediately before its broadcast, listeners had been advised that it included "sensitive language which might be regarded as offensive to some." Pacifica characterized George Carlin as "a significant social satirist" who "[is] not mouthing obscenities, [but] using words to satirize as harmless and essentially silly our attitudes towards those words." Pacifica stated that it was not aware of any other complaints about the broadcast. [The] Commission issued a declaratory order granting the complaint. [It] did not impose formal sanctions, but it did state that the [complaint] would be "associated with the station's license [file]." . . .

The Commission characterized the language used in the Carlin monologue as "patently offensive," though not necessarily obscene, and expressed the opinion that it should be regulated by principles analogous to those found in the law of nuisance where the

> law generally speaks to *channeling* behavior more than actually prohibiting it. [The] concept of "indecent" is intimately connected with the exposure of children to language that describes, in terms patently offensive as measured by contemporary community standards for the broadcast medium, sexual or excretory activities

---

*[According to Carlin, there are seven such words: "shit, piss, fuck, cunt, cocksucker, motherfucker, and tits. Those are the ones that will curve your spine [and] grow hair on your hands." — EDS.]

and organs, at times of the day when there is a reasonable risk that children may be in the audience. . . .

Applying these [considerations], the Commission concluded [that] the language as broadcast was indecent and prohibited by 18 U.S.C. [§]1464 [prohibiting the broadcasting of "obscene, indecent or profane language"]. . . .

The United States Court of Appeals for the District of Columbia Circuit reversed. [We reverse and thus sustain the Commission's action.]

IV

B

The question in this case is whether a broadcast of patently offensive words dealing with sex and excretion may be regulated because of its content.[18] Obscene materials have been denied the protection of the First Amendment because their content is so offensive to contemporary moral standards. [*Roth*.] But the fact that society may find speech offensive is not a sufficient reason for suppressing it. Indeed, if it is the speaker's opinion that gives offense, that consequence is a reason for according it constitutional protection. For it is a central tenet of the First Amendment that the government must remain neutral in the marketplace of ideas. If there were any reason to believe that the Commission's characterization of the Carlin monologue as offensive could be traced to its political content — or even to the fact that it satirized contemporary attitudes about four-letter words[22] — First Amendment protection might be required. But that is simply not this case. These words offend for the same reasons that obscenity offends.[23] Their place in the hierarchy of First Amendment values was aptly sketched by Mr. Justice Murphy when he said: "[S]uch utterances are no essential part of any exposition of ideas, and are of such slight social value as a step to truth that any benefit that may be derived from them is clearly outweighed by the social interest in order and morality." [*Chaplinsky*.]

Although these words ordinarily lack literary, political, or scientific value, they are not entirely outside the protection of the First Amendment. Some uses of even the most offensive words are unquestionably protected. [Indeed], we may

18. A requirement that indecent language be avoided will have its primary effect on the form, rather than the content, of serious communication. There are few, if any, thoughts that cannot be expressed by the use of less offensive language. [Relocated footnote — Eds.]

22. The monologue does present a point of view; it attempts to show that the words it uses are "harmless" and that our attitudes toward them are "essentially silly." [The] Commission objects, not to this point of view, but to the way in which it is expressed. The belief that these words are harmless does not necessarily confer a First Amendment privilege to use them while proselytizing, just as the conviction that obscenity is harmless does not license one to communicate that conviction by the indiscriminate distribution of an obscene leaflet.

23. The Commission stated: "Obnoxious, gutter language describing these matters has the effect of debasing and brutalizing human beings by reducing them to their mere bodily functions. . . ." Our society has a tradition of performing certain bodily functions in private, and of severely limiting the public exposure or discussion of such matters. Verbal or physical acts exposing those intimacies are offensive irrespective of any message that may accompany the exposure.

assume, arguendo, that this monologue would be protected in other contexts. Nonetheless, the constitutional protection accorded to a communication containing such patently offensive sexual and excretory language need not be the same in every context. It is a characteristic of speech such as this that both its capacity to offend and its "social value," to use Mr. Justice Murphy's term, vary with the circumstances. Words that are commonplace in one setting are shocking in another. To paraphrase Mr. Justice Harlan, one occasion's lyric is another's vulgarity. Cf. [*Cohen*].[25]

In this case it is undisputed that the content of Pacifica's broadcast was "vulgar," "offensive," and "shocking." Because content of that character is not entitled to absolute constitutional protection under all circumstances, we must consider its context in order to determine whether the Commission's action was constitutionally permissible.

C

We have long recognized that each medium of expression presents special First Amendment problems. [The] broadcast media have established a uniquely pervasive presence in the lives of all Americans. Patently offensive, indecent material presented over the airwaves confronts the citizen, not only in public, but also in the privacy of the home, where the individual's right to be left alone plainly outweighs the First Amendment rights of an intruder. [*Rowan.*] Because the broadcast audience is constantly tuning in and out, prior warnings cannot completely protect the listener or viewer from unexpected program content. To say that one may avoid further offense by turning off the radio when he hears indecent language is like saying that the remedy for an assault is to run away after the first blow.[27]

[Moreover], broadcasting is uniquely accessible to children, even those too young to read. Although Cohen's written message might have been incomprehensible to a first grader, Pacifica's broadcast could have enlarged a child's vocabulary in an instant. Other forms of offensive expression may be withheld from the young without restricting the expression at its source. Bookstores and motion picture theaters, for example, may be prohibited from making indecent material available to children. [Citing *Ginsberg*, section D4 supra.][28] The ease with which

---

25. The importance of context is illustrated by the *Cohen* case. [So] far as the evidence showed, no one in the courthouse was offended by his jacket. . . .

In holding that criminal sanctions could not be imposed on Cohen for his political statement in a public place, the Court rejected the argument that his speech would offend unwilling viewers; it noted that "there was no evidence that persons powerless to avoid [his] conduct did in fact object to it." [In] contrast, in this case the Commission was responding to a listener's strenuous complaint, and Pacifica does not question its determination that this afternoon broadcast was likely to offend listeners. It should be noted that the Commission imposed a far more moderate penalty on Pacifica than the state court imposed on Cohen. Even the strongest civil penalty at the Commission's command does not include criminal prosecution. . . .

27. Outside the home, the balance between the offensive speaker and the unwilling audience may sometimes tip in favor of the speaker, requiring the offended listener to turn away. See [*Erznoznik*].

28. The Commission's action does not by any means reduce adults to hearing only what is fit for children. Cf. [Butler v. Michigan, section D4 supra]. Adults who feel the need may purchase tapes and records or go to theaters and nightclubs to hear these words. In fact, the Commission has not unequivocally closed even broadcasting to speech of this sort; whether broadcast audi-

children may obtain access to broadcast material, coupled with the concerns recognized in *Ginsberg*, amply justify special treatment of indecent broadcasting.

It is appropriate, in conclusion, to emphasize the narrowness of our holding. This case does not involve a two-way radio conversation between a cab driver and a dispatcher, or a telecast of an Elizabethan comedy. We have not decided that an occasional expletive in either setting would justify any sanction or, indeed, that this broadcast would justify a criminal prosecution. The Commission's decision rested entirely on a nuisance rationale under which context is all-important. The concept requires consideration of a host of variables. The time of day was emphasized by the Commission. The content of the program in which the language is used will also affect the composition of the audience, and differences between radio, television, and perhaps closed-circuit transmissions, may also be relevant. As Mr. Justice Sutherland wrote, a "nuisance may be merely a right thing in the wrong place, — like a pig in the parlor instead of the barnyard." [We] simply hold that when the Commission finds that a pig has entered the parlor, the exercise of its regulatory power does not depend on proof that the pig is obscene.

[Reversed.]

MR. JUSTICE POWELL, with whom MR. JUSTICE BLACKMUN joins, concurring in part and concurring in the judgment. . . .

I [agree] with much that is said in Part IV of Mr. Justice Stevens' opinion, and with its conclusion that the Commission's holding in this case does not violate the First Amendment. Because I do not subscribe to all that is said in Part IV, however, I state my views separately. . . .

[The] Commission sought to "channel" the monologue to hours when the fewest unsupervised children would be exposed to it. [This] consideration provides strong support for the Commission's holding.

The Court has recognized society's right to "adopt more stringent controls on communicative materials available to youths than on those available to adults." [This] recognition stems in large part from the fact that "a child [is] not possessed of that full capacity for individual choice which is the presupposition of First Amendment guarantees." [At] the same time [offensive] speech may have a deeper and more lasting negative effect on a child than on an adult. . . .

The Commission properly held that [the] language involved in this case is as potentially degrading and harmful to children as representations of many erotic acts. In most instances, the dissemination of this kind of speech to children may be limited without also limiting willing adults' access to it. [The] difficulty is that such a physical separation of the audience cannot be accomplished in the broadcast media. [In] my view, the Commission was entitled to give substantial weight to this difference [between the broadcast and other media] in reaching its decision in this case.

A second difference [is] that broadcasting [comes] directly into the home, the one place where people ordinarily have the right not to be assaulted by uninvited and offensive sights and sounds. [This] is not to say [that] the Commission has an unrestricted license to decide what speech, protected in other media, may be

---

ences in the late evening contain so few children that playing this monologue would be permissible is an issue neither the Commission nor this Court has decided.

banned from the airwaves in order to protect unwilling adults from momentary exposure to it in their homes. Making the sensitive judgments required in these cases is not easy. But this responsibility has been reposed initially in the Commission, and its judgment is entitled to respect. [Moreover, the] Commission's holding does not prevent willing adults from purchasing Carlin's record, from attending his performances, or, indeed, from reading the transcript reprinted as an appendix to the Court's opinion. On its face, it does not prevent respondent Pacifica Foundation from broadcasting the monologue during late evening hours when fewer children are likely to be in the audience, nor from broadcasting discussions of the contemporary use of language at any time during the day. [On] the facts of this case, the Commission's order did not violate respondent's First Amendment rights. . . .

[I] do not join Part IV-B [of Justice Stevens' opinion] because I do not subscribe to the theory that the Justices of this Court are free generally to decide on the basis of its content which speech protected by the First Amendment is most "valuable" and hence deserving of the most protection, and which is less "valuable" and hence deserving of less protection. [In] my view, the result in this case does not turn on whether Carlin's monologue, viewed as a whole, or the words that constitute it, have more or less "value" than a candidate's campaign speech. This is a judgment for each person to make, not one for the judges to impose upon him.

The result turns instead on the unique characteristics of the broadcast media, combined with society's right to protect its children from speech generally agreed to be inappropriate for their years, and with the interest of unwilling adults in not being assaulted by such offensive speech in their homes. Moreover, I doubt whether today's decision will prevent any adult who wishes to receive Carlin's message in Carlin's own words from doing so. [These] are the grounds upon which I join the judgment of the Court as to Part IV.

MR. JUSTICE BRENNAN, with whom MR. JUSTICE MARSHALL joins, dissenting. . . .

Without question, the privacy interests of an individual in his home are substantial and deserving of significant protection. [But in] finding these interests sufficient to justify the content regulation of protected speech [the] Court misconceives the nature of the privacy interests involved where an individual voluntarily chooses to admit radio communications into his home [and] it ignores the constitutionally protected interests of both those who wish to transmit and those who desire to receive broadcasts that many — including the FCC and this Court — might find offensive.

"The ability of government, consonant with the Constitution, to shut off discourse solely to protect others from hearing it is . . . dependent upon a showing that substantial privacy interests are being invaded in an essentially intolerable manner. . . ." [Cohen.] [A]n individual's actions in switching on and listening to communications transmitted over the public airways and directed to the public at large do not implicate fundamental privacy interests, even when engaged in within the home. Instead, [these] actions are more properly viewed as a decision to take part, if only as a listener, in an ongoing public discourse. [Moreover], the very fact that [the individual's privacy] interests are threatened only by a radio broadcast precludes any intolerable invasion of privacy; for unlike other intrusive modes of communication, such as sound trucks, "[t]he radio can be turned off." . . .

The [Court] fails to accord proper weight to the interests of listeners who wish to hear broadcasts the FCC deems offensive. It permits majoritarian tastes completely to preclude a protected message from entering the homes of a receptive, unoffended minority. No decision of this Court supports such a result. . . .

[The] government unquestionably has a special interest in the well-being of children and consequently "can adopt more stringent controls on communicative materials available to youths than on those available to adults." [But] "[s]peech that is neither obscene as to youths[2] nor subject to some other legitimate proscription cannot be suppressed solely to protect the young from ideas or images that a legislative body thinks unsuitable for them." [*Erznoznik.*] [Thus, today's] result violates in spades the principle of Butler v. Michigan [that government may not] "reduce the adult population [to] reading only what is fit for children." . . .

[T]he factors relied on by [Justices Stevens and Powell are] plagued by a common failing: the lack of principled limits on their use as a basis for FCC censorship. [My] Brother Powell is content to rely upon the judgment of the Commission while my Brother Stevens deems it prudent to rely on this Court's ability accurately to assess the worth of various kinds of speech.[6] [I] would place the responsibility and the right to weed worthless and offensive communications from the public airways where it belongs and where, until today, it resided: in a public free to choose those communications worthy of its attention from a marketplace unsullied by the censor's hand. . . .

My Brother Stevens [takes] comfort in his observation[s] that "[a] requirement that indecent language be avoided will have its primary effect on the form, rather than the content, of serious communication," [and] that "[t]here are few, if any, thoughts that cannot be expressed by the use of less offensive language." [The] idea that the content of a message [can] be divorced from the words that are the vehicle for its expression is transparently fallacious. A given word may have a unique capacity to capsule an idea, evoke an emotion, or conjure up an image. [Justice] Harlan, speaking for the Court, recognized [in *Cohen*] that a speaker's choice of words cannot surgically be separated from the ideas he desires to express [and that] even if an alternative phrasing may communicate a speaker's abstract ideas as effectively as those words he is forbidden to use, it is doubtful that the sterilized message will convey the emotion that is an essential part of so many communications. . . .

[Moreover, the suggestion] that "[a]dults who feel the need may purchase tapes and records or go to theaters and nightclubs to hear [the tabooed] words," [displays] both a sad insensitivity to the fact that these alternatives involve the ex-

---

2. Even if the monologue appealed to the prurient interest of minors, it would not be obscene as to them unless, as to them, "the work, taken as a whole, lacks serious literary, artistic, political, or scientific value." [*Miller.*] [Relocated footnote — EDS.]

6. Although ultimately dependent upon the outcome of review in this Court, the approach taken by my Brother Stevens would not appear to tolerate the FCC's suppression of any speech, such as political speech, falling within the core area of First Amendment concern. The same, however, cannot be said of the approach taken by my Brother Powell, which, on its face, permits the Commission to censor even political speech if it is sufficiently offensive to community standards. A result more contrary to rudimentary First Amendment principles is difficult to imagine.

penditure of money, time, and effort that many of those wishing to hear Mr. Carlin's message may not be able to afford, and a naive innocence of the reality that in many cases, the medium may well be the message. . . .

[There] runs throughout the opinions of my Brothers Powell and Stevens [a] depressing inability to appreciate that in our land of cultural pluralism, there are many who think, act, and talk differently from the Members of this Court, and who do not share their fragile sensibilities. It is only an acute ethnocentric myopia that enables the Court to approve the censorship of communications solely because of the words they contain. . . .

MR. JUSTICE STEWART, with whom MR. JUSTICE BRENNAN, MR. JUSTICE WHITE, and MR. JUSTICE MARSHALL join, dissenting. . . .

[I] think that "indecent" should properly be read as meaning no more than "obscene." Since the Carlin monologue concededly was not "obscene," I believe that the Commission lacked statutory authority to ban it. . . .

SABLE COMMUNICATIONS, INC. v. FCC, 492 U.S. 115 (1989).

The Court unanimously held unconstitutional a federal statute prohibiting the interstate transmission of "indecent" commercial telephone messages ("dial-a-porn" services). In an opinion by Justice White, the Court distinguished the "emphatically narrow holding" of *Pacifica*, which did not deal with a total ban on broadcasting indecent material and involved the unique intrusiveness of broadcasting. The Court explained that telephone communications are different, for they require the caller to take "affirmative steps" to receive the message: "Placing a telephone call is not the same as turning on a radio and being taken by surprise by an indecent message." Moreover, the government's interest in protecting children could be served by various technical means other than a total ban of the transmission of such messages; although some limited numbers of children might be able to defeat these devices, the prohibition "has the invalid effect of limiting the content of adult telephone conversations to that which is suitable for children to hear."

DENVER AREA EDUCATIONAL TELECOMMUNICATIONS CONSORTIUM, INC. v. FCC, 518 U.S. 727 (1996).

In the Cable Act of 1984, Congress required cable operators to reserve approximately 15 percent of their channels for commercial lease. The act expressly prohibited cable operators from exercising any editorial control over the content of programs broadcast on "leased access" channels. In this case, the Court considered the constitutionality of several provisions of the Cable Television Consumer Protection and Competition Act of 1992, which altered this scheme with respect to "indecent programming," defined as programming that depicts or describes "sexual activities or organs in a patently offensive manner."

Section 10(a). This provision authorized cable operators to prohibit programming they "believe to be indecent," as defined above, on leased access channels. In defense of this provision, the FCC argued that a cable operator is analogous to a newspaper, which, as a private actor, can refuse to carry such material without violating the first amendment. The FCC maintained that section 10(a) does nothing more than give a cable operator, also a private actor, the same authority as a newspaper. Petitioners (a consortium of leased access channel programmers) offered a different view of the matter. Noting that section 10(a) is an exception to the general statutory prohibition against cable operators exercising editorial control over leased access programming, they argued that section 10(a) is an unconstitutional content-based discrimination against "indecent" speech because it authorizes cable operators to exercise editorial control over *only* this form of expression. In a seven-to-two decision, the Court upheld this provision.

In a plurality opinion, Justice Breyer, joined by Justices Stevens, O'Connor, and Souter, concluded that section 10(a) does not violate the first amendment. Noting "the changes taking place in the law, the technology, and the industrial structure related to telecommunications," Breyer maintained that the Court should "decide this case . . . narrowly, by closely scrutinizing §10(a) to assure that it properly addresses an extremely important problem, without imposing [an] unnecessarily great restriction on speech."

Applying that approach, Justice Breyer invoked several considerations to justify his conclusion. First, "the provision [serves] an extremely important justification — the need to protect children from exposure to patently offensive sex-related material." Second, "the provision arises in a very particular context — congressional permission to regulate programming that, but for a previous Act of Congress, would have [no access to such channels] free of an operator's control." Third, "the problem Congress addressed here is remarkably similar to the problem addressed [in] *Pacifica*." Fourth, "the permissive nature of §10(a) means that it likely restricts speech less than, not more than, the ban at issue in *Pacifica*," for cable operators need not exercise the authority granted them under the act. In light of these considerations, Breyer concluded that "the permissive nature of the provision, coupled with its viewpoint-neutral application, [suggests that section 10(a) is] a constitutionally permissible way to protect [children]."

Justice Thomas, joined by Chief Justice Rehnquist and Justice Scalia, concurred in the result.

Justice Kennedy, joined by Justice Ginsburg, dissented. In Kennedy's view, the issue here is "straightforward." Kennedy emphasized that in section 10(a) "Congress singles out one sort of speech for vulnerability to private censorship in a context where [it does not otherwise permit] content-based discrimination." Specifically, section 10(a) expressly disadvantages "nonobscene, indecent programming, a protected category of expression, [citing *Sable*], on the basis of its content." Kennedy argued that in such circumstances "strict scrutiny applies," and however "compelling Congress' interest in shielding children from indecent programming," section 10(a) "cannot survive this exacting review." This is so, Kennedy argued, because "to the extent cable operators prohibit indecent programming on access channels, not only children but adults will be deprived of it," and in light of the availability of other means of regulating such expression, such as blocking mechanisms available to individual subscribers, the government "has no legitimate interest in making access channels pristine."

Section 10(b). This section of the act required cable operators who choose to carry "indecent" programming to segregate such programming on a single channel, to block that channel from viewer access, and to unblock it only on a subscriber's written request. The Court, in a six-to-three decision, invalidated this provision. Justice Breyer delivered the opinion of the Court. At the outset, the Court noted that this provision "significantly differs" from section 10(a) because "it does not simply permit, but rather requires cable operators to restrict [such] speech." The Court observed that this provision has "obvious restrictive effects" on the access of individuals to this sort of programming, including the potential chilling effect of the "written notice" requirement on subscribers who may "fear for their reputations should the operator, advertently or inadvertently, disclose the list of those who wish to watch the 'patently offensive' channel."

Although agreeing with the government that the "protection of children is a 'compelling interest,'" the Court concluded that this provision is nonetheless invalid because "it is not a 'least restrictive alternative,'" is "not 'narrowly tailored,'" and is "'more extensive than necessary.'" The most important consideration leading the Court to this conclusion was the availability of other, less speech-restrictive, means to achieve the objective of the provision. Other legislation, for example, governing channels other than leased access channels, "requires cable operators to [scramble] such programming"; requires cable operators to "honor a subscriber's request to block any, or all, programs on any channel to which he or she does not wish to subscribe"; requires cable operators to provide subscribers, on request, with a "lockbox," which enables parents "to 'lock out' those programs or channels that they [do] not want their children to see"; and requires "manufacturers, in the future, [to] make television sets with a so-called 'V-chip' — a device that will be able automatically to identify and block sexually explicit or violent programs." Although not deciding "whether these [alternative] provisions are themselves lawful," the Court emphasized that "they are significantly less restrictive than the provision here at issue." The Court "conceded" that "no provision, [short] of an absolute ban, can offer certain protection against assault by a determined child," but emphasized that it has not "generally allowed this fact alone to justify 'reduc[ing] the adult population [to] only what is fit for children.'"

Justice Thomas, joined by Chief Justice Rehnquist and Justice Scalia, dissented. Although conceding that "§10(b) must be subjected to strict scrutiny and can be upheld only if it furthers a compelling governmental interest by the least restrictive means available," Thomas concluded that section 10(b) satisfies this standard. After asserting that "Congress has 'a compelling [interest in]' shielding minors from the influence of [indecent speech] that is not obscene by adult standards," Thomas turned to his disagreement with the Court: "The Court strikes down §10(b) by pointing to alternatives, such as reverse-blocking and lockboxes, that it says are less [restrictive]. Though these methods attempt to place in parents' hands the ability to permit their children to watch as little, or as much, indecent programming as the parents think proper, they do not effectively support parents' authority to direct the moral upbringing of their children. [Because] indecent programming on leased access channels is 'especially likely to be shown randomly or intermittently between non-indecent programs,' [parents] armed with only a lockbox must carefully monitor all leased-access programming and constantly reprogram the lockbox to keep out undesired programming. [This] characteristic of leased access channels makes lockboxes and reverse-blocking largely ineffective."

Justice Thomas also dismissed the Court's concern that section 10(b) requires subscribers who want access to indecent programming to give written consent. Thomas argued that if a segregation and blocking scheme is otherwise permissible, then it can hardly be invalidated because subscribers must request access, for any "request for access to blocked programming — by whatever method — ultimately will make the subscriber's identity knowable. But this is hardly the kind of chilling effect that implicates the First Amendment."

RENO v. AMERICAN CIVIL LIBERTIES UNION, 521 U.S. 844 (1997). In an opinion by Justice Stevens, the Court invalidated two sections of the Communications Decency Act of 1996 (CDA) that were designed to protect minors from "indecent" and "patently offensive" communications on the Internet. Section 223(a) prohibited any person from making any communication over the Internet "which is . . . indecent, knowing that the recipient of the communication is under eighteen years of age." Section 223(d) prohibited any person from knowingly sending over the Internet any communication that will be available to a person under 18 years of age and "that, in context, depicts or describes, in terms patently offensive as measured by contemporary community standards, sexual or excretory activities or organs."

At the outset, the Court distinguished *Pacifica*: "[T]here are significant differences between the order upheld in *Pacifica* and the CDA. First, the order in *Pacifica*, issued by an agency that had been regulating radio stations for decades, targeted a specific broadcast that represented a rather dramatic departure from traditional program content in order to designate when — rather than whether — it would be permissible to air such a program in that particular medium. The CDA's broad categorical prohibitions are not limited to particular times and are not dependent on any evaluation by an agency familiar with the unique characteristics of the Internet. Second, unlike the CDA, the Commission's declaratory order was not punitive; we expressly refused to decide whether the indecent broadcast 'would justify a criminal prosecution.' Finally, the Commission's order applied to a medium which as a matter of history had 'received the most limited First Amendment protection,' in large part because warnings could not adequately protect the listener from unexpected program content. The Internet, however, has no comparable history. Moreover, [the] risk of encountering indecent material [on the Internet] by accident is remote because a series of affirmative steps is required to access specific material."

The Court next noted "the many ambiguities" concerning the act's coverage, which "render it problematic" for purposes of the first amendment: "For instance, each of the two parts of the CDA uses a different linguistic form. The first uses the word 'indecent,' while the second speaks of material that 'in context, depicts or describes, in terms patently offensive as measured by contemporary community standards, sexual or excretory activities or organs.' Given the absence of a definition of either term, this difference in language will provoke uncertainty among speakers about how the two standards relate to each other and just what they mean. Could a speaker confidently assume that a serious discussion about birth control practices, homosexuality, the First Amendment issues raised by the [text of the broadcast at issue in *Pacifica*], or the consequences of prison rape would not violate the CDA? This uncertainty undermines the likelihood that the CDA has been carefully tailored to the congressional goal of protecting minors from potentially harmful materials."

The Court found this "lack of precision" fatal: "In order to deny minors access to potentially harmful speech, the CDA effectively suppresses a large amount of speech that adults have a constitutional right to receive and to address to one another. That burden on adult speech is unacceptable if less restrictive alternatives would be at least as effective in achieving the legitimate purpose that the statute was enacted to serve. In evaluating the free speech rights of adults, we have made it perfectly clear that '[s]exual expression which is indecent but not obscene is protected by the First Amendment.' [It] is true that we have repeatedly recognized the governmental interest in protecting children from harmful materials. [Citing *Ginsberg; Pacifica.*] But that interest does not justify an unnecessarily broad suppression of speech addressed to adults. As we have explained, the Government may not 'reduc[e] the adult population [to] only what is fit for children.'"

Finally, the Court noted that in enacting these provisions the government had not used the "least restrictive means" for achieving its goal: "The arguments in this Court have referred to possible alternatives such as requiring that indecent material be 'tagged' in a way that facilitates parental control of material coming into their homes, making exceptions for messages with artistic or educational value [and] regulating some portions of the Internet — such as commercial web sites — differently than others, such as chat rooms. Particularly in the light of the absence of any detailed findings by the Congress, or even hearings addressing the special problems of the CDA, we are persuaded that the CDA is not narrowly tailored if that requirement has any meaning at all."

UNITED STATES v. PLAYBOY ENTERTAINMENT GROUP, INC., 527 S. CT. 1062 (2000). Section 505 of the Telecommunications Act of 1996 requires cable operators who provide channels "primarily dedicated to sexually-oriented programming" either to "fully scramble" those channels or to limit their transmission to between 10 P.M. and 6 A.M. Even before the enactment of section 505, cable operators used scrambling to ensure that only paying customers had access to such programming, but the technology of scrambling is imperfect and the scrambled programs occasionally "bleed" through to the viewer. The purpose of section 505 was to shield children from exposure to sexually oriented "signal bleed." Because the technology to "fully" eliminate signal bleed is very expensive, most cable operators conformed to the requirements of section 505 by limiting transmission to only the eight authorized hours.

In a five-to-four decision, the Court invalidated section 505. Justice Kennedy wrote the opinion of the Court: "[The statute] is content-based [because it] applies only to channels primarily dedicated to 'sexually explicit adult programming or other programming that is indecent.' [Moreover, the] overriding justification for the regulation is concern for the effect of the [content] on young viewers. . . .

"[The] only reasonable way for a substantial number of cable operators to comply with [section 505] is to time channel, which silences the protected speech for two-thirds of the day in every [home], regardless of the presence or [absence] of children or of the wishes of the viewers. According to the District Court, 30% to 50% of all adult programming is viewed by households prior to 10 P.M. [To] prohibit this much speech is a significant restriction of communication. [It] is of no moment that the statute does not impose a complete prohibition. The distinction between laws burdening and laws banning speech is but a matter of degree. The

Government's content-based burdens must satisfy the same rigorous scrutiny as its content-based bans.

"Since section 505 is a content-based speech restriction, it can stand only if it [is] narrowly tailored to promote a compelling Government interest. If a less restrictive alternative would serve the Government's purpose, the legislature must use that alternative. [Citing *Reno*.] Where the designed benefit of a content-based speech restriction is to shield the sensibilities of listeners, the general rule is that the right of expression prevails. [Citing *Cohen; Erznoznik; Bolger*.] . . .

"There is [a] key difference between cable television and the broadcasting media, which is the point on which this case turns: Cable systems have the capacity to block unwanted channels on a household-by-household basis. The option to block reduces the likelihood, so concerning to the Court in *Pacifica*, that traditional First Amendment scrutiny would deprive the Government of all authority to address this sort of problem. The corollary, of course, is that targeted blocking enables the Government to support parental authority without affecting the First Amendment interests of speakers and willing listeners. [Simply] put, targeted blocking is less restrictive than banning, and the Government cannot ban speech if targeted blocking is a feasible and effective means of furthering its compelling interests. . . .

"[In this case,] a less restrictive alternative is available: Section 504 [of the same Act] requires cable operators to [fully] block undesired channels at individual households upon request, [with no limitation as to whether the programming is sexually oriented or indecent]. [This alternative approach] is narrowly tailored to the Government's goal of supporting parents who want those channels blocked. [When such] a plausible, less restrictive alternative is offered to a content-based restriction, it is the Government's obligation to prove that the alternative will be ineffective to achieve its goals. The Government has not met that burden here. . . .

"[Finally,] the Government [argues] that society's independent interests will be unserved if parents fail to act [by failing to use the section 504 alternative]. [But even] upon the assumption that the Government has an interest in substituting itself for informed and empowered parents, its interest is not sufficiently compelling to justify this widespread restriction on speech. The Government's argument stems from the idea that parents do not know their children are viewing the material on a scale or frequency to cause concern, or if so, that parents do not want to take affirmative steps to block it and their decisions are to be superceded. [The] Government has not [shown, however,] that [the section 504] alternative [would] be insufficient to secure its objective, or that any overriding harm justifies its intervention."

Justice Breyer, joined by Chief Justice Rehnquist and Justices O'Connor and Scalia, dissented: "The specific question is whether section 504's 'opt-out' [alternative] amounts to a 'less restrictive,' but *similarly* practical and *effective*, way to accomplish section 505's child-protecting objective. As *Reno* tells us, a 'less restrictive alternative' must be 'at least as effective in achieving the legitimate purpose that the statute was enacted to serve.' [Section 504] is not a similarly effective alternative. [Section 504] gives parents the power to tell cable operators to keep any channel out of their home. Section 505 does more. Unless parents explicitly consent, it inhibits the transmission of adult cable channels to children whose parents may be unaware of what they are watching, whose parents cannot easily supervise television viewing habits, whose parents do not know of the section 504 'opt-out' rights, or whose parents are simply unavailable at critical times. In this respect, section 505 serves the same interests as the laws that deny children access to adult cabarets or X-rated movies. These laws, and section 505, all act in the absence of direct parental supervision. [Section] 504's 'opt-out' [is] *not* similarly effective in achieving the legitimate goals that the statute was enacted to serve."

Note: The Problem of "Indecent" Expression

1. Reno: *right result, wrong reason?* Consider Volokh, Freedom of Speech, Shielding Children, and Transcending Balancing, 1997 Sup. Ct. Rev. 141, 148-149, 165-166:

> The CDA is invalid, the Court said, because it is possible to protect speech in this context without *any* sacrifice of shielding of children. [But] the Court is wrong. None of the Court's proposed alternatives to the CDA [would] have been as effective [in protecting children] as the CDA's more or less total ban. [This] error is more than just a harmless misstatement, [for the] pregnant negative in the Court's reasoning is that, had there really been no equally effective alternatives, the CDA should have been upheld. [This view] is unsound. As Butler v. Michigan [section D4 supra] correctly holds, the government may not reduce adults to reading only what is fit for children. This is true even though letting adults access indecent material would necessarily sacrifice a great deal of shielding of children — even though a total ban would genuinely be the only means to effectively further the interest. [Thus, the correct approach would provide that if] the law imposes a substantial burden on generally protected speech, then it is per se impermissible, even if this means we must sacrifice a significant amount of shielding of children. [Under this approach, the] CDA would be unconstitutional because [banning such] communications substantially burdens speech to adults, [even if there are no less restrictive alternatives].

2. *Indecent expression and subsidies for the arts.* In considering the constitutionality of government regulations of "indecent" expression, to what extent should it matter whether the government directly restricts such expression (as in *Reno, Pacifica,* and *Sable*) or merely refuses to subsidize it in a government-sponsored grant program? See National Endowment for the Arts v. Finley, section E2d infra, in which the Court upheld against both overbreadth and vagueness challenges a federal statute that directs the National Endowment for the Arts, in establishing procedures to judge the artistic merit of grant applications, to take "into consideration general standards of decency." The subsidy issue is closely related to the issue of "unconstitutional conditions." See Chapter 9, section E, infra.

Young v. American Mini-Theatres

427 U.S. 50 (1976)

MR. JUSTICE STEVENS delivered the opinion of the Court.

Zoning ordinances adopted by the city of Detroit [require] that [adult] theaters be dispersed. Specifically, an adult theater may not be located within 1,000 feet of any two other "regulated uses" or within 500 feet of a residential area.[3]

[A] theater [is classified] as "adult" [if it] is used to present "material distinguished or characterized by an emphasis on matter depicting, describing or relating to 'Specified Sexual Activities' or 'Specified Anatomical Areas.'"[4]

[These] ordinances were amendments to an "Anti-Skid Row Ordinance" which had been adopted 10 years earlier. [In] the opinion of urban planners and real estate experts who supported the ordinances, the location of several [regulated uses] in the same neighborhood tends to attract an undesirable quantity and quality of transients, adversely affects property values, causes an increase in crime, especially prostitution, and encourages residents and businesses to move elsewhere.

Respondents, [two] operators of adult motion picture theaters, [sought] a declaratory judgment that the ordinances were unconstitutional and an injunction against their enforcement. [The Court of Appeals held the ordinances unconstitutional. We reverse.]

II

The ordinances are not challenged on the ground that they impose a limit on the total number of adult theaters which may operate in the city of Detroit. There is no claim that distributors or exhibitors of adult films are denied access to the market or, conversely, that the viewing public is unable to satisfy its appetite for sexually explicit fare. Viewed as an entity, the market for this commodity is essentially unrestrained.

[Moreover,] we have held that [a] municipality [whose regulations do not restrain the market for speech] may control the location of theaters as well as the location of other commercial [establishments]. [Thus,] apart from the fact that the ordinances treat adult theaters differently from other theaters and the fact that the classification is predicated on the content of material shown in the respective theaters, the regulation of the place where such films may be exhibited does not offend the First Amendment. We turn, therefore, to the question whether the classification is [unconstitutional because it turns on content].

---

3. In addition to adult motion picture theaters and "mini" theaters, which contain less than 50 seats, the regulated uses include adult bookstores; cabarets (group "D"); establishments for the sale of beer or intoxicating liquor for consumption on the premises; hotels or motels; pawnshops; pool or billiard halls; public lodging houses; secondhand stores; shoeshine parlors; and taxi dance halls.

4. These terms are defined as follows:

For the purpose of this Section, "Specified Sexual Activities" is defined as:

1. Human Genitals in a state of sexual stimulation or arousal;
2. Acts of human masturbation, sexual intercourse or sodomy;
3. Fondling or other erotic touching of human genitals, pubic region, buttock or female breast.

And "Specified Anatomical Areas" is defined as:

1. Less than completely and opaquely covered: (a) human genitals, pubic region, (b) buttock, and (c) female breast below a point immediately above the top of the areola; and
2. Human male genitals in a discernibly turgid state, even if completely and opaquely covered.

III

A remark attributed to Voltaire characterizes our zealous adherence to the principle that the government may not tell the citizen what he may or may not say. Referring to a suggestion that the violent overthrow of tyranny might be legitimate, he said: "I disapprove of what you say, but I will defend to the death your right to say it." The essence of that comment has been repeated time after time in our decisions invalidating attempts by the government to impose selective controls upon the dissemination of ideas. . . .

[But the Detroit ordinances draw a line] on the basis of content without violating the government's paramount obligation of neutrality in its regulation of protected communication. For the regulation of the places where sexually explicit films may be exhibited is unaffected by whatever social, political, or philosophical message a film may be intended to communicate; whether a motion picture ridicules or characterizes one point of view or another, the effect of the ordinances is exactly the same.

Moreover, even though we recognize that the First Amendment will not tolerate the total suppression of erotic materials that have some arguably artistic value, it is manifest that society's interest in protecting this type of expression is of a wholly different, and lesser, magnitude than the interest in untrammeled political debate that inspired Voltaire's immortal comment. Whether political oratory or philosophical discussion moves us to applaud or to despise what is said, every schoolchild can understand why our duty to defend the right to speak remains the same. But few of us would march our sons and daughters off to war to preserve the citizen's right to see "Specified Sexual Activities" exhibited in the theaters of our choice. Even though the First Amendment protects communication in this area from total suppression, we hold that the State may legitimately use the content of these materials as the basis for placing them in a different classification from other motion pictures.

The remaining question is whether the line drawn by these ordinances is justified by the city's interest in preserving the character of its neighborhoods. [The] record discloses a factual basis for the Common Council's conclusion that this kind of restriction will have the desired effect.[34] It is not our function to appraise the wisdom of its decision to require adult theaters to be separated rather than concentrated in the same areas. In either event, the city's interest in attempting to preserve the quality of urban life is one that must be accorded high respect. Moreover, the city must be allowed a reasonable opportunity to experiment with solutions to admittedly serious problems.

Since what is ultimately at stake is nothing more than a limitation on the place where adult films may be exhibited,[35] even though the determination of whether

34. The Common Council's determination was that a concentration of "adult" movie theaters causes the area to deteriorate and become a focus of crime, effects which are not attributable to theaters showing other types of films. It is this secondary effect which these zoning ordinances attempt to avoid, not the dissemination of "offensive" speech. In contrast, in [*Erznoznik*] the justifications offered by the city rested primarily on the city's interest in protecting its citizens from exposure to unwanted, "offensive" speech. The only secondary effect relied on to support that ordinance was the impact on traffic — an effect which might be caused by a distracting open-air movie even if it did not exhibit nudity.

35. The situation would be quite different if the ordinance had the effect of suppressing, or greatly restricting access to, lawful speech. Here, however, the District Court specifically found

a particular film fits that characterization turns on the nature of its content, we conclude that the city's interest in the present and future character of its neighborhoods adequately supports its classification of motion pictures. . . .

Reversed.

MR. JUSTICE POWELL, concurring.

Although I agree with much of what is said in the Court's opinion, and concur in [Part II], my approach to the resolution of this case is sufficiently different to prompt me to write separately.[1] I view the case as presenting an example of innovative land-use regulation, implicating First Amendment concerns only incidentally and to a limited extent. . . .

[The] primary concern of the free speech guarantee is that there be full opportunity for expression in all of its varied forms to convey a desired message. Vital to this concern is the corollary that there be full opportunity for everyone to receive the message. . . .

The inquiry for First Amendment purposes [thus] prompts essentially two inquiries: (i) Does the ordinance impose any content limitation on the creators of adult movies or their ability to make them available to whom they desire, and (ii) does it restrict in any significant way the viewing of these movies by those who desire to see them? On the record in this case, these inquiries must be answered in the negative. At most the impact of the ordinance on these interests is incidental and minimal. . . .

In these circumstances, it is appropriate to analyze the permissibility of Detroit's action under the four-part test of United States v. O'Brien, [section E3 infra].* Under that test, a governmental regulation is sufficiently justified, despite its incidental impact upon First Amendment interests, "if it [furthers] an important or substantial governmental interest; if the governmental interest is unrelated to the suppression of free expression; and if the incidental restriction [on] First Amendment freedoms is no greater than is essential to the furtherance of that interest." . . .

There [is] no question that [the] interests furthered by this ordinance are both important and substantial. [Moreover, it is clear] that Detroit has not embarked on an effort to suppress free expression. [Indeed] it is not seriously challenged [that] the governmental interest prompting the [ordinance] was wholly unrelated to any suppression of free expression.[4] Nor is there reason to question that the degree of incidental encroachment upon such expression was the minimum necessary to further the purpose of the ordinance. The evidence presented to the

---

that "[t]he Ordinances do not affect the operation of existing establishments but only the location of new ones. There are myriad locations in the City of Detroit which must be over 1000 feet from existing regulated establishments. This burden on First Amendment rights is slight." . . .

1. I do not think we need reach, nor am I inclined to agree with, the holding in Part III (and supporting discussion) that nonobscene, erotic materials may be treated differently under First Amendment principles from other forms of protected expression. . . .

*[In O'Brien, the Court upheld the constitutionality of a conviction for burning a draft card — EDS.]

4. [The] Common Council simply acted to protect the economic integrity of large areas of its city against the effects of a predictable interaction between a concentration of certain businesses and the responses of people in the area. If it had been concerned with restricting the message purveyed by adult theaters, it would have tried to close them or restrict their number rather than circumscribe their choice as to location.

Common Council indicated that the urban deterioration was threatened [only] by a concentration of those [movie theaters] that elected to specialize in adult movies. The case would present a different situation had Detroit brought within the ordinance types of theaters that had not been shown to contribute to the deterioration of surrounding areas. . . .[6]

MR. JUSTICE STEWART, with whom MR. JUSTICE BRENNAN, MR. JUSTICE MARSHALL, and MR. JUSTICE BLACKMUN join, dissenting. . . .

This case does not involve a simple zoning ordinance, or a content-neutral time, place, and manner restriction, or a regulation of obscene expression or other speech that is entitled to less than the full protection of the First Amendment. The kind of expression at issue here is no doubt objectionable to some, but that fact does not diminish its protected status any more than did the particular content of the "offensive" expression in [*Erznoznik* or *Cohen*].

What this case does involve is the constitutional permissibility of selective interference with protected speech whose content is thought to produce distasteful effects. It is elementary that a prime function of the First Amendment is to guard against just such interference. By refusing to invalidate Detroit's ordinance the Court rides roughshod over cardinal principles of First Amendment law, which require that time, place, and manner regulations that affect protected expression be content neutral except in the limited context of a captive or juvenile audience. In place of these principles the Court invokes a concept wholly alien to the First Amendment. Since "few of us would march our sons and daughters off to war to preserve the citizen's right to see 'Specified Sexual Activities' exhibited in the theaters of our choice," [the] Court implies that these films are not entitled to the full protection of the Constitution. This stands "Voltaire's immortal comment," [on] its head. For if the guarantees of the First Amendment were reserved for expression that more than a "few of us" would take up arms to defend, then the right of free expression would be defined and circumscribed by current popular opinion. The guarantees of the Bill of Rights were designed to protect against precisely such majoritarian limitations on individual liberty.[6] . . .

CITY OF RENTON v. PLAYTIME THEATRES, 475 U.S. 41 (1986). The ordinance at issue in *Renton* prohibited adult motion picture theaters from locating within 1,000 feet of any residential zone, single- or multiple-family dwelling, church, park, or school. In an opinion by Justice Rehnquist, the Court upheld the ordinance.

At the outset, the Court observed that "the resolution of this case is largely dictated by [*Young*]." After noting the distinction between "regulations enacted for the purpose of restraining speech on the basis of its content," which "pre-

---

6. In my view Mr. Justice Stewart's dissent misconceives the issue in this case by insisting that it involves an impermissible time, place, and manner restriction based on the content of expression. It involves nothing of the kind. We have here merely a decision by the city to treat certain movie theaters differently because they have markedly different effects upon their surroundings. . . .

6. [The] Court stresses that Detroit's content-based regulatory system does not preclude altogether the display of sexually oriented films. But [this] is constitutionally irrelevant, for "'one is not to have the exercise of his liberty of expression in appropriate places abridged on the plea that it may be exercised in some other place.'" [Quoting Schneider v. State, 308 U.S. 147 (1939), section E1 infra.]

sumptively violate the First Amendment," and "'content-neutral' time, place, and manner regulations," which "are acceptable so long as they are designed to serve a substantial governmental interest and do not unreasonably limit alternative avenues of communication," the Court concluded that, because "the Renton ordinance is aimed not at the *content* of the films, [but] at the *secondary effects* of such theaters on the surrounding community," it is "completely consistent with our definition of 'content-neutral' speech regulations as those that 'are *justified* without regard to the content of the regulated speech.'"

This being so, the Court held that the Renton ordinance must be tested as a content-neutral restriction. Applying that standard, the Court echoed its finding in *Young* that "a city's 'interest in attempting to preserve the quality of urban life is one that must be accorded high respect.'" The Court then rejected three distinct arguments against the ordinance. First, the Court rejected the argument that the city had enacted the ordinance without the benefit of studies specifically demonstrating the need to disperse adult theaters in Renton, holding that the city could reasonably rely on studies that had been produced by other cities. Second, the Court rejected the argument that the ordinance was underinclusive because it failed to regulate other kinds of adult businesses that were likely to produce similar "secondary effects," such as bars, massage parlors, and adult bookstores, holding that the city's decision "first to address the potential problems created by one particular kind of adult business in no way suggests that the city has 'singled out' adult theaters for discriminatory treatment." And third, the Court rejected the argument that the ordinance did not leave "reasonable alternative avenues of communication" because it left only 5 percent of the area of the city available for adult theaters, "some of which was already occupied by existing businesses" and none of which was "commercially viable" for adult theaters, holding that the first amendment does not compel "the Government to ensure that adult theaters, or any other kinds of speech-related business," will be able to obtain sites at "bargain prices."

Justice Brennan, joined by Justice Marshall, dissented. At the outset, Justice Brennan lamented the Court's "misguided" conclusion that the Renton ordinance was "content-neutral." In Justice Brennan's view, the "fact that adult movie theaters may cause harmful 'secondary' land use effects" may be relevant in assessing the strength of the city's justifications for the regulation but does not mean that the regulation is content-neutral. To the contrary, because the ordinance explicitly "discriminates on its face against certain forms of speech based on content," it must be tested as a content-based restriction. Justice Brennan added, however, that, even if the ordinance "should be treated like a content-neutral time, place, and manner restriction," it should still be invalidated because, unlike the ordinance upheld in *Young*, the Renton ordinance "'greatly restrict[s] access [to] lawful speech.'"

Note: *Zoning and Nude Dancing*

1. *The rationale of* Young *and* Renton. Presumably, the Court would not uphold a law authorizing cable operators to exclude only Nazi or Socialist programming or restricting the location of theaters that show racist or antiwar films. What, then, explains these decisions? Is it that "indecent" (but non-obscene)

speech is of only "low" first amendment value? Is it that regulations of such expression are "viewpoint-neutral"? Is it that this sort of expression causes distinctive harms that warrant greater regulation?

2. Renton *and content-neutrality.* Do you agree with the Court that the ordinance upheld in *Renton* was "content-neutral"? Does it make sense to treat a law that expressly "discriminates on its face against certain forms of speech based on content" more leniently than other content-based laws because it is "justified" in terms of the "secondary effects" of the speech? The issue of content-neutrality is taken up in section E infra.

3. *Zoning the Internet.* Suppose Congress enacts legislation prohibiting any person to put sexually explicit, indecent speech on the Internet, except in a special "domain") (e.g., .com, .edu, .gov, and .sex). Would such a law be constitutional after *Young* and *Renton?*

4. *Nude dancing.* In Schad v. Borough of Mt. Ephraim, 452 U.S. 61 (1981), appellants, who operated an adult bookstore, installed a coin-operated mechanism permitting a customer to watch a live dancer, usually nude, performing behind a glass panel. Appellants were convicted of violating a Mount Ephraim zoning ordinance prohibiting all live entertainment within the borough. The Court, in an opinion by Justice White, held the ordinance invalid. The Court noted that, as a form of entertainment, "nude dancing is not without its First Amendment protections from official regulation." The Court found it unnecessary, however, to define precisely how much "First Amendment protection should be extended to nude dancing," holding instead that the ordinance's prohibition on *all* live entertainment was constitutionally overbroad. It explained that "this case is not controlled by *Young*," for unlike the situation in *Young*, there was "no evidence" in *Schad* "that the kind of entertainment appellants wish to provide is available in reasonably nearby areas." Chief Justice Burger, joined by Justice Rehnquist, dissented, observing that "to invoke the First Amendment to protect the activity involved in this case trivializes and demeans that great Amendment."

See also California v. LaRue, 409 U.S. 109 (1972) (upholding as "reasonable" under the twenty-first amendment an administrative regulation prohibiting nude dancing in bars and nightclubs that are licensed to sell liquor because of administrative findings that such explicitly sexual performances in establishments licensed to sell liquor tend to promote rape and prostitution and often result in the commission by customers of unlawful public acts of sexuality); New York State Liquor Authority v. Bellanca, 452 U.S. 714 (1981) (upholding a statute prohibiting nude dancing in establishments licensed by the state to sell liquor for on-premises consumption); Newport v. Iacobucci, 479 U.S. 92 (1986) (same); 44 Liquormart, Inc. v. Rhode Island, 517 U.S. 484 (1996) (disavowing *LaRue's* reliance on the twenty-first amendment and concluding that the twenty-first amendment does not qualify the first amendment's prohibition against laws abridging the freedom of speech).

In Barnes v. Glen Theatre, Inc., 501 U.S. 560 (1991), the Court upheld an Indiana statute prohibiting any person to appear "in a state of nudity" in any "public place" as applied to establishments that present nude dancing as entertainment. Although there was no opinion of the Court, a majority of the justices concluded that nude performance dancing "is expressive conduct within the outer perimeters of the First Amendment." A majority also concluded, however, that the requirement that such dancers wear pasties and a G-string does not violate the first amendment because the nudity statute was not directed at nude dancing and thus had only an "incidental effect" on constitutionally protected activity. See also City of Erie v. Pap's A.M., 529 S. Ct. 277 (2000) (upholding a city ordinance banning public nudity, as applied to nude performance dancing). For a fuller account of *Barnes* and *Pap's* A.M., see section E3 infra.

6. *Hate Speech and Pornography*

Beauharnais v. Illinois

343 U.S. 250 (1952)

[Beauharnais, president of the White Circle League, organized the distribution of a leaflet setting forth a petition calling on the mayor and city council of Chicago "to halt the further encroachment, harassment and invasion of white people, their property, neighborhoods and persons, by the Negro." The leaflet called for "[o]ne million self respecting white people in Chicago to unite" and added that, "[i]f persuasion and the need to prevent the white race from becoming mongrelized by the negro will not unite us, then the aggressions, [rapes], robberies, knives, guns and marijuana of the negro surely will." Attached to the leaflet was an application for membership in the White Circle League. As a result of his participation in the distribution of this leaflet, Beauharnais was convicted under an Illinois statute declaring it unlawful for any person to [distribute] any publication that "portrays depravity, criminality, unchastity, or lack of virtue of a class of citizens, of any race, color, creed or religion, which [publication] exposes the citizens of any race, color, creed or religion to contempt, derision, or obloquy or which is productive of breach of the peace or riots." At Beauharnais's trial, the judge refused to instruct the jury that, in order to convict, they must find "that the article complained of was likely to produce a clear and present danger of a serious substantive evil that rises far above public inconvenience, annoyance or unrest." The trial judge also refused to consider Beauharnais's offer of proof on the issue of truth, for under Illinois law, the defense of truth is unavailable in a prosecution for criminal libel unless "the truth of all facts in the utterance [be] shown together with good motive for publication." The Supreme Court, in a five-to-four decision, affirmed the conviction.]

MR. JUSTICE FRANKFURTER delivered the opinion of the Court. . . .

Libel of an individual was a common-law crime, and thus criminal in the colonies. Indeed, at common law, truth or good motives was no defense. In the first decades after the adoption of the Constitution, this was changed by judicial decision, statute or constitution in most States, but nowhere was there any suggestion that the crime of libel be abolished. [As we have observed, "libelous] utterances are no essential part of any exposition of ideas, and are of such slight social value as a step to truth that any benefit that may be derived from them is clearly outweighed by the social interest in order and morality. . . ." [*Chaplinsky.*]

No one will gainsay that it is libelous falsely to charge another with being a rapist, robber, carrier of knives and guns, and user of marijuana. The precise question before us, then, is whether the [Constitution] prevents a State from punishing such libels — as criminal libel has been defined, limited and constitutionally recognized time out of mind — directed at designated collectivities and flagrantly disseminated. [If] an utterance directed at an individual may be the object of criminal sanctions, we cannot deny to a State power to punish the same utterance directed at a defined group, unless we can say that this is a willful and purposeless restriction unrelated to the peace and well-being of the State.

Illinois did not have to look beyond her own borders or await the tragic experience of the last three decades to conclude that wilful purveyors of falsehood concerning racial and religious groups promote strife and tend powerfully to obstruct the manifold adjustments required for free, ordered life in a metropolitan, polyglot community. From the murder of the abolitionist Lovejoy in 1837 to the Cicero riots of 1951, Illinois has been the scene of exacerbated tension between races, often flaring into violence and destruction. In many of these outbreaks, utterances of the character here in question, so the Illinois legislature could conclude, played a significant part. . . .

In the face of this history and its frequent obligato of extreme racial and religious propaganda, we would deny experience to say that the Illinois legislature was without reason in seeking ways to curb false or malicious defamation of racial and religious groups, made in public places and by means calculated to have a powerful emotional impact on those to whom it was presented. . . .

It may be argued, and weightily, that this legislation will not help matters; that tension and on occasion violence between racial and religious groups must be traced to causes more deeply embedded in our society than the rantings of modern Know-Nothings. Only those lacking responsible humility will have a confident solution for problems as intractable as the frictions attributable to differences of race, color or religion. This being so, it would be out of bounds for the judiciary to deny the legislature a choice of policy, provided it is not unrelated to the problem. . . .

[It] is not within our competence to confirm or deny claims of social scientists as to the dependence of the individual on the position of his racial or religious group in the community. [Moreover, it would be] quite outside the scope of our authority [for] us to deny that the Illinois legislature may warrantably believe that a man's job and his educational opportunities and the dignity accorded him may depend as much on the reputation of the racial and religious group to which he willy-nilly belongs, as on his own merits. This being so, we are precluded from saying that speech concededly punishable when immediately directed at individuals cannot be outlawed if directed at groups with whose position and esteem in society the affiliated individual may be inextricably involved.

We are warned that the choice open to the Illinois legislature here may be abused, [that] prohibiting libel of a creed or of a racial group [is] but a step from prohibiting libel of a political party.[18] Every power may be abused, but the possibility of abuse is a poor reason for denying Illinois the power to adopt measures against criminal libels sanctioned by centuries of Anglo-American law. "While this Court sits" it retains and exercises authority to nullify action which en-

---

18. It deserves emphasis that there is no such attempt in this statute. The rubric "race, color, creed or religion" which describes the type of group libel of which is punishable, has attained too fixed a meaning to permit political groups to be brought within it. If a statute sought to outlaw libels of political parties, quite different problems not now before us would be raised. For one thing, the whole doctrine of fair comment as indispensable to the democratic political process would come into play. . . .

croaches on freedom of utterance under the guise of punishing libel. Of course discussion cannot be denied and the right, as well as the duty, of criticism must not be stifled. . . .

As to the defense of truth, Illinois in common with many States requires a showing not only that the utterance state the facts, but also that the publication be made "with good motives and for justifiable ends." Both elements are necessary if the defense is to prevail. [The] teaching of a century and a half of criminal libel prosecutions in this country would go by the board if we were to hold that Illinois was not within her rights in making this combined requirement. Assuming that defendant's offer of proof directed to a part of the defense was adequate,[21] it did not satisfy the entire requirement which Illinois could exact.[22]

Libelous utterances not being within the area of constitutionally protected speech, it is unnecessary, either for us or for the State courts, to consider the issues behind the phrase "clear and present danger." Certainly no one would contend that obscene speech, for example, may be punished only upon a showing of such circumstances. Libel, as we have seen, is in the same class.

We find no warrant in the Constitution for denying to Illinois the power to pass the law here under attack. . . .

Affirmed.

MR. JUSTICE BLACK, with whom MR. JUSTICE DOUGLAS concurs, dissenting. . . .

The Court condones this expansive state censorship by painstakingly analogizing it to the law of criminal libel. As a result of this refined analysis, the Illinois statute emerges labeled a "group libel law." This label may make the Court's holding more palatable for those who sustain it, but the sugar-coating does not make the censorship less deadly. However tagged, the Illinois law is not that criminal libel which has been "defined, limited and constitutionally recognized time out of mind." For as "constitutionally recognized" that crime has provided for punishment of false, malicious, scurrilous charges against individuals, not against huge groups. This limited scope of the law of criminal libel is of no small importance. It has confined state punishment of speech and expression to the narrowest of areas involving nothing more than purely private feuds. Every expansion of the law of criminal libel so as to punish discussions of matters of public concern means a corresponding invasion of the area dedicated to free expression by the First Amendment. . . .

The Court's reliance on [Chaplinsky] is also misplaced. New Hampshire had a state law making it an offense to direct insulting words at an *individual* on a pub-

---

21. Defendant offered to show (1) that crimes were more frequent in districts heavily populated by Negroes than in those where whites predominated; (2) three specific crimes allegedly committed by Negroes; and (3) that property values declined when Negroes moved into a neighborhood. It is doubtful whether such a showing is as extensive as the defamatory allegations in the lithograph circulated by the defendant.

22. The defense attorney put a few questions to the defendant on the witness stand which tended toward elaborating his motives in circulating the lithograph complained of. When objections to these questions were sustained, no offer of proof was made, in contrast to the rather elaborate offer which followed the refusal to permit questioning tending to show the truth of the matter. Indeed, in that offer itself, despite its considerable detail, no mention was made of the necessary element of good motive or justifiable ends. In any event, the question of exclusion of this testimony going to motive was not raised by motion in the trial court, on appeal in Illinois, or before us.

lic street. Chaplinsky had violated that law by calling a man vile names "face-to-face." We pointed out in that context that the use of such "fighting" words was not an essential part of exposition of ideas. Whether the words used in their context here are "fighting" words in the same sense is doubtful, but whether so or not they are not addressed to or about *individuals*. Moreover, the leaflet used here was also the means adopted by an assembled group to enlist interest in their efforts to have legislation enacted. And the fighting words were but a part of arguments on questions of wide public interest and importance. Freedom of petition, assembly, speech and press could be greatly abridged by a practice of meticulously scrutinizing every editorial, speech, sermon or other printed matter to extract two or three naughty words on which to hang charges of "group libel." The *Chaplinsky* case makes no such broad inroads on First Amendment freedoms. . . .

If there be minority groups who hail this holding as their victory, they might consider the possible relevancy of this ancient remark: "Another such victory and I am undone."

Mr. Justice Douglas, dissenting. . . .

My view is that if in any case other public interests are to override the plain command of the First Amendment, the peril of speech must be clear and present, leaving no room for argument, raising no doubts as to the necessity of curbing speech in order to prevent disaster. . . .

[Dissenting opinions of Justices Reed and Jackson are omitted.]

Note: Group Defamation and "Hate Speech"

1. *The* Skokie *controversy.* Reconsider the *Skokie* controversy, section B3 supra, in light of *Beauharnais.* Does the display of a swastika constitute "group libel"?

2. *Group defamation as "libel."* Central to Justice Frankfurter's analysis was the conclusion that "group libel," as defined in the Illinois statute, is not "within the area of constitutionally protected speech" and thus need not be tested by the clear and present danger standard. In justifying this conclusion, Justice Frankfurter relied primarily on *Chaplinsky's* characterization of "libelous" utterances as "unprotected" speech. In New York Times v. Sullivan, however, the Court held that "libel can claim no talismanic immunity from constitutional limitations." Morever, the concept of "group libel," held in *Beauharnais* to be "unprotected" expression, was not limited to false statements of fact. Subsequent opinions, however, such as *New York Times, Hepps, Milkovich* (section D1 supra), and *Hustler,* have unequivocally held that "libel" is of "low" first amendment value only insofar as it consists of false statements of fact. These decisions have thus generally been understood to pull the rug out from under *Beauharnais*. See, e.g., Collin v. Smith, 578 F.2d 1197 (7th Cir. 1978) (the "approach sanctioned [in] *Beauharnais* would [not] pass constitutional muster today").

3. *False statements of fact.* Suppose the Illinois statute prohibited only false statements of fact that portray "depravity, criminality, unchastity, or lack of virtue of a class of citizens, of any race, color, creed or religion." Are the interests threatened by such expression too diffuse to warrant restriction? Given the statements in the *Beauharnais* leaflet, what sort of showing would be necessary to establish "truth" or "falsity"? Consider Arkes, Civility and the Restriction of Speech: Re-

discovering the Defamation of Groups, 1974 Sup. Ct. Rev. 281, 301: "One can think of few things worse than having a jury pronounce on the 'truth' of Beauharnais's charges, with all the solemnity and authority of the legal process. [These] are not the kinds of questions that we typically trust to the judgment of juries."

4. *Other bases for "low" value status.* If the conclusion that group libel constitutes "low" value speech can no longer be sustained solely by invocation of the term "libel," is there any other basis for attributing to such expression only "low" first amendment value? Consider the following arguments:

a. The group libel doctrine is a logical extension of the fighting words doctrine. The fighting words doctrine declares the malicious use of personal epithets to be of "low" first amendment value, see section B3 supra; the group libel doctrine accords equivalent treatment to the similarly malicious use of what amount to epithets directed against groups.

b. Group libel is of only "low" first amendment value because it operates not by persuasion but by insidiously undermining social attitudes and beliefs, as evidenced by the experience of Nazi Germany. See Riesman, Democracy and Defamation: Control of Group Libel, 42 Colum. L. Rev. 727 (1942). (Interestingly, Germany of the 1920s and 1930s had and generally enforced strict anti-hate speech laws that prohibited religious insults, including insults designed to provoke anti-Semitic behavior. Indeed, during the fifteen years before Hitler came to power, there were more than 200 prosecutions based on anti-Semitic speech. See A. Neier, Defending My Enemy (1979).) For a description of contemporary anti-Nazi legislation in Germany, see Stein, History against Free Speech: The New German Law against the "Auschwitz" — and Other — Lies, 85 Mich. L. Rev. 277 (1986).

c. It cannot seriously be maintained that the first amendment was intended to protect speech that maliciously "portrays depravity, criminality, unchastity, or lack of virtue of a class of citizens, of any race, color, creed or religion." Just as express language of incitement is incompatible with the fundamental assumptions of our democratic system, and is thus of "low" first amendment value, group libel is likewise of "low" value because it is incompatible with our fundamental commitment to human dignity and equality. Indeed, this issue poses a clash of constitutional rights and calls for the first amendment to be interpreted and applied in light of the fourteenth amendment's equally important guarantee of "equal protection of the laws." For a similar problem, involving a "clash" of first and sixth amendment rights, recall *Bridges*, section B2 supra. Consider also Lawrence, If He Hollers, Let Him Go: Regulating Racist Speech on Campus, 1990 Duke L.J. 431, 439-440:

> The key [to] understanding [Brown v. Board of Education] is that the practice of segregation [was] speech. *Brown* held that segregation is unconstitutional [primarily] because of the message [it] conveys — the message that black children are an untouchable caste, unfit to be educated with white children. Segregation serves its purpose by conveying an idea. It stamps a badge of inferiority upon blacks, and this badge communicates a message [that] is injurious to blacks. Therefore, *Brown* can be read as regulating the content of racist speech. As [such], the decision is an exception to the usual rule that regulation of speech content is presumed unconstitutional.

d. Matsuda, Public Response to Racist Speech: Considering the Victim's Story, 87 Mich. L. Rev. 2320, 2332, 2336-2337, 2357, 2359 (1989):

The claim that a legal response to racist speech is required stems from a recognition of the structural reality of racism in America. Racism, as used here, comprises the ideology of racial supremacy and the mechanisms for keeping selected victim groups in subordinated positions. [Victims of] hate propaganda have experienced [fear, nightmares], post-traumatic stress disorder, hypertension, psychosis, and suicide. [In] order to avoid receiving hate messages, victims [of such speech] have had to quit jobs, forego education, leave their homes, avoid certain public places, curtail their own exercise of free speech rights, and otherwise modify their behavior. . . .

Racist speech is best treated as a *sui generis* category, presenting an idea so historically untenable, so dangerous, and so tied to perpetuation of violence and degradation [that] it is properly treated as outside the realm of protected discourse. [The] identifying characteristics [of] racist hate [speech are]: 1. The message is of racial inferiority; 2. The message is directed against a historically oppressed group; and 3. The message is persecutorial, hateful, and degrading. . . .

How can one argue for censorship of racist hate messages without encouraging a revival of McCarthyism? There is an important difference that comes from human experience, our only source of collective knowledge. [The] doctrines of racial supremacy and racial hatred [are] uniformly rejected. [We] have fought wars and spilled blood to establish [this principle]. The universality of this principle, in a world bereft of agreement on many things, is a mark of collective human progress.

In light of Matsuda's argument that hate speech causes its victims to "curtail their own exercise of free speech rights," can it be said that the regulation of hate speech is justified because it maximizes free expression in the aggregate?

Consider also Powell, As Justice Requires/Permits: The Delimitation of Harmful Speech in a Democratic Society, 16 Law & Inequality 97, 103, 147-149 (1998):

[T]he insights proffered by critical race and post-modern theorists [suggest] that the classic remedy for harmful speech — that is, more speech — will, in some instances, perpetuate disparities of power and destabilize our sense of self. The marketplace of ideas cannot self-regulate so long as objections to lack of participatory access are subsumed by claims that the liberty interest in expression is primary to the equality interest in participatory access. A self-regulating marketplace presupposes an equal starting line — an assumption that has never been a reality in American political life.

[A decision of the Canadian Supreme Court, Regina v. Keegstra, 2 W.W.R. 1 (1991), illustrates] an alternative way of using democratic principles to valorize liberty and equality. [In *Keegstra*, a Canadian high school teacher was convicted of "communicating statements [that] willfully promote hatred against any identifiable group" for communicating anti-Semitic statements to his students. The Canadian Supreme Court rejected Keegstra's claim that his conviction violated the Canadian Charter of Rights and Freedoms because his speech] was not expression that "serves individual and societal values in a free and democratic society." [This decision reflects] a commitment to both liberty and equality, and mediates between these values by recourse to a collective concern for the underlying values and principles of the society, including social justice. [Commenting] that it is destructive of free expression values themselves, as well as other democratic values, "to treat all expression as equally crucial to those principles at the core" of free expression, the Court suggested that democratic principles recommend viewing free expression as a function of three underlying goals. These goals are truth attainment, ensuring [the] development of self-identity, and most importantly, [the] guarantee that the opportunity for participation in the democratic process is open to all. The Court simultaneously supports these rationales with the observations that hate speech can impede the search for truth, impinge on the autonomy necessary to individual development and subvert the democratic process. Cognizant that the regulation "muzzles the participation of a [few]," the Court remains certain that the loss of that voice is not substantial. [What] is most instructive about the decision is that the Court was willing to employ a democratic calculus.

e. Graber, Old Wine in New Bottles: The Constitutional Status of Unconstitutional Speech, 48 Vand. L. Rev. 349, 352, 364, 367-368, 371-372 (1995):

Scholars who would ban [hate speech] insist that government can regulate certain expressions of prejudice without violating First Amendment values [because] the First Amendment does not fully protect unconstitutional speech — speech that denies or threatens the realization of fundamental constitutional values. [But what proponents of hate speech regulation] fail to realize is that the leading opponents of free speech in every generation [have] insisted that the First Amendment does not fully protect the right to deny or criticize what their generation regards to be fundamental constitutional values.

[The leading] proponents of restrictions on speech during World War I, [for example, maintained] that persons had no constitutional right to attack what they believed to be the essential principles of republican government. [Similarly,] proponents of the freedom of contract [argued] that the First Amendment did not protect [attacks] on private property because such advocacy [was] unconstitutional speech, [and proponents of restricting the speech of communists asserted] that "[n]o democratic or constitutional principle is violated [when] a democracy acts to exclude those groups from entering the struggle for political power which, if victorious, will not permit that struggle to continue in accordance with the democratic way."

f. Post, Racist Speech, Democracy, and the First Amendment, 32 Wm. & Mary L. Rev. 267, 312-317 (1991):

[If] representations in the current literature are accepted as true, [the members of victim groups] confront in public discourse an undifferentiated complex of circumstances in which they are systematically demeaned, stigmatized, ignored; in which the very language of debate resists the articulation of their claims; in which they are harassed, abused, intimidated, and systematically [injured] both individually and collectively. The question [posed is] whether this unacceptable situation would be cured by restraints on speech. . . .

Bluntly expressed, the argument requires us to balance the integrity of public discourse [against] the importance of enhancing the experience [of] members of victim groups. The argument thus reiterates the position that public discourse ought to be subordinated to the egalitarian ideals of the fourteenth amendment. [This] invitation to balance ought to be declined [because] the temptation to balance rests on what might be termed the fallacy of immaculate isolation. The effect on public discourse is acceptable only if it is de minimis, and it is arguably de minimis only when a specific claim is evaluated in isolation from other, similar claims. But no claim is in practice immaculately isolated in this manner. As the flag burning [issue] suggests, there is no shortage of powerful groups contending that uncivil speech [ought] to be "minimally" regulated for highly pressing symbolic reasons. [This] is already plain in the regulations that have proliferated on college campuses, which commonly proscribe not merely speech that degrades persons on the basis of their race, but also [on] the basis of their "color, national origin, religion, sex, sexual orientation, age, handicap, or veteran's status." The claim of de minimis impact loses credibility as the list of claimants to special protection grows longer.

g. Fried, A New First Amendment Jurisprudence: A Threat to Liberty, 59 U. Chi. L. Rev. 225, 245-255 (1992):

The ideas that [university hate speech regulations] condemn are false and offensive, but universities do not condemn all false and offensive ideas. For example, an invective condemning the United States as an oppressor nation or condemning capitalism as a form of exploitation may be repeated with impunity. [Individuals] within the community may not espouse some forms of race and gender superiority, but may espouse others. [And] none of these codes would condemn burning the American flag, even to affront a gathering of veterans or the widows and orphans of soldiers killed in battle. [This] discrimination makes clear that those who promulgate these regulations assign to themselves the authority to determine which ideas are false and which false ideas people may not express as they choose. [The] ban is an exercise of power. It shows who is boss. Thus the holders of [some] noxious ideas are suppressed and the rest of the community is impressed and intimidated by this display of political might.

h. In Doe v. University of Michigan, 721 F. Supp. 852 (E.D. Mich. 1989), the court invalidated as unconstitutionally "overbroad" a university regulation that prohibited any person from stigmatizing an individual on the basis of race, religion, gender, or sexual orientation when the "reasonably foreseeable effect" may be to interfere with the victim's "academic efforts." Do you agree? Consider the narrower code adopted by Stanford University:

Speech or other expression constitutes [prohibited] harassment by personal vilification if it:
(a) is intended to insult or stigmatize an individual or a small number of individuals on the basis of their sex, race, color, handicap, religion, sexual orientation, or national and ethnic origin; and
(b) is addressed directly to the individual or individuals whom it insults or stigmatizes; and
(c) makes use of insulting or "fighting" words or non-verbal symbols . . . "which by their very utterance inflict injury . . ." [and] are commonly understood to convey direct and visceral hatred or contempt for human beings on the basis of their sex, race, color, handicap, religion, sexual orientation, or national and ethnic origin.

Is this regulation consistent with first amendment principles? Is it defensible by analogy to the fighting words doctrine? See Delgado, Words That Wound: A Tort Action for Racial Insults, Epithets and Name-Calling, 1982 Harv. C.R.-C.L. L. Rev. 133 (arguing that such a restriction is consistent with first amendment principles); Strossen, Regulating Racist Speech on Campus: A Modest Proposal?, 1990 Duke L.J. 484 (arguing that such a restriction is inconsistent with first amendment principles). In 1992, California enacted a law that prohibits private universities from disciplining students for speech unless public universities could prohibit the same speech. A state court, relying on R.A.V. v. City of St. Paul, infra, concluded that the Stanford code would violate the first amendment if Stanford were a public university and therefore held the code invalid.

R.A.V. v. City of St. Paul

505 U.S. 377 (1992)

JUSTICE SCALIA delivered the opinion of the Court.

[After allegedly burning a cross on a black family's lawn, petitioner, a teenager, was charged under the St. Paul, Minnesota, Bias-Motivated Crime Ordinance, which prohibits the display of a burning cross, a swastika, or other symbol that one knows or has reason to know "arouses anger, alarm or resentment in others" on the basis of race, color, creed, religion, or gender. The state supreme court rejected a claim that the ordinance was unconstitutionally overbroad because the phrase "arouses anger, alarm or resentment in others" had been construed in earlier state cases to limit the ordinance's reach to fighting words within the meaning of *Chaplinsky*. It also rejected the claim that the ordinance was impermissibly content-based because it was narrowly tailored to serve a compelling governmental interest. The U.S. Supreme Court reversed.]

I

[We] accept the Minnesota Supreme Court's authoritative statement that the ordinance reaches only those expressions that constitute "fighting words" within the meaning of *Chaplinsky*. Petitioner [urges] us to modify the scope of the *Chaplinsky* formulation, thereby invalidating the ordinance as "substantially overbroad." We find it unnecessary to consider this issue. Assuming, arguendo, that all of the expression reached by the ordinance is proscribable under the "fighting words" doctrine, we nonetheless conclude that the ordinance is facially unconstitutional in that it [prohibits] speech solely on the basis of the subjects the speech addresses.

The First Amendment generally prevents government from proscribing speech [because] of disapproval of the ideas expressed. Content-based regulations are presumptively invalid. From 1791 to the present, however, our society [has] permitted restrictions upon the content of speech in a few limited areas, which are "of such slight social value as a step to truth that any benefit that may be derived from them is clearly outweighed by the social interest in order and morality." [*Chaplinsky*.] [We] have sometimes said that these categories of expression are "not within the area of constitutionally protected speech." [Such] statements must be taken in context, however. [What] they mean is that these areas of speech can, consistently with the First Amendment, be regulated because of their constitutionally proscribable content (obscenity, defamation, etc.)—not that they are categories of speech entirely invisible to the Constitution, so that they may be made the vehicles for content discrimination unrelated to their distinctively proscribable content. Thus, the government may proscribe libel; but it may not make the further content discrimination of proscribing only libel critical of the government, [and although a city may proscribe obscenity, it may not prohibit] only those legally obscene works that contain criticism of the city government. . . .

Even the prohibition against content discrimination [is] not absolute. It applies differently in the context of proscribable speech than in the area of fully protected speech. [When] the basis for the content discrimination consists entirely of the very reason the entire class of speech at issue is proscribable, no significant danger of idea or viewpoint discrimination exists. Such a reason, having been adjudged neutral enough to support exclusion of the entire class of speech from First Amendment protection, is also neutral enough to form the basis of distinction within the class. To illustrate: A State might choose to prohibit only that obscenity which is the most patently offensive in its prurience — i.e., that which involves the most lascivious displays of sexual activity. But it may not prohibit, for example, only that obscenity which includes offensive political messages. And the Federal Government can criminalize only those threats of violence that are directed against the President — since the reasons why threats of violence are outside the First Amendment (protecting individuals from the fear of violence, from the disruption that fear engenders, and from the possibility that the threatened violence will occur) have special force when applied to the person of the President. But the Federal Government may not criminalize only those threats against the President that mention his policy on aid to inner cities. And to take a final example, [a] State may choose to regulate price advertising in one industry but not in others, because the risk of fraud (one of the characteristics of commercial speech that justifies depriving it of full First Amendment protection), is in its view greater there. But a State may not prohibit only that commercial advertising that depicts men in a demeaning fashion. . . .

Another valid basis for according differential treatment to even a content-defined subclass of proscribable speech is [that] words can in some circumstances violate laws not directed against speech but against [conduct]. Thus, for example, sexually derogatory "fighting words," among other words, may produce a violation of Title VII's general prohibition against sexual discrimination in employment practices. Where the government does not target conduct on the basis of its expressive content, acts are not shielded from regulation merely because they express a discriminatory idea or philosophy. [See section E3 infra.] . . .

II

Applying these principles to the St. Paul ordinance, we conclude that, even as narrowly construed by the Minnesota Supreme Court, the ordinance is facially unconstitutional. Although the phrase in the ordinance, "arouses anger, alarm or resentment in others," has been limited by the Minnesota Supreme Court's construction to reach only those symbols or displays that amount to "fighting words,"the remaining, unmodified terms make clear that the ordinance applies only to "fighting words" that insult, or provoke violence, "on the basis of race, color, creed, religion or gender." Displays containing abusive invective, no matter how vicious or severe, are permissible unless they are addressed to one of the specified disfavored topics. Those who wish to use "fighting words" in connection with other ideas — to express hostility, for example, on the basis of political affiliation, union membership, or homosexuality — are not covered. The First Amendment does not permit St. Paul to impose special prohibitions on those speakers who express views on disfavored subjects.

In its practical operation, moreover, the ordinance goes even beyond mere content discrimination, to actual viewpoint discrimination. Displays containing some words — odious racial epithets, for example — would be prohibited to proponents of all views. But "fighting words" that do not themselves invoke race, color, creed, religion, or gender — aspersions upon a person's mother, for example — would seemingly be usable ad libitum in the placards of those arguing in favor of racial, color, etc. tolerance and equality, but could not be used by that speaker's opponents. One could hold up a sign saying, for example, that all "anti-Catholic bigots" are misbegotten; but not that all "papists" are, for that would insult and provoke violence "on the basis of religion." St. Paul has no such authority to license one side of a debate to fight freestyle, while requiring the other to follow Marquis of Queensbury Rules.

What we have here, it must be emphasized, is not a prohibition of fighting words that are directed at certain persons or groups (which would be facially valid if it met the requirements of the Equal Protection Clause); but rather, a prohibition of fighting words that contain (as the Minnesota Supreme Court repeatedly emphasized) messages of "bias-motivated" hatred and in particular, as applied to this case, messages "based on virulent notions of racial supremacy." One must wholeheartedly agree with the Minnesota Supreme Court that "it is the responsibility, even the obligation, of diverse communities to confront such notions in whatever form they appear," but the manner of that confrontation cannot consist of selective limitations upon speech. St. Paul's brief asserts that a general "fighting words" law would not meet the city's needs because only a content-specific measure can communicate to minority groups that the "group hatred" aspect of such speech "is not condoned by the majority." The point of the First Amendment is that majority preferences must be expressed in some fashion other than silencing speech on the basis of its content.

Despite the fact that the Minnesota Supreme Court and St. Paul acknowledge that the ordinance is directed at expression of group hatred, Justice Stevens suggests that this "fundamentally misreads" the ordinance. It is directed, he claims, not to speech of a particular content, but to particular "injuries" that are "qualitatively different" from other injuries. This is word-play. What makes the anger, fear, sense of dishonor, etc. produced by violation of this ordinance distinct from the anger, fear, sense of dishonor, etc. produced by other fighting words is nothing other than the fact that it is caused by a distinctive idea, conveyed by a distinctive message. The First Amendment cannot be evaded that easily. . . .

The content-based discrimination reflected in the St. Paul ordinance [does] not fall within the exception for content discrimination based on the very reasons why the particular class of speech at issue (here, fighting words) is proscribable. [The] reason why fighting words are categorically excluded from the protection of the First Amendment is not that their content communicates any particular idea, but that their content embodies a particularly intolerable (and socially unnecessary) mode of expressing whatever idea the speaker wishes to convey. St. Paul has not singled out an especially offensive mode of expression — it has not, for example, selected for prohibition only those fighting words that communicate ideas in a threatening (as opposed to a merely obnoxious) manner. Rather, it has proscribed fighting words of whatever manner that communicate messages of racial, gender, or religious intolerance. Selectivity of this sort creates the possibility that the city is seeking to handicap the expression of particular ideas. . . .

Finally, St. Paul [argues] that, even if the ordinance regulates expression based on hostility towards its protected ideological content, this discrimination is nonetheless justified because it is narrowly tailored to serve compelling state interests. Specifically, [it asserts] that the ordinance helps to ensure the basic human rights of members of groups that have historically been subjected to discrimination, including the right of such group members to live in peace where they wish. We do not doubt that these interests are compelling, and that the ordinance can be said to promote them. But the "danger of censorship" presented by a facially content-based statute requires that that weapon be employed only where it is "necessary to serve the asserted [compelling] interest." The existence of adequate content-neutral alternatives thus "undercuts significantly" any defense of such a statute, casting considerable doubt on the government's protestations that "the asserted justification is in fact an accurate description of the purpose and effect of the law." The dispositive question in this case, therefore, is whether content discrimination is reasonably necessary to achieve St. Paul's compelling interests; it plainly is not. An ordinance not limited to the favored topics, for example, would have precisely the same beneficial effect. In fact the only interest distinctively served by the content limitation is that of displaying the city council's special hostility towards the particular biases thus singled out. That is precisely what the First Amendment forbids. . . .

Let there be no mistake about our belief that burning a cross in someone's front yard is reprehensible. But St. Paul has sufficient means at its disposal to prevent such behavior[1] without adding the First Amendment to the fire.

The judgment of the Minnesota Supreme Court is reversed. . . .

JUSTICE WHITE, with whom JUSTICE BLACKMUN and JUSTICE O'CONNOR join, and with whom JUSTICE STEVENS joins except as to Part I(A), concurring in the judgment. . . .

I

A

This Court's decisions have plainly stated that expression falling within certain limited categories so lacks the values the First Amendment was designed to protect that the Constitution affords no protection to that expression. [Nevertheless], the majority holds that the First Amendment protects those narrow categories of expression long held to be undeserving of First Amendment protection — at least to the extent that lawmakers may not regulate some fighting words more strictly than others because of their content. [It] is inconsistent to hold that the government may proscribe an entire category of speech because the content of that speech is evil; but that the government may not treat a subset of that category differently without violating the First Amendment; the content of the subset is by definition worthless and undeserving of constitutional protection. . . .

C

The Court has patched up its argument with an apparently nonexhaustive list of ad hoc [exceptions]. For instance, if the majority were to give general application

---

1. The conduct might have violated Minnesota statutes [prohibiting "terrorist threats," arson, or criminal damage to property]. [Relocated footnote — EDS.]

to the rule on which it decides this case, today's decision would call into question the constitutionality of the statute making it illegal to threaten the life of the President. Surely, this statute, by singling out certain threats, incorporates a content-based distinction; it indicates that the Government especially disfavors threats against the President as opposed to threats against all others. But because the Government could prohibit all threats and not just those directed against the President, under the Court's theory, the compelling reasons justifying the enactment of special legislation to safeguard the President would be irrelevant, and the statute would fail First Amendment review.

To save the statute, the majority has engrafted the following exception onto its newly announced First Amendment rule: Content-based distinctions may be drawn within an unprotected category of speech if the basis for the distinctions is the very reason the entire class of speech at issue is proscribable. [The] exception swallows the majority's rule. Certainly, it should apply to the St. Paul ordinance, since "the reasons why [fighting words] are outside the First Amendment . . . have special force when applied to [groups that have historically been subjected to discrimination]." . . .

II

Although I disagree with the Court's analysis, I do agree with its conclusion: The St. Paul ordinance is unconstitutional. However, I would decide the case on overbreadth grounds. [In] construing the St. Paul ordinance, the Minnesota Supreme Court drew upon the definition of fighting words that appears in *Chaplinsky* — words "which by their very utterance inflict injury or tend to incite an immediate breach of the peace." [The court also stated, however,] "the ordinance censors only those displays that one knows or should know will create anger, alarm or resentment based on racial, ethnic, gender or religious bias." [Our] fighting words cases have made clear, however, that such generalized reactions are not sufficient to strip expression of its constitutional protection. The mere fact that expressive activity causes hurt feelings, offense, or resentment does not render the expression unprotected. [Citing, e.g., Cohen v. California; Terminiello v. Chicago.] [Thus, although] the ordinance reaches conduct that is unprotected, it also makes criminal expressive conduct that causes only hurt feelings, offense, or resentment, and is protected by the First Amendment. The ordinance is therefore fatally overbroad and invalid on its face. . . .

JUSTICE BLACKMUN, concurring in the judgment.

I regret what the Court has done in this case. [I] fear that the Court has been distracted from its proper mission by the temptation to decide the issue over "politically correct speech" and "cultural diversity," neither of which is presented here. [I] see no First Amendment values that are compromised by a law that prohibits hoodlums from driving minorities out of their homes by burning crosses on their lawns, but I see great harm in preventing the people of Saint Paul from specifically punishing the race-based fighting words that so prejudice their community.

I concur in the judgment, however, because I agree with Justice White that this particular ordinance reaches beyond fighting words to speech protected by the First Amendment.

JUSTICE STEVENS, concurring in the judgment. . . .

[T]he St. Paul ordinance regulates [fighting words] not on the basis of [content], but rather on the basis of the harm the speech causes. [Contrary] to the Court's suggestion, the ordinance regulates [a] subcategory of expression that causes injuries based on "race, color, creed, religion or gender," not a subcategory that involves discussions [of] those characteristics. [Moreover], even if the St. Paul ordinance did regulate fighting words based on its subject matter, such a regulation would, in my opinion, be constitutional. [Subject matter restrictions] generally do not raise the same concerns of government censorship and the distortion of public discourse presented by viewpoint regulations. [Contrary] to the suggestion of the majority, the St. Paul ordinance does not regulate expression based on viewpoint. [The] St. Paul ordinance is evenhanded. In a battle between advocates of tolerance and advocates of intolerance, the ordinance does not prevent either side from hurling fighting words at the other on the basis of their conflicting ideas, but it does bar both sides from hurling such words on the basis of the target's "race, color, creed, religion or gender." To extend the Court's pugilistic metaphor, the St. Paul ordinance simply bans punches "below the belt" — by either party. It does not, therefore, favor one side of any debate. . . .

WISCONSIN v. MITCHELL, 508 U.S. 476 (1993). After viewing the motion picture Mississippi Burning, in which a white man beat a young black who was praying, Mitchell, who is black, urged a group of blacks to assault a young white boy who happened to be walking by. The group, including Mitchell, beat the white boy severely. Mitchell was convicted of aggravated battery, which ordinarily carries a maximum sentence of two years' imprisonment. But because the jury found that Mitchell had intentionally selected his victim because of the boy's race, the maximum sentence for his offense was increased to seven years under the state's hate-crime penalty enhancement statute, which enhances the maximum penalty for an offense whenever the defendant "intentionally selects the person against whom the crime . . . is committed . . . because of the race, religion, color, disability, sexual orientation, national origin or ancestry of that person." The Court overturned the holding of the Wisconsin Supreme Court that the statute violated the first amendment. Chief Justice Rehnquist delivered the opinion for a unanimous Court:

"[A] physical assault is not by any stretch of the imagination expressive conduct protected by the First Amendment. [But this does not end the matter, for] although the statute punishes criminal conduct, it enhances the maximum penalty for conduct motivated by a discriminatory point of view more severely than the same conduct engaged in for some other reason or for no reason at all. Because the only reason for the enhancement is the defendant's discriminatory motive for selecting his victim, Mitchell argues (and the Wisconsin Supreme Court held) that the statute violates the First Amendment by punishing offenders' bigoted beliefs. [But] motive plays the same role under the Wisconsin statute as it does under federal and state antidiscrimination [laws]. Title VII, for example, makes it unlawful for an employer to discriminate against an employee 'because of such individual's race, color, religion, sex, or national origin.' [In Hishon v. King & Spalding, 467 U.S. 69 (1984), we] rejected the argument that Title VII infringed employers' First Amendment rights. . . .

"Nothing in our decision last Term in *R.A.V.* compels a different result here, [for] whereas the ordinance struck down in *R.A.V.* was explicitly directed at expression (i.e., 'speech' or 'messages'), the statute in this case is aimed at conduct unprotected by the First Amendment. Moreover, the Wisconsin statute singles out for enhancement bias-inspired conduct because this conduct is thought to inflict greater individual and societal harm. For example, according to the [State], bias-motivated crimes are more likely to provoke retaliatory crimes, inflict distinct emotional harms on their victims, and incite community unrest. The State's desire to redress these perceived harms provides an adequate explanation for its penalty-enhancement provision over and above mere disagreement with offenders' beliefs or biases."

Note: *R.A.V. and* Mitchell

1. *The nature of the content-based restriction in* R.A.V. The Court in *R.A.V.* held that a content-based distinction within a category of expression that can constitutionally be restricted violates the first amendment. Is that sensible? Why does the content-based distinction trouble the Court? Should it matter whether the distinction is based on "subject matter" or "viewpoint"? Consider C. Sunstein, Democracy and the Problem of Free Speech 188-193 (1993):

[The ordinance in *R.A.V.* did] not draw a line between prohibited and permitted points of view. It has not said that one view on an issue [is] permitted, and another proscribed. [To the contrary,] antiwhite and antiblack statements are [treated alike]. In this respect, the law is content-based but viewpoint-neutral. [It] has regulated on the basis of subjects for discussion, not on the basis of viewpoint.

[Of course, the Court in *R.A.V.*] offers a tempting and clever response. [But] the short answer [to the Court's "Marquis of Queensbury" argument] is that the ordinance [does] not embody viewpoint discrimination as that term is ordinarily understood. Viewpoint discrimination occurs if the government takes one side in a debate; it is not established by the fact that in some hypotheticals one side has greater means of expression than another. . . .

We can make the point by reference to statutes that make it a federal crime to threaten the life of the President. The [Court] said in *R.A.V.* that such statutes are permissible. [But] the presidential threat statute involves the same kind of de facto viewpoint discrimination as in *R.A.V.* Imagine the following conversation: John: "I will kill the President." Jill: "I will kill anyone who threatens to kill the President." John has committed a federal crime; Jill has not. . . .

[What *R.A.V.* does involve is a subject matter restriction.] As a class, subject matter restrictions [occupy] a point somewhere between viewpoint-based restrictions and content-neutral ones. [A] subject matter restriction on unprotected speech should probably be upheld if the legislature can plausibly argue that it is counteracting harms rather than ideas. [This standard is easily satisfied in *R.A.V.* because the kinds of fighting words covered by the ordinance have] especially severe social consequences, [and there] is nothing partisan or illegitimate in recognizing that distinctive harms are produced by this unusual class of fighting words.

Assuming a city can constitutionally prohibit all solicitation of contributions within its subway cars, may it permit solicitation of contributions only by groups that address issues relating to abortion? After *R.A.V.*, how would you assess the constitutionality of this policy? This issue, and the issue of subject matter restrictions, are addressed more fully in sections E2c and E2d infra.

2. *Variations on* R.A.V. a. Consider the following law: "No public official may sue for libel for any statement concerning the performance of her official duties." Is this distinguishable from *R.A.V.?* If so, is it because the "content discrimination is based on the very reason why the particular class of speech at issue is proscribable"? Is it because the state can adequately justify the exemption of defamatory statements concerning the performance of a public official's duties from the "content-neutral" alternative of restricting all defamatory statements governed by New York Times v. Sullivan? Note that in *R.A.V.* the Court explained its result in part on the ground that the city could not adequately justify its decision not to restrict fighting words concerning matters other than "race, color, creed, religion or gender." Was the Court right to undertake such an inquiry?

b. After *R.A.V.*, how would you assess the constitutionality of 18 U.S.C. §241, which prohibits any person to "injure, oppress, threaten, or intimidate" others in the enjoyment of their civil rights, as applied to a white who burns a cross in front of a black's home? See Note, Federal Prosecution of Cross-Burners, 107 Harv. L. Rev. 1729 (1994) (concluding that the statute is content-discriminatory within the meaning of *R.A.V.* but is nonetheless constitutional because "the content discrimination is based on the very reason the particular class of speech at issue is proscribable").

c. The civil rights laws prohibit an employer from firing an employee because of her race, even though the employer may fire her for many other reasons. Are the civil rights laws invalid after *R.A.V.* because they penalize the employer for his political convictions? That is, if the employer fires an employee because he does not like blacks he is penalized, but if he fires an employee because he does not like Democrats or gays, he is not. Why is *R.A.V.* different? Because the employer is not engaged in "speech"? Because the government's interest in the civil rights context is unrelated to whether the employer is engaged in speech?

3. Mitchell *and* R.A.V. On what principle is *Mitchell* consistent with *R.A.V.?* Is the difference that, unlike the defendant in *Mitchell*, the cross-burner was engaged in "speech"? This seemingly obvious distinction is problematic on at least three counts. First, although the cross-burner was prosecuted for his expression, that expression consisted of fighting words, which are not protected "speech" within the meaning of the first amendment. In what *meaningful* sense, then, was the defendant in *R.A.V.* engaged in "speech"?

Second, the act of beating an individual "because of his race" can be a form of expression. After all, the assault does "communicate" the defendant's views both to the victim and to observers. Is the assault not "speech" within the meaning of the first amendment because the communication is achieved by conduct rather than by words? If so, what of cross-burning? Is the difference that in *R.A.V.* the harm was caused by the communicative element of the conduct, whereas in *Mitchell* the harm was caused directly by the conduct itself? On the problem of symbolic expression, see section E3 infra.

Third, consider the "harms" identified by the Court in *Mitchell* that are said to justify the enhanced punishment. Would any of them arise if the actor did not *communicate* a message of racial hatred? If not, how can this statute be said not to regulate speech? See generally Tribe, The Mystery of Motive, Private and Public: Some Notes Inspired by the Problems of Hate Crime and Animal Sacrifice, 1993 Sup. Ct. Rev. 1.

4. *Harassment in the workplace.* Title VII of the 1964 Civil Rights Act prohibits discrimination in conditions of employment by race, religion, national origin, and sex. Courts have held that various kinds of harassment at work can be so severe that an employee effectively suffers from "discrimination" within the meaning of title VII. Such harassment generally takes two forms. First, there is quid pro quo harassment. This typically arises when an employer conditions an individual's hiring, promotion, or continued employment on sexual involvement, as when a supervisor tells an employee that he will fire her unless she has sex with him. This sort of harassment is generally regarded as an explicit threat that, at least in this context, is not protected by the first amendment.

The second form of harassment is more complex. It may arise when an employer or coworker creates a situation in which the working environment becomes hostile or abusive. Consider the following situations: (a) A white supervisor repeatedly says that his black workers are lazy. (b) A male employee repeatedly compliments a female employee on her appearance. (c) Christian employees post pictures of Jesus at their workstations, over the objections of Jewish employees. (d) Male employees post pictures of naked women at their workstations, over the objections of female employees. To what extent, and on what theories, may such forms of expression be prohibited?

Consider the following arguments: (a) Workplace harassment is not speech. It is discrimination. (b) The workplace is for work, not speech. (c) Workplace harassment is private conversation, not public discourse. (d) Workers are a captive audience. (e) Workplace harassment is of "low" first amendment value.

For a "contextualist" approach to this issue, consider Fallon, Sexual Harassment, Content-Neutrality, and the First Amendment Dog That Didn't Bark, 1994 Sup. Ct. Rev. 1, 42-44:

> [Sexual] harassment involves speech [of] a sexual nature that is by definition unwelcome and that creates an unequal work environment based on gender. [The] government has a compelling interest in eradicating discrimination of this kind. [Narrowly] targeted, face-to-face expression has often received less constitutional protection than words [in] other contexts [because speech] of this kind is less likely to have public or political value than speech directed to larger audiences. Even more important, individually targeted, face-to-face speech is especially likely to have the purpose of being, and to be experienced as, invasive, threatening, or coercive. [Characteristic] features of the workplace provide additional reasons for allowing a legal prohibition against sexually harassing speech. [For many], employment is a practical necessity, and the economic and other costs of changing jobs would often be prohibitive. [No] one should have to endure a gauntlet of discriminatory insult or ridicule or suffer discriminatorily demeaning sexualization as a condition of employment.

Fallon recognizes several limitations, however, on the sorts of speech that can be prohibited in this context: (1) Hostile environment claims "must meet an objective standard," that is, the speech "must be sufficiently 'severe or pervasive' to create [an] environment that a *reasonable person* would find hostile." (2) Government may not in this context prohibit speech "that is 'reasonably designed or intended' to contribute to reasoned debate on issues of public concern." Id. at 45-47.

For further discussion of workplace harassment, see K. Greenawalt, Fighting Words 77-96 (1995); Browne, Title VII as Censorship: Hostile Environment Harassment and the First Amendment, 52 Ohio St. L.J. 481 (1991); Estlund, Freedom of Expression in the Workplace and the Problem of Discriminatory Harassment, 75 Tex. L. Rev. 687 (1997); Strauss, Sexist Speech in the Workplace, 25 Harv. C.R.-C.L. L. Rev. 1 (1990); Volokh, Freedom of Speech and Workplace Harassment, 39 UCLA L. Rev. 1791 (1992).

Note: *Pornography and the Victimization of Women*

1. *A model statute*. Consider the constitutionality of the following law:

Pornography is the sexually explicit subordination of women, graphically depicted, whether in words or pictures, that also includes one or more of the following: (i) women are presented dehumanized as sexual objects, things or commodities; (ii) women are presented as sexual objects who enjoy pain, humiliation or rape; (iii) women are presented as sexual objects tied up or cut up or mutilated or physically hurt; (iv) women are presented in postures of sexual submission or sexual servility, including by inviting penetration; or (v) women are presented as whores by nature. No person may sell, exhibit, or distribute pornography.

2. *Evaluation*. Consider the following views:
a. MacKinnon, Not a Moral Issue, 2 Yale L. & Soc. Poly. Rev. 321, 322-324 (1984):

Obscenity law is concerned with morality, specifically morals from the male point of view, meaning the standpoint of male dominance. The feminist critique of pornography is politics, specifically politics from the women's point of view, meaning the standpoint of the subordination of women to men. Morality here means good and evil; politics means power and powerlessness. Obscenity is a moral idea; pornography is a political practice. The two concepts represent entirely different things. Nudity, explicitness, excess of candor, [these] qualities bother obscenity law when sex is depicted or portrayed. [Sex] forced on real women so that it can be sold at a profit to be forced on other real women; women's bodies trussed and maimed and raped and made into things to be hurt and obtained and accessed and this presented as the nature of women; the coercion that is visible and the coercion that has become invisible — this and more bothers feminists about pornography. Obscenity as such probably does little harm; pornography causes attitudes and behaviors of violence and discrimination which define the treatment and status of half of the population.

b. Clark, Liberalism and Pornography, in Pornography and Censorship 52-57 (D. Copp and S. Wendells eds. 1983):

[Pornography] has very little to do with sex, [but] it has everything to do with [the] use of sexuality as an instrument of active oppression. [Pornography is] a species of hate literature. [It depicts] women [as inviting] humiliating, degrading, and violently abusive [treatment]. [It feeds] traditional male phantasies [and glorifies] the traditional advantages men have enjoyed in relation to exploitation of female sexuality. [Pornography] is a method of socialization; [it] "teaches society to view women as less than human." [It is thus an] affront to [the dignity of women] as equal persons. [Moreover,] role modeling has a powerful effect on human behavior. [People] tend to act out and operationalize the behavior that they see typically acted out around them. [While] the liberal principle behind opposition to censorship is based on a recognition that desirable social change requires public access to information which challenges the beliefs and practices of the status quo, what it does not acknowledge is that information which supports the status quo through providing role models which advocate the use or threat of coercion as a technique of social control directed at a clearly identifiable group depicted as inferior, subordinate, and subhuman, works against the interest both of desirable social change and of the members of the subgroup so identified.

See also A. Dworkin, Pornography: Men Possessing Women (1981); Take Back the Night: Women on Pornography (L. Lederer ed. 1980).

c. MacKinnon, Pornography, Civil Rights, and Speech, 20 Harv. C.R.-C.L. L. Rev. 1, 52-54 (1985):

Recent experimental research on pornography shows that [pornographic material may cause] measurable harm to women through increasing men's attitudes and behaviors of discrimination in both violent and nonviolent forms. Exposure to [pornography] increases men's immediately subsequent willingness to aggress against women under laboratory conditions. It [significantly] increases attitudinal measures known to correlate with rape, [such as] hostility toward women, [condoning] rape, and predicting that one would rape [if] one knows one would not get caught. [As] to that pornography [in] which normal research subjects seldom perceive violence, long-term exposure still makes them see women as more worthless, trivial, non-human, and object-like, i.e., the way those who are discriminated against are seen by those who discriminate against them.

d. Note, Anti-Pornography Laws and First Amendment Values, 98 Harv. L. Rev. 460, 470-472, 475 (1984):

The Supreme Court denies [some categories of expression] full first amendment protection because they do not serve the values [of self-government, search for truth, and self-fulfillment that underlie] the first amendment. Pornography may likewise fail to serve such values. [Opponents] of pornography argue that it presents false and degrading images of women [and that it] is as harmful as, and no more valuable than, defamatory falsehoods. Proponents of pornographers' first amendment rights argue that pornography is intended not as a statement of fact, but as an opinion or fantasy about male and female sexuality [that] cannot be prohibited on the basis of its truthfulness or falsity. [But] the argument over whether pornography should be viewed as a statement of fact or an opinion assumes that sexually explicit images communicate "ideas" in the same way that nonsexually explicit words or images do. Feminists argue that men are influenced by pornography not because [it] prompts conscious testing of its depictions of sexuality [but] because [it] conditions men to associate harmful attitudes and actions towards women with sexual excitement. To the extent that any form of expression influences its audience through means that bypass the process of conscious deliberation, [it] cannot be said to [further] self-government [or] the search for truth. Some [argue that the] importance of self-expression as a means of [achieving] individual dignity and choice [supports the pornographer's] right to express his view of the world [and] his [customer's] right to receive those [images]. But the self-expression argument is double-edged. Those who oppose pornography assert that pornography denies women *their* right to individual dignity and choice. They maintain that pornography forces the state to choose whose right to individual dignity and choice it will protect.

e. How would you evaluate the claim that pornography produces harms equal to or greater than those produced by speech falling within existing categories of "low" value expression? Why isn't counterspeech an effective remedy in the pornography context? Note that some defenses of the antipornography ordinance, instead of (or in addition to) operating within the traditional doctrinal framework, reveal ambivalence about conventional approaches to freedom of speech. Such defenses claim that, when social power is distributed to dominant groups, free speech, understood in traditional terms, tends to perpetuate the dominance of such groups. In light of widespread social and economic inequality, the notion of a "marketplace of ideas" breaks down. Consider Baat-Ada, Freedom of Speech as Mythology, or Quill Pen and Parchment Thinking in an Electronic Environment, 8 N.Y.U. Rev. L. & Soc. Change 271, 275, 278-279 (1978-1979):

> Contemporary mass media techniques have made the "free marketplace" into American folk mythology. [Were] those [who] oppose pornography able to present [their] case as fully as pornographers present theirs, the pornography industry would be in a precarious position. [Pornography] receives the support it does, however, because [the] pornographic environment is so profitable that [those who oppose pornography are effectively denied equal] access to the public through mass media communication forums.

See also C. MacKinnon, Feminism Unmodified: Discourses on Life and Law 155-156 (1987) ("Laissez faire might be an adequate theory of the social preconditions for knowledge in a nonhierarchical society. But in a society of gender inequality, the speech of the powerful impresses its view upon the world, concealing the truth of powerlessness."). See also the challenge to "marketplace" theories set out in section A supra. Would these sorts of arguments compel a substantial rethinking of first amendment doctrine? Would that be a good or a bad idea?

f. West, The Feminist-Conservative Anti-Pornography Alliance and the 1986 Attorney General's Commission on Pornography Report, 1987 Am. B. Found. Res. J. 681, 686, 691-692:

> A woman-centered conception of pornography [has] two dimensions: for many women (perhaps most), pornography is primarily victimizing, threatening and oppressive, [but] for others [it] is on occasion liberating and transformative. [Indeed, some pornography assaults] a source of oppression: the marital, familial, productive, and reproductive values that the conservative wrongly identifies as necessary to the creation of a virtuous life and a virtuous society. [According] to women who enjoy pornography, the validation of pleasure, desire, and sexuality found in some pornography is [a] healthy attack on a stifling and oppressive societal denial of female sexuality. [It can be] something to celebrate, rather than something to condemn.

g. In American Booksellers Association v. Hudnut, 771 F.2d 323 (7th Cir. 1985), the Court of Appeals for the Seventh Circuit held unconstitutional an Indianapolis antipornography ordinance similar to the model antipornography law set forth above. The court of appeals accepted the factual premises of the ordinance, conceding that "depictions of subordination tend to perpetuate subordination," and that the "subordinate status of women in turn leads to affront and lower pay at work, insult and injury at home, battery and rape on the streets." The court of appeals observed, however, that "racial bigotry, anti-semitism, violence on television [and other forms of expression also] influence the culture and shape our socialization. [Yet] all is protected speech, however insidious. Any other answer leaves the government in control of all of the institutions of culture, the great censor and director of which thoughts are good for us." Moreover, the court of appeals rejected the argument that pornography, as defined in the ordinance, is "low" value speech: "True, pornography and obscenity have sex in common. But Indianapolis left out of its definition any reference to literary, artistic, political, or scientific value. [Moreover, although the Supreme] Court sometimes balances the value of speech against the costs of its restriction, [it] does this by category of speech and not by the content of particular works." The Court emphasized that the Indianapolis ordinance expressly discriminated against a particular viewpoint: "Under the ordinance graphic sexually explicit speech is 'pornography' or not depending on the perspective the author adopts. Speech that 'subordinates' women [is] forbidden, [but speech] that portrays women in positions of equality is [lawful]. This is thought control. [Those] who espouse that approved view may use sexual images; those who do not, may not." The court of appeals concluded that, because the ordinance "created an approved point of view," it could not be defended as a restriction of only "low" value speech. See also Stone, Anti-Pornography Legislation as Viewpoint Discrimination, 9 Harv. J.L. & Pub. Poly. 701 (1986). For the Supreme Court's summary affirmance of *Hudnut*, see 475 U.S. 1001 (1986). The Canadian Supreme Court has unanimously upheld legislation that is similar to the model antipornography ordinance. See Butler v. Regina, File No. 22191 (1992).

h. The conclusion that antipornography legislation is impermissible because it is viewpoint discrimination has been challenged. Consider Sunstein, Pornography and the First Amendment, 1986 Duke L.J. 589, 612:

> The initial response to a claim that antipornography legislation is viewpoint-based should be straightforward. The legislation aimed at pornography [is] directed at harm rather than at viewpoint. Its purpose [is] to prevent sexual violence and discrimination, not to suppress expression of a point of view. Only pornography — not sexist material in general or material that reinforces notions of female subordination — is regulated. Because of its focus on harm, antipornography legislation [does] not pose the dangers associated with viewpoint-based restrictions.

For the opposing view, consider L. Tribe, American Constitutional Law 925-926 (2d ed. 1988):

> It is an inadequate response to argue [that antipornography] ordinances take aim at harms, not at expression. *All* viewpoint-based regulations are targeted at some supposed harm, whether it be linked to an unsettling ideology like Communism [or] to socially shunned practices like adultery. [It] is beyond dispute that government may choose to outlaw the incitement of various acts independently deemed crimes — including murder, rape, or, indeed, the violent overthrow of government.

Likewise, government may surely outlaw the direct incitement of sexual violence against women. [It] is, however, altogether different, and far more constitutionally tenuous, for government to outlaw [the] incitement of violence against women *only* when such incitement is caused by words or pictures that express a particular point of view: that women are meant for domination. The analogue would be a ban on anti-capitalist speeches that incite robbery, leaving other equally effective incitements to robbery unprohibited.

See also Kagan, Regulation of Hate Speech and Pornography after *R.A.V.*, 60 U. Chi. L. Rev. 873, 879 (1993) ("Contrast an ordinance punishing abortion advocacy [with] an ordinance punishing any speech that might induce a woman to get an abortion. To sever these pairs of statutes would be to transform the First Amendment into a formal rule of legislative drafting, concerned only with appearance.").

For a rejoinder, consider Sunstein, Neutrality in Constitutional Law (with Special Reference to Pornography, Abortion, and Surrogacy), 92 Colum. L. Rev. 1, 28-29 (1992):

[F]irst Amendment law contains several categories of [low value] speech that are subject to ban or regulation even though they are nonneutral in precisely the same way as antipornography legislation. Consider, for example, labor law, where courts have held that government may ban employers from speaking unfavorably about the effects of unionization in the period before a union election if the unfavorable statements might be interpreted as a threat. [Citing *Gissel.*] Regulation of such speech is unquestionably nonneutral, since employer speech favorable to unionization is not proscribed. Similarly, the State may prohibit truthful television and radio advertisements for casinos and cigarettes. [Citing *Posadas.*] This is so even though speech that takes the opposite side is freely permitted, in advertisements or elsewhere. Even regulation of bribery is nonneutral. One may not offer $100 to tempt a person to commit a tort, although a $100 offer to refrain from committing a tort is permissible. In all of the cases, the partisanship of the regulation is not apparent because there is so firm a consensus on the presence of real-world harms that the objection from neutrality does not even register. [Similarly,] we could imagine a society in which the harms produced by pornography were so widely acknowledged and so generally condemned that an antipornography ordinance would not be regarded as viewpoint-based at all.

3. *Alternative approaches.* Consider the following:

a. Suppose a city enacted an ordinance that prohibited obscenity, which is concededly of "low" first amendment value, only insofar as it is also pornographic, within the meaning of the ordinance invalidated in *Hudnut.* Would such a law be constitutional? Recall *R.A.V.*

b. In light of *Ferber,* could the antipornography ordinance be justified on the ground that pornography harms women participants in the same way that child pornography harms children? Consider Note, Anti-Pornography Laws and First Amendment Values, 98 Harv. L. Rev. 460, 473 (1984): "Because the Court is probably not disposed to presume that adult models are incapable of refusing to participate in pornographic films or photographs, it is unlikely to reason that adult pornography [can] be banned irrespective of a work's social merit."

c. Many states have enacted antipandering laws to prevent profiteering in prostitution. Can such laws constitutionally be used to prosecute producers of pornography who pay individuals to engage in sex on screen? See Barnes v. Glen Theatre, section E3, in which the Court upheld a public indecency statute, which prohibits any person to appear "in a state of nudity" in any "public place," as applied to establishments that present nude dancing as entertainment. See also Kagan, supra, at 887-888 (arguing that the application of pandering statutes to the producers of pornography is "questionable" because of the "potential for applying such statutes to large amounts of speech at the core of constitutional protection"); People v. Freeman, 46 Cal. 3d 419, 758 P.2d 1128, 250 Cal. Rptr. 598 (1988) (reversing the pandering conviction of a film producer who had paid actors to copulate on screen).

4. *Street harassment.* Consider the constitutionality of the following statute, proposed in Bowman, Street Harassment and the Informal Ghettoization of Women, 106 Harv. L. Rev. 517, 575 (1993):

> It shall be a misdemeanor [to] engage in street harassment. Street harassment occurs when one or more unfamiliar men accost one or more women in a public place [and] intrude or attempt to intrude upon the woman's attention in a manner that is unwelcome to the woman, with language that is explicitly or implicitly sexual. Such language includes, but is not limited to, references to male or female genitalia or to female body parts or to sexual activities, solicitation of sex, or reference by word or action to the target of the harassment as the object of sexual desire, or similar words that by their very utterance inflict injury or naturally tend to provoke violent resentment, even if the woman did not herself react with violence. The harasser's intent, except his intent to say the words or engage in the conduct, is not an element of this offense. This section does not apply to any peaceable activity intended to express political views or provide public information to others.

Note: "Low" Value Speech — Final Thoughts

Has the doctrine of "low" value speech injected the Court "into value judgments [foreclosed] to it by the basic theory of the First Amendment"? T. Emerson, The System of Free Expression 326 (1970). Reconsider the various categories of "low" or arguably "low" value expression — express incitement, fighting words, threats, technical military information, false statements of fact, nonnewsworthy invasions of privacy, commercial speech, obscenity, offensive language, offensive sexually oriented expression, group defamation, hate speech, pornography. Has the Court developed a coherent theory of first amendment "value"? What considerations are relevant in deciding whether particular categories of expression constitute "low" value speech?

Consider Sunstein, Pornography and the First Amendment, 1986 Duke L.J. 589, 603-604:

> [In] determining whether speech qualifies as low-value, the cases suggest that four factors are relevant. First, the speech must be far afield from the central concern of the first amendment, which, broadly speaking, is effective popular control of public affairs. [Second], a distinction is drawn between cognitive and noncognitive aspects of speech. [Third], the purpose of the speaker is relevant: if the speaker is seeking to communicate a message, he will be treated more favorably than if he is not. Fourth, the various classes of low-value speech reflect judgments that in cer-

tain areas, government is unlikely to be acting for constitutionally impermissible reasons or producing constitutionally troublesome harms.

Does this four-factor analysis adequately explain the Court's decisions? If so, are they the right factors to consider? Should the Court define the high value/low value distinction more explicitly in terms of the distinction between political and nonpolitical expression?

How would you assess the overall impact of the "low" value doctrine? Have any of the restrictions upheld under this doctrine seriously threatened the system of free expression? Consider the following evaluations: (1) The "low" value doctrine demonstrates the sharply limited efficacy of judicial controls on censorship by the majority, for it defines speech as unworthy of protection in precisely those cases where it most seriously threatens majority values and where protection is thus most needed. (2) The "low" value doctrine has served a salutary function, for it has operated as a critical "safety valve," enabling the Court to deal sensibly with somewhat harmful, but relatively insignificant, speech without running the risk of diluting the protection accorded expression at the very heart of the guarantee. (3) The Court's use of the "low" value theory "has been marked by vacillation and uncertainty." It is a highly "result-oriented" approach that is susceptible to an endless expansion of the list of "low" value categories "whenever another kind of expression [gains] a renewed disfavor." To the extent that fighting words, commercial speech, obscenity, and libel are "subject to regulation, it should be because they cause harm and not because they are presumed to be low in communicative value." Shaman, The Theory of Low-Value Speech, 48 S.M.U. L. Rev. 297, 339, 348 (1995).

E.   CONTENT-NEUTRAL RESTRICTIONS: LIMITATIONS ON THE MEANS OF COMMUNICATION AND THE PROBLEM OF CONTENT-NEUTRALITY

Content-neutral restrictions limit expression without regard to its content. They turn neither on their face nor as applied on the content or communicative impact of speech. Such restrictions encompass a broad spectrum of limitations on expressive activity, ranging from a prohibition on the use of loudspeakers, to a ban on billboards, to a limitation on campaign contributions, to a prohibition on the mutilation of draft cards.

To what extent, and in what manner, do content-neutral restrictions implicate the concerns and values underlying the first amendment? How do they differ in this regard from content-based restrictions? Should the doctrines devised to govern content-based restrictions also govern content-neutral restrictions? In exploring these and related questions, this section begins with a search for general principles and then examines four specific areas: the right to a public forum; symbolic speech; regulation of the electoral process; and litigation, association, and the right not to speak. Throughout, this section questions the meaning of "content-neutrality" and tests the occasionally elusive line between content-based and content-neutral restrictions.

1.   General Principles

SCHNEIDER v. STATE, 308 U.S. 147 (1939). Appellants distributed leaflets on a public street announcing a protest meeting. Although appellants themselves did not scatter any of the leaflets, some of those to whom the leaflets were handed threw them on the sidewalk and street. Appellants were convicted of violating an ordinance prohibiting any person to distribute leaflets in "any street or way." The Court held the ordinance invalid. Justice Roberts delivered the opinion:

"Municipal authorities, as trustees for the public, have the duty to keep their communities' streets open and available for movement of people and property, the primary purpose to which the streets are dedicated. So long as legislation to this end does not abridge the constitutional liberty of one rightfully upon the street to impart information through speech or the distribution of literature, it may lawfully regulate the conduct of those using the streets. For example, a person could not exercise this liberty by taking his stand in the middle of a crowded street, contrary to traffic regulations, and maintain his position to the stoppage of all traffic; [nor] does the guarantee of freedom of speech or of the press deprive a municipality of power to enact regulations against throwing literature broadcast in the streets. Prohibition of such conduct would not abridge the constitutional liberty since such activity bears no necessary relationship to the freedom to speak, write, print or distribute information or opinion.

"This court has characterized the freedom of speech and freedom of press as fundamental personal rights and liberties. [Mere] legislative preferences or beliefs respecting matters of public convenience may well support regulation directed at other personal activities, but be insufficient to justify such as diminishes the exercise of rights so vital to the maintenance of democratic institutions. And so, as cases arise, the delicate and difficult task falls upon the courts to weigh the circumstances and to appraise the substantiality of the reasons advanced in support of the regulation of the free enjoyment of the rights.

"[The] legislation under attack [is designed to prevent littering]. Although the alleged offenders were not charged with themselves scattering paper in the streets, their convictions were sustained upon the theory that distribution by them [resulted] in such littering. We are of opinion that the purpose to keep the streets clean and of good appearance is insufficient to justify an ordinance which prohibits a person rightfully on a public street from handing literature to one willing to receive it. Any burden imposed upon the city authorities in cleaning and caring for the streets as an indirect consequence of such distribution results from the constitutional protection of the freedom of speech and press. This constitutional protection does not deprive a city of all power to prevent street littering. There are obvious methods of preventing littering. Amongst these is the punishment of those who actually throw papers on the streets. . . .

"It is suggested that the [ordinance is] valid because [its] operation is limited to streets and alleys and leaves persons free to distribute printed matter in other places. [But] the streets are natural and proper places for the dissemination of information and opinion; and one is not to have the exercise of his liberty of expression in appropriate places abridged on the plea that it may be exercised in some other place."

Justice McReynolds dissented.

MARTIN v. CITY OF STRUTHERS, 319 U.S. 141 (1943). Appellant, a Jehovah's Witness, went to the homes of strangers, knocking on doors and ringing doorbells in order to distribute leaflets advertising a religious meeting. She was convicted of violating a municipal ordinance prohibiting any person "to ring the door bell [or] otherwise summon the inmate [of] any residence [for] the purpose of [distributing] handbills." The Court held the ordinance invalid. Justice Black delivered the opinion of the Court:

"We are faced [with] the necessity of weighing the conflicting interests of the appellant in the civil rights she claims, as well as the right of the individual householder to determine whether he is willing to receive her message, against the interest of the community which by this ordinance offers to protect the interests of all its citizens, whether particular citizens want that protection or not. [In] considering legislation which thus limits the dissemination of knowledge, we [must] 'weigh the circumstances [and] appraise the substantiality of the reasons advanced in support of the regulation.' [*Schneider.*] . . .

"While door to door distributors of literature may be either a nuisance or a blind for criminal activities, they may also be useful members of society engaged in the dissemination of ideas in accordance with the best tradition of free discussion. The widespread use of this method of communication by many groups espousing various causes attests its major importance. [Door] to door distribution of circulars is essential to the poorly financed causes of little people.

"Freedom to distribute information to every citizen whenever he desires to receive it is so clearly vital to the preservation of a free society that, putting aside reasonable police and health regulations of time and manner of distribution, it must be fully preserved. [Traditionally] the American law punishes persons who enter onto the property of another after having been warned by the owner to keep off. [Thus], the city may make it an offense for any person to ring the bell of a householder who has appropriately indicated that he is unwilling to be disturbed. This or any similar regulation leaves the decision as to whether distributors of literature may lawfully call at a home where it belongs — with the homeowner himself. [Because] the dangers of distribution can so easily be controlled by traditional legal methods, [the challenged ordinance] can serve no purpose but that forbidden by the Constitution, the naked restriction of the dissemination of ideas."

Justice Frankfurter filed a separate opinion: "[The] ordinance before us [penalizes only] the distribution of 'literature.' [It does not penalize door-to-door canvassing for other purposes, such as the sale of pots and pans.] The Court's opinion leaves one in doubt whether prohibition of [*all* door-to-door canvassing] would be deemed an infringement of free speech. It would be fantastic to suggest that a city has power [to] forbid house-to-house canvassing generally, but the Constitution prohibits the inclusion in such prohibition of door-to-door [distribution of] printed matter."

Justice Reed dissented.

KOVACS v. COOPER, 336 U.S. 77 (1949). In *Kovacs*, the Court, in a five-to-four decision, upheld a city ordinance prohibiting any person to use any sound truck or other instrument that emits "loud and raucous noises" on any public street. Justice Reed, joined by Chief Justice Vinson and Justice Burton, wrote a plurality opinion: "City streets are recognized as a normal place for the exchange of [ideas]. But this does not mean the freedom is beyond all control. We think it is a permissible exercise of legislative discretion to bar sound [trucks], amplified to a loud and raucous volume, from the public ways of municipalities. On the business [streets] such distractions would be dangerous to traffic at all hours useful for the dissemination of information, and in the residential thoroughfares the quiet and tranquility so desirable for city dwellers would likewise be at the mercy of advocates of particular religious, social or political persuasions. . . .

"The right of free speech is guaranteed every citizen that he may reach the minds of willing listeners and to do so there must be opportunity to win their attention. [But the] freedom of speech [does] not require legislators to be insensible to claims by citizens to comfort and convenience. To enforce freedom of speech in disregard of the rights of others would be harsh and arbitrary in itself. That more people may be more easily and cheaply reached by sound trucks [is] not enough to call forth constitutional protection for what those charged with public welfare reasonably think is a nuisance when easy means of publicity are open. [The ordinance does not] restrict the communication of ideas or discussion of issues by the human voice, by newspapers, by pamphlets, by dodgers. We think that the need for reasonable protection in the homes or business houses from the distracting noises of vehicles equipped with such sound amplifying devices justifies the ordinance."

Justice Frankfurter concurred in the result. At the outset, Justice Frankfurter referred to his earlier opinion in Saia v. New York, 334 U.S. 558 (1948), in which he had maintained that "modern devices for amplifying the range and volume of the voice [afford] easy, too easy, opportunities for aural aggression. If uncontrolled, the result is intrusion into cherished privacy. [Surely] there is not a constitutional right to force unwilling people to listen." Justice Frankfurter thus concluded in *Kovacs* that "[s]o long as a legislature does not prescribe what ideas may be noisily expressed, [it] is not for us to supervise the limits it may impose in safeguarding the steadily narrowing opportunities for serenity and reflection." Justice Jackson also concurred in the result.

Justice Black, joined by Justices Douglas and Rutledge, dissented: "The basic premise of the First Amendment is that all present instruments of communication, as well as others that inventive genius may bring into being, shall be free from governmental censorship or prohibition. Laws which hamper the free use of some instruments of communication thereby favor competing channels. Thus, [laws] like [this] ordinance can give an overpowering influence to views of owners of legally favored instruments of communication. [There] are many people who have ideas that they wish to disseminate but who do not have enough money to own or control publishing plants, newspapers, radios, moving picture studios, or chains of show places. [Transmission] of ideas through public speaking is [thus] essential to the sound thinking of a fully informed citizenry. [And] it is an obvious fact that public speaking today without sound amplifiers is a wholly inadequate way to reach the people on a large scale. . . .

"I am aware that the 'blare' of this new method of carrying ideas is susceptible of abuse and may under certain circumstances constitute an intolerable nuisance. But ordinances can be drawn which adequately protect a community from unreasonable use of public speaking devices without absolutely denying to the community's citizens all information that may be disseminated or received through this new avenue for trade in ideas. [A] city ordinance that reasonably restricts the volume of sound, or the hours during which an amplifier may be used, does not, in my mind, infringe the constitutionally protected area of free speech. [But the challenged] ordinance [is] an absolute prohibition of all uses of an amplifier on any of the streets of [the city]."

Justice Murphy also dissented.

METROMEDIA, INC. v. SAN DIEGO, 453 U.S. 490 (1981). A San Diego ordinance banned virtually all outdoor advertising display signs. Four justices concluded that the ordinance was an unconstitutional "content-based" restriction and thus found it unnecessary to decide whether a content-neutral ban on *all* outdoor advertising "would be consistent with the first amendment." The five remaining justices did address that question. Justice Brennan, joined by Justice Blackmun, concurred in the invalidation of the ordinance:

"[The] *practical* effect of the San Diego ordinance is to eliminate the billboard as an effective medium of communication. [Thus, it is necessary to assess] the 'substantiality of the governmental interests asserted' and 'whether those interests could be served by means that would be less intrusive on activity protected by the First Amendment.' [*Schneider; Struthers.*] Applying that test to the instant case, I would invalidate the San Diego ordinance. [First], although I have no quarrel with the substantiality of the city's interest in traffic safety, the city has failed to come forward with evidence demonstrating that billboards actually impair traffic safety in San Diego. [Second], the city has failed to show that its asserted interest in aesthetics is sufficiently substantial in the commercial and industrial areas of San Diego. . . .

"It is no doubt true that the appearance of certain areas of the city would be enhanced by the elimination of billboards, but 'it is not immediately [apparent]' that their elimination in all other areas as well would have more than a negligible impact on aesthetics. [A] billboard is not *necessarily* inconsistent with oil storage tanks, blighted areas, or strip development. Of course, it is not for a court to impose its own notion of beauty on San Diego. But before deferring to a city's judgment, a court must be convinced that the city is seriously and comprehensively addressing aesthetic concerns with respect to its environment. Here, San Diego has failed to demonstrate a comprehensive coordinated effort in its commercial and industrial areas to address other obvious contributors to an unattractive environment. In this sense the ordinance is underinclusive."

Justice Stevens dissented: "[The] net effect of the city's ban on billboards will be a reduction in the total quantity of communication in San Diego. [But that does not in itself render the ordinance invalid.] Graffiti [is] an inexpensive means of communicating [to] large numbers of people; some creators of graffiti have no effective alternative means of publicly expressing themselves. Nevertheless, I believe a community has the right to decide that its interests in protecting property from damaging trespasses and in securing beautiful surroundings outweigh the countervailing interest in uninhibited expression by means of words and pictures in public places. If the First Amendment categorically protected the marketplace of ideas from any quantitative restraint, a municipality could not outlaw graffiti.

"I therefore assume that some total prohibitions may be permissible. It seems to be accepted by all that a zoning regulation excluding billboards from residential neighborhoods is justified by the interest in maintaining pleasant surroundings and enhancing property values. The same interests are at work in commercial and industrial zones, [for the] character of the environment affects property values and the quality of life not only for the suburban resident but equally so for the individual who toils in a factory or invests his capital in industrial properties.

"Because the legitimacy of the interests [is] beyond dispute, [the] constitutionality of the prohibition of outdoor advertising involves two separate questions. First, is there any reason to believe that the regulation is biased in favor of one point of view? Second, is it fair to conclude that the market which remains open for the communication [of] ideas is ample and not threatened with gradually increasing restraints? In this case, there is not even a hint of bias or censorship in the city's actions. Nor is there any reason to believe that the overall communications market in San Diego is inadequate. [Thus,] nothing in this record suggests that the ordinance poses a threat to the interests protected by the First Amendment."

Chief Justice Burger also dissented: "[The] messages conveyed on San Diego billboards [can] reach an equally large audience through a variety of other [media]. True, these other methods may not be so 'eyecatching' — or so cheap — as billboards, but there has been no suggestion that billboards [advance] any particular viewpoint or issue disproportionately to advertising generally. Thus, the ideas billboard advertisers have been presenting are not relatively disadvantaged vis-à-vis the messages of those who heretofore have chosen other methods of spreading their views. [It] borders on the frivolous to suggest that the San Diego ordinance infringes on freedom of expression, given the wide range of alternative means available."

Justice Rehnquist also dissented.

CITY OF LADUE v. GILLEO, 512 U.S. 43 (1994). In a unanimous opinion, the Court held that a city could not constitutionally prohibit homeowners from displaying signs on their property. The purpose of the ordinance was to minimize "visual clutter." At issue was respondent's desire to place on her front lawn a 24-by-36-inch sign printed with the words "Say No to War in the Persian Gulf, Call Congress Now." Justice Stevens delivered the opinion of the Court:

"Ladue has almost completely foreclosed a venerable means of communication that is both unique and important. [Although] prohibitions foreclosing entire media may be completely free of content or viewpoint discrimination, the danger they pose to freedom of speech is readily apparent — by eliminating a common means of speaking, such measures can suppress too much speech. . . .

"Ladue contends, however, that its ordinance is a mere regulation of the 'time, place, or manner' of speech because residents remain free to convey their desired messages by other means, such as hand-held signs, 'letters, handbills, flyers, telephone calls, newspaper advertisements, bumper stickers, speeches, and neighborhood or community meetings.' However, even regulations [of] time, place, or manner [must] 'leave open ample alternative channels for communication.' In this case, we are not persuaded that adequate substitutes exist for the important medium of speech that Ladue has closed off.

"Displaying a sign from one's own residence often carries a message quite distinct from placing the same sign someplace else, or conveying the same text or picture by other means. Precisely because of their location, such signs provide information about the identity of the 'speaker.' [Moreover, residential] signs are an unusually cheap and convenient form of communication. Especially for persons of modest means or limited mobility, a yard or window sign may have no practical substitute. . . .

"A special respect for individual liberty in the home has long been part of our culture and our law; that principle has special resonance when the government seeks to constrain a person's ability to speak there. Most Americans would be understandably dismayed, given that tradition, to learn that it was illegal to display from their window [a] sign expressing their political views. . . .

"Our decision [by] no means leaves the City powerless to address the ills that may be associated with residential signs. [We] are not confronted here with mere regulations short of a ban. [We] are confident that more temperate measures could in large part satisfy Ladue's stated regulatory needs without harm to the First Amendment rights of its citizens. As currently framed, however, the ordinance abridges those rights."

NAACP v. ALABAMA, 357 U.S. 449 (1958). Alabama has a statute, similar to those of many other states, that requires out-of-state corporations to qualify before doing business in the state. For membership organizations, this requirement includes disclosure of the names and addresses of all Alabama members of the organization. In an opinion by Justice Harlan, the Court held at the height of the civil rights movement in the South that this otherwise valid requirement could not constitutionally be applied to the NAACP:

"It is hardly a novel perception that compelled disclosure of affiliation with groups engaged in advocacy may constitute [an effective] restraint on freedom of association. [There is a] vital relationship between freedom to associate and privacy in one's associations. [Inviolability] of privacy in group association may in many circumstances be indispensable to preservation of freedom of association, particularly where a group espouses dissident beliefs. . . .

"We think that the production order [must] be regarded as entailing the likelihood of a substantial restraint upon the exercise by petitioner's members of their right to freedom of association. Petitioner has made an uncontroverted showing that on past occasions revelation of the identity of its rank-and-file members has exposed these members to economic reprisal, loss of employment, threat of physical coercion, and other manifestations of public hostility. Under these circumstances, we think it apparent that compelled disclosure of petitioner's Alabama membership is likely to affect adversely the ability of petitioner and its members to pursue their collective effort to foster beliefs which they admittedly have the right to advocate, in that it may induce members to withdraw from the Association and dissuade others from joining it because of fear of exposure of their beliefs shown through their associations and of the consequences of this exposure. . . .

"We turn to the final question whether Alabama has demonstrated an interest in obtaining the disclosures it seeks from petitioner which is sufficient to justify the deterrent effect which we have concluded these disclosures may well have on the free exercise by petitioner's members of their constitutionally protected right of association. [Whatever] interest the State may have in obtaining names of ordinary members has not been shown to be sufficient to overcome petitioner's constitutional objections to the production order."

Note: The Search for Principles

1. *Balancing.* Is "balancing" underprotective of free speech? Should content-neutral restrictions be governed by the same standards as content-based restric-

tions? Consider Redish, The Content Distinction in First Amendment Analysis, 34 Stan. L. Rev. 113, 128 (1981):

> The most puzzling aspect of the distinction between content-based and content-neutral restrictions is that either restriction reduces the sum total of information or opinion disseminated. That governmental regulation impedes all forms of speech, rather than only selected viewpoints or subjects, does not alter the fact that the regulation impairs the free flow of expression. Whatever rationale one adopts for the constitutional protection of speech, the goals behind that rationale are undermined by *any* limitation on expression, content-based or not.

Consider the following responses: (a) Content-based restrictions generally are more dangerous than content-neutral restrictions because they are more likely significantly to distort the "marketplace of ideas." (b) Content-based restrictions are more dangerous than content-neutral restrictions because they are more likely to be enacted for the constitutionally impermissible purpose of suppressing "erroneous," "undesirable," or "unpopular" ideas. (c) Content-based restrictions are more dangerous than content-neutral restrictions because they are more likely to restrict speech because of its "communicative impact" (i.e., because of government's fear of how people will react to the content of the speaker's message).

For analysis of the distortion argument, consider Baker, Turner Broadcasting: Content-Based Regulation of Persons and Presses, 1994 Sup. Ct. Rev. 57, 85-86:

> There is no "natural" version of public dialogue that the First Amendment could prohibit the government from distorting. The content and quality of public dialogue depend on many factors, including the overall legal order and legally established resource allocations. The government even participates, massively and purposefully, in the debate itself. [Government's] recognized role in structuring society in ways that affect public dialogue and its discretionary participation in that dialogue make it unclear why anything called "distortion" could be constitutionally objectionable. These facts also mean that there can be no standard with which to compare the effect of governmental policies in order to describe these effects as "distortions."

Consider also C. Sunstein, The Partial Constitution 227-228 (1993):

> [The] idea of [distortion] depends on taking the marketplace as unobjectionable in its current form. [But] it would be exceptionally surprising [if] there were no such [distortion already built into the existing marketplace of ideas, for that marketplace is itself] a function of existing law. [On the other hand], the existence of an unjust status quo should probably not be a reason to allow regulation of the content of speech, [for such regulation] is probably beyond governmental capacity. There is a serious risk that [governmental] decisions about the relative power of various groups [will] be biased or unreliable.

For further commentary on the content-based/content-neutral distinction, see Ely, Flag Desecration: A Case Study in the Roles of Categorization and Balancing in First Amendment Analysis, 88 Harv. L. Rev. 1482 (1975); Stephan, The First Amendment and Content Discrimination, 68 Va. L. Rev. 203 (1982); Stone, Content-Neutral Restrictions, 54 U. Chi. L. Rev. 46 (1987); Williams, Content Discrimination and the First Amendment, 139 U. Pa. L. Rev. 615

(1991); Kagan, Private Speech, Public Purpose: The Role of Governmental Motive in First Amendment Doctrine, 63 U. Chi. L. Rev. 415, 446-463 (1996) (arguing that the concern with improper government motivation best explains the content-based/content-neutral distinction); Brownstein, Rules of Engagement for Culture Wars: Regulating Conduct, Unprotected Speech, and Protected Expression in Anti-Abortion Protests, 29 U.C. Davis L. Rev. 553 (1996). For a critique of balancing, see Aleinikoff, Constitutional Law in the Age of Balancing, 96 Yale L.J. 943 (1987).

2. *Striking the balance.* If content-neutral restrictions are tested by "balancing," what factors should be weighed in the balance? Consider the following propositions:

a. Although "the purpose to keep the streets clean and of good appearance is insufficient to justify" a prohibition on leafleting, the first amendment does not "deprive a municipality of power to enact regulations against throwing literature broadcast in the streets [since] such activity bears no necessary relationship to the freedom to speak, write, print or distribute information or opinion."

b. "[One] is not to have the exercise of his liberty of expression in appropriate places abridged on the plea that it may be exercised in some other place." Suppose a city permits soapbox orators to make public speeches in only four of its six municipal parks.

c. "That more people may be more easily and cheaply reached by sound trucks [is] not enough to call forth constitutional protection for what those charged with public welfare reasonably think is a nuisance when [alternative] means of publicity are open." Is this consistent with b? Should the existence of alternative means of communication affect the balance?

d. "The dangers of [door-to-door distribution of leaflets] can so easily be controlled by traditional legal methods [that] stringent prohibition can serve no purpose but [the] naked restriction of the dissemination of ideas." Should it matter that the state may be able to achieve part or all of its goals through alternative means that may have a less restrictive effect on expression?

e. "It would be fantastic to suggest that a city has power [to] forbid house-to-house canvassing generally, but that the Constitution prohibits the inclusion in such prohibition of door-to-door [distribution of] printed matter." Should it matter whether a law specifically restricts expression or restricts a broader range of activities in a manner that has only an incidental effect on expression?

f. "There has been no suggestion that billboards heretofore have advanced any particular viewpoint or issue disproportionately. . . . Thus, the ideas billboard advertisers have been presenting are not *relatively* disadvantaged vis-à-vis the messages of those who heretofore have chosen other methods of spreading their views." Should it matter whether a content-neutral restriction has "content-differential" effects? Consider NAACP v. Alabama.

3. *Regulation versus prohibition. Schneider, Struthers, Kovacs, Metromedia,* and *Gilleo* focused primarily on government efforts to *prohibit* completely or at least substantially the use of particular means of communication. Often, however, government attempts merely to *regulate* the use of particular means of communication. Should the same general principles govern? In light of the opinions set out above, how would you rule on the constitutionality of the following laws?

a. "It is unlawful for any person to ring the door bell or otherwise summon the inmate of any residence for the purpose of canvassing between the hours of 8:00 P.M. and 8:00 A.M."

b. "The use of sound amplification equipment is prohibited within
of any hospital, school, church, courthouse, or residence."

c. "No sign larger than 800 square inches may be displayed on residential
property."

Note: The Meaning of "Content-Neutrality"

In most cases, a law's content-neutrality is self-evident. There are several situations, however, in which the matter is more complex:

1. *Communicative impact.* A law may be content-neutral on its face but may turn in application on communicative impact — that is, "on how people will react to what the speaker is saying." J. Ely, Democracy and Distrust 111 (1980). Consider, for example, a law declaring it unlawful for any person to "disturb the peace" by making any public speech that "may cause a hostile audience response." Although such laws are "neutral" on their face, the Court has analyzed them as content-based because it is the content of the message that triggers the restriction. Recall, for example, *Terminiello, Cantwell,* and *Edwards,* section B3 supra. For analysis of this issue, see Stone, Content Regulation and the First Amendment, 25 Wm. & Mary L. Rev. 189, 207-217 (1983).

2. *Secondary effects.* A law may be content-based on its face but may be defended in terms that are unrelated to communicative impact. In *Renton,* section D5 supra, for example, the Court characterized a zoning ordinance that restricted the location of movie theaters that exhibit movies emphasizing "specified sexual activities" as "content-neutral" because it was defended not in terms of the communicative impact of the restricted expression but in terms of "the secondary effects of such theaters on the surrounding community."

In a separate concurring opinion in Boos v. Barry, 485 U.S. 312 (1988), Justice Brennan elaborated on his *Renton* dissent:

> I [register] my continuing disagreement with the proposition that an otherwise content-based restriction on speech can be recast as "content-neutral" if the restriction "aims" at "secondary effects" of the speech. [Such] secondary effects offer countless excuses for content-based suppression of political speech. No doubt a plausible argument could be made that the political gatherings of some parties are more likely than others to attract large crowds causing congestion, that picketing for certain causes is more likely than other picketing to cause visual clutter, or that speakers delivering a particular message are more likely than others to attract an unruly audience. [The] *Renton* analysis [plunges] courts into [a morass of] notoriously hazardous and indeterminate inquiry. [This] indeterminacy is hardly *Renton*'s worst [flaw, however], for the root problem [is that *Renton*] relies on the dubious proposition that a statute which on its face discriminates based on the content of speech aims not at content but at some secondary effect that does not itself affect the operation of the statute.

In decisions since *Renton,* the Court seems to have backed away from the *Renton* analysis or at least interpreted *Renton* narrowly. In *Boos,* for example, the Court, in invalidating an ordinance prohibiting the display of any sign within 500 feet of a foreign embassy if the sign tends to bring the foreign government into disrepute, rejected the government's argument that the ordinance was "content-neutral" under *Renton* because "the real concern is a secondary effect, namely, our international law obligation to shield diplomats from speech that offends their dignity."

The Court visited the issue again in City of Cincinnati v. Discovery Network, 507 U.S. 410 (1993), in which the Court invalidated a prohibition on the use of newsracks on public property for the distribution of commercial handbills. Although the ordinance on its face distinguished between commercial and non-commercial publications, the city argued that the challenged prohibition was content-neutral "because the [city's] interests in safety and esthetics [are] entirely unrelated to the content of [the] publications." The Court, in an opinion by Justice Stevens, rejected this argument:

> The argument is unpersuasive because the very basis for the regulation is the difference in content between ordinary newspapers and commercial speech. [Under] the city's newsrack policy, whether any particular newsrack falls within the ban is determined by the content of the publication resting inside the newsrack. Thus, by any commonsense understanding of the term, the ban [is] "content-based." [The city's] reliance on Renton is misplaced. [We] upheld the regulation [in Renton] largely because it was justified, not by an interest in suppressing adult films, but by the city's concern for the "secondary effects" of such theaters on the surrounding neighborhoods. In contrast to the speech at issue in Renton, there are no secondary effects attributable to newsracks [containing commercial handbills] that distinguish them from the newsracks Cincinnati permits to remain on its sidewalks.

For another application of the secondary effects doctrine, see City of Erie v. Pap's A.M., 529 U.S. 277 (2000) (upholding an ordinance banning public nudity, as applied to nude performance dancing).

3. *Impermissible motive.* A law may be content-neutral on its face but may have been enacted with the purpose of suppressing a particular message. Consider, for example, a law prohibiting any person to destroy a draft card, enacted for the purpose of punishing those individuals who publicly burn their draft cards to protest national policy. For analysis of this issue, see section E3 infra.

4. *Content-differential effects.* Some laws are content-neutral on their face but have content-differential effects. Recall, for example, Justice Black's observation in *Struthers* that "door to door distribution of circulars is essential to the poorly financed causes of little people." To what extent should this factor convert a content-neutral regulation into one that is treated as content-based? See Williams, Content Discrimination and the First Amendment, 139 U. Pa. L. Rev. 615 (1991) (disparate impact should trigger content-based analysis); Stone, Content-Neutral Restrictions, 54 U. Chi. L. Rev. 46, 81-86 (1987) (disparate impact should merely be a relevant factor in content-neutral analysis). In NAACP v. Alabama, should the Court have invalidated the statute in its entirety or only as applied to the NAACP? Could the statute constitutionally be applied to the Republican Party? Note that a decision exempting only the NAACP would have the anomalous effect of converting a content-neutral regulation into one that is essentially content-based. See Stone and Marshall, Brown v. Socialist Workers: Inequality as a Command of the First Amendment, 1983 Sup. Ct. Rev. 583.

5. *Speaker-based restrictions.* Is an injunction prohibiting specifically named antiabortion protestors from demonstrating near an abortion clinic content-based or content-neutral? In Madsen v. Women's Health Center, Inc., 512 U.S. 753 (1994), the Court held that such an injunction, issued after the specifically

named petitioners had previously violated a narrower order enjoining them from blocking access to the clinic, was content-neutral:

> We [reject] petitioners' contention that the [order is content-based because it] restricts only the speech of antiabortion protestors. [The] injunction, by its very nature, applies only to a particular group. [It] does so, however, because of the group's past actions in the context of a specific dispute. [The] fact that the injunction in the present case did not prohibit activities of those demonstrating in favor of abortion is justly attributable to the lack of any similar demonstrations by those in favor of abortion, and of any consequent request that their demonstrations be regulated by injunction. There is no suggestion [that] Florida law would not equally restrain similar conduct directed at a target having nothing to do with abortion; none of the restrictions [were] directed at the contents of petitioners' message. [The] state court imposed restrictions on petitioners incidental to their abortion message because they repeatedly violated the court's original order. That petitioners all share the same viewpoint regarding abortion does not in itself demonstrate that some invidious content or viewpoint-based purpose motivated the issuance of the order. It suggests only that those in the group whose conduct violated the court's order happen to share the same opinion regarding abortions being performed in the clinic.

Suppose the injunction had prohibited "any antiabortion protestor from demonstrating within thirty-six feet of an abortion clinic"? Would that be content-neutral? Speaker-based restrictions, which treat some speakers differently than others but define the distinction in terms other than content, do not fit neatly within the Court's content-based/content-neutral distinction. For example, suppose a city bans all door-to-door canvassing after 8:00 P.M., except for canvassing by veterans groups. How should such a law be analyzed? For commentary on speaker-based restrictions, see Stone, Content Regulation, supra, at 244-251. See also Regan v. Taxation with Representation, Perry Educators' Assocation v. Perry Local Educators'Association, and Cornelius v. NAACP Legal Defense and Educational Fund, sections E2c and E2d infra.

6. *Content-neutrality: another look.* In Hill v. Colorado, 120 S. Ct. 2480 (2000), the Court upheld as a "content-neutral" time, place, or manner regulation a Colorado statute that makes it unlawful for any person within 100 feet of a health care facility to "knowingly approach" within eight feet of another person, without that person's consent, in order to pass "a leaflet or handbill to, [display] a sign to, or [engage] in oral protest, education, or counseling with, such other person." Is this law content-based or content-neutral?

Consider Justice Scalia's argument in dissent that the law is content-based: "A speaker wishing to approach another for the purpose of communicating *any* message except one of protest, education, or counseling may do so without first securing the other's consent. Whether a speaker must obtain permission before approaching within eight feet — and whether he will be sent to prison for failing to do so — depends entirely on *what he intends to say* when he gets there. [Moreover,] when applied, as it is here, at the entrance to medical facilities, [such a law is clearly] a means of impeding speech against abortion. The Court's confident assurance that the statute poses no special threat to First Amendment freedoms because it applies alike to 'used car salesmen, animal rights activists, fundraisers, environmentalists, and missionaries,' . . . is a wonderful replication (except for its lack of sarcasm) of Anatole France's observation that '[t]he law, in its majestic equality, forbids the rich as well as the poor to sleep under bridges. . . .'"

Consider the Court's response: "[The statute] seeks to protect those who enter a health care facility from the harassment, the nuisance [and] the implied threat of physical touching that can accompany an unwelcome approach within eight feet of a patient by a person wishing to argue vociferously face-to-face and perhaps thrust an undesired handbill upon her. The statutory phrases, 'oral protest, education, or counseling,' distinguish speech activities likely to have those consequences from speech activities [that] are most unlikely to have those consequences. The statute does not distinguish among speech instances that are similarly likely to raise the legitimate concerns to which it responds. Hence, the statute cannot be struck down for failure to maintain 'content neutrality.' [Similarly], the contention that a statute is 'viewpoint based' simply because its enactment was motivated by the conduct of the partisans on one side of a debate is without support. [The] statute is not limited to those who oppose abortion. It applies to all 'protest,' to all 'counseling,' and to all demonstrators whether or not the demonstration concerns abortion, and whether they oppose or support the woman who has made an abortion decision. That is the level of neutrality that the Constitution demands."

2. Speech on Public Property: The Public Forum

In what circumstances, if any, does the first amendment guarantee the individual the right to commandeer publicly owned property for the purpose of exercising the freedoms of speech, press, assembly, and petition? The Court has been highly solicitous of the right of owners of *private* property to prevent others from using their property for speech purposes. In *Struthers*, for example, the Court left no doubt that the city could constitutionally "punish those who call at a home in defiance of the previously expressed will of the occupant." More generally, the Court has accepted the view that in most circumstances "an uninvited guest may [not] exercise general rights of free speech on property privately owned," for it "would be an unwarranted infringement of property rights to require them to yield to the exercise of First Amendment rights." Lloyd Corp. v. Tanner, 407 U.S. 551, 568, 567 (1972). To what extent, then, does the first amendment supersede the "property rights" of the state? Must the state "subsidize" speech by allowing individuals to use publicly owned property for speech purposes?

For commentary on the "public forum," see Cass, First Amendment Access to Government Facilities, 65 Va. L. Rev. 1287 (1979); Kalven, The Concept of the Public Forum: Cox v. Louisiana, 1965 Sup. Ct. Rev. 1; Stone, Fora Americana: Speech in Public Places, 1974 Sup. Ct. Rev. 233.

Public forum theory has evolved along two separate, but related, lines — one governing streets and parks, the other governing all other publicly owned property. The materials in the first two parts of this section track this distinction. The remaining two parts of this section examine the problem of inequality of access to public property for speech purposes.

a. The Public Forum: Streets and Parks

COMMONWEALTH v. DAVIS, 162 MASS. 510, 39 N.E. 113 (1895), aff'd sub nom. DAVIS v. MASSACHUSETTS, 167 U.S. 43 (1897). Davis, a preacher whose congregation apparently consisted of the crowds on the Boston Common, was convicted under a city ordinance that forbade, among other things, "any public address" on any publicly owned property "except in accordance with a permit from the mayor." The Supreme Judicial Court of Massachusetts, speaking through Justice Holmes, affirmed the conviction. Justice Holmes explained that Davis's argument was premised on the "fallacy" that "the ordinance is directed against free speech generally, [whereas] in fact it is directed toward the modes in which Boston Common may be used." Justice Holmes reasoned that, "as representative of the public," the legislature "may and does exercise control over the use which the public may make of such places," and for "the Legislature absolutely or conditionally to forbid public speaking in a highway or public park is no more an infringement of the rights of a member of the public than for the owner of a private house to forbid it in his house." Since the legislature "may end the right of the public to enter upon the public place by putting an end to the dedication to public uses," it necessarily "may take the lesser step of limiting the public use to certain purposes."

On appeal, the Supreme Court unanimously embraced Justice Holmes's position. Chief Justice White, speaking for the Court, maintained that the federal Constitution "does not have the effect of creating a particular and personal right in the citizen to use public property in defiance of the constitution and laws of the State." Indeed, the "right to absolutely exclude all right to use, necessarily includes the authority to determine under what circumstances such use may be availed of, as the greater power contains the lesser." *

Is this a satisfactory resolution of the public forum issue? Consider Stone, Fora Americana: Speech in Public Places, 1974 Sup. Ct. Rev. 233, 237: "[Under] the Holmes-White approach, the state possessed the power absolutely to prohibit the exercise of First Amendment rights [on] public property simply by asserting the prerogatives traditionally associated with the private ownership of land. [The] problem of the public forum had been 'solved' by resort to common law concepts of private property."

HAGUE v. CIO, 307 U.S. 496 (1939). Forty-two years later, the Court reopened the question. In *Hague*, the Court considered the constitutionality of a municipal ordinance forbidding all public meetings in the streets and other public places without a permit. The city maintained that the ordinance was clearly constitutional under *Davis*. Although the Court did not directly decide the question, Justice Roberts, in a plurality opinion, flatly rejected the city's contention in a dictum that has played a central role in the evolution of public forum theory:

"Wherever the title of streets and parks may rest, they have immemorially been held in trust for the use of the public and, time out of mind, have been used for

---

* [At the time of *Davis*, the Court had not as yet held the first amendment applicable to the states, thus undermining the precedential force of *Davis* as a "free speech" decision. It appears that the primary constitutional issue before the Court concerned dictum in Yick Wo v. Hopkins, 118 U.S. 356 (1886), suggesting that the equal protection clause prohibited all forms of standardless licensing. This dictum was rejected more clearly in a series of subsequent decisions. See Lieberman v. Van de Carr, 199 U.S. 552 (1905); Gundling v. Chicago, 177 U.S. 183 (1900); Wilson v. Eureka, 173 U.S. 32 (1899). — EDS.]

purposes of assembly, communicating thought between citizens, and discussing public questions. Such use of the streets and public places has, from ancient times, been a part of the privileges, immunities, rights, and liberties of citizens. The privilege of a citizen of the United States to use the streets and parks for communication of views on national questions may be regulated in the interest of all; it is not absolute, but relative, and must be exercised in subordination to the general comfort and convenience, and in consonance with peace and good order; but it must not, in the guise of regulation, be abridged or denied."

Consider Stone, supra, at 238:

> Perhaps the most interesting aspect of the Roberts dictum is its implicit acceptance of the underlying premise of the Holmes-White position — that the public forum issue must be defined in terms of the common law property rights of the state. Rather than challenging that premise head-on, Roberts conveniently adapted it to his own advantage, predicating the public forum right upon established common law notions of adverse possession and public trust. [In effect, Roberts concluded that] the streets, parks, and similar public places are subject to what Professor Kalven has termed "a kind of First-Amendment easement." [Citing Kalven, The Concept of the Public Forum: Cox v. Louisiana, 1965 Sup. Ct. Rev. 1, 13.] Since such places have been used, "time out of mind," for purposes of speech and assembly, the Constitution now requires that their continued use for these purposes not "be abridged or denied."

Is this a sound rationale for the right to a public forum? Note that the Roberts rationale creates by implication two distinct classes of public property. Although streets, parks, and similar public places may constitute public fora, publicly owned property that cannot satisfy the "time out of mind" requirement remains subject to the *Davis* dictum, and access to such places for purposes of speech and assembly may thus be denied absolutely upon the state's naked assertion of title. Would it be preferable to base public forum theory on the notion that access to public property for speech purposes is essential to effective exercise of first amendment rights?

SCHNEIDER v. STATE, 308 U.S. 147 (1939). In *Schneider*, section E1 supra, decided only eight months after *Hague*, the Court held that a city's interest in keeping "the streets clean and of good appearance" was "insufficient" to justify a municipal ordinance prohibiting the distribution of leaflets on public property. Although the Court did not explicitly address the status of *Davis*, the impact of *Hague* and *Schneider* was made clear several years later in Jamison v. Texas, 318 U.S. 413 (1943), in which the Court, following *Schneider*, invalidated a city ordinance prohibiting the dissemination of leaflets. Relying on *Davis*, the city maintained that "it has the power absolutely to prohibit the use of the streets for the communication of ideas." The Court responded: "This same argument, made in reliance upon the same decision, has been directly rejected by this Court. [Citing Justice Roberts's concurring opinion in *Hague*.]"

Consider Kalven, supra, at 18-21:

The result [in *Schneider*] had an impressive bite. Leaflet distribution in public places in a city is a method of communication that carries as an inextricable and expected consequence substantial littering of the streets, which the city has an obligation to keep clean. It is also a method of communication of some annoyance to a majority of people so addressed; that its impact on its audience is very high is doubtful. Yet the constitutional balance in *Schneider* was struck emphatically in favor of keeping the public forum open for this mode of communication. [At stake in *Schneider* was] the immemorial claim of the free man to use the streets as a forum. [The state], the Court was telling us, must recognize the special nature and value of that claim to be on the street. [The] operative theory of the Court, at least for the leaflet situation, is that [the] right to use the streets as a public forum [cannot] be prohibited and can be regulated only for weighty reasons.

How does the *Hague/Schneider* theory of the public forum relate to the analysis of content-neutral restrictions generally? Consider the following propositions:

1. Although the *Hague/Schneider* theory holds that the property rights of the state do not in themselves permit the state absolutely to exclude expression from public property that has been used "time out of mind" for speech purposes, it does not hold that government property rights are irrelevant. Thus, content-neutral restrictions governing streets and parks should be tested by more lenient standards of justification than content-neutral restrictions that do not implicate the property rights of the state.

2. The *Hague/Schneider* theory holds that government property rights are irrelevant when the property has been used "time out of mind" for speech purposes. Thus, content-neutral restrictions governing streets and parks should be tested by the same standards of justification that are used to test content-neutral restrictions that do not implicate the property rights of the state.

3. The *Hague/Schneider* theory holds that the streets and parks are "public fora" in which the state must be especially solicitous of free expression. Thus, content-neutral restrictions governing streets and parks should be tested by more stringent standards of justification than content-neutral restrictions that do not implicate "public forum" rights.

Note: Regulating the Public Forum

1. *Signs near a courthouse.* In United States v. Grace, 461 U.S. 171 (1983), the Court invalidated a federal statute prohibiting any person to display on the public sidewalks surrounding the Supreme Court building "any flag, banner, or device designed [to] bring into public notice any party, organization or movement." The Court explained that the "public sidewalks forming the perimeter of the Supreme Court grounds [are] public forums," and that "the government's ability" to restrict expression in such places "is very limited." Indeed, "the government may enforce reasonable time, place, and manner restrictions" in public forums only if "the restrictions 'are content-neutral, are narrowly tailored to serve a significant government interest, and leave open ample alternative channels of communication,'" and it may absolutely prohibit "a particular type of expression" only if the prohibition is "narrowly drawn to accomplish a compelling governmental interest."

The Court held that this statute could not be justified as a means "to maintain proper order and decorum" near the Supreme Court, for a "total ban" was not necessary to achieve these ends. And the restriction could not be justified as a means to prevent the appearance "that the Supreme Court is subject to outside influence," for the restriction did not "sufficiently serve" that purpose "to sustain its validity."

Recall Cox v. Louisiana, section B2 supra, in which the Court, in dictum, upheld a statute prohibiting any person, "with the intent of interfering with, obstructing, or impeding the administration of justice, or with the intent of influencing any judge, juror, witness, or court officer, in the discharge of his duty," to picket or parade "in or near a building housing a court." Does this aspect of Cox survive Grace?

2. *Noise near a school.* In Grayned v. Rockford, 408 U.S. 104 (1972), approximately 200 demonstrators marched on a public sidewalk about 100 feet from a public high school to protest the school's racial policies. Appellant, a participant in the demonstration, was convicted of violating a Rockford ordinance prohibiting any "person, while on public or private grounds adjacent to any building in which a school or any class thereof is in session, [to make] any noise or diversion which disturbs or tends to disturb the peace or good order of such school." The Court, in an eight-to-one decision, affirmed the conviction.

The Court explained that, although "the public sidewalk adjacent to school grounds may not be declared off limits for expressive activity, [such] activity may be prohibited if it 'materially disrupts classwork or involves substantial disorder or invasion of the rights of others.'" In this case, the Court held that the "antinoise" ordinance "is narrowly tailored to further Rockford's compelling interest in having an undisrupted school session conducive to the students' learning"; "punishes only conduct which disrupts or is about to disrupt normal school activities"; requires that the "decision [be] made [on] an individualized basis"; and "gives no license to punish anyone because of what he is saying." The Court concluded that "such a reasonable regulation is not inconsistent with the First and Fourteenth Amendments."

3. *Picketing near a home.* In Frisby v. Shultz, 487 U.S. 474 (1988), a group varying in size from eleven to forty people picketed in protest on six occasions within one month on the public street outside the residence of a doctor who performed abortions. The picketing was orderly and peaceful. Thereafter, the town enacted an ordinance that prohibited residential picketing that focuses on and takes place in front of a particular residence. The Court, in a six-to-three decision, upheld the ordinance.

Although emphasizing that "a public street does not lose its status as a traditional public forum because it runs through a residential neighborhood," the Court nonetheless concluded that the ordinance was constitutional because it left "open ample alternative channels of communication" and was "narrowly tailored to serve a significant government interest." The Court found the first requirement "readily" satisfied because the ordinance left protestors free to march, proselytize door-to-door, leaflet, and even picket in a manner that did not focus exclusively on a particular residence.

As to the second requirement, the Court observed that "privacy of the home is [of] the highest order in a free and civilized society." Moreover, the "type of picketers banned by [this ordinance] generally do not seek to disseminate a message to the general public, but to intrude upon the targeted resident, and to do so in an especially offensive way. [And] even if some such picketers have a broader communicative purpose, their activity nonetheless inherently and offensively intrudes on residential privacy." Indeed, the Court noted that "even a solitary picket can invade residential privacy, [for the] target of the focused picketing banned by [this] ordinance is [a] 'captive,' [figuratively], and perhaps literally, trapped within the home." The Court thus concluded that the ordinance was "narrowly tailored" because "the 'evil' of targeted residential picketing, 'the very presence of an unwelcome visitor at the home,' is 'created by the medium of expression itself.'" Justices Brennan, Marshall, and Stevens dissented.

4. *Sleeping in a park.* In Clark v. Community for Creative Non-Violence, 468 U.S. 288 (1983), the National Park Service permitted CCNV to erect symbolic tent cities, consisting of between twenty and forty tents, in Lafayette Park and on the Mall in Washington, D.C., for the purpose of conducting a round-the-clock demonstration designed to dramatize the plight of the homeless. Pursuant to a National Park Service regulation prohibiting "camping" in these parks, however, the Park Service prohibited CCNV demonstrators from sleeping overnight in the tents. The Court assumed arguendo "that overnight sleeping in connection with the demonstration is expressive conduct protected [by] the First Amendment," but upheld the regulation as a "reasonable time, place, and manner restriction."

The Court emphasized that the regulation is "content neutral," that it does not prevent CCNV from demonstrating the "plight of the homeless [in] other ways," and that it "narrowly focuses on the Government's substantial interest in maintaining the parks [in] an attractive and intact condition." The Court rejected CCNV's argument that, once the Park Service decided to permit "the symbolic city of tents," the "incremental benefit to the parks was insufficient to justify the ban on sleeping." Justice Marshall, joined by Justice Brennan, dissented.

5. *Noise in a park.* In Ward v. Rock against Racism, 491 U.S. 781 (1989), the Court upheld a New York City regulation requiring the use of city-provided sound systems and technicians for concerts in the Bandshell in Central Park. The principal justification for the regulation was the city's desire to control noise levels to avoid undue intrusion into other areas of the park and adjacent residential areas. The Court held that government clearly "'ha[s] a substantial interest in protecting its citizens from unwelcome noise,'" and that the regulation clearly leaves "open ample alternative channels of communication." The more difficult issue concerned the requirement that the regulation be "narrowly tailored," for the court of appeals had invalidated the regulation on the ground that "there were several alternative methods of achieving the desired end that would have been less restrictive [of] First Amendment rights"; for example, the city could have regulated the volume of noise but left control of the sound equipment and selection of the technicians to the performers. The Court rejected this approach:

[A] regulation of the time, place, or manner of protected speech must be narrowly tailored to serve the government's legitimate content-neutral interests, but [it] need not be the least-restrictive or least-intrusive means of doing so. Rather, the requirement of narrow tailoring is satisfied "so long as [the] regulation promotes a substantial governmental interest that would be achieved less effectively absent the regulation." [This] does not mean that a time, place, or manner regulation may burden substantially more speech than is necessary to further the government's legitimate interests. Government may not regulate expression in such a manner that a substantial portion of the burden on speech does not serve to advance its goals. [But so] long as the means chosen are not substantially broader than necessary to achieve the government's interest, [the] regulation will not be invalid simply because a court concludes that the government's interest could be adequately served by some less-speech-restrictive alternative.

Justice Marshall, joined by Justices Brennan and Stevens, dissented.

6. *Demonstrating near an abortion clinic.* In Madsen v. Women's Health Center, Inc., 512 U.S. 753 (1994), after petitioners repeatedly violated an injunction prohibiting them from blocking access to an abortion clinic and engaging in other activities that harassed patients and doctors both at the clinic and at their homes, a state court issued a new injunction prohibiting the petitioners from, inter alia, demonstrating within thirty-six feet of the clinic; making excessive noise near the clinic by "singing, chanting, whistling, shouting, yelling, use of bullhorns, auto horns [or] sound amplification equipment"; exhibiting "images observable" by patients within the clinic; approaching patients within 300 feet of the clinic who did not voluntarily indicate a desire to speak with them; and demonstrating within 300 feet of the residence of any of the clinic's employees.

The Court upheld the thirty-six-foot buffer zone around the clinic primarily because the original injunction, which had established no such buffer zone, "did not succeed in protecting access to the clinic." Although conceding that the "need for a complete buffer zone may be debatable," the Court concluded that "some deference must be given to the state court's familiarity with the facts and the background of the dispute." The Court also upheld the restriction on excessive noise because noise "control is particularly important around hospitals and medical facilities."

On the other hand, the Court invalidated the restriction on exhibiting "images observable" to patients within the clinic. The Court explained that the proper remedy is for the clinic to "pull its curtains." The Court also invalidated that portion of the injunction that prohibited petitioners from "approaching any person seeking services of the clinic 'unless such person indicates a desire to communicate' in an area within 300 feet of the clinic." The Court held that, "[a]bsent evidence that the protesters' speech is independently proscribable (i.e., 'fighting words' or threats), [this] provision cannot stand." Finally, the Court invalidated the provision enjoining petitioners from demonstrating within 300 feet of the residences of clinic staff. The Court explained that "the 300-foot zone [is] much larger than the zone [upheld] in *Frisby*. [A] limitation of the time, duration of picketing, and number of pickets outside a smaller zone could have accomplished the desired result."

Justice Scalia, joined by Justices Kennedy and Thomas, dissented from the upholding of the thirty-six-foot buffer zone and the restriction against excessive noise near the clinic. Justice Stevens dissented from the invalidation of the restriction on "physically approaching" clients within 300 feet of the clinic without their consent.

7. *Demonstrating near an abortion clinic II.* In Schenck v. Pro-Choice Network of Western New York, 519 U.S. 357 (1997), several abortion clinics in upstate New York were subjected to a series of large-scale blockades in which antiabortion protesters marched, stood, knelt, or lay in clinic parking lots and doorways, blocking cars from entering the lots and interfering with patients and clinic employees who attempted to enter the clinics. Smaller groups of protesters, called "sidewalk counselors," crowded, jostled, pushed, and yelled and spit at women

entering the clinics. Police officers who attempted to control the protests often were harassed by the protesters both verbally and by mail. A federal district court issued an injunction against fifty individuals and three organizations (including Operation Rescue), which, among other things, (a) prohibited them from demonstrating within fifteen feet of clinic doorways, parking lots, and driveways ("fixed buffer zones"); (b) prohibited them from demonstrating within fifteen feet of any person or vehicle seeking access to or leaving a clinic ("floating buffer zones"); and (c) permitted them to have two "sidewalk counselors" inside the buffer zones on the condition that they "cease and desist" their "counseling" if the person with whom they are speaking so requests.

Applying *Madsen*, the Court asked whether these provisions of the injunction "burden more speech than necessary to serve a significant governmental interest." In upholding the "fixed buffer zones" as appropriate means of ensuring "that people and vehicles trying to enter or exit the clinic property [can] do so," the Court rejected the claim that such zones were unnecessary in light of other provisions of the injunction prohibiting the protesters from "blocking, impeding or obstructing access to" the clinics. The Court explained that, in light of the prior conduct of the protesters, the district court "was entitled to conclude" that fixed buffer zones were necessary to prevent the protesters from doing "what they had done before: aggressively follow and crowd individuals right up to the clinic door and then refuse to move, or purposefully mill around parking lot entrances in an effort to impede or block the progress of cars."

On the other hand, the Court invalidated the "floating buffer zones." The Court was particularly concerned that, because sidewalks near the clinics are usually only seventeen feet wide, protesters wishing to communicate with an individual entering or leaving a clinic would either have to walk in the street, walk fifteen feet behind the individual, or walk backwards fifteen feet in front of the individual. The Court concluded that this was "hazardous" and would effectively prevent protesters "from communicating a message from a normal conversational distance or handing leaflets to people entering or leaving the clinics [on] the public sidewalks."

Finally, the Court upheld the "cease and desist" provision that "limits the exception for sidewalk counselors in connection with the fixed buffer zone." At the outset, the Court cast doubt on the district court's explanation that this provision was designed "to protect the right of the people approaching and entering the facilities to be left alone," noting that "as a general matter, we have indicated that in public debate [our] citizens must tolerate insulting, and even outrageous, speech in order to provide adequate breathing space to the freedoms protected by the First Amendment." But the Court nonetheless upheld the "cease and desist" provision because "the entire exception for sidewalk counselors was an effort to enhance [the] speech rights" of the protesters.

Justice Scalia, joined by Justices Kennedy and Thomas, dissented from the upholding of the fixed buffer zones and the "cease and desist" provision. Justice Breyer dissented from the invalidation of the floating buffer zones.

8. *Demonstrating near an abortion clinic III.* In Hill v. Colorado, 120 S. Ct. 2480 (2000), the Court, in a six-to-three decision, upheld a Colorado statute that makes it unlawful for any person within 100 feet of a health care facility to "knowingly approach" within eight feet of another person, without that person's consent, in order to pass "a leaflet or handbill to, [display] a sign to, or [engage] in

oral protest, education, or counseling with, such other person." Citing *Frisby*, the Court explained that although the right to free speech "includes the right to attempt to persuade others to change their views, and may not be curtailed simply because the speaker's message may be offensive to his audience," the "protection afforded to offensive messages does not always embrace offensive speech that is so intrusive that the unwilling audience cannot avoid it." Indeed, "no one has a right to press even 'good' ideas on an unwilling recipient," and "none of our decisions has minimized the enduring importance of 'the right to be free' from persistent 'importunity, following and dogging' after an offer to communicate has been declined." The Court thus concluded that the statute "is a valid time, place, and manner regulation [because it] serves governmental interests that are significant and legitimate and [is] 'narrowly tailored' to serve those interests and . . . leaves open ample alternative channels for communication."

Justice Scalia, joined by Justice Thomas, dissented. Scalia argued that the "burdens this law imposes upon the right to speak are substantial," for "most of the 'counseling' and 'educating' likely to take place outside a health care facility cannot be done at a distance and at a high-decibel level," and "leafletting will be rendered utterly ineffectual by a requirement that the leafletter obtain from each subject permission to approach." Scalia maintained that "that simply is not how it is done," for "a leafletter, whether he is working on behalf of Operation Rescue [or] Bubba's Bar-B-Que, stakes out the best piece of real estate he can, and then walks a few steps toward individuals passing in his vicinity, extending his arm and making it *as easy as possible* for the passerby, whose natural inclination is generally not to seek out such distributions, [to] accept the offering. Few pedestrians are likely to give their 'consent' to the approach of a handbiller (indeed, by the time he requested it they would likely have passed by)." Justice Kennedy also dissented.

9. *Unattended structures.* Does an individual have a constitutional right to erect an unattended display in a public park? Suppose, for example, an individual wants to construct a statue, or a cross, or a billboard in such a park. Can the state prohibit this completely? If prohibition is impermissible, what sorts of regulations would be appropriate? In Capitol Square Review and Advisory Board v. Pinette, 515 U.S. 753 (1995), the Court strongly suggested, but did not decide, that "a ban on all unattended displays" might be constitutional. As Justice Stevens explained in a separate opinion, such a display "creates a far greater intrusion on government property and interferes with the Government's ability to differentiate its own message from those of private individuals."

Note: Devices for Regulating the Public Forum

1. *Licensing.* In Cox v. New Hampshire, 312 U.S. 569 (1941), a group of Jehovah's Witnesses were convicted of violating a state statute prohibiting any "parade or procession" upon a public street without first obtaining a permit. The Court, in a unanimous decision, affirmed the convictions. Chief Justice Hughes, speaking for the Court, explained that, "as regulation of the use of the streets for parades and processions is a traditional exercise of control by local government, the question in a particular case is whether that control is exerted so as not to deny or unwarrantedly abridge the right of assembly and the opportunities for the

communication of [thought] immemorially associated with resort to public places."

The Court emphasized that the state court had "construed the statute" as authorizing "the licensing authority" to take into account only "considerations of time, place and manner so as to conserve the public convenience." Such a limited permit requirement had the "obvious advantage" of "giving the public authorities notice in advance so as to afford opportunity for proper policing" and, "in fixing time and place, '[to] prevent confusion by overlapping parades or processions, to secure convenient use of the streets by other travelers, and to minimize the risk of disorder.'" Moreover, the Court emphasized that the state court had stressed that "the licensing board was not vested with arbitrary power [and] that its discretion must be [exercised] 'free [from] unfair discrimination.'" The Court concluded that under this construction of the statute, it is "impossible to say that the limited authority conferred by the licensing provisions [contravened] any constitutional right." For a critical view, see Baker, Unreasoned Reasonableness: Mandatory Parade Permits and Time, Place, and Manner Regulations, 78 Nw. U.L. Rev. 937 (1983). For analysis of licensing generally, see section C2 supra. Is *Cox* consistent with the general presumption against "prior restraints"? Does *Cox* "symbolize the ideal of Robert's Rules of Order for use of the public forum"? Kalven, The Concept of the Public Forum: Cox v. Louisiana, 1965 Sup. Ct. Rev. 1, 26, 28-29. For further analysis, see Blasi, Prior Restraints on Demonstrations, 68 Mich. L. Rev. 1481 (1970).

2. *Fees.* To what extent may the state charge for use of the public forum? In Murdock v. Pennsylvania, 319 U.S. 105 (1943), the Court held that the state may not impose a "flat license tax [as] a condition to the pursuit of activities whose enjoyment is guaranteed by the First Amendment" where the tax "is not a nominal fee imposed as a regulatory measure to defray the expenses of policing the activities in question." In Cox v. New Hampshire, supra, the licensing statute provided that "every licensee shall pay in advance" a fee ranging from a nominal amount to $300 per day. The state court construed the statute as requiring "a reasonable fixing of the amount of the fee." That is, the amount of the fee must in each instance turn on the size of the "parade or procession," the size of the crowd, and the "public expense of policing" the event. The state court explained that the fee was "not a revenue tax, but one to meet the expense incident to the administration of the Act and to the maintenance of public order in the matter licensed." The Court held that in such circumstances "there is nothing contrary to the Constitution in the charge of a fee limited to the purpose stated." Moreover, the Court rejected "the suggestion that a flat fee should have been charged," explaining that it is difficult to frame "a fair schedule to meet all circumstances," and that there is "no constitutional ground for denying to local governments that flexibility of adjustment of fees which in the light of varying conditions would tend to conserve rather than impair the liberty sought."

Consider Goldberger, A Reconsideration of Cox v. New Hampshire: Can Demonstrators Be Required to Pay the Costs of Using America's Public Forums?, 62 Tex. L. Rev. 403, 412-413 (1983):

> The Court's approval of [license fees] in *Cox* results from the Court's erroneous assumption that the relationship between a speaker and the government can be treated like a two-party business relationship. [The Court assumes] that the speaker

is the primary beneficiary of his use of a public forum. [This] assumption ignores the benefit of the speaker's activities for the entire society. His activities are part of the process by which a democratic society makes informed decisions. [A] proper distribution of costs [would] allocate the costs generated by speech activities to the society as a whole.

Is there a danger that, if the state "is forced to defray administrative costs, it is likely to be more resistant to permit requests"? Blasi, supra, at 1527.

During the Skokie controversy, section B3 supra, the village enacted an ordinance requiring applicants for parade or public demonstration permits to procure public liability insurance in the amount of $350,000 and property damage insurance in the amount of $50,000. Is this ordinance constitutional under the doctrine of *Cox*? Consider Forsyth County, Georgia v. The Nationalist Movement, 505 U.S. 123 (1992), in which the Court invalidated a municipal ordinance that authorized permit fees for parades, demonstrations, marches, and similar activities, up to a maximum of $1,000, based in part on the anticipated expense necessary to maintain the public order. The Court, in an opinion by Justice Blackmun, explained that under this scheme the fee "will depend on the administrator's measure of the amount of hostility likely to be created by the speech." As a result, those "wishing to express views unpopular with bottle throwers [may] have to pay more for their permit." The Court announced that speech "cannot be financially burdened, any more than it can be punished or banned, simply because it might offend a hostile mob," and that "regulations which permit the Government to discriminate on the basis of the content of the message cannot be tolerated under the First Amendment."

3. *Disclosure.* To what extent may the state, in order to prevent abuse, require speakers to disclose their identities? In Talley v. California, 362 U.S. 60 (1960), a distributor of handbills protesting employment discrimination was prosecuted for violating a Los Angeles ordinance prohibiting any person to distribute "any hand-bill [which] does not have printed on [the] face thereof, the name and address of [the] person who printed, wrote, compiled, or manufactured [it]." The Court held the ordinance invalid:

> [It is] urged that this ordinance is aimed at providing a way to identify those responsible for fraud, false advertising and libel. [But] such an identification requirement would tend to restrict freedom to distribute information and thereby freedom of expression. [Anonymous] pamphlets, leaflets, brochures and even books have played an important role in the progress of mankind. Persecuted groups [throughout] history have been able to criticize oppressive practices [either] anonymously or not at all. [Identification] and fear of reprisal might deter perfectly peaceful discussions of public matters of importance. This broad Los Angeles ordinance is subject to the same infirmity.

Justice Clark, joined by Justices Frankfurter and Whittaker, dissented: "[There] is neither allegation nor proof that Talley [would] suffer 'economic reprisal, loss of employment, threat of physical coercion [or] other manifestations of public hostility.' Talley makes no showing whatever to support his contention that a restraint upon his freedom of speech will result from the enforcement of the ordinance. The existence of such a restraint is necessary before we can strike the ordinance down."

See also McIntrye v. Ohio Elections Commission, 514 U.S. 334 (1995), in which the Court invalidated a state statute prohibiting the distribution of campaign literature that does not contain the name and address of the person issuing the literature: "Under our Constitution, anonymous pamphleteering is not a pernicious, fraudulent practice, but an honorable tradition of advocacy and of dissent. Anonymity is a shield from the tyranny of the majority. It thus exemplifies the purpose behind the Bill of Rights, and of the First Amendment in particular: to protect unpopular individuals from retaliation — and their ideas from suppression — at the hand of an intolerant society." See also Buckley v. American Constitutional Law Foundation, 525 U.S. 182 (1999) (invalidating a state law requiring petition circulators to wear a badge identifying them by name).

Are there any circumstances in which compelled disclosure is constitutional? See Buckley v. Valeo, section E4 infra, (upholding compelled disclosure of campaign contributions). Are there any circumstances in which compelled disclosure is generally constitutional, but is unconstitutional as applied to particular speakers who can demonstrate a meaningful risk of "economic reprisal, loss of employment, threat of physical coercion [or] other manifestations of public hostility"? Recall NAACP v. Alabama, 357 U.S. 449 (1958) (invalidating an Alabama statute requiring disclosure of the names of members of registered organizations, as applied to the NAACP); see also Brown v. Socialists Workers '74 Campaign Committee, 459 U.S. 87 (1982) (invalidating the statute compelling disclosure of campaign contributions that had been upheld in *Buckley*, as applied to the Socialist Workers Party).

b. The Public Forum: Other Publicly Owned Property

If there is a first amendment right to use streets and parks for purposes of expression, to what extent, if any, is there an analogous right to use other publicly owned property, ranging from the grounds surrounding a jail, to a military base, to a state fair? Does the *Hague* dictum's definition of the right to a "public forum" in terms of the common law property rights of the state suggest that the right does not extend to property that has not been used "time out of mind" for speech purposes?

Adderley v. Florida
385 U.S. 39 (1966)

[About 200 Florida A. & M. students marched to the county jail to protest the arrest the previous day of several of their schoolmates who had engaged in a civil rights demonstration. The protestors went directly to the jail entrance, where they were met by a deputy sheriff who explained that they were blocking the entrance to the jail and asked them to move back. The protestors moved back part of the way, where they stood or sat, singing, clapping, and dancing, on the jail driveway and on an adjacent grassy area on the jail premises. This jail entrance and driveway were normally used not by the public, but by the sheriff's department for transporting prisoners and by commercial concerns for servicing the jail. Even after their partial retreat, the protestors continued to block vehicular passage over this driveway. Shortly thereafter, the county sheriff, who was legal custodian of the jail and jail grounds, tried to persuade the students to leave. When this failed, he ordered them to leave and informed them that, if they did not leave within ten minutes, he would arrest them for trespassing. Some protestors left, but 107 others, including petitioners, remained and were arrested. They were convicted of violating a Florida statute declaring unlawful "every trespass upon the property of another, committed with a malicious and mischievous intent." The Court, in a five-to-four decision, affirmed the convictions.]

MR. JUSTICE BLACK delivered the opinion of the Court. . . .

[Petitioners maintain that conviction under the trespass statute] unconstitutionally deprives [them] of their rights to freedom of speech, press, assembly, or petition. We hold that it does not. The sheriff, as jail custodian, had power [to] direct that this large crowd of people get off the grounds. There is not a shred of evidence in this record that this power was exercised [because] the sheriff objected to what was being sung or said by the demonstrators or because he disagreed with the objectives of their protest. The record reveals that he objected only to their presence on that part of the jail grounds reserved for jail uses. There is no evidence at all that on any other occasion had similarly large groups of the public been permitted to gather on this portion of the jail grounds for any purpose. Nothing in the Constitution of the United States prevents Florida from even-handed enforcement of its general trespass statute against those refusing to obey the sheriff's order to remove themselves from what amounted to the curtilage of the jailhouse. The State, no less than a private owner of property, has power to preserve the property under its control for the use to which it is lawfully dedicated. For this reason there is no merit to the petitioners' argument that they had a constitutional right to stay on the property, over the jail custodian's objections, because this "area chosen for the peaceful civil rights demonstration was not only 'reasonable' but also particularly appropriate. . . ." Such an argument has as its major unarticulated premise the assumption that people who want to propagandize protests or views have a constitutional right to do so whenever and however and wherever they please. [We] reject [that concept]. The United States Constitution does not forbid a State to control the use of its own property for its own lawful nondiscriminatory purpose.

These judgments are affirmed.

MR. JUSTICE DOUGLAS, with whom THE CHIEF JUSTICE, MR. JUSTICE BRENNAN, and MR. JUSTICE FORTAS concur, dissenting. . . .

The jailhouse, like an executive mansion, a legislative chamber, a courthouse, or the statehouse itself [is] one of the seats of government, whether it be the Tower of London, the Bastille, or a small county jail. And when it houses political prisoners or those who many think are unjustly held, it is an obvious center for protest. The right to petition for the redress of grievances has an ancient history and is not limited to writing a letter or sending a telegram to a congressman; it is not confined to appearing before the local city council, or writing letters to the President or Governor or Mayor. [Conventional] methods of petitioning may be, and often have been, shut off to large groups of our citizens. [Those] who do not control television and radio, those who cannot afford to advertise in newspapers or circulate elaborate pamphlets may have only a more limited type of access to public officials. Their methods should not be condemned as tactics of obstruction and harassment as long as the assembly and petition are peaceable, as these were.

There is no question that petitioners had as their purpose a protest against the arrest of Florida A. & M. students for trying to integrate public theatres. [There] was no violence; no threat of violence; no attempted jail break; no storming of a prison; no plan or plot to do anything but protest. . . .

We do violence to the First Amendment when we permit this "petition for redress of grievances" to be turned into a trespass action. [To] say that a private owner could have done the same if the rally had taken place on private property is to speak of a different case, as an assembly and a petition for redress of grievances run to government, not to private proprietors.

The Court forgets that prior to this day our decisions have drastically limited the application of state statutes inhibiting the right to go peacefully on public property to exercise First Amendment rights. [Citing Justice Roberts's plurality opinion in *Hague*. There] may be some public places which are so clearly committed to other purposes that their use for the airing of grievances is anomalous. There may be some instances in which assemblies and petitions for redress of grievances are not consistent with other necessary purposes of public property. A noisy meeting may be out of keeping with the serenity of the statehouse or the quiet of the courthouse. No one, for example, would suggest that the Senate gallery is the proper place for a vociferous protest rally. And in other cases it may be necessary to adjust the right to petition for redress of grievances to the other interests inhering in the uses to which the public property is normally put. [See Cox v. New Hampshire.] But this is quite different from saying that all public places are off limits to people with grievances. . . .

Note: "No Less Than a Private Owner of Property"?

1. Davis *revisited?* Does *Adderley* turn on Justice Black's assertion that "the State, no less than a private owner of property, has power to preserve the property under its control for the use to which it is lawfully dedicated"? Does *Adderley* undervalue the interest of the speaker in selecting a "particularly appropriate" location for his speech?

2. *The* Grayned *dictum.* In Grayned v. Rockford, section E2a supra, decided in 1972, the Court, although upholding the antinoise ordinance as a reasonable time, place, and manner regulation, offered the following analysis of the public forum issue:

The nature of a place, "the pattern of its normal activities, dictate the kinds of regulations of time, place, and manner that are reasonable." [The] crucial question is whether the manner of expression is basically incompatible with the normal activity of a particular place at a particular time. Our cases make clear that in assessing the reasonableness of a regulation, we must weigh heavily the fact that communication is involved; the regulation must be narrowly tailored to further the State's legitimate interest.

What are the implications of *Grayned?* Does it reject the central premise of *Adderley?* Consider Stone, Fora Americana: Speech in Public Places, 1974 Sup. Ct. Rev. 233, 251-252:

> In [the *Grayned* dictum], the right to a public forum came of age. No longer does the right to effective freedom of expression turn on the common law property rights of the state, and no longer does it turn on whether the particular place at issue has historically been dedicated to the exercise of First Amendment rights. The streets, parks, public libraries, and other publicly owned places are all brought under the same roof. In each case, the "crucial question is whether the manner of expression is basically incompatible with the normal activity of a particular place at a particular time."

As events turned out, this celebration proved premature. Consider the following post-*Grayned* decisions.

3. *A military base.* The Fort Dix Military Reservation is a U.S. Army post. Although the federal government exercises exclusive jurisdiction over the base, civilian vehicular traffic is permitted on paved roads within the reservation, and civilians are freely permitted to visit unrestricted areas of the base. In 1972, Benjamin Spock, the People's Party's candidate for President of the United States, requested permission to enter the base to hold a meeting to discuss election issues with service personnel and their dependents. The commanding officer of the base rejected the request, citing a Fort Dix regulation providing that "demonstrations, picketing, sit-ins, protest marches, political speeches and similar activities are prohibited and will not be conducted on the Fort Dix Military Reservation."

In Greer v. Spock, 424 U.S. 828 (1976), the Court, in a six-to-two decision, upheld the regulation. In an opinion by Justice Stewart, the Court rejected "the principle that whenever members of the public are permitted freely to visit a place owned or operated by the Government, then that place becomes a 'public forum' for purposes of the First Amendment." Quoting *Adderley,* the Court explained that "'[t]he State, no less than a private owner of property, has power to preserve the property under its control for the use to which it is lawfully dedicated.'" The Court added that it is "the business of a military installation like Fort Dix to train soldiers, not to provide a public forum," and that the challenged regulation reflects "a considered [policy], objectively and evenhandedly applied, of keeping official military activities [free] of entanglement with partisan political campaigns of any kind [in order to insulate] the military [from] both the reality and the appearance of acting as a handmaiden for partisan political causes or candidates."

Justice Brennan, joined by Justice Marshall, dissented. Justice Brennan maintained that the Court's emphasis on whether the base was a "public forum" was misplaced, for "the determination that a locale is a 'public forum' has never been erected as an absolute prerequisite to all forms of demonstrative First Amendment activity." What is needed, Justice Brennan explained, is a "flexible approach [for] determining when public expression should be protected." Justice Brennan reasoned that the speech in this case was "basically compatible with the activities otherwise occurring" at the base, and he rejected the contention that the interest in "military neutrality" could justify the restriction, for "it borders on casuistry to contend that by evenhandedly permitting public expression to occur in unrestricted portions of a military installation, the military will be viewed as sanctioning the causes there espoused."

4. *A state fair.* The Minnesota State Fair is conducted each year on a 125-acre site. The average daily attendance exceeds 100,000. Minnesota State Fair Rule 6.05 prohibits the sale or distribution of any merchandise, including printed or written material, except from a booth rented from the state. Booths are rented to all comers in a nondiscriminatory manner on a first-come, first-served basis. The rental charge is based on the size and location of the booth. The International Society for Krishna Consciousness (ISKCON), an international religious society espousing the views of the Krishna religion, challenged Rule 6.05 on the ground that it would impair ISKCON's ability effectively to distribute its literature.

In Heffron v. International Society for Krishna Consciousness, 452 U.S. 640 (1981), the Court upheld the rule. In an opinion by Justice White, the Court rejected ISKCON's effort to analogize "the fairgrounds [to] city streets which have 'immemorially been [used] for purposes [of] assembly [and] discussing public questions'": "A street is continually open, often uncongested, [and] a place where people may enjoy the open air or the company of friends [in] a relaxed environment. The Minnesota Fair [is] a temporary event attracting great numbers of visitors who come to the event for a short period to see [the] host of exhibits [at] the Fair. The flow of the crowd and the demands of safety are more pressing in the context of the Fair. As such, any comparisons to public streets are necessarily inexact." The Court thus concluded that, given the "threat to the State's interest in crowd control if [all] organizations [could] move freely about the fairgrounds distributing and selling literature and soliciting funds at will, [the] State's interest in confining distribution, selling, and fund solicitation activities to fixed locations is sufficient to satisfy the requirement that a place or manner restriction must serve a substantial state interest."

Justice Brennan, joined by Justices Marshall and Stevens, concurred in part and dissented in part. Although conceding that "the State has a significant interest in maintaining crowd control on its fairgrounds," Justice Brennan concluded that the "booth rule is an overly intrusive means of achieving [that interest]." "A state fair," Justice Brennan maintained, "is truly a marketplace of ideas and a public forum for the communication of ideas and information." Thus, Rule 6.05 constitutes a "significant restriction on First Amendment rights," for "by prohibiting distribution of literature outside the booths, the fair officials sharply limit the number of fairgoers to whom the proselytizers [can] communicate their messages." Moreover, although "the State contends that if fairgoers are permitted to distribute literature, large crowds will gather, blocking traffic lanes and causing safety problems," it "has failed to provide any support for these assertions." The state, Justice Brennan maintained, may not impose "a significant restriction on [the] ability to exercise core First Amendment rights" on the basis of "a general, speculative fear of disorder."

5. *A mailbox.* In U.S. Postal Service v. Council of Greenburgh Civic Associations, 453 U.S. 114 (1981), the Court upheld a federal statute prohibiting the deposit of unstamped "mailable matter" in a letter box approved by the U.S. Postal Service, as applied to appellee civic association, which routinely delivered its messages by placing unstamped notices in the letter boxes of private homes. In an opinion by Justice Rehnquist, the Court explained: "There is neither historical nor constitutional support for the characterization of a letter box as a public

forum. [At least since 1934, when the statute was promulgated,] access to [letter boxes] has been unlawful except under the terms and conditions specified by Congress and the Postal Service. As such, it is difficult to accept appellees' assertion that because it may be somewhat more efficient to place their messages in letter boxes there is a First Amendment right to do so. [Indeed,] it is difficult to conceive of any reason why this Court should treat a letter box differently for First Amendment [purposes] than it has in the past treated the military base in [*Greer* or] the jail [in *Adderley*]." The Court added: "What we hold is the principle reiterated by cases such as [*Adderley*] and [*Greer*], that property owned or controlled by the government which is *not* a public forum may be subject to a prohibition of speech, leafleting, picketing, or other forms of communication without running afoul of the First Amendment. Admittedly, the government must act reasonably in imposing such restrictions [and] the prohibition must be content-neutral. [But] this statute is both a reasonable and content-neutral regulation." Justices Marshall and Stevens dissented.

6. *A public utility pole.* In Members of the City Council of Los Angeles v. Taxpayers for Vincent, 466 U.S. 789 (1984), the Court upheld a Los Angeles ordinance prohibiting the posting of signs on public property as applied to individuals who tied political campaign signs to public utility poles. Justice Stevens delivered the opinion: "The ordinance [diminishes] the total quantity of [appellees'] communication in the City. [But] the state [may] curtail speech [in a content-neutral manner if the restriction] 'furthers an important or substantial governmental interest [and if the] restriction on [free speech] is no greater than is essential to the furtherance of that interest.' [It is undisputed that the] problem addressed by this ordinance — the visual assault [on] citizens [presented] by an accumulation of signs posted on public property — constitutes a significant substantive evil. [Moreover, the] restriction on appellees' expressive activity is [no] broader than necessary to protect the City's interest. [By] banning these signs, the City did no more than eliminate the exact source of the evil it sought to remedy. [Appellees] suggest that the public property covered by the ordinance is [a] 'public forum,' [but they] fail to demonstrate the existence of a traditional right of access respecting such items as utility poles for purposes [of] communication comparable to that recognized for public streets and parks. [The] mere fact that government property can be used as a vehicle for communication does not mean that the Constitution requires such uses to be permitted." Justice Brennan, joined by Justices Marshall and Blackmun, dissented.

Is *Vincent* consistent with *Schneider?* Consider Justice Stevens's answer in *Vincent:* "It is true that the esthetic interest in preventing [litter] cannot support a prophylactic prohibition against [leafleting. But the] rationale of *Schneider* is inapposite in the context of this case. [In *Schneider*,] an anti-littering statute could have addressed the substantive evil without prohibiting expressive activity. [Here], the substantive evil — visual blight — is not merely a possible by-product of the activity, but is created by the medium of expression itself. [Thus, the] ordinance curtails no more speech than is necessary to accomplish its purpose." Is *Vincent* consistent with *Gilleo?*

7. *A post office sidewalk.* In United States v. Kokinda, 497 U.S. 720 (1990), respondents, members of a political advocacy group, set up a table on a sidewalk near the entrance to a United States Post Office to distribute literature and solicit contributions. The sidewalk, which is located entirely on Postal Service property,

is the sole means by which customers may travel from the parking lot to the post office building. Respondents were convicted of violating a federal regulation prohibiting any person from soliciting contributions "on postal premises." The Court upheld the regulation as applied.

Justice O'Connor, in a plurality opinion joined by Chief Justice Rehnquist and Justices White and Scalia, explained that the "postal sidewalk [does] not have the characteristics of public sidewalks traditionally open to expressive activity." Rather, "the postal sidewalk was constructed solely to provide for the passage of individuals engaged in postal business." Although conceding that individuals had generally "been permitted to leaflet, speak, and picket on postal premises," Justice O'Connor argued this did "not add up to the dedication of postal property to speech activities." Justice O'Connor therefore concluded that "the regulation [must] be analyzed under the standards set forth for nonpublic fora: it must be reasonable and 'not an effort to suppress expression merely because public officials oppose the speaker's view.'" Applying that standard, Justice O'Connor noted that, "based on its long experience with solicitation," the Postal Service had concluded that "solicitation is inherently disruptive of the postal service's business" because it "impedes the normal flow of traffic" and "is more intrusive and intimidating than an encounter with a person giving out information." Justice O'Connor concluded that the challenged regulation therefore "passes constitutional muster under [the] usual test for reasonableness." Justice Kennedy concurred in the result. Justice Brennan, joined by Justices Marshall, Blackmun, and Stevens, dissented.

What about an airport terminal?

INTERNATIONAL SOCIETY FOR KRISHNA CONSCIOUSNESS v. LEE, 505 U.S. 672 (1992). The Port Authority of New York and New Jersey, which owns and operates three major airports in the New York City area, forbids within the airport terminals the repetitive solicitation of money and the repetitive sale or distribution of any merchandise, "including but not limited to jewelry, food stuffs, candles, flowers, . . . flyers, brochures, pamphlets, books or any other printed or written material." The regulation governs only the terminal buildings. It does not restrict such activities on the public sidewalks outside the buildings. In a bewildering array of opinions, the Court upheld the ban on solicitation but invalidated the ban on the sale or distribution of literature.

Solicitation. Chief Justice Rehnquist delivered the opinion of the Court upholding the ban on solicitation. The Court explained that airport terminals are not traditional public fora because, "given the lateness with which the modern air terminal has made its appearance, it hardly qualifies for the description of having 'immemorially . . . time out of mind' been held in the public trust and used for purposes of expressive activity." Moreover, such terminals have not "been intentionally opened by their operators to such activity." To the contrary, "the frequent and continuing litigation evidencing the operators' objections belies any such claim." Moreover, "airports are commercial establishments funded by use fees and designed to make a regulated profit." The Court thus concluded that, "because it cannot fairly be said that an airport terminal has as a principal purpose 'promoting the free exchange of ideas,'" it is not a public forum.

This being so, the prohibition of solicitation "need only satisfy a requirement of reasonableness," a standard the Court held was easily satisfied because of "the disruptive effect that solicitation may have on business." Specifically, the Court observed that solicitation impedes "the normal flow of traffic," and that such "delays may be particularly costly in this setting, as a flight missed by only a few minutes can result in hours worth of subsequent inconvenience." Moreover, "face to face solicitation presents risk of duress" and "fraud," and it may be especially difficult for airport authorities to enforce rules against such abuses because passengers "frequently are on tight schedules" and are "unlikely to stop and formally complain." Finally, the prohibition is reasonable because solicitation is permitted on the "sidewalk areas outside the terminals," where the "overwhelming" majority of airport users can be reached.

Justice Kennedy, joined by Justices Blackmun, Stevens, and Souter, offered a very different approach to the public forum issue and, contrary to the majority, concluded that airport terminals are public fora. Justice Kennedy complained that "our public forum doctrine ought [not] convert what was once an analysis protective of expression into one which grants the government authority to restrict speech by fiat." Justice Kennedy observed that the Court's analysis, which "holds that traditional public forums are limited to public property which have as their 'principal purpose . . . the free exchanges of ideas,'" as "evidenced by a longstanding historical practice of permitting speech," leaves "the government with almost unlimited authority to restrict speech on its property," for "the critical step in the Court's analysis" is "the government's own definition or decision, unconstrained by an independent duty to respect the speech its citizens can voice" on public property. Justice Kennedy argued that this view "is contrary to the underlying purposes of the public forum doctrine," for "at the heart of our jurisprudence lies the principle that in a free nation citizens must have the right to gather and speak with other persons in public places."

Justice Kennedy therefore argued that the purposes of the public forum doctrine "cannot be given effect unless we recognize that open, public spaces and thoroughfares which are suitable for discourse may be public forums, whatever their historical pedigree and without concern for a precise classification of the property." Indeed, "without this recognition our forum doctrine retains no relevance in times of fast-changing technology and increasing insularity," and the Court's failure to "recognize the possibility that new types of government property may be appropriate forums for speech will lead to a serious curtailment of our expressive activity." Justice Kennedy thus maintained that, "if the objective, physical characteristics of the property at issue and the actual public access and uses which have been permitted by the government indicate that expressive activity would be appropriate and compatible with those uses, the property is a public forum."

Turning to the issue of airport terminals, Justice Kennedy observed that "in these days an airport is one of the few government-owned spaces where people have extended contact with other members of the public." Although an "airport corridor [is] not a street," it bears important "physical similarities" to a street, the relevant areas "are open to the public without restriction," and the "recent history of airports [demonstrates] that when adequate time, place, and manner regulations are in place, expressive activity is quite compatible with the uses of major airports." Justice Kennedy thus found that the public areas of an airport terminal constitute a public forum.

Despite this disagreement with the Court, Justice Kennedy, writing only for himself, concurred that the ban on solicitation was constitutional as "a reasonable time, place, and manner restriction" because of the risks of fraud and duress. Justice Souter, joined by Justices Blackmun and Stevens, adopted Justice Kennedy's analysis of the general public forum issue but dissented on the constitutionality of the ban on solicitation. In Justice Souter's view, "the claim to be preventing coercion is weak" because, "while a solicitor can be insistent," a pedestrian on the street or airport concourse can simply "walk away." Moreover, Justice Souter found the claim to be preventing fraud unpersuasive because, once it is accepted that the terminal is a public forum, the absolute ban on solicitation does not meet "the requirement of narrow tailoring."

Sale or distribution of literature. In a plurality opinion, Justice Kennedy, joined by Justices Blackmun, Stevens, and Souter, concluded that the ban on the sale or distribution of literature violated the first amendment. After finding, for the reasons set forth above, that airport terminals are public fora, Justice Kennedy explained that the ban was invalid because "the right to distribute flyers and literature lies at the heart of the liberties guaranteed" by the first amendment, the challenged "regulation is not drawn in narrow terms [and] does not leave open ample alternative channels for communication," and the "Port Authority's concerns with the problem of congestion can be addressed through narrow restrictions on the time and place of expressive activity."

Justice O'Connor concurred in the result. Although agreeing with the dissent that airport terminals are not public fora, she nonetheless concluded that the ban on the sale or distribution of literature was invalid because it was an "unreasonable" restriction. Justice O'Connor explained that "leafletting does not necessarily entail the same kinds of problems presented by face-to-face solicitation." Indeed, "with the possible exception of avoiding litter, it is difficult to point to any problems intrinsic to the act of leafletting that would make it naturally incompatible with a large, multipurpose forum such as those at issue here."

Chief Justice Rehnquist, joined by Justices White, Scalia, and Thomas, dissented. Having found that airport terminals are not public fora, Chief Justice Rehnquist reasoned that "the distribution ban, no less than the solicitation ban, is reasonable." He argued that "the weary, harried or hurried traveler may have no less desire and need to avoid the delays generated by having literature foisted upon him than he does to avoid delays from a financial solicitation." Moreover, like solicitation, leafletting can cause congestion. Finally, leafletting is even worse than solicitation insofar as leafletting may produce litter, thereby "creating an eyesore, a safety hazard, and additional clean-up work for the airport staff."

Note: Modern Public Forum Doctrine

1. *Deference to regulators.* Consider Goldberger, Judicial Scrutiny in Public Forum Cases: Misplaced Trust in the Judgment of Public Officials, 32 Buff. L. Rev. 175, 206-207, 217-218 (1983):

By employing [low] levels of scrutiny in [these cases], the Court [assumes] that regulatory decision making is [generally] trustworthy. [The] Court has failed to recognize [that] public officials [often] have strong incentives to overregulate. [These incentives come] from two sources. First, there is the tendency of forum regulators to be disproportionately sensitive to threats of [disruption]. Second, forum regulators tend to be particularly sensitive toward protecting public services [when] the communication is controversial or is of interest to only a small segment of the population. [To compensate for these incentives, the Court in these cases should have required state] officials to prove that the activities regulated were as disruptive [as] claimed.

For an excellent analysis of deference in this context, see Post, Between Governance and Management: The History and Theory of the Public Forum, 34 UCLA L. Rev. 1713, 1809-1824 (1987).

2. *Evaluation.* Consider the following assessment: The dispute over access to nonpublic forum public property turns on a conflict between two competing views. Under one view, the first amendment requires government to permit the widest possible opportunity for free expression. The greater the opportunity for free expression, the healthier the marketplace of ideas. Thus, any law that restricts free expression must be invalidated unless the government interest served by the restriction outweighs the effect on free expression. Under the competing view, the traditional means of expression — radio, television, newspapers, speeches, parades, picketing, leaflets, and the like — provide ample opportunity for free expression. Although access to nonpublic forum public property might make some speech marginally more effective, a denial of access to such property poses no real threat to the marketplace of ideas. But to require such access would necessarily interfere with competing government interests and involve the courts in an endless series of highly subjective and unpredictable judgments. Thus, the costs of such inquiries far exceed the benefits. In recent years, the Court has embraced this second view.

Note: The Right to a "Private" Forum

To what extent, if any, does the first amendment guarantee the individual a right to commandeer some other person's private property for speech purposes? Do the property rights of private owners absolutely preclude such an interpretation of the first amendment? Does the state action requirement foreclose such an interpretation? On the state action doctrine, see Chapter 9.

1. *The company town.* In Marsh v. Alabama, 326 U.S. 501 (1946), the Court considered whether a state could constitutionally "impose criminal punishment on a person who undertakes to distribute religious literature on the premises of a company-owned town contrary to the wishes of the town's management." The town, a suburb of Mobile, Alabama, known as Chickasaw, was owned by the Gulf Shipbuilding Corporation. The town was freely used by the public, and there was "nothing to distinguish [it] from any other town [except] the fact that the title to the property [belonged] to a private corporation." Appellant, a Jehovah's Witness, attempted to distribute literature on one of the town's sidewalks. She was informed that, pursuant to a formal corporation policy, she could not distribute literature without a permit, and that no permit would be issued her. When asked to leave, she declined. She was eventually convicted of violating a state statute pro-

hibiting any person to enter or remain on the premises of another after having been warned not to do so.

The Court overturned the conviction. Justice Black, speaking for the Court, observed:

> Had the title to Chickasaw belonged not to a private, but to a municipal corporation [it] would have been clear that appellant's conviction must be reversed. [The] State urges [that] the corporation's right to control the inhabitants of Chickasaw is coextensive with the right of a homeowner to regulate the conduct of his guests. We cannot accept that contention. Ownership does not always mean absolute dominion. The more an owner, for his advantage, opens up his property for use by the public in general, the more do his rights become circumscribed by the statutory and constitutional rights of those who use it. [In] our view the circumstance that the property rights to the premises where the deprivation of liberty, here involved, took place, were held by others than the public, is not sufficient to justify the State's permitting a corporation to govern a community of citizens so as to restrict their fundamental liberties and the enforcement of such restraint by the application of a state statute.

2. *Privately owned shopping centers.* Suppose a privately owned shopping center bans all leafleting in the shopping center. Does that violate the first amendment? Consider the following argument:

> [The] similarities between the business block in *Marsh* and the [modern day] shopping center [are] striking. [The] shopping center premises are open to the public to the same extent as the commercial center of a normal town. [Because the] shopping center [is] clearly the functional equivalent of the business district of Chickasaw involved in *Marsh*, [the] State may not delegate the power, through the use of its trespass laws, wholly to exclude those members of the public wishing to exercise their First Amendment rights on the premises in a manner and for a purpose generally consonant with the use to which the property is actually put.

Food Employees Local 590 v. Logan Valley Plaza, 391 U.S. 308 (1968) (holding that the "peaceful [labor] picketing of a business enterprise located within a shopping center" cannot constitutionally be prohibited by the owner of the shopping center). In Hudgens v. NLRB, 424 U.S. 507 (1976), the Court overruled *Logan Valley*. For a critical evaluation, consider C. Sunstein, The Partial Constitution 208 (1993):

> The [Court] has said that the First Amendment is not implicated [in cases like *Hudgens* because] no government regulation of speech is involved. All that has happened is that private property owners have barred people from their land. [But] this is a poor way to understand the situation. [The] owners of the shopping center are able to exclude the protestors only because government has conferred on them a legal right to do so. The conferral of that right is an exercise of state power. It is this action that restricts the speech of the protestors. Surely it is a real question whether the grant of exclusionary power violates the First Amendment.

3. *Does the appropriation of private property for speech purposes violate the constitutional rights of owners?* Suppose the state, in an effort to promote free expression, grants the individual a right under state law to enter on private property

for speech purposes. Might that in itself violate the property or speech rights of the property owner? In PruneYard Shopping Center v. Robins, 447 U.S. 74 (1980), a group of high school students who sought to solicit support for their opposition to a United Nations resolution against Zionism set up a card table in the PruneYard Shopping Center and asked passersby to sign petitions. Pursuant to a policy prohibiting any visitor to engage in any publicly expressive activity not directly related to the shopping center's commercial purposes, a security guard ordered the students to leave. The California Supreme Court held that the California Constitution protects "speech and petitioning, reasonably exercised, in shopping centers even when the centers are privately owned." The U.S. Supreme Court rejected PruneYard's contention that the California Supreme Court's decision violated the federal constitutional rights of the shopping center owner.

The Court explained:

> [PruneYard contends] that a right to exclude others underlies the Fifth Amendment guarantee against the taking of property without just compensation. [But] "not every destruction or injury to property by governmental action has been held to be a 'taking' in the constitutional sense." [Here, there] is nothing to suggest that preventing [PruneYard] from prohibiting this sort of activity will unreasonably impair the value or use of [the] property as a shopping center. [PruneYard contends further] that a private property owner has a First Amendment right not to be forced by the State to use his property as a forum for the speech of others. [Although there are circumstances in which] a State may not constitutionally require an individual to participate in the dissemination of an ideological message by displaying it on his private property, [this is not such a case. First, PruneYard is] a business establishment that is open to the public to come and go as they please. The views expressed by members of the public in passing out pamphlets or seeking signatures for a petition thus will not likely be identified with those of the owner. Second, no specific message is dictated by the State to be displayed. [There] consequently is no danger of governmental discrimination for or against a particular message. Finally, [PruneYard] can expressly disavow any connection with the message by simply posting signs in the area where the speakers or handbillers stand.

On the right "not to speak," see section E5 infra. On the problem of "takings," see Chapter 6.

c.   The Public Forum: Unequal Access and the Problem of Content-Neutrality

As we saw above, there are many situations in which government can constitutionally restrict expression on public property in a content-neutral manner. Suppose, however, government in such circumstances decides voluntarily to permit some, but not all, speech? For example, as the Court held in *Lee*, government can constitutionally prohibit all solicitation in airport terminals. Suppose government decides voluntarily to permit such solicitation by antiabortion groups, or local political candidates, or groups interested in issues relating to air travel?

The issue is one of "underinclusion." That is, such a regulation restricts *less* speech than a broader and concededly constitutional content-neutral restriction. But in so doing, it adopts a potentially problematic inequality. To avoid this inequality, the regulation could be broadened to restrict *more* speech. Can it be that a law that restricts *more* speech is constitutional but a law that restricts *less* speech is unconstitutional? Recall *R.A.V.*, section D6 supra.

Consider Kagan, The Changing Faces of First Amendment Neutrality, 1992 Sup. Ct. Rev. 38-40:

> Such underinclusion [is] a particular kind of content-based restriction. . . . In [most] cases of content-based restrictions, the question [is] the permissibility of the burden placed on the speech affected. Consider, for example, [a] statute that [criminalizes] seditious advocacy. In deciding [on the constitutionality of such a statute], the Court usually will not ask whether the government has a sufficient reason to treat speech of one kind (seditious advocacy) differently from speech of another; rather, the Court will ask merely whether the government has a sufficient reason to restrict the speech actually affected. [In] such a case, the issue is not underinclusion, for the government could not cure the constitutional flaw by extending the restriction to [other speech]. By contrast, in a content-based underinclusion case, equality is all that is at issue.

Police Department of Chicago v. Mosley

408 U.S. 92 (1972)

MR. JUSTICE MARSHALL delivered the opinion of the Court.

At issue in this case is the constitutionality of [a] Chicago ordinance [providing that a] "person commits disorderly conduct when he knowingly [pickets] or demonstrates on a public way within 150 feet of [any] school building while the school is in [session], provided that this subsection does not prohibit the peaceful picketing of any school involved in a labor dispute. . . ."

[For] seven months prior to the enactment of [this ordinance], Earl Mosley, a federal postal employee, [frequently] picketed Jones Commercial High School in Chicago. During school hours and usually by himself, Mosley would walk the public sidewalk adjoining the school, carrying a sign that read: "Jones High School practices black discrimination. Jones High School has a black quota." His lonely crusade was always peaceful, orderly, and quiet, and was conceded to be so by the city of Chicago.

[Mosley brought this action] seeking declaratory and injunctive relief. [We] hold that the ordinance is unconstitutional because it makes an impermissible distinction between labor picketing and other peaceful picketing.

Because Chicago treats some picketing differently from others, we analyze this ordinance in terms of the Equal Protection Clause of the Fourteenth Amendment. Of course, the equal protection claim in this case is closely intertwined with First Amendment interests; the Chicago ordinance affects picketing, which is expressive conduct; moreover, it does so by classifications formulated in terms of the subject of the picketing. As in all equal protection cases, however, the crucial question is whether there is an appropriate governmental interest suitably furthered by the differential treatment.

The central problem with Chicago's ordinance is that it describes permissible picketing in terms of its subject matter. Peaceful picketing on the subject of a school's labor-management dispute is permitted, but all other peaceful picketing is prohibited. The operative distinction is the message on a picket sign. But, above all else, the First Amendment means that government has no power to restrict expression because of its message, its ideas, its subject matter, or its content. [Citing Cohen v. California; New York Times v. Sullivan; Terminiello v. Chicago.] . . .

Necessarily, then, under the Equal Protection Clause, not to mention the First Amendment itself, government may not grant the use of a forum to people whose views it finds acceptable, but deny use to those wishing to express less favored or more controversial views. And it may not select which issues are worth discussing or debating in public facilities. There is an "equality of status in the field of ideas," and government must afford all points of view an equal opportunity to be heard. Once a forum is opened up to assembly or speaking by some groups, government may not prohibit others from assembling or speaking on the basis of what they intend to say. Selective exclusions from a public forum may not be based on content alone, and may not be justified by reference to content alone. . . .

This is not to say that all picketing must always be allowed. We have continually recognized that reasonable "time, place and manner" regulations of picketing may be necessary to further significant governmental interests. [Cox v. New Hampshire; Adderley v. Florida.] Conflicting demands on the same place may compel the State to make choices among potential users and uses. And the State may have a legitimate interest in prohibiting some picketing to protect public order. But these justifications for selective exclusions from a public forum must be carefully scrutinized [and such discriminations] among pickets must be tailored to serve a substantial governmental interest.

In this case, the ordinance itself describes impermissible picketing not in terms of time, place, and manner, but in terms of subject matter. The regulation "thus slip[s] from the neutrality of time, place, and circumstance into a concern about content." This is never permitted. In spite of this, Chicago urges that the ordinance is not improper content censorship, but rather a device for preventing disruption of the school. [Although] preventing school disruption is a city's legitimate concern, Chicago itself has determined that peaceful labor picketing during school hours is not an undue interference with school. Therefore, under the Equal Protection Clause, Chicago may not maintain that other picketing disrupts the school unless that picketing is clearly more disruptive than the picketing Chicago already permits. "Peaceful" nonlabor picketing, [however], is obviously no more disruptive than "peaceful" labor picketing. . . .

Similarly, we reject the city's argument that, although it permits peaceful labor picketing, it may prohibit all nonlabor picketing because, as a class, nonlabor picketing is more prone to produce violence than labor picketing. Predictions about imminent disruption from picketing involve judgments appropriately made on an individualized basis, not by means of broad classifications, especially those based on subject matter. [Some] labor picketing is peaceful, some disorderly; the same is true of picketing on other themes. [Given] what Chicago tolerates from labor picketing, the excesses of some nonlabor picketing may not be controlled by a broad ordinance prohibiting both peaceful and violent picketing. Such excesses "can be controlled by narrowly drawn statutes," [focusing] on the abuses and dealing even handedly with picketing regardless of subject matter. [Far] from being tailored to a substantial governmental interest, the discrimination among pickets is based on the content of their expression. Therefore, under the Equal Protection Clause, it may not stand.

Affirmed.

MR. JUSTICE BLACKMUN and MR. JUSTICE REHNQUIST concur in the result.

Note: Mosley *and the "Equality" of Ideas*

1. *Equality and underinclusion.* Is the Chicago ordinance, absent the labor picketing exemption, a permissible content-neutral restriction? Recall Grayned v. Rockford, section E2a supra. If the ordinance is constitutional absent the labor-picketing exemption, should the exemption render it invalid? Is it anomalous that under the Court's reasoning the ordinance would be more likely to be constitutional if it restricted *more* speech? Consider the following arguments:

(a) The city's willingness to enact the labor exemption undermines the credibility of its asserted justifications for the restriction of nonlabor speech. Thus, even under the ordinary standards of content-neutral review, the restriction of nonlabor picketing may be invalid, even though a restriction of all picketing might be valid.

(b) The standard of review should be higher when the city distinguishes between labor and nonlabor speech than when it acts in a content-neutral manner. That is, from a constitutional perspective, the inequality between labor and nonlabor picketing is more problematic than the broader, but more "equal," restriction of all picketing near a school. (On the other hand, consider the following argument: The standard of review should be especially *lenient* in a case like *Mosley* because the ordinance was designed not to restrict but to expand the opportunities for free expression.)

2. *Equal protection versus the first amendment.* Note the Court's reliance on the equal protection clause. Consider Stone, Content Regulation and the First Amendment, 25 Wm. & Mary L. Rev. 189, 206 (1983): "The degree of scrutiny that is appropriate in [testing] content-based restrictions [is] fundamentally a first amendment issue. Invocation of the equal protection clause adds nothing constructive to the analysis. It may, however, deflect attention from the central constitutional issue."

3. *Subject matter restrictions.* Note that in *Mosley* the content-based restriction was directed not against a particular viewpoint but against an entire subject of discussion — all nonlabor expression. Should the first amendment's hostility to content-based regulation extend not only to restrictions on particular viewpoints but also to restrictions on entire topics? Recall the debate on this issue in R.A.V. v. City of St. Paul, section D6 supra. Consider Stone, Restrictions of Speech because of Its Content: The Peculiar Case of Subject-Matter Restrictions, 46 U. Chi. L. Rev. 81, 83, 108 (1978):

[Although] "subject-matter" distinctions unquestionably regulate content, they [do] not fit neatly within the Court's general framework. [The] Court's rigorous approach to content-based restrictions stems in part from the realization that such restrictions generally have an especially potent viewpoint-differential impact upon the "marketplace of ideas." [Because] they are at least facially viewpoint-neutral, [however, subject-matter restrictions] do not have the same sort of skewing effect on "the thinking process of the community" as restrictions directed against speech taking a particular side in an ongoing debate. Moreover, because of their apparent viewpoint-neutrality, subject-matter restrictions seem much less likely than other forms of content-based restrictions to be the product of government hostility to the ideas suppressed. In general, one is more likely to be hostile to speech espousing a specific point of view than to speech about an entire subject. As a result, one [might] argue that subject-matter restrictions are in general less threatening than other sorts of content-based restrictions and, like content-neutral restrictions, need not be subjected to the most stringent standards of review.

4. *The reach of* Mosley: *residential picketing.* In Carey v. Brown, 447 U.S. 455 (1980), appellees participated in a peaceful demonstration in front of the home of the mayor of Chicago, protesting his alleged failure to support the busing of school children to achieve racial integration. As a result of this demonstration, appellees were convicted of violating an Illinois statute declaring it "unlawful to picket before or about the residence [of] any person, except when the residence" is "a place of employment involved in a labor dispute."

The Court held that the residential picketing statute was "constitutionally indistinguishable from the ordinance invalidated in *Mosley*":

[The] Act accords preferential treatment to the expression of views on one particular subject; information about labor disputes may be freely disseminated, but discussion of all other issues is restricted. [When] government regulation discriminates among speech-related activities in a public forum, the Equal Protection Clause mandates that the legislation be finely tailored to serve substantial state interests, and the justifications offered for and distinctions it draws must be carefully scrutinized. [*Mosley.*] . . .

Justice Rehnquist, joined by Chief Justice Burger and Justice Blackmun, dissented.

5. *The reach of* Mosley: *universities and the problem of religious expression.* The University of Missouri at Kansas City, which officially recognizes more than 100 student groups and routinely permits such groups to meet in university facilities, adopted a regulation prohibiting the use of university buildings for "purposes of religious worship or religious teaching." Several university students who were members of an organization of evangelical Christian students challenged the regulation.

In Widmar v. Vincent, 454 U.S. 263 (1981), the Court invalidated the regulation. The Court observed:

[The] campus of a public university, at least for its students, possesses many of the characteristics of a public forum. [At] the same time, however, [a] university differs in significant respects from public forums such as streets or parks. [A] university's mission is education, and [it may] impose reasonable regulations compatible with that mission upon the use of its campus and facilities. [Here, through] its policy of accommodating their meetings, the University has created a forum generally open for use by student groups. [The] Constitution forbids a State to enforce certain exclusions from a forum generally open to the public, even if it was not required to create the forum in the first place. [In] order to justify discriminatory exclusion from a public forum based on the religious content of a group's intended speech, the University [must] show that its regulation is necessary to serve a compelling state interest and that it is narrowly drawn to achieve that end. See [Carey v. Brown]. In this case the University claims a compelling interest in maintaining a strict separation of church and state. [We] agree that the interest of the University in complying with its constitutional obligations may be characterized as compelling. It does not follow, however, that an "equal access" policy would be incompatible with [the establishment clause]. It is possible — perhaps even foreseeable — that religious groups will benefit from access to University facilities. But [a] religious organization's enjoyment of merely "incidental" benefits does not violate the prohibition against the "primary advancement" of religion.

Justice Stevens concurred in the judgment. Justice White dissented.

See also Lamb's Chapel v. Center Moriches Union Free School District, 508 U.S. 384 (1993) (relying on *Widmar* to invalidate a school district rule permitting school property to be used after school for social, civic, and recreational uses, but prohibiting the use of such property for religious purposes); Rosenberger v. Rector and Visitors of the University of Virginia, 515 U.S. 819 (1995) (relying on *Lamb's Chapel* to invalidate a University of Virginia policy authorizing payment from the Student Activities Fund for the printing costs of a variety of student publications, but prohibiting payment for any student publication that "primarily promotes or manifests a particular belief in or about a deity or an ultimate reality").

6. *Religious expression and the establishment clause.* Are there any circumstances in which the establishment clause would justify (or require) governmental exclusion of religious speech from public property? Consider Capitol Square Review and Advisory Board v. Pinette, 515 U.S. 753 (1995), in which the Court invalidated an administrative decision that denied permission to the Ku Klux Klan to erect a large, unattended cross in Capitol Square, a public forum located in front of the Ohio Statehouse, because observers might conclude that the state endorsed the religious beliefs embodied in the cross. In a plurality opinion, Justice Scalia, speaking for four justices, argued that the establishment clause is violated in these circumstances only if the government engages in religious expression itself or discriminates in favor of religious expression. He maintained that there is no violation of the establishment clause where, as here, the government enacts "neutral policies that happen to benefit religion." Justice Scalia therefore concluded that, because the government could constitutionally have permitted the Klan to erect its cross on the same terms on which it would have permitted any other speaker to erect a speech-related display in Capitol Square, the establishment clause did not justify the government's decision to deny access to the Klan because of the religious nature of the expression.

In concurring opinions, Justices O'Connor, Souter, and Breyer disagreed with Justice Scalia that the establishment clause could not be violated by "neutral policies that happen to benefit religion." In their view, even neutral policies could violate the establishment clause if the circumstances are such "that the community would think that the [State] was endorsing religion." As applied to this case, however, these justices concluded that this problem was not present both because "the reasonable observer would [be] fully aware that Capitol Square is a public space in which a multiplicity of groups, both secular and religious, engage in expressive conduct" and because the reasonable observer would "be able to read and understand an adequate disclaimer."

Justice Stevens dissented on the ground that the establishment clause "prohibits government from allowing [unattended] displays that take a position on a religious issue [in] front of the seat of government," for "viewers reasonably will assume that [government] approves of them." Moreover, a disclaimer would not be sufficient to satisfy this concern, for even with a disclaimer, the "inference would remain." Justice Ginsburg also dissented.

After *Pinette*, could the government constitutionally require only religious speakers to affix disclaimers to their unattended displays on public property? Is the government constitutionally required to order *all* religious speakers who use public property to display disclaimers — those who distribute handbills on public streets as well as those who erect displays in public parks?

In Board of Education of Westside Community Schools v. Mergens, Chapter 8, section D, infra, the Court upheld against a challenge under the establishment clause the federal Equal Access Act, which makes it unlawful for any public secondary school that receives federal financial assistance and that allows one or more noncurriculum-related student groups to meet on school premises during noninstructional time to deny equal access to any students who wish to conduct meetings on similar terms because of the religious, political, philosophical, or other content of their speech.

7. *The reach of* Mosley: *the "careful scrutiny" standard.* Are there circumstances in which a content-based law, like the ones invalidated in *Mosley, Carey,* and *Widmar,* can withstand "careful scrutiny"? See Burson v. Freeman, 504 U.S. 191 (1992) (upholding a law prohibiting the solicitation of votes and the display or distribution of campaign materials within 100 feet of the entrance to a polling place).

Lehman v. City of Shaker Heights

418 U.S. 298 (1974)

MR. JUSTICE BLACKMUN announced the judgment of the Court and an opinion, in which THE CHIEF JUSTICE, MR. JUSTICE WHITE, and MR. JUSTICE REHNQUIST join.

This case presents the question whether a city which operates a public rapid transit system and sells [commercial and public service] advertising space for car cards on its vehicles is required by the First and Fourteenth Amendments to accept paid political advertising on behalf of a candidate for public office.

[Petitioner, a candidate for the office of state representative,] sought to promote his candidacy by purchasing car card space on the Shaker Heights Rapid Transit System for the months of August, September, and October.

[He] was informed [that], although space was then available, [the] city did not permit political advertising. The system, however, accepted ads from cigarette companies, banks, savings and loan associations, liquor companies, retail and service establishments, churches, and civic and public-service oriented groups. . . .

When petitioner did not succeed in his effort to have his copy accepted, he sought declaratory and injunctive relief in the state courts of Ohio without success. . . .

It is urged that the car cards here constitute a public forum protected by the First Amendment, and that there is a guarantee of nondiscriminatory access to such publicly owned and controlled areas of communication "regardless of the primary purpose for which the area is dedicated." [We] disagree.

[This situation is] different from the traditional settings where First Amendment values inalterably prevail. [Although] American constitutional jurisprudence, in the light of the First Amendment, has been jealous to preserve access to public places for purposes of free speech, the nature of the forum and the conflicting interests involved have remained important in determining the degree of protection afforded by the Amendment to the speech in question. . . .

Here, we have no open spaces, no meeting hall, park, street corner, or other public thoroughfare. Instead, the city is engaged in commerce. It must provide rapid, convenient, pleasant, and inexpensive service to the commuters of Shaker Heights. The car card space, although incidental to the provision of public transportation, is a part of the commercial venture. In much the same way that a newspaper or periodical, or even a radio or television station, need not accept every proffer of advertising from the general public, a city transit system has discretion to develop and make reasonable choices concerning the type of advertising that may be displayed in its vehicles. . . .

Because state action exists, however, the policies and practices governing access to the transit system's advertising space must not be arbitrary, capricious, or invidious. Here, the city has decided that "[p]urveyors of goods and services saleable in commerce may purchase advertising space on an equal basis, whether they be house builders or butchers." This decision is little different from deciding to impose a 10-, 25-, or 35-cent fare, or from changing schedules or the location of bus stops. [Revenue] earned from long-term commercial advertising could be jeopardized by a requirement that short-term candidacy or issue-oriented advertisements be displayed on car cards. Users would be subjected to the blare of political propaganda. There could be lurking doubts about favoritism, and sticky administrative problems might arise in parceling out limited space to eager politicians. In these circumstances, the managerial decision to limit car card space to innocuous and less controversial commercial and service oriented advertising does not rise to the dignity of a First Amendment violation. . . .

[The] city consciously has limited access to its transit system advertising space in order to minimize chances of abuse, the appearance of favoritism, and the risk of imposing upon a captive audience. These are reasonable legislative objectives advanced by the city in a proprietary capacity. [There] is no First or Fourteenth Amendment violation.

[Affirmed.]

MR. JUSTICE DOUGLAS, concurring in the judgment. . . .

[If] the streetcar or bus were a forum for communication akin to that of streets or public parks, considerable problems would be presented. [But] a streetcar or bus is plainly not a park or sidewalk or other meeting place for discussion.

[It] is only a way to get to work or back home. The fact that it is owned and operated by the city does not without more make it a forum.

[If] we are to turn a bus or streetcar into either a newspaper or a park, we take great liberties with people who because of necessity become commuters and at the same time captive viewers or listeners.

In asking us to force the system to accept his message as a vindication of his constitutional rights, the petitioner overlooks the constitutional rights of the commuters. While petitioner clearly has a right to express his views to those who wish to listen, he has no right to force his message upon an audience incapable of declining to receive it. In my view the right of the commuters to be free from forced intrusions on their privacy precludes the city from transforming its vehicles of public transportation into forums for the dissemination of ideas upon this captive audience. . . .

I do not view the content of the message as relevant either to petitioner's right to express it or to the commuters' right to be free from it. Commercial advertisements may be as offensive and intrusive to captive audiences as any political message. But the validity of the commercial advertising program is not before us since we are not faced with one complaining of an invasion of privacy through forced exposure to commercial ads. Since I do not believe that petitioner has any constitutional right to spread his message before this captive audience, I concur in the Court's judgment.

MR. JUSTICE BRENNAN, with whom MR. JUSTICE STEWART, MR. JUSTICE MARSHALL, and MR. JUSTICE POWELL join, dissenting. . . .

In the circumstances of this case, [we] need not decide whether public transit cars *must* be made available as forums for the exercise of First Amendment rights. By accepting commercial and public service advertising, the city effectively waived any argument that advertising in its transit cars is incompatible with the rapid transit system's primary function of providing transportation. A forum for communication was voluntarily established when the city installed the physical facilities for the advertisements [and] created the necessary administrative machinery for regulating access to that forum.

The plurality opinion, however, contends that as long as the city limits its advertising space to "innocuous and less controversial commercial and service oriented advertising," no First Amendment forum is created. I find no merit in that position. Certainly, noncommercial public service advertisements convey messages of public concern and are clearly protected by the First Amendment. And while it is possible that commercial advertising may be accorded *less* First Amendment protection than speech concerning political and social issues of public importance, [it] is "speech" nonetheless, often communicating information and ideas found by many persons to be controversial. [Once] such messages have been accepted and displayed, the existence of a forum for communication cannot be gainsaid. To hold otherwise, and thus sanction the city's preference for bland commercialism and noncontroversial public service messages over "uninhibited, robust, and wide-open" debate on public issues, would reverse the traditional priorities of the First Amendment.

Once a public forum for communication has been established, both free speech and equal protection principles prohibit discrimination based *solely* upon subject matter or content. See, e.g., [*Mosley*]. That the discrimination is among entire classes of ideas, rather than among points of view within a particular class, does not render it any less odious. Subject matter or content censorship in any form is forbidden. [Few] examples are required to illustrate the scope of the city's policy and practice.[10]

The city contends that its ban against political advertising is bottomed upon its solicitous regard for "captive riders" of the rapid transit system, who are "forced to endure the advertising thrust upon [them]." Whatever merit the city's argument might have in other contexts, it has a hollow ring in the present case, where the city has voluntarily opened its rapid transit system as a forum for communication. In that circumstance, the occasional appearance of provocative speech should be expected. . . .

The line between ideological and nonideological speech is impossible to draw with accuracy. By accepting commercial and public service advertisements, the city opened the door to "sometimes controversial or unsettling speech" and determined that such speech does not unduly interfere with the rapid transit system's primary purpose of transporting passengers. In the eyes of many passengers, certain commercial or public service messages[11] are as profoundly disturbing as some political advertisements might be to other passengers. There is certainly no evidence in the record of this case indicating that political advertisements, as a class, are so disturbing when displayed that they are more likely than commercial or public service advertisements to impair the rapid transit system's primary function of transportation. . . .

Moreover, even if it were possible to draw a manageable line between controversial and noncontroversial messages, the city's practice of censorship for the benefit of "captive audiences" still would not be justified. [The] advertisements accepted by the city [are] not broadcast over loudspeakers in the transit cars. The privacy of the passengers is not, therefore, dependent upon their ability "to sit and to try *not* to listen." [Rather], all advertisements accepted for display are in *written* form. [Should] passengers chance to glance at advertisements they find offensive, they can "effectively avoid further bombardment of their sensibilities

---

10. In declaring unconstitutional an advertising policy remarkably similar to the city's policy in the present case, the California Supreme Court detailed "the paradoxical scope of the [transit] district's policy [banning political advertising]" in the following manner:

> A cigarette company is permitted to advertise the desirability of smoking its brand, but a cancer society is not entitled to caution by advertisement that cigarette smoking is injurious to health. A theater may advertise a motion picture that portrays sex and violence, but the Legion for Decency has no right to post a message calling for clean films. A lumber company may advertise its wood products, but a conservation group cannot implore citizens to write to the President or Governor about protecting our natural resources. An oil refinery may advertise its products, but a citizens' organization cannot demand enforcement of existing air pollution statutes. An insurance company may announce its available policies, but a senior citizens' club cannot plead for legislation to improve our social security program. Advertisements for travel, foods, clothing, toiletries, automobiles, legal drugs — all these are acceptable, but the American Legion would not have the right to place a paid advertisement reading, "Support Our Boys in Viet Nam. Send Holiday Packages."

Wirta v. Alameda-Contra Costa Transit District, 63 Cal. 2d 51, 57-58, 434 P.2d 982, 986-987 (1967).

11. For example, the record indicates that *church advertising* was accepted for display on the Shaker Heights Rapid Transit System.

simply by averting their eyes." [Cohen v. California.] Surely that minor inconvenience is a small price to pay for the continued preservation of so precious a liberty as free speech.

The city's remaining justification is equally unpersuasive. The city argues that acceptance of "political advertisements [would] suggest [that] the candidate so advertised is being supported or promoted by the government of the City." Clearly, such ephemeral concerns do not provide the city with *carte blanche* authority to exclude an entire category of speech from a public forum. . . .

Moreover, neutral regulations, which do not distinguish among advertisements on the basis of subject matter, can be narrowly tailored to allay the city's fears. The impression of city endorsement can be dispelled by requiring disclaimers to appear prominently on the face of every advertisement. And while problems of accommodating all potential advertisers may be vexing at times, the appearance of favoritism can be avoided by the even-handed regulation of time, place, and manner for all advertising, irrespective of subject matter. . . .

Note: Lehman *and the Limits of* Mosley

1. *Lehman.* In *Mosley*, the Court announced that laws granting unequal access to government property for speech purposes "must be carefully scrutinized" and "must be tailored to serve a substantial governmental interest." But in *Lehman*, Justice Blackmun, speaking for the plurality, upheld such a law because it was not "arbitrary, capricious, or invidious." Is Justice Blackmun's analysis in *Lehman* consistent with *Mosley*? Consider the following:

a. *In its operation of the transit system and its sale of advertising space, "the city is engaged in commerce."* Consider Wells and Hellerstein, The Governmental-Proprietary Distinction in Constitutional Law, 66 Va. L. Rev. 1073, 1116 (1980):

> As a regulator of the general public, the government must base its proscription of an activity on the premise that the proscription will act to enhance the general welfare. [As] a procurer or provider of goods and services, however, it may assert a different, more specific kind of interest — the interest of an employer who needs an efficient workforce, a landlord who would prefer not to deal with tenants who do not pay rent, or a purchaser who wishes to contract with a trustworthy seller. This quasi-business interest may adequately support regulation that a court might strike down if applied to the public at large and the state supported it with arguments that it promotes the general welfare. [That government acts in a proprietary capacity, however,] legitimately serves only to identify a state interest not present when the state regulates the general public. It should be but one element in the analysis and should not by itself determine the outcome.

See also International Society for Krishna Consciousness, Inc. v. Lee, supra (invoking the proprietary/governmental distinction in upholding a ban on solicitation in airport terminals); United States v. Kokinda, section E2b supra (invoking the distinction in upholding a Postal Service regulation prohibiting any person from soliciting contributions on post office property).

b. *Streetcar passengers are a "captive audience."* Recall Cohen v. California, section D5 supra: "The ability of government, consonant with the Constitution, to shut off discourse solely to protect others from hearing it is [dependent] upon a showing that substantial privacy interests are being invaded in an essentially intolerable manner." Is that test satisfied in *Lehman*? If so, is the exclusion of all political speech an appropriate device for protecting the sensibilities of captive commuters? Suppose that, after polling its commuters, the city finds that, although the vast majority do not object to the ideas of Democratic and Republican candidates, they "deeply resent" the views expressed by Socialist candidates. Based on this finding, may the city permit Democratic and Republican candidates to purchase car card space to espouse their "inoffensive" ideas, while excluding the "offensive" Socialist messages? For analysis of the "captive" audience, see section D5 supra.

c. *"No First Amendment forum is here to be found."* Do you agree with Justice Brennan that, even if the car card space did not inherently constitute a public forum, the city's acceptance of commercial and public service advertisements "created" such a forum? Recall *Widmar*. Consider Emerson, The Affirmative Side of the First Amendment, 15 Ga. L. Rev. 795, 813 (1981): "The dissenters fail to recognize the complications arising when the government is affirmatively promoting expression by providing facilities for a selected area of expression. They argue that, once the 'forum' has been opened, the government may not regulate on the basis of content. The issue before the Court, however, was what the scope of the forum was."

Would any of these "explanations" of *Lehman* justify a content-based restriction defined in terms of viewpoint rather than subject matter?

2. *The reach of* Lehman: *military bases.* In Greer v. Spock, section E2b supra, the base commander of the Fort Dix Military Reservation, acting under the authority of a regulation prohibiting "demonstrations, picketing, sit-ins, protest marches, political speeches and similar activities" on the base, denied the request of a political candidate to make a speech on the base to discuss election issues with service personnel and their dependents. The candidate maintained that the regulation was invalid because the ban on civilian access to the base for expressive purposes was not content-neutral: "Civilian speakers have occasionally been invited to the base to address military personnel. The subjects of their talks have ranged from business management to drug abuse. Visiting clergymen have, by invitation, participated in religious services at the base chapel. Theatrical exhibitions and musical productions have also been presented on the base."

The Court upheld the regulation. Although the base was generally open to the public, the Court explained that "the business of a military installation [is] to train soldiers, not to provide a public forum." Moreover, the Court emphasized that there was "no claim that the military authorities discriminated in any way among candidates for public office based upon the candidates' supposed political views." In such circumstances, the ban on partisan political expression was not unconstitutional. Justices Brennan and Marshall dissented. Is *Greer* reconcilable with *Mosley* and *Widmar*?

PERRY EDUCATORS' ASSOCIATION v. PERRY LOCAL EDUCATORS' ASSOCIATION, 460 U.S. 37 (1983). The school district of Perry Township, Indiana, operates an interschool mail system to transmit messages among the teachers and between the teachers and the school administration. In addition, some private organizations, such as the YMCA and the Cub Scouts, have been permitted to use the system. After the Perry Educators' Association (PEA) was certified as the exclusive bargaining representative of the district's teachers, the school district and PEA entered into a collective bargaining agreement granting PEA, but no other union, access to the mail system. The Perry Local Educators' Association (PLEA), a rival union, brought this suit claiming that the district's access policy violated the Constitution.

The Court, in a five-to-four decision, upheld the challenged policy. Justice White delivered the opinion: "The existence of a right of access to public property [depends] on the character of the property at issue. [First, there are the] streets and [parks]. In these quintessential public forums, the government may not [enforce] a content-based exclusion [unless the exclusion] is necessary to serve a compelling state interest and [is] narrowly drawn to achieve that end. [*Mosley; Carey.*] [A] second category consists of public property which the state has [voluntarily] opened for use by the public as a place for expressive activity. [Although] a state is not required to indefinitely retain the open character of [such facilities], as long as it does so it is bound by the same standards as apply in a traditional public forum. [*Widmar.*] [A third category consists of public] property which is not by tradition or designation a forum for public communication. [The] state may reserve [such property] for its intended purposes, communicative or otherwise, so long as the regulation of speech is reasonable and not an effort to suppress expression merely because public officials oppose the speaker's view. . . .

"The school mail facilities [fall] within the third category. [The] interschool mail system is not a traditional public forum [and it] is not held open to the general public. [PLEA argues, however,] that the school mail facilities have become a 'limited public forum' from which it may not be excluded because of the periodic use of the system by private non-school connected groups, [such as] the YMCA, Cub Scouts, and other civic and church organizations. [The] use of the [mail system] by [such] groups [is] no doubt a relevant consideration. [Indeed, had the school district] opened its mail system for indiscriminate use by the general public, then PLEA could justifiably argue a public forum [had] been created. [But that] is not the case. [And the] type of selective access [involved here] does not transform government property into a public forum. [*Greer; Lehman.*] Moreover, even if [the grant of] access to the Cub Scouts, YMCAs, and parochial schools [had] created a 'limited' public forum, the constitutional right of access [would] extend only to other entities of similar character. While the school mail facilities thus might be a forum generally open for [other] organizations that engage in activities of interest [to] students, they would not [be] open to an organization such as PLEA, which is concerned with the terms and conditions of teacher employment. . . .

"[PLEA argues further that by allowing PEA and not PLEA to use the mail facilities,] the access policy [favors] a particular viewpoint, that of the PEA, on labor relations, and consequently must be strictly scrutinized regardless of whether a public forum is involved. There is, however, no indication that the school board intended to discourage one viewpoint and advance another. [It] is more accurate to characterize the access policy as based on the *status* of the respective unions rather than their views. Implicit in the concept of the nonpublic forum is the right to make distinctions in access on the basis of subject matter and speaker identity. These distinctions may be impermissible in a public forum but are inherent and inescapable in the process of limiting a nonpublic forum to activities compatible with the intended purpose of the property. The touchstone for evaluating these distinctions is whether they are reasonable in light of the purpose which the forum at issue serves. [Access to the] mail service [clearly] could be restricted to those with teaching and operational responsibility in the schools. [By] the same token — and upon the same principle — the system was properly opened to PEA, when it [was] designated the collective bargaining agent for all teachers in the Perry schools. PEA thereby assumed an official position in the operational structure of [the schools]. [The] differential access provided PEA and PLEA is reasonable because it is wholly consistent with the district's legitimate interest in 'preserv[ing] the property [for] the use to which it is lawfully dedicated.'"

Justice Brennan, joined by Justices Marshall, Powell, and Stevens, dissented: "In focusing on the public forum issue, the Court disregards the First Amendment's central proscription [against] viewpoint discrimination, in any forum, public or nonpublic. [As the] Court of Appeals [noted], 'the access policy [favors] a particular viewpoint on labor relations in the Perry schools: the teachers inevitably will receive from [PEA] self-laudatory descriptions of its activities [and] will be denied the critical perspective offered by [PLEA].' [Indeed], the only reason for [PEA] to seek an exclusive access policy is to deny its rivals access to an effective channel of communication. [In effect, the school district] has agreed to amplify the speech of [PEA], while repressing the speech of [PLEA] based on [PLEA's] point of view. [Such viewpoint discrimination] can be sustained 'only if the government can show that the regulation is a precisely drawn means of serving a compelling state interest.' [The state interests here] are not sufficient to sustain the [challenged] policy."

Note: Perry *and the Limits of* Lehman

1. *The reach of* Perry: *distinctions among charities.* The Combined Federal Campaign (CFC) is an annual charitable fund-raising drive conducted in the federal workplace during working hours largely through the voluntary efforts of federal employees. In Cornelius v. NAACP Legal Defense & Educational Fund, 473 U.S. 788 (1985), the Court, in a four-to-three decision, upheld an executive order limiting participation in the CFC to voluntary, tax-exempt, nonprofit charitable agencies that provide direct health and welfare services to individuals and expressly excluding legal defense and political advocacy organizations.

In an opinion by Justice O'Connor, the Court first held that the CFC is a nonpublic forum:

Respondents argue [that] the Government created a limited public forum for use by all charitable organizations to solicit funds from federal employees. [We do not agree.] The Government's consistent policy has been to limit participation in the CFC to "appropriate" voluntary [agencies]. Such selective access, unsupported by evidence of a purposeful designation for public use, does not create a public forum. [Nor] does the history of the CFC support a finding that the Government was motivated by an affirmative desire to provide an open forum for charitable solicitation, [for the] historical background indicates that the Campaign was designed to minimize the disruption to the workplace that had resulted from unlimited ad hoc solicitation activities by *lessening* the amount of expressive activity occurring on federal property. [Finally,] the nature of the government property involved strengthens the conclusion that the CFC is a nonpublic forum, [for the] federal workplace, like any place of employment, exists to accomplish the business of the employer [and] the Government has the right to exercise control over access to the [workplace] to avoid interruptions to the performance of the duties of its employees. [We therefore] conclude that the CFC is a nonpublic forum.

Citing *Perry*, the Court next explained that "control over access to a nonpublic forum can be based on subject matter and speaker identity so long as the distinctions drawn are reasonable in light of the purpose served by the forum and are viewpoint neutral." The Court held that the challenged limitation was reasonable because "the President could reasonably conclude" that (1) "a dollar directly spent on providing food or shelter to the needy is more beneficial than a dollar spent on litigation that might or might not result in aid to the needy"; (2) the participation of legal defense and political advocacy groups would generate controversy and thus "be detrimental to the Campaign and disruptive of the federal workplace"; and (3) the exclusion of legal defense and political advocacy groups would "avoid the reality and the appearance of government favoritism or entanglement with particular viewpoints." Finally, noting that "the purported concern to avoid controversy excited by particular groups may conceal a bias against the viewpoint advanced by the excluded speakers," the Court remanded for a determination whether the regulation "is in reality a facade for viewpoint-based discrimination."

Justice Blackmun, joined by Justice Brennan, dissented. Justice Blackmun maintained that the "Court's analysis empties the limited public forum concept of meaning, [for if] the Government does not create a limited public forum unless it intends to provide an 'open forum' for expressive activity, and if the exclusion of some speakers is evidence that the Government did not intend to create such a forum, no speaker [will] ever be able to prove that the forum is a limited public forum." Justice Blackmun concluded that the regulation was unconstitutional because the government's justifications for excluding legal defense and political advocacy organizations from the CFC "neither reserve the CFC for expressive activity compatible with the property nor serve any other compelling governmental interest." Justice Stevens also dissented.

2. *The reach of* Perry: *distinctions among different means of expression.* In United States v. Kokinda, section E2b supra, respondents, members of a political advocacy group, set up a table on a sidewalk near the entrance to a United States Post Office to distribute literature and solicit contributions. The sidewalk is located entirely on post office property and is the sole means by which customers travel from the parking lot to the post office building. Respondents were convicted of violating a regulation prohibiting any person from soliciting contributions on postal premises. The Court upheld the regulation as applied.

In a plurality opinion, Justice O'Connor, joined by Chief Justice Rehnquist and Justices White and Scalia, concluded that the sidewalk is not a "traditional" public forum because the "postal sidewalk at issue does not have the characteristics of public sidewalks traditionally open to expressive activity." Justice O'Connor then rejected the claim that the sidewalk, which was available for all conventional forms of expressive activity other than solicitation, was a "limited-purpose" public forum:

The Postal Service has not expressly dedicated its sidewalks to any expressive activity. [Although] individuals or groups have been permitted to leaflet, speak, and picket on postal premises, [the] practice of allowing some speech activities on postal property [does] not add up to the dedication of postal property to speech activities. ["The] government does not create a public forum by . . . *permitting* limited discourse, but only by intentionally opening a nontraditional forum for public discourse."[*Cornelius*]. [It] is anomalous [to suggest] that the Service's allowance of some avenues of speech would be relied upon as evidence that it is impermissibly suppressing other speech. If anything, the Service's generous accommodation of some types of speech testifies to its willingness to provide as broad a forum as possible, consistent with its postal mission. [Any other view] would create, in the name of the First Amendment, a disincentive for the Government to dedicate its property to any speech activities at all.

Justice Kennedy concurred in the result. Justice Brennan, joined by Justices Marshall, Blackmun, and Stevens, dissented. Would it be constitutional for the post office to permit only charities eligible to participate in the CFC to distribute literature on this sidewalk?

3. *The reach of* Perry: *distinctions concerning religious expression.* In Lamb's Chapel v. Moriches Union Free School District, 508 U.S. 384 (1993), the Court considered the constitutionality of a school district rule that permitted after-school social, civic, and recreational uses of school property but prohibited the use of such property for religious purposes. Applying this rule, the school district rejected Lamb's Chapel's request to show on school property religious-oriented films concerning family values and childrearing. The lower courts upheld the rule on the theory that the school property was "a limited public forum open only for designated purposes" and that access to such a forum "can be based on subject matter [so] long as the distinctions drawn are reasonable [and] viewpoint neutral." The Supreme Court accepted this analysis but nonetheless invalidated the rule because it was not "viewpoint neutral."

In reaching this result, the Court rejected the lower courts' conclusion that the challenged rule was based on subject matter, rather than viewpoint, "because it [would] be applied in the same way to all uses of school property for religious purposes." Although conceding that "all religions and all uses for religious purposes are treated alike under the rule," the Court observed that this "does not answer the critical question" whether it constitutes discrimination "on the basis of viewpoint to permit the school property to be used for the presentation of all views about family issues [except] those dealing with the subject matter from a religious standpoint." The Court reasoned that the "film involved here [dealt] with a subject otherwise permissible under [the rule], and its exhibition was denied solely because the film dealt with the subject from a religious standpoint." The Court therefore concluded that the rule "violates the First Amendment" because it denied "access to a speaker solely to suppress the point of view he espouses on an otherwise included subject." Is this conception of viewpoint discrimination consistent with the analyses in *Lehman* and *Perry*?

Consider Stone, The Equal Access Controversy: The Religion Clauses and the Meaning of "Neutrality," 81 Nw. U.L. Rev. 168, 169-170 (1986):

The protection of political speech, like religious speech, lies at the very core of the first amendment. The Court often has recognized, however, that government may grant special benefits to nonpolitical speech without extending those benefits to political speech, so long as it does not expressly favor any particular political viewpoint. [Citing *Lehman; Greer; Cornelius.*] This is so because policies that disadvantage political speech as a class are less threatening to first amendment values than laws that expressly disadvantage specific points of view.

A similar principle [should govern] religious expression. As the Supreme Court has long recognized, the "clearest command" of the religion clauses is that "one religious denomination cannot be officially preferred over another." [Denominational] discrimination in the religious context is the analog of viewpoint discrimination in the political context. [The] corollary is also true, however. Governmental policies that grant special benefits to nonreligious expression as a class should be tested by the same — less demanding — standards that the Court uses to test the constitutionality of governmental policies that grant special benefits to nonpolitical expression as a class. In the religious, as in the political, realm the broader subject-matter classification is less threatening to core first amendment values.

4. Lamb's Chapel *revisited: further debate on the meaning of viewpoint-neutrality.* In Rosenberger v. Rector and Visitors of University of Virginia, 515 U.S. 819 (1995), the Court, in a five-to-four decision, invalidated a University of Virginia policy authorizing payment from the Student Activities Fund for the printing costs of a variety of student publications but prohibiting payment for any student publication that "primarily promotes or manifests a particular belief in or about a deity or an ultimate reality." The suit was brought by a student organization that was denied funding because it publishes a journal that "offers a Christian perspective on both personal and community issues," such as "racism, crisis pregnancy, [and] homosexuality."

The Court, in an opinion by Justice Kennedy, explained that, although the "necessities of confining a forum to the limited and legitimate purposes for which it was created may justify the State in reserving it for certain groups or for the discussion of certain topics," it may not "discriminate against speech on the basis of its viewpoint." The Court then observed that these "same principles apply" to the Student Activities Fund, which the Court described as a "forum," albeit "more in a metaphysical than in a spatial or geographic sense."

Acknowledging that the definition of viewpoint discrimination "is not a precise one," the Court nonetheless concluded that "here, as in *Lamb's Chapel*, viewpoint discrimination is the proper way to interpret the University's" policy. The Court explained that this was so because it was the religious "perspective" of the journal, rather than the "subjects discussed," such as racism, pregnancy, or homosexuality, that resulted in the university's refusal to pay the journal's printing costs.

In dissent, Justice Souter, joined by Justices Stevens, Ginsburg, and Breyer, maintained that the "issue whether a distinction is based on viewpoint does not turn simply on whether a government regulation happens to be applied to a speaker who seeks to advance a particular viewpoint," but "on whether the burden on speech is explained by reference to viewpoint." Thus, citing *Lehman*, Justice Souter observed that "a municipality's decision to prohibit political advertising on bus placards" does not "amount to viewpoint discrimination when in the course of applying this policy it denies space to a person who wishes to speak in favor of a particular political candidate."

Justice Souter argued that it is the "element of taking sides in a public debate that identifies viewpoint discrimination and makes it the most pernicious of all distinctions based on content." Justice Souter reasoned that, given this understanding, there was "no viewpoint discrimination" in this case:

> If the [policy] were written [so] as to limit [only] Christian advocacy, [the] discrimination would be based on viewpoint. But that is not what the regulation authorizes; it applies to Muslim and Jewish and Buddhist advocacy as well as Christian. And since it limits funding to activities promoting or manifesting a particular belief not only "in" but "about" a deity or ultimate reality, it applies to agnostics and atheists as well as [to] deists and theists. [Thus, the policy does] not skew debate by funding one position but not its competitors. [It simply denies] funding for hortatory speech that "primarily promotes or manifests" any view on the merits of religion; [it denies] funding for the entire subject matter of religious apologetics.

Justice Souter concluded that if the policy at issue in this case "amounts to viewpoint discrimination, the Court has all but eviscerated the line between viewpoint and content."

Recall the debate over a similar issue in R.A.V. v. City of St. Paul, section D6 supra. In light of the Court's reasoning in *Lamb's Chapel* and *Rosenberger*, does it follow that the regulation of "obscenity" is also impermissibly viewpoint-based "because it is justified by moral objections to the ideas or messages that sexual speech is said to convey"? Heins, Viewpoint Discrimination, 24 Hast. Const. L.Q. 99, 103 (1996).

5. *Speaker-based restrictions.* Note that *Perry* and *Cornelius* involve "speaker-based" restrictions. Such restrictions, which treat some speakers differently than others, but define the distinction in terms other than content, do not fit neatly within the Court's content-based/content-neutral distinction. In cases such as *Perry* and *Cornelius*, the Court sharply distinguished speaker-based from viewpoint-based restrictions and, at least in the nonpublic forum context, tested speaker-based restrictions by a standard of reasonableness. But speaker-based restrictions often have clear viewpoint-differential effects. In *Perry*, for example, the challenged policy unquestionably favored some viewpoints over others, for recognized bargaining agents are likely to take consistent and predictable positions on particular issues. Indeed, in some instances, speaker-based restrictions may correlate almost perfectly with viewpoint. Consider, for example, laws granting special subsidies to veterans' organizations or denying tax deductions to individuals who contribute to the Communist Party. How should we deal with such restrictions? See Stone, Content Regulation and the First Amendment, 25 Wm. & Mary L. Rev. 189, 244-251 (1983).

6. *Majoritarian control over access.* Suppose a school district authorizes the students of a public high school or university to elect a student to speak for three minutes at the beginning of each home football game. Does this create a public forum? Suppose the students consistently elect very conservative student speakers. Cf. Board of Regents of University of Wisconsin v. Southworth, 529 U.S. 217 (2000) ("access to a public forum [does] not depend upon majoritarian consent").

7. *Evaluation.* Consider the Court's categorization of "quintessential," "limited," and "non" public forums. Do these categories make sense? Do you agree that the Court in *Perry* "indulged in a shell game, [throwing] out a circular definition of the public forum"? L. Tribe, Constitutional Choices 207 (1985). Consider the following views:

a. Like viewpoint-based restrictions, subject matter classifications should be subjected to the same standard of scrutiny whether they occur in "quintessential" public forums, "limited" public forums, or "non" public forums.

b. Whether a particular public facility constitutes a "limited" public forum, rather than a "non" public forum, should turn on the amount of speech the government has allowed. If the government allows almost all speech, and excludes only a narrow category, as in *Widmar*, it has created a public forum. If it excludes almost all speech, and allows only a narrow category, as in *Lehman*, *Greer*, and *Perry*, it has not created a public forum.

c. "Classification of public places as various types of forums has only confused judicial opinions by diverting attention from the real first amendment [issues]. Constitutional protection should depend not on labeling the speaker's physical location but on the first amendment values and governmental interests involved in the case." Farber and Nowak, The Misleading Nature of Public Forum Analysis: Content and Context in First Amendment Adjudication, 70 Va. L. Rev. 1219, 1234 (1984).

ARKANSAS EDUCATIONAL TELEVISION COMMISSION v. **FORBES, 523 U.S. 666 (1998).** The AETC is a state agency that owns and operates a network of five noncommercial television stations in the state. In 1992, the AETC planned a series of debates between candidates for federal office. Given the time constraints of such debates, the AETC decided to limit participation "to the major party candidates or any other candidate who had strong popular support." Forbes, an independent candidate for Congress, had satisfied the Arkansas requirement that he obtain 2,000 signatures to qualify him to appear on the ballot, but the AETC nonetheless refused to include him in the debates because he "had not generated appreciable voter support" and "was not regarded as a serious candidate by the press." It was undisputed that the AETC did not exclude Forbes because of any "disagreement with his views." Forbes claimed that his exclusion violated the first amendment.

The Court, in an opinion by Justice Kennedy, rejected this claim. After noting that exclusions from such "candidate debates" are governed by the public forum doctrine, and that a public broadcaster therefore "cannot grant or deny access [on] the basis of whether it agrees with a candidate's views," the Court next turned to the question whether the debate was properly characterized as a designated public forum or a nonpublic forum: "To create a [designated public forum], the government must intend to make the property 'generally available' to a class of speakers. [A] designated public forum is not created when the government allows selective access for individual speakers rather than general access for a class of speakers. [Citing *Perry* and *Cornelius*.] These cases illustrate the distinction between 'general access,' which indicates the property is a designated public forum, and 'selective access,' which indicates the property is a nonpublic forum. On the one hand, the government creates a designated public forum when it makes its property generally available to a certain class of speakers, as the university made its facilities generally available to student groups in *Widmar*. On the other hand, the government does not create a designated public forum when it does no more than reserve eligibility for access to the forum to a particular class of speakers, whose members must then, as individuals, 'obtain permission' to use it. For instance, the [government] did not create a designated public forum in *Cornelius* when it reserved eligibility for participation in the CFC drive to charitable agencies, and then make individual, non-ministerial judgments as to which of the eligible agencies would participate. [This] distinction [furthers] First Amendment interests. By recognizing the distinction, we encourage the government to open its property to some expressive activity in cases where, if faced with an all-or-nothing choice, it might not open the property at all."

Applying this analysis, the Court held that the "AETC debate was not a designated public forum": "Here, the debate did not have an open-microphone format. [The] AETC did not make its debate generally available to candidates for [this congressional] seat. Instead, [just] as the government in *Cornelius* made agency-by-agency determinations as to which of the eligible agencies would participate in the CFC, the AETC made candidate-by-candidate determinations as to which of the eligible candidates would participate in the debate. 'Such selective access, unsupported by evidence of a purposeful designation for public use, does not create a public forum.' Thus the debate was a nonpublic forum." To bolster this conclusion, the Court observed that a contrary holding "would result in less speech, not more" because "a public television editor might, with reason, decide that the inclusion of all ballot-qualified candidates [in the debates] would 'actually undermine the educational value and quality of debates'" and therefore cancel the debates altogether. Applying the standard for exclusion from a nonpublic forum, the Court concluded that the decision to exclude Forbes "because he had generated no appreciable public support" was constitutionally permissible because it was not "based on the speaker's viewpoint" and was "reasonable in light of the purpose of the property."

Justice Stevens, joined by Justices Souter and Ginsburg, dissented. Although agreeing with the general analysis of the Court, Justice Stevens objected that the broad "flexibility of AETC's purported standard" for excluding individual candidates gave it "nearly limitless discretion to exclude Forbes from the debate based on ad hoc justifications."

The Court concluded in *AETC* that the candidate debate was a nonpublic forum, in which viewpoint discrimination was prohibited. But what about the public television station itself? In deciding what programming to present, may the state agency select among the viewpoints it will present? May it present television documentaries that celebrate the civil rights movement but not the Ku Klux Klan?

In his opinion for the Court in *AETC*, Justice Kennedy concluded that, as a general matter, the public forum doctrine is inapplicable to the activities of a state-owned television station: "In the case of television broadcasting, [broad] rights of access for outside speakers would be antithetical, as a general rule, to the discretion that stations [must] exercise to fulfill their journalistic purpose. [The] nature of editorial discretion counsels against subjecting [even public] broadcasters to claims of viewpoint discrimination. Programming decisions would be particularly vulnerable to claims of this type because even principled exclusions, rooted in sound journalistic judgment, can often be characterized as viewpoint-based. [Much] like a [public] university selecting a commencement speaker, [or] a public school prescribing its curriculum, a broadcaster by its nature will facilitate the expression of some viewpoints instead of others." Thus, "as a general matter," a state-owned television station is not a nonpublic forum, it is "not a forum at all," and the ordinary requirement of viewpoint-neutrality, which governs even nonpublic forums, does not apply. Does this make sense? Consider the following section.

d.   Unequal Access to Other Forms of Government Property: Auditoriums, Libraries, Tax Exemptions, and Government Grants

To what extent, if any, should the principles and doctrines that govern access to public parks, airport terminals, and military bases also govern public auditoriums, school libraries, and government-funded programs to support the arts?

SOUTHEASTERN PROMOTIONS v. CONRAD, 420 U.S. 546 (1975). Petitioner, a promoter of theatrical productions, applied to a municipal board charged with managing a city auditorium and a city-leased theater to present the musical "Hair" at the theater. Although no conflicting engagement was scheduled, the board, based on reports that the musical involved nudity and "obscenity," rejected the application because the production would not be "in the best interest of the community." The Court held that this action constituted an unconstitutional prior restraint. Justice Blackmun, speaking for the Court, explained:

"The elements of prior restraint [were] clearly present in the system by which [the] board regulated the use of its theaters. One seeking to use a theater was required to apply to the board. The board was empowered to determine whether the applicant should be granted permission — in effect, a license or permit — on the basis of its review of the content of the proposed production. [The board's] action was no less a prior restraint because the public facilities under [its] control happened to be municipal theaters. The Memorial Auditorium and the [city-leased theater] were public forums designed for and dedicated to expressive activities. [Thus, in] order to be held lawful, [the board's] action [must] have been accomplished with procedural safeguards that reduce the danger of suppressing constitutionally protected speech. [We] held in [Freedman v. Maryland, section C2 supra], that a system of prior restraint runs afoul of the First Amendment if it lacks certain safeguards. [Such] safeguards were lacking here."

Justice Douglas dissented in part and concurred in the result in part: "The critical flaw in this case lies, not in the absence of procedural safeguards, but rather in the very nature of the content screening in which respondents have engaged. [A] municipal theater is no less a forum for the expression of ideas than is a public park, or a sidewalk. [As] soon as municipal officials are permitted to pick and choose [between] those productions which are 'clean and healthful and culturally uplifting' in content and those which are not, the path is cleared for a regime of censorship under which full voice can be given only to those views which meet with the approval of the powers that be."

Justice White, joined by Chief Justice Burger, dissented: "[The District Court described] the play as involving not only nudity but repeated 'simulated acts of anal intercourse, frontal intercourse, heterosexual intercourse, homosexual intercourse, and group intercourse.' Given this description of 'Hair,' the First Amendment in my view does not compel municipal authorities to permit production of the play in municipal facilities. Whether or not a production as described by the District Court is obscene and may be forbidden to adult audiences, it is apparent to me that the [State] could constitutionally forbid exhibition of the musical to children, [Ginsberg v. New York, section D4 supra], and that [the city] may reserve its auditorium for productions suitable for exhibition to all citizens of the city, adults and children alike."

Justice Rehnquist also dissented: "[Until] this case the Court has not equated a public auditorium, which must of necessity schedule performances by a process of inclusion and exclusion, with public streets and parks. [Moreover, here] we deal with municipal [action], not prohibiting or penalizing the expression of views in dramatic form [in privately owned theaters], but rather managing its municipal auditorium. [If] it is the desire of the citizens of [the city], who presumably have paid for and own the facilities, that the attractions to be shown there should not be of the kind which would offend any substantial number of potential theatergoers, I do not think the policy can be described as arbitrary or unreasonable. [May] an opera house limit its production to operas, or must it also show rock musicals? May a municipal theater devote an entire season to Shakespeare, or is it required to book any potential producer on a first come, first served basis? These questions are real ones in light of the Court's opinion. [A] municipal theater may not be run by municipal authorities as if it were a private theater, free to judge on a content basis alone which plays it wishes to have performed and which it does not. [But] I do not believe fidelity to the First Amendment requires the exaggerated and rigid procedural safeguards which the Court insists upon in this case."

What substantive standards should govern the use of municipal auditoriums? Consider Shiffrin, Government Speech, 27 UCLA L. Rev. 565, 584 (1980): "*Conrad* does not appreciate the complicated relationships between public forum doctrine and government interests in speech. *Conrad* supposes that the government could not choose between competing applicants on a content basis. Yet such a supposition denies any legitimate government speech interest." What is the city's "speech interest" in *Conrad*? May the city limit use of the auditorium to the presentation of Shakespeare? To "family" productions? To "competently performed" productions?

Suppose a city allocates $50,000 per year to "promote the arts." What factors may it consider in awarding its grants? Consider the following statute, which was proposed by Senator Jesse Helms in 1990:

> None of the funds authorized to be appropriated pursuant to this Act may be used by [the National Endowment for the Arts] to promote, disseminate, or produce —
>
>   (1) obscene or indecent material, including but not limited to depictions of sadomasochism, homo-eroticism, the exploitation of children, or individuals engaged in sex acts; or
>
>   (2) material which denigrates the objects or beliefs of the adherents of a particular religion or non-religion; or
>
>   (3) material which denigrates, debases, or reviles a person, group, or class of citizens on the basis of race, creed, sex, handicap, age, or national origin.

Are government subsidies of expression less problematic than government restrictions? Is the ordinance in *Mosley* a subsidy or a restriction?

BOARD OF EDUCATION, ISLAND TREES UNION FREE SCHOOL DISTRICT v. PICO, 457 U.S. 853 (1982). In 1975, several members of the petitioner Board of Education attended a conference sponsored by a politically conservative organization at which they obtained lists of books described as "objectionable" and as "improper fare for school students." Thereafter, the board removed eleven of the listed books from the district's school libraries "so that Board members could read them." In a press release justifying this action, the board characterized the books as "anti-American, anti-Christian, anti-Semitic, and just plain filthy." Among the books removed were Slaughterhouse Five, by Kurt Vonnegut, Jr.; The Naked Ape, by Desmond Morris; Best Short Stories of Negro Writers, edited by Langston Hughes; Soul on Ice, by Eldridge Cleaver; and Go Ask Alice, of anonymous authorship. The board appointed a Book Review Committee, consisting of parents and teachers, to recommend whether the books should be retained. Although the committee recommended that most of the books should be retained, the board decided to remove nine of the books and to make one other available subject to parental approval. Respondents, students in the Island Trees school system, brought this action claiming that the board's decision violated the first amendment. The district court, finding that the board acted not on religious or political principles, but "on its belief that the [books] were irrelevant, vulgar, immoral, and in bad taste," granted summary judgment to the board. The court of appeals reversed and remanded for a trial on the merits. The Supreme Court affirmed. Justice Brennan delivered an opinion joined by Justices Marshall and Stevens and joined in part by Justice Blackmun:

"[Although petitioners] rightly possess significant discretion to determine the content of their school [libraries, that] discretion may not be exercised in a narrowly partisan or political manner. If a Democratic school board, motivated by party affiliation, ordered the removal of all books written by or in favor of Republicans, few would doubt that the order violated the [first amendment]. The same conclusion would surely apply if an all-white school board, motivated by racial animus, decided to remove all books authored by blacks or advocating racial equality and integration. Our Constitution does not permit the official suppression of *ideas*. Thus, whether petitioners' removal of the books from their school libraries [violated the first amendment] depends upon the motivation behind petitioners' actions. If petitioners *intended* by their removal decision to deny respondents access to ideas with which petitioners disagreed, and if this intent was the decisive factor in petitioners' decision, then petitioners have exercised their discretion in violation of the Constitution. On the other hand, [an] unconstitutional motivation would *not* be demonstrated if it were shown that petitioners had decided to remove the books at issue because those books were pervasively vulgar [or educationally unsuitable. Such motivations] would not carry the danger of an official suppression of ideas, and thus would not violate respondents' First Amendment rights."

Justice Blackmun filed a concurring opinion: "[Our decisions] yield a general [first amendment] principle: the State may not suppress exposure to ideas — for the sole *purpose* of suppressing exposure to those ideas — absent sufficiently compelling reasons. [I] do not suggest that the State has any affirmative obligation to provide students with information and ideas. [Instead], I suggest that certain forms of state discrimination *between* ideas are improper. [The] State may not act to deny access to any idea simply because state officials disapprove of that idea for partisan or political reasons." Justice White concurred in the judgment.

Justice Rehnquist, joined by Chief Justice Burger and Justice Powell, filed a dissenting opinion: "[When the government] acts as an educator, at least at the elementary and secondary school level, [it] is engaged in inculcating social values and knowledge in relatively impressionable young people. Obviously there are innumerable decisions to be made as to what courses should be taught, what books should be purchased, or what teachers should be employed. [In my view,] it is 'permissible and appropriate for local boards to make educational decisions based upon their personal, social, political and moral views.' [When the managers of a school district decide to remove a book from a school library,] they are not proscribing it as to the citizenry in general, but are simply determining that it will not be included in [the] library. [Actions] by the government as educator do not raise the same First Amendment concerns as actions by the government as sovereign." Chief Justice Burger and Justices Powell and O'Connor also filed dissenting opinions.

Do you agree with the plurality that a school board cannot constitutionally remove books "simply because they dislike the ideas" espoused? Consider Justice Powell's evaluation, set forth in his *Pico* dissent: "[Under the plurality's approach, books] may not be removed because they are indecent; extoll violence, intolerance and racism; or degrade the dignity of the individual. [I] would not *require* a school board to promote ideas and values repugnant to a democratic society." May a public library block access on its own computers to Internet sites that carry sexually explicit material? See Mainstream Loudoun v. Board of Trustees of Loudoun Country Library, 2 F. Supp. 2d 783 (E.D. Va. 1998) (holding such a policy unconstitutional).

REGAN v. TAXATION WITH REPRESENTATION OF WASHINGTON, 461 U.S. 540 (1983). In a unanimous decision, the Court upheld a federal statute providing that contributions to an otherwise tax-exempt organization, other than a tax-exempt veterans' organization, are not tax deductible if a substantial part of the organization's activities consists of attempts to influence legislation. Justice Rehnquist delivered the opinion of the Court:

"Congress is not required by the First Amendment to subsidize lobbying. [Respondent contends, however, that the challenged provision is unconstitutional because of its distinction between veterans' and other tax-exempt organizations. We do not agree.] The case would be different if Congress were to discriminate invidiously in its subsidies in such a way as to '"aim[] at the suppression of dangerous ideas."' [But] veterans' organizations [receive] tax-deductible contributions regardless of the content of [their speech]. We find no indication that the statute was intended to suppress any ideas or any demonstration that it has had that effect. . . .

"It [is] not irrational for Congress to decide that, even though it will not subsidize substantial lobbying by charities generally, it will subsidize lobbying by veterans' organizations. Veterans have [made a unique contribution to the nation]. Our country has a long standing policy of compensating veterans for [this contribution] by providing them with numerous advantages. This policy has 'always been deemed to be legitimate.'"

Justice Blackmun, joined by Justices Brennan and Marshall, filed a concurring opinion: "Because [the] discrimination between veterans' organizations and charitable organizations is not based on the content of their speech, [it] does not deny charitable organizations equal protection of the law. [As] the Court says, a statute designed to discourage the expression of particular views would present a very different question."

Consider the following: (a) "No organization, other than a veterans' organization, may demonstrate on a military base." (b) "Contributions to an otherwise tax-exempt organization are not deductible if the organization engages in substantial lobbying activities, unless those activities concern the subject of abortion." (c) "Contributions to an otherwise tax-exempt organization are not deductible if the organization advocates the violent overthrow of government."

In FCC v. League of Women Voters, 468 U.S. 364 (1984), the Court invalidated section 399 of the Public Broadcasting Act of 1967, which prohibited any noncommercial educational station that receives a grant from the Corporation for Public Broadcasting to "engage in editorializing." The Court distinguished *Taxation with Representation* on the ground that, under the statute at issue in *Taxation with Representation*, "a charitable organization could create [an] affiliate to conduct its non-lobbying activities using tax-deductible contributions, and, at the same time, establish [a] separate affiliate to pursue its lobbying efforts without such contributions," whereas in *League of Women Voters* "a noncommercial educational station that receives [even] 1% of its overall income from [the CPB] is barred absolutely from all editorializing." Thus, in *Taxation with Representation* the law only prevented the use of *government funds* for lobbying, whereas in *League of Women Voters* the law prohibited any station that accepted government funds from editorializing, whether or not the editorializing was paid for with government funds.

Consider Kreimer, Allocational Sanctions: The Problem of Negative Rights in a Positive State, 132 U. Pa. L. Rev. 1293, 1300-1301 (1984):

> [In analyzing issues of subsidy and discrimination,] courts must distinguish between threats and offers. Threats are allocations that make a citizen worse off than she otherwise would be because of her exercise of a constitutional right. Offers merely expand her range of options, leaving the citizen better off. For example, an offer by the National Endowment for the Arts to provide grants to citizens who choose to write symphonies rather than jazz differs fundamentally from a threat to withdraw welfare payments if the citizen chooses jazz over symphonies. Both allocations influence a constitutionally protected choice, but a threat abridges first amendment rights in ways an offer does not. The crucial task is to specify an appropriate baseline against which to determine whether the proposed allocation improves or worsens the citizen's situation.

In attempting to specify an appropriate baseline in each case, Kreimer would consider three factors: deviation from the status quo ante (has the complainant lost something she previously had?); equality (has the complainant been singled out for treatment less favorable than that accorded most comparable groups?); and prediction (what would be the normal course of events if government could not impose the condition or take the exercise of constitutional rights into account?). For additional commentary, see Epstein, Foreword: Unconstitutional Conditions, State Power, and the Limits of Consent, 102 Harv. L. Rev. 4 (1988);

Sullivan, Unconstitutional Conditions, 102 Harv. L. Rev. 1413 (1988); Symposium, Unconstitutional Conditions, 26 San Diego L. Rev. 175 (1989).

RUST v. SULLIVAN, 500 U.S. 173 (1991). Title X of the Public Health Service Act, enacted in 1970, provides that none of the federal funds appropriated under the act for family planning services "shall be used in programs where abortion is a method of family planning." In 1988, respondent, the Secretary of Health and Human Services, issued new regulations attaching three conditions on the grant of federal funds for title X projects. First, a "[t]itle X project may not provide counseling concerning the use of abortion or provide referral for abortion as a method of family planning," even upon request. Second, a title X project may not engage in activities that "encourage, promote or advocate abortion as a method of family planning." Forbidden activities include lobbying for legislation and disseminating materials, providing speakers, and using legal action to increase the availability of abortion. Third, title X projects must be organized so that they are "physically and financially separate" from prohibited abortion activities.

Petitioners, title X grantees and doctors suing on behalf of themselves and their patients, challenged these regulations. The Court, in a five-to-four decision, upheld the regulations. Chief Justice Rehnquist delivered the opinion of the Court:

"Petitioners contend that the regulations violate the first amendment by impermissibly discriminating based on viewpoint because they prohibit 'all discussion about abortion as a lawful option — including counseling, referral, and the provision of neutral and accurate information about ending a pregnancy — while compelling the clinic or counselor to provide information that promotes continuing a pregnancy to term.' [In] Maher v. Roe, [432 U.S. 464 (1977)], we upheld a state welfare regulation under which Medicaid recipients received payments for services related to childbirth, but not for nontherapeutic abortions. The Court rejected the claim that this unequal subsidization worked a violation of the Constitution. We held that the government may 'make a value judgment favoring childbirth over abortion, and . . . implement that judgment by the allocation of public funds.' Here the Government is exercising the authority it possesses under *Maher* [to] subsidize family planning services [while] declining to 'promote or encourage abortion.' The Government can, without violating the Constitution, selectively fund a program to encourage certain activities it believes to be in the public interest, without at the same time funding an alternate program which seeks to deal with the problem in another way. In so doing, the Government has not discriminated on the basis of viewpoint; it has merely chosen to fund one activity to the exclusion of the other. '[A governmental] decision not to subsidize the exercise of a fundamental right does not infringe that right.' [Quoting *Taxation with Representation*.] The challenged regulations [are] designed to ensure that the limits of the federal program are observed. [This] is not a case of the Government 'suppressing a dangerous idea,' but of a prohibition on a project grantee or its employees from engaging in activities outside of its scope.

"To hold that the Government unconstitutionally discriminates on the basis of viewpoint when it chooses to fund a program dedicated to advance certain permissible goals, because the program in advancing those goals necessarily discourages alternate goals, would render numerous government programs constitutionally suspect. When Congress established a National Endowment for Democracy to encourage other countries to adopt democratic principles, it was not constitutionally required to fund a program to encourage competing lines of political philosophy such as Communism and Fascism. Petitioners' assertions ultimately boil down to the position that if the government chooses to subsidize one protected right, it must subsidize analogous counterpart rights. But the Court has soundly rejected that proposition. [Citing *Taxation with Representation; Maher.*] Within far broader limits than petitioners are willing to concede, when the government appropriates public funds to establish a program it is entitled to define the limits of that program. [We] have here not the case of a general law singling out a disfavored group on the basis of speech content, but a case of the Government refusing to fund activities, including speech, which are specifically excluded from the scope of the project funded.

"[Relying on *League of Women Voters*, petitioners] contend that the restrictions on the subsidization of abortion-related speech [are] impermissible because they condition the receipt of a benefit [on] the relinquishment of [the constitutional] right to engage in abortion advocacy and counseling. [Petitioners'] reliance on [this case] is unavailing, however, because here the Government is not denying a benefit to anyone, but is instead simply insisting that public funds be spent for the purposes for which they were authorized. The [regulations] do not force the Title X grantee to give up abortion-related speech; they merely require that the grantee keep such activities separate and distinct from Title X activities. [By] requiring that the Title X grantee engage in abortion-related activity separately from activity receiving federal funding, Congress has, consistent with our teaching in *League of Women Voters* and *Taxation with Representation*, not denied it the right to engage in abortion-related activities. Congress has merely refused to fund such activities out of the public fisc. . . .

"This is not to suggest that funding by the Government, even when coupled with the freedom of the fund recipients to speak outside the scope of the Government-funded project, is invariably sufficient to justify government control over the content of expression. For example, this Court has recognized that the existence of a Government 'subsidy,' in the form of Government-owned property, does not justify the restriction of speech in areas that have 'been traditionally open to the public for expressive activity' [or] have been 'expressly dedicated to speech activity.' [Citing *Kokinda; Hague; Perry.*] In [the] circumstances [of this case, however], the general rule that the Government may choose not to subsidize speech applies with full force."

Justice Blackmun, joined by Justices Marshall and Stevens, dissented: "Until today, the Court has never upheld viewpoint-based suppression of speech simply because that suppression was a condition upon the acceptance of public funds. [Nothing in *Taxation with Representation*] can be said to challenge this long-settled understanding. In [*Taxation with Representation*], the Court upheld a content-neutral provision [and emphasized that the] 'case would be different if Congress were to discriminate invidiously in its subsidies in such a way as to "[aim] at the suppression of dangerous ideas."' [The regulations at issue here are] clearly viewpoint-based. [Indeed, if] a client asks directly about abortion, a Title X physician or counselor is required to say, in essence, that the project does not consider abortion to be an appropriate method of family planning. [The] regulations pertaining to 'advocacy' are even more explicitly viewpoint-based. [The] majority's reliance on the fact that the regulations pertain solely to funding decisions simply begs the question. Clearly, there are some bases upon which government may not rest its decisions to fund or not to fund. For example, [the] majority surely would agree that government may not base its decision to support an activity upon considerations of race. [Our] cases make clear that ideological viewpoint is a similarly repugnant ground upon which to base funding decisions. . . .

"In the cases at bar, the speaker's interest in the communication is both clear and vital. In addressing the family planning needs of their clients, the physicians and counselors who staff Title X projects seek to provide them with the full range of information and options regarding their health and reproductive freedom. Indeed, the legitimate expectations of the patient and the ethical responsibilities of the medical profession demand no less. [When] a client becomes pregnant, the full range of therapeutic alternatives includes the abortion option, and Title X counselors' interest in providing this information is compelling. The Government's articulated interest in distorting the doctor/patient dialogue — ensuring that federal funds are not spent for a purpose outside the scope of the program — falls far short of that necessary to justify suppression of truthful information and professional medical opinion regarding constitutionally protected conduct. [Indeed], it is of no small significance that the speech the Secretary would suppress is truthful information regarding constitutionally protected conduct of vital importance to the listener. One can imagine no legitimate governmental interest that might be served by suppressing such information." Justice O'Connor dissented on statutory grounds.

Note: The Implications of Rust

1. *Abortions v. smoking.* Suppose government establishes a program to give grants to organizations that help people quit smoking. Does the first amendment require government also to give grants to organizations that encourage people to smoke? Consider the following argument: The cigarette regulation is constitutional, even though *Rust* was wrong. This is so because in the cigarette case the information relates only to the individual's decision whether to smoke, whereas in *Rust* the information relates to the individual's decision whether to exercise a constitutional right (abortion). Along these lines, suppose the government instructs all public defenders not to advise their clients of their rights under the fourth amendment exclusionary rule. Is *Rust* distinguishable? After *Rust*, could the government constitutionally fund the Democratic, but not the Republican, Convention?

2. *Government speech.* At least part of the Court's argument in *Rust* turned on the notion that government does not unconstitutionally discriminate "on the basis of viewpoint when it chooses to fund a program dedicated to advance certain permissible goals." Consider Rosenberger v. Rector and Visitors of University of Virginia, 515 U.S. 819 (1995), in which the Court invalidated a University of Virginia policy authorizing payment from the Student Activities Fund for the printing costs of a variety of student publications but prohibiting payment for any student publication that "primarily promotes or manifests a particular belief in or about a deity or an ultimate reality." Citing *Rust*, the University argued that it "must have substantial discretion in determining how to allocate scarce resources

to accomplish its educational mission," and that the challenged policy was reasonably designed to serve the permissible goal of preserving the separation of church and state. The Court rejected this argument:

> [W]e have permitted the government to regulate the content of what is or is not expressed when it is the speaker or when it enlists private entities to convey its own message. [In *Rust*, for example,] the government did not create a program to encourage private speech but instead used private speakers to transmit specific information pertaining to its own program. We recognized that when the government appropriates public funds to promote a particular policy of its own it is entitled to say what it wishes [and] it may take [appropriate] steps to ensure that its message is neither garbled nor distorted by the grantee. It does not follow, however, [that] viewpoint-based restrictions are proper when the [government] does not itself speak or subsidize transmittal of a message it favors but instead expends funds to encourage a diversity of views from private speakers. [The] distinction between the University's own favored message and the private speech of students is evident in the case before us. [The] University declares that the student groups eligible for Student Activities Fund support are not the University's agents, are not subject to its control, and are not its responsibility. Having offered to pay [the printing costs] of private speakers who convey their own messages, the University may not silence the expression of selected viewpoints.

On the other hand, consider Capitol Square Review and Advisory Board v. Pinette, 515 U.S. 753 (1995), in which the Court invalidated an administrative decision denying permission to erect a large, unattended cross in Capitol Square, a public forum located in front of the Ohio Statehouse. In a plurality opinion, Justice Scalia made clear that, because of the establishment clause, the display of the cross would be unconstitutional if it was the government's own expression, but constitutional if it was purely private expression occurring on public property under "neutral policies." Is this consistent with *Rust*? With *Rosenberger*?

3. *What's wrong with* Rust? Consider Redish and Kessler, Government Subsidies and Free Expression, 80 Minn. L. Rev. 543, 576-577 (1996):

> The problem with the [Court's analysis in *Rust*] is that it allows the government to define its subsidization programs in a wholly unchecked, self-referential manner. [The] fallacy of [this approach] becomes clear if one visualizes the subsidization of private expression exclusively in favor of such ideas as a free-market economic philosophy, or the political theories of Mao Zedong or Rush Limbaugh. [Government] may appropriately choose neutrally to fund works on family planning, on the viability of free-market economic philosophy, or on the wisdom of Mao Zedong's or Rush Limbaugh's political thought. Each of these subsidies would foster First Amendment values by adding to the public's knowledge. [But] government may not foster public acceptance of its own viewpoints on these issues by manipulating private expression [in a viewpoint-based manner].

Consider also Post, Subsidized Speech, 106 Yale L.J. 151, 152-174 (1996):

> . . . Subsidized speech [forces] us to determine whether subsidies should be characterized as government regulations imposed on persons or instead as a form of government participation in the marketplace of ideas. [The] Court's point [in *Rosenberger*] is that when the state itself speaks it may adopt a determinate content and viewpoint, even "when it enlists private entities to convey its own message."

But when the state attempts to restrict the independent contributions of citizens to public discourse, even if those contributions are subsidized, First Amendment rules prohibiting content and viewpoint discrimination will apply. The reasoning of *Rosenberger* thus [suggests that] substantive First Amendment analysis will depend on whether the citizen who speaks is characterized as a public functionary or as an independent participant in public discourse. . . .

[Critical to this distinction are what I have called "managerial domains," within which] the state organizes its resources so as to achieve specified ends. [Managerial] domains are necessary so that a democratic state can actually achieve objectives that have been democratically agreed upon. [Viewpoint] discrimination occurs frequently within managerial domains. To give but a few obvious examples: the president may fire cabinet officials who publicly challenge rather than support administration policies; the military may discipline officers who publicly attack rather than uphold the principle of civilian control over the armed forces; [and] public defenders who prosecute instead of defend their clients may be sanctioned. . . . Viewpoint discrimination occurs within managerial domains whenever the attainment of legitimate managerial objectives requires it.

[In *Rust*, it is at least] superficially plausible to locate [the speech of the Title X clinics and their employees] within a managerial domain established by Title X. [The argument] would be that Congress enacted Title X to accomplish certain purposes, that these purposes are legitimate, and that the HHS regulations function within this managerial domain to regulate speech so as to achieve these purposes. [By] upholding the HHS regulations, [the] Court in *Rust* in effect stated that [even "viewpoint discriminatory"] regulations within managerial domains would not be deemed [unconstitutional] so long as they were necessary to accomplish legitimate managerial ends.

Post concludes, however, that "the Court in *Rust* lacked justification for its implicit decision to allocate medical counseling to the managerial domain" because if the government "were to control the independent judgment" of the physician, the government's control "might conflict with the [physician's] primary and unequivocal duty [as a professional] to exercise his or her independent judgment." Because "neither the role of physician nor that of patient warrants any inference of acceptance of such a purely instrumental orientation," the "viewpoint discrimination inherent in the HHS regulations cannot be justified by reference to managerial authority."

4. Rust *and* R.A.V. For another twist on the problem of underinclusive, content-based restrictions, see R.A.V. v. City of St. Paul, section D6 supra. Although it may seem that *R.A.V.* and *Rust* pose quite different questions, consider Kagan, The Changing Faces of First Amendment Neutrality, 1992 Sup. Ct. Rev. 29, 31-32:

Rust and R.A.V. both raise the same question: If, in a certain setting, the government need not protect or promote any speech at all, may the government choose to protect or promote only speech with a certain content? *Rust* is easily seen in this light. The government [is] not constitutionally required to promote speech through the use of federal funds. May the government then fund whatever speech it wants? [The] question is similar in *R.A.V.* The government is not constitutionally required to tolerate any "fighting words" at all. May the government then permit some but not all fighting words? The question posed in each case is in an important sense the question of First Amendment neutrality in its starkest form: when speech [has] no claim to government promotion or protection, what limitations does the government face in voluntarily advancing some messages, but not all? [Although] the cases have a similar structure, implicate an identical question, and fall within a single [category] of First Amendment [cases, the justices deciding them saw no connection at all].

NATIONAL ENDOWMENT FOR THE ARTS v. FINLEY, 524 U.S. 569

(1998). Since its creation by Congress in 1965, the NEA has made more than 100,000 grants, totaling some three billion dollars, to promote "public knowledge, education, understanding and appreciation of the arts." In 1989, two provocative works that were supported by NEA grants — a series of homoerotic photographs by Robert Mapplethorpe and a photograph by Andres Serrano that depicted a crucifix immersed in urine ("Piss Christ") — prompted a public controversy that led to a congressional reevaluation of the NEA's funding priorities and procedures. Thus, in 1990 Congress enacted section 954(d)(1), which directs the NEA, in establishing procedures to judge the artistic merit of grant applications, to "tak[e] into consideration general standards of decency and respect for the diverse beliefs and values of the American public." In implementing this provision, the NEA concluded that it was not required to do anything more than ensure that its peer review panels were constituted in such a way as to represent geographic, ethnic, and aesthetic diversity.

The Court, in an opinion by Justice O'Connor, held that section 954(d)(1) is not unconstitutional "on its face": "Respondents argue that the provision is a paradigmatic example of viewpoint discrimination. [But the challenged provision merely] adds 'considerations' to the grant-making process; it does not preclude awards to projects that might be deemed 'indecent' or 'disrespectful,' [or] even specify that those factors be given any particular weight in reviewing an application. . . .

"[Moreover], the considerations that the provision introduces [do] not engender the kind of directed viewpoint discrimination that would prompt this Court to invalidate a statute on its face. [The considerations enumerated in section 954(d)(1) are] susceptible to multiple interpretations, [and particularly because the NEA considers grant applications through the decisions of many diverse review panels], the provision does not introduce considerations that, in practice, would effectively preclude or punish the expression of particular views."

Although acknowledging that the provision could conceivably be applied in ways that could violate the first amendment, the Court was "reluctant . . . to invalidate legislation 'on the basis of its hypothetical application to situations not before the Court,'" particularly where, as here, there are numerous "constitutional applications" for both the "decency" and "respect" criteria. For example, "educational programs are central to the NEA's mission," and "it is well-established that 'decency' is a permissible factor where 'educational suitability' motivates its consideration. [Citing *Pico*.]" And "permissible applications of the mandate to consider 'respect for the diverse beliefs and values of the American public' are also apparent, [for the] agency expressly takes diversity into account, giving special consideration to 'projects and productions . . . that reach, or reflect the culture of, a minority, inner city, rural, or tribal community.'"

The Court was unpersuaded that "the language of §954(d)(1) itself will give rise to the suppression of protected expression": "Any content-based considerations that may be taken into account in the grant-making process are a consequence of the nature of arts funding. The NEA has limited resources and it must deny the majority of the grant applications that it receives, including many that propose 'artistically excellent' projects. The agency may decide to fund particular projects for a wide variety of reasons, 'such as the technical proficiency of the artist, the creativity of the work, the anticipated public interest in or appreciation of the work, the work's contemporary relevance, its educational value, its suitability for or appeal to special audiences (such as children or the disabled), its service to a rural or isolated community, or even simply that the work could increase public knowledge of an art form.' [The] very 'assumption' of the NEA is [that] absolute neutrality is simply 'inconceivable.'"

The Court therefore distinguished its decision in *Rosenberger* on the ground that, in "the context of arts funding, in contrast to many other subsidies, the Government does not indiscriminately 'encourage a diversity of views from private speakers.' The NEA's mandate is to make aesthetic judgments, and the inherently content-based 'excellence' threshold for NEA support sets it apart from the subsidy issue in *Rosenberger* — which was available to all student organizations that were 'related to the educational purpose of the University' — and from comparably objective decisions on allocating public benefits, such as access to a school auditorium or a municipal theater [citing *Lamb's Chapel* and *Southeastern Promotions*]."

The Court emphasized that "we have no occasion here to address an as-applied challenge in a situation where the denial of a grant may be shown to be the product of invidious viewpoint discrimination. If the NEA were to leverage its power to award subsidies on the basis of subjective criteria into a penalty on disfavored viewpoints, then we would confront a different case. [Even] in the provision of subsidies, the Government may not 'ai[m] at the suppression of dangerous ideas,' and if a subsidy were 'manipulated' to have a 'coercive effect,' then relief could be appropriate. In addition, as the NEA itself concedes, a more pressing constitutional question would arise if government funding resulted in the imposition of a disproportionate burden calculated to drive 'certain ideas or viewpoints from the marketplace.'"

Justice Scalia, joined by Justice Thomas, concurred in the result: "[Under the challenged provision, to] the extent a particular applicant exhibits disrespect for the diverse beliefs and values of the American public or fails to comport with general standards of decency, the likelihood that he will receive a grant diminishes. [This] unquestionably constitutes viewpoint discrimination. That conclusion is not altered by the fact that the statute does not 'compel' the denial of funding, any more than a provision imposing a five-point handicap on all black applicants for civil service jobs is saved from being race discrimination by the fact that it does not compel the rejection of black applicants. [And] the conclusion of viewpoint discrimination is not affected by the fact that what constitutes 'decency' or 'the diverse beliefs and values of the American people' is difficult to pin down, any more than a civil-service preference in favor of those who display 'Republican-party values' would be rendered nondiscriminatory by the fact that there is plenty of room for argument as to what 'Republican-party values' might be. [I] turn, then, to whether such viewpoint discrimination violates the Constitution. . . .

"[The challenged provision does] not *abridge* the speech of those who disdain the beliefs and values of the American public, nor [does] it *abridge* indecent speech. Those who wish to create indecent and disrespectful art are as unconstrained now as they were before the enactment of this statute. [They] are merely deprived of the [satisfaction] of having the [public] taxed to pay for it. It is preposterous to equate the denial of taxpayer subsidy with measures 'aimed at the *suppression* of dangerous ideas.' 'The reason that denial of participation in a tax exemption or other subsidy scheme does not necessarily "infringe" a fundamental right is that — unlike direct restriction or prohibition — such a denial does not, as a general rule, have any significant coercive effect.' . . .

"Respondents, relying on [*Rosenberger*], argue that viewpoint-based discrimination is impermissible unless the government is the speaker or the government is 'disburs[ing] public funds to private entities to convey a governmental message.' It is impossible to imagine why that should be so; one would think that directly involving the government itself in the viewpoint discrimination [would] make the situation even worse. [But it] is the very business of government to favor and disfavor points of view, [and] it makes not a bit of difference, insofar as either common sense or the Constitution is concerned, whether these officials further their (and in a democracy, our) favored point of view by achieving it directly (having government-employed artists paint pictures); or by advocating it officially (establishing an Office of Art Appreciation); or by giving money to others who achieve or advocate it (funding private art classes). None of this has anything to do with abridging anyone's speech. [*Rosenberger*] found the viewpoint discrimination unconstitutional, not because funding of 'private' speech was involved, but because the government had established a limited public forum — to which the NEA's granting of highly selective [awards] bears no resemblance. The nub of the difference between me and the Court is that I regard the distinction between 'abridging' speech and funding it as a fundamental divide, on this side of which the First Amendment is inapplicable."

Justice Souter dissented: "The decency and respect proviso mandates viewpoint-based decisions in the disbursement of government subsidies, and the Government has wholly failed to explain why the statute should be afforded an exemption from the fundamental rule of the First Amendment that viewpoint discrimination in the exercise of public authority over expressive activity is unconstitutional. ['If] there is a bedrock principle underlying the First Amendment, it is that the government may not prohibit the expression of an idea simply because society finds the idea itself offensive or disagreeable.' [Because] this principle applies not only to affirmative suppression of speech, but also to disqualification for government favors, Congress is generally not permitted to pivot discrimination against otherwise protected speech on the offensiveness or unacceptability of the views it expresses. [Citing *Rosenberger* and *Lamb's Chapel*.] One need do nothing more than read the text of [this] statute to conclude that Congress's purpose in imposing the decency and respect criteria was to prevent the funding of art that conveys an offensive message; the [provision] on its face is quintessentially viewpoint-based, [for] it penalizes [art] that disrespects the ideology, opinions, or convictions of a significant segment of the American [public, but not] art that reinforces those values. . . .

"[Another] basic strand in the Court's [analysis], and the heart of Justice Scalia's, in effect assumes that whether or not the statute mandates viewpoint discrimination, [government] art subsidies fall within a zone of activity free from First Amendment restraints. [This argument] calls attention to the roles of government-as-speaker and government-as-buyer, in which the government is of course entitled to engage in viewpoint discrimination: if the Food and Drug Administration launches an advertising campaign on the subject of smoking, it may condemn the habit without also having to show a cowboy taking a puff on the opposite page; and if the Secretary of Defense wishes to buy a portrait to decorate the Pentagon, he is free to prefer George Washington over George the Third.

"[But the government] neither speaks through the expression subsidized by the NEA, nor buys anything itself with NEA grants. On the contrary, [in this context] the government acts as a patron, financially underwriting the production of art by private artists [for] independent consumption. [And] outside of the contexts of government-as-buyer and government-as-speaker, we have held time and again that Congress may not 'discriminate invidiously in its subsidies in such a way as to aim at the suppression of ideas.' [As we held in *Rosenberger*, when] the government acts as patron, subsidizing the expression of others, it may not prefer one lawfully stated view over another. [The Court attempts] to distinguish *Rosenberger* on the ground that the student activities funds in that case were generally available to most applicants, whereas NEA funds are disbursed selectively and competitively to a choice few. But the Court in *Rosenberger* [specifically] rejected just this distinction when it held [that] '[t]he government cannot justify viewpoint discrimination among private speakers on the economic fact of scarcity.' Scarce money demands choices, of course, but choices 'on some acceptable [viewpoint] neutral principle,' like artistic excellence; 'nothing in our decision[s] indicates that scarcity would give the State the right to exercise viewpoint discrimination that is otherwise impermissible.'"

3.   *Symbolic Conduct*

This section explores the use of nonverbal conduct — such as burning a draft card or mutilating a flag — as a means of "symbolic" expression. In what circumstances, if any, does such nonverbal conduct constitute protected "speech" within the meaning of the first amendment? Consider Henkin, Foreword: On Drawing Lines, 82 Harv. L. Rev. 63, 79-80 (1968): "A constitutional distinction between speech and conduct is specious. Speech *is* conduct, and actions speak. There is nothing intrinsically sacred about wagging the tongue or wielding a pen; there is nothing intrinsically more sacred about words than other symbols. [The] meaningful constitutional distinction is not between speech and conduct, but between conduct that speaks, communicates, and other kinds of conduct." In fact, the Court has long recognized that at least some forms of conduct may constitute "speech" within the meaning of the first amendment. In West Virginia State Board of Education v. Barnette, 319 U.S. 624 (1943), for example, Justice Jackson explained that "symbolism is a primitive but effective way of communicating ideas. [It] is a short cut from mind to mind." See also Hurley v. Irish-American Gay, Lesbian and Bisexual Group of Boston, 515 U.S. 557 (1995) (parades); R.A.V. v. City of St. Paul, section D6 supra (cross-burning); Tinker v. Des Moines Independent Community School District, 393 U.S. 503 (1969) (black armbands); Brown v. Louisiana, 383 U.S. 131 (1966) (sit-in); Stromberg v. California, 283 U.S. 359 (1931) (red flag).

If it is assumed that some forms of nonverbal conduct may constitute "speech," the question remains, how are we to determine what nonverbal conduct merits first amendment protection? At one level, it seems clear that "[e]verything that one does, every action that one takes or fails to take, 'speaks' to anyone who is interested in looking for a message." That is, "all behavior is *capable of being understood* as communication." F. Haiman, Speech and Law in a Free Society 31 (1981). Surely, however, not all behavior that is "capable of being understood as communication" constitutes "speech," for that would bring all conduct within the ambit of the first amendment.

Consider Nimmer, The Meaning of Symbolic Speech under the First Amendment, 21 UCLA L. Rev. 29, 36 (1973):

> A further element must be added to the mix before conduct may be considered to be speech. Whatever else may or may not be true of speech, as an irreducible minimum it must constitute a communication. That, in turn, implies both a communicator and a communicatee — a speaker and an audience. [Without] an actual or potential audience there can be no first amendment speech right. Nor may the first amendment be invoked if there is an audience but no actual or potential "speaker." [Unless] there is a human communicator intending to convey a meaning by his conduct, it would be odd to think of it as conduct constituting a communication protected by the first amendment.

Does all nonverbal conduct that is intended to communicate constitute "speech"? Note that such a doctrine might create a serious "imposter problem." That is, it would invite fraudulent claims by "criminals" that their actual intent was to communicate. Should courts be in the business of inquiring into the sincerity of individuals who claim to have exercised first amendment rights? Is there any way to avoid such inquiries? The issue of inquiry into sincerity in the religion context is examined in Chapter 8, section C, infra. Note also that, depending on the circumstances, nonverbal conduct that is intended to communicate may range across the entire spectrum of human behavior. It may include assassination, refusal to pay taxes, public nudity, flag burning, and urination on the steps of the state capitol. Does all such conduct constitute constitutionally protected "speech" so long as the actor intended to communicate?

United States v. O'Brien

391 U.S. 367 (1968)

MR. CHIEF JUSTICE WARREN delivered the opinion of the Court.

On the morning of March 31, 1966, David Paul O'Brien and three companions burned their Selective Service registration certificates on the steps of the South Boston Courthouse. A sizable crowd, including several agents of the Federal Bureau of Investigation, witnessed the event. Immediately after the burning, [O'Brien] stated to FBI agents that he had burned his registration certificate because of his beliefs, knowing that he was violating federal law.

For this act, O'Brien was indicted, tried, convicted, and sentenced in the United States District Court for the District of Massachusetts. He did not contest the fact that he had burned the certificate. He stated in argument to the jury that he burned the certificate publicly to influence others to adopt his antiwar beliefs, as he put it, "so that other people would reevaluate their positions with Selective Service, with the armed forces, and reevaluate their place in the culture of today, to hopefully consider my position."

The indictment upon which he was tried charged that he "willfully and knowingly did mutilate, destroy, and change by burning [his] registration Certificate [in] violation of [§462(b)(3) of the Universal Military Training and Service Act of 1948]." Section 462(b)(3) [was] amended by Congress in 1965 (adding the words italicized below) so that at the time O'Brien burned his certificate an offense was commited by any person, "who forges, alters, *knowingly destroys, knowingly mutilates,* or in any manner changes any such certificate. . . ." (Italics supplied.) . . .

[T]he Court of Appeals [held] the 1965 Amendment unconstitutional as a law abridging freedom of speech. At the time the Amendment was enacted, a regulation of the Selective Service System required registrants to keep their registration certificates in their "personal possession at all times." 32 C.F.R. §1617.1 (1962). [The] Court of Appeals [was] of the opinion that conduct punishable under the 1965 Amendment was already punishable under the nonpossession regulation, and consequently that the Amendment served no valid purpose; further, that in light of the prior regulation, the Amendment must have been "directed at public as distinguished from private destruction." On this basis, the court concluded that the 1965 Amendment ran afoul of the First Amendment by singling out persons engaged in protests for special treatment. [We] hold that the 1965 Amendment is constitutional both as enacted and as applied. . . .

[The] 1965 Amendment plainly does not abridge free speech on its face, and we do not understand O'Brien to argue otherwise. Amended §12(b)(3) on its face deals with conduct having no connection with speech. It prohibits the knowing destruction of certificates issued by the Selective Service System, and there is nothing necessarily expressive about such conduct. The Amendment does not distinguish between public and private destruction, and it does not punish only destruction engaged in for the purpose of expressing views. Compare Stromberg v. California, 283 U.S. 359 (1931). A law prohibiting destruction of Selective Service certificates no more abridges free speech on its face than a motor vehicle law prohibiting the destruction of drivers' licenses, or a tax law prohibiting the destruction of books and records.

O'Brien nonetheless argues that the 1965 Amendment is unconstitutional in its application to him, and is unconstitutional as enacted because what he calls the "purpose" of Congress was "to suppress freedom of speech." We consider these arguments separately.

II

O'Brien first argues that the 1965 Amendment is unconstitutional as applied to him because his act of burning his registration certificate was protected "symbolic speech" within the First Amendment. His argument is that the freedom of expression which the First Amendment guarantees includes all modes of "communication of ideas by conduct," and that his conduct is within this definition because he did it in "demonstration against the war and against the draft."

We cannot accept the view that an apparently limitless variety of conduct can be labeled "speech" whenever the person engaging in the conduct intends thereby to express an idea. However, even on the assumption that the alleged communicative element in O'Brien's conduct is sufficient to bring into play the First Amendment, it does not necessarily follow that the destruction of a registration certificate is constitutionally protected activity. This Court has held that when "speech" and "nonspeech" elements are combined in the same course of conduct, a sufficiently important governmental interest in regulating the nonspeech element can justify incidental limitations on First Amendment freedoms. To characterize the quality of the governmental interest which must appear, the Court has employed a variety of descriptive terms: compelling; substantial; subordinating; paramount; cogent; strong. Whatever imprecision inheres in these terms, we think it clear that a government regulation is sufficiently justified if it is within the constitutional power of the Government; if it furthers an important or substantial governmental interest; if the governmental interest is unrelated to the suppression of free expression; and if the incidental restriction on alleged First Amendment freedoms is no greater than is essential to the furtherance of that interest. We find that the 1965 Amendment [meets] all of these requirements, and consequently that O'Brien can be constitutionally convicted for violating it.

The constitutional power of Congress to raise and support armies and to make all laws necessary and proper to that end is broad and sweeping. [Pursuant] to this power, Congress may establish a system of registration for individuals liable for training and service, and may require such individuals within reason to cooperate in the registration system. The issuance of certificates indicating the registration and eligibility classification of individuals is a legitimate and substantial administrative aid in the functioning of this system. And legislation to insure the continuing availability of issued certificates serves a legitimate and substantial purpose in the system's administration. . . .

1. The registration certificate serves as proof that the individual described thereon has registered for the draft. The classification certificate shows the eligibility classification of a named but undescribed individual. Voluntarily displaying the two certificates is an easy and painless way for a young man to dispel a question as to whether he might be delinquent in his Selective Service obligations. [Additionally] in a time of national crisis, reasonable availability to each registrant of the two small cards assures a rapid and uncomplicated means for determining his fitness for immediate induction, no matter how distant in our mobile society he may be from his local board.

2. The information supplied on the certificates facilitates communication between registrants and local boards, simplifying the system and benefiting all concerned. To begin with, each certificate bears the address of the registrant's local board, an item unlikely to be committed to memory. Further, each card bears the registrant's Selective Service number, and a registrant who has his number readily available so that he can communicate it to his local board when he supplies or requests information can make simpler the board's task in locating his file. . . .

3. Both certificates carry continual reminders that the registrant must notify his local board of any change of address, and other specified changes in his status. . . .

The many functions performed by Selective Service certificates establish beyond doubt that Congress has a legitimate and substantial interest in preventing their wanton and unrestrained destruction and assuring their continuing availability by punishing people who knowingly and wilfully destroy or mutilate them. And we are unpersuaded that the pre-existence of the nonpossession regulations in any way negates this interest.

In the absence of a question as to multiple punishment, it has never been suggested that there is anything improper in Congress' providing alternative statutory avenues of prosecution to assure the effective protection of one and the same interest. [Here], the pre-existing avenue of prosecution was not even statutory. Regulations may be modified or revoked from time to time by administrative discretion. Certainly, the Congress may change or supplement a regulation.

Equally important, a comparison of the regulations with the 1965 Amendment indicates that they protect overlapping but not identical governmental interests, and that they reach somewhat different classes of wrongdoers. The gravamen of the offense defined by the statute is the deliberate rendering of certificates unavailable for the various purposes which they may serve. Whether registrants keep their certificates in their personal possession at all times, as required by the regulations, is of no particular concern under the 1965 Amendment, as long as they do not mutilate or destroy the certificates so as to render them unavailable. . . .

We think it apparent that the continuing availability to each registrant of his Selective Service certificates substantially furthers the smooth and proper functioning of the system that Congress has established to raise armies [and] that the 1965 Amendment specifically protects this substantial governmental interest. We perceive no alternative means that would more precisely and narrowly assure the continuing availability of issued Selective Service certificates than a law which prohibits their wilful mutilation or destruction.

[Moreover,] both the governmental interest and the operation of the 1965 Amendment are limited to the noncommunicative aspect of O'Brien's conduct. The governmental interest and the scope of the 1965 Amendment are limited to preventing harm to the smooth and efficient functioning of the Selective Service System. When O'Brien deliberately rendered unavailable his registration certificate, he wilfully frustrated this governmental interest. For this noncommunicative impact of his conduct, and for nothing else, he was convicted.

The case at bar is therefore unlike one where the alleged governmental interest in regulating conduct arises in some measure because the communication allegedly integral to the conduct is itself thought to be harmful. In Stromberg v. California, 283 U.S. 359 (1931), for example, this Court struck down a statutory phrase which punished people who expressed their "opposition to organized government" by displaying "any flag, badge, banner, or device." Since the statute there was aimed at suppressing communication it could not be sustained as a regulation of noncommunicative conduct. . . .

In conclusion, we find that because of the Government's substantial interest in assuring the continuing availability of issued Selective Service certificates, because amended §462(b) is an appropriately narrow means of protecting this interest and condemns only the independent noncommunicative impact of conduct within its reach, and because the noncommunicative impact of O'Brien's act of burning his registration certificate frustrated the Government's interest, a sufficient governmental interest has been shown to justify O'Brien's conviction.

III

O'Brien finally argues that the 1965 Amendment is unconstitutional as enacted because what he calls the "purpose" of Congress was "to suppress freedom of speech." We reject this argument because under settled principles the purpose of Congress, as O'Brien uses that term, is not a basis for declaring this legislation unconstitutional.

It is a familiar principle of constitutional law that this Court will not strike down an otherwise constitutional statute on the basis of an alleged illicit legislative motive. . . .

Inquiries into congressional motives or purposes are a hazardous matter. When the issue is simply the interpretation of legislation, the Court will look to statements by legislators for guidance as to the purpose of the legislature, because the benefit to sound decision-making in this circumstance is thought sufficient to risk the possibility of misreading Congress' purpose. It is entirely a different matter when we are asked to void a statute that is, under well-settled criteria, constitutional on its face, on the basis of what fewer than a handful of Congressmen said about it. What motivates one legislator to make a speech about a statute is not necessarily what motivates scores of others to enact it, and the stakes are sufficiently high for us to eschew guesswork. We decline to void [legislation] which could be reenacted in its exact form if the same or another legislator made a "wiser" speech about it. . . .

We think it not amiss, in passing, to comment upon O'Brien's legislative-purpose argument. There was little floor debate on this legislation in either House. Only Senator Thurmond commented on its substantive features in the Senate. [After] his brief statement, and without any additional substantive comments, the [bill] passed the Senate. [In] the House debate only two Congressmen addressed themselves to the Amendment — Congressmen Rivers and Bray. [The] bill was passed after their statements without any further debate by a vote of 393 to 1. It is principally on the basis of the statements by these three Congressmen that O'Brien makes his congressional-"purpose" argument. We note that if we were to examine legislative purpose in the instant case, we would be obliged to consider not only these statements but also the more authoritative reports of the Senate and House Armed Services Committees. [While] both reports make clear a concern with the "defiant" destruction of so-called "draft cards" and with "open" encouragement to others to destroy their cards, both reports also indicate that this concern stemmed from an apprehension that unrestrained destruction of cards would disrupt the smooth functioning of the Selective Service System.

IV

Since the 1965 Amendment to §12(b)(3) of the Universal Military Training and Service Act is constitutional as enacted and as applied, the Court of Appeals should have affirmed the judgment of conviction entered by the District Court. . . .

Mr. Justice Marshall took no part in the consideration or decision of these cases.

MR. JUSTICE HARLAN, concurring. . . .

I wish to make explicit my understanding that this [decision] does not foreclose consideration of First Amendment claims in those rare instances when an "incidental" restriction upon expression, imposed by a regulation which furthers an "important or substantial" governmental interest and satisfies the Court's other criteria, in practice has the effect of entirely preventing a "speaker" from reaching a significant audience with whom he could not otherwise lawfully communicate. This is not such a case, since O'Brien manifestly could have conveyed his message in many ways other than by burning his draft card.

MR. JUSTICE DOUGLAS, dissenting. . . .

[Justice Douglas maintained that the "underlying and basic [issue] in this case [is] whether conscription is permissible in the absence of a declaration of war." Justice Douglas therefore suggested that "this case should be put down for re-argument" on that question. Justice Douglas briefly addressed the symbolic conduct issue in his concurring opinion the following term in Brandenburg v. Ohio, section B1 supra: "Action is often a method of expression and within the protection of the First Amendment. Suppose one tears up his own copy of the Constitution in eloquent protest to a decision of this Court. May he be indicted? Suppose one rips his own Bible to shreds to celebrate his departure from one 'faith' and his embrace of atheism. May he be indicted? [This] Court's affirmance of [O'Brien's conviction for burning the draft card] was not, with all respect, consistent with the First Amendment."]

Note: Draft Card Burning and the First Amendment

1. *Is draft card burning "speech"?* Did the Court decide that question? How would you decide it? Why was Chief Justice Warren reluctant in *O'Brien* to "accept the view that an apparently limitless variety of conduct can be labeled 'speech' whenever the person engaging in the conduct intends thereby to express an idea"? Consider the following propositions: (a) If nonverbal conduct that is intended "to express an idea" constitutes "speech," government may not restrict that conduct unless it poses a "clear and present danger" within the meaning of the Holmes/Brandeis formulation. (b) Even if nonverbal conduct that is intended to communicate constitutes "speech," the first amendment does not "afford the same kind of freedom to those who would communicate ideas by conduct [as it affords] to those who communicate by pure speech." Cox v. Louisiana, 379 U.S. 536, 555 (1965).

2. *Symbolic conduct and the content-based/content-neutral distinction.* Should a distinction be drawn between laws that restrict symbolic conduct because of its content and laws that restrict symbolic conduct for reasons unrelated to content? Compare, for example, a law prohibiting "any person to urinate in public" with

a law prohibiting "any person to urinate on a public building as a symbolic act of opposition to city government." Does the content-based/content-neutral distinction provide a useful framework for analyzing the constitutionality of such laws? Does *O'Brien* adopt such an analysis?

3. *Restrictions related "to the suppression of free expression"*: Stromberg, Tinker, *and* Schacht. In Stromberg v. California, discussed in *O'Brien*, the Court invalidated a statute prohibiting any person to display "a red flag [in] any public place [as] a [symbol] of opposition to organized government." The Court explained that the law might be construed to prohibit "peaceful and orderly opposition to government by legal means" and thus curtail "the opportunity for free political discussion."

In Tinker v. Des Moines Independent Community School District, 393 U.S. 503 (1969), decided a year after *O'Brien*, school officials, fearing possible disruption of school activities, suspended three public school students because they wore black armbands to school to protest the government's policy in Vietnam. In invalidating the suspensions, the Court observed that "the wearing of an armband for the purpose of expressing certain views is the type of symbolic act that is within [the] First Amendment" and is "closely akin to 'pure speech.'" The Court observed further that "the school authorities did not purport to prohibit the wearing of all symbols of political or controversial significance; [rather], a particular symbol — black armbands worn to exhibit opposition to this Nation's involvement in Vietnam — was singled out for prohibition." Consider Ely, Flag Desecration: A Case Study in the Roles of Categorization and Balancing in First Amendment Analysis, 88 Harv. L. Rev. 1482, 1498 & n.63 (1975): "[In] *Tinker* the state regulated [the armbands] because it feared the effect that the message those armbands conveyed would have on the other children. [*Tinker*] would have been quite a different case had it arisen [in] the context of a school regulation banning armbands in woodworking class along with all other sartorial embellishments liable to become safety hazards."

In Schacht v. United States, 398 U.S. 58 (1970), petitioner, who participated in a skit demonstrating opposition to American involvement in Vietnam, was convicted of violating 18 U.S.C. §702, which made criminal the unauthorized wearing of an American military uniform. The Court reversed the conviction. Citing *O'Brien*, the Court observed that section 702 "is, standing alone, a valid statute on its face." The Court noted, however, that another statute, 10 U.S.C. §772(f), authorized the wearing of an American military uniform in a theatrical production "if the portrayal does not tend to discredit [the armed forces]." Finding that petitioner's skit constituted a "theatrical production" within the meaning of section 772(f), the Court concluded: "[Petitioner's] conviction can be sustained only if he can be punished for speaking out against the role of our Army and our country in Vietnam. Clearly punishment for this reason would be an unconstitutional abridgement of freedom of speech. [Section 772(f)], which leaves Americans free to praise the war in Vietnam but can send persons like [petitioner] to prison for opposing it, cannot survive in a country which has the First Amendment."

4. *An intermediate case*: Mitchell. In Wisconsin v. Mitchell, section D6 supra, which involved a racially motivated assault, the Court upheld a state statute enhancing the maximum penalty for an offense whenever the defendant "intentionally selects the person against whom the crime [is committed] because of the

race, religion, color, disability, sexual orientation, national origin or ancestry of that person." The Court noted that "a physical assault is not by any stretch of the imagination expressive conduct protected by the First Amendment." But suppose X assaults Y to express his view that whites should not enter his neighborhood, this "message" is clearly understood by the "audience," and the relevant law authorizes enhanced punishment whenever an individual "physically assaults another as an expression of racial antagonism." Is it still clear that "a physical assault is not by any stretch of the imagination expressive conduct protected by the First Amendment"?

Note also that, in upholding the statute actually at issue in *Mitchell*, the Court observed that "the statute singles out for enhancement bias-inspired" crimes because such "crimes are more likely to provoke retaliatory crimes, inflict distinct emotional harms on their victims, and incite community unrest." Is this statute "related" or "unrelated" to the suppression of free expression? Note that the harms identified by the Court arise *only* if the victim or others know that the defendant committed a hate crime. In such circumstances, is the law "related" to the suppression of free expression because the harm sought to be prevented occurs only if the defendant has in some way communicated his motive?

5. *Restrictions "unrelated to the suppression of free expression."* O'Brien's analysis of restrictions that are "unrelated to the suppression of free expression" applies the general principles of content-neutral balancing to the specific context of symbolic conduct. Is *O'Brien's* application of those principles sufficiently speech-protective?

Consider Alfange, The Draft-Card Burning Case, 1968 Sup. Ct. Rev. 1, 23, 26:

> [As] the Court's own inventory of possible draft-card uses indicates, [the certificates] serve functions of dispensable convenience rather than urgent necessity. The Court's use of "substantial," therefore, is more appropriate if the term is understood in its sense of "having substance" or "not imaginary," rather than the sense of "considerable" or "large." [Moreover, the Court should have weighed] the importance of the government's interest against the impact of the draft law amendment on freedom of speech.

Should the Court have "balanced" the competing interests in *O'Brien*? How would you assess the importance of the draft law amendment's impact on free speech? Consider the following arguments:

a. "In view of the fact that the amendment does not punish dissent per se, but merely forbids one very specific means of conveying the expression of dissent, it cannot seriously be contended that the amendment's effect upon speech is anything but minor." Id. at 27.

b. "Burning a draft card [is] the ordinary person's way of attracting the attention of the national news media. [To] [prohibit] such an effective form of propagating one's views [is] to greatly diminish the effectiveness of the individual's right [to] make his dissent known." Velvel, Freedom of Speech and the Draft Card Burning Cases, 16 U. Kan. L. Rev. 149, 153 (1968).

c. "[Symbolic] conduct deserves a high degree of constitutional protection. [The] kind of stimulus necessary to activate the political conscience of [the] populace sometimes can be created only by transcending rationality and appealing to more primitive, more basic instincts. [The] communication achieved by the wave of draft-card burnings at the height of the United States involvement in Vietnam represents a paradigm example of the 'speech' with which the First Amendment is concerned." Blasi, The Checking Value in First Amendment Theory, 1977 Am. B. Found. Res. J. 521, 640.

d. "[Much] of the effectiveness of O'Brien's communication [derived] precisely from the fact that it was illegal. Had there been no law prohibiting draft card [burning], he might have attracted no more attention than he would have by swallowing a goldfish." Ely, supra, at 1489-1490.

e. "As applied to expression, the [O'Brien] statute had [a] disparate impact on those who opposed government policy, for who would destroy a draft card as an expression of *support* for government policy? [Indeed], in practical effect, the statute had essentially the same content-differential effect as a law prohibiting any person [to destroy] a draft card 'as a symbolic expression of protest against government policy.'" Stone, Content Regulation and the First Amendment, 25 Wm. & Mary L. Rev. 189, 222-223 (1983).

Is the Court's analysis of symbolic expression in *O'Brien* consistent with its analysis of content-neutral restrictions generally? Consider Ely, supra, at 1488-1489: "What was unconsciously going on in *O'Brien* [was] a reservation [of] serious balancing [for] relatively familiar [means] of expression, such as pamphlets, pickets, public speeches and rallies, [and a relegation of] other, less orthodox modes of communication to the [highly deferential approach] that sustained the draft card burning law." Is there anything wrong with this set of priorities?

6. *"Incidental" restrictions on free speech*. Note that, unlike most content-neutral restrictions, such as laws prohibiting leafleting, the law at issue in *O'Brien* was not directed at expressive activity. Its effect on speech was merely "incidental." Should it matter whether a content-neutral law specifically restricts expression or restricts a broader range of activities, but has only an incidental effect on free speech? In addition to *O'Brien*, see Arcara v. Cloud Books, 478 U.S. 697 (1986) (upholding as an "incidental" restriction on speech a law requiring the closure of any building used for prostitution as applied to an "adult" bookstore); Wayte v. United States, 470 U.S. 598 (1985) (upholding as an "incidental" restriction on speech the government's policy of enforcing the Selective Service registration requirement only against those men who advised the government that they had failed to register or who were reported by others as having failed to register); United States v. Albertini, 477 U.S. 675 (1985) (upholding as an "incidental" restriction on speech a federal statute prohibiting any person to reenter a military base after being ordered not to do so as applied to an individual who sought to reenter a base for speech purposes). For analysis of incidental restrictions, see Stone, Content-Neutral Restrictions, 54 U. Chi. L. Rev. 46, 99-114 (1987); Shane, Equal Protection, Free Speech, and the Selective Prosecution of Draft Nonregistrants, 72 Iowa L. Rev. 359 (1987); Kagan, Private Speech, Public Purpose: The Role of Governmental Motive in First Amendment Doctrine, 63 U. Chi. L. Rev. 415, 494-508 (1996) (arguing that the distinction between direct and incidental restrictions in first amendment analysis can be explained largely in terms of the concern with avoiding possible improper governmental motivation); Dorf, Incidental Burdens on Fundamental Rights, 109 Harv. L. Rev. 1175 (1996) (arguing that although "sound reasons can be advanced for taking direct burdens more seriously than incidental burdens," this does not mean "that incidental burdens should never count as constitutional infringements," but con-

cluding that only "*substantial* incidental burdens" raise "a bona fide constitutional problem"). When is an incidental burden "substantial"? Consider Stone, supra, at 114: "The general presumption is that incidental restrictions do not raise a question of first amendment review. The presumption is waived, however, whenever an incidental restriction either has a highly disproportionate impact on [particular viewpoints or] significantly limits the opportunities for free expression."

For an example of a (relatively rare) decision in which the Court has invalidated an incidental restriction on expression, recall NAACP v. Alabama, 357 U.S. 449 (1958), in which the Court held that an Alabama statute requiring that all out-of-state corporations doing business in the state must disclose the names and addresses of all Alabama "members" was invalid as applied to the NAACP because "on past occasions revelation of the identity of [the NAACP's] rank-and-file members has exposed these members to economic reprisal, loss of employment, threat of physical coercion, and other manifestations of public hostility." The Court concluded that, "under these circumstances, [compelled] disclosure of [the NAACP's] Alabama membership is likely to affect adversely the ability of [the NAACP] and its members to pursue their [constitutional rights]."

7. *The problem of legislative motivation.* Should the Court in *O'Brien* have invalidated the 1965 amendment because "the 'purpose' of Congress was 'to suppress freedom of speech'"? As the Court noted, only two Representatives and one Senator commented directly on the legislation. Congressman Bray's comments are representative: "The need of this legislation is clear. Beatniks and so-called 'campus cults' have been publicly burning their draft cards to demonstrate their contempt for the United States and our resistance to Communist takeovers. [If] these 'revolutionaries' are permitted to deface and destroy their draft cards, our entire Selective Service System is dealt a serious blow."

Consider Alfange, supra, at 15, 16: "[What] emerges with indisputable clarity from an examination of the legislative history of the amendment is that the intent of its framers was purely and simply to put a stop to this particular form of antiwar protest, which they deemed extraordinarily contemptible and vicious — even treasonous — at a time when American troops were engaged in combat. [The Court's contrary conclusion blinked] the facts."

The Court has often inquired into the motivation underlying executive and administrative decisions. See, e.g., Cornelius v. NAACP Legal Defense & Educational Fund, 473 U.S. 788 (1985) ("the existence of reasonable grounds for limiting access to a nonpublic forum [will] not save a regulation that is in reality a facade for viewpoint-based discrimination"); Mt. Healthy City School District Board of Education v. Doyle, 429 U.S. 274 (1977) (although untenured teacher can be dismissed for "no reason whatever," he cannot be fired for exercise of first amendment rights); Keyes v. School District No. 1, 413 U.S. 189 (1973) (Denver schools held unlawfully segregated because school board decisions concerning the location of schools were motivated by racial considerations); Yick Wo v. Hopkins, 118 U.S. 356 (1886) (licensing law invalidated because of discriminatory administration). As indicated in *O'Brien*, however, the Court has been reluctant to inquire into the motivation underlying legislative actions. Three explanations have usually been offered for this reluctance: the difficulty of ascertaining the "actual" motivation of a collective body; the futility of invalidating a law that could be reenacted with a show of "wiser" motives; and the inappropriateness of impugning the integrity of a coordinate branch of government. Are these explanations sufficiently weighty to justify the conclusion that "the purpose of Congress [is] not a basis for declaring [legislation] unconstitutional"? See generally Alfange, supra, at 27-51; Brest, Palmer v. Thompson: An Approach to the Problem of Unconstitutional Legislative Motive, 1971 Sup. Ct. Rev. 95; Ely, Legislative and Administrative Motivation in Constitutional Law, 79 Yale L.J. 1205 (1970); Symposium, Legislative Motivation, 15 San Diego L. Rev. 925 (1978). For more on the problem of "motivation," see Chapter 5, section C2, supra.

Note: Flag Desecration and Misuse

1. *Flag burning.* In Street v. New York, 394 U.S. 576 (1969), appellant, after hearing a news report that civil rights leader James Meredith had been shot, took his American flag out of a drawer, carried it to a nearby street corner, and lit it with a match. As it burned on the pavement, appellant said to a group of onlookers, "We don't need no damn flag. [If] they let that happen to Meredith we don't need an American flag." Appellant was convicted of violating a New York statute declaring it a misdemeanor "publicly [to] mutilate, deface, defile, trample upon, or cast contempt upon either by words or acts [any flag of the United States]." The Court, in a five-to-four decision, overturned appellant's conviction. The Court found it unnecessary, however, to address appellant's assertion "that New York may not constitutionally punish one who publicly destroys or damages an American flag as a means of protest," holding instead that the statute "was unconstitutionally applied in appellant's case because it permitted him to be punished merely for *speaking* defiant or contemptuous *words* *about* the American flag."

Chief Justice Warren and Justices Black, White, and Fortas dissented. Chief Justice Warren chastised the Court for ducking "the basic question presented" — "'whether the deliberate act of burning an American flag in public as a "protest" may be punished as a crime.'" On that question, Chief Justice Warren concluded that "the States and the Federal Government [have] the power to protect the flag from acts of desecration and disgrace." In a separate dissenting opinion, Justice Fortas elaborated:

> If a state statute provided that it is a misdemeanor to burn one's shirt [on] the public thoroughfare, it could hardly be asserted that the citizen's constitutional right is violated. [And if] the arsonist asserted that he was burning his shirt [as] a protest against the Government's fiscal policies, [it] is hardly possible that his claim to First Amendment shelter would prevail against the State's claim of a right to avert danger to the public and to avoid obstruction to traffic as a result of the fire. [If], as I submit, it is permissible to prohibit the burning of personal property on the public sidewalk, there is no basis for applying a different rule to flag burning. And the fact that the law is violated for purposes of protest does not immunize the violator. [Citing *O'Brien.*]

Suppose Street had been convicted of violating a law prohibiting any person to make any "open fire in public." Is the flag desecration statute distinguishable?

2. *Contemptuous treatment.* In Smith v. Goguen, 415 U.S. 566 (1974), appellee, who wore a small cloth replica of the United States flag sewn to the seat of

his trousers, was convicted of violating a Massachusetts statute prohibiting any person to "publicly mutilate, trample upon, deface or treat contemptuously the flag of the United States." The Court, in an opinion by Justice Powell, overturned the conviction. The Court found it unnecessary to decide whether the statute was unconstitutionally overbroad, holding instead that it was "void for vagueness." The Court emphasized that appellee was charged not "with any act of physical desecration," but with "'publicly [treating] contemptuously the flag of the United States.'" Noting that "the flag has become 'an object of youth fashion and high camp,'" and that "casual treatment of the flag in many contexts has become a widespread contemporary phenomenon," the Court concluded that this aspect of the statute was "inherently vague" and hence violative of due process. Chief Justice Burger and Justices Blackmun and Rehnquist dissented.

3. *Flag misuse.* In Spence v. Washington, 418 U.S. 405 (1974), appellant, to protest the invasion of Cambodia and the killings at Kent State University, displayed a United States flag, which he owned, out of the window of his apartment. Affixed to the flag was a large peace symbol made of removable tape. Appellant was convicted under Washington's "flag misuse" statute, which prohibited the exhibition of a United States flag to which is attached or superimposed "any word, figure, mark, design, drawing, or advertisement." The Court held, in a per curiam opinion, that, "as applied to appellant's activity," which the Court described as "a pointed expression of anguish by appellant about [the] affairs of his government," the Washington statute "impermissibly infringed free expression":

[The state maintains that it] has an interest in preserving the national flag as an unalloyed symbol of our country. [This] interest might be seen as an effort to prevent the appropriation of a revered national symbol by an individual, interest group, or enterprise where there was a risk that association of the symbol with a particular product or viewpoint might be taken erroneously as evidence of governmental endorsement. [Alternatively], the interest [may be understood as] based on the uniquely universal character of the national flag as a symbol. [If] it may be destroyed or permanently disfigured, it [could] lose its capability of mirroring the sentiments of all who view it.

[We] need not decide in this case whether the interest advanced by the [state] is valid. We assume, arguendo, that it is. [But even if] it is valid, [it] is directly related to expression in the context of activity like that undertaken by appellant. For that reason [the] four-step analysis of [*O'Brien*] is inapplicable. [We hold that the statute is] unconstitutional as applied to appellant's activity. There was no risk that appellant's acts would mislead viewers into assuming that the Government endorsed his viewpoint. [Moreover, appellant] did [not] permanently disfigure the flag or destroy it. [And] his message was direct, likely to be understood, and within the contours of the First Amendment. [The] conviction must be reversed.

Justice Rehnquist, joined by Chief Justice Burger and Justice White, dissented:

[The] Court's treatment [of the state's interest] lacks all substance. The suggestion that the State's interest somehow diminishes when the flag is decorated with *removable* tape trivializes something which is not trivial. The State [is] hardly seeking to protect the flag's resale value. [The] true nature of the State's interest in this case is [one] of preserving the flag as "an important symbol of nationhood and unity." [It] is the character, not the cloth, of the flag which the State seeks to protect. "[The] flag is a national property, and the Nation may regulate those who would make, imitate, sell, possess, or use it.". . .

[That] the State has a valid interest in preserving the character of the flag does not mean, of course, that it can employ all conceivable means to enforce it. It certainly could not require all citizens to own the flag or compel citizens to salute one. [It] presumably cannot punish criticism of the flag, or the principles for which it stands, any more than it could punish criticism of this country's policies or ideas. But the statute in this case demands no such allegiance. Its operation does not depend upon whether [the] use of the flag is respectful or contemptuous. [It] simply withdraws a unique national symbol from the roster of materials that may be used as a background for communications. [The] Constitution [does not prohibit] Washington from making that decision.

Is *Spence* consistent with *O'Brien*? Do you agree with the Court that the interests underlying flag misuse statutes are "directly related to expression," and that the *O'Brien* standard thus should not govern? Consider Ely, Flag Desecration: A Case Study in the Roles of Categorization and Balancing in First Amendment Analysis, 88 Harv. L. Rev. 1482, 1503-1504, 1506-1508 (1975):

[The flag misuse statute is] ideologically neutral on its face, and would proscribe the superimposition of "Buy Mother Fletcher's Ambulance Paint" [as] fully as it would the addition of a swastika. Such "improper use" provisions are [thus] more complicated constitutionally than the ideologically tilted "desecration" provisions. [In the flag misuse context], the state may assert an interest [similar] to that asserted in [defense of a content-neutral law prohibiting any person to interrupt a public speaker]. The state's interest in both of these cases might be characterized as an interest in preventing the [defendant] from interfering with the expression of others. [As with interruption of a public speaker, the] state does not care what message the defendant is conveying by altering the flag: all that matters is that he is interrupting the message conveyed by the flag. [There is, however, an answer to this argument, for] although improper use statutes do not single out certain messages for proscription, they *do* single out one set of messages, namely the set of messages conveyed by the American flag, for protection. That, of course, is not true of a law that generally prohibits the interruption of speakers. [In reality, then, an improper use statute] is, at best, analogous to a law prohibiting the interruption of patriotic speeches, and that is a law that is hardly "unrelated to the suppression of free expression."

4. *Flag desecration.* The Court directly confronted the issue of flag desecration in Texas v. Johnson, 491 U.S. 397 (1989). During the 1984 Republican National Convention, Johnson burned an American flag as part of a political demonstration protesting the policies of the Reagan administration. Johnson was arrested and convicted of violating a Texas flag desecration statute, which made it a crime for any person to "deface, damage or otherwise physically mistreat" the flag "in a way that the actor knows will seriously offend one or more persons likely to observe or discover his action." The Court, in a five-to-four decision, overturned the conviction.

In an opinion by Justice Brennan, the Court began by concluding that "Johnson's flag-burning was 'conduct' sufficiently imbued with elements of 'communication' to implicate the First Amendment." After rejecting the claim that the statute could be justified in terms of the state's interest in "preventing breaches of the peace," see section B3 supra, the Court turned to the heart of the issue:

The Government generally has a freer hand in restricting expressive conduct than it has in restricting the written or spoken word. It may not, however, proscribe particular conduct *because* it has expressive elements. [Thus], although we have recognized that where "'speech' and 'nonspeech' elements are combined in the same course of conduct, a sufficiently important governmental interest in regulating the nonspeech element can justify incidental limitations on First Amendment freedoms," [*O'Brien*], we have limited the applicability of *O'Brien's* relatively lenient standard to those cases in which "the governmental interest is unrelated to the suppression of free expression." . . .

The State [asserts] an interest in preserving the flag as a symbol of nationhood and national unity. [We are] persuaded that this interest is related to expression in the case of Johnson's burning of the flag. The State, apparently, is concerned that such conduct will lead people to believe either that the flag does not stand for nationhood and national unity, but instead reflects other, less positive concepts, or that the concepts reflected in the flag do not in fact exist, that is, we do not enjoy unity as a Nation. These concerns blossom only when a person's treatment of the flag communicates some message, and thus are related "to the suppression of free expression" within the meaning of *O'Brien*. . . .

It remains to consider whether the State's interest in preserving the flag as a symbol of nationhood and national unity justifies Johnson's conviction. [Johnson] was prosecuted because he knew that his politically charged expression would cause "serious offense." [The] Texas law is thus not aimed at protecting the physical integrity of the flag in all circumstances, but is designed instead to protect it only against impairments that would cause serious offense to others. [Whether] Johnson's treatment of the flag violated Texas law thus depended on the likely communicative impact of his expressive conduct. [Because] this restriction [is] content-based, [we must] subject the State's asserted interest [to] "the most exacting scrutiny." . . .

If there is a bedrock principle underlying the First Amendment, it is that the Government may not prohibit the expression of an idea simply because society finds the idea itself offensive or disagreeable. We have not recognized an exception to this principle even where our flag is involved. [Citing *Street*; *Spence*; and *Goguen*.] [Nothing] in our precedents suggests that a State may foster its own view of the flag by prohibiting expressive conduct related to it. [If] we were to hold that a State may forbid flag-burning wherever it is likely to endanger the flag's symbolic role, but allow it wherever burning a flag promotes that role — as where, for example, a person ceremoniously burns a dirty flag — we would be saying that when it comes to impairing the flag's physical integrity, the flag itself may be used as a symbol [only] in one direction. We would be permitting a State to "prescribe what shall be orthodox" by saying that one may burn the flag to convey one's attitude toward it and its referents only if one does not endanger the flag's representation of nationhood and national unity.

We never before have held that the Government may ensure that a symbol be used to express only one view of that symbol or its referents. [Citing *Schacht*.] To conclude that the Government may permit designated symbols to be used to communicate only a limited set of messages would be to enter territory having no discernible or defensible boundaries. Could the Government, on this theory, prohibit the burning of state flags? Of copies of the presidential seal? Of the Constitution? . . .

Chief Justice Rehnquist, joined by Justices White and O'Connor, dissented:

The flag is not simply another "idea" or "point of view" competing for recognition in the marketplace of ideas. [Flag burning is] no essential part of any expression of ideas, [citing *Chaplinsky*], and [Johnson's] act [conveyed] nothing that could not have been conveyed [in] a dozen different ways. [Far] from being a case of "one picture being worth a thousand words," flag burning is the equivalent of an inarticulate grunt or roar that [is] most likely to be indulged in not to express any particular idea, but to antagonize others. [The] Texas statute deprived Johnson of only one rather inarticulate symbolic form of protest — a form of protest that was profoundly offensive to many — and left him with a full panoply of other symbols and every conceivable form of verbal expression to express his deep disapproval of national policy. Thus, in no way can it be said that Texas is punishing him because his hearers — or any other group of people — were profoundly opposed to the message that he sought to convey. [It] was Johnson's use of this particular symbol, and not the idea that he sought to convey by [it], for which he was punished.

Justice Stevens also dissented.

5. *Flag desecration revisited.* Almost immediately after the decision in *Johnson*, Congress enacted the Flag Protection Act of 1989, which made it a crime for any person knowingly to mutilate, deface, physically defile, burn, maintain on the floor or ground, or trample upon any flag of the United States. The government maintained that this act was constitutional because, unlike the statute addressed in *Johnson*, the act was designed to protect "the physical integrity of the flag under all circumstances," did "not target expressive conduct on the basis of the content of its message," and proscribed "conduct (other than disposal) that damages or mistreats a flag, without regard to the actor's motive, his intended message, or the likely effects of his conduct on onlookers." In United States v. Eichman, 486 U.S. 310 (1990), the Court, in a five-to-four decision, invalidated this act. Justice Brennan delivered the opinion:

Although the [Act] contains no explicit content-based limitation on the scope of prohibited conduct, it is nevertheless clear that the Government's asserted *interest* is "related to the suppression of free expression" and concerned with the content of such expression. The Government's interest in protecting the "physical integrity" of a privately owned flag rests upon a perceived need to preserve the flag's status as a symbol of our Nation and certain national ideals. But the mere destruction or disfigurement of a particular physical manifestation of the symbol, without more, does not diminish or otherwise affect the symbol itself in any way. For example, the secret destruction of a flag in one's own basement would not threaten the flag's recognized meaning. Rather, the Government's desire to preserve the flag as a symbol for certain national ideals is implicated "only when a person's treatment of the flag communicates [a] message" to others that is inconsistent with those ideals.

Moreover, the precise language of the Act's prohibitions confirms Congress' interest in the communicative impact of flag destruction. The Act criminalizes the conduct of anyone who "knowingly mutilates, defaces, physically defiles, burns, maintains on the floor or ground, or tramples upon any flag." Each of the specified terms — with the possible exception of "burns" — unmistakably connotes disrespectful treatment. . . .

Although Congress cast the [Act] in somewhat broader terms than the Texas statute at issue in *Johnson*, the Act still suffers from the same fundamental flaw: it suppresses expression out of concern for its likely communicative impact. Despite the Act's wider scope, its restriction on expression cannot be "'justified without reference to the content of the regulated speech.'" The Act therefore must be subjected to "the most exacting scrutiny," and for the reasons stated in *Johnson*, the Government's interest cannot justify its infringement on First Amendment rights.

Justice Stevens, joined by Chief Justice Rehnquist and Justices White, O'Connor, dissented.

Central to the Court's reasoning in *Eichman* is its assertion that the Flag Protection Act was "related to the suppression of free expression" because "the Government's desire to preserve the flag as a symbol for certain national ideals" is implicated "only when a person's treatment of the flag 'communicates [a] message' to others that is inconsistent with those ideals." Is that assertion persuasive? Suppose Congress enacts the following statute: "No person may knowingly impair the physical integrity of the American flag." Do *Johnson* and *Eichman* require the invalidation of this law? See Stone, Flag Burning and the Constitution, 75 Iowa L. Rev. 111 (1989). Could government constitutionally protect the flag as a matter of copyright law? See Kmiec, In the Aftermath of *Johnson* and *Eichman*, 1990 B.Y.U. L. Rev. 577.

BARNES v. GLEN THEATRE, INC., 501 U.S. 560 (1991). Respondents, two Indiana establishments that present nude dancing as entertainment, brought suit to enjoin enforcement of Indiana's public indecency statute, which prohibits any person to appear "in a state of nudity" in any "public place." The state courts interpreted the statute as requiring nude dancers in such establishments to wear pasties and a G-string. The Court, in a five-to-four decision, rejected the claim that this statute, as applied to respondents, violates the first amendment.

Chief Justice Rehnquist, joined by Justices O'Connor and Kennedy, delivered the plurality opinion: "[N]ude dancing of the kind sought to be performed here is expressive conduct within the outer perimeters of the First Amendment, though we view it as only marginally so. [Indiana], of course, has not banned nude dancing as such, but has proscribed public nudity across the board. [Applying] the four-part *O'Brien* test, we find that Indiana's public indecency statute is justified despite its incidental limitations on some expressive activity. The public indecency statute is clearly within the constitutional power of the State and furthers substantial governmental interests. [Such statutes, which] are of ancient origin, and presently exist in at least 47 States, [reflect] moral disapproval of people appearing in the nude among strangers in public places. [The] traditional police power of the States is defined as the authority to provide for the public health, safety, and morals, and we have upheld such a basis for legislation. [Citing *Roth*, section D4 supra; *Paris Adult Theatre*, section D4 supra.]

"This interest is unrelated to the suppression of free expression. [Respondents contend] that even though prohibiting nudity in public generally may not be related to suppressing expression, prohibiting the performance of nude dancing is related to expression because the state seeks to prevent its erotic message. [But] we do not think that when Indiana applies its statute to the nude dancing in these nightclubs it is proscribing nudity because of the erotic message conveyed by the dancers. Presumably numerous other erotic performances are presented at these establishments [without] any interference from the state, so long as the performers wear a scant amount of clothing. Likewise, the requirement that the dancers don pasties and a G-string does not deprive the dance of whatever erotic message it conveys; it simply makes the message slightly less graphic. The perceived evil that Indiana seeks to address is not erotic dancing, but public nudity. The appearance of people of all shapes and sizes in the nude at a beach, for example, would convey little if any erotic message, yet the state still seeks to prevent it. Public nudity is the evil the state seeks to prevent, whether or not it is combined with expressive activity. . . ."

Justice Scalia filed a separate concurring opinion: "[T]he challenged regulation must be upheld [because], as a general law regulating conduct and not specifically directed at expression, it is not subject to First Amendment scrutiny at all. [Virtually] every law restricts conduct, and virtually any prohibited conduct can be performed for an expressive purpose — if only expressive of the fact that the actor disagrees with the prohibition. It cannot reasonably be demanded, therefore, that every restriction of expression incidentally produced by a general law regulating conduct pass normal First Amendment scrutiny, or even — as some of our cases have suggested, see, e.g., *O'Brien* — that it be justified by an 'important or substantial' government interest. . . .

"This is not to say that the first amendment affords no protection to expressive conduct. Where the government prohibits conduct precisely because of its communicative attributes, we hold the regulation unconstitutional. See, e.g., *Eichman*; *Johnson*; *Spence*. [In] each of the foregoing cases, we explicitly found that suppressing communication was the object of the regulation of conduct. Where that has not been the case, however — where suppression of communicative use of the conduct was merely the incidental effect of forbidding the conduct for other reasons — we have allowed the regulation to stand. [All] our holdings (though admittedly not some of our discussion) support the conclusion that 'the only First Amendment analysis applicable to laws that do not directly or indirectly impede speech is the threshold inquiry of whether the purpose of the law is to suppress communication. If not, that is the end of the [matter].' We have explicitly adopted such a regime in another First Amendment context: that of Free Exercise. [Citing Employment Division, Department of Human Resources v. Smith, Chapter 8, section C, infra.] I think we should avoid wherever possible [a] mode of analysis that requires judicial assessment of the 'importance' of government interests — and especially of government interests in various aspects of morality."

Justice Souter also filed a concurring opinion: "[I] agree with the plurality that the appropriate analysis to determine the actual protection required by the First Amendment is the four-part enquiry described in *O'Brien*. [I rest my concurrence, however,] not on the possible sufficiency of society's moral views [but] on the State's substantial interest in combating the secondary effects of adult establishments of the sort typified by respondents' establishments. [In] my view, the interest [in] preventing prostitution, sexual assault, and other criminal activity, although presumably not a justification for all applications of the statute, is sufficient under *O'Brien* to justify the State's enforcement of the statute against the type of adult entertainment at issue here. [Citing *Renton* and *Young*, section D5 supra.] [This] justification of the statute may not be ignored merely because it is unclear to what extent this purpose motivated the Indiana Legislature in enacting the statute. Our appropriate focus is not an empirical enquiry into the actual intent of the enacting legislature, but rather the existence [of a] governmental interest in the service of which the challenged application of the statute may be constitutional. [The] secondary effects rationale on which I rely would be open to question if the State were to seek to enforce the statute by barring expressive nudity in classes of productions that could not readily be analogized to the adult films at issue in *Renton*. It is difficult to see, for example, how the enforcement of

Indiana's statute against nudity in a production of 'Hair' or 'Equus' somewhere other than in an 'adult' theater would further the State's interest in avoiding harmful secondary effects. . . ."

Justice White, joined by Justices Marshall, Blackmun, and Stevens, dissented: "The purpose of forbidding people from appearing nude in parks, beaches, hot dog stands, and like public places is to protect others from offense. But that could not possibly be the purpose of preventing nude dancing in theaters and barrooms since the viewers are exclusively consenting adults who pay money to see these dances. The purpose of the proscription in these contexts is to protect the viewers from what the State believes is the harmful message that nude dancing communicates. [This] being the case, it cannot be that the statutory prohibition is unrelated to expressive conduct. [It] is only because nude dancing performances may generate emotions and feelings of eroticism and sensuality among the spectators that the State seeks to regulate such expressive activity, apparently on the assumption that creating or emphasizing such thoughts and ideas in the minds of the spectators may lead to increased prostitution and the degradation of women. But generating thoughts, ideas, and emotions is the essence of communication. The nudity element of nude dancing performances cannot be neatly pigeonholed as mere 'conduct' independent of any expressive component of the dance. That fact dictates the level of First Amendment protection to be accorded the performances at issue here. [Content] based restrictions 'will be upheld only if narrowly drawn to accomplish a compelling governmental interest.' [Neither] the Court nor the State suggests that the statute could withstand scrutiny under that standard."

Consider Justice Scalia's response to Justice White's dissent: "The dissent confidently asserts that the purpose of restricting nudity in public places in general is to protect nonconsenting parties from offense; and argues that since only consenting, admission-paying patrons see respondents dance, that purpose cannot apply and the only remaining purpose must relate to the communicative elements of the performance. Perhaps the dissenters believe that 'offense to others' ought to be the only reason for restricting nudity in public places generally, but there is no basis for thinking that our society has ever shared that Thoreauvian 'you-may-do-what-you-like-so-long-as-it-does-not-injure-someone-else' beau ideal — much less for thinking that it was written into the Constitution. The purpose of Indiana's nudity law would be violated, I think, if 60,000 fully consenting adults crowded into the Hoosierdome to display their genitals to one another, even if there were not an offended innocent in the crowd. Our society prohibits, and all human societies have prohibited, certain activities not because they harm others but because they are considered in the traditional phrase, 'contra bonos mores,' i.e., immoral. [The] purpose of the Indiana statute [is] to enforce the traditional moral belief that people should not expose their private parts indiscriminately, regardless of whether those who see them are disedified. Since that is so, the dissent has no basis for positing that, where only thoroughly edified adults are present, the purpose must be repression of communication."

Consider the constitutionality, after *Barnes*, of the application of Indiana's public nudity statute to movies, art exhibits, and television productions depicting nudity. For the argument that "the outcome in *Barnes* would have been different" had Indiana attempted to apply its "statute to accepted media for the communication of ideas, as for example by attempting to prohibit nudity in movies or in the theater," see Post, Recuperating First Amendment Doctrine, 47 Stan. L. Rev. 1249, 1255-1259 (1995), arguing that "[c]rucial to the result in *Barnes* [is] the distinction between what the Court is prepared to accept as a medium for the communication of ideas and its implicit understanding of nude dancing in nightclubs."

CITY OF ERIE v. PAP'S A.M., 529 U.S. 277 (2000). Erie, Pennsylvania, enacted an ordinance banning public nudity. The preamble stated that the "purpose" of the ordinance was to respond to "a recent increase in nude live entertainment within the City, which activity adversely impacts . . . the public health, safety and welfare by providing an atmosphere conducive to violence, sexual harassment, public intoxication, prostitution, the spread of sexually transmitted diseases and other deleterious effects." The ordinance was challenged by the owner of Kandyland, a nude dancing establishment. Does the existence of this preamble distinguish this case from *Barnes?* The Court, in a six-to-three decision, upheld the ordinance.

Justice O'Connor delivered a plurality opinion, joined by Chief Justice Rehnquist and Justices Kennedy and Breyer: "The ordinance here, like the statute in *Barnes,* is on its face a general prohibition on public nudity. [It] bans all public nudity, regardless of whether that nudity is accompanied by expressive activity. [Moreover, the] State's interest in preventing harmful secondary effects is not related to the suppression of expression. In trying to control the secondary effects of nude dancing, the ordinance seeks to deter crime and the other deleterious effects caused by the presence of such an establishment in the neighborhood. [Citing *Renton.*]

"[E]ven if Erie's public nudity ban has some minimal effect on the erotic message by muting that portion of the expression that occurs when the last stitch is dropped, [erotic dancers] are free to perform wearing pasties and G-strings. Any effect on the overall expression is *de minimis.* . . .

"[This] case is, in fact, similar to [*O'Brien*]. The justification for the government regulation in each case prevents harmful 'secondary' effects that are unrelated to the suppression of expression. [While] the doctrinal theories behind 'incidental burdens' and 'secondary effects' are, of course, not identical, there is nothing objectionable about a city passing a general ordinance to ban public nudity (even though such a ban may place incidental burdens on some protected speech) and at the same time recognizing that one specific occurrence of public nudity — nude erotic dancing — is particularly problematic because it produces harmful secondary effects. . . .

"We conclude that Erie's asserted interest in combating the negative secondary effects associated with adult entertainment establishments [is] unrelated to the suppression of the erotic message conveyed by nude dancing. The ordinance [is] therefore valid if it satisfies the four-factor test from *O'Brien* for evaluating restrictions on symbolic speech." Justice O'Connor then went on to find that the ordinance did, indeed, satisfy the *O'Brien* test.

Justice Scalia, joined by Justice Thomas, concurred in the judgment, reaffirming his position in *Barnes* that because the public nudity ordinance is "a general law regulating conduct and not specifically directed at expression, it is not subject to First Amendment scrutiny at all." Justice Scalia argued further that the existence of the preamble is irrelevant to the constitutionality of the ordinance because it neither "make[s] the law any less general in its reach nor demonstrate[s] that what the municipal authorities *really* find objectionable is expression rather than public nakedness."

Justice Stevens, joined by Justice Ginsburg, dissented: "The Court relies on the so-called 'secondary effects' test to defend the ordinance. [But] never before have we approved the use of that doctrine to justify a total ban on protected First Amendment expression. [The ordinances upheld in *Young* and *Renton* did] not ban adult theaters altogether, but merely 'circumscribe[d]' their choice as to location.' [The] reason we have limited our secondary effects cases to zoning and declined to extend their reasoning to total bans is [that a] dispersal [is] a minimal imposition whereas a total ban is the most exacting of restrictions. The State's interest in fighting presumed secondary effects is sufficiently strong to justify the former, but far too weak to support the latter, more severe burden. . . .

"The Court is also quite mistaken in equating our secondary effects cases with the 'incidental burdens' doctrine applied in cases such as *O'Brien*. [Either] Erie's ordinance was not aimed at speech and the Court may attempt to justify the regulation under the incidental burdens test, or Erie has aimed its law at the secondary effects of speech, and the Court can try to justify the law under that doctrine. But it cannot conflate the two. . . .

"The censorial purpose of Erie's ordinance precludes reliance on [*Barnes*]. As its preamble forthrightly admits, the ordinance's 'purpose' is to 'limit' a protected form of speech. [Moreover,] Erie's ordinance differs from the statute in *Barnes* in another respect, [for in] an earlier proceeding in this case, [the city stipulated that it had] permitted a production of [the play] Equus to proceed without prosecution [even though it included public nudity]. [Thus, unlike the statute in *Barnes*, the Erie] ordinance is deliberately targeted at Kandyland's type of nude dancing (to the exclusion of plays like Equus). [And this] narrow aim is confirmed by the expressed views of the Erie City Councilmembers who voted for this ordinance, [each of whom stated] that the ordinance was aimed specifically at nude adult establishments, and not at more mainstream forms of entertainment that include total nudity, nor even at nudity in general. [Given] that the Court has not even tried to defend the ordinance's total ban on the ground that its censorship of protected speech might be justified by an overriding state interest, it should conclude that the ordinance is patently invalid."

In her plurality opinion, Justice O'Connor offered the following response to Justice Stevens's argument about the purpose of the ordinance: "The argument that the ordinance is 'aimed' at suppressing expression through a ban on nude dancing — an argument [supported] by pointing to statements [that] the public nudity ban was not intended to apply to 'legitimate' theater productions — is really an argument that the city council [had] an illicit motive in enacting the ordinance. [But] this Court will not strike down an otherwise constitutional statute on the basis of an alleged illicit motive. [Citing *O'Brien*.]"

Justice Souter also dissented, arguing that the appropriate level of scrutiny in this case requires the "government to make some demonstration of an evidentiary basis for the harm it claims to flow from the expressive activity, and for the alleviation expected from the restriction imposed." Justice Souter maintained that "the record before us today is deficient in its failure to reveal any evidence on which Erie may have relied, either for the seriousness of the threatened harm or for the efficacy of its chosen remedy." Finally, Justice Souter confessed that his "dissent rests on a demand for an evidentiary basis that I failed to make when I concurred in *Barnes*," explaining that "I have come to believe that a government must toe the mark more carefully than I first insisted."

In response to this argument, Justice O'Conner noted that cases like *Barnes*, *Renton*, and *O'Brien* did not require such specific evidentiary proof, and that in this situation Erie could reasonably rely upon information "generated by other cities" and "the experience of the local government."

Note: Political Boycotts

Suppose an antiabortion group boycotts all manufacturers who sell supplies to abortion clinics. Is such a concerted refusal to deal "speech"? May the group constitutionally be punished under a statute that prohibits "two or more persons, acting in concert, to refuse to deal with any merchant in an effort to induce such merchant to adopt a policy it would not otherwise choose to adopt"? Suppose the group boycotts all local merchants who will not contribute funds to the group? Consider the following views:

a. Note, The Political Boycott: An Unprivileged Form of Expression, 1983 Duke L.J. 1076:

> A political boycott uses economic coercion to force its victims to speak or act politically in a way that furthers the goals, not necessarily of the [victim], but of the boycotter. Although attempts to persuade individuals to act are usually protected by the first amendment, attempts to *coerce* individuals to act are not so immunized. [Indeed, government has] a strong interest in protecting innocent parties from unprovoked [economic] harm [and] in protecting the free speech and association of individuals from economic coercion. [Moreover, these interests are clearly unrelated] to the suppression of free expression. [Thus], a law [prohibiting] political boycotts should survive the *O'Brien* test.

b. Harper, The Consumer's Emerging Right to Boycott, 93 Yale L.J. 409, 425 (1984):

> The coercive power of a group of consumers who boycott a supporter of a particular [political] cause is limited to the aggregation of those consumers' economic votes. [The] coercion inherent in [such] boycotts is simply an exercise of the influence that citizens as consumers should be encouraged to exercise. [An] analogy to electoral voting is illuminating. By threatening to remove elected officials from office, electoral voting may "coerce" those officials to reject political causes in which [they] believe. Yet such "coercion" is an accepted part of governmental decisionmaking. Consumer "coercion" of businessmen [should] also be acceptable.

See NAACP v. Claiborne Hardware Co., 458 U.S. 886 (1982), in which the Court invalidated a civil judgment against the NAACP for instituting a boycott of white merchants designed to induce business and civic leaders to adopt a number of reforms, including the desegregation of all public facilities, the hiring of black policemen, and an end to verbal abuse by law enforcement officers. The Court explained that "speech does not lose its protected character . . . simply because it may . . . coerce [others] into action." And while "States have broad powers to regulate economic activity, we do not find a comparable right to prohibit peaceful political activity such as that found in the boycott in this case." See also International Longshoremen's Association v. Allied International, 456 U.S. 212 (1982), in which a longshoremen's union, in protest against the Soviet Union's invasion of Afghanistan, refused to handle cargoes arriving from or destined for the Soviet Union. The Court held that the union's conduct constituted a secondary boycott in violation of the National Labor Relations Act. Characterizing the boycott as "conduct designed not to communicate but to coerce," the Court held that the boycott was not "protected activity under the First Amendment." The Court explained that the "labor laws reflect a careful balancing of interests," and that there "are many ways in which a union and its individual members may express their opposition to Russian foreign policy without infringing upon the rights of others."

4.   *Regulation of Political Solicitation, Contribution, Expenditure, and Activity*

It has been suggested that the "critical problem for contemporary First Amendment theory is the unequal access that wealth can buy." Carter, Technology, Democracy, and the Manipulation of Consent, 93 Yale L.J. 581 (1984). This section explores that "problem." To what extent is the solicitation, contribution, or expenditure of money "speech" within the meaning of the first amendment? To what extent may government regulate or restrict such activities in order to "enhance" the quality of public debate?

   VILLAGE OF SCHAUMBURG v. CITIZENS FOR A BETTER ENVIRONMENT, 444 U.S. 620 (1980). A Schaumburg ordinance prohibited door-to-door and on-street solicitation of contributions by charitable organizations that do not use at least 75 percent of their receipts for "charitable purposes." The village maintained that the ordinance did not pose a "free speech" issue, for it "deals only with solicitation" and leaves every charity "free to propagate its views [so] long as it refrains from soliciting money." The Court rejected the village's contention:

   "[Charitable] appeals for funds [involve] a variety of speech interests — communication of information, the dissemination and propagation of views and ideas, and the advocacy of causes — that are within the protection of the First Amendment. Soliciting financial support is undoubtedly subject to reasonable regulation but the latter must be undertaken with due regard for the reality that solicitation is characteristically intertwined with information and perhaps persuasive speech seeking support for particular causes or for particular views on economic, political, or social issues, and for the reality that without solicitation the flow of such information and advocacy would likely cease. Canvassers in such contexts are necessarily more than solicitors for money."

   Consider Marshall, Village of Schaumburg v. Citizens for a Better Environment and Religious Solicitation: Freedom of Speech and Freedom of Religion Converge, 13 Loy. L.A.L. Rev. 953, 960, 973 (1980):

The Court's conclusion [does] not follow from [its] premise. [That] there are elements of first amendment concern within a given activity does [not] dictate that the activity as a whole should be construed as protected speech. [A better explanation for holding solicitation protected by the first amendment is that solicitation] is not merely an appeal for money, [but] an exhortation to the person solicited to show his support. [The] grant or denial of a contribution is itself an expression of advocacy.

If solicitation is "speech," is the sale of flowers or the operation of a car wash to raise funds for a charitable or political organization also "speech"? Is panhandling "speech"?

Assuming that solicitation is "speech," is the Schaumburg ordinance constitutional? The Court invalidated the ordinance:

[The ordinance] is a direct and substantial limitation on protected activity [and] cannot be sustained unless it serves a sufficiently strong, subordinating interest that the Village is entitled to protect. [The Village maintains that] any organization using more than 25 percent of its receipts on fundraising, salaries, and overhead is not a charitable, but [a] for profit enterprise and that to permit it to represent itself as a charity is fraudulent. [Although] such reasoning might apply to charitable organizations whose primary purpose is to provide money or services to the poor or to others worthy of charity, it does not apply to organizations, like CBE, whose primary purpose is [to] advocate positions on matters of public concern, [for such organizations] necessarily spend more than 25 percent of their budget on salaries and administrative expenses. [Although the] Village may serve its legitimate interests, [it] must do [so] without unnecessarily interfering with First Amendment freedoms.

See also Secretary of State of Maryland v. Joseph H. Munson Co., 467 U.S. 947 (1984) (invalidating a statute prohibiting any charitable organization from paying expenses of more than 25 percent of the amount raised in any fund-raising activity); United States v. Kokinda, section E2b supra (upholding a regulation prohibiting any person from soliciting contributions on post office property); International Society for Krishna Consciousness v. Lee, section E2b supra (upholding a ban on solicitation in airport terminals).

Buckley v. Valeo

424 U.S. 1 (1976)

Per Curiam.

These appeals present constitutional challenges to the key provisions of the Federal Election Campaign Act of 1971 (Act), and related provisions of the Internal Revenue Code of 1954, all as amended in 1974. . . .

[The] statutes at issue [contain] the following provisions: (a) individual political contributions [and expenditures] "relative to a clearly identified candidate" are limited, [and] campaign spending by candidates for various federal offices [is] subject to prescribed limits; (b) contributions and expenditures above certain threshold levels must be reported and publicly disclosed; (c) a system for public funding of Presidential campaign activities is established; [and] (d) a Federal Election Commission is established to administer and enforce the legislation. . . .

[The Court upheld the constitutionality of the individual contribution limits, the disclosure and reporting provisions, and the public financing scheme. The Court invalidated the composition of the Federal Election Commission and the limitations on expenditures. The following excerpts relate to the contribution and expenditure limitations.]

I. Contribution and Expenditure Limitation

The intricate statutory scheme adopted by Congress to regulate federal election campaigns includes restrictions on political contributions and expenditures that apply broadly to all phases of and all participants in the election process. The major contribution and expenditure limitations in the Act prohibit individuals from contributing more than $25,000 in a single year or more than $1,000 to any single candidate for an election campaign and from spending more than $1,000 a year "relative to a clearly identified candidate." Other provisions restrict a candidate's use of personal and family resources in his campaign and limit the overall amount that can be spent by a candidate in campaigning for federal office. . . .

A. GENERAL PRINCIPLES

The Act's contribution and expenditure limitations operate in an area of the most fundamental First Amendment activities. Discussion of public issues and debate on the qualifications of candidates are integral to the operation of the system of government established by our Constitution. . . .

In upholding the constitutional validity of the Act's contribution and expenditure provisions on the ground that those provisions should be viewed as regulating conduct, not speech, the Court of Appeals relied upon [O'Brien].

We cannot share the view that the present Act's contribution and expenditure limitations are comparable to the restrictions on conduct upheld in O'Brien. The expenditure of money simply cannot be equated with such conduct as destruction of a draft card. Some forms of communication made possible by the giving and spending of money involve speech alone, some involve conduct primarily, and some involve a combination of the two. Yet this Court has never suggested that the dependence of a communication on the expenditure of money operates itself to introduce a nonspeech element or to reduce the exacting scrutiny required by the First Amendment. . . .

Even if the categorization of the expenditure of money as conduct were accepted, the limitations challenged here would not meet the O'Brien test because the governmental interests advanced in support of the Act involve "suppressing communication." The interests served by the Act include restricting the voices of people and interest groups who have money to spend and reducing the overall scope of federal election campaigns. Although the Act does not focus on the ideas expressed by persons or groups subject to its regulations, it is aimed in part at equalizing the relative ability of all voters to affect electoral outcomes by placing a ceiling on expenditures for political expression by citizens and groups. Unlike O'Brien, where the Selective Service System's administrative interest in the preservation of draft cards was wholly unrelated to their use as a means of communication, it is beyond dispute that the interest in regulating the alleged "conduct" of giving or spending money "arises in some measure because the communication allegedly integral to the conduct is itself thought to be harmful.". . . .

Nor can the Act's contribution and expenditure limitations be sustained, as some of the parties suggest, by reference to the constitutional principles reflected in such decisions as [Adderley v. Florida and Kovacs v. Cooper, supra]. Those cases stand for the proposition that the government may adopt reasonable time, place, and manner regulations, which do not discriminate among speakers or ideas, in order to further an important governmental interest unrelated to the restriction of communication. [In] contrast to *O'Brien*, where the method of expression was held to be subject to prohibition, [*Adderley*] and *Kovacs* involved place or manner restrictions on legitimate modes of expression — picketing, parading, demonstrating, and using a soundtruck. The critical difference between this case and those time, place, and manner cases is that the present Act's contribution and expenditure limitations impose direct quantity restrictions on political communication and association by persons, groups, candidates, and political parties in addition to any reasonable time, place, and manner regulations otherwise imposed.[17]

A restriction on the amount of money a person or group can spend on political communication during a campaign necessarily reduces the quantity of expression by restricting the number of issues discussed, the depth of their exploration, and the size of the audience reached.[18] This is because virtually every means of communicating ideas in today's mass society requires the expenditure of money. . . .

The expenditure limitations contained in the Act represent substantial rather than merely theoretical restraints on the quantity and diversity of political speech. The $1,000 ceiling on spending "relative to a clearly identified candidate," [for example,] would appear to exclude all citizens and groups except candidates, political parties, and the institutional press from any significant use of the most effective modes of communication.[20] . . .

By contrast with a limitation upon expenditures for political expression, a limitation upon the amount that any one person or group may contribute to a candidate or political committee entails only a marginal restriction upon the contributor's ability to engage in free communication, [for] it permits the symbolic expression of support evidenced by a contribution but does not in any way infringe the contributor's freedom to discuss candidates and issues. While contri-

---

17. The nongovernmental appellees argue that just as the decibels emitted by a sound truck can be regulated consistently with the First Amendment, [*Kovacs*,] the Act may restrict the volume of dollars in political campaigns without impermissibly restricting freedom of speech. [This] comparison underscores a fundamental misconception. The decibel restriction upheld in *Kovacs* limited the *manner* of operating a soundtruck, but not the *extent* of its proper use. By contrast, the Act's dollar ceilings restrict the extent of the reasonable use of virtually every means of communicating information. . . .

18. Being free to engage in unlimited political expression subject to a ceiling on expenditures is like being free to drive an automobile as far and as often as one desires on a single tank of gasoline.

20. The record indicates that, as of January 1, 1975, one full-page advertisement in a daily edition of a certain metropolitan newspaper cost $6,971.04 — almost seven times the annual limit on expenditures "relative to" a particular candidate imposed on the vast majority of individual citizens and associations by [the Act].

butions may result in political expression if spent by a candidate or an association to present views to the voters, the transformation of contributions into political debate involves speech by someone other than the contributor.

Given the important role of contributions in financing political campaigns, contribution restrictions could have a severe impact on political dialogue if the limitations prevented candidates and political committees from amassing the resources necessary for effective advocacy. There is no indication, however, that the contribution limitations imposed by the Act would have any dramatic adverse effect on the funding of campaigns and political associations.[23] The overall effect of the Act's contribution ceilings is merely to require candidates and political committees to raise funds from a greater number of persons and to compel people who would otherwise contribute amounts greater than the statutory limits to expend such funds on direct political expression, rather than to reduce the total amount of money potentially available to promote political expression. . . .

In sum, although the Act's contribution and expenditure limitations both implicate fundamental First Amendment interests, its expenditure ceilings impose significantly more severe restrictions on protected freedoms of political expression and association than do its limitations on financial contributions.

B. CONTRIBUTION LIMITATIONS

Section 608(b) provides, with certain limited exceptions, that "no person shall make contributions to any candidate with respect to any election for Federal office which, in the aggregate, exceed $1,000." . . .

[The] primary First Amendment problem raised by the Act's contribution limitations is their restriction of one aspect of the contributor's freedom of political association. The Court's decisions involving associational freedoms establish that the right of association is a "basic constitutional freedom," [and that] governmental "action which may have the effect of curtailing the freedom to associate is subject to the closest scrutiny." Yet, it is clear that "Neither the right to associate nor the right to participate in political activities is absolute." [Even] a "'significant interference' with protected rights of political association" may be sustained if the State demonstrates a sufficiently important interest and employs means closely drawn to avoid unnecessary abridgment of associational freedoms. . . .

It is unnecessary to look beyond the Act's primary purpose — to limit the actuality and appearance of corruption resulting from large individual financial contributions — in order to find a constitutionally sufficient justification for the $1,000 contribution limitation. [The] increasing importance of the communications media and sophisticated mass-mailing and polling operations to effective campaigning make the raising of large sums of money an ever more essential ingredient of an effective candidacy. To the extent that large contributions are given to secure a political quid pro quo from current and potential office holders, the integrity of our system of representative democracy is undermined. . . .

Of almost equal concern [is] the appearance of corruption stemming from [the] opportunities for abuse inherent in a regime of large individual financial

---

23. Statistical findings agreed to by the parties reveal that approximately 5.1% of the $73,483,613 raised by the 1,161 candidates for Congress in 1974 was obtained in amounts in excess of $1,000. . . .

contributions. [Congress] could legitimately conclude that the avoidance of the appearance of improper influence [is] "critical [if] confidence in the system of representative Government is not to be [eroded]." . . .

Appellants contend that the contribution limitations must be invalidated because bribery laws and narrowly drawn disclosure requirements constitute a less restrictive means of dealing with "proven and suspected quid pro quo arrangements." But laws making criminal the giving and taking of bribes deal with only the most blatant and specific attempts of those with money to influence governmental action. And while disclosure requirements serve [many salutary purposes] Congress was surely entitled to conclude that disclosure was only a partial measure, and that contribution ceilings were a necessary legislative concomitant to deal with the reality or appearance of corruption. . . .

We find that, under the rigorous standard of review established by our prior decisions, the weighty interests served by restricting the size of financial contributions to political candidates are sufficient to justify the limited effect upon First Amendment freedoms caused by the $1,000 contribution ceiling.

[Appellants argue further, however,] that the contribution limitations work [an] invidious discrimination between incumbents and [challengers].[33] [But] there is [no] evidence [that] contribution limitations [discriminate] against major-party challengers to incumbents, [and although] the charge of discrimination against minor-party and independent candidates is more troubling, [the] record provides no basis for concluding that the Act invidiously disadvantages such candidates. [Indeed, in some circumstances] the restriction would appear to benefit minor-party and independent candidates relative to their major-party opponents because major-party candidates receive far more money in large contributions. . . .

In view of these considerations, we conclude that the impact of the Act's $1,000 contribution limitation on major-party challengers and on minor-party candidates does not render the provision unconstitutional on its face.

[For similar reasons, the Court also upheld the $5,000 limit on contributions by "political committees," the limits on volunteers' incidental expenses, and the $25,000 limit on total political contributions by an individual during a single calendar year.]

C. EXPENDITURE LIMITATIONS

The Act's expenditure ceilings impose direct and substantial restraints [on] the quantity of campaign speech by individuals, groups, and candidates. The re-

---

33. In this discussion, we address only the argument that the contribution limitations alone impermissibly discriminate against nonincumbents. We do not address the more serious argument that these limitations, in combination with the limitation on expenditures [invidiously] discriminate against major-party challengers and minor-party candidates.

Since an incumbent is subject to these limitations to the same degree as his opponent, the Act, on its face, appears to be evenhanded. The appearance of fairness, however, may not reflect political reality. Although some incumbents are defeated in every congressional election, it is axiomatic that an incumbent usually begins the race with significant advantages. [In some circumstances] the overall effect of the contribution and expenditure limitations enacted by Congress could foreclose any fair opportunity of a successful challenge.

However, since we decide in Part I-C, infra, that the ceilings on [expenditures] are unconstitutional under the First Amendment, we need not express any opinion with regard to the alleged invidious discrimination resulting from the full sweep of the legislation as enacted.

strictions, while neutral as to the ideas expressed, limit political expression "at the core of our electoral process and of the First Amendment freedoms." . . .

1. The $1,000 Limitation on Expenditures "Relative to a Clearly Identified Candidate"

Section 608(e)(1) provides that "[n]o person may make any expenditure . . . relative to a clearly identified candidate during a calendar year [which] exceeds $1,000." [Appellants maintain] that the provision is unconstitutionally vague. [The] use of so indefinite a phrase as "relative to" a candidate fails to clearly mark the boundary between permissible and impermissible [speech]. "Such a distinction offers no security for free [discussion]." [To] preserve the provision against invalidation on vagueness grounds, §608(e)(1) must be construed to apply only to expenditures for communications that in express terms advocate the election or defeat of a clearly identified candidate for federal office.

We turn then to the basic First Amendment question — whether §608(e)(1), even as thus narrowly and explicitly construed, impermissibly burdens the constitutional right of free expression. . . .

The discussion in Part I-A supra, explains why the Act's expenditure limitations impose far greater restraints on the freedom of speech and association than do its contribution limitations. . . .

We find that the governmental interest in preventing corruption and the appearance of corruption is inadequate to justify §608(e)(1)'s ceiling on independent expenditures. [First], §608(e)(1) prevents only some large expenditures. So long as persons and groups eschew expenditures that in express terms advocate the election or defeat of a clearly identified candidate, they are free to spend as much as they want to promote the candidate and his views. The exacting interpretation of the statutory language necessary to avoid unconstitutional vagueness thus undermines the limitation's effectiveness. . . .

Second, [although the] parties defending §608(e)(1) contend that it is necessary to prevent would-be contributors from avoiding the contribution limitations [by] paying directly for media advertisements or for other portions of the candidate's campaign activities, [such] coordinated expenditures are treated as contributions rather than expenditures under the Act [and are thus limited by the] contribution ceilings. [Thus], §608(e)(1) limits [only] expenditures [made] totally independently of the candidate and his campaign. [But the] absence of [coordination with respect to such expenditures] undermines the value of the expenditure to the candidate [and] alleviates the danger that expenditures will be given as a quid pro quo for improper commitments. [Thus,] §608(e)(1) severely [restricts] independent advocacy despite its substantially diminished potential for abuse. . . .

It is argued [further, however, that the] governmental interest in equalizing the relative ability of individuals [to] influence the outcome of elections [justifies the] expenditure ceiling. But the concept that government may restrict the speech of some [in] order to enhance the relative voice of others is wholly foreign to the First Amendment, which was designed "to secure 'the widest possible dissemination of information from diverse and antagonistic sources.'" [The] First Amendment's protection against governmental abridgment of free expression cannot properly be made to depend on a person's financial ability to engage in public discussion. [Section] 608(e)(1)'s [expenditure] limitation is unconstitutional under the First Amendment.

2. Limitation on Expenditures by Candidates from Personal or Family Resources

The Act also [limits] expenditures by a candidate "from his personal funds, or the personal funds of his immediate family, in connection with his campaigns during any calendar year." . . .

The ceiling on personal expenditures by candidates on their own [behalf] imposes a substantial restraint on the ability of persons to engage in protected First Amendment expression. The candidate, no less than any other person, has a First Amendment right to engage in the discussion of public issues and [to] advocate his own election. . . .

The [interest] in equalizing the relative financial resources of candidates competing for elective office is clearly not sufficient to justify the provision's infringement of fundamental First Amendment rights. . . .

3. Limitations on Campaign Expenditures

Section 608(c) places limitations on overall campaign expenditures by candidates seeking nomination for election and election to federal office. [For example, the] Act imposes blanket $70,000 limitations on both primary campaigns and general election campaigns for the House of Representatives. . . .

No governmental interest that has been suggested is sufficient to justify the restriction on the quantity of political expression imposed by §608(c)'s campaign expenditure limitations. [The] interest in alleviating the corrupting influence of large contributions is served by the Act's contribution limitations and disclosure provisions, [and the] interest in equalizing the financial resources of candidates [is not a] convincing justification for restricting the scope of federal election campaigns. [The] campaign expenditure ceilings appear to be designed primarily to [reduce] the allegedly skyrocketing costs of political campaigns. [But the] First Amendment denies government the power to determine that spending to promote one's political views is wasteful, excessive, or unwise. In the free society ordained by our Constitution it is not the government, but the people — individually as citizens and candidates and collectively as associations and political committees — who must retain control over the quantity and range of debate on public issues in a political campaign.

For these reasons we hold that §608(c) is constitutionally invalid.

In sum, the provisions of the Act that impose a $1,000 [limitation on contributions] are constitutionally valid. These limitations [serve] the basic governmental interest in safeguarding the integrity of the electoral process without directly impinging upon the rights of individual citizens and candidates to engage in political debate and discussion. By contrast, the First Amendment requires the invalidation of the Act's independent expenditure [ceilings]. These provisions place substantial and direct restrictions on the ability of candidates, citizens, and associations to engage in protected political expression, restrictions that the First Amendment cannot tolerate. . . .

[Affirmed] in part and reversed in part.

MR. CHIEF JUSTICE BURGER, concurring in part and dissenting in part. . . .

[The contribution limitations are unconstitutional. Contributions] and expenditures are two sides of the same First Amendment coin. [Limiting] contributions, as a practical matter, will limit expenditures and will put an effective ceiling on the amount of political activity [that] the Government will permit to take place. . . .

The Court's attempt to distinguish the communication inherent in political *contributions* from the speech aspects of political *expenditures* simply "will not wash." We do little but engage in word games unless we recognize that people — candidates and contributors — spend money on political activity because they wish to communicate ideas, and their constitutional interest in doing so is precisely the same whether they or someone else utters the words. [Moreover, the contribution] restrictions are hardly incidental in their effect upon particular campaigns. [Such restrictions] will foreclose some candidacies,[9] [and] alter the nature of some electoral contests drastically.[10]

At any rate, the contribution limits are a far more severe restriction on First Amendment activity than the sort of "chilling" legislation for which the Court has shown such extraordinary concern in the past. See, e.g., [Cohen v. California, section D5 supra]. If such restraints can be justified at all, they must be justified by the very strongest of state interests. . . .

MR. JUSTICE WHITE, concurring in part and dissenting in part. . . .

I dissent [from] the Court's view that the expenditure limitations [violate] the First Amendment. . . .

The congressional judgment [was that expenditure limitations are necessary] to counter the corrosive effects of money in federal election campaigns. [The] Court strikes down [§608(e)], strangely enough claiming more [knowledge] as to what may improperly influence candidates than is possessed by the majority of Congress that passed this bill and the President who signed it. [I] would take the word of those who know — that limiting independent expenditures is essential to prevent transparent and widespread evasion of the contribution limits. . . .

The Court also rejects Congress' judgment manifested in §608(c) that the federal interest in limiting total campaign expenditures by individual candidates justifies the incidental effect on their opportunity for effective political speech. I disagree. . . .

[The] argument that money is speech and that limiting the flow of money to the speaker violates the First Amendment proves entirely too much. Compulsory bargaining [has] increased the labor costs of those who publish newspapers, [and] taxation directly removes from company coffers large amounts of money that might be spent on larger and better newspapers. [But] it has not been suggested [that] these laws, and many others, are invalid because they siphon [off] large sums that would otherwise be available for communicative activities.

[The] judgment of Congress was that reasonably effective campaigns could be conducted within the limits established by the Act. [There] is no sound basis for invalidating the expenditure limitations, so long as the purposes they serve are legitimate and sufficiently substantial, which in my view they are.

---

9. Candidates who must raise large initial contributions in order to appeal for more funds to a broader audience will be handicapped. . . .

10. Under the Court's holding, candidates with personal fortunes will be free to contribute to their own campaigns as much as they like, since the Court chooses to view the Act's provisions in this regard as unconstitutional "expenditure" limitations rather than "contribution" limitations. . . .

[Expenditure] ceilings reinforce the contribution limits and help eradicate the hazard of corruption. [Without] limits on total expenditures, campaign costs will [inevitably] escalate, [creating an incentive to accept unlawful contributions. Moreover,] the corrupt use of money by candidates is as much to be feared as the corrosive influence of large contributions. There are many illegal ways of spending money to influence elections. [The] expenditure limits could play a substantial role in preventing unethical practices. There just would not be enough of "that kind of money" to go around. . . .

It is also important to [restore] public confidence in federal elections. It is critical to obviate [the] impression that federal elections are purely and simply a function of money. [The] ceiling on candidate expenditures represents the considered judgment of Congress that elections are to be decided among candidates none of whom has overpowering advantage by reason of a huge campaign war chest. [This] seems an acceptable purpose and the means chosen a common-sense way to achieve it. . . .

I also disagree with the Court's judgment that §608(a), which limits the amount of money that a candidate or his family may spend on his campaign, violates the Constitution. [By] limiting the importance of personal wealth, §608(a) helps to assure that only individuals with a modicum of support from others will be viable candidates. [This] would tend to discourage any notion that the outcome of elections is primarily a function of money. Similarly, §608(a) tends to equalize access to the political arena, encouraging the less wealthy [to] run for political office. [Congress] was entitled to determine that personal wealth ought to play a less important role in political campaigns than it has in the past. Nothing in the First Amendment stands in the way of that determination. . . .

MR. JUSTICE MARSHALL, concurring in part and dissenting in part.

[The] Court invalidates §608(a), [which limits the amount a candidate may spend from personal or family funds], as violative of the candidate's First Amendment Rights. [I] disagree.

[The] perception that personal wealth wins elections may not only discourage potential candidates without significant personal wealth from entering the political arena, but also undermine public confidence in the integrity of the electoral process.[1]

The concern that candidacy for public office not become, or appear to become, the exclusive province of the wealthy assumes heightened significance when one considers the impact of §608(b), which the Court today upholds. That provision prohibits contributions from individuals and groups to candidates in excess of $1,000, and contributions from political committees in excess of $5,000. While the limitations on contributions are neutral there can be no question that large contributions generally mean more to the candidate without a substantial personal fortune to spend on his campaign. Large contributions are the less wealthy candidate's only hope of countering the wealthy candidate's immediate access to substantial sums of money. [Section 608(a) thus provides] some symmetry to a regulatory scheme that otherwise enhances the natural advantage of the wealthy. . . .

---

1. "In the Nation's seven largest States in 1970, 11 of the 15 major senatorial candidates were millionaires. The four who were not millionaires lost their bid for election." . . .

MR. JUSTICE BLACKMUN, concurring in part and dissenting in part.

I am not persuaded that the Court makes [a] principled constitutional distinction between the contribution limitations [and] the expenditure limitations. [I] therefore do not join Part I-B of the Court's opinion or those portions of Part I-A that are consistent with Part I-B. As to those, I dissent. . . .

Note: Buckley *and the Problem of Abridging Speech to* "Enhance" *the Electoral Process*

1. *The problem of unequal resources.* In upholding the expenditure and contribution limitations in *Buckley*, the court of appeals explained: "[The] statute taken as a whole affirmatively enhances First Amendment values. By reducing in good measure disparity due to wealth, the Act tends to equalize both the relative ability of all voters to affect electoral outcomes, and the opportunity of all interested citizens to become candidates for elective federal office. This broadens the choice of candidates and the opportunity to hear a variety of views." 519 F.2d 817, 841 (D.C. Cir. 1975). A fundamental question presented in *Buckley*, then, was "this: in a situation where the speech opportunities of a group in the aggregate, or of the average member of a group, could be maximized, enhanced, or even made initially possible only by abridging the speech of an individual, what (if anything) does the First Amendment command to be done?" Polsby, Buckley v. Valeo: The Nature of Political Speech, 1976 Sup. Ct. Rev. 1, 5. Do you agree that, if the purpose and "net effect of the legislation [are] to enhance freedom of speech, the exacting review reserved for abridgements of free speech is inapposite"? L. Tribe, American Constitutional Law 1135 (2d ed. 1988). Do you agree with the Court that "the concept that government may restrict the speech of some elements of our society in order to enhance the relative voice of others is wholly foreign to the First Amendment"?

Note that *Buckley* posed a conflict between two conceptions of a properly functioning system of free expression, and between two conceptions of the role of the state. Under one view, government should take the "private" status quo for granted and all persons, no matter their resources, are free to press their interests on the political process. If some people have more money than others, and if their greater resources permit more speech, that result is something for which government is not itself responsible and which cannot be "remedied" consistent with the first amendment. The role of government is to remain "neutral" as people in the private sphere compete in the political marketplace.

Under the competing view, a system of free expression is one in which there is fair deliberation on what the public good requires, and inequality of resources, which can seriously distort that deliberation, is understood to be at least in part the product of governmental choices. If government permits the process of political deliberation to become distorted by this inequality of resources, the result is inconsistent with first amendment aspirations. Under this view, government "inaction" is equivalent to government action, and governmental efforts to equalize resources are permitted and perhaps even required in order to promote a more fair public debate. See Balkin, Some Realism about Pluralism: Legal Realist Approaches to the First Amendment, 1990 Duke L.J. 375, 410-412 ("[I]t is not only wrong but also incoherent for opponents of campaign finance reform to contend that the government should not regulate access to the political process. Government already regulates access to the political process — the first amendment simply demands that it do so fairly.").

For an elaboration of this view, consider Sunstein, Free Speech Now, 59 U. Chi. L. Rev. 255, 263-267, 272, 291-292 (1992):

> Perhaps we need a New Deal for speech [that] would parallel what the New Deal provided for property rights during the 1930's. [Before] the New Deal, the Constitution [was] often invoked to prohibit governmental interference with existing distributions of rights and entitlements. Hence minimum wage and maximum hour laws were seen as unjustifiable [takings] from employers for the benefit of employees and the public at large. [The] pre-New Deal framework treated the existing distribution of resources and opportunities as prepolitical, when in fact it was not. [The] New Dealers pointed out that this sphere was actually a creation of law. Rules of property, contract, and tort produced the set of entitlements that ultimately yielded market hours and wages. [Viewed in this light], minimum wage laws [merely] substituted one form of regulation for another. . . .
>
> These ideas have played little role in the law of free speech. [*Buckley*, for example,] reflects pre-New Deal understandings. We should view it as the modern-day analogue of *Lochner*: a decision [that takes] the market status quo as just and prepolitical, and [uses it] to invalidate democratic efforts at reform. Reliance on [existing distributions] is [taken as] governmental neutrality. [But] it should be clear that elections based on those distributions [are] made possible and constituted through law. That law consists, first, in legal rules protecting the present distribution of wealth, and more fundamentally, in legal rules allowing candidates to buy speech rights through markets.

Consider also Wright, Politics and the Constitution: Is Money Speech?, 85 Yale L.J. 1001, 1005, 1015-1019 (1976):

> Nothing in the First Amendment prevents us, as a political community, from [choosing] to move closer to the kind of community process that lies at the heart of the First Amendment conception — a process wherein ideas and candidates prevail because of their inherent worth, not because [one] side puts on a more elaborate show of support. [The] picture of the political process that emerges from [*Buckley*] corresponds [to the] pluralist model. [To] the pluralist, the political process consists [of] the pulling and hauling of various competing interest groups. [Force] collides with counterforce, [and] the strongest force [determines] the outcome of [the] process. [By this] line of reasoning, the First Amendment's highest function is to let group pressure run its course unimpeded, lest we skew the process that determines for us the public interest. [This model] gives undeserved weight [to] highly organized and wealthy groups [and drains] politics of its moral and intellectual content. [Unlike the pluralist conception, the First Amendment] is founded on [a] model of how self-governing people [make] their decisions [that emphasizes] considerations of justice and morality — considerations absent from the pluralist approach. [What] the pluralist rhetoric obscures is that *ideas*, and not intensities, form the heart of the expression which the First Amendment is designed to protect.

On the other hand, consider BeVier, Money and Politics: A Perspective on the First Amendment and Campaign Finance Reform, 73 Cal. L. Rev. 1045, 1066-1068, 1071, 1076 (1985):

Advocates of judicial deference begin their argument by equating first amendment objectives with a substantive vision of an ideal political process. [They] assert that the actual political process departs significantly from the posited ideal. [They then argue that because the proposed] reforms "promote" first amendment values, [they] ought not to require strict judicial scrutiny. [But] it is difficult to understand how, without strict judicial scrutiny of the actual effects of the statue, the Court could confidently reach a conclusion that its "net effect . . . is to enhance freedom of speech." [Moreover, the] values generally invoked in behalf of reform do not seem capable of generating nonarbitrary, workable criteria for evaluating political reality. When has the public received "enough" information to satisfy the constitutional value of an "informed public"? [What] is the constitutional norm against which "distortions" of election outcomes can be said to occur? [Moreover, commentators] who defend lenient scrutiny for campaign finance reform legislation [fail] to acknowledge that regulation of the political process might be a context warranting distrust of elected officials. [They] ignore any systematic possibility that legislators will behave in self- rather than public-interested ways.

Consider Kagan, Private Speech, Public Purpose: The Role of Governmental Motive in First Amendment Doctrine, 63 U. Chi. L. Rev. 415, 467-475 (1996):

In what has become one of the most castigated passages in modern First Amendment case law, the Court pronounced in *Buckley* that "the concept that government may restrict the speech of some elements of our society in order to enhance the relative voice of others is wholly foreign to the First Amendment. . . ." [The] *Buckley* principle emerges not from the view that redistribution of speech opportunities is itself an illegitimate end, but from the view that governmental actions justified as redistributive devices often (though not always) stem partly from hostility or sympathy toward ideas — or, even more commonly, from self-interest. [The] nature of [such] regulations, as compared with other content-neutral regulations, creates [a special problem]: that governmental officials (here, legislators) more often will take account of improper factors. [This] increased probability of taint arises [from] the very design of laws directed at equalizing the realm of public expression. Unlike most content-neutral regulations, these laws not only have, but are supposed to have, content-based effects. . . . In considering such a law, a legislator's own views of the ideas (or speakers) that the equalization effort means to suppress or promote may well intrude, consciously or not, on her decisionmaking process. [Thus,] there may be good reason to distrust the motives of politicians when they apply themselves to reconstructing the realm of expression.

Consider also Strauss, Corruption, Equality, and Campaign Finance, 94 Colum. L. Rev. 1369, 1383-1386 (1994):

[The principle] "one person, one vote" is [the] decisive counterexample to the suggestion [in *Buckley*] that the aspiration [of equalizing "speech"] is foreign to the First Amendment. We do not think of "one person, one vote" as an example of reducing the speech of some to enhance the relative speech of others, but that is only because the principle seems so natural. When legislatures were malapportioned, rural voters had a more effective voice than urban voters. Reapportionment reduced their influence in order to enhance the relative influence of others. We might unreflectively say that the rural voters were deprived of voting power that was not rightfully theirs, while my ability to make a campaign contribution is rightfully [mine]. But this formulation begs the question. We have to explain why superior spending power is rightfully mine but superior voting power is not. . . .

The problem with promoting equality in campaign finance occurs not at the level of aspiration, as [Buckley] suggests, but at the level of institutional specifics. [If] "one person, one vote" shows why Buckley's dictum about equality is incorrect, then a different analogy to voting rights — gerrymandering — shows why Buckley's conclusion is not so easily rejected. Reapportionment [has] apparently been a success story, in the sense that there are no longer any grossly malapportioned legislatures. [But the] experience with gerrymandering has been the opposite. It is notoriously difficult to define administrable standards to control gerrymandering. The result has been [a] system in which incumbent protection is the order of the day. Unless campaign finance reform reflects a clear and plausible conception of equality, we may well end up with the gerrymandering experience, rather than the reapportionment experience. That is, simply turning Congress loose to promote "equality" [could] just lead to measures that give even more protection to political incumbents or other favored interests. In fact it would be surprising if it did not lead to such a result.

Can you think of a "clear and plausible conception of equality" that would avoid this problem? Consider the following proposal: "The principle of equal-dollars-per-voter means that each eligible voter should receive the same amount of financial resources for the purpose of participating in electoral politics. [The] only money that voters would be permitted to [spend or contribute] would be the money they receive from the government." Foley, Equal-Dollars-Per-Voter: A Constitutional Principle of Campaign Finance, 94 Colum. L. Rev. 1204, 1206-1207 (1994). Are there "principled" as well as "pragmatic" justifications for Buckley's "dictum"?

Consider also the following views:

a. Blasi, How Campaign Spending Limits Can Be Reconciled with the First Amendment, 7 The Responsive Community 1, 5-8 (1996-1997):

Buckley was a defensible decision when it was rendered in 1976. Enter next the law of unintended consequences. The combination of strict limits on the size of direct financial contributions to candidates (upheld in Buckley) and no limits on candidate spending (the result of Buckley's invalidation of spending limits) left standing an incoherent patchwork regime of campaign finance regulation. Then came breakthroughs in expensive but effective electoral techniques such as focus group research, tracking polls, Madison Avenue-style advertising, and demographically targeted direct mail. Today candidates need a great deal of money if they are to compete, but they cannot raise it in the traditional, relatively efficient way, i.e., from a small number of large donors. So instead challengers and incumbents alike must beat the bushes — day after day, week after week, year after year — to accumulate dizzying numbers of small contributions.

This is a terrible way for representatives and would-be representatives to be spending their time. [Opponents] of spending limits no doubt will argue that the government has no more business deciding how large a role fundraising should play in the electoral process than it has prescribing a "balanced" public discourse. . . . As a matter of First Amendment principle, however, the two objectives are very different. Any effort to balance public debate or protect voters from too much campaign speech places government in the role of saving listeners from their own cognitive susceptibilities. Such paternalism in the realm of ideas is [constitutionally disfavored]. When campaign spending is regulated in order to reduce candidate fundraising chores rather than protect audiences, the traditional First Amendment antipaternalism principle is not implicated. [What] makes the fundraising-control rationale for spending limits constitutionally legitimate is that the harm sought to be remedied is a product not of the communicative impact of speech but of the practices that generate the speech. Legislatures have far more leeway to regulate such practices than to attempt to forestall or alter communicative effects.

It is often said that a major part of the problem in financing modern political campaigns is the cost of television. How would you assess the constitutionality of a law prohibiting all paid political advertising on television during an election period? Such legislation exists in the United Kingdom, France, Norway, Sweden, the Netherlands, Denmark, Austria, Israel, and Japan. Would this be more attractive if broadcasters were required to make free time available to candidates? If so, how would the free time be allocated among competing candidates? For a comparative perspective, see Australian Capital Television v. Commonwealth of Australia, 177 C.L.R. 106 (1992) (Australian High Court invalidates such legislation). For more on the regulation of the media to improve the marketplace of ideas, see section F4 infra.

b. Baker, Campaign Expenditures and Free Speech, 33 Harv. Civ. Rts.-Civ. Lib. L. Rev. 1, 21-25, 46 (1998):

> Within institutions of democratic governance, acceptable regulation of speech, including content regulation, is ubiquitous. Restrictions occur, for example, [in] Congress and before its committees. [Similarly, in a courtroom], a combination of court rules and the judge's discretion [determines] who speaks and whether particular content is barred. . . . [The] electoral process [should] be viewed as a special governmental institution [designed] to further the governing process. [Thus], the determinative issue in a First Amendment challenge to a restriction on campaign speech should be the restriction's effect on the openness and fairness of the electoral process. [Under this approach], candidates enter campaigns the way trial participants enter a courtroom, officials enter a legislative hall, or witnesses appear before an agency hearing. Their speech can be legally restricted [by] rules that further the proper functioning of the particular institution. [This] approach does not abandon constitutional protection for speech in the campaign context, [but it significantly] changes the First Amendment analysis [from that employed in *Buckley*].

c. Sullivan, Political Money and Freedom of Speech, 30 U.C. Davis L. Rev. 663, 664, 667-673 (1997):

> [T]he view that political money should be limited has become mainstream orthodoxy. [Currently] on the table are three types of reform proposals to impose new restrictions on political money. One advocates further limiting campaign contributions. The second proposes more conditioning of benefits upon corresponding "voluntary" limits on private spending. The third would place outright restrictions on campaign expenditures. [Arguments] for greater limits on political contributions and expenditures typically suggest that any claims for individual liberty to spend political money ought yield to an overriding interest in a well-functioning democracy. But what is meant by democracy here?
>
> [For example, one] argument for campaign finance limits is that they further individual rights to political equality among voters in an election. [Reformers] often proceed from the premise of equal suffrage in elections to the conclusion that equalization of speaking power in electoral campaigns is similarly justifiable in furtherance of democracy. [The extreme version of this principle] would be one per-

son, one vote, one dollar. [But there] is an alternative possibility: that political finance more resembles political speech than voting. That is the analogy drawn by the *Buckley* Court, [and] the choice of analogy is crucial. In the formal realm of voting — like other formal governmental settings, such as legislative committee hearings and trials in court — speech may be constrained in the interest of the governmental function in question. For example, at a town meeting, Robert's Rules of Order govern to ensure that orderly discussion may take place; at a trial, witnesses testify [subject] to rules of evidence. . . . Likewise, one voter does not get ten votes merely because he feels passionately about a candidate or issue. By contrast, in the informal realm of political speech — the kind that goes on continuously between elections as well as during them — conventional First Amendment principles generally preclude a norm of equality of influence.

2. *Subsidizing speech to "improve" the electoral process: public financing of campaigns. Buckley* concluded that, absent extraordinary circumstances, government cannot constitutionally *restrict* an individual's or corporation's speech in order to eliminate imbalance in the marketplace. What other means, if any, might government employ to achieve this objective? Consider Powe, Mass Speech and the Newer First Amendment, 1982 Sup. Ct. Rev. 243, 268-269, 282-283: "[To] attempt to tone down a debate [in] the interests of enhancing the marketplace [is] wildly at odds with the normal First Amendment belief that more speech is better. [If the problem is that] the wealthy are too powerful, [we should provide] significant additional public funding [for] electoral campaigns, so that the advantages of wealth can [be] minimized."

In *Buckley*, the Court considered the constitutionality of subtitle H of the Internal Revenue Code, which established a scheme of campaign "subsidies" to equalize the financial resources of political candidates. Under subtitle H, major political parties (those that had received more than 25 percent of the vote in the preceding presidential election) qualified for subsidies of up to $20 million for their candidates' presidential campaigns. Minor parties (those that had received between 5 and 25 percent of the vote in the preceding presidential election) qualified for subsidies proportional to their share of the vote in the preceding or current election, whichever was higher. All other political parties qualified for subsidies only if they received more than 5 percent of the vote in the current election. Subtitle H provided for public financing of primaries and party nominating conventions on similar terms. All subsidies were indexed to inflation. Major party candidates were eligible for public funding only if they agreed to forgo all private contributions and to limit their expenditures to the amount of the subsidy. Other candidates who accepted subsidies were permitted to supplement their public funding with private contributions as long as they agreed to limit their total expenditures to the amount of the major party subsidy.

The Court upheld the public financing provisions: "Subtitle H is a congressional effort, not to abridge, restrict, or censor speech, but rather to use public money to facilitate and enlarge public discussion and participation in the electoral process, goals vital to a self-governing people. Thus, Subtitle H furthers, not abridges, pertinent First Amendment values." Is this consistent with the Court's analysis in other parts of the opinion?

The Court held further that subtitle H's requirement that a candidate who accepts public financing agree to limit total campaign expenditures to the amount of the major party subsidy did not independently violate the first amendment:

"Congress [may] condition acceptance of public funds on an agreement by the candidate to abide by specified expenditure limitations. Just as a candidate may voluntarily limit the size of the contributions he chooses to accept, he may decide to forgo private fundraising and accept public funding." Consider Polsby, supra, at 26: "[No] sooner does the Court resolve a most fundamental First Amendment question [concerning the constitutionality of expenditure limitations] in a manner highly favorable to the interest in personal liberty, then it takes it all back again, letting expenditure ceilings in the back door by allowing them as a condition to the candidate's accepting public financing. [The] clash of the holdings is startling."

3. *Equality and the first amendment.* Another issue posed in *Buckley* was whether "as constructed public financing invidiously discriminates [against non-major party candidates]." In *Buckley*, the Court rejected the equal protection challenge:

Subtitle H does not prevent any candidate from getting on the ballot or any voter from casting a vote for the candidate of his choice; the inability, if any, of minor-party candidates to wage effective campaigns will derive not from lack of public funding but from their inability to raise private contributions. [Third parties have historically been] incapable of matching the major parties' ability to raise money and win elections. Congress was [thus] justified in providing both major parties full funding and all other parties only a percentage of the major-party entitlement. Identical treatment of all [parties] would [make] it easy to raid the United States Treasury [and] artificially foster the proliferation of splinter parties. [Finally, there has been no showing] that the election funding plan disadvantages nonmajor parties by operating to reduce their strength below that attained without any public financing. [We thus] conclude that the general election funding system does not work an invidious discrimination against candidates of nonmajor parties.

Other aspects of the intersection of equal protection and free expression are explored in sections E2c and E2d supra.

4. *Disclosure.* To what extent is disclosure of the identity of contributors an effective and constitutional means of preventing undue influence? The Federal Election Campaign Act of 1971 requires every political candidate and "political committee" to maintain records of the names and addresses of all persons who contribute more than $10 in a calendar year and to make such records available for inspection by the Federal Election Commission. Moreover, the act provides that such reports are to be available "for public inspection and copying." In *Buckley*, the Court upheld these provisions:

The governmental interests sought to be vindicated by the disclosure requirements [fall] into three categories. First, disclosure provides the electorate with information "as to where political campaign money comes [from]" in order to aid the voters in evaluating those who seek federal office. [Second,] disclosure requirements deter actual corruption and avoid the appearance of corruption by exposing [contributions] to the light of publicity. [Third, such] requirements are an essential means of gathering the data necessary to detect violations of the contribution limitations. [Thus, the] disclosure requirements [directly] serve substantial governmental interests. . . .

Appellants contend that the Act's requirements are [nonetheless unconstitutional] insofar as they apply to contributions to minor parties [because] the governmental interest in this information is minimal and the danger of significant infringement on First Amendment rights is greatly increased. [It is true that the] Government's interest in deterring the "buying" of elections and the undue influence of large contributors on officeholders [may] be reduced where contributions to a minor party [are] concerned, for it is less likely that the candidate will be victorious. [Moreover, these] movements are less likely to have a sound financial base and thus are more vulnerable to falloffs in contributions. In some instances fears of reprisal may deter contributions to the point where the movement cannot survive. [Thus, there] could well be a case [where] the threat to the exercise of First Amendment rights is so serious and the state interest furthered by disclosure so insubstantial that the Act's requirements cannot be constitutionally applied. But no appellant in this case has tendered record evidence of [that] sort. . . .

In Brown v. Socialist Workers '74 Campaign Committee, 459 U.S. 87 (1982), the Court held that the disclosure provisions of the Ohio campaign reporting law could not constitutionally be applied to the Socialist Workers Party, "a minor political party which historically has been the object of harassment by government officials and private parties."

Consider Stone and Marshall, Brown v. Socialist Workers: Inequality as a Command of the First Amendment, 1983 Sup. Ct. Rev. 583, 619:

In *Buckley*, the Court, applying ordinary content-neutral balancing, held that campaign disclosure requirements are constitutional because they "directly serve substantial governmental interests." In *Brown*, the Court held that such disclosure requirements cannot constitutionally be applied to [the Socialist Workers Party]. What, though, is the appropriate remedy in *Brown*? Is it to leave the disclosure requirements intact for all organizations that do not qualify for the constitutionally compelled exemption or is it to invalidate the requirements in their entirety? In *Buckley* and *Brown*, the Court, without explanation, endorsed the former approach. But suppose that, after *Brown*, the Republican Party challenges the disclosure requirements, modified by the constitutionally compelled exemption, as an unconstitutional content-based restriction. Are the requirements, as modified, constitutional?

FIRST NATIONAL BANK OF BOSTON v. BELLOTTI, 435 U.S. 765 (1978). A Massachusetts statute prohibited any corporation to make contributions or expenditures "for the purpose [of] influencing or affecting the vote on any question submitted to the voters, other than one materially affecting any of the property, business or assets of the corporation." The statute specified further that "[n]o question submitted to the voters solely concerning the taxation of the income, property or transactions of individuals shall be deemed materially to affect the property, business or assets of the corporation." The state court, in upholding the statute, held that the first amendment rights of a corporation are limited to issues that materially affect its business, property, or assets.

The Court, in a five-to-four decision, reversed. In an opinion by Justice Powell, the Court explained that the state court had "posed the wrong question." The proper question "is not whether corporations 'have' First Amendment rights and, if so, whether they are coextensive with those of natural persons, [but] whether [the statute] abridges expression that the First Amendment was meant to protect." The statute is directed against speech that is "indispensable to decisionmaking in a democracy," and that lies "at the heart of the First Amendment's protection."

Moreover, the Court could "find no support in the First [Amendment], or in the decisions of this Court, for the proposition that speech that otherwise would be within the protection of the First Amendment loses that protection simply because its source is a corporation that cannot prove, to the satisfaction of a court, a material effect on its business or property."

The state maintained that the statute was necessary to preserve "the integrity of the electoral process." The participation of corporations in the electoral process, the state argued, "would exert an undue influence on the outcome of a referendum vote, and — in the end — destroy the confidence of the people in the democratic process and the integrity of government." Corporations, the state explained, "are wealthy and powerful and their views may drown out other points of view."

The Court gave this argument short shrift: "To be sure, corporate advertising may influence the outcome of the vote; this would be its purpose. But the fact that advocacy may persuade the electorate is hardly a reason to suppress it. [As we noted in *Buckley*,] 'the concept that government may restrict the speech of some elements of our society in order to enhance the relative voice of others is wholly foreign to the First [Amendment.]' [Moreover,] the people in our democracy are entrusted with the responsibility for judging and evaluating the relative merits of conflicting arguments. They may consider, in making their judgment, the source and credibility of the advocate. But if there be any danger that the people cannot evaluate the information and arguments advanced by [corporations], it is a danger contemplated by the Framers of the First Amendment."

Justice White, joined by Justices Brennan and Marshall, dissented. At the outset, Justice White observed that "what some have considered to be the principal function of the First Amendment, the use of communication as a means of self-expression, self-realization and self-fulfillment, is not at all furthered by corporate speech." Moreover, "the restriction of corporate speech concerned with political matters impinges much less severely upon the availability of ideas to the general public than do restrictions upon individual speech," for even "the complete curtailment of corporate communications concerning political or ideological questions not integral to day-to-day business functions would leave individuals, including corporate shareholders, employees, and customers, free to communicate their thoughts." It is thus "unlikely," White maintained, "that any significant communication would be lost by such a prohibition."

Justice White then turned to the central question: "[The] special status of corporations has placed them in a position to control vast amounts of economic power which may, if not regulated, dominate not only the economy but also the very heart of our democracy, the electoral process. Although [*Buckley*] provides support for the position that the desire to equalize the financial resources available to candidates does not justify the limitation upon the expression of support which a restriction upon individual contributions entails, the interest of Massachusetts [is] quite different. It is not one of equalizing the resources of opposing candidates or opposing positions, but rather of preventing institutions which have been permitted to amass wealth as a result of special advantages extended by the State for certain economic purposes from using that wealth to acquire an unfair advantage in the political process. [The] State need not permit its own creation to consume it."

Justice Rehnquist also dissented: "'A corporation is an artificial being, [existing] only in contemplation of law. Being the mere creature of law, it possesses only those properties which the charter of creation confers upon it, either expressly, or as incidental to its very [existence].' [When] a State charters a corporation for the purpose of publishing a newspaper, it necessarily assumes that the corporation is entitled to the liberty of the press essential to the conduct of its business. [Similarly, the] right of commercial speech [might be] necessarily incidental to the business of a commercial corporation. [But it] cannot be so readily concluded that the right of political expression is equally necessary to carry out the functions of a corporation organized for commercial purposes. A State grants to a business corporation the blessings of potentially perpetual life and limited liability to enhance its efficiency as an economic entity. It might reasonably [conclude] that those properties, so beneficial in the economic sphere, pose special dangers in the political sphere."

AUSTIN v. MICHIGAN CHAMBER OF COMMERCE, 494 U.S. 652 (1990). The Court, in a six-to-three decision, upheld section 54(1) of the Michigan Campaign Finance Act, which prohibited corporations from using corporate treasury funds for independent expenditures in support of or in opposition to any candidate for state office, but allowed corporations to make such expenditures from segregated funds used solely for political purposes.

In an opinion by Justice Marshall, the Court observed that "the unique legal and economic characteristics of corporations" — such as "limited liability, perpetual life, and favorable treatment of the accumulation and distribution of assets" — enable corporations "to use 'resources amassed in the economic marketplace' to obtain 'an unfair advantage in the political marketplace.'" The Court explained that "the political advantage of corporations is unfair because '[t]he resources in the treasury of a business corporation [are] not an indication of popular support for the corporation's political ideas. They reflect instead the economically motivated decisions of investors and customers. The availability of these resources may make a corporation a formidable political presence, even though the power of the corporation may be no reflection of the power of its ideas.'"

Noting that section 54(1) was designed to deal with "the corrosive and distorting effects of immense aggregations of wealth that are accumulated with the help of the corporate form and that have little or no correlation to the public's support for the corporation's political ideas," rather than "'to equalize the relative influence of speakers on elections,'" the Court held that "the State has articulated a sufficiently compelling rationale to support its restriction on independent expenditures by corporations."

The Court also held that the act is "sufficiently narrowly tailored to achieve its goal" because it is "precisely targeted to eliminate the distortion caused by corporate political spending while also allowing corporations to express their political views [through] separate segregated funds." The Court explained that because "persons contributing to such funds understand that their money will be used solely for political purposes, the speech generated accurately reflects contributors' support for the corporation's political views."

Justice Scalia dissented: "[Corporations] are, to be sure, given special advantages, [but] so are other associations and private individuals, [ranging] from tax breaks to contract awards to public employment to outright cash subsidies. It is rudimentary that the State cannot exact as the price of those special advantages the forfeiture of First Amendment rights. [Moreover], the fact that corporations

'amas[s] large treasuries' [is] not sufficient justification for the suppression of political speech, unless one thinks it would be lawful to prohibit men and women
whose net worth is above a certain figure from endorsing political candidates.
[The] Court's opinion ultimately rests upon [the] proposition [that] expenditures
must 'reflect actual public support for the political ideas espoused.' [But why] is
it perfectly all right if advocacy by an individual billionaire is out of proportion
with 'actual public support' for his positions? There is no explanation. [The] object of the law we have approved today is not to prevent wrongdoing but to prevent speech. Since those private associations known as corporations have so
much money, they will speak so much more, and their views will be given inor-
dinate prominence in election campaigns. This is not an argument that our democratic traditions allow."

Justice Kennedy, joined by Justices O'Connor and Scalia, also dissented: "The
argument that the availability of a PAC as an alternative means can save a restriction on independent corporate expenditures [is undermined by the fact that
it is] a costly and burdensome disincentive to speech. [Between] 25 and 50 percent of a PAC's funds are required to establish and administer the PAC. While the
corporation can direct the PAC to make expenditures on behalf of candidates,
the PAC can be funded only by contributions from shareholders, directors, officers, and managerial employees, and cannot receive corporate treasury funds.
[This] secondhand endorsement structure [debases] the voice [of] corporate
speakers."

Note: Additional Regulation of the Electoral Process

1. *Regulating political action committees.* The Court has handed down several
decisions concerning political action committees (PACs) and related organizations. See, e.g., Federal Election Commission v. National Conservative Political Action Committee, 470 U.S. 480 (1985) (invalidating a statute prohibiting
any independent political action committee to spend more than $1,000 to fur-
ther the election of a presidential candidate who receives public financing); Federal Election Commission v. National Right to Work Committee, 459 U.S. 197
(1982) (upholding a statute prohibiting nonstock corporations from soliciting
contributions from persons other than their "members" for the purpose of generating funds to be spent in federal election campaigns); Citizens against Rent
Control v. Berkeley, 454 U.S. 290 (1981) (invalidating an ordinance imposing a
$250 limit on contributions to committees formed to support or oppose ballot
measures submitted to a popular vote); California Medical Association v. Federal
Election Commission, 453 U.S. 182 (1981) (upholding a statute prohibiting individuals and unincorporated associations from contributing more than $5,000
per year to any multicandidate political committee).

2. *Regulating political parties.* After *Buckley,* can the government constitutionally limit the amount a political party can spend in support of its own candidates? Are such expenditures "contributions" or "expenditures" within the meaning of *Buckley?* See Colorado Republican Federal Campaign Committee v.
Federal Election Commission, 518 U.S. 604 (1996), in which the Court held
that the first amendment prohibits the application of a provision of the Federal
Election Campaign Act that imposes dollar limits on political party "expendi-

tures in connection with the general election campaign of a [congressional] candidate," at least where the political party makes the expenditures "independently, without coordination with a candidate."

3. *Prohibiting paid petitioners.* In Meyer v. Grant, 486 U.S. 414 (1988), the Court invalidated a Colorado statute prohibiting the use of paid circulators to obtain signatures for petitions to qualify proposed state constitutional amendments for inclusion on the general election ballot:

> The refusal to permit appellees to pay petition circulators restricts political expression in two ways: First, it limits the number of voices who will convey appellees' message and the hours they can speak and, therefore, limits the size of the audience they can reach. Second, it makes it less likely that appellees will garner the number of signatures necessary to place the matter on the ballot, thus limiting their ability to make the matter the focus of statewide attention. [Colorado's] prohibition of paid petition circulators restricts access to the most effective, fundamental, and perhaps economical avenue of political discourse, direct one-on-one communication. That it leaves open "more burdensome" avenues of communication does not relieve its burden on First Amendment expression. The First Amendment protects appellees' right not only to advocate their cause but also to select what they believe to be the most effective means for so doing. [We] are not persuaded [that] the prohibition is justified by its interest in making sure that an initiative has sufficient grass roots support to be placed on the ballot, or by its interest in protecting the integrity of the initiative process.

See also Buckley v. American Constitutional Law Foundation, 525 U.S. 182 (1999), in which the Court, relying upon *Meyer,* invalidated a state law providing that (a) only registered voters may circulate ballot initiative petitions; (b) petition circulators must wear a badge identifying them by name; and (c) ballot initiative proponents must file a report listing each petition circulator by name and stating the amount paid to each circulator.

4. *Regulating campaign promises.* In Brown v. Hartlage, 456 U.S. 46 (1982), petitioner, a candidate for local office in Kentucky, promised the voters that, if elected, he would reduce the salary of the office "to a more realistic level." Petitioner was elected, but a state court declared the election void on the ground that petitioner had violated Kentucky's Corrupt Practices Act. The Court reversed:

> The [Act] prohibits a political candidate from giving, or promising to give, anything of value to a voter in exchange for his vote or support. In many of its possible applications, this provision would appear to present little constitutional difficulty, for a State may surely prohibit a candidate from buying votes. [But] it is equally plain that there are constitutional limits on the State's power to prohibit candidates from making promises in the course of an election campaign. [Candidate] commitments enhance the accountability of government officials [and] assist the voters in predicting the effect of their vote. . . .
>
> [Here, petitioner's promise] was made openly, subject to the comment and criticism of his political opponent and to the scrutiny of the voters. [He] did not offer the voters a payment from his personal funds. His was a declaration of intention to exercise the fiscal powers of government office within what he believed [to] be the recognized framework of office. [Moreover, the] benefit was to extend beyond those voters who cast their ballots for [petitioner], to all taxpayers and citizens. [Thus, like] a promise to lower taxes, to increase efficiency in government, or indeed to increase taxes in order to provide some group with a desired public benefit or public

service, [petitioner's] promise to reduce his salary cannot be deemed beyond the reach of the First Amendment, or considered as inviting the kind of corrupt arrangement the appearance of which a State may have a compelling interest in avoiding. See [*Buckley*].

5. *Ballot access and the role of political parties.* See, e.g., Anderson v. Celebrezze, 460 U.S. 780 (1983) (invalidating a statute requiring independent candidates to file their nominating petitions in mid-March in order to qualify for the ballot in the November election); Tashjian v. Republican Party, 479 U.S. 208 (1987) (invalidating a statute prohibiting independents from voting in party primaries); Eu v. San Francisco County Democratic Central Committee, 490 U.S. 214 (1989) (invalidating a statute prohibiting political parties from endorsing, supporting, or opposing candidates in primary elections); Burdick v. Takushi, 504 U.S. 428 (1992) (upholding a statute prohibiting write-in voting); Timmons v. Twin Cities Area New Party, 520 U.S. 351 (1997) (upholding a ban on multi-party, or "fusion," candidacies); California Democratic Party v. Jones, 120 S. Ct. 2402 (2000) (invalidating a state law permitting individuals who are not members of a political party to vote in that party's primary).

6. *State contribution limits and the future of* Buckley. In Nixon v. Shrink Missouri Government PAC, 523 U.S. 666 (2000), the Court upheld a Missouri statute imposing limits ranging from $275 to $1,075 on contributions to candidates for state offices (different limits were applicable to different offices). In an opinion by Justice Souter, the Court held that *Buckley* "is authority for state limits on contributions to state political candidates" and that it authorizes "comparable state regulation, which need not be pegged to *Buckley*'s dollars." The Court rejected the argument that "*Buckley* set a minimum constitutional threshold for contribution limits, which in dollars adjusted for loss of purchasing power are now well above the lines drawn by Missouri." Rather, in "*Buckley*, we specifically rejected the contention that $1,000, or any other amount, was a constitutional minimum below which legislatures could not regulate. [W]e referred instead to the outer limits of contribution regulation by asking whether there was any showing that the limits were so low as to impede the ability of candidates to 'amas[s] the resources necessary for effective advocacy.'" The Court found no such showing in this case.

Justice Kennedy dissented: "[T]he compromise the Court invented in *Buckley* set the stage for a new kind of speech to enter the political system. It is covert speech. The Court has forced a substantial amount of political speech underground, as contributors and candidates devise ever more elaborate methods of avoiding contribution limits, limits which take no account of rising campaign costs. The preferred method has been to conceal the real purpose of the speech. Soft money may be contributed to political parties in unlimited amounts, and is often used to fund so-called issue advocacy, advertisements that promote or attack a candidate's positions without specifically urging his or her election or defeat. Issue advocacy, like soft money, is unrestricted, while straightforward speech in the form of financial contributions paid to a candidate, speech subject to full disclosure and prompt evaluation by the public, is not. [This] mocks the First Amendment. [I] would overrule *Buckley*. . . ."

Justice Thomas, joined by Justice Scalia, also dissented: "[O]ur decision in *Buckley* was in error, and I would overrule it. I would subject campaign contribution limitations to strict scrutiny, under which Missouri's contribution limits are patently unconstitutional. ['P]reventing corruption or the appearance of corruption' are [legitimate] and compelling interests, [but] the State's contribution limits are not narrowly tailored to that harm. The limits directly suppress the political speech of both contributors and candidates, and only clumsily further the governmental interests that they allegedly serve. They are crudely tailored because they are massively overinclusive, prohibiting all donors who wish to contribute in excess of the cap from doing so and restricting donations without regard to whether the donors pose any real corruption risk. [Moreover], the government has less restrictive means of addressing its interest in curtailing corruption. Bribery laws bar precisely the *quid pro quo* arrangements that are targeted here. And disclosure laws 'deter actual corruption and avoid the appearance of corruption by exposing large contributions and expenditures to the light of publicity.' [In] the end, contribution limits find support only in the proposition that other means will not be as effective at rooting out corruption. But when it comes to a significant infringement on our fundamental liberties, that some undesirable conduct may or may not be deterred is an insufficient justification to sweep in vast amounts of protected political speech. [Citing Martin v. Struthers; Schneider v. State, both section E1 supra.]"

Note: *Regulating the Political Activities of Public Employees*

1. *Partisan political activity.* U.S. Civil Service Commission v. National Association of Letter Carriers, 413 U.S. 548 (1973), concerned the constitutionality of §9(a) of the Hatch Act, now codified in 5 U.S.C. §7324(a)(2), which prohibits federal employees from taking "an active part in political management or in political campaigns." Specifically, the act prohibits federal employees from soliciting contributions for a partisan political purpose, taking an active part in a political campaign, soliciting votes for any candidate, or endorsing any candidate. The Court, in an opinion by Justice White, expressly reaffirmed United Public Workers v. Mitchell, 330 U.S. 75 (1947), and upheld the Act:

> [Until] after the Civil War, the spoils system under which federal employees came and went depending upon party service and changing administrations, was the prevalent basis for governmental employment and advancement. [That] system did not survive. [It is now] the judgment of Congress, the Executive, and the country [that] partisan political activities by federal employees must be limited if the Government is to operate effectively and fairly, elections are to play their proper part in representative government, and employees themselves are to be sufficiently free from improper influences. The restrictions [imposed] on federal employees are not aimed at particular parties, groups, or points of view, but apply equally to all partisan activities of the type described. . . .
>
> [The] problem in any case is to arrive at a balance between the interests of the [employee] and the [interests] of the [government]. Although Congress is free to strike a different balance than it has, [we] think the balance it [has] struck is sustainable by the obviously important interests sought to be served by [the] Hatch Act.
>
> It seems fundamental [that] employees [of] the Government [should] administer the law in accordance with the will of Congress, rather than in accordance with

[the] will of a political party. [Moreover,] it is not only important that [Government] employees in fact avoid practicing political justice, but [also] that they appear to the public to be avoiding it, if confidence in the system of representative Government is not to be eroded. [Another] major concern [is] the conviction that the rapidly expanding Government work force should not be employed to build a powerful, invincible, and perhaps corrupt political machine. [A] related concern [is] to make sure that Government employees [are] free from pressure [to] vote in a certain way or perform political chores in order to curry favor with their superiors rather than to act out of their own beliefs. It may be urged that prohibitions against coercion are sufficient protection; but for many years the joint judgment of the Executive and Congress has been that to protect the rights of federal employees [it] is not enough merely to forbid one employee to attempt to influence or coerce another. [Perhaps] Congress at some time will come to a different view of the realities of political life and Government service; but that is its current view of the matter, and we are not now in any position to dispute it. [In light of these interests,] identifiable acts of political management and political campaigning on the part of federal employees may constitutionally be prohibited. . . .

Justice Douglas, joined by Justices Brennan and Marshall, dissented: "The Hatch Act [prohibits] federal employees from taking 'an active part in political management or in political campaigns.' [No] one could object if employees were barred from using office time to engage in outside activities whether political or otherwise. But it is of no concern of Government what an employee does in his spare time, [unless] what he does impairs efficiency or other facets of the merits of his job. Some [activities may] affect the employee's job performance. But his political creed, like his religion, is irrelevant. In the areas of speech, like religion, it is of no concern what the employee says in private to his wife or to the public in Constitution Hall."

In Broadrick v. Oklahoma, 413 U.S. 601 (1973), decided on the same day as *Letter Carriers*, the Court upheld Oklahoma's Merit System of Personnel Administration Act, which "serves roughly the same function as the analogous provisions of the other 49 States, and is patterned on §9(a) of the Hatch Act." Appellants, several state employees charged with violating the Oklahoma act, maintained that the act was unconstitutionally overbroad because it had been construed to prohibit public employees from wearing political buttons and displaying political bumper stickers. Finding that appellants' own activities could clearly be proscribed, and that the act was not "substantially" overbroad, the Court found it unnecessary to decide the overbreadth issue. See section C1 supra. Can Oklahoma constitutionally prohibit its public employees from wearing political buttons and displaying political bumper stickers? For an interesting variation, see United States v. National Treasury Employees Union, 513 U.S. 454 (1995) (invalidating a provision of the Ethics in Government Act that prohibited a broad class of government employees from accepting any compensation for making speeches or writing articles without regard to whether the subject of the speech or article or the person or group paying the honorarium had any connection with the employee's official duties).

2. *Criticizing government policy.* In Pickering v. Board of Education, 391 U.S. 563 (1968), a teacher was dismissed from his position by the Board of Education for sending a letter to a local newspaper in connection with a recently proposed tax increase that was critical of the way in which the board and the district su-

perintendent of schools had handled past proposals to raise new revenue for the schools. The teacher's dismissal resulted from a determination by the board, after a full hearing, that the publication of the letter was "detrimental to the efficient operation and administration of the schools of the district." The Court, in an opinion by Justice Marshall, held that the teacher's right to freedom of speech had been violated:

> The problem in any case is to arrive at a balance between the interests of the teacher, as a citizen, in commenting upon matters of public concern and the interest of the State, as an employer, in promoting the efficiency of the public services it performs through its employees. . . .
>
> An examination of the statements in appellant's letter objected to by the Board reveals that [they] consist essentially of criticism of the Board's allocation of school funds between educational and athletic programs. [The] statements are in no way directed towards any person with whom appellant would normally be in contact in the course of his daily work as a teacher. Thus no question of maintaining either discipline by immediate superiors or harmony among coworkers is presented here. Appellant's employment relationships with the Board and, to a somewhat lesser extent, with the superintendent are not the kind of close working relationships for which it can persuasively be claimed that personal loyalty and confidence are necessary to their proper functioning. Accordingly, to the extent that the Board's position here can be taken to suggest that even comments on matters of public concern that are substantially correct [may] furnish grounds for dismissal if they are sufficiently critical in tone, we unequivocally reject it.

Suppose the teacher's speech had been personal in nature — for example, suppose the teacher had made statements critical of another teacher's driving, causing tension between them. Would *Pickering* govern? See Connick v. Meyers, 461 U.S. 138 (1983) ("when employee expression cannot fairly be considered as relating to any matter of political, social, or other concern to the community, [but concerns only matters of personal interest,] officials should enjoy wide latitude in managing their offices, without intrusive oversight by the judiciary in the name of the First Amendment"); Rankin v. McPherson, 483 U.S. 378 (1987) (*Pickering* rather than *Connick* governs in a situation in which a clerical employee in the office of a county constable was fired because, after hearing of an assassination attempt against the President, she remarked to a coworker, "If they go for him again, I hope they get him," because the remark constituted speech "on a matter of public concern").

Suppose the teacher's statements in *Pickering* had been false? The Court noted in *Pickering* that "in a case such as this, absent proof of false statements knowingly or recklessly made by him, a teacher's exercise of his right to speak on issues of public importance may not furnish the basis for his dismissal from public employment." On related issues, see Waters v. Churchill, 511 U.S. 661 (1994) (there is no violation of the first amendment when a government employer fires an employee for constitutionally protected speech if the employer reasonably believed that the speech was unprotected); Board of County Commissioners, Wabaunsee County, Kansas v. Umbehr, 518 U.S. 668 (1996) (independent contractors are governed by *Pickering*); O'Hare Truck Service, Inc. v. City of Northlake, 518 U.S. 712 (1996) (same); Gentile v. State Bar of Nevada, 501 U.S. 1030 (1991) (government licensees, such as attorneys participating in judicial proceedings, are governed by *Pickering*).

3. *Patronage.* In December 1970, the Sheriff of Cook County, Illinois, a Republican, was replaced by Richard Elrod, a Democrat. At that time, respondents, all Republicans, were non-civil service employees of the Cook County Sheriff's Office. Respondent Burns was a process server; respondent Vargas was a bailiff and security guard. Following prior practice, Sheriff Elrod discharged respondents from their employment solely because they did not support and were not members of the Democratic Party. In Elrod v. Burns, 427 U.S. 347 (1976), the Court held this practice unconstitutional. In a plurality opinion, Justice Brennan explained:

> The [practice] of dismissing employees on a partisan basis [is] one form of the general practice of political patronage. Patronage practice is not new to American politics. It has existed at the federal level at least since the Presidency of Thomas Jefferson. [More] recent times have witnessed a strong decline in its use, [however, and] merit systems have increasingly displaced the practice. [The] cost of the practice of patronage is the restraint it places on freedoms of belief and association. In order to maintain their jobs, respondents were required to pledge their political allegiance to the Democratic Party, work for the election of other candidates of the Democratic Party, contribute a portion of their wages to the Party, or obtain the sponsorship of a member of the Party, usually at the price of one of the first three alternatives. [An] individual who is a member of the out-party maintains affiliation with his own party at the risk of losing his job. He works for the election of his party's candidates and espouses its policies at the same risk. The financial and campaign assistance that he is induced to provide to another party furthers the advancement of that party's policies to the detriment of his party's views and ultimately his own beliefs....
>
> One interest which has been offered in justification of patronage is the need to insure effective government and the efficiency of public employees. It is argued that employees of political persuasions not the same as that of the party in control of public office will not have the incentive to work effectively and may even be motivated to subvert the incumbent administration's efforts to govern effectively. We are not persuaded. [It] is doubtful that the mere difference of political persuasion motivates poor performance. [At] all events, less drastic means for insuring government effectiveness and employee efficiency are available to the State. Specifically, employees may always be discharged for good cause, such as insubordination or poor job performance, when those bases in fact exist....
>
> A second interest advanced in support of patronage is the need for political loyalty of employees [to] the end that representative government not be undercut by tactics obstructing the implementation of policies of the new administration, policies presumably sanctioned by the electorate. The justification is not without force, but is nevertheless inadequate to validate patronage wholesale. Limiting patronage dismissals to policymaking positions is sufficient to achieve this governmental end. Nonpolicymaking individuals usually have only limited responsibility and are therefore not in a position to thwart the goals of the in-party....
>
> It is argued that a third interest supporting patronage dismissals is the preservation of the democratic process. [This] is certainly an interest the protection of which may in some instances justify limitations on First Amendment freedoms. See [*Buckley; Letter Carriers*]. But however important preservation of the two-party system [may be,] we are not persuaded that the elimination of patronage practice [will] bring about the demise of party politics. Political parties existed in the ab-

sence of active patronage practice [and] they have survived substantial reduction
in their patronage power through the establishment of merit systems. [The] gain to
representative government provided by the practice of patronage, if any, would be
insufficient to justify its sacrifice of First Amendment rights. . . .

Justice Powell, joined by Chief Justice Burger and Justice Rehnquist, dissented:

[Patronage] hiring practices have contributed to American democracy by stimulat-
ing political activity and by strengthening parties, thereby helping to make government accountable. It cannot be questioned seriously that these contributions
promote important state interests. [For example,] election campaigns for lesser
offices [usually] attract little attention from the media. [Unless] the candidates for
these offices are able to dispense the traditional patronage that has accrued to the
offices, they also are unlikely to attract donations of time or money from voluntary
groups. [Thus, the] activities of [patronage supporters] are often the principal
source of political information for the voting public. [It] is naive to think that these
types of political activities are motivated at these levels by some academic interest
in "democracy" or other public service impulse. For the most part, as every politician knows, the hope of some reward generates a major portion of the local political activity supporting parties.

See also Branti v. Finkel, 445 U.S. 507 (1980) (the position of assistant public
defender is not a "policymaking" position within the meaning of *Elrod* and the
first amendment therefore prohibits the discharge of two assistant public defenders solely because they were Republicans and were unable to provide the necessary Democratic sponsorship when a Democratic Public Defender took office);
Rutan v. Republican Party of Illinois, 497 U.S. 62 (1990) (rejecting the argument
that "only those employment decisions that are the 'substantial equivalent of a
dismissal' violate a public employee's rights under the first amendment" and
holding that *Elrod* also governs decisions about hiring, "promotions, transfers
and recalls after layoffs based on political affiliation or support"); O'Hare Truck
Service, Inc. v. City of Northlake, 518 U.S. 712 (1996) (*Elrod* protects independent contractors as well as government employees).

Precisely how does patronage impair the first amendment interests of public
employees? In *Elrod,* the plurality noted that patronage may both prevent an employee from supporting the party of his choice and "compel" him to support a
party he opposes. Which concern, if either, is dominant? Is there a first amendment right not to support the promulgation of views with which one disagrees?
The right not to speak is examined in section E5 infra.

5.   *Other Means of Expression: Litigation, Association, and the Right* Not *to Speak*

NAACP v. BUTTON, 371 U.S. 415 (1963). For more than a decade, the Virginia Conference of the NAACP had financed litigation aimed at ending racial
segregation in the public schools of Virginia. In 1956, the Virginia legislature enacted chapter 33, which prohibited any organization to retain a lawyer in connection with litigation to which it was not a party and in which it had no pecu-

niary right or liability. The Supreme Court held that, as applied to the NAACP's activities, chapter 33 violated the first amendment. Justice Brennan delivered the opinion:

"In the context of NAACP objectives, litigation is not a technique of resolving private differences; it is a means for [achieving] equality of treatment [for] the members of the Negro [community]. It is [a] form of political expression. Groups which find themselves unable to achieve their objectives through the ballot frequently turn to the courts. [Moreover,] there is no longer any doubt that the First and Fourteenth Amendments protect certain forms of orderly group activity. Thus we have affirmed the right 'to engage in association for the advancement of beliefs and ideas.' [The] NAACP is not a conventional political party; but [for the group] it assists, [association] for litigation may be the most effective form of political association.

"[Under] Chapter 33, [a] person who advises another that his legal rights have been infringed and refers him to a particular attorney [for] assistance has committed a [crime]. There thus inheres in the statute the gravest danger of smothering all discussion looking to the eventual institution of litigation on behalf of the rights of members of an unpopular minority. [We] cannot close our eyes to the fact that the militant Negro civil rights movement has engendered the intense resentment and opposition of the politically dominant white community of Virginia; litigation assisted by the NAACP has been bitterly fought. In such circumstances, a statute broadly curtailing group activity leading to litigation may easily become a weapon of oppression, however even-handed its terms appear. Its mere existence could well freeze out of existence all such activity on behalf of the civil rights of Negro citizens.

"It is apparent, therefore, that Chapter 33 as construed limits First Amendment freedoms. [This] Court has consistently held that only a compelling state interest [can] justify limiting First Amendment freedoms. [However] valid may be Virginia's interest in regulating the traditionally illegal practices of barratry, maintenance and champerty, that interest does not justify the prohibition of the NAACP activities disclosed by this record. Malicious intent was the essence of the common-law offenses of fomenting or stirring up litigation. [The exercise] of First Amendment rights to enforce constitutional rights through litigation, as a matter of law, cannot be deemed malicious. . . ."

Justice White concurred in part and dissented in part.

Justice Harlan, joined by Justices Clark and Stewart, dissented: "Freedom of expression embraces more than the right of an individual to speak his mind. It includes also his right to advocate and his right to join with his fellows in an effort to make that advocacy effective. And just as it includes the right jointly to petition the legislature for redress of grievances, so it must include the right to join together for purposes of obtaining judicial redress. . . .

"But to declare that litigation is a form of conduct that may be associated with political expression does not resolve this case. [For this Court has repeatedly held that] 'general regulatory statutes, not intended to control the content of speech but incidentally limiting its unfettered exercise,' are permissible 'when they have been found justified by subordinating valid governmental interests.' . . .

"The interest which Virginia has asserted is that of maintaining high professional standards among those who practice law within its borders. [The Court's analysis of this interest is] too facile. [When] an attorney is employed by an asso-

ciation [to] represent individual litigants, [the] lawyer necessarily finds himself
with a divided allegiance — to his employer and to his client — which may prevent full compliance with his basic professional obligations. [For example], it
may be in the interest of the [NAACP] in every case [to] press for an immediate
breaking down of racial [barriers]. But in a particular litigation, [a] Negro parent,
concerned that a continued frontal attack could result in schools closed for years,
might prefer to wait [a] longer time for good-faith efforts by the local school board
than is permitted by the centrally determined policy of the NAACP. [Is the]
lawyer, retained and paid by petitioner and subject to its directions on matters of
policy, able to advise the parent with that undivided allegiance that is the hallmark of the attorney-client relation? I am afraid not. . . .

"The important function of organizations like petitioner in vindicating constitutional rights is [not] substantially impaired by this statute. [This] enactment
[does] not in any way suppress [advocacy] of litigation in general or in particular.
[Moreover, it does not] prevent petitioner from recommending the services of attorneys who are not subject to its directions and control. [It] prevents only the solicitation of business for attorneys subject to petitioner's control, and as so limited, should be sustained."

Note: Litigation and the First Amendment

1. Button *in context.* Consider H. Kalven, The Negro and the First Amendment 66-69, 75-79 (1965):

> One of the most distinctive features of the Negro revolution [of the 1950s and
> 1960s was] its almost military assault on the Constitution via the strategy of sys-
> tematic litigation. [To] a South hostile to [Brown v. Board of Education], the
> NAACP appeared, and accurately, as a militant army led by lawyers determined to
> see to it that "all deliberate speed" [would] have some meaning. [Chapter 33 was
> designed] to slow down [NAACP litigation]. Unless the NAACP [could go] out and
> sign up the client, pay for the case, and deliver the client to one of its expert lawyers,
> it [would have been] unable to recruit the needed flow of litigation. Unless it
> [could] control the timing and line of attack in the litigation once it was begun, its
> grand strategy of war by lawsuit [would have been] frustrated. [The] case thus raised
> a profound question for our scheme of constitutional adjudication.

2. *Litigation as "speech."* Why does *Button* pose a first amendment issue? Because the law might be discriminatorily applied against persons espousing a
particular view? Because association for the purpose of litigation is "speech"? Because litigation is "speech"? Because litigation is "speech" when it attempts to enforce constitutional rights?

3. *The reach of* Button: Primus. In In re Primus, 436 U.S. 412 (1978), an
ACLU "cooperating lawyer" wrote a letter to a woman who had been sterilized,
informing her of the ACLU's willingness to provide free legal representation to
women in her position in a proposed lawsuit challenging the constitutionality of
an alleged program of sterilizing pregnant mothers as a condition of their continued receipt of Medicaid benefits. The Disciplinary Board of the South Carolina Supreme Court reprimanded the ACLU lawyer for violating a disciplinary

rule prohibiting any "lawyer who has given unsolicited advice to a layman that he should [take] legal action [to] accept employment resulting from that advice."

The Court held the reprimand unconstitutional. The Court emphasized that "for the ACLU, as for the NAACP, 'litigation is not a technique of resolving private differences'; it is 'a form of political expression' and 'political association.'" To justify a restriction on such "'core First Amendment rights,'" the state must demonstrate that the attorney's "activity in fact involved the type of misconduct at which South Carolina's [prohibition on solicitation] is said to be directed." Since the record did "not support [the state's] contention that undue influence, overreaching, misrepresentation, or invasion of privacy [had] actually occurred," the reprimand violated the first amendment.

See also United Transportation Union v. State Bar of Michigan, 401 U.S. 576 (1971) (invalidating an injunction prohibiting the union from recommending attorneys to its members only if the attorneys agreed that their fees would not exceed 25 percent of the recovery); United Mine Workers v. Illinois Bar Association, 389 U.S. 217 (1967) (invalidating an injunction prohibiting the union from employing a salaried attorney to assist its members with workers' compensation claims); Brotherhood of Railroad Trainmen v. Virginia State Bar, 377 U.S. 1 (1964) (invalidating an injunction prohibiting a union from recommending lawyers to its members to represent them in railroad personal injury litigation).

4. *The reach of* Button: Ohralik. In Ohralik v. Ohio State Bar Association, 436 U.S. 447 (1978), decided on the same day as *Primus*, appellant, an attorney, after learning about an automobile accident, personally contacted two young women who had been injured in the accident and arranged to represent them in subsequent litigation. As a result of this "ambulance chasing," Ohralik was suspended by the Ohio State Bar for violation of a disciplinary rule prohibiting any "lawyer who has given unsolicited advice to a layman that he should obtain counsel" to accept "employment resulting from that advice."

The Court upheld the suspension. The Court explained that *Ohralik* was not governed by *Button* and *Primus*, for appellant's "approaches to the young women [did not involve] political expression or an exercise of associational freedom '[to] secure constitutionally guaranteed civil rights.'" Moreover, *Ohralik* was not governed by the union cases, for "[appellant cannot] compare his solicitation to the mutual assistance in asserting legal rights that was at issue [in those cases]." Indeed, a "lawyer's procurement of remunerative employment is a subject only marginally affected with First Amendment concerns. It falls within the State's proper sphere of economic and professional regulation." Appellant's conduct, the Court added, was analogous to commercial expression, which occupies only a "subordinate position in the scale of First Amendment values." Accordingly, it was unnecessary for the state to prove that appellant's act of solicitation involved any actual abuse or caused any actual harm to his "clients." Rather, the prohibition could constitutionally be applied wherever, as in *Ohralik*, an attorney for remunerative purposes "personally solicits an unsophisticated, injured, or distressed lay person," for in such circumstances there is present a "potential for overreaching," and the solicitation is thus "likely to result in the adverse consequences the State seeks to avert."

ROBERTS v. U.S. JAYCEES, 468 U.S. 609 (1984). The Jaycees is a nonprofit membership corporation whose objective is to provide young men with an "opportunity for personal development and achievement and an avenue for intelligent participation [in] the affairs of [the] community." Regular membership in the Jaycees is limited to men between the ages of eighteen and thirty-five. Associate membership is open to older men and to women. Associate members may not vote, hold office, or participate in certain leadership training programs. The Minnesota Department of Human Rights found that the Jaycees' membership policy violated the Minnesota Human Rights Act, which prohibits discrimination on the basis of sex. The Court held that the act does not violate the first amendment right of association. Justice Brennan delivered the opinion of the Court:

"[We have long] recognized a right to associate for the purpose of engaging in those activities protected by the First Amendment, [for an] individual's freedom to speak [and] to petition the Government for the redress of grievances could not be vigorously protected [unless] a correlative freedom to engage in group effort toward those ends were not also guaranteed. [There] can be no clearer example of an intrusion into the internal structure [of] an association than a regulation that forces the group to accept members it does not desire. . . .

"The right to associate for expressive purposes is not, however, absolute. Infringements on that right may be justified by regulations adopted to serve compelling state interests, unrelated to the suppression of ideas, that cannot be achieved through means significantly less restrictive of associational freedoms. [We] are persuaded that Minnesota's compelling interest in eradicating discrimination against its female citizens justifies the impact that application of the statute to the Jaycees may have on the male members' associational freedoms. . . .

"[The challenged act] does not aim at the suppression of speech [and it] does not distinguish between prohibited and permitted activity on the basis of viewpoint. [The] Act reflects the State's strong historical commitment to eliminating [discrimination]. That goal, which is unrelated to the suppression of expression, plainly serves compelling state interests of the highest order. . . .

"[Moreover], the Jaycees have failed to demonstrate that the Act imposes any serious burdens on the male members' freedom of expressive association. [To] be sure, [a] 'not insubstantial part' of the Jaycees' activities constitutes protected expression on political, economic, cultural, and social affairs. [There] is, however, no basis [for] concluding that admission of women as full voting members will impede the organization's ability to engage in these protected activities or to disseminate its preferred views. The Act requires no change in the Jaycees' creed of promoting the interests of young men, and it imposes no restrictions on the organization's ability to exclude individuals with ideologies [different] from those of its existing members. . . .

"It [is] arguable that, insofar as the Jaycees is organized to promote the views of young [men], admission of women as voting members will change the message communicated by the group's [speech]. [In] claiming that women might have a different attitude about such issues as the federal budget, school prayer, voting rights, and foreign relations, [the] Jaycees rely solely on unsupported generalizations about the relative interests and perspectives of men and women. Although such generalizations may or may not have a statistical basis in fact with respect to particular positions adopted by the Jaycees, we have repeatedly condemned legal decisionmaking that relies uncritically on such assumptions. [In] the absence of a showing far more substantial than that attempted by the Jaycees, we decline to indulge in the sexual stereotyping that underlies the [contention] that, by allowing women to vote, the [act] will change the content or impact of the organization's speech."

Justices O'Connor and Rehnquist concurred in the judgment. Chief Justice Burger and Justice Blackmun did not participate.

Note: Association and the First Amendment

1. *Incidental restrictions.* Note that analytically *Roberts* is a variant of *O'Brien.* That is, in both cases a law that arguably was not directed at expression was challenged on the ground that it had an incidental effect on speech. Recall NAACP v. Alabama and *Barnes.* In what circumstances does a law that has only an incidental effect on speech violate the first amendment?

2. *The reach of* Roberts: *social and business clubs.* In Board of Directors of Rotary International v. Rotary Club of Duarte, 481 U.S. 537 (1987), the Court unanimously upheld a California antidiscrimination statute that required the Rotary Club to admit women. The Court explained that, although "the right to engage in activities protected by the First Amendment implies 'a corresponding right to associate with others in pursuit of a wide variety of political, social, economic, educational, religious, and cultural ends,' [the] evidence [in this case] fails to demonstrate that admitting women to Rotary Clubs will affect in any significant way the existing members' ability to carry out their various purposes." See also New York State Club Association, Inc. v. City of New York, 487 U.S. 1 (1988) (upholding a New York City human rights law that banned discrimination on the basis of race, creed, or sex in any institution, club, or place of accommodation that has more than 400 members, provides regular meal service, and regularly receives payment from nonmembers for the furtherance of trade or business).

3. *The reach of* Roberts: *political associations.* After *Roberts,* can a state prohibit the Nazi Party of America from excluding Jews? Is that case different because the Nazis, unlike the Jaycees, are engaged principally in political expression? Is it different because the admission of Jews would *symbolically* interfere with the essential message of the party? In *Roberts,* the Court rejected the argument that the act was invalid as applied to the Jaycees because the admission of women would interfere with the symbolic message inherent in an all-male organization: "[Even] if enforcement of the Act causes some incidental abridgment of the Jaycees' protected speech, that effect is no greater than is necessary to accomplish the State's legitimate purposes. [Like] violence or other types of potentially expressive activities that produce special harms distinct from their communicative impact, [discrimination on the basis of gender is] entitled to no constitutional protection."

After *Roberts,* can a state permit Republicans to vote in a Democratic primary? See California Democratic Party v. Jones, 120 S. Ct. 2402 (2000), in which the Court held that a state may not permit individuals who are not members of a political party to vote in that party's primary. The Court explained that such a law "forces political parties to associate with — to have their nominees and hence their positions, determined by — those who, at best, have refused to affiliate with the party, and, at worst, have expressly affiliated with a rival." The Court explained that "freedom of association would prove an empty guarantee if associations could not limit control over their decisions to those who share the interests and persuasions that underlie the association's being."

Cf. Rosario v. Rockefeller, 410 U.S. 752 (1973) (upholding a New York statute requiring voters to register their party affiliation eleven months prior to the next party primary in order to inhibit "party raiding"); Storer v. Brown, 415 U.S. 724 (1974) (upholding a California statute forbidding ballot position to an independent candidate who "had a registered affiliation with [any] political parties at any time within one year prior to the immediately preceding primary election"); Tashjian v. Republican Party, 479 U.S. 208 (1987) (invalidating a state law prohibiting independents from voting in party primaries).

4. *The reach of* Roberts: *the Boy Scouts.* In Boy Scouts of America v. Dale, 120 S. Ct. 2446 (2000), Dale's position as an adult scoutmaster in the Boy Scouts was revoked when the Boy Scouts learned that he is an "avowed homosexual" and a gay rights activist. New Jersey's public accommodations law, which prohibits discrimination on the basis of sexual orientation, was interpreted by the New Jersey courts to prohibit the Boy Scouts from revoking Dale's position. The Court, in a five-to-four decision, held that this application of the New Jersey public accommodations law violates the Boy Scouts' first amendment right of expressive association. Chief Justice Rehnquist delivered the opinion of the Court:

> The forced inclusion of an unwanted person in a group infringes the group's freedom of expressive association if the presence of that person affects in a significant way the group's ability to advocate public or private viewpoints. [But] the freedom of expressive association, like many freedoms, is not absolute. We have held that the freedom could be overridden "by regulations adopted to serve compelling state interests, unrelated to the suppression of ideas, that cannot be achieved through means significantly less restrictive of associational freedoms." [*Roberts.*]
>
> To determine whether a group is protected by the First Amendment's expressive associational right, we must determine whether the group engages in "expressive association." The First Amendment's protection of expressive association is not reserved for advocacy groups. But to come within its ambit, a group must engage in some form of expression, whether it be public or private. . . .
>
> The Boy Scouts is a private, nonprofit organization. According to its "mission statement," [the] general mission of the Boy Scouts is "[t]o instill values in young people." The Boy Scouts seeks to instill these values by having its adult leaders spend time with the youth members, instructing and engaging them in activities like camping, archery, and fishing. During the time spent with the youth members, the scoutmasters and assistant scoutmasters inculcate them with the Boy Scouts' values — both expressly and by example. It seems indisputable that an association that seeks to transmit such a system of values engages in expressive activity. . . .
>
> Given that the Boy Scouts engages in expressive activity, we must determine whether the forced inclusion of Dale as an assistant scoutmaster would significantly affect the Boy Scouts' ability to advocate public or private viewpoints. This inquiry necessarily requires us first to explore, to a limited extent, the nature of the Boy Scouts' view of homosexuality. [Although the] Boy Scout Oath and Law do not expressly mention sexuality or sexual orientation, [the] Boy Scouts asserts that it "teach[es] that homosexual conduct is not morally straight" [and] that it does "not want to promote homosexual conduct as a legitimate form of behavior." [We] accept the Boy Scouts' assertion. . . .

We must then determine whether Dale's presence as an assistant scoutmaster would significantly burden the Boy Scouts' desire to not "promote homosexual conduct as a legitimate form of behavior." As we give deference to an association's assertions regarding the nature of its expression, we must also give deference to an association's view of what would impair its expression. [That] is not to say that an expressive association can erect a shield against antidiscrimination laws simply by asserting that mere acceptance of a member from a particular group would impair its message. But here Dale, by his own admission, is one of a group of gay Scouts who have "become leaders in their community and are open and honest about their sexual orientation." Dale was the co-president of a gay and lesbian organization at college and remains a gay rights activist. Dale's presence in the Boy Scouts would, at the very least, force the organization to send a message, both to the youth members and the world, that the Boy Scouts accepts homosexual conduct as a legitimate form of behavior.

The New Jersey Supreme Court determined that the Boy Scouts' ability to disseminate its message was not significantly affected by the forced inclusion of Dale as an assistant scoutmaster because "Boy Scout members do not associate for the purpose of disseminating the belief that homosexuality is immoral." [We] disagree with the New Jersey Supreme Court's [reasoning]. First, associations do not have to associate for the "purpose" of disseminating a certain message in order to be entitled to the protections of the First Amendment. An association must merely engage in expressive activity that could be impaired in order to be entitled to protection. Second, [the] First Amendment simply does not require that every member of a group agree on every issue in order for the group's policy to be "expressive association." The Boy Scouts takes an official position with respect to homosexual conduct, and that is sufficient for First Amendment purposes. . . .

Having determined that the Boy Scouts is an expressive association and that the forced inclusion of Dale would significantly affect its expression, we inquire whether the application of New Jersey's public accommodations law to require that the Boy Scouts accept Dale as an assistant scoutmaster runs afoul of the Scouts' freedom of expressive association. We conclude that it does. . . .

We recognized in cases such as *Roberts* [that] States have a compelling interest in eliminating discrimination against women in public accommodations. But in each of these cases we went on to conclude that the enforcement of these statutes would not materially interfere with the ideas that the organization sought to express. In *Roberts*, we said "[i]ndeed, the Jaycees has failed to demonstrate [any] serious burden on the male members' freedom of expressive association." We thereupon concluded in each of these cases that the organizations' First Amendment rights were not violated by the application of the States' public accommodations laws.

[We] have already concluded that a state requirement that the Boy Scouts retain Dale as an assistant scoutmaster would significantly burden the organization's right to oppose or disfavor homosexual conduct. The state interests embodied in New Jersey's public accommodations law do not justify such a severe intrusion on the Boy Scouts' rights to freedom of expressive association. That being the case, we hold that the First Amendment prohibits the State from imposing such a requirement through the application of its public accommodations law.

Justice Stevens, joined by Justices Souter, Ginsburg, and Breyer, dissented:

[Until] today, we have never once found a claimed right to associate in the selection of members to prevail in the face of a State's antidiscrimination law. To the contrary, we have squarely held that a State's antidiscrimination law does not violate a group's right to associate simply because the law conflicts with that group's exclusionary membership policy. [Citing *Roberts*.]

Surely there are instances in which an organization that truly aims to foster a belief at odds with the purposes of a State's antidiscrimination laws will have a First Amendment right to association that precludes forced compliance with those laws. But that right is not a freedom to discriminate at will, nor is it a right to maintain an exclusionary membership policy simply out of fear of what the public reaction would be if the group's membership were opened up. It is an implicit right designed to protect the enumerated rights of the First Amendment, not a license to act on any discriminatory impulse. To prevail in asserting a right of expressive association as a defense to a charge of violating an antidiscrimination law, the organization must at least show it has adopted and advocated an unequivocal position inconsistent with a position advocated or epitomized by the person whom the organization seeks to exclude. . . .

Dale's inclusion in the Boy Scouts [sends] no cognizable message to the Scouts or to the world. [If] there is any kind of message being sent, [it] is by the mere act of joining the Boy Scouts. [The] only apparent explanation for the majority's holding [is] that homosexuals are simply so different from the rest of society that their presence alone — unlike any other individual's — should be singled out for special First Amendment treatment. Under the majority's reasoning, an openly gay male is irreversibly affixed with the label "homosexual." [Reliance] on such a justification is tantamount to a constitutionally prescribed symbol of inferiority. . . .

Furthermore, it is not likely that BSA would be understood to send any message, either to Scouts or to the world, simply by admitting someone as a member. Over the years, BSA has generously welcomed over 87 million young Americans into its ranks. In 1992 over one million adults were active BSA members. [The] notion that an organization of that size and enormous prestige implicitly endorses the views that each of those adults may express in a non-Scouting context is simply mind boggling. Indeed, in this case there is no evidence that the young Scouts in Dale's troop, or members of their families, were even aware of his sexual [orientation]. It is equally farfetched to assert that Dale's open declaration of his homosexuality, reported in a local newspaper, will effectively force BSA to send a message to anyone simply because it allows Dale to be an Assistant Scoutmaster.

Should *Dale* have been governed by *Roberts* or by *California Democratic Party*? Is the Boy Scouts more of an "expressive association" than the Jaycees? Is the compelled inclusion of a gay Boy Scout more intrusive upon the right of expressive association than the compelled inclusion of a woman Jaycee? Is *Dale* reconcilable with *O'Brien*? Because the government's interests in preventing the destruction of draft cards are more important that its interests in preventing discrimination against gays? Because it is more important for the Boy Scouts to discriminate against gays than it is for antiwar protesters to burn draft cards?

Can a private association that is authorized by a city to conduct the St. Patrick's Day parade exclude from the parade an organization formed for the purpose of expressing its members' pride in their Irish heritage as openly gay, lesbian, and bisexual individuals because the association does not wish to be associated with that message, despite a finding that the exclusion violates a state law prohibiting discrimination on the basis of sexual orientation? See Hurley v. Irish-American Gay, Lesbian and Bisexual Group of Boston, 515 U.S. 557 (1995) (holding that the private association has a right under the first amendment not to be compelled "to propound" this message).

5. *The reach of* Roberts: dance halls. In City of Dallas v. Stanglin, 490 U.S. 19 (1989), the Court unanimously upheld a Dallas ordinance restricting admittance to certain dance halls to persons between the ages of fourteen and eighteen: "[The opportunities to dance with adults, and for adults to dance with minors] do not involve the sort of expressive association that the First Amendment has been held to protect. The hundreds of teenagers who congregate each night at this particular dance hall are not members of any organized association; they are patrons of the same business establishment. Most are strangers to one another, and the dance hall admits all who are willing to pay the admission fee. [These patrons do not] 'take positions on public questions,' or perform any of the other [activities that constitute First Amendment expression]. The activity of these dance-hall patrons — coming together to engage in recreational dancing — is not protected by the First Amendment. Thus this activity [does not qualify] as a form of 'expressive association' as [that term was used] in *Roberts.*"

PRUNEYARD SHOPPING CENTER v. ROBINS, 447 U.S. 74 (1980). The PruneYard is a privately owned shopping center containing more than seventy-five shops and restaurants. It prohibits any visitors or tenants from engaging in any publicly expressive activity, including the circulation of petitions. Several high school students seeking support for their opposition to a United Nations resolution against Zionism set up a card table in PruneYard's central courtyard. They distributed leaflets and asked passersby to sign petitions. They were asked to leave and thereafter filed suit to enjoin PruneYard from denying them access to the premises for the purpose of circulating their petitions. The California Supreme Court held that the California Constitution protects "speech and petitioning, reasonably exercised, in shopping centers even when the centers are privately owned." Appellants, the owners of PruneYard, maintained that "a private property owner has a First Amendment right not to be forced by the State to use his property as a forum for the speech of others." The Court, in an opinion by Justice Rehnquist, rejected appellants' claim:

"[T]he shopping center [is] a business establishment that is open to the public. [The] views expressed by members of the public in passing out pamphlets or seeking signatures for a petition thus will not likely be identified with those of the owner. [Moreover], no specific message is dictated by the State. [There] consequently is no danger of governmental discrimination for or against a particular message. Finally, [appellants] can expressly disavow any connection with the message by simply posting signs [disclaiming] any sponsorship of the message and [explaining] that the persons are communicating their own messages by virtue of state law. [Appellants here are not] compelled to affirm their belief in any governmentally prescribed position or view, and they are free to publicly dissociate themselves from the views of the speakers or handbillers." Justice Powell, joined by Justice White, concurred in the result.

Note: *Compelled Affirmation, Expression, and Association: The Right Not to Speak*

1. *Conscientious sensibilities.* Consider Cantor, Forced Payments to Service Institutions and Constitutional Interests in Ideological Non-Association, 36 Rutgers L. Rev. 3, 26, 16 (1984):

Americans often have money extracted from them and used to promote objects which they ideologically oppose. The most obvious example is the taxpayer. Despite moral objections, pacifists' taxes are used to support war efforts, anarchists' funds help support government, and "right to life" advocates' monies are used to further birth control and abortions. [The] explanation is not that freedom of conscience [is] unimportant, [but] that pure peace of mind cannot be accorded high constitutional status in an organized society. [Any other result would cause insurmountable] administrative tangles, [for the] range of conscientious sensibilities is limitless.

2. *The pledge of allegiance.* Are there any circumstances in which there is a right not to be compelled to support or express ideas with which one disagrees? This right first received articulation in West Virginia State Board of Education v. Barnette, 319 U.S. 624 (1943), in which the Court overruled its prior decision in Minersville School District v. Gobitis, 310 U.S. 586 (1940), and held unconstitutional a state law requiring all children in the public schools to salute and pledge allegiance to the flag of the United States. Justice Jackson, speaking for the Court, explained:

[The] compulsory flag salute and pledge requires affirmation of a belief and an attitude of mind. [To] sustain the compulsory flag salute we are required to say that a Bill of Rights which guards the individual's right to speak his own mind, left it open to public authorities to compel him to utter what is not in his mind. [But if] there is any fixed star in our constitutional constellation, it is that no official, high or petty, can prescribe what shall be orthodox in politics, nationalism, religion, or other matters of opinion or force citizens to confess by word or act their faith therein. If there are any circumstances which permit an exception, they do not now occur to us.

Justice Frankfurter dissented. Is *PruneYard* reconcilable with *Barnette*? In *PruneYard,* the Court explained that "*Barnette* is inapposite because it involved the compelled recitation of a message containing an affirmation of belief," whereas in *PruneYard* "no specific message [was] dictated by the State."

Is *Barnette* wrong because reasonable observers would understand that the speech was compelled? Consider Greene, The Pledge of Allegiance Problem, 64 Fordham L. Rev. 451, 473, 482 (1995):

For an act to be considered expressive, and thus worthy of prima facie protection under the Free Speech Clause, that act must involve (or appear to a reasonable observer to involve) the communication of the speaker's internal mental state, such as her beliefs, attitudes or convictions. [Neither] a law compelling the utterance of the pledge of allegiance nor a law compelling a left turn signal requires the agent to reveal the contents of her mind. . . . [Because] a reasonable observer [would] understand the teacher-led pledge of allegiance, with no opt-out provision, as compelled and thus as not reflective of the beliefs of the [students, there is no violation of the free speech clause].

3. *"Live free or die."* In Wooley v. Maynard, 430 U.S. 705 (1977), the Court, in an opinion by Chief Justice Burger, held that New Hampshire could not criminally punish individuals who covered up the state motto "Live Free or Die" on their passenger vehicle license plates because the motto was repugnant to their moral, political, and religious beliefs:

[Here,] as in *Barnette*, we are faced with a state measure which forces an individual, as part of his daily life [to] be an instrument for fostering public adherence to an ideological point of view he finds unacceptable. [Thus, we must] determine whether the State's countervailing interest is sufficiently compelling to justify requiring appellees to display the state motto on their license plates. The two interests advanced by the State are that display of the motto (1) facilitates the identification of passenger [as distinct from other] vehicles, and (2) promotes appreciation of history, individualism, and state pride. [The first argument is insufficient] "in the light of less drastic means for achieving the same basic purpose." [The] State's second claimed interest is not ideologically neutral. [The State's interest in disseminating an ideology] cannot outweigh an individual's First Amendment right to avoid becoming the courier for such message.

Justice Rehnquist, joined by Justice Blackmun, dissented:

For First Amendment principles to be implicated, the State must place the citizen in the position of either apparently or actually "asserting as true" the message. This was the focus of *Barnette*, and clearly distinguishes this case from that one. [Here,] there is nothing in state law which precludes appellees from displaying their disagreement with the state motto as long as the methods used do not obscure the license plates. Thus appellees could place on their bumper a conspicuous bumper sticker explaining in no uncertain terms that [they] disagree with the connotations of [the] motto. Since any implication that they affirm the motto can be so easily displaced, I cannot agree that the statute may be invalidated under the fiction that appellees are unconstitutionally forced to affirm, or profess belief in, the state motto.

In *PruneYard*, the Court distinguished *Wooley* as follows: "[In *Wooley*,] the government itself prescribed the message, required it to be displayed openly on appellee's personal property that was used 'as part of his daily life,' and refused to permit him to take any measures to cover up the motto even though the Court found that the display of the motto served no important state interest."

4. *A St. Patrick's Day parade.* The City of Boston authorized the South Boston Allied War Veterans Council to organize the annual St. Patrick's Day Parade. The council refused a place in the parade to GLIB, an organization formed for the purpose of expressing its members' pride in their Irish heritage as openly gay, lesbian, and bisexual individuals. GLIB filed suit claiming that this refusal violated a Massachusetts law prohibiting discrimination on account of sexual orientation in places of public accommodation. In Hurley v. Irish-American Gay, Lesbian and Bisexual Group of Boston, 515 U.S. 557 (1995), the Court, in a unanimous opinion by Justice Souter, held that application of the statute in this context violated the first amendment rights of the council.

The Court explained that, because "every participating unit affects the message conveyed by the private organizers," application of the statute in this context effectively required the council "to alter the expressive content" of its parade. The Court declared that "this use of the State's power violates the fundamental rule" that "a speaker has the autonomy to choose the content of his own message." Thus, if the council "objects," for example, to GLIB's implicit assertion that homosexuals and bisexuals are entitled to full and equal "social acceptance," it has a right "not to propound" this message.

The Court held that *PruneYard* was distinguishable because (1) the proprietors of the shopping center "were running 'a business establishment that [was] open to the public,'" (2) they "could 'expressly disavow any connection with the message by simply posting signs in the areas where the speakers or handbillers stand,'" and (3) the shopping center owners' own right to speak was not implicated because they "did not even allege that [they] objected to the content" of the speech. On the disclaimer issue, the Court observed that disclaimers would not be sufficient to protect the interests of the council because "such disclaimers would be quite curious in a moving parade."

5. *Union dues.* May a state compel government employees to pay union dues? See Abood v. Detroit Board of Education, 431 U.S. 209 (1977) (upholding a state statute authorizing unions representing government employees to charge members dues insofar as the dues are used to support collective bargaining and related activities, but invalidating the statute insofar as the union uses the dues "to contribute to political candidates and to express political views unrelated to its duties as exclusive bargaining representative"); Ellis v. Brotherhood of Railway, Airline & Steamship Clerks, 466 U.S. 85 (1984) (compelled contributions may constitutionally be used to pay for union conventions, social activities, and publications); Keller v. State Bar of California, 496 U.S. 1 (1990) (an integrated state bar association may not use compulsory dues to finance political and ideological activities with which particular members disagree when such expenditures are not "necessarily or reasonably incurred for the purpose of regulating the legal profession or improving the quality of legal services"); Lehnert v. Ferris Faculty Association, 500 U.S. 507 (1991) (a union may constitutionally charge dissenting employees only for those activities that are (1) "germane" to collective bargaining; (2) justified by the government's interests in labor peace and avoiding free riders; and (3) not significantly burdening of speech).

6. *Student activity fees.* Board of Regents of the University of Wisconsin System v. Southworth, 529 U.S. 217 (2000), concerned the constitutionality of the University of Wisconsin's requirement that all full-time students pay an annual activities fee, part of which is allocated by the student government to support registered student organizations that engage in a broad range of expressive and other activities. Examples of the more than 600 registered student organizations at the University of Wisconsin are the College Democrats, the College Republicans, the International Socialist Organization, and the Future Financial Gurus of America. Citing *Abood*, respondents challenged the constitutionality of this program on the ground that by compelling them financially to support political and ideological expression with which they disagree, the program violates their first amendment right "not to speak."

In an unanimous decision, the Court rejected this challenge. Justice Kennedy authored the opinion of the Court:

> In *Abood* [the] constitutional rule took the form of limiting the required subsidy to speech germane to the purposes of the [union]. The standard of germane speech as applied to student speech at a university is [unworkable]. The speech the University seeks to encourage in the program before us is distinguished not by discernable limits but by its vast, unexplored bounds. To insist upon asking what speech is germane would be contrary to the very goal the University seeks to pursue. It is not for the Court to say what is or is not germane to the ideas to be pursued in an institution of higher learning. . . .
>
> It is all but inevitable that the fees will result in subsidies to speech which some students find objectionable and offensive to their personal beliefs. If the standard

of germane speech is inapplicable, then, it might be argued the remedy is to allow each student to list those causes which he or she will or will not support. If a university decided that its students First Amendment interests were better protected by some type of optional or refund system it would be free to do so. We decline to impose a system of that sort as a constitutional requirement, however. The restriction would be so disruptive and expensive that the program to support extracurricular speech would be ineffective.

The University may determine that its mission is well served if students have the means to engage in dynamic discussion of philosophical, religious, social and political subjects in their extracurricular campus life outside the lecture hall. If the University reaches this conclusion, it is entitled to impose a mandatory fee to sustain an open dialogue to these ends.

The University must provide some protection to its students' First Amendment interests, however. [The] principal standard of protection for objecting students [is] the requirement of viewpoint neutrality in the allocation of funding support. When a university requires its students to pay fees to support the extracurricular speech of other students, all in the interest of open discussion, it may not prefer some viewpoints to others. [We] conclude that the University of Wisconsin may sustain the extracurricular dimensions of its program by using mandatory student fees with viewpoint neutrality as the operational principle.

There was one aspect of the university's program that the Court found more problematic. In addition to authorizing the student government to make funding decisions (subject to a university-imposed requirement of viewpoint-neutrality), funding decisions could also be made through student referenda: "[It] appears that by majority vote of the student body a given [registered student organization] may be funded or defunded. It is unclear to us what protection, if any, there is for viewpoint neutrality in this part of the process. To the extent the referendum substitutes majority determinations for viewpoint neutrality it would undermine the constitutional protection the program requires. The whole theory of viewpoint neutrality is that minority views are treated with the same respect as are majority views. Access to a public forum, for instance, does not depend upon majoritarian consent. That principle is controlling here. A remand is necessary [to] resolve this point."

Justice Souter, joined by Justices Stevens and Breyer, filed a concurring opinion, noting that "a cast-iron viewpoint neutrality requirement" may not be appropriate in this setting because the very nature of universities may make such a requirement inappropriate.

7. *The right not to publish or broadcast.* In what circumstances, if any, may government constitutionally compel a broadcaster or publisher to broadcast or publish material? See Denver Area Education Telecommunications Consortium, Inc. v. FCC, 518 U.S. 727 (1996) (considering the constitutionality of several provisions of the Cable Television Consumer Protection and Competition Act of 1992 concerning the broadcasting of "indecent" programming on public access and leased access channels); Turner Broadcasting System Inc. v. FCC, 512 U.S. 622 (1994) (upholding "must carry" provisions for cable television); Columbia Broadcasting System v. FCC, 453 U.S. 367 (1981) (upholding an FCC rule requiring broadcasters "to allow reasonable access [by] a legally qualified candidate for Federal elective office on behalf of his candidacy"); Miami Herald Publishing Co. v. Tornillo, 418 U.S. 241 (1974) (invalidating a "right of reply" statute requiring any newspaper that "assails" the character of a political candidate to print

the candidate's reply); Red Lion Broadcasting Co. v. FCC, 395 U.S. 367 (1969) (upholding the FCC's "fairness doctrine"). See section F infra.

8. *Additional decisions.* For additional decisions on the right not to speak, see Boy Scouts of America v. Dale, 120 S. Ct. 2446 (2000) (a law prohibiting the Boy Scouts from excluding gays does violate the first amendment right of expressive association); California Democratic Party v. Jones, 120 S. Ct. 2402 (2000) (invalidating a state law permitting individuals who are not members of a political party to vote in that party's primary); Glickman v. Wileman Brothers & Elliott, Inc., 512 U.S. 1145 (1997) (upholding an order of the Secretary of Agriculture requiring California agricultural producers to pay assessments to help defray the cost of generic advertising of California fruits because this does not involve an objection based "on political or ideological disagreement with the content of the message"); Pacific Gas & Electric Co. (PG&E) v. Public Utilities Commission, 475 U.S. 1 (1986) (invalidating an order of a state public utilities commission directing a privately owned electric company to permit private advocacy groups to include in the company's monthly billing envelopes their own communications with the customers of the company because the order "is not content-neutral," but awards access "only to those who disagree with [the company's] views and who are hostile to its interests"); Roberts v. Jaycees, 468 U.S. 609 (1984) (a law prohibiting the Jaycees from excluding women does not violate the right of expressive association); Branti v. Finkel, 445 U.S. 507 (1980) (invalidating patronage programs requiring government employees, as a condition of employment, to support the incumbent political party); and Elrod v. Burns, 427 U.S. 347 (1976).

9. *Assessment.* Consider Jacobs, Pledges, Parades and Mandatory Payments, 52 Rutgers L. Rev. 123, 183-184 (1999):

> [Compelled] expression analysis should look to whether the government's purpose is to manipulate the marketplace of ideas or whether its purpose is not related to expression. Where the government acts to manipulate the marketplace of ideas [e.g., *Barnette*; *PG&E*; *Wooley*], strict scrutiny applies. . . . Where the government acts for a nonspeech purpose but incidentally compels expression or compels contributions, some of which are used to fund expression, [e.g., *Hurley*; *Abood*], the government's nonspeech purpose invokes mid-level balancing review.

Note: Content-Neutral Restrictions — Final Thoughts

Consider the following evaluation: The Court has long recognized that by limiting the availability of particular means of communication, content-neutral restrictions can significantly impair the ability of individuals to communicate their views to others. This is a central first amendment concern. The Court generally tests content-neutral restrictions with an implicit balancing approach: The greater the interference with the opportunities for free expression, the greater the burden on government to justify the restriction. When the challenged restriction has a relatively severe effect, the Court invokes strict scrutiny. See, e.g., *Button*; *Buckley* (expenditure limitations); *Roberts*. When the challenged restriction has a significant, but not severe, effect, the Court employs intermediate scrutiny. See, e.g., *Schneider*; *Buckley* (contribution limitations); *Martin*. And when the restriction has a relatively modest effect, the Court applies deferential scrutiny. See, e.g., *O'Brien*; *Heffron*, section E2b supra; *Clark*, section E2a. There are exceptions to this pattern, and the exceptions are often quite revealing, for they suggest the impact of additional factors, such as "public property" or "incidental effect," that may trump the central concern of content-neutral analysis. But the general pattern is clear: As the restrictive effect increases, the standard of review increases as well.

Is this an accurate description of the Court's analysis? If so, does it reflect a satisfactory approach? See Stone, Content-Neutral Restrictions, 54 U. Chi. L. Rev. 46 (1987); Lee, Lonely Pamphleteers, Little People, and the Supreme Court: The Doctrine of Time, Place, and Manner Regulations of Expression, 54 Geo. Wash. L. Rev. 757 (1986); Bhagwat, Purpose Scrutiny in Constitutional Analysis, 85 Cal. L. Rev. 297 (1997) (arguing that the "Court should abandon its current distinction between content-based and content-neutral regulations" because the distinction is "a poorly-suited tool" for what "appears to be" its primary task — "to identify improperly motivated regulations").

Consider also S. Fish, There's No Such Thing as Free Speech 15-16, 110 (1994):

> Short of an absolutely absolutist position (which no one holds or defends), a line must be drawn between protected speech and speech that might in some circumstances be regulated, and that line will always reflect a *political* decision to [value] some kinds of verbal behavior and devalue others. [The] point is obvious if the line is drawn between so-called high-value and low-value speech, for someone must decide what is high and what is low, and someone else, were he or she in power, would decide otherwise; but the point holds even when the line is specifically drawn to rule out political considerations, as in the distinction between content regulation [and] time-manner-place regulation. Supposedly the latter is indifferent to ideas and is merely a matter of maintaining order, [but] as the many challenges to such regulations show, their effect is almost always either to maximize the speech opportunities of certain favored groups [or] to minimize the speech opportunities of less favored groups.
>
> [The] moral is [that the] First Amendment [will] display the political "spin" of whatever group has its hand on the interpretative machinery. [People] cling to First Amendment pieties because they do not wish to face what they correctly take to be the alternative. That alternative is *politics*, the realization [that] decisions about what is and is not protected in the realm of expression [rest] not on principle [or] doctrine but on the ability of some persons to [interpret] principle and doctrine in ways that lead to the protection of speech they want heard and the regulation of speech [they] want silenced. (That is how [conservatives] can argue *for* flag-burning statutes and *against* hate-speech codes.) When the First Amendment is successfully invoked, the result is not a victory for free speech [but a] victory won by the party that has managed to wrap its agenda in the mantle of free speech.

F.   FREEDOM OF THE PRESS

This section examines the first amendment's guarantee of "freedom [of] the press." The focus is on four questions. First, in what circumstances, if any, is the press, because of its constitutionally protected status, exempt from laws of otherwise general application? Second, to what extent, if any, does the first amendment guarantee a right to "gather" news? Third, in what circumstances, if any, may government treat the press differently from other institutions? Fourth, in what circumstances, if any, may government regulate the press in order to improve the "marketplace of ideas"?

1. A "Preferred" Status for the Press?

The first amendment prohibits any law "abridging the freedom of speech, or of the press." Does the press clause confer any rights that would not be conferred by the speech clause alone? Consider the views of Justice Stewart and Chief Justice Burger.

a. Stewart, "Or of the Press," 26 Hastings L.J. 631, 633-634 (1975):

[The] Free Press guarantee is, in essence, a *structural* provision of the Constitution. Most of the other provisions in the Bill of Rights protect specific liberties or specific rights of individuals. [The] Free Press Clause extends protection to an institution. The publishing business is the only organized private business that is given explicit constitutional protection. [If] the Free Press guarantee meant no more than freedom of expression, it would be a constitutional redundancy. [By] including both [the speech and press] guarantees in the First Amendment, the Founders quite clearly recognized the distinction between the two. [In] setting up the three branches of the Federal Government, the Founders deliberately created an internally competitive system. [The] primary purpose of the constitutional guarantee of a free press was [to] create a fourth institution outside the Government as an additional check on the three official branches. [The] relevant metaphor [is that] of the Fourth Estate. [The first amendment thus protects] the institutional autonomy of the press.

b. First National Bank of Boston v. Bellotti, 435 U.S. 765, 797-801 (1978) (Burger, C.J., concurring):

[There are those] who view the Press Clause as somehow conferring special and extraordinary privileges or status on the "institutional press." [I] perceive two fundamental difficulties with [such a] reading of the Press Clause. First, although certainty on this point is not possible, the history of the Clause does not suggest that the authors contemplated a "special" or "institutional" privilege. [Most] pre-First Amendment commentators "who employed the term 'freedom of speech' [used] it synonymously with freedom of the press." [The] second fundamental difficulty with interpreting the Press Clause as conferring special status on a limited group is one of definition. [The] very task of including some entities within the "institutional press" while excluding others [is] reminiscent of the abhorred licensing system [that] the First Amendment was intended to ban. [In my view,] the First Amendment does not "belong" to any definable category of persons or entities: It belongs to all who exercise its freedoms.

Consider also Associated Press v. NLRB, 301 U.S. 103 (1937). The Associated Press is a cooperative organization whose members in 1937 included approximately 1,350 newspapers. It collects, compiles, and distributes news to its members. The NLRB found that the Associated Press discharged an employee in violation of section 7 of the National Labor Relations Act, which confers on employees the right to organize and to bargain collectively. The Court, in a five-to-four decision, held that application of section 7 to the Associated Press did not violate the first amendment:

> The business of the Associated Press is not immune from regulation because it is an agency of the press. The publisher of a newspaper has no special immunity from the application of general laws. He has no special privilege to invade the rights and liberties of others. He must answer for libel. He may be punished for contempt of court. He is subject to the anti-trust laws. Like others he must pay equitable and nondiscriminatory taxes on his business. The regulation here in question has no relation whatever to the impartial distribution of news.

See also Dun & Bradstreet v. Greenmoss Builders, section D1 supra (the media are not entitled to any greater protection against actions for libel than other speakers); Citizen Publishing Co. v. United States, 394 U.S. 131 (1969) (Sherman Antitrust Act); Oklahoma Press Publishing Co. v. Walling, 327 U.S. 186 (1946) (Fair Labor Standards Act); cf. Grosjean v. American Press Co., 297 U.S. 233 (1936) (taxation).

Are these decisions consistent with Justice Stewart's contention that the "publishing business is the only organized private business that is given explicit constitutional protection"? Are there *some* circumstances in which the first amendment exempts the press from tax, labor, antitrust, or other laws of general application?

2.   A Right to "Gather" News?

Branzburg v. Hayes

408 U.S. 665 (1972)

Opinion of the Court by Mr. Justice White. . . .

[Branzburg, a newspaper reporter, published several articles describing unlawful drug activities in Frankfort, Kentucky. He refused, on first amendment grounds, to disclose to a state grand jury the identities of the persons whose activities he had described.]

The issue in these cases is whether requiring newsmen to appear and testify before state or federal grand juries abridges the freedom of speech and press guaranteed by the First Amendment. We hold that it does not.

Petitioners [press] First Amendment claims that may be simply put: that to gather news it is often necessary to agree either not to identify the source of information published or to publish only part of the facts revealed, or both; that if the reporter is nevertheless forced to reveal these confidences to a grand jury, the source so identified and other confidential sources of other reporters will be measurably deterred from furnishing publishable information, all to the detriment of the free flow of information protected by the First Amendment. Although the newsmen [do] not claim an absolute privilege against official interrogation in all circumstances, they assert that the reporter should not be forced either to appear or to testify before a grand jury or at trial until and unless sufficient grounds are shown for believing that the reporter possesses information relevant to a crime the grand jury is investigating, that the information the reporter has is unavailable from other sources, and that the need for the information is sufficiently compelling to override the claimed invasion of First Amendment interests occasioned by the disclosure. [The] heart of the claim is that the burden on news gathering resulting from compelling reporters to disclose confidential information outweighs any public interest in obtaining the information.

We do not question the significance of free speech, press, or assembly to the country's welfare. Nor is it suggested that news gathering does not qualify for First Amendment protection; without some protection for seeking out the news, freedom of the press could be eviscerated. But these cases involve no [restriction] on what the press may publish, and no express or implied command that the press publish what it prefers to withhold. [The] use of confidential sources by the press is not forbidden or restricted. [The] sole issue before us is the obligation of reporters to respond to grand jury subpoenas as other citizens do and to answer questions relevant to an investigation into the commission of crime. . . .

[The] First Amendment does not invalidate every incidental burdening of the press that may result from the enforcement of civil or criminal statutes of general applicability. [Citing Associated Press v. NLRB; Oklahoma Press Publishing Co. v. Walling]. . . .

It has generally been held that the First Amendment does not guarantee the press a constitutional right of special access to information not available to the public generally. [In Zemel v. Rusk, 381 U.S. 1 (1965)], for example, the Court sustained the Government's refusal to validate passports to Cuba even though that restriction "render[ed] less than wholly free the flow of information concerning that country." The ban on travel was held constitutional, for "[t]he right to speak and publish does not carry with it the unrestrained right to gather information."

Despite the fact that news gathering may be hampered, the press is regularly excluded from grand jury proceedings, our own conferences, the meetings of other official bodies gathered in executive session, and the meetings of private organizations. Newsmen have no constitutional right of access to the scenes of crime or disaster when the general public is excluded, and they may be prohibited from [attending] trials if such restrictions are necessary to assure a defendant a fair trial before an impartial tribunal. . . .

It is thus not surprising that the great weight of authority is that newsmen are not exempt from the normal duty of appearing before a grand jury and answering questions relevant to a criminal investigation. [The] prevailing constitutional view of the newsman's privilege is very much rooted in the ancient role of the grand jury. [Because] its task is to inquire into the existence of possible criminal conduct and to return only well-founded indictments, its investigative powers are necessarily broad. [On] the records now before us, we perceive no basis for holding that the public interest in law enforcement and in ensuring effective grand jury proceedings is insufficient to override the consequential, but uncertain, burden on news gathering that is said to result from insisting that reporters, like other citizens, respond to relevant questions put to them in the course of a valid grand jury investigation or criminal trial.

This conclusion [does not] threaten the vast bulk of confidential relationships between reporters and their sources. [Only] where news sources themselves are implicated in crime or possess information relevant to the grand jury's task need they or the reporter be concerned about grand jury subpoenas. Nothing before us indicates that a large number or percentage of *all* confidential news sources falls into either category and would in any way be deterred by our holding. . . .

[Moreover, although the] argument that the flow of news will be diminished by compelling reporters to aid the grand jury in a criminal investigation is not [irrational, we] remain unclear how often and to what extent informers are actually deterred from furnishing information when newsmen are forced to testify before a grand jury. [The] evidence fails to demonstrate that there would be a significant constriction of the flow of news to the public if this Court reaffirms the prior common-law and constitutional rule regarding the testimonial obligations of newsmen.[33]

[Moreover, the] administration of a constitutional newsman's privilege would present practical and conceptual difficulties of a high order. Sooner or later, it would be necessary to define those categories of newsmen who qualified for the privilege, a questionable procedure in light of the traditional doctrine that liberty of the press is the right of the lonely pamphleteer [just] as much as of the large metropolitan publisher. [Almost] any author may [assert] that he is contributing to the flow of information to the public, that he relies on confidential sources of information, and that these sources will be silenced if he is forced to make disclosures before a grand jury.

In each instance where a reporter is subpoenaed to testify, the courts would also be embroiled in preliminary factual and legal determinations with respect to whether the proper predicate had been laid for the reporter's appearance: Is there probable cause to believe a crime has been committed? Is it likely that the reporter has useful information gained in confidence? Could the grand jury obtain the information elsewhere? Is the official interest sufficient to outweigh the claimed privilege? . . .

Finally, as we have earlier indicated, news gathering is not without its First Amendment protections, and grand jury investigations if instituted or conducted other than in good faith, would pose wholly different issues for resolution under the First Amendment. Official harassment of the press undertaken not for purposes of law enforcement but to disrupt a reporter's relationship with his news sources would have no justification. Grand juries are subject to judicial control and subpoenas to motions to quash. We do not expect courts will forget that grand juries must operate within the limits of the First Amendment. . . .

Mr. Justice Powell, concurring.

I add this brief statement to emphasize what seems to me to be the limited nature of the Court's holding. The Court does not hold that newsmen, subpoenaed to testify before a grand jury, are without constitutional rights with respect to the gathering of news or in safeguarding their sources. . . .

As indicated in the concluding portion of the opinion, the Court states that no harassment of newsmen will be tolerated. If a newsman believes that the grand

33. In his Press Subpoenas: An Empirical and Legal Analysis, Study Report of the Reporters' Committee on Freedom of the Press 6-12, Prof. Vince Blasi [found] that slightly more than half of the 975 reporters questioned said that they relied on regular confidential sources for at least 10% of their stories. Of this group of reporters, only 8% were able to say with some certainty that their professional functioning had been adversely affected by the threat of subpoena; another 11% were not certain whether or not they had been adversely affected. [Relocated footnote. — Eds.]

jury investigation is not being conducted in good faith he is not without remedy. Indeed, if the newsman is called upon to give information bearing only a remote and tenuous relationship to the subject of the investigation, or if he has some other reason to believe that his testimony implicates confidential source relationships without a legitimate need of law enforcement, he will have access to the court on a motion to quash and an appropriate protective order may be entered. The asserted claim to privilege should be judged on its facts by the striking of a proper balance between freedom of the press and the obligation of all citizens to give relevant testimony with respect to criminal conduct. The balance of these vital constitutional and societal interests on a case-by-case basis accords with the tried and traditional way of adjudicating such questions.

In short, the courts will be available to newsmen under circumstances where legitimate First Amendment interests require protection.

MR. JUSTICE DOUGLAS, dissenting. . . .

Today's decision will impede the wide-open and robust dissemination of ideas and counterthought which a free press both fosters and protects and which is essential to the success of intelligent self-government. . . .

I see no way of making mandatory the disclosure of a reporter's confidential source of the information on which he bases his news story. . . .

MR. JUSTICE STEWART, with whom MR. JUSTICE BRENNAN and MR. JUSTICE MARSHALL join, dissenting.

The Court's crabbed view of the First Amendment reflects a disturbing insensitivity to the critical role of an independent press in our society. [While] Mr. Justice Powell's enigmatic concurring opinion gives some hope of a more flexible view in the future, the Court in these cases holds that a newsman has no First Amendment right to protect his sources when called before a grand jury. The Court thus invites state and federal authorities to undermine the historic independence of the press by attempting to annex the journalistic profession as an investigative arm of government. . . .

A corollary of the right to publish must be the right to gather news. [The] right to gather news implies, in turn, a right to a confidential relationship between a reporter and his source. [Informants] are necessary to the news-gathering process as we know it today. [And] the promise of confidentiality may be a necessary prerequisite to a productive relationship between a newsman and his informants. . . .

The impairment of the flow of news cannot, of course, be proved with scientific precision, as the Court seems to demand. [But] we have never before demanded that First Amendment rights rest on elaborate empirical studies demonstrating beyond any conceivable doubt that deterrent effects exist. . . .

Rather, on the basis of common sense and available information, we have asked, often implicitly, (1) whether there was a rational connection between the cause (the governmental action) and the effect (the deterrence or impairment of First Amendment activity), and (2) whether the effect would occur with some regularity, i.e., would not be de minimis. [Citing, e.g., NAACP v. Alabama; New York Times v. Sullivan.] Once this threshold inquiry has been satisfied, we have then examined the competing interests in determining whether there is an unconstitutional infringement of First Amendment freedoms. . . .

Surely [the] claim of deterrence here is as securely grounded in evidence and common sense as the claims in the cases cited above. [To] require any greater burden of proof is to shirk our duty to protect values securely embedded in the Constitution. . . .

Posed against the First Amendment's protection of the newsman's confidential relationships in these cases is society's interest in the use of the grand jury to administer justice fairly and effectively. [To] perform these functions the grand jury must have available to it every man's relevant evidence. [But] the longstanding rule making every person's evidence available to the grand jury is not absolute. The rule has been limited by the Fifth Amendment, the Fourth Amendment, and the evidentiary privileges of the common law. . . .

In striking the proper balance between the public interest in the efficient administration of justice and the First Amendment guarantee of the fullest flow of information, we must begin with the basic proposition [that] First Amendment rights require special safeguards. . . .

Accordingly, when a reporter is asked to appear before a grand jury and reveal confidences, I would hold that the government must (1) show that there is probable cause to believe that the newsman has information that is clearly relevant to a specific probable violation of law; (2) demonstrate that the information sought cannot be obtained by alternative means less destructive of First Amendment rights; and (3) demonstrate a compelling and overriding interest in the information. . . .

No doubt the courts would be required to make some delicate judgments in working out this accommodation. But that, after all, is the function of courts of law. Better such judgments, however difficult, than the simplistic and stultifying absolutism adopted by the Court in denying any force to the First Amendment in these cases. . . .

Note: A Right to Gather News?

1. *Newsgathering*. Does the first amendment guarantee the press a right to gather as well as to publish the news? Has the press a first amendment right to gather news through such practices as deception, burglary, wiretapping, and the bribing of sources? Suppose a reporter breaks into a government official's home to uncover evidence of corruption. Can the reporter be prosecuted? See Note, And Forgive Them Their Trespasses: Applying the Defense of Necessity to the Criminal Conduct of the Newsgatherer, 103 Harv. L. Rev. 890 (1990) (suggesting an exemption when the harm prevented by the newsgatherer's illegal conduct outweighs the harm it causes, the prevented harm is imminent, there is no alternative legal method for the newsgatherer to achieve the same end, and the newsgatherer reasonably believes the illegal conduct will abate a greater evil); Bezanson, Means and Ends and Food Lion: The Tension between Exemption and Independence in Newsgathering by the Press, 47 Emory L.J. 895 (1998) (suggesting that the press should be exempt from a law of otherwise general application if it can demonstrate that its otherwise unlawful act was taken "to avoid imminent harm," that "no reasonable legal alternatives existed," that the harm of the act "was not disproportional to the harm avoided," and "that there was a di-

rect causal relationship between the act and the harm avoided"). If the reporter can be prosecuted for the break-in, can the newspaper be restrained from publishing the information? Recall the *Pentagon Papers* case, section B4 supra.

2. *Branzburg.* Does *Branzburg* recognize a right to gather news? In light of Justice Powell's concurring opinion, is it fair to say that the Court divided "by a vote of four and a half to four and a half"? Stewart, "Or of the Press," 26 Hastings L. Rev. 631, 635 (1975). Since *Branzburg,* a majority of states have enacted some form of "shield" law to protect the confidentiality of press sources.

3. *Newsroom searches.* In Zurcher v. Stanford Daily, 436 U.S. 547 (1978), the Daily, a student newspaper, published articles and photographs concerning a violent clash on campus between demonstrators and police. Thereafter, the police obtained a warrant for an immediate search of the newspaper's offices for negatives, films, and pictures that might enable them to identify some of the demonstrators. The Daily's photographic laboratories, filing cabinets, desks, and wastepaper baskets were searched, but the police found only those photographs that had already been published. The Daily brought this civil action on the theory that the decision of the police to conduct a search, rather than to proceed by subpoena duces tecum, violated the first amendment. The Daily maintained that, unlike subpoenas, "searches of newspaper offices for evidence of crime [will] seriously threaten the ability of the press to gather, analyze, and disseminate news." In a five-to-three decision, the Court, in an opinion by Justice White, rejected this argument:

> Properly administered, the preconditions for a warrant — probable cause, specificity with respect to the place to be searched and the things to be seized, and overall reasonableness — should afford sufficient protection against the harms that are assertedly threatened by warrants for searching newspaper offices. There is no reason to believe, for example, that magistrates cannot guard against searches of the type, scope, and intrusiveness that would actually interfere with the timely publication of a newspaper [or enable] officers to rummage at large in newspaper files. [Nor] are we convinced, any more than we were in [*Branzburg*], that confidential sources will disappear. [Whatever] incremental effect there may be in this regard [does] not make a constitutional difference.

In the Privacy Protection Act of 1980, 42 U.S.C. §2000aa, Congress prohibited any government officer to search for work product or other documents of any "person reasonably believed to have a purpose to disseminate to the public a newspaper, book, broadcast, or other similar form of public communication," unless there is either probable cause to believe that the person is involved in the crime being investigated or there is otherwise reason to believe that giving notice by subpoena would result in the loss of the evidence.

4. *Breach of promise.* In Cohen v. Cowles Media Co., 501 U.S. 663 (1991), petitioner, who was associated with one party's campaign during the 1982 Minnesota gubernatorial race, gave court records disclosing derogatory information about another party's candidate to respondent newspapers after receiving a promise of confidentiality from the reporters. Despite this promise, the newspapers identified him in their stories, and petitioner was thereafter fired from his job. In a five-to-four decision, the Court held that the first amendment does not bar petitioner's state law action for damages for breach of promise. Justice White delivered the opinion of the Court:

Generally applicable laws do not offend the First Amendment simply because their enforcement against the press has incidental effects on its ability to gather and report the news. [There] can be little doubt that the Minnesota doctrine of promissory estoppel is a law of general applicability. It does not target or single out the press. [The] First Amendment does not forbid its application to the press.

Justice Souter, joined by Justices Marshall, Blackmun, and O'Connor, dissented:

["There] is nothing talismanic about neutral laws of general applicability," for such laws may restrict First Amendment rights just as effectively as those directed specifically at speech itself. [In this case, there] can be no doubt that the fact of [petitioner's] identity expanded the universe of information relevant to the choice faced by Minnesota voters in that State's 1982 gubernatorial election, the publication of which was thus of the sort quintessentially subject to strict First Amendment protection. [Indeed, the election could conceivably have turned on just such information. In such circumstances] I believe the State's interest in enforcing a newspaper's promise of confidentiality insufficient to outweigh the interest in unfettered publication.

As a member of the press, would you prefer a rule that made your promises of confidentiality enforceable against you or unenforceable? Recall the argument of the press in *Branzburg*.

5. *Does the press have a right to publish someone else's "property"?* Consider Zacchini v. Scripps-Howard Broadcasting Co., 433 U.S. 562 (1977), in which petitioner's fifteen-second "human cannonball" act, in which he is shot from a cannon into a net some 200 feet away, was, without his consent, filmed in its entirety at a county fair and shown on a television news program later the same day. Petitioner filed a damage action alleging an "unlawful appropriation" of his "professional property." The Court held that the first amendment did not bar petitioner's action: "[The first amendment does not give the media a right to] broadcast a performer's entire act without his consent. The Constitution no more prevents a State from requiring respondent to compensate petitioner for broadcasting his act on television than it would privilege respondent to film and broadcast a copyrighted dramatic work without liability to the copyright owner."

See also Harper & Row, Publishers v. Nation Enterprises, 471 U.S. 539 (1985) (a magazine's unauthorized publication of verbatim quotes from President Ford's unpublished memoirs constituted an actionable copyright infringement). See generally Volokh and McDonnell, Freedom of Speech and Independent Judgment Review in Copyright Cases, 107 Yale L.J. 2431 (1998); Patterson, Free Speech, Copyright, and Fair Use, 40 Vand. L. Rev. 1 (1987); Note, Copyright, Free Speech and the Visual Arts, 93 Yale L.J. 1565 (1984). For an interesting twist on this problem, see Simon & Schuster, Inc. v. Members of the New York State Crime Victims Board, 502 U.S. 428 (1991) (invalidating New York's Son of Sam law, which required any entity contracting with a person convicted of a crime to publish any depiction of the crime to turn over any income under the contract to the Crime Victims Board, which was then required to deposit the payments in an escrow account for the benefit of any victims).

6. *A right of access?* To what extent, if any, does the press have a first amendment right of access to information from the government? For example, do

members of the press ever have a constitutional right to be present during military operations, to interview prisoners, to demand information from government officials, or to attend criminal trials? Consider the following.

PELL v. PROCUNIER, 417 U.S. 817 (1974). Three professional journalists brought this suit to challenge the constitutionality of section 415.071 of the California Department of Corrections Manual, which prohibits face-to-face interviews between press representatives and individual inmates whom they specifically request to interview. This restriction was adopted in 1971. According to the Department of Corrections, prior to the promulgation of section 415.071, every journalist had virtually free access to interview any individual inmate whom he might wish. In practice, it was found that this policy resulted in press attention being concentrated on a relatively small number of inmates who, as a result, became virtual "public figures" within the prison society and gained a disproportionate degree of notoriety and influence among their fellow inmates. Because of this notoriety and influence, these inmates often became the source of severe disciplinary problems. Section 415.071 was adopted to mitigate the problem. The Court, in an opinion by Justice Stewart, held that this policy did not violate the first amendment:

"The First and Fourteenth Amendments bar government from interfering in any way with a free press. The Constitution does not, however, require government to accord the press special access to information not shared by members of the public generally. It is one thing to say that a journalist is free to seek out sources of information not available to members of the general public, that he is entitled to some constitutional protection of the confidentiality of such sources, cf. [*Branzburg*], and that government cannot restrain the publication of news emanating from such sources. Cf. [*Pentagon Papers*, section B4 supra]. It is quite another thing to suggest that the Constitution imposes upon government the affirmative duty to make available to journalists sources of information not available to members of the public generally. That proposition finds no support in the words of the Constitution or in any decision of this Court. Accordingly, since §415.071 does not deny the press access to sources of information available to members of the general public, we hold that it does not abridge the protections that the First and Fourteenth Amendments guarantee."

Justice Douglas, joined by Justices Brennan and Marshall, dissented: "In dealing with the free press guarantee, it is important to note that the interest it protects [is] the right of the people, the true sovereign under our constitutional scheme, to govern in an informed manner. [Prisons,] like all other public institutions, are ultimately the responsibility of the populace. [The] public's interest in being informed about prisons is thus paramount. [It is] not enough to note that the press [is] denied no more access to the prisons than is denied the public generally. [In my view,] the absolute ban on press interviews with specifically designated [inmates] is far broader than is necessary to protect any legitimate governmental interests and is an unconstitutional infringement on the public's right to know protected by the free press guarantee of the First Amendment."

Justice Powell also dissented, noting that "I would hold that California's absolute ban against prisoner-press interviews impermissibly restrains the ability of the press to perform its constitutionally established function of informing the people on the conduct of their government." Powell expressly invoked his dissenting opinion in Saxbe v. Washington Post Co., 417 U.S. 843 (1974).

In *Saxbe*, decided on the same day as *Pell*, the Court sustained a U.S. Bureau of Prisons policy virtually identical to the regulation upheld in *Pell*. Dissenting in *Saxbe*, Justice Powell, joined by Justices Brennan and Marshall, argued as follows:

> [Although it] goes too far to suggest that the government must justify under the stringent standards of First Amendment review every regulation that might affect in some tangential way the availability of information to the news [media, it] is equally impermissible to conclude that no governmental inhibition of press access to newsworthy information warrants constitutional scrutiny. At some point official restraints on access to news sources, even though not directed solely at the press, may so undermine the function of the First Amendment that it is both appropriate and necessary to require the government to justify such regulations in terms more compelling than discretionary authority and administrative convenience. It is worth repeating our admonition in *Branzburg* that "without some protection for seeking out the news, freedom of the press could be eviscerated." . . .
>
> In seeking out the news the press [acts] as an agent of the public at large. It is the means by which the people receive that free flow of information and ideas essential to intelligent self-government. [The] Bureau's absolute prohibition of prisoner-press interviews negates the ability of the press to discharge that function and thereby substantially impairs the right of the people to a free flow of information and ideas on the conduct of their Government. The underlying right is the right of the public. . . .

HOUCHINS v. KQED, 438 U.S. 1 (1978). In 1975, KQED reported the suicide of a prisoner in the Greystone portion of the Santa Rita jail. Thereafter, KQED requested and was denied permission to inspect and take pictures within the Greystone facility. KQED brought this action claiming that the refusal to permit public or media access to the jail violated the first amendment. Shortly after the action was filed, Sheriff Houchins modified his "no-access" policy and instituted a series of monthly tours of the jail. Each tour was limited to twenty-five persons, including representatives of the press. The tours did not include the Greystone facility. No cameras or tape recorders were allowed, and those on the tours were not permitted to interview inmates. The district court rejected the sheriff's contention that such a restrictive policy was necessary to protect inmate privacy and to minimize security and administrative problems. It therefore preliminarily enjoined the sheriff from denying KQED and other "responsible representatives" of the press "access to the Santa Rita facilities, including Greystone, 'at reasonable times and hours' and 'from preventing [them] from utilizing photographic and sound equipment [and] inmate interviews in providing full and accurate coverage of the Santa Rita facilities.'" The court of appeals affirmed. In a three-one-three decision, the Supreme Court, Justices Marshall and Blackmun not participating, affirmed in part and reversed in part. Chief Justice Burger, joined by Justices White and Rehnquist, found *Pell* controlling:

"This Court has never intimated a First Amendment guarantee of a right of access to all sources of information within government control. [There] is an undoubted right to gather news 'from any source by means within the law,' but that affords no basis for the claim that the First Amendment compels others — private persons or governments — to supply information."

Justice Stewart concurred in the judgment: "The First and Fourteenth Amendments do not guarantee the public a right of access to information generated or controlled by government, nor do they guarantee the press any basic right of access superior to that of the public generally. The Constitution does no more than assure the public and the press equal access once government has opened its doors. Accordingly, I agree substantially with [the opinion of the Chief Justice. However, whereas] he appears to view 'equal access' as meaning access that is identical in all respects, I believe that the concept of equal access must be accorded more flexibility in order to accommodate the practical distinctions between the press and the general public.

"When on assignment, a journalist does not tour a jail for his own edification. He is there to gather information to be passed on to others, [and our] society depends heavily on the press for [its] enlightenment. [Thus,] the terms of access that are reasonably imposed on individual members may, if they impede effective reporting without sufficient justification, be unreasonable as applied to journalists who are there to convey to the general public what the visitors see."

Applying this standard, Justice Stewart agreed with the district court's findings that "the press required access to the jail on a more flexible and frequent basis than scheduled monthly tours if it was to keep the public informed," and that "the media required cameras and recording equipment for effective presentation to the viewing public of the conditions at the jail seen by individual visitors." Justice Stewart found the injunction "overbroad," however, insofar as it "ordered the Sheriff to permit reporters into the [Greystone] facility and [to] interview randomly encountered inmates," for in "both these respects, the injunction gave the press access to areas and sources of information from which persons on the public tours had been excluded, and thus enlarged the scope of what the [sheriff] had opened to public view."

Justice Stevens, joined by Justices Brennan and Powell, dissented. Justice Stevens maintained that the "preservation of a full and free flow of information to the general public has long been recognized as a core objective of the First Amendment." Moreover, without "some protection for the acquisition of information about the operation of public institutions [by] the public at large, the process of self-governance [would] be stripped of its substance." Although conceding that there are "occasions when governmental activity may properly be carried on in complete secrecy," Justice Stevens observed that "there is no legitimate penological justification for concealing from citizens the conditions in which their fellow citizens are being confined." Justice Stevens thus concluded that an "official prison policy of concealing [knowledge about the operation of a prison] by arbitrarily cutting off the flow of information at its source abridges the [First Amendment]."

Note: A Press Right of Access to Government Information?

1. *Right of access.* Does the first amendment guarantee the press a right of access to government information? If the right of the press to *publish* information

about the activities of government is central to the first amendment, isn't the right of the press to *obtain* such information equally central? Consider the following:

a. BeVier, An Informed Public, An Informing Press: The Search for a Constitutional Principle, 68 Cal. L. Rev. 482, 498-499 (1980):

> The effect on the flow of information [of] government denials of access to information [is] similar to the [effect of such direct restrictions on publication as punishment and censorship. But] the failure of government to [grant] access cannot be credibly argued to be the constitutional equivalent of [such direct restrictions. Punishment and censorship] interfere quite directly with the freedom to publish. When the government denies access to information, however, it poses no threat to freedom, at least if that word is given its ordinary legal meaning. [Punishment and] censorship directly undermine the value of *free* speech, while the denial of access to information undermines [only] the value of *well-informed* speech.

Recall the problem of access to public property for speech purposes, section E2 supra.

b. A. Bickel, The Morality of Consent 80, 87 (1975):

> [Government] may guard mightily against [leaks], and yet must suffer them if they occur. [It] is a disorderly situation, surely. But if we ordered it we would have to sacrifice one of two contending values — privacy or public discourse — which are ultimately irreconcilable. [Thus, to effect a compromise, the First Amendment] ordains an unruly contest between the press [and] government.

Recall the problem of restrictions on the disclosure of confidential information, section B4 supra.

If there is a first amendment right of press access to government information, what are its limits? Is government under a constitutional obligation to make public all information that might enhance "the ability of our people through free and open debate to consider and resolve their own destiny"? Is it "impossible to conceive of a court making case-by-case determinations of the 'necessity' of nondisclosure in any way that would bear even the faintest resemblance [to] 'reasoned elaboration'"? BeVier, supra, at 510.

2. *"Offensive" and "defensive" press rights: a theory of press autonomy?* Consider Blasi, The Checking Value in the First Amendment, 1977 Am. B. Found. Res. J. 521, 596:

> [In his opinions in *Branzburg* and *Zurcher*, on the one hand, and *Pell* and *Houchins*, on the other, Justice Stewart] drew a sharp distinction between the claim to freedom from government interference with source relationships that reporters have established on their own and the contention "that the Constitution imposes upon government the affirmative duty to make available to journalists sources of information not available to members of the public generally." Since this [distinction] would not seem to be of pivotal importance if the overriding consideration is the amount and quality of information available to the public, Justice Stewart's heavy reliance on [it] suggests that his principal concern [was] the institutional autonomy of the press.

Does the "institutional autonomy of the press" provide a more satisfactory basis for interpreting the press clause than the public's "right to know"? Consider

Baker, Press Rights and Government Power to Structure the Press, 34 U. Miami L. Rev. 819, 839-845 (1980):

> Testimonial privileges, protection against searches and seizures, and most protections against regulation are defensive rights: they protect the [press] against destruction, interference, or appropriation by government. Special access to information is an offensive right, a special privilege to engage in activities relevant to press functions. [The] justifications for institutional protection of the press — (1) the need to preserve an outside source that can expose government practices and abuses and (2) the importance of nongovernmentally controlled sources of information [and opinion — suggest] that the press clause rationale is persuasive only for defensive rights. [The] checking function of the press clearly requires independence from government; it requires rights that give the press a defense against government intrusions. [Offensive rights are more problematic. Although] a right of access to government facilities or information furthers the press's capacity to inform and [expose,] constitutionally based access privileges are not as necessary to the protection of the press's integrity.

3. *Are there potential dangers in recognizing a "preferred" status for the press?* Consider Van Alstyne, The First Amendment and the Free Press: A Comment on Some New Trends and Some Old Theories, 9 Hofstra L. Rev. 1, 19-23 (1980):

> [If] journalists may assert access to certain public facilities [in] "first amendment preference" to laypersons, [it] may follow symmetrically that the ensuing published story must meet a standard of professionalism commensurate with the privileged standing of the reporter. [The press operates] most effectively and most legitimately precisely because it forms no part of government. [The] security of the [press] from the encumbrance of public regulation [may] be at risk if one's accent is not on the freedom of the press but is, rather, on the public's right to know. [We] have already imposed upon radio and television substantial "public" obligations — in exchange for exclusive, cost-free licensing privileges. [There] is no reason to suppose that the matter will be different for newspapers should they, too, "succeed" in securing particular rights [that others] cannot claim under a single and indivisible amendment.

4. *Access to judicial proceedings:* Gannett. In Gannett v. DePasquale, 443 U.S. 368 (1979), the defendants in a murder prosecution requested that the public and the press be excluded from a pretrial hearing on a motion to suppress allegedly involuntary confessions. The district attorney did not oppose the request, and the trial judge, finding that the adverse publicity might jeopardize the defendants' right to a fair trial, granted the closure motion. In upholding this order, the Court focused primarily on the claim that the order violated the sixth amendment's guarantee that "[i]n all criminal prosecutions, the accused shall enjoy the right to a [public] trial."

Justice Stewart delivered the opinion of the Court. Although conceding that "there is a strong societal interest in public trials," the Court concluded that the sixth amendment guarantee "is personal to the accused," and that "members of the public" thus "have no constitutional right under the Sixth [Amendment] to attend criminal trials." Turning to the first amendment, the Court found it unnecessary to decide "in the abstract" whether there was a first amendment right of the press or public to attend criminal trials, for "even assuming arguendo, that the [first amendment] may guarantee such access in some situations, [this] putative right was given all appropriate deference by the state [court] in the present case." In reaching this conclusion, the Court noted that the trial judge had concluded that an open proceeding would pose a "reasonable probability of prejudice" to the defendants, so that the closure decision was based "on an assessment of the competing social interests involved [rather] than on any determination that First Amendment freedoms were not implicated." Justice Blackmun, joined by Justices Brennan, White, and Marshall, dissented on sixth amendment grounds.

Richmond Newspapers v. Virginia
448 U.S. 555 (1980)

MR. CHIEF JUSTICE BURGER announced the judgment of the Court and delivered an opinion, in which MR. JUSTICE WHITE and MR. JUSTICE STEVENS joined.

The narrow question presented in this case is whether the right of the public and press to attend criminal trials is guaranteed under the United States Constitution.

[In 1976, Stevenson was convicted of murder. The conviction was reversed, however, and two subsequent trials ended in mistrials. At the outset of his fourth trial, Stevenson moved that the proceeding be closed to the public. Neither the prosecutor nor anyone else present, including two of appellant's reporters, objected to the motion. The trial judge, acting pursuant to a Virginia statute authorizing the court, "in its discretion," to "exclude from the trial any persons whose presence would impair the conduct of a fair trial," ordered "that the Courtroom be kept clear of all parties except the witnesses when they testify." Later that day appellant moved to vacate the closure order. In defense of the order, Stevenson argued that he "didn't want information to leak out," be published by the media, perhaps inaccurately, and then be seen by the jurors. The trial judge, noting also that "having people in the Courtroom is distracting to the jury," denied the motion to vacate and ordered the trial to continue "with the press and public excluded." The following day the trial judge excused the jury and found Stevenson "not guilty." As soon as the trial ended, tapes of the proceeding were made available to the public.]

We begin consideration of this case by noting that the precise issue presented here has not previously been before this Court for decision. In [Gannett], the Court was not required to decide whether a right of access to trials, as distinguished from hearings on pretrial motions, was constitutionally guaranteed. . . .

The origins of the proceeding which has become the modern criminal trial in Anglo-American justice can be traced back beyond reliable historical records. [Throughout] its evolution, the trial has been open to all who cared to observe. [This] is no quirk of history; rather, it has long been recognized as an indispensable attribute of an Anglo-American trial. [Such openness gives] assurance that the proceedings [are] conducted fairly to all concerned, and it [discourages] perjury, the misconduct of participants, and decisions based on secret bias or partiality.

[Moreover,] public trials [have] significant community therapeutic value. [When] a shocking crime occurs, a community reaction of outrage and public protest often follows. Thereafter the open processes of justice serve an important prophylactic purpose, providing an outlet for community concern, hostility, and emotion. . . .

The Bill of Rights was enacted against the backdrop of the long history of trials being presumptively open. [In] guaranteeing freedoms such as those of speech and press, the First Amendment can be read as protecting the right of everyone to attend trials so as to give meaning to those explicit guarantees. "[T]he First Amendment goes beyond protection of the press and the self-expression of individuals to prohibit government from limiting the stock of information from which members of the public may draw." Free speech carries with it some freedom to listen. "In a variety of contexts this Court has referred to a First Amendment right to 'receive information and ideas.'" What this means in the context of trials is that the First Amendment guarantees of speech and press, standing alone, prohibit the government from summarily closing courtroom doors which had long been open to the public at the time that Amendment was adopted. . . .

It is not crucial whether we describe this right to attend criminal trials to hear, see, and communicate observations concerning them as a "right of access,"[11] or a "right to gather information," for we have recognized that "without some protection for seeking out the news, freedom of the press could be eviscerated." [*Branzburg.*] The explicit, guaranteed rights to speak and to publish concerning what takes place at a trial would lose much meaning if access to observe the trial could, as it was here, be foreclosed arbitrarily.[12] . . .

We hold that the right to attend criminal trials[17] is implicit in the guarantees of the First Amendment; without the freedom to attend such trials, which people have exercised for centuries, important aspects of freedom of speech and "of the press could be eviscerated."

Having concluded there was a guaranteed right of the public under the First and Fourteenth Amendments to attend the trial of Stevenson's case, we return to the closure order challenged by appellants. [The] trial judge made no findings to support closure; no inquiry was made as to whether alternative solutions would have met the need to ensure fairness; there was no recognition of any right under the Constitution for the public or press to attend the trial. In contrast to the pretrial proceeding dealt with in *Gannett*, there exist in the context of the trial itself various tested alternatives to satisfy the constitutional demands of fairness. There was no suggestion that any problems with witnesses could not have been dealt with by their exclusion from the courtroom or their sequestration during the trial. Nor is there anything to indicate that sequestration of the jurors would not have guarded against their being subjected to any improper information. All of the alternatives admittedly present difficulties for trial courts, but none of the factors relied on here was beyond the realm of the manageable. Absent an overriding

11. *Procunier* and *Saxbe* are distinguishable in the sense that they were concerned with penal institutions which, by definition, are not "open" or public places. Penal institutions do not share the long tradition of openness. . . .

12. That the right to attend may be exercised by people less frequently today when information as to trials generally reaches them by way of print and electronic media in no way alters the basic right. Instead of relying on personal observation or reports from neighbors as in the past, most people receive information concerning trials through the media whose representatives "are entitled to the same rights [to attend trials] as the general public."

17. Whether the public has a right to attend trials of civil cases is a question not raised by this case, but we note that historically both civil and criminal trials have been presumptively open.

interest articulated in findings, the trial of a criminal case must be open to the public.[18]

Accordingly, the judgment under review is [reversed].

Mr. Justice Powell took no part in the consideration or decision of this case.

MR. JUSTICE BRENNAN, with whom MR. JUSTICE MARSHALL joins, concurring in the judgment. . . .

Customarily, First Amendment guarantees are interposed to protect communication between speaker and listener. [But] the First Amendment embodies more than a commitment to free expression and communicative interchange for their own sakes; it has a *structural* role to play in securing and fostering our republican system of self-government. Implicit in this structural role is not only "the principle that debate on public issues should be uninhibited, robust, and wide-open," but the antecedent assumption that valuable public debate [must] be informed. The structural model links the First Amendment to that process of communication necessary for a democracy to survive, and thus entails solicitude not only for communication itself, but also for the indispensable conditions of meaningful communication.

However, because "the stretch of this protection is theoretically endless," it must be invoked with discrimination and temperance. [At] least two helpful principles may be sketched. First, the case for a right of access has special force when drawn from an enduring and vital tradition of public entree to particular proceedings or information. Such a tradition commands respect in part because the Constitution carries the gloss of history. More importantly, a tradition of accessibility implies the favorable judgment of experience. Second, the value of access must be measured in specifics. Analysis is not advanced by rhetorical statements that all information bears upon public issues; what is crucial in individual cases is whether access to a particular government process is important in terms of that very process.

To resolve the case before us, therefore, we must consult historical and current practice with respect to open trials, and weigh the importance of public access to the trial process itself. [Tradition], contemporaneous state practice, and this Court's own decisions manifest a common understanding that "[a] trial is a public event." [As] a matter of law and virtually immemorial custom, public trials have been the essentially unwavering rule in ancestral England and in our own Nation. Such abiding adherence to the principle of open trials "reflect[s] a profound judgment about the way in which law should be enforced and justice administered." [Moreover, publicity] serves to advance several of the particular purposes of the trial (and, indeed, the judicial) process. Open trials play a fun-

18. We have no occasion here to define the circumstances in which all or parts of a criminal trial may be closed to the public, but our holding today does not mean that the First Amendment rights of the public and representatives of the press are absolute. Just as a government may impose reasonable time, place, and manner restrictions upon the use of its streets in the interest of such objectives as the free flow of traffic, see, e.g., Cox v. New Hampshire, [section E2a supra], so may a trial judge, in the interest of the fair administration of justice, impose reasonable limitations on access to a trial. [Moreover], since courtrooms have limited capacity, there may be occasions when not every person who wishes to attend can be accommodated. In such situations, reasonable restrictions on general access are traditionally imposed, including preferential seating for media representatives. . . .

damental role in furthering the efforts of our judicial system to assure the criminal defendant a fair and accurate adjudication of guilt or innocence; [public] access is essential [if] trial adjudication is to achieve the objective of maintaining public confidence in the administration of justice; [and public] access to trials acts as an important check [on] our system of government. . . .

[Thus,] our ingrained tradition of public trials and the importance of public access to the broader purposes of the trial process tip the balance strongly toward the rule that trials be open. What countervailing interests might be sufficiently compelling to reverse this presumption of openness need not concern us now,[24] for the statute at stake here authorizes trial closures at the unfettered discretion of the judge and parties.[25] Accordingly, [the statute] violates the First and Fourteenth Amendments, and the decision of the Virginia Supreme Court to the contrary should be reversed.

MR. JUSTICE STEWART, concurring in the judgment. . . .

Whatever the ultimate answer [with] respect to pretrial suppression hearings in criminal cases, the First and Fourteenth Amendments clearly give the press and the public a right of access to trials themselves, civil as well as criminal. [It] has for centuries been a basic presupposition of the Anglo-American legal system that trials shall be public trials. [With] us, a trial is by very definition a proceeding open to the press and to the public.

In conspicuous contrast to a military base, Greer v. Spock, [section E2b supra]; a jail, Adderley v. Florida, [section E2b supra]; or a prison, [*Pell*], a trial courtroom is a public place. Even more than city streets, sidewalks, and parks as areas of First Amendment activity, a trial courtroom is a place where representatives of the press and of the public are not only free to be, but where their presence serves to assure the integrity of what goes on.

But this does not mean that the First Amendment right of members of the public and representatives of the press to attend civil and criminal trials is absolute. Just as a legislature may impose reasonable time, place, and manner restrictions upon the exercise of First Amendment freedoms, so may a trial judge impose reasonable limitations upon the unrestricted occupation of a courtroom by representatives of the press and members of the public. . . .

Since in the present case the trial judge appears to have given no recognition to the right of representatives of the press and members of the public to be present at the Virginia murder trial over which he was presiding, the judgment under review must be reversed. . . .

MR. JUSTICE BLACKMUN, concurring in the judgment.

My opinion and vote in partial dissent last Term in [*Gannett*] compels my vote to reverse the judgment of the Supreme Court of Virginia. . . .

MR. JUSTICE REHNQUIST, dissenting. . . .

24. For example, national security concerns about confidentiality may sometimes warrant closures during sensitive portions of trial proceedings, such as testimony about state secrets. Cf. United States v. Nixon, 418 U.S. 683, 714-716 (1974).

25. Significantly, closing a trial lacks even the justification for barring the door to pretrial hearings: the necessity of preventing dissemination of suppressible prejudicial evidence to the public before the jury pool has become, in a practical sense, finite and subject to sequestration.

[I] do not believe that [the Constitution] requires that a State's reasons for denying public access to a trial, where both the prosecuting attorney and the defendant have consented to an order of closure approved by the judge, are subject to any additional constitutional review at our hands. . . .

The issue here is not whether the "right" to freedom of the press conferred by the First Amendment to the Constitution overrides the defendant's "right" to a fair trial conferred by other Amendments to the Constitution; it is instead whether any provision in the Constitution may fairly be read to prohibit what the trial judge in the Virginia state-court system did in this case. Being unable to find any such prohibition in the First, Sixth, Ninth, or any other Amendment to the United States Constitution, or in the Constitution itself, I dissent.

GLOBE NEWSPAPER CO. v. SUPERIOR COURT, 457 U.S. 596 (1982). To protect the minor victims of sex crimes from further trauma and embarrassment and to encourage such victims to come forward and testify in a truthful and credible manner, section 16A of chapter 278 of Massachusetts General Laws requires trial judges, at trials for specified sexual offenses involving a victim under age eighteen, to exclude the press and general public from the courtroom during the testimony of the victim. The Court, in a six-to-three decision, held section 16A unconstitutional. Justice Brennan delivered the opinion of the Court:

"*Richmond Newspapers* firmly established for the first time that the press and general public have a constitutional right of access to criminal trials. [Two] features of the criminal justice system, emphasized in the various opinions in *Richmond Newspapers*, together serve to explain why a right of access to *criminal trials* in particular is properly afforded protection by the First Amendment. First, the criminal trial historically has been open to the press and general public. [Second,] the right of access to criminal trials plays a particularly significant role in the functioning of the judicial process and the government as a whole.

"[The Commonwealth] argues that criminal trials have not always been open to the press and general public during the testimony of minor sex victims. [Even] if [this is correct], the argument is unavailing. [Whether] the First Amendment right of access to criminal trials can be restricted in the context of any particular criminal trial [depends] not on the historical openness of that type of criminal trial but rather on the state interests assertedly supporting the restriction. . . .

"Where, as in the present case, the State attempts to deny the right of access in order to inhibit the disclosure of sensitive information, it must be shown that the denial is necessitated by a compelling governmental interest, and is narrowly tailored to serve that interest. . . .

"We agree [that the Commonwealth's interest in] safeguarding the physical and psychological well-being of a minor [is] a compelling one. But as compelling as that interest is, it does not justify a *mandatory*-closure rule, for it is clear that the circumstances of the particular case may affect the significance of the interest. A trial court can determine on a case-by-case basis whether closure is necessary to protect the welfare of a minor victim. Among the factors to be weighed are the minor victim's age, psychological maturity and understanding, the nature of the crime, the desires of the victim, and the interests of parents and relatives. [Section] 16A cannot be viewed as a narrowly tailored means of accommodating the State's asserted interest. . . .

"Nor can §16A be justified on the basis of the Commonwealth's [interest in] the encouragement of minor victims of sex crimes to come forward and provide accurate testimony. The Commonwealth has offered no empirical support for the claim that the rule of automatic closure [will] lead to an increase in the number of minor sex victims coming forward and cooperating with state authorities. . . ."

Justice O'Connor concurred in the judgment.

Chief Justice Burger, joined by Justice Rehnquist, dissented: "In *Richmond Newspapers*, we [emphasized] that criminal trials were generally open to the public throughout this country's history. [Today] Justice Brennan ignores the weight of historical practice. There is clearly a long history of exclusion of the public from trials involving sexual assaults, particularly those against minors.

"[Moreover, the] Commonwealth has not denied the public or the media access to information as to what takes place at trial. [Massachusetts] does not deny the press and the public access to the trial transcript or to other sources of information about the victim's testimony. Even the victim's identity is part of the public record. [The] purpose of [section 16A] was to give assurance to parents and minors that they would have this moderate and limited protection from the trauma, embarrassment and humiliation of having to reveal the intimate details of a sexual assault in front of a large group of unfamiliar spectators — and perhaps a television audience — and to lower the barriers to the reporting of such crimes which might come from the victim's dread of public testimony. [For] me, it seems beyond doubt, considering the minimal impact of the law on First Amendment rights and the overriding weight of the Commonwealth's interest in protecting child rape victims, that the Massachusetts law is not unconstitutional. . . ." Justice Stevens dissented on other grounds.

Note: Variations on the Press Right of Access

1. *Voir dire hearings.* In Press-Enterprise Co. v. Superior Court, 464 U.S. 501 (1984), the Court held that a state court order closing the voir dire examination of prospective jurors in a criminal trial violated the first amendment. The Court explained that the "presumption of openness may be overcome only by an overriding interest based on findings that closure is essential to preserve higher values and is narrowly tailored to serve that interest." Although conceding that the "jury selection process may, in some circumstances, give rise to a compelling [privacy] interest of a prospective juror when interrogation touches on deeply personal matters," the Court concluded that the trial court in this case had not adequately considered the alternatives to closure. See also Press-Enterprise Co. v. Superior Court, 478 U.S. 1 (1986) (holding that a newspaper has a first amendment right of access to the transcript of a preliminary hearing).

In what circumstances, if any, does the first amendment guarantee the media a right to televise criminal trials? Cf. Chandler v. Florida, 449 U.S. 560 (1981) (for a state to permit television coverage of a criminal trial does not constitute a per se violation of the defendant's right to a fair trial).

2. *Conditioned access to information.* Despite *Richmond Newspapers*, government is under no general constitutional obligation to disclose information to the press or public and indeed may ordinarily prohibit its employees from disclosing "confidential" information. To what extent, then, may government condition its voluntary disclosure of information on the press's agreement not to publish?

Consider Seattle Times Co. v. Rhinehart, 467 U.S. 20 (1984). In a defamation action against the Seattle Times, a state court ordered the plaintiff to disclose certain information in discovery. The state court entered a protective order pursuant to a state rule modeled on Rule 26(c) of the Federal Rules of Civil Procedure. The order prohibited the newspaper from using the disclosed information, which included the names of contributors to a controversial religious group, for any purpose other than trial of the case. The Supreme Court unanimously rejected the newspaper's claim that the order violated the first amendment:

> [The newspaper] gained the information [only] by virtue of the trial court's discovery processes. [It had] no First Amendment right of access to [the information]. [Moreover, the] protective order prevents [the dissemination only of] information obtained through [discovery. The newspaper is free to] disseminate the identical information [if it obtains it] through means independent of the court's processes. [Thus], continued court control over the discovered information does not raise the same spectre of government censorship that such control might suggest in other situations. [We] therefore hold that where [a] protective order is entered on a showing of good cause as required by Rule 26(c), is limited to the context of pretrial civil discovery, and does not restrict the dissemination of the information if gained from other sources, it does not offend the First Amendment.

3.   *Differential Treatment of the Press*

Consider the constitutionality of the following laws: (1) A sales tax of 4 percent on all sales of goods. This is challenged by a newspaper publisher who argues that, as applied to his sales, the tax constitutes an impermissible "tax on the press." (2) A sales tax of 4 percent on all sales of goods, except that sales of newspapers, books, and periodicals are taxed at the rate of 6 percent. (3) A sales tax of 4 percent on all sales of goods, except that sales of newspapers, books, and periodicals are taxed at the rate of 2 percent. (4) A sales tax of 4 percent on all sales of goods, except that sales of newspapers are taxed at the rate of 2 percent. This is challenged by a publisher of magazines. (5) A sales tax of 4 percent on all sales of goods, except that sales of newspapers, books, and periodicals are taxed at 2 percent if the publisher has an annual profit of less than $1 million. This is challenged by the only publisher in the state who has an annual profit of more than $1 million.

MINNEAPOLIS STAR & TRIBUNE CO. v. MINNESOTA COMMISSIONER OF REVENUE, 460 U.S. 575 (1983). Minnesota imposes a sales tax on retail sales. To avoid double taxation, sales of components to be used in the production of goods that will themselves be sold at retail are exempt from the sales tax. Minnesota also imposes a use tax on the use or consumption of goods that were purchased without payment of the sales tax. The use tax is designed to eliminate the incentive of residents to buy goods in states with lower sales taxes. Until 1971, periodic publications were exempt from both the sales and the use taxes. In 1971, however, Minnesota imposed a use tax on the cost of paper and ink products consumed in the production of periodic publications. As a result, ink and paper used in such publications became the only components of goods to be sold at retail subject to the use tax. In 1974, Minnesota amended the use tax to exempt the first $100,000 worth of ink and paper consumed by a publication in any calendar year. After enactment of the $100,000 exemption, eleven publishers, producing fourteen of the 388 newspapers in Minnesota, incurred a tax liability in 1974. Appellant was one of the eleven. Because of its size, it paid approximately $600,000, or about two-thirds of the total revenue raised by the tax. The Court held that this taxing scheme violated appellant's rights under the first amendment. Justice O'Connor delivered the opinion of the Court:

"Minnesota has [created] a special tax that applies only to certain publications protected by the First Amendment. [We] must determine whether the First Amendment permits such special taxation. [There] is substantial evidence that differential taxation of the press would have troubled the Framers of the First Amendment. [The] fears of the [framers] were well-founded. [When] a State singles out the press [for special taxation], the political constraints that prevent a legislature from passing crippling taxes of general applicability are weakened, and the threat of burdensome taxes becomes acute. That threat can operate as effectively as a censor to check critical comment by the press. [Differential] taxation of the press, then, places such a burden on the interests protected by the First Amendment and we cannot countenance such treatment unless the State asserts a counterbalancing interest of compelling importance that it cannot achieve without differential taxation. . . .

"Minnesota invites us to look beyond the form of the tax to its substance. The tax is, according to the State, merely a substitute for the sales tax, which, as a generally applicable tax, would be constitutional as applied to the press. [But] the State has offered no explanation of why it chose to use a substitute for the sales tax rather than the sales tax itself.

"[The State argues further] that this scheme actually *favors* the press over other businesses, because the same rate of tax is applied, but, for the press, the rate applies to the cost of components rather than to the sales price. [But we] would be hesitant to fashion a rule that automatically allowed the State to single out the press for a different method of taxation as long as the effective burden was no different from that on other taxpayers or the burden on the press was lighter than that on other businesses. One reason for this reluctance is that the very selection of the press for special treatment threatens the press not only with the current *differential* treatment, but with the possibility of subsequent differentially *more burdensome* treatment. Thus, even without actually imposing an extra burden on the press, the government might be able to achieve censorial effects, for '[t]he threat of sanctions may deter [the] exercise of [First Amendment] rights almost as potently as the actual application of sanctions.' [A] second reason to avoid the proposed rule is that courts as institutions are poorly equipped to evaluate with precision the relative burdens of various methods of taxation. [The] possibility of error inherent in the proposed rule poses too great a threat to concerns at the heart of the First Amendment, and we cannot tolerate that possibility.[13] Min-

13. If a State employed the same *method* of taxation but applied a lower *rate* to the press, so that there could be no doubt that the legislature was not singling out the press to bear a more burdensome tax, we would, of course, be in a position to evaluate the relative burdens. And, given the clarity of the relative burdens, as well as the rule that differential methods of taxation are not automatically permissible if less burdensome, a lower tax rate for the press would not raise the threat that the legislature might later impose an extra burden that would escape detection by the courts.

nesota, therefore, has offered no adequate justification for the special treatment of newspapers. . . .

"Minnesota's ink and paper tax violates the First Amendment not only because it singles out the press, but also because it targets a small group of newspapers. The effect of the $100,000 exemption [is] that only a handful of publishers pay any tax at [all]. The State explains this exemption as part of a policy favoring an 'equitable' tax system, [but] there are no comparable exemptions for small enterprises outside the press. [We] think that recognizing a power in the State [to] tailor the tax so that it singles out only a few members of the press presents such a potential for abuse that [Minnesota's interest in an 'equitable' tax system cannot] justify the scheme. [The] tax violates the First Amendment."

Justice Rehnquist dissented: "The Court recognizes [that] Minnesota could avoid constitutional problems by imposing on newspapers [the same] sales tax that it imposes on other retailers. Rather than impose such a tax, however, the Minnesota legislature decided to provide newspapers with an exemption from the sales tax and impose a use tax on ink and paper. [The] problem the Court finds too difficult to deal with is whether this difference in treatment results in a significant burden on newspapers. The record reveals that in 1974 [appellant had total sales of] $46,498,738. Had a 4% sales tax been imposed, [appellant] would have been liable for $1,859,950. [The] record further indicates that [appellant] paid $608,634 in use taxes in 1974. We need no expert testimony [to] determine that the [use tax] is significantly less burdensome than the [sales tax]. Ignoring these calculations, the Court concludes that 'differential treatment' alone [requires] that the [tax] be found 'presumptively unconstitutional' and declared invalid 'unless the State asserts a [compelling justification].' The 'differential treatment' standard [is] unprecedented and unwarranted. [No] First Amendment issue is raised unless First Amendment rights have been infringed. . . .

"Wisely not relying solely on its inability to weigh the burdens of the [tax] scheme, the Court also says that even if the resultant burden on the press is lighter than on others '[t]he very selection of the press for special treatment threatens the press [with] the possibility of subsequent differentially *more burdensome* [treatment].' Surely the Court does not mean what it seems to say. [This] Court is quite capable of dealing with changes in state taxing laws which are intended to penalize newspapers. [Furthermore], the Court itself intimates [in footnote 13 that certain forms of differential treatment are permissible, even though they too have the] potential for 'the threat of sanctions,' because the legislature could at any time raise the taxes to the higher rate. . . .

"[In my view, the] State [in this case] is required to show [only] that its taxing scheme is rational. [In] this case that showing can be made easily. [There] must be few such inexpensive items sold in Minnesota in the volume of newspaper sales. [The] legislature could have concluded that paper boys, corner newsstands, and vending machines provide an unreliable and unsuitable means for collection of a sales tax. [The] reasonable alternative Minnesota chose to impose [was] the use tax on ink and paper. [The Court also] finds [that] the exemption newspapers receive for the first $100,000 of ink and paper [used] violates the First Amendment because the result is that only a few of the newspapers actually pay a use tax. I cannot agree. [Absent] any improper motive on the part of the Minnesota legislature in drawing the lines of this exemption, it cannot be construed as violating the First Amendment. [There] is no reason to conclude that the State [acted] other than reasonably and rationally to fit its sales and use tax scheme to its own local needs and usages."

Justice White concurred in part and dissented in part.

Note: Differential Treatment

1. *Preserving press neutrality.* Consider Bezanson, Political Agnosticism, Editorial Freedom, and Government Neutrality toward the Press, 72 Iowa L. Rev. 1359, 1371 (1987): "[A sound] reason for making constitutionally suspect any formal singling out of the press [is] to protect the political neutrality of the press [and to] prevent the government from undermining the [neutrality of the press] by forcing [it] to engage actively in the political process [to] protect its own self-interest." Does this mean that even a law expressly benefiting the press, such as an exemption from a state's sales tax, should be invalid? Consider footnote 13 in *Minneapolis Star.*

2. *Beneficial differentiation.* A Michigan statute prohibits corporations, excluding "media corporations," from using general treasury funds for independent expenditures in connection with state elections. Assuming the restriction on such corporate political expenditures is constitutional because it reduces the threat that corporate treasuries, which are amassed with the aid of favorable state laws and have little or no correlation to the public's support for the corporation's political ideas, will be used unfairly to influence election outcomes, is the exemption of "media corporations" constitutional after *Minneapolis Star?* In Austin v. Michigan Chamber of Commerce, 494 U.S. 652 (1990), the Court upheld this exemption on the ground that it served a "compelling state purpose" in light of "the unique role that the press plays in 'informing and educating the public, offering criticism, and providing a forum for discussion and debate.'" Suppose the Michigan statute had not exempted media corporations. Would such an exemption be constitutionally compelled by the first amendment?

3. *Content-based differentiation.* The Court relied on *Minneapolis Star* in Arkansas Writers' Project, Inc. v. Ragland, 481 U.S. 221 (1987), to invalidate an Arkansas statute that imposed a state sales tax on general interest magazines but exempted religious, professional, trade, and sports journals. In an opinion by Justice Marshall, the Court held that selective taxation of the press — either by singling out the press as a whole or by singling out individual members of the press — posed particular dangers of governmental abuse. Moreover, the Arkansas statute evidenced an even more disturbing use of selective taxation than the statute invalidated in *Minneapolis Star* because the discrimination was "content-based." Justice Scalia, joined by Chief Justice Rehnquist, dissented.

4. *Intermedia differentiation: Leathers.* In Leathers v. Medlock, 499 U.S. 439 (1991), the Court considered the constitutionality of the Arkansas Gross Receipts Act, which imposes a 4 percent tax. The act expressly exempts receipts from subscription and over-the-counter newspapers and magazine sales but imposes the tax on cable television. The Court, in an opinion by Justice O'Connor, rejected petitioners' argument that such "intermedia discrimination" violates the first amendment. The Court explained that such a tax is "suspect" only if it "threatens to suppress the expression of particular ideas or viewpoints," "singles out the press," "targets a small group of speakers," or "discriminates on the basis [of] con-

tent." Because the "Arkansas tax [presents] none of these types of discrimination," the Court concluded that Arkansas's "extension of its generally applicable sales tax to [cable television], while exempting the print media, does not violate the First Amendment."

Justice Marshall, joined by Justice Brennan, dissented:

> Because cable competes with [the print] media in the larger information market, the power to discriminate between these media triggers the central concern underlying the nondiscrimination principle: the risk of covert censorship. [By] imposing tax burdens that disadvantage one information medium relative to another, the State can favor those media that it likes and punish those that it dislikes. [The] State bears the burden of demonstrating that "differential treatment" of cable television is justified by some "special characteristic" of that particular information medium or by some other "counterbalancing interest of compelling importance that [the State] cannot achieve without differential taxation." [The] only justification that the State asserts for taxing cable operators more heavily than newspapers [and magazines] is its interest in raising revenue. This interest is not sufficiently compelling to overcome the presumption of unconstitutionality under the nondiscrimination principle.

5. *Intermedia discrimination:* Turner. In Turner Broadcasting Inc. v. FCC, 512 U.S. 622 (1994), section F4 infra, the Court upheld "must carry" provisions for cable television that favored broadcast over cable programmers. The Court observed:

> Regulations that discriminate among media, or among different speakers within a single medium, often present serious First Amendment concerns. [Citing *Minneapolis Star* and *Arkansas Writers' Project.*] It would be error to conclude, however, that the First Amendment mandates strict scrutiny for any speech regulation that applied to one medium (or a subset thereof) but not others. [The] taxes invalidated in *Minneapolis Star* and *Arkansas Writers' Project* [targeted] a small number of speakers [and] were structured in a manner that raised suspicions that their objective [was] the suppression of certain ideas.
>
> But such heightened scrutiny is unwarranted [where, as here,] the differential treatment [is] not structured in a manner that carries the inherent risk of undermining First Amendment interests. The [must carry] regulations [apply] to almost all cable systems in the country, rather than just a select few. As a result, [they] do not pose the same dangers of suppression and manipulation that were posed by the more narrowly targeted regulations in *Minneapolis Star* and *Arkansas Writers' Project*.

4. Regulating the Press to "Improve" the Marketplace of Ideas

In what circumstances, if any, is it appropriate for government to regulate the media in order to "improve" the system of free expression? Recall the discussion of this issue in the electoral context in section E4 supra.

MIAMI HERALD PUBLISHING CO. v. TORNILLO, 418 U.S. 241 (1974). In *Tornillo*, the Court considered the constitutionality of a Florida "'right of reply' statute which [provided] that if a candidate for [political office] is assailed regarding his personal character or official record by any newspaper, the candidate has the right to demand that the newspaper print, free of cost to the candidate, any reply the candidate may make to the newspaper's charges. The reply must appear in as conspicuous a place and in the same kind of type as the charges which prompted the reply, provided it does not take up more space than the charges." The Court, in a unanimous decision, held the statute invalid. Chief Justice Burger delivered the opinion of the Court:

"[Advocates] of an enforceable right of access to the press [urge] that at the time the First Amendment [was ratified] the press was broadly representative of the people it was serving. [Entry] into publishing was inexpensive [and a] true marketplace of ideas existed in which there was relatively easy access to the channels of communication. Access advocates submit that [the press of today is] very different. [Newspapers] have become big business and [the press] has become noncompetitive and enormously powerful and influential in its capacity to manipulate popular opinion. [The] result of these vast changes has been to place in a few hands the power to inform the American people and shape public opinion. [There] tends to be a homogeneity of editorial opinion, commentary, and interpretative analysis. [The] obvious solution [would] be to have additional newspapers. But [economic factors] have made entry into the marketplace of ideas served by the print media almost impossible. [The] First Amendment interest of the public in being informed is said to be in peril. . . .

"However much validity may be found in these arguments, [the] implementation of a remedy such as an enforceable right of access necessarily [brings] about a confrontation with the express provisions of the First Amendment. [The] argument that the Florida statute does not amount to a restriction of [the newspaper's] right to speak because 'the statute in question here has not prevented [the newspaper] from saying anything it wished' begs the core question. Compelling editors or publishers to publish that which '"reason" tells them should not be published' is what is at issue in this case. The Florida statute operates as a command in the same sense as a statute or regulation forbidding [the newspaper] to publish specified matter. [The] Florida statute exacts a penalty on the basis of the content of a newspaper. The first phase of the penalty [is] exacted in terms of the cost in printing [and] in taking up space that could be devoted to other material the newspaper may have preferred to print. [Faced with such a penalty,] editors might well conclude that the safe course is to avoid controversy. [Thus, the government-enforced] right of access inescapably 'dampens the vigor and limits the variety of public debate.' . . .

"[Moreover, even] if a newspaper would face no additional costs to comply with a compulsory access law and would not be forced to forgo publication of news or opinion by the inclusion of a reply, the Florida statute fails to clear the barriers of the First Amendment because of its intrusion into the function of editors. A newspaper is more than a passive receptacle or conduit for news, comment, and advertising. The choice of material to go into a newspaper [constitutes] the exercise of editorial control and judgment. It has yet to be demonstrated how governmental regulation of this crucial process can be exercised consistent with First Amendment guarantees of a free press as they have evolved to this time."

Consider the possibility that the law in *Tornillo* was a kind of "candidate protection act," and illegitimate because its purpose and effect were to insulate political figures from criticism. In a concurring opinion in *Tornillo*, Justice Brennan asserted that "the Court's opinion [implies] no view upon the constitutionality of 'retraction' statutes affording plaintiffs able to prove defamatory falsehoods a statutory action to require publication of a retraction." Do you agree? Suppose, instead of a "right-of-reply" law, Florida adopted a "right-of-access" law, requiring every newspaper to set aside one page each issue for letters to the editor, not to exceed 500 words, to be selected for publication without regard to content. Would such a law be invalid under *Tornillo?* Recall *PruneYard*, section E5 supra.

Red Lion Broadcasting Co. v. FCC
395 U.S. 367 (1969)

[In *Red Lion*, the Court considered the constitutionality of the Federal Communication Commission's fairness doctrine and its component regulations governing personal attacks and political editorializing. The fairness doctrine, which originated "very early in the history of broadcasting," imposes "on radio and television broadcasters the requirement that discussion of public issues be presented on broadcast stations, and that each side of those issues must be given fair coverage." The personal attack rule requires that when, "during the presentation of views on a controversial issue of public importance, an attack is made upon the honesty, character, integrity or like personal qualities of an identified person or group," the attacked person or group must be given notice, a transcript, and a reasonable opportunity to respond. The political editorializing rule requires that when, in an editorial, a broadcaster endorses or opposes a political candidate, the broadcaster must notify the opposed candidate or the opponents of the endorsed candidate and give them a "reasonable opportunity" to reply.]

JUSTICE WHITE delivered the opinion of the Court. . . .

The broadcasters challenge the fairness doctrine and its specific manifestations in the personal attack and political editorial rules on conventional First Amendment grounds, alleging that the rules abridge their freedom of speech and press. Their contention is that the First Amendment protects their desire to use their allotted frequencies continuously to broadcast whatever they choose, and to exclude whomever they choose from ever using that frequency. No man may be prevented from saying or publishing what he thinks, or from refusing in his speech or other utterances to give equal weight to the views of his opponents. This right, they say, applies equally to broadcasters.

Although broadcasting is clearly a medium affected by a First Amendment interest, differences in the characteristics of new media justify differences in the First Amendment standards applied to them. . . .

Where there are substantially more individuals who want to broadcast than there are frequencies to allocate, it is idle to posit an unabridgeable First Amendment right to broadcast comparable to the right of every individual to speak, write, or publish. If 100 persons want broadcast licenses but there are only 10 frequencies to allocate, all of them may have the same "right" to a license; but if there is to be any effective communication by radio, only a few can be licensed and the rest must be barred from the airwaves. It would be strange if the First Amendment, aimed at protecting and furthering communications, prevented the Government from making radio communication possible by requiring licenses to broadcast and by limiting the number of licenses so as not to overcrowd the spectrum. . . .

By the same token, as far as the First Amendment is concerned those who are licensed stand no better than those to whom licenses are refused. A license permits broadcasting, but the licensee has no constitutional right to be the one who holds the license or to monopolize a radio frequency to the exclusion of his fellow citizens. There is nothing in the First Amendment which prevents the Government from requiring a licensee to share his frequency with others and to conduct himself as a proxy or fiduciary with obligations to present those views and voices which are representative of his community and which would otherwise, by necessity, be barred from the airwaves.

[The] people as a whole retain their interest in free speech by radio and their collective right to have the medium function consistently with the ends and purposes of the First Amendment. It is the right of the viewers and listeners, not the right of the broadcasters, which is paramount. [It] is the right of the public to receive suitable access to social, political, esthetic, moral, and other ideas and experiences which is crucial here. . . .

[We cannot] say that it is inconsistent with the First Amendment goal of producing an informed public capable of conducting its own affairs to require a broadcaster to permit answers to personal attacks occurring in the course of discussing controversial issues, or to require that the political opponents of those endorsed by the station be given a chance to communicate with the public. Otherwise, station owners and a few networks would have unfettered power to make time available only to the highest bidders, to communicate only their own views on public issues, people and candidates, and to permit on the air only those with whom they agreed. There is no sanctuary in the First Amendment for unlimited private censorship operating in a medium not open to all. . . .

It is strenuously argued, however, that if political editorials or personal attacks will trigger an obligation in broadcasters to afford the opportunity for expression to speakers who need not pay for time and whose views are unpalatable to the licensees, then broadcasters will be irresistibly forced to self-censorship and their coverage of controversial public issues will be eliminated or at least rendered wholly ineffective. Such a result would indeed be a serious matter, for should licensees actually eliminate their coverage of controversial issues, the purposes of the doctrine would be stifled.

At this point, however, as the Federal Communications Commission has indicated, that possibility is at best speculative. [And] if experience with the administration of these doctrines indicates that they have the net effect of reducing rather than enhancing the volume and quality of coverage, there will be time enough to reconsider the constitutional implications. The fairness doctrine in the past has had no such overall effect.

That this will occur now seems unlikely, however, since if present licensees should suddenly prove timorous, the Commission is not powerless to insist that they give adequate and fair attention to public issues. It does not violate the First Amendment to treat licensees given the privilege of using scarce radio frequencies as proxies for the entire community, obligated to give suitable time and attention to matters of great public concern. To condition the granting or renewal of licenses on a willingness to present representative community views on controversial issues is consistent with the ends and purposes of those constitutional provisions forbidding the abridgment of freedom of speech and freedom of the press. . . .

It is argued that even if at one time the lack of available frequencies for all who wished to use them justified the Government's choice of those who would best serve the public interest by acting as proxy for those who would present differing views, or by giving the latter access directly to broadcast facilities, this condition no longer prevails so that continuing control is not justified. To this there are several answers.

Scarcity is not entirely a thing of the past. Advances in technology, such as microwave transmission, have led to more efficient utilization of the frequency spectrum, but uses for that spectrum have also grown apace. [Nothing] in this record, or in our own researches, convinces us that the resource is no longer one for which there are more immediate and potential uses than can be accommodated. . . .

Even where there are gaps in spectrum utilization, the fact remains that existing broadcasters have often attained their present position because of their initial government selection in competition with others before new technological advances opened new opportunities for further uses. Long experience in broadcasting, confirmed habits of listeners and viewers, network affiliation, and other advantages in program procurement give existing broadcasters a substantial advantage over new entrants, even where new entry is technologically possible. These advantages are the fruit of a preferred position conferred by the Government. Some present possibility for new entry by competing stations is not enough, in itself, to render unconstitutional the Government's effort to assure that a broadcaster's programming ranges widely enough to serve the public interest.

In view of the scarcity of broadcast frequencies, the Government's role in allocating those frequencies, and the legitimate claims of those unable without governmental assistance to gain access to those frequencies for expression of their views, we hold the [regulations] constitutional.[28] . . .

[Not having heard argument, Justice Douglas did not participate.]

Note: Regulating the Airwaves

1. Buckley *and* Red Lion. Note that *Red Lion*, like Buckley v. Valeo, section E4 supra, involves a conflict between competing theories of the role of government and of the appropriate conception of a system of freedom of expression. Under one view, government is permitted and may even have an obligation to in-

---

28. We need not deal with the argument that even if there is no longer a technological scarcity of frequencies limiting the number of broadcasters, there nevertheless is an economic scarcity in the sense that the Commission could or does limit entry to the broadcasting market on economic grounds and license no more stations than the market will support. Hence, it is said, the fairness doctrine or its equivalent is essential to satisfy the claims of those excluded and of the public generally. A related argument, which we also put aside, is that quite apart from scarcity of frequencies, technological or economic, Congress does not abridge freedom of speech or press by legislation directly or indirectly multiplying the voices and views presented to the public through time sharing, fairness doctrines, or other devices which limit or dissipate the power of those who sit astride the channels of communication with the general public. . . .

tervene in order to prevent the distorting effects on deliberative processes that are created by the operation of the "private" sphere. Under the competing view, government should accept the private sphere "as is" and may not consider inequalities that derive therefrom as "distortions" at all. Why do *Buckley* and *Red Lion* resolve what is in many respects the same dispute in such different ways? See C. Sunstein, Democracy and the Problem of Free Speech (1993) (approving *Red Lion*, criticizing *Buckley*, and calling for greater regulation of the media to promote free expression).

2. *Licensing the airwaves.* In the Communications Act of 1934, the government, "to maintain the control of the United States over [the channels of] radio transmission; and to provide for the use of such channels, but not the ownership thereof, by persons for limited periods of time," established the FCC and granted it broad power to license and regulate the broadcast spectrum "as public convenience, interest, or necessity requires." In National Broadcasting Co. v. United States, 319 U.S. 190 (1943), the Court held that such government licensing did not violate the first amendment because, "[u]nlike other modes of expression, radio inherently is not available to all." Consider the following arguments:

a. Powe, "Or of the [Broadcast] Press," 55 Tex. L. Rev. 39, 55-56 (1976):

> As a theory, scarcity begins with the premise [that] information sources do not compete effectively with each other. This premise is not successfully explained, and seems contradictory to the normal first amendment assumption. [Moreover,] if one looks to actual numbers [there are more radio and television stations in the United States than daily newspapers].

b. Coase, The Federal Communications Commission, 2 J.L. & Econ. 1, 14-18 (1959):

> [The Court] seems to believe that federal regulation is needed because radio frequencies are limited in number and people want to use more of them than are available. But it is a commonplace of economics that almost all resources used in the economic system (and not simply radio and television frequencies) are limited in amount and scarce, in that people would like to use more than exists. [It] is true that some mechanism has to be employed to decide who [should] be allowed to use the scarce resource. But the way this is usually done [is] to employ the price mechanism, and this allocates resources to users without the need for government regulation. [An] administrative agency which attempts to perform the function normally carried out by the pricing mechanism [cannot], by the nature of things, be [fully aware] of the preferences of consumers. [Allocation by means of the pricing mechanism is thus more likely than allocation by administrative action to serve the "public convenience, interest, or necessity."]

c. Van Alstyne, The Mobius Strip of the First Amendment: Perspectives on *Red Lion*, 29 S.C. L. Rev. 539, 562 (1978):

> The [Coase] argument is appealing, but it is based on a fatal myopia in its failure to see how clearly freedom of speech [is] abridged by a government policy that adheres only to a private property system and a market-pricing mechanism in determining who shall be able to speak. [Allocation by means of the pricing mechanism would winnow] the field of otherwise eligible applicants strictly according to their ability to pay; it [would eliminate] from the licensing competition those who lack dollars to put in an effective bid.

d. Bollinger, Freedom of the Press and Public Access: Toward a Theory of Partial Regulation of the Mass Media, 75 Mich. L. Rev. 1, 26-36 (1976):

[The] Court's decisions on the question of access [to the print and broadcast media] exhibit fundamental good sense. The good sense, however, derives not from the Court's treatment of broadcasting as being somehow special, but rather from its apparent desire to limit the over-all reach of access regulation. [There] are good first amendment reasons for being both receptive to and wary of access regulation. [Only under a partial regulatory scheme,] with a major branch of the press remaining free of regulation, will the costs and risks of regulation be held at an acceptable level. [By] permitting different treatment of the two institutions, the Court can facilitate realization of the benefits of two distinct constitutional values, both of which ought to be fostered: access in a highly concentrated press and minimal governmental intrusion. [The] Court has imposed a compromise — a compromise, however, not based on notions of expediency, but rather on a reasoned, and principled, accommodation of competing first amendment values.

e. Logan, Getting Beyond Scarcity: A New Paradigm for Assessing the Constitutionality of Broadcast Regulation, 85 Cal. L. Rev. 1687, 1709-1714 (1997):

If the Supreme Court were to reject the scarcity rationale, the public forum doctrine could provide an alternative basis for upholding broadcast content regulation. [The] central premise of this argument is that broadcasters have been granted the exclusive use of a valuable resource — the electromagnetic spectrum — which Congress has deemed to be public property. [Because] access to the spectrum [has traditionally been] limited to those broadcasters who have received a license to use the airwaves, and they [have traditionally been allowed to] program their channels as they see fit as long as they abide by their public interest obligations, [the] broadcast spectrum is best characterized as a limited designated public forum, [in which the] government may impose content-based restrictions [provided] they are "reasonable in light of the purpose served by the forum" and do not "discriminate against speech on the basis of its viewpoint."

3. *Regulating the airwaves.* Assuming licensing of the airwaves is not itself unconstitutional, what factors may the FCC consider in its allocation of licenses?
a. May the FCC prohibit the common ownership of a radio or television station and a daily newspaper located in the same community? In FCC v. National Citizens Committee for Broadcasting, 436 U.S. 775 (1978), the Court sustained such regulations:

In making [its] licensing decisions between competing applicants, the Commission has long given "primary significance" to "diversification of control of the media of mass communications." [This policy is consistent] with the statutory scheme [and with] the First Amendment goal of achieving "the widest possible dissemination of information from diverse and antagonistic sources." [Petitioners argue that the regulations are invalid because they seriously restrict the opportunities for expression of both broadcasters and newspapers. But as] we stated in *Red Lion*, "to deny a station license because 'the public interest' requires it 'is not a denial of free speech.'" [The] regulations are a reasonable means of promoting the public interest in diversified mass communications; thus they do not violate the First Amendment rights of those who will be denied broadcast licenses pursuant to them.

b. May the FCC compel an applicant for a broadcast license to ascertain the problems, needs, and interests of his community and to provide programming to meet those needs? See Ascertainment of Community Problems by Broadcast Applicants Primer, 57 F.C.C.2d 418 (1976). May the FCC, for example, deny a license to an applicant for a radio station in a community with a substantial black population unless the applicant agrees to devote a substantial portion of her programming to information and entertainment designed specifically for the black community?

c. May the FCC prohibit broadcasters from airing programs that contain profanity? May it prohibit programs that incite to crime? That are sexually explicit? That depict a racial or religious group in a degrading manner? Recall FCC v. Pacifica Foundation, section D5 supra.

d. Consider the following proposal made by Reed Hundt, then-chair of the FCC, in Hundt, The Public's Airwaves: What Does the Public Interest Require of Television Broadcasters?, 45 Duke L.J. 1089, 1099-1100, 1105-1106 (1996):

> In the aggregate, political candidates at all levels spent [$500 million in 1996] on media advertising. [The] cost of television advertising makes fundraising an enormous entry barrier for candidates seeking public office, an oppressive burden for incumbents seeking reelection, a continuous threat to the integrity of our political institutions, and a principal cause of the erosion of public respect for public service. [To address this problem,] broadcasters should be required, [as] a condition of their licenses, to provide free airtime for political candidates. . . . [This could be accomplished by requiring] broadcasters [to] donate [$500-million worth of] airtime to [a time] bank and [authorizing] candidates [to] draw airtime from the bank during their campaigns. [How] would we divide the time contributed to a time bank? One approach would be to grant each eligible candidate a right to a specific dollar amount of free time. Candidates would then negotiate with broadcasters for advertising time, just as they currently do, but would pay with time bank credits rather than actual dollars. Why would broadcasters accept credits? Because they would be required to provide free time worth, say, 2 percent of their annual advertising revenues as a condition of using the public airwaves for free. Indeed, it would be important for broadcasters to provide time to candidates lest they lose their licenses.

4. *Related issues.* See FCC v. League of Women Voters, 468 U.S. 364 (1984) (invalidating section 399 of the Public Broadcasting Act of 1967, which prohibited any noncommercial educational station that receives a grant from the Corporation for Public Broadcasting to "engage in editorializing"); CBS v. FCC, 453 U.S. 367 (1981) (upholding the constitutionality of FCC rules interpreting section 312(a)(7) of the Communications Act, which requires broadcasters to permit "a legally qualified candidate for Federal elective office" to purchase "reasonable amounts of time" on "behalf of his candidacy"); FCC v. Midwest Video Corp., 440 U.S. 689 (1979) (FCC rules requiring cable systems to hold out dedicated channels for all users on a first-come, nondiscriminatory basis violate section 3(h) of the Communications Act, which provides that "a person engaged [in] broadcasting shall not [be] deemed a common carrier"); Columbia Broadcasting System v. Democratic National Committee, 412 U.S. 94 (1973) (the first amendment does not itself require broadcast licensees to sell advertising time to groups or individuals wishing to express their views on controversial issues of public importance).

5. *Repeal of the fairness doctrine. Red Lion* has been the subject of considerable criticism. See, e.g., Karst, Equality as a Central Principle in the First Amendment, 43 U. Chi. L. Rev. 20, 49 (1975) ("Any process of continuing governmental surveillance over broadcasting content presents truly grave dangers. [Even] the right-of-reply portion of the fairness [doctrine, although] less threatening than the doctrine's more general insistence on fair coverage of issues, [will] give added encouragement to an editorial blandness already promoted by the broadcasters' commercial advertisers; broadcasters will simply minimize the number of newscasts to which a fairness doctrine obligation will attach."); Van Alstyne, supra, at 574 ("In yielding to the fear of licensee abuse, the fairness doctrine may ultimately betray a lack of confidence in the presuppositions of the first amendment itself. [What] can possibly be plainer than that the luminescence of the first amendment itself is dimmed whenever freedom for passionate expression is systematically discouraged by state-imposed duties of fiduciary obligation and the yellow light of self-restraint?").

In 1987, the FCC repealed the fairness doctrine, asserting that the doctrine was unconstitutional because it "chilled" the first amendment rights of broadcasters. Reflecting the FCC's market-oriented position at the time it repealed the fairness doctrine, Chair Mark Fowler remarked that "television is just another appliance. It's a toaster with pictures."

The issues surrounding the fairness doctrine highlight the conflict implicit in the first amendment visions of Justices Holmes and Brandeis — with Justice Holmes emphasizing the "free trade in ideas" and Justice Brandeis focusing on the "deliberative process" and the need for a system in which "public discussion is a political duty." See section B1 supra. Consider, for example, Justice Brandeis's observation that "the greatest menace to freedom is an inert people." Does this suggest that government regulation of the marketplace is appropriate if the market otherwise provides too little attention to public issues and too much in the way of senationalism? If television is, in the words of former FCC Chair Newton Minow, "a vast wasteland," what government responses are appropriate? See N. Minow and C. LaMay, Abandoned in the Wasteland (1985).

6. *A paradox?* Could Congress constitutionally reserve all television time for news and public affairs programming? Could it limit "entertainment" to two hours per day? Consider R. Collins and D. Skover, The Death of Discourse 3-4 (1996):

[T]he First Amendment is still grounded in eighteenth-century fears of government's tyrannical censorship. It is ill-equipped to deal [with the problems posed by] late twentieth-century America['s] insatiable appetite for amusement. [T]he forces of capitalism now encourage exploitation of highly-advanced electronic technology to accelerate the age-old human drive for self-gratification. The consumptive thrust of unchecked capitalism [is] most apparent in the culture of commercial television, [which] provides unceasing mass amusement. [Public] talk is increasingly taking a distinctive and aestheticized form consistent with the look and feel of commercial television. [Where] amusement and commerce mark the boundaries for much public discourse, traditional First Amendment values — which include serious dialogue and civic participation — are overshadowed. [In addressing this problem], we encounter a paradox: To save itself, the traditional First Amendment must destroy itself. [To] guard against censorship, the First Amendment must [constrain] most governmental controls over expression, including those over the commercial use of electronic media. [But] if the First Amendment [gives such protection to commercial television], the modern obsession with self-amusement can trivialize public expression and thereby undermine the traditional aims of the First Amendment.

7. *Regulating the media to achieve a "more advanced democratic society."* Consider L. Bollinger, Images of a Free Press 133-145 (1991):

[Under the image of freedom of the press established in New York Times v. Sullivan], the goal of press freedom [was] viewed as the creation of a vast space for "uninhibited, robust, and wide-open" public discussion [and it was] assumed that the role of the Supreme Court is to stand guard against government intervention. [This approach is] insensitive to problems affecting the quality of public discussion that are posed by a laissez-faire system of modern mass media. [What is needed is a] more fundamental understanding [of press freedom].

[To achieve this more fundamental understanding, we] must address the nature of our own behavior in the discussion of public questions. [A] democratic society, like an individual, should strive to remain conscious of the biases that skew, distort, and corrupt its own thinking about public issues. [Even] in a world in which the press is entirely free and open to all voices, with a perfect market in that sense, human nature would still see to it that quality public debate and decisionmaking would not rise naturally to the surface but would [need] the buoyant support of some form of collective action [involving] public institutions.

[In our criminal justice system, for example,] we go to great lengths to ensure the decisionmaking process is purified of biases, and we recognize that an entire laissez-faire system is likely to produce great injustice. [We accept the constraints in this context, exemplified by the rules of evidence], because we understand that the stakes are so high for the individual defendant. [We should think the same way about democracy.]

[Although the mass media may] give viewers and readers what they "want" [through] the expression of their preferences in the marketplace, [it is nonetheless imaginable] that we — the same "we" that issue our marketplace votes for what we get — might be very concerned about [what] choices we are making in that system. [Accordingly, we may] decide together, through public regulation, that we would like to alter [the] demands we find ourselves making in that market context, [for we may] recognize that if we are left to choose on our own whether and how to inform ourselves, too many will neglect to undertake the burdens of self-education, choosing instead to pursue more pleasant things. [It] would be a more [advanced] democratic society that could act to correct deficiencies arising out of [the] citizens themselves.

Consider also Stone, Imagining a Free Press, 90 Mich. L. Rev. 1246, 1262-1263 (1992):

Bollinger's analogy to the criminal justice system is especially powerful. As Bollinger notes, we exclude all sorts of evidence from the consideration of the jury [because we believe] jurors are more likely to reach a fair and accurate result if they are denied access to the evidence. Consider the following extension of the analogy. Traditionally, the press did not report information about the private sexual conduct of political candidates. In exercising such discretion, the press acted like a judge in a criminal trial, preventing the people — the jurors — from learning information that arguably would distort their judgment and distract their attention from more important matters. Today, however, as part of a general breakdown of journalistic standards, the press, driven by rampant commercialism, routinely sensationalizes such information to the (arguable) detriment of the political process.

In its defense, the press argues that it would be irresponsible not to report such information, pointing to polls indicating that perhaps fifteen percent of the public would not vote for a candidate who engaged in such activity. [There] must be some limit, however, and this limit must be designed not only to respect the legitimate privacy interests of candidates, but also to reflect our right, as a society, to decide that some matters simply should not play a significant role in our political process, even if some of our fellow citizens disagree. And our right to make such a decision should be strongest when, as in the trial context, the information has a greater potential to distract and distort than to inform our better judgment. As in the trial context, we should be able to protect the political process against our own failures of judgment. But, of course, there remains the question: Who decides?

8. *Exclusive cable franchises.* Does the scarcity theory apply to cable television? Does the first amendment permit a municipality to award an exclusive franchise to a single cable operator? To condition a franchise on the willingness of the operator to provide public access or make particular programming decisions? In City of Los Angeles v. Preferred Communications, Inc., 476 U.S. 488 (1986), the Court declined to answer these questions in the absence of a fully developed factual record. However, Justice Rehnquist's opinion for the Court stated that the activities of cable operators "plainly implicate First Amendment interests."

TURNER BROADCASTING SYSTEM INC. v. FCC, 512 U.S. 622 (1994). The "must carry" provisions of the Cable Television Consumer Protection and Competition Act of 1992 require cable television systems to devote a portion of their channels, free of charge, to the transmission of local broadcast television stations. The rationale of these provisions was explained by the Court:

"Cable technology affords two principal benefits over broadcast. First, it eliminates the signal interference sometimes encountered in over-the-air [broadcasting]. Second, it is capable of transmitting many more channels than are available through broadcasting. [Congress] enacted the 1992 Cable Act after conducting three years of [hearings]. Congress concluded that [the] overwhelming majority of cable operators exercise a monopoly over cable service [and that] this market position gives cable operators the power and the incentive to harm broadcast competitors. The power derives from the cable operator's ability [to refuse to transmit broadcast signals]. The incentive derives from the economic reality that '[c]able television systems and broadcast systems increasingly compete for television advertising revenues.' By refusing carriage of broadcasters' signals, cable operators [can] reduce the number of households that have access to the broadcasters' programming, and thereby capture advertising dollars that would otherwise go to broadcast stations. [In such circumstances], Congress concluded that unless cable operators are required to carry local broadcast stations, '[t]here is a substantial likelihood [that] the economic viability of free local broadcast television [will] be seriously jeopardized.' [Congress] sought to avoid the elimination of broadcast television [because] '[s]uch programming is . . . free to those who own television sets and does not require cable transmission to receive broadcast signals.' [The] provisions are designed to [ensure] that every individual with a television set can obtain access to free television programming."

Although the Court divided sharply on the constitutionality of the "must carry" provisions, it was unanimous in holding that the regulation of cable television should not be governed by the same constitutional standards as broadcast regulation. Justice Kennedy delivered the opinion of the Court:

"[The] rationale for applying a less rigorous standard of First Amendment scrutiny to broadcast regulation [does] not apply in the context of cable regulation. The justification for our distinct approach to broadcast regulation rests upon the unique physical limitations of the broadcast medium. As a general matter, there are more would-be broadcasters than frequencies available in the electromagnetic spectrum. And if two broadcasters were to attempt to transmit over the same frequency in the same locale, they would interfere with one another's signals, so that neither could be heard at all. The scarcity of broadcast frequencies thus required the establishment of some regulatory mechanism to divide the electromagnetic spectrum and assign specific frequencies to particular broadcasters. [The] broadcast cases are inapposite in the present context because cable television does not suffer from the inherent limitations that characterize the broadcast medium. Indeed, given the rapid advances in fiber optics and digital compression technology, soon there may be no practical limitation on the number of speakers who may use the cable medium. Nor is there any danger of physical interference between two cable speakers attempting to share the same channel. In light of these fundamental technological differences between broadcast and cable transmission, application of the more relaxed standard of scrutiny adopted in *Red Lion* [is] inapt when determining the First Amendment validity of cable regulation. . . .

"Although the Government acknowledges the substantial technological differences between broadcast and cable, it advances a second argument for application of the *Red Lion* framework to cable regulation. It asserts that the foundation of our broadcast jurisprudence is not the physical limitations of the electromagnetic spectrum, but rather the 'market dysfunction' that characterizes the broadcast market. Because the cable market is beset by a similar dysfunction, the Government maintains, the *Red Lion* standard of review should also apply to cable. While we agree that the cable market suffers certain structural impediments, the Government's argument is flawed in two respects. First, as discussed above, the special physical characteristics of broadcast transmission, not the economic characteristics of the broadcast market, are what underlies our broadcast jurisprudence. Second, the mere assertion of a dysfunction or failure in a speech market, without more, is not enough to shield a speech regulation from the First Amendment standards applicable to nonbroadcast media."

In his opinion for the Court, Justice Kennedy conceded that the "must carry" "provisions interfere with cable operators' editorial discretion by compelling them to offer carriage [to] broadcast stations," but emphasized that "the extent of the interference does not depend upon the content of the cable operators' programming." Justice Kennedy therefore concluded that "the appropriate standard by which to evaluate the constitutionality of [the 'must carry' provisions] is [not 'the most exacting level' of first amendment scrutiny, but] the intermediate level of scrutiny applicable to content-neutral restrictions that impose an incidental burden on speech," invoking the standard set forth in United States v. O'Brien, section E3 supra.

Applying this standard, Justice Kennedy, writing at this point only for himself and three other justices, remanded for further fact-finding on whether the "must carry" rules are in fact "necessary to protect the viability of broadcast television." Justice Kennedy explained that the government "must demonstrate that the recited harms are real, not merely conjectural, and that the regulation will in fact alleviate these harms in a direct and material way." Although agreeing that "courts must accord substantial deference to the predictive judgments of Congress," Justice Kennedy nonetheless concluded that the courts have an "obligation to exercise independent judgment when First Amendment rights are implicated [to] assure that, in formulating its judgments, Congress has drawn reasonable inferences based on substantial evidence." In this case, without "a more substantial elaboration [of] the predictive or historical evidence upon which Congress relied, or the introduction of some additional evidence to establish [that] broadcasters would be at serious [risk], we cannot determine whether the threat to broadcast television is real enough to overcome the challenge to the provisions. . . ."

In a concurring opinion, Justice Stevens agreed "with most of Justice Kennedy's reasoning," but concluded that the "must carry" provisions should be upheld without a remand: "[T]he question for us is merely whether Congress could fairly conclude that cable operators' monopoly position threatens the continued viability of broadcast television and that must carry is an appropriate means of minimizing that risk. [Accorded] proper deference, the [congressional] findings [are] sufficient to sustain the must carry [provisions]. An industry need not be in its death throes before Congress may act to protect it from economic harm. . . ."

Justice O'Connor, joined by Justices Scalia, Thomas, and Ginsburg, dissented in part. At the outset, Justice O'Connor observed that the act "implicates the First Amendment rights of two classes of speakers": "First, it tells cable operators which programmers they must [carry]. Second, [it] deprives [cable programmers] of access to over one-third of an entire medium. Cable programmers may compete only for those channels that are not set aside by the must carry provisions. [It] is as if the government ordered all movie theaters to reserve at least one-third of their screening for films made by American production companies, or required all bookstores to devote one-third of their shelf space to nonprofit publishers."

Justice O'Connor argued further that the "must carry" provisions are content-based, rather than content-neutral, because various congressional findings supporting the legislation expressed "[p] references for diversity of viewpoints, for localism, for educational programming, and for news and public affairs." Although the Court concluded that such findings showed "nothing more than the recognition that the services provided by broadcast television have some intrinsic value and, thus, are worth preserving against the threats posed by cable," Justice O'Connor argued that the "controversial judgment at the heart of the statute is not that broadcast television has some value, [but] that broadcasters should be preferred over cable programmers" because of the content of broadcast programming. In Justice O'Connor's view, the government's "interest in ensuring access to a multiplicity of diverse and antagonistic sources of information [is] directly tied to the content of what the speakers will likely say." Justice O'Connor therefore reasoned that the "must carry" provisions must be tested by "exacting" standards of content-based analysis and must be "narrowly tailored to a compelling state interest." Applying this standard, Justice O'Connor concluded that the provisions could not withstand constitutional scrutiny.

Note: Turner *and the Regulation of Cable*

1. Turner *and the problem of content.* Consider Justice O'Connor's argument that the "must carry" regulations are content-based because they were designed in part to promote "access to a multiplicity of diverse and antagonistic sources of information." Is a city council's decision to permit individuals to display messages in the interior of city-owned buses "content-based" because the city council's goal is to promote "access to a multiplicity of diverse and antagonistic sources of information"? Should it make a difference whether the challenged provision attempts to achieve this goal (a) by expanding opportunities for free expression in a facially content-neutral manner or (b) by providing expanded speech opportunities for particular, otherwise underrepresented, viewpoints in an explicitly content-based manner?

For another perspective on the content issue in *Turner,* consider Baker, *Turner Broadcasting:* Content-Based Regulation of Persons and Presses, 1994 Sup. Ct. Rev. 57, 61, 66, 72, 91:

> [B]oth the majority and the dissent were wrong to assume [in *Turner*] that a content-motivation is objectionable. [Cable] operators [are] business enterprises that take a corporate [form]. Speech is their business. [They thus] differ from individuals who speak as an aspect [of] making personal choices for themselves. [Because] structural regulation of [such] instrumentally created, collective entities in ways that affect their speech [does not impinge personal autonomy, the first amendment should be understood to] allow even facially content-based [though perhaps not viewpoint-based] laws imposed on the media as long as the law does not suppress expression or undermine the media's integrity. [For] example, the government could require broadcasters to include children-oriented programming or to cover controversial issues.

2. *The purpose of the "must carry" rules.* The Court and the dissent each offer a theory for the enactment of the "must carry" rules. But consider another possibility — that the rules were "simply a product of the political power of the broadcasting industry." Indeed, it seems at least plausible that "the broadcasting industry was trying to protect its economic interests at the expense of cable." To the extent this was so, "there is a large lesson for the future": "New regulations, ostensibly defended as public-interested or as helping viewers and consumers, will often be a product of private self-interest, and not good for the public at all. [Whether] and to what extent this is a constitutional (as opposed to a political) problem may be disputed. But it points to a distinctive and legitimate concern about governmental regulation of the communications industry." Sunstein, The First Amendment in Cyberspace, 104 Yale L.J. 1757, 1767-1768 (1995).

3. *Does* Turner *offer a new "model" for free speech analysis?* Because of its analysis of the scarcity issue, the Court in *Turner* clearly rejected the broadcasting model as an appropriate analogy for the regulation of cable. But the Court may not have applied the competing "print" model either. Consider Sunstein, supra, at 1774:

> There is now a third model — the *Turner* model — of what government may do. [The] new model has four simple components. Under *Turner,* (a) government may

regulate [new] speech sources so as to ensure access for *viewers* who would otherwise be without free programming *and* (b) government may require owners of
speech sources to provide access to *speakers*, at least if the owners are not conventional speakers too; *but* (c) government must do all this on a content-neutral basis;
but (d) government may support its regulation [by] invoking such democratic goals
as the need to ensure "an outlet for exchange on matters of local concern" and "access to a multiplicity of information sources." [This new approach] is likely to have
continuing importance in governmental efforts to control the information super-
highway so as to ensure viewer and listener access.

4. Turner *revisited*. In Turner Broadcasting System Inc. v. FCC, 520 U.S. 180
(1997) (*Turner II*), the Court, in a five-to-four decision, upheld under "intermediate scrutiny" the constitutionality of the must-carry provisions at issue in *Turner I*,
affirming the district court's decision that the expanded record presented to it on
remand from *Turner I* contained substantial evidence supporting Congress' predictive judgment that the must-carry provisions further important governmental
interests in preserving cable carriage of local broadcast stations, and that the provisions are narrowly tailored to promote those interests.

In reaching this conclusion, the Court, in an opinion by Justice Kennedy, emphasized that "we owe Congress' findings deference [because Congress] 'is far
better equipped than the judiciary to "amass and evaluate the vast amounts of
data" bearing upon' legislative questions." Moreover, the Court observed, "this
principle has special significance in cases, like this one, involving congressional
judgments concerning regulatory schemes of inherent complexity and assessments about the likely interaction of industries undergoing rapid economic and
technological change." Thus, the Court concluded, "the issue before us is
whether, given conflicting views of the probable development of the television industry, Congress had substantial evidence for making the judgment that it did.
We need not put our imprimatur on Congress' economic theory in order to validate the reasonableness of its judgment," nor should we "re-weigh the evidence
de novo" or "replace Congress' factual predictions with our own."

In a concurring opinion, Justice Stevens emphasized that "if this statute regulated the content of speech, rather than the structure of the market, our task
would be quite different." In a separate concurring opinion, Justice Breyer noted
that, unlike the plurality, which concluded that the must-carry provisions were
justified in terms of each of three "important" government interests — "preserving the benefits of free, over-the-air local broadcast television; promoting the
widespread dissemination of information from a multiplicity of sources; and promoting fair competition in the market for television programming" — he rested
his conclusion only on the first two of these interests.

Justice O'Connor, joined by Justices Scalia, Thomas, and Ginsburg, dissented.
Justice O'Connor argued that "the Court errs in two crucial respects." First, by
failing to understand that the must-carry rules are content-based, "the Court
adopted the wrong analytic framework" in *Turner I*. "Second, the Court misapplies the 'intermediate scrutiny' framework it adopts." With respect to her second
objection, Justice O'Connor argued that, although "Congress' reasonable conclusions are entitled to deference, [in] the course of our independent review we
cannot ignore sharp conflicts in the record that call into question the reasonableness of Congress' findings." And, in this case, "the record on remand does not
permit the conclusion [that] Congress could reasonably have predicted serious

harm to a significant number of stations in the absence of must-carry." In Justice O'Connor's view, "the principal opinion" fails "to closely scrutinize the logic of the regulatory scheme," and exhibits "an extraordinary and unwarranted deference for congressional judgments, a profound fear of delving into complex economic matters, and a willingness to substitute untested assumptions for evidence." As a consequence, the principal opinion "trivializes the First Amendment issue at stake in this case."

5. *Regulation of cable: another look.* In Denver Area Educational Telecommunications Consortium, Inc. v. FCC, section D5 supra, the Court considered the constitutionality of several provisions of the Cable Television Consumer Protection and Competition Act of 1992 regulating public access and leased access channels. In a plurality opinion, Justice Breyer, joined by Justices Stevens, O'Connor, and Souter, maintained that, in light of "the changes taking place in the law, the technology, and the industrial structure related to telecommunications," the Court should adopt a narrow, highly contextual, and fact-specific approach, rather than articulate hard-and-fast rules or import into this new and complex area doctrines developed in other areas of first amendment jurisprudence. Is this a wise approach? Consider the following views, expressed in separate opinions in this case:

a. Justice Souter:

All of the relevant characteristics of cable are presently in a state of technological and regulatory flux. [In such circumstances], we should be shy about saying the final word today about what will be accepted as reasonable tomorrow. [Not] every nuance of our old standards will necessarily do for the new technology. [Thus], the job of the courts [in this area will be to recognize] established First Amendment interests through a close analysis that constrains [government], without wholly incapacitating [it], maintaining the high value of open communication, measuring the costs of regulation by exact attention to fact, and compiling a pedigree of experience with the changing subject. These are familiar judicial responsibilities in times when we know too little to risk the finality of precision, and attention to them will probably take us through the communications revolution. Maybe the judicial obligation to shoulder these responsibilities can itself be captured by a much older rule, familiar to every doctor of medicine: "First, do no harm."

b. Justice Kennedy, joined by Justice Ginsburg:

The plurality opinion [is] adrift. The opinion [applies] no standard, and by this omission loses sight of existing First Amendment doctrine. When confronted with a threat to free speech in the context of an emerging technology, we ought to have the discipline to analyze the case by reference to existing elaborations of constant First Amendment principles. [Rather] than undertake this task, however, the plurality just declares that, all things considered, [the challenged provision] seems fine. [The] novelty and complexity of the case is a reason to look for help from other areas of our First Amendment jurisprudence, not a license to wander into uncharted areas of the law with no compass other than our own opinions about good policy. [Justice] Souter recommends to the Court the precept, "First, do no harm." The question, though, is whether the harm is in sustaining the law or striking it down. If the plurality is concerned about technology's direction, it ought to begin by allowing speech, not suppressing it.

c. Justice Thomas, joined by Chief Justice Rehnquist and Justice Scalia:

For many years, we have failed to articulate how and to what extent the First Amendment protects cable operators, programmers, and viewers from state and federal regulation. I think it is time we did so, and I cannot go along with the plurality's assiduous attempts to avoid addressing that issue openly. [Our] First Amendment distinctions between media, dubious from their infancy, placed cable in a doctrinal wasteland in which regulators and cable operators alike could not be sure whether cable was entitled to the substantial First Amendment protections afforded the print media or was subject to the more onerous obligations shouldered by the broadcast media. [In] *Turner,* by adopting much of the print paradigm, and by rejecting *Red Lion,* we adopted with it a considerable body of precedent that governs the respective First Amendment rights of competing speakers. In *Red Lion,* we [legitimized] consideration of the public interest and emphasized the rights of viewers, at least in the abstract. Under that view, "[i]t is the right of the viewers and listeners, not the right of broadcasters, which is paramount." After *Turner,* however, that view can no longer be given any credence in the cable context. It is the operator's right that is preeminent.

6. *Cable operators v. cable programmers.* In the Cable Act of 1984, Congress authorized local governments to require cable operators to set aside a certain number of channels for "public, educational, or governmental use." The act expressly prohibited cable operators from exercising any editorial control over the content of programs broadcast on such "public access" channels. In the Cable Television Consumer Protection and Competition Act of 1992, Congress altered this scheme and authorized cable operators to restrict on public access channels programming that depicts or describes "sexual activities or organs in a patently offensive manner." In Denver Area Educational Telecommunications Consortium, Inc. v. FCC, section D5 supra, the Court invalidated this provision. Consider the argument of Justice Thomas, joined by Chief Justice Rehnquist and Justice Scalia, in dissent:

[Programmers have no first amendment] right to transmit over an operator's cable system. [Accordingly], when there is a conflict, a programmer's asserted right to transmit over an operator's cable system must give way to the operator's editorial discretion. [Citing *Tornillo.*] Drawing an analogy to the print media, [the] author of a book [has] no right to have the book sold in a particular bookstore without the store owner's consent. [Thus], the proper question [posed by this regulation is not whether the act violates the] free speech rights [of programmers because it authorizes operators to restrict indecent expression, but whether the] public access requirements [are] improper restrictions on the operators' free speech rights. [This being so, the programmers cannot] reasonably assert that the Court should strictly scrutinize [the act] in a way that maximizes their ability to speak [and], by necessity, minimizes the operators' discretion.

Note: The First Amendment in Cyberspace

1. *New technologies and the first amendment.* As new technologies revolutionize communication, questions inevitably arise about how the first amendment should apply. *Red Lion* struggled with the novel challenges posed by broadcasting, and *Denver Area* wrestled with how to assess the special issues posed by cable.

The Court encountered similar difficulties when it first considered motion pictures and sound trucks. Recall Kovacs v. Cooper, section E1 supra. What, then, of cyberspace? Consider the following views:

a. Berman and Weitzner, Abundance and User Control: Renewing the Democratic Heart of the First Amendment in the Age of Interactive Media, 104 Yale L.J. 1619, 1624 (1995):

Unlike the channelized networks of today's mass media, open-access networks are decentralized: No single point is designated for the origination of content. A single user can send information to [millions] of other users on the networks, without any advance negotiation or special arrangement with the network operator. [With no] centralized distribution point on the network, it is much harder for a network operator — or any other entity — to stifle independent information sources. [The] abundance generated by such an open-access network eliminates one of the key First Amendment diversity difficulties found in mass media. Instead of network operators or government regulators allocating a small number of channels among a large number of information sources, all information providers [will] have the opportunity to speak. . . .

b. Fiss, In Search of a New Paradigm, 104 Yale L.J. 1613, 1614-1615 (1995):

[Much of current First Amendment analysis is premised] on an outmoded paradigm: the street corner speaker. [By the 1980s it was clear that] we needed to move from the street corner to CBS. Reexamining free speech controversies from this new vantage point [would make] it possible [to] better appreciate some of the crucial factors shaping public discourse today, including the scarcity of channels of communication and the high cost of speech. Also, with CBS in mind, we could see how the old lines between speaker and censor, or between the state and the private sphere, had to be redrawn. [A] body of doctrine that did no more than protect the street corner speaker from the menacing reach of the police would leave the values served by the First Amendment vulnerable [and] largely unfulfilled. [But we are now already] on the edge of a new technological revolution. [What] is happening is nothing less than a redefinition of the way we read and write, the way we talk to and correspond with one another [and] how we perform our roles as citizens. [We must begin the process of thinking] through the implications for the First Amendment of the technological revolution through which we are now living.

c. Krattenmaker and Powe, Converging First Amendment Principles for Converging Communications Media, 104 Yale L.J. 1719, 1721, 1725, 1726, 1740 (1995):

No matter how often one repeats the statement, it cannot be true that "[d]ifferent communications media [should be] treated differently for First Amendment purposes." Should everything we knew about regulation of books have been discarded once talking motion pictures were invented? Did discovery of the personal computer [render] obsolete everything the courts said about the First Amendment and broadcasting, or cable, or telephones? [Past] complaints will be prologue for future complaints about what creators place on, and users receive from, [cyberspace]. Some will complain that an insufficient amount of the appropriate type or quality of information is available. Others [will] complain that users may be accessing information they ought not have. [In responding to these familiar issues,] only a unitary First Amendment for all media will do. [The] general principles underlying regulation of the [traditional print] media should apply fully to the new as well as the old electronic communications media.

2. *The first amendment in cyberspace — some specific issues.* What sorts of regulations of expression should be permissible in the realm of cyberspace? Is there a need for more or less regulation of content? Consider the following: (a) Congress imposes liability on America On-Line for any libelous material that it transmits over the Internet. Is the issue different from the situation in which the New York Times prints libelous material? Is it different from making the telephone company liable for threats made over the phone? (b) Congress prohibits any person to post instructions on how to build a bomb on the Internet. Does *Brandenburg* apply? (c) Congress bans sexually explicit material from the Internet. Is the issue different from the situation in which the FCC regulates such material on radio and television?

Consider also the following:

a. Berman and Weitzner, supra, at 1634:

[Because modern] user-control technologies enable customers (in particular, parents) to limit access to certain kinds of material, [the] goal of indecency regulations [could] be achieved without intrusive government restrictions. In interactive media, the reasoning of *Pacifica* [section D5 supra] would not justify content regulation at all, whether it is regulation of sexual expression, violence, commercial speech, or other controversial materials.

b. Branscomb, Anonymity, Autonomy, and Accountability: Challenges to the First Amendment in Cyberspace, 104 Yale L.J. 1639, 1652-1653 (1995):

[Whose] community rules should govern a cyberspace controversy? [Consider the Amateur Action case.] The Amateur Action BBS was a subscription bulletin board where users, consenting adults within an electronically mediated environment, could access [sexually explicit] materials. The images [at issue in this obscenity prosecution] were uploaded in California and were downloaded [in] Tennessee. [The] case raises the important issue of which local community's standards should apply — [California's, Tennessee's, or those of] the virtual community on the electronic network.

c. Lessig, The Path of Cyberlaw, 104 Yale L.J. 1743, 1750, 1752 (1995):

[We] can see many good reasons why someone would want to remain anonymous. [One] wants to contribute to a political discussion without suffering the costs of unpopular views; one wants to find information without revealing that one needs that information; one wants to assume a role in certain discussion groups to explore an alternative identity. [Not] all anonymity, however, is so benign. Perfect anonymity makes perfect crime possible. The ability to appear invisibly on the network [certainly] will increase the incidence of those on the network who slander, or harass or assault. [A careful] balance will have to be drawn. [Already] the extremes are well staked, with some arguing that no regulation [of anonymity] should be permitted, and others arguing that only with regulation should [anonymity] be allowed.

3. *Indecency on the Internet.* In Reno v. American Civil Liberties Union, section D5 supra, the Court invalidated provisions of the Communications Decency Act of 1996 (CDA) that prohibited any person from sending over the Internet in a way that would be available to a person under eighteen years of age any "indecent" material or any material that "depicts or describes, in terms patently offensive as measured by contemporary community standards, sexual or excretory activities or organs." In distinguishing the Internet from broadcasting, the Court explained:

[We have] observed that "[e]ach medium of expression . . . may present its own problems." Thus, some of our cases have recognized special justifications for regulation of the broadcast media that are not applicable to other speakers [citing, e.g., *Red Lion; Pacifica*]. In these cases, the Court relied on the history of extensive government regulation of the broadcast medium, the scarcity of available frequencies at its inception, and its "invasive" nature.

Those factors are not present in cyberspace. Neither before nor after the enactment of the CDA have the vast democratic fora of the Internet been subject to the type of government supervision and regulation that has attended the broadcast industry. Moreover, the Internet is not as "invasive" as radio or television. The District Court specifically found that "[c]ommunications over the Internet do not 'invade' an individual's home or appear on one's computer screen unbidden. Users seldom encounter content 'by accident.'" [Finally], unlike the conditions that prevailed when Congress first authorized regulation of the broadcast spectrum, the Internet can hardly be considered a "scarce" expressive commodity. It provides relatively unlimited, low cost capacity for communication of all kinds. [Our] cases provide no basis for qualifying the level of First Amendment scrutiny that should be applied to this medium.

4. *The liability of cable and Internet carriers for the speech of users.* In what circumstances, if any, should cable or Internet carriers be liable for the libelous, obscene, or otherwise actionable speech they carry? Consider the liability of (a) a store that sells typewriters for the messages typed by purchasers; (b) a telephone company for the speech of callers; (c) a bookstore for the contents of the books it sells; (d) a news vendor for the contents of the newspapers it sells; (e) a newspaper or magazine for the statements made by guest columnists; (f) a cable operator for the programs it carries; and (g) a computer network, such as CompuServe, for the messages it transmits. Should the standards of liability differ across these different situations? Should it matter whether the defendant exercises "editorial" control? Should the defendants in all or some of these cases be liable only "if they have actual notice that the speech has previously been adjudicated illegal or unprotected"? Myerson, Authors, Editors, and Uncommon Carriers: Identifying the "Speaker" within the New Media, 71 Notre Dame L. Rev. 79, 122 (1995).

Note: *Free Expression — Final Thoughts*

Consider Post, Recuperating First Amendment Doctrine, 47 Stan. L. Rev. 1249, 1249-1250 (1995):

Contemporary First Amendment doctrine [is] striking chiefly for its superficiality, its internal incoherence, its distressing failure to facilitate constructive judicial engagement with significant contemporary social issues connected with freedom of speech. . . . [It] has become increasingly a doctrine of words merely, and not of things.

Consider also Nagel, How Useful Is Judicial Review in Free Speech Cases?, 69 Cornell L. Rev. 302, 303, 335-338 (1984):

The dominant consensus that has prevailed for the last [seventy] years holds that the adjudication of individual cases can promote the level and quality of public debate. [The] assumptions upon which this [consensus] rests are largely unproven and often doubtful. [Indeed, a] general assessment of free speech cases is not reassuring. [Since 1919], much of the admiration for judges as protectors of free speech is predicated upon eloquent [dissents]. There are numerous major decisions in which the Court has subordinated free speech values to other social [interests]. Even in the cases that ultimately protect free speech, the Court often achieves the protection by [indirection]. In the relatively few decisions resting directly on free speech considerations, the Court often hedges its rulings with enough cautions and limitations to put into question the scope of the Court's commitment to free speech. [Moreover, judicial] efforts — such as those to protect corporate expenditures, nude dancing, and advertising — erode popular support by breeding resentment and bringing into question the utility of free speech. [Indeed,] the Court's program, taken as a whole, has done great damage to the public's understanding and appreciation of free speech by making it seem trivial, foreign, and unnecessarily costly.

On the other hand, consider S. Shiffrin, The First Amendment, Democracy, and Romance 159 (1990):

American citizens not only feel a deep emotional attachment to the country, but also [a] sense of pride about the first amendment. The first amendment speaks to the kind of people we are and the kind of people we aspire to be. [It] plays an important role in the construction of an appealing story, a story about a nation that promotes independent people, a nation that affords a place of refuge for peoples all over the globe, a nation that welcomes the iconoclast, a nation that respects, tolerates, and even sponsors dissent. [The] image called up by this national picture [encourages] us to picture Walt Whitman's citizenry — vibrant, diverse, vital, stubborn, and independent. It encourages us to believe with Emerson that "America is the idea of emancipation."

VIII

The Constitution
and Religion

The first amendment bars Congress from making laws "respecting an establishment of religion, or prohibiting the free exercise thereof." In addition to discussing doctrinal approaches to church/state issues, this chapter examines whether the relative clarity of the constitutional text, or its history, eases the task of constitutional adjudication or reduces the necessity for other theoretical underpinnings to the constitutional law of religion.

The chapter has four sections. The first provides historical background and outlines the general approaches that courts and commentators have taken to the religion clauses. The second examines problems of establishment, highlighting the tension between the idea that the establishment clause requires some degree of separation between church and state and a history that includes substantial state support of religious activities. The third section deals with problems of free exercise, focusing on the degree to which government must or may adjust its programs to claims that the programs burden the free exercise of religion. The fourth section deals with the constitutional status of legislative efforts to accommodate religion through laws that arguably relieve burdens on the free exercise of religion.

A. INTRODUCTION: HISTORICAL AND ANALYTICAL OVERVIEW

EVERSON v. BOARD OF EDUCATION, 330 U.S. 1 (1947). New Jersey authorized its local school boards to repay parents with children in private schools for the cost of bus transportation to the schools. Most of the private schools were Roman Catholic parochial institutions. By a five-to-four vote, the Court upheld the statute against an establishment clause challenge, concluding that the state could pay the fares "as part of a general program under which it pays the fares of pupils attending public and other schools." This satisfied the first amendment's requirement that "the state [be] neutral in its relations with groups of religious believers and non-believers." Justice Black's opinion for the Court "[reviewed] the background and environment of" the first amendment:

"A large proportion of the early settlers of this country came here from Europe to escape the bondage of laws which compelled them to support and attend government-favored churches. The centuries immediately before and contemporaneous with the colonization of America had been filled with turmoil, civil strife, and persecutions, generated in large part by established sects determined to maintain their absolute political and religious supremacy. With the power of government supporting them, at various times and places, Catholics had persecuted Protestants, Protestants had persecuted Catholics, Protestant sects had persecuted other Protestant sects, Catholics of one shade of belief had persecuted Catholics of another shade of belief, and all of these had from time to time persecuted Jews. In efforts to force loyalty to whatever group happened to be on top and in league with the government of a particular time and place, men and women had been fined, cast in jail, cruelly tortured, and killed. . . .

"These practices of the old world were transplanted to and began to thrive in the soil of the new America. The very charters granted by the English Crown to the individuals and companies designated to make the laws which would control the destinies of the colonials authorized these individuals and companies to erect religious establishments which all, whether believers or non-believers, would be required to support and attend. An exercise of this authority was accompanied by a repetition of many of the old-world practices and persecutions. Catholics found themselves hounded and proscribed because of their faith; Quakers who followed their conscience went to jail; Baptists were peculiarly obnoxious to certain dominant Protestant sects; men and women of varied faiths who happened to be in a minority in a particular locality were persecuted because they steadfastly persisted in worshipping God only as their own consciences dictated. And all of these dissenters were compelled to pay tithes and taxes to support government-sponsored churches whose ministers preached inflammatory sermons designed to strengthen and consolidate the established faith by generating a burning hatred against dissenters.

"These practices became so commonplace as to shock the freedom-loving colonials into a feeling of abhorrence. The imposition of taxes to pay ministers' salaries and to build and maintain churches and church property aroused their indignation. It was these feelings which found expression in the First Amendment. [Virginia,] where the established church had achieved a dominant influence in political affairs and where many excesses attracted wide public attention, provided a great stimulus and able leadership for the movement. The people there, as elsewhere, reached the conviction that individual religious liberty could be achieved best under a government which was stripped of all power to tax, to support, or otherwise to assist any or all religions, or to interfere with the beliefs of any religious individual or group.

"The movement toward this end reached its dramatic climax in Virginia in 1785-86 when the Virginia legislative body was about to renew Virginia's tax levy for the support of the established church. Thomas Jefferson and James Madison led the fight against this tax. Madison wrote his great Memorial and Remonstrance against the law. In it, he eloquently argued that a true religion did not need the support of law; that no person, either believer or non-believer, should be taxed to support a religious institution of any kind; that the best interest of a society required that the minds of men always be wholly free; and that cruel persecutions were the inevitable result of government-established religions. Madison's Remonstrance received stronger support throughout Virginia, and [when] the proposed tax measure [came] up for consideration [it] not only died in committee, but the Assembly enacted the famous 'Virginia Bill for Religious Liberty' originally written by Thomas Jefferson. The preamble to that Bill stated among other things that

> Almighty God hath created the mind free; that all attempts to influence it by temporal punishments or burthens, or by civil incapacitations, tend only to beget habits of hypocrisy and meanness, and are a departure from the plan of the Holy author of our religion, who being Lord both of body and mind, yet chose not to propagate it by coercions on either . . . ; that to compel a man to furnish contributions of money for the propagation of opinions which he disbelieves, is sinful and tyrannical; that even the forcing him to support this or that teacher of his own religious persuasion, is depriving him of the comfortable liberty of giving his contributions to the particular pastor, whose morals he would make his pattern. . . .

And the statute itself enacted

> That no man shall be compelled to frequent or support any religious worship, place, or ministry whatsoever, nor shall be enforced, restrained, molested, or burthened in his body or goods, nor shall otherwise suffer on account of his religious opinions or belief. . . .

"[The] provisions of the First Amendment, in the drafting and adoption of which Madison and Jefferson played such leading roles, had the same objective and were intended to provide the same protection against governmental intrusion on religious liberty as the Virginia statute. . . ."

The opinion summarized the meaning of the establishment clause: "[It] means at least this: Neither a state nor the Federal Government can set up a church. Neither can pass laws which aid one religion, aid all religions, or prefer one religion over another. Neither can force nor influence a person to go to or to remain away from church against his will or force him to profess a belief or disbelief in any religion. No person can be punished for entertaining or professing religious beliefs or disbeliefs, for church attendance or non-attendance. No tax in any amount, large or small, can be levied to support any religious activities or institutions, whatever they may be called, or whatever form they may adopt to teach or practice religion. Neither a state nor the Federal Government can, openly or secretly, participate in the affairs of any religious organizations or groups and vice versa. In the words of Jefferson, the clause was intended to erect 'a wall of separation between Church and State.' Reynolds v. United States [94 U.S. at 164]."

The dissenters agreed with Justice Black's description of the relevant history, but argued that the New Jersey statute breached the "wall" of separation. Questions regarding state aid to nonpublic education are discussed in more detail in section B4 infra.

Note: The History of the Religion Clauses

1. *Two views of the Memorial and Remonstrance.* In Rosenberger v. Rectors and Visitors of the University of Virginia, 515 U.S. 819 (1995), Justices Thomas (con-

curring) and Souter (in dissent) offered competing interpretations of the establishment clause's history.

Summarizing the view of legal commentators, Justice Thomas wrote, "For
some, the experience in Virginia is consistent with the view that the Framers saw
the Establishment Clause simply as a prohibition on governmental preferences
for some religious faiths over others. Other commentators have rejected this
view, concluding that the Establishment Clause forbids not only government
preferences for some religious sects over others, but also government preferences
for religion over irreligion." Justice Thomas found "much to commend the former view. [The] funding provided by the Virginia assessment was to be extended
only to Christian sects, and the Remonstrance seized on this defect: 'Who does
not see that the same authority which can establish Christianity, in exclusion of
all other Religions, may establish with the same ease any particular sect of Christians, in exclusion of all other Sects.'" He continued:

> [Even] if Madison believed that the principle of nonestablishment of religion pre-
> cluded government financial support for religion per se (in the sense of govern-
> ment benefits specifically targeting religion), there is no indication that at the time
> of the framing he took the [extreme] view that the government must discriminate
> against religious adherents by excluding them from more generally available finan-
> cial subsidies.

Justice Thomas pointed to "historical examples of funding that date back to
the time of the founding. [Both] Houses of the First Congress elected chaplains."
There were "other, less familiar examples of what amount to direct funding [in]
early Acts of Congress. See, e.g. Act of Feb. 20, 1833 (authorizing the State of
Ohio to sell 'all or any part of the lands heretofore reserved and appropriated by
Congress for the support of religion within the Ohio Company's . . . purchases . . .
and to invest the money arising from the sale thereof, in some productive fund;
the proceeds of which shall be for ever annually applied . . . for the support of religion within the several townships for which said lands were originally reserved
and set apart, and for no other use or purpose whatsoever')."

Justice Souter offered a different interpretation of Madison's position. "[The]
bill [to which the Remonstrance was directed would] have allowed a taxpayer
to refuse to appropriate his levy to any religious society, in which case the legislature was to use these unappropriated sums to fund 'seminaries of learning.'
While some of these seminaries undoubtedly would have been religious in character, others would not have been, as a seminary was generally understood at the
time to be 'any school, academy, college or [university.'] N. Webster, An American Dictionary of the English Language (1st ed. 1828). [The] fact that the bill, if
passed, would have funded secular as well as religious instruction did nothing to
soften Madison's opposition to it."

Justice Souter continued, "Nor is it fair to argue that Madison opposed the bill
only because it treated religious groups unequally. [Madison] strongly inveighed
against the proposed aid for religion for a host of reasons [and] many of those
reasons would have applied whether or not the state aid was being distributed
equally among sects, and whether or not the aid was going to those sects in the
context of an evenhanded government program. See, e.g., ¶1 ('In matters of Religion, no man's right is abridged by the institution of Civil Society, and . . . Religion is wholly exempt from its cognizance'); ¶7 ('Experience witnesseth that

ecclesiastical establishments, instead of maintaining the purity and efficacy of Religion, have had a contrary operation'). [Madison's] Remonstrance did not argue for a bill distributing aid to all sects and religions on an equal basis, and the outgrowth of the Remonstrance and the defeat of the Virginia assessment was not such a bill; rather, it was the Virginia Bill for Establishing Religious Freedom, which [proscribed] the use of tax dollars for religious purposes."

2. *Some historical detail.* Justice Souter's concurring opinion in Lee v. Weisman, 505 U.S. 577 (1992), offered this view of the First Amendment's background and early history:

> When James Madison arrived at the First Congress with a series of proposals to amend the National Constitution, one of the provisions read that "the civil rights of none shall be abridged on account of religious belief or worship, nor shall any national religion be established, nor shall the full and equal rights of conscience be in any manner, or on any pretext, infringed." Madison's language [was] sent to a Select Committee of the House, which, without explanation, changed it to read that "no religion shall be established by law, nor shall the equal rights of conscience be infringed." Thence the proposal went to the Committee of the Whole, which was in turn dissatisfied with the Select Committee's language and adopted an alternative proposed by Samuel Livermore of New Hampshire: "Congress shall make no laws touching religion, or infringing the rights of conscience." . . .
>
> The House rewrote the amendment once more before sending it to the Senate, this time adopting, without recorded debate, language derived from a proposal by Fisher Ames of Massachusetts: "Congress shall make no law establishing Religion, or prohibiting the free exercise thereof, nor shall the rights of conscience be infringed." [The] House rejected the Select Committee's version, which arguably ensured only that "no religion" enjoyed an official preference over others, and deliberately chose instead a prohibition extending to laws establishing "religion" in general. . . .
>
> [In] September 1789, the Senate [briefly] entertained this language: "Congress shall make no law establishing One Religious Sect or Society in preference to others, nor shall the rights of conscience be infringed." After rejecting two minor amendments to that proposal, the Senate dropped it altogether. [Six] days later, the Senate went half circle and adopted its narrowest language yet: "Congress shall make no law establishing articles of faith or a mode of worship, or prohibiting the free exercise of religion." The Senate sent this proposal to the House. . . .
>
> [The] House rejected the Senate's version of the Establishment Clause. [The] House conferees ultimately won out, persuading the Senate to accept [the] final text of the Religion Clauses. [Unlike] the earliest House drafts or the final Senate proposal, the prevailing language is not limited to laws respecting an establishment of "a religion," "a national religion," "one religious sect," or specific "articles of faith."[2] . . .
>
> What we thus know of the Framers' experience underscores the observation [that] confining the Establishment Clause to a prohibition on preferential aid "requires a premise that the Framers were extraordinarily bad drafters — that they be-

---

2. Some commentators have suggested that by targeting laws respecting "an" establishment of religion, the Framers adopted the very nonpreferentialist position whose much clearer articulation they repeatedly rejected. See, e.g., R. Cord, Separation of Church and State 11-12. Yet the indefinite article before the word "establishment" is better seen as evidence that the Clause forbids any kind of establishment, including a nonpreferential one. [See] Laycock, "Nonpreferential" Aid to Religion: A False Claim About Original Intent, 27 Wm. & Mary L. Rev. 875, 884-885 (1986).

lieved one thing but adopted language that said something substantially different, and that they did so after repeatedly attending to the choice of language." Laycock, "Nonpreferential" Aid. . . .[3]

While some argue that the Framers added the word "respecting" simply to foreclose federal interference with State establishments of religion, the language sweeps more broadly than that. In Madison's words, the Clause in its final form forbids "everything like" a national religious establishment, and after incorporation, it forbids "everything like" a State religious establishment. The sweep is broad enough that Madison himself characterized congressional provisions for legislative and military chaplains as unconstitutional "establishments." . . .

The Framers adopted the Religion Clauses in response to a long tradition of coercive state support for religion, particularly in the form of tax assessments, but their special antipathy to religious coercion did not exhaust their hostility to the features and incidents of establishment. Indeed, Jefferson and Madison opposed any political appropriation of religion, and [they] did not always temper their rhetoric with distinctions between coercive and noncoercive state action. When, for example, Madison criticized Virginia's general assessment bill, he invoked principles antithetical to all state efforts to promote religion. An assessment, he wrote, is improper not simply because it forces people to donate "three pence" to religion, but, more broadly, because "it is itself a signal of persecution. It degrades from the equal rank of Citizens all those whose opinions in Religion do not bend to those of the Legislative authority." J. Madison, Memorial and Remonstrance. . . .

[Early] Presidents included religious messages in their inaugural and Thanksgiving Day addresses. [However, Americans] today find such proclamations less controversial than did the founding generation. President Jefferson [steadfastly] refused to issue Thanksgiving proclamations of any kind, in part because he thought they violated the Religion Clauses. Letter from Thomas Jefferson to Rev. S. Miller (Jan. 23, 1808) . . . :

> It is only proposed that I should recommend, not prescribe a day of fasting & prayer. That is, that I should indirectly assume to the U.S. an authority over religious exercises which the Constitution has directly precluded from them. It must be meant too that this recommendation is to carry some authority, and to be sanctioned by some penalty on those who disregard it; not indeed of fine and imprisonment, but of some degree of proscription perhaps in public opinion.

By condemning such noncoercive state practices that, in "recommending" the majority faith, demean religious dissenters "in public opinion," Jefferson necessarily condemned what, in modern terms, we call official endorsement of religion. He accordingly construed the Establishment Clause to forbid not simply state coercion, but also state endorsement, of religious belief and observance.[5] And if he

---

3. In his dissent in Wallace v. Jaffree, 472 U.S. 38 (1985), the Chief Justice rested his nonpreferentialist interpretation partly on the post-ratification actions of the early national government. Aside from the willingness of some (but not all) early Presidents to issue ceremonial religious proclamations, which were at worst trivial breaches of the Establishment Clause, he cited such seemingly preferential aid as a treaty provision, signed by Jefferson, authorizing federal subsidization of a Roman Catholic priest and church for the Kaskaskia Indians. But this proves too much, for if the Establishment Clause permits a special appropriation of tax money for the religious activities of a particular sect, it forbids virtually nothing. See Laycock, "Nonpreferential" Aid 915. Although evidence of historical practice can indeed furnish valuable aid in the interpretation of contemporary language, acts like the one in question prove only that public officials [can] turn a blind eye to constitutional principle.

5. [The] "proscription" to which Jefferson referred was [by] the public and not the government, whose only action was a noncoercive recommendation. [Jefferson's] position straightforwardly contradicts the claim that a showing of "coercion," under any normal definition, is prerequisite to a successful Establishment Clause claim. At the same time, Jefferson's practice, like Madison's,

opposed impersonal presidential addresses for inflicting "proscription in public opinion," all the more would he have condemned less diffuse expressions of official endorsement.

During his first three years in office, James Madison also refused to call for days of thanksgiving and prayer, though later, amid the political turmoil of the War of 1812, he did so on four separate occasions. Upon retirement, in an essay condemning as an unconstitutional "establishment" the use of public money to support congressional and military chaplains, he concluded that "religious proclamations by the Executive recommending thanksgivings & fasts are shoots from the same root with the legislative acts reviewed. Altho' recommendations only, they imply a religious agency, making no part of the trust delegated to political rulers." . . .

Madison's failure to keep pace with his principles in the face of congressional pressure cannot erase the principles. He admitted to backsliding, and explained that he had made the content of his wartime proclamations inconsequential enough to mitigate much of their impropriety. . . .

To be sure, the leaders of the young Republic engaged in some of the practices that separationists like Jefferson and Madison criticized. The First Congress did hire institutional chaplains, and Presidents Washington and Adams unapologetically marked days of "public thanksgiving and prayer." Yet in the face of the separationist dissent, those practices prove, at best, that the Framers simply did not share a common understanding of the Establishment Clause, and, at worst, that they, like other politicians, could raise constitutional ideals one day and turn their backs on them the next. . . .

3. *A challenge to originalist approaches.* Consider these observations by Justice Brennan, concurring in Abington School District v. Schempp, 374 U.S. 203 (1963), which held unconstitutional the practice of devotional Bible-reading in public schools:

[An] awareness of history and an appreciation of the aims of the Founding Fathers do not always resolve concrete problems. [A] more fruitful inquiry [is] whether the practices [threaten] those consequences which the Framers deeply feared; whether, in short, they tend to promote that type of interdependence between religion and state which the First Amendment was designed to prevent. . . .

[Our] religious composition makes us a vastly more diverse people than were our forefathers. They knew differences chiefly among Protestant sects. Today the Nation is far more heterogeneous religiously. [In] the face of such profound changes, practices which may have been objectionable to no one in the time of Jefferson and Madison may today be highly offensive to many persons, the deeply devout and the nonbelievers alike.

Consider the proposition that social change, such as the expansion of government, ought to affect the interpretation of both religion clauses: When government was confined to the enforcement of the common law and relatively little else, its potential for adversely affecting religious exercises was small, and a regime of government neutrality with respect to religion might have allowed religious liberty to flourish; an expansive government means that neutral government rules may interfere substantially with religious liberty. To what extent do current controversies implicate a concern not to repeat the past? See Chief Jus-

---

sometimes diverged from principle, for he did include religious references in his inaugural speeches. Homer nodded. . . .

tice Burger's observations in Lynch v. Donnelly, section B below, and Justice Powell's, quoted in Mueller v. Allen, section B4 below.

4. *Other traditions.* L. Tribe, American Constitutional Law 1158-1160 (2d ed. 1988), describes another tradition:

> [The] evangelical view (associated primarily with Roger Williams) [was] that "worldly corruptions [might] consume the churches if sturdy fences against the wilderness were not maintained." . . . Roger Williams saw separation largely as a vehicle for protecting churches against the state. To the extent that it was possible to accept state aid without state control, he urged cooperation; indeed, he argued that the state must "countenance, encourage, and supply" those in religious service. Thus, his view has been called one of positive toleration, imposing on the state the burden of fostering a climate conducive to all religion.
>
> Thomas Jefferson, in contrast, saw separation as a means of protecting the state from the church. [It] was Jefferson's conviction that only the complete separation of religion from politics would eliminate the formal influence of religious institutions and provide for a free choice among political views; he therefore urged the strictest "wall of separation between church and state."
>
> James Madison believed that both religion and government could best achieve their high purposes if each were left free from the other within its respective sphere; he thus urged that the "tendency to a usurpation on one side or the other, or to a corrupting coalition or alliance between them, will be best guarded against by an entire abstinance [sic] of the Government from interference in any way whatever, beyond the necessity of preserving public order, & protecting each sect against trespass on its legal rights by others."

For a recent analysis of Roger Williams's views, see Hall, Roger Williams and the Foundations of Religious Liberty, 71 B.U. L. Rev. 455 (1991).

5. *Federalism and incorporation.* Recall that the bill of rights was adopted to allay fears that the Constitution's grants of power might authorize Congress to act in matters that should be left to the states. When the first amendment was adopted, several states had churches established by law. See W. Katz, Religion and American Constitutions 8-10 (1964) (arguing that the religion clauses were designed to bar Congress from interfering with existing establishments in the states).

The framers' concern for federalism and the language of the fourteenth amendment pose some problems for the use of the amendment to make the religion clauses applicable to the states. Consider Justice Brennan's argument in *Schempp*:

> It has been suggested [that] absorption of the First Amendment's ban against congressional legislation "respecting an establishment of religion" is conceptually impossible because the Framers meant the Establishment Clause also to foreclose any attempt by Congress to disestablish the existing official state churches. [But] the last of the formal state establishments was dissolved more than three decades before the Fourteenth Amendment was ratified, and thus the problem of protecting official state churches from federal encroachments could hardly have been any concern of those who framed the post-Civil War Amendments. [The] Fourteenth Amendment created a panoply of new federal rights from the protection of citizens of the various States. And among those rights was freedom from such state governmental involvement in the affairs of religion as the Establishment Clause had originally foreclosed on the part of Congress.

It has also been suggested that the "liberty" guaranteed by the Fourteenth Amendment logically cannot absorb the Establishment Clause because that clause is not one of the provisions of the Bill of Rights which in terms protects a "freedom" of the individual. [This] contention [underestimates] the role of the Establishment Clause as a co-guarantor, with the Free Exercise Clause, of religious liberty. The Framers did not entrust the liberty of religious beliefs to either clause alone. . . .

Finally, it has been contended that absorption of the Establishment Clause is precluded by the absence of any intention on the part of the Framers of the Four-teenth Amendment to circumscribe the residual powers of the States to aid reli-gious activities and institutions in ways which fell short of formal establishments. That argument relies in part upon the express terms of the abortive Blaine Amend-ment — proposed several years after the adoption of the Fourteenth Amendment — which would have added to the First Amendment a provision that "[n]o State shall make any law respecting an establishment of religion. . . ." Such a restriction would have been superfluous, it is said, if the Fourteenth Amendment had already made the Establishment Clause binding upon the States.

The argument proves too much, for the Fourteenth Amendment's protection of the free exercise of religion can hardly be questioned; yet the Blaine Amendment would also have added an explicit protection against state laws abridging that lib-erty. [Further,] the religious liberty embodied in the Fourteenth Amendment would not be viable if the Constitution were interpreted to forbid only establish-ments ordained by Congress.

Note: General Approaches to the Religion Clauses

The preceding material indicates that the religion clauses deal with the gen-eral area of religious liberty, though in differing ways. Is it useful to develop an overall approach to their interpretation? In considering the following efforts at synthesis, it may help to keep in mind the following questions about each approach: Would the approach permit Congress to exempt from the Social Se-curity or income tax those who base their objections to payment on religious grounds? Would it require Congress to do so? Would the approach permit Con-gress to subsidize the operation of social services by church-related institutions? Would it require Congress to do so?

1. *Strict separation.* The clauses could be read to erect an absolute barrier to formal interdependence of religion and the state. Religious institutions could receive no aid whatever, direct or indirect, from the state. Nor could the state adjust its secular programs to alleviate burdens the programs placed on believers.

Strict separation has been questioned under both clauses. As to establishment, the Court in *Everson* argued that

state-paid policemen, detailed to protect children going to and from church schools from the very real hazards of traffic, would serve much the same purpose and accomplish much the same result as state provisions intended to guarantee free transportation of a kind which the state deems to be best for the school children's welfare. And parents might refuse to risk their children to the danger of traffic ac-cidents going to and from parochial schools, the approaches to which were not pro-tected by policemen. Similarly, parents might be reluctant to permit their children to attend schools which the state had cut off from such general government services as ordinary police and fire protection, connections for sewage disposal, public highways and sidewalks. Of course, cutting off church schools from these services, so separate and so indisputably marked off from the religious function, would make it far more difficult for the schools to operate. But [the] First Amendment [requires] the state to be a neutral in its relations with groups of religious believers and non-believers; it does not require the state to be their adversary. State power is no more to be used so as to handicap religions than it is to favor them.

2. *Strict neutrality.* Kurland, Of Church and State and the Supreme Court, 29 U. Chi. L. Rev. 1, 5 (1961): "[Religion] may not be used as a basis for classification for purposes of governmental action, whether that action be the conferring of rights or privileges or the imposition of duties or obligations." Thus, states must use purely secular criteria as the basis for their actions. Strict neutrality does not permit, much less require, accommodation of secular programs to religious belief. It does permit aid to religious institutions that satisfy the purely secular criteria for participation in the program, at least if the courts are unwilling to conclude that the criteria were not concealed methods of using religion as a basis for the program.

3. *Noncoercion and anti-indoctrination.* Consider Schwarz, No Imposition of Religion: The Establishment Clause Value, 77 Yale L.J. 692, 693 (1968): The establishment clause prohibits "only aid which has as its motive or substantial effect the imposition of religious belief or practice." More broadly, the religion clauses prohibit the government from influencing religious choice. See Gianella, Religious Liberty, Nonestablishment, and Doctrinal Development, 80 Harv. L. Rev. 1381 (1967), 81 Harv. L. Rev. 513 (1968). Consider Gianella's argument that a society's institutions provide the structure within which choice is made, that different structures produce different choices, and that, in a society in which much is done in collective institutions, voluntarism requires aid to religion. 81 Harv. L. Rev. at 522-526. For example, the system of public education might be said to affect the values students come to acquire and might therefore influence their choices among religions or between religion and nonreligion. Is that an "imposition of religious belief"? If so, does it follow that state aid to religious schools, or a voucher system in which parents receive a specified sum from the state to use for the education of their children in public or private schools, is required by the Constitution? Alternatively, consider whether the use of taxes to provide aid to religious institutions is coercive or influences religious choice.

4. *Nonpreferentialism.* According to nonpreferentialist views, government may not favor one religion over another, nor may it disfavor any particular religious view (including antireligious views), but it may support religion in general. In a religiously pluralist society, what forms of aid are nondiscriminatory? Consider the observation by Justice Souter, in Lee v. Weisman, supra, that "a nonpreferentialist who would condemn subjecting public school graduates to, say, the Anglican liturgy would still need to explain why the government's preference for Theistic over non-Theistic religion is constitutional."

Should the religion clauses protect the interests of nonbelievers? Can they do so without creating a regime of hostility to religion? In a society with wide government involvement in subsidizing social activities, are refusals to subsidize religious institutions discriminatory against religion?

5. *Voluntarism and separatism.* L. Tribe, supra, at 1160-1161, argues that the religion clauses rest on "a pair of fundamental [principles:] voluntarism and separatism." As to voluntarism,

[t]he free exercise clause was at the very least designed to guarantee freedom of conscience by preventing any degree of compulsion in matters of belief. It prohibited not only direct compulsion but also any indirect coercion which might result from subtle discrimination; hence it was offended by any burden based specifically on one's religion. So viewed, the free exercise clause is a mandate of religious voluntarism. The establishment clause [can] be understood as designed in part to assure that the advancement of a church would come only from the voluntary support of its followers and not from the political support of the state. Religious groups, it was believed, should prosper or perish on the intrinsic merit of their beliefs and practices. . . .

Separatism [calls] for much more than the institutional separation of church and state; it means that the state should not become involved in religious affairs or derive its claim to authority from religious sources, that religious bodies should not be granted governmental powers, and — perhaps — that sectarian differences should not be allowed unduly to fragment the body politic. Implicit in this ideal of mutual abstinence was the principle that under no circumstance should religion be financially supported by public taxation: "for the men who wrote the Religion Clauses [the] 'establishment' of a religion connoted sponsorship, financial support, and active involvement of the sovereign in religious activity."

Is the result in *Everson* consistent with these principles? When might the principles conflict with each other? Consider whether nondiscriminatory aid involves "indirect coercion" or "political support" of "a church" that might displace voluntary support by its members.

6. *Religious pluralism and the political process.* Consider White, J., dissenting in Widmar v. Vincent, 454 U.S. 263 (1981): "[Just] as there is room under the Religion Clauses for state policies that may have some beneficial effect on religion, there is also room for state policies that may incidentally burden religion. In other words, [the] states [have] a good deal [of freedom] to formulate policies that affect religion in divergent ways." Why should states have that freedom? Consider whether a justification lies in the contemporary political process: The United States is a religiously pluralist society in which most religious groups are tolerant of views that diverge from their own. As proposals work their way through the political process, religiously based interest groups will affect their contours. It might be unlikely that programs threatening the values with which the religion clauses are concerned will emerge from that process.

Is this sketch of the political process accurate? Are there programs on which substantial majorities can agree that disregard intense views of religious minorities, and that have substantial religious components? Consider the range of programs the Court has examined: state-supported nativity scenes, devotional prayer in public schools, tax support to nonpublic education, tax exemptions for churches.

What might be the limits of a state's freedom to formulate policies that affect religion? Justice White "[did not] suppose that [a state] could prevent students from saying grace before meals in the school cafeteria." Could it require them to do so? Is either the prohibition or the requirement likely to be adopted in any state in the near future? Could the public schools require that students take a course on religion? On Christianity?

7. *Baselines.* Douglas Laycock, The Underlying Unity of Separation and Neutrality, 46 Emory L.J. 43, 49, 69-71 (1997), discusses the "no aid" and "equal access" theories, similar to strict separation and nonpreferentialism:

In the no-aid theory, the baseline is government inactivity, because doing nothing neither helps nor hurts religion. Any government aid to a religion is a departure from that baseline, and thus a departure from neutrality. In the nondiscrimination theory, the baseline is the government's treatment of analogous secular activities; a government that pays for medical care should pay equally whether the care is provided in a religious or a secular hospital.

Laycock argues for a standard of "minimizing government influence":

[The] underlying criterion for choosing among baselines depends on the incentives that government creates. If government says that it will pay for your soup kitchen if and only if you secularize it, that is a powerful incentive to secularize. [In] this context, the baseline of analogous secular activity is substantively neutral: if government will pay both religious and secular providers, it creates no incentive for either to change. [In] the regulatory context, substantive neutrality generally requires the baseline of government inactivity. If government says it will send you to jail if you consume peyote in a worship service, that is a powerful disincentive to religious behavior. But an exemption for religious behavior rarely encourages people to join the exempted church. [When] the claim to religious exemption is not contaminated by secular self-interest, exemption minimizes government influence on religion. [If] government were free to praise or condemn religion, celebrate religious holidays, or lead prayers or worship services, government could potentially have enormous influence on religious belief and liturgy. Government is large and highly visible; for better or worse, it would model one form of religious speech or observance as compared to others.

8. *Why protect religion?* Is the constitutional text alone sufficient to justify giving religion special protection? Must we also have reasons for thinking that religion ought to be specially protected? Consider these observations: (a) Laycock, Religious Liberty as Liberty, 7 J. of Contemp. Legal Issues 313, 317 (1996): "First, in history that was recent to the American founders, government attempts to suppress disapproved religious views had caused vast human suffering. [Second], beliefs about religion are often of extraordinary importance to the individual — important enough to die for, to suffer for, to rebel for, to emigrate for, to fight to control the government for. [Third], beliefs at the heart of religion [are] of little importance to the civil government." Are the first and second reasons distinctive to religion? Is the third reason true? (b) Garvey, An Anti-Liberal Argument for Religious Freedom, 7 J. of Contemp. Legal Issues 275 (1996): "We protect it because religion is important."

Note: *Defining Religion*

In its decisions under the free speech clause, the Supreme Court has sometimes considered whether a form of expression is "speech" within the meaning of the clause. Similarly, the religion clauses require the courts to determine whether a form of belief is a "religion" within their meaning. If the free exercise clause requires the state to accommodate its secular programs to religious, but not to nonreligious (e.g., political), belief, courts must decide whether an objector's belief is religious. The courts may be asked to decide whether the teaching of evolution or of creationism is an establishment of religion. What general considerations might guide the definitional effort?

1. *Unitary or variable definitions?* Rutledge, J., dissenting in *Everson*, above:

"Religion" appears only once in the [First] Amendment. But the word governs two prohibitions and governs them alike. It does not have two meanings, one narrow to forbid "an establishment" and another, much broader, for securing "the free exercise thereof." "Thereof" brings down "religion" with its entire and exact content, no more and no less, from the first into the second guaranty, so that Congress and now the states are as broadly restricted concerning the one as they are regarding the other.

L. Tribe, American Constitutional Law 826-828 (1st ed. 1978):

At least through the nineteenth century, religion was given the same fairly narrow reading in the two clauses: "religion" referred to theistic notions respecting divinity, morality, and worship, and was recognized as legitimate and protected only insofar as it was generally accepted as "civilized" by Western standards. . . .

[But religion] in America, always pluralistic, has become radically so in the latter part of the twentieth century. [There] are, of course, many traditionally theistic American theologians, but for many others there has been a shift in religious thought from a theocentric, transcendental perspective to forms of religious consciousness that stress the immanence of meaning in the natural order. . . .

[Clearly,] the notion of religion in the free exercise clause must be expanded beyond the closely bounded limits of theism to account for the multiplying forms of recognizably legitimate religious exercise. It is equally clear, however, that in the age of the affirmative and increasingly pervasive state, a less expansive notion of religion was required for establishment clause purposes lest all "humane" programs of government be deemed constitutionally suspect. Such a twofold definition of religion — expansive for the free exercise clause, less so for the establishment clause — may be necessary to avoid confronting the state with increasingly difficult choices that the theory of permissible accommodations [could] not indefinitely resolve. . . .

Is Tribe's approach consistent with the language of the Constitution? In the second edition of his treatise, Tribe calls this proposal "a dubious solution to a problem that [may] not exist at all" because courts can and should focus on the more important ideas of tolerance and establishment. L. Tribe, American Constitutional Law 1186-1187 (2d ed. 1988).

2. *An expansive definition by the Supreme Court: the conscientious objector cases.* The Court's most extended consideration of the definition of religion occurred in a series of cases interpreting a federal statute granting an exemption from compulsory military service to any person "who, by reason of religious training and belief, is conscientiously opposed to participation in war in any form" and defining "religious training and belief" as "an individual's belief in relation to a Supreme Being involving duties superior to those arising from any human relation, but [not] any essentially political, sociological, or philosophical views or a merely personal moral code." (The reference to a "Supreme Being" was deleted in 1967.)

The Court interpreted these provisions in United States v. Seeger, 380 U.S. 163 (1965). Seeger stated on his draft form that he "preferred to leave the question as to his belief in a Supreme Being open," and that he had a "belief in and devotion to goodness and virtue for their own sakes, and a religious faith in a purely ethical creed [without] belief in God, except in the remotest sense." The Court unanimously found that Seeger qualified for the statutory exemption. The test was "whether a given belief that is sincere and meaningful occupies a place in the life of its possessor parallel to that filled by the orthodox belief in God of one who clearly qualifies for the exemption. Where such beliefs have parallel positions in the lives of their respective holders we cannot say that one is 'in relation to a Supreme Being' and the other is not." The Court mentioned "the richness and variety of spiritual life in our country."

Would granting an exemption on religious grounds to a group more narrowly defined than that in *Seeger* violate the establishment clause? Is the exemption as interpreted in *Seeger* nondiscriminatory? See Greenawalt, All or Nothing at All, 1971 Sup. Ct. Rev. 31.

Justice Douglas, concurring in *Seeger*, thought that a broadly defined exemption was required by the free exercise clause and by concepts of equal protection. The plurality in Welsh v. United States, 398 U.S. 333 (1970), applied the *Seeger* test to grant an exemption to someone who crossed off the word "religious" on the draft form. Justice Harlan concurred only in the result. He argued that *Seeger* had stretched the statutory language to its limit. "Congress [could eliminate] *all* exemptions for conscientious objectors. Such a course would be wholly 'neutral.' [However,] having chosen to exempt, it cannot draw the line between theistic or nontheistic religious beliefs on the one hand and secular beliefs on the other." To do so would violate the establishment clause.

In Gillette v. United States, 401 U.S. 437 (1971), the Court held that the statutory exemption was unavailable to those who had religious objections "relating to a particular conflict." It rejected the claim that the free exercise clause required that the exemption be available to such "selective" objectors and concluded that an exemption limited to objectors to all wars was sufficiently neutral to avoid establishment clause problems. The "de facto discrimination among religions" was not an establishment of religion because the discrimination "serves a number of purposes having nothing to do with a design to foster or favor any sect, religion, or cluster of religions [such] as the hopelessness of converting a sincere conscientious objector into an effective fighting man." The "interest in maintaining a fair system" might be defeated by requiring the draft system to inquire into the "enormous number of variables" that make selective objection "ultimately subjective." "There is a danger that as between two would-be objectors, both having the same complaint against a war, that objector would succeed who is more articulate, better educated, or better counseled." This danger was greater "the more discriminating and complicated the basis of classification." Justice Douglas dissented.

For an argument that protection should be extended to claims based on conscience as well as religion, see Smith, Converting the Religious Equality Amendment into a Statute with a Little "Conscience," 1996 BYU L. Rev. 645.

3. *The futility of definition?* Commentators, drawing on modern theology, have suggested that religion must involve "ultimate concern" or belief in "extra-temporal consequences" or in a "transcendent reality." See, e.g., Note, Toward a Constitutional Definition of Religion, 91 Harv. L. Rev. 1056 (1978); Choper, Defining "Religion" in the First Amendment, 1982 U. Ill. L. Rev. 579. Are the following belief systems religions? Does it matter whether the issue is free exercise or establishment? (a) Transcendental meditation (see Malnak v. Yogi, 592

F.2d 197 (3d Cir. 1979), finding that a school board established religion when it authorized the teaching of TM in the public schools); (b) pantheism (see Africa v. Pennsylvania, 662 F.2d 1025 (3d Cir. 1981), finding a system strongly resembling pantheism not a religion when its adherent sought to require prison officials to provide him with a diet of raw foods only); (c) secular humanism (see Grove v. Mead School District, 753 F.2d 1528 (9th Cir. 1985), finding no establishment clause violation in allowing public school students to satisfy requirements by reading a book said to advance secular humanism).

Consider Freeman, The Misguided Search for the Constitutional Definition of "Religion," 71 Geo. L.J. 1519, 1553, 1556 (1983): A "religious belief system" has some of the following "relevant features": belief in a supreme being, belief in a transcendent reality, a moral code, a worldview accounting for people's role in the universe, sacred rituals, worship and prayer, a sacred text, membership in a social organization. But "there is no single feature or set of features that constitutes the essence of religion." Rather, "a belief system [may] be more or less religious depending on how closely it resembles [the] paradigm" having all eight features.

How can the religion clauses be interpreted unless there is a definition of religion? Consider whether it would be possible to develop doctrines by accepting all sincerely proffered claims that a belief is religious and then determining whether the state's secular goals justify imposing a burden on that belief or whether the state's secular goals justify its adopting the program at issue. Freeman suggests that such doctrines might be unacceptable because the courts would be unable to distinguish between belief systems at the core of the concept of religion and those at its periphery; distaste for granting a free exercise exemption to the peripheral religion might distort the doctrines dealing with the balance between secular goals and burdens on religion.

4. *Determining sincerity.* In United States v. Ballard, 322 U.S. 78 (1944), the leaders of the "I Am" religion were indicted for mail fraud. The religion, an offshoot of the theosophy movement, was centered in the western states. Its founder, Guy Ballard, was said to have met a Master Saint Germain, who used Ballard as a messenger. Ballard's widow and son were charged with making representations that they knew were false regarding their power to cure diseases. The Supreme Court held that the jury could not be allowed to determine the truth or falsity of the representations about the Ballards' ability to cure. It could determine only whether the Ballards believed the representations they made. "Men may believe what they cannot prove. [Religious] experiences which are as real as life to some may be incomprehensible to others. [If] one could be sent to jail because a jury in a hostile environment found [his] teachings false, little indeed would be left of religious freedom." Justice Jackson would have gone further:

> I do not see how we can separate an issue as to what is believed from considerations as to what is believable. [Any] inquiry into intellectual honesty in religion raises profound psychological problems. [It] seems to me an impossible task for juries to separate fancied [religious experiences] from real ones, dreams from happenings, and hallucinations from true clairvoyance. [Further,] I do not know what degree of skepticism or disbelief in a religious representation amounts to an actionable fraud. [Religious] symbolism is even used by some with the same mental reservations one has in teaching of Santa Claus or Uncle Sam or Easter bunnies or dispassionate judges.

Chief Justice Stone, whose dissent was joined by Justices Roberts and Frankfurter, countered, "[If] it were shown that a defendant [had] asserted [that] he had physically shaken hands with St. Germain in San Francisco on a day named, or that [by] the exertion of his spiritual power he 'had in fact cured [hundreds] of persons . . . ,' it would be open to the Government to submit to the jury proof that he had never been in San Francisco and that no such cures had ever been effected." Justice Jackson agreed that a church leader could be prosecuted for fraud if he or she "represents that funds are being used to build a church when in fact they are being used for personal purposes." How does that differ from what the Ballards were charged with?

Note that inquiries into sincerity may be a disguised attempt to question whether the underlying belief is religious at all. Would that justify or cast doubt on the propriety of inquiries into sincerity?

B.   THE ESTABLISHMENT CLAUSE

In Lemon v. Kurtzman, 403 U.S. 602 (1971), the Court identified three "tests" for determining whether a statute violates the establishment clause: "First, the statute must have a secular legislative purpose; second, its principal or primary effect must be one that neither advances nor inhibits religion; finally, the statute must not foster 'an excessive government entanglement with religion.'" Are these criteria adequate to deal with the variety of problems that arise under the establishment clause? Can they be sensibly applied?

The so-called *Lemon* test has not been formally repudiated by the Supreme Court. A majority of the justices sitting in 2000 have criticized it, and it has not been relied on by a majority to invalidate any practice since 1985. In a concurring opinion in Lamb's Chapel v. Center Moriches Union Free School District, 508 U.S. 384 (1993), Justice Scalia criticized the *Lemon* test by analogizing it to "a ghoul in a late-night horror movie that repeatedly sits up in its grave and shuffles abroad, after being repeatedly killed and buried. [It] is there to scare us [when] we wish it to do so, but we can command it to return to the tomb at will. When we wish to strike down a practice it forbids, we invoke it; when we wish to uphold a practice it forbids, we ignore it entirely. [Such] a docile and useful monster is worth keeping around, at least in a somnolent state; one never knows when one might need him." For an overview of developments, see Lupu, The Lingering Death of Separationism, 62 Geo. Wash. L. Rev. 230 (1994).

1.   *The Anticoercion Principle*

Lee v. Weisman

505 U.S. 577 (1992)

JUSTICE KENNEDY delivered the opinion of the Court.

School principals in the public school system of the city of Providence, Rhode Island, are permitted to invite members of the clergy to offer invocation and benediction prayers as part of the formal graduation ceremonies for middle schools and for high schools. The question before us is whether including clerical members who offer prayers as part of the official school graduation ceremony is consistent with the Religion Clauses of the First Amendment, provisions the Fourteenth Amendment makes applicable with full force to the States and their school districts. . . .

[Following the school district's custom, a middle school principal invited a member of the clergy, Rabbi Leslie Gutterman, to deliver prayers at the school's graduation exercises. The principal gave Rabbi Gutterman a pamphlet, "Guidelines for Civic Occasions," prepared by the National Conference of Christians and Jews. The pamphlet recommended that prayers at civic ceremonies be "inclusive[]" and "sensitiv[e]." Rabbi Gutterman's invocation was:

> God of the Free, Hope of the Brave. For the legacy of America where diversity is celebrated and the rights of minorities are protected, we thank You. May these young men and women grow up to enrich it. For the liberty of America, we thank You. May these new graduates grow up to guard it. For the political process of America in which all its citizens may participate, for its court system where all may seek justice we thank You. May those we honor this morning always turn to it in trust. For the destiny of America we thank You. May the graduates of Nathan Bishop Middle School so live that they might help to share it. May our aspirations for our country and for these young people, who are our hope for the future, be richly fulfilled.

The benediction was similar in tone and content. Deborah Weisman, a student at the school, challenged the practice of having prayers at public school graduations.]

These dominant facts mark and control the confines of our decision: State officials direct the performance of a formal religious exercise at promotional and graduation ceremonies for secondary schools. Even for those students who object to the religious exercise, their attendance and participation in the state-sponsored religious activity are in a fair and real sense obligatory, though the school district does not require attendance as a condition for receipt of the diploma. . . .

[It] is beyond dispute that, at a minimum, the Constitution guarantees that government may not coerce anyone to support or participate in religion or its exercise, or otherwise act in a way which "establishes a [state] religion or religious faith, or tends to do so." [Lynch v. Donnelly, infra.] The State's involvement in the school prayers challenged today violates these central principles.

That involvement is as troubling as it is undenied. A school official, the principal, decided that an invocation and a benediction should be given; this is a choice attributable to the State, and from a constitutional perspective it is as if a state statute decreed that the prayers must occur. The principal chose the religious participant, here a rabbi, and that choice is also attributable to the State. The reason for the choice of a rabbi is not disclosed by the record, but the potential for divisiveness over the choice of a particular member of the clergy to conduct the ceremony is apparent.

Divisiveness, of course, can attend any state decision respecting religions, and neither its existence nor its potential necessarily invalidates the State's attempts to accommodate religion in all cases. The potential for divisiveness is of particular relevance here though, because it centers around an overt religious exercise in a secondary school environment where [subtle] coercive pressures exist and where the student had no real alternative which would have allowed her to avoid the fact or appearance of participation.

The State's role did not end with the decision to include a prayer and with the choice of clergyman. Principal Lee provided Rabbi Gutterman with a copy of the "Guidelines for Civic Occasions," and advised him that his prayers should be nonsectarian. Through these means the principal directed and controlled the content of the prayer. "[It] is a cornerstone principle of our Establishment Clause jurisprudence that it is no part of the business of government to compose official prayers for any group of the American people to recite as a part of a religious program carried on by government," Engel v. Vitale, 370 U.S. 421, 425 (1962), and that is what the school officials attempted to do.

Petitioners argue [that] the directions for the content of the prayers were a good-faith attempt by the school to ensure that the sectarianism which is so often the flashpoint for religious animosity be removed from the graduation ceremony. The concern is understandable, as a prayer which uses ideas or images identified with a particular religion may foster a different sort of sectarian rivalry than an invocation or benediction in terms more neutral. [The] question is not the good faith of the school in attempting to make the prayer acceptable to most persons, but the legitimacy of its undertaking that enterprise at all when the object is to produce a prayer to be used in a formal religious exercise which students, for all practical purposes, are obliged to attend.

We are asked to recognize the existence of a practice of nonsectarian prayer, prayer within the embrace of what is known as the Judeo-Christian tradition. [There] may be some support, as an empirical observation, to the statement [that] there has emerged in this country a civic religion, one which is tolerated when sectarian exercises are not. Note, Civil Religion and the Establishment Clause, 95 Yale L.J. 1237 (1986). If common ground can be defined which permits once conflicting faiths to express the shared conviction that there is an ethic and a morality which transcend human invention, the sense of community and purpose sought by all decent societies might be advanced. But though the First Amendment does not allow the government to stifle prayers which aspire to these ends, neither does it permit the government to undertake that task for itself.

The First Amendment's Religion Clauses mean that religious beliefs and religious expression are too precious to be either proscribed or prescribed by the State. The design of the Constitution is that preservation and transmission of religious beliefs and worship is a responsibility and a choice committed to the private sphere, which itself is promised freedom to pursue that mission. [While] concern must be given to define the protection granted to an objector or a dissenting nonbeliever, these same Clauses exist to protect religion from government interference. . . .

These concerns have particular application in the case of school officials, whose effort to monitor prayer will be perceived by the students as inducing a participation they might otherwise reject. [Our precedents] caution us to measure the idea of a civic religion against the central meaning of the Religion Clauses of the First Amendment, which is that all creeds must be tolerated and none favored. The suggestion that government may establish an official or civic religion as a means of avoiding the establishment of a religion with more specific creeds strikes us as a contradiction that cannot be accepted.

The degree of school involvement here made it clear that the graduation prayers bore the imprint of the State and thus put school-age children who objected in an untenable position. . . .

[It] is argued that [high] school students no doubt have been required to attend classes and assemblies and to complete assignments exposing them to ideas they find distasteful or immoral or absurd or all of these. Against this background, students may consider it an odd measure of justice to be subjected during the course of their educations to ideas deemed offensive and irreligious, but to be denied a brief, formal prayer ceremony that the school offers in return. This argument cannot prevail, however. It overlooks a fundamental dynamic of the Constitution.

The First Amendment protects speech and religion by quite different mechanisms. Speech is protected by insuring its full expression even when the government participates, for the very object of some of our most important speech is to persuade the government to adopt an idea as its own. The method for protecting freedom of worship and freedom of conscience in religious matters is quite the reverse. In religious debate or expression the government is not a prime participant, for the Framers deemed religious establishment antithetical to the freedom of all. The Free Exercise Clause embraces a freedom of conscience and worship that has close parallels in the speech provisions of the First Amendment, but the Establishment Clause is a specific prohibition on forms of state intervention in religious affairs with no precise counterpart in the speech provisions. The explanation lies in the lesson of history that was and is the inspiration for the Establishment Clause, the lesson that in the hands of government what might begin as a tolerant expression of religious views may end in a policy to indoctrinate and coerce. A state-created orthodoxy puts at grave risk that freedom of belief and conscience which are the sole assurance that religious faith is real, not imposed.

The lessons of the First Amendment are as urgent in the modern world as in the 18th Century when it was written. One timeless lesson is that if citizens are subjected to state-sponsored religious exercises, the State disavows its own duty to guard and respect that sphere of inviolable conscience and belief which is the mark of a free people. To compromise that principle today would be to deny our own tradition and forfeit our standing to urge others to secure the protections of that tradition for themselves.

[There] are heightened concerns with protecting freedom of conscience from subtle coercive pressure in the elementary and secondary public schools. [What] to most believers may seem nothing more than a reasonable request that the nonbeliever respect their religious practices, in a school context may appear to the nonbeliever or dissenter to be an attempt to employ the machinery of the State to enforce a religious orthodoxy.

[The] school district's supervision and control of a high school graduation ceremony places public pressure, as well as peer pressure, on attending students to stand as a group or, at least, maintain respectful silence during the Invocation and Benediction. This pressure, though subtle and indirect, can be as real as any overt compulsion. Of course, in our culture standing or remaining silent can signify adherence to a view or simple respect for the views of others. And no doubt some persons who have no desire to join a prayer have little objection to standing as a sign of respect for those who do. But for the dissenter of high school age, who has a reasonable perception that she is being forced by the State to pray in a manner her conscience will not allow, the injury is no less real. [For] many, if not most, of the students at the graduation, the act of standing or remaining silent was an expression of participation in the Rabbi's prayer. That was the very point of the religious exercise. It is of little comfort to a dissenter, then, to be told that for her the act of standing or remaining in silence signifies mere respect, rather than participation. What matters is that, given our social conventions, a reasonable dissenter in this milieu could believe that the group exercise signified her own participation or approval of it.

Finding no violation under these circumstances would place objectors in the dilemma of participating, with all that implies, or protesting. [We] think the State may not, consistent with the Establishment Clause, place primary and secondary school children in this position. Research in psychology supports the common assumption that adolescents are often susceptible to pressure from their peers towards conformity, and that the influence is strongest in matters of social convention. To recognize that the choice imposed by the State constitutes an unacceptable constraint only acknowledges that the government may no more use social pressure to enforce orthodoxy than it may use more direct means.

The injury caused by the government's action [is] that the State, in a school setting, in effect required participation in a religious exercise. [The] embarrassment and the intrusion of the religious exercise cannot be refuted by arguing that these prayers [are] of a de minimis character. To do so would be an affront to the Rabbi who offered them and to all those for whom the prayers were an essential and profound recognition of divine authority. [That] the intrusion was in the course of promulgating religion that sought to be civic or nonsectarian rather than pertaining to one sect does not lessen the offense or isolation to the objectors. At best it narrows their number, at worst increases their sense of isolation and affront.

There was a stipulation in the District Court that attendance at graduation and promotional ceremonies is voluntary. [Law] reaches past formalism. And to say a teenage student has a real choice not to attend her high school graduation is formalistic in the extreme. [Everyone] knows that in our society and in our culture high school graduation is one of life's most significant occasions. A school rule which excuses attendance is beside the point. [A] student is not free to absent herself from the graduation exercise in any real sense of the term "voluntary," for absence would require forfeiture of those intangible benefits which have motivated the student through youth and all her high school years. . . .

The importance of the event is the point the school district [relies] upon to argue that a formal prayer ought to be permitted, but it becomes one of the principal reasons why [the] argument must fail. [The] contention [is] that the prayers are an essential part of these ceremonies because for many persons an occasion of this significance lacks meaning if there is no recognition, however brief, that human achievements cannot be understood apart from their spiritual essence. We think the Government's position [fails] to acknowledge that what for many of Deborah's classmates and their parents was a spiritual imperative was for Daniel and Deborah Weisman religious conformance compelled by the State. While in some societies the wishes of the majority might prevail, the Establishment

Clause of the First Amendment is addressed to this contingency and rejects the balance urged upon us. The Constitution forbids the State to exact religious conformity from a student as the price of attending her own high school graduation. This is the calculus the Constitution commands.

The Government's argument gives insufficient recognition to the real conflict of conscience faced by the young student. The essence of the Government's position is that with regard to a civic, social occasion of this importance it is the objector, not the majority, who must take unilateral and private action to avoid compromising religious scruples, here by electing to miss the graduation exercise. This turns conventional First Amendment analysis on its head. It is a tenet of the First Amendment that the State cannot require one of its citizens to forfeit his or her rights and benefits as the price of resisting conformance to state-sponsored religious practice. To say that a student must remain apart from the ceremony at the opening invocation and closing benediction is to risk compelling conformity in an environment analogous to the classroom setting, where we have said the risk of compulsion is especially high. . . .

We do not hold that every state action implicating religion is invalid if one or a few citizens find it offensive. People may take offense at all manner of religious as well as nonreligious messages, but offense alone does not in every case show a violation. We know too that sometimes to endure social isolation or even anger may be the price of conscience or nonconformity. But, [the] conformity required of the student in this case was too high an exaction to withstand the test of the Establishment Clause. The prayer exercises in this case are especially improper because the State has in every practical sense compelled attendance and participation in an explicit religious exercise at an event of singular importance to every student, one the objecting student had no real alternative to avoid. . . .

[Our] society would be less than true to its heritage if it lacked abiding concern for the values of its young people, and we acknowledge the profound belief of adherents to many faiths that there must be a place in the student's life for precepts of a morality higher even than the law we today enforce. We express no hostility to those aspirations, nor would our oath permit us to do so. A relentless and all-pervasive attempt to exclude religion from every aspect of public life could itself become inconsistent with the Constitution. We recognize that, at graduation time and throughout the course of the educational process, there will be instances when religious values, religious practices, and religious persons will have some interaction with the public schools and their students. But these matters, often questions of accommodation of religion, are not before us. The sole question presented is whether a religious exercise may be conducted at a graduation ceremony in circumstances where, as we have found, young graduates who object are induced to conform. No holding by this Court suggests that a school can persuade or compel a student to participate in a religious exercise. That is being done here, and it is forbidden by the Establishment Clause of the First Amendment.

For the reasons we have stated, the judgment of the Court of Appeals is affirmed.

JUSTICE BLACKMUN, with whom JUSTICE STEVENS and JUSTICE O'CONNOR join, concurring. . . .

[It] is not enough that the government restrain from compelling religious practices: it must not engage in them either. . . .[6]

Our decisions have gone beyond prohibiting coercion, [because] the Court has recognized that "the fullest possible scope of religious liberty," *Schempp* (Goldberg, J., concurring) [section A supra], entails more than freedom from coercion. The Establishment Clause protects religious liberty on a grand scale; it is a social compact that guarantees for generations a democracy and a strong religious community — both essential to safeguarding religious liberty. "Our fathers seem to have been perfectly sincere in their belief that the members of the Church would be more patriotic, and the citizens of the State more religious, by keeping their respective functions entirely separate." Religious Liberty, in Essays and Speeches of Jeremiah S. Black 53 (C. Black ed. 1885) (Chief Justice of the Commonwealth of Pennsylvania). . . .

[A concurring opinion by Justice Souter, joined by Justices Stevens and O'Connor, is omitted.]

JUSTICE SCALIA, with whom THE CHIEF JUSTICE, JUSTICE WHITE, and JUSTICE THOMAS join, dissenting. . . .

[In] holding that the Establishment Clause prohibits invocations and benedictions at public-school graduation ceremonies, the Court [lays] waste a tradition [that] is a component of an even more longstanding American tradition of nonsectarian prayer to God at public celebrations generally. . . .

I . . .

From our Nation's origin, prayer has been a prominent part of governmental ceremonies and proclamations. The Declaration of Independence "[appealed] to the Supreme Judge of the world for the rectitude of our intentions" and avowed "a firm reliance on the protection of divine Providence." In his first inaugural address, after swearing his oath of office on a Bible, George Washington deliberately made a prayer a part of his first official act as President:

> it would be peculiarly improper to omit in this first official act my fervent supplications to that Almighty Being who rules over the universe, who presides in the councils of nations, and whose providential aids can supply every human defect, that His benediction may consecrate to the liberties and happiness of the people of the United States a Government instituted by themselves for these essential purposes.

Such supplications have been a characteristic feature of inaugural addresses ever since. . . .

Our national celebration of Thanksgiving likewise dates back to President Washington. [This] tradition of Thanksgiving Proclamations — with their reli-

---

6. As a practical matter, of course, anytime the government endorses a religious belief there will almost always be some pressure to conform. "When the power, prestige and financial support of government is placed behind a particular religious belief, the indirect coercive pressure upon religious minorities to conform to the prevailing officially approved religion is plain." Engel v. Vitale, 370 U.S. 421, 431 (1962). [Relocated footnote — EDS.]

gious theme of prayerful gratitude to God — has been adhered to by almost every President. . . .

II

The Court presumably would separate graduation invocations and benedictions from other instances of public "preservation and transmission of religious beliefs" on the ground that they involve "psychological coercion." [A] few citations of "research in psychology" that have no particular bearing upon the precise issue here cannot disguise the fact that the Court has gone beyond the realm where judges know what they are doing. The Court's argument that state officials have "coerced" students to take part in the invocation and benediction at graduation ceremonies is, not to put too fine a point on it, incoherent.

A

[According] to the Court, students at graduation who want "to avoid the fact or appearance of participation," in the invocation and benediction are psychologically obligated "[to] stand as a group or, at least, maintain respectful silence" during those prayers. This assertion [does] not say [that] students are psychologically coerced to bow their heads, place their hands in a Drer-like prayer position, pay attention to the prayers, utter "Amen," or in fact pray. [It] claims only that students are psychologically coerced "to stand . . . or, at least, maintain respectful silence." Both halves of this disjunctive [merit] particular attention.

[The] Court's notion that a student who simply sits in "respectful silence" during the invocation and benediction [has] somehow joined — or would somehow be perceived as having joined — in the prayers is nothing short of ludicrous. We indeed live in a vulgar age. But surely "our social conventions" have not coarsened to the point that anyone who does not stand on his chair and shout obscenities can reasonably be deemed to have assented to everything said in his presence. Since the Court does not dispute that students exposed to prayer at graduation ceremonies retain [the] free will to sit, there is absolutely no basis for the Court's decision. . . .

But let us assume the very worst, that the nonparticipating graduate is "subtly coerced" . . . to stand! Even that half of the disjunctive does not remotely establish a "participation" (or an "appearance of participation") in a religious exercise. [If] it is a permissible inference that one who is standing is doing so simply out of respect for the prayers of others that are in progress, then how can it possibly be said that a "reasonable dissenter . . . could believe that the group exercise signified her own participation or approval"? [Maintaining] respect for the religious observances of others is a fundamental civic virtue that government [can] and should cultivate — so that even if [the] displaying of such respect might be mistaken for taking part in the prayer, I would deny that the dissenter's interest in avoiding even the false appearance of participation constitutionally trumps the government's interest in fostering respect for religion generally.

[The] Court itself has not given careful consideration to its test of psychological coercion. For if it had, how could it observe [that] students stood for the Pledge of Allegiance, which immediately preceded Rabbi Gutterman's invocation? [Recital] of the Pledge would appear to raise the same Establishment Clause issue as the invocation and benediction. [Must] the Pledge therefore be barred from the public schools (both from graduation ceremonies and from the classroom)? . . .

III . . .

[The] coercion that was a hallmark of historical establishments of religion was coercion of religious orthodoxy and of financial support by force of law and threat of penalty. Typically, attendance at the state church was required; only clergy of the official church could lawfully perform sacraments; and dissenters, if tolerated, faced an array of civil disabilities. . . .

The Establishment Clause was adopted to prohibit such an establishment of religion at the federal level (and to protect state establishments of religion from federal interference). I will further acknowledge for the sake of argument that, as some scholars have argued, by 1790 the term "establishment" had acquired an additional meaning — "financial support of religion generally, by public taxation" — that reflected the development of "general or multiple" establishments, not limited to a single church. But that would still be an establishment coerced by force of law. And I will further concede that our constitutional tradition [has], with a few aberrations, ruled out of order government-sponsored endorsement of religion — even when no legal coercion is present, and indeed even when no ersatz, "peer-pressure" psycho-coercion is present — where the endorsement is sectarian, in the sense of specifying details upon which men and women who believe in a benevolent, omnipotent Creator and Ruler of the world, are known to differ (for example, the divinity of Christ). But there is simply no support for the proposition that the officially sponsored nondenominational invocation and benediction read by Rabbi Gutterman — with no one legally coerced to recite them — violated the Constitution of the United States. To the contrary, they are so characteristically American they could have come from the pen of George Washington or Abraham Lincoln himself. . . .

IV . . .

[Given] the odd basis for the Court's decision, invocations and benedictions will be able to be given at public-school graduations next June [so] long as school authorities make clear that anyone who abstains from screaming in protest does not necessarily participate in the prayers. All that is seemingly needed is an announcement, or perhaps a written insertion at the beginning of the graduation Program, to the effect that, while all are asked to rise for the invocation and benediction, none is compelled to join in them, nor will be assumed, by rising, to have done so. That obvious fact recited, the graduates and their parents may proceed to thank God, as Americans have always done, for the blessings He has generously bestowed on them and on their country. . . .

The reader has been told much in this case about the personal interest of Mr. Weisman and his daughter, and very little about the personal interests on the other side. They are not inconsequential. Church and state would not be such a difficult subject if religion were, as the Court apparently thinks it to be, some purely personal avocation that can be indulged entirely in secret, like pornography, in the privacy of one's room. For most believers it is not that, and has never been. Religious men and women of almost all denominations have felt it necessary to acknowledge and beseech the blessing of God as a people, and not just as individuals, because they believe in the "protection of divine Providence," as the Declaration of Independence put it, not just for individuals but for societies; because they believe God to be, as Washington's first Thanksgiving Proclamation put it, the "Great Lord and Ruler of Nations." One can believe in the effectiveness of such public worship, or one can deprecate and deride it. But the long-standing American tradition of prayer at official ceremonies displays with unmistakable clarity that the Establishment Clause does not forbid the government to accommodate it. . . .

I must add one final observation: The founders of our Republic knew the fearsome potential of sectarian religious belief to generate civil dissension and civil strife. And they also knew that nothing, absolutely nothing, is so inclined to foster among religious believers of various faiths a toleration — no, an affection — for one another than voluntarily joining in prayer together, to the God whom they all worship and seek. Needless to say, no one should be compelled to do that, but it is a shame to deprive our public culture of the opportunity, and indeed the encouragement, for people to do it voluntarily. The Baptist or Catholic who heard and joined in the simple and inspiring prayers of Rabbi Gutterman on this official and patriotic occasion was inoculated from religious bigotry and prejudice in a manner that can not be replicated. To deprive our society of that important unifying mechanism, in order to spare the nonbeliever what seems to me the minimal inconvenience of standing or even sitting in respectful nonparticipation, is as senseless in policy as it is unsupported in law.

For the foregoing reasons, I dissent.

Note: The Noncoercion Principle

1. *Defining coercion.* Does treating the psychological impact of a practice on dissenters as coercive create a "dissenter's veto"? Does Justice Scalia's treatment of coercion overlook the possibility that some student, in the face of the graduation prayer, will engage in a prayer that he or she would not otherwise have engaged in? Is that accurately described as coercion? If not, is it more accurate to describe the problem in *Lee* as one of government endorsement of religion, which on the margin induces someone to engage in prayer, rather than one of government coercion? Should there be a parallel concern (under the free exercise clause?) for the "coercion" of some religious students when presented with material — about evolution, for example — inconsistent with their religious beliefs? Consider this perspective on *Lee*:

[The] harm inflicted by government-sponsored religious exercises is two-fold. First, civic religious exercises force religious minorities to sever civil communion to avoid spiritual pollution. [The] second harm is that civic religious exercises wound the civil community by compelling the severance of religious minorities and thus fracturing community. [In] contrast with Justice Scalia's proposed inoculation against bigotry, [a] very different view of toleration [does] not necessarily engender affection among believers of different stripes, but simply civil cooperation. [Roger Williams] and the Separatists [remind] us that we must deny to ecumenical impulses any right to a smug place of preeminence in the history of religious freedom in America.

T. Hall, Separating Church and State: Roger Williams and Religious Liberty 158, 159-160 (1998).

2. *The scope of the principle.* Walz v. Tax Commission, 397 U.S. 664 (1970), held constitutional the practice of granting churches exemptions from the property tax. Chief Justice Burger's opinion for the Court said that the "purpose of a property tax exemption is neither the advancement nor the inhibition of religion. [The state] has not singled out one particular church [or] even churches as such; rather, it has granted exemption to all houses of worship within a broad class of property owned by nonprofit, quasi-public corporations [which the state considers] beneficial and stabilizing influences in community life." After describing the ways in which denial of tax exemption would "expand the involvement of government" with religion, the Court said, "The exemption creates only a minimal and remote involvement between church and state. [It] restricts the fiscal relationship between [them], and tends to complement and reinforce the desired separation insulating each from the other." Fiscal support of religion through the tax system is thus not the imposition of religion on nonbelievers.

In Engel v. Vitale, 370 U.S. 421 (1962), a public school allowed those who objected to state-written prayers recited at the beginning of classes to remain silent or be excused from attendance. The Court said, "When the power, prestige and financial support of government is placed behind a particular religious belief, the indirect coercive pressure upon religious minorities to conform to the prevailing officially approved religion is plain." Justice Stewart would have remanded a similar case for development of the facts involving coercion:

[The] dangers of coercion involved in the holding of religious exercises in a schoolroom differ qualitatively from those presented by the use of similar exercises or affirmations in ceremonies attended by adults. Even as to children, however, the duty laid upon government in connection with religious exercises in the public schools is that of refraining from so structuring the school environment as to put any kind of pressure on a child to participate in those exercises; it is not that of providing an atmosphere in which children are kept scrupulously insulated from any awareness that some of their fellows may want to open the school day with prayer, or of the fact that there exist in our pluralistic society differences of religious belief. [Certain] types of exercises would present situations in which no possibility of coercion on the part of secular officials could be claimed to exist. Thus, if such exercises were held either before or after the official school day, or if the school schedule were such that participation were merely one among a number of desirable alternatives, it could hardly be contended that the exercises did anything more than to provide an opportunity for the voluntary expression of religious belief. [If] the exercises were held during the school day, and no equally desirable alternative were provided by the school authorities, the likelihood that children might be under at least some psychological compulsion to participate would be great. In such a case as the latter, however, I think we would err if we *assumed* such coercion in the absence of any evidence.

School District of Abington Township v. Schempp, 374 U.S. 203, 316-318 (1963).

Consider the argument of Carter, Parents, Religion, and Schools: Reflections on *Pierce*, 70 Years Later, 27 Seton Hall L. Rev. 1194, 1214 (1997):

> [If] beginning the school day with a prayer is unconstitutional because it prefers religion over nonreligion, then why is not a curriculum devoid of any religious observance unconstitutional because it prefers non-religion over religion? [By] compelling school attendance, [the] state as much as announces that what occurs in its schools is of vital importance. So if none of the material is religious, children will receive the message that the state deems religion unimportant. [The] ban on prayer must be intended to help individuals to make up their own minds [about] what religions to follow. But prayer and other formal religious instruction are hardly the only things that can do that. [If] our concern is for state interference with religious choice, we would surely want to take a hard look at the curriculum and rid it of other topics of instruction that make it difficult for individuals to make up their own minds about what religions to follow.

3. *Coercion, free exercise, and free speech.* The free exercise and free speech clauses protect against coercion *away from* a person's beliefs. Would it violate a student's free exercise right to compel her to stand respectfully during the benediction? Her free speech right? If neither right would be violated, the anticoercion principle might guard against direct violations that are difficult to identify on a case-by-case basis. Should such a principle be regarded as an establishment clause or a free exercise/free speech principle? If free exercise and free speech rights are not implicated, the establishment clause might deal with structural relations between religion and government rather than with individual rights. How could the Court identify impermissible structural relations except by referring to individual rights?

4. *Prayers at football games.* Sante Fe Independent School District v. Doe, 530 U.S. 290 (2000), held unconstitutional a district's policy that authorized students to vote, first, whether to allow "invocations" at high school football games, and then to choose a person to deliver them. Relying on Board of Regents v. Southworth, Chapter 7, section E5, supra, Justice Stevens, writing for six justices, concluded that the speech the selected student gave would not be private speech because of the policy authorizing an election in which a majority would determine whether to have invocations. The Court then held that an invocation at a high school football game violated the principle established in *Lee*. The establishment clause was designed "to remove debate over this kind of issue from governmental supervision or control." Some students, such as cheerleaders and team members, were compelled to attend the games, and other students would feel "immense social pressure" and "truly genuine desire" to attend the games. The delivery of a religious invocation would therefore coerce them in the way condemned in *Lee*. Chief Justice Rehnquist and Justices Scalia and Thomas dissented.

2.   *The Nonendorsement Principle and De Facto Establishments*

Lynch v. Donnelly

465 U.S. 668 (1984)

THE CHIEF JUSTICE delivered the opinion of the Court. . . .

Each year, in cooperation with the downtown retail merchants' association, the City of Pawtucket, Rhode Island, erects a Christmas display as part of its observance of the Christmas holiday season. The display is situated in a park owned by a nonprofit organization and located in the heart of the shopping district. The display is essentially like those to be found in hundreds of towns or cities across the Nation — often on public grounds — during the Christmas season. The Pawtucket display comprises many of the figures and decorations traditionally associated with Christmas, including, among other things, a Santa Claus house, reindeer pulling Santa's sleigh, candy-striped poles, a Christmas tree, carolers, cutout figures representing such characters as a clown, an elephant, and a teddy bear, hundreds of colored lights, a large banner that reads "SEASONS GREETINGS," and the crèche at issue here. All components of this display are owned by the City. . . .

[The court of appeals held that the crèche violated the establishment clause.]

[Rather] than mechanically invalidating all governmental conduct or statutes that confer benefits or give special recognition to religion in general or to one faith — as an absolutist approach would dictate — the Court has scrutinized challenged legislation or official conduct to determine whether, in reality, it establishes a religion or religious faith, or tends to do so. . . .

In each case, the inquiry calls for line drawing; no fixed, *per se* rule can be framed. . . .

In the line-drawing process we have often found it useful to inquire whether the challenged law or conduct has a secular purpose, whether its principal or primary effect is to advance or inhibit religion, and whether it creates an excessive entanglement of government with religion. [*Lemon.*] But, we have repeatedly emphasized our unwillingness to be confined to any single test or criterion in this sensitive area. . . .

[In] this case, the focus of our inquiry must be on the crèche in the context of the Christmas season. . . .[12]

[When] viewed in the proper context of the Christmas Holiday season, it is apparent that, on this record, there is insufficient evidence to establish that the inclusion of the crèche is a purposeful or surreptitious effort to express some kind of subtle governmental advocacy of a particular religious message. In a pluralistic society a variety of motives and purposes are implicated. The City, like the Congresses and Presidents, however, has principally taken note of a significant historical religious event long celebrated in the Western World. . . .

12. Justice Brennan states that "by focusing on the holiday 'context' in which the crèche appear[s]," the Court seeks to "explain away the clear religious import of the crèche," and that it has equated the crèche with a Santa's house or a talking wishing well. Of course this is not true. [Relocated footnote. — EDS.]

The narrow question is whether there is a secular purpose for Pawtucket's display of the crèche. The display is sponsored by the City to celebrate the Holiday and to depict the origins of that Holiday. These are legitimate secular purposes. . . .

The dissent asserts some observers may perceive that the City has aligned itself with the Christian faith by including a Christian symbol in its display and that this serves to advance religion. We can assume, *arguendo,* that the display advances religion in a sense; but our precedents plainly contemplate that on occasion some advancement of religion will result from governmental action. [Here,] whatever benefit to one faith or religion or to all religions, is indirect, remote and incidental; display of the crèche is no more an advancement or endorsement of religion than the Congressional and Executive recognition of the origins of the Holiday itself as "Christ's Mass," or the exhibition of literally hundreds of religious paintings in governmentally supported museums. . . .

The Court has acknowledged that the "fears and political problems" that gave rise to the Religion Clauses in the 18th century are of far less concern today. [*Everson.*] We are unable to perceive the Archbishop of Canterbury, the Vicar of Rome, or other powerful religious leaders behind every public acknowledgment of the religious heritage long officially recognized by the three constitutional branches of government. Any notion that these symbols pose a real danger of establishment of a state church is far-fetched indeed. . . .

[Reversed.]

JUSTICE O'CONNOR, concurring. . . .

I

The Establishment Clause prohibits government from making adherence to a religion relevant in any way to a person's standing in the political community. Government can run afoul of that prohibition in two principal ways. One is excessive entanglement with religious institutions, which may interfere with the independence of the institutions, give the institutions access to government or governmental powers not fully shared by nonadherents of the religion, and foster the creation of political constituencies defined along religious lines. The second and more direct infringement is government endorsement or disapproval of religion. Endorsement sends a message to nonadherents that they are outsiders, not full members of the political community, and an accompanying message to adherents that they are insiders, favored members of the political community. Disapproval sends the opposite message. . . .

III

The central issue in this case is whether Pawtucket has endorsed Christianity by its display of the crèche. To answer that question, we must examine both what Pawtucket intended to communicate in displaying the crèche and what message the City's display actually conveyed. The purpose and effect prongs of the *Lemon* test represent these two aspects of the meaning of the City's action.

The meaning of a statement to its audience depends both on the intention of the speaker and on the "objective" meaning of the statement in the community.

Some listeners need not rely solely on the words themselves in discerning the speaker's intent: they can judge the intent by, for example, examining the context of the statement or asking questions of the speaker. Other listeners do not have or will not seek access to such evidence of intent. They will rely instead on the words themselves; for them the message actually conveyed may be something not actually intended. If the audience is large, as it always is when government "speaks" by word or deed, some portion of the audience will inevitably receive a message determined by the "objective" content of the statement, and some portion will inevitably receive the intended message. Examination of both the subjective and the objective components of the message communicated by a government action is therefore necessary to determine whether the action carries a forbidden meaning.

The purpose prong of the *Lemon* test asks whether government's actual purpose is to endorse or disapprove of religion. The effect prong asks whether, irrespective of government's actual purpose, the practice under review in fact conveys a message of endorsement or disapproval. An affirmative answer to either question should render the challenged practice invalid.

A

The purpose prong of the *Lemon* test requires that a government activity have a secular purpose. That requirement is not satisfied [by] the mere existence of some secular purpose, however dominated by religious purposes. The proper inquiry under the purpose prong of *Lemon* [is] whether the government intends to convey a message of endorsement or disapproval of religion.

Applying that formulation to this case, I would find that Pawtucket did not intend to convey any message of endorsement of Christianity or disapproval of non-Christian religions. The evident purpose of including the crèche in the larger display was not promotion of the religious content of the crèche but celebration of the public holiday through its traditional symbols. Celebration of public holidays, which have cultural significance even if they also have religious aspects, is a legitimate secular purpose. . . .

B

[Under the effect prong, what] is crucial is that a government practice not have the effect of communicating a message of government endorsement or disapproval of religion. It is only practices having that effect, whether intentionally or unintentionally, that make religion relevant, in reality or public perception, to status in the political community.

Pawtucket's display of its crèche, I believe, does not communicate a message that the government intends to endorse the Christian beliefs represented by the crèche. Although the religious and indeed sectarian significance of the crèche [is] not neutralized by the setting, the overall holiday setting changes what viewers may fairly understand to be the purpose of the display — as a typical museum setting, though not neutralizing the religious content of a religious painting, negates any message of endorsement of that content. The display celebrates a public holiday. [The] holiday itself has very strong secular components and traditions. Government celebration of the holiday [generally] is not understood to endorse the religious content of the holiday, just as government celebration of Thanksgiving is not so understood. The crèche is a traditional symbol of the holiday that is very commonly displayed along with purely secular symbols, as it was in Pawtucket.

These features combine to make the government's display of the crèche in this particular physical setting no more an endorsement of religion than such governmental "acknowledgments" of religion as [printing] of "In God We Trust" on coins, and opening court sessions with "God save the United States and this honorable court." Those government acknowledgments of religion serve, in the only ways reasonably possible in our culture, the legitimate secular purposes of solemnizing public occasions, expressing confidence in the future, and encouraging the recognition of what is worthy of appreciation in society. For that reason, and because of their history and ubiquity, those practices are not understood as conveying government approval of particular religious beliefs. The display of the crèche likewise serves a secular purpose — celebration of a public holiday with traditional symbols. It cannot fairly be understood to convey a message of government endorsement of religion. It is significant in this regard that the crèche display apparently caused no political divisiveness prior to the filing of this lawsuit, although Pawtucket had incorporated the crèche in its annual Christmas display for some years. For these reasons, I conclude that Pawtucket's display of the crèche does not have the effect of communicating endorsement of Christianity.

JUSTICE BRENNAN, with whom JUSTICE MARSHALL, JUSTICE BLACKMUN, and JUSTICE STEVENS join, dissenting. . . .

I . . .

[The] nativity scene, unlike every other element of the Hodgson Park display, reflects a sectarian exclusivity that the avowed purposes of celebrating the holiday season and promoting retail commerce simply do not encompass. [The] inclusion of a distinctively religious element like the crèche [demonstrates] that a narrower sectarian purpose lay behind the decision to include a nativity scene.

The "primary effect" of including a nativity scene in the City's display is [to] place the government's imprimatur of approval on the particular religious beliefs exemplified by the crèche. Those who believe in the message of the nativity receive the unique and exclusive benefit of public recognition and approval of their views. For many, the City's decision to include the crèche as part of its extensive and costly efforts to celebrate Christmas can only mean that the prestige of the government has been conferred on the beliefs associated with the crèche, thereby providing "a significant symbolic benefit to religion. . . ." [Larkin v. Grendel's Den, section D infra.] The effect on minority religious groups, as well as on those who may reject all religion, is to convey the message that their views are not similarly worthy of public recognition nor entitled to public support. . . .

[The] Court, by focusing on the holiday "context" in which the nativity scene appeared, seeks to explain away the clear religious import of the crèche. [It] blinks reality to claim [that] by including such a distinctively religious object as the crèche in its Christmas display, Pawtucket has done no more than make use of a "traditional" symbol of the holiday, and has thereby purged the crèche of its religious content and conferred only an "incidental and direct" benefit on religion. . . .

[The] City has done nothing to disclaim government approval of the religious significance of the crèche, to suggest that the crèche represents only one religious symbol among many others that might be included in a seasonal display truly aimed at providing a wide catalogue of ethnic and religious celebrations, or to disassociate itself from the religious content of the crèche. . . .

Finally, [even] in the context of Pawtucket's seasonal celebration, the crèche retains a specifically Christian religious meaning. I refuse to accept the notion implicit in today's decision that non-Christians would find that the religious content of the crèche is eliminated by the fact that it appears as part of the City's otherwise secular celebration of the Christmas holiday. The nativity scene [is] the chief symbol of the characteristically Christian belief that a divine Savior was brought into the world and that the purpose of this miraculous birth was to illuminate a path toward salvation and redemption. For Christians, that path is exclusive, precious and holy. But for those who do not share these beliefs, the symbolic re-enactment of the birth of a divine being who has been miraculously incarnated as a man stands as a dramatic reminder of their differences with Christian faith. [To] be so excluded on religious grounds by one's elected government is an insult and an injury that, until today, could not be countenanced by the Establishment Clause. . . .

When government decides to recognize Christmas day as a public holiday, it does no more than accommodate the calendar of public activities to the plain fact that many Americans will expect on that day to spend time visiting with their families, attending religious services, and perhaps enjoying some respite from pre-holiday activities. [When public] officials participate in or appear to endorse the distinctively religious elements of this otherwise secular event, they encroach upon First Amendment freedoms. For it is at that point that the government brings to the forefront the theological content of the holiday, and places the prestige, power and financial support of a civil authority in the service of a particular faith.

[Unlike] such secular figures as Santa Claus, reindeer and carolers, a nativity scene represents far more than a mere "traditional" symbol of Christmas. The essence of the crèche's symbolic purpose and effect is to prompt the observer to experience a sense of simple awe and wonder appropriate to the contemplation of one of the central elements of Christian dogma — that God sent His son into the world to be a Messiah. [The] crèche is far from a mere representation of a "particular historic religious event." It is, instead, best understood as a mystical re-creation of an event that lies at the heart of Christian faith. To suggest, as the Court does, that such a symbol is merely "traditional" and therefore no different from Santa's house or reindeer is not only offensive to those for whom the crèche has profound significance, but insulting to those who insist for religious or personal reasons that the story of Christ is in no sense a part of "history" nor an unavoidable element of our national "heritage." . . .

II . . .

Intuition tells us that some official "acknowledgment" is inevitable in a religious society if government is not to adopt a stilted indifference to the religious life of the people. It is equally true, however, that if government is to remain scrupulously neutral in matters of religious conscience, as our Constitution requires, then it must avoid those overly broad acknowledgments of religious practices that may imply governmental favoritism toward one set of religious beliefs. This does not mean, of course, that public officials may not take account, when necessary, of the separate existence and significance of the religious institutions and practices in the society they govern. . . .

[At] least three principles — tracing the narrow channels which government acknowledgments must follow to satisfy the Establishment Clause — may be identified. First, although the government may not be compelled to do so by the Free Exercise Clause, it may, consistently with the Establishment Clause, act to accommodate to some extent the opportunities of individuals to practice their religion. [That] principle would justify government's decision to declare December 25th a public holiday.

Second, [while] a particular governmental practice may have derived from religious motivations and retain certain religious connotations, it is nonetheless permissible for the government to pursue the practice when it is continued today solely for secular reasons. [The] mere fact that a governmental practice coincides to some extent with certain religious beliefs does not render it unconstitutional. Thanksgiving Day, in my view, fits easily within this principle, for despite its religious antecedents, the current practice of celebrating Thanksgiving is unquestionably secular and patriotic. . . .

Finally, we have noted that government cannot be completely prohibited from recognizing in its public actions the religious beliefs and practices of the American people as an aspect of our national history and culture. While I remain uncertain about these questions, I would suggest that such practices as the designation of "In God We Trust" as our national motto, or the references to God contained in the Pledge of Allegiance can best be understood [as] a form a "ceremonial deism," protected from Establishment Clause scrutiny chiefly because they have lost through rote repetition any significant religious content. Moreover, these references are uniquely suited to serve such wholly secular purposes as solemnizing public occasions, or inspiring commitment to meet some national challenge in a manner that simply could not be fully served in our culture if government were limited to purely non-religious phrases. . . .

The crèche fits none of these categories. . . .

III . . .

The intent of the Framers with respect to the public display of nativity scenes is virtually impossible to discern primarily because the widespread celebration of Christmas did not emerge in its present form until well into the nineteenth century. Carrying a well-defined Puritan hostility to the celebration of Christ's birth with them to the New World, the founders of the Massachusetts Bay Colony pursued a vigilant policy of opposition to any public celebration of the holiday. To the Puritans, the celebration of Christmas represented a "Popish" practice lacking any foundation in Scripture. . . .

During the eighteenth century, sectarian division over the celebration of the holiday continued. As increasing numbers of members of the Anglican and the Dutch and German Reformed churches arrived, the practice of celebrating

Christmas as a purely religious holiday grew. But denominational differences continued to dictate differences in attitude toward the holiday. [Many] nonconforming Protestant groups, including the Presbyterians, Congregationalists, Baptists, and Methodists, continued to regard the holiday with suspicion and antagonism well into the nineteenth century. This pattern of sectarian division concerning the holiday suggests that for the Framers of the Establishment Clause, who were acutely sensitive to such sectarian controversies, no single view of how government should approach the celebration of Christmas would be possible. . . .

Furthermore [the] public display of nativity scenes as part of governmental celebrations of Christmas does not come to us supported by an unbroken history of widespread acceptance. It was not until 1836 that a State first granted legal recognition to Christmas as a public holiday. [Congress] did not follow the States' lead until 1870 when it established December 25th, along with the Fourth of July, New Year's Day, and Thanksgiving, as a legal holiday in the District of Columbia. . . .

[The] City's action should be recognized for what it is: a coercive, though perhaps small, step toward establishing the sectarian preferences of the majority at the expense of the minority, accomplished by placing public facilities and funds in support of the religious symbolism and theological tidings that the crèche conveys. . . .

I dissent.

JUSTICE BLACKMUN, with whom JUSTICE STEVENS joins, dissenting. . . .

The crèche has been relegated to the role of a neutral harbinger of the holiday season, useful for commercial purposes, but devoid of any inherent meaning and incapable of enhancing the religious tenor of a display of which it is an integral part. The city has its victory — but it is a Pyrrhic one indeed.

The import of the Court's decision is to encourage use of the crèche in a municipally sponsored display, a setting where Christians feel constrained in acknowledging its symbolic meaning and non-Christians feel alienated by its presence. Surely, this is a misuse of a sacred symbol. . . .

Note: The Nonendorsement Principle

1. *Applying the nonendorsement principle.* In County of Allegheny v. American Civil Liberties Union, 492 U.S. 573 (1989), a majority of the Court joined Justice Blackmun's opinion adopting Justice O'Connor's "no endorsement" analysis as a general guide in establishment clause cases. Shifting majorities on the Court held unconstitutional a freestanding display of a nativity scene on the main staircase of a county courthouse, but upheld the display of a Jewish menorah placed next to the city's Christmas tree and a statement declaring the city's "salute to liberty." One majority concluded that the "setting" of the nativity scene, which was the "single element" in the display, "celebrate[d] Christmas in a way that has the effect of endorsing a patently Christian message."

Justice Blackmun, writing for himself, concluded that the display of the menorah was permissible. "The menorah's message is not exclusively religious," and it stood next to a Christmas tree and a sign saluting liberty, with the effect of "creat[ing] an 'overall holiday setting' that represents both Christmas and Chanukah — two holidays, not one." Justice O'Connor agreed that the display of the menorah was permissible. Although the menorah had religious content, she said, the overall display "sends a message of pluralism and freedom to choose one's own beliefs." Justices Brennan, Marshall, and Stevens dissented as to the menorah. Justice Brennan argued that the Christmas tree was a religious symbol, and that Chanukah was not a holiday with secular dimensions. The government's message in the "salute to liberty" was not religious, but "patriotic," and "the government's use of religion to promote its own cause is undoubtedly offensive to those whose religious beliefs are not bound up with their attitude toward the Nation."

Justice Kennedy, joined by Chief Justice Rehnquist and Justices White and Scalia, rejected the majority's adoption of the "no endorsement" test, saying that it "reflects an unjustified hostility toward religion." He argued that the establishment clause "permits government some latitude in recognizing and accommodating the central role religion plays in our society." To him, the Court's decisions

> disclose two limiting principles: government may not coerce anyone to support or participate in any religion or its exercise; and it may not, in the guise of avoiding hostility or callous indifference, give direct benefits to religion in such a degree that it in fact "establishes a [state] religion or religious faith, or tends to do so." [Lynch.] [Symbolic] recognition or accommodation of religious faith may violate the Clause in an extreme case, [such as] the permanent erection of a large Latin cross on the roof of city hall [because] such an obtrusive year-round religious display would place the government's weight behind an obvious effort to proselytize on behalf of a particular religion. [Absent] coercion, the risk of infringement of religious liberty by passive or symbolic accommodation is minimal.

Are the ceremonial or symbolic endorsements of religion at issue in these cases more or less important for the principle of antiestablishment than monetary subsidies to church-related education? Than the practice of prayer in the public schools?

2. *Justifying the nonendorsement principle.* Leedes, Rediscovering the Link between the Establishment Clause and the Fourteenth Amendment: The Citizenship Declaration, 26 Ind. L. Rev. 469 (1993), suggests that the "citizenship declaration" in the first sentence of the fourteenth amendment "prohibits the federal and state governments from subverting a citizen's status in the political community because of his or her creed or lack of religious commitment." According to Leedes, "[T]he immunity associated with citizen status does *not* need to come into play when nonpreferential, noncoercive state aid to religion advances legitimate secular objectives and does not stigmatize members of religious outgroups. It needs to come into play if, and only if, noncoercive state aid to religion marginalizes citizens who do not share the creed of the aided religion."

Consider this defense of religious liberty founded on the principle of "equal regard": "[The] government is obliged to treat the deep religious commitments of members of minority religious faiths with the same regard as it treats the deep commitments of other members of the society. [Government] policy must be justified by [secular] reasons [in] principle endorsable by [any] person committed to living in a pluralist society governed by the precepts of equal regard. [Government] must not act so as to divide the community along lines of religious affiliation." Eisgruber and Sager, Unthinking Religious Freedom, 74 Tex. L. Rev. 577,

600-601 (1996). The criticism that this "amounts to a 'secular establishment'" overlooks "the distinction between a secular constitution and a secular faith. One can reject the idea that the civil government should presuppose the truth of some religious faith without thereby rejecting religion. Many religious views [are] consistent with the idea that constitutional principles should be justified on secular grounds." Id. at 604. Does this approach offer equal regard to religious views that are inconsistent with that idea?

3. *The appropriate perspective.* Justice O'Connor would prohibit actions reasonably perceived as endorsement or disapproval. Perceived by whom? If by religious minorities, is she correct in concluding that reasonable Jews would not perceive the crèche as endorsement of Christianity? Consider the observation of Feldman, Principle, History, and Power: The Limits of the First Amendment Religion Clauses, 81 Iowa L. Rev. 833, 863 (1996): "In *Lynch*, the Court supported its conclusion by noting that [nobody] had complained about the crèche even though it had been publicly displayed for forty years. To the Court, this silence meant that the crèche had not generated dissension. [The] Court overlooked the possibility [that] Christian cultural imperialism had produced the silence of religious outgroup members. Silence often demonstrates domination, not consensus."

Suppose the government does not intend to endorse religion, but an observer might infer endorsement from the government's actions. How much must that person know about the government's real position?

In Capitol Square Review and Advisory Board v. Pinette, 515 U.S. 753 (1995), the Court divided over whether, and under what circumstances, an unattended display of a privately owned cross on public property could constitute an unconstitutional endorsement of religion. The Ku Klux Klan applied for a permit to display a cross in Capitol Square, the plaza surrounding Ohio's Statehouse. The square is a public forum that has been used for speeches and demonstrations. Before the Klan's application, unattended displays owned by private parties had been placed on the square three times: a "thermometer" showing the progress of a United Way fund drive, some booths during an arts festival, and a menorah.

Justice Scalia, writing for a plurality of four justices, concluded that the Constitution prohibited government endorsement of religion, but not "the government's neutral treatment of *private* religious expression." The plurality agreed that "giving sectarian religious speech preferential access to a forum close to the seat of government (or anywhere else for that matter) would violate the Establishment Clause." It "could conceive of a case in which a governmental entity manipulates its administration of a public forum [in] such a manner that only certain religious groups take advantage of it, creating an impression of endorsement *that is in fact accurate.*" But "private religious speech cannot be subject to veto by those who see favoritism where there is none."

Justices O'Connor, Souter, and Breyer concurred in the judgment. Justices O'Connor and Souter both stressed the importance of having "a sign disclaiming government sponsorship or endorsement" on the cross, which would "[help] remove doubt about State approval of [the] religious message." According to Justice O'Connor, "[w]hen the reasonable observer would view a government practice as endorsing religion, [it] is our *duty* to hold the practice invalid. [The Establishment] Clause is more than a negative prohibition against certain narrowly defined forms of government favoritism; it also imposes affirmative obligations that may require a State [to] take steps to avoid being perceived as supporting or endorsing a private religious message. [The Clause] forbids a State from [remaining] studiously oblivious to the effects of its actions." To determine whether "the State's own actions [*actually*] *convey* a message of endorsement," courts must conduct the inquiry "from the perspective of a hypothetical observer who is presumed to possess a certain level of information that all citizens might not share." The reasonable observer "must be deemed aware of the history and context of the community and forum in which the religious display occurs [and] the general history of the place in which the cross is displayed. [An] informed member of the community will know how the public space in question has been used in the past."

Justice Souter argued that "[given] the domination of the square by the government's own displays, one would not be a dimwit as a matter of law to think that an unattended religious display here was endorsed by the government." He found the permit denial unconstitutional only because the board had failed to grant the application "subject to the condition that the Klan attach a disclaimer sufficiently clear and large to preclude any reasonable inference that the cross was there to 'demonstrat[e] the government's allegiance to, or endorsement of, Christian faith.'"

Justice Stevens dissented. He argued, "If a reasonable person could perceive a government endorsement of religion from a private display, then the State may not allow its property to be used as a forum for that display. [So] it is with signs and symbols left to speak for themselves on public property. The very fact that a sign is installed on public property implies official recognition and reinforcement of its message. That implication is especially strong when the sign stands in front of the seat of the government itself. The reasonable observer of any symbol placed unattended in front of any capitol in the world will normally assume that the sovereign which is not only the owner of that parcel of real estate but also the lawgiver for the surrounding territory has sponsored and facilitated its message."

Justice Ginsburg also dissented, arguing that the display at issue in the case had an inadequate disclaimer. She reserved judgment on whether "a sturdier disclaimer" would have been sufficient.

4. *De facto establishments.* Consider M. Howe, The Garden and the Wilderness 11-12 (1965):

[Roger Williams's] principle of separation endorsed a host of favoring tributes to faith [so] substantial that they have produced in the aggregate what may fairly be described as a de facto establishment of religion [in which] the religious institution as a whole is maintained and activated by forces not kindled directly by government. [Some] elements of our religious establishment are, of course, reinforced by law. Whenever that situation prevails, as it does, for instance, when the law secures the sanctity of Sunday, the courts are apt to seek out a secular justification for the favoring enactment and, by this evasive tactic, meet the charge that an establishment de jure exists. [The] persistence of the de facto establishment [is] owing in large part to the fact that throughout our history the evangelical theory of separation has demanded that the de facto establishment be respected. The hold of that theory is so strong that it is almost inconceivable that any branch of government, whether local, state, or national, could today acknowledge that its objective is the destruction of this establishment. Yet the Supreme Court, by pretending that the American principle of separation is predominantly Jeffersonian and by purporting to outlaw even those aids in religion which do not affect religious liberties, seems to have endorsed a governmental policy aimed at the elimination of de facto establishments.

For an argument that most aspects of "ceremonial deism" violate the Court's establishment clause doctrine, see Epstein, Rethinking the Constitutionality of Ceremonial Deism, 96 Colum. L. Rev. 2083 (1996).

In McGowan v. Maryland, 366 U.S. 420 (1961), the Court rejected an establishment clause challenge to laws requiring that most large-scale commercial enterprises remain closed on Sundays. The Court's review of history demonstrated that Sunday closing laws were originally efforts to promote church attendance. "But, despite the strongly religious origin of these laws, nonreligious arguments for Sunday closing began to be heard more distinctly." The Court said that the Constitution "does not ban federal or state regulation of conduct whose reason or effect merely happens to coincide with the tenets of some or all religions." It concluded that, "as presently written and administered, most [Sunday closing laws] are of a secular rather than of a religious character." They "provide a uniform day of rest for all citizens. [To] say that the States cannot prescribe Sunday as a day of rest for these purposes solely because centuries ago such laws had their genesis in religion would give a constitutional interpretation of hostility to the public welfare rather than one of mere separation of church and State." As of 1961, was Howe's characterization of Sunday closing laws more accurate than the Court's? As of the present?

5. *History as a guide.* In Walz v. Tax Commission, section B1 supra, the Court noted that every state had a property tax exemption for churches, and that the federal income tax has since its inception exempted religious organizations. It found "significant" that Congress exempted churches from real estate taxes in 1802. "[An] unbroken practice of according the exemption to churches, openly and by affirmative state action, not covertly or by state inaction, is not something to be lightly cast aside." Justice Brennan, concurring, agreed that "the existence from the beginning of the Nation's life of a practice [is] a fact of considerable import in the interpretation of abstract constitutional language. [The] more long-standing and widely accepted a practice, the greater its impact upon constitutional interpretation." He found two "secular purposes" for the exemption: Churches, like other exempt groups, "contribute to the well-being of the community in a variety of nonreligious ways," and they "uniquely contribute to the pluralism of American society."

Marsh v. Chambers, 463 U.S. 783 (1983), relied on a "unique history" to uphold the constitutionality of opening legislative sessions with prayers led by a state-employed chaplain. The history ran from colonial times to the present and included the first Congress's hiring a chaplain in 1789, only three days before it reached final agreement on the language of the first amendment:

[Historical] evidence sheds light not only on what the draftsmen intended the Establishment Clause to mean, but also on how they thought that Clause applied to the practice authorized by the First Congress — their actions reveal their intent. [In] light of the unambiguous and unbroken history of more than 200 years, there can be no doubt that the practice of opening legislative sessions with prayer has become part of the fabric of our society.

Justice Brennan, joined by Justice Marshall, dissented. He argued that "legislative prayer [intrudes] on the right to conscience by forcing some legislators either to participate in a 'prayer opportunity' with which they are in basic disagreement, or to make their disagreement a matter of public comment by declining to participate. [It] has the potential for degrading religion by allowing a religious call to worship to be intermeshed with a secular call to order." He criticized the Court's reliance on the actions of the first Congress: "Legislators, influenced by the passions and exigencies of the moment, the pressure of constituents and colleagues, and the press of business, do not always pass sober constitutional judgment on every piece of legislation they enact." James Madison, who voted for the bill in the first Congress, later said that the practice was unconstitutional. This "may not have represented so much a change of *mind* as a change of *role*, from a member of Congress engaged in the hurly-burly of legislative activity to a detached observer engaged in unpressured reflection."

Did *Lynch* rely on history in an appropriate way? Did *Walz* and *Marsh*? Is Justice Brennan correct in distinguishing *Lynch* from *Walz* and *Marsh*? Is he consistent in seeking the "lessons of history" while insisting that the Court should rely only on the history of the particular practices at issue? In *Walz*, the Court stated that tax exemptions had not "given the remotest sign of leading to an established church," and in *Marsh*, it said that the fear that "prayer in this context risks the beginning of the establishment the founding Fathers feared [was] not well-founded." Is that the "lesson of history" with respect to de facto establishments?

6. *Religious pluralism and the political process.* What does the Court mean in *Lynch* by saying that the crèche must be considered "in the proper context"? Is Justice Blackmun correct in his claim that religion's victory is Pyrrhic? Consider Kurland, The Religion Clauses and the Burger Court, 34 Cath. U.L. Rev. 1, 13-14 (1984):

> The crèche opinion was sleazy. [It] would seem that the crèche was really only a device to attract commercial activity, a passive record of an historical event, to be analogized to religious paintings that occupy the walls of many a municipal museum. To suggest that the crèche [is] not a religious symbol clearly demeans the religion of those who erected it. [Such] treatment of the crèche symbol further detracts from the religious significance of the Christmas holiday. [I] would think that devout Christians might take umbrage at the government, in the form of the judiciary, for labeling a depiction of the birth of the Christ child as a nonreligious symbol, like a Christmas tree or a banner proclaiming "Seasons Greetings."

Does the emphasis on context suggest that there is no religious content to the use of the crèche? Or that the undeniable religious content is relatively modest? Should the Court insist that permissible de facto establishments have a low level of religious content? Consider the following argument: Contemporary society is pluralist in religion and in politics. Some religious groups oppose all governmental support of religion; others would support sectarian aid but oppose nondenominational aid; and others would support nondenominational aid. As some of these groups seek to secure legislation, they will have to adjust their programs to obtain majority support. The likely outcome of pluralist political bargaining in contemporary society on matters relating to religion is legislation having relatively modest religious content. The political process is therefore sufficient to guard against the evils at which the establishment clause is directed. Does this argument under-

degree to which a "least common denominator" religion may raise
cern about establishment?

crèche in *Lynch* demonstrate less governmental support for religion than nondenominational voluntary school prayer? Than student-led prayer
groups held in school buildings before or after school hours? Is it sufficient to say
that the Court regarded the school prayer cases as involving statutes that had *no*
secular purposes?

7. *Nondiscrimination.* In *Walz,* Justice Harlan's concurring opinion stated that
"[the] Court must survey meticulously the circumstances of governmental categories to eliminate [religious] gerrymanders. [The] critical question is whether
the circumference of legislation encircles a class [sufficiently] broad." What is the
basis for choosing between defining the class in *Lynch* as the crèche alone or defining it as the entire holiday display?

3. *Impermissible Purposes: The School Prayer Cases*

Stone v. Graham, 449 U.S. 39 (1980), held unconstitutional a Kentucky statute
requiring that a copy of the Ten Commandments be posted on the walls of each
public classroom. The Court found that this requirement had "no secular legislative purpose": The commandments were "undeniably a sacred text in the Jewish and Christian faiths," and "if the posted copies [are] to have any effect at all,
it will be to induce the school children to read, meditate upon, perhaps to vener-
ate and obey, the Commandments. However desirable this might be as a matter
of private devotion, it is not a permissible state objective under the Establishment
Clause." Justice Rehnquist's dissent relied on a statement in the statute that its
purpose was secular and argued that the requirement had a secular purpose because "the Ten Commandments have had a significant secular impact on the development of secular legal codes of the Western World."

Stone relied heavily on the school prayer cases. In Engel v. Vitale, 370 U.S. 421
(1962), the New York Board of Regents drafted and recommended that school
districts have classes recite aloud the following prayer: "Almighty God, we acknowledge our dependence upon Thee, and beg Thy blessings upon us, our parents, our teachers and our Country." Justice Black, writing for the Court, stated
that "in this country it is no part of the business of government to compose official
prayers for any group of the American people to recite as a part of a religious program carried on by government."

In Abington School District v. Schempp, 374 U.S. 203 (1963), the Court held
unconstitutional a state law requiring that ten verses from the Bible be read aloud
at the opening of each public school day. Justice Clark's opinion for the Court
stated that Bible-reading had a religious character and found the state's policy of
permitting nonattendance was not "consistent with the contention that the Bible
is here used either as an instrument for nonreligious moral inspiration or as a reference for the teaching of secular subjects." Justice Stewart dissented, finding "a
substantial free exercise claim" that "a compulsory state educational system so
structures a child's life that if religious exercises are held to be an impermissible activity in schools, religion is placed at an artificial and state-created disadvantage."

Wallace v. Jaffree, 472 U.S. 38 (1985), held unconstitutional an Alabama statute authorizing schools to set aside one minute at the start of the school day "for

meditation or voluntary prayer." The statute amended an earlier one authorizing a moment of silence "for meditation." The Court drew on Madison and *Everson* to conclude that "the individual freedom of conscience [embraces] the right to select any religious faith or none at all" because "religious beliefs worthy of respect are the product of free and voluntary choice by the faithful." The bill's sponsor stated that it was "an 'effort to return voluntary prayer' to the public schools." The Court said that the statute served "*no* secular purpose" not already served by the "meditation" statute. It noted that the statute could not be a permissible accommodation of religion because, prior to its enactment, "there was no governmental practice impeding students from silently praying for one minute at the beginning of the school day. [What] was missing [was] the State's endorsement and promotion of religion and a particular religious practice."

Justice O'Connor concurred in the judgment on the ground that the statute's "purpose and likely effect [were] to endorse and sponsor voluntary prayer in the public schools." She argued that simple "moment of silence" statutes were constitutional because "a moment of silence is not inherently religious [and because] a pupil who participates in a moment of silence need not compromise his or her belief." Thus, the "State does not necessarily endorse any activity that might occur during the period. Even if a statute specifies that a student may choose to pray silently during a quiet moment, the State has not thereby encouraged prayer over other specified alternatives. [The] crucial question is whether the state has conveyed or attempted to convey the message that children should use the moment of silence for prayer." She also wrote, "[A] legislature [might] enunciate a sham secular [purpose, but] our courts are capable of distinguishing a sham secular purpose from a real one."

Chief Justice Burger dissented, noting that the bill's sponsor testified that "one of his purposes [was] to clear up a widespread misunderstanding that a schoolchild is legally *prohibited* from [praying] once he steps inside a public school building."

Note: Problems with a "Purpose" Test

1. *Determining impermissible legislative purposes.* Is it accurate to say that each of the statutes described above had no purpose other than the promotion of religion? Alternatively, do the statutes have no *substantial* secular purposes? Consider whether the purposes discussed in Lynch v. Donnelly are substantial.

2. *Determining legislative purpose: nondiscrimination and gerrymandering.* Larson v. Valente, 456 U.S. 228 (1982), involved a Minnesota statute imposing reporting requirements on religious organizations that solicit more than 50 percent of their funds from nonmembers. The legislative history included one legislator's statement that "what you're trying to get at here is the people who are running around streets and soliciting people" and another's that he was "not sure why we're so hot to regulate the Moonies anyway." Five members of the Court, in an opinion by Justice Brennan, held that the statute violated "the clearest command of the Establishment Clause [— that] one religious denomination cannot be officially preferred over another." Such "denominational preferences" must be "justified by a compelling governmental interest, and [be] closely fitted to further that interest." The state's "interest in protecting its citizens from abusive practices"

might be compelling, but the 50 percent rule was not closely fitted to preventing abuse. The distinctions in the statute "engender a risk of politicizing religion" and "led the Minnesota legislature to discuss the characteristics of various sects with a view towards 'religious gerrymandering.'" Justice White, joined by Justice Rehnquist, dissented on the ground that the statute was not "a deliberate and explicit preference for some religious denominations over others" because it "names no churches or denominations. [Some] religions will qualify and some will not, but this depends on the source of their contributions, not on their brand of religion."

3. *A critique of the search for impermissible purposes.* In his dissenting opinion in Edwards v. Aguillard, 482 U.S. 578 (1987), Justice Scalia offered this critique of the "purpose" test:

[While] it is possible to discern the objective "purpose" of a statute (i.e., the public good at which its provisions appear to be directed), or even the formal motivation for a statute where that is explicitly set forth, [discerning] the subjective motivation of those enacting the statute is, to be honest, almost always an impossible task. The number of possible motivations, to begin with, is not binary, or indeed even finite. In the present case, for example, a particular legislator [may] have thought the bill would provide jobs for his district, or may have wanted to make amends with a faction of his party he had alienated on another vote, or he may have been a close friend of the bill's sponsor, or he may have hoped the Governor would appreciate his vote and make a fund-raising appearance for him, or he may have been pressured to vote for a bill he disliked by a wealthy contributor or by a flood of constituent mail, or he may have been seeking favorable publicity, or he may have been reluctant to hurt the feelings of a loyal staff member who worked on the bill, or he may have been settling an old score with a legislator who opposed the bill, or he may have been mad at his wife who opposed the bill, or he may have been intoxicated and utterly *un*motivated when the vote was called, or he may have accidentally voted "yes" instead of "no," or, of course, he may have had (and very likely did have) a combination of some of the above and many other considerations. To look for *the sole purpose* of even a single legislator is probably to look for something that does not exist.

Putting that problem aside, however, where ought we to look for the individual legislator's purpose? We cannot of course assume that every member present [agreed] with the motivation expressed in a particular legislator's pre-enactment floor or committee statement. [Can] we assume, then, that they all agree with the motivation expressed in the staff-prepared committee reports they might have [read]? Should we consider post-enactment floor statements? Or post-enactment testimony from legislators, obtained expressly for the lawsuit? Should we consider media reports on the realities of the legislative bargaining? [Legislative] histories can be contrived and sanitized, favorable media coverage orchestrated, and post-enactment recollections conveniently distorted. Perhaps most valuable of all would be more objective indications — for example, evidence regarding the individual legislators' religious affiliations. And if that, why not evidence regarding the fervor or tepidity of their beliefs?

Having achieved, through these simple means, an assessment of what individual legislators intended, we must still confront the question [how] *many* of them must have the invalidating intent. If a state senate approves a bill by vote of 26 to 25, and only one of the 26 intended solely to advance religion, is the law unconstitutional? What if 13 of the 26 had that intent? What if 3 of the 26 had the impermissible intent, but 3 of the 25 were simply attempting to "balance" the votes of their impermissibly motivated colleagues? Or is it possible that the intent of the bill's sponsor is alone enough to invalidate it — on a theory, perhaps, that even though everyone else's intent was pure, what they produced was the fruit of a forbidden tree?

Are inquiries into legislative purposes easier or more difficult in this context than in the equal protection setting?

4. *A critique of the "ban" on impermissible purposes.* Does the ban on impermissible purposes imply that a legislator may not rely on religious convictions as a reason for supporting or opposing legislation?

In Harris v. McRae, 448 U.S. 297 (1980), the Court rejected an establishment clause attack on a statute restricting public financing of abortions. The challengers argued that the statute "incorporates into law the doctrines of the Roman Catholic Church." The Court responded that "the fact that the funding restrictions [may] coincide with the religious tenets of the Roman Catholic Church does not, without more, contravene the Establishment Clause." It mentioned that many statutory prohibitions, such as those against larceny, similarly coincided with religious tenets. Are such prohibitions distinguishable on the ground that more religious traditions converge in condemning them than condemn abortion? What more would be needed to establish a first amendment violation? Suppose the challengers showed that religious motivations not broadly shared among many religions played a substantial part in the enactment. Should the burden shift to the state to show a substantial secular purpose?

Consider these observations:

> Legislation must be justified in terms of secular objectives, but when people reasonably think that shared premises of justice and criteria for determining truth cannot resolve critical questions of fact, fundamental questions of value, or the weighing of competing benefits and harms, they do appropriately rely on religious convictions that help them answer these questions. Not only is such reliance appropriate for ordinary citizens, legislators in similar instances may also rely on their own religious convictions and those of their constituents, and occasionally such reliance is warranted even for judges. Though reliance on religious convictions may be appropriate in these settings, argument in religious terms is often an inapt form of public dialogue.

K. Greenawalt, Religious Convictions and Political Choice 12 (1988).

On the use of "argument in religious terms," S. Carter, The Culture of Disbelief 23 (1993), observes, "One good way to end a conversation — or start an argument — is to tell a group of well-educated professionals that you hold a political position (preferably a controversial one, such as being against abortion or pornography) because it is required by your understanding of God's will." How might the conversation continue?

5. *Course selection: the creationism controversy.* Consider Epperson v. Arkansas, 393 U.S. 97 (1968). In 1928, Arkansas enacted a statute prohibiting "the teaching in its public schools and universities of the theory that man evolved from other species of life." The Court held the statute, "a product of the upsurge of 'fundamentalist' religious fervor of the twenties," unconstitutional. The law "selects from a body of knowledge a particular segment which it proscribes for the sole reason that it is deemed to conflict with a particular religious doctrine. [The] First Amendment does not permit the State to require that teaching and learning

must be tailored to the principles or prohibitions of any religious sect or dogma," despite the "State's undoubted right to prescribe the curriculum for its public schools." The Court said that "[n]o suggestion has been made that [the statute] may be justified by considerations of state policy other than the religious views of some of its citizens." Justice Black, concurring, would distinguish *Epperson* from the case of "a state law prohibiting all teaching of human development." Suppose such a prohibition was motivated (a) by a new upsurge of fundamentalism that viewed the subject as inculcating antireligious values or (b) by a judgment that, as Justice Black put it, "it would be best to remove this controversial subject from its schools."

In Edwards v. Aguillard, 482 U.S. 578 (1987), the Court, in an opinion by Justice Brennan, held unconstitutional a Louisiana statute requiring public schools to teach "creation science" whenever they taught the theory of evolution. Examining the structure of the statute and statements made in the course of its adoption, the Court concluded that the statute had no secular purpose despite the statement in the statute's text that it was designed to promote "academic freedom." The Court stated that the statute would not promote academic freedom in the sense of "enhancing the freedom of teachers to teach what they will" or even "teaching all the evidence" in part because it required that curriculum guides be developed for creation science but not for evolution. The Court also stressed that the case presented "[the] same historic and contemporaneous antagonisms between the teachings of certain religious denominations and the teaching of evolution" that it had found in *Epperson*. "The preeminent purpose of the Louisiana legislature was clearly to advance the religious viewpoint that a supernatural being created humankind." The Court's analysis concluded:

> We do not imply that a legislature could never require that scientific critiques of prevailing scientific theories be taught. [Teaching] a variant of scientific theories about the origins of humankind to school children might be validly done with the clear secular intent of enhancing the effectiveness of science instruction. But because the primary purpose of the [Louisiana] Act is to endorse a particular religious doctrine, the Act furthers religion in violation of the Establishment Clause.

Justice Powell's concurring opinion, in which Justice O'Connor joined, agreed that the statute had no secular purpose. Justice Scalia wrote a long dissent, in which Chief Justice Rehnquist joined. His examination of the legislative history led him to conclude that one purpose of the statute was to advance academic freedom, as it stated, in the sense of enhancing "*students'* freedom from *indoctrination*," which the legislature believed was occurring in biology courses that presented only the theory of evolution.

Could a legislature prohibit the teaching of evolution because it was a scientifically questionable theory whose acceptance by many scientists resulted from their antireligious biases? What sort of legislative hearings or findings would be required? Could a judge reassess the legislature's evaluation of the scientific status of the theory of evolution? Is this a case of a "religion-specific" subject, analogous to the "race-specific" classifications discussed in Chapter 5, section C3, supra? In the absence of an illicit motivation of the sort found in *Aguillard*, does the Constitution require states to teach only the truth in matters of science? Political theory?

4.   *Facially Neutral Statutes That Incidentally Aid Religion: Permissible and Impermissible Effects*

The school prayer cases indicate that, de facto establishments aside, legislation with the sole (or predominant?) purpose of aiding religion is unconstitutional. Sometimes the Court will treat legislation that does not use religion as a basis for classification as a religious gerrymander, inferring an impermissible purpose from the statute's structure and history. More complex problems arise when the Court is unwilling to infer an impermissible purpose for a statute that does not use religion as a basis for classification, yet the legislation substantially aids religious institutions.

The Court has examined this problem most extensively in cases questioning legislative efforts to support nonpublic education. Below the college level, nearly all such education occurs in schools affiliated with churches, so that usually 75 percent or more of the aid goes to church-related schools. The Court's first substantial decision was *Everson*. The Court said that the first amendment "requires the state to be a neutral in its relations with groups of religious believers and non-believers; it does not require the state to be their adversary." It should not be interpreted "to prohibit [the state] from extending its general state law benefits to all its citizens without regard to their religious belief." The bus transportation statute "does no more than provide a general program to help parents get their children, regardless of their religion, safely and expeditiously to and from accredited schools."

Justice Rutledge's dissent was joined by Justices Frankfurter, Jackson, and Burton. He contended that the first amendment "broadly forbids state support, financial or other, of religion in any guise, form or degree. It outlaws all use of public funds for religious purposes." In this case, "parents pay money to send their children to parochial schools and funds raised by taxation are used to reimburse them. This not only helps the children to get to school and the parents to send them. It aids them in a substantial way to get [religious] training and teaching" in part because "transportation [is] as essential to education as any other element." He argued that it was impossible to apportion the expenditures between the parochial schools' religious instruction and their instruction in secular subjects.

The transportation subsidy makes it less expensive for parents to provide their children with a comprehensive religious education. In this sense, the subsidy "supports" or "aids" religion. But if the legislation is truly neutral, should this kind of support violate the Constitution? Is it distinguishable from the provision of general police and fire protection to churches and parochial schools, which could purchase private security services to provide those protections? In Rosenberger v. Rectors and Visitors of the University of Virginia, 515 U.S. 819 (1995), Justice Souter, for four dissenters, argued that these forms of aid should be limited to "essential public benefits." Justice Thomas, in a separate concurring opinion, responded that to do so would be inconsistent with "[our] Nation's tradition of allowing religious adherents to participate in evenhanded government programs."

Since 1968, the Court has decided over a dozen cases involving public aid to nonpublic education. For earlier decisions, see McCollum v. Board of Education, 333 U.S. 203 (1948) (invalidating a program in which public school students were released from their classes to participate in religious education programs conducted in public school classrooms; nonparticipants were required to remain in school); Zorach v. Clauson, 343 U.S. 306 (1952) (upholding a program in which students were dismissed from school to attend religious education classes conducted in nonschool buildings; nonparticipants were required to remain in school).

The Court held the following forms of aid unconstitutional: (a) statutes reimbursing nonpublic schools for salaries, textbooks, and instructional materials used in secular courses and paying teachers of secular subjects in nonpublic schools a 15 percent salary supplement, Lemon v. Kurtzman, 403 U.S. 602 (1971); (b) a tuition tax scheme providing tax credits to low-income parents of children in nonpublic schools and a tax deduction to higher-income parents with children in such schools, Committee for Public Education v. Nyquist, 413 U.S. 756 (1973); (c) a statute reimbursing parents for $75 or $150 in tuition paid to elementary or secondary nonpublic schools, Sloan v. Lemon, 413 U.S. 825 (1973); (d) a statute reimbursing nonpublic schools for their expenses in administering state-required and teacher-prepared tests, Levitt v. Committee for Public Education, 413 U.S. 472 (1973).

The Court upheld the following forms of aid: (a) a statute lending textbooks in secular subjects to students in nonpublic schools, Board of Education v. Allen, 392 U.S. 236 (1968); (b) statutes authorizing the use of public school personnel to administer standardized tests and to provide diagnostic speech, hearing, and psychological services at nonpublic schools and to provide therapeutic, remedial, and guidance services at neutral sites, such as public schools and mobile units, for students enrolled in nonpublic schools, Wolman v. Walter, 433 U.S. 229 (1977); (c) a statute reimbursing nonpublic schools for the cost of administering state-mandated and state-composed tests and for the cost of maintaining state-required records, Committee for Public Education v. Regan, 444 U.S. 646 (1980).

Laycock, A Survey of Religious Liberty in the United States, 47 Ohio St. L.J. 409, 443-446 (1986), describes six theories that "have been endorsed by one or more justices." They are (a) the "no-aid theory: that any state money paid to a religious school or its students expands the school's budget and thereby aids religion"; (b) the "purchase-of-services theory: that state money paid to a religious school is simply a purchase of educational services"; (c) the "equal-treatment theory[, which] holds that government is obligated to pay for the secular aspects of education in religious schools [or] that government is free to make such payments if it wishes"; (d) the "child-benefit theory: that the state can provide educational benefits directly to children or their parents, even if the benefits are used at or in connection with a religious school [but] cannot provide the same aid directly to the school"; (e) the "tracing theory, [which] tries to trace each dollar of government money to see what the school spent it on"; and (f) the "little-bit theory[: that] a little bit of aid to religious schools is permissible, but it must be structured in a way that keeps it from becoming too much." Which of these theories explains which of the cases? Which, if any, makes sense of the Constitution?

Mueller v. Allen

463 U.S. 388 (1983)

[Minnesota's income tax statute permitted taxpayers to deduct from their gross income actual expenses incurred for "tuition, textbooks and transportation" for the education of their children in elementary and secondary schools. The deduction, available for expenses incurred in sending children to public as well as non-public schools, was limited to $500 per child in elementary school and $700 per child in secondary school. About 820,000 children attended public schools in Minnesota, while about 91,000 attended nonpublic schools, 95 percent of them in religiously affiliated schools. The court of appeals held that the statute did not violate the establishment clause.]

JUSTICE REHNQUIST delivered the opinion of the Court. . . .

One fixed principle in this field is our consistent rejection of the argument that "any program which in some manner aids an institution with a religious affiliation" violates the Establishment Clause. Hunt v. McNair, 413 U.S. 734, 742 (1973). For example, [a] state may reimburse parents for expenses incurred in transporting their children to school [*Everson*], and [it] may loan secular textbooks to all schoolchildren within the state [Board of Education v. Allen, supra]. . . .

A state's decision to defray the cost of educational expenses incurred by parents — regardless of the type of schools their children attend — evidences a purpose that is both secular and understandable. An educated populace is essential to the political and economic health of any community, and a state's efforts to assist parents in meeting the rising cost of educational expenses plainly serves this secular purpose of ensuring that the state's citizenry is well educated. Similarly, Minnesota, like other states, could conclude that there is a strong public interest in assuring the continued financial health of private schools, both sectarian and nonsectarian. By educating a substantial number of students such schools relieve public schools of a correspondingly great burden — to the benefit of all taxpayers. In addition, private schools may serve as a benchmark for public schools, in a manner analogous to the "TVA yardstick" for private power companies. . . .

We turn therefore to the more difficult but related question whether the Minnesota statute has "the primary effect of advancing the sectarian aims of the nonpublic schools." [*Lemon.*] In concluding that it does not, we find several features of the Minnesota tax deduction particularly significant. First, an essential feature of Minnesota's arrangement is the fact that §290.09, subd. 22, is only one among many deductions [available] under the Minnesota tax laws. [The] Minnesota legislature's judgment that a deduction for educational expenses fairly equalizes the tax burden of its citizens and encourages desirable expenditures for educational purposes is entitled to substantial deference.[6]

Other characteristics of §290.09, subd. 22, argue equally strongly for the provision's constitutionality. Most importantly, the deduction is available for educational expenses incurred by *all* parents, including those whose children attend public schools and those whose children attend nonsectarian private schools or

6. Our decision in [*Nyquist*] is not to the contrary on this point. [The] outright grants to low-income parents did not take the form of ordinary tax benefits. As to the benefits provided to middle-income parents, the Court said:

> The amount of the deduction [is] apparently the product of a legislative attempt to assure that each family would receive a carefully estimated net benefit, [comparable] to, and compatible with, the tuition grant for lower income families.

[While] the economic consequences of the program in *Nyquist* and that in this case may be difficult to distinguish, we have recognized on other occasions that "the form of the [State's assistance to parochial schools must be examined] for the light that it casts on the substance." [*Lemon.*] The fact that the Minnesota plan embodies a "genuine tax deduction" is thus of some relevance. . . .

sectarian private [schools:] "the provision of benefits to so broad a spectrum of groups is an important index of secular effect."

In this respect, as well as others, this case is vitally different from the scheme struck down in *Nyquist*. There, public assistance amounting to tuition grants was provided only to parents of children in *nonpublic* schools. [Unlike] the assistance at issue in *Nyquist*, §290.09, subd. 22, permits *all* parents — whether their children attend public school or private — to deduct their childrens' educational expenses. [A] program, like §290.09, subd. 22, that neutrally provides state assistance to a broad spectrum of citizens is not readily subject to challenge under the Establishment Clause.

We also agree [that,] by channeling whatever assistance it may provide to parochial schools through individual parents, Minnesota has reduced the Establishment Clause objections to which its action is subject. It is true, of course, that financial assistance provided to parents ultimately has an economic effect comparable to that of aid given directly to the schools attended by their children. It is also true, however, that under Minnesota's arrangement public funds become available only as a result of numerous, private choices of individual parents of school-age children. [It] is noteworthy that all but one of our recent cases invalidating state aid to parochial schools have involved the direct transmission of assistance from the state to the schools themselves. The exception [was] *Nyquist*, which [is] distinguishable from this case on other grounds. Where, as here, aid to parochial schools is available only as a result of decisions of individual parents no "imprimatur of State approval" [*Widmar*, section A supra] can be deemed to have been conferred on any particular religion, or on religion generally.

We find it useful [to] compare the attenuated financial benefits flowing to parochial schools from the section to the evils against which the Establishment Clause was designed to protect. These dangers are well-described by our statement that "[w]hat is at stake as a matter of policy [in Establishment Clause cases] is preventing that kind and degree of government involvement in religious life that, as history teaches us, is apt to lead to strife and frequently strain a political system to the breaking point." [*Nyquist*.] It is important, however, to "keep these issues in perspective":

> At this point in the 20th century we are quite far removed from the dangers that prompted the Framers to include the Establishment Clause in the Bill of Rights. The risk of significant religious or denominational control over our democratic processes — or even a deep political division along religious lines — is remote, and when viewed against the positive contributions of sectarian schools, any such risk seems entirely tolerable in light of the continuing oversight of this Court.

[*Wolman*] (Powell, J., concurring in part, concurring in the judgment in part, and dissenting in part). The Establishment Clause of course extends beyond prohibition of a state church or payment of state funds to one or more churches. We do not think, however, that its prohibition extends to the type of tax deduction established by Minnesota. The historic purposes of the clause simply do not encompass the sort of attenuated financial benefit, ultimately controlled by the private choices of individual parents, that eventually flows to parochial schools from the neutrally available tax benefit at issue in this case.

Petitioners argue that, notwithstanding the facial neutrality of §290.09, subd. 22, in application the statute primarily benefits religious institutions. Petitioners rely [on] a statistical analysis of the type of persons claiming the tax deduction. They contend that most parents of public school children incur no tuition expenses and that other expenses deductible under §290.09, subd. 22, are negligible in value; moreover, they claim that 96% of the children in private schools in 1978-1979 attended religiously-affiliated institutions. Because of all this, they reason, the bulk of deductions taken under §290.09, subd. 22, will be claimed by parents of children in sectarian schools. . . .

[We] would be loath to adopt a rule grounding the constitutionality of a facially neutral law on annual reports reciting the extent to which various classes of private citizens claimed benefits under the law. [The] fact that private persons fail in a particular year to claim the tax relief to which they are entitled — under a facially neutral statute — should be of little importance in determining the constitutionality of the statute permitting such relief.

Finally, [if] parents of children in private schools choose to take especial advantage of the relief provided by §290.09, subd. 22, it is no doubt due to the fact that they bear a particularly great financial burden in educating their children. More fundamentally, whatever unequal effect may be attributed to the statutory classification can fairly be regarded as a rough return for the benefits [provided] to the state and all taxpayers by parents sending their children to parochial schools. In the light of all this, we believe it wiser to decline to engage in the type of empirical inquiry into those persons benefited by state law which petitioners urge. . . .

Turning to the third part of the *Lemon* inquiry, we have no difficulty in concluding that the Minnesota statute does not "excessively entangle" the state in religion. The only plausible source of the "comprehensive, discriminating, and continuing state surveillance" necessary to run afoul of this standard would lie in the fact that state officials must determine whether particular textbooks qualify for a deduction. In making this decision, state officials must disallow deductions taken [for] "instructional books and materials used in the teaching of religious tenets, doctrines or worship, the purpose of which is to inculcate such tenets, doctrines or worship." Making decisions such as this does not differ substantially from making the types of decisions approved in earlier opinions of this Court. In [Board of Education v. Allen], for example, the Court upheld the loan of secular textbooks to parents or children attending nonpublic schools; though state officials were required to determine whether particular books were or were not secular, the system was held not to violate the Establishment Clause. The same result follows in this case. . . .

[Affirmed.]

JUSTICE MARSHALL, with whom JUSTICE BRENNAN, JUSTICE BLACKMUN, and JUSTICE STEVENS join, dissenting.

I . . .

A

[Direct] government subsidization of parochial school tuition is impermissible because "the effect of the aid is unmistakably to provide desired financial support for nonpublic, sectarian institutions." "[A]id to the educational function of [parochial] schools . . . necessarily results in aid to the sectarian enterprise as a whole" because "[t]he very purpose of those schools is to provide an integrated secular and religious education." [Meek v. Pittenger, 421 U.S. 349 (1973).] . . .

Indirect assistance in the form of financial aid to parents for tuition payments is similarly impermissible. [By] ensuring that parents will be reimbursed for tuition payments they make, the Minnesota statute requires that taxpayers in general pay for the cost of parochial education and extends a financial "incentive to parents to send their children to sectarian schools." [Nyquist.] . . .

B . . .

1

The majority first attempts to distinguish *Nyquist* on the ground that Minnesota makes all parents eligible. . . .

That the Minnesota statute makes some small benefit available to all parents cannot alter the fact that the most substantial benefit provided by the statute is available only to those parents who send their children to schools that charge tuition. [The] statute is little more than a subsidy of tuition masquerading as a subsidy of general educational expenses. The other deductible expenses are *de minimis* in comparison to tuition expenses.

[The] bulk of the tax benefits afforded by the Minnesota scheme are enjoyed by parents of parochial school children not because parents of public school children fail to claim deductions to which they are entitled, but because the latter are simply *unable* to claim the largest tax deduction that Minnesota authorizes. [Parents] who send their children to free public schools are simply ineligible to obtain the full benefit of the deduction except in the unlikely event that they buy $700 worth of pencils, notebooks, and bus rides for their school-age children. Yet parents who pay at least $700 in tuition to nonpublic, sectarian schools can claim the full deduction even if they incur no other educational expenses. . . .

2

The majority also asserts that the Minnesota statute is distinguishable from the statute struck down in *Nyquist* in another respect: the tax benefit available under Minnesota law is a "genuine tax deduction," whereas the New York law provided a benefit which, while nominally a deduction, also had features of a "tax credit." . . .

This is a distinction without a difference. [The] deduction afforded by Minnesota law was "designed to yield a [tax benefit] in exchange for performing a specific act which the State desires to encourage." [Nyquist.] . . .

Note: *From* Aguilar *to* Mitchell

1. *Aguilar.* Aguilar v. Felton, 473 U.S. 402 (1985), invalidated New York's system for delivering federal financial assistance to educationally deprived children in low-income areas under Title I of the Elementary and Secondary School Act of 1965. The state provided Title I services, including remedial reading and arithmetic classes and guidance services, to parochial school students in their schools. The services were provided by public school employees who volunteered to

teach in the parochial schools. The teachers were "directed to avoid involvement with religious activities [and] to bar religious materials." They were supervised by a system of unannounced visits. The administrators of the parochial schools were "required to clear the classrooms used by the public school personnel of all religious symbols."

The Court, in an opinion by Justice Brennan, held the program unconstitutional. "[Publicly] funded instructors teach classes composed exclusively of private school students in [religiously affiliated] private schools." The supervisory system used to prevent the program from being used to inculcate religious beliefs "inevitably results in the excessive entanglement of church and state." Here, "the aid is provided in a pervasively sectarian environment[, and] because assistance is provided in the form of teachers, ongoing inspection is required to ensure the absence of a religious message." "Agents of the state must visit and inspect the religious school regularly, alert for the subtle or overt presence of religious matter in Title I classes. In addition, the religious school must obey these same agents when they make determinations as to what is and what is not a 'religious symbol' and thus off limits in a Title I classroom. [As] government agents must make these judgments, the dangers of political divisiveness along religious lines increase."

Justice Powell's concurring opinion found

> [the] risk of entanglement [compounded] by the additional risk of political divisiveness. [There] remains a considerable risk of continuing political strife over the propriety of direct aid to religious schools and the proper allocation of limited governmental resources. [In] states such as New York that have large and varied sectarian populations, one can be assured that politics will enter into any state decision to aid parochial schools. [Any] proposal to extend direct governmental aid to parochial schools alone is likely to spark political disagreement from taxpayers who support the public schools, as well as from non-recipient sectarian groups, who may fear that needed funds are being diverted from them.

He also believed that Title I had the prohibited effect of "a state subsidy of the parochial [schools,] by relieving those schools of the duty to provide the remedial and supplemental education their children require."

Chief Justice Burger, Justice White, and Justice Rehnquist filed brief dissents, the latter noting that the Court "[took] advantage of the 'Catch-22' paradox of its own creation, whereby aid must be supervised to ensure no entanglement but the supervision itself is held to cause an entanglement." Justice O'Connor's dissent emphasized that the record contained no evidence that, during the nineteen-year experience with Title I in New York, any Title I teacher had attempted to indoctrinate children in religion. She found the explanation in the fact that the teachers "are professional educators who can and do follow instructions not to inculcate religion in their classes." Thus, "the degree of supervision required to manage [the] risk" of indoctrination "has been exaggerated."

2. *Witters.* In Witters v. Washington Department of Services for the Blind, 474 U.S. 481 (1986), the Court held that the "effects" branch of the *Lemon* test was not violated by a statute authorizing payment to a visually handicapped person for vocational rehabilitation services where the recipient planned to use the funds to pay his tuition at a Christian college to prepare himself for a career as a minister. The Court found "central" to its analysis the fact that the payments were made "directly to the student, who transmits it to the educational institution

of his or her choice." Thus, "any aid provided under [the] program that ultimately flows to religious institutions does so only as a result of the genuinely independent and private choices of aid recipients." The program

> creates no financial incentive for students to undertake sectarian education [and] does not tend to provide greater or broader benefits for recipients who apply their aid to religious education. [Further], and importantly, nothing [indicates] that [any] significant portion of the aid expended under the [program] as a whole will end up flowing to religious education.

Justice Powell, joined by Chief Justice Burger and Justice Rehnquist, wrote a concurring opinion arguing that *Mueller* meant that "state programs that are wholly neutral in offering educational assistance to a class defined without reference to religion do not violate the second part of the [*Lemon*] test."

3. *Zobrest.* Zobrest v. Catalina Foothills School District, 509 U.S. 1 (1993), held that the establishment clause would not be violated if a school district paid the salary of a sign-language interpreter for a deaf student attending a Roman Catholic high school. Chief Justice Rehnquist's opinion for the Court, relying on *Mueller* and *Witters*, held that "government programs that neutrally provide benefits to a broad class of citizens defined without reference to religion are not readily subject to an Establishment Clause challenge just because sectarian institutions may also receive an attenuated financial benefit." The sign-language interpreter was provided as "part of a general government program that distributes benefits neutrally to any child qualifying as 'handicapped' [without] regard to the 'sectarian-nonsectarian, or public-nonpublic nature' of the school the child attends." Because the statute "creates no financial incentive for parents to choose a sectarian school, an interpreter's presence there cannot be attributed to state decision-making. [Indeed,] this is an even easier case than *Mueller* and *Witters* in the sense that [no] funds traceable to the government ever find their way into sectarian schools' coffers. The only indirect economic benefit a sectarian school might receive [is] the handicapped child's tuition — and that is, of course, assuming that the school makes a profit on each student; that, without an [interpreter,] the child would have gone to school elsewhere; and that the school, then, would have been unable to fill that child's spot."

Justice Blackmun, joined by Justice Souter, dissented. According to Justice Blackmun, the Court's decision "authorized a public employee to participate directly in religious indoctrination." Unlike *Witters* and *Mueller*, "where governmental involvement ended with the disbursement of funds or lessening of tax[, this] case [involves] ongoing, daily, and intimate governmental participation in the teaching and propagation of religious doctrine."

4. *Rosenberger.* In Rosenberger v. Rectors and Visitors of the University of Virginia, 515 U.S. 819 (1995), the Court held that the university would not violate the establishment clause by providing payments from a mandatory student activity fee account to printers hired by a student group to print their religious magazine. "Any benefit to religion is incidental to the government's provision of secular services for secular purposes on a religion-neutral basis. Printing is a routine, secular, and recurring attribute of student life." Responding to concerns expressed by four dissenters, Justice Kennedy's opinion said that the decision "cannot be read as addressing an expenditure from a general tax fund. [This] is a far cry from a general public assessment designed and effected to provide financial

support for a church." Further, the case did not involve "direct money payments to an institution or group that is engaged in religious activity" because the payments were made to the printer.

Justice Souter's dissent, joined by Justices Stevens, Ginsburg, and Breyer, argued that it was not enough that the student activities fees were "available on an evenhanded basis to secular and sectarian applicants alike." Rather, "whenever affirmative government aid ultimately benefits religion, the Establishment Clause requires some justification beyond evenhandedness on the government's part; [direct] public funding of core sectarian activities, even if accomplished pursuant to an evenhanded program, would be entirely inconsistent with the Establishment Clause and would strike at the very heart of the Clause's protection. [In] the doubtful cases (those not involving direct public funding), [evenhandedness] serves to weed out those laws that impermissibly advance religion by channelling aid to it exclusively. Evenhandedness is therefore a prerequisite to further enquiry into the constitutionality of a doubtful law, but evenhandedness [does] not guarantee success under Establishment Clause scrutiny." He distinguished *Mueller* on the ground that it involved only indirect public funding.

5. *Agostini.* Agostini v. Felton, 521 U.S. 203 (1997), overruled *Aguilar.* Justice O'Connor, writing for the Court, said that the Court would not presume "that the placement of public employees on parochial school grounds inevitably results in the impermissible effect of state-sponsored indoctrination or constitutes a symbolic union between government and religion." Nor would it assume "that the presence of a public employee on private school property creates an impermissible 'symbolic link' between government and religion." In addition, the Court said, not "all government aid that directly aids the educational function of religious schools is invalid [*Witters*]."

> First, there is no reason to presume that, simply because she enters a parochial school classroom, a full-time public employee such as a Title I teacher will depart from her assigned duties and instructions and embark on religious indoctrination, any more than there was a reason in *Zobrest* to think an interpreter would inculcate religion by altering her translation of classroom lectures. Certainly, no evidence has ever shown that any New York City Title I instructor teaching on parochial school premises attempted to inculcate religion in students. Thus, both our precedent and our experience require us to reject respondents' remarkable argument that we must presume Title I instructors to be "uncontrollable and sometimes very unprofessional." . . .
>
> *Zobrest* also repudiates [the] assumption that the presence of Title I teachers in parochial school classrooms will, without more, create the impression of a "symbolic union" between church and state. [Title] I services may be provided to sectarian school students in off-campus locations, even though that notion necessarily presupposes that the danger of "symbolic union" evaporates once the services are provided off-campus. Taking this view, the only difference between a constitutional program and an unconstitutional one is the location of the classroom. [We] do not see any perceptible (let alone dispositive) difference in the degree of symbolic union between a student receiving remedial instruction in a classroom on his sectarian school's campus and one receiving instruction in a van parked just at the school's curbside. . . .

The Court then addressed "the criteria by which an aid program identifies its beneficiaries":

[The] criteria might themselves have the effect of advancing religion by creating a financial incentive to undertake religious indoctrination. This incentive is not present, however, where the aid is allocated on the basis of neutral, secular criteria that neither favor nor disfavor religion, and is made available to both religious and secular beneficiaries on a nondiscriminatory basis. Under such circumstances, the aid is less likely to have the effect of advancing religion. See Widmar v. Vincent, 454 U. S. 263, 274 (1981) ("The provision of benefits to so broad a spectrum of groups is an important index of secular effect"). [Title] I services are allocated on the basis of criteria that neither favor nor disfavor religion. The services are available to all children who meet the Act's eligibility requirements, no matter what their religious beliefs or where they go to school. The Board's program does not, therefore, give aid recipients any incentive to modify their religious beliefs or practices in order to obtain those services.

Finally, the Court addressed the argument "that New York City's Title I program resulted in an excessive entanglement between church and state. [The] factors we use to assess whether an entanglement is 'excessive' are similar to the factors we use to examine 'effect.'" The Court concluded that it should treat entanglement as "an aspect of the inquiry into a statute's effect." The opinion continued: "Not all entanglements [have] the effect of advancing or inhibiting religion. Interaction between church and state is inevitable, and we have always tolerated some level of involvement between the two. Entanglement must be 'excessive' before it runs afoul of the Establishment Clause." Neither "administrative cooperation" nor the danger of political divisiveness created excessive entanglement, particularly in light of the fact that they would be present even if the Title I services were offered off-campus. And, given the Court's refusal to assume that public school teachers working in parochial schools "would be tempted to inculcate religion," there was no need for "pervasive monitoring." The unannounced monthly visits were not excessive entanglement.

Justice Souter, joined by Justices Stevens and Ginsburg and in part by Justice Breyer, dissented. In the portion of the dissent that Justice Breyer did not join, Justice Souter said that the Court decision "authorize[d] direct state aid to religious institutions on an unparalleled scale, in violation of the Establishment Clause's central prohibition against religious subsidies by the government. [This] rule expresses the hard lesson learned over and over again in the American past and in the experiences of the countries from which we have come, that religions supported by governments are compromised just as surely as the religious freedom of dissenters is burdened when the government supports religion." According to Justice Souter, the New York plan allowed the city's school system to

[assume] a teaching responsibility indistinguishable from the responsibility of the [private] schools themselves. The obligation of primary and secondary schools to teach reading necessarily extends to teaching those who are having a hard time at it, and the same is true of math. Calling some classes remedial does not distinguish their subjects from the schools' basic subjects, however inadequately the schools may have been addressing them. [There] is simply no line that can be drawn between the instruction paid for at taxpayers' expense and the instruction in any subject that is not identified as formally religious. While it would be an obvious sham, say, to channel cash to religious schools to be credited only against the expense of "secular" instruction, the line between "supplemental" and general education is likewise impossible to draw. If a State may constitutionally enter the schools to

teach in the manner in question, it must in constitutional principle be free to assume, or assume payment for, the entire cost of instruction provided in any ostensibly secular subject in any religious school.

Justice Souter suggested that "off-premises teaching is arguably less likely to open the door to relieving religious schools of their responsibilities for secular subjects simply because these schools are less likely [to] dispense with those subjects from their curriculums or to make patently significant cut-backs in basic teaching within the [schools]; if the aid is delivered outside of the schools, it is less likely to supplant some of what would otherwise go on inside [them]. On top of that, the difference in the degree of reasonably perceptible endorsement is substantial."

Justice Breyer joined the section of Justice Souter's dissent that stated that "even-handedness is a necessary but not a sufficient condition for an aid program to satisfy constitutional scrutiny. [If] a scheme of government aid results in support for religion in some substantial degree, or in endorsement of its value, the formal neutrality of the scheme does not render the Establishment Clause helpless."

Justice Ginsburg, joined by Justices Stevens, Souter, and Breyer, also dissented on procedural grounds.

6. *Mitchell.* Justice Thomas, writing for a plurality in Mitchell v. Helms, 530 U.S. 793 (2000), proposed that statutes providing aid to "religious, irreligious, and areligious" institutions should generally be constitutional because "no one would conclude that any indoctrination that any particular recipient conducts has been done at the behest of the government. [If] the government is offering assistance to recipients who provide [a] broad range of indoctrination, the government itself is not thought responsible for any particular indoctrination." *Mitchell* upheld a statute that provided funds for state education agencies to lend computers, including software, and library books, to nonpublic schools. The amount available to each school was determined by each school's enrollment. Justice Thomas's opinion rejected as "arbitrary" the distinction between direct and indirect aid to the religious missions of religious schools. It also found irrelevant the possibility that some forms of aid might be diverted to religious uses: "So long as the governmental aid is not itself 'unsuitable for use in the public schools because of religious content,' [Board of Education v. Allen], and eligibility for aid is determined in a constitutionally permissible manner, any use of that aid to indoctrinate cannot be attributed to the government, and is thus not of constitutional concern. [A] concern for divertibility, as opposed to improper content, is misplaced [because] it is boundless [and] thus has only the most attenuated [link] to any realistic concern for preventing an 'establishment of religion.'"

Justice O'Connor, joined by Justice Breyer, concurred in the judgment. She criticized the plurality's "near-absolute position with respect to neutrality." She also believed "significant" the "distinction between a per-capita school-aid program and a true private-choice program. [In] terms of public perception, a government program of direct aid to religious schools based on the number of students attending each school differs meaningfully from the government distributing aid directly to individual students who, in turn, decide to use the aid at the same religious schools. In the former example, if the religious school uses the aid to inculcate religion in its students, it is reasonable to say that the government has communicated a message of endorsement." She found the program in *Mitchell* constitutional because it provided sufficient guarantees that the aid would not be diverted to religious uses and because the evidence of actual diversion was de minimis. Justices Souter, Stevens, and Ginsburg dissented.

Note: *Purpose and Effect in Aid to Nonpublic Education — Benevolent Neutrality?*

1. *Vouchers.* What lines of analysis in the Court's opinions support the constitutionality of "voucher" programs that provide public funds that students (or their parents) can use to pay tuition at nonpublic schools, including religiously affiliated schools? What lines of analysis in those opinions support the argument that such programs are unconstitutional?

2. *The meaning of neutrality.* Will a requirement of neutrality increase the cost of providing aid to nonpublic schools and thereby alter the political dimensions of the issue? Consider this justification for upholding direct appropriations to private schools: Public schools are subsidized through ordinary appropriations; neutrality is achieved by the separate appropriations to private schools. Finding the latter to violate neutrality artificially divides a unitary system of state-supported education that, taken as a whole, is neutral. Consider the proposal in Choper, The Establishment Clause and Aid to Parochial Schools, 56 Cal. L. Rev. 260, 266 (1968), that aid should be allowed "so long as such aid does not exceed the value of the secular educational service rendered by the school." How likely is it that a legislature, constrained by pluralist politics and tax limitations, would enact a program that violated this test? Does it simply restate the requirement of neutrality?

Berg, Religion Clause Anti-Theories, 72 Notre Dame L. Rev. 693, 703-704 (1997), argues that "[government] should, as much as possible, minimize the effect it has on the voluntary, independent religious decisions of the people as individuals and in voluntary groups. The baseline against which effects on religion should be compared is a situation in which religious beliefs and practices succeed or fail solely on their merits — as those merits are presented and judged by individuals and groups, not by government." Consider the assumptions implicit in the term "the merits" in this formulation.

For a discussion of the problem of identifying an appropriate baseline, see Gedicks, The Rhetoric of Church and State: A Critical Analysis of Religion Clause Jurisprudence 57-58, 60 (1995): "How does one identify the baseline measure of religious neutrality? [In] the modern welfare state, [government] aid to both individuals and organizations is widespread and pervasive. Since in the United States most persons and entities are entitled to some kind of government aid, religious neutrality would generally seem to require that this aid not be denied to otherwise qualified recipients simply because they are religious. Indeed, to deny aid to such persons and entities constitutes a tax on religious exercise which skews private choice *away* from religion. [If] one were to imagine a world of minimalist government in which secular public schools did not exist, then government action mandating religious instruction [would] violate neutrality." Berg discusses some implications of Gedicks's position: "[If] a system of subsidized secular public schools does, in fact, discourage religiously informed education, why can't government include religious teaching in the public school curriculum? [Any] statement the government makes is bound to favor one faith over another." Berg, supra, at 743.

3. *Indirect v. direct aid.* Do the cases support a distinction between direct aid — payments or donations of goods and services made to religiously affiliated schools — and indirect aid — payments made to parents who then use the funds to pay such schools? Would it be constitutional for a state to pay a portion of the salary of mathematics teachers in nonpublic schools as part of a "general program" of paying the salaries of all mathematics teachers? In *Rosenberger,* Justice Souter argued that the Court's approach "would permit a State to pay all the bills of any religious institution." Justice Kennedy's opinion for the Court responded that the student publication involved was "not a religious institution, at least in the usual sense of that term." After *Rosenberger,* must a state include religiously affiliated schools in any voucher program it adopts? What is the basis for the proposition that direct aid to religious institutions is impermissible?

4. *Monetary v. nonmonetary aid.* Justice Thomas's opinion in *Mitchell* noted that prior cases had found "'special Establishment Clause dangers' when *money* is given to religious schools or entities directly rather than [indirectly]. But [we] refuse to allow a 'special' case to create a rule for all cases." Justice O'Connor wrote, "If [a] per-capita-aid program is identical in relevant constitutional respects to a true private-choice program, then there is no reason that [the] government should be precluded from providing direct money payments to religious organizations [based] on the number of persons belonging to each organization." If the distinction between direct and indirect aid is "arbitrary" when nonmonetary resources are involved, is it less arbitrary when money is involved?

5. *Administrative and political entanglement.* Administrative entanglement occurs when public officials are required to scrutinize the use of public funds to assure that they are not used for sectarian purposes. *Lemon* also discussed political entanglement. Public funds completely devoted to secular purposes result in an equal amount of nonpublic funds becoming available for sectarian purposes. Are direct and unrestricted grants to nonpublic schools therefore constitutional? *Lemon* argued that such grants had a "divisive political potential," as partisans would force candidates "to declare" on issues that will lead people to "find their votes aligned with their faith." Although political division is "normal and healthy," division "along religious lines was one of the principal evils against which the First Amendment was intended to protect. [To] have States [divide] on [these] [would] tend to confuse and obscure other issues of great urgency." Political fragmentation is "likely to be intensified" where "successive and very likely permanent annual appropriations that benefit relatively few religious groups" are involved.

Is the idea of political entanglement misconceived? *Mueller* stated that the language in *Lemon* about political entanglement must be "confined to cases where direct financial subsidies are paid." Is the distinction between direct subsidies and indirect tax benefits consistent with the realities of the legislative process? Note that legislatures must determine annual levels of direct subsidies. Would the use of some formula — for example, a stated proportion of the appropriations for public schools — avoid the political entanglement problems raised in *Lemon?*

Is the use of political divisiveness as a criterion completely misguided? How is political divisiveness to be measured? Is there any reason to regard interest groups organized around religion as different, and more suspect, actors in the political process than interest groups organized around economic interests?

6. *Aid to "pervasively sectarian" institutions.* In Bowen v. Kendrick, 487 U.S. 589 (1988), the Court considered the constitutionality of the Adolescent Family Life Act, which authorizes federal grants to public and private organizations, including organizations with institutional ties to religious denominations, for counseling services and research in the area of premarital adolescent sexual relations and pregnancy. Applying the *Lemon* standard, the Court held that the act on its face did not violate the establishment clause. "[It] is clear from the face of the statute that the [act] was motivated primarily, if not entirely, by a legitimate secular purpose — the elimination or reduction of social and economic problems caused by teenage sexuality, pregnancy, and parenthood." Further, the "services to be provided under the [act] are not religious in character." Moreover, although the act "takes a particular approach toward dealing with adolescent sexuality and pregnancy — for example, two of its stated purposes are to 'promote self-discipline' [and] to 'promote adoption as an alternative' [to abortion —], that approach is not inherently religious." Although conceding that "the Establishment Clause '[prohibits] government-financed [indoctrination] into the beliefs of a particular religious faith,'" the Court reasoned that, when the aid flows to religiously affiliated institutions that are not pervasively sectarian, "we [will not] presume that it [will] be used in a way that would have the primary effect of advancing religion." The Court remanded for a determination whether the act was unconstitutional "as applied," which would turn on such determinations as whether any of the grantees under the act were "pervasively sectarian" and whether any of the "aid has been used to fund 'specifically religious activit[ies] in an otherwise substantially secular setting.'"

Justice Thomas's plurality opinion in *Mitchell* concluded that the doctrine barring pervasively sectarian institutions from receiving aid that was otherwise permissible should be rejected. "The pervasively sectarian recipient has not received any special favor, and it is most bizarre that the Court would [reserve] special hostility for those who take their religion seriously, who think that their religion should affect the whole of their lives, or who make the mistake of being effective in transmitting their views to children." In addition, "the inquiry into the recipient's religious views [is offensive]." Finally, "hostility to aid to pervasively sectarian schools has a shameful pedigree that we do not hesitate to disavow." That pedigree involved hostility to Catholic parochial schools. Justice O'Connor's opinion concurring in the judgment did not address the doctrine; the dissent treated the question of the degree of an institution's sectarianism as relevant to constitutional analysis.

Note: Concluding Observations

Consider these observations from K. Karst, Law's Promise, Law's Expression 149 (1994): "Today the risk of religious polarization does seem to have lessened in the resource-allocation context, where the issues can be seen as part of the everyday grist of the political mill. [Issues] concerning governmental deployments of the symbols of religion [have] a greater capacity to polarize [because] they are not the subject of multilateral negotiation and they do not invite com-

promise [and because] any such symbol has a diffuse meaning, ar̶
handy referent for a whole world view." Does this reconcile *Mue̶*
and *Lee?* Does it justify the Court's decisions?

C.   THE FREE EXERCISE CLAUSE: REQUIRED ACCOMMODATIONS

The Court's discussions of required accommodations of religion have tended to ignore examination of the intentions of the drafters of the first amendment, except by referring in general terms to their interest in religious liberty. McConnell, The Origins and Historical Understanding of Free Exercise of Religion, 103 Harv. L. Rev. 1409, 1512 (1990), concludes on the basis of an examination of pre-1787 practice, the debates over the Constitution and the bill of rights, and contemporaneous political theory that "exemptions were not common enough to compel the inference that the term 'free exercise of religion' necessarily included an enforceable right to exemption. [Without] overstating the force of the evidence, however, it is possible to say that the [doctrine] of free exercise exemptions is more consistent with the original understanding than is a position that leads only to the facial neutrality of legislation." How do legislative practices of exemption support a constitutional requirement of exemption? For a study of the same materials coming equally cautiously to the opposite conclusion, see Hamburger, A Constitutional Right of Religious Exemption: An Historical Perspective, 60 Geo. Wash. L. Rev. 915 (1992). Justices Scalia and O'Connor examined the historical materials in their separate opinions in City of Boerne v. Flores, 521 U.S. 507 (1997), with the latter concluding that the historical materials showed that the free exercise clause placed limits on government's ability to adopt neutral laws that adversely affected religious practices, and the former disagreeing.

Until 1963, the Supreme Court had not squarely held that the free exercise clause protects religious beliefs differently, or more extensively, than the free speech clause protects political beliefs. Reynolds v. United States, 98 U.S. 145 (1879), upheld a conviction of a Mormon for bigamy, rejecting a free exercise defense. The Court said that under the first amendment "Congress was deprived of all legislative power over mere opinion, but was left free to reach actions which were in violation of social duties or subversive of good order. [Laws] are made for the government of actions, and while they cannot interfere with mere religious belief and actions, they may with practices." In Cantwell v. Connecticut, 310 U.S. 296 (1940), the Court said that the free exercise clause "embraces two concepts, — freedom to believe and freedom to act. The first is absolute, but in the nature of things, the second cannot be. Conduct remains subject to regulation for the protection of society. [*Reynolds.*] [In] every case the power to regulate must be so exercised as not [unduly] to infringe the protected freedom."

BRAUNFELD v. BROWN, 366 U.S. 599 (1961). Pennsylvania's law requiring that businesses be closed on Sundays was challenged on free exercise grounds by Orthodox Jews, whose religion required that they close their stores on Saturdays. They alleged that the Sunday closing laws placed them at a competitive disadvantage so severe as to force them out of business. Chief Justice Warren's plurality opinion rejected the free exercise claim. Citing *Reynolds*, it said, "[T]he statute [does] not make criminal the holding of any religious belief or opinion, nor does it force anyone to embrace any religious belief. [It simply] make[s] the practice of their religious beliefs more expensive. [To] strike down [legislation] which imposes only an indirect burden on the exercise of religion [would] radically restrict the operating latitude of the legislature. [We] are a cosmopolitan nation made up of people of almost every conceivable religious preference. [Consequently,] it cannot be expected, much less required, that legislators enact no law regulating conduct that may in some way result in an economic disadvantage to some religious sects and not to others because of the special practices of the various religions. [If] the State regulates conduct by enacting a general law within its power, the purpose and effect of which is to advance the State's secular goals, the statute is valid despite its indirect burden on religious observance unless the State may accomplish its purposes by means which do not impose such a burden." An exemption for Saturday-observers was not required because it "might well undermine the State's goal of providing a day that, as best possible, eliminates the atmosphere of commercial noise and activity. [Enforcement] problems would be more difficult [and Saturday-observers] might well [receive] an economic advantage over their competitors who must close on that day."

Justice Brennan, in dissent, described the state's interest as "the mere convenience of having everyone rest on the same day" and called the plurality's concern about a system allowing exemptions "fanciful." This "[exalts] administrative convenience to a constitutional level high enough to justify making one religion economically disadvantageous." Justice Stewart's dissent said that the law "compels an Orthodox Jew to choose between his religious faith and his economic survival. That is a cruel choice. It is a choice which I think no State can constitutionally demand. For me this is not something that can be swept under the rug and forgotten in the interest of enforced Sunday togetherness."

SHERBERT v. VERNER, 374 U.S. 398 (1963). Mrs. Sherbert, a Seventh-Day Adventist, was fired by her employer because she would not work on Saturday, her church's Sabbath. She was unable to find other employment in her town that would allow her to observe her Sabbath. She sought unemployment compensation, which was denied because she had lacked good cause to refuse suitable work. (The unemployment systems in most states, but not Sherbert's, treated inability to find work that would allow observance of the worker's Sabbath to be "good cause" for refusing to accept job offers.)

The Supreme Court, in an opinion by Justice Brennan, held that the denial of unemployment compensation violated the free exercise clause. The denial "imposes [a] burden on the free exercise" of religion. "Here not only is it apparent that appellant's declared ineligibility for benefits derives solely from the practice of her religion, but the pressure upon her to forego that practice is unmistakable. The ruling forces her to choose between following the precepts of her religion and forfeiting benefits, on the one hand, and abandoning one of the precepts of her religion in order to accept work, on the other hand. Governmental imposition of such a choice puts the same kind of burden upon the free exercise of religion as would a fine imposed against appellant for her Saturday worship."

The Court then considered "whether some compelling state interest [justifies] the substantial infringement of appellant's First Amendment right." The only interest asserted was prevention of the filing of fraudulent claims, but, according to the Court, the Constitution required that the state demonstrate that "no alternative forms of regulations would combat such abuses without infringing First Amendment rights." Unlike *Braunfeld*, where allowing exemptions would necessarily impair the interest in preserving a uniform day of rest, here exemptions could be administered without undermining the unemployment compensation system.

Justice Stewart concurred in the result. "The guarantee of religious liberty embodied in the Free Exercise Clause affirmatively requires government to create an atmosphere of hospitality and accommodation to individual belief or disbelief. [Our] Constitution commands the positive protection by government of religious freedom [for] each of us."

Justice Harlan, joined by Justice White, dissented. The Court's holding, he said, meant that "the State [must] *single out* for financial assistance those whose behavior is religiously motivated, even though it denies such assistance to others whose identical behavior [is] not religiously motivated." Justice Harlan believed that the state could choose "to create an exception to its eligibility requirements for persons like the appellant," but he could not "subscribe to the conclusion that the State is constitutionally *compelled* to carve out an exception to its general rule of eligibility in the present case. Those situations in which the Constitution may require special treatment on account of religion are, in my view, few and far between. [Such] compulsion in the present case is particularly inappropriate in light of the indirect, remote, and insubstantial effect of the decision below on the exercise of appellant's religion and in light of the direct financial assistance to religion that today's decision requires."

WISCONSIN v. YODER, 406 U.S. 205 (1972). Yoder, a member of the Old Order Amish, was fined $5 for refusing to send his children to school after they had completed the eighth grade. His children were ages fourteen and fifteen; Wisconsin required school attendance until age sixteen. The Amish object to high school education because of their desire to live in a "church community separate and apart from the world." They believe that high schools expose children to worldly matters and emphasize "intellectual and scientific accomplishments, self-distinction, competitiveness, worldly success, and social life with other students," in contrast to the Amish desire for "informal learning-through-doing [and] wisdom, rather than technical knowledge; community welfare, rather than competition." Basic education is acceptable to them because it prepares children "to read the Bible [and] to be good farmers and citizens." The state supreme court held that the conviction violated the free exercise clause, and the Supreme Court affirmed.

Chief Justice Burger's opinion for the Court acknowledged the state's "interest in universal education," but required that it be balanced "when it impinges on fundamental rights and interests" to assure that "there is a state interest of sufficient magnitude to override the [free exercise] interest." "[Only] those interests of the highest order and those not otherwise served can overbalance legitimate claims of free exercise of religion." The Court first asked whether the Amish claim was "rooted in religious belief. [If] the Amish asserted their claims because of their subjective evaluation and rejection of the contemporary secular values accepted by the majority, much as Thoreau rejected the social values of his time and isolated himself at Walden Pond, their claims would not rest on a religious basis. Thoreau's choice was philosophical and personal rather than religious, and such belief does not rise to the demands of the Religion Clauses." But the Amish way of life was "one of deep religious conviction, shared by an organized group and intimately related to daily living." Compulsory high school education required the Amish "to perform acts undeniably at odds with fundamental tenets of their religious beliefs" and "[carried] with it a very real threat of undermining the Amish community."

The Court rejected the state's effort to rely on the distinction between belief and action; "in this context belief and action cannot be neatly confined in logic-tight compartments." Nor was it dispositive that the requirement was facially neutral, for even such a regulation "may offend the constitutional requirement for governmental neutrality if it unduly burdens the free exercise of religion [Sherbert]." The Court accepted the state's argument that "some degree of education is necessary to prepare citizens to participate effectively and intelligently in our open political system [and] to be self-reliant and self-sufficient participants in society." But the additional one or two years of formal high school education "would do little to serve those interests." The state also argued that the Amish fostered ignorance, but the Court said that the record showed "that the Amish community has been a highly successful social unit within our society, even if apart from the conventional 'mainstream.' Its members are productive and very law-abiding members of society; they reject public welfare in its usual modern forms." The Court also rejected as "highly speculative" the state's claim that its requirement served the interest in providing those Amish children who eventually leave the community with an adequate basis for "making their way in the world." It said that "there is nothing in this record to suggest that the Amish qualities of reliability, self-reliance, and dedication to work would fail to find ready markets in today's society." The Court emphasized that it was "not dealing with a way of life and mode of education by a group claiming to have recently discovered some 'progressive' or more enlightened process for rearing children for modern life." In light of the Amish's "long history as a successful and self-sufficient segment of American society," and their showing of "the adequacy of their alternative mode of continuing informal vocational education in terms of precisely those overall interests that the State advances," a showing "that probably few other religious groups or sects could make, and weighing the minimal difference between what the State would require and what the Amish already accept, it was incumbent on the State to show with more particularity how its admittedly strong interest in compulsory education would be adversely affected by granting an exemption to the Amish."

Justice Douglas's dissent focused on the potential conflict of interest between Amish parents and their children, some of whom might wish to attend high school in order to be in a position to choose whether to adhere to or "to break from the Amish tradition." The Court replied that, in the absence of evidence of actual conflicts, allowing the state to compel high school attendance because of "the potential" that some parents might "act contrary to the best interests of their children by foreclosing their opportunity to make an intelligent choice between the Amish way of life and that of the outside world" would create "such an intrusion by a State into family decisions in the area of religious training" as itself to raise "grave questions of religious freedom."

Note: Problems of Mandatory Accommodation

1. *Unemployment cases.* The Court followed *Sherbert* in three later unemployment compensation cases, which presented minor variations on the basic claim. In Hobbie v. Unemployment Appeals Commission, 480 U.S. 136 (1987), the claimant's beliefs had changed during the course of her employment, but the Court held that "the timing of [the] conversion is immaterial." Frazee v. Illinois Department of Employment Security, 489 U.S. 829 (1989), applied *Sherbert* to a person who was not a member of an established religious sect or church, one of whose tenets was a prohibition on Sunday work, but who sincerely believed that "as a Christian, he could not work on 'the Lord's Day.'" See also Thomas v. Review Board, 450 U.S. 707 (1981).

2. *Taxation.* United States v. Lee, 455 U.S. 252 (1982), rejected a claim for a constitutionally required exemption from paying the Social Security tax. Lee, a member of the Old Order Amish, was a self-employed farmer and carpenter, who did not pay the Social Security tax for his Amish employees because "the Amish believe it sinful not to provide for their own elderly and therefore are religiously opposed to the national social security system." The Court found that the limitation on religious liberty was "essential to accomplish an overriding governmental interest." Mandatory participation in the Social Security system was "indispensable to [its] fiscal vitality." Chief Justice Burger's opinion for the Court said, "Unlike [*Yoder*], it would be difficult to accommodate the comprehensive social security system with myriad exceptions flowing from a wide variety of religious beliefs. [There] is no principled way [to] distinguish between general taxes and those imposed under the Social Security Act. If, for example, a religious adherent believes war is a sin, and if a certain percentage of the federal budget can be identified as devoted to war-related activities, such individuals would have a similarly valid claim to be exempt from paying that percentage of the income tax. The tax system could not function if denominations were allowed to challenge the tax system because tax payments were spent in a manner that violates their religious belief."

Justice Stevens concurred in the judgment but criticized the Court for overstating the risk that "a myriad of other claims" would occur. He noted that "in the typical case [of general taxes], the taxpayer is not in any position to supply the government with an equivalent substitute for the objectionable use of his money." Justice Stevens noted that, "if tax exemptions were dispensed on religious grounds, every citizen would have an economic motivation to join the favored sects [while no] comparable economic motivation could explain the conduct of the [employee] in *Sherbert*," where employer-dictated changes in work arrangements forced Sherbert out of a job.

3. *Restricted environments.* a. *The military.* Goldman v. Weinberger, 475 U.S. 503 (1986), rejected a free exercise challenge to an air force regulation prohibiting the wearing of headgear while indoors as applied to an orthodox Jewish officer who was disciplined for wearing a yarmulke. Writing for the Court, Justice Rehn-

quist emphasized the deference owed to military judgments concerning the need to "foster instinctive obedience, unity, commitment, and esprit de corps. [The] desirability of dress regulations in the military is decided by the appropriate military officials, and they are under no constitutional mandate to abandon their considered professional judgment."

Justice Stevens, joined by Justices White and Powell, wrote a concurring opinion. Although acknowledging that petitioner presented "an especially attractive case for an exception" from the regulations, Justice Stevens worried about the application of such an exemption to members of other religious groups, wishing to wear turbans, saffron robes, and dreadlocks:

> The very strength of [petitioner's] claim creates the danger that a similar claim on behalf of a Sikh or a Rastafarian might readily be dismissed as "so extreme, so unusual, or so faddish an image that public confidence in his ability to perform his duties will be destroyed" [quoting from Justice Brennan's dissenting opinion.] If exceptions from dress code regulations are to be granted on the basis of a multifactored test[, inevitably] the decisionmaker's evaluation of the character and the sincerity of the requestor's faith — as well as the probable reaction of the majority to the favored treatment of a member of that faith — will play a critical part in the decision. [The] Air Force has no business drawing distinctions between such persons when it is enforcing commands of universal application.

In a dissenting opinion joined by Justice Marshall, Justice Brennan found "totally implausible" the claim that the group identity of the air force would be threatened by the wearing of yarmulkes. "To the contrary, a yarmulke worn with a United States military uniform is an eloquent reminder that the shared and proud identity of United States servicemen embraces and unites religious and ethnic pluralism." Although turbans, saffron robes, and dreadlocks were not before the Court, Justice Brennan noted that "a reviewing court could legitimately give deference to dress and grooming rules that have a *reasoned* basis in, for example, functional utility, health and safety considerations, and the goal of a polished, professional appearance. It is the lack of any reasoned basis for prohibiting yarmulkes that is so striking here."

In a separate dissenting opinion, Justice Blackmun acknowledged that the air force could consider not only the costs of allowing petitioner to wear a yarmulke but also the cumulative costs of accommodating other requests for religious exemptions. He also acknowledged that "to allow noncombat personnel to wear yarmulkes but not turbans or dreadlocks because the latter seem more obtrusive [would] be to discriminate in favor of this country's more established, mainstream religions." Nevertheless, he rejected the air force's argument because it "simply has not shown any reason to fear that a significant number of enlisted personnel and officers would request religious exemptions that could not be denied on neutral grounds such as safety, let alone that granting these requests would noticeably impair the overall image of the service."

b. *Prisons.* O'Lone v. Estate of Shabazz, 482 U.S. 342 (1987), concerned a challenge by Muslim prisoners to a prison policy that prevented them from attending Jumu'ah, a weekly Muslim congregational service mandated by the Koran. Prison regulations, adopted for security reasons, prevented prisoners with respondents' classification from being inside the building where the service was held. The Court held that in a prison context alleged infringements on free exercise interests "are judged under a 'reasonableness' test less restrictive than that ordinarily applied to [infringements] of fundamental constitutional rights." Applying this reasonableness test to the facts before it, the Court concluded that the restriction was justified by security concerns.

4. *The concept of burdens: internal government operations.* When does a statute burden the exercise of religion? Lupu, Where Rights Begin: The Problem of Burdens on the Free Exercise of Religion, 102 Harv. L. Rev. 933, 935, 966 (1988), proposes a principle derived from the common law for defining free exercise burdens: "Whenever religious activity is met by intentional government action analogous to that which, if committed by a private party, would be actionable under general principles of law, a legally cognizable burden on religion is present." Is there a constitutionally cognizable burden in the following cases?

Bowen v. Roy, 476 U.S. 693 (1986), rejected religious-based objections to a federal statute requiring applicants for certain welfare benefits to provide the states with their Social Security numbers and requiring the states to use the numbers in administering the program. Appellees had applied for such benefits, including food stamps. They contended that providing a Social Security number for their two-year-old daughter and use of that number by the government would violate their religious beliefs.

Writing for eight justices, Chief Justice Burger rejected appellee's claim that the free exercise clause was infringed when the government used the number. "Never to our knowledge has the Court interpreted the First Amendment to require the Government *itself* to behave in ways that the individual believes will further his or her spiritual development. [The] Free Exercise Clause affords an individual protection from certain forms of governmental compulsion; it does not afford an individual a right to dictate the conduct of the Government's internal procedures." The Court did not definitively rule on the claim that appellants could not be required to apply for Social Security numbers, though a majority of the justices indicated that, were the Court to reach the issue, they would hold that free exercise required that they could not be so required.

Lyng v. Northwest Indian Cemetery Protective Association, 485 U.S. 439 (1988), rejected a free exercise challenge to the Forest Service's plan to permit timber harvesting and road construction in part of a national forest that was traditionally used by various Indian tribes as sacred areas for religious rituals. The Court held, in an opinion by Justice O'Connor, that the government did not have to show a compelling need to engage in the relevant projects:

> In both [*Roy* and *Lyng*] the challenged governmental action would interfere significantly with private persons' ability to pursue spiritual fulfillment according to their own religious beliefs. In neither case, however, could the affected individuals be coerced by the Government's action into violating their religious beliefs; nor would either governmental action penalize religious activity by denying any person an equal share of the rights, benefits, and privileges enjoyed by other citizens.

The Court acknowledged that

> indirect coercion or penalties on the free exercise of religion, not just outright prohibitions, are subject to scrutiny under the First Amendment. [But] this [cannot] imply that incidental effects of government programs, which may make it more difficult to practice certain religions but which have no tendency to coerce individu-

als into acting contrary to their religious beliefs, require government to bring forward a compelling justification for its otherwise lawful actions. The crucial word
in the constitutional text is "prohibit."

The Court noted that the projects at issue "could have devastating effects on traditional Indian religious practices . . . intimately and inextricably bound up with
the unique features" of the area, but it concluded that "government simply could
not operate if it were required to satisfy every citizen's religious needs and desires."

In a dissenting opinion joined by Justices Marshall and Blackmun, Justice
Brennan criticized the Court's conception of "coercion":

> Ultimately, the Court's coercion test turns on a distinction between governmental
> actions that compel affirmative conduct inconsistent with religious belief, and
> those governmental actions that prevent conduct consistent with religious belief.
> [The] crucial word in the constitutional text, as the Court itself acknowledges, is
> "prohibit," a comprehensive term that in no way suggests that the intended protec-
> tion is aimed only at governmental actions that coerce affirmative conduct. [Reli-
> gious] freedom is threatened no less by governmental action that makes the prac-
> tice of one's chosen faith impossible than by governmental programs that pressure
> one to engage in conduct inconsistent with religious belief.

In what sense is the land in *Lyng* more "the government's" than was the money
in *Sherbert?* Note that in *Lyng* there was even greater coercion than in *Sherbert* — an across-the-board foreclosure rather than a financial inducement to
abandon religious practice. Lupu, supra, at 973-976, suggests that the tribes
might be seen as having acquiring an interest analogous to a common law easement by prescription.

Employment Division, Department of Human Resources v. Smith

494 U.S. 872 (1990)

JUSTICE SCALIA delivered the opinion of the Court.

This case requires us to decide whether the Free Exercise Clause of the First
Amendment permits the State of Oregon to include religiously inspired peyote
use within the reach of its general criminal prohibition on use of that drug, and
thus permits the State to deny unemployment benefits to persons dismissed from
their jobs because of such religiously inspired use. . . .

[Smith was a member of the Native American Church, which has as part of its
religious ritual the supervised consumption of peyote. Peyote is a "controlled substance" under Oregon law, possession of which is a criminal offense. Smith was
fired from his job at a private drug rehabilitation clinic because he ingested peyote as part of his church's ritual. He sought unemployment benefits, which were
denied because he had been discharged for work-related misconduct. On his appeal from the denial of benefits, the Oregon Supreme Court held that state law
did not contain an exemption from its criminal statute for religious consumption
of peyote, that the criminal ban was unconstitutional as applied to the consumption of peyote in this setting, and that Smith was therefore entitled to unemployment compensation.]

II

Respondents' claim for relief rests on our decisions [which held] that a State could not condition the availability of unemployment insurance on an individual's willingness to forgo conduct required by his religion. [However,] the conduct at issue in those cases was not prohibited by law. . . .

A

[The] free exercise of religion means, first and foremost, the right to believe and profess whatever religious doctrine one desires. . . .

[The] "exercise of religion" often involves not only belief and profession but the performance of (or abstention from) physical acts: assembling with others for a worship service, participating in sacramental use of bread and wine, proselytizing, abstaining from certain foods or certain modes of transportation. [A] state would be "prohibiting the free exercise [of religion]" if it sought to ban such acts or abstentions only when they are engaged in for religious reasons, or only because of the religious belief that they display. It would doubtless be unconstitutional [to] prohibit bowing down before a golden calf.

Respondents in the present case, however, seek to carry the meaning of "prohibiting the free exercise [of religion]" one large step further. They contend that their religious motivation for using peyote places them beyond the reach of a criminal law that is not specifically directed at their religious practice, and that is concededly constitutional as applied to those who use the drug for other reasons. They assert, in other words, that "prohibiting the free exercise [of religion]" includes requiring any individual to observe a generally applicable law that requires (or forbids) the performance of an act that his religious belief forbids (or requires). As a textual matter, we do not think the words must be given that meaning. It is no more necessary to regard the collection of a general tax, for example, as "prohibiting the free exercise [of religion]" by those citizens who believe support of organized government to be sinful, than it is to regard the same tax as "abridging the freedom . . . of the press" of those publishing companies that must pay the tax as a condition of staying in business. It is a permissible reading of the text [to] say that if prohibiting the exercise of religion [is] not the object of the tax but merely the incidental effect of a generally applicable and otherwise valid provision, the First Amendment has not been offended.

[That] reading is the correct one. We have never held that an individual's religious beliefs excuse him from compliance with an otherwise valid law prohibiting conduct that the State is free to regulate. On the contrary, the record of more than a century of our free exercise jurisprudence contradicts that proposition. [We] first had occasion to assert that principle in [Reynolds]. . . .

Subsequent decisions have consistently held that the right of free exercise does not relieve an individual of the obligation to comply with a "valid and neutral law of general applicability on the ground that the law proscribes (or prescribes) conduct that his religion prescribes (or proscribes)." United States v. Lee (Stevens, J., concurring in judgment). . . .

The only decisions in which we have held that the First Amendment bars application of a neutral, generally applicable law to religiously motivated action have involved not the Free Exercise Clause alone, but the Free Exercise Clause in conjunction with other constitutional protections, such as freedom of speech and of the press, see [*Cantwell*], or the right of parents, acknowledged in Pierce v. Society of Sisters, 268 U.S. 510 (1925), to direct the education of their children, see Wisconsin v. Yoder. . . .[1]

The present case does not present such a hybrid situation, but a free exercise claim unconnected with any communicative activity or parental right. Respondents urge us to hold [that] when otherwise prohibitable conduct is accompanied by religious convictions, not only the convictions but the conduct itself must be free from governmental regulation. We have never held that, and decline to do so now. "[Our] cases do not at their farthest reach support the proposition that a stance of conscientious opposition relieves an objector from any colliding duty fixed by a democratic government." Gillette v. United States.

B

Respondents argue that even though exemption from generally applicable criminal laws need not automatically be extended to religiously motivated actors, at least the claim for a religious exemption must be evaluated under the balancing test set forth in Sherbert v. Verner. [We] have never invalidated any governmental action on the basis of the *Sherbert* test except the denial of unemployment compensation. Although we have sometimes purported to apply the *Sherbert* test in contexts other than that, we have always found the test satisfied. In recent years we have abstained from applying the *Sherbert* test (outside the unemployment compensation field) at all [citing *Roy, Lyng, Goldman,* and *O'Lone*].

Even if we were inclined to breathe into *Sherbert* some life beyond the unemployment compensation field, we would not apply it to require exemptions from a generally applicable criminal law. The *Sherbert* test [was] developed in a context that lent itself to individualized governmental assessment of the reasons for the relevant conduct. [Our] decisions in the unemployment cases stand for the proposition that where the State has in place a system of individual exemptions, it may not refuse to extend that system to cases of "religious hardship" without compelling reason.

Whether or not the decisions are that limited, they at least have nothing to do with an across-the-board criminal prohibition on a particular form of conduct. [The] government's ability to enforce generally applicable prohibitions of socially harmful conduct, like its ability to carry out other aspects of public policy, "cannot depend on measuring the effects of a governmental action on a religious objector's spiritual development." [*Lyng.*] To make an individual's obligation to obey such a law contingent upon the law's coincidence with his religious beliefs, except where the State's interest is "compelling" — permitting him, by virtue of his beliefs, "to become a law unto himself" [*Reynolds*] — contradicts both constitutional tradition and common sense.[2]

---

1. Both lines of cases have specifically adverted to the non-free exercise principle involved. . . .

2. Justice O'Connor seeks to distinguish *Lyng* [and] *Roy*, on the ground that those cases involved the government's conduct of "its own internal affairs," which is different because, as Justice Douglas said in *Sherbert*, "the Free Exercise Clause is written in terms of what the government cannot do to the individual, not in terms of what the individual can exact from the government." [It] is hard to see any reason in principle or practicality why the government should have to tailor its health and safety laws to conform to the diversity of religious belief, but should not have to tailor its management of public lands, or its administration of welfare programs.

The "compelling interest" requirement seems benign, because it is familiar from other fields. But using it as the standard that must be met before the government may accord different treatment on the basis of race, or before the government may regulate the content of speech, is not remotely comparable to using it for the purpose asserted here. What it produces in those other fields — equality of treatment, and an unrestricted flow of contending speech — are constitutional norms; what it would produce here — a private right to ignore generally applicable laws — is a constitutional anomaly.[3]

Nor is it possible to limit the impact of respondents' proposal by requiring a "compelling state interest" only when the conduct prohibited is "central" to the individual's religion. It is no more appropriate for judges to determine the "centrality" of religious beliefs before applying a "compelling interest" test in the free exercise field, than it would be for them to determine the "importance" of ideas before applying the "compelling interest" test in the free speech field. What principle of law or logic can be brought to bear to contradict a believer's assertion that a particular act is "central" to his personal faith? Judging the centrality of different religious practices is akin to the unacceptable "business of evaluating the relative merits of differing religious claims." United States v. Lee (Stevens, J., concurring). [Repeatedly] and in many different contexts, we have warned that courts must not presume to determine the place of a particular belief in a religion or the plausibility of a religious claim.[4]

If the "compelling interest" test is to be applied at all, then, it must be applied across the board, to all actions thought to be religiously commanded. Moreover, if "compelling interest" really means what it says (and watering it down here would subvert its rigor in the other fields where it is applied), many laws will not meet the test. Any society adopting such a system would be courting anarchy, but that danger increases in direct proportion to the society's diversity of religious beliefs, and its determination to coerce or suppress none of them. Precisely because "we are a cosmopolitan nation made up of people of almost every conceivable religious preference," Braunfeld v. Brown, and precisely because we value and protect that religious divergence, we cannot afford the luxury of deeming presumptively invalid, as applied to the religious objector, every regulation of conduct that does not protect an interest of the highest order. The rule respondents favor would open the prospect of constitutionally required religious exemptions from civic obligations of almost every conceivable kind — ranging from compulsory military service, to the payment of taxes, to health and safety regulation such as manslaughter and child neglect laws, compulsory vaccination laws, drug laws,

---

3. [Just] as we subject to the most exacting scrutiny laws that make classifications based on race, or on the content of speech, so too we strictly scrutinize governmental classifications based on religion, see McDaniel v. Paty, 435 U.S. 618 (1978). But we have held that race-neutral laws that have the effect of disproportionately disadvantaging a particular racial group do not thereby become subject to compelling-interest analysis under the Equal Protection Clause, see Washington v. Davis, and we have held that generally applicable laws unconcerned with regulating speech that have the effect of interfering with speech do not thereby become subject to compelling-interest analysis under the First Amendment. . . .

4. [Dispensing] with a "centrality" inquiry is utterly unworkable. It would require, for example, the same degree of "compelling state interest" to impede the practice of throwing rice at church weddings as to impede the practice of getting married in church. There is no way out of the difficulty that, if general laws are to be subjected to a "religious practice" exception, both the importance of the law at issue and the centrality of the practice at issue must reasonably be considered.

and traffic laws, to social welfare legislation such as minimum wage laws, child labor laws, animal cruelty laws, environmental protection laws, and laws providing for equality of opportunity for the races. The First Amendment's protection of religious liberty does not require this.

Values that are protected against government interference through enshrinement in the Bill of Rights are not thereby banished from the political process. Just as a society that believes in the negative protection accorded to the press by the First Amendment is likely to enact laws that affirmatively foster the dissemination of the printed word, so also a society that believes in the negative protection accorded to religious belief can be expected to be solicitous of that value in its legislation as well. It is therefore not surprising that a number of States have made an exception to their drug laws for sacramental peyote use. But to say that a nondiscriminatory religious-practice exemption is permitted, or even that it is desirable, is not to say that it is constitutionally required, and that the appropriate occasions for its creation can be discerned by the courts. It may fairly be said that leaving accommodation to the political process will place at a relative disadvantage those religious practices that are not widely engaged in; but that unavoidable consequence of democratic government must be preferred to a system in which each conscience is a law unto itself or in which judges weight the social importance of all laws against the centrality of all religious beliefs.

[Reversed.]

JUSTICE O'CONNOR, with whom JUSTICE BRENNAN, JUSTICE MARSHALL, and JUSTICE BLACKMUN join as to [Part] II, concurring in the judgment. . . .

II . . .

A

[Because] the First Amendment does not distinguish between religious belief and religious conduct, conduct motivated by sincere religious belief, like the belief itself, must therefore be at least presumptively protected by the Free Exercise Clause.

[A] law that prohibits [conduct] that happens to be an act of worship for someone [manifestly] does prohibit that person's free exercise of his religion. A person who is barred from engaging in religiously motivated conduct is barred from freely exercising his religion. Moreover, that person is barred from freely exercising his religion regardless of whether the law prohibits the conduct only when engaged in for religious reasons, only by members of that religion, or by all persons. It is difficult to deny that a law that prohibits religiously motivated conduct, even if the law is generally applicable, does not at least implicate First Amendment concerns.

The Court responds that generally applicable laws are "one large step" removed from laws aimed at specific religious practices. The First Amendment, however, does not distinguish between laws that are generally applicable and laws that target particular religious practices. Indeed, few States would be so naive as to enact a law directly prohibiting or burdening a religious practice as such. Our free exercise cases have all concerned generally applicable laws that had the effect of significantly burdening a religious practice. If the First Amendment is to have any vitality, it ought not be construed to cover only the extreme and hypothetical situation in which a State directly targets a religious practice. . . .

To say that a person's right to free exercise has been burdened, of course, does not mean that he has an absolute right to engage in the conduct. Under our established First Amendment jurisprudence, we have recognized that the freedom to act, unlike the freedom to believe, cannot be absolute. Instead, we have respected both the First Amendment's express textual mandate and the governmental interest in regulation of conduct by requiring the Government to justify any substantial burden on religiously motivated conduct by a compelling state interest and by means narrowly tailored to achieve that interest. The compelling interest test effectuates the First Amendment's command that religious liberty is an independent liberty, that it occupies a preferred position, and that the Court will not permit encroachments upon this liberty, whether direct or indirect, unless required by clear and compelling governmental interests "of the highest order" [*Yoder*]. . . .

[In] each of the [cases] cited by the Court to support its categorical rule, we rejected the particular constitutional claims before us only after carefully weighing the competing interests. That we rejected the free exercise claims in those cases hardly calls into question the applicability of First Amendment doctrine in the first place. Indeed, it is surely unusual to judge the vitality of a constitutional doctrine by looking to the win-loss record of the plaintiffs who happen to come before us.

B . . .

[The] essence of a free exercise claim is relief from a burden imposed by government on religious practices or beliefs, whether the burden is imposed directly through laws that prohibit or compel specific religious practices, or indirectly through laws that, in effect, make abandonment of one's own religion or conformity to the religious beliefs of others the price of an equal place in the civil community. . . .

Legislatures, of course, have always been "left free to reach actions which were in violation of social duties or subversive of good order." [*Reynolds.*] Yet because of the close relationship between conduct and religious belief, "[i]n every case the power to regulate must be so exercised as not, in attaining a permissible end, unduly to infringe the protected freedom." [*Cantwell.*] Once it has been shown that a government regulation or criminal prohibition burdens the free exercise of religion, we have consistently asked the Government to demonstrate that unbending application of its regulation to the religious objector "is essential to accomplish an overriding governmental interest" [*Lee*], or represents "the least restrictive means of achieving some compelling state interest" [*Thomas*]. To me, [the] approach more consistent with our role as judges to decide each case on its individual merits [is] to apply this test in each case to determine whether the burden on the specific plaintiffs before us is constitutionally significant and whether the particular criminal interest asserted by the State before us is compelling. Even if, as an empirical matter, a government's criminal laws might usually serve a compelling interest in health, safety, or public order, the First Amendment at least requires a case-by-case determination of the question, sensitive to the facts of each particular claim. Given the range of conduct that a State might legitimately make criminal, we cannot assume, merely because a law carries criminal sanctions and is generally applicable, that the First Amendment never requires the State to grant a limited exemption for religiously motivated conduct. . . .

[The cases] cited by the Court for the proposition that we have rejected application of the *Sherbert* test outside the unemployment compensation field are distinguishable because they arose in the narrow, specialized contexts. [That] we did not apply the compelling interest test in these cases says nothing about whether the test should continue to apply in paradigm free exercise cases such as the one presented here.

[There] is nothing talismanic about neutral laws of general applicability or general criminal prohibitions, for laws neutral toward religion can coerce a person to violate his religious conscience or intrude upon his religious duties just as effectively as laws aimed at religion. Although the Court suggests that the compelling interest test, as applied to generally applicable laws, would result in a "constitutional anomaly," the First Amendment unequivocally makes freedom of religion, like freedom from race discrimination and freedom of speech, a "constitutional nor[m]," not an "anomaly." [As] the language of the Clause itself makes clear, an individual's free exercise of religion is a preferred constitutional activity. See, e.g., McConnell, Accommodation of Religion, 1985 Sup. Ct. Rev. 1, 9 ("[T]he text of the First Amendment itself 'singles out' religion for special protections."). A law that makes criminal such an activity therefore triggers constitutional concern — and heightened judicial scrutiny — even if it does not target the particular religious conduct at issue. Our free speech cases similarly recognize that neutral regulations that affect free speech values are subject to a balancing, rather than categorical, approach. The Court's parade of horribles not only fails as a reason for discarding the compelling interest test, it instead demonstrates just the opposite; that courts have been quite capable of applying our free exercise jurisprudence to strike sensible balances between religious liberty and competing state interest.

Finally, the Court today suggests that the disfavoring of minority religions is an "unavoidable consequence" under our system of government and that accommodation of such religions must be left to the political process. In my view, however, the First Amendment was enacted precisely to protect the rights of those whose religious practices are not shared by the majority and may be viewed with hostility. The history of our free exercise doctrine amply demonstrates the harsh impact majoritarian rule has had on unpopular or emerging religious groups such as the Jehovah's Witnesses and the Amish. [The] compelling interest test reflects the First Amendment's mandate of preserving religious liberty to the fullest extent possible in a pluralistic society. For the Court to deem this command a "luxury" [is] to denigrate "[t]he very purpose of a Bill of Rights."

[Part III of Justice O'Connor's opinion concluded that Oregon's prohibition satisfied the compelling state interest test. She agreed that the prohibition placed a "severe burden" on the free exercise of religion, but said that the state had a "significant interest" in controlling drug use. Finding the question close, she concluded that "uniform application" of the prohibition is "essential to accomplish" the overriding purpose of preventing physical harm caused by drug use. Selective exemptions for religious believers would "seriously impair" the state's interest.]

Justice Blackmun, with whom Justice Brennan and Justice Marshall join, dissenting. . . .

I

In weighing respondents' clear interest in the free exercise of their religion against Oregon's asserted interest in enforcing its drug laws, it is important to articulate in precise terms the state interest involved. It is not the State's broad interest in fighting the critical "war on drugs" [but] the State's narrow interest in refusing to make an exception for the religious, ceremonial use of peyote. [Failure] to reduce the competing interests to the same plane of generality tends to distort the weighing process in the State's favor.

The State's interest in enforcing its prohibition, in order to be sufficiently compelling to outweigh a free exercise claim, cannot be merely abstract or symbolic. The State cannot plausibly assert that unbending application of a criminal prohibition is essential to fulfill any compelling interest, if it does not, in fact, attempt to enforce that prohibition. In this case, the State actually has not evinced any concrete interest in enforcing its drug laws against religious users of peyote. Oregon has never sought to prosecute respondents, and does not claim that it has made significant enforcement efforts against other religious users of peyote. The State's asserted interest thus amounts only to the symbolic preservation of an unenforced prohibition. But a government interest in "symbolism, even symbolism for so worthy a cause as the abolition of unlawful drugs," Treasury Employees v. Von Raab, 489 U.S. 656 (1989) (Scalia, J., dissenting), cannot suffice to abrogate the constitutional rights of individuals. . . .

The State proclaims an interest in protecting the health and safety of its citizens from the dangers of unlawful drugs. It offers, however, no evidence that the religious use of peyote has ever harmed anyone. . . .

[Moreover,] 23 States, including many that have significant Native American populations, have statutory or judicially crafted exemptions in their drug laws for religious use of peyote. Although this does not prove that Oregon must have such an exception too, it is significant that these States, and the Federal Government, all find their (presumably compelling) interests in controlling the use of dangerous drugs compatible with an exemption for religious use of peyote.

The carefully circumscribed ritual context in which respondents used peyote is far removed from the irresponsible and unrestricted recreational use of unlawful drugs.[6] The Native American Church's internal restrictions on, and supervision of, its members' use of peyote substantially obviate the State's health and safety concerns. . . .[7]

The State's apprehension of a flood of other religious claims is purely speculative. Almost half the States and the Federal Government have maintained an exemption for religious peyote use for many years, and apparently have not found themselves overwhelmed by claims to other religious exemptions.[8] Allowing an exemption for religious peyote use would not necessarily oblige the State to grant

---

6. [Respondents'] use of peyote seems closely analogous to the sacramental use of wine by the Roman Catholic Church. During Prohibition, the Federal Government exempted such use of wine from its general ban on possession and use of alcohol. However compelling the Government's then general interest in prohibiting the use of alcohol may have been, it could not plausibly have asserted an interest sufficiently compelling to outweigh Catholics' right to take communion.

7. The use of peyote is, to some degree, self-limiting. The peyote plant is extremely bitter, and eating it is an unpleasant experience, which would tend to discourage casual or recreational use.

8. Over the past years, various sects have raised free exercise claims regarding drug use. In no reported case, except those involving claims of religious peyote use, has the claimant prevailed.

a similar exemption to other religious groups. The unusual circumstances that make the religious use of peyote compatible with the State's interests in health and safety and in preventing drug trafficking would not apply to other religious claims. Some religions, for example, might not restrict drug use to a limited ceremonial context, as does the Native American Church. Some religious claims involve drugs such as marijuana and heroin, in which there is significant illegal traffic, with its attendant greed and violence, so that it would be difficult to grant a religious exemption without seriously compromising law enforcement efforts. . . .

III . . .

[Respondents] believe, and their sincerity has never been at issue, that the peyote plant embodies their deity, and eating it is an act of worship and communion. Without peyote, they could not enact the essential ritual of their religion.

If Oregon can constitutionally prosecute them for this act of worship, they, like the Amish, may be "forced to migrate to some other and more tolerant region." [Yoder.] This potentially devastating impact must be viewed in light of the federal policy — reached in reaction to many years of religious persecution and intolerance — of protecting the religious freedom of Native Americans.

The American Indian Religious Freedom Act [42 U.S.C. §1996], in itself, may not create rights enforceable against government action restricting religious freedom, but this Court must scrupulously apply its free exercise analysis to the religious claims of Native Americans, however unorthodox they may be. Otherwise, both the First Amendment and the stated policy of Congress will offer to Native Americans merely an unfulfilled and hollow promise. . . .

Note: Should Accommodation Be Required?

1. *Free exercise and free speech.* United States v. O'Brien, Chapter 7, section E3, supra, held that facially neutral statutes serving important purposes unrelated to suppression of speech are constitutional if the incidental impact on speech is no greater than necessary. Is the Court correct in stating that *Smith* transfers the *O'Brien* approach to the free exercise area? Gedicks, The Normalized Free Exercise Clause, 75 Ind. L.J. 77 (2000), argues that *Smith* adopts a "rational basis" standard of review and thereby "contradicts the Court's Speech Clause doctrine governing [incidental] burdens on speech occurring as the result of otherwise legitimate government regulations of conduct or the time, place, or manner of expression," which requires that such regulations satisfy an intermediate standard of review. Is Gedicks's description of free speech doctrine accurate?

2. *The scope of* Smith. How broadly does *Smith* undermine a doctrine of mandatory accommodation?

a. *Individualized determinations.* Was the unemployment commission in *Sherbert* in a position to balance the impairment of free exercise against the prevention of fraudulent claims?

b. *Hybrid claims.* Is the Court's explanation of *Yoder* persuasive? Consider the proposition that, because there is no substantive due process right, independent of a religious claim, to keep children out of school, and there is no religious claim, independent of a due process claim, to do so, the two inadequate arguments taken together cannot add up to a valid claim.

c. *Expressive association rights.* Suppose a state adopts an antidiscrimination statute, creating civil liability and prohibiting discrimination on the basis of gender. Must a church-related school comply with that statute by hiring a teacher with a one-year-old child if the church's tenets demand that women with small children raise them at home and not participate in the paid workforce? Does the Court's discussion of cases in which free exercise claims are joined with other claims, such as freedom of association, adequately deal with this problem?

d. *The political process.* Although the political process protected the sacramental use of wine during Prohibition, it has not fully protected the sacramental use of peyote. What limitations does this suggest on reliance on the political process to protect religious liberty interests? (Congress responded to *Smith* with the Religious Freedom Restoration Act, found unconstitutional in City of Boerne v. Flores, 521 U.S. 507 (1997), Chapter 2, section D4, supra.)

e. *Invidious motivation.* Church of the Lukumi Babalu Aye v. City of Hialeah, 508 U.S. 520 (1993), invalidated a city's ban on "ritual slaughter" as applied to animal sacrifices conducted by the church as part of its practice of the Santeria religion. The Court found that the background of the ban, and its specific language and exemptions, demonstrated that "suppression of the central element of the Santeria worship service was the object of the ordinances." The background "demonstrates animosity to Santeria adherents and their religious practices; the ordinances by their own terms target this religious exercise; the texts of the ordinances were gerrymandered with care to proscribe religious killings of animals but to exclude almost all secular killings; and the ordinances suppress much more religious conduct than is necessary to achieve the legitimate ends asserted in their defense." The ordinances did not satisfy the "rigorous scrutiny" required of regulations that are not neutral or of general application because they were "not drawn in narrow terms to accomplish" the objectives of protecting animals from inhumane slaughter or avoiding unhealthy methods of disposing of animal carcasses. Justice Blackmun, joined by Justice O'Connor, concurred in the judgment, saying that, "when a law discriminates against religion as such, [it] automatically will fail strict scrutiny [because] by definition, [it] is not precisely tailored to a compelling governmental interest."

Is *Hialeah* best understood as involving an impermissibly motivated antireligious gerrymander, that is, a statute that, though neutral on its face, actually reaches only religious activities? For the suggestion that the Court's approach, following *Smith*'s "focus[] on persecutory motivation, [elicits] the same kind of *ad hominem* argumentation that is reflected in 'purpose' cases under the Establishment Clause," see Smith, Free Exercise Doctrine and the Discourse of Disrespect, 65 U. Colo. L. Rev. 519, 558 (1994).

3. *(Implicit) denominational preferences?* Williams and Williams, Volitionalism and Religious Liberty, 76 Cornell L. Rev. 769, 772, 777, 908 (1991), argue that *Smith* resulted from "the Court's profound discomfort with nonvolitionalist beliefs" that "acknowledge the possibility that some religious consequences for individuals may be caused by activities or events over which they had no free choice or control," as in *Lyng* and Bowen v. Roy. On their analysis, free exercise claims lie along a spectrum ranging from "exemption" claims to "ordering" claims, "the remedy for which consists primarily of reordering some aspect of the

nment's program not limited in application to the individual claimant." suggest that under a pre-*Smith* analysis, "ordering" claims, which typify those made by people with nonvolitionalist beliefs, "are, as a practical matter, likely to impose greater burdens on the government than will exemption claims." Does this raise questions about denominational preference? Note that, on some views, neither religious belief in general nor commitment to Christianity in particular results from volitional choices. See Garvey, An Anti-Liberal Argument for Religious Freedom, 7 J. of Contemp. Legal Issues 275, 278 (1996): "The individual does not have complete control over choosing the religious option. It is God who makes the choice."

Greene, The Political Balance of the Religion Clauses, 102 Yale L.J. 1611 (1993), argues that the establishment clause bars "enacting legislation for the express purpose of advancing the values believed to be commanded by religion," and that "precisely because religion should be excluded from politics in this way, [the] Free Exercise Clause requires the recognition of religious faith as a ground for exemption from legal obligation. [These] exemptions are merely the appropriate remedy for the damage that precluding religious values from grounding law causes religious people." The establishment clause ban arises because, when legislation is enacted for the express purpose of advancing religious values, "a nonbeliever is effectively denied participation in the political process because the nonbeliever cannot discuss the matter on the terms that the religious believers have set." According to Greene, because one type of argument is thereby excluded from political negotiations, those who would make it are entitled to a compensatory offset.

D. PERMISSIBLE ACCOMMODATION

Statutes that attempt to accommodate the concerns of adherents of religion lie at the borderland of the free exercise and establishment clauses. They promote "free exercise values," in the sense that they allow believers to pursue their religious beliefs without hindrance, but legislatures are rarely compelled by the free exercise clause to adopt statutory accommodations. Such statutes are in tension with some formulations of the requirements of the establishment clause because they have the purpose of advancing religion in the sense just specified. Are such accommodations constitutional? If so, why?

Consider these positions:

a. There is no tension. No regulation promoting free exercise values can violate antiestablishment values, and no statute promoting antiestablishment values impairs free exercise ones. But consider Thornton v. Caldor, infra.

b. There is no tension. Only statutory accommodations required by the free exercise clause are constitutional, and all other efforts to serve "free exercise values" are unconstitutional. Why should a legislature ever enact a statutory accommodation if this is the test? If the free exercise clause requires some accommodation, what reasons are there to think that court-devised accommodations will be more appropriate than legislative ones?

c. The tension should be resolved by preferring free exercise values to antiestablishment ones. The expansive role of the modern state creates many opportunities for facially neutral statutes to burden religious belief and reduces the role previously played by many religious institutions. Religious intolerance poses serious threats in a religiously diverse society, so that when legislation advances free exercise values, it should be encouraged. Consider the extent to which the problems discussed in section B supra, and especially the issue of state aid to religious schools, could be recast as efforts by the state to advance free exercise values.

d. The tension should be resolved by preferring antiestablishment values to free exercise ones. Mainstream religions have a powerful advantage in the political process over marginal religions and over nonreligion. Legislation is likely to enhance the positions of mainstream religions. In the long run, religious minorities will be better off under a regime of strict separation, even though the application of neutral regulations may sometimes affect them adversely.

e. There need be no tension. If states are barred from using religion as a basis for either conferring benefits or imposing burdens, legislators will be required to use neutral rules to accomplish their goals, and the legislation resulting from a political process constrained by a requirement of neutrality will threaten neither free exercise nor antiestablishment values.

Corporation of Presiding Bishop of the Church of Jesus Christ of Latter-Day Saints v. Amos

483 U.S. 327 (1987)

JUSTICE WHITE delivered the opinion of the Court.

Section 702 of the Civil Rights Act of 1964 exempts religious organizations from Title VII's prohibition against discrimination in employment on the basis of religion. The question presented is whether applying the §702 exemption to the secular nonprofit activities of religious organizations violates the Establishment Clause of the First Amendment. The District Court held that it does. . . .

[The appellee was a janitor at the Deseret Gymnasium, a nonprofit facility, open to the public, run by the Mormon church. He was fired after he failed to qualify for a certificate stating that he was a member of the church eligible to attend its temples because he observed the church's standards involving church attendance, tithing, and abstinence from coffee, tea, alcohol, and tobacco.]

"This Court has long recognized that the government may (and sometimes must) accommodate religious practices and that it may do so without violating the Establishment Clause." [*Hobbie*, section C supra.] It is well established, too, that "[t]he limits of permissible state accommodation to religion are by no means co-extensive with the noninterference mandated by the Free Exercise Clause." [*Walz*, section B1 supra.] There is ample room under the Establishment Clause for "benevolent neutrality which will permit religious exercise to exist without sponsorship and without interference." At some point, accommodation may devolve into "an unlawful fostering of religion" [*Hobbie*], but these are not such cases, in our view. . . .

Lemon requires first that the law at issue serve a "secular legislative purpose." This does not mean that the law's purpose must be unrelated to religion — that would amount to a requirement "that the government show a callous indifference to religious groups," Zorach v. Clauson, 343 U.S. 306, 314 (1952), and the

Establishment Clause has never been so interpreted. Rather, *Lemon's* "purpose" requirement aims at preventing the relevant governmental decisionmaker — in this case, Congress — from abandoning neutrality and acting with the intent of promoting a particular point of view in religious matters.

Under the *Lemon* analysis, it is a permissible legislative purpose to alleviate significant governmental interference with the ability of religious organizations to define and carry out their religious missions. Appellees argue that there is no such purpose here because §702 provided adequate protection for religious employers [when] it exempted only the religious activities of such employers from the statutory ban on religious discrimination. We may assume for the sake of argument that [that] exemption was adequate in the sense that the Free Exercise Clause required no more. Nonetheless, it is a significant burden on a religious organization to require it, on pain of substantial liability, to predict which of its activities a secular court will consider religious. The line is hardly a bright one, and an organization might understandably be concerned that a judge would not understand its religious tenets and sense of mission. Fear of potential liability might affect the way an organization carried out what it understood to be its religious mission. [Congress's] purpose was to minimize governmental "interfer[ence] with the decision-making process in religions." [This] purpose does not violate the Establishment Clause.

The second requirement under *Lemon* is that the law in question have "a principal or primary effect . . . that neither advances nor inhibits religion." Undoubtedly, religious organizations are better able now to advance their purposes than they were prior to the 1972 amendment to §702. [A] law is not unconstitutional simply because it allows churches to advance religion, which is their very purpose. For a law to have forbidden "effects" under *Lemon*, it must be fair to say that the government itself has advanced religion through its own activities and influence. . . .

The District Court appeared to fear that sustaining the exemption would permit churches with financial resources impermissibly to extend their influence and propagate their faith by entering the commercial, profit-making world. The cases before us [involve] a nonprofit activity instituted over 75 years ago. [Moreover], we find no persuasive evidence in the record before us that the Church's ability to propagate its religious doctrine through the Gymnasium is any greater now than it was prior to the passage of the Civil Rights Act in 1964. In such circumstances, we do not see how any advancement of religion achieved by the Gymnasium can be fairly attributed to the Government, as opposed to the Church.[15]

We find unpersuasive the District Court's reliance on the fact that §702 singles out religious entities for a benefit. Although the Court has given weight to this

---

15. Undoubtedly, [appellee's] freedom of choice in religious matters was impinged upon, but it was the Church[, and] not the Government, who put him to the choice of changing his religious practices or losing his job. This is a very different case than Estate of Thornton v. Caldor, Inc., 472 U.S. 703 (1985). In *Caldor*, the Court struck down a Connecticut statute prohibiting an employer from requiring an employee to work on a day designated by the employee as his Sabbath. In effect, Connecticut had given the force of law to the employee's designation of a Sabbath day and required accommodation by the employer regardless of the burden which that constituted for the employer or other employees. . . .

consideration in its past decisions, it has never indicated that statutes that give special consideration to religious groups are per se invalid. [Where], as here, government acts with the proper purpose of lifting a regulation that burdens the exercise of religion, we see no reason to require that the exemption come packaged with benefits to secular entities. . . .

[In] a case such as this, where a statute is neutral on its face and motivated by a permissible purpose of limiting governmental interference with the exercise of religion, we see no justification for applying strict scrutiny to a statute that passes the *Lemon* test. The proper inquiry is whether Congress has chosen a rational classification to further a legitimate end. [As] applied to the nonprofit activities of religious employers, §702 is rationally related to the legitimate purpose of alleviating significant governmental interference with the ability of religious organizations to define and carry out their religious missions.

[Reversed.]

JUSTICE BRENNAN, with whom JUSTICE MARSHALL joins, concurring in the judgment.

I write separately to emphasize that my concurrence in the judgment rests on the fact that these cases involve a challenge to the application of §702's categorical exemption to the activities of a nonprofit organization. I believe that the particular character of nonprofit activity makes inappropriate a case-by-case determination whether its nature is religious or secular.

[Any] exemption from Title VII's proscription on religious discrimination necessarily has the effect of burdening the religious liberty of prospective and current employees. An exemption says that a person may be put to the choice of either conforming to certain religious tenets or losing a job opportunity, a promotion, or, as in this case, employment itself. The potential for coercion created by such a provision is in serious tension with our commitment to individual freedom of conscience in matters of religious belief.

At the same time, religious organizations have an interest in autonomy in ordering their internal affairs, so that they may be free to "select their own leaders, define their own doctrines, resolve their own disputes, and run their own institutions. Religion includes important communal elements for most believers. They exercise their religion through religious organizations, and these organizations must be protected by the [Free Exercise Clause.]" Laycock, Towards a General Theory of the Religion Clauses: The Case of Church Labor Relations and the Right to Church Autonomy, 81 Colum. L. Rev. 1373, 1389 (1981). For many individuals, religious activity derives meaning in large measure from participation in a larger religious community. Such a community represents an ongoing tradition of shared beliefs, an organic entity not reducible to a mere aggregation of individuals. Determining that certain activities are in furtherance of an organization's religious mission, and that only those committed to that mission should conduct them, is thus a means by which a religious community defines itself. Solicitude for a church's ability to do so reflects the idea that furtherance of the autonomy of religious organizations often furthers individual religious freedom as well.

The authority to engage in this process of self-definition inevitably involves what we normally regard as infringement on free exercise rights, since a religious organization is able to condition employment in certain activities on subscription to particular religious tenets. We are willing to countenance the imposition of such a condition because we deem it vital that, if certain activities constitute part of a religious community's practice, then a religious organization should be able to require that only members of its community perform those activities.

This rationale suggests that, ideally, religious organizations should be able to discriminate on the basis of religion only with respect to religious activities, so that a determination should be made in each case whether an activity is religious or secular. This is because the infringement on religious liberty that results from conditioning performance of secular activity upon religious belief cannot be defended as necessary for the community's self-definition. Furthermore, the authorization of discrimination in such circumstances [puts] at the disposal of religion the added advantages of economic leverage in the secular realm. As a result, the authorization of religious discrimination with respect to nonreligious activities [has] the effect of furthering religion in violation of the Establishment Clause.

What makes the application of a religious-secular distinction difficult is that the character of an activity is not self-evident. As a result, determining whether an activity is religious or secular requires a searching case-by-case analysis. This results in considerable ongoing government entanglement in religious affairs. Furthermore, this prospect of government intrusion raises concern that a religious organization may be chilled in its free exercise activity. While a church may regard the conduct of certain functions as integral to its mission, a court may disagree. A religious organization therefore would have an incentive to characterize as religious only those activities about which there likely would be no dispute, even if it genuinely believed that religious commitment was important in performing other tasks as well. As a result, the community's process of self-definition would be shaped in part by the prospects of litigation. A case-by-case analysis for all activities therefore would both produce excessive government entanglement with religion and create the danger of chilling religious activity.

The risk of chilling religious organizations is most likely to arise with respect to nonprofit activities. [Nonprofits] historically have been organized specifically to provide certain community services, not simply to engage in commerce. Churches often regard the provision of such services as a means of fulfilling religious duty and of providing an example of the way of life a church seeks to foster.

Nonprofit activities therefore are most likely to present cases in which characterization of the activity as religious or secular will be a close question. [This] substantial potential for chilling religious activity makes inappropriate a case-by-case determination of the character of a nonprofit organization, and justifies a categorical exemption for nonprofit activities. Such an exemption demarcates a sphere of deference with respect to those activities most likely to be religious. It permits infringement on employee free exercise rights in those instances in which discrimination is most likely to reflect a religious community's self-definition. While not every nonprofit activity may be operated for religious purposes, the likelihood that many are makes a categorical rule a suitable means to avoid chilling the exercise of religion. . . .

JUSTICE O'CONNOR, concurring in the judgment. . . .

In Wallace v. Jaffree, I noted a tension in the Court's use of the *Lemon* test to evaluate an Establishment Clause challenge to government efforts to accommodate the free exercise of religion: "On the one hand, a rigid application of the

Lemon test would invalidate legislation exempting religious observers from generally applicable government obligations. By definition, such legislation has a religious purpose and effect in promoting the free exercise of religion. On the other hand, judicial deference to all legislation that purports to facilitate the free exercise of religion would completely vitiate the Establishment Clause. Any statute pertaining to religion can be viewed as an 'accommodation' of free exercise rights."

In my view, the opinion for the Court leans toward the second of the two unacceptable options described above. [The] Court seems to suggest that the "effects" prong of the *Lemon* test is not at all implicated as long as the government action can be characterized as "allowing" religious organizations to advance religion, in contrast to government action directly advancing religion.

This distinction seems to me to obscure far more than to enlighten. Almost any government benefit to religion could be recharacterized as simply "allowing" a religion to better advance itself, unless perhaps it involved actual proselytization by government agents. . . .

The necessary first step in evaluating an Establishment Clause challenge to a government action lifting from religious organizations a generally applicable regulatory burden is to recognize that such government action does have the effect of advancing religion. The necessary second step is to separate those benefits to religion that constitutionally accommodate the free exercise of religion from those that provide unjustifiable awards of assistance to religious organizations. [The] inquiry [should] be "whether government's purpose is to endorse religion and whether the statute actually conveys a message of endorsement." . . .

[These] cases involve a government decision to lift from a nonprofit activity of a religious organization the burden of demonstrating that the particular nonprofit activity is religious as well as the burden of refraining from discriminating on the basis of religion. Because there is a probability that a nonprofit activity of a religious organization will itself be involved in the organization's religious mission, in my view the objective observer should perceive the government action as an accommodation of the exercise of religion rather than as a government endorsement of religion.

It is not clear, however, that activities conducted by religious organizations solely as profit-making enterprises will be as likely to be directly involved in the religious mission of the organization. . . .

[An opinion by Justice Blackmun, concurring in the judgment, is omitted.]

TEXAS MONTHLY v. BULLOCK, 489 U.S. 1 (1989). A sharply divided Court held unconstitutional a statute that exempted religious publications from a state sales tax. Justice Brennan's opinion, joined by Justices Marshall and Stevens, said that "government policies with secular objectives [may] incidentally benefit religion. The nonsectarian aims of government and religious groups often overlap, and this Court has never required that public authorities refrain from implementing reasonable measures to advance legitimate secular goals merely because they would thereby relieve religious groups of costs they would otherwise incur [citing Widmar v. Vincent, 454 U.S. 263 (1981), and *Walz*]." However, in such cases, "the benefits derived by religious organizations flowed to a large number of nonreligious groups as well. Indeed, were those benefits confined to religious organizations, they could not have appeared other than as state sponsorship of religion." The exemption for religious publications "lacks sufficient breadth to pass scrutiny under the Establishment Clause. [Insofar] as [the] subsidy is conferred upon a wide array of nonsectarian groups as well as religious groups in pursuit of some legitimate secular end, the fact that religious groups benefit incidentally does not deprive the subsidy of the secular purpose and primary effect mandated by the Establishment Clause. However, when government directs a subsidy exclusively to religious organizations that is not required by the Free Exercise Clause and that either burdens nonbeneficiaries markedly or cannot reasonably be seen as removing a significant state-imposed deterrent to the free exercise of religion, [it] 'provide[s] unjustifiable awards of assistance to religious organizations' and cannot but 'conve[y] a message of endorsement' to slighted members of the community [Amos]. This is particularly true where, as here, the subsidy is targeted at writings that *promulgate* the teachings of religious faiths." If the state subsidized groups contributing to the community's "cultural, intellectual, and moral betterment," the exemption for religious publications would be permitted, but "if Texas sought to promote reflection and discussion about questions of ultimate value and the contours of a good and meaningful life, then a tax exemption would have to be available to an extended range of associations whose publications were substantially devoted to such matters."

Justice Scalia's dissent, joined by Chief Justice Rehnquist and Justice Kennedy, argued that the tax exemption was a permissible accommodation of religion. For him, breadth of coverage is relevant only where the state justifies its legislation on entirely secular grounds, but "where accommodation of religion is the justification, by definition religion is being singled out." Although "it is not always easy to determine when accommodation slides over into promotion, and neutrality into favoritism," the tax exemption was an easy case because imposing a general sales tax on the sale of religious publications was at least arguably unconstitutional as a burden on religion. (Does this argument survive *Smith*, section C supra?) Justice Brennan's opinion rejected this argument on the ground that it was obviously not unconstitutional to impose a general sales tax on religious publications. For Justice Brennan, accommodations must not "impose substantial burdens on nonbeneficiaries [or must be] designed to alleviate government intrusions that might significantly deter adherents of a particular faith from conduct protected by the Free Exercise Clause." The tax exemption did burden nonbeneficiaries by increasing their tax bills and did not alleviate a "demonstrated and possibly grave imposition on religious activity sheltered by the Free Exercise Clause."

Justice Blackmun, whose opinion concurring in the result was joined by Justice O'Connor, expressed more sympathy with the accommodation argument. He argued that the tax exemption was unconstitutional because it was "limited to the sale of religious literature by a religious organization." How is this different from Justice Brennan's concern about the breadth of the exemption? (Justice White also concurred in the result, relying on Arkansas Writers' Project v. Ragland, Chapter 7, section F3, supra.)

BOARD OF EDUCATION OF KIRYAS JOEL VILLAGE SCHOOL DISTRICT v. GRUMET, 512 U.S. 687 (1994). The village of Kiryas Joel in New York is a religious enclave of Satmar Hasidim, a group of Orthodox Jews "who make few concessions to the modern world and go to great lengths to avoid assimilation." Most children in the village are educated in private religious schools. Educating handicapped children in such schools is quite expensive, and the village residents arranged to have a public school system provide education for their handicapped children in an annex to one of the religious schools. That arrangement ended after the Court's decision in Aguilar v. Felton, section B4 supra. The children were then sent to schools in the neighboring public school system. The village residents found the education there unsatisfactory in part because the children suffered "panic, fear and trauma" from "leaving their own community and being with people whose ways were so different." In 1989, the New York legislature enacted a statute designating the village of Kiryas Joel as a separate school district. The Supreme Court held the statute unconstitutional.

Justice Souter's opinion for the Court stated, "The fact that this school district was created by a special and unusual Act of the legislature [gives] reason for concern whether the benefit received by the Satmar community is one that the legislature will provide equally to other religious (and nonreligious) groups." For the Court, "[the] fundamental source of constitutional concern [is] that the legislature itself may fail to exercise governmental authority in a religiously neutral way. The anomalously case-specific nature of the legislature's exercise of state authority in creating this district for a religious community leaves the Court without any direct way to review such state action for the purpose of safeguarding a principle at the heart of the Establishment Clause, that government should not prefer one religion to another, or religion to irreligion." The difficulty was that Kiryas Joel had not received its authority "simply as one of many communities eligible for equal treatment under a general law," so the Court could not be sure "that the next similarly situated group seeking a school district of its own will receive one; [a] legislature's failure to enact a special law is itself unreviewable." The Court agreed that the state could "accommodate religious needs by alleviating special burdens," but creating a separate district "singles out a particular religious sect for special treatment" and thereby violated the principle that "neutrality as among religions must be honored."

Justice Stevens, joined by Justices Blackmun and Ginsburg, added that, to meet the concerns about "panic, fear and trauma," the state "could have taken steps to alleviate the children's fear by teaching their schoolmates to be tolerant and respectful of Satmar customs. Action of that kind would raise no constitutional concerns and would further the strong public interest in promoting diversity and understanding in the public schools." But the state's response, "a solution that affirmatively supports a religious sect's interest in segregating itself and preventing its children from associating with their neighbors," was unconstitutional. It "increased the likelihood that they would remain within the fold, faithful adherents of their parents' religious faith," and thereby "provided official support to cement the attachment of young adherents to a particular faith."

Justice Kennedy, concurring, argued that "[the] real vice of the school district [is] that New York created it by drawing political boundaries on the basis of religion." He criticized the Court's broader analysis. "[By] creating the district, New York did not impose or increase any burden on non-Satmars, compared to the burden it lifted from the Satmars, that might disqualify the District as a genuine accommodation." There was no evidence "that the legislature has denied another religious community like the Satmars its own school district under analogous circumstances. The legislature, like the judiciary, is sworn to uphold the

Constitution, and we have no reason to presume that the New York Legislature would not grant the same accommodation in a similar future case. The fact that New York singled out the Satmars for this special treatment indicates nothing other than the uniqueness of the handicapped Satmar children's plight. It is normal for legislatures to respond to problems as they arise — no less so when the issue is religious accommodation."

Justice O'Connor argued that "[the] Satmars' living arrangements were accommodated by their right — a right shared with all other communities, religious or not, throughout New York — to incorporate themselves as a village." In her view, "one's religion ought not affect one's legal rights or duties or benefits," even when the government was "acting to accommodate religion." Permissible accommodations could not involve "discriminations based on sect. [A] draft law may exempt conscientious objectors, but it may not exempt conscientious objectors whose objections are based on theistic belief (such as Quakers) as opposed to nontheistic belief (such as Buddhists) or atheistic belief." The New York statute "benefits one group" and should be treated "as a legislatively drawn religious classification." It was, for Justice O'Connor, "a close question, because the Satmars may be the only group who currently need this particular accommodation. The legislature may well be acting without any favoritism, so that if another group came to ask for a similar district, the group might get it on the same terms as the Satmars. But the nature of the legislative process makes it impossible to be sure of this. [A] group petitioning for a law may never get a definite response, or may get a 'no' based not on the merits but on the press of other business or the lack of an influential sponsor. Such a legislative refusal to act would not normally be reviewable by a court. Under these circumstances, it seems dangerous to validate what appears to me a clear religious preference." According to Justice O'Connor, "A district created under a generally applicable scheme would be acceptable even though it coincides with a village which was consciously created by its voters as an enclave for their religious group."

Justice Scalia's dissent was joined by Chief Justice Rehnquist and Justice Thomas. "[The] Founding Fathers would be astonished to find that the Establishment Clause [has] been employed to prohibit characteristically and admirably American accommodation of the religious practices (or more precisely, cultural peculiarities) of a tiny minority sect." As he saw it, "[T]he Court's 'no guarantee of neutrality' argument is an assertion of this Court's inability to control the New York Legislature's future denial of comparable accommodation. [Most] efforts at accommodation seek to solve a problem that applies to members of only one or a few religions. Not every religion uses wine in its sacraments, but that does not [require] the State granting such an exemption to explain in advance how it will treat every other claim for dispensation from its controlled-substances laws." The Court should not require "some 'up front' legislative guarantee of equal treatment for [other] sects."

Note: When — If Ever — Should Accommodations of Religion Be Permitted?

1. *The attractions of a doctrine of permissible accommodation.* Consider McConnell, Accommodation of Religion, 1985 Sup. Ct. Rev. 1, 1-3:

The much-discussed "tension" between the two Religion Clauses largely arises from the Court's substitution of a misleading formula (the three-part *Lemon* [test]) and subsidiary, instrumental, values (especially the separation of church and state) in place of the central value of religious liberty. [Between] the accommodations compelled by the Free Exercise Clause and the benefits to religion prohibited by the Establishment Clause there exists a class of permissible government actions toward religion, which have as their purpose and effects the facilitation of religious liberty. [Only] an interpretation of the Religion Clauses based on religious liberty [satisfactorily] distinguishes permissible accommodations from impermissible establishments.

See also McConnell, Accommodation of Religion: An Update and a Response to the Critics, 60 Geo. Wash. L. Rev. 685 (1992).

2. *Permissible accommodations and antidiscrimination legislation.* Thornton v. Caldor, 472 U.S. 703 (1985), held unconstitutional a Connecticut statute providing, "No person who states that a particular day of the week is observed as his Sabbath may be required by his employer to work on that day." Chief Justice Burger's opinion for the Court said that the statute imposes "an absolute duty to conform [business] practices to the particular religious practices of the employee. [The] State thus commands that Sabbath religious concerns automatically control over all secular interests at the workplace; the statute takes no account of the convenience or interests of the employer or those of other employees who do not observe a Sabbath." Justice O'Connor, joined by Justice Marshall, concurred, objecting to the "special and [absolute] protection" given to Sabbath observers over those with other "ethical and religious beliefs and practices." "The message conveyed is one of endorsement of a particular religious belief, to the detriment of those who do not share it."

Why are the statute's absolute nature and targeting on a particular religious practice impermissible? Consider the implications of Justice Brennan's emphasis in *Texas Monthly* that permissible accommodations must be sufficiently broad: The broader the accommodation, the more significantly it impairs the majority's ability to accomplish the substantive aims it seeks — raising revenue, for example. A requirement of breadth therefore makes permissible accommodations self-limiting, reducing the possibility that serious erosions of the antiestablishment value will occur.

Consider 42 U.S.C. §§2000e-2(a), 2000e(j):

> It shall be an unlawful employment practice for an employer to [discriminate] against any individual with respect to his compensation, terms, conditions, or privileges of employment [because] of such individual's [religion; the] term "religion" includes all aspects of religious observance and practice, as well as belief, unless an employer demonstrates that he is unable to reasonably accommodate an employee's [religious] observance or practice without undue hardship on the conduct of the employer's business.

These provisions were construed in Trans World Airlines v. Hardison, 432 U.S. 63 (1977), as not requiring an employer to adjust its seniority system to allow junior employees to avoid work on their Sabbaths by displacing senior employees entitled by the system to work on the other days. "To require TWA to bear more than a de minimis cost in order to give Hardison Saturdays off is an undue hardship."

In *Thornton*, Justice O'Connor's opinion distinguished Title VII because it required reasonable, not absolute, accommodation of all religious beliefs and practices. "[An] objective observer would perceive it as an anti-discrimination law rather than an endorsement of religion or a particular religious practice."

The opinions suggest that the more a statutory accommodation places a burden on nonbeneficiaries, the less likely it is a permissible accommodation. Consider the argument that, to the contrary, the greater the burden, the more permissible the accommodation because those feeling the burden will have more political influence in striking an appropriate balance. For a discussion of balancing interests in religious liberty against harms to third parties, see Lipson, On Balance: Religious Liberty and Third-Party Harms, 84 Minn. L. Rev. 589 (2000).

3. *Permissible accommodations and sect preference.* Lupu, The Lingering Death of Separationism, 62 Geo. Wash. L. Rev. 230, 270 (1994), says that New York in *Kiryas Joel* "predictably responded to the circumstances and political strength of the affected sect. [Is] it imaginable that New York State would create a new public school district at the behest of an insular group of Branch Davidians or members of the Unification Church?" If the presumption is that the legislature would not do so, how can the courts ever learn whether the legislature is in fact willing to act in a sect-neutral manner?

Does *Kiryas Joel* raise serious questions about state laws protecting the practice of labeling certain foods kosher (i.e., satisfying certain religious requirements) by making it a fraudulent practice to label a food as kosher when it has not received the approval of a specific religious institution? For a discussion, see Greenawalt, Religious Law and Civil Law: Using Secular Law to Assure Observance of Practices with Religious Significance, 71 S. Cal. L. Rev. 781, 793-796 (1998).

4. *The doctrine's justification.* On what theory of the establishment clause are statutory accommodations of religious practices permissible? Note that statutory accommodations have the purpose of benefiting religious belief as against nonbelief. Consider these possibilities:

a. Justice Souter's concurring opinion in Lee v. Weisman, section B1 supra, observed, "[Accommodation] must lift a discernible burden on the free exercise of religion. Concern for the position of religious individuals in the modern regulatory state cannot justify official solicitude for a religious practice unburdened by general rules. [Religious] students cannot complain that omitting prayers from their graduation ceremony would, in any realistic sense, 'burden' their spiritual callings." Note that the Court in *Amos* concedes that the church's free exercise rights would not be violated by requiring it to comply with the ban on religious discrimination as to the employees there. "Burden," thus, means some impairment of free exercise values short of a violation of free exercise rights.

b. Statutory accommodations are permissible solely to alleviate burdens that violate the free exercise clause, but legislatures have some leeway to determine what an appropriate balance is, or to devise accommodations that differ from judicially devised ones because of institutional differences between courts and legislatures.

c. Legislatures have substantial discretion to promote "free exercise values" by enacting statutory accommodations. Why is not voluntary devotional prayer in public schools a permissible accommodation? Consider also Chief Justice Burger's argument in dissent in *Jaffree*, section B3 supra, that Alabama's moment of silence statute "accommodates the purely private, voluntary religious choices of the individual pupils who wish to pray while at the same time creating a time for nonreligious reflection for those who do not choose to pray." Are such practices insufficiently broad to satisfy the doctrine's requirements?

Can any of these theories support the accommodation in *Kiryas Joel?*

Gedicks, The Normalized Free Exercise Clause, 75 Ind. L.J. 77 (2000), argues that the doctrine of permissible accommodations is inconsistent with equal protection doctrine dealing with affirmative action, which subjects assertedly benign legislation based on suspect traits to strict scrutiny. With which account of the doctrine of permissible accommodations is equal protection doctrine inconsistent?

Note: Free Exercise, Free Speech, and the Right of Expressive Association

What, if anything, does the free exercise clause add to the first amendment? Many activities associated with religion are forms of expression, either expressly (prayer) or as action that can be described as symbolic speech (some or all religious rituals). Would the analysis of the restriction on the use of peyote in *Smith* differ were that use characterized as symbolic speech? Could the restriction on ritual sacrifice invalidated in *Hialeah* be characterized as discrimination against expressive activity based on its content? Epps, What We Talk About When We Talk About Free Exercise, 30 Ariz. St. L.J. 563, 577-578 (1998), argues that distinctive free exercise issues arise only in connection with "rituals that are of a concededly religious nature with symbolic content but for which there is an empirical basis to believe that [the] ritual action may also have permanent consequences in the physical world."

1. *Content- or viewpoint-based discrimination.* Widmar v. Vincent, 454 U.S. 263 (1981), invoked the free speech clause to require a state university to make its facilities available to a student prayer group, just as it would make them available to other groups seeking to use the public forum it created. The Court held that a policy of "nondiscrimination against religious speech" would not violate the establishment clause. See also Lamb's Chapel v. Center Moriches Union Free School District, 508 U.S. 384 (1993), invalidating a school district's restriction on the after-hours use of its facilities by religious groups, finding the restriction viewpoint-based; Rosenberger v. Rector and Visitors of the University of Virginia, 515 U.S. 819 (1995), invalidating a university policy authorizing payment from the Student Activities Fund for the printing costs of a variety of student publications, but prohibiting payment for any student publication that "primarily promotes or manifests a particular belief in or about a deity or an ultimate reality." These cases find no establishment clause problem because, according to *Lamb's Chapel,* "There would have been no realistic danger that the community would think that the District was endorsing religion or any particular creed." See also Capitol Square Review and Advisory Board v. Pinette, 515 U.S. 753 (1995), finding no establishment clause violation in allowing a private group to display a Latin cross on public property and therefore requiring the board to permit the display.

Justice White, the only dissenter in *Widmar,* criticized the Court for arguing that "religious worship *qua* speech is not different from any other variety of protected speech. [This] proposition is plainly wrong. Were it right, the Religion Clauses would be emptied of any independent meaning in which religious practice took the form of speech." He would have distinguished between "verbal acts of worship and other verbal acts," saying that "the line may be difficult to draw in many cases," but that doing so was necessary in order to avoid the result that the university could "offer a class entitled 'Sunday Mass,' [indistinguishable] from a class entitled 'The History of the Catholic Church.'" The Court responded by noting that the distinction between worship and speech about religion had no "intelligible content" because "there is no indication when 'singing hymns, reading scripture, and teaching biblical principles' cease to be ['speech,'] despite their religious subject matter [and] become 'worship.'"

The Equal Access Act, 20 U.S.C. §4071 (1984), provides, "It shall be unlawful for any public secondary school which receives Federal financial assistance and which has a limited open forum to deny equal access [to] any students who wish to conduct a meeting within that limited open forum on the basis of the religious, political, philosophical, or other content of the speech at such meetings." A limited open forum is created when the school allows "noncurriculum related student groups to meet on school premises during noninstructional time." The Court upheld the constitutionality of the Equal Access Act in Board of Education of Westside Community Schools v. Mergens, 496 U.S. 226 (1990). Justice O'Connor's plurality opinion on the constitutional question concluded that "the logic of *Widmar* applies" to the Equal Access Act. Prohibiting discrimination on the basis of political as well as religious speech was a secular purpose under *Lemon*. Equal access would not have the effect of conveying a message of government endorsement of religion. "We think that secondary school students are mature enough and are likely to understand that a school does not endorse or support student speech that it merely permits on a nondiscriminatory basis." Congress had made a similar determination, and Justice O'Connor said that the Court should not "lightly second-guess [legislative] judgments, particularly where the judgments are based in part on empirical determinations," as this one was. She noted that "the broad spectrum of officially recognized student groups [counteracts] any possible message of official endorsement of or preference for religion or a particular religion. [To] the extent that a religious club is merely one of many different student-initiated voluntary clubs, students should perceive no message of government endorsement of religion."

2. *Religion in politics*. a. *Church members as political actors*. Torcaso v. Watkins, 367 U.S. 488 (1961), invalidated a provision in the Maryland Constitution requiring state officials to declare their belief in the existence of God. "[Neither] a State nor the Federal Government can constitutionally force a person 'to profess a belief or disbelief in any religion' [and] neither can aid those religions based on a belief in the existence of God as against those religions founded on different beliefs."

In McDaniel v. Paty, 435 U.S. 618 (1978), the Court invalidated, without dissent, a provision of the Tennessee Constitution barring ministers from serving as legislators or as delegates to the state's constitutional convention. Chief Justice Burger's plurality opinion reviewed the history of such disqualifications, which were in effect in seven of the original states and which were adopted by six states later admitted to the Union. Disqualification was designed "to assure the success of a new political experiment, the separation of church and state." But "as the value of the dis-establishment experiment was perceived, 11 of the 13 States [gradually] abandoned that limitation," until by 1900 only Maryland and Tennessee retained it. The opinion continued, "[T]he right to the free exercise of religion unquestionably encompasses the right to preach [and] to be a minister." If the disqualification "were viewed as depriving the clergy of a civil right solely because of their religious beliefs," *Torcaso* would control. But the disqualification was triggered by the minister's status, defined "in terms of conduct and activity rather than in terms of belief." Thus, the relevant precedent was *Yoder*, which required an "interest of the highest order." But the state had "failed to demonstrate that [the] dangers of clergy participation in the political process have not lost whatever validity they may once have enjoyed. [The] American experience provides no persuasive support for the fear that clergymen in public office will be less careful of anti-establishment interests or less faithful to their oaths of civil office than their unordained counterparts."

Justice Brennan, joined by Justice Marshall, and Justice Stewart submitted separate concurring opinions arguing that *Torcaso* controlled. Justice Brennan wrote, "[F]reedom of belief [embraces] freedom to profess or practice that belief, even including doing so to earn a livelihood." Tennessee's rule was therefore "absolutely prohibited," and no balancing of interests was required. Justice Brennan argued that

> public debate of religious ideas [may] arouse emotion, [but] the mere fact that a purpose of the Establishment Clause is to reduce or eliminate religious divisiveness or strife, does not place religious discussion, association, or political participation in a status less preferred than rights of [political] participation generally. [In] short, government may not as a goal promote "safe thinking" with respect to religion and fence out from political participation those [whom] it regards as overinvolved in religion. Religionists no less than members of any other group enjoy the full measure of protection afforded speech. [The] antidote which the Constitution provides against zealots who would inject sectarianism into the political process is to subject their ideas to refutation in the market-place of ideas and their platforms to rejection at the polls. With these safeguards [and] with judicial enforcement of the Establishment Clause, any measure of success they achieve must be short-lived, at best.

Justice White concurred in the judgment, relying on the equal protection clause rather than the free exercise clause, because he did not see how the minister "has been deterred in the observance of his religious beliefs."

What result in *McDaniel* under the free speech clause? Is the confidence expressed by Chief Justice Burger and Justice Brennan in the political process warranted? Should a state be precluded from taking a more jaundiced view of the efficacy of the political process in matters of religion?

b. *Churches as political actors.* Larkin v. Grendel's Den, 459 U.S. 116 (1982), held unconstitutional a statute granting churches and schools the power to veto the issuance of liquor licenses to restaurants within 500 feet of the church or school buildings. The Court acknowledged the "interest in being insulated from certain kinds of commercial establishments," but found that delegating the veto power to churches had the effect of advancing religion and "provides a significant symbolic benefit to religion in the minds of some." Further, the statute "enmeshes churches in the exercise of substantial governmental powers." Note that delegation of similar authority to other private organizations is unlikely to raise federal constitutional questions.

Justice Souter, writing only for a plurality in *Kiryas Joel*, regarded the New York statute as a delegation of state power to a religious institution, barred by *Larkin*. Justice Scalia's dissent called "breathtaking" this "steamrolling of the difference between civil authority held by a church, and civil authority held by members of a church." It "boils down to the quite novel proposition that any group of citizens (say, the residents of Kiryas Joel) can be invested with political power, but not if they all belong to the same religion. Of course such disfavoring of religion is positively antagonistic to the purposes of the Religion Clauses."

3. *The right of expressive association.* Had Congress not exempted it from regulation, would the right to expressive association of the church employer in *Amos* be violated by applying the antidiscrimination law to its workers in the nonprofit gymnasium? In a profit-making activity associated with the church? What accommodations, permissible under the Court's doctrine, would be required not by the free exercise clause as interpreted in *Smith* but by the right of expressive association? For a discussion of the right of expressive association, see Chapter 7, section E, supra.

Note: Concluding Observations

Do the preceding materials demonstrate that contemporary religion clause doctrine is hostile to religion in the name of neutrality? In a religiously pluralist nation with an expansive government, is neutrality toward religion possible? Are the two religion clauses incompatible in such a nation? The establishment clause requires (some sort of) neutrality, while the free exercise clause requires (some sort of) preference to religion and may permit other preferences. Does the concept of benevolent neutrality reconcile the clauses? When does a permissible benevolence become a prohibited encouragement? Consider whether the religion clauses are incompatible because of religious pluralism: Any purported benevolent encouragement of some or many religions will discourage others; given the range of actions required by some religions and prohibited by others, no regulation can be neutral in its effects as between some religions and others or between religion and nonreligion.

Consider the application of the "interest-convergence" thesis by Feldman, Principle, History, and Power: The Limits of the First Amendment Religion Clauses, 81 Iowa L. Rev. 833, 871-872 (1996): "[Outgroup] religions benefit only when their interests happen to converge [with] the interests of Christians. The benefits to outgroups [are] merely *incidental*, while the *primary* benefits of separation of church and state flow [to] Christianity. [While] the accrual of primary benefits to Christianity occasionally entails incidental benefits for outgroup religions, it also [imposes] certain costs on those [religions]. [The] principle of separation of church and state [benefits] Christianity and harms minority religions by furnishing a facade of governmental neutrality and religious freedom that hides and legitimates [Christian] cultural imperialism."

IX

The Constitution, Baselines, and the Problem of Private Power

It is a commonplace that the commands of the Constitution are directed to governmental entities, not to private parties. Is there a good reason for this limitation on the Constitution's reach? On a standard view, the limitation is based on the judgment that government generally has more power than private entities and has a monopoly on the use of force to accomplish its objectives.

Note that for at least two reasons, the state action limitation may tell us less than we might think. First, any meaningful constitutional right requires government to respond when rights are invaded. For example, The Civil Rights Cases, section A infra, hold that the thirteenth amendment prohibits purely private acts of enslavement. In this sense, the thirteenth amendment seems to be an exception to the proposition that the Constitution applies only to government. But to have practical meaning, the amendment must require public entities — government — to do something to outlaw the "prohibited" acts.

Second, the statement that the Constitution controls only government conduct *tells us nothing about what the Constitution requires the government to do.* Perhaps some constitutional provisions require government to control private conduct. For example, even if a private person's denial of equal treatment to blacks does not itself violate the fourteenth amendment, the state's decision to permit private persons to deny equal treatment to blacks *might* violate that amendment. Whether it does depends on what the fourteenth amendment means. The state action doctrine says that the government and not some private person must be the defendant. But it does not say that the government is under no obligation to stop private people from injuring other people.

To have meaning, then, the state action doctrine must be supplemented by some substantive ideas about the meaning of relevant constitutional provisions. This chapter examines the Court's efforts to develop such ideas.

A. STATE ACTION, FEDERALISM, AND INDIVIDUAL AUTONOMY

A state action requirement might be thought to define an area that must remain beyond the reach of national power — at least national judicial power. Consider, for example, Lugar v. Edmondson Oil Co., 457 U.S. 922, 936 (1982): "Careful adherence to the 'state action' requirement preserves an area of individual freedom by limiting the reach of federal law and federal judicial power. [A] major consequence is to require the courts to respect the limits of their own power as directed against state governments and private interests. Whether this is good or bad policy, it is a fundamental fact of our political order."

The notion that "limiting the reach of federal law" serves to "preserve individual freedom" is a controversial one. The fourteenth amendment, for example, was premised to some degree on the opposite assumption — that an extension of federal law was essential to the preservation of individual rights. See Chapter 5, section A, supra. Nonetheless, the Court's analysis of the state action issue has long been influenced by the assumed link among individual freedom, state action requirements, and restrictions on federal power. Indeed, this "fundamental fact of our political order" was arguably central to the Court's earliest effort to articulate a state action doctrine.

1.   State Action and Federalism

The modern Court has held that state action is a prerequisite to the assertion of rights contained in both the first eight amendments (originally applicable only to the federal government) and the fourteenth amendment (applicable to the states). But historically the requirement attracted little attention until passage of the Reconstruction amendments after the Civil War.

After the ratification of these amendments, the Court was required to decide the extent to which they changed the traditional balance between state and federal authority. One view was that the new amendments gave the federal government plenary authority to protect individual rights — against both public and private actors. A second view was that the amendments left untouched the states' traditional functions and authorized federal intervention only when the states defaulted in their primary obligations. See Chapter 5, section A2, supra.

The Court's earliest state action decision looked to principles of federalism to give content to the doctrine.

THE CIVIL RIGHTS CASES, 109 U.S. 3 (1883). The Civil Rights Act of 1875 provided that all persons were "entitled to the full and equal enjoyment of the accommodations, advantages, facilities, and privileges of inns, public conveyances, on land or water, theatres, and other places of public amusement; subject only to the conditions and limitations established by law, and applicable alike to citizens of every race and color, regardless of any previous condition of servitude." Private persons violating these rights were subject to civil damages and criminal penalties. The constitutionality of the act was challenged on the ground that it was not authorized by any substantive grant of power to the federal government. In an eight-to-one decision, the Court agreed and invalidated the act.

Justice Bradley delivered the Court's opinion: "Has Congress constitutional power to make such a law? Of course, no one will contend that the power to pass it was contained in the Constitution before the adoption of the [thirteenth, fourteenth, and fifteenth] amendments. . . .

"[The fourteenth amendment is prohibitory in its character, and prohibitory upon the states. [Individual] invasion of individual rights is not the subject matter of the amendment. . . .

"[The Civil Rights Act, in contrast,] proceeds ex directo to declare that certain acts committed by individuals shall be deemed offences, and shall be prosecuted and punished by proceedings in the courts of the United States. It does not profess to be corrective of any constitutional wrong committed by the states. [It] applies equally to cases arising in States which have the justest laws respecting the personal rights of citizens, and whose authorities are ever ready to enforce such laws, as to those which arise in States that may have violated the prohibition of the amendment. In other words, it steps into the domain of local jurisprudence and lays down rules for the conduct of individuals in society towards each other, and imposes sanctions for the enforcement of those rules, without referring in any manner to any supposed action of the State or its authorities. . . .

"The wrongful act of an individual, unsupported by any [State] authority is simply a private wrong, or a crime of that individual; an invasion of the rights of the injured party, it is true, whether they affect his person, his property, or his reputation; but if not sanctioned in some way by the State, or not done under State authority, his rights remain in full force, and may presumably be vindicated by resort to the laws of the State for redress. An individual cannot deprive a man of his right to vote, to hold property, to buy and sell, to sue in the courts, or to be a witness or a juror; he may, by force or fraud, interfere with the enjoyment of the right in a particular case; [but] unless protected in these wrongful acts by some shield of State law or State authority, he cannot destroy or injure the right; he will only render himself amenable to satisfaction or punishment; and amenable therefor to the laws of the State where the wrongful acts are committed."

Defenders of the act also relied on Congress's power to enforce the thirteenth amendment, which abolished slavery. The Court agreed that the thirteenth amendment, unlike the fourteenth, authorized legislation that was "primary and direct in its character; for the amendment is not a mere prohibition of State laws establishing or upholding slavery, but an absolute declaration that slavery or involuntary servitude shall not exist in any part of the United States."

Nonetheless, the Court concluded that the statute was not authorized under the thirteenth amendment because the refusal to serve a person in a public accommodation was no more than an ordinary civil injury and not a badge of slavery. "[Such] an act of refusal has nothing to do with slavery or involuntary servitude, and [if] it is violative of any right of the party, his redress is to be sought under the laws of the State; or if those laws are adverse to his rights and do not protect him, his remedy will be found in the corrective legislation which Congress has adopted, or may adopt, for counteracting the effect of State laws, or State action, prohibited by the Fourteenth Amendment. It would be running the slavery argument into the ground to make it apply to every act of discrimination which a person may see fit to make as to the guests he will entertain, or as to the people he will take into his coach or cab or car, or admit to his concert or theatre, or deal with in other matters of intercourse or business. . . .

"When a man has emerged from slavery, and by the aid of beneficent legislation has shaken off the inseparable concomitants of that state, there must be some stage in the progress of his elevation when he takes the rank of a mere citizen, and ceases to be the special favorite of the law, and when his rights as a citizen, or a man, are to be protected in the ordinary modes by which other men's rights are protected."

Only Justice Harlan dissented from the Court's opinion: "The [majority] opinion in these cases proceeds, it seems to me, upon grounds entirely too narrow and artificial. I cannot resist the conclusion that the substance and spirit of the recent amendments of the Constitution have been sacrificed by a subtle and ingenious verbal criticism. . . .

"[Since] slavery [was] the moving or principal cause of the adoption of [the thirteenth] amendment, and since that institution rested wholly upon the inferiority, as a race, of those held in bondage, their freedom necessarily involved immunity from, and protection against, all discrimination against them, because of their race, in respect of such civil rights as belong to freemen of other races. Congress, therefore, under its express power to enforce that amendment, by appropriate legislation, may enact laws to protect that people against the deprivation, *because of their race*, of any civil rights granted to other freemen in the same State; and such legislation may be of a direct and primary character, operating upon States, their officers and agents, and, also upon, at least, such individuals and corporations as exercise public functions and wield power and authority under the State. . . .

"The assumption that [the fourteenth] amendment consists wholly of prohibitions upon State laws and State proceedings in hostility to its provisions, is unauthorized by its language. The first clause of the first section — 'All persons born or naturalized in the United States, and subject to the jurisdiction thereof, are citizens of the United States, and of the State wherein they reside' — is of a distinctly affirmative character. . . .

"The citizenship thus acquired by [the black] race, in virtue of an affirmative grant from the nation, may be protected, not alone by the judicial branch of the government, but by congressional legislation of a primary direct character; this, because the power of Congress is not restricted to the enforcement of prohibitions upon State law or State action. It is, in terms distinct and positive, to enforce 'the *provisions* of *this article*' of the amendment; not simply those of a prohibitive character, but the provisions — *all* of the provisions — affirmative and prohibitive, of the amendment. . . .

"It is, I submit, scarcely just to say that the colored race has been the special favorite of the laws. The statute of 1875, now adjudged to be unconstitutional, is for the benefit of citizens of every race and color. What the nation, through Congress, has sought to accomplish in reference to that race is, — what had already been done in every State of the Union for the white race — to secure and protect rights belonging to them as freemen and citizens; nothing more.

"[Today] it is the colored race which is denied, by corporations and individuals wielding public authority, rights fundamental in their freedom and citizenship. At some future time, it may be that some other race will fall under the ban of race discrimination. If the constitutional amendments be enforced, according to the intent with which, as I conceive, they were adopted, there cannot be, in this republic any class of human beings in practical subjection to another class, with power in the latter to dole out to the former just such privileges as they may choose to grant."

Note: Federalism and the Substantive Content of the State Action Doctrine

The Court has read The Civil Rights Cases to establish "the essential dichotomy [between] deprivation by the State, subject to scrutiny under [the fourteenth amendment,] and private conduct [against] which the Fourteenth Amendment offers no shield." Jackson v. Metropolitan Edison Co., 419 U.S. 345, 349 (1974). And the Court in The Civil Rights Cases did assert that "[i]ndividual invasion of individual rights is not the subject matter of the [fourteenth] amendment." But by itself this proposition tells us little about what should count as a *state* invasion of individual rights. Perhaps it counts as a state invasion of individual rights for a state *to fail to remedy* acts of racial discrimination undertaken by owners of public accommodations who are required by state law to serve the public. Consider in this regard the Court's argument in The Civil Rights Cases that a wrongful act, unsupported by state authority, cannot by itself violate legal rights so long as the victim can look to state law for redress; consider especially its complaint that the 1875 act "applies equally to cases arising in States which have the justest laws respecting the personal rights of citizens, and whose authorities are ever ready to enforce such laws, as to those which arise in States that may have violated the prohibition of the amendment." Is the Court suggesting that the national government might control private discrimination if the states are failing to do so?

Consider also Justice Bradley's comments on the fourteenth amendment in correspondence with Circuit Judge (later Justice) Wood, written twelve years before he authored the majority opinion in The Civil Rights Cases: "[The fourteenth amendment] not only prohibits the making or enforcing of laws which shall abridge the privileges of the citizen; but prohibits the states from denying to all persons within its jurisdiction the equal protection of the laws. [Denying] includes inaction as well as action. And denying the equal protection of the laws includes the omission to protect, as well as the omission to pass laws for protection." (The correspondence is quoted in Bell v. Maryland, 378 U.S. 226, 309-310 (1964) (Goldberg, J., concurring).)

Under this view of the matter, The Civil Rights Cases may stand for the proposition that the states are the primary guarantors of the rights of their citizens, and that the federal government may protect those rights if — but only if — the states fail to do so. Note that this position suggests both a broad and a narrow conception of federal power. It is broad in the sense that it treats state failures to act as state action for purposes of the fourteenth amendment; it is narrow in the sense that it incorporates a federalism-based limit on the federal government's power to act.

This view was, however, severely qualified, and perhaps even rejected, in United States v. Morrison, 120 S. Ct. 1740 (2000), where the Court held that the Violence against Women Act was beyond congressional power under the fourteenth amendment. Congress defended the act, which created a federal cause of action by victims against perpetrators of "a crime of violence motivated by gender," in part on the ground that states had not provided sufficient "protection" against such crimes, and hence a federal cause of action was necessary to ensure equal protection of the laws. The Court acknowledged legislative findings of bias in state criminal justice systems, but emphasized that Congress could not reach private conduct, which the act purported to do, by making ordinary people defendants, not state actors. This appears to be an authoritative ruling that Congress cannot reach private conduct under section 5 of the fourteenth amendment.

To the claim that the civil action was necessary to counteract state discrimination, the Court said that the remedy did not have a "congruence and proportionality" to the injury sought to be prevented. The act "visits no consequence whatever on any" state official "involved in investigating or prosecuting" sex-related crimes. Because it did not punish state officials, and because it "applies uniformly throughout the nation," it was different from other cases in which Congress was allowed, under section 5 of the fourteenth amendment, to proceed prophylactically.

Question: If states in fact fail to provide "equal protection" to women who are subject to violence, why isn't a federal civil rights action against private actors a perfectly reasonable response, not to private action, but to violations of "equal protection" on the part of the states?

2.   *State Action and Individual Autonomy*

Might we look to principles about the appropriate scope of individual autonomy to give content to the state action requirement? According to this view, the Constitution is designed primarily to protect individual freedom. Without some sort of state action doctrine, private autonomy would be subject to the same limitations as government autonomy. Instead of *protecting* individual rights from *legislative* interference, the Constitution might *subject* them to *judicial* interference. It is easy to imagine the extreme consequences that might follow. Newspapers might be prohibited from exclusively promoting a particular point of view. Private homeowners might be precluded from choosing their guests on racial or political grounds. (Note that whether these consequences would follow would depend on the Court's interpretation of the relevant constitutional provisions.)

Consider in this regard Columbia Broadcasting System (CBS) v. Democratic National Committee, 412 U.S. 94 (1973). Respondents claimed that the refusal of broadcasters to accept their editorial advertisements violated the first amendment. The Federal Communications Commission rejected this contention and refused to require that broadcasters accept such advertisements. The Court agreed with the commission.

In a portion of his plurality opinion joined by only two other justices, Chief Justice Burger argued that the first amendment claim failed because the broadcasters' decision could not be attributed to the government:

> Were we to read the First Amendment to spell out governmental action in the circumstances presented here, few licensee decisions on the content of broadcasts or the processes of editorial evaluation would escape constitutional scrutiny. . . .
>
> [It] would be anomalous for us to hold, in the name of promoting the constitutional guarantees of free expression, that the day-to-day editorial decisions of broadcast licensees are subject to the kind of restraints urged by respondents. To do so in the name of the First Amendment would be a contradiction. Journalistic discretion would in many ways be lost to the rigid limitations that the First Amendment imposes on Government. Application of such standards to broadcast licensees would

be antithetical to the very ideal of vigorous, challenging debate on issues of public interest.

Is the result in *CBS* really protective of private autonomy? Note that the result maximizes the journalistic freedom of broadcasters, who need not account to a court or government agency for their editorial decisions. But it arguably does so at the expense of the freedom of those wishing to present editorial advertisements, who may be prevented from securing a forum.

Note also that a finding of no state action means only that the Constitution does not of its own force regulate the activity. It does not follow from such a finding that the private actor is constitutionally immune from legislative regulation. Private discriminators are not subject to the Constitution, but they are subject to civil rights statutes. For example, in Hudgens v. NLRB, 424 U.S. 507 (1976), the Court held that the decision of a privately owned shopping center to exclude peaceful picketers could not be attributed to the government and therefore did not violate the first amendment, but in PruneYard Shopping Center v. Robins, 447 U.S. 74 (1980), the Court rejected a shopping center owner's first amendment objection when a state chose to outlaw such exclusions.

B. PURE INACTION AND THE THEORY OF GOVERNMENTAL NEUTRALITY

Typically the Court has organized the state action inquiry under two rubrics. (1) Sometimes the Court finds that a private actor must be subject to constitutional requirements because the state has delegated a traditional state (or "public") function to a private entity. (2) Sometimes the Court finds that a private actor must be subject to constitutional requirements (a) because the state has become entangled with a private entity or (b) because it has approved, encouraged, or facilitated private conduct. When the state itself is acting — when, in other words, the state's involvement *is* "immediately obvious" — no further inquiry is necessary. We now turn to what seems to be the simplest case: "pure" state inaction.

1. Pure Inaction

DESHANEY v. WINNEBAGO COUNTY DEPARTMENT OF SOCIAL SERVICES, 489 U.S. 189 (1989). When petitioner Joshua DeShaney was one-year-old, a Wyoming court granted his parents a divorce and awarded custody to his father. Shortly thereafter the father moved to Winnebago County, Wisconsin. Two years later respondent social workers working for Winnebago County began receiving reports that the father was physically abusing Joshua. The caseworkers carefully noted each of these reports, as well as Joshua's suspicious injuries, but took no action to remove him from his father's custody. Eventually, when Joshua was four years old, his father beat him so severely that he suffered permanent brain injuries that left him profoundly retarded and confined to an institution for life. This was an action brought by Joshua and his mother claiming that the state's conduct deprived him of his liberty in violation of the due process clause of the fourteenth amendment.

Justice Rehnquist delivered the Court's opinion: "[Nothing] in the language of the Due Process Clause itself requires the State to protect the life, liberty, and property of its citizens against invasion by private actors. The Clause is phrased as a limitation on the State's power to act, not as a guarantee of certain minimal levels of safety and security. [Nor] does history support such an expansive reading of the constitutional text. [Its] purpose was to protect the people from the State, not to ensure that the State protected them from each other. The Framers were content to leave the extent of governmental obligation in the latter area to the democratic political processes. . . .

"Petitioners contend, however, that even if the Due Process Clause imposes no affirmative obligation on the State to provide the general public with adequate protective services, such a duty may arise out of certain 'special relationships' created or assumed by the State with respect to particular individuals. . . .

"We reject this argument. It is true that in certain limited circumstances the Constitution imposes upon the State affirmative duties of care and protection with respect to particular individuals. . . .

"[But these cases] stand only for the proposition that when the State takes a person into its custody and holds him there against his will, the Constitution imposes upon it a corresponding duty to assume some responsibility for his safety and general well-being. [The] affirmative duty to protect arises not from the State's knowledge of the individual's predicament or from its expressions of intent to help him, but from the limitation which it has imposed on his freedom to act on his own behalf.

"Judges and lawyers, like other humans, are moved by natural sympathy in a case like this to find a way for Joshua and his mother to receive adequate compensation for the grievous harm inflicted upon them. But before yielding to that impulse, it is well to remember once again that the harm was inflicted not by the state of Wisconsin, but by Joshua's father. [In] defense of [the state officials] it must also be said that had they moved too soon to take custody of the son away from the father, they would likely have been met with charges of improperly intruding into the parent-child relationship, charges based on the same Due Process Clause that forms the basis for the present charge of failure to provide adequate protection."

Justice Brennan, joined by Justices Marshall and Blackmun, dissented: "It may well be, as the Court decides, that the Due Process Clause as construed by our prior cases creates no general right to basic governmental services. That, however, is not the question presented here. . . .

"In a constitutional setting that distinguishes sharply between action and inaction, one's characterization of the misconduct alleged [may] effectively decide the case. Thus, by leading off with a discussion (and rejection) of the idea that the Constitution imposes on the States an affirmative duty to take basic care of their citizens, the Court foreshadows — perhaps even preordains — its conclusion that no duty existed even on the specific facts before us. . . .

"The Court's baseline is the absence of positive rights in the Constitution and a concomitant suspicion of any claim that seems to depend on such rights. From this perspective, the DeShaneys' claim is first and foremost about inaction (the failure, here, of respondents to take steps to protect Joshua), and only tangentially about action (the establishment of a state program specifically designed to help children like Joshua). And from this perspective, holding these Wisconsin officials liable — where the only difference between this case and one involving a general claim to protective services is Wisconsin's establishment and operation of a program to protect children — would seem to punish an effort that we should seek to promote.

"I would begin from the opposite direction. I would focus first on the action that Wisconsin *has* taken with respect to Joshua and children like him, rather than on the actions that the State failed to take. . . .

"Wisconsin law invites — indeed, directs — citizens and other governmental entities to depend on local departments of social services such as respondent to protect children from abuse. . . .

"In these circumstances, a private citizen, or even a person working in a government agency other than [the Department of Social Services] would doubtless feel that her job was done as soon as she had reported her suspicions of child abuse to [the department]. If [the department] ignores or dismisses these suspicions, no one will step in to fill the gap. [Conceivably], then, children like Joshua are made worse off by the existence of this program when the persons and entities charged with carrying it out fail to do their jobs."

Justice Blackmun also filed a dissenting opinion.

Flagg Brothers v. Brooks

436 U.S. 149 (1978)

MR. JUSTICE REHNQUIST delivered the opinion of the Court.

The question presented by this litigation is whether a warehouseman's proposed sale of goods entrusted to him for storage, as permitted by New York Uniform Commercial Code §7-210, is an action properly attributable to the State of New York. [Section 7-210 provides that after proper notification, a warehouseman may satisfy a lien on goods in his possession by selling the goods.]

I

[When respondent Brooks was evicted from her apartment, the city marshal arranged for storage of her possessions in petitioner's warehouse. After a series of disputes over the validity of petitioner's charges for moving and storage, petitioner sent Brooks a letter threatening sale of the possessions. Brooks thereupon initiated this action, claiming, inter alia, that the sale pursuant to section 7-210 without a prior judicial hearing would violate the due process clause. She relied on a series of decisions in which the Court had held that due process requires that debtors be afforded a hearing before a creditor can utilize remedies involving the deprivation of property. See North Georgia Finishing, Inc. v. Di-Chem, Inc., 419 U.S. 601 (1975); Fuentes v. Shevin, 407 U.S. 67 (1972); Sniadach v. Family Finance Corp., 395 U.S. 337 (1969). Brooks was later joined in her action by respondent Jones, whose goods had also been stored by petitioner following her eviction.]

II

[It] must be noted that respondents have named no public officials as defendants in this action. The city marshal, who supervised their evictions, was dismissed from the case by the consent of all the parties. This total absence of overt official involvement plainly distinguishes this case from earlier decisions imposing procedural restrictions on creditors' remedies such as [*North Georgia Finishing; Fuentes*; and *Sniadach*]. In those cases, the Court was careful to point out that the dictates of the Due Process Clause "attac[h] only to the deprivation of an interest encompassed within the Fourteenth Amendment's protection." [*Fuentes.*] While as a factual matter any person with sufficient physical power may deprive a person of his property, only a State or a private person whose action "may be fairly treated as that of the State itself," [Jackson v. Metropolitan Edison Co., 419 U.S. 345 (1974)], may deprive him of "an interest encompassed within the Fourteenth Amendment's protection," [*Fuentes*]. Thus, the only issue presented by this case is whether Flagg Brothers' action may fairly be attributed to the State of New York. We conclude that it may not.

III

Respondents' primary contention is that New York has delegated to Flagg Brothers a power "traditionally exclusively reserved to the State." [*Jackson.*] They argue that the resolution of private disputes is a traditional function of civil government, and that the State in §7-210 has delegated this function to Flagg Brothers. Respondents, however, have read too much into the language of our previous cases. While many functions have been traditionally performed by governments, very few have been "exclusively reserved to the State." . . .

[The] proposed sale by Flagg Brothers under §7-210 is not the only means of resolving this purely private dispute. Respondent Brooks has never alleged that state law barred her from seeking a waiver of Flagg Brothers' right to sell her goods at the time she authorized their storage. Presumably, respondent Jones, who alleges that she never authorized the storage of her goods, could have sought to replevy her goods at any time under state law. The challenged statute itself provides a damages remedy against the warehouseman for violations of its provisions. This system of rights and remedies, recognizing the traditional place of private arrangements in ordering relationships in the commercial world, can hardly be said to have delegated to Flagg Brothers an exclusive prerogative of the sovereign.[10]

10. It is undoubtedly true, as our Brother Stevens says in dissent, that "respondents have a property interest in the possessions that the warehouseman proposes to sell." But that property interest is not a monolithic, abstract concept hovering in the legal stratosphere. It is a bundle of rights in personalty, the metes and bounds of which are determined by the decisional and statutory law of the State of New York. The validity of the property interest in these possessions which respondents previously acquired from some other private person depends on New York law, and the manner in which that same property interest in these same possessions may be lost or transferred to still another private person likewise depends on New York law. It would intolerably broaden, beyond the scope of any of our previous cases, the notion of state action under the Fourteenth Amendment to hold that the mere existence of a body of property law in a State, whether decisional or statutory, itself amounted to "state action" even though no state process or state officials were ever involved in enforcing that body of law.

This situation is clearly distinguishable from cases such as [*North Georgia Finishing; Fuentes;*

Whatever the particular remedies available under New York law, we do not consider a more detailed description of them necessary to our conclusion that the settlement of disputes between debtors and creditors is not traditionally an exclusive public function.[11] . . .

IV

Respondents further urge that Flagg Brothers' proposed action is properly attributable to the State because the State has authorized and encouraged it in enacting §7-210. [This] Court, however, has never held that a State's mere acquiescence in a private action converts that action into that of the State.

[It] is quite immaterial that the State has embodied its decision not to act in statutory form. If New York had no commercial statutes at all, its courts would still be faced with the decision whether to prohibit or to permit the sort of sale threatened here the first time an aggrieved bailor came before them for relief. [If] the mere denial of judicial relief is considered sufficient encouragement to make the State responsible for those private acts, all private deprivations of property would be converted into public acts whenever the State, for whatever reason, denies relief sought by the putative property owner.

[Here,] the State of New York has not compelled the sale of a bailor's goods, but has merely announced the circumstances under which its courts will not interfere with a private sale. Indeed, the crux of respondents' complaint is not that the State *has* acted, but that it has *refused* to act. This statutory refusal to act is no different in principle from an ordinary statute of limitations whereby the State declines to provide a remedy for private deprivations of property after the passage of a given period of time.

[Reversed.]

Mr. Justice Brennan took no part in the consideration or decision in these cases.

[Justice Marshall's dissenting opinion is omitted.]

---

and *Sniadach*]. In each of those cases a government official participated in the physical deprivation of what had concededly been the constitutional plaintiff's property under state law before the deprivation occurred. The constitutional protection attaches not because, as in *North Georgia Finishing*, a clerk issued a ministerial writ out of the court, but because as a result of that writ the property of the debtor was seized and impounded by the affirmative command of the law of Georgia. The creditor in *North Georgia Finishing* had not simply sought to pursue the collection of his debt by private means permissible under Georgia law; he had invoked the authority of the Georgia court, which in turn had ordered the garnishee not to pay over money which previously had been the property of the debtor. See Virginia v. Rives, 100 U.S. 313, 318 (1880); Shelley v. Kraemer, 334 U.S. 1 (1948). . . .

11. It may well be, as my Brother Stevens' dissent contends, that "[t]he power to order legally binding surrenders of property and the constitutional restrictions on that power are necessary correlatives in our system." But here New York, unlike Florida in *Fuentes*, Georgia in *North Georgia Finishing*, and Wisconsin in *Sniadach*, has not ordered respondents to surrender any property whatever. It has merely enacted a statute which provides that a warehouseman conforming to the provisions of the statute may convert his traditional lien into good title. There is no reason whatever to believe that either Flagg Brothers or respondents could not, if they wished, seek resort to the New York courts in order to either compel or prevent the "surrenders of property" to which that dissent refers, and that the compliance of Flagg Brothers with applicable New York property law would be reviewed after customary notice and hearing in such a proceeding.

MR. JUSTICE STEVENS, with whom MR. JUSTICE WHITE and MR. JUSTICE MAR-SHALL join, dissenting. . . .

[The] question is whether a state statute which authorizes a private party to de-prive a person of his property without his consent must meet the requirements of the Due Process Clause of the Fourteenth Amendment. This question must be an-swered in the affirmative unless the State has virtually unlimited power to trans-fer interests in private property without any procedural protections. . . .

In determining that New York's statute cannot be scrutinized under the Due Process Clause, the Court reasons that the warehouseman's proposed sale is solely private action because the state statute "*permits* but does not compel" the sale, (emphasis added), and because the warehouseman has not been delegated a power "*exclusively* reserved to the State" (emphasis added). Under this approach a State could enact laws authorizing private citizens to use self-help in countless situations without any possibility of federal challenge. A state statute could autho-rize the warehouseman to retain all proceeds of the lien sale, even if they far ex-ceeded the amount of the alleged debt; it could authorize finance companies to enter private homes to repossess merchandise; or indeed, it could authorize "any person with sufficient physical power," to acquire and sell the property of his weaker neighbor. An attempt to challenge the validity of any such outrageous statute would be defeated by the reasoning the Court uses today: The Court's ra-tionale would characterize action pursuant to such a statute as purely private ac-tion, which the State permits but does not compel, in an area not exclusively re-served to the State.

As these examples suggest, the distinctions between "permission" and "com-pulsion" on the one hand, and "exclusive" and "nonexclusive," on the other, can-not be determinative factors in state-action analysis. There is no great chasm between "permission" and "compulsion" requiring particular state action to fall within one or the other definitional camp. [In] this case, the State of New York, by enacting §7-210 of the Uniform Commercial Code, has acted in the most ef-fective and unambiguous way a State can act. This section specifically authorizes petitioner Flagg Brothers to sell respondents' possessions; it details the proce-dures that petitioner must follow; and it grants petitioner the power to convey good title to goods that are now owned by respondents to a third party.

[Cases] such as *North Georgia Finishing* must be viewed as reflecting this Court's recognition of the significance of the State's role in defining *and control-ling* the debtor-creditor relationship. The Court's language to this effect in the var-ious debtor-creditor cases has been unequivocal. In Fuentes v. Shevin the Court stressed that the statutes in question "abdicate[d] effective state control over state power." And it is clear that what was of concern in *Shevin* was the *private* use of state power to achieve a nonconsensual resolution of a commercial dispute.

[It] is important to emphasize that, contrary to the Court's apparent fears, this conclusion does not even remotely suggest that "all private deprivations of prop-erty [will] be converted into public acts whenever the State, for whatever reason, denies relief sought by the putative property owner." The focus is not on the pri-vate deprivation but on the state authorization. "[W]hat is always vital to remem-ber is that it is the *state*'s conduct, whether action or inaction, not the *private* con-duct, that gives rise to constitutional attack." Friendly, The Dartmouth College Case and The Public-Private Penumbra, 12 Texas Quarterly, No. 2, p. 17 (1969) (Supp.) (emphasis in original). The State's conduct in this case takes the concrete form of a statutory enactment, and it is that statute that may be challenged. . . .

Finally, it is obviously true that the overwhelming majority of disputes in our society are resolved in the private sphere. But it is no longer possible, if it ever was, to believe that a sharp line can be drawn between private and public actions.

[In] the broadest sense, we expect government "to provide a reasonable and fair framework of rules which facilitate commercial transactions. . . ." This "framework of rules" is premised on the assumption that the State will control nonconsensual deprivations of property and that the State's control will, in turn, be subject to the restrictions of the Due Process Clause. The power to order legally binding surrenders of property and the constitutional restrictions on that power are necessary correlatives in our system. In effect, today's decision allows the State to divorce these two elements by the simple expedient of transferring the implementation of its policy to private parties. Because the Fourteenth Amendment does not countenance such a division of power and responsibility, I respectfully dissent.

LUGAR v. EDMONDSON OIL CO., 457 U.S. 922 (1982). Lugar was indebted to Edmondson Oil, who sued him in state court. Ancillary to that action, and pursuant to state law, Edmondson Oil filed an ex parte petition for prejudgment attachment of certain of Lugar's property. Acting on the petition, the clerk of the state court issued a writ of attachment, which was executed by the county sheriff. This effectively sequestered Lugar's property, although he remained in possession of it. The state court subsequently held a hearing on the propriety of the attachment and ordered it dismissed because Edmondson had failed to establish the statutory grounds for it. Lugar thereupon brought this federal action, alleging that Edmondson had acted jointly with the state to deprive him of his property without due process of law. In a five-to-four decision, the Court distinguished *Flagg Brothers* and held that Lugar had alleged sufficient state involvement to make out a due process violation.

Justice White delivered the Court's opinion: "Beginning with [*Sniadach*], the Court has consistently held that constitutional requirements of due process apply to garnishment and prejudgment attachment procedures whenever officers of the State act jointly with a creditor in securing the property in dispute. [In] each of these cases state agents aided the creditor in securing the disputed property; but in each case the federal issue arose in litigation between creditor and debtor in the state courts and no state official was named as a party. Nevertheless, in each case the Court entertained and adjudicated the defendant-debtor's claim that the procedure under which the private creditor secured the disputed property violated federal constitutional standards of due process. Necessary to that conclusion is the holding that private use of the challenged state procedures with the help of state officials constitutes state action for purposes of the Fourteenth Amendment. . . .

"Our cases have [insisted] that the conduct allegedly causing the deprivation of a federal right be fairly attributable to the State. These cases reflect a two-part approach to this question of 'fair attribution.' First, the deprivation must be caused by the exercise of some right or privilege created by the State or by a rule of conduct imposed by the State or by a person for whom the State is responsible. [Second], the party charged with the deprivation must be a person who may fairly be said to be a state actor. This may be because he is a state official, because he has acted together with or has obtained significant aid from state officials, or because his conduct is otherwise chargeable to the State. Without a limit such as this, private parties could face constitutional litigation whenever they seek to rely on some state rule governing their interactions with the community surrounding them. . . .

"*Flagg Brothers* focused on the [second] component of the state-action principle. [Undoubtedly] the State was responsible for the statute [authorizing Flagg Brothers' conduct]. The response of the Court, however, focused not on the terms of the statute but on the character of the defendant: [Action] by a private party pursuant to this statute, without something more, was not sufficient to justify a characterization of that party as a 'state actor.' . . .

"While private misuse of a state statute does not describe conduct that can be attributed to the State, the procedural scheme created by the statute obviously is the product of state action. . . .

"[We] have consistently held that a private party's joint participation with state officials in the seizure of disputed property is sufficient to characterize that party as a 'state actor' for purposes of the Fourteenth Amendment."

Justice Powell, joined by Justices Rehnquist and O'Connor, dissented: "[The Court] holds that respondent, a private citizen who did no more than commence a legal action of a kind traditionally initiated by private parties, thereby engaged in 'state action.' This decision is as unprecedented as it is implausible. It is plainly unjust to the respondent, and the Court makes no argument to the contrary. Respondent, who was represented by counsel, could have had no notion that his filing of a petition in state court, in the effort to secure payment of a private debt, made him a 'state actor' liable in damages for allegedly unconstitutional action by the Commonwealth of Virginia. . . .

"[It] is not disputed that the Virginia Sheriff and Clerk of Court, the state officials who sequestered petitioner's property in the manner provided by Virginia law, engaged in state action. Yet petitioner, while alleging constitutional injury from this action by state officials, did not sue the State or its agents. . . .

"From the occurrence of state action taken by the Sheriff who sequestered petitioner's property, it does not follow that respondent became a 'state actor' simply because the Sheriff was. This Court, until today, has never endorsed this non sequitur."

Chief Justice Burger filed a separate dissenting opinion.

Note: *The Problem of the Passive State*

1. *"Pure" inaction.* At the beginning of his opinion for the Court in *DeShaney*, Justice Rehnquist characterizes the due process clause as "a limitation on the State's power to act, [rather than] a guarantee of certain minimal levels of safety and security." Similarly, in *Flagg Brothers* he observes that "the crux of respondents' complaint is not that the State *has* acted, but that it has *refused* to act." Even if we assume that the state's involvement in these disputes can be fairly characterized as a "mere" refusal to act, why should that fact make a constitutional difference? Does the Constitution always permit the government to acquiesce passively in an existing state of affairs? Consider the view that whether the Constitution permits government to do this is a question about the meaning of the relevant constitutional provision, and that any "state action" doctrine is unhelpful in answering that question.

Consider also Strauss, Due Process, Government Inaction, and Private Wrongs, 1989 Sup. Ct. Rev. 53, 59:

> Suppose a plaintiff seeking, say, to enjoin a trespass by a private party, loses his or her case because the judge is biased. (Suppose the judge has a financial interest aligned with the defendant.) That is a clear violation of the Due Process Clause. In what sense, however, is this an instance of government action, as opposed to inaction? The case is just like *DeShaney* [except] that the official who refused to intervene against the private wrongdoing is a judge instead of a social worker. Thus the *DeShaney* approach leads to a wholly implausible conclusion in connection with an issue that goes to the core of the Due Process Clause, the right to trial before an impartial judge.

Many equal protection cases can be characterized as involving state inaction. For example, in Plyler v. Doe, Chapter 6, section E5, supra, the Court held that the state's failure to provide public education for "undocumented" immigrant children violated the equal protection clause. Although the Court was narrowly divided on the substantive equal protection issue, not even the dissenters claimed that the challenge should fail because of the absence of state action. Of course, the state's failure to act in these situations is embedded in a context where the state is also acting; discrimination claims involve selective inaction. But is it fair to characterize New York and Wisconsin as wholly passive with regard to the disputes in *DeShaney* and *Flagg Brothers?* Didn't the state take some affirmative steps?

2. *Natural law and "invisible" state action.* None of the *DeShaney* opinions focused on the most direct way in which state action "positively" contributed to Joshua DeShaney's injury: the network of statutes and common law rules that grant custody and control of minor children to their biological parents. (State responsibility for this outcome is particularly obvious on the facts of *DeShaney*, where a state court, albeit in Wyoming rather than in Wisconsin, had adjudicated a custody dispute regarding the boy in connection with his parents' divorce.) Consider whether the state action doctrine has embedded within it unarticulated baselines, in the form of natural law assumptions about the "rightness" of certain initial allocations — such as the allocation of children to their biological parents — and whether these assumptions blind the court to state action that creates or maintains this "natural" state of affairs. Consider the possibility that the state action doctrine thus depends not at all on whether there has been state action, but on whether the state has deviated from a course of action that seems natural or desirable.

Compare *DeShaney* to Baltimore City Department of Social Services v. Bouknight, 493 U.S. 549 (1990), where the Court rejected the argument that a parent of a child under court supervision could invoke the fifth amendment privilege against compelled incrimination to refuse to produce the child. *Bouknight*, like *DeShaney*, involved a parent who had previously abused her biological child and who was under court supervision. But whereas in *DeShaney* the Court deemed irrelevant the governmental conduct relating to child custody decisions, that conduct was crucial to the result in *Bouknight*. The Court analogized childrearing to heavily regulated industries, where the fifth amendment privilege has generally been available in only diluted form:

> When a person assumes control over items that are the legitimate object of the government's non-criminal regulatory powers, the ability to invoke the privilege is re-

duced. . . . Once Maurice was adjudicated a child in need of assistance, his care and safety became the particular object of the States' regulatory interests. . . . The government demands production of the very public charge entrusted to a custodian, and makes the demand for compelling reasons unrelated to criminal law enforcement and as part of a broadly applied regulatory regime.

The *Bouknight* Court did not cite *DeShaney* — a case decided a year earlier. Are the two cases consistent?

Compare Reitman v. Mulkey, 387 U.S. 369 (1967). Between 1959 and 1963, California enacted various fair housing acts that prohibited racial discrimination in the sale or rental of private dwellings. In 1964, through the initiative process California voters enacted Proposition 14, which amended the state's constitution to prohibit the state from denying the "right of any person [to] decline to sell, lease or rent [property] to such person or persons as he, in his absolute discretion, chooses." Respondents, alleging that petitioners had refused to rent them an apartment because of their race, brought an action in state court based on the fair housing acts. They contended that Proposition 14, which had the effect of repealing the acts, violated the equal protection clause. The California Supreme Court ruled in their favor, and in a five-to-four decision, the U.S. Supreme Court affirmed.

The Court, in an opinion by Justice White, agreed with petitioners that the mere repeal of a statute prohibiting racial discrimination was not unconstitutional. (The Court did not make entirely clear whether this would be because the repeal would not implicate sufficient state action or whether it would be because it would not violate the equal protection clause.) But the California Supreme Court had not

read either our cases or the Fourteenth Amendment as establishing an automatic constitutional barrier to the repeal of an existing law prohibiting racial discrimination in housing. [The state court] held the intent of [Proposition 14] was to authorize private racial discrimination in the housing market, to repeal the [fair housing acts] and to create a constitutional right to [discriminate]. . . .

[Private] discriminations in housing were now not only free from [the antidiscrimination statutes] but they also enjoyed far different status than was true before the passage of those statutes. The right to discriminate, including the right to discriminate on racial grounds, was now embodied in the State's basic charter, immune from legislative, executive, or judicial regulation at any level of the state government. Those practicing racial discriminations need no longer rely solely on their personal choice. They could now invoke express constitutional authority, free from censure or interference of any kind from official sources.

Justice Harlan, joined by Justices Black, Clark, and Stewart, dissented:

[A]ll that has happened is that California has effected a pro tanto repeal of its prior statutes forbidding private discrimination. This runs no more afoul of the Fourteenth Amendment than would have California's failure to pass any such antidiscrimination statutes in the first instance. The fact that such repeal was also accompanied by a constitutional prohibition against future enactment of such laws by the California Legislature cannot well be thought to affect, from a federal constitutional standpoint, the validity of what California has done. The Fourteenth Amendment does not reach such state constitutional action any more than it does a simple legislative repeal of legislation forbidding private discrimination.

Consider some possible readings of *Reitman*. (a) A state may fail to ban racial discrimination; it may repeal any such ban; but it may not erect special barriers to laws forbidding racial discrimination. When it does so, it interferes in a constitutionally relevant way with ordinary political processes. (b) The measure in *Reitman* was unconstitutional because it was motivated by racial animus. (c) The measure in *Reitman* would encourage private racial discrimination by expressly putting the state's weight behind such discrimination. This would not be true of a mere repeal.

3. Flagg Brothers *and* Lugar. Does *Lugar* provide an adequate explanation for the result in *Flagg Brothers?* The Court's opinion in *Lugar* at least has the virtue of recognizing the obvious — that is, that the conduct of the state legislature in enacting a statute is "state action" for purposes of the Constitution. But according to *Lugar,* the state action problem in *Flagg Brothers* was created by the fact that the actual defendant before the Court was a private actor who was merely invoking his statutory rights. In *Lugar,* of course, the defendant was also a private party. But, there, the defendant had relied on state assistance to assert his rights, and this joint conduct was sufficient to make the private party a state actor for constitutional purposes.

Does this distinction make sense? How did the private petitioners in *Reitman* rely on state assistance in asserting their rights? Recall that the state activity in *Lugar* did not involve any actual shift in possession of the property in question. The sheriff merely served on Lugar a piece of paper announcing Lugar's legal obligations. Would the situation be functionally different if these obligations were embodied in a statute and Lugar read of them in a codification printed by the state?

4. *Tarkanian.* Compare *Flagg Brothers* and *Lugar* with National Collegiate Athletic Association v. Tarkanian, 488 U.S. 179 (1988). The case arose out of a National Collegiate Athletic Association (NCAA) investigation of the University of Nevada, Las Vegas (a state university) and its highly successful basketball coach, Tarkanian, for violations of NCAA rules. Under pressure from the NCAA, the university removed Tarkanian, who thereupon sued both the NCAA and the university, claiming that their conduct violated his rights to substantive and procedural due process. The lower courts found that the NCAA's conduct constituted state action subject to constitutional restraint, and that both the NCAA and the university had violated Tarkanian's constitutional rights. In a five-to-four opinion written by Justice Stevens, the Supreme Court reversed the lower court insofar as it had held the NCAA constitutionally liable.

The Court began its analysis by noting that the situation "uniquely mirrors the traditional state action case," and that it required the court "to step through an analytical looking glass to resolve it." In more typical cases, such as *Lugar* and *Flagg Brothers*, a private party has taken steps that cause harm to the plaintiff, and the issue is whether the state was sufficiently involved to treat this private conduct as state action. Here, in contrast, the university — concededly a state actor — had suspended Tarkanian. "Thus, the question is not whether [the university] participated to a critical extent in the NCAA's activities, but whether [the university's] actions in compliance with the NCAA rules and recommendations turned the NCAA's conduct into state action."

The Court concluded that university compliance did not transform the NCAA into a state actor. "It would be ironic indeed to conclude that the NCAA's imposition of sanctions against [the university] — sanctions that [the university] and its counsel steadfastly opposed during protracted adversary proceedings — is fairly attributable to the State of Nevada. It would be more appropriate to conclude that [the university] had conducted its athletic program under the color of policies adopted by the NCAA, rather than that those policies were developed and enforced under color of Nevada law."

5. *Pope.* Consider also the Court's reading of *Lugar* and *Flagg Brothers* in Tulsa Professional Collection Services v. Pope, 485 U.S. 478 (1988). Oklahoma's probate laws require that claims arising under a contract be presented to the executor of the estate within two months of the publication of a notice advising creditors of the commencement of probate proceedings. A creditor who had not received actual notice and failed to file a claim within two months argued that the constructive notice provision violated due process. In an opinion by Justice O'Connor, the Court held that the creditor had a property interest that was protected by the due process clause. It went on to note, however, that the fourteenth amendment protected this interest only from deprivation by state action. On the state action question, it summarized the holdings of *Lugar* and *Flagg Brothers* as follows:

> Private use of state sanctioned private remedies and procedures does not rise to the level of state action, see, e.g., [*Flagg Brothers*]. Nor is the state's involvement in the mere running of a general statute of limitation generally sufficient to implicate due process. [But] when private parties make use of state procedures with the overt, significant assistance of state officials, state action may be found. See, e.g., [*Lugar*].

The Court went on to hold that, although the mere state promulgation of the limitation period would not constitute state action (what does this mean?), the probate court's "pervasive and substantial" involvement with the probate proceedings was sufficient.

It may appear that *Pope's* "pervasive and substantial" involvement test is inconsistent with *Lugar.* Consider the possibility that *Pope* is distinguishable because the creditor was invoking the Constitution to secure the affirmative assistance of the state in *Pope*, while the debtor was invoking the Constitution to ward off state interference in *Lugar.* Taken together, do *Pope* and *Lugar* mean Ms. Brooks could have broken into Flagg Brothers' warehouse, stolen the furniture, and then successfully asserted the unconstitutionality of section 7-210 as a defense to a criminal prosecution?

2. *Judicial Action and the Theory of Government Neutrality*

Shelley v. Kraemer

334 U.S. 1 (1948)

Mr. Chief Justice Vinson delivered the opinion of the Court.

These cases present for our consideration questions relating to the validity of court enforcement of private agreements, generally described as restrictive covenants, which have as their purpose the exclusion of persons of designated race or color from the ownership or occupancy of real property. Basic constitutional issues of obvious importance have been raised. . . .

[In each of the two cases before the Court, black families had purchased homes burdened by restrictive covenants, signed by property owners in the neighborhood, that prohibited occupancy by nonwhites. Respondents brought these actions in state court seeking to specifically enforce the covenant provisions. In each case, the state court upheld the provision and ruled that respondents were entitled to an injunction prohibiting petitioners from occupying the property.]

It cannot be doubted that among the civil rights intended to be protected from discriminatory state action by the Fourteenth Amendment are the rights to acquire, enjoy, own and dispose of property. Equality in the enjoyment of property rights was regarded by the framers of that Amendment as an essential precondition to the realization of other basic civil rights and liberties which the Amendment was intended to guarantee. Thus, [42 U.S.C. §1982], derived from §1 of the Civil Rights Act of 1866 which was enacted by Congress while the Fourteenth Amendment was also under consideration, provides:

> All citizens of the United States shall have the same right, in every State and Territory, as is enjoyed by white citizens thereof to inherit, purchase, lease, sell, hold, and convey real and personal property. . . .

It is likewise clear that restrictions on the right of occupancy of the sort sought to be created by the private agreements in these cases could not be squared with the requirements of the Fourteenth Amendment if imposed by state statute or local ordinance. We do not understand respondents to urge the contrary. . . .

But the present cases [do] not involve action by state legislatures or city councils. Here the particular patterns of discrimination and the areas in which the restrictions are to operate, are determined, in the first instance, by the terms of agreements among private individuals. Participation of the State consists in the enforcement of the restrictions so defined. The crucial issue with which we are here confronted is whether this distinction removes these cases from the operation of the prohibitory provisions of the Fourteenth Amendment.

Since the decision of this Court in the Civil Rights Cases, the principle has become firmly embedded in our constitutional law that the action inhibited by the first section of the Fourteenth Amendment is only such action as may fairly be said to be that of the States. That Amendment erects no shield against merely private conduct, however discriminatory or wrongful.

We conclude, therefore, that the restrictive agreements standing alone cannot be regarded as violative of any rights guaranteed to petitioners by the Fourteenth Amendment. So long as the purposes of those agreements are effectuated by voluntary adherence to their terms, it would appear clear that there has been no action by the State and the provisions of the Amendment have not been violated.

But here there was more. These are cases in which the purposes of the agreements were secured only by judicial enforcement by state courts of the restrictive terms of the agreements.

[That] the action of state courts and judicial officers in their official capacities is to be regarded as action of the State within the meaning of the Fourteenth Amendment, is a proposition which has long been established by decisions of this Court. . . .

One of the earliest applications of the prohibitions contained in the Fourteenth Amendment to action of state judicial officials occurred in cases in which

Negroes had been excluded from jury service in criminal prosecutions by reason of their race or color. These cases demonstrate, also, the early recognition by this Court that state action in violation of the Amendment's provisions is equally repugnant to the constitutional commands whether directed by state statute or taken by a judicial official in the absence of statute. Thus, in Strauder v. West Virginia, 100 U.S. 303 (1880), this Court declared invalid a state statute restricting jury service to white persons as amounting to a denial of the equal protection of the laws to the colored defendant in that case. In the same volume of the reports, the Court in Ex parte Virginia, [100 U.S. 339 (1880)], held that a similar discrimination imposed by the action of a state judge denied rights protected by the Amendment, despite the fact that the language of the state statute relating to jury service contained no such restrictions.

The action of state courts in imposing penalties or depriving parties of other substantive rights without providing adequate notice and opportunity to defend, has, of course, long been regarded as a denial of the due process of law guaranteed by the Fourteenth Amendment.

In numerous cases, this Court has reversed criminal convictions in state courts for failure of those courts to provide the essential ingredients of a fair hearing. . . .

But the examples of state judicial action which have been held by this Court to violate the Amendment's commands are not restricted to situations in which the judicial proceedings were found in some manner to be procedurally unfair. It has been recognized that the action of state courts in enforcing a substantive common-law rule formulated by those courts, may result in the denial of rights guaranteed by the Fourteenth Amendment, even though the judicial proceedings in such cases may have been in complete accord with the most rigorous conceptions of procedural due process. . . .

Against this background of judicial construction, extending over a period of some three-quarters of a century, we are called upon to consider whether enforcement by state courts of the restrictive agreements in these cases may be deemed to be the acts of those States; and, if so, whether that action has denied these petitioners the equal protection of the laws which the Amendment was intended to insure.

We have no doubt that there has been state action in these cases in the full and complete sense of the phrase. The undisputed facts disclose that petitioners were willing purchasers of properties upon which they desired to establish homes. The owners of the properties were willing sellers; and contracts of sale were accordingly consummated. It is clear that but for the active intervention of the state courts, supported by the full panoply of state power, petitioners would have been free to occupy the properties in question without restraint.

These are not cases, as has been suggested, in which the States have merely abstained from action, leaving private individuals free to impose such discriminations as they see fit. Rather, these are cases in which the States have made available to such individuals the full coercive power of government to deny to petitioners, on the grounds of race or color, the enjoyment of property rights in premises which petitioners are willing and financially able to acquire and which the grantors are willing to sell. The difference between judicial enforcement and nonenforcement of the restrictive covenants is the difference to petitioners between being denied rights of property available to other members of the community and being accorded full enjoyment of those rights on an equal footing.

Respondents urge, however, that since the state courts stand ready to enforce restrictive covenants excluding white persons from the ownership or occupancy of property covered by such agreements, enforcement of covenants excluding colored persons may not be deemed a denial of equal protection of the laws to the colored persons who are thereby affected. This contention does not bear scrutiny. The parties have directed our attention to no case in which a court, state or federal, has been called upon to enforce a covenant excluding members of the white majority from ownership or occupancy of real property on grounds of race or color. But there are more fundamental considerations. The rights created by the first section of the Fourteenth Amendment are, by its terms, guaranteed to the individual. The rights established are personal rights. It is, therefore, no answer to these petitioners to say that the courts may also be induced to deny white persons rights of ownership and occupancy on grounds of race or color. Equal protection of the laws is not achieved through indiscriminate imposition of inequalities.

Nor do we find merit in the suggestion that property owners who are parties to these agreements are denied equal protection of the laws if denied access to the courts to enforce the terms of restrictive covenants and to assert property rights which the state courts have held to be created by such agreements. The Constitution confers upon no individual the right to demand action by the State which results in the denial of equal protection of the laws to other individuals. And it would appear beyond question that the power of the State to create and enforce property interests must be exercised within the boundaries defined by the Fourteenth Amendment. Cf. Marsh v. Alabama, 326 U.S. 501 (1946). . . .

For the reasons stated, the judgment of the Supreme Court of Missouri and the judgment of the Supreme Court of Michigan must be reversed.

Reversed.

Mr. Justice Reed, Mr. Justice Jackson, and Mr. Justice Rutledge took no part in the consideration or decision of these cases.

Note: *Shelley v. Kraemer, State Inaction, and the Theory of Government Neutrality*

1. *State action as a nonissue.* Chief Justice Vinson devotes virtually all of his opinion to a demonstration that judicial action is "state action" within the meaning of the fourteenth amendment. But how could anyone doubt that there is state action when a state judge issues an injunction enforceable by the state marshal and ultimately supported by the threat of contempt and incarceration in a state institution?

Compare Shelley v. Kraemer with New York Times v. Sullivan, Chapter 7, section D, supra, where the Court held that the first amendment required proof of "actual malice" to support libel judgments in favor of public officials. *Sullivan*, like *Shelley*, concerned the constitutionality of a state common law rule invoked in the course of private litigation. Yet in *Sullivan* the Court never doubted that judicial enforcement of the rule was state action and devoted all its attention to the substantive question of its constitutionality. Why is the state action question controversial in *Shelley* but not in *Sullivan*?

2. *The real issue in* Shelley? After completing his lengthy discourse on the state action question, Chief Justice Vinson devotes a single paragraph to petitioners' substantive contention that the enforcement of restrictive covenants violates the equal protection clause. But surely this is a hard question — and perhaps it is the real issue in the case. On this view, the state action question was simple; of course judicial enforcement of contracts is state action. The difficult issue was one of equal protection law. On what theory does a rule requiring uniform enforcement of any privately made covenant deny equality? Why does Chief Justice Vinson think that it is relevant that only whites have chosen to use the rule? What does he mean when he says that the equal protection clause bars the "indiscriminate imposition of inequalities"?

3. *State action and the Washington v. Davis problem.* Consider the following argument: In cases such as *Shelley*, focusing analysis on whether or not there is "state action" is unproductive and misleading, since, as *Shelley* itself illustrates, it will always be possible to find some state actor implicated in the alleged constitutional violation. The appropriate question to ask is whether, as a substantive matter, this governmental action is unconstitutional. When one asks this question in *Shelley*, the reason for the controversy over the Court's holding becomes clearer. Recall that in Washington v. Davis, page 514 supra, the Court held that a statute neutral on its face should not be subject to heightened scrutiny simply because of its disproportionate racial impact. Such statutes need satisfy only low-level review unless they were enacted for a discriminatory purpose. See Chapter 5, section C2, supra.

If this is so, the question becomes: Was Missouri law regarding restrictive covenants neutral on its face in the Washington v. Davis sense? Consider L. Tribe, Constitutional Choices 260 (1985):

> Like other states, Missouri treats most restraints on alienability of real estate as judicially unenforceable: to enforce any such restraint, a state court must first find that the *substance* of the restraining covenant is reasonable and consistent with public policy. Therefore, the issue is not whether *any* judicial enforcement of racially invidious private arrangements constitutes racially invidious state action, but whether a state may *choose* automatically to enforce restrictive covenants that discriminate against blacks *while generally regarding alienability restraints as anathema*. The real "state action" in *Shelley* was Missouri's facially discriminatory body of common and statutory law — the quintessence of a racist state policy.

Compare Strauss, Discriminatory Intent and the Taming of *Brown*, 56 U. Chi. L. Rev. 935, 968 (1989):

> [This] selective enforcement argument is not a satisfactory theoretical justification of *Shelley*. The argument makes *Shelley* contingent: it implicitly concedes that *Shelley* would not be correct in any state that happened to enforce all, or most, restrictive covenants. The holding of *Shelley* is not limited in this way, and the moral appeal of the result in *Shelley* [would] be very strong even in a state that enforced all restrictive covenants.

Perhaps *Shelley* is nonetheless consistent with Washington v. Davis because the decision to enforce restrictive covenants is infected by a racially discriminatory purpose. Consider Strauss, supra, at 970, 973-974, 990:

[Under] the discriminatory intent standard, the party challenging the restrictive covenant in *Shelley* could make the following argument: An act of private discrimination by a white against a black in America inflects great harm, both material and psychological. . . .

The only reason the state tolerates these serious injuries [is] that they fall on blacks. The state would never allow harms of that severity to fall on whites. . . .

In short, if one rigorously applies the discriminatory intent standard to *Shelley*, the question is essentially: suppose the entire situation of blacks and whites in America had been reversed; suppose blacks had done everything to whites that in fact whites did to blacks. Now suppose that blacks entered into a restrictive racial covenant. Would Missouri enforce it?

The first thing one notices about this question is that any answer would be highly speculative. . . .

There is a conceptual problem as well: in an important sense, [the] question may be meaningless. It may be meaningless because being a long-term victim of discrimination may be part of what it *means* to be black in the United States. . . .

A conception of discrimination that [included] elements of the effects-based approaches would provide a more satisfactory way of analyzing these issues. The problematic character of *Shelley* is the result not of judicial activism but of the impoverished conception of discrimination that is reflected in the intent test.

As you read the remaining material, consider the extent to which the controversy over "state action" in the equal protection context is really a controversy concerning the meaning and scope of Washington v. Davis and the principle of governmental neutrality that it embodies. When the Court says that there is no "state action," is it really saying that the state action is facially neutral and therefore not subject to heightened review?

4. *The reach of* Shelley. It would also be a mistake to read some of the more sweeping language in *Shelley* literally. There are certainly situations in which an individual can invoke judicial processes to effectuate a discriminatory intent. It is safe to assume that no court would inquire into the racist motives of an individual invoking state trespass laws against uninvited dinner guests at a private home.

Is there something about *Shelley* that makes the invocation of judicial processes especially troublesome? Is it relevant that a network of restrictive covenants operates as the functional equivalent of zoning laws and therefore serves an essentially "governmental" function? (The "public function" strand of state action jurisprudence is discussed at section D infra.) That the state's enforcement of the covenant prevented a willing buyer and seller from dealing with each other?

a. *Governmental neutrality and the problem of money damages.* Consider, for example, the award of money damages for violation of restrictive covenants. Does *Shelley* apply if a court imposes damages on a white seller but does not prevent the black purchaser from securing possession? In Barrows v. Jackson, 346 U.S. 249 (1953), respondent entered a restrictive covenant prohibiting the use or occupancy of his property by nonwhites. He then violated the covenant by permitting nonwhites to move into the premises. Petitioners, property owners in the same neighborhood who were also parties to the covenant, sued for damages. The Court held that *Shelley* barred the suit:

To compel respondent to respond in damages would be for the State to punish her for her failure to perform her covenant to continue to discriminate against non-Caucasians in the use of her property. [If] the State may thus punish respondent for her failure to carry out her covenant, she is coerced to continue to use her property in a discriminatory manner, which in essence is the purpose of the covenant. Thus, it becomes not respondent's voluntary choice but the State's choice that she observe her covenant or suffer damages. The action of a state court at law to sanction the validity of the restrictive covenant here involved would constitute state action as surely as it was state action to enforce such covenants in [equity].

Chief Justice Vinson, the author of *Shelley*, was the sole dissenter:

The *Shelley* case, resting on the express determination that restrictive covenants are valid between the parties, dealt only with a state court's attempt to enforce them directly against innocent third parties whose right to enjoy their property would suffer immediate harm. [In] this case, the plaintiffs have not sought such relief. The suit is directed against the very person whose solemn promise helped to bring the covenant into existence. The plaintiffs ask only that respondent do what she in turn had a right to ask of plaintiffs — indemnify plaintiffs for the bringing about of an event which she recognized would cause injury to the plaintiffs.

b. *State enforcement of discriminatory testamentary and inter vivos dispositions of property*. Consider Pennsylvania v. Board of Directors of City Trusts, 353 U.S. 230 (1957). In a will probated in 1831, Stephen Girard left a fund to be held in trust for erection and operation of a school for "poor white male orphans." The will named the city of Philadelphia as the trustee, and the school was administered by a state agency. When petitioners were denied admission to the school because of their race, they brought this action. The state court denied relief, but the Supreme Court, in a brief per curiam opinion, reversed: "The Board which operates Girard College is an agency of the State of Pennsylvania. Therefore, even though the Board was acting as a trustee, its refusal to admit [petitioners] to the college because they were Negroes was discrimination by the State."

On remand in *City Trusts*, the state court appointed private trustees in order to comply with the terms of Girard's will. In Pennsylvania v. Brown, 392 F.2d 120 (3d Cir.), cert. denied, 391 U.S. 921 (1968), the court of appeals held that the substitution was unconstitutional.

Compare *City Trusts* with Evans v. Newton, 382 U.S. 296 (1966). In 1911, U.S. Senator Augustus O. Bacon executed a will that devised to the Mayor and City Council of Macon, Georgia, a tract of land to be used as a park. The will provided that the park should be used by white people only and was to be under the control of a board of managers, all of whom were to be white. At first, the city ran the park on a segregated basis, but when it began to admit blacks, members of the board of managers brought this suit asking that the city be removed as trustee. The city thereupon resigned as trustee, and the state court appointed new, private trustees to run the park. Black intervenors challenged this decision. The Supreme Court held that the park could not be run on a racially segregated basis. The Court, in an opinion by Justice Douglas, stated:

If a testator wanted to leave a school or center for the use of one race only and in no way implicated the State in the supervision, control, or management of that facility, we assume arguendo that no constitutional difficulty would be encountered. [This] park, however, is in a different posture. For years it was an integral part of the City of Macon's activities. [The] momentum it acquired as a public facility is certainly not dissipated ipso facto by the appointment of "private" trustees. So far as this record shows, there has been no change in municipal maintenance and concern over this facility. [If] the municipality remains entwined in the management or control of the park, it remains subject to the restraints of the Fourteenth Amendment.

The Court went on to suggest that the park should be treated as a public institution because it was serving a "public function" and was "municipal" in character. (The "public function" strand of the state action doctrine is considered in section D infra.) Justice White concurred in the result on the ground that the trust was tainted by state legislation that validated racially discriminatory conditions. Justices Black, Harlan, and Stewart dissented.

On remand, the state court held that Senator Bacon's intention to provide a park for whites only had become impossible to fulfill. Since this limitation was, in the court's view, central to Bacon's intention, it declined to reform the trust and held instead that the trust had failed, and that the parkland reverted to the testator's heirs. In Evans v. Abney, 396 U.S. 435 (1970), the Court affirmed in a six-to-two decision. Justice Black, a dissenter in Newton, wrote for the Court: "We are of the opinion that in ruling as they did the Georgia courts did no more than apply well-settled general principles of Georgia law to determine the meaning and effect of a Georgia will." Justices Douglas and Brennan dissented.

The Court maintained that Shelley was "easily distinguishable" because "[h]ere the effect of the Georgia decision eliminated all discrimination against Negroes in the park by eliminating the park itself, and the termination of the park was a loss shared equally by the white and Negro citizens of Macon since both races would have enjoyed a constitutional right of equal access to the park's facilities had it continued." Compare Justice Brennan's dissenting opinion:

> Shelley v. Kraemer stands at least for the proposition that where parties of different races are willing to deal with one another a state court cannot keep them from doing so by enforcing a privately devised racial restriction. . . .
>
> [So] far as the record shows, this is a case of a state court's enforcement of a racial restriction to prevent willing parties from dealing with one another. The decision of the Georgia courts thus, under Shelley v. Kraemer, constitutes state action denying equal protection.

The Court in Abney rejected petitioners' argument that

> the action of the Georgia court violates the United States Constitution in that it imposes a drastic "penalty," the "forfeiture" of the park, merely because of the city's compliance with the constitutional mandate expressed by this Court in Evans v. Newton. [We] think [that] the will of Senator Bacon and Georgia law provide all the justification necessary for imposing such a "penalty." . . .
>
> [The] Georgia Supreme Court [interpreted] Senator Bacon's will as embodying a preference for termination of the park rather than its integration. Given this, the Georgia court had no alternative under its relevant trust laws, which are long standing and neutral with regard to race, but to end the Baconsfield trust and return the property to the Senator's heirs.

Compare Justice Brennan's views: "When it is as starkly clear as it is in this case that a public facility would remain open but for the constitutional command that it be operated on a nonsegregated basis, the closing of that facility conveys an un-ambiguous message of community involvement in racial discrimination."

Recall Palmer v. Thompson, Chapter 5, section C2, supra, decided only a year after *Abney*. In *Palmer*, Justice Black, again writing for the Court, held that a municipality's decision to close a swimming pool, rather than comply with court-ordered integration, was constitutionally permissible. Given *Palmer*, does anything turn on the state action analysis in *Abney*, or is the *Abney* decision, once again, fully explicable in terms of substantive equal protection doctrine?

c. *State enforcement of trespass laws.* Does *Shelley* prohibit judicial enforcement of facially neutral trespass laws at the behest of a property owner who attempts to exclude the defendants for racial reasons? This issue was posed in a series of cases involving sit-in demonstrations in racially segregated restaurants in the early 1960s. Although the Court managed to reverse all the resulting convictions, it never reached the *Shelley* issue. See, e.g., Bell v. Maryland, 378 U.S. 226 (1964) (convictions reversed and remanded for consideration of the effect of an intervening change in state law); Peterson v. Greenville, 373 U.S. 244 (1963) (conviction reversed because official state policy encouraged segregation). But although no majority opinion reached the issue, individual justices engaged in spirited debate about the relevance of *Shelley*. Consider, for example, the views of Justice Black in Bell v. Maryland, supra. Justice Black argued that

> [t]he [Fourteenth] Amendment does not forbid a State to prosecute for crimes committed against a person or his property, however prejudiced or narrow the victim's views may be. [Such] a doctrine would [severely] handicap a State's efforts to maintain a peaceful and orderly society. Our society has put its trust in a system of criminal laws to punish lawless conduct. [Instead] of attempting to take the law into their own hands, people have been taught to call for police protection to protect their rights wherever possible. It would betray our whole plan for a tranquil and orderly society to say that a citizen, because of his personal prejudices, habits, attitudes, or beliefs, is cast outside the law's protection and cannot call for the aid of officers sworn to uphold the law and preserve the peace.

Justice Black distinguished *Shelley*:

> It seems pretty clear that the reason judicial enforcement of the restrictive covenants in *Shelley* was deemed state action was not merely the fact that a state court had acted, but rather that it had acted "to deny to petitioners, on the grounds of race or color, the enjoyment of property rights in premises which petitioners are willing and financially able to acquire and which the grantors are willing to sell." [Quoting from *Shelley*.] [This] means that the property owner may, in the absence of a valid statute forbidding it, sell his property to whom he pleases and admit to that property whom he will; so long as *both* parties are willing [parties]. [But] equally, when one party is unwilling, as when the property owner chooses *not* to sell to a particular person or *not* to admit that person, then [he] is entitled to rely on the guarantee of due process of law, that is, "law of the land," to protect his free use and enjoyment of property and to know that only by valid legislation, passed pursuant to some constitutional grant of power, can anyone disturb this free use.

Shortly after *Bell* the public accommodations controversy was mooted when Congress enacted the 1964 Civil Rights Act, which, inter alia, prohibited racial discrimination in most places of public accommodation. In Heart of Atlanta Motel v. United States, 379 U.S. 241 (1964), and Katzenbach v. McClung, 379 U.S. 294 (1964), the Court unanimously upheld the constitutionality of the act. See Chapter 2, section C, supra.

C.   CONSTITUTIONALLY IMPERMISSIBLE DEPARTURES FROM NEUTRALITY: STATE SUBSIDIZATION, APPROVAL, AND ENCOURAGEMENT

1.   State Subsidization of Private Conduct

Burton v. Wilmington Parking Authority

365 U.S. 715 (1961)

MR. JUSTICE CLARK delivered the opinion of the Court.

In this action for declaratory and injunctive relief it is admitted that the Eagle Coffee Shoppe, Inc., a restaurant located within an off-street automobile parking building in Wilmington, Delaware, has refused to serve appellant food or drink solely because he is a Negro. The parking building is owned and operated by the Wilmington Parking Authority, an agency of the State of Delaware, and the restaurant is the Authority's lessee. Appellant claims that such refusal abridges his rights under the Equal Protection Clause of the Fourteenth Amendment to the United States Constitution. The Supreme Court of Delaware has held that Eagle was acting in "a purely private capacity" under its lease; that its action was not that of the Authority and was not, therefore, state action within the contemplation of the prohibitions contained in that Amendment. [We conclude] that the exclusion of appellant under the circumstances shown to be present here was discriminatory state action in violation of the Equal Protection Clause of the Fourteenth Amendment. . . .

[The City of Wilmington created the Wilmington Parking Authority for the purpose of constructing parking facilities. Before beginning construction of the facility at issue here, the parking authority entered into a series of long-term leases with commercial tenants in order to provide needed capital for its debt service requirements. One such lease was made with Eagle for a period of twenty years, renewable for another ten years. The space leased to Eagle was directly accessible from the street and had no marked public entrance leading from the parking portion of the facility into the restaurant. The parking authority agreed to complete construction expeditiously, including decorative finishing of the leased premises and necessary utility connections. Eagle, in turn, spent some $220,000 to make the space suitable for its operation, and to the extent such improvements were attached to the realty, it enjoyed the parking authority's tax exemption. The lease contained no requirement that restaurant services be made available to the general public on a nondiscriminatory basis, although the parking authority had statutory authority to adopt rules respecting the use of its facilities so long as they would not impair the security of its bondholders. When the building was completed, the parking authority placed official signs in appropriate places indicating the public character of the building and flew from mast-heads on the roof both the state and national flags.

[On being refused service by Eagle because of his race, appellant filed this lawsuit. The trial court granted his motion for summary judgment, but the Delaware Supreme Court reversed.]

[To] fashion and apply a precise formula for recognition of state responsibility under the Equal Protection Clause is an "impossible task" which "This Court has never attempted." Kotch v. Pilot Commrs., 330 U.S. 552, 556. Only by sifting facts and weighing circumstances can the nonobvious involvement of the State in private conduct be attributed its true significance. . . .

[The] Delaware Supreme Court seems to have placed controlling emphasis on its conclusion [that] only some 15% of the total cost of the facility was "advanced" from public funds; that the cost of the entire facility was allocated three-fifths to the space for commercial leasing and two-fifths to parking space; that anticipated revenue from parking was only some 30.5% of the total income, the balance of which was expected to be earned by the leasing; that the Authority had no original intent to place a restaurant in the building, it being only a happenstance resulting from the bidding; that Eagle expended considerable moneys on furnishings; that the restaurant's main and marked public entrance is on Ninth Street without any public entrance direct from the parking area; and that "the only connection Eagle has with the public facility . . . is the furnishing of the sum of $28,700 annually in the form of rent which is used by the Authority to defray a portion of the operating expense of an otherwise unprofitable enterprise." While these factual considerations are indeed validly accountable aspects of the enterprise upon which the State has embarked, we cannot say that they lead inescapably to the conclusion that state action is not present. Their persuasiveness is diminished when evaluated in the context of other factors which must be acknowledged.

The land and building were publicly owned. As an entity, the building was dedicated to "public uses" in performance of the Authority's "essential governmental functions." 22 Del. Code, §§501, 514. The costs of land acquisition, construction, and maintenance are defrayed entirely from donations by the City of Wilmington, from loans and revenue bonds and from the proceeds of rentals and parking services out of which the loans and bonds were payable. Assuming that the distinction would be significant, the commercially leased areas were not surplus state property, but constituted a physically and financially integral and, indeed, indispensable part of the State's plan to operate its project as a self-sustaining unit. Upkeep and maintenance of the building, including necessary repairs, were responsibilities of the Authority and were payable out of public funds. It cannot be doubted that the peculiar relationship of the restaurant to the parking facility in which it is located confers on each an incidental variety of mutual benefits. Guests of the restaurant are afforded a convenient place to park their automobiles, even if they cannot enter the restaurant directly from the parking area. Similarly, its convenience for diners may well provide additional demand for the Authority's parking facilities. Should any improvements effected in the leasehold by Eagle become part of the realty, there is no possibility of increased taxes being passed on to it since the fee is held by a tax-exempt government agency. Neither can it be ignored, especially in view of Eagle's affirmative allegation that for it to serve Negroes would injure its business, that profits earned by discrimination not only contribute to, but also are indispensable elements in, the financial success of a governmental agency.

Addition of all these activities, obligations and responsibilities of the Authority, the benefits mutually conferred, together with the obvious fact that the restaurant is operated as an integral part of a public building devoted to a public parking service, indicates that degree of state participation and involvement in discriminatory action which it was the design of the Fourteenth Amendment to condemn. It is irony amounting to grave injustice that in one part of a single building, erected and maintained with public funds by an agency of the State to serve a public purpose, all persons have equal rights, while in another portion, also serving the public, a Negro is a second-class citizen, offensive because of his race, without rights and unentitled to service, but at the same time fully enjoys equal access to nearby restaurants in wholly privately owned buildings. [In] its lease with Eagle the Authority could have affirmatively required Eagle to discharge the responsibilities under the Fourteenth Amendment imposed upon the private enterprise as a consequence of state participation. But no State may effectively abdicate its responsibilities by either ignoring them or by merely failing to discharge them whatever the motive may be. It is of no consolation to an individual denied the equal protection of the laws that it was done in good faith. [By] its inaction, the Authority, and through it the State, has not only made itself a party to the refusal of service, but has elected to place its power, property and prestige behind the admitted discrimination. The State has so far insinuated itself into a position of interdependence with Eagle that it must be recognized as a joint participant in the challenged activity, which, on that account, cannot be considered to have been so "purely private" as to fall without the scope of the Fourteenth Amendment.

Because readily applicable formulae may not be fashioned, the conclusions drawn from the facts and circumstances of this record are by no means declared as universal truths on the basis of which every state leasing agreement is to be tested. Owing to the very "largeness" of government, a multitude of relationships might appear to some to fall within the Amendment's embrace, but that, it must be remembered, can be determined only in the framework of the peculiar facts or circumstances present. [Specifically] defining the limits of our inquiry, what we hold today is that when a State leases public property in the manner and for the purpose shown to have been the case here, the proscriptions of the Fourteenth Amendment must be complied with by the lessee as certainly as though they were binding covenants written into the agreement itself. . . .

Reversed and remanded.

MR. JUSTICE STEWART, concurring.

[In] upholding Eagle's right to deny service to the appellant solely because of his race, the Supreme Court of Delaware relied upon a statute of that State which permits the proprietor of a restaurant to refuse to serve "persons whose reception or entertainment by him would be offensive to the major part of his customers. . . ." There is no suggestion in the record that the appellant as an individual was such a person. The highest court of Delaware has thus construed this legislative enactment as authorizing discriminatory classification based exclusively on color. Such a law seems to me clearly violative of the Fourteenth Amendment.

[A dissenting opinion by Justice Frankfurter is omitted.]

MR. JUSTICE HARLAN, whom MR. JUSTICE WHITTAKER joins, dissenting.

The Court's opinion, by a process of first undiscriminatingly throwing together various factual bits and pieces and then undermining the resulting structure by an equally vague disclaimer, seems to me to leave completely at sea just what it is in this record that satisfies the requirement of "state action."

I find it unnecessary, however, to inquire into the matter at this stage, for it seems to me apparent that before passing on the far-reaching constitutional questions that may, or may not, be lurking in this judgment, the case should first be sent back to the state court for clarification as to the precise basis of its decision. . . .

If the Delaware court construed this state statute "as authorizing discriminatory classification based exclusively on color," I would certainly agree, without more, that the enactment is offensive to the Fourteenth Amendment. [If], on the other hand, the state court meant no more than that under the statute, as at common law, Eagle was free to serve only those whom it pleased, then, and only then, would the question of "state action" be presented in full-blown form.

Note: Subsidies, Penalties, and the Search for a Baseline

1. *The meaning of* Burton. *Burton* seems to be a case about governmental entanglement with private discrimination. But note that, in one sense at least, the policy of the Wilmington Parking Authority was "neutral" with regard to racial discrimination by its tenants. It did not seek tenants who would discriminate or encourage them to do so. One way to restate the holding of *Burton*, then, is that in this context, state inaction in the face of private discriminatory conduct is constitutionally unacceptable. Does the Court identify what it is about this context that triggers this affirmative obligation? Did the government somehow facilitate or encourage discrimination?

2. *State subsidization.* Does *Burton* stand for the general proposition that state subsidization of discriminatory conduct is unconstitutional? On this view, the state is not obligated to prohibit or penalize such conduct, but neither is it permitted to accord benefits to those who engage in it. Is this position tenable? Surely it is not unconstitutional, for example, for the state to provide police and fire protection to establishments that discriminate. Some subsidies or benefits are acceptable. Moreover, any theory that makes "subsidies" of discriminatory conduct unconstitutional, but does not require government to impose "penalties" on such conduct, ultimately rests on our ability to distinguish between the withholding of a benefit, on the one hand, and the imposition of a burden, on the other.

Consider, for example, Norwood v. Harrison, 413 U.S. 455 (1973), in which the Court confronted a constitutional challenge to a Mississippi statutory program under which textbooks were purchased by the state and lent to students in both public and private schools, without reference to whether any participating private school had racially discriminatory policies. The Court unanimously struck down the program as applied to discriminatory schools. Defenders of the program relied on Pierce v. Society of Sisters, 268 U.S. 510 (1925), which had established the constitutional right of parents to provide private education for their children. They argued that *Pierce* rights would be infringed by lending free textbooks to public school children but withholding them from certain private school children. The Court rejected this argument: "In *Pierce*, the Court affirmed the right of private schools to exist and to operate; it said nothing of any supposed right of private or parochial schools to share with public schools in state largesse, on an equal basis or otherwise. [It] is one thing to say that a State may not prohibit the maintenance of private schools and quite another to say that such schools must, as a matter of equal protection, receive state aids."

Having disposed of appellees' argument that the textbook aid was constitutionally required, the Court went on to hold that it was constitutionally impermissible: "A State may not grant the type of tangible financial aid here involved if that aid has a significant tendency to facilitate, reinforce, and support private discrimination." The Court was careful to note, however, that its holding did not extend to all types of state assistance:

> Textbooks are a basic educational tool and, like tuition grants, they are provided only in connection with schools; they are to be distinguished from generalized services government might provide to schools in common with others. Moreover, the textbooks provided to private school students by the State in this case are a form of assistance readily available from sources entirely independent of the State. [The] State has neither an absolute nor operating monopoly on the procurement of school textbooks; anyone can purchase them on the open market.

After *Norwood*, would it be unconstitutional for the state to grant the same tax-exempt status to discriminatory private schools that it grants to other charitable and nonprofit institutions? See McGlotten v. Connally, 338 F. Supp. 448 (D.D.C. 1972) (tax-exempt status of discriminatory fraternal orders unconstitutional). Cf. Bob Jones University v. United States, 461 U.S. 574 (1983) (Internal Revenue Service decision to deny tax-exempt status to private schools engaging in racial discrimination permissible as matter of statutory construction). Is there a constitutionally relevant distinction between tax exemptions for discriminatory institutions and direct monetary subsidies to them? (For a more detailed discussion of these issues in connection with the establishment and free exercise clauses of the first amendment, see Chapter 8, section B4, supra.)

One year after *Norwood* the Court again considered whether the provision of "generalized" government services to private discriminatory groups constituted an impermissible departure from neutrality. Gilmore v. City of Montgomery, 417 U.S. 556 (1974), arose out of the fifteen-year struggle of blacks in Montgomery, Alabama, to desegregate the city's public parks. After protracted litigation involving repeated efforts by the city to avoid the original desegregation order, the district court enjoined the city from allowing use of city-owned recreational facilities by any private group that was racially segregated or had a racially discriminatory admissions policy. The court of appeals sustained this order insofar as it restrained the use of city facilities by private schools when the use was "exclusive" and not in common with other citizens. With respect to "nonexclusive" use by private school children and use by nonschool groups, however, the court of appeals reversed.

The Supreme Court, in an opinion by Justice Blackmun, affirmed that portion of the court of appeals decision prohibiting exclusive use of city facilities by segregated private schools. Emphasizing the city's affirmative duty to desegregate its public schools, the Court argued that "the city's actions significantly enhanced the attractiveness of segregated private schools, formed in reaction against the federal court school order, by enabling them to offer complete athletic programs.

[We] are persuaded [that] this assistance significantly tended to undermine the federal court order mandating the establishment and maintenance of a unitary school system in Montgomery."

With regard to nonexclusive use by school groups and use by nonschool groups, however, the Court found that the record was insufficiently developed to render a decision. To guide the district court on remand, the Court noted that non-exclusive access by segregated school groups might well undermine outstanding school desegregation orders. "For example, all-white private school basketball teams might be invited to participate in a tournament conducted on public recreational facilities with desegregated private and public school teams. [Such] assistance, although proffered in common with fully desegregated groups, might so directly impede the progress of court-ordered school desegregation within the city that it would be appropriate to fashion equitable relief."

Use by segregated nonschool groups might also undermine the outstanding decree to desegregate park facilities:

> For example, the record contains indications that there are all-white private and all-Negro public Dixie Youth and Babe Ruth baseball leagues for children, all of which use city-provided ballfields. [Were] the District Court to determine that this dual system came about as a means of evading the parks decree, or of serving to perpetuate the separate-but-equal use of city facilities on the basis of race, through the aid and assistance of the city, further relief would be appropriate.

The Court cautioned, however, that

> [t]raditional state monopolies, such as electricity, water, and police and fire protection — all generalized governmental services — do not by their mere provision constitute a showing of state involvement in invidious discrimination. The same is true of a broad spectrum of municipal recreational facilities: parks, playgrounds, athletic facilities, amphitheaters, museums, zoos, and the like. It follows, therefore, that the portion of the District Court's order prohibiting the mere use of such facilities by *any* segregated "private group, club, or organization" is invalid because it was not predicated upon a proper finding of state action.
>
> If, however, the city or other governmental entity rations otherwise freely accessible recreational facilities, the case for state action will naturally be stronger than if the facilities are simply available to all comers without condition or reservation. Here, for example, petitioners allege that the city engages in scheduling softball games for an all-white church league and provides balls, equipment, fields, and lighting. The city's role in that situation would be dangerously close to what was found to exist in *Burton*, where the city "elected to place its power, property and prestige behind the admitted discrimination." We are reminded, however, that the Court has never attempted to formulate "an infallible test for determining whether the State . . . has become significantly involved in private discriminations" so as to constitute state action [quoting *Reitman*, section B1 supra].

3. *State dependence on discriminatory conduct.* Justice Clark points out in *Burton* that "profits earned by discrimination not only contribute to, but also are indispensable elements in, the financial success of a governmental agency." Should the result in *Burton* have been different if Eagle were able to show that its refusal to serve blacks resulted in reduced profits? If the parking authority had charged it a lower rent so as not to capture any of the profits earned from Eagle's discrimi-

natory conduct? Justice Clark's opinion relies on the "mutual benefits" conferred by Eagle and the parking authority on each other. Note that there is a tension between the need to avoid conferring benefits on the private actor and the need to avoid public capture of the benefits from discrimination. For example, the state could avoid benefiting from the discriminatory conduct by not taxing the profits attributable to the discrimination. But by pursuing this policy, the state would in effect subsidize the discriminatory conduct. Does the need to avoid this dilemma explain the constitutional requirement that the state divorce itself entirely from discriminatory private entities when the benefits conferred are "mutual"?

   4. *State action as symbolism.* Does the result in *Burton* depend on the "message" sent to the general public when a discriminatory private entity rents space in a public building? Notice Justice Clark's emphasis on the state and federal flags that flew over the parking facility. In these circumstances, is there a risk that the public would interpret Eagle's presence in the building as connoting state approval of its policies? That it would perceive Eagle as a state entity? Should the parking authority prominently post signs stating that it did not approve of the racial policies of its tenants?

   RENDELL-BAKER v. KOHN, 457 U.S. 830 (1982). Petitioners were employees of the New Perspectives School, a privately owned institution specializing in "problem" students. Nearly all the school's students were referred to it by public institutions. It was heavily regulated by public authorities, and between 90 and 99 percent of its operating budget came from public funds. Petitioners were discharged after disagreeing with certain school policies. They claimed that their discharge violated their constitutional rights to free speech and procedural due process. Chief Justice Burger wrote the Court's opinion:

   "[The] Court of Appeals concluded that the fact that virtually all of the school's income was derived from government funding was the strongest factor to support a claim of state action. But [we] conclude that the school's receipt of public funds does not make the discharge decisions acts of the State.

   "The school [is] not fundamentally different from many private corporations whose business depends primarily on contracts to build roads, bridges, dams, ships, or submarines for the government. Acts of such private contractors do not . become acts of the government by reason of their significant or even total engagement in performing public contracts. . . .

   "[The] decisions to discharge the petitioners were not compelled or even influenced by any state regulation. Indeed, in contrast to the extensive regulation of the school generally, the various regulators showed relatively little interest in the school's personnel matters. . . .

   "[Petitioners] argue that there is a 'symbiotic relationship' between the school and the State similar to the relationship involved in [*Burton*]. [But] in *Burton*, the Court [stressed] that the restaurant was located on public property and that the rent from the restaurant contributed to the support of the garage. In response to the argument that the restaurant's profits, and hence the State's financial position, would suffer if it did not discriminate, the Court concluded that this showed that the State profited from the restaurant's discriminatory conduct. The Court viewed this as support for the conclusion that the State should be charged with the discriminatory actions. Here the school's fiscal relationship with the State is not different from that of many contractors performing services for the government. No symbiotic relationship such as existed in *Burton* exists here."

Justice White wrote a separate opinion concurring in the judgment.

Justice Marshall, with whom Justice Brennan joined, dissented: "The State has delegated to the New Perspectives School its statutory duty to educate children with special needs. The school receives almost all of its funds from the State, and is heavily regulated. This nexus between the school and the State is so substantial that the school's action must be considered state action. I therefore dissent."

SAN FRANCISCO ARTS & ATHLETICS, INC. v. UNITED STATES OLYMPIC COMMITTEE, 482 U.S. 522 (1987). The Amateur Sports Act of 1978 gave the United States Olympic Committee the exclusive right to use the term "Olympic." When petitioner organized and began to promote the "Gay Olympic Games," the committee brought suit under the statute to enjoin petitioner from using the word "Olympic." Petitioner responded by pointing out that the committee had allowed other groups to use the word "Olympic." It argued that the committee's discriminatory selection of such groups violated the equal protection component of the fifth amendment due process clause.

In a five-to-four decision, the Supreme Court held that the committee's selection of groups permitted to use the term was not state action. Justice Powell delivered the Court's opinion: "The fact that Congress granted [the committee] a corporate charter does not render [it] a government agent. All corporations act under charters granted by a [government]. [Nor] is the fact that Congress has granted the [committee] exclusive use of the word 'Olympic' dispositive. All enforceable rights in trademarks are created by some governmental [act]. . . .

"The [committee's] choice of how to enforce its exclusive right [simply] is not a governmental decision. There is no evidence that the Federal Government coerced or encouraged the [committee] in the exercise of its rights. At most, the Federal Government, by failing to supervise the [committee's] use of its rights, can be said to exercise '[m]ere approval of or acquiescence in the initiatives' of the [committee]. [This] is not enough to make the [committee's] actions those of the Government."

Justice Brennan, joined by Justice Marshall, dissented: "The [committee] and the Federal Government exist in a symbiotic relationship sufficient to provide a nexus between the [committee's] challenged action and the Government. First, as in *Burton*, the relationship here confers a variety of mutual benefits. [The] Act gave the [committee] authority and responsibilities that no private organization in this country had ever held. . . .

"Second, in the eye of the public, [the] connection between the decisions of the United States Government and those of the United States Olympic Committee is profound. . . .

"Even more importantly, there is a close financial and legislative link between the [committee's] alleged discriminatory exercise of its word-use authority and the financial success of both the [committee] and the Government. It would certainly be 'irony amounting to grave injustice' if, to finance the team that is to represent the virtues of our political system, the [committee] were free to employ government-created economic leverage to prohibit political speech. [*Burton*.]"

Justice O'Connor, joined by Justice Blackmun, also dissented from the Court's state action determination.

Note: State Action as Coercion or Significant Encouragement

1. United States Olympic Committee *and* Burton. Does *United States Olympic Committee* help explain what factors triggered the finding of state action in *Burton?* Justice Powell's opinion relies on an earlier decision, Blum v. Yaretsky, 457 U.S. 991 (1982), where the Court rejected a procedural due process challenge to the decisions, made without hearings by state-subsidized nursing homes, to downgrade the level of treatment for patients receiving Medicaid payments. Although Medicaid regulations required the nursing home to maintain different levels of care for patients and to transfer patients when necessary, and although the state responded to the transfers by reducing Medicaid payments, the Court held that no state action was present because the state was not responsible for the individual transfer decisions. The Court summarized the law as follows:

> [Although] the factual setting of each case will be significant, our precedents indicate that a State normally can be held responsible for a private decision only when it has exercised coercive power or has provided such significant encouragement, either overt or covert, that the choice must in law be deemed to be that of the State. Mere approval of or acquiescence in the initiatives of a private party is not sufficient to justify holding the State responsible for those initiatives under the terms of the Fourteenth Amendment.

2. Rendell-Baker *and* Burton. According to *Rendell-Baker, Burton* stands for the proposition that the state may not profit from discriminatory conduct. Is that a fair reading of *Burton?* Assuming that it is, might not the school in *Rendell-Baker* pass on to the state some of the savings it realizes from avoiding the cost of due process hearings just as the restaurant in *Burton* passed on some of the profits derived from racial discrimination?

3. Rendell-Baker *and the recognition of public actors.* The Court begins its analysis in *Rendell-Baker* with the assumption that the New Perspectives School is "private." If the school were itself a "public" institution, there would be no doubt that its decision to discharge petitioners would be "state action." But given the fact that the school received virtually all of its funds from public sources, why does the Court begin with the assumption that it is "private"?

Presumably what makes the New Perspectives School private is the fact that the state exercises less pervasive control over it than it would over a state instrumentality; thus, the state did not produce the objectionable conduct at issue. But the very issue in dispute in *Rendell-Baker* was the degree of control the state was obligated to exercise. Surely the acts of state police officers would be attributable to the state even if state law left them largely unconstrained in exercising their discretion.

Compare *Rendell-Baker* with Ex parte Virginia, 100 U.S. 339 (1880), where a state judge discriminated against blacks in the selection of juries in violation of state law. The Court rejected the defendant's argument that he was not a state actor because the state had prohibited the conduct in question. "[As] he acts in the name and for the State, and is clothed with the State's power, his act is that of the State. This must be so, or the constitutional prohibition has no meaning." See also Screws v. United States, 325 U.S. 91 (1945) (state police officer who exceeds his authority under state law is nonetheless a state actor acting under color of law). Is the *Rendell-Baker* "coercion or significant encouragement" test consistent with Ex parte Virginia and *Screws?*

Compare *Rendell-Baker* to West v. Atkins, 487 U.S. 42 (1988), where the Court held that a private physician, under contract with the state to provide medical services for inmates at a state prison, was a state actor for constitutional purposes. Writing for eight justices, Justice Blackmun rejected the argument that the doctor's actions were not attributable to the state because he was exercising independent medical judgment. In a footnote, the Court distinguished *Rendell-Baker* and *Blum* as follows:

> Where the issue is whether a *private* party is engaged in activity that constitutes state action, it may be relevant that the challenged activity turned on judgments controlled by professional standards, where those standards are not established by the State. The Court has held that "a State normally can be held responsible for a private decision only when it has exercised coercive power or has provided such significant encouragement, either overt or covert, that the choice must in law be deemed to be that of the State." [*Blum; Rendell-Baker.*] In both *Blum* and *Rendell-Baker*, the fact that the private entities received state funding and were subject to state regulation did not, without more, convert their conduct into state action. . . .
>
> This determination cannot be transformed into the proposition that no person acts under color of state law where he is exercising independent professional judgment. [*Blum*] and *Rendell-Baker* provide no support for respondent's argument that a physician, employed by the State to fulfill the State's constitutional obligations, does not act under color of state law merely because he renders medical care in accordance with professional obligations.

Why wasn't the New Perspectives School "employed by the State to fulfill the State's constitutional obligations"?

4. *Amtrak.* For an extended discussion of the distinction between private and government actors, see Lebron v. National Railroad Passenger Corp., 513 U.S. 374 (1995). The controversy arose when Lebron sought to rent a huge, illuminated billboard known as the "Spectacular" in New York's Pennsylvania Station. Lebron wished to use the space to display a photo montage parodying Coors beer commercials and attacking the brewery for its alleged support for right-wing causes. Pennsylvania Station was owned by Amtrak, a corporation created by Congress to avert the threatened extinction of passenger train service. The United States owned all of Amtrak's preferred stock, and the President appointed a majority of its board of directors. When Amtrak refused to rent the space to Lebron, he sued, claiming that his first amendment rights had been violated. The court of appeals held that Amtrak was not a government actor and therefore rejected Lebron's claim. In an eight-to-one decision, the Supreme Court reversed.

Writing for the majority, Justice Scalia began by noting that, although the Court had "held once [see *Burton*] and said many times that actions of private entities can sometimes be regarded as governmental action for constitutional purposes," it was unnecessary "to traverse this difficult terrain in the present case, since [Amtrak] is not a private entity but the Government itself."

In reaching this conclusion, the Court found irrelevant Congress's own declaration that Amtrak was not a government actor. Nor was Amtrak's corporate form determinative. "It surely cannot be that government [is] able to evade the most solemn obligations imposed in the Constitution by simply resorting to the corporate form. On that thesis, ~~Plessy v. Ferguson can be resurrected~~ by the simple device of having the State of Louisiana operate segregated trains through a state-owned Amtrak." Amtrak was a government actor because it was "established and organized under federal law for the very purpose of pursuing federal governmental objectives, under the direction and control of federal governmental appointees."

5. *Edmonson.* In Edmonson v. Leesville Concrete Co., 500 U.S. 614 (1991), the Court, in a opinion by Justice Kennedy, held that a private civil litigant who utilized peremptory challenges to exclude jurors on account of race was a state actor for constitutional purposes. The Court based this conclusion in part on the "overt, significant assistance of state officials" in the discriminatory conduct:

> [A] private party could not exercise its peremptory challenges absent the overt, significant assistance of the court. The government summons jurors, constrains their freedom of movement, and subjects them to public scrutiny and examination. [Without] the direct and indispensable participation of the judge, who beyond all question is a state actor, the peremptory challenge system would serve no purpose. By enforcing a discriminatory peremptory challenge, the court "has not only made itself a party to the [biased act], but has elected to place its power, property and prestige behind the [alleged] discrimination." [*Burton.*]

Justice O'Connor, joined by Chief Justice Rehnquist and Justice Scalia, dissented:

> It is the nature of a peremptory that its exercise is left wholly within the discretion of the litigant. [The] peremptory is, by design, an enclave of private action in a government-managed proceeding. . . .
>
> That [government activity] may be necessary to a peremptory challenge — in the sense that there could be no such challenge without a venire from which to select — no more makes the challenge state action than the building of roads and provision of public transportation makes state action of riding on a bus. . . .
>
> The government "normally can be held responsible for a private decision only when it has exercised coercive power or has provided such significant encouragement, either overt or covert, that the choice must in law be deemed to be that of the State" [*Blum*]. . . .
>
> A judge does not "significantly encourage" discrimination by the mere act of excusing a juror in response to an unexplained request.

2. State Licensing and Authorization

PUBLIC UTILITIES COMMISSION v. POLLAK, 343 U.S. 451 (1952). Capital Transit Company was a privately owned corporation providing bus and streetcar service in the District of Columbia under a franchise from Congress. In 1948, it began experimenting with a "music as you ride" program under which radio programs were amplified through loudspeakers in the streetcars and buses. In 1949, the Public Utilities Commission, which regulated Capital, ordered an investigation of the program to determine whether it was "consistent with public convenience, comfort and safety." The commission concluded that the use of radios was not inconsistent with the public interest and dismissed its investigation. Some of Capital's passengers thereupon appealed the commission's decision, and the court of appeals reversed, holding that the broadcasts deprived passengers of liberty without due process of law. Justice Burton delivered the Court's opinion:

"It was held by the court below that the action of Capital Transit in installing and operating the radio receivers, coupled with the action of the Public Utilities Commission in dismissing its own investigation of the practice, sufficiently involved the Federal Government in responsibility for the radio programs to make the First and Fifth Amendments [applicable] to this radio service. . . .

"[We agree. In reaching this result,] we do not rely on the mere fact that Capital Transit operates a public utility on the streets of the District of Columbia under authority of Congress. Nor do we rely upon the fact that, by reason of such federal authorization, Capital Transit now enjoys a substantial monopoly of street railway and bus transportation in the District of Columbia. We do, however, recognize that Capital Transit operates its service under the regulatory supervision of the Public Utilities Commission of the District of Columbia which is an agency authorized by Congress. We rely particularly upon the fact that that agency, pursuant to protests against the radio program, ordered an investigation of it and, after formal public hearings, ordered its investigation dismissed on the ground that the public safety, comfort and convenience were not impaired thereby.

"We, therefore, find it appropriate to examine into what restriction, if any, the First and Fifth Amendments place upon the Federal Government under the facts of this case, assuming that the action of Capital Transit in operating the radio service, together with the action of the Commission in permitting such operation, amounts to sufficient Federal Government action to make the First and Fifth Amendments applicable thereto."

The Court held that the broadcasts were not unconstitutional.

Moose Lodge No. 107 v. Irvis

407 U.S. 163 (1972)

MR. JUSTICE REHNQUIST delivered the opinion of the Court.

[Appellant Moose Lodge is a local branch of a national fraternal organization. Lodge policy restricts membership to whites and prohibits members from bringing black guests to the lodge dining room and bar. When appellee, a black, was refused service because of his race, he filed this action, naming as defendants both Moose Lodge and the Pennsylvania Liquor Authority. He claimed that, because the liquor authority had issued Moose Lodge a license that authorized the sale of alcoholic beverages on its premises, the refusal of service was "state action." He sought an injunction requiring the liquor authority to revoke Moose Lodge's license so long as it continued its discriminatory practices. The court below ruled in his favor.]

The Court has never held, of course, that discrimination by an otherwise private entity would be violative of the Equal Protection Clause if the private entity receives any sort of benefit or service at all from the State, or if it is subject to state regulation in any degree whatever. Since state-furnished services include such necessities of life as electricity, water, and police and fire protection, such a holding would utterly emasculate the distinction between private as distinguished from state conduct set forth in The Civil Rights Cases and adhered to in subsequent decisions. Our holdings indicate that where the impetus for the discrimination is private, the State must have "significantly involved itself with invidious discriminations," [*Reitman*], in order for the discriminatory action to fall within the ambit of the constitutional prohibition. . . .

Here there is nothing approaching the symbiotic relationship between lessor and lessee that was present in [*Burton*]. Unlike *Burton*, the Moose Lodge building is located on land owned by it, not by any public authority. Far from apparently holding itself out as a place of public accommodation, Moose Lodge quite ostentatiously proclaims the fact that it is not open to the public at large. Nor is it located and operated in such surroundings that although private in name, it discharges a function or performs a service that would otherwise in all likelihood be performed by the State. In short, while Eagle was a public restaurant in a public building, Moose Lodge is a private social club in a private building.

With the exception hereafter noted, the Pennsylvania Liquor Control Board plays absolutely no part in establishing or enforcing the membership or guest policies of the club that it licenses to serve liquor. There is no suggestion in this record that Pennsylvania law, either as written or as applied, discriminates against minority groups either in their right to apply for club licenses themselves or in their right to purchase and be served liquor in places of public accommodation. The only effect that the state licensing of Moose Lodge to serve liquor can be said to have on the right of any other Pennsylvanian to buy or be served liquor on premises other than those of Moose Lodge is that for some purposes club licenses are counted in the maximum number of licenses that may be issued in a given municipality. . . .

The District Court was at pains to point out in its opinion what it considered to be the "pervasive" nature of the regulation of private clubs by the Pennsylvania Liquor Control Board. . . .

However detailed this type of regulation may be in some particulars, it cannot be said to in any way foster or encourage racial discrimination. Nor can it be said to make the State in any realistic sense a partner or even a joint venturer in the club's enterprise. The limited effect of the prohibition against obtaining additional club licenses when the maximum number of retail licenses allotted to a municipality has been issued, when considered together with the availability of liquor from hotel, restaurant, and retail licensees, falls far short of conferring upon club licensees a monopoly in the dispensing of liquor in any given municipality or in the State as a whole. We therefore hold that, with the exception hereafter noted, the operation of the regulatory scheme enforced by the Pennsylvania Liquor Control Board does not sufficiently implicate the State in the discriminatory guest policies of Moose Lodge to make the latter "state action" within the ambit of the Equal Protection Clause of the Fourteenth Amendment.

The District Court found that the regulations of the Liquor Control Board adopted pursuant to statute affirmatively require that "[e]very club licensee shall adhere to all of the provisions of its Constitution and By-Laws." . . .

The effect of this particular regulation on Moose Lodge under the provisions of the constitution placed in the record in the court below would be to place state sanctions behind its discriminatory membership rules. . . .

Even though the Liquor Control Board regulation in question is neutral in its terms, the result of its application in a case where the constitution and bylaws of a club required racial discrimination would be to invoke the sanctions of the State to enforce a concededly discriminatory private rule. State action, for purposes of the Equal Protection Clause, may emanate from rulings of administrative and regulatory agencies as well as from legislative or judicial action. [*Shel-*

ley] makes it clear that the application of state sanctions to enforce such a rule would violate the Fourteenth Amendment. . . .

[Appellee] was entitled to a decree enjoining the enforcement of [the] regulations promulgated by the Pennsylvania Liquor Control Board insofar as [they require] compliance by Moose Lodge with provisions of its constitution and bylaws containing racially discriminatory provisions. He was entitled to no more. . . .

Reversed and remanded.

MR. JUSTICE DOUGLAS, with whom MR. JUSTICE MARSHALL joins, dissenting.

[The] fact that a private club gets some kind of permit from the State or municipality does not make it *ipso facto* a public enterprise or undertaking, any more than the grant to a householder of a permit to operate an incinerator puts the householder in the public domain. We must, therefore, examine whether there are special circumstances involved in the Pennsylvania scheme which differentiate the liquor license possessed by Moose Lodge from the incinerator permit. . . .

[Liquor] licenses in Pennsylvania, unlike driver's licenses, or marriage licenses, are not freely available to those who meet racially neutral qualifications. There is a complex quota system. [What] the majority neglects to say is that the quota for Harrisburg, where Moose Lodge No. 107 is located, has been full for many years. No more club licenses may be issued in that city.

This state-enforced scarcity of licenses restricts the ability of blacks to obtain liquor, for liquor is commercially available *only* at private clubs for a significant portion of each week. . . .

I would affirm the judgment below.

MR. JUSTICE BRENNAN, with whom MR. JUSTICE MARSHALL joins, dissenting.

When Moose Lodge obtained its liquor license, the State of Pennsylvania became an active participant in the operation of the Lodge bar. Liquor licensing laws are only incidentally revenue measures; they are primarily pervasive regulatory schemes under which the State dictates and continually supervises virtually every detail of the operation of the licensee's business. Very few, if any, other licensed businesses experience such complete state involvement. Yet the Court holds that such involvement does not constitute "state action" making the Lodge's refusal to serve a guest liquor solely because of his race a violation of the Fourteenth Amendment.

[Plainly,] the State of Pennsylvania's liquor regulations intertwine the State with the operation of the Lodge bar in a "significant way [and] lend [the State's] authority to the sordid business of racial discrimination." . . .

I therefore dissent and would affirm the final decree entered by the District Court.

Jackson v. Metropolitan Edison Co.

419 U.S. 345 (1974)

MR. JUSTICE REHNQUIST delivered the opinion of the Court. . . .

[Metropolitan Edison, a privately owned utility, holds a certificate of public convenience issued by a state utility commission authorizing it to provide electricity to its customers. As a condition for holding this certificate, it is subject to extensive state regulation. Under a provision of its general tariff filed with the state commission, it has the right to discontinue service to a customer on reasonable notice of nonpayment of bills. After a lengthy dispute, Metropolitan Edison terminated Jackson's service for alleged nonpayment. Jackson thereupon brought this action, claiming that the termination constituted state action depriving her of property in violation of the due process clause of the fourteenth amendment.]

[The] mere fact that a business is subject to state regulation does not by itself convert its action into that of the State for purposes of the Fourteenth Amendment. Nor does the fact that the regulation is extensive and detailed, as in the case of most public utilities, do so. [*Pollak.*] It may well be that acts of a heavily regulated utility with at least something of a governmentally protected monopoly will more readily be found to be "state" acts than will the acts of an entity lacking these characteristics. But the inquiry must be whether there is a sufficiently close nexus between the State and the challenged action of the regulated entity so that the action of the latter may be fairly treated as that of the State itself. [*Moose Lodge.*] The true nature of the State's involvement may not be immediately obvious, and detailed inquiry may be required in order to determine whether the test is met. [*Burton*]. . . .

[Petitioner] first argues that "state action" is present because of the monopoly status allegedly conferred upon Metropolitan by the State of Pennsylvania. As a factual matter, it may well be doubted that the State ever granted or guaranteed Metropolitan a monopoly.[8] But assuming that it had, this fact is not determinative in considering whether Metropolitan's termination of service to petitioner was "state action" for purposes of the Fourteenth Amendment. In *Pollak*, [we] expressly disclaimed reliance on the monopoly status of the transit authority. Similarly, although certain monopoly aspects were presented in *Moose Lodge No. 107*, we found that the Lodge's action was not subject to the provisions of the Fourteenth Amendment. In each of those cases, there was insufficient relationship between the challenged actions of the entities involved and their monopoly status. There is no indication of any greater connection here.

We also reject the notion that Metropolitan's termination is state action because the State "has specifically authorized and approved" the termination practice. In the instant case, Metropolitan filed with the Public Utility Commission a general tariff — a provision of which states Metropolitan's right to terminate service for nonpayment. This provision has appeared in Metropolitan's previously filed tariffs for many years and has never been the subject of a hearing or other scrutiny by the Commission. Although the Commission did hold hearings on portions of Metropolitan's general tariff relating to the general rate increase, it never even considered the reinsertion of this provision in the newly filed general tariff. The provision became effective 60 days after filing when not disapproved by the Commission. . . .

The case most heavily relied on by petitioner is [*Pollak*]. [It] is not entirely clear whether the Court alternatively held that Capital Transit's action was action of the "state" for First Amendment purposes, or whether it merely assumed, argu-

---

8. [As] petitioner admits, such public utility companies are natural monopolies created by the economic forces of high threshold capital requirements and virtually unlimited economy of scale. Regulation was superimposed on such natural monopolies as a substitute for competition and not to eliminate it. . . .

endo, that it was and went on to resolve the First Amendment question adversely to the bus riders.[16] In either event, the nature of the state involvement there was quite different than it is here. The District of Columbia Public Utilities Commission, on its own motion, commenced an investigation of the effects of the piped music, and after a full hearing concluded not only that Capital Transit's practices were "not inconsistent with public convenience, comfort, and safety," but also that the practice "in fact, through the creation of better will among passengers, . . . tends to improve the conditions under which the public ride." Here, on the other hand, there was no such imprimatur placed on the practice of Metropolitan about which petitioner complains. The nature of governmental regulation of private utilities is such that a utility may frequently be required by the state regulatory scheme to obtain approval for practices a business regulated in less detail would be free to institute without any approval from a regulatory body. Approval by a state utility commission of such a request from a regulated utility, where the commission has not put its own weight on the side of the proposed practice by ordering it, does not transmute a practice initiated by the utility and approved by the Commission into "state action." At most, the Commission's failure to overturn this practice amounted to no more than a determination that a Pennsylvania utility was authorized to employ such a practice if it so desired. Respondent's exercise of the choice allowed by state law where the initiative comes from it and not from the State, does not make its action in doing so "state action" for purposes of the Fourteenth Amendment.

[Affirmed.]

[Dissenting opinions by Justices Douglas and Brennan are omitted.]

MR. JUSTICE MARSHALL, dissenting.

When the State confers a monopoly on a group or organization, this Court has held that the organization assumes many of the obligations of the State. Even when the Court has not found state action based solely on the State's conferral of a monopoly, it has suggested that the monopoly factor weighs heavily in determining whether constitutional obligations can be imposed on formally private entities. . . .

The majority distinguishes this line of cases with a cryptic assertion that public utility companies are "natural monopolies." The theory behind the distinction appears to be that since the State's purpose in regulating a natural monopoly is not to aid the company but to prevent its charging monopoly prices, the State's involvement is somehow less significant for state-action purposes. I cannot agree that so much should turn on so narrow a distinction. [It] is far from obvious that an electric company would not be subject to competition if the market were unimpeded by governmental restrictions. . . .

I dissent.

16. At one point the Court states:

"We find in the reasoning of the court below a sufficiently close relation between the Federal Government and the radio service to make it necessary for us to consider those Amendments." Later, the opinion states: "We, therefore, find it appropriate to examine into what restriction, if any, the First and Fifth Amendments place upon the Federal Government . . . *assuming* that the action of Capital Transit . . . amounts to sufficient Federal Government action to make the First and Fifth Amendments applicable thereto." (Emphasis added.)

Note: Licensing and Authorization as State Action

1. Pollak *and the failure to regulate.* If Congress had chosen not to regulate bus and railway service at all, the Court presumably would have held that the decision of a private company to install radio service was not "state action." Why does the government's refusal to prohibit this practice become state action when it is part of a pervasive pattern of regulation? (a) Perhaps licensing justifies a state action finding because it eliminates competitive pressures that otherwise might prevent the private entity from engaging in the challenged conduct. (b) Perhaps the absence of an alternative source for the service increases the costs of the challenged conduct to those objecting to it. Note that *Pollak* rejects Capital Transit's monopoly status as a basis for finding state action.

Is the symbolic significance of the state's affirmative imprimatur on the activity dispositive? Recall that in *Flagg Brothers*, the Court treats a statute authorizing Flagg Brothers' sale as "immaterial" because it merely "embodied [the state's] decision not to act in statutory form."

2. *Licensing and government neutrality.* Is the requirement of government neutrality relevant to the *Pollak* problem? Was the action of the Public Utilities Commission a departure from neutrality? Does it matter that its statutory mandate required it to prohibit the radio broadcast if it found that the practice was not in the public interest?

In Columbia Broadcasting System v. Democratic National Committee, 412 U.S. 94 (1973), the Federal Communications Commission refused to require broadcast licensees to accept editorial advertising. The Court rejected a first amendment attack on the broadcasters' practice. In a portion of his opinion joined by only two other justices, Chief Justice Burger argued that the Federal Communications Commission decision did not make the actions of the broadcasters "state action." He distinguished *Pollak* as follows:

> [In *Pollak*] Congress had expressly authorized the agency to undertake plenary intervention into the affairs of the carrier and it was pursuant to that authorization that the agency investigated the challenged policy and approved it on public interest standards. [Here], Congress has not established a regulatory scheme for broadcast licensees as pervasive as the regulation of public transportation in *Pollak*. More important, [Congress] has affirmatively indicated in the Communications Act that certain journalistic decisions are for the licensee, subject only to the restrictions imposed by evaluation of its overall performance under the public interest standard. In *Pollak* there was no suggestion that Congress had considered worthy of protection the carrier's interest in exercising discretion over the content of communications forced on passengers.

Did the regulatory schemes in *Moose Lodge* and *Jackson* depart from the requirement of governmental neutrality? Both schemes are facially neutral in the Washington v. Davis sense. Do government-enforced monopolies in these contexts nonetheless constitute subsidies for conduct that threatens constitutional values? Answering this question presumably involves a comparison between the status quo and the situation that would exist if the government were completely passive. Is such a comparison meaningful?

3. *Political parties.* What implications does *Jackson* hold for the treatment of political parties as state actors? The Court debated this issue in Morse v. Repub-

lican Party of Virginia, 517 U.S. 186 (1996). The case presented the court with a question of statutory construction — whether the Virginia Republican Party was obligated under the 1965 Voting Rights Act to obtain preclearance before changing the qualifications for participation in a state nominating convention. In the course of answering this question (in the affirmative), the Court had occasion to distinguish its prior state action precedent:

> In [*Jackson*] and [*Flagg Brothers*] this Court concluded that the defendants were not acting under authority explicitly or implicitly delegated by the State when they carried out the challenged actions. In this case, however, . . . the Party acted under the authority conferred by the Virginia election code. It was the Commonwealth of Virginia — indeed only Virginia — that had exclusive power to reserve one of the two special ballot provisions for the Party.

Compare Justice Thomas's dissent:

> The Party's selection of a candidate at a convention does not satisfy [the exclusive public function] test. [We] have carefully distinguished the "conduct" of an election by the State from the exercise of private political rights within that State-created framework. Providing an orderly and fair process for the selection of public officers is a classic exclusive state function. . . .
>   [By] contrast, convening the members of a political association in order to select the person who can best represent and advance the group's goals is not, and historically has never been, the province of the State — much less its exclusive province.
>   To be sure, the Party takes advantage of favorable State law when it certifies its candidate for automatic placement on the ballot. Nevertheless, according to our state action cases, that is no basis for treating the Party as the State. The State's conferral of benefits upon an entity — even so great a benefit as monopoly status — is insufficient to convent the entity into a State actor. See [*Jackson*].

D. CONSTITUTIONALLY REQUIRED DEPARTURES FROM NEUTRALITY? THE PUBLIC FUNCTION DOCTRINE

Marsh v. Alabama

326 U.S. 501 (1946)

MR. JUSTICE BLACK delivered the opinion of the Court.

In this case we are asked to decide whether a State, consistently with the First and Fourteenth Amendments, can impose criminal punishment on a person who undertakes to distribute religious literature on the premises of a company-owned town contrary to the wishes of the town's management. The town, a suburb of Mobile, Alabama, known as Chickasaw, is owned by the Gulf Shipbuilding Corporation. Except for that it has all the characteristics of any other American town. The property consists of residential buildings, streets, a system of sewers, a sewage disposal plant and a "business block" on which business places are situated. A deputy of the Mobile County Sheriff, paid by the company, serves as the town's policeman. Merchants and service establishments have rented the stores and business places on the business block and the United States uses one of the places as a post office [and] according to all indications the residents use the business block as their regular shopping center. To do so, they now, as they have for many years, make use of a company-owned paved street and sidewalk located alongside the store fronts in order to enter and leave the stores and the post office. Intersecting company-owned roads at each end of the business block lead into a four-lane public highway which runs parallel to the business block at a distance of thirty feet. There is nothing to stop highway traffic from coming onto the business block and upon arrival a traveler may make free use of the facilities available there. In short the town and its shopping district are accessible to and freely used by the public in general and there is nothing to distinguish them from any other town and shopping center except the fact that the title to the property belongs to a private corporation.

Appellant, a Jehovah's Witness, came onto the sidewalk [and] undertook to distribute religious literature. In the stores the corporation had posted a notice which read as follows: "This Is Private Property, and Without Written Permission, No Street, or House Vendor, Agent or Solicitation of Any Kind Will Be Permitted." Appellant was warned that she could not distribute the literature without a permit and told that no permit would be issued to her. She protested that the company rule could not be constitutionally applied so as to prohibit her from distributing religious writings. When she was asked to leave the sidewalk and Chickasaw she declined. The deputy sheriff arrested her and she was charged in the state court with violating [a state statute] which makes it a crime to enter or remain on the premises of another after having been warned not to do so. Appellant contended that to construe the state statute as applicable to her activities would abridge her right to freedom of press and religion contrary to the First and Fourteenth Amendments to the Constitution. This contention was rejected and she was convicted. . . .

Had the title to Chickasaw belonged not to a private but to a municipal corporation and had appellant been arrested for violating a municipal ordinance rather than a ruling by those appointed by the corporation to manage a company town it would have been clear that appellant's conviction must be reversed. [Our] question then narrows down to this: Can those people who live in or come to Chickasaw be denied freedom of press and religion simply because a single company has legal title to all the town?

[We] do not agree that the corporation's property interests settle the question. [Ownership] does not always mean absolute dominion. The more an owner, for his advantage, opens up his property for use by the public in general, the more do his rights become circumscribed by the statutory and constitutional rights of those who use it. Thus, the owners of privately held bridges, ferries, turnpikes and railroads may not operate them as freely as a farmer does his farm. Since these facilities are built and operated primarily to benefit the public and since their operation is essentially a public function, it is subject to state regulation. . . .

Whether a corporation or a municipality owns or possesses the town the public in either case has an identical interest in the functioning of the community in such manner that the channels of communication remain free. [The] managers appointed by the corporation cannot curtail the liberty of press and religion of these people consistently with the purposes of the Constitutional guarantees, and a state statute, as the one here involved, which enforces such action by criminally punishing those who attempt to distribute religious literature clearly violates the First and Fourteenth Amendments to the Constitution.

Many people in the United States live in company-owned towns. These people, just as residents of municipalities, are free citizens of their State and country. Just as all other citizens they must make decisions which affect the welfare of community and nation. To act as good citizens they must be informed. In order to enable them to be properly informed their information must be uncensored. There is no more reason for depriving these people of the liberties guaranteed by the First and Fourteenth Amendments than there is for curtailing these freedoms with respect to any other citizen.

When we balance the Constitutional rights of owners of property against those of the people to enjoy freedom of press and religion, as we must here, we remain mindful of the fact that the latter occupy a preferred position. [In] our view the circumstance that the property rights to the premises where the deprivation of liberty, here involved, took place, were held by others than the public, is not sufficient to justify the State's permitting a corporation to govern a community of citizens so as to restrict their fundamental liberties and the enforcement of such restraint by the application of a state statute.

[Reversed and remanded.]

Mr. Justice Jackson took no part in the consideration or decision of this case.

[Justice Frankfurter's concurring opinion is omitted.]

Mr. Justice Reed, dissenting. . . .

What the present decision establishes as a principle is that one may remain on private property against the will of the owner and contrary to the law of the state so long as the only objection to his presence is that he is exercising an asserted right to spread there his religious views. This is the first case to extend by law the privilege of religious exercises beyond public places or to private places without the assent of the owner. . . .

[Chief Justice Vinson] and Mr. Justice Burton join in this dissent.

Note: The "Public Function" Theory and the Passive State

1. Marsh *and* Shelley. Note that Justice Black might have written an opinion in *Marsh* that paralleled the Court's analysis two years later in *Shelley.* He might have focused attention on state court enforcement of Alabama's trespass statute and held that this judicial conduct violated the first amendment. But although Justice Black makes brief reference to the state prosecution, his analysis focuses on the conduct of the company town rather than on the conduct of the state court. Why should decisions of this "private" entity be treated as if they were state decisions? Would the town's actions have been unconstitutional if its owners had physically ejected Marsh without resorting to the state's legal processes?

2. *"Public functions" and private power.* Some language in *Marsh* supports the view that the town was subject to constitutional constraint because it was acting "like" a state. Thus, Justice Black points out that, except for its private ownership, Chickasaw had "all the characteristics of any other American town." Why is this relevant?

To the extent that the opinion rests on this premise, it seems to stand for the proposition that there are limits on the extent to which the state may escape constitutional restraints by "delegating" to private parties functions traditionally performed by the state. Does the opinion make clear what those limits are or why they were exceeded in this case?

Some passages in *Marsh* suggest that the difficulty was not with the state's delegation of public functions to a private entity, but with its failure to act in the face of widespread violation of constitutional values. Viewed in this light, the opinion is a rare acknowledgment that individual freedom may on occasion be threatened as much by private as by public action. From this perspective, Gulf Shipbuilding's status was "public" because its power rivaled that of the state rather than because of any particular function it had assumed. Whereas constitutional liberty is normally associated with limits on governmental authority, in *Marsh* the Court arguably thought that the Constitution required the government to intervene actively in order to control exercises of private power.

3. *The reach of the public function doctrine.* In what other circumstances should the state's delegation of governmental power to private entities — or failure to control exercises of private power — be subject to constitutional constraint? Consider the following applications of the public function doctrine:

a. *The "white primary" cases.* In a series of cases involving the effective exclusion of blacks from Texas elections, the Court held that the discriminatory policies of "private" political organizations could be attributed to the state. Nixon v. Herndon, 273 U.S. 536 (1927), held that the fourteenth amendment had been violated when blacks were denied ballots in the state Democratic Party primary pursuant to a Texas statute that stated, "[I]n no event shall a Negro be eligible to participate in a Democratic Party primary election held in the State of Texas." Texas thereupon rewrote the statute to provide that the State Executive Committee of the party in power could prescribe the qualifications of its members for voting. In Nixon v. Condon, 286 U.S. 73 (1932), the Court once again found that the denial of the franchise to blacks was unconstitutional. Since the committee was acting under authority expressly delegated by the state, the Court reasoned that its decisions could be attributed to the state.

In Grovey v. Townsend, 295 U.S. 45 (1935), however, where the policy of racial exclusion had been adopted by the state party convention without specific statutory authorization, the Court held that there was no state action and therefore no constitutional violation. In the Court's view, the exclusionary policy was voluntarily adopted by the Democratic Party, which was not an organ of the state. The policy was no more than a refusal of party membership with which "the State need have no concern."

Grovey was overruled in Smith v. Allwright, 321 U.S. 649 (1944). The Court stated that "[t]he privilege of membership in a party may be, as this Court said in [*Grovey*,] no concern of a State. But when, as here, that privilege is also the essential qualification for voting in a primary to select nominees for a general election, the State makes the action of the party the action of the State."

Although the Court was unambiguous in holding that the Democratic Party's exclusionary policy could be attributed to the state, the exact basis for the attribution was less clear. In part, the state action finding seemed to rest on the "public function" performed by party officials. Thus, the Court wrote that "the place of the primary in the electoral scheme makes clear that state delegation to a party of the power to fix the qualifications of primary elections is delegation of a state function that may make the party's action the action of the State."

But the state action finding seemed to rest as well on actual state involvement in the primary election process:

> When primaries become a part of the machinery for choosing officials, state and national, as they have here, the same tests to determine the character of discrimination or abridgement should be applied to the primary as are applied to the general election. If the State requires a certain electoral procedure, prescribes a general election ballot made up of party nominees so chosen and limits the choice of the electorate in general elections for state offices, practically speaking, to those whose names appear on such a ballot, it endorses, adopts and enforces the discrimination against Negroes, practiced by a party entrusted by Texas law with the determination of the qualifications of participants in the primary.

Finally, another passage in the opinion suggested that the state had an affirmative constitutional obligation to prevent private organizations from abridging electoral rights:

> The United States is a constitutional democracy. Its organic law grants to all citizens a right to participate in the choice of elected officials without restriction by any State because of race. This grant to the people of the opportunity for choice is not to be nullified by a State through casting its electoral process in a form which permits a private organization to practice racial discrimination in the election. Constitutional rights would be of little value if they could be thus indirectly denied.

Although the Court maintained virtual unanimity in *Smith*, controversy over which strand of the opinion was determinative erupted nine years later in Terry v. Adams, 345 U.S. 461 (1953), the last in this series of cases. *Terry* concerned the exclusion of blacks from "pre-primaries" held by the Jaybird Democratic Association, a Texas political organization. The Jaybirds maintained that they were not a political party at all but rather a self-governing voluntary club. Their election was not regulated by the state, and there was no legal connection between victory in that election and nomination by the Democratic Party to run in the subsequent general election. As a practical matter, however, white voters generally abided by the "recommendations" of the Jaybirds, and the Jaybird president testified that a purpose of his organization was to exclude blacks from the voting process. The Jaybirds were so successful in this endeavor that victors in the Jaybird primary had almost without exception run and won without opposition in the Democratic primaries and the general election that followed.

Although eight justices agreed that exclusion of blacks from the Jaybird primary violated the fifteenth amendment, no opinion attracted a majority. Writing for three justices, Justice Black focused on the state's failure to control private conduct that effectively deprived blacks of political power:

> The only election that has counted in this Texas county for more than fifty years has been that held by the Jaybirds from which Negroes were excluded. The Democratic primary and the general election have become no more than the perfunctory ratifiers of the choice that has already been made in Jaybird elections from which Negroes have been excluded. It is immaterial that the state does not control that part of this elective process which it leaves for the Jaybirds to manage. [The] effect of the whole procedure, Jaybird primary plus Democratic primary plus general election, is to do precisely that which the Fifteenth Amendment forbids —

strip Negroes of every vestige of influence in selecting the officials who control the local county matters that intimately touch the daily lives of citizens.

Writing only for himself, Justice Frankfurter found state involvement because state election officials had participated as voters in the Jaybird primary. The four other justices who found the requisite state action joined an opinion by Justice Clark. In his view, the record established that the Jaybirds operated, "as part and parcel of the Democratic Party, an organization existing under the auspices of Texas law." It followed that the result was dictated by Smith v. Allwright. "[When] a state structures its electoral apparatus in a form which devolves upon a political organization the uncontested choice of public officials, that organization itself, in whatever disguise, takes on those attributes of government which draw the Constitution's safeguards into play." Justice Minton cast the sole dissenting vote.

If the state had attempted to control participation in the Jaybird primary, might not the Jaybirds have had a plausible first amendment complaint?

Compare *Terry* to Tashjian v. Republican Party, 479 U.S. 208 (1986). In *Tashjian*, the Court upheld the Republican Party's constitutional challenge to a state law that prohibited nonparty members from participating in party primaries. (The Republicans had adopted a party rule permitting independents to vote in its primaries.) The Court held that

> [the] Party's attempt to broaden the base of public participation in and support for its activities is conduct undeniably central to the exercise of the right of association. [The] freedom to join together in furtherance of common political beliefs "necessarily presupposes the freedom to identify the people who constitute the association." Democratic Party of the United States v. Wisconsin, 450 U.S. 107, 122 (1981).

Why wasn't the Jaybirds' "freedom to identify the people who constitute the association" constitutionally protected?

When private groups effectively secure the power normally associated with the state, why shouldn't they be subject to the same restrictions? Is it relevant that the Jaybirds were able to wield this power only because of the voluntary decision by most white voters to adhere to the result of the Jaybird primary? Recall that on one theory, this sort of "voluntary" exclusion of discrete and insular minorities from private coalitions is precisely why laws discriminating against such minorities are subject to heightened scrutiny. See Chapter 5, section C1, supra. If the results of such exclusionary coalitions are constitutionally suspect, is it reasonable to think that the Constitution places no limits on the ability to form the coalitions in the first place?

b. *Private property and public functions.* Does the public function doctrine help to explain other cases where the Court has placed constitutional limits on the owners of private property? Does it explain *Shelley?*

In Evans v. Newton, section B2 supra, the Court's opinion invalidating the exclusion of blacks from the park created by Senator Bacon's will rested in part on the public character of the facility:

> The service rendered even by a private park of this character is municipal in nature. It is open to every white person, there being no selective element other than race. Golf clubs, social centers, luncheon clubs, schools such as Tuskegee was at least in origin, and other like organizations in the private sector are often racially

oriented. A park, on the other hand, is more like a fire department or police department that traditionally serves the community. Mass recreation through the use of parks is plainly in the public domain; and state courts that aid private parties to perform that public function on a segregated basis implicate the State in conduct proscribed by the Fourteenth Amendment.

The public function doctrine also played a role for at least some of the justices in analyzing state responsibility for the racial exclusions at issue in the sit-in cases. See section B2 supra. For example, in a long concurring opinion in Bell v. Maryland, section B2 supra, Justice Goldberg argued that restaurants were places of "public accommodation" that the framers of the fourteenth amendment assumed would be subject to governmental control:

> Prejudice and bigotry in any form are regrettable, but it is the constitutional right of every person to close his home or club to any person or to choose his social intimates and business partners solely on the basis of personal prejudice including race. These and other rights pertaining to privacy and private association are themselves constitutionally protected liberties. [But the] broad acceptance of the public in this and in other restaurants clearly demonstrates that the proprietor's interest in private or unrestricted association is slight. The relationship between the modern innkeeper or restaurateur and the customer is relatively impersonal and evanescent. [As] the history of the common law and, indeed, of our own times graphically illustrates, the interests of proprietors of places of public accommodation have always been adapted to the citizen's felt need for public accommodations, a need which is basic and deep-rooted.

Note that the opinion for the Court in *Evans* and Justice Goldberg's concurrence in *Bell* both emphasize the strand in *Marsh* that focused on the "inherently" public or private character of the activity involved. Both opinions tend to underplay the strand that focused on the degree to which private entities exercise the kind of coercive power normally associated with the state. Which version of the public function doctrine is more persuasive?

4. *Retreat from* Marsh? In the last three decades, the Court has demonstrated a growing reluctance to burden private entities with constitutional requirements through the public function doctrine. Very few functions are now "public" for purposes of the state action doctrine. In the Court's current formulation, a function must be traditionally an *exclusive* state function in order to be subject to the Consitution. Thus, although shopping centers are generally as open to the public as parks, the Court has held that their owners are not bound by the first amendment. See Hudgens v. NLRB, infra this section. Although major utilities arguably exercise coercive power rivaling that of the state, the Court has refused to impose the requirements of procedural due process on them. See Jackson v. Metropolitan Edison Co., infra this section. And in *Flagg Brothers*, section B1 supra, the Court rejected respondents' argument that "dispute resolution" was a public function. But it did find it necessary to warn that

> there are a number of state and municipal functions not covered by our election cases or governed by the reasoning of *Marsh* which have been administered with a greater degree of exclusivity by States and [municipalities]. Among these are such functions as education, fire and police protection, and tax collection. We express no view as to the extent, if any, to which a city or State might be free to delegate to

private parties the performance of such functions and thereby avoid the strictures of the Fourteenth Amendment.

As you read the material below, consider which version of the public function doctrine the modern court has adopted. In its current form, does the doctrine take sufficient account of the need to leave "private space" free from government control? Is it sufficiently attentive to the risk that constitutional values will be undermined by private coercion?

JACKSON v. METROPOLITAN EDISON CO., 419 U.S. 345 (1974). This case, which is summarized in more detail at section C2 supra, arose when Metropolitan, a privately owned utility holding a certificate of public convenience issued by the Pennsylvania Public Utility Commission, terminated Jackson's electrical service for alleged nonpayment of bills. Jackson claimed that her due process rights were violated because she was not accorded a hearing prior to the termination. Justice Rehnquist delivered the Court's opinion:

"Petitioner [urges] that state action is present because respondent provides an essential public service required to be supplied on a reasonably continuous basis by [state law], and hence performs a 'public function.' We have, of course, found state action present in the exercise by a private entity of powers traditionally exclusively reserved to the State. [Nixon v. Condon; *Marsh*; Evans v. Newton.] If we were dealing with the exercise by Metropolitan of some power delegated to it by the State which is traditionally associated with sovereignty, such as eminent domain, our case would be quite a different one. But while the Pennsylvania statute imposes an obligation to furnish service on regulated utilities, it imposes no such obligation on the State. The Pennsylvania courts have rejected the contention that the furnishing of utility services is either a state function or a municipal duty.

"Perhaps in recognition of the fact that the supplying of utility service is not traditionally the exclusive prerogative of the State, petitioner invites the expansion of the doctrine of this limited line of cases into a broad principle that all businesses 'affected with the public interest' are state actors in all their actions.

"We decline the invitation for reasons stated long ago in Nebbia v. New York, 291 U.S. 502 (1934), in the course of rejecting a substantive due process attack on state legislation: It is clear that there is no closed class or category of businesses affected with a public interest. . . . The phrase "affected with a public interest" can, in the nature of things, mean no more than that an industry, for adequate reason, is subject to control for the public good. In several of the decisions of this court wherein the expressions "affected with a public interest," and "clothed with a public use," have been brought forward as the criteria . . . it has been admitted that they are not susceptible of definition and form an unsatisfactory test. . . .

"Doctors, optometrists, lawyers, Metropolitan, and Nebbia's upstate New York grocery selling a quart of milk are all in regulated businesses, providing arguably essential goods and services, 'affected with a public interest.' We do not believe that such a status converts their every action, absent more, into that of the State."

Justice Douglas filed a dissenting opinion: "I agree that doctors, lawyers, and grocers are not transformed into state actors simply because they provide arguably essential goods and services and are regulated by the State. In the present case, however, respondent is not just one person among many; it is the only public utility furnishing electric power in the city. When power is denied a householder, the home, under modern conditions, is likely to become unlivable."

Justice Marshall also filed a dissenting opinion: "[The] fact that Metropolitan Edison Co. supplies an essential public service that is in many communities supplied by the government weighs more heavily for me than for the majority. The Court concedes that state action might be present if the activity in question were 'traditionally associated with sovereignty,' but it then undercuts that point by suggesting that a particular service is not a public function if the State in question has not required that it be governmentally operated. This reads the 'public function' argument too narrowly. The whole point of the 'public function' cases is to look behind the State's decision to provide public services through private parties. See [Evans v. Newton; Terry v. Adams; *Marsh*]. In my view, utility service is traditionally identified with the State through universal public regulation or ownership to a degree sufficient to render it a 'public function.' . . .

"Private parties performing functions affecting the public interest can often make a persuasive claim to be free of the constitutional requirements applicable to governmental institutions because of the value of preserving a private sector in which the opportunity for individual choice is maximized. Maintaining the private status of parochial schools [advances] just this value. In the due process area, a similar value of diversity may often be furthered by allowing various private institutions the flexibility to select procedures that fit their particular needs. But it is hard to imagine any such interests that are furthered by protecting privately owned public utility companies from meeting the constitutional standards that would apply if the companies were state owned. The values of pluralism and diversity are simply not relevant when the private company is the only electric company in town."

Note: Public Functions as "Exclusive Prerogatives" of the State

1. *Post-*Jackson *developments.* In a series of decisions since *Jackson,* the Court has rejected "public function" arguments in many contexts:

a. *Shopping centers.* In Amalgamated Food Employees Union v. Logan Valley Plaza, 391 U.S. 308 (1968), a pre-*Jackson* decision, the Court held that shopping centers were covered by the *Marsh* principle. The case arose out of peaceful picketing of a supermarket located in a privately owned shopping mall. Noting that the "similarities between the business block in *Marsh* and the shopping center in the present case are striking," the Court saw "no reason why access to a business district in a company town [should] be constitutionally required, while access for the same purpose to property functioning as a business district should be limited simply because the property surrounding the 'business district' is not under the same ownership." Four years later the Court sharply limited the reach of *Logan Valley.* In Lloyd Corp. v. Tanner, 407 U.S. 551 (1972), the Court held that *Logan Valley* was inapplicable to handbilling protesting the Vietnam War and conducted at a privately owned shopping center. The Court noted that *Logan Valley* was distinguishable because picketers there would have been effectively denied the opportunity to convey their message to patrons of the store in question had they been denied access to the shopping center. The Lloyd Center, in contrast, was surrounded by public sidewalks where handbilling would have been permitted. Moreover, *Logan Valley*, unlike *Lloyd*, involved first amendment activity "directly related [to] the use to which the shopping center property was being put."

Lloyd purported merely to distinguish *Logan Valley*. In a post-*Jackson* case, however, the Court announced that "the reasoning [in] *Lloyd* cannot be squared with the reasoning [in] *Logan Valley.*" Hudgens v. NLRB, 424 U.S. 507 (1976). Accordingly, "the constitutional guarantee of free expression has no part to play in a case such as this." Justice Marshall, joined by Justice Brennan, dissented.

b. *Dispute resolution.* As noted above, in Flagg Brothers v. Brooks, section B1 supra, the Court held that resolution of disputes between creditors and debtors is not a "public function." The Court focused primarily on the "exclusivity" requirement. "Creditors and debtors have had available to them historically a far wider number of choices than has one who would be an elected public official, or a member of Jehovah's Witnesses who wished to distribute literature in Chickasaw, Ala., at the time *Marsh* was decided."

c. *Schools.* In Rendell-Baker v. Kohn, section C1 supra, the Court held that a private school for "maladjusted" high school students was not subject to constitutional constraints. The Court reached this conclusion despite the fact that students were placed in the program by public officials and virtually all of the school's funding came from public sources. With regard to petitioners' public function argument, the Court conceded that "[t]here can be no doubt that the education of maladjusted high school students is a public function." But in the Court's view, that was "only the beginning of the inquiry." It must further be shown that the function has been "traditionally the *exclusive* prerogative of the State. [Quoting from *Jackson*.]" Here, the state had elected to provide services for these students at public expense, but "[t]hat legislative policy choice in no way makes these services the exclusive province of the State. [That] a private entity performs a function which serves the public does not make its acts state action." Justice Marshall, joined by Justice Brennan, dissented.

d. *Nursing homes.* In Blum v. Yaretsky, section C1 supra, a case decided on the same day as *Rendell-Baker*, the Court announced that nursing homes in receipt of federal Medicaid payments were not performing a public function when they decided on the level of care for their patients. The Court rejected respondents' argument that the Medicaid statute and state law made the state responsible for providing every Medicaid patient with nursing home services. Moreover, "[e]ven if respondents' characterization of the State's duties were correct, [it] would not follow that decisions made in the day-to-day administration of a nursing home are the kind of decisions traditionally and exclusively made by the sovereign for and on behalf of the public." Justice Brennan, joined by Justice Marshall, dissented.

e. *Amateur sports.* In San Francisco Arts & Athletics, Inc. v. United States Olympic Committee, section C1 supra, the Court, in an opinion by Justice Powell, held that the United States Olympic Committee was not a state actor. The Amateur Sports Act of 1978 created the committee as a "private [corporation] established under Federal law." The act imposed certain requirements on the committee, provided for some funding for it, and granted it exclusive use of the word "Olympic." The Court held that

> [the act] merely authorized the [committee] to coordinate activities that always
> have been performed by private entities. Neither the conduct nor the coordination
> of amateur sports has been a traditional governmental function.

Compare Justice Brennan's dissenting opinion:

> In the Amateur Sports Act of 1978, Congress placed the power and prestige of the United States Government behind a single, central sports organization. Congress delegated to the [committee] functions that Government actors traditionally perform — the representation of the Nation abroad and the administration of all private organizations in a particular economic sector. The representation function is of particular significance here [because] an organization that need not adhere to the Constitution cannot meaningfully represent this Nation. The Government is free, of course, to "privatize" some functions it would otherwise perform. But such privatization ought not automatically release those who perform government functions from constitutional obligations.

f. *Peremptory challenges.* In Edmonson v. Leesville Concrete Co., 500 U.S. 614 (1991), the Court relied in part on the public function doctrine to hold that private litigants in civil cases were state actors for constitutional purposes when they utilized peremptory challenges to eliminate jurors on the basis of race. Writing for six justices, Justice Kennedy argued that

> [t]he peremptory challenge is used in selecting an entity that is a quintessential governmental body, having no attributes of a private actor. . . .
> If a government confers on a private body the power to choose the government's employees or officials, the private body will be bound by the constitutional mandate of race-neutrality. [At] least a plurality of the Court recognized this principle in [Terry v. Adams]. There we found state action in a scheme in which a private organization known as the Jaybird Democratic Association conducted whites-only elections to select candidates to run in a Democratic primary [election]. . . .
> The principle that the selection of state officials, other than through election of all qualified voters, may constitute state action applies with even greater force in the context of jury selection through peremptory challenges. Though the motive of a peremptory challenge may be to protect a private interest, the objective of jury selection proceedings is to determine representation on a governmental body.

Justice O'Connor, joined by Chief Justice Rehnquist and Justice Scalia, dissented:

> Peremptory challenges are not a traditional governemnt function; the "tradition" is one of unguided private choice. . . .
> In order to constitute state action under [the governmental function] doctrine, private conduct must not only comprise something that the government traditionally does, but something that *only* the government traditionally does. Even if one could fairly characterize the use of a peremptory strike as the performance of the traditional government function of jury selection, it has never been exclusively the function of the government to select juries; peremptory strikes are older than the Republic.

See also Georgia v. McCollum, 505 U.S. 42 (1992) (holding that a defense attorney in a criminal trial who utilizes peremptory strikes on a racially discriminatory basis is a government actor for constitutional purposes).

In J.E.B. v. Alabama ex rel. T.B., 511 U.S. 127 (1994), the Court held that the equal protection clause barred the use of peremptory challenges on the basis of gender.

2. Jackson *and the legacy of* Marsh. Recall that the public function doctrine, as first stated in *Marsh*, seemed to rest on two interlocking rationales. First, constitutional restraints were appropriate because company towns had the power to undermine freedom as effectively as the state. Second, state intervention to control this power was not itself subversive of individual liberty because company towns were already open to the public and serving public functions. Much of the debate in the post-*Marsh* cases stems from disagreement about which of these rationales is dominant. Does either of the original *Marsh* rationales survive *Jackson?* The emphasis on alternative means of dispute resolution in *Flagg Brothers* arguably relates to the degree of coercive power possessed by creditors. And the "limited invitation" argument in the shopping center cases seems responsive to the "open to the public" rationale. More generally, however, the Court now appears ready to exempt "private" entities from constitutional responsibilities even in situations in which both of the *Marsh* requirements are satisfied.

Instead of inquiring into the power of the private entity and its claim to individual autonomy, the *Jackson* court asked whether its function has "traditionally" been performed by the state and whether it is the "exclusive" prerogative of the state. Even if this test is workable (see below), why should the "state action" question turn on these factors? Note, for example, that even the municipal functions at stake in *Marsh* were hardly the "exclusive" prerogatives of the state. Indeed, Justice Black argued that constitutional constraints were necessary precisely because "[m]any people in the United States live in company-owned towns." Would it have made an important difference if such towns were a new development or had existed for a long time?

3. *Public functions, baselines, and natural law.* What does it mean for a function to be traditionally the exclusive prerogative of the state? Whether a function is "exclusively" the state's may depend on how the function is characterized. In *Flagg Brothers*, for example, it may make an important difference whether one thinks of the function as "dispute resolution" (nonexclusive) or as the transfer of property interests (arguably exclusive). And why should it matter whether the relevant function has been exclusively the state's?

Does the *Jackson* test ultimately depend on a platonic or "natural law" view of the functions appropriately attributable to state and individual? Consider in this connection the *Jackson* Court's reliance on Nebbia v. New York, 291 U.S. 502 (1934). In *Nebbia*, which marked the beginning of the end of the "*Lochner* era," the Court upheld the constitutionality of state legislation fixing the price of milk. See Chapter 6, section D, supra. Before the demise of *Lochner*, the Court treated the private sphere as a preconstitutional given that neither legislature nor court had the power to alter. In more recent years, the Court has generally followed *Nebbia* and, at least in the area of "social and economic legislation," treated the division between public and private as a matter of legislative discretion. Is the use of *Nebbia* ironic in light of the fact that something like *Lochner* is plausibly at work in Justice Rehnquist opinion itself? Does a version of *Lochner* survive as a "natural" barrier to judicial, as opposed to legislative, invasions of the private sphere? Is there good reason to treat legislative and judicial invasions differently?

E.   UNCONSTITUTIONAL CONDITIONS AND THE BENEFIT/BURDEN DISTINCTION

At many places in this book, we have seen the problem of "unconstitutional conditions" — the problem that arises when government attaches constitutionally troublesome "strings" to government benefits, such as housing, employment, money, or licenses. Suppose, for example, the government says that only Democrats may work in the State Department, or that members of the Central Intelligence Agency must agree not to write about their activities, or that welfare beneficiaries must allow searches of their homes, or that medical facilities receiving federal funds must agree not to perform certain medical procedures. The question raised by the problem of unconstitutional conditions is how, and whether, these sorts of cases should be treated differently from "ordinary" constitutional cases.

The general problem is ubiquitous. It has clear connections to the state action doctrine because, as we shall see, it raises similar questions about appropriate baselines for deciding whether government has behaved neutrally. The following cases have been considered in other parts of this book. We offer excerpts from the majority opinions (notably all four produced divided courts) in order to give a sense of why they all involved arguably unconstitutional conditions.

RUST v. SULLIVAN, 500 U.S. 173 (1991). In this case, the Court upheld a new administrative interpretation of a statute. The statute said that federal funds for family services shall not "be used in programs where abortion is a method of family planning." The new administrative interpretation was that federal funds could not be used not only for abortion itself but also for all activities that "encourage, promote or advocate abortion as a method of family planning." In an opinion by Chief Justice Rehnquist, the Court said:

"The Government can, without violating the Constitution, selectively fund a program to encourage certain activities it believes to be in the public interest, without at the same time funding an alternate program which seeks to deal with the problem in another way. In so doing, the Government has not discriminated on the basis of viewpoint; it has merely chosen to fund one activity to the exclusion of the other. . . .

"[Petitioners'] assertions ultimately boil down to the position that if the government chooses to subsidize one protected right, it must subsidize analogous counterpart rights. But the Court has soundly rejected that proposition. Within far broader limits than petitioners are willing to concede, when the government appropriates public funds to establish a program it is entitled to define the limits of that program. . . .

"Petitioners also contend that the restrictions on the subsidization of abortion-related speech contained in the regulations are impermissible because they condition the receipt of a benefit . . . on the relinquishment of a constitutional right, the right to engage in abortion advocacy and counseling. [P]etitioners argue that 'even though the government may deny [a] . . . benefit for any number of reasons, there are some reasons upon which the government may not rely. It may not deny a benefit to a person on a basis that infringes his constitutionally protected interests — especially, his interest in freedom of speech.'

"Petitioners' reliance on these cases is unavailing, however, because here the government is not denying a benefit to anyone, but is instead simply insisting that public funds be spent for the purposes for which they were authorized. The Secretary's regulations do not force the Title X grantee to give up abortion-related speech; they merely require that the grantee keep such activities separate and distinct from Title X activities. . . .

"In contrast, our 'unconstitutional conditions' cases involve situations in which the government has placed a condition on the *recipient* of the subsidy rather than on a particular program or service, thus effectively prohibiting the recipient from engaging in the protected conduct outside the scope of the federally funded program. In [FCC v. League of Women Voters, infra this section,] we invalidated a federal law providing that noncommercial television and radio stations that receive federal grants may not 'engage in editorializing.' Under the law, a recipient of federal funds was 'barred absolutely from all editorializing' because it 'is not able to segregate its activities according to the source of its funding' and thus 'has no way of limiting the use of its federal funds to all noneditorializing activities.' . . .

"Similarly, in [Regan v. Taxation with Representation of Washington, infra this section,] we held that Congress could . . . reasonably refuse to subsidize the lobbying activities of tax-exempt charitable organizations by prohibiting such organizations from using tax-deductible contributions to support their lobbying efforts. In so holding, we explained that such organizations remained free 'to receive deductible contributions to support . . . nonlobbying activit[ies].' . . . The condition that federal funds will be used only to further the purposes of a grant does not violate constitutional rights. . . .

"The same principles apply to petitioners' claim that the regulations abridge the free speech rights of the grantee's staff. . . . The regulations, which govern solely the scope of the Title X project's activities, do not in any way restrict the activities of those persons acting as private individuals. The employees' freedom of expression is limited during the time that they actually work for the project; but this limitation is a consequence of their decision to accept employment in a project, the scope of which is permissibly restricted by the funding authority."

MAHER v. ROE, 432 U.S. 464 (1977). The Court upheld a state regulation granting Medicaid benefits for childbirth, but denying such benefits for nontherapeutic abortions (i.e., abortions that are not "medically necessary"). Justice Powell delivered the opinion of the Court:

"The Constitution imposes no obligation on the States to pay the pregnancy-related medical expenses of indigent women, or indeed to pay any of the medical expenses of indigents. But when a State decides to alleviate some of the hardships of poverty by providing medical care, the manner in which it dispenses benefits is subject to constitutional limitations. Appellees' claim is that [the State] must accord equal treatment to both abortion and childbirth, and may not evidence a policy preference by funding only the medical expenses incident to childbirth. This [presents] a question [under] the Equal Protection Clause. . . .

"This case involves no discrimination against a suspect class. An indigent woman desiring an abortion does not come within the limited category of [suspect classes]. Nor does the fact that the impact of the regulation falls upon those who cannot pay lead to a different conclusion.

"The [regulation] before us is different in kind from the laws invalidated in our previous [decisions. It] places no obstacles — absolute or otherwise — in the pregnant woman's path to an abortion. An indigent woman who desires an abortion suffers no disadvantage as a consequence of [the State's] decision to fund childbirth; she continues as before to be dependent on private sources for the service she desires. The State may have made childbirth a more attractive alternative, thereby influencing the woman's decision, but it has imposed no restriction on access to abortions that was not already there. The indigency that may make it difficult — and in some cases, perhaps, impossible — for some women to have abortions is neither created nor in any way affected by [the] regulation. [The challenged] regulation does not impinge upon the fundamental right recognized in *Roe*.

"[Appellees] rely on [Shapiro v. Thompson, infra this section, and Memorial Hospital v. Maricopa County, 415 U.S. 250 (1974)]. Appellees' reliance on the penalty analysis of [those decisions] is misplaced. [*Shapiro*] and *Maricopa County* recognized that denial of welfare to one who had recently exercised the right to travel [was] sufficiently analogous to a criminal fine to justify strict judicial scrutiny. If [the State] denied general welfare benefits to all women who had obtained abortions and who were otherwise entitled to the benefits, we would have a close analogy [to] *Shapiro*, and strict scrutiny might be [appropriate]. But the claim here is that the State 'penalizes' the woman's decision to have an abortion by refusing to pay for it. *Shapiro* and *Maricopa County* did not hold that States would penalize the right to travel [by] refusing to pay the bus fares of the indigent [travelers]. Sherbert v. Verner [see Chapter 8, section C, supra] similarly is inapplicable here. . . .

"Our conclusion signals no retreat from [*Roe*]. There is a basic difference between direct state interference with a protected activity and state encouragement of an alternative [activity]. Constitutional concerns are greatest when the State attempts to impose its will by force of law; the State's power to encourage actions deemed to be in the public interest is necessarily far broader. . . ."

SOUTH DAKOTA v. DOLE, 483 U.S. 203 (1987). Here, the Court upheld a federal statute directing the Secretary of Transportation to withhold a portion of federal highway funds from states that do not prohibit the purchase of alcohol by people under the age of twenty-one. In an opinion by Chief Justice Rehnquist, the Court said that this was not an unconstitutional condition:

"[O]ur cases have suggested (without significant elaboration) that conditions on federal grants might be illegitimate if they are unrelated to 'the federal interest in particular national projects or programs.' . . . [But, here,] the State itself, rather than challenging the germaneness of the condition, admits that it 'has never contended that the congressional action was . . . unrelated to a national concern in the absence of the Twenty-first Amendment.' Indeed, the condition imposed by Congress is directly related to one of the main purposes for which highway funds are expended — safe interstate travel. . . .

"Our decisions have recognized that in some circumstances the financial inducement offered by Congress might be so coercive as to pass the point at which 'pressure turns into compulsion.' Here, however, Congress has directed only that a State desiring to establish a minimum drinking age lower than 21 lose a relatively small percentage of certain federal highway funds. . . .

"Here Congress has offered relatively mild encouragement to the State to enact higher minimum drinking ages than they would otherwise choose. But the enactment of such laws remains the prerogative of the States not merely in theory but in fact. Even if Congress might lack the power to impose a national drinking age directly, we conclude that the encouragement to state action . . . is a valid use of the spending power."

NOLLAN v. CALIFORNIA COASTAL COMMISSION, 483 U.S. 825 (1987). In this case, the California Coastal Commission conditioned the grant of a permit to rebuild appellants' house on their transfer to the public of an easement across their beachfront property. The Court held that the attempt to impose this condition was a taking in the form of an unconstitutional condition. Justice Scalia wrote for the Court:

"Justice Brennan [suggests] that the Commission's public announcement of its intention to condition the rebuilding of houses on the transfer of easements of access caused the Nollans to have 'no reasonable claim to any expectation of being able to exclude members of the public' from walking across their beach. . . . But the right to build on one's own property — even though its exercise can be subjected to legitimate permitting requirements — cannot remotely be described as a 'government benefit.' [Nor] are the Nollans' rights altered because they acquired the land well after the Commission had begun to implement its policy. So long as the Commission could not have deprived the prior owners of the easement without compensating them, the prior owners must be understood to have transferred their full property rights in conveying the lot.

"Given, then, that requiring uncompensated conveyance of the easement outright would violate the Fourteenth Amendment, the question becomes whether requiring it to be conveyed as a condition for issuing a land use permit alters the outcome. . . .

"[If] the Commission attached to the permit some condition that would have protected the public's ability to see the beach notwithstanding construction of the new house — for example, a height limitation, a width restriction, or a ban on fences — so long as the Commission could have exercised its police power (as we [assume] it could) to forbid construction of the house altogether, imposition of the condition would also be constitutional. Moreover, [the] condition would be constitutional even if it consisted of the requirement that the [appellants] provide a viewing spot on their property for passersby with whose sighting of the ocean their new house would interfere. Although such a requirement [would] have to be considered a taking if it were not attached to a development permit, the Commission's assumed power to forbid construction of the house in order to protect the public's view of the beach must surely include the power to condition construction upon some concession by the owner, even a concession of property rights, that serves the same end. . . .

"The evident constitutional propriety disappears, however, if the condition substituted for the prohibition utterly fails to further the end advanced as the justification for the prohibition. When that essential nexus is eliminated, the situation becomes the same as if California law forbade shouting fire in a crowded theater, but granted dispensations to those willing to contribute $100 to the state treasury. [In] short, unless the permit condition serves the same governmental purpose as the development ban, the building restriction is not a valid regulation of land use but 'an out-and-out plan of extortion.' . . ."

Note: Benefits, Burdens, and Coercion

1. *Origins of the unconstitutional conditions doctrine.* The cases suggest that some, but not at all, conditions on government benefits are constitutionally troublesome. But this is a relatively new development. For a long time, courts concluded that the government could accompany benefits with whatever conditions it chose. This position was reflected in many opinions by Justice Holmes, who, in a case involving a discharge of a police officer for his political views, responded: "The petitioner may have a constitutional right to talk politics, but he has no constitutional right to be a policeman. . . . The servant cannot complain, as he takes the employment on the terms that are offered him." McAuliffe v. Mayor of New Bedford, 155 Mass. 216, 220, 29 N.E. 517, 518 (1892). Eventually the Court concluded that this position was too broad. Suppose, for example, access to federally funded highways was limited to people with a certain political view; surely this could not be acceptable. Before the New Deal, the Court invalidated a state's effort to allow companies to use public highways only after receiving a permit certifying that the business was for the "public convenience and necessity." Frost & Frost Trucking Co. v. Railroad Commission, 271 U.S. 583 (1926). Thus, the Court started to give birth to the idea — recognized in Rust v. Sullivan — that government may not use its "greater power" to deny a benefit altogether as a justification for exercising the "lesser power" to grant the benefit on such terms as it chooses. See Van Alstyne, The Demise of the Right-Privilege Distinction in Constitutional Law, 81 Harv. L. Rev. 1439 (1968).

2. *The "greater power" and the question of waiver.* The Court's general repudiation of Holmes's position raises many questions, especially because that position seems quite logical. Exactly *why* is government prohibited from exercising "the lesser power"? And how can someone who has voluntarily waived her constitutional rights be heard to complain about the waiver? See Easterbrook, Insider Trading, Secret Agents, Evidentiary Privileges, and the Production of Information, 1981 Sup. Ct. Rev. 309, for a qualified defense of Holmes's position. Consider these possible answers.

a. The Constitution limits the reasons for government action. If the government says that welfare recipients must vote for the President, it has acted for an illegitimate reason. The illegitimacy of the reason dooms the law. Hence, both the "greater power" and the "waiver" arguments are unconvincing.

b. The government may not do indirectly what it may not do directly. It may not bring about what is in the end a constitutionally forbidden result by using its power over dollars, jobs, and licenses. See Sullivan, Unconstitutional Conditions, 102 Harv. L. Rev. 1413 (1989), for general discussion of this argument and argument *a* above.

c. "[The waiver argument] ignores monopoly and collective action problems, which also induce individuals to take actions that benefit their private, but not the social interest. . . . The reasons that lead us not to enforce some private bargains can thus explain why certain bargains between the government and the individual are not enforced. . . . [L]imits on the types of gains that the state can hope to extract by bargaining with its citizens can limit the social loss associated with strategy behavior. . . . The imposition of a condition on a grant is often an attempt to shift some portion of [the general social surplus] from some persons or interest groups to others. . . . The bargain that is made with one citizen may have the effect of freezing other citizens out of the market or setting them at a competitive disadvantage." Epstein, Foreword: Unconstitutional Conditions, State Power, and the Limits of Consent, 102 Harv. L. Rev. 4, 14, 102-103 (1988).

d. The problem with the waiver argument is that in many cases, a seemingly individual waiver has serious systemic effects, extending far beyond the single case. Individual citizens may often find it in their interest to give up the right of free speech in return for government benefits. But if government is permitted to obtain a number of individual waivers of the free speech right, the aggregate effect on free speech could be substantial, and the deliberative processes of the community could be skewed. See R. Epstein, Bargaining with the State (1994), for general discussion of this and related points.

3. *The shape of the doctrine.* The cases suggest three points that seem to organize much of current law:

a. Government is under no obligation to *subsidize* activity, including, for example, speech, voting, or abortion. Refusals to subsidize are by themselves acceptable, even if people have a constitutional right to do the relevant activity and to be free from coercion in so doing. See, e.g., Harris v. McRae, 448 U.S. 297 (1980); *Rust*; Regan v. Taxation with Representation of Washington, 461 U.S. 540 (1983) (upholding a federal statute saying that contributions to an otherwise tax-exempt organization, other than a tax-exempt veterans' organization, are not tax deductible if a substantial part of the organization's activities consists of attempts to influence legislation).

b. In the first amendment context, government may speak however it wishes. Public officials may say whatever they want. See *Rust*.

c. Government may not use its power over funds or other benefits so as to pressure people to relinquish rights that they "otherwise have," or so as to "penalize" the exercise of constitutional rights. Government cannot say that, as a condition for receiving welfare, poor people must agree to vote for a certain political party. It cannot tell you that if you want a driver's license, you must agree not to criticize the President or not to have an abortion. See FCC v. League of Women Voters, 468 U.S. 364 (1983); Shapiro v. Thompson, 394 U.S. 618 (1969) (holding that government may not condition receipt of welfare benefits on willingness to work on the Sabbath); Sherbert v. Verner, 374 U.S. 398 (1963) (holding that government may not condition receipt of unemployment benefits on recipient's willingness to work on the Sabbath).

4. *Mere subsidies.* These propositions raise a number of questions. For one thing, it may be hard to know in which of the three categories a certain case falls. When do we have a mere failure to subsidize, and when do we have an impermissible penalty? A useful guide comes from FCC v. League of Women Voters, supra, and Regan v. Taxation with Representation, supra. In the first case, the Court said that government could not prohibit noncommercial education stations from engaging in editorializing, even those stations that received money from the Corporation for Public Broadcasting. In the second case, the Court said that it was permissible for the government not to subsidize — through a tax deduction — attempts to influence legislation. The difference between the cases came

in the fact that *Taxation with Representation* involved a ban on the use of taxpayer funds, whereas *League of Women Voters* involved a ban on the use of private as well as taxpayer funds. This is the basic point on which the Court is insisting in Rust v. Sullivan.

But sometimes this distinction is not so clear. The majority in Rust v. Sullivan thought that the case fell in category *a*; the dissenters thought that it fell in category *c*. But it might even be urged that the relevant category was *b*. Government consists, after all, of its employees, and perhaps anyone who accepts money is to that extent a government employee. Can you respond to the argument that *Rust* was an easy case because it involved government speech?

5. *Baselines.* The trickiest category may well be *c*. How do we know whether the right is something that someone "otherwise" has? To answer this question, it may be necessary to identify some counterfactual world that would exist if not for the allegedly unconstitutional condition. Here, again, *Rust* is relevant, but it is especially useful to consider Harris v. McRae, 448 U.S. 297 (1980), involving a prohibition on the use of federal Medicaid funds for the performance of medically necessary abortions. See Chapter 6, section F2, supra. In *Harris*, the Court, following *Maher*, said that it was dealing with a mere failure to subsidize: "[A] woman's freedom of choice [does not carry] with it a constitutional entitlement to the financial resources to avail herself of the full range of protected choices." Justice Marshall said that poor women would "otherwise" receive Medicaid payments: "Appellees have met the statutory requirements for eligibility, but they are excluded because the treatment that is medically necessary involves the exercise of a fundamental right." In a footnote, the Court responded: "A substantial constitutional question would arise if Congress had attempted to withhold all Medicaid benefits from an otherwise eligible candidate because that candidate had exercised her constitutionally protected freedom to terminate her pregnancy by abortion. . . . [But a] mere refusal to fund protected activity, without more, cannot be equated with the imposition of a 'penalty' on that activity." In short, Justice Marshall thought the case involved a penalty, whereas the Court thought it was dealing with a mere refusal to subsidize.

Who gets the better of the argument? And how does the Court tell whether there is a subsidy or a penalty? The answer must depend on the identification of the normal or natural state of affairs — just as in the distinction between a "threat" and an "offer." Thus, the problem "lies in the challenge to specify an appropriate normal course of events from which to judge deviations." See Kreimer, Allocational Sanctions, 132 U. Pa. L. Rev. 1293, 1359 (1984); see also Nozick, Coercion, in Philosophy, Science, and Method 440, 447 (S. Morgenbesser et al. eds. 1969), suggesting that threats involve a departure from a baseline of the "normal course of events." Should the "normal course" be determined by asking what has been done historically? By asking what would in fact be done if the condition were invalidated? See Kreimer, supra, for discussion. Here, there is a question about government neutrality that runs parallel to the questions in the state action area. For a suggestion that the subsidy/penalty distinction is impossible to administer and constitutionally irrelevant, see C. Sunstein, The Partial Constitution 298-301 (1993).

6. *The search for legitimate motivations.* Perhaps one can make sense of the cases not by asking about baselines, but by asking *whether the government has a legitimate motivation for the condition that is said to be unconstitutional.* If, for ex-

ample, government said that companies that operate nuclear power plants must agree to allow inspections — and thus to waive their fourth amendment rights — in return for a license, the condition would almost certainly be constitutional. It would be seen as a legitimate effort to ensure safety. See in this regard Snepp v. United States, 444 U.S. 507 (1980), discussed in Chapter 7, section B4, supra, which upholds the CIA secrecy agreement on the ground that it is a legitimate effort to promote national security interests. By contrast, if government says that welfare beneficiaries must agree to vote for the President, no legitimate motivation is apparent. Instead the government is trying to regulate political behavior.

If the cases are explored in this way, there is no unitary unconstitutional conditions doctrine but instead a set of results that depend on the particular constitutional provision at issue — on what sorts of motivations it allows government to have. And if the issue is explored in this way, the question involves the meaning of the relevant provision, as (arguably) in the state action context. See, for pertinent discussion, Sullivan, supra; Epstein, Foreword, supra; Sunstein, Why the Unconstitutional Conditions Doctrine Is an Anachronism, 70 B.U. L. Rev. 593 (1990); McConnell, The Selective Funding Problem: Abortions and Religious Schools, 104 Harv. L. Rev. 989 (1991). And consider the suggestion that this line of thought leads to the conclusion that "[i]n a crucial sense, all constitutional cases are unconstitutional conditions cases. Ordinary property rights are created by a government. . . . When the government says that it will take your property if you do something, it is, in essence, imposing a condition on a right that it has conferred." Sunstein, The Partial Constitution, supra, at 293.

7. *Selective subsidies and the limits of Rust v. Sullivan.* Should *Rust* be read for all that it is worth? Suppose government decides to fund the Democratic convention but not the Republican convention — or to subsidize broadcasters only to the extent that they are praising the current government. Wouldn't this be acceptable in light of *Rust*? If such selective subsidies would be unconstitutional, how can they be distinguished by funding speech opposing the use of illegal drugs but not speech favoring the use of illegal drugs? Does it matter that the speech in *Rust* was ancillary to conduct that government sought not to fund?

The Court has shed some light on these questions in subsequent cases. In Rosenberger v. Rector and Visitors of the University of Virginia, 515 U.S. 819 (1995), the Court struck down a University of Virginia policy authorizing university subsidies of some student publications but forbidding subsidies for student publications that "primarily promotes or manifests a particular belief in or about a diety or an ultimate reality." The University cited *Rust*, which appears strongly supportive of the selective subsidy. But the Court distinguished and narrowed its prior decision in such a way as to leave unsettled the status of viewpoint discrimination in government funding.

The Court explained that government can "regulate the content of what is or is not expressed when it is the speaker or when it enlists private entities to convey its own message." Thus, *Rust* was merely a case in which the government "used private speakers to transmit specific information pertaining to its own program." This means that a government appropriation of "public funds to promote a particular policy of its own" can legitimately be accompanied by appropriate "steps to ensure that its message is neither garbled nor distorted by the grantee." But it does not follow that government may impose "viewpoint-based restrictions" when the government "does not itself speak or subsidize transmittal of a message it favors but instead expends funds to encourage a diversity of views from private speakers." In this case, the University of Virginia did not contend that those who were eligible for university support are the university's agents; student organizations "are not subject to its control and are not its responsibility." Thus, when the university has decided to pay private speakers "who convey their own messages," it "may not silence the expression of selected viewpoints."

There is obvious tension between *Rust* and *Rosenberger*, and the implications of the two cases, taken together, are far from clear. The distinction seems to be that in *Rosenberger* the university did not contend that it was attempting to "convey its own message" or implement "its own program." But what if the university said that its funding policies involved "its own program," broadly speaking? What if the university denied that its purpose was "to encourage a diversity of views from private speakers"? What if the university said that it sought to encourage diversity, but subject to certain restrictions, on the ground that some funding decisions would create too much entanglement between the state and religion? In any case *Rosenberger* could be understood broadly or very narrowly, and as the opinion is written, it is not clear that it stands as a barrier to a government decision to refuse to fund art that it deems offensive, even on the basis of viewpoint.

Compare in this regard the Court's most sustained encounter with the question of government funding of the arts, National Endowment for the Arts v. Finley, 524 U.S. 569 (1998). There the Court was asked to assess a statute asking the NEA, in establishing procedures to assess the artistic merit of applicants, to "take into consideration general standards of decency and respect for the diverse beliefs and values of the American public." The Court upheld the statute against facial attack; but what is especially important here is what the Court did not say. The Court did not conclude that government could give out taxpayer funds however it chose. It did not accept a "strong" reading of *Rust v. Sullivan*, which would allow government to choose, in its discretion, its preferred candidates for public subsidization. Instead, the Court found it necessary to emphasize that the statute at issue was not, in fact, a form of viewpoint discrimination. Thus, the Court said that the considerations listed in the statute are "susceptible to multiple interpretation," and nothing in the law was introduced that "in practice, would effectively preclude or punish the expression of particular views." Both the "decency" and the "respect" criteria could be understood in a constitutional fashion, as, for example, attempting to give special consideration to "projects and productions . . . that reach, or reflect the culture of, a minority, inner city, rural, or tribal community." Because artistic funding was necessarily based on content discrimination, this case was not covered by *Rosenberger*, which was (in the Court's view) an indiscriminate effort to encourage a diversity of views from the private sphere. And the Court left open the possibility that in particular cases, "the denial of a grant may be shown to be the product of invidious viewpoint discrimination." Thus, any "penalty on disfavored viewpoints" would present "a different case." Justice Souter dissented on the ground that this was in fact a form of viewpoint discrimination; Justice Scalia, joined by Justice Thomas, concurred in the result, invoking a strong reading of *Rust* and suggesting that government may "earmark NEA funds for projects it deems to be in the public interest without thereby abridging speech."

It is not easy to reconstruct the law as constituted by *Rust*, *Rosenberger*, and *Finley*. The strong version of *Rust* appears to have been rejected by the Court; unambiguous viewpoint discrimination appears to be impermissible, even with respect to the allocation of government funds for art. On the other hand, government may itself speak as it wishes, and if government wants to create a "program" for a proposed point of view, and to enlist private speakers in the endeavor, it is permitted to do exactly that. Thus, for example, government might have a project for democracy, or a project for the reduction of smoking among teenagers, and it might pay private speakers to help. It might even be possible for government to have a special artistic project whose purpose is to encourage (for example) celebration of the nation's natural beauty. In such cases, *Rust* would probably govern. But where the government is engaged in a general funding process for art, it is unlikely to be permitted to discriminate on the basis of viewpoint. Of course, the distinction between a specific program and a general funding process is very far from transparent.

8. *Examples.* Test your understanding of unconstitutional conditions by exploring the following cases. (a) Government funds public schools but not private schools. Are parents of children attending private schools being subjected to an unconstitutional condition? See McConnell, supra, for discussion. (b) Suppose there is a great deal of criminal activity in a public housing project in Los Angeles. The government asks all tenants to sign — as a condition for subsidized housing — an agreement that random searches will be allowed in homes. Is this an unconstitutional condition? What if 90 percent, or 60 percent, or 10 percent of the tenants are in favor of this proposal? (c) The government decides not to fund artistic activity containing nudity. May an artist complain if his work has not been funded because it contains nudity? (d) The national government tells the states that unless they meet national clean air standards, all national highway subsidies will be cut off. Is this an unconstitutional condition distinguished from the *Dole* case? (e) May the government say that Medicaid benefits will be unavailable for any medical expense related to reproduction? (f) May the government say that, as a condition for receiving a permit to build an expansion of your house near the National Seashore, you will allow access to the beach? See Dolan v. City of Tigard, 512 U.S. 687 (1994), and *Nollan*, supra.

F. SOME FINAL THOUGHTS

A pervasive question is whether there is, or should be, a state action doctrine, and whether instead the Court is, and should be, asking about the reach of the particular constitutional provision at issue. Some commentators have concluded that the state action requirement need never prevent a litigant from securing a decision on the merits of a constitutional claim. On this view, it will always be possible to find some government actor and through good lawyering to structure litigation that will challenge the constitutionality of that official's conduct. Note that, even if this is so, the state action doctrine might perform an important function by making it clear that private actors are not subject to the Constitution. But is the state really passive, and legitimately free from constitutional restraints, when it "merely" acquiesces in private decisions, or creates the property rights that allow private markets to function, and private choices to turn out as they do?

Table of Cases

Italic type indicates principal and intermediate cases.

Table of Authorities

Index